India

written and researched by

David Abram, Devdan Sen, Nick Edwards, Mike Ford and Beth Wooldridge

with additional contributions by

Simon Lewis and Charles Young

ROUGH GUIDES

www.roughguides.com

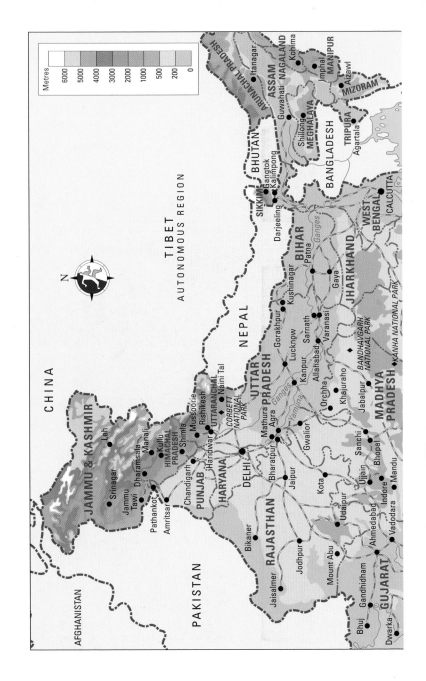

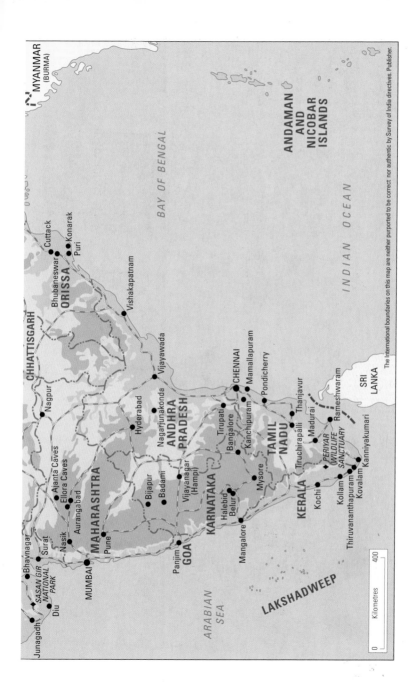

The international boundaries on this map are neither purported to be correct nor authentic by Survey of India directives. Publisher.

iii

Introduction to

India

"Unity in Diversity" was the slogan chosen when India celebrated fifty years of Independence in 1997, a declaration replete with as much optimism as pride. Stretching from the frozen barrier of the Himalayas to the tropical greenery of Kerala, and from the sacred Ganges to the sands of the Thar desert, the country's boundaries encompass incomparable variety. Walk the streets of any Indian city and you'll rub shoulders with representatives of several of the world's great faiths, a multitude of castes and outcastes, fair-skinned, turbanned Punjabis and dark-skinned Tamils. You'll also encounter temple rituals that have been performed since the time of the Egyptian Pharaohs, onion-domed mosques erected centuries before the Taj Mahal was ever dreamt of, and quirky echoes of the British Raj on virtually every corner.

 That so much of India's past remains discernible today is all the more astonishing given the pace of change since Independence in 1947. Spurred by the free-market reforms of the early 1990s, the economic revolution started by Rajiv Gandhi has transformed the country with new consumer goods, technologies and ways of life. Now the land where the Buddha lived and taught, whose religious festivals are as old as the rivers that sustain them, is the second-largest producer of computer software in the world, with its own satellites and nuclear weapons.

However, the presence in even the most far-flung market towns of internet cafés and Japanese hatchbacks has thrown into sharp relief the problems that have bedevilled the subcontinent since long before it became the world's largest secular democracy. Rooted in the monolithic hierarchy of caste,

Fact file

● The Republic of India, whose capital is New Delhi, borders Afghanistan, China, Nepal and Bhutan to the north, Bangladesh and Myanmar (formerly Burma) to the east and Pakistan to the west.

● The world's seventh-largest country, covering more than 3 million square kilometres, it is second only to China in terms of population, which stands at over a billion. Hindus comprise 83 percent of the population, Muslims 12 percent and there are millions of Christians, Sikhs, Buddhists and Jains. Eighteen major languages and more than 1000 minor languages and dialects are spoken; Hindi is the language of forty percent of the population, but English is widely spoken.

● The caste system is all-pervasive and although it is integral to Hindu belief, also encompasses non-Hindus. A system of social hierarchy that holds especial sway in rural areas, it may dictate where a person lives and what their occupation is.

● The Congress Party, whose members included Mahatma Gandhi and Jawaharlal Nehru, was traditionally the most powerful political force in India, but went into decline following corruption allegations in the 1990s. Its successors are the secular socialist Janata Dal and the Hindu Bharatiya Janata (BJP).

● Literacy extends to 69 percent of males and 42 percent of females: 56 percent of the total population.

For all its jarring juxtapositions, intractable paradoxes and frustrations, India remains an utterly compelling destination

poverty remains a harsh fact of life for around forty percent of India's inhabitants. No other nation on earth has slum settlements on the scale of those in Delhi, Mumbai and Calcutta, nor so many malnourished children, uneducated women and homes without access to clean water and waste disposal.

Many first-time visitors find themselves unable to see past such glaring disparities. Others come expecting a timeless ascetic wonderland and are surprised to encounter one of the most materialistic societies on the planet. Still more find themselves intimidated by what may seem, initially, an incomprehensible and bewildering continent. But for all its jarring juxtapositions, intractable paradoxes and frustrations, India remains an utterly compelling destination. Intricate and worn, its distinctive patina – the stream of life in its crowded bazaars, the ubiquitous *filmi* music, the pungent melange of *beedi* smoke, cooking spices, dust and cow dung – casts a spell that few forget from the moment they step off a plane. Love it or hate it – and most travellers oscillate between the two – India will shift the way you see the world.

Where to go

T he best Indian itineraries are the simplest. It just isn't possible to see everything in a single expedition, even if you spent a year trying. Far better, then, to concentrate on one or two specific regions and, above all, to be flexible. Although it requires a deliberate change of pace to venture away from the urban centres, rural India has its own very distinct pleasures. In fact, while Indian cities are undoubtedly adrenalin-fuelled, upbeat places, it is possible – and certainly less stressful – to travel for months around the subcontinent and rarely have to set foot in one.

The most-travelled circuit in the country, combining spectacular monuments with the flat, fertile landscape that for many people is archetypally Indian, is the so-called "Golden Triangle" in the north: Delhi itself, the colonial capital; Agra, home of the Taj Mahal; and the Pink City of Jaipur in Rajasthan. Rajasthan is probably the single most popular state with travellers, who are drawn by its desert scenery, by the imposing medieval forts

India's sacred geography

It's hard to think of a more visibly religious country than India. The very landscape of the subcontinent – its rivers, waterfalls, trees, hilltops, mountains and rocks – comprises a vast sacred geography for adherents of the dozen or more faiths rooted here. Connecting the country's countless holy places is a network of pilgrimage routes along which tens of thousands of worshippers may be moving at any one time – on regular trains, specially decorated *darshan* (ritual viewing) buses, tinsel-covered bicycles, barefoot, alone or in noisy family groups. For the visitor, joining devotees in the teeming temple precincts of the south, on the *ghats* at Varanasi, at the Sufi shrines of Ajmer and Delhi, before the naked Jain colossi of Saravanbelgola, or at any one of the innumerable religious festivals that punctuate the astrological calendar is to experience India at its most intense.

Kashmir

Few civil wars on earth can have been fought against a more idyllic backdrop than the current troubles in Kashmir. During the run-up to Partition in 1947, when the local Hindu Maharaja threw the lot of this Muslim-majority valley in with India instead of neighbouring Pakistan, he sowed the seeds of a conflict that would erupt into a full-scale uprising forty years later, between various factions of Islamic, Pakistani-backed militants and the Indian state.

Since 1989, some 25,000 Kashmiri separatists, Indian troops and civilians have died in a campaign of appalling violence that has, on several occasions, brought south Asia's two nuclear powers to the brink of all-out war. Although technically open to visitors, the Kashmir Valley, for all its undeniable beauty, remains a war zone we strongly recommend you steer clear of – hence the absence of a chapter on the region in this book. For more background, see p.1498.

and palaces of Jaisalmer, Jodhpur, Udaipur and Bundi, and by the colourful traditional dress.

East of Delhi, the River Ganges meanders through some of India's most densely populated regions to reach the extraordinary holy Hindu city of Varanasi (also known as Benares), where to witness the daily rituals of life and death focused around the waterfront *ghats* (bathing places) is to glimpse the continuing practice of India's most ancient religious traditions. Further east still is the great city of Calcutta, the capital until early this century of the British Raj, and now a teeming metropolis that epitomizes contemporary India's most pressing problems.

The majority of travellers follow the well-trodden Ganges route to reach Nepal, perhaps unaware that the Indian Himalayas offer superlative trekking and mountain scenery to rival any in the range. With Kashmir effectively off the tourist map since the escalation of its civil war, Himachal Pradesh – where Dharamsala is the home of a Tibetan community that includes the Dalai Lama himself – and the remote province of Ladakh, with its mysterious lunar landscape and cloud-swept monasteries, have become the major targets for journeys into the mountains. Less visited, but possessing some of Asia's highest peaks, is the niche of

Uttaranchal bordering Nepal, where the glacial source of the sacred River Ganges has attracted pilgrims for over a thousand years. At the opposite end of the chain, Sikkim, north of Bengal, is another low-key trekking destination, harbouring scenery and a Buddhist culture similar to that of neighbouring Bhutan. The Northeast Hill States, connected to eastern India by a slender neck of land, boast remarkably diverse landscapes and an incredible fifty percent of India's biodiversity.

Heading south from Calcutta along the coast, your first likely stop is Konarak in Orissa, site of the famous Sun Temple, a giant carved pyramid of stone that lay submerged under sand until its rediscovery at the start of the twentieth century. Tamil Nadu, further south, has its own tradition of magnificent architecture, with towering *gopura* gateways dominating towns whose vast temple complexes are still the focus of everyday life. Of them all, Madurai, in the far south, is the most stunning, but you could spend months wandering between the sacred sites of the Cauvery Delta and the fragrant Nilgiri Hills, draped in the tea terraces that have become the hallmark of South Indian landscapes. Kerala, near the southernmost tip of the subcontinent on the western coast, is India at its most tropical and relaxed, lush backwaters teeming

Spices

Aromatic herbs and seeds, whole or ground into fine powders, have been essential flavouring agents in India for several thousand years, and today Indians still like their food hot and spicy. Even an innocuous samosa can knock your block off in the land of a myriad masalas (spices). That said, the subtlety and variety of Indian cuisine may come as a revelation to aficionados of British curry houses.

One thing travellers to India rarely complain about is the food, which is invariably delicious, available fresh in the most unlikely places and, in spite of what you may have heard, generally healthy.

The Eating section on p.55 tells you all you need to know before you tuck in.

Indian railways

India's railways, which daily transport millions of commuters, pilgrims, animals, and hessian-wrapped packages between the four corners of the subcontinent, are often cited as the best thing the British Raj bequeathed to its former colony. And yet, with its hierarchical legion of clerks, cooks, *coolis*, bearers, ticket inspectors, stations managers and ministers, the network has become a quintessentially Indian institution. Travelling across India by rail – whether you rough it in dirt-cheap second-class, or pamper yourself with starched cotton sheets and hot meals in an air-con carriage – is likely to yield some of the most memorable moments of your trip. Open around the clock, the stations in themselves are often great places to watch the world go by, with hundreds of people from all walks of life eating, sleeping, buying and selling, regardless of the hour. This is also where you'll grow familiar with one of the unforgettable sounds of the subcontinent: the robotic drone of the chai-wallah, dispensing two-rupee cups of hot, sweet tea. For the practical low-down on train travel see p.41.

with simple wooden craft of all shapes and sizes, and red-roofed towns and villages all but invisible beneath a canopy of palm trees. Further up the coast is Goa, the former Portuguese colony whose hundred-kilometre coastline is fringed with beaches to suit all tastes and budgets, from upmarket package tourists to long-staying backpackers, and whose towns hold whitewashed Christian churches that might have been transplanted from Europe.

North of here sits Mumbai, an ungainly beast that has been the major focus of the nationwide drift to the big cities. Centre of the country's formidable popular movie industry, it reels along on an undeniable energy that, after a few days of acclimatization, can prove addictive. Beyond Mumbai is the state of Gujarat, renowned for the unique culture and crafts of the barren Kutch region. Traditionally the wealthiest state in India, Gujarat was ravaged by an earthquake in 2001 that killed around thirty thousand people and virtually destroyed the ancient town of Bhuj.

Some of India's most memorable monuments lie far inland, on long-forgotten trading routes across the heart of the peninsula – the abandoned city of Vijayanagar (or Hampi) in Karnataka, whose ruins are scattered across a primeval boulder-strewn landscape; the painted and sculpted Buddhist caves of Ajanta and Ellora in Maharashtra; the erotic temples of Khajuraho and palaces of Orchha in Madhya Pradesh.

> **Some of India's most memorable monuments lie far inland, on long-forgotten trading routes across the heart of the peninsula**

On a long trip, it makes sense to pause and rest every few weeks. Certain places have fulfilled that function for generations, such as the Himalayan resort of Manali, epicentre of India's hashish-producing area, and the many former colonial hill stations that dot the country, from Ootacamund (Ooty), in the far south, to that archetypal British retreat, Simla, immortalized in the writing of Rudyard Kipling. Elsewhere, the combination of sand and the sea, and a picturesque rural or religious backdrop – such as at Varkala in Kerala, Gokarna in Karnataka, and the remoter beaches of Goa – are usually enough to loosen even the tightest itineraries.

When to go

ndia's weather is extremely varied, something you must take into account when planning your trip. The most influential feature of the subcontinent's climate is the wet season, or monsoon. This breaks on the Keralan coast at the end of May, working its way northeast across the country over the following month and a half. While it lasts, regular and prolonged downpours are interspersed with bursts of hot sunshine, and the pervasive humidity can be intense. At the height of the monsoon – especially in the jungle regions of the northwest and the low-lying delta lands of Bengal – flooding can severely disrupt communications, causing widespread

destruction. In the Himalayan foothills, landslides are common, and entire valley systems can be cut off for weeks.

By September, the monsoon has largely receded from the north, but it takes another couple of months before the clouds disappear altogether from the far south. The east coast of Andhra Pradesh and Tamil Nadu, and the south of Kerala, get a second drenching between October and December, when the "northwest" or "retreating" monsoon sweeps in from the Bay of Bengal. By December, however, most of the subcontinent enjoys clear skies and relatively cool temperatures.

The International boundaries on this map are neither purported to be correct nor authentic by Survey of India directives. Publisher.

Mid-winter sees the most marked contrasts between the climates of north and south India. While Delhi, for example, may be ravaged by chill winds blowing off the snowfields of the Himalayas, the Tamil plains and coastal Kerala, more than 1000km south, still stew under fierce post-monsoon sunshine. As spring gathers pace, the centre of the subcontinent starts to heat up again, and by late March thermometers nudge 33°C across most of the Gangetic Plains and Deccan plateau. Temperatures peak in May and early June, when anyone who can retreats to the hill stations. Above the baking subcontinental land mass, hot air builds up and sucks in humidity from the southwest, causing the onset of the monsoon in late June, and bringing relief to millions of overheated Indians.

The best time to visit most of the country, therefore, is during the cool, dry season, between November and March. Delhi, Agra, Varanasi and the northern states, including Rajasthan and Madhya Pradesh, are ideal at this time, and temperatures in Goa and central India remain comfortable. The heat of the south is never less than intense but it becomes stifling in May and June, so aim

to be in Tamil Nadu and Kerala between January and March. From this time onwards, the Himalayas grow more accessible, and the trekking season reaches its peak in August and September while the rest of the subcontinent is being soaked by the rains.

Average temperature and rainfall

	Jan	Feb	Mar	Apr	May	June	July	Aug	Sept	Oct	Nov	Dec
Ahmedabad (Guj)												
Av daily max (°C)	29	31	36	40	41	38	33	32	33	36	33	30
Rainfall (mm)	4	0	1	2	5	100	316	213	163	13	5	1
Bangalore (Kar)												
Av daily max (°C)	28	31	33	34	33	30	28	29	28	28	27	27
Rainfall (mm)	4	14	6	37	119	65	93	95	129	195	46	16
Calcutta (WB)												
Av daily max (°C)	26	29	34	36	36	34	32	32	32	31	29	27
Rainfall (mm)	13	22	30	50	135	263	320	318	253	134	29	4
Chennai (TN)												
Av daily max (°C)	29	31	33	35	38	37	35	35	34	32	29	28
Rainfall (mm)	24	7	15	25	52	53	83	124	118	267	309	139
Darjeeling (WB)												
Av daily max (°C)	9	11	15	18	19	19	20	20	20	19	15	12
Rainfall (mm)	22	27	52	109	187	522	713	573	419	116	14	5
Delhi												
Av daily max (°C)	21	24	30	36	41	40	35	34	34	35	29	23
Rainfall (mm)	25	22	17	7	8	65	211	173	150	31	1	5
Hyderabad (AP)												
Av daily max (°C)	29	31	35	37	39	34	30	29	30	30	29	28
Rainfall (mm)	2	11	13	24	30	107	165	147	163	71	25	5
Jaisalmer (Raj)												
Av daily max (°C)	24	28	33	38	42	41	38	36	36	36	31	26
Rainfall (mm)	2	1	3	1	5	7	89	86	14	1	5	2
Kochi (Ker)												
Av daily max (°C)	31	31	31	31	31	29	28	28	28	29	30	30
Rainfall (mm)	9	34	50	139	364	756	572	386	235	333	184	37
Mumbai (M)												
Av daily max (°C)	31	32	33	33	33	32	30	29	30	32	33	32
Rainfall (mm)	0	1	0	0	20	647	945	660	309	17	7	1
Panjim (Goa)												
Av daily max (°C)	31	32	32	33	33	31	29	29	29	31	33	33
Rainfall (mm)	2	0	4	17	18	580	892	341	277	122	20	37
Puri (Ori)												
Av daily max (°C)	27	28	30	31	32	31	31	31	31	31	29	27
Rainfall (mm)	9	20	14	12	63	187	296	256	258	242	75	8
Shimla (HP)												
Av daily max (°C)	9	10	14	19	23	24	21	20	20	18	15	11
Rainfall (mm)	65	48	58	38	54	147	415	385	195	45	7	24
Varanasi (UP)												
Av daily max (°C)	23	27	33	39	41	39	33	32	32	32	29	25
Rainfall (mm)	23	8	14	1	8	102	346	240	261	38	15	2

40

things not to miss

It's not possible to see everything that India has to offer in one trip – and we don't suggest you try. What follows is a selective taste of the country's highlights: outstanding buildings, natural wonders, spectacular festivals and unforgettable journeys. They're arranged alphabetically in five colour-coded categories, which you can browse through to find the very best things to see and experience. All highlights have a page reference to take you straight into the guide, where you can find out more.

01 **Ajanta caves** Page **813** • Extraordinarily beautiful murals, dating from 200 BC to 650 AD, adorn the walls of caves chiselled into basalt cliffs.

02 **Amritsar** Page **656** • Site of the fabled Golden Temple, the Sikhs' holiest shrine.

03 **Ashrams** Page **383** • Brush up on your yoga and meditation in the holy town of Rishikesh on the Ganges, where the Beatles came to meet Maharishi Yogi.

04 **Bandhavgarh National Park** Page **492** • Deep in the eastern tracts of Madhya Pradesh, this park is rich in animal and birdlife, including tigers and leopards.

05 **Boating on the backwaters of Kerala** Page **1326** • Lazy boat trips wind through the lush tropical waterways of India's deep south.

06 Camel trekking in the Thar Page **236** • A wonderfully romantic if utterly touristy way to experience the Great Indian Desert. Most visitors trek out of Jaisalmer, but Bikaner offers more variety.

07 Chauragarh Mountain, Pachmarhi Page **445** • Thousands of Shivaite tridents are carried by pilgrims to the summit of this holy peak, from where the views are stupendous.

08 Cricket Page **70** • The nation's favourite sport is played everywhere, from the Oval Maidan in Mumbai to Eden Gardens in Calcutta, the hot cauldron of Indian cricket.

09 Dharamsala Page **542** • Perched on the edge of the Himalayas, this is the home of the Dalai Lama and Tibetan Buddhism in exile.

10 Durga Puja Page **69** • An exuberant festival held in September or October, when every street and village erects a shrine to the goddess Durga. Calcutta has the most lavish festivities.

11 Ellora caves Page **805** • Buddhist, Hindu and Jain caves, and the colossal Hindu Kailash temple, carved from a spectacular volcanic ridge at the heart of the Deccan plateau.

12 Fatehpur Sikri Page **303** • The Moghul Emperor Akbar's elegant palace complex now lies deserted on a ridge near Agra, but remains one of India's architectural masterpieces.

13 **Gangotri** Page **390** ● An atmospheric village on the Ganges that serves as a base for the trek into the heart of the Hindu faith – Gomukh, the source of the Ganges.

15 **Hampi/Vijayanagar** Page **1442** Deserted capital of the last great Hindu empire, scattered over a bizarre landscape of giant golden-brown boulders.

14 **Gokarn** Page **1435** ● The beautiful beaches on the edge of this temple town are popular with budget travellers fleeing the commercialism of nearby Goa.

16 **Jaisalmer** Page **229** • Honey-coloured citadel, emerging from the sands of the Thar Desert.

17 **Keoladeo National Park, Bharatpur** Page **202** • Asia's most famous bird reserve, where millions of migrants nest each winter. The perfect antidote to the frenzy and pollution of nearby Agra and Jaipur.

18 **Kathakali** Page **1355** • Kerala is the place to experience Kathakali and other esoteric ritual theatre forms.

19 **Kaziranga National Park** Page **1052** • Take a dawn elephant ride as the mists slowly lift: sightings of the one-horned rhino, symbol of Assam, are virtually guaranteed.

20 Khajuraho
Page **468** ●
Immaculately preserved temples renowned for their uncompromisingly erotic carvings.

21 **Kochi** Page **1343** ● The Keralan capital's atmospheric harbourside is strung with elegant Chinese fishing nets.

22 **Konarak** Page **1120** ● A colossal thirteenth-century temple, buried under sand until its rediscovery by the British.

23 **Madurai** Page **1256** ● Definitive South Indian city, centred on a spectacular medieval temple.

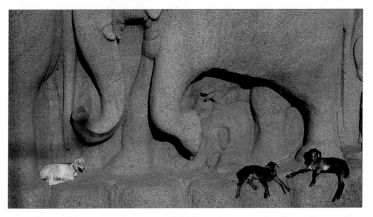

24 **Mamallapuram** Page **1211** • A fishing and stone-carving village, with magnificent boulder friezes, shrines and the sea-battered Shore Temple.

25 **Manali–Leh Highway**
Page **587** • India's epic Himalayan road trip, along the second-highest road in the world.

26 **Movies** Page **778** • Take in the latest Bollywood blockbuster at one of Mumbai's mega movie houses, which feature huge screens, wrap-around sound and rowdy audiences.

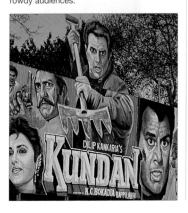

27 **Meherangarh Fort, Jodhpur** Page **224** • The epitome of Rajput power and extravagance, its ramparts towering above a labyrinthine, blue-painted old city.

28 Mysore market Page **1402** • Jaggery, incense and garlands are made and veggies and kitsch paraphernalia are sold in Mysore's covered market.

29 Palolem Page **908** • Exquisite crescent-shaped beach in Goa's relaxed south, famous for its dolphins and local alcoholic spirit, feni.

30 Pushkar camel mela Page **218** • November sees the largest livestock market on earth, where 200,000 Rajasthani herders in traditional costume converge on the desert oasis of Pushkar to trade and bathe in the sacred lake.

31 Rafting on the Indus Page **612** • A relatively sedate way to enjoy the grandiose scenery of the northwest Himalaya's most spectacular high-altitude valley.

32 Rajasthani handicrafts

Page **170** • The teeming bazaars of the Pink City in Jaipur burst with vibrant cloth, jewellry, Persian-style pottery and semi-precious stones. Simply the best place to shop in the subcontinent.

33 Rath Yatra, Puri Page 1114

• Three colossal chariots with brightly coloured canopies are pulled by crowds of devotees through the streets of eastern India's holiest town.

34 Taj Mahal Page 289 • Simply the world's greatest building: Shah Jahan's monument to love fully lives up to all expectations.

35 Thrissur Puram

Page **1362** • More than one hundred sumptuously caparisoned elephants march in Kerala's biggest temple festival, accompanied by ear-shattering South Indian drum orchestras.

xxiii

36 Tikse Page **614** • One of many dramatic monasteries within striking distance of Leh.

37 Udaipur Page **256** • Arguably the most romantic city in India, with ornate Rajput palaces floating in the middle of two shimmering lakes.

38 Varanasi Page **340** • City of Light, founded by Shiva, where the bathing ghats beside the Ganges teem with pilgrims.

39 Varkala Page **1317** • Kerala's low-key alternative to Kovalam boasts sheer red cliffs, amazing sea views and a legion of Ayurvedic masseurs.

40 Zanskar Page **636** • A barren moonscape with extraordinary scenery and challenging trails over the high passes.

contents

using the Rough Guide

We've tried to make this Rough Guide a good read and easy to use. The book is divided into five main sections, and you should be able to find whatever you want in one of them.

front section

The front colour section offers a quick tour of India. The **introduction** aims to give you a feel for the place, with suggestions on where to go. We also tell you what the weather is like and include a basic country fact file. Next, our authors round up their favourite aspects of India in the **things not to miss** section – whether it's a great market, an amazing sight or a dramatic festival. Right after this comes the Rough Guide's full **contents** list.

basics

You've decided to go and the Basics section covers all the **pre-departure** nitty-gritty to help you plan your trip. This is where to find out which airlines fly to your destination, what paperwork you'll need, what to do about money and insurance, about internet access, food, security, public transport, car rental – in fact just about every piece of **general practical information** you might need.

guide

This is the heart of the Rough Guide, divided into user-friendly chapters, each of which covers a specific region. Every chapter starts with a list of **highlights** and an **introduction** that helps you to decide where to go, depending on your time and budget.

Likewise, introductions to the various towns and smaller regions within each chapter should help you plan your itinerary. We start most town accounts with information on arrival and accommodation, followed by a tour of the sights, and finally reviews of places to eat and drink, and details of nightlife. Longer accounts also have a directory of practical listings. Each chapter concludes with **public transport** details for that region.

contexts

Read Contexts to get a deeper understanding of what makes India tick. We include a brief **history**, articles about **development** and **music** among other topics, a detailed further reading section that reviews dozens of **books** relating to the country, a **language** section which gives useful guidance for speaking Hindi, and a glossary of words and terms that are peculiar to the country.

index + small print

Apart from a **full index**, which includes maps as well as places, this section covers publishing information, credits and acknowledgements, and also has our contact details in case you want to send in updates and corrections to the book – or suggestions as to how we might improve it.

contents ▶

basics ▶

guide ▶

1 Delhi **2** Rajasthan **3** Uttar Pradesh **4** Uttaranchal **5** Madhya Pradesh
6 Himachal Pradesh **7** Ladakh **8** Haryana and Punjab **9** Gujarat **10** Mumbai
11 Maharashtra **12** Goa **13** Calcutta and West Bengal **14** Bihar and Jharkhand
15 Sikkim **16** The Northeast **17** Orissa **18** Andhra Pradesh **19** The Andaman Islands
20 Tamil Nadu **21** Kerala **22** Karnataka

contexts ▶

index ▶

chapter map of **India**

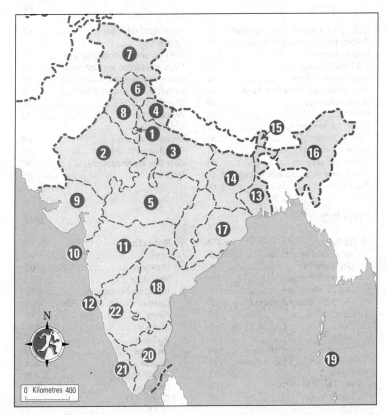

N

0 Kilometres 400

contents

colour section

i–xxiv

Colour map ii
Where to go vii
When to go xi
40 things not to miss xiv

basics

9

Getting there from Britain and Ireland ..11
Getting there from North America 16
Getting there from Australia
& New Zealand 20
Visas and red tape 22
Information, websites and maps 24
Travel insurance 28
Health 29
Costs, money and banks 37
Getting around 41
Accommodation 51
Eating and drinking 54
Telephones, mail and internet access 64
The media 66
Festivals and holidays 67
Sports 70
Trekking and outdoor pursuits 71
Yoga, meditation and ashrams 74
Crime and personal safety 76
Cultural hints and etiquette 78
Shopping 81
Women travellers 85
Gay travellers 87
Disabled travellers 88
Travelling with children 89
Voluntary organizations 90
Directory 91

guide

93

❶ Delhi   96–156
Arrival and information 103
City transport 105
Accommodation 151
Central New Delhi 114
Old Delhi (Shahjahanabad) 123
South Delhi 130
Eating 138
Shopping 142
Nightlife and entertainment 146
Sports and outddoor activities ..148
Listings 148
Moving on from Delhi 152
Travel details 156

❷ Rajasthan   158–279
Jaipur 167
Shekhawati 186
Bharatpur 201
Keoladeo National Park 202
Ranthambore National Park 205
Ajmer 208
Pushkar 215
Jodhpur 221
Jaisalmer 229
Bikaner 242
Mount Abu 249
Udaipur 256
Chittaurgarh 271

Kota 274
Bundi 276
Travel details 279

❸ Uttar Pradesh   280–363
Agra 283
Fatehpur Sikri 303
Mathura 310
Vrindavan 314
Kanpur 316
Lucknow 318
Ayodhya 327
Allahabad 329
Jhansi 335
Varanasi 340
Sarnath 355
Gorakhpur 359
Travel details 362

❹ Uttaranchal   364–419
Garhwal 368
Dehra Dun 369
Mussoorie 373
Haridwar 377
Rishikesh 381
Yamunotri 388
Gangotri 390
The Valley of the Flowers 400
Nanda Devi Sanctuary 401
Kumaon 403
Corbett National Park 407
Travel details 419

❺ Madhya Pradesh   420–513
Bhopal 424
Sanchi 435
Pachmarhi 445
Gwalior 451
Shivpuri 460
Orchha 463
Khajuraho 468
Jabalpur 482
Kanha National Park 489
Bandhavgarh National Park 492
Indore 495
Mandu 500
Ujjain 505
Omkareshwar 510
Travel details 512

❻ Himachal Pradesh   514–589
Shimla 519
Mandi 538
Dharamsala 542
McLeodganj 542
Dalhousie 553

The Kullu valley 559
Kullu 561
The Parvati Valley 564
Nagar 566
Manali 569
Lahaul 581
Spiti 583
The Manali–Leh Highway 587
Travel details 589

❼ Ladakh   590–641
Leh 597
Tikse 614
Hemis 615
Chemrey 616
Thak Thok 617
Nubra Valley 619
Spitok 623
Lamayuru 628
Kargil 631
The Suru Valley 633
Zanskar 636
Travel details 640

❽ Haryana and Punjab   643–665
Chandigarh 646
Pathankot 656
Amritsar 656
Travel details 665

❾ Gujarat   666–737
Ahmedabad 672
Kutch 690
Bhuj 692
Saurashtra 698
Jamnagar 701
Dwarka 704
Porbandar 705
Junagadh 708
Somnath 713
Gir National Park 714
Diu 715
Bhavnagar 720
Palitana 723
Vadodara (Baroda) 725
Champaner 729
Travel details 736

❿ Mumbai   738–786
Arrival and information 745
City transport 748
Accommodation 750
Colaba 754
Downtown Mumbai 757
Marine Drive and Chowpatty
  Beach 762

Malabar Hill 764
The central bazaars 767
Elephanta 769
Uptown and the outskirts 770
Eating 773
Nightlife and entertainment 776
Shopping 779
Listings 781
Moving on from Mumbai 783
Travel details 786

⑪ **Maharashtra**   788–851
Aurangabad 793
Daulatabad 801
Ellora 805
Ajanta 813
Lonar 821
Nasik 823
Nagpur 828
Matheran 833
Pune (Poona) 840
Kolhapur 849
Travel details 851

⑫ **Goa**   852–916
Panjim 860
Old Goa 868
Ponda 872
Candolim 875
Calangute 879
Baga 883
Anjuna 885
Vagator 889
Chapora 893
Vasco da Gama 897
Margao (Madgaon) 898
Colva 902
Benaulim 904
Canacona 908
Palolem 908
Travel details 917

⑬ **Calcutta and West
   Bengal**   918–991
Arrival and information 927
City transport 929
Accommodation 932
The Maidan, New Market
   and the Park Street area 935
Central Calcutta 939
North Calcutta 941
Howrah and the River Hooghly 943
South Calcutta...........................945
East Calcutta 947
Eating and drinking 948
Culture and entertainment 951

Shopping 952
Sports 954
Listings 954
The Sunderbans
Tiger Reserve 961
Siliguri and New Jalpaiguri 969
Jaldapara Wildlife Sanctuary 973
Darjeeling 973
Ghoom 985
Kalimpong 986
Travel details 990

⑭ **Bihar and Jharkhand**..992–1013
Patna 995
The road to Nepal 1001
Bodhgaya 1003
Jharkhand 1011
Ranchi 1011
Travel details 1013

⑮ **Sikkim**   1014–1039
Gangtok 1019
Rumtek 1027
Ghezing 1030
Pemayangtse 1031
Pelling 1033
Travel details 1039

⑯ **The Northeast**   1040–1087
Assam 1044
Meghalaya 1060
Tripura 1067
Mizoram 1071
Manipur 1074
Arunachal Pradesh 1077
Nagaland 1083
Travel details 1087

⑰ **Orissa**   1088–1135
Bhubaneswar 1092
Dhauli 1106
Puri 1107
Konarak 1120
Cuttack 1125
Travel details 1135

⑱ **Andhra Pradesh**   1136–1159
Hyderabad and Secunderabad 1138
Warangal 1148
Nagarjunakonda 1149
Vijayawada 1151
Tirupati 1154
Travel details 1158

⑲ The Andaman Islands 1160–1185

Port Blair 1168
Madhuban 1176
Neill 1177
Havelock 1177
Long Island 1178
Middle Andaman 1179
Interview Island 1180
North Andaman 1181
Smith Island 1182
Cinque Island 1184
Barren Island 1184
Little Andaman 1184
Travel details 1185

⑳ Tamil Nadu 1186–1291

Chennai 1191
Mamallapuram (Mahabalipuram) 1211
Kanchipuram 1222
Tiruvannamalai 1226
Pondicherry 1229
Auroville 1234
Chidambaram 1236
Kumbakonam 1239
Gangaikondacholapuram 1243
Thanjavur 1244
Tiruchirapalli 1252
Madurai 1256
Rameshwaram 1269
Kanniyakumari 1272
The Ghats 1274
Kodaikanal 1274
Coimbatore 1279
Coonoor 1281
Udhagamandalam
  (Ootacamund) 1283
Mudumalai Wildlife Sanctuary 1288
Travel details 1289

㉑ Kerala 1292–1379

Thiruvananthapuram 1297
Kovalam 1305
Varkala 1317
Kollam (Quilon) 1321
Karunagapalli 1324
Alappuzha 1324
Kottayam 1330
Periyar Wildlife Sanctuary 1334
Kumily 1337
The Cardamom Hills 1339
Munnar 1340
Kochi (Cochin) 1343
Fort Cochin 1351
Ernakulam 1353
Thripunitra 1353
Thrissur 1358
Kozhikode (Calicut) 1372
Lakshadweep 1376
Travel details 1378

㉒ Karnataka 1380–1468

Bangalore 1385
Mysore 1398
Bandipur National Park 1409
Nagarhole National Park 1410
Hassan 1411
Halebid 1413
Belur 1416
Sravanabelgola 1417
Kodagu (Coorg) 1420
Madikeri (Mercara) 1422
Mangalore 1426
Udupi 1431
Jog Falls 1433
Gokarn 1436
Hospet 1439
Hampi (Vijayanagar) 1442
Badami 1452
Aihole 1455
Bijapur 1457
Travel details 1468

contexts

1469–1579

History 1471
Religion 1504
Indian women 1524
Wildlife 1531
Development and green issues 1541

Music 1549
Books 1561
Language 1569
Glossary 1573

map symbols

Maps are listed in the full index using coloured text.

REGIONAL MAPS

- Main road
- Minor road
- Railway
- Track/trail
- Coastline/river
- Ferry
- International boundary
- State boundary
- Chapter boundary
- Mountains
- Peak
- Rocks
- Cave
- Pass
- Waterfall
- Viewpoint
- Airport
- Point of interest
- Church
- Bugyal
- Hut
- Lighthouse
- Palm trees
- Mudflats
- Marshland
- Glacier
- Forest
- Beach

STREET MAPS

- Main road
- Secondary road
- Railway
- Track
- Steps
- Path
- Wall
- Tourist office
- Post office
- Internet access
- Statue
- Petrol station
- Hospital
- Bus/taxi stand
- Metro/underground station
- Stadium
- Accommodation
- Restaurant
- Building
- Church
- Cemetery

COMMON SYMBOLS

- Mosque/Muslim monument
- Buddhist temple
- Hindu/Jain temple
- Haveli
- Palace
- Ghat
- Park

basics

basics

Getting there from Britain and Ireland 11

Getting there from North America 16

Getting there from Australia & New Zealand 20

Visas and red tape 22

Information, websites and maps 24

Travel insurance 28

Health..29

Costs, money and banks...37

Getting around 41

Accommodation..51

Eating and drinking...54

Telephones, mail and internet access 64

The media 66

Festivals and holidays...67

Sports..70

Trekking and outdoor pursuits..71

Yoga, meditation and ashrams 74

Crime and personal safety..76

Cultural hints and etiquette...78

Shopping...81

Women travellers 85

Gay travellers 87

Disabled travellers..88

Travelling with children...89

Voluntary organizations..90

Directory..91

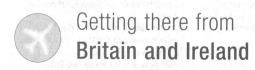

Getting there from Britain and Ireland

British Airways and Air India fly nonstop from Britain to Delhi and Mumbai (Bombay), and fly direct to Chennai (Madras), Calcutta and Ahmedabad; feeder flights from Air India and the extensive domestic airline network can link you to any number of Indian cities. Discounted return fares on these vary from just under £450 in low season (roughly Jan–June, except Easter, & Nov) to upwards of £600 in high season (July, Aug & Dec).

A cheaper option is to take an **indirect flight** which involves a change of plane and inevitably takes a few hours longer, though the airline may also allow you the option of a stopover, usually going via their national hub, on the way out or back. Cheaper fares – down to as little as £320 return out of season – can usually be found on indirect flights with airlines such as Aeroflot, Tarom, Air Uzbekistan, or Syrian Arab Airlines. However, these flights can involve tedious and inconvenient changes of planes, long waits and, on rare occasions, multi-day stopovers. Passengers have been known to be stranded for days on these airlines (as well as others like Air India), waiting for a seat on the return flight, so confirm your return departure as soon as possible – at least three days in advance. For more comfort try Gulf Air, Royal Jordanian, Emirates or Royal Brunei.

For short stays only, there are also ever-increasing numbers of **charter flights to Goa**. However you go, though, be sure to shop around, as prices can vary wildly between agents.

Flights from regional airports and Ireland

No direct flights to India are available from regional **British airports**. From Manchester, your best bet is to fly with Emirates or Gulf Air to Delhi or Mumbai via Dubai for £420–550, depending on season. You can also pick up KLM flights to India by flying first to Amsterdam; either fly KLM from Belfast, Birmingham, Bristol, Cardiff or Manchester (for the same price as from London), or KLM

UK from Aberdeen, Edinburgh, Glasgow, Humberside, Leeds/Bradford, Norwich, or Newcastle. Similarly, Air France flies to Paris from Birmingham, Bristol, Edinburgh and Glasgow; in general, both KLM and Air France beat BA by £50–100, with return tickets often discounted to as low as £420.

There are no direct flights to India **from Ireland**. Apart from BA via London, **Dublin** is also served by KLM via Amsterdam, Air France via Paris and Swissair via Zurich. The best high-season fare to Mumbai or Delhi is around IR£600. Royal Jordanian is by far the best deal from Ireland with a flight out of **Shannon** in low season for IR£350 return (rising to IR£700 in high season). Aeroflot's daily flight from Shannon, at around IR£500 all year round, is another cheap alternative.

Airlines and agents in Britain and Ireland

As well as the agents listed below, check out the travel supplements of national papers, regional listings magazines and the *Evening Standard* in London and free giveaways like *TNT*. The web is also a good source: try ⊛ www.ebookers.com, ⊛ www.travelocity.co.uk, ⊛ www.expedia.co.uk and ⊛ www.deckchair.com.

Aeroflot ☏ 020/7355 2233, ⊛ www.aeroflot.com. Some of the cheapest fares around but you will have to change at Moscow for flights to Delhi, which are nearly always full, and Calcutta.

Air France ☏ 0845/0845 111, ⊛ www.airfrance.fr. Fly to Paris and change for flights to Delhi and Mumbai. Competitively priced efficiency if you shop around.

Air India ☏ 020/8560 9996 or 8745 1000, ⊛ www.airindia.com. Nonstop flights to Delhi and

Mumbai and a feeder network to Chennai, Bangalore and Ahmedabad and other Indian cities; the Calcutta connection involves a long wait in Mumbai.

Air Lanka, ☏ 020/7930 4688,
ⓦ www.airlanka.com. A good and reasonably priced airline for those going to south India. Change at Colombo for flights to Chennai, Tiruchirapalli and Thiruvananthapuram (Trivandrum).

Biman Bangladesh Airlines ☏ 020/7629 0252. Cheap flights especially suitable for those travelling to Calcutta, but you'll have to change at Dhaka.

British Airways London ☏ 020/7828 4895 (all enquiries ☏ 0845/722 2111.
ⓦ www.britishairways.com. Not many bargains but the advantage of direct flights to Delhi (daily), Mumbai (daily), Chennai (thrice weekly) and Calcutta (weekly).

Egyptair ☏ 020/7734 2395. A little-used but cheap option with a fare that doesn't fluctuate seasonally; stop over in Cairo for an extra £100 or so.

Emirates Airlines ☏ 0870/243 2222
ⓦ www.emirates.com. Good connections through Dubai to Delhi, Mumbai and Kerala.

Gulf Air ☏ 020/7408 1717, ⓦ www.gulfairco.com. Popular and reasonably priced flights with connections from Manchester and London through Muscat, Bahrain and Abu Dhabi to Mumbai, Delhi and Kerala.

KLM Royal Dutch Airlines ☏ 08705/074 074, ⓦ www.klm.com. An excellent service to Delhi, Mumbai and Calcutta with a change in Amsterdam, but it's not cheap.

KLM UK ☏ 08705/074 074, ⓦ www.klmuk.com. KLM recently bought Air UK, and the new KLM UK flies from virtually all British airports to a variety of European destinations; change in Amsterdam for KLM flights to India.

Lufthansa ☏ 0845/773 7747,
ⓦ www.lufthansa.co.uk. Efficient connections through Frankfurt to Delhi and Mumbai.

Pakistan International Airlines (PIA)
☏ 020/7499 5500, ⓦ www.fly-pia.com. Change in Karachi for connections to Delhi and Mumbai.

Royal Brunei Airlines ☏ 020/7584 6660, ⓦ www.bruneiair.com. Some cheap tickets through discount agents on this good airline with a stop in the Gulf and connections to Delhi and Calcutta.

Royal Jordanian ☏ 020/7878 6341,
ⓦ www.rja.com.jo. Very reasonably priced airline with connections from Shannon and London through Amman to Delhi (thrice weekly), Mumbai (twice weekly) and Calcutta (one a week). Some

return flights involve an all-inclusive stopover in Amman.

Swissair Swiss Centre ☏ 020/7434 7300,
ⓦ www.swissair.com. Good for connections through Zurich to Delhi and Mumbai.

Syrian Arab Airlines ☏ 020/7493 2851
A cheap flight with connections through Damascus to Delhi.

Tarom Romanian Airlines ☏ 020/7224 3693, ⓦ www.tarom.digirow.net. Cheap, indirect flights through Bucharest.

Thai International ☏ 0870/606 0911,
ⓦ www.thaiair.com. A highly reputed airline with connections to India through Bangkok; not cheap but attractive if you want to take in Thailand as well.

Virgin Atlantic Airways ☏ 01293/747747, ⓦ www.virgin-atlantic.com. In conjunction with Air India, with two direct flights a week to Delhi (Wed & Fri).

United Airlines ☏ 0845 8444 777,
ⓦ www.unitedairlines.co.uk. Daily flights leaving Heathrow every morning for Delhi, with connections from Manchester, Edinburgh, Glasgow, Leeds/Bradford, Dublin and Belfast.

Air Uzbekistan 72 Wigmore St, London W1
☏ 020/7935 1899,
ⓦ www.uzbekistanairways.com. Flights to Tashkent and then change for Delhi and Amritsar. Reasonably priced but not as cheap as Aeroflot. Book through their agent HY Travel ☏ 020/7935 4775.

Discount agents

The best deals on tickets to India are normally to be found through **discount agents**, who sell off excess seats for airlines at rock-bottom prices. Some of these (such as STA, Usit Campus, and Trailfinders) specialize in youth and student travel.

Smaller agents, or **bucket shops**, also known as "consolidators", generally offer unbeatable prices, but are not always reliable. It's best to use a company that's a member of ATOL, as this guarantees you a refund if the company goes bust. At the very least, ensure you get a printed receipt with your full travel itinerary as soon as you pay for your ticket.

At certain times (Christmas for one), the best-value flights can get booked up weeks, even months, in advance, so plan ahead.

Discount agents in Britain and Ireland

Arrowguide Ltd 29 Dering St, London W1 ☎020/7629 9516, ⊛www.arrowguide.co.uk. A long-established and reliable consolidator that specializes in cheap flights to Asia.

Bridge the World, 47 Chalk Farm Rd, London NW1 8AN ☎020/7911 0900, ⊛www.bridgetheworld.com. Specializing in round-the-world tickets, with good deals aimed at the backpacker market.

Flightbookers, 177–178 Tottenham Court Rd, London W1P 0LX ☎020/7757 2444, ⊛www.ebookers.com. Low fares on an extensive offering of scheduled flights.

The London Flight Centre
⊛www.topdecktravel.co.uk. 131 Earls Court Rd, London SW5 9RH ☎020/7244 6411; 47 Notting Hill Gate, London W11 3JS ☎020/7727 4290; Shop 33, The Broadway Centre, Hammersmith tube, London W6 9YE ☎020/8748 6777. Long-established agent dealing in discount flights.

North South Travel, Moulsham Mill Centre, Parkway, Chelmsford, Essex CM2 7PX ☎&℻ 01245/608 291, ⊛www.northsouthtravel.co.uk. Friendly, competitive travel agency, offering discounted fares worldwide – profits are used to support projects in the developing world, especially the promotion of sustainable tourism.

STA Travel London call centre worldwide ☎020/7361 6144, northern call centre ☎0161/830 4713, ⊛www.statravel.co.uk; 86 Old Brompton Rd, London SW7 3LH; 117 Euston Rd, London NW1 2SX; 38 Store St, London WC1E 7BZ; 11 Goodge St, London W1P; 38 North St, Brighton ☎01273/728 282; 25 Queens Rd, Bristol BS8 1QE ☎0117/929 4399; 38 Sidney St, Cambridge CB2 3HX ☎01223/366 966; 75 Deansgate, Manchester M3 2BW ☎0161/834 0668; 88 Vicar Lane, Leeds LS1 7JH ☎0113/244 9212; 78 Bold Street, Liverpool L1 4HR ☎0151/707 1123; 9 St Mary's Place, Newcastle-upon-Tyne NE1 7PG ☎0191/233 2111; 36 George St, Oxford OX1 2OJ ☎01865/792 800; 27 Forrest Rd. Edinburgh ☎0131/226 7747; 184 Byres Rd, Glasgow G1 1JH ☎0141/338 6000; 30 Upper Kirkgate, Aberdeen ☎0122/465 8222; plus over 40 branches including on many university campuses. Worldwide specialists in low-cost flights and tours for students and under-26s, though other customers welcome. Also over 200 offices abroad.

Trailfinders ⊛www.trailfinders.co.uk; 1 Threadneedle St, London EC2R 8JX ☎020/7628 7628; 42–50 Earls Court Rd, London W8 6FT

☎020/7938 3366; 194 Kensington High St, London, W8 7RG ☎020/7938 3939; 58 Deansgate, Manchester M3 2FF ☎0161/839 6969; 254–284 Sauchiehall St, Glasgow G2 3EH ☎0141/353 2224; 22–24 The Priory Queensway, Birmingham B4 6BS ☎0121/236 1234; 48 Corn St, Bristol BS1 1HQ ☎0117/929 9000. One of the best-informed and most efficient agents for independent travellers; they produce a very useful quarterly magazine worth scrutinizing for round-the-world routes (for free copy call ☎020/7938 3366); all branches open daily until 6pm, Thurs until 7pm.

Travel Cuts, 295a Regent St, London W1R 7YA ☎020/7255 2082, ⊛www.travelcuts.co.uk; 229 Great Portland St, W1N 5HD ☎020/7436 0459; 44 Queensway, London, NW2 3RS ☎020/7792 3770. Established in Canada in 1974, Travel Cuts specialize in budget, student and youth travel and round-the-world tickets, with offices in London and abroad.

Usit Campus, national call centre ☎0870/240 1010, ⊛www.usitcampus.co.uk; 52 Grosvenor Gardens, London SW1W 0AG ☎020/7730 8111; 541 Bristol Rd, Selly Oak, Birmingham B29 6AU ☎0121/414 1848; 61 Ditchling Rd, Brighton BN1 4SD ☎01273/570 226; 37–39 Queen's Rd, Clifton, Bristol BS8 1QE ☎0117/929 2494; 5 Emmanuel St, Cambridge CB1 1NE ☎01223/324 283; 53 Forest Rd, Edinburgh EH1 2QP ☎0131/225 6111; 122 George St, Glasgow G1 1RF ☎0141/553 1818; 166 Deansgate, Manchester M3 3FE ☎0161/833 2046, telesales 273 1721; 105–106 St Aldates, Oxford OX1 1DO ☎01865/242 067. Student/youth travel specialists, with 51 branches, including in YHA shops and on university campuses all over Britain.

USIT Now 19-21 Aston Quay, O'Connell Bridge, Dublin 2, Ireland ☎01/602 1700, ⊛www.usitnow.ie. Student and youth specialists for flights and trains, with branches in Belfast, Cork, Galway, Limerick and Waterford.

Charter flights

Various package specialists (see overleaf) operate winter (Oct–May) **charters to Goa and Kerala**. Leaving from Gatwick, Manchester, Glasgow and Newcastle, these are usually for stays of two weeks (though 1–6 weeks are also possible) and often work out cheaper than a standard scheduled deal to Mumbai. Your fare must include some form of accommodation, which you can occupy on arrival and then ditch when you're ready to move on. Charter tickets are generally sold through

13

high-street travel agents, and are also advertised in the travel pages of newspapers.

Packages and organized tours

A large number of operators run **package holidays** to India, covering such activities as trekking and safaris as well as sightseeing and sunbathing. Specialist minority-interest tours range from steam locomotives and war history to religion and food. Even if you book a general sightseeing tour, most firms have a good range of options, usually including the "Golden Triangle" of Delhi, Agra and Jaipur; a tour of Rajasthan; or a southern tour taking in Bangalore, Hyderabad, Chennai and Kochi. Some also offer wildlife tours; the Palace on Wheels train journey (see p.45); take in Nepal or Bhutan; or have various combinations of all these. In addition, many companies will arrange **tailor-made tours**, and can help you plan your own itinerary.

Of course, any package holiday is a lot easier than going under your own steam, particularly if you only have a short time and don't want to use it up on making your own travel bookings. On the other hand, a typical sightseeing tour can rather isolate you from the country, shutting you off in air-conditioned hotels and buses. Specialist trips such as trekking and tailor-made tours will work out rather expensive, compared to what you'd pay if you organized everything independently, but they do cut out a lot of hassle. However, Goa beach holidays, and packages to Kovalam in Kerala, particularly with charter operators, can work out cheaper than a normal flight, and usually offer tour options as extras. One-week packages to Goa including flights and accommodation, for example, are available for around £450 with discounts off season.

Package tour operators to India available through high-street travel agents include the largest tour operator to India, Kuoni Travel (☏01306/742888), Hayes and Jarvis (☏020/8748 5050) and the two Kerala and Goa specialists, Manos (☏020/7216 8070) and Inspirations (☏01293/822244).

Specialist tour operators in Britain

Abercrombie and Kent ☏ 020/7730 9600, 🖳 www.abercrombiekent.com. Upmarket

sightseeing and tailor-made holidays, trekking and wildlife trips.
Asian Journeys ☏ 01604/234401, 🖳 www.asianjourneys.com. Tailor-made itineraries and tours of Varanasi, combined with guided sailing on the Ganges, trips to the Sonepur elephant fair, wildlife safaris and so on.
Chandertal Tours ☏ 01323/422213, 🖳 www.steali.co.uk/chandertal-tours. Flexible and friendly agency, specializing in Himachal Pradesh and Ladakh as well as mahseer fishing holidays; options include trekking and rafting. Great value.
Coromandel ☏ 01572/821330. Car tours, textile trips to village craft workshops, plus David Sayer's botanical and horticultural tours, and Himalaya treks.
Cox & Kings ☏ 020/7873 5000, 🖳 www.coxandkings.com. Tailor-made itineraries with operators established in the days of the Raj.
Discover India ☏ 020/8429 3300 Tailor-made trips including pilgrimages, cricket, golf and football tours and flights.
Essential India ☏ 01225/868544, 🖳 www.essential-india.co.uk. Courses in India on a wide range of subjects, from writing, painting, and pottery to Buddhism and outdoor pursuits, for individuals or groups.
Exodus ☏ 020/8675 5550, 🖳 www.exodustravels.co.uk. Experienced specialists in small group itineraries, treks and overland tours.
Global Link ☏ 020/7409 7766. Gourmet food tours, wildlife as well as standard, budget and tailor-made sightseeing.
High Places ☏ 0114/275 7500, 🖳 www.highplaces.co.uk. Specialists in trekking and mountaineering.
Himalayan Kingdoms Ltd ☏ 01453/844400, 🖳 www.himalayankingdom.co.uk. Trekking in Sikkim, Garhwal, Himachal Pradesh, Ladakh and Arunachal Pradesh, and trekking and rafting in Zanskar.
Indian Encounters ☏ 01929/481421. Theme tours including golf, painting, textiles, plus camel safaris and tailor-made itineraries.
Kambala ☏ 01803/732488. One of the few operators specializing in tours for the over-50s. General sightseeing and hobby holidays (textiles and painting in rural Rajasthan).
KE Adventure Travels ☏ 017687/73966, 🖳 www.keadventure.com. Well-organized, high-altitude trekking and mountaineering.
Munjeeta Travel ☏ 01483/773331. Homestay holidays lodging with Indian families.
Partnership Travel ☏ 020/8343 3446, 🖳 www.partnershiptravel.co.uk. Specialists in mid-

and upmarket tailor-made itineraries in South India and strong on Kerala.

Pettitts India ☎ 01892/515966,

Ⓦ www.pettitts.co.uk. Tailor-made holidays off the beaten track.

The Romance of India by Rail

☎ 02890/329477. Set itineraries and tailor-made tours by train.

Somak Holidays ☎ 020/8423 7857,

Ⓦ www.somak.co.uk. Goa beach holidays with optional sightseeing and wildlife trips.

Soul of India ☎ 01902/561485,

Ⓦ www.soulofindia.com. Guided tours (set or tailor-made) of sacred India, including the source of the Ganges, Sikh shrines, the Hindu and Christian south, and landmarks associated with Buddha and Gandhi – for individuals or groups.

Steppes East Ltd ☎ 01285/810267,

Ⓦ www.steppeseast.co.uk. Packaged and tailor-made itineraries.

Trans Indus Travel ☎ 020/8566 2729,

Ⓦ www.transindus.co.uk. Fixed and tailor-made tours from various Indian cities: specialists in wildlife, fishing and trekking.

Western & Oriental Travel ☎ 020/7313 6600,

Ⓔ info@westernoriental.com. Well-researched, award-winning upmarket agency with tailor-made itineraries covering all of India but especially strong on Goa and Rajasthan.

Round-the-world tickets

Other possibilities include taking in India as a stopover while flying, for example, between Britain and Australia, or on a **round-the-world ticket**, which makes a lot of sense if you are planning a long trip with several stops in Asia. A typical one, say with Qantas and BA (£950–1500), open for a year, would depart and return to London, taking in Delhi, Mumbai, Singapore, Sydney, Honolulu and LA; variations could include doing a leg from Delhi to Kathmandu overland.

Overland routes to India

The classic Asia **overland trip** is still alive and kicking, despite periodic rerouteings in the face of political circumstances. Leaving Europe at Istanbul, the usual route traverses Turkey, angles down through Iran (check beforehand that this route is open, and note that it still difficult for US citizens to obtain Iranian visas), entering Pakistan via Quetta (Afghanistan is still off-limits), thence to Lahore and across into India at Amritsar.

Alternative routes could include the **Trans-Siberian express** to China, from there down the Karakoram Highway – if it's open – into Pakistan and then India; another idea might be to negotiate a ride on a dhow from the Gulf to Karachi. It may just be possible to find a cargo ship or a private yacht to take you from the Red Sea or East Africa, but don't count on it.

If you are considering coming by car, motorbike or bicycle, you'll find further information on pp.49–50.

Overland expedition operators in the UK (see below) run six- to eighteen-week trips in special vehicles along the overland trail, most finishing in Kathmandu, Nepal. Expect to pay £1000–3500 for the one-way trip from London, depending on the length of the journey (some detour around the Middle East) and the level of luxury.

Overland expedition operators in Britain

Dragoman 97 Camp Green, Debenham, Stowmarket IP14 6LA ☎ 01728/861133,

Ⓦ www.dragoman.co.uk. Fifteen- and sixteen-week trips in expedition vehicles (customized Mercedes trucks) departing London in June and September with prices from £2390 (plus food), shorter tours within India and an eleven-week full circuit of the country.

Exodus ☎ 020/8675 5550,

Ⓦ www.exodustravels.co.uk. The Ultimate Asia Tour is a thirty-week adventure leaving London in March and terminating in Singapore, with three to four weeks in India (£5555 all inclusive). There's also an eleven-week tour of India, and a four-week "Ganges Explorer".

Hinterland Travel 12 The Enterdent, Godstone, Surrey RH9 8EG ☎ 01883/743584,

Ⓔ hinterland@tinyworld.co.uk. Hinterland organize a fifty-day London to Delhi trip via Istanbul, almost entirely by train, which costs £900 plus food and accommodation. The three-month London to Kathmandu overland route by bus (three weeks in India) costs £1400, and there are also two- and six-week tours within India.

Top Deck Travel 131–135 Earls Court Rd, London SW5 9RH ☎ 020/7244 8641,

Ⓦ www.topdecktravel.co.uk. Seventy-four-day tour departing from London to Kathmandu in early September and returning in the new year; the trip (£1399 plus £599 for food) can also be done in segments.

Getting there from North America

India is on the other side of the planet from North America. If you live on the East Coast it's somewhat shorter to go via Europe, and from the West Coast it's shorter via the Pacific, but either way it's a long haul, involving one or more intermediate stops, and you'll arrive fresher and less jet-lagged if you can manage to fit in a few days' layover somewhere en route.

Most North American travellers arrive at either **Delhi** or **Mumbai** (Bombay), India's busiest – and, in general, cheapest – air gateways. Either one makes a good starting/ending point for a tour of the whole country or of the popular north and west. You can also get flights from North America to **Chennai** (Madras), the main port of entry for the south, to **Calcutta** in the east, and to **Thiruvananthapuram** (Trivandrum) in the far south.

There are no **nonstop flights** to India from North America, but Air India has **direct** flights from New York and Chicago to Mumbai, via London, and Air Canada has a direct flight from Vancouver to Delhi via London.

Many more airlines offer services to India from North America with a change of planes either in Asia or Europe. Your choice of airline is likely to be limited by whether you fly from the east or the west (with the exception of the above-mentioned Vancouver–Delhi direct flight), with a variety of Asian airlines making the trip from the West Coast, and several European and Middle Eastern carriers doing the trip from the Midwest and the East Coast (for more details see p.18).

Air fares from North America to India are highest from the beginning of June to late August. They drop during the "shoulder" seasons (Sept to early Dec and the last half of May), but you'll get the best deals during low season (mid-Dec to mid-May, excluding Christmas). Direct flights are no more expensive than those where you'll have to change planes, but flying on weekends ordinarily adds about $100 to the round-trip fare; price ranges quoted in the sections below assume midweek travel.

If India is only one stop on a longer journey, you might want to consider buying a **round-the-world ticket**. Some travel agents can sell you an "off-the-shelf" RTW ticket, touching down in about half a dozen cities (Delhi is on most itineraries); tailor-made RTW tickets usually work out more expensive. Figure on paying at least $1500 for a regular RTW ticket including India and Europe. A more extensive RTW ticket will cost up to $3000.

Shopping for tickets

Airline tickets are sold through many channels, and there's no magic rule for predicting which will be cheapest. Whatever the airlines are offering, however, any number of specialist travel agents set out to beat it. These are the outfits you'll see advertising in the Sunday newspaper travel sections, and they come in several forms.

Consolidators buy up large blocks of tickets to sell at a discount. Besides being cheap, they don't normally impose advance purchase requirements (although in busy times you'll want to book ahead to be sure of getting a seat), but they do often charge very stiff fees for date changes; note also that airlines generally won't alter tickets after they've gone to a consolidator, so you can only make changes through the consolidator. Also, as these companies' margins are pretty tiny, they make their money by dealing in volume – don't expect them to entertain lots of questions.

Discount agents also wheel and deal in blocks of tickets offloaded by the airlines, but typically offer a range of other travel-related services such as insurance, youth and student ID cards, car rentals, tours and the like. They tend to be most worthwhile to students and under-26s. **Discount travel clubs**, offering money off air tickets, car rental and the like, are an option if you travel a lot. Most, including those we've listed below, charge annual membership fees.

Another way of finding cut-price flights is via the **internet**. Websites such as ⓦwww .airticketsindia.com, ⓦwww.cheaptickets .com, ⓦwww.flynow.com, and, best of all, ⓦwww.travelocity.com have connections to dozens of airlines to provide competitive discounts. All you have to do is key in the dates you want to travel and their search engines will dig up the cheapest fares.

Finally, don't automatically assume that tickets bought through a travel specialist will be cheapest – once you get a quote, check with the airlines and you may turn up an even cheaper promotion. Never deal with a company that demands cash up front or refuses to accept credit cards.

Airlines in North America

Aeroflot ⓣ1-888/340-6400; in Canada, ⓣ514/288-2125, ⓦwww.aeroflot.com.
Air Canada ⓣ1-800/263-0882 in Canada; 1-800/776-3000 in US, ⓦwww.aircanada.ca.
Air France ⓣ1-800/237-2747; in Canada, ⓣ1-800/667-2747, ⓦwww.airfrance.fr.
Air India ⓣ1-800/223-2250 or ⓣ212/751-6200, ⓦwww.airindia.com.
Air Lanka ⓣ1-800/247-5265, ⓦwww.airlanka.com.
All Nippon Airways ⓣ1-800/235-9262, ⓦwww.fly-ana.com.
Asiana Airlines ⓣ1-800/227-4262, ⓦwww.flyasiana.com.
British Airways ⓣ1-800/247-9297, ⓦwww.british-airways.com.
Canadian Airlines in Canada, ⓣ1-800/665-1177; in US, ⓣ1-800/426-7000, ⓦwww.cdnair.ca.
Cathay Pacific ⓣ1-800/233-2742, ⓦwww.cathay-usa.com.
Czech Airlines ⓣ1-800/223-2365 or 212/765-6022, ⓦwww.csa.cz.
EgyptAir ⓣ1-800/334-6787 or 212/315-0900, ⓦwww.egyptair.com.eg.
El Al ⓣ1-800/223-6700, ⓦwww.elal.com.
Emirates Air ⓣ1-800/777-3999, ⓦwww.ekgroup.com.
Gulf Air ⓣ1-800/553-2824, ⓦwww.gulfairco.com.

KLM/Northwest in US, ⓣ1-800/447-4747; in Canada, ⓣ1-800/361-5073, ⓦwww.klm.com.
Kuwait Airways ⓣ1-800/458-9248 or 212/308-5454, ⓦwww.kuwait-airways.com.
Lufthansa in US, ⓣ1-800/645-3880; in Canada, ⓣ1-800/563-5954, in Canada, ⓦwww.lufthansa.com.
Malaysia Airlines ⓣ1-800/552-9264, ⓦwww.malaysiaair.com.
Malev Hungarian Airlines ⓣ1-800/223-6884 or 212/757-6446, ⓦwww.malev.hu.
Northwest/KLM Airlines domestic, ⓣ1-800/225-2525; international, ⓣ1-800/447-4747, ⓦwww.nwa.com.
Pakistan International Airlines ⓣ1-800/221-2552 or 212/370-9150, ⓦwww.piac.com.
Polynesian Airlines ⓣ1-800/644-7659, ⓦwww.pacificislands.com.
Qantas Airways ⓣ1-800/227-4500, ⓦwww.qantas.com.
Royal Jordanian Airlines ⓣ1-800/223-0470 or 212/949-0050, ⓦwww.rja.com.jo.
Royal Nepal Airlines ⓣ1-800/266-3725, ⓦwww.royalnepal.com.
Sabena ⓣ1-800/955-2000, ⓦwww.sabena-usa .com.
Singapore Airlines ⓣ1-800/742-3333, ⓦwww.singaporeair.com.
Swissair in US, ⓣ1-800/221-4750, ⓦwww.swissair.com.
Tarom Romanian Air ⓣ212/687-6013, ⓦwww.tarom.digiro.net.
Thai Airways International in US, ⓣ1-800/426-5204; in Canada, ⓣ1-800/668-8103, ⓦwww.thaiair.com.
TWA domestic, ⓣ1-800/221-2000; international, ⓣ1-800/892-4141, ⓦwww.twa.com.
United Airlines, ⓣ1-800-241-6522, ⓦwww.unitedairlines.com.
Virgin Atlantic Airways ⓣ1-800/862-8621, ⓦwww.virgin-atlantic.com.

Discount agents, consolidators and travel clubs in North America

Air Brokers International ⓣ1-800/883-3273 or ⓣ415/397-1383, ⓦwww.airbrokers.com. Round-the-world ticket specialist with good rates for itineraries that include India.
Council Travel ⓣ1-800/226-8624, ⓦwww.counciltravel.com. Student/budget travel agency.
Discount Airfares Worldwide On-Line ⓦwww.etn.nl/discount.htm. A hub of consolidator and discount agent web links, maintained by the nonprofit European Travel Network.

Educational Travel Centre ☎ 1-800/747-5551
or 608/256-5551, ⊛ www.edtrav.com.
Student/youth and consolidator fares.
Hari World Travel ☎ 212/997-3300,
⊛ www.hariworld.com. Biggest Indian consolidator,
the agent for Indrail passes.
High Adventure Travel ☎ 1-800/350-0612 or
415/912-5600, ⊛ www.airtreks.com. Round-the-
world and Circle Pacific tickets. The extensive
website features an interactive database called
"Farebuilder" that lets you create your own RTW
itinerary.
HighTime Travel ☎ 212/684-7700. Consolidator
specializing in tickets to India.
**International Travel Network/Airlines of the
Web** ⊛ www.flyaow.com. Online air travel info and
reservations site.
Jaya Travels ☎ 312/606 9600,
⊛ www.jayatravels.com. Chicago-based India
specialist with offices nationwide.
Now Voyager, 74 Varick St, Suite 307, New York,
NY 10013; ☎ 212/431-1616,
⊛ www.nowvoyagertravel.com. Courier flight-broker
and consolidator.
Rupa Travel ☎ 1-888 438 7872,
⊛ www.rupatravel.com. New Jersey/NY India ticket
consolidator.
STA Travel ☎ 1-800/777-0112 or 1-800/781-
4040, ⊛ www.sta-travel.com. Branches in most
major US cities, including: 10 Downing St, New
York, NY 10014 ☎ 212/627-3111; 7202 Melrose
Ave, Los Angeles, CA 90046 ☎ 323/934-8722; 51
Grant Ave, San Francisco, CA 94108 ☎ 415/391-
8407; 297 Newbury St, Boston, MA 02115
☎ 617/266-6014; 429 S Dearborn St, Chicago, IL
60605 ☎ 312/786-9050; 3701 Chesnut St,
Philadelphia, PA 19104 ☎ 215/382-2928; 317 14th
Ave SE, Minneapolis, MN 55414 ☎ 612/615-1800.
Worldwide discount travel firm specializing in
student/youth fares.
Travel CUTS ☎ 1-800/667-2887 Canada only, or
☎ 416/979-2406, ⊛ www.travelcuts.com.
Organization specializing in student fares, IDs and
other travel services.
Travelers Advantage ☎ 1-800/548-1116,
⊛ www.travelersadvantage.com. Discount
travel club; annual membership of $59.95
required.
Travelocity ⊛ www.travelocity.com. Online
consolidator whose website has a special India
section, where you'll find tour operators,
accommodation options and cheap air fares.
Worldwide Discount Travel Club, 1674
Meridian Ave, Suite 206, Miami Beach, FL 33139
☎ 305/534-2082. Discount travel club, with annual
membership fee of $80.

From eastern and central USA

Flying east, you'll stop over somewhere in
Europe (most often London), the Gulf, or
both. Figure on at least eighteen hours' total
travel time from the **East Coast**.

Air India and PIA discount their tickets
heavily through a few specialist, understaffed
New York consolidators. Marked-down tickets on European carriers – notably British
Airways, Air France, KLM/Northwest and
Lufthansa – are frequently sold by other discount agents. Other airlines flying between
the eastern US and India include
KLM/Northwest, Air France, Virgin Atlantic,
Aeroflot, Gulf Air, Kuwait Airways and Egypt
Air. Or you can simply hop on any of the
dozens of airlines that fly to London and pick
up a flight to India from there.

Prices are most competitive out of **New
York**, where the cheapest low-season consolidated fares to Mumbai/Delhi hover
around $1400 in low season and rise to
$1750 in high season. From **Washington** or
Miami, figure on $1600 in low season to
$1850 in high season; from **Chicago** $1600
to $2000; and from **Dallas/Fort Worth**
$1800 to $3000. Add on roughly $100 for
an onward domestic leg from Mumbai to
Goa; $180 for Thiruvananthapuram; $145
for Chennai; and $180 for Delhi to Calcutta.

From the West Coast

From the **West Coast**, it takes about as long
to fly east or west – a minimum of 22 hours'
total travel time – and if you're booking
through a consolidator there may not be
much difference in price. Thai Airways,
Cathay Pacific, Northwest, Malaysia Airlines
and Singapore Airlines are the main carriers
flying over the Pacific to India, via their
respective hubs. Air India doesn't do the
trans-Pacific route, but can book passengers on Northwest to any of several Asian
capitals and then fly them the rest of the
way.

From **Los Angeles** or **San Francisco**,
you're looking at a minimum of $1400 to fly
to Delhi or Mumbai in low season, and up to
$1700 in high season. For domestic con-
nections booked in the US or Canada, count
on around $100 for Mumbai to Goa, $180 to
Thiruvananthapuram, $145 to Chennai and
$180 from Delhi to Calcutta.

From Canada

The only direct flight from **Canada** to India is Vancouver–Delhi on Air Canada (via London, and taking under 20hr). All other routeings involve a plane change and more layover time. Air Canada flies during shoulder and high season from all major Canadian cities to London, where passengers can join the Vancouver–Delhi flight; the rest of the year they fly through Zurich. Other airlines offering services to India, via their capitals, include British Airways, Air France, Lufthansa, KLM and Aeroflot. This list doesn't convey the full range of possibilities, however. A discount agent will probably break the journey into two, using one of dozens of carriers for the transatlantic (or trans-Pacific) leg.

Typical discounted low and high season fares to Delhi or Mumbai from Montreal, Toronto and Vancouver are CDN$2200/ $2500. Add CDN$140 for domestic tickets from Mumbai to Goa; CDN$260 for Thiruvananthapuram; CDN$220 for Chennai; and CDN$270 from Delhi to Calcutta.

Packages and organized tours

Wrapping India up into a tidy **package** makes it less daunting and more comprehensible for many first-time tourists. A tour company can also shield you from the subcontinent's many little frustrations, enabling you to cover more ground than if you were going it alone. Of course, you'll have to be prepared to forgo independence and spontaneity, and accept that there will be only fleeting and predominantly mercenary encounters with local people.

Tours of India work best when they focus on one region of the country, or when based on an activity or a special interest. A fairly standard bestseller list is offered by many companies: Rajasthan palaces, Rajasthan camel safaris (often timed to coincide with the Pushkar Camel Fair), Agra–Varanasi–Khajuraho (often packaged with a few days in Nepal), wildlife parks, Goa, temples and/or beaches of the south and the Palace on Wheels railway. Quite a few companies specialize in trekking in the Himalayas, although they invariably offer many more itineraries in Nepal than in India.

Tour prices are always wildly out of line with the cost of living in India, and whether you take one will depend on which is tighter, your budget or your schedule. Excluding air fare, a two-week tour is likely to cost at least $2200, and a three-week trip with all the bells and whistles can cost $3500 or more. Your local travel agent should be able to book any tour for you at no additional cost.

Specialist tour operators in North America

Above the Clouds ☎ 1-800/233-4499, 🌐 www.aboveclouds.com. Ladakh mountain trek over the Parang La mountain range.

Adventure Center ☎ 1-800/227-8747, 🌐 www.adventurecenter.com. Trekking and cultural tours.

Cox & Kings ☎ 1-800/999-1758, 🌐 www.coxandkings.com. Deluxe and special-interest sightseeing.

Geographic Expeditions ☎ 1-800/777-8183, 🌐 www.geoex.com. Remote mountain treks and unusual tours including sea kayaking in the Andamans.

Himalayan Travel ☎ 1-800/225-2380, 🌐 www.gorp.com/himtravel.htm. Tailor-made regional tours and organized treks.

Journeyworld International ☎ 1-800/635-3900. Fifteen- and twenty-day regional tours across the country, some including Sri Lanka and Nepal.

Mercury Travels Limited ☎ 1-800/223-1474. A variety of regional and custom tours to each region of India.

Mountain Travel/Sobek ☎ 1-800/227-2384, 🌐 www.mtsobek.com. Trekking and camel safaris and cultural trips to Ladakh.

Myths and Mountains ☎ 1-800/670-6984 or 775-832-5454, 🌐 www.mythsandmountains.com. Special-interest trips, tailor-made or group, with emphasis on culture, crafts, religion and traditional medicine.

Nature Expeditions International ☎ 1-800/ 869-0639 or 503/484-6529, 🌐 www.naturexp.com. Wildlife and cultural tours.

Rama Tours ☎ 1800/223-2474 A full-service operator to India, offering individual packages to Goa among its range of regional tours.

Tours of Distinction ☎ 1-800/888-8634. Regional and all-India tours.

Wilderness Travel ☎ 1-800/368-2794, 🌐 www.wildernesstravel.com. Rajasthan camel safaris and elephant-research expeditions.

Worldwide Quest Adventures ☎ 1-800/387-1483, 🌐 www.worldwidequest.com. Sightseeing plus trekking, cycling, camel safaris and cultural tours.

Getting there from
Australia & New Zealand

There are no nonstop flights to India from either Australia or New Zealand; you have to make at least one change of plane in a Southeast Asian hub city (usually Kuala Lumpur, Singapore or Bangkok). The choice of routes and airlines is bewildering, and most agents will offer you a combination of two or more carriers to get the best price.

Bear in mind when you're shopping around which city you want to fly into; your point of arrival may well affect your eventual itinerary, and there's no point in saving a few dollars on the cost of an air ticket only to lose them on an expensive or time-consuming ride across the country to get to the part of India you want to explore first.

Flying west, the main, and cheapest, India gateway city tends to be Chennai (Madras), with Mumbai (Bombay) and Delhi not far behind. As a rule of thumb, the best-value tickets from Australia are on departures from the east coast. Flying from Perth to Chennai in **low/shoulder season** (Feb 1–Nov 21) costs A$1100–1300 with Singapore Airlines, Sri Lanka Airlines, Malaysia, Ansett or Air India, and from around A$1700 during **high season** (Nov 22–Jan 31). Qantas/British Airways also offers a competitive low-season fare from the east coast to Mumbai of around A$1400, and there are daily departures connecting with these flights from most Australian cities, with less frequent departures from Cairns and Darwin (2–3 times a week). Coming from the west coast – Sydney, Melbourne or Brisbane – typically costs A$50–100 more.

Flying **from New Zealand**, the cheapest fares to India are generally with Singapore Airlines, Thai Airways, Air New Zealand and Air India (or more probably a combination of all four). Tickets range from just under NZ$2000 to around NZ$2250 if you leave from Auckland; add on approximately NZ$150 for flights from Wellington or Christchurch.

Round-the-world fares from Australia and New Zealand using the above airlines can take in India; for example, Thai Airways,

Air New Zealand, Qantas and Malaysia Airlines can route you through Delhi or Mumbai as part of a RTW deal from around A$2200/NZ$2600.

Shopping for tickets

Buying a **scheduled ticket** direct with the airline is the most expensive way to fly and most people book through an established **discount agent**, whose fares may undercut those offered by the airlines by as much as fifty percent. See the box opposite for a list of recommended agents. It is also a good idea to check out the ads in the national Sunday papers or in listings magazines, and to check out online agents such as ⓦwww.travel.com.nz or ⓦwww.planit .com.au.

Many of the companies advertising in newspapers and magazines are **bucket shops** (also known as "consolidators") who are able to offer extremely cheap deals, but who don't necessarily belong to an official bonding scheme such as ABTA or IATA, which means that if they go bust you won't get a refund. For this reason, never deal with a company that demands cash upfront or refuses to accept payment by credit card. If you're unsure about your agent, give the ABTA or IATA a ring quoting the company's number (listed under the logo).

Students and **under-26-year-olds** may be able to get further discounts on flight prices, especially through agents like Trailfinders or STA (although for India there's often little difference between a youth fare and a regular discounted one). Bear in mind, too, that the lower-priced tickets will often come with restrictions (length of stay, advance booking requirements) and that penalties for changing your plans can be stiff.

Airlines in Australia and New Zealand

Air France in Australia ℡ 02/9244 2100; New Zealand ℡ 09/308 3352, Ⓦ www.airfrance.fr.

Air India Australia ℡ 02/9299 2022; New Zealand ℡ 09/303 1301, Ⓦ www.airindia.com.

Air New Zealand Australia ℡ 13 2476; New Zealand ℡ 0800 737 000, ℡ 09/357 3000, Ⓦ www.airnewzealand.com.

Ansett Australia, Australia ℡ 13 1414, ℡ 02/9352 6707; New Zealand ℡ 09/336 2364, Ⓦ www.ansett.com.au.

Ansett New Zealand Australia ℡ 1800 022 146; New Zealand ℡ 09/526 8300, Ⓦ www.ansett.com.au.

British Airways Australia ℡ 02/8904 8800; New Zealand ℡ 09/356 8690, Ⓦ www.british-airways .com.

Cathay Pacific Australia ℡ 13 1747; New Zealand ℡ 09/379 0861, Ⓦ www.cathaypacific.com.

KLM Australia ℡ 1300 303 747; New Zealand ℡ 09/302 1452, Ⓦ www.klm.com.

Lufthansa Australia ℡ 1300 655 727, ℡ 02/9367 3887; New Zealand ℡ 09/303 1529, ℡ 008/945 220, Ⓦ www.lufthansa.com.

Malaysia Airlines Australia ℡ 13 2627; New Zealand ℡ 09/373 2741 or ℡ 008/657 472, Ⓦ www.malaysiaairlines.com.

Qantas Australia ℡ 13 1313; New Zealand ℡ 09/357 8900 & ℡ 0800/808 767, Ⓦ www.qantas.com.

Royal Jordanian Airlines Australia (℡ 02/9244 2701); New Zealand ℡ 03/365 3910, Ⓦ www.rja.com.jo.

Singapore Airlines Australia ℡ 13 1011 or ℡ 02/9350 0262; New Zealand ℡ 09/379 3209 or ℡ 0800/808 909, Ⓦ www.singaporean.com.

Air Lanka/Sri Lanka Airlines Australia ℡ 02/9244 2234; New Zealand ℡ 09/308 3353, Ⓦ www.airlanka.com.

Swissair Australia ℡ 02/9232 1744 & 1800 221 339; New Zealand ℡ 09/358 3216, Ⓦ www.swissair.com.

Thai Airways Australia ℡ 1300 651 960; New Zealand ℡ 09/377 3886, Ⓦ www.thaiair.com.

Travel agents in Australia and New Zealand

Anywhere Travel ℡ 02/9663 0411, ℡ 018 401 014, Ⓔ anywhere@ozemail.com.au.

Asian Travel Centre ℡ 03/9245 0747, Ⓦ www.planit.com.au.

Australia: Adventure World ℡ 02/956 7766

Budget Travel ℡ 09/366 0061 & 0800/808 040

Flight Centres Australia: Australia ℡ 02/9235 3522, nearest branch ℡ 13 1600. New Zealand ℡ 09/358 4310, plus branches nationwide, Ⓦ www.flightcentre.com.au.

Northern Gateway ℡ 08/8941 1394, Ⓔ oztravel@norgate.com.au.

STA Travel, Australia, nearest branch ℡ 13 1776, fastfare telesales ℡ 1300 360 960; New Zealand ℡ 09/309 0458, fastfare telesales ℡ 09/366 6673, Ⓦ www.statravel.com.au.

Student Uni Travel ℡ 02/9232 8444, Ⓔ sydney@backpackers.net.

Thomas Cook, Australia ℡ 02/9231 2877 or for local branch ℡ 13 1771, Thomas Cook Direct telesales ℡ 1800/801 002; New Zealand ℡ 09/379 3920, Ⓦ www.thomascook.com.au.

Trailfinders, ℡ 02/9247 7666 or ℡ 07/3229 0887 or ℡ 07/4041 1199, Ⓦ www.trailfinders.com/au.

Travel.com.au ℡ 02/9249 5444 or 1-800 000 447, Ⓦ www.travel.com.au.

Usit Beyond New Zealand ℡ 09/379 4224 or ℡ 0800/788 336 plus branches in Christchurch, Dunedin, Palmerston North, Hamilton and Wellington, Ⓦ www.usitbeyond.co.nz.

Packages and organized tours

Wrapping India up into a tidy **package** makes it less daunting and more comprehensible to many first-time tourists. A tour company can also shield you from the subcontinent's many little frustrations, enabling you to cover more ground than if you were going it alone. Of course, you'll have to be prepared to forgo independence and spontaneity, and accept that there will be only fleeting and predominantly mercenary encounters with local people.

Tours of India work best when they focus on one region of the country, or when based on an activity or a special interest. A fairly standard bestseller list is offered by many companies: Rajasthan palaces, Rajasthan camel safaris (often timed to coincide with the Pushkar Camel Fair), Agra–Varanasi–Khajuraho (often packaged with a few days in Nepal), wildlife parks, Goa, temples and/or beaches of the south and the Palace on Wheels railway. Quite a few companies specialize in trekking in the Himalayas, although they invariably offer many more itineraries in Nepal than in India.

Tour prices are always wildly out of line with the cost of living in India, and whether you take one will depend on which is tighter, your budget or your schedule. Excluding air fare, a two-week tour is likely to cost at least A$2200, and a three-week trip with all the bells and whistles can cost $3500 or more.

Tour operators in Australia and New Zealand

Abercrombie and Kent 90 Bridport St, Albert Park, Victoria ☎ 03/9699 9766, www.abercrombiekent.co.uk. Specialist in individual mid- to upmarket holidays, away from the main tourist trails.
Adventure World 73 Walker St, Sydney ☎ 02/9956 7766, toll-free 1800/221 931, plus branches in Melbourne, Adelaide, Brisbane and Perth; 101 Great South Rd, Remuera, Auckland ☎ 09/524 5118. Tailor-made air and accommodation packages, rail passes and regional tours. NZ agents for Peregrine.

Classic Oriental Tours, 4th Floor, 491 Kent St, Sydney ☎ 02/9266 3988, ⓦ www.classicoriental.com.au/india.htm. Wide choice of tours ranging from three-day city breaks to 22-day itineraries, with some adventure options.
India Nepal Travel Centre, 2/84 Pitt St, Sydney ☎ 02/9223 6000, ⓦ www.indianepaltravelcentre.com.au.
Peregrine Adventures 258 Lonsdale St, Melbourne ☎ 03/9663 8611; offices in Brisbane, Sydney, Adelaide and Perth. Trekking specialists with a wide range of tailored group and individual tours.
San Michele Travel, 83 York St, Sydney ☎ 02/9299 1111 & 1800/222 244, plus a branch in Melbourne, ⓦ www.asiatravel.com.au. Budget and upmarket air and accommodation packages, rail tours and tailor-made land tours for groups or individual travellers.
Travel.com.au, 76 Clarence St, Sydney ☎ 01/800 000 447, ⓦ www.travel.com.au. Agent for a broad range of tour operators. You can select set itineraries or tailor-make your own packages on their website.

Visas and red tape

Gone are the days when Commonwealth nationals could stroll visa-less into India and stay for as long as they pleased: now everybody needs a visa, except citizens of Nepal and Bhutan.

If you're going to India on business or to study, you'll need to apply for a special student or business visa, otherwise a **standard tourist visa** will suffice. These are **valid for six months** from the date of issue (not of departure from your home country or entry into India), and cost £30/US$60/ CDN$62/A$55/NZ$55. As you're asked to specify whether you need a single-entry or a **multiple-entry visa**, and the same rates apply to both, it makes sense to ask for the latter, just in case you decide to make a side trip to Nepal or another neighbouring country.

Much the best place to get a visa is in your country of residence, from the embassies and high commissions listed on pp.23–24;

you should be able to download forms from the embassy and consulate websites (ⓦ http://passport.nic.in/vspassport/missions .htm). In Britain and North America, you'll need a passport valid for at least six months, two passport photographs and an application form, obtainable in advance by post or on the day; address applications to the Postal Visa Section of the consulate in question. In Australia and New Zealand, one passport-sized photo and your flight/travel itinerary are required, together with the visa application form. As a rule, visas are issued in a matter of hours, although embassies in India's neighbouring countries often drag their feet, demand letters of recommendation from your embassy (expensive if you are, for example, British), or make you wait and pay for them to send your application to Delhi. In the US, postal applications take a month as opposed to a same-day service if you do it in person – check with your nearest embassy, high commission or consulate. Make sure that your visa is signed by someone at the embassy, as you may be refused entry into the country otherwise.

It's also possible in many countries to pay a **visa agency** to process the visa on your behalf, which in the UK costs from around £25 (plus the price of the visa). In Britain, try The Visa Service, 2 Northdown St, Kings Cross, London N1 (☏ 0990/343638 premium rate calls, ⓦ www.visaservice.co.uk) who offer a 48hr service; you could also try Visa Express, 31 Corsham St, London N1 (☏ 020/7251 4822, ⓔ visaexpress @cwcom.net). In the US, try Express Visa Service, 2150 Wisconsin Ave, Suite 20, Washington DC (☏ 202/337-2442, ⓦ www.expressvisa.com) who charge $45 and normally take six days or charge $120 for a next-day service.

Visa extensions

It is no longer possible to **extend a visa** in India, though exceptions may be made in special circumstances. Most people whose standard six-month tourist visas are about to expire head for Colombo, capital of neighbouring Sri Lanka, or the Nepalese capital, Kathmandu, or Bangkok, and apply for a new one. However, in recent years this has been something of a hit-and-miss business, with some tourists having their requests turned down for no apparent reason. The Indian High Commission in Kathmandu is particularly notorious for this; you can telephone them to check their current policy, but don't expect the story to be the same when you arrive there. Try to find out from other travellers what the visa situation is, and always allow enough time on your current permit to re-enter India and catch a flight out of the country in case your request is refused.

If you do stay more than 180 days, before you leave the country you are supposed to get a **tax clearance certificate**, available at the foreigners' section of the income-tax department in every major city. They are free, but you should take bank receipts to show you have changed your money legally. In

practice, tax clearance certificates are rarely demanded, but you never know.

For details of other kinds of visas – fiveyear visas can be obtained by foreigners of Indian origin, business travellers and even students of yoga – contact your nearest Indian embassy.

Indian embassies

Australia High Commission: 3–5 Moonah Place, Yarralumla, Canberra, ACT 2600 ☏ 02/6273 3999, ⓕ 6273 1308, ⓔ hicanb@ozemail.com.au. Consulates: Level 27, 25 Bligh St, Level 27, Sydney, NSW 2000 ☏ 02/9223 9500, ⓕ 9223 9246, ⓔ indianc@enternet.com.au; 15 Munro St, Coburg, Melbourne, Vic 3058 ☏ 03/9384 0141, ⓕ 9384 1609. Honorary Consulates: Level 1, Terrace Hotel, 195 Adelaide Terrace, East Perth WA 6004, Australia (mailing address: PO BOX 6118 East Perth WA 6892, Australia) ☏ 08/9221 1485, ⓕ 9221 1206, ⓔ india@vianet.net.au; Brisbane ☏ 07/3260 2825, ⓕ 3260 2826.
Bangladesh House 120, Rd 2, Dhanmondi Residential Area, Dhaka ☏ 02/503606, ⓕ 863662; 1253–1256 Nizam Road, Mehdi Bagh, Chittagong ☏ 031/211007, ⓕ 225178.
Burma (Myanmar) Oriental Assurance Building, 545–547 Merchant St (PO Box 751), Rangoon ☏ 01/82550.
Canada High Commission: 10 Springfield Rd, Ottawa, ON K1M 1C9 ☏ 613/744 3751, ⓕ 744 0913, ⓦ www.docuweb.ca/india. Consulates: 2 Bloor St W, #500, Toronto, ON M4W 3E2 ☏ 416/960 0751; 325 Howe St, 2nd floor, Vancouver, BC V6C 1Z7 ☏ 604/662 8811, ⓦ www.cgivancouver.com.
Japan 2-11, Kudan Minami 2-Chome, Chiyoda-ku, Tokyo 102 ☏ 03/3262 2391, ⓕ 3234 4866.
Malaysia 2 Jalan Taman Dlita (off Jalan Duta), PO Box 10059, 50704 Kuala Lumpur ☏ 03/253 3504, ⓕ 253 3507.
Nepal Lainchaur (off Lazimpath), PO Box 92, Kathmandu ☏ 01/410900, ⓕ 413132, ⓦ www.south-asia.com/Embassy-India. Allow a week – plus extra fee – to fax Delhi; British nationals and some Europeans need letters of recommendation. Mon–Fri 9.30–11am.
New Zealand Indian High Commission: 180 Molesworth St (PO Box 4005), Wellington ☏ 04/473 6390, ⓕ 499 0665.
Pakistan G-5, Diplomatic enclave, Islamabad ☏ 051/814371, ⓕ 820742; India House, 3 Fatima Jinnah Rd (PO Box 8542), Karachi ☏ 021/522275, ⓕ 568 0929.

Singapore India House, 31 Grange Rd (PO Box 9123), Singapore 0923 ☏737 6777, ☏732 6909.
Sri Lanka 36–38 Galle Rd, Colombo 3
☏01/421605, ☏446403, ☞www.indiahcsl.org; 31 Rajapihilla Mawatha, PO Box 47, Kandy
☏08/24563.
Thailand ☞www.indiaemb.or.th.
46 Soi 23 (Prasarn Mitr), Sukhumvit Road, Bangkok 10110 ☏02/258 0300, ☏258 4627; 113 Bumruangrat Road, Chiang Mai 50000
☏053/243066, ☏247879. Visas take five working days to issue.
UK ☞www.hcilondon.org. High Commission: India House, Aldwych, London WC2B 4NA ☏020/7836 8484, ☏7836 4331. Consulates: 20 Augusta St, Jewellery Quarter, Hockley, Birmingham B18 6GL ☏0121/212 2782; 17 Rutland Square, Edinburgh EH1 2BB ☏0131/229 2144. All open Mon–Fri 8.30am–noon.
USA Embassy of India (Consular Services): 2107 Massachusetts Ave NW, Washington DC 20008
☏202/939-7000, ☏939-7027. Consulates: 3 East 64th St, New York, NY 10021 ☏212/774-0600, ☏861-3788, ☞www.indiacgny.org; 540 Arguello Blvd, San Francisco, CA 94118 ☏415/668-0683, ☏668-9764; 455 North Cityfront Plaza Drive, Suite 850, Chicago IL 60611 ☏312/595 0405 (ext 22 for visas), ☏595 0416, ☞www.indianconsulate.com; 201 St Charles Ave, New Orleans, LA 70170
☏504/582-8106; 2051 Young St, Honolulu, HI 96826 ☏808/947-2618.

Special permits

In addition to a visa, **special permits** may be required for travel to certain areas of the country – notably Sikkim, parts of Ladakh,
the Andaman Islands, Lakshadweep, the far west of the Thar desert beyond Jaisalmer, and some northeastern hill states.

There are two types of permits: those for **restricted areas** such as Sikkim, and the **Inner Line Permit** required by both foreigners and Indians intending to visit politically sensitive border areas of Ladakh, parts of the northeast, and north and east Sikkim. Inner Line Permits are usually issued by the District Magistrate (see chapters for more detail). Some areas (parts of Sikkim, and the Indo-Chinese-Pak border region in Jammu-Kashmir for example) remain completely out of bounds to tourists. If you have some special reason for going to any of these latter areas, apply for a permit to the Ministry for Home Affairs Foreigners' Section, Lok Nayak Bhavan, Khan Market, New Delhi 110 003, at least three months in advance.

Permits for those areas of Sikkim that are open to tourists are easily available at all foreigners' registration offices, immigration offices at the main international airports, all Indian embassies, consulates and high commissions abroad and at offices in Darjeeling and Siliguri; a two-day permit is instantly available at the checkpoint on the Sikkim border. Sikkim is the only place where you need a special **trekking permit** (see p.1019).

Should you get your hands on a visa for Bhutan, you'll also need a transit permit for the border area from the Ministry of External Affairs.

For details of permit requirements to other areas, see the relevant chapters of this book.

Information, websites and maps

The Indian government maintains a number of tourist offices abroad, where you can pick up a range of pamphlets. Their main purpose is to advertise rather than inform, but they can be extremely helpful and knowledgeable. Other sources of information include travel agents (who are in business for themselves, so their advice may not always be totally unbiased), and the Indian Railways representatives listed on p.46.

Inside India, both national and local governments run **tourist information offices**, providing general travel advice and handing out an array of printed material, from city maps to glossy leaflets on specific destinations. The Indian government's tourist department, whose main offices are on Janpath in New Delhi and opposite Churchgate railway station in Mumbai, has branches in most regional capitals. These, however, operate independently of the **state government information counters** and their commercial bureaux run by the state tourism development corporations, usually referred to by their initials (eg MPTDC in Madhya Pradesh and RTDC in Rajasthan), who offer a wide range of travel facilities, including guided tours, car rental and their own hotels (which we identify with the relevant acronyms throughout this book).

Just to confuse things further, the Indian government's tourist office has a go-ahead corporate wing too. The **Indian Tourism Development Corporation (ITDC)**, is responsible for the Ashok chain of hotels, and operates tour and travel services, frequently competing with its state counterparts.

Indian government tourist offices

Australia Level 2, Piccadilly, 210 Pitt St, Sydney NSW ☏ 02/9264 4855, ℱ 9264 4860, ℮ sydney@tourismindia.com; Level 1, 17 Castle Reagh, Sydney, NSW 2000 ☏ 02/9232 1600, ℱ 9223 3003, ℮ sydney@tourismindia.com.
Canada 60 Bloor St (West), #1003, Toronto, Ontario M4W 3B8 ☏ 416/ 962-3787, ℱ 962 6279, ℮ toronto@tourismindia.com.
Netherlands Rokin 9–15, 1022 KK, Amsterdam ☏ 020/620 8991, ℱ 638 3059, ℮ amsterdam@tourismindia.com.
Singapore 20 Karamat Lane, 01–01A United House, Singapore 0922 ☏ 065/235 3800, ℱ 235 8677, ℮ singapore@tourismindia.com.
Thailand Singapore Airlines Bldg, 3rd floor, 62/5 Thaniya Rd (Silom), Bangkok ☏ 02/235 2585 & 235 6670, ℱ 236 8411.
UK 7 Cork St, London W1X 2LN ☏ 020/7437 3677, ℱ 7454 1048, ℮ london@tourismindia.com.
USA 3550 Wilshire Blvd, Suite #204, Los Angeles, CA 90010 ☏ 213/380-8855, ℱ 380-6111, ℮ la@tourismindia.com; Suite 1808, 1270 Ave of Americas, New York NY 10020 ☏ 212/751-6840, ℱ 582-3274, ℮ ny@tourismindia.com.

India online

India has one of the highest levels of IT awareness on the planet and this has helped fuel the growth of home-grown resources on the **internet**. Today there are several excellent India-specific **websites** and portals, or gateway sites, covering a vast range of topics. We list relevant websites throughout the Guide; the recommendations below are more general, and are a good place to start your navigating.

The internet has had a major impact, with sites like ⓦ www.tehelka.com responsible for explosive stories such as the cricket scandal of 2000 that saw the downfall of several illustrious cricketers involved with bribes, including Hansie Cronjie and Azharuddin.

General

ⓦ **www.indya.com** One of the best-developed India portals with links to a huge variety of subjects as well as a good search engine; their astrology page is excellent.
ⓦ **www.rediff.com** Another leading India-specific portal with great search facilities and a site plan that stretches from news to travel.
ⓦ **www.123india.com** India-specific portal with a useful search engine and great links to a wide choice of India-related websites.
ⓦ **www.indiangenie.com** Slick portal with a wide range of features including articles, film reviews and excellent links to music, culture and even matrimonial sites and services.
ⓦ **www.bharatguru.com** A WAP enabled portal offering everything from news to film gossip, romance, cooking and horoscopes, all in several Indian languages as well as in English.
ⓦ **www.britannicaindia.com** Highly informative general site on India, part of the famous encyclopedia chain.

News and media

ⓦ **www.samachar.com** One of the best news gateway sites, featuring headlines and excellent links to leading Indian newspapers, and other portals including the BBC.

ⓦ **www.timesofindia.com**
ⓦ **www.thehinduonline.com**
ⓦ **www.hindustantimes.com**
The websites of some of India's leading papers with detailed national coverage.

Tourism

ⓦ **www.tourismindia.com** A very useful site providing a vast range of information, including rail and air travel timetables, and details and dates of festivals.

ⓦ **www.tourindia.com** The website of the US Government of India Tourist Office, which is easier to navigate than the main site.

ⓦ **www.shubhyatra.com** Well-designed India-dedicated travel website with a host of features including online booking, hotel deals and airline and train schedules.

Travel advice

ⓦ **www.fco.gov.uk/travel** The British Foreign Office website is useful for checking potential or actual dangerous areas.

ⓦ **http://travel.state.gov/travel_warnings .html** The US State Department's travel advice regarding potential hot spots.

Culture

ⓦ **http://www.artindia.net** Great site for dance, music, cinema and fine art: http://artindia.net/hope.html links to the homepages of various well-known dancers, artists and musicians.

ⓦ **www.themusicmagazine.com** A music "e-zine" with an incredible range, from Bob Dylan to ghazal.

ⓦ **www.carnaticmusic.com** Very well-organized site which explores Carnatic (South Indian) classical music.

ⓦ **www.sruti.com**
The e-zine of a very informative and in-depth music and dance magazine devoted to India's rich tradition of classical performing arts.

ⓦ **http://movies.sify.com** Devoted to Indian and international films.

ⓦ **www.stardustindia.com** The place for Bollywood gossip.

Sport

ⓦ **http://www.khel.com** A Great sports site, especially strong on cricket.

Maps

Getting good **maps** of India, in India, can be difficult; the government – in an archaic suspicion of cartography – forbids the sale of detailed maps of border areas, which include the entire coastline. In theory, certain maps, especially detailed ones of border areas skirting Tibet and Pakistan, are illegal, so use them very discreetly. These maps are available outside India, and useful if you are going to be trekking in places like Ladakh, Spiti, Sikkim and Garhwal.

It makes sense to bring a basic map of India with you, such as Bartholomew's 1:4,000,000 map of South Asia, which has coloured contours and serves as a reliable route map of the whole country; a handful of other publishers produce a similar map, including the Daily Telegraph World Series map of India; while the Lascelles map on the same scale is also good. Geocentre produces an excellent three-set map of India at a scale of 1:2,500,000, showing good road detail.

Nelles covers parts of the country with 1:1,500,000 regional maps. These are generally excellent, with colour contours, road distances, inset city plans and even the tiniest places marked, but cost a fortune if you buy the complete set. Their double-sided map of the Himalayas is useful for roads and planning and has some detail but is not sufficient as a trekking map. Ttk, a Chennai-based company, publishes basic state maps which are widely available in India, and in some specialized travel and map shops in the UK such as Stanfords; these are poorly drawn but useful for road distances. The Indian Railways map at the back of the publication *Trains at a Glance* is useful for planning railway journeys.

If you need larger-scale **city maps** than the ones we provide in this book – which are keyed to show recommended hotels and restaurants – you can sometimes get them from tourist offices. Both Ttk and the official Indian mapping organization, the Survey of India (Janpath Barracks A, New Delhi 110 001; ☏011/332 2288), have town plans at scales of 1:10,000 and 1:50,000. Some of the city and regional maps they have for sale are grossly out of date.

As for **trekking maps**, the US Army Map Service produced maps in the 1960s which, with a scale of 1:250,000, remain sufficiently accurate on topography, but are of course outdated on the latest road developments. Most other maps that you can buy are based on their work. Their maps of Kanchenjunga, Leh, Palampur (including Bara Bangal, Manali and Lahaul), Tso Moriri (including Tabo, Kaza and Kibber) and Chini (including Kinnaur and the Baspa valley) are some of the best you can get. One exception is the superb Swiss Stiftung für Alpine Forschunger map of the Sikkim Himalayas at a scale of 1:150,000. The Survey of India, recognizing the competition, has come out with a version of the Sikkim map that is not particularly accurate. Leomann Maps (1:200,000) cover Srinagar, Zanskar, West Ladakh, Leh and around, Dharamsala, Kulu with Lahaul and Spiti, Garhwal and Kumaon. These are not contour maps and are therefore better for planning and basic reference than as reliable trekking maps. The Survey of India publishes a rather poor 1:250,000 series for trekkers in the Uttar Pradesh Himalayas; they are simplified versions of their own infinitely more reliable maps, produced for the military, which it is absolutely impossible for an outsider to get hold of.

Book and map outlets in the UK and Ireland

Blackwell's Map and Travel Shop, 53 Broad St, Oxford OX1 3BQ ☎01865/792792, ⊛www.blackwell.bookshop.co.uk.

Daunt Books, 83 Marylebone High St, W1M 3DE ☎020/7224 2295, ⓕ020/7224 6893; 193 Haverstock Hill, NW3 4QL ☎020/7794 4006.

Heffers Map and Travel, 20 Trinity St, Cambridge, CB2 1TJ ☎01223/586 586, ⊛www.heffers.co.uk.

John Smith and Sons, 26 Colquhoun Ave, Glasgow, G52 4PJ ☎0141/221 7472, ⊛www.johnsmith.co.uk.

James Thin Melven's Bookshop, 29 Union St, Inverness, IV1 1QA ☎01463/233500, ⊛www.jthin.co.uk.

The Map Shop, 30a Belvoir St, Leicester, LE1 6QH ☎0116/2471400

National Map Centre, 22–24 Caxton St, SW1H 0QU ☎020/7222 2466, ⊛www.mapsnmc.co.uk.

Newcastle Map Centre, 55 Grey St, Newcastle upon Tyne, NE1 6EF ☎0191/261 5622, ⊛www.newtraveller.com.

Stanfords, ⊛www.stanfords.co.uk: 12–14 Long Acre, WC2E 9LP ☎020/7836 1321; British Airways office, 156 Regent St, W1R 5TA ☎020/7434 4744; 29 Corn St, Bristol BS1 1HT ☎0117/929 9966

The Travel Bookshop, 13–15 Blenheim Crescent, W11 2EE ☎020/7229 5260, ⊛www.thetravelbookshop.co.uk.

Waterstone's, 91 Deansgate, Manchester, M3 2BW ☎0161/837 3000, ⓕ835 1534, ⊛www.waterstonesbooks.co.uk.

Book and map outlets in the USA

ADC Map and Travel Center, 1636 I St NW, Washington DC 20006 ☎202/628 2608.

Adventurous Traveler Bookstore, PO Box 64769, Burlington, VT 05406 ☎1-800/282-3963, ⊛www.adventuroustraveler.com.

Book Passage, 51 Tamal Vista Blvd, Corte Madera, CA 94925 ☎415/927-0960, ⊛www.bookpassage.com.

The Complete Traveler Bookstore, 199 Madison Ave, New York, NY 10016 ☎212/685-9007; 3207 Fillmore St, San Francisco, CA 92123 ☎415/923-1511.

Distant Lands, 56 S Raymond Ave, Pasadena, CA 91105 ☎626/449-3220, ⊛www.distantlands.com.

Elliott Bay Book Company, 101 S Main St, Seattle, WA 98104 ☎206/624-6600, ⊛www.elliottbaybook.com.

Map Link, 30 S La Petera Lane, Unit #5, Santa Barbara, CA 93117 ☎805/692-6777, ⊛www.maplink.com.

Phileas Fogg's Books & Maps, #87 Stanford Shopping Center, Palo Alto, CA 94304 ☎1-800/533-FOGG, ⊛www.foggs.com.

Rand McNally, ⊛www.randmcnally.com: 444 N Michigan Ave, Chicago, IL 60611 ☎312/321-1751; 150 E 52nd St, New York, NY 10022 ☎212/758-7488; 595 Market St, San Francisco, CA 94105 ☎415/777-3131; 7988 Tysons Corner Center, McLean, VA 22102 ☎703/556-8688; ☎1-800/333-0136 ext 2111 for other locations or for mail order.

Sierra Club Bookstore, 730 Polk St, San Francisco, CA 94110 ☎415/977-5653, ⊛www.sierraclubbookstore.com.

Travel Books & Language Center, 4437 Wisconsin Ave NW, Washington, DC 20016 ☎1-800/220-2665

Traveler's Choice Bookstore, 22 W 52nd St, New York, NY 10019 ☎212/941-1535, ⓔ tvlchoice@aol.com.

Book and map outlets in Canada

Open Air Books and Maps, 25 Toronto St, Toronto, ON M5R 2C1 ☎416/363-0719.

Ulysses Travel Bookshop, 4176 St-Denis, Montreal ☎514/843-9447, ⊛www.ulysses.ca.

World of Maps, 1235 Wellington St, Ottawa, ON K1Y 3A3 ☎613/724-6776, ⊛www.worldofmaps.com.

World Wide Books and Maps, 552 Seymour St, Vancouver, BC V6B 3J5 ☎604/687-3320, ⊛www.itmb.com.

Book and map outlets in Australia and New Zealand

Mapland, 372 Little Bourke St, Melbourne, VIC 3000 ☎03/9670 4383
The Map Shop, 16a Peel St, Adelaide, SA 5000 ☎08/8231 2033
Perth Map Centre, 884 Hay St, Perth, WA 6000 ☎08/9322 5733

Speciality Maps, 58 Albert St, Auckland ☎09/307 2217
Travel Bookshop, Shop 3, 175 Liverpool St, Sydney, NSW 2000 ☎02/9261 8200
Worldwide Maps and Guides, 187 George St, Brisbane, QLD 4000 ☎07/3221 4330
Mapworld, 173 Gloucester Street, Christchurch ☎03/374 5399, fax 03/374 5633, ⊚www.mapworld.co.nz.

Travel insurance

In the light of the potential health risks involved in a trip to India – see opposite – travel insurance is too important to ignore. In addition to covering medical expenses and emergency flights, it also insures your money and belongings against loss or theft. A typical travel insurance policy usually provides cover for the loss of baggage, tickets and – up to a certain limit – cash or cheques, as well as cancellation or curtailment of your journey. Most of them exclude so-called dangerous sports unless an extra premium is paid: in India this can mean trekking, mountaineering, skiing, whitewater rafting and scuba-diving, though probably not Jeep safaris.

Read the small print and benefits tables of prospective policies carefully; coverage can vary wildly for roughly similar premiums. Many policies can be chopped and changed to exclude coverage you don't need – for example, sickness and accident benefits can often be excluded or included at will. If you do take **medical coverage**,

Rough Guide travel insurance

Rough Guides now offers its own **travel insurance**, customized for our readers by a leading UK broker and backed by a Lloyds underwriter. It's available for anyone, of any nationality or age, travelling anywhere in the world.

There are two main Rough Guide insurance plans: **Essential**, for basic, no-frills cover (£23.03 worldwide) for two weeks; and **Premier** – with more generous and extensive benefits (£28.79 worldwide). Alternatively, you can take out annual **multi-trip insurance**, which covers you for any number of trips throughout the year (with a maximum of 60 days for any one trip) at £83.99 (worldwide). Unlike many policies, the Rough Guides schemes are calculated by the day, so if you're travelling for 27 days rather than a month, that's all you pay for. If you intend to be away for the whole year, the **Adventurer** policy will cover you for 365 days from £160 (worldwide excluding USA and Canada) and £200 (worldwide including USA and Canada). Each plan can be supplemented with a "Hazardous Activities Premium" if you plan to indulge in sports considered dangerous, such as trekking, mountaineering, skiing or scuba-diving.

For a **policy quote**, call the Rough Guide Insurance Line on UK freefone ☎0800 015 0906, US freefone ☎ 1-866/220 558 or, if you're calling from outside Britain, on (☎44/1243 621 046). Alternatively, get a quote and buy online at ⊚www.roughguides.com/insurance.

ascertain whether benefits will be paid as treatment proceeds or only after return home, and whether there is a 24-hour medical emergency number. When securing baggage cover, make sure that the per-article limit – typically under £500 equivalent – will cover your most valuable possession.

If you need to make a claim, you should keep **receipts** for medicines and medical treatment and, in the event you have anything stolen, you must obtain an official police report. Bank and credit cards often have certain levels of medical or other insurance included; you may automatically get travel insurance if you use a major credit card to pay for your trip. Keep photocopies of everything you send to the insurer and don't allow months to elapse before informing them. Write immediately and tell them

what's happened; you can usually claim later.

If you have a good all-risks home insurance policy it may cover your possessions against loss or theft even when overseas. Many private medical schemes such as BUPA or PPP also offer coverage plans for abroad, including baggage loss, cancellation or curtailment and cash replacement as well as sickness or accident.

Travellers from the **US** and **Canada** should carefully check their current insurance policies before taking out a new one. You may discover that you are already covered for medical and other losses while abroad. Holders of ISIC cards are entitled to be reimbursed for $3000-worth of accident coverage and sixty days of inpatient benefits of up to $100 a day for the period the card is valid.

Health

A lot of visitors get ill in India, and some of them get very ill. However, if you are careful, you should be able to get through the country with nothing worse than a mild dose of "Delhi belly", an almost obligatory introduction to the country. The important thing is to keep your resistance high and to be very aware of health risks such as poor hygiene, untreated water, mosquito bites and undressed open cuts.

What you **eat** and **drink** is crucial: a poor diet lowers your resistance. Ensure you eat a balance of protein, energy, vitamins and minerals. Meat and fish are obvious sources of protein for non-vegetarians in the West, but not necessarily in India: eggs, pulses (lentils, peas and beans), rice and curd are all protein sources, as are nuts. Overcooked vegetables lose a lot of their vitamin content; eating plenty of peeled fresh fruit helps keep up your vitamin and mineral intake. With all that sweating, too, make sure you get enough salt (put extra on your food) and drink enough water. It's also worth taking daily multi-vitamin and mineral tablets with you. Above all, make sure you eat enough – an unfamiliar

diet may reduce the amount you eat – and **get enough sleep** and rest: it's easy to get run down if you're on the move a lot, especially in a hot climate.

It's worth knowing, if you are ill and can't get to a doctor, that almost any medicine can be bought over the counter without a prescription.

Precautions

The lack of sanitation in India can be exaggerated. It's not worth getting too worked up about it or you'll never enjoy anything, but a few **common-sense precautions** are in order, bearing in mind that things such as bacteria multiply far more quickly in a tropical climate, and your body will have little immunity to Indian germs.

For details on the **water**, see the box on p.32. When it comes to **food**, it's quite likely that tourist restaurants and Western dishes will bring you grief. Be particularly wary of prepared dishes that have to be reheated – they may have been on display in the heat and the flies for some time. Anything that is boiled or fried (and thus sterilized) in your presence is usually all right, though meat can sometimes be dodgy, especially in towns or cities where the electricity supply (and thus refrigerators) frequently fails; anything that has been left out for any length of time is definitely suspect. Raw unpeeled fruit and vegetables should always be viewed with suspicion, and you should avoid salads unless you know they have been soaked in an iodine or potassium permanganate solution. Wiping down a plate before eating is sensible, and avoid straws as they are usually dusty or secondhand. As a rule of thumb, stick to cafés and restaurants that are doing a brisk trade, and where the food is thus freshly cooked, and you should be fine.

Be vigilant about **personal hygiene**. Wash your hands often, especially before eating, keep all cuts clean, treat them with iodine or antiseptic, and cover them to prevent infec-

tion. Be fussier than usual about sharing things like drinks and cigarettes, and never share a razor or toothbrush. It is also inadvisable to go around barefoot – and best to wear flip-flop sandals even in the shower.

Advice on avoiding **mosquitoes** is offered under "Malaria" below. If you do get bites or itches try not to scratch them: it's hard, but infection and tropical ulcers can result if you do. Tiger balm and even dried soap may relieve the itching.

Finally, especially if you are going on a long trip, have a **dental check-up** before you leave home – you don't want to go down with unexpected tooth trouble in India. If you do, and it feels serious, head for Delhi, Mumbai or Calcutta, and ask a foreign consulate to recommend a dentist.

Vaccinations

No **inoculations** are legally required for entry into India, but meningitis, typhoid, and hepatitis A jabs are recommended, and it's worth ensuring that you are up to date with tetanus, polio and other boosters. All vaccinations can be obtained in Delhi, Mumbai and other major cities if necessary; just make sure the needle is new.

Hepatitis A is not the worst disease you can catch in India, but the frequency with which it strikes travellers makes a strong case for immunization. Transmitted through contaminated food and water, or through saliva, it can lay a victim low for several months with exhaustion, fever and diarrhoea – and may cause liver damage. The Havrix vaccine has been shown to be extremely effective; though expensive, it lasts for up to ten years. The protection given by gamma-globulin, the traditional serum of hepatitis antibodies, wears off quickly and the injection should therefore be given as late as possible before departure: the longer your planned stay, the larger the dose.

Symptoms by which you can recognize hepatitis include a yellowing of the whites of the eyes, nausea, general flu-like malaise, orange urine (though dehydration could also cause that) and light-coloured stools. If you think you have it, avoid alcohol, try to avoid passing it on, and get lots of rest. More serious is **hepatitis B**, passed on like AIDS through blood or sexual contact. There is a vaccine, but it is only recommended for those planning to work in a medical environment.

A travellers' first-aid kit

Below are items you might want to take, especially if you're planning to go trekking – all are available in India itself, at a fraction of what you might pay at home:

❏ Antiseptic cream
❏ Insect repellent and cream such as Anthisan for soothing bites
❏ Plasters/band aids
❏ A course of Flagyl antibiotics
❏ Water sterilization tablets or water purifier
❏ Lint and sealed bandages
❏ Knee supports
❏ Imodium (Lomotil) for emergency diarrhoea treatment
❏ A mild oral anaesthetic such as Bonjela for soothing ulcers or mild toothache
❏ Paracetamol/aspirin
❏ Multi-vitamin and mineral tablets
❏ Rehydration sachets
❏ Hypodermic needles and sterilized skin wipes

Typhoid, also spread through contaminated food or water, is endemic in India, but rare outside the monsoon. It produces a persistent high fever with malaise, headaches and abdominal pains, followed by diarrhoea. Vaccination can be by injection (two shots are required, or one for a booster), giving three years' cover, or orally – tablets are more expensive but easier on the arm.

Cholera, spread the same way as hepatitis A and typhoid, causes sudden attacks of watery diarrhoea with cramps and debilitation. It is endemic in the Ganges basin, but only during periodic epidemics. If you get it, take copious amounts of water with rehydration salts and seek medical treatment. There is currently no effective vaccination against cholera.

Most medical authorities now recommend vaccination against meningitis too. Spread by airborne bacteria (through coughs and sneezes for example), it attacks the lining of the brain and can be fatal. Symptoms include fever, a severe headache, stiffness in the neck and a rash on the stomach and back.

You should have a tetanus booster every ten years whether you travel or not. Tetanus (or lockjaw) is picked up through contaminated open wounds and causes severe muscular spasms; if you cut yourself on something dirty and are not covered, get a booster as soon as you can.

Assuming that you were vaccinated against polio in childhood, only one (oral) booster is needed during your adult life. Immunizations against mumps, measles, TB and rubella are a good idea for anyone who wasn't vaccinated as a child and hasn't had the diseases.

Rabies is a problem in India. The best advice is to give dogs and monkeys a wide berth, and not to play with animals at all, no matter how cute they might look. A bite, a scratch or even a lick from an infected animal could spread the disease; wash any such wound immediately but gently with soap or detergent, and apply alcohol or iodine if possible. Find out what you can about the animal and swap addresses with the owner (if there is one) just in case. If the animal might be infected or the wound begins to tingle and fester, act immediately to get treatment – rabies is invariably fatal once symptoms appear. There is a vaccine, but it is expensive, which serves only to shorten the course of treatment you need anyway, and is only effective for a maximum of three months.

Medical resources for travellers

For up-to-the-minute information, make an appointment at a **travel clinic**. These clinics also sell travel accessories, including mosquito nets and first-aid kits. Information about specific diseases and conditions, drugs and herbal remedies is provided at ⑩http://health.yahoo.com, as well as advice from health experts. You could also consult the *Rough Guide to Travel Health* by Dr Nick Jones.

UK

British Airways Travel Clinics Operates several clinics located in London including 156 Regent St, London W1 ⑦020/7439 9584 (Mon–Fri 9.30am–5.15pm, Sat 10am–4pm; no appointment necessary). There are appointment-only branches at 101 Cheapside, London EC2 ⑦020/7606 2977, and at the BA terminal in London's Victoria Station ⑦020/7233 6661. Call ⑦01276/685040 for your nearest clinic, or check out ⑩www.britishairways.com; BA operates around 28 regional clinics throughout the country. The clinics provide vaccinations, tailored advice from their online database and a complete range of travel health-care products.

Hospital for Tropical Diseases Travel Clinic, 2nd floor, Mortimer Market Centre, off Capper Street, London WC1E 6AU (Mon–Fri 9am–5pm by appointment only; ⑦020/7388 9600). A consultation costs £15 which is waived if you have your injections here. Their recorded Health Line (⑦09061/337 733; 50p per min) gives hints on hygiene and illness prevention as well as listing appropriate immunizations.

Malaria Helpline 24-hr recorded message (t0891/600 350; 60p per minute).

MASTA (Medical Advisory Service for Travellers Abroad), London School of Hygiene and Tropical Medicine. Operates a prerecorded 24-hour Travellers' Health Line (t0906/822 4100, 60p per min), giving written information tailored to your journey by return of post.

Nomad Pharmacy, surgeries 40 Bernard St, London, WC1 opposite Russell Square tube station; and 3–4 Turnpike Lane, London N8 (Mon–Fri 9.30am–6pm ⑦020/7833 4114 to book appointment). Advice is free if you go in person, and the telephone helpline is ⑦09068/633 414 (60p a minute). They can give information tailored to your travel needs.

Trailfinders No-appointments-necessary immunization clinics at the 194 Kensington High St branch in London (Mon–Fri 9am–5pm except Thurs to 6pm, Sat 9.30am–4pm; ☎ 020/7938 3999).

North America

Canadian Society for International Health, 1 Nicholas St, Suite 1105, Ottawa, ON K1N 7B7 ☎ 613/241-5785, ⓦ www.csih.org. Distributes a free pamphlet, *Health Information for Canadian Travellers*, containing an extensive list of travel health centres in Canada.

Centers for Disease Control, 1600 Clifton Rd NE, Atlanta, GA 30333 ☎ 404/639-3311, ⓦ www.cdc.gov. Publishes outbreak warnings, suggested inoculations, precautions and other background information for travellers. The website is very useful, as well as their International Travelers Hotline: ☎ 1/888-232-3228.

International Association for Medical Assistance to Travellers (IAMAT), 417 Center St, Lewiston, NY

What about the water?

One of the chief concerns of many prospective visitors to India is whether the water is safe to drink. To put it simply, it's not, though your unfamiliarity with Indian micro-organisms is generally more of a problem rather than any great virulence in the water itself.

As a rule, it is not a good idea to drink **tap water**, although in big cities it is usually chlorinated. However, you'll find it almost impossible to avoid untreated tap water completely: it is used to make ice, which may appear in drinks without being asked for, to wash utensils and so on. Bottled **mineral water** is widely available and cheap. Always check that the seal is intact, as refilling bottles is not uncommon; some brands are better than others with Bisleri being the best, though you don't always have a choice. Always crush bottles after use and dispose of them properly. Note that plastic is a real menace to the environment especially in fragile areas such as the mountains; try to recycle where possible, or purify your own water.

If you plan to go somewhere with no access to bottled drinks (which really only applies to travellers venturing well off the beaten track) you'll need to find an appropriate method of **treating water**, whether your source is tap water or natural ground water such as a river or stream. Boiling it for a minimum of five minutes (longer at higher altitudes) is sufficient to kill micro-organisms, but is not always practical and does not remove unpleasant tastes. **Chemical sterilization** is cheap and convenient, but dirty water remains dirty, and still contains organic matter or other contamination. You can sterilize water by using chlorine or iodine tablets, but these leave a nasty aftertaste (which can be masked with lemon or lime juice). Pregnant women, babies and people with thyroid problems should avoid using iodine sterilizing tablets or iodine-based purifiers, or use an additional iodine-removal filter. The various kinds of filter only remove visible impurities and the larger pathogenic organisms (most bacteria and cysts); however fine the filter, it will not remove viruses.

Purification, a two-stage process involving both filtration and sterilization, gives the most complete treatment. The Aqua Pure Traveller water bottle (£34.99) has a filter top that turns contaminated water into safe, clean drinking water. Tested and approved by the London School of Hygiene and Tropical Medicine, it uses replaceable filters to strain out even the smallest viruses and pathogens. Each one lasts for 350 litres, making it money saving as well as environmentally friendly. ⓦ www.thirstpoint.com. Another supplier of water purifiers is Pre-Mac – for suppliers contact:

Pre-Mac Ltd Unit 5 Morewood Close, Sevenoaks, Kent TN13 2HU, England ☎ 01732/460333, ⓦ www.pre-mac.com.

All Water Systems Ltd Unit 2018, Citywest Business Campus, Faggart, Dublin, Ireland ☎ 01/466 0133.

Travel Medicine 351 Pleasant St, Suite 312, Northampton, MA 01060, US ☎ 1-800/872-8633, ⓦ www.travmed.com.

Nomad Travellers Store and Medical Centre 3–4 Wellington Terrace, Turnpike Lane, London N8 0PX ☎ 020/8889 7014, ⓕ 8889 9529, ⓦ www.nomadtravel.co.uk.

14092 ⊕ 716/754-4883; 40 Regal Rd, Guelph, ON N1K 1B5 ⊕ 519/836-0102,
ⓦ www.sentex.net/~iamat. A nonprofit organization supported by donations, it can provide a list of English-speaking doctors in India, climate charts and leaflets on various diseases and inoculations.
International SOS Assistance, PO Box 11568, Philadelphia, PA 19116 ⊕ 1-800/523-8930,
ⓦ www.intsos.com. Members receive pre-trip medical referral info, as well as overseas emergency services designed to complement travel insurance coverage.
Travel Medicine, 351 Pleasant St, Suite 312, Northampton, MA 01060 ⊕ 1-800/872-8633,
ⓦ www.travmed.com. Sells first-aid kits, mosquito netting, water filters and other health-related travel products.
Travelers Medical Center, 31 Washington Square West, New York, NY 10011 ⊕ 212/982-1600. Consultation service on immunizations and treatment of diseases for people travelling to developing countries.

Australia and New Zealand

Auckland Hospital, Park Road, Grafton ⊕ 09/797 440. General traveller health advice.
Travel-Bug Medical and Vaccination Centre, 161 Ward St, North Adelaide ⊕ 08/8267 3544. Consultations, inoculations, first-aid/medical kits, post-travel examinations.
Travellers' Immunization Service, 303 Pacific Hwy, Lindfield, Sydney ⊕ 02/9416 1348. Offers inoculations and general advice.
Travellers' Medical and Vaccination Centre Australia: Level 7, 428 George St, Sydney ⊕ 02/9221 7133; Level 2, 393 Little Bourke St, Melbourne ⊕ 03/9602 5788; Level 6, 29 Gilbert Place, Adelaide ⊕ 08/8212 7522; Level 6, 247 Adelaide St, Brisbane ⊕ 07/3221 9066; 5 Mill St, Perth ⊕ 08/9321 1977. New Zealand: 1/170 Queen St ⊕ 09/373 3531; 6 Washington Way, Christchurch ⊕ 03/379 4000. General info/health line: ⊕ 1902/261 560 (Australia). Inoculations/medications, area-specific advice, lists of English-speaking doctors in India, first-aid/medical kits and post-travel examinations. A full rundown of their branches, along with general travellers' health advice, appears on ⓦ www.tmvc.com.au.

Malaria

Protection against **malaria** is absolutely essential. The disease, caused by a parasite carried in the saliva of female **Anopheles mosquitoes**, is endemic everywhere in India except high-altitude regions of Ladakh, Himachal Pradesh, Kashmir and Sikkim, and is nowadays regarded as the big killer in the subcontinent. It has a variable incubation period of a few days to several weeks, so you can become ill long after being bitten. Programmes to eradicate the disease by spraying mosquito-infested areas and distributing free preventative tablets have proved disastrous; within a short space of time, the Anopheles develop immunities to the insecticides, while the malaria parasite itself constantly mutates into drug-resistant strains, rendering the old cures ineffective.

It is vital for travellers to take **preventative tablets** according to a strict routine, and to cover the period before and after your trip. The drug used is **chloroquine** (trade names include Nivaquin, Avloclor and Resochin), usually two tablets weekly, but India has chloroquine-resistant strains, and you'll need to supplement it with daily proguanil (**Paludrine**) or weekly **Maloprim**. In India chloroquine is easy to come by but proguanil isn't, so stock up before you arrive. Unfortunately, the highly effective weekly anti-malarial **Larium** (**Mefloquine**), can cause horrible side effects (see below). Australian authorities are now prescribing the antibiotic **Doxycycline** instead of Mefloquine. As the malaria parasite can incubate in your system without showing symptoms for more than a month, it is essential to continue to take preventative tablets for at least four weeks after returning home: the most common way of catching malaria is by forgetting to do this.

Side-effects of anti-malaria drugs may include itching, rashes, hair loss and sight problems. In the case of Larium some people may experience disorientation, depression and sleep disturbance; if you're intending to use Larium you should begin to take it two weeks before you depart to see whether it will agree with your metabolism, though normally you only need to begin taking anti-malaria medication a week before your departure date. If you plan on diving, you should perhaps avoid Mefloquine, as there is a worry about possible side effects for divers.

Malarial symptoms

The first **signs of malaria** are remarkably similar to a severe flu, and may take months to appear: if you suspect anything go to a hospital or clinic immediately. The shivering, burning fever and headaches come in waves, usually in the early evening. Anyone who develops such symptoms should get to a doctor for a blood test as soon as possible. Malaria is not infectious, but some strains are dangerous and occasionally even fatal when not treated promptly, in particular, the chloroquine-resistant **cerebral malaria**. This virulent and lethal strain of the disease, which affects the brain, is treatable, but has to be diagnosed early. Erratic body temperature, lack of energy and aches are the first key signs.

Preventing mosquito bites

The best way of combating malaria is of course to stop yourself getting bitten: malarial mosquitoes are active from dusk until dawn and during this time you should use **mosquito repellent** and take all necessary precautions. Sleep under a **mosquito net** if possible – one which can hang from a single point is best (you can usually find a way to tie a string across your room to hang it from), burn **mosquito coils** (widely available in India, but easy to break in transit) or electrically heated repellents such as All Out. An Indian brand of repellent called Odomos is widely available and very effective, though most travellers bring their own from home, usually one containing the noxious but effective compound **DEET**. DEET can cause rashes and a strength of more than thirty percent is not advised for those with sensitive skin. If you do have sensitive skin, a natural alternative is **citronella** or, in the UK, Mosi-guard Natural, made from a blend of **Eucalyptus oils**, though still use DEET on clothes and nets. Mosquito "buzzers" are pretty useless but wrist and ankle bands are as effective as spray and a good alternative for sensitive skin. Though active from dusk till dawn, female Anopheles mosquitoes prefer to bite in the evening, so be especially careful at that time. Wear long sleeves, skirts and trousers, avoid dark colours, which attract mosquitoes, and put repellent on all exposed skin.

Dengue fever and Japanese encephalitis

Another illness spread by mosquito bites is **dengue fever**, whose symptoms are similar to those of malaria, plus aching bones.

There is no vaccine available and the only treatment is complete rest, with drugs to assuage the fever. **Japanese encephalitis**, yet another mosquito-borne viral infection causing fever, muscle pains and headaches, has been on the increase in recent years in wet rural rice-growing areas. However, there have been no reports of travellers catching the disease, and you shouldn't need the vaccine (which is expensive and has several potentially nasty side-effects) unless you plan to spend much time around paddy fields during and immediately after the monsoons.

Intestinal troubles

Diarrhoea is the most common bane of travellers. When mild and not accompanied by other major symptoms, it may just be your stomach reacting to unfamiliar food. Accompanied by cramps and vomiting, it could well be food poisoning. In either case, it will probably pass of its own accord in 24–48 hours without treatment. In the meantime, it is essential to replace the fluids and salts you're losing, so take lots of water with oral **rehydration salts** (commonly referred to as ORS, or called Electrolyte in India). If you can't get ORS, use half a teaspoon of salt and eight of sugar in a litre of water, and if you are too ill to drink, seek medical help immediately. Travel clinics and pharmacies sell double-ended moulded plastic spoons with the exact ratio of sugar to salt.

While you are suffering, it's a good idea to avoid greasy food, heavy spices, caffeine and most fruit and dairy products. Some say bananas and pawpaws are good, as are kitchri (a simple dhal and rice preparation) and rice soup and coconut water, while curd or a soup made from Marmite or Vegemite (if you happen to have some with you) are forms of protein that can be easily absorbed by your body when you have the runs. Drugs like Lomotil or Imodium simply plug you up – undermining the body's efforts to rid itself of infection – though they can be useful if you have to travel. If symptoms persist for more than a few days, a course of antibiotics may be necessary; this should be seen as a last resort, following medical advice.

Sordid though it may seem, it's a good idea to look at what comes out when you go to the toilet. If your diarrhoea contains blood or mucus and if you are suffering other symptoms including rotten-egg belches and farts, the cause may be **dysentery** or giardia. With a fever, it could well be caused by **bacillic dysentery**, and may clear up without treatment. If you're sure you need it, a course of antibiotics such as tetracycline should sort you out, but they also destroy "gut flora" in your intestines (which help protect you – curd can replenish them to some extent). If you start a course, be sure to finish it, even after the symptoms have gone. Similar symptoms, without fever, indicate **amoebic dysentery**, which is much more serious, and can damage your gut if untreated. The usual cure is a course of Metronidazole (Flagyl) or Fasigyn, both antibiotics which may themselves make you feel ill, and must not be taken with alcohol. Symptoms of **giardia** are similar – including frothy stools, nausea and constant fatigue – for which the treatment is again Metronidazole. If you suspect that you have either of these, seek medical help, and only start on the Metronidazole (750mg three times daily for a week for adults) if there is definitely blood in your diarrhoea and it is impossible to see a doctor.

Finally, bear in mind that oral drugs, such as malaria pills, and the Pill, are likely to be largely ineffective if taken while suffering from diarrhoea.

Bites and creepy crawlies

Worms may enter your body through skin (especially the soles of your feet), or food. An itchy anus is a common symptom, and you may even see them in your stools. They are easy to treat: if you suspect you have them, get some worming tablets such as Mebendazole (Vermox) from any pharmacy.

Biting **insects** and similar animals other than mosquitoes may also aggravate you. The obvious suspects are bed bugs – look for signs of squashed ones around cheap hotel beds. An infested mattress can be left in the hot sun all day to get rid of them, but they often live in the frame or even in walls or floors. Head and body **lice** can also be a nuisance, but medicated soap and shampoo (preferably brought with you from home) usually see them off. Avoid scratching bites, which can lead to infection. Bites from ticks

and lice can spread typhus, characterized by fever, muscle aches, headaches, and, later, red eyes and a measles-like rash. If you think you have it, seek treatment (tetracycline is usually prescribed).

Snakes are unlikely to bite unless accidentally disturbed, and most are harmless in any case. To see one at all, you need to search stealthily – walk heavily and they usually oblige by disappearing. If you do get bitten, remember what the snake looked like (kill it if you can), try not to move the affected part, and seek medical help: anti-venoms are available in most hospitals. A few **spiders** have poisonous bites too. Remove **leeches**, which may attach themselves to you in jungle areas, with salt or a lit cigarette: never just pull them off.

Heat trouble

The sun and the heat can cause a few unexpected problems. Many people get a bout of **prickly heat** rash before they've acclimatized. It's an infection of the sweat ducts caused by excessive perspiration that doesn't dry off. A cool shower, zinc oxide powder (sold in India) and loose cotton clothes should help. **Dehydration** is another possible problem, so make sure you're drinking enough liquid, and drink rehydration salts frequently, especially when hot and/or tired. The main danger sign is irregular urination (only once a day for instance); dark urine definitely means you should drink more (although it could also indicate hepatitis).

The **sun** can burn, or even cause sunstroke, and a high-factor sun block is vital on exposed skin, especially when you first arrive, and on areas newly exposed by haircuts or changes of clothes. A light hat is also a very good idea, especially if you're doing a lot of walking around in the sun.

Finally, be aware that overheating can cause **heatstroke**, which is potentially fatal. Signs are a very high body temperature, without a feeling of fever but accompanied by headaches and disorientation. Lowering body temperature (taking a tepid shower for example) and resting in an air-conditioned room is the first step in treatment.

Altitude sickness

At high altitudes, you may develop symptoms of **acute mountain sickness (AMS)**.

Just about everyone who ascends to around 4000m or more experiences mild symptoms, but serious cases are rare. The simple cure – descent – almost always brings immediate recovery.

AMS is caused by the fact that at high elevations there is not only less oxygen, but also lower atmospheric pressure. This can have all sorts of weird effects on the body: it can cause the brain to swell and the lungs to fill with fluid, and even bring on uncontrollable farting. The syndrome varies from one person to the next, but symptoms include breathlessness, headaches and dizziness, nausea, difficulty sleeping and appetite loss. More extreme cases may involve disorientation and loss of balance, and the coughing up of pink frothy phlegm.

AMS strikes without regard for fitness – in fact, young people seem to be more susceptible, possibly because they're more reluctant to admit they feel sick and they dart about more energetically. Most people are capable of acclimatizing to very high altitudes but the process takes time and must be done in stages. The golden rule is not to go too high, too fast; or if you do, spend the night at a lower height ("Climb High, Sleep Low"). Above 3000m, you should not ascend more than 500m per day; take mandatory acclimatization days at 3500m and 4000m – more if you feel unwell – and try to spend these days day-hiking higher.

The general symptoms of AMS can be treated with the drug acetazolamide (Diamox) but this is not advised as it will block the early signs of severe AMS, which can be fatal. It is better to stay put for a day or two, eat a high carbohydrate diet, drink plenty of water (three litres a day is recommended), take paracetamol or aspirin for the headaches, and descend if the AMS persists or worsens. If you fly direct to a high-altitude destination such as Leh, be especially careful to acclimatize (plan for three days of initial rest); you'll certainly want to avoid doing anything strenuous at first.

Other precautions to take at high altitudes include avoiding alcohol and sleeping pills, drinking more liquid, and protecting your skin against UV solar glare.

HIV and AIDS

The rapidly increasing presence of **AIDS** has only recently been acknowledged by the Indian government as a national problem. The reluctance to address the issue is partly due to the disease's association with sex, a traditionally closed subject in India. As yet only NGOs and foreign agencies such as the WHO have embarked on awareness and prevention campaigns. As elsewhere in the world, high-risk groups include prostitutes and intravenous drug users. It is extremely unwise to contemplate casual sex without a condom – carry some with you (preferably brought from home as Indian ones may be less reliable; also, be aware that heat affects the durability of condoms), and insist upon using them.

Should you need an injection or a transfusion in India, make sure that new, sterile equipment is used; any blood you receive should be from voluntary rather than commercial donor banks. If you have a shave from a barber, make sure he uses a clean blade, and don't submit to processes such as ear-piercing, acupuncture or tattooing unless you can be sure that the equipment is sterile.

Getting medical help

Pharmacies can usually advise on minor medical problems, and most doctors in India speak English. Also, many hotels keep a doctor on call; if you do get ill and need medical assistance, take advice as to the best facilities around. Basic medicaments are made to Indian Pharmacopoea (IP) standards, and most medicines are available without prescription (always check the sell-by date). Hospitals vary in standard: **private clinics** and mission hospitals are often better than state-run ones, but may not have the same facilities. Hospitals in the big cities, including university or medical-school hospitals, are generally pretty good, and cities such as Delhi, Mumbai and Bangalore boast state-of-the-art medical facilities, but at a price. Many hospitals require patients (even emergency cases) to buy necessities such as medicines, plaster casts and vaccines, and to pay for X-rays, before procedures are carried out.

However, **government hospitals** provide all surgical and after-care services free of charge and in most other state medical institutions, charges are usually so low that for minor treatment the expense may well be lower than the initial "excess" on your insur-

Ayurvedic medicine

Ayurved, a Sanskrit word meaning the "knowledge for prolonging life", is a five-thousand-year-old holistic medical system that is widely practised in India. Ayurvedic doctors and clinics in large towns deal with foreigners as well as their usual patients, and some **pharmacies** specialize in Ayurvedic preparations, including toiletries such as soaps, shampoos and toothpastes.

Ayurved assumes the fundamental sameness of self and nature. Unlike the allopathic medicines of the West, which depend on finding out what's ailing you and then killing it, Ayurved looks at the whole patient: disease is regarded as a symptom of **imbalance**, so it's the imbalance that's treated, not the disease. Ayurvedic theory holds that the body is controlled by three forces, which reflect the forces within the self: *pitta*, the force of the sun, is hot, and rules the digestive processes and metabolism; *kapha*, likened to the moon, the creator of tides and rhythms, has a cooling effect, and governs the body's organs; and *vata*, wind, relates to movement and the nervous system. The healthy body is one that has the three forces in balance. To diagnose an imbalance, the Ayurvedic **viad** (doctor) responds not only to the physical complaint but also to family background, daily habits and emotional traits.

Imbalances are typically treated with herbal remedies designed to alter whichever of the three forces is out of whack. Made according to traditional formulae, using indigenous plants, Ayurvedic medicines are cheaper than branded or imported drugs. In addition, the doctor may prescribe various forms of yogic cleansing to rid the body of waste substances. To the uninitiated, these techniques will sound rather off-putting – for instance, swallowing a long strip of cloth, a short section at a time, and then pulling it back up again to remove mucus from the stomach. Ayurvedic **massage** with herbal oils is especially popular in Kerala where courses of treatments are available to combat a wide array of ailments.

ance. You will, however, need a companion to stay, or you'll have to come to an arrangement with one of the hospital cleaners, to help you out in hospital – relatives are expected to wash, feed and generally take care of the patient. Beware of scams by private clinics in tourist towns such as Agra where there have been reports of overcharging and misdiagnosis by doctors to claim insurance money. Addresses of foreign consulates (who will advise in an emergency), and of clinics and hospitals, can be found in the Listings sections in the accounts of major towns in this book.

Costs, money and banks

India is still one of the least expensive countries for travellers in the world; a little foreign currency can go a long way. You can be confident of getting good value for your money, whether you're setting out to keep your budget to a minimum or to enjoy the opportunities that spending a bit more will make possible.

While we attempt below to suggest the kind of sums you can expect to pay for varying degrees of comfort, it is vital not to make a rigid assumption at the outset of a long trip that whatever money you bring to India will last for a certain number of weeks or months. On any one day it may be possible to spend very little, but cumulatively you

Entrance fees

In 2000, the Archeological Survey of India announced a **double-tiered entry system**, with foreign visitors (including non-resident Indians) required to pay $5–20 or its rupee equivalent to enter major archeological sites. This means that foreigners can find themselves paying forty times the entrance fee levied to domestic visitors. Due to considerable outcry from tour agencies and tourists, the Indian government is currently reviewing this policy, and discount pass schemes may emerge; ask at a Government of India tourist office for the latest.

Foreign visitors may be charged in either dollars or rupees; where, as is the case at some sites, foreigners are charged in dollars at that day's exchange rate, we give the dollar rate current at the time of going to press, so bear in mind that this may fluctuate. Throughout the Guide, we list the price for Indian visitors in square brackets.

won't be doing yourself any favours if you don't make sure you keep yourself well rested and properly fed. As a foreigner in India, you will find yourself penalized by double-tier entry prices to museums and historic sites (see box) as well as in upmarket hotels and air fares, both of which are levied at a higher rate and in dollars.

What you spend depends on you: where you go, where you stay, how you get around, what you eat and what you buy. On a budget of as little as $8/£5 per day, you'll manage if you stick to the cheapest of everything and don't move about too much; double that, and you can permit yourself the odd splurge meal, the occasional mid-range hotel, and a few souvenirs. If you're happy spending $20–30 (£15–20) per day, however, you can really pamper yourself; to spend much more than that, you'd have to be doing a lot of travelling, consistently staying in the best hotel in town and eating in the top restaurants. At the top of the range expect to pay international prices for food and accommodation.

Accommodation ranges from a basic $2/£1.50 per night upwards (see p.51), while a vegetarian meal in an ordinary restaurant is unlikely to cost even that much. Rice and dhal can be had for well under 50¢/30p, but you wouldn't want to live on that alone. Transport in town costs pennies (even by taxi), while a twelve-hour train journey might cost $5 (£3) in second class, $20 (£15) in first.

Where you are makes a difference: Mumbai is notoriously pricey, especially for accommodation, while tourist enclaves like the Goa beaches will not be cheap for things like food, and there will be more souvenirs to tempt you. Delhi, too, is substantially more

costly than most parts of the country. Out in the sticks, on the other hand, and particularly away from your fellow tourists, you will find things incredibly cheap, though your choice will obviously be more limited.

Some independent travellers tend to indulge in wild and highly competitive **penny-pinching**, which Indian people find rather pathetic – they know how much an air ticket to Delhi or Mumbai costs, and they have a fair idea of what you can earn at home. Bargain where appropriate, but don't begrudge a few rupees to someone who's worked hard for them: consider what their services would cost at home, and how much more valuable the money is to them than it is to you. Even if you get a bad deal on every rickshaw journey you make, it will only add a minuscule fraction to the cost of your trip. Remember too, that every pound or dollar you spend in India goes that much further, and luxuries you can't afford at home become possible here: sometimes it's worth spending more simply because you get more for it. At the same time, don't pay well over the odds for something if you know what the going rate is. Thoughtless extravagance can, particularly in remote areas that see a disproportionate number of tourists, contribute to inflation, putting even basic goods and services beyond the reach of local people.

Currency

India's unit of currency is the **rupee**, usually abbreviated "Rs" and divided into a hundred **paise**. Almost all money is paper, with notes of 10, 20, 50, 100, 500 and, recently, 1000 rupees: a few notes of 1, 2 and 5 are still in circulation. Coins start at 5 paise then range up to 10, 20, 25 and 50 paise, and 1, 2 and 5 rupees.

Banknotes, especially lower denominations, can get into a terrible state, but don't accept **torn banknotes**; no one else will be prepared to take them, so you will be left saddled with the things, though you can change them at the Reserve Bank of India and large branches of other big banks. Don't pass them on to beggars; they can't use them either, so it amounts to an insult.

Large denominations can also be a problem, as change is usually in short supply. Many Indian people cannot afford to keep much lying around, and you shouldn't necessarily expect shopkeepers or rickshaw-wallahs to have it (and they may – as may you – try to hold onto it if they do). Paying for your groceries with a Rs100 note will probably entail waiting for the grocer's errand boy to go off on a quest to try and change it. Larger notes – like the Rs500 note – are good for travelling with and can be changed for smaller denominations at hotels and other suitable establishments. A word of warning – the Rs500 note looks remarkably similar to the Rs100 note.

At the time of writing, the **exchange rate** was approximately Rs68 to £1, or Rs45 to $1.

Travellers' cheques, credit cards and ATMs

In addition to your cash, carry some **travellers' cheques** to cover all eventualities, with a few small denominations for the end of your trip, and for the odd foreign-currency purchase such as tourist-quota rail tickets which can be bought with American Express travellers' cheques. US dollars are the easiest **currency** to convert, with pounds sterling a close second. Major hard currencies can be changed easily in tourist areas and big cities, less so elsewhere. If you enter the country with more than $10,000 or the equivalent, you are supposed to fill in a currency declaration form.

Travellers' cheques aren't as liquid as cash, but obviously more secure (and you get a slightly better exchange rate for them at banks). Not all banks, however, accept them, and those that do can be quirky about exactly which ones they will change. Well-known brands such as Thomas Cook and American Express are your best bet, but in some places

even American Express is only accepted in US dollars and not as pounds sterling.

A **credit card** is a handy back-up, as an increasing number of hotels, restaurants, large shops and tourist emporia as well as airlines now take plastic; American Express, Access/Mastercard, Visa and Diners Club are the most commonly accepted brands. If you have a selection of cards, take them all; you'll get much the same exchange rate as you would in a bank, and bills can take a surprisingly long time to be charged to your account at home. The Bank of Baroda and Standard Chartered Grindlays issue rupees against a Visa card at all their branches. Train tickets can now be paid for by credit card, but only in the major cities.

Several banks now have **ATM machines** but only in the cities, and not all ATMs will accept foreign cards even if they sport Visa and Mastercard signs; you are best advised to enquire first before sticking your card into the slot. Delhi and Mumbai branches of the Hong Kong Bank and Bank of America have 24hr ATMs that take Visa and Mastercard, while some of Standard Chartered Grindlays banks also have foreigner-friendly ATM machines.

It is illegal to carry rupees (besides spending money) into or out of India, and you won't get them at a particularly good rate in the West anyhow (though you might in Thailand, Malaysia or Singapore).

Both American Express and Thomas Cook have offices in other major cities throughout India; see the relevant accounts in the guide and collect a full list when you purchase your travellers' cheques.

Travellers' cheques and credit card contacts

American Express

@www.americanexpress.com.
Lost and stolen cards ☏011/614 5920 or 687 5050 (open 24hr)
Bangalore ☏080/227 1485
Janardhan Tower, 2 Residency Rd
Calcutta ☏033/248 8570 and 248 9570
21 Old Court House St
Chennai ☏044/852 3628 & 852 3573
G-17, Spencer Plaza, 768–769 Anna Salai
Mumbai ☏022/204 8291-5
Regal Cinema Building, Chatrapati Shivaji Maharaj Rd, Colaba

Delhi ☎ 011/332 4119
Wenger House, "A" Block, Connaught Place

Thomas Cook

🌐 http://64.27.75.224/index.html
Lost and stolen cards ☎ 0044-1733/294451
Bangalore ☎ 080/558 8038
70 Mahatma Gandhi Rd & 55 Mahatma Gandhi Rd
(☎ 080/559 4168)
Calcutta ☎ 033/247 4560 & 247 5378
Chitrakoot Building, 2nd Floor, 230A AJC Bose Rd
Chennai ☎ 044/855 3276 & 855 4913
Ceebros Centre, 45 Montieth Rd, Egmore
Jaipur ☎ 0141/360940
Mirza Ismail Road
Mumbai ☎ 022/204 8556-7
Dr Dadabhai Naoroji Road, Fort
Delhi ☎ 011/374 7404
Rishsya Mook Building, 85-A Panchkuin Rd and
Hotel Imperial, Janpath (☎ 336 8561)

Banks

Changing money in regular **banks**, especially government-run banks such as the State Bank of India (SBI), can be a time-consuming business, involving lots of form-filling and queuing at different counters, so change substantial amounts at any one time. Banks in main cities are likely to be most efficient, though not all change foreign currency, and some won't take **travellers' cheques** or currencies other than dollars or sterling (banks usually charge a percentage of the transaction while Grindlays charge Rs200). You'll have no such problems with **private companies** such as Thomas Cook and American Express who have offices in most state capitals.

In the major cities and the main tourist centres, there are usually several **licensed currency exchange bureaus** where the rates are not usually as good as at a bank but where there's generally a lot less hassle. In small towns, the SBI is your best bet but you may want to ask around for an alternative. Note that if you arrive at a minor airport you may not be able to change anything except cash US dollars or sterling.

Outside **banking hours** (Mon–Fri 10am till 2–4pm, Sat 10am–noon), large hotels may change money, probably at a lower rate, and exchange bureaus have longer opening hours. Banks at Delhi, Mumbai, Calcutta and Chennai **airports**, and at the Ashok Hotel in Delhi, stay open 24 hours but none of these

is very conveniently located. Otherwise, there's always the black market if you're desperate.

Hold on to **exchange receipts** ("encashment certificates"); they will be required if you want to change back any excess rupees when you leave the country, and to buy air tickets and reserve train berths with rupees. The State Bank of India now charges for tax clearance forms (see p.23 to find out if you'll need one.)

Wiring money to India is a lot easier than it used to be. Indian banks with branches abroad, such as the State Bank of India and the Bank of Baroda, can wire money by telex from those branches to large ones in India in two working days. Western Union (information on ☎ 1-800/325-6000 in the US or ☎ 0800/833833 in the UK) can transfer cash or banker's drafts paid into their overseas branches to any one of 43 offices in India within fifteen minutes, for a typical fee of around 7.5 percent of the total amount; similar services are offered by American Express, Thomas Cook, and foreign banks with branches in India such as Standard Chartered (and Standard Chartered Grindlays) and HSBC.

The black market

A **black market** still exists, but only in the major tourist areas of the biggest cities, with little if any premium over the bank rate, though it is a lot faster. You shouldn't need to use it, as the change facilities, especially in the major cities, are far improved. If you do use the black market, small denominations are not popular, with the best rates given for notes of $100, £50 or DM1000; you will, of course, have to haggle.

Always do this kind of business with shopkeepers rather than shady "hello my friend" types on the street, and proceed with caution. Never hand over your pile until you yourself have counted and checked the rupees and have them in your hand; make sure they really are the denominations you think. Unusually high rates suggest a con, as does any attempt to rush you, or sudden claims that the police are coming. Remember that what you are doing is illegal; you can be arrested and you may be set up.

At one or two of India's land borders (notably Bangladesh), unofficial money-changers may be your only option; as their rates will not be good, however, only change as much as you need to get you to a bank.

Baksheesh

As a presumed-rich sahib or memsahib, you will, like wealthy Indians, be expected to be liberal with the **baksheesh**, which takes three main forms.

The most common is tipping: a small reward for a small service, which can encompass anyone from a waiter or porter to someone who lifts your bags onto the roof of a bus or keeps an eye on your vehicle for you. Large amounts are not expected – ten rupees should satisfy all the aforementioned. Taxi drivers and staff at cheaper hotels and restaurants do not necessarily expect tips, but always appreciate them, of course, and they can keep people sweet for the next time you call. Some may take liberties in demanding baksheesh, but it's often better just to acquiesce rather than spoil your mood and cause offence over trifling sums.

More expensive than plain tipping is paying people to **bend the rules**, many of which seem to have been invented for precisely that purpose. Examples might include letting you into a historical site after hours, finding you a seat or a sleeper on a train that is "full", or speeding up some bureaucratic process. This should not be confused with bribery, a more serious business with its own risks and etiquette, which is best not entered into.

The last kind of baksheesh is **alms giving**. In a country without a welfare system, this is an important social custom. People with disabilities and mutilations are the traditional recipients, and it seems right to join local people in giving out small change to them. Kids demanding money, pens, sweets or the like are a different case, pressing their demands only on tourists. In return for a service it is fair enough, but to yield to any request encourages them to go and pester others.

Getting around

Inter-city transport in India may not be the fastest or the most comfortable in the world, but it's cheap, goes more or less everywhere, and generally gives you the option of train or bus, sometimes plane, and occasionally even boat. Transport around town comes in even more permutations, ranging in Calcutta, for example, from rickshaws still pulled by men on foot to a spanking new metro system.

Whether you're on road or rail, public transport or your own vehicle, India offers the chance to try out some classics: narrow-gauge railways, steam locomotives, the Ambassador car and the Enfield Bullet motorbike, they're all here. Some people come to India for these alone.

By train

Travelling by train is one of the great experiences of India. It's a system which looks like chaos, but it works, and well. Trains are

often late of course, sometimes by hours rather than minutes, but they do run, and with amazing efficiency too: when the train you've been waiting for rolls into the station, the reservation you made halfway across the country several weeks ago will be on a list pasted to the side of your carriage, and when it's time to eat, the packed meal you ordered down the line will be ready at the next station, put on the train and delivered to your seat.

It's worth bearing in mind, with journeys frequently lasting twelve hours or more, that

Travel details

At the end of each chapter in this book, you'll find a Travel Details section summarizing major transport connections in the relevant state. In addition, boxes at the end of each major city detail moving on from that city.

an **overnight train** can save you a day's travelling and a night's hotel bill, assuming you sleep well on trains. While sleeper carriages can be more crowded during the day, between 9pm and 6am anyone with a bunk reservation is entitled to exclusive use of their bunk. When travelling overnight, always padlock your bag to your bunk; an attached chain is usually provided beneath the seat of the lower bunk.

Routes, classes and fares

The railway network covers almost the entire country; only a few places (such as Sikkim, Ladakh, Uttaranchal and most of Himachal Pradesh, all mountainous) are inaccessible by train. **Inter-city** trains, called "express" or "mail", vary a lot in the time taken to cover the same route. Slow by Western standards, they're still much faster than local **"passenger" trains**, which you need only use to get right off the beaten track. Note that express and mail trains cost a fair amount more than ordinary passenger trains, so if travelling unreserved you must buy the right ticket to avoid being fined. There are also an increasing number of special **"super-fast"** air-conditioned trains – the Rajdhani expresses link distant cities to New Delhi while the Shatabdi expresses are daytime trains which connect major cities within an eight-hour travelling distance. Bottled water, snacks and good meals are included in the much higher ticket prices of the "super-fast" trains.

Most lines are either metre-gauge or broad-gauge (1.676m, or 4'6"), the latter being faster; many metre-gauge lines are now being converted to broad-gauge. There are also a few narrow-gauge lines (often referred to as "toy trains"), notably to the hill stations of Darjeeling (now a World Heritage line), Shimla, Matheran and Ootacamund. Although being phased out, **steam locomotives** are still used on the first and last (the latter on Sundays only) of these, and you may well see some in use in shunting yards,

but they are fast disappearing. Almost all trains nowadays are diesel-hauled, although some main and suburban lines are electric.

Classes of train travel

Indian Railways (IR, @ www.indianrailway .com) distinguishes between no fewer than seven **classes** of travel, though you'll seldom have more than four to choose from on mainline services: second-class unreserved, second-class sleeper, first, and air-conditioned first (or air-conditioned sleeper with two or three bunks, referred to as two- or three-tier: pronounced "tyre"). In general, most travellers (not just those on low budgets) choose to travel second class, and prefer not to be in a/c compartments; an open window keeps you cool enough, and brings you into contact with the world outside, while air-conditioning by definition involves being sealed away behind glass, often virtually opaque. Doing without a sleeper on an overnight journey is, however, a false economy. **Bed rolls** (sheet, blanket and pillow) are available in first class and a/c second for that extra bit of comfort – book these with your ticket, or before you board the train.

Second-class unreserved is painfully crowded and noisy with no chance of a berth overnight, but incredibly cheap: just Rs77 (that's under $2 or just over £1) for a thousand-kilometre journey. However, the crush and hard wooden seats (if you are lucky or nifty enough to get one) make it viable only for short hops or for the extremely hardy. Far more civilized and only around fifty percent more expensive is **second-class sleeper** (from Rs119 for 1000km), which must be booked in advance even for daytime journeys. If you have an unreserved ticket and travel in a sleeper carriage, even if it is not full, you will be charged a Rs60 fine as well as the difference in fare. Second-class sleepers can be pretty crowded during the day but never lack activity, with peanut-, chai- and coffee-sellers, travelling musicians, beggars or sweepers passing through the carriages. Overnight trips in second-class sleeper compartments are reasonably comfy (provided the berths are foam and not wooden), and there's the option of more privacy for women in ladies' compartments on most long-haul journeys.

First class, in comfortable if ageing compartments of two to four berths, used mainly by English-speaking business travellers, costs about 3.5 times as much as sleeper class (from Rs914 for 1000km on express and mail trains). Not always available on passenger trains and gradually being phased out, first class insulates you to a certain extent from the chaotic hustle and bustle.

Air-conditioned travel, unavailable on "passenger trains", falls into five categories but only one or two will be available on any particular service, except for the Rajdhani which has three. The best value is the **a/c chair car** (often denoted as CC), with comfortable reclining seats at only twice the price of second-class sleeper class. The "super-fast" Shatabdi expresses are exclusively chair car but come in two classes – ordinary a/c chair car and, for double the price, an executive a/c chair car. Very occasionally, a/c chair cars appear on express or mail trains. **Air-conditioned three-tier sleepers** (3AC) cost slightly less than normal first class but cost more on the Rajadhani. Three-tier can feel a bit cramped, especially with loads of luggage, but represents good value (Rs783 for 1000km); they are, however, not as common as the **a/c two-tier sleepers** (2AC) which cost half as much again as first class – Rs1253 for 1000km, and more for Rajdhani. Top of the tree is **a/c first class** (1AC), which offers shared compartments for two or four and has a little more luxury with carpeting and more presentable bathrooms, but at Rs2506 for 1000km and more on the Rajdhani, this is not much cheaper than flying. Bed linen is provided free on most a/c services while meals are also included on Rajdhani and Shatabdi trains.

Ladies' compartments exist on all overnight trains for women travelling on their own or with other women; they are usually small and can be full of noisy kids, but can give untold relief to women travellers who otherwise have to endure incessant staring in the open section of the carriage. They can be a good place to meet Indian women, particularly if you like (or are with) children. Some stations also have ladies-only waiting rooms.

Train fares

To give a rough idea of **typical fares** on express or mail trains: Mumbai–Ahmedabad in an express or mail (490km) costs Rs106 in second-class unreserved, Rs165 in second-class sleeper, and Rs557 in ordinary first class; Delhi–Varanasi (760km) costs Rs231 in second-class sleeper, Rs783 in ordinary first class, Rs1073 in 2AC and Rs1870 in 1AC. The fare on the Shatabdi from New Delhi to Agra (199km) costs Rs390 and Rs760 for executive class; the fare on the Rajdhani from New Delhi to Howrah (Calcutta; 1441km) via Gaya is Rs1500 (3AC), Rs2470 (2AC) and Rs4270 (1AC).

Rail records

Comprising 42,000 miles (over 60,000km) of track and 14,000 locomotives that daily transport an average of 12 million passengers, India's rail network is the second largest in the world. It's also the biggest employer on the planet, with a workforce of around 1.6 million.

One record the country's transport ministers are somewhat less proud of, however, is the accident rate. Four to five hundred crashes occur annually in India, causing between seven and eight hundred fatalities, which makes this the most dangerous rail network in the world, by a long chalk.

The world's worst rail disaster took place in Ferozabad, near Delhi, in 1995, when a cyclone blew a train of a bridge, killing 800. In August 1999, another 350 passengers died when two trains – carrying a total off 2500 people – collided head on in West Bengal. On both occasions, as in sixty percent of Indian rail accidents, human error was cited as the cause. In reality, lack of adequate training, maintenance and investment at government level are the real roots of the problems facing India's ageing network.

Train passengers, however, can take solace in the fact that travelling by rail in India is considerably safer than using the buses. An average of 1,500 people die on the country's roads every day.

Timetables and tickets

Indian Railways publish an annual **timetable** of all mail and express trains – in effect, all the trains you are likely to use. Called *Trains at a Glance*, it is available from information counters and newsstands at all main stations, and from IR agents abroad. Thomas Cook's *International Timetable Vol II* (the blue one) has a limited selection of timetables, while the elusive monthly Indian *Bradshaw* covers every scheduled train in the country. In theory, this is available at major stations, but it is often difficult to get hold of (Calcutta seems to be the best place); complete regional timetables are widely available, however. You can also access rail timetables and fares at ⓦ www.indianrailway.com.

All rail fares are calculated according to the exact **distance** travelled. *Trains at a Glance* prints a chart of fares by kilometres, and also gives the distance in kilometres of stations along each route in the timetables, making it possible to calculate what the basic fare will be for any given journey.

Each individual train has its own name and number, prominently displayed in station booking halls. When buying a second-class ticket, it makes sense to pay the tiny extra fee to reserve a seat or sleeper (the fee is already included in the price of the higher classes). To do so, you fill in a form specifying the train you intend to catch, its number, your date of travel, and the stations you are travelling to and from, plus, amusingly to most travellers, your age and sex (this helps conductors to determine who you are). Most stations have **computerized booking counters** (these are listed in *Trains at a Glance*), and you will be told immediately whether or not seats are available.

Reserving tickets

Reservation offices in the main stations are often in a separate building and generally open from Monday to Saturday from 8am to 8pm, and on Sunday to 2pm. In larger cities, the major stations have special **tourist sections** to cut the queues for foreigners and Indian citizens resident abroad buying tickets, with helpful English-speaking staff; however, if you don't pay in pounds sterling or dollars (travellers' cheques or cash), you must produce an encashment certificate to back up your rupees. Elsewhere, buying a ticket can often involve a long wait, though

women get round this at ticket counters which have **"ladies' queues"**; travelling in a mixed group or couple, a woman will find it easier to get a ticket. Some stations also operate a number system of queuing, allowing you to repair to the chai stall or check the timetable until your number is called. Alternatively, many travel agents will secure tickets for a reasonable Rs25–50 fee. Failure to buy a ticket at the point of departure will result in a stiff penalty when the ticket inspector (known as the "TT") finds you.

It's important to plan your train journeys in advance, as the demand often makes it impossible to buy a long-distance ticket on the same day that you want to travel. Travellers following tight itineraries tend to buy their departure tickets from particular towns the moment they arrive, to avoid having to trek out to the station again. At most large stations, it's possible to reserve tickets for journeys starting elsewhere in the country. You can even book tickets for specific journeys (if you buy an Indrail pass; see p.45) before you leave home, with Indian Railways representatives abroad (see p.46). They accept bookings up to six months in advance, with a minimum of one month for first class, and three months for second.

If there are no places available on the train you want, you have a number of choices. First, some seats and berths are set aside as a **"tourist quota"** – ask at the tourist counter if you can get in on this, or else try the stationmaster. This quota is available in advance but usually only at major or originating stations. Failing that, other special quotas, such as one for VIPs, only released on the day of travel, may remain unused – however, if you get a booking on the VIP quota and a pukka VIP turns up, you lose the reservation. Alternatively, a "reservation against cancellation" (RAC) ticket will give you priority if sleepers do become available – the ticket clerk should be able to tell you your chances. With an RAC ticket you are allowed onto the train and can sit until the conductor can find you a berth. The worst sort of ticket to have is a **wait-listed** one which will allow you onto the train but not in a reserved compartment; in this case go and see the ticket inspector as soon as possible to persuade him to find you a place if one is free: something usually is, but you'll be stuck in unreserved if it isn't. Wait-listed ticket holders are not allowed onto Shatabdi and

Rajdhani trains. In practice, if your number is not too far down the order on the waiting list, you have a good chance of getting a place; each station has its own quota of tickets so ask in the ticket inspector's office at the station before the train gets in. Alternatively, and especially if you get on where the train starts its journey, **baksheesh** may persuade a porter to "reserve" you an unreserved seat or, better still, a luggage rack where you can stretch out for the night. You could even fight your way on and grab one yourself, although we don't rate your chances. As for attempting to **travel unreserved**, for journeys of any length it's too uncomfortable to be worth seriously considering on any major route.

Cancelling tickets

If you have to **cancel** your ticket, the fare is refunded up to a day before departure, minus a fee for the reservation (Rs10 in second class, Rs20 in sleeper, Rs30 a/c chair car or first and Rs50 in a/c first). Between a day and four hours before scheduled departure, you get 75 percent back; you can still claim a fifty percent refund if you present your ticket up to twelve hours after the train actually leaves on a journey of more than 500km, six hours on 200–500km trips, or three hours after a short journey.

Tourist trains

Inspired by the Orient Express, Indian Railways runs four luxury **tourist trains** on packaged holidays with exorbitant prices charged in dollars. The flagship of the scheme is the **Palace on Wheels,** with luxurious ex-maharajas' carriages updated into modern air-conditioned coaches, still decorated with the original designs. The all-inclusive, one-week whistle-stop tour (Sept–April weekly) starts from Delhi and tours through Jaipur and Jodhpur to the sands of Jaisalmer before turning south to Udaipur and returning via Agra; prices start at around US$350 per person per day with discounts off season (Sept & April).

Other alternatives include the **Fairy Queen**, driven by one of the oldest working steam engines in the world, which travels

Indrail passes

Indrail passes, sold to foreigners and Indians resident abroad, cover all fares and reservation fees for periods ranging from half a day to ninety days. Even if you travel a lot, this works out considerably more expensive than buying your tickets individually (especially in second class), but it will save you queuing for tickets, allow you to make and cancel reservations with impunity (and without charge), and generally smooth your way in, for example, finding a seat or berth on a "full" train: passholders, for example, get priority for tourist quota places. Indrail passes are available, for sterling or US dollars, at main station tourist counters in India, and outside the country at IR agents (see opposite). If you're travelling from Britain, Dr Dandapani of SD Enterprises Ltd (see opposite) is an excellent contact, providing information on all aspects of travel on Indian railways.

	a/c First Class Sleeper, or a/c Chair Car		First Class or a/c		Second Class	
	Adult	Child	Adult	Child	Adult	Child
1 day*	$95	$48	$43	$22	$19	$10
4 days*	$220	$110	$110	$55	$50	$25
7 days	$270	$135	$135	$68	$80	$40
15 days	$370	$185	$185	$95	$90	$45
21 days	$396	$198	$198	$100	$100	$50
30 days	$495	$248	$248	$125	$125	$63
60 days	$800	$400	$400	$200	$185	$95
90 days	$1060	$530	$530	$265	$235	$120

Children under 5 travel free

*For sale outside India only; half-day and two-day pass also available.

Indian railways sales agents abroad

Australia Adventure World, 73 Walker St (PO Box 480), N Sydney, NSW 2059 ☎ 02/8913 0755 & 9956 7766, ⓦ www.adventureworld.com.au.

Bangladesh Omaitrans International, 70/1 Inner Circular Rd, Kakrail, Dhaka ☎ 02/834401.

Canada Hari World Travel Inc, 1 Financial Place, Adelaide St East, Toronto M5C 2V8 ☎ 416/366-2000.

Malaysia City East West Travels, 23 Jalan Yao Ah Shak, 50300 Kuala Lumpur ☎ 03/293 0569 or 491 8070.

South Africa , 13 M K Bobby Naidoo Travel Agency, PO Box 2878, Durban, South Africa 44001 ☎ 021/309 3628.

Thailand SS Travels Service, 10/12–13, SS Building, Convent Rd, Bangkok 10500 ☎ 02/236 7188 & 235 1195.

UK SD Enterprises Ltd, 103 Wembley Park Drive, Wembley, Middx HA9 8HG ☎ 020/8903 3411, ⓦ www.indiarail.co.uk.

USA Hari World Travels Inc, 25 W 45th St # 1003 New York, NY 10036 ☎ 212/957-3000; additional locations in Atlanta ☎ 404/233-5005 and Chicago ☎ 773/381-5555.

through eastern Rajasthan (Oct–Feb twice monthly; around $300 per day); while the **Royal Orient** with thirteen lavishly decorated saloon cars, travels from Delhi through southern Rajasthan to Gujarat (Oct–March, $150 per day). In a completely different vein, the **Buddha Parikrama Express** starts at Calcutta and takes rich pilgrims (mostly Japanese) around the Buddhist sites of Bihar and Uttar Pradesh. Bookings for these trains can be made through Indian Railway representatives abroad, and tour operators who peg on additional excursions.

In addition, the *Palace on Wheels* can be booked through RTDC, Bikaner House, Pandara Road, New Delhi (☎ 011/338 1884); the *Fairy Queen* through the Tourism Directorate, Rail Bhavan, New Delhi (☎ 011/338 3000); the *Royal Orient* through the Tourism Corporation of Gujarat, II Floor, A-6, State Emporia Building, Baba Kharak Singh Marg, New Delhi (☎ 011/336 4724); and the *Buddha Parikrama Express* through ITDC, Room 305, III Floor, 27 Barakhamba Rd, New Delhi (☎ 011/331 3233).

Cloakrooms

Most stations in India have **"cloakrooms"** (sometimes called parcel offices) for passengers to leave their baggage. These can be extremely handy if you want to go sightseeing in a town and move on the same day. In theory, you need a train ticket or Indrail pass to deposit luggage, but they don't always ask; they may, however, refuse to take your bag if you can't lock it. Losing your reclaim ticket causes problems; the clerk will be assumed to have stolen the bag if he can't produce it, so there'll be untold running around to obtain clearance before you can get your bag without it. Make sure, when checking baggage in, that the cloakroom will be open when you need to pick it up. The standard charge is currently Rs7 per 24 hours.

By air

Considering the huge distances involved in getting around the country, **flying** will come as an attractive option until you consider the cost. India has some of the highest domestic **air fares** in the world, which is why a lot of wealthier Indians now actually find it cheaper to fly abroad on a package holiday than to see their own country.

On top of that, **foreigners** and nonresident Indians are penalized by having to pay in dollars (or show equivalent exchange receipts) and the price is invariably higher than for Indians – around fifteen percent. There are no return flight deals and while short flights can cost as little as $50, longer ones prove exorbitant. For example, a Delhi–Chennai flight costs over $230 (though it takes a mere 2hr 30min by plane compared to 36 hours' hard train travel). Delays and cancellations can whittle away the time advantage, especially over small distances, but if you're short of time and plan to cover a lot of ground, you should definitely consider flying for longer journeys.

India has just one national internal air carrier, **Indian Airlines** or IA (ⓦ www.nic.in /indian-airlines), which serves over 140 routes, and also flies to several Southeast Asian and Gulf destinations. In addition, Air India runs feeder services between several major cities and its hub, Mumbai, to connect with its international flights.

Jet Airways (@www.jetairways.com) flies many of the major routes covered by IA, and generally provides a more efficient, slicker service than the national carrier. Amongst the other private airlines, Sahara runs an efficient service but only on a handful of main routes like Delhi–Mumbai, where operators such as Jagson, Archana and Gujarat Airways offer links with smaller towns such as Porbander, Kullu, Dharamsala and Jaisalmer. All are very convenient, but at least as expensive as IA.

Both IA and Jet Airways have a number of special deals that are worth knowing about. IA offers 25 percent discount for under-30s and students, and 50 percent for over-65s. Both airlines offer multi-flight discounts (see box below).

One problem with flying is that you may have to spend a massive amount of time queuing at the airline office to get a **reservation**; it's often quicker to book through a hotel or travel agent, which is the norm for booking on private carriers. If you haven't got a confirmed seat, be sure to get to the airport early and keep checking your position in the queue; even if you have got a confirmed seat, be sure to always reconfirm 72 hours before your flight.

Airlines have offices or representatives in all the places they fly to; all are listed in this book in the relevant city sections. IA tickets must be paid for in hard currency or with a **credit card** (not accepted in smaller towns like Leh). Children under 12 pay half fare, and under-twos (one per adult) pay ten percent. There are no **cancellation charges** if you pay in foreign currency, but tickets are not replaceable if lost. **Timetables** for all internal flights (with fares) are published in *Divan* and *Excel* magazines, in city listings magazines and newspaper supplements, shown on teletext, and posted on the airlines' websites.

By bus

Although trains are the definitive form of transport in India, and generally more comfortable than **buses**, there are places (such as most Himalayan valleys) where trains don't go, where they are inconvenient, or where buses are simply faster (as in most of Rajasthan and other places without broadgauge track). Buses go almost everywhere, more frequently than trains (though mostly in daylight hours).

Services vary somewhat in price and standards. Government-run ramshackle affairs, packed to the gunnels with people, livestock and luggage, cover most routes. In addition, popular trunk routes between large cities, towns and resorts are usually covered by **private buses**. These tend to be more comfortable, with extra legroom, tinted windows and padded reclining seats. In some states, notably Rajasthan, they are also considerably cheaper. Smaller private bus companies may be only semi-legal and have little backup in case of breakdown.

The description of the service usually gives some clue about the level of comfort. "Ordinary" buses usually have minimally padded, bench-like seats with upright backs. "Deluxe" or "luxury" are more or less interchangeable terms but sometimes the term deluxe signifies a luxury bus past its sell-by date; occasionally a bus will be described as a "2 by 2" which means a deluxe bus with just two seats on either side of the aisle. When applied to government services, these may hardly differ from "ordinary" buses, but with private companies, they should guarantee a softer, individual seat. It's worth asking when booking if your bus will have a video or music system (a "video bus"), as their deafening noise ruins any chances of sleep. Always try to avoid the back seats – they accentuate bumpy roads.

Luggage travels in the hatch of private buses – for which you will have to part with about Rs5 as "security" for the safekeeping of your bags. On state-run buses, you can usually squeeze it into an unobtrusive corner,

---

Multi-flight deals

These fares only work on a circular route and don't allow intentional backtracking.

Indian Airlines
Discover India Fare Unlimited travel on all internal flights: 15 days $500; 21 days $750 (no single route twice)
India Wonderfare Seven days' travel in one given region; $300

Jet Airways
Visit India Fare Unlimited travel on their routes: 15 days $550; 21 days $800; 7 days regional fare (either north or south India) $330

although you may sometimes be requested to have it travel on the roof (you may be able to travel up there yourself if the bus is too crowded, though it's dangerous and illegal); check that it's well secured (ideally, lock it there) and not liable to get squashed. Baksheesh is in order for whoever puts it up there for you.

Buying a bus ticket is usually less of an ordeal than buying a train ticket, although at large city bus stations there may be twenty or so counters, each assigned to a different route. When you buy your ticket you'll be given the registration number of the bus and, sometimes, a seat number. As at railway stations, there is usually a separate, quicker, ladies' queue, although the sign to indicate it may not be in English. You can always get on ordinary state buses without a ticket, and at bus stands outside major cities you can usually only pay on board, so you have to be sharp to secure a seat. Prior booking is usually available and preferable for express and private services and it is a good idea to check with the agent exactly where the bus will depart from. You can usually pay on board private buses too, though that reduces your chances of a seat.

By boat

Apart from river ferries, few **boat services** run in India. The Andaman Islands are connected to Calcutta and Chennai by boat – as well as to each other – and there are luxury services between Kochi and Lakshadweep. Kerala has a regular passenger service with a number of services operating out of Alappuzha and Kollam, including the popular "backwater trip" between the two. The Sunderbans in the delta region to the south of Calcutta is only accessible by boat.

By car

It is much more usual for tourists in India to be driven than it is for them to drive; **car rental** firms operate on the basis of supplying **chauffeur-driven vehicles**, and taxis are available at cheap daily rates. Arranged through tourist offices, local car rental firms, or branches of Hertz, Budget or Europcar, a chauffeur-driven car will run to about $30 per day. On longer trips, the driver sleeps in

the car. The big international chains are the best bet for self-drive car rental; in India they charge around thirty percent less than chauffeur-driven, with a Rs1000 deposit against damage, though if you pay in your home country it can cost a whole lot more.

Driving in India is not for beginners. If you do drive yourself, expect the unexpected, and expect other drivers to take whatever liberties they can get away with. **Traffic** circulates on the left, but don't expect **road regulations** to be obeyed; generally the vehicle in front seems to have right of way so at busy intersections or roundabouts (rotaries) drivers try and get out in front as soon as possible with prudence. Another unstated law of the road is that might is right.

Traffic in the cities is heavy and undisciplined; vehicles cut in and out without warning, and pedestrians, cyclists and cows wander nonchalantly down the middle of the road as if you didn't exist. In the country the roads are narrow, in terrible repair, and hogged by overloaded Tata trucks that move aside for nobody, while something slow-moving like a bullock cart or a herd of goats can easily take up the whole road. To overtake, sound your **horn** (an essential item on Indian roads) – the driver in front will signal if it is safe to do so; if not, he will wave his hand, palm downwards, up and down. A huge number of potholes don't make for a smooth ride either. Furthermore, during the monsoon roads can become flooded and dangerous; rivers burst their banks and bridges get washed away. Ask local people before you set off, and proceed with caution, sticking to main highways if possible.

You should have an **international driving licence** to drive in India, but this is often overlooked if you have your licence from home (but beware of police in Goa, who are quick to hand out fines). **Insurance** is compulsory, but not expensive. Car **seat belts** are not compulsory but very strongly recommended. Accident rates are high, and you should be on your guard at all times. It is particularly dangerous to drive at night – not everyone uses lights, and bullock carts don't have any. If you have an **accident**, it might be an idea to leave the scene quickly and go straight to the police to report it; mobs can assemble fast, especially if pedestrians or cows are involved.

Fuel is reasonably cheap compared to home, but the state of the roads will take its toll, and mechanics are not always very reliable, so a knowledge of **vehicle maintenance** is a help, as is a checkup every so often to see what all those bone-shaking journeys are doing to your conveyance. Luckily, if you get a flat tyre, puncture-wallahs can be easily found almost everywhere.

To import a car or motorbike into India, you'll have to show a **carnet de passage**, a document intended to ensure that you don't sell the vehicle illegally. These are available from foreign motoring organizations such as the AA. It's also worth bringing a few basic spares, as spare parts for foreign makes can be hard to find in India, although low-quality imitations are more widely available. All in all, the route is arduous (see p.15), and bringing a vehicle to India something of a commitment.

The classic Indian automobile is the **Hindustan Ambassador** (basically a Morris Oxford), nowadays largely superseded by more modern vehicles such as the Maruti Suzuki. Renting a car, you'll probably have a choice of these two or others such as the Land Rover-like Tata Sumo popular in hill regions. If you're interested in buying one, the Ambassador is not famed for its mod cons or low mpg, but has a certain style and historical interest; later models make little sense as prices are higher and quality lower than in the West.

By motorbike

Riding a motorbike around India has become increasingly popular but is not without its hazards. Beside the appalling road conditions encountered (see above) and the ensuing fatigue, **renting a bike**, unless you are well versed in maintenance, can be a bit of a nightmare, with breakdowns often in the most inconvenient places. If you do breakdown in the middle of nowhere, you may need to flag down an empty truck to transport the bike to the nearest town for repairs. Motorbike rental is available in some tourist towns and useful for local use, but the quality of the bikes is never assured. You could bring your own but then you will need to consider spares. Helmets are best brought from home.

Buying a motorbike in India is a much more reasonable proposition, and again, if it's

an old British classic you're after, the Enfield Bullet (350 model), sold cheapest in Pondicherry, on the Tamil Nadu coast, leads the field (check one of several motoring magazines for details and reviews). If low price and practicality are your priorities, however, a smaller model, perhaps even a moped or a scooter, might better fit the bill. Many Japanese bikes are now made in India, as are Vespas and Lambrettas, and motorcycles of various sorts can easily be bought new or **secondhand**. Garages and repair shops are a good place to start; see Delhi Listings for details of the city's Karol Bagh area, renowned for its motorcycle shops, as well as Bales Road in Chennai. Obviously, you will have to **haggle** for the price, but you can expect to pay half to two-thirds the original price for a bike in reasonable condition. Given the right bargaining skills, you can sell it again later for a similar price – perhaps to another foreign traveller, by advertising it in hotels and restaurants. A certain amount of bureaucracy is involved in transferring vehicle ownership, but a garage should be able to put you on to a broker ("auto consultant") who, for a modest commission (around Rs300), will help you find a seller or a buyer, and do the necessary paperwork. A motorbike can be taken in the luggage car of a **train** for the same price as a second-class passenger fare (get a form and pay a small fee at the station luggage office).

Some knowledge of mechanics is necessary to ensure that you are not being sold a pup, so if you are not too savvy yourself, make sure you take someone who is to give the once-over to important parts like the engine, forks, brakes and suspension. Experienced overlanders often claim that making sure the seat is comfy is the crucial element to an enjoyable trip.

If you are unsure of negotiating your own bike or travelling around on your own you may consider joining one of several **motorbike tours**:

Blazing Trails UK☏ 01293/533338,
ⓦ www.jewelholidays.com.
Classic Bike Adventure "Casa Tres Amigos", Assagao 403 507 ☏ 0832/244467,ⓕ 262076
ⓦ www.classic-bike-india.com.
Himalayan Motorcycle Tours US☏ 1-303/440 6482, UK☏ 01256/770775.
ⓔ patrickmoffat@yahoo.com
ⓦ www.himalanmotorcycles.com.
Himalayan Roadrunners UK☏ 01233/733001

By bicycle

Ever since Dervla Murphy's *Full Tilt*, a steady but increasing trickle of travellers have either themselves done the overland trip **by bicycle**, or else bought a bike in India and ridden it around the country. In many ways it is the ideal form of transport, offering total independence without loss of contact with local people. You can camp out, though there are cheap lodgings in almost every village – take the bike into your room with you – and, if you get tired of pedalling, you can put it on top of a bus as luggage, or transport it by train.

Bringing a bike from abroad requires no carnet or special paperwork, but spare parts and accessories may be of different sizes and standards in India, and you may have to improvise. Bring **basic spares** and **tools**, and a **pump**. **Panniers** are the obvious thing for carrying your gear, but fiendishly inconvenient when not attached to your bike, and you might consider sacrificing ideal load-bearing and streamlining technology for a backpack you can lash down on the rear carrier.

Buying a bike in India presents no great difficulty; most towns have cycle shops and even cycle markets. The advantages of a local bike are that spare parts are easy to get, locally produced tools and parts will fit, and your vehicle will not draw a crowd every time you park it; although when covered with dust it should not present problems. Disadvantages are that Indian bikes tend to be heavier and less state-of-the-art than ones from abroad; in cities and bigger towns mountain bikes are beginning to appear, but they're not worth buying, with insufficient gears and a low level of equipment. Selling should be quite easy: you won't get a tremendously good deal at a cycle market, but you may well be able to sell privately, or even to a rental shop.

Bicycles can be **rented** in most towns, usually for local use only: this is a good way to find out if your legs and bum can survive the Indian bike before buying one. Rs10–25 per day is the going rate, occasionally more in tourist centres, and you may have to leave a deposit, or even your passport as security. Several adventure tour operators such as Exodus and Chandertal (see p.14) offer bicycle tours of the country with most customers bringing their own bicycles.

As for **contacts**, International Bicycle Fund, 4887 Columbia Drive S, Seattle, WA 98108-1919 (℡206/767-0848, ⊛www.ibike.org), publishes information and offers advice on bicycle travel around the world, and maintains a useful website. In India, the Cycle Federation of India, C-5A/262, DDA Flats, Janak Puri, New Delhi 110058 (℡011/553006), is the main cycle-sports organization.

City transport

Transport around town takes various forms, with **buses** the most obvious. These are usually single-decker, though double-deckers (some articulated) exist in Mumbai and elsewhere. City buses can get unbelievably crowded, so beware of pickpockets, razor-armed pocket-slitters, and "Eve-teasers" (see p.85); the same applies to **suburban trains** in Mumbai (Chennai is about the only other place where you might want to use trains for local city transport). Any visitor to Calcutta will be amazed by the clean efficiency of India's only metro.

You can also take **taxis**, usually rather battered Ambassadors (painted black and yellow in the large cities) and Maruti omnivans. With luck, the driver will agree to use the **meter**; in theory you're within your rights to call the police if he doesn't, but the usual compromise is to agree a **fare** for the journey before you get in. Naturally, it helps to have an idea in advance what the fare should be, though any figures quoted in this or any other book should be treated as being the broadest of guidelines only. From places such as main stations, you may be able to find other passengers to share a taxi to the town centre; many stations, and certainly most airports, operate prepaid taxi schemes with set fares that you pay before departure; more expensive prepaid limousines are also available.

The **auto-rickshaw**, that most Indian of vehicles, is the front half of a motor-scooter with a couple of seats mounted on the back. Cheaper than taxis, better at nipping in and out of traffic, and usually metered (again, in most places they probably won't use them and you should agree a fare before setting off), auto-rickshaws are a little unstable and their drivers often rather reckless, but that's all part of the fun. In major tourist centres rickshaw-wallahs can, however, hassle you endlessly on the street, often shoving themselves right in your path to prevent you from ignoring them, and once you're inside they may take you to several shops before reaching your destination. Moreover, agreeing a price before the journey will not necessarily stop your rickshaw-wallah reopening discussion when the trip is under way, or at its end. In general it is better to hail a rickshaw than to take one that's been following you, and to avoid those that hang around outside posh hotels.

One or two cities also have larger versions of auto-rickshaws known as **tempos** (or Vikrams), with six or eight seats behind, which usually ply fixed routes at flat fares. Here and there, you'll also come across horse-drawn carriages, or **tongas**. Tugged by underfed and often lame horses, these are the least popular with tourists.

Slower and cheaper still is the **cycle rickshaw** – basically a glorified tricycle. Foreign visitors often feel uncomfortable about travelling this way; except in the major tourist cities, cycle rickshaw-wallahs are invariably emaciated pavement dwellers who earn only a pittance for their pains. In the end, though, to deny them your custom on those grounds is spurious logic; they will earn even less if you don't use them. Also you will invariably pay a bit more than a local would. Only in Calcutta do the rickshaw-wallahs continue to haul the city's pukka rickshaws on foot.

If you want to see a variety of places around town, consider hiring a taxi, rickshaw or auto-rickshaw for the day. Find a driver who speaks English reasonably well, and agree a price beforehand. You will probably find it a lot cheaper than you imagine: the driver will invariably act as a guide and source of local knowledge, and tipping is usually in order.

Accommodation

There are far more Indians travelling around their own country at any one time – whether for holidays, on pilgrimages, or for business – than there are foreign tourists, and a vast infrastructure of hotels and guesthouses caters for their needs. On the whole, accommodation, like so many other things in India, provides good value for money, though in the major cities, especially, expect to pay international prices for luxury establishments that provide Western-style comforts and service.

Throughout this book we recommend places to stay in cities, towns and villages that range from lavish lakeside palaces to the most basic dormitory accommodation.

Inexpensive hotels

While accommodation prices in India are generally on the up, there's still an abundance of **cheap hotels**, catering for backpacking tourists and less well-off Indians. Most charge Rs150–250 for a double room, and some outside the big cities have rates below Rs100 (£1.50/$2.50). The cheapest option is usually in a dormitory of a hostel or hotel, where you'll be charged anything from Rs30 to 100. Cheaper options include hostels run by religious establishments and pilgrim guesthouses (see below).

Budget accommodation varies from filthy fleapits to homely guesthouses and, naturally, tends to be cheaper the further you get off the beaten track; it's most expensive in Delhi and Mumbai, where prices are at least double those for equivalent accommodation in most other cities.

Cold showers or "bucket baths" are the order of the day – not really a problem in

Accommodation price codes

All accommodation prices in this book are coded using the symbols below. The prices given are for a double room; in the case of dorms, we give the price in rupees. Most mid-range and all expensive and luxury hotels charge a luxury tax of around ten to fifteen percent, and a local tax of around five percent. All taxes are included in the prices we quote.

India doesn't have a tourist season as such, and most accommodation keeps the same prices throughout the year. Certain resorts however, and some spots on established tourist trails, do experience some variation and will be more expensive, or less negotiable, when demand is at its peak. For the hill stations, this will be in the summer (April–July); for Goa and other beach resorts in the south, it'll be the winter, especially around Christmas and New Year. We indicate such fluctuations where appropriate.

➊ up to Rs100	➍ Rs300–400	➐ Rs900–1500
➋ Rs100–200	➎ Rs400–600	➑ Rs1500–2500
➌ Rs200–300	➏ Rs600–900	➒ Rs2500 and upwards

most of India for most of the year – and it's always wise to check out the state of the bathrooms and toilets before taking a room. Bed bugs and mosquitoes are other things to check for – splotches of blood around the bed and on the walls where people have squashed them are tell-tale signs.

If a taxi driver or rickshaw-wallah tells you that the place you ask for is full, closed or has moved, it's more than likely that it's because he wants to take you to a hotel that pays him commission – added, in some cases, to your bill. Hotel touts operate in some major tourist spots, working for commission from the hotels they take you to; this can become annoying, but sometimes paying the little extra can be well worth it, especially if you arrive alone in a new place at night. One way to avoid the hassle is to stay put – some of the airports have retiring rooms and so do most of the larger railway stations.

Mid-range hotels

Even if you value your **creature comforts**, you don't need to pay through the nose for them. A large clean room, freshly made bed, your own spotless (often sit-down) toilet, and hot and cold running water can still cost under Rs350 ($7/£5). Extras that bump up the price include local taxes, TV, mosquito nets, a balcony, and, above all, **air-conditioning**. Abbreviated in this book and in India itself as **a/c**, air-conditioning is not necessarily the advantage you might expect – in some hotels you can find your-self paying double for a system that is so dust-choked, wheezy and noisy as to preclude any possibility of sleep – but providing it entitles a hotel to consider itself mid-range. Some also offer a halfway-house option known as **air-cooled**, which is found only in drier climes as coolers do not work in areas of extreme humidity such as along the coasts of south India and the Bay of Bengal. Many medium-priced hotels also have attached restaurants, and even room service.

New hotels tend to be lined inside, on floors and walls, with marble (or some imitation), which can make them feel totally characterless. They are, however, much cleaner than older hotels, where dirt and grime clings to cracks and crevices, and damp quickly devours paint. Some mid-range hotels feel compelled to furnish their rooms with wall-to-wall carpeting which often smells due to the humidity and damp caused by heavy rains.

Most state governments run their own "tourist bungalows", similar to mid-range hotels, but often also offering pricier a/c rooms and cheaper dorms. They are usually good value, though they vary a lot from state to state and even within states. Rajasthan's, for example, tend to be rather run-down, whereas Madhya Pradesh's are as a rule very well kept, and some of those in Kerala are positively luxurious. If you're on a medium budget, it's not a bad idea to think first of staying in the state-run hotel in any town; to make that easier, we've indicated such places throughout this guide by including the state acronym in the name – eg MPTDC

Palace. The "TDC" stands for Tourist Development Corporation and most states have one. Bookings for state-run hotels can be made in advance by telephone, or through the state tourist offices throughout the country.

Upmarket hotels

Most **luxury hotels** in India fall into one of two categories: old-fashioned institutions brimming with class, and modern jet-set chain hotels, largely confined to large cities and tourist resorts.

The faded grandeur of the **Raj** lingers on in the venerable edifices of British imperial hangouts such as Calcutta and the hill stations. These can be well worth seeking out for their old-world charm, and their knack of being somehow more quintessentially British than the British ever managed. In addition, in states such as Rajasthan, Uttar Pradesh and Madhya Pradesh, magnificent **old forts** and **palaces** (*thikanas*) from feudal estates, and **havelis**, the former homes of aristocratic families, have been designated **heritage hotels**. Some old stately homes and forts in Himachal Pradesh have also been converted into hotels.

Modern deluxe establishments – slicker, brighter, faster and far more businesslike – tend to belong to **chains**, as often Indian as international. The *Taj* in Mumbai, for example, the country's grandest hostelry, has a number of offshoots, including former palaces in Rajasthan; some Taj hotels rank amongst the best and certainly the most expensive in the world. Other chains include Oberoi, Hilton International, Meridien, Hyatt and Sheraton, the Welcomgroup and the India Tourist Development Corporation's Ashok chain. You'll find such hotels in most state capitals and some resorts favoured by rich Indian and foreign tourists. It's becoming more common for these to quote tariffs in US dollars, starting at $80, but sometimes bringing the price for a double room up to an astonishing $500. In palaces and heritage hotels, however, you'll still get excellent value for money, with rates only just beginning to approach those of their counterparts back home.

Bookings for many of the larger hotel chains can be made in offices around the world; you can also find **discounts** through travel agencies such as the Travel Corporation of India who offer up to sixty percent off certain luxury hotels, depending on the season. The Taj, Oberoi and Sheraton chains are among those with outlets in the UK and the US.

Other options

Many **railway stations** have **"retiring rooms"** where passengers can sleep – if they can put up with station noises. These rooms can be particularly handy if you're catching an early morning train, but tend to get booked up well in advance. They vary in price, but generally charge roughly the same as a budget hotel, and have large, clean, if somewhat institutional rooms; dormitories, where you can bank on being woken at the crack of dawn by a morning chorus of throat-clearing, are often available. Occasionally you may come across a main station with an air-conditioned room, in which case you will have found a real bargain.

In one or two places, you can rent rooms in people's **homes**. In Rajasthan, the state tourist development corporation runs a "paying guest scheme" to place tourists with families offering lodging, while Munjeeta Travel in London (see p.14) organize "homestay tours" across India – an excellent way to get to know an Indian family and see how they live. **Servas** (www.servas.org), established in 1949 as a peace organization, is devoted to providing homestays. There are currently 626 hosts in India; you have to join before travelling by applying to the local Servas secretary (located via the website) – you then get a list of hosts to contact in the place you are visiting. Some people provide free accommodation, others are just day hosts. There is no guarantee a bed will be provided – it's up to the individual.

Camping is possible too, although in most of the country it's hard to see why you'd want to be cooped up in a tent overnight when you could be sleeping on a cool charpoi (a sort of basic bed) on a roof terrace for a handful of rupees – let alone why you'd choose to carry a tent around India in the first place. Except possibly on treks, it's not usual simply to pitch a tent in the countryside, though many hotels allow camping in their grounds. The YMCA run a few sites, as do state governments

(Maharashtra in particular), and the Scouts and Guides.

YMCAs and **YWCAs**, confined to big cities, are plusher and pricier, comparable to a mid-range hotel. They are usually good value, but are often full, and some are exclusively single-sex. Official and non-official **youth hostels**, some run by state governments, are spread haphazardly across the country. They give HI cardholders a discount, but rarely exclude non-members, nor do they usually impose daytime closing. Prices match the cheapest hotels; where there is a youth hostel, it usually has a dormitory and may well be the best budget accommodation available – which goes especially for the **Salvation Army** ones.

Finally, religious institutions, particularly Sikh **gurudwaras**, offer accommodation for pilgrims and visitors, and may put up tourists; a donation is often expected, and certainly appreciated but some of the bigger ones charge a fixed, nominal fee. Pilgrimage sites, especially those far from other accommodation, also have **dharamshalas** where visitors can stay – very cheap and very simple, usually with basic, communal washing facilities but some charitable institutions even have rooms with attached if simple bathrooms. *Dharamshalas*, like *gurudwaras*, offer accommodation either on a donations system or charge a nominal fee which can be as low as Rs20.

Accommodation practicalities

Check-out time is often noon, but confirm this when you arrive: some expect you out by 9am, but many others operate a 24-hour system, under which you are simply obliged to leave by the same time as you arrived. Some places let you use their facilities after the official check-out time, sometimes for a small charge, others won't even let you leave your baggage after then unless you pay for another night.

Unfortunately, not all hotels offer **single rooms**, so it can often work out more expensive to be travelling alone; in hotels that don't, you may be able to negotiate a slight discount. It's not unusual to find rooms with three or four beds however – great value for families and small groups.

In cheap hotels and hostels, you needn't expect any additions to your basic bill, but as you go up the scale, you'll find **taxes** and **service charges** creeping in, sometimes adding as much as a third on top of the original tariff. Service is generally ten percent, but taxes are a matter for state governments and vary from state to state.

Like most other things in India, the price of a room may well be open to **negotiation**. If you think the price is too high, or if all the hotels in town are empty, try haggling. You may get nowhere – but nothing ventured, nothing gained.

Eating and drinking

Indian food has a richly deserved reputation throughout the world for being aromatic and delicious. If you're a vegetarian, you've come to the right place. Indians are used to people having special dietary requirements: yours will be respected, and no one will think you strange for having them. Indeed, some of the very best food India has to offer is vegetarian, and even confirmed meat-eaters will find themselves tucking into delicious dhals and veg curries with relish.

Most religious Hindus, and the majority of people in the south, do not consume the flesh of animals, while some orthodox Brahmins will not eat food cooked by anyone outside their household (or onions or garlic, as they inflame the baser instincts), and Jains are even stricter. **Veganism** is not common, however; if you're vegan, you'll have to keep your eyes open for eggs and dairy products.

Many eating places state whether they are vegetarian or non-vegetarian either on signs outside or at the top of the menu. The terms used in India are **"veg"** and **"non-veg"**, and we have adopted these throughout our eating reviews. You'll also see "pure veg" which means that no eggs or alcohol are served. As a rule, meat-eaters should exercise caution in India: even when meat is available, especially in the larger towns, its quality is not assured except in the best restaurants and you won't get much in a dish anyway – especially in railway canteens where it's mainly there for flavouring. Hindus, of course, do not eat beef and Muslims shun pork, so you'll only find those in a few Christian enclaves such as the beach areas of Goa, and Tibetan areas. Note that what is called **"mutton"** on menus is in fact goat.

Broadly speaking, there are four types of eating establishments: *dhabas* and *bhojanalayas*, restaurants, tourist restaurants and fast-food joints. *Dhabas* and *bhojanalayas* are **cheap Indian diners**, where food is basic but often good, consisting of vegetable curry, dhal (a lentil soup pronounced "da'al"), rice or Indian bread (the latter more standard in the north) and sometimes meat. Often found along the sides of highways, *dhabas* traditionally cater to truck drivers, and one way of telling a good *dhaba* from a distance is to judge from the number of trucks parked outside. *Bhojanalayas*, common in towns around the north and centre of the country, tend to be vegetarian, especially those signed as "Vaishno". Both *dhabas* and *bhojanalayas* can be grubby – look them over before you commit yourself – and they tend to pile on the garam masala as a substitute for fresh spices. They do, on the other hand, have the advantage of being dirt cheap.

Restaurants as such vary in price and quality, and can be veg or non-veg, offering a wide choice of dishes, much like Indian restaurants anywhere else in the world.

For advice on drinking water in India, see p.32.

Deluxe restaurants such as those in five-star hotels can be very expensive by Indian standards, but they offer a chance to try classic Indian cooking of very high quality: rich, subtle, mouthwatering, and still a fraction of the price you'd pay for such delights at home – assuming you could find Indian food that good. Try a meal in one at least once.

The third type of eating place caters specifically for foreign travellers with unadventurous tastebuds: the **tourist restaurant**, found in beach resorts, hill stations and travellers' meccas across India. Here you can get pancakes and fritters, omelettes and toast, chips, fried prawns, cereal and fruit salad. The downside is that they tend to be pricey, some miss the mark by a long way, and they are not, of course, authentically Indian.

The fourth type is international **fast food** including burgers (without beef) as well as pizzas, which seem to have taken cosmopolitan India by storm with familiar household names available in most major cities.

Finally, should you be lucky enough to be invited into someone's home, you will get to taste the most authentically Indian food of all. Most Indian women are professional cooks and housewives, trained from childhood by mothers, grandmothers and aunties, and aided by daughters and nieces. They can quite easily spend a whole day cooking, grinding and mixing the spices themselves, and using only the freshest ingredients.

Indian food

What Westerners call a **curry** covers a variety of dishes, each made with a different masala, or mix of spices. Curry powder does not exist in India, the nearest equivalent being garam masala ("hot mix"), a combination of dried ground black pepper and other spices, in theory added to a dish at the last stage of cooking to spice it up, but often used as a substitute for other aromatics. Commonly used **spices** include chilli, turmeric, garlic, ginger, cinnamon, cardamom, cloves, coriander – both leaf and seed – cumin and saffron. These are not all added at the same time, and some are used whole, so beware of chewing on them. The spice that gives British and Caribbean curry powder its distinctive taste, fenugreek, is actually used much more sparingly in India.

It's the Indian penchant for **chilli** that alarms many Western visitors. The majority of foreigners develop a tolerance for it; if you don't, you'll just have to stick to mild dishes such as kurma and biryani where meat or vegetables are cooked with rice, and eat plenty of chapati. Indians tend to assuage the effects of chilli with chutney, dhai (curd) or raita (curd with mint and cucumber, or other herbs and vegetables). Otherwise, **beer** is one of the best things for washing chilli out of your mouth; the essential oils that cause the burning sensation dissolve in alcohol, but not in water.

Vegetarian curries are usually identified (even on menus in English) by the Hindi names of their main ingredients. Terms like "curry" and "masala" don't really tell you what to expect; meat curries are more often given specific names such as kurma or dopiaza, to indicate the kind of masala used or the method of cooking.

Regional variety is vast: Bengalis love fish and cook a mean *mangsho* (meat) curry as well as exotic vegetable dishes such as *mocha* – cooked banana flower. They also like to include fish bones for added flavour in their vegetable curries – a nasty surprise for vegetarians. Biharis were known for their *satu* – a staple flour used instead of rice – but *satu* has become unfashionable outside the rural communities. Tibetans and Bhotias from the Himalayas have a simple diet of *thukpa* (meat soup), and *momo* (meat dumplings), as well as a salty tea made with either rancid yak butter where available, or with ordinary butter. In Punjab and much of northern India, home cooking consists of dhal and vegetables along with roti (bread) and less rice than the Bengalis. Food in Gujarat, predominantly veg, is often cooked with a bit of sugar.

In the north of India especially, but as far south as Hyderabad, the influence of the Moghuls lives on in the form of Mughlai cooking. Mostly non-veg, the food is extremely rich, using ingredients such as cream, almonds, sultanas and saffron. Mughlai as the name of a masala normally indicates a mild, creamy one. *Mughlai paratha* is spicy fried bread with egg.

The other big northern style is tandoori. The name refers to the deep clay oven (tandoor) in which the food is cooked. Tandoori chicken is marinated in yoghurt, herbs and spices before cooking. Boneless pieces of meat, marinated and cooked in the same way are known as tikka; they may be served in a medium-strength masala (tikka masala), one thickened with almonds (pasanda), or in a rich butter sauce (*murg makhani* or butter chicken). Breads such as naan and roti are also baked in the tandoor.

Certain combinations are traditional and seasonally repeated, such as *makki ki roti* (fried corn bread) with *sarson ka sag* (mustard-leaf greens) around Punjab and other parts of north India. *Baingan bharta* (puréed roast aubergine) is commonly eaten with plain yoghurt and roti (plain bread). In good Muslim cooking from the north, delicately thin *rumali roti* (handkerchief bread) often accompanies rich meat and chicken dishes. Dhal is a safe bet with almost any meat or vegetable dish, and easy to eat with rice or bread.

Set meals are quite common in the north, and even more so in the south, where they are generally referred to simply as **"meals"**. They generally consist of a mound of rice surrounded by various delicious vegetable curries, sambar dhal, chutney and curd, and usually accompanied by poppadums, *vadas* and *rasam*, a hot pepper water. Traditionally served on a round metal tray or **thali** (also found in north India), with each side dish in a separate metal bowl, set meals are sometimes served up on a rectangle of banana leaf instead. In most traditional restaurants, you can eat as much as you want, and staff circulate with refills of everything. In the south even more than elsewhere, eating with your fingers is *de rigueur* (you want to feel the food as well as taste it) and cutlery may be unavailable.

Wherever you eat, remember to use only your right hand, and wash your hands before you start. Try and avoid getting food on the palm of your hand by eating with the tips of your fingers.

Snacks and street food

Feeling peckish should never be a problem, with all sorts of **snack meals** and finger food to choose from. Of the sit-down variety, *chana puri*, a chick-pea curry with a *puri* (or

Paan

You may be relieved to know that the red stuff people spit all over the streets isn't blood, but juice produced by chewing **paan** – a digestive, commonly taken after meals, and also a mild stimulant, found especially in the northeast where it is fresh and much stronger.

A paan consists of chopped or shredded nut (always referred to as betel nut, though in fact it comes from the areca palm), wrapped in a leaf (which does come from the betel tree) that is first prepared with ingredients such as *katha* (a red paste), *chuna* (slaked white lime), *mitha masala* (a mix of sweet spices, which can be ingested) and *zarda* (chewing tobacco, not to be swallowed on any account, especially if made with *chuna*). The triangular package thus formed is wedged inside your cheek and chewed slowly, and in the case of *chuna* and *zarda* paans, spitting out the juice as you go.

Paan, and paan masala, a mix of betel nut, fennel seeds, sweets and flavourings, are sold by paan-wallahs, often from tiny stalls squeezed between shops. Paan-wallahs develop big reputations; those in the tiny roads of Varanasi are the most renowned, asking astronomical prices for paan made to elaborate specifications including silver and even gold foil. Paan is an acquired taste; novices should start off, and preferably stick with, the sweet and harmless *mitha* variety, which is perfectly alright to ingest.

sometimes other breads) to dunk, is a great favourite in the north of the country; *iddli sambar* – lentil and vegetable sauce with rice cakes to dunk – is the southern equivalent. But the great snack meal of the south is masala dosa, a potato and vegetable curry wrapped in a crispy rice pancake.

Street finger food includes *bhel puris* (a Mumbai speciality of small vegetable-stuffed puris with tamarind sauce), *pani puris* (the same puris dunked in peppery and spicy water – only for the seasoned), bhajis (deep-fried cakes of vegetables in chick-pea flour), samosas (meat or vegetables in a pastry triangle, fried), and pakoras (vegetables or potato dipped in chick-pea flour batter and deep-fried). Kebabs are common in the north, most frequently seekh kebab, minced lamb grilled on a skewer, but also shami kebab, small minced lamb cutlets. Kebabs rolled into griddle-fried bread, known as *kathi* rolls, originated in Calcutta but are now available in other cities as well. With all street snacks, though, remember that food left lying around attracts germs – make sure it's freshly cooked. Be especially careful with snacks involving water, such as *pani puris*, and cooking oil, which is often recycled. Generally, it's a good idea to acclimatize to Indian conditions before you start eating street snacks.

You won't find anything called "Bombay mix" in India, but there's no shortage of dry spicy snack mixes, often referred to as *channa chur*. Jackfruit chips are sometimes sold as a savoury snack – though they are rather bland – and cashew nuts are a real bargain. Peanuts, also known as "monkey nuts" or *mumfuli*, usually come roasted and unshelled. Look out for gram vendors who sell dry roasted chickpeas.

Non-Indian food

Chinese food has become widespread in large towns, where it is generally cooked by Indian chefs and not what you'd call authentic. However in a few cities, like Calcutta, that have large Chinese communities, you can get very good Chinese cuisine.

Western food is often dire, and expensive compared to Indian food, although the international chains serve the same standard fare as elsewhere in the world at much cheaper prices. Branches of *Pizza Hut*, *Domino's*, *KFC* and *McDonald's* can be found in Delhi, Mumbai, Calcutta, Chennai, Pune and Bangalore in ever-increasing numbers. *Wimpy*, home-grown chains such as *Nirula* and *Kwality* and independently owned fast-food cafés can be found in any town. Tourist centres such as Leh, Goa and Kovalam offer a fair choice of Western food, from patisseries serving cakes and croissants to restaurants serving lasagne on candle-lit terraces. Small cheese factories are beginning to emerge, providing an alternative to the dreary processed cheese produced by Amul. Delhi and Mumbai also offer a choice Tex-Mex, Thai, Japanese, Italian and French cuisine – usually in restaurants of luxury hotels.

Breakfast

Unreconstructed Westerners seem to get especially homesick around **breakfast** time, but getting fry-ups and hash browns is likely to be a problem. *Chana puri* is an option in the north, if a little spicy for some, and *alu paratha* with dhal is another traditional start to the day. *Iddli sambar* and masala dosa is the most common equivalent in the south, where members of the *India Coffee House* chain can be depended upon for some decent coffee and toast.

In those towns which have established a reputation as hang-outs for "travellers", budget hotels and restaurants serve up the usual hippy fare – banana pancakes, muesli, etc – as well as omelettes, toast, porridge (not always oatmeal), cornflakes, and even bacon and eggs.

Sweets

Most Indians have rather a sweet tooth and Indian **sweets**, usually made of milk, can be very sweet indeed. Of the more solid type, *barfi*, a kind of fudge made from milk which has been boiled down and condensed, varies from moist and delicious to dry and powdery. It comes in various flavours from plain creamy white to *pista* (pistachio) in livid green and is often sold covered with silver leaf (which you eat). Smoother-textured, round *penda* and thin diamonds of *kaju katri*, plus *moist sandesh* and the harder *paira*, both popular in Bengal, are among many other sweets made from *chhana* or boiled-down milk. Crunchier *mesur* is made with chick peas; numerous types of gelatinous *halwa*, not the Middle Eastern variety, include the rich *gajar ka halwa* made from carrots and cream.

Getting softer and stickier, those circular orange tubes dripping syrup in sweet-shop windows, called *jalebis* and made of deep-fried treacle, are as sickly as they look. *Gulab jamuns*, deep-fried cream cheese sponge balls soaked in syrup, are as unhealthy. Common in both the north and the south, *ladu* consists of balls made from semolina flour with raisins and sugar and flour, sometimes made of other grains and flour, while among Bengali sweets, widely consid-

ered to be the best are *rasgullas*, rosewater-flavoured cream cheese balls floating in syrup. *Ras malai*, found throughout north India, is similar but soaked in cream instead of syrup.

Chocolate is improving rapidly in India and you'll find various Cadbury's and Amul bars. None of the various indigenous brands of imitation Swiss and Belgian chocolates appearing on the cosmopolitan markets are worth eating.

Among the large ice-cream vendors, Kwality (now owned and branded as Walls), Vadilal's, Gaylord and Dollops stand out. Uniformed men push carts of ice cream around and the bigger companies have many imitators, usually quite obvious. Some have no scruples – stay away from water ices unless you have a seasoned constitution. Ice-cream parlours selling elaborate concoctions including sundaes have really taken off; Connaught Circus in Delhi has several. Be sure to try kulfi, a pistachio- and cardamom-flavoured frozen sweet which is India's answer to ice cream; bhang kulfi (not available everywhere but popular during the festival of Holi) is laced with cannabis and has an interesting kick to it, but should be approached with caution.

Fruit

What fruit is available varies with region and season, but there's always a fine choice. Ideally, you should **peel all fruit** including apples (*sev*), or soak them in strong iodine or potassium permanganate solution for half an hour. Roadside vendors sell fruit which they often cut up and serve sprinkled with salt and even masala – don't buy anything that looks like it's been hanging around for a while.

Mangoes (*aam*) of various kinds are usually on offer, but not all are sweet enough to eat fresh – some are used for pickles or curries. Indians are picky about their mangoes, which they feel and smell before buying; if you don't know the art of choosing the fruit, you could be sold the leftovers. Among the species appearing at different times in the season, which lasts from spring to summer, look out for Alphonso and Langra. Bananas (*kela*) of one sort or another are also on sale all year round, and oranges and tangerines are generally easy to come by, as are sweet melons and thirst-quenching watermelons.

A glossary of food terms

General terms and requests

bhat	cooked rice
chamach	spoon
chawal	uncooked rice
cheeni	sugar
cheeni mat dhalna	do not put sugar (eg in tea)
cheeni nehin	no sugar!
chhoori	knife
dahi	yoghurt
dudh	milk
garam	hot
gosht	meat, usually mutton
hath dhoney ka pani	water for washing hands
jaggery	unrefined sugar
jhaal	chilli hot
kala mirch	black pepper
kam or kamti	less – eg jhaal kam (less hot)
kanta	fork
khaana	food
lal mirch	red pepper
macchi	fish
mehti	fenugreek
mirch	pepper
murgi	chicken
namak	salt
pani	water
peeney ka pani	drinking water (not mineral water)
plate	plate
sabji	any vegetable curry
thanda	cold
ziadah or awr	more

Vegetables

adrak	ginger
alu	potatoes
baingan or brinjal	eggplant (aubergine)
bhindi	okra (ladies finger)
chana	chick peas (garbanzo beans)
dhal	lentils
gaajar	carrot
gobi	cauliflower
kadoo	pumpkin
karela	bitter gourd
lasoon	garlic
mattar	peas
paalak or saag	spinach

paneer	Indian cheese
piaz	onions
sabzi	literally greens; used for all vegetables
saag or palak	various varieties of spinach
tamatar	tomato

Dishes and cooking terms

alu baingan	potato and aubergine; mild to medium
alu methi	potato with fenugreek leaves; usually medium-hot
baingan bharta	baked and mashed aubergine mixed with onions; best with dhal and roti
bhindi bhaji	fried okra; gently spiced
bhuna	roasted first and thickened-down medium-strength curry
biryani	rice baked with saffron or turmeric, whole spices, and meat (sometimes vegetables), and often hard-boiled egg; rich
Bombay duck	dried bummelo fish
chingri	prawns
chop	minced meat or vegetable surrounded by breaded mashed potato
cutlet	cutlet – often minced meat or vegetable – fried in the form of a flat cake
dahi maach	fish curry with yoghurt, ginger and turmeric; a mild Bengali dish
dhal gosht	meat cooked in lentils; hot
dhansak	meat and lentil curry, a Parsi speciality; medium-hot
dopiaza	with onions added at two different stages of cooking; medium-mild
dum	steamed in a casserole; the most common dish is alu dum with potatoes
jalfrezi	with tomatoes and green chilli; medium-hot
jeera	cumin; a masala so described will usually be medium-hot

karahi	cast-iron wok which has given its name to a method of cooking meat with dry masala to create dishes of medium strength
karhi	a dhal-like dish made from dahi and gram flour; popular in the north, especially in Punjab and Gujarat
keema	minced meat
kofta	balls of minced vegetables or meat in a curried sauce
korma	meat braised in yoghurt sauce; mild
maacher jhol	mild fish stew, often made with the entire fish – a Bengali delicacy
malai kofta	vegetable kebabs in a rich cream sauce; medium-mild
molee	curry with coconut, usually fish, originally Malay (hence the name), now a speciality of Kerala; hot
mulligatawny	curried vegetable soup, a classic Anglo-Indian dish rumoured to have come from "Mulligan Aunty" but probably south Indian; medium-strength
pathia	thickened curry with lemon juice; hot
pomfret	a flatfish popular in Mumbai and Calcutta
pulau	rice, gently spiced and prefried
rogan josh	deep red lamb curry, a classic Mughlai dish; medium-hot
sambar	soupy lentil and vegetable curry with asafoetida and tamarind
stew or estew	stew with a distinct Keralan twist (contains chilli and coconut); there's also a north Indian Muslim version)
subje	white coconut chutney often served with vada
tarka dhal	lentils with a masala of fried garlic, onions and spices

vindaloo	Goan vinegared meat (sometimes fish) curry, originally pork; very hot (but not as hot as the kamikaze UK version)

Breads and pancakes

appam*	rice pancake speckled with holes, soft in the middle; a speciality of the Malabar coast of Kerala
batura	soft bread made of white flour and traditionally accompanying chana; common in Delhi
chapati	unleavened bread made of wholewheat flour and baked on a round griddle-dish called a tawa
dosa*	rice pancake; should be crispy; when served with a filling it is called a masala dosa and when plain, a sada dosa
iddli*	steamed rice cake, usually served with sambar
kachori	small thick cakes of salty deep-fried bread; especially good in Varanasi and Calcutta
loochi	delicate puri often mixed with white flour; cooked in Bengalnan white leavened bread kneaded with yogurt and baked in a tandoor
papad or poppadum	crisp, thin, chick-pea flour cracker
paratha or parantha	wholewheat bread made with butter, rolled thin and griddle-fried; a little bit like a chewy pancake, sometimes stuffed with meat or vegetables
phulka	A chapati that has been made to puff out by being placed directly on the fire
puri	crispy, puffed-up, deep-fried wholewheat bread
roti	loosely used term; often just another name for chapati, though it should be thicker, chewier, and baked in a tandoor
uttapam*	thick rice pancake often cooked with onions
vada*	doughnut-shaped, deep-fried lentil cake

*South Indian terminology; all other terms are either in Hindi or refer to north Indian cuisine.

Tropical fruits such as coconuts, papayas (pawpaws) and pineapples are more common in the south, while things such as lychees and pomegranates are very seasonal. In the north, temperate fruit from the mountains can be much like that in Europe and North America, with strawberries, apricots and even rather soft apples available in season.

Among less familiar fruit, the *chiku*, which looks like a kiwi and tastes a bit like a pear, is worth a mention, as is the watermelon-sized jackfruit, whose spiny green exterior encloses sweet, slightly rubbery yellow segments, each containing a seed. Individual segments are sold at roadside stalls.

Soft drinks

India sometimes seems to run on **tea** or **chai**, grown in Darjeeling, Assam and the Nilgiri Hills, and sold by chai-wallahs on just about every street corner. However, although it was introduced from China by the East India Company in 1838, its use was only popularized by a government campaign in the 1950s.

Tea is usually made by putting tea dust, milk and water in a pan, boiling it all up, straining it into a cup or glass with lots of sugar and pouring back and forth from one cup to another to stir. Ginger and/or cardamoms are often added. If you're quick off the mark, you can get them to hold the sugar. English tea it isn't, but most travellers get used to it. Sometimes, especially in tourist spots, you might get a pot of European-style "tray" tea, generally consisting of a tea bag in lukewarm water – you'd do better to stick to the pukka Indian variety, unless, that is, you are in a traditional tea-growing area.

Instant coffee is becoming increasingly common, and in some cases is more popular than tea. At street stalls and on trains the familiar cry of "garam chai" (hot tea) is giving way to "kofi", while the *bhand*, a disposable mud teacup, is gradually disappearing in preference to inferior plastic cups. In the north, most coffee is instant, even that advertised as "espresso". Good vacuum-packed filter coffee from Coorg (Kodargu) in Karnataka is now available but is yet to have an impact in cafés and restaurants. Café society has finally arrived in the major cities, and Delhi and Mumbai now have a fair share

of trendy coffee shops serving real cappuccino and espresso.

In the south, **coffee (kofi)** is just as common as tea, and far better than it is in the north. One of the best places to get it is in outlets of the *India Coffee House* chain, found in every southern town, and occasionally in the north. A whole ritual is attached to the drinking of milky Keralan coffee in particular, poured in flamboyant sweeping motions between tall glasses to cool it down.

With **bottled water** so widely available, you may have no need of **soft drinks** (known as cold drinks in India). These have long been surprisingly controversial in India. Coca Cola and Pepsi returned to India in the early nineties after being banned from the country for seventeen years. That policy was originally instigated, in part, to prevent the expatriation of profits by foreign companies; since their return, militant Hindu groups such as the RSS have threatened to make them the focus of a boycott campaign against multinational consumer goods. The absence of Coca Cola and Pepsi spawned a host of Indian colas such as Campa Cola (innocuous), Thums Up (not unpalatable), Gold Spot (fizzy orange), and Limca (rumoured to have dubious connections to Italian companies, and to contain additives banned there). All contain a lot of sugar but little else: adverts for Indian soft drinks have been known to boast "Absolutely no natural ingredients!" None will quench your thirst for long.

More recommendable are straight water (treated, boiled or bottled; see also p.32), and cartons of Frooti Jumpin, Réal and similar brands of fruit juice drinks, which come in mango, guava, apple and lemon varieties. If the carton looks at all mangled, it is best not to touch it as it may have been recycled. At larger stations, there will be a stall on the platform selling Himachali apple juice. Better still, **green coconuts**, common around coastal areas especially in the south, are cheaper than any of these, and sold on the street by vendors who will hack off the top for you with a machete and give you a straw to suck up the coconut water (you then scoop out the flesh and eat it). You will also find street stalls selling freshly made sugarcane juice: delicious, and not in fact too sweet, but not always as safe healthwise as you might like.

India's greatest cold drink, **lassi**, is made with beaten curd and drunk either sweetened with sugar, salted, or mixed with fruit. It varies widely from smooth and delicious to insipid and watery, and is sold at virtually every café, restaurant and canteen in the country. Freshly made milk shakes are also commonly available at establishments with blenders. They'll also sell you what they call a fruit juice, but which is usually fruit, water and sugar (or salt) liquidized and strained; also, street vendors selling fresh fruit juice in less than hygienic conditions are apt to add salt and garam masala. With all such drinks, however appetizing they may seem, you should exercise great **caution** in deciding where to drink them: find out where the water is likely to have come from.

Alcohol

Prohibition, once widespread in India, is now only fully enforced in Gujarat and some of the northeastern hill states, although Tamil Nadu, Andhra Pradesh and some other states retain partial prohibition in the form of "dry" days, high taxes, restrictive licences, and health warnings on labels ("Liquor – ruins country, family and life," runs Tamil Nadu's). Even in areas where alcohol is readily available, dry days are often observed once a week (usually Thursday), and liquor shops remain shut.

Most Indians drink to get drunk as quickly as possible, and this trend has had a terrible toll on family life especially among the working classes and peasantry. Because of this, politicians searching for votes have from time to time played the prohibition card. The government in Haryana introduced prohibition in 1996 which, in a state that produces huge amounts of liquor, led to lost revenue and, as is common in all prohibition areas, the rapid growth of a highly organized illicit trade, but no evidence of less drinking. Haryana is no longer dry, but in states like Tamil Nadu, which persist with these policies, every now and then papers report cases of mass contamination from illicit stills that have led tragically to an extraordinary number of deaths.

Alcoholic enclaves in prohibition states can become major drinking centres: Daman and Diu in Gujarat, and Pondicherry and Karaikal in Tamil Nadu are the main ones. Goa, Sikkim and Mahé (Kerala) join them as places where the booze flows especially freely and cheaply. Interestingly, all were out-side the British Raj. **Liquor permits** – free, and available from Indian embassies, high commissions and tourist offices abroad, and from tourist offices in Delhi, Mumbai, Calcutta and Chennai, and even at airports on arrival – allow those travellers who bother to apply for one to evade certain restrictions in prohibition states like Gujarat.

Beer is widely available, if rather expensive by local standards. Price varies from state to state, but you can usually expect to pay Rs40–70 for a 650ml bottle. A pub culture, not dissimilar to that of the West, has taken root amongst the wealthier classes in cities like Bangalore and Mumbai and also in Delhi. Kingfisher and Black Label are the leading brands, but there are plenty of others. All lagers, which tend to contain chemical additives including glycerin, are usually pretty palatable if you can get them cold. In certain places, notably unlicensed restaurants in Tamil Nadu, beer comes in the form of "special tea" – a teapot of beer, which you pour into and drink from a teacup to disguise what it really is. A cheaper, and often delicious, alternative to beer in Kerala and one or two other places is *toddy* (palm wine). In Bengal it is made from the date palm, and is known as *taddy*. Sweet and nonalcoholic when first tapped, it ferments within twelve hours. In the Himalaya, the Bhotia people, of Tibetan stock, drink *chang*, a beer made from millet, and one of the nicest drinks of all – *tumba*, where fermented millet is placed in a bamboo flask and topped with hot water, then sipped through a bamboo pipe.

Spirits usually take the form of "Indian Made Foreign Liquor" (IMFL), although the recently legitimized foreign liquor industry is expanding rapidly. Some Scotch, such as Seagram's Hundred Pipers, is now being bottled in India and sold at a premium, and so is Smirnoff vodka amongst other known brands. Some of the brands of Indian whisky are not too bad and are affordable in comparison; gin and brandy can be pretty rough, while Indian rum is sweet and distinctive. In Goa, *feni* is a spirit distilled from coconut or cashew fruit. Steer well clear of illegally distilled *arak* however, which often contains methanol (wood alcohol) and other poisons. A look through the press, especially at festival times, will soon reveal numerous cases of blindness and death as a result of drinking bad hooch (or "spurious liquor" as it's called). Licensed country liquor, sold in several states under such names as *bangla*, is an acquired taste. Unfortunately, the Indian wine industry, though slowly improving with vineyards such as Grovers, is not up to scratch and the wines are pricey, while foreign wine available in upmarket restaurants and luxury hotels comes with an exorbitant price-tag.

Telephones, mail and internet access

There is no need to be out of touch with the rest of the world while you're in India. International phone calls are surprisingly easy, the mail service is pretty reliable, if a little slow, and cybercafés are common in the major cities and in many tourist centres.

Telephones

Privately run **phone services** with international **direct dialling** facilities are very widespread. Advertising themselves with the acronyms **STD/ISD** (standard trunk dialling/international subscriber dialling), they are extremely quick and easy to use; some stay open 24 hours. Both national and international calls are dialled direct. To call abroad, dial the international access code (00), the code for the country you want – 44 for the UK, for example – the appropriate area code (leaving out any initial zeros), and the number you want; then you speak, pay your bill, which is calculated in seconds, and leave. Prices vary between private places and are slightly cheaper at official telecommunications offices; many have fax machines too. Calling from hotels is usually more expensive. "Call back" (or "back call", as it is often known) is possible at most phone booths and hotels, although check before you call and be aware that, in the case of booths, this facility rarely comes without a charge of Rs3–10 per minute.

Direct dialling **rates** are very expensive during the day – Monday to Saturday 8am to 7pm – but this falls to half rate on Sundays, national holidays, and daily from 7am to 8am and 7pm to 8.30pm, after which the charge is reduced further.

Home country direct services are now available from any phone to the UK, the USA, Canada, Ireland, Australia, New Zealand, and a growing number of other countries. These allow you to make a collect or telephone credit card call to that country via an operator there. If you can't find a phone with home country direct buttons, you can use any phone toll-free, by dialling 000, your country code, and 17 (except Canada which is 000-127).

To **call India** from abroad, dial the international access code, followed by 91 for India, the local code minus the initial zero, then the number you want.

When you land and switch on your **mobile phone**, your network will search for a local partner, you confirm that you want to use

International dialling codes

	From India:	To India:
UK	☎ 00 44	☎ 00 91
Irish Republic	☎ 00 353	☎ 00 91
US and Canada	☎ 001	☎ 011 91
Australia	☎ 00 61	☎ 0011 91
New Zealand	☎ 00 64	☎ 00 91

them, then you can use the phone as usual. It's worth investigating costs before deciding to take your mobile to India, but bear in mind that it may be useful in an emergency. **Prepaid cards** for pay-as-you-go phones are handy and available in most of the major cities and towns; prices start from Rs1000 and as low as Rs500 for a top-up card.

Mail services

Mail can take anything from three days to four weeks to get to or from India, depending largely on where you are; ten days is about the norm. Stamps are not expensive, and aerogrammes and postcards cost the same to anywhere in the world. Ideally, you should have mail franked in front of you. Most post offices keep the same opening hours (Mon–Fri 10am–5pm & Sat 10am–noon), but big city GPOs, where the Poste Restante is usually located, are open longer (Mon–Fri 9.30am–6pm, Sat 9.30am–1pm). You can also buy stamps at big hotels.

Poste Restante (General Delivery) services throughout the country are pretty reliable, though exactly how long individual offices hang on to letters is more or less at their own discretion; for periods of longer than a month, it makes sense to mark mail with your expected date of arrival. Letters are filed alphabetically; in larger offices, you sort through them yourself. To avoid misfiling, your name should be printed clearly, with the surname in large capitals and underlined, but it is still a good idea to check under your first name too, just in case. Have letters addressed to you c/o Poste Restante, GPO (if it's the main post office you want), and the name of the town and state. In Delhi, you will probably want to specify "GPO, New Delhi", since "GPO, Delhi" means Old Delhi GPO, a lot less convenient for most tourists. Sometimes too, as in Calcutta and Chennai, local tourist offices might be more convenient than the GPO. Don't forget to take ID with you to claim your mail. American Express offices also keep mail for holders of their charge card or travellers' cheques.

Having **parcels** sent out to you in India is not such a good idea – chances are they'll go astray. If you do have a parcel sent, have it registered.

Sending a parcel out of India can be quite a performance. First you have to get it cleared by customs at the post office (they often don't bother, but check), then you take it to a tailor and agree a price to have it wrapped in cheap cotton cloth (which you may have to go and buy yourself), stitched up and sealed with wax. In big city GPOs, people offering this service will be at hand. Next, take it to the post office, fill in and attach the relevant customs forms (it's best to tick the box marked "gift" and give its value as less than Rs1000 or "no commercial value", to avoid bureaucratic entanglements), buy your stamps, see them franked, and dispatch it. Parcels should not be more than 1m long, nor weigh more than 20kg. Surface mail is incredibly cheap, and takes an average of six months to arrive – it may take half, or four times that, however. It's a good way to dump excess baggage and souvenirs, but don't send anything fragile this way.

As in Britain, North America and Australia and New Zealand, books and magazines can be sent more cheaply, unsealed or wrapped around the middle, as **printed papers** ("book post"). Alternatively, there are numerous courier services but it is safest to stick to known international companies such as DHL. Packages sent by air are expensive. **Couriers** are not as reliable as they should be and there have been complaints of packages going astray. Remember that all packages from India are likely to be suspect at home, and searched or X-rayed: don't send anything dodgy.

Internet and email

In all the large cities and in many tourist towns there are **internet** and **email** facilities accessible to the general public, usually at **cybercafés**, though many hotels and STD booths offer this service as well. Charges for internet use range from Rs10 to Rs80 per hour for reading mail and browsing, and extra for printing; most centres offer membership deals which can cut costs. You should make constant checks to see whether your connection is still alive; in the main cities faster connections through ISDN are now common: check this before you start using the service. The shops that advertise email alongside unrelated business concerns are cheaper, but you have to send and receive mail through their own private account, which means your messages are open to public scrutiny, and the service is invariably slow.

The media

With over one billion people and a literacy rate of around fifty percent, India produces a staggering 4700 daily papers in over 300 languages and another 39,000 journals and weeklies. There are a large number of English-language daily newspapers, both national and regional. The most prominent of the nationals are The Hindu, The Statesman, the Times of India, The Independent, the Economic Times and the Indian Express (usually the most critical of the government). All are pretty dry and sober, and concentrate on Indian news; The Independent and the Calcutta Telegraph tend to have better coverage of world news than the rest. Asian Age, published simultaneously in India, London and New York, is a conservative tabloid that sports a motley collection of the world's more colourful stories. All the major Indian newspapers have websites (see p.25), with the Times of India, The Hindu and the Hindustan Times providing the most up-to-date and detailed news services.

India's press is the freest in Asia and attacks on the government are often quite outspoken. However, as in the West, most papers can be seen as part of the political establishment, and are unlikely to print anything that might upset the "national consensus".

In recent years, a number of *Time/Newsweek*-style **news magazines** have hit the market, with a strong emphasis on politics. The best of these are *India Today* and *Frontline*, published by *The Hindu*. Others include *Outlook*, which presents the most readable, broadly themed analysis, *Sunday* and *The Week*. As they give more of an overview of stories and issues than the daily papers, you will probably get a better idea from them of what is going on in Indian politics, and most tend to have a higher proportion of international news too. *Business India* is more financially oriented and *The India Magazine* more cultural. Film **fanzines** and gossip mags are very popular (*Screen* and *Filmfare* are the best, though you'd have to be reasonably au fait with Indian movies to follow a lot of it), but magazines and periodicals in English cover all sorts of popular and minority interests, so it's worth having a look through what's available. One publication of special interest is Amar Chitra Katha's series of Hindu legends, Indian history and folk tales in comic form for children.

Foreign publications such as the *International Herald Tribune*, *Time*, *Newsweek*, *The Economist* and the international edition of the British *Guardian* are all available in the main cities, and in the most upmarket hotels, but they are rather costly. For a read through the British press, try the British Council in Delhi, Mumbai, Calcutta and Chennai; the USIS is the American equivalent. Expat-oriented bookstalls, such as those in New Delhi's Khan Market, stock slightly out-of-date and expensive copies of magazines like *Vogue* and *NME* for homesick Westerners.

BBC World Service radio can be picked up on short wave on 15.31MHz (19.6m) between about 8.30am and 10.30pm (Indian time). Alternative frequencies if reception is poor include 17.79MHz (16.9m), 15.56MHz (19.3m) and 11.96MHz (25.1m).

The government-run **TV** company, Doordarshan, which broadcasts a sober diet of edifying programmes, has tried to compete with the onslaught of mass access to **satellite TV**. The main broadcaster in English is Rupert Murdoch's Star TV network, which incorporates the BBC World Service and Zee TV (with Z News), a progressive blend of Hindi-oriented chat, film, news and music programmes. Star Sports and ESPN churn out a mind-boggling amount of cricket with an occasional sprinkling of other sports. Others include CNN, some sports channels, the Discovery Channel, the immensely popular Channel V, hosted by scantily clad Mumbai models and DJs, and a couple of American soap and chat stations. There are now several local-language channels as well.

Festivals and holidays

Virtually every temple in every town or village across the country has its own festival. The biggest and most spectacular include Puri's Rath Yatra festival in June or July, the Hemis festival in Ladakh also held in June or July, Pushkar's camel fair in November, Kullu's Dussehra, Madurai's three annual festivals, and of course the Kumbh Mela, held at Allahabad, Haridwar, Nasik and Ujjain. While mostly religious in nature, merrymaking rather than solemnity are generally the order of the day, and onlookers are usually welcome. Indeed, if you are lucky enough to coincide with a local festival, it may well prove to be the highlight of your trip.

Alas, we cannot list here every festival in every village across India, but local festivals are listed throughout the body of the guide. The following pages feature a list of the main national and regional celebrations, which requires a little explanation. Hindu, Sikh, Buddhist and Jain festivals follow the Indian **lunar calendar** and their dates therefore vary from year to year against the plain old Gregorian calendar. Determining them more than a year in advance is a highly complicated business best left to astrologers. Each lunar cycle is divided into two *paksa* (halves): "bright" (waxing) and "dark" (waning), each consisting of fifteen *tithis* ("days" – but a *tithi* might begin at any time of the solar day). The paksa start respectively with the new moon (*ama* or *bahula* – the first day of the month) and the full moon (*purnima*). Lunar festivals, then, are observed on a given day in the "light" or "dark" side of the month. The lunar calendar adds a leap month every two or three years to keep it in line with the seasons. Muslim festivals follow the **Islamic calendar**, whose year is shorter and which thus loses about eleven days per annum against the Gregorian.

You may, while in India, have the privilege of being invited to a **wedding**. These are jubilant affairs with great feasting, always scheduled on auspicious days. A Hindu bride dresses in red for the ceremony, and marks the parting of her hair with red *sindhur* and her forehead with a *bindu*. She wears gold or bone bangles, which she keeps on for the rest of her married life. Although the practice is officially illegal, large dowries often change hands. These are usually paid by the bride's family to the groom, and can be contentious; poor families feel obliged to save for years to get their daughters married.

Funeral processions are private affairs, and should be left in peace. In Hindu funerals, the body is normally carried to the cremation site within hours of death by white-shrouded relatives (white is the colour of mourning). The eldest son is expected to shave his head and wear white following the death of a parent. At Varanasi and other places, you may see cremations; such occasions should be treated with respect, and photographs should not be taken.

Principal Indian holidays

India has only four national public holidays as such: Jan 26 (Republic Day); Aug 15 (Independence Day); Oct 2 (Gandhi's birthday); and Dec 25 (Christmas Day). Each state, however, has its own calendar of public holidays; you can expect most businesses to close on the major holidays of their own religion (marked with an asterisk below).

The Hindu calendar months are given in brackets below as most of the festivals listed are Hindu.

Key: B=Buddhist; C=Christian; H=Hindu; J=Jain; M=Muslim; N=nonreligious; P=Parsi; S=Sikh.

Jan–Feb (Magha)

H Pongal (1 Magha): Tamil harvest festival celebrated with decorated cows, processions and rangolis (chalk designs on the doorsteps of houses). Pongal is a sweet porridge made from newly harvested rice and eaten by all, including the cows. The festival is also known as Makar Sankranti, and celebrated in Karnataka, Andhra Pradesh and the east of India.

H Ganga Sagar: Pilgrims come from all over the country to Sagar Dwip, on the mouth of the Hooghly 150km south of Calcutta, to bathe during Makar Sankranti.

H Vasant Panchami (5 Magha): One-day spring festival in honour of Saraswati, the goddess of learning, celebrated with kite-flying, yellow saris, and the blessing of schoolchildren's books and pens by the goddess.

N Republic Day (Jan 26): A military parade in Delhi typifies this state celebration of India's republic-hood, followed on Jan 29 by the "Beating the Retreat" ceremony outside the Presidential Palace in Delhi.

N Goa Carnival: Goa's own Mardi Gras features float processions and *fenni*-induced mayhem in the state capital, Panjim.

N International Kite Festival at Aurangabad (Maharashtra).

H Floating Festival (16 Magha) at Madurai (Tamil Nadu).

N Elephanta Music and Dance Festival (Mumbai).

Feb–March (Phalguna)

B Losar (1 Phalguna): Tibetan New Year celebrations among Tibetan and Himalayan Buddhist communities, especially at Dharamsala (HP).

H Shivratri (10 Phalguna): Anniversary of Shiva's *tandav* (creation) dance, and his wedding anniversary. Popular family festival but also a *sadhu* festival of pilgrimage and fasting, especially at important Shiva temples.

H Holi (15 Phalguna)*: Water festival held during Dol Purnima (full moon) to celebrate the beginning of spring, most popular in the north. Expect to be bombarded with water, paint, coloured powder and other mixtures; they can permanently stain clothing, so don't go out in your Sunday best.

N Khajuraho (Madhya Pradesh) Dance Festival.

C Carnival (Mardi Gras): The last day before Lent, 40 days before Easter, is celebrated in Goa, as in the rest of the Catholic world.

March–April (Chaitra)

H Gangaur (3 Chaitra): Rajasthani festival (also celebrated in Bengal and Orissa) in honour of Parvati, marked with singing and dancing.

H Ramanavami (9 Chaitra)*: Birthday of Rama, the hero of the Ramayana, celebrated with readings of the epic and discourses on Rama's life and teachings.

C Easter (movable feast)*: Celebration of the Resurrection of Christ. Good Friday in particular is a day of festivity.

P Pateti: Parsi new year, also known as No Ruz, celebrating the creation of fire. Feasting, services and present-giving.

P Khorvad Sal (a week after Pateti): Birthday of Zarathustra (aka Zoroaster).

H Chittirai, Madurai (Tamil Nadu): Elephant-led procession.

April–May (Vaisakha)

HS Baisakhi (1 Vaisakha): To the Hindus, it's the solar new year, celebrated with music and dancing; to the Sikhs, it's the anniversary of the foundation of the Khalsa (Sikh brotherhood) by Guru Gobind Singh. Processions and feasting follow readings of the Granth Sahib scriptures.

J Mahavir Jayanti (13 Vaisakha)*: Birthday of Mahavira, the founder of Jainism. The main Jain festival of the year.

H Puram Festival, Thrissur (Kerala): frenzied drumming and elephant parades.

B Buddha Jayanti (16 Vaisakha)*: Buddha's birthday. He achieved enlightenment and nirvana on the same date. Sarnath (UP) and Bodh Gaya (Bihar) are the main centres of celebration.

May–June (Jyaishtha)

H Ganga Dussehra (10 Jyaishtha): Bathing festival to celebrate the descent to earth of the goddess of the Ganges.

June–July (Ashadha)

H Rath Yatra (2 Ashadha): Festival held in Puri (and other places, especially in the south) to commemorate Krishna's (Lord Jaggernath's) journey to Mathura.

H Teej (3 Ashadha): Festival in honour of Parvati, to welcome the monsoon. Celebrated particularly in Rajasthan.

B Hemis Festival, Leh (Ladakh): Held sometime between late June and mid-July, this spectacular festival features *chaam* (lama dances) to signify the victory of Buddhism over evil.

July–Aug (Shravana)

H Naag Panchami (3 Shravana): Snake festival in honour of the naga snake deities. Mainly celebrated in Rajasthan and Maharashtra.

H Raksha Bandhan/Narial Purnima (16 Shravana): Festival to honour the sea god Varuna. Brothers and sisters exchange gifts, the sister tying a thread known as a *rakhi* to her brother's wrist. Brahmins, after a day's fasting, change the sacred thread they wear.

N Independence Day (15 Aug): India's biggest secular celebration, on the anniversary of independence from Britain.

Aug–Sept (Bhadraparda)

H Ganesh Chaturthi (4 Bhadraparda): Festival dedicated to Ganesh, especially celebrated in Maharashtra. In Mumbai, huge processions carry images of the god to immerse in the sea.

H Onam: Keralan harvest festival, celebrated with snake-boat races. The Nehru Trophy snake-boat race at Alappuzha (held on the second Saturday of August) is the most spectacular, with long boats each crewed by 150 rowers.

H Janmashtami (23 Bhadraparda)*: Krishna's birthday, an occasion for fasting and celebration, especially in Agra, Mumbai, Mathura (UP) and Vrindaban (UP).

H Avani Mula festival, Madurai (Tamil Nadu): Celebration of the coronation of Shiva.

Sept–Oct (Ashvina)

H Dussehra (1–10 Ashvina)*: Ten-day festival (usually two days' public holiday) associated with vanquishing demons, in particular Rama's victory over Ravana in the Ramayana, and Durga's over the buffalo-headed Mahishasura (particularly in West Bengal, where it is called Durga Puja). Dussehra celebrations include performances of the Ram Lila (life of Rama). Best in Mysore (Karnataka), Ahmedabad (Gujarat) and Kullu (Himachal Pradesh). Durga Puja is best seen in Calcutta where it is an occasion for exchanging gifts, and every locality has its own competing street-side image.

N Mahatma Gandhi's Birthday (2 Oct): Solemn commemoration of Independent India's founding father.

Oct–Nov (Kartika)

H Diwali (Deepavali) (15 Kartika)*: Festival of lights, and India's biggest, to celebrate Rama and Sita's homecoming in the Ramayana. Festivities include the lighting of oil lamps and firecrackers, and the giving and receiving of sweets and gifts. Diwali coincides with Kali Puja, celebrated in temples dedicated to the wrathful goddess, especially in Bengal, and often accompanied by the ritual sacrifice of goats.

J Jain New Year (15 Kartika): Coincides with Diwali, so Jains celebrate alongside Hindus.

S Nanak Jayanti (16 Kartika)*: Guru Nanak's birthday marked by prayer readings and processions, especially in Amritsar and in the rest of the Punjab, and at Patna (Bihar).

Nov–Dec (Margashirsha, or Agrahayana)

H Sonepur Mela: World's largest cattle fair at Sonepur (Bihar).

N Pushkar (Rajasthan) Camel Fair.

N Hampi Festival (Karnataka): Government-sponsored music and dance festival.

Dec–Jan (Pausa)

CN Christmas (Dec 25)*: Christian festival celebrated throughout the world, popular in Christian areas of Goa and Kerala, and in big cities.

N Posh Mela (Dec 27): Held in Shantiniketan near Calcutta, a festival renowned for *baul* music.

Movable

H Kumbh Mela: Major three-yearly festival held at one of four holy cities: Nasik (Maharashtra), Ujjain (MP), Haridwar (UP), or Prayag (Maharashtra) as well as at Allahabad (UP). The Maha Kumbh Mela or "Great" Kumbh Mela, the largest religious fair in India, is held every twelve years in Allahabad (UP); the next festival is due to take place in 2013.

M Ramadan (first day: Dec 9, 2000; Nov 28, 2001): The start of a month during which Muslims may not eat, drink or smoke from sunrise to sunset, and should abstain from sex. Towards the end of the month it takes its toll, so be gentle with Muslims you meet at this time.

M Id ul-Fitr (Jan 8, 2000; Dec 28, 2001)*: Feast to celebrate the end of Ramadan, after 28 days.

M Id ul-Zuha: Pilgrimage festival to commemorate Abraham's preparedness to sacrifice his son Ismail. Celebrated with slaughtering and consumption of sheep.

M Muharram: Festival to commemorate the martyrdom of the (Shi'ite) Imam, the Prophet's grandson and popular saint, Hussain.

Sports

India is not perhaps a place that most people associate with sports (India only achieved one bronze medal in the Sydney Olympics in 2000), but cricket, hockey and football (soccer, that is) all have their place.

Cricket is by far the most popular of these, and a fine example of how something quintessentially British (well, English) has become something quintessentially Indian. Travellers to India will find it hard to get away from cricket – it is everywhere and especially on television. Cricketing heroes such as the batting maestro Sachin Tendulkar live under the constant scrutiny of the media and public. Expectations are high and disappointments acute; India versus Pakistan matches are especially emotive. In 1999, the right-wing Hindu group, Shiv Sena, threatened to disrupt Pakistan's tour of India and even dug up the pitch in Delhi. Despite riots at Calcutta's famous but volatile Eden Gardens, however, caused not by politics but by an umpiring decision, the tour was a resounding success and one of the most exciting and eagerly fought cricketing contests ever held between the two sides. Since then, due to politics, the two sides have not played each other on home soil.

India's faith in cricket was dramatically tested in 2000, when match-fixing allegations fuelled by Indian-led betting interests – first exposed in the cyber media by tehelka.com – shocked the international cricketing world. The revelations led to the disgrace and resignations of two illustrious cricketing captains: Mohammed Azharuddin of India and Hansie Cronjie of South Africa.

Test matches are rare but interstate cricket is easy to catch – the most prestigious competition is the Ranji Trophy. Besides spectator cricket, you'll see games being played on open spaces all around the country. Occasionally, in cities like Calcutta, you may even come across a match blocking a road, and will have to be patient as the players begrudgingly let your vehicle continue.

Horse racing can be a good day out, especially if you enjoy a flutter. Calcutta's racecourse is the most popular, often attracting crowds of over 50,000, especially on New Year's Day. There are several other racecourses around the country, mostly in larger cities such as Mumbai, Delhi, Pune, Hyderabad, Mysore, Bangalore and Ooty. Other (mainly) spectator sports include **polo**, originally from upper Kashmir, but taken up by the British to become one of the symbols of the Raj. Princes of Rajasthan, such as the late Hanut Singh of Jodhpur, were considered in the Thirties, Forties and Fifties to be the best polo players in the world, but since the Sixties, when the privy purses were cut, they have been unable to maintain their stables, and the tradition of polo has declined. Today, it is mainly the army who plays the game; the best place to catch a match is at the Delhi Gymkhana during the winter season. Polo, in more or less its original form, is still played on tiny mountain ponies in Ladakh and a good place to catch a match is in Leh during the Ladakh Festival in early September.

After years in the doldrums, Indian **hockey**, which used to regularly furnish India with Olympic medals, is making a strong comeback. The haul of medals dried up in the Sixties when international hockey introduced Astro-turf which was, and still is, a rare surface in India. However hockey is still very popular, especially in schools and colleges and, interestingly, amongst the tribal girls of Orissa, who supply the Indian national team with a regular clutch of players. Indian **athletics** are improving all the time and, today the country can boast some world-class women sprinters who bagged several medals at the 1998 Asian Games.

Volleyball is very popular throughout India, and you may even see army men playing at extraordinary altitudes on the road to Leh. Standards aren't particularly high and joining a game should be quite easy. **Football** (soccer) is similarly popular with a keenly contested national championship. The best teams are based in Calcutta and include three legendary clubs – Mohan Bagan, East Bengal and Mohamadan Sporting – who all command fanatical support. Unlike most of the league, these teams employ professional players and even include some minor internationals mostly from Africa. International soccer tournaments are becoming increasingly common.

Tennis in India has always been a sport for the middle classes. The country boasts a player or two of world-class standing, such as the duo of Bhupati and Paes who briefly achieved a world number-one ranking in the mens' doubles in 1999. Motorsport is popular in the south and there is a popular racetrack on the outskirts of Chennai. **Golf** is extremely popular and relatively inexpensive in India, again amongst the middle classes; the second-oldest golf course in the world is in Calcutta, and one of the highest in the world at Simla.

One indigenous sport you're likely to see in north India is **kabadi**, played on a small (badminton-sized) court, and informally on any suitable open area. The game, with seven players in each team, consists of a player from each team alternately attempting to "tag" as many members of the opposing team as possible in the space of a single breath (cheating is impossible; the player has to maintain a continuous chant of kabadikabadikabadikabadi etc), and getting back to his/her own side of the court without being caught. The game can get quite rough, with slaps and kicks in tagging allowed, and the defending team must try to tackle and pin the attacker so as not to allow him or her to even touch the dividing line. Tagged victims are required to leave the court. Although still an amateur sport, kabadi is taken very seriously with state and national championships, and now features in the Asian Games.

Popular with devotees of the monkey god, Hanuman, Indian **wrestling**, or **kushti**, has a small but dedicated following. Wrestlers are known as pahlwaans or "strong men" and can be seen exercising early in the morning with traditional instruments along river *ghats* such as those in Varanasi or Calcutta.

Trekking and outdoor pursuits

India offers an increasing number of opportunities for adventure sports, including trekking, mountaineering, white-water rafting, caving and diving. A word of warning though – if you plan to do any of these activities during your trip, make sure you take out a comprehensive insurance policy (see p.28).

Trekking

Though **trekking** in India is not nearly as commercialized as in neighbouring Nepal, there are some highly rewarding routes, especially in the Ladakh and Zanskar Himalayas, where the mountain passes are mostly in excess of 5000m. Himalayan routes are not all extreme, with relatively gentle short trails exploring the Singalila range around Darjeeling, low-level forest walks through the rhododendron-clad hillsides of Sikkim and the well-beaten pilgrim trails of Garhwal. Hiring a guide is recommended whenever possible, especially on more difficult and less frequented routes; you must carry all necessary equipment and supplies and research the route in advance.

One or two operators run **package trekking holidays**, and trekking agencies exist at such places as Manali, Leh, Darjeeling and Gangtok, but in most cases it is possible to go under your own steam and organize guides, plus porters or ponies, pri-

Specialist **tour operators** are listed in the various Getting There sections of Basics.

vately. A trek normally lasts a week or two; the longer it is, in general, the more you'll get out of it.

Himachal Pradesh, which issues trekking maps, brochures and trekking guides, is the most efficient state in which to trek; the Mountaineering Institute is on hand in Dharamsala to offer advice. **Uttaranchal** sees fewer trekkers, but there are plenty of opportunities to wander off the beaten track and escape the hordes of pilgrims or join them on their way to the sacred sites of Badrinath, Gangotri, Joshimath and Kedarnath. It is not advisable to venture into Kashmir at present, but there are exciting and exotic high-mountain trekking opportunities in the ancient Buddhist kingdoms of **Ladakh** and **Zanskar** where trails can vary in length from short four-day excursions to epics of ten days or more. At the eastern end of the Himalayas, **Darjeeling** makes a good base from which to explore the surrounding mountains. Neighbouring **Sikkim** has the greatest variations in altitude, from steamy river valleys to the third highest massif in the world; there are a number of high-altitude treks which require a permit, readily available in the capital Gangtok through government-recognized guides charging fees in dollars. Shorter and less strenuous treks are available in the Ghats and the Nilgiri hills of southern India.

Having the right **equipment** for a trek is important, but high-tech gear isn't essential – bring what you need to be comfortable but keep weight to a minimum. In some places, such as Leh and Darjeeling, you can rent equipment, but otherwise, you'll have to buy what you need or bring it with you. Make sure everything (zips for example) is in working order before you set off. Clothes should be lightweight and versatile, especially considering the range of temperatures you might encounter: dress in layers for maximum flexibility.

Mountaineering

Mountaineering is a more serious venture, requiring planning and organization; if you've never climbed, don't start in the Himalayas. Mountaineering institutes at Darjeeling, Uttarkashi and Dharamsala, run training courses, though only the one in Dharamsala is open to foreigners; it also organizes high-altitude treks (see p.552). Permission for mountaineering expeditions should be sought at least six months in advance from the Indian Mountaineering Federation, Anand Niketan, Benito Juarez Road, New Delhi 110021 (☎011/467 7935, ⓦwww.indmount.com). Peak fees range from $1500 to $4000, according to height, and expeditions must be accompanied by an IMF liaison officer equipped to the same standard as the rest of the party. The IMF can also supply lists of local mountaineering clubs; climbing with such clubs enables you to get to know local climbers, and obtain permits for otherwise restricted peaks.

Skiing

Despite the mammoth spread of the Himalayas, **skiing** in India remains relatively undeveloped. The only option for organized skiing is the western Himalayas, in particular Uttaranchal and Himachal Pradesh; the eastern Himalayas have unreliable snowfall at skiing altitudes.

The ski area at **Auli**, near Joshimath in Uttaranchal, has had money poured into it with a gondola lift system and a handful of surface tows but it suffers from a short season, limited though cheap skiing and non-existent après-ski activity. Auli also lies in a "dry zone", so you won't find a bar after a hard day on the slopes.

In Himachal Pradesh, the skiing in the vicinity of **Shimla** is far too underdeveloped to warrant a detour but the possibilities around Manali are more enticing because of the prospect of virgin powder: two or three surface tows operate in the **Solang Nala** for three months every winter.

There are two options for back-country skiing – the first is to plan your own ski-tour and bring your own equipment, but you should never go alone. The other way to float down trackless slopes is to go heli-skiing (see p.574), but at around US$500 a day, you'd have to be pretty well off to explore what aficionados describe as some of the best powder in the world. The other place where you can do back-country skiing is Kashmir, but the political situation there is far too dangerous to consider it.

White-water rafting

Though not as well known as some of the mighty rivers of Nepal, the rivers Chenab and Beas in **Himachal Pradesh**, Rangit and Teesta in **Sikkim**, Zanskar and Indus in **Ladakh**, and Ganges in upper Uttar Pradesh all combine exciting waters with magnificent scenery. Kullu, Manali, Leh, Gangtok and Rishikesh are among the main rafting centres. Prices start at around Rs500 per day including food, but it's worth sounding out a few agents to find the best deals. For more details see the relevant accounts in the guide.

Caving

Meghalaya has the best caving potential of all the Indian states. Tucked away in the northeast of India, it offers extensive limestone regions and boasts the two wettest places on earth – Mawsynram and Cherrapunjee. The three main areas for caving are: the **East Khasi hills**, the **Jainta hills** and the **South Garo hills**. Krem Umlawan, 60km from Jowai in the Jainta hills, used to be considered the longest (6381m) and deepest (107m) cave in India. That is, until cavers found a link from this cave to the nearby Krem Kotsati (another interesting cave with eight entrances, the main one being through a deep pool with some beautiful river passages), making the combined Krem Kotsati–Umlawan cave the longest system in mainland Asia, measuring 21.4km. A small cave entrance in Nengkhong village (South Garo hills) leads to a 5330m cave which is the second longest in India. The third largest system, near the village of Siju, has some of the best river sections anywhere in the world, and is the most explored cave in India. Half a kilometre west of Cherrapunjee, Krem Mawmluh (4500m) measures up in fourth place. For potholing contacts in Meghalaya, see p.1062.

Diving and snorkelling

Because of the number of rivers draining into the sea around the subcontinent, India's coastal waters are generally silt-laden and too murky for decent **diving** or **snorkelling**. However, in many areas abundant hard coral and colourful fish make up for the relatively poor visibility. India also counts two beautiful tropical island archipelagos in its territory,

both surrounded by exceptionally clear seas. Served by well-equipped and reputable diving centres, the Andaman islands, and Lakshadweep offer world-class diving on a par with just about anything in Asia. Don't come here expecting rock-bottom prices though. Compared to Thailand, India's dive schools are pricey, typically charging around Rs15,000 ($350) for a four-day PADI-approved open-water course.

For independent travellers, the most promising destination for both scuba-diving and snorkelling is the **Andaman islands** (see p.1167) in the Bay of Bengal, around 1000km east of the mainland. Part of a chain of submerged mountains that stretch north from Sumatra to the coast of Burma (Myanmar), this isolated archipelago is ringed by gigantic coral reefs whose crystal-clear waters are teeming with tropical fish and other marine life. Given the prohibitively high cost of diving courses, most visitors stick to snorkelling, but if you already have your PADI permit, it's well worth renting equipment from one of the two dive schools in the capital, Port Blair, and joining an excursion to an offshore dive site such as Cinque Island or the Mahatma Gandhi Marine Reserve. If you want to do an open-water course, book ahead as places tend to be in short supply especially during the peak season, between December and February.

The other group of Indian islands surrounded by clear seas and abundant marine life is **Lakshadweep** (see p.1376), a classic coconut palm-covered atoll, some 400km west of Kerala in the Arabian Sea. The shallow lagoons, extensive coral reefs and exceptionally good visibility make this a perfect option for both first-timers and more experienced divers.

For anyone on a limited budget, a better option is Goa, where two dive schools (see p.853) currently offer a full range of courses, and equipment rental for qualified divers. Visibility is not so great along this stretch of coast, but you can escape the worst of the silt by heading further out to sea by boat, where a handful of islands and two wrecks shelter prolific fish life. Most of the dive sites are shallow (between 10 and 20m), and thus ideal for beginners.

As with other countries, qualified divers should take their current certification card and/or logbook; if you haven't used it for one year or more, expect to have to take a short test costing around Rs300 ($7).

Yoga, meditation and ashrams

Most first-time visitors to India opt for a cocktail – temples, trekking, palaces, wildlife parks, beaches, and, to balance the indulgences and hedonism, a spiritual element in whatever form. From basic yoga and pranayama classes to residential meditation retreats, India has no equal in terms of tradition and opportunity.

Yoga is taught virtually everywhere in India and there are several internationally known yoga centres where you can train to become a teacher. **Meditation** is similarly practised all over the country and specific courses are available in temples, meditation centres, monasteries and ashrams. **Ashrams** are communities where people work, live and study together, drawn by a common, usually spiritual, goal. Adopting a guru is a completely different experience to simply attending a few classes, and whether you choose to do so will ultimately depend on your deep personal commitment and on how comfortable you feel being around a specific guru, but be careful in your choice.

Details of yoga and meditation courses and ashrams are provided throughout this guide section of this book. Most centres offer courses that you can enrol on at short notice, but many of the more popular ones, listed opposite, need to be booked well in advance.

Yoga

The word **yoga** literally means "to unite" and the aim of the discipline is to help the practitioner unite his or her individual consciousness with the divine. This is achieved by raising awareness of one's self through spiritual, mental and physical discipline. Hatha yoga is based on physical postures called **asanas**, and although the most popular form in the West, it is traditionally just the first step leading to more subtle stages of meditation which commence when the energies of the body have been awakened and sensitized by stretching and relaxing. Other forms of yoga include *raja* yoga, which includes moral

discipline and *bhakti* yoga, the yoga of devotion, which entails a commitment to one's guru or teacher. *Jnana* yoga (the yoga of knowledge) is centred around the deep philosophies that underlie Hindu spiritual thinking; the greatest body of Hindu philosophic treatises are known as the Upanishads (c.1000 BC) which came to be embodied in the philosophical discipline of Vedanta. **Rishikesh** and **Varanasi**, both in Uttar Pradesh, are the two traditional centres for yoga, but numerous institutions throughout the country have good teachers and advanced practitioners. In many of the travellers' haunts such as Pushkar, Dharamsala, Goa, and Kovalam, posters in cafés advertise local teachers, although many offer dubious qualifications and may well be seasonal. Ask other tourists for a teacher of quality and repute, or ask the teacher if you can do a trial session.

Meditation

Meditation is often practised after a session of yoga, when the energy of the body has been awakened, and is an essential part of both Hindu and Buddhist practice. In both religions, meditation is considered the most powerful tool for understanding the true nature of mind and self, an essential step on the path to enlightenment. In **Vedanta**, meditation's aim is to realize the true self as nondual Brahman or godhead – the foundation of all consciousness and life. *Moksha* (or liberation – the Nirvana of the Buddhists), achieved through disciplines of yoga and meditation, eventually helps believers release the soul from endless cycles of birth and rebirth.

Vipassana meditation is a technique originally taught by the Buddha, whereby practitioners learn to become more aware of physical sensations and mental processes. Courses last for a minimum of ten days and are austere – involving 4am kick-offs, around ten hours of meditation a day, no solid food after noon, segregation of the sexes, and no talking for the duration (except with the leaders of the course). Courses are free for all first-time students, to allow everyone an opportunity to learn and benefit from the technique. Vipassana is taught in more than 25 centres throughout India including in Bodhgaya, Bangalore, Chennai, Hyderabad and Jaipur.

Tibetan Buddhist meditation is attracting more and more followers around the world. With its four distinct schools, Tibetan Buddhism incorporates a huge variety of meditation practices, including Vipassana, known as **shiné** in Tibetan, and various visualization techniques involving the numerous deities that make up the complex and colourful Tibetan pantheon. India, with its large Tibetan diaspora, has become a major centre for those wanting to study Tibetan Buddhism and medicine. Dharamsala in Himachal Pradesh, home to the Dalai Lama and Tibetan government-in-exile, is the main centre for Tibetan studies, offering numerous opportunities for one-on-one study with the Tibetan monks and nuns who live there. Other major Tibetan diaspora centres in India include Darjeeling in West Bengal and Bylakuppe near Mysore in Karnataka. For further details of courses available locally, see the relevant chapters of the guide.

Ashrams

Ashrams can range in size from several thousand people to just a handful, and their rules, regulations and restrictions vary enormously. Some offer on-site accommodation, others will require you to stay in the nearest town or village. Some charge Western prices, others local prices, and some simply operate on a donation basis. Many ashrams run specific courses and have set programmes each day including meditation and *bhakti* yoga, while others are less structured, providing self-study facilities and offering guidance and teaching as and when requested.

Courses and ashrams

Astanga Yoga Nilayam 876 1st Cross, Lakshmipuram, Mysore, Karnataka 570 004. Run by Pattabhi Jois, courses last at least a month and need to be booked in advance. The great yoga master Sri Tirumalai Krisnamacharya taught here until his death in 1989. Dynamic yoga affiliated with martial arts.

Divine Life Society PO Shivanandanagar, Munir ki Reti, Rishikesh, District Tehri Garhwal, Uttaranchal ☏0135/430040, ℻433101,🖳www.sivanandadlshq.org. The original Sivananda ashram – well organized if institutional, with several retreats and courses on all aspects and forms of yoga. The strength of Sivananda's yoga, however, was his deep understanding of Advaitya Vedanta – the philosophy of non-duality.

International Society for Krishna Consciousness (ISKCON) 🖳www.iskcon.org. 3c Albert Road, Calcutta ☏033/247 3757; Bhaktivedanta Swami Marg, Raman Reti, Vrindavan ☏0565/442478. Large well-run international organization with major ashrams and temples in Mayapur, north of Calcutta in West Bengal, Vrindavan in west UP and centres in several major Indian cities and abroad. Promotes *bhakti* yoga (the yoga of devotion) through good deeds, right living and chanting – a way of life rather than a short course.

Osho Commune International 17 Koregaon Park, Pune, Maharashtra 411 001 ☏020/612 6655, ℻613 9955, 🖳www.osho.com. The centre, established by the enigmatic Osho who generated a huge following of both Western and Indian devotees, is set in 31 acres of beautifully landscaped gardens and offers a variety of courses in personal therapy, healing and meditation. For full details see p.845. There are numerous other Indian and international centres.

Prasanthi Nilayam, Puttaparthi, Andhra Pradesh ☏08555/87583,🖳www.sathyasai.org. The ashram of Sathya Sai Baba, one of India's most revered and popular gurus who has a worldwide following of millions despite the deaths of four followers in mysterious circumstances in 2000. The ashram is four or five hours by bus from Bangalore. Visitors sometimes comment on the strict security staffing and rigid rules and regulations. Cheap accommodation is available in dormitories or "flats" for four people. There is no need to book in advance though you should phone to check availability; see p.1158 for more details. Sai Baba also has a smaller ashram in Bangalore and one in Kodaikanal.

Root Institute for Wisdom Culture Bodhgaya, Bihar ☏0631/400714, ℻400548,

www.rootinstitute.com. An important meditation and teaching centre linked to the Foundation for the Preservation of the Mahayana Tradition (FPMT). Regular seven- to ten-day courses are held here and there are facilities for individual retreats. Accommodation for longer stays should be booked well in advance. See p.1006 for further details.

Saccidananda Ashram, Thanneepalli, Kullithalai, near Tiruchirapelli, Tamil Nadu ℡ 04323/22260, 🖷 22280, 🖳 www.bedegriffiths.com. Also known as Shantivanam (meaning Peace Forest in Sanskrit), it is situated on the banks of the sacred River Cauvery. Founded by Father Bede Griffiths, a visionary Benedictine monk, it presents a curious but sympathetic fusion of Christianity and Hinduism. Visitors can join in the services and rituals or just relax here. Accommodation is in simple huts dotted around the grounds and meals are communal. Very busy during the major Christian festivals.

Sivananda Yoga Vedanta Dhanwanthari Ashram PO Neyyar Dam, Thiruvananthapuram Dist, Kerala, 695 576 ℡ 0471/273493, 🖷 272493, 🖳 www.sivananda.org. An offshoot of the original Divine Life Society, a yoga-based ashram where yoga

postures (asanas), breathing techniques (pranayama) and meditation are taught. They also run teacher-training programmes. There are two other branches in India: Sivananda Kutir (near Siror bridge), PO Netala, Uttar Kashi Dist. Uttar Pradesh 249193 ℡ 01374/2624), and Sivananda Guha, Gangotri, PO Uttar Kashi Dist, Uttar Pradesh. Both are in the Himalayas.

Tushita Meditation Centre McLeod Ganj, Dharamsala 176219, Himachal Pradesh ℡ 01892/21866, 🖷 21246, 🖳 http://come.to/tushita Offers a range of Tibetan meditation courses. A ten-day course costs in the region of Rs3500; book well in advance.

Vipassana International Academy Dhamma Giri, PO Box 6, Igatpuri, Dist. Nasik, Maharashtra 422 403 ℡ 025/538 4076, 🖷 538 4176, 🖳 www.dhamma.org. The main centre for Vipassana in India; they can also provide contact details for other centres. Vipassana is a form of Theravada Buddhism meditation and is usually taught through short intensive retreats which most find difficult but immensely rewarding.

Crime and personal safety

In spite of the crushing poverty and the yawning gulf between rich and poor, India is on the whole a safe country in which to travel. As a tourist, however, you are an obvious target for the tiny number of thieves (who may include some of your fellow travellers), and stand to face serious problems if you do lose your passport, money and ticket home. Common sense, therefore, suggests a few precautions.

If you can tolerate the encumbrance, carry valuables in a money belt or a pouch around your neck at all times. In the latter case, the cord should be hidden under your clothing and not be easy to cut through. Beware of **crowded locations**, such as packed buses or trains, in which it is easy for pickpockets to operate – slashing pockets or bags with razor blades is not unheard of in certain locations, and itching powder can used to distract the unwary – and don't leave valuables unattended on the beach

when you go for a swim. Backpacks in dormitory accommodation are also obvious targets.

Budget travellers would do well to carry a **padlock**, as these are usually used to secure the doors of cheap hotel rooms and it's reassuring to know you have the only key; strong combination locks are ideal. You can also use them to lock your bag to seats or racks in trains, for which a length of chain also comes in handy. Don't put valuables in your luggage for bus or plane

Future is black if sugar is brown
Indian anti-drugs poster

India is a centre for the production of cannabis and to a lesser extent opium, and derivatives of these drugs are widely available. *Charas* (hashish) is produced all along the Himalayas. The use of cannabis is frowned upon by respectable Indians – if you see anyone in a movie smoking a *chillum*, you can be sure it's the baddie. *Sadhus*, on the other hand, are allowed to smoke ganja (marijuana) legally as part of their religious devotion to Shiva, who is said to have originally discovered its narcotic properties. If you indulge as a foreigner, it is best to be discreet, even if you see others behaving more openly.

Bhang (a preparation made from marijuana leaves, which it is claimed sometimes contains added hallucinogenic ingredients such as datura) is legal and widely available in *bhang* shops: it is used to make sweets and drinks such as the notoriously potent *bhang* lassis which have waylaid many an unwary traveller. *Bhang* shops also frequently sell ganja, low-quality *charas*, and opium (*chandu*), mainly from Rajasthan and Madhya Pradesh. Its derivatives, morphine and heroin, are widespread too, with addiction an increasing problem among the urban poor. "Brown sugar" that you may be offered on the street is grade three heroin; Varanasi is becoming notorious for its heroin problem. Use of other illegal drugs such as LSD, ecstasy and cocaine is largely confined to tourists in party locations such as Goa.

All of these drugs except *bhang* are strictly controlled under Indian law, with a minimum sentence of ten years for possession. Anyone arrested with less than five grams of cannabis which they are able to prove is for their own use is liable to a six-month maximum, but cases can take years to come to trial (two is normal, and eight not unheard of). Police raids and searches are particularly common at the following places: Manali, the Kullu valley and Almora, and on buses from those places to Delhi, especially at harvest time; buses and trains crossing certain state lines, notably between Gujarat and Maharastra; budget hotels in Delhi's Paharganj; the beach areas of Goa; and around Idukki and Kumily in Kerala. "Paying a fine now" may be possible with one or two officers on arrest (though it will probably mean all the money you have), but once you are booked in at the station, your chances are slim; a minority of the population languishing in Indian jails are foreigners on drugs charges.

journeys: keep them with you at all times. If your baggage is on the roof of a bus, make sure it is well secured. On trains and buses, the prime time for theft is just before you leave, so keep a particular eye on your gear then, beware of deliberate diversions, and don't put your belongings next to open windows. Remember that routes popular with tourists tend to be popular with thieves too; knifepoint muggings are on the increase in Goa. Druggings leading to theft and worse are rare but not unheard of and so you are best advised to politely **refuse food and drink** from fellow passengers or passing strangers, unless you are completely confident it's the family picnic you are sharing or have seen the food purchased from a vendor.

However, don't get paranoid; the best way of enjoying the country is to stay relaxed but with your wits about you. Crime levels in India are a long way below those of Western countries, and violent crime against tourists is extremely rare. Virtually none of the people who approach you on the street intend any harm: most want to sell you something (though this is not always made apparent immediately), some want to practise their English, others (if you're a woman) to chat you up, while more than a few just want to add your address to their book or have a snap taken with you. Anyone offering wonderful-sounding moneymaking schemes, however, is almost certain to be a con artist.

If you do feel threatened, it's worth looking for help. In 1999, the Indian Government established a special "tourism police", with plans to assign officers to major tourist sites in cities such as Delhi, Jaipur, Varanasi and Agra in the hope that an increased **police** presence would deter potential offenders. Tourism police are found sitting in clearly marked booths in the main railway stations, especially in big tourist centres, where they will also have a booth in the main bus station. They may also have a marked booth outside major tourist sites.

Be wary of **credit card fraud**; a credit card can be used to make duplicate forms to which your account is then billed for fictitious transactions, so don't let shops or restaurants take your card away to process – insist they do it in front of you or follow them to the point of transaction. Even **monkeys** rate a mention here – it is not unknown for them to steal things from hotel rooms with open windows, or even to snatch bags from unsuspecting shoulders.

It's not a bad idea to keep $100 or so separately from the rest of your money, along with your travellers' cheque receipts, insurance policy number and phone number for claims, and a photocopy of the pages in your passport containing personal data and your Indian visa. This will cover you in case you do lose all your valuables.

If the worst happens and you get robbed, the first thing to do is report the theft as soon as possible to the local police. They are very unlikely to recover your belongings, but you need a report from them in order to claim on your travel insurance. Dress smartly and expect an uphill battle – city cops in particular tend to be jaded from too many insurance and travellers' cheque scams.

Losing your passport is a real hassle, but does not necessarily mean the end of your trip. First, report the loss immediately to the police, who will issue you with the all-important "complaint form" that you need to be able to travel around and check into hotels, as well as claim back any expenses incurred in replacing your passport from your insurer. A complaint form, however, will not allow you to change money or travellers' cheques. If you've run out of cash, your best bet is to ask your hotel manager to help you out (staff will have seen your passport when you checked in, and the number will be in the register). The next thing to do is telephone your nearest embassy or consulate in India. Normally, passports have to be applied for and collected in person, but if you are stranded, it is usually possible to arrange to receive the necessary forms in the post. However, you still have to go to the embassy or consulate to pick up your new passport. "Emergency passports" are the cheapest form of replacement, but are normally only valid for the few days of your return flight. If you're not sure when you're leaving India, you'll have to obtain a more costly "full passport"; these can only be issued by embassies and larger consulates in Delhi or Mumbai, and not those in Chennai, Calcutta or Panjim.

Cultural hints and etiquette

Cultural differences extend to all sorts of little things. While allowances will usually be made for foreigners, visitors unacquainted with Indian customs may need a little preparation to avoid causing offence or making fools of themselves. The list of do's and don'ts here is hardly exhaustive: when in doubt, watch what the Indian people around you are doing.

Eating and the right-hand rule

The biggest minefield of potential faux pas has to do with **eating**. This is usually done with the fingers, and requires practice to get absolutely right. Rule one is: **eat with your right hand only**. In India, as right across Asia, the left hand is for wiping your bottom, cleaning your feet and other unsavoury functions (you also put on and take off your shoes with your left hand), while the right hand is for eating, shaking hands, and so on.

Quite how rigid individuals are about this tends to vary, with brahmins (who at the top of the hierarchical ladder are one of the two "right-handed castes") and southerners likely to be the strictest. While you can hold a cup or utensil in your left hand, and you can usually get away with using it to help tear your chapati, you should not eat, pass food or wipe your mouth with your left hand. Best is to keep it out of sight below the table.

This rule extends beyond food. In general, do not pass anything to anyone with your left hand, or point at anyone with it either; and Indians won't be impressed if you put it in your mouth. In general, you should accept things given to you with your right hand – though using both hands is a sign of respect.

The other rule to beware of when eating or drinking is that your lips should not touch other people's food – *jhuta* or sullied food is strictly taboo. Don't, for example, take a bite out of a chapati and pass it on. When drinking out of a cup or bottle to be shared with others, don't let it touch your lips, but rather pour it directly into your mouth. This custom also protects you from things like hepatitis. It is customary to wash your hands before and after eating.

Temples and religion

Religion is taken very seriously in India; it's important always to show due respect to religious buildings, shrines, images, and people at prayer. When entering a temple or mosque, remove your shoes and leave them at the door (socks are acceptable and protect your feet from burning-hot stone ground). Some temples – Jain ones in particular – do not allow you to enter wearing or carrying leather articles, and forbid entry to menstruating women. When entering a religious establishment, dress conservatively (see below), and try not to be obtrusive.

In a mosque, you'll not normally be allowed in at prayer time and women are sometimes not let in at all. In a Hindu temple, you are not often allowed into the inner sanctum; and at a Buddhist stupa or monument, you should always walk round clockwise (ie, with the stupa on your right). Hindus are very superstitious about taking **photographs** of images of deities and inside temples; if in doubt, desist. Do not take photos of funerals or cremations.

Dress

Indian people are very conservative about **dress**. Women are expected to dress modestly, with legs and shoulders covered. Trousers are acceptable, but shorts and short skirts are offensive to many. Men should always wear a shirt in public, and avoid shorts (a sign of low caste) away from beach areas. These rules go double in temples and mosques. Cover your head with a cap or cloth when entering a *dargah* (Sufi shrine) or Sikh *gurudwara*; women in particular are also required to cover their limbs. Men are similarly expected to dress appropriately with their legs and head covered. Caps are usually available on loan, often free, for visitors, and sometimes cloth is available to cover up your arms and legs.

Never mind sky-clad Jains or *naga sadhus*, **nudity** is not acceptable in India. The mild-mannered people of Goa may not say anything about nude bathing (though it is in theory prohibited), but you can be sure they don't like it.

In general, Indians find it hard to understand why rich Western sahibs should wander round in ragged clothes or imitate the lowest ranks of Indian society, who would love to have something more decent to wear. Staying well groomed and dressing "respectably" vastly improves the impression you make on local people, and reduces sexual harassment too.

Other possible gaffes

Kissing and **embracing** are regarded in India as part of sex: do not do them in public. It is not even a good idea for couples to hold hands, though Indian men can sometimes be seen holding hands as a sign of "brotherliness". Be aware of your feet. When entering a private home, you should normally remove your shoes (follow your host's example); when sitting, avoid pointing the soles of your feet at anyone. Accidental contact with one's foot is always followed by an apology.

Indian English can be very formal and even ceremonious. Indian people may well call you "sir" or "madam", even "good lady" or "kind sir". At the same time, you should be aware that your English may seem rude to them. In particular, swearing is taken rather seriously in India, and casual use of the F-word is likely to shock.

Meeting people

Westerners have an ambiguous status in Indian eyes. In one way, you represent the rich sahib, whose culture dominates the world, and the old colonial mentality has not completely disappeared: in that sense, some Indians may see you as "better" than them. On the other hand, as a non-Hindu, you are an outcaste, your presence in theory polluting to an orthodox or high-caste Hindu, while to members of all religions, your morals and your standards of spiritual and physical cleanliness are suspect: in that sense Indians may see themselves as "better" than you. Even if you are of Indian origin, you may be considered to suffer from Western corruption, and people may test you out on that score.

As a traveller, you will constantly come across people who want to strike up a **conversation**. English not being their first language, they may not be familiar with the conventional ways of doing this, and thus their opening line may seem abrupt if at the same time very formal. "Excuse me good gentleman, what is your mother country?" is

a typical one. It is also the first in a series of questions that Indian men seem sometimes to have learnt from a single book in order to ask Western tourists. Some of the questions may baffle at first ("What is your qualification?" "Are you in service?"), some may be queries about the ways of the West or the purpose of your trip, but mostly they will be about your family and your job.

You may find it odd or even intrusive that complete strangers should want to know that sort of thing, but these subjects are considered polite conversation between strangers in India, and help people place one another in terms of social position. Your family, job, even income, are not considered "personal" subjects, and it is completely normal to ask people about them. Asking the same questions back will not be taken amiss – far from it. Being curious does not have the "nosey" stigma in India that it has in the West.

Things that Indian people are likely to find strange about you are lack of religion (you could adopt one), travelling alone, leaving your family to come to India, being an unmarried couple (letting people think you are married can make life easier), and travelling second class or staying in cheap hotels when, as a tourist, you are relatively rich. You will probably end up having to explain the same things many times to many different people; on the other hand, you can ask questions too, so you could take it as an opportunity to ask things you want to know about India. English-speaking Indians and members of the large and growing middle class in particular are usually extremely well informed and well educated, and often far more *au fait* with world affairs than Westerners, so you may even be drawn into conversations that are way out of your depth.

Shopping

So many beautiful and exotic souvenirs are on sale in India, at such low prices, that it's sometimes hard to know what to buy first. On top of that, all sorts of things (such as made-to-measure clothes) that would be vastly expensive at home are much more reasonably priced in India. Even if you lose weight during your trip, your baggage might well put on quite a bit – unless of course you post some of it home.

Where to shop

Quite a few items sold in tourist areas are made elsewhere and, needless to say, it's more fun (and cheaper) to pick them up at source. Best buys are noted in the relevant sections of the guide, along with a few specialities that can't be found outside their regions. India is awash with **street hawkers**, often very young kids. Although they can be annoying and should be dealt with firmly if you are not interested, do not write them off completely as they sometimes have decent souvenirs at lower than shop prices and are open to hard bargaining.

Virtually all the state governments in India run handicraft **"emporia"**, most with branches in the major cities such as Delhi, Mumbai, Chennai and Calcutta. There are also Central Cottage Industries Emporiums in Delhi, Chennai, Calcutta and Mumbai. Goods in these places are generally of a high quality, even if their fixed prices are a little expensive, and they are worth a visit to get an idea of what crafts are available and how much they should cost.

Bargaining

Whatever you buy (except food and cigarettes), you will almost always be expected to **haggle** over the price. Bargaining is very much a matter of personal style, but should always be lighthearted, never acrimonious. There are no hard and fast rules – it's really a question of how much something is worth to you. It's a good plan, however, to have an idea of how much you want, or ought, to pay. "Green" tourists are easily spotted, so try and look like you know what you are up to, even on your first day, or leave it till later;

you could wait and see what an Indian might pay first.

Don't worry too much about the first quoted prices. Some guidebooks suggest paying a third of the opening price, but it's a flexible guideline depending on the shop, the goods and the shopkeeper's impression of you. You may not be able to get the seller much below the first quote; on the other hand, you may end up paying as little as a tenth of it. If you bid too low, you may be hustled out of the shop for offering an "insulting" price, but this is all part of the game, and you'll no doubt be welcomed as an old friend if you return the next day.

Don't start haggling for something if you know you don't want it, and never let any figure pass your lips that you are not prepared to pay. It's like bidding at an auction. Having mentioned a price, you are obliged to pay it. If the seller asks you how much you would pay for something, and you don't want it, say so.

Sometimes rickshaw-wallahs and taxi drivers stop unasked in shops; they get a small commission simply for bringing customers. In places like Jaipur and Agra where this is common practice, tourists often strike a deal with their drivers – agreeing to stop at five shops and splitting the commission for the time wasted. Obviously if you're taken to a shop by a tout or driver and you buy something, you pay around fifty percent extra. Stand firm about not entering shops and getting to your destination if you have no appetite for such shenanigans.

Metalware and jewellery

Artisans have been casting **bronze statues** of Hindu gods for more than a thousand years. The images are produced by the lost-wax process, in which a model is first carved out of wax, then surrounded in clay, and finally fired. The wax melts to leave a terracotta mould. Small pieces can be cast from a single mould, but larger ones have to be assembled from up to a dozen pieces, the joins concealed by ornate ornamentation. The best-quality images will have carefully detailed fingers and eyes, and the metal should not have pits or spots. The south is one major area for them (dancing Shivas, known as Nataraj, are a favourite here – check out the quality in the palace art gallery at Thanjavur), the Himalayas another. Dokra, a speciality of West Bengal and Orissa, uses this very same lost-wax technique to produce charming figurines, often depicting animals.

Brass and copperware can be very finely worked, with trays, plates, ashtrays, cups and bowls among products available. The best trays – which should be forty years old or more – are from Varanasi. In the north, particularly in Rajasthan, enamel inlays (*meenakari*) are common. *Bidri* work, named after Bidar (Karnataka), where it originated, is a method of inlaying a gunmetal alloy with fine designs in brass or silver, then blackening the gunmetal with sal-ammoniac, to leave the inlay work shining. *Bidri* jewellery boxes, dishes and hookah pipes, among other things, are widely sold, especially in Karnataka and Andhra Pradesh; while the Orissan filigree *tarakashi* is worth looking out for. **Stainless steel** is less decorative and more workaday: thali sets and spice tins are among the possible buys, available throughout the country.

Among precious metals, silver is generally a better buy than **gold** but is difficult to distinguish from cheap white metal often palmed off in curio shops as silver. Gold is usually 22 carat and very yellow, but relatively expensive due to taxes (smuggling from the Gulf to evade them is rife) and to its popularity as a form of investment – women traditionally keep their wealth in this form, and a bride's jewellery is an important part of her dowry. **Silver** varies in quality, but is usually reasonably priced, with silver jewellery generally heavier and rather more folksy than gold. Rajasthan and Bengal are its main centres, and Tibetan silver jewellery is also popular. Gold and silver are usually sold by weight, the workmanship costing very little.

Buying gemstones can be something of a minefield; scams abound, and you would be most unwise to even consider buying gems for resale or as an investment without a basic knowledge of the trade. That said, some precious and semiprecious stones can be a good buy in India, particularly those which are indigenous, such as garnets, black stars and moonstones. Jaipur is a major centre for gems (and con tricks), while Hyderabad specializes in sorting pearls, which can therefore be picked up at low prices.

Woodwork, ceramics and stone

Wooden furniture, if a little heavy to carry with you, can be a real bargain, and is especially good in the mountainous areas of the north. Carvings of gods (often in sandalwood) are particularly common in the south, and those of elephants are always a favourite. Old wooden carvings from houses or temples that are being refurbished are usually available at reasonable prices, if sometimes a little weathered.

Terracotta figures are a speciality of Bengal and Bihar, but the finest **ceramic** work is the glazed pottery of Jaipur, Kurja, and Delhi. Brightly painted clay and plaster gods are another souvenir possibility, while marble and soapstone are both used for sculpture (though big pieces weigh a ton), and marble items inlaid in the style of the Taj Mahal are popular souvenirs in Agra. The stone carvings of Mahabalipuram prove excellent value for small pieces, which are all you will want to carry. Somewhat less weighty than these are papier-mâché items sold in Kashmiri shops that have sprung up around the country (most of which seem to get their supplies in Delhi).

Carpets and rugs

If you get dragged into a Kashmiri arts shop, chances are it's a **carpet** they really want to sell you. Kashmiri rugs are among the best in the world (up there with those from Iran) and, given a little caution and scepticism, you can get yourself a bargain in India (though you can also get shafted if you're not careful). A pukka Kashmiri carpet should have a label on the back stating that it is made in Kashmir, what it is made of (wool, silk, or "silk touch", the latter being wool combined with a little cotton and silk to give it a sheen), its size, density of knots per square inch (the more the better), and the name of the design. To tell if it really is silk, scrape the carpet with a knife and burn the fluff – real silk shrivels to nothing and has a distinctive smell. Even producing the knife should cause the seller of a bogus silk carpet to demur.

The best way to ensure a carpet reaches home is to take it away and post it yourself; a seller may offer to post it to you and bill you later, which is fair enough, but your carpet will be sent immediately, whatever you say (will someone be there to receive it?), and if you use a credit card, your account will also be billed immediately, whatever is said. Be aware of import tax being levied on arrival. Choose your shop carefully as there have been complaints of shipped carpets never arriving (or perhaps never having been shipped in the first place).

Dhurries (woven carpets or kilims), traditionally made of wool, are an older art form, and a less expensive one. UP is the main centre for these, particularly Agra and Mirzapur, but they are also made in Rajasthan, Gujarat, the Punjab, and Andhra Pradesh. Recent revelations have exposed the widespread use of child labour, especially in Mirzapur, but NGOs are proving successful in providing education and other basic facilities in the mills.

Tibetan rugs are available in areas with a large Tibetan community, such as Himachal Pradesh. Many foreigners prefer carpets in "tasteful" earthy colours, assuming them to be traditional and therefore "ethnic". In fact, Indian carpets traditionally come in bright colours, though the synthetic dyes used nowadays are of course newfangled.

Textiles and clothing

Textiles are so much a part of Indian culture that Gandhi wanted a spinning wheel put on the national flag. The kind of cloth he had in mind was the plain white homespun material worn by Nehru, whose hat, jacket and dhoti remain a mark of support for the Congress Party to this day. Homespun, handloom-woven hand-printed cloth is called **khadi**, and is sold in the government shops called Khadi Gramodyog that are

found all over India. Methods of dyeing and printing this and other cloth vary from the tie-dyeing (*bhandani*) of Rajasthan to block printing and screen printing of calico (from Calicut – now Kozhikode, Kerala) cotton, and of silk.

Saris are normally made of cotton for everyday use, although **silk** is used for special occasions, and quite common in the south. Western women are notoriously inept at wearing this most elegant of garments – it takes years of practice to carry one properly – but silk is usually a good buy in India, provided you make sure it is the real thing (the old test was to see whether it was possible to pull the whole garment straight through a wedding ring; however, some synthetics apparently go through too, so burn a thread and sniff it to be sure). Though Varanasi silk is world famous, the best nowadays comes from Kanchipuram and Madurai in Tamil Nadu; silk from Mysore is also prized but has recently had a bad press due to accusations concerning child labour.

Other popular fabrics include the heavy mirror-embroidered cloth of Rajasthan, Bengali *baluchari* brocade, and Indonesian-style ikat and batik from Orissa, Madhya Pradesh and Gujarat, while clothing to take home includes lunghis in the south (as much sheets as garments), thick Tibetan sweaters from Darjeeling, and *salwar kamise*, the elegant pyjama suits worn by Muslim women, with trousers (pyjamas) of various styles. Long loose shirts – preferably made of *khadi*, and known as *kurta* or *panjabi* – are practical in the heat of India, and traditionally worn, by men, with white pyjamas. Tourist shops sell versions in various fabrics and colours. Block-printed bedsheets, as well as being useful, make good wall-hangings, as do Punjabi *phulkari* (originally wedding sheets), but every region has its own fabrics and its own methods of colouring them and making them up – the choice is endless.

On top of this, with **tailoring** so cheap in India, you can choose the fabric you want, take it to a tailor, and have it made into whatever you fancy. For formal Western-style clothes, you'll want to see quite a posh tailor in a big city, but tailors in almost every village in the country can run you up a shirt or a pair of pyjama-type trousers in next to no time. Many tailors will also copy a garment you already have.

Paintings and antiques

Art and antiques are another field where only experts should look for an investment, but where a souvenir hunter is very likely to find a bargain. Silk and cotton paintings are popular in Rajasthan and the north, but vary vastly in quality, so check out a few before you buy. The village of Kishangarh (Rajasthan) is known for them; they are also sold in Udaipur. The striking black lines and primary colours depicting mythological and religious themes easily distinguish Madhuvani paintings, also known as Mithila paintings after the district in Bihar where they are made. The folk art, which makes ideal gifts, first started as decoration on huts but is now marketed widely through emporia, using handmade paper.

Most Tibetan **thangkas** (Buddhist religious paintings mounted on brocaded silk) are mass produced (usually in Nepal) and modern, whatever the seller says, but even the cheapest boast the dense Buddhist symbolism inherent in the form. You'll find them in the north, where there are Tibetan communities, and a little investigation of the range of styles is well worthwhile.

Leaf skeleton paintings, originally from southern Kerala, are much cheaper and widely available, though they too vary somewhat in quality. **Miniatures** in the traditional style, often masquerading as antiques, are common in tourist shops too, but subject to the same provisos as *thangkas*.

When it comes to **antiques**, if they really are genuine – and, frankly, that is unlikely – you'll need a licence to export them, which is virtually impossible to get. The same applies to "art treasures". Age and status can be verified by the Archaeological Survey of India, Janpath, New Delhi 110011 (℡011/301 8614); Sion Fort, Sion, Mumbai 400022 (℡022/407 1102); 4th floor, Block DF, Sector 1, Salt Lake City, Calcutta 700064 (℡033/334 3775); Fort St George, Chennai 600009 (℡044/560396); Old Town, Bhubaneshwar 751002, Orissa (℡0674/430590); 5th floor, F Wing, Kendriya Sadan, 17th Main Rd, Keramangala, Bangalore 560034 (℡080/553 7348). These offices also issue export clearance certificates.

Odds and sods

Of course, not everything typically Indian is old or traditional. **CDs, tapes or records** of classical, bhangra, *filmi*, and Western music are very cheap and popular. **Videos** too are widely available; southern films are more likely to be subtitled than Hindi ones.

Publishers thrive in India and **books** are excellent buys, whether by Indian writers (see Contexts) or writers from the rest of the English-speaking world. International publishers market books in India at discounted prices and they are likely to be much cheaper than at home. Books printed and published in India tend to be not so well printed or bound but there is a growing market for upmarket coffee-table books and old rare books. Hardback volumes of Indian sacred literature are particularly good value.

Leatherware can be very cheap and well-made, though the leather doesn't normally come from cows, of course. Rajasthani camel-hide *mojadi* slippers go down well, as do *chappal* (sandals) and the distinctive *kho-lapuri* slippers, which need to be broken in; pointed *juttes* popular around Delhi and the Punjab also need some perseverance. Otherwise, buffalo-hide belts and bags can be very reasonable compared to similar items made of cowhide in the West; Chennai and Pondicherry are good places to go looking. Upmarket shops offer a range of good-quality leather goods, from handbags and briefcases to clothes at reasonable prices. Recent campaigns in the West have called for the boycotting of Indian leather goods due to poor treatment of animals.

Bamboo flutes are incredibly cheap, while other **musical instruments** such as tabla, sitar and sarod are heavy to carry and available in the West anyway, though usually of lower quality and higher price. The quality is crucial; there's no point going home with a sitar that is virtually untuneable, even if it does look nice. Students of music purchase their instruments from master craftsmen or established shops; get advice before you buy, and never buy one from a tourist shop.

Other possibilities include kitchen implements like tiffin boxes, wind-up clockwork tin toys, film posters, tea (especially from Darjeeling, Assam and Nilgiri), coffee, spices, peacock feather fans (though these are considered unlucky), and anything which reminds you of India – which needn't be expensive or arty.

Things not to bring home include ivory and anything made from a rare or protected species, including snakeskin and turtle products. As for drugs – don't even think about it.

Women travellers

India is not a country that provides huge obstacles to women travellers, petty annoyances being more the order of the day. In the days of the Raj, upper-class eccentrics started a tradition of lone women travellers, taken up enthusiastically by the flower children of the hippy era. Women today still do it, and most come through the challenge perfectly unscathed. However, few women get through their trip without any hassle, and it's good to prepare yourself to be a little thick-skinned.

Indian streets are almost without exception male-dominated – something that may take a bit of getting used to, particularly when you find yourself subjected to incessant staring, whistling and name calling. This can usually be stopped by ignoring the gaze and quickly moving on, or by firmly telling the offender to stop looking at you. Most of your fellow travellers on trains and buses will be men who may start up most unwelcome conversations about sex, divorce and the freedom of relationships in the West. These cannot often be avoided, but demonstrating too much enthusiasm to discuss such topics can lure men into thinking that you are easy about sex, and the situation could become threatening. At its worst in larger cities, all this can become very tiring. You can get round it to a certain extent by joining women in public places, and you'll notice an immense difference if you join up with a male travelling companion. In this case, expect Indian men to approach him (assumed, of course, to be your husband – an assumption it is sometimes advantageous to go along with) and talk to him about you quite happily as if you were not there. Beware, however, if you are (or look) Indian with a non-Indian male companion: this may well cause you grief and harassment, as you will be seen to have brought shame on your family by adopting the loose morals of the West.

In addition to staring and suggestive comments and looks, **sexual harassment**, or "Eve teasing" as it is bizarrely known, is likely to be a nuisance, but not generally a threat. North Indian men are particularly renowned for their disregard of women's rights, and it is on the plains of Uttar Pradesh and Bihar that you are most likely to experience physi-

cal hassle. Expect to get groped in crowds, and to have men "accidentally" squeeze past you at any opportunity. It tends to be worse in cities than in small towns and villages, but anywhere being followed can be a real problem.

In time you'll learn to gauge a situation – sometimes wandering around on your own may attract so much unwanted attention that you may prefer to stay in one place until you've recharged your batteries or your male fan club has moved on. It's always best to dress modestly – a *salwar kamise* is perfect, as is any baggy clothing – and refrain from smoking and drinking in public, which only reinforces suspicions that Western women are "loose" and "easy".

Returning an unwanted touch with a punch or slap is perfectly in order (Indian women often become aggressive when offended), and does serve to vent a little frustration. It should also attract attention and urge someone to help you, or at least deal with the offending man – a man transgressing social norms is always out of line, and any passer-by will want to let him know it. If you feel someone getting too close in a crowd or on a bus, brandishing your left shoe in his face can be very effective.

To go and watch a Bollywood movie at the cinema is a fun and essential part of your trip to India, but unfortunately such an occasion is rarely without hassle. The crowd is predominantly male and mostly young at that. If you do go to the cinema, go with a group of people and/or sit in the balcony area – it's a bit more expensive but the crowd is much more sedate up there.

Violent sexual assaults on tourists are extremely rare, but unfortunately the num-

For more on **Indian women**, see Contexts, p.1524.

ber of reported cases of rape is rising. Though no assault can be predicted, you can take precautions: at night avoid quiet, dimly lit streets and alleys, if you find a trustworthy rickshaw/taxi driver in the day keep him for the night journey, and try to get someone to accompany you to your hotel whenever possible. While Indian women are still quite timid about reporting rape – it is considered as much a disgrace to the victim as to the perpetrator – Western victims should always report it to the police, and before leaving the area try to let other tourists, or locals, know, in the hope that pressure from the community may uncover the offender and see him brought to justice. At present there's nowhere for tourists who've suffered sexual violence to go for sanctuary; most victims seek support from other travellers, or go home.

The **practicalities of travel** take on a new dimension for lone women travellers. Often you can turn your gender to your advantage. For example, on buses the driver and conductor will often take you under their wing, watch out for you and buy you chai at each stop, and there will be countless other instances of kindness wherever you travel. You'll also be more welcome in some private houses than a group of Western males, and may find yourself learning the finer points of Indian cooking round the family's clay stove. Women frequently get preference at bus and railway stations where they can join a separate "ladies' queue", and use ladies' waiting rooms. On overnight trains the enclosed ladies' compartments are peaceful havens (unless filled with noisy children); you could also try to share a berth section with a family where you are usually drawn into the security of the group and are less exposed to lusty gazes. In hotels watch out for "peep-holes" in your door (and in the common bathrooms), be sure to cover your window when changing and when sleeping, and avoid the sleazy permit-room hotels of the southern cities.

Lastly, bring your own supply of tampons,

as these are not widely available outside Indian cities.

Womens' organizations in India

The Centre for Feminist Legal Research, B-12 Maharani Bagh, New Delhi 110065 ☎011/691 8923, ✆rk.cflr@rkpslaw.sprintrpg.sprint.com. Promotes women's rights and human rights by conducting workshops, training and seminars for women and the development of feminist legal research.

Forum against the Oppression of Women 29 Bhatia Bhawan, Babrekan Rd, Gokale Rd (North), Dadar, Mumbai 400028 ☎022/422 2436 Support centre which also organizes workshops.

Indian Council of Social Science Research (ICSSR) 3F Shah Rd, New Delhi 110001 ☎011/383186, ✆www.icssr.org. Organizes workshops and symposia on feminist themes and runs a women's studies programme.

Indian Social Institute (ISI) Programme for Women's Development, 10 Lodi Rd, New Delhi 110003 ☎011/462 5051 Runs courses and conferences.

Jagori C-54 Defence Colony, New Delhi ☎011/625 7015 Runs workshops, conferences and has a good reference library and contemporary resource centre.

Kali for Women B1/8 Haus Khas Bhag, New Delhi, 110006 ☎011/685 2530 Feminist publisher that produces a range of very readable books on the Indian women's movement.

SANHITA c/o Sanlaap, 89B Raja Basanta Roy Rd, Calcutta 700029 ☎033/466 2150 Very prominent association spearheading women's empowerment in eastern India.

Self-Employed Women's Association (SEWA) Textile Workers' Union Building, opposite Victoria gardens, Ahmedabad, Gujarat. Self-help union that helps rural women organize income-generating projects; see also p.680.

Streelekha (International Feminist Bookshop and Information Centre), 15/55, 1st floor, Cambridge, Jeevan Kendra Layout, Bangalore 560 008, Karnataka. Stocks books, journals, posters; provides space for women to meet.

Women's Centre 104B Sunrise Apartments, Nehru Rd, Valoka, Santa Cruz East, Mumbai 400055 ☎022/614 0403 A drop-in centre for women to meet, hold workshops and gain access to literature on women's issues.

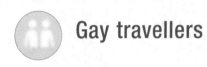

Gay travellers

Homosexuality is not generally open or accepted in India. "Carnal intercourse against the order of nature" (anal intercourse) is a ten-year offence under article 377 of the penal code, while laws against "obscene behaviour" can be used to arrest gay men for cruising or liaising anywhere that could be considered a public place. The same law could in theory be used against lesbians.

The homosexual scene in India was brought into the spotlight in 1998 with the nationwide screening of the highly controversial film *Fire* by Deepa Mehta, about two sisters-in-law living together under the same roof who become lesbian lovers. Flying in the face of the traditional emphasis on heterosexual family life, the film created a storm. Right-wing extremists attacked cinemas that showed it, and in the wake of the attacks, many gay men and lesbians came out into the open for the first time to hold candle-lit protest vigils in Delhi, Mumbai, Calcutta, Chennai and Bangalore – all cities known for their more open-minded younger generations.

For lesbians, making contacts is rather difficult; even the Indian women's movement does not readily promote lesbianism as an issue that needs confronting. The only public faces of a hidden scene are the organizations listed below and a few of the nationwide women's organizations (see opposite).

For gay men, homosexuality is no longer solely the preserve of the alternative scene of actors and artists, and is increasingly accepted by the middle-line urban middle and upper classes. If you keep your finger on the social pulse of the larger cities, especially Bangalore and Mumbai, you will soon discover which nightclubs and bars have a gay scene. Also, the organizations listed below can tell you about gay events and parties.

Bombay Dost (Rs50; ⊕ www.bombay-dost.com) is a quarterly with news, views and useful information on gay and lesbian issues. The magazine is available in Delhi at The People Tree; and in Mumbai at Danai Bookshop at Khar-Danda Road and at 105A Veena-Beena Shopping Centre.

Gay contacts

Write in advance for information – most addresses are PO boxes:

Arambh c/o Aalok, PO Box 9522, New Delhi 110095. Gay support group.

Bombay Dost 105A Veena-Beena Shopping Centre, Bandra Station Rd, Bandra (West), Mumbai 400050. Publish a newsletter and have contacts nationwide.

Friends of India PO Box 59, Mahanagar, Lucknow 226006 ⊕ 0522/247009 Local gay support group.

Gay Info Centre c/o Owais, PO Box 1662, Secunderabad HPO 500003, Andhra Pradesh. Provides literature, contacts and resources on homosexuality in India.

Good As You 201 Samaraksha, 2nd Floor Royal Corner, 1–2 Lalbang Rd, Bangalore. Gay support group.

Khush Club PO Box 573551, Mumbai 400058. Organizes gay social events regularly in Mumbai.

Men India Movement PO Box 885, Kochi 682005, Kerala. Gay men's support group.

Saathi PO Box 571, Putlibowli PO, Hyderabad, Andhra Pradesh. Gay support group.

Shakhi PO Box 3526, Lajpat Nagar, New Delhi 110065. Lesbian guesthouse and resource centre.

Sneha Sangama PO Box 3250, Bangalore 560032. Gay men's support group.

Stree Sangam PO Box 16613, Matunga, Mumbai 400019. A support group for lesbian and bisexual women.

The Counsel Club PO Bag 10237, Calcutta 700016. Support and meeting centre for homosexuals.

Disabled travellers

Disability is common in India; many conditions that would be curable in the West, such as cataracts, are permanent disabilities here because people can't afford the treatment. Disabled people are unlikely to get jobs (though there is a famous blind barber in Delhi), and the choice is usually between staying at home being looked after by your family, and going out on the street to beg for alms.

For the **disabled traveller**, this has its advantages: disability doesn't get the same embarrassed reaction from Indian people that it does from some able-bodied Westerners. On the other hand, you'll be lucky to see a state-of-the-art wheelchair or a disabled loo (major airports usually have both, though the loo may not be in a useable state), and the streets are full of all sorts of obstacles that would be hard for a blind or wheelchair-bound tourist to negotiate independently. Kerbs are often high, pavements uneven and littered, and ramps nonexistent. There are potholes all over the place and open sewers. Some of the more expensive hotels have ramps for the movement of luggage and equipment, but if that makes them accessible to wheelchairs, it is by accident rather than design.

If you walk with difficulty, you will find India's many street obstacles and steep stairs hard going. Another factor that can be a problem is the constant barrage of people proffering things (hard to wave aside if you are for instance on sticks or crutches), and all that queuing, not to mention heat, will take it out of you if you have a condition that makes you tire quickly. A light, folding camp-stool is one thing that could be invaluable if you have limited walking or standing power.

Then again, Indian people are likely to be very helpful if, for example, you need their help getting on and off buses or up stairs. Taxis and rickshaws are easily affordable and very adaptable; if you rent one for a day, the driver is certain to help you on and off, and perhaps even around the sites you visit. If you employ a guide, they may also be prepared to help you with steps and obstacles.

If complete independence is out of the question, going with an able-bodied companion might be on the cards. Contact one of the specialist organizations listed below

for further advice on planning your trip. Otherwise, some package tour operators try to cater for travellers with disabilities – Bales and Somak among them – but you should always contact any operator and discuss your exact needs with them before making a booking. You should also make sure you are covered by any insurance policy you take out.

Contacts for disabled travellers

Britain and Ireland

Can Be Done 7–11 Kensington High St, London W8 5NP ☎020/8907 2400. Specialist tour operators for the disabled.

Carefree Holidays 64 Florence Rd, Northampton NN1 4NA ☎01604/634301. Specialist tour operators for the disabled.

Holiday Care Service 2nd Floor, Imperial Buildings, Victoria Rd, Horley, Surrey RH6 7PZ ☎01293/774535. Provides information and lists of tour operators and should be able to help you get in touch with someone.

National Rehabilitation Board 25 Clyde Rd, Ballsbridge, Dublin 4 ☎01/668 4181.

Tripscope, Alexandra House, Albany Road, Brentford, Middlesex TW8 0NE ☎08457/585 641, ⒺLtripscope@cableinet.co.uk, ⓌLwww.justmobility .co.uk/tripscope. This registered charity provides a national telephone information service offering free advice on UK and international transport for those with a mobility problem.

US and Canada

Jewish Rehabilitation Hospital 3205 Place Alton Goldbloom, Chomedy Laval, Quebec, H7V 1RT ☎450/688-9550 ext.226. Their medical library provides guidebooks and travel information on India and various other countries for travellers with disabilities.

Society for the Advancement of Travel for the Handicapped (SATH) 347 Fifth Ave, Suite 610, New York, NY 10016 ☎212/447-7284, ⓦ www.sittravel.com.
Travel Information Service Moss Rehab Hospital, 1200 West Tabor Rd, Philadelphia PA 19141 ☎215/456-9600
Twin Peaks Press Box 129, Vancouver, WA 98666 ☎ 360/694-2462 or 1-800/637-2256
Publisher of *Directory of Travel Agencies for the Disabled*, *Travel for the Disabled*, *Directory of Accessible Van Rentals* and *Wheelchair Vagabond*, which is loaded with personal tips.

Australia and New Zealand

ACROD PO Box 60, Curtin, ACT 2605 ☎02/6682 4333.
Barrier Free Travel 36 Wheatley St, North Bellingen, NSW 2454 ☎02/6655 1733.
Disabled Persons Assembly 173 Victoria St, Wellington ☎04/801 9100.

India

India Rehabilitation Co-ordination – India A–2 Rasadhara Co-operation Housing Society, 385 SVP Rd, Mumbai 400004.

Travelling with children

Travelling with kids can be both challenging and rewarding. Indians are very tolerant of children so you can take them almost anywhere without restriction, and they always help break the ice with strangers.

The main problem with children, especially small children, is their extra vulnerability. Even more than their parents, they need protection from the sun, unsafe drinking water, heat and unfamiliar food. All that chilli in particular may be a problem, even with older kids, if they're not used to it. Remember too, that diarrhoea, perhaps just a nuisance to you, could be dangerous for a child: rehydration salts (see p.34) are vital if your child goes down with it. Make sure too, if possible, that your child is aware of the dangers of rabies; keep children away from animals, and consider a rabies jab.

For babies, nappies (diapers) and places to change them can be a problem. For a short visit, you could bring disposable ones with you; for longer journeys, consider going over to washables. A changing mat is another necessity. And if your baby is on powdered milk, it might be an idea to bring some of that: you can certainly get it in India, but it may not taste the same. Dried baby food too could be worth taking – any café or chai-wallah should be able to supply you with boiled water.

For touring, hiking or walking, child-carrier backpacks are ideal. If the child is small enough, a fold-up buggy is also well worth packing, even if you no longer use a buggy at home, as kids tire so easily in the heat. If you want to cut down on long journeys by flying, remember that children under 2 travel for ten percent of the adult fare, and under-12s for half price.

Voluntary organizations

While in India, you may consider doing some voluntary charitable work. Several charities welcome volunteers on a medium-term commitment, say over two months.

If you do want to spend your time working for an **NGO (Non-Government (voluntary) Organization)**, you should make arrangements before you arrive by contacting the body in question. If you are working within the time limit of an ordinary tourist visa and are not working anywhere sensitive that may require a special permit, you shouldn't need to apply for a special visa. Missionaries, however, do require a special visa (consult the Indian consulate).

Voluntary work resources

The following organizations provide useful resources:

Charities Aid Foundation (CAF), Kings Hill, West Malling, Kent ME19 4TA, UK ☏ 01732/520 000, ⓦ http://www.cafonline.org/cafindia/i_search .cfm. CAF provides useful information and contacts for numerous NGOs and aid agencies working in India; their online database is very useful.

Indev, The British Council, 17 Kasturba Gandhi Marg, New Delhi 110 001 ☏ 011/371 1401, ⓦ www.indev.org. Indev, an initiative of the British Council, provides useful resources through discussions and a mammoth databank, accessed through their website, with over 1000 Indian NGOs.

Peace Corps of America ☏ 1-800/424 8580, ⓦ www.peacecorps.gov. The US-government sponsored aid and voluntary organization, with projects all over the world.

Voluntary Service Overseas (VSO), 317 Putney Bridge Road, London SW15 2PN, UK ☏ 020/8780 2266 & 878 7200, ⓦ www.vso.org.uk. A British government-funded organization that places volunteers on various projects around the world and in India.

Voluntary Service Overseas (VSO) ⓦ www.vsocan.com. Canada 806-151 Slater Street, Ottawa ON K1P 5H3 Canada (☏ 1-888-VSO-2911 (1-888-876-2911). Canadian-based organization affiliated to the British VSO.

Charities

Here are just some of the charities that accept voluntary workers:

Denjong Padma Choeling Academy, c/o Sonam Yongda, Pemayengtse Gompa, West Sikkim 737 113 ☏ 03595/50760 & 50141 The academy, with around 200 orphans and destitute children, relies on donations and welcomes voluntary teachers. Sikkim is a restricted area, so you will have to make arrangements with the academy to get a special permit.

The Farm Project, International Society for Ecology and Culture (ISEC), Apple Barn, Week, Totnes, Devon TQ9 6JP, UK ☏ 01803/868650; ISEC/Ladakh Project, PO Box 9475, Berkely, CA 94709, USA ☏ 1-510-527-3873; ⓦ www.ecovillage.org/india/ladakh. The Farm Project is part of the Ladakhi Women's Alliance and set up by ISEC to help promote the rehabilitation of traditional Ladakhi agriculture. The project uses volunteers on two- to three-month agricultural projects; experience helps but is not a prerequisite.

The Missionaries of Charity, International Committee of Co-Workers, 41 Villiers Rd, Southall Middlesex UB1 3BS, UK ☏ 020/8574 1892; or the Mother House, 54A AJC Bose (Lower Circular) Rd, Calcutta. Mother Teresa's Missionaries of Charity has numerous charitable institutions throughout India, some of which use casual volunteers. Contact the International Committee of Co-Workers to find out more.

SECMOL (Students' Educational and Cultural Movement of Ladakh), Leh, Ladakh ☏ 01982/52421. SECMOL was set up to protect Ladakh's culture against the detrimental effects of modernization and strives to increase awareness of developmental issues amongst the young. Qualified English teachers are welcome, especially during their summer schools.

SOS Children's Villages of India, A-7 Nizamuddin (West), New Delhi 110 013 ☏ 0111/464 7835 & 464 9734, ⓦ www.soscvindia.org. SOS has 32 villages and numerous allied projects in different parts of India, including Karnataka and Rajasthan, giving shelter to distressed children by providing a healthy

environment and education including vocational training. Volunteers are welcomed at some of their centres – contact them first.

Directory

CIGARETTES Indian cigarettes, such as Wills, Gold Flake, Four Square and Charms, are OK once you get used to them, and hardly break the bank (Rs10–30 per pack), but if you find them too rough, stock up on imported brands such as Marlboro and Benson and Hedges, or some rolling tobacco, available in the bigger towns and cities. One of the great smells of India is the *bidi*, the cheapest smoke, made of a single low-grade tobacco leaf. If you smoke roll-ups, stock up on good papers as Indian Capstan cigarette papers are thick and don't stick very well and Rizlas, where available, are pretty costly.

DUTY FREE ALLOWANCE Anyone over 17 can bring in one US quart (0.95 litre – but nobody's going to quibble about the other 5ml) of spirits, or a bottle of wine and 250ml spirits; plus 200 cigarettes, or 50 cigars, or 250g tobacco. You may be required to register anything valuable on a tourist baggage re-export form to make sure you can take it home with you, and to fill in a currency declaration form if carrying more than $10,000 or the equivalent. There is a market for duty free spirits in big cities: small retailers are the best people to approach.

ELECTRICITY Generally 220V 50Hz AC, though direct current supplies also exist, so check before plugging in. Most sockets are triple round-pin (accepting European-size double round-pin plugs). British, Irish and Australasian plugs will need an adaptor, preferably universal; American and Canadian appliances will need a transformer too, unless multi-voltage. Power cuts and voltage variations are very common; voltage stabilizers should be used to run sensitive appliances such as laptops.

INITIALS AND ACRONYMS Widely used in Indian English. Thus, the former Prime Minister, Vishwana Pratap Singh, was always "VP", and many middle-class Indian men bear similar monikers. The United Provinces, renamed Uttar Pradesh after independence, have always been UP. More recently, and less universally, Himachal Pradesh is HP, Madhya Pradesh MP, and Andhra Pradesh (not

Arunchal Pradesh) AP. State and national organizations such as ITDC, RTDC and so on are always known by their acronyms. MG Road means Mahatma Gandhi Road, CST Terminus in Mumbai is Chatrapathi Shivaji Terminus, and the only reason Calcutta has come to accept the new name for Dalhousie Square is because they can call it BBD Bagh (that's Benoy Badal Dinesh).

LAUNDRY In India, no one goes to the laundry: if they don't do their own, they send it out to a dhobi-wallah. Wherever you are staying, there will either be an in-house dhobi-wallah, or one very close by to call on. The dhobi-wallah will take your dirty washing to a *dhobi ghat*, a public clothes-washing area (the bank of a river for example), where it is shown some old-fashioned discipline: separated, soaped and given a damn good thrashing to beat the dirt out of it. Then it is hung out to dry in the sun and, once dried, taken to the ironing sheds where every garment is endowed with razor-sharp creases and then matched to its rightful owner by hidden cryptic markings. Your clothes will come back from the dhobi-wallah absolutely spotless, though this kind of violent treatment does take it out of them: buttons get lost and eventually the cloth starts to fray. For more on dhobi-wallahs, see the box on p.767 in the Mumbai chapter; if you'd rather not entrust your Savile Row made-to-measure to their tender mercies, there are dry-cleaners in large towns.

NAME CHANGES There is a growing politically motivated trend to rename some of the major Indian cities and towns to eradicate anglicized spellings and names. In the 1990s, Bombay became Mumbai, Madras became Chennai, Poona became Pune, Shimla became Simla and Banaras became Varanasi. In the latest major name change, which came into effect in early 2001, Calcutta became Kolkata. However, the new official name isn't yet widely in use, so we've stuck with Calcutta throughout the guide.

NUMBERS A hundred thousand is a *lakh* (written 1,00,000); ten million is a *crore* (1,00,00,000). Millions, billions and the like are not in common use.

OPENING HOURS Standard shop opening hours in India are Mon–Sat 9.30am–6pm. Most big stores, at any rate, keep those hours, while smaller shops vary from town to town, religion to religion, and one to another, but usually keep longer hours. Government tourist offices are open Mon–Fri 9.30am–5pm, Sat 9.30am–1pm, closed on the third Sat of the month, and occasionally also the second Sat of the month; state-run tourist offices are likely to be open Mon–Fri 10am–5pm.

PHOTOGRAPHY Beware of pointing your camera at anything that might be considered "strategic", including airports and anything military, but even at bridges, railway stations and main roads. Remember too that some people prefer not to be photographed, so it is wise to ask before you take a snapshot of them. More likely, you'll get people, especially kids volunteering to pose. Camera film, sold at average Western prices, is widely available in India (but check the date on the box, and note that false boxes containing outdated film are often sold – Konica have started painting holograms on their boxes to prevent this). It's fairly easy to get films developed, though they don't always come out as well as they might at home; Konica and Kodak film laboratories are usually of a good standard. If you're after slide film, slow film or fast film, buy it in the big cities, and don't expect to find specialist brands such as Velvia; it is rare to find a dealer who keeps film refrigerated. Also, remember to guard your equipment from dust – reliable repair is extremely hard to come by in India.

TIME India is all in one time zone: GMT+5hr 30min. This makes it 5hr 30min ahead of London, 10hr 30min ahead of New York, 13hr 30min ahead of LA, 4hr 30min behind Sydney and 6hr 30min behind NZ; however, summer time in those places will vary the difference by an hour. Indian time is referred to as IST (Indian Standard Time, which cynics refer to as "Indian stretchable time").

TOILETS A visit to the loo is not one of India's more pleasant experiences: toilets can be filthy and stink. They are also major potential breeding grounds for disease. And then there is the squatting position to get used to; the traditional Asian toilet has a hole in the ground and two small platforms for the feet, instead of a seat. Paper, if used, often goes in a bucket next to the loo rather than down it. Indians use instead a jug of water and their left hand, a method you may also come to prefer, but if you do use paper, keep some handy – it isn't usually supplied, and it might be an idea to stock up before going too far off the beaten track as it is not available everywhere. Travelling is especially difficult for women as facilities are limited or nonexistent, especially when travelling by road. However, toilets in the a/c carriages of trains are usually kept clean as those in mid-range and a/c restaurants. In the touristy areas, most hotels offer Western-style loos, even in budget lodges. The latest development is tourist toilets at every major historical site. They cost Rs2 and you get water, mirrors, toilet paper and a clean sit-down loo.

Things to take

Most things are easy to find in India and cheaper than at home, but here is a list of useful items worth bringing with you bearing in mind that your bags should not get too heavy:

- ❏ A padlock and chain (to lock rooms in budget hotels, and attach your bag to train fittings)
- ❏ A universal electric plug adaptor and a universal sink plug (few sinks or bathtubs have them)
- ❏ A mosquito net
- ❏ A sheet sleeping bag (made by sewing up a sheet – so you don't have to worry about the state of the ones in your hotel room)
- ❏ A pillowcase
- ❏ A small flashlight and spare bulbs
- ❏ Earplugs (for street noise in hotel rooms and music on buses)
- ❏ High-factor sunblock (difficult to find in India)
- ❏ A pocket alarm clock
- ❏ An inflatable neck-rest, to help you sleep on long journeys
- ❏ A multipurpose penknife
- ❏ A needle and some thread (but dental floss is better than cotton for holding baggage together)
- ❏ Plastic bags (to sort your baggage, make it easier to pack and unpack, and keep out damp and dust)
- ❏ A small umbrella (available in Indian cities)
- ❏ Tampons
- ❏ Condoms
- ❏ Multi-vitamin and mineral tablets

guide

guide

1 Delhi 96–156

2 Rajasthan 158–279

3 Uttar Pradesh 280–363

4 Uttaranchal 364–419

5 Madhya Pradesh 420–513

6 Himachal Pradesh 514–589

7 Ladakh 590–641

8 Haryana and Punjab 643–665

9 Gujarat 666–737

10 Mumbai 738–786

11 Maharashtra 788–851

12 Goa 852–916

13 Calcutta and West Bengal 918–991

14 Bihar and Jharkhand 992–1013

15 Sikkim 1014–1039

⑯ The northeastern states 1040–1087

⑰ Orissa 1088–1135

⑱ Andhra Pradesh 1136–1159

⑲ The Andaman Islands 1160–1185

⑳ Tamil Nadu 1186–1291

㉑ Kerala 1292–1379

㉒ Karnataka 1380–1468

CHAPTER 1 # Highlights

✳ **Rajpath** The centrepiece of Lutyen's imperial New Delhi, epitomizing the spirit of the British Raj. See p.115

✳ **National Museum** India's finest museum, with exhibits from over 5000 years of Indian culture. See p.120

✳ **Red Fort** Delhi's most famous monument is an imposing sandstone fort, a ghostly vestige of Moghul splendour. See p.123

✳ **Jami Masjid** Shah Jahan's great mosque, with huge minarets offering birds' eye views over the old city. See p.126

✳ **Bazaars of Old Delhi** A warren of chaotic Moghul-era lanes, each one dedicated to a different trade. See pp.128–129

✳ **Hazrat Nizamuddin** A Sufi shrine in a deeply traditional Muslim quarter, where hypnotic *qawwali* music is performed each Friday. See p.132

✳ **Humayun's Tomb** An elegant red-brick forerunner of the Taj Mahal, whose lovely gardens are an escape from the heat. See p.133

✳ **Qutb Minar** The ruins of this twelfth-century city, Delhi's first incarnation, are dominated by the Qutb Minar Victory Tower. See p.136

Delhi

Delhi is the symbol of old India and new . . . even the stones here whisper to our ears of the ages of long ago and the air we breathe is full of the dust and fragrances of the past, as also of the fresh and piercing winds of the present.

Jawaharlal Nehru

On first impressions, **DELHI**, with its jam-packed streets, tower blocks and temples, forts, mosques and colonial mansions, can be disorienting and fascinating. It certainly takes a while to find your feet, as you attempt to weave a path through buses, trucks, nippy modern cars, mopeds, rickshaws, cows, bullock carts, hand-pulled trolleys and the occasional elephant being ridden along with the flow of traffic. You'll find unlikely juxtapositions are everywhere you look: suit-and-tie businessmen rub shoulders with traditionally dressed orthodox Hindus and Muslims; groups of young Delhi-ites wearing Levis pile into burger-joints, bars and discos; turbaned snake charmers tease hypnotizing moans out of curved pipes; pundits pontificate while *sadhus* smoke their *chillums*; and ragged beggars clutching dusty children plead for a little help towards a meal.

The daunting scale of Delhi becomes more manageable as you start to appreciate that geographically as well as historically it consists of several distinct cities – if anything, more than the **Seven Cities** of tradition. The hub of the metropolis is **Central New Delhi**, an orderly plan of wide roads lined with sturdy colonial buildings which was established soon after the imperial capital of **British India** moved here in 1911. Many of the city's hotels are here, concentrated amid the columned facades of **Connaught Place**, and just north of the parliamentary buildings, the architectural jewels in the Imperial crown. **Old Delhi**, Shah Jahan's seventeenth-century capital (**Shahjahanabad**), lies 2km or so further north. This is Delhi at its most quintessentially Indian, where the traditional lifestyle of its predominantly Muslim population has changed little over two hundred years. A visit to Old Delhi's mighty **Red Fort** and **Jami Masjid**, India's largest mosque, is a must, and should be combined with a stroll through the old city's **bazaars**, a warren of clustered houses, buzzing with commotion, and infused with aromatic smells drifting from open-fronted restaurants, spice shops and temples.

The other five of Delhi's ex-capitals, further south, are today all but deserted, standing as impressive reminders of long-vanished dynasties. Among them you'll find the towering free-standing column erected by Qutb-ud-din Aibak, the **Qutb Minar** (twelfth century), that marks the first capital, **Dhillika**, and that signalled the development of the city that visitors see today. Walls and dilapidated pillars survive from the fourteenth-century city of **Tughluqabad**,

DELHI ❶

Anand Vihar ISBT ▲

Yamuna River

Vijay Ghat

Shanti Vana

Raj Ghat

Firoz Shah Kotla & Ashoka Pillar

Foreigners Registration Office

Pragati Maidan

Humayun's Tomb

Sunder Nagar

Zoo

Red Fort

National Gallery of Modern Art

Crafts Museum

Delhi Gate

Bengali Market

Museum of Natural History

India Gate

Golf Club

Old Delhi GPO

Jami Masjid

Interstate Bus Station

Kashmiri Gate

National Museum

Gurudwara

Sangeet Natak Akademi

Nepalese Embassy

Rabindra Bhavan

Khan Market

Old Delhi Railway Station

Ajmeri Gate

New Delhi Railway Station

Jantar Mantar

National Museum

Fatehpuri Mosque

Bangla Sahib

Connaught Place

Lodi Gardens

Indira Gandhi Memorial

PAHARGANJ

Main Bazaar

GPO Poste Restante

Parliament

Rashtrapati Bhavan

Secretariat

Nehru Museum

Lakshmi Narayan Mandir

Delhi Sarai Rohilla Station

Buddha Jayanti Park

Mahavir Jayanti Park

Santushti

Santa

GRAND TRUNK RD

MAHATMA GANDHI RD

SHAMNATH MARG

RANI JHANSI RD

GURU GOBIND SINGH MARG

SADHU VASWANI MARG

DESHBANDHUGUPTA RD

QUTUB RD

CHANDNI CHOWK

MANDIR MARG

FAIZ RD

RANI JHANSI RD

ROHTAK RD

SHANKAR RD

DR VITHAL BHAI PATEL RD

NAJAFGARH RD

UPPER RIDGE RD

TODAPUR RD

PANCHKUIN RD

ASHOKA RD

JANPATH

SANSAD MARG

RAFI MARG

RAJPATH

AKBAR RD

KASTURBA GANDHI MARG

TILAK MARG

MATHURA RD

VIKAS MARG

MAHATMA GANDHI RD

MAULANA AZAD RD

AURANGZEB RD

SHAHJAHAN RD

SHER SHAH RD

❶ & Majnu Ka Tilla ▲

ACCOMMODATION

Ambassador	7
Ashok Country Resort	22
Claridges	10
Hyatt Regency	18
ITDC Ashok	13
ITDC Kanishka	4
ITDC Lodi	16
ITDC Samrat	13
La Sagrita	11
Le Meridien	5
Maharani Guest House	8
Master Paying Guest House	3
Maurya Sheraton & Towers	14
New Krishna Guest House	19
Oberoi	12
Oberoi Maidens	2
Park Royal	17
Qutab	23
Raddison	21
Taj Mahal	6
Taj Palace	15
Tarra Inn	20
Wongdhen House	1
Youth Hostel	9

THE SEVEN CITIES OF DELHI

☆ Qila Rai Pithora
☆☆ Siri
☆☆☆ Tughluqabad
☆☆☆☆ Jahanpanah
☆☆☆☆☆ Firozabad
☆☆☆☆☆☆ Shergarh
☆☆☆☆☆☆☆ Shahjahanabad

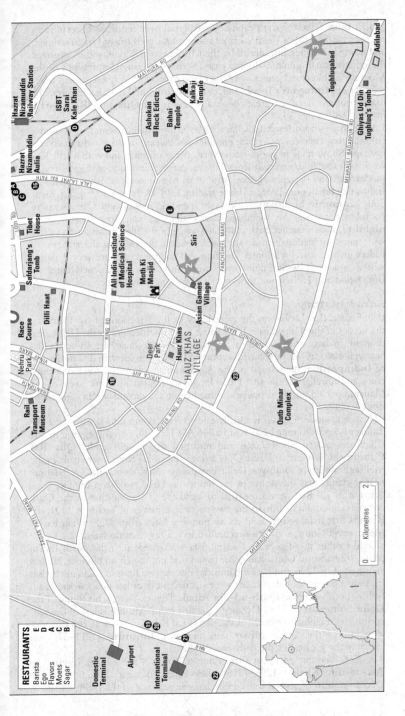

RESTAURANTS
Barista E
Ego D
Flavors A
Moets C
Sagar B

Tughluqabad

Adilabad

MATHURA RD

Hazrat
Nizamuddin
Railway Station

ISBT
Sarai
Kale Khan

Hazrat
Nizamuddin
Aulia

Ashokan
Rock Edicts

Bahai
Temple

Kalkaji
Temple

Ghiyas Ud Din
Tughluq's Tomb

MEHRAULI BADARPUR RD

LALA LAJPAT RAI PATH

Tibet
House

Safdarjang's
Tomb

Siri

PANCHSHEEL MARG

All India Institute
of Medical Science
Hospital

Moth Ki
Masjid

Asian Games
Village

LODI RD

Dilli Haat

Race
Course

Nehru
Park

VINAY MARG

RING RD

SHANTIPATH

Deer
Park

Hauz Khas

HAUZ KHAS
VILLAGE

SRI AUROBINDO MARG

AFRICA AVE

OUTER RING RD

Rail
Transport
Museum

SANT PATEL MARG

Qutb Minar
Complex

MEHRAULI RD

Domestic
Terminal

Airport

International
Terminal

NH-8

0   1   2

Kilometres

99

and **Purana Qila**, the sixth capital. Interspersed between these historic ruins are the grand tombs of Delhi's former rulers, plus a plethora of Hindu temples, and domed mosques, introduced by the Muslims, which dramatically changed the conventional mould of Indian cities. Perhaps the finest expressions of the Moghuls' architectural genius were the grand *charbagh* (quartered garden) mausoleums of **Humayun's Tomb**, and, most famously, the Taj Mahal in Agra. The major monument of the great Moghul period is **Lal Qila**, the **"Red Fort"**, in Old Delhi.

As befits a national capital, Delhi, with its many **museums** and art treasures, cultural performances and crafts, provides a showcase of the country's diverse heritage. Shops trade in goods from every corner of India, and with a little legwork you can find anything from Tibetan carpets, antiques, and jewellery to modern art and designer clothes. After years of economic isolation caused by India's draconian post-Independence trading laws, Delhi is enjoying a tremendous **economic boom**. With plenty of spending money and a new sense of confidence among the wealthier classes, the city can now boast a great **nightlife**, with designer bars, chic cafés and good clubs. Its auditoria host a wide range of national music and dance events, drawing on the richness of India's great classical traditions. The film and theatre scenes are very dynamic with a choice of plays in English every week, and smart new cinemas that show Bollywood and Hollywood movies to a film-hungry audience.

Some history

Belief has it that Delhi was the capital city of the Kingdom of the Pandavas, the heroes of the *Mahabharata*. The earliest known settlement in the Delhi area, thought to have stood close to the River Yamuna (near the Purana Qila) between 1000 BC and the fourth century AD, has been identified with the city of **Indraprastha**, mentioned in the *Mahabharata*. Unearthed terracotta pots, coins and jewellery show that Delhi lay on an important trunk route of the Mauryan period, and Ptolemy, who came here in the second century AD, mentions "Dilli".

However, modern Delhi is usually said to have come into being when the Tomara Rajputs founded **Lal Kot** in 736 AD. In 1180, a rival Rajput clan, the Chauhans, ousted the Tomaras and renamed the walled citadel **Qila Rai Pithora**, the first city of Delhi. Only a few walls of Lal Kot now remain, in the Mehrauli suburb of southwest Delhi, but a stone inscription at the Qutb Minar nearby claims that the stones of the numerous Hindu and Jain temples constructed in Lal Kot were later used to build the Great Mosque in the Qutb complex. Soon afterwards, in the two successive battles of Tarain in 1191, the Rajputs first managed to hold off an invading force from Afghanistan led by Muhammad Ghuri, and then succumbed to it a few months later.

Unlike other invaders from Central Asia who swept into the north Indian plains, Muhammad Ghuri had come to stay and not merely to plunder. He was assassinated in 1206 and his kingdom did not survive long in Afghanistan, but his Indian provinces, palaces and forts remained more or less intact in the hands of his Turkish general, **Qutb-ud-din Aibak**. This ex-slave, who founded the **Delhi Sultanate** (or Slave Dynasty – the first major Muslim rulers of the subcontinent), established himself at the site of Lal Kot, and commenced the construction of the **Qutb Minar**. His successor, **Iltutmish** (1211–27), was arguably the greatest of the early Delhi sultans.

In 1290, another group of Turks came to power – the Khaljis. Inspired by **Ala-ud-din Khalji** (1296–1316), they extended their dominion to the Deccan plateau of central India. His reign, the pinnacle of the Delhi Sultanate, was marked by agrarian reforms, and the establishment in 1303 of **Siri**, the second city of Delhi, built in characteristically ornate marble and red sandstone. Near present-day Hauz Khas, it grew into a flourishing commercial centre. Ala-ud-din died a disappointed man, however, as cracks appeared in his dream of empire; the ensuing period of confusion only ended when **Ghiyas-ud-din Tughluq** proclaimed himself Sultan in 1320.

Ghiyas-ud-din in turn built a city fortress, at **Tughluqabad**, 8km east of Qutb, but Delhi's third city was occupied for just five years from 1321, when the capital was shifted 1100km south to Daulatabad in Maharashtra at great human cost. Apart from the ramparts encompassing the crumbling ruins, and the odd building and tomb, little now remains of this third settlement. Water scarcity drove the Tughluqs back to Delhi in 1327, and as a recompense for the mistake, a new city, **Jahanpanah**, was built between Lal Kot and Siri by the eccentric Muhammad bin Tughluq to protect the vulnerable open plain. The energies of the next sultan, Firuz Shah, were taken up with suppressing rebellion, as the Sultanate began to disintegrate, but his reputation as an iconoclast is belied by his keen interest in Indian culture and history. Fascinated by the Ashokan pillars of Meerut and Topra, he had them moved to the new capital, the fifth city of **Firozabad**, built beside the river in 1354.

The Tughluq line came to an end in 1398, when Timur (Tamerlane), a Central Asian Turk, sacked Delhi. His successors, the **Sayyids** (1414–44), were ousted by **Buhlul Lodi** who established a dynasty that left behind the fine tombs and mosques still to be seen in the beautiful Lodi Gardens. As the Lodi sultans became more absolute, they made many enemies among the nobles, especially the governors of Punjab and Sind, who invited Babur (a descendant of Genghis Khan) and Timur, who was seeking his fortune in Afghanistan, to come to their aid. The Lodi dynasty ended when Sultan Ibrahim Lodi died in battle, fighting the brilliant and enigmatic Babur on the plain of Panipat just north of Delhi in 1526. Babur's victory marked the dawn of the Moghul (a derivative of Mongol) dynasty, whose lengthy sojourn in power led to the eventual realization of the dream of an Indian empire that had so eluded the earlier Delhi Sultans. Babur's reign was brief, and he moved his capital to Agra not long after taking Delhi; his *Babarnama*, a chronicle of the times, makes fascinating reading.

Babur was succeeded in 1530 by his son, **Humayun**, a scholar and astronomer who moved to Delhi in 1534. All the signs indicated that Humayun's reign would be prosperous, but in 1540, he was driven to Persia for fifteen years by the Afghan King **Sher Shah** of Ser, who quickly built the fort, **Din-Panah**, or Asylum of Faith, which still stands on the banks of the Yamuna in the southwest of modern Delhi and is known as **Purana Qila**. Sher Shah was surrounded by bickering power-thirsty relatives, all of whom were overcome when Humayun returned from Kabul to retake Delhi in 1555. When Humayun died in a fall in 1556, his wife Banu Begum built a sandstone garden tomb for him in Nizamuddin, in the style that was to set the pattern for the development of Moghul mausoleum architecture. His son **Akbar** (who could not read or write) took over as emperor, and the capital was moved once more to Agra.

Delhi once again became capital under Prince Khurrum, Akbar's grandson, in 1628, who assumed the title **Shah Jahan**, "Ruler of the Universe", and began a fruitful and extravagant reign that oversaw the construction of some of the finest Moghul monuments, including the Taj Mahal in Agra. The new walled capital of **Shahjahanabad**, the seventh city, which is now Old Delhi, incorporated the mighty **Red Fort** with its opulent courts and the huge **Jami**

Although sixty percent of Delhi-ites are born elsewhere, the city's **population** has grown over forty percent in the last decade and now stands at around fourteen million. Rapid growth has seen Delhi spilling into the surrounding states, creating satellite developments such as Gurgaon to the south. The city has been attracting its fare share of **industrial development** in the last two decades, with an influx of technocrats, specialists and fortune seekers to match. In a heady atmosphere of optimism, around 9000 new industrial units sprang up every year during the 1990s. Despite this new-found affluence, a staggering third of the city's population lives in the notorious *jhuggies* – slums often seen clinging to the edge of new developments. With a daily average of around 200 major incidents of **crime**, including mindless cases of murder accompanying simple robberies, Delhi has gained the dubious reputation of being the crime capital of the country. The poor aren't the only perpetrators of crime – the city's nouveau riche young, burdened with more money than sense, have been responsible for some of the most notorious recent cases.

The authorities are trying, at last, to check the terrible **pollution** that smothers the city, especially in winter when vehicle fumes mix with the fires of the *jhuggies* to create a thick blanket of smog. Many small-scale industrial units are being forced out of the city, and, in 1998, cars over ten years old were banned. Further draconian measures were introduced in 2001, when all diesel-powered buses, taxis and autos were outlawed in favour of **natural gas-powered vehicles**. Still, with over 4,000,000 cars battling through the city's streets (more than Mumbai, Chennai and Calcutta put together), the new ecological awareness may be too little too late. While some checks are being made to counter air pollution, an appalling seventy percent of the effluents draining into the River Yamuna still remain untreated. Delhi's growth pangs are far from over.

Masjid or Friday Mosque, fringed by bazaars. Shah Jahan was deposed (and imprisoned in Agra) by his ruthless son, Aurangzeb, who ruled from Delhi until 1681, when he transferred the capital to the Deccan plateau until his death in 1707.

For the next sixty years, Delhi's government was controlled by courtiers, and the city fell victim to successive invasions. In 1739, Nadir Shah, the emperor of Persia, swept across north India and overcame Muhammad Shah in the Red Fort, taking away precious booty and wiping out much of the local population. The relatively plain tomb of Safdarjung (near the Lodi Gardens), built in 1754 for Emperor Mirza Khan in the same style as the Taj, yet lacking the marble and rich decoration, demonstrates the decline of Moghul power. Soon after, in 1760, the Hindu Marathas and Jats, in the wake of fading Moghul supremacy, combined forces against the rulers and besieged and looted the Red Fort, but did not take power.

The Moghul rulers were reduced to puppet kings, and the **British**, who had already gained footholds in Madras and Bengal under the guise of the East India Company, moved to Delhi in 1803 during the reign of the Moghul emperor, **Bahadur Shah**. They swiftly took control, leaving Bahadur Shah with his palace and his pension, but no power. British forces fended off a number of Maratha attacks in the next decade, and faced determined opposition during 1857 when the Indian Mutiny (or "First War of Independence") broke out. Bahadur Shah was proclaimed Hindustani emperor in the Red Fort, and it took much bloodshed before the British regained the city.

The British retained a hold on Delhi while administering affairs of state from their capital in Calcutta. When King George V came to India from England to be crowned as emperor in 1911, it was decided to make Delhi India's new **cap-**

ital. Fervent construction of sprawling bungalows, parliamentary buildings and public offices followed, and in 1931 Delhi was officially inaugurated as the capital of Britain's largest colonial possession.

With India's declaration of **Independence** in 1947, the British, represented in Delhi by the viceroy, Lord Mountbatten, lost all authority, and the democratically elected Congress government came to power with **Nehru** at its head. Independence saw a mass migration of Muslims from Delhi to newly created Pakistan, taking with them a cultural ambience that the subsequent influx of Punjabis have failed to replace. Today, Delhi is one of the fastest growing cities in the world, with spiralling population growth and pollution to match.

Arrival and information

Delhi is India's main point of arrival for overseas visitors, and has two **airports**, one domestic and one international. State **buses** from all over the country pull into the Inter-state Bus Terminal in Old Delhi, while private buses stop in the more central location close to New Delhi railway station. **Trains** arrive at the railheads in Old or New Delhi, both well connected to Connaught Place, the commercial centre of the city, by rickshaw and taxi.

For a summary of the kinds of **accommodation** available in different areas of the city, which may well determine where you head first, see p.107. In short, **Connaught Place**, the heart of New Delhi, packed with banks, restaurants and shops, caters for all pockets, while there are budget options in **Paharganj**, close to New Delhi railway station, and **Old Delhi**.

By air

International flights land at **Indira Gandhi International Airport** (℡011/569 6021 or 565 2011), also known as Terminal 2, 23km southwest of the centre (formerly Palam airport). The State Bank of India and Thomas Cook in the airport offer 24hr moneychanging facilities; be sure to get some small change for taxis and rickshaws. If you need to book accommodation, 24hr desks, including ITDC in the departure hall and Delhi Tourism (DTTDC), have a list of approved hotels and will secure reservations by phone. Beware of bogus booking counters: there have been several cases of trickery and overcharging. Not all budget hotels accept telephone bookings; for these you'll have to make your own way into town. ITDC and DTTDC also operate desks at the **domestic airport** (℡011/566 5181), 8km away to the north on the opposite side of the shared runway to IGI Airport; there are two terminals, 1A & 1B. **Retiring rooms** at both airports are convenient if you need to make an early connection but are issued on a first-come, first-served basis (Rs660). A free AAI **shuttle** bus (20min) runs between the two airports every hour and there's a shuttle every twenty minutes between the two domestic terminals.

From the international airport, the least expensive and least convenient way to get into Delhi is by **bus**. Tickets for the ex-servicemen's shuttle (EATS) are issued in the departure hall, while State Transport buses wait outside; both take roughly thirty minutes to reach their terminal point at F Block in Connaught Place in the city centre. Expect to pay Rs50 from either airport, plus an additional Rs5 for luggage. All buses go via the domestic terminal, from where it's a twenty-minute ride into the city (18 daily), and stop at Janpath in New Delhi. The driver may be able to drop you close to your chosen hotel.

Taxis are faster and more comfortable, and should certainly be taken if you arrive late at night, to save you from having to search for your hotel in the dark. Book at the official prepaid kiosk in the restricted area outside the arrival hall. Fixed rates (Rs300) apply, with a 25 percent surcharge between 11pm and 5am. Beware of touts also offering prepaid taxis and avoid the non-registered taxis near the bus rank; these often ask extortionate prices and may even claim that your hotel is full, closed, or even burnt down. Ignore such assertions and remember it's best to phone ahead to your accommodation. The **rickshaws** that wait in line at the departure gate are less expensive than taxis (Rs100–150), but constitute the most precarious and least reliable form of transport from the airport, especially at night. Many tourists have complained of being taken to a hotel other than the one requested, and being hassled for more money on arrival. It makes sense to settle in for a while before you try using one.

By train

Delhi has two major **railway stations**. **New Delhi Station** is east of Paharganj (Main Bazaar), and within walking distance of many of the area's budget hotels, though tourists burdened with luggage often prefer to hail a cycle rickshaw to reach their hotel, which shouldn't cost more than Rs20 – negotiate the fare in advance. If you're heading for hotels south of the station, however, bear in mind that cycle rickshaws cannot enter Connaught Place. The station has two exits, with the Paharganj exit the more popular, useful for Connaught Place and most points south, and the Ajmeri Gate exit, more convenient for Old Delhi. You can take an auto-rickshaw (insist the meter is turned on or negotiate a price before you jump in). However, the most reliable option is to book a prepaid rickshaw at the booth, close to the main road at the front of the railway station on the Paharganj side. Autos to Connaught Place cost from Rs20, and to Old Delhi from Rs35 though, unfortunately, pressure from touts has meant that the prepaid taxi service rarely operates. Some taxis, especially those parked at the exit opposite Ajmeri Gate, have their meters rigged and you can be assured that the touts who approach you as you exit the station will be bad news. **Delhi Station** in Old Delhi, west of the Red Fort, is connected to the city hotels by taxis (not prepaid) and auto-rickshaws. Both stations have **retiring rooms** (Rs100–250), and are notorious for theft:

Delhi scams

Delhi can prove a headache for the first-time visitor, with several scams to entrap the unwary. Arrival is always the most difficult, but for those arriving at New Delhi railway station a special word of warning is to avoid all touts and the false tourist offices opposite the Paharganj entrance to the New Delhi railway station, which have brought grief to many an unsuspecting traveller. Similarly, steer clear of those along Janpath that claim to be "government authorized" – there is no such authorization and you're likely to end up paying well over the odds for any services. Shoe-shine boys have been known to dump dung onto shoes when their victim is distracted and then charge the earth to clean the shoes for them. For shopaholics, beware that several shops pretend to be official "government" shops and taxi, auto and rental-car drivers get a commission for just leading you in – this will be added to your bill.

don't take your eyes off your luggage for a moment. Lesser stations in the Delhi area include **Hizrat Nizamuddin**, south of the centre on the main line into New Delhi and the point of departure for passenger trains to Agra (except the Shatabdi Express).

By bus

State buses pull in at the Inter-state Bus Terminal (ISBT), north of the railway station in Old Delhi. Auto-rickshaws to New Delhi or Paharganj take about fifteen minutes (around Rs50), cycle rickshaws twice that (around Rs30). **Private buses** from all over India terminate outside New Delhi railway station; some will drop passengers in Connaught Place if they pass that way.

Information

There are reasonably helpful tourist offices at the international and domestic airports, railway stations and bus terminals, and the **Government of India tourist office** at 88 Janpath, just south of Connaught Place (Mon–Fri 9am–6pm, Sat 9am–4.30pm; ☎011/332 0005 or 333 0008), is a good place to pick up information on Delhi's sites, city tours, shopping, cultural events and accommodation. They also provide free maps of the city; you'll find the same ones sold in the streets at negotiable prices. The information counter at the less busy **DTTDC** (Delhi Tourism and Transport Development Corporation) office, Bombay Life Building, Middle Circle (Mon–Fri 9am–6pm, Sat 9am–1pm; ☎011/331 4229) has an extremely useful office, where you can change money, book trains and reserve accommodation.

For details of exhibitions or cultural events in Delhi, pick up a local **magazine** from any bookstore or street stall (and see p.147). The excellent weekly *Delhi Diary* lists useful information on current events, lectures, exhibitions, films and TV listings and has a comprehensive directory and map. Monthly *First City* is far more readable though, with feature articles, a comprehensive city directory, reviews and listings.

Travel tips, train and airline timetables for Delhi and further afield and, more crucially, taxi and auto-rickshaw fare tables, can be found in the monthlies *City Companion*, *Travel Links* and *Delhi City*. *City Scan* also features a range of topical issues, from sports and arts to politics and industry.

City transport

In the absence of the underground metro system promised for 2004, Delhi's **public transport** remains ill-equipped to cope with the city's size and ever-increasing complexity. Roads have to support diverse and conflicting forms of transport and there aren't any motorways to connect the satellite communities that keep cropping up around the metropolis. A mammoth new road-building project to construct 34 new flyovers by 2004 to help ease the horrendous traffic jams has in the meantime caused further misery, especially at rush hour. Buses and a few suburban trains carry most of the burden of public transport, though many visitors prefer to pay more for auto-rickshaws and taxis.

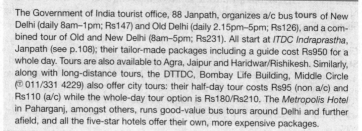

The Government of India tourist office, 88 Janpath, organizes a/c bus **tours** of New Delhi (daily 8am–1pm; Rs147) and Old Delhi (daily 2.15pm–5pm; Rs126), and a combined tour of Old and New Delhi (8am–5pm; Rs231). All start at *ITDC Indraprastha*, Janpath (see p.108); their tailor-made packages including a guide cost Rs950 for a whole day. Tours are also available to Agra, Jaipur and Haridwar/Rishikesh. Similarly, along with long-distance tours, the DTTDC, Bombay Life Building, Middle Circle (☎ 011/331 4229) also offer city tours: their half-day tour costs Rs95 (non a/c) and Rs110 (a/c) while the whole-day tour option is Rs180/Rs210. The *Metropolis Hotel* in Paharganj, amongst others, runs good-value bus tours around Delhi and further afield, and all the five-star hotels offer their own, more expensive packages.

Buses

Despite running more than three hundred different routes, the Delhi Transport Corporation's vast centralized **bus network** can seem totally inadequate. The *Latest Guide to Delhi, Old, and New* (published by Lal Chand and Sons; Rs10) is in English and has the most comprehensive DTC bus route listings available. You can buy it from magazine vendors in Connaught Place or Paharganj. The first digit of each three-digit route number shows the direction of each bus – thus routes starting with "5" head south from the centre towards Mehrauli, and those starting with "4" travel southeast towards Kalkaji through Nizamuddin, while those starting with "1" go north through Old Delhi.

Specific services useful for tourists include #454 between Connaught Place and Nizamuddin, #505 from Ajmer Gate to Mehrauli and the Qutb Minar, #602 and #620 to Chanakyapuri, and #101 and #139 between the Regal Cinema bus stand (beside *Park Hotel*) and the Red Fort. Another handy route is #450 from Paharganj, via Connaught Place and India Gate, to Lodi Road, near Tibet House and Lodi Gardens. **Night buses** start with the digit "0", such as #055 which passes Nizamuddin on its way to Connaught Place. All buses are liable to get hideously overcrowded – **women** travellers will appreciate the row of seats which is reserved exclusively for their use.

Minibuses and private buses, such as the "**Green**" and the slightly more expensive "**White**" lines ply many of the same routes, and are often less congested. A Ring Service runs around the Ring Road, both clockwise (marked with a "+") and anti-clockwise ("–"). **Railway specials** connect outlying stations with the centre; the #42 to Tughluqabad is handy for visitors to the ancient fort. The most useful service however, is provided by the maroon-coloured minibuses of the **Phatphat Seva** that run from Palika Bazaar to Old Delhi. This service replaced the majestic old Harley-Davidson motorcycle taxis (hence "phatphat") which plied this route for years until forced off the streets by Delhi's new antipollution traffic laws, which forbid vehicles over ten years old.

Auto-rickshaws and cycle rickshaws

Auto-rickshaws (or "autos") – scooters converted into three-wheeler taxis – can be extremely useful in Delhi's chaotic traffic, though they catch the worst of the polluting exhaust fumes since their open sides are level with larger vehicles' exhaust pipes. Autos are now, however, finding themselves in the forefront of the recent ecological drive, with most new vehicles being fitted with natural gas-powered engines instead of the old diesel ones. In theory autos should charge what's shown on the meter, but even on the rare occasions when their meters are working, the rates tend to be out of date, and liable to supplements according to a table which drivers are required to carry but sometimes don't. For most journeys, it's simplest just to agree on a price before you set out; by way of example, at the time this book went to press, Paharganj to Connaught Place cost Rs20 maximum, while Red Fort to Connaught Place is more like Rs40. Try to avoid catching the rickshaws that hang around major tourist centres: even crossing the road from a hotel entrance can make for a better price.

Cycle rickshaws are not allowed in Connaught Place and parts of New Delhi, but are handy for short routes in outlying areas and in Paharganj, and nippier than motorized traffic in Old Delhi. Serious bargaining is required to get the going rate, which should be much less than an auto.

Taxis

Black and yellow taxis, which charge around fifty percent more than auto-rickshaws – thus Red Fort to Connaught Place costs in the region of Rs80 – are considered to be the most reliable mode of transport. Drivers belong to local taxi stands, where you can make bookings and fix prices; if you flag a taxi down on the street you're letting yourself in for some hectic haggling. Between 11pm and 5am, there is a surcharge of around 25 percent. A new service, **Dial-a-Cab** (T 1920), offers convenience and luxury with air-conditioned cars and tamper-proof digital meters, but at a price.

Car and cycle rental

For local sightseeing and journeys beyond the city confines, the cheapest and most reliable outlets for chauffeur-driven **cars** are the tourist office, 88 Janpath, and the booths at the southern end of the Tibetan Market on Janpath, most of which are willing to negotiate a price. Expect to pay from Rs500 a day which includes 80km mileage; in the high season the price rises to around Rs800 a day. Private travel agencies throughout Delhi usually charge more. If you want the option of **self-drive**, and don't mind paying extra to brave Delhi's notoriously dangerous roads, try Budget, G3 Arunchal Building, Barakhamba Road (T 011/331 8600), which charges from $50 per day for self-drive and $70 for a chauffeur. Other international names include Europcar Inter Rent (T 011/641 1601) and Hertz (T 011/619 7188). Alternatively, Wheels, 4–5 Kanchenjunga Building, Barakhamba Road (T 011/331 8695), offer slightly lower self-drive rates from around $40 per day.

Cycling in the large avenues of New Delhi takes some getting used to and can be dangerous for those not used to chaotic traffic. **Bicycle rental** is surprisingly difficult to come by; try Mehta Cycles at 5109/10 Main Bazaar, Paharganj, next door but one to the *Khosla Café*.

Accommodation

Delhi has a great range of **accommodation**, from dirt-cheap lodges to extravagant international hotels. Bookings for upmarket hotels can be made at the tourist desks at airports and railway stations, but budget travellers have to do their own searching. If you want to stay in comfort, try booking your ticket through the Travel Corporation of India (TCI; T 011/336 5181), which offers substantial **discounts** on double rooms in select upmarket hotels (see p.151).

Accommodation price codes

All accommodation prices in this book have been categorized using the price codes below. Prices given are for a double room, and all taxes are included. For more details, see p.52.

- **①** up to Rs100
- **②** Rs100–200
- **③** Rs200–300
- **④** Rs300–400
- **⑤** Rs400–600
- **⑥** Rs600–900
- **⑦** Rs900–1500
- **⑧** Rs1500–2500
- **⑨** Rs2500 and upwards

The hotels of **Connaught Place** cover all price ranges, are handy for banks, restaurants and shops, and have good transport connections to all the main sights. North of Connaught Place, the busy market area of **Paharganj** and the adjacent Ram Nagar, close to New Delhi railway station, feature the best of the budget accommodation, and **Old Delhi** has some even cheaper hotels. The main youth hostel is in the **south**, where you'll also find most of Delhi's top **luxury hotels**, complete with bars, discos, swimming pools and health clubs, and charging upwards of $250 a night. If you're leaving on an early flight, you might want to opt for one of the hotels near the international airport.

Connaught Place and Central Delhi

Within the curved colonial lanes of **Connaught Place** you'll find moderately priced hotels of varying standards. Further south, grander hotels on and around **Janpath** and along **Sansad Marg** cater mainly for business travellers and tourist groups. Most of these have plush restaurants and bars and include meals, and some have pools – all add heavy taxes to their bills, which we have included in our price guide, and many require non-Indian residents to pay in foreign currency, although Visa cards and travellers' cheques will also be accepted. However, the inexpensive lodges, huddled around the north end of Janpath, near the Government of India tourist office, offer dorms as well as rooms, are cramped but friendly, and often full.

The hotels listed below are marked on the **map** of Connaught Place on p.118 and on the general Delhi map on pp.98–99.

Alka, 16/90 P-Block, Connaught Place ☎ 011/334 4328. Stuffy but comfortable carpeted rooms, all with TV and a/c, few with windows. Excellent in-house vegetarian restaurant as well as a bar and coffee shop. **⑨**

Central Court, N-Block, Connaught Place ☎ 011/331 5013. Large, clean rooftop establishment with nice terraces, although the balcony rooms are very noisy. **⑦**

Gandhi Guest House, 80 Tolstoy Lane, behind Scindia House ☎ 011/332 1113. Less cramped than some of the neighbouring lodges, with a tiny roof area. Shared baths with hot water in winter. **③**

Imperial, Janpath ☎ 011/334 1234, ℮ hotel@imperialindia.com. Plush rooms in the recently renovated Delhi landmark. Large gardens with palms, a swimming pool plus shops, a beauty parlour, English pub and several restaurants. Rooms start at $205. **⑨**

Inter-Continental, Barakhamba Avenue ☎ 011/332 0101, ℮ newdelhi@interconti.com. Plush, monolithic hotel with comfortable rooms and all mod cons including a choice of restaurants, bars and a disco. Prices start from $285. **⑨**

ITDC Kanishka, 19 Ashoka Rd ☎ 011/334 4422. One of the better government-run hotels in the area. Comfortable but unimaginative rooms on eighteen storeys, all with TV and clean bathrooms. Features a swimming pool, bars and food halls and a rooftop restaurant. Its neighbouring sister hotel, *Indraprastha*, is shabby. **⑨**

Janpath, Janpath ☎ 011/334 0070. Moderate hotel with large, clean carpeted rooms and some exceptionally good restaurants as well as foreign exchange, shops and a travel counter. **⑨**

Le Meridien, Windsor Place ☎ 011/371 0101, ⓦ www.lemeridien-newdelhi.com. Posh, glitzy hotel, with taxes on everything. Facilities include a swimming pool, a health club and a choice of restaurants and bars. Prices start at $240 per double; it's cheaper booked through the TCI. **❾**

Master Paying Guest House, R-500 New Rajendra Nagar ☎ 011/574 1089 or 5850914, ⓔ urvashi@del2.vsnl.net.in. Comfortable, secure and relaxing family guesthouse with secluded roof terrace, on the edge of the green belt only 10min by rickshaw from CP. The cheaper rooms have shared bathrooms; those on the roof are larger with optional a/c. Book ahead. **❻–❼**.

Madras Hotel, 23 P-Block, Connaught Place ☎ 011/336 3652. Busy South Indian establishment with small but clean rooms and a dorm (Rs60) behind the huge no-frills restaurant. **❹**

Marina, 59 G-Block, Connaught Place ☎011/332 4658. Long-established business hotel, convenient for the railway station, with sizeable rooms and good service, at inflated rates. Rooms facing the road are constantly invaded by traffic noise. Has an efficient travel counter and a 24hr coffee shop. **❾**

Metro, 49 N-Block, Connaught Place ☎ 011/331 3856. Despite visible ageing and lack of maintenance, the large, shabby but clean rooms and restaurant of this once grand hotel retain a little of their charm, and the staff are friendly. **❼–❽**

Nirula's, L-Block, Connaught Place ☎ 011/335 2419. Smart hotel, with a handful of small, cosy rooms with a/c and TV and a variety of restaurants. Often full. **❾**

Palace Heights, D-Block, Connaught Place ☎ 011/332 1419. Central but rundown with small rooms, some with windows, some a/c, and a pleasant balcony terrace. **❺–❻**

Park, 15 Sansad Marg ☎ 011/373 3737. Comfortable but soulless and overpriced carpeted rooms, with bathtubs, fridges, TV and room service, and views over Jantar Mantar from the front. A swimming pool, health club and disco spice the place up, though overall it's not one of the best in this category. Prices start at $275 for a double but it's cheaper through the TCI. **❾**

Ringo Guest House, 17 Scindia House ☎ 011/331 0605. Cramped but friendly lodge, popular for its rooftop dorms (Rs90) and restaurant. Individual rooms are poky and airless but clean, and they offer privacy and undisturbed sleep. Open 24hr – knock if you arrive after midnight. **❸–❺**

Royal Guest House, 44 Janpath above the Royal Nepal Airlines office ☎ 011/332 9485. A veritable warren, but quiet and clean, with spacious singles. Some a/c rooms. **❸–❺**

Sunny Guest House, 152 Scindia House ☎ 011/331 2909. Similar layout to *Ringo Guest House*, with friendly staff, a sociable rooftop restaurant and a range of dorm beds (Rs90) and rooms, some with a/c. Clean bathrooms, hot showers and booking facilities for private buses. Open 24hr. **❸–❺**

YMCA Tourist Hostel, Jai Singh Road ☎ 011/336 1915. A staid and sterile place with good restaurants, a swimming pool and attractive gardens. Ordinary and a/c rooms, and a reliable hot-water supply in both the common and private bathrooms; the price includes breakfast. **❻–❼**

YWCA International Guest House, 10 Sansad Marg ☎ 011/336 1561. Clean and airy a/c rooms with private bathrooms, and set meals in the hostel's restaurant. Women are given priority but men can also stay. Foreign currency preferred; the price includes breakfast. **❼**

Paharganj

The **Paharganj** area running west from New Delhi railway station, a popular hunting ground for inexpensive and mid-range accommodation, has a lively scene – see p.119 – that you'll miss if you stay in Connaught Place, just ten minutes' walk south. It's also a place where you can buy from other travellers things they no longer need: Enfield motorbikes, rucksacks, camping gear, malaria tablets and so forth. However, some hotels, particularly those with all-night restaurants, are becoming more like 24hr parties, so if you want to sleep, choose carefully.

Lodges at knock-down prices are invariably poky, stuffy and grubby, with rickety beds, moth-eaten mattresses and thin partition walls, but if you're intent on finding a budget room, there are exceptions on and around the **Main Bazaar**, which runs west from New Delhi railway station for nearly 1km. The area is crowded and noisy, unlike the spacious surrounds of the hotels south of Connaught Place, but staying here makes you feel more a part of the throbbing city.

Note, too, that Paharganj is notorious for hotel **touts**, and it's not uncommon for rickshaw drivers to announce that the hotel you're heading for has burnt

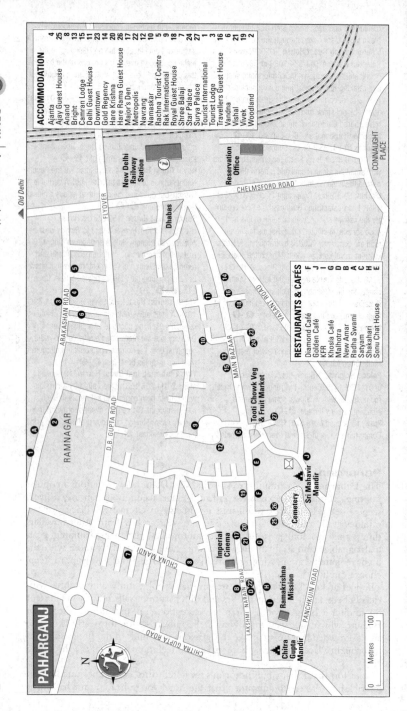

PAHARGANJ

ACCOMMODATION

Ajanta	4
Ajay Guest House	25
Anand	8
Bright	13
Camran Lodge	15
Delhi Guest House	11
Downtown	23
Gold Regency	14
Hare Krishna	20
Hare Rama Guest House	26
Major's Den	17
Metropolis	22
Navrang	12
Namaskar	10
Rachna Tourist Centre	5
Rak International	9
Royal Guest House	18
Shree Balaji	7
Star Palace	24
Surya Palace	27
Tourist International	1
Tourist Lodge	3
Travellers Guest House	16
Vandna	6
Vishal	21
Vivek	19
Woodland	2

RESTAURANTS & CAFÉS

Diamond Café	F
Golden Café	J
KFR	I
Khosla Café	G
Malhotra	D
New Amar	B
Radha Swami	A
Satyam	C
Shakahari	H
Sonu Chat House	E

New Delhi Railway Station

Reservation Office

CHELMSFORD ROAD

CONNAUGHT PLACE

Old Delhi

FLYOVER

Dhabas

ARAKASHAN ROAD

RAMNAGAR

D.B. GUPTA ROAD

MAIN BAZAAR

VASANT ROAD

Tooti Chowk Veg & Fruit Market

Imperial Cinema

CHUNA MANDI

LAKSHMI NARAIN ROAD

Cemetery

Sri Mahavir Mandir

Ramakrishna Mission

PANCHKUIN ROAD

CHITRA GUPTA ROAD

Chitra Gupta Mandir

N

Metres

0   100

down, gone bankrupt, changed its name, or simply never existed. Be firm and stand your ground.

The hotels listed below are marked on the Paharganj **map** opposite.

Ajay Guest House, 5084-A Main Bazaar ☏ 011/354 3125. Marble decor and clean, small rooms, most with baths but no windows. Boasts good-value dorms (Rs60) and a 24hr bakery downstairs. ❷–❹

Anand, 2537/48 Chuna Mandi ☏ 011/352 1755. A grotty but cheap lodge north of *Imperial Cinema*, with long balconies on each floor. Some rooms with fridge, all with bath. ❷–❸

Bright, 1089–1090 Main Bazaar ☏ 011/355 0182. Basic and dirt-cheap lodge spread over three buildings, one with a courtyard. Extra charges for blankets and hot water. ❶–❷

Camran Lodge, 1116 Main Bazaar ☏ 011/352 6053. Small lodge built into a late-Moghul period mosque; some character despite being dim and a little poky. Good-value singles. ❷–❹

Delhi Guest House, Gali Halwaian ☏ 011/367 6864. Spread over three ramshackle old houses, this place is cramped and grubby but as cheap as they come and handy for the station. ❶–❷

Downtown, 4583 Main Bazaar ☏ 011/355 5815. A good value option, with small clean rooms and friendly management; it also houses a good internet café. ❷–❸

Gold Regency, opposite New Delhi railway station ☏ 011/354 0101. Overpriced a/c rooms within a stone's throw of the station; convenient with a 24hr coffee shop, restaurant, money change and a cheap internet café open round the clock. ❻–❼

Hare Krishna, 1572–1573 Main Bazaar ☏ 011/352 9188. Friendly, clean and cosy, and fairly quiet with a pleasant rooftop café. ❸

Hare Rama Guest House, 298 Main Bazaar ☏ 011/352 1413. Modern, marble-slab lodge with a 24hr rooftop restaurant, popular with the Israeli party crowd. Clean rooms and dorms, as well as helpful service, left-luggage facilities and airport taxis. ❸–❺

Major's Den, 2314 Lakshmi Narain St ☏ 011/362 9599. Hotel run by a cheerful ex-army officer, offering large carpeted rooms in an old house full of character. Very homely, and safe for women travelling on their own. ❹–❺

Metropolis, 1634 Main Bazaar ☏ 011/753 1794. Main Bazaar's most upmarket and comfortable hotel. Dorms are a bit pricier and quieter than elsewhere, with lockers provided. Some double rooms have a/c, large windows and a shower with constant hot water. No singles. Two good restaurants. ❻–❼

Navrang, 644-C Mahalla Bowali, 6 Tooti Chowk ☏ 011/753 1922. One of the cheapest options, a basic, friendly lodge tucked off the main street but pretty cramped and grubby. ❷

Namaskar, 917 Chandiwalan, Main Bazaar ☏ 011/362 1234. You are in safe hands with brothers Surinder and Rajinder; they have simple but clean rooms and are also one of the best tour operators in Paharganj, offering airport pickup with prior notice. ❸–❺

Rak International, Tooti Chowk, 820 Main Bazaar ☏ 011/355 0478. Friendly, extremely good-value, newly converted hotel. Rooms are smart and on the large side, all with phone, TV, fridge and hot water. ❹–❻

Royal Guest House, 4464 Main Bazaar ☏ 011/753 5880. Clean and friendly, with a selection of a/c and non-a/c rooms, all with private bathroom. Often full. ❷–❺

Shree Balaji, 2204 Chuna Mandi ☏ 011/353 2212. Clean modern building and one of the better hotels along this strip. All rooms with TV and carpet. Good-value singles. ❸

Star Palace, 4590 Main Bazaar ☏ 011/362 8585. One of Paharganj's more salubrious hotels, with a good restaurant and decent rooms arranged round a central well. The more expensive ones with carpets and a/c are better value. If full, they can take you to their similar sister establishment, the *Star View*. ❸–❺

Surya Palace, 4826–28 Main Bazaar ☏ 011/351 5816. Adequate, average place, tucked off the vegetable market. One of the better cheap options. ❷

Travellers Guest House, 4360 Main Bazaar ☏ 011/354 4849. A smart, well-kept hotel above Madan's Store near the railway station, with unremarkable decor but friendly service. ❷–❹

Vishal, 1600 Main Bazaar ☏ 011/753 2079. Unoriginal marble decor, but clean and comfortable, with a good restaurant and larger rooms than similar lodges. ❸–❺

Vivek, 1534–1550 Main Bazaar ☏ 011/351 2900. Popular place, with a 24hr rooftop restaurant, and unremarkable rooms. Most feature attached baths and hot water, and room service is available. The best rooms, some a/c, have windows facing the street. ❸–❻

Ram Nagar

Directly north of Paharganj, five minutes' walk from New Delhi railway station and just beyond the flyover section of D.B. Gupta Road, is **Ram Nagar**, lined with hotels and a few restaurants. Within easy reach of the bazaar, but spared the incessant noise and commercial atmosphere, hotels in Ram Nagar are worth considering if you want to stay near the station, but don't fancy Paharganj. However, crossing D.B. Gupta Road to get to the Main Bazaar can be more than nerve-wracking; it's wise to go the long way round, under the flyover. The hotels listed below are marked on the map of Paharganj on p.110.

Ajanta, 36 Arakashan Rd ☏011/362 0925. Clean and efficiently run place with spacious rooms, some a/c, but not much atmosphere. Good attached restaurant/ice-cream bar. ❺–❻

Rachna Tourist Lodge, 8510 Arakashan Rd ☏011/361 5355. Simple, good-value rooms, including deluxe ones with TV and air-coolers. Cheaper than most here and near the station. ❷–❸

Tourist International, 8197/6 Arakashan Rd ☏011/361 7754. Good standards and comfortable rooms, all with TV and fridge, plus a travel desk and internet access. ❹–❻

Tourist Lodge, 26 Arakashan Rd ☏011/353 2990. Sizeable rooms with attached bathrooms. Reasonably clean, and typical of the higher-standard establishments along this strip. ❺–❻

Vandna, 47 Arakashan Rd ☏011/362 8821. Just off the main road, with some a/c rooms that are especially good value. ❸–❺

Woodland, 8235/6 Multani Danda, Arakashan Road ☏011/361 2980. Comfortable, popular hotel with smart rooms and good facilities. ❸–❻

Old Delhi and north of Connaught Place

If you find Paharganj too much of a travellers' hang-out, or Connaught Place too impersonal, head for **Old Delhi**, where foreign tourists seldom stay. Here you'll find yourself swamped by the noise and smells of the least modernized area of the capital. Prices are low and standards not very high, but the hotels are well sited for visits to the Red Fort and Jami Masjid, and you can guarantee constant activity on the crowded streets, excellent food at long-established restaurants and superb sweets from roadside stalls. If the noise of Chandni Chowk proves too much, you could opt for a bit more luxury and still retain access to the bazaars and the atmosphere of the old city. Sadly, the much-loved *New Delhi Tourist Camp* is no more.

The hotels listed below are marked on the **map** of Old Delhi on p.123.

Broadway, Asaf Ali Road ☏011/327 3821, ⓔbroadway@oldworldhospitality.com. Midway between Old and New Delhi, close to Delhi Gate, this is a great top-range hotel with high standards, an excellent restaurant specializing in Kashmiri feasts, and two bars. Some rooms look out over the Jami Masjid. Tours through Old Delhi can be organized for guests. ❼–❽

Naaz, motor market, behind Jami Masjid ☏011/326 2525. One of the small, friendly hotels behind the mosque; the rooms are basic but clean, some even have a/c and there's a restaurant. ❸–❹

New India Hotel, 172 Katra Bariyan, Fatehpuri ☏011/392 3040. Old house, opposite Fatehpuri mosque, where large simple rooms, steeped in the

character of the old city, open onto a central courtyard: some double rooms have their own balcony. Basic communal washing facilities. ❸–❺

Oberoi Maidens, 7 Sham Nath Marg ☏011/397 5464, ⓦ.www.oberoihotels.com/odelhim.htm. Quiet luxury hotel in a colonnaded colonial mansion north of Old Delhi, close to the Inter-state Bus Terminal. Pleasant rooms, but now showing their age. Leafy gardens, swimming pool, a fine restaurant and a bar open till midnight. Doubles from $96. ❾

Star Guest House, 186 Katra Bariyan, Fatehpuri ☏011/392 1127. Poky, characterless rooms in a fairly new hotel overlooking the narrow street that

winds past Fatehpuri mosque. Worth considering if you can't get into *New India Hotel*. ④
Wongdhen House, 15-A New Tibetan Colony, Majnu Ka Tilla ☎011/391 6689. A clean and safe traveller-friendly guesthouse with a restaurant and terrace and some rooms overlooking the River Yamuna. A 15min auto ride to the north of Old Delhi railway station, the Tibetan refugee colony makes a pleasant change from the grime of the city. ②–⑥

South Delhi

Most of the accommodation **south of Connaught Place** lies firmly in the luxury category, although there are a few guesthouses in Sundernagar, the odd mid–range hotel tucked away in a residential area and a modern **youth hostel** near the exclusive diplomatic enclave. The five-star hotels provide Delhi's best restaurants, bars, health centres, nightclubs and most exclusive discos. As a result, the city's high society uses them to entertain, be seen in and hold lavish weddings, cocooned from the outside world. Prices here are some of the highest in India; those in this section encompass a range from $16 to over $1000.

The hotels listed below appear on the general Delhi **map** on pp.98–99.

Ambassador, Sujan Singh Park ☎011/463 2600, ⓦwww.tajhotels.com. Next to Khan Market, and recently acquired by the Taj Group, this is a comfortable and friendly place with no frills and large old-fashioned rooms. The restaurants and disco are popular with locals. Rates start at $160. ⑨

Claridges, 12 Aurangzeb Rd ☎011/301 0211, ⓔclaridges.hotel@gems.vsnl.net.in. An elegant Thirties-style facade leads into the marble foyer of one of Delhi's oldest and finest establishments. Facilities include tennis courts, restaurants and a swimming pool. From $210 for a double. ⑨

Hyatt Regency, Bhikaiji Cama Place, Ring Road ☎011/679 1234, ⓦwww.delhi.hyatt.com. Smart, elegant and not too brash, with all the comforts of this renowned chain. Excellent eating, plus a fitness and health centre and the best pub in town. Prices start at $250. ⑨

ITDC Ashok, Chanakyapuri ☎011/611 0101. A landmark in the grand pseudo-Moghul style, finished in red sandstone. Fading luxury run by this ailing group. ⑨

ITDC Lodi, Lala Lajpat Rai Marg ☎011/436 2422. A once grand hotel built in mock-Tughluq style but now falling apart, though it does have an open-air swimming pool and a fantastic South Indian restaurant. From $52 for a double. ⑧

ITDC Samrat, Kautiliya Marg, Chanakyapuri ☎011/611 0606. Comfortable place, behind the *Ashok*, with pretentious five-star treatment aimed at business users. ⑨

La Sagrita, 14 Sundernagar ☎011/469 4541. One of a handful of private guesthouses in this exclusive colony away from the din of central Delhi. Quiet and clean with room service and central a/c. ⑦–⑧

Maharani Guest House, 3 Sundernagar ☎011/469 3128. Experience residential Delhi in a pleasantly sited colony with a good shopping arcade. An alternative to the usual luxury hotels, with several similar guesthouses around the corner including *La Sagrita*. ⑧–⑨

Maurya Sheraton and Towers, Diplomatic Enclave ☎011/611 2233, ⓦwww.welcomgroup.com/mauryasheraton. Extremely plush, with an imposing range of individually designed luxury rooms, great restaurants and a nightclub. Rooms start at around $270 per night. ⑨

Oberoi, Dr Zakir Hussain Marg ☎011/436 3030, ⓦwww.oberoihotels.com/delhim.htm. One of Delhi's first in the super league; manages to retain its elegance without being loud and brash. Highly recommended if you can afford it. Rates start at $370. ⑨

Park Royal, Nehru Place ☎011/622 3344, ⓦwww.theparkhotels.com. Over-the-top opulence that is meant to bowl you over and does, with all mod cons, a great coffee shop, restaurants, bars but a dismal location. From $290. ⑨

Qutab, off Sri Aurobindo Marg ☎011/652 1010. Concrete and characterless, but otherwise comfortable. Top facilities including tennis courts, swimming pool and a bowling alley. ⑨

Taj Mahal, 1 Man Singh Rd ☎011/302 6162, ⓦwww.tajhotels.com/luxury/tajpalace_delhi/new.htm. Also known as the *Taj Man Singh*, ornate and luxurious in the typical grand style of the Taj Group, with a marble foyer and chandeliers, and an excellent choice of restaurants. Expect to pay at least $350 a night. ⑨

Taj Palace, 1 Sardar Patel Marg ℡ 011/611 0202, ℮ palace.delhi@tajhotels.com. Grand, imposing, very comfortable and exclusive, but otherwise lacking the character of the flagship *Taj Mahal*, though similarly priced from around $350. ❾

Youth Hostel, 5 Naya Marg, Chanakyapuri ℡ 011/611 6285. Away from the bustling city centre, this ultramodern building in grey concrete, with dorms (Rs50) and doubles, is the showpiece-cum-administration centre of the Indian YHA. ❻

Near the IGI Airport

There are **retiring rooms** at both airports, but if you are in for a long wait, head for the hotels clustered around the turn-off for the **international airport**. Several good *dhabas* can be found around there too; the *Banaz* restaurant next to the *International Inn* serves good Chinese and tandoori food, while the *Radisson* boasts a cake shop and seven cafés, bars and restaurants where you can while away the time agreeably.

Ashok Country Resort, Rajokri Road, Kapashera ℡ 011/556 4590, ℮ sahnihtl@del2.vsnl.net.in. Just off the Jaipur road, spacious carpeted rooms in four-star comfort, with a pleasant lawn and a swimming pool but low-key service. ❽
New Krishna Guest House, M.R. Complex, Gurgoan Road ℡ 011/678 4266. Clean doubles with attached bathrooms but no food. One of several mid-range hotels along this strip. ❻–❼
Radisson, NH8, Mahipalpur ℡ 011/612 9191, ℗ www.radisson.com. A luxury hotel that's the

best around the airport, with a friendly atmosphere, health club, bars and Italian and Tex-Mex restaurants amid exhibitions of contemporary Indian art. The rooms are deluxe with all mod cons. From $275. ❾
Tarra Inn, A-55 NH8, Mahipalpur ℡ 011/678 3677. The best of the budget hotels along this stretch, with colourful rooms, huge beds, friendly staff and a good restaurant. Open 24hr. ❹–❺

The City

Delhi is both daunting and alluring, a sprawling metropolis with a stunning backdrop of ancient architecture. Once you've found your feet and got over the initial impact of the commotion, noise, pollution and sheer scale of the place, the city's geography slowly slips into focus. Monuments in sandstone and marble, which stand in assorted states of repair, make Delhi a veritable museum of Indo-Islamic architecture, seen at its best in the frenetic streets of **Old Delhi** and the venerable sites of **South Delhi**. Delhi today, however, as experienced by its many thousands of visitors, centres very much around the imperial city built by the British from 1911 onwards. Most foreign travellers to India find it necessary to call in at some of the myriad of administrative offices that fill the formal buildings of **Connaught Place**, the heart of **New Delhi**. From here it's easy to visit one of many outstanding **museums**, stocked with artistic treasures from all over the country and recording the lives of India's political figureheads.

Central New Delhi

The modern area of **CENTRAL NEW DELHI**, with its wide tree-lined avenues and solid colonial architecture, has been the seat of central government since 1931. At its hub, the royal mall, **Rajpath**, runs from palatial **Rashtrapati Bhavan**, in the west, to the **India Gate** war memorial in the east. At the north edge of the new capital lies the thriving business centre, **Connaught Place**, where neon advertisements for Wimpy, American Express, hotels and countless airline offices adorn the flat roofs and colonnaded verandas of high white buildings that curve around a central park to form an almost perfect circle. Central New Delhi also has its fair share of more recent high-rise offices and hotels, standing close to pre-British constructions such as the open-air observatory, **Jantar Mantar**, and a generous smattering of excellent museums covering arts and crafts and the lives of India's post-Independence politicians.

Rashtrapati Bhavan and Rajpath

After George V, king of England and emperor of British India, decreed in 1911 that Delhi should replace Calcutta as the capital of India, the talented and ambitious English architect **Edwin Lutyens** was commissioned to plan the new governmental centre. **Rashtrapati Bhavan**, the official residence of the president of India, is one of the largest and most grandiose of the Raj constructions, built by Lutyens and Sir Herbert Baker between 1921 and 1929. Originally the Viceroy's House, this salmon-pink H-shaped structure on the gentle slope of Raisina Hill was built to dominate: a symbol asserting imperial power in the face of its doomed struggle against Indian nationalism, it was home to Lord Mountbatten, appointed viceroy in 1947 to supervise the transition to Independence. Its grandeur was considered nothing more than "vulgar ostentation and wasteful extravagance" by Motilal Nehru, while Mahatma Gandhi claimed that the construction of such "architectural piles" was "in conflict with the best interests of the nation".

Despite its classical columns, Moghul-style domes and *chhatris*, and Indian filigree work, the whole building is unmistakably British in character. The majestic proportions are best appreciated from India Gate to the east, from where you can see the perfectly balanced residence slightly raised on the hill, flanked in pleasing symmetry by the two Secretariat buildings below – though with increasing pollution, the view is often clouded by a smoggy haze. At closer quarters, the height and multitude of pillars supporting the front verandas are clearly seen, while the immensity of the central crowning copper dome, the dominating feature of the whole complex, is quite overwhelming. Between the entrance gates and the east side of the residence, the slender **Jaipur Column**, donated by the Maharaja of Jaipur, rises to a height of 145m, piercing the sky with a glass star balanced on a bronze lotus blossom. Close to its base, an early plan of New Delhi is etched onto a square panel. Troops and guards parade before the iron-grille gates each Saturday (9.35–10.15am) in a ceremony that is Delhi's answer to London's Changing of the Guard.

The apartments inside are strictly private, but the **gardens** at the west side are open to the public each February. Modelled on Moghul pleasure parks, with a typically ordered square pattern of quadrants dissected by waterways and refreshed by fountains, Lutyens' gardens extend beyond the normal confines to include eight tennis courts, butterfly enclosures, vegetable and fruit patches and a swimming pool. The immaculate flowerbeds contain many English varieties, and the trees lining the walkways are trimmed into perfect oblongs. In 1947, 418 staff worked in the gardens, fifty of whom were specifically employed to frighten away birds.

The **Secretariats** on the north and south side of Raisina Hill are an interesting synthesis of Moghul and colonial styles, topped with baroque domes overlaid with low-relief lotus motifs and elephants. Built by Baker, today they house the Home and Finance Ministries and the Ministry of Foreign Affairs.

Vijay Chowk, immediately in front of Rashtrapati Bhavan, leads into **Rajpath**, the wide straight road once known as King's Way, flanked with gardens and fountains that are floodlit at night, and the scene of annual **Republic Day** celebrations (Jan 26). Rajpath runs directly east to **India Gate**, the "All India War Memorial" designed by Lutyens in 1921. The high arch, reminiscent of the Arc de Triomphe in Paris, commemorates 90,000 Indian soldiers killed fighting for the British in World War I, and bears the names of more than 3000 British and Indian soldiers who died on the Northwest frontier and in the Afghan War of 1919. The extra memorial beneath the arch honours the lives lost in the Indo-Pakistan War of 1971.

Parliament House (Sansad Bhavan)

Northeast of Rashtrapati Bhavan at the end of Sansad Marg is **Parliament House**, now known as **Sansad Bhavan**. Planned by Lutyens and built under the supervision of Baker, the low circular structure covers more than five acres. Obliged to respond to complaints about its extravagant design and large costs, Baker himself referred to the unusual building as a "merrie-go-round", but successfully completed a momentous project. From outside, Parliament House presents an unbroken circle of high buff pillars, and a higher storey (not originally planned) that screens a central dome.

Inside, three semicircular chambers were built to house the Council of State, the Assembly Chamber and the Council of Princes. Today, the latter, where leaders from India's princely states gathered until Independence, contains a

The parliament of India

The **Indian Parliament** in Delhi was formed under the British in 1931, and later tailored to the needs of the newly independent nation under the leadership of Jawaharlal Nehru. Today, Delhi's parliament closely follows the English model. It is made up of a politically neutral president, an upper house, the **Rajya Sabha** ("Council of States"), and a lower house, the **Lok Sabha** (literally "People's House"). Members represent all India's seventeen states and ten Union Territories, in numbers proportionate to each district's population. Thanks in part to the influence of Mahatma Gandhi, a quota of seats is reserved for "untouchables", or Harijans. Members of the Lok Sabha are elected every five years, and every two years elections replace one-third of the Rajya Sabha.

The Lok Sabha, the larger of the two houses, comprises up to 525 members, at least fifty of whom must be present to propose and pass bills. Only two or three times a year does the whole house attend. While bills may be put forward in either house, most originate in the Lok Sabha, and are passed to the Rajya Sabha for approval. Taxation, spending, budgets and government economy are discussed only in the lower house. Each day in the Lok Sabha begins with an hour of questions to the speaker, when government policies are clarified, and opposition parties criticize and push for change.

The smaller Rajya Sabha, with 250 members, serves as more of an advisory body. It does, however, have the power to create or abolish states and alter boundaries – issues that were of particular importance between 1953 and 1956, when 562 principalities acceded and Congress demanded that territories should be determined by common language. In the Sixties the formation of Punjab and Nagaland states and the Union Territory of Himachal Pradesh was also determined by the Rajya Sabha and, in 2000, the new states of Chhattisgarh, Uttaranchal and Jharkand.

Despite their separate roles, the two houses meet for collective votes on bills that have not been passed by a majority, and to elect the parliamentary president. While the large membership and exhaustive screening of bills ensures the fullest consideration of political issues, government critics argue that the two-house system wastes energy, and thickens India's already stifling web of bureaucratic confusion.

library with a comprehensive collection of books and records detailing political history from the 1920s onwards. Visitors can look round when parliament is not in session; ask one of the desk clerks in reception for permission. It's suitably formal, stuffy even, its walls overlaid with convex teak panels positioned at a downward angle to improve acoustics, and the coats of arms of India's royal families. The **Lok Sabha** now meets in the Assembly Chamber, and with permission from the reception office on Raisina Road (and a letter of introduction for foreigners from a relevant embassy), visitors can watch debates from seats in the public gallery.

Connaught Place

The hub of New Delhi, **Connaught Place** could not be more different from the crowded centre of Old Delhi that it replaced. Conceived by Robert Tor Russell, chief architect of the Government of India, it is one of the few areas of the new city that was not designed by Lutyens, though its lofty facades and classical columns are derivative of the style he established with Rashtrapati Bhavan. Originally designed in the shape of a horseshoe, Connaught Place now forms a full circle, divided into blocks A–N by seven radial roads and rimmed by a busy outer Ring Road known as **Connaught Place**. Note also that the whole area, from Plaza Cinema in the north to Jantar Mantar and Tolstoy Marg in the south, is commonly referred to as Connaught Place.

Connaught Place is rather grand for a commercial centre, with shops and offices housed in colonnaded buildings almost as splendid as the parliamentary headquarters further south. Unsurprisingly, considering its wealth of tourist facilities, including a glut of hotels and many of Delhi's best restaurants, the area buzzes with touts and salesmen, selling anything from airline tickets to five-metre-long leather whips.

From Connaught Place, **Sansad Marg** runs southwest to the parliamentary buildings, while southbound **Janpath**, with the busy Tibetan Market at its northern end, is lined with several modern hotels, Russell's majestic Eastern and Western Courts, and the Central Post and Telegraph offices. The park at the core of Connaught Place, and the grassy area over the underground Palika Bazaar, close to Janpath, offer respite from the busy streets, and provide the perfect arena for Delhi's ice-cream sellers, shoe-shiners, masseurs and flower-vendors, who peddle their wares from dawn to dusk.

Jantar Mantar

Between Connaught Place and Rashtrapati Bhavan on Sansad Marg, **Jantar Mantar** (daily 9am–7pm) stands little changed since its construction in 1725 as the first of five open-air observatories designed by the ruler of Jaipur, Jai Singh II (see p.167). Huge deep-red and white slanting stone structures loom over palm trees and neat flower beds – these giant sundials cast shadows formerly used to calculate time, solar and lunar calendars and astrological movements, all with an admirable degree of accuracy.

Lakshmi Narayan Mandir

Directly west of Connaught Place on Mandir Marg, **Lakshmi Narayan Mandir** is a large modern temple also known as Birla Mandir after its sponsors, the wealthy Marwari Birla merchants. The extravagant temple with its striking white, cream and brown domes makes for a good introduction to modern Hinduism. There is a special reception room where foreigners can leave their shoes before climbing the steps to the large open courtyard in

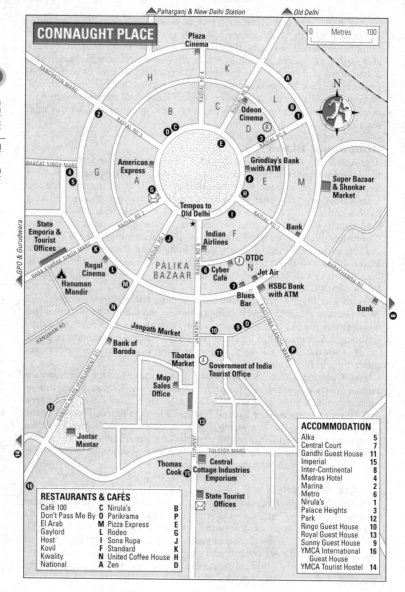

front of the main shrine dedicated to Lakshmi (appropriately the goddess of wealth). The rest of the complex is spread over several raised tiers and includes smaller shrines to Hanuman (the monkey god), and beloved Ganesh (the elephant-headed god). At the back of the second-largest carpeted hall, you'll hear gentle devotional music and chanting in a tiny, ornate chamber decorated with coloured stones and mirrors and dedicated to Krishna.

Throughout the temple, the walls are decorated with various symbols and quotations from the *Bhagavad Gita* and *Upanishads*, some of them translated into English. For many Westerners, this is the first place in India where they are confronted with the, to them, incongruous sight of multiple swastikas. The original meaning of the sign, an ancient Aryan symbol of the striving for perfection, is explained on one wall. The pleasant gardens behind the temple are reached by a separate entrance and contain a variety of large sculptures, shelters, fountains and seats, set amid welcome greenery.

Bangla Sahib Gurudwara

Just off Ashoka Road near the poste restante, the huge white marble structure of **Bangla Sahib Gurudwara**, Delhi's principal *gurudwara*, topped by golden onion-shaped domes, is visible from some distance. As in all Sikh places of worship, visitors of all denominations are welcome. You can deposit shoes, collect brochures, and enlist the services of a free guide in the information centre near the main entrance. To go into the main complex, you'll need to cover your head and wear conservative clothes that cover legs and shoulders.

The large **main hall** is unelaborate except for the open central shrine, where a sculpted bronze cupola hangs over a smaller golden dome under which silk sheets are spread out and covered in flowers. This shrine is the scene of constant devotional music (vocals, harmonium and *tabla* played by blue-turbaned priests), whose ethereal tones are relayed throughout the entire complex.

The other main features of the temple are the vast **bathing tank**, home to numerous fish, and the **dining hall**, where visitors are welcome to join in the simple meal of dhal and chapatis served three times daily. All you need to do is follow the crowd, sit in line on the long rows of coarse carpet, and wait for the bucket to come round.

Colonial churches

No British governmental centre could be complete without a church, and in 1927 work began on the **Church of the Redemption**, east of Parliament House. Designed by Russell's successor, Henry Medd, the robust structure owes more than a passing nod to Lutyens with its high curved vaults, and subtle yet dominant domed tower – it appealed so much to the then-viceroy, Lord Irwin, that it became known as "Viceroy's Church". The exterior is plain and boldly linear, while within, high rounded arches and shafts of strong light streaming through crescent windows impart an overwhelming sense of space. A company of angels looks down from the curved roof above the altar.

Further north, at the south end of Bhai Vir Singh Marg, is one of Medd's more ambitious projects, the Roman Catholic **Church of the Sacred Heart**. This betrays a strong Italianate influence, with a facade of white pillars supporting a canopy set against a dark brick background, and circular colonnaded turrets rising above the roof to each side of the entrance porch. The lofty interior has a towering curved roof, polished stone floors and broad arches set into smooth walls, and is far grander than would be expected from the largely stark and unadorned facade.

Paharganj

With buzzing **Main Bazaar** as its centrepiece, the lively area of **Paharganj**, immediately west of New Delhi railway station, is a fascinating area to stroll around and, for many budget travellers, their first experience of the subcontinent. Renowned for its cheap hotels (see p.109), it's also packed with restaurants, cafés, internet cafés, travel agents and shops selling anything from plastic toys and hardware to psychedelic clothing, carvings, bronzes and perfumed san-dalwood. There's a busy fruit and vegetable market halfway along, a multitude of stalls dishing up tasty snacks, and itinerant hawkers keen to sell you drums, sleeping bags or even whips at the "best prices". A constant stream of cycle and auto-rickshaws, handcarts, cows and the odd taxi squeeze through impossible gaps without the flow ever coming to a complete standstill. The winding alleys where children play among chickens and pigs seem worlds away from the com-mercial city centre only just around the corner.

Spend a bit of time shopping or lounging in cafés here and you'll see invet-erate old Western hippies, groups of Russians and lost-looking newly arrived backpackers, but be warned that you may well be approached by some charac-ters best avoided. The worst offenders are drug-dealers, and Kashmiri touts who will assure you that the Kashmir valley is a safe haven once more and try to sell you irresistible houseboat packages. By comparison, the relatively inno-cent hotel and ticket touts are easy to spot and brush off.

National Museum

The **National Museum** (11 Janpath; Tues–Sun 10am–5pm; guided tours daily 10.30am, 11.30am, noon, 2pm & 3pm; Rs150 [Rs5], camera Rs300), Delhi's largest, provides the best general overview of Indian culture and history. Packed with exhibits ranging over five thousand years, it takes several hours to get around the whole place, which follows a circular plan, with galleries arranged around a central courtyard. A small shop in the entrance hall sells postcards, books and souvenirs, and has details of daily film shows (2.30pm; in English).

The **ground floor** is dominated by architectural displays, setting off with simple stone **Neolithic** tools (3000–1500 BC), and shell and bone jewellery excavated from **Indus Valley civilization** sites such as Mohenjo Daro and Harappa in Pakistan, Lothal (Gujarat) and Kalibangan (Rajasthan). Carved pil-lars and statues from the **Mauryan** empire (250 BC) feature typical designs such as the emperor Ashoka's lion motif and common Buddha symbols: lotus blossoms, *bodhi* trees, stupas, footprints and wheels. An assortment of **Gupta** (400 AD) terracottas includes imposing statues of the river goddesses, Ganga and Yamuna, who stand with water vessels in their hands, and can often be seen guarding temple sanctuaries. **South Indian** temple architecture is repre-sented by a series of bold rounded sandstone figures from Pallava temples, dominated by Shiva and his consort, and some more intricate dark grey stone friezes from later Chola constructions. Stone and bronze **Buddhist** statues from India are set beside exquisitely designed Thai figurines, such as the ele-gant Tara (goddess of wisdom), fashioned in jade and crowned with a jewelled tiara. Take a little time to absorb the complexity of the Tibetan manuscripts, painted in sweeping black-ink characters and illustrated in extraordinarily minute detail.

Another gallery on the ground floor holds a superb collection of bejewelled clothes, dark-wood boxes inlaid with mother-of-pearl, fierce swords, daggers and spears, silk tapestries and ivory ornaments, all of which belonged to the powerful **Moghul** rulers who combined art forms from Persia, Afghanistan and India to create a unique and elaborate style. The Moghul theme is continued on the **first floor**, where Persian and Arabic manuscripts include the hand-written memoirs of Emperor Jahangir (1605–27). Other paintings on this floor show the work of several Indian schools, the most distinctive of which are the **Pahari** miniatures of the Himalayan regions of Gharwal and Kangra – simple yet striking scenes of courtly life and loving couples, whose fine lines were often drawn using a single hair. Continuing through the first-floor galleries you'll come across a section devoted entirely to models and masks made in **Nagaland**, whose long straight noses, square-set faces and slanted eye-slits evoke Peruvian art; the assorted masks and religious statues from Morocco, Peru and Costa Rica on the second floor make for interesting comparison. Also tucked away on the upper floor are several thick-set and intricately carved wooden doors, lintels and window shutters, examples of the elaborate carpentry that remains a strong tradition in **Gujarat**. The three hundred musical instruments on display in the adjoining gallery represent only part of India's vast musical tradition – it's a good collection, but if you want an even better insight into Indian music, head for Sangeet Natak Akademi (see overleaf).

Nehru Memorial Museum and Library

Built in 1930 as the residence for the British commander-in-chief, the grand and sombre Teen Murti House on Teen Murti Marg later became home to India's first prime minister, Jawaharlal Nehru, and is now the **Nehru Memorial Museum and Library** (Tues–Sun 9.30am–4.45pm; free). A tour of the house leads through rooms laden with photographs recording Nehru's life, from his childhood and student years at Harrow and Cambridge to his formal appointment as leader of India's government in the presence of the king and queen of England in 1948. The years between were dominated by the growth of the Congress party and calls for Independence, decisive periods in India's history that are documented here with excellent displays and reference to all the political activists involved. While Nehru's political life is brought to the fore, his personal effects in a simple bedroom, office and sitting room give some idea of the character of the father of a dynasty that hasn't left the political arena since Independence. Even Sonia Gandhi, reluctant to enter politics, is now something of a figurehead for many Indians.

Another of Nehru's passions was astronomy, an interest reflected in the **planetarium** (Rs1; daily astronomy shows in English at 11.30am & 3pm, Rs10) in the formal grounds of the house. The exhibition has little of striking interest, save the descent module used by the first Indian cosmonaut in 1984, its heatshield charred by re-entry into the atmosphere.

Indira Gandhi Memorial Museum

Although at times uncompromisingly harsh in her politics, Indira Gandhi was a much loved mother-figure during the long years of her leadership, and it is with deep respect that she is remembered at the **Indira Gandhi Memorial Museum**, 1 Safdarjung Rd (Tues–Sun 9.30am–5pm; free). It was in this house that she was assassinated by her own Sikh bodyguards in 1984; her bloodstained sari, which has been chemically preserved, is on display. The collection of letters, press cuttings, photos (many taken by Rajiv) and possessions is both informative and moving. It's supplemented by a section devoted to Rajiv, including the clothes he was wearing when he was assassinated in 1991, that winds up the exhibition on a rather tragic note. The tastefully decorated and furnished study, drawing room and dining room conjure up images of how the family must have lived, in great style but not overt opulence. So popular is the former Gandhi home that you may well find yourself caught up in a fast moving line of Indian tourists, especially at weekends; arrive early so you can view the exhibition at a leisurely pace.

National Gallery of Modern Art

Once the residence of the Maharaja of Jaipur, the extensive **National Gallery** (daily 10am–5pm; Rs5) housed in Jaipur House, near India Gate, is a rich showcase of Indian contemporary art. The permanent displays, focusing on post-1930s work, have many of the best exhibits, including pieces by the "Bengali Renaissance" artists Abanendranath Tagore and Nandalal Bose, the great poet and artist, Rabindranath Tagore, and Jamini Roy, whose work, reminiscent of Modigliani, reflects the influence of Indian folk art. Also on show are the romantic paintings and etchings of Thomas Daniell and his nephew William, British artists of the Bombay or Company School. The newly converted ground-floor galleries are used for temporary exhibitions of twentieth-century art from all over the subcontinent. An **Art Reference Library**, also on the ground floor, has a good collection of art books, journals and periodicals. The sculpture garden at the back features a selection of fairly uninspiring works, set out in regimental lines around the lawn.

National Museum of Natural History

The galleries at the **National Museum of Natural History**, FICCI Building, Barakhamba Road (daily except Sat 10am–5pm; free), house exhibitions on natural resources and ecology projects from all over the world, with a particular focus on India. Along with models of dinosaurs, stuffed animals and birds and fossils, there are supervised activity rooms in which children learn to model animals and handle specimens. Such appreciation of ecological issues is all too rare in India, where forests and natural habitats are fast disappearing, and the list of endangered species is growing rapidly.

National Philatelic Museum

To locate the **National Philatelic Museum**, at Dak Bhavan, Post Office, Sansad Marg (Mon–Fri 9.30am–12.30pm & 2.30–4.30pm; free), go to the entrance by the car park at the back of the post office on Sansad Marg and report to reception, where you will be given a pass to go up to the first floor and view the extensive collection of rare stamps. These include first-day covers and special cancellations from the pre- and post-Independence eras. A booth in the main post office sells special commemorative stamps to liven up your letters.

Sangeet Natak Akademi

India's premier institution for music (*sangeet*), dance (*natak*), and the performing arts, **Sangeet Natak Akademi**, Rabindra Bhavan, Firoz Shah Road (Mon–Fri 9.30am–6pm; free), is more of a resource centre than a museum, with a large audiovisual archive. A gallery also displays an extensive collection of folk and classical musical instruments, masks and costumes, while its library holds all sorts of rare and otherwise unobtainable volumes.

Crafts Museum

Immediately north of Purana Qila on Bhairon Road, the **Crafts Museum** (daily 10am–5pm; free) is a uniquely dynamic exhibition of the rural arts and crafts of India. Its village complex displays an assortment of building traditions, bringing together cultures from across the subcontinent to provide a unique if artificial insight into rural life. Authentically constructed mud huts are beautifully decorated with folk art, and exhibits include woodcarvings, paintings, papier-mâché, embroidery and a full-sized wooden *haveli* from Gujarat. Live demonstrations by the artisans offer close-up glimpses of the folk arts that can be all too difficult to obtain elsewhere in the country. You can buy ritual objects, ornaments, rugs, shawls and books from the craftsmen and women or from the excellent museum shop.

Old Delhi (Shahjahanabad)

Although it's not in fact the oldest part of Delhi, the seventeenth-century city of **Shahjahanabad**, built by the Moghul emperor, Shah Jahan, is known as **OLD DELHI**. The original city walls spread for seven miles, enclosing the sprawling fort, **Lal Qila**, and the formidable **Jami Masjid**, or "Friday Mosque". Old Delhi's main thoroughfare, **Chandni Chowk**, a seething mass of hooting, pushing cars, tempos, cycle rickshaws and ox carts, was once a sublime canal lined with trees and some of the most opulent bazaars of the East. Today the city walls have crumbled, and houses and shops have long since spilled beyond the remaining five of the fourteen old gates.

On the west bank of the River Yamuna northeast of the modern centre, Old Delhi resembles an overgrown village of tight-knit communities, alive with intriguing contradictions and contrasts. Photographers huddled at the east end of Chandni Chowk using rickety equipment left over from the days of the Raj are overlooked by garish film boards and advertisements for sex clinics, while the bazaars in the back alleys have changed little since the eighteenth and nineteenth centuries. It's a fascinating area, but you'll need stamina, patience and time to endure the crowds and traffic.

Lal Qila (Red Fort)

The largest of Old Delhi's monuments is **Lal Qila**, or Red Fort (daily dawn to dusk; $5 [Rs5]), whose thick red sandstone walls, bulging with turrets and bastions, rise above a wide dry moat in the northeast corner of the original city of Shahjahanabad. The fort covers a semi-octagonal area of almost 2km, its longest walls facing the town in the west and the River Yamuna in the east. Work was started on the fort – modelled on the royal citadel in Agra – in 1639, and it was completed by 1648. It contains all the expected trappings of the cen-

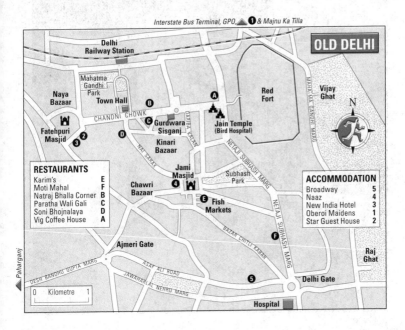

tre of Moghul government: halls of public and private audience, domed and arched marble palaces, plush private apartments, a mosque, and elaborately designed gardens. Today the Yamuna no longer flows close to the east wall, the "Stream of Paradise" no longer trickles through each palace, copper-plated domes have been replaced with plainer marble domes, and there are few signs of the precious stones and gems once set into the marble walls. Nevertheless, the fort remains an impressive testimony to Moghul grandeur, despite being attacked and plundered by the Persian emperor Nadir Shah in 1739, and by British soldiers during the battles of 1857 – as well as being rubbed, touched and worn down by thousands of marvelling tourists.

Entrance to the fort is through the mighty three-storey **Lahori Gate** in the centre of the west wall. A booking office sells tickets just outside, and eager guides will offer their services at negotiable prices (Rs30–50) – generally more than twice the price that you'd pay within. The main entrance opens onto **Chatta Chowk**, a covered street flanked with arched cells that used to house Delhi's most talented jewellers, carpet-makers, goldsmiths and silk-weavers, but now stock the usual souvenirs: miniatures, hookahs, brass ornaments, stone and woodcarvings and low-quality jewellery. Just beyond a small restaurant at the end of Chatta Chowk, the road stretches past the military colony into the heart of the fort, coming to an end at **Naubhat Khana**, the erstwhile "drum house", where music was once played five times a day and which now bears scant remains of its original painting.

From Naubhat Khana, a path runs east through wide lawns to the hall of public audience, the **Diwan-i-Am**. This lofty hall, with sturdy pillars supporting its roof and its floor raised on a high platform, was the scene of daily public appearances by the emperor until the custom was stopped by Aurangzeb. When in use, it was strewn with silk carpets and partitioned with hanging tapestries and curtains. Set against the west wall is "the seat of the shadow of God", a marble throne surrounded by twelve panels inlaid with precious stones. It was designed by an artist from Bordeaux, whose frieze of the Greek god Orpheus with his lute makes a surprising departure from the more usual floral designs of the Moghuls. Lord Curzon, viceroy of India from 1898 to 1905, restored the hall and returned the emperor's seat from the British Museum in 1909.

The **palaces** in the fort along the east wall face spacious gardens in the west and overlook the banks of the Yamuna, once the scene of animal fights laid on to entertain the royal occupants. Immediately east of the Diwan-i-Am, **Rang Mahal**, the "Palace of Colour", housed the emperor's wives and mistresses. "The crowning jewel of Shah Jahan's seraglio" was crowned with gilded turrets, delicately painted and decorated with intricate mosaics of mirrors, and with a ceiling overlaid with gold and silver that was reflected in a central pool in the marble floor. Unfortunately, it was greatly defaced when the British used it as an Officers' Mess after the Mutiny, and today is a shadow of its former glory. The similar **Mumtaz Mahal**, south of the main *zenana*, or women's quarters, and probably used by princesses, is now a **museum** (daily except Fri 10am–5pm) housing weaponry, textiles, carpets, ornate chess sets and hookahs.

On the northern side of Rang Mahal, the marble **Khas Mahal** was the personal palace of the emperor, divided into separate apartments for worship, sleeping and sitting. The southern chamber, **Tosh Khana** (robe room), has a stunning marble filigree screen on its north wall, carved with the scales of justice. Viewing the screen from the north you'll see suns surrounding the scales, but from the south these look more like moons. The octagonal tower project-

Sound and light shows

Each night a **Sound and Light** show takes place in the **Red Fort**: the palaces are dramatically lit, and a historical commentary blares from crackly loudspeakers. The show starts after sunset and lasts an hour (in Hindi Feb–April & Sept–Oct 7pm, May–Aug 7.30pm, Nov–Jan 6pm; in **English** Feb–April & Sept–Oct 8.30pm, May–Aug 9pm, Nov–Jan 7.30pm; Rs30; ☎011/327 4580). The mosquitoes are ferocious, so bring repellent. Heavy monsoon rains may affect summer shows.

ing over the east wall of the Khas Mahal was used by the emperor, who would appear here daily before throngs gathered on the riverbanks below. In 1911, when Delhi was declared capital, King George V (emperor of India) and Queen Mary sat here before the citizens of Delhi.

North of Khas Mahal, in the large **Diwan-i-Khas** (hall of private audience), the emperor would address the highest nobles of his court. Today it's the finest building in the fort, a marble pavilion shaded by a roof raised on stolid pillars embellished with amber, jade and gold, meeting in ornate scalloped arches. On the north and south walls you can still make out the Persian inscription attributed to Shah Jahan's prime minister:

Agar Firdaus bar ru-e-zamin ast
Hamin ast o hamin ast o hamin ast.

(If there be paradise on the face of earth,
It is this, Oh, it is this, Oh, it is this.)

A marble and gold peacock throne inlaid with rubies, sapphires and diamonds once stood on the central pedestal, bypassed by a "Stream of Paradise" that gurgled through the cool chamber. It took seven years to construct, and was the pride of the fort, but the Persian Nadir Shah took it back to his kingdom as booty after a raid in 1739.

A little further north are the **hammams**, or baths, sunken into the marble floor inlaid with delicate patterns of precious stones, and dappled in jewel-coloured light that filters through stained-glass windows. The western chamber contained hot baths while the eastern apartment, with fountains of rose-water, was used as a dressing room.

West of the baths the tiny **Moti Masjid**, built by Aurangzeb, is beautifully proportioned, but desperately in need of maintenance. In the gardens beyond, pavilions stand among symmetrical flowerbeds and neat lawns intersected by stream-beds that once bubbled with water drawn from the Yamuna.

Jami Masjid

Old Delhi's red and white **Jami Masjid** (Rs10; Rs50 extra for camera), dominating the surrounding markets around 500m to the west of the Red Fort, may look huge from a distance, but feels nothing short of immense once you've climbed the wide staircases to the arched gateways and entered the open courtyard, large enough to accommodate the bending bodies of up to 25,000 worshippers. This is India's largest mosque, designed by the eminent architect Shah Jahan, and built by a workforce of 5000 between 1644 and 1656. Originally called Masjid-i-Jahanuma ("mosque commanding a view of the world"), this grand structure stands on Bho Jhala, one of Shahjahanabad's two hills, and looks east to the sprawling Red Fort, and down on the seething streets of Old Delhi all around. Broad red sandstone staircases lead to gateways on the east, north and southern sides, where all visitors must remove their shoes and pay the entrance fee. If you're wearing shorts, you'll have to rent a *lunghi* to wrap around your legs and hide your knees.

Once inside the stadium-like courtyard, your eyes will be drawn to the three bulbous marble domes crowning the **main prayer hall** on the west side (facing Mecca), fronted by a series of high cusped arches, and sheltering the mihrab, the central niche in the west wall reserved for the prayer leader. Worshippers use the prayer hall on most days, extending into the courtyard and even filling it on Fridays and other holy days. The pool in the centre is used for washing feet, hands and faces before prayer. At each corner of the square yard a slender minaret crowned with a marble dome rises to the sky, and it's well worth climbing the **tower** south of the main sanctuary (Rs10; Rs5 extra for camera) for an unrivalled view over Delhi, ancient and modern. In the northeast corner a white shrine protects a collection of Muhammad's relics, shrouded in pungent rose petals and watched over by keepers who are keen to reveal the contents, for a small baksheesh: two sections of the Koran written on deerskin by relatives of the prophet, a red beard-hair of Muhammad's, his sandals, and his "footprint" miraculously embedded in a marble slab.

Digambara Jain temple and Jain Bird Hospital

Delhi's oldest **Digambara Jain temple**, directly opposite the entrance to the Red Fort, at the east end of Chandni Chowk, was built in 1526, but has been modified and added to ever since, and remains a haven of tranquillity amid the noise and chaos of the main street. Though not as ornate as the fine temples in Gujarat and Rajasthan, it does boast detailed carvings, and gilded paintwork in the antechambers surrounding the main shrine to Parshvanath, the twenty-third *tirthankara*. You'll have to remove your shoes, and hand them over with your bags and all leather articles to a kiosk before entering.

The **Jain Bird Hospital** (free but donations are appreciated), in the temple courtyard, puts into practice the Jain principle that all life is sacred, admitting up to sixty sick birds per day. It serves as a rescue sanctuary for partridges, caught and wounded by fowlers and bought in bulk by Jain merchants who bring them here to recover, and there are separate wards for pigeons, parrots, sparrows (notoriously vulnerable to deadly whirring ceiling fans) and domestic fowl. Squirrels, who will not hurt the birds, are also treated here, but birds of prey are seen on a strictly outpatient basis, as they are not vegetarian. Most of the cages are home to pigeons with a disease that brings on paralysis. As their condition improves they are moved to larger cages closer to the roof, and eventually released.

Gauri Shankar temple

Tucked behind fragrant mounds of marigolds, roses and jasmine blossoms sold on Chandni Chowk just west of the Jain temple, the large marble **Gauri Shankar temple**, dominated by its eight-hundred-year-old *lingam*, is Delhi's holiest Shiva temple. Devotees enter up a narrow flight of marble steps, flanked by pillars carved with chains and bells, that opens onto a spacious courtyard, always a scene of animated devotional activity. Inside, offerings for sale include *bilva* (wood apple) leaves, *chandan* (sandalwood paste), marigolds, red powder, rice, and cotton threads. The main sanctuary holds bejewelled statues of Gauri (Parvati) and Shankar (Shiva) standing beneath a silver canopy, and the ancient brown stone *lingam* resting on a marble *yoni* encased in silver and draped with silver serpents. Shrines to other deities line the south wall.

The bazaars of old Delhi

Old Delhi's trading is carried out in bustling **bazaars**, where shops huddle together in open houses or beneath makeshift awnings, and between them stock an incredible array of goods ranging from fish and spices to currency garlands and giant candles. If you take time to amble down streets branching off **Chandni Chowk** and running south of the mosque, you'll come across lively markets of all kinds, each concentrating on one particular trade.

Chor Bazaar A curious bazaar behind the old ramparts of the Red Fort, which comes to life on Sundays to trade a mix of "secondhand" and allegedly stolen goods.

Kinari Bazaar A colourful street set behind the *guradwara* on Chandni Chowk, and connected to the main road by Dariba Kalan, "the street of incomparable pearl", which is the centre for jewellers. The shops in Kinari Bazaar overflow with bright wedding finery, including garlands made of rupee notes, grooms' turbans, rosettes and glistening tinsel used by Hindus, Christians and Muslims in vivid and noisy marriage ceremonies. In October (the month of Ram Lila) the shops stock props for the annual theatre productions – bows and arrows, cardboard swords and fake heads for the evil nine-headed King Ravana.

Naya Bazaar Spice market on Khari Baoli, near Fatehpuri Masjid, clouded with the fine dust of flour and spices, and heavy with rich aromas. The nuts, spices and dried fruits sold here are said to be the best in Delhi, and many are sold to wholesalers by the sack; weighed-down porters load their burdens onto ox carts which trundle off to other parts of the city through the mass of motorized traffic. The covered **Gadodia Market**, just off Khari Baoli, is a gathering place for wholesalers who weigh their goods on huge old-fashioned scales. Among the spices and condiments you can find aniseed, turmeric, pomegranate, dried mangoes, ginger, saffron, reetha nuts (used for washing hair and cleaning silver), lotus seeds, pickles, sugars, chutneys and edible leaves of silver paper used to coat sweets and cakes.

Raj Ghat

When Shah Jahan established his city in 1638, its eastern edges bordered the River Yamuna, and a line of *ghats*, or steps leading to the water, was installed along the riverbanks. *Ghats* have been used in India for centuries, primarily for worship, but also for washing clothes and bathing, and for the final ritual, cremation. **Raj Ghat**, the site of the cremations of three of modern India's most revered figures, Mahatma Gandhi (1948), Indira Gandhi (1984) and her son Rajiv (1991), is more of a park than a *ghat*, lying well away from the river bank. The Mahatma's *samadhi*, a low black plinth, receives the attentions and prayers of an almost constant stream of visitors. Walk northwards from here to the quieter memorials of the two former prime ministers, Rajiv remembered in a striking frieze and his mother marked by a red-grey stone monolith. You can continue through the park all the way to the southern end of the Red Fort, roughly 1km to the north.

Mahatma Gandhi is further remembered at his *samadhi* by prayers held every Friday evening, and on the anniversaries of his birth and death (Oct 2 & Jan 30), and by the small **Gandhi Memorial Museum** (daily except Thurs 9.30am–5.30pm) opposite Raj Ghat. On Sundays you can watch a film on

Meena Bazaar A distinctively Islamic bazaar of cramped shops clustered around the base of the Jami Masjid, full of clothes, domestic implements and smells not found in Hindu regions of the city. Here you can buy *burquas*, *dupattas*, *topis*, caged chickens, bangles, kebabs, sticky sweetmeats and devotional pictures for shrines.

Car Parts Bazaar South of the Jami Masjid, the stalls that make up this bazaar stock, or rather pile high, new and secondhand automobile parts from all models, ranging from speedometers and the all-important horn to complete engines.

Chawri Bazaar Named after the Marathi word *chawri* (meeting place), this street, running west from the Jami Masjid, was once flanked by huge mansions which were destroyed by the British after the Mutiny. In the nineteenth century it was famous for its "dancing girls", who looked into the streets below from arched windows and balconies and beckoned men with enticing glances; they were moved out by the Delhi Municipal Corporation in the twentieth century. Today the shops specialize in copper and brass Buddhas, Vishnus, Krishnas, bells, lamps, ashtrays, masks and boxes.

The long road, **Nai Sarak**, which connects Chawri Bazaar with Chandni Chowk, is lined with nineteenth- and twentieth-century buildings whose lower storeys are used for making and selling paper, and houses shops stocking educational books and stationery.

Kalan Mahal A small market street further south of the Jami Masjid near the Kalan Masjid, Kalan Mahal is the gathering place for brass polishers, and also has stalls displaying intricately carved bone necklaces.

Poultry and Fish Markets East of Kalan Mahal the air is filled with the unmistakable smell of fish. Piled high on lorries and stored in barrels of ice, transported between cramped stalls on the heads of porters, every imaginable kind of fish is traded here before finding its way onto plates all over the city. In between fish stalls, chickens lie cramped in stacked cages before being slaughtered and plucked. Head towards **Netaji Subash Marg** to get into the thick of the poultry scene, and watch out for the "cul-de-sacs" in the fish market. While most traders sleep at the back of their pungent patches, few visitors can stand more than half an hour in Old Delhi's smelliest corner.

Gandhi's political and personal life (March–Oct Hindi 6pm, English 7pm; Nov–Feb 4 & 5pm) after taking in the displays of photographs and writings in the museum.

Firoz Shah Kotla

The prosperous fifth city of Delhi, **Firozabad**, founded in 1354, stretched from the north ridge to Hauz Khas in the south; today few traces survive save the remains of the palace of Firoz Shah Kotla, set amid ornamental gardens 500m east of Delhi Gate. Its most incongruous and yet distinctive element is the single polished sandstone **Ashokan Column** (third century BC), carried down the Yamuna by raft from Ambala to grace a palace that is now a crumbling ruin. The 14m-high column, the second brought to Delhi, continues to protrude above the surroundings, withstanding the ravages of time and dominating the ill-kept gardens. Next to a *baoli* (step-well) lie the massive ruins of a mosque which once accommodated over 10,000 worshippers; Timur (Tamerlane) is said to have been so impressed by it that it served as the model for his great mosque in Samarkand. Today, surrounded by large and busy roads, the gardens and their monuments lie almost forgotten, and few tourists stop by.

North of the Old City

Just north of Old Delhi, not far from the Inter-state Bus Terminal, the peaceful **Qudsia Gardens** are a fading reminder of the magnificent pleasure gardens commissioned in the mid-eighteenth century by Queen Qudsia, favourite mistress of Muhammad Shah, and mother of Ahmed Shah. The original mosque still stands, but part of the park was taken over by the British Freemasons, who built a hall and banned Indians from entering the park in the afternoons. There's also a Hindu monument here; a mounted figure represents the valiant Pratap Singh who is famed for his unfaltering defiance of Akbar. Near the gardens, on Commissioner's Lane, is **Mother Teresa's Orphanage**, "Missionaries of Charity" where voluntary help is welcomed (see p.90).

Just west of Qudsia Gardens, on Qudsia Road, is Delhi's oldest burial ground, **Nicholson Cemetery**, named after Brigadier General John Nicholson, who led the attacks on Delhi in 1857 when the British were striving to regain the city from the Nationalists. The graveyard is still used, but most of the headstones show the names of British residents killed defending this outpost of the British Empire, or stricken as young children by fatal diseases at the beginning of the twentieth century.

South Delhi

Most of the early settlements of Delhi, including its first cities, are to be found not in "Old Delhi" but in **SOUTH DELHI**, the area south of Connaught Place and Rajpath. Although the rapid expansion of suburban Delhi is swallowing up the countryside, the area remains littered with monuments from the past, and pockets of almost untouched rural peace make it a fascinating blend of the contemporary, the pastoral and the historic. This mix of urban and rural is at its most startling in the housing enclaves and shopping precincts, such as the fashionable **Hauz Khas**, that have sprung up over the last few years throughout the vast area of South Delhi.

While the first Muslim kingdoms built their cities on the foundations of those settlements they conquered, shaping the **Qutb Minar Complex**, later dynasties created their own capitals at **Siri**, **Tughluqabad**, and **Jahanpanah** as well as Firozabad (see p.129), north along the river, and **Shergarh**, around the **Purana Qila**. **Humayun's Tomb**, which heralded the great Moghul period in architecture, is not far from the elegant **Lodi Gardens** and one of the holiest shrines of Sufism, **Hazrat Nizamuddin**. Today, the chaotic and rampant development of South Delhi has engulfed many of its ancient monuments leaving some to rack and ruin and others isolated deep within urban sprawl. Only the most spectacular and robust of Delhi's monuments are protected from the city's immutable urge to grow.

Purana Qila

The majestic fortress of **Purana Qila** (daily dawn to dusk; Rs2), whose crumbling ramparts dominate busy **Mathura Road**, 4km southeast of Connaught Place, is often said to stand on the site of **Indraprastha**, the city of the Pandavas, of *Mahabharata* fame. More certainly, it was the centre of the sixth city of Delhi, created by Humayun, the second Moghul emperor, as **Din-Panah**, and renamed **Shergarh** by Sher Shah, who briefly displaced him. Purana Qila is served by buses between Delhi Gate and Sundernagar, such as #423 and #438. The #411 continues to Nizamuddin, and #482 goes on to Kalkaji.

Two principal buildings survive to hint at the former glories of the fortress. The **Qila-i-Kuhna Masjid** is one of Sher Shah's finest monuments.

Constructed in 1541 in the Afghan style, influenced by Indo-Islamic architecture, it consists of five elegant arches, embellished with white and black marble to complement the red sandstone. The **Sher Mandal**, a red sandstone octagonal observatory and library, was the scene of the death of Humayun, just a year after he defeated Sher Shah and returned to power. He stumbled down its treacherously steep steps in 1556 as he answered the *muezzin's* call to prayer; visitors today can climb to the top for panoramic views of Delhi and the River Yamuna to the east. The fortress is entered through the lofty south gate, **Lal Darwaza**, just inside which a small museum houses sculpture from the Mauryan era (daily 8am–6.30pm; free).

The few other remains of the once-extensive sixth city include the grey and red arch known as **Sher Shah's Gate**, and **Khair-ul-Manzil Masjid**, built in 1561 during the reign of Akbar for use as a *madrasa* or seminary, whose cloistered courtyard is reached via an elegant large sandstone gateway opposite Lal Darwaza and the zoo.

The Yamuna formerly flowed along the eastern base of Purana Qila; the moats it fed are now dry, save a lake to the west used for boating. During the painful Partition of India in 1947, hordes of Muslim refugees gathered within the confines of the fort, in extremely unhygienic conditions and amid great trepidation, to await transportation to the newly created nation of Pakistan.

Delhi Zoo

Below the southern ramparts of the Purana Qila, the open-air enclosures and cages of **Delhi Zoo** (daily except Fri: April–Oct 8am–6pm; Nov–March 9am–5pm; Rs40 [Rs5], Rs50 extra for video camera) cover an extensive area. A little toy train chugs through the grounds, stopping regularly so you can hop on and off as you like. The white tigers are the longstanding attraction but animal-lovers will be disappointed by the conditions in which the big cats are kept.

Lodi Gardens

The leafy, pleasant **Lodi Gardens** off Lodi Road (previously Lady Willingdon Park; daily 5am–8pm; free), 4km south of Connaught Place, form part of a belt of fifteenth- and sixteenth-century monuments that now stand incongruously amid golf greens, large bungalows and privileged estates. The park is especially full in the early mornings and early evenings, when middle-class fitness enthusiasts come for brisk walks or to jog through the manicured gardens against a backdrop of much-graffitied medieval monuments. The gardens, a Rs15 **auto** ride from India Gate, also contain the **National Bonsai Park**, which has a fine selection of diminutive trees. The best time to come is at sunset, when the light is soft and the tombs are all lit up.

Near the centre of the gardens is the imposing **Bara Gumbad** (large dome), a square late-fifteenth-century tomb capped by the eponymous dome. While its monotonous exterior is relieved by grey and black stones, the inside is adorned with painted stuccowork. The mosque alongside was built in 1494, with a rectangular prayer hall faced by five arched openings. Heavily ornamented with coloured tiles, foliage and Koranic inscriptions, the tapering Tughluq-style minarets next to the mihrab seem to herald the octagonal towers of the coming Sur and Moghul periods. **Shish Gumbad** (glazed dome), a similar tomb 50m north, still bears a few traces of the blue tiles liberally used to form friezes below the cornice and above the entrance. Inside, plasterwork is inscribed with ornate Koranic inscriptions.

The octagonal **tomb of Muhammad Shah** (1434–44) of the Sayyid dynasty, stands 300m southwest of Bara Gumbad, surrounded by verandas and pierced by arches and sloping buttresses. Accented by turrets at each corner, a sixteen-sided drum supports a majestic dome. Enclosed within high walls and a square garden, 300m north of Bara Gumbad, the **tomb of Sikandar Lodi** (1517–18) repeats the octagonal theme, with a central chamber encircled by a veranda. **Athpula** (eight piers), a sixteenth-century ornamental bridge, lies east, in the northwest corner of the park.

Tibet House

Tibet House, 1 Institutional Area, Lodi Road (Mon–Fri 9.30am–1pm & 2–5.30pm; free), a cultural centre that organizes seminars and monthly lectures mostly in Hindi, also has a small and limited museum of Tibetan art, worth a visit if only for its beautiful *thangkas* (painted scrolls; admission Rs5). Other objects on display include old currency notes, costumes, objects of prayer and musical instruments; the shop sells the usual mix of clothes, jewellery, medicines, incense and curios.

Nizamuddin

Now engulfed by a busy road network and plush suburbs, the *mahalla* (neighbourhood) of **Nizamuddin** is almost isolated from the rest of the city; to enter it is like passing through a time warp into the Middle Ages. The heart of the village is just off the busy Mathura Road, 6km south of Connaught Place, and easily accessible by public transport such as the #454 bus, which passes Paharganj and Palika Bazaar. At the centre of the village lies one of Sufism's greatest shrines, pulsating with life and drawing devotees from far and wide through its narrowing arteries.

Alleys lead past busy restaurants catering for a steady stream of pilgrims and with shops selling flowers and accoutrements of worship, to arrive through a narrow gateway at the marble courtyard of **Hazrat Nizamuddin Dargah**, the tomb of the fourth saint of the Chistiya order, Sheikh Nizamuddin Aulia (1236–1325). The shrine was built the year the sheikh died, but has been through several renovations, and the present mausoleum dates from 1562. A distinctive white marble dome, ornamented with vertical black lines, crowns its small square chamber surrounded by marble-faced verandas. Lattice screens and arches in the inner sanctum surround the actual tomb, enclosed by a marble rail and a canopy of mother-of-pearl. Religious song and music play an important role among the Chistiyas, and *qawwals* (bards) gather to sing in the evenings (especially on Thursdays and feast days). Sheikh Nizamuddin's disciple, the poet and chronicler **Amir Khusrau** – considered to be the first Urdu poet and the founder of *khyal*, the most common form of north Indian classical music – lies in a contrasting red sandstone tomb in front of his master's mausoleum.

Anyone entering either building should cover their legs, shoulders and heads (handkerchiefs or caps can be bought or borrowed from one of the stalls selling offerings). Sheikhs hover about ready to assist and take donations from visitors. Twice a year, on the anniversaries of the deaths of Sheikh Nizamuddin and Amir Khusrau, an *urs* (religious fair) draws thousands of pilgrims, and Nizamuddin resounds to the sound of *qawwali*.

The oldest building in the area, the red sandstone mosque of **Jam-at Khana Masjid**, looms over the main *dargah* on its western side (closed to women). It was built in 1325 by Khizr Khan, the son of Ala-ud-din-Khalji. Enclosed by marble lattice screens next to Amir Khusrau's mausoleum, the tomb of **Princess Jahanara**, the favourite daughter of Shah Jahan, is topped by a hollow filled with grass in compliance with her wish to have nothing but grass covering her grave. At the north gate of the *dargah*'s compound is a holy *baoli* (step-well), next to the mosque **Chini-ka-Burj** (tower of tiles) named for its upper chamber profusely decorated with coloured tiles.

Prominent Muslims buried in Nizamuddin include **Mirza Ghalib**, the nineteenth-century poet whose work lives on in *ghazals* (devotional and love poetry, often set to music) popular throughout the Urdu-speaking world. Alongside is the elegant marble pavilion of **Chausath Khamba** (sixty-four pillars), built in 1625.

Humayun's Tomb

Close to the medieval Muslim centre of **Nizamuddin** and 2km from Purana Qila, **Humayun's Tomb** (daily dawn to dusk; Rs5) stands at the crossroads of the Lodi and Mathura roads, 500m from Nizamuddin railway station which is one stop from New Delhi station on the suburban line. Delhi's first Moghul tomb was constructed from 1564 onwards, after the death of the second Moghul emperor, under the watchful eye of Haji Begum, Humayun's senior widow and mother of Akbar, who camped here for the duration. The grounds were later used to inter several prominent Moghuls, and served as a refuge for the last emperor, Bahadur Shah II, captured here by the British in 1857.

Though later eclipsed by the Jami Masjid and the Taj Mahal, its sombre, Persian-style elegance marks this as one of Delhi's finest historic sites. Constructed of red sandstone, inlaid with black and white marble, on a commanding podium looking towards the Yamuna, it stands in the centre of the formal *charbagh*, or quartered garden. The enclosure is dissected into quarters by causeways and channels, and each square is further quartered. Rising on an arcaded platform, the octagonal structure is crowned with a double dome that soars to a height of 38m – the inner shell forms the vaulted ceiling.

Qawwali

Of all Indian art forms, qawwali, whose prime purpose is to gain *hal* (spiritual ecstasy) through devotional song, is among the most adaptable and versatile, appearing as popular entertainment at modern weddings and on concert platforms. The form has been embraced by the world music scene: the late Nusrat Fateh Ali Khan gained an international reputation with a *qawwali* repertoire that ranged from the traditional to experimental fusion. Musically, *qawwali* is linked to the north Indian classical form of vocal music, *khyal*, deriving its melody from such sources as classic *ragas* (modal compositions) and its own modal systems based on central Asian roots. Comprising a chorus led by solo singing accompanied by clapping and usually a harmonium combined with *dholak* (double-membraned barrel drum) and *tabla* (paired hand-drums), the resulting hypnotic rhythm can inspire its audience into a state of *mast* (spiritual intoxication), manifested by wild swaying and swinging of the head. The simple but effective drum patterns used include *qawwali tal*, *dadra* and *keherwa* – respectively four-, six- and eight-beat rhythmic cycles.

Most performers, or *qawwals*, are hereditary musicians who trace their lineage back to **Amir Khusrau**, to whom several songs are attributed. Some compositions have become universal hymns, such as the haunting *Dam-a-dam mast Qalandar* (constantly intoxicated Qalandar) and the robust *hamd* (a eulogy in praise of God, the Prophet, or a saint), *Allah Hu*. Musical gatherings, or *Mehfil-e Sama*, are held regularly, usually on Thursday evenings, in the main *dargahs* of Delhi such as Nizamuddin and Mehrauli, with especial poignancy during the *urs* (anniversary) of the saint in question. *Qawwali* in front of the shrine is rarely as elaborate as that on stage, but far more moving in its powerful and simple devotion.

Porches on each side rise to 12.2-metre-high pointed arches, flanked by outer bays and recessed windows with lattice screens of stone and marble. Below the cenotaph, inside the building, are the graves of Humayun and Haji Begum.

Among tombs of uncertain origin nearby is **Nila Gumbad** (blue dome), an octagonal tomb with a dome of blue tiles, to the southeast outside the enclosure. Nila Gumbad was supposedly built by one of Akbar's nobles to honour a faithful servant but may possibly predate Humayun's Tomb. Within the grounds southeast of the main mausoleum, another impressive square tomb has a double dome and two graves inscribed with verses from the Koran. It is tentatively considered to be that of **Babur**, the first Moghul emperor and father of Humayun. Immediately south of Bu Halima's Garden (who exactly Bu Halima was remains a mystery), which marks the entrance to Humayun's Tomb, the central dome of the tomb of **Isa Khan**, a nobleman of Sher Shah, rises from a 32-sided drum.

Safdarjang's Tomb

The tomb of **Safdarjang** (daily dawn to dusk; Rs5), the Moghul viceroy of Avadh under Muhammad Shah (1719–48), and the father of the Nawab of Avadh, Shuja-ud-Daula, stands at the junction of Lodi Road and Aurobindo Marg, 5km southwest of Connaught Place; take bus #560 from Jantar Mantar. Built between 1753 and 1774, it is one of the last in the tradition of Moghul garden tombs. At the centre of another *charbagh*, reached through a grand double-storeyed gateway off a busy main road to the east, the double-storeyed mausoleum, built of red and buff sandstone and relieved by marble, rises on a dramatic platform overlooking the adjacent airport of the Delhi Flying Club. However, its inordinate height and bulbous dome somehow lack the grandeur of Humayun's Tomb. A single cenotaph in the square central hall marks the underground tombs of Safdarjang and his wife. Immediately to the south is the site of the battlefield where Timur (Tamerlane) routed Muhammad Shah Tughluq in 1398.

Hauz Khas

Hauz Khas, the Soho of Delhi, is a wealthy suburban development, packed with boutiques and restaurants, 12km southwest of Connaught Place. The "village", as it is known, is just off Aurobindo Marg (or the Delhi–Mehrauli Road), which leads from the centre to the Qutb Minar Complex, and adjacent to a pleasant deer park. The road through the shopping enclave leads to the ruins of Ala-ud-din-Khalji's large tank (enclosed reservoir) known as Hauz-i-Alai, built early in the fourteenth century to supply the inhabitants of Siri, Delhi's second city. It was expanded almost fifty years later by Firoz Shah Tughlak, who added a two-storey *madrasa* (seminary), and a mosque at its northern end. The L-shaped *madrasa* providing grand views of the tank was constructed with latticed windows, and deep stone niches for books.

In among the anonymous tombs scattered throughout the area is that of Firoz Shah himself, situated on the edge of the tank. Its high walls, lofty dome, and doorway spanned by a lintel with a stone railing outside, are fine examples of Indian traditions effectively blended with Islamic architecture. At dawn every day, the surrounding woodlands and the bed of the immense tank, once the site of Timur's camp, come alive with Delhi-ites out walking, practising yoga and jogging; in the evenings, Hauz Khas's salubrious restaurants attract diners from all over the city (see p.141).

Moth-ki-Masjid

The **Moth-ki-Masjid**, built during the reign of Sikandar Lodi (1488–1517), is now all but abandoned, isolated in a rural setting within the rapidly spreading suburbs of south Delhi, 2km from Hauz Khas off the Delhi–Mehrauli Road. A milestone in the evolution of the Moghul mosque, its three-domed prayer hall, ornate mihrab and arches stand on a raised plinth, enclosed by walls pierced by an elegant red sandstone gate to the east. Legend has it that Sikandar Lodi picked a grain of *moth* (a type of lentil) which was then sown by his minister Miyan Bhuwa; the bumper crop multiplied again and again and so financed the construction of the mosque. Some houses in the village of the same name still have mangers.

Khirki-ki-Masjid

Firoz Shah's **Khirki-ki-Masjid**, "The Mosque of Windows", famous for its heavy stone lattice windows, lies in the middle of one of South Delhi's villages close to the site of Jahanpanah, Delhi's fourth city, 4km east of Qutb Minar and 13km south of Connaught Place. The battered bastions of the squat double-storeyed mosque, flanked by short minarets, give it a fortress-like aspect. Its unusual roof – there are only two covered mosques in north India – consisting of 25 squares capped by domes and flat sections, is open at the centre to allow light into a dark pillared courtyard, plagued by bats.

Baha'i Temple and Kalkaji

Often compared to the Sydney Opera House, on open ground atop Kalkaji Hill 12km southeast of Connaught Place, Delhi's modern **Baha'i Temple** (daily: April–Sept 9am–7pm; Oct–March 9.30am–5.30pm; closed to tourists during morning and evening prayers Tues–Sun 10am–4pm) has become yet another symbol of the city attracting a steady stream of visitors. Dominating the haphazard suburban sprawl, 27 spectacular giant white petals of Rajasthani Macrana marble in the shape of an unfolding lotus spring from nine pools and walkways, to symbolize the nine unifying spiritual paths of the Baha'i faith. You're welcome to meditate inside the impressive but plain central hall, which rises to a height of 34.27m without the distraction of supporting columns. In each of the petal alcoves are thought-provoking extracts of the Baha'i holy scriptures. Set amid well-maintained gardens, the temple is at its most impressive when the rays of the setting sun catch the lotus petals. You'll be asked to remove your shoes on entering, and remain silent, although don't expect solitude as this is a popular place.

The domed twelve-sided *shakti* **Kalkaji** temple (also known as Kalika or Kalka Devi) lies on the same hill as the Baha'i temple. Though of no architectural significance, this popular Kali shrine is at the heart of a village that has somehow ignored the march of time, and the Hindu worship of its *mahants* (important *sadhus*) makes a fascinating contrast with the brash new faith of the Baha'is. There is a festival at the temple every October, drawing thousands of devotees. Kalkaji is a major bus depot – among buses from the centre are #433 and #440 from Connaught Place.

Ashoka's Rock Edict

The emperor **Ashoka's Rock Edict** was discovered in 1966, engraved on a rock overlooking the Yamuna near Srinivaspuri, 11km southeast of Connaught Place, not far from Kalkaji. A ten-line epigraph in the ancient Brahmi script, one of many such placed at important sites and crossroads throughout Ashoka's vast empire, the inscription proves that Delhi was occupied during the

Mauryan period, prior to both Muslim and Rajput settlement. It states that the emperor's exertions in the cause of *dharma* had brought the people of India (Jambudvipa) closer to the gods; and that through their efforts, irrespective of their station, this attainment could be increased even further.

Tughluqabad

On a rocky escarpment, 8km east of Qutb Minar and 15km southeast of Connaught Place on the Mehrauli–Badarpur Road, stand the crumbling 6.5-kilometre-long battlements of the third city of Delhi, **Tughluqabad**, built during the short reign of Ghiyas-ud-din Tughluq (1321–25). After the king's death the city was deserted, probably due to the lack of a clean water source nearby. The huge ruins are almost entirely abandoned, overgrown with scrubland and home to nomadic Gujars and rhesus monkeys – which is seen by some as a fulfilment of a curse by the Sufi saint, Sheikh Nizamuddin Aulia.

Divided into three main portions, Tughluqabad had its high-walled citadel to the south near the present entrance off the main road; only a long underground passage, the ruins of several halls and a tower now remain. The grid pattern of some of the city streets to the north is still traceable, while the palace area is to the southwest. The southernmost of its thirteen gates still looks down on a causeway, breached by the modern road, which rises above the flood plain, to link the fortress with **Ghiyas-ud-din Tughluq's tomb**. Itself resembling a small fortress, it has withstood the ravages of time, rising beyond a massive red sandstone gateway on a high plinth, surrounded by pentagonal stone walls. The distinctive mausoleum consists of sloping walls topped with a marble dome and contains the graves of Ghiyas-ud-din, his wife, their son Muhammad Shah II, and even what is purported to be Ghiyas-ud-din's favourite dog – although dogs are traditionally held to be unclean. The later fortress of **Adilabad**, built by Muhammad Shah II in much the same style as his father's citadel and now in ruins, can be seen on a hillock to the southeast.

Tughluqabad is awkward to get to by **bus**; either take #460 from Jantar Mantar to Badarpur, and change onto a Mehrauli-bound service, or take #505 to Mehrauli/Qutb Minar Complex, and catch a bus going east.

Qutb Minar Complex

Above the foundations of **Lal Kot**, settled in the eighth century by the Tomara Rajputs and developed in the twelfth century by the Chauhans, the first monuments of Muslim India, now known as the **Qutb Minar Complex** (daily dawn to dusk; Rs10), stand in well-tended grounds 13km south of Connaught Place; to get here take bus #505 from Ajmeri Gate. One of Delhi's most famous landmarks, the fluted red sandstone tower of the Qutb Minar tapers upwards from the ruins, covered with intricate carvings and deeply inscribed verses from the Koran, to a height of 72.5m.

Work on the Qutb Minar started in 1199 as Qutb-ud-din Aibak's victory tower, celebrating the advent of the Muslim dominance of Delhi (and much of the subcontinent) that was to endure until 1857. For Qutb-ud-din, who died four years after gaining power, it marked the eastern extremity of the Islamic faith, casting the shadow of God over east and west. It was also a minaret, from which the *muezzin* called the faithful to prayer. Only the first storey of the Qutb Minar has been ascribed to Qutb-ud-din's short reign; the other four were built by his successor Iltutmish, and the top was restored in 1369 by Firoz Shah, who used marble to face the red sandstone. Access to the balconies via the staircase inside has been closed after a spate of accidents and suicides.

Adjacent to the tower lie the ruins of India's first mosque, **Quwwat-ul-Islam** ("the might of Islam"), built by Qutb-ud-din using the remains of 27 Hindu and Jain temples and the help of Hindu artisans – their influence can be seen in the detail of the masonry and the indigenous corbelled arches. Steps lead to an impressive courtyard flanked by cloisters and supported by pillars unmistakably taken from a Hindu temple and adapted to accord with strict Islamic law forbidding iconic worship – all the faces of the decorative figures carved into the columns have been removed. Especially fine ornamental arches, rising as high as 16m, remain of what was once the prayer hall. Beautifully carved sandstone screens, combining Koranic calligraphy with the Indian lotus, form a facade immediately to the west of the mosque, facing Mecca. Iltutmish and his successors extended the mosque, enlarging the prayer hall and the cloisters and introducing such Islamic architectural traditions as geometric designs, calligraphy, glazed tiles set in brick, and squinches (arches set diagonally to a square to support a dome).

In complete contrast to the mainly Islamic surroundings, an **Iron Pillar** (7.2m) stands in the corner of the mosque, bearing fourth-century Sanskrit inscriptions of the Gupta period attributing it to the memory of King Chandragupta II (373–413). Once topped with an image of the Hindu bird god, Garuda, the extraordinary and virtually rust-free pillar, made of 98 percent pure iron, is a puzzle to metallurgists. It must have been transplanted here, but its origins remain hazy. Tradition has it that anyone who can encircle the column with their hands behind their back will have their wishes granted, although today the pillar is fenced off from eager fortune-seekers.

Ala-i-Darwaza, a mausoleum-like gateway with stone lattice screens, was added by Ala-ud-din Khalji (1296–1316). Its inlaid marble embellishments are owed to an influx of Pathan artisans from Byzantine Turkey, and the import of Seljuk influences – the true arches were the first in India. The south entrance to the complex is marked by yet another tower, **Alai Minar**. Planned as grander and larger than the Qutb Minar, it was left abandoned after the construction of its 24.5-metre-high first storey.

On a plinth west of Quwwat-ul-Islam, the **tomb of Iltutmish**, built in 1235 by the ruler himself, was the first Muslim mausoleum in India – something new to the subcontinent, as Hindus cremate their dead rather than bury them. A relatively plain exterior blending Indian and Muslim styles, with three ornate arches, hides an interior 9m square with geometric arabesque patterns combined with calligraphy and lotus and wheel motifs. The square red sandstone chamber was once covered by the dome that now lies in pieces around the site; only its corbelled squinches bear witness to a flawed method of early Indo-Islamic building.

Ala-ud-din Khalji's tomb and **madrasa** (theological college), lie on the southwest perimeter of Quwwat-ul-Islam, their L-shaped structure reflecting the Seljuk influence. To the southeast of the Ala-i-Darwaza is the small and attractive tomb of the Sufi saint Imam Muhammad Ali, better known as **Imam Zamin**, a native of Turkestan who came to India during the reign of Sikandar Lodi (1488–1517).

The octagonal Moghul tomb of Muhammad Quli Khan, one of Akbar's courtiers, perched above the scrubland 150m southeast of the Qutb Minar, was occupied and converted by **Charles Metcalfe**, resident at the Moghul court, into a country house but is now in ruins. Another crumbling Raj-era house nearby still boasts a very ornamental English fireplace and swimming tank. Outside the complex, north of the Qutb Minar, **Adham Khan's tomb** stands on the remains of the walls of Lal Kot. A general in Akbar's army, Khan was hurled from the ramparts of Agra Fort on the orders of the emperor after some murderous court feuding. You can get a particularly good view of both the tomb and the Qutb complex from the roof of the Church of St John, an incongruous little chapel with an Anglican nave, monastic cloisters and a Hindu *chhapra* (tower), tucked down a lane opposite the tomb entrance.

Rail Transport Museum

Venerable trains remain in use throughout the country, but to see the cream of India's royal coaches and her oldest engines, you should head for the **Rail Transport Museum** in Chanakyapuri (Tues–Sun 9.30am–5.30pm; Rs5, Rs10 extra for camera); it's on bus route #620 from New Delhi railway station. Outside, 27 locomotives and 17 carriages, including an armoured train, stand on short tracks in the open air. Look out for the ornate gold-painted saloon car of the Maharaja of Baroda (1886), the teak carriage of the Maharaja of Mysore, trimmed in gold and ivory, and the cabin used by the Prince of Wales in 1876. Steps beside each carriage enable visitors to peer in without damaging the well-preserved interiors.

The covered section of the museum is a delight for train buffs, with models of famous engines and coaches, explanations of the workings of narrow- and broad-gauge lines, displays of old tickets, and even the skull of an elephant hit by a train near Calcutta in 1894. The pride of the museum is a model of India's very first train, a steam engine which made its inaugural journey of 21 miles from Mumbai to Thane in 1853. Trainspotters who wish to delve deeper can ask the curators to open the library.

Eating

Delhi-ites love to eat out and have a large variety of **restaurants** and cuisine from all over the world from which to choose. There's something for every budget, from delicious Indian snacks at **roadside** stalls in Paharganj, Palika Bazaar and Janpath, to traditional north Indian cuisine at one of Delhi's many celebrated restaurants, to **Western** food at the likes of instantly recognizable names such as *Wimpy*, *McDonald's*, *Pizza Express*, *TGIF* and *Pizza Hut*. The vast **buffets** of luxury hotels are worth the splurge, their **coffee shops** are surprisingly affordable and, if you can afford it, their restaurants superlative; their **bakeries** are also excellent (open to non-guests). Many specialist restaurants regularly demonstrate expert cooking with themed food festivals (check media listings for current festivals).

Although locals tend to eat around nine, they do not linger; most restaurants close around eleven, but those with bars usually stay open until midnight. If you're looking for a late-night meal, you can either eat in a top hotel, try a snack in Paharganj's round-the-clock rooftop cafés, or head to the markets of south Delhi. Wherever you eat, be careful of the water and salads.

Connaught Place and Central Delhi

Connaught Place has snack bars for quick stops, and plenty of upmarket restaurants, as well as budget sit-down joints that attract a largely Western clientele. Even if you can't afford a meal in an expensive restaurant, it's worth going into air-conditioned comfort and treating yourself to silver-service tea, filter coffee, or a cool milkshake. For patties, sandwiches and take-out meat and veg dishes, head behind the market at the top of Janpath, where you'll find great snacks at incredibly good value. Several familiar fast-food joints are represented in CP and elsewhere in Delhi and there is a new *TGIF*. CP's larger restaurants remain closed on Sunday mornings. Food malls are beginning to be fashionable, with the likes of *Dilli Haat* in south Delhi (see p.141) and *Anarkali Food Plaza*, unfortunately located at the sterile exhibition ground of Pragati Maidan (Gate 3), which comes alive at show time and weekends (5pm–11pm; closed in winter).

The restaurants listed below are marked on the **map** of Connaught Place on p.118.

Café 100, B-Block, Connaught Place. Ice creams galore, plus pizzas, burgers and fries to take away or eat in (standing). Long lunchtime queues; buy a meal ticket before you reach the counter.

Don't Pass Me By, 79 Scindia House. Friendly, inexpensive and tasty veg and non-veg Chinese restaurant just off Janpath, popular with travellers staying nearby. Go early for full-on breakfasts. They also run a reliable travel service.

El Arab, Sansad Marg. Great place for Middle-Eastern dishes on the corner of Sansad Marg and the outer ring of Connaught Place, with prices ranging from medium to high. Tasty hummus, *baba ghanoush* and Lebanese salads in an excellent-value daily lunchtime buffet.

Gaylord, Connaught Place, off Sansad Marg. Originally Delhi's top nightclub, now limited to serving standard but expensive Indian dishes in plush surroundings lit by glittering chandeliers.

Host, F-Block. Air-con relief from the Indian heat, and a good place to sit with a beer, silver-service tea, or strong filter coffee. The standard multi-cuisine, however, is unexciting and meals are over-priced.

Kovil, 2 E-Block, Connaught Place. Fresh, no-smoking restaurant and takeaway serving exclusively south Indian veg dishes, with great *dosas*, and delicious full thalis (around Rs150) at lunchtime.

Kwality, Regal Building, Sansad Marg. High standards of service and hygiene, with good but unspectacular international cuisine; renowned for its *channa batura*, a particular speciality of Delhi.

National, opposite L-Block, Connaught Place. The best of a bunch of inexpensive sit-down restaurants, with great fiery curries, and an endless supply of chapatis.

Nirula's, 135 L-Block, Connaught Place. Choose from the downstairs snack bar (serving packed lunches), the Chinese or tasty multi-cuisine rooms upstairs, or sample some of the fifty flavours of delicious ice cream in the parlour. A second branch on N-Block, near the *Wimpy*, is a popular snack bar with smooth ice-cream shakes.

Parikrama, Kasturba Gandhi Marg. Novel and expensive Indian and Chinese cuisine in a revolving restaurant worth a visit only for the superb views over Delhi; a single rotation takes 100 minutes.

Pizza Express, D-10 Connaught Place. An ambience and menu identical with their restaurants abroad; so are the prices, which makes it expensive for Delhi, especially their drinks menu.

Rodeo, 12 A-Block, Connaught Place. New-Mexican restaurant with Wild West waiters, crooning karaoke, swinging saddle bar stools, pitchers of beer, cocktails, excellent *fajitas* and moderate prices.

Sona Rupa, 46 Janpath. Good Indian and Chinese food, extremely popular with families. No-nonsense prices, and dramatic *dosa*-flinging in the open-fronted kitchen downstairs. Beer and north Indian food upstairs; buy a food ticket at the till and present it to the cooks.

Spice Route, *Hotel Imperial*, Janpath. The beautifully decorated and expensive restaurant specializes in spicy Thai and Kerala cuisine and is widely considered to be one of the best restaurants in Asia.

Standard, 44 Regal Buildings, Connaught Place. Close to the Regal Cinema, with two food halls, one for the best-value south Indian thalis in town, and the other for north Indian and tandoori specials and chilled beer on tap.

Surang, *Alka Hotel*, 16-90 P-Block, Connaught Place. A minor treat – delicious tandoori and Mughlai specialities. Vegetarians should try the *Vega* restaurant (also in the *Alka Hotel*), where purest Indian veg dishes are served with ginger *kulcha*.

United Coffee House, 15 E-Block, Connaught Place. Together with the *Host*, this is a long-standing favourite, and does great coffee and cold beer. The food is very good and portions are ample, but as a whole it's overpriced.

Zen, 25 B-Block, Connaught Place. Excellent Chinese and Japanese meals served in a leisurely and traditional style, with chopsticks, and Western snacks (3–7pm). Distinctly upper-class, with prices to match, and a selection of wines, spirits and beers.

Paharganj and Ram Nagar

Food comes inexpensive and unelaborate in the lively market area of **Paharganj**, where the smell of pungent spices wafts from numerous eating places. You can guarantee finding some excellent wholly Indian joints, particularly in the alleys opposite the railway station, where *channa batura* stalls do a raging business trading on their celebrated reputation, despite the flies. Restaurants geared to tourists offer typically poor Western imitations and under-spiced "curries", but are popular hangouts, and good for a tame breakfast of toast, porridge, muesli or cereal if you can't stomach chillies too early. Many of the hotels in the centre of the main street have cafés serving light meals through the night. Look out too, for meat cuts hanging in shop fronts where you can choose a piece to be grilled or tandooried, and mobile stalls dishing out French fries seasoned with masala, salt, pepper and lemon juice, and served in a bowl made of dried leaves. Roadside juice stalls stock Mars bars, Snickers, Yoplait yoghurt, European cheeses, and all brands of international cigarettes. For great lassis, try the stalls on the corner of Main Bazaar and Chuna Mandi. Eating options in **Ram Nagar** are more limited, with simple cafés and run-of-the mill restaurants.

The restaurants listed below are marked on the **map** of Paharganj on p.110.

Appetite, *Hotel Vishal*, 1600 Main Bazaar. Popular travellers' restaurant serving pizzas in addition to the usual Indo-Western food. Cable TV is switched on during international sports matches.

Diamond Café, opposite *Hotel Vivek*. Small and simple café-cum-restaurant; good for snacks, breakfast and street-watching.

Golden Café, opposite Sri Mahavir Mandir. Cheap and cheerful Chinese and Indian fare in cramped surroundings.

Hare Krishna, Main Bazaar. Pleasant rooftop restaurant in the hotel of the same name. Passable Italian and Thai dishes supplement the usual menu.

KFR, near Chitra Gupta Mandir, Main Bazaar. Cheap Tamil Nadu restaurant serving thalis, *idlis*, *sambar* and *dosas* as well as Chinese food.

Khosla Café, Main Bazaar. Another well-subscribed meeting place serving simple snacks, breakfasts and drinks, with an inside section as well as pavement seating.

Malhotra, Laksmi Narain Street. Popular restaurant, one of the best in Paharganj, with tasty Chinese and Indian food at cheaper than average prices especially in the basement; there is now a more comfortable a/c wing.

Metropolis, 1634 Main Bazaar. Cosy a/c ground-floor restaurant in the hotel of same name.

Paharganj's priciest venue serves full breakfasts, great curries and tandoori specials on a rooftop terrace, plus Western dishes and beer.

New Amar, Chuna Mandi, opposite the Imperial Cinema. Tiny café with simple meals and the best-value Western breakfasts in Paharganj.

Radha Swami, 8183/6 Arakashan Rd, Ram Nagar. A new café with good north Indian vegetarian cooking and a limited but classic menu including *aloo gobi* and *roti*.

Satyam, 659 Main Bazaar, Six Tooti Chowk. Mediocre Chinese and Indian food but a great site overlooking the busy fruit and vegetable market, with a good breakfast menu.

Shakahari, Main Bazaar, opposite the *Metropolis*. Excellent ultra-cheap veg *dhaba* with tasty fare on offer in huge roadside pots. Sign only in Hindi, but some dish names are written in English.

Sonu Chat House, Main Bazaar. Noodles, soup, samosas and red-hot curries in cramped but clean surroundings. Also good for south Indian dishes such as masala and *dosa*.

Vivek, Main Bazaar. 24hr rooftop restaurant in the hotel of the same name, with a wide selection of Eastern and Western food. Specialities include duck, pork and goulash.

Old Delhi

Among the shops, offices and houses in **Old Delhi**'s crowded streets, simple, grubby, unadvertised hole-in-the-wall food halls serve surprisingly good, and invariably fiery, Indian dishes for less than Rs20. There are few upmarket places in the heart of Old Delhi, but a number of larger, cleaner restaurants on the outskirts offer surroundings more conducive to leisurely and relaxed eating. The restaurants listed below are marked on the **map** of Old Delhi on p.123.

Chor Bizarre, *Hotel Broadway*, 4/15 Asaf Ali Rd. Pure, but pricey, Kashmiri *tarami* and *wazwan*, made all the more enjoyable by imaginative decor and a servery made from a 1927 vintage Fiat.

Karim's, Matya Mahal. In a side street opposite the south gate of the Jami Masjid, with the best and widest range of meat dishes (as well as the usual veg) in the city. Four eating halls round a courtyard all serve delicious fresh kebabs, hot breads and curries. Has been a favourite of Delhi-ites for years; there are other branches in Delhi including the more expensive one in Nizamuddin.

Moti Mahal, Netaji Shubash Marg, Darya Ganj. On the noisy main road south of Jami Masjid, this once smart restaurant, established in 1947, may have seen better days but is still renowned as the home of tandoori chicken.

Natraj Bhalla Corner, Chandni Chowk. Right next to the Central Bank, midway along Chandni Chowk. Cosy first-floor snack bar with a few window seats and a limited menu comprising Indian, Western and Chinese options.

Paratha Wali Gali, Chandni Chowk. Opposite the Central Bank, down an alley that leads behind Kanwarji Raj Kumar Sweet Shop. Follow the smell of rich ghee (the lane's hallmark from more than a century dedicated to *paratha*-making) to any of the several tiny rooms squeezed behind counters displaying pure veg food. Here you choose a *paratha* to go with standard veg dishes, filled with anything from *paneer* and *gobi* to *mutter* and mooli, all cooked to order, a culinary treat that will set you back around Rs30.

Soni Bhojnalaya, Nai Sarak. First-floor restaurant at the top of a yellow staircase opposite Bina Musical Stores, 30m off Chandni Chowk. Great thalis in typically Indian unfussy surroundings.

Vig Coffee House, Chandni Chowk. A small snack stall just over from the Red Fort serving excellent coffee, cold drinks, samosas, toasties and veg burgers.

South Delhi

The enclaves and villages spread across the vast area of **South Delhi** offer countless eating options. Trendy **Hauz Khas**, with its *Village Bistro* restaurant complex comprising several eateries, is renowned as one of Delhi's best areas for dining out. **Chanakya market** holds a cluster of Tibetan *dhabas* selling excellent *momos* (dumplings) and *thukpa* (soup). The alleys and lanes of the medieval village of **Nizamuddin** conceal cafés and a range of restaurants, while **Pandara Road Market**'s restaurants and snack bars, close to India Gate, stay open until 2am, and the expensive coffee shops in the five-star hotels are all 24hr.

Asian Games Village, Siri Fort, Khelgoon Road. A clutch of restaurants including *Angeethi*, with desert decor and live Rajasthani music in the evenings, specializing in delicious tandoori dishes; *ACS*, a coffee shop with a Mexican theme good for snacky meals and a cold beer; and *Chopsticks*, a smart Chinese restaurant.

Barista, M Block Market, Greater Kailash II. Trendy young café with a snacky menu: good cakes and coffee. *Fab Café* next door is equally good but a little more formal.

Basil & Thyme, Santushti Shopping Complex. Popular with Delhi's "ladies who lunch", serving Western and Parsi food at reasonable prices, despite the chic location.

Bengali Sweet House, Bengali Market. More than a sweet shop: a busy café whose menu ranges from *dosas* to onion *kulcha* and *channa* (bread and chickpeas), plus ice creams and milk shakes. Also takeaway *makki-ki-roti* (cornbread) with *sarson ka sag* (mustard-leaf spinach) and yoghurt in winter.

Dasaprakash, *Ambassador Hotel*, Sujan Singh Park. Considered by many Delhi-ites to be one of the best south Indian restaurants in Delhi, dishing up terrifc *dosas*. Expensive.

The Dhaba, *Claridges Hotel*, 12 Aurangzeb Rd. Designed to look like a trucker's café, with a reconstructed truck to add atmosphere – for those who want really good *dhaba* cooking without the grime of a roadside truck stop.

Dilli Haat, Safdarjang. Shop and snack at the exhibition ground popular with Delhi-ites, at small, inexpensive restaurants from every state in India, although standards vary.

Ego, Community Centre, New Friend's colony. Authentic and imaginative Italian, with good beer, cocktails and loud music.

Flavours, 52c Moolchand Flyover, Banks Complex, Defence Colony. Well-kept Delhi secret near Humayun's Tomb, serving excellent Italian food including risotto and delicious tiramisu; run by a Naga-Italian couple.

Fujiya, Malcha Marg Market, Chanakyapuri. A pilgrimage place for homesick Chinese tourists and well worth the queues. Superb, piping-hot Chinese dishes and fast service.

Karim's, Nizamuddin. Unmissable Mughlai cooking, although not as good as its Old Delhi counterpart. The sumptuous food is very rich, offering much-renowned specialities, plus kebabs, korma and *rumali roti* (super-thin bread).

Moets, Defence Colony Market. This very popular restaurant serves excellent Kashmiri – try the *dum aloo*, *paneer shashlik* and *mirchi korma* – plus Mughlai and Thai cuisine; another branch can be found on Mathura Road.

Nathu Sweets, 23–25 Bengali Market. Popular and clean, recently revamped inexpensive vegetarian café with an assorted menu including great thalis, masala dosas on banana leafs and a mean *kulfi falooda*. They also have a patisserie a few doors down good for snacks and cold coffee.

Osaka, Main Square, Hauz Khas Village. Chinese and Japanese food with a pleasant ambience; gentle on the pocket.

Rampur Kitchen, 8A Khan Market. A must for connoisseurs of Muslim haute cuisine, run by a famous chef. The food can be very rich indeed; order half-portions to sample the dishes and if the biriyani is too rich try some of the breads to soak up the spices.

Sagar, Defence Colony Market. Delicious, inexpensive south Indian food – sample the *dahi vadas*, and the masala dosas. The service is fast and the decor nondescript but it is popular; there's another branch at the *Lodi Hotel* where you need to book ahead.

Tea House of the August Moon, *Taj Palace Hotel*, 2 Sardar Patel Marg. Named in honour of the *Goon Show*, this place serves excellent Chinese cooking and does a good-value lunch including a glass of wine or beer for around Rs50.

TGIF, Modern Bazaar, Vasant Vihar. Tex-Mex, pasta, burgers and ribs and the best cocktails in town – the happy hour every evening from 6pm–7.30pm is especially good value. There's a new branch at CP.

Triveni Kala Sangam, 205 Tansen Marg, near Bengali Market. Small art-centre café serving Indian food. Go for lunch, but be prepared to share a table and put up with indifferent service.

Village Bistro Complex, Hauz Khas Village. Choose excellent Indian cuisine from any of the three menus offered in six different dining-halls. The outdoor *Top of the Village* balcony is the most pleasant, with good views over South Delhi.

Yellow Brick Road, *Ambassador Hotel*, Sujan Singh Park. Themed coffee shop with an excellent snack menu: a great place for a coffee after shopping at Khan Market next door.

Shopping

Although the traditional places to **shop** in Delhi are around **Connaught Place** and **Chandni Chowk**, a number of suburbs created by the rapid growth of the city are emerging as fashionable shopping districts. The shopping area of **Hauz Khas Village**, 12km southwest of Connaught Place, with numerous boutiques, jewellery shops and galleries, some pretentious and others well worth a browse, has, due to over-popularity, lost some of its charm. Outrageous rents and uncontrolled building have ruined the ambience and forced boutiques out, some to the yet-to-be-developed village of **Shahpur Jat**, a short distance away.

The garden setting of **Santushi Shopping Complex**, just inside Wellington Barracks next to the *Samrat Hotel* in Chanakyapuri, and run by Air Force officers' wives, is a trendy place, patronized by embassy officials but now threatened with closure. If you are looking for hand-spun cotton clothes, **Greater Kailash** and **South Extension I & II** are the hot spots for designer "ethnic chic" as well as Western chain brand names. Elsewhere, self-contained local precincts ranging from bookshops to European imported food include **Khan Market**, 1km south of India Gate, and **Bengali Market**, off Barakhamba Road, which is especially renowned for its sweet shops and large bustling cafés. Unlike the markets of Old Delhi (see pp.128–129), most shops in New Delhi take credit cards. In general, beware of touts who want to drag you into false "government shops" for a commission.

Art, antiques, crafts and jewellery

Much the best area to go shopping for **art** and **antiques** – even if sceptics do consider it vastly overpriced and rarely authentic – is the small **Sunder Nagar Market**, in a wealthy residential area near Purana Qila and the zoo. However, you shouldn't expect a bargain – the antique and art trade in India is a cut-throat business. Bear in mind that it is illegal to take art objects over one hundred years old out of the country and, strictly speaking, antiques should be registered and trading in them is against the law (see p.84).

Elsewhere, curio shops aimed at tourists sell everything from carpets and fabrics to handicrafts and collectors' items. Few locals bother to venture to the stretch of Janpath known as **Tibetan Market**, packed with vendors feeding off the tourist trade. In fact its shops (few still run by Tibetans) have a fine assortment of **jewellery**, using **semiprecious stones** and even **silver**. Be sure you can tell the difference between silver and white metal, and bargain hard. A concentration of **state government emporia** with fixed but fair prices can be found on Baba Kharak Singh Marg near Connaught Place. **Dilli Haat**, Safdarjang, has a similar selection of shops and cafés to complement the shopping.

Central Cottage Industries Emporium, Jawahar Vyapar Bhawan, Janpath. Popular and convenient multistorey government-run complex, with handicrafts, carpets, leather and reproduction miniatures at fixed (if fractionally high) rates. Jewellery ranges from tribal silver anklets to costume jewellery and precious stones.

Cottage of Arts and Jewels, 50 Hauz Khas Village ☎011/696 7418. Interesting, eccentric mix with jewellery, curios and papier-mâché. But the best of Mrs Jain's collection, including miniatures and precious stones, is not on display: you'll have to ask to see it.

Ellora, Shop 9, Sunder Nagar. Silver specialists selling jewellery and Indian handicrafts.

Friends Oriental Arts & Electric Company, Shops 15 & 25, Sunder Nagar Market. One shop devoted to an interesting range of art and handicrafts, the other specializing in brassware and things electric.

Jain Super Store, 172 Palika Bazaar, Gate 6. Perfumes, bottles, tea, incense, spices and the like at very reasonable prices.

Lotus Eaters, Santoshi Shopping Complex. Fashion boutique with a mixed bag including good-quality silver trinkets and jewellery.

M Zee Handicrafts, 48 Palika Bazaar, Gate 3, Connaught Place. Good for silver jewellery.

Natesans, 13 Sunder Nagar Market. An established and reliable name in Indian art and antiquities with quality assured, but at a price.

Nav-Rattan Arts, Shop 26, Sunder Nagar Market. As the name ("nine gems") suggests, an emphasis on gems, jewellery, silver, bronze, tapestries, and antique perfume bottles.

Neemrana Shop, F-580 Lado Sarai, near Qutab Complex. Run by the renowned hotel group of the same name, the shop has a chic clientele and offers a range of lifestyle products as well as a small collection of antiques and *objets d'art*.

Plutus, 10 Hauz Khas Village. An attractively presented shop selling replicas, bronzes and an assorted collection of silver and gold jewellery.

Poonam Backliwal, Shop 5, Sunder Nagar Market. Established in 1880, Poonam Backliwal specializes in miniatures, bronze and stone sculptures, Tanjore glass paintings and medieval jewellery.

R-Expo, 1115 Main Bazaar, Paharganj. Aromatic oils, bath stuff, scented candles, sandalwood, massage implements, *chillums*, solid and liquid perfumes. It's all of rather dubious quality, but beautifully presented.

Books

Delhi has a wide selection of places to buy **books** and **magazines**. Pavement vendors around Connaught Place will sell you anything from Sidney Sheldon to Vivekananda, as well as guidebooks. Bookshops – of which the best are in Khan Market, 4km south of Connaught Place – generally lack the Western trivia, but sell all kinds of publications in English, Hindi, and other European languages. The shops of South Extension, a short distance further south, are gradually superseding those of Khan Market. You'll find books on all aspects of Indian history and culture, and an ever-growing supply of short works by Indian authors published by Penguin India. Upmarket hotels often have their own bookshops, which usually tend towards the coffee-table market: **Khazana**, at the *Taj Mahal*, and **Jainson's** at *Janpath Hotel*, are worth perusing. Several budget hotels have multilingual collections of secondhand books for sale, swap or part exchange.

Amrit Book Co, 21 N-Block, Connaught Place. Vast stock of novels and books on history, philosophy and religion.

Bahri & Sons, Khan Market ☎ 011/469 4610, ⊚ bahrisons@vsnl.com. Legendary shop with books piled to the ceiling, covering every possible subject; if you find the cramped shop confusing ask one of the helpful assistants. Bahri's will order books and ship them abroad and are reliable.

The Bookshop, Khan Market. Small but good selection in this popular market renowned for its bookshops, with all the latest titles and a comprehensive section on Indian literature, religion and travel.

Book Mark, A/2 Ring Road, South Extension 1. A modern bookshop with a growing reputation and a varied selection, from fiction to travel.

Book World, Shop 7, Palika Bazaar. A wealth of glossy hardbacks, architectural books, travelogues and novels. Credit cards accepted.

Crossword, 2nd floor, Ebony, D-4 South Extension 2. Modern bookshop in a department store, with plenty of elbow room to browse: popular titles, reference and a good magazine section.

English Book Store, 17 L-Block, Connaught Place. A good place to get Western blockbusters and books on adventure sports and yoga.

Full Circle, Khan Market. A pleasant and versatile bookshop with an emphasis on New Age titles, as well as general travel and guidebooks, and music and a café upstairs.

Galgotia & Sons, 17-B Connaught Place. Cavernous room stacked with new and second-hand books and out-of-print titles. Topics range from cookery to travel, and it's well worth a browse.

Moti Lal Benarsi Das, Nai Sarak, Chandni Chowk. One of India's premier publishing institutions, retailing as well as publishing academic books on India.

New Book Depot, 18 B-Block, Connaught Place. Well-stocked shop with international titles, bargain hardbacks and a good selection of books covering religion, the environment and society in India.

RS Books & Prints, A-40 South Extension 2. A selection of antiquarian books, with interesting old maps and prints.

Rajiv Book House, Shop 30, Palika Bazaar. Expensive photo-packed hardbacks, great for gifts and collections, and often reduced in price, as well as cheaper novels and paperbacks.

Timeless, 46 Housing Society, South Extension 1. A beautiful shop with tasteful piles of coffee-table books, some published by Timeless itself. Complementary herbal tea or coffee for customers.

Fabrics and clothes

In Delhi you can buy anything from high-quality silks, homespun cottons and Kashmiri jackets and shawls to traditional everyday wear and multicoloured tie-dyed Western-style outfits. Buyers are expected to bargain in most street-side stalls, which can make shopping all the more fun – start at fifty percent of the quoted price and slowly increase. Be wary of high prices – the same item is often available in different shops at varying rates. Shops with fixed prices should have a sign to prove it. For Western-style trousers, skirts and shirts, try **Paharganj**, the **Tibetan Market** at the north end of Janpath, the export-seconds market (watch out for "Kevin Clein" and "Ralphe Lawren" labels) at **Sarojini Nagar** in Chanakyapuri and buy leather at **Palika Bazaar** or **Chanakya Market**. Roadside stalls behind the Tibetan Market off Janpath sell lavishly embroidered and mirrored spreads from Rajasthan and Gujarat, but you'll need to bargain. Beautiful silks and fine cotton are best bought in **government emporia**, most of which are on Baba Kharak Singh Marg.

Delhi also holds a few upmarket boutiques, trading in designer labels and furnishings; some, such as **Anokhi**, now have branches all around the world.

Anokhi, Santushti Shopping Complex and Khan Market. Sells soft cotton and raw silk clothes and soft furnishings; particularly renowned for hand-block printed cottons combining traditional and contemporary designs.

Bata, 16 B-Block, Connaught Place. Reliable and hardy sandals, trainers and smarter leather shoes, that will survive in India much longer than the flimsy leather flip-flops sold in most bazaars.

Cashmeir Galleri, 50 Hauz Khas Village. Kashmiri-run shops with handmade Oriental carpets in silk and wool, chain-stitch rugs, shawls and papier-mâché.

Central Cottage Industries Emporium, Jawahar Vyapar Bhawan, Janpath. A multistorey government-run shop with a good range of raw silk and cotton lengths; they also stock traditional Indian outfits, silk ties and finely tailored jackets and suits (particularly for women), leather handbags and coats.

Darzi, 4A Shahpur Jat. Ethnic chic with a good selection of ready-made garments for women including *kurta* and *salwar kamise*.

Dastkar, 45-B Shahpur Jat. Recently relocated from Hauz Khas, Dastkar stocks reasonably priced terracotta, block prints, saris, patchwork, toys, leather, basketry, weaves and beautiful Madhubani folk-art prints on cloth.

Fabindia, Greater Kailash. Spread through several shops in the market with a range from furnishings and interiors to ethnic chic including cotton clothing for men, women and children and wearable block-printed cottons.

Handloom House, 9 A-Block, Connaught Place. An all-India co-operative with exquisite silks; they offer assured quality and fixed prices, but it's not cheap.

Khadi Gramodyog Bhavan, 24 Regal Building, corner of Sansad Marg and Connaught Place. Great place to pick up hardy, lightweight travelling clothes. Reasonably priced, ready-made traditional Indian garments include *salwar kamise* (trousers and shirt), woollen waistcoats, *kurta pygama*, shawls and caps, plus rugs, material by the metre, incense, cards and tablecloths.

People Tree, 8 Regal Buildings, Sansad Marg, CP. Alternative Delhi, with an emphasis on T-shirts, ethnic chic and jewellery as well as pamphlets on topics covering poverty, the environment, health, politics and women's issues. Also a notice board with details of forthcoming films and lectures at centres such as the Max Mueller Bhavan.

Tibetan Carpets and Handicrafts, HH the Dalai Lama's Charitable Trust Handicraft Exports, 16 Jor Bagh, Lodi Road. Carpets of all sizes, seamless and runners, woollen pullovers, jackets, bags, *chuba* (Tibetan women's dress), incense and other gifts.

Musical instruments, cassettes and CDs

Delhi has a lively classical **Indian music** scene; the Triveni arts centre (see p.147) is a good place to catch live performances as well as to get information on instrument-makers. Among classical recordings, both the Music Today and Maestro's Choice series have an excellent collection of north and south Indian classical music. For popular Western music on tape and CD at bargain prices, head to any of the music stalls in Palika Bazaar or Khan Market.

Blue Bird & Co, 9 Regal Buildings, Sansad Marg. Cassettes, CDs, videos and hi-fis.

Lahore Music House, Netaji Subhash Marg, Darya Ganj. Long-established North Indian musical instrument-makers who have a reputation for quality.

The Music Shop, Khan Market. Every type of music with good quality CDs, cassettes and videos and helpful, well-informed staff.

Planet M, E-3 South Extension 2. The trendy four-storey music shop which tries to cater for everything but is especially strong on pop and holds pop-related events in-store as well as elsewhere in the city; there's a pleasant café on the top floor.

Rangarsons, Outer Circle, Connaught Place. Extraordinary shop that once boasted regiments of the British Indian army among its patrons. A collection of brass and other marching band instruments as well as contemporary tablas and sitars.

Rhythm Corner, 16 N-Block, Connaught Place. Much like Blue Bird; copious quantities of CDs, cassettes, and videos of contemporary and classical music, including international chart hits.

Rikhi Ram, G-Block, Marina Arcade, Outer Circle, Connaught Place. Once sitar makers to the likes of Ravi Shankar, they maintain their exclusive air. Top-quality instruments (sitar, tablas and more) available and an interesting cabinet with their own unique instrumental inventions on view. Expect to pay more than bazaar prices.

Nightlife and entertainment

The **nightlife** scene in Delhi is in full swing, with the advent of pubs and private nightclubs. During the week, the clubs are empty – stick to central restaurants and the well-stocked bars at upmarket hotels if you want some atmosphere. Come the weekend, though, bars are full by 9pm and clubs take off at midnight. Most clubs are in five-star hotels and operate couples-only policies at the door; women usually get in free, and men pay Rs400. Another option is to take an auto to **India Gate** and Rajpath any night after 8pm for a nightly people's party that attracts huge crowds who mill about, snacking and eating ice cream; women on their own are likely to encounter hassle.

The city fares well on the cultural front. A range of indoor and outdoor venues host performances of classical dance such as Bharatnatyam and Kathakali; one Sunday a month a classical concert is held free of charge in Nehru Park – but you'll have to be there very early to get in. Check any of the listings magazines detailed on p.105 to see what's on at **India International Centre**, a good place to catch art exhibitions, lectures and films on all aspects of Indian culture and environment. The colossal new **India Habitat Centre**, the **British Council** and the **art** and **theatre auditoria** around India Gate are all renowned for their innovative shows and high-standard drama in both Hindi and English mediums. If you crave a Hollywood or a Bollywood hit, there are a number of good **cinemas**, such as the **Regal** in Connaught Place and the **Chanakya** in Chanakyapuri – this has just been refurbished, is safe for women on their own and shows recent Hollywood blockbusters, as do the PVR Priya in Vasant Vihar and the PVR Anupam in Saket.

Bars

Blues, N-17 Connaught Place. A snazzy bar and restaurant, offering an eclectic range of loud music but little in the way of blues and jazz. The bar staff are all pros at mixing extravagant cocktails.

Djinns, *Hyatt Regency Hotel*, Bhikaiji Cama Place. A huge bar, pool table, darts, live bands from Europe and the Caribbean, innovative Indian snacks and pitchers of beer and cocktails. Packed on Wednesday and the weekend with the Delhi jet-set, so get in early. No entrance after 11pm, even though it stays open until 2am.

Geoffries, Ansal Plaza. A very popular "English" pub with bar meals and beer on tap.

Jazz Bar, *Maurya Sheraton Hotel*, Diplomatic Enclave. Live jazz of varying standards from Indian musicians. Serves beer in pitchers and cocktails.

Maikada, *Hotel Marina*, 59 G-Block, Connaught Place. Comfortable bar with a small outside terrace but pricey drinks.

Le Meridien, Windsor Place. Two exclusive and rather staid bars, *Aloha* and *Henri's*, with extortionate prices but nothing less than five-star treatment.

Park Baluchi, Deer Park, Hauz Khas. Pleasant restaurant-bar situated in a leafy corner; a great place for a beer after hectic shopping.

Patiala Peg, *Hotel Imperial*, Janpath. A plush but cosy atmosphere, offering imported and local beers, spirits and great cocktails.

Pegasus Pub, Nirulas, 135 L-Block, Connaught Place. Part of the Nirulas complex, a reproduction English pub with a plush a/c ambience and expensive beer outside the happy hour (6–8pm).

Radisson, NH8, Mahipalpur. The sports bar at the *Radisson* (near the airport) is a great bar to kill a few hours if you are waiting for a plane– there are four top-notch bowling alleys, billiards and snooker, nonstop TV coverage of the match of the day, and lots of beer and cocktails

Rodeo, 12 A-Block, Connaught Place. Bustling atmosphere in restaurant-bar serving a full range of drinks, including tequila slammers. Mock-saddle seats at the bar play on the rodeo theme; Tuesday is karaoke night. The early evening happy hours are great value.

Saqi, *Hotel Alka*, 16-90 P-Block, Connaught Place. Very dimly lit bar that's a little sleazy, but you can take your drink out onto a small veranda.

Discos

Most, if not all, of the **discos** popular with elite Delhi-ites are in the luxury hotels; many now are free but you have to buy at least one drink.

Ghungroo, *Maurya Sheraton* ☏011/611 2233. Delhi's oldest Western-style disco, with very Eighties decor – a flashing dance floor – but it plays the latest dance and trance. Restricted entry for nonresidents of the hotel.
Mirage, *Surya Palace*, 4826-28 Main Bazaar ☏011/683 5070. A studenty club with an emphasis on the latest dance tracks, rather than the cheesy classics; ladies' night on Wednesdays.
My Kind of Place, *Taj Palace*, 1 Sardar Patel Marg ☏011/611 0202. One of Delhi's most popular clubs, especially with the expats and especially on Saturday nights, with hip-hop, drum'n'bass and reggae. Occasional theme nights such as belly dancing. Closed Mon & Tues.
Someplace Else, *Park*, 15 Sansad Marg ☏011/373 3737. Popular place for those who want cheaper beer; and a DJ who is willing to play requests, especially more alternative tracks. Jazz night on Wednesday.

Dance and drama

Dances of India, Parsi Anjuman Hall, Bahadur Shah Zafar Marg ☏011/623 4689. Excellent classical, folk and tribal dance. Daily 7–8pm.
Habitat World, India Habitat Centre, Lodhi Road ☏011/469 1920. Popular venue for dance, music and theatre as well as talks and exhibitions; look up the local press for listings or enquire by phone.
Kamani Auditorium, Copernicus Marg ☏011/338 8084. Concerts and theatre; check local press.
Triveni Kala Sangam, 205 Tansen Marg ☏011/371 8833. A popular venue for dance shows by professionals and talented student groups.

Cultural centres and libraries

There is nearly always some cultural activity going on in Delhi – check at the tourist office, or get hold of local newspapers and publications like *First City* and *Delhi Diary*.

Alliance Française, D13 NDSE Part II ☏011/625 8128. Hosts film shows and has an art gallery.
British Council, 17 Kasturba Gandhi Marg ☏011/371 1401 & 371 0111. Talks, film shows and concerts, plus a good library and reading room and internet.
India International Centre, 40 Lodi Estate ☏011/461 9431. Daily films, lectures, dance, and music performances; look up listings magazines (see p.105) or enquire by phone.
Lalit Kala Akademi, Rabindra Bhavan, 35 Firoz Shah Rd ☏011/338 7241. Delhi's premier art academy, with an extensive collection of paintings, sculpture, frescoes and drawings. Also hosts films and seminars, and has a photographic section and a sales counter.
Max Mueller Bhavan, 3 Kasturba Gandhi Marg ☏011/332 9506. Along with hosting concerts and exhibitions which include Indian artists, this German government cultural centre also has a library.
Sahitya Akademi, Rabindra Bhavan, Firoz Shah Road ☏011/338 7064. An excellent library devoted to Indian literature through the ages, with some books and periodicals in English.
Sangeet Natak Akademi, Rabindra Bhavan, Firoz Shah Road ☏011/338 7246. The premier performing arts institution, with a large archive and collection (see p.122).

Cinemas

After gloriously hyped releases, **Bollywood** movies make their way to the capital where there is passionate enthusiasm for burly heroes and red-lipped maidens. If you're interested in enjoying a classic Indian experience, the best cinemas to head for are the **Regal**, **Odeon** and **Plaza** in Connaught Place. All show popular films with the compulsory goodies and baddies, a generous dose of manly courage and shy love, much singing and dancing, and happy endings.

An alternative branch of Bollywood has recently emerged, producing films in English that ooze attitude, with sex scenes and lots of designer wear. Suburban cinemas, such as the **Priya** in Vasant Vihar, the Chanakya in Chanakyapuri and the **PVR Anupam** in Saket, provide a diet of relatively recent **Hollywood** films (in English, with Hindi subtitles) with digital surround sound and superb popcorn. In addition, many of the cultural centres listed above run international film festivals.

Sports and outdoor activities

The recreational activity most likely to appeal to visitors in the pre-monsoon months has to be a dip in one of Delhi's **swimming pools** (see p.151). Other local diversions include **bowling**, **golf**, and even **rock climbing**, on crags on the outskirts of the city, during the cooler months.

Bowling Alley, *Qutb Hotel*, off Sri Aurobindo Marg ☏011/652 1010; Xanadu Bowling Lanes, South Delhi Club, Greater Kailash 1 ☏011/647 3988.
Delhi Flying Club, Safdarjang Airport ☏011/461 8161. Temporary membership available.
Delhi Gliding Club, Safdarjang Airport ☏011/463 6052. Call for details of a day's flying.
Delhi Golf Club, Dr Zakir Hussein Marg ☏011/436 2768. Busy and beautiful 220-acre golf course on the fifteenth-century estate of the Lodi dynasty, planted with over two hundred varieties of trees, which also acts as a bird sanctuary. Monuments and mausoleums, such as the ruined *barakhamba* on a hillock next to the seventh green, dot the grounds. Temporary membership is available.
Delhi Lawn Tennis Association, Africa Avenue ☏011/619 3955.

Delhi Riding Club, Safdarjang Road ☏011/301 1891. Morning rides start at 6.30am and afternoon rides at 2pm; open to the public by prior arrangement through the Club Secretary.
Delhi Tourism, N-36 Bombay Life Building, Middle Circle, Connaught Place ☏011/331 4229. Local activities such as rock climbing, paragliding and water sports, plus treks as far afield as Sikkim.
Indian Mountaineering Foundation, Benito Juarez Marg ☏011/467 7935. Official organization governing mountaineering and permits throughout India, with a library and an outdoor climbing wall. Some equipment can be rented here, and you can get information on local crags and climbing groups.

Listings

Airport enquiries International ☏011/565 2011; domestic ☏011/566 5121.
Airlines, domestic Indian Airlines main office: Safdarjang Airport ☏011/462 2220, open 24hr; general enquiries ☏141, prerecorded information ☏142, departures ☏143; booking offices: PTI Building, Sansad Marg (Mon–Sat 10am–5pm; ☏011/371 9168; Malhotra Building, Janpath (daily except Sat 10am–5pm; ☏011/331 0517; Kanchenjunga Building, Barakhamba Road (Mon–Sat 10am–5pm; ☏011/331 3732. Archana Airways, 41A Friends Colony East, Mathura Road ☏011/684 2001. Jagson Airlines, 12E Vandhana, 11 Tolstoy Marg ☏011/372 1593. Jet Airways,

main office: Jetair House, 13 Community Centre, Yusuf Sarai ☏011/651 7443; booking offices: N-40 Outer Circle, Connaught Place ☏011/685 3700. Sahara Indian Airlines, Ambadeep Building, Kasturba Gandhi Marg ☏011/332 6851. UP Air, A2 Defence Colony ☏011/464 6290.
Airlines, international Aeroflot, Tolstoy House, 15-17 Tolstoy Marg ☏011/372 3241; Air Canada, 1st floor, ALPs Building, 56 Janpath ☏011/372 0014; Air France, 7 Atma Ram Mansion, Scindia House, Connaught Place ☏011/331 7054; Air India, Jeevan Bharati Building, opposite Palika Bazaar, Connaught Place ☏011/373 1225; Air Lanka, Room 1, *Hotel Janpath*, Janpath ☏011/332

6843; Air Ukraine, C-37, Hauz Khas ☏011/686 7545; Alitalia, 2H, DCM Bldg, 16 Barakhamba Rd ☏011/372 1006; American Airlines, 105 Indra Prakash Building, Barakhamba Road ☏011/332 5876; Bangladesh Biman, World Trade Centre, Babar Road, Connaught Place ☏011/335 4401; British Airways, 1A DLF Centre, Sansad Marg ☏011/332 7428; Cathay Pacific, Ashoka Estate ☏011/332 3332; Egypt Air, GF-I, Ansal Bhawan, Kasturba Gandhi Marg ☏011/335 4493; El-Al Israel Airlines, 7th floor, Prakash Deep Building, Tolstoy Marg ☏011/335 7965; Emirates, Kanchenjunga Building, 18 Barakhamba Rd ☏011/332 4665; Ethiopian Airlines, GF-I, Ansal Bhawan, Kasturba Gandhi Marg ☏011/335 4491; Gulf Air, G-12 Marina Arcade, Connaught Place ☏011/332 7814; Japan Airlines, 36 Chandralok Building, Janpath ☏011/332 7104; KLM, 7 Prakash Deep, Tolstoy Marg ☏011/332 4489; Kuwait Airways, 2C, DCM Building, 16 Barakhamba Rd ☏011/335 4373; Lufthansa, 56 Janpath ☏011/332 3310; Malaysia Airlines, 10th floor, Ashoka Estate Building, Barakhamba Road ☏011/331 3448; Qantas Airways, Mohandev Building, 13 Tolstoy Marg ☏011/332 9027; Royal Jordanian, G-56 Connaught Place ☏011/332 7418; Royal Nepal Airlines, 44 Janpath ☏011/332 1164; SAS, Amadeep Building Kasturba Gandhi Marg ☏011/335 2299; Saudi Arabian Airlines, Hansalaya Building, 15 Barakhamba Rd ☏011/331 0464; Singapore Airlines, G-11 Connaught Place ☏011/335 6281; Swissair, DLF Centre, Sansad Marg ☏011/332 5511; TAROM, 16 GF Antrikash Building, 22 Kasturba Gandhi Marg ☏011/335 4422; Thai Airways, *Park Royal Hotel*, American Plaza, Nehru Place ☏011/623 9988; Uzbekistan Airways, 3 Prakash Deep Building, 7 Tolstoy Marg ☏011/335 8687.

Banks and currency exchange You can exchange money at the international airport, at the 24hr State Bank of India or Thomas Cook, but there are no facilities for withdrawing money on a credit card. Changing money in the city is far easier than a few years ago, with several banks (Mon–Fri 10am–2pm, Sat 10am–noon or 1pm) sporting ATM machines which accept Visa and Mastercard; try Standard Charter Grindlays (Visa encashments and ATM), 10 E-Block, Connaught Place; Andhra Bank, 35 M-Block, Connaught Place; Bank of Baroda (Visa encashments); and the State Bank of India, Sansad Marg. Thomas Cook is located in the *Hotel Imperial* on Janpath (Mon–Fri 9.30am–8pm, Sat 9.30am–6pm) and American Express on A-Block, Connaught Place (Mon–Sat 9.30am–6.30pm). Hong Kong Bank (ECE House, Kasturba Gandhi Road) has a 24hr ATM cash machine that takes Visa and Mastercard. In addition, you can change money at the DTTDC office, Middle Circle, Connaught Place, and all major hotels have exchange facilities. Numerous authorized exchange bureaux are available, particularly in Paharganj, including Cheque Point, just past the *Star Palace Hotel* on Main Bazaar (daily 9.30am–8.30pm). For money transfers, the Western Union office is at Sita World Travel, F-12 Connaught Place ☏011/331 1122; it also has a forex counter.

Bus enquiries Delhi Transport Corporation ☏011/251 5543 & 335 4518, will also provide enquiry numbers for buses run by other state transport corporations.

Churches Church of the Redemption, Church Road; Sacred Heart Free Church, Parliament Street.

Embassies & consulates Australia, 1/50-G Shanti Path, Chanakyapuri ☏011/688 8223; Bangladesh, 56 Ring Rd, Lajpat Nagar III ☏011/683 4668; Bhutan, Chandragupta Marg, Chanakyapuri ☏011/688 9230; Canada, 7/8 Shanti Path, Chanakyapuri ☏011/687 6500; China, 50-D Shanti Path, Chanakyapuri ☏011/687 1585; European Commission, 65 Golf Links ☏011/462 9237; Indonesia, 50A Chanakyapuri ☏011/611 8642; Iran, 5 Baraljaba Rd ☏011/332 9600; Malaysia, 50-M Satya Marg, Chanakyapuri ☏011/611 1291; Nepal, Barakhamba Road ☏011/332 8191; Netherlands, 6/50-F Shanti Path, Chanakyapuri ☏011/688 4951; New Zealand, 50-N Nyaya Marg ☏011/688 3170; Pakistan, 2/50G Shanti Path, Chanakyapuri ☏011/467 6004; Singapore, E6 Chandragupta Marg, Chanakyapuri ☏011/688 5659; Sri Lanka, 27 Kautilya Marg, Chanakyapuri ☏011/301 0201; South Africa, B-18 Vasant Vihar ☏011/614 9411; Thailand, 56-N Nyaya Marg, Chanakyapuri ☏011/611 8103; UK, Shanti Path, Chanakyapuri ☏011/687 2161; USA, Shanti Path, Chanakyapuri ☏011/419 8000.

Hospitals All India Institute of Medical Sciences, Ansari Nagar, Sri Aurobindo Marg ☏011/686 4851, 24hr emergency service and good treatment; East West Medical Centre, 38 Golf Links Rd ☏011/462 3738, good private clinic; Dr Ram Manohar Lohia Hospital, Baba Kharak Singh Marg ☏011/336 1014, also private; Lok Nayak Jaya Prakash Hospital, Jawaharlal Nehru Marg, Old Delhi ☏011/323 2400, a government hospital near Delhi Gate.

Internet access Prices range from a mere Rs10 per hour to around Rs100 per hour but make sure you check your connection by surfing first. The British Council, 17 Kasturba Gandhi Marg ☏011/371 1401 & 371 0111, is by far the most reliable but there are several other good options including *Cyber Café*, N-9/II Connaught Place (daily 9.30am–8.30pm; ☎011/335 7986. A short distance away you'll find the small but friendly *Bainson Café internet*, 17/98 Scindia House, Connaught Lane. Paharganj teems with internet cafés, all with very competitive rates, including *Cyber Station* at *Downtown Hotel* off the Main Bazaar and close to the New Delhi station gates, while the internet café at the *Hotel Gold Regency* is almost as lively as the streets outside.

Left luggage Left luggage counters at the railway stations cost Rs5 per day. To deposit your bags long-term ask at your hotel; most charge Rs2–5 per day. Hotels *Hare Rama*, *Anoop* and *Ajay* in Paharganj offer access to a 24hr lockup, for a maximum period of six months.

Maps The Survey of India Map Sales Office, in Janpath, sells guide maps of a number of cities and states, some of which are grossly out of date and lack detail (see Basics, pp.26–28).

Mother Teresa hostels The orphanage inspired by Mother Teresa close to Qudsia Gardens north of Old Delhi accepts voluntary help with teaching, which should be prearranged. Contact Missionaries of Charity, 12 Commissioner's Lane, Shishu Bhavan, Delhi 110054, or call ☎011/251 8457.

Motorcycles The Karol Bagh area is known for its many good motorcycle shops specializing in new or secondhand Enfields. The most reliable and recommended of these is Inder Motors, 1744/1755 Hari Singh Nalwa St, Abdul Aziz Road ☎011/572 8579, while Lucky Auto Accessories, 53/1767 Shri Kishan Dass Rd ☎011/73 8815, also offers excellent renovations of secondhand (ex-army) Enfield Bullets.

Opticians Bon-Ton Opticians, 13 Janpath Market, and Lawrence & Mayo, 76 Janpath, both offer good, expensive glasses and sunglasses; Medikos Opticians, 1588 Main Bazaar, Paharganj, has cheap computerized eye-tests, prescription lenses and sunglasses made up in half a day.

Pharmacies Nearly every market has at least one pharmacy. Those in Super Bazaar, Connaught Place, and the All India Medical Institute, Ansari Nagar, Sri Aurobindo Marg, are open 24hr.

Photographic studios Delhi Photo Company, 78 Janpath, for high-quality developing, printing, and slide processing, is second only to Kinsey Brothers beneath the *India Today* offices at 2-A Block, Connaught Place.

Police ☎100 (national number). If you have any problem that needs to involve the police, your hotel reception or the Government of India tourist office will direct you to the appropriate station.

Postal services Poste restante (Mon–Sat 10am–4.30pm) is available at the GPO on the roundabout at the intersection of Baba Kharak Singh Marg and Ashoka Road (known as Gole PO) and the Foreign Post Office, nearby on Bhai Vir Singh Marg, about fifteen minutes' walk from Connaught Place. You must show your passport to claim mail, and check the register for parcels. Letters sent to "Poste Restante, Delhi", rather than to New Delhi, may end up in Old Delhi GPO, north of the railway line on Mahatma Gandhi Road. You can also have mail sent to the Government of India tourist office, 88 Janpath, who pass any parcels to the main Gole GPO. Other post offices are on Janpath, Sansad Marg and A-Block, Connaught Place; all have a speed post service, and you can guarantee next-day delivery of parcels and papers to all international destinations with Overnite Express Pvt Ltd, whose office is in Kanishka Shopping Plaza, Janpath.

State tourist offices Andaman and Nicobar Islands, F105 Curzon Road Hostel, Kasturba Gandhi Marg ☎011/378 2904; Andhra Pradesh, Andhra Bhavan, 1 Ashoka Rd ☎011/338 1293; Arunachal Pradesh, Arunchal Bhawan, Kautilya Marg ☎011/301 3915; Assam, State Emporia Complex, Baba Kharak Singh Marg ☎011/336 5897; Bihar, 216 Kanishka Shopping Plaza, 19 Ashoka Rd ☎011/372 3371; Goa, Goa Sadan, 8 Amrita Shergill Marg ☎011/462 9967; Gujarat, A6 State Emporia Building, Baba Kharak Singh Marg ☎011/373 4015; Haryana, Chandralok Building, 36 Janpath ☎011/332 4911; Himachal Pradesh, Chanderlok Building, 36 Janpath ☎011/332 5320; Jammu & Kashmir, 202 Kanishka Shopping Plaza, 19 Ashoka Rd ☎011/332 5373; Karnataka, C4 State Emporia Building, Baba Kharak Singh Marg ☎011/336 3862; Kerala, Information Centre, 219 Kanishka Shopping Plaza ☎011/336 6541; Madhya Pradesh, 204–205 Kanishka Shopping Plaza ☎011/332 1187; Maharashtra, A8 State Emporia Building, Baba Kharak Singh Marg ☎011/336 3773; Manipur, C7 State Emporia Building, Baba Kharak Singh Marg ☎011/336 4026; Meghalaya, Meghalaya House, 9 Aurangzeb Rd ☎011/301 5503; Mizoram, Mizoram Bhawan, Circular Road, Chanakyapuri ☎011/301 5951; Nagaland, Government of Nagaland, 29 Aurangzeb Rd ☎011/301 5638; Orissa, B4 State Emporia Building, Baba Kharak Singh Marg ☎011/336 4580; Punjab, 214–215 Kanishka Shopping Plaza ☎011/332 3055; Rajasthan, Bikaner House, near India Gate ☎011/338 9525; Sikkim, New Sikkim House, 14 Panch Sheel Marg, Chanakyapuri ☎011/301 5346; Tamil Nadu, C1 State Emporia Building, Baba Kharak Singh Marg ☎011/336

3913; Tripura, Tripura Bhavan, Kautilya Marg, Chanakyapuri ☎011/301 4607; Uttar Pradesh, Chanderlok Building, 36 Janpath ☎011/332 2251; West Bengal, A/2 State Emporia Building, Baba Kharak Singh Marg ☎011/373 2840.

Swimming pools Most luxury hotels are making it impossible or prohibitively expensive for non-residents to use their pools with fees in the region of Rs700. The city's main public swimming baths are the NMDC Pools, in Nehru Park, Chanakyapuri, and the Talkatora Pool on Talkatora Road.

Telephones and faxes Making international telephone calls from Delhi is easy with STD booths, marked with yellow signs, sporting direct-dialling facilities and LCD displays showing the length and cost of each call. Several will allow you to receive incoming calls, usually for a small charge. Most STD booths now have fax machines and the booths in Paharganj operate round the clock and store incoming faxes until collection. You can also send faxes from post offices and outlets in Connaught Place. Rates are usually Rs30 per page plus the cost of the call, with around Rs10 charged for incoming faxes.

Visa extensions and permits For visa renewal and permits for restricted states, go to the Foreigners' Registration office, Hans Bhavan, Mathura Road, near Tilak Bridge railway station (Mon–Fri 9.30am–1.30pm & 2–4pm; ☎011/331 9489 & 331 9781, with four passport photographs. Be sure to wait in the right queue – to pay either

Travel agents and tour operators

NB: Booking flights and excursions through street-side touts, particularly along Janpath, is not recommended, even if they claim to be "government recognized". For the issue or renewal of ISIC cards, head to STIC, opposite *Imperial Hotel*. American Express, A-Block, Connaught Place ☎011/332 4119: expensive, tailor-made tours of the capital, and sites further afield – card-holders only; Cox and Kings, Indira Palace, Connaught Place ☎011/332 0067: international operators offering expensive and exclusive tailor-made tours; Don't Pass Me By Tours and Travels, 79 Scindia House, nr Janpath ☎011/335 2942: reliable and inexpensive tour operator specializing in road trips to Agra and through Rajasthan; Hans Travel Service, 1600 *Vishal Hotel*, Main Bazaar, Paharganj ☎011/332 7629: friendly and reasonably priced taxi rental, private long-distance buses and tours by private car; Journeys, 4-B Jangpura, Mathura Road ☎011/432 3523, ⓔjourneys@giasdl01.vsnl.net.in: excellent tailor-made tours that can be arranged via email; specialists on Rajasthan but with a wider all-India coverage; Namaskar, *Hotel Namaskar*, 917 Chandiwalan, Main Bazaar ☎011/362 1234: brothers Surinder and Rajinder offer a reliable service including very competitively priced tours of Rajasthan; Rajasthan Tourism Development Corporation, Bikaner House, Pandara Road ☎011/338 9525: package tours of Rajasthan by bus or car, including wildlife tours of Sariska, Ranthambore and Bharatpur, plus the legendary luxury train, *Palace on Wheels*; Rajshree Tours and Travels, 53 Kamdhen Apartment, Plot 51, Sector 9, Rohini ☎011/740 0746: specialize in renting out well-fitted motor caravans with the (recommended) option of having a chauffeur; this is a unique way to tour Rajasthan; Sita World Travel, F-12 Connaught Place ☎011/331 1122: well-established operators specializing in international and domestic flights, package tours and money change; Student Travel Information Centre, STIC Travels PVT, 1st floor, Chandralok Building, opposite *Imperial Hotel*, Janpath ☎011/332 0239: excellent organization who will book your tours and travel, and sort out any travel problems giving unbiased advice; Thomas Cook, *Hotel Imperial*, Janpath ☎011/332 8468: comprehensive travel service from a well-established operator; Travelite, 5H & 6E Vandana Building, Tolstoy Marg ☎011/331 3541: efficient tour group, organizing any kind of trip, from the Golden Triangle to extensive tours of India and Nepal; Travel Corporation of India, *Hotel Metro*, N49 Connaught Place ☎011/335 6167): efficient tour operators and travel agents now owned by Thomas Cook, who book train and air tickets, run tours and provide bargain rates for select luxury hotels in Delhi and elsewhere in India; Trip Travels, 13 Tolstoy Lane, behind tourist office ☎011/375 5194: popular and trustworthy travel service dealing with international airlines and sometimes offering discounts; Y's Tours & Travels, *YMCA*, Jai Singh Road ☎011/336 1915, ext 4426: you can avoid queues by obtaining train tickets here; Youth Hostelling International, 5 Nyaya Marg, Chanakyapuri ☎011/301 6250: extremely good-value treks in the mountains of Himachal Pradesh.

in rupees (backed up by exchange certificates), or foreign currency – and take plenty of change. For longer renewals, you'll have to first liaise with the Ministry of Home Affairs, Lok Nayak Bhavan, Khan Market (Mon–Fri 10am–noon; ☎011/467 7648. If you've been in India more than 120 days, you'll need to get a tax clearance certificate before you can leave, from the foreign section of the Income Tax Office, Indraprastha Estate (Mon–Fri 10am–1pm & 2–5pm; ☎011/331 7826) in the

Central Revenue Building next to the FRO; bring bank certificates.
Yoga centres Sivananda Yoga Vedanta Nataraja Centre, A41 Kailash Colony ☎011/648 0869. Tushita Mahayana Meditation Centre, 9 Padmini Enclave, Hauz Khas ☎011/651 3400. Yoga Shakti Mission, 14–20 Ajit Arcade, Kailash Colony ☎011/641 2379; Yoga Vishwatayan, Ashoka Road ☎011/371 8866. Yoga and Natural Health Care Centre ☎011/619 2687.

Moving on from Delhi

Delhi has good domestic and international travel connections. Anyone heading from the south to the western Himalayas (Himachal Pradesh, Kullu, Manali, Ladakh) will pass through Delhi; it seldom takes more than a day to arrange the onward journey. Scores of **travel agents** (see box p.151) sell bus and air tickets, and many hotels (budget or otherwise) will book private buses for you; **touts**, concentrated at the top of Janpath, waylay tourists with promises of cheap fares, but can't always be trusted.

Travel within India

Whichever direction you're heading in, there'll be a plane, train or bus to get you there. Buses leave Delhi extremely frequently, and tourists are usually ensured places on trains in a reserved **tourist quota**. Flights should be booked as far in advance as possible, but since most routes are covered daily, nobody should have to wait too long.

By air
Indian Airlines, whose main office is in the Malhotra Building on F-Block, Connaught Place, near *Wimpy*, operate the largest network of **internal flights**, though private carriers (see p.148) serve more destinations: tickets can be bought through travel agents or the main offices. All flights leave from the domestic terminal, 15km southwest of town, easily reached by the convenient EATS bus service (Rs50 plus Rs5 for luggage; 30min) that departs from Palika Bazaar, just opposite *Wimpy*. Rickshaws and taxis are more expensive, but slightly quicker. Passengers on domestic flights must check in two hours prior to departure. A simple food counter sells tea, coffee and snacks.

For a summary of flights from Delhi, see the Travel Details at the end of this chapter.

By train
Delhi's main railhead, **New Delhi Station** at the eastern end of Paharganj, less than 1km north of Connaught Place, has regular departures to all corners of India, and a very efficient **booking office** (Mon–Sat 8am–5pm) for foreign tourists, on the first floor of the main departure building. They'll give you advice on the fastest trains, and you should have little difficulty finding a seat or berth: **women** travelling alone in second class may prefer to ask for a berth in the ladies' carriage. Foreigners must show passports, and pay in foreign cur-

Recommended trains from Delhi

The trains below are recommended as the fastest and/or most convenient for specific cities. All are daily if not otherwise marked.

Destination	Name	No.	From	Departs	Total time
Agra	Shatabdi Express*	#2002	ND	6am	1hr 55min
	Punjab Mail	#2138	ND	5am	3hr 25min
	Mangala Express	#2618	HN	9.55am	2hr 33min
	Taj Express	#2180	HN	7.15am	2hr 47min
	A.P. Express	#2724	ND	5.50pm	2hr 40min
Ahmedabad	Ashram Express	#2916	OD	3.05pm	17hr
	Rajdhani Express (Tue, Thur & Sat)	#2958	ND	2.40pm	12hr 5min
Ajmer	Shatabdi Express‡*	#2015	ND	6.15am	6hr 30min
	Ahmedabad Mail	#9106	OD	10.50pm	8hr 30min
Calcutta	Rajdhani Express* (Except Mon & Fri)	#2302/	ND	5.15pm	17hr 30min
	Rajdhani Express* (Mon & Fri)	#2306	ND	5.00pm	19hr 40min
	Kalka–Howrah Mail	#2312	OD	6.30am	24hr 15min
Chandigarh	Himalayan Queen	#4095	ND	6.10am	4hr 15min
	Shatabdi Express*	#2011	ND	7.35am	3hr 10min
	Shatabdi Express*	#2005	ND	5.15pm	3hr 15min
Chennai	Tamil Nadu Express	#2622	ND	10.30pm	32hr 25min
	Chennai Rajdhani (Wed & Fri only)	#2434		3.30pm	27hr 35min
Jaipur	Shatabdi Express‡*	#2015	ND	6.15am	4hr 15min
	Ahmedabad Mail	#9106	OD	10.50pm	5hr 25min
Jhansi	Shatabdi Express*	#2002	ND	6.00am	4hr 25min
	Punjab Mail	#2138	ND	5.30am	6hr 25min
	Mangala Express	#2618	HN	9.55am	5hr 43min
Mumbai	Rajdhani Express§*	#2952	ND	4.00pm	16hr 35min
Haridwar¬	Shatabdi Express*	#2017	ND	7.10am	4hr 12min
	Mussoorie Express	#4041	OD	10.15pm	7hr 30min
Udaipur	Chetak Express	#9615	SR	2.10pm	21hr 15min
Varanasi	Kashi Vishwanath Express	#4258	ND	1.30pm	15hr 50min
	Farrakka Express	#3414 & 3484	OD	9.45pm	15hr 40min
Vasco da Gama	Goa Express†	#2780	HN	3pm	36hr 45min

OD Old Delhi   **ND** New Delhi   **HN** Hazrat Nizamuddin   **SR** Sarai Rohilla

†Change to connecting train at Miraj
¬Change for Rishikesh
‡ Does not run Sun
§ Does not run Tues
*A/c only

rency or in rupees backed up by exchange certificates. **Ignore** roadside advice to book train tickets elsewhere, and don't try buying one at the reservations building down the road, a confusion of queues and crowds. Also, ignore warnings that the tourist booking office is closed during the above hours.

Most **southbound** trains leave from New Delhi, many stopping also at **Old Delhi station**, where you can board the train if it's more convenient. All trains to **Rajasthan**, except those to Bharatpur, Kota and Sawai Madhopur, begin their journey at Old Delhi or **Sarai Rohilla station**, which is several kilometres to the west of Old Delhi railway station. Bookings can be made at the tourist office in New Delhi station and at the bus terminal. Quite a few trains to south and central India originate at **Hazrat Nizamuddin station**, a rickshaw ride away, southeast of Purana Qila, so check carefully when you buy your ticket.

See the box on p.153 for recommended trains from Delhi, and the Travel Details at the end of this chapter for a summary of the main train services from the capital.

By bus

Delhi is at the centre of an extensive **bus** network covering much of north India's neighbouring states. Buses can often be quicker than trains, but the long-distance ones especially tend to be uncomfortable. On long-distance routes there's usually a choice between ramshackle state-run buses and smart soft-seated coaches run by tourist offices, hotels and private agents. Use these as much as you can – outside the main cities, all buses are state-run.

The vast majority of **state-run buses** depart from the **Inter-state Bus Terminal** near Kashmiri Gate in Old Delhi (☎011/296 8836), which has a café and left-luggage counter. However, services for some UP hill stations like Nainital, Almora and Ramnagar (for Corbett National Park) leave from Anand Vihar ISBT (☎011/215 2431) across the Yamuna towards Ghaziabad. Buses to Agra, Mathura, Bharatpur, Vrindavan, Gwalior, Jaipur, Ajmer and Pushkar leave from the Sarai Kale Khan ISBT (☎011/463 8092) south of Hazrat Nizamuddin. However, for Jaipur and other points in Rajasthan, the Rajasthan Roadways terminal at Bikaner House, India Gate (☎011/338 6698) has by far the best service, with a range that includes comfortable deluxe buses. If leaving from the ISBT, be sure to arrive up to an hour before departure to allow time to find the correct counter (there are thirty or so) and book your ticket. Ask for the numbers of both platform and licence plate to ensure you board the right bus.

Private **deluxe buses**, in theory faster and more comfortable than state buses, usually depart from near the Ramakrishna Mission at the end of Main Bazaar, Paharganj, but some pick up passengers at hotels. Popular destinations include Kullu, Manali, and Dharamsala, which are not accessible by train, as well as towns in the UP hills, and Pushkar. Typical prices include: Rs375 to Jaipur, Rs400 to Manali, Rs400 to Dharamsala, Rs300 to Nainital and Rs400 to Pushkar. You can easily book tickets a day or two in advance at the agencies in Paharganj or Connaught Place. HPTDC run tourist coaches to Shimla and Manali from behind their office at Chandralok Building, 36 Janpath, and are slightly more expensive but not much better than the competition.

Leaving India

Most travellers leave India by **plane**, while the most likely overland destination from Delhi is Pakistan, and it's not uncommon to head straight for Nepal.

Anyone travelling to a country that requires a **visa** should get the necessary documentation from the embassy concerned (see Listings, p.149). Before going to the embassy, call to check opening hours, how many photos you'll need, and the likely waiting period.

By air

If you don't already have a ticket for a **flight** out of India, you'll have little trouble finding one, except between December and March when it may be difficult to get a flight at short notice. While you can buy tickets directly from the airlines, who all have offices around Connaught Place, it saves time and legwork to book through an **agency** (see p.151); reputable agents abound in Paharganj, and there are several on Janpath. The cheapest deals are to be had from touts on the street; make sure they're genuine by ringing the airline (see p.148) to check you have a seat. In any case, confirm your flight 72 hours before leaving.

Make sure you arrive two hours prior to departure for all **international flights**. The obligatory Rs500 airport tax is now supposed to be automatically levied in the ticket price but there is no harm in checking this with the airline when you reconfirm your flight. Most tourists taking night-time flights book a **taxi** in advance (Rs250–350) to avoid sleeping at the airport, where there's only a minimal food stall. It's a good idea to take a little food and drink in any case – delays are very common. If you're travelling on your own, you should have no difficulty finding someone who will share a taxi. Otherwise, **airport buses** to the international airport, running from outside the Indian Airlines office at the top of Janpath, cost Rs50 plus Rs5 per item of baggage. You can book tickets in advance at the small office next to Indian Airlines. The journey takes around 40 minutes. Departures are as follows: 4am, 5.30am, 7.30am, 2pm, 3.30pm, 6pm, 7.30pm, 9pm, 10.10pm and 11.30pm.

Overland travel

For journeys to neighbouring countries, there's always the alternative of **overland** travel, a long haul by train and/or bus. Crossings to **Pakistan** should be made from Amritsar, ten hours by train from Delhi, where buses cross the border and head to Lahore (lifts with trucks are no longer easy to find). The twice-weekly direct Delhi–Lahore bus, inaugurated by Prime Minister Vajpayee in 1998, was short-lived, terminated by the Kargil War of 1999; check with tourist information or the ISBT in Old Delhi. Those travelling overland to **Nepal** should make for **Gorakhpur**, to pick up a bus to the border, which is easier to cross on foot so as to have a choice of Kathmandu buses on the other side. In addition, several agencies now offer direct bus services to Kathmandu from Delhi – a gruelling two- or three-day journey that is convenient, but rarely comfortable, so you're probably better off making your own arrangements. Connections east to **Bangladesh** can be made via Calcutta or Chittagong.

Travel details

Trains

To **Rajasthan**: Abu Road (3–4 daily; 11hr 10min–14hr 15min); Ajmer (5–6 daily; 7hr 10min–11hr 5min); Bharatpur (5 daily; 2hr 50min–4hr 15min); Bikaner (3 daily; 10hr 20min–11hr 40min); Chittaurgarh (2 daily; 16hr 30min); Jaipur (10–12 daily; 4hr 25min–11hr 35min); Jodhpur (2 daily; 10hr 55min–13hr 40min); Kota (7–9 daily; 4hr 40min–10hr 45min); Sawai Madhopur (7 daily; 5hr 15min–8hr 15min); Udaipur (2 daily; 15hr 10min–21hr 15min).

To **Uttar Pradesh**: Agra (18–20 daily; 1hr 55min–4hr 40min); Allahabad (10–12 daily; 7–14hr); Dehra Dun (2–3 daily; 5hr 25min–10hr 20min); Gorakhpur (4–5 daily; 13hr 30min–22hr 5min); Kanpur (18–22 daily; 4hr 25min–8hr 20min); Lucknow (5–6 daily; 6hr–9hr 10min); Mathura (15–16 daily; 1hr 55min–2hr 45min); Varanasi (6–12 daily; 10hr 50min–18hr).

To **The east**: Bhubaneshwar (2–3 daily; 21hr 25min–35hr 15min); Cuttack (2–3 daily; 24hr 20min–34hr 10min); Gaya (9–10 daily; 11hr 15min–17hr); Guwahati (3–4 daily; 27hr 30min–40hr 40min); Howrah, Calcutta (7 daily; 17hr 45min–34hr 15min); Puri (2 daily; 31hr 30min–38hr 10min); Vijayawada (6 daily; 22hr 10min–31hr 35min).

To **Punjab and Himachal Pradesh**: Ambala Cantt (24 daily; 2hr 20min–3hr 30min); Amritsar (9 daily; 7hr 20 min–12hr); Chandigarh (5 daily; 3hr 10min–5hr); Firozpur (2 daily; 8hr 30min); Jammu Tawi (8–9 daily; 8hr 55min–15hr); Kalka, for Shimla (3 daily; 3hr 55min–6hr 15min); Ludhiana (12 daily; 3hr 45min–8hr 25min); Pathankot (5 daily; 10–12hr).

To **Central India**: Bhopal (20–22 daily; 7hr 45min–15hr 15min); Gwalior (21–24 daily; 3hr 15min–6hr); Indore (2 daily; 13hr 35min–17hr 50min); Jhansi (21–24 daily; 4hr 25min–8hr 10min).

To **Gujarat and Mumbai**: Ahmedabad (3–4 daily; 13hr 5min–19hr 45min); Mumbai (7–9 daily; 16hr 30min–29hr).

To **The south**: Bangalore (1–2 daily; 34hr 5min–50hr 55min); Chennai (4–5 daily; 28hr 10min–46hr 35min); Ernakulam (2–3 daily; 46hr 40min–52hr); Hyderabad (2–3 daily; 21hr 35min–34hr 45min); Kanyakumari (1 daily; 60hr); Pune (1 daily; 26hr 30min); Thiruvananthapuram (2

daily; 52hr 25min–57hr 30min); Vasco Da Gama (1 daily; 36hr 45min; change at Miraj).

Buses

Only state buses are included in this summary; for details of private buses see p.154.

To **Rajasthan**: Ajmer (every 30min; 9hr); Alwar (every 20min; 4hr); Bikaner (3 daily; 11hr); Chittaurgarh (1 daily; 11hr); Jaipur (every 30min; 6hr); Jodhpur (3 daily; 12hr); Kota (3 daily; 12hr); Pushkar (1 daily; 10hr).

To **Uttar Pradesh**: Agra (every 30min; 5hr); Almora (2 daily; 12hr); Dehra Dun (every 30min; 7hr); Haridwar (every 30min; 5hr 30min); Mussoorie (3 daily; 8hr 30min); Nainital (4 daily; 9hr); Ramnagar, for Corbett National Park (hourly; 7–8hr); Rishikesh (hourly; 6hr 30min).

To **Haryana & Punjab and Himachal Pradesh**: Amritsar (9 daily; 10hr); Chandigarh (every 20min; 5–6hr); Dharamsala (6 daily; 12hr); Manali (2 daily; 16hr); Shimla (9 daily; 10hr).

Flights

For a list of **airline addresses** and **travel agents**, see p.148 and p.151 respectively. In the listings below, IA represents Indian Airlines, JA is Jet Airways, and SA Sahara Indian Airlines.

Delhi to: Agra (IA 4 weekly; 35min); Ahmedabad (IA, JA 3–5 daily; 1hr 25min); Amritsar (IA 5 weekly; 50min); Aurangabad (IA 1 daily; 3hr 25min); Bagdogra, for Siliguri and Darjeeling (JA 1–2 daily; 1hr 55min–3hr 25min); Bangalore (IA, JA, SA 7 daily; 2hr 30min); Bhopal (IA 1–2 daily; 1hr 10min–2hr); Bhubaneshwar (IA 1 daily; 1hr 55min); Calcutta (IA, JA 4–5 daily; 2–3hr 40min); Chandigarh (IA, JA 3 weekly; 40min); Chennai (IA, JA, SA 6–7 daily; 2hr 25min–3hr 45min); Goa (IA 2 daily; 2hr 25min); Guwahati (IA, JA 2–3 daily; 2hr 5min–2hr 25min); Gwalior (IA 4 weekly; 45min); Hyderabad (IA 2 daily; 2hr); Indore (JA 1–2 daily; 1hr 45min–3hr); Jaipur (IA, JA 2–4 daily; 30–45min); Jaisalmer (IA 3 weekly; 2hr 5min); Jammu (IA 1 daily; 1hr 10min); Jodhpur (IA 3 weekly; 55min–1hr 50min); Khajuraho (JA 4 weekly; 1hr–1hr 55min); Kochi (IA 1 daily; 4hr); Kullu (JGA 2 daily; 1hr 30min–1hr 50min); Leh (IA

4 weekly; 1hr 15min); Lucknow (JA 3–4 daily; 50min–1hr); Mumbai (IA, JA, SA 18–21 daily; 2–4hr); Nagpur (IA 1 daily; 1hr 25min); Patna (IA 2–3 daily; 1hr 25min–2hr 15min); Pune (IA, JA 2 daily; 2hr); Ranchi (IA 1 daily; 2hr 50min); Shimla (IA 1 daily; 1hr); Thiruvananthapuram (IA 1 daily; 4hr 35min); Udaipur (IA, JA 1–2 daily; 1hr 55min); Vadodara (IA 1 daily; 1hr 25min); Varanasi (IA, JA 2–3 daily; 1hr 15min–2hr 55min).

CHAPTER 2

Highlights

✳ **Keoladeo national park, Bharatpur**
Rare Siberian cranes number among the thousands of birds and animals that flock to this amazing park in the winter. **See p.201**

✳ **Ranthambore national park** A wonderfully atmospheric wildlife park, where you're virtually guaranteed a tiger sighting. **See p.205**

✳ **Saivitri temple, Pushkar**
For optimum views of the famous lake and white-washed holy town, climb to the hilltop Saivitri temple at sunset. **See p.216**

✳ **Meherangarh Fort, Jodhpur** The most impressive citadel in Rajasthan, offering maximum impact views of the blue city below.
See p.224

✳ **Camel trekking** There's no better way to experience the Thar desert than by riding a camel through it. **See p.236**

✳ **Udaipur** Fabulous palaces, slender temple spires and intricately carved balconies adorn this lake-side city.
See p.256

✳ **Shilpgram**, near Udaipur. A great place to catch traditional folk music and dance from around the state, against a photogenic village backdrop. **See p.264**

2

Rajasthan

ndia's largest state, **RAJASTHAN**, emerged after Partition from a mosaic of eighteen feudal kingdoms, known in the British era as **Rajputana**, "Land of Kings". Running northeast from Mount Abu, near the border with Gujarat, to within a stone's throw of the ruins of ancient Delhi, its backbone is formed by the bare brown hills of the Aravalli Range, which divide the fertile Dhundar basin from the shifting sands and *khejri*-covered flats of the mighty Thar Desert, one of the driest places on earth. As the site of India's recent nuclear tests, this western flank of the country, forming the sensitive border with Pakistan, has become one of the world's most notorious geopolitical hotspots. However, the flat terrain, combined with the lure of the lucrative trans-Thar trade routes, rendered it vulnerable to invasion long before Partition. By taxing the movement of silk, spices and precious stones across their territories, successive rulers – from the Hindu **Rajputs** to their medieval Muslim overlords, the Moghuls – amassed vast fortunes, which they poured into ever more ambitious building projects.

Rajasthan's extravagant **palaces**, **forts** and finely carved **temples** today comprise one of the country's richest crop of historic monuments, visited in greater numbers than any other apart from Agra. But these exotic buildings are far from the only legacy of the region's prosperous and militaristic past. Centuries of Rajput rule created a hierarchy of rigid **caste** distinctions as monolithic as any in the country, bound by codes of chivalry and honour powerful enough to have driven the female population of whole cities to mass suicide, or *johar*. The Rajputs remain the landowners, dominating the state's political and economic life, while the lot of the lower castes has altered little since feudal times. In recent years, these disparities have led to violent inter-caste confrontations across Rajasthan, sparked off by Rajput resentment at the government's introduction of job and university place quotas for members of oppressed castes.

For visitors, however, Rajasthan's strong adherence to the traditions of the past is precisely what makes it a compelling place to travel. Swaggering moustaches, heavy silver anklets, bulky red, yellow or orange turbans, pleated veils and mirror-inlaid saris may be part of the complex language of caste, but to most outsiders they epitomize India at its most exotic. Nowhere is this traditional flamboyance more vividly expressed than at the annual camel fair at **Pushkar**, when hundreds of thousands of villagers converge on a sacred lake in the Aravalli Hills to buy and sell livestock, their almost luminous costumes striking against the muted hues of the desert.

Colour also distinguishes Rajasthan's most important tourist cities. Because of the reddish colourwash applied to its ornate facades and palaces in the nineteenth century, **Jaipur**, the chaotic state capital, is known as the "Pink City". One day's journey to the southwest, **Jodhpur**'s labyrinthine old walled town, whose sky-blue painted mass of cubic houses is overlooked by India's most

The International boundaries on this map are neither purported to be correct nor authentic by Survey of India directives. Publisher.

PAKISTAN

Kali Bangan

Bikaner
Gajner
Kolayat
Deshnok
Nokha

Kishangarh

Bhuttewala

Ramgarh

Thar Desert Indira Gandhi Canal

(Great Indian Desert)

Phalodi

R A J

Jaisalmer

Pokaran

Osian

Sam
Lodurva
Khuhri

Dechhu

Mandor

Jodhpur

Shiv

Balotra

Luni

Barmer

Pali
Marwar

Jalor
Sanderav

Ranakpur

Sirohi

NH-15

Sanchor

Mt Abu
Abu Rd

Nagda
Udaipur

Rishdeo

Palanpur

Dungarpur

Rann of Kutch

G U J A R A T

Himatnagar

Little Rann of Kutch

Ahmedabad

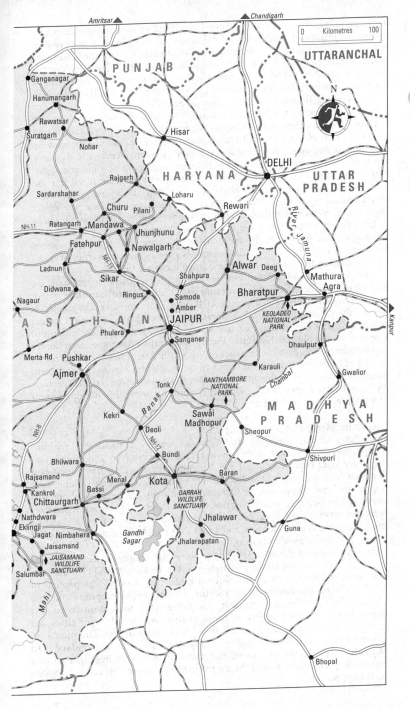

imposing hilltop fort, is called the "Blue City". Further west, the remote desert outpost of **Jaisalmer**, built from a local sandstone that glows in the evening light, is the "Golden City" – birthplace, and undisputed king, of the Rajasthani **camel safari**. In the far south of the state, **Udaipur** hasn't gained a colour tag yet, but it could be called the "White City": coated in decaying limewash, its waterside palaces and *havelis* (mansions) are perfectly reflected in the still waters of Lake Pichola, framed by a distant vista of desert hills.

As an extension to the "Golden Triangle" of Delhi–Agra–Jaipur, the route stringing together these four cities has become the most trodden tourist trail in India. From November until March, thousands of visitors may be moving around it at any one moment, and you'll find the same faces – and the same kinds of souvenir shops, hotels and restaurants – cropping up time and again. But with dependable accommodation and transport available in all but the most out-of-the-way places, it's easy enough to step off the merry-go-round of established sights into more remote areas. Northwest of Jaipur, the desert region of **Shekhawati** is littered with atmospheric little market towns whose richly painted *havelis*, castles and mausolea see barely a trickle of visitors. The same is true of **Bundi**, in the far south of the state, where one of western India's most imposing hilltop palaces presides over a compact warren of traditional buildings that have barely altered since medieval times.

Other incentives to venture into less frequented corners of the state are Rajasthan's wonderful **wildlife sanctuaries**. Of these, **Ranthambore**, where you can watch tigers prowling around Rajput ruins and lakeside jungles, is deservedly the most famous, but **Sariska**, between Jaipur and Agra, boasts almost as many big cats and equally serene landscapes. For sheer profusion, however, the **Keoladeo National Park** at **Bharatpur**, on the eastern border of Rajasthan near Agra, is unmatched in South Asia. Literally hundreds of species of birds, from giant saras cranes to tiny scarlet finches and incandescent kingfishers, feed here in the winter months, creating an unforgettable spectacle and a welcome respite from the frenetic cities that inevitably dominate most visitors' itineraries in this state.

Visiting Rajasthan

Rajasthan's climate reaches the extremes common to desert regions. Temperatures can rise unbearably to over 45°C between May and June, before the heavy skies over central and east Rajasthan break with a fierce monsoon that revitalizes the arid land and fills empty river beds. The fierce summer heat lingers until mid-September or October, when night temperatures drop considerably. The best time to visit is between November and February, when daytime temperatures rarely exceed 30°C; in midwinter, you'll need a shawl or thick jumper if you're outdoors, and a thin sleeping bag for night journeys and hotels that don't provide blankets.

Getting around the state is rarely problematic, though there's no avoiding some tedious long hauls. The state-run bus company, RSTDC, has regular services between cities, but since it hiked its prices by fifty percent in 1997, **private operators** have become a more popular option, offering cheaper fares and greater comfort. For those who don't want to subject themselves to sleepless nights on buses, **trains** connect all major cities and many smaller towns – always book ahead for night journeys. The most luxurious way to travel in Rajasthan, however, has to be the **Palace On Wheels**, a rolling five-star hotel that takes in the state's highlights over a week-long whistle-stop tour. More information about this service appears in Basics, on p.45.

Accommodation price codes

All accommodation prices in this book have been categorized using the price codes below. Prices given are for a double room, and all taxes are included. For more details, see p.51.

- ❶ up to Rs100
- ❷ Rs100–200
- ❸ Rs200–300
- ❹ Rs300–400
- ❺ Rs400–600
- ❻ Rs600–900
- ❼ Rs900–1500
- ❽ Rs1500–2500
- ❾ Rs2500 and upwards

Thanks to massive government tax incentives, **luxury accommodation** is big business in Rajasthan. Cashing in on the kudos of their royal connections, the region's maharajas have ditched their former squeamishness about business to open their family homes as "heritage" or **palace hotels**. While some have been insensitively converted under the auspices of large chains, others retain their former charm and, by comparison with the cost of five-stars in other parts of the world, offer excellent value for money. At the opposite end of the scale, the state's laudable **paying guest scheme**, Rajasthan's equivalent of B&B accommodation, provides a great opportunity to get to know an Indian family. Tourist offices across the state keep names and addresses of local families who take part in the scheme, along with details of family members, languages spoken and diet (veg or non-veg). Prices range from Rs150 per night, to around Rs750, depending on the location and levels of comfort offered.

Some history

People of the Indus Valley Civilization are known to have spread into western India as far as the Gujarati coast, from their base of Mohenjo Daro in Pakistan, but few Rajasthani sites – such as Kali Bangan in the north, thought to have been settled by the **Harappans** before 2500 BC – have been discovered. Similarly, the Buddhist influence of the powerful Mauryan empire, who rose to prominence in Gujarat between 360 BC and 210 BC, touched only the southernmost districts of Rajasthan.

The turbulent history of Rajasthan, characterized by courtly intrigue and inter-state warfare, only really begins in the sixth and seventh centuries AD, with the emergence of warrior clans such as the Sisodias, Chauhans, Kuchwahas and Rathores – the **Rajputs** ("sons of princes"). These heroic fighters seem originally to have been denied positions of power by a rigid caste system, due to low social status or foreign birth, but claimed to be able to cleanse themselves of impurities by complex fire rituals. Never exceeding eight percent of the population, they were to rule the separate states of **Rajputana** for centuries. Their code of honour set them apart from the rest of society – as did the popular belief that they were descended from the sun and moon – but did not invite excessive hostility. The Rajputs provided land, employment and trading opportunities for their subjects, and are still praised as gods in some communities.

The Rajput codes of chivalry that lay behind endless clashes between clans and family feuds found their most savage expression in battles with Muslims. **Muhammad of Ghori**, the first to march his troops through Rajasthan, met with the fierce defiance of the Chauhan Rajputs at Ajmer; however, the success of his second onslaught gained him the foothold that enabled him to establish the **Sultanate** in Delhi. During the 350 years that followed, much of central, eastern and western India came under the control of the sultans, but, despite all the Muslims' efforts and victories, Rajput resistance

Festivals in Rajasthan

Rajasthan's vibrant local costumes are at their most dazzling during the state's festivals, which accompany cattle markets and celebrate nationwide religious events, local folk heroes and village deities. Most also feature traditional dancing, singing and folk music. Some, such as Jaisalmer's Desert Festival, are geared particularly towards foreign visitors, and many of the most important celebrations fall in the tourist season (the cool months between November and March). For dates of specific events, ask at tourist offices; most festivals fall on days determined by the lunar calendar.

Also held during the winter, weddings in Rajasthan tend to be ostentatious, noisy affairs whose most conspicuous feature is the raucous groom's procession, or *baraat*. Led by out-of-tune bands and lines of urchins carrying mobile strip-lights, dancing male relatives process through the streets, waving wads of rupees ahead of the gold-turbaned bridegroom, seated on a white horse.

Nagaur Fair (Feb). The state's largest livestock market after Pushkar is a week-long fair, attracting thousands of camels, cattle, horses and donkeys and their owners to a lakeside location 135km northeast of Jodhpur. It's a grittier and less colourful *mela* than Pushkar's (mostly because few women attend), but correspondingly free of tourists.

Desert Festival (Feb). Jaisalmer's own two-day event, when camel races, folk dances and competitions are laid on primarily to attract tourists and promote local handicrafts.

Elephant Festival (March). Parades of caprisoned and brightly painted elephants process through the streets of Jaipur and into the City Palace to the accompaniment of drums and trumpets. The event concludes with an extraordinary "elephants versus mahoots" tug-o-war.

Mewar Festival (March & April). The Ranas of Udaipur celebrate Holi with the lighting of a sacred fire, traditional dance from local tribals and music from the city's famous bagpipe orchestra, followed by a swish society bash in the *Shiv Niwas Palace* hotel.

---

precluded them from ever undermining family solidarity and taking over Rajputana.

Ghori's successors were pushed out of Delhi in 1483 by the Moghul Babur, whose grandson **Akbar** came to power in 1556. Aware of the futility of using force against the Rajputs, Akbar chose instead to negotiate in friendship, and married Rani Jodha Bai, a princess from the Kuchwaha family of Amber. As a result, Rajputs entered the Moghul courts, and the influence of Moghul ideas on art and architecture remains evident in palaces, mosques, pleasure gardens and temples throughout the state.

When the Moghul empire began to decline after the accession of Aurangzeb in 1658, so too did the power of the Rajputs. Aurangzeb sided with a new force, the **Marathas**, who plundered Rajput lands and extorted huge sums of protection money from territories as strong as Mewar, whose capital was Udaipur, and Marwar, whose ruling family in Jodhpur had never submitted to any other power. The Rajputs eventually turned for help to the Marathas' chief rivals, the **British**, and signed formal treaties as to mutual allies and enemies. Although in theory the residents who represented British authority in each state were supposed to be neutral communicators, they soon wielded more power than the Rajput princes. However, the Rajputs were never denied their royal status, and relations were so amicable that few joined the Mutiny of 1857. Wealth from overland trade enabled them to festoon their palaces with silks,

Gangaur (April). A festival unique to Rajasthan, when women pray for their husbands, and unmarried girls wish for good ones. Excellent in Jaisalmer, when the local Raja heads the procession amid an entourage of camels, and in Mt Abu, where effigies of Gauri (Parvati) and Isa (Shiva) – the ideal couple – are carried through the streets along with potted rice and flowers which hark back to the days when this was primarily a harvest festival.

Rani Sati Mela (Aug). Vast crowds gather for this day of prayers and dances in Jhunjhunu (northern Shekhawati), in memory of a merchant's widow who committed *sati*, sacrificing her life on her husband's pyre, in 1595.

Urs Mela (Oct). Tens of thousands of Muslims converge on the Dargah in Ajmer for the subcontinent's largest Islamic festival, commemorating the life of the Sufi saint and teacher Muin-ud-din Chishti, who died here in 1236. For weeks before it, you'll see busloads of pilgrims and *pirs* (wandering holy men) heading towards the shrine, where worship culminates in performances by India and Pakistan's top *qawwali* singers.

Diwali (Nov). A five-day festival of lights celebrated across India but of particular importance to the merchant community, especially in Shekhawati, since it marks the start of the financial year and includes a day of praises to Lakshmi, goddess of wealth. Hundreds of delicious sweets are cooked and exchanged by families and friends.

Pushkar Camel Fair (Nov). Rajasthan's largest and most colourful festival attracts an estimated 200,000 people and 50,000 camels, camped in the dunes around the sacred lake at Pushkar, where a holy dip at this time is considered especially auspicious. Still an unmissable spectacle, despite the vastly inflated accommodation prices and tourist deluge.

Chandrabhaga Fair (Nov). The full moon of Kartika is celebrated in Jhalawar at the temples on the banks of the Chandrabhaga, and devotees bathe in the river.

carpets, jewels and furnishings far beyond the imagination of most ordinary citizens, while the prosperous **Marwari** merchants of the northwest built and decorated stylish mansions, temples and meeting halls. Murals depicting British ministers with Indians, British hunting parties, ladies, motor cars and black-capped bobbies are firm reminders of the strong alliance between the two ruling powers.

The nationwide clamour for Independence in the years up to 1947 eventually proved stronger in Rajasthan than Rajput loyalty; when British rule ended, the Rajputs were left out on a limb. With persuasion from the new Indian government including the offer of "privy purses", they agreed one by one to join the Indian Union, and in 1949 the 22 states of Rajputana finally merged to form the state of **Rajasthan**.

But for three brief years of Janata domination from 1977 onwards, Congress held sway over Rajasthan from its first democratic elections in 1952 until 1994, when the **BJP** won a decisive victory. Central control soon exposed the Rajputs' neglect of their subjects, whom they had entrusted to power-thirsty landowners (*jaghidars*), and village councils (*panchayats*) were set up to organize local affairs. Nonetheless, several princes still maintain splendid households. Since 1947 the literacy rate among men has risen from 9 percent to 25 percent, and several universities have been established. New industries benefit from an increased electricity supply that once only met the needs of palaces, but now reaches most villages, while irrigation schemes such as the Indira Gandhi Canal, which brings water from Punjab across the northern deserts to Bikaner and Jaisalmer, have improved crop production, and provided relief in times of inadequate monsoon.

The **modernization** of Rajasthan, however, has been an uphill struggle, and this remains among the poorest and most staunchly traditional regions of India. As Rajasthanis are apt to remind you: "*Delhi door ast*", "Delhi is far away", particularly in its attitude to women. Feminist groups in the capital created a publicity storm in the 1980s over the *sati* case of Roop Kanwar, an eighteen-year-old from a village near Jaipur who burned to death on her husband's funeral pyre (see p.1529), but more revealing of the everyday problems faced by Rajasthani women are the rates of female mortality and illiteracy, far higher here than in any other state in the country.

Drought in Rajasthan

The succession of violent cyclones that devastated eastern India during the monsoons of 1999 and 2000, in which tens of thousands died and millions were left homeless, somewhat eclipsed a less dramatic, but no less serious, climate crisis in India's northwest. Since the failure of the 1997 rains, **drought** has brought the parched desert regions of Rajasthan to their knees. Millions of farmers have lost cattle and crops, while in the blazing summer of 2000, when temperatures in the Thar soared to well above 50 degrees for weeks on end, many wells ran dry, forcing streams of desperate rural poor to flee the worst affected areas.

Unprepared for the scale of the disaster, the government was slow to respond. But after pictures of emaciated Rajasthani refugees and bony cattle lying dead by the roadside hit the newspapers, Prime Minister Vajpayee made a televised appeal for public donations, and later announced a Rs9.5 billion (£138 million) relief package: trainloads of fodder were dispatched to feed starving animals, along with convoys of subsidized grain, and tankers of water.

Meanwhile, the Indian drought was starting to make international headlines. Commentators evinced amazement that the country Microsoft had just selected to site its multimillion-dollar Hi-Tech City, which boasted the world's largest film industry, and which had recently developed its own nuclear bomb, was incapable of providing adequate water supplies for an estimated fifty million farmers.

What few picked up on, however, was that the Indian government's water policies were, after the failure of the rains, among the main causes of shortages. Since Independence, huge dam and canal projects have been pushed forward by successive administrations to irrigate the dry regions. For the twelve years after 1985, when rainfall levels were good, these lived up to expectations, but when the monsoons failed in the late 1990s, the expensive irrigation network was found wanting.

Rajasthan is no stranger to drought. In the past, however, villagers would capture what little rain fell in the desert, maintaining ancient, stone-lined wells in pond bottoms and river beds. But the advent of seemingly inexhaustible supplies of piped water put paid to this traditional knowledge. Instead of remaining self-reliant, people relaxed their traditionally frugal attitude to water and relied on the government to meet their needs. Thus, when the drought started to bite, poor farmers had to rely on supplies tanked in by private hauliers. To pay for it, they borrowed money at usurious rates from the local landowners, putting up their fields and homes as security – which is why so many thousands ended up on the road in 2000.

The Indian government's relief efforts may have alleviated the worst of the suffering, but its long-term policies, determined more by the demands of big business and corrupt officialdom than the basic needs of Rajasthan's 23,400 drought-prone villages, look hopelessly inadequate under the relentlessly cloudless skies of the Thar.

Jaipur and around

A flamboyant showcase of Rajasthani architecture, the **Pink City** of **JAIPUR** has long been established on tourist itineraries as the third corner of India's "Golden Triangle", just 300km southwest of Delhi and 200km west of Agra. Though the "Pink City" label applies specifically to the old walled quarter of the state capital, in the northeast of town, exuberant eighteenth- and nineteenth-century palaces are scattered throughout the whole urban area. These, and the salmon-coloured facades of the city's ornately decorated vernacular buildings, form an appropriately exotic backdrop for the swirl of typically Rajasthani street life below. A vast storehouse of traditional crafts, the orderly **bazaars** of the old town rank among the most vibrant in Asia, renowned above all for hand-dyed and embroidered textiles, jewellery, and the best selection of precious stones and metals in India. For all its colour, however, Jaipur's heavy traffic, combined with the aggression of over-eager traders and touts, tends to reduce the appeal of a long stay. Few travellers find it easy to relax here, and most leave craving the fresher air and laid-back pace of Bharatpur or the Thar Desert towns.

Lying on the bed of a long-dry lake, Jaipur sprawls to hills in the north, east and west, and south across the open plains towards Bundi. Getting and keeping your bearings is simple; even if you can't see the high walls of the Pink City, the hills behind it in the northeast, topped by **Nawalgarh Fort**, are always conspicuous. The **Pink City** houses the principal tourist attractions – the Palace of Winds or **Hawa Mahal**, and Jai Singh's **City Palace** and **Jantar Mantar Observatory** – while the **Ram Niwas Garden**, **zoo**, and **Albert Hall** (Central Museum) are a short way south of the walls, within easy walking distance of its gates. Broad and widely spaced roads in the newer areas outside the walls accommodate the industries and businesses that underlie the economy of the modern city, as well as most of Jaipur's hotels. **Mirza Ismail (MI) Road** is the main route from west to east (south of the old city), on which you'll find the GPO, hotels and restaurants and some of the larger boutiques and jewellery shops. **Station Road** runs from the railway station in the west, past the bus stand and on to Chand Pole, the westernmost gate of the old city

If you're anywhere near Jaipur in March, don't miss the **Elephant Festival**, one of India's most flamboyant parades, celebrated with full Rajput pomp during Holi (March).

Some history

Jaipur is one of Rajasthan's younger cities, founded in 1727. In 1700, **Jai Singh II** succeeded at the tender age of thirteen to the throne of the **Kuchwaha Rajputs** in Ajmer, inheriting a realm that encompassed Shekhawati to the north, and spread east to the borders of the kingdom of the Jats at Bayana, south to Aligarh, and west to Kishangarh where its boundaries met the mighty kingdoms of the Mewars (Udaipur) and Marwars (Jodhpur). Although the Kuchwaha Rajputs had been the first to ally themselves with the Moghuls, in 1561, thereby inviting contempt from other Rajput clans, the free flow of trade, art and ideas with their obliging overlords had by this time won them great prosperity. Jai Singh's sharp wit greatly impressed the Moghul emperor Aurangzeb, who bestowed upon him the title of "Sawai" (one and a quarter), to imply his superlative potential. Jai Singh proved his distinction, excelling in battle, politics and learning, and quickly showing an aptitude for astronomy and an extraordinary passion for symmetry.

JAIPUR

RESTAURANTS

Annapurna	J
Anoka Gaon	A
Chanakya	E
Copper Chimney	F
Four Seasons	K
Indian Coffee House	H
Lassiwalla	G
LMB	D
Mediterraneo	B
Natraj	I
Niro's	I
Pizza Hut	C

ACCOMMODATION

Anurag	9
Arya Niwas	13
Atithi	16
Bissau Palace	2
Dewi Niwas	21
Diggi Palace	22
Evergreen Guest House	19
Jai Mahal	20
Jaipur Inn	10
Kaiser-I-Hind	14
Kantichandra Palace	12
Karni Niwas	15
Madhuban	6
Mansingh & Mansingh Towers	17
Meghniwas	1
Narain Niwas	24
New Pink City	18
Raj Mahal	23
Raj Palace	7
Rambagh Palace	25
Sajjan Niwas	4
Samode Haveli	3
Shahpura House	8
Tara Niwas	11
Umaid Bhavan	5

Galta

Gaitor & Amber

Nahargarh

Suraj Pole Gate

Zarawar Singh Gate

THE PINK CITY

Talkatora Tank

Govind Devji

City Palace & Museum

Jantar Mantar

Hawa Mahal

Jami Masjid

Sanganeri Gate

Elephant Owners' Area

Chand Pole

HPO

Rajmandir Cinema

Bus Stand

Thomas Cook

Sita World Travels

Jaipur Railway Station

Police Station

New Gate

Ajmeri Gate

Zoo (Birds)

Central Museum

Ram Niwas Gardens

Zoo (Mammals & Reptiles)

SMS Hospital

Museum of Indology

Anokhi

Delhi

Ajmer

Sanganer & Airport (15 km)

A & Sikar

0   Metres   500

N

When Jai Singh decided to move his capital south from the cramped hilly area of Amber, he drew up plans for the new city of Jaipur, named after himself, in accordance with the ancient Hindu treatise *Vastu Sashtra*, a formal exposition on architecture written soon after the compilation of the *Vedas*. With the aid of the superb Bengali architect Vidyadhar Chakravati, he had the city built in less than eight years. The **City Palace** was also designed by him, as was **Jantar Mantar**, the largest stone-built observatory in the world.

After Jai Singh's fruitful 43-year reign came an inevitable battle for succession between the offspring he had fathered with 28 wives and four concubines, and the state was thrown into turmoil. Much of its territory was lost to Marathas and Jats, and the British quickly moved in to take advantage of Rajput infighting, gaining power for themselves while forming alliances with the Rajputs to avoid inconvenient conflict. Unlike their neighbours in Delhi and Agra, the rulers of Jaipur remained loyal to the British during the bloody uprisings of 1857. Following Independence, Jaipur merged with the states of Bikaner, Jodhpur and Jaisalmer; it became capital of Rajasthan in 1956. Today, with a population bordering on two million, the state's most advanced commercial and business centre is as prosperous as ever.

The growing affluence, however, has brought with it mounting **environmental problems**. With 25 percent of Rajasthan's 1.22 million vehicles registered here, air pollution in the Pink City exceeds the World Health Organization's permissable limits by three times. Recently, the municipality took the radical step of banning three-wheelers, but this has had little impact on air quality, which is worsened by emissions from two large industrial areas on the outskirts. Water quality is also poor due to the lack of adequate sewage disposal systems, and the fact that around one third of the city's inhabitants live in slum dwellings without toilets. As a result, infectious diseases are rapidly increasing, notably **hepatitis** (a real problem here at the start of the hot season in March and April) and **malaria** (seventy percent of cases reported in one hospital in 1997 were of the deadly Falciparum strain). The civic authority's inability to respond effectively to Jaipur's public health problems was epitomized in June 1996 when an anti-malarial "fogging operation" in the walled old town led to hospitalization of 2700 people with breathing problems and bronchitis.

Arrival and information

Jaipur's Sanganer **airport**, 15km south of the centre, is served by domestic Indian Airlines and Jet Airways flights from Delhi and Mumbai. An airport bus into town costs Rs30; taxis charge more like Rs250.

The **railway station** is 1km west of the Pink City, very close to the main concentration of hotels, while state buses from all over Rajasthan and further afield pull in at the more central Inter-state Bus Terminal on Station Road. Arriving from Delhi, you skirt the south side of the city, stopping briefly at an intersection called Narayan Circle, where rickshaw-wallahs frequently board the bus saying it's the end of the line ("bus going to yard"); it isn't, only a ploy to get you on to their rickshaws and into a hotel that pays generous commission. Rackets like this thrive in Jaipur, so brace yourself for a barrage of auto-rickshaw drivers wherever you arrive.

Information

RTDC has a handy **tourist information offiice** on Platform 1 of the railway station (daily 6am–8pm; ✆0141/315714). There's a second branch at the

If you come across an Indian handicraft object or garment abroad, chances are it will have been bought in Jaipur. Foreign buyers and wholesalers from all over the world flock in their thousands to the Pink City to shop for textiles, clothes, jewellery, miniature paintings, puppets and pottery. As a regular tourist, you'll find it harder to hunt out the best merchandise and fairest prices, but it can be fun trying. As a source of souvenirs, nowhere else in India – not even Delhi – comes close.

In keeping with Maharaja Jai Singh's original city divisions, different streets are reserved for purveyors of different goods. For clothes and cloth, including Jaipur's famous **blockprint** work and *bhandani* **tye-dye**, recently pedestrianized **Bapu bazaar**, on the south side of the Pink City is the best place. This is also where you'll find those pointy-toed camel-leather *jootis*, and traditional glass, laquer and inlaid bangles. On the opposite side of town, along Amber Road just beyond Zorawar Gate, rows of emporia are stacked with gorgeous patchwork wallhangings, embroidery and traditional or antique Rajasthani costumes; these places do a steady trade with bus parties of wealthy tourists, so be prepared to haggle hard. The same is true of the outlets of the city's renowned **blue potteries**, further along Amber Road, where you can buy old-style Persian-influenced vases, in additional to tiles, plates, candleholders and a host of other Westerner-oriented nick-nacks. For top-quality blue pottery, though, visit the shop of Jaipur's most famous ceramist, Kripal Singh, at B-18A Shiv Marg (near the *Jaipur Inn*), Bani Park. Bear in mind that Jaipur's blue pottery is essentially decorative; none of it – in spite of what some shop owners tell you – may be used for hot food as the glazes are unstable and poisonous.

For silver **jewellery** and **gemstones**, **Chameliwala Market**, southwest of the old city, is in a league of its own. It is also one of the hardest places to shop in peace, thanks to a particularly slippery breed of scam merchant, known locally as **lapkars**. Usually young lads in their late teens or early twenties, smartly dressed in Western clothes, these smooth operators speak excellent English, which they use to befriend foreigners in the street. Offers of trips to local beauty spots are invariably followed by a stop at a "relative's" art studio, pottery or carpet-weaving workshop. The sting comes when the visitor is pressured into buying something with a credit card, which is deftly whisked into a backroom and used to run off a few blank dockets. One is signed on the spot; the others are filled in and completed with a forged signature later.

When buying gemstones, you should also be extremely suspicious of anyone offering an address in your own country where, it is claimed, you'll be able to sell them at a huge profit. This is nonsense, of course, but by the time you realize this you'll be thousands of miles away wondering where the mysterious entries on your credit card bill came from. So if you're paying for gemstones or jewellery with a credit card in Jaipur, don't let it out of your sight, and certainly don't agree to leaving a docket as security.

One place you're guaranteed to have no such problems is the opulent **Anokhi** showroom at 2 Tilak Marg, in the Civil Lines area, southwest of the city centre. Started by a British designer, who now employs hundreds of workers in the Jaipur area to produce garments for her high-street stores in the UK, this is the place to buy high-quality "ethnic" Indian evening wear, tastefully patterned *salwar camise* and block-printed or batique men's shirts. They also do lovely bedspreads and cushion covers, although you can find similar textiles at much lower prices in the shops lining the west side of the ground floor of Ganpati Plaza, on MI Road.

Finally, it's worth knowing that any stuff you've bought in Jaipur, but don't wish to cart around, may be sent ahead to Delhi or Mumbai. Silverwing Roadways, at Mandawa House, Sansar Chandra Road, 200m north of *Hotel Arya Niwas* (℡0141/367542 or 376151) will truck parcels securely bound in cotton (which you can have done in the lobby of the Head Post Office on MI Road) to their little warehouses in Kamla Market, Delhi and Clive Road, Mumbai, where you can collect them weeks (or months) later. They charge around Rs100 for a large suitcase-sized package.

Tourist Hotel (☏0141/360328), and an unusually hopeless Government of India tourist office at the *Khasa Kothi* hotel (Mon–Fri 9am–6pm, Sat 9am–1.30pm; ☏0141/315461). To find out what's on, you're better off consulting the monthly **Jaipur Vision**, available at Books Corner on MI Road (Rs25).

Changing money can be time-consuming at the city's banks, but there are plenty of private exchange places in Jaipur offering more or less the same rates, where you can cash travellers' cheques quickly and easily in air-conditioned comfort. Best of the bunch are Thomas Cook on the first floor of Jaipur Towers, on MI Road (Mon–Sat 9.30am–6pm), American Express, in the next building down MI Road from Ganpati Plaza, (Mon–Sat 9.30am–6pm) and LKP Merchant Financing, on the first floor of Sunil Sadan, 2 MI Road (Mon–Sat 9.30am–6pm).

City transport

Jaipur's frenzied flow of vehicles is at its heaviest during the morning and evening peak periods; it's best to avoid rush hours if you want to enjoy the sights and street activity. The city itself, particularly its modern part, is very spread out, and although it's pleasant to walk around the Pink City, you may need some form of transport to get you there.

Unmetered yellow-top **taxis** have stands on MI Road, and there are countless auto-rickshaws buzzing around at all times of day and night. Fares, as ever, should be fixed in advance.

Given Jaipur's chronic pollution problems, it makes sense to opt for cycle power while you're in the city. **Cycle rickshaws** travel no slower through the congestion than autos, and are much cleaner and cheaper. As long as you keep your wits about you, the city is also a fun place to explore by **bicycle**. Many budget hotels rent bikes out to their guests; failing that, you can rent one for Rs25–30 a day from a place in the passage by 286 Kishan Pole Bazaar, about 100m north of the Ajmeri Gate, and from the Muslim cycle repair-shop just off Nirwan Marg, near the *Jaipur Inn*.

Cars with drivers can be rented most cheaply and reliably through the *Arya Niwas Hotel*, or RTDC at the *Tourist Hotel*, MI Road. Typical costs are around Rs375 return to Amber, or Rs675 to Samode. For destinations not covered by fixed fares, expect to pay around Rs75–100 per hour, plus Rs4.5 per kilometre.

City tours

One efficient, though somewhat rushed, way to see Jaipur's main attractions is on a **guided tour**. **Half-day** tours, starting from the railway station and the RTDC *Tourist Hotel* on MI Road, take in Hawa Mahal, the Observatory, the City Palace and Museum, Amber Fort, Jaigarh Fort and the Central Museum (daily 8am, 11.30am & 1.30pm; 5hr, book the day before; Rs75). The **full-day** tour (daily 9.30am–5.30pm; Rs125, Rs150 a/c) also includes the Central Museum, Birla Mandir and Gaitor – getting to the fort alone costs more than the tour itself, unless you walk. ITDC Ashok Travels and Tours at the gates of the *Khasa Kothi* hotel offer full-day tours (daily 9.30am–5.30pm; Rs125, Rs150 a/c) which also take in Amber.

Accommodation

As a major tourist and business centre, Jaipur has a wide selection of **hotels**, many of them offering exceptional value for money. For once this is especially true at the bottom of the range, thanks largely to the **paying guest scheme** introduced by the local tourist office, which enables you to stay in small family guesthouses that are far friendlier than most hotels. That said, the city also boasts some of India's most impressive and opulent **palace hotels**, as well as a batch of thoroughly dilapidated former mansions offering more atmosphere than creature comforts. Wherever you choose to stay, it's prudent to book ahead, particularly around the Pushkar camel *mela* (early Nov) and the Elephant Festival (first half of March).

Inexpensive

Anurag, D-249 Devi Marg, Bani Park ☎ 0141/201679. Clean, sedate guesthouse in quiet residential area, with large rooms and a relaxing lawn. Meals available. ❸–❹

Dewi Niwas near Dhuleshwar Garden, Sadar Patel Marg, C Scheme ☎ 0141/363727, ✆ singh_kd@hotmail.com. Homely paying guesthouse in 300-year-old yellow-washed *haveli*, marooned amid Jaipur's concrete southern suburbs. Large rooms, sunny courtyard (with incongruous grass huts for candlelit meals), and cold beers. Mrs Singh also serves delicious home-cooked food. ❷–❸

Diggi Palace, Diggi House, Shivaji Marg, Hospital Road ☎ 0141/374265, ✆ 370359, ✆ diggihtl@datainfosys.net. This lofty 200-year-old *haveli* made national headlines a few years back when its owner was arrested for hashish smuggling, since when standards have dropped noticeably, but it's still among the few "heritage" hotels in the budget category. Rooms range from basic to larger "standards" (Rs300), a/c suites and cottages facing lawns (Rs600). ❷–❻

Evergreen Guest House, Chameliwala Mkt, MI Road ☎ 0141/363446, ✆ 204234, ✆ evergreen34@hotmail.com. Famous budget ghetto that's claustrophobic and seedy, or totally cool depending on your point of view. Its poorly maintained rooms are stacked on three storeys around a large, leafy garden, with adjacent pool (Rs75 non-guests) and café-restaurant. ❷–❸

Jaipur Inn, B-17 Shiv Marg, Bani Park ☎ 0141/201121. Along with *Evergreen*, Jaipur's most popular backpackers' hostel. Thanks to years of undeserved guidebook recommendations, an air of complacency hangs over the place, compounded by the ugly modern architecture. Its Rs400 rooms are pleasant enough, but dorms are stuffy and cramped, and the "non-attached" cells ludicrously overpriced. ❶–❹

Kaiser-I-Hind, Palace Road, opposite the *Sheraton Rajputana* ☎ 0141/200195. Once Jaipur's top hotel, though now sadly dilapidated. Deep verandas and a peacock-filled garden still evoke the Raj era, but most travellers find the huge suites and musty doubles too grubby. Illustrious former guests include Gandhi, Nehru, Khrushchev, Rockefeller and Mark Twain, who complained in his autobiography about the bedsprings in room #6 (they haven't been replaced yet). For die-hard romantics only. ❸

Kantichandra Palace, Vivek Nagar, off Station Road ☎ 0141/204473. Quirky old *haveli*, within easy walking distance of the bus stand, that has somehow lapsed to become an obscure, grubby budget hotel. Some of the rooms are much larger and airier than others, so check a few out first. Huge lawn and no hasslers. Good value. ❷–❸

New Pink City, opposite GPO, Pink City Lane ☎ 0141/363774. A row of large, fairly well-kept "attached" rooms fronting a spacious garden that's used in the winter for wedding parties (check to make sure there isn't one on while you're there). Very central, good value, and their peacocks are cute, but you'll need a mozzie net. Not recommended for lone women travellers, as the approach is down a narrow, unlit lane. ❷

Moderate

Arya Niwas, behind Amber Complex, Sansar Chandra Road ☎ 0141/372456, ✆ 364376, ✆ aryahotl@jp1.dot.net.in. Impeccably clean, family-run place that's larger and more impersonal than a guesthouse, which some people will like. All rooms have attached baths and hot water. The restaurant is excellent (see Eating), and there's a bar and reading room overlooking a lawn strewn with wicker furniture, where you can relax over coffee or tiffin. Tours, bicycles and fairly priced car rental. Arguably the best hotel in Rajasthan in this bracket. Book ahead. ❺–❻

Atithi, 1 Park House Scheme, opposite All India Radio ☎ 0141/378679, ✆ atithijaipur@hotmail.com. Centrally located, spotlessly clean guesthouse boasting a leafy raised terrace and relaxing lawn. All rooms with private bathrooms, soap and towels; the pricier ones have balconies. Excellent guests-only restaurant, email facilities, courteous staff and genuinely hospitable management. If it's full, you'll be better off in the nearby *Karni Niwas* than at the *Aangan* next door. ❹–❻

Karni Niwas, C-5 Motilal Atal Road, behind the *Neelam Hotel* ☎0141/365433, ℻375034, ℮karniniwas@hotmail.com. Pleasant and deservedly popular little guesthouse, run by four burly brothers, that takes the overspill from the *Atithi*. The pricier rooms (some a/c) have lacquered furniture and great verandas. ④–⑤

Madhuban, D-237 Behari Marg, Bani Park ☎0141/200033 or 205427, ℻202344, ⓦwww.madhuban.net. A very comfortable option at this price: large standard rooms at the back around a lovely garden, or plusher deluxe ones in the main building (two with Jacuzzis). Spotless and secure, complimentary pickup from station (phone ahead) and the food is good too. ⑤–⑧

Meghniwas, C-9 Sawai Jai Singh Highway, Bani Park ☎0141/202034 or 5 or 6, ℻201420, ⓦwww.meghniwas.com. Grand family house in the posh part of town, with pleasant furniture, a pool and a croquet lawn. All the facilities of a four-star hotel (including a/c) at a fraction of the price, and still with the personal touch of a family-run place. ⑦–⑧

Sajjan Niwas, Bank Road, behind the Collectorate, Bani Park ☎0141/311544, ℻206029, ⓦwww.sajjanniwas.com. Large, immaculate marble-lined rooms in a new suburban building. The pricier front-side ones open onto a quiet lawn; all are more spacious and lighter than those in the more popular *Umaid Bhawan* next door. ③–⑥

Shahpura House, D-257 Devi Marg, Bani Park ☎0141/202293 or 203069, ℻201494, ℮shapurahous@usa.net. Smart, respectable suburban hotel run by a descendant of the Shahpura royal family. Recently renovated and excellent value, with tastefully furnished rooms (one has a big sun terrace and fancy mirrorwork), wonderful colonial-era arms and sepia photos on the walls, as well as attentive staff. ⑤–⑧

Tara Niwas, B-22-B Shiv Marg, Bani Park ☎0141/2206823, ℮aryahotl@jp1.dot.net.in. New place pitched at foreign buyers and other longer-staying visitors, with sliding rates that offer unbeatable value (Rs2000 per week or Rs6000 per month for non-a/c doubles); daily tariffs comparable with Arya Niwas, but you get a lot more for your money here. The rooms (all en suite; some a/c) are huge and scrupulously clean, the food excellent and the area quiet. ④–⑥

Umaid Bhavan, D1-2A Bani Park ☎0141/316184, ℻207445, ⓦwww.umaidbhawan.com. Large and labyrinthine, but clean and well-managed, guesthouse in quiet suburb, with sunny garden and small pool. Congenial and good value. ④–⑦

Expensive

Bissau Palace, Khetri House Road, outside Chand Pole ☎0141/304371, ℻304628, ⓦwww.bissaupalace.com. The summer home of the Thakurs of Bissau, built 1787–1919 and decorated with artefacts of the heroic fighting days before Independence. Rajasthan's first heritage hotel, with tastefully furnished rooms, recent erotic murals (ask to see the ones in the Prince's Suite), some a/c, plus gardens, and a swimming pool. Adequate parking space, and dining facilities. ⑦–⑧

Jai Mahal, Jacob Road, Civil Lines ☎0141/371616, ℻365237. Palatial former residence of the Jaipur state PM, now run as a plush hotel by the Taj Group. Regal atmosphere, a swimming pool, gardens and a restaurant. ⑨

Mansingh, Sansar Chandra Road ☎0141/378771, ℻377582. Luxurious a/c rooms with large windows, a swimming pool, health club, restaurant and bar. The newer *Mansingh Towers* next door (same ☎&℻ and price range) is a spectacular fusion of plate-glass and sculpted Moghul stone; the lobby alone is worth a visit for the "giant-miniature" painting by acclaimed Bikaner artist Mahaveer Swami. $275 gets you a suite with its own Jacuzzi. ⑥–⑧

Narain Niwas Palace, Kanota Bagh, Narayan Singh Road ☎0141/561291, ℻561045, ⓦwww.narainniwas.com. Gaudily restored grand *haveli*, 2km from the old city, with individually styled rooms and a classy new pool in huge, shady gardens. No longer the good deal it used to be, but a comfortable option. ⑧–⑨

Raj Mahal Palace, Sardar Patel Marg ☎0141/381757, ℻381887. Elegant former palace of Jai Singh's favourite maharana, converted into Neoclassical style pad by the British for their agent general. Lawns, peacocks, a pool and all the trimmings, though an air of neglect hangs over the place. Rooms start at $180 per night. ⑨

Raj Palace, Chomu *haveli*, Zorawar Singh Gate, Amber Road ☎ & ℻0141/634077, ⓦwww.raj-palace.com. The most recently converted of Jaipur's grand old *havelis*, and the only one with central a/c and wheelchair ramps throughout. Each room is individually designed, mixing new and antique Indian furniture: the upper floor features a penthouse honeymoon suite with an exclusive courtyard and superb views. No pool yet, though. Rooms $165–385. ⑨

Rambagh Palace, Bhawani Singh Marg ☎0141/381919, ℻381098, ⓦwww.tajhotels.com. Indisputably the grandest palace hotel in Jaipur, if not in India. A vast, thoroughly Rajasthani complex set amid 47 acres of beautiful gardens. Prince Charles and Princess Diana stayed here, and it's a

favourite with Bollywood stars. Even if you can't afford a room, call in for a coffee and walk around the grounds. Rooms $250–930. ❾
Samode Haveli, Gangapole ☎ & ℱ 0141/632407, ⓦ www.samodehaveli.com. Exquisite old *haveli* in the northeastern corner of the city, formerly a residence of the Rawals of Samode. Opulent, traditional Rajput decor, *fin-de-siècle* furniture and top service, but its rates ($66–94) reflect its fame. The best rooms are in the *zenana* portion of the building (ask to see the richly mirrored *sheesh mahal* suites). No pool. ❾

The Pink City

Jaipur's most famous monuments – the **Hawa Mahal** and **Jantar Mantar Observatory** – both lie within the **City Palace Complex**, at the heart of the **Pink City**. For anyone familiar with Indian cities, the grid-plan may come as a surprise. Instead of a maze of narrow winding alleys, the spacious streets of the quarter are completely straight and laid out at right angles in accordance with the *Vastu Shastras*, ancient Hindu architectural manuals, carefully adapted and applied by the local maraharaja in the eighteenth century. However, the city's single most striking feature, its **pink colour**, did not form part of Jai Singh's original design. Although many people think the rosy hue is as old as the buildings themselves, they were in fact originally a sallow yellow. Pink is traditionally the colour of hospitality in Rajasthan, but the wash, now regularly reapplied, has only been compulsory since the city was spruced up in preparation for the visit of Prince Albert from England in 1856.

Another face-lift preceded the visit, in 2000, of Bill Clinton and daughter. The chief minister of Rajasthan ordered that the colonnaded walkways lining the old city's main streets be cleared of hawkers, chai stalls and beggars. No one believed he was serious until he sent in bulldozers to enforce the deadline, and the Pink City has looked a lot smarter (and pinker) since, with shop fronts now bearing the regulation black Hindi graphics on white backgrounds. In addition, a couple of streets (notably Bapu Bazaar) were even permanently closed to traffic – unheard of in India.

In keeping with the prescriptions of the *Shastras*, each quarter in the Pink City is home to a particular centre of activity or commerce. **Suraj Pole Bazaar** in the southeast corner houses elephants and their owners; **Nehru Bazaar** (closed Tues) and **Bapu Bazaar** (closed Sun) are special centres for textiles, perfumes and locally styled camelskin shoes; shops in **Tripolia Bazaar** and **Chaura Rasta** sell textiles and household utensils. For more advice on shopping in Jaipur, see p.170.

Hawa Mahal

Jaipur's most acclaimed landmark, the tapering **Hawa Mahal**, or "Palace of Winds" (daily 9am–4.30pm; Rs2, Rs50 extra for camera, Rs100 extra for video), stands to the west of the City Palace, where it exudes an orangey-pink glow in the rays of the rising sun (8–9am is the best time for photographs). Built in 1799 to enable the women of the court to watch street processions while remaining in a strict state of purdah, its five-storey facade, decked with no less than 593 finely screened windows and balconies, makes the building seem far larger than it really is; in fact it is little more than one room thick in most parts.

Though the primary source of its appeal is undoubtedly the fantastic honeycomb pink and white face, visitors can go inside (enter from the back) to see exactly where the women sat, and take a close look at the detailed stone-work.

The Pink City's overall **design** follows some of the strictest principles of town planning ever devised. Meticulously laid out in accordance with rules set down in ancient texts, the grid plan actually forms a giant magical diagram, or mandala, designed to infuse daily human life with the overarching harmony of the cosmos.

No one knows for sure from where the tenets of the old architectural texts, or **Vastu Shastras** originally derive, but they're thought to have provided the blueprints for the now lost cities of the Vedic age, three thousand years ago. Since this time, Hindu buildings, from humble hermitages to giant temple towns like Madurai, have traditionally followed the proportions and lines of mandalas. At one level, these sacred diagrams represent the laws governing the universe; at another, they are abstract depictions of the Hindu creator god, Brahma, in the form of the primeval being, Parusha. Simply put, the architects and town planners saw a parallel between their work and the creation of the earth and of existence by Brahma.

In the *Vastu Shastras*, it is written that towns should conform to one of 32 possible mandala patterns. These basic outlines can then be divided and subdivided into smaller sectors, or *padas*, in sacred sequences of 4, 9, 16, 25, 36, 49, 64 and 81, each corresponding to a different part of Brahma's body. Under the guidance of his chief architect, the Bengali brahmin Vidyadhar Chakravati, Maharaja Jai Singh decided Jaipur would be in the form of the Vastu Purusha mandala, whose form bears an external resemblance to the Indian horoscope, with twelve squares for the different signs of the Zodiac. Being a capital city of a temporal ruler, this grid had to be rectangular, not square (as with sacred precincts), while the *padas* (known in Rajasthani as *chowka*, or squares) were assigned to specific castes and sub-castes. This explains why, to this day, the bazaars and residential districts of the Pink City remain strictly divided according to caste and occupation, with brahmins in the north, *kshatryas* (Rajputs) in the east, *vaishyas* in the south and *shudras* in the west, and different sectors or streets for cloth merchants, dyers, weavers, silversmiths, shoemakers and so on. Streets were built to prescribed widths, and houses to regulation heights. Notable exceptions were the lofty maharaja's palace, which occupies the most central position in the *pada* most closely associated with Brahma, the *Brahma-sthana*.

Although a lot of painstaking planning clearly preceded the construction of Jaipur, no blueprints have survived. Chakravati's explanatory notes disappeared when the same philistine descendant of Jai Singh who ditched the grid plan sold off chunks of the maharaja's legendary library to be used as wrapping paper.

City Palace

The magnificent **City Palace** (daily 9.30am–4.45pm; Rs110 includes camera and video), open to the public as the **Sawai Man Singh Museum**, stands enclosed by a high wall in the centre of the city amid fine gardens and courtyards. The royal family still occupies part of the palace, advancing in procession on formal occasions through the grand **Tripolia Gate** in the centre of the southern wall. Less regal visitors must enter through **Atish Gate** left of the main gate or **Nakkar Gate** in the west, passing the food stalls and souvenir shops in Jalebi Chowk.

The palace was conceived and built by Jai Singh, but many of the apartments and halls were added by his successors. The exhibits and interior design have lost none of the pomp and splendour of their glory days. Each door and gateway is heavily decorated, each chandelier intact and each hall guarded by turbaned retainers decked in full royal livery, so that Jaipur's palace impresses upon the visitor the continuity of a living royal presence.

An ornate gateway in the southwest corner of the complex leads into the first courtyard, with the solid marble **Mubarak Mahal** in its centre. This elegant

palace, built in 1890, holds the **textile section** of the museum, whose treasures include antique *pashmina* shawls from Kashmir, throne carpets and a pink padded jacket worn by Madho Singh I (one of Jai Singh's sons) who stood a full 2m tall. Opulently decorated ritual objects and musical instruments used to entertain the rulers are also on display, but the real highlight is the former maharani's richly gilded black Diwali outfit, covered in elaborate *gota* appliqué work. The first floor of the building next to the Mubarak Mahal houses the royal **arsenal**. Inside what was once the harem, with its delicate paintings on the walls and mirrors glittering on the ceilings, is laid out a menacing array of spears, swords, shields, daggers with handles carved from jade, crystal, silver and gold, and two inscribed swords that belonged to the Moghul emperor Shah Jahan.

As you enter the second courtyard you're confronted by the raised **Diwani-i-Khas**, the Hall of Private Audience, built in sandstone and marble. Open-sided, with its roof raised on marble pillars, the hall contains two silver urns, or *gangajalis*, listed in the *Guinness Book of Records* as the largest crafted silver objects in the world, each more than 1.5m high with a capacity of 8182 litres. When Madho Singh II went to England to attend the coronation of King Edward VII in 1901, he was so reluctant to trust the water in the West that he had these urns filled with Ganges water and took them along with him.

Mujra

Long before the age of hip-thrusting Hindi-movie stars, Jaipur was the centre of a subtly suggestive Rajasthani dance form known as mujra. Based on Sufi-influenced *kathak*, the dance was not performed in temples, but in *kothas* – special *havelis* in the walled old town belonging to families of the dancers. Reclining on bolsters (*masnad*) and ornate appliqué mattresses, an exclusively male audience would gather in the late evening to be served betel on silver trays, while the women dancers, or *tawaifs*, performed, accompanied by tabla, harmonium and percussion. Their costumes were similar to those worn by *kathak* dancers: calf-length pleated *ghoomar* skirts that swirled open during spins, and long silk pyjama trousers with cuffs of small bells tied around the ankles to emphasize elaborate footwork.

Only certain families performed *mujra* in Jaipur, handing down the tradition from mother to daughter. Through the generations, they retained relationships with well-to-do families in the city who would send their sons to the *kotha* to gain experience of music and poetry, as well as dance. For although it was not uncommon for *tawaifs* to become mistresses of their clients, the Jaipuri *kothas* were regarded primarily as repositories of fine manners and courtesies.

The drift from studied suggestiveness to clumsy eroticism really only began with the advent of cinema, after which the graceful moves of traditional *mujra* became increasingly debased by Bollywood groin-grinding and Hindi karaoke. By the 1950s, *tawaif* had become a synonym for "whore" and most *kothas* were basically brothels, while the few serious establishments left were forced out of business by constant anti-prostitution raids by the police. Of the 37 *kothas* open in 1957, only a dozen or so remain today, and most of these are pretty tawdry affairs. Dressed in garish Western-style clothes or bright *salwar-kurta*, the *tawaifs* now do routines from hit Hindi movies, bending on their knees to pull bank notes from punters' lips with their teeth.

Claims by a Delhi-based group set up to monitor the Indian sex industry that teenage *mujra* dancers were being smuggled into the UK to work in illicit Asian clubs were proven to be true in 2000. In the course of an enquiry into the murder of a London restaurateur, Scotland Yard's Clubs and Vice section discovered that *mujra* was being used as a front for prostitution in several British cities.

In the centre of the compound, with balconies and windows studding its seven-storey facade, **Chandra Mahal** is the residence of the royal family. You can see it best from **Pritam Niwas Chowk**, known as Peacock Courtyard, to the west of the Diwan-i-Khas. Against the ochre walls of this court, four gateways provide a shock of dazzling colour, decorated with peacocks and regular patterns in red, green, blue and gold.

The last and largest section of the museum is housed in the **Diwan-i-Am**, once the Hall of Public Audience, where ornate pillars support the high ceilings. The walls, intricately painted with touches of deep red and gold, provide perfect mounts for immense medieval Afghan and Persian carpets. Miniatures from the Moghul and Jaipur schools, and Jai Singh's translations in Arabic and Sanskrit of the astronomical treatises of ancient scientists such as Euclid and Ptolemy, are displayed in glass cases.

Jantar Mantar

The incredible brick curves, slants, circles and pillars of Jai Singh's astronomical **observatory** (daily 9am–4.30pm; Rs2, free Mon, Rs50 extra for camera, Rs100 extra for video), overlaid with sherbet-yellow gypsum, are solidly planted in the southern courtyard of the palace complex. A total of eighteen instruments were erected between 1728 and 1734 by Jai Singh; some are triangular, some are circular or semicircular, and all are very large. Although the Maharaja was influenced by the works of foreign astrologers and the advice of his teachers – one of whom was his mother – many of the devices were of his own invention.

It's a good idea to pay (Rs30–50) for the services of a **guide** to explain how the observatory works. The instruments are built so that shadows fall onto marked surfaces, identifying the position and movement of stars and planets, telling the time, and even predicting the intensity of the monsoon. The time calculated is unique to Jaipur, between ten and forty-one minutes (depending on the time of year) behind Indian standard time, but is used to calculate the Hindu (lunar) calendar. Probably the most impressive of Jai Singh's constructions is the sundial, **Samrat Yantra**. Its slanting centrepiece, or *gnomon*, reaches a height of 27m, casting shadows onto curved stone faces that are graduated in hours. Each hour is divided into thirty parts, so the time calculated is accurate to within two minutes.

A more original device, the **Jaiprakash Yantra**, consists of two hemispheres laid in the ground, each composed of six curving marble slabs with a suspended ring in the centre, whose shadow marks the day, time and zodiac symbol. This is vital for the calculations of auspicious days for marriage; when unfavourable planets are in influential positions, for example between August and October, marriages have always been avoided.

Outside the Pink City

A handful of museums, temples and cenotaphs, scattered around Jaipur's less congested suburbs, offer welcome respite from the relentless traffic and crowds of the Pink City. The **Albert Hall museum**, housed in a grand British building that somewhat eclipses the collection inside, presides over a swathe of formal parkland, the **Ram Niwas Public Gardens**, south of the centre near the **Museum of Indology**, home to a fascinating hoard of quirky Indian artefacts. As a target for day walks out of town, the hilltop "Tiger Fort" at **Nawalgarh**, overlooking Jaipur from the rocky ridge north of the Pink City, is a strenuous option. Offering equally impressive views over the eastern fringes of the city, the old pilgrims' path to **Galta**, passing the "monkey temple" en route to a famous Hindu bathing tank, is less strenuous, although correspondingly more popular. **Gaitor**, where Jaipur's royal family have erected marble memorial *chhatris*, is best visited on the way to Amber.

Ram Niwas Public Gardens

South of the Pink City, on the road leading out of New Gate, lie 36 acres of lush gardens named **Ram Niwas Public Gardens** after the planner, Ram Singh, who ruled Jaipur from 1835 to 1880. The gardens represent but a small fraction of Ram Singh's successful efforts to improve public services, and originally covered 76 acres.

As well as providing green space for the citizens, the gardens now house a number of institutions, the most notable being the **Albert Hall**, in which you'll find the **Central Museum** (daily except Fri 9.30am–4.30pm; Rs5, free on Mon), designed by the British architect Sir Samuel Jacob. This remarkable stately construction, built over several years from 1867, drew heavily on contemporary British models, but its arched verandas and rooftop domed pavilions hint at the Moghul background of its artisans. The exhibits within, which include miniature paintings, rocks, clothes and ornamental wooden boxes, may not be quite as inspiring as the building itself, but it's worth seeking out the highly original display of yoga postures demonstrated by tiny clay *sadhus*. Also within the gardens is a **zoo** (daily except Tues: summer 8am–6pm; winter 8am–5.30pm), with an aviary on one side, an animal section on the other, and a small crocodile-breeding farm. The beasts are kept in the usual grim conditions.

To the south of these, off Jawaharlal Nehru Road, the **Museum of Indology** (daily 10am–5pm; Rs40 including guided tour) holds an outrageous collection of assorted curiosities maintained by writer and painter Acharya Vyakul, including a map of India painted on a grain of rice, letters written on a hair, a glass bed and the largest collection of Tantric art in the world, as well as a gallery of modern art. A larger premises is planned 7km out on the road to Amber.

Gaitor

A short distance north of the City Palace, and just over 6km from central Jaipur on the road to Amber, the walled complex of **Gaitor** contains the stately marble *chhatris* of Jaipur's ruling family. Built by Jai Singh II, the complex contains memorials to himself and his successors, including his son and grandson, with a room set aside for a future memorial to the present head of the family.

Unless a ruler should happen to die an untimely death, the construction of his cenotaph is normally well under way during his lifetime, and traditionally each ruler takes exceptional pains to ensure that the marble carving on his own tomb is of a high standard. That of Jai Singh is inlaid with scenes from Hindu mythology, and processions from his reign, depicting among other things the Hawa Mahal.

Nawalgarh

Teetering on the edge of the hills 3km northeast of Jaipur, **Nawalgarh**, or "Tiger Fort" (10am–4.30pm; Rs4) was built by Jai Singh II in 1734 as a retreat for his wives, the maharanis. Its unique design, regular and repetitive, stands in contrast to the other royal dwellings in Jaipur, and the views are breathtaking.

All the queens' apartments are identical, arranged around the central courtyard in perfect symmetry, each with a room for a personal maidservant. Ram

Singh, who in 1868 built more apartments on the upper floor, continued Jai Singh's tradition of orderly design by constructing another set of identical rooms. These bear traces of paintings and slightly damaged stained-glass windows.

Vehicles of any kind can only get to the fort along a road that branches off Amber Road, a nine-kilometre journey from Jaipur. However, if you're feeling energetic, it's possible to **walk** there along a two-kilometre footpath that starts northwest of the City Palace. A very reasonably priced café by the fort serves meals and snacks.

If you want to **stay** somewhere a little out of the ordinary, the old buildings next to the fort hold one double room for rent (℡0141/320538, best booked in advance; ❹): the room is simple but the views spectacular, with six windows facing west and south.

Galta

Nestling in a steep-sided valley 3km west of Jaipur, **Galta** is a picturesque collection of 250-year-old temples grouped around a sacred water tank. You can either get there by road, following a route that winds around the hills for 10km, or walk for around 45min from town, leaving by **Suraj Pole** and climbing steeply up to the Surya temple on the crest of the hill above. From here, a cobbled track zigzags down to the main temple complex on the valley floor.

Galta owes its sacred status in large part to a freshwater spring that seeps constantly through the rocks in the otherwise dry valley, keeping two **tanks** fresh and full, and hordes of monkeys (associated with the monkey god Hanuman) happy. Humans bathe in the upper water tank, while monkeys jump and splash in the lower pool.

The **temples** themselves are intricately and vividly painted. Friezes around the top of pavilions that face the monkeys' tank show scenes from religious festivals and stately occasions; behind one procession the City Palace is sketched in dubious proportions. Inside the roofs, swirling red, yellow and blue clouds ring more of Michelangelo than of traditional Hindu style.

Follow the surfaced road beyond the temples for around ten minutes and you'll come across a sign for the **Dhammathali Vipassana Centre**, one of fifty centres across the world set up to promote the practice of Vipassana **meditation**. For more information on courses, see Basics, p.75.

Beyond the Vipassana centre, the road passes the **Sisodia Rani-ka-Bagh** (daily 8am–6pm; Rs2), 8km east of Jaipur. Landscaped with fountains and painted pavilions, these gardens are part of a palace complex built in the eighteenth century by Jai Singh II for the Udaipur princess he married to secure relations with his neighbouring Sisodia Rajputs.

Temples at the back of the gardens, coated with the sherbet-yellow wash that covers the whole compound – the original colour of the Pink City – and enhanced with naturalistic designs, are open midday and early evening for worship.

Eating and drinking

Jaipur has an excellent choice of quality **restaurants**, both veg and non-veg, although options are more limited at the bottom of the range. If you're on a tight budget and staying at a small or family-run guesthouse, eat in where the food is likely to be fresher and more tailored for tourists' sensitive taste buds. Whatever your budget, though, find time for a *lassi* at the legendary *Lassiwalla* pavement café on MI Road.

Annapurna, down the lane behind *Raj Mandir* cinema on Bhagwan Das Road (look for the red sign in Gujarati). Keep-it-coming, tasty Gujarati veg thalis at low prices (Rs50). The best cheap meal in Jaipur, although the dining room's a bit gloomy. Open noon–3pm & 7–10pm.

Anokha Gaon, 14 Vishwakarm Road, opposite Jodla Power House, 12km north of town along Sikar Road. Unquestionably the best and most authentic Rajasthani restaurant in town. The approach (through an industrial estate) is unpromising and the furniture rudimentary (you sit in rows on the floor and eat with your hands off leaf plates set on low plank tables) but the food, prepared on wood fires and old clay ovens, is out of this world. Rs90 for the full works, including four kinds of *rotis* and wonderful *keer* (saffron-flavoured rice pudding). For kids, there's a desultory puppet show and camel rides.

Chanakya, MI Road. Top-notch pure veg restaurant specializes in carefully prepared Rajasthani thalis (though you can also order dishes and breads separately). For a quick snack, try their superb stuffed *parathas*. Open noon–11pm.

Chitra Café, *Arya Niwas Hotel*, Sansar Chandra Road. Busy self-service restaurant that does good-value veg thalis (Rs70), and a range of delicious side dishes (with display samples so you know what you're getting). Also cold drinks, tea and coffee, and delicious mango *lassi*, on the lawn.

Copper Chimney, MI Road. Swish glass-fronted restaurant on the main drag, renowned for its top-notch Mughlai cuisine (including a matchless *rogan josh*). They also offer a better-than-average choice of Western dishes, and all the north Indian standards. Count on Rs250 per head.

Chowki Dhani, 22km south of Jaipur on the Tonk Road. Well-heeled Jaipuris flock in droves to this famous out-of-town restaurant. The Rs150 entrance fee covers a slap-up traditional thali and cabaret (folk dance, acrobats, musicians and puppetry). Well worth the long drive for the atmosphere, but the food's not as good as *Anokha Gaon's*. Taxis charge around Rs400 for the round trip (Rs250 for auto-rickshaw). Open Mon–Sat 6.30–11pm & Sun from 2.30pm.

Four Seasons, D-43A Subhash Marg, C-Scheme. The most popular vegetarian restaurant in town, tucked away in a residential area that's well off the tour group trail. Its south Indian *dosas* and *utta-pams* are as good as you'll eat anywhere, and they serve a full selection of top north Indian specialities, snacks, ice creams and shakes. Most dishes cost around Rs80. Expect a short wait for a table.

Indian Coffee House, MI Road, 100m west of Ajmeri Gate. The usual fine coffee (try their "special"), south Indian snacks, and decent breakfast options (including unusually good plain toast), dished up by waiters in cotton cummerbunds. Open 7.30am–9pm.

Lassiwalla, opposite *Niro's*, MI Road. A gastronomic institution in Jaipur (during the summer, you have to queue for thirty minutes to be served), famous for its sublime lassis, still served in old-style, hygienic terracotta mugs. Be sure to order one without ice.

LMB, Johari Bazaar. Scrupulously pure-veg, high-caste cooking ("No onions, No garlic"), served in a large, cool dining hall whose classic early Peter Sellers movie-set decor was, tragically, under threat of renovation when we last looked. This has long been regarded as the best restaurant in town, but the food is no longer what it was, drenched in sickly *deshi ghee* and too spicy for most tastes. However, their famous *paneer ghewar* (honeycomb cake soaked in treacle) and potato-and-cashew nut *tikkis* dished up piping hot (in spicy mango sauce) at the sweet counter outside are a must. Open 11.30am–3.30pm & 7–11pm, snacks only 4–7pm.

Mediterraneo, *Hotel Vijeet Palace*, Sansar Chandra Road. Lively Italian terrace restaurant with views of the fort. Their pizzas (Rs120–200) are wood-fired, their pasta dishes fresh every day, and the coffee excellent. Beer is served in Prohibition-style teapots pending a liquor licence.

Natraj, MI Road. The *Chanakya's* main competitor, famed for its *paneer* dishes and superb sweets (try their melt-in-the-mouth *rasmala*, flavoured with cardamom and saffron).

Niro's, MI Road. Along with *Copper Chimney*, this place gets the local vote for best non-veg food in Jaipur, although they offer a full multi-cuisine and veg menu, too. No alcohol. Open 10am–11.30pm.

Pizza Hut, 109 Ganpati Plaza, MI Road ☏0141/388627. Doubtless not what you came to Jaipur for, but the food and decor's just the same as back home, the prices low by comparison (Rs100–200), and they'll deliver free to your hotel room or guesthouse.

Listings

Airlines Indian Airlines, Nehru Place, Tonk Road, the southward continuation of Sawai Ram Singh Road ☏0141/514500. Jet's agents are Travel-Care, E-4, Ground Floor, Jaipur Tower, MI Road ☏0141/371832. For ANA, Continental, Royal Brunei, Royal Nepal, Sri Lankan and Thai go to

Jaipur is the main transport hub for Rajasthan and has daily air and train services to most major Indian cities. Buses are also frequent to destinations in and around the state. If your nerves are up to it, short journeys to destinations like Agra, Bharatpur, Ajmer (for Pushkar) and towns in Shekhawati are best made by road; one exception is Sawai Madhopur, the jumping-off place for Ranthambore National Park, which is most easily reached by train. Heading west for **Jaisalmer**, think about breaking the 631-kilometre trip at Pushkar and/or Jodhpur; otherwise brace yourself for a long overnight bus journey (depart 9.45pm, arrive 9.45am the next day), or a change of trains at Jodhpur (there are no direct rail services to Jaisalmer from Jaipur). For a full summary of transport services from Jaipur, giving departure frequencies and journey times, see Travel Details at the end of this chapter.

By air

Indian Airlines fly to six destinations nationwide (listed in Travel Details on p.279) in competiton with Jet Airways on their most popular routes to Delhi, Mumbai and Udaipur, and Air India, who fly daily to Mumbai. Jet are a shade pricier than the two national carriers, but offer a much swisher service. Tickets may be booked direct through the airlines' offices or with an accredited travel agent (see Listings on p.184).

By bus

Frequent RSRTC **buses** to most destinations reachable by road from Jaipur leave from the Inter-state Bus Station on Station Road. For longer routes, faster (but less frequent) "deluxe" services guarantee seats. Enquiries can be made by phone (℡0141/206143), but it's less hassle to turn up at the bus stand and head for the relevant booking office (destinations are listed outside each cabin). The deluxe services have their own separate booking hatch behind platform 3 (open 24 hrs). **Private bus services** are a slightly cheaper alternative, although they tend to cram too many passengers on board and make unnecessary stops at *dhabas* along the way. You can book tickets for these at the string of agents on Station Road, but avoid desperately uncomfortable **video buses**. A reliable company for **direct buses to Pushkar** is Jai Ambay Travels, next door to the Bank of Punjab on MI Road (℡0141/205177 or 214777), whose comfortable twenty-seater coach leaves at 9.30am and 1pm; you can buy tickets (Rs80) just prior to departure, but it's a good idea to get them in advance. The same outfit also runs buses to Ajmer (11.30am, 5pm & 6pm; Rs85), Jodhpur (3 daily; 7hr; Rs110), Jaisalmer (1 daily; 12hr; Rs225), Udaipur (1 nightly; 9hr; Rs120) and Agra (hourly; 5hr 30min; Rs95).

STIC Travels, 4th Floor Ganpati Plaza, MI Road ℡0141/372965. El Al, Korean and Malaysia operate through a shared office at 304 Ganpati Plaza, MI Road ℡0141/374038. In the same building, you'll also find the Air India office ℡0141/368569. Just down the road, British Airlines are at G-2 Usha Plaza, MI Road ℡0141/361065. With the exception of Lufthansa, who are at Sharangi Mansion, New Gate ℡0141/582822, the remaining airlines are all based in the Jaipur Tower, on MI Road: Austrian Airlines ℡0141/377695; Air France ℡0141/370509; Gulf Air ℡0141/375430; Kuwait Airlines ℡0141/372896; KLM ℡0141/367772; PIA ℡0141/361460; Royal Jordanian ℡0141/375430; Syrian Arab Airines ℡0141/377062; and Thai Airways ℡0141/360188.

Beauty parlours Jaipur is renowned for its herbal beauty parlours, where you can pamper yourself with a healing body massage or marrow-and-turmeric pack facial. The most famous is the Shahnaz Hussain Institute, at S-55 Ashok Marg in C Scheme (℡0141/378444), which has separate clinics for men and women; if it's fully booked, try the less expensive Kaya Kalp, at 55 Chander Bhawan, behind the Rajput Sabha Bhawan, near St Xavier's school, Ashok Marg (also with separate clinics).

By train

Some train services from Jaipur have been disrupted over the past few years by track work, so check your departure and arrivals times when you buy your ticket. Bookings should be made at least a day in advance at the computerized reservations hall in the main station (Mon–Sat 8am–8pm, Sun 8am–2pm; ☏ 0141/201401); there's a special "Foreign Tourist and Freedom Fighter" counter.

Recommended trains from Jaipur

The following daily trains are recommended as the fastest and/or most convenient from Jaipur. Bear in mind that timetables change, so check the departure time when you buy your ticket (it'll be printed on it).

Destination	Name	No.	Departs	Total time
Ajmer	Jaipur–Ajmer Link Express	#2413A	11.15am	2hr 30min
Agra	Marudhar (Jodhpur–Varanasi Express)	#4864/4854	1.25pm	6hr 55min
	Jodhpur–Howrah Express	#2308	11.20pm	7hr 20min
Bikaner	Jaipur–Bikaner Intercity Express	#2468	3pm	6hr 50min
Delhi	Jodhpur–Delhi Express	#4860	6am	5hr 25min
	Shatabdi Express*†	#2016	5.55pm	4hr 20min
Jodhpur	Delhi–Jodhpur Express	#4859	11.30pm	6hr 10min
	Intercity Express	#2465	5.30pm	5hr 15min
Mumbai	Superfast Express	#2956	1.30pm	16hr 30min
	Jaipur–Mumbai Express	#9708	7am	24hr
Sawai Madhopur	(for Ranthambore National Park) Superfast Express	#2956	1.30pm	2hr 5min
Udaipur	Chetak Express	#9615	10.10pm	12hr 15min
Varanasi	(Moghul Sarai) Marudhar (Jodhpur–Varanasi Express)	#4864/4854	1.25pm	18hr 50min

* a/c only
† Does not run Sun

Bookstores The boutique in *Hotel Arya Niwas* stocks a good selection of titles in English, most of them about, or set in, India. Books Corner, on MI Road just past *Niro's* has up-to-date magazines, newspapers and books in all major European languages, while *Evergreen Guest House* also has a secondhand stall.

Cinemas If you go to the cinema only once while you're in India, it should be at the *Raj Mandir* on Bhagwan Das Road just off MI Road, which boasts India's most kitsch, over-the-top decor and hefty sound system. Most movies have four daily show-

ings, and there's always a long queue, so get your tickets an hour or so before the show starts.

Dance Several of the big five-stars, including the *Rambagh Palace* and *Sheraton Rajputana Palace*, host nightly culture shows, featuring folk dance, music and traditional puppetry. These can be a lot of fun, especially if they're held outdoors. Expect to pay around Rs150. Another music and dance venue is *Choowki Dhani*, 22km south of the city (see p.181).

Hospitals The largest in Jaipur is Santokba Durlabhji Memorial Hospital (SDMH), Bhawani Singh Marg ☏ 0141/566251.

Internet Access costs Rs30–50 per hour. The majority of hotels listed above are online. Otherwise, try one of the many internet offices around town: one of the best is Communicator on the ground floor of the Jaipur Towers, opposite All India Radio, MI Road, who charge less than average for offline work.

Music Jaipur's not a particularly good place to buy musical instruments (those made here are of medium or inferior quality), but plenty of travellers take sitar lessons while they're in the city. A recommended teacher is Mr Ghasi Lal Sharma, who can be contacted through the Sharma Music Centre, on Nawalgarh Road.

Photography Fuji outlet on Kishan Pole Bazaar, near Ajmeri Gate; Konica on MI Road almost opposite Niro's, Kodak by Sweet Dream hotel, and various others.

Police stations The main police post is on Station Road opposite the railway station ☎0141/311677.

Post For poste restante, go to the GPO on MI Road (Mon–Sat 9am–6pm). Parcels and registered mail are kept at the sorting office behind the main desks; packages are cotton-wrapped and sewn at the concession by the main entrance.

Swimming pools Evergreen Guest House charge nonresidents Rs75 for use of their pool, but you may prefer to pay more (Rs150–175) at posher establishments such as the Jai Mahal, Jaipur Ashok or Raj Mahal, where lawns, deck chairs and refreshments are available.

Tailors One of the best tailors in town, patronized by no less than the maharaja himself, is Jodhpur Tailors, behind Neela Hotel, near Ganpati Plaza (MI Road). This is a good place to get suits made, as well as traditional Indian shirts and pukka Jodhpur riding breeches, and they're not at all expensive.

Travel agents GSA Janta Travels, MI Road ☎0141/368569. Sita World Travels, Station Road ☎0141/368226 or 361404, ☎321522, an agent for Indian Airlines and also Western Union, deals with international and domestic flights very efficiently.

Yoga Jaipur has several reputable yoga schools, among them: the Rajasthan Yoga Centre, 2km north of Bani Park in Shastri Nagar; the Yoga and Naturopathy Centre, opposite Rajasthan University, C Scheme, in the southwest of the city; and Samarpan, #1 Road, VKI Area, which is run by a disillusioned allopathic doctor. If you need somewhere to convalesce after a chronic illness (such as hepatitis), a place well worth checking out is the Navneet Natrupathy Centre, 30km south along the Agra road, in the village of Bassi.

Around Jaipur

Forts, palaces, temples and ruins from a thousand years of Kuchwaha history adorn the hills and valleys near Jaipur. The superb palaces of **Amber** provide the most obvious destination for a day-trip, but you can also visit **Amber Fort** – or Jaigarh – which crowns the hills to the north of the city, or travel south to search out the traditional potters, block printers and dyers of **Sanganer**.

Organized tours visit Amber and Jaigarh in a day; Amber is accessible by public transport, and minibuses run to Sanganer.

Amber

On the crest of a rocky hill behind Maota Lake, 11km north of Jaipur, the Rajput stronghold of **AMBER** was the capital of the Kuchwaha Rajputs from 1037 until 1728. Fortified by natural hills, high ramparts and a succession of gates along a cobbled road, Amber's magnificent palaces are distinctly Rajput, but it's clear that Moghul ideas crept in to influence the design. The practice of covering walls with mosaics of mirrors is purely Moghul, first introduced to India at Agra and Fatehpur Sikri.

It's worth visiting Amber independently, as there's so much to see; tour groups rarely get enough time to view the entire compound, let alone to scramble into the village behind it, dotted with fascinating temples and ruins. To avoid the big bus parties, get here early in the day. Regular **public buses** to Amber (#113) leave from outside Jaipur's Hawa Mahal, stopping on the main road below the palaces, where there's a **tourist office**. From there you can either enjoy a pleasant twenty-minute uphill walk, take a jeep for Rs75 (up to four people), or waddle like the royals of yesteryear on an elephant for Rs300 (again, four people). For a cheaper, longer elephant ride, wait around the entrance to the palace complex on the main road at end of the afternoon, when the mahoots head home to the "elephant sleeping place" near the Jal Mahal palace. You can hitch a ride with them, arriving at the lakeside shortly before sunset.

The palace complex

Entering the **palace complex** (daily 9am–4.30pm; Rs100, Rs50 extra for camera, Rs100 extra for video) from the east through Suraj Pole (Sun Gate), you step into the main courtyard, **Jaleb Chowk**, where there's another opportunity to ride an elephant (Rs80 for a turn around the courtyard). In its southwest corner, the Shri Sila Devi temple is the Kuchwaha shrine to the goddess of war, Sila, an aspect of Kali; the image inside was brought to Amber from Bengal in 1604. Next to this, at the head of a flight of steps, Singh Pole (Lion Gate) provides access to the palaces.

The lofty Hall of Public Audience, **Diwan-i-Am**, used by Raja Jai Singh I and his successors from 1639, stands in the entrance courtyard, while opposite, in the south wall of the yard, the exquisitely painted **Ganesh Pole** leads through narrow passages into the charming royal apartments. Here, protruding from the east wall, the dazzling **Sheesh Mahal** houses what were the private chambers of the maharaja and his queen. Shards of mirror and coloured glass form an intricate mosaic that entirely covers the inner and outer walls and ceilings of the rooms. From a distance they seem to be covered in jewels, tinted with pastel shafts of sunlight that seep through the Arabic-style stained-glass windows. Above the Sheesh Mahal, the small chamber of the brilliant **Jas Mandir** radiates with the light and colour of similar mosaics. Guarded from the glare of the sun in the east by delicate marble screens, it served as a cool refuge in summer.

A fountained garden separates the mirrored palace from the "pleasure palace" opposite, **Sukh Mahal**, where marble rooms are cooled by water cascading through fine perforations in the centre of the wall – an early and very efficient system of air-conditioning. The doors are inlaid with ivory and sandalwood.

The oldest part of the complex, the **Palace of Man Singh I**, lies south of the main quadrangle. The pillared *biradiri* in the centre of the courtyard was once a meeting area for the maharanis, shrouded from men's eyes by flowing curtains. Narrow passages and stairwells connect small rooms and open balconies on all sides.

Walking down the hill behind the palace complex – via the elephant stable in the western corner of Jaleb Chowk – brings you to the temples and ruined mansions of **Amber village**.

Amber Fort

The mighty **Amber Fort** (Jaigarh), built in 1600, stands high on the hill behind Amber (daily 9am–4.30pm; Rs50, Rs25 extra for camera, Rs100 extra for video). As the Kuchwahas were on friendly terms with the Moghuls, the fort saw few battles, and its immense cannon – the largest in Asia, which needed one hundred kilos of gunpowder for one shot and could send a ball 35km – was never fired in anger. The small museum collection displaying artillery, old maps, medals, stamps and photographs, plus the odd fifteenth-century spitoon, is unspectacular, but has an interesting hand-drawn floor plan of the palaces at Amber. The fort is also renowned as the most likely hiding place of the Kuchwahas' famous **lost treasure**. A huge hoard of gemstones and jewellery disappeared after Independence, probably to prevent its confiscation by the government. Income tax officials scoured the building with metal detectors in 1977 but found nothing.

Most people walk to Amber Fort from the village, but it's quite a long climb; the alternative is to descend to the valley and follow by vehicle the much longer road that leads to both Jaigarh and Nawalgarh.

Sanganer

SANGANER, 16km south of Jaipur, is the busiest centre for handmade **textiles** in the region, and the best place to watch traditional block printers in action. There are a couple of large factories here, but most of the printing is done in family homes as a cottage industry. This is also a great place to shop for traditional textiles; prices are much lower than in Jaipur.

Sanganeri craftsmen and women also decorate **pottery** in Rajasthan's distinctive style; graceful floral designs in white or deep sea-green are painted over a traditional inky-blue glaze. Within the town itself, there are ruined palaces and a handful of elegant Jain **temples**, most notably the Shri Digamber temple near the Tirpolia Gate. Minibuses and tempos (Rs6) leave for Sanganer from Chand Pole, or you can take city bus #113 from Ajmeri Gate.

Samode

Hidden among the scrubby Aravalli Hills, **SAMODE**, on the outskirts of Shekhawati, is notable for its impeccably restored eighteenth-century **palace**, which became famous in the 1980s as the setting for the hit Raj-romance movie *The Far Pavilions*. It's possible to come here on a day-trip from Jaipur, 42km southeast, but if your budget can stretch to it, spend a night in one of the palace's uncompromisingly romantic rooms, plastered with murals and filled with antiques and ornate stonework. Nonresidents have to shell out a hefty Rs100 to visit, but it's worth it just to see the beautiful **Sheesh Mahal**, or Hall of Mirrors, on the south side of the building.

Samode village itself is a centre for block printing and lacquered bangle making, and you can climb the three hundred steps leading from the palace to a hilltop **fort**, the maharaja's ruined former residence, for impressive views over the surrounding countryside. Sections of it have been converted into a luxury heritage hotel, the *Samode Palace* (℡01423/4114, ℻4123; ❾). The same owners also have fifty richly appointed tents, 3km southeast of Samode at *Samode Bagh* (❾), in a campus with its own swimming pool, croquet lawns and tennis courts. Bookings both for this and the palace can be made in Jaipur through *Samode Haveli*, Gangapole (℡ & ℻0141/632407).

North of Jaipur: Shekhawati

Beyond the last ripples of the Aravalli range, north of Jaipur, lies the easternmost extent of the Thar Desert, where small sand-blown towns nestle between dunes and sprawling expanses of parched land. Before the rise of Bombay and Calcutta (and the arrival of railways) diverted the trans-Thar trade south and eastwards, this region, known as **Shekhawati**, lay on an important caravan route connecting Delhi and Sind (now in Pakistan) with the Gujarati coast.

SHEKHAWATI

The merchant Marwari and landowning *thakur* castes of its small market towns grew rich on trade and taxes from the through traffic, but instead of erecting impressive temples and supporting religious institutions, spent their fortunes competing with each other to build grand, ostentatiously decorated *havelis*. Many have survived, and now collectively comprise one of the richest artistic and architectural legacies in all India: an incredible number of mansions, palaces and cenotaphs plastered inside and out with elaborate and colourful **murals**. Executed between the 1770s and the 1930s, these depict not only traditional themes, scenes from folk tales and religious stories, animals and local customs, but also faraway cities, merchants and their families, British sahibs of the Raj, and Victorian technology, each mural bordered with ornate floral designs. Sadly, nowadays, most are faded, defaced, covered with posters or even just whitewashed over, but there are so many – and the towns are so small – that you cannot fail to see a work of art virtually everywhere you look.

Considering the wealth of traditional art here, and the region's proximity to Jaipur, Shekhawati feels surprisingly far off the tourist trail – few local people speak English, accommodation is thin on the ground, and there's little prospect of Western food. But this ranks among the most rewarding parts of Rajasthan to explore: the towns are compact, the air clear and fresh and local people still pleasantly surprised to see foreigners. Of the few independent travellers who find their way up here, most invariably stay longer than planned, using **Nawalgarh** as a base for day-trips or leisurely walks into the desert.

Only the main towns have been covered in the following account, but – ideally with the help of Ilay Cooper's excellent *The Painted Towns of Shekhawati*, published by Mapin and available in Delhi, Jaipur and Mandawa – you should be able to find interesting sites in any town or village you pass through. Most of the buildings are still privately owned, and many of them are homes; ask permission to enter any house, and respect the custom of removing your shoes before you do so.

Some history

The first people to settle the lands north of Jaipur, Muslims of the Khaimkani clan, established two small states based at **Jhunjhunu** and **Fatehpur** in 1450. Their hold on the region was broken in 1730, when the Rajput **Sardul Singh** of the Shekawat clan took over Jhunjhunu. Two years later he consolidated

The havelis of Shekhawati

The magnificent houses built by the rich merchants of Shekhawati were called **havelis** after the Persian word for "enclosed space". Each house, anything from one to four storeys high, is entered from the street through huge arched porches with carved brass or wooden doors. Inside, you come into the forecourt, where visitors were received. Beyond, through the most ornate doorway of the house, is the main courtyard, where the women of the family could live in purdah, shielded from the eyes of the street. The forecourt is flanked by large pillared reception areas called *baithak*, each surmounted by a gallery where the women could if they wanted be privy to the business conducted below, and there is often a window by the door to the inner courtyard so that they could see whomever came in. More extravagant Marwari mansions might have up to four large courtyards, as well as grand domed facades and overhanging upper storeys supported on sturdy stone brackets. The tradition of woodcarving that produced the imposing doors and window shutters is still strong, particularly in Churu.

The meticulous painting of the interiors was executed by craftsmen from outside the region, using a vast array of intense hues, often highlighted with gold or silver leaf and mirrored designs. Religious themes, especially episodes from the life of Krishna, were common, and often feature along the lintels above the main doors. The outer walls were usually decorated by the masons who built the *haveli*, employing bolder designs and weather-hardy green, maroon and yellow ochres, with the occasional flash of blue.

However, what set the Shekhawati murals aside from virtually all others in India are the seemingly incongruous, naive depictions of machines, events and contemporary fashions they invariably include, from scenes of British redcoats marching into battle against the Moghuls, to eccentric Victorian flying devices, steam trains, motor cars and Edwardian memsahibs in big hats. When painted, these were all features of a faraway world that the women and poor townsfolk of Shekhawati had never seen with their own eyes. The wealthy men of the region wanted to share with their compatriots the extraordinary phenomena encountered on their travels trading in the great cities of the Raj, and commissioned artists to paint their houses, even though these artists had probably never seen the newfangled European novelties they were asked to depict.

Shekhawati rule by helping his brother (already ruler of Sikar) to seize Fatehpur from its Muslim Nawab.

Although the area is known as Shekhawati, the Shekawat Rajputs were only responsible for the construction of the forts in each town. The caravan route known as the "spice road" passed through the region on its way between China and the coast of Gujarat, and it was the local **merchants** – the Marwaris, Hindus of the *vaisya* caste, and Jains – who funded the building and painting of family houses, temples, wells and rest houses. The Marwaris were often rivals in influence to the local Rajputs, and it was this that led the Shekawats to turn a blind eye to, and even sponsor, brigandry against them. In response, the merchants formed an alliance with the British, ever eager for means to get a foothold in this fiercely independent region. In 1835, and with funding from the maharajas of Jaipur and Bikaner (to whom the Marwaris had also applied for help), a small force of cavalry called the Shekhawati Brigade was set up under the command of Henry Forster and based in Jhunjhunu to control the brigands. This gave the Marwaris the security they needed to build their magnificent *havelis*, and though many of them moved, encouraged by the British, to Bombay, Madras and especially Calcutta, they continued to send their profits back to Shekhawati, erecting elaborate buildings either to prove their worth as prospective bridegrooms, or simply as aid projects during times of famine.

When the British left India a number of Marwaris bought British industries, and such names as Birla and Poddar remain prominent in business today. However, many merchant families have now left Shekhawati and settled more permanently in the major urban centres, which is why so many of their buildings have been allowed to deteriorate. The region's current inhabitants continue to rear goats and sheep for their wool, and coax crops of winter wheat, mustard and millet from the dry earth, while maintaining traditional crafts: tie-dyeing, screen printing, lacquer working, woodcarving and silverwork.

Arrival and local transport

Shekhawati is crossed by a mainline railway, linking the major towns with Delhi, Jaipur and Bikaner, but services are all hopelessly slow, unreliable and run at inconvenient times of the night; basically, you're better off travelling into the region by bus. **From Jaipur**, the first town in Shekhawati you come to is **Sikar**, an unprepossessing market town two hours away by road (110km) that's only worth stopping in to pick up transport northwest to **Nawalgarh**, where you'll find better hotels and a more relaxed, rural atmosphere. Buses also run from Jaipur to **Fatehpur** (48km north of Sikar) – approaching **from Bikaner**, this will almost certainly be your point of arrival. Travelling from **Delhi**, the first town in Shekhawati worth stopping at is **Jhunjhunu** (245km southwest of Delhi and 180km north of Jaipur).

Unless you happen to coincide with the right train, **travelling around Shekhawati** by rail is far less convenient than by bus; slow and infrequent trains arrive at stations on the outskirts of towns. Fairly regular local **buses**, always overcrowded, also usually stop on the outskirts of town; few operate after dark. **Jeeps** run according to demand, picking up as many passengers as physically possible. For less congested and precarious transport, you can rent a Jeep in Nawalgarh, but by far the most comfortable (and most costly) way to get round the area is by **taxi** from Jaipur; for a three-day/two-night tour, most Jaipuri travel agents charge around Rs1600 for a diesel Ambassador, or Rs2200 for a more luxurious a/c model.

Nawalgarh

NAWALGARH, 25km north of Sikar, came into its own in 1737, when the Shekawat Nawal Singh claimed what was then a small village as the site for a fort. Thick stone walls, pierced by four gateways, were erected to encircle Nawalgarh, now a lively little market surrounded by miles of yellow desert and *khejri* scrub. For tourists, this is by far the most congenial base for the Shekhawati region, with a bumper crop of painted *havelis*, a picturesque, relatively traffic-free bazaar, good transport connections and some of the best budget accommodation in Rajasthan.

Nawalgarh is the home town of the wealthy and influential Poddar family, merchants who emigrated south to become Bombay-based industrialists and who have, over the years, sponsored the construction of schools and colleges across the country, including here. One of the town gates, formerly the **Nansa Gate**, has been renamed after Ramilas Poddar. It's the first you come to when approaching the town from the bus stand: turn left just inside it and follow the street round for about 250m, and you'll come to an enclosure on your left, surrounded by painted walls, many of which form part of **Aath Haveli**, a complex of seven *havelis*. The murals here feature trains, carts, false windows (very common in Nawalgarh) and barbers at work. Taking a right turn just inside Nansa Gate and then the second right, brings you to the **Surajmal Chhauchharia Haveli**, where murals include a picture of Europeans floating past in a hot-air balloon. The painter took some playful licence as to the mechanics involved: the two passengers blow into the balloon to power their journey.

The third right turn after entering Nansa Gate leads to the **fort**, housing banks and offices around a central yard crowded with vegetable vendors. The building marked "Hotel Rajendra", next to the State Bank of Bikaner and Jaipur, boasts the magnificent mirrored **Sheesh Mahal**, with a ceiling mural that includes maps of Nawalgarh and Jaipur. Despite its name, the building is a sweet shop; they will let you see the Sheesh Mahal for Rs10. Heading straight on from the Nansa Gate takes you, after 300m, to a little square, beyond which stands the colourful **Lakshminarayan temple**. A right turn at the square brings you to the **eastern gateway**, called Poddar Gate.

Other *havelis* in Nawalgarh include **Goenka Haveli**, in the north of town near Bowri Gate, and the magnificent **Anandi Lal Poddar Haveli**, east beyond Poddar Gate (follow the main road, bearing left and then round to the right after 50m, past a trio of rather delapidated *havelis*, and it's down a turning on your right). Built in 1920 and now a school, this is one of the few *havelis* in Shekhawati to have been restored to its original glory. Admission to the *haveli* itself costs Rs20, which includes a short but informative tour; all proceeds go towards maintenance of the building.

Practicalities

Nawalgarh's **bus** and **jeep** stand is about 2km west of town, served by buses from Jhunjhunu (every 30min; 1hr) via Dundlod (15min) and Mukundgarh (20min); Sikar (every 30min; 40min); Jaipur (every 30min; 3hr 30min), and Ajmer (1 daily; 5hr). Jeeps leave when they're full. The **railway station** is about 500m west, with four daily services in each direction from Sikar to Jhunjhunu (three from Jaipur). Incoming trains tend to arrive in the dead of night (when all the hotels are shut), but you can catch a conveniently timed service from here **to Delhi** at around 10pm (the Shekhawati Express; #9734), which joins up with the Link Express from Bikaner (#4710) to arrive at Delhi's Sarai Rohilla station at 5.30am the following morning.

For trips around the region, you can either jump on and off cheap, cramped village-to-village **Jeeps**, or rent a vehicle for the day, at very reasonable rates that include the services of a knowledgable English-speaking guide, through Ramesh Jangid at *Apani Dhani* (see below). **Cycles** can also be rented (Rs3/hr) from the small repair shop just north of the big Doordarshan transmitter mast on the northwest edge of town.

Accommodation

Although plentiful compared with most towns in Shekhawati, **accommodation** can be in short supply in the winter and should be booked a day or two in advance.

Apani Dhani, northwest edge of town, on the main Jhunjhunu road ☎ 01594/22239, ℱ 22129, ⊚ www.apanidhani.com Environmentally friendly campus of traditional-style round huts made with local materials. Home-grown vegetarian food, open-air kitchen and dining area, and hospitable owners. Excellent value, but popular with groups so book ahead. ❻

DS Bungalow, near *Roop Niwas*, on the eastern edge of town ☎ 01594/22703 or 23326. The best budget option after *Ramesh Jangid's*. Rooms (jazzed up with carpets and old wine bottles) are set around a sandy courtyard in a friendly family house. ❹–❺

Nawal Hotel, next to the bus stand and train station ☎ 01594/22155. Run-down lodge that's only worth considering if you arrive late and can't get into *Ramesh Jangid's*. ❷

Ramesh Jangid Tourist Pension, on the west edge of town, just north of Maur Hospital ☎ 01594/24060 or 22239. Immaculate, inexpensive en-suite rooms opening onto a sunny roof terrace, in a warm brahmin family home. Delicious pure-veg food available, as well as Jeep transport and expert advice on day-trips. One of the most congenial places of its kind in the country. ❷

Roop Niwas, 1km east of the bazaar ☎ 01594/22008, ℱ 23388. Nawalgarh's only upscale place is a rambling Raj-era mansion, with comfortably furnished rooms, set in extensive grounds. Wonderful sepia photos from the 1930s hang on the walls, along with moth-eaten hunting trophies; there's also a pool in summer. ❼

Around Nawalgarh: Dunlod and Parasrampura

The most obvious target for a day-trip from Nawalgarh is nearby **DUNLOD**, 7km north and the site of an old fort and some large *havelis*. It's possible to get there by bus, but most people walk across the fields – a leisurely amble that's enjoyable save for the last two kilometres, which you have to cover via a rough sandy track linking the village with the main road. The **fort**, like most others in the region, has been converted into a luxury hotel, the *Dunlod Castle* (☎ 01594/52519 or book through Jaipur ☎ 0141/361611; ❾), but its murals are mediocre and the rather shabby rooms, which have been tackily restored, lack the atmosphere of those at Mandawa and Mahansar. Radiating from its south-eastern walls, the village streets harbour several interesting *havelis*, painted around the turn of the twentieth-century, and the delicate **Chhatri of Ram Dutt Goenka**, a cenotaph erected in 1888 with vibrant friezes lining its dome.

More painted buildings are dotted around the serene hamlet of **PARAS-RAMPURA**, 20km southeast of Nawalgarh, amid some of the most attractive desert scenery between here and Jaisalmer. Buses run every half-hour or so, or you could cycle (although be warned, if you do, that several stretches of the track degenerate into soft sand). Monuments include the **Gopinath temple**, built in 1742, whose murals include depictions of the torments of hell (a common theme in the eighteenth century), and images of the local Rajput ruler, Sardul Singh, with his five sons; flocks of Persian-style angels look down from the ceilings. Some of the paintings are unfinished, as the artists were diverted to decorate the *chhatri* of Rajul Singh, who died that same year. The large dome of his exquisite cenotaph, supported by twelve pillars, contains a flourish of lively and well-preserved murals. Once again there are images of hell, and of Sardul Singh with his sons; this time he's also seen smoking a hookah and enjoying a tiger hunt. Parasrampura's modest **fort**, in reasonable repair, is on the west bank of the dry riverbed.

Jhunjhunu

JHUNJHUNU, taken over by the Shekawats in 1730 as the capital of their newly formed territory, is the principal entry point to Shekhawati if you're travelling southwest from Delhi. Spreading in a mass of brick and concrete from the base of a bare rocky hill, it's a busy, largely unprepossessing town these days, whose raucous traffic tends to make a more lasting impression than its painted *havelis*, which aren't a patch on those elsewhere in the region. Lots of visitors make the mistake of basing themselves here, but it's a better idea to stop long enough only to take in the highlights and then carry on another hour or so to Nawalgarh.

The most impressive private mansions are grouped around Nehru bazaar, five minutes by rickshaw north of the main bus stand along Station Road. Beginning at Gandhi Chowk, at the far east end of the market, walk west until you reach a pair of *havelis* facing each other from opposite sides of a lane running north. Known as the **Modi Havelis**, they contain some of the finest murals and woodcarving in the town. Above the nearby vegetable stalls, the **Kaniram Narsinghdas Tibrewala Haveli** boasts coloured-glass windows around the top of its *baithak*, or pillared reception area, while the **Bihari temple**, further up the same lane, features some of the oldest Shekhawati murals, painted in 1776 in vegetable pigments. Dating to a time before the Marwaris took over from the Rajputs as the dominant social class, they feature Sardul Singh's five sons, each of whom built a fort in the town.

Further west, the unique **Khetri Mahal**, built in 1760, is ageing and empty, but there's no mistaking the originality of its design: sandstone pillars stand in place of walls wherever possible, and a covered ramp, wide enough for horses, winds up to the roof. Views over Jhunjhunu from here stretch to the old Muslim quarter, **Pirzada Mahalla**, where a grand mosque is surrounded by tombs dating back to 1500. Many of Jhunjhunu's Muslims – still an important sector of the population – were wealthy merchants who built painted *havelis* of their own. A wander through Pirzada Mahalla leads past mosques, *dargahs* and meat markets, as well as neat rows of shops painted in pastel greens, blues and pinks unlike anywhere else in Shekhawati.

West of the Khetri Mahal, at the foot of the conical Kana Pahar hill, are **Badalgarh** – the only fort remaining from the Nawab period – and the **Dargah of Kamaruddin Shah**, with a mosque, *madrasa* and collection of tombs enclosed in a small complex. Behind the *madrasa* stands a monument to the infant son of Henry Forster, commander of the British-run Shekhawati Brigade, who died in 1841. Only one of the five gates of "Forster Gunge", the Shekhawati Brigade's cantonment, survives.

In the north of Jhunjhunu, the **Mertani Baori** is the region's most impressive step-well. If you head up there, make the short detour east to the extraordinary **Rani Sati Mandir**. Few foreigners ever visit this shrine, but, as the centre of a phenomenally popular Sati Mata cult, it is reputedly the richest in the country after Tirupati (in Andhra Pradesh), receiving hundreds of thousands of pilgrims each year and millions of rupees in donations. Its immense popularity bears witness to the enduring awe with which **satis** – women who commit ritual suicide by climbing on the funeral pyre of their husband – are viewed in the state. Although banned by the British in 1829, the practice has survived in parts of rural Rajasthan; forty cases are known to have occurred since Independence – the latest, and most infamous, being that of Roop Kanwar, a beautiful eighteen-year-old Rajput girl who committed self-immolation in 1987 in the village of Deorala, near Jaipur. The *sati* commemorated here was performed by a merchant's wife in 1595. Her image, rendered in tile- and mirror-work, adorns the ceiling of the main prayer hall, while a sequence of panels on the north wall relates the legend surrounding the events of her death.

Practicalities

Buses from the chaotic government stand in the south of town run to Nawalgarh (every 30min; 40min–1hr) and towns throughout Shekhawati, as well as to Bikaner (5 daily; 5hr 30min), Jaipur (every 30min; 5hr) and Delhi. The stand for private buses is east of the main bazaar; tempos and shared auto-rickshaws run between the two via Gandhi Chowk. Four **train** services arrive at the station on the southern edge of town from Sikar via Nawalgarh (three of them from Jaipur), and there are four services running the other way from Loharu (one of which starts in Delhi), but they get in at inconvenient times of the night, or else are passenger trains that are slower than buses.

The local **tourist office**, attached to the RTDC *Tourist Bungalow*, occupies a new building on the western outskirts that's amazingly large considering it

---

The khejri tree

A defining feature of Shekhawati's arid landscape and of the whole Thar Desert region, is the khejri tree (*Prosopis cinerasia*), whose dark knobbly branches and small, olive-green leaves dot the dunes and scrubby sand flats from here all the way to Sind. Possessing exceptionally deep roots, it is among the few plants that can survive in this drought-prone area, and is an essential resource for north and western Rajasthan's subsistence farmers, who use its rock-hard wood for ploughs and its leaves as precious fodder for goats and camels. During November and early December, the desert is filled with villagers pruning trees and binding bundles of freshly cut *khejri* to cart home. Fruit from the tree is gathered and eaten raw (*khoka*), or cooked as a curry vegetable (*sangri*) to be relished with *rotis*, while the sap (*rayee*), which is believed to be good for arthritis and aching joints, is used to sweeten tea in the winter.

The key role played by *khejri* in the desert peasants' economy explains why the tree is revered as a religious object by the infamous Bishnoi tribe (see p.226) of Jodhpur district. Their beliefs came to the political forefront in 1730, when the Maharaja of Jodhpur ordered his men to collect wood for a new palace. Despite the pleas of the Bishnois, felling commenced in the small village of Khejadali, near Jodhpur. In a desperate bid to halt the axe-men, Amritdevi, a Bishnoi woman, hugged a *khejri* tree, but the fellers, assuming that the maharaja's request was to be respected, ignored her plea. She and 362 of her fellow people lost their lives trying to protect the forests. On hearing the news the maharaja recalled his men and accorded state sanction to the Bishnoi religion, a turning point in history remembered each September when thousands attend a festival at Khejadali. At this time, red threads associated with the goddess Lakshmi, whom the *khejri* is believed to incarnate in the same way as the *peepal* embodies Vishnu, are tied to trees as petitions for the long life of husbands.

The Bishnois' *khejri* festival has become somewhat controversial in recent years, amid allegations that it has been hijacked by the Congress (I) party to whip up anti-feudal feeling, and thus votes, among the notoriously rebellious tribals.

has nothing more to offer visitors than maps of other places. Jhunjhunu is quite spread out, and walking around can be tiring, but many of the streets of the old town are too narrow for cars; **rickshaws** operate as taxis, picking up as many passengers as they can. **Bicycles** can be rented from a small shop near the park in the south. **Taxis** to explore further afield gather at a rank outside the bus stand, costing around Rs4 per kilometre.

The best budget **accommodation** is the *Hotel Sangam* (☎01592/32544; ❷), which has clean, spacious rooms. It's set back from the bus stand, so doesn't get the noise that infiltrates the nearby *Naheen* (☎01592/32527; ❷), which is pretty basic. Further east, the *Shiv Shekhawati* (☎01592/32651, ℻32603; ❺), is a much smarter, well-maintained hotel with large, clean rooms, a restaurant and relaxing lawn; nearby, on a hilltop overlooking the eastern edge of town, the same owner has opened the more swanky *Jamuna Resort* (☎01592/32871, ℻32603; ❻), popular with Delhi-ites for its pool and panoramic views. A less pretentious alternative on the south side of Jhunjhunu is the *Shekhawati Heritage* (☎01592/35727; ❹–❺), which has a range of plain but comfortable rooms tucked away in a quiet residential suburb.

With the exception of the *Sangam* and *Naheen*, all of the above hotels have good **restaurants** attached to them that are the best places to eat in town. There are also the usual rows of cheap food stalls concentrated around the bus stand, and basic sit-down joints such as *Nehru's Hotel* in Gandhi Chowk.

Mandawa

Rising from a flat, featureless landscape roughly midway between Jhunjhunu and Fatehpur, **MANDAWA** was founded by the Shekawats in 1755, though most of its paintwork dates from the early nineteenth century. The town's imposing **fort**, right in the centre, now houses the most famous **hotel** in the region (see below), whose prominence on the upmarket tour-group trail has made this a more tourist-oriented place than anywhere else in Shekhawati. However, the handicraft shops, touts and guides clustered around its cannonball-chipped walls detract very little from the dilapidated beauty of the nearby mansions, and you could well find yourself tempted to stay a day or two. In addition to some fine monuments, Mandawa harbours a better-than-average batch of hotels, among them one of the few genuine *havelis* run as a budget guesthouse.

The outer walls, jutting balconies, alcoves and overhanging upper storeys of the **Goenka Double Haveli** in the west of town are replete with patterns and paintings, ranging from traditional Rajasthani women and religious motifs to Europeans in stylish hats and Victorian finery. In the **Nand Lal Murmuria Haveli** next door, the paintings of trains, cars, George V, and Venice were executed during the 1930s by Balu Ram, one of the last working artists of the region. Murals in the **Thakurji temple** opposite these two mansions include soldiers being shot from the mouths of cannons, a reflection of the horrors of the Mutiny. Further west are a couple of *chhatris*, and a step-well, still used today and bearing paintings inside its decorative corner domes.

Another *haveli* worth asking for by name is **Gulab Rai Wadia Haveli**, in the south of town, where the decoration of the outer and inner walls is perhaps the finest in Shekhawati. Blue washes here and there betray twentieth-century censorship of the erotic scenes that had been commonly acceptable one hundred years earlier. Just south of here, the **Chowkhadi Haveli** is unique in the region for having twin wings. Its murals are particularly beautiful and well preserved; look for the miserable British soldiers and *chillum*-smoking *sadhu* on the walls in the recess of the facade.

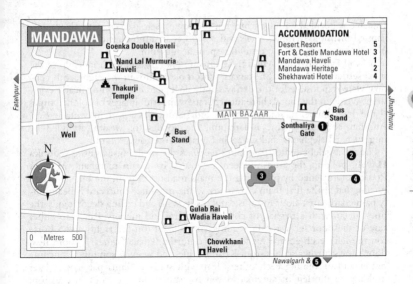

ACCOMMODATION

Desert Resort	5
Fort & Castle Mandawa Hotel	3
Mandawa Haveli	1
Mandawa Heritage	2
Shekhawati Hotel	4

Nawalgarh & ⑤ ▼

RAJASTHAN | Shekhawati

Practicalities

Buses from Jhunjhunu and Nawalgarh (at least hourly), as well as Jaipur and Bikaner (3 daily) stop at Sonthalia Gate in the east of town. From Fatehpur, most buses pull in at a stand in the centre, just off the main bazaar. Jeeps ply the same routes. Mandawa's **accommodation** covers the full range and is plentiful, although you'll save yourself a march around town by phoning ahead as the hotels and guesthouses are spread out.

Castle Mandawa ☏01592/23124, ℻23171, ⊛www.castlemanadawa.com. The castle is the real thing and the rooms, complete with alcoved sitting areas, murals and period furniture, are luxurious enough, but there's something hollow about the whole experience. Turbaned Nepali waiters perform nightly Rajasthani cabarets for tour groups, and the approaches are filled with shops selling fake antiques. ⑨

Desert Resort, 1km south of town ☏01592/23151 or 23514. Award-winning "tourist hamlet", sealed off from the outside world, with its own pool. The kind of place, with its expensively designed cow-dung covered walls, that looks exquisite in interiors magazines (the "tribal" murals are wonderful) but feels contrived here in rural Rajasthan. ⑧–⑨

Mandawa Haveli, near Sonthaliya Gate ☏01592/23088,

ⓔhotelmandawahaveli@yahoo.com. Comfortable rooms, all en suite and luxuriously furnished, in recently renovated *haveli*. The suites on the upper storey (especially "Nilas") are much the nicest. ⑦

Mandawa Heritage, Mukandgarh Road ☏01592/23742, ℻23243. A turn-of-the-twentieth-century mansion with attractively furnished rooms, on the quiet south side of town. The quoted tariffs are a bit steep, but a feigned walk-out will bring them down. ④–⑥

Shekhawati, near Government Veterinary Hospital, Mukandgarh Road ☏01592/23036. Small, friendly budget guesthouse run by a garrulous retired banker. His rooms (en suite or cheaper non-attached) are neat and clean, but again, the prices are a touch ambitious. Tasty meals on request. ②–④

Fatehpur

Lying just off NH-11, **FATEHPUR** is the closest town in Shekhawati to Bikaner, 116km west, and a good place to stop overnight if you're taking the northern route across the Thar to or from Jaisalmer. The only accommodation available is decidedly uninspiring, but the town itself, packed with elaborately painted mansions, temples, wells and *chhatris*, is an atmospheric little place that in parts has the feel of a crumbling open-air museum.

In 1450 Fateh Khan, a Muslim Khaimkani Nawab, claimed leadership of the small settlement, but the Shekawats, who took control in the eighteenth century, were responsible for the extravagantly decorated *havelis* lining nearly every street. Many of the murals here incorporate wonderful images of colonial times – the king emperor, soldiers, trains and parties of *angrezi* in vintage cars. Another common theme is Lakshmi, the goddess of wealth, attended by mighty, regal elephants, and set against a rich azure background.

The most celebrated of Fatehpur's *havelis* is the small but exquisite **Goenka Haveli**, built in the mid-nineteenth century by a Jain merchant, Mahavir Prasad, and reached by following the main road north from the bus stand and turning left at the first main crossroads. While the inner courtyard is beautifully painted, the first-floor room is dazzling, its walls and ceiling decorated in the finest detail with a myriad of colours, gold leaf and mirrors. Panels to either side of the door show Krishna riding an elephant (on the right) and a horse (on the left), each animal made up of contorted female figures. A room next door shows further scenes from Krishna's life, and women spinning, churning butter and decorating each other's feet with spidery henna patterns. A later building to the left of Goenka Haveli has superb mirror work in the front porch. If you rejoin the main northbound road at the crossroads, and turn right after 20m, you'll come to **Nand Lal Devra Haveli**, whose splendid ceiling panels in the reception area were copied by many other merchant families. The murals on the courtyard walls, and the complex carving of the wooden doors and shutters, are equally impressive.

To the north of town, distinctive Shekhawati **wells** (*baoris*) stand raised on square platforms, with domed shelters on each corner, so they could be seen from afar. Once the lifeline of the community, and still common meeting places, these wells have not suffered the decay seen elsewhere since the advent of more sophisticated plumbing.

Practicalities

Fatehpur has two **bus stands**, both close together in the centre of town on the main Sikar–Churu (north–south) road. Buses from the government Roadways stand, the one furthest south, serve Jaipur (25 daily; 3hr 30min), Ramgarh (hourly) and Bikaner (14 daily; 3hr 30min–4hr), as well as Delhi (5 daily; 6hr). Private buses, most of them handsome old snub-nosed Tata Mercedes vehicles, run from the stand further north along the bazaar to Mandawa (every 2hr; 30min), Jhunjhunu (every 30min; 1hr), Mahansar (4 daily; 45min) and Ramgarh (hourly; 30min). The **railway station**, east of town, has four daily **trains** to Churu, one continuing to Bikaner, and four to Sikar, of which two go on to Jaipur; these, however, run at inconvenient times.

A kilometre south of town, just off NH-11, is the modern RTDC *Hotel Haveli* (℡01571/20293; ❺–❻), the town's only commendable **hotel**. The rooms, some of which have a/c or air-coolers, are large and light, but in other respects this is a typical government-run place with dodgy plumbing, a noisy television hall on the ground floor and less-than-helpful staff. It's also a fair walk from the bazaar and bus stand; if you aim to catch the early morning (6.30am) express service to Bikaner, note that rather than lug your gear up to the Roadways stand, you can flag the bus down from the roadside next to the hotel. For **food**, you've a less than inspiring choice between the RTDC *Hotel Haveli*'s hit-and-miss, overpriced menu (whose only redeeming feature is its cold beers), or the row of basic *dhabas* near the bus stand.

Mahansar, Ramgarh and Lakshmangarh

Some of the most outstanding murals and Hindu monuments in the region are scattered across three small towns in the far north and west of Shekhawati: **Mahansar**, **Ramgarh** and **Lakshmangarh**. Of these, only Mahansar has any accommodation (an old fort that's been converted into a characterful, and relatively inexpensive, heritage hotel), but you can reach the other two easily enough on day-trips from Fatehpur.

Mahansar

The relative inaccessibility of **MAHANSAR**, marooned amid a sea of scrub and drifting sand 27km northeast of Fatehpur, has ensured that its monuments, which include a fortress and some of the most elaborate and accomplished interior paintings in Shekhawati, rank among the least visited in the region. A ribbon of hopelessly potholed tarmac leads out here from Mandawa, and another runs due west to Ramgarh, but aside from sporadic buses, the only traffic along them are camel carts and herds of goats. This makes Mahansar an eminently peaceful and pleasant place to hole up for a day or two, and a much more enticing prospect than more touristy Mandawa, a thirty-minute Jeep ride south.

Twelve **rooms** of varying standards are available at the fort, built in 1768 by Thakur Nahar Singh and converted recently by his descendent, Thakur Typal Singh, into the quirky *Narayan Niwas* (℡01595/64322, or through Delhi ℡011/648 6807; ❻). Room #1 is the most romantic, with old rugs, bolsters, ancient carved wooden doors and raised sitting alcoves with views. It's a more informal, slapdash establishment than other heritage hotels in the area, but this lends it a certain charm. Budget travellers should note that the *thakur* also has a couple of inexpensive rooms (❷–❸) tucked away in less frequented corners of the castle, although he is generally reluctant to advertise the fact.

Once you've explored the fort, there's little more to do other than wander around the village looking for painted buildings. Mahansar's most beautiful murals, however, are locked away out of sight in the **Sona Ki Dukan Haveli**, next to the main crossroads (ask around the shops for the key). The ceiling of the entrance hall to this mansion is exquisitely decorated with painted and richly gilded scenes from the *Ramayana* and *Gita Govinda*. To fully appreciate the colours and mass of detail, you'll need a pocket light. A small donation of around Rs10 is expected for each visit.

Ramgarh

RAMGARH, 20km north of Fatehpur, was founded in 1791 and developed almost as a status symbol by the Poddar merchant family, who made every effort to make their new town outshine nearby Churu, which they left following a dispute with the local *thakur* over wool tax. They were successful; there's hardly a bare wall in town, even among the shops in the bazaar. Most of the grand Poddar **chhatris** beside the main Churu–Sikar road preserve vibrant turquoise and vermillion murals depicting scenes from the *Ramayana* within their domes, but to see them you'll have to ask for the key at the sweet shop just outside (communal tensions have resulted in some of the paintings being defaced in recent years). The Poddar family *havelis* in the north of town, west of Churu Gate, are decorated with scenes from local folk stories, and a three-fish motif that is unique to Ramgarh. Temples such as Natwar Niketan, Ram Lakshman and Ganga Mandir harbour accomplished depictions of scenes from the Hindu epics and local legends; the **Shani temple** in the northwest of town also holds some elaborate mirror work.

Lakshmangarh

The most imposing feature of **LAKSHMANGARH**, 20km south of Fatehpur, is the nineteenth-century **fort**, hewn from steep, smooth grey rocks, that dominates the west side of town. It is now empty and dim inside, though you can climb the ramp to the summit to enjoy a spectacular view. Lakshmangarh is easy to explore, thanks to a symmetrical street grid inspired by that of Jaipur. It holds three principal squares, several wells and temples, and plenty of richly painted *havelis*. Just below the fort, near the bus stand, stands the huge **Char Chowk Haveli**. Built around four large courtyards (*chowks*), it remains in private ownership, and access is therefore restricted. In any case, it's best seen from the fort, from where its peculiar design can be appreciated.

To see other excellent – and amusing – frescoes in Lakshmangarh search out the heavily painted **Kyal** and **Naria** *havelis* in the southeast of town, the scenes of European women on walls near the clock tower, and **Sanganeeria Haveli**, east of the Radha Murlimanohar temple. In the far east of town, near a *chhatri* and a well, the bright but dilapidated **Pansari Haveli** shelters a semiperma-nent settlement of *lohars*, nomadic ironworkers.

East of Jaipur

The fertile area **east of Jaipur**, interspersed with the forested slopes of the Aravalli Hills, holds an inviting mixture of historic towns and wildlife sanctu-aries. The fortified town of **Alwar** to the northeast, fought over for centuries before its incorporation into Rajasthan in 1949, served as refuge for the exiled Pandava brothers of the *Mahabharata* during their thirteenth year of hiding, before Krishna helped them in the fierce battle against their cousins, the Kauravas, chronicled in the *Bhagavad Gita*.

Not far from Alwar, **Sariska Wildlife Sanctuary** is renowned for its tigers, while further east are the former princely capitals of **Deeg** and **Bharatpur**, and India's finest bird sanctuary, **Keoladeo National Park**. The wildlife sanc-tuary at **Ranthambore**, southeast of Jaipur, offers the best chance of spotting wild tigers in India, against a backdrop of idyllic scenery.

Alwar

Roughly 140km northeast from Jaipur towards Delhi, **ALWAR** rests peaceful-ly in a valley, overlooked by a fortress that stretches along a high craggy ridge to the northwest. Alwar was not always so calm. Traditionally the northern gateway to Rajasthan, its strategic position on the Rajput border resulted in incessant warfare between the Jats of Bharatpur and the Kuchwahas of Amber, from the tenth to the seventeenth century. Jai Singh, the flamboyant, eccentric grandfather of the present incumbent, became notorious during the British era for his outrageous behaviour. Official reports in the 1930s describe him bury-ing his luxury Hispano-Suiza cars when he tired of them, and dousing his favourite polo pony in petrol and setting fire to it; rumours also circulated suggesting a predilection for young boys. One visiting ruler claimed he climbed into bed one night only to discover a naked lad, who produced from his bottom a pristine silk handerchief as proof of his cleanliness.

The fort, now a radio station, can only be visited with police permission; the buildings within are in any case unspectacular, but the climb is worthwhile for the views. Construction of Alwar's Indo-Islamic **Vinay Vilas Palace** began under Bhaktawar Singh, Pratap Singh's successor. Although time has worn away much of its glory, it remains flamboyant, with domed roofs, lavish verandas decorated in gold leaf, and delicate balconies facing a huge tank flanked by symmetrical *ghats* and pavilions. The stately sandstone and marble **Moosi Maharani Chhatri** here was built in memory of Bhaktawar Singh's mistress, who sacrificed her life on his funeral pyre. A **museum** on the top floor of the palace (daily except Fri 10am–4.30pm; Rs3) houses a collection of courtly memorabilia, including remarkable Arabic and Sanskrit manuscripts, tenth-century statues, ivory ornaments, fine embroidery and the inevitable weapons and stuffed animals.

Much of the palace is now taken up with government offices; in the main courtyard, used as the venue for the local courts, typists, lawyers and advisers huddle round rickety tables under banyan trees, drinking tea and filing through endless piles of paper. If you've time to kill, scale the steps leading uphill from the grounds behind the palace to the **Gopi Billib-ka Temple**, which affords fine views over the town.

Practicalities

The **bus stand** in the west of Alwar sees services to and from Deeg and Bharatpur (every 15min), and Sariska (every 30min or so). Frequent buses also run north to Delhi and south to Jaipur (both 2–3hr). Several food stalls at the bus stand sell drinks and fiery curries, and there's a **bike rental** shop near the exit. The **railway station**, receiving trains from Delhi, Jaipur, Jodhpur, Ahmedabad, Deeg and Ajmer, is a few kilometres away on the east side of town, and has retiring rooms. You can **change** currency and travellers' cheques, albeit at a thumb-chewingly slow speed, at the State Bank of Bikaner and Jaipur, in the centre of town.

The **tourist office**, just south of the station exit on the opposite side of Nehru Marg (Mon–Sat 10am–5pm; ☎0144/21868), has dusty piles of aged leaflets about Rajasthan, but little else. Your best bet for budget **accommodation** is a group of five hotels of varying standards, all owned by five brothers and grouped together on the corner of Manu Marg, ten minutes' walk up Vivekananda Marg from the railway station. The *Ankur* (☎0144/333025; ❸–❺) is just about the best of the bunch, but there's little to choose between them and all invariably have vacancies. For more comfort, try the *Aravali*, a couple of doors down from the railway station on Nehru Marg (☎0144/332883, ℱ332011; ❸–❺), which has seen better days, but boasts a bar and pool in summer. With your own transport, a more atmospheric upscale choice is the *Hill Fort Kesroli*, 12km east of town (☎0144/81312; ❼–❾), where a wonderful little fourteenth-century fort has been impeccably restored and converted into a hotel. Centred on a lush inner courtyard filled with palms and bougainvillea, its rooms, set in the forbidding outer walls, have great views over Kesroli village and the surrounding countryside.

Back in town, the *Aravali* has a gloomy but serviceable **restaurant**, but for crispy *dosas*, tasty *channa batura* and other hot snacks, the *South India* café, opposite the State Bank of Bikaner and Jaipur, is hard to beat. The only competition comes from the clean and pleasant *Siddartha* vegetarian restaurant, just south of the *Imperial Hotel* on Manu Marg.

Sariska

Alwar is the jumping-off point for the beautiful **Sariska Tiger Reserve and National Park**, a former maharaja's hunting ground managed since 1979 by Project Tiger (see p.1532). Like its more famous counterpart Ranthambore, the sanctuary encompasses abundant woodland dotted with evocative ruins, including a popular Hanuman temple (only open to the public two days per week) and an old fort. **Wildlife** here includes sambar, *nilgai* and *chital,* wild boar, mongooses, monkeys, peacocks, parrots and other birds, but poaching has regrettably decimated Sariska's population of **tigers** and sightings are less frequent than at Ranthambore. The poaching problem came to a head in the mid-1980s, when numbers plummeted from 45 to 16 in a single year. A local tribesman was arrested and confessed to the shootings, which he'd carried out with an old muzzle-loader, aided by poorly paid Forest-department staff.

The best prospect of seeing a tiger is around the artificial **water holes** placed along the main road through the park to attract animals in the dry season. Access to the park (closed July & Aug, when the animals retreat to higher ground) is limited to daylight hours (dawn to dusk), to protect tigers from night poaching.

Practicalities

The 37-kilometre journey by **bus** to Sariska from Alwar (1hr) can be very crowded. Tours run by the *Aravali Hotel* in Alwar cost well over the odds for a trip in a packed minibus that rushes through the park, with a minimal chance of any sightings.

If you choose to **stay** in Sariska there are two options. RTDC *Hotel Tiger Den* (☏0144/41342; ❶–❻), set in peaceful gardens right next to the park entrance, offers well-kept spacious rooms and a cheap dorm. Otherwise, get your credit card out and head for the totally extravagant *Sariska Palace* (☏0144/41322, ☏41323; ❽), the former maharaja's hunting lodge, which charges Rs3000 per night for its luxurious rooms (ask for one in the main block or you'll find yourself in the far less appealing converted stable annexe). The hotel has a gorgeous pool, manicured grounds and a television room with videotapes of BBC wildlife documentaries about tigers.

Tours of the park leave twice each day, at 7am and 3pm, and last around three hours. Unlike Ranthambore, only Gypsy Jeeps operate in Sariska. The cost depends on which vehicle you choose. For a quieter petrol Jeep, count on paying Rs825 (which includes rental and admission charges), or Rs725 for a diesel one. Don't, however, arrange a safari through your hotel, as they'll slap a Rs200 surcharge on top of these prices.

Deeg

DEEG (also spelt Dig), 30km northwest of Bharatpur, is a grim little market town midway between Agra and the Aravallis which, as the second capital of the local ruling Rajputs, was the scene of bloody encounters with the Moghul overlords in the mid-1700s. The only reason you might want to come here these days is to see the town's much-photographed palace en route between the Bharatpur bird sanctuary and Sariska tiger reserve near Alwar, 50km west. Fusing Moghul and Hindu elements, it's an undeniably beautiful building, but doesn't really warrant a special day-trip.

Construction of the royal retreat began in 1730, when the Jat ruler Badan Singh established Deeg as the second capital of Bharatpur state. There's a commanding view from the high fortified walls of his citadel, and you can still see some of the original cannons. The delicate design of the **palaces** or *bhawans* (daily 8am–noon & 1–7pm), with arches, pillars and domes reflected in surrounding water tanks, and the leafy gardens interspersed with two thousand fountains, is typical of the Jats. Most were built by the king Surajmal in 1756, and even the oldest, **Purana Mahal**, still bears traces of wall paintings. The largest, **Gopal Bhawan**, near the entrance to the complex, was Surajmal's summer residence. Its spacious, plushly furnished hall is gracefully proportioned, with majestic archways, sculpted pillars and intricate balconies overlooking the tank, or **Gopal Sagar**. A pavilion stands on either side of the *bhawan*; the deliberate resemblance of the whole ensemble to a pleasure barge is best appreciated from the west.

In the east of the complex, overlooking Rup Sagar, **Kesav Bhawan** is an open-sided square pavilion, designed to re-create the freshness of the monsoon. In Surajmal's time, fountains played within it, producing a shimmering rainbow in the sunshine, while cooling water showered from the roof to the accompaniment of artificial rolls of thunder. The reservoir for the fountains took a week to fill and only a matter of hours to empty, and nowadays they are only switched on during local festivals.

Deeg fell into decline along with the Jat rulership at the beginning of the nineteenth century, and remains very small, though it is served by bus (every 15min; 1hr 30min) and train (daily; 2hr) from Alwar. Permission to **stay** at the *Dak Bungalow* (❶) must be obtained in advance from the overseer in the Public Works Department office, Kama Darwaja. Otherwise, the only place to stay in the area is RTDC's featureless *Motel Deeg* (☎05641/21000; ❹), on the main road to Mathura near the bus stand.

Bharatpur and Keoladeo National Park

The walled town of **BHARATPUR** is just a stone's throw from the border with Uttar Pradesh, 150km east of Jaipur, and a mere 18km from Fatehpur Sikri, Akbar's deserted capital. Though it may not hold any especially distinguished attractions, it's fun to explore by bike or on foot, with traditional markets, mosques, temples and a massive fort encircled by a wide and murky moat.

However, the real reason to come here is to visit India's most famous bird sanctuary, the **Keoladeo National Park**, just a short way south of the town. Even if you're not particularly interested in ornithology, this extraordinary site deserves at least a night or two. Few places in the world, let alone ones so easily accessible, boast such a profusion of wildlife in so confined an area. During the winter months, hundreds of thousands of indigenous and migratory birds congregate on land flooded in the late nineteenth century by the local maharaja to create a giant hunting reserve. Cycling around the sanctuary's quiet, shady paths, you're almost certain to glimpse several species of large mammals such as black buck and deer, as well as lizards and pythons, and some of the most startlingly exotic birds you'll ever see – a perfect antidote to the fumes and frenzy of the nearby cities.

The Town

Bharatpur itself was founded by the Jat king Surajmal, who built the virtually impregnable **Lohagarh Fort** at its heart in 1732; known as the eastern gateway to Rajasthan, it soon developed into a busy market centre. Although the original moat, 45m wide and up to 15m deep, still encircles the town, little remains of the thick eleven-kilometre walls that protected it – the British spent

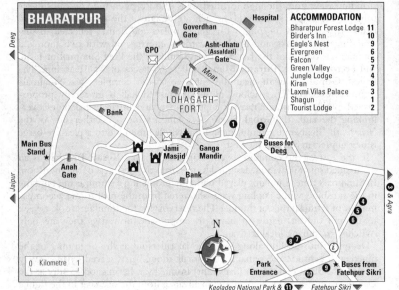

BHARATPUR

Goverdhan
Gate

Hospital

GPO

Asht-dhatu
(Assaldati)
Gate

Moat

Museum
LOHAGARH
FORT

Bank

Main Bus
Stand

Anah
Gate

Jami
Masjid

Ganga
Mandir

Bank

Buses for
Deeg

ACCOMMODATION
Bharatpur Forest Lodge	11
Birder's Inn	10
Eagle's Nest	9
Evergreen	6
Falcon	5
Green Valley	7
Jungle Lodge	4
Kiran	8
Laxmi Vilas Palace	3
Shagun	1
Tourist Lodge	2

▲ *Deeg*   ▲ *Jaipur*   ▶ ❸ *& Agra*

N

0   Kilometre   1

Park
Entrance

★ Buses from
Fatehpur Sikri

Keoladeo National Park & ⓫ ▼   *Fatehpur Sikri* ▼

four months in 1805 trying in vain to penetrate them, before suffering their
heaviest defeat in Rajasthan.

As you enter the fort from the north, through Assaldati Gate, you'll see a jumble of old and new buildings, among them the three palaces built by the Jats
between 1730 and 1850. Of these, the **Maharaja's Palace** with its stone lattice windows, painted walls and a curious collection of *hammams* (sunken
baths) on the ground floor, is the most aesthetically appealing. The **Kamra
Palace** in the west of the fort now houses the government **museum** (daily
except Fri 10.30am–5pm), with a well-stocked gallery of Jain sculptures, a
copious assortment of weaponry and graphic manuscripts in Arabic and
Sanskrit. Among its collection of statues from the region is a figurine of a *yaksha* from the first century BC. From the shade of a lofty pavilion on the roof
of the palace, you can enjoy great views of the surrounding countryside.

South of the fort, in the main market area, lie the **Jami Masjid**, fronted by
a magnificent arched portal, and **Ganga Mandir**, a large, elaborate temple of
pure sandstone.

Keoladeo National Park
KEOLADEO NATIONAL PARK (daily 6am–6.30pm; Rs100 [Rs20]), formerly known as Bharatpur Bird Sanctuary, was for sixty years a royal hunting
reserve. However, against the odds, the avian population survived and the area
became a sanctuary in 1956, receiving total protection in 1981 when it was
recognized as a national park. Today, Keoladeo's 29 square kilometres of swamp
and lakes constitute one of the most important breeding and migratory areas
in the world. Species include the majestic saras crane, which stands as tall as a
man, and a staggering two thousand painted storks, whose nesting cries, from
Bharatpur's partially submerged trees, create a constant background din to
wanderings around the park. Other residents include snake-like darters, spoon-

bills, pink flamingos, white ibis, grey pelicans and around thirty species of birds of prey, among them vultures, marsh harriers, peregrine falcons and ospreys. Some are vegetarian, but many feed on frogs, beetles and fish, and soon after the breeding season (July–Oct), birds of prey home in on the vulnerable fledglings to supplement their usual diet.

Between October and March, the 200 species of Indian birds who live in the park year-round are joined by a further 130 species from as far afield as the Russian steppes and Central Asia. The finest and rarest of these migratory birds, all of whom spend the winter in Bharatpur building up reserves of fat before the long flights back to their breeding grounds, are the five pairs of **Siberian cranes** who nest in the south of the park each winter. Only 125 such cranes, pure white with crimson bills and facial patches, are estimated to survive in the entire world. This group flies over five thousand miles from its summer breeding grounds around the Ob River in Siberia, crossing the Himalayas en route. After they failed to reappear in the winters of 1995 and 1996, it was feared the Bharatpur "sibes" had fallen foul of hunters in the mountains, but four finally showed up two years and two months late in 1996, and now the population seems stable. They're easy enough to spot, and tend to feed in pairs just off the main Ghana Canal, a short way southwest of the Keoladeo temple in the centre of the park; just look for the gaggle of khaki-clad birdspotters with metre-long lenses.

You also stand a good chance of glimpsing wild boar, mongoose, *chital, nilgai* and sambar along the paths, and spotting elusive jungle cats, hyenas, jackals, otters and Indian black buck. Languorous rock pythons sun themselves at Python Point, just past Keoladeo temple, and in the dry bush land off the main road close to the entrance barrier. Believe it or not, you might also catch a glimpse of a **tiger** if you venture into the more remote grassland areas of the park. In August 2000, villagers spotted a large, three- to four-year-old female who'd wandered into Keoladeo from the Sawai Madhopur/Ranthmabore region. The sighting was confirmed soon after, but at the time of writing the park authorities were in a quandary over what to do about their exotic new resident, whose presence in the Colar Dehar zone makes this key site for ornithologists unsafe to explore on foot or by bike.

Keoladeo is at its most picturesque at dawn and dusk, and fullest between October and March. In summer you miss the migratory flocks, but should catch some busy nesting activity. A single metalled road passes through the sanctuary; numerous small paths lined with *babul* trees cut across lakes and marshes and provide excellent cover for bird-watching. The free **map** handed out at the park entrance is useful for finding your way around. If you need help identifying the birds, or finding vantage points, you can hire a **guide** at the gate (Rs35/hr for up to 5 people), who will probably have binoculars. The best way to get around is by bike, which are also available at the sanctuary gate, or by cycle rickshaw (Rs30/hr) – drivers are very clued up and know the main nesting areas. Tongas (Rs50/hr) carry up to six people. During the winter, gondola-style **boats** provide a superb opportunity to get really close to the birds in the heart of the wetland.

Practicalities

Bharatpur's **bus stand** is in the west of town near Anah Gate, just off NH-11. If you're arriving **from Fatehpur Sikri**, get off well before, when the bus stops at the crossroads on the opposite side of town near the park gates, as this is nearer all the hotels and guesthouses. From the main bus stand, services run to all major centres in Rajasthan (including Jaipur) and to Delhi, Agra and

Fatehpur Sikri. Two kilometres northwest, the **railway station** lies on the main Delhi–Mumbai line. There are also two fast trains to Agra (2hr) and one to Amritsar (14hr), and an express service to Sawai Madhopur (2hr 30min). The town's **tourist office** (Mon–Sat 10am–5pm), where you can pick up good state maps and information on Bharatpur and the sanctuary, stands at the cross-roads near the park entrance where Fatehpur Sikri buses pull in.

Cycle rickshaws are the main form of transport within the city, but fares for the long haul in and out of town soon mount up, and it makes sense to rent a **bicycle**, either from your hotel (around Rs35/day) or the shop on NH-11 outside the *Spoonbill Restaurant*. If you need to **change money**, head for the State Bank of Bikaner and Jaipur, Binarayan Gate (Mon–Fri 10am–2pm, Sat 10am–noon).

Accommodation and eating

Few people stay in Bharatpur proper – the entrance to the park is 7km south of the railway station on the far side of town, so to be well placed for an early start it's a better idea to spend the night in one of several assorted **hotels** and **guesthouses** along NH-11, which skirts the northern edge of the park. Best of the bunch for budget travellers are the *Kiran* and the four guesthouses just north of the main crossroads, run by four brothers and their families. Further up the scale, the options are more limited, with most hotels ranged along the noisy highway, giving them a motel-like feel that's not at all in keeping with wildlife watching. Wherever you stay, in peak season (mid-Nov to late Feb) it's a good idea to book a room in advance, as places fill up early in the day.

Bharatpur Forest Lodge, in the park ☏05644/22760. This is the only hotel actually inside the park grounds. You pay well over the odds for the privilege, but the rooms are very comfortable, with a/c and balconies that are great for bird-watching. Book in advance. ❾

Birders' Inn, NH-11 ☏05644/27346, ℻ 25265. Newest of the mid-price places along the main road, with large, scrupulously clean rooms set well back from the traffic, large, modern tiled bathrooms and a quality restaurant. ❻

Eagle's Nest, NH-11 ☏05644/25144. Impersonal but efficient mid-range hotel on the main highway. The rooms are spacious and clean, with attached bathrooms and 24hr hot water, and the restaurant is one of the best in town, serving mainly north Indian specialities, and chilled beer. ❺

Evergreen, near the tourist office ☏05644/25917. Congenial family-run guesthouse near the highway junction. Immaculate rooms (most with bathroom), relaxing roof terrace and good home cooking (try their delicious *misi rotis* for breakfast, cooked on a wood-and-dung fire in the back garden). Bikes and binoculars available. ❷–❸

Falcon, 1km northwest of RTDC *Saras* ☏05644/23815. Set back from the main road junction on a quiet suburban street, this modern guesthouse has a range of spotlessly clean and comfortable rooms on two floors (those on the

upper storey are best, with more space and thick mattresses) and a small lawn-side restaurant with an open fire in the back garden. The best choice in this price bracket. ❷–❹

Green Valley, 376 Rajendra Nagar, Bharatpur ☏05644/29576. Very friendly family guesthouse, with clean, airy en-suite rooms and spacious garden ten minutes' walk from the park gates. The three resident daughters make this a particularly commendable option for women travellers. ❷–❸

Jungle Lodge, Govi Shankar ☏05644/25622. Pleasant rooms facing a green marble-floored veranda and flower-filled garden. Friendly and well managed. Cycles, binoculars and two 500cc Enfields for rent, and they have a nice little restaurant. ❸

Kiran, 364 Rajendra Nagar ☏05644/23845. Tucked away 300m northeast of the park gates, on the same peaceful suburban backstreet as *Babbler's*. Only five rooms, but they're very large, clean and comfortable, and the home cooking, served on an intimate rooftop terrace, is superb. Beer, bikes and binoculars available. ❷–❸

Laxmi Vilas Palace, Kakji Ki Kothi ☏05644/25323, ℻ 25259. Former prince's palace, set amid fifty acres of grounds and mustard fields on the outskirts of town. Although somewhat gar-ishly converted, it's still a romantic place to stay, with a secluded inner courtyard and colourful

Rajasthani murals. Their "deluxe" rooms are small, but the suites are large and sumptuously furnished, and the restaurant serves gourmet food. **7**–**8**

Shagun, Mathura Gate ☏ 05644/29202. Hidden away deep in the old town, this tiny budget guesthouse has only four rooms, and a pair of thatched huts in the garden. The rates are low, the location atmospheric and the owner very pleasant, but conditions are cramped, to say the least. Meals available. **2**

Tourist Lodge, Mathura Gate, off Gol Bagh Road ☏ 05644/23742. Higgledy-piggledy blue-painted backpackers' enclave on the edge of the market area, with rock-bottom rates for their small but passably clean rooms, and a small courtyard restaurant. Foreigners only. **1**–**3**

Sawai Madhopur and Ranthambore National Park

In no Indian nature reserve are you guaranteed a tiger sighting, but at **Ranthambore National Park**, 10km west of the rail junction and market town of **SAWAI MADHOPUR**, the odds are probably better than anywhere else. This has less to do with the size of the population, which is perilously small due to a recent spate of poaching, than because the tigers themselves are famously unperturbed by humans, hunting in broad daylight and rarely shying from cameras or Jeep-loads of tourists. Combine the big cats' bravado with the park's proximity to the Delhi–Agra–Jaipur "Golden Triangle" (Bharatpur is only 180km northeast of Delhi), and you'll understand why Ranthambore attracts the numbers of visitors it does. For anyone accustomed to the tranquillity of the tiger sanctuaries in Madhya Pradesh, the crowds here, crammed into open-top Canter buses and fleets of nippy Gypsy Jeeps, can be off-putting, to say the least. However, even if there were no wildlife, the landscape alone would make the park worth a visit. One of the last sizeable swathes of verdant bush in Rajasthan, Ranthambore is fed by several perennial rivers that have been dammed to form **lakes**, haunted by crocodiles and dotted with delicate pavilions and decaying, creeper-covered Rajput palaces. At sunset or in the mists of early morning, these can be ethereal, while the ruined tenth-century Chauhan **fort**, towering above the forest canopy from atop a dramatic crag, is straight out of Rudyard Kipling's *Jungle Book*.

The fort was conquered by Ala-ud-din Khalji's army in 1031, and Akbar in 1569, but for most of its existence Ranthambore has been controlled by the Rajputs, and was set aside by the rulers of Jaipur for royal hunting jaunts. Soon after Independence the area was declared a sanctuary, becoming a fully fledged national park under **Project Tiger** (see Contexts) in 1972. Over time, Ranthambore became world-renowned for its "friendly tigers", who were the subject of some memorable wildlife documentaries in the 1980s (the most famous of which featured remarkable footage of a young male hunting sambar in the shallows of the lake). Its reputation as Project Tiger's flagship operation, however, took a severe dent a decade later when it transpired some of Ranthambore's own wardens were involved in **poaching**, and that, as a result, the tiger population here had plummeted to single figures. Since then, rigorous policing is said to have brought the problem under control, and numbers have recovered to somewhere between sixteen and twenty.

In addition to tigers, Ranthambore is still home to very healthy populations of *chital*, *nilgai*, jackals, panthers, jungle cats and a wide array of birds, among which you may see crested serpent eagles, paradise flycatchers and more common peacocks and painted storks. One of the best places for bird-watching is the fort, which is also the site of a temple to Ganesh, where people from all over the country write to the elephant-headed god to invite him to their weddings. All the letters are read aloud to Ganesh (or at least to his image) by the temple priest.

Ranthambore is open from October to June, but the **best time to visit** is during the dry season (Jan–April), when the lack of water entices the larger animals out to the lakeside. During and immediately after the monsoons, they are more likely to remain in the forest.

Practicalities

Sawai Madhopur is served by **trains** on the main Mumbai–Delhi line, and is thus easily accessible from Bharatpur, Agra, Jaipur and Delhi, as well as destinations further south, such as Kota. The train tracks divide the main residential side of town to the north from the industrial zone, known as **Sawai Madhopur City**, to the south (where you arrive when travelling from Shivpuri). The **station** is midway between the two, close to the **bus stand** and bustling Bazriya market area, near the cheapest lodges. About 100m southwest along the train lines (towards Mumbai and Jaipur) is a flyover carrying the road to Ranthambore (left) and Sawai Madhopur City. Just beyond it is the very helpful and friendly **tourist office** (Mon–Sat 10am–5pm; ☏07462/20808), which hands out inexpensive fold-up **maps** of town and is a good place to check transport timings. Opposite the tourist office and beneath the flyover, a lane peels left off the main road and runs parallel with the train tracks to the **Project Tiger office** (same day booking, daily 5.30–7.30am & 12.30–2.30pm; advanced booking, Mon–Sat 10am–noon & 3–5pm; ☏07462/20223), where you have to book seats on Jeeps and Canters for tours of the park.

Park transport

To visit Ranthambore, you will either have to rent a five-passenger **Jeep** (referred to as a Gypsy), for Rs875 (including compulsory guide and Jeep entrance fee; maximum five people), or else pay Rs110 for a place on a twenty-seater open truck called a **Canter**. Seats on both must be booked at the Project Tiger office, from the hatch on the road side of the building, preferably a day in advance. Jeeps can be booked for any time, but only ten can enter the park at once. Canters enter the park at 6.30am and 3.30pm in summer (March–June), 7am and 2.30pm in winter (Oct–Feb) for the three-hour jaunt; they will pick up from any hotel on the Ranthambore Road, but not from those in Sawai Madhopur, so if you're staying there, you'll have to get to the

Dastkar Craft Centre

Around 3km beyond the turning for Ranthambore National Park, near the village of Kutalpura, is the excellent **Dastkar Crafts Centre**, where local low-caste women are trained to make patchwork quilting and appliqué. Most of the pieces they produce are sent off to be sold in Delhi, but there's a small shop in the centre showcasing beautiful block-printed bedspreads, pottery and an assortment of handmade clothes; the work is of an exceptionally high standard, and the prices very fair. This is a laudable attempt to combat poverty in villages bordering the park by ensuring money goes directly to the women instead of the men. It is hoped that in the long run this may lessen the hardships that, in the past, have pushed villagers into illegal poaching. While you're in the area, have a wander around the houses on the opposite side of the road, whose walls are decorated with some wonderful traditional murals.

Project Tiger office before departure time. Jeep fees do not include **park entrance fees** (Rs200, video Rs200).

Ranthambore's Canters are run by private contractors and are of varying standards, with some older and more clapped out than others. Although engine noise doesn't seem to bother the animals, it can definitely detract from your enjoyment of the landscape, and this is worth considering when you book. Lack of space is another drawback with Canters (especially for anyone with long legs), as is the fact that whenever animals are sighted, everyone on that side of the vehicle stands up, obscuring the view for those sitting on the other side. With plans afoot to ban all vehicles in the park except Canters, you may not have the option of renting a Jeep, but if you do and can afford it, then splash out on one; they're much quieter and more manoeuvrable, and allow you to get away from the crowds.

Also worth bearing in mind is that visitors staying in one or other of the luxury hotels have priority over access to park transport. With visitor numbers nowadays far exceeding the established limits, this can a real bonus if you happen to be travelling five-star, but highly frustrating if you're not and find all the tickets booked in advance. **Saturdays** tend to be worst for this, when the *Palace on Wheels* pulls into town and monopolizes all the available Jeeps and Canters.

To **visit the fort**, book an early morning safari and ask to be dropped at the main park entrance on the way out, from where you can climb an old paved path to the ruins. After spending the middle of the day exploring, it's possible to meet up with your Canter or Jeep back at the entrance gates for the evening tour (although note that you'll have to pay for your afternoon admission ticket in advance to do this).

Accommodation and eating

The range of **hotels** in Sawai Madhopur includes something for all budgets, generally increasing in price and luxury the closer you get to the park. RTDC hotels are often cheaper between April and June. Though the **food** isn't special in the cheaper lodges, you'll be glad it's there at all; there's precious little alternative other than two small *dhabas* on the main bazaar, between the train and bus stations. Of the pair, the *Hotel Argawal* looks the less hygienic, but serves the best food, including delicious *alu paratha* with fresh curd for breakfast, and the usual gamut of curried seasonal vegetables and hot chapati during the rest of the day.

Ankur Resort, Ranthambore Road, 1.5km from town ☎07462/20792, ℗20697. Modern complex of clean, comfortable rooms with baths in the main building, or pricier, more spacious chalets with verandas around the back. Filling meals served in its dining room. Discounts out of season, when the overland groups who usually stay here dry up. ❺–❻

Chinkala, 14 Indira Colony, Civil Lines ☎07462/20340 or 22642. Mostly large, but poorly maintained rooms in a suburban house on the southwest side of town. Similar standard to the *Vishal*, although slightly more expensive because of the quieter location. ❷–❸

Hammir Wildlife Resort, Ranthambore Road, 7km from town ☎07462/20562, ℗20697.

Reasonable fall-back if the *Ankur* is full; the rooms are far better value than the outside "cottages". ❻

RTDC Castle Jhoomar Baori, on a hillside 7km out of town ☎07462/20495. Former royal hunting lodge on a great hilltop site inside the park, with views from a roof terrace over woodland and escarpment. The rooms are plain but good value. The only drawback is the food, which is a lot less inspiring than the location. Book ahead; discounts April–June. ❻–❼

RTDC Vinayak, Ranthambore Road, 8km from town ☎07462/21333. Somewhat austere modern building, with large, simply furnished rooms that are a good deal considering their peaceful location and proximity to the park. ❼

Sawai Madhopur straddles the main train line, but many of the services from here are painfully slow passenger ones, so check timings at the tourist office before you book, or you could spend unnecessary hours travelling. For **Jaipur**, take the Mumbai–Jaipur Express (#2955) at 10.35am (2hr 15min). There are also direct services to **Bharatpur**, of which the quickest is the Golden Temple Mail (#2903) leaving at 1pm (2hr 30min), and daily departures to **Jodhpur** (8hr 30min), and **Agra** (5hr).

Buses, slower and less comfortable, run to Jaipur (2 daily; 5hr), Kota (4 daily; 4hr), and Ajmer (3 daily; 8hr) from a stand on the market area's main street, just before the bridge. For Shivpuri (Madhya Pradesh), however, you'll have to trek out to the city bus stand in Sawai Madhopur City.

Sawai Madhopur Lodge, Ranthambore Road ☎07462/20541, ℻20718, ⒲www.tajhotels.com/other/sawai_madhopur. Stylish 1930s hunting lodge, formerly belonging to Maharaja Sawai Man Singh II but now run as a luxury heritage hotel by the Taj Group. Elegant lawns and tasteful period decor, and what must be the most expensive camping accommodation in India. Prices start at $165 for double rooms, or $123 for tents (includes full board). ⑨

Sher Bagh, on the edge of the park ☎011/331 6534, ℮sherbagh@vsnl.com. Ten luxury tents (each with own toilet and running hot water), camp fires in the evening, and excellent Rajasthani food, made with organic vegetables from surrounding farms. Safaris and trips to local development proj-ects optional. Full board at around Rs7000 per person. ⑨

Tiger Moon, 2km northeast of Ranthambore village (reservations through 257 SV Road, Bandra, Mumbai ☎022/640 8742, ℻640 6399. Hidden down a dirt track in shady woodland, and the most secluded of the upscale resorts, although poor value for money at $115 per head. Pool, restaurant, and park tours included in their "Jungle Plan" rates. ⑨

Vishal, main road, market area, about 500m northeast of the railway station ☎07462/20504. The most popular option among foreign backpackers: charmless, but acceptably clean, and the rates are low. If it's full, try the less salubrious *Swagat* two doors down. In both, the upstairs rooms are by far the best. ❷

Ajmer

As you head west from Jaipur, or north from Chittor and Bundi, the flat, arid expanse of the Dhundar plains are dramatically interrupted by the Aravallis, running in a bare brown ridge towards Mount Abu and the Gujarat border. A reference point for millions of pilgrims over the centuries, this steeply shelving spur, known locally as the Nag Pahar (Snake Mountain), forms an appropriately epic backdrop for **AJMER**, famous throughout India as the former home of the Sufi **Khwaja Muin-ud-din Chishti**, founder of the Chishtiya order. He died here in 1236, at a time when Ajmer was under Muslim rule, the forces of the fearsome Mahmud Ghazni and Muhammad of Ghor having successfully besieged what was previously a stronghold of the Rajput Chauhans in 1191. To this day, the Chishti's tomb, or **Dargah**, remains one of the holiest Muslim shrines in the country, attracting streams of pilgrims and dervishes (it is believed that seven visits here are the equivalent of one to Mecca), especially during Muharram and Id, and the Chishti's anniversary day, or **Urs Mela** in October/November. For Hindus and foreign travellers, however, Ajmer is important primarily as a jumping-off place for **Pushkar**, a twenty-minute bus ride away across the hills.

Weighed down with luggage, you're unlikely to want to pause here for longer than it takes to catch a bus out of town, but it's definitely worth mak-

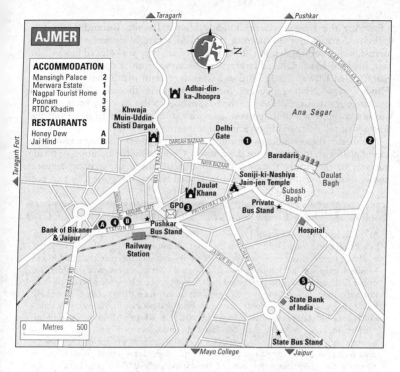

ing time for a visit before you leave the area. Although Ajmer's dusty main streets are choked with traffic, the narrow lanes of the bazaars and residential quarters around the Dargah retain an almost medieval character, with lines of rose-petal stalls and shops selling prayer mats, beads and lengths of gold-edged green silk offerings. Finely arched Moghul gateways, some bearing fragments of blue and green glazed tilework, still stand at the main entrances to the old city, whose skyscape of whitewashed mosque minarets and domes is overlooked from on high by the crumbling crenellations of what was for centuries India's most strategically important fortress, the mighty **Taragarh**. Ajmer is also one of the few sacred Islamic sites in the country where you can be pretty certain of catching **qawwali** singers in action (see p.132).

The Khwaja-ud-din Chishti Dargah

The revered Sufi, Khwaja Muin-ud-din Chishti, who died in Ajmer in 1236, was buried in a small brick tomb that is today engulfed by a large marble complex known as the **Dargah**, reached via the bazaars winding north off Station Road and west from Delhi Gate. Founded in the thirteenth century by Sultan Iltutmish of the slave dynasty, and completed under the sixteenth-century Moghul emperor Humayun, the Dargah contains structures erected by many Muslim rulers. But it was under the imperial patronage of the three great Moghuls – Shah Jahan, Jahangir and, most crucially, Akbar, who visited the shrine on numerous occasions and even walked here twice from Agra – that this became the most important Muslim shrine in India.

Entering the Dargah via the mightly blue-and-white **Buland Darwaza** gateway, donated by the Nizam of Hyderabad, you're likely to be stopped by stern-looking young men in tall black hats saying they are "official guides". In fact, they are *khadims*, hereditary priests descended from a disciple of Khwaja Sahib called Khwaja Fakhrudin, and who operate in much the same way as Hindu *pujaris*, leading pilgrims through rituals in the sacred precinct in exchange for donations. Despite their assurances to the contrary, their services are not compulsory, although you may wish to employ one to point out the features of religious and historical significance inside.

The first of these are the two immense cauldrons, known as **degs**, resting on raised platforms to the right of the gateway. Continuing the tradition of giving succour to the needy that was so important to the saint, arriving pilgrims throw money into them, which is later shared among the poor. The two pots

Khwaja Muin-ud-din Chishti

At the height of the communal troubles in 1992–3, Ajmer's main bazaar, which runs in a straight line from Delhi Gate to the front entrance of the Dargah, was widened by the army to ensure easier access for its troops. All over the country, Hindus and Muslims were on the rampage, and this devout Islamic enclave was considered a prime flashpoint. The expected blood bath, however, never happened. While most of northern India suffered the worst communal unrest since Partition, Ajmer's curfew held firm. No one had any doubt that peace prevailed because of the enduring influence of the Sufi saint enshrined at the heart of the city, Khwaja Muin-ud-din Chishti.

Born in 1156, in Afghanistan, Muslim India's most revered saint, also known as Khwaja Sahib or Garib Nawaz, began his religious career at the age of 13, when he distributed his inheritance among the poor and adopted the simple, pious life of an itinerant Shia *fakir* (the equivalent of the Hindu *sadhu*). Wandering between the *madrasas* of Persia and Samarkand, he soaked up the teachings of the great Central Asian Sufis, whose emphasis on mysticism, ecstatic states and pure devotion as a path to God were revolutionizing Islam during this period.

By the time he came to India with the invading Afghan armies at the end of the twelfth century, Khwaja Sahib had already established a following of his own. But his reputation as a divinely inspired prophet really snowballed after he and his disciples settled in Ajmer, while the holy man was in his fifties. Withdrawing into a life of meditation and fasting, he preached a message of renunciation, affirming that personal experience of God was attainable to anyone who relinquished their ties to the world with an an open heart. More radically, he also insisted on the fundamental unity of all religions: mosques and temples, he asserted, were merely material manifestations of a single divinity, with which all men and women could commune.

In this way, Khwaja Sahib became one of the first religious figures to bridge the gap between India's two great faiths. With its wandering holy men, emphasis of mysticism and miracles, and devotional worship involving music, dance and states of trance, Sufism would have been intelligible to many Hindus. Moreover, it readily absorbed and integrated aspects of Hindu worship into its own beliefs and rituals. After Khwaja Sahib died at the age of 97, his followers lauded the Bhagavad Gita as a sacred text, and even encouraged Hindu devotees to pray using names of God familiar to them, equating Ram with "Rahman", the Merciful Aspect of Allah.

The spirit of acceptance and unity central to the founder of the Chishti order's teachings explains why his shrine in Ajmer continues to be loved by adherents of all faiths. Nor does it seem to matter that the tomb was probably erected over the ruins of a Hindu temple. This is one sacred site in India where the rantings of right-wing Hindu extremists are drowned out by a more inclusive, ecstatic kind of religious fervour.

are also the focus of an extraordinary ritual during the Urs mela, in which a huge gruel is cooked from rice, sugar, coconut, barley, almonds and lentils, paid for by wealthy patrons. When it is ready, a mad scramble begins as the devout, dressed in heat-protective plastic bags, dive head first into the bubbling *degs* to fill their buckets with the porridge, regarded by the faithful as *tabarruk* (equivalent of the Hindu *prasad*, or Christian "consecrated"). The best place from which to view this spectacle is the platform above the main entrance archway, which you can usually gain a place on by slipping a tip to one of the *khadims*.

To the right of the *degs* is the marble mosque donated by Akbar, and to the left stands an assembly hall for the homeless. Other subsidiary shrines inside the enclosure include those of Khwaja Sahib and Shah Jehan's daughters, a handful of generals and governors, and companions of the saint from Afghanistan. Look out, too, for the small white marble tomb on the eastern side of the complex, commemorating the famous *bhishti*, or water carrier, who saved the life of Humayun when he nearly drowned in the Ganges after his defeat by Afghan leader, Sher Shah, in 1590. To thank the water wallah for the timely loan of his inflated waterskin, Humayun ordered that he be placed on the Moghul throne for an afternoon. Much to the abject horror of his ministers, leather coins are even said to have been struck to mark the event. Originally the *bhishti's* tomb was covered in precious stones, but Aurangzeb had them removed after he mistook the grave for that of the saint himself.

These days, it's impossible to miss Khwaja Sahib's final resting place. Surrounded by silver railings, it is surmounted by a large gilt dome, near the magnificent mosque of Shah Jehan. Devotees file past with brilliant *chadars*, gilt-brocaded silk covers for the saint's grave, carried on beds of rose petals in flat, round head-baskets. Visitors are asked by the hawk-eyed *khadims* for donations, offered blessings, lightly brushed with peacock feathers and given the chance to touch the cloth covering the tomb. The continual murmur of prayer and the heady scent of rose attar, and uplifting *qawwali* music being performed before the shrine (from an hour so or before sunset until 9pm), exactly as it has been for seven hundred years, create an unforgettable atmosphere.

Islamic monuments

Often overlooked by visitors, the **Adhai-din-ka-Jhonpra**, or "two-and-a-half-day mosque", 400m north of the Dargah, is the oldest surviving monument in the city and unquestionably one of the finest examples of medieval architecture in Rajasthan. Originally built in 1153 as a Hindu college by the first Chohan emperor, Raja Visaldeva, it was destroyed forty years later by the Afghan Ghors, who later renovated it. Tradition holds that the mosque's name derived from the speed with which it was constructed, but in fact the reconstruction took fifteen years, using bricks and finely sculpted panels plundered from Hindu and Jain temples (including the Visaldeva's college). Motifs of pre-Muslim origin are still clearly discernible on the pillars and ceilings. However, the mosque's most beautiful feature is the bands of Koranic calligraphy decorating its arched facade. Writing in the nineteenth century, shortly after the building had been restored by the Scindias, the dilettante and architectural historian, James Ferguson, claimed that "nothing in Cairo or in Persia is so exquisite in detail, and nothing in Spain or Syria can approach [the inscriptions] or beauty of surface decoration".

A more recent Islamic relic is the squat sandstone **Daulat Khana**, also known as the **Magazine**, a massive rectangular palace at the heart of the city that was used by Akbar and his son Jahangir during their visits to the Dargah.

A panel outside it records that here, in 1615, **Sir Thomas Roe** became the first British ambassador to be granted an official audience, after four years of trailing between the emperor's encampments. The effort, however, bore fruit. By granting the British East India Company trading privileges in exchange for naval protection, Jahangir effectively paved the way for future British power. In spite of his diplomatic coup, Roe was none too impressed by Ajmer, which had never fully recovered from the first Muslim onslaughts in the twelfth century. The makeover initiated by the Moghals was continued by the British, whose residents and army took shelter in the Magazine during the 1857 Mutiny. Today, the old palace houses a small **museum** (daily except Fri 10am–4.30pm; Rs3), displaying mainly Hindu Rajasthani statues dating from the eighth century.

The huge artificial lake sprawling northwest of Ajmer beside the road to Pushkar, known as **Ana Sagar**, was laid out by the Hindu Raja Anaji between 1135 and 1150. A long embankment, or *bund*, on its southwest shore moderated the flow of the river through the city and it was on top of this parapet, exposed to the cooling breezes off the water, that Shah Jehan chose to erect a line of exquisite white marble pavilions as summer shelters. Modelled on the Diwan-I-Am in Delhi's Red Fort, the five **Baradaris** were later converted into offices, libraries and houses, before Curzon had them restored in 1899. Today, four remain beautifully preserved, standing in the shade of trees and ornamental gardens (the former **Daulat Bagh**) planted by Jehangir. To find them, turn left at the bottom of the hill as you arrive in Ajmer from Pushkar, and left again 400m later, through the park. The best time to come is an hour or so before sunset, when the colours on the lake and polished stone of the Baradaris are sublime.

The Taragarh

Just visible on the ridge high above the city, the **Taragarh** was for two thousand years the most important *point d'appui* for invading armies in northwest India. Any ruler who successfully breached its walls, rising from a ring of forbidding escarpments, effectively controlled the region's trade. Few, however, were able to do so by mounting a siege; the fortress even repulsed the indomitable Mahmud Ghazni in 1024. It's now badly ruined, enclosing no visible remnants of its pre-Muslim past, but is still visited in large numbers by pilgrims, who come to pay their respects at what must be one of the few shrines in the world devoted to a tax inspector, the **Dargah of Miran Sayeed Hussein Khangsawar**. Akbar's court chronicler, Abdul Fazal, records that Mahmud of Ghori's chief revenue collector numbered among the many slain in the Rajput attack of 1202, when – following one of the fort's rare defeats – the entire Muslim population of the fort was put to the sword. Today, a vestigal Muslim community still survives in a tumbledown village inside the walls, clustered around the whitewashed Dargah. For non-Muslims, the main incentive to venture up here is the superb **views** across the plains and neighbouring hills, and an exceptionally rewarding **hike** along the ancient paved pathway from Ajmer.

To pick up the trailhead, follow the lane behind the Khwaja Sahib Dargah, past the Adhai-din-ka-Jhonpra and on towards the saddle in the ridge visible to the south. Lined by red-bearded *pir-zadas*, perfumiers, gemstone sellers, amulet hawkers, beggars and hashish-smoking dervishes, this old path can't have changed much since the days of the Moghuls, when Jehangir used to ride up to it en route to a summer palace he built in the hills southwest of the fort.

Near the top, look out for a limewashed boulder called the **Adhar Silla**, which Muslims believe the Rajputs charmed and used to attack the fort in 1202. When one renowned holy man, Miran Sahib, saw it falling through the air towards him, he is said to have shouted "if thou art come from God fall on my head!". It didn't, but squashed his horse; the *khadims* will show you marks believed to have been left by his finger and stick.

The hike to Taragarh takes around one-and-a-half hours. Carry plenty of water with you (and pockets full of change for the many beggars who line the route). Inside the battlements, the only places to eat are a handful of fly-infested non-veg cafés. To return to Ajmer, you can either follow the path back downhill, or catch a **Jeep** (Rs20) from the lot at the northeast side of the village, near the Dargah. Heading in the other direction, the Jeeps leave from a *chowk* on the western edge of Ajmer; ask for the rickshaw wallah for the "Ta-ra-garh jeeps", pronouncing all the syllables clearly, or you'll end up at the main Khwaja Sahib Dargah.

Other attractions

When Ajmer came under British control in 1818, it was one of the few cities in Rajputana outside the hegemony of the princely states. Monuments still standing as echoes of its colonial past include the **Jubilee clock tower** opposite the railway station, the **King Edward Memorial Hall** a little to the west and the famous **Mayo College**, originally built as a school for princes, and now a leading educational institution known in society circles as the "Eton of the East".

Perhaps the most bizarre sight in Ajmer is the mirrored **Soniji-ki-Nashiya** hall adjoining the Nashiyan Jain temple, or "red temple" (daily 8am–5pm; Rs2). Constructed in the 1820s by an Ajmeri diamond magnate, the hall commemorates the life of Rishabha (or Adinath), the first Jain *tirthankara*, believed to have lived countless aeons in the past. From the uppermost of the three storeys that surround it, you can look down on musicians flying above the sacred Mount Sumeru on swans, peacocks and elephants suspended on rods and strings. The display, sealed in behind dust-blocking glass panels and doors, is made from 1000kg of gold, extravagantly detailed in fantastic proportions appropriate to the realm of legend. Admission to the main temple alongside is restricted to Jains.

Practicalities

Ajmer's **railway station** is in the centre of town, with regular services from Delhi, Jaipur, Ahmedabad, Udaipur, Cittor and Kota. See the box opposite for a list of recommended trains for onward travel. The state **bus stand**, with an exhaustive array of routes, is inconveniently situated on the northeast edge of town, 2km from the railway station. Tempos and auto-rickshaws connect the two; auto-rickshaws cost around Rs25. Approaching town from the south, most buses stop at a string of large intersections en route, but don't be tempted to get off before the bus stand as transport into town from these places can be thin on the ground. Buses to **Pushkar** leave every fifteen minutes or so from outside Gandhi Bhawan, a few hundred metres east of the railway station (you can buy tickets in advance from the little hatch by the roadside). Seats on private buses – many of which have connecting services from Pushkar – can be reserved at Ajmer bus station, Pushkar hotels, or at any of the travel agents along Kutchery Road between the state bus stand and railway station.

The **tourist office** (Mon–Sat 8am–noon & 3–6pm) adjoins RTDC *Hotel Khadim*, not far from the state bus stand, but typically too far from the centre to be of use unless you happen to be in the area. The State Bank of India, bewteen the tourist office and state bus stand, will **change** Thomas Cook and American Express (but not Visa) travellers' cheques. A more central place to change money is the Bank of Bikaner and Jaipur, on Station Road.

Ajmer's chief attractions lie within walking distance of each other, in the centre of town, and are easily visited in half a day. To rent a **bicycle**, there are a couple of places just west of Delhi Gate (expect to pay about Rs3/hr). Fares for cycle rickshaws, more popular here than auto-rickshaws, should be negotiated in advance. If you want to dump your gear while you look around, head for the **left luggage** cloakroom just inside the main entrance at the railway station.

Accommodation

With long-distance bus and train departures conveniently timed so that you can make them from Pushkar, it's hard to think of a reason to spend a night in Ajmer. However, the town has many **hotels** to house the flow of pilgrims visiting the Dargah, and although most are chock-full during Urs Mela, at other times rooms are in plentiful supply. A collection of cheap lodges stand opposite the railway station, and there are also a few hotels in the bazaar area.

Mansingh Palace, Ana Sagar Circular Road ☎0145/425702. Luxury hotel in ideal surroundings, a few kilometres northwest of town on the shores of Ana Sagar. ⑨

Nagpal Tourist Home, Station Road ☎0145/429503. Bright and breezy modern hotel close to the station, where the cheaper rooms have TV but no hot water. ④

Poonam, near Sadar Kotwali Khailana ☎0145/621711. The best value cheapie in town – much cleaner and quieter than the competition, though you may have to haggle the tariff down. ②–③

RTDC Khadim, near the bus stand ☎0145/52490. Good-value place, with cheap dorm, but well away from the centre. ④–⑥

Moving on from Ajmer

Ajmer is on the main Delhi–Ahmedabad train line, but there are considerable variations between the journey times of services passing through here. For Delhi, by far the fastest and most comfortable option is the air-conditioned Ajmer–New Delhi Shatabdi Express (#2016; Mon–Sat), which departs at 3.30pm and arrives 6hr 45min later at 10.15pm. There's also a slower overnight service, the Ahmedabad–Delhi Mail (#9105), leaving at 8.33pm and arriving at 5.20am the following morning, but the easiest train to get a reservation for at short notice is Porbander–Delhi Express (#9263; Tues & Sat only), which leaves at 11am and reaches Delhi Sarai Rohilla 9hrs later.

Of the seven or eight daily trains to Jaipur, the Shatabdi Express is once again the quickest, taking just under two hours; alternatively, catch the cheaper Ajmer–Jaipur Link Express (#2414A) at 1.45pm, which takes just thirty minutes longer. Heading in the opposite direction, the Delhi Sarai Rohilla–Ahmedabad Express (#9943) is the best train for Udaipur, starting from Ajmer at 7.50am and arriving 10hr 10min later at 6pm.

The computerized reservations hall is on the first floor of the main railway station's south wing; get there early in the morning to avoid long queues, or shell out a little extra for a travel agent to buy your ticket through the back door.

Eating

In addition to the snack and fruit juice places around Dargah Bazaar and Delhi Gate, Ajmer has a handful of larger **restaurants**.

Bhola, in the hotel of the same name, Agra Gate, Subzi Mandi. Excellent pure veg food, including good-value thalis. Open 8am–11pm.

Honey Dew, Station Road. Veg, non-veg and pizza at middling prices, next to the King Edward Memorial. Garden restaurant serving a good selection of Indian, Chinese and Continental food (including passable pizzas), as well as shakes and Kwality ice cream. Open 7am–11pm.

Jai Hind, Station Road, tucked in an alley directly opposite the station's main exit. Opened in 1949 by Hindu refugees from Sind. Very good veg food, including delicious *alu-paratha-curd* "breakfast thalis" and *dosas*. Open 8.30am–10.30pm.

Mansingh Palace Hotel, Ana Sagar Circular Road. Pricey international cuisine served in a/c comfort by the lakeside. Open 12.30–3pm & 7.30–11pm.

Pushkar

According to the *Padma* (Lotus) *Purana*, **PUSHKAR**, 15km northwest of Ajmer, came into existence when Lord Brahma, the Creator, dropped his lotus flower (*pushpa*) to earth from his hand (*kar*) to kill a demon. At the three spots where the petals landed, water magically appeared in the midst of the desert to form three small blue lakes, and it was on the banks of the largest of these that Brahma subsequently convened a gathering of some 900,000 celestial beings – the entire Hindu pantheon. Surrounded by whitewashed temples and bathing *ghats*, the lake is today revered as one of India's most sacred sites: *Pushkaraj Maharaj*, literally "Pushkar King of Kings". During the auspicious full-moon phase of October/November (the anniversary of the gods' mass meeting, or *yagya*), its waters are believed to cleanse the soul of all impurities, drawing pilgrims from all over the country. Alongside this annual religious festival, Rajasthani villagers also buy and sell livestock at what has become the largest **camel market** (*unt mela*) in the world, when more than 200,000 dealers, tourists and traders fill the dunes to the west of the lake.

The legendary colour of the camel *mela*, combined with the beautiful desert scenery and heady religious atmosphere of the temples and *ghats* have inevitably made Pushkar a prime tourist destination. In fact, it's hard to think of anywhere else in India, apart from perhaps Manali, Kovalam and the resorts of Goa, that has been so thoroughly transformed by mass tourism over the past decade. The main bazaar, which only fifteen years ago comprised a string of stalls selling traditional *puja* paraphernalia, is now a kilometre-long line of shops crammed with hippy trinkets, full-moon-party fluoro outfits, jewellery and fusion CDs, while the streetside cafés churn out banana pancakes and mind-blowing *bhang lassis* for a clientele clad in gaudy Glastonbury gear. Arriving from less budget-traveller-oriented parts of the country, this may come as a welcome break, but if you've travelled here hoping for a taste of the east, the ravers and relentless didgeridoo music can be a stark disappointment.

That said, Pushkar has not been entirely spoilt. Wander away from the bazaar to the more tranquil fringes of the lake, or into the surrounding hills, and the magical atmosphere that attracted travellers here in the first place survives undiminished. At sunset, with the sound of temple bells and drums drifting across the water, this can still feel like one of the most exotic places on earth.

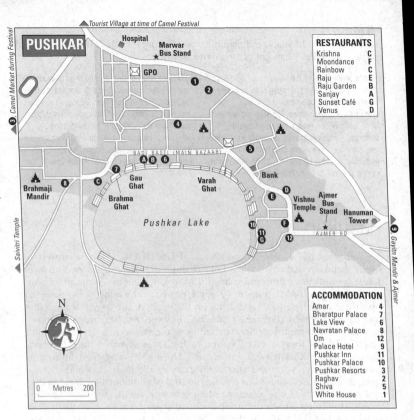

Tourist Village at time of Camel Festival

Camel Market during Festival ③

Savitri Temple ▲

Gaytri Mandir & Ajmer ⑨

PUSHKAR

Hospital

Marwar
★Bus Stand

✉ GPO

❶
❷

❹ ▲

▲ ✉ ❺

BADI BASTI (MAIN BAZAAR)
Ⓐ Ⓑ Ⓖ

❼ Gau
Ⓒ Ghat

Brahmaji
Mandir ▲ ❽ Ⓒ

Brahma
Ghat

Varah
Ghat

Bank

Ⓓ

Ⓔ Vishnu Ajmer
   Temple Bus
          Stand Hanuman
                 Tower ●

Pushkar Lake

❿
⓫ Ⓕ
Ⓖ ⓬ _AJMER RD_

▲

N

0 Metres 200

RESTAURANTS

Krishna	C
Moondance	F
Rainbow	C
Raju	E
Raju Garden	B
Sanjay	A
Sunset Café	G
Venus	D

ACCOMMODATION

Amar	4
Bharatpur Palace	7
Lake View	6
Navratan Palace	8
Om	12
Palace Hotel	9
Pushkar Inn	11
Pushkar Palace	10
Pushkar Resorts	3
Raghav	2
Shiva	5
White House	1

Temples

There are five hundred temples in and around Pushkar; many had to be rebuilt after pillaging during the merciless rule of Moghul Emperor Aurangzeb (1656–1708), while others are recent additions. Some, like the splendid **Vishnu temple**, on your right as you enter the village from Ajmer, are out of bounds to non-Hindus.

Pushkar's most important temple, **Brahmaji Mandir**, houses a four-headed image of Brahma in its main sanctuary. Raised on a stepped platform in the centre of a courtyard, the chamber is surrounded on three sides by smaller subsidiary shrines topped with flat roofs providing views across the desert west to **Saivitri Mandir** on the summit of a nearby hill. The one-hour climb to the top of that hill is rewarded by matchless vistas over the town, surrounded on all sides by desert, and is best done in the evening, to reach the summit for sunset. **Gayitri Mandir**, on the other hand, set on a hill east of the town, faces east and should ideally be visited at sunrise.

The lake and ghats

Pushkar **lake** is ringed by five hundred beautiful whitewashed temples, connected to the water by 52 *ghats* – one for each of Rajasthan's maharajas, who

Brahma, Saivitri and Gayitri

Brahma, revered as the Creator from later Vedic times onwards, was seen as one of the most important gods, together with Shiva (Destroyer) and Vishnu (Preserver). The three served in anthropomorphic terms to represent the powerful, non-conceptual Brahman – an unchanging and eternal force associated with cosmic unity. As the concept of *samsara* came to be at the heart of Hindu philosophy, however – and life was envisaged as endless transmigration with no beginning – Brahma's role as Creator was questioned by later philosophers. His importance as a cult god dwindled in the nineteenth century, though he is still regarded as a major divinity.

Stories of Brahma's exploits are still told and retold in Pushkar, site of a temple dedicated exclusively to the deity. One such tale reveals the significance of the temples named after Brahma's wives, **Saivitri** and **Gayitri**. At the great *yagya* gathering of deities, Lord Brahma was to marry Saivitri, but she was busy dressing for the ceremony and failed to show up on time. Without a wife, the Creator could not perform the *yagya* at the auspicious moment, so he had to ask Indra, the god of fire, to find another consort. The only unmarried woman available was a shepherdess of the untouchable Gujar caste, whom the gods hastily purified by passing her through the mouth of a cow; *gaya* means "cow", and *tri*, "passed through". When Saivitri finally arrived, she was furious that Brahma had married someone else and cursed him, saying that henceforth he would be worshipped only at Pushkar. She also pronounced that the Gujar caste would gain liberation after death only if their ashes were scattered on Pushkar lake – a belief which has persisted to this day. After casting her curses, disgruntled Saivitri flew off to establish a temple on the highest hill above the town, while Gayitri occupied the lower hill on the opposite, eastern side of the lake.

built separate guesthouses and employed their own private *pujaris* (priests) to perform rituals during their stays here. Each is named after an event or person, and three in particular bear special significance. Primary among them is **Gau Ghat,** sometimes called Main Ghat, where visiting ministers and politicians come to worship, and from which ashes of Mahatma Gandhi, Jawaharlal Nehru and Shri Lal Bahadur Shastri were sprinkled into the lake. **Brahma Ghat** marks the spot where Brahma himself is said to have worshipped, while at the large **Varah Ghat**, just off the market square, Vishnu is believed to have appeared in the form of Varaha (a boar), one of his nine incarnations. At all the *ghats*, it is a respected and unspoken request that visitors should remove their shoes at a reverential distance from the lake, and refrain from smoking and taking photos.

Indian and Western tourists alike are urged by local brahmin priests to worship at the lake, that is, to make **Pushkar Puja**. This involves the repetition of prayers while scattering rose petals into the lake, and then being asked for a donation (these days often an astronomically high one) which usually goes to temple funds, or to the priest who depends on such benefaction. On completion of the *puja*, a red thread taken from a temple is tied around your wrist. Labelled the "Pushkar passport" by locals, this simple token means that you'll no longer attract pushy Pushkar priests, and can wander unhindered onto the *ghats*.

In years past, the lake used to be prowled by dozens of man-eating **crocodiles** that would often pick off unwary pilgrims. Elderly brahmins can still recall the days when they regularly used to have to beat the rapacious reptiles on the head with long sticks before entering the water, but their strict vegetarian principles prevented them from doing anything about the problem. Eventually, the British intervened by fishing the crocodiles out with nets and transporting them to a nearby reservoir.

Hindus visit Pushkar year-round to take a dip in the redemptory waters of the lake, but there is one particular day when bathing here is believed to relieve devotees of all their sins, and ultimately free them from the bonds of *samsara*: the full moon (*purnima*) of the **Kartika** month (usually Nov). For five days leading up to and including the full moon, Pushkar hosts thousands of celebrating devotees, following prescribed rituals on the lakeside and in the Brahma Mandir. To add to the flurry of colour and activity, a large **camel fair** is held at around the same time in the sand dunes west of the town, when hordes of herders from all over Rajasthan gather to parade, race and trade their livestock. The transformation of Pushkar from a peaceful desert town is complete and overwhelming – the streets are packed with swarms of pilgrims, hawkers and thousands of tourists; hotels and restaurants are chock-a-block, and prices soar. Families from all over Rajasthan struggle through the crowded lanes laden with children, blankets, food and makeshift tents, setting up camp in the dunes where night fires, delicious open-air cooking smells and traditional folk music drifting through the starlit night create an unforgettable experience.

Once trading is under way, camels and cattle are meticulously groomed, lined up and auctioned, while women dressed in mirrored skirts and vivid shawls lay out embroidered cloth, jewellery, pots and ornaments beside the herds, stopping trade occasionally to gather dung to fuel the evening fires. Cattle, poultry, sheep and goats are entered for competitions, and prizes given for the best displays of fruit and vegetables. Away from the main activity, the dusty ground is stirred up by vigorous **camel races**, noisily urged on by gamblers. Things become even more animated as acrobats balance precariously on tightropes and cartwheel between the crowds.

Aside from its overwhelming size, the most striking feature of the Pushkar camel fair from a foreign visitor's point of view is that it is attended by equal numbers of men and women. With the harvest safely in the bag and the surplus livestock sold, the villagers, for this brief week or so, have a little money to spend enjoying themselves, which creates a lighthearted atmosphere that's generally absent from most other Rajasthani livestock fairs. As a result, photo opportunities are endless. Proudly

Practicalities

Most long-distance journeys to and from Pushkar have to be made via Ajmer. Pushkar does not have a railway station. The **Ajmer bus stand** in the east of town is served by buses from Ajmer and Jaipur, while travellers from destinations further afield, such as Delhi, Jodhpur and Bikaner, arrive in the north of town at **Marwar bus stand**, to be besieged by accommodation touts. The lack of rickshaws means that you'll have to walk to your hotel (though there are **bicycles** for rent right by the Ajmer bus stand, and hand carts for transporting luggage).

Pushkar doesn't have a **tourist office**. The **GPO** for parcels and poste restante is in the north of town, and there's a smaller branch on the market square. The State Bank of Bikaner and Jaipur (Mon–Fri 11am–3pm) in the square near Varah Ghat offers **currency exchange**, but you can cash travellers' cheques and change cash more quickly at any of the private money-changers in the main bazaar.

In addition to the state **buses**, a number of **private firms** run daily buses to Delhi, Agra, Jaipur, Mount Abu, Jaisalmer, Udaipur, Jodhpur and Ahmedabad, and some have connecting services from Pushkar. That said, we've had numerous letters complaining about some of these outfits, with

dressed in their most colourful clothes and jewellery, both the menfolk and their wives and daughters tend to be happy to pose for the camera, being as interested in you as you are in them. The presence of so many exotic foreigners milling around in the crowd all adds to the holiday feel for the herders, for whom Pushkar represents the highlight of the year, eagerly looked forward to throughout the heat of summer and the hard work of the harvest.

The fair typically attracts up to 200,000 people. In recent years, however, numbers have dwindled due to the drought. Only a fraction of the normal number of herders showed up in November 2000, because so many of them had no animals to sell (see our box on 'Drought in Rajasthan', p.166). More than ever, therefore, if you're coming to see the camels and traditional costumes, the **best time to come** is at least a week or so before the final weekend, when most of the buying and selling is done. By the full moon, the bulk of the herders tend to have packed up and gone home (unless the local tourist office has managed to induce them to stick around with the lure of free fodder, as it has done for the past few fairs), leaving crowds of pilgrims from neighbouring districts to enjoy the religious celebrations.

Hotels hike their rates at least a fortnight before the full moon, and are usually full well before the start of the fair, but extra **accommodation** is provided by RTDC in tented compounds outside town where there's a choice between dormitory beds (❸), deluxe tents (❹), or huts (❷) complete with private bathrooms. Be sure to book well ahead by contacting the RTDC office in Jaipur (☎ & ℡0141/316045) or by writing to the Manager, CRO, RTDC, Usha Niwas, Kalyan Path, Jaipur. The tent village has an information counter (☎0145/772074), exchange facilities, safes, shops and a medical centre. Additional luxury camping, complete with carpets, furniture, running water and Western toilets, is offered by the local maharaja's *Royal Desert Camp*, out on the Motisar Road (❷); for reservations, contact the *Hotel Pushkar Palace* (see Accommodation).

The **dates** given by Rajasthan Tourism for the next few camel fairs are: 2001, 27–30 November; 2002, 16–19 November; and 2003, 5–8 November; but bear in mind our earlier advice and get here at least one week before these times to see the *mela* in full swing.

tourists frequently finding their seats double-booked when they arrive in Ajmer; Ekta Travels seems to be prime offender, but is far from unique. The same outfits will also arrange onward **train** journeys from Ajmer for a small charge, and book, cancel or confirm air tickets (which should be carefully checked before you leave the office; make sure there's no 'W', for 'Waitlist' in front of your seat number). Otherwise go to Ajmer to book for yourself well in advance; services to Delhi in particular are often reserved days ahead. A list of recommended trains from Ajmer appears in the Moving On box on p.214.

Accommodation

Pushkar has numerous *dharamshalas* for pilgrims. For the ever-growing influx of Western tourists, there's a wide choice of **hotels** and **guesthouses**, many of them in family homes. Views over the lake are rare, but many have rooftops looking across Pushkar to the distant hills. Note that **prices** double or triple during the camel fair.

Amar, in the centre of town ☎0145/772809. A delightful little place, with ground-floor rooms facing a lush jasmine-filled garden, and a secluded terrace restaurant. ❷
Bharatpur Palace, Brahma Mandir Road

☎0145/772320. Rambling old lakeside house overlooking the *ghats*, with spacious roof area and simple rooms. Ask for the (pricier) "Maharaja Room", which has windows on all sides (but no bathroom). ❷–❹

Lake View, Main Bazaar ☏ 0145/772106, ⓦ www.pushkarraj.com. Simple rooms opening on to a large rooftop, right by the lake, with beautiful views and low single-occupancy rates. A little run-down, but plenty of atmosphere. ❷–❸

Navratan Palace, Brahma Mandir Road ☏ 0145/772145, ⓕ 772225. New, somewhat characterless place with large comfy en-suite rooms and great views towards the hills. Some a/c, and a big pool. ❸–❺

Om, Ajmer Road ☏ 0145/772672. Basic rooms, with or without bathroom, close to the bazaar and Vishnu temple. Relaxing garden, but the pool doesn't look much more inviting than the lake. ❶–❸

Palace Hotel, Ajmer Road ☏ 0145/772403, ⓕ 772226, ⓔ hppalace@datainfosys.net. Huge luxury hotel on the outskirts, incorporating masonry plundered from an old fort, but superbly reconstructed with elaborate wall paintings, gilt inlay and period fittings. Sweeping views, huge pool and walled garden with a "rose walk". ❽

Pushkar Inn, next to the *Sunset Café* ☏ 0145/772010. A row of large, clean rooms (7 simple; 6 en suite) between the lakeside and a marigold patch, next door to the *Sunset Café*. ❸

Pushkar Palace ☏ 0145/772001 or 72401, ⓕ 72226, ⓔ hppalace@datainfosys.net. Former maharaja's palace on the east side of the lake, with panoramic views from a peaceful terrace garden. Rooms range from tiny and basic bathroomless cells to tastefully furnished rooftop suites with verandas. The most stylish option overlooking the lake. ❸–❽

Pushkar Resorts, Motisur Road, Gankera village ☏ 0145/72017 or 72944, ⓕ 72946, ⓔ pushkar@pushkarresorts.com. Modern resort 5km out of town in the desert, comprising 40 swish a/c chalets set around a kidney-shaped pool in 15 acres of grounds. Optional extras include nocturnal camel rides (with candles and telescopes), and putting on a golf green. Their top-notch restaurant is the only one hereabouts with a non-veg menu, and an alcohol licence. Advance booking recommended. ❽

Raghav, near the Marwar bus stand ☏ 0145/772207. A modern building set in a huge garden on the north side of town. The rooms are plain but large and clean, with narrow balconies and comfy mattresses, and there's a cool rooftop terrace shaded by a sprawling tree canopy. Quiet, and good value. ❷

Shiva, on the road leading off the market square by the post office ☏ 0145/772120. A popular, friendly and dependable cheapie with a leafy courtyard, rooftop and resident tortoises, but small rooms. If full, try the similarly priced *Sai Baba* and *Shanti Palace* across the street. ❷–❹

White House, near the Marwar bus stand ☏ 0145/772147, ⓕ 772950, ⓔ hotelwhitehou7@hotmail.com. A cut above most guesthouses in this bracket: neat, clean and well run, with attached bathrooms, rooftop restaurant (see Eating), internet and ISD phone facilities, and warm family atmosphere. ❷–❸

Eating

As Pushkar is sacred to Lord Brahma, all food (with the exception of the *Pushkar Resort*) is strictly veg: meat, eggs and alcohol are banned, and taking drugs is considered highly offensive. However, its **restaurants** cater for both Indian and foreign palates, offering national dishes as well as pizza, spaghetti and apple pie. Be wary of the many buffets offering tempting all-you-can-eat menus; most are likely to consist of terribly unhealthy reheated food, and it's safer to stick to the more expensive places. This does not apply to **buffet breakfasts**, however, with unlimited supplies of cereal, toast and curd – try the *Omshiva Buffet*, on the fourth floor, above *Hotel VK*, near the *Pushkar Palace*. One other word of **warning**: think twice before downing a **bhang lassi** at one of the stalls in the bazaar. Although *bhang* (ground cannabis leaves; see p.77) is legal here, it can cause intense, and protracted, psychological distress if you're not used to its mind-altering properties.

Krishna, Brahma Mandir Road. Tasty Indian dishes, including south Indian *dosas* at breakfast, and Israeli-style felafel and hummus. Open 8am–10.30pm.

Moondance, opposite the Vishnu temple. Nepali-run, with nothing Indian on the menu. Attempts at Thai and "Maxican" food are tasty but nothing like the real thing; the pizza and pasta is the best in town. Open 8.30am–11pm.

Rainbow, Brahma Mandir Road. Rooftop restaurant above the *Krishna*, serving veg curries, pasta, pizza, felafel, Chinese dishes and even attempts at *enchiladas* and *moussaka*. Open 8am–midnight.

Raju, Ajmer Road. Not to be confused with *Raju Garden Restaurant*, this small basic place serves very cheap curries and good thalis. Open 7am–10pm.

Raju Garden Restaurant, off Main Bazaar near Ram Ghat. Delicious Indian, Chinese and Western food of a standard rarely matched by other restaurants. Particularly renowned for its vegetarian shepherd's pie, and baked potatoes with peanut butter, garlic cheese and imported Marmite fillings. Open 8am–11pm.

Sanjay, Main Bazaar. Rooftop seating overlooking the lake; the food – veg curries, thalis, pizza – is nothing special, but the buffet breakfasts (Rs40) are good. Open 7am–noon.

Sunset Café, east side of the lake near the *Pushkar Palace*. As its name implies, an ideal spot from which to enjoy Pushkar's legendary lakeside sunsets, offering German-bakery snacks and cakes, in addition to a main menu.

Venus, Ajmer Road. Set back from the lake, with a garden and roof terrace overlooking the main bazaar. Currently the most popular restaurant in town. Sumptuous "sizzlers" are the house speciality, but they do a full range of Indian dishes, and Western pizzas and pastas that seem to improve each year. Open 7am–10.30pm.

White House, near Marwar bus stand. Standard budget travellers' menu, made from home-grown vegetables and served on rooftop terrace with good views over the town and Gayitri temple. Their speciality is delicious mango tea, and they also lay on *pukka* brahmin food if given a little advanced warning.

Jodhpur

On the eastern fringe of the Thar Desert, **JODHPUR**, dubbed "the Blue City" after the colour-wash of its old town houses, sprawls across the arid terrain, overlooked by the mighty Meherangarh fort, whose ramparts rise from a sheer-sided sandstone outcrop. It was once the centre of Marwar, the largest princely state in Rajputana, and today has a population close to 800,000.

Most of the tourists that stop in Jodhpur only stay for a day, squeezing in a visit to the fort before heading west to Jaisalmer (300km) or east to Jaipur (320km). It's a shame to rush the place though. Getting lost in the blue maze of the old city you'll stumble across Muslim tie-dyers, lacquer bangle and puppet makers and traditional spice markets, while Jodhpur's famed cubic roofscape, best viewed at sunset, is a photographer's paradise. In addition, the encroaching desert beyond the blue city is dotted with small settlements where you escape the congestion and pollution for a taste of rural Rajasthan.

Some history

In 1459, Rao Jodha of the Rathore clan moved the capital of Marwar state several kilometres from the exposed site of **Mandore** to a massive steep-sided escarpment, where he named his new capital after himself. The high barricaded fort proved virtually impregnable, and the city soon amassed great wealth from trade en route to the ports of Gujarat. Not surprisingly, the Moghuls were eager to take over Jodhpur, but realizing there was little prospect of that, they presented treaties and riches to the Rathores in exchange for military aid in their onslaught on Gujarat. A marriage alliance between Udai Singh's sister and Akbar in 1561 ensured the most friendly of terms.

However, the tide turned in the mid-seventeenth century, after Jaswant Singh joined Shah Jahan's forces in an unsuccessful bid for power against his fellow Moghul Aurangzeb. Aurangzeb set out to purge his enemies, and demanded the death of Jaswant's young son, **Ajit Singh**. That demand was not satisfied, but Jodhpur was sacked in 1678 and its inhabitants forcibly converted to Islam. In the finest romantic tradition, Ajit Singh eventually recaptured his rightful king-

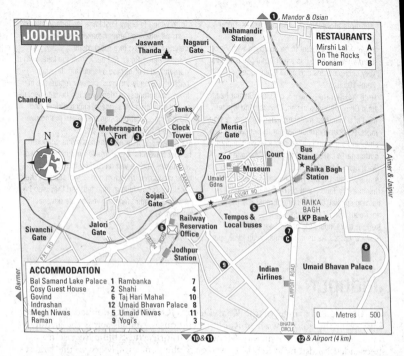

JODHPUR

, Mandor & Osian

RESTAURANTS
Mirshi Lal **A**
On The Rocks **C**
Poonam **B**

Jaswant Thanda
Nagauri Gate
Mahamandir Station

Chandpole

Meherangarh Fort

Jaswant Thanda

Tanks

Clock Tower

Mertia Gate

Zoo

Court

Museum

Bus Stand

Raika Bagh Station

Ajmer & Jaipur

Umaid Gdns

RAIKA BAGH

Sojati Gate

HIGH COURT RD

Tempos & Local buses

LKP Bank

Sivanchi Gate

Jalori Gate

Railway Reservation Office

Indian Airlines

Umaid Bhavan Palace

Jodhpur Station

AIRPORT ROAD

BHATIA CIRCLE

0 Metres 500

Barmer

ACCOMMODATION
Bal Samand Lake Palace	**1**	Rambanka	**7**
Cosy Guest House	**2**	Shahi	**4**
Govind	**6**	Taj Hari Mahal	**10**
Indrashan	**12**	Umaid Bhavan Palace	**8**
Megh Niwas	**5**	Umaid Niwas	**11**
Raman	**9**	Yogi's	**3**

10 & 11

12 & Airport (4 km)

dom after thirty years in hiding. The performance of *sati* on his funeral pyre by six wives and fifty-eight concubines in 1731 may seem shocking now, but at the time was testimony to his heroism. The eighteenth century saw many bloody battles between Jodhpur, Jaipur and Udaipur, despite their policy of unification against the Moghuls. At its close, Jodhpur passed first into the hands of the Marathas and then the British; the signing of a friendship treaty with the East India Company in 1818 guaranteed its safety, albeit at great cost to Rathore honour.

The last maharaja before Independence, **Umaid Singh**, is commemorated by his immense Umaid Bhawan Palace; he set 3000 citizens to work for sixteen years on its construction, in part to alleviate problems during a severe famine by creating employment. Jodhpur is now a democratic union within the independent India, but its social fabric remains tinged with feudalism and a medieval atmosphere prevails.

Arrival and information

Jodhpur's main **railway station** is in the south of town, a couple of kilometres west of the state **bus stand**. Private buses drop you near the main railway station. From the **airport**, 4km south, an auto-rickshaw into town costs Rs50; taxis charge around Rs200 (go to the RTDC prepaid taxi counter in the arrivals lounge). In town, these are supplemented by tempos that follow fixed routes along the main roads. **Bicycles** can be rented from shops near the railway station (Rs3/hr).

The excellent **tourist office** (Mon–Sat 7am–8pm), in the RTDC *Goomar Tourist Bungalow* on High Court Road, has timings for private bus services and keeps lists of families offering paying guest accommodation. The State Bank of India is behind the Collectorate, off High Court Road (Mon–Fri 10am–2pm, Sat 10am–noon), but you can **change money** more quickly at LKP, 1 Mahavir Place, opposite the Circuit House (near *Hotel Ajit Bhawan*), or Ritco Travels, opposite *Arun Hotel*, Police Chowk, Sojati Gate, not far from the railway station.

The **Head Post Office**, for poste restante and parcel packing, is opposite the *Govind Hotel* on Station Road. **Internet access** is widely available these days, even amid the medieval labyrinth of the old city. A convenient and competitive place to head for is *Sweet Dreams* in the lobby of the RTDC *Goomar Tourist Bungalow* on High Court Road, who use several different ISPs and are thus more likely to have a dependable connection.

Jodhpur's best English-language **bookstore** is Khazanza Books, in the *Taj Hari Mahal*, on Residency Road (see Accommodation).

Accommodation

Jodhpur has plenty of pleasant places to stay in all brackets, but getting to most of them involves breaking through a particularly vociferous posse of touts, *lapkars* and rickshaw-wallahs, who will all want to take you to the *Haveli Guest House*, which pays them whopping commissions. The best way around this problem is to phone ahead to **book a room**, in which case some guesthouse owners will pick you up from your arrival point. With the exception of the *Govind*, where most backpackers end up, the hotels outside the railway station on Station Road are grim and best avoided.

Bal Samand Lake Palace, Mandore Road ☎0291/571991, ℱ571240. Heritage hotel converted from the maharaja's lakeside summer palace. Their run-of-the-mill standard rooms (in an old stable block; Rs3500) are nothing special, but if your budget can stretch to Rs4000, go for a suite in the main building: they're huge, airy and exquisitely furnished. Among the most attractive hotels of its kind in the state, and you get the run of an enormous garden pool and croquet lawn. ⑨

Cosy Guest House (formerly *Joshi's Blue House*), Novechokiya Road, Brahm Puri ☎0291/612066. A mid-fifteenth-century *haveli* in the thick of the old city, due west of the fort. Variously priced and sized rooms (some with attached bathrooms and air coolers), great rooftop terrace, home cooking, family atmosphere and garrulous host, all at rock bottom rates. About as blue as the Blue City gets. ②–③

Govind, Station Road ☎0291/622758. Popular budget hotel opposite the GPO (look for the tree in front), near the station. Clean and central, with helpful, genuinely friendly management and a busy rooftop restaurant, but the location suffers from traffic noise and pollution. ②–③

Indrashan, 593 High Court Colony ☎0291/438593, ℱ440665, ℯrajdisk@datainfosys.net. Outstandingly comfortable, hospitable paying guesthouse, 3km from the centre. Well out of town, but the family are per-fect hosts and the food is excellent. Single occupancy rates available. ⑤

Megh Niwas, 30 Umed Club Rd ☎0291/510530, ℱ511560, ℯmeghniwas@usa.net. Air-cooled or cheaper rooms in comfortable, secluded paying guesthouse outside the centre, run by a retired army colonel and his extrovert helper, Baghira. ⑤–⑥

Raman, opposite Kesar Bagh, Shiv Road, Ratananda ☎0291/620380. This place is what the paying guest scheme is all about: inexpensive, clean rooms (some attached), home-cooked food, kids charging around and optional turban-tying lessons. ②–③

Rambanka, near Circuit House ☎0291/512800, ℱ512800, ℯrambank@ndf.vsnl.net.in. Following a family squabble, the maharaja of Jodhpur's younger brothers split their wonderful nineteenth-century palace down the middle to make two hotels. This one is much the most elegant of the pair, with loads of period charm: wood and marble floors, stylish repro furniture, beautiful pool and lawns overlooked by polo stables. Rooms start at around Rs2000. ⑨

Shahi, Gandhi Street, near Sadar Police Thana, Old City ☎0291/623589. Quirky 350-year-old *haveli* buried deep in the warren of lanes beneath the fort's southwest wall. The en suite rooms are cavernous, with interconnecting annexes and shuttered windows overlooking narrow streets below. Full of atmosphere, though hard to find. Head for the Balaji temple and ask again. ④–⑤

Taj Hari Mahal, 5 Residency Rd ℡ 0291/439700, ⓕ 614451, ⓔ thmbc.jodh@tajhotels.com. Sumptuous, sensitively designed new 5-star on the edge of the city, blending traditional Rajasthani features with state-of-the-art comforts that include a huge outdoor pool. Competitive rates April–Oct ($83), but thereafter $236. ⑨

Umaid Bhawan Palace, southeast of town ℡ 0291/510101, ⓕ 510100, ⓔ ubp@ndf.vsnl.net.in. The Maharaja of Jodhpur's princely pile (see p.225) ranks among the world's grandest hotels. Each of its 98 rooms and suites is individually styled, with original Art-Deco furniture and fittings. The rest of the building, guarded by teams of turbaned old retainers, is crammed with hunting trophies and royal memorabilia. Nonresidents can visit the veranda café and museum (see Eating, p.226). Given the competition, room tariffs are high (from $200); one night in the former royal apartments will set you back a cool $825. ⑨

Umaid Niwas, 40-B/1 PWD Colony ℡ 0291/644352, ⓕ 201276, ⓔ umaid-bhawan @yahoo.com. Large suburban paying guesthouse offering good value round-houses and cooler a/c rooms in main building. Calm, secure and welcoming. Meals available. ④–⑥

Yogi's, Rajpurohitji Ki Haveli, Nayabas ℡ 0291/643436. Compact, welcoming and clean budget guesthouse in old blue-painted walled compound at the foot of the fort. Relaxing chill-out space with fan, mattresses and pillows, and rooftop café that catches the morning sun. ②–③

The City

Life in Jodhpur focuses very much around the fort, still almost completely encircled by the strong walls erected by Rao Maldeo in the 1500s. The blue wash applied to most of the houses huddled beneath it is often erroneously said to denote high-caste brahmin residences. In fact, it originally resulted from the addition of copper sulphate to white limewash, thought to protect the buildings from termites and other insect pests. Over time the distinctive colour caught on and there's now even a blue-wash mosque on the road from the Jalori Gate, west of the fort.

The bazaars of the old city are gathered around the tall **clock tower**, with different areas assigned to different trades. Locally made goods include tie-dye, puppets and lacquered jewellery. **Jalori Gate** and **Sojati Gate** lead out of the old city to the south, near the railway station, GPO and hospital. Beyond the walls, more modern buildings spread east and west of the old boundaries, the domes of **Umaid Bhawan** dominating the scene to the southeast.

Meherangarh Fort

Jodhpur's **Meherangarh Fort** (daily: summer 8.30am–5.30pm; winter 9am–5pm; Rs50, Rs50 extra for camera, Rs100 extra for video, Rs10 elevator), provides what must be the most authentic surviving taste of the ceaseless round of war, honour and extravagance that characterized Rajputana. Unlike the fort in Jaisalmer, it is uninhabited, its paths trodden only by visitors to the temples and palaces within its high crenellated walls. Allow at least a couple of hours for a tour (guides Rs100 for 1–5 people, Rs150 for 6 or more) of the various exhibitions inside the palace, followed by a stroll out to the Durga temple, perched on the far southern tip of the precipice, from where the views over the old city are superb. A good place to steel yourself for the visit, or recover afterwards, is the fort's cool little **restaurant**, just inside the main entrance.

On the wall next to **Loha Pole**, the sixth of seven gates designed to hinder the ascent of enemies up a steep winding cobbled road, are the handprints of Maharaja Man Singh's widows. Following the Rajput code of honour, they voluntarily ended their lives in 1843 on their husband's pyre, in defiance of the law against *sati* passed in 1829 by the British. As you stop to look at them, musicians and dancers will strike up in the hope of receiving a tip.

Beyond the massive **Suraj Pole**, the final gate, lie the palaces that now serve as the **Meherangarh Museum** (same opening hours as fort but closed 1–2.30pm). From the courtyards, you can see the fantastic *jali* (lattice) work that almost entirely covers their sandstone walls and balconies. The exotic names of the palaces evoke a courtly society that in between fighting violent battles loved to indulge in beauty and elegance. In the **Jhanki Mahal**, or "Queen's Palace", there's a colourful array of cradles of former rulers, while **Moti Mahal** (Pearl Palace) houses the majestic marble coronation seat upon which all the rulers apart from Jodha have been, and still are, crowned. One prize exhibit in the museum is a 250-year-old pure silk tent seized during a raid on the Moghul court in Delhi. The most elaborate of the apartments is **Phool Mahal** (Flower Palace), a dancing hall for the entertainment of the maharaja and his guests. Pictures of dancers, deities and rulers look out from its walls and wooden ceilings, brightly painted with touches of gold. Other palaces have sandalwood ceilings, mirrored walls and decorated archways, and the last section displays solid silver *howdahs* (elephant seats) and palanquins, perfectly carved and very, very heavy.

The fascinating walk up to the fort from the old city passes through busy bazaars and communal living areas, with some streets so narrow that pedestrians must advance in single file, vying for right of way with goats and chickens. You can also reach the fort by taxi or rickshaw along the much longer road (5km) that enters the old city at Nagauri Gate.

Jaswant Thanda

North of the fort, and connected to it by road, **Jaswant Thanda** is a pillared marble memorial to the popular ruler Jaswant Singh II (1878–95), who purged Jodhpur of dacoits, initiated irrigation systems and boosted the economy. The cenotaphs of members of the royal family who have died since Jaswant are close by his memorial; those who preceded him are remembered by *chhatris* at Mandor (see p.228). This south-facing spot is also the best place from which to photograph the fort, looming above the sheer rocky Meherangarh plateau.

Umaid Bhawan Palace

Dominating the city's southeast horizon is the **Umaid Bhawan Palace**, a colossal Indo-Sarcenic pile commissioned by Maharaja Umaid Singh in 1929 as a famine relief project. One of the largest and most opulent royal abodes in Asia, it kept three thousand labourers gainfully employed for sixteen years and remains a potent symbol of Rajput megalomania, lording it over the modern city from a scrub-covered hill on the outskirts. Surmounted by a helmet-shaped dome, its austere pink sandstone walls and monumental scale recall the Presidential Palace in New Delhi (whose designer, Sir Edwin Lutyens, was much admired by Umaid Bhawan's chief architect, Henry Lanchester). When it was completed in 1944, the building boasted 347 rooms, among them a cinema and indoor swimming pool. The maharaja had little time to savour his achievement, however; only three years after the work was finished he died.

The present incumbent, Maharaja Gaj Singh, occupies only one-third of the palace; the rest is given over to a luxury **hotel** (see Accommodation, p.224) and a small **museum** (daily 9am–5pm; Rs50), housed in the old, mural-lined Durbar Hall. Ranks of glass cases, guarded by a retinue of elderly turbaned retainers, enclose the usual array of old clocks, weapons, miniature paintings, porcelain, portraits, silverware and stately garb. While you're here, have a nose around the hotel, whose furniture and fittings are nearly all original 1930s Art Deco, enlivened with lashings of typically Rajasthani gilt and sweeping staircases.

Eating

Jodhpur's **restaurants** cater for all tastes and all budgets. **Local specialities** include *mawa* sweets and *dhood fini*, a sweet mixture of wheat strands and milk. The best place to sample these is in shops such as *Janta Sweet* and *Poker Sweet*, both on Nai Sarak near the corner of High Court Road (look for the crowds). These places also sell *mirchi bada*, a chilli in wheatgerm and potato, deep-fried like a *pakora*, available at *samosa* stalls elsewhere in Rajasthan, but originally from here.

Also worth a visit while you're in Jodhpur is Mohanlal Verhomal's **spice shop**, at 209-B Kirana Merchant Vegetable Market, near the clock tower (℡0291/615846, ℡615846). After a cup of appropriately spicy *masala* chai and a dose of Mr Verhomal's inimitable sales patter, you can select fragrant packets of home-ground spices to be sent home. His "pay-on-receipt" mail-order service is very reliable.

Fort View, on the roof of the *Govind* hotel, Station Road. A cut above the usual tourist places, with good veg curries, thalis, Chinese food and great views of the fort. It's open round the clock, and you can hang out here while waiting for the bus or train (baggage storage facilities available). Try their sublime *makhania lassis*.

Josi's, *Cosy Guest House*, Novechokiya Road, Brahm Puri ℡0291/612066. Nonresidents are welcome to eat on the small but highly atmospheric roof terrace of this family-run guesthouse, in the bluest part of the blue city. Their delicious, inexpensive home-cooked thalis are freshly prepared to order, so phone ahead if you're not staying here.

Marwar, Taj Hari Mahal. The best place in town to sample traditional Marwari cuisine, such as *Jodhpuri mas* (a spicy mutton dish) or *gatta di subzi* (its veg equivalent), rounded off with *mawa ki kachori* (basically chocolate truffle with ice cream). Count on around Rs400–450 per head for two courses.

Mirshi Lal, in the gateway just south of the clock tower. The most famous purveyor of *makhania lassi*, made with cream, saffron and cardomom, but in fact theirs is rather sickly – the lighter version available at the Fort View restaurant is better.

On the Rocks, Hotel Ajit Bhawan, Airport Road. Delicious evening buffets (7–10.30pm; Rs250) accompanied by live folk music and dance. Buffet lunches also available, but must be pre-booked.

The Pillars, Umaid Bhawan Palace. The veranda café at the maharaja's palace gives you the excuse to wander around the hotel's absurdly grand interior. It's also a relaxing place for a sundowner, with peacocks on the lawn and sweeping views of the distant city. Rs50 cover charge payable on entry.

Poonam, High Court Road. The best south Indian vegetarian in town: huge paper *dosas* and delicious *rawa masala dosas*. The generous set dishes are carefully prepared, too, although the enclosed, rather gloomy interior is less than inspiring.

Around Jodhpur

Should you stay in Jodhpur for longer than a day, and be tempted to see more than the fort and the bazaars, you can visit the gardens in the old capital of **Mandor** on the northern outskirts of town, where former rulers are remembered by elaborate temple-like constructions, or a remarkable collection of early Jain and Hindu temples further afield at **Osian**, an hour's drive away.

Jodhpur's arid surroundings can also be explored on organized "**village safaris**", which take small groups of tourists out into rural Rajasthan for a taste of traditional life. The tours usually include four or five stops at villages set in scrubland where the rare black buck, a beautiful indigenous antelope that is a menace to crops, is protected by the local **Bishnoi** tribe. In desert dwellings, mostly circular thatched huts, you can taste traditional food, learn about herbal remedies, and watch crafts such as spinning and carpet-making. The maharaja

Moving on from Jodhpur

As the principal staging post on the long haul to and from Jaisalmer, Jodhpur stands at the nexus of Rajasthan's main tourist routes, with connections northeast to Jaipur, Pushkar and Delhi, and south to Udaipur and Ahmedabad. Although the city is well served by trains, most journeys from here (for example to Bikaner, Udaipur, Ajmer/Pushkar and Mt Abu) are quicker by road. Buses travel the tedious 275km to Jaisalmer between ninety minutes and two-and-a-half hours faster than the train, but the sleeper rail service is much the most relaxing way to cross the Thar. Take plenty of warm clothing and a thick sleeping bag with you, as temperatures drop to just below zero at night crossing the desert; it may even be worth buying an extra blanket for this trip. You should also stay alert for thieves and con merchants on this train. *Lapkars* from Jaislamer routinely bribe the conductors to be allowed on board, where they attempt to recruit customers for their dodgy hotels and desert safaris.

By bus

Private buses depart year round from Jodhpur to Delhi, Agra, Ajmer/Pushkar, Jaipur, Mumbai, Udaipur, Bikaner, Abu Road and Jaisalmer. The best place to book tickets and consult the latest timetables is the reception of the *Govind Hotel* on Station Road, opposite the Head Post Office, which acts as an agent for all the main private bus companies. For goverment buses, which tend to be slower but safer, turn up at the bus stand an hour or so before depature time to buy a ticket. For timetable information, ask your hotel or guesthouse to ring on your behalf.

By plane

Indian Airlines operate daily flights from Jodhpur to Delhi ($105), Mumbai ($150), Jaipur ($80) and Udaipur ($65). Book tickets through an agent in town, or direct with IA at their office on Airport Road, 3km south of the centre, near the *Hotel Ajit Bhawan* (daily 10am–1pm & 2–4.30pm; ☎0291-510758 or 512617).

By train

Train tickets should be booked at least a day in advance at the computerized reservations hall (Mon–Sat 8am–8pm, Sun 8am–2pm), just north of the station behind the Head Post Office, or at the new Northern Railways bookings counter at the tourist office on High Court Road (Mon–Sat 10am–5pm). If you're a foreigner, you're entitled to use the International Tourist Waiting Room on the ground floor of the main station building. Its toilets are decidedly grim, but there are clean shower facilities.

Recommended trains from Jodhpur

The following trains from Jodhpur are recommended as the fastest or most convenient for the destinations listed on the left; all are daily services. Departure times were correct at the time of writing, but check them when you buy your ticket.

Destination	Name	No.	Departs	Total time
Abu Road	Jodhpur–Bangalore Express	#6507	6am	5hr
Agra	Bikaner–Howrah Express	#2308	5.15pm	13hr 10min
	Marudhar Express	#4864/4854	7am	13hr
Ahmedabad	Jodhpur–Bangalore Express	#6507	6am	10hr
Delhi	Jodhpur–Delhi Express	#4860	11pm	12hr 25min
Jaipur	Jaipur Intercity Express	#2466	5.45am	5hr
	Jodhpur–Delhi Express	#4860	11pm	6hr 45min
Jaisalmer	Jaisalmer Express	#4810	11.15pm	6hr 15min
	Jailsalmer Passenger	#2JPJ	8.20am	8hr 40min
Udaipur	Udaipur Passenger	#251	10pm	12hr
Varanasi	Marudhar Express	#4864	9am	26hr

encourages the fair sale of Bishnoi handicrafts in the hope that they can thereby avoid the emigration to the city that has destroyed the traditional way of life of so much of India's rural population. These tours get mixed reviews; some enjoy the experience, others find it totally contrived. A lot depends on the integrity of the operators and the relations they have with the villagers. Three inexpensive, commendable companies are: RTDC, based at the tourist office on High Court Road; the *Govind Hotel* on Station Road (☎0291/622758); and Joshi, at *Cosy Guest House*, Novechokiya Road, Brahm Puri (☎0291/612066). Rates start at around Rs400 per head for a group of five and it's a good idea to opt for a translator-guide, although this bumps the price up a little. Book at least one day in advance.

Mandor

Most of Jodhpur's minibuses head for the royal cenotaphs, or *dewals*, of the maharajas in the fertile gardens 9km north of the city at **MANDOR**, the capital of the Parihar Rajputs between the sixth and fourteenth centuries. The Parihars were ousted when the Rathore Rao Chauhan established the seat of government for his new kingdom at Mandor in 1381, and little remains of their fortified city. The dark red sandstone *chhatris*, memorials to Jodhpur's rulers, grew in size and grandeur as the Rathore kingdom prospered, culminating with the last and largest, that of **Maharaja Dhiraj Ajit Singh** (died 1763). It is Shaivite in style, fronted by a balustraded porch and topped with a towering roof crowned with four faces of Shiva. By the *chhatris*, opposite a rather dull museum, you'll find the **Hall of Heroes**, a strange display of life-sized gods and Rajput fighters that were hewn out of the rock face early in the eighteenth century.

A path leads over the hill behind the gardens to another set of cenotaphs, seemingly neglected on a sandy slope among twisted cacti. These commemorate the ranis of Jodhpur and, though smaller, are more stately than those of the men, with exquisitely detailed carving on the pillars and domed roofs.

Osian

Rajasthan's largest group of early Jain and Hindu temples lies on the outskirts of the small town of **OSIAN**, 64km north of Jodhpur. Half-hourly buses (1hr 30min) drop you on the main road south of town; the railway station (served by the Jodhpur–Jaisalmer train, 2hr 30min out of Jodhpur) is 1km west. Alternatively, get a group together and book a Jeep through RTDC (Rs650 for up to five people, or Rs950 for four people and a guide).

The oldest group, the **Vishnu and Harihara temples**, built in the Pratihara period of the eighth and ninth centuries, are right by the bus stop. All three retain a considerable amount of decorative carving. Where the main road from Jodhpur to Phalodi bends round to the right, the smaller road straight ahead leads to the town centre, where you'll find the **Sachiya Mata temple**, at the top of a large staircase, overlooking the whole of Osian, and still used for worship. This temple dates back to the twelfth century, and features a hall for large gatherings. The main shrine, to Sachiya, an incarnation of Durga, is surrounded by smaller, earlier ones to Ganesh and Shankar (an aspect of Shiva), and, on the right, to Surya and Vishnu.

As you leave the Sachiya Mata temple, the third group of temples, rather more spread out, lies roughly straight ahead. The first is the **Mahavira Jain temple**, built in the eighth century, and renovated in the tenth. The gateway embellished with figurines was added in 1015. Twenty elegantly carved pillars hold up the main portico. The usual rules (no leather, don't enter during menstruation) apply. Fifty metres beyond is the **Surya temple**, surrounded by gargoyle-like projecting elephants. Its inner sanctum contains an image of Surya, flanked by Ganesh and Durga. Another 50m brings you to the **Sun temple**, where the carvings around the doorway have suffered the ravages of time (and graffiti), but those in the surrounding niches are very fine. A little way behind it is a massive Pratihara period step-well, currently under restoration.

For **accommodation**, you've a choice between a very basic guesthouse run by a brahmin priest opposite the Mahavira temple (☏02922/74232; ❷–❸), or a more luxurious tent at *The Camel Camp*, straddling a sand dune on the village outskirts (book in advance through The Safari Club in Jodhpur on ☏0291/437023; ❹–❻).

Jaisalmer

In the remote westernmost corner of Rajasthan, a good 100km beyond its closest neighbour Pokaran, **JAISALMER** is a desert town *par excellence*, its sand-yellow ramparts rising out of the arid Thar like a vision from *Scheherazade*. Put off by reports of rampant commercialism, many travellers never make the long detour out here, but in spite of all the souvenir shops, hotel touts and large tour groups, the town remains one of India's most enchanting destinations. Villagers from outlying settlements, dressed in dazzling red and orange *odinis* or voluminous turbans, still outnumber foreigners in the bazaar, while the town's exquisite sandstone architecture is quite unlike anything else in India. Staring west at sunset time, when the palace, 99 bastions and delicately sculpted temple towers of the citadel are suffused with honey-coloured light, you'll see how Jaisalmer came to be known as the "Golden City".

Rawal Jaisal of the Bhatti clan founded the town in 1156 as a replacement for his less easily defensible capital at nearby Loduvra, 16km west. A brahmin hermit had told him that Lord Krishna and Arjuna came here once, and that they'd prophesied a ruler would one day build a fort along the ridge, known at that time as Trikuta, "Triple-Peaked Hill". There were constant wars with the neighbouring Rajput states of Jodhpur and Bikaner until eventually, in 1294, Muslim invaders attacked and conquered Jaisalmer, inducing large-scale *johar* (voluntary death by sword and fire) by the warriors and their womenfolk. In the fourteenth century the Bhatti Rajputs retook the city, but provoked a second sacking when they challenged the Muslims at Ajmer. Relations with the Muslims improved, and in 1570 the ruler of Jaisalmer married one of his daughters to Akbar. From the seventeenth century the town prospered as a market centre for traders on the overland routes between India and Central Asia; the magnificent *havelis* of the merchants bear witness to those times. However, with the emergence of Bombay and Surat as major ports, overland trade diminished, and so did Jaisalmer's wealth. The financial problems were compounded by the usurious taxes imposed on merchants by a particularly greedy prime minister, **Salim Singh Mehta**, in the nineteenth century. Many of the wealthiest Jain families moved out as a result, while the royal family, who were also in debt to the Mehtas, lacked the funds to modernize Jaisalmer and reverse its decline. The death blow came with Partition, when its life-line trade route was severed by the new, highly sensitve Pakistani border.

JAISALMER

▲ Ramgarh

▲ Jodhpur

⑪ & Barmer

ACCOMMODATION

Fort Rajwada	11
Gorbandh Palace	5
Jaisal Palace	8
Jawahar Niwas	1
Maru Palace	12
Mandir Palace	7
Nachana Haveli	6
Ratan Palace	3
Renuka	2
Residency Centre Point	4
RTDC Moomal	9
Shri Giriraj Palace	10

Bus Stand ★

Railway Station

BARMER ROAD

Gadi Sagar Tank

Desert Culture Museum

Folklore Museum

Gadi Sagar Pole

⑫

GADI SAGAR ROAD

Salim Singh's Haveli

Patwon-Ki-Haveli ④

Nathmalji-Ki-Haveli ⑤

LKP Forex

"Sunset Point"

Amar Sagar Pole

GANDHI CHOWK

Local Buses ★

② ③

⑥

State Bank of India ★

Private Buses ★

Palace

⑦ ⑧

GOPA CHOWK

⑩

MAIN CHOWK

SHIV MARG

Laxminath Temple

Palace

Jain Temples

Fort

See Jaisalmer Fort Map

▶ Khuhri

Telegraph Office

Hospital

AMAR SAGAR

District Magistrate

⊠

Government Museum ⑨

RESTAURANTS

Kalpana	B
Natraj	C
Seema	D
Trio	A

N

Metres

0   250

Jaisalmer in jeopardy

Sign boards, banners and electric wires may have horribly disfigured Jaisalmer, but the tourist boom has created a far more serious, potentially irreversible threat to the town's survival. Erected on a base of soft clay, sand and sandstone, the foundations of Rajasthan's most picturesque citadel are rapidly eroding because of huge increases in water consumption. At the height of the tourist season, around 120 litres per head are pumped into the area – twelve times the quantity used fifteen years ago. Most of the resulting waste pours through an inadequate drainage system of open gulleys, seeping through cracks into the hillside and leaving chronic subsidence in its wake. The retaining wall below the citadel has burst in several places, many of the bastions are on the verge of collapse and around 250 buildings inside the fort have partially disintegrated, among them the sixteenth-century Maharani's Palace. In recognition of the urgency of the town's repair, Jaisalmer is listed among the World Monument Fund's 100 Most Endangered Sites.

An international campaign, **Jaisalmer in Jeopardy**, has been set up to raise funds for the restoration of the Maharani's Palace, where a new Heritage Centre will house an exhibition on desert culture, focusing on women and traditional architecture. Dozens of houses are being stabilized, facades repaired, and seams of grey cement replaced with traditional material. The campaign relies substantially on donations. If you'd like to help, contact Sue Carpenter at 31 Alpha House, Santley Street, London SW4 7QN (☎/℻+44 2077374948, ⊛www.jaisalmer-in-jeopardy.org). Bear in mind, too, that you can make a small difference by not staying in the fort or, if you do, by conserving water as much as possible while you're there.

Jaisalmer's location, however, gave it renewed strategic importance during the Indo-Pak wars of 1965 and 1971, and it is now a major military outpost, with helicopters and jet aircraft roaring past the ramparts at intervals throughout the day. The area's other main source of income, of course, is tourism. Visitor numbers increased dramatically throughout the 1990s, partly as a result of the air-force base being cleared for civil traffic (which rendered it accessible to package-tour groups from the Delhi–Agra–Jaipur "Golden Triangle" trail), and partly because of the glowing reputation Jaisalmer earned over the preceding two decades as a backpackers' destination. The sign-board war that has spiralled with the booming camel safari and guesthouse business has transformed Jaisalmer almost beyond recognition. To recapture the feeling of remoteness and tranquility that once defined the town, you'll have to head into the depths of the desert by camel.

Arrival and information

Jaisalmer's **railway station** is 2km east of the city. Overeager touts, hoping to entice you onto a shoddy and overpriced camel safari, accost arriving passengers with offers of free Jeep taxi services and low rents at their hotels. To sidestep, walk or pay Rs10 to get into town by auto-rickshaw and choose a hotel yourself. Arriving at the **RSRTC bus stand** nearby, you will not be met with quite such a gauntlet of touts, rickshaw-wallahs and commission agents; the **private bus stand** by Amar Sagar Pole in the west of town is within easy walking distance of most accommodation. There are **bike rental** shops in the main street, and opposite *Fort View Hotel*.

RTDC's **tourist office** (Mon–Sat 8am–6pm; ☎02922/52406) is inconveniently situated southeast of town not far from Gadi Sagar Pole. The **Head Post Office**, with poste restante, is west of town, 100m south of the private bus stand; a more convenient office stands shaded by a huge banyan tree in Gopa Chowk in the centre. **Banks** are concentrated on Gandhi Chowk; the Bank of Baroda changes cash and travellers' cheques, as does the State Bank of India, inside the courtyard of *Nachana Haveli*.

Accommodation

Jaisalmer has plenty of places to stay in all categories. Almost all offer **camel treks**, which vary in standard and price, and some managers can be uncomfortably pushy if you don't want to arrange a safari through them, suddenly hiking room rates or turfing you out in the middle of the night. In general you should avoid anyone touting for business at the station or bus stand. All of the hotels listed below are reputable and relaxed. Many visitors prefer the peaceful, atmospheric guesthouses among the jumble of sandstone houses and *havelis* within the **fort**, whose roofs offer splendid desert vistas. Due to the problems caused by increased water consumption in the citadel, however, you may prefer to make a more ethical choice and stay below the fort in the **town**, where lovely roof terraces and great views of the citadel make up for the comparative blandness of the hotels. Over the past few years, a crop of lookalike luxury resorts have also appeared on fringes of Jaisalmer to service tour groups. Stiff competition between them has held room tariffs in check, so you now enjoy five-star poolside luxury in the desert for around $70 per double room (or less off-season).

In the fort

Chandra Niwas, near Laxminath temple ☎ 02922/54477. Run by English/Indian couple; relaxed, immaculately clean, and with a great roof terrace right next to the temple towers. Good value. ❷–❸

Desert, northwest side of the fort ☎ 02922/50602). Not to be confused with the very dodgy *Desert Boys* nearby (nor the *Desert Guest House* recommended below). Tiny budget place with only six clean and comfortable rooms (2 doubles) and friendly owner. ❷

Desert Guest House, near Jain temples ☎ 02922/51555, ✉ g.sharma2002@yahoo.com. An established and popular budget guesthouse. Variously sized, cavernous stone-walled rooms, with old durries on the floor, tiny windows and some attached bathrooms. ❷

Ishar Palace, Kunda Padda, near Laxminath temple ☎ 02922/53062. Pleasant little paying guesthouse, deep in a tangle of lanes at the centre of the fort. Ask for the front room – their only *pukka* one; the others are "huts" on the roof. Welcoming family; particularly recommended for women travellers. ❷

Killa Bhawan, 445 Kotri Badda ☎ 02922/51204 or 54517. Created by French fashion designer and like something out of an interiors magazine: supremely tasteful decor (silk bed-covers, embroidery wall hangings, antique ornaments and furniture) and the perfect roof terrace. The only catch is

the cheaper rooms (Rs1350) share a (beautifully appointed) bathroom. If you treat yourself only once in Rajasthan, it should be here. ❼–❽

Moti Palace ☎ 02922/53493, ✉ jorasaith@gd.com. New place in prime location overlooking the main gate with outstanding views from its large, new rooms. One has been done up with traditional mud floors and old shutters. All have modern, spacious bathrooms with hot showers and Western toilets. ❸–❻

Paradise, off the Main Chowk ☎ 02922/52674 or 52417. Well-run, comfortable hotel in an old *haveli* with a leafy courtyard and some excellent rooms. The larger ones have views and bathrooms; budget options with common baths on the ground floor. Large roof terrace with live folk music each evening at sunset. ❸–❻

Suraj, near the Jain temples ☎ 02922/51623. Superbly carved sandstone *haveli*. Five spacious, comfortable rooms all with hot shower and some with original wall-paintings, in a family atmosphere. Excellent rooftop view. ❺–❻

Suraja, Kotri Barra, southeast tip of the fort ☎ 02992/50617. Good-sized rooms, most with sitouts or projecting *jhokaras* (#2 is the most romantic). Scruffy roof space, but fine views and lovely family. ❷–❺

Surya, Kotri Barra ☎ 02922/50647. Superb views over the town and a characterful old courtyard are the hallmarks of this restored *haveli*. A touch overpriced considering the cramped conditions and proximity of rooms to restaurant, but some will think the decor and situation worth the extra. ③–④

In and around the town

Fort Rajwada, Jodhpur–Barmer Road ☎ 02992/53533, ℻ 53733, ⓦ www.fortrajwada.com. Among the new resort hotels on the outskirts, this place is in a league of its own. It's worth coming out here just to see the massive marble lobby, which includes chunks of richly filagreed sandstone plundered from the old city. All the facilities of a five-star (huge pool, gourmet restaurant and coffee shop), but at lower tariffs. Rooms start at Rs3300. ⑨

Jaisal Palace, behind the royal palace ☎ 02922/52717 or 51417, ℻ 50257, ⓔ jaisalpalace@yahoo.com. Modern and a bit bland, but the smallish, simply furnished rooms are immaculately clean and the beds comfortable. Ask for one on an upper storey; the ground floor can be a bit dingy. A/c Rs300 extra. ⑤

Mandir Palace, Gandhi Chowk ☎ 02992/52788 or 52951, ℻ 51677, ⓔ mandirpalace@hotmail.com. Richly carved former palace with lots of character, whose most prominent feature is the Escher-like Badal Vilas tower – one of the town's main landmarks. Well-ventilated, comfortably furnished en-suite rooms, with ornate silver chairs and ceramic tiles. Phone ahead for a complimentary jeep from the station/airport. ⑧

Maru Palace, near Fort Gate ☎ 02992/50713, ℻ 52259. Airy, clean en-suite rooms, laundry facilities, ISD phone with complimentary call-back and a great chill-out area on the rooftop. Camel safaris are offered, but you're under no pressure to accept. Plenty of rooms. ①–④

Nachana Haveli, Gandhi Chowk ☎ 02992/52110 or 51910, ℻ 52778, ⓔ nachana_haveli@yahoo.com. Quiet, secluded and tastefully furnished with antiques, but the rooms are a little small for the price, and not very light. ⑧

Ratan Palace, off Gandhi Chowk ☎ 02992/51119 or 53615. Same owners and high standards as *Renuka* (see below) but newer and more spacious rooms with large, marble-lined bathrooms. A notch more expensive than their old property, but worth the extra. ③

Renuka, off Gandhi Chowk ☎ 02992/52757. Among the best budget options in this part of town. Fifteen rooms, some with two windows, all with attached bathrooms and running water, and a relaxing rooftop restaurant. Free pick-up from the station, and a "no pressure" policy regarding camel treks. ①–②

Residency Centre Point, around the corner from the Patwon-ki-Haveli, Kumbhara Para ☎ 02992/52883. Opened in late 2000 and a great deal in this bracket, especially their first-floor front room ("Mahendre-ka-Mole"), which incorporates original stonework. Rear-side rooms are well-aired but lack external windows. All attached bathrooms. Good rooftop area. ②

RTDC Moomal Tourist Bungalow, Amar Sagar Road ☎ 02992/52392. Clean, spacious rooms in a more comfortable than average government-run hotel. Less pricey round huts in the grounds, each with double room and bathroom, and there's a dorm. Noon checkout. ①–⑤

Shri Giriraj Palace, near Gopa Chowk ☎ 02992/52268 or 51519. Small, but ornately carved *haveli* near First Gate, with pleasant rooms and courteous management. A dependable budget choice in the heart of the bazaar. ②–③

The Town

Getting lost in the narrow winding streets of Jaisalmer is both easy and enjoyable, though the town is so small that it never takes long to find a familiar landmark. Main roads lead around the base of the fort from the central market square, **Gopa Chowk**, east to **Gadi Sagar Tank**, and west to **Gandhi Chowk**. Within the fort the streets are narrower still, but orientation is simple: head west from the main *chowk* and **Maharawal's Palace** to reach the **Jain temples** and hotels nestled within the walls. Along the way, expect your progress to be blocked at regular intervals by Jaisalmer's imperious stray cows, some of which are almost as wide as the lanes they inhabit. Finally, for optimum **views**, head for "Sunset Point" north of the main bazaar area, which overlooks the town. As the name of this far western end of the Trikuta ridge implies, the panorama is most impressive around sunset time. Alternatively, try the rooftop of the *Paradise Hotel*, where you can watch the sun slipping over the desert horizon accompanied by live folk music.

Jaisalmer's flourishing tourist trade has made it one of the best places in India to shop for **souvenirs**. Prices are comparatively high and the salesmen notoriously hard at work, but the choice of stuff on sale puts the town on a par with Pushkar and Jaipur. Good buys include woven jackets, tie-dyed cloth, wooden boxes and ornaments, camel-leather slippers (*jhoolis*) and Western-style clothes. **Puppets** are sold inside Number One (aka "First Fort") Gate, but you'll get better prices buying direct from the puppet-makers' quarter north of town, immediately below the "Sunset Point"; to find it, pick your way through Bhatia Bazaar and follow the main arterial road north past the *Narayan Niwas Palace* hotel, turning left when you reach a junction that drops downhill past a row of painted mud-and-thatch houses.

Every conceivable kind of traditional Rajasthani **textile** is sold at shops in and around the fort. Most of the pieces on offer are specially made for the tourist trade at craft centres such as Sanganer near Jaipur, but you can occasionally find older garments, or patches worked into wall-hangings, at the more established dealers. The best place to start looking is the Barmer Embroidery House, near the Patwon-ki-Haveli, Gangana Para, in the north of town. The stock here ranges from standard Jaipuri block-printed bedspreads and mirror work or appliqué cushion covers to rare door-hangings (*torans*), ornately embroidered cradle covers, sari blouses (*choli*), Lamani *chillum* pouches, camel tack, and silk-woven *mashru* skirts from the remote Muslim villages of Kutch. Even if you aren't buying, it's worth coming to see what the village women of western India used to make and wear before the advent of mass-produced day-glo polyester. The shop owner, Mr Abhimanyu Rathi, has actively encouraged the revival of traditional motifs and techniques by loaning some of his better preserved antique pieces to local craftswomen for them to copy. The results are stored on bulging shelves in his first-floor showroom.

Also worth a visit are the various government-run Khadi Gramodyog shops dotted around town (biggest branches at Gadi Sagar Gate and Gandhi Chowk). The best bargains, and most authentically regional pieces, are the tough, richly patterned handloom shawls and woollen blankets from Khuri and other villages near the Pakistani border, all sold at fixed prices.

Jaisalmer fort

Every part of Jaisalmer **fort**, from its outer walls to the palace, temples and houses within, is made of soft yellow Jurassic sandstone. The narrow winding streets are flanked with carved sandy facades, and from the barrel-sided bastions, some of which still bear cannons, you can see the thick walls that drop almost 100m to the town below. Two thousand people live inside it; seventy percent of them are brahmins and the rest predominantly Rajput caste.

A paved road punctuated by four huge gateways winds up to the fort, built when the city was founded in 1156. By the second gate stands a "death well", down which traitors and criminals were thrown to their doom back in days of yore. The fourth gateway leads into **Main Chowk**, which these days becomes a crowded mass of colour and life during festive celebrations, but was once the scene of the gathering of troops, marriage parties, horse sacrifices (*arsha puja*) and the terrible act of *johar* when women chose death rather than dishonour for themselves and their children after their husbands left for the battlefield. The *chowk* is dominated by the old **palace of the Maharawal** (daily 10am–3pm), whose five-storey facade of balconies and windows displays some of the finest masonry work in Jaisalmer, while the interior is painted and tiled in typical Rajput style. The monarch would address his troops and issue orders from the large ornate marble throne to the left of the palace entrance.

Although the fort holds temples dedicated to Surya, Lakshmi, Ganesh, Vishnu and Shiva, none are as impressive as the **Jain temples** (daily 7am–noon; free, Rs25 extra for camera, Rs50 extra for video; usual restrictions on leather and menstruation apply), built between the twelfth and fifteenth centuries in the familiar Jurassic sandstone, with their yellow and white marble shrines. Walls, ceilings and pillars bear exquisite sculpted motifs, and small corridors and stairways connect one temple to another. In a vault beneath the Sambhavnath temple, the **Gyan Bhandar** (daily 10–11am) contains Jain manuscripts, paintings and astrological charts dating back to the eleventh century, among them one of India's oldest surviving palm-leaf books, a copy of Dronacharya's *Oghaniryaktivritti* (1060). It was saved, along with most of the rest of the library's contents, from Muslim iconoclasts in 1443.

The havelis

The streets of Jaisalmer are flanked with numerous honey-pale facades, covered with latticework and floral designs, but the city's real showpieces are its **havelis**. Each of these extravagant mansions, comprising three or more storeys around a central courtyard, was commissioned by a wealthy merchant during the eighteenth or nineteenth century. Their stonework was the art of *silavats*, a community of masons responsible for much of Jaisalmer's unique sculpture.

The large **Patwon-ki-Haveli** (daily 10am–5pm; Rs10), not far from *Narayan Niwas Hotel* in the north of town, was constructed over fifty years by the Patwa merchants, traders in brocades and opium. Five separate suites with individual entrances facing a narrow street are connected from within, and all have flat

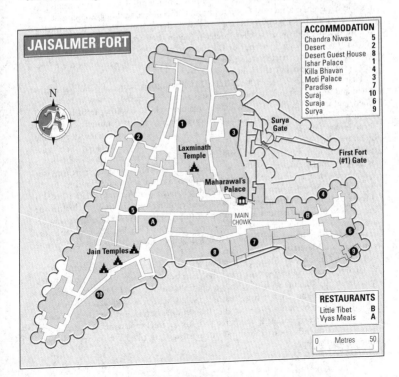

Few visitors who make it as far as Jaisalmer pass up the opportunity to go on a **camel trek**, which provides an irresistibly romantic chance to cross the barren sands on a sturdy ship of the desert, sleeping under what must rank as one of the starriest skies in the world. Sandstorms, sore backsides and camel farts aside, the safaris are usually great fun.

Although you can travel for up to two weeks by camel from Jaisalmer to Bikaner, treks normally last from one to four days, at **prices** varying from Rs200 to Rs1500 per night. In general the less you spend the less you get, in terms of food, blankets, fitness of camel, and so forth. A lot depends on whether the guides are friendly, how big the group is, and what expectations you have. Freelance camel owners, working for extremely low prices, may stop you in the street and offer their services, but increased demand has resulted in high prices and very poor service from some. All in all, you'll do better to go through an established agency or hotel. A couple of reputable operators are mentioned below, and you should also check with other travellers. Make sure you'll be provided with an adequate supply of blankets, to sleep on and under (it can get very cold at night); a quota of fruit if you're paying anything over the average; and a campfire. As a precaution, have the deal fixed on paper, giving the maximum size of the group, details of the food you'll be getting, transport and anything else you've arranged. If you're only going for a day, none of this applies, but wear a broad-brimmed hat and take high-factor sun-protection lotion.

Following government restrictions on **routes**, most safaris head west of Jaisalmer through places such as Sam sand dunes, Lodurva, Amar Sagar, Bada Bagh and assorted small villages. Some visitors feel this puts too much emphasis on sightseeing; it's possible to arrange a few days' amble through the desert without stopping at any monuments. Taking a **jeep** at the start or end of the trek enables you to go further in a short time, and some travellers prefer to begin their trek at Khuri (see p.240). Longer treks to Pokaran, Jodhpur or Bikaner can also be arranged (see p.244). Firms running treks into restricted areas (see Around Jaisalmer, p.238) should fix the necessary permits for you, but check in advance.

Thar Safari (℡0292/54295, ℻52722) in Gandhi Chowk is one of the oldest-established and most reputable **agencies**, offering a range of safaris, many with tents provided, and reliable guides. They will also organize treks to Jaisalmer from Pokaran if given at least ten days' notice, and are among the few agents genuinely concerned about protecting the desert environment. Less expensive, but equally dependable operators include Sahara Travels in Gopa Chowk near the First Fort gate (℡02922/52609). Of the **hotels which organize camel safaris**, *Paradise* has a deservedly good reputation, while the *Jaisal Palace* is recommended for short trips (for Rs650–750 you'll be pampered with comfy beds and restaurant-standard food). Among the budget alternatives, the friendly *Renuka* (see Accommodation, p.233) offers excellent value for money. They've been running trips for more than a decade into a stretch of drifting dunes north of Sam that only a couple of other operators are allowed into. This means you can enjoy optimum Thar landscape without the contrived atmosphere that prevails when a dozen or more groups descend on the same patch of desert at the same time.

However much you intend to spend on a trek, don't book anything until you get to Jaisalmer. Unscrupulous touts trawl the train from Jodhpur, and even try to pick up tourists in Udaipur with offers of cheap deals, but they, and the barrage of safari operators at the bus and railway stations, usually represent dodgy outfits, most of which are based at one or other of the small budget hotels north of the fort. Some offer absurdly cheap rooms if you agree to book a camel trek with them, but guesthouse notice boards (not to mention our postbags) are filled with sorry stories by tourists who accepted.

roof areas – the views are excellent. Traces of stylish wall-paintings survive in some rooms. The building's most striking features, however, are its exuberantly carved *jarokhas*, or protruding balconies. To ensure a clear view of them from the street, Indira Gandhi had one of the more modern buildings opposite demolished (its owners were compensated) following a visit here.

Salim Singh's small *haveli* provides Jaisalmer's only favourable memory of the tyrannical Salim Singh Mohta, who became prime minister in 1800 after his father was murdered for publicly challenging a Rajput prince to repay a loan. From an early age, Salim seemed hell-bent on avenging this crime, impoverishing Jaisalmer's citizens through vigorous taxation and extortion rackets, and holding the royal family to ransom by raising interest rates on their huge loans. He was eventually stabbed by a furious Rajput, and his wife made sure the wound wouldn't heal by infesting it with poison. Their curious family home is topped with small blueish domes; its upper floor, enclosed by a protruding balcony, is best seen from the roof of *Natraj Restaurant*. The house is still lived in, but you can go inside. On the road to Malka Pole, you pass the decorative facade of the late-nineteenth-century **Nathmalji-ki-Haveli**, also built for a prime minister of Jaisalmer. No visitors are allowed, so you won't be able to view the skilful paintings on the interior walls.

Gadi Sagar Tank and the Folklore Museum

South of the city through an imposing triple gateway, **Gadi Sagar Tank**, built in 1367, was once Jaisalmer's sole water supply. Its north and east banks are flanked with *ghats* and temples whose sandstone bricks glow with a warm deep ochre in the evening light. This peaceful place is the focus of the festival of Gangaur in March, when women fling flowers into the lake and pray for a good husband, and the Maharawal heads a procession amid a pomp and splendour unchanged for generations.

The delightful little **Folklore Museum** near the tank's main gate (daily 8am–7pm; Rs10) has some interesting displays of folk art, much of it religious. The locally styled wooden statues of Krishna and Radha, musical instruments, paintings and travelling temples (*kavad*) are all from the personal collection of its proprietor, who will probably be on hand, and happy to talk about them. You'll find much the same selection of local curiosities at the **Desert Culture Museum** (daily 8am–7pm; Rs10), opened by the same family at larger premises next to the tourist office on the main road.

Eating

Being so popular with foreign tourists, Jaisalmer offers peanut butter, Vegemite, Marmite, pizza, pancakes, apple pie and cakes on its menus alongside typical Indian dishes. The choice of **places to eat** is thin. Many are rooftop restaurants with a view, often attached to hotels, but officially these have been banned because they are eyesores, although it remains to be seen how far that ban will be enforced. If you're on a tight budget, a good place to fill up on freshly cooked, spicy food is the little *pao bhaji* stall on Gopa Chowk (opposite the bhang-lassi-wallah), which does a roaring trade in the evening. Afterwards, stroll through the bazaar for a glass of hot *badam* (milk, flavoured with cardamom and whole almonds), from the huge bubbling vats on the roadside between Amar Sagar Pole and Hanuman Circle.

Note that restaurants situated inside the fort are shown on the Jaislamer Fort map on p.235.

Moving on from Jaisalmer

Jaisalmer's only train connection is to Jodhpur, more than 250km east. Two trains cover the route each day; the fastest is the 10.30pm departure, which gets in to Jodhpur at 5.30am the following morning. The slower passenger train leaves at 7.15am, and arrives at 3.15pm. Book tickets at the station, or save yourself the trip down there by reserving through a reputable agent such as the *Paradise Hotel*. If you catch the night train, take along plenty of warm clothes and a sleeping bag as temperatures drop to almost freezing point in the winter.

All other long-distance trips involve tedious bus journeys. The RSRTC bus stand, round the corner from the station, has departures for Jaipur, Jodhpur, Bikaner, Barmer, Mount Abu and Ahmedabad. "Deluxe" private buses are the best option, and leave from the crossroads just outside Amar Sagar Gate, where you'll find the booking offices. There are buses to Jodhpur (hourly; 5hr 30min), Barmer (hourly; 3hr), Bikaner (3 daily; 7hr) and one or two daily to Jaipur (13hr), Delhi (20hr), Mumbai (30hr), Ajmer (12hr 30min), Pushkar (8hr 30min), Mount Abu (11hr) and Udaipur (14hr). Frequent but much slower local buses, which can't be booked, use the stand a little northeast of the crossroads. They include three daily to Khuhri (1hr 30min).

The airport, 8km west of town on the Sam road, has been closed to domestic services since the recent intensification of troubles with neighbouring Pakistan, but you can reconfirm and book flights to and from other cities at the Indian Airlines office in the RTDC *Moomal Tourist Bungalow*, on the west edge of town (daily 9.30am–1pm & 2–5.30pm; ☎&☏02922/51912).

Jaisal Palace, behind the royal palace. Popular tourist restaurant on the top floor of a midscale hotel, with a long pure-veg menu strong on Rajasthani specialities, including *dal-batti-churma* (crumbly lentil cake flavoured with ghee), *sangari* (spicy beans and local vegetables) with *gatta* (dhal-flour dumplings). They also have a great chill-out terrace with optimum fort views.

Little Tibet, Fort. Scrupulously clean travellers' café-restaurant run by a team of smart young Tibetans. Their extensive menu includes all the usual Indian/Chinese choices, plus tasty enchilladas, pasta and Tibetan *momos*. Careful, hygenic cooking (their veg are washed in iodized water), and a good venue for breakfast.

Natraj, facing the top floor of Salim Singh's *haveli*. Pleasant rooftop and indoor non-veg restaurant, famous for its *malai* chicken and *malai kofta*. The quality food is soft on spices and moderately priced. Open 8am–11pm.

Seema, opposite Salim Singh's *haveli*. This place looks pretty run-of-the-mill, but it serves some of the town's top tandoori food, at a fraction of *Trio*'s prices. Delicious korma, tikka and piping hot naan bread.

Surya, *Surya Guest House*, southeast side of the fort. The thalis served in this tiny hotel restaurant, at the top of a beautifully weathered old *haveli*, are mediocre, but the romantic decor, low tables, bolsters and candlelight make it a memorable place to dine. Best to book ahead, as space is limited.

Trio, Gandhi Chowk. Sumptuous Mughlai food, antique decor, snappy service and live folk music make this a wonderful place to eat; excellent value for its price range. The safari soup is, as the menu claims, memorable. Open 7.30am–10pm, meals noon–3pm & 6.30–10pm.

Vyas Meals, in the fort by the handicraft shops on the way to the Jain temples. Small, unpretentious place run by an elderly couple who do superb home-style veg thalis and snacks at unbeatable prices. Eat in or takeaway. Open 10am–10pm.

Around Jaisalmer

The sandy, barren terrain around Jaisalmer harbours some unexpected monuments, dating from the Rajput era when this area lay on busy caravan routes.

Infrequent buses negotiate the dusty roads, and you can rent a Jeep through RTDC, who also offer inexpensive day-trip **tours** to the main sights, but the best way to visit these places, and see villages and abandoned towns inaccessible by road, is on a camel trek (see p.236). Being close to the Pakistani border, the area west of Highway NH-15 is a **restricted area**. Tourists are allowed to visit Amar Sagar, Sam, Bada Bagh, Lodurva, Akal fossil park, Khuri, Rampunda and Kuldera without a permit, but if you want to go anywhere beyond those places, you should apply to the District Magistrate's Office just west of the private bus stand in Jaisalmer (Mon–Fri & sometimes Sat 10am–5pm). On the few camel treks where this is necessary, however, the organizers will usually get permits for you.

Amar Sagar, Sam and Barra Bagh

A short distance northwest of Jaisalmer, **AMAR SAGAR** is a small peaceful town set around a large lake (empty during the dry season). A former palace and large complex of Jain temples, recently restored to their former magnificence, stand on the lake edges.

The huge, rolling sand dunes 40km west of Jaisalmer are known as **SAM**, though strictly this is the name of a small village further west. The dunes are so famous in Rajasthan that most tourists don't realize that there are others throughout the desert; consequently they have become a prime attraction. There's even an RTDC tourist bungalow, the *Hotel Sam Dhani* (☎02922/52392; ❸), bookable through the RTDC *Moomal Tourist Bungalow* in Jaisalmer, but given the inexorable advance rate of the dunes, it will probably be buried by sand within the next decade. Sunset at Sam can be breathtaking, though drink-sellers, musicians, piles of plastic rubbish and numerous camel trains and bus parties somewhat dilute the romance. The undulating sandscape also looks spectacular at sunrise, so it's worth sleeping the night here if you're on a camel safari. A **bus** does run to Sam, but it doesn't return until the next day. Those visitors who aren't travelling on camels usually make the journey by Jeep.

Six kilometres north of Jaisalmer, in the fertile area of **Barra Bagh**, a collection of cenotaphs built in memory of Jaisalmer's rulers stand clustered on a hill.

The lovers of Lodurva

Lodurva is the scene of Rajasthan's answer to *Romeo and Juliet*, the story of **Moomal** and **Mahendra**. Moomal was a princess whose legendary beauty brought her many suitors, none of whom succeeded in gaining her affections, until the handsome Prince Mahendra, with the aid of Moomal's maid, was able to reach her bedroom and win her heart. Every night he visited her, and in the morning he left. One day Moomal's sister, who was dying to meet him, persuaded Moomal to let her attend the bedchamber disguised as a minstrel. That night however, Mahendra's wives, suspicious of his absence, kept him from leaving, and he didn't arrive at Moomal's until dawn. On finding her asleep in bed with a minstrel boy, he stormed out in disgust, and in the months that followed, though ill from grief, refused to so much as open her letters. Finally, Moomal disguised herself as a man and set out to find him. She eventually tracked him down and, joining him in a game of *chokar* (a board game), noticed that he was crying and asked him why. "It's the birthmark on your hand", he explained, "it reminds me of my lost true love". Revealing her identity, Moomal explained to Mahendra what had happened, and they fell into each others' arms. But alas, it was too much for them, and they both died there and then from the emotion of it all. Scant remains of Moomal's palace can still be seen by the bank of the River Kak, which they say has never flowed since that day.

Domed roofs shade small marble or sandstone slabs bearing inscriptions and equestrian statues. The green oasis below is where most of the fruit and vegetables of the region used to be grown – a surreal sight amid the hostile waste of sand and scrub.

Lodurva

Another 10km north of Bada Bagh, **LODURVA** was the capital of the Bhatti rulers until the foundation of Jaisalmer in the twelfth century. Of the city's fine buildings, only a few **Jain temples**, rebuilt in the 1970s, remain (8am–6pm; Rs40 extra for camera, Rs75 extra for video). The *toran* (archway) at the entrance to the temple compound is the most exquisite in the Jaisalmer area. The main structure has detailed tracery work in the stone walls and a finely carved exterior. A smaller temple, built on a series of diminishing square platforms, stands to its right.

Akal Fossil park

The scattered remains of Jurassic tree fossils up to 180 million years old in the **fossil park**, 17km south of Jaisalmer (daily: Nov–Feb 8am–5pm; March–Oct 8am–6pm) are of interest only to the most avid paleobotanists. Eighteen trees, none of them standing, and most of them pretty shattered, lie around the site. Buses to Barmer pass through, but for a quicker visit it's best to take a Jeep, which costs about Rs300 for the round trip.

Khuhri

Though most camel treks start in Jaisalmer, a handful of travellers prefer to begin their safari out in the desert at the village of **KHUHRI**, just 1km from the dunes. It can be reached on three daily buses (90min) from the local bus stand in Jaisalmer. The village harbours a handful of basic guesthouses. The oldest is *Mama's* (☏02992/9267 5423; ❸–❻), which offers overpriced "traditional" huts with common bathrooms or plainer, cheaper rooms for Rs325. *Khuri Guest House* (☏02992/75444; ❷–❸), near the bus stand, is a better budget option, offering shared or en-suite shower-toilets. This is one of the most accessible places in the region to see traditional **desert architecture**. Many of the houses are still made of mud and thatch instead of concrete, and their exterior surfaces are beautifully decorated with ornate white murals. If you're lucky enough to be invited inside one, you'll see some superb moulded mud shelves and fireplaces, inlaid with mica- and mirror work.

Barmer

BARMER, 158km south of Jaisalmer, is another important desert outpost, but has little to offer tourists. It's usually a dusty backwater, where the manufacture of **handicrafts**, its main export, occupies much of the population. In January however, the place is transformed during the hectic **Tilwara Cattle Fair**, held on the banks of a saltwater river nearby. This is the largest cattle market in Rajasthan, attended by villagers and traders from all over the state.

Accommodation and **food** stalls in Barmer are scarce; if you need to stay the night, try the basic *Krishna Hotel* (☏02982/20785; ❸–❺) near the railway station, or the rather better *Hotel Kailash Sarowar* (☏02982/20730; ❷–❹). The best accommodation in town, however, is RTDC's *Khartal* tourist bunglaow (☏02982/22956; ❹), which has just four rooms.

Buses run to Barmer from Jaisalmer (hourly; 3hr), and there are two expresses (5hr) and a passenger train (7hr) from Jodhpur.

Pokaran

POKARAN, with its red-sandstone fort and superb *havelis*, is a quiet, seldom-visited desert town 110km east of Jaisalmer, situated at the road and rail junctions between Jodhpur, Bikaner and the west. Once included in the territory of Jodhpur, it passed into the huge state of Jaisalmer after Independence. Pokaran became the unlikely object of world attention in

The Pokaran N-tests

At around 3.45pm on May 11, 1998, three massive explosions erupted 200m beneath the sands of Thar Desert, 20km northwest of Pokaran. Villagers in the area felt the ground sway under their feet as a cloud of mysterious brown dust blew through their settlements, only a stone's throw north of the main Bikaner–Jaisalmer highway. The bombs were small by modern standards – 20 kilotonnes, Hiroshima-sized – but their political shockwaves resounded from western Rajasthan to Islamabad, Beijing and Washington. By May 13, after two more detonations, India's transition from so-called "threshold state" to fully fledged atomic power was complete. As one British expert commented, Delhi now had the capacity to "put a sizeable crater in the centre of Lahore".

The nuclear tests at the Pokaran Range were hailed by India's vehemently anti-Pak press as "A Moment of Pride" and "The Road to Resurgence". Celebratory fireworks lit the skies of the capital, and some fanatical BJP workers announced they were beginning a pilgrimage to the test site to collect dust in ceremonial urns, which would be blessed in a nearby temple and distributed throughout Rajasthan.

The widespread euphoria, however, temporarily faltered when the scale of the international outcry became apparent. Caught completely unawares by the explosions (the CIA officials charged with monitoring India's nuclear programme were reportedly asleep when the satellite pictures came in), the US immediately announced that it was suspending all aid to India, and recommended a freeze in IMF and World Bank loans. Sanctions were opposed by Japan, the UK and other EU countries, but the American threats alone were enough to sober up the Delhi government, which owes \$40 billion to the US, and had been promised a further \$3 billion in aid that year.

Despite government assurances that the timing of the N-tests was purely a matter of foreign policy, the Pokaran explosions were widely interpreted as a response to the internal wrangling that had paralysed prime minister Vajpayee's beleagured BJP coalition since it came to power the previous March. Encouraged by his shadowy backers, the RSS (a grass-roots Hindu extremist organization), Vajpayee hoped the nuclear card would restore confidence in his rule and bring the regional parties on side. But the barely disguised triumphalism that followed the Pokaran tests evaporated two weeks later when Pakistan detonated its own thermo-nuclear devices. India was suddenly locked into a spiralling nuclear arms race in one of the most geopolitically sensitive parts of the world. The rupee took a severe tumble, plummeting to an all-time low against the dollar, as did tourist bookings.

Yet within India, few dissenting voices were heard. Among the only high-profile critics of the government was Booker-prize winner Arundhati Roy, who, comparing India's pride at the tests with its track record on tackling poverty, wrote in *Frontline* and *Outlook*: "For India to demand the status of a superpower is as ridiculous as demanding to play in the World Cup finals simply because we have a ball. Never mind that we haven't qualified, or that we don't play much soccer and haven't got a team." Lesser known opponents of the N-tests are to be found in the villages surrounding the site of the explosions, where hundreds of poor farmers and their families have fallen ill since May. Official doctors visiting the scene claim the sudden outbreak of sickness was caused by "the high summer temperatures".

May 1998, when five nuclear bombs were detonated at the army test range 20km northwest of town (see box on p.241). Previously, a few tourists used to stop here en route to or from Jaisalmer, but despite the Indian government's insistence that there has been no ground-water contamination, most wisely stay on the bus these days, and hope the dust blowing through the windows isn't radioactive.

Phalodi and Keechen

The main highway and broad-gauge train wind in tandem east from Jaisalmer across the desert, separating at the small junction settlement of **PHALODI**, almost exactly midway between Jaisalmer and Bikaner. This scruffy salt-extraction colony would be entirely forgettable were it not the jumping-off place for one of Rajasthan's most beautiful natural sights. Sheltered by a swathe of soft yellow dunes, the village of **Keechen**, 4km further east on the opposite side of the main road, hosts a 7000-strong flock of **demoiselle cranes** (*Anthropoides virgo*), who migrate here each winter from their breeding grounds on the Central Asian steppes. Known locally as *kurja*, the birds are encouraged to return by the villagers, who scatter specially donated grain for them to feed on twice each day – a custom which has persisted for 150 years or more. At feeding times (6.30am & 3.30–4pm), the flock descends en masse on a football-pitch-sized patch of level ground just outside the village, where you can watch and photograph them at close quarters. Should you arrive in the middle of the day, head into the nearby dunes, being careful not to scare the birds, or pick your way north through the village to the small reservoir where thousands of cranes congregate between feeds. Watching them circle in noisy, undulating formations overhead, or stepping gingerly across the sands, has to be one of the great spectacles of the Thar region, and you shouldn't miss the chance to call here if you're passing.

From Phalodi, the best way to get to Keechen is to rent a bicycle from one of the stalls near the bus stand – a pleasant, mostly flat four-kilometre ride on well-surfaced roads. Alternatively, jump in a Jeep for Rs100; Ambassador taxis queue outside the railway station. If you want to store gear while you're crane-watching, ask at the *Hotel Chetnya Palace* (℗02925/23945; ❷–❹), next to the bus stand, which has **left-luggage lockers** in a rear-side dorm. The Rs25 fee will entitle you to a bed in the same room, but they also have more comfortable en-suite rooms for Rs150–300, the pricier ones with air coolers. The hotel's bright, clean **restaurant** at the front of the building is the most hygienic place in town to **eat**, serving inexpensive *parathas* and rice-plate vegetarian meals to order, as well as the usual hot and cold drinks. If you're only stopping for a couple of hours en route to or from Jaisalmer, **check bus times** before you head off to Keechen, as services can be sporadic.

Bikaner and around

The commercial city of **BIKANER** may not quite possess the aesthetic attraction of its more venerable neighbour, Jaisalmer, over 300km southwest, but it does boast a spectacular fort and an old city dotted with *havelis* and surrounded by 7km of high walls. In addition, simply because Rajasthan's fourth largest city receives fewer visitors than other major settlements, it has a certain unspoilt feel. Most foreign tourists only spend one night here en route to

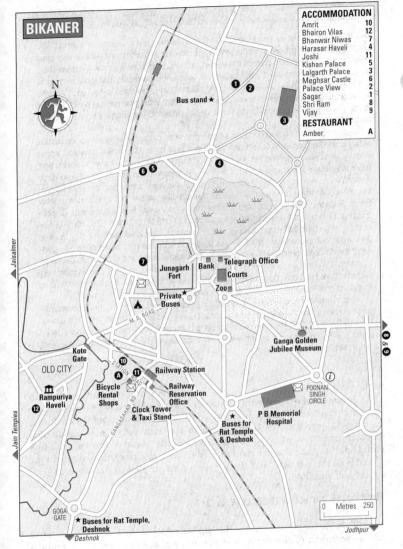

ACCOMMODATION

Amrit	10
Bhairon Vilas	12
Bhanwar Niwas	7
Harasar Haveli	4
Joshi	11
Kishan Palace	5
Lalgarth Palace	3
Meghsar Castle	6
Palace View	2
Sagar	1
Shri Ram	8
Vijay	9

RESTAURANT

Amber	A

or from Jaisalmer, but extend your stay and you can visit the famous **rat temple** at nearby Deshnok, and the government **camel-breeding farm**, 10km south.

The city was founded in 1486 as a link in the overland trading route, by **Bika**, one of fourteen sons of Rao Jodha, the Rathore king who established Jodhpur as the centre of the state of Marwar. Two emissaries he had sent in search of a site for his new capital had met a shepherd called Ner (whence the town's name) who claimed to have watched one of his sheep fend off seven wolves under a *khair* bush; the spot was selected in the belief it would inspire courage

Camel safaris from Bikaner

Camel treks are not as established in Bikaner as they are in Jaisalmer (see p.236), but the growing numbers of visitors who opt for a safari from here are invariably glad they did so. This eastern part of the desert, while just as scenic as the western Thar, is not nearly as congested with fellow trekkers, with the result that local people in the villages along the route are genuinely pleased and surprised to see you. Wildlife in the area is also abundant, and during a three-day safari you can be pretty sure of spotting demoiselle cranes, black buck, *nilgai*, desert foxes, monitor lizards and the odd chameleon.

When it comes to finding and booking an operator, the same advice applies as that outlined in the Camel Safaris from Jaisalmer box on p.236: make sure you know exactly what you're getting for your money, down to the food they plan to serve, and have the details listed in a contract before you part with any cash. You'll also have a much more rewarding time if your guide speaks at least a little English – not always the case. Currently offering the best all-round value safaris out of Bikaner is Vijay Singh Rathore (aka "Camel Man"), based at *Vijay Guest House* (opposite Sophia School), 5km out of town along the Jaipur road (℗0151/231244, ℗525150). His itineraries range from half-day trips and village visits to full-blown fourteen-day treks to Jaislamer, complete with camel cart to transport luggage and crash out on (a godsend for novices) and, when within range of Bikaner, fresh ice and drinks delivered to camp by Jeep each evening. The food is also varied and his camel men very experienced. His basic daily rate, which includes all meals, mattresses and travel to and from starting and finishing points, is around Rs450.

Other dependable operators in a similar price bracket, and who get consistently good reviews from readers, include Vino Desert Safari, opposite the Gopeshwar temple (℗0151/270445, ℗www.vinodesertsafari.com), and the improbably named Bubble's Safaris, based at the *Hotel Harasar Haveli* (℗0151/209891, ℗525150, ℗harasar_haveli@yahoo.com).

---

in the people who lived there. Under Rai Singh, who came to the throne in 1573, **Junagarh Fort** was built and closer ties were forged with the Moghuls; Rai Singh gave his daughter in marriage to one of Akbar's sons. Later, during the fifty-six-year reign of Ganga Singh in the early 1900s, new agricultural schemes, irrigation work, town planning and the construction of a rail link with Delhi helped Bikaner's economic advance; it has long since outgrown the confines of the city wall, and the population has tripled in size since 1947 to almost half a million.

Arrival and information

Rickshaws ply the route between the **bus stand**, opposite Lalgarh Palace a few kilometres north of the centre, and the south of town, where you'll find the railway station and most hotels. The very helpful **tourist office** (daily 10am–5pm; ℗0151/544125 or 1913) is in the RTDC *Dholamaru Hotel* at Pooran Singh Circle. For trips around town, use any of the cycle or auto-rickshaws, or rent a bike; you'll find two **cycle rental shops** outside the **post office** on Station Road. **Travellers' cheques** can be changed at the State Bank of Bikaner and Jaipur (Mon–Fri 10am–2.30pm) opposite the entrance to the fort. Booths have opened up all over town offering **internet access**, but the best equipped cybercafé is behind the *Amber Restaurant* on Station Road. If you're staying at the *Shri Ram* or somewhere else in the east of the centre, head for Cyber City at A-52 Sadul Ganj.

Accommodation

Bikaner boasts a surprisingly good selection of **hotels**, with plenty of choice in all price ranges. The only area to avoid if you can help it is the one outside the railway station, which – unlike most of the town – is unpleasantly congested and polluted.

Amrit, Station Road ☏0151/544451. Standard lodge very near the station. Clean enough, but cramped and often full with Jaisalmer-bound backpackers. ❷–❹

Bhairon Vilas, next to Lalgarh Fort ☏&℻0151/544751, ℗www.hbhaironvilas.tripod.com. Terracotta and ochre-coloured *haveli* overlooking the fort, owned by maharaja's younger brother and now a typical Rajput heritage hotel, with antiques and family curios adding period atmosphere. Rooms #109 & 110 have best views. ❽

Bhanwar Niwas, old city ☏0151/201043 or 529323, ℻200830, ℗sunilrampuri@usa.net. Bikaner's most ostentatious *haveli*, originally built for a textile tycoon in the late 1920s and now run as an independent heritage hotel. Crammed with original fittings and furniture, it's a kitsch period piece, complete with Italian tiles and a vintage car in the lobby. Vegetarian café-restaurant open to nonresidents. Rs3600 per double room. ❾

Harasar Haveli, near Karni Singh Stadium ☏0151/209891, ℻525150, ℗harasar_haveli@yahoo.com. Comfortable, clean and airy rooms (the "standard" ones are best value) in a large new purpose-built block overlooking the stadium. Great views from rooftop terrace restaurant. ❸–❺

Joshi, Station Road ☏0151/527700. Smartest in this pretty grim area. Clean carpeted rooms, some a/c. ❹–❻

Kishan Palace, 8-B Gajner Jaisalmer Rd ☏0151/527762, ℻522041. Impeccably clean budget guesthouse on the main highway, west of the centre. A far better option than anywhere outside the station, and with lower rates and a nice garden. ❶–❸

Lalgarh Palace ☏0151/540201–8, ℻522253, ℗gm.bikaner@itchotels.co.in. This huge maharaja's palace, one of India's most opulent heritage hotels, perfectly preserves the dowdy feel of the interwar years, with old photos, hunting trophies and a billiards room. The tariffs are phenomenally expensive for walk-in clients, but it's worth coming for coffee. Room #20 is the nicest. ❾

Meghsar Castle, 9 Gajner Rd ☏0151/527315, ℻522041, ℗meghsarcastle@yahoo.com. Pleasant mid-scale hotel on the main Jaisalmer road, just north of city centre. Hospitable owner, fresh food, quiet rear garden and good-value rates, although too close to the highway for a long stay (you can ask to be dropped off here if arriving by bus from Jaisalmer). ❹–❺

Palace View, Lalgarh Palace Campus ☏0151/543625, ℻522741. An excellent choice at this price: spotless rooms (ask for one on the upper floor with views of the palace from the veranda), good food and a friendly family. Close to the bus stand. ❹–❻

Sagar, Lalgarh Palace Campus ☏0151/520677, ℻201877, ℗hsagar@nda.vsnl.net.in. Modern hotel, attractively designed in local Dholpur colours, and with well-appointed rooms, including (cheaper) Rajasthani round houses in the rear garden. Restaurant, foreign exchange and credit cards accepted. Very near the bus stand. ❺–❻

Shri Ram, Sadul Ganj, 500m east of the tourist office ☏0151/522651 or 521320, ℻209181. Respectable suburban guesthouse with a range of comfortable en-suite rooms, from large sunny ones on the roof to smaller options out the back. This place gets rave reviews, primarily for its hospitable owner, a retired brigadier who's an authority on local history and culture. The food is excellent, too, and they keep a stock of chilled beers. ❷–❻

Vijay, opposite Sophia School, 5km east of centre along the Jaipur Highway ☏0151/529344. Slightly eccentric, pleasantly scruffy but very cheap family guesthouse that's geared for overlanders. Some rooms are huge; all have attached shower-toilets; and there's camping/parking space. Free cycle or scooters on request. ❶–❸

The City

It's worth spending a day or two just wandering around Bikaner, watching dyers at work, visiting the ancient **Jain temples**, and exploring **Junagarh Fort**. Bikaner is also famous for its skilled lacquer work and handicrafts, sold in the bazaar for a fraction of Jaisalmer's inflated "tourist prices", and for its hand-woven woollen shawls and blankets. The best place to buy the latter is the **Abhivyakti** shop just inside the main gate of the fort.

Junagarh Fort

Built on ground level, defended only by high walls and a wide moat, **Junagarh Fort** (daily except Fri 10am–4.30pm; Rs50, Rs50 extra for camera, Rs100 extra for video) is not as immediately imposing as the mighty hill forts elsewhere in Rajasthan. But the decorative interiors and sculpted stone of the palaces, temples and 37 pavilions within its walls are almost unrivalled in their magnificence. Outside the main gate, a barrage of "guides" offer their services, but you can ignore them as a guided tour is included in fort admission.

The fort was built between 1587 and 1593, during the rule of Rai Singh, and later rulers added their own palatial suites, temples and plush courtyards. Although never conquered, the bastion was attacked – handprints set in stone near the second gate, **Daulat Pole**, bear witness to the voluntary deaths of royal women, remembered as *satis*, whose menfolk had lost their lives in battle.

Opening onto the main courtyard, the **Karan Mahal**, with gold-leaf paintings adorning its pillars and walls, was built in the seventeenth century to commemorate a victory over the Moghul emperor Aurangzeb, while the dazzling **Phool Mahal** was erected by Gaj Singh, a hundred years later. Stained-glass windows, finely carved stone and wood balconies, and brightly painted walls and ceilings around the fort demonstrate the extravagant tastes of these rulers. The **Anup Mahal** is the grandest construction, with wooden ceilings inlaid with mirrors, Italian tiles and delicate latticework on the windows and balconies. The huge carpet is one of many made by inmates of Bikaner jail, a manufacturing tradition that has only recently ceased. At some point in the tour, your guide may offer to unlock the door of the **Chandra Mahal**, normally out of bounds to visitors. Don't let the demands for baksheesh put you off; this is the most opulent room in the fort, filled with gilded deities and precious-stone encrusted paintings.

The tour generally winds up in the huge **Ganga Singh Hall**. The most recent part of the fort, dating from 1937, it houses part of the **museum**, whose exhibits include the inevitable weaponry and an unexpected World War II aeroplane, still in tip-top condition.

The old city

Kote Gate at the west end of MG Road is the main entrance through the high walls into Bikaner's atmospheric **old city**. The main attractions here are some extraordinary **havelis** whose idiosyncratic architecture is an unlikely fusion of indigenous sandstone carving with turn-of-the-twentieth century red-brick

Abhivyakti

The rulers of Bikaner have always objected to commercial exploitation of their heritage, and have therefore forbidden traders to set up shop in the fort. However, the royal principles have been relaxed for a good cause in the case of a handicrafts shop, Abhivyakti, inside the main fort gate. Abhivyakti was established with the aid of funding from the local Urmul Trust and from Oxfam in England. The high-quality rugs, bags, clothes, cushion-covers, shawls and stools sold here are made in 150 villages around Bikaner. In the past, all proceeds from sales of these unique handicrafts went directly to the villagers who produced them. Sadly, it seems that these days the dark hand of the commission racket is at work, with rickshaw-wallahs and middlemen routinely taking their cut.

municipal Britain. Adorned with busts of the British king and queen emperors, the most impressive specimens stand in the heart of the old city; ask for **Rampuriya Haveli**, or the more famous **Bhanwar Niwas Haveli**, further down the same street, which was built in 1927 for the heir to a vast textile and real estate fortune, and is now a plush hotel (see Accommodation, p.245).

Continue south past Barra Bazaar towards the southeast corner of the old city, and you'll eventually reach Bikaner's two **Jain temples** (daily 7am–1pm & 5–8pm). Built by two merchant brothers, both are remarkable for the sheer mass of colour and intricate wall paintings. The ground floor of **Bhandreshwar temple** (1571) has a cluster of pillars; some are decorated with gilded floral designs known as *usta* typical of Muslim artisans, others with embossed male and female sculptures common in medieval India. A statue of Lord Suminath, the fifth *tirthankara*, stands on the second floor. Steps lead up the tower, from where you get a great view over the old city. **Sandeshwar temple**, dedicated to Neminath (the 22nd *tirthankara*) and dated to 1536, houses rows of saints shaped from solid marble, and has enamel and gold-leaf paintings on the walls.

The sixteenth-century **Laxminath temple** nearby was built by Lunkaran Singh, the third ruler of Bikaner, on the edge of the high city wall. It overlooks a Muslim community of dyers and screen printers, with the barren desert in the distance.

Lalgarh Palace and Ganga Golden Jubilee Museum

The sturdy red-sandstone **Lalgarh Palace** in the north of the town is home to the royal family of Bikaner, although parts now serve as a hotel. It was built during the reign of Ganga Singh, who lived there from 1902, using the fort only for private business, and despite some detailed carving, its modern aspect makes it fairly ugly in comparison to other Rajasthani palaces. The **Shri Sadul Museum** (Mon–Sat 10am–5pm; Rs20) houses an enormous collection of old photographs showing various viceregal visits and royal processions that will fascinate any Rajophiles. If you've time, also worth a look is the **Anup Sanskrit Library** (same hours; free) which has a small selection of unique and well-preserved manuscripts, parchments and engraved copper, plus gold and silver plaques.

The small **Ganga Golden Jubilee Museum** (daily except Fri 10am–4.30pm; Rs3) on NH-8 not far from the *Dhola Maru Hotel* contains a moderately interesting display of costumes, weapons, ornaments, ancient statues and paintings, one of which depicts the signing of the Versailles Treaty by Ganga Singh. Older exhibits include terracottas from the Gupta period (fourth and fifth centuries)

Eating

Most visitors eat at their hotels or guesthouses while in Bikaner. If you fancy eating out, try *Harasar Haveli*, which is a popular meeting place for Western travellers and has the best rooftop views.

Amber, Station Road. A cleaner than average (although somewhat dingy) thali house that's popular with Westerners. Full veg menu and refreshing masala chai.

Harasar Haveli, near Karni Singh Stadium. Open-air rooftop terrace restaurant with panoramic views, top *tandoori* and non-veg Mughlai food and cold beers.

Joshi, Station Road. The most salubrious of the eating places near the station. Filling, cheap rice-plate meals and arguably the town's best-value thalis, served in a busy ground-floor restaurant (12.30–3pm & 7.30–10pm); also recommended for *paratha*-curd breakfasts, from 6am.

Mehfil, *Bhanwar Niwas Hotel*, old city. Sumptuous veg food stylishly served in evocative fin-de-siècle surroundings. Have a nose around the hotel while you're there. Around Rs200–250 per head.

Moving on from Bikaner

RSTRC buses operate out of the main bus stand on the north side of town. **Private buses** leave from MG Road, just below the fort. **Trains** include three to Delhi Sarai Rohilla (two by night, one by day; 10hr 30min) via Churu (4hr). Services to Jaipur include the fast early-morning Intercity Express #2467 (7hr 30min) and the slow overnight Bikaner–Jaipur Express #4738 (10hr 30min). The latter also serves Churu, Fatehpur and Sikar. The best train to Jodhpur is the Kalka Express #4887, leaving around midday.

Around Bikaner

Several places of interest close to Bikaner can be visited in a day. The most unusual are the **camel-breeding farm** and **Karni Mata temple**, a scurrying mass of sacred rats.

The Deshnok Devi

Regarded by Hindus as one of India's most potent *shakti* shrines, the Karni Mata temple at Deshnok is unusual for being dedicated not to a conventional Puranic deity, but to a historical figure. Karniji was a female bard – a *Charani* – born into a wealthy landowning family at a village near Phalodi in 1387. Traditionally poets and court chroniclers, members of the *Charan* caste believe that incarnations of the goddess Durga periodically appear among them. One kind, known as *sagats*, feature in each generation and are blessed with healing powers (there are currently three of these in Rajasthan); the other, more powerful and charismatic *purn avatars*, are said to emerge only in times of crisis. From birth, Karni exhibited many of the traits associated with this latter, messianic incarnation of the *devi*. The seventh successive daughter in her family, she was dark, incredibly tough and ugly, and possessed miraculous powers, reputedly fusing the fingers of her aunt's hand together after she expressed disappointment at the birth of another baby girl.

In spite of performing such miracles as water divination and bringing the dead back to life, her family insisted Karniji marry instead of following the path of celibacy essential for *purn avatars*. However, she was able to avoid consummating her marriage by turning herself into a lion on her wedding night (and by having her sister marry her husband at the same time) and soon went on to become the region's most powerful cult leader, worshipped primarily by the Jats and low-caste farmers.

The rise in Karniji's popularity, dating from her family's move north to Deshnok, mirrored that of the Rathore clan, whose constant raids were causing great instability in the region at the end of the fourteenth century. Rao Bika, the founder of Bikaner, realized that he and the Deshnok *devi* could forge a formidable alliance, and wooed her during repeated pilgrimages with promises of tax exemptions and tutelary deity status if she gave his clan her stamp of approval. When her eventual endorsement came it turned Bika's fortunes, quadrupling the size of his army. After he finally defeated the local warlords, Karniji was accorded the honour of laying the foundation stone of Junagarh fort, and Bika regularly consulted her throughout his reign – a connection with the ruling family that has endured to this day. The Bikaner flag sports Karniji's colours, and she is the patron goddess of the Bikaner camel corps, who still march into battle crying "Shree Karniji!". The *devi*'s intercession is also believed to have spared members of the 19th Rajputs, which included Bikaner soldiers, from being massacred in the storming of the Golden Temple in 1984, when the unenviable task of spearheading the assault on the Sikh's holiest shrine was given to another regiment at the last minute.

What is probably Asia's largest camel-breeding farm (Mon–Fri 3–5pm) lies out in the desert 10km south of Bikaner, an easy round trip by rickshaw that should cost around Rs60 (including waiting time of 30min). Although Bikaner has long been renowned for its famously sturdy beasts, and the camel corps was a much-feared component of the imperial battle formation, the farm itself was only founded in 1975. Its propagation programme has been so successful that it now provides fifty percent of India's camels, hundreds of whom, young and old, can be seen strutting their knock-kneed way across the sands.

Devotees at the unique Karni Mata temple (daily 7am–9pm; free; Rs20 extra for camera, Rs50 extra for video) in **Deshnok**, 30km south of Bikaner, believe that departing souls are saved from the wrath of Yama, the god of death, by being reincarnated as **rats**. Teeming hordes of free-roaming holy rodents, known as *kabas*, are accordingly worshipped and fed by visitors; the experience of having one run over your feet is considered a great privilege, but don't whatever you do tread on one or you'll have to donate a gold model of a rat to placate the deity. It is also deemed auspicious to eat *prasad* (blessed food from the main shrine) after it has been nibbled by the *kabas*.

Made of rough stone and logs cut from sacred *jal* trees, the rustic innermost shrine housing the yellow-marble image (*pratima*) of Karniji is encased by a much grander marble building erected by Bika Rao's grandson after he defeated the Moghuls. It is entered through a stunning set of solid silver doors, donated by Maharaja Ganga Singh, the penultimate ruler of Bikaner. Other shrines in the complex are dedicated to Manu Bhai (Karni's grandaughter); and, to the right of the main entrance, Deshrath Meghwat, a shepherd boy who was killed protecting Karni's cattle.

To get to Deshnok by **bus from Bikaner**, wait at the southwest exit of the large roundabout near the PB Memorial Hospital, or at Goga Gate Circle, just outside the southeast corner of the old city.

Mount Abu

Rajasthan's ruling caste, the "twice-born" Rajputs, trace their mythological origins back to a powerful fire ceremony, or *yagna agnikund*, conducted by the sage Vashista after the fall of the Gupta empire in the eighth century AD. The ritual is believed to have taken place at the top of a huge rocky massif in the southwest corner of the state, near the present-day border with Gujarat. More than a thousand years later, the British, attracted by the same outcrop's cool air and clear light, founded a sanitarium on the high plateau at its centre. Thereafter, **MOUNT ABU** became a permanent hot-season retreat for the region's maharajas, who built summer palaces that made the most of the views and cooling breezes. As the state's only bona fide hill station, the town, sprawling over the sides of a wooded basin, remains a major resort, popular above all with **honeymooners**, who flock here during the winter wedding season to smooch around in woolly jumpers and unflattering hats while they get to know each other.

Among foreign tourists, opinion tends to be divided as to whether or not Mount Abu merits a visit. While some welcome the fresh air, panoramic views over the plains and good food on offer at the many restaurants, others find the tacky middle-class Indian holiday culture less than relaxing. One sight, however, tips the scales – at least for art and history buffs. Hidden in

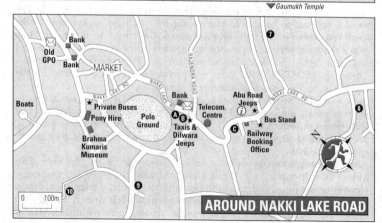

MOUNT ABU

Achalgarh & Guru Shikar

Dilwara Temples

Adhar Devi Temple

DILWARA ROAD

PILGRIM ROAD

①

The Crags

CRAGS ROAD

Anadhra-Ganesh Temple

Honeymoon Point

②

Om Shanti Bhawan
③

SUBHASH ROAD

④

State Museum

⑤ ⑥

Nakki Lake

St Lawrence

Nilkanth Temple

Toad Rock

Raghunath Temple

RAJENDRA ROAD

PILGRIM ROAD

Sunset Point

See inset map

NAKKI LAKE RD

Polo Ground

Bus Stand

LAKE RESIDENCY

Abu Road (28 km)

ACCOMMODATION
Cama Rajputana	2
Chandravati Palace	7
Connaught House	6
Hillock	8
Kesar Bhavan Palace	9
Lake Residency	3
Mount Hotel	4
Palace Hotel	1
Shree Ganesh	10
Sudhir	5

RESTAURANTS
Jodhpur Bhojnalaya	B
Kanak Dining Hall	C
Veena	A

0   Metres   500

Gaumukh Temple

AROUND NAKKI LAKE ROAD

Bank

Old GPO

Bank

MARKET

⑦

RAJENDRA ROAD

Boats

Private Buses

Pony Hire

Polo Ground

Bank

Telecom. Centre

NAKKI LAKE RD

Abu Road Jeeps

ⓘ

NAKKI LAKE RD

⑧

Ⓐ Ⓑ

Taxis & Dilwara Jeeps

Ⓒ

Bus Stand

Brahma Kumaris Museum

Railway Booking Office

⑨

⑩

0   100m

thick woodland north of the town, the **Jain temples** at **Dilwara** are architectural gems, decorated with what is thought to be the most intricate marble carving in the world. Anyone happy to rock hop and follow unmarked trails will also find plenty of scope for **hikes** and scrambles amid the granite boulders and wooded ridges high above the town, where dozens of tiny caves, connected by a tangle of dirt paths, shelter a transient community of semi-nomadic, *chillum*-smoking *sadhus* – a reminder of the area's great religious importance.

According to Hindu mythology, the focal point of Mount Abu, **Nakki Lake**, was formed when the gods scratched away at the mountain with their fingernails (*nakh*). These days, the waterside is cluttered by far more pedalos and ice-cream parlours than pilgrims, but the temple marking the site of the famous *yagna agnikund* at Gaumukh, 3km north of Mount Abu on the road up from the plains, still sees streams of devotees. In addition, around Mount Abu itself you'll come across many white-clad **Brahma Kumaris**, members of an international spiritual movement whose headquarters are situated in a quiet valley behind the lake.

In order to get the most benefit from Mount Abu's scenery and climate, it's essential to **time your visit** carefully. Bear in mind that during the peak months of April–June, and almost any major festival time (especially Diwali in November) the place is heaving. Room rates double, or triple, and peace and quiet is at a premium.

Arrival and information

Mount Abu is accessible only by road. Aim to spend as little time as possible in the grim bazaar town of **Abu Road**, the nearest railhead, where travellers pick up buses for the forty-five-minute ascent from the plains. Entering Mount Abu itself, you have to pay a Rs5 fee.

Passengers arriving at the main **bus stand** in the southeast of Mount Abu are swamped by hotel touts and would-be luggage porters pushing pram-like trolleys. Turn right to get to the more expensive hotels, such as the *Mount Regency*; left for the large central polo ground, the main bazaar, budget hotels and restaurants, and the lake (the road up the east side of the polo ground is the quickest route).

Details on local sights are available at the **tourist office**, opposite the main bus stand (Mon–Sat 10am–1.30pm & 2–5pm); they can also direct you to the best guides. To **change travellers' cheques** the best bet is the Union Bank of India, at the northern end of the bazaar behind the State Bank of India. The Bank of Baroda at the junction southeast of the polo ground gives cash against Visa or Mastercard. Next door to it stands the main **post office**.

Accommodation

The steady stream of pilgrims and honeymoon couples ensures that Mount Abu has plenty of **hotels**. Lots of them offer luxuries for newlyweds in special "couple rooms"; the *Samrat International*, for example, takes pride in its curtained four- or six-poster beds and deep marble bathtubs, and even boasts swings for two in some rooms. Though in **low season** you can live in stylish comfort for little more than you might otherwise pay for rock-bottom accommodation, prices rocket in **high season** (April–June & Nov–Dec), reaching their peak during Diwali (Oct & Nov). We have indicated below where the difference in seasonal rates is drastic.

Note that **checkout** time is usually 9am, and the flow of hot water can be sporadic.

Cama Rajputana, Dilwara Road ☏02974/38205–6, ☏38412. Grand colonial building recently converted into a sporty upscale hotel, with a pool, squash court, billiards room, gym and health club. ➑

Chandravati Palace, up the lane opposite the bus stand ☏02974/38219). Excellent little paying guesthouse, tucked away up a quiet side road. The rooms are impeccable, and have good-sized balconies and hill views. ➋–➌

Connaught House, Rajendra Road ☏02974/38560, ☏542240, ☏ welcom@ndf.vsnl.net.in. This former Maharaja of Jodhpur's bolthole is a typically British-era retreat, boasting cosy rooms in the building, or newer ones in the modern block above, with a sunny veranda, flowery garden and sweeping views. Its unique asset is the venerable octogenarian retainer, Takhur Barney Singh, who regails guests with tales of the Raj from his bench under an old mango tree. ➑

Hillock, Abu Road ☏02974/38463, ☏38467. Swish high-rise hotel with grounds like the ones in the fantasy posters you see in cheap lodges all over India. Carpeted rooms are immaculately clean, and provide great views over the Abu hills. Restaurant, bar, small pool and parking facilities. Good value at this price, with 50 percent off-peak discounts. ➏–➑

Kesar Bhavan Palace, Sunset Road ☏02974/38647. New-ish mid-scale place set behind the polo ground in a quiet location. The rooms are spacious and well furnished, and large individual sitouts have green views over the tree tops. ➎–➏

Lake Residency, near Arya Samaj Mandir ☏02974/43209. Charming little paying guest-house, with 4 bright, scrupulously clean rooms (2 triple-bed) tucked away in quiet spot near the lake. Gorgeous family, leafy garden (great for birders) and wholesome home cooking. ➋–➌

Mount Hotel, Dilwara Road ☏02974/43150. Charming former British *burrasahib*'s bungalow that has a lot of period charm, but somewhat ambitious tariffs, so be prepared to haggle.➎

Palace Hotel, Bikaner House ☏02974/38673, ☏38674. Half a kilometre before the Dilwara temples, the Maharaja of Bikaner's former summer palace has private lawns and tennis courts, plus its own lake. The rooms are tastefully furnished and have their own cosy little sitting rooms. Some discounts off-season. Easily the most elegant option in the area, though its friendly staff appear to have been trained in the Basil Fawlty school of hotel management. ➑–➒

Shree Ganesh, near Sophia High School ☏02974/43591 or 37292, ☏s_ganesh @datainfosys.net. Overlooked by the Maharaja of Jaipur's summer palace, this is the best-value budget hotel in town, with satellite TVs in rooms, cheap internet facility, hill views, in-house shop and home-cooked thalis served on a relaxing rooftop. They also offer complimentary guided walks and tours of Abu's temples. Geared primarily for foreign budget travellers. ➋–➌

Sudhir, opposite *Connaught House*, Rajendra Road ☏02974/43120 or 43311. Very good-value place above the bazaar. The best deals are the eight upper-floor rooms, facing west with separate balconies (ask for #208–213). Clean, spacious and efficient. ➌–➍

The Town

Mount Abu has a significant number of religious sites but all are some way out of town. Nearer the centre, **Nakki Lake** is where everyone converges in the late afternoon for pony and pedalo rides, and to dress up in fake peasant clothes to have their photos taken. Of several panoramic viewpoints on the fringes of town above the plains, **Sunset Point** is the favourite – with its hordes of holiday-makers, peanut sellers, camel drivers, cart pushers and horse owners, it has to be the noisiest and least romantic place imaginable to watch the sun sink over the horizon. **Honeymoon Point**, also known as Ganesh Point (after the adjacent temple), and Anadhra Point offer breathtaking views over the plain at any time of day, and tend to be more peaceful; 4pm is a good time to be there.

Dotted around the plateau outside town are several Hindu shrines and the spectacular Jain **Dilwara temples**. Forget the rushed tours touted by the tourist office and make your own way up there, allowing a good one or two hours to pick your way through the extraordinary wealth of intricate carving.

Dilwara temples

Jains consider temple building to be an act of devotion, and without fail their houses of worship are lovingly adorned and embellished, but even by Jain standards, the **Dilwara temples**, 3km northeast of Mount Abu (daily noon–6pm; free; no leather, cameras, transistors, tape recorders, or menstruating women), are some of the most beautiful in India. All five are made purely from marble, and the carving, especially in the two main structures, is breathtakingly intricate, unparalleled in its lightness and delicacy. Each little section stands on its own as a work of art, inspiring a stunned response from even the most temple-jaded tourists. For sheer aesthetic splendour, only the temples at Ranakpur 200km northwest (see p.268) come close.

The oldest temple, **Vimala Vasahi**, named after the Gujarati minister who funded its construction in 1031AD, is dedicated to Adinath, the first *tirthankara*, whose image sits cross-legged in the central sanctuary guarded by tall statues of Parshvanath (the 23rd *tirthankara*). Although the exterior is simple, inside not one wall, column or ceiling is unadorned; the work, carried out by almost 2000 labourers and sculptors, took fourteen years to complete. Eight of the forty-eight pillars in the front hall form an octagon that supports a domed ceiling arranged in eleven concentric circles, alive with dancers, musicians, elephants and horses. Within the sanctuary and the cloisters that surround it, small shrines, countless pillars, brackets and wall niches are imaginatively decorated, and each section of the roof is adorned.

The later **Neminath temple** (1231 AD) imitates that dedicated to Adinath, but its carvings are yet more precise and detailed. The large dome over the entrance hall is unprecedented. Friezes etched into the walls depict cosmological themes, stories of the *jinas* (saints) and grand processions. Sculptures near the entrance porch commemorate the temple's patrons, the two brothers Vastupala and Tejapala. Said in legend to have discovered a huge treasure, they were advised by their wives – also portrayed here – to build temples, and funded many on the holy hill of Shatrunjaya in Gujarat.

The remaining three fifteenth-century temples are less spectacular. Although the **Adinath templ**e – not to be confused with Vimala Vasahi – which houses a four-and-a-half-ton brass image of the *tirthankara*, has some fine carving, much of it unfinished; the one consecrated to Parshvanath has ornate ceilings and *jinas* etched into the outer walls, and is topped by a high grey stone tower.

To **get to Dilwara**, you can charter a Jeep (Rs50), or take a place in a shared one (Rs4), from the main junction at the southeastern end of Mount Abu's polo ground. The walk up there is also pleasant, though many prefer to save their energies for the downhill walk back into town.

Hindu temples

Beyond the Brahma Kumaris University, about 3km northeast of town, a flight of more than four hundred steps climbs up to **Adhar Devi temple** (dedicated to Durga), cut into the rocky hilltop. The milk-coloured water of the **Doodh Baori** well at the foot of the steps is considered to be a source of pure milk (*doodh*) for gods and sages.

A further 8km northeast, the temple complex at **ACHALGARH** is dominated by the **Achaleshwar Mahadeo** temple, believed to have been created

Brahma Kumaris

The spiritual sect **Brahma Kumaris** (children of Brahma) preach that all religions reach for the same goal, but label it differently. Based at about 5000 centres around the world they teach *raja* yoga – meditation that directs people to knowledge of an inner light, the "divine spark" or soul, that is part of, and one with, the all-encompassing soul, Shiva. Belief in the five evils – anger, ego, attachment, greed and lust – is shared with Buddhism and Hinduism, with the ultimate goal being their elimination, and the advent of a **Golden Age** of peace, prosperity and purity.

The **Brahma Kumaris Spiritual University** at **Om Shanti Bhawan** to the north of Nakki Lake (☎02974/38268) aims to foster awareness, tolerance, love and "God-consciousness" in a meditative atmosphere where smoking, alcohol, meat and sex are avoided. Classes range from three-day *raja* yoga camps to advanced six-month courses; lectures are translated into eighteen languages. The **Brahma Kumaris Museum** by the private bus stand between the polo ground and the lake (daily 8am–8pm; free) holds daily meditation classes.

when Lord Shiva placed his toe on the spot to still an earthquake. Its sanctuary holds neither an image of Shiva nor a *lingam*, only a *yoni* with a hole in it said to reach into the netherworld, watched over by figures of Parvati and Ganesh on the walls. Statues of Parvati flank the entrance, faced by an unusually large metal Nandi bull. Subsidiary shrines include one dedicated to Vishnu, in which detailed plaques depict the familiar reclining Vishnu and his nine incarnations. The large tank lined with stone buffaloes outside the temple, intended to contain purifying water, is the legendary scene of the slaying of demons disguised as buffaloes who stole purifying *ghee* from the tank. Nearby,

Hiking in Mount Abu

The views over the plains from the hilltops around Mount Abu town are a revelation. Down in the market area, you gain little sense of the wonderfully wild landscape enfolding the town, but head for a few minutes up one of the many trails threading through the rocks and undergrowth around the sides of the plateau, and it is easy to see why the area has inspired sages, saints and pilgrims for centuries.

In recent decades, the forest has been decimated by woodcutters, but a recently imposed, and strictly enforced, ban on wood gathering seems to be heralding a recovery. Abu's other environmental menace is the lantana plant. Introduced by the maharaja of Alwar early in the last century, this fragrant flowering weed has invaded most of the slopes, squeezing out many of the eighteen highly prized medicinal herbs listed as growing here in ancient Hindu scriptures. A standard way to occupy schoolkids from the town is to dispatch them into the hills on lantana weeding detail.

Also under pressure from the changing forest ecology have been fragile populations of bear and leopard. However, sightings of both are still not uncommon and you should take great care while trekking not to disturb any encountered along the trails. Bears, in particular, can be dangerous if surprised, or when with young. A couple of years back, two unwary French tourists were mauled during an evening scramble around the rocks above Nakki Lake. Menstruating women are especially at risk.

Most of the mountain peaks and rock outcrops visible from the town are accessible on foot, but finding the trails to them amid the undergrowth can be very difficult, particularly after the monsoons. The best way to enjoy the mountains, therefore, is to sign up for one of the free walking tours organized by Lalit Kanojia at the *Shree Ganesh Hotel* (☎02974/43591 or 37292, @s_ganesh@datainfosys.net), a nature enthusiast and keen trekker who leads small groups of tourists to Abu's more remote hilltops and hidden lakes.

the **Jamadagni Ashram** is site of the **Agnikund**, where the sage Vashista presided over the fire ritual that produced the four Rajput clans (the Parmars, Parihars, Solankis and Chauhans).

The lesser visited, but more dramatically situated, **Gaumukh temple** lies 7km south of the market area. Reached via a steep flight of 750 steps (which you drop down initially), the small pool inside the shrine is believed to hold water from the sacred Sarawati Ganga river. Pilgrims come here to perform *Gauda puja*, to invoke the blessings of India's two greatest Rishis (sages), Vashista and Vishwamitra, who are thought to have meditated and conducted a famous metaphysical debate on the spot.

The last important Hindu pilgrimage site on Mount Abu is the Atri Rishi temple at **Guru Shikar**, 15km northeast of town, which at 1772m above sea level marks the highest point in Rajasthan. Depending on how energetic you're feeling, you can enjoy superb panoramic vistas either from the temple itself, or from the drinks stall at the bottom of the steps that lead up to it.

Eating and drinking

Mount Abu's predominantly middle-class Indian visitors are typically hard to please when it comes to food, so standards are exceptionally high and prices

---

Moving on from Mount Abu

Buses leave Mount Abu for Abu Road every hour until 9pm; Jeeps leave when full (from opposite the bus stand), and taxis are available on request (from the junction at the southeastern corner of the polo ground; Rs200 for a full car).

For train travellers, there's an information and booking office, or "Out Agency" (Mon–Sat 9am–1pm & 2–4pm) directly opposite the police station, next to the bus stand. It has quotas for services to Delhi, Jaipur, Ajmer, Ahmedabad and Mumbai, but *not* Jodhpur, so if you're heading northeast towards Jaisalmer, you'll have to head back down to Abu Road railway station to book an onward ticket. The most convenient service to Ahmedabad is the daily Delhi–Ahmedabad Mail #9106, which passes through at 1.10pm and arrives 4hr 20min later. In the other direction, of the three trains to Delhi, by far the fastest is the Rajdhani Express #2958, which leaves Abu Road at 8.35pm and arrives in New Delhi at 7.50am the following morning. En route it calls at Ajmer (4hr 20min) and Jaipur (6hr 20min), but at inconvenient hours of the night; the same applies to the four other express services covering this route, so for these two destinations you're better off catching the bus, which will get you in at a more civilized hour. For Jodhpur, the only daily train is the Suryanagari Express #4846, which departs at 1.50am. To catch it, you'll have to take the last (9pm) bus to Abu Road, and hole up in one of the station's grim little waiting rooms – or catch a bus.

Government buses, 50 percent pricier, 30 percent slower, but 100 percent safer than their private counterparts, run services from the state bus stand, about 200m southeast of the polo ground on the main road. Most buses to Ahmedabad go via Palanpur (3hr, change for Bhuj) and Mehsana (4hr), with a couple continuing to Vadodara (9hr), and one to Surat (12hr). Other destinations include Udaipur, Jaipur via Ajmer (7hr 30min) and Chittaurgarh (2 daily; 9hr), with morning departures to Delhi, Jodhpur, and Jaisalmer via Barmer (8hr).

Mount Abu's private buses run to Ahmedabad (6 daily; 6hr), Udaipur (2 daily; 4hr 30min), Jaipur (1 nightly; 11hr 30min), Ajmer (1 nightly; 9hr 30min), Jodhpur (1 nightly; 9hr 30min), and Mumbai (1 nightly; 17hr). For timings and information, go to Gujarat Travels in the main bazaar, just along from the state bus stand.

low in the numerous **restaurants** dotted along Nakki Road. Competition is stiffest between the squeaky-clean pure-veg Gujarati thali joints, most of which have indoor seating, but you can eat top-notch south Indian snacks and spicy rice-plate meals al fresco at the terrace cafés between the bazaar and the lake, and there are plenty of busy ice-cream stalls towards the waterfront. The classier hotels serve **alcohol**, also available at the wine and beer shops opposite the *Veena* at the bottom of town.

Kanak Dining Hall, near the bus stand. Arguably the best Gujarati thalis in town; at Rs50 per head, not the cheapest option, but impecccably hygienic, carefully prepared dishes, and "unlimited" portions.

Jodhpur Bhojnalaya, near taxi stand. The only place in town where you can eat authentic Rajasthani food, famous for its defintive *dal batti*, which comes with full veg thali and *churma* (crumbly, sweet wheat-flour balls flavoured with car-

damom) for Rs40. Highly recommended, but very heavy on *ghee* and spices.

Veena, Nakki Lake Road. Open-air seating next to the main road. Quintessentially tacky Mount Abu (bright lights and the latest *filmi* hits blaring out), but the fast food is second to none, and they have a welcome open fire on the terrace most evenings. Try their tangy *pao bhaji* or melt-in-the-mouth paper *dosas*, praised by no less than the PM himself, who eats here during his annual holidays.

Udaipur

The valley of Oodipur, the most diversified and most romantic spot on the continent of India

Col. James Tod, *Annals and Antiquities of Rajasthan* (1829)

Despite the last twenty years of unchecked ferro-concrete construction, James Tod's assessment of **UDAIPUR** still holds true. Reflected in the shimmering waters of Pichola Lake, the city's skyline of whitewashed *havelis* and tapering temple *shikharas*, surmounted by the domes and ornately carved balconies of the famous Rajput city palace, has managed to keep its head above the rising tide of hotels and terrace restaurants, and remains one of Asia's most exotic spectacles. Enjoying it from a boat at water level, or on a rooftop in the cool of the evening, many travellers are tempted to forget their tight itineraries. In any case, it takes at least a week to explore the city's monuments, and the temples, forts, palaces and scenery of the hills and valleys nearby.

The smooth rolling hills that surround Udaipur like sleeping armadillos were once covered with forests. Widespread felling, instigated by the Indian government in the 1970s after it took possession of the Mewar lands, left them irreversibly barren and have added to the dry and dusty desert conditions of the Udaipur valley.

Some history

Udaipur takes pride in having been the capital of the state of **Mewar**, the only one of the seven major Rajput states to uphold its Hindu allegiance in the face of Muslim invasions and political compromises. Its present ruler is the seventy-sixth in the unbroken line of Mewar suzerains, which makes the Mewar household the longest lasting of all ruling powers in Rajasthan, and perhaps the oldest surviving dynasty in the world.

The history of Udaipur itself stretches back far beyond its foundation in the sixteenth century, for the actions and policies of its Sisodia maharanas follow a code of honour laid down by the very first in line, **Guhil**, who established

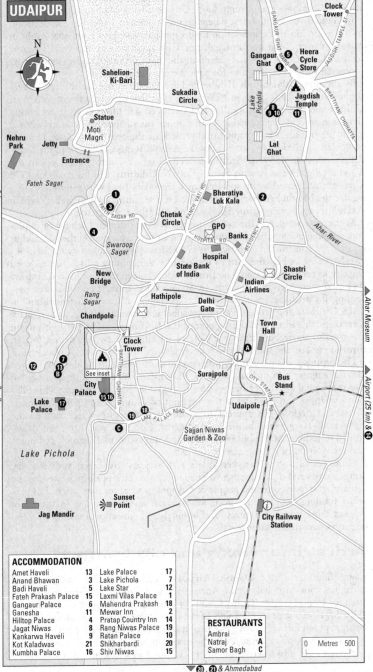

UDAIPUR

N

Clock Tower

Heera Cycle Store

Gangaur Ghat

Jagdish Temple

Lal Ghat

Lake Pichola

Sahelion-Ki-Bari

Sukadia Circle

Statue
Moti Magri

Nehru Park

Jetty

Entrance

Fateh Sagar

Bharatiya Lok Kala

Chetak Circle

GPO

Banks

Hospital

State Bank of India

Indian Airlines

Shastri Circle

Swaroop Sagar

New Bridge

Rang Sagar

Hathipole

Delhi Gate

Chandpole

Clock Tower

Town Hall

See inset

City Palace

Surajpole

Bus Stand

Udaipole

Lake Palace

Lake Pichola

Sajjan Niwas Garden & Zoo

Jag Mandir

Sunset Point

City Railway Station

▲ Shilpgram

◄ Saijangarh "Monsoon Palace" ◄

Ahar River

▶ Ahar Museum

▶ Airport (25 km) & ⑩

▼ ⑳, ㉑ & Ahmedabad

ACCOMMODATION

Amet Haveli	13	Lake Palace	17
Anand Bhawan	3	Lake Pichola	7
Badi Haveli	5	Lake Star	12
Fateh Prakash Palace	15	Laxmi Vilas Palace	1
Gangaur Palace	6	Mahendra Prakash	18
Ganesha	11	Mewar Inn	2
Hilltop Palace	4	Pratap Country Inn	14
Jagat Niwas	8	Rang Niwas Palace	19
Kankarwa Haveli	9	Ratan Palace	10
Kot Kaladwas	21	Shikharbardi	20
Kumbha Palace	16	Shiv Niwas	15

RESTAURANTS

Ambrai	B
Natraj	A
Samor Bagh	C

0   Metres   500

Mewar in 568 AD. Legend claims that Guhil was of local stock, but he seems at the time to have been fleeing south Gujarat during Muslim invasions. Either way, Guhil dwelt in the forest where he was trained in leadership and devotion by a hermit. His successors set up their capital at **Nagda**, which now stands in ruins just over 30km north of Udaipur. Chittaurgarh (also known as Chittor; see p.271) replaced Nagda as capital in the eighth century, and its hilltop fort protected the Sisodia Rajputs for almost eight hundred years.

By the time **Udai Singh II** inherited the throne of Mewar and the leadership of the Sisodia Rajputs in 1537, it was clear that the magnificent fortress of Chittor was doomed; his mother had sacrificed her life two years previously during its second major sacking. Udai scanned the surrounding countryside for a suitable site for a new capital, and settled for the area beside Lake Pichola, protected on all sides by outcrops of the Aravalli Range. Having laid the foundation stones in 1559, he fled the battlefield when Chittor finally fell to the Moghuls eight years later to his new city of **Udaipur**. On his death in 1572 Udai was succeeded by his son **Pratap**, a legendary hero whose refusal to recognize the Moghul **Akbar** as emperor led to the battle of Haldighati, in which Akbar's forces were outwitted and peace in Udaipur was guaranteed.

As the city prospered, the arts flourished; Mewar's superior school of miniature painting became firmly rooted and the awesome palaces on the lake and its shore were constructed. However, in 1736 Mewar was attacked by the destructive Marathas and by the turn of the century the ensuing pillage had reduced the city to poverty and ruin. The British, whose role in the East India Company had until then been purely commercial, stepped in to pick up the pieces, presenting the maharana with a treaty of "perpetual alliance and friendship" in 1818. Guaranteeing protection from invaders and restoration of all its hereditary territories, this treaty and the support of the British helped to put Udaipur on the road to recovery. Yet the principle of refusing to bow down to a foreign power persisted and the maharanas never allowed the British to displace them.

The promises of "perpetual" protection had of course to be dissolved when Britain withdrew from India in 1947. The maharana of Udaipur spearheaded the movement by the princely states to join the new democratic and independent India, and was later at the forefront of a campaign to persuade Indira Gandhi's Congress government to retain the privy purses that funded the upkeep of Rajputana's historic monuments. Congress was, however, determined to reduce the Rajput princes to the status of normal citizens, and political recognition of royalty came to an end.

Centuries of loyalty between rulers and subjects have been kept alive by songs, stories and paintings; the maharana may now lack political power, but he remains as respected by the people of Udaipur as were his forefathers. His personal funding and income from tourism are invested in the Maharana of Mewar Trust, which subsidizes local hospitals and educational institutions, and supports environmental projects.

Arrival, information and city transport

Daily flights connect **Dabok Airport** (☎0294/655453), 25km east of Udaipur, with Mumbai, Delhi, Aurangabad and Jaipur. Taxis run to the city itself for around Rs200. **Trains** from Delhi and Ahmedabad pull in at **Udaipur City Station** a little to the south of the town centre (don't get off at Udaipur Station, much further north). The **bus stand** is a few hundred metres north of here, directly opposite **Udai Pole**, the easternmost gate of the old city. The easiest way to get into town from either is to jump in a rickshaw or tonga.

The town's grand but largely ineffectual **tourist office** (Mon–Sat 10am–5pm; ☎0294/411535) is situated well away from the main tourist sights, on the east side of the city at Surajpole, but there are also branch offices at the airport (☎0294/655433) and City railway station (Mon–Sat 7.30–11.30am & 4–7pm).

The cheapest and most efficient places to **change money** are Thomas Cook in the City Palace compound (daily 9.30am–5.30pm; ☎&☎0294/411663), and the registered agent for American Express, TSG Tours & Travels, across town on Chetak Circle (daily 9.30am–7.30pm; ☎0294/529661). For Visa withdrawals, go to Bank of Baroda, opposite the Town Hall on Bapu Bazaar; card transactions (on the mezzanine floor upstairs) are charged at one percent. You can also change currency and travellers' cheques at the State Bank of Bikaner and Jaipur, Chetak Circle, and the State Bank of India, between Hathi Pol and Chetak Circle (both Mon–Fri 10am–2pm, Sat 10am–noon), but transactions take a lot longer.

Poste restante in Udaipur is notoriously unreliable; in principle, it should be addressed to the Postmaster at Shastri Circle Post Office; however, some ends up at the GPO, just off Chetak Circle (Mon–Sat 10am–1pm & 1.30–7pm, Sun 10am–3pm). Note that **parcels** may only be posted Mon–Fri 10am–4pm & Sat 10am–1pm.

Most of the hotels listed in Accommodation offer **internet access** for Rs40–80/hr, and there are plenty of privately run STD bureaux around the Jagdish temple where you send and receive email. One of the cheapest places in town is Arena, near the Jet Airways office at Madhuban.

City transport

Rickshaws and **taxis** are the usual means of transport. Rickshaw prices are relatively high and it's worth renting a **bicycle**: try Heera Cycle Store, at 86 Gangaur Ghat Rd, whose rates are the lowest at Rs25 per day. The same firm also has a fleet of well-maintained Scooty 50cc mopeds (Rs200/day) and a couple of 150cc Vespa-style motorcycles (Rs250/day) – ideal for trips outside the city.

RTDC, based at the tourist office, offers car rental and **tours** around the city (daily 8am–1pm; Rs74), and to Haldighati, Nathdwara and Eklingji (daily 2–7pm; Rs105). In addition, some of Udaipur's **travel agencies** – mostly located around Lalghat, Lake Palace Road and Chetak Circle (a selection is listed on p.266) offer city tours (Rs40–50), airport transfer (Rs200), private car rental, and booking services for trains and buses. All offer "fixed rates" to most destinations around the city, listed on handouts, but you can nearly always negotiate a reduction on these. Count on around Rs1000 for a full-day or long-haul trip.

Accommodation

Sandwiched between the City Palace and Jagdish temple on the **east side of Lake Pichola**, countless guesthouses vie for views of the water with elegant *havelis* and royal palaces. Cut-throat competition in this area has meant perennially low tariffs for punters in most categories. But it has also sparked off a destructive building boom as hoteliers scramble to attract customers with better views from ever loftier tower blocks. The result is a mass of hideous concrete that threatens to engulf the very skyline tourists flock here to see. In 1999, the High Court ruled that no further building should take place in the area, but the ban seems to have had little effect. The only sure way of slowing down the degradation is for tourists to boycott the offending hotels.

Dotted along the busy main road running due east (inland) from the foot of the City Palace, **Lake Palace Road**'s hotels have larger rooms and gardens but lack views across the lake. Those on the opposite **western side of Lake Pichola**, by contrast, occupy prime spots with optimum views of the palace complex. Note that most of the cheaper hotels in Udaipur have 10am **check-out**.

Jagdish temple area/east side of Lake Pichola

Badi Haveli, 86 Gangaur Ghat Marg ⓉO294/412588, Ⓕ520008. Delightful hotel in a labyrinthine 350-year-old *haveli* with individual rooms, a garden restaurant, relaxing courtyard and excellent views of the lake and palace. Rickshaw-wallahs won't take you there, so jump off at the Jagdish temple and walk down the hill until you see their signboard. ❸–❹

Fateh Pakash Palace, City Palace ⓉO294/528016–9, Ⓕ528006, Ⓔresv@udaipur.hrindia.com. Seven royal suites and nine "deluxe" rooms, crammed with miniature paintings and traditional furniture, on the lake-facing side of the City Palace, all with spellbinding views. Cosier than *Shiv Niwas*, whose facilities (including pool) you can use if staying here. Rooms start at $150. ❾

Ganesha, 7 Jagdish Chowk (no phone). Five simple rooms with comfortable beds and a rooftop restaurant, in a very welcoming family home. All with attached bathrooms and hot and cold water. ❶–❷

Gangaur Palace, 3 Gangaur Ghar Road ⓉO294/422303. Currently the best of the budget hotels in this densely developed tourist enclave, in spite of its insensitive rooftop expansion. Clean, bright, ochre-washed rooms in traditional *haveli*, some lake-facing and with original stucco arches and niches. ❷–❹

Jagat Niwas, 24–25 Lalghat ⓉO294/415547 or 418512, Ⓕ560414, Ⓔjagatniwas@yahoo.com. Beautifully restored seventeenth-century *haveli* right on the lakeside, entered down a narrow alley. Quiet, comfortable and relaxing, with shady courtyards, rooftop and restaurant, but not as good value as the *Kankarwa* next door. ❼

Kankarwa Haveli, 26 Lalghat ⓉO294/411457, Ⓕ521403, Ⓔkhaveli@yahoo.com. Atmospheric, immaculately maintained old *haveli*, slap on the waterfront, with a range of variously priced, comfortable rooms. ❺–❼

Lake Palace, Lake Pichola ⓉO294/527961 or 73. Among the most romantic luxury hotels in India, seemingly afloat on the lake opposite City Palace. The pricier suites, ranged around an ornamental pool and garden, are individually styled, with antique fittings and private terraces, but furnishings in the standard ones are showing signs of wear and tear. Double rooms $229–420 per night. Book at least one month ahead. ❾

Ratan Palace, 21 Lalghat ⓉO294/561153. Clean and homely, with modern rooms on three storeys opening onto the original courtyard, and great lake views from the rooftop. ❹–❺

Shiv Niwas, City Palace ⓉO294/528016 or 7, Ⓕ528006. Former guesthouse of Merwar royal family, and now the flagship of Maharaja Arvind Singh Merwar's HRH hotel chain. Opulently furnished rooms and even more luxurious "historic suites", overlooking the lake or city, and a dreamy pool in the courtyard (open to nonresidents for Rs300). Ask for a peek at the "Imperial Suite". $150–720. ❾

Along Lake Palace Road

Kumbha Palace, 104 Bhatiyani Chotta ⓉO294/422702. One of Udaipur's best-value budget hotels, hidden under the east walls of City Palace. Spacious rooms for the price (all attached), with views and wall-hangings, and a great rooftop restaurant. If it's full, try the equally dependable *Mona Lisa* next door (ⓉO294/561562). ❷

Mahendra Prakash, Lake Palace Road ⓉO294/522993 or 422090. Arguably the best mid-price deal in town: not the most inspiring situation, but you get a large, comfortable en-suite room, plus the use of a well-kept pool, for under Rs350 – a bargain. Pricier rooms in new block are also good value. Some a/c. Pool table and internet facilities. ❹–❻

Rang Niwas Palace, Lake Palace Road, opposite the gate leading to *Shiv Niwas* ⓉO294/523890 or 1, Ⓕ527884, Ⓔrangniwas@hotmail.com. Again, an unpromising location next to the main road, but inside is a palatial old building with attractively furnished rooms and luxurious suites. The large garden, friendly atmosphere and pool (Rs125 nonresidents) make up for the lack of views. ❻–❾

West side of Lake Pichola

Amet Haveli, Chandpole ⓉO294/431085, Ⓕ522447, Ⓔregiudr@datainfosys.net. Newly renovated wing of an old *haveli*, occupying a perfect spot on the waterfront, with spectacular views of the city and palaces out of arched windows. The six en-suite rooms are simply furnished to retain the building's original character, with marble floors and stained glass that makes the most of the reflected light off the water. Quality restaurant adjacent. Top value. ⑥–⑦

Lake Pichola, Chandpole ☏ 0294/431197, ⊕ 430575, ✉ reservation@lakepicholahotel.com. Grand waterfront hotel, recently constructed in traditional style, with "deluxe" lake-facing rooms and a roof terrace boasting superb views of the palace. Moneychanging, boat rides and room service. Accepts credit cards. ⑧

Lake Star, 80 Naga Nagri, beyond Chandpole (no phone). A friendly budget guesthouse on the less polluted, more tranquil Chandpole side of the lake. The rooms are large and clean, with attached shower-toilets, comfy foam mattresses and beautiful views, and there's an excellent roof terrace. Self-catering rooms for families on request. Very good value. If it's full, try the pleasant-enough *Sudha* (☏ 0294/431870; ②) behind. ②–③

Around Fateh Sagar

Anand Bhawan, off Fateh Sagar Road ☏ 0294/523256, ⊕ 523247. Pricey government-run hilltop hotel, with commanding views from its lawns and terraces, but nowhere near as much panache as the *Laxmi Vilas* nearby. ⑧

Hilltop Palace, Ambavgarh ☏ 0294/432245, ⊕ 432136, ✉ hilltop@ad1.vsnl.net.in. Most swish and modern of the upscale places above Fateh Sagar, with superb views, panoramic rooftop bar (see Eating p.266) and restaurant, and the best pool in town. Their lake-facing rooms cost double, but ask for a discount. ⑥–⑧

Laxmi Vilas Palace, off Fateh Sagar Road ☏ 0294/529711 or 2, ⊕ 526273. Gopal Singh's nineteenth-century hilltop guesthouse, overlooking Fateh Sagar Lake, is now run by ITDC. Although marginally less pricey than other palace hotels, it's still sumptuously furnished and has a pool (Rs165 for nonresidents), gourmet restaurant and bar. $140 per night. ⑨

Outside the city centre

Karni Bhavan Fort, Bambora, 30km south ☏ 0291/512101 or 2, ⊕ 512105, ✉ karani@jpl.dot.net.in. Tranquil upscale accommodation in a recently restored Rajput fort with fine views and a superb pool featuring spouting marble elephants. Horse safaris and a range of worthwhile trips into the surrounding countryside available on request. Among the nicest hotels of its kind on the region. ⑨

Kot Kaladwas, Motiyon Wali Magri, Rani-Ji-Ki-Bawdi, Jhamarkotra Road, Kaladwas Village ☏ & ⊕ 0294/493075, ✉ billaedwards@btinternet.com. Very posh campsite in idyllic rural setting, 8km southeast of the city in the Aravallis. The tents, pitched next to an old Rajput family house and Marwari stables, have en-suite showers and toilets, lockers, beds and sitouts. Guided horse riding (Rs2250/day), birdwatching and Jeep drives (Rs1750/day). Tariff includes all meals, one Jeep ride and picnic. ⑧

Mewar Inn, 42 Residency Rd ☏ 0294/522090. Backpackers' hostel north of the lake and city centre; a touch grimy, and too close to the main road for comfort, but ultra-cheap. Facilities include OSHO-run rooftop restaurant, left luggage, ticketing service, laundry and inexpensive cycle rental. Rickshaw-wallahs will say it's full or closed, but be persistent, or take a tonga. Dorm beds only Rs20. ①

Pratap Country Inn, Titardhi village ☏ 0294/583138, ⊕ 583058. Secluded, shabby rural guesthouse, 8km out of town. Differently priced rooms in various states of disrepair, ranged around an equally ramshackle courtyard, roamed by dogs and chickens. Recommended for horse-lovers (they offer pony trekking safaris into the Aravallis for Rs400), but otherwise inconveniently far from town. ③–⑤

Shikharbadi, Goverdhan Vilas ☏ 0294/583201 or 2 or 3, ⊕ 584841, ✉ resv@udaipur.hrindia.com. Former royal hunting lodge set in the lower Aravallis (5km south on Ahmedabad road, NH-8), with own pool, lake, polo pitch, deer park and stud farm. Less ostentatious and more peaceful than the palaces in town. Suites in the 1930s block have more character than the newer a/c "cottages". ⑨

The City

The original settlement of Udaipur focused around the grand **City Palace**, bordering the west shore of **Lake Pichola**. Immediately north is the maze of tightly winding streets that constitute the **old city**. It takes a few days of wandering before this labyrinth becomes intelligible; start by getting acquainted with the gates and circles that form traffic islands at the major crossroads. From the **clock tower** that marks the northern edge of the old city, roads lead east to the tourist information office and Ahar, west to the lake, and north to the GPO at Chetak Circle. Continuing north, the road passes the **Bharatiya Lok Kala** folk art museum, and heads to **Sahelion-ki-Bari**, the gardens of the royal ladies.

The road that encircles **Lake Fateh Sagar** north of Lake Pichola carries on west to the excellent crafts village of **Shilpgram**, a showcase for all types of traditional Indian art. It's a good cycling route; you can stop off at **Pratap Memorial Gardens** on the eastern shore of the lake, visit **Nehru Park** in its centre and cool off with an ice cream or drink from mobile stands near the jetty. In the far west of the city, **Sajjangarh** – the "Monsoon Palace" – commands superb views, while to the east both the royal cenotaphs and **Ahar museum** with its fifth-century BC relics can be visited in a morning.

Lake Pichola
The serene lakeside location chosen by Udai for his new capital made a welcome change from the craggy heights of Chittaurgarh. He enlarged the lake, which drew water from mountains up to 160km away, and now covers eight square kilometres. Later rulers added dams and canals to prevent flooding during the monsoon.

The two islands in the lake, topped with the ivory-white domes and arches of private palaces, are the most familiar and photogenic features of Udaipur. **Jag Niwas**, now the **Lake Palace Hotel**, is the larger of the two, built as a summer palace during the reign of Jagat Singh (1628–52). If you aren't staying here, you can visit the palace for lunch, dinner or afternoon tea; the price includes the boat ride from the mainland (booking advisable; see p.265).

The larger **Jag Mandir**, on the island to the south, has changed little since its construction by Karan Singh in 1615. It takes its name from Jagat Singh who added to the initial structure. Intended as a small Rajput palace, it was never used as such; Karan Singh offered refuge here to the Moghul prince Khurum (later Emperor Shah Jahan), exiled by his father, Emperor Jahangir, in the 1620s. Khurum succeeded his father while still in Udaipur, and the Moghul gathering for the occasion defied the established code of Rajput–Moghul enmity. During the 1857 Mutiny the island once again served as a safe haven, this time for European women and children.

The main building facing the City Palace has detailed stone inlay work within its domed roof. In front of it a green marble *chhatri* carved with vines and flowers is the centrepiece of a garden guarded by stone elephants. Jag Mandir's only inhabitants other than flocks of birds are three royal servants who tend the gardens and grow flowers for the maharana's celebrations.

Half-hour **boat rides** around the lake depart from the jetty behind the City Palace (hourly: April–Sept 8–11am & 3–6pm; Oct–March 10am–noon & 2–5pm; Rs75), while an hour's trip (hourly 2–6pm; Rs150) includes a stop at Jag Mandir. The view of the palaces and shoreline from the lake at sunset is one of the most memorable images of Rajput splendour. To make the most of them by boat, however, you'll have to sit on the side facing the palace (they usually run anticlockwise around the lake, so check when you get on).

The City Palace
Udaipur's fascinating **City Palace** stands moulded in soft yellow stone on a rocky promontory on the northwest shore of Lake Pichola, its thick windowless base crowned with ornate turrets and canopies. Eleven constituent *mahals* (palaces), constructed by successive maharanas during the three hundred years

that followed the foundation of Udaipur in 1559, and characterized through-out by their exemplary workmanship, together form the largest royal complex in Rajasthan.

Part of the palace is now a museum (daily 9.30am–4.30pm; Rs100, Rs100 extra for camera, Rs300 extra for video), entered through **Toran Pole** from the massive courtyard where elephants once lined up for inspection before battle. Although **guided tours** (Rs70 for a non-Indian language) are not compulsory, they do serve to illuminate the chronology of the palaces, the significance of the paintings, and details of the lives of the maharanas.

Everywhere you look the marble and granite walls are laden with brilliant miniature paintings, decorated with tiles or overlaid with spangling mosaics of coloured glass and mirrors, and each room glows with sunlight filtering through stained-glass windows. Narrow low-roofed passages connect the different *mahals* and courtyards, creating a haphazard effect, designed to prevent surprise intrusion by armed enemies.

Each of the three large peacocks (*mor*) set into the walls of the seventeenth-century **Mor Chowk**, placed there by Sajjan Singh two hundred years after the palace was built, is composed of 5000 pieces of glass, glittering in green, gold and blue. The pillared apartments that face Mor Chowk are adorned with scenes from Krishna legends, a favourite theme of the paintings in the **Zenana Mahal**, the women's quarters. With alcoves, balconies, coloured windows, tiled walls and floors, these are the most splendid rooms in the palace. Other chambers include **Kanchi-ki-Burj**, decorated throughout with a mosaic of mirrors, and **Chandra Chowk** (Moon Square) which although right at the top of the palace manages to enclose its own garden – it rests on the crest of a hill that rises in the heart of the palace. **Krishna Vilas**, an apartment full of miniatures, honours a nineteenth-century Udaipur princess who poisoned herself to avoid the dilemma of choosing a husband from the two rival households of Jodhpur and Jaipur.

Adjoining the palace, the dusty **Government Museum** (daily except Fri 10am–5pm; Rs2) displays clothes, unlabelled relics and a stuffed and decaying two-headed deer. It's worth passing through to the last room to see a good selection of temple statues, dating back to the eighth century, but otherwise the museum does not merit a detour.

Jagdish temple

Raised above the main crossroads a little north of the City Palace, **Jagdish temple** is a centre of constant activity. Built in 1652 and dedicated to Lord Jagannath, an aspect of Vishnu, its outer walls and towering *shikhara* are heavily carved with figures of Vishnu, scenes from the life of Krishna, and dancing *apsaras* (nymphs). The spacious *mandapa* leads to the sanctuary where a black stone image of Jagannath sits shrouded in flowers, while a small raised shrine in front of the temple protects a bronze Garuda, the half-man, half-bird vehicle of Vishnu. Smaller shrines to Ganesh and Hanuman stand to either side of the main temple.

Bharatiya Lok Kala

Since the opening of Shilpgram, the **Bharatiya Lok Kala** on Panch Vati Road just north of Chetak Circle (daily 9am–6pm; Rs10, Rs10 extra for camera, Rs50 extra for video), has been squarely upstaged, and its hard to think of a reason why anyone would want to look at tired models and bleached-out photographs of the state's folk traditions when the genuine article can be experienced live across town. That said, visitors interested in puppetry will find some inspiration here. Short amusing **puppet shows** (free) are staged throughout the day, while longer performances take place between noon and 1pm and 6pm and 7pm (Rs30). In addition, the museum runs short courses in puppet-making and theatre; call in for details.

Sahelion-ki-Bari

The "garden of the maids of honour", **Sahelion-ki-Bari**, roughly 2km north of Hathi Pole (daily 9am–7.30pm; Rs3), was laid out by Sangram Singh early in the eighteenth century for the diversion and entertainment of the ladies of the royal household. Surrounding a shady courtyard, the fountained garden must once have made a delightful retreat, but today the fountains only play at the request of visitors, and the focus of attention is the wide range of indigenous trees and flowers. During the monsoon the lotus pond behind the court-yard is ablaze with colour.

Fateh Sagar

Not far west of Sahelion-ki-Bari is **Fateh Sagar**, a lake fringed by sharp hills and connected to Lake Pichola by a canal built shortly after the turn of the twentieth century. At the jetty on the western shore, you can hop on the boat that ferries tourists across the water to **Nehru Park** in the centre of the lake (daily: summer 8am–6.30pm; winter 8am–6pm; Rs3). The park, constructed in 1937 as a famine relief project, is nothing special, but pleasant enough if you want to get away from the bustle of the town.

Shilpgram

The road running around the north of Fateh Sagar leads to the rural arts and crafts centre of **Shilpgram** (daily 9.30am–6pm; Rs10), near the village of Havala, 5km out from town and best reached by bike. This exemplary crafts village – one of the best in the country – was set up to promote and preserve the traditional architecture, music and crafts of the tribal people of western India, and holds displays of the diverse traditional lifestyles and customs of India's rural population.

Dwellings arranged in the compound include a solid two-storey wooden house from northern Gujarat, exquisitely carved throughout, circular painted huts from Kutch (Gujarat), thick-walled low-roofed houses from the Rajasthani deserts, and Goan potters' huts. Musicians and dancers – *hijras* (eunuchs) among them – perform around the houses, while weaving, potting, puppetry and embroidery continue as they would in their original localities. Allow at least an hour to walk around the compound; the best time to go is at weekends, when the centre is filled with artisans.

Sajjangarh

High on a hill 5km west of the city, the "Monsoon Palace", **Sajjangarh**, was abandoned by the royal family soon after its construction in 1880. It had been found to be impossible to pump water to the palace, which is now used as Udaipur's radio station and closed to visitors. The views over Udaipur from the courtyards of the palace are unrivalled, however, especially if you can make it there for sunrise, when the surrounding countryside looks its most magical. That said, getting up the hill requires a bit of effort, as the climb is too steep to tackle by bicycle. The journey takes a good fifteen minutes by rickshaw or taxi, and costs more than Rs150 for the round trip; if you can handle the traffic, rent a moped or motorcycle from Heera Cycles, just down the hill from the Jagdish temple on Gangaur Ghat Road (see p.263).

Royal cenotaphs and Ahar museum

Across the narrow Ahar River, 2km east of Udaipur, domed cenotaphs huddle together on the site of the royal cremation ground. Raised on platforms, some of which are decorated with *shivalingams*, many of the *chhatris* are falling into disrepair, and the site is pretty dirty. Even so, it's a good place to pick up on local history, featuring an ornate memorial to the prodigious builder Jagat Singh (1628–52) and the cenotaph of Amar Singh (died 1620) who contributed so much to the City Palace, embellished with friezes depicting the immolation of his wives.

Less than 1km south of here, archeological exhibits at the **Ahar museum** (daily except Fri 10am–5pm; Rs4) include locally unearthed pottery from the first millennium BC. Among more recent statues is a handsome tenth-century Surya image.

Eating

The place to eat in Udaipur has long been the Lake Palace's romantic dining terrace, reached by launch from the *Fateh Prakash Palace Hotel*. The closest most visitors get to it, however, are the rooftop **restaurants** stacked behind Lal and Gangaur Ghats, whose gastronomic shortcomings and generally inflated prices are more than offset by spellbinding views over Pichola Lake to the distant Aravallis. Many of the cheaper places in this area advertise free screenings of the James Bond movie *Octopussy*, with its manic boat and auto-rickshaw chases around the city's landmarks, beginning every evening, usually at 7pm. Thankfully, you can escape Roger Moore and his big balloon by heading across the lake for a tandoori at the *Ambrai Restaurant*, or across the bazaar to the *Natraj*, Udaipur's most popular thali joint.

Ambrai, *Amet Haveli Hotel*, Chandpole. One of the few lakeside restaurants whose cooking lives up to its location, on a spit of land facing the City Palace. Perfect for a sundowner, and their tandoori, prepared by the royal family's former chef, is second to none. Full multi-cuisine menu, with plenty of veg options, cold beer and live Hindustani music. Rs200 for two courses.

Fateh Pakash Palace, City Palace. English-style "high tea" served in an elegant, sunny gallery (3–5pm daily), with live Indian classical music and sublime lake views. Count on Rs175–250 for the full Monty – hotel-made jam, cream, scones and sandwiches. An absolute must for cream-tea addicts.

Kumbha Palace, 104 Bhatiyani Chotta. Better-than-average budget tourist grub (pizzas, baked potatoes, Marmite, homemade cakes), dished up on a rooftop terrace below the town-facing east wall of the City Palace. Pleasant views, big portions, very reasonable prices, and a friendly dog.

Lake Palace, Lake Pichola. Nonresidents can visit the *Lake Palace* for a candle-lit buffet dinner at what must rank among the world's most romantic restaurants, open 7.30–10pm. Reserve a table one day in advance through the *Fateh Prakash Hotel*, and dress smartly (they'll say they're fully booked

if you don't). Rs750 covers dinner (Rs650 lunch), plus Rs25 if you want to look around the hotel. As a one-off extravagance, the whole experience is hard to beat, even though the food can be disappointing.

Natraj, New Bapu Bazaar, behind *Ashok Cinema*. Udaipur's top thali joint for over twenty years, but well off the tourist trail because it's fiendishly hard to find (head down Barra Bazaar from the clock tower, and ask the way when you get to Suraj Pole). Easily the best cheap meal in town: Rs45 for unlimited portions of five different vegetables, dhal, rice, *papad*, fresh chapatis and pickle.

Samor Bagh, near Gulab Bagh and Tibetan market, Lake Palace Road. Mostly Indian and Chinese dishes (including excellent non-veg tandoori), served on a spacious lawn beneath the City Palace, a ten-minute stroll down Lake Palace Road from the Jagdish temple. Careful, delicious cooking (their butter chicken is to die for) and a relaxed atmosphere, with fairy lights and live music or dance daily. 8am–10.30pm.

Shikarbadi, Goverdhan Vilas, 5km south along NH-8. Top-notch Mewari cuisine served on the terrace of the maharaja's former hunting lodge, on the slopes of the Aravallis. If you can, get here for 4.30pm when hordes of deer, blue buck (*nilgai*), langur monkeys and wild boar mass to be fed. Lunch Rs250; dinner Rs350 per head; drinks cost extra.

Zannat, *Hotel Hilltop Palace*, Ambavgarh, above Fateh Sagar. Rooftop restaurant of swanky modern hotel (open to nonresidents). Their multi-cuisine menu is standard (go for the tandoori or Indian veg options), but the panoramic views are matchless, especially from the bar, whose terrace is the highest vantage point in the city. Most main courses under Rs100.

Listings

Bookshops The best-stocked bookstore in town is the one just inside the City Palace complex (no ticket required). For general India-related paperbacks and fiction in English, browse the shops around the Jagdish temple and along Lake Palace Road.

Cultural entertainment The best place to hear live Rajasthani folk music is Shilpgram (see p.264). Folk dance performances are staged at Meera Kala Mandir, Meera Bhawan, Sector 11, on the Ahmedabad road (Mon–Sat 7pm; Rs60). For tickets, book direct (☎0294/583176), or through Meera Cycles on Gangaur Ghat Road, just below the Jagdish temple.

Hospital The (private) Udaipur Hospital, Gulab Bagh Road (0294/420223 or 420322, mobile 98290/42190), has a 24hr casualty service and pharmacy.

Music Sitar and tabla lessons are offered to beginners on a weekly or hourly basis by the enthusiastic and experienced Rajesh Prajapat, contactable through the Prem Musical Instrument shop, opposite Hotel Gangaur Palace, Gangaur Ghat (☎0294/430599).

Pharmacies Bansal Department Stores, inside Surajpole (20m west of the gate); Vijay Medical Store, opposite the hospital entrance on Hospital Road. Laxmi General Store, Bhattiyani Chohatta, 300m coming from Jagdish temple, on the right, is a useful general pharmacy selling almost anything you could need, including Marmite, tiger balm and Rizlas.

Travel agents Reliable travel agents to choose from include the very efficient Comfort Travels and Tours, inside the City Palace (☎0294/419746), and Gangaur Tours and Travels, 28 Gangaur Ghat Marg (☎0294/411476). Details of airline offices appear below.

Yoga Ashtanga Yoga Ashram (aka "Raiba House"), at Chandpole ☎0294/524872, ✉jaswanttank@yahoo.com.

Moving on from Udaipur

Indian Airlines **flies** to Jaipur, Jodhpur, Delhi and Mumbai. Book tickets direct at their office in the LIC Building, opposite *Hotel Air Palace*, Delhi Gate (Mon–Sat 10am–1pm & 2–5pm; ☎0294/410999). Jet Airways also fly to Jaipur, Delhi and Mumbai, but not to Jodhpur. Their office is north of the centre at the Blue Circle Business Centre, 1C Madhuban (Mon–Sat 9am–6pm ☎0294/561105–6).

Udaipur is poorly served by **trains**, with just one daily departure to Ahmedabad (#9943; depart 9.15pm), where you can pick up connecting services to Mumbai. Heading north, two trains run to Delhi each day. The fastest is the #9616 Chetak Express (depart 6.10pm), which also serves as a night train to Jaipur, but for Ajmer you're better off taking the #9944 Ahmedabad–Delhi Express, which leaves in the morning at 8am and arrives just in time to catch a connecting bus to Pushkar – if you're lucky.

Government **buses** work out of the main RSTRC bus stand at Udai Pole. Make sure when you buy your ticket that you're booked on an express bus, not a slow passenger service. More comfortable, cheaper **private buses** operate daily services to the same range of destinations (also Pushkar), departing from Town Hall Road by Taldar Travels, who can supply tickets and departure times. **Local buses** to destinations such as Nagda, Eklingi, Nathwarda, Kankroli and Kumbalgarh leave from the main government bus stand at regular intervals throughout the day.

Around Udaipur

You'd need to have a lot of time on your hands to see more than a fraction of the ruins, palaces, temples, forts, lakes and wildlife sanctuaries that abound in the countryside around Udaipur.

Day-trips northeast of the city can take in the important historic temples of **Nagda**, **Eklingji**, **Nathdwara**, and **Kankroli** along NH-8 towards Bhilwara, or the peaceful wooded surroundings of **Ranakpur** and **Kumbalgarh**, which also make appealing stopovers before you join NH-15 en route to Jodhpur. Renting a car saves time, but regular and efficient local buses, as well as private tour companies, serve both routes.

Nagda and Eklingji

The ragged remnants of the ancient capital of Mewar, **NAGDA**, which date back to 626 AD, stand next to a lake 20km northeast of Udaipur, a couple of kilometres short of Eklingji. Buses from Udaipur set down passengers for Nagda shortly before the road drops into the valley that shelters the Eklingji temple, beside a chai stall and bicycle shop. Nagda itself is a short ride away, west of the lake. Most of the buildings were either destroyed by Moghul zealots or submerged by the lake, which has naturally accumulated over the centuries. All that survives is a majestic pair of tenth-century Vaishnavite temples, known as **Saas-Bahu** – literally "Mother-in-law" and "Daughter-in-law". The larger (Mother-in-law) has an astounding wealth of carving in its interior. Within the *mandapa*, a marriage area is marked by four pillars bearing images of the gods to which a couple must pay homage: Brahma, Vishnu, Shiva and Surya. On the northeast pillar you can make out representations of Sita's trial by fire, a favourite episode from the *Ramayana*, while scenes from the *Mahabharata* cover the ceilings. The outer walls of both temples display images of the entire Hindu pantheon, nubile *apsaras* (heavenly maidens), and even a few couples engaged in erotic acts.

The quickest route to **EKLINGJI** from the chai stall where the bus drops you off is along a path that leads behind the old protective walls and downhill, passing shaded tanks and half-preserved muddy-brown temples. The god **Eklingji**, a manifestation of Shiva, has been the protective deity of the rulers of Mewar ever since the eighth century, when Bappa Rawal was bestowed with the title *darwan* (servant) of Eklingji by his guru. To this day, the Maharana of Udaipur still visits his temples at the eponymous town every Monday evening – the day traditionally celebrated all over India as being sacred to Shiva. Lesser mortals can make the straightforward half-hour trip northeast of Udaipur by taxi, or on very frequent buses from the main bus stand. The milky-white marble main temple (daily 4.30–6.30am, 10.30am–1.30pm & 5.30-6.45pm), dominating the compound with an elaborate two-storey *mandapa* guarded by stone elephants, surrounds a four-faced black marble *lingam* that marks the precise spot where Bappa Rawal received his accolade. Images of Shiva and his fellow deities, *apsaras* and musicians are etched into the walls both outside and within. The temple had to be rebuilt under Maharana Raimal at the end of the fifteenth century, and again two hundred years later after the ravages of Aurangzeb's iconoclastic forces.

Nathdwara

The temple dedicated to Krishna – known also as **Nath**, the favourite *avatar* (incarnation) of Vishnu – at **NATHDWARA**, "Gateway to God", is said to be the second richest temple in India after Tirupati (in Andhra Pradesh, see p.1154). The site was known as Sihar until the moment in the seventeenth century when a chariot laden with an image of Krishna became stuck in the mud 26km north of Eklingji. The idol was being carried from Krishna's birthplace Mathura to Udaipur to spare it almost certain destruction by Aurangzeb; its bearers interpreted the event as a divine sign and established a new temple where it had stopped.

Nathdwara is on NH-8, and sees a constant flow of buses en route north and south, as well as two daily trains to Udaipur. Although the area around the bus stand is grim, a short ride west on a rickshaw brings you to narrow streets where stalls display incense, beads, perfumes and small Krishna statues, and blossom with the pinks, yellows and reds of temple decorations. In the centre of town the **Shri Nathji temple** opens for worship eight times daily, when the image is woken, dressed, washed, fed and put to bed. The most elaborate session, *aarti*, takes place between 5pm and 6pm. Don't miss the radiant *pichwai* paintings in the main sanctuary, made of hand-spun cloth and coloured with strong vegetable pigments; these original hangings possess a brilliance unmatched by the numerous copies available all over Rajasthan.

Rooms are at a premium during the festivals of **Janmasthami** (Aug & Sept) and **Diwali** (Oct & Nov). Hotels in Nathdwara and the surrounding valley, whose primary function is to serve the needs of pilgrims, include the RTDC *Hotel Gokul* (☎02953/30917; ❶–❺) in the north of town overlooking Lal Bagh, and the posher *Shree Resort* (☎02953/40341; ❻), which boasts the town's best restaurant.

Kankroli and Rajsamand

Northeast of Nathdwara, NH-8 winds through another 17km of undulating scrub before reaching **KANKROLI**, 65km from Udaipur. This dusty little market town stands on the shores of the vast **Rajsamand Lake**, whose construction was commissioned by Maharana Raj Singh in the seventeenth century after a terrible drought swept Rajasthan.

On the lake's western shore, a few kilometres out of town, is **Nauchowki**, a collection of nine *chowks* (pavilions), on platforms above the steps leading to the water. With carved pillars and ceilings showing scenes from the life of Krishna, these *chowks* were erected by Raj Singh to commemorate his marriage to Princess Charumati of Kishangarh, an act that saved her from the matrimonial clasp of Aurangzeb.

The **Dwarkadish temple** overlooking the southern shore houses an image of Krishna installed by Raj Singh in 1676, and has a sanctuary similar to that at Nathdwara. It forms part of an old palace whose passages wind through low-ceilinged rooms to covered walkways beside the lake. On steps descending to the water you can buy grain to feed the flocks of pigeons who survive on the charity of pilgrims.

The best views of the lake are to be had from the **Digambara Jain temple**, dedicated to Adinath, which crowns a steep hill between Nauchowki and the bus stand. From here you can see the Dwarkadish temple, Nauchowki, scattered old palaces on the nearby hills, and the Aravalli landscape rolling south as far as the eye can see.

Ranakpur

The complex of **Jain temples** at **RANAKPUR**, 60km north of Udaipur, is the largest of its kind in India, boasting marble work on a par with that of the more famous Dilwara shrines at Mount Abu (see p.253) and Shatrunjaya near Palitana in Gujarat (see p.723). Unlike the latter two hilltop sites, however, this sacred spot is hidden at the base of a wooded valley. The land, deep in the Aravalli range, was originally gifted to the Jain community in the fifteenth-century by Rana Kumbha, the Hindu ruler of Mewar.

Ranakpur's isolated position has kept it well off the foreign tourist trail, but if you're working your way between Jodhpur and Udaipur on country buses, this is an excellent place to break the journey. Regular buses connect the village with Udaipur, and the main Ajmer–Mount Abu highway to the north, and you can hike here through a tract of protected forest from Kumbalgarh (see below). Catering for the hundreds of Jain pilgrims who pour through daily, a small crop of hotels also provides a choice of accommodation.

The main temple (10am–5pm) is dedicated to the first *tirthankara* **Adinath**, whose four-faced image is enshrined in its central sanctuary. Built in 1439 on land donated to the Jains by Rana Kumbha, the temple is two or three storeys high in parts, and its roof, topped with five large *shikharas*, undulates with tiny spires that crown the small shrines to Jain saints lining the temple walls. Within, 29 halls, some octagonal and many more than one storey high, are dissected by 1444 pillars, each sculpted with unique designs. The carving on the walls, columns and the domed ceilings is superb. Friezes depicting the life of the *tirthankara* are etched into the walls, while musicians and dancers have been modelled out of brackets between the pillars and the ceiling.

Two smaller temples dedicated to **Parshvanath** and **Neminath** nestle among the trees close by; the sculptures within are of a similarly high standard. Also in the compound is a contemporary Hindu temple dedicated to **Surya**, inside which carvings depict racing chariots commanded by the solar deities.

Practicalities

Ranakpur is a bumpy three-hour journey on regular buses from Udaipur. You can also get here from Jodhpur, via the market town of **Falna** on NH-14, and there are a couple of express connections to Abu Road. If you're intending to visit Kumbalgarh as well, though, think about **trekking** between the two sites, which are separated by one of the few remaining forested areas in the Aravallis. As Kumbalgarh is on the top of the range, it's much easier to hike from there down to Ranakpur (for more on this route see p.270), but guides may be arranged through *The Castle Hotel* (see below) for the six-hour uphill climb in the other direction.

For budget **accommodation** in Ranakpur, you've a choice between the rundown RTDC *Hotel Shilpi* (☎02934/3674; ❶–❹) or the much more congenial *Shivika Lake Hotel* (☎-2934/85078; ❸–❹), 2km south of the temples near a small lake. There are also a couple of pricier hotels in the area. Nearest to the temples and offering the best value for money is *The Castle* (☎02934/85133; ❻), a small resort complex with twenty well-appointed rooms, buffet restaurant and pool. Further down the road from the temples, the swisher *Maharani Bagh* (☎0934/85105; ❽) is part of the Maharaja of Jodhpur's luxury chain, with a stock-in-trade of large tour groups. Buffet lunches, served from 12.30–3pm by waiters in traditional garb and accompanied by local folk musicians, cost a whopping Rs350.

Kumbalgarh

The remote hilltop fort of **KUMBALGARH**, 84km north of Udaipur, is the most formidable of the 32 constructed by Maharana Kumbha in the fifteenth century. Protected by a series of seven thick ramparts, it was only successfully besieged once, when a confederacy led by Akbar poisoned the Sisodias' water supply – the Moghul emperor later returned it to them anyway. Aside from the impressive fortifications and ancient monuments they enclose, the main reason to venture out here is to experience the idyllic Aravalli countryside. Winding through a string of tribal villages and picturesque valleys, the Udaipur road alone more than repays the effort, and once you've reached the top of the range the views are superb.

The most memorable panorama of all is the one from the pinnacle of Kumbalgarh **palace**, crowning the summit of the fort. A guide will show you through the series of gateways and residential quarters to the room where Udai Singh was raised by his nurse after fleeing Chittaurgarh in 1535, and the top-most Cloud Palace (so named because during the monsoons it sits in the clouds), restored and furnished by Udaipur's Fateh Singh early this century. From the rooftops, you gain striking birds' eye views over the Jain and Hindu **temples** scattered across the plateau. The oldest of them are thought to date from the second century; the **tombs** of Kumbha (murdered by his eldest son) and his grandson Prithviraj (poisoned by his brother-in-law) stand to the east.

Provided you're equipped with good shoes and ample provisions, the best way to explore these more remote monuments is on foot, via the old walls. Some 36km of crenellated ramparts wind around the rim of the hilltop, and it is possible to complete a circuit in two comfortable days, sleeping rough mid-way around. You won't need a guide, but be sure to take food and water as there are no permanent settlements.

Lining the deep valley that plunges west from the fort down to the plains, the **Kumbalgarh Wildlife Sanctuary** comprises a dense swathe of woodland that's a stronghold for wolves, leopards and panthers. With a local guide, you can trek through it to Ranakpur, an excellent hike of between four and five hours. Entry to the sanctuary costs Rs50 (plus Rs50 for cameras); foreigners need **permits**, obtainable from the District Forest Officer at nearby **Kelwara,** or through either of the upmarket hotels if you're staying in one. Both the *Aodhi* and *Kumbalgarh Fort* can also arrange guides for the trek, but you'll save a lot of money by contacting one yourself: ask at the café just inside the fort gates.

Practicalities

Taxis regularly run tourists out to Kumbalgarh and Ranakpur in a day-trip from Udaipur, but it's best to take your time and travel at a more leisurely pace, staying for a night or two in one of the hotels that lie within walking distance of the fort. A couple of express buses leave Udaipur's RSRTC stand in the morning (3hr 30min). Competent motorcyclists may also consider riding out here on a rented bike, which would allow you to explore this particularly scenic stretch of road in more depth. Ranakpur lies a long, winding journey away on a route served by infrequent country buses. The most congenial way to reach the Jain shrines, therefore, is on foot via the Wildlife Sanctuary (see above).

Clinging to the hillside near the base of the citadel, the *Aodhi* (☏02954/4222, ☏4348; ⑨) is a swish heritage hotel, complete with gourmet restaurant and pool, run by the Maharana of Udaipur's HRH chain, with 20–30 percent discounts April–July. From the hotel you can take a six-hour horse trek (Rs1500 per person) or five-hour jeep safari (Rs1750) through the sanctuary and on to Ranakpur. Bookings can be made through the *Aodhi* hotel direct, or the *Shiv Niwas Palace* in Udaipur. Another great place to unwind is the more modern

Kumbalgarh Fort Hotel (☎02954/42057, ⊕432136, ⊜hilltop@ad1.vsnl.net.in; ⑨), 5km along the Kelwara road, with fifty percent discounts April to July. From its garden terraces and poolside, you get superb hill views, and they have a few cycles for rent. Guides and horses can also be arranged here for treks through the wildlife sanctuary. Choice for budget travellers is limited to the much less inspiring *Ratnadeep* (☎02954/42255, ⊕42340; ❸–❹), a standard budget hotel 9km from the fort in Kelwara village.

East of Udaipur

The belt of hilly land east of Udaipur is the most fertile in Rajasthan, watered by several perennial rivers. Although you need your own vehicle to penetrate the countryside, the historic town of **Chittaurgarh**, which preceded Udaipur as the seat of Mewar's rulers, is easily accessible by bus. Further east, clusters of crumbling temples mark the sites of still older cities. In the far southeast, the heartland of the princely state of Kota, palaces and forts in **Kota** and **Bundi** stand sentinel over fields of wheat, groundnut, castor-oil plants and opium poppies. A prime crop here for centuries, **opium** is nowadays grown for the pharmaceutical industry according strict government quotas, but the legal cultivation masks a much larger illicit production overseen by Mumbai drug barons. An estimated one in five men in the area are addicts.

Chittaurgarh

Of all the former Rajput capitals, **CHITTAURGARH** (or Chittor), 115km northeast of Udaipur, was the strongest bastion of Hindu resistance against the Muslim invaders. No less than three mass suicides (*johars*) were committed over the centuries by the female inhabitants of its fort, whose husbands watched their wives, sisters and mothers burn alive before smearing ash from the sacred funeral pyres over their bodies and riding to their deaths on the battlefield below. An air of desolation still hangs over the honey-coloured ramparts, temples, towers and palaces of the old citadel, which sprawls over a rocky plateau high above the Mewar Valley. Though less imposing than Jodhpur's Meherangarh fort, the ruins evoke more vividly than any other in Rajasthan the zeal of medieval Rajput chivalry.

Below the fort, the modern town, whose population of 85,000 is spread over both banks of the River Ghambiri, holds little to detain travellers beyond the narrow bazaars of its old quarter, and some tourists choose to squeeze a tour of Chittaurgarh into a day-trip, or en route between Bundi and Udaipur. A one-night stop, however, leaves time for a more leisurely visit to the fort and a stroll through the town.

Some history

The uncompromising policy of death before submission followed by Chittor's **Sisodia** overlords ensured that its history is replete with tales of loyalty and terrible sacrifice. In 1303, during the reign of **Rana Ratan Singh**, a devastating attack was launched by **Ala-ud-din-Khalji**, the fiercest of the Delhi sultans. Having besieged the city, he offered to withdraw on condition that he be permitted to glimpse Ratan's legendarily beautiful queen, **Padmini**. After being admitted alone into the palace to view the queen's reflection in a lotus lake, however, the sultan contrived to have Ratan ambushed just as he was showing him out. But Padmini devised a plan to recapture him. Sending word that she would give herself up to the sultan, the queen left the fort accompanied by troops disguised as maids of honour. Once inside the Muslim camp, the transvestite commandos managed to rescue Rana Ratan, but 7000 of them were killed in the process. As a result, the defence of the fort foundered and the Rajputs lost the ensuing battle. Thirteen thousand women, led by Padmini, committed *johar* by throwing themselves and their children onto a huge funeral pyre, whereupon the angry sultan destroyed most of the fort's temples and palaces.

After returning to Rajput hands in 1326, Chittaurgarh enjoyed two hundred years of prosperity. However, in 1535, an unexpected onslaught led by **Sultan Bahadur Shah** from Gujarat once again decimated the Rajput ranks, and the women surrendered their lives in another ghastly act of *johar*. The young Rajput heir, **Udai Singh**, who had been whisked away to Kumbalgarh fort by his nursemaid Panna Dai, returned to Chittaurgarh at the age of 13. Aware of its vulnerability, he searched for a new site for his capital, and in 1559 founded Udaipur on the shore of Lake Pichola. This proved to be a prescient decision. **Akbar** laid siege to Chittaurgarh in 1567. His forces killed 30,000 of the fort's inhabitants; the women once again sacrificed themselves on a raging pyre, and many of the buildings within the fort were devastated. Although Chittaurgarh was ceded back to the Rajputs in 1616, the royal family never resettled there.

The fort

The ascent to the fort, protected by massive bastions, begins at **Padan Pole** in the east of town and winds upwards through a further six gateways (*poles*). Close to the second *pole* stand the *chhatris* of Kalla and Jaimal, heroic fighters who lost their lives in the final sacking of 1567. The houses of the small community that still inhabits the fort are huddled together near the final gate, **Rama Pole**.

As you enter the fort you pass the fifteenth-century **Shingara Chauri Mandir**, a highly adorned Jain temple dedicated to Shantinath, the sixteenth *tirthankara*. Ahead of this, the slowly deteriorating fifteenth-century **Palace of Rana Kumbha** – built by the ruler who presided over the period of Mewar's greatest prosperity – remains a classic example of Rajput architecture, and is immortalized as one of the scenes of *johar*. Nearby, the modern **Fateh Prakash Palace**, built for the maharana in the 1920s, is the site of a small, dimly lit **archeological museum**, filled with weapons (daily 10am–4.30pm; Rs3). Also in the palace compound is the **Kumbha Shyama temple**, crowned by a pyramidal roof and lofty tower, whose eighth-century sanctuary enshrines an image of Varaha, the boar incarnation of Vishnu. Slightly to the south, a smaller temple with a delicate curved tower, also constructed by Rana Kumbha, is dedicated to **Meerabai**, a Jodhpur princess and poet famed for her devotion to Krishna.

The main road within the fort continues south to its focal point, **Jaya Stambh**, the soaring "tower of victory", erected by Kumbha to commemorate his 1437 victory over the Muslim Sultan Mehmud Khilji of Malwa. This magnificent sand-coloured tower, whose nine storeys rise 36m, took a decade to build; its walls are lavishly carved with mythological scenes and images from all Indian religions, including Arabic inscriptions in praise of Allah. You can climb the dark narrow stairs to the very summit for Rs1 (daily dawn to dusk; free on Fri).

A path leads from the tower through more fine but ruined temples to **Gaumukh Kund**, a large reservoir fed by an underground stream that trickles through carved mouths (*mukh*) of cows (*gau*). This quiet spot, away from the main road, commands superb views across the plains. Buildings further south include the **Kalika Mata Temple**, originally dedicated to **Surya** in the eighth century, but rededicated to the Mother Goddess after renovations in 1568. Carvings on the outer wall include images of Surya, the guardians of the eight directions, and friezes depicting the churning of the ocean by the gods and demons, a popular creation myth. An image of Surya guards the main entrance to the temple. **Padmini's Palace**, now rather dilapidated, stands opposite, in the centre of the pool that allegedly revealed the queen to Ala-ud-din-Khalji.

The road continues south past the deer park to the point used for hurling traitors to their deaths, and returns north along the eastern ridge. Several temples line the route, but the most impressive monument is **Kirti Stambh**. The inspiration for the tower of victory, this smaller "tower of fame" was built by Digambaras as a monument to the first *tirthankara* Adinath, whose unclad image is repeated throughout its six storeys.

Practicalities

Chittaurgarh's **railway station** is in the western corner of the city. From here it's about 2km north to the **Roadways** (aka "**Kothwali**") **bus stand** on the west bank of the Ghambiri, and a further 2km east to the base of the fort.

RTDC's forlorn **tourist office**, where you can obtain free maps of the town (but little else), stands just north of the railway station on Station Road (Mon–Sat 10am–5pm; ☎01472/41089). The **Head Post Office** (Mon–Sat 10am–6pm) is on Shri Gurukul Road near the *Pratap Palace Hotel*.

Tours of the fort are most easily made by rickshaw (Rs75–100), complete with jangly pop music and silky curtains, or tonga (Rs50). However, tours tend to take in only the most famous monuments rather than the entire fort, which is 5km long and 1km wide. The best way to see the whole thing – which takes a good three hours – is to rent a **bike** from the shop on the road leading west from the crossroads outside the station. The initial climb is steep, but most of the roads on the plateau itself are flat.

Accommodation and eating

While Chittaurgarh's mid- and upper-range **hotels** cost a little more than elsewhere, places at the lower end of the price scale are pretty dingy. This is one place budget travellers might want to splash out. As for **food**, both the *Pratap Palace* and *Meera* have popular non-veg restaurants, of the dimly lit variety where travelling businessmen indulge in chicken eating and beer drinking. A more respectable, and cheaper, option is the *Ratu Raj Vatika*, across town. They specialize in traditional wedding feasts, but also have an excellent little pure-veg restaurant inside with tables spread over a lawn. The *paneer* dishes are particularly good, and you can get a range of delicious thalis for under Rs50. To find it, head up the insalubrious-smelling lane opposite the bus stand and follow the signboards in red Hindi writing.

Chetak, Neemuch Road, opposite the railway station ☎01472/41588 or 9. A notch more comfortable than the *Shalimar* opposite, with larger rooms and uniformed room boys, and a busy little restaurant downstairs. Best of the bunch immediately outside the railway station. ❹–❺

Meera, Neemuch Road, 500m south of the *Chetak* ☎01472/40266, ☎41427. The *Pratap*'s main competitor: larger, and with a more institutional decor. "Special deluxe" rooms have bathtubs. Good restaurant. ❺–❻

Moving on from Chittaurgarh

Moving on, there are two express trains a day to Udaipur: the #9615 Chetak Express at 6.50am (3hr 30min), and the #2915 Delhi Sarai Rohilla–Ahmedabad Express at 1.45pm (4hr 15min); both invariably leave late. In the opposite direction, the same two expresses go to Delhi (15hr–16hr); for Jaipur take the overnight Chetak Express (8hr), or the slightly faster #9770 Purna–Jaipur Express, which leaves early in the morning at 5.50am, arriving at 2pm the same day. The latter service is also the best for Ajmer (4hr 30min).

Travelling east to Bundi, you're better off catching the 2.30pm train, which follows a far more scenic route (try for a window seat on the north/left side of the carriage) and takes one-and-a-half hours less than the bus.

Padmini, Chanderiya Road ☎ 01472/41718. On the Ajmer road, just across the Bairach River. Chittor's biggest hotel is a modern wedding *bhavan* on the outskirts, with large but overpriced rooms and views of the concrete factory. Fifty percent discounts if you haggle. ⑤–⑥

Pratap Palace, Shri Gurukul Road, opposite the GPO ☎ 01472/40099, ℗ 41042. Frayed around the edges, but acceptable, with a relaxing garden and popular restaurant. Their "deluxe" rooms boast raunchy Krishna murals and plum-coloured satin bed covers, but the "ordinary" ones are much better value. ④–⑥

RTDC Panna, Station Road ☎ 01472/41238. One of RTDC's shabbier places, although the deluxe rooms are passable. Hopeless restaurant. ①–⑥

Kota

KOTA, 230km south of Jaipur on a fertile plain fed by Rajasthan's largest river, the Chambal, is one of the state's dirtier and less stimulating cities, and foreign visitors are sufficiently unusual to attract stares in the streets. But it does have some beautiful gardens, and its old palaces house one of the best museums in Rajasthan.

In the seventeenth century, when Kota was declared capital of a newly independent princely state by the Moghul emperor Jahangir, it was ruled by Rao Madho Singh of the Hadachauhan Rajputs. Today, with a population nudging 650,000, it is one of Rajasthan's major commercial and industrial cities, with hydro, atomic and thermal power stations lining the banks of the Chambal, alongside Asia's largest fertilizer plant. The nuclear plant of Rawat Bhata, protected by stringent security 60km southwest, is notorious for its impact on local villagers.

Greatly prized saris from the village of **Kaithoon**, 20km southeast of Kota, are sold in all the bazaars. Made of tightly woven cotton or silk, and often highlighted with golden thread, they are known here as *masooria* and elsewhere as *Kota doria* saris.

The City

The residential areas, bazaars, fort, City Palace and museum east of the Chambal face harsh buildings and factory smokestacks across the river. **Kishor Sagar**, an artificial lake built in 1346, gives picturesque relief. The red and white palace in its centre, **Jag Mandir**, was commissioned by Prince Dher Deh of Bundi in 1346 and can be visited only with permission from the Superintendent Engineer of Kota; ask at the tourist office. Gardens to the north of the tank are lush with mango trees, dahlias and palms, and crocodiles and gharial sun themselves in a shallow pond in the **Chambal Gardens** on the edge of the river a few kilometres south of the fort.

In the Brijvilas Palace on the northern edge of the lake, the **Government Museum** (daily except Fri 10am–5pm; Rs2) has a small collection of clothes, weapons and miniature paintings and a fascinating hand-drawn plan of Kota's manoeuvres during the Mutiny of 1857 that shows positions of defence and attack in minute detail.

Kota's **fort**, raised above the flat bank of the Chambal 2km south of the bus stand, was built in 1264 by Rajkumar Jait Singh of Bundi. Construction of the **City Palace** and offices of state within the fortifications began in 1625, and continued sporadically until the early years of this century. Although the older fort ramparts are falling into disrepair, the palaces are still in excellent condition. Apartments in the heart of the palaces house the excellent **Maharao Madho Singh Museum** (daily except Fri 11am–5pm; Rs50; Rs50 extra for camera, Rs75 extra for video). Among a vast collection of carefully decorated weapons, the size and severity of which is out of this world, you'll see shields adorned with the solar symbol of the Hadachauhan Rajputs, large enough to protect an elephant. Solid silver artefacts and fading sepia photographs of viceroys, maharajas, polo teams and Queen Victoria record the extravagance of royalty, and there are some outstanding examples of *Kota Kamba*, miniatures from Kota's school of painting. The most spectacular apartment is **Raj Mahal**, which contains the royal throne.

Practicalities

Kota's **railway station** is in the north of town, a few kilometres from the central **bus stand**. The **tourist office** (Mon–Sat 8am–6pm; ☎0744/327695) is in the RTDC *Chambal Hotel*, Nayarpura, not far from the bus stand. Changing **money** is a time-consuming process. The State Bank of India on Aerodrome Circle will change travellers' cheques: other banks do not. The **post office** is on Station Road (Mon–Sat 6am–6pm).

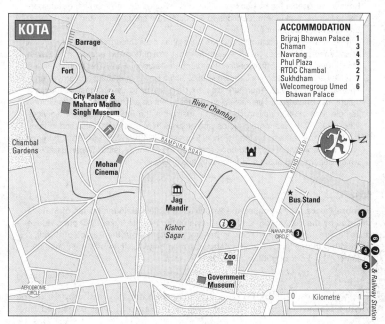

Accommodation and eating

Kota's **hotels** cater mainly for passing business travellers, and the cheaper rest-houses reflect the dustiness and neglect that prevails in the town. Inexpensive dives are grouped around the railway station and the areas known as Civil Lines and Nayapura close to the bus stand and main market. In addition to the hotel **restaurants** – the *Navrang* and *Chaman* both have reasonable dining rooms open to nonresidents – try the cheap but good veg *Barkha Restaurant* on Nayapura Circle. Failing that, you'll have to settle for a roadside stall – there are a couple of decent ones outside the *Phul Plaza*.

Brijraj Bhawan Palace ☏ 0744/450529, ℗ 450057. Former British Residency, now home to the Maharao of Kota; an oasis of calm in beautiful gardens on the banks of the Chambal. Lovely rooms and suites, plus a restaurant for residents; full board available. ❼–❽

Chaman, Nayapura ☏ 0744/323377. One of cheapest lodges in town; the surface dirt makes it look worse than it is. Quieter rooms at the back, away from the road. ❷

Navrang, Station Road, near the Post Office ☏ 323294, ℗ 450044. Dependably clean mid-scale hotel ranged around a central courtyard, with some a/c rooms and a little restaurant. ❺–❻

Phul Plaza, Civil Lines ☏ 0744/329350, ℗ 322614. Newish hotel with a wide range of

rooms; best fallback if the *Navrang* next door is full. ❹–❻

RTDC Chambal, Kshar Bagh ☏ 0744/326527. Typically shabby government-run place, with uninspiring but spacious rooms. ❹–❻

Sukhdham, near *Umed Bhawan Palace* ☏ 0744/320081 or 332661, ℗ 327781. Congenial family-run guesthouse in a sandstone colonial mansion, set amid three acres of gardens. The best choice in this class. Meals available. ❻–❼

Welcomegroup Umed Bhawan Palace, Station Road, Khetri Phatak ☏ 0744/325262, ℗ 451110. Former palace converted into swish four-star hotel, with original Edwardian furniture and ostentatious European-Rajput fusion architecture. Rooms start at Rs1850. ❽

Moving on from Kota

Kota is well connected by **bus** to destinations in Rajasthan and across the state border to Bhopal and Indore. Services to Bundi leave more or less every half an hour, taking around one hour.

Travellers heading northeast towards **Agra** often pass through Kota to pick up the main broad-gauge line, which is also the most straightforward approach to **Sawai Madhopur**, jumping-off place for Ranthambore National Park. The recommended service here is the Paschim Express #2955, which leaves at 8.50am and arrives one-and-a-half hours later. There are also six daily **trains** to **Delhi** (most of them via Jaipur and Bharatpur). The easiest one to get a seat on at short notice is the Golden Temple Mail #2903, leaving daily at 11.30am, but the Rajdhani Express services #2951/2953/2431 are more punctual and quicker. To **Mumbai** (via Ujjain and Indore), the fastest trains are again the Rajdhani Expresses #2432/2952/2954, but for **Jaipur** you'll probably find it easier to book a seat on the Mumbai–Jaipur Superfast #2955, which departs at 8.50am and takes only two hours.

Bundi

Jeypore Palace may be called the Versailles of India; Udaipur's House of State is dwarfed by the hill round it and the spread of the Pichola Lake; Jodhpur's House of strife, grey tower on red rock, is the work of giants, but the Palace of Bundi, even in broad daylight, is such a palace as men build for themselves in uneasy dreams – the work of goblins rather than of men.

Rudyard Kipling

The walled town of **BUNDI**, 37km north of Kota, lies in the north of the former Hadaoti state, shielded on the north, east and west by jagged outcrops of the Vindhya Range. Visible only from the south and guarded by the tremendous **Taragarh** or "star fort" high in the north of town, the site made a perfect capital for the Hadachauhans, perched in their immense turreted **palace**, beneath the lofty walls of the fort. Although settled in 1241, 25 years before Kota, Bundi never amounted to more than a modest market centre, and remains relatively untouched by modern developments. Yet its palace alone ranks among the most spectacular monuments in Rajasthan, while the almost complete absence of intrusive modern structures within the **old walled town**, site of several impressive step-wells and crumbling stucco *havelis*, make this a far more appealing destination than other more famous landmarks in the state.

ACCOMMODATION

Haveli Braj Bushanjee	4	RTDC Vrindawati	1
Haveli Kartoun	2	Uma Megh	5
Ishwari Niwas	7	**RESTAURANT**	
Kishan Niwas	6		
Lake View	3	Diamond	A

The Town

In his *Annals and Antiquities of Rajasthan* (1829), Col James Tod, the first British official ever to explore the region, wrote that the "coup d'oeil of the castellated palace of Bundi, from which ever side you approach it, is perhaps the most striking in India". Walking north through the bazaar today, with the creamy stone domes, cupolas and bleached walls of the **palace** spilling down the hillside ahead, you'll doubtless agree. Built during the sixteenth and seventeenth centuries in authentic Rajput style, this was one of the few royal abodes in Rajasthan untainted by Moghul influence. Its appearence is surprisingly homogeneous considering the number of times it was added to over the years, although some wings are virtually derelict now, including the one that harbours Bundi's greatest art treasures: its famous **murals**. As some of these are hidden behind locked doors, it's a good idea to arrange a guide to show you around; the *Haveli Braj Bhushanjee* can put you in touch with a good one.

A short steep path winds to the entrance, **Hathi Pole**, flanked by the elephants that are so common in the Hadaoti region. From the small courtyard within, steps lead to **Ratan Daulat**, the Diwan-i-Am or Hall of Public Audience, with its simple marble throne. Shrine rooms and the womens' quarters above it contain the cream of Bundi's murals, but these lie within the so-called "closed portion" of the palace and you'll need prior permission (or a good guide) to see them. Other wall-paintings, however, may be viewed in the **Chittra Shala**, a courtyard enclosed by cloisters whose sides swirl with elaborate blue, green, turquoise and white images of battles, court scenes and religious tableaux. Views over Bundi from the projecting balconies take in the **Nawal Sagar** tank with its half-submerged temple. The best views of all are from the Taragarh, though it's a steep climb to see them.

A walk from the palace westwards through the walled bazaar and old gateways takes you to Rajasthan's most spectacular step-well, **Raniji-ki-Baori**, built in 1699 by Nathwati, wife of Rao Raja Singh. One among a hundred such wells in Bundi, it lies deep beneath the surface of a small park, reached by a flight of steps punctuated by platforms and embellished pillars. As you descend, look for the beautifully carved panels showing the ten *avatars* of Lord Vishnu which line the side walls.

East of town, a few kilometres by rickshaw, the beautiful **Sukh Mahal** – Rao Raja Vishun Singh's summer palace – on the northern shore of **Jait Sagar** tank, is where Rudyard Kipling wrote *Kim*. Now the regional water authority's rest house, it is generally closed to visitors, but you can take a pleasant stroll in the gardens further along the west side of the lake, the **Sahr Bagh**, which encloses sixty crumbling royal cenotaphs. If the door to it is locked, ask for the key at the *chowkidar*'s hut, on your left just after the gateway over the main road.

Practicalities

Buses run between Kota and Bundi (1hr) every half-hour, and cover the journey **to Chittaurgarh** (5hr) three times a day, two of them continuing to Udaipur; better still, jump on the 8.10am train from the station on the southern edge of town (only 3hr 30min). Coming **from Chittaurgarh**, you can avoid a long and tedious road journey by catching the 2.30pm train, which gets you in here at 6pm. Bundi is also connected by hourly buses to Ajmer (165km; 4hr), Jaipur (210km; 8hr) and Jodhpur (11hr). For Pushkar, there are three daily direct buses (7hr 30min); Sawai Madhopur (for Ranthambore National Park) can also be reached by road (5hr), but it's quicker to travel down to Kota and pick up a train connection there (see p.276).

Note that as yet, there is nowhere in Bundi to **change money**; the nearest bank with a foreign exchange facility is in Kota (see p.275).

Accommodation and eating

With its lake and palace views, and traffic- and tout-free backstreets, Bundi makes a relaxing place to **stay**; many travellers find themselves moving on well after they'd intended. Most of the accommodation is in old *havelis* that for once offer a good choice of budget rooms. Pick of the bunch has to be the *Haveli Braj Bhushanjee*, just below the palace, but there are plenty of cheaper fall-backs further up the lane. Book in advance and you can be sure of an evening meal, otherwise the best **restaurant** is the modest *Garden*, next to the *Lake View*, whose speciality is "Rajasthani Pizza", served on a lakeside lawn. The only other option is the run-of-the-mill *Diamond*, just south of Chogan Gate in the bazaar, which serves cheap rice and veg meals.

Haveli Braj Bhushanjee, just below the palace ☎0747/442322, ℱ442142, ℮res@kiplingsbundi .com. The former home of the Bundi prime minister's elder brother, this 150-year-old *haveli* is full of character, with original murals and family portraits on the walls. Comfortable, tastefully furnished rooms at various prices, and delicious home-cooked food, served in the dining hall or an outside terrace with superb views of the palace. Well worth splashing out on if this is normally above your budget. ❹–❼

Haveli Katoun, near Gopal Mandir Balchandpara ☎0747/444311. Smallish rooms (some with bathrooms) in new block of an old *haveli*. Leafy garden; meals available on request. ❸

Ishwari Niwas, 1 Civil Lines ☏0747/442414.
Well-appointed rooms (some a/c) in a period building on the south side of town. Comfortable enough, and they serve passable food, but too far from the palace. ❻

Kishan Niwas, near Lakshmi Nath temple ☏0747/445807, ✉ dilipparasher@hotmail.com.
Very rudimentary, but genuinely hospitable, paying guesthouse in the thick of the bazaar. Attached bathrooms, home cooking and rock-bottom rates.
❶–❷

Lake View, Bohra Meghwahan Ji-ki-Haveli, opposite Nawal Sagar tank ☏0747/442326. Another ramshackle *haveli* whose owners claim descent from the Diwan of Bundi: deservedly popular,

friendly, near the lake and palace, with simple, clean rooms. Home-made thalis for Rs50. ❶–❷

RTDC Vrindawati, Jait Sagar tank
☏0747/442473. Run-of-the-mill government hotel in a great location on the west shore of Jait Sagar, near the Sukh Mahal. Good-value rooms, but a characterless option compared with the *havelis* across town. ❹–❻

Uma Megh, Balchandpara ☏0747/442040 or 442191. Best of the budget options, with a range of inexpensive rooms in *haveli* of former diwan (prime minister). The best of them, on the upper floor, have large windows overlooking the lake and attached bathrooms. This place has seen better days, but the rooftop views and warm family welcome more than compensate. ❶–❸

RAJASTHAN | Travel details

Travel details

Trains

Jaipur to: Agra (2 daily; 7hr); Ahmedabad (2 daily; 14hr); Ajmer (5 daily; 2–3hr); Alwar (7 daily; 2hr 35min–4hr); Bikaner (3 daily; 6hr 30min–10hr); Calcutta (2 daily; 29hr); Chittaurgarh (2 daily; 7hr 40min–8hr 15min); Churu (3 daily; 5hr 20min); Delhi (8 daily; 4hr 20min–6hr 30); Jhunjhunu (3 daily; 4hr 40min–6hr); Jodhpur (4–5 daily; 5hr–6hr 10min); Kota (3 daily; 3hr 45min); Mount Abu (3 daily; 8–9hr); Mumbai (2 daily; 16hr 30min–22hr); Sawai Madhopur (2–3 daily; 2hr–3hr 20min); Sikar (5 daily; 3hr); Udaipur (2 daily; 10–12hr).

Jodhpur to: Abu Road (3 daily; 5hr); Agra (2 daily; 13hr); Ahmedabad (3 daily; 10hr); Barmer (2 daily; 4hr 30min–5hr); Bikaner (1 daily; 5hr); Delhi (3 daily; 11–13hr); Jaipur (4–5 daily; 5–7hr); Jaisalmer (2 daily; 6hr 15min–8hr40min); Osian (1 daily; 2hr 30min); Udaipur (2 daily; 12hr 30min).

Udaipur to: Ahmedabad (1 daily; 9hr 20min); Ajmer (2 daily; 8hr–12hr 50min); Chittaurgarh (2 daily; 3hr 30min–4hr 30min); Delhi (2 daily; 19–23hr); Jaipur (2 daily; 10–12hr); Jodhpur (2 daily; 12hr 30min).

Buses

Jaipur to: Abu Road (2 daily; 11hr); Agra (12 daily; 5hr); Ahmedabad (1 daily; 16hr); Ajmer (hourly; 1hr 55min–2hr 30min); Alwar (hourly; 4hr); Bharatpur (every 30min; 4hr 30min); Bikaner (11 daily; 7hr 30min); Calcutta (4 weekly; 24hr); Chittaurgarh (7 daily; 7hr 15min); Churu (every 30min; 4hr 30min); Delhi (every 15 min; 6hr); Jaisalmer (2 daily; 13–15hr); Jhunjhunu (every 30min; 5hr); Jodhpur (every 30min; 7–8hr); Kota (12 daily; 6hr);

Nawalgarh (hourly; 3hr); Pushkar (9 daily; 3hr 30min–4hr); Sawai Madhopur (2 daily; 4hr 30min); Sikar (every 15min; 3hr); Udaipur (hourly; 10hr).

Jaisalmer to: Ajmer (1 daily; 12hr); Barmer (hourly; 3hr 30min); Bhuj (1 daily; 16hr); Bikaner (3 daily; 7hr); Jaipur (2 daily; 13–15hr); Udaipur (1 daily; 15hr).

Jodhpur to: Agra (1 daily; 10hr); Ahmedabad (4 daily; 11hr); Ajmer (hourly; 5hr); Bharatpur (2 daily; 10hr); Bikaner (13 daily; 6hr); Delhi (3 daily; 11–12hr); Jaipur (6 daily; 7hr); Jaisalmer (hourly; 5hr 30min); Mount Abu (1 daily; 9hr 30min); Mumbai (3 daily; 22hr); Osian (every 30min; 2hr); Udaipur (9 daily; 9–10hr).

Udaipur to: Ahmedabad (hourly; 7hr); Ajmer (hourly; 7hr); Bikaner (1 daily; 12hr); Bundi (10 daily; 7hr); Chittaurgarh (hourly; 3hr–3hr 30min); Delhi (2 daily; 15hr); Jaipur (hourly; 10hr); Jaisalmer (1 daily; 15hr); Jodhpur (9 daily; 9–10hr); Kota (10 daily; 6hr); Mount Abu (8 daily; 7hr); Mumbai (daily; 2hr 15min); Ranakpur (6 daily; 3hr).

Flights

Jaipur to: Ahmedabad (3 weekly; 1hr); Calcutta (6 weekly; 2hr–3hr 50min); Delhi (3 daily; 40min–1hr); Jodhpur (1 daily; 40min); Mumbai (2 daily; 1hr 30min); Udaipur (2 daily; 1hr 15min–1hr 50min).

Jodhpur to: Delhi (daily; 1hr 50min); Jaipur (1 daily; 40min); Mumbai (2 daily; 2hr 10min); Udaipur (daily; 40min).

Udaipur to: Delhi (22 weekly; 1hr 55min); Jaipur (2 daily; 1hr 15min–1hr 50min); Jodhpur (daily; 40min); Mumbai (daily; 2hr 15min).

279

CHAPTER 3

Highlights

＊ **Taj Mahal**
The highest expression of Moghul culture, which you can see for free from the far bank of the Yamuna River in Agra. See p.289

＊ **Akbar's mausoleum, Sikandra**
The great Moghul's tomb looks just as it does in old miniatures, with tame monkeys and deer wandering in its ornamental gardens. See p.298

＊ **Fatehpur Sikhri**
An awesomely grand deserted palace complex, straddling an arid ridge near the Rajasthani border. See p.303

＊ **Kalinjar Fort**
Remote fortifications in UP's dusty badlands, far from the tourist trail. See p.338

＊ **Varanasi**
Take a boat on the Ganges before dawn to watch the sun rise over India's most ancient and sacred city. See p.339

＊ **Sarnath**
Evocative ruins on the site of Buddha's first sermon. See p.355

3

Uttar Pradesh

U **TTAR PRADESH**, "the Northern State", known as **UP** since the days of the United Provinces, under the Raj, is the heartland of Hinduism and Hindi, dominating the nation in culture, religion, language and politics. A vast steamy plain of the Ganges, its history is very much the history of India, and its temples and monuments – Buddhist, Hindu and Muslim – are among the most impressive in the country.

Not far from Delhi, in the west of the state, **Agra**, home of the Taj Mahal, and deserted **Fatehpur Sikri** stand as poignant reminders of the great Moghuls. Nearby, on the other hand, somehow sheltered from successive waves of Muslim conquest, the much-mythologized Hindu land of **Braj**, centred on **Mathura** and **Vrindavan**, was the childhood playground of the god Krishna.

Central UP, and especially **Lucknow**, the state capital, is redolent with memories of the lavish and ultimately decadent last days of Muslim rule, when the Kingdom of Avadh faded away before the advance of the British imperialists in the nineteenth century. The scars of the First War of Independence, the "Mutiny", a despairing reaction to the British usurpation of power, have in places yet to heal. To the east, **Allahabad** is the site of one of the world's largest religious fairs, when millions congregate at the confluence of the Ganges and the Yamuna rivers to mark the auspicious occasion of **Kumbh Mela**. Along the southern borders of the state, the rugged Vindhya Mountains mark the end of the Deccan plateau. Once the domain of the Chandela Rajputs, the belt known as **Bundelkhand** harbours forgotten fortresses such as gigantic **Kalinjar**; the fort at **Jhansi** remains a symbol of the struggle for Independence.

The Ganges meanders across the vast plains of **Eastern UP** to the holiest Hindu city of all – the sacred *tirtha* (crossing-place) of **Varanasi**, where death transports the soul to final liberation. Even before Hinduism, this land was sacred; the Buddha himself, and Mahavira, the founder of Jainism, frequented Varanasi, and the whole state, from Mathura to **Sarnath**, on the outskirts of Varanasi, and beyond to the great schools of learning in Bihar, was long under the influence of Buddhism.

Accommodation price codes

All accommodation prices in this book have been categorized using the price codes below. Prices given are for a double room, and all taxes are included. For more details, see p.51.

❶ up to Rs100	❹ Rs300–400	❼ Rs900–1500
❷ Rs100–200	❺ Rs400–600	❽ Rs1500–2500
❸ Rs200–300	❻ Rs600–900	❾ Rs2500 and upwards

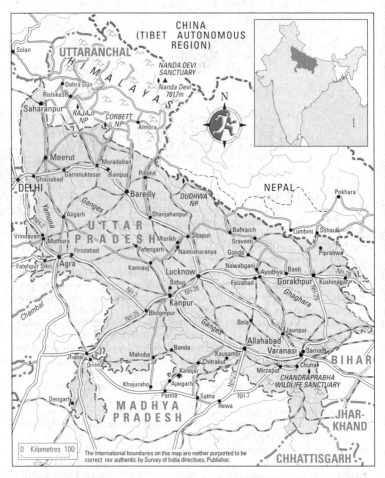

Although UP was once a thriving centre of Islamic jurisprudence and culture, many Muslims departed during the painful years after Independence, and the Muslim population now comprises just sixteen percent. In recent years, **Gangetic UP**, known derisively elsewhere as the "cow belt", has been plagued by caste politics and is dominated by the right-wing Hindu BJP, who control its government. The state acquired an unfortunate reputation as the focus of bitter communal tensions, most notoriously in the wake of the destruction of the Babri Masjid mosque in **Ayodhya** in 1992.

With an efficient if basic state bus system and an excellent railway network, **travelling around** the state is generally straightforward (except in Bundelkhand in the south). The major tourist cities, **Agra** and **Varanasi**, have been coping with visitors and pilgrims for centuries; and today have good transport connections and all the facilities the traveller could require.

Western UP

Western Uttar Pradesh, on the fringes of Delhi, and serving as the gateway to the heartland of the subcontinent, has always been close to the centre of power in India. Once the Moghul capital, **Agra** is renowned for the most stunning mausoleum in the world – the **Taj Mahal** – as well as the stupendous battlements and palaces of the **Agra Fort**. Not far away, the sandstone pavilions of **Fatehpur Sikri**, built by the Moghul emperor Akbar and abandoned after only fifteen years, remain perfectly preserved in the dry desert-like air.

The earliest records of the area date back 2500 years, when Gautama Buddha visited the ancient city of **Mathura**, whose strategic position at the junction of several major trade routes had already earned it the prosperity that was to attract numerous adventurers and conquerors. Later, Mathura was incorporated at the centre of the Hindu mythological landscape of **Braj**, associated with the childhood of Krishna.

Immediately north and east of Delhi, an industrial belt of commercial and administrative towns on busy road and railway networks includes **Meerut**, which is only noteworthy as the place where the Mutiny of 1857 began.

Agra

The splendour of **AGRA** – capital of all India under the Moghuls – remains undiminished, from the massive fort to the magnificent **Taj Mahal**. Along with Delhi, 204km northwest, and Jaipur in Rajasthan, Agra is the third apex of the "Golden Triangle", India's most popular tourist itinerary. It fully merits that status; the Taj effortlessly transcends all the frippery and commercialism that surrounds it, and continues to have a fresh and immediate impact on all who see it.

That said, Agra city itself can be an intense experience, even for seasoned India hands. Years of corruption and political neglect have reduced its infrastructure to a shambles: filthy water and open sewers are ubiquitous, power cuts routine, and the traffic pollution appalling (some mornings you can barely see the sun through the fog of fumes). Moreover, as a tourist you'll have to contend with often overwhelming crowds at the major monuments, absurdly high admission fees, and some of Asia's most persistent touts, commission merchants and rickshaw-wallahs. Don't, however, let all this put you off. Although it's possible to see Agra on a day-trip from Delhi, the Taj alone deserves so much more – a fleeting visit would miss the subtleties of its many moods, as the light changes from sunrise to sunset – while the warren of old streets and bazaars around it offers glimpses of an Indo-Muslim way of life that, in many respects, has altered little since the time of the Moghuls.

Some history

Little is known of the pre-Muslim history of Agra; one of the earliest chronicles, dated to the Afghan invasion under Ibrahim Ghaznavi in 1080 AD, describes a robust fort occupying a chain of hills, with a flourishing city strategically placed at the crossroads between the north and the centre of

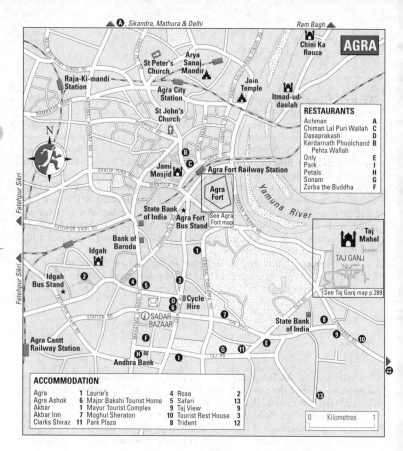

RESTAURANTS

Achman	A
Chiman Lal Puri Wallah	C
Dasaprakash	D
Kerdarnath Phoolchand	B
Pehta Wallah	
Only	E
Park	I H G
Petals	
Sonam	F
Zorba the Buddha	G

ACCOMMODATION

Agra	1	Laurie's	4	Rose	2
Agra Ashok	6	Major Bakshi Tourist Home	5	Safari	13
Akbar	1	Mayur Tourist Complex		Taj View	9
Akbar Inn	7	Moghul Sheraton	10	Tourist Rest House	3
Clarks Shiraz	11	Park Plaza	8	Trident	12

India. However, Agra remained a minor administrative centre until 1504, when the Sultan of Delhi, **Sikander Lodi**, moved his capital here, to keep a check on the warring factions of his empire. The ruins of the Lodis' great city can still be seen on the eastern bank of the Yamuna. After defeating the last Lodi Sultan, Ibrahim Lodi, at Panipat in 1526, **Babur**, the founder of the Moghul empire, sent ahead his son **Humayun** to capture Agra. In gratitude for their benevolent treatment at his hands, the family of the Raja of Gwalior rewarded the Moghul with jewellery and precious stones – among them the legendary **Koh-i-noor Diamond**, now among the crown jewels of England.

Agra's greatest days arrived during the reign of Humayun's son, **Akbar the Great** (1556–1605), with the construction of Agra Fort. The city maintained its position as the capital of the empire for over a century; even when **Shah Jahan**, Jahangir's son and successor, built a new city in Delhi, his heart remained in Agra. He pulled down many of the earlier red-sandstone structures in the fort, replacing them with his hallmark – exquisite marble buildings. Although the empire flourished under his heir Aurangzeb (1658–1707), his intolerance towards non-Muslims stirred a hornets' nest. Agra was occupied successively by the Jats, the Marathas, and eventually the British.

After the uprising in 1857, the city lost the headquarters of the government of the Northwestern Provinces and the High Court to Allahabad. Agra began to decline, but its medieval treasures ensured its survival, and today the city is once again prospering, as an industrial and commercial centre as well as a tourist destination.

Arrival and information

Agra has no less than six **railway stations**. The busiest is **Agra Cantonment (Cantt)**, in the southwest, which serves Delhi, Gwalior, Jhansi and points south, has a tourist information counter, and is near most hotels. Trains from Rajasthan pull in close to the Jami Masjid at **Agra Fort Station**, further from the main hub of hotels. Don't be persuaded to get off at Agra City Station, an expensive rickshaw ride away from town.

To get to a hotel, use the prepaid auto-rickshaw/taxi booth at Agra Cantonment Station (Rs40/90) or flag down one of the cycle rickshaws (Rs25) that wait in the forecourt outside; avoid the drivers who dash onto the platform to find passengers. They invariably demand an inflated price and can get quite aggressive. Bear in mind, too, that most cycle rickshaw and auto-rickshaw drivers will try and gain commission by taking you to a hotel and may even tell you that the hotel of your choice is closed.

Buses usually stop at **Idgah bus stand** close to Agra Cantonment station, though services from Mathura arrive at the more chaotic **Agra** Fort **bus stand**, just west of the fort. Some buses from Delhi stop outside the fort gate, where you'll have no trouble finding a rickshaw.

Information
Agra has two **tourist offices**, one run by the Government of India, at 191 The Mall (Mon–Fri 9am–5.30pm, Sat 9am–1pm; ℡0562/363959), and one run by UP Tourism, close to the *Clarks Shiraz,* at 64 Taj Rd (same hours; ℡0562/360517); there is also an information booth at Cantonment station. The Government of India office is better organized and provides information about other destinations, though both supply information on hotels and local sights, and details of **tours** that start and end at Agra Cantonment railway station.

City transport

Plans are being considered to create a two-kilometre pollution-free exclusion zone around the Taj banning the petrol and diesel-powered vehicles which choke the city and spoil its architecture. At present, however, only a 500-metre ban is enforced (on scooters, auto-rickshaws and taxis), while the only environment-friendly initiative in operation is an **electric bus** for tourists, connecting the fort to the Taj (Rs1), and the fleet of green-painted tempos and auto-rickshaws, whose exhaust fumes are no less noxious for the "Clean Agra, Green Agra" slogans daubed across their backs. Although becoming fairly scarce, **tongas**, horse-drawn carriages, may also be encouraged as part of the pollution-control scheme, but the sight of skinny near-lame horses, often covered in open sores, tends to put most people off.

Another alternative is the city's dwindling fleet of **cycle rickshaws**, whose persistent drivers invariably offer their services for day tours; more often than not they'll have a book full of encouraging comments from delighted tourists. Apart from being cleaner and greener than autos, they provide a livelihood for

Tours

There are currently two official tours run by UP Tourism, designed to coincide with the main train connections on the Taj Express to and from Delhi. Pickup for both starts at 9.30am at the Government of India tourist office on The Mall, with the second stop at Agra Cantonment railway station at 10.20am. The main tour (Rs750, including all admission charges) then proceeds to Fatehpur Sikri before returning to the *Taj Kheema* hotel for lunch (not included in the price) at 2pm; the other tour just goes to Fatehpur Sikri before returing to Agra in time to catch the Taj Express to New Delhi Nizamudddin at 6.25pm. Though useful for those with limited time, the tours are rather rushed and don't cover Akbar's mausoleum and the tomb of Itmad-ud-Daulah ("Baby Taj").

some of the city's poorest inhabitants. An American-backed NGO has been attempting to improve the lot of Agra's rickshaw-wallahs by introducing new, lightweight, super-strong cycle-rickshaws, complete with raised passenger seats and two-speed gears. You'll come across these in the more touristy areas of town, where their drivers are encouraged to buy them using zero-interest bank loans, paid back at a manageable rate of Rs5 per day – considerably less than the rental fees most rickshaw-wallahs have to pay to their bosses.

Auto-rickshaws are faster, but contribute in no small part to Agra's traffic and pollution problems. Fares, including waiting time, are reasonable as long as you bargain hard, although the trip out to Akbar's tomb and other monuments on the outskirts of the city can cost up to Rs100. **Taxis** are handy for longer trips to the airport or Fatehpur Sikri. Expensive hotels have their own fleet of vehicles, and there are taxi ranks at the stations and airport.

Whichever form of transport you choose, expect to have to haggle hard. Agra sees so many "fresh" tourists that the drivers will always quote high prices. Also, note that many rickshaw- and taxi-drivers will stop at jewellers, marble shops and the like to earn **commission**; some will even quote you a lower fare if you agree to visit a couple of emporiums en route. Don't consent to this (their commission will only be added to your bill should you buy something).

The best way to sidestep the hassle of public transport is to rent a **bicycle**, and do everything at your own pace. Try the rental shop near the *Taj View Hotel* or the Raja Cycle Stall near the tonga stand in Taj Ganj; charges should be around Rs4 per hour, and no more than Rs35 per day. If you **walk**, expect an unending stream of offers from cycle- and auto-rickshaw-wallahs.

Whatever form of transport you opt for, an early start for the Taj is essential; book rickshaws and taxis the night before.

Accommodation

Taj Ganj, the grid of narrow lanes immediately south of the Taj, is where most budget travellers end up in Agra. With their matchless rooftop views, laid-back terrace cafés and rock-bottom room rates, its little guesthouses can be great places to stay. Their downside is the constant hassle at street level, and the fact that the whole Taj Ganj tourist "scene" can completely eclipse the traditional feel of the area. In this case, you may be happier in the more modern **Tourist Complex** district, southwest of Taj Ganj, or the leafier, greener **Cantonment**, near Agra Cantonment railway station, which has places to suit every budget, from overlanders' camp sites to luxurious five-star hotels.

Taj Ganj

The hotels and guesthouses listed below are all marked on the **map** of Taj Ganj on p.289.

Host, West Gate ☎ 0562/361010. Simple, small rooms, most of them with air-coolers, and a view of the Taj from the roof. Their sheets are holed, but this is otherwise a well-maintained place that's ideal as an overspill for the *Siddhartha* next door. Ask for rooms #200 or 201. ②–③

India, South Gate ☎ 0562/330909. Tiny, ultra-basic place whose rudimentary rooms (the one on the upper storey is best) are worth enduring for the warm hospitality of the proprietress, Mrs Nirmal. ①

Indo, 2/9 South Gate (no phone). Another pint-size family guesthouse with rock-bottom rates, cell-like, dark rooms and friendly (mostly female) management. ①

Kamal, Chowk Kagzi, South Gate ☎ 0562/360126. Run-of-the-mill attached rooms in a dull concrete building, but right in the thick of things and with a great view from the rooftop restaurant. ②–④

Noorjahan, South Gate ☎ 0562/333034. Closest to the south gate of the Taj, the rooms here are small and very basic (some without attached bathrooms). To sample the acclaimed view, you'll have to climb a ladder to the roof. ①–②

Shah Jahan, South Gate ☎ 0562/331159. Variously priced, mostly clean and cosy rooms with tiny bathrooms, run by an elderly Muslim gentleman who looks like he just arrived from Samarkand. The best are on the top floor, and there's a café with great views on the roof. ②–③

Shanti Lodge, Chowk Kagzi, South Gate ☎ 9837/17984. One of the most popular back-packers' places in Taj Ganj: avoid the poky rooms with smelly shower-toilets in the old block, and ask for one in the new annexe around the back, which are large, well ventilated and have clean tiled bathrooms. From the rooftop restaurant, the views of the Taj are the best in this area. ③

Sheela, East Gate ☎ 0562/333074 or 331194, ⓔ hotelsheela@yahoo.com. Easily the best budget hotel in Taj Ganj: secluded, impeccably clean rooms only 200m from the Taj (inside the "no pollution zone"), ranged around a lovely little garden; the air-cooled options are larger and only slightly more expensive. Dependably hygienic restaurant (see Eating) and friendly Alsatian dog called Tiger add to its charm. Advanced telephone bookings accepted. ②–④

Shyam Palace, next to the Central Bank ☎ 0562/331599 or 331482. Large, clean, marble-floored rooms opening onto a peaceful courtyard garden that doubles as a low-key restaurant; all with fresh linen, attached bathrooms and 24hr hot water power showers. Very good value, but check your bill carefully for extra "service charges". ③

Siddhartha, West Gate ☎ 0562/331238 or 330931. A clean and popular guesthouse with plain, spacious rooms, set around a leafy courtyard café that includes fragments of medieval walls. The best rooms (Rs275) on the top floor come with air-coolers. ②–④

UPTDC Taj Kheema, East Gate ☎ 0562/330140. Misconceived, overpriced government-run hotel with a small handful of uninspiring airless rooms, some a/c. Superb views of the Taj from a grassy mound in the gardens, but nonresidents have to pay Rs25 just to sit there. ⑤–⑦

Cantonment

The hotels listed below are all marked on the **map** of Agra on p.284.

Agra, F M Cariappa Road ☎ 0562/363331, ⓕ 265830. Former British *burra-sahib*'s bungalow that's retained some of its old-world charm in spite of general shabbiness. The rooms (some a/c) are dim and musty but spacious, with large bathrooms and hot showers. ③–④

Agra Ashok, 6B The Mall ☎ 0562/361223, ⓕ 265830. Rather dowdy government-run luxury hotel with gardens and a swimming pool; offers a choice of high-standard expensive restaurants. This is the least pricey option in the four- to five-star bracket. ⑨

Akbar, 196 FM Cariappa Rd ☎ 0562/269438, ⓕ 226691. Budget rooms in the annexe of a run-down cantonment bungalow, set amid peaceful gardens close to Agra Fort. The more expensive rooms (Rs300 double) are well worth the extra. ②–④

Akbar Inn, 21 Mall Rd ☎ 0562/226836. Deservedly popular budget rooms surrounding a lawn, deep in the cantonment green belt. The rock-bottom options are some of the cheapest rooms in Agra (Rs60), but ultra-basic and airless. The pricier ones are much larger, and open onto a long veranda where simple meals are served. ①–④

Clarks Shiraz, 54 Taj Rd ☎ 0562/226221, ⓕ 226128, ⓦ www.clarkraz@nde.vsnl.net.in. Huge tower-block five-star hotel in a pleasant cantonment setting with extensive grounds, swimming pool, golf green, restaurants, bar, shopping arcade, banks and travel services on the premises. Rooms start at around $100. ⑨

Laurie's, Mahatma Gandhi Road ⓣ 0562/364536, ⓕ 268045. One of Agra's legendary hotels, dating from the British era, but which has definitely seen better days. Open-air swimming pool (filled intermittently and in a poor state) and pleasant grounds and gardens; as well as camping facilities popular with overland groups. ⑥

Major Bakshi Tourist Home, 33–38 Ajmer Rd ⓣ 0562/363829 or 363991. Since the demise of its famously hospitable owners, this Sikh-run guesthouse, renowned for its home cooking (and for having once accommodated Julie Christie), has gone a bit downhill, though it's still clean enough, quiet and handy for the bus stand. ⑤

Rose, 21 Old Idgah Colony ⓣ 0562/369786, down

a quiet lane behind the *Sakura*. Mr Gulati goes out of his way to welcome foreigners – this is among the best options in the Idgah bus stand area. The cheaper rooms are good value and there's a dorm. You can just about see the Taj from the rooftop café. ②–⑤

Tourist Rest House, Baluganj ⓣ 0562/363961, ⓕ 366910, ⓔ trh@nde.vsnl.com. The best value, most welcoming budget hotel in this area, if not in all Agra: some of its rooms are on the small side, but immaculately clean, with attached bathrooms & 24hr running hot water. Meals are served in the sociable, leafy ground-floor courtyard or in new dining hall. There's also a phone booth, internet facilities and back-up generator. Rickshaw-wallahs don't get commission here, so will try to take you to one of the "soundalikes". Telephone bookings accepted. ②–④

South of Taj Ganj

The hotels listed below are all marked on the **map** of Agra on p.284.

Amar Yatri Niwas, Fatehbad Road ⓣ 0562/331885, ⓕ 333805, ⓔ amaragra@vsnl.com. Modern, multistorey hotel with all mod cons including a health club and swimming pool. Central and well maintained, but bland. ⑦–⑧

Moghul Sheraton, Fatehbad Road ⓣ 0562/331701, ⓕ 331730. Opulent chain five-star on the edge of town. Gourmet restaurants, bar and a large pool, but the fake Moghul splendour feels overdone. Rooms start at $115. ⑨

Park Plaza, Fatehbad Road ⓣ 0562/331870, ⓕ 330408, ⓔ hppi@nde.vsnl.net.in. Smart and central, with a pool and a relaxing restaurant. Aimed primarily at business clients, and thus a good deal at this price (from $50). ⑧

Safari, Shaheed Nagar, Shamsabad Road ⓣ 0562/333029 or 360110. Friendly and relaxed hotel formerly under the same management as the

Tourist Rest House. Most rooms are a bit run-down and the area's badly polluted, but the tariffs are low, and you get views of the distant Taj from the rooftop café. If it's full, don't be tempted into the *Gypsy* next door, which is shabby and overpriced. ②–③

Taj View, Fatehbad Road, Taj Ganj ⓣ 0562/331841, ⓕ 361860, ⓔ tajagra @taj hotels.com. All the hallmarks of the Taj Group of luxury hotels, including an inlaid-marble lobby and swish rooms (the pricier ones have views of distant Taj – just about). Rooms from $145. ⑨

Trident, Tajnagri, Fatehbad Road ⓣ 0562/331818, ⓕ 331827, ⓔ reservations@tridentag.com. Among the most attractive of the modern upscale hotels, in mock-Moghul style with a large pool and multi-cuisine brasserie. Usually swamped with tour groups. Recommended for disabled travellers. Rooms start at $120. ⑨

The City

Agra's densely populated heart is the sprawling labyrinth of bazaars, alleys and cramped, crumbling tenements clustered around the onion domes of the Jami Masjid, but the most useful landmark in the city is the **fort** immediately south of the mosque, rising above the sharp bend in the River Yamuna where it changes its course to flow past the **Taj Mahal,** 2km east. While budget travellers tend to congregate in the enclave of **Taj Ganj,** directly south of the Taj, most of the mid- and upper-range hotels, restaurants and other tourist amenities are dotted around the leafier commercial centre of **Sadar Bazaar,** and the old British military **Cantonment** area, insulated from the mayhem of the centre by a swathe of open parkland.

Of the city's monuments, **Agra Fort** provides the best insight into the private lives of the Moghuls, its high sandstone ramparts crowded with golden pavilions and richly inlaid marble apartments. Immediately across the river, the tranquil tomb of **Itmad-ud-daulah**, is even more ornately decorated, while **Akbar's Mausoleum** at Sikandra, 10km northwest, and the abandoned capital of **Fatehpur Sikri**, 40km west, are further unforgettable echoes of the most grandiloquent chapter in Indian history.

The Taj Mahal

Described by the poet Rabindranath Tagore as a "tear on the face of eternity", the **Taj Mahal** (daily dawn to dusk, except Fri; Rs960 [Rs10]), is undoubtedly the zenith of Moghul architecture and quite simply one of the world's most marvellous buildings. Volumes have been written on its perfection, and its image adorns countless glossy brochures and guidebooks; nonetheless, the reality never fails to overwhelm all who see it, and few words can do it justice.

The glory of the monument is strangely undiminished by the crowds of tourists who visit, as small and insignificant as ants in the face of this immense and captivating monument. That said, the Taj is at its most alluring in the relative quiet of early morning, shrouded in mists and bathed with a soft red glow. As its vast marble surfaces fall into shadow or reflect the sun, its colour changes, from soft grey and yellow to pearly cream and dazzling white; it's well worth visiting at different times. This play of light is an important decorative device, symbolically implying the presence of Allah, who is never represented in anthropomorphic form.

Overlooking the River Yamuna, and visible from the fort in the west, the Taj Mahal stands at the northern end of vast gardens enclosed by walls. Though its layout follows a distinctly Islamic theme, representing Paradise, it is above all a monument to romantic love. **Shah Jahan** built the Taj to enshrine the body of

TAJ GANJ

Taj Mahal

Agra Fort

Museum

EAST GATE

Shahjahan Park

WEST GATE

SOUTH GATE

SHAHJAHAN GARDENS ROAD

Cantonment

TAJ RD

FATEHBAD ROAD

ACCOMMODATION
Host	4
India	5
Indo	3
Kamal	7
Noorjahan	3
Shah Jahan	9
Shanti	8
Sheela	1
Shyam Palace	10
Siddartha	6
Sikander	3
UPTDC Taj Kheema	2

RESTAURANT
Sheela	A

N

0 Metres 100

his favourite wife, Arjumand Bann Begum, better known as Mumtaz Mahal ("Elect of the Palace"), who died shortly after giving birth to her fourteenth child, in 1631. The Shah was devastated by her death, and set out to create an unsurpassed, eternal monument to her memory. Of all the Moghuls, only Shah Jahan, who had been designing palaces and forts since the age of sixteen, could have come up with such a magnificent design. The name of the chief architect is unknown, but Amanat Khan, who had previously worked on Akbar's tomb, was responsible for the calligraphic inscriptions that adorn the gateways, mosque and tomb. Construction by a workforce of some 20,000 men from all over Asia commenced in 1632, and the mausoleum was completed in 1653. Marble was brought from Makrana, near Jodhpur in Rajasthan, and precious stones for decoration – onyx, amethyst, lapis lazuli, turquoise, jade, crystal, coral and mother-of-pearl – were carried to Agra from Persia, Russia, Afghanistan, Tibet, China and the Indian Ocean.

The story is given an exquisite poignancy by the fate of Shah Jahan himself, who became a tragic and inconsolable figure. Eventually, his devout and austere son Aurangzeb seized power, and Shah Jahan was interned in Agra Fort, where as legend would have it he lived out his final years "gazing wistfully at the Taj Mahal" in the distance (although the truth is somewhat less poetic: see p.293). He died there in January 1666, with his daughter, Jahanara Begum, at his side; his body was carried across the river to lie alongside his beloved wife in his peerless tomb.

The complex

The walled complex is approached from the south through a red sandstone forecourt, Chowk-i Jilo Khana, whose wide paths, flanked by arched kiosks, run to high gates in the east and west. The original entrance, a massive arched gateway topped with delicate domes and adorned with Koranic verses, stands at the northern edge of Chowk-i Jilo Khana, directly aligned with the Taj, but shielding it from the view of those who wait outside.

Once beyond the southern wall, you'll see the mighty marble tomb at the end of superb gardens designed in the *charbagh* style so fashionable among Moghul, Arabic and Persian architects. Dissected into four quadrants by waterways, they evoke the Islamic image of the Gardens of Paradise, where rivers flow with water, milk, wine and honey. The "rivers" converge at a marble tank in the centre that corresponds to *al-Kawthar*, the celestial pool of abundance mentioned in the Koran. Today only the watercourse running from north to south is filled, and then only for special occasions, and its precise, glassy reflection of the Taj is a favourite photographic image. Views from the paths lining the east–west canal, lined with lofty trees, ferns and deep red and pink flowers, are equally sublime. To the west of the tomb is a domed red-sandstone mosque, and to the east a replica (*jawab*), probably built to house visitors, and necessary to achieve perfect symmetry.

Essentially square in shape, with peaked arches cut into its sides, the Taj Mahal surmounts a square marble platform marked at each corner by a high minaret. Topped with a huge central dome, it rises for over 55m, its height accentuated by a crowning brass spire, itself almost 17m high. Steps lead to the platform, and visitors must remove their shoes before climbing to the tomb. The marble floor can be icy cool in the morning, but at midday it gets extremely hot – you may want to wear socks, or rent a cloth foot-cover from the shoe attendants. On approach, the tomb looms ever larger and grander, but not until you are close do you appreciate both its awesome magnitude and the extraordinarily fine detail of relief carving, highlighted by floral patterns of precious stones.

Pollution threatening the Taj Mahal

Although the Taj Mahal may appear to the untrained eye almost as perfect as the day it was completed, the marble is undeniably sullen and yellow in parts, and empty casings here and there betray lost precious stones. These are the early effects of the threat posed by pollution from traffic and industry, and the millions of tourists who visit the tomb year-round. While marble is all but impervious to the onslaught of wind and rain that erodes softer sandstone, it has no natural defence against the sulphur dioxide that lingers in a dusty haze and shrouds the monument; sometimes the smog is so dense that the tomb cannot be seen from the fort. Sulphur dioxide mixes with atmospheric moisture and settles as sulphuric acid on the surface of the tomb, making the smooth white marble yellow and flaky, and forming a subtle fungus that experts have named "marble cancer".

The main sources of pollution are the 1700 factories in and around Agra, and the continuous flow of vehicles along the national highways that skirt the city. Chemical effluents belched out of factory chimneys are well beyond safety limits laid down by environmental committees. Despite laws demanding the installation of pollution-control devices, the imposition of a ban on all petrol- and diesel-fuelled traffic within 200m of the Taj Mahal, and an exclusion zone marking 10,400 square kilometres around the complex that should be free of any new industrial plants, pollutants in the atmosphere have continued to rise, and new factories have been set up illegally. In 1993, the Supreme Court finally took action and ordered nearly three hundred plants to shut down until emissions fell to legal limits.

Cleaning work on the Taj Mahal rectifies the problem to some extent, but the chemicals used will themselves eventually affect the marble. Already attendants shine their torches on repaired sections of marble to demonstrate that they have lost their translucency. The doubtful methods of the Archaeological Survey of India, such as scrubbing with toothbrushes, may prove disastrous in the long term. Hopes for proper care of the Taj Mahal have been raised since the government turned its attention to the plight of India's greatest monument, and entry fees for foreign visitors have been increased substantially, amid great controversy, to regulate the flow of tourists and generate much needed income, but the fate of the Taj Mahal hangs in the balance.

For more on the admission fee controversy, see Viewing Practicalities, p.292.

Carved vases of flowers including roses, tulips and narcissi, rise subtly out of the marble base, a pattern repeated more colourfully and inlaid with precious stones around the four great arched recesses (*pishtaqs*) on each side. Arabic verses praising the glory of Paradise fringe the archways, proportioned exactly so that each letter appears to be the same size when viewed from the ground.

The south face of the tomb is the main entrance to the **interior**: a high, echoing octagonal chamber flushed with pallid light reflected by yellowing marble surfaces. A marble screen, cut so finely that it seems almost translucent, and decorated with precious stones, scatters dappled light over the cenotaph of Mumtaz Mahal in the centre of the tomb, and that of Shah Jahan next to it. Inlaid stones on the marble tombs are the finest in Agra; attendants gladly illuminate the decorations with torches. No pains were spared in perfecting the inlay work – each petal or leaf may comprise up to sixty separate stone fragments. Ninety-nine names of Allah adorn the top of Mumtaz's tomb, and set into Shah Jahan's is a pen box, the hallmark of a male ruler. These cenotaphs, in accordance with Moghul tradition, are only representations of the real coffins, which lie in the same positions in an unadorned and humid crypt below that's heavy with the scent of heady incense and rose petals. Have a few coins ready as a respectful donation to an attendant priest who will lay the offering on the graves.

If you're spending a full day at the Taj and want a break from the sun, make a small detour to the **museum** (daily 10am–5pm) in the western wall of the enclosure. The interior contains exquisite miniatures, two marble pillars believed to have come from the fort, and portraits of Moghul rulers including Shah Jahan and Mumtaz Mahal. Further into the building a gallery shelters architectural drawings of the Taj Mahal, a display of elaborate porcelains, seventeenth-century coins and examples of stone inlay work, though you'll more than likely have seen enough of that in the Taj.

Taj Mahal viewing practicalities

India's most famous monument became the centre of heated controversy in December 2000, when the Agra Municipality and Archaeological Survey of India (ASI) jointly imposed a "hike" in **admission charges** from Rs15 to a whopping Rs960 for a day ticket. The increase only applies to foreigners; Indian visitors pay Rs10.

Further disputes followed the announcement in January, 2001, that the Taj would be **closed on Fridays** (instead of Mondays, as it had been previously) – a move strongly resisted by Agra's vociferous Muslim community, many of whom visit the Taj to pray on the Islamic sabbath. The profit-boosting measures would, it was claimed, generate revenue for "essential renovation work". Few in the local tourist industry, however, take such reassurances seriously. In a city renowned throughout India for its corrupt politicians, little of the extra cash is likely to be "ploughed back into the upkeep of the Taj", or any other of the 3606 monuments on India's critical list. Nor, if the authority's track record is anything to go by, will much of it be spent improving access roads and beautifying the green belt around the complex to reduce the damaging effects on the building of traffic pollution.

Galling though this price increase is, comparatively few visitors refuse to pay it; fewer still regard the expense as money wasted once they are inside. That said, foreign tourists these days rarely visit the Taj on several consecutive days. To appreciate the famous play of light on the building, you'll have to stick around from dawn until dusk (ticket valid all day, but only for one entrance). Thankfully, the gardens are the most blissful place to spend a day in Agra. Hawkers and salesmen are not allowed in, and official guides are not available on site, so no one is likely to pester you while you're dozing or reading on the lawns.

The only ways to **see the Taj for free** are by climbing onto a Taj Ganj hotel rooftop (see p.287), or, better still, by heading across the Yamuna to **Katchpura** village. From the opposite bank of the river, where Shah Jahan planned to erect his mirror-image "Black Taj" (see box opposite), the view is breathtaking, especially at dawn. **Boats** ferry foot passengers across from the *ghats* just east of the Taj at first light, charging what they can get away with (anything from Rs100 to Rs1000, depending on the size of your camera). Alternatively, hire a rickshaw-wallah for the trip, or cycle there yourself. Cross the river on the road bridge north of Agra Fort, and turn right when you reach the far bank, following the metalled road until it enters the village of Katchpura, where it becomes a rough track that eventually emerges at a small Dalit shrine on the riverside, directly opposite the Taj. The Municipality is supposed to be developing this area, with floodlights and walkways, but for the time being you should have it pretty much to yourself.

The secret symbolism of the Taj Mahal

Inextricably associated with the royal love legend of Shah Jahan and his wife Mumtaz, the Taj Mahal is regarded by most modern visitors as *the* symbol of eternal love. Recent historical research, however, suggests the world's most famous tomb complex encodes a somewhat less poetic and poignant vision – one more revealing of the Moghul emperor's megalomania and unbridled vanity than his legendary romantic disposition.

The clues to the Taj's **hidden symbolism** lie in the numerous Islamic **inscriptions** which play a key part in the overall design of the building. Fourteen chapters of the Koran are quoted at length here, dealing with two principal themes: the Day of Judgement, and the pleasures of Heaven. The first appears in the broad band of intricate calligraphy over the main gateway. Citing the last phrase of chapter 89, it invites the faithful to "Enter thou My Paradise". This is one of only two occasions in the Islamic scriptures when God speaks directly to man, and the quotation stresses the dual function of the Taj as both a tomb garden and replica of Heaven, complete with the four Rivers of Paradise and central Pool of Abundance.

In a dramatic break with tradition, the actual tomb is situated not in the middle of the gardens, as was customary, but at the far end of a rectangle. Recently, the theory of symbolic association has been taken a step further with the rediscovery of an enigmatic diagram contained in an **ancient Sufi text**, *The Revelations of Mecca* by renowned medieval mystic, Ibn al 'Arabi. Entitled *The Plain of Assembly on the Day of Judgement*, the diagram, which scholars know Shah Jahan's father had a copy of in his library, corresponds exactly to the layout of the Taj Mahal complex, proving beyond doubt, they now claim, that the tomb was intended as a reproduction of God's throne. Given that the emperor's remains are enshrined within it, the inevitable conclusion is that, aside from being an extravagant romantic, Shah Jahan possessed an opinion of his own importance that knew no bounds.

The one possible flaw in this theory comes in the form of a legend that the emperor intended his own body to lie not alongside that of his wife, but in a separate **Black Taj**, on the opposite bank of the Jamuna. The black-marble version would have been a perfect mirror image of its white forerunner. However, no one regarded such rumours as anything more than fanciful until archeologists recently unearthed ruins on the far river bank at Katchpura. Comprising formal Moghul gardens and foundations of exactly the same size as the Taj, they lend credence to the theory that Shah Jahan began work on his own black tomb but never finished it, either because of lack of funds, or due to his prelonged incarceration in Agra Fort.

While scholars continue to debate the symbolism of the Taj, and the possible existence of its black counterpart, they are united in disbelieving the popular, but wholly apocryphal, image of Shah Jahan's last days as propounded by the tour guides. Far from spending his old age gazing whimsically down the river to the tomb of his beloved wife, the Moghuls' most decadent emperor expired after a protracted bout of sex and drug-taking (see p.307). His death in 1666, at the ripe old age of 74, was brought about not by grief, but by a massive overdose of opium and aphrodisiacs.

Agra Fort

The high red-sandstone ramparts of **Agra Fort** (dawn to dusk; Rs505 [Rs20]) dominate a bend in the River Yamuna, 2km northwest of the Taj Mahal. Akbar laid the foundations of this majestic citadel, built between 1565 and 1573 in the form of a half moon, on the remains of earlier Rajput fortifications. Agra Fort developed as the seat and stronghold of the Moghul empire for successive generations: Akbar constructed the walls and gates, his grandson, Shah Jahan, had most of the principal buildings erected, and Aurangzeb, the last great emperor, was responsible for the ramparts.

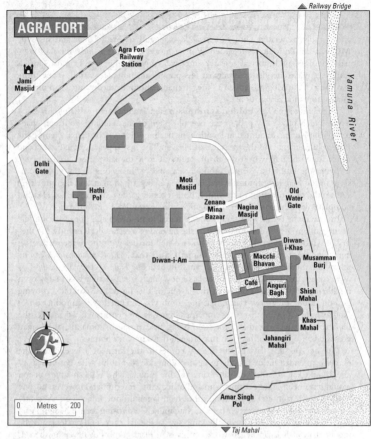

AGRA FORT

Railway Bridge

Agra Fort
Railway
Station

Jami
Masjid

Yamuna River

Delhi
Gate

Moti
Masjid

Old
Water
Gate

Hathi
Pol

Zenana
Mina
Bazaar

Nagina
Masjid

Diwan-
i-Khas

Diwan-i-Am

Macchi
Bhavan

Musamman
Burj

Café

Anguri
Bagh

Shish
Mahal

N

Khas
Mahal

Jahangiri
Mahal

0   Metres   200

Amar Singh
Pol

Taj Mahal

The curved bastions of the sandstone battlements are interrupted by massive gates, of which only the **Amar Singh Pol** is open to the public. Ornamented with glazed tiles, and with impressive double walls and a forecourt, it was used by the victorious General Lake when he entered the fort in 1803. The original and grandest entrance, however, was through the western **Delhi Gate**, leading to the inner portal, **Hathi Pol** or "Elephant Gate", now flanked by two red-sandstone towers faced in marble, but once guarded by colossal stone elephants with riders – destroyed by Aurangzeb in 1668.

Access to much of the fort is restricted, so masterpieces of Moghul architecture such as Shah Jahan's beautiful **Moti Masjid** (Pearl Mosque) are out of bounds to visitors. Only those parts open to the public are described in detail below, working in an anticlockwise direction from Shah Jahan's Hall of Public Audience to the private apartments.

Diwan-i-am and the great courtyard

Once through the Amar Singh Gate, ignore, for the time being, the complex of ornately carved buildings on your right and continue straight ahead through a second gate to a spacious enclosure dominated by the graceful **Diwan-i-Am** (Hall of Public Audience). Open on three sides, the sandstone pillared hall, which replaced an earlier wooden structure, was constructed by Shah Jahan in 1628 and, after use as an arsenal by the British, was restored in 1876 by Sir John Strachey. Three rows of white polished stucco pillars topped by peacock arches support a flat roof; the elegance of the setting would have been enhanced by the addition of brocade, carpets and satin canopies for audiences with the emperor. The ornate throne alcove is inlaid in marble decorated with flowers and foliage in bas-relief, and connects to the royal chambers within. Encrusted with diamonds, rubies and emeralds, the **Peacock Throne** which it was built to house was removed to the Red Fort in Delhi when Shah Jahan shifted his court there; it eventually ended up in Persia after the fort was looted by Nadir Shah in 1739. Adjacent to the alcove, the Baithak, a small marble block, is where ministers would have sat to deliver petitions and receive commands. This is also where trials would have been conducted, and justice speedily implemented. The East India naval commander, William Hawkins, who attended Jehangir's court between 1609 and 1611, noted the presence next to the emperor of his "master hangman, who is accompanied with forty hangmen, with an hatchet on their shoulders; and others with sorts of whips being there, readie to do what the King commandeth".

An incongruous intrusion in the centre of the great courtyard is a gothic Christian tomb marking the **grave of John Russel Colvin**, the Lieutenant-Governor of the Northwestern Provinces who died here during the Mutiny of 1857.

The royal pavilions

Clustered around a high terrace overlooking the river, the **royal pavilions** were designed to catch the cool breezes blowing across the Yamuna – and for ease of access to a water supply. The **Macchi Bhavan** (Fish Palace), approached through the alcove in the Diwan-i-Am, has suffered through the ages. During the period of Jat control, the Maharaja of Bharatpur removed some of its marble fixtures to his palace in Deeg; later, the zealous evangelist Lord William Bentinck (governor-general from 1828–35) auctioned off much of the original mosaic and fretwork, including parts of the **Hammam-i-Shahi**, the royal bath. The palace was once strewn with fountains and flowerbeds, interspersed with tanks and water channels stocked with fish for the angling pleasure of the emperor and courtiers. In the northwest corner of the enclosure, the exquisite little **Nagina Masjid** (Gem Mosque) is entirely made of marble. Capped with three domes and approached from a marble-paved courtyard, it was built by Shah Jahan for the ladies of the *zenana* (harem). Below it, overlooked by a beautiful marble balcony with carved lattice screens and peacock arches, is the **Inner** or **Zenana Mina Bazaar**, where ladies of the court could look at goods such as silk, jewellery and brocade offered by merchants, without being seen themselves.

The **Chittor Gate**, salvaged by Akbar as a trophy from the horrific sacking of the Rajput stronghold of Chittor (now Chittaurgarh in southeast Rajasthan; see p.271) and installed in 1568, leads to the **Mandir Raja Ratan**, erected in 1768 during the Jat occupation of the fort. Past this is the Hall of Private Audience, the **Diwan-i-Khas**, where the emperor would have received kings, dignitaries and ambassadors, and where recently completed paintings or architectural plans were submitted for his approval. Erected in 1635, the building was badly damaged when it came under bombardment by General Lake in 1803, but the hall – with its ornate pillars and arches inlaid with lapis lazuli and jasper – survives. Two thrones adorn the large terrace in front of the Diwan-i-Khas, one of black slate and the other of white marble. Shah Jahan apparently took his evening repose in the white throne; from the black one, the emperor would amuse himself by watching elephant fights in the eastern enclosure.

A doorway from the rear of the Diwan-i-Khas leads to a two-storeyed pavilion or tower known as **Musamman Burj**, famous in Moghul legend as the spot where, in the open octagonal chamber atop the highest of the riverside bastions, Shah Jahan caught his last glimpse of the Taj Mahal before he died. Surrounded by a veranda, the elegant pavilion has a lattice-screen balustrade with ornamental niches; exquisite *pietra dura* inlay covers almost every surface, and a marble *chhatri* adds the finishing touch. In front of the tower a courtyard, paved with marble octagons, centres on a *pachisi* board where the emperor, following his father's example at Fatehpur Sikri, played a rather bizarre version of the game (a form of backgammon) using dancing girls as pieces.

To the south of Musamman Burj lies the marble building known as **Khas Mahal** (Private Palace), possibly used as a drawing room or the emperor's sleeping chamber. Designed essentially for comfort, it incorporates cavities in its flat roofs to insulate against the searing heat of an Agra summer, and affords soothing riverside and garden views. The palace is flanked by two Golden Pavilions, their curved roofs covered with gilded copper tiles, in a style inspired by the thatched roofs of Bengali village huts. Stretching in front of the Khas

Kabootas

Look up from any Taj Ganj roof terrace around 4pm, when the sun is low and the city's bulbous onion domes and minarets glow pale orange, and you'll see a side of local life of which very few tourists are even aware. Pigeons, or kabootas, wheel above clusters of men and boys staring skywards from their flat rooftops, shouting, whistling and waving sticks at the birds. Agra's pigeon fanciers, known as *kaboota baz*, don't race their pigeons, but fly them in flocks, controlling them with a code of high-pitched whistles and calls that are as much a feature of Muslim districts like Taj Ganj as the *muezzin*'s call to prayer. The waving of sticks is supposed to keep the lazier pigeons in the air, although a couple of sleepy specimens can usually be spotted hiding on nearby satellite dishes, waiting for their owners to scatter soaked grain for them to feed on. When this happens, the rest of the flock drops back to ground in a cloud, and pecks around the roof of their coop, or *kaboota kanna*, for the grain. This five- or ten-minute cycle is then repeated for an hour or so until the pigeons have been well exercised.

Pigeon fancying is an established tradition in Agra, and cities such as Old Delhi and Lucknow, where there are sizeable Muslim communities (Hindus rarely indulge in the sport). Its techniques were set down by Akbar's poet laureate, Abu'l Fazl, for the Moghul court who considered it a noble pastime, and to this day men and boys across Urdu-speaking parts of India still take their *kaboota* flying very seriously. Thoroughbred birds change hands for more than Rs5000, a fortune considering the average income of most *kaboota baz*. Owning a large flock brings with it a certain cachet, and the coveted title of *Barra Kaboota Baz*, literally "Big Pigeon Fancier". Once a man is deemed to have mastered the plethora of tricks and subtleties of this ancient sport, he may even be known among his peers as a *Khalifa*, or "Great Master". Only *Khalifas* can direct their flocks in perfect parabolic curves, or single files across the sky, or command them to encircle a neighbours' flock and drive it to ground.

Four or five flocks fly above Taj Ganj each day. You can watch them from your guesthouse rooftop, but if you'd like to get closer to the action, ask around for an introduction to a *kaboota baz* – the manager of the *Shah Jahan Lodge* on South Gate can arrange for you to meet his neighbour, Danesh Khan, a *Barra Kaboota Baz* who keeps his birds on an adjacent roof.

Mahal to the west is Anguri Bagh (Grape Garden), a miniature *charbagh*, with its quarters delineated by wide marble pavements. In the northeast corner, the Shish Mahal (Palace of Mirrors) was where royal women bathed in the soft lamplight reflected from the mirror-work mosaics that covered the walls and ceiling. Connected to the Khas Mahal by an extensive corridor, the Shah Jahani Mahal (Shah Jahan's Palace) is supported by wooden beams; its four chambers were originally painted in bright colours and embossed in gold.

The palaces of Jahangir and Akbar

Immediately southwest of the Shah Jahani Mahal is the robust, square **Jahangiri Mahal**. This red-sandstone palace, built either by Jahangir or by Akbar on his son's behalf, is almost entirely Hindu in its interior design. In the Assembly Hall, carved ornamental brackets support beams, wide eaves and ceilings with struts; the serpentine form being emitted from a dragon's mouth is reminiscent of a Gujarati temple.

Rooms to the west are thought to have been the temple and drawing room of Akbar's Rajput wife Jodhbai. Below the palace, three storeys of basement chambers were used to escape the heat. **Jahangir's Hauz** or cistern, a giant bowl made in 1611 from a single block of porphyry and inscribed in Persian, was unearthed in the nineteenth century and stands in the courtyard in front of the Jahangiri Mahal. Filled with rose water, it would have been used by the emperor as a bathtub.

Returning towards Amar Singh Gate to the left, an assembly hall, a veranda overlooking the river and excavations are all that remain of the southernmost palace, the once extensive **Akbari Mahal**, built in 1571.

Jami Masjid and the bazaars

Opposite the fort and overlooking Agra Fort railway station, the **Jami Masjid** or "Friday Mosque" was built by Shah Jahan in 1648 and dedicated to his favourite daughter, Jahanara Begum. Standing on a high plinth approached by stairs, and with five arched entrances to the courtyard, the mosque is crowned by three large sandstone domes distinguished by their zigzag bands of marble. Along the wings of the main prayer wall, panels of beautifully inlaid sandstone similar to those decorating the main gateway of the Taj Mahal, add an appropriately feminine touch. Still in use today, the mosque is one of the city's main landmarks, and serves as a useful reference point when exploring the crowded **bazaars** that sprawl from its base. These are laid out in a street plan that's barely altered since Moghul days, and is best negotiated on foot. Opposite the northeast corner of the complex, look out for the **pehta-wallahs**, purveyors of Agra's most famous sweets, which are made from crystallized pumpkins (and devoured with relish by the wasps living in the eves of the mosque *mihrab* arches).

The Jama Masjid can be reached from the road running northwest from the fort; alternatively, avoid the traffic by approaching through the station, taking a shortcut through the mail office on the far platform. For photography, the optimum time to visit is between 7 and 8am, when the morning sun accentuates the warm reds of the stonework.

Itmad-ud-daulah

Itmad-ud-daulah (dawn–dusk; Rs235 [Rs10]), the beautiful tomb of Mirza Ghiyath Beg – an important member of Akbar's court and later *wazir* (chief minister) to, and father-in-law of, Emperor Jahangir – stands amid gardens with scampering monkeys on the east bank of the Yamuna, less than 3km from the city. The first building to be built of white inlaid marble in Moghul India, this charming two-storey mausoleum, which Agra's rickshaw-wallahs misleadingly call the **"Baby Taj"**, is small but perfectly executed, with translucent stones set into its walls and tracery-work. It's unmistakeably feminine, having been designed by Ghiyath Beg's daughter, the favourite queen of Jahangir, and the most powerful woman in Moghul history, named Nur Jahan, "Light of the World", by Jahangir. He respected her intellect and talent so much that he ordered coins to be minted in her name, and by the time of her father's death in 1622 she had substantial control over the empire.

The square mausoleum, with an octagonal turret at each corner, foreshadows the Taj Mahal in its exclusive use of marble, but is more daintily proportioned, and has a pavilion on its roof rather than a dome. However, recent "restoration" work has resulted in poor-quality plaster obscuring some of the exquisite detail, and in other places semiprecious stones that were once embedded into the marble have been winkled out and stolen. Ghiyath Beg's grave is underground, next to his wife's sarcophagus, shrouded in flowers. A pierced and intricately carved wall in front of the entrance to the grave casts a soft hazy light over paintings of flowers, cypresses, vases and wine vessels, all symbols of paradise, in the inner chamber.

Chini-ka-rauza

Less than 1km north of Itmad-ud-daulah is **Chini-ka-rauza**, built in 1635 and reputed to be the mausoleum of Afzal Khan, a Persian poet and Shah Jahan's prime minister. Neglected and decaying, its soft brown stone is victim to the elements and is now crumbling away into the riverbank. Topped with an Afghan-style bulbous dome, the dull earth-coloured tomb is a far cry from Nur Jahan's delicate work, but is distinctive as Agra's sole Persian construction. Parts of the walls are still covered with the coloured enamel tiles (*chini*) that once enhanced the whole of the exterior and gave the tomb its name, while traces of paintings and Islamic calligraphy can still be made out on the high domed ceiling.

Ram Bagh

Ram Bagh, laid out by Babur in 1528 and probably the first pleasure garden of its kind, is just a few kilometres north of Chini-ka-rauza. Reputedly the resting place of Babur's body before it was taken to Kabul, the garden is now dilapidated and overgrown, and only a few tattered columns and walls remain of the stone pavilions that once sheltered the royal family. Its original name, Aram Bagh (Garden of Rest), was corrupted to Ram, after the Hindu god.

Akbar's mausoleum

Given the Moghul tradition of building magnificent tombs for men and women of high status, it comes as no surprise that the mausoleum of the most distinguished Moghul ruler was one of the finest and most ambitious structures of its time. **Akbar's mausoleum** (daily dawn to dusk; Rs235), a majestic composition of deep-red sandstone and cool marble designed by the emperor himself and modified in 1605 by his son, Jahangir, borders the roadside at Sikandra, 10km northwest of Agra. Rickshaws charge at least Rs60 to make the round trip, or you could hop on any bus bound for Mathura from the Agra Fort bus stand.

Although neither as grand nor as awesome as the indomitable Taj, this stately structure possesses a serenity sometimes absent among the throngs of tourists at Agra's most visited monument. It also marks the important transition in

Moghul design after Akbar's death, when his bold, masculine red stone monuments were superseded by more ethereal and sensuous marble buildings, epitomized and perfected in the Taj Mahal itself.

The most overwhelming feature of the complex is its huge south gate, **Buland Darwaza**, "Gateway of Magnificence" – so high that it obstructs any view to the tomb beyond. Surmounted by four tapering marble minarets, and overlaid with marble and coloured tiles set in repetitive geometrical patterns, it bears the Koranic inscription "These are the gardens of Eden, enter them and live forever." Buy a ticket at the office set into the left face of the gate, then walk through to the gardens, divided by wide paved walkways into four equal quadrants in typical Moghul fashion, and enclosed by high walls. Along the paths, friendly long-tailed langur monkeys laze in the sunshine and groom one another, and black buck roam through the tall grasses, just as they do in the Moghul miniature paintings dating from the era when the tomb was constructed.

In the centre of the gardens, directly in front of Buland Darwaza, the broad-based square mausoleum has arcaded cloisters along each side and pavilions enhanced by delicate marble domes rising above its centre. A high marble gateway in the southern face draws attention to meticulous lattice screens shielding a small vestibule, once painted with rich sea-blue frescoes and Koranic verses. From here a ramp leads to a subterranean crypt, where Akbar's grave lies sprinkled with rose petals and bathed in a cool yellow light.

Eating

Considering the number of tourists that pass through, Agra suffers from a dearth of good **places to eat**. With a few notable exceptions, the best restaurants are all in the upscale hotels, where, at a price, you can sample the city's speciality, **Mughlai** cooking. Imitated in Indian curry houses throughout the world, Agra's traditional Persian-influenced cuisine is renowned for its rich cream and curd-based sauces, kebabs, *nan* and tandoori breads roasted in earthen ovens, *pulao* rice dishes and milky sweets such as *kheer*. However, you'll be hard pushed to find more than pale imitations in the cramped cafés and rooftop terrace restaurants of **Taj Ganj**. These places may serve much cheaper meals than you'll find further south in **Sadar Bazaar** and the **Tourist Complex** area, but because of the recent spate of poisoning incidents (see box on p.300), the overall **poor standards of hygiene** in this district, and the fact that most "restaurants" are merely set up as a means for touts and shop owners to hook customers, we strongly recommend you steer clear of them. The one exception is the *Sheela*, near the East Gate, reviewed below.

Achman, By-Pass Road, Dayal Bagh. Among Agra-wallahs, the most rated restaurant in the city, famous above all for its *navratan korma* (a mildly spiced mix of nuts, dried fruit and *paneer*), *malai kofta* and chickpea *masala*, as well as wonderful stuffed naans. Well off the tourist trail in the north of the city, but ideally placed for dinner on your way home from Sikandra. Most mains around Rs75.

Chiman Lal Puri Wallah, opposite northeast wall of Jami Masjid. An institution in Agra for five generations, this much-loved little café-restaurant looks a touch grubby from the outside, but serves delicious *puri*-thalis, with two veg dishes and melt-in-the-mouth saffron-flavoured *kheer*

(Mughlai rice pudding) – all for Rs20. Ideal pit stop after visiting the mosque.

Dasaprakash, Meher Theatre Complex, 1 Gwalior Rd, close to the *Hotel Agra Ashok*. Offshoot of the famous Chennai restaurant, serving a limited menu of top-notch south Indian food (their onion *rawa masala dosas* and cheese *uttapams* are sublime), and an extensive ice cream menu (the "Hot fudge bonanza split" wins by a nose). Count on Rs150 per head for the works.

Kedarnath Phoolchand Pehta Wallah, Johri Bazaar, five minutes' walk north of Jami Masjid. Agra's most famous sweet and *namkeen* shop, source of the city's definitve *pehta*, or crystallized pumpkin (the pricier orange stuff, flavoured with saffron, is best). They also do delicious *dal mot*, crunchy mix made with black lentils.

Lakshmi Villas, Sadar Bazaar. Unpretentious south Indian café on the posh side of town, offering the usual *idly-dosa-uttapam* menu, with delicious *chatni-sambar*, and much lower prices than *Dasaprakash*.

Only, 45 Taj Rd, Phool Syed Crossing. Should be renamed "Only for Tourists". Packed with bus parties from the five-stars, and unwary travellers lured here by commission-hungry rickshaw-wallahs; the food is mediocre and way overpriced, and the atmosphere wincingly contrived.

Park Restaurant, Sadar Bazaar. A newcomer that has quickly gained a reputation, among tourists and locals alike, for its careful cooking. The dining hall is sparsely furnished but immaculately kept and, if you're here in the hot season, blissfully air-conditioned. Dishes come in three gravies: ultra-mild "white" cashew, medium "onion", and red-hot "tomato", served with delicious garlic naans and cold Kingfishers. Main dishes Rs70–120; half portions available.

Petals, Gopi Chand Shivare Road, Sadar Bazaar. A quality multi-cuisine menu snappily served in squeaky clean a/c comfort; the house specialities are kebabs and chicken tikka. Reservations necessary on Sun evening.

Sheela, East Gate, Taj Ganj. One of the few genuinely dependable, inexpensive and pleasant places to eat near the Taj. Their menu features a good choice of simple (mostly vegetarian) Indian dishes, as well as drinks and snacks, and the fruit-and-nut lassis are a must. Seating outside in shady garden, or in narrow café.

Sonam, 51 Taj Rd. Mid-price garden restaurant and bar. Another infamous tourist trap, but at least their food is good. The Indian options are best, attempting to re-create medieval Mughlai cuisine. Also buffets in winter, and a budget section featuring thalis. Credit cards accepted.

Tourist Rest House, Baluganj. Atmospheric garden restaurant, with beaten-earth floors, candle light and mature trees, serving a modest selection of copious breakfasts and tasty Indian dishes to a sedate clientele of foreign backpackers. Try their tasty cheese *malai kofta*, rounded off with fruit custard like you never ate at school. All mains under Rs50.

Zorba the Buddha, E-13 Shopping Arcade, Gopi Chand Shivare Rd, Sadar Bazaar. A very popular, no-smoking, Westerner-oriented veg restaurant run by Osho devotees. The food is fussy Indian with lashings of fresh fruit and nuts – imaginative and healthy, but overpriced. Worth at least one visit, though. Open noon–3pm & 6–9pm.

Warning

Agra has long been renowned for its con-tricksters, but over the past couple of years some dodgy operators in Taj Ganj have come up with a scam so cynical it makes phoney policemen and fake gemstone pedlars look pedestrian.

The first sign of something amiss is when, shortly after a meal at a **Taj Ganj** café, you suddenly fall ill. As luck would have it, the rickshaw-wallah taking you back to your hotel, or some other seemingly sympathetic person such as your hotel manager, happens to know a good doctor nearby, who makes a prompt diagnosis, checks you into his private "clinic" and prescribes some pills. While you're throwing up with a drip in your arm, he faxes your medical insurers and starts claiming a huge sum of money for daily health-care costs. What you don't know, though, is that the drugs you're taking are the reason why, days later, you're still ill, and that the "doctor" has all along been in cahoots with both the rickshaw driver and restaurant.

In November 1998, dozens of so-called "clinics" were raided and their records scrutinized after a young British couple who'd been poisoned went to the Agra press with their experience. The story was soon picked up by the national dailies in Delhi and an investigation begun, but so far no one has been convicted. This may sound like drastic advice, but all you can do until the police have caught up with the phoney doctors and their accomplices is avoid the restaurants in Taj Ganj (unless they're listed in our Eating reviews). Failing that, stick to your hotel restaurant (although some tourists have been poisoned in their own hotels) and if you do get sick, go to a reputable hospital, not a backstreet clinic (see Listings opposite).

An information service (ⓦ www.agrapolice.com) is provided by the local police department to warn visitors about corrupt businesses in the city.

Shopping

Agra is renowned for its **marble** tabletops, vases and trays, inlaid with semi-precious stones in ornate floral designs, in imitation of those found in the Taj Mahal. It is also an excellent place to buy **leather**: Agra's shoe industry supplies all India, and its tanneries export bags, briefcases and jackets. **Carpets** and **dhurries** are manufactured here too, and traditional embroidery continues to thrive. *Zari* and *zardozi* are brightly coloured, the latter building up three-dimensional patterns with fantastic motifs; *chikan* uses more delicate overlay techniques.

There are several large emporiums such as the official-sounding Cottage Industries Exposition on the Fatehabad Road, which is well presented but outrageously expensive; it is one of the places you're likely to be taken to by a commission-seeking driver. Shops in the big hotels may be pricey, but their quality and service are usually more reliable. UP Handicrafts Palace, 49 Bansal Nagar, has a wide selection of marble; other state emporia round the Taj include UP's Gangotri, which has fixed prices. Close to the East Gate, Shilpgram is an extensive crafts village with arts and handicrafts from all over India, and occasional live music and dance performances.

Shopping or browsing around the Mall, MG Road, Munro Road, Kinari Bazaar, Sadar Bazaar and the Taj Complex is fun, but you need to know what you're buying and be prepared to haggle; you should also be wary of ordering anything to be sent overseas. Commission payable by shops to rickshaw- and taxi-drivers and tour guides inflate prices. You are advised never to let your credit card out of your sight, even for the card to be confirmed, and you should make sure that all documentation regarding the card is filled in correctly and fully so as not to allow unauthorized later additions. A large number of serious cases of **credit-card fraud** have been reported in Agra, even in some of the most popular tourist restaurants. A list of emporia against whom complaints have been lodged is maintained by the local police department.

Listings

Banks and exchange The State Bank of India is just south of Taj Gaj in the Cantonment (Amex travellers' cheques not accepted); Andhra Bank is over in Sadar Bazaar; and the Allahabad is in the *Hotel Clarks Shiraz*). Money transfers can also be arranged through Sita World Travel, on Taj Road (T 0562/363013). If you get caught out by a public holiday, you could always try one of the private exchange offices in the Tourist Complex Area, around *Pizza Hut* (LKP Forex, opposite the *Amar Hotel* on the Fatehbad Road, are always reliable and fast), but if you're changing a large amount it's always worth shopping around to find the best rate.

Internet access Offered by an ever-growing number of hotels, guesthouses and email booths around town, despite the notoriously undependable connection in Agra. At the time of writing, the lowest rates in Taj Ganj were offered by the STD/ISD office on the corner of West Gate and the main street (South Gate) through the bazaar (Rs55/hr).

Hospitals The Upadhyay Hospital, Shahid Nagar Crossing (T 0562/368844, F 361111), has been recommended by readers as clean and dependable, with competent English-speaking doctors.

Photography Agra Color Lab, E6–7 Shopping Arcade, Sadar Bazaar, and 34/2 Sanjay Place, opposite Soor Sadan, offers one-hour processing.

Post The Head Post Office is on the Mall, near the Government of India tourist office; there are smaller sub-post offices in the Taj Mahal complex and in Taj Ganj. Poste restante at the Head Post Office is inefficient and you may be better off using the Government of India tourist office's address on the Mall, instead.

Swimming Agra's exclusive hotels sometimes let nonresidents swim in their pools, for daily fees. Best of the bunch is the *Clarks Shiraz* (Rs200) and the *Moghul Sheraton* (Rs200), followed by the *Agra Ashok* and the *Mayur* (Rs150).

By air

Indian Airlines flights from Agra's Kheria airport, 7km out of the centre, have been suspended while the airport is upgraded to take international traffic. However, you can still book and re-confirm tickets at the company's office in the *Clarks Shiraz* (daily 10am–1.15pm & 2–5pm; ☎0562/226820, 821823), which also hosts the Jet Airways and Lufthansa counters.

By train

Train tickets, especially to the capital, should be booked well in advance at either Agra Cantonment or Agra Fort stations, which both have fully computerized booking offices with separate tourist counters. The fastest and most expensive service to Delhi is the fully a/c Shatbadi Express #2001 (8.10am; 2hr); in the other direction as #2002 (8.17am), it travels to Gwalior (1hr 15min) and on to Jhansi (2hr 25min) from where you can catch a bus to Khajuraho. A convenient early-morning service to New Delhi is the A P Express #2723 (5.30am; 3hr 10min); the fastest midday train is the Kerala Express #2625 (depart 12.18pm; 3hr 25min). Although the Udyan Abha Toofan Express #3008 travels all the way to Calcutta (12.50pm; 30hr) via Moghul Sarai and Patna, it is nearly always late. The best train for Varanasi is the nightly #4854/4864 Marudhar Express (9.05pm; 13hr 45min).You can also pick up trains to Chennai and Thiruvananthapuram. For Goa, return to Delhi and catch the super-fast #2432 Trivandrum Rajdhani (depart 11am; 25hr).

Agra's principal Rajasthan train is the #4853/4863 Marudhar Express, which leaves Agra Cantonment daily at 7.15am for Jaipur (7hr) and Jodhpur (13hr). Others depart from Agra Fort station but the line is currently being upgraded; check to see if regular services have been reinstated. Also from Agra Fort, the daily #5311 Lalkuan Kumaun Express (departs 9.30pm) travels to Lalkua and Kathgodam, the nearest railhead to the hill station of Nainital in northern Uttar Pradesh. Regular daily trains connect Agra Fort with Kanpur and Lucknow.

By bus

Travelling by bus along the main highways, especially to the capital on the Grand Trunk road and to Jaipur on NH-11, is considerably more hair-raising than travelling the same routes by train. Accidents, most of them head-on collisions with other buses or trucks, are disconcertingly frequent.

For those unable to get hold of a rail ticket, seats on Rajasthan Roadways buses, which leave from Idgah bus stand in the southwest of town, should be booked at the bus stand itself: for any destinations further afield than Jaipur, take a bus to Jaipur (via Bharatpur) and pick up a connecting service from there. One exception is Ajmer, jumping off town for Pushkar, which has its own direct service (10hr). Deluxe and a/c services for Jaipur (5hr) leave from the forecourt of *Hotel Shakpura*, next to the bus stand. There's a booking office in the lodge for fast and direct private buses to Delhi (5–6hr) and Gwalior (3hr 30min), and early morning departures for Khajuraho (12hr), Lucknow (9hr 30min) and Nainital (10hr). Additional buses to the same destinations leave from the tourist office on Taj Road: book a day in advance at the office. If you're heading southwest towards Bharatpur via Fatehpur Sikri, catch one of the regular services from the Idgah bus stand (1hr).

Agra Fort bus stand, chaotic, dusty and potholed, has frequent services (several each hour) on rickety, often windowless buses heading for Delhi, Mathura, Haridwar, Rishikesh and Dehra Dun, and as afar afield as Lucknow. Tickets are sold on the buses. Unless you fly, getting to Khajuraho involves a twelve-hour bus journey (daily; 5am), or a train to Jhansi (2hr 45min–3hr 50min), and then a six-hour bus ride from there.

Fatehpur Sikri

The ghost city of **FATEHPUR SIKRI**, former imperial capital of the great Moghul emperor **Akbar**, straddles the crest of a rocky ridge, 40km southwest of Agra. Built between 1569 and 1585, it has lain silent for almost four centuries; by 1600, its meagre water supply had proved incapable of sustaining the population, and Akbar shifted the court to Lahore. Now deserted, it is almost perfectly preserved – a masterpiece in sandstone, glowing in subtly changing shades of pink and red as the day progresses and the light fades.

The plan to move the court here was conceived by a ruler who, tired of the crowds and congestion of Agra, wanted to create a new capital that was both an appropriate symbol of imperial power, and a sympathetic backdrop for the philosophical debates and artistic pursuits that were his passion. An astute diplomat as well as a gifted military strategist, Akbar consolidated his territorial gains in the north and west by promoting a policy of religious tolerance developed through discussions with representatives of the major faiths. He abolished the much hated poll-tax on non-Muslims (*jizya*), and was the first Moghul ruler to marry a Hindu (a Rajput princess from Jaipur). By gaining the allegiance of local rulers (often through marriage), he was also able to install the most efficient system of revenue collection ever seen in the empire, and it was this that enabled Akbar to build Fatehpur Sikri – a palace complex that would become the very embodiment of his unorthodox court, fusing Hindu and Muslim artistic traditions. Hindu buildings such as **Birbal's Palace** and **Jodhbai's Palace** mingle with the pavilions and halls of the grand court, while the **Jami Masjid**, the only building of exclusively Muslim derivation, houses one of the most exquisite mausoleums of the Moghul period, the marble **Tomb of Sheikh Salim Chishti**.

Fatehpur Sikri was originally intended to be joint capital with Agra; although it receives only a fraction of the visitors of its rival, the stunning elegance of its palace, mosque and courts ensure that it remains as powerful a testimony to Moghul grandeur. As long as you don't mind modest amenities (and salty water), it's also an enjoyably atmospheric place to stay, with a scattering of simple guesthouses huddled in the village below the ruins. The one drawback is the overall filthiness of the bazaar area, which many travellers find too high a price to pay for the awesome sight of the Buland Darwaza at sunrise.

The Royal Palace

Shunning the Hindu tradition of aligning towns with the cardinal points (as dictated by ancient canonical texts on architecture, the *Shilpa Shastras*), Akbar chose to construct his new capital following the natural features of the terrain. This is why the principal thoroughfare, town walls, and many of the most important buildings inside it (including the mint, treasury, baths and caravanserai) face southwest or northeast. The mosque and most private apartments, on the other hand, do not follow the main axis, but face west towards Mecca, according to Muslim tradition, with the palace crowning the highest point on the ridge

Although unused and uninhabited since its abandonment, the main **Royal Palace** and court complex (daily dawn to dusk; Rs460 [Rs10]), remains largely intact, thanks to extensive restoration work carried out by British archeologists before Independence. The entrance is via the ASI ticket kiosk at the centre of the site. Offical guides offer their services at the booking office for around Rs75–100.

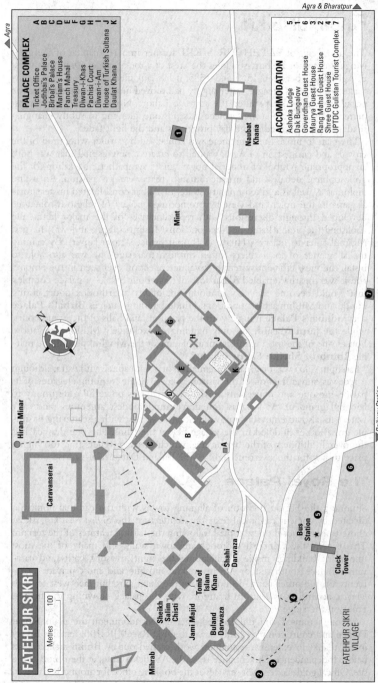

FATEHPUR SIKRI

Metres
0   100

Agra

Agra & Bharatpur

N

Caravanserai

Hiran Minar

Mint

Naubat Khana

Railway Station

Mihrab

Sheikh Salim Chisti

Jami Majid

Buland Darwaza

Tomb of Islam Khan

Shahi Darwaza

Clock Tower

Bus Station

FATEHPUR SIKRI VILLAGE

PALACE COMPLEX

Ticket Office   A
Jodhbai's Palace   B
Birbal's Palace   C
Mariam's House   D
Panch Mahal   E
Treasury   F
Diwan-i-Khas   G
Pachisi Court   H
Diwan-i-Am   I
House of Turkish Sultana J
Daulat Khana   K

ACCOMMODATION

Ashoka Lodge   5
Dak Bungalow   1
Goverdhan Guest House   6
Maurya Guest House   3
Rang Mahal Guest House   2
Shree Guest House   4
UPTDC Gulistan Tourist Complex 7

Diwan-i-Am

The logical place to begin a tour of the palace complex, whose layout is thought to have been inspired by the form of a Moghul camp, is the **Diwan-i-Am** (Hall of Public Audience), at the far northeast edge of the enclosure (follow the walkway from the ticket booth). Surrounded by colonnades, cloisters and exquisite pierced-stone *jali* screens, this was where important festivals were held, and where citizens could exercise their right to petition the king, whose throne would have occupied the raised pavilion at its west side. Note the position of the royal platform in relation to the enclosure's main entrance, set at an angle which forced the emperor's subjects to approach him from the side in an attitude of humility.

The Diwan-i-Khas courtyard

An insignificant seeming doorway in the northwest corner of the Diwan-i-Am leads to a second courtyard, at the top of which stands the Hall of Private Audience, or **Diwan-i-Khas**. The centrepiece of this chamber is an extraordinary carved column known as the **Throne Pillar**, supporting a large circular platform from which four balustraded bridges radiate outwards. Seated upon this throne, the emperor would hold discussions with representatives of diverse religions – orthodox Muslim leaders (*ulema*), Jesuit priests from Goa, Hindu brahmins, Jains and Zoroastrians – ranged around the walls of the balcony. Through such discussions, Akbar sought to synthesize India's religions and the pillar symbolizes this project by incorporating motifs drawn from Hinduism, Buddhism, Islam and Christianity. Eventually, however, the *ulemas* became alienated by the discussions held here and instigated an uprising, which Akbar ruthlessly crushed in 1581. Thereafter, the emperor evolved a concept of divine kingship, which the overall architecture of the Diwan-i-Khas, with its axial pillars radiating from a central point, serves to underline.

Access to the pillar and balconies is via steps on the exterior of the building. Close by lies the three-roomed **Treasury**, its brackets embellished by mythical sea creatures, guardians of the treasures of the deep; it was apparently used to play the game of *ankh michauli* (hide and seek), the origin of the building's other name. Next to it is the Astrologer's Seat, a small pavilion embellished with elaborate Jain carvings.

In the middle of the courtyard, separating the Diwan-i-Khas from the buildings on the opposite (south) side of the complex, is the **Pachisi Court**, a giant stone board for the game known as *pachisi* (or *chawpai*), which is similar to ludo. Akbar is said to have been a fanatical player, using slave girls dressed in colourful costumes as live pieces. Abu'l Fazl, the court chronicler, related that "[at] times more than two hundred persons participated in [*pachisi*] and no one was allowed to go home until he had played sixteen rounds. This could take up to three months. If one of the players lost his patience and became restless, he was made to drink a cupful of wine. Seen superficially, this appears to be just a game. But His Majesty pursues higher objectives. He weighs up the talents of his people and teaches them to be affable."

House of the Turkish Sultana

Immediately southwest of the *pachisi* board, the **Anup Talao Pavilion**, also known as the **House of the Turkish Sultana**, is thought to have been the palace of one of Akbar's favourite wives, the Sultana Ruqayya Begum. With balconies and Kashmiri-style woodcarvings, this exquisite building betrays Persian, Turkish and even Chinese influences, and may have been a *hammam* (bath) or pleasure pavilion. Legend has it that the great musician **Mian Tansen** once sang *Deepak*, the *raag* of fire, on its central dais. So effective was his performance that he grew hotter and hotter, until his daughter had to come to the rescue by performing the rain *raag*, *Malhar*. Understandably nervous at this great responsibility, she faltered on the seventh note of the scale, thereby creating one of the most famous and stirring *raags* of north India – *Mian ki Malhar*. Happily, the *raag* had the desired effect; rain fell, and Tansen was saved. The southern aspect overlooks the Anup Talao or "Peerless Pool" where, on a central dais surrounded by perfumed water, Akbar is believed to have taken repose.

The Daulat Khana and Panch Mahal

Facing the Turkish Sultana's house from the other side of the gardens are Akbar's private quarters, the **Daulat Khana** (Abode of Fortune). These comprise a series of buildings distinguished by exquisite stone *jali* screens, elaborate brackets, broad eaves, and columns mounted on carved bell-shaped pedestals. The room on the ground floor with alcoves in its walls was the emperor's library, where he would be read to (he himself was illiterate) from a collection of 50,000 manuscripts he allegedly took everywhere with him. Behind the library, the beautiful imperial sleeping chamber, the **Khwabgah** (House of Dreams), is decorated with faded inscriptions of Persian verse.

One of Fatehpur Sikri's most famous structures, the **Panch Mahal** or Five-Storeyed Palace, looms northwest of here. The palace tapers to a final single kiosk and is supported by 176 columns of varying designs; the ground floor contains 84 pillars – an auspicious number in Hindu astrology. At one time, the Panch Mahal also had stone lattice screens, which would have been augmented by layers of dampened *khas*, a scented grass still harvested and used to cool verandas throughout northern India.

The women's quarters

Next to the Daulat Khana, a courtyard garden reserved for the *zenana*, the ladies of the harem, signals the start of the **women's area** of the palace complex. The adjoining **Sunahra Makan** (Golden House) is variously thought to have been the home of the emperor's mother or the palace of one of Akbar's wives – hence its alternative names of the **Palace of the Christian Queen** and **Mariam's House** – although no record exists of Akbar's marriage to a Christian called Mariam. Once adorned with gilded murals, the only ornamentation that survives are some inscriptions of verse penned by Abu'l Fazl.

Solemnly presiding over the whole complex, the main harem, known as **Jodhbai's Palace**, blends elements of traditional Islamic architecture with Hindu influences from Gujarat and Gwalior, incorporating an elegant tulip motif characteristic of Fatehpur Sikri. Surrounding the central courtyard are four self-contained raised terraces; those on the north and south sides are surmounted by unusual roofs, thought to imitate the shape of bamboo and thatch, with traces of blue-glazed tile that forms a striking, distinctly Persian counterpoint to the building's beautiful red local sandstone. The **Hawa Mahal** (Palace of the Winds), a small screened tower with a delicately carved chamber, was designed to catch the evening breeze, while a covered walkway gave the imperial ladies of the court access to a lake which has now dried up.

The third women's palace, part of the **Haram Sara** (Imperial Harem) is called **Birbal's Palace** – a misnomer, as Birbal, Akbar's favourite courtier, was a man and would have been most unwelcome in this area. It may in fact have been the residence of two of Akbar's senior wives. The palace's profuse carvings include a ceiling crafted to resemble a canopy of blossoms.

Although remembered primarily for his liberal approach to religion, Akbar was typically Moghul in his attitudes to women, whom he collected in much the same way as an obsessive philatelist amasses stamps. At its height of splendour, the royal harem at Fatehpur Sikri held around five thousand women, guarded by a legion of eunuchs. Its doors were closed to outsiders, but rumours permeated the sandstone walls and several notable travellers were smuggled inside the Great Moghuls' seraglios, leaving for posterity often lurid accounts of the emperors' private lives.

The size of Akbar's harem grew in direct proportion to his empire. With each new conquest, he would be gifted by the defeated rulers and nobles their most beautiful daughters, who, together with their maidservants, would be installed in the luxurious royal *zenana*. In all, the emperor is thought to have kept three hundred wives; their ranks were swollen by a constant flow of concubines (*kaniz*), dancing girls (*kanchni*) and female slaves (*bandis*), or "silver bodied damsels with musky tresses" as one chronicler described them, purchased from markets across Asia. Screened from public view by ornately pierced stone *jali* windows were women from the four corners of the Moghul empire, as well as Afghanis, Turks, Iranis, Arabs, Tibetans, Russians and Abyssinians, and even one Portuguese Christian, sent as presents or tribute.

The eunuchs who presided over them came from similarly diverse backgrounds. While some were hermaphrodites, others had been forcibly castrated, either as punishment following defeat on the battlefield, or after having been donated by their fathers as payment of backdated revenue – an all too common custom at the time.

Akbar is said to have consumed prodigious quantities of Persian wine, local *araq* distilled from sugar cane, *bhang* (prepared from cannabis) and opium in the drinkable form known as *majun*. The lavish dance recitals held in the harem, as well as sexual liaisons conducted on the top pavilion of the Panch Mahal and in the *zenana* itself, would have been fuelled by these substances. Over time, Akbar's hedonistic ways incurred the disapproval of his highest clerics – the *Ulema*. The Koran expressly limits the number of wives a man may take to four, but one verse also admits a lower form of marriage, known as *muta*, which was more like an informal pact, and could be entered into with non-Muslims. Akbar's abuse of this long lapsed law was heavily criticized by his Sunni head priest during their religious disquisitions.

What life must actually have been like for the women who lived in Akbar's harem one can only imagine, but it is known that alcoholism and drug addiction were widespread, and that some also risked their lives to conduct illicit affairs with male lovers, smuggled in disguised as physicians or under heavy Muslim veils. If the reports of a couple of foreign adventurers who secretly gained access to Jehangir's seraglio are to be believed, the eunuchs were also required to intercept anything (other than the emperor) that might excite the women's passion.

In fact, the notion that the harem was a gilded prison whose inmates whiled their lifetimes away in idle vanity and dalliance is something of a myth. Many of the women in the *zenana* were immensely rich in their own right, and wielded enormous influence on the court. Jehangir's wife, Nur Jahan, virtually ran the empire from behind the screen of *purdah* during the last five years of her husband's ailing reign, while her mother-in-law owned a ship that traded between Surat and the Red Sea, a tradition continued by Shah Jahan's daughter, who grew immensely wealthy through her business enterprises.

Partly as a result of the money and power at the women's disposal, jealousies in the harem were also rife, and the work of maintaining order and calm among the thousands of foster mothers, aunties, the emperor's relatives and all his wives, minor wives, paramours, musicians, dancers, amazons and slaves, was a major preoccupation. As Akbar's court chronicler wryly observed, "the goverment of the kingdom is but an amusement compared with such a task, for it is within the (harem) that intrigue is enthroned".

Jami Masjid

At the southwestern corner of the palace complex, with the village of Fatehpur Sikri nestling at its base, stands the **Jami Masjid**, or Dargah Mosque. The alignment of the entire palace complex, which faces west instead of following the ridge, was determined by the orientation of the mosque's *mihrab* (prayer niche) towards Mecca. Housing the tomb of Sheikh Salim Chishti, the mosque is unusual in that it is also a living Sufi shrine.

The main approach is through the imposing **Buland Darwaza** (Great Gate), though you may choose to use the Shahi Darwaza to escape the attentions of touts, unofficial guides and hawkers. Built around 1576, possibly to commemorate Akbar's brilliant campaign in Gujarat, the spectacular gate reaches a height of 54m and is scaled by an impressive flight of steps. Flanked by domed kiosks, the archway of the simple sandstone memorial is inscribed with a message from the Koran: "Said Jesus Son of Mary (peace be on him): The world is but a bridge – pass over without building houses on it. He who hopes for an hour hopes for eternity; the world is an hour – spend it in prayer for the rest is unseen."

Before entering the mosque itself, visitors are required to remove their shoes, but cloth sandals can be borrowed for a small fee. The gate leads into a vast cloistered courtyard containing the **Zenana Rauza** (Tomb of the Royal Ladies), and the lattice-screen **Tomb of Islam Khan**, one of many nobles buried here. The focus of the Sufi shrine or *dargah* is the relatively small but exquisite **Tomb of Sheikh Salim Chishti**, much of which was originally crafted in red sandstone and only later faced in marble: the lattice screens are among the most intricate and beautiful in the world, with striking serpentine brackets supporting the eaves.

Sheikh Salim played a crucial role in the founding of Fatehpur Sikri by prophesizing the birth of a son to the emperor. When one of Akbar's wives, Rani Jodh Bai, a Hindu Rajput princess from Amber, became pregnant she was sent here until the birth of her son Salim, who later became the emperor Jahangir. Fatehpur Sikri was constructed in the saint's honour. The Dargah still attracts women who come here to pray for offspring, tying string onto the marble screen; when entering the main chamber, visitors cover their heads with cloth as a mark of respect. During Ramadan, an *urs* is held here, attracting *qawwals* (singers of Sufi songs; see p.132) from all over the country.

Practicalities

Buses to and from Agra run every half-hour from about 5.45am until 6.30pm, and take between forty minutes and one hour. Regular buses also leave for Bharatpur (approx every 30min; 30min); if you're in a rush, consider renting one of the jeeps that wait outside the bus stand for around Rs300–400.

Though it's well worth spending a day or two here, Fatehpur Sikri has a limited choice of places to **stay**. Unless you've pre-booked a room in the *Dak Bungalow* (see below), by far the best of the bunch is the *Goverdhan Guest House*, just east of the bus stand on Buland Gate Road (☎05619/882222 or 882643; ❷–❸), whose spacious rooms (all en suite) open onto a lawn, and are good value, if a little grubby. This is also a dependable place to **eat**; unlike every other restaurant in the village, the food and hot drinks here are all made with filtered or mineral water (Fatehpur Sikri's ground water is extremely salty). Just over 1km further out of town on the Agra Road, the UPTDC *Gulistan Tourist Complex* (☎05619/41837; ❺–❻), a slightly impersonal state-run complex with en-suite rooms and a run-of-the-mill restaurant, is the best fallback. Fatehpur

Sikri's three budget guesthouses are all grouped immediately below the Buland Darwaza. The *Maurya* (℡ 05619/882348; **❷–❸**) makes the most of the prime location with its atmospheric roof terrace, but the rooms are a bit poky and overpriced, and there's no hot water, which can be inconvenient in the middle of winter. It was also closed for while in 2000, reputedly after a Taj-Ganj-style poisoning incident. In a similar mould is the *Rang Mahal* (℡ 0562/882218; **❷**), next to the car park below the Buland Darwaza, and the very basic *Shree* (℡ 0562/882276; **❶–❷**), down the hill on the lane leading from the bazaar. The dingy lodges immediately beside the bus stand, notably the *Ashoka*, are best avoided, as their airless, dark rooms suffer from traffic noise and fumes until well into the evening. In this bracket, you won't do better than the *Dak Bungalow* (**❶**), located 2km northeast of the bazaar on a hill overlooking the old road into the palace complex, whose large, comfortably furnished rooms are an unbeliev-able bargain at Rs10; the one drawback with this place is that you have to book ahead through the Archaeological Survey, at 22 Mall Rd in Agra (although if you arrive late in the day and slip the *chowkidar* a tip, he may offer a booking on spec).

For **food**, eat either at the *Goverdhan* or *RTDC Gulistan*; local rumours sug-gest the Maurya is less than hygienic (see above). Not to be missed, by con-trast, are Fatephur Sikri's delicious **biscuits**, which you can savour hot out of the oven each evening at the bakeries on the lane leading up from the bazaar to the Jami Masjid. Nearby, next to the fork in the lane, is the **liquor shop** which, aside from the *RTDC Gulistan*, is this predominantly Muslim village's only source of chilled beers.

Braj: Mathura and Vrindavan

The holy land of **BRAJ** can be precisely located on the map – centred around the city of **Mathura**, it lies in the southwestern corner of the Gangetic valley, extending 75km north to south and 50km east to west, with its northern boundary roughly 80km south of Delhi. However, its prime significance is metaphysical, as the mythological land where the Hindu god **Krishna** spent his idyllic childhood.

Early texts mention only Mathura itself – Krishna's birthplace – the forest tract of **Vrindavan**, the hill of **Govardhan**, and the **River Yamuna**. However, in the sixteenth century, Bhakti saints (Krishna devotees) such as Chaitanya and Vallabha "rediscovered" the geographical features and bound-aries of the holy area and identified it with "Braj", Krishna's legendary pas-toral playground. By then Vrindavan had already been decimated by defor-estation, but they gave the myths a new spatial reality by mapping out the sites of Krishna's youthful adventures, pinpointing twelve smaller "forests", various woods, and assorted lakes and ponds that he might have played in. The fact that Braj lay between Delhi and Agra, and thus had borne the brunt of the Muslim conquests, provided a historical explanation for the previous "loss" of these sacred sites.

Braj became, and remains, one of the most important pilgrimage centres for devotees of Krishna, who tour the twelve forests – now reduced to groves on the outskirts of towns and villages – on foot. This great circular pilgrimage, known as the Ban Yatra (forest pilgrimage), or the **Chaurosi Kos Parikrama** (which refers to the circumambulatory distance of 84 *kos*, equivalent to

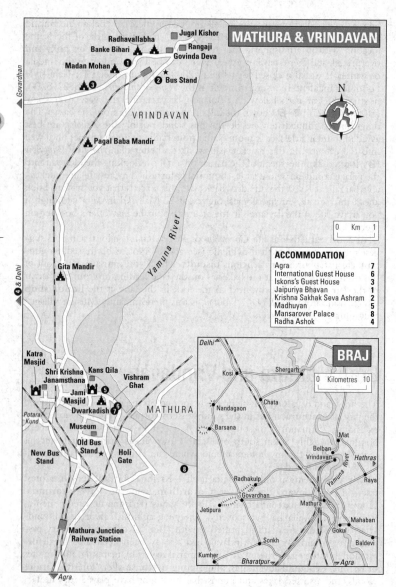

MATHURA & VRINDAVAN

ACCOMMODATION

Agra	7
International Guest House	6
Iskons's Guest House	3
Jaipuriya Bhavan	1
Krishna Sakhak Seva Ashram	2
Madhuyan	5
Mansarover Palace	8
Radha Ashok	4

BRAJ

224km), can take several weeks. Less energetic or devout visitors may prefer to explore the major sites by bus.

Mathura

The sprawling city of **MATHURA**, 141km south of Delhi and 58km north-west of Agra, is celebrated above all as the place where Krishna was born, on the banks of the River Yamuna that features so prominently in tales of his boyhood. Hindu mythology claims that it was founded by Satrugna, the youngest brother of Rama – hero of the *Ramayana* and incarnation of the godhead Vishnu. However, Mathura's earliest historical records date back around 2500 years, before the conquests of Alexander. Buddha himself founded monasteries here, in what was known to later Greeks as Madoura ton Theon (Mathura of the Gods). The city reached an early peak under the Indo–Bactrian Kushan people, whose greatest ruler Kanishka came to power in 78 AD. Fa Hian, the Chinese pilgrim, reported that in 400 AD it held twenty Buddhist monasteries, with about three thousand resident monks.

The enduring prosperity and sophistication of Mathura, which lay on a busy trade route, attracted such adventurers as the Afghan Mahmud of Ghazni in 1017, whose plundering and destruction signalled the death knell of Buddhism. Sikander Lodi from Delhi wrought further havoc in 1500, as did Aurangzeb. With a population nearing 275,000, Mathura has expanded rapidly in recent years, incorporating the teeming **old city** with its many Krishna-associated sites, a vast British military cantonment known as the **Civil Lines** to the south, and haphazard industrial development on the outskirts.

The Town

Despite its prominent history and its religious heritage, Mathura today must be one of the most crowded and dusty cities in India. The recently restored sandstone **Holi Gate** at the entrance to the old city is Mathura's major landmark, surrounded by similarly decorative temples boasting Moghul cusped arches and intricate carvings of flowers and deities. To the east, the riverfront, with its many temples haphazardly crowding the *ghats*, is minute compared with Varanasi. Flanking each temple are shops selling Krishna dolls and assorted outfits to dress them in, and other equipment necessary for devotional activites. Along the river towards the north lie the remains of **Kans Qila**, a fort built by Raja Man Singh of Amber and rebuilt by Akbar – little is left apart from the foundations.

To the south, the brightly coloured **Vishram Ghat** is the "*ghat* of rest", where Krishna is said to have recuperated after killing the evil Kamsa. You must remove your shoes before entering the temple complex or visiting the *ghats*, no matter how muddy they are. **Boats** for river excursions (Rs25 per head) can be rented here.

Heading through the network of lanes from Vishram Ghat you come to Radha Dhiraj Bazaar, and the large and ostentatious turn-of-the-twentieth-century **Dwarkadhish** temple. A little way north, the **Jami Masjid**, on a plinth raised above street level, was completed in 1661 by Aurangzeb's governor Abd-un-Nabi. It has long since lost its original vivid glazed tiles, but remains surrounded by four minarets and assorted outer pavilions. Around 500m west stands another of Aurangzeb's mosques, the impressive red-sandstone **Katra Masjid**. This was erected on the foundations of the once-famous Kesava Deo temple, destroyed by the Moghul emperor, which had itself been built on the ruins of a Buddhist monastery. Some traces of the Hindu temple can be seen around the back, where the **Shri Krishna Janamsthan** or Janambhoomi complex (daily dawn to noon & 4pm to dusk; free) now stands. Directly behind the mosque, approached through a corridor, a shrine marks Krishna's exact birthplace (*janamsthan*); its cage-like surround signifies that he was born in captivity, when his parents were prisoners of the tyrant king Kamsa. Inside the adjacent **Bhagwat Bhavan** – a flamboyantly modern, towering hulk also known as **Gita Mandir** – a garishly painted ceiling depicts scenes from Krishna's life. No cameras are allowed into the complex, where, although the shops and shrines combine to produce a park-like atmosphere, nothing obscures the heavy paramilitary presence – a reminder of underlying Hindu–Muslim tensions. Nearby, the impressive stepped sandstone tank of **Potara Kund** is believed to have been used to wash Krishna's baby clothes.

Close to the centre of Mathura in Dampier Park, the **Archeological Museum** (Tues–Sat 10.30am–4.30pm; free), places a particular emphasis on Buddhist and Jain sculpture, dating from the Kushan (first–third centuries AD) and Gupta periods (fourth–sixth centuries). Known collectively as the **Mathura school**, it is characterized by its spotted red sandstone and reflects the assimilation of early primitive cults within the successive Jain, Buddhist and Hindu pantheons. The museum's highlight, one of the finest examples of Gupta art, is a miraculously intact standing Buddha. Shown with a beautiful benign expression, an ornate halo, and delicate fluted robes, he is making the Abhaya *mudra* (fearless) hand gesture. Both this and a seated Buddha, this time depicted as the Enlightened One, are thought to have been created by the monk Dinna around 434 AD. Kushana art on display includes a headless image of King Kanishka in a foreign-styled tunic and boots, and some exquisite railings carved with floral motifs and human figures.

Practicalities

The city's principal **railway station** lies southwest of the centre, around 4km from Holi Gate and the old city. It's on the main Delhi–Agra line, 1hr 45min from Delhi Nizamuddin on the fast Taj Express #2180, and only 50min short of Agra; Mathura is also served by several Delhi–Mumbai trains such as the Punjab Mail #2138 via Agra and the fast Kerala Express #2626; the Pashchim Express #2926 stops at Sawai Madhopur (for the wildlife park of Ranthambore; see p.205) and Kota.

Mathura has two bus stands; the **Old Bus Stand**, near Holi Gate, has hourly connections to Agra and serves **Govardhan**, 25km west, while the **New Bus Stand**, a little way west, is used by Delhi and Jaipur, Bharatpur and Deeg buses as well as more Agra services.

Cycle and auto-rickshaws are always on hand for local journeys, and shared tempos and horse-drawn tongas are also available. The **tourist office** (Mon–Sat 9.30am–5pm) at the Old Bus Stand is not worth seeking out; **foreign exchange** is handled by the State Bank of India, Railway Station Road (Mon–Fri 10am–2pm, Sat 10am–noon).

Accommodation

Despite being an important pilgrimage centre and a large industrial and military city, Mathura offers a very limited choice of **accommodation**, and none of its upmarket hotels is especially worthy of recommendation. Neighbouring Vrindavan (see p.314) also has a small, basic range of accommodation.

Agra, Bengali Ghat ☎0565/403318. Charming, small place established in 1930, overlooking the river in the old city and redolent of the atmosphere of the *ghats*. Bengali food, and a choice of clean air-cooled rooms. Some a/c. ❷–❹
International Guest House, Shri Krishna Janamsthan ☎0565/405888. Large institution-like building set in beautiful gardens beside the temple. Very affordable and clean, with a good *bhojanalaya*, or vegetarian café. ❶

Madhuvan, Krishna Nagar ☎0565/404064, ℻401884. The top hotel in the city centre has 28 rooms and a pool (open to nonresidents). ❼–❽
Mansarovar Palace, State Bank Crossing ☎0565/408686. 22 well-appointed rooms, most with a/c and TV. Facilities include a good multi-cuisine restaurant and a foreign exchange desk. ❻–❼
Radha Ashok, Masani By-Pass Road ☎0565/40557, ℻409557. Swish but cosy

four-star on the outskirts of town, 4km northeast on the Delhi road. The most comfortable option in the area, with a/c and a pool. **8**

Eating

Due to the city's spiritual significance, restaurants and cafés in Mathura tend to serve **vegetarian** food only. Aside from the hotel restaurants, the numerous sweetshops and *dhabas* around Holi Gate and the Shri Krishna Janamsthan serve snacks and thalis.

Brijwasi Mithai Wala, opposite Shri Krishna Janamsthan. Very clean sweetshop with a number of other branches in Mathura. Offers a huge range of fresh sweets and snacks.

Kwality, near Old Bus Stand. Formerly part of the famous chain, and retaining much of its typical look and feel, but now poorly maintained and run by indifferent management. Serves veg food.

Prakash Hotel, next to Holi Gate. A *dhaba* serving delicious thalis and Thai-style *chana masala*.

Around Mathura

At the very heart of Braj, Mathura is the obvious base for peregrinations into the pastoral landscape associated with the adolescent Krishna, where the sacred temple-crowned hills of **Govardhan**, **Barsana** and **Nandagaon** stand in striking contrast to the prevailing flatness. Very little survives of its idyllic legendary forests, and only serious pilgrims would choose to walk rather than catch one of the numerous local buses.

Mahaban and Gokul

Across the Yamuna from Mathura, 10km southeast of the city and reachable by boat, rickshaw or bus, **Mahaban** and **Gokul** are associated with Krishna's foster parents, Nanda and Yashoda. There is a cluster of temples at **MAHABAN**, "the Great Forest", of which the most interesting is **Nanda's Palace**, also known as **Assi Khamba** or "Eighty Pillars", an amalgam of several influences including Buddhist. Rebuilt as a mosque under Aurangzeb, the temple's pillars resemble the Qutb Minar in Delhi, and probably date back to the tenth century.

On a high bank overlooking the river 2km from Mahaban, **GOKUL**, the cowherd encampment to which the newborn Krishna was smuggled, is the headquarters of the followers of the sixteenth-century saint Vallabha. This is where Krishna first revealed his divinity to his foster mother Yashoda − she made him open his mouth after catching him eating earth, only to peer in and see the entire universe. All of Gokul's sixteenth- and seventeenth-century temples are in a very bad state of repair.

Govardhan

GOVARDHAN, 25km west of Mathura, is significant as Krishna is said to have lifted the hill of the same name on the tip of one finger, to shelter the inhabitants of Braj from a deluge caused by the wrath of the god Indra. A popular Vaishnavite icon, the entire hill is circumambulated by thousands of pilgrims each year. The eponymous town is clustered close to a masonry tank known as Mansi Ganga, in a gap towards the hill's northern end. Two impressive **cenotaphs** immediately opposite the tank commemorate the Randhir Singh and Baladeva Singh, two of the Bharatpur rajas, while the temple of **Hari Deva**, founded during the reign of Akbar, lies nearby.

Barsana and Nandagaon

The hill sites of **Barsana** and **Nandagaon**, 25km and 32km north of Govardhan respectively, were originally dedicated to Brahma and Shiva before being appropriated into the Krishna myth. An impressive stone staircase leads from the town at the base of the hill at **BARSANA** to an extensive ridge, where temples include that of **Lali Ji**, a local name for Krishna's mistress, Radha.

The eighteenth-century temple of **Nand Rae** dominates the smaller hill and town of **NANDAGAON**, identified as the village of Krishna's foster father Nanda. A curious local ritual takes place each year during the spring festival of Holi. First the menfolk of Nandagaon invade Barsana, to taunt the women with lewd songs and be beaten with long wooden staffs for their pains; then on the next day the procedure is reversed, and the men of Barsana pay courting calls to the women of Nandagaon.

Vrindavan

VRINDAVAN, a dusty little town on the banks of the Yamuna, 11km north of Mathura, is among the most important pilgrimage sites in Braj, attracting an estimated 500,000 pilgrims each year. In practice, most of these come during the spring Holi festival, which hereabouts is extended for up to a month, and during the two months of celebrations for the birthdays of Krishna and Radha, his mythical mistress, in the autumn.

Although Vrindavan is in theory a *tirtha* or holy crossing place on the Yamuna, in fact the town has been progressively abandoned by the river, as it meanders away from the original 2km-long waterfront, and all but five of its 38 *ghats* are now without water. Neither is there much trace of the forests of the Krishna legend, and only a few sacred basil groves remain at the spot where he cavorted with the *gopis*. Nevertheless, as a *tirtha*, the town attracts elderly Vaishnavas who believe that to die here earns them instant *moksha* or liberation. Along with its many *dharamshalas*, Vrindavan holds several "**widow houses**", maintained by wealthy devotees, which provide food and shelter for the poor women, clad in white saris, who find solace in devotion to Krishna. Two thousand of them congregate in the Mirabai Ashram twice a day to sing *bhajans* (devotional songs).

Though it may not boast the several thousand temples of popular exaggeration, the town does hold numerous shrines, many of them now neglected and crumbling or overrun with monkeys. Close to the centre, on the main Mathura–Vrindavan road, **Govinda Deva**, known locally as "Govindji", is one of northern India's most impressive medieval Hindu edifices, though worship here is low-key in comparison to some of the other shrines of Vrindavan. Erected by Raja Man Singh in 1590, its main tower is said to have once been seven storeys high; the three storeys that survived the depredations of Aurangzeb leave it with a squat and truncated look.

Although of much later design, and rebuilt in the nineteenth century, **Banke Bihari** (9am–noon & 6–9pm; free), off Purana Bazaar, is the town's most popular temple, renowned for impressive floral decorations of the deity. Stalls on the corner of the lane leading to it serve excellent *malai* (cream) and *kesar* (saffron) *lassis* in *bhands* (unfired clay cups).

Opposite Govinda Deva, across the main road, lies the lavish new south Indian-style temple of **Shri Ranganatha**, also known as **Rangaji Temple**, where ostentatious displays include the numerous gold-plated embellishments that crown its lofty *shikhara*, and the gold-plated **Dhwaja Stambha** column in the inner courtyard (no admittance to non-Hindus). An electronic puppet show of the Hindu epics enlivens the entrance gate, and a small museum inside houses processional images and chariots (Rs0.50).

The widows of Vrindavan

Walk around the bazaars and temples of Vrindavan and you cannot fail to notice the overwhelming numbers of shaven-headed women dressed in ragged white-cotton saris, shuffling between shops, shrines and ashrams with their begging bowls. These are the widows of Vrindavan – women who, after the death of their husbands, have left home so as not to be a burden on their families, or who have been forced into destitution by cruel relatives.

Based on the tenets of the ancient *Shastras* and *Manu-Smirti*, Hindu tradition accords no status to a widow. If she outlives her husband, a Hindu woman is regarded as a curse; she is expected to destroy her marriage bangles and jewellery, abstain from wearing colour and *kohl* under her eyes, *kunkum* vermillion in her hair parting and *mehendi* on her hands, and to spend the rest of her days in fasting and prayer for her deceased spouse.

When the ostracization and ignominy of life among the in-laws gets too much, Vrindavan is one of the religious centres to which widows travel in search of succour. Here, by chanting in ashrams and begging for alms from pilgrims, they can at least expect to obtain a bowl of rice and a few rupees. It is estimated that as many as nine thousand women subsist in this way in Vrindavan alone, living off the charity of ashrams, in whose huge halls you can see them intoning mantras and *kirtans* for eight-hour shifts. The widows are becoming increasingly vulnerable to unscrupulous landlords and the sex industry, and it is also rumoured that some of the ashrams are little more than fronts for money laundering.

Women's rights and support groups from the capital have tried alleviate the suffering of Vrindavan's widows, but their efforts are swamped by the ever-increasing numbers of women pouring in.

ISKCON, the International Society of Krishna Consciousness, also has a lavish new temple complex in Vrindavan, the **Krishna Balaram Mandir**, around 3km west of town at Raman Reti. Built in Bengal Renaissance style with bright frescoes depicting episodes from Krishna's life, the temple incorporates a marble mausoleum in honour of the society's founder, Swami Prabhupada, who died in 1977. His private chambers have been made into a museum.

Among the new temples springing up along the Mathura–Vrindavan road is the **Gita Mandir** which houses the Gita Stambh, a pillar with the entire *Bhagavad Gita* carved on its surface. The imposing temple, built by one of the country's leading industrial families, the Birlas, is overshadowed by the outrageous multistoreyed, spaceship-like edifice known as the **Pagal Baba Mandir** just down the road.

Practicalities

Buses, shared tempos, and taxis run out to Vrindavan from Mathura for about Rs70 per head one way. Three local **trains** also cover the same route, leaving from Mathura Junction (6.30am, 3.40pm & 7.40pm) for the station in the south of Vrindavan (they return at 7.30am, 4.35pm & 8.05pm). Besides the numerous *dharamshalas*, several ashrams offer good-value **accommodation** at fixed rates, as well as **food**. Some are, however, open only to Indian pilgrims. Away from the centre, the *Krishna Sadhak Seva Ashram* on Gurukul Road (❶–❸), set in extensive grounds, is quiet and has comfortable suites; more central is the large, friendly *Jaipuriya Bhavan* (❶–❸), built around a pleasant garden courtyard. ISKCON's *Guest House* (☎0565/442478; ❷), immediately behind their temple, offers rooms to all, whether a devotee or not, and you may need to book ahead as it can get busy. Their vegetarian restaurant serves excellent meals, pitched at the Western palate.

Central UP

Large tracts of **CENTRAL UP**, along the fertile flood plains of the Doab, constituted the nineteenth-century **Kingdom of Avadh**. Destined eventually to become little more than puppets of the British, its wealthy nawabs (governors) focused their attentions on the arts, and created a unique civilization centred around **Lucknow**. Monuments from those days, and traces of the bitter fighting of the "Mutiny" or "First War of Independence" that coincided with the final eclipse of Avadh, are scattered throughout both city and region. Today central UP has become a Hindu stronghold as the BJP extends its grip from its seat in the state capital, Lucknow. East of Lucknow, the holy town of **Ayodhya**, once the royal seat that Rama fought for in the *Ramayana*, is now better known as a flashpoint of Hindu militancy since the destruction of the Babri mosque in 1992. Industrialized **Kanpur**, southwest of Lucknow, was as "Cawnpore" the scene of some of the bloodiest moments of the rebellion of 1857, now worth visiting to explore its near-neighbour **Bithur**, a miniature and forgotten Varanasi beside the Ganges. Further east, the holy river flows towards **Allahabad**, and the sacred confluence at **Prayag**, where it meets the Yamuna and the mythical Saraswati that flows from heaven.

Kanpur and around

The teeming metropolis of **KANPUR**, 438km east of Delhi and 190km west of Allahabad, is among the most polluted cities in the world, and most visitors are there solely for business. Kanpur has been a textile-manufacturing centre since its cotton mills were established in 1869, and together with its twin city, Lucknow, 76km northeast, it dominates the industrial heartland of Uttar Pradesh. Unlike other points along the Ganges, the riverside is of little significance; its *ghats* are run down, and only those at **Bithur**, 20km upstream, are worth exploring.

The Town

The focus of modern Kanpur is north of the station, where the large avenue known as **the Mall** threads east to west to form a hub for the more pleasant and cosmopolitan sectors of the city. Further north and west, beyond the exclusive Civil Lines area, is the river.

Cawnpore, among the most vital of the British East India Company's garrisons along the Ganges, was a major focus of the wild revolt of 1857 – what the British called the **Indian Mutiny**, and Indians the **First War of Independence**. One thousand or so British residents were besieged throughout June by the forces of Nana Sahib of Bithur, their numbers whittled away by disease, starvation and enemy sharpshooting. Only a few hundred were still alive when Brigadier-General Wheeler finally managed to negotiate a truce. However, as they boarded boats at Satichaura Ghat, to carry them to Allahabad, they were mown down by gunfire, and any survivors put to the sword. When relief under Brigadier-General Havelock reached Kanpur a few days later, on

July 17, they found that two hundred imprisoned women and children had been butchered. Terrifying reprisals by the British included executions of innocent civilians, the razing of villages, and the shooting of captives spreadeagled across the mouths of cannons.

Aside from the historical significance of Kanpur, there is really nothing in the way of sites or buildings of interest for the visitor. Around 1.5km east of the station, close to the run-down Kanpur Club, broad tree-lined streets lead to the red-brick **All Saints' Memorial Church**. Erected in 1875, near the site of General Wheeler's original entrenchment, it serves as a tribute to the British dead. Within an enclosure east of the church, the Memorial Garden has a Gothic screen designed by Sir Henry Yule, and a touching epitaph in stone by Baron Carlo Marochetti.

Practicalities

Trains on the main Delhi–Calcutta line, including the superfast Shatabdi Express #2003 (1 daily) pull in regularly at **Kanpur Central**, in the most congested part of the city. **Buses** from Lucknow and points east terminate at the **Collectorganj Bus Stand** (☎0512/61705) in Sadar Bazaar, a short way east, while services from Delhi, Agra, Haridwar and the west arrive at **Chunniganj** (☎0512/210646), 3km west of the Mall. Few people fly to Kanpur, as rail connections, especially with Delhi, are good, but there's an **airport** 12km to the east, a taxi-ride (Rs100) or an auto-rickshaw ride (Rs30) from the centre. Indian Airlines have offices opposite MG College, Civil Lines (☎0512/211430) and at the airport (☎0512/42642).

Local buses use stands such as Ghanta Ghar, near the Mall; **taxis** are plentiful near the station; cars can be rented through the larger hotels or from the main taxi stand at Canal Road Crossing on the Mall; and cycle and auto-rickshaws abound. Noisy diesel-powered Vikrams and tempos operate along fixed routes, and horse-drawn tongas can be rented on a shared or exclusive basis. As the government does not consider Kanpur to be a tourist destination, the city has no official information centre. The **GPO** is at Bara Chaurha on the Mall, and money can be changed nearby at ANZ Grindlays **bank**.

Accommodation

Several of Kanpur's better **hotels** can be found in and around the Mall, while cheaper accommodation is concentrated near the Central railway station – which itself has reasonable retiring rooms.

Ganges, 51/50 Nayaganj ☎0512/352853. Cheap and basic, not far from the station, with a mediocre restaurant attached. ❷

Gaurav, 18/54 the Mall ☎0512/368616. Central hotel, four doors down from the better-known *Geet*, but not as loud, a little newer, and a lot more pleasant. ❻–❼

The Landmark, 10 the Mall ☎0512/317601. Behind Som Dutt Plaza; the closest Kanpur comes to luxury. Features include currency exchange, coffee shop, health suite and travel centre. ❾

Meghdoot, the Mall ☎0512/311999. Popular business-class hotel opposite Company Bagh, with a small rooftop swimming pool, health club, several restaurants and a bar. ❽

Natraj, 71/150 Suterkhana ☎0512/366907. Reasonable budget accommodation close to the railway station. Some rooms with shared baths and some small but expensive a/c. ❶–❹

Station View, opposite the railway station, city side ☎0512/366138. Reasonably priced basic, budget hotel with air-cooled rooms. ❶–❸

Eating

Few of the high-street **eating places** can be recommended, but several of Kanpur's better hotels such as the *Landmark* and the *Meghdoot* have good restaurants.

Budhsen, Virhana Road, Nayaganj. A popular restaurant with an adjacent sweetshop which, along with the posh *Haveli*, is one of several options on this busy and central shopping street.
Kailash Misthan Bhandar, GT Road, Gumti 5. The best of a couple of roadside cafés near Moti Jheel, serving snacks such as *dosas* to locals who come here to take the evening air.

Shanghai, the Mall. In the centre of town, popular with well-heeled locals, many of whom take their children to sample the exotic Chinese cuisine.
Treat, behind *The Landmark*, Navin Market, the Mall. Popular café in a shopping precinct, with a flexible menu including basic Chinese and south Indian food and ice creams.

Bithur

Some Hindus consider the charming little town of **BITHUR**, set in rich farming country beside the Ganges, 20km west of Kanpur, to be the centre of the world. However, few pilgrims, let alone tourists, come to this miniature Varanasi, where many of the *ghats* have been reclaimed by the river since being devastated by the British bombardment that followed the uprising of 1857. Bithur's principal shrine, at the main *ghat*, is one of the few in the Hindu world to be dedicated to Brahma. The town is also connected to the *Ramayana*, and specifically with Rama's wife Sita – this is where her sons were born, and where she died when the earth opened and swallowed her. Much the best way to enjoy the peaceful ambience of the place is to rent a boat at the main *ghat* and slowly drift up the river watching the devoted busy at their puja.

Three local **trains** a day connect Brahmavart, 2km from Bithur, with Kanpur Central, while buses and shared auto-rickshaws travel between Kanpur and Mandhana, where local transport to Bithur can be picked up. For the moment, the only way to arrange food and lodging is through the pleasant and helpful *pandas*. During the full moon of Kartika Purnima (Oct/Nov), Bithur plays host to a large and colourful rustic fair.

Lucknow

In the approximate centre of Uttar Pradesh, 516km east of Delhi, the state capital **LUCKNOW** is best remembered for the ordeal of its British residents during the five-month **siege** of 1857. However, the city had earlier witnessed the last heady days of Muslim rule in India, before the final capitulation to the British. In fact the summary British deposition of the incompetent last Nawab of **Avadh** – or of Oudh, the British name for the kingdom – Wajid Ali Shah, is usually numbered among the root causes of the "Mutiny". Today, Lucknow's fading nineteenth-century monuments bear the scars of the fighting, and of the destruction wreaked by the British army when they regained control.

The centre of Muslim power shifted gradually from Delhi to Avadh from the middle of the eighteenth century onwards, as the Moghul empire declined. The later nawabs of Avadh are a byword in India for indolence and decadence, but under their rule the arts flourished. Cocooned from the responsibilities of government, Avadh became a magnet for poets and artists, where Hindus and Muslims worked in harmony, fuelled by wealth and plentiful leisure time. Lucknow was also an important repository of Shi'a culture and Islamic jurisprudence, with its Farangi Mahal school of law attracting students from as far afield as China and Central Asia.

The patronage of the Shi'a nawabs also produced new expressions of the faith – the annual **Muharram** processions, in memory of the martyrdom of Hussain

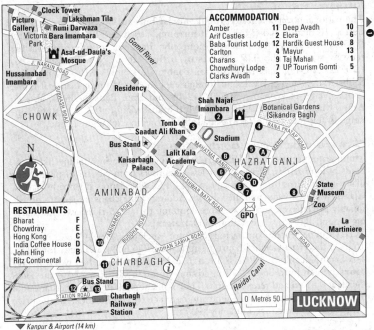

Within the map:

ACCOMMODATION

Amber	11	Deep Avadh	10
Arif Castles	2	Elora	6
Baba Tourist Lodge	12	Hardik Guest House	8
Carlton	4	Mayur	13
Charans	9	Taj Mahal	1
Chowdhury Lodge	7	UP Tourism Gomti	5
Clarks Avadh	3		

RESTAURANTS

Bharat	F
Chowdray	E
Hong Kong	C
India Coffee House	D
John Hing	B
Ritz Continental	A

Map labels: Clock Tower, Picture Gallery, Lakshman Tila, Rumi Darwaza, Victoria Park, Bara Imambara, Gomti River, Asaf-ud-Daula's Mosque, J. NARAIN ROAD, Hussainabad Imambara, SUBHASH ROAD, Residency, CHOWK, Shah Najaf Imambara, Botanical Gardens (Sikandra Bagh), Tomb of Saadat Ali Khan, RANA PRATAP ROAD, Bus Stand, Stadium, MAHATMA GANDHI ROAD, Kaisarbagh Palace, Lalit Kala Academy, HAZRATGANJ, BISHESHWAR NATH ROAD, ASHOK MARG, AMINABAD, State Museum, Zoo, AMINABAD ROAD, BUDDHA ROAD, GPO, La Martiniere, PARK ROAD, VIDHAN SABHA ROAD, CHARBAGH, Haidar Canal, 0 Metres 50, **LUCKNOW**, Bus Stand, STATION ROAD, Charbagh Railway Station

▼ *Kanpur & Airport (14 km)*

and his two sons, developed into elaborate affairs with **tazia**, ornate reproductions in paper of the Shi'a Imam's shrine at Karbala in southern Iraq, being carried to the local Karbala for burial. During the rest of the year the *tazia* images are kept in Imambara ("houses of the Imam"); these range from humble rooms in poor Shi'a households to the **Great Imambara** built by Asaf-ud-Daula in 1784.

Extraordinary sandstone monuments, now engulfed by modern Lucknow, still testify to the euphoric atmosphere of this unique culture. European-inspired edifices too are prominent on the skyline, often embellished with flying buttresses, turrets, cupolas and floral patterns, but the brick and mortar with which they were constructed means that they are not ageing as well as the earlier stone buildings, and old Lucknow is, literally, crumbling away.

Arrival, information and transport

From **Amausi Airport** (☎0522/436132), 16km south on the Kanpur Road, a taxi to the centre of Lucknow costs around Rs150. Airport buses connect with flights.

Lucknow's main **Charbagh Railway Station** (☎0522/259932 for computerized reservations), 4km southwest of the central hub of Hazratganj, is itself a remarkable building, with prominent *chhatris* above the entrance arcade and a roof inspired by chess pieces. Most **buses**, including those from Varanasi, Allahabad, Agra, Jhansi and Kanpur, arrive at the main **Charbagh Bus Stand** alongside, while some buses from the Nepal border at Sonauli and from Gorakhpur, Faizabad and Ayodhya pull in at the **Kaisarbagh stand**, near Hazratganj.

Information

The national government's **regional tourist bureau**, close to the railway station at 10 Station Rd (Mon–Sat 10am–5pm, closed 2nd Sat of each month; ☏0522/246205), provides information only; they also operate a stand at the railway station. The **UP Tourism office**, at 3 Newal Kishore Rd (☏0522/228349), has an information counter. Lucknow's **GPO** is on Vidhan Sabha Marg. Among **banks** for foreign exchange are Punjab National Bank, Ashok Marg, Hazratganj (☏0522/21290), and State Bank of India, also on Ashok Marg (☏0522/21341) and at Moti Mahal Marg (☏0522/220186). Top-range hotels such as the *Taj Mahal* also have foreign exchange facilities.

City transport and guided tours

Multi-seater **tempos** and **Vikrams**, their diesel engines sounding like hundreds of loud rattles, have more or less taken over from city buses, plying regular routes such as from Charbagh to the GPO, with depots at Janpath Market, Clarks Avadh Crossing and the Chowk. Adding to the chaos are legions of reasonably priced cycle rickshaws, more common than auto-rickshaws and charging around Rs5 from the station to Hazratganj.

Cars can be rented from various operators, including *Hotel Clarks Avadh*, UP Tours at the *Hotel Gomti*, 6 Sapru Marg (☏0522/232659), and Aliza Tours Ltd, 4-A Saran Chambers, 5 Park Rd (☏0522/238357). Comprehensive daily **city tours**, which must be booked in advance through UP Tours, leave the *Hotel Gomti* at 9.45am and return at 2pm. They will also pick up from the station (at 8.30am) and various hotels. Guide and entrance fees are included in the price except for the expensive residency (Rs75).

The performing arts of Lucknow

In the eighteenth and nineteenth centuries, Muslim Lucknow saw the emergence of an astounding range of music and dance forms that remain prominent in the performing arts of north India. The period is still considered a Golden Age of artistic achievement.

Apart from the musicians of the court, and courtiers – among them some of the nawabs themselves – tawwaif (courtesans) took on a vital role in the cultural life of the city, becoming proficient as poets and in dance and song. While *khyal* and *dhrupad* remained the mainstay of classical music, thumri – love songs amalgamating classical *ragas* and folk melodies – developed a high degree of sophistication, and forms such as *dadra, tappa* and *hori*, influenced by folk traditions, also became widely popular. Often referred to as "semi" or "light" classical music, these latter forms are fading from the repertoire of modern musicians.

Kathak, the main genre of north Indian classical dance, developed under nawabs such as Shuja-ud-Daula (1756–75) and Asaf-ud-Daula (1775–97). The theme of Krishna cavorting with the milkmaids (*gopis*) became especially important within performances that otherwise rely on strong and energetic footwork around *laikari*, intricate rhythmic compositions accompanied by *tabla* or hand-drums. Some of Avadh's great Gharana (schools) of dance and music – including those at Lucknow, Farrakhabad and Rampur – are gradually being assimilated into a new system of patronage, now dependent on the middle classes.

The Lucknow Festival, held in February, gives visitors an excellent opportunity to sample the city's vibrant traditions of music and dance. For information, contact UP Tourism.

Accommodation

Budget and mid-range **hotels** are concentrated in the **Charbagh** area, around the bus and railway stations, and along Vidhan Sabha Marg, the main artery feeding into the city centre around the GPO. The more cosmopolitan **Hazratganj** district holds a few bargains. Top-range hotels include the *Taj Mahal* in Gomti Nagar and *Arif Castles*.

Amber, Naka Hindola ℡ 0522/215658. Spacious air-cooled rooms, with clean Indian-style toilets. ③–⑤

Arif Castles, 4 Rana Pratap Marg, near Shah Najaf ℡ 0522/211317. Comfortable but ostentatious; dripping with chandeliers and reminiscent of a Hindi film set. Standard luxury hotel with all facilities, including a good bakery. ⑦–⑧

Baba Tourist Lodge, Charbagh Railway Station ℡ 0522/454357. A stone's throw from the station – turn left and walk 300m; pleasantly quiet and reasonably clean Sikh-run option with a range of rooms from shared baths to a/c. ②–⑤

Carlton, Shah Najaf Road ℡ 0522/224021. Fabled Lucknow address, a *fin-de-siècle* Euro-Avadhi edifice with big rooms, ancient plumbing and musty hunting trophies. Expensive for what it is. ⑥–⑦

Charans, 16 Vidhan Sabha Marg ℡ 0522/227219. Mid-range and quiet, even though it lies just off the main road, with a choice of air-cooled or a/c rooms and a new restaurant. ⑤–⑥

Chowdhury Lodge, 3 Vidhan Sabha Marg ℡ 0522/221911. Close to the GPO, well-priced, pleasant, and justifiably popular. The cheapest rooms are very good value. ①–③

Clarks Avadh, 8 Mahatma Gandhi Marg ℡ 0522/220131. An imposing if characterless landmark in the centre of Lucknow, which has lost its crown as the best in town to the *Taj* (see opposite). ⑨

Deep Avadh, Naka Hindola, Aminabad Road ℡ 0522/216521. New place, with a good multi-cuisine restaurant and a travel desk, in an interesting part of town, close to the station. ③–⑤

Elora, 3 Lalbagh ℡ 0522/211307. Friendly, architecturally eccentric place popular with travellers, in the busy heart of Lucknow. The misshapen rooms are dominated by monolithic a/c units, and some corridors are very low; the prices, however, are a bit high. ④–⑦

Hardik Guest House, 16 Rana Pratap Marg, near Jopling Road Crossing ℡ 0522/209497. Clean, comfortable little guesthouse, with a/c rooms and food. ⑤–⑦

Mayur, Charbagh ℡ 0522/451824. Opposite the station, next to the Charbagh Bus Stand and above the *Bharat Restaurant*. Unattractive cheaper rooms, while those at the other end of the range are much too expensive for what they are. ④–⑤

Taj Mahal, Vipin Khand, Gomti Nagar ℡ 0522/393939. Recently built in Avadhi style, this is easily Lucknow's most elegant and comfortable hotel with a swimming pool and a range of restaurants, but inconveniently situated far out of town. ⑨

UP Tourism Gomti, 6 Tej Bahadur Sapru Marg ℡ 0522/220624. This crumbling high-rise is so devoid of character it resembles a hospital. UP Tours are billeted here, and so are their unlucky tour groups. ⑤–⑦

The Town

Most of Lucknow's monuments are spread along or near the southern bank of the Gomti, a sluggish weed-covered stream that most of the year swells with the monsoon, and becomes crowded with the small dugout boats of local fishermen. Close to the main central bridge lies the modern commercial centre of **Hazratganj**, with the **Shah Najaf Imambara** to its north near the riverbank. Further west, beyond the ruins of the **Residency**, the road passes the majestic **Bara Imambara**, leading through the large gate of **Rumi Darwaza** to the **Hussainabad Imambara**. South of Hussainabad, between Hazratganj and Charbagh, the old city sector of **Aminabad** holds a maze of busy streets and fascinating markets.

Hussainabad

In the west of the city, in the vicinity of Hardinge Bridge around "old" Lucknow, lie several crumbling relics of the nawabs of Avadh. Chief among them is the Great or **Bara Imambara** (daily except during Muharram 8am–6.30pm; ticket includes Hussainabad Imambara and Picture Gallery, Rs10), which boasts one of the largest vaulted halls in the world – 50m long and 15m high. Flat on top, slightly arched inside, and built by Asaf-ud-Daula in 1784 without the aid of a single iron or wooden beam, the roof was constructed using a technique known as *kara dena*, in which bricks are broken and angled to form an interlocking section and then covered with concrete – here several metres thick. The arcaded structure is approached through what must have been an extravagant gate, now pockmarked and on the verge of collapse. Two successive courtyards lead from the gates to the unusually festive-looking Imambara itself. Steps lead up to a labyrinth of chambers known as *bhulbhulaiya* – the "maze". Adjacent to the Bara Imambara and overlooking it is **Asaf-ud-Daula's Mosque**, set upon a two-tiered arcaded plinth with two lofty minarets. Closed to non-Muslims, it can be readily viewed from the Victoria Gardens that adjoin it to the west (daily except Fri dawn to dusk; Rs6).

Straddling the main road west of the main gates, the colossal **Rumi Darwaza** is an ornamental victory arch modelled on one of the gates to Asia Minor in Istanbul (known to the Islamic world in Byzantine times as "Rumi"). Now decaying, it sports elaborate floral patterns and a few extraordinary trumpets. Steps lead up to open chambers that command a general prospect of the monuments of Hussainabad.

A short distance further west, the lavish **Hussainabad Imambara** is also known as the Chota ("small") Imambara, or the Palace of Lights, thanks to its fairy-tale appearance when decorated and illuminated for special occasions. The raised tank in front of it, which is approached via a spacious courtyard, adds to the overall festive atmosphere. A central gilded dome dominates the whole ensemble, busy with minarets, small domes and arches and even a crude miniature Taj Mahal. Built in 1837 by Muhammad Ali Shah (1837–42), partly to provide famine relief through employment, the Imambara houses a silver-faced throne, plus the tombs of important Avadhi personalities. The dummy gate opposite the main entrance was used by ceremonial musicians, while the unfinished watchtower is known as the Satkhanda or "Seven Storeys", even though only four were ever constructed. West of the Imambara, and surrounded by ruins, are the two soaring minarets and three domes of the **Jami Masjid**, completed after the death of Muhammad Ali Shah, which does not admit non-Muslims.

Beyond the Hussainabad Tank, east of the Hussainabad Imambara, the isolated 67-metre-high **Hussainabad Clocktower**, an ambitious Gothic tower completed in 1887, carries the largest clock in India. Close to this bizarre monolith lies **Taluqdar's Hall**, built by Muhammad Ali Shah to house the offices of the Hussainabad Trust, and the dusty **Picture Gallery**, also known as the **Muhammad Ali Shah Art Gallery**. The portraits of Nawabs, arranged chronologically, graphically demonstrate the decline of their civilization, as the figures become progressively portlier. In a famous image, the androgynous-looking last nawab, Wajid Ali Shah (1847–56), is shown in a daringly low-cut top that reveals his left nipple. **Aurangzeb's Mosque**, on the high ground towards Hardinge Bridge known as **Lakshman Tila**, was the site of Lucknow's original fifteenth-century settlement.

The Residency

The blasted **Residency** (daily dawn to dusk; Rs250 [Rs10]) rests in peace amid landscaped gardens southeast of Hardinge Bridge – a battle-scarred ruin left exactly as it stood when the siege was finally relieved by Sir Colin Campbell on November 17, 1857. Its cannonball-shattered tower became a shrine to the tenacity of the British in India, and continued to be maintained as such even after Independence.

During the siege, every building in the complex was utilized for the hard-fought defence of the compound. The **Treasury**, on the right through the **Baillie Guard Gate**, served as an arsenal, while the sumptuous **Banqueting Hall**, immediately west, was a makeshift hospital, and the extensive single-storey **Dr Fayrer's House**, just south, housed women and children. Most of the original structures, such as **Begum Kothi**, were left standing to impede direct fire from the enemy. On the lawn outside Begum Kothi, a large cross honours the astute Sir Henry Lawrence, responsible for building its defences, who died shortly after hostilities began.

The pockmarked Residency itself holds a small **museum**. On the ground floor, the **Model Room** (daily 9am–4.30pm), the only one with its roof intact, houses a large model of the defences and of the Residency, and a small but excellent collection of images, including etchings showing wall breaches blocked up with billiard tables and a soldier blacking up in preparation for a dash across enemy lines.

Kaisarbagh

Isolated by the noise and bustle of modern Lucknow, the nineteenth-century monuments around **Kaisarbagh**, south of the Residency, stand forlorn and

The siege of the Residency of Lucknow

The mutinous sepoys who poured across the River Gomti into Lucknow on June 30, 1857 found the city rife with resentment against the recent British takeover of the kingdom of Avadh. The tiny, isolated, British garrison, under the command of Sir Henry Lawrence, took refuge in the Residency, which became the focus of a fierce struggle for survival.

Less than a thousand of the three thousand British residents and loyal Indians who crammed into the Residency survived the relentless war of attrition. So unhygienic were their living conditions that those who failed to succumb to gangrenous and tetanus-infected wounds were liable to fall victim to cholera and scurvy. While a barrage of heavy artillery was maintained by both sides, a simultaneous subterranean battle was being fought. The sepoys pinned their hopes of breaching the defences on tunnelling and laying mines, but the British were far more adept at such methods. The skills of the ex-miners of the 32nd (Cornish) Regiment enabled them to follow the sounds of enemy chipping and defuse mines, and even blow up several sepoy-controlled buildings on the peripheries of the complex.

Morale remained high among the 1400 noncombatants, who included fifty schoolboys from La Martinière, and class distinctions were upheld throughout. While the wives of European soldiers and noncommissioned officers, children and servants took refuge in the *tikhana* (cellar), the "ladies" of the Residency occupied the higher and airier chambers, until the unfortunate loss of Miss Palmer's leg on July 1 persuaded them of the gravity of their predicament. Sir Henry Lawrence was fatally wounded the next day.

The wealthier officers managed to maintain their own private hoard of supplies, living in much their usual style. Matters improved when after three months Brigadier General Sir Henry Havelock arrived with reinforcements, and the normal round of visits and invitations to supper was resumed despite the inconvenient shortage of good food and wine. Not until November 17 was the siege finally lifted by the forces of Sir Colin Campbell. When the Highlanders liberated the Residency, their offers of tea were turned down by the women; they were used to taking milk in their tea, which the soldiers could not supply.

unattended. Large chunks of the **Kaisarbagh Palace**, built in 1850 by Wajid Ali Shah and intended to be the eighth wonder of the world, have vanished, while the nearby **Chattar Manzil**, once the United Services Club, has lost most of its roof. Within the grounds of the Kaisarbagh, beside the grave of his wife **Khurshid Zadi**, is the tomb of **Saadat Ali Khan** (1798–1814). Now overgrown and often locked, it is distinguished by black-and-white marble paving, beneath which a dark narrow stairway drops down to the vault.

Kaisarbagh's **Folk Art Museum** is a large hall devoted to the contemporary arts of UP. Nearby, the former coronation hall on Lal Baradari is now the **Lalit Kala Academy** (Mon–Fri 9am–5pm; free), the gallery for the government school of art.

Hazratganj

Along the river, opposite the *Carlton Hotel*, on Rana Pratap Marg, squats the huge dome of the **Shah Najaf Imambara** (daily except Fri dawn to dusk; donations), named after the tomb of Ali in Iraq and at its best when adorned with lights during Muharram. Its musty interior holds some incredibly garish chandeliers used in processions, several *tazia*, and the silver-faced tomb of the decadent and profligate Ghazi-ud-din-Haidar (1814–27), buried with three of his queens.

The Imambara was commandeered as a sepoy stronghold in 1857, and the crucial battle that enabled the British to relieve the Residency was fought in the adjacent pleasure gardens of **Sikandrabagh** on November 16. It took one and a half hours of bombardment for the soldiers of Sir Colin Campbell to breach the defences of the two thousand sepoys; then the Sikhs and 93rd Highlanders poured through. There was no escape for the terrified sepoys, some of whom are said to have believed the bloodstained, red-faced, kilted Scots to be the ghosts of the murdered European women of Kanpur. Driven against the north wall, they were either bayoneted or shot, and the dead and dying piled shoulder-high. Tranquil once again, Sikandrabagh is now home to the National Botanical Research Institute and the beautiful **Botanical Gardens** (daily 6am–5pm; free), with their conservatories, nurseries, herb, rose and bougainvillea gardens, and manicured lawns.

Towards the east of Lucknow, an extraordinary chateau-like building has become almost a symbol of the city – **La Martinière**, remains to this day an exclusive public school in the finest colonial tradition. It was built as a country retreat by Major-General Claude Martin, a French soldier-adventurer taken prisoner by the British in Pondicherry in 1761. The enigmatic Martin later joined the East India Company, made his fortune in indigo, and served both the British and the nawabs of Avadh. The building is an outrageous but intriguing amalgam, crowned by flying walkways; Greco-Roman figures on the parapets give it a busy silhouette, gigantic heraldic lions gaze across the grounds, and a large bronze cannon graces the front. Martin himself is buried in the basement. During the siege, La Martiniere was occupied by rebels, while its boys were evacuated to the Residency. Entry to the building is by prior arrangement with the principal.

Close to the centre of Hazratganj, its grounds dotted with derelict Avadhi monuments, Lucknow's small **zoo** also serves as an amusement park with a miniature train to view the animals (Tues–Sun dawn to dusk; Rs5). Head through the large zoo gardens to reach the **State Museum** (Tues–Sun 10.30am–4.30pm; Rs100, Rs5 extra for camera), with its delicate, speckled-red-sandstone sculpture from the Mathura school of the Kushana and Gupta periods (first to sixth centuries AD). Besides sculpture from Gandhara, Mahoba,

Indian Airlines flights from Lucknow include daily flights to Varanasi, Mumbai and Calcutta via Patna, and several to Delhi. Indian Airlines have offices at *Hotel Clarks Avadh*, 8 Mahatma Gandhi Marg (☎0522/220927), and at the airport at Amausi (☎0522/436132; information ☎142). Sahara India Airlines, Sahara India Tower, 7 Kapoorthala Complex (☎0522/377675) also fly to Mumbai, Varanasi and Delhi.

By rail, the excellent all a/c Shatabdi Express #2003 goes to Delhi (Daily 3.20pm; 7hr); cheaper alternatives include the Gomti Express #2419 (daily except Tues; 5.25am, 8hr), and the slower overnight Lucknow Mail #4229 (10pm; 9hr 45min). The best choice to Agra is the Avadh Express #5063 (8.55pm; 7hr). The Kushinagar Express #1016 travels to Mumbai (daily; 12.50am; 30hr). Calcutta is served by several trains, such as the Amritsar–Howrah Mail #3006 (10.50am; 22hr 15min) and the slower Amritsar–Howrah Express #3050 (11.40am; 28hr). Trains to Varanasi include the fast evening Lucknow– Varanasi Varuna Express #4228 (6pm; 7hr), the overnight Kashi–Vishwanatha Express #4058 (11.20pm; 8hr), the Dehra Dun–Varanasi Express #4266 (8am; 8hr 30min) and the Doon Express #3010; the last two in the opposite direction head for Dehra Dun (14hr) via Haridwar. Satna, the jumping-off point for Khajuraho, is serviced by trains such as the Chitrakoot Express #5010 (5.25pm; 11hr), which stops at Chitrakut Dham in the middle of the night.

Trains such as the Vaishali #2554, Kushinagar #1015 and Sabarmati #9165 expresses travel to Gorakhpur (5hr), where you can catch a bus to the Nepal border at Sonauli – the choice of buses to Kathmandu and Pokhara is better on the Nepalese side. This may seem a convoluted way to get to Nepal, but is more comfortable than a single long gruelling direct bus. If you're content to make the 11- to 12-hour journey by road, several buses leave from Kaisarbagh and Charbagh bus stands, from where buses also go to Gorakhpur and to Faizabad. Kaisarbagh also offers Delhi buses, and an efficient night service to Nainital.

Agents for air, rail and bus tickets include Travel Corporation of India, Videocon Building, 1st Floor, Jopling Road (☎0522/207550); and the efficient, friendly UP Tours, *Hotel Gomti*, 6 Sapru Marg (☎0522/212659).

Finally, if you're heading for the UP hills, Lucknow holds offices of both GMVN, Khushnuma Complex, Old Hyderabad (☎0522/207844), and KMVN, near Kirpa Automobiles, 2 Gopal Khera House, Sarojini Naidu Marg (☎0522/239434), who organize tours of, and accommodation in, Garhwal and Kumaon respectively. For more on both, see p.368 and p.403.

Nalanda and Sravasti, it boasts a gallery of terracotta artefacts and even an Egyptian mummy. Musical instruments, paintings and costumes provide atmosphere in the Avadh Gallery, while the natural history section is a taxidermist's dream.

Eating

The rich traditional **Lucknavi cuisine** – featuring such Mughlai dishes as *shami kebabs*, *mughlai parathas*, *sheekh kebabs*, chicken musallam and *boti kebab* – is available from food stalls throughout the city, in places such as Shami Avadh Bazaar, near the K D Singh Babu Stadium, and behind the Tulsi Theatre in Hazratganj. Standard a/c restaurants are found mostly in Hazratganj, while, of course, hotel restaurants such as the expensive *Clarks Avadh* and the *Taj Mahal* serve excellent but pricey food.

Bharat Restaurant, Charbagh. Cheap open-air *dhaba* opposite the station. Good *dosas* and thalis.
Chowdray, Mahatma Gandhi Marg, Hazratganj. Excellent Lucknavi cuisine in a busy restaurant;

locals say that this is *the* place to come to for lunch. The sweet shop at the front serves delicious lemon and cardamon *rasgulla*.

Dominos Pizza, MG Road ☎0522/111123.
Pizzas from 11am to 11pm and they'll deliver to
your hotel room.
Hong Kong, Mahatma Gandhi Marg, Hazratganj.
Popular restaurant with standard Indian versions of
Chinese food.
India Coffee House, Ashok Marg. Once a hotbed
of Lucknow's political intelligentsia and nicknamed
the maternity ward for the ideas it has given birth
to. Still popular with the faithful – who complain
that these days their politicians are more likely to
haunt bars or brothels – but now dingy and a bit
run down. Serves south and north Indian snacks
and coffee that you can sit over for an afternoon.
Take a paper.
John Hing, opposite Sahu Cinema, Mahatma
Gandhi Marg, Hazratganj. One of the few reasonable Chinese restaurants in Lucknow.
Ritz Continental, Ashok Marg. An upmarket
place, popular with middle-class families. Western
food is available but the local cuisine is much better. Try the baked vegetables.

Shopping

Chikan is a long-standing Lucknavi tradition of embroidery, in which designs
are built up to form delicate floral patterns along edges on saris and on neck-
lines and collars of *kurtas*. Workshops can be found around the Chowk, the
market area of old Lucknow, and shops and showrooms in Hazratganj, Janpath
Market, Nazirabad and Aminabad. **Bhagwat Das & Sons** are reputable dealers with two shops – one at the Chowk and the other at Husseinganj
Chaurhai; **Tandon's**, 17/1 Ashok Marg, Hazratganj, is another good outlet.
The fixed prices at **Gangotri**, the UP government emporium in Hazratganj,
are more expensive than those in the markets, but the quality is assured and you
don't have to haggle.

Lucknow is also renowned for its **ittar** (or *attar*), concentrated perfume sold
in small vials – an acquired (and expensive) taste. Small balls of cotton wool are
daubed with the scent and placed neatly within the top folds of the ear; musicians believe that the aroma heightens their senses. Popular *ittar* are *ambar* from
amber, *khus* from a flowering plant and *ghulab* from rose.

Ayodhya and around

The small town of **AYODHYA**, on the south bank of the River Ghaghara,
130km east of Lucknow and 6km east of Faizabad, was catapulted to world
prominence by the destruction in 1992 of the Babri Masjid mosque by Hindu
fanatics. Few tourists venture out here (especially around the December 6
anniversary). Though the town is safe to visit nowadays, check in the press for
reports of any renewed communal tensions, and ignore the Kar Sevaks, or "volunteers", who mingle with the pilgrims and visitors pretending to be guides
while dishing out propaganda.

The embattled and heavily guarded site of the vandalized **Babri Masjid** –
what Hindus call the Ram Janmabhumi – stands just south of the shrine
known as **Janam Sthana**, the "birthplace", where Rama is said to have been
born. The contentious site is opened to the public twice a day (7–10am and
3–5pm) attracting huge crowds who throw flowers at the barbed-wire-
adorned ruins. Other sites associated with the Rama legend include
Lakshmana Ghat, a river landing near the bridge north of the town, where
Rama's brother Lakshmana is said to have committed suicide after breaking a
vow. Not far away, on the banks of a rivulet, is the prominent and much venerated temple of **Kala Rama**, while the nineteenth-century **Kanak Bhavan**

Babri Masjid and Ram Janmabhumi

Although legend tells of Ayodhya as the birthplace of Rama – an incarnation of Vishnu and hero of the epic *Ramayana* – archeologists have found no proof of the existence of the king or his capital. They have however shown that Ayodhya was inhabited in the seventh century BC, and a Jain settlement dating from the fourth century BC is among the oldest known, said to be the home of the first and fourth Jain *tirthankaras*. The Buddha is also said to have visited the town, but there is little evidence that Ayodhya had any significance prior to the Muslim invasion in the fifteenth century.

Rama has been hijacked as the champion of fundamentalist Hindus, orchestrated by political parties such as the Vishwa Hindu Parishad (VHP) and the Bharatiya Janata Party (BJP) to advance their campaign for a Hindu homeland or "Hindutva", as opposed by the secularism of the Congress Party. They focused attention on the then quiet and barely used Babri Masjid mosque, constructed by the first Moghul emperor Babar in the fifteenth century, which has coexisted for many years alongside the shrine known as Ram Janmabhumi, which was long considered to be the spot where Rama was born. This has been disputed since 1998, when Indus seals, unearthed in the town of Banawali on the River Saraswati in Haryana, identified Rama as Ramachandra, king of the Indus valley from 1753 to 1693 BC.

After two years of ugly confrontation, Babri Masjid was attacked in 1992 by thousands of Hindu fanatics, who tore it down with their bare hands. Television footage of the onslaught inspired "communalist" riots throughout India, especially in Mumbai and Gujarat, leaving hundreds dead. Repercussions were felt wherever in the world Hindus and Muslims live side-by-side, including Britain, and there were violent demonstrations in a number of Muslim countries. In 1994, the egalitarian *purohit* (priest) of Ram Janmabhumi – according to whom Hindus and Muslims had shared the premises peacefully for years until the right-wing parties manipulated the issue – was murdered by unknown persons. The issue is still causing debate and the central government of India has yet to carry out its declared intention of reconstructing the mosque alongside a Hindu shrine.

temple in the centre of the town is devoted to Rama and his wife Sita. Further south, towards the railway station 1km east of the Ram Janmabhumi, the **Hanuman Gadhi** temple ("Hanuman's Fortress"), approached by an impressive flight of stairs, is enclosed within a quadrangle protected by massive white bastion-like walls. Embossed silver doorways lead to several shrines of Rama's monkey-companion, Hanuman, and one of Sita. Shops on the street below sell religious paraphernalia, gifts and postcards, some of which, clearly aimed by the VHP to shock, are gruesome and graphic photographs of Kar Sevaks killed during police firing – in fact the police largely colluded in the destruction.

Annual festivals held in Ayodhya to celebrate the life of Rama include the **Ramnavami** in March/April, the **Parikrama** in October/November and the **Rama Virah** in November. The staff at the UP tourist bungalow can tell you the specific dates nearer the time.

Practicalities

Though Ayodhya has a small **railway station** of its own, most visitors come for the day from busy Faizabad (see below), on buses and auto-rickshaws from the station there. If you want to **stay** in Ayodhya, the tourist bungalow *Hotel Saket* (℡05278/32435; ❷–❸), next to the station, has a dorm (Rs50) and a wide range of rooms, as well as a poorly managed restaurant. Alternatively, the *Birla Dharamsala* (❶), on the main road, has very decent and cheap accommodation in its "VIP" rooms. Ayodhya is a **vegetarian** town.

Faizabad

During the reign of Shuja-ud-Daula (1756–75), as the Moghul empire disintegrated, **FAIZABAD**, 6km southwest of Ayodhya, attracted craftsmen, artists and musicians from Delhi. However, the first capital of Avadh declined in tandem with the rise of Lucknow. Among the few monuments to survive is the lofty white marble **Tomb of Bahu Begum**, widow of Shuja-ud-Daula, close to the the nawab's own mausoleum. Faizabad's cantonment area is a legacy of British rule – caught up in the rebellion of 1857, it was thankfully spared the bloodshed seen in Kanpur and Lucknow.

Cheap central **accommodation** can be found near the *chowk* in the *Hotel Abha*, Moti Bagh (☏05278/32550; ❷), the best of a handful along this quiet lane; the *Shan-e-Awadh* (☏05278/33586; ❸–❺), Civil Lines, near the bus stand, has more comfortable a/c rooms, while the adjacent *Tirupati* (☏05278/33231; ❸–❺) is newer, with a good restaurant. Faizabad is practically equidistant from Lucknow, Allahabad, Varanasi and Gorakhpur. **Buses** to all these cities take three to five hours, and there are regular trains to Lucknow and Varanasi.

Allahabad and around

The administrative and industrial city of **ALLAHABAD**, 135km west of Varanasi and 227km southeast of Lucknow, is also known as **Prayag** ("confluence"), as the point where the rivers Yamuna and Ganges meet the mythical Saraswati. Sacred to Hindus, the **Sangam** (which also means "confluence"), east of the city, is one of the great pilgrimage destinations of India. Allahabad comes alive during its *melas* (fairs); the annual **Magh Mela** (Jan/Feb), and the colossal **Maha Kumbh Mela**, held every twelve years (the next is due to take place in 2013).

The Kumbh Mela

Hindus traditionally regard river confluences as auspicious places, and none more so than the Sangam at Allahabad, where the Yamuna and the Ganges meet the River of Enlightenment, the mythical subterranean Saraswati. According to legend, Vishnu was carrying a *kumbha* (pot) of *amrita* (nectar), when a scuffle broke out between the gods, and four drops were spilled. They fell to earth at the four *tirthas* of Prayag, Haridwar, Nasik, and Ujjain. The event is commemorated every three years by the Kumbh Mela, held at each *tirtha* in turn; the Allahabad Sangam is known as Tirtharaja, the "King of *tirthas*", and its *mela*, held once every twelve years, is the greatest and holiest of all.

The Maha Kumbh Mela – the "Great" Kumbh Mela – is the largest religious fair in India, attended by an astonishing seventeen million pilgrims at the last *mela* in 2001. The vast flood plains and riverbanks adjacent to the confluence are overrun by tents, organized in almost military fashion by the government, the local authorities and the police. The *mela* is especially renowned for the presence of an extraordinary array of religious ascetics – *sadhus* and *mahants* – enticed from remote hideaways in forests, mountains and caves. Once astrologers have determined the propitious bathing time or *kumbhayog*, the first to hit the water are legions of Naga Sadhus or Naga Babas, the ferocious-looking members of the "snake sect" who cover their naked bodies with ash, and wear their hair in dreadlocks. The *sadhus*, who see themselves as guardians of the faith, approach the confluence at the appointed time with all the pomp and bravado of a charging army.

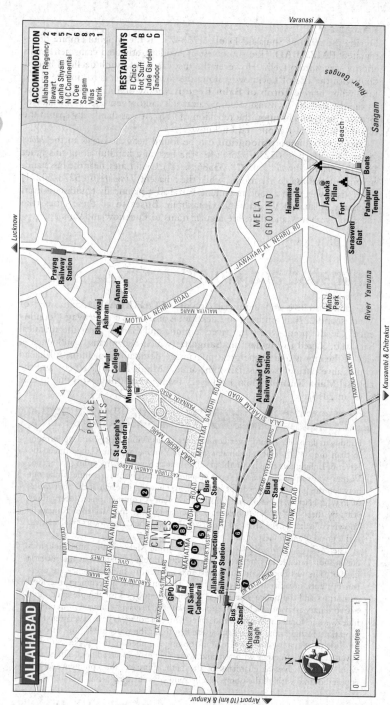

ALLAHABAD

Varanasi

River Ganges

Sangam

Beach

MELA
GROUND

Hanuman
Temple

Ashoka
Pillar

Fort

Saraswati Ghat

Patalpuri
Temple

Boats

JAWAHARLAL NEHRU RD

Prayag
Railway
Station

Anand
Bhavan

Bharadwaj
Ashram

MOTILAL NEHRU ROAD

MALVIYA MARG

Muir
College

Minto
Park

River Yamuna

Museum

PANNALAL ROAD

Allahabad City
Railway Station

YAMUNA BANK RD

LALA SITARAM ROAD

Kausambi & Chitrakut

POLICE
LINES

St Joseph's
Cathedral

KASTURBA GANDHI MARG

KAMLA NEHRU MARG

MAHATMA GANDHI ROAD

SWAMI VIVEKANAND MARG

Bus
Stand

Bus
Stand

ZERO RD

MAHARSHI DAYANAND MARG

TASHKENT MARG

CIVIL LINES

CIVIL
LINES

SARDJINI NAIDU MARG

MUIR ROAD

LAL BAHADUR SHASTRI MARG

GPO

All Saints
Cathedral

NAWAB YUSUF ROAD

SMITH RD

LEADER ROAD

DR KATJU ROAD

GRAND TRUNK ROAD

Allahabad Junction
Railway Station

Bus
Stand

Khusrau
Bagh

N

Kilometres

0   1

Lucknow

Airport (10 km) & Kanpur

① ② ③ ④ ⑤ ⑥ ⑦ ⑧
Ⓐ Ⓑ Ⓒ Ⓓ

ACCOMMODATION

Allahabad Regency	2
Ilawart	4
Kanha Shyam	5
N C Continental	7
N Cee	6
Sangam	8
Vilas	3
Yatrik	1

RESTAURANTS

El Chico	A
Hot Stuff	B
Jade Garden	C
Tandoor	D

Allahabad is a pleasant city to visit, with vast open riverside scenery and good amenities, but is without major temples or monuments. At the junction of the fertile Doab, the "two-river" valley between the Yamuna and the Ganges, it did however possess a crucial strategic significance; its massive **fort**, built by the emperor Akbar in 1583, is still used by the military. Another Moghul, Jahangir's son Khusrau, was murdered here by his brother Shah Jahan, who went on to become emperor and build the Taj Mahal.

Allahabad played a vital role in the emergence of modern India. After the Mutiny of 1857, the British moved the headquarters of their Northwestern Provinces here from Agra, and the formal transfer of power from the East India Company to the crown took place here the following year. Well-preserved relics of the British impact include **Muir College** and **All Saints' Cathedral**. The city also witnessed the first Indian National Congress in 1885, and the inauguration of Mahatma Gandhi's nonviolent movement in 1920. **Anand Bhavan**, the home of Pandit Jawaharlal Nehru, is now a shrine to the Independence movement.

The Town

As the railway line crosses the centre, it splits Allahabad in two, with the chaotic and congested **old city** or **Chowk** south of the main station, and the well-defined grid of the **Civil Lines** to the north.

One kilometre north of the station, the yellow-and-red sandstone bulk of the Gothic **All Saints' Cathedral** dominates the surrounding avenues. Designed by Sir William Emerson, architect of the Victoria Memorial in Calcutta, the cathedral retains much of its stained glass and an impressive altar of inlaid marble. Plaques provide interesting glimpses of Allahabad in the days of the Raj, while flying buttresses and snarling gargoyles on the exterior add to the effect of an English county town – though the impression is subverted by the palm trees in the garden. Sunday services continue to attract large congregations; so too do Masses at the flamboyant **St Joseph's Roman Catholic Cathedral**, a short distance northwest.

On the edge of the pleasant **Chander Shekhar Azad Park**, also in the Civil Lines, the grounds of the **Allahabad Museum** (Tues–Sun 10am–5pm, closed 2nd Sat each month; Rs100) are dotted with pieces of ancient sculpture. Inside, you'll find early terracotta artefacts, eighth-century sculptures from the Buddhist site of Kausambi, and a striking twelfth-century image from Khajuraho of Shiva and Parvati. A copious collection of modern Indian art includes work by Haldar, Sajit Khastgir and Rathin Mitra, as well as Jamini Roy, who was inspired by folk art. European paintings concentrate on spiritual themes, with bright, naive canvases by the Russian artist Nicholas Roerich, and pieces by the Tibetologist Lama Angarika Govinda. A natural history section features stuffed animals and birds, and photographs and documents cover the Independence struggle.

North of the museum rise the nineteenth-century sandstone buildings of **Allahabad University**, and the Gothic **Muir College**, built in 1870. A 61m-high tower accompanies domes clad with blue and white glazed tiles (some of which are missing), and a quadrangle with tall and elegant arches. Just beyond the college, in beautiful grounds roughly 1km northeast of the museum, is **Anand Bhavan** (Tues–Sun 9.30am–5pm; Rs5 allows entry to the first floor). This ornate Victorian building, with Indo-Saracenic effects finished in grey and white trim, and crowned by a *chhatri*, was the boyhood home of the first prime minister of an independent India, Jawaharlal **Nehru**. It is now maintained as a museum, allowing queues of visitors to peer through plate glass into the opulent interior and see how well the first family lived. More diverting than Nehru's spoons and trousers is the stuffy English court document recording his trial for making salt. Nehru was the father of one assassinated prime minister, Indira Gandhi, who was born here, and the grandfather of another, Rajiv Gandhi; Mahatma Gandhi (no relation of the family) stayed here when he visited the city. Also within the grounds, as at the Nehru Memorial Museum in Delhi (see p.121), is a **planetarium**, which puts on four shows per day (Rs10; 1hr long, all in Hindi with a 30min lecture prior to the show).

Not far from Anand Bhavan, down a small road next to a children's park, the **Bharadwaj Ashram** is not an ashram as such but a collection of small temples. None is particularly old, but the ashram is named after the philosopher, scientist and ascetic Bharadwaj, said in the *Ramayana* to have had his hermitage here, and to have been visited by Rama. Legend relates that the ashram once had ten thousand students. Unusually, women are numbered among its *purohits* (priests), and act as caretakers.

A short way south of the main railway station, a lofty gateway leads to the attractive walled gardens of **Khusrau Bagh**, where the remains of Jahangir's tragic son Khusrau rest in a simple sandstone mausoleum, completed in 1622. Khusrau made an unsuccessful bid for power that ended in death at the hands of his brother Shah Jahan, and is buried far from the centre of Moghul power. His mother's two-storeyed mausoleum is a short way west, beyond a tomb reputed to be that of his sister. Once Jahangir's pleasure garden, today much of Khusrau Bagh has been made into an orchard, famous for its guavas, and a rose nursery, but parts are unkempt and overgrown.

The river frontage

Most of Allahabad's river frontage is along the Yamuna, to the south, where women perform *arati* or evening worship at **Saraswati Ghat** by floating *diya*, small oil-filled lamps, downstream. Immediately to the west, in **Minto Park**, a memorial marks the exact spot where the British Raj came into being, when India was taken away from the East India Company in 1858 and placed under the auspices of the Crown.

East of Saraswati Ghat, close to the Sangam, loom the huge battlements of Akbar's **Fort** – best appreciated from boats on the river. Much of the fort remains in military occupation, and public access is restricted to the leafy corner around the **Patalpuri temple**, approached through one of the three massive gates that puncture the fort's defences. The catacombs occupied by the temple have been converted into a sort of religious supermarket; its religious figures and deities are reminiscent of an extended Punch and Judy show. A sapling is said to be descended from the infamous **Akshaya Vata** or "Undying Tree", visited by the Chinese pilgrim Xuan Zhang in the seventh century, from which desperate pilgrims threw themselves to their deaths in order to gain instant *moksha* (salvation). According to some reports the tree itself is bricked away beyond public access. Much of the superstructure of the fort is neglected; the **Zenana** with its columned hall does survive, but can only be viewed with prior permission. At the main gates to the fort stands a poorly restored polished stone **Ashoka Pillar**, inscribed with the emperor's edicts and dated to 242 BC.

Where the eastern battlements of the fort meet the river, a muddy *ghat* is busy with boatmen jostling for custom from the steady stream of pilgrims heading to the Sangam. Inland along the base of the fort, with the vast flood plain of the Sangam to the right, a road leads past rows of stalls catering to pilgrims to the brightly painted **Hanuman temple**. Unusually the large sunken image of

The Sangam

Around 7km from the centre of the Civil Lines, overlooked by the eastern ramparts of the fort, wide flood plains and muddy banks protrude towards the sacred Sangam. At the point at which the brown Ganges meets the greenish Yamuna, *pandas* (priests) perch on small platforms to perform puja and assist the devout in their ritual ablutions in the shallow waters. Beaches and *ghats* are littered with the shorn hair of pilgrims who come to offer *pind* for their deceased parents, and women sit around selling cone-shaped pyramids of bright red and orange *tilak* powder.

Boats to the Sangam, used by pilgrims and tourists alike, can be rented at the *ghat* immediately east of the fort, for the recommended government rate of Rs12 per head. However, most pilgrims pay around Rs36 and you can be charged as much as Rs150. Official prices for a whole boat are between Rs100 and Rs120 but can soar to more than Rs250 during peak seasons. On the way to the Sangam, high-pressure aquatic salesmen loom up on the placid waters selling offerings such as coconuts for pilgrims to discard at the confluence. Once abandoned, the offerings are fished up and sold on to other pilgrims.

the monkey god inside the temple is reclining rather than standing erect; the story goes that during the annual floods the waters rise to touch his feet before once again receding.

Practicalities

Allahabad has four **railway stations** (including Prayag, City and Daraganj), but major trains on the broad-gauge Delhi–Kanpur–Calcutta line arrive at the main **Allahabad Junction**. Most of the city's hotels are nearby; be sure to use the exit appropriate to the area where you plan to stay.

Leader Road bus stand, used by buses from western destinations such as Agra, Lucknow, Kanpur, Kausambi and Delhi, is just outside the station's south gates on the city side, while the smaller **Zero Road** bus stand, serving Mahoba and Satna and Chitrakut to the south – the railheads for Khajuraho – is 1km southeast. Buses from all over and especially points east, including Varanasi, arrive at the **MG Marg** bus stand, next to the *Tourist Bungalow*, about 1km east of the Civil Lines, the area that corresponds to the residential quarter of the Raj military town. There are no **flights** currently operating in and out of Bamrauli Airport, 18km west on the road to Kanpur.

Taxis are widely available around the station, but cycle and auto-rickshaws are the most common modes of transport; a trip to the Sangam from the Civil Lines crossing costs around Rs25 (hang on to your vehicle for the return journey). **Car rental** through general travel agencies such as Kant Travel (℡0532/605699) and Krishna Travel (℡0532/602832), both at 936 Daraganj, costs in the region of Rs500 per day plus mileage. Other reputable travel agents are Varuna Travels, Maya Bazaar, MG Marg (℡0532/624323).

The **tourist information office**, at the *Hotel Ilawart*, 35 MG Marg, Civil Lines (Mon–Sat 10am–5pm; ℡0532/601873), is very helpful and in particular can provide useful information during the *melas*. Allahabad's **post office** (known as the GPO or HPO), is at Sarojini Naidu Marg, near All Saints' Cathedral in the Civil Lines.

Accommodation

Allahabad has **hotels** to suit most budgets and temperaments, with cheaper options generally in the old Chowk area to the south, and the mid-range and more expensive ones in the Civil Lines.

Allahabad Regency, 16 Tashkent Marg, Civil Lines ☎0532/601519. Comfortable, colonial bungalow place with a decent garden restaurant, plus a sauna, Jacuzzi, swimming pool and well-kitted gym. ⑥–⑦

Ilawart, 35 MG Marg, Civil Lines ☎0532/601440. Run by UP tourism. The comfortable, cylindrical new block, built around a central well, overlooks the bus stand; choose your room carefully to avoid round-the-clock noise. The older block, now showing its age, is less noisy. Friendly restaurant has slow and haphazard service, but the food is good when it arrives. The hotel bar is popular with locals. ③–⑤

Kanha Shyam, Civil Lines ☎0532/420281. New starred hotel with luxury rooms and every facility, including a swimming pool and rooftop bar overlooking all of Allahabad. The restaurant is the place for a splurge with very different variations on the usual multi-cuisine theme. ⑧–⑨

N C Continental, Dr Katju Road ☎0532/652058. Good, clean accommodation south of the railway lines and very handy for the station. A bit more spacious than the *N Cee*. ②–⑤

N Cee, Leader Road ☎0532/401166. Sister to *N C Continental*, south of the railway line in the busy bazaar area. The rooms are small, but it's a pleasant and friendly place. ②–③

Sangam, Johnstonganj Crossing ☎0532/402667. Basic budget accommodation in the old city. ①–②

Vilas, 22C Sardar Patel Marg, Civil Lines ☎0532/622878. Moderately priced and central, but otherwise quite ordinary with a new restaurant. Telephones in the bathroom allow you to call room service while using the toilet. ④–⑤

Yatrik, 33 Sardar Patel Marg, Civil Lines ☎0532/601713. Never mind the ugly name, or that of its restaurant – "The Bhoj" – this is the best of the upmarket places, with fewer facilities but more character than its rival the Kanha. Popular, well run and with a beautiful garden graced with elegant palms. Sometimes booked out by tour groups. ⑦–⑧

Eating

Most of the better **cafés** and **restaurants** are in the Civil Lines area, within walking distance from each other close to the main crossing. In the early evening, the snack stalls along MG Marg entice the populace with their individual and often legendary specialities.

El Chico, MG Marg, Civil Lines. One of the city's best, a smart place with good Indian, Chinese and Western cuisine. Tasty fried chicken.

Hot Stuff, 15 Elgin Rd, Civil Lines. Popular hang-out for Allahabad's young and trendy, with burgers, shakes, Chinese food and ice creams.

Jade Garden, MG Marg, Civil Lines. Small thatched garden restaurant, strong on Chinese food.

Tandoor, MG Marg. Tucked into a shopping precinct opposite *El Chico*. Comfortable and upmarket, it preserves a reputation as one of the best places in the city for Indian food.

Around Allahabad

Just 63km south of Allahabad, on the banks of the Yamuna, are the extensive ruins of **Kausambi**, a major Buddhist centre where the Buddha himself came to preach. The city flourished between the eighth century BC and the sixth century AD; archeological evidence suggests even earlier habitation. According to legend, it was founded by descendants of the Pandavas, after floods destroyed their city of Hastinapur. Mud ramparts, originally faced with brick, tower over the fields, running along an irregular 6km perimeter, and sections remain of a defensive moat. Within the complex, excavations have revealed a paved road, brick houses, wells, tanks and drains, a monastery with cloisters and a large stupa, and the remains of a palace in the southeast corner. The only standing feature is a damaged sandstone column ascribed to **Ashoka** – a second column, moved by the Moghuls, now graces the gates of the fort at Allahabad.

If you have your own vehicle or hire a taxi, Kausambi is a straightforward day-trip from Allahabad. Otherwise, there is a direct bus every day from Leader Road bus station (Rs25). The Buddhist pilgrimage circuit is developing rapidly, so it's worth consulting local tourist authorities for a package they may have tailored.

Allahabad also makes a good base from which to venture into the remoter parts of **Bundelkhand** to the south. The pilgrimage town of **Chitrakut** (see p.339) is 132km south, and easily accessible by both train and bus; the hilltop fort of **Kalinjar** (see p.338) is 150km away.

Southern UP: Bundelkhand

BUNDELKHAND – the area defined by the craggy Vindhya Mountains, which stretch across southern UP – was carved by the ninth-century Chandella Rajputs into a mighty kingdom that included **Khajuraho** in Madhya Pradesh (see p.468). Today, it abounds in relics of the past – the colossal astrologically aligned fortress at **Kalinjar** that was the Chandella capital of Mahoba, the Vaishnavite pilgrimage centre of **Chitrakut**, and the fortified town of **Jhansi**, scene of epic nineteenth-century resistance to the British. However, the sheer harshness of the terrain, and the all but unbearable heat in the summer, make this the most difficult, if intriguing, region of the state to explore.

In fact, the labyrinthine hills and valleys along the border with Madhya Pradesh are also the most difficult region to govern, and even today are home to infamous bands of outlaw **dacoits**. Many of these brigands have become folk-heroes among local villagers, who shelter them from the almost equally brutal police force. The most celebrated in recent years was **Phoolan Devi**, the "Bandit Queen", who was kidnapped by a dacoit gang, became the leader's lover, and took over from him after he was killed. She eventually surrendered to the police, was released in 1994, and is now an MP. The past couple of years has seen the rise of a fledgling and uncertain movement for a semi-autonomous region of Bundelkhand, separate from both UP and Madhya Pradesh.

Jhansi

Unless you harbour a passion for seventeenth-century forts, you'll find the rail- and road-junction town of **JHANSI**, located in an anomalous promontory of UP that thrusts south into Madhya Pradesh, unremittingly dull. Most visitors only stop long enough to catch a connecting bus to **Khajuraho**, 175km further southeast in Madhya Pradesh.

Until 1742, Jhansi was a sleepy satellite village of the Bundela capital at nearby **Orchha**, 18km southeast. When the local raja died without a male heir in 1853, the British enacted the controversial Principle of Lapse to wrest control of the town from his widow. Four years later, resentment at this colonial opportunism bubbled over into a full-blown **rebellion**, sparked off by the Mutiny at Kanpur (see p.316). Once the uprising had been put down by the British, they handed Jhansi over to Maharaja Scindia in 1861, in exchange for Gwalior, only to reclaim it 25 years later.

The Town

In common with many former British cities, Jhansi is divided into two distinct areas: the wide tree-lined avenues, leafy gardens and bungalows of the **Cantonment** and **Civil Lines** to the west, and the clutter of brick and concrete cubes, narrow lanes, minarets and *shikharas* of the **old town** to the east.

Dominating it all from a bare brown craggy hill, **Jhansi fort** (daily dawn to dusk; Rs0.25; Fri free) is the obvious place to head if you've time to kill – but be careful of the vicious monkeys. Built in 1613 by one of the Orchha rajas, Bir Singh Joo Deo, it's worth visiting primarily for the **views** from the lofty ramparts – down to the densely packed old town on one side, and out across a dusty *maidan* and the Cantonment to the other. The legendary **Rani of Jhansi** was supposed to have leapt over the west wall on horseback when she escaped from the British – if so, she must have had a very athletic horse. Inside the fort are a couple of unremarkable temples, plus an old cistern and the ruins of a palace.

The new **state archeological museum** (Tues–Sun 10.30am–4.30pm) stands to the left of the road as you head back into town, with an unremarkable collection of Hindu **sculpture** saved from the area's ruined medieval temples.

Once the palace of the Rani of Jhansi, the **Rani Lakshmi Mahal** (Tues–Sun 10am–5pm) is a small stately home in "Bundela style" (lots of ornate balconies and domed roofs), two minutes' walk from the roundabout directly below the fort. This was the scene of a brutal massacre in 1858, when British troops bayoneted all its occupants. These days, the building is a memorial museum-cum-archeological warehouse, with unlabelled fragments of antique stone sculpture littered around its attractive interior courtyard.

The grounds of a pleasant seminary in the Cantonment area hold one of the most important Catholic pilgrimage sites in India, **St Jude's Shrine**. A bone belonging to Jude the Apostle, the patron saint of hopeless causes, is said to be buried in the foundations of the sombre grey and white cathedral. On his feast day, October 28, thousands come to plead their own special causes.

The Rani of Jhansi

Rani Lakshmi Bhai, better known as the Rani, or Queen, of Jhansi, was one of the great nationalist heroines of pre-Independence India. Born the daughter of a Benares brahmin, she was married off to Raja Gangadhar of Jhansi, but never bore him children – a fact exploited by the British to force her and her adopted baby son into retirement in 1853. The rani retaliated in 1857, the year of the Mutiny, by leading her personal bodyguard of five hundred Afghan-Pathan warriors to seize Jhansi fort. The British dispatched troops to see off the insurgents, but took seventeen days to blow a breach in the walls of the citadel. Three days of fierce hand-to-hand fighting ensued, in which five thousand soldiers were killed. With her son strapped tightly to her back, the Rani somehow managed to slip through the British net and rejoin the main rebel army at Gwalior, where she rode to her death, "dressed as a man . . . using her sword with both hands and holding the reins of her horse in her mouth". Statues of Rani Jhansi in this heroic pose stand all over northern India. For many in the Independence movement, she was India's Joan of Arc; a martyr whose example set in motion the struggle that eventually removed the subcontinent's colonial rulers.

Practicalities

Trains on both of the Central Railway branches that converge on Jhansi pull in at the station on the west side of town, near the Civil Lines area. Both of the two state **tourist information** kiosks on platform one are useless but MP Tourism's (℡0517/442622) does give out leaflets on the most up-to-date methods of transport on to Khajuraho. In town, the **Regional Tourist Office**, *Hotel Veerangana* (℡0517/442402), provides literature and information on Bundelkhand and the route to Khajuraho (Mon–Sat 10am–5pm, closed every 2nd Sat).

Jhansi is the most convenient main railway station for Khajuraho, Orchha and Deogarh. From the railway station, the express **deluxe bus** (daily 11am; 7–8hr) and **local buses** (3 daily starting at 5.30am), leave for **Khajuraho**. One local bus for Khajuraho departs from the Kanpur Road bus stand (daily 11.15am). This is also the place to pick up buses for Datia, Deogarh and Gwalior; **tempos** for **Orchha** (faster than local buses, at 45min, and more frequent) wait alongside. **Car rental** is available through the larger hotels, as well as Baghel Travels, Nehru Market (℡0517/441255) and Ruby Travels, near Elite Crossing (℡0517/441136).

If you need to **change money**, the State Bank of India (Mon–Fri 10am–2pm, Sat 10am–noon; ℡0517/440534), stands on Jhokan Bagh Road beside the busy intersection in the centre of town, exactly halfway between the railway station and the bus stand.

Accommodation

With Orchha just down the road, it's hard to see why you might stay in Jhansi unless you arrive too late to move on. Most of its **hotels** are too far from the railway and bus stations to be easily reached on foot. The cheaper ones operate 24-hour check-out, as opposed to noon in the mid-price and more expensive hotels.

Jhansi, Shastri Marg ℡0517/470360. Former haunt of British *burra-sahibs*. Comfortable rooms, some a/c, plus satellite TV, verandas, and a big garden. There is a well-stocked and atmospheric colonial bar and restaurant. ❺

Prakash, Station Road, Civil Lines ℡0517/448822. Pleasant if basic bungalow accommodation including some a/c rooms, set around a small garden and very handy for the station. ❷–❹

Raj Palace, near GPO, Shastri Marg ℡0517/470554. Clean, comfortable and handy for the bus stand. Rooms have attached bathrooms and hot water. Some a/c. 24hr check-out. ❸–❹

Sita, Shivpuri Road ℡0517/442956. Comfortable international-style hotel close to the station, with well-appointed rooms and a good restaurant. Credit cards accepted. Some a/c. ❺–❻

UPTDC Veeranganga, near Exhibition Ground, Shivpuri Road ℡0517/442402. Shabby and unfriendly government-run hotel, five minutes by scooter from the station. Plain rooms, some a/c, plus dorms, a restaurant and a bar serving ice-cold beer. ❶–❺

Eating

With the exception of the cheaper lodges, nearly all of Jhansi's hotels have their own **restaurants**. For a cheap alternative, try the *Railway Refreshment Rooms* in the station, which serve freshly cooked ten-rupee thalis and budget breakfasts.

Holiday, Shastri Marg. Posh but not all that expensive a/c restaurant, east of the *Jhansi Hotel*. Low light, tablecloths, attentive service and classy Indian and Western food.

Nav Bharat, Shastri Marg. Western-style fast food and Indian snacks, behind the post office, and a proper restaurant greatly patronized by locals just down the road. Both closed on Tuesday.

Sharma Sweets, Shastri Marg. Hygienic sweet shop selling delicious take-out *rasgulla, gulabja-*

mun, jalebi and *barfi*.

Sita, Shivpuri Road. Spotlessly clean, upmarket hotel restaurant with a wide selection of Indian (and some Continental) dishes. The place for a splurge.

Kalinjar

Deep in the heart of Bundelkhand, in a remote region 150km west of Allahabad and 53km south of Banda, the abandoned star-shaped fortress of **KALINJAR** looks down on the Gangetic valley from the final escarpments of the craggy Vindhya hills. Little remains of its huge fortifications, save sections of battlements around the rim of the high forested plateau. Overlooking the dusty town of the same name, much of the fort has been reclaimed by dry shrubby forest, populated by monkeys. Once-grand avenues are now rocky footpaths that wind through the few remaining crumbling yet ornately carved buildings. Kalinjar has no tourist facilities to speak of – most of those who do come are either on day-trips from Chitrakut or Allahabad, or stay in Banda, which is on major train and bus routes and is connected to Kalinjar by local buses.

Possibly one of the oldest forts in India, referred to by Ptolemy as Kanagora, Kalinjar may have started life as a hill shrine before it was converted into a fortress; now devoid of military significance, it is once again becoming a place of worship. Kalinjar is known to have been a stronghold of the Chandellas (ninth to twelfth centuries AD), the creators of Khajuraho, who left their mark in stone sculptures around the temple of Nilkantha, below the western battlements. This strategic location attracted repeated Muslim onslaughts; Mahmud of Ghazni laid unsuccessful siege in 1023, Qutb-ud-din-Aibak destroyed several temples in his conquest of 1202, and Humayun spent fifteen years trying to capture the fort. After Sher Shah Suri, who temporarily wrested power from the Moghuls, died when an exploding shell ignited gunpowder as he attacked Kalinjar in 1545, his son went on to take the fortress. Even the British occupied it for a while, before its strategic importance was finally exhausted, and it was left to decay.

The fortress

Each of the seven gates, sheltered by barbicans, that pierces the walls of Kalinjar symbolizes one of the seven planets. Steep steps lead straight up for 3km from Kalinjar village, in the valley at the northern base of the fort, to the main gate, known as the **Alam Darwaza**. To the southeast, an unkempt boulder-strewn road gradually climbs across the hillside to approach the southernmost **Panna Gate**, where rock carvings depict seven deer. Beyond Lal Darwaza to the east, the **Bara Darwaza** or "Large Gate" is flanked by two iron cannons. Beneath it, in the artificial cave of **Sita Sej**, a stone couch dating from the fourth century holds some of Kalinjar's earliest inscriptions.

Colossal rambling battlements provide sweeping views of the Gangetic plain to the north and the Vindhya hills to the south, hiding the crumbling remains of a fortress that is almost 1.5km long. Tracing the faint marks of the old avenues, you arrive at its heart, littered with roofless and devastated buildings. **Kot Tirth**, a ceremonial tank with stone steps, is the largest of several bodies of water on the plateau, and still in frequent use by villagers and pilgrims. Above it, beyond a small and very beautiful Hanuman shrine, stands the well-preserved, palace-like **Raja Mansingh Mahal**. Further west, beside the bougainvillea-fringed road that passes the PWD bungalow (❸), which also has dorm accommodation (Rs50). The small British graveyard holds a monument to Andrew Wauchope, the first commissioner of Bundelkhand. Paths through desultory woodland head to a gate overlooking the western flank, where steep steps flanked by rock carvings wind down from the massive stone battlements to the temple of **Nilkantha** – the "Blue Throated One", an epithet of Shiva. To the left of the main shrine, within the temple compound, a five-metre-high low-relief rock carving, of primeval intensity, portrays Bhairava, the wrathful emanation of Shiva as Destroyer, sporting four arms and brandishing weapons. A gap in the retaining wall provides access to the steps back down to the village.

Chitrakut

The large sprawling town of **CHITRAKUT** stands on the banks of the Mandakini, 128km southwest of Allahabad and 116km east of Mahoba. Together with its twin town of **Karbi**, 8km east, Chitrakut, known also as Sitapur or Chitrakut Dham, is a major Vaishnavite pilgrimage centre. In the *Ramayana*, Rama, his wife Sita, and his brother Lakshmana, sought refuge in a forest that covered this entire area, after being banished from Ayodhya.

Most of Chitrakut's religious and leisure activity revolves around the small, charming, and very central **Ramghat**, where boats with electric-blue mattresses and pillows create a pretty picture against a backdrop of ashrams and *ghats* to either side of the narrow, slow-moving river. Half-hour boat trips cost around Rs2 per person or Rs12 per boat.

Practicalities

For the few tourists in this region, Chitrakut serves as a centre for catching connecting **buses** and **trains** between Allahabad, Kalingar and Khajuraho. Long-distance transport connections are best made via **Karbi**. From the main Karbi Bus Stand numerous daily buses run to Allahabad (3–4hr), passing through Serai Akil, 15km from the Buddhist ruins of Kausambi, and also to historic Mahoba, a possible stopoff en route to Khajuraho. The **railway station** at Karbi has services to Allahabad and Mahoba, as well as Varanasi, 374km northeast (9hr). From the **Satna Bus Stand** in Chitrakut, buses head south into Madhya Pradesh; connecting buses from Satna itself can also carry you to Khajuraho.

Unless you read Hindi, you may not find the information provided by the **UP Tourist Office**, at Karbi Road, Sitapur (Mon–Sat 10am–5pm, closed every 2nd Sat; ☎05197/652219), all that helpful. UPTDC's drab and poorly maintained *Tourist Bungalow* alongside (☎05197/682219; ❷–❺), has some a/c rooms, and provides food in its restaurant if you order several hours in advance. MP Tourism's old-fashioned *Tourist Bungalow*, at Satna bus stand in Chitrakut (☎05197/685326; ❸–❹) is more welcoming, and serves basic Indian food. Other accommodation can be found in the railway **retiring rooms** (❶) at the station.

Eastern UP

Flowing beyond Allahabad across the plains of **EASTERN UP**, the Ganges turns sharply north at **Chunar** and traces a great arc through ancient **Varanasi**. Even before the Hindus declared this to be the most sacred spot on earth, it stood at the centre of the Buddhist universe, linked by trading routes from Rajgir in Bihar to Mathura near Delhi. It was on the outskirts of Varanasi, at the deer park at **Sarnath**, that the Buddha delivered his first sermon. North of Varanasi, the much-travelled road to **Nepal** passes through the large administrative town of **Gorakhpur**, not far from **Kushinagar**, where the Buddha achieved final enlightenment.

Varanasi

Older than history, older than tradition, older even than legend, and looks twice as old as all of them put together. Mark Twain

The great Hindu city of **VARANASI**, also known as **Banaras** or **Benares**, stretches along the crescent of the River Ganges, its waterfront dominated by long flights of stone steps known as *ghats*, literally "landings", where thousands of pilgrims and residents come for their daily ritual ablutions. Known to the devout as **Kashi**, the Luminous – the City of Light, founded by Shiva – Varanasi is one of the oldest living cities in the world. It has maintained its religious life since the sixth century BC in one continuous tradition, in part by remaining outside the mainstream of political activity and historical development of the subcontinent, and stands at the centre of the Hindu universe, the focus of a religious geography that reaches from the Himalayan cave of Amarnath in Kashmir, to Kanyakumari, the southern tip of India, Puri to the east, and Dwarka to the west. Located next to a ford on an ancient trade route, Varanasi is among the holiest of all *tirthas* – "crossing places", that allow the devotee access to the divine and enable gods and goddesses to come down to earth. It has attracted pilgrims, seekers, *sanyasins*, and students of the *Vedas* throughout its history, including sages such as the Buddha, Mahavira, the founder of the Jain faith, and the great Hindu reformer Shankara.

Anyone who dies in Varanasi attains instant *moksha* or enlightenment. Widows and the elderly come here to seek refuge or to live out their final days, finding shelter in the temples and assisted by alms given by the faithful. Western visitors since the Middle Ages have marvelled at the strangeness of this most alien of Indian cities – at the tight mesh of alleys, the accoutrements of religion, the host of deities, and at the proximity of death.

Arrival, information and city transport

An airport bus (Rs25) connects with flights landing at **Babatpur Airport**, 22km northwest of the city, and goes to the Indian Airlines office, via the Government of India Tourist Office, both in the Cantonment area. Taxis charge around Rs200–250 for the same journey.

Tout dodging

Like Agra and Delhi, Varanasi is rife with touts, and you will have to be careful of scams, especially on arrival. Most hotels pay a commission of up to eighty percent of the room rate (for every day you stay) to whoever takes you to the door – a cost that is passed on to you.

All English-speaking rickshaw drivers are part of this racket, and avoiding it takes persistence. At the railway station, first visit the very helpful tourist office (see below) and telephone your hotel of choice. They'll send someone to pick you up. If you want to make your own way to the hotels of the old town, walk away from the bus or railway station to the main road, find a non-English-speaking rickshaw driver, and ask to be taken to Godaulia, 3km southeast – a Rs10–15 cycle rickshaw ride. Rickshaws are unable to penetrate the maze of lanes around Vishwanatha Temple and are banned from the central part of Godaulia. Again, you should telephone a hotel from here and they'll come and find you – if you attempt to get to a hotel yourself, someone will attach himself and claim a commission on arrival. The only hotels in the old town that don't pay commission to touts are the *Vishnu*, *Shanti* and *Yogi Lodge* (see box, opposite), so it's common to hear that these places have "burned down" or "flooded".

Varanasi lies on the main east–west axis between Delhi and Calcutta, and is actually served by two stations: **Varanasi Cantonment** in the town itself, and **Mughal Sarai**, 17km out of town. Varanasi Cantonment is the most conveniently located, but depending on where you are travelling from, you may find yourself using the Mughal Sarai line. There are retiring rooms at Mughal Sarai and local buses and taxis regularly make the 17km-trip to Varanasi. Most **buses** terminate a couple of hundred metres east of the railway station along the main (Grand Trunk) road and in the **Cantonment bus station** where the chaos, confusion and noise is much the same as on the Grand Trunk Road but enclosed. Buses from Nepal are met by the rickshaw mafia – see below.

Information

The main **UPTDC tourist office** is at their *Tourist Bungalow* on Parade Kothi (℡0542/343413) though their **tourist information counter** (℡0542/346370) inside the railway station is far more efficient and on the ball – the boss, Uma Shankar, seems to regard the protection of tourists as a personal crusade. Both book accommodation and provide free maps. The shabby **Bihar Government Tourist Office** at Englishia Market, Sher Shah Suri Marg, Cantonment (℡0542/343821), is useful if you're heading east towards the Buddhist centres.

The **Government of India Tourist Office** languishes in the leafy suburbs of the Cantonment, a long way from the main attractions of the old city and the *ghats*, at 15B the Mall (Mon–Sat 9.30am–5pm; ℡0542/343744). Its primary function is to dish out information on the whole of India, but the staff can assist with booking accommodation. They also maintain a booth at the airport during flight times.

To experience the *ghats* at sunrise, or the peace of Sarnath, you're best off eschewing guided tours and making your own arrangements. If your time is very limited, official tour **guides** can be organized through the Government of India tourist office.

City transport

Cycle rickshaws are the easiest way to get around Varanasi, and often defy death and traffic jams by cycling up the wrong side of the road; a ride from

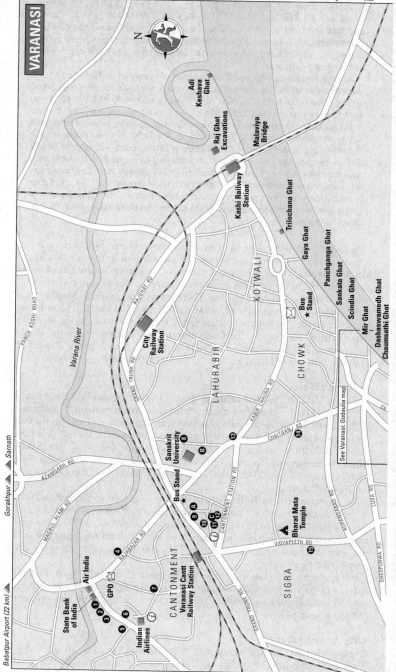

VARANASI

Mughal Sarai

Babatpur Airport (22 km) Gorakhpur Sarnath

Adi Keshava Ghat

Raj Ghat Excavations

Malaviya Bridge

Kashi Railway Station

Trilochana Ghat

Gaya Ghat

Panchganga Ghat

Sankata Ghat

Scindia Ghat

Mir Ghat

Dashaswamedh Ghat

Chaumsathi Ghat

KOTWALI

Bus Stand

CHOWK

See Varanasi: Godaulia map

PANCH KOSHI ROAD

Varana River

RAJGHAT RD

City Railway Station

LAHURABIR

GRAND TRUNK RD

KABIR CHAURA RD

CHAITGANJ RD

AZAMGARH RD

MASBUL ALAM RD

Sanskrit University

CANTONMENT STATION RD

Bharat Mata Temple

AURANGABAD RD

LUXA RD

Bus Stand

SIGRA

VIDYAPEETH RD

SHEOPURWA RD

GRAND TRUNK RD

State Bank of India

Air India

GPO

RAJABAZAR RD

Indian Airlines

CANTONMENT

Varanasi Cantt Railway Station

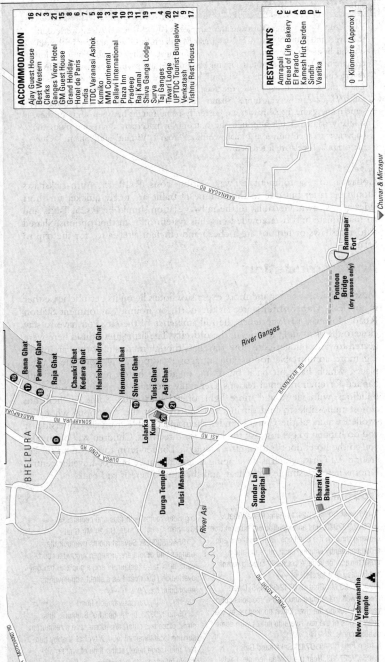

ACCOMMODATION

Ajay Guest House	16
Best Western	2
Clarks	3
Ganges View Hotel	21
GM Guest House	15
Grand Holiday	8
Hotel de Paris	6
India	7
ITDC Varanasi Ashok	5
Kumiko	18
MM Continental	3
Pallavi International	14
Plaza Inn	10
Pradeep	13
Raj Kamal	11
Shiva Ganga Lodge	19
Surya	1
Taj Ganges	4
Tiwari Lodge	20
UPTDC Tourist Bungalow	12
Venkatesh	9
Vishnu Rest House	17

RESTAURANTS

Amrapali	C
Bread of Life Bakery	E
El Parador	A
Kamesh Hut Garden	B
Sindhi	D
Vaatika	F

0 Kilometre (Approx) 1

► Chunar & Mirzapur

Ramnagar Fort

Pontoon Bridge
(dry season only)

River Ganges

RAMNAGAR RD

Rana Ghat
Pandey Ghat
Raja Ghat
Chauki Ghat
Kedara Ghat
Harishchandra Ghat
Hanuman Ghat
Shivala Ghat
Tulsi Ghat
Asi Ghat

MADANPURA
SONARPURA RD
BHELPURA
DURGA KUND RD
ASI RD

Lolarka Kund

Durga Temple
Tulsi Manas

River Asi

Sundar Lal Hospital

Bharat Kala Bhavan

New Vishwanatha Temple

PANCH KOSHI RD

RAJA MOTICHAND RD

► Allahabad

What's in a name?

The **Yogi Lodge** (near Vishwanatha temple), **Vishnu Rest House** (overlooking the river) and **Shanti Guest House** (near Manikarnika Ghat) are three of the oldest and best-run places in the old city. Unfortunately they are all facing dubious competition from other hotels copying their names and paying rickshaw-wallahs to divert customers. Four other "Vishnu" lodges have sprung up – the *Old Vishnu Lodge*, the *Vishnu Guest House*, the *Real Vishnu Guest House* and the *New Vishnu Guest House*. And several more "Shanti" lodges and "Yogi" lodges are playing the same name game. Legal battles are currently being fought between some of these similarly named hotels although the outcome is uncertain as no one owns the copyright to such universal Indian words as "Yogi", "Vishnu" and "Shanti". Only the original hotels are listed below.

Godaulia to Cantonment railway station costs Rs10–15. Auto-rickshaws should be faster but due to the volume of traffic are rarely quicker for short rides across town. Godaulia to the railway station should be Rs25. **Taxis** and an inadequate and overcrowded city bus system offer further options. Shared auto-rickshaws or tempos are a cheap and efficient alternative for the trip to Sarnath.

Accommodation

Most of Varanasi's better and more expensive hotels lie on its peripheries, either in the leafy **Cantonment** area in the north or around Cantonment Station Road. However, to experience the full ambience of the city, you have to stay close to the *ghats* and the lanes of the **old city**. The little guesthouses here were geared towards budget-conscious travellers though increasingly they are offering more comfortable rooms and attracting custom away from the classier places, which have hit back by trying to get all hotels near the riverbank banned for environmental reasons. Generally speaking, the top floors of these buildings, with views and more light, offer better value. Some of them are almost impossible to find during and shortly after the monsoons when the swollen waters of the Ganges render them inaccessible from the waterside. If you do happen to get lost, ask the locals for directions. Children will often take you to the hotel door – for a little *baksheesh*. Longer-term tourists tend to stay around Asi Ghat, which is developing as an alternative budget-traveller centre. Rooms here are simple and cheap and the atmosphere is laid back.

Godaulia

Ajay Guest House, D21/11 Rana Mahal Ghat ☏ 0542/327970. Has an extraordinary banyan tree growing through the buildings, with monkeys and a dog constantly winding each other up and a great terrace for yoga. A couple of superb rooms but in need of a facelift. ❷–❹

Alka, D3/23 Mir Ghat ☏ 0542/328445. Clean rooms, well maintained and with a spacious courtyard overlooking the river. Often booked up by tour groups. One of the few riverside hotels with some quality rooms. ❷–❻

Ganga Fuji Home, D7/21 Sakarkand Gali ☏ 0542/327333. Near the Golden Temple. Fairly big clean rooms with fans and coolers. ❷–❹

Ganpati Guest House, D3/24 Mir Ghat ☏ 0542/390059. Several rooms overlook the Ganges and others are arranged around a courtyard; also has a restaurant and a sociable balcony overlooking the river. Has a slight edge over its neighbour, the *Alka*. ❷–❺

La–Ra India, Dashaswamedh Road ☏ 0542/320323. In the heart of Godaulia, this small place has smart a/c rooms, and a restaurant serving local Varanasi food. A typical shabby genteel mid-range hotel, at the time of writing bizarrely infested with butterflies. ❸–❺

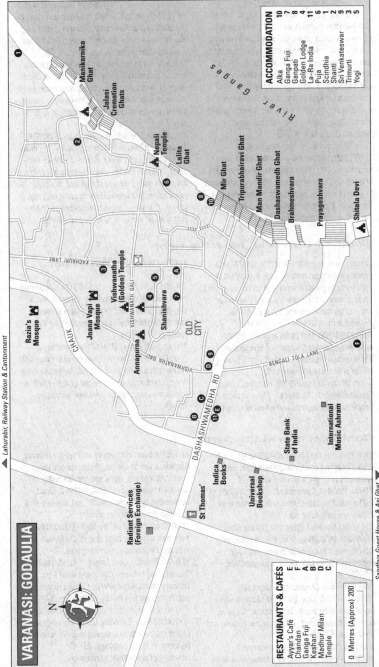

◀ Lahurabir, Railway Station & Cantonment

VARANASI: GODAULIA

N

RESTAURANTS & CAFÉS
Ayyar's Café	E
Chandan	F
Ganga Fuji	A
Keshari	B
Madhur Milan	D
Temple	C

0 Metres (Approx) 200

Radiant Services
(Foreign Exchange)

St Thomas'

Indica
Books

Universal
Bookshop

State Bank
of India

International
Music Ashram

DASHASHWAMEDHA RD

BENGALI TOLA LANE

Razia's
Mosque

CHAUK

KACHAURI LANE

Jnana Vapi
Mosque

Vishwanatha
(Golden) Temple

VISHWANATH GALI

Annapurna

Shanishvara

VISHWANATHA GALI

OLD
CITY

Manikarnika
Ghat

Jalasi
Cremation Ghats

Nepali
Temple

Lalita
Ghat

Mir Ghat

Tripurabhairavi Ghat

Man Mandir Ghat

Dashaswamedh Ghat

Brahmeshvara

Prayageshvara

Shitala Devi

River Ganges

ACCOMMODATION
Alka	10
Ganga Fuji	7
Ganpati	8
Golden Lodge	4
La-Ra India	11
Puja	6
Scindhia	1
Shanti	2
Sri Venkateswar	9
Trimurti	3
Yogi	5

Sandhya Guest House & Asi Ghat ▶

Puja Guest House, D1/45 Lalita Ghat ☎0542/326102. Overlooking the Nepali temple with excellent rooftop views and a restaurant. Offers a range of rooms in a new upmarket wing. The top floor rooms with balconies (surrounded by anti-monkey mesh) are the best value. ❶–❻

Scindhia Guest House, Scindhia Ghat ☎0542/320319. Near Manikarnika Ghat, this guesthouse is easy to find at low tide but well hidden after the monsoon when the riverside path is closed. Clean, some rooms with balconies. Excellent river views. ❷–❸

Shanti Guest House, Manikarnika Ghat ☎0542/392568. An old favourite tucked away near the burning *ghats*. Large building with loads of generally clean rooms with attached bathrooms. In need of a lick of paint but offers the cheapest dorm beds (Rs25) in the city. Excellent views from the lively rooftop restaurant. ❶–❸

Sri Venkateswar Lodge, D5/64 Dashaswamedh Rd ☎0542/322357. Simple but clean and close to the *ghats* and to Vishwanatha Temple, capturing the ambience of the old city. Lovely courtyard but a shame about all the broken furniture. ❶–❷

Trimurti Guest House, 35/12 Saraswati Phatak, near Vishwanatha Temple ☎0542/323554. Good range of rooms (some air-cooled), which can be on the small side. Views of the golden temple from the terrace are so good that photography is forbidden. ❶–❷

Yogi Lodge, D8/29 Kalika Gali ☎0542/392588. An old favourite with budget travellers in the heart of the old city; very well run, with a safe for valuables. Spotless kitchen, clean rooms and attractive dorms. As one of the few places that don't pay commission, it is unpopular with touts, who regularly rip down the signposts necessary to find it. Ring and get someone to fetch you. ❶–❷

South of Godaulia, near the river

Ganges View, Asi Ghat ☎0542/313218. A great veranda looking out onto the river, a lobby full of good books, a pleasant ambience and an interesting landlord mean this popular place is often booked up with visiting musicians and scholars. ❹–❼

Kumiko House, D24/26 Pandey Ghat ☎0542/324308. Run by an eccentric, affable Japanese-speaking Bengali who operates an 11pm curfew. Pleasantly located with a small choice of atmospheric rooms. ❷

Shiva Ganga Lodge, B3/155 Niranjani Akhara, Shivala Ghat ☎0542/314689. Peaceful place with simple rooms, a veranda and a lush enclosed gar-

den. Next to the Shiva temple with great river views. ❶

Tiwari Lodge, Asi Ghat ☎0542/31512. Appealing family-run lodge, built around a shrine, aimed at long-term guests. Simple rooms have kitchen spaces attached. You have to provide your own bedding. ❶

Vishnu Rest House, D24/17 Pandey Ghat ☎0542/329206. One of the nicest of the riverside lodges with a lovely patio and café overlooking the Ganges, best approached via the *ghats* – south of Dashaswamedh. Popular and often booked up. ❶–❸

Cantonment and the peripheries

Best Western, the Mall ☎0542/348091. Next to *Clarks*, new and comfortable chain hotel with a swimming pool, bar and a restaurant. ❽

Clarks, the Mall, Cantonment ☎0542/348501 to 9. Plush and well presented, with all mod cons including a swimming pool. ❾

GM Guest House, 1 Chandrika Colony, Sigra ☎0542/222638. Away from the old town, but easy to reach. Good-value rooms, large and air-cooled with clean bathrooms, plus good food. ❷–❻

Grand Holiday, Dhoopchandi, Jagatganj ☎0542/343792. Near the Sanskrit University. Small homely hotel with large rooms, run by an eccentric family. Lovely garden, home cooking and good value. ❸–❺

Hotel de Paris, 15 the Mall, Cantonment ☎0542/346601. Founded by a Frenchman at the

turn of the twentieth century, and set in extensive gardens, it has an old-world atmosphere. Large comfortable rooms, some with marble baths. ❼

India, 59 Patel Nagar ☎0542/342912. Smart, comfortable hotel with a health and fitness centre, a rooftop bar and two restaurants. ❼

ITDC Varanasi Ashok, the Mall ☎0542/346020. New, well-run chain hotel next to *Clarks* with all mod cons including a swimming pool. ❾

MM Continental, Cantonment ☎0542/345272. Tucked away between *Clarks* and *Ideal Tops*. Ordinary rooms with baths and deluxe rooms without. Restaurant and rooftop coffee shop. ❼

Pallavi International, Hathwa Place, Chetganj ☎0542/356939. Extensive former maharaja's palace behind a busy shopping mall – ornate but a bit tacky; used for weddings. ❺–❽

Plaza Inn, Parade Kothi, Cantonment

3

☎0542/348210. Two hundred metres from the railway station, new hotel with 63 a/c rooms, all with baths and TV. ❼

Pradeep, Jagatganj ☎0542/344963. Comfortable, quite smart and popular with tour groups; away from the *ghats* but within striking distance. Attractive multi-cuisine *Poonam* restaurant. ❺–❻

Railway Retiring Rooms. Convenient, with cheap a/c rooms and dorms with free lockers. Often booked up. ❶

Raj Kamal, Parade Kothi, Cantonment ☎0542/346514. Budget options near the railway station, just outside the *Tourist Bungalow* gates. No atmosphere, but useful for early and late train departures. ❷–❸

Surya, S20/51, A5 Nepali Kothi, Varuna Bridge, Cantonment ☎0542/343014. A good restaurant and reasonable prices make this place popular

with overland groups, who maintain the illusion of roughing it by camping in the garden. Will be a lot more pleasant when the present refurbishment is finished. ❸–❻

Taj Ganges, Nadesar Palace Grounds, Raja Bazaar Road ☎0542/345100. Top hotel, in the grand *Taj* style. Excellent facilities – two restaurants, a bar and a swimming pool – but lacking the character of *Clarks*. ❾

UPTDC Tourist Bungalow, Parade Kothi, Cantonment ☎0542/343413. Handy for the bus and railway station. Large institutional complex with a garden, bar and restaurant. Wide range of rooms including a dorm. ❸–❺

Venkatash, ☎0542/345777, opposite *El Parador* restaurant near the *Tourist Bungalow*, Cantonment. Cheapest option in the area, good for late arrivals and early departures as it's just a few minutes' walk from the railway station. ❶–❷

The ghats

The great riverbanks at Varanasi, built high with eighteenth- and nineteenth-century pavilions and palaces, temples and terraces, are lined with a chain of stone steps – the **ghats** – progressing along the whole of the waterfront, altering in appearance with the dramatic seasonal fluctuations of the river level. Each of the hundred *ghats*, big and small, is marked by a *lingam*, and occupies its own special place in the religious geography of the city. Some have crumbled over the years, others continue to thrive, with early-morning bathers, brahmin priests offering puja, and people practising meditation and yoga. Hindus regard the Ganges as *amrita*, the elixir of life, which brings purity to the living and salvation to the dead. Actually the river is scummy with effluent – don't be tempted to join the bathers; never mind the chemicals and human body parts, it's the level of heavy metals, dumped by factories upstream, that are the real cause for concern. Whether Ganga water still has the power to absolve sin if sterilized is a contentious point; current thinking has it that boiling is acceptable but chemical treatment ruins it.

For centuries, pilgrims have traced the perimeter of the city by a ritual circumambulation, paying homage to shrines on the way. Among the most popular routes is the **Panchatirthi Yatra**, which takes in the *pancha* (five) *tirthi* (crossings) of Asi, Dashaswamedh, Adi Keshava, Panchganga and finally Manikarnika. To gain merit or appease the gods, the devotee, accompanied by a *panda* (priest), recites a *sankalpa* (statement of intent) and performs a ritual at each stage of the journey. For the casual visitor, however, the easiest way to see the *ghats* is to follow a south–north sequence either by boat or on foot.

Boat trips on the Ganges

All along the *ghats*, and especially at the main ones such as Dashaswamedh, the prices of **boat** (*bajra*) rental are highly inflated, with local boatmen under pressure from touts to fleece tourists and pilgrims. There's a police counter at the top of Dashaswamedh, but the lack of government tourist assistance means that renting a boat to catch the dawn can be a bit of a free-for-all, and haggling is essential. A few boatmen operate on a fixed rate, determined by UP Tourism, of about Rs50 per hour.

Asi Ghat to Kedara Ghat

At the clay-banked **Asi Ghat**, at the confluence of the Asi and the Ganges, pilgrims bathe prior to worshipping at a huge *lingam* under a *peepal* tree. Another *lingam* visited is that of **Asisangameshvara**, the "Lord of the Confluence of the Asi", in a small marble temple just off the *ghat*. Traditionally, pilgrims continued to **Lolarka Kund**, the "Trembling Sun", a rectangular tank 15m below ground level, approached by steep steps. Now almost abandoned, except during the Lolarka Mela fair (Aug/Sept), when thousands come to propitiate the gods and pray for the birth of a son, Lolarka Kund is among Varanasi's earliest sites, one of only two remaining sun sites linked with the origins of Hinduism. Equated with the twelve *adityas* or divisions of the sun, which predate the great deities of modern Hinduism, it was attracting bathers in the days of the Buddha.

Much of the adjacent **Tulsi Ghat** – originally Lolarka Ghat, but renamed in honour of the poet Tulsi Das, who lived nearby in the sixteenth century – has crumbled. Continuing north, above **Shivala Ghat**, **Hanuman Ghat** is the site of a new temple built by the *ghat's* large south Indian community. Considered by many to be the birthplace of the fifteenth-century Vaishnavite saint, Vallabha, who was instrumental in the resurgence of the worship of Krishna, the *ghat* also features a striking image of **Ruru**, one of the eight forms of the dog **Bhairava**, a ferocious and early form of Shiva.

Named after a legendary king who gave up his entire kingdom in a fit of self-abnegation, **Harishchandra Ghat**, one of Varanasi's two cremation or burning *ghats*, is easily recognizable from the smoke of its funeral pyres.

Further north, the busy **Kedara Ghat** is ignored by pilgrims on the Panchatirthi Yatra. Above its steps, a red-and-white-striped temple houses the **Kedareshvara lingam**, an outcrop of black rock shot through with a vein of white. Mythologically related to Kedarnath in the Himalayas, Kedara and its *ghat* become a hive of activity during the sacred month of Sravana (July/Aug), the month of the rains.

Chauki Ghat to Chaumsathi Ghat

Northwards along the river, **Chauki Ghat** is distinguished by an enormous tree that shelters small stone shrines to the *nagas*, water-snake deities, while at the unmistakeable **Dhobi** (Laundrymen's) **Ghat**, clothes are still rhythmically pulverized in pursuit of purity. Past smaller *ghats* such as **Manasarovara Ghat**, named after the holy lake in Tibet, and **Narada Ghat**, honouring the divine musician and sage, lies **Chaumsathi Ghat**, where impressive stone steps lead up to the small temple of the **Chaumsathi** (64) **Yoginis**. Images of Kali and Durga in its inner sanctum represent a stage in the emergence of the great goddess as a single representation of a number of female divinities. Overlooking the *ghats* here is Peshwa Amrit Rao's majestic sandstone *haveli* (mansion), built in 1807 and currently used for religious ceremonies and occasionally as an auditorium for concerts.

Dashaswamedh Ghat

Dashaswamedh Ghat, the second and busiest of the five *tirthas* on the Panchatirthi Yatra, lies past the plain, flat-roofed building that houses the shrine of **Shitala**. Extremely popular, even in the rainy season when devotees have to wade to the temple or take a boat, Shitala represents both benign and malevolent aspects – ease and succour as well as disease, particularly smallpox.

Dashaswamedh is Varanasi's most popular and accessible bathing *ghat*, with rows of *pandas* sitting on wooden platforms under bamboo umbrellas, masseurs plying their trade and boatmen jostling for custom. Its name, "ten horse sacrifices", derives from a complex series of sacrifices performed by Brahma to test King Divodasa: Shiva and Parvati were sure the king's resolve would fail, and he would be compelled to leave Kashi, thereby allowing them to return to their city. However, the sacrifices were so perfect that Brahma established the **Brahmeshvara** *lingam* here. Since that time, Dashaswamedh has become one of the most celebrated *tirthas* on earth, where pilgrims can reap the benefits of the huge sacrifice merely by bathing.

Man Mandir Ghat to Lalita Ghat

Man Mandir Ghat is known primarily for its magnificent eighteenth-century observatory, equipped with ornate window casings, and built for the Maharaja of Jaipur. Pilgrims pay homage to the important *lingam* of Someshvara, the lord of the moon, alongside, before crossing **Tripurabhairavi Ghat** to **Mir Ghat** and the **New Vishwanatha Temple**, built by conservative brahmins who claimed that the main Vishwanatha *lingam* was rendered impure when Harijans (untouchables) entered the sanctum in 1956. Mir Ghat also has a shrine to **Vishalakshi**, the Wide-Eyed Goddess, on an important *pitha* – a site marking the place where various parts of the disintegrating body of Shakti fell as it was carried by the grief-stricken Shiva. Also here is the **Dharma Kupa**, the Well of Dharma, surrounded by subsidiary shrines and the *lingam* of **Dharmesha**, where it is said that Yama, the Lord of Death, obtained his jurisdiction over all the dead of the world – except here in Varanasi.

Immediately to the north is **Lalita Ghat**, renowned for its **Ganga Keshava** shrine to Vishnu and the Nepali Temple, a typical Kathmandu-style wooden temple which houses an image of **Pashupateshvara** – Shiva's manifestation at Pashupatinath, in the Kathmandu Valley – and sports a small selection of erotic carvings.

Manikarnika Ghat

North of Lalita lies Varanasi's pre-eminent cremation ground, **Manikarnika Ghat**. Such grounds are usually held to be inauspicious, and located on the fringes of cities, but the entire city of Shiva is regarded as **Mahashmashana**, the Great Cremation Ground for the corpse of the entire universe. The *ghat* is perpetually crowded with funeral parties, as well as the **Doms**, its Untouchable guardians, busy and preoccupied with facilitating final release for those lucky enough to pass away here. Seeing bodies being cremated so publicly has always exerted a great fascination for visitors to the city, but photography is strictly taboo; even having a camera visible may be construed as intent, and provoke hostility. Wood touts descend on tourists at the *ghat* explaining the finer metaphysical points of transmutation ("cremation is education") before subtly shifting to the practicalities of how much wood is needed to burn one body, the never-ending cycle of inflation and would you like to give a donation. The amounts written down in their "ledgers" are unbelievable.

Lying at the centre of the five *tirthas*, Manikarnika Ghat symbolizes both creation and destruction, epitomized by the juxtaposition of the sacred well of **Manikarnika Kund**, said to have been dug by Vishnu at the time of creation, and the hot, sandy ash-infused soil of cremation grounds where time comes to an end. In Hindu mythology, Manikarnika Kund predates the arrival of the Ganga and has its source deep in the Himalayas. Vishnu carved the *kund* with his discus, and filled it with perspiration from his exertions in creating the world, at the behest of Shiva. When Shiva quivered with delight, his earring fell into this pool, which as Manikarnika – "Jewelled Earring" – became the first *tirtha* in the world. Every year, after the floodwaters of the river have receded to leave the pool caked in alluvial deposits, the *kund* is re-dug. Its surroundings are cleaned and painted with bright folk art depicting the presiding goddess, **Manikarni Devi**.

Scindhia Ghat

Bordering Manikarnika to the north is the picturesque **Scindia Ghat**, with its tilted Shiva temple lying partially submerged in the river, having fallen in as a result of the sheer weight of the *ghat's* construction around 150 years ago. Above the *ghat*, several of Varanasi's most influential shrines are hidden within the tight maze of alleyways of the area known as **Siddha Kshetra** (the "Field of Fulfilment"). Vireshvara, the Lord of all Heroes, is especially propitiated in prayer for a son; the Lord of Fire, Agni, was supposed to have been born here.

Panchganga Ghat to Adi Keshava Ghat

Beyond Lakshmanbala Ghat, with its commanding views of the river, lies one of the most dramatic and controversial *ghats*, **Panchganga Ghat**, dominated by Varanasi's largest riverside building, the great **Mosque of Alamgir**, known locally as Beni Madhav-ka-Darera. With its minarets now much shortened, the mosque stands on the ruins of the **Bindu Madhava**, a Vishnu temple that extended from Panchganga to Rama Ghat before it was destroyed by Aurangzeb and replaced by the mosque. Panchganga also bears testimony to more favourable Hindu–Muslim relations, being the site of the initiation of the medieval saint of the Sufi-Sant tradition, Kabir, the son of a humble Muslim weaver who is venerated by Hindus and Muslims alike. Along the riverfront lies a curious array of three-sided cells, submerged during the rainy season, some with *lingams*, others with images of Vishnu, and some empty and used for meditation or yoga.

Above **Trilochana Ghat**, further north, is the holy ancient *lingam* of the three (*tri*)-eyed (*lochana*) Shiva. Beyond it, the river bypasses some of Varanasi's oldest precincts, now predominantly Muslim in character; the *ghats* themselves gradually become less impressive and are usually of the *kaccha* (clay-banked) variety.

At **Adi Keshava Ghat** (the "Original Vishnu"), on the outskirts of the city, the Varana flows into the Ganga. Unapproachable during the rainy season, when it is completely submerged, it marks the place where Vishnu supposedly landed as an emissary of Shiva, and stands on the original site of the city before it spread southwards; around Adi Keshava are a number of Ganesha shrines.

The old city

At the heart of Varanasi, between Dashaswamedh Ghat and Godaulia to the south and west and Manikarnika Ghat on the river to the north, lies the **old city** (or Vishwanatha Khanda), a maze of ramshackle alleys. The whole area rewards exploration, with shrines and *lingams* tucked into every corner and buzzing with the activity of pilgrims, *pandas* and stalls selling offerings to the faithful. Watch for cow jams in the narrow lanes and if you get lost head for the river.

Approached through labyrinthine alleys and the **Vishwanatha Gali** (or Lane), the temple complex of **Vishwanatha** or **Visheshwara**, the "Lord of All", is popularly known as the **Golden Temple**, due to the massive gold plating on its *shikhara* (spire). Hidden behind a wall, the opulent complex is closed to non-Hindus, who have to make do with glimpses from adjacent buildings.

Vishwanatha's history has been fraught. Sacked by successive Muslim rulers, the temple was repeatedly rebuilt, until the grand edifice begun in 1585 by Todar Mal, a courtier of the tolerant Moghul Akbar, was finally destroyed by Aurangzeb. Its simple white domes tower over the **Jnana Vapi** ("Wisdom Well"), immediately north, housed in an open arcaded hall built in 1828, where Shiva cooled his *lingam* after the construction of Vishwanatha. Adjacent to the temple, guarded by armed police to protect it from Hindu fanatics, stands the **Jnana Vapi Mosque**, also known as the Great Mosque of Aurangzeb. Slightly north, across the main road, the thirteenth-century **Razia's Mosque** stands atop the ruins of a still earlier Vishwanatha temple, destroyed under the Sultanate.

Close by, the temple of **Annapurna Bhavani** is dedicated to Shakti, the divine female energy. Manifest in many forms, including the awesome Kali and Durga with their weapons and gruesome garlands of skulls, here she is seen as the provider of sustenance and carries instead a cooking pot. A subsidiary shrine, open for just three days a year, houses a solid gold representation of Annapurna. Nearby is a stunning image, faced in silver against a black surround, of **Shani** or Saturn. Anyone whose fortunes fall under his shadow is stricken with bad luck – a fate devotees try to escape by worshipping here on Saturdays.

The rest of the city

Varanasi holds a few other sites of interest, especially in the area south of Godaulia, just beyond Asi Ghat. The **Durga Temple** here, and the Bharat Kala Bhavan museum of **Benares Hindu University** (BHU) are easily accessible, while just across the river, **Ramnagar** and its impressive fort continue to play an important role in the life of the city.

Bharat Mata
About 3km northwest of Godaulia, outside the old city, the modern temple of **Bharat Mata** (Mother India), inaugurated by Mahatma Gandhi, is unusual in that it has a huge relief map in marble of the whole of the Indian subcontinent and the Tibetan plateau, with mountains, rivers and the holy *tirthas* all clearly visible. Pilgrims circumambulate the map before viewing it in its entirety from the second floor. The temple can be reached by rickshaw from Godaulia for around Rs7.

South of the Old City: the Durga Temple and the Hindu University
The nineteenth-century **Durga Temple** – stained red with ochre, and known among foreign travellers as the Monkey Temple, thanks to its aggressive and irritable monkeys – stands within a walled enclosure 4km south of Godaulia, not far from Asi Ghat. It was built in a typical north Indian style, with an ornate *shikhara*, consisting of five segments symbolizing the elements, and supported by finely carved columns. The whole ensemble is best seen from across Durga *kund*, the adjoining tank. Permeated by a stark primeval atmosphere, it is devoted to Durga, the terrifying aspect of Shiva's consort, Parvati, and the embodiment of **shakti** or female energy. A forked stake in the courtyard is used during festivals to behead sacrificial goats.

Non-Hindus are admitted to the courtyard, but not the inner sanctum, of the Durga temple, but access to the **Tulsi Manas Temple** alongside is unrestricted (daily 5am–noon & 3pm–midnight). Built in 1964 of white-streaked marble, its walls are inscribed with verses by the poet and author of the *Ramcharitmanas*, the Hindi equivalent of the great Sanskrit epic *Ramayana*.

A little further south, the **Bharat Kala Bhavan** museum (Mon–Sat: May & June 7.30am–12.30pm; July–April 11am–4.30pm; Rs100, Rs10 extra with camera) has a fabulous collection of miniature paintings, sculpture, contemporary art and bronzes. Dedicated to the city of Varanasi, a gallery with a stunning nineteenth-century map has a display of the recent Raj Ghat excavations and old etchings of the city. Along with Buddhist and Hindu sculpture and Moghul glass, galleries are devoted to foreign artists who found inspiration in India, such as Nicholas Roerich and Alice Boner. Jamini Roy, the Bengali renaissance painter so influenced by folk art, is also well represented.

Bharat Kala Bhavan forms part of BHU, the campus of which also holds the **New Vishwanatha Temple** (daily 4am–noon & 1–9pm), distinguished by its lofty white-marble *shikhara*. The brainchild of Pandit Malaviya, founder of the university and a great believer in an egalitarian and casteless Hindu revival, it was built by the Birlas, a wealthy Marwari industrial family. Although supposedly modelled on the original temple destroyed by Aurangzeb, the building displays characteristics of the new wave of temple architecture, amalgamating influences from various parts of India with a garish interior. Teashops, flower-sellers and other vendors in the small market outside the gates cater for a continuous flow of visitors.

Ramnagar

The residence of the Maharaja of Varanasi, **Ramnagar Fort** looks down upon the Ganges not far south of the Asi Ghat. The best views of the fortifications – especially impressive in late afternoon – are to be had from the other side of the river, which is reached by a road heading south from the BHU area and over a rickety pontoon bridge. During the monsoon the bridge is dismantled and replaced by a ferry, still preferable to the long main road that crosses the main Malaviya bridge in the north before heading down the eastern bank of the river. It can also be reached by chartering a boat from Dashaswamedh Ghat.

Inside, the fort bears testimony to the wealth of the maharaja and his continuing influence. A dusty and poorly kept **museum** (daily 9am–noon & 2–5pm; Rs5) provides glimpses of a decadent past: horse-drawn carriages, old motor cars, palanquins, gilded and ornate silver *howdahs* (elephant seats), *hookahs*, costumes and old silk in a sorry state are all part of the collection, along with an armoury, a collection of minute ivory carvings, an astronomical clock and hunting trophies. Some visitors have reported having tea with the affable maharaja after chance encounters.

Across the courtyard, a section is devoted to the **Ram Lila** procession and festivities, held during Dussehra (Oct). Varanasi is renowned for its Ram Lila, during which episodes from the *Ramayana* are re-enacted throughout the city and the maharaja sponsors three weeks of elaborate celebrations.

Eating

Most of the old city **cafés** are veg, and alcohol is not tolerated, but the newer Cantonment area is less constrained by religious mores, and some of the more expensive hotels have bars. After a trip on the boats in the early morning, try *kachori*, savoury deep-fried pastry bread, a traditional snack found in the old city next to the *ghats* – but avoid the chai stalls here as the cups are washed in the river. Varanasi is also renowned for its sweets and *paan* (betel leaf). *Bhang*, a potent form of cannabis, sometimes mixed in *lassis*, is available from government-licensed shops, along with weak weed and ropey opium.

Stomach disorders are a common phenomenon in Varanasi, so stick to bottled or treated water and be careful when choosing where you eat. In December 1998, two young Irish travellers died from **food poisoning** here, and allegations have been made suggesting that they were victims of a bizarre scam involving unscrupulous restaurateurs and medical staff poisoning customers in order to claim medical costs from the victim's insurance company. For more details on a similar scam in Agra, see the box on p.300. There are some excellent restaurants around, and your hotel restaurant (if it has one) should be fairly safe if only because an entire guesthouse full of dying travellers may arouse suspicion. The *Vishnu Rest House* on Pandey Ghat does excellent thalis; the *Shanti* has an extensive menu including a host of Israeli food; and the *Yogi Lodge* near Vishwanatha temple must have the cleanest kitchen in the old city – all the travellers' favourites but not a lot of spice.

Amrapali, next to the *Tourist Bungalow*, Parade Kothi, Cantonment. Smart a/c restaurant with very reasonable prices.

Ayyar's Café, Dashaswamedh Road. At the back of a shopping arcade, a small, cheap café serving south Indian food, including masala dosas, filter coffee and delicious milk drinks.

Bread of Life Bakery, B3/322 Shivala. Bakery providing brown bread, cinnamon rolls, muffins and confectionery, with a small clean restaurant serving Western food such as tuna burger and crème caramel. Its not cheap at around Rs200 a head, but it's good for a splurge and the profits go to charity.

El Parador, Maldahia Road. Round the corner from the *Tourist Bungalow*. Remarkable menu ranging from Mexican to Italian, with good pasta, chocolate cake and pancakes. Popular with travellers but not cheap.

Ganga Fuji, D5/8 Kalika Gali, near Vishwanatha, Dashaswamedh. Odd name for a pleasant little café serving multi-cuisine and with live classical Indian music in the evenings.

Kamesh Hut Garden Restaurant, C27/111

Jagatganj near the *Hotel Pradeep*. Indian, Chinese and Continental food served either indoors or in their pleasant garden. Reasonable rates.

Keshari, off Dashaswamedh Road, down a small alley beyond the Bank of Baroda building as you approach from the river. Cool clean and very popular with the locals, so arrive early at meal times. *Paneer* dishes, good-value thalis and pizza.

Madhur Milan Café, Dashaswamedh Road, just past Vishwanatha Lane. Cheap and very popular with locals. Good for samosas, sweets and *kachoris*.

Poonam, *Hotel Pradeep*, Jagatganj. Good though expensive Mughlai food served in a comfortable environment.

Sindhi, Bhelupur Thana. One of Varanasi's most popular restaurants, 1.5km from Godaulia. The rickshaw ride (Rs5–10) is rewarded by excellent veg food.

Temple, *Hotel Ganges*, Bank of Baroda Building, Dashaswamedh Road. Familiar menu with balcony tables overlooking the busy main drag.

Vaatika, Asi Ghat. A leafy terrace right on the ghat serving good pizza to travellers.

Shopping

With hustlers and rickshaw drivers keen to drag tourists into shops offering commission, **shopping in Varanasi** can be a nightmare – but it's worth seeking out the city's rich silk-weaving and brasswork. The best areas to browse are the Thatheri Bazaar (for brass), or Jnana Vapi and the Vishwanatha Gali with its Temple Bazaar (for silk brocade and jewellery). State-run emporia in Godaulia, Lahurabir and the Chowk – the three UP Handlooms outlets at Lahurabir, Nadesar and Neechi Bag, and Mahatex in Godaulia – offer fixed prices and assured quality. Housed in a former palace opposite the *Taj Hotel* in the Cantonment, the CIE has a large and impressive selection but, despite its official-sounding name, is an outrageously expensive Kashmiri-run chain aimed exclusively at the five-star market.

Sales pitches tend to become most aggressive when it comes to **silk**, and you need to be wary of the hard sell. Qazi Sadullahpura, near the *Chhavi Mahal Cinema*, lies at the heart of a fascinating Muslim neighbourhood devoted to the production of silk. Upica, the government-run emporium, has the advantage of fixed prices, with outlets at Godaulia and opposite the *Taj Hotel*, Cantonment. Handloom House, D64/132K Sigra, another government-sponsored chain, is one of the best and safest places to buy silk and the Mehrotra silk factory (☏0542/345289) near the railway station is also recommended. Ask at the station tourist office for precise directions. For tailoring, try Paraslakshmi Exports, 71 Chandrika Colony, Sigra (☏0542/221496), a silk business providing a good and prompt service; they'll deliver to your hotel, and also offer ready-made waistcoats and boxer shorts.

Listings

Airlines Air India are in *Hotel Clarks* (☏0542/346326). Indian Airlines are behind the *Hotel de Paris*, Cantonment (Mon–Fri 10am–1pm & 2–5pm; ☏0542/345959), and they also have an airport office (☏0542/343742). Sahara Airlines are at Mint House, opposite the *Taj Hotel* (☏0542/342355).

Banks and exchange Most foreign-currency branches of the major banks are located in the Cantonment area. The State Bank of India behind *Best Western Hotel*, the Mall (Mon–Fri 10am –2pm; Sat 10am–noon) will change travellers' cheques but doesn't advance cash on Visa cards. The Allahabad Bank is near *Takshal Cinema*. Most of the top hotels also have foreign exchange facilities. Down at Dashaswamedh, there is a branch of the State Bank of India past the *Garden Restaurant* on Madanpura road, but it will not change American Express travellers' cheques; the Bank of Baroda in the *Hotel Ganges* building accepts credit cards but not travellers' cheques; Radiant Services near the main Godaulia junction (near St Thomas' church) changes travellers' cheques and cash– they charge a higher commission than banks but stay open long hours (daily 9am–8pm; 6 percent commission on Visa).

Bookshops Amit (University) Book House, University Road, Lanka, with another branch at Asi Ghat, have a good range of novels and coffee-table books on India; Indica Books, D40/18 Godaulia, have a good selection of religion and philosophy and also provide a useful parcel mailing service; Nandi, Varanasi Ashok, has a good selection including secondhand books which you can also sell here. A secondhand bookshop on Vishwanath Lane, outside the golden temple, will do exchanges.

Car rental at around Rs700 per day is available from ITDC in the *Hotel Varanasi Ashok*, the Mall (☏0542/346032); Travel Corporation of India,

Hotel Clarks, the Mall (☏0542/348501); and the Government of India tourist office (☏0542/343744).

Hospitals Sir Sunderlal Hospital, Benares Hindu University (☏0542/312542 to 45); Shiv Prasad Gupta Hospital (government-run), Kabir Chaura (☏0542/333723); Marwari Hospital, Godaulia (☏0542/321456); Ram Krishna Mission Hospital, Luxa (☏0542/321727).

Internet access Internet cafés aimed at travellers and costing around Rs60/hr cluster around Kachauri Lane.

Motorcycles Jagatganj, near the Sanskrit University. Mechanics and workshops specializing in Enfields are clustered in this area; ask around for a secondhand bike.

Music The International Music Ashram, D33/81 Kalishpura, old city, is an excellent place to get a few lessons in tabla, sitar and theory.

Opticians Gupta Optical, Godaulia (10am–7pm).

Pharmacies The 24hr Singh Medical pharmacy is near the *Prakash Cinema*, Lahurabir, a couple of kilometres north of Godaulia.

Photography Bright Studio, Godaulia; Passi Studio, Lahurabir; Veer Studio, Jagatganj, in front of Queen's College.

Post The main post office is in the Cantonment area. Other branches are located in *Hotel Clarks*; down by the river on the Dashaswamedh road 100m beyond Vishwanatha Lane and the *Madhur Milan dhaba*; and near Kotwali police station at the top end of Chowk.

Travel agencies General travel agencies, selling train, plane and bus tickets, include the ITDC, at the *Ashok*, the Mall (☏0542/346032); the friendly Nova International on Shubhash Nagar, near Parade Kothi (☏346903); Sita Travels (☏0542/342447) and Travel Corporation India (☏0542/346209), both at *Hotel Clarks*; and Varuna Travels, Pandey Haveli (☏0542/323370).

Visa extensions The Foreigners Registration Office is on Srinagar Colony, Sigra (℡0542/351968).

Yoga There is a yoga institute at the Benares Hindu University, but the Yoga Ashram Academy (D 5/4 *Ganesha Guest House*, Saraswati Phatak) in Godaulia is more central. Vag Yoga Consciousness Institute (B 3/13A, Shivala; ℡0542/311706), is based near Shivala Ghat. Many traveller-oriented hotels and cafés have leaflets advertising classes and venues.

Moving on from Varanasi

Indian Airlines' daily flight to Kathmandu gets very heavily booked in winter; there are two daily flights to Delhi, one via Khajuraho and Agra and two to Mumbai. Sahara India Airlines fly daily from Varanasi to Delhi, and Patna, and from Patna to Lucknow and Mumbai. Allow at least ninety minutes from the Old City to the airport due to gridlock.

Most of the super-fast trains on the main east–west line between Delhi and Calcutta such as the Rajdhani, bypass Varanasi but stop at Mughal Sarai, an arduous 45 minutes away by road or a short train ride. Varanasi station has a reservations desk (daily 8am–2pm & 2.30–7pm; ℡0542/343404). The daily Mahanagri Express #1094 is the fastest service to Mumbai (11.35am; 28hr). For Calcutta via Patna, the daily choice is between the Amritsar–Howrah Express #3050 (7.50pm; 20hr) or the Amritsar–Howrah Mail #3006 (4.45pm; 20hr). The #3010 Dehra Dun–Howrah train leaves at 4pm and arrives in Calcutta at 7am. Two good trains run to Delhi: the AC Express #2381 (Wed, Thurs & Sun, 7.45pm; 14hr), and the Neelachal Express #8474 (Mon, Wed & Sat; 6.55am; 14hr). For the mountains of UP, the Dehra Dun–Varanasi Express #4265 (8.40am; 24hr) and the Doon Express #3009 (11.30am; 20hr) are the best options. Three trains daily leave for Nepal via Gorakhpur (6–8hr); they're not main-line services, so are subject to infuriating delays. For Khajuraho, take a train to Satna (best is the #1028 Gorakhpur–Dader Express; 11.05am; 8hr 45min), and change onto a bus (6am, 7am, 12 noon and 3pm) for the four-hour journey.

UPSRTC run morning and evening buses, including overnight services, to the border at Sonauli (10hr) via Gorakhpur, from the Cantonment Bus Stand. Slightly more luxurious private buses travel through Sonauli to Kathmandu (tickets include basic overnight accommodation), but from Sonauli you get a better choice of buses across the border to Pokhara or Kathmandu. Several buses depart for Gaya, near Bodh Gaya (7hr) after 6am. Regular services ply the Grand Trunk Road east to Patna, and there are good deluxe buses for Allahabad, which is an excellent rail link. There are also regular bus services to Lucknow (9hr), Faizabad, Ayodhya (7hr) and Jaunpur (2hr).

Sarnath

SARNATH, 10km north of Varanasi, is a place of pilgrimage for Buddhists, and has also become popular with day-trippers from Varanasi who picnic among its ruins and parklands. It was in a quiet grove here, in the sixth century BC, that Siddhartha Gautama – who came to be known as the **Buddha**, the "Awakened One" – gave his first sermon, and set in motion the Wheel of Law, the *Dharmachakra*. During the rainy season, when the Buddha and his followers sought respite from their round of itinerant teaching, they would retire to Sarnath. Also known as **Rishipatana**, the place of the *rishis* or sages, or **Mrigadaya**, the deer park, its name derives from *Saranganatha*, the Lord of the Deer.

Over the centuries, Sarnath flourished as a centre of Buddhist art and teaching, particularly for **Hinayana** Buddhism (the "Lesser Vehicle"). In the seventh

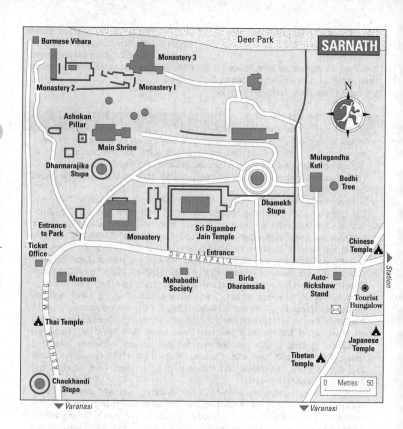

century, the Chinese pilgrim Xuan Zhang recounted seeing thirty monasteries, supporting some 3000 monks, and a life-sized brass statue of the Buddha turning the Wheel of Law.

Buddhism in India floundered under the impact of Muslim invasions and the rise of Hinduism, and except for the vast bulk of the Dhamekh Stupa much of the site lay in ruins for almost a millennium. Prey to vandalism and pilfering, Sarnath remained abandoned until 1834, when Major-General Sir Alexander Cunningham, the head of the Archaeological Survey, visited the site. Today it is once more an important Buddhist centre, and its avenues house missions from all over the Buddhist world.

The main site and the Dhamekh Stupa

Dominated by the huge bulk of the Dhamekh Stupa, the extensive archeological excavations of the main site of Sarnath are maintained within an immaculate park (daily 9am–5pm; $5 [Rs2]). Entering from the southwest, the pillaged remains of the **Dharmarajika Stupa** lie immediately to the north: within its core the stupa concealed a green marble casket full of human bones and precious objects, including decayed pearls and gold leaf. Commemorating the spot where the Buddha delivered his first sermon, the stupa is attributed to the reign of Ashoka in the third century BC, but was extended a further six times.

Adjacent to Dharmarajika Stupa are the ruins of the **Main Shrine**, where Ashoka is said to have meditated. To the west stands the lower portion of an **Ashokan Pillar** – minus its famous capital, now housed in the museum. The ruins of four monasteries, dating from the third to the twelfth centuries, are also contained within the compound; all bear the same hallmark of a central courtyard surrounded by monastic cells.

Most impressive of all is the **Dhamekh Stupa**, also known as the **Dharma Chakra Stupa**, which stakes a competing claim as the exact spot of the Buddha's first sermon. The stupa is composed of a cylindrical tower rising 33.5m from a stone drum, ornamented with bas-relief foliage and geometric patterns; the eight arched niches halfway up may once have held statues of the Buddha. It dates from the Gupta period, but with evidence of earlier Mauryan construction; some archeologists have conjectured that the stupa's upper brick-work may originally have been plastered over.

The **Sri Digamber Jain Temple**, or **Shreyanshnath Temple** – which can be visited by entering another gate without paying the outrageous entrance fee – is believed to mark the birthplace of Shreyanshnath, the eleventh *tirthankara*. Built in 1824, the interior houses a large image of the Jain saint, as well as attractive frescoes depicting the life of Lord Mahavira, the founder of the religion and contemporary of the Buddha.

Museum

Opposite the gates to the main site, the **museum** (daily except Fri 10am–5pm; Rs2, Rs25 extra with video), designed to look like a *vihara* (monastery), has a small but renowned collection of Buddhist and Brahmanist antiquities, consisting mostly of sculpture of Chunar sandstone.

The most famous exhibit is the **lion capital**, removed here from the Ashokan column on the main site. Constructed by Ashoka (273–232 BC), the great Mauryan king and convert to the *dharma*, it has become the emblem of modern India: four alert and beautifully sculpted lions guard the four cardinal points, atop a circular platform. Belonging to the first and second centuries AD are two impressive life-size standing *bodhisattvas* – one has a stone parasol with fine ornamentation and emblems of the faith. Among the large number of fifth-century figures is one of the **Buddha**, cross-legged and with his hands in the *mudra* gesture. Perfectly poised, with his eyes downcast in deep meditation, and a halo forming an exquisite nimbus behind his head, the Buddha is seated above six figures, possibly representing his companions, with the Wheel of Law in the middle, to signify his first sermon. Later sculptures, dating from the tenth to twelfth centuries, include an exceptionally delicate image of the deity **Avalokiteshvara** with a lotus, and another of **Lokeshvara** holding a bowl.

Chaukhandi Stupa

The dilapidated brick remains of the **Chaukhandi Stupa**, 1km south of the main site, date from the Gupta period (300–700 AD), and are said to mark the spot where the Buddha was reunited with the Panchavargiya Bikshus, his five ascetic companions who had previously deserted him. Standing on a terraced rectangular plinth, the stupa is capped by an incongruous octagonal Moghul tower, built by Akbar in 1589 AD to commemorate his father's visit to the site.

Mulagandha Kuti Vihara and modern sites

To the east of the Dhamekh Stupa, the lofty church-like **Mulagandha Kuti Vihara** (free) was built in 1931 with donations from the international Buddhist community. Run by the Mahabodhi Society, it drew devotees from all over the world to witness its consecration, and has become one of Sarnath's greatest attractions for pilgrims and tourists alike. The entrance foyer is dominated by a huge bell – a gift from Japan – and the interior houses a gilded reproduction of the museum's famous image of the Buddha, surrounded by fresco-covered walls depicting scenes from his life.

A little way east, shielded by a small enclosure, Sarnath's **bodhi tree** is an offshoot of the tree at Bodh Gaya, in Bihar, under which the Buddha attained enlightenment. Sangamitta, Emperor Ashoka's daughter, took a branch from the original tree in 288 BC and planted it in Anuradhapura, in Sri Lanka, where its offshoots have been nurtured through the ages.

Buddhist communities from other parts of the world are well represented in Sarnath. In addition to the long-established **Mahabodhi Society**, the **Central Institute of Tibetan Studies** (☎0542/385142), founded in 1967, offers degree courses in Tibetan philosophy and the ancient language of Pali. Close to the *Tourist Bungalow* is the traditional-style **Tibetan Temple** with frescoes and a good collection of *thangkas* (Tibetan Buddhist paintings): its central image is a colossal Shakyamuni, or "Buddha Calling the Earth to Witness" (his enlightenment). The **Chinese Temple** lies 200m east of the main gates; to the west, the **Burmese Temple** houses a white marble image of the Buddha flanked by two disciples. Behind the *Tourist Bungalow* are the **Japanese Temple** and the **Thai Temple**, the latter run by the Mrigdayavana Mahavihara Society.

Practicalities

Sarnath is easily reached by road from Varanasi. Blue **buses** depart regularly from outside Varanasi Cantonment railway station and cost Rs4 but can get very crowded. Shared auto-rickshaws also run from the station for around Rs8 per person and are quicker and more comfortable. The main sites can be quite easily – and pleasantly – explored on foot; the so-called guides who linger outside the main gates and near the museum aren't really necessary.

Close to the main gate, the UPTDC *Tourist Bungalow* (☎0542/386965; ❸) has reasonable **rooms** and a dorm (Rs50). Some of the monasteries, such as the pleasant *Burmese Vihara*, north of the main site, have basic rooms where visitors can stay, for a donation. Right in front of the Mahabodhi Temple gates, the *Birla Dharamsala* (❶), is a very central option. There are a few simple **cafés** and **restaurants** outside the main gates near the Mulagandha Kuti Vihara, and a rather institutional restaurant serving thalis at the *Tourist Bungalow*. Also at the *Tourist Bungalow* is the UP **tourist bureau** (Mon–Sat 10am–5pm). The main **post office** is opposite.

Chunar and Jaunpur

From their vantage point at the northern extremity of the Kaimur Hills, the impressive sandstone battlements of **CHUNAR** overlook a bend in the Ganges before the river curves north to Varanasi, 22km away. Evidence of the earliest occupation of the site dates from Vikramaditya of Ujjain in 56 BC. Chunar sandstone has been used for centuries, most famously in Ashokan pillars – highly polished for sheen and longevity – and is still quarried, leaving the surrounding hills ravaged in places.

The almost impregnable citadel, protected by massive Moghul ramparts, looks down onto the river, graced by a beautiful beach of silver sand during the dry season; the views at sunset are stunning. Akbar stormed the fortress in 1575, and it was presided over by the nawabs of Avadh until the British took it in 1764. Chunar is also associated with Warren Hastings, who took refuge here from an uprising in 1781; a large British graveyard lies near the western gate by the river. The ramparts and huge gates aside, the buildings themselves are unremarkable, except for a picturesque pavilion, built as a gatehouse and now a PWD bungalow, it makes an atmospheric and inexpensive stopover (❶–❷), bookable through the PWD at Mizrapur or by a private arrangement with the *choukidar* (caretaker) who may also be able to arrange food.

The best way to get to Chunar is by local bus from Godaulia to Chunar Ghat, 22km south, from where a pontoon bridge crosses to Balu Ghat, at the base of the fortress. During the rainy season, the bridge is dismantled and a ferry takes its place.

Few tourists visit the large dusty town of **JAUNPUR**, 65km northwest of Varanasi, and founded by Feroz Shah in 1360. The city flourished until a ruthless onslaught by Sikander Lodi spared only its remarkable **mosques** – built in a unique hybrid style, using the remains of previous Hindu and Buddhist structures – and later returned to prominence under the Moghuls.

The River Gomti, which bisects Jaunpur, is spanned by the massive sixteenth-century **Akbari Bridge** congested with hawkers and choked with traffic. Designed by an Afghan architect, the stone structure's fifteen arches have withstood floods and earthquakes; at its southern end, a large sculpture of a lion tussling with an elephant doubles as a provincial milestone.

The older sector, north of the river, is the site of Feroz Shah's original **Fort**, whose stone walls still show traces of coloured and glazed-brick cladding, and the remnants of masonry from an earlier Hindu temple. Little remains of its towers, blown up by the British in 1857. Around 350m north of the bridge, **Atala Mosque** is the earliest and finest example of the architecture of the independent Sharqi dynasty. Built by Sultan Ibrahim Sharqi in 1408, and incorporating the remains of the temple of Atala Devi, it holds two-storeyed cloisters, large arches and an open-pillared veranda. Along with three handsome gateways, the most impressive feature of the mosque is the three pylons of the prayer hall's central arch.

Less than 1km north, the ambitious **Jami Masjid** (Friday Mosque), built by Sultan Hussain Shah Sharqi (1458–79), sits on a high plinth. Approached by steep steps, its prayer hall has an imposing square chamber capped with a lofty dome, with remnants of Hindu structures embedded in the cloisters and walls. Around 6km northwest of Akbari Bridge, the squat **Lal Darwaza Mosque**, built around 1450 by Bibi Raji, the queen of Sultan Muhammad Shah (1436–58), is a cut-down version of Atala Mosque, with just one dome over its prayer hall and an almost square arch.

What basic accommodation and food is available is concentrated around the Fort. Most visitors come from Varanasi for the day: both trains and buses take two hours.

Gorakhpur

GORAKHPUR, 230km north of Varanasi, which rose to prominence as a way-station on a pilgrim route linking Kushinagar (the place of Buddha's enlightenment) and **Lumbini** (his birthplace, across the border in Nepal), is now known primarily as a gateway to Nepal. It was named after the Shaivite yogi **Gorakhnath**, and holds a large ashram and temple dedicated to him. Tourists and pilgrims tend to hurry through, their departure hastened by the town's

Getting to Nepal

Gorakhpur is a convenient jumping-off point for western Nepal, offering access to Pokhara and even Kathmandu. Direct **buses** to **Kathmandu** and **Pokhara** are not a very good deal – your best bet is to enter Nepal at the 24-hour crossing at **Sonauli** where there is a better choice of transport.

Buses for Sonauli (3hr) depart from the bus stand near Gorakhpur railway station between 4.30am and 9pm: deluxe buses leave from in front of the railway station. Take one of the earliest if you want to get a connecting bus to Pokhara (10hr) or Kathmandu in daylight, to enjoy the views; night buses also ply the routes. Private buses leave Sonauli almost hourly in the mornings, between 5am and 11am. The most popular service for Kathmandu, the government-run Saja, actually operates from **Bhairawa**, 5km away in Nepal; the booking office is near Bhairawa's *Yeti Hotel*. Local buses cover the 24km from Bhairawa to Lumbini (Nepal), the birthplace of the Buddha. If you want to **break your journey**, UPT's *Hotel Niranjana* (❶–❺) in Sonauli, 1km short of the border, has a dorm (Rs50) and air-cooled rooms. There's more choice over the border in Nepal; in Bhairawa, 5km up the road from the border, the *Yeti* and the *Himalayan Inn* are popular.

Nepalese **visas**, which you can get at the border, cost $30. There is a State Bank of India on the Indian side of the border. Moneychangers across the border will also cash travellers' cheques. Note that Indian Rs500 notes are illegal in Nepal; yours may be "confiscated".

infamous flies and mosquitoes; if you do get stranded, there's a bustling bazaar, adequate amenities and a few passable hotels.

Practicalities

There are three **bus** stands – the main Railway bus stand, 1km north of the centre, for buses from the Nepalese border at **Sonauli** and **Kushinagar**; the Kacheri bus stand, 1km southwest of the station, for services from **Allahabad**, **Lucknow** and **Varanasi**; and the main bus stand for **Varanasi** (6hr) and Nepal–Varanasi buses, at Pedleyganj, 2km southeast of the station.

Major daily **trains** servicing Gorakhpur include the fast Vaishali Express #2553 to **Lucknow** and **Delhi** (5.10pm) and the Gorakhpur–Dadar Express #1028 for **Mumbai** via Varanasi (5am); among trains to **Varanasi** (6hr) are the fast Kashi Express #1028 (5am) and the Chauri–Chaura Express #5004 (10.10pm). Station facilities include pleasant retiring rooms, a basic restaurant and a **tourist information** booth (theoretically Mon–Sat 9am–5pm but usually closed).

Rickshaws are the main means of **transport**, with few hotels more than 1km from the station. **Car rental** can be arranged through India Tours and Travels (℡0527/336645) in the Ellora Building, opposite the railway station; beware of ticket touts and poor service from most of the travel agents around here. The main **GPO** is in Golghar, to the southwest. The State Bank of India is on Bank Road; foreign-exchange facilities can also be found at some of the more expensive hotels.

Accommodation and eating

Gorakhpur has a wide range of **hotels** from the budget-type near the station to the mid-range in the dull commercial hub around Golghar, 1km southwest. During the hot months, air-cooled or the more expensive a/c rooms are welcome, especially if you have just come down from the mountains. Cheap *dhabas* can be found in the vicinity of the station; a row of them stand outside the station gates. Elsewhere, the best **eating** is in the more expensive hotels or the new multi-cuisine *Bobos* restaurant in Golghar.

Bobina, Nepal Road ⊕0551/336663. About 2km from the station; a tacky pastel-coloured and uniquely depressing museum of kitsch that may be familiar from your nightmares. Visit the lobby out of curiosity, then leave. Facilities include foreign exchange, a garden, restaurant and bar. ❸–❼

Elolra, opposite the railway station ⊕0551/200647. One of the best of the station hotels, with a range of rooms including a/c and air-cooled. The best rooms are at the back, away from the station. ❸–❻

Ganges, *Tarang Cinema* crossing, towards Gorakhnath Temple ⊕0551/333530. Pronounced *gang-ez*, one of Gorakhpur's better hotels. All the mod cons, including two good restaurants and friendly staff. Shame about the decor but it's no worse than anywhere else in town. ❸–❻

Ganges Deluxe, Cinema Road, Golghar ⊕0551/336330. Newish with all a/c rooms at same price. ❺

Marina, Golghar ⊕0551/337630. Tucked away behind the *President Hotel* in the same compound, this place is older, less ostentatious and more pleasant. Room service but no restaurant. ❸–❹

Retiring Rooms, railway station. Good value with a cheap dorm, ordinary and a/c rooms; recommended if you need to catch an early train. ❷–❹

Standard, Station Road ⊕0551/336439. Reminiscent of station retiring rooms but good-value. Opposite the station gates. ❷–❸

Yark Inn, MP Building, Golghar ⊕0551/33233. One of several similarly and reasonably priced establishments along this stretch. ❸–❺

Kushinagar

Set against a pastoral landscape, the small hamlet of **KUSHINAGAR**, 53km west of Gorakhpur, is revered as the site of Buddha's **Mahaparinirvana**, his death and cremation that marked his final liberation from the cycles of death and rebirth. During the Buddha's lifetime, **Kushinara**, as it was then called, was a small kingdom of the Mallas, surrounded by forest. It remained forgotten until the late nineteenth century when archeologists rediscovered the site, and began excavations – based on the writings of the seventh-century Chinese pilgrims, including Xuan Zhang.

Set in a leafy park in the heart of Kushinagar, the **Nirvana Stupa**, dated to the reign of Kumaragupta I (413–455 AD), was extensively rebuilt by Burmese Buddhists in 1927. Within the accompanying shrine lies a large gilded **reclining Buddha**, reconstructed from the remains of an earlier Malla image, and the surrounding area is strewn with stupas erected by pious pilgrims, as well as the ruins of four monasteries. At a crossing immediately southwest, excavations continue at the **Mathakunwar** shrine, where a stunning tenth-century blue schist Buddha has been unearthed. About 1.5km southeast of the main site – surrounded by fields of rice, wheat and cane – the crumbling bricks of the **Ramabhar Stupa** are thought to be the original **Mukutabandhana Stupa** erected to mark the spot of the Buddha's cremation.

Today Kushinagar is rediscovering its roots as a centre of international Buddhism, and is home to many *viharas* (monasteries), including a Tibetan *gompa* devoted to Shakyamuni (the historical Buddha), a Burmese *vihara*, and temples from China and Japan. The strikingly simple **Japanese Temple**, built by Atago Isshin World Buddhist Cultural Association, consists of a single circular chamber housing a great golden image of the Buddha, softly lit through small, stained-glass windows. In May an annual festival – the **Bukkha Mahotsav** – is held in Kushinagar to celebrate the occasion of the Buddha Purnima.

Practicalities

Regular **buses** link Kushinagar with **Gorakhpur** (2hr) and **Varanasi** (8hr). Shared **taxis** and Jeeps also travel to and from Gorakhpur, but are a lot less comfortable. The airport is closed to commercial flights. **UP Tourism** maintains a low-key office and information desk at the tourist bungalow, *Pathik Niwas* (℡ 0556/37138). Both the Government of India and UP Tourism run comprehensive **tours** of the whole "Buddhist Circuit" of Uttar Pradesh, which can be booked either at the tourist office in Kushinagar or in Delhi.

Accommodation is available in rooms for visiting pilgrims at some of the temples such as the *Myanmar Buddhist Temple* (❶, as donation); the *Birla Dharamshala* (❶) opposite, is similarly basic while the *International Buddhist Guest House* (❶), opposite the Tibetan *gompa*, is poorly maintained but otherwise quiet and pleasant. The relatively expensive state-run tourist bungalow, *Pathik Niwas* (℡ 0556/37138; ❺–❻), has a/c rooms, luxury cottages called "American Huts" and a canteen-like **restaurant**. Food stalls at the Kasia crossing provide inexpensive snacks.

Travel details

Trains

Note that most important trains to Varanasi stop at Moghul Sarai, requiring a change of trains or a connecting bus or taxi.

Agra to: Ahmedabad (1 weekly; 27hr 30min); Alwar (1 daily; 4hr); Bhopal (16–19 daily; 5hr 30min–9hr); Bhubaneshwar (1 daily; 39hr); Chennai (1–2 daily; 34hr–42hr); Delhi (15 daily; 2hr–4hr 15min); Gwalior (15–19 daily; 1hr 15min–2hr); Indore (1 daily; 14hr 25min); Jaipur (3 daily; 7hr); Jalgaon (3–4 daily; 14hr 20min–19hr); Jhansi (15–19 daily; 2hr 25min–5hr); Jodhpur (3 daily; 13hr); Kanpur (4 daily; 7hr); Kolkota (Calcutta) (1 daily; 30hr); Lucknow (3 daily; 7hr–8hr 30min); Mathura (12 daily; 1hr 30min–2hr); Mumbai (2 daily; 23hr 30min–27hr); Nainital (1 daily; 11hr); Puri (1 daily; 40hr); Thiruvananthapuram (1–2 daily; 50hr 30min–52hr 40min); Ujjain (2 daily; 14hr 30min–17hr 30min); Varanasi (2 daily; 13hr 45min–16hr).

Varanasi to: Agra (2 daily; 15hr); Allahabad (6–8 daily; 2hr 30min–4hr); Ahmedabad (4 weekly; 43hr); Bhubaneshwar (3 weekly; 23hr); Calcutta (5–8 daily; 11–18hr); Chennai (2 weekly; 36–42hr); Dehra Dun (2 daily; 20hr); Delhi (10 daily; 14–16hr); Gaya (6–8 daily; 3hr 30min–5hr); Gorakhpur (4 daily; 5–10hr); Gwalior (1 daily; 19hr); Haridwar (2 daily; 19hr); Jabalpur (7 daily; 8hr 30min–11hr); Jalgaon (4 daily; 18–22hr); Jhansi (2 daily; 17–19hr); Kanpur (4 daily; 8–9hr); Lucknow (8 daily; 5–7hr); Mumbai (3 weekly; 30–33hr); New Jalpaiguri (3 daily; 12–17hr); Patna (2 daily; 5hr); Puri (3 weekly; 24hr); Ujjain (1 daily; 33hr).

Jhansi to: Agra (2 daily; 15hr); Calcutta (4 weekly; 23hr 25min); Chennai (5 daily; 28–38hr); Delhi (16–20 daily; 4hr 25min–9hr); Goa (1 daily; 35hr); Indore (1 daily; 10hr 45min); Khajuraho (4 daily; 7–8hr); Mumbai (4 daily; 19–23hr); Orchha (3 daily; 15min); Ujjain (2–3 daily; 8–14hr).

Lucknow to: Agra (3 daily; 8hr); Calcutta (5–6 daily; 21hr 45min–28hr); Dehra Dun (2 daily; 14–18hr); Delhi (17 daily; 6hr 30min–9hr 45min); Gorakhpur (13 daily; 5hr); Haridwar (3 daily; 10–12hr); Kanpur (15 daily; 1hr); Mumbai (2 daily; 26hr 30min–30hr); Kulu (1 daily; 3hr 15min); Kathgodam for Nainital (1 daily; 9hr 15min); Patna (4 daily; 9hr); Sonauli (for Nepal; 8 daily; 10–12hr); Varanasi (2 daily; 13hr 45min–16hr).

Buses

Agra to: Delhi (hourly; 5–6hr); Fatehpur Sikri (every 25min; 1hr–1hr 30min); Gwalior (3 daily; 3hr 30min); Haridwar (2 daily; 10hr); Jaipur (every 15min; 5–6hr); Kanpur (1 daily; 10hr); Khajuraho (1 daily; 12hr); Lucknow (4 daily; 9hr 30min); Mathura (hourly; 1hr 30min); Nainital (1 daily; 10hr); Pushkar (2 daily; 10hr).

Varanasi to: Allahabad (every 30min; 2hr 30min); Delhi (1 nightly; 18hr); Gaya (4 daily; 6hr); Kanpur (7 daily; 10hr); Lucknow (frequent; 8hr); Patna (7 daily; 6hr); Varanasi (every 30min; 8hr).

Jhansi to: Orchha (hourly; 30min).

Lucknow to: Agra (2 daily; 10hr); Delhi (2 daily; 9hr); Haridwar (4 daily; 10hr); Kanpur (hourly; 1hr 15min); Nainital (4 daily; 10hr).

Flights

Agra to: Delhi (4 weekly; 40min); Khajuraho (4 weekly; 40min); Varanasi (4 weekly; 2hr).

Varanasi to: Delhi (2 daily; 1hr 15min–2hr 55min); Kathmandu (daily; 1hr 10min); Khajuraho (daily; 40min); Patna (3 weekly; 45min).

Lucknow to: Calcutta (9 weekly; 2hr 20min–3hr 40min); Delhi (2–4 daily; 1hr); Mumbai (1–2 daily; 2hr–3hr 30min); Patna (3 weekly; 1hr).

CHAPTER 4

Highlights

✳ **Char Dham** The pilgrim circuit around the four holy sites of Garwhal, coverable by bus, reveals a cross-section of the Indian Himalayas' most superb scenery. See p.369

✳ **Rishikesh** This busy pilgrimage place on the banks of the turquoise Ganges is a renowned yoga and meditation centre. See p.381

✳ **Gangotri** Hole up at the source of the Ganges, high in the mountains, where *sadhus* offer accommodation for spiritual retreats. See p.390

✳ **Valley of the Flowers** A hidden valley, discovered only in 1931, whose lush meadows are a botanist's dream: hike here after the monsoons. See p.401

✳ **Curzon Trail** A ten-day trail over the Kuari Pass, offering stunning views of the Great Himalayan Watershed. See p.402

✳ **Corbett National Park** Established in the 1930s, India's most famous nature reserve is renowned for its population of tigers. See p.407

✳ **The Panchulis** The magnificent "Five Cooking Pots" peaks, plumes of snow perennially blowing from them, are visible from Munsiyari. See p.418

4

Uttaranchal

ortheast of Delhi, bordering Nepal and Tibet, the mountains of Garwhal and Kumaon rise from the fertile sub-Himalayan plains. Together they form the new state of **UTTARANCHAL**, also known as Uttarkhand, which was recently shorn free from lowland Uttar Pradesh after years of agitation. The region has its own distinct languages and cultures, and successive deep river valleys shelter fascinating micro-civilizations, where Hinduism meets animism and the Buddhist influence is never too far away. The area is progressively opening up to visitors, with the slow demilitarization of the Tibetan border regions to the north. Although not as high as the giants of Nepal, further east, or the Karakoram, the snow peaks here rank among the most beautiful mountains of the inner Himalayas, forming an almost continuous chain that culminates in **Nanda Devi**, at 7816m the highest mountain in India.

Garwhal is the more visited region, busy with pilgrims who flock to its holy spots. At **Haridwar**, the Ganges thunders out from the foothills on its long journey to the sea. The ashram town of **Rishikesh** nearby is familiar from one of the classic East-meets-West images of the 1960s; it was where the Beatles came to stay with the Maharishi. From here pilgrims set off for the high temples known as the Char Dham – **Badrinath**, **Kedarnath**, **Yamunotri** and **Gangotri**, the source of the Ganges. Earthier pursuits are on offer at **Mussoorie**, a British hill station that's now a popular Indian resort. The lesser visited **Kumaon** is more unspoilt, and boasts pleasant small towns famed for mountain views and hill walks, such as **Kausani** and **Ranikhet**, as well as its own Victorian hill station, **Nainital**, whose promenade throngs with refugees from the heat of the plains. Further down, the forests at **Corbett National Park** offer the chance to go tiger-spotting from the back of an elephant. Both districts are full of classic **treks**, many leading through the high alpine meadows known as bugyals – summer pastures, where rivers are born and paths meet.

Facilities are good in the big towns of the foothills, and if you are aiming to ascend make the most of foreign exchange facilities, internet services and

Accommodation price codes

All accommodation prices in this book have been categorized using the price codes below. Prices given are for a double room, and all taxes are included. For more details, see p.51.

❶ up to Rs100	❹ Rs300–400	❼ Rs900–1500
❷ Rs100–200	❺ Rs400–600	❽ Rs1500–2500
❸ Rs200–300	❻ Rs600–900	❾ Rs2500 and upwards

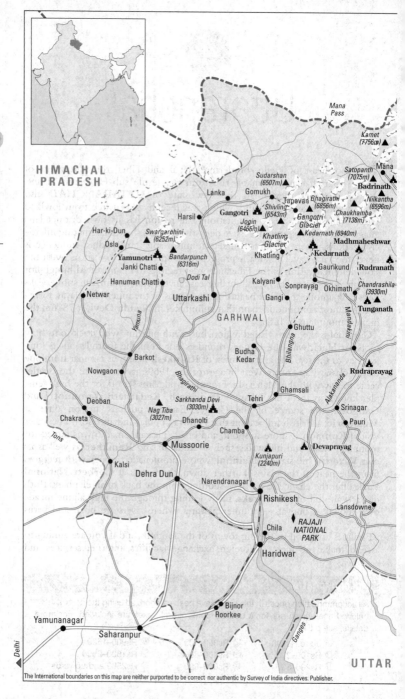

4

HIMACHAL
PRADESH

Mana
Pass

Kamet
(7756m) ▲

Satopanth
(7075m) ▲   Mana

Sudarshan
(6507m) ▲   Nilkantha
(6596m) ▲   **Badrinath**

Lanka   Gomukh

Tapovan   Bhagirathi
(6856m) ▲

Shivling
(6543m) ▲   Chaukhamba
(7138m) ▲

Harsil   **Gangotri**   Gangotri
Glacier

Har-ki-Dun   Jogin
(6465m) ▲   Kedarnath (6940m) ▲

Swargarohini
(6252m) ▲   Khatling
Glacier   **Madhmaheshwar**
▲

Osla

Yamunotri   Bandarpunch
(6316m) ▲   Khatling   **Kedarnath**   **Rudranath**
▲

Janki Chatti ●

Hanuman Chatti ●   Dodi Tal   Gaurikund   Chandrashila
(3930m)

● Netwar   Kalyani   Sonprayag   Okhimath   **Tunganath**
▲ ▲

Gangi   **Mandakini**

Uttarkashi   Ghuttu

GARHWAL

Budha
Kedar   Ghamsali   **Rudraprayag**
▲

● Barkot   **Bhilangna**

Nowgaon ●   **Bhagirathi**

Deoban ●   Sarkhanda Devi
(3030m) ▲   Tehri   **Alakananda**

Chakrata   Nag Tiba
(3027m) ▲   Dhanolti   Srinagar ●

Pauri ●

Chamba ●

● Kalsi   Mussoorie   Kunjapuri
(2240m) ▲   **Devaprayag**
▲

Dehra Dun   Narendranagar

Tons   Rishikesh
Lansdowne ●

Chila   RAJAJI
NATIONAL
PARK

Haridwar

Bijnor
Roorkee ●

Yamunanagar ●   Saharanpur

Ganges

UTTAR

366

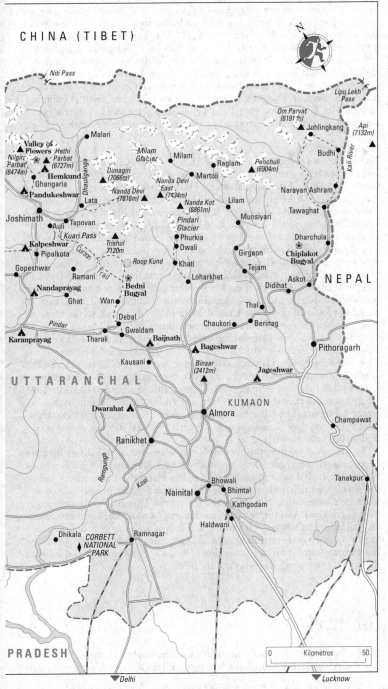

CHINA (TIBET)

Niti Pass

Lipu Lekh
Pass

Om Parvat
(6191 m)

Johlingkang

Api
(7132m)

Malari

Budhi

Valley of
Flowers

Hathi
Parbat
(6727m)

Milam
Glacier

Milam

Raglam

Panchuli
(6904m)

Narayan Ashram

Kali River

Nilgiri
Parbat
(6474m)

Hemkund

Dunagiri
(7066m)

Martoli

Ghangaria

Nanda Devi
East
(7434m)

Lilam

Tawaghat

Pandukeshwar

Lata

Nanda Devi
(7816m)

Nanda Kot
(6861m)

Dharchula

Joshimath

Auli

Tapovan

Kuari Pass

Trishul
7120m

Pindari
Glacier

Phurkia

Munsiyari

Chiplakot
Bugyal

Dhauliganga

Kalpeshwar

Pipalkota

Curzon
Trail

Dwali

Girgaon

Askot

NEPAL

Gopeshwar

Ramani

Roop Kund

Khati

Tejam

Didihat

Nandaprayag

Bedni
Bugyal

Loharkhet

Ghat

Wan

Thal

Pindar

Debal

Chaukori

Berinag

Karanprayag

Gwaldam

Tharali

Baijnath

Bageshwar

Pithoragarh

Kausani

Binsar
(2412m)

Jageshwar

UTTARANCHAL

KUMAON

Dwarahat

Almora

Champawat

Ranikhet

Ramgunga

Kosi

Bhowali

Tanakpur

Nainital

Bhimtal

Kathgodam

Haldwani

Dhikala

CORBETT
NATIONAL
PARK

Ramnagar

PRADESH

0   Kilometres   50

367

▼Delhi

▼Lucknow

satellite TV here as there's little chance of any of that elsewhere in the state. In the mountains, roads are good – maintained by the army which has a large presence up here thanks to the proximity of the Chinese border – but getting around is not always easy as the monsoon (Aug–Sept) causes landslides and avalanches which block the roads. There are buses, but, especially high up, most locals get around by shared Jeep, with many vehicles crammed to bursting (women and foreigners inside, local youths hanging off the back). Compared to the plains, there's little caste strife (most mountain people are high-caste rajput or brahmin) and you'll see few beggars other than religious mendicants. A few words of Hindi are certainly handy as the mountain people usually speak little English.

Some history

The first known inhabitants of the UP Hills were the **Kuninda** in the second century BC, who seem to have had a close affinity with contemporary Indo-Greek civilization. Essentially a central Himalayan tribal people, practising an early form of Shaivism, they traded in salt with Tibet. A second-century Ashokan edict at Kalsi in western Garhwal shows that Buddhism made some inroads in the region, but Garhwal and Kumaon remained Brahmanical. The Kuninda eventually succumbed to the **Guptas** around the fourth century AD, who despite controlling much of the north Indian plains failed to make a lasting impact in the hills. Between the seventh and the fourteenth centuries, the Shaivite **Katyuri** dominated lands of varying extent from the Katyur-Baijnath valley in Kumaon, where their stone temples still stand. Under them **Jageshwar** was a major pilgrimage centre, and Brahmanical culture flourished. Eastern Kumaon prospered under the **Chandras**, from the thirteenth to the fifteenth century, when learning and art took on new forms and the Garhwal school of painting was developed. Later on, the westward expansion of the Gurkha empire was brought to an end by British annexation in the nineteenth century.

Since Independence, Garhwal and Kumaon were part of Uttar Pradesh but failure by the administration in Lucknow to develop the region led to increasingly violent calls for a separate state. Things came to a head in October 1994 when a peaceful protest march to Delhi was **violently** disrupted in Mussoorie by the UP police. The separatist cause was taken up by the sympathetic high-caste BJP when they came to power in March 1998 and the new state was created in November 1999.

The process of creating this new state was somewhat acrimonious; there are deep cultural differences between Garhwal and Kumaon and both regions wanted the capital to sit in their patch, and in Haridwar – culturally a part of the plains – farmers took to the streets to demand things remain as they are. Kumaonis were upset that Dehra Dun, a city in Garhwal, was provisionally chosen as capital. And the new administration now faces serious environmental problems. Deforestation is causing the loss of arable land in the hills and higher up, glaciers are retreating at an alarming rate as a result of global warming, causing water shortages lower down. Some scientists predict that most of the region's rivers will have run dry by 2035.

Garhwal

As the sacred land that holds the sources of the mighty Ganges and Yamuna rivers, **GARWHAL** has been the heartland of Hindu identity since the ninth century when, in the wake of the decline of Buddhism in northern India, the reformer Shankara incorporated many of the mountains' ancient shrines into the fold of Hinduism. He founded the four main **yatra** (pilgrimage) temples, deep within the Himalayas, known as the **Char Dham** – **Badrinath**, **Kedarnath**, and the less-visited pair of **Gangotri** and **Yamunotri**. Each year, between May and November, once the snows have melted, streams of pilgrims penetrate high into the mountains, passing by way of **Rishikesh**, the land of *yogis* and ashrams.

For more than a millennium, the *yatris* (pilgrims) came on foot. However, the annual event has been transformed in the last few years; roads blasted by the military through the mountains during the war against China in the early 1960s are now the lifelines for a new form of motorized *yatra*. Eastern Garhwal in particular is getting rich, and the fabric of hill society is changing rapidly. Visitors hoping to experience the old Garhwal should spend at least part of their time well away from the principal *yatra* routes.

Not far north of Delhi is the pleasant cantonment town of **Dehra Dun**. The hill station of **Mussoorie** rises behind, affording the traveller first sight of the Himalayan snows. Further south, near Rishikesh, holy **Haridwar** marks where the Ganges emerges from the hills onto the Indian plains.

Garwhal is a challenging place to travel around, with extremely long and often nerve-wracking bus and Jeep rides being the order of the day. However, you are rewarded with spectacular views of snowy peaks offset by gaudily painted Garhwali villages in deep valleys. Most visitors stop at Rishikesh, leaving inner Garhwal to the *sadhus* and Hindu pilgrims, heading up to the holy Char Dham. In addition to their spiritual significance, the hills are now becoming established as a centre for **adventure sports**, offering all levels of trekking, white-water rafting, paragliding, skiing and climbing.

All the tourist bungalows in Garhwal are operated by Garhwal Mandal Vikas Nigam – **GMVN**. Most are concentrated along the pilgrimage routes, although their network has been expanding both in areas right off the beaten track and in new destinations such as the ski resort of Auli. Standards vary widely, but most hotels offer a range of rooms and dorms to suit most budgets, along with a restaurant. GMVN also organizes **tours** (often overpriced and inefficient), and offers expensive **car rental**. The GMVN headquarters is in Dehra Dun (☏0135/653217), although you will get more help from their office in Delhi (☏011/332 2251). The GMVN Trekking and Mountaineering Division is based in Rishikesh (☏01364/430799, ⓦwww.gmvn.com).

Dehra Dun

The newly crowned capital of Uttaranchal, **DEHRA DUN**, 255km north of Delhi, tends to be seen simply as a staging post on the way to the hill station of Mussoorie, 34km north, and the Garhwal interior. Pleasantly located at just below 700m, as the Himalayan foothills begin their dramatic rise, Dehra Dun never gets too hot in summer, and snows only rarely in winter. With its vast open spaces and colonies such as the Cantonment, this popular retirement spot is renowned for its elite public schools and prestigious institutions. Although occupied in turn by Sikhs, Moghuls, and Gurkhas, it is clearly an overgrown British town, with its Raj roots always showing.

Dehra Dun stands at the centre of the 120km-long **Doon Valley** (*dun* or *doon* literally means "valley"), famous for its long-grain rice – basmati – and unique in being hemmed in by the Yamuna to the west and the Ganges at Rishikesh to the east. Also in the east is **Rajaji National Park**, known for its wild elephants, while the low-forested Shivalik hills separate the valley from the dusty plains to the south. The locals are fighting back against devastating deforestation; the springs are returning to life and with them the dry riverbeds that criss-cross the valley. Those tracts of forests that remain are best seen at its eastern and western extremities.

The Town and around

Most of Dehra Dun's busy markets lie near the tall Victorian **Clock Tower**, from where Rajpur Road, the lifeline to Mussoorie, stretches northwards. Four kilometres along is the vast leafy colony occupied by the **Survey of India**, founded in 1767. Its greatest achievement was to determine the height of Mount Everest – and name it after the surveyor general, Sir George Everest. Most of the stock in its **map shop** is old and out of date, and their new trekking series of the UP hills is very poor.

Crossing the rainy-season riverbed of Bindal Rao, Kaulagarh Road progresses northwest past Dehra Dun's top private school, the **Doon School**, to the expansive grounds of the chateau-like **Forest Research Institute** (Mon–Fri 10am–5pm; free), devoted to the preservation of India's much-threatened woodlands. There's a large and interesting museum, holding wood samples, insects, furniture, pickled animal embryos and the like. A second museum further into the complex holds an anthropological exhibition on hill tribes. The curator knows his stuff and is happy to show visitors around. The Botanical Survey of India, in the next building, is open to visitors with a prior appointment (℡ 0135/753433) and would only interest the specialist.

Somewhat further afield, **Rajpur**, 12km to the north, past the Survey of India and well connected by Vikrams, has a sizeable Tibetan community with a striking *gompa* – the **Shakya Centre** – decorated with ornate frescoes and a centre of Tibetan medicine next door. Another *gompa* is located on the main road around 5km towards Mussoorie.

Practicalities

The **railway station** is on Gandhi Road, just south of the **City Bus Stand** and the **post office**, which is next to the Clock Tower in the centre of town. The State Bank of India, Convent Road (Mon–Fri 10am–2pm, Sat 10am–noon) changes travellers' cheques, as do several of the state banks that line Rajpur Road. Dehra Dun is the best place in the state for **internet** access as the region's only server is here; there's a cybercafé in the mall at 17 Rajpur Rd (daily 7.30am–11pm; Rs50/hr).

Moving on from Dehra Dun

Jolly Grant airport, 24km east of Dehra Dun, is currently not served by any airline and is unlikely to resume operations for commercial flights in the near future.

Major trains down to the plains include the Dehra Dun–Varanasi Express #4266 through Lucknow to Varanasi, the Howrah Express #3010 through Varanasi to Calcutta, the Mussoorie Express #4042 to Delhi, the Mumbai Express #9020, and the Ujjain–Dehra Dun Ujjaini Express #4310, which stops at Agra. Train reservations are available at the computerized booking office, opposite the railway station.

Hourly buses from the Mussoorie (City) Bus Stand near the station gates head to Mussoorie, while buses to Delhi leave from the Gandhi Road Bus Stand; a deluxe bus costs around Rs120. You can also get buses to Shimla, Dharamsala, Chandigarh, Kullu, Manali, as well as numerous services to Rishikesh and Haridwar, and one early morning bus to Nainital.

See Travel Details at the end of this chapter for more information on journey frequencies and durations.

The helpful **Regional Tourist Office**, at the GMVN *Hotel Drona*, 45 Gandhi Rd (Mon–Sat 10am–5pm; ☎0135/653217), covers all Garhwal. Drona Travels (☎0135/654371), within the same complex, books GMVN accommodation and tours, and rents cars. Abundant local transport includes cycle and auto-rickshaws and multi-seater Vikrams.

If you're looking to fix up a **trek**, try Garhwal Tours and Trekking, 151 Araghar (☎0135/627769), run by KP Sharma, an established and experienced organization used to working with tour groups such as Exodus. Paramount, 16 Moti Market, behind Paltan Bazaar, are the best trekking and mountaineering **equipment** dealers in the entire region.

Accommodation

Dehra Dun has a good selection of mid-range **hotels**, many of them strung along Rajpur Road as it heads north to Mussoorie. What little budget accommodation there is can be found near the town centre – or in the old-fashioned railway retiring rooms.

Ajanta, Rajpur Road, opposite *Great Value* ☎0135/744596. Comfortable, clean and well managed, with an excellent restaurant and pleasant bar. The only hotel with a swimming pool. ⑦–⑧

Embassy, 18 Dhamawala ☎0135/654439. Down a series of lanes, not far from the centre and well worth seeking out. A good range of rooms. ③

GMVN Drona, 45 Gandhi Rd ☎0135/654371. Drab government-run hotel that resembles a giant beehive. Government drones hand out information at the tourist office on site. Central and close to all amenities. The range of accommodation includes a cheap men-only dorm (Rs50) and a/c rooms. ②–⑥

Great Value, 74C Rajpur Rd ☎0135/744086. Large, well-run chain hotel with good facilities including a nice garden, bars and live music in the restaurant. ⑦–⑧

Kwality, 19 Rajpur Rd ☎0135/657230. A landmark near the centre of Dehra Dun, established in the motel-influenced 1960s, with large, comfortable, if old-fashioned, rooms, a good restaurant and a bar. ⑤–⑥

Madhuban, 47 Rajpur Rd ☎0135/749990. A large, imposing upmarket hotel with two popular restaurants, a bar, and a travel desk; some consider it Dehra Dun's best and it is certainly the most expensive. A favourite with the few tour groups that come through. ⑧

Meedo, 71 Gandhi Rd ☎0135/626870. Close to the station gates. Reasonably priced and moderately comfortable with the best rooms at the back away from the sleazy bar in front. ③

Nishima, 59 Gandhi Rd ☎0135/629470. Reasonable if ordinary budget accommodation close to the station and bus stand; slightly better than the poky *Dinex* next door. ②

Osho Resorts, 111 Rajpur Rd ☎0135/749544. Weird place on the road to Mussoorie – part hotel, part restaurant and part ashram – with wooden cottages and eager, unblinking staff. The piped audiovisual channels include lectures by Osho, formerly known as Bhagwan Rajneesh. Offers meditation and billiards. ⑤–⑦

Victoria, 70 Gandhi Rd, near railway station ☎0135/623486. Simple, central, lodge, with a courtyard. ②

White House, 15/7 Lytton Rd ☎0135/652765. Rambling old Raj residence, with huge verandas, lofty ceilings, sturdy furniture and moody plumbing. A peaceful retreat from the centre of Dehra Dun yet only a few minutes' walk away. Recommended ③–④

Eating

Dehra Dun has several commendable mid-priced **eating places** and a bunch of adequate cheaper cafés around the bus and train stations.

Bossa Nova, Astley Hall, Rajpur Road. Swanky American-style outlet serving Western fast food. There is a *Baskin-Robbins* ice-cream parlour at the entrance.

Gary's, 25 Rajpur Rd. Tasty pizzas (Rs45–75) and fast food in a *faux* US atmosphere. You might have to ask them to turn the music down.

Kumar Veg, 15B Rajpur Rd. Excellent veg cooking at reasonable prices in comfortable surroundings. Very popular.

Kwality, 19 Rajpur Rd. Good and reliable multi-cuisine chain restaurant with bar, next to the motel of the same name.

Kundan Palace, opposite the hotel *Madhuban*, Rajpur Road. Open-air multi-cuisine place, popular with locals.

Tripti, 72 Gandhi Rd. Clean *dhaba* opposite the station gates with ordinary cooking and tough competition from similar thali places, such as *Samman Veg Restaurant*, close by.

The Veg, Astley Hall, Rajpur Road. South Indian and Punjabi cooking in a cavernous Soviet-style canteen.

Yeti, 55A Rajpur Rd. Interesting Chinese and Thai veg and non-veg menus, including spicy Sichuan cuisine. Pretensions to upmarket sophistication are somewhat shattered by its location beside a petrol station forecourt. Expect to pay around Rs150 per head.

Mussoorie

Spreading for 15km along a high serrated ridge, **MUSSOORIE** is the closest hill station to Delhi, just 278km north of the capital, and 34km north of Dehra Dun (from where it is clearly visible). At an altitude of 2000m, it gives travellers from the plains their first glimpse of the snow-covered Himalayan **peaks** of western Garhwal, as well as dramatic views of the Dehra Dun valley below. Established in 1823 by a certain Captain Young, Mussoorie soon became a typical Victorian resort, centring on its long promenade – the **Mall** – and boasting an Anglican church, library and club.

These days, Mussoorie is a very popular weekend retreat for middle-class Indians up from the plains. The centre is cluttered with souvenir shops, but it is easy to escape the bazaars and ramble around the atmospheric cantonment of Landour or head to the surrounding woods. Most foreign visitors come to Mussoorie to **study** Hindi at the excellent Landour Language School, but the town is also a useful base camp for **treks** into the western interior of Garwhal. Dominated by the long Banderpunch Massif (6316m), with Swargarohini (6252m) in the west and the Gangotri group in the east, Mussoorie's mountain panorama may not be as dramatic as some other hill stations, but it forms a pleasant backdrop to the busy holiday town.

The Town

Surprisingly, the Mall and the main hub face away from the snows towards Dehra Dun; the distant peaks can best be seen from the flat summit of **Gun Hill**, which rises like a volcano from central Mussoorie. This can be ascended on foot or pony on a bridle path that forks up from the Mall, or on the 400-metre "Ropeway" **cable-car** ride from the Mall (Rs25 return). Alternative prospects of the mountains can be had on a peaceful stroll or ride around the three-kilometre-long **Camel's Back Road**, which girdles the northern base of Gun Hill, passing by the distinctive Camel's Rock and an old British cemetery with inscriptions on the graves that give a fascinating insight into life in the town during the Raj. Another vantage point, the highest in the immediate vicinity, is **Childer's Lodge**, 5km east of the Mall above Landour.

Just below the Mall, beside the *Padmini Nivas* hotel, a **Tibetan street market** has become something of a fixture, with traders selling sweaters and woollens to unprepared tourists. **Kulri Bazaar** (also known as **Picture Palace**), at the eastern end of the Mall, is more upbeat and full of attractions to lure the urbane Indian tourist. The pool halls – including one at *Clarks Hotel* and one by the *Vikas Hotel* – charge around Rs100 per hour. Of the new video game arcades, the one opposite *Clarks* is the most sophisticated, offering Virtua Cop for only Rs10 a go. The **Rink**, reputedly India's largest indoor rollerskating rink (Rs30 plus skate hire) is in an old British theatre. Wear plenty of padding as the uneven wooden floor is treacherous.

Beyond Kulri Bazaar, the road winds steeply upwards for 5km through the

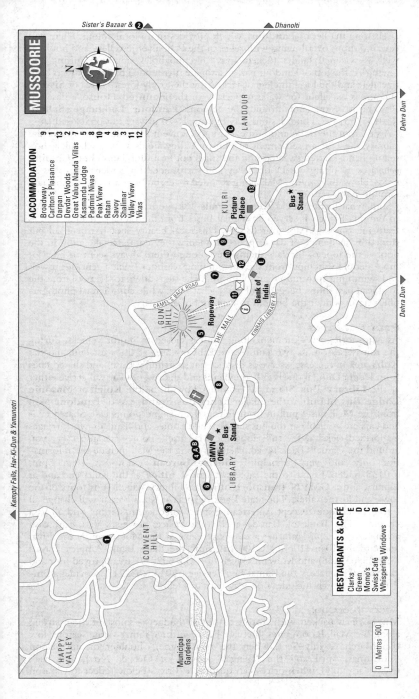

MUSSOORIE

ACCOMMODATION

Broadway	9
Carlton's Plaisance	1
Darpan	13
Devdar Woods	2
Great Value Nanda Villas	7
Kasmanda Lodge	5
Padmini Nivas	8
Peak View	10
Ratan	4
Savoy	6
Shalimar	3
Valley View	11
Vikas	12

RESTAURANTS & CAFÉ

Clarks	E
Green	D
Momo's	C
Swiss Café	B
Whispering Windows	A

Sister's Bazaar & ② ▲

▲ Dhanolti

◀ Kempty Falls, Har-Ki-Dun & Yamunotri

LANDOUR

KULRI

Picture Palace

Bus Stand ★

CAMEL'S BACK ROAD

GUN HILL

Ropeway

THE MALL

Bank of India

KINRAIG LIBRARY RD

CONVENT HILL

LIBRARY

GMVN Office

Bus Stand ★

HAPPY VALLEY

Municipal Gardens

Dehra Dun ▶

Dehra Dun ▶

0 Metres 500

fascinating market of **Landour**, which provides more local colour. There you can find shops overflowing with relics of the Raj, silver jewellery and books as well as wizened tailors tucked away in cubbyholes snipping, cutting and sewing. At the top of Landour bazaar, a square surrounded by cafés attracts both travellers and the local intelligentsia. Nearby, the lovely forested area of **Sister's Bazaar** is excellent for walks, especially to the **Haunted House**, a deserted Raj-era mansion, and around the famous **Landour Language School** (☎0135/631467; Hindi lessons Rs50 group, Rs70 private tuition; closed Jan).

Away from the noise and bustle, close to Convent Hill and 3km west of the Library, the Tibetan settlement of **Happy Valley** holds a large school, a shop selling hand-knitted sweaters and the small but beautiful **Tchechen Choling** *gompa* overlooking the Doon valley and surrounded by gardens. It makes an enjoyable walk from the Mall along wooded roads, but you can also catch a taxi (around Rs60 return).

Somewhat further afield, **Kempty Falls**, 18km northwest on the road down to Yamuna Bridge, is served by regular buses from the Library stand as well as featuring on a GMVN tour (Rs25). This local beauty spot has been all but ruined by its deluge of day-trippers. In theory they come to take a dip in the pool at the foot of the falls themselves, though there always seem to be a lot more people watching from the surrounding teashops (which rent out towels and swimming costumes) than swimming. The steps down to the pool from the road lead past shops, beggars and snake-charmers, while commercial photographers lie in wait at the bottom to capture holiday snaps.

Practicalities

As Mussoorie's two-kilometre-long **Mall** is closed to motor vehicles during the tourist season, its two ends – the **Library** area at the west end, and the **Kulri** area in the east – serve as distinct transport hubs. Buses and shared taxis from Dehra Dun (about Rs50), the plains and the rest of Garhwal arrive either at the **Library Bus Stand** at Gandhi Chowkh, or the **Kulri** or **Masonic Lodge Bus Stand**. At the smaller **Tehri Bus Stand**, east of **Landour** 5km from the Mall, buses pull in from Tehri, Chamba and points east. Shared taxis and cars are available at the bus stands, while ponies and hand-drawn carriages – glorified rickshaws – run along the Mall itself. Ponies can also carry you around the Camel's Back Road. Facilities along the Mall include the information-only and very unhelpful **tourist bureau** (Mon–Sat 10am–5pm, ☎0135/632863) next to the cable car, a **post office** at the Kulri end and at Library, and a **GMVN transport office** at Library which runs tours of the town and further afield. The State Bank of India at Kulri Bazaar will change all travellers' cheques except American Express cheques in sterling and all Visa cheques. The Bank of Baroda at Picture Palace processes Visa card cash advances until 2pm. Internet access is available at the Mousetrap by the *Vikas Hotel* (daily 10am–10pm; Rs100/hr), near the State Bank. Ambica Travels (☎0135/632238) and Kulwant Travels (☎0135/632717) are approved tour and **car rental** operators; the Kamal Taxi Service (☎0135/632717) provides a similar service which includes one-way trips to Delhi.

Accommodation

Mussoorie is packed with **hotels** to suit all budgets – most of them strung along the Mall. Room rates fluctuate between three rather vague seasons; low (Jan–March & July–Sept, when the rains come), shoulder or mid-season (Christmas, April and the "Bengali season" of Oct & Nov), and peak (May–early July), when prices can quadruple. Prices below reflect low season with an indication of high-season fluctuations. The town suffers from severe **water shortages**, which may affect some of the cheaper hotels.

Porters from either the Library or the Kulri bus stands charge under Rs20 to carry luggage to most locations along the Mall.

Broadway, Camel's Back Road, Kulri Bazaar ☏ 0135/634423. Rambling old guesthouse which perches on the edge of the Bazaar, with charming bright window-boxes and lovely views. A good bet for budget travellers. Price includes a morning cup of tea. ② – ④

Carlton's Plaisance, Happy Valley Road ☏ 0135/632800. An old Raj-era house plus a more modern building, both stuffed full of Victorian drapes and memorabilia. Sir Edmund Hillary stayed here and recommended it. Lovely gardens and an ideal base for gentle rambles away from the town. ④ – ⑦

Darpan, Landour Road, near Picture Palace, Kulri ☏ 0135/632483. Reasonable and clean, with mountain views and a good Gujarati veg restaurant. ③ – ⑥

Devdar Woods, Sister's Bazaar ☏ 0135/632644. Large old hotel situated on a high and secluded site, recently refurbished with a large restaurant. Often full due to its proximity to the language school, so book well in advance – you may even get picked up from the bus stop. Prices include breakfast. ⑤

Great Value Nanda Villa, Camel's Back Road ☏ 0135/632088. Comfortable modern chain hotel with good views. Reasonably priced for its range, close to all amenities and quiet. ⑦ – ⑧

Kasmanda Lodge, opposite *Vasu* cinema, the Mall ☏ 0135/632424. A short but stiff climb leads to an ex-maharaja's summer palace now opened as a period hotel. Comfortable and quiet with beautiful gardens. ⑧

Padmini Niwas, Library, the Mall ☏ 0135/632793. Just below the Mall with beautiful gardens and buildings and excellent views. One of Mussoorie's more established and classier addresses. ⑦ – ⑨

Peak View, opposite the State Bank of India, Camel's Back Road (☏ 0135/632052). Quiet budget hotel close to all amenities. Comfortable with an open terrace and views of the snowy peaks. ③

Ratan, Gandhi Chowkh ☏ 0135/632719. In the busy Library area, clean and friendly, with a roof terrace, and rooms graded according to their views. ② – ⑤

Savoy Hotel, the Mall ☏ 0135/632010. Above the Library, a long driveway leads to this collapsing Victorian pile. It's certainly atmospheric and steeped in history, and with peeling wallpaper and decaying animal heads on the walls might make a good location for a ghost story. Agatha Christie based her first novel, *The Mysterious Affair at Styles*, on a celebrated poisoning that took place here. Not a good-value place to stay but it's worth having a look around, or to have a cocktail at the bar. ⑧ – ⑨

Shalimar, Charliville Road ☏ 0135/632410. A refurbished old British hotel, set away from the town in peaceful grounds with good views. ⑤ – ⑥

Valley View, the Mall ☏ 0135/632324. Towers over the Mall with sunny terraces overlooking the Doon valley and a good restaurant; clean and close to all amenities. ③ – ⑥

Eating

Cafés and **restaurants** all along the Mall and around Kulri serve everything from hotdogs to Chinese specialities; in addition to those recommended below, there are good restaurants in many of the hotels including the *Devdar Woods*, the *Padmini Nivas*, the *Valley View* and the crumbling *Savoy*.

Clarks, the Mall, Kulri. Multi-cuisine restaurant that is continually being expanded, yet maintains its period atmosphere; also has a bar and a bakery.

Green, the Mall, Kulri. Justifiably popular restaurant; go early at mealtimes or you will have to queue. The menu is Indian and Chinese, serving up very tasty thalis and biryanis using locally grown basmati rice.

Momo's, Landour Bazaar. A small but funky café serving excellent Tibetan food.

Prakash's Store, Sister's Bazaar. A gastronomic pilgrimage site for those in the know – home-made breads, jams, peanut butter and cheddar cheese.

Swiss Cafe, Gandhi Chowkh. Inexpensive veg and non-veg multi-cuisine; the coffee is superb.

Whispering Windows, Gandhi Chowkh. Also a hotel, one of Mussoorie's better restaurants – great views, piped music and a bar.

A relatively undemanding but superb trek from Mussoorie takes three days (plus one on the bus) to reach the sparsely populated "Valley of the Gods", HAR-KI-DUN, in the Fateh Parvat region of northwestern Garhwal. The valley trails are open from mid-April until mid-November, but the mountain passes only in mid-June. All the trails on the trek are clear, and villagers will happily point you in the right direction. Recommended maps of the trail and region include those published by Leomann – sheet 8 covers Garwhal – and the Ground Survey of India map of the area available from any major UP tourist office. In the valley itself, if not higher in the mountains, accommodation is widely available, and food can usually be bought.

The rivers and streams of Har-ki-dun drain the glaciers and snowfields of the peaks of Swargarohini (the "Ascent to Heaven"; 6252m) and Bandarpunch (the "Monkey's Tail"; 6316m). Local people trace their lineage back to the *Mahabharata*, claiming descent from Duryodhana and his followers. Like the Pandavas of the epic, they practise a form of polyandry and follow intriguing religious customs, including witchcraft. Worship at Taluka's Duryodhana temple, for example, consists of throwing shoes at the idol; at Pakola, the image has its back to the congregation. Their distinctive alpine buildings have beautifully carved wooden doors and windows, with the mortar construction punctuated by wooden slats.

The trek to Har-ki-Dun

Starting out from Mussoorie on DAY 1, catch a Yamunotri bus (1 daily; 10am) at the Library Bus Stand and change at Nowgaon to continue via Netwar (9km short of Barkot, from where a road climbs to Hanuman Chatti) to Purola – a total of 154km. Set amid a patchwork of wheat and rice terraces in Purola, is a PWD bungalow, where accommodation is available, and where you can obtain permission to stay at the forest bungalows further on. Simple cafés can be found around the bus stand.

Early the next morning – DAY 2 – take the bus to the roadhead at Sankri, which also has a bungalow. A gentle trail from here leads 12km through deodar and sycamore woods to Taluka (1900m), where there is another bungalow serving simple food.

On DAY 3, the trail descends to follow the River Tons through beautiful forests. Although you can get tea at the hamlet of Gangari, no food is available until you've walked the full 11km to Osla (2259m). The forest bungalow, GMVN hotel and *dhaba* stalls are all on the main trail in an area know as Seema, below Osla; from here on you have to carry your food, so stock up.

A steep climb of 14km from Osla on DAY 4 brings you finally to the campground at Har-ki-Dun (3560m) – an excellent base from which to explore the *bugyals* below the Swargarohini to the east, and the Jaundhar Glacier (3910m) at the head of the valley.

Across Yamunotri Pass

From the head of Har-ki-Dun valley, a challenging trail – only to be tackled by fully equipped and acclimatized trekkers, with local guides – winds for 30km over the Yamunotri Pass (4890m). Take the trail that forks off above Osla, and head 10km east along the Ruinsar Nala gorge to the mountain lake of Ruinsara Tal (3350m). From here, it takes a full day to climb to a campsite just below the pass at 4135m; on the second day you cross the pass and camp on the far side at 4000m; the third day ends at Yamunotri itself (see p.388).

From here, the gentle fourteen-kilometre trek outlined on p.387 leads down to Hanuman Chatti (2134m), from where you can either embark on the Dodi Lal trek to create a two-week expedition through stunning mountain scenery, or catch a bus out.

Haridwar

At **Haridwar** – the Gates (*dwar*) of God (*Hari*) – 214km northeast of Delhi, the **River Ganges** emerges from its final rapids past the Siwalik Hills to start the long slow journey across northern India to the Bay of Bengal. Stretching for roughly 3km along a narrow strip of land between the craggy wooded hills to the west and the river to the east, Haridwar is especially revered by Hindus, for whom the **Har-ki-Pairi** *ghat* (literally the "Footstep of God") marks the exact spot where the river leaves the mountains. As you look north along the vast Doon Valley, the faint lines of the Himalayan foothills can be discerned rising above Rishikesh in the distance, while Haridwar itself faces east across the river to the Rajaji National Park. A major road and rail junction, Haridwar links Delhi and the Gangetic plains with the mountains of Uttaranchal and their holy pilgrimage (*yatra*) network. Along with Nasik (see p.823), Ujjain (see p.505), and the holiest of them all, Prayag in Allahabad (see p.228), Haridwar is

HARIDWAR

Rishikesh (24km), Dehra Dun, Sapta Rishi Ashram ▲

Rishikesh ▲ & Dehra Dun

Bhimgoda ▲

N

River Ganges

Mansa Devi ▲

Chair Lift

Har-Ki-Pairi ▲

Barrage

Bara Bazaar

See inset map

GPO

UPPER RD

Shri Mayadevi ▲

Canal

NEW LALITA RAO BRIDGE

Railway Station

RAILWAY ROAD

Upper Ganges

Bus Stand

Moti Bazaar

GPO

UPPER ROAD

Canara Bank

Vishnu Ghet

Shri Mayadevi ▲

State Bank of India

RAILWAY ROAD

SADHU BELA MARG

Upper Ganges

Canal

NEW LALITA RAO BRIDGE

◀ 🔟 & Delhi

◀ Delhi

Daksha Mahadev (6km) ◀

Chandi Devi (5km) & Chila (13km) ▶

ACCOMMODATION

Aarti	5
Inder Kutir Guest House	9
Jai Ram Ashram	1
Kailash	6
Midtown	4
Prem Nagar Ashram	10
Raj Deluxe	3
Shiv Vishram Grah Lodge	2
Suvidha	8
Tourist Bungalow	12
Tourist Villa	7
Up Tourism Rahi Motel	11

RESTAURANTS

Ahaar	C
Chotiwala	D
Hoshiyarpuri	A
Kwality	B
Shiwalik	E

0 — Metres — 200

one of the four holy *tirthas* or "crossings" that serve as the focus of the massive **Kumbh Mela** festival (see p.329). Every twelve years, thousands of pilgrims come to bathe at a preordained moment in the turbulent waters of the channelled river around Har-ki-Pairi. Haridwar's next Kumbh Mela is due to take place in 2013. Busy at the best of times, Haridwar can become unbearably congested during the Mela, when surging crowds around the bathing *ghats* can create stampedes.

The Town

Split by a barrage north of Haridwar, the **Ganges** flows through the town in two principal channels, divided by a long sliver of land. The main natural stream lies to the east, while the embankment of the fast-flowing canal to the west holds *ghats* and ashrams. Promenades, river channels and bridges create a pleasant riverfront ambience, with the major *ghats* and religious activity clustered around **Har-ki-Pairi**, which looks like a railway station. Bridges and walkways connect the various islands, and metal chains are placed in the river to protect bathers from being swept away by ferocious currents.

Non-Hindus are not allowed onto the actual Har-ki-Pairi *ghat,* but the platform-like island opposite it, topped by a clock tower, provides an excellent vantage point, especially during evening worship. At dusk, the spectacular daily ceremony of **Ganga Arati** – devotion to the life-bestowing goddess Ganga – draws a crowd of thousands onto the islands and bridges. Lights float down the river and priests perform elaborate choreographed movements while swinging torches to the accompaniment of gongs and music. As soon as they've finished the river shallows fill up with people looking for coins thrown in by the devout.

Haridwar's teeming network of **markets** is the other main focus of interest. **Bara Bazaar**, at the top of town, is strong on brass, cane and bamboo-ware – a good place to buy a *danda* (bamboo staff) for treks in the mountains. Stalls in the colourful **Moti Bazaar** on the Jawalapur road sell everything from clothes to spices.

High above Haridwar, on the crest of a ridge, the gleaming white *shikhara* of the **Mansa Devi** temple dominates both town and valley. The temple is easily reached by **cable car** (daily 8am–noon & 2–5pm; Rs20 return, Rs45 combined ticket for Mansa Devi and Chanda Devi temple), from a base station off Upper Road in the heart of town, though the steep 1.5-kilometre walk is pleasant enough early in the morning. None of the shrines and temples up top holds any great architectural interest, but you do get excellent views along the river. An elaborate queuing system leads pilgrims to a *darshan* of the main image, showing Mansa Devi – a triple-headed image of Shakti as the goddess Durga. Photography is forbidden.

The tacky modern seven-storeyed **Bharat Mata** temple, 5km north of Haridwar and reachable in shared Vikrams for around Rs10, is dedicated to "Mother India". A temple with a similar name and purpose can be found in Varanasi, but this one is much newer, and much more garish. Each of its various floors – connected by lifts – is dedicated to a celestial or political theme, and populated by lifelike images of heroes, heroines and Hindu deities.

The **Shri Dakheshwar** temple, also known as **Daksha Mahadev**, 6km south of Haridwar in Khankhal and reachable by Vikram for around Rs10, is beautifully situated with large trees above a *ghat*. The new main temple contains a gilded image of a snake symbolizing Shiva; legend relates that Shiva's wife Sati was so enraged when her father snubbed Shiva by failing to invite him to a sacrifice performed on this spot that she sacrificed herself by self-immolation.

Practicalities

Haridwar's **railway station** and **Station Bus Stand**, southwest of the centre, face each other across the main thoroughfare that channels all the traffic through to meet the river at Har-ki-Pairi. **Trains** and **buses** connect Haridwar with Rishikesh, Dehra Dun and the mountains, and run back down to Delhi. You can also get to Rishikesh in shared taxis, while Vikrams and tempos ply the few roads in town. To arrange a **tour** of Garwhal by bus or car, call in at Konark Tourist Service, Jassa Ram Road (℡0133/427210).

A UP Tourism information booth at the station operates at arrival times. Information is also availaible at the **GMVN Tourist Office** (Mon–Sat 10am–5pm; ℡0133/427025), near Lalita Rao Bridge on Upper Road, and at the **UP Tourist Information Bureau** (Mon–Sat 10am–5pm, closed the 2nd Sat of each month; ℡0133/427370), near the bus stand at *Rahi Motel*, Station Road. There's a **post office** on Upper Road, opposite Ram Panjawani (℡0133/427025), the local agents for Indian Airlines. You can change **money** at the State Bank of India on Sadhu Bela Marg (℡0133/427672), or at Canara Bank, Railway Road (℡0133/427208) whose foreign exchange is open 10am to 2pm. A small **internet** café 100m east of the *Midtown Hotel* charges Rs120 per hour and is open 10am–7pm.

Accommodation

Although it has no luxury hotels, Haridwar has **accommodation** to suit most budgets, including a number of ashrams – two of which are included in the list below. Only the UP and GMVN tourist hotels and *Shankar Niwas* have fixed prices, so the rates below are subject to change with seasonal discounts and hard bargaining. It's a small place, so wherever you stay the river and the bazaars are never too far away. Most hotels are a Rs5 rickshaw ride northeast of the station; some are within walking distance.

Aarti, Railway Road ℡0133/427456. Quite a reasonable, clean hotel on a busy main road, convenient for the railway station and bus stand. ④–⑥

Inder Kutir Guest House, Sharwan Nath Nagar ℡0133/426336. A family home near the river, with small rooms off a terrace and a pleasant central sitting room. ③

Jai Ram Ashram, Bhimgoda ℡0133/427335. Basic room at a government-recommended nominal rate of Rs50 per night. ①

Kailash, Shiv Murti ℡0133/427789. Central hotel near the railway station, with a handy counter for rail and bus tickets. Around 70 rooms, some air-cooled, and a veg restaurant. ②–③

Midtown, in an alley off Railway Road, opposite *Chotiwallah* restaurant ℡0133/249401. Best-value mid-range hotel, with clean rooms in pastel colours and friendly staff. Rooms at the front have balconies. ③–④

Prem Nagar Ashram, Jawalapur Road, 2km west of the station ℡0133/426345. Basic room at a government-recommended nominal rate of Rs50 per night. ①

Raj Deluxe, Vishnu Ghat ℡0133/427755. Large, busy and moderately comfortable hotel at the heart of a busy market, close to the river and bridge. ④–⑥

Shiv Vishram Grah Lodge, Upper Road, near Har-ki-Pairi ℡0133/427618. Large, quiet courtyard with a monkish atmosphere near the busiest part of town, with reasonable, air-cooled, budget rooms. ②

Suvidha, Sharwan Nath Nagar, behind Chitra Talkies cinema ℡0133/427423. Pleasant location, near the river, away from the bustle of the bazaars and main roads. Comfortable and plush. ⑤

Tourist Bungalow, Belwala, on the main island ℡0133/426379. One of the few places on the east bank, in a pleasant garden overlooking the river away from the noise. Rooms range from a cheap dorm (Rs50) to a/c comfort. ④–⑥

Tourist Villa, Himalaya Depot Gali, Sharwan Nath Nagar ℡0133/426391. Popular and quite new with a range of rooms. The ones at the top are less noisy. Food available as room service only. ②–⑥

UP Tourism Rahi Motel, Jawalapur Haridwar Road ℡0133/426430. Large modern bungalow next to the bus stand, with a dorm (Rs60) plus a restaurant set in pleasant gardens. ⑤–⑦

Eating

Haridwar is a strictly veg town; if you're happy with that, the food is very good, whether in the **cafés** around Har-ki-Pairi or the **restaurants** of Upper Road and Railway Road.

Ahaar, Railway Road. Mid-range Sikh-run restaurant, with a wood-panelled ambience, and serving good thalis, Chinese food and superb Punjabi cuisine such as the traditional and seasonal *makki-ki-roti* (corn *paratha*) with *sarson ka saag* (mustard-leaf spinach).

Chotiwala, Lalita Rao Bridge, near *Big Town Hotel*, Railway Road. Next to *Ahaar* this offers Indian food and good thalis. Established in 1937, and with two branches in Swarg Ashram, Rishikesh, it's still one of the best around. Its many imitators include one near Har-ki-Pairi.

Hoshiyarpuri, Upper Road. Legendary and popular *dhaba*-like restaurant close to Har-ki-Pairi Ghat. Busy and friendly place with delicious Indian (especially Punjabi) and Chinese food.

Kwality, Upper Road, near the *Shankar Niwas* hotel. A new branch of this standard multi-cuisine chain of restaurants.

Shiwalik, Railway Road. One of a row of three good restaurants. Don't take its breakfast sign too seriously as it tends to open late; tasty south Indian snacks include *dosas*.

Moving on from Haridwar

Major trains passing through include the Mussoorie Express #4042 between Dehra Dun and Delhi, which leaves Haridwar at 10.50pm and takes 7hr to reach Delhi. Other trains to Delhi include the costly but air-conditioned and fast Dehra Dun Shatabdi Express #2018, which leaves at 6pm and takes 5hr (food is included in the price), and the Dehra Dun–Mumbai Express #2020; the Ujjain–Dehra Dun Express #4310 stops at Agra. The Dehra Dun–Varanasi Express #4266 covers the 850km to Varanasi in 20hr. Local trains on the branch line to Rishikesh aren't that useful in view of the excellent and more frequent road connections.

Buses to Delhi leave from Station Bus Stand almost every half-hour (5–6hr; fare roughly Rs100). Five or six buses per day leave for Agra, 368km south (10hr; around Rs110). Similarly, numerous buses leave for Rishikesh, 24km north (Rs12), and Dehra Dun 57km northwest, as well as Shimla, Nainital and Almora. The Taxi Association near the railway station sets prices slightly higher than those quoted elsewhere; a taxi to Delhi costs Rs1300, and Rs300 to Rishikesh. Shared Vikrams or tempos ply the route to Rishikesh and provide a cheap if cramped alternative for Rs10. Travellers heading into the mountains should go to Rishikesh to pick up onward transport.

See Travel Details at the end of this chapter for more information on journey frequencies and durations.

Rajaji National Park and around

Around 830 square kilometres of the Himalayan foothills immediately east of Haridwar are taken up by **RAJAJI NATIONAL PARK** (mid-Nov to mid-June; Rs100 for three days, Rs50 each additional day, plus Rs20 per vehicle, Rs500 with video camera), which belongs to the same forest belt as Corbett National Park, 180km east. Although not geared for tourism to the same extent as Corbett, the park is absolutely beautiful, with a similar range of wildlife – most notably elephants, but also antelope, leopard and even a rare species of anteater – although no tigers. There are eight entry gates into the national park including **Kunnao** close to Rishikesh and the main gates at **Chila**, 9km east of Haridwar by road, across the Ganges. **Accommodation** is available at four forest rest houses within the park and is bookable through the Rajaji National Park Office, 5/1 Ansari Marg, Dehra Dun (☎ 0135/621669). However, visitors don't have to go into the core area to experience the jungles, as it's possible to venture in from Chila or Rishikesh, or from the road between the two, which runs parallel to the canal marking the boundary of the huge fringe forest.

Chila

To get to **CHILA** from Haridwar, catch a Kandi- or Kandra-bound **bus** from the stand opposite the railway station, or a shared **Jeep** from Chandi Ghat opposite Har-ki-Pairi. You could even **walk**; Chila is visible from Haridwar, and taking a short cut from Har-ki-Pairi via the riverbeds and a bridge makes it a journey of just 4km east. The town itself is neither attractive nor interesting, located right beside the Ganges barrage and its massive electricity pylons. However, it makes a good base for explorations of the park, and **Chila Beach** – occasionally used by large river turtles – lies within walking distance through the woods, 1km north along the Ganges. **Elephant rides** from here cost **around Rs200 for two hours.**

Accommodation is available at the large GMVN *Chila Tourist Centre* (℡ 0135/420343; ❷–❹), which has a dorm (Rs100), standard and a/c rooms, huts and camping facilities.

Bindevasani and forest trails

Along the Kimsar road, which penetrates the deep *sal* forests northeast of Chila, visitors have a reasonable chance of glimpsing **wild elephant**. Elephant herds migrate here seasonally from as far away as Corbett, and can sometimes be seen in the forests behind Swarg Ashram in Rishikesh. The tiny hamlet of **BINDEVASANI**, 14km northeast of Chila and linked to both Chila and Haridwar by regular buses, stands at the foot of steep hills. Besides a small *dharamshala* and a teashop, there's little here to detain travellers, but it's possible to camp in the covered forecourt of the small clifftop Durga temple, which affords dramatic views over the confluence of the Bindedhara and Nildhara rivers. For around 4km before Bindevasani, the road follows a vast riverbed, dry and extremely hot in summer and fordable during the rainy season.

A copious network of **trails** laces through the hills around Bindevasani. Possible routes include one to the village and temple of **Nilkantha** (14km north; one to **Lakshmanjhula** (20km northwest), the bridge and roadhead near Rishikesh; and one to the remote hamlet of **Yamkeshwar** (22km northeast), where a small Shiva temple on the banks of the Ravasan is surrounded by deep forest.

Rishikesh and around

RISHIKESH, 238km northeast of Delhi and 24km north of Haridwar, lies at the point where the wooded mountains of Garhwal rise abruptly from the low valley floor and the Ganges crashes onto the plains. The centre for all manner of New Age and Hindu activity, its many ashrams – some ascetic, some opulent – continue to draw devotees and followers of all sorts of weird, wonderful and occasionally fraudulent gurus, with the large **Shivananda Ashram** in particular renowned as a yoga centre.

Rishikesh has one or two ancient shrines, but its main role has always been as a way-station for *sannyasin, yogis* and *sadhus* heading for the high Himalayas. The arrival of the Beatles, who came here to meet the Maharishi in 1968, was one of the first manifestations of the lucrative expansion of the *yatra* pilgrimage circuit; these days it's easy to see why Ringo thought it was "just like Butlin's". By far the best times to visit are in winter and spring, when the

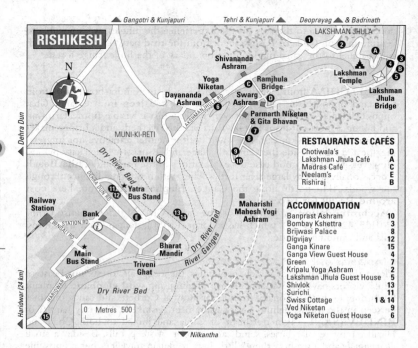

▲ Gangotri & Kunjapuri   Tehri & Kunjapuri ▲   Deoprayag ▲ & Badrinath

RISHIKESH

LAKSHMAN JHULA

N

Shivananda Ashram

Yoga Niketan

Dayananda Ashram

Ramjhula Bridge

Swarg Ashram

Lakshman Temple

Lakshman Jhula Bridge

Parmarth Niketan & Gita Bhavan

MUNI-KI-RETI

Dry River Bed

GMVN ⓘ

Yatra Bus Stand

Railway Station

Bank

Maharishi Mahesh Yogi Ashram

Main Bus Stand

Bharat Mandir

Triveni Ghat

Dry River Bed

River Ganges

Dry River Bed

0 Metres 500

RESTAURANTS & CAFÉS

Chotiwala's	D
Lakshman Jhula Café	A
Madras Café	C
Neelam's	E
Rishiraj	B

ACCOMMODATION

Banprast Ashram	10
Bombay Kshettra	3
Brijwasi Palace	8
Digvijay	12
Ganga Kinare	15
Ganga View Guest House	4
Green	7
Kripalu Yoga Ashram	2
Lakshman Jhula Guest House	5
Shivlok	13
Surichi	11
Swiss Cottage	1 & 14
Ved Niketan	9
Yoga Niketan Guest House	6

▼ Nilkantha

mountain temples are shut by the snows. In the absence of the *yatra* razzmatazz, you can get a sense of the tranquillity that was the original appeal of the place. At other times, a walk upriver leads easily away from the bustle to secluded spots among giant rocks ideally suited for yoga, meditation or an invigorating dip in the cold water.

Confusingly, the name Rishikesh is applied to a loose association of five distinct sections, encompassing not only the town but also hamlets and settlements on both sides of the river: **Rishikesh** itself, the commercial and communications hub; sprawling suburban **Muni-ki-Reti**; **Shivananda Nagar**, just north; the assorted ashrams around **Swarg Ashram** on the east bank, and the riverbank temples of **Lakshmanjhula**, a little further north.

The **telephone codes** for Rishikesh are ☏ 0135 and ☏ 01364 unless you're dialling within a 75km radius of Rishikesh, in which case the ☏ 0135 code changes to ☏ 92135.

The Town

Most of the pilgrims who pass through Rishikesh on their way to the Himalayan shrines of the Char Dham pause for a dip and puja at what is left of the large sandy expanse of **Triveni Ghat**, close to the centre of town. Large, outlandish statues of the heroes of Hinduism have recently sprouted up along the *ghat* giving it an air of a theme park. The river here looks especially spectacular during *arati* (evening worship), when *diya* lights float on the water. Nearby, at **Bharat Mandir**, Rishikesh's oldest temple, a black stone image of

Ashrams, yoga and meditation

Due to an ongoing dispute with the government, Maharishi Mahesh Yogi's beautifully situated ashram, home to the Beatles in 1968, is not presently open to foreigners; it stands empty on a high forested bluff above the river. However, plenty of other ashrams in Rishikesh welcome students of yoga, and offer courses of varying duration – from one day to several months – and cost. In addition, a **Yoga Week** is held at the *Hotel Ganga Kinare* (☏ 01364/431658; ring to confirm location) every year around the first week in February. The intensive course, based on Iyengar Yoga, costs $600 per head, which includes all accommodation and food. Cheaper yoga courses are available at Sri Ved Niketan Ashram (Rs300/week).

Shivananda Ashram. Large institution, with branches all over the world, run by the Divine Life Society and founded by the remarkable Swami Shivananda (who passed into what his followers refer to as *maha samadhi*, final liberation, in 1963). It places an emphasis on the philosophy of Advaitya Vedanta, based on the belief of the non-dual Brahman, or godhead as the undivided self, and has a well-stocked library, a forest retreat, and a charitable hospital with allopathic, homeopathic and Ayurvedic treatment. Courses in meditation and other forms of yoga, plus other activities, are always going on. To arrange a long-term stay, contact the Secretary two months in advance (Divine Life Society, PO Shivanandanagar 249162, Tehri District, Garwhal, UP, ℱ 01364/430040).

Brahma Niwas. Towards the river near Kailash Gate in Muni-ki-Reti, Swami Kaivalyananda delivers a no-nonsense, shoot-from-the-hip interpretation of Vedanta that may not agree with some.

Dayananda Vedanta Ashram. Near Shivananda Ashram; lectures on Vedanta and yoga classes.

Omkarananda Ashram. Above Yoga Niketan, and also known as Durga Mandir; kindergarten school, plus classes which include classical Indian music and dance. Morning and evening tours.

Vanamli Gita Yogashram. On an idyllic site overlooking the river at Tapovan near Lakshman Jhula and offering short courses on different aspects of yoga (☏ 01364/431316).

Ved Niketan Huge Ashram. Across the river south of Swarg Ashram. Yoga classes early in the morning and evening lectures (☏ 01364/430279).

Yoga Niketan. Meditation centre. Reached by a path adjacent to Shivananda Ashram. Founded by the late Swami Yogeshwarananda, it offers a range of courses, with accommodation if necessary (☏ 01364/430227).

Yoga Study Centre. Reputable school for the Iyengar form of Hatha yoga, 1km south of central Rishikesh at Koyelgati (☏ 01364/431196).

Vishnu is supposed to have been consecrated by Shankara in the ninth century; the event is commemorated during Basant Panchami, to mark the first day of spring.

The dense-knit complex of cafés, shops and ashrams collectively known as **Swarg Ashram**, opposite Shivananda Ashram backs on to forest-covered hills where caves are still inhabited by *sadhus*. The river can be crossed at this point either on the Ram Jhula footbridge, or on **ferries**, which operate between 8am and 7pm according to demand (Rs4 one-way, Rs6 return). Women on either side sell ultra-small change to give to the many beggars, and kids sell fish food to throw off the bridge for the fat carp. Swarg Ashram itself, popularly referred to as Kale Kumbli Wale, was founded in honour of Swami Vishudhanand, who came here in 1884 and habitually wore a black (*kala*) blanket (*kumble*). The most conspicuous of the other ashram-temples is **Parmarth Niketan**, whose large courtyard is crammed with brightly clad gods and goddesses. **Gita Bhavan** runs a free Ayurvedic dispensary here, as well as selling books and *khadi*, handloom cloth.

Around 2km north of Swarg Ashram, a path skirts the east bank of the river, and beautiful sandy beaches sheltered by large boulders, en route to **Lakshmanjhula**. A footbridge spans the river here as it negotiates its final rocky course out of the mountains. It's the most appealing part of Rishikesh, although made less so by ugly temples and ashrams, for example the huge **Kailashananda Ashram** which resembles a gaudy multistorey car park. The attractive landscape and turquoise river are best appreciated from the German bakery on the west side where travellers spend days watching daredevil monkeys cavorting on the bridge.

Practicalities

Far more visitors arrive in Rishikesh by road or rail than at the airport, 18km west. The **Main Bus Stand**, used by Haridwar and Dehra Dun government buses, as well as direct services to and from Delhi (6hr), is on Bengali Road, close to the centre; buses for the Garhwal hills use the **Yatra Bus Stand**, also known as the **Tehri Bus Stand**, off the Dehra Dun Road. Rishikesh is at the end of a small branch **railway** line, served by trains to and from Haridwar. Advance reservations can be made from the station, which only has a small quota of seats.

Local transport connecting the main areas includes cycle and auto-rickshaws and shared Vikrams; the fare from Rishikesh to Lakshmanjhula is Rs40 (Rs4 shared ride). Some head south towards Haridwar, but few go all the way. **Cars** and **taxis** can be rented through the reliable Ajay Travels, at the *Hotel Nilkanth*,

---

Panch Prayag – the five holy confluences

Legend relates that as Ganga descended to earth at the behest of the gods to deliver penance to the mortal people, she fell onto Shiva's head and flowed down his matted locks; these strands are the mountain valleys whose churning rivers eventually meet to form the holy river Ganges before she emerges onto the plains of northern India. Five sacred confluences and tributaries mark the successive stages of her journey.

The Alaknanda, which rises near Badrinath, meets the Dhauli Ganga river 10km north of Joshimath at Vishnuprayag, in a deep valley hidden from the sun for most of the day. A few shrines are all that mark the dramatic, rocky confluence. At the small town of Nandprayag on the Uttarkashi road, the river is joined by the Nandakini tributary. The Alaknanda meets the Pindar 21km later, dropping from Nanda Devi, at the market town of Karnaprayag, named after a character in the Mahabharata.

The Alaknanda continues on its turbulent way down to the town of Rudraprayag where it joins the Mandakini river, flowing from its source at Kedarnath; the bustling commercial centre is also famous as the place where Jim Corbett (see p.409) shot a man-eating leopard. The Alaknanda then descends through the open valley of Srinagar before its final and most dramatic mountain confluence, Deoprayag. Here it meets the Bhagirathi, a river of equal importance, which descends from Gomukh on the glacier above Gangotri, and the two become the Ganges as it heads first to Rishikesh, 68km away, and then to Haridwar, where it emerges onto the northern plains. The two mighty rivers meet with great force at a promontory of rock, where temples and a *ghat* extend into the confluence.

Haridwar Road (℡01364/430644), or through the UP Tourism-approved Mahamaya Travels, Urvasi Complex, Dehra Dun Road (℡01364/432968). Rishikesh, like many of the hill towns, is increasingly turning to seasonal tourism, and a negative impact of this has been the dramatic rise of unregulated tour and **travel operators** with no insurance cover for their drivers and cars, or for you. Ask for recommended travel agents at your hotel or at the tourist office. Long-distance journeys can be booked at Triveni Travels, Shop No 1, opposite the Garwhal Co-op Bank, Haridwar Road (℡01364/430989).

The friendly and helpful **UP Tourist Office**, Nehru Park, Station Road (Mon–Sat 10am–5pm, closed 2nd Sat of each month; ℡01364/430209), provides information only. **GMVN** on Lakshmanjhula Road in theory exists to promote tourism in the region from their headquarters in Muni-ki-Reti (℡01364/430372), but in practice restrict themselves to selling their own tours or to booking accommodation in one of their tourist lodges. Their **Mountaineering and Trekking** division (℡01364/430799), however, rents basic equipment, arranges guides, and provides information which may not always be conclusive; they also organize ski trips to Auli (see p.399). You may find one of the private operators situated around here such as Vicky Tiwari at the Tourist Information and Facilitation Desk, opposite the Punjab National Bank, Muni-ki-Reti (℡01364/431654), more use; they also organize **rafting** on the Ganges. Most of the established river camps on the Ganges above Rishikesh operate from the end of September to mid-December, and from mid-February until late April; they can arrange rafting excursions varying in length from one-day runs to extended camping-rafting expeditions, but they must be booked in Delhi. Two very reputable operators are Himalayan River Runners (℡011/685 2602, ✉hrr@ndb.usn1.net.in), who offer three-day packages for around Rs5000, and Snow Leopard (℡011/689 1473, 🌐www.snowleopardadventure.com).

Banks in town include the State Bank of India, Railway Lok, near *Inderlok Hotel* (℡01364/430114), and the Bank of Baroda, Dehra Dun Road (both Mon–Sat 10am–2pm) for Visa card withdrawals.

Accommodation

Rishikesh town has plenty of hotels but it's a noisy and polluted place and the only reason to stay here is to be near the bus station and amenities. Muni-ki-Reti is not too far and slightly more pleasant. New Agers tend to stay around Swarg Ashram and the east bank of the river, away from the noise and near the ashrams, while budget travellers head for the cheap little guesthouses of Lakshmanjhula, which feature hot water by bucket.

Banprast Ashram, next to Ved Niketan, Swarg Ashram (no phone). Well-maintained bungalows at very good rates, in attractive grounds within a walled enclosure. Entry is discretionary. Close to the river and quiet. ①

Bombay Kshettra, Lakshmanjhula (no phone). Basic accommodation with shared baths off a leafy courtyard catering for the discerning ascetic. Handy for exploring the unspoilt upper reaches of this stretch of the river. ①

Brijwasi Palace, Swarg Ashram ℡01364/435918. New hotel next to the *Green* and built, one suspects, to take its overflow. Large airy rooms with huge double beds in a rather anonymous complex. The garden is quite nice though. ②

Digvijay, Yatra Bus Stand ℡01364/431528. Good value, pleasant and roomy – possibly the best of the budget hotels around the bus stand. ②

Ganga View Guesthouse, Lakshmanjhula. Budget place perched voyeuristically above a *ghat* beside the bridge. Tiny rooms with poky bathrooms but cheap. ①

Green, Swarg Ashram ℡01364/431242. Popular little traveller hotel tucked behind *Gita Bhavan* ashram with a roof terrace. All rooms have attached baths, and a restaurant serves underspiced Indian and Italian food. ②–③

Kripalu Yoga Ashram, Lakshmanjhula Road ℡01364/430599. An Italian-American initiative, situated high on the hillside in lovely woods.

Simple ashram rooms around leafy gardens dotted with open hut areas for eating, yoga and meditation. ●

Lakshmanjhula Guesthouse, Lakshmanjhula Road (no phone). New, friendly, basic place with a rooftop restaurant. and hot water by bucket. One of many small new budget hotels in the area, all pretty similar. ●–②

Shivlok, Lakshmanjhula Road, Muni-ki-Reti ☎ 01364/431055. Moderately comfortable, mid-priced hotel lying close to the bridge and handy for town. ③–④

Surichi, Yatra Bus Stand ☎ 01364/432269. Modern and well-maintained hotel, with a good restaurant. Convenient for buses for the Char Dham, if a bit far from the river. ④–⑥

Swiss Cottage, Chandra Bhaga (no phone). Run by the affable Swami Brahmananda, once one of Swami Shivananda's inner group of disciples. Near the bridge and down unnamed lanes towards the river, a small but peaceful haven with nine rooms in a motley selection of buildings. Not an ashram, but popular with long-term visitors, and extremely good value, so often booked up. ●

Ved Niketan, Swarg Ashram. Enormous and gaudy ashram, far south on the east bank of the river, and very popular with low-budget Westerners. ●

Yoga Niketan Guesthouse, Laksh manjhula Road ☎ 01364/433537. You don't have to involve yourself in any of the ashram activities to stay here, though guests are asked to obey an 11pm curfew and not to smoke. Spotlessly clean, good value and right next to the river, so worth considering. ③

Eating

In addition to the **restaurants** in the larger hotels, Rishikesh has plenty of cafés and *dhabas*. Rishikesh is a vegetarian town.

Chotiwala's, Swarg Ashram. Two neighbouring establishments with the same name vie for custom and constantly attempt to outdo each other; their latest marketing gimmick is to have a man outside dressed and painted as the mythical *choti wallah* and ringing a bell. The one closest to the river has slightly better service and a congenial roof terrace. Both places are large, busy and open at 7am for breakfast. An extensive menu includes ice cream, sweets and cold drinks, while a thali costs around Rs35.

Laksh manjhula Cafe, Laks manjhula. Just above the bridge on the town side of the river. An outlet of the German bakery chain, where you can enjoy superb cakes and coffee as you watch the Ganges and the pilgrims flow past. Also a New Age bookshop.

Madras Cafe, Shivananda Nagar. Near the ferry and the tempo stand. Strong on south Indian food but a little pricier than it should be.

Neelam's, off Haridwar Road. Towards the bridge and Muni-ki-Reti, this legendary Sikh-run *dhaba* is always filled with foreign travellers. It's easy to miss – look for the small sign on the left just before the bridge. The Western-oriented food is worth braving the crowds for, and the manager, Mr Singh, is extremely helpful. The only place in town that will make an omelette (discreetly of course).

Rishiraj, Lakshmanjhula Road, New, big and very professional traveller place with pizza and macaroni (Rs60), and its own bakery with cinammon rolls and the like. Has a pleasant terrace and a noticeboard. It gets busy so service can be slow.

Char Dham buses

During the April to November pilgrimage season, when the **Char Dham** temples are open in the Garhwal Hills, direct buses connect Rishikesh's Yatra Bus Stand with **Badrinath** (297km), **Kedarnath** (210km, via Gaurikund), **Gangotri** (250km), and **Yamunotri** (280km, via Hanuman Chatti). Book at least a day in advance as buses start to leave around 4am and few complete the journey in a day; the roads are treacherous and tedious, so you might prefer to break the journey along the way.

GMVN in Muni-ki-Reti organizes **package tours** (a four-day trip to Badrinath, including bus, food and lodging, costs around Rs2000), as well as very expensive car rental. Sharma Travels, Haridwar Road (☎ 01364/430364), has a fleet of press cars leaving around 5am to carry newspapers to various points in the mountains including Joshimath and Uttarkashi. Slightly more expensive and often cramped and uncomfortable, this is nevertheless a much faster way of getting to the interior than by bus.

Around Rishikesh: local treks

Although a road has now been blasted through the forest to the small Shiva shrine in the hamlet of **Nilkanth Mahadev** or simply Nilkantha, east of Rishikesh, it's still possible to walk there along the old pilgrim path. This beautiful forest track rises through the forests behind Swarg Ashram, passes Mahesh Yogi's ashram, and eventually crosses a spur before descending to Nilkantha. There's a chance you may encounter wildlife along the way; keep a safe distance from wild elephants. Nilkantha itself is changing, as an ever-growing number of pilgrims travel along the new road that has cut a swathe through the forests from Lakshmanjhula. Its small bazaar and *dharamshala* become especially animated for around a month from mid-July, when pilgrims flock to the temple, which commemorates the time when the god drank the poison of creation and ended up with a blue (*nil*) throat (*kantha*). The motorable track north of Lakshmanjhula follows the river, passing several good beaches before arriving at the beautiful ashram of Phulcchatti (10km) on a bend in the river with giant boulders and excellent swimming.

Another hike leads high above Lakshmanjhula for ten kilometres to the small white Shakti temple of **Kunjapuri**, at the sharp point of an almost perfectly conical hill with stupendous views of the Himalayas to the north and towards Haridwar to the south. Try to catch the sunrise from the top, before the haze seeps into the atmosphere. A less strenuous alternative is to take the bus to Hindola Khal on the road to Tehri and walk the remaining 3km to the temple.

The trek to Yamunotri

Cradled in a deep cleft in the lap of Bandarpunch, and thus denied mountain vistas, the temple of **Yamunotri** (3291m), 223km northeast of Rishikesh, marks the source of the Yamuna, India's second holiest river after the Ganges. The least dramatic but most beautiful of the four *dhams* (temples) of Garhwal, it's also the most unspoiled and the least commercial, and the undemanding fourteen-kilometre (5hr) trek up to it from **Hanuman Chatti** is one of the region's most popular short hikes. The trail leads through attractive countryside, following the turbulent ice-blue river as it runs below terraced fields, with snowy peaks in the distance. The trek can also be combined with the longer Dodi Tal trek linking Hanuman Chatti to Uttarkashi (see the box on p.389).

Hanuman Chatti

The bleak roadhead for the Yamunotri trek, **Hanuman Chatti**, is connected by bus with Dehra Dun, Mussoorie, and Rishikesh. Some routes require a change at **Barkot**, 29km short, which has a GMVN *Tourist Bungalow* (❷–❺) and several other basic hotels. Buses and shared taxis (about Rs30) run the last leg up from there along a road which is prone to landslides. Hanuman Chatti itself also holds a large GMVN *Tourist Bungalow* (❷–❺) with good dorms, pleasantly situated down by the river, and a couple of basic hotels up at the bus stand. Most trekkers pass straight through, however, and stay in the more hospitable and sunny village of **Janki Chatti**. Simple meals are available either at the bungalow or at cafés around the bus stand.

The path to Yamunotri leads up across a bridge from Hanuman Chatti to meet the trail to Dodi Tal (see p.389), then veers left along the Yamuna for 6km to **Phul Chatti** where a couple of teashops serve basic food. If you're planning any more ambitious trekking than the hike up to Yamunotri, you're strongly advised to secure the aid of a local **guide**; Tota Ram and the older Shankar

Singh are based in Phul Chatti from May until October, and others can be found in Hanuman Chatti.

Janki Chatti

The main trail from Phul Chatti continues along the river and over a bridge. A short and narrow section then traverses a landslide high above the river, before widening to reach **JANKI CHATTI**. Its GMVN *Tourist Bungalow* (❷–❺) is friendly, and has its own café. GMVN also runs a simpler hostel with dormitories (Rs100), down by the river. Also along the main trail, the *Ganga Jamuna* (❸) and the cheaper *Arvind Ashram* (❶–❷) are alternatives, and there are a number of decent restaurants offering thalis, cold drinks and snacks. While you're in Janki Chatti, it's worth making the one-kilometre detour across the river to the traditional Garhwali village of **Kharsali**, home to the *pandas* (pilgrim priests) of Yamunotri. Amongst the drystone buildings with their beautifully carved wooden beams stands a unique three-storey Shiva temple – dedicated to Someshwar, lord of the mythical intoxicant Soma.

Yamunotri

A short way beyond Janki Chatti, the trail becomes much steeper but increasingly dramatic and beautiful as it passes through rocky forested crags to **YAMUNOTRI**. Sited near the river, around three piping-hot sulphur springs, Yamunotri's temple is new and architecturally uninteresting; it has to be completely rebuilt every few years due to the impact of heavy winter snows and monsoon rains. Its main shrine – actually part of the top spring, worshipped as the source of the river – holds a small silver image of the goddess Yamuna, bedecked with garlands. The daughter of Surya, the sun, and Sangya, consciousness, Yamuna is the twin sister of Yama, the lord of death; all who bathe in her waters are spared a painful end, while food cooked in the water is considered to be *prasad* (divine offering). If you choose to **stay** in Yamunotri, there's a simple dormitory (Rs50) at the GMVN *Tourist Bungalow* (❹–❻) near the temple. Probably the best of the few *dharamshalas* is the *Ramananda Ashram* (Rs100), commanding good views from the hill above the temple, and owned by the head priest. Simple food arrangements can be made through the ashrams and the bungalow. Below the temple, a bridge leads across the river to a small complex of tea stalls and shops selling paraphernalia for worship.

Technically, the source of the Yamuna is the glacial lake of **Saptarishi Kund**. This is reached via a hard twelve-kilometre trek, which heads straight up the mountain alongside the river until finally easing towards the base of Kalinda Parbat. Both this trek, and the route over the challenging Yamunotri Pass to Har-ki-Dun (see p.376) necessitate at least one day's acclimatization, adequate clothing, supplies and a guide.

Uttarkashi

The largest town in the interior of Garhwal, **UTTARKASHI** was little-known to the outside world until its unhappy association with the massive nearby earthquake in 1992. The town occupies the flat and fertile valley floor of the Bhagirathi; most pilgrims and tourists stop here to break the long journey between Rishikesh, 148km south, and Gangotri, 100km northeast. Uttarkashi's busy and well-stocked market is ideal for picking up supplies before high-altitude treks, and the town is also a good place to contact experienced mountain guides – mostly graduates of its Nehru Institute of

The relatively short Dodi Tal trek, which links the Gangotri and Yamunotri regions without straying into high glacial terrain, is one of Garhwal's all-time classics. It's not a difficult hike, but local villagers are keen to offer their services as porters or guides, and you should definitely avail yourself of their help if you want to wander off the beaten track and visit the villages. Carry as much of your own food as possible, and also your own tent. The best maps for this trek are the Ground Survey map of Garhwal, and Leomann map (sheet 7 in the India Series), both available from major UP tourism offices.

The trek is described below from east to west, starting from Uttarkashi on the way to Gangotri, and ending at Hanuman Chatti, the roadhead for Yamunotri.

On DAY 1, catch one of the three daily buses from Uttarkashi to Kalyani (1829m) via Gangotri (the first is at 7am, and takes 1hr). From Kalyani, a good but steep trail rises through open fields to Agoda (2286m), 7km on. Stop for the night at the basic *Tourist Bungalow* (❶), at the far end of the village, however tempted you may be to press on. You'll need a carry-mat to sleep on.

On DAY 2, the trail from Agoda climbs beside a river and then zigzags steadily upwards through lush pine and spruce forests, with a couple of chai shops en route. After 14km and a final undulation, it arrives at Dodi Tal (3024m), a lake set against a backdrop of thickly forested hills. Near the basic forest bungalow in the clearing are chai shops and areas for camping.

Some trekkers consider the full 18km from Dodi Tal to Shima on DAY 3 too long and arduous, and prefer to split it into two days. Follow the well-marked path along (and often across) the stream that feeds Dodi Tal, which can get steep and entail scrambling; continue straight ahead, ignoring tracks that cross the trail, until you emerge above the treeline. After a further 1.5km the trail heads left to a small pass then zigzags up scree to Darwa Top (4130m). This is the highest point of the trek, providing superb panoramas of the Srikanta Range. If you're ready to rest here, a leftward path beyond the top leads to camping and water. The main route goes down to a valley and then climbs sharply again. Shima, where you rejoin the tree-line, has basic hut accommodation; bring your own food.

The beautiful twelve-kilometre trail down from Shima on DAY 4 kicks off with a steep 1.5km scramble alongside a stream, then eases past forest and *bugyal*, where shepherds have their huts. A well-defined rocky path drops steadily through two villages and zigzags down to the Hanuman Ganga river. It emerges at Hanuman Chatti (see p.387) from where buses run via Barkot to Uttarkashi, Mussoorie and other points in Garhwal. The Dodi Tal trek can easily be tied in with hikes in the Har-ki-Dun and Yamunotri areas; see also p.376.

Mountaineering. The going rates stand at around Rs150 per porter and Rs300–350 for a guide. Specialist operators include Mount Support, PO Box 2, B D Nautial Bhawan, Bhatwari Road (℡01374/2419), on the main road near the bus stand, who also have equipment for rent.

Practicalities

All **buses** to and from Uttarkashi – which has hourly services to both Gangotri and Rishikesh between May and November – stop on the main highway, near the bazaar between the road and the river. **Taxis** can be picked up in the market area; a seat in a shared Jeep to Gangotri costs Rs100 per person. On the main drag, the information-only **tourist office** (Mon–Sat 10am–5pm; ℡01374/2290) is almost hidden behind the queues of noisy buses.

Good and reasonably priced **lodges** in the quieter lanes off the main road include the *Meghdoot* (❷–❹), with some a/c rooms. GMVN's poorly run *Tourist Bungalow* (❺), around 1km away near the bridge, is a large faceless complex with a garden, cheap dorms (Rs50) and spacious rooms with attached baths; the GMVN *Travellers Lodge* (②–④) tucked behind the tourist office is much better value. Of the many lodges that line the main road, the *Bandhari* (②–③) has a range of clean doubles, some with hot water and TV, and a restaurant. Among the many *bhojanalaya* (veg cafés), in central Uttarkashi, *Roopam* on the main road serves healthy local cuisine with dhal and fresh roti.

Gangotri and around

Set amid tall *deodar* pine forests at the head of the Bhagirathi gorge, 248km north of Rishikesh at 3140m, **Gangotri** is the most remote of the four *dhams* (pilgrimage sites) of Garhwal. Although the wide Alaknanda, which flows past Badrinath, has in some ways a better claim to be considered the main channel of the Ganges, Gangotri is for Hindus the spiritual source of the great river, while its physical source is the ice cave of **Gomukh** on the Gangotri Glacier, 14km further up the valley. From here, the **River Bhagirathi** begins its tempestuous descent through a series of mighty gorges, carving great channels and cauldrons in the rock and foaming in white-water pools.

From Uttarkashi, frequent buses, taxis and Jeeps head up to Gangotri; walking is also a pleasant albeit slow option. A shared Jeep should cost no more than Rs120 per head and is probably the most enjoyable way of making the journey, stopping for chai at little hamlets along the way. Parts of the road beyond Gangnani, where the vast and fertile Bhagirathi flood plain is famous for its apple orchards, were damaged by the earthquake in 1992; gigantic blocks of rock almost dammed the river and created a lake. Off the main road down a rough track 31km along, **Harsil** marks the bottom limit of the Gangotri gorge. The village itself is grubby and depressing, with a large army base, but there's a *Tourist Bungalow* (②–⑤; no phone) pleasantly situated beside the river. A stone path leads along the valley floor and over a couple of bridges to an appealing Bhotia village. Prayer flags flutter over the small Buddhist temple of Vagori, standing amid the apple trees in a small garden. Ten kilometres beyond Harsil, the road crosses the deep Bhagirathi gorge at **Lanka**, on a dramatic bridge said to be among the highest in the world. This is an army area, so don't take any photographs. At the hamlet of **Bhaironghati**, 3km further on and 11km short of Gangotri, the Rudragaira emerges from its own gorge to meet the Bhagirathi. A small temple stands in towering *deodar* forests, and there are a few teashops as well as a barely used GMVN *Tourist Bungalow* with dorm accommodation (Rs100).

Gangotri ashrams

Although most of the so-called "ashrams" in Gangotri are in reality boarding houses, a few *sadhus* offer rooms on a donation basis for visitors looking for a quiet retreat. The simple, atmospheric **Kailash Ashram**, overlooking the confluence of the Kedar Ganga and the Bhagirathi, is run (along with a small Ayurvedic clinic) by the affable Bhim Yogi, who welcomes guests for medium- and long-term stays. Nearby, **Nani Mata's Ashram** belongs to an English *mataji* (female *sadhu*), who has lived in Gangotri for many years and is held in high esteem. Above Kailash Ashram, the larger **Yoga Niketan Ashram**, set in an attractive garden, operates along much more regimented lines, with fixed meal times and meditation periods, and a fixed fee of Rs200, which includes morning yoga classes.

Gangotri

Although most of the nearby snow peaks are obscured by the desolate craggy mountains looming immediately above **GANGOTRI**, the town itself is redolent of the atmosphere of the high Himalayas, populated by a mixed cast of Hindu pilgrims and foreign trekkers. Its unassuming **temple**, overlooking the river just beyond a small market on the left bank, was built early in the eighteenth century by the Gurkha general Amar Singh Thapa. Capped with a gilded roof, consisting of a squat *shikhara* surrounded by four smaller replicas, it commemorates the legend that the goddess Ganga was enticed to earth by acts of penance performed by King Bhagirath, who wanted her to revitalize the ashes of his people. As she fell from heaven, Shiva braced the impact by entangling her in his locks; she was released by Brahma in answer to further prayers from the pious king. Inside the temple is a silver image of the goddess, while a slab of stone adjacent to the temple is venerated as **Bhagirath Shila**, the spot where the king meditated. Steps lead down to the main riverside *ghat*, where the devout bathe in the freezing waters of the river to cleanse their bodies and souls of sin.

Across the river, a loose development of ashrams and guesthouses dwarfed by great rocky outcrops and huge trees leads down to **Dev Ghat**, overlooking the confluence with the Kedar Ganga. Not far beyond, at the impressive waterfall-fed pool of **Gaurikund**, the twenty-kilometre-long gorge starts to get into its stride. Beautiful forest paths lead through the dark *deodar* woods and past a bridge along the edge of the gorge to a flimsy rope-bridge, commanding great views of the ferocious torrent below.

GMVN's *Tourist Bungalow* (②–⑤), over the footbridge from the bus stand, has a reasonably cheap dorm (Rs100). Next to the main cantilever bridge, the large and popular *Ganga Niketan* (①–③) has a café and supplies shop overlooking the river, and the *Himalaya* (①–③) along the riverside opposite the temple offers basic, friendly accommodation with fantastic views up the valley to the snow peaks. The most attractive of the bungalows, the *Forest Guest House* (①) is a beautiful new log cabin set in immaculate gardens; it can only be booked through the Forestry Department in Uttarkashi. A number of *dhabas* and cafés on both sides of the river serve thalis, good breakfasts and much-needed warming chai.

Gomukh and Gangotri Glacier

A flight of steps alongside the temple at Gangotri leads up to join a large pony path that rises gently, providing stunning mountain vistas, towards the Gangotri Glacier, which has long been regarded as one of the most beautiful and accessible glaciers in the inner Himalayas. Sadly, it is retreating at the rate of almost 1km a year. Two kilometres into the trek, the forest **checkpoint** demands Rs100 (refunded on return) and rather disconcertingly also searches your rucksack, allegedly for potential litter.

Approaching the oasis of **Chirbasa**, 7km out of Gangotri, the skyline is dominated by magnificent buttresses and glass-like walls, culminating in the sharp pinnacles of Bhagirathi 3 (6454m) and Bhagirathi 1 (6856m). Chirbasa amounts to no more than a few chai stalls, which can also provide you with a roof and simple food. The path then climbs above the treeline, continuing along the widening valley to enter a high mountain desert. Just beyond Chirbasa, the trail across a cliff face has badly deteriorated and gusts of wind tend to send small rocks cascading down onto the narrow path, so great care is called for. Soon after crossing a stream, the path rounds a shoulder to offer a glimpse of the glacier's snout near **Gomukh** ("the cow's mouth"), the ever-

present Bhagirathi peaks, and the huge expanse of the Gangotri Glacier – 24km long, and up to 4km wide – sweeping like a gigantic highway through the heart of the mountains.

Down below on the flat valley bottom, 5km from Chirbasa, is the cold grey hamlet of **Bhojbasa**, cowering in the shadow of the beautiful **Shivling Peak** (6543m), where most visitors spend the night before heading on to Gomukh and beyond. If you are planning on trekking any further than Gomukh, then this is a good point at which to stop and acclimatize. The GMVN *Tourist Bungalow* here (❸–❹) provides a dormitory (Rs100), basic double rooms (some with attached bathrooms), and chilly but rodent-free tents. Guests huddle in the evening in the small but friendly café, which is the place to arrange a mountain guide if you plan to cross the glaciers. Accommodation is also available in dorms at the nearby dark and dismal *Ramola* (❶), or at *Lal Baba's Ashram* (❶) which is even more basic – just mattresses on the floor – though food is included in the price here. There is a good campground down by the river if you have your own tent.

If you've stayed in Bhojbasa, it really is worth braving the cold to walk to Gomukh for sunrise. A good track continues from Bhojbasa for 5km to Gomukh, where the river emerges with great force from a cavern in the glacier. The ice is in a constant state of flux, so the huge greyish-blue snout of the glacier continually changes appearance as chunks of ice tumble into the gushing water – be careful of standing above the cave. Two or three chai shops near here provide food and basic shelter, and there are many flat areas for camping.

Tapovan and Nandanvan

The campsites of **Tapovan** and **Nandanvan**, 6km beyond Gomukh on slightly divergent glacier-side routes, are popular objectives for lightweight trekking and mountaineering, and as a rule best attempted using guides engaged from Gangotri or Bhojbasa.

A difficult track leads past the last teashop at Gomukh to ascend the moraine on the left edge of the glacier, following it for 1km before crossing the glacier diagonally towards a high point in the middle, in line with Shivling. Depending on the season, this stage can be confusing and dangerous; heavy snow can conceal deep crevasses and the cairns that mark the way. From the high point, you should be able to see a stream coming down the high bank opposite. Use this as a marker; an extremely steep and strenuous climb up unstable ground runs to its left, to top out eventually on the grassy meadow of **TAPOVAN**, where you're greeted by the fantastic sight of Shivling (6543m) towering above. With its herds of grazing, almost tame *bharal* (mountain goats), and a tranquil stream, the meadow makes a bizarre contrast to the sea of ice below.

Many trekkers arrive in Tapovan without camping equipment, expecting to shelter in either of its two ashrams. However, although Mataji, a female *sadhu* who lives here throughout the year, and Shimla Baba do indeed have small hermitages with blankets, and are prepared to feed visitors, their resources are greatly stretched. Whether or not you stay with them, please carry supplies, which will always be welcome, and bring camping and cooking equipment if you plan to be here more than a day or two.

NANDANVAN lies on a similar but less frequented meadow below the Bhagirathi Peaks, at the junction of the glacier known as the Chaturang Bamak and the Gangotri Glacier. From here you get magnificent views of Bhagirathi, Shivling, and the huge snowy mass of **Kedar Dome** (6831m), hiding a steep sheer rocky face. The trail up follows the same path from Gomukh, but instead of the diagonal slant towards Tapovan, continues across the Raktaban Glacier

Trekking in Tehri Garhwal: Khatling Glacier

The **Khatling Glacier**, source of the Bhilangana, lies at the head of a remote valley between the Gangotri and Kedarnath regions. It forms a huge watershed, with Jaonli (6632m) to the west, the Jogin group (6465m) to the north, and the striking peaks of Kirti Stambh (6270m) and Bharte Kunta (6578m) to the east. The upper Bhilangana valley is virtually unspoiled, with vast tracts of forest, beautiful waterfalls, and mountain streams descending from high *bugyals*.

Trails radiate from the nearest roadhead, **Ghuttu**, 147km north of Rishikesh, to the Bhagirathi to the west, and Sonprayag and the Mandakini valley to the east, while high mountain routes lead to Kedarnath via Khatling, and Uttarkashi via Gomukhi Tal.

Most long-distance bus journeys to Ghuttu involve a change at **Ghansyali** on the Uttarkashi Rudraprayag road, three hours' drive west of Tehri (served by regular buses to and from Rishikesh). Simple hotels and cafés can be found at Ghansyali and Ghuttu.

The Khatling Glacier trail

Day 1 of the moderately strenuous trail up to Khatling Glacier is a gentle introduction, with a mild ascent in the 10km hike from Ghuttu (1524m) to Reeh (2132m). You can stay above **Reeh** in the *Forest Rest House* (❶) at Buranshchauri. An arduous trek of 10km on **Day 2** brings you to the last inhabited village of the valley, **Gangi** (2500m). Continue 6km to camp at Kalyani, a village used by shepherds during the grazing season. **Day 3** leads 14km from **Kalyani**, beyond Kharsoli, to **Bhelbagi** – at 3110m, the base camp for the glacier. On **Day 4**, follow a rough trail up to Khatling Glacier (3658m) for a grand view (weather permitting) of the amphitheatre of snow peaks. Alas, the glacier itself has all but vanished, a victim of global warming. The trip back to **Bhelbagi** is 14km.

On to Kedarnath

Using local guides, acclimatized and well-equipped trekkers can continue past Bhelbagi, beyond Khatling Glacier to **Kedarnath** (see p.397), past a succession of mountain lakes. From Behlbagi, a difficult track leads 7km to **Maser Tal** (4572m),

and follows the left bank of the Gangotri Glacier. If you do get confused and find yourself in Nandanvan by mistake, an indistinct 3km trail across Gangotri Glacier leads back to Tapovan.

Kedar Tal

Kedar Tal, the source of the Kedar Ganga – an emerald lake 5000m above sea level, surrounded by a grand amphitheatre of mountains – makes a challenging objective. Although it's only 17km from Gangotri, the 2000m climb to such an altitude means that trekkers should be well equipped and fully acclimatized to the height.

A steep rough trail through the forest from Dandi Chetra, near Gangotri's Dev Ghat, follows the right bank of the Kedar Ganga for 7.5km to the meadow of **Bhoj Kharak**. At this point – a good campground – the pine woods give way to *bhoj* (birch), whose bark was used to write on before the introduction of paper. Continuing along a stretch made treacherous by rockfall and avalanche, the path rises for 4km above the treeline to reach another *bugyal* (meadow) suitable for camping – **Kedar Kharak**.

From Kedar Kharak, the gruelling 5km ascent to Kedar Tal scrambles over difficult loose terrain directly towards the rocky pinnacle of Thalesagar. Surrounding the beautiful glacial lake at the head of the valley, the cirque of

where pilgrims bathe in the freezing waters. Camping here is recommended, as the icy conditions get extreme at the high Pain Tal (5629m), 7km further on. From there, a track descends through rough terrain for 6km to Vasuki Tal (4328m); you could camp here, but if you're going well and are dying for a chai shop and a good bed, Kedarnath is just 9km further along a well-marked pony track. However, the descent to 3584m can be hard on the legs. From Kedarnath a 14km pony track, often full of pilgrims, leads to the pleasant little town of Gaurikund (see p.396) and the Sonprayag roadhead.

Sahastra Tal

The seven small lakes known as Sahastra Tal lie close to each other, high on the divide between the Bhilangana valley in Tehri Garhwal and the Philangana valley in Uttarkashi, and cradled within rough rocky ground, covered with snow for much of the year. The lakes are venerated by local people in the belief that the Pandavas of the *Mahabharata* inhabited their shores, and built the natural stone terraces to sow their grain. During the rainy season, villagers from both sides of the divide carry deities to the lakes in an annual pilgrimage and perform ceremonies for their dead ancestors.

Although the lakes can be reached along a 35km trek from Malla on the Uttarkashi–Gangotri road, via Shilla and the simple refuge of Dharamshala, the path from Gangi to the highest lake – Gomukhi Tal, on the Bhilangana side – is shorter, and can be combined with the trip to Khatling Glacier. From Kalyani (see above), a rough track that becomes progressively harder to discern rises for 8km to the campsite at Tari Udiyar.

The Sonprayag trail

The major pilgrim path that linked the Gangotri and Uttarkashi region with Kedarnath until the motor road opened leads east from Ghuttu to Sonprayag, with simple shelter and food available along the way. The first stop is the village of Panwali Kanta, 10km out of Ghuttu. Maggu is 6km further on, and the popular temple village of Triyugi Narayan, with its eternal flame, is 5km beyond that. A rough motor road connects Triyugi Narayan to the main road, and a trail of around 3km cuts through the forest to Sonprayag.

mountains include, from left to right, Bhrigupanth (6772m), Thalesagar (6904m) and the Jogin group.

The route to Kedarnath

It's hard to imagine a more dramatic setting for a temple than **Kedarnath**, 223km north of Rishikesh, close to the source of the Mandakini at 3583m above sea level, and overlooked by tumbling glaciers and huge buttresses of ice, snow and rock. Kedarnath – the "field" (*kedara*) where the crop of *moksha* (liberation) is sown – is the most important shrine in the Himalayas, and among the major Shiva temples of all India. According to the *Puranas* (Hindu tales), when the Pandavas were searching for Shiva to grant them absolution, they succeeded in tracking him down to Kedarnath, where he disguised himself as a bull in a herd of cattle. One of the brothers, Bhim, then straddled the valley and allowed the herd to pass beneath him, reasoning that the only bull to refuse must be Shiva himself. When Shiva was unmasked, he dived into the ground; Bhim grabbed him from behind, and held on tight. However, all that remained of the god was his rear; his *lingam* appeared in Varanasi (Kashi), while assorted other pieces of his anatomy are commemorated by the **Panch Kedar temples**. Kedarnath is the third of the sacred Char Dham sites, and as one of India's twelve *jyotrilinga* – *lingams* of light – attracts hordes of Hindu Pilgrims (*yatri*) in the summer months. The area makes a refreshing change from the rocky and desolate valleys of west Garwhal, with lush hanging gorges, immaculately terraced hillsides and abundant apple orchards. Kedarnath is also a good base for short treks to the beautiful lakes of Vasuki Tal and Gandhi Sarovar.

Gaurikund

GAURIKUND, a friendly and bustling small town perched above the roadhead for Sonprayag, marks the starting point of the trek up to the **temple of Kedarnath**, although there are plans to extend the road as far as Rambara. En route to or from chilly Kedarnath, a dip in its **Tapt Kund** hot springs can be very welcome, although sadly they are not well maintained. The small temple of Gauri Devi, adjacent to the pool, is dedicated to Parvati.

Direct **buses** run to Gaurikund all the way from Rishikesh, but most visitors arrive on local buses and taxis from the larger bus terminal at **Guptkashi**, 29km lower down. This receives services from Rudraprayag, 109km south on the busy main Rishikesh–Joshimath–Badrinath route, and Gopeshwar, 138km southeast.

Inexpensive *dharamshalas* and **hotels** in Gaurikund itself include the large grey *Bharat Seva Ashram* (❶), and the *Vijay Tourist Lodge* (❶) which is on the main bazaar road and has clean if basic rooms. Opposite, the *Annapurna* (❷–❹) has large carpeted doubles with sunny balconies and dorms. The squat GMVN *Tourist Centre* (❶–❺) has pricier but cosy doubles, and a cheap dorm. The *Gauri's Grand* **restaurant** is a complete culture shock, with MTV piped through the sound system – however, it is comfortable and clean, and its wide-ranging menu even extends as far as veggie burgers.

The trail from Gaurikund

So popular is Kedarnath on the *yatra* trail that the path up from Gaurikund has been all but stripped of vegetation, used for fuel and to feed the ponies that

---

Shankara in Garhwal

Immediately behind the temple at Kedarnath, towards the glacier, a gigantic hand holding an ascetic's staff protrudes from a marble wall. This modern monument – which, it has to be said, is a complete eyesore – commemorates the ninth-century Hindu philosopher and reformer, **Shankara**, who is said to have died here.

Shankara travelled through the region as the Buddhist era came to a close, introducing sweeping reforms that helped to create the order of *sanyas* (monkhood). Much of his philosophy adheres to the principles of Advaitya Vedanta and its belief in non-dual Brahman or unified consciousness which some modern philosophers see as borrowing heavily from Buddhism.

In Garhwal, he converted fertility and animist cults into Shaivite and Vaishnavite shrines, and helped to establish the great pilgrimage centres such as Kedarnath. The five most sacred of these shrines are collectively known as the **Panch Kedar**. They represent the five (*panch*) parts of Shiva's body that were left protruding from the earth when he escaped the Pandavas by fleeing into the underworld. **Kedarnath** is the receptacle of Shiva's *lingam*; **Madhmaheshwar** in northwest Garhwal holds his navel; Shiva's arms appeared at Tunganath, at 3680m the highest temple in India; his face is said to be found at **Rudranath** and his hair below **Kalpeshwar**, which overlooks the Alknanda valley in the east.

Today, the **Rawal**, who heads both Badrinath and Kedarnath, continues to be chosen from the same Nambudiri sect of Keralan brahmins that Shankara belonged to. Among the four major seats of learning set up by Shankara in the four corners of India, one was nearby in Joshimath.

carry wealthier pilgrims. Chai shops that provide food and shelter along the route, especially in the upper sections, add to the environmental damage.

A large pony track, dotted with chai shops, climbs from Gaurikund, traversing the hillside through the disappearing forests, to the village of **Rambara**, 7km up and halfway to Kedarnath. With its many cafés and rest houses (and open sewers), Rambara signals the end of the treeline and the start of the alpine zone. Several conspicuous short cuts scar the hillside as the track rises steeply to **Garur Chatti**, then levels off roughly 1km short of Kedarnath. Suddenly, rounding a corner, you come face to face with the incredible south face of the peak of Kedarnath (6940m) at the end of the valley, with the temple town dwarfed beneath it and almost insignificant in the distance.

Kedarnath: town and treks

KEDARNATH is not in itself a very attractive town – in fact it's almost unbearable at the height of the pilgrimage season (May, June & Sept). It's a grey place, consisting of a central thoroughfare stretching for 500m between the temple and the bridge, lined with rest houses and *dharamshalas,* pilgrim shops, and administrative offices. However, the sheer power of its location tends to sweep away any negative impressions, and it's always possible to escape to explore the incredible high-altitude scenery.

At the head of the town, the imposing **temple** is constructed along simple lines in stone, with a large *mandapa* (fore-chamber) housing an impressive stone image of Shiva's bull, Nandi. Within the inner sanctum, open to all, *pandas* sit around a rock considered to be Shiva's upraised arse, left here as he plunged head-first into the ground. Mendicant *sadhus* congregate in the elevated courtyard in front of the temple.

A solid path from near the main bridge, before the town, crosses the Mandakini to the left of the valley, and ends 4km away at the **glacier**. At its edge, the **Chorabari Tal** lake is now known as **Gandhi Sarovar**, as some of Mahatma Gandhi's ashes were scattered here. Close by, around 800m before the lake, is the source of the Mandakini; it emerges from a hole in the moraine on extremely suspect ground, which should not be approached. You could also cross the river by the small bridge behind the temple, and scramble up the rough boulder-strewn moraine to meet the main track.

East of town, a well-marked path rises diagonally along the hillside to the prayer flags that mark a small shrine of the wrathful emanation of Shiva – **Bhairava**. The cliff known as **Bhairava Jhamp** is said to be somewhere nearby; until the British banned the practice in the nineteenth century, fanatical pilgrims used to leap to their deaths from it in the hope of gaining instant liberation.

The most challenging of all the Kedarnath excursions is the nine-kilometre trek to the lake of Vasuki Tal (4328m). From the *Tourist Bungalow,* a well-marked pony track zigzags in clear view of Kedarnath, heading up the hill for around 1km before negotiating scree and rough ground near the crest, and descending slightly to Vasuki Tal (see p.395).

Practicalities

Kedarnath's GMVN *Tourist Bungalow* (⊕0137286/6210; ❶–❺), standing like a disused railway station before the bridge that leads into town, has a cheap dorm and standard double rooms. Alternatives include the clean and comfortable *Bharat Seva Ashram* (❶), a large red building beyond the temple on the left; the pleasantly located bungalow of *Modi Bhavan* (❷), behind and above the temple near the monument, which has large rooms and kitchenettes; and *Punjab Sindh* (❶–❷), next to the post office.

Food in the cafés along Kedarnath's main street is simple but expensive, as all supplies have to be brought up from the valley on horseback. The canteen run by the temple committee, *Shri Badrinath Kedarnath Mandi Samiti*, behind the temple, serves meals and *alu paratha*. It is also a good place to contact a mountain **guide**, if you plan to attempt the Vasuki Tal and Khatling crossing.

Joshimath and Auli

The scattered administrative town of **JOSHIMATH** clings to the side of a deep valley 250km northeast of Rishikesh, with tantalizing glimpses of the snow peaks high above, and the prospect far below of the road disappearing into a sunless canyon at Vishnu Prayag, the confluence with the Dhauli Ganga. Few of the thousands of pilgrims who pass through en route to Badrinath linger here, but Joshimath has close links with **Shankara**, the ninth-century reformer, who attained enlightenment here beneath a mulberry tree, before going on to establish **Jyotiramath**, one of the four centres of Hinduism (*dhams*) at the four cardinal points. In winter, when Badrinath is closed, the Rawal, the head priest of both Badrinath and Kedarnath, resides at Joshimath.

Joshimath consists of a long drawn-out upper bazaar, and, around 1km from the main square on the Badrinath road, a lower bazaar which holds the colourful **Narsingh**, **Navadurga**, **Vasudev** and **Gauri Shankar** temples.

Practicalities

Most **buses** and **Jeeps** up to Joshimath stop in the upper bazaar. All motorized transport onwards to Badrinath – and there are plenty of buses during the *yatra* season – is obliged to move in **convoys**. A gate system controls traffic in each direction, in two equal 24-kilometre stages – the first between Joshimath and Pandukeshwar, the second between Pandukeshwar and Badrinath. Several convoys leave Joshimath each day, the first at 6.30am and the last at 4.30pm from the Narsingh temple complex in the lower bazaar. At night the road remains closed.

The local **tourist office** (Mon–Sat 10am–5pm) at Gandhi Maidan is helpful, but for more specific trekking and skiing advice, head for Nanda Devi Mountain Travel, *Hotel Nanda Devi*, Upper Bazaar (℡01389/22170), a local operator that organizes treks and river rafting, and provides guides and equipment.

Rooms at the prison-like GMVN *Tourist Rest House* (℡01389/22118; ❷–❹), at the north end of the upper bazaar, include a dorm (Rs50); a café serves simple meals. Just up from the *Nanda Devi*, *Shailja* (℡01389/22208; ❶–❷) is popular with travellers as the prices are negotiable, and it has a new restaurant serving the usual multi-cuisine in a pleasant courtyard. Small hotels around the main square include the basic *Kamet* (℡01389/22155; ❶–❸): rooms facing the square are the cheapest. A short way south, the friendly *Jyoti Lodge* (℡01389/22123; ❷–❹) is excellent value and has its own trekking agency down in the main bazaar, while the older *Neelkanth* (℡01389/22131; ❷–❹), opposite, has quiet pleasant rooms overlooking the valley. Further south of the centre, *Dronagiri* (℡01389/22254; ❹–❻) may be characterless but it's the most comfortable in town, with good views and a clean restaurant. The traveller-friendly *Paradise* café, next to the *Tourist Rest House*, has a good range of multi-cuisine plus porridge for breakfast, while down at the main square the *Marwari* is a busy and reasonable veg *dhaba* with a small hotel upstairs.

Auli

A rough road winds 15km up through the *deodar* forest from Joshimath to **AULI**, which has recently been developed as a **ski** resort, partly in the hope of replacing the ski areas rendered inaccessible by the war in Kashmir. The longest cable car in Asia, or the **trolley** as it is known locally, connects Joshimath with **Gorson**, above Auli (Rs150 return, no singles). A short distance beyond Gorson lies the hill of Gorson Top, which provides excellent mountain vistas and is on the 24-kilometre trail to Kuari Pass (see p.402). From Gorson, Auli's only chairlift travels to the base lodge (Rs50), a small building marking the start of the ski-runs. At present, all the pistes empty into one central three-kilometre run, arriving at the badly sited GMVN *Tourist Centre*, which faces the wrong way and has no views. Skiing here is cheap – Rs2800 for a seven-day course or a day-trip for around Rs250, including lift charges and the equipment rental. Unfortunately equipment is poor and there are few medical facilities, which is pertinent if you're thinking of trying out the paragliding on offer. Auli's season is short, running from around New Year until March. For up-to-date information on skiing, contact UP Tourism in Delhi (℡011/3322251), or GMVN at Rishikesh (℡01364/430372).

The *Tourist Centre* (℡01389/2226; ❷–❻) has two large dorms with lockable cubicles, and comfortable, if pricey, rooms and suites in its outbuildings. The friendly staff in the dining hall try their best, but don't expect any après-ski activity.

Badrinath

The most popular of the four main temples of Garhwal, 298km northeast of Rishikesh and just 40km south of Tibet, is that of **BADRINATH**, "Lord of the Berries". One of Hinduism's holiest sites, it was founded by Shankara in the ninth century, not far from the source of the Alaknanda, the main tributary of the holy Ganga. Although the temple has a stunning setting, deep in a valley beneath the sharp snowy pyramid of Nilkantha (6558m), the town that has grown up around it is grey, grubby and unattractive.

Until a few years ago, Badrinath was a remote and evocative place, where legends spoke of mysterious *sadhus* such as the Englishman who lived high in the mountains amid the snow and ice. Now, however, it has grown out of all proportion to its infrastructure. The army-built road up from Joshimath, 48km south, brings endless convoys of **buses** and **taxis**, and the temple turns over astronomical amounts of money. Pilgrims crowd in, the streets are lined with mendicant *sadhus* and beggars, and roadside stalls sell all sorts of religious paraphernalia.

Badrinath is still presided over by a Nambudiri brahmin from Kerala – the Rawal, who also acts as the head priest for Kedarnath. According to myth, the two temples were once close enough together for the priest to worship at both on the same day. The **temple** itself, also known as **Badri Narayan**, is dedicated to Vishnu, who is said to have done penance in the mythical Badrivan ("Forest of Berries"), that once covered the mountains of Uttaranchal. Unusually, it is made of wood; the entire facade is repainted each May, once the snows have receded and the temple opens for the season. From a distance, its bright colours, which contrast strikingly with the concrete buildings, snowy peaks and deep blue skies, resemble a Tibetan *gompa*; there's some debate as to whether the temple was formerly a Buddhist shrine. Inside, where photography is strictly taboo, the black stone image of **Badri Vishal** is seated like a *bodhisattva* in the lotus position (some Hindus regard the Buddha as an incarnation of Vishnu). *Pandas* (pilgrim priests) sit around the cloisters carrying on the business of worship and a booth enables visitors to pay in advance for *darshan* (devotional rituals) chosen from a long menu.

This site, on the west bank of the turbulent Alaknanda, may well have been selected because of the sulphurous **Tapt Kund** hot springs on the embankment right beneath the temple, which are used for ritual bathing. Immediately south of the temple, the old **village** of Badrinath is still there, its traditional stone buildings and a small market seeming like relics from a bygone age. A sign on the main road north of Badrinath prohibits foreigners from proceeding further towards Tibet. However, visitors can normally – check the current situation – take local buses 4km on to the end of the road where the intriguing Bhotia village of **Mana** nestles. It's also possible to walk to Mana along a clear footpath by the road. The village itself consists of a warren of small lanes and buildings piled virtually on top of each other; the local Bhotia people, Buddhists of Tibetan origin who formerly traded across the high Mana Pass, now tend livestock and ponies and sell yak meat and brightly coloured, handmade carpets. A path drops from the village to cross a bridge, then continues west along the side valley towards the mountain of Satopanth on the divide between the Mana and Gangotri regions, to the base of the impressive high waterfall of **Vasudhara**. Dropping from a hanging valley, this is considered to be the source of the Alaknanda, where it falls from heaven.

Practicalities

At the **information centre**, run by Badrinath's **Temple Committee**, on the east bank opposite the temple, you can book **rooms** in the various pilgrim rest houses they manage, such as the nearby *Modi Bhavan* (❷), and *Gujarat Bhavan* (❷), next to the temple on the more atmospheric west bank. *Kale Kambli Wale's Ashram* (❶), behind the temple, is also excellent value. The most comfortable option in town is the large GMVN *Devlok* (❷–❻), behind the post office, with accommodation ranging from dorms to deluxe rooms, plus gardens and a restaurant. There are two other GMVN establishments near the new, space-age-style bus stand: the tourist hostel provides simple dorm accommodation (❶–❷); the *Garwhal*, cosy and carpeted doubles and triples (❷–❹). The most atmospheric area for **cafés** and chai shops is the old section close to the temple, but the more commercial east bank holds a few more upmarket neon-lit restaurants, such as *Kwality* and *Saket*, along with numerous *dhabas*, none of them very special.

Traffic back down to Joshimath, including the regular local buses, moves in the same convoy system as on the way up (see p.398). Long-distance buses run direct to Rishikesh – the nearest railway station – with an overnight halt en route, and to Gaurikund near Kedarnath (14hr), bookable at the bus stand office above the town.

Hemkund and the Valley of the Flowers

Starting from the hamlet of **Govind Ghat**, 28km south of Badrinath on the road to Joshimath (local buses will stop on request), an important pilgrim trail winds for 21 steep kilometres up to the snow-melt lake of **Hemkund** (4329m). In the Sikh holy book, the *Guru Granth Sahib*, Govind Singh, recalled meditating at a lake surrounded by seven high mountains; only in the twentieth century was Hemkund discovered to be that lake. A large *gurudwara* (Sikh temple), and a small shrine to Lakshmana, the brother of Rama of *Ramayana* fame, now stand alongside. However, to protect the *deodar* forests along the trail, visitors can no longer spend the night.

Instead, the overgrown village of **Ghangaria**, 6km below Hemkund, serves as a base for day-hikes. It has several chai shops, basic lodges, *gurudwaras* and even a GMVN *Tourist Bungalow*, complete with dormitory (mid-April to mid-Nov; ❷–❺). Govind Ghat too has a large *gurudwara*, run on a donations system.

An alternative trail forks left from Ghangaria, climbing 5km to the mountain *bugyals* of the Bhyundar valley – the **Valley of the Flowers**. Starting at an altitude of 3352m, the valley was discovered in 1931 by the visionary mountaineer, Frank Smythe, who named it, not surprisingly, for its multitude of rare and beautiful plants and flowers. The meadows are at their best towards the end of the monsoons, in early September; they too have suffered at the hands (or rather feet) of large numbers of visitors, so camping is not allowed here either. As a result, it is not possible to explore the ten-kilometre valley in its entirety, in the space of a day's hike from Ghangaria.

Nanda Devi Sanctuary

The majestic twin peaks of **Nanda Devi** – at 7816m, the highest complete mountain in India – dominate a large swathe of northeastern Garhwal and Kumaon. The eponymous goddess is the most important deity for all who live in her shadow, a fertility symbol also said to represent Durga, the virulent form of Shakti. Surrounded by an apparently impenetrable ring of mountains, the fastness of Nanda Devi was long considered inviolable; when mountaineers Eric Shipton and Bill Tilman finally traced a way through, along the difficult **Rishi Gorge**, in 1934, it was seen as a defilement of sacred ground. A string of catastrophes followed; as recently as 1976, an attempt on the mountain by the father and daughter team of Willi and Nanda Devi Unsoeld ended in tragedy, when Nanda Devi Unsoeld died below the summit after which she was named.

The beautiful wilderness around the mountain now forms the **Nanda Devi Sanctuary**. In theory, it's a magnificent place to camp, but it has been closed since 1983 for environmental reasons. Although the Indian Mountaineering Foundation in Delhi has declared the sanctuary open, local wardens do not allow access into the inner sanctuary past Lata Kharak and the Dharansi Pass. As the entire area lies comfortably in India, away from the Tibetan frontier, there is hope that the current easing of border tensions may soon lead to the reopening of the sanctuary; check with KMVN or GMVN in Rishikesh (who also arrange a 15-day trek to the Nanda Devi base camp in the sanctuary), and don't try to go it alone. If the trail does reopen, be prepared for a gruelling sixty-kilometre haul from the village of **Lata**, on the Joshimath–Malari road.

Gwaldam and Roop Kund

Straddling a pass between Garhwal and Kumaon, surrounded by pine forests 61km east of Karnprayag, the peaceful hamlet of **GWALDAM** looks down upon the beautiful valley of the Pindar, a world away from the hectic *yatra* trails. This picturesque spot, with stunning views of the triple-pointed peak, **Trisul** (7120m), used to be a tea plantation; now, thanks to its position on the main road to Almora, 90km southeast, it makes an ideal base for treks, especially following the ten-day **Curzon Trail** across the high mountain *bugyals* of northeastern Garhwal, over **Kuari Pass** to Tapovan and Joshimath. The unassuming little Buddhist **Khamba Temple**, or **Drikung Kagyu Lhundrup Ling**, stands alongside orchards in the middle of a Tibetan settlement about 1.5km from Gwaldam's main crossroads. On the ridge above the village, the

Kuari Pass and the Curzon Trail

Named after a British Viceroy who trekked parts of the **Curzon Trail**, and renamed after Independence as the **Nehru Trail**, the long route over **KUARI PASS** (4268m), in northeastern Garhwal provides some stunning mountain views. Traversing the high ranges without entering the permanent snowline, the ten-day trail starts on the border with Kumaon at Gwaldam above the River Pindar and ends around 150km north, at the hot springs of Tapovan in the Dhauli Ganga valley near Joshimath. Numerous variations and shorter trails approaching the pass include one of around 24km from Auli. The whole route, and connected hikes, is mapped out on the Leomann map of Kumaon–Garhwal (sheet 8 in the India Series). The best time to go is from May to June and mid-September to November.

An ideal expedition for those not equipped to tackle glacial terrain, the trail over Kuari Pass follows alpine meadows and crosses several major streams, skirting the outer western edge of the Nanda Devi Sanctuary. Along the way you'll get excellent views of Trisul (7120m), the trident, Nanda Ghunti (6309m), and the elusive tooth-like Changabang (6864m), while to the far north on the border with Tibet rises the unmistakeable pyramid of Kamet (7756m).

On a major bus route between Karnaprayag and Almora and with comfortable accommodation, **Gwaldam** makes a good base for the start of the trek. Camping equipment is needed, especially on the pass. Guides can be negotiated here, available at several points along the route. You can either take local transport from Gwaldam, including shared Jeeps via Tharali, or trek down through beautiful pine forests and cross the River Pindar to **Debal** 8km away, where there is a forest rest house and a tourist lodge. Motorized transport is available from Debal to **Bagrigadh**, just below the beautiful hamlet of Lohajung, which has a pleasant tourist lodge. Also here is the shrine of *lohajung* – a rusted iron bell suspended from a cypress tree and rung to announce your arrival to the *devta* or local spirit.

Following the river Wan for 10km the trail arrives at the large village of **Wan**, where there's a choice of accommodation, including a GMVN *Tourist Bungalow* (**❶**) and a forest rest house. The small village of **Sutol** is 14km from Wan, along a trail following pleasant cypress and *deodar* forests. From Sutol to **Ramni**, a gentle 10km trail passes through several villages. A steep trail rises for 4km through dense forest from Ramni to the pass of **Sem Kharak** before descending for a further 9km to the small village of **Jhenjhenipati**, from where a rough track continues to the village of Panna 12km away, passing the beautiful **Gauna Lake**. From Panna a relentlessly steep trail rises for 12km to **Kuari Pass** (4298m) on the high divide between the lesser and the greater Himalayas, with rewarding views of Nanda Devi and Trisul.

Using Kuari Pass as a base, a climb to the peak of **Pangerchuli** (5183m), 12km up and down, is thoroughly recommended – the views from the summit reveal almost the entire route, including breathtaking mountain vistas. Although snow may be encountered on the climb, it is not a technical peak and no special equipment is necessary, save a good stick. From Kuari, a gruelling, knee-grinding 22-kilometre descent brings you straight down to the small village of **Tapovan**, overlooking the Dhauli Ganga, which has a hot-spring-fed tank. From here, local buses run to Joshimath, 11km away with several bus connections back down towards Karnaprayag and Rishikesh. An alternative descent from Kuari Pass is the long but picturesque route through forest to the ski centre of **Auli** via Chitrakantha – a trek of 24km – that avoids the dramatic decrease in altitude to Tapovan.

small shrine of **Badhangari**, dedicated to the goddess Durga and not far from the remnants of a Chand stone fort, commands superb views of the mountains of Kumaon and Garhwal. To reach it, take a bus for 4km to the village of Tal, then trek another 4km – some of which is quite steep – through rhododendron forests.

The GMVN *Tourist Rest House* (❹), above the crossroads in Gwaldam, has an old cottage equipped with two exceptionally comfortable suites, and a new block with ordinary **rooms** and dorms (Rs50); only limited food is available. This is the place to arrange guides for local treks. Alternatively try the good-value *Trishul* (❶–❸), where a pleasant little garden offers views of the snows. The new extension upstairs is more luxurious but less characterful.

Roop Kund: the mysterious lake

The high mountain lake of **Roop Kund** (4778m), a few days out of Gwaldam, lies in the lap of Mount Trisul. Though it is the goal of the Raj Jat Yatra, a pilgrimage from the village of Nauti, led by a four-horned ram and held every twelve years, Roop Kund is not one of the most attractive spots in the mountains; during the short summer thaw, when the snow and ice on its surface melts, it reveals a grisly secret. Three hundred **skeletons**, thought to be six hundred years old, can be seen in the water. Some say that they are what remains of the army of a Dogra general, Zorawar Singh, who tried to invade Tibet, but they probably belonged to a party of royal pilgrims caught by bad weather while making the Nanda Jat pilgrimage to the lake of **Hom Kund**, 13km away, to propitiate the goddess Nanda Devi. The route from Gwaldam to Roop Kund passes through **Wan** and the beautiful alps of **Badni Bugyal**, taking in some of the finest scenery of the region and should not be attempted without a local guide and adequate supplies.

Kumaon

The Shaivite temples of **Kumaon**, such as **Jageshwar**, **Bhageshwar** and **Baijnath**, do not attract the same fervour as their equivalents in Garhwal. Instead they remain frozen in time, undisturbed by the throngs from the plains. In fact, the Kumaon's comparative unholiness is probably an advantage as there is much less tourist traffic, so villages are largely unspoilt and trekking routes unlittered. Hill towns like **Almora**, **Ranikhet** and **Kausani** have a charm of their own, with views towards the snows, while in **Corbett National Park**, southeast of the resort of **Nainital**, vast jungles continue to protect tiger and huge herds of wild elephant. To the east, Kumaon's border with Nepal follows the Kali valley to its watershed with Tibet; threading through it is the holy trail (closed to foreigners) to the ultimate pilgrimage site, Mount Kailash in Tibet, the abode of Shiva and his consort Parvati. Kumaon Mandal Vikas Nigam, or **KMVN**, are in charge of tourism in Kumaon, providing a similar (and equally patchy) range of services to GMVN in Garhwal. The electricity supply is capricious, with cuts occurring almost daily, so hotels without generators are listed. Note too that the only places to change money are Nainital and Almora (which won't change cash). A few places offer internet use but the nearest server is in Dehra Dun and the connection is tortuously slow.

Nainital

The dramatic crater lake of **Nainital** (*tal* means lake), set in a mountain hollow at an altitude of 1938m, 277km north of Delhi, gives its name to the largest and most important town in Kumaon. Discovered for Europeans in 1841 by

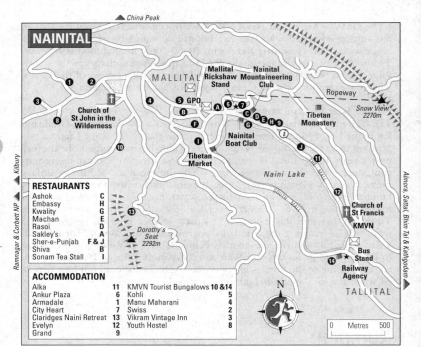

RESTAURANTS

Ashok	C
Embassy	H
Kwality	G
Machan	E
Rasoi	D
Sakley's	A
Sher-e-Punjab	F & J
Shiva	B
Sonam Tea Stall	I

ACCOMMODATION

Alka	11	KMVN Tourist Bungalows	10 &14
Ankur Plaza	6	Kohli	5
Armadale	1	Manu Maharani	4
City Heart	7	Swiss	2
Claridges Naini Retreat	13	Vikram Vintage Inn	3
Evelyn	12	Youth Hostel	8
Grand	9		

Mr Barron, a wealthy sugar merchant, **NAINITAL** swiftly became a popular escape from the summer heat of the lowlands, and continues to be one of India's main hill stations. Throughout the year, and especially between March and July, hordes of tourists and honeymooners pack the **Mall**, the promenade that links **Mallital** (head of the lake), the older colonial part of Nainital at the north end, with **Tallital** (foot of the lake).

Nainital's position within striking range of the inner Himalayas – visible from vantage points above town – makes it a good base for exploring Kumaon: Corbett National Park, Almora and Ranikhet are all within easy access. When the town's garish commercialism gets a bit much, it's always possible to escape into the beautiful surrounding country, to lakes such as **Sat Tal** where the foothills begin their sudden drop towards the plains to the south, or to the forested ridges around **Kilbury**.

The Town

Most of the activity around the lake of Nainital takes place along the 1.5-kilometre-long **Mall**, a promenade of restaurants, hotels and shops selling souvenirs and jumpers. Cycle rickshaws charge a standard Rs5 to go from one end to the other. Basic **boat rental** starts at around Rs30 per hour out of season but can shoot up to Rs200 per hour in the summer; dinghies (or yacht, as they are locally called) arranged at the boat club on the northwest corner of the lake in Mallital, cost in the range of Rs75 per hour. You can join the club on a three-day membership for Rs750 for a couple, for which you get access to the elegant old colonial clubhouse and all its facilities, including the card tables and billiards room.

The boat club stands on the large plain known as the **Flats**, the result of a huge landslide in 1880, which buried the *Victoria Hotel* along with 150 people. Now the area hosts sporting events, and you are likely to catch a football or hockey game. Also here, the **Tibetan Market** sells clothing to shivering tourists up from the plains. The name is a little misleading – there's nothing ethnic for sale; it's mostly expensive fake designer fleeces.

A ropeway climbs from near the *Mayur* restaurant on the Mall to **Snow View** (2270m); the return ticket covers a one-hour stay (7am–1pm & 2–6pm; Rs50 return, Rs35 single). Otherwise it's a two-kilometre hike along a choice of steep trails, which can also be undertaken on ponies for Rs40. At the top, which gets overcrowded in season, you'll find a promenade, cafés and a viewpoint; views of the snow peaks are most assured early in the morning. Trails lead on for five kilometres to **Naina Peak** (2611m) one of the best vantage points around, and to the isolated **China Peak** (pronounced "Cheena"), the craggy rise to the west. About halfway up to Snow View, conspicuous thanks to its abundant prayer flags, lies the small Tibetan *gompa* (monastery) of **Gadhan Kunkyop Ling**, which has recently been rebuilt in traditional *gompa* style. Three kilometres out of town along the Almora Road, Hanuman Garh, a temple full of monkeys and young priests monkeying around, is a popular place to watch the sunset.

Practicalities

Two main highways approach Nainital from opposite ends; one arrives at Mallital from Ramnagar and Corbett National Park, the other, which brings in most of the traffic, comes in at Tallital in the south. **Buses** and **taxis** from Tallital travel with great frequency to the closest railhead at **Kathgodam** near Haldwani, 40km south. The nearest airport, at **Pantnagar**, 72km south, is rarely used and best reached by taxi.

Parvat Tours and Tourist Information Centre, Tallital (☏05942/35656), run by KMVN, organizes tours, car rental and books accommodation at all KMVN lodges. Cars can also be rented from agencies along the Mall, such as Hina Tours & Travels (☏05942/35860), though cycle rickshaws are the most convenient means of local transport. The **UP tourist office**, on the Mall near the Mallital end (Mon–Sat 10am–5pm; ☏05942/35337), hands out leaflets and has a KMVN representative who books tours. A tourist office by the bus station sells leaflets and book hotels but specializes in being patronizing and unhelpful. For specialist advice on **trekking** and **mountaineering**, call in at Nainital Mountaineering Club, CRST Inter College Building (☏05942/36209), or their representative Anit Sah at the Allied Stores, the Mall, Mallital. **Banks** in town include the State Bank of India and Allahabad Bank, on the Mall in Mallital. It is advisable to change travellers' cheques here if you are moving on into the mountains, as it is very difficult to find any authorized exchange outlets further north. Cash advances are accepted at the Bank of Baroda. Internet access is available at the *Cybercafé* by *Shakley's Restaurant* (9.30am–10pm; Rs120/hr).

Accommodation

As a holiday town, Nainital is full of **hotels**; however, budget accommodation is hard to come by, and a hefty fifteen percent tax is levied onto prices almost everywhere. Rates are high between March and July, peaking between mid-April and mid-June, but you can normally find discounts at other times. On the whole, rooms are cheaper in Tallital than in Mallital. The price codes indicated overleaf are for the low season but with an indication of the high season rates.

Alka, the Mall ☎05942/35220. Ornate, large and comfortable, perhaps a little heavy on the marble, with a restaurant strong on Gujarati and Punjabi food. Rates are lower in the annexe, 300m towards Mallital. ❻–❽

Ankur Plaza, above Mallital rickshaw stand ☎05942/35448. Good value especially low-season, with friendly management. Vases of plastic flowers on the cisterns at least shows attention to detail if not great taste. The best rooms are off a great roof terrace overlooking the lake. ❸–❺

Armadale, Waverley Road, Mallital ☎05942/36205. Quiet location. Reasonably comfortable mid-range rooms and a good-value dorm (Rs100), with free transport on arrival. ❻–❽

City Heart, above Mallital rickshaw stand ☎05942/35228. Upper rooms are overpriced during the high season, but have superb lake views. No food, but it's close to amenities, and worth coming to just to meet the eccentric manager, a bass guitarist in a local band and wildlife photographer. ❸–❼

Claridges Naini Retreat, Ayarpatta Slopes ☎05942/35105. Beautifully situated high above the lake, with extensive and immaculate grounds, and a great terrace for barbecues. The best Nainital can offer. ❾

Evelyn, the Mall ☎05942/05942 or 2457. Overlooking the lake, with excellent views from the large roof patio. Some rooms have giant red beds. The claim made in hotel literature – "all rooms fitted with CCTV" is mercifully untrue. The cheaper rooms at the top have their own terrace. Popular with visitors to the Ramgarh ashram 25km down the road. ❹–❻

Grand, the Mall (☎05942/35406). One of Nainital's oldest establishments, where time seems to stand still – period atmosphere but a bit musty. ❺–❼

Kohli, Mallital (☎05942/36368). Well-located small-budget place. Rooms have a common balcony decorated with pot plants and satellite TV inside, unusual for the price range. Rooms at the top overlook the lake and are a little more expensive. Excellent value. ❷–❺

KMVN Tourist Bungalows, booked through Parvat Tours, the Mall ☎05942/35400. Two lodges with rooms and cheap dorms (Rs100) at either end of town, and a cottage at *Snow View* ☎05942/35772. The lodge at Tallital is the most conveniently situated, near the bus stand. ❸–❼

Manu Maharani, Grasmere Estate ☎05942/37341. Standard luxury hotel, with all mod cons, including the only bar in town, a discotheque, and good Szechuan food in the *Lotus Garden* restaurant. Excellent buffet breakfasts. ❾

Swiss, Mallital ☎05942/36013. Popular family-run converted Raj mansion. Huge old-fashioned rooms with giant cupboards, wood panelling and eccentric plumbing; they vary widely so ask to see a selection. Atmospheric if chaotic. ❼–❽

Vikram Vintage Inn, Mallital ☎05942/36177. Full-featured hotel; billiards, snooker, and smart comfortable rooms. No views, but surrounded by pines and away from the bustle. ❽–❾

Youth Hostel, Mallital ☎05942/35353. Forty-four dorm beds (Rs42) in a charming secluded spot above Mallital; with lovely gardens and friendly staff. Likely to be either deserted or jammed with schoolkids. Slightly more expensive for non-YHA members. Excellent value but no generator. ❶

Eating

Nainital has plenty of places to **eat**, with restaurants and fast-food options along the Mall geared to tourists (some close in the low season), and everyday *dhabas* (which serve cheap and tasty fish curry) in the bazaars at either end.

Ashok, near the Boat House, the Mall, Mallital. Good veg *dhaba*; cheap considering its location.

Embassy, the Mall, Mallital. One of Nainital's better restaurants with wood-panelled interior; serves pizzas and baked dishes, but strongest on Mughlai cooking. About the only place with a selection of desserts.

Kwality, the Mall, Mallital. Lakeside restaurant; tables overlook the water. The usual standard multi-cuisine.

Machan, just west of the Embassy, a new and well run upstairs restaurant that's good for people watching on the promenade below. A clay oven, Bronze Age chic decor and dedicated management.

Rasoi, the Mall, towards Mallital. Mid-priced veg cooking but otherwise unexceptional.

Sakley's, the Mall, Mallital. Versatile restaurant, with Western food on the menu, including passable pizza, plus a bakery and confectioners.

Sher-e-Punjab, the Mall. Good Indian food, halfway along between Mallital and Tallital. A second, bigger branch, near the main bazaar of Mallital, is just as good, a bit cheaper, and popular with locals.

Shiva, Bara Bazaar, Mallital. Cheap but good and popular *dhaba* in the bazaar with tasty palak paneer and the usual casual attitude to electrical safety.

Sonam Tea Stall, Tibetan Market, Mallital.
Roadside café in the covered section of the market

selling *momos* (steamed meat dumplings) and
thukpa (soup).

Moving on from Nainital

Shared taxis and jeeps regularly ply the route between Tallital, Haldwani and Kathgodam which is the main railway station for Nainital. Buses leave every thirty minutes and take around 1hr 30min to Haldwani. The Road cum Railway Out Agency (℡05942/35518), at the Tallital bus stand, handles railway reservations. Among the trains that depart from Kathgodam are the Delhi–Kathgodam Express #5014 to New Delhi, the Kathgodam–Howrah Express #3020 passing through Lucknow to Calcutta, and the Kumaon Express #5312 to Agra; the Nainital Express #5307 is a convenient overnight train to Lucknow leaving from Lalkuan, 14km south.

Delhi is an eight-hour ride away with either UPSRTC buses (6, 7.30 & 8.30am) or the Delhi Transport Corporation (8.45am & 7.30pm), while private operators run more comfortable coaches at around twice the price (you'll have to put up with non-stop videos). Almora, 67km north, is served by hourly direct buses (2hr 30min) and shared taxis from Bhowali (Rs40), 11km from Nainital. In Almora, you can catch onward sevices for Pithoragarh (9hr) and Kausani (5hr). There is one direct bus to Kausani at 8am (7hr) and one direct bus to Dehra Dun (11hr) and Mussoorie (13hr), with a stop at Haridwar (9hr). There is an early morning bus to Song – the start of the route to Pindari Glacier.

To get to Corbett National Park, 113km southwest, take the 7am bus for 66km to Ramnagar (3hr), from where local transport is available (see p.409). KMVN's Parvat Tours (℡05942/35656) organizes cheap package tours of Corbett from Rs165 per head per day.

See Travel Details at the end of this chapter for more information on journey frequencies and durations.

Corbett National Park

Corbett National Park, based at **Ramnagar**, 250km northeast of Delhi and 63km southwest of Nainital, is one of India's premier wildlife reserves. Established in 1936 by Jim Corbett among others, as the Hailey National Park, India's first, and later renamed in his honour, it is one of Himalayan India's last expanses of wilderness. Almost the entire 521-square-kilometre park, spread over the foothills of Kumaon, is sheltered by a buffer zone of mixed deciduous and giant *sal* forests, which provide impenetrable cover for wildlife. Most of the Core Area of 330 square kilometres at its heart remains out of bounds, and safaris on foot are only permissible in the fringe forests.

Corbett is most famous for its big cats, and in particular the **tiger** – this was the first designated Project Tiger Reserve, in 1973 – but its tigers are extremely elusive. Sightings are very far from guaranteed, and should be regarded as an unlikely bonus. Nonetheless, although there have been problems elsewhere with the project, and the very survival of the tiger in India is in serious jeopardy (see Contexts), Corbett does at least seem to be prioritizing the needs of tigers over those of other wildlife – and of tourists – and claims to have poaching under control.

The park holds a great assortment of other animals. Large **elephant** herds have been confined within its boundaries since the construction of the Ramganga reservoir blocked migratory routes that formerly ranged as far as Rajaji National Park, 200km west. The best place to see them is around the

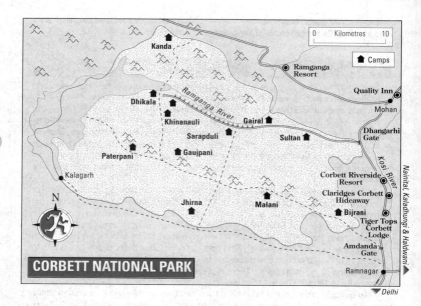

CORBETT NATIONAL PARK

picturesque Dhikala camp near the reservoir, especially in spring, when the water level drops and the animals have more space to roam. The reservoir shelters populations of **gharial**, a long-snouted, fish-eating crocodile, and **maggar**, a large marsh crocodile, and other reptiles. Jackal are common, and wild boar run through the camps in the evenings. The grasslands around Dhikala are home to deer species such as the spotted deer known as **chital**, **hog deer** and the larger **sambar**. Rhesus and common langur are both abundant, representing the two main classes of Indian monkeys. Bird life ranges from water birds such as the pied kingfisher to **birds of prey**, including the crested serpent eagle, Pallas's fishing eagle and Himalayan greyheaded fishing eagle.

Getting to and from Corbett National Park

Ramnagar is served by frequent **buses** to and from Nainital and Ranikhet, 112km north. Buses arrive every half-hour or so after the eight-hour trip from **Delhi**; Delhi Transport Corporation run a semi-deluxe service (Rs90), and most of the alternatives are pretty basic. The only direct **train** to Delhi leaves at 8pm and arrives at 6.30am, with interminable stops along the way. For faster

---

Entry into Corbett National Park

All visitors to Corbett National Park have to obtain **permits** from the park administration centre at Ramnagar. Indians pay less than overseas visitors. At present it costs Rs350 for the first three days at Dhikala, excluding board and lodging. Each additional day is Rs175. To take a minibus into the park costs Rs250, a private car Rs100 and a motorbike Rs50. Use of a video camera is Rs5000. Elephant rides are Rs100 per head or Rs400 per elephant.

Note that Corbett is **closed** between June 16 and November 14, when the monsoons flood the riverbeds and cut the fragile road links.

Jim Corbett – hunter of man-eating tigers, photographer, conservationist and author – was born in Nainital of English and Irish parentage. A childhood spent around the Corbett winter home of Kaladhungi (halfway between Nainital and Ramnagar, and now a rather disappointing memorial to him) brought young Jim into close communion with nature and to an instinctive understanding of jungle ways. After working on the railways, he joined the Indian army in 1917 at the age of 40, rising to the rank of Lieutenant Colonel, and seeing action in Flanders at the head of the 70th Kumaon Company.

Known locally as "Carpet Sahib", a mispronunciation of his name, Jim Corbett was called upon time and time again to rid the hills of Kumaon of man-eating tigers and leopards. Normally shy of human contact, such animals become man-eaters when infirmity brought upon by old age or wounds renders them unable to hunt their usual prey. Many of those killed by Corbett were found to have suppurating wounds caused by porcupine quills embedded deep in their paws; tigers always seem to fall for the porcupine's simple defensive trick of walking backwards in line with its lethal quills.

One of Corbett's most memorable exploits was the killing of the Rudraprayag leopard, which accounted for 125 human lives between 1918 and 1926, and was bold enough to steal its victims from the midst of human habitation; he also terminated the careers of the Chowgarh tigress, the Talla Des and the Mohan man-eaters. Corbett described his adventures in books such as *My India*, *Jungle Lore* and *Man-Eaters of Kumaon*; Martin Booth's *Carpet Sahib* is an excellent biography of a remarkable man. Awarded the Order of the British Empire in recognition of his lifelong work with nature, Jim Corbett was unhappy in post-Independence India, and left to settle in East Africa.

trains and connections to other parts change at Moradabad. The nearest airport, at Pantnagar, 80km southeast, is rarely used.

The closest of the various **gates** into the park, 1km from central Ramnagar, is Amdanda on the road to **Bijrani camp**, 11km away, a base for day-trips. **Dhangarhi Gate**, 18km along the highway north to Ranikhet, provides access to the northern and northwestern portion of the park along the Ramganga river valley, and to the main camp of **Dhikala**.

Jeeps, the most convenient way to travel within the park, can be rented for around Rs800 per day in Ramnagar from the KMVN *Tourist Lodge* (☏05945/85225) and other agencies such as *Bharat Hotel* (☏05945/85775) near the bus stand. There is no longer a public bus from Ramnagar to **Dikhala**, and the conducted bus trip is expensive at Rs1200. The Jeeps which are readily available are better value, and can be hired for 24hrs for around Rs1000.

KMVN's Parvat Tours (☏05942/35656) organizes cheap package tours (from Nainital) of Corbett from Rs165 per head per day.

Ramnagar

Situated in the rich farm-belt of the *terai*, on the southeastern fringes of the great forests, the busy market town of **RAMNAGAR** is the main administrative centre for **Corbett National Park** and **Project Tiger**. There's little to do around Ramnagar itself except go **fishing** (Oct 1–June 30). At Lohachaur, 15km north along the River Kosi, good anglers are in with a chance of landing the legendary *mahseer*, a redoubtable battling river carp. Permits to have a go must be sought from the Project Tiger office in Ramnagar; most resorts also arrange all-inclusive fishing trips.

Although most tourists head straight to Dhikala in the park as soon as they arrive, Ramnagar does have some **accommodation**. The KMVN *Tourist Lodge* (⊤ 05945/85225; ❶–❺), next to the Project Tiger offices, is not bad as such places go, with a dorm as well as basic doubles, while the *Everest* (❶–❸), at the bus stand, has a variety of decent good-value rooms. On the main road opposite the bus stand, *Govindas* is a surprisingly good multi-cuisine **restaurant**, strongest on Indian food. Across from the *Tourist Lodge*, *Corbett Jungle Outpost*, more of a bar than a restaurant, is good for a cold beer and serves food.

Dhikala

Corbett's main camp, **DHIKALA**, beautifully situated overlooking the Ramganga reservoir and the forested hills beyond, is 40km northwest of Ramnagar. As you can only stray beyond the confines of the camp under armed guard, on elephant-back or in a car or Jeep, the whole place has something of the air of a military encampment. **Accommodation** ranges from the 24 bunk beds in the *Log Huts* (Rs100) and other assorted spartan huts (❺), to more comfortable bungalows and cabins (❼) which sleep two. **Food** is available in a canteen either per day, with higher prices for Western food, or on a *janta* ("peoples") meal basis. There is also a *dhaba*, frequented by the park staff who sit and tell of their adventures and latest sightings. The food here is fantastic (apparently it drew the late prime minister Rajiv Gandhi back to the park time and time again), although you need to order well in the morning if you require an evening meal. There's also a library and reading room where film shows on wildlife are run.

It's normally possible to see plenty of animals and birds from the **lookout tower** beside a waterhole 1km from the camp; bring binoculars, remain quiet, and don't wear bright colours or perfume. Chital, sambar, and various other deer species find refuge in the savannah grasslands known as the *maidan*, behind the camp to the south, and tigers are occasionally drawn in looking for prey. Two-hour **elephant rides** (Rs100 per head, fifty percent less for Indian citizens; in theory, rides are first-come-first-served) explore this sea of grass, rarely penetrating far into the deep jungles beyond; try to convince your *mahout* (elephant driver) to venture in, as they can be quite magical. Come at dusk or dawn; in the heat of the day you probably won't come across much more than deer among the tall grass. Tiger sightings are few and far between, count yourself lucky if you see fresh pug marks.

On the way to Dhikala from the Dhangarhi gate, the road passes through magnificent forest – if you have your own transport, stop at the **High Bank** vantage point, and try to spot crocodile or even elephant on the river below. The *Sultan* (❺), *Gairal* (❺–❻) and *Sarapduli* (❺–❻) forest rest houses on the road are bookable through Project Tiger, but you have to make your own food arrangements and there is no electricity. The bungalows are surrounded by deep forest; as movement on foot is restricted, you'll only see wild animals that stray close to or into the compound. The beautifully sited *Kanda* (❺) rest house stands on a hill above the Ramganga reservoir and Dhikala.

Resort accommodation around Corbett

A number of self-contained **resorts** are springing up on the fringes of Corbett, providing a higher standard of accommodation – at a price – as well as guides for expeditions in the forests, which can be as rich in wildlife as the park, without the restrictions. Impossible to get to without prearranged transport, the most secluded is the *Ramganga Resort*, 13km off the main road from Mohan.

Claridges Corbett Hideaway, Garija, Ramnagar
(☎ 05945/85959; reservations 011/3010211).
Luxurious with all mod cons; pretending to be rustic without success. Terracotta huts dotted around
a pleasant orchard on a bluff overlooking the river.
Safaris and the usual tours arranged. **⑨**
Corbett Riverside Resort, Garija, Ramnagar
(☎ 05945/85960). A picturesque setting, 10km
north of Ramnagar, looking across the River Kosi to
forest-covered cliffs. Much of the complex was
washed away not long ago, when the river dramatically changed course. Now rebuilt, with some
buildings sited on a ledge above the extensive
beach area, the rustic-looking huts are luxurious
inside and expensive. Safaris arranged; full board;
off-season discounts. **⑧–⑨**

Quality Inn Corbett Jungle Resort, Kumeria
Reserve Forest, Mohan (☎ 05945/85219). Wood-
panelled stone cottages in a leafy mango orchard
above the Kosi, 29km from Ramnagar on the road
north to Ranikhet, 9km beyond the Dhangarhi
gate. Elephant rides into the forest and safaris into
the park itself; full board; good off-season discounts from June to November. **⑨**
Tiger Tops Corbett Lodge, Dhikala, Ramnagar
(☎ 05945/85279). Corbett's most ostentatious
resort, overlooking the Kosi and the forested hills
beyond. Large comfortable rooms, a library, a well-
stocked bar and a swimming pool. Activities
include nature trails with the resort's own naturalists, jungle rides, fishing, trekking and films. Not
related to the famous Tiger Tops in Nepal. **⑨**

Ranikhet

The small and deliberately undeveloped town of **RANIKHET**, 50km west of
Almora, is one of UP's most pleasant hill stations. Essentially, it's an army cantonment, the home of the Kumaon Rifles. New construction is confined to
the **Sadar Bazaar** area, while the rest of the town above it, climbing up
towards the crest of the hill, retains atmospheric leafy pine woods. Beautiful
forest trails abound, including short cuts from the bazaar to the Mall; leopards
still roam some of the more remote areas within the town boundaries, despite
efforts by army officers to prove their skill at hunting. Ranikhet is for some
reason only marginally popular with Indian tourists, so it's unspoilt and an ideal
place for a quiet break.

Ranikhet's "Mall", 3km above the town, is something of a misnomer; it is simply a quiet road running along the wooded crest of the ridge, with few buildings apart from officers' messes. Though there's a strong army presence – everything, even the flowerpots at the side of the road, is painted in the regimental
colours of green and yellow – it never feels overbearing, and the sense of rigorous military order is subverted by the many gambolling monkeys. For a taste
of Indian military life, you can join the Ranikhet Officers' Club (Rs50 per day),
half-way up the hill, which has a rather fine bar, restaurant and billiards room
and features men with grand moustaches calling each other chaps. Other traces
of the colonial past remain in the form of large bungalows and church steeples.

At the **Shawl & Tweed Factory and Outlet**, above the Narsingh Stadium
Parade Ground – an old church equipped with looms and wheels – you can
ask to watch the weavers in action, a fascinating display of concentration, dex-
terity and counting. The herringbone and houndstooth tweeds are sold in the
shop next door. Kumaon has a tradition of weaving, and the Gandhi Ashram
in the bazaar has a selection of local fabric including *pankhis*, plain shawls for
men. A signpost near here directs you to the well-kept and beautifully situated
nine-hole **golf course** 3km away, within view of the Himalayan snows.

The military influence wanes towards the top of the hill, where a few secluded hotels nestle. Exploring the many trails around here that lead into the deep
dark woods around could keep you occupied for weeks, but if you do fancy
venturing further afield, local tourist authorities promote the idea of a visit to
the orchards of **Chaubatia**, 10km east beyond the Mall. It's a scenic enough
spot, with good views of the snows, and a pleasant short walk leads along a lofty
pine-covered ridge to the small lake of **Bhaludam**.

Practicalities

Buses from all over Kumaon, including the railhead at Kathgodam, 84km away, arrive at the bazaar, at either of two bus stops. The KMOU stand, on the Haldwani road, is the base for buses to Haldwani (10–12 daily; 4hr), the nearest town to Kathgodam; the Kausani–Pithoragarh bus departs (2 or 3 daily; 4hr) from this stand; to get to Nainital, change at Bhowali, or take one of the three daily direct services (10am, 11am & 4pm; 3hr). The Roadways (Almora) Bus Stand, 500m on, is used by regular services to Almora (2hr) with shared Jeeps providing a crowded but slightly faster alternative. There's a **map** of the local area painted on the wall opposite the Rajdeep Hotel. A few hundred metres uphill from here is the town's taxi rank.

KMVN provides the usual Kumaon-wide services from their *Tourist Bungalow* on the Mall (℡ 05966/2297), while the **UP Tourist Bureau**, above the Almora Bus Stand, offers a haphazard assortment of leaflets. The **post office** is at the top of the Mall.

Accommodation and eating

Hotels in Ranikhet readily divide into two sections, but there's really no point staying around the busy bazaar when you can stay in the woods at the top of the Mall. Seasonal fluctuations can double prices especially around June and July. The prices listed here apply to low season. Choice of **eating** is pretty limited; the best food is found in the better hotels, but there are a few simple cafés and *dhabas* in the market area.

Forest Guesthouse, the Mall ℡ 05966/20893. Follow the sign from the Meghdoot and it's half a kilometre down the forest track in a beautiful wooded spot. A well-kept complex of bungalows with a cheap dorm (Rs60). **③**–**④**

Himadri Tourist Rest House, Chilianaula ℡ 05966/2588. A new and modern KMVN-run bungalow next to the Haidarkhan complex, 7km from town; with a range of rooms at high rates but also a very cheap dorm (Rs50). Well located and very quiet. **③**–**④**

Meghdoot, the Mall ℡ 05966/2475. Comfortable suites full of potted plants and flowers, with running hot water, parking and room service, plus a good mid-price restaurant that serves up a range of very tasty biriyani and *pulao*, in particular. **④**–**⑤**

Norton's, the Mall ℡ 05966/2377. Family-run hotel with a huge and very cosy lounge and dining room featuring paintings by previous guests. The friendly manager still remembers the Raj and the atmosphere is very Anglo-Indian; the architecture and furniture is English in style but the bright colour schemes are decidedly local. Opposite the *Meghdoot*. **②**–**④**

Rajdeep, Bazaar ℡ 05966/2447. The best budget hotel in the bazaar area and nearly always busy. A bit noisy but clean with long verandas facing the snow peaks. The arrival of room service is announced by a spooky door buzzer that chimes "may I come in?". **①**–**②**

Rosemount, the Mall ℡ 05966/3489. Newly opened hotel in an old Raj mansion, 2km away from the main road and deep in the woods. Lavishly restored rooms, restaurant, and gardens complete with lawn tennis, croquet, badminton and snow views. **⑦**–**⑨**

West View, Mahatma Gandhi Road ℡ 05966/2261. Grand old-world establishment in an idyllic spot among the pines on the outskirts of town. Spacious if a bit musty, with fireplaces, restaurant, and extensive gardens. **⑦**–**⑨**

Almora and around

ALMORA, 67km north of Nainital, is one of the rare Kumaoni towns that conspicuously predates the Raj, with its cobbled alleyways and wood and stone buildings. Founded by the Chand dynasty in 1560, and occupied successively by the Gurkhas and the British, it remains a major market town, and is considered the cultural capital of the region. Set at a pleasant altitude of 1646m on rambling ridges that look towards the inner Himalayan snows, Almora's peaceful environs have attracted an eclectic assortment of visitors over the years, such as Swami Vivekananda, Timothy Leary and the Tibetologist and author of *The Way of the White Clouds*, Lama Angarika Govinda.

Although most of Almora's official business is conducted along the **Mall**, the **market area** immediately above and parallel to it along the crest of the saddle, holds much more of interest. Exploring its well-stocked bazaars, knitted together with lanes flanked by beautifully carved wooden facades, you feel as though you're drifting into the distant past. Among items you might want to buy are *khadi* (home-spun) cotton textiles and ready-mades from the Gandhi Ashram near the bus stands, and local woollens from Garur Woollens or Kumaon Woollens on the Mall. However, the great local tradition is the manufacture of **tamta**, beaten copper pots plated with silver, which are sold in the busy Lala Bazaar and the Chowk area at the northeast end of the market.

Towards the top of town, beyond Chowk, a compound holds a group of Chand-period stone **temples**. The main one, a squat single-storey structure, is dedicated to **Nanda Devi**, the goddess embodied in the region's highest mountain. More typical of Kumaoni temple architecture are two larger Shaivite painted stone temples, capped with umbrella-like wooden roofs covering their stone *amalaka* (circular crowns). During Sravana (July/Aug), a large fair is held here in honour of Nanda Devi.

Enclosures amid the tall pine woods of Deer Park, a pleasant three-kilometre walk northeast of the Mall, house assorted deer, as well as Himalayan black bear and sorry-looking leopards. Following the Mall southwest for three kilometres, on the other hand, brings you to the hill called **Bright End Corner**, where you may, weather permitting, catch views of the hills and vales of Kumaon, and the distant snow peaks.

Moving on 8km east of Almora, a pleasant walk or Jeep ride away, the small Durga temple of **Kasara Devi**, surrounded by pines, on a commanding hill above the Binsar Road is an idyllic spot, where Swami Vivekananda meditated and gained enlightenment.

Practicalities

Almora has regular **bus** connections with Nainital (3 daily; 3hr), Ranikhet (5 daily; 2hr 30min), Kathgodam, the nearest railhead (2 daily; 4hr), and Kausani (6 daily; 2hr 30min). Most buses use either of two adjacent stands on the Mall, which has a **taxi stand** close by if you're heading for distant accommodation, such as the *Holiday Home*. However, most hotels are within walking distance. Access to much of the centre, including the market area above the Mall, is restricted to pedestrians. Another bus stand at Dharanaula, on the other side of the market, is for buses to the interior of Kumaon, with most leaving in the afternoon.

UP Tourism maintains a helpful information-only **tourist office** next to the *Savoy Hotel* above the GPO (Mon–Sat 10am–5pm; ☏05962/30180). The KMVN HQ is at the *Holiday Home*; another office near the Gandhi statue at Chaudhan Pata, the Mall (☏05962/30706), assists in booking their packages and accommodation throughout Kumaon. The best places to find out about **treks** or hire equipment and guides are Discover Himalaya (☏05962/31470) and High Adventure (☏05962/32277), both on the Mall. The State Bank of India on the Mall will only change American Express travellers' cheques. Nainital is the nearest town that will change currency and other cheques.

Accommodation

Accommodation in Almora itself is largely centred along the Mall. However, it is also possible to go native in village houses in the region around Kasar Devi; enquire about places to rent at the chai shops in Kalimath nearby.

Deodar Holiday-Inn, Sister Nivedita Cottage, the Mall ☏ 05962/31295. Home to Swami Vivekananda and his disciple Nivedita between 1890 and 1898, which time seems to have forgotten and where little has changed. The rooms are basic and the garden is tranquil with a log fire at night. ❸

Kailash, east end of the Mall, above the GPO ☏ 05962/30624. Quaint, brightly coloured but filthy place, whose owner, Mr Shah, has been known to use his charm and good reputation among travellers to extract as much money as possible from his guests by adding hidden extras to the bill. Mrs Shah concocts excellent herbal teas and dishes up a good thali. No generator. ❶

Konark, the Mall ☏ 05962/301217. The lobby may be full of funky furniture but the rooms are simple, clean and tasteful. Good value – one of the best in its range – and well located. ❹–❺

KMVN Holiday Home, the Mall ☏ 05962/30250. Set in a nice garden 2km west of the centre, this characterless tourist bungalow has a main building and cottages, and a good-value dorm (Rs100). ❹

Savoy, Police Line, above the GPO ☏ 05962/30329. A quiet place with pleasant gardens, away from the noise of the Mall and the markets, but handy for all amenities. Spacious rooms, veranda and a fantastic albeit slow restaurant; good off-season discounts. ❺

Shikhar, the Mall ☏ 05962/30253. Almora's central landmark. Don't be put off by the exterior or expensive reputation; a wide range of rooms, some at very reasonable prices, most with private balconies. The reasonable restaurant serves good breakfasts. ❸–❻

Eating

Cafés and **restaurants** are strung along the Mall, especially around the bazaar area at its northern end. There should be something for everybody. Locally grown and prepared Kumaon rice and black dhal are particularly delicious. Hotels such as the *Savoy* can produce a feast of Kumaoni dishes, if given plenty of advance warning.

Bansal Expresso Bar, Lala Bazaar. An Italian-style café, complete with marble-topped tables. Serves up the best coffee, chai and shakes in town; freshly made snacks are also available.

Dolma, Kalimath, 5km west of the town. A café run by Tibetans that shows the locals how it's done. Located at a beauty spot with a view of the Himalayas. *Momos*, beer and outdoor seating.

Glory, near *Shikhar*, the Mall. Multi-cuisine café-cum-restaurant, strong on north Indian cooking.

Madras Café, opposite the *Glory*, the Mall. The name is misleading, as the emphasis is on good-value north Indian food. Tasty coffee, too.

Soni Dhaba, the Mall bus stand. Excellent, Sikh-run *dhaba* which can get crowded.

Swagat, opposite the *Shikhar*, the Mall. Large café, with *dosas* and other snacks as well as meals.

Binsar and Jageshwar

Both **BINSAR** and **JAGESHWAR** are in easy reach of Almora and can be visited as a day-trip (around Rs400 return for a taxi) although its well worth overnighting at both places as they are lovely spots. Binsar, known locally as Jhandi Dhar, the forest-clad hill, 34km north of Almora, rises in isolation to a commanding 2412m. A steep road leads 11km up from the main Almora–Bageshwar highway, to a new tourist complex near the top of the hill (❺–❻). This was the summer capital of the Chands, but today little remains in the area except the bulbous stone Shiva temple of **Bineshwar** 3km below the summit. Most visitors come for the 300-kilometre panorama of Himalayan peaks along the northern horizon, including from west to east Kedarnath, Chaukhamba, Trisul, Nandaghunti, Nanda Devi, Nandakot, and Panchuli. Closer at hand, you can enjoy quiet forest walks through oak and rhododendron woods. Recently designated a nature reserve, Binsar is rich in alpine flora, ferns, hanging moss and wild flowers.

JAGESHWAR, 34km northeast of Almora, is the very heart of Kumaon, a place where language and customs seem to have resisted change. An idyllic small river meanders through dark pines into this ancient world, 3km off the main road from Artola, stumbling onto a complex of 124 ancient shrines and temples which cluster at the base of venerable deodar trees like so many stone mushrooms. Jageshwar village retains much of its traditional charm, with stone-paved lanes and beautifully carved wooden doors and windows painted in green, turquoise and other striking colours. **Accommodation** can be found either in the large, comfortable KMVN *Tourist Bungalow* (❷–❺), or there's a very basic but atmospheric *dharamshala* (❶) in a traditional building. Jageshwar has a sprinkling of simple *dhabas*. Good local **walks** include the steep three-kilometre ascent through beautiful pine forests to the small hamlet and stone temples of **Vriddha** or **Briddh Jageshwar** (Old Jageshwar), with an extensive panorama from the mountains of Garhwal to the massifs of western Nepal. A trail from here leads 12km along an undulating ridge to Binsar (see above); the trail finally emerges from the woods near the stone temple of **Bineshwar**.

Kausani and around

Spreading from east to west along a narrow pine-covered ridge, 52km north-west of Almora, the village of **KAUSANI** boasts a spectacular Himalayan panorama and as a result has become a popular resort. It's a simple day-trip from Almora, though as the peaks – Nanda Choti, Trisul, Nanda Devi and Panchol – are at their best at dawn and dusk, its worth staying overnight. There are several ashrams, including one that once housed Mahatma Gandhi, who walked here in 1929, thirty years before the road came through. Gandhi-ism continues to be a major influence in these hills and his symbol of self-reliance, the spinning wheel, is still used in homes in the area. There are numerous possibilities for short day-hikes in the woods and valleys around Kausani, as well as longer excursions to the important pilgrimage sites of Baijnath and Bageshwar.

Practicalities

Kausani is well connected by **bus** to Almora and Ranikhet, and Bageshwar and Gwaldam further north. The tourist scene is growing and a number of new hotels and restaurants have sprung up in recent years to cater for the very seasonal demand. The fanciest place to **eat** is the *Hill Queen*, a mid-priced but very good-value multi-cuisine restaurant below the Anashakti Ashram. The owner also serves as the unofficial tourist officer and is a mine of information about the area. The new *Ashok* and *Sunrise* restaurants nearby serve inexpensive multi-cuisine dishes.

Accommodation

The prices indicated are for the **low season**, but go up by fifty percent in high season (April 15–June 15 & Oct 1–Nov 15). Rooms with views are much more expensive than those without.

Anashakti Ashram, above the Mall on Snow View Road. Guests prepared to observe ashram rules, such as not smoking, are welcome to stay at Gandhi's pleasant but spartan former ashram. A great place to watch the mountains blush and fade at sunset. No generator. ❶
KMVN Tourist Bungalow, ☎ 05962/45006. The

usual tourist lodge atmosphere but it is at least secluded, and surrounded by pine forests. ❶–❻
Himalaya Mount View, ☎ 05962/45033. In the valley below the ridge, this place is very quiet and rather pleasant, with chunky but elegant wooden furnishings and tile floors. Little English is spoken. Follow the winding main road out of town for

about three hundred metres. **⑤**
Hotel Uttarkhand, below the *Hill Queen*.
Precariously perched on the side of the hill, with
simple doubles and a great roof terrace. The new
second-storey rooms with satellite TV and bidet

toilets are the best value. Recommended. **①**–**③**
Krisdhna, ☎ 05962/45008. A huge place that falls
short of its aspirations to luxury, but good views of
the snows through the telescope in the garden and
a friendly manager. **⑤**

Baijnath and Bageshwar

BAIJNATH is halfway between Kausani, 20km southeast, and Gwaldam to
the west. The road (served by occasional buses) drops down to a broad valley
and to eleventh-century stone temples, standing at a bend in a beautiful river.
This was once an important town of the Katyurs, who ruled much of Garhwal
and Kumaon; now it's more like a park. Unusually, the main temple is devoted
to Parvati, the consort of Shiva, rather than Shiva himself; its 1.5-metre image
of the goddess is one of the few in the complex to have withstood the ravages
of time. The only **amenities** are KMVN's modern *Tourist Rest House* (**②**) and
a couple of simple cafés.

BAGESHWAR, nestled in a steamy valley 90km north of Almora, is one of
Kumaon's most important pilgrimage towns. The lush Gomti River valley
around is lovely, so it's a shame the town is a dump. Its market is a good place

---

The trek to Pindari Glacier

One of the most accessible and varied treks into the heart of the Kumaoni Himalayas
leads from Bageshwar through forests, valleys and high *bugyals* right up to the
Pindari Glacier, 3820m above sea level in the shadow of Nanda Devi. Unless you
want to spend a night at the glacier itself, there's no need to carry a tent or stove,
as the route is amply supplied with KMVN bungalows. These should be booked in
advance through the *Tourist Bungalow* in Bageshwar, which can also provide
trekking equipment and information.

On **Day 1**, take a local bus from **Bageshwar** either to **Bharari**, where there is a
basic hotel and a PWD bungalow, and walk for 16km from there along the Sarayu
valley to **Song**, or catch the bus all the way. From Song, continue for 3km on foot
to **Loharkhet**, which has a basic KMVN *Tourist Bungalow* overlooking the village,
and a PWD bungalow.

Day 2 is considerably more gruelling, involving around 1000m of ascent along a
good forest track for 11km over Dhakuri Pass (2835m), which has superb mountain
views, before dropping 2km down to the KMVN *Tourist Bungalow* at **Dhakuri**.

Day 3 consists of an 8km walk along the Pindar valley to **Khati**, where the Pindar
and Sunderdhanga rivers meet. The last major village along the trail, Khati too has
a bungalow.

Continuing beside the Pindar on **Day 4**, you follow a forested trail past bamboo,
fern and spectacular waterfalls, for 11km to **Dwali**, where there is more KMVN
accommodation (a trail right from here, with no further facilities of any kind, leads
13km to **Kafni Glacier**, near the base of the elegant 6860m peak of Nanda Kot). For
an early start for Pindari Glacier, head another 5km from Dwali to **Phurkia**, where the
treeline gives way to *bugyal*, used for summer pastures, and there's a KMVN *Tourist
Bungalow*.

Although it's just 8km from Phurkia up to the glacier, **Day 5** can prove long and
exhausting, because if you don't have a tent you'll have to get back down to Phurkia
by nightfall. **Zero Point** (3820m), marks the foot of the Pindari Glacier, which consists of two sections; the bottom is dry and crevassed, with a large rubble-strewn
lateral moraine, while the top is a severely broken ice-fall, topped by a snowfield
known as **Traill's Pass**. Some maps show a route up to the pass, but only expert
mountaineers should attempt it.

Trekking restrictions in eastern Kumaon

With the gradual shrinking of the Inner Line and the removal of restrictions, the mountains of Pithoragarh District are being opened up to trekkers. Ironically, while on certain routes, foreigners do not require **permits**, Indians, including trekking agents, still do. Starting at Tawaghat, the trail via Nue to Johlingkang near the base of Om Parvat (6191m) aka Chotta ("small") Kailash, is currently open. Although the main Kailash trail to Tibet also starts at Tawaghat, access is allowed, via the idyllic Narayan Ashram, only as far as Budhi. Milam Glacier (see p.418) north of Munsiyari has also been derestricted. If the local tourist office and local trekking agencies can't provide the necessary information regarding current regulations, contact the Sub-Divisional Magistrates (SDM) at Pithoragarh, Dharchula or Munsiyari, who are responsible for issuing permits.

to stock up on provisions and it's used by trek groups as the base for the trek to Pindari – although they'd be better off in the nicer villages of Song or Loharkhet. Most foreigners stay at the large, ugly, KMVN *Tourist Bungalow* (**2**), 2km south of the bus station across a bridge, though there are also basic *dharamshalas* and *dhabas* around the temple.

Pithoragarh

PITHORAGARH, the headquarters of the easternmost district of Kumaon, in the beautiful sprawling Sore valley, 188km northeast of Nainital, is a busy administrative and market town which acts as a gateway to the mountains. While the town itself is not particularly attractive and only worth stopping at to stock up on provisions for expeditions, the fringes remain charming with terraced cultivation at an altitude of around 1650m offering glimpses of Panchuli and the remote mountains of western Nepal.

Above Pithoragarh, in the pine-wooded slopes of the **Leprosy Mission** at Chandag 7km north, a large cross overlooks the valley, commanding views of the Saipal and Api massifs in western Nepal. It makes a pleasant walk up from the *Tourist Bungalow*, or you can take local buses en route for Bans.

Practicalities

UPT's low-key **tourist office** at the top of the town, at Siltham (Mon–Fri 10am–5pm; ☎05964/25527), is useful for information on current trekking restrictions. Hill **buses** and shared **taxis** stop here at the main **Roadways Bus Stand**, close to the centre below the bazaar; the smaller, **KMOU Bus Stand** 1km to the north, also services hill destinations. Private bus companies and UPSRTC buses connect the town with **Nainital** (8hr; 1 daily) and **Almora** (6hr; 3 daily), as well as the railheads of **Tanakpur**, 151km south, and **Kathgodam**, 212km southeast. Although amenities in town remain limited, Pithoragarh's busy markets are worth a browse for trek supplies.

Hotel **accommodation** is basic and, for once, the KMVN *Tourist Lodge* (☎05964/22434; **2**–**4**), tucked away in the woods 1.5km above the bazaar on the Chandag Road, comes out tops. The more central *Ulka Priyadarshani* (☎05964/22596; **1**–**2**), in the top bazaar close to the Roadways bus stand, is a very decent clean budget hotel while the cheaper *Trishul* (**1**), nearby, is poky. Along with simple **cafés** and *dhabas* in the bazaars, *Cooks*, Link Road, above Roadways, is about the best that Pithoragarh can offer. *Meghnath*, in Simalgair Bazaar, is a large, decent and very popular snack bar specializing in sweets and *masala dosa*.

Munsiyari

The sprawling village of **MUNSIYARI** stands at the threshold of the inner Himalayas, 154km north of Pithoragarh, looking down on the Gori River gorge and deep valleys branching up into the high mountains. Vantage spots throughout the area offer breathtaking views of the five almost-symmetrical **Panchuli Peaks**, which owe their name – the "five cooking pots" – to their plumes of wind-blown snow. These are notorious for their bad weather, but on clear days at Munsiyari you feel you could almost reach out and touch them.

Among spectacular local high-mountain walks, which are being increasingly derestricted, is the gentle 11km trail up to the **Kalika Pass** (2700m), where a small Shakti temple stands amid dark pines. More difficult trails lead, via the small village of **Matkot**, 12km away, to the glaciers in the Panchuli group, and 30km away to the large alpine meadows of **Chiplakot Bugyal**, dotted with tiny lakes, as well as up to the Milam Glacier and the Johar valley (see below).

Many of the local people are **Bhotias**, of Tibetan stock, who have over the ages absorbed Indian religious and cultural practices, though their origins can be seen in their weaving of carpets, adorned with the ubiquitous dragon motif, and in cultural practices such as animal sacrifice – a festive and a bloody picnic to all and sundry. Carpets are sold in Munsiyari by Pratpsing Pangtey, an elderly gentleman who runs a small carpet factory just below the bus stand.

Munsiyari is at the end of the road, so few buses come this way and those that do are very basic; there are daily departures to **Pithoragarh** (5.30am; 8hr) and **Almora** (5am; 11hr). Most people arrive here by shared Jeep; you'll have to change at Thul for the last four hours of the journey. Along with KMVN's brand new *Tourist Lodge* (**❶–❸**), there are a couple of simple **lodges** near the bus stand and the PWD *Bungalow* (**❶**) has four very comfortable suites with hot water geysers. Most foreigners stay at the pleasant **Martolia Lodge**, a

Trekking in Milam Glacier and the Johar valley

The Milam trail from Munsiyari sets out to explore the beautiful and remote **Johar valley**, in the vicinity of the magnificent peak of Nanda Kot (6860m). Lying near the border with Tibet, and policed by the Indo-Tibetan Border Police, Milam has been closed to visitors until quite recently. Foreigners are allowed to follow the main trails but not to stray off them; check current regulations before setting out.

Day 1 consists of a total walk of 12km. Follow the pony trail from **Munsiyari** down to **Jemighat**, and then along the River Gori until a final forested rise for 3km to **Lilam**, a village which has a PWD bungalow, plus a couple of tea shops and cafés.

Another 12km walk on **Day 2** continues from Lilam beside the Gori along a forested trail for 8km to **Railgari** (whose unusual name means "railway train"), where simple cafés offer very basic accommodation in season. **Bugdiar**, 4km further on, has a PWD guesthouse with a kitchen, a few very limited cafés – and an Indo-Tibet Border Police checkpoint.

A steady but gentle rise from Bugdiar on **Day 3** leads for 7km to mountain *bugyals* and the hamlet of **Manpanga**, which also has a seasonal teashop. Press on for 5km to **Railkot**, where there is limited seasonal accommodation and food.

Set off from Railkot on **Day 4** up a gentle path that reaches the treeline after 6km at the large village of **Burfu**, where basic accommodation includes a hotel. From Burfu a gentle track leads for 4km to **Bilju**, with a teashop and views of Nanda Kot. A further 3km brings you to the large village of **Milam**, home to the Rawats and other groups of Hindu Bhotias; Milam also has a large ITBP presence and a checkpoint where you may be asked to leave your camera. Milam Glacier is 2km further on.

simple homestay 2km from the bus stand with excellent food. Unfortunately it is run by an old goat who tries to charm as much money as he can out of his guests. Payment is "as you like"; Rs200 per day for meals and a room is reasonable.

A handful of **trekking agencies** are cropping up around the bazaar including Panchuli Trekking (☎059612/262554), while Prem Ram, of Gram Bunga, Tala, Nayabasti, is a recommended guide who can organize treks including cooks and porters, from around Rs150 per head per day.

Travel details

Trains
Haridwar to: Calcutta (1 daily; 33hr); Dehra Dun (8 daily; 2hr); Delhi (4 daily; 4hr 30min–8hr); Mumbai (1 daily; 40hr); Kathgodam (3 daily; 4hr 30min–8hr); Rishikesh (2 daily; 30min).
Kathgodam (railhead 3hr from Nainital) to: Calcutta (1 daily; 40hr); Delhi (2 daily; 8hr).

Buses
Almora to: Nainital (4 daily; 3hr); Delhi (2 daily; 11hr).
Dehra Dun to: Delhi (6 daily; 8hr); Kullu/Manali (1 daily; 14hr); Mussoorie (every 30min; 1hr); Nainital (1 daily; 11hr); Rishikesh (every 30min; 1hr 30min)

Haridwar to: Dehra Dun (hourly; 1hr 15min); Delhi (4–6 daily; 5–6hr); Rishikesh (20 daily; 30min).
Mussoorie to: Dehra Dun (every 30min; 1hr); Delhi (2 daily; 9hr); Haridwar (every 30min; 3hr); Rishikesh (every 30min; 4hr); Uttarkashi (2 daily; 7hr).
Nainital to: Almora (4 daily; 3hr); Dehra Dun (1 daily; 10hr 30min); Delhi (4 daily; 8hr); Kausani (4 daily; 5hr); Ramnagar (4 daily; 3hr 30min); Ranikhet (4 daily; 3hr).
Rishikesh to: Haridwar (every 30min; 1hr); Dehra Dun (every 30min; 1hr 30min); Nainital (1 daily; 9hr); Hanumanchatti for Yamunotri (4 daily; 10hr).

✷ **Sanchi** A finely restored
   Buddhist stupa complex,
   complete with intricately
   carved gateways.
   See p.435

✷ **Pachmarhi** The only hill
   station in central India,
   where you can trek to
   the top of a sacred Shiva
   peak, hunt out prehis-
   toric rock art and chill in
   the cool air. See p.445

✷ **Orchha** Central India at
   its most exotic: crum-
   bling riverside tombs,
   ornate Rajput palaces
   and flocks of green parakeets. See p.463

✷ **Khajuraho** Two groups of
   temples swathed in bla-
   tantly erotic sculpture,
   lost for centuries in thick
   jungle but now beautifully restored. See p.468

✷ **Kanha and
   Bandhavgarh national
   parks** Archetypal Kipling
   country, teeming with
   wildlife, including tigers
   and leopards. See p.489
   and p.492

✷ **Mandu** A Moghul fort,
   atop a plateau where the
   emperor got down to
   serious pleasure-seeking
   in his vast harem, theatre, steam baths and
   pavilions. See p.501

5

Madhya Pradesh

Hot, dusty **MADHYA PRADESH** is a vast landlocked expanse of scrub-covered hills, sun-parched plains and dense tree cover that accounts for one third of India's forests. Stretching from beyond the headwaters of the mighty **River Narmada**, at the borders of Orissa and Bihar, to the fringes of the Western Ghats, it's a transitional zone between the Gangetic lowlands in the north and the high dry **Deccan plateau** to the south.

Despite its diverse array of exceptional attractions, ranging from ancient temples and hilltop forts to superb, isolated wildlife reserves, Madhya Pradesh receives only a fraction of the tourist traffic that pours between Delhi, Agra and Varanasi, and the South. For those that do make the effort, this relatively secret gem of a state is both culturally rewarding and largely hassle-free – a welcome break after Rajasthan. While interest from tour groups is rising, the only place you're likely to meet more than a handful of tourists is the palace at Orchha and Khajuraho, one of India's most celebrated temple sites.

Any exploration of central India will be illuminated if you have a grasp of its long and turbulent **history**. Most of the marauding armies that have swept across the peninsula over the last two millennia passed along this crucial corridor, leaving in their wake a bumper crop of monuments. The very first traces of settlement in Madhya Pradesh are the 10,000-year-old paintings on the lonely hilltop of **Bhimbetka**, a day-trip south of the sprawling capital **Bhopal**. Aboriginal rock art was still being created here during the Mauryan emperor Ashoka's evangelical dissemination of Buddhism, in the second century BC. The immaculately restored stupa complex at nearby **Sanchi** is the most impressive relic of this era, ranking among the finest early Buddhist remains in Asia. Nearby, the rock-cut Jain and Hindu caves at **Udaigiri** recall the dynasties that succeeded the Mauryans, from the Andhras to the Guptas in the fourth century.

Accommodation price codes

All accommodation prices in this book have been categorized using the **price codes** below. Prices given are for a double room, and all taxes are included. For more details, see p.51.

❶ up to Rs100	❹ Rs300–400	❼ Rs900–1500
❷ Rs100–200	❺ Rs400–600	❽ Rs1500–2500
❸ Rs200–300	❻ Rs600–900	❾ Rs2500 and upwards

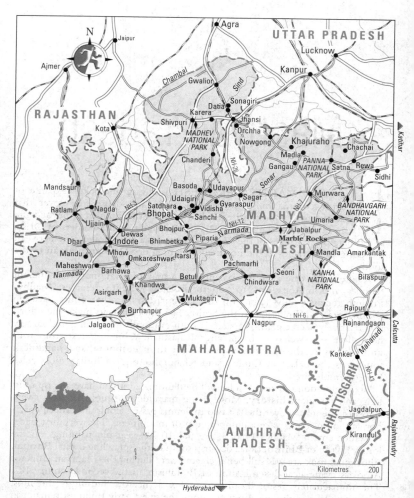

By the end of the first millennium AD, central India was divided into several kingdoms. The Paramaras, whose ruler Raja Bhoj founded Bhopal, controlled the southern and central area, known as **Malwa**, while the **Chandellas**, responsible for some of the subcontinent's most exquisite temples, held sway in the north. Lost deep in the countryside, equidistant from Agra and Varanasi, their magnificent erotica-encrusted sandstone shrines at **Khajuraho** were erected sufficiently far from the main north–south route to have been overlooked by the iconoclastic warriors who marched past in the eleventh and twelfth centuries. Today, the site is as far off the beaten track as ever; its many visitors either fly in, or make the five- to six-hour bus journey from the nearest railheads at **Satna**, to the east, or **Jhansi**, in an anomalous sliver of Uttar Pradesh to the west. Just south of Jhansi, the atmospheric ruined capital of the Bundella rajas at **Orchha** merits a short detour from the highway.

Monuments associated with the long Muslim domination of the region are much easier to visit. The romantic ghost-town of **Mandu**, capital of the Malwa sultans, can be reached in a day from the industrial city of **Indore**, in western Madhya Pradesh. Meanwhile **Gwalior**, whose hilltop fort-palace was the linchpin of both the Delhi Sultanate's and the Moghuls' southward expansion, straddles the main Delhi–Mumbai railway in the far north.

Under the **British**, the middle of India was known as the "Central Provinces", and administered jointly from Nagpur (now in Maharashtra), and the summer capital **Pachmarhi** near Bhopal, the state's highest hill station. Madhya Pradesh, or **"MP"**, only came into being after Independence, when the Central Provinces were amalgamated with a number of smaller princedoms. Since then, the 93-percent-Hindu state, with a substantial rural and tribal population, has remained more stable than neighbouring Uttar Pradesh and Bihar. Major civil unrest was virtually unheard of until the Bhopal riots of 1992–93, sparked off by events in Ayodhya, Uttar Pradesh. Despite this sudden assertion of Hindu fundamentalism, a subsequent backlash against the BJP-led central government in 1998 resulted in Congress reasserting itself as the leading local party. Now that Hindu-Muslim relations are cordial once more, the state has turned to focus on the latest enemy – recurring drought across the poverty-stricken plains and the social and environmental consequences of the damming of the great Narmada river (see p.1546). In November 2000, the boundaries of Madhya Pradesh were redrawn; its elongated eastern portion, which is bereft of sights and does not feature in this guide, became Chhattisgarh.

Visiting Madhya Pradesh

In addition to its historic sites, Madhya Pradesh boasts a number of **wildlife reserves**, of which two are amongst the finest on the subcontinent. In the sparsely populated east, remote savannah grasslands are an ideal habitat for deer and bison, while the shady *sal* forests and *tarai* swamplands that surround the *maidans* provide perfect cover for larger predators such as the **tiger**. Of the **national parks** hidden away in this area, **Kanha** is deservedly popular, though tiger sightings here are on the decline. For the big cats, trek out to **Bandhavgarh** national park to the north.

Getting around Madhya Pradesh without your own vehicle normally involves a lot of bone-shaking bus journeys, usually under the auspices of MPSRTC, the state road transport authority, although deluxe buses ply the main tourist routes too. For longer distances, trains are the best way to go. The Central Railway, the main broad-gauge line between Mumbai and Calcutta, scythes straight through the middle of the state, forking at **Itarsi** junction. One branch veers north towards Bhopal, Jhansi, Gwalior and Agra, while the other continues northeast to Varanasi and eastern India via Jabalpur. In the far west, at Indore and the holy city of **Ujjain**, you can pick up the Western Railway, which heads up through eastern Rajasthan to Bharatpur and Delhi.

The **best time to visit** Madhya Pradesh is during the relatively cool winter months between November and February. In April, May and June the region heats up like a furnace, and daytime temperatures frequently exceed 40°C. If you can stand the heat, this is the best time to catch glimpses of tigers in the parks. The increasingly meagre rains finally sweep in from the southeast in late June or early July.

Central Madhya Pradesh

All roads through the central regions of Madhya Pradesh lead to the state's capital, and its largest and fastest growing city – **Bhopal**. The city itself may come as a pleasant surprise; amidst the dust and chaos of a metropolitan centre there are plenty of quiet parks around its two lakes. Bhopal is also a good place to break the long journey between south and north; within a couple of hours reach is the unmissable Buddhist stupa complex at **Sanchi**, and there are other, lesser monuments in the area. The prehistoric site of **Bhimbetka** is just 45km south of Bhopal, while at the attractive, but rarely visited hill station of **Pachmarhi**, further southeast, enjoyable hikes lead through craggy mountains and thick forests littered with ancient rock-art sites.

Bhopal

With well over a million inhabitants, **BHOPAL**, the capital of Madhya Pradesh, has a skyline of minarets jutting from tightly packed streets and sprawling from the eastern shores of a huge artificial lake. Yet to the west there are verdant hills hiding nouveau-riche suburbs and the more expensive hotels. Below them on Upper Lake, little fishing boats bob along the shore, while middle-class families get down to some serious pedalo action.

In addition to the nineteenth-century **mosques** that bear witness to Bhopal's enduring Muslim legacy, the packed **bazaars** of the walled old city are well worth a visit. Elsewhere, excellent archeological **museums** house large hoards of ancient sculpture. **Bharat Bhavan**, on the lakeside, is one of India's premier centres for performing and visual arts, with an unrivalled collection of contemporary painting, sculpture and *adivasi* (tribal) art, while the **Museum of Man** is an excellent open-air exhibition of *adivasi* houses, culture and technology which aims to challenge prevailing stereotypes of the country's many indigenous groups.

Some history

Bhopal's name is said to derive from the eleventh-century **Raja Bhoj**, who was instructed by his court gurus to atone for the murder of his mother by linking up the nine rivers flowing through his kingdom. A dam, or *pal*, was built across one of them, and the ruler established a new capital around the two resultant lakes – **Bhojapal**. By the end of the seventeenth century, **Dost Mohammed Khan**, an opportunistic ex-soldier of fortune and erstwhile general of Aurangzeb, had occupied the now-deserted site to carve out his own kingdom from the chaos left in the wake of the Moghul empire. The Muslim dynasty he established eventually became one of central India's leading royal families. Under the Raj, its members were among the select few to merit the accolade of a nineteen-gun salute from the British – a consequence of the help given to General Goddard in his march against the Marathas in 1778. In the nineteenth century, Bhopal was presided over largely by women rulers. Holding court from behind the wicker screen of purdah, successive begums revamped the city with noble civic works, including the three sandstone **mosques** which still dominate the skyline.

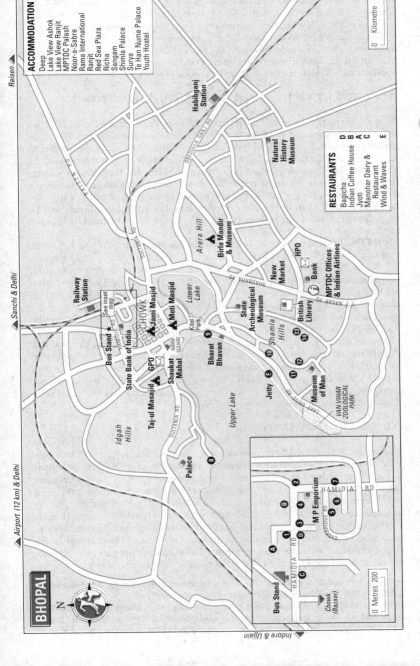

BHOPAL

ACCOMMODATION

Deep	7
Lake View Ashok	11
Lake View Ranjit	10
MPTDC Palash	13
Noor-a-Sabre	8
Rama International	4
Ranjit	3
Red Sea Plaza	2
Richa	1
Sangam	6
Shimla Palace	9
Surya	5
Te Han Numa Palace	12
Youth Hostel	14

RESTAURANTS

Bagicha	D
Indian Coffee House	B
Jyoti	A
Manohar Dairy & Restaurant	C
Wind & Waves	E

Bhojpur, Bhimbetka & Itarsi ▲

Raisen ◀

Sanchi & Delhi ◀

Airport (12 km) & Delhi ◀

Indore & Ujjain ◀

Habibganj Station

Natural History Museum

Arera Hill

Birla Mandir & Museum

HPO

New Market

Bank

MPTDC Offices & Indian Airlines

Railway Station

See inset map

CHOWK

Jami Masjid

Moti Masjid

Lower Lake

State Archeological Museum

British Library

Shamla Hills

Kilol Park

Bus Stand

State Bank of India

GPO

Shaukat Mahal

IQBAL SQUARE

Bharat Bhavan

Jetty

Museum of Man

VAN VIHAR ZOOLOGICAL PARK

Taj-ul Masjid

Idgah Hills

Upper Lake

Palace

0 Kilometre 1

N

Inset map:

Bus Stand

Chowk (Bazaar)

M P Emporium

HAMIDIA RD

0 Metres 200

425

Today, Bhopal carries the burden of the appalling Union Carbide factory gas disaster of 1984 (see p.428), with residents quick to remind you of their continuing legal and medical plight. More recently, in 1992, Hindu-Muslim rioting broke out following the destruction of the Babri Masjid in Ayodhya (see p.328), leading to a record eleven-day curfew being imposed. In spite of the inter-communal violence, however, the many tales of Hindus sheltering their Muslim friends from the mobs at this time and vice versa, demonstrate the long tradition of religious tolerance which exists in the city.

Arrival, information and city transport

Bhopal's **airport**, served by daily Indian Airlines flights from Delhi, Gwalior and Mumbai, is around 12km by taxi or auto-rickshaw from the city. The main **railway station**, by contrast, is within easy walking distance of the centre; to reach the hotel district, leave by the exit on platforms 4 or 5, and head past the tonga rank until you reach the busy corner of **Hamidia Road**. Approaching Bhopal from the south, most trains also stop briefly at **Habibganj station**, a long way out – only get off here if you intend to stay in one of the expensive hotels in Shamla Hills or the New Market area. The main **bus stand**, used by long-distance buses from Indore, Jabalpur, Pachmarhi, Sanchi and Ujjain is ten minutes' walk west of the railway station.

MPTDC has helpful **tourist information** counters in the arrivals hall at the station (platform 1 exit), and on the fourth floor of the Gangotri Building on TT Nagar, New Market (℡0755/774340,℗www.madhyapradeshtourism.com), fifteen minutes south of the railway station by auto-rickshaw. They don't hand out street maps or run a city tour, but they're a useful source of travel information for the whole state, and can pre-book any MPTDC accommodation for you. They also rent out minibuses and Ambassador or Maruti cars for around Rs1000 per day.

Most of Bhopal's principal places of interest are so far apart that the best way of **getting around** has to be by metered **auto-rickshaws**, all of which sport smart interior upholstery and uniformed drivers (perhaps the reason for their slightly above average fares). **Taxis** can be found outside all of the top hotels, or else arranged through MPTDC. There's also a prepaid taxi and auto-rickshaw booth outside the station on Hamidia Road.

Accommodation

Visitors not too bothered by the roar of traffic and its accompanying pollution need look no further than **Hamidia Road** for a **place to stay**. Bhopal's busy main thoroughfare, within easy walking distance of the bus and railway stations (leave the latter via platforms 4 and 5), is crammed with hotels. These range from grim, menonly fleapits to modern Western-style establishments with porters and glitzy reception desks; we have only included the cleanest and safest hotels in the area. Bargains are thin on the ground; all, even the dingiest dives, will slap a ten-percent "luxury" tax and an equally stiff "service charge" on your bill. Most of Bhopal's **top hotels** favour congenial locations close to **Upper Lake**, a fifteen-minute ride from the railway station. Checkout in all of the following is 24hr unless otherwise stated.

Jehan Numa Palace, 57 Shamla Hills ℡ 0755/540100, ℗ 540720. The heritage hotel of Bhopal, in a palazzo-style building set around a central courtyard, in spacious grounds with topnotch restaurant, coffee shop, pastry shop, internet, bar and foreign exchange, but no lake view. Noon checkout. ❽–❾

Lake View Ashok, Shamla Hills ℡ 0755/541600. Ugly building and stuffy management, but in a prime site overlooking the lake. The rooms are comfortable, and there are the usual facilities including moneychanging, swish restaurant and shops. **⑧–⑨**

Lake View Ranjit, Lake Drive Road ①0755/660600, ②660321. A new hotel right on the shores of Upper Lake. Every one of the well-appointed rooms has a wall of glass to enjoy panoramic views of the water, and the roof-terrace restaurant and 24hr coffee shop are cooled by lake breezes. Foreign-exchange and free station and airport pick-up/drop-off available. The tariff includes buffet breakfast. **⑧**

MPTDC Palash, TT Nagar, near New Market ①0755/553006. Pleasant and popular, with 33 variously priced, large rooms around a lawn. There is a good restaurant, café and bar. Tourist information is readily available and other MPTDC hotels can be reserved from here. Book ahead. Noon checkout. **⑥–⑦**

Noor-a-Sabre, Palace Grounds ①0755/74910. The old imperial palace has been recently revamped and turned into a plush five-star with rooms looking down to the lake across tropical gardens. Home to the most expensive restaurant in town serving predictably good and safe multi-cuisine. **⑨**

Rama International, Hamidia Road ①0755/535542. Walk though a courtyard off the main road to this relatively peaceful and rambling hotel. The rooms are simple and clean, with some cheap a/c rooms. **②–④**

Ranjit, Hamidia Road ①0755/533511. One of the best along the stretch, with light and clean rooms (all with attached bathrooms and cable TV), a terrace bar and a popular, cheap restaurant downstairs. **③–④**

Red Sea Plaza, Hamidia Road ①0755/741518. A large, functional hotel that is conveniently close to the railway station, but poorly maintained with overpriced grubby rooms. A fall-back option only. **③–⑤**

Richa, 1 Hamidia Rd ①0755/532564. Clean, efficient and very good value, with satellite TV and hot water in all rooms. **④–⑤**

Sangam, Overbridge Road ①0755/542382. Big building with variously priced, clean rooms on different floors. Good standards and all have cable TV, but the deluxe rooms aren't worth the extra. **②–③**

Shimla Palace, 31 Shimla Rd ①0755/546987. Very pleasant, family-run place in a quiet suburban backstreet overlooking the lake. The rooms, some with views, are neat and spacious. **②–④**

Surya, Hamidia Road ①0755/741701. Better than most in the area but more pricey; the clean standard rooms are the best value. Noon checkout. **④–⑥**

Youth Hostel, TT Nagar, New Market ①0755/553670. Absolutely no-frills institutional hostel, but in an excellent location for sightseeing and moneychanging. The dorms (Rs40) are dismal, but the basic and excellent-value doubles are clean and all have air-coolers. The communal bathrooms are all well-maintained. **②**

The City

Bhopal has two separate centres. Spread over the hill to the south of the lakes, the **New Market** area, as its name implies, is a recent extension of the city – a modest agglomeration of shopping arcades, cybercafés, ice-cream parlours, cinemas and modern office blocks. Once you've squeezed through the strip of land that divides the Upper and (smaller) Lower lakes, sweeping avenues, civic buildings and pleasure gardens quickly give way to the more heavily congested **old city**. Focused around the **Jami Masjid** mosque, the **bazaar**, in the area known as **Chowk**, occupies the dense grid of streets between **Moti Masjid Square** to the south and the most chaotic stretches of Hamidia Road to the north. The art **galleries** and **museums** are all tucked down side-roads off New Market, or along the hilly southern edge of the Upper Lake.

Chowk

Bhopal's vibrant bazaar (closed Mon & Fri), situated in the old **Chowk** district, comes as a very welcome splash of colour after the dismal, traffic-filled streets around the railway station. Famous for "*zarda, purdah, garda and namarda*" (tobacco, veils, dust and eunuchs), its bustling back lanes have retained a strong Muslim ambience with overhanging balconies intricately carved with Islamic geometric designs. Many of the women only venture out in long black *burkhas*,

The Bhopal gas tragedy

Bhopal is notorious as the site of the world's worst industrial disaster. Late at night, on December 2, 1984, a lethal cloud of Methyl Iso-Cynate (MIC), a toxic chemical used in the manufacture of pesticides, exploded from a tank at the huge **Union Carbide** plant on the northern edge of the city.

MIC is a highly reactive chemical that has to be kept under constant pressure and at a temperature of zero degrees centigrade, but regardless of the hazard, cost-conscious officials had reduced the pressure in order to save about $40 a day. The danger was heightened when water entered Tank 610 through badly maintained and leaking valves to contaminate the MIC, and a massive reaction was triggered. Cool wind dispersed the gas throughout densely populated residential districts and shanty settlements. There was no warning siren and no emergency procedures to put in place, leaving the thick cloud of burning gas to blind and suffocate its victims. The leak killed 1600 instantly (according to official figures) and about 6000 in the aftermath, but the figure now totals over 20,000 in the years since the incident. Over 500,000 people were exposed to the gas, of whom about one-fifth have been left with chronic and incurable health problems, often passed on to children born since the disaster.

The factory officials and their "medical experts" initially said that the effect of MIC was akin to tear gas, causing only temporary health problems. They accepted moral responsibility for the disaster, but blamed the Indian government for inadequate safety standards when it came to the issue of compensation. Only in 1989, did Union Carbide agree to pay an average of Rs15,000 to each adult victim – a paltry sum which didn't even cover loans for the medical bills in the first five years, let alone compensate for the loss of life and livelihoods, and other consequences of the disaster. Relatives of only 6000 of the victims who died have received compensation; the rest have been rejected on grounds that the death was not related to gas exposure, rather it was a result of "personal injury". Government and factory authorities have been keen to sweep the whole catalogue of disasters under the carpet – both US and Indian officials charged with serious offences, including manslaughter, have escaped their sentences to date.

The incidence of TB, cancers, infertility and cataracts in the affected area is way above the national average, yet the government has failed to complete any of the proposed specialist hospitals for the gas victims, who are forced to use ill-qualified and expensive local private practitioners. As if the suffering was not already enough, the water in the community pumps of the affected residential areas is contaminated with dangerous toxic chemicals that seeped out from the now-deserted factory. Union Carbide has reinvented itself elsewhere in India under the name of Eveready Industries India Ltd.

The Union Carbide factory now stands desolate and overgrown, but widespread suffering continues daily. If you are interested in learning more about the disaster or volunteering your services in the affected communities, contact the Sambhavna Trust at 44, Sant Kanwar Ram Nagar, Berasia Road, Bhopal 462 018 ☎ 0755/730914, @ sambavna@bom.6.vsnl.net.in.

while the older men, sporting *kurta pajama*, crocheted skull-caps and henna-ed beards, spend much of the day sitting cross-legged on their raised wooden shop fronts or *haveli* balconies murmuring verses from the Koran. Each of the narrow streets radiating from the central market square specializes in a different type of merchandise. One has a monopoly on brocaded "Chanderi" silk saris, another, west of the square, is given over to the bass drums and wailing clarinets of Bhopali wedding bands; others deal in brassware, spices and shoes. Particular specialities of the bazaar include *tussar* silk, silver jewellery and the gaudily beaded women's purses for which Bhopal is renowned.

The most straightforward way to approach the northern – Hamidia Road – end of the bazaar is via the lane leading south off the busy crossroads by the main bus stand. Bear right at the bottom and you'll eventually come out near a large **fortified gateway** – one of the last remaining fragments of the walls that once encircled the old city. At the very centre of the bazaar, the rich red sandstone walls and stumpy minarets of the **Jami Masjid** appear at the end of the street. Built in 1837 by Kudsia Begum, the mosque boasts neither age nor great architectural merit, but its whitewashed domes and gleaming gilded pinnacles lend an exotic air to proceedings in the square below.

Imam Square to the Tajul Masajid

A short way southwest of the Chowk area, **Imam Square** was once the epicentre of royal Bhopal. Nowadays, it's little more than a glorified traffic island, only worth stopping at to admire the **Moti Masjid** on its eastern edge. The "Pearl Mosque", erected in 1860 by Sikander Begum, Kudsia's daughter, is a diminutive and much less imposing version of Shah Jahan's Jami Masjid in Old Delhi, notable more for its slender, gold-topped minarets and sandstone cupolas than its size.

Lining the opposite, northern side of the square near the ceremonial archway is a markedly more eccentric nineteenth-century building. The **Shaukat Mahal** was originally designed by a French architect (allegedly descended from the Bourbon royal family) and is an unlikely fusion of Italian, Gothic and Islamic influences. Unfortunately, both the palace and the elegant **Sadar Manzil** (Hall of Public Audience) have been converted into government offices and are closed to visitors.

Leaving Imam Square by the archway to the west, a five-minute walk brings you to the foot of Bhopal's most impressive monument. With its matching pair of colossal pink minarets soaring high above the city skyline, the **Darul Uloom Tajul Masajid** (daily except Fri and during Id ul-Fitr) certainly lives up to the epithet of "mother of all mosques", as denoted by the extra "a" in its name. Whether it also deserves to be dubbed the biggest in India, as locals claim, is rather less certain. The main entrance, along the west side, opens onto a large walled courtyard with a square *dukka* – the fountain and water tank used for ritual ablutions – to the south. At the opposite end, the bulbous white domes and multi-tiered towers flanking the facade are at their most imposing. Work on the building commenced under the auspices of Sultan Jehan Begum (1868–1901), the eighth ruler of Bhopal. After the death of the domineering sultan, his widow embarked on a spending spree that left the city with a postal system, new schools and a railway, but which all but impoverished the royal family – the reason the Tajul Masajid was never completed. If you plan to go inside, make sure you come suitably dressed.

The state archeological museum

Hidden away near Raj Bhavan, just south of Lower Lake, the modest, poorly labelled collection of ancient sculpture, bronzes and Moghul miniatures at the **state archeological museum**, or *Rajkiya Sangrahalaya* (Tues–Sat 10am–5pm; Ⓦwww.mparchaeology.com; free), is only likely to inspire real enthusiasts. If you do end up here, among the more noteworthy exhibits in the main gallery are the second-century BC *yakshis* (female fertility figures), the standing Buddha in black granite and the fifth-century statue of Karttikeya, the Hindu god of war. The far wall in the last gallery holds a reproduction of the famous – but now badly damaged – Bagh frescoes, contemporary with those at Ajanta in Maharashtra. On your way out through the main foyer, have a look at the plaster-cast souvenir copies of the exquisite *salabhanjika* figurine from Gyaraspur. The original, one of India's most valuable pieces of stone sculpture, is in Gwalior museum (see p.455). To the left of the foyer, there is an *adivasi* gallery with a brave attempt at the reconstruction of a Warli house and some fine exhibits of the colourful and descriptive wall art common throughout rural Madhya Pradesh.

The Birla Mandir museum

Much to the chagrin of the state museum, the **Birla Mandir** collection (Tues–Sun 9am–noon & 2–6pm; Rs3) comprises some of the finest stone sculpture in Madhya Pradesh. It's also more informatively displayed, with explanatory panels in English in the main galleries. The museum is in a detached house beside Birla Mandir, the garish modern Hindu Lakshmi Narayan temple that stands high on the hill overlooking Lower Lake. The temple gardens overlook the city sprawl and are a fine place to watch the sun setting behind the minarets.

As usual, the exhibition is divided between Vishnu, the mother goddesses and Shiva. The **Vishnu** section contains some interesting representations of the god's diverse and frequently bizarre reincarnations (*avatars*), though the portly Rajnavahara – the wild boar whose form he adopted in order to rescue the earth from the depths of the primordial ocean – hardly oozes with the panache one might expect of a cosmic superhero. In the **Devi** gallery next door, a cadaverous Chamunda (the goddess Durga in her most terrifying aspect) stands incongruously amid a row of voluptuous maidens and fertility figures. Note the dying man writhing at her feet. The **Shiva** room, by contrast, is altogether more subdued. Many of the beautifully carved bas-reliefs show the god of preservation and destruction enjoying moments of marital bliss on Mount Kailash with his consort Parvati – an icon known as *Uma-Maheshwar*.

Finally, have a look at the replicas of the 3500-year-old **Harappan** artefacts encased under the stairs. One of the seals bears an image of the pre-Aryan god Rudra, seated in the lotus position; archeologists believe he was the ancient forerunner of Shiva.

Bharat Bhavan

Inaugurated in 1982 as part of a national bid to promote visual and performing arts, **Bharat Bhavan** (Tues–Sun: Feb–Oct 2–8pm; Nov–Jan 1–7pm; Rs5) was originally intended as one of several such institutions set up in state capitals throughout the country. After Indira Gandhi's death the initiative fizzled out, but Bhopal's contribution has become established as provincial India's most outstanding arts centre.

Once you're within range, the building isn't hard to find, standing on the hill above the lake. Charles Correa's campus of concrete domes and dour brickwork was designed, apparently, to "merge in exquisite harmony with the landscape, creating a visual impact of spacious and natural elegance"; it would have looked less out of place on the Maginot Line. Fortunately, the prospect improves when you step inside. There are temporary exhibitions as well as a large split-level permanent collection of modern Indian painting and sculpture. Rather incongruously placed in the midst of complex abstract offerings is an eighteenth-century gilt-framed "landscape" by the Daniells – the uncle-nephew duo employed as a part of the "Company School of Painting" during the Raj. Company artists had to churn out beautiful and romantic paintings of India for those back home in Britain who could not imagine the nature of the subcontinent. Bharat Bhavan has one gallery devoted exclusively to **adivasi**

art, in search of which talent scouts spent months roaming remote regions. Among their more famous discoveries was the Gond painter **Jangarh Singh Shyam**, featured by veteran BBC correspondent Mark Tully in his book *No Full Stops In India*. A number of Jangarh's works are on display here, along with a colourful assemblage of masks, terracottas, woodcarvings and ritual paraphernalia. The absence of background information is intentional – the exhibition is intended to represent the objects as works of art in their own right, rather than merely anthropological curios.

If you're wondering how to spend an evening in Bhopal, scan the posters in the foyer for forthcoming **events** at Bharat Bhavan such as theatre productions and music and dance recitals. The pleasant café, to the right of the main building, is just the place to pen a couple of the tribal art **postcards** on sale in the office next to the gate.

The Museum of Man

The story of India's indigenous minorities – the *adivasis*, literally "original inhabitants" – is all too familiar. Dispossessed of their land by large-scale "development" projects or exploitative moneylenders, the "tribals" have seen a gradual erosion of their traditional culture – a process hastened by proselytizing missionaries and governments that tend at best to regard tribal people as anachronistic and, at worst, as an embarrassment. The **Museum of Man**, properly known as the *Rashtriya Manav Sangrahalaya* (Tues–Sun: March–Aug 11am–6.30pm; Sept–Feb 10am–5.30pm; free), is an enlightened attempt to redress the balance, setting out to provide genuine insights into ways of life few see at first hand. The aim is twofold: to expose city people to the overall richness and ingenuity of India's tribal culture and to foster greater respect for their heritage among the *adivasis* themselves.

Overlooking New Market on one side and the majestic sweep of Upper Lake on the other, the two-hundred-acre hilltop site includes a reconstructed Keralan coastal village, and a winding, mythological trail where each tribal group from the state has contributed their own interpretation of the creation (with clear English translations). A large exhibition hall draws on all the daily and ritual elements in the *adivasi* lifestyle, although the focus is on one group at a time. Dotted amongst the forest scrub are a botanical trail, a research centre and, as its centrepiece, a permanent open-air exhibition of traditional *adivasi* houses, compounds and religious shrines collectively known as the "**tribal habitat**". Specialist *adivasi* craftsmen and women from all corners of India were brought in to construct and maintain authentic replicas of these buildings, using only tools and materials available in their home environments.

Before tackling the exhibition, have a quick look at the **introductory gallery** in the small building opposite the main entrance (the approach from New Market). From here, a flight of steps leads underneath a thatched gateway (a structure adapted from the "youth dormitory" of the Ao-Naga from Nagaland) up to the top of the hill, where the seventeen or so dwelling complexes are scattered. On a quiet day, the empty mud huts, corral and beaten-earth courtyards form a striking contrast to the teeming city all around. Nearly all the house **interiors** contain original tools, cooking utensils, baskets and musical instruments, while some are beautifully decorated with intricate **murals**, mouldings and carved beams. Of particular note are the multicoloured paintings of horses adorning the walls of the Rathwa huts (look out for the picture of the train that carried the artists from their village in Gujarat); the ochre, red, black and yellow rectangular designs inside the Gadaba buildings (from Orissa); and the famous Warli wedding paintings of northern

Maharashtra, which show the tribal fertility goddess Palghat framed by complex geometrical patterns.

The only way of **getting to the museum** without your own vehicle is by auto-rickshaw; drivers will probably insist on double the meter rate for the twenty-minute ride from the railway station as they're unlikely to pick up a return fare, so negotiate a flat rate for the round trip, taking at least an hour's waiting time into consideration. A cheaper option is to take a bus or *tempo* from the railway station to New Market and pick up a rickshaw there. The museum has nowhere to buy snacks or drinks, so come with an ample supply as it can be hot work.

Museum of Natural History

The newly constructed **Regional Museum of Natural History** (Tues–Sun 10am–5pm; free) is several kilometres southeast of New Market, so again the only real option is to go by auto-rickshaw. Around a courtyard with model dinosaurs and colourful murals there are attractive and well-written displays on biodiversity and ecosystems, and on the geological history of the earth. There are also temporary exhibitions, a discovery centre (10.30am–noon & 2.30–4pm) and a film show at 4pm.

Van Vihar Zoological Park

If you haven't made it to Madhya Pradesh's bona fide national parks, or if you have, but missed the big cats, it's well worth visiting **Van Vihar Zoological Park** (daily 7–11am & 2–5.30pm; Rs100 [Rs10], free for children under 5; Rs25 extra with camera, Rs200 extra with video; for transport around the park, a rickshaw is Rs100-150 plus Rs10 entrance fee, bicycle Rs3 entrance fee). A trip round the five-square-kilometre sanctuary ties in nicely with a visit to the Museum of Man next door – keep the same rickshaw for the whole trip. The star of the park is a regal white tiger, but you can also see tortoises, long-nosed *gharial*, leopards, Himalayan bears and Indian tigers. The best chance of sightings is from 4pm onwards, when the mighty felines pad and drool close to the boundaries of their enclosures, waiting for their daily feed. Sambar (deer) munch the grass nearby, while egrets, herons, cormorants and ducks take in the evening light on the lake shore. You can get a longer and more peaceful look at the birds by taking a boat from the jetty, half a kilometre from the park gate (9am–sunset; pedal and rowing boats Rs30–35 per 30min). Set back from the jetty, MPTDC's *Wind and Waves Restaurant* is close at hand for refreshment.

Eating

Restaurants in Bhopal's larger hotels serve uniformly spicy north Indian food with a few Continental and Chinese dishes thrown in for good measure; the strip-light-and-formica cafés opposite the bus stand do thalis and hot platefuls of *subzi*, rice and dhal for next to nothing. For breakfast try the state's favourite food, *poha* – a light steamed rice dish served piping hot in newspaper from every street corner, followed by their famous *katchoris* (a fried snack stuffed with lentils) and a chai. Stalls in New Market serve big glasses of frothy fresh juice, and there are lots of cheap fruit shops nearby to stock up on those vitamins.

Bagicha Bar and Restaurant, Hamidia Road. Mostly Mughlai and Punjabi dishes served al fresco in a courtyard. Pleasant, but quite pricey.

Bharat Bhavan Café, Bharat Bhavan Arts Centre. Refreshingly mixed crowd of artists, workers and visitors lounge around in this friendly and relaxed café, which serves up tea, coffee, cold drinks and light snacks. The terrace is a great place to put your legs up and watch the sunset (bring mozzie repellent).

Indian Coffee House, Hamidia Road. Bhopal's big breakfast venue offers tasty south Indian snacks, eggs and filter coffee served with great style. Open 7.30am until late evening.

Jehan Numa Palace, Shamla Hills. Fine Mughlai cuisine and barbecue specialities in a beautiful Rajera mansion. The Western menu is also excellent.

Jyoti, 53 Hamidia Rd. Popular hotel-restaurant specializing in traditional (mild, pure-veg) Gujarati food. Lunchtime thalis are particularly good value.

Manohar Dairy & Restaurant, Hamidia Road. South Indian snacks, speciality sweets and *namkeen*, plus a full range of ice cream – the perfect antidote to chilli.

Mehfil, below *Ranjit Hotel*, Hamidia Road. Exceedingly dark restaurant and bar serving up generous piles of no-nonsense northern food to discerning office workers.

Palash, TT Nagar, New Market. Upstairs there is a cheap and tasty south Indian Café (open 11am–11pm). In the popular restaurant downstairs, the multi-cuisine menu may be standard, but the food is absolutely delicious, especially the Indian veg and fish dishes. Reserve in advance at weekends.

Wind and Waves, just up from the boathouse on the lake. Sample the same old MPTDC menu in a better-than-usual setting that is conveniently close to the lakeside museums. Opens at 11am until late.

Listings

Airlines Indian Airlines has an office in the Gangotri complex on Bhadbada Road, New Market (Mon–Sat 9am–5pm, Sun 9am–noon; ☎ 0755/550480), and a booking counter at the airport.

Banks and exchange Apart from the top hotels, only the main New Market branches of some banks do foreign exchange. Banks such as IBIB bank in New Market have ATMs which accept Visa and Mastercard. The most efficient and convenient place is the State Bank of India (Mon–Fri 10.30am–2pm, Sat 10.30am–12.30pm), next to the GPO.

Bookstores The two English-language bookstores at the top of Bhadbada Road in New Market stock a reasonable range of paperbacks (mostly popular fiction and Indian authors in translation). A more limited selection is available from the newsstand on platform 1 at the railway station.

Hospital Bhopal's main Hamidia hospital (☎ 0755/540222) is on Sultania Road, between Imam Square and the Darul Uloom Tajul Masajid. The small private Hajela Hospital (☎ 0755/773392) on TT Nagar is excellent. Doctors are best arranged through the top hotels.

Internet access By far the best email and internet facilities are available at the British Library (see below). The service is extremely fast and efficient, although a steep Rs60 per hour.

Left luggage Most hotels will look after your bags free of charge. If not, try the parcel office at the railway station.

Library The British Council has a library in the GTB Complex on Roshanpura Naka, New Market (Tues–Sat 11am–7pm; ☎ 0755/553767). Non-members are welcome to peruse their collection of British newspapers, magazines and periodicals.

Post office The Head Post Office is on TT Nagar in New Market, or there's a GPO on Sultania Road near the Darul Uloom Tajul Masajid (both Mon–Fri 10am–5pm, Sat 10am–noon). To receive mail, have it sent to the Head Post Office well in advance – the poste restante at the GPO is unreliable.

Shopping Chowk (closed Mon & Fri) is the best place for silk and silver; New Market (Tues–Sat) has some bigger stores, including Mrignayani for handicrafts, men's calico shirts and trendy ethnic *salwar kamises*. The MP State Emporium on Hamidia Road is the place to buy batiks, *dokra* metalwork, *khadi* clothes, bedspreads and silk saris, although the fixed prices are not cheap. Check the street stalls on Overbridge Road for bargains.

Around Bhopal

Within a couple of hours' journey from Bhopal lie a wealth of ancient monuments, all of which are generally more impressive than the state capital's own his-

Bhopal is on one of the two broad-gauge train lines between Delhi and Mumbai. If you're heading north via Jhansi (for Orchha/Khajuraho), Gwalior or Agra, you have a choice between a good twelve or so regular services; and the super-fast, completely a/c Shatabdi Express #2001 which leaves Bhopal at 2.50pm promptly and arrives in Delhi a mere 7hr 45min later. The one train to avoid on this route is the super-slow Amritsar–Dadar Express #1457. In the other direction, the 5.25pm Punjab Mail #2138 is the best for Mumbai (14hr 55min). The nightly service to Jabalpur, Narmada Express #8233, leaves at 11pm and gets in at 5.50am, leaving time to pick up a connecting bus to Kanha. You'll have to change at Itarsi Junction, 92km south, for Calcutta and Varanasi.

Most journeys from Bhopal are easier and quicker by train, but the city's good bus connections are especially useful for Indore, which can be reached either on frequent state buses or the daily MPSRTC super-fast luxury service, which connects with the arrival of the Shatabdi Express (for Ujjain, get off at Dewas and pick up a local bus for the remaining 37km); tickets are sold at the MPTDC counter in the railway station. There are several daily buses to Pachmarhi (5–6hr), which leave from the state bus stand on Hamida Road, the fastest of which departs at 7am.

Daily trains to Sanchi leave Bhopal at 8am (45min) and 10.05am (55min); there are also hourly buses (1hr 30min–2hr).

toric sights. To the northeast, the third-century BC stupas at **Sanchi** can be seen in an easy day-trip from Bhopal, or as a stopover as you head north on the Central Railway. Sanchi's peaceful setting and good facilities make it an ideal base for visits to more stupas at **Satdhara,** or to **Udaigiri's** rock-cut caves and the nearby Column of Heliodorus at **Besnagar.** Avid templo-philes with the luxury of their own vehicle may also be enticed by the remote Gupta ruins at **Udayapur.**

Close to the main road south towards Hoshangabad and the Narmada Valley, the prehistoric cave paintings at **Bhimbetka** can be visited in a day by bus. If you rent a car, the eleventh-century Shiva temple at **Bhojpur,** with its monolithic *shivalingam,* is also worth checking out along the way.

Satdhara

Set among verdant rolling hills 30km north of Bhopal, **SATDHARA** ("seven streams") is well worth the detour for stupa enthusiasts, although you'll need your own vehicle to get there. Heading north from Bhopal, a signpost about 13km south of Sanchi points west down a motorable seven-kilometre dirt-track leading to the excavated site. There are no less than thirty-four **stupas** dating from the Mauryan period in the third century BC, several of which are in good condition, and fourteen **monasteries**, three of which have substantial foundations still visible. Under the auspices of UNESCO, a number of the stupas and two of the monasteries have now been reconstructed using original methods and materials, and others including the huge **stupa 1** are currently under excavation and renovation.

A path down to the left of the makeshift car park leads directly to a line of well-restored stupas, perched on the cliff edge of a dramatic ravine. No human bones have been discovered in any of these mounds, unlike their counterparts at Sanchi. Past **stupas 6, 7,** and **8** you come to the largest and most impressive of them all, known simply as **stupa 1**, standing 13m high and with a *medhi* (broad circumambulatory path) around the base. Some of its sculpted **toranas** (gateways) have been moved a short distance away for restoration work, but remain on view. Immediately behind it is the imposing 3m-tall foundation platform of **Monastery 1**, whilst to the right are two circular **mills**, where oxen still push a great stone around a rut to crush the lime, sand and stone rubble for cement – the technique used by the original architects.

Alongside the numerous subsidiary stupas and monasteries, the remains of **apsidal temples** from the second century BC Gupta period bear inscriptions in Brahmi script. A multitude of coins, tools and terracotta objects have been unearthed and removed for cataloguing and eventual display. If you do make it here, you're virtually guaranteed to have the atmospheric site all to yourself.

Sanchi

From a distance, the smooth-sided hemispherical object that appears on a hillock overlooking the main train line at **SANCHI**, 46km northeast of Bhopal, has the surreal air of a space station or an upturned satellite dish. In fact, the giant stone mound stands as testimony to a much older means of communing with the cosmos. Quite apart from being India's finest surviving Buddhist monument, the **Great Stupa** is one of the earliest religious structures in the subcontinent. It presides over a complex of ruined temples and monasteries that collectively provide a rich and unbroken record of the development of Buddhist art and architecture from the faith's first emergence in central India during the third century BC, until it was eventually squeezed out by the resurgence of Brahmanism during the medieval era.

A visit to Sanchi, however, is no dry lesson in South Asian art history. The main stupa is surrounded by some of the richest and best-preserved ancient **sculpture** you're ever likely to see *in situ*, while the site itself, floating serenely above a vast expanse of open plains, has pre-

SANCHI

Vidisha & Udaigiri Caves

Railway Station
Mahabodhi Society Guest House
Jaiswal Hotel
Bus Stand
Cycle Rental
Dhabas
Government Rest House
MPTDC Cafeteria
Ticket Kiosk
Archeological Museum
MPTDC Travellers Lodge
Tank
New Temple
Stupa 2
Stupa 3
Vihara 45
Vihara 51
The Great Stupa
Ashok's Pillar
Temple 18
Temple 17

Bhopal
Bhopal

N

0   Metres   300

served the tranquillity that must have attracted its original occupants. Most visitors find a couple of hours more than sufficient to explore the ruins, although you could spend several days poring over the four exquisite gateways, or **toranas**, that surround the Great Stupa. Paved walkways and steps lead around the hilltop enclosure (daily 8am–6pm; $10 [Rs5]), dotted with interpretive panels and shady trees to relax under if the heat gets the better of you.

The site is connected to the small village at the foot of the hill by a metalled road. Once you've bought an entrance ticket from the roadside booth outside the **museum**, head up the stone steps on the right, past the welcoming posse of postcard-wallahs, to the main entrance. From here, the central walkway runs alongside the new Sri Lankan Buddhist temple and a cold-drinks stall, before leading straight to the Great Stupa.

Some history

Unlike the other famous Buddhist centres in eastern India and Nepal, Sanchi has no known connection with the life of Buddha himself. It first became a place of pilgrimage when the Mauryan emperor **Ashoka**, who married a woman from nearby **Besnagar** (see p.443), erected a polished stone pillar and brick-and-mortar stupa here midway through the third century BC. The complex was enlarged by successive dynasties, but after the eclipse of Buddhism Sanchi lay deserted and overgrown until its rediscovery in 1818 by General Taylor of the Bengal Cavalry. In the years that followed, a swarm of heavy-handed treasure hunters invaded the site, eager to crack open the giant stone eggs and make off with what they imagined to be their valuable contents. In fact, only Stupas 3 and 4 yielded anything more than rubble; the soapstone relic caskets containing bone fragments are displayed in the new temple for one day each December. These amateur archeologists, however, left the ruins in a sorry state. Deep gouges gaped from the sides of stupas 1 and 2, a couple of ceremonial gateways completely collapsed, and much of the masonry was plundered by the villagers for building materials (one local landlord is alleged to have carted off Ashoka's pillar to use as a roller in his sugar cane press).

Restoration work made little impact until the archeologist John Marshall and the Buddhist scholar Albert Foucher took on the job in 1912. The jungle was hacked away, the main stupas and temples were rebuilt, lawns and trees planted and a museum erected to house what sculpture had not been shipped off to Delhi or London.

The Great Stupa

Stupa 1, or the **Great Stupa**, stands on a stretch of level ground at the western edge of the plateau. Fragments of the original construction, a much smaller version built in the third century BC by Ashoka, still lie entombed beneath the thick outer shell of lime plaster added a century later. The **Shungas** were responsible for the raised processional balcony, and the two graceful staircases that curve gently around the sides of the drum from the paved walkway at ground level, as well as the aerial-like *chhattra* and its square enclosure which crown the top of the mound. Four elaborate gateways were added by the **Satavahanas** in the first century BC, followed by the four serene **meditating Buddhas** that greet you as you pass through the main entrances. Carved out of local sandstone, these were installed during the Gupta era, around 450 AD, by which time figurative depictions of Buddha had become acceptable (elsewhere in Sanchi, the Master is euphemistically represented by an empty throne, a wheel, a pair of footprints or even a parasol).

As you move gradually closer to the stupa, the extraordinary wealth of sculpture adorning the **toranas** slips slowly into focus. Staring up at these masterpieces from below, you can see why archeologists believe them to have been the work of ivory craftsmen. Every conceivable nook and cranny of the eight-metre upright posts and three curving cross-bars teems with delicate figures of humans, demigods and goddesses, birds, beasts and propitious symbols. Some of the larger reliefs depict narratives drawn from the lives of Gautama Buddha and his six predecessors, the *Manushis*, while others recount Ashoka's dissemination of the faith. In between are purely decorative panels and illustrations of heaven intended to inspire worshippers to lead meritorious lives on earth. Start with the *torana* on the south side, which is the oldest, and proceed in a clockwise direction around the stupa – as is the custom at Buddhist monuments.

Southern torana

Opening directly onto the ceremonial staircase, the **southern torana** was the Great Stupa's principal entrance, as is borne out by the proximity of the stump of Ashoka's original stone pillar. Over the years, some of the panels with the best sculpture have dropped off the gateway (and are now housed in the site museum), but those that remain on the three crossbeams are still in reasonable condition. A carved frieze on the middle architrave shows Ashoka, complete with royal retinue, visiting a stupa in a traditional show of veneration. On the reverse side, the scene switches to one of the Buddha's previous incarnations. For the **Chhaddanta Jataka**, the *bodhisattva* adopts the guise of an elephant who, in extreme selflessness, helps an ivory hunter saw off his own (six) tusks.

Stupas

The hemispherical mounds known as **stupas** have been central to Buddhist worship since the sixth century BC, when Buddha himself modelled the first prototype. Asked by one of his disciples for a symbol to help disseminate his teachings after his death, the Master took his begging bowl, teaching staff and a length of cloth – his only worldly possessions – and arranged them into the form of a stupa, using the cloth as a base, the upturned bowl as the dome and the stick as the projecting finial, or spire.

Originally, stupas were simple burial mounds of compacted earth and stone containing relics of the Buddha and his followers. As the religion spread, however, the basic components multiplied and became imbued with **symbolic significance**. The main dome, or **anda** – representing the sacred mountain, or "divine axis" linking heaven and earth – grew larger, while the wooden railings, or **vedikas**, surrounding it were replaced by massive stone ones. A raised ambulatory terrace, or **medhi**, was added to the vertical sides of the drum, along with two flights of stairs and four ceremonial entrances, carefully aligned with the cardinal points. Finally, crowning the tip of the stupa, the single spike evolved into a three-tiered umbrella, or **chhattra**, standing for the Three Jewels of Buddhism: the Buddha, the Law and the community of monks.

The *chhattra*, usually enclosed within a low square stone railing, or **harmika** (a throwback to the days when sacred *bodhi* trees were surrounded by fences) formed the topmost point of the axis, directly above the reliquary in the heart of the stupa. Ranging from bits of bone wrapped in cloth, to fine caskets of precious metals, crystal and carved stone, the reliquaries were the "seeds" and their protective mounds the "egg". Excavations of the 84,000 stupas scattered around the subcontinent have shown that the solid interiors were also sometimes built as elaborate **mandalas** – symbolic patterns that exerted a beneficial influence over the stupa and those who walked around it. The ritual of circumambulation, or **pradhakshina**, which enabled the worshipper to tap into cosmic energy and be transported from the mundane to the divine realms, was always carried out in a clockwise direction from the east, in imitation of the sun's passage across the heavens.

Of the half-dozen or so giant stupa sites dotted around ancient India, only **Sanchi** has survived to the present day. To see one in action, however, you have to follow in the footsteps of Ashoka's missionaries southwards to Sri Lanka, northwards to the Himalayas and the Tibetan plateau, or across the Bay of Bengal to Southeast Asia, where, as "**dagobas**", "**chortens**" and "**chedis**", stupas are still revered as repositories of sacred energy.

Western torana

The **western torana** collapsed during the depredations of the nineteenth century, but has been skilfully restored. Some of Sanchi's liveliest sculpture appears around its two square posts. In the top right panel, a troop of monkeys scurries across a bridge over the Ganges, made by the *bodhisattva*, their leader, from his own body to help them escape a gang of soldiers (seen below). According to the **Mahakapi Jataka**, the troops were dispatched by the local king to capture a coveted mango tree from which the monkeys had been feeding. You can also just about make out the final scene, where the repentant monarch gets a stern ticking-off from the *bodhisattva* under a *peepal* tree. High on the top crossbeam, the eight Buddhas, including Maitreya, the Buddha-to-come, appear as a line of *bodhi* trees and stupas.

One of the most frequently represented episodes from the life of the Buddha features on the first two panels of the left-hand post facing the stupa. In the **Temptation of Mara**, the Buddha, who has vowed to remain under the *bodhi* tree until he attains enlightenment, heroically ignores the attempts of the evil demon Mara to distract him with threats of violence and seductive women (Mara's beautiful daughters). Notice the contrast at the end between Mara's agitated troops and the solemn-faced procession of angels who accompany the Buddha after he has achieved his goal.

Northern torana

Crowned with a fragmented Wheel of the Law and two tridents symbolizing the Buddhist trinity, the **northern torana** is the most elaborate and best-preserved of the four gateways. Scenes crammed onto its two vertical posts include Buddha performing an aerial promenade – one of many stunts he pulled to impress a group of heretics – and a monkey presenting the Master with a bowl of honey. Straddling the two pillars, a bas-relief on both faces of the lowest crossbeam depicts the **Vessantara Jataka**, telling of a *bodhisattva*-prince banished by his father for giving away a magical rain-making elephant. During his exile, the over-generous Vessantara was persuaded to part with everything else that was dear to him, including his wife and children, before finally being forgiven by the king. A better view of the inner, south-facing side of the plaque can be had from the balcony of the stupa's raised terrace. Note the little tableau on the far right showing the royal family trudging through the jungle; the prince's son is holding his father's hand, while his daughter clings to her mother's hip. The four **elephants** sculpted from the capital supporting the architraves are also very realistic, as are other, smaller elephants, horses and female wood-nymphs separating the three beams.

Eastern torana

Leaning languorously into space from the right capital of the **eastern torana** is Sanchi's most celebrated piece of sculpture, the sensuous **salabhanjika**, or wood-nymph. The full-breasted fertility goddess is one of several such figures that once blessed worshippers as they entered the Great Stupa. Only a few, however, still remain in place, others having been removed to Los Angeles and London. Her *tribhanga*, or hip-shot stance, is a classical dance pose which, from this moment onwards, was to become a distinctive feature of all Indian religious sculpture.

Panels on the inner face of the pillar below the *salabhanjika* depict scenes from the life of the Buddha, including his conception when the *bodhisattva* entered the body of his mother, Maya, in the form of a white elephant, shown astride a crescent moon. The front face of the middle architrave picks up the tale some years later, when the young Buddha, represented by a riderless horse, makes his **Great Departure** from the palace where he grew up to begin the life of a wandering ascetic. The reverse side shows the fully enlightened Master, now symbolized by an empty throne, with a crowd of celestial beings and jungle animals paying their respects.

Elsewhere around the enclosure

Of the dozens of other numbered ruins around the 400-metre enclosure, only a handful are of more than passing interest. Smaller, plainer and graced with only one ceremonial gateway, the immaculately restored **Stupa 3**, immediately northeast of Stupa 1, is upstaged by its slightly older cousin in every way but one. In 1851, a pair of priceless reliquaries were discovered deep in the middle of the mound. Turned on a lathe from fine marble-like soapstone called steatite, the caskets were found to contain relics belonging to two of Buddha's closest disciples. In one, fragments of bone were encased with beads made from pearls, crystal, amethyst, lapis lazuli and gypsum, while on the lid, the initial of the saint they are thought to have belonged to, Sariputra, was painted in ink. Once in the British Museum, along with other treasures pilfered from Sanchi, both are now safely locked in the new Buddhist temple outside the stupa enclosure, and are brought out for public view for one day each December (ask at any MPTDC tourist office for details). On this day, Sanchi is transformed from a lonely open-air museum into a bustling pilgrimage site, with devotees from as far afield as Sri Lanka and Japan.

From Stupa 3, pick your way through the clutter of pillars, small stupas and exposed temple floors nearby to the large complex of interconnecting raised terraces at the far **eastern edge** of the site. The most intact monastery of the bunch, **Vihara 45**, dates from the ninth and tenth centuries, and has the usual layout of cells ranged around a central courtyard. Originally, a colossal, richly decorated sanctuary tower soared high above the complex, but this collapsed, leaving the inner sanctum exposed. The river goddesses Ganga and Yamuna number among the skilfully sculpted figures flanking the entrance to the shrine itself – testimony to the mounting popularity of Brahminism at the start of the medieval era. Inside, however, Buddha still reigns supreme. Regally enthroned on a lotus bloom, his right hand touches the ground to call upon the earth goddess to witness the moment of his enlightenment.

The enclosure's tenth-century eastern **boundary wall** is the best place from which to enjoy Sanchi's serene **views**, especially at sunset. To the northeast, a huge, sheer-sided rock rises from the midst of Vidisha, near the site of the ancient city that sponsored the monasteries here (traces of the **pilgrimage trail** between Besnagar and Sanchi can still be seen crossing the hillside below). South from the hill, a wide expanse of well-watered wheat-fields, dotted with clumps of mango and palm trees, stretches off towards the angular sandstone ridges of the Raisen escarpment on the distant horizon.

The southern area

The **southern area** of the enclosure harbours some of Sanchi's most interesting **temples**. Pieces of burnt wood dug from the foundations of **Temple 40** prove that the present apsidal-ended *chaitya* was built on top of an earlier structure contemporary with the Mauryan Stupa 1. **Temple 17** is a fine example of early Gupta architecture and the precursor of the classical Hindu design developed later in Orissa and Khajuraho. Its small, flat-roofed sanctum is entered via an open-sided porch held up by four finely carved pillars with lion capitals. Nearby, directly opposite the Great Stupa's southern entrance, the tall slender pillars of **Temple 18** lend it a distinctly Greek air, but in fact, the temple layout follows the usual design for rock-cut Buddhist *chaitya* halls, and resembles the apsidal plan of the caves at Karle and Bhaja (see p.838). Rebuilt several times since its original construction, the present structure dates from the seventh century.

Before leaving the enclosure, hunt out the stump of **Ashoka's pillar** (#10) to the right of Stupa 1's southern *torana*. Columns such as this were erected by the Mauryan emperor all over the empire to mark sacred sites and pilgrims' trails (see Contexts). Its finely polished shaft (made, like all Ashokan pillars, with a sandstone known as Chunar after a quarry on the Ganges near Varanasi) was originally crowned with the magnificent lion capital now housed in the site museum. The inscription etched around its base is in the Brahmi script, recording Ashoka's edicts in Pali, the early Buddhist language and forerunner of Sanskrit.

The western slope

A flight of steps beside Stupa 1 leads down the **western slope** of Sanchi hill to the village, passing two notable monuments. The bottom portions of the thick stone walls of **Vihara 51** have been carefully restored to show its floor-plan of 22 cells around a paved central courtyard. Further down, the second-century BC **Stupa 2** stands on an artificial ledge, well below the main enclosure – probably because its relics were less important than those of Stupas 1 and 3. The ornamental railings and gateways around it are certainly no match for those up the hill, although the carvings of lotus medallions and mythical beasts (including some bizarre horse-headed women) that decorate them are worth checking out. The straps that dangle from some of the horse riders' saddles are believed to mark the first appearance in India of stirrups. The lotus designs covering the interior wall of the enclosure are remarkable in that each flower is of a different design and pattern.

The archeological museum

Sanchi's small **archeological museum** (daily except Fri 10am–5pm; Rs5), just behind the admission kiosk to the left of the road up to the hilltop, houses a modest collection of artefacts, mostly fragments of sculpture recovered during successive excavations. Its **main hall** contains the most impressive pieces, including the famous Ashokan lion-capital (see above) and two damaged *salabhanjikas* from the gateways of Stupa 1. Also of note are the distinctive Mathuran red-sandstone Buddhas, believed to have been sent to Sanchi from Gandhara in the far northwest of India – source of the first figurative representations of the Master. The best preserved of them dates from the Gupta period around the fourth century AD. Gallery 1 contains more large pieces of sculpture, while the remaining sections are devoted to smaller antiquities – votive terracotta figurines, stone plaques, jewellery, pottery, weapons and tools.

Practicalities

Although Sanchi is on the main Delhi–Mumbai train line and less than an hour from Bhopal, **getting there by train** involves a choice of only two morning services at 8am and 10.05am. Return services to Bhopal leave at 5.16am, 8.45am and 10.06am, and 4.10pm and 7pm. First-class passengers who have come at least 161km can also arrange to make a "special halt" at Sanchi – except for the "superfast" a/c chair services, like the Shatabdi Express, which stop only at Bhopal. The nearest main-line station is **Vidisha**, 10km northeast and connected by plenty of local buses; there are two daily trains to Mumbai and six to Delhi from here.

Buses from Bhopal to Sanchi depart from the main city bus stand every twenty minutes between 6am and 6pm, then every forty minutes thereafter, taking around ninety minutes to complete the journey. All buses pull into the centre of the tiny bazaar, a handful of wooden stalls surrounding the bus stand. The low, whitewashed houses of the village proper are on the other side of the main road, huddled below the stupa-covered hill. Finally, **bicycles** – good for a trip to the nearby Udaigiri caves – can be rented for around Rs20 per day from a small shop in the bazaar.

Power cuts are a daily occurrence in Sanchi, often stretching through the day and night, so make sure you have a good torch and spare batteries, otherwise candles can be bought in the bazaar area.

Accommodation

Cheap **accommodation** can be found in the unusually good *Retiring Room* at the railway station (❶–❷), or else at the nearby *Sri Lanka Mahabodhi Society Guest House* (☎07482/62739; ❶) which has basic doubles facing into a peaceful flower-filled courtyard. There is a communal bathroom, and no restaurant. Opposite, the friendly *Jaiswal* restaurant (☎07482/63908; ❶) had two simple rooms in the family house at the time of writing, and is currently building more next door. Moving up the scale, the MPTDC *Tourist Cafeteria* (☎07482/62743; ❸), next door to the museum, has two plain, clean rooms with attached shower-toilets. By far the most comfortable option in Sanchi, however, has to be the MPTDC *Travellers Lodge* (☎07482/62723; ❸–❹), five minutes' walk south of the crossroads. Their eight spacious and spotless rooms (two a/c) are excellent value, but often booked; try to reserve at least five days in advance through any MPTDC office or hotel, or in Delhi (see p.150). As a last resort, try the *Government Rest House* (❶–❷), behind the MPTDC *Cafeteria*, but the offer of a room depends entirely on the mood of the staff, and if you do stay make sure you have a couple of padlocks as the rooms all have several entrances.

Eating

MPTDC has the monopoly on good **places to eat** in Sanchi. If you're staying in the *Travellers Lodge* you can take your dinner at leisure in the courtyard, otherwise the MPTDC *Tourist Cafeteria* offers the same menu and garden ambience. This is also a good base for toast-and-egg breakfast. The *Jaiswal* serves up tasty home-cooked thalis in the evenings (order in advance), as do the rather less hygienic *dhabas* at the far south end of the bus stand; at *Gopal*'s a generous thali will set you back Rs35. Steaming chai, *puri* and *jalebi* are dished up in the stalls by the bus stand from 7am, as well as the local speciality – sweet *samosa* stuffed with coconut.

Vidisha

The main reason to call in at the bustling railway and market town of **VIDISHA**, a straightforward 56-kilometre train or bus ride from Bhopal, and also served by buses from nearby Sanchi, is to hop on a tonga to the archeological sites at Udaigiri and Besnagar. However, if you're not pushed for time, the place merits a closer look.

In front of the station, the Hindu temple, painted in loud pinks, yellows and blues and decorated with twinkling mirrors, has a fancy racing chariot flying across its roof, commandeered by Lord Rama (of the *Ramayana* myth); inside, a gloriously orange Ganesh stands guard in front of the shrine. All around the temple is the cheerful bazaar, which spreads out in front of the whitewashed houses of the old town. Beyond this, the River Betwa, dappled with *ghats*, white-domed temples and commemorative *sati* stones, signals the edge of town and the route to Udaigiri.

The small **museum** (Tues–Sun 10am–5pm; free), hidden away behind the railway station in the east of town, is also worth a quick visit. The majority of its prize pieces, such as Kubera Yaksha, the three-metre, pot-bellied male fertility figure in the hallway, are second-century Hindu artefacts unearthed at Besnagar. Attractive Jain *tirthankaras* and lumps of masonry salvaged from the district's plethora of ruined Gupta temples litter the garden.

Vidisha is also known for having financed a prolific third-century BC spate of stupa construction, including much of the work at Sanchi. By the sixth century AD however, it lay deserted and in ruins, remaining so until the arrival of the Muslims three hundred years later when a settlement, called **Bhilsa**, was founded around the flat-topped hill in the centre of the modern town. Vidisha's other rather tenuous claim to fame is that the bricks of a nearby second-century BC Vishnu temple were stuck together with lime mortar, believed to be the world's oldest cement.

Udaigiri and Besnagar

A modest collection of ruined temples and fifth-century rock-cut caves stand just 6km west of Vidisha, at **UDAIGIRI**. The caves, many decorated by Hindu and Jain mendicants, lie scattered around a long, thin outcrop of sandstone that rises from the surrounding patchwork of yellow and green wheat-fields. It's a congenial area to explore, particularly on one of the tongas that hang around outside Vidisha's bus stand (Rs40–50 round trip), though the site is also an easy cycle ride from Vidisha (bikes are available from shops on the outskirts of the bazaar) or, if your legs are up to it, from Sanchi (1–2hr). It's a good idea to bring supplies of food and water as there are no shops after Vidisha.

Heading out from Vidisha, a left turn just after crossing the River Betwa 5km short of Besnagar leads along a gently undulating tree-lined avenue for 2–3 km. As it approaches the hillside, the road takes a sharp left turn towards the village. Get off at this corner, at the base of the near-vertical rock face, to climb a steep flight of steps to **Cave 19** which has worn but attractive reliefs of gods and demons around the doorways, and a **Jain cave temple** on the northern edge of the ridge. Inside the temple, at the base of an uneven flight of steps, there are Gupta inscriptions in the pre-Sanskrit script of Parkrit and damaged *tirthankaras* on the back wall look through a natural balcony to the countryside below. From here, a path follows the backbone of the ridge, past a hilltop ruin (possibly a Hindu temple), to the most interesting caves, opposite the small terracotta-roofed village. An ASI *chowkidar* should be around to unlock the doors for you.

The site's *pièce de résistance*, a four-metre image of the boar-headed hero Varaha, stands carved into **Cave 5**. Vishnu adopted the guise of this long-snouted monster to rescue the earth-goddess, Prithvi (perched on a lotus next to his right shoulder) from the churning primordial ocean – depicted by delicate wavy lines. Varaha's left foot rests on a Naga king wearing a hood of thirteen cobra heads, while the river goddesses Ganga and Yamuna hold water vessels on either side. In the background you can see Brahma and Agni, the Vedic fire-god, plus sundry sages and musicians. The scene, prominent in many contemporary Hindu monuments, is seen as an allegory of the emperor Chandra Gupta II's conquest of northern India. Walking around the back of Cave 5 you'll see the waves and curves of Brahmi script etched into the rock, dating from 401AD. Around the corner, **Cave 7** contains Brahmi script that details the stay of Emperor Chandra Gupta II, and further around, **Cave 13** contains a three-metre-high sculpture of Vishnu reclining on a cobra. **Cave 4** contains a unique *lingam* in which the faces of Shiva and his consort Parvati have been combined in a single carving. To the south, porticoed **Cave 1**, constructed in the fourth century, is probably the earliest hermit hide-out here.

The ruins of ancient **BESNAGAR**, known locally as **Khambaba**, lie couched in a tiny village down the main road from Vidisha, 5km after the Udaigiri turn-off. During the time of the Mauryan and Shunga empires, between the third and first centuries BC, a thriving provincial capital overlooked the confluence of the Bes and Betwa rivers. The emperor Ashoka himself was governor here at one time, and even married a local banker's daughter. Nowadays, a few mounds and some scattered pieces of masonry are all that remain of the houses, stupas, temples and streets. One small monument, however, makes the short detour worthwhile. According to the inscription etched around its base and sixteen-sided column, the stone pillar in an enclosed courtyard, known as the **Column of Heliodorus**, was erected in 113 BC by a Bactrian-Greek envoy from Taxila, the capital city of Gandhara (now the northwest frontier region of Pakistan). The shaft, dedicated to Krishna's father Vasudeva, was originally crowned with a statue of Vishnu's vehicle Garuda. Heliodorus converted to the local Vaishnavite cult during his long diplomatic posting here. Most of the other archeological finds dug up on the site – including a colossal fertility god, Kubera Yaksha (see opposite) – are now at the museum in Vidisha and the archeological museum in Gwalior.

Udayapur

Remote, rural **UDAYAPUR**, 73km northeast of Bhopal, is the site of one of Madhya Pradesh's least-visited architectural gems. Unfortunately, to get there from Bhopal or Vidisha you have to catch a train to **Basoda** and then a local bus for the final 10km. Check the return times carefully before leaving, as there's nowhere to stay in the town, with the possible exception of the first-class waiting room at the railway station.

The magnificent **Neelkantheswara temple**, built in 1080 AD by the Paramara king Udayadita, took 22 years to complete and is considered to be on a par with its illustrious cousins at Khajuraho, even if its sculpture is rather more restrained. Its sandstone *shikhara* soars high above the surrounding clutter of dusty streets. Some of the best stonework is to be found in the niches around the huge curved sanctuary tower. A large panel on the front face frames a dancing Shiva, **Nataraj**, surmounted by a sea monster with bulging eyes and the seven mother goddesses, the Sapta Matrikas. The doorways of the three entrance porches of the pyramidal-roofed *mandapa* assembly hall are also richly carved with demigods and goddesses, including several amorous couples. Inside, the pillars are encrusted with garlands of flowers and bells, in marked contrast to the bare shrine room, which houses a *shivalingam*.

Bhojpur

Raja Bhoj's legendary mania for hydraulic experiments was by no means confined to Bhopal. At **BHOJPUR**, 28km southeast of the capital (and devoid both of direct bus services and of any accommodation), the eleventh-century Paramara ruler created a 400-square-kilometre tank from the waters of the

River Betwa. The dam was breached – and the lake destroyed – by the invading army of Hoshang Shah, the second sultan of Mandu, and Bhojpur's only real attraction these days is its colossal **Shiva temple** – another of the Raja's large-scale projects. The **Bhojeshwar Mandir** rests unfinished and dishevelled, but not entirely forlorn, due to its imposing centrepiece – a 2.5-metre-tall polished limestone *shivalingam*, maintained as a living shrine. It rests on an even more enormous pedestal (*yonipatha*), from which the resident *pujari* dispenses smudges of vermillion powder to worshippers. Currently under restoration, enterprising devotees use the scaffolding to hang their offerings of garlands and wooden snakes. A stone's throw north, beyond a jumble of boulders and collapsed masonry, the ASI have fenced off a flat rock onto which the raja's architects chiselled their original plans for the temple. This is also a good place to view the remnants of the earthen **ramp** they used to raise chunks of unworked stone up to the roof.

Bhimbetka

Shortly after NH-12 peels away from the main Bhopal–Hoshangabad road, 45km southeast of the state capital, a long line of boulders appears high on a scrub-covered ridge to the west. The hollows, overhangs and crevices eroded over the millennia from the crags of this malleable sandstone outcrop harbour one of the world's largest collections of **prehistoric rock art**. Discovered in 1957 by the archeologist Dr V.S. Wankaner, **BHIMBETKA** (sunrise-sunset; free) is South Asia's equivalent of the cave complexes at Lascaux in southwest France and Altamira in Spain, or the rock paintings of aboriginal Australia. If you have your own transport, or are prepared to do a bit of walking to get there, this rarely visited site makes a fascinating day-trip from Bhopal. Initially, the paintings are hard to find and decipher but the *chowkidars* sitting at the entrance to the cave area are pleased to show you around for a bit of baksheesh.

Of the thousand **shelters** so far catalogued along the ten-kilometre hilltop, around half contain rock paintings. These date from three different periods, each with its own distinctive style. The oldest fall into two categories: green outline drawings of human figures, and large red images of animals. Lumps of hematite (from which the red pigment was manufactured) unearthed amid the deepest excavations on the site have been carbon-dated to reveal origins in the Upper Paleolithic era, around 10,000 years ago. The second, and more prolific phase accounts for the bulk of Bhimbetka's rock art, and took place in the **Late Mesolithic** era – the "Stone Age" – between 8000 and 5000 BC. These friezes depict dynamic hunting scenes full of rampaging animals, initiation ceremonies, burials, masked dances, sports, wars, pregnant women, an arsenal of different weapons and even what seems to be a drinking party. No one is sure why these sophisticated communities of hunter-gatherers decorated their temporary abodes in this way. One theory is that the cave art served the ritual or **magical** function of ensuring a plentiful supply of game; but while abundant depictions of bison, wild boar, antelope and deer lend credence to that notion, animals that were not on the Mesolithic menu, such as tigers and elephants, also appear.

Shards of pottery found amid the accumulated detritus on the rock-shelter floors show that Bhimbetka's third and final spate of cave painting took place during the early historic period, after its inhabitants had begun to trade with settled agriculturalists. Their stylized, geometric figures bear a strong resemblance to the art still produced by the region's *adivasi*, or tribal groups.

From the car park at the top of the hill, a paved pathway winds through the jumble of rocks containing the most striking and accessible of Bhimbetka's paintings. As you wander around, look out for the Paleolithic images in green, the wonderful "X-ray" animals filled in with cross-hatching and complex geometric designs, and the recurrent image of a bull chasing a human figure and a crab – a motif believed to represent a struggle between the totemic heroes of three different tribes. At the bottom of the track, on the base of a tall column of sandstone not included in the guide's whistle-stop tour, there's also a very fine wild boar in black and red.

Practicalities

The only way of getting to the caves at Bhimbetka is by private vehicle or **taxi**. From Bhopal, take NH-12, and 7km after the market town of Obaidullaganj, take a left when you see a sign in Hindi with "3.2" written on it. Cross the railway line and the caves are 3km further on along the road. There's nowhere to **eat** or **drink** for miles around Bhimbetka, so bring a day's supply of food and water with you.

The Pachmarhi Plateau

Halfway between Bhopal and Jabalpur, a forbidding wall of weird, blackened sandstone peaks, precipitous ravines and impenetrable forest rears along the south side of the Narmada Valley. The **Mahadeo Hills** were among the last tracts of central India charted by the British. Not until 1857 did the first column of redcoated Bengal Lancers hack their way up from the sweltering plains. Led by the infamous explorer and big-game hunter Captain J Forsyth, the sun-weary troops were astonished to discover, deep in this wilderness of *sal* trees and sheer red-sandstone cliffs, an idyllic saucer-shaped plateau strewn with huge boulders and crisscrossed by perennial clear-water streams.

The **PACHMARHI** plateau was inhabited long before Forsyth's "discovery" and the subsequent development of a fashionable hill station retreat for Nagpur's British contingent. Abundant **prehistoric rock art** scattered across a wide area of remote hills and valleys suggests that this northern spur of the Satpuras harboured a population of hunter-gatherers as long ago as the late Stone Age. Finding "the paintings" can be difficult, but enjoyable, involving lots of scrambling through dense forests.

The majority of visitors who venture up to Pachmarhi are Gujarati and Bengali families, taking a reviving spell in the clear, cool air – although rarely do they manage much more than a sedate stroll or Jeep excursion. The army has a strong presence here, adding a reminder of the Raj, although their primary concern appears to be practising military anthems and marches from dawn to dusk, in competition with the large guide and scout contingents that insist on more upbeat musical drills. The result is an interesting cacophony of music drifting across the lake and through the bazaars.

One of the few times the sleepy hill station sees any real action is during the annual **Shivratri mela** (Feb/March), when *lakhs* of pilgrims are drawn to ancient shrines hidden in the gorges and on the peaks surrounding the plateau. The trail trodden by the exuberant crowds of ragged *yatris* (pilgrims) winds through spectacular scenery to the top of **Chauragarh mountain**. Out of season, it makes an excellent **day-hike** from the town, or alternatively, a number of less strenuous saunters along woodland tracks offer a rewarding way to sample the area's abundant flora and fauna. A similar *mela* takes place during **Nag Panchmi** in August, when pilgrims visit the cave shrines on a circular trail around Nagdwari, a two-hour climb down from the northern shoulder of **Dhupgarh**, MP's highest point at 1350m. The **Satpura National Park** to the north and west of town, encompasses a 600-square-kilometre swathe of old-growth *sal,* teak and bamboo forest, and supports a wide array of wildlife, including Indian bison (*gaur*), barking deer, sambar, *barasingha*, jackals, wild dogs and a handful of elusive tigers and leopards.

The best **time to visit** Pachmarhi is between September and May, when the cool, clear mountain air makes a refreshing change from the heat and dust at lower elevations. It's especially worth trying to be here for the *melas*, although the bus journeys up from the plains can be nightmarish when the festivals are in full swing. It is also best to avoid long holiday weekends when popular spots such as **Bee Falls** and Dhupgarh (famed for its sunsets) attract large crowds.

The Town

At over 1000m above sea level, the plateau had one quality that strongly appealed to the homesick British – deliciously cool air. Within five years Forsyth was back, this time with a gang of surveyors to push a road through the hills from the railhead at **Piparia**. A military sanitorium was established, quickly followed by bungalows, churches, clubhouses, a racecourse, a polo pitch and a network of cart tracks through the woods. By the end of the century, India's newest hill station had become the summer capital of the entire Central Provinces.

The town of **PACHMARHI** is clean, green and pleasant, with a very laid-back feel. Unlike India's larger and better-known hill stations, it retains a colonial ambience enhanced by the elegant British bungalows and Victorian church spires that nose incongruously above the tropical tree line. In the evenings families stroll and picnic in the parklands, while retired army officers, with handlebar moustaches and in their cleanest whites, take a brisk walk, with their *salwar kameez*-clad wives puffing behind.

Practicalities

The nearest railhead for Pachmarhi is the busy market town of **Piparia,** 52km northeast and one hour away by bus (frequent services). Piparia is on the Mumbai–Howrah (via Allahabad, Varanasi and Itarsi) line. If you are coming from the north, Bhopal or the south, you will need to get off at **Itarsi junction** and then catch a bus (3hr) or train (several daily; 1–2hr) to Piparia. The train from Itarsi that will arrive in time to catch the last bus up the hill is the Itarsi-Bina Express #1271 (departs 4.20pm). If you arrive after the last bus (6pm) has left, the only decent place to stay is the MPTDC *Tourist Motel* (℡07576/22299; ❷), behind the station. However share taxi-Jeeps usually keep running till later. **Buses** also connect Pachmarhi with Bhopal (3 "Express direct" daily; 6hr), Chindwara (2 daily; 4–5hr), en route to Nagpur, and Indore (1 daily; 12hr).

Pachmarhi's small bus stand has an MPTDC **information** counter (Mon–Sat 10.30am–2.30pm, although it appears to be closed most of the time) which can book accommodation; their **maps** are wildly inaccurate.

Most of the private budget accommodation lies a short walk up the hill in the bazaar and in a cluster close to the bus stand, but a few of the more comfortable MPTDC hotels are a five-minute Jeep or rickshaw ride south on the far side of a lotus-filled lake, near the military training area, **Tehsil**. For longer excursions, negotiate with a jeep driver, or rent a **car** (with driver) through the main MPTDC office (℡ 07578/52100), next to the *Amaltas Hotel*, 1.5km south of the bus stand.

Neither the State Bank of India nor any of the hotels have foreign exchange facilities. The nearest places to **change money** are in Bhopal, Jabalpur or Nagpur.

Accommodation

Finding **accommodation** in Pachmarhi is a problem during the *melas* and during May and June, when visitors flock to escape the heat of the plains. The tourist information counter at the bus stand can tell you which of the eight MPTDC hotels have vacancies; otherwise several pleasant and friendly private places in the bazaar are good alternatives. These independent establishments will all negotiate good discounts outside the October to March high season; MPTDC offers a twenty-percent "monsoon discount".

Evelyn's Own (just before MPTDC Satpura Retreat ℡ 07578/52056. Homely rooms in a beautiful colonial bungalow, set in gardens with a tennis court and pool. Retired Colonel "Bunny" Rao, has a fascinating library and is a mine of local information. Delicious meals are served by prior arrangement. ❺–❻

MPTDC Amaltas, near Tehsil ℡ 07578/52098. Small hotel in an old British house with a range of different sized rooms, each with attached bath and fans. Room no. 1 is particularly grand with circular walls, marble fireplace and a sweeping private veranda. The bar-restaurant is very average. ❺–❻

MPTDC Holiday Homes, near SADA Barrier, about 600m before the bus stand ℡ 07578/52099. No-frills cottages with private verandas and little gardens. The attached bathrooms across a courtyard are extremely chilly in the winter. ❸

MPTDC Panchvati Cottages, near Tehsil ℡ 07578/52096. Five pricey, self-contained chalets in their own gardens, aimed mainly at honeymooners. ❻

MPTDC Panchvati Huts, near Tehsil ℡ 07578/52096. Good-value, well-run hotel set in pleasant grounds with spacious rooms, attached shower-toilets, and on-site restaurant. ❺

MPTDC Rock End Manor ℡ 07578/52079. The top hotel in Pachmarhi in a well-restored pukka British bungalow. Six very comfortable, old-fashioned rooms, huge tiled bathrooms and views over the hills and a flower garden from easy chairs on the veranda both the hotel and the restaurant are very popular with visiting VIPs, so book both in advance. ❽

Pachmarhi, Patel Marg, opposite *Saket* ℡ 07578/52170. One of a batch of budget hotels in the same road. A large institutional place with unexciting, clean rooms at assorted prices, with a good restaurant. ❸–❺

Saket, Patel Marg ℡ 07578/52165. Close to the State Bank in the heart of the bazaar, five minutes from bus stand. Friendly, clean and very good value, with fans and attached bathrooms. Some rooms have cable TV. ❷

Sapna, 2min walk south of the bus stand ℡ 07578/52209. In this self-acclaimed "house of sweet dreams", the reception is in a higgledy-piggledy shop; there are several basic doubles with attached bathrooms, behind the scenes. ❷

Eating

All the MPTDC hotels have restaurants serving the same safe but tasty Indian and Chinese menus, and the quintessential Raj-era charm of *Rock End Manor* certainly adds ambience to the affair. The *dhabas* along the main road serve generous and very cheap thalis, although hygiene is not always a top priority. If you plan to go on a trek all day, get a *dhaba* to prepare some *aloo parathas* and pickle for a picnic lunch.

Amaltas, near Tehsil. Quiet restaurant with a predictable MPTDC multi-cuisine menu and the town's only bar.

China Bowl, near *Panchvati Huts*. Standard MPTDC restaurant, with a few extra soups, *chop sueys* and *chow meins* thrown in. Open for breakfast – mainly cutlets and eggs.

Indian Coffee House, main road, just before the

bus stand. Open from 8.30am for *dosas* and cof-fee. All day the relaxed café serves up "south Indian fast food" and cold drinks.
Kalsa, bottom end of bazaar off the main road. Inexpensive, delicious Punjabi and Chinese dishes served inside under strip lights or in the garden.

Beer is available in a side room. Recommended.
Mrignayani, Gandhi Chowk. The most hygienic of the cheap thali joints in the bazaar, serving no-nonsense, fiery, pure-veg curries and piping hot *rotis* from large vats.

Pachmarhi hikes

The web of forest tracks and pilgrim trails that thread their way around Pachmarhi's widely dispersed archeological and religious sites make for excellent **walking**, but few, if any, routes are marked in English. By far the best maps and **trekking information** are available at the *Tola Trekking Club* (☎07578/52256, ✉trekpachmarhi@hotmail.com), run by Vinay Sahu from *Hotel Saket*. This very reliable outfit will organize both day (Rs150 per person; extra for Jeep hire to trailheads) and overnight treks (Rs250), where you camp in the *adivasi* villages hidden in the hills. The **guides** in the *Tola Trekking Club* are all young tribal men from the villages hidden in the surrounding hills; they have expert knowledge of the area and the fees go directly to the guides and their villages.

All foreigners are required to buy **permits** (Rs100 per day) to enter all areas outside Pachmarhi town, including Bee Falls, Duchess Falls and Dhupgarh. These permits, and the further permit required for overnight halts in the forest, are issued (Mon–Sat 10am–5pm) at the office of the Director of the Forestry Commission, next to the MPTDC *Almatas* hotel. **Bikes**, rented from the bazaar or the repair shop just below the Government Gardens (around Rs25 per day), are an alternative (and cheaper) way of getting to the trailheads, but make sure you carry a chain and padlock and hide the bicycle in the bushes while you are trekking.

As all the longer treks are extremely hard to follow without a guide, we have described only the short or very distinct treks from the town. If you want to attempt more difficult trekking, we suggest that you contact the *Tola Trekking Club* (see above), who will happily dispense trekking maps and detailed advice about hidden waterfalls, gorges and great cycle routes.

Short hikes

Popular shorter excursions include the fifteen-minute climb up from the whitewashed Muslim shrine in the Babu Lines area of town (1km southwest of the bus stand) to the top of **Pachmarhi Hill**. From here you have a fine panoramic view over Pachmarhi town on one side, and the thickly forested valley of **Jambu Dwip** on the other. The craggy cliffs lining the north side of the uninhabited gorge below are riddled with hidden rock-shelters and caves.

Alternatively, a 30-minute walk follows a well-beaten track from the bus stand, twisting north from the main bazaar into the hillside through a narrow steep-sided canyon to **Jatashankar**, a sacred cave under a mass of loose boulders, and a prominent point in the Shivratri *yatra*.

Treks from Reechgarh

The twelve kilometre trek to the hidden gorge of **Sunder Kund** begins at the trailhead of **Reechgarh** (literally, "fortress of the bears"), 7km west of the bazaar. Walk north from the car park and follow the wide path that winds around the hill to the right. A number of viewpoints show where the valley drops dramatically away below, only to rise again as sheer cliff faces and distant blue-tinged mountains. A chai shop, selling refreshing lemon tea, signals the sharp left turn down to **Duchess Falls**. The path is difficult and very steep but at the bottom you are greeted by the frantic rush of frothy water swirling around the shallow pools that catch the falls. It is not advised that you drink the water, but there is some great splashing about to be done; try and get here in the morning, before hordes of people arrive by Jeep. From here you can either continue for 2km to Sunder Kund, or return to the chai stall and continue the walk around Astachal hill.

To reach **Sunder Kund**, you need to cross the stones in the big pool at the bottom of Duchess Falls, then follow the upper path through the jungle; the path is a very narrow ledge cut into the hillside and overgrown, so care should be taken. After 1.5km the path drops down to Sunder Kund, a secret little stretch of river that you are practically guaranteed to have to yourself. The river here is clean and a deliciously cooling swim is a great way to end the trek.

To walk around **Astachal** (or "Monte Rosa") – the fourth highest in Pachmarhi – turn left at the chai stall and follow the track. Just before the car park, halfway along this stretch, is a left turn that leads down to **Draupadi Dweep** rock shelter, containing some of the best rock paintings in Pachmarhi, although contemporary graffiti has ruined much of the art. However, you can see a depiction of a human figure with an elephant head, which may well be an interpretation of Ganesh. There are other paintings of humans, a tiger and a rearing horse, all painted in the red and white pigments typical of the cave paintings found in the region (see p.444). To return to the main track, climb the steps hewn into the rock face near the cave entrance, and take time out to enjoy breathtaking views across the gorge.

En route, in a small cluster of prehistoric rock-shelters just off the path, **Harper's cave** is named for a seated figure of a man playing a harp, and also holds an unusual portrait, painted in white and outlined in red, of a man riding an X-shaped horse. From the clearing below Harper's cave, the path picks its way past small temples and a lurid blue effigy of Shiva emerging from a large wayside boulder, to the head of a dark chasm. The **Jatashankar cave** itself lies deep in the bowels of the mountain at the foot of a long flight of stone steps. Lord Shiva is said to have fled here through a secret passageway under the Mahadeo range to escape the evil demon Bhasmasur. The grotto's name, which literally means "Shiva's hairstyle", derives from the rock formation around a natural *lingam* on the cave floor, supposed to resemble the god's matted dreadlocks. Above the *lingam* the rocks resemble a cluster of snakes, *naga*, forming a reverential parasol over the deity. During the week of the *mela*, the claustrophobic cleft in the rock resounds with the ringing of *puja* bells and the raised voices of *yatris* and *sadhus*, whose fires and incense offerings have blackened the sides of the cliff. Off-season, a lone *pujari* tends the *shivalingam* inside the tiny cave.

From here, continuing along the track will bring you back to the main bazaar.

Pandav caves, Fairy Pool and Big Falls

A two-to-three-hour walk around the eastern fringes of the plateau strings together a small cluster of interesting sights. First head up to the *Panch Pandav*, or **Pandav caves** (40min), which occupy a knobbly sandstone hillock just east of the road between the ATC cantonment and the petrol pump. Hindu mythology tells that these five (*panch*) simple cells (*marhi*), from which the name Pachmarhi derives, sheltered the famous Pandava brothers of *Mahahbarata* fame (see p.1508) during their thirteen-year exile. Archeologists however maintain that the bare stone chambers and pillared verandas were excavated by a group of Buddhist monks around the first century BC.

Rejoin the metalled road in front of the caves and head around the back of the hill to the melancholy **British cemetery**. Beyond that, the road becomes a dirt track leading to a small car park. From here, take the footpath down the hill through the woods for about twenty minutes till the trail flattens out, and turn right at a fork to descend to **Apsara Vihar**, or "Fairy Pool" – an often crowded bathing place and picnic spot at the foot of a small waterfall. Troupes of black-faced langur monkeys crash through the canopy overhead as you approach the 150-metre **Rajat Prapat**, or "Big Falls", about a five-minute scramble over the boulders downstream from the Fairy Pool. If you walk back to the fork and continue along the trail, a five-minute walk brings you to a railing facing the 105m falls. Beyond this point you will need a guide to find the two-kilometre trail down to the deep cold pool at the bottom, best swum in when the sun is directly on it in the mornings.

Chauragarh

The first 8km of the climb to the sacred summit of **Chauragarh mountain**, on the south rim of the Pachmarhi plateau, can be done on bike. From the bazaar, head south across the lake towards the crossroads in front of the MPTDC *Amaltas Hotel*. Heaped around the trunk of a mango tree nearby are a collection of spatula-shaped wooden memorial plaques placed here by members of the local Gond tribe. Beautifully carved with traditional designs, they're part of the Gonds' ancestor-worship cult and should not be disturbed.

From here take the road to **Mahadeo Cave**. After 2km, it's worth stopping at the railings, just off the road to the left, to peer down the beginning of the deep, narrow ravine of **Handi Kho**, supposedly created by Lord Shiva as a prison for a giant serpent that once inhabited the nearby lake. To punish the snake for harassing pilgrims, Shiva drank the lake, gouged out the ravine with a mighty wallop of his trident and forced the evil reptile inside. It's often suggested that this legend may be rooted in the events of the sixth and seventh centuries AD, when the plateau's Buddhist occupants, referred to by the *Vedas* as "Snakes", were ousted by Hindus.

Continuing, leave your bike hidden in the bushes just before the road makes it's first sharp descent at the turn-off for **Priyadarshini**, or "Forsyth's Point". From here there's another spectacular view of Handi Kho, where it broadens out and turns sharply east. The walk from Priyadarshini is tough, as the road switchbacks up some steep, thickly wooded hills. Eventually, it emerges at the head of a sweeping valley, with the striking profile of the Chauragarh peak rising high above the treetops. At the height of the Shivratri *mela*, the bare conical summit that crowns the near-vertical flanks of the mountain shimmers and glints with immense crowds.

The **footpath** proper begins at the very bottom of the valley, after the road has plunged down another sequence of hairpin bends. Before setting off, make a brief diversion up the *khud* behind the modern **temple** to the Mahadeo cave, where pilgrims take a purifying dip in the cool perennial springwater that gushes through its pitch-black interior. From here, a strenuous two-hour climb follows an ancient trail to the top of the holy mountain. At the very summit, after a flight of concrete steps, a bright blue statue of Shiva is surrounded by a thicket of orange tridents, and a nearby temple houses the all-powerful Chauragarh *lingam*. The view over the verdant Satpuras, to the dusty scrubland and distant flat-topped mountains, is suitably sublime.

Northern Madhya Pradesh

The remoteness of the famous temples at **Khajuraho**, with their superbly carved erotic sculptures, means that many visitors find themselves passing through a large tract of **northern Madhya Pradesh**. Few choose to linger in the region, however, preferring to return to the main Delhi–Agra artery or move onto Varanasi. Yet this much-trodden trail passes within striking distance of several other sights which are well worth taking time out to see. Foremost among them is the hill-fort at **Gwalior**. In addition to the immaculately restored palaces and ancient Hindu temples within the fort itself, the city also boasts an extravagant European-style palace crammed with quirky art treasures and curios. A short bus ride west, at **Shivpuri**, you can enjoy classical *ragas* at dusk in a richly inlaid mausoleum.

To the east, **Jhansi**, in UP (see p.335), is the main jumping-off point both for Khajuraho and the medieval ghost-village of **Orchha**, where architecture enthusiasts may also want to visit one of the few Indian monuments admired by Lutyens, the brain behind imperial New Delhi. The multistorey fort-palace at **Datia**, 27km northwest of Jhansi, stands within sight of an even more rarely visited monument, the Jain hilltop temple complex and pilgrimage site of **Sonagiri**.

The region's major rail and road routes arc north from Bhopal, passing through the jigsaw joint with neighbouring Uttar Pradesh at Jhansi, before heading north to Agra and Delhi. In the east, the Central Railway connects the state capital with **Satna**, the nearest railhead to Khajuraho, then veers northeast towards Varanasi and the Ganges basin. Cutting between the two train lines on the busy back-country road to Khajuraho enables you to take in Orchha on the way.

Gwalior

Straddling the main Delhi–Mumbai train line, **GWALIOR** is the largest city in northern Madhya Pradesh and the site of India's most spectacular hilltop **fort**. The old sandstone citadel, with its temples and palaces, peers down from the edge of a sheer-sided plateau above a haze of petrol fumes, busy streets and cubic concrete houses. Once you've checked out the **archeological museum**, and the rock-cut **Jain colossi** at the foot of the cliff, the city's other unmissable attraction is the supremely kitsch **Jai Vilas palace** belonging to the local ruling family, the **Scindias**. Their personalities and influence are everywhere, from the grand hospital and the **Chhatris** (memorial halls) north of Jiyaji Chowk to the nearby excellent **Sarod Ghar** museum that celebrates the long tradition of royal patronage of classical music in the city.

Despite its proximity to Agra, 119km north, Gwalior sees few foreigners; in truth, with its drab modern centre and gritty bazaar, it does lack the charm of its counterparts in nearby Rajasthan. Nevertheless, it can be a worthwhile place to pause for a day, particularly around late November and early December, when the old **Moghul tombs** in Gwalior's Muslim quarter host one of the premier Indian classical **music festivals**.

▲ Airport (9 km), Agra & Delhi

GWALIOR

RESTAURANTS
Indian Coffee House **A**
Kwality **B**

Jami Masjid

Gujuri Mahal
& Museum

FORT RD

Karam
Mandir

Vikram
Mandir

Ghaus Muhammed
& Tansen's Tombs

Man
Mandir

Urwahi Valley &
Jain Sculptures

Sasbahu
Temples

TV
Mast

Suraj Kund

Teli-Ka-Mandir

Sikh
Gurudwara

Railway
Station

State
Bus
Stand

Jain Sculptures

Rani
Jhansi
Memorial

Indian
Airlines
Office

MPTDC
Tourist Office

Sarod Ghar
Museum

LAKSHMIGANJ NEW RD

MAHARANI LAKSHMI BAI RD

BHAI LAL BAI RD

Jai Vilas Palace
& Museum

ACCOMMODATION

Ambika	3
Banjara	11
D.M.	2
Fort View	9
Gwalior Regency	5
India	1
Landmark	8
Man Mandir	11
Tansen	7
Regency Square	4
Shelter	6
Ushan Kiran Palace	10

State
Bank

Sarafa
Bazaar

Jayaji
Chowk

GPO

NAI SARAK RD

PALACE RD

JHANSI RD

0 Metres 500

Private
Bus Stand

▼ Shivpuri ▼ Jhansi

Some history

A donative inscription unearthed in a now-defunct sun temple proves that
Gwalior was first occupied in the sixth century BC by Hun invaders from the
north. Local legend, however, attributes the founding of the fort to the
Kuchwaha prince **Suraj Sen**, said to have been cured of leprosy during the
tenth century by the hermit **Gwalipa** after whom the city is named. The water
tank where the miracle took place, the Suraj Kund, remains intact, as do a pair
of ornate temples, the Sasbahu Mandirs, erected by the Rajput clan. The
Kuchwahas' successors, the Parihars, were brutally overthrown in 1232 by
Iltutmish, following an eleven-month siege. Before the fort eventually fell to
the Muslim army, the Rajput women trapped inside committed mass suicide
by self-immolation. Afterwards, the Delhi sultan added to the carnage by ordering the execution, outside his tent, of all seven hundred prisoners taken in the
battle.

A third Rajput dynasty, the **Tomars**, retook Gwalior in 1398, and ushered in
the city's "golden age". Under **Man Singh**, who ascended to the Tomar *gadi*
(throne) in 1486, the hilltop gained the magnificent palaces and fortifications
that were to earn it the epithet "the pearl in the necklace of the castles of

Hind". Skirmishes with neighbouring powers dogged the Rajputs' rule until 1517, however, when the **Lodis** from Delhi besieged the fort for a second time. On this occasion they were successful. Man Singh was slain, and his son, who managed to fend off the attackers for another twelve months, finally surrendered. Thereafter, Gwalior was ruled by a succession of Muslim overlords, including Babur, Humayun and Sher Shah, before falling to Akbar.

With the decline of the Moghuls, the **Marathas** – a confederacy of Hindu dynasties from the Deccan region – worked their way northwards into the power vacuum. Gwalior became the base of the most powerful of the four Maratha clans, the **Scindias**, in 1754. Twenty-six years later, wily British East India Company troops conquered the fort in an audacious night raid, using rope ladders and socks stuffed with cotton to muffle the sound of their approach. Within hours, the citadel was overrun, and Gwalior became a British feudatory state ruled by a succession of puppet rajas. The most famous of these, the immensely rich Jayaji Rao Scindia (1843–86), remained loyal to the British during the 1858 Mutiny, although 6500 of his troops joined the opposing forces led by Tantia Topia and the infamous **Rani Lakshmi Bai** of Jhansi (see p.332). Both rebel leaders were killed in the ensuing battle, and the maharaja quickly resumed his role as host of some of the grandest viceregal dinners, royal visits and tiger hunts ever witnessed by the Raj. The Scindias remained influential after Independence, and still live in Gwalior; the maharaja is a high-ranking minister in the Congress Party. The royal family's political fortunes, quarrels and marriages continue to provide fodder for voracious gossip columnists, although a less exalted native of Gwalior, **Atal Vajpayee**, has enjoyed far more political power as BJP leader and prime minister.

Arrival and information

Gwalior's main-line **railway station**, linked to Delhi, Agra, Jhansi and Bhopal by the fast Shatabdi Express, lies in the east of the city, just around the corner from the **state bus stand**. Most of the decent accommodation is within walking distance of the station, with more places an auto-rickshaw ride away to the west, down the busy MLB (Maharani Lakshmi Bai) Road. If you're travelling light, you could save on the fare by squeezing into one of the inexpensive *tempos* that run along Station Road. Gwalior **airport**, 9km to the northeast of the centre, is served by taxis and auto-rickshaws. The **private bus stand** is inconveniently situated on the southwestern edge of town.

MPTDC has a helpful **information** counter at their *Hotel Tansen* (℡0751/340370 or 342606), less than ten minutes' walk south of the railway station on Gandhi Road. To book onward transport, accommodation and flights, authorized travel agents include Travel Bureau (℡0751/340103) at 220 Jiwaji Chowk, and Touraids Travel Service (℡0751/423293) at Moti palace. If you need to **change money**, and are not staying in a hotel with a foreign exchange facility, the State Bank of India (Mon–Fri 10am–2pm, Sat 10am–noon) is at the heart of the bazaar district, on **Jayaji Chowk**, near the **GPO**.

Accommodation

Most of Gwalior's **hotels** are strung between the railway station and Lashkar, the main bazaar area, along the hectic MLB Road. Standards at the cheaper end of the market are particularly low, with cramped windowless cells the norm; those we have listed have attached baths (but not all have hot water) and 24hr checkout, and offer cheaper rates for single travellers. Most of the moderate to expensive hotels whack ten-percent "luxury" tax and ten-percent service charge on top of the tariff.

Ambika, Tansen Road, Padav ☎ 0751/410551. Reasonably clean budget hotel five minutes from the railway station; walk over the flyover, then take an immediate right turn back towards the station up a lane. The rooms at the back escape the noise from the flyover. ❷

Banjara, High Court Lane ☎ 0751/321637. Slightly hard to find, but central and welcoming hotel with large clean rooms, all with attached bath and some a/c. ❹–❻

Fort View, MLB Road ☎ 0751/331586. Plain, but comfortable and well managed, with bright rooms, Star TV and some a/c. "Regular" rooms are particularly good value. ❸–❻

D.M., near state bus stand ☎ 0751/342038. The most pleasant of the budget hotels in the area, this small lodge is quiet, clean and friendly. The rooms all have attached baths and 24hr hot water; the slightly more pricey "deluxe" rooms are particularly good value. ❷–❸

Gwalior Regency, near state bus stand ☎ 0751/340671. Modern and ritzy, with Star TV, foreign exchange, nightclub, health club (with Jacuzzi) and a pool. ❼

India, Station Road ☎ 0751/341983. Friendly, no-frills lodge run by the Indian Coffee Workers' Co-op. Clean, but rooms overlooking the main street are noisy. Deluxe rate gets you a Western toilet. Handy for the station. ❷–❸

Landmark, Manik Vilas ☎ 0751/345780. A new hotel that offers the top accommodation in the station area, with comfortable rooms and central a/c, internet (Rs60/hr and open to nonresidents) and foreign exchange facilities, plus a bar and a restaurant. ❻

Man Mandir, High Court Lane ☎ 0751/321442. A recent drop in standards makes this basic hotel a real fall-back, but it's central for the sights and cheap. Cooler hire is Rs30. ❷

MPTDC Tansen, 6-A Gandhi Rd ☎ 0751/340370. Large, efficient hotel in its own grounds near the station, with plain rooms (some a/c) and a good restaurant. Popular with tour groups, so advance booking is recommended. The MP Tourism office is also housed here. ❺–❻

Regency Square, next to state bus stand ☎ 0751/344116. Cheaper version of its sister hotel, *Gwalior Regency*; the well-appointed rooms (some a/c) all face onto a central lawn, that becomes a pleasant open-air restaurant in the evening. ❺

Shelter, Padav ☎ 0751/326209. Smart hotel only 5min from the station, with comfortable rooms, smart bar, and a swimming pool. A/c rooms are only slightly more pricey than non-a/c. Bed tea and a buffet breakfast are included in the room tariff. ❻–❼

Ushan Kiran Palace, Jayendraganj, Lakshar ☎ 0751/323993. Former maharaja's guesthouse now run by Welcomgroup as an opulent five-star. Period furnishings, intricate lattice friezes, large verandas, and a lawn with wicker chairs preserve some of its original *fin-de-siècle* feel. Pay in dollars only. ❾

The fort

Gwalior's imposing **fort** (daily 8am–6pm; Rs0.20) sprawls over a 3km-long outcrop of sandstone to the north of the modern city. Its mighty turreted battlements encompass no less than six palaces, three temples and several water tanks and cisterns, as well as a prestigious public school and a shiny new Sikh *gurudwara*.

Two routes wind up the hill. In the west, a motorable track climbs the steep gorge of the **Urwahi valley**, passing a line of rock-cut Jain statues along the way. The other, more accessible entrance is on the northeast corner of the cliff, at the head of a long, stepped ramp. The two can be combined by taking a rickshaw to the Urwahi side, then walking up and across the plateau and dropping down via the northeastern entrance to the museum and Jami Masjid, from where it's easier to pick up a rickshaw or *tempo* back into town.

You can pick up an official **guide** (approximately Rs180 for a 3hr tour) at the Urwahi gate or at the cold drinks shop at the entrance to the palace complex. There is a new 45-minute **son-et-lumière** show (English show starts at 7.30pm Nov–Feb, 8.30pm March–Oct; Rs100 [Rs20], children half price) each night at the Man Mandir. The narrative traces the history and culture of the fort, complemented by evocative Indian classical music and very professional lighting effects that bathe the palace in ethereal colours as it rises above the evening smog of the city.

The northeastern approach and museum

The **northeastern approach** to the fort leads under five successive fortified **gateways**. The first, **Alamgiri gate**, was built by Matamad Khan in 1660, in honour of the Moghul emperor Aurangzeb. Beyond its small courtyard, the **Badalgarh gate**, named after Man Singh's uncle Badal, and also known as the "**Hindola**" after the *hindol*, or "swing", that used to hang from it, is in the same Hindu style as the hilltop palace, with two round turrets raised above its doorway.

The small two-storeyed **Gujuri Mahal**, to the right of the Badalgarh gate, was built by Man Singh to woo his favourite rani, Mrignayani, when she was still a peasant girl. According to legend, the raja first became smitten with the "fawn-eyed" Gujur tribeswoman when he saw her wrestle apart a pair of water buffalo during an expedition in the forest; but she would not agree to marry him until he supplied the new palace with water from her village well – the source of her superhuman strength. The elegant sandstone palace now houses Gwalior's **archeological museum** (daily except Friday 10am–5pm; Rs2), where the large exhibition of sculpture, inscriptions and painting is well worth a look, even if the labels are woefully uninformative. Highlights include the twin Ashoka lion capitals from Vidisha in gallery two; the massive lintel carved with a depiction of "the humbling of Bali" in gallery seven; and gallery nine's erotic bas-relief, in which a prince is shown gently removing the top of his beloved's sari. However, the best piece is the priceless **Salabhanjika**, a small, exquisitely carved female figurine found in the ruins of the temple at Gyaraspur. Noted for her sensuous curves and sublime facial expression, the statue is often dubbed "India's *Mona Lisa*".

The next gateway up the hill, the **Ganesh gate**, dates from the mid-fifth century. Close by stands an old pigeon coop, or *kabutar khana*, and, on the far side of the arch, a modern Hindu shrine assembled from the ruins of an earlier one dedicated to the sage **Gwalipa**, which Muhamad Khan replaced with a mosque in 1664. Before arriving at the **Lakshman gate**, you pass a restructured ninth-century Vishnu temple, the **Chatarbhunj** ("four-armed") **Mandir**; a Muslim memorial to one of Ibrahim Lodi's nobles who died during the siege of Gwalior in 1518; and a flight of steps up to some unremarkable Jain rock-cut statues. The fifth and final gateway, the **Hathiya** ("elephant") **Paur**, the most spectacular in the series, forms the entrance to the Man Mandir. Its twin turrets and ornate blue tilework are contiguous with the rest of the massive stone facade.

The Man Mandir

Towering above the northeastern approach to the fort, the **Man Mandir** (daily 8am–5pm; $5 [Rs2]) has to be one of the finest early Hindu palaces in India. Built between 1486 and 1517 by the Tomar ruler Man Singh, it's also known as the Chit Mandir, or "painted palace", for the rich ceramic **mosaics** that encrust its facade. The best-preserved fragments of tilework, on its south side, can be seen from the bank left of the main Hathiya Paur gateway. Spread in luxurious bands of turquoise, emerald-green and yellow across the ornate stonework are tigers, elephants, peacocks, banana palms and crocodiles brandishing flowers.

By contrast, the **interior** of the four-storeyed palace is very plain. Some of the larger halls, however, do contain fine pierced-stone *jali* screens, behind which the women of the palace would assemble to receive instruction from Gwalior's great music gurus. The circular chambers in the lower storeys were formerly the palace dungeons. Prisoners incarcerated here in Moghul times were fed on a preparation made with boiled poppy heads called *poust* – a cruelly ingenious form of torture that ensured a protracted and painful death from malnourishment and drug addiction.

Around the Man Mandir

The **Vikram Mandir** (1516), next door to the Man Mandir, is joined to Man Singh's palace by a network of passages hidden in the thick outer walls. The **Karam Mandir**, a two-storeyed Hindu building with a long colonnaded hall at its centre, stands further to the north, a short walk from the remnants of the now-derelict Jehangiri and Shah Jahan palaces. In the far northwestern corner of the enclosure is the large **Jauhar Kund**, the water tank where, in 1232, the women of the Parihar court performed mass suicide by self-immolation, to avoid capture by Iltutmish's advancing army. A small modern **archeological museum** (daily 8am–5pm; Rs2) on a mound behind the Man Mandir contains more sculpture including a fine temple doorframe and the usual collection of deities and celestial beauties in provocative poses.

The Teli-ka-Mandir and Suraj Kund

The 30m-tall **Teli-ka-Mandir**, on the south side of the plateau, is the oldest surviving monument in the fort. Dating from the mid-eighth century, it consists of a huge rectangular sanctuary tower capped with an unusual vaulted-arch roof, whose *peepal*-leaf shape derives from the *chaitya* windows of much earlier rock-cut Buddhist caves. In the aftermath of the Gwalior Mutiny in 1858, the temple, dedicated to Vishnu, was used by the British as a soda factory. The ASI is now carrying out extensive restoration work.

Set back from the road at the head of the Urwahi ravine, just north of the Teli-ka-Mandir, the **Suraj Kund** is the 100m-long tank whose magical waters are supposed to have cured the tenth-century ruler Suraj Sen, later Suraj Pal, of leprosy.

The Sasbahu mandirs and Sikh gurudwara

The **Sasbahu**, or "mother- and daughter-in-law", temples overlook the city from the eastern edge of the fort, near the unsightly TV mast. The larger of the pair has a three-storey *mandapa* (assembly hall), supported by four intricate pillars, while the smaller one consists of an open-sided porch with a pyramidal roof. Both were erected late in the eleventh century and are dedicated, like the Teli-ka-Mandir, to Vishnu.

The huge, gold-tipped, white-domed marble building to the south is a modern **Sikh gurudwara**. Built to commemorate a Sikh hero who was imprisoned in the fort, the temple attracts a constant stream of pilgrims, most of whom drive here in specially converted "Public Carrier" trucks from the Punjab. Along the road leading to it, you'll pass groups of men clad in the traditional garb of Sikh warriors – long blue *kurtas*, bulky turbans, daggers, and spears held over their shoulders – filing along like foot-soldiers from a bygone era. The *gurudwara*'s cool marble courtyard, filled with the strains of devotional music, makes an atmospheric place to escape the heat. Before entering, make sure you cover your arms, legs and head, remove your socks and shoes, and wash your feet in the tank at the bottom of the steps. Tobacco is strictly prohibited inside the complex.

The rock-cut Jain sculptures

The sheer sandstone cliffs around the fort harbour some imposing **rock-cut Jain sculpture**. Carved between the seventh and fifteenth centuries, most of the figures are large honey-coloured icons of the 24 Jain teacher-saviours – the *tirthankaras*, or "Crossing Makers" – depicted in their characteristic poses: standing with their arms held stiffly at their sides, or sitting cross-legged, the palms of their hands upturned, staring serenely into the distance. Many lost their faces and genitalia when Moghul Emperor Babur's iconoclastic army descended on the city in 1527.

The larger of the two main groups lines the southwestern approach to the fort, along the sides of the **Urwahi** ravine. The largest image, to the side of the road near Urwahi Gate, portrays Adinath, 19m tall, with decorative nipples, a head of tightly curled hair and drooping ears, standing on a lotus bloom beside several smaller statues. Worshippers leave flowers and incense at his colossal feet. The group is well-preserved and the statues, including elephants and heavenly *apsaras*, are more or less intact. A little further from the fort, on the other side of the road, another company of *tirthankaras* enjoys a more dramatic situation, looking over a natural gorge. All have lost their faces, save a proud trio sheltered by a delicate canopy.

The third collection stands on the southeast corner of the plateau, overlooking the city from a narrow ledge. To get there, follow Gwalior Road north along the foot of the cliff from Phool Bagh, near the **Rani Jhansi memorial**, until you see a paved path winding up the hill from behind a row of houses on the left. Once again, the *tirthankaras*, which are numbered, occupy deep recesses hewn from the rock wall. One of the few not defaced by the Muslim invaders, **no. 10** is still visited by Gwalior's small Jain community as a shrine. After bathing in the spring in **cave 1**, devotees leave offerings of flowers and rice at the *tirthankara*'s gigantic feet.

The old town and south of the fort

A number of interesting Islamic monuments are tucked away down the narrow, dusty backstreets of Gwalior's predominantly Muslim **old town**, clustered around the north and northeast corners of the hill. The **Jami Masjid** stands close to the Gujuri Mahal, near the main entrance to the fort. Erected in 1661 by Mohammad Khan, using sandstone quarried from the plateau above, the beautifully preserved mosque has two slender minarets and three bulbous onion domes crowned with golden spires.

The city's most famous Muslim building, however, is set amid balding lawns and unruly bougainvillea bushes 1km further east. The sixteenth-century **Tomb of Ghaus Mohammed**, an Afghan prince who helped Babur take Gwalior fort, is a fine specimen of early Moghul architecture, and a popular local shrine. Elegant hexagonal pavilions stand at each of its four corners; in the centre, the large central dome was formerly covered with blue-glazed tiles. The tomb's walls are inlaid with exquisite pierced-stone *jali* screens, whose complex geometric patterns are best admired from the incense-filled interior.

The second and smaller of the tombs in the gardens is that of the famous Moghul singer-musician **Tansen**, one of the "Nine Jewels" of Emperor Akbar's court. Every year, performers and aficionados from all over India flock here for Gwalior's annual **music festival** (Nov–Dec). At other times, impromptu recitals of *qawwali*, Islamic devotional singing accompanied on the harmonium (see p.132), take place on the terrace outside. Local superstition holds that the leaves of the **tamarind tree** growing on the plinth nearby have a salutary effect on the singing voice, which explains why its bottom branches have been stripped bare. **To get there** from the station, take a rickshaw (Rs15) or a *tempo* bound for Hazira (Rs2).

The Jai Vilas palace

Due south of the fort, in the heart of Gwalior's upper-class neighbourhood, the **Jai Vilas palace** (daily except Wed 9.30am–5pm; Rs175 [Rs10]; Rs25 extra with camera, Rs75 extra with video. Guides charge about Rs50 per tour) is one of India's most grandiose and eccentric nineteenth-century relics, although the extremely steep entry fee and total lack of labelling and information make this an unsatisfactory experience.

The palace was built in 1875 during the reign of Maharaja Jayaji Rao Scindia. Wanting his residence to rival those of his colonial overlords in Britain, he dispatched his friend Colonel Michael Filose – "Mikul Sahib", the descendant of an Italian mercenary – on a grand tour of Europe to seek inspiration. A year or so later, Filose returned with a vast shipment of furniture, fabric, paintings, tapestries and cut glass, together with the blueprints for a building that borrowed heavily from Buckingham Palace, Versailles, and a host of Greek ruins and Italian-Baroque stately homes. The result is an improbable blend of Doric, Tuscan and Corinthian architecture, with one of the most shamelessly over-the-top interiors you're likely to see outside Hollywood.

The Scindias, who still occupy a part of the palace, have opened two wings to the public. Eager to maintain the sense of a family home, they have placed innumerable photographs of their richly clad clan members on every available surface throughout the first wing, a **museum** of the more valuable and extraordinary artefacts accumulated by the rulers of Gwalior. Collecting dust in the dozens of rooms and creaky wood-panelled corridors are countless Moghul paintings, Persian rugs, gold and silver ornaments, and antique furniture that had originally belonged to the estate of Louis XVI before the French Revolution. Elsewhere, you'll come across a swing made from Venetian cut glass which the royal family used to celebrate Krishna's birthday, and a room full of stuffed tigers and sepia photographs that show the maharaja posing stiffly with rows of pipe-smoking, pith-helmeted British guests. Finally, a room upstairs is given over to **erotica**. The *chowkidar* will gleefully point out its centrepiece, a life-size marble statue of a woman succumbing with some élan to the amorous advances of a swan.

The palace's most extravagant wing lies across the courtyard from the museum. The **durbar hall** was where the maharaja entertained important visitors, among them the Prince of Wales (later Edward VII), who descended on Gwalior in 1875 with an entourage of a thousand people. Displayed in the banquet hall on the ground floor is a silver toy train used by Jayaji Rao Scindia to dispense brandy and cigars after dinner; the maharaja would tease anyone he didn't like by not stopping the electric locomotive when it reached them. A sweeping Belgian glass staircase leads from the lobby to the gargantuan assembly hall upstairs. Suspended from its ceiling are the world's biggest **chandeliers**. At over three and a half tonnes apiece, they could not be installed until the strength of the roof had been tested with eight elephants – a feat that necessitated the construction of a 500m-long earth ramp. The rug lining the floor of the hall is equally enormous. Woven by inmates of Gwalior jail, it took twelve years to complete and, at over 40m in length, is the largest handmade carpet in Asia.

Sarod Ghar

Tucked away in the west of the city, the new **Sarod Ghar** museum (Tues–Sun 10am–1pm & 2–5pm; free; ⓦwww.sarod.com) is on Ustad Hafiz Ali Khan Marg, Jiwaji Ganj. Either take a rickshaw directly to the house, or a *tempo* (Rs3) to Jiwyaji, a five-minute walk north of Jayaji Chowk (circle). The museum is in the beautiful ancestral home of the Bagnash family, which is worth a visit in its own right, with rose sandstone walls aligned in pure symmetry and delicate sculptural detail around a marble courtyard, still used for musical recitals (check newspaper listings or at the MPTDC tourist office). The Bagnash ancestors were originally Afghan horse traders who settled in India and produced a dynasty of musical virtuosos, including **Ustad Hafiz Ali Khan** and his son **Ustad Amjad Ali Khan**.

The museum traces the rich **musical legacy** that modern Gwalior is justifiably proud of, from the fame of Tansen, who played in the court of Moghul Emperor Akbar, to the first formal school of Indian music, established in the palace of Man Singh. In the nineteenth and twentieth centuries, the Scindia rajas faithfully continued the local tradition of royal patronage of the arts; the musical talents of the Bagnash family flourished and Gulam Ali Khan Bagnash created a new instrument – the **sarod**. Combining the harsh sound of the *rabab* with the more flowing and melodious nature of the sitar, which is used to play the classical ragas of India, the sarod is a wooden plucked instrument with a large, conical bell-shaped base and long neck. At the top end of the neck, behind the tuning screws, there is a tamba – a second, smaller bell that produces the highly refined pitch of the notes.

As sarod music drifts around the museum, the informative galleries take you through the development of the instrument. The last gallery contains a hoard of classical Indian instruments donated by famous artists. These include sets of tabla (drums), the violin – which is very similar to the European version but played from the chest rather than the chin – and the *sur-mandal* (harp). There is also a small shop where you can stock up on books and recordings of some of the finest performances of Indian classical music.

The Scindia Chhatris

If you've developed an interest in the ostentatious Scindia family, the two monumental sandstone **chhatris** (mausoleums) a short *tempo* ride north of Jayaji Chowk are yet another lavish display of their wealth and egotism. Although the *chhatris* are a shadow of their outstanding counterparts in Shivpuri (see p.460), the intricate stone-carvings and ornate paintings of life inside the Maratha royal court in the nineteenth century deserve a look. If the *chhatris* are shut there is a *chowkidar* who will open them up.

You enter a courtyard, where the largest *chhatri* is on your immediate right. Built in 1817 to commemorate Maharaja Jiyaji Rao Scindia, it is most remarkable for the ornate outside panelling of interwoven flowers. The interior is a large hall traditionally used for musical recitals, although dust and pigeons have got the better of it and the dressed marble effigy of the maharaja stares out into the gloom.

The second *chhatri* is reached through a yellow and white arch to the left of the courtyard, and is a more compact and finely detailed version of the former. Constructed in 1843 for the newly departed Maharaja Janakaji Scindia, the sculptures and carvings depict the hectic lifestyle of a king. There are little stone elephants, each bejewelled and covered with a unique silk canopy, plodding in a line around the platform to symbolize the power of the maharaja, and the door is guarded by two solemn soldiers in full Maratha regalia. As an antidote to the warring reputation of the Maratha rulers, numerous panels outside depict the life of Krishna surrounded by his many pleasure-seeking beauties, and inside the *chhatri* there are painted frescoes of princesses and court dances, as well as life-size marble effigies of the maharaja and his three wives.

Eating

With a couple of exceptions, all the best **places to eat** in Gwalior are in the mid- and top-of-the-range hotels, where main dishes set you back anywhere between thirty and a hundred rupees. More basic, and much **cheaper** dhal, *subzi* and *roti* meals are doled out on stainless-steel plates at the row of dodgy *dhabas* outside the railway station. Look out too for the **juice bars** dotted around the station and Jayaji Chowk, over in the west end of town, which serve glasses of refreshing, freshly squeezed fruit juice (ask for no ice).

Banjara, High Court Lane. Very dim lighting, but a good range of mainly Indian dishes, imaginative daily specials, and efficient service. Western and south Indian breakfasts.

Indian Coffee House, Station Road. Delicious *dosas* and other south Indian snacks, plain or with "special" nut and veg fillings. Opens 7.30am for breakfast – *iddlis* and large omelettes with good coffee and the newspapers.

Kwality, MLB Road, near *Fort View Hotel*. Part of the north Indian restaurant chain serving up tasty veg and non-veg Indian dishes from a particularly long menu.

Landmark, Manik Vilas. The usual modestly priced multi-cuisine menu with an emphasis on Mughlai specialities; the main attraction however, is the live Indian classical music every evening.

MPTDC Tansen, 6-A Gandhi Rd. Good Western breakfasts, and the standard, safe MPTDC Indian/Chinese menu; the biriyani dishes are particularly good.

Ushan Kiran Palace, Jayendraganj, Lakshar. Modest selection of (expensive) gourmet Indian and Western food, with lots of mouthwatering Mughlai-style dishes. The buffet lunches are good for a splurge.

Shivpuri

SHIVPURI, the former summer capital of the Scindias, lies 114km southwest of Gwalior, at a crossroads on the main Jhansi–Jaipur highway. Local rulers from the Moghuls onwards were drawn here by the abundance of game in the area's lush deciduous forests. These days, however, only a few fragments of woodland remain, and the small market town is now marooned in a landscape of shaly scrub, dried-up riverbeds and escarpments peppered with dusty brown trees. Apart from a couple of nineteenth-century cenotaphs and a minor-league national park, little remains of Shivpuri's princely past.

The town's main monuments, the **chhatris** of the Scindia family (8am–8pm; Rs1, Rs5 extra with camera, Rs30 extra with video), stand a two-kilometre tonga ride from the bus stand, by the side of the road leading to the MPTDC *Tourist Village*. Facing each other across an ornamental garden, the cenotaphs fuse Hindu and Islamic styles, juxtaposing slender temple *shikharas* with Moghul domes and pavilions. The larger of the pair, dedicated to the dowager queen Maharani Raje Scindia, boasts a grand double-storey facade that opens onto a water tank intersected by walkways. Her son Madho Rao Scindia's *chhatri* is even more ornate, standing on a raised platform on the opposite side of the tank. The porch is flanked by ersatz Victorian street lamps; its intricately carved walls are inlaid with lapis lazuli and onyx and the doors are solid silver. Both enshrine life-size effigies of the Scindias, each served and dressed daily by two manservants, and regaled with devotional music in the evenings (6.30–8pm). This atmospheric occasion is well worth attending.

Shivpuri's other attraction, the **Madhav national park** (also known as Shivpuri National Park), is not worth bothering with unless you have your own vehicle. Even then you have to pay Rs200 for entry and mandatory guide (Rs25), and the most exciting animals you're likely to spot are run-of-the-mill Indian deer: *cheetal, chinkara, nilgai*, sambar and *chausingha*. One advantage, however, is that Madhav is open all year round. Jeeps can be rented through MPTDC, at the reception desk of the *Tourist Village*; a two-hour tour costs Rs350 and includes the unexciting **tiger safari** (the animals are captive). Birdwatchers may find Madhav marginally more inspiring, however, as its large artificial (and crocodile-infested) lakes attract several species of migratory wildfowl during the winter. The rare Indian bustard also nests 40km away to the east, in the **Karera bird sanctuary**, which is only accessible by car.

Practicalities

Shivpuri can be reached by hourly **buses** from both Gwalior and Jhansi, 84km east, as well as from Datia (with a change at Karera). Tongas and more expensive unmetered auto-rickshaws are on hand at the bus stand in the middle of town to ferry visitors out to Shivpuri's **hotels**. The lakeside MPTDC *Tourist Village* (☎07492/23760; ❺–❻), 3km from the bus stand, is peaceful with spacious and modern chalets decorated with *adivasi* art, with attached bathrooms and a/c on request. Ideally, you should reserve at least five days in advance (through any MPTDC office). *Vanasthali* (☎07492/33057; ❷–❸) is the best of the basic hotels along AB Road, close to the bus stand; the new all-a/c *Hotel Delhi* (☎07492/33093; ❻), just off the roundabout by the bus stand, is overpriced but comfortable.

The MPTDC hotel with delicious tandoori dishes or the pure-veg *Hotel Delhi* are the best places to **eat**. If you're on a tight budget, there is a handful of *dhabas* on the main street near the bus stand.

Datia

Constructed by Bir Singh Deo at the height of the Bundela's "golden age", the majestic multistoreyed palace at **DATIA**, 30km northwest of Jhansi, is regarded as one of the finest Rajput buildings in India. Although few of the visitors who spy the exotic hulk of yellow-brown ramparts, cupolas and domed pavilions from the nearby train line actually stop here, those that do are rarely disappointed. The palace presides from the top of a rocky outcrop at the edge of a busy market town, overlooking a mass of white- and blue-washed brick houses, packed tightly onto a saucer-shaped depression in the plains.

The **Nrsing Dev Palace** (dawn to dusk) stands in the north of town, separated from the railway and bus stations by narrow streets and lanes. Decorated with paintings and stone carving, the main entrance leads into the gloomy bowels of the building under a massive five-storey facade. Half the fun of visiting the labyrinthine palace is trying to find a path from its pitch-black subterranean chambers, hewn out of the solid base of the hill for use during the hot season, to the rani's airy apartment on the top floor. In between, a maze of cross-cutting corridors, flying walkways, walls encrusted with fragments of ceramic tiles, latticed screens and archways, hidden passages, pavilions and suites of apartments lead you in ever-decreasing circles until you eventually run out of staircases. The views from the upper storeys are breathtaking.

Scattered around the town below are several other Rajput monuments, including a sprawling fort, the **Bharat Garh**, and the stately home of Datia's present ruling family. Although not officially open, you can stroll into the compound where the obliging *chowkidar* may show you round the dusty and disorganized durbar hall, which stands next to a multi-domed whitewashed Govind Mandir (Krishna temple). Immediately to the north, a large tank, the **Karna Sagar**, stands amid *dhobi ghats* and the ruins of temples and *chhatris*. The white pinnacles of Sonagiri are also visible on the horizon.

Nearer the bus stand, the less impressive of Datia's two hilltop palaces, the **Raj Garh**, houses a small **museum** (Tues–Sat 10am–5pm; free), whose dull collection of sculpture and painting is far less inspiring than the views from its balcony.

Practicalities

Datia, on the main Delhi–Mumbai train line, is most often visited as a day-trip from Jhansi, or as a break in the journey to Gwalior, 71km to the northwest. Buses run from both cities every half hour and there are ten trains daily. If you're coming from Shivpuri, 97km west, you'll have to change buses at Karera. Tongas and cycle rickshaws ferry passengers into town from the small **railway station**, 2km southwest, while **buses** pull in at a lot on the south side of the centre. Bicycles can be hired at minimal cost from a shop on the corner of the main road and the road to the bus stand, near Raj Garh Palace. You can get simple food and cold drinks in the *dhabas*.

Sonagiri

SONAGIRI, 61km southeast of Gwalior, is among the more ethereal landmarks punctuating the Delhi–Mumbai rail journey. Flowing down the east-facing slope of a solitary hillock, deep in the central Indian countryside, 84 gleaming white shrines mark the spot where the legendary King Nanganang Kumar, together with five-and-a-half *crore* of his followers, achieved liberation from the cycle of rebirth. Today the site, sacred to **Digambar** ("sky-clad") **Jains**, makes an atmospheric pause for a couple of hours en route to one of the nearby cities.

Minibuses to Sonagiri from the mainline station pull in at the "manager's office" in a small **village square**, where you can check that it's OK to visit. From here, most pilgrims make for the "**mirror temple**", down the lane to the left, in which artists can be seen fashioning mosaics of *tirthankaras* from coloured glass and mirrors. More sombre spiritual pursuits take place in the seminary at the back of the square, next to the main entrance. Old Digambar monks conduct religious discussions with pilgrims in the courtyard, their distinctive, yellow wooden water pots (*dariyes*) and peacock-feather whisks beside them. For most of the year, these ascetics wander naked around the country, returning to monasteries for a few months to give and receive teachings. More secular Jains notch up credits on the cosmic balance sheet by making gifts to religious establishments instead – as evidenced by the dozens of donatory plaques set in the **marble walkway** leading up the hill. Crowning the summit of Sonagiri, the main **temple** houses a colossal *tirthankara* icon, while below it, a ceramic scale model of **Mount Meru**, the axial mountain said by Jains, Buddhists and Hindus to support the cosmos, looks out over the cascade of whitewashed spires and fluttering yellow pennants to the distant plains.

Without your own vehicle, the only way to get to Sonagiri is by **train**. Check the timings of onward services carefully before leaving the station, as only three trains in each direction actually stop here and there's very little **accommodation**. If you get stuck, the office in the main square will fix you a dorm bed for a night in the Jain *dharamshala*, or you can try the railway retiring rooms. Pure-veg **food**, snacks, chai and cold drinks are available at the insanitary-looking stall opposite the bus stand.

Orchha

ORCHHA, literally "hidden place", certainly lives up to its name. Languishing amid a tangle of scrubby *dhak* forest, 18km southeast of Jhansi, the former capital of the **Bundela** dynasty has become an essential halt for the tourist traffic bound for Khajuraho on the nearby highway. The deserted medieval town is an architectural gem where guano-splashed temple *shikharas*, derelict palaces, *havelis* and weed-choked sandstone cenotaphs lie neglected by the banks of the tranquil River Betwa – home to troupes of black-faced langurs, vultures and wheeling flocks of bright green parakeets.

Clustered around the foot of the exotic ruins, the sleepy village of neatly painted houses, market stalls, and a couple of attractive hotels makes an excellent spot to unwind after the hassle of northern cities.

Some history

According to one legend, the name of Orchha's founding dynasty, the **Bundelas**, derives from an eleventh-century ancestor who sacrificed five severed heads (or five drops of his own blood) to the mountain goddess Vindhyabatha – a deed that earned him the epithet of "Vindhyela", or "he who offered blood". Expelled by his brothers from their homeland near Varanasi, Vindhyela and his descendants roamed central India until finally settling at **Garkhundar**, the first capital of Bundelkhand. Pushed on by the Delhi Sultan Tuqluq late in the fifteenth century, the Bundelas decamped 45km to a more remote and defensible jungle site. The old Malwan outpost at **Orchha**, astride an island formed by a sharp bend in the River Betwa, proved an ideal platform from which to dominate the region when the Tuqluqs' power eventually declined.

Work on Orchha's magnificent fortifications, palaces and temples was started by Raja **Rudra Pratap** soon after the move, and continued after he was killed in 1531 trying to wrestle a cow from the clutches of a tiger. Thereafter, the dynasty's fortunes depended on the goodwill of their mighty neighbours, the **Moghuls**. After being defeated in battle by Akbar, the proud and pious **Madhukar Shah** nearly signed his clan's death warrant by showing up at the imperial court with a red *tilak* smeared on his forehead – a mark banned by the staunchly Muslim emperor. Luckily for the Bundelas, however, Madhukar's bold gesture earned Akbar's respect, and the two became friends – an alliance fostered in the following years by Orchha's most illustrious raja, **Bir Singh Deo**. Long before he acceded to the throne, the ambitious young Bundela saw the value of keeping on the right side of his counterpart in Delhi, Prince Salim. In 1601, he assassinated the latter's much-loathed adversary, **Abdul Fazal**, and sent Salim the decapitated head on a platter. The murder infuriated Akbar but was never forgotten by his son, who, when he became Emperor

Jahangir in 1605, rewarded Bir Singh Deo's brutal act by helping him to seize the Bundela throne from his elder brother Ram Shah.

During his 22-year rule, Bir Singh Deo erected a total of 52 forts and palaces across the region, including the citadel at **Jhansi**, the rambling Nrsing Dev at **Datia**, and many of Orchha's finest buildings. In 1627, he was killed by bandits while returning from the Deccan with a camel train full of booty. Afterwards, Bundelkhand's relations with the Moghuls rapidly deteriorated. Attacks by the armies of Shah Jahan, Aurangzeb, and the Marathas ensued, and a spate of eighteenth-century Jat peasant uprisings finally forced the Bundelas to flee Orchha for the comparative safety of **Tikamgarh**. Apart from the *Sheesh Mahal*, now converted into a small hotel, the magnificent monuments have lain virtually deserted ever since.

Arrival and information

Tightly packed **tempos** from Jhansi bus station run frequently to Orchha's main crossroads, 18km away, or there are five daily **buses**. Both take 20 to 40 minutes (depending on the number of stops), and cost Rs6–8 (plus Rs10 for luggage in a *tempo*). An **auto-rickshaw** from Jhansi railway or bus station will set you back around Rs120; it costs more at night. Coming from **Khajuraho**, you can ask to be dropped at the Orchha turning on the main road and pick up a *tempo* for the remaining 7km.

If you're heading in the other direction, don't bet on flagging down the express MPSRTC coaches on the highway, as they're often full. Instead, get to Jhansi early and arrange a ticket before the Delhi/Agra trains get in; the Shatabdi Express deluxe coach leaves Jhansi railway station at 10.40am and takes four hours. More comfortable private **Jeeps** (with drivers) cut the journey time to Khajuraho – they cost upwards of Rs1200 (one-way), and can be rented at the bus station, or through the manager of the MPTDC *Sheesh Mahal* hotel, who can also arrange day-trips (Rs1400-1600). You can change **travellers' cheques** only at Canara Bank in the main square, otherwise Jhansi also has moneychanging facilities.

Accommodation and eating

Orchha has an increasing number of **places to stay**. Cheap accommodation has proliferated in the last couple of years, ranging from the original and extremely cheap and soulless state-run **rest houses** in the main bazaar to the typical backpacker hangouts with communal and/or attached bathrooms, 24hr hot water and even generators for the frequent power cuts.

The smartest **place to eat**, and an attractive place to hang out in the evenings, is the colonnaded dining hall in the *Sheesh Mahal*, which serves a good mix of veg and non-veg food, and tandoori specials at lunch time. Alternatively, at *Betwa Cottages*, the Indian veg dishes are delicious (order an hour in advance). There are also a few simple *dhabas* in the bazaar, serving very cheap thalis, and a congenial café on the corner of the junction between the track to the *Sheesh Mahal* and the main road through the bazaar, which serves great pancake, thali and lassi fare. The delicious local speciality, Orchha milk-cake, can be bought from the small stalls around the gate to the Ram Raja temple forecourt.

Fortview, on the main road ☎07680/52701. Airy and clean doubles, with one facing the palace, and the peaceful little garden is on the banks of the

river. An excellent option. **❷**
MPTDC Betwa Cottages ☎07680/52618. A cheerful place by the river, whose interior design

celebrates Moghul tradition with period painting and furniture. In the gardens there are a/c or non-a/c cottages each with a double room, modern bathroom and veranda. ❺–❻

MPTDC Sheesh Mahal ☎07680/52624. Formerly the local raja's country bolt hole, this small, very friendly hotel has one cheap single (Rs190) and seven non-a/c doubles – all excellent value, with attached bathrooms and superb views. If you can afford it, treat yourself to a romantic night in the royal apartment. Perks include candlelit dinner on your private veranda, a vast marble bathtub, and the ultimate loo with a view. Advance booking is recommended. ❺–❾

Orchha Resort ☎07680/52678, a brand new, characterless hotel by the river with all mod cons, including foreign exchange, a health club and pool, but it's very overpriced – especially the buffet meals. ❾

Rama Mandir, along a terrace overlooking the bazaar. A friendly place with simple doubles, and a more pleasant option than the more dingy and basic *Shri Mahant Guest House* opposite. ❶

SADA Mansarover, main bazaar near Rama Raja mandir. Very basic and dingy doubles and a communal bathroom; a fall-back only. ❶

Sharma, on the main road past the bazaar, is by far the best of the lodges, with spotless sunny yellow rooms around a quiet and shady courtyard and communal bathrooms; some more expensive a/c rooms are currently being constructed. ❶

The monuments

Though the best-preserved of Orchha's scattered palaces, temples, tombs and gardens (daily 9am–5pm; "day passport" for all monuments: Rs30 [Rs10]; still Rs20 extra with camera, Rs50 extra with video) lie within comfortable walking distance of the village and can be seen – at breakneck speed – in a day, to get the most out of a trip you should plan on staying the night. If you want to catch up on the history of the palaces and the significance of their wall paintings, it's worth using MPTDC's excellent **walkman tour** of the highlights (2hr; Rs50, plus Rs500 deposit – available from the main ticket office and the reception at the *Sheesh Mahal*). It sets a lively scene, with medieval Indian music and an easy-to-follow commentary.

The Raj Mahal and the Rai Praveen Mahal

The first building you come to across Orchha's medieval granite bridge, the **Raj Mahal**, was started by Rudra Pratap, and completed by one of his successors, the indomitable Madhukar Shah. From the end of the bridge, bear left at the main entrance, and then right before reaching the *Sheesh Mahal* hotel. Of the two rectangular courtyards inside, the second, formerly used by the Bundela ranis, is the most dramatic. Opulent royal quarters, raised balconies and interlocking walkways rise in symmetrical tiers on all four sides, crowned by domed pavilions and turrets; the apartments projecting into the quadrangle on the ground floor belonged to the most-favoured queens. As you wander around, look out for the fragments of mirror inlay and vibrant **painting** plastered over their walls and ceilings. Some of the friezes are still in remarkable condition, depicting Vishnu's various outlandish incarnations, court and hunting scenes, and lively festivals involving dancers, musicians and jugglers. The resident *chowkidar* is an excellent guide.

Reached via a path that leads from the Raj Mahal around the northern side of the hill, the **Rai Praveen Mahal** is a small, double-storeyed brick apartment built by Raja Indramani for his concubine in the mid-1670s. The gifted poetess, musician and dancer, Rai Praveen, beguiled the Moghul emperor Akbar when she was sent to him as a gift, but was eventually returned to Orchha to live out her remaining days. Set amid the well-watered lawns of the **Anand Mahal gardens**, it has a main assembly hall on the ground floor (used to host music and dance performances), a boudoir upstairs, and cool underground apartments.

The Jahangir Mahal

Orchha's single most admired palace, the **Jahangir Mahal**, was built by Bir Singh Deo as a monumental welcome present for the Moghul emperor when he paid a state visit here in the seventeenth century. Jahangir had come to invest his old ally with the sword of Abdul Fazal – the emperor's erstwhile enemy whom Bir Singh had murdered some years earlier. Entered through an ornate ceremonial gateway, the main, east-facing facade is still encrusted with turquoise tiles. Two stone elephants flank the stairway, holding bells in their trunks to announce the arrival of the raja. Once again, three storeys of elegant hanging balconies, terraces, apartments and onion domes are piled around a central courtyard. This palace, however, has a much lighter feel, with countless windows and pierced stone screens looking out over the exotic Orchha skyline to the west, and a sea of treetops and ruined temples in the other direction.

The Sheesh Mahal

Built during the early eighteenth century, long after Orchha's demise, the **Sheesh Mahal** ("Palace of Mirrors") was originally intended as an exclusive country retreat for the local raja, Udait Singh. Following Independence, however, the property was inherited by the state government, who have converted it into a hotel. The rather squat palace stands between the Raj Mahal and the Jahangir Mahal, at the far end of an open-sided courtyard. Covered in a coat of whitewash and stripped of most of its Persian rugs and antiques, the building retains little of its former splendour, though it does offer stunning views from its upper terraces and turrets. The only rooms worth a peep – assuming they're not occupied (check with reception) – are the palatial nos. 1 and 2, which contain original bathroom fittings.

Around the village

Dotted **around the village** below the hill are several other interesting monuments. The **Ram Raja Mandir** stands at the end of the small bazaar, in a cool marble-tiled courtyard. Local legend has it that Madhukar Shah constructed the building as a palace for his wife, Rani Ganesha, and it only became a temple after a Rama icon, which the queen had dutifully carried all the way from her home town of Ayodhya, could not be lifted from the spot where she first set it down. The god, it seems, had only consented to the move on condition that he be immediately enshrined in his own purpose-built temple. When she got back to Orchha, however, the rani was dismayed to find the Chatturbuj temple still unfinished. True to its word, when the time came to transport the deity over to the new shrine, it remained stuck to the floor, where it has stood ever since. Nowadays, the pink and yellow Ram Raja Mandir is a popular pilgrimage site. During major Rama festivals, thousands of worshippers gather in front of its ornate silver doors to await *darshan* of the garlanded deity inside.

With its huge pointed *shikharas* soaring high above the village, the temple originally built to house Rani Ganesha's icon, **Chatturbuj Mandir**, seems, on the face of it, well worthy of that honour. In cruciform shape, representing the four-armed Vishnu, with seven storeys and spacious courtyards ringed by arched balconies, it epitomizes the regal Bundelkhand style inspired by the Moghuls, but is also influenced by Rajput, Persian and European tastes. It's unusual for a Hindu temple, with very few carvings and a wealth of space – perhaps to accommodate followers of the **bhakti** cult (a form of worship involving large congregations of people rather than a small elite of priests). You can climb up the narrow staircases between storeys to the temple's roof, pierced by an ornate *shikhara* whose niches shelter nesting vultures.

On the other side of Ram Mandir, a path leads through the Moghul-style **Phool Bagh** ornamental garden to **Hardaul ka Baithaka**, a grand pavilion where Bir Singh Deo's second son, Hardaul, ally of Jahangir and romantic paragon, once held court. Newlyweds come here to seek blessing from Hardaul; he was poisoned by his jealous brother who accused him of intimacy with his sister-in-law. The tall towers rising above the gardens like disregarded bridge supports are *dastgirs* (literally "wind-catchers"), Persian-style cooling towers that provided air-conditioning for the neighbouring palace, Palkhi Mahal; they're probably the only ones of their kind surviving in India.

The Lakshminarayan Mandir

The lone **Lakshminarayan Mandir** crowns a rocky hillock just under 1km west of Orchha village, at the end of a long, paved pathway. From the square directly behind the Ram Raja temple, a leisurely fifteen-minute stroll is rewarded with fine views, and excellent seventeenth- and nineteenth-century paintings. For a small tip, the resident *chowkidar* will lead you through the galleries inside the temple. Look out for the frieze depicting the battle of Jhansi, in which the rani appears in an upper room of the fort next to her horse, while musket-bearing British troops scuttle about below. Another great battle scene is the epic encounter between the ten-headed, twenty-armed demon Ravana and Rama's army of monkey soldiers. Elsewhere, episodes from the much-loved Krishna story crop up, as do portraits of the Bundela rajas and their military and architectural achievements. Finally, a side pillar bears a sketch of two very inebriated English soldiers – as much a parody of the colonials' curious customs as an invective against the evils of drink.

The chhatris

A solemn row of pale brown weed-choked domes and spires, the riverside **chhatris** are Orchha's most melancholy ruins and a fitting place to end a tour of the village. The fourteen cenotaphs, memorials to Bundelkhand's former rulers, are best viewed from the narrow road bridge or, better still, from the boulders on the opposite bank, where you get the full effect of their reflection in the still waters of the Betwa.

Khajuraho

The resplendent Hindu temples of **KHAJURAHO**, immaculately restored after almost a millennium of abandonment and neglect, are among the most essential stops on any itinerary of India's historic monuments. Famed above all for the delicate sensuality – and forthright **eroticism** – of their sculpture, they were built between the tenth and twelfth centuries AD as the greatest architectural achievement of the **Chandella** dynasty. Mysteriously, the Chandellas appear to have forgotten about the temples soon afterwards, and it took "rediscovery" by the British before these masterpieces were fully appreciated in India, let alone internationally. Even today, excavations continue with a new temple – and possibly the biggest – unearthed in 1998-9 in the area of the Southern group.

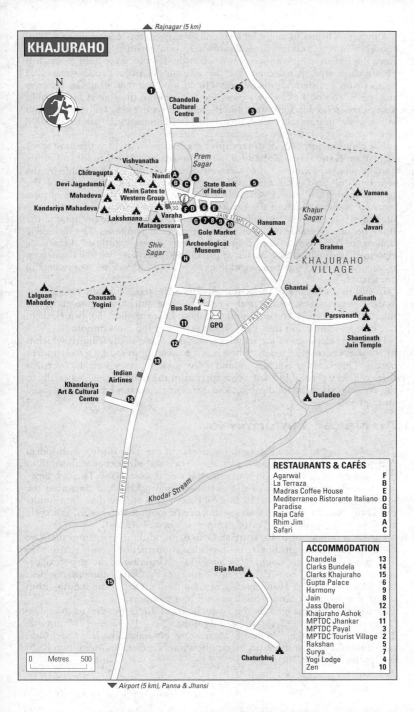

KHAJURAHO

▲ Rajnagar (5 km)

N

① Chandella Cultural Centre

②
③

Prem Sagar

Vishvanatha
Chitragupta
Devi Jagadambi
Mahadeva
Kandariya Mahadeva
Nandi Ⓐ
Ⓑ
Ⓒ ④
State Bank of India ⑤

Ⓘ
MAIN SQ
Ⓕ Ⓓ
Main Gates to Western Group
Lakshmana
Varaha
Ⓖ ⑥ Ⓔ
JAIN TEMPLES ROAD
Matangesvara
Ⓖ ⑦ ⑧ ⑨ ⑩
Hanuman
Gole Market
Archeological Museum
Ⓗ

Shiv Sagar

▲ Vamana

Khajur Sagar

▲ Javari

▲ Brahma

KHAJURAHO VILLAGE

Lalguan Mahadev
Chausath Yogini
Bus Stand
★
GPO
Ghantai ▲
BY-PASS ROAD
Adinath
Parsvanath
Shantinath Jain Temple

⑪
⑫
⑬
Indian Airlines
Khandariya Art & Cultural Centre
⑭
▲ Duladeo

AIRPORT ROAD

Khodar Stream

⑮

Bija Math ▲

Chaturbhuj ▲

RESTAURANTS & CAFÉS

Agarwal	F
La Terraza	B
Madras Coffee House	E
Mediterraneo Ristorante Italiano	D
Paradise	G
Raja Café	B
Rhim Jim	A
Safari	C

ACCOMMODATION

Chandela	13
Clarks Bundela	14
Clarks Khajuraho	15
Gupta Palace	6
Harmony	9
Jain	8
Jass Oberoi	12
Khajuraho Ashok	1
MPTDC Jhankar	11
MPTDC Payal	3
MPTDC Tourist Village	2
Rakshan	5
Surya	7
Yogi Lodge	4
Zen	10

▼ Airport (5 km), Panna & Jhansi

Although Khajuraho might look central on maps of the subcontinent, 400km southeast of Agra and the same distance west of Varanasi, it remains as remote from the Indian mainstream as it was when the temples were built – which is presumably what spared them the depredations of marauders, invaders and zealots who devastated so many early Hindu sites. No train routes as yet cross this extended flood plain, set against the backdrop of the jagged Dantla hills, and visitors who don't fly straight here are faced with a long bus journey from either of the nearest railheads. A branch line to Mahoba was begun in late 1998 but it's not expected to be open until 2003 at the earliest.

The exquisite intricacy of the **temples** themselves – of which the most spectacular are **Kandariya Mahadeva**, **Vishvanatha** and **Lakshmana**, all in the conglomeration known as the **Western Group** – was made possible by the soft buff-coloured sandstone used in their construction. Considering the propensity of such stone to crumble, they have withstood the ravages of time remarkably well. Much of the ornate **sculpture** that adorns their walls is in such high relief as to be virtually three-dimensional, with strains of pink in the stone helping to imbue the figures with gentle flesh-like tones. The incredible skill of the artisans is evident throughout, with friezes as little as 10cm wide crammed with naturalistic details of ornaments, jewellery, hairstyles and even manicured nails. A huge congregation of gods and goddesses are everywhere in attendance.

To add to the beauty of the whole ensemble, the temples subtly change hue as the day progresses, passing from a warm pink at sunrise, to white under the midday sun, and back to warm pink at sunset. Dramatic floodlights pick them out in the evening, and they glow white beneath a luminous moon.

The sheer splendour of the temples rather overshadows the **village**, which is increasingly becoming a rash of hotels and trinket shops fed by a daily tourist invasion. However, if you stay around a few days, you may well discover that there is a slow pace of life that exists apart from the temple scene, especially in the evening when the local market and open-air restaurants create a very social atmosphere.

Arrival and information

The easiest way to get to Khajuraho is on one of the daily **flights** with Indian Airlines from Delhi (via Agra), or Varanasi. The local **airport** is 5km south of the main square of Khajuraho town; the taxi ride in costs Rs80. The two nearest railheads are at **Jhansi** to the northwest (see p.335), and **Satna** to the southeast; both are connected by bus. All buses terminate less than 1km southeast at the bus stand, within walking distance of most central hotels, or a cycle rickshaw will set you back Rs10, an auto-rickshaw Rs15.

The Government of India **Tourist Office**, round the corner from the *Raja Cafe*, is efficient although it provides information only (Mon–Fri 9am–5.30pm, Sat 8am–noon; ☎07686/72347); a counter at the airport operates at flight times. The MP Tourism Office is in the State Museum, out near Hotel Payal (Mon–Sat 10am–5pm; closed 2nd and 3rd Sat of the month), from where you can book accommodation and hire transport.

Money can be changed at the State Bank of India on the main square (Mon–Fri 10.45am–2.45pm & 4–5pm; Sat 10.45am–12.45pm & 2.30–3.30pm), and there's a post office near the bus stand. The *Red Cyber Café*, on Airport Road near the main bazaar offers internet facilities (minimum Rs20 for 15min, Rs80 for 1hr).

City transport and tours

Khajuraho is no more than an overgrown cluster of villages, without public **transport**, and visitors are dependent on the various rented vehicles in competition with each other. **Taxis** and **rental cars** are available at the main square; through *Raja Cafe*, or from operators such as the reliable Sanjay Jain of the *Hotel Jain* (☎07686/72352), Khajuraho Tours (☎07686/72343), in the Maqbara building, or Travel Bureau (☎07686/74037), on Jain Temples Road, near the square. Typical costs are Rs500 for half a day, and Rs600 plus Rs5 per km for longer journeys. **Cycle rickshaw** drivers ask around Rs30 per hour; trips to the Eastern or Southern groups from town are Rs40, and a tour of all the temples costs Rs100. **Auto-rickshaws** charge Rs150 for a half-day, or Rs250 for a full day of temple-spotting. By far the most enjoyable way of getting around, with virtually empty roads, is by **bicycle**; most budget hotels stock them, as do some restaurants (try *Assi Restaurant* on Jain Temples Road) and the stall outside the *Raja Cafe*, charging around Rs15–20 per day.

Among recommended and highly experienced **guides** who can help you make sense of Khajuraho is Ganga, the owner of *Hotel Harmony* (☎07686/74135), and the reputable Mr D.S. Rajput, who can be contacted through the *Raja Café*. Guide rates are set by the government at Rs255 for one–four people for a half-day, or Rs380 for a full day; for tours in languages other than Hindi and English, there is a Rs125 surcharge. Tour operators such as Khajuraho Tours, Travel Bureau (see above) and *Raja Café* can also arrange explorations further afield (see below).

Accommodation

There is a hotel in Khajuraho to suit every budget; and not a single fleapit in sight. Khajuraho's exclusive deluxe **hotels** are all virtually identical and a bit secluded, whereas the mid-range and budget accommodation is around the town centre, near the Western Group. In the low summer season, you can negotiate a good discount on the room tariff in all hotels (MPTDC offers twenty percent). There's a daily power cut from 4pm to 6pm, but the nights seem to be relatively free of the inconvenience.

A good alternative to Khajuraho itself is *Gilles' Tree House* in Madla, 24km southeast (see p.481), which can be booked through the two sisters who run the *Raja Café*.

Chandela, Airport Road ☎07686/72355. Khajuraho's grandest address, with every amenity and all the hallmarks of the Taj Group, from superb restaurant, pool and beautiful gardens to the glamorous shops. Nonresidents can use the pool for Rs150. Puppet shows are held in the evenings. ❽

Clarks Bundela, Airport Road ☎07686/72386. Posh hotel with all mod cons, lush gardens and a large pool. Down the road is an identical sister outfit, the all-new *Clarks Khajuraho*, opposite the airport. Pay in dollars. Both ❾.

Gupta Palace, Jain Temples Road, opposite Gole market ☎07686/742009. Yet another new establishment, with very smart budget and more expensive a/c rooms ranged along a terrace overlooking the market. Good value. ❷–❺

Harmony, Jain Temples Road ☎07686/74135. Claims to be "a real substitute to the five stars", which is an exaggeration but the Mediterranean influence in the design lends an air of spaciousness. The rooms are neat and clean – ask for one facing the small garden. Run by Ganga, an expert local guide. ❸–❻

Jain, Jain Temples Road ☎07686/72352. Close to the heart of Khajuraho, a popular hotel with reasonable air-cooled rooms, good-value singles, and good veg food. Very similar to the slightly more expensive *Gem* next door. ❷–❸

Jass Oberoi, By-Pass Road ☎07686/72344. Elegant but pleasantly friendly and understated top-of-the-range place, with tennis courts, swimming pool, a quality shopping arcade, and a good restaurant. Pay in dollars. ⑨

Khajuraho Ashok, Airport Road Ⓣ07686/74024. Long-established comfortable hotel popular with tour groups, and the President of India, who came to enjoy the millennium celebrations here. Carpeted en-suite rooms look over a swimming pool (nonresidents Rs100) to the spires of the Western Group. The helpful staff can arrange itineraries and car rental. ⑧

MPTDC Jhankar, near the *Jass Oberoi* Ⓣ07686/74063. The best of the MPTDC options; clean, with a good restaurant, but otherwise plain. ④–⑥

MPTDC Payal, across the fields northeast of the centre Ⓣ07686/74076. Typical, mid-range government place north of the bazaar; but the rooms are spacious with great a/c, and a veranda opens onto gardens. The campsite alongside can be booked through reception. ④–⑥

MPTDC Tourist Village, near MPTDC *Payal* Ⓣ07686/74128. Mud huts neo-tribal style with comfortable carved furniture and wall designs, and a modern bathroom; spread out in imitation of a small village. ③

Rakshan, Sevagram, off Jain Temples Road Ⓣ07686/74475. A new friendly, little hotel away from the bustle of the market, in a small village area; the rooms are simple but clean and all have attached bath, and there is a small garden restaurant. ①

Surya, Jain Temples Road Ⓣ07686/74145. Good-value place with variously priced rooms on different floors. There is a large verdant garden where free yoga classes are held daily (residents only) and tasty meals are served alfresco under the stars. ②–④

Yogi Lodge, in a small cul-de-sac between the row of shops behind *Raja Cafe* Ⓣ07686/74158. Very popular and excellent-value budget accommodation with a small courtyard, terrace restaurant and internet facilities. The owner offers free instruction to all at his ashram 2km north. Similar lodges on either side include *Vikram*, *Marco Polo* and *Natraj*. ①–②

Zen, Jain Temples Road Ⓣ07686/74228. Ultra-cool and clean marble hotel managed by an intense Oshoite, who will also take you on tours of the temples. The comfortable double bedrooms look down to the Zen-influenced courtyard. Great value. ②–⑤

The town and village

Facilities for visitors are concentrated in the uncluttered avenues of the small modern town of **Khajuraho**; the gates of the Western Group of temples open immediately onto its main square, which is surrounded by budget hotels and cafés. Curio shops sell everything from clothes, film and jewellery to Tibetan *thangkas*, but the sales pitch of their owners can be aggressive and it makes sense to be wary of buying anything. The brand new Kandariya **Art and Cultural Centre**, 1km south of the centre, is an upmarket emporium selling quality goods at fixed prices and has an auditorium with evening dance shows at 6.30 and 8.30pm daily (Rs250).

On the south side of the square, the small **Archeological Museum** (daily except Fri 10am–5pm; Rs5) is principally noteworthy for a remarkable sculpture of a pot-bellied dancing Ganesh, his trunk swinging with a vibrant sense of motion. Other items include assorted friezes, brackets and pieces of carving, such as a panel depicting the transportation and cutting of stone used to build the temples. The ubiquitous Vishnu reclines on the endless serpent, Anantha, with a lotus rising from his navel supporting Brahma the originator, and nearby there's the only seated Buddha found in Khajuraho; and of course some erotica.

Most local people live a pleasant 1.5-kilometre walk or cycle ride away to the east, in the more rustic setting of **Khajuraho Village**, near the **Eastern Group**. Three further temples, loosely termed the **Southern Group**, lie some distance out. Water is a prominent feature of the landscape, with the lakes or tanks of **Shiv Sagar** just south of the Western Group, **Khajur Sagar** to the east before the village, and the large **Prem Sagar** on the right to the north of the main square.

Khajuraho is transformed from a fairly sleepy place to a bustling epicentre during Phalguna (Feb/March), when the festival of **Maha Shivratri** draws pilgrims from all over the region to commemorate the marriage of Shiva. It also sees one of India's premier dance events, the **Khajuraho Festival of Dance** – a showcase for all forms of classical dance with some performances staged against the stunning backdrop of the Western Group (though most take place at the more prosaic Chandella Cultural Centre). Precise dates for the festival tend to be confirmed late so check with Government of India tourist authorities, and book early, as this is the one time of year when Khajuraho is busy. Tickets for specific events cost between Rs40 and Rs200. A season ticket costs Rs500.

The Western Group

Stranded like a fleet of stone ships, amid pristine lawns and flowerbeds fringed with bougainvillea, Khajuraho's **Western Group** of temples (daily sunrise-sunset; $10 [Rs5]) seem oddly divorced from their past. With the exception of **Matangesvara**, just outside the main complex, all are now virtually devoid of religious significance, and they only spring back to life during Shivratri (see above). Visitors must remove their shoes before entering individual temples. MPTDC offers **Walkman tours** of the Western Group (around 45min; Rs50 plus Rs500 deposit), which are available from any of their hotels, the tourist offices or at the temple booking office.

There is an excellent *son-et-lumière* show in the grounds of the Western group, using Indian classical music and stunning technicoloured floodlighting to give ambience to the history of the temples, as narrated by the "master sculptor". The fifty-minute show was inaugurated on millennium eve, and runs nightly in both Hindi and English (English show: March–Aug 7.30pm; Sept–Feb 7pm; Rs200 per person).

Varaha

Just inside the complex is a small open *mandapa* pavilion built between the tenth and eleventh centuries, housing a huge, highly polished sandstone image of **Vishnu** as the boar – **Varaha**. Carved in low relief on its body, 674 figures in neat rows represent the major gods and goddesses of the Hindu pantheon. Lord of the earth, water and heaven, the alert boar straddles Shesha the serpent, accompanied by what T. S. Burt (see p.474) conjectured must have been the most beautiful form of **Prithvi**, the earth goddess – all that remains are her feet, and a hand on the neck of the boar. Above the image the lotus ceiling stands out in relief. Archeologists suggest that Varaha belonged to the earlier Gupta period, and was brought here from elsewhere, or that the artisans of Khajuraho may simply have admired the Gupta style and chosen to emulate it.

Lakshmana

Beyond Varaha, adjacent to the Matangesvara temple across the boundary wall, the richly carved **Lakshmana** temple, dating from around 950 AD, is the oldest of the Western Group. It stands on a high plinth covered with processional friezes of horses, elephants and camels, as well as soldiers, domestic scenes, musicians and dancers. Among explicit sexual images is a man buggering a horse, flanked by shocked female onlookers. The sheer energy of the work gives the whole temple an astounding sense of movement and vitality.

While the plinth depicts the human world, the temple itself, the *adhisthana*, brings one into contact with the celestial realm. Two tiers of carved panels

The erotic art of Khajuraho

Prurient eyes have been hypnotized by the unabashed **erotica** of Khajuraho ever since the "rediscovery" of the site in February 1838. A young British officer of the Bengal Engineers, **T.S. Burt**, alerted by the talk of his *palki* (palanquin) bearers, had deviated from his official itinerary when he came upon the ancient temples all but engulfed by jungle – "They reared their sun-burnt tops above the huge trees by which they were surrounded, with all the pride of superior height and age. But the chances are, the trees (or jungle rather) will eventually have the best of it."

Frank representations of oral sex, masturbation, copulation with animals, and such acts may have fitted into the mores of the tenth-century Chandellas, but were hardly calculated to meet with the approval of the upstanding officers of Queen Victoria:

> I found . . . seven Hindoo temples, most beautifully and exquisitely carved as to workmanship, but the sculptor had at times allowed his subject to grow a little warmer than there was any absolute necessity for his doing; indeed some of the sculptures here were extremely indecent and offensive, which I was at first much surprised to find in temples that are professed to be erected for good purposes, and on account of religion. But the religion of the ancient Hindoos can not have been very chaste, if it induced people under the cloak of religion, to design the most disgraceful representations to desecrate their ecclesiastical erections. The palki bearers, however, appeared to take great delight at those, to them, very agreeable novelties, which they took care to point out to all present.

Burt found the inscription on the steps of the Vishvanatha temple that enabled historians to attribute the site to the Chandellas, and to piece together their genealogy, but it was several more years before Major General Sir Alexander Cunningham produced detailed plans of Khajuraho, drawing the distinction between "Western" and "Eastern" groups that is still applied today. For Cunningham, "all [the sculptures] are highly indecent, and most of them disgustingly obscene".

The erotic images remain the subject of a disproportionate amount of contro-

decorate its exterior, with gods and goddesses attended by *apsaras*, "celestial nymphs", and figures in complicated sexual acts on the lower tier and in the recesses. Fine detail includes a magnificent dancing Ganesh on the south face, a master architect with his students on the east, and heavenly musicians and dancers.

Successive pyramidal roofs over the *mandapa* and the porch rise to a clustered tower made of identical superimposed elements. Small porches with sloping eaves project from the *mandapa* and passageway, with exquisite columns, each with eight figures, at each corner of the platform supported by superb brackets in the form of *apsaras*. The inner sanctum, the *garbha griha*, is reached through a door whose lintel shows Vishnu's consort **Lakshmi**, accompanied by **Brahma** and **Shiva**; a frieze depicts the **Navagraha**, the nine planets. Inside, the main image is of Vishnu as the triple-headed, four-armed Vaikuntha, attended by his incarnations as boar and lion.

Kandariya Mahadeva

Sharing a common platform with other temples to the rear of the enclosure, the majestic **Kandariya Mahadeva** temple, built between 1025 and 1050 AD, is the largest and most imposing of the Western Group. A perfect consummation of the five-part design instigated in Lakshmana and Vishvanatha, this Shiva temple represents the pinnacle of Chandellan art, its ornate roofs soaring dramatically to culminate 31m above the base in a *shikhara* that consists of 84 smaller replicas.

versy and debate among academics and curious tourists alike. The task of explanation is made more difficult by the fact that even the Chandellas themselves barely
mentioned the temples in their literature, and the very name "Khajuraho" may be
misleading, simply taken from that of the nearby village.

Among attempts to account for the sexual content of the carvings have been
suggestions of links with **Tantric** cults, which use sex as a pivotal part of worship.
Some claim that they were inspired by the **Kama Sutra**, and similarly intended to
serve as a manual on love, while others argue that the sculptures were designed to
entertain the gods, divert their wrath, and thus protect the temples against natural
calamities. Alternatively, the geometric qualities of certain images have been put
forward as evidence that each represents a *yantra*, a pictorial form of a mantra, for
use in meditation.

The sixteen large panels depicting sexual union that appear along the northern
and southern aspects of the three principal temples – Kandariya Mahadeva,
Lakshmana and Vishvanatha – are mostly concerned with the junction of the male
and the female elements of the temples, the *mandapa* and the *garbha griha* (the
"womb" – see p.476). They might therefore have been intended as a visual pun,
elaborated by artistic licence.

A radical new approach that ties history and architecture with living traditions
has been proposed by Shobita Punja, in her book *Divine Ecstasy* (Penguin, 1992).
Citing historic references to Khajuraho under the name of *Shivpuri* – the "City of
Shiva" – she uses ancient Sanskrit texts to suggest that the dramatic temples and
their celestial hordes represent the **marriage party of Shiva and Parvati**, taking
place in a mythical landscape that stretches along the Vindhya hills to Kalinjar in the
east. Thus Punja argues that the lower panel on Vishvanatha's southern walls shows
Shiva as a bridegroom accompanied by his faithful bull, Nandi, while the intertwined limbs of the panel above – the couple locked in *mithuna*, assisted by a maid-
en to either side – show the consummation, with the lustful Brahma a pot-bellied
voyeur at their feet.

Kandariya Mahadeva is especially popular with visitors for the extraordinarily energetic and provocative **erotica** that ornaments its three tiers, covering
almost every facet of the exterior. Admiring crowds can always be found in
front of a particularly fine image of a couple locked in **mithuna** (sexual intercourse) with a maiden assisting on either side. One of Khajuraho's most familiar motifs, it seems to defy nature, with the male figure suspended upside down
on his head; only when considered as if from above do the sinuous intertwined
limbs begin to make sense.

An elaborate garland at the entrance to the temple, carved from a single
stone, acts as a *torana*, the ritual gateway of a marriage procession. Both inside
and out, lavish and intricate images of gods, goddesses, musicians and nymphs
celebrate the occasion; within the sanctuary a dark passage leads to the *garbha
griha*, and its central *shivalingam*. Niches along the exterior contain images of
Ganesh, **Virabhadra** and the **Sapta Matrikas**, the Seven Mothers responsible for dressing the bridegroom, Shiva. Wrathful deities and fearsome protectors, the seven consist of Brahmi, a female counterpart of Shiva, seated on the
swan of Brahma; a three-eyed Maheshvari on Shiva's bull Nandi; Kumari;
Vaishnavi, seated on the bird Garuda; Varahi, the female form of Vishnu as the
boar; Narasimhi, the female form of Vishnu as lion; and the terrifying
Chamunda, the slayer of the *asuras* or "demons" Chanda and Munda, the only
one of the Sapta Matrikas who is not a female representation of a major male
god.

Devi Jagadambi

North of Kandariya Mahadeva along the platform, the earlier **Devi Jagadambi** temple is a simpler structure, whose outer walls lack projecting balconies. Originally dedicated to Vishnu, its prominent *mandapa* is capped by a massive pyramidal roof. Three *bhandas* (belts) bind the *jangha* (body), adorned with exquisite and sensuous carvings; the erotica on the third is arguably the finest in Khajuraho. Vishnu appears throughout the panels, all decorated with sinuous figures of nymphs, gods and goddesses, some in amorous embrace. Some consider the image in the temple sanctum to be a standing Parvati, others argue that it is the black goddess Kali, known here as Jagadambi.

Between Kandariya Mahadeva and Jagadambi, the remains of **Mahadeva** temple shelter a metre-high lion accompanied by a figure of indeterminate sex. Recurring throughout Khajuraho, the highly stylized lion motif, seen here rearing itself over a kneeling warrior with drawn sword, may have been an emblem of the Chandellas.

Chitragupta

Beyond the platform, and similar to its southern neighbour, Jagadambi, the heavily (and in places clumsily) restored **Chitragupta** temple is unusual in being dedicated to **Surya**, the sun god. Once again its design emphasizes the *mandapa*, which here has large projecting balconies, rather than the main temple. Ornate depictions of hunting scenes, nymphs and dancing girls accompany processional friezes, while on the southern aspect a particularly vigorous ten-headed Vishnu embodies all his ten incarnations. Within the inner chamber, the fiery Surya rides a chariot driven by seven horses.

The small and relatively insignificant temple in front of Chitragupta, also heavily restored and now known as **Parvati**, may originally have been a Vishnu temple, but holds an interesting image of the goddess Ganga riding on a crocodile.

Vishvanatha

Laid out along the same lines as Lakshmana, **Vishvanatha**, in the northeast corner of the enclosure – the third of the three main Western Group shrines –

The body and the womb

The *jangha*, or body, of each temple at Khajuraho – the walls between the base (*adisthana*) and the crowning spire (*shikhara*) – is the realm of the celestial. Its support and protection of the whole structure is symbolized by the strange composite animals, embodying strength and intelligence, depicted on two or three ornate encircling belts known as *bhandas*. Despite the popular belief that the copulating couples of Khajuraho represent the lives of ordinary people, according to Shobita Punja the *jangha* here in fact shows the marriage of Shiva and Parvati. She argues that the beautiful nymphs caught in naturalistic everyday poses are expressing surprise and wonder at seeing the god and the wedding party.

The construction of every temple echoes the creation of life itself, developing from a single seed (*bindu*) placed within its foundations. The central image of the temple, be it a *lingam* or a manifestation in human form, is positioned directly over this seed, and immediately under the highest point, the *shikhara*, in the sacred room known as the **garbha griha** – the womb. Though surrounded by the diverse manifestations and shapes of the world of matter – most obviously, on the external walls of the temple – the womb remains simple and without ornamentation, a representation of the dark generative nucleus of life.

can be precisely dated to 1002 AD, as the work of the ruler Dhangadeva. Unlike some other temples at Khajuraho, which may have changed their presiding deities, Vishvanatha is most definitely a Shiva temple, as confirmed by the open *mandapa* pavilion in front of the main temple, where a monolithic seated **Nandi** waits obediently. Hundreds of small *shikharas* resembling miniature temples decorate the *mandapa* roof, sweeping up towards the climax of the main tower. Large panels between the balconies once more show *mithuna*, with amorous couples embracing among the sensuous nymphs. Idealized representations of the female form include women in such poses as writing letters, playing music and fondling babies. Decorative elephant motifs appear to the south of Vishvanatha, and lions guard its northern aspect.

Matangesvara

The simplicity of the **Matangesvara** temple, outside the complex gates, shows it to be one of Khajuraho's oldest structures, but although built early in the tenth century it remains in everyday use. Deep balconies project from the walls of its circular sanctuary, inside which a pillar-like *shivalingam* emerges from the pedestal *yoni*, the vulva – the recurring symbol of the union of Shiva. During the annual festival of Shivratri, the great wedding of Shiva and Parvati, the shrine becomes a hive of activity, drawing pilgrims for ceremonies that hark back to Khajuraho's distant past.

Shiv Sagar

A short way south of the complex, a few hundred metres from Matangesvara, the **Shiv Sagar** tank is surrounded by a motley assortment of buildings and open space. The steps down to it are animated with pilgrims bathing and collecting water from the "Ocean of Shiva". Cunningham's original map of the temples showed a body of water that ran north to divide the Western Group into two sections; crossing it to the temples may have represented a symbolic transition from the finite to the celestial.

Chausath Yogini

Beyond Shiv Sagar, to the southwest, lie the remains of the curious temple of **Chausath Yogini** – the "Sixty-Four Yoginis". Dating from the ninth century, Chausath Yogini consists of 35 small granite shrines clustered around a quadrangle; there were originally 64 shrines, with the presiding goddess's temple at the centre. Only fourteen other temples, all in northern India, are known to have been dedicated to these wrathful and bloodthirsty female attendants of the goddess Kali; art historians surmise that the site was used by an esoteric Tantric group. Around 1km further west lie the ruins of **Lalguan Mahadev**, a small temple dedicated to Shiva.

The Eastern Group

The two separate networks of temples that make up Cunningham's "Eastern Group" are reached via the two forks of the road east of town. One is the tightly clustered **Jain Group** (daily sunrise–sunset), while slightly north, scattered in the vicinity of Khajuraho Village, there are a number of shrines and two larger temples, Vamana and Javari.

Left of the road just beyond town, a comparatively new temple holds a two-metre-high image of the monkey god **Hanuman** that may predate all of Khajuraho's temples and shrines. As the road forks left along the eastern shore of the murky Khajur Sagar lake, at the edge of Khajuraho village, it passes the remains of a single-room temple erroneously referred to as the **Brahma** temple. Often considered to be a Vishnu temple, it is in fact a shrine to Shiva, as demonstrated by its *chaturmukha* – "four-faced" – *lingam*. While the eastern and western faces carry benign expressions, and the north face bears the gentler aspect of Uma, the female manifestation of Shiva, the ferocious southern face is surrounded by images of death and destruction. Crowning the *lingam* is the rounded form of **Sadashiva**, Shiva the Infinite at the centre of the cosmos.

The dirt road continues to the small **Javari** temple, set on a plain terrace and featuring a double porch and a slender *shikhara*, similar to Chaturbhuj of the Southern Group. Built late in the eleventh century, it may not have the exuberance seen elsewhere but nevertheless contains some fine sculpture, including alluring nymphets in classic Khajuraho style.

The largest of the Khajuraho village temples, **Vamana**, stands alone in a field 200m further north. Built slightly earlier than Javari, in a fully evolved Chandella style, Vamana has a simple uncluttered *shikhara* that rises in bands covered with arch-like motifs. Figures including seductive celestial nymphs form two bands around the *jangha*, the body of the temple, while a superb doorway leads to the inner sanctum, which is dedicated to Vamana, an incarnation of Vishnu. On the way to the Jain Group, the road runs near what survives of a late-tenth-century temple, known as **Ghantai** for its fine columns sporting bells (*ghantai*), garlands and other motifs.

The temple of **Parsvanath**, dominating the walled enclosure of the **Jain Group**, is probably older than the main temples of Khajuraho, judging by its relatively simple ground plan. Its origins are a mystery; although officially classified as a Jain monument, and jointly administered by the Archeological Survey and the Jain community, it may have been a Hindu temple that was donated to the Jain community which settled there at a later date. Certainly, the animated sculpture of Khajuraho's other Hindu temples is well represented on the two horizontal bands around the walls, and the upper one is crowded with Hindu gods in intimate entanglements. Among Khajuraho's finest work, they include Brahma and his consort; a beautiful Vishnu; a rare image of the god of love, **Kama**, shown with his quiver of flower arrows embracing his consort **Rati**; and two graceful female figures, one applying kohl to her eyes and another removing a thorn from her foot. A narrow strip above the two main bands depicts celestial musicians (*gandharvas*) playing cymbals, drums, stringed instruments and flutes, some carrying garlands, cleverly caught in mid-flight with billowing robes. Inside, beyond an ornate hall, a black monolithic stone is dedicated to the Jain lord Parsvanath, inaugurated as recently as 1860 to replace an image of another *tirthankara*, Adinath.

Immediately north of Parsvanath, **Adinath**'s own temple, similar but smaller, has undergone drastic renovation. Three tiers of sculpture surround its original structure, of which only the sanctum, *shikhara* and vestibule survive; the incongruous *mandapa* is a much later addition. Inside the *garbha griha* stands the black image of the *tirthankara* Adinath himself. The huge 4.5-metre-high statue of the sixteenth *tirthankara*, **Shantinath**, in his newer temple, is the most important image in this working Jain complex. With its slender beehive *shikharas*, the temple attracts pilgrims from all over India, including naked *sadhus*.

Sculpture in the small circular **Jain Museum**, at the entrance to the Jain temples, includes representations of all twenty-four *tirthankaras* (Mon-Sat 7am–6pm; Rs2).

The Southern Group

What is generally referred to as Khajuraho's **Southern Group** consists of three widely separated temples. The nearer to town, **Duladeo**, is down a dirt track south of the Jain Group, 1.5km from the main square – an isolation that stops it achieving the same impact as the great Western Group temples. Built early in the twelfth century, Duladeo in any case bears witness to the decline of temple architecture in the late Chandellan period, noticeable above all in sculpture that lacks the hallmark fluidity of Khajuraho. Nevertheless, its main hall does contain some exquisite carving, and the angular rippled exterior of the main temple is unique to Khajuraho. Rising on a star-shaped ground plan, on which the square inner sanctum dedicated to Shiva is extended by a multifaceted geometrical design, its complex architectural themes are developed only at the expense of becoming rather tediously repetitive. The entire structure, especially the *shikhara* and the pyramidal roof of the *mandapa*, has been extensively renovated.

Across the Khodar stream on the way south towards the airport, a small road leads left to the disproportionately tall, tapering **Chaturbhuj**, around 5km south of Khajuraho – the *shikhara* is visible for miles above the trees. A forerunner to Duladeo, built around 1100 AD and bearing some resemblance to the Javari temple of the Eastern Group, Chaturbhuj is plainer than Duladeo and devoid of erotica. A remarkable 2.7-metre-high image of Vishnu graces its inner sanctum.

To reach the third temple, **Bija Math**, return to the cluster of houses before Chaturbhuj and take a right along the dirt track through the hamlet. Until 1998, it was buried underneath a suspiciously large mound of mud (*tela*), until the ASI undertook an excavation project and discovered the delicately carved platform. Excavation has only just begun, but it is believed to be the largest temple discovered so far; unfortunately, the temple itself has disintegrated into the debris of ornate sculpture lying strewn around the site. You can go and watch the archeologists at work, patiently brushing the mud away to reveal parading elephants, intertwined lovers and rearing horses.

Eating

Khajuraho is surprisingly good for **food**; it even has several places serving good Italian dishes among its well-priced restaurants and cafés. The budget choices are good although the fare is becoming increasingly standard multi-cuisine, with a cold beer or a lassi never too far away, and the top hotels all provide reasonable to excellent eating. During the day, carts around Gole market serve glasses of freshly squeezed fruit juice.

Agrawal, Gole Market. If you eat one thali in India, have it here. The absolutely delicious unlimited "special thali" (Rs80) is a vast array of *kofta*, fresh veg preparations, tandoori roti and *pulao*.

Jass Oberoi, By-Pass Road ☎ 07686/72344. Comfortably stylish multi-cuisine restaurant in luxury hotel; works out as good value when paid for in foreign currency. Highly recommended.

La Terraza, off main square. Standard mish-mash of Eastern and Western cuisine, with good Kashmiri home cooking. The rooftop has a fine view.

Paradise, Airport Road, Shiv Sagar. Typical pancake and non-spicy thali menu, with little tables and lanterns on a roof terrace, overlooking the waterlilly lake.

Madras Coffee House, main square. Reliable south Indian fare at north Indian prices, with great *dosas*. Opens at 7.30am for pre-bus journey breakfasts.

Mediterraneo Ristorante Italiano, Jain Temples Road. This pleasant, leafy roof terrace café and beer bar is a Mecca for those craving fresh pasta and pizza baked in a wood-fired oven; it makes a welcome change – but you'll miss the wine.

Raja Cafe, main square. Where it all happens in Khajuraho, under the aegis of two Swiss ladies who circulate among the guests tucking into good tandoori, pancakes and chocolate cake. Have one of their famous waffles while you pick up guides, information, and cold beers, and there's a bookstore and curio shop too.

Rhim Jim, just past the tourist office on the main road. Decent Indian and Western snacks and meals in a sunken courtyard with unobstructed temple views.

Safari, Jain Temples Road. Popular among travellers, serving chicken and chips, extensive breakfasts, and a big range of lassis to the strains of Bob Marley.

Zen, Jain Temples Road. A very chilled-out courtyard café with a Zen garden, or the roof-terrace restaurant serving Italian and Korean specialities.

Moving on from Khajuraho

The first daily express MPSTRC bus leaves at 9am for Jhansi (4hr), 175km west then moves directly on to Gwalior and Agra (8hr). Alternatively, the most comfortable bus leaves for Jhansi at 11.15am to connect with night trains north and express trains running to Delhi and Agra, or Bhopal and Mumbai. The super-fast a/c Shatabdi Express #2001 train via Gwalior and Agra, to Delhi (departs from Jhansi at 5.55pm). A number of private buses also run the Jhansi route, departing at 5.30am, 1.30pm, 3.15pm and 4.15pm and a MPSTRC bus leaves at 6pm daily for Bhopal. Agents and hotels all display bus timetables.

Between 8.30am and 4pm daily, five buses set out for Satna (4hr), 125km east, which is served by trains on the Mumbai–Varanasi–Calcutta network, as well as to Gorakhpur, from where buses head for the Nepal border. If you're heading to Varanasi, 415km east, either take the 4pm overnight bus from Khajuraho, or expect a long wait in Satna: night trains (8hr) leave daily at 7.50pm and, on most days, at 1.25am as well, while the daily morning departure (7–8hr) leaves at 7.05am. The best train for Jabalpur is the Mahanagiri Express #1094, which leaves Satna daily at 5.55pm (3hr).

An alternative route to Varanasi is to take one of the five daily buses north to Mahoba (first bus 7.30am, last 4pm; 3hr; Rs30), from where the #1107 train to Varanasi departs at 10.35pm (12hr).

There is an extremely efficient computerized train booking office at the bus stand (daily 8am–5pm). All train tickets can be reserved up to five days in advance for journeys, and it saves the long queues in Jhansi, Mahoba or Satna.

To avoid tediously long overland journeys from Khajuraho, Indian Airlines (☎07686/74035; airport ☎74036) has daily flights to Varanasi at 1.15pm (45min), as well as to Agra at 3.35pm (1hr) continuing to Delhi (1hr 45min). The frequency of these services is reduced in the monsoon season. Since the time of research, flights to Jaipur and Calcutta have begun; see a booking agent for details. Jet Airways (☎07686/74407), whose office is in the airport, only run one daily flight to Varanasi, leaving at 1.20pm.

Flights can be heavily booked, and note that with a late reservation you may be promised a confirmation, but can only be sure of a place on the flight at the airport, shortly before departure; allow a little leeway in case your flight is delayed, and be patient.

Panna National Park

The vast **PANNA NATIONAL PARK** (Nov–June; Rs100 including obligatory guide, vehicle extra), known for its large cats (including tiger), deer and antelope (*nilgai*), lies a short way east of Khajuraho, spreading across a landscape of rocky hills and ravines covered mostly by scrubby deciduous forest. Access is easier than in some of India's better-known sanctuaries – you can even go in on foot if you take along an armed guide. It's best visited in winter, as the entire area gets extremely hot during summer – though there is a better chance then of seeing tigers as they emerge in search of water. Flowing north through the park towards the Ganges, the **River Ken**, whose rocky islands are bare during the lean seasons, harbours both major species of Indian crocodile, the *magar* and the long-snouted *gharial*.

The exquisite lake of **Pandava Falls**, couched in a hollow and fed by a waterfall, is 11km east of Madla. Legend has it that the Pandavas of *Mahabharata* fame spent time here. A short road leads left off the main road to a car park and teashop that overlook a rocky escarpment and the lake. It's an idyllic spot, set within the deep emerald cover of the Panna forest, and offers a good chance of spotting wildlife – tigers are said to frequent the lake to drink. If you descend to the lake and follow a rough track, you'll emerge after a short distance beneath dripping cliffs, where caves have been hewn out of the rock to form shrines.

Park practicalities: Madla

The village of **MADLA**, 24km southeast of Khajuraho near a bridge across the picturesque River Ken, is the most convenient point of access to the park, and has the nearest **accommodation**.

Gilles' Tree House (**4**–**5**), booked through the *Raja Cafe* in Khajuraho, is a fairly professional operation and serves meals (order all food at least 4hr before leaving Khajuraho). You can sleep on the beautiful open platform of the branches or camp by the riverbank below. Car hire (also from *Raja Café*) for the roundabout trip to the *Tree House* is Rs500. Madla's more upmarket *Ken River Lodge* (**7**) consists of comfortable modern mud cottages overlooking the river, near the bridge, with package deals including meals and a visit to the national park, or longer safaris. Book through Vandhya Tours in Khajuraho (☎07686/74087).

Car rental for a comprehensive tour of the national park costs around Rs2000, and is best booked at Khajuraho – facilities at Madla are extremely limited. To get to Madla by **bus** from Khajuraho, take any Panna- or Chhatarpur-bound bus, then change at the T-junction 12km south of Khajuraho and pick up a jeep or a bus east. Allow plenty of time if you want to get from Khajuraho to Pandava Falls and back within a day; there's no accommodation near the falls apart from a friendly caretaker's lodge at the crossing on the main road.

En route to Madla, the Chhatarpur–Panna road passes 1km north of the rambling white **Rajgarh Palace**, perched high on the commanding spur of a hill overlooking the valley, where visitors are allowed to wander the battlements.

Satna

Although the busy market town of **SATNA**, 125km east of Khajuraho, holds little or no interest for the traveller, its strategic position as the nearest **railhead** to Khajuraho and the awkwardness of some of the connections make it very likely that you will end up staying the night here. Adequate **accommodation** can be found in the vicinity of the railway station and the bus stand, 2km apart. Turn right onto the main road in front of the railway station to reach the small, clean and friendly *Hotel Paradise*, five minutes' walk away on Pannilal Chowk (☎07672/23666; **2**–**3**), and the nearby *Hotel Pavan* (☎07672/23082; **2**–**3**).

Just off the road running between the station and the bus stand, *Hotel Yogesh* (⌕ 07672/22345; ❷–❸) has plain rooms; at the crossroads near the bus stand *Hotel India* (⌕ 07672/22482; ❷–❸) is more comfortable than the dingy exterior suggests. There are few eating options, but the reliable *Indian Coffee House* can be found at both ends of town. For onward **transport connections**, see the box on p.480.

Eastern Madhya Pradesh

On the tourist trail, Eastern Madhya Pradesh is singularly and justifiably famous for its amazing abundance of **wildlife**. Amid the rolling terraced plains and craggy cliffs are hidden two of the country's finest **national parks**, **Kanha** and **Bandhavgarh.** In the few remaining fragments of a forest that until 150 years ago extended right across central India, the reserves are among the last strongholds for many endangered species of birds and mammals, including the **tiger**, **gaur** (bison) and **barasingha** (swamp deer).

The whole eastern area is deep in *adivasi* country; the villages of the Gond and Barga tribes dot the scrubby hills. Lining the roads to the parks are the picturesque Barga villages, each a cluster of white and turquoise-blue mud houses with low tiled roofs, usually dripping with marrow vines. To the visitor, this may appear to be quintessential rural India, but behind the scenes of a slow, simple daily life, the *adivasi* in this area are largely a marginal and impoverished lot, constantly threatened with drought, heavy loans, and a lack of access to education and health care.

Two major **rail networks** cut through the region. The Central Railway heads straight up the Narmada Valley from Bhopal to **Jabalpur**, the springboard for Kanha National Park, before veering north to Satna (4hr from Khajuraho) and the Gangetic plains. The other main route, traced by the Southeastern Railway, skirts the top of Bastar district (the remote and poor southern extension of the state, dovetailing with Maharashtra, Andhra Pradesh and Orissa), passing through the grim industrial cities of Raipur and Bilaspur at the head of the Chhattisgarh Valley. From here, the three big rivers that rise in the coal-rich hills to the north flow eastwards, while the train makes for the Orissan border.

Jabalpur and around

After running in tandem across an endless expanse of wheat fields and tribal villages, the main Calcutta to Mumbai road and train line converge on eastern Madhya Pradesh's largest city. Though an important provincial capital, **JABALPUR**, 330km east of Bhopal, harbours little of interest beyond a half-decent museum, some stalwart Raj-era buildings and the **marble rocks**

JABALPUR

RESTAUARANTS	
Blue Moon	E
Indian Coffee House	A&B
Sahni	C
SSS	D
Tasty Bite	F

ACCOMMODATION	
Jackson's	3
MPTDC Hotel Kalchuri	8
Rahul	1
Rishi Regency	4
Sambriya Inn	5
Samdariya	9
Shivalaya Lodge	2
Siddharth	7
Utsav	6

BAZAAR

gouged by the River Narmada nearby. It's only really worth visiting en route
to the national parks and tiger reserves, Kanha and Bandhavgarh, both half a
day's journey to the east.

The city as it stands today is of comparatively recent origin. Formerly,
access to the fertile Narmada Valley (and its lucrative trade routes) was controlled from the ancient capital at **Tripuri**, 9km west. The site, occupied from
around 2000 BC onwards, rose to prominence under the Kushanas at the
start of the Christian era. The Satavahanas (or "Andhras") followed, picking
up what pieces their predecessors hadn't frittered away on court intrigues
and unbridled debauchery. It was under the powerful and militaristic
Kalchuri (or "Chedi") dynasty, however, that the city emerged as the
region's dominant force. Pre-eminence on the battlefield enabled successive
rulers to extend their borders westwards almost to within sight of the
Arabian Sea before they were finally swept aside in the eleventh century by the
Gonds, descendants of Tripuri's aboriginal inhabitants. Based at **Garha**, on
the outskirts of modern Jabalpur, Gond rule gradually spread down the
Narmada to Bhopal before it was challenged in 1564 by Asaf Khan, one of
Akbar's more ambitious governors. Despite some brave resistance from **Rani
Durgavati**, a sixteenth-century Rajput Boadicea, Gondwana was overwhelmed by the imperial army and Asaf Khan installed as its overlord. The
Garha–Mandla Gonds, as the new ruling dynasty became known, were in
turn ousted from their new capital at Mandla by the Marathas late in the
eighteenth century, and they by the British, who established a military cantonment and administrative centre in Jabalpur in 1819. A strong missionary
presence here led to the proliferation of English schools and hospitals which
continue to thrive today.

The little city prospers, due largely to its location at the centre of India, and
these days is experiencing a period of intense and chaotic growth, driven by an
influx of migrant workers from the poorer rural districts to the east.

Thugs

With their potholes, unlit bullock carts and suicidal drivers, trunk roads in Madhya Pradesh can be trying at the best of times. For travellers in past centuries, however, a much more sinister threat lurked along the highways of central India. A secret sect of bandits and Kali-worshippers known as thugs used to express their devotion to the jet-black four-armed goddess of death (usually shown splattered with blood, wearing a necklace of skulls and a belt of dead men's hands) by committing ritual murders on her behalf. The *thugs* would fall in with hapless travellers, gain their confidence, then summarily throttle them with silk scarves. Any pieces of the corpse not required for offerings were dumped in wells or buried in large pits.

Fear of retribution, and the belief among local rulers and village headmen that *thugee* was in some way the sacred will of the goddess herself, allowed the killing to continue unchecked for generations. Then, in 1830, the British dispatched the zealous sleuth Colonel – later Sir – William Sleeman to eradicate the sect. His tactics were ruthless and effective. Using promises of lenient prison sentences, Sleeman recruited a network of "supergrass" informers to expose the identities of the clandestine stranglers. In all, some 4000 *thugs* were captured during the twenty-year campaign, many of whom had notched up three hundred or more murders – one even confessed to killing 931 people in the course of his career. Special courts sent a total of four hundred convicted *thugs* to the gallows and many more to jail or penal colonies in places such as the Andaman Islands. As for the informers, most ended up with their families in the purpose-built "School of Industry" (now a reform school) at Jabalpur where they were taught to turn their hands from silk scarves to carpet weaving. The word "thug" passed into common usage thanks to the characteristically macabre interest in the phenomenon shown by the British press.

The City

With few real sights to speak of, the best way to kill time in Jabalpur **city** itself is a leisurely tour by bicycle or rickshaw. To the south of the train line you'll find the remains of the former colonial enclave – now a peaceful suburb of leafy streets, bungalows, churches, British-style boarding schools and barracks. The underpass east of the station opens onto the far end of Collectorate Road. Head west from here, past Madhya Pradesh's Victorian **High Court** building, and you'll eventually arrive at the **clock tower** at the start of Jabalpur's large **bazaar** district. An intricate grid of long dusty streets lined with small shops, factories and disintegrating wooden buildings, the commercial hub is drab by Indian standards, and flooded with raucous traffic.

Due south of the bazaar, a short way down a side-road off Russel Chowk, the **Rani Durgavati Museum** (Mon–Sat 10am–5pm; free) preserves sculpture and inscriptions in the nineteenth-century home of the local maharaja. The scruffy garden outside contains Hindu and Jain pieces, the finest being a partially damaged depiction of Shiva and Parvati (as Uma-Maheshwar), to the right of two large Jain statues. Inside, the ground-floor galleries are divided between Shiva and Parvati, Vishnu, and Jain *tirthankaras*, while the upstairs rooms are mostly devoted to bronze plates and seals recording regional dynastic histories. In the last room on the first floor, the *adivasi* exhibition attempts to celebrate aspects of local village culture, from female fertility rites to tattooing. The real highlights though are the many dummies in "authentic" dress and poses.

Three kilometres west of the centre, the main highway runs alongside a large tank lined with bathing *ghats*, banyan trees and a picturesque row of Hindu shrines crumbling into the water. Opposite, on top of a moraine of enormous granite boulders, stand the ruins of the **Madan Mahal** (pronounced *M'den M'hel*) – a fortress-cum-pleasure-palace built by the Gond ruler Madan Shah in 1116. Nowadays, the stony slopes around the bottom of the hill also shelter a sprawl of ramshackle dwellings belonging to a community of potters (whose wares you can see piled up on the roadside) and a couple of immaculately whitewashed **Jain temples**.

The left fork in the main road, 1km or so further on, drops down to an impressive bridge spanning the River Narmada. Known locally as **Tilwara Ghat**, the handful of shrines near the water's edge below marks one of the sacred places where Mahatma Gandhi's ashes were scattered. The right fork takes you out towards the Marble Rocks.

Practicalities

Central Railway **trains** arrive at the city's only **railway station**, 2km east of the centre. From here, it's a five-minute auto-rickshaw ride into town; less if you plan to stay in either of the slightly more expensive hotels at the top end of the cantonment district. The shambolic city **bus stand** is more in the thick of things, a short way south of the bazaar and west of Naudra Bridge, site of several cheaper hotels.

MPTDC's friendly and efficient **tourist office**, inside the main arrivals hall at the railway station (Mon–Fri 6am–10pm; ℡0761/322111), can provide the usual range of hand-outs, give advice on travel arrangements, and inform you of vacancies in their hotels in Kanha or Bandhavgarh.

English-language newspapers and magazines are only available on the *Jackson's* hotel campus or from platform 1 in the railway station. The **post office** is a five-minute walk south of the railway station, just past the *Hotel Kalchuri*. If you need to **change money** (there are no exchange facilities in either national park), you can cash travellers' cheques at the State Bank of India (Mon–Fri 10am–2pm, Sat 10am–noon) just under 1km west of the railway station, or at the *Rishi Regency* opposite, which has a 24hr exchange counter. The *Samdariya* or *Jackson's* hotels may also agree to help out in emergencies, though officially they're only supposed to change money for residents.

Jabalpur teems with **auto-** and **cycle rickshaws**, while the rarer Ambassador **taxis** can usually be found in front of the *Samdariya*. Vehicles for day-trips can be rented through the top hotels. Otherwise, **bicycles** make a good way to get about the city; ask in the repair shops opposite *Hotel Kalchuri*, or on Malvna Chowk in the main bazaar. The dilapidated **tempos** and **minibuses** that chug through the centre of town serve outlying suburbs and are only useful for travelling out to the marble rocks.

Accommodation

The majority of Jabalpur's **hotels** are within easy reach of the bus stand – handy for early departures to Kanha. Watch out for "luxury taxes" and "service charges" levied by the pricier places. If you're on a tight budget and don't fancy a seedy windowless cell, try the "economy" rooms in the mid-range hotels. The railway station has **retiring rooms** (❶–❷) and cheap dorms.

Jackson's, Civil Lines ℡ 0761/323412. Dating from the 1920s, the building has long seen its heyday and now has large and clean but drab and dark rooms. The compensation is friendly manage-ment, two good restaurants, foreign exchange, a pool table and bar, a lovely garden and the only travel agents in Jabalpur on site. Some a/c rooms. ❺–❼

MPTDC Kalchuri, Residency Road, Civil Lines
℡ 0761/321491. Welcoming hotel around the corner from the railway station. The rooms are spacious and the deluxe ones have a/c. ⑥–⑦
Rahul, opposite Jyoti Cinema, Naudra Bridge
℡ 0761/325525. A slight improvement on rock-
bottom, but not much, though the rooms are surprisingly clean. Most of the cheaper ones are windowless; the more expensive ones have a/c. Ask
for a quieter room at the back. ②–③
Rishi Regency, Civil Lines ℡ 0761/321804.
Between the railway station and town, opposite
the bank. Three-star hotel with smart interiors and
rooms, foreign exchange and a speciality barbecue
restaurant. ⑥–⑨
Samdariya, off Russel Chowk ℡ 0761/316800.
Plush and friendly hotel, close to the roundabout,
with a marble lobby and TVs in all rooms. An offshoot, the nearby *Samdariya Inn* (℡ 0761/324896;

④–⑦) offers similar quality, but lacks the central
a/c. Both have excellent restaurants; the *Inn* has a
Baskin Robbins ice-cream parlour, while the other
hotel has a coffee shop ⑥–⑧
Shivalaya Lodge, opposite Jyoti Cinema, Naudra
Bridge ℡ 0761/325188. If you avoid the dirty but
most expensive rooms on the first floor, the rooms
on the second and third floors are extremely simple, clean and have attached bathrooms. The
cooler charge is Rs40. ②
Siddharth, off Russel Chowk ℡ 0761/409247.
Well run and central, with simple, light, good-value
"standard" rooms, some of which are a/c. ④–⑥
Utsav, Russel Chowk ℡ 0761/414038. Large,
friendly hotel bang in the centre of town. The
mostly a/c rooms all have satellite TV, attached
bathrooms and hot water, and range from excellent-value "economy" to "super-deluxe" with bathtubs. Avoid the restaurant. ②–⑥

Eating

With a few exceptions, the best **places to eat** in Jabalpur are the hotels. Prices
are reasonable and most menus varied, though not all of the restaurants serve
alcohol.

Indian Coffee Houses, both in the bazaar district.
Great for cheap *dosas, iddlis, uttapams* and other
light snacks. They open at 8.30am for breakfast.
Kalchuri, Residency Road, Civil Lines. Dimly lit,
with starched table cloths and the usual MPTDC
menu: a selection of their standard, delicious
meat, veg and Chinese dishes. Tandoori after
7.30pm only. A cold beer makes the place
markedly more cheerful.
The Rooftop Bar and Restaurant and **Grub
Room**, *Jackson's Hotel*, Civil Lines. The new multi-
cuisine *Rooftop Bar and Restaurant* claims to be
the best place to eat in Jabalpur – at least you can
have a game of pool while you wait for your butter
chicken or *malai kofta*. The *Grub Room* has rather
jaded and spartan decor, but the moderately priced
veg and non-veg grub is good. Some Chinese and
adventurous Western options.
Roopmali, Opposite Naudra Bridge. Hidden behind
a most excellent snacks shop, the very popular

family place serves up a pure-veg "plate system".
Inexpensive and delicious.
Sahni, Naudra Bridge. Bustling, unpretentious and
cheap. Generous heaps of spicy Punjabi food
served to a mainly office crowd. The a/c family
room (*Eskimo*) next door is alcohol-free.
Samdariya, off Russel Chowk. The place to splash
out on top-notch Indian and Chinese veg food –
their unlimited thalis are particularly great value at
Rs70 for an array of their best dishes. A Western-
style coffee shop also does delicious south Indian
snacks.
SSS (Satyam Shivam Sundaram), near *Jyoti
Cinema*, Naudra Bridge. Don't be put off by the
bizarre rococo interior. The inexpensive, strictly veg
food, including thalis and some set menus, is excellent value and some tables overlook the street.
Tasty Bite, Russel Chowk. Brightly lit, good-value
fast food-style restaurant serving great burgers
and excellent Indian and Chinese meals.

The marble rocks

**In a bustling, dusty, Oriental land, the charm of coolness and quiet belonging to
these pure cold rocks, and deep and blue yet pellucid waters, is almost entrancing.**
Captain J Forsyth, *The Highlands of Central India* (1889).

West of Jabalpur, the River Narmada suddenly narrows, plunges over a series
of dramatic waterfalls, then squeezes through a seam of milky-white marble
before continuing on its westward course across the Deccan. The thirty-metre
cliffs and globulous shapes worn by the water out of the rock may not exact-

ly rank as one of the seven wonders of the natural world, but the **MARBLE ROCKS**, known locally as **Bheraghat**, are as good a place as any to while away an idle afternoon.

Bheraghat **village** itself, overlooking the gorge, is a sleepy little place, with few signs of activity beyond the ringing of chisels in the workshops of its many **marble-carvers**. Most pieces on display in the shop fronts are heavy-duty Hanumans, *shivalingams* and other deities, destined for sites around India – the local translucent white marble is much in demand for new temples and shrines.

From the main street, a flight of steps leads down to the river and the **ghats**, where **rowing boats** (Rs210 per boat, Rs10 per head on a shared basis) are on hand to ferry visitors up the gorge, although these do not run during the monsoon (July to mid-Oct). Trips take thirty to forty minutes, depending on the water level (if the dams upstream are open, the current can be too strong for boats to pass), though you're more likely to spend at least that long waiting for a minimum of fifteen passengers to show up. Avoid the boatmen who try and squeeze in twenty-five: the boats are old and are theoretically designed only for ten people.

Once under way, the boatman begins his spiel, pointing out the more interesting **rock formations**. The most appreciative noises from the other passengers are not reserved for the "footprint of the celestial elephant", however, or even the "monkey's leap" (jumped over by Hanuman on his way to Lanka), but for the places where Hindi movie-stars posed in well-known films shot on location here. Look out for the enormous **bees' nests** dangling from the crevices in the rock. One nineteenth-century guidebook urged its readers to refrain from "smoking or firing guns" in the gorge, as an angry swarm once attacked a party of English army engineers who were carrying out survey work for a new railway here. A memorial plaque, still visible on top of the cliffs, was erected to one of their number who drowned trying to shake the bees off. During the evenings the formations are floodlit.

Not surprisingly, Bheraghat is also something of a religious site. From the fork in the river, 107 stone steps lead up to the tenth-century **Mandapur temple**, a circular building known for the 64 beautifully carved Tantric goddesses, or *Chausath Yogini*, which stand in its enclosure.

Beyond the temple, at the far end of the gorge, the **Dhaundhar**, or "Smoke Cascade" waterfall, is particularly dramatic when shrouded in spray after the monsoons. It's reached either by following the main street out through the village, or else via the goat-track that twists along the top of the cliffs below the MPTDC motel. Just above the waterfall, you pass a string of stalls loaded with locally carved marble goods – among them some fine pocket-sized pieces of religious kitsch; they can even carve out your name in a piece of marble while you're out in the boat. *Tempos* back to Jabalpur start from the open space between the stalls and the village.

Practicalities

Getting to Bheraghat under your own steam from Jabalpur involves picking up a **tempo** (Rs10), from the bus stand next to the museum. The 45-minute stop-and-start trip on a *tempo* can be excruciating; you need to clamber off when you see a row of cold drink and souvenir stalls lining a sharp left-hand bend in the main street. Auto rickshaws (Rs350 return) can be negotiated anywhere in Jabalpur, or a private taxi can be arranged in any of the hotels, at a rate of Rs500 for up to five people. The only other alternative is a tedious bicycle ride along a busy main road.

Accommodation is available if you want to stay the night. Just off the road out to the falls, MPTDC has converted a colonial bungalow, complete with veranda, well-kept lawn and easy chairs, into the very pleasant four-roomed *Motel Marble Rocks* (☎0761/83424; ❺). The garden looks out over the gorge and a small **restaurant** serves a standard veg and non-veg menu. The only other option is at the slightly cheaper *Shagun Resorts* (❹), a motley collection of little huts, each with a veranda, air-cooler and attached bath, in a scrubby garden opposite the brightly painted Jain temple on the main street (sign in Hindi). There is a basic veg restaurant in the garden, if you don't mind being surrounded by adolescent couples escaping here for some privacy.

Moving on from Jabalpur

Kanha National Park is most travellers' next move after Jabalpur. Direct MPSRTC services leave the central bus stand twice daily for the main gate at Kisli; the first, at 7am, is faster (5–6hr); the second (6–7hr) leaves at 11am. Buses to Mandla, halfway to the park, leave hourly. Bandhavgarh is harder to reach; you need to catch a train (4–6 daily; 1hr 20min) or bus (1–2 hourly; 2hr) to Murwara, then travel down the Eastern Railway line to Umaria, where you can pick up a local bus to the park gate.

To get to Khajuraho, you can catch either the 4am express (3hr) or the later slow passenger train to Satna, where you can pick up direct state buses. Alternatively, take one of the more frequent afternoon express trains and stay overnight in Satna. Varanasi is on the main Mumbai–Calcutta line. Aim for the Kurla–Varanasi Express #1065 (departs at 10.45pm on Mon, Wed & Thurs; arrives 8am), or the daily Dadar-Gorakhpur Express #1027 (departs 1.15am, arrives 12.55pm). Daily trains from Jabalpur to Patna help travellers en route to Nepal.

Of the five or six daily express trains to Mumbai, the Howrah–Mumbai Mail #3003 is the most convenient (departs 5.35pm; 16hr). For Delhi (20hr), take the daily Mahakosal Express #1449 at 5.40pm, or travel down to Itarsi junction to pick up the more frequent northward services via Bhopal, Gwalior and Agra. There are also 1–2 daily trains to Chennai (23hr 45min–32hr).

From Jabalpur towards Kanha

From Jabalpur, the four-hour bone-shaking bus ride to Kanha takes you into some of eastern Madhya Pradesh's most isolated rural districts. When Captain J Forsyth and his Bengal Lancers pushed through en route to the uncharted interior at the end of the nineteenth century, this landscape was a virtually unbroken tract of *sal* forest teeming with Indian bison, deer and tigers. Since then, the local Barga tribals have taken up the plough, and all but a few patches of forest clinging to the ridges of nearby hillsides have been logged, cleared for farmland or simply burned as firewood by the burgeoning populations of sharecroppers.

Shortly after **Narayanganj**, a junction where the bus halts for a ten-minute chai stop, the road rejoins the Narmada River again, twisting through the patchwork of ripening wheat and sugar cane planted in the well-watered alluvial soil that lines the riverbanks. Along the way, look out for the two-tiered terracotta roofs on the village huts – a local design inherited from earlier thatching techniques.

It was around these parts, in 1564, that **Rani Durgavati**, the warrior queen of Gondwana, was defeated in battle by Asaf Khan, one of Akbar's right-hand men. When she heard that the viceregal army was advancing on her kingdom,

Durgavati rounded up her troops from the harvest, and marched north on ele-phant-back to waylay the attackers. But unable to hold off the better-armed Moghuls, the Gonds were soon forced to retreat to a place near Mandla where, with the swollen river blocking their only escape, they were finally routed. Asaf Khan allegedly captured 101 cooking pots full of gold and jewels, though not Durgavati, who stabbed herself through the heart to avoid the ignominy of being incarcerated in his harem.

The only big town en route to Kanha, is **Mandla**, the district centre and a bustling market town. If you have taken the train to Mandla from Nagpur or Jabalpur, head over to the bus stand for a bus or shared Jeep to Kanha; the last bus departs at 2pm. If you get dropped here on your return from Kanha, buses leave for Jabalpur every thirty minutes. The State Bank of India (Mon–Fri 10am–2pm, Sat 10am–noon) will exchange cash only, and is the nearest place to Kanha with this facility.

Kanha National Park

Widely considered the greatest of India's wildlife reserves, **KANHA NATIONAL PARK** encompasses nearly 2000 square kilometres of decidu-ous forest, savanna grassland, hills and gently meandering rivers – home to lit-erally hundreds of species of animals and birds, including a stable population of **tigers**. Despite the arduous overland haul to the park, few travellers are disap-pointed by its beauty, particularly poignant at dawn, though many feel hard done by when it comes to tiger-spotting: you will need several forays into the park to ensure a chance of at least one good sighting.

Central portions of the Kanha Valley were designated as a wildlife sanctuary as long ago as 1933. Prior to this, the whole area was one enormous viceregal hunting ground, its game the exclusive preserve of high-ranking British army officers and civil servants seeking trophies for their colonial bungalows. Not until the 1950s though, after a particularly voracious hunter bagged thirty tigers in a single shoot, did the government declare Kanha a bona fide nation-al park. Kanha was one of the original participants in Indira Gandhi's **Project Tiger** (see p.1532), and since then, animal numbers have recovered dramati-cally to currently stand at 110 tigers (according to the official census of 1999). As part of the long-term project, the park has expanded to encompass a large protective buffer zone – a move not without its opponents among the local tribal community, who depend on the forest for food and firewood. Over the years, the authorities have had a hard time reconciling the needs of the villagers with the demands of conservation and tourism; but for the time being at least, an equitable balance seems to have been struck. The **poaching** record has been successfully reduced – although not completely stopped – and Kanha upholds its reputation as a model in wildlife management and research. Even if you don't spot a cat, it's a congenial environment in which to enjoy some of cen-tral India's most unspoiled and quintessentially Kiplingesque countryside.

The Park

From the main gates, at **Kisli**, in the west, and **Mukki**, 35km away in the south, a complex network of motorable dirt tracks fans out across the park, taking in a good cross-section of its diverse terrain. Which animals you see from your open-top Jeep largely depends on where your guide decides to take you. Kanha is perhaps best known for the broad sweeps of grassy rolling meadows, or **maidans**, along its river valleys, which support large concentrations of **deer**. The park has several different species, including the rare "twelve-horned" **barasingha** (swamp deer), plucked from the verge of extinction in the 1960s, and a handful of **hiran** (black buck), now perforce enclosed by tall jackal-proof fences. The ubiquitous **chital** (spotted deer – the staple diet of Kanha's tigers), congregates in especially large numbers during the rutting season in early July, when it's not uncommon to see 4000 at one time.

The **woodland** carpeting the spurs of the Maikal Ridge that taper into the core zone from the south consists of *sal*, teak and moist deciduous forest oddly reminiscent of northern Europe. Troupes of black-faced langur monkeys crash through its canopy, while **gaur,** India's tallest wild buffalo, forage through the fallen leaves. Years of exposure to snap-happy humans seem to have left the awesome, hump-backed bulls impervious to camera flashes, but it's still wise to keep a safe distance. Higher up, you may catch sight of a spiky-horned **nilgai** (blue cow), porcupines, pythons, sloth bears, wild boar, mouse deer or secretive sambar – a favourite snack for the nocturnal predators that prowl through the trees. Sightings of **leopards** are not an outside impossibility, although these shy animals tend to steer well clear of motor vehicles.

Kanha also boasts an exotic and colourful array of **birds**, including Indian rollers, bee-eaters, golden orioles, paradise flycatchers, egrets, some outlandish **hornbills** and numerous kingfishers and birds of prey. Enthusiasts should head for the **River Banjar** area near the Mukki entrance, where the majority of the different species of water birds hang out.

Kanha's **tigers**, though, are its biggest draw, and the Jeep drivers, who are well aware of this, scan the sandy tracks for pug marks and respond to the agitated alarm calls of nearby animals. After an hour or so of mooching around the park, every Jeep congregates at Kanha, a purpose-built centre in the heart of the park. While visitors can check out the excellent museum (free), spot a few birds on the nearby lake and have a chai, the drivers wait for the call of a tiger sighting by field scouts on elephants. If one is sighted, a rush for the Jeeps ensues and the car park empties in seconds in a whirlwind of dust. This kind of "chase" gives you an idea of the thrill of the hunt that led so many to track the cats, but rarely ends in a sighting. If you're intent on seeing one in the flesh, reckon on making at least two to five excursions, and try to persuade your driver to travel at a slower pace. Staying still for a while may give you the time to spot a tiger relaxing in camouflaging brakes of bamboo or the tall elephant grass lining streams and waterholes, and it will definitely improve bird-spotting prospects. One place you're guaranteed to see tigers is on film, at the nightly audiovisual show at the **visitors' centre**, by the park gate in Kisli (6.30pm; free).

Park practicalities

Kanha is **open** from dawn to dusk (closes for three or four hours around noon; Rs200 [Rs10], vehicle Rs100, compulsory guide Rs90, Rs25 extra with camera, Rs200 extra with video) from November 1 until the monsoon arrives at the end of June. During peak season (Nov–Feb), the nights and early mornings can get very **cold**, and there are frequent frosts, so bring a jumper – without one, an open-top Jeep safari quickly gets to be a real endurance test. The **heat** between March and June keeps visitor numbers down, but tiger sightings are more common then, when the cats are forced to come out to the waterholes and streams.

The most straightforward way to **get to Kanha** is via Jabalpur, which is well connected by **rail** to most other parts of the country. If you're coming from **Orissa**, take a direct train to Katni on the main Mumbai–Calcutta line and change there. The nearest airport with scheduled domestic **flights** is at Nagpur, 226km away. Daily **buses** leave Jabalpur for **Kisli** (via Mandla) at 7am (5–6hr) and 11am (6–7hr). Both stop briefly at the barrier in **Khatia**, 4km down the road from Kisli; you must register with the park office here. Buses back to Jabalpur leave Khatia at 8am and 12.30pm. If you want to visit the park by **car** (around Rs2500 for the round trip from Jabalpur, with a night halt) taxis can be arranged at the MPTDC tourist office in Jabalpur (see p.485).

The main way to get around the park is by Jeep, leaving from Kisli every day at dawn (usually 6am) and in the afternoon. The fare, worked out according to distance and the fee for the obligatory guide, usually comes to around Rs500–700. Most of the moderate to expensive hotels have jeeps for the exclusive use of their residents. If you are at the budget hotels try and get a group (up to a maximum of five, though four is more comfortable) together from your hotel and book a Jeep direct at the park gate a day in advance. If not, ask your hotel manager about spare seats – he should be able to find you a place. Walking inside the park is strictly forbidden, but you can enquire at the park gates whether you can arrange an evening elephant ride, occasionally the ranger will let a maximum of four people spend an hour tracking tigers at a rather steep Rs300 per head.

If you arrive on the early bus and feel up to an evening safari, try asking groups on their way through the main Kisli barrier if they have a spare place.

Accommodation and eating

MPTDC has two lodges in **Kisli**, both situated in an atmospheric location inside the park proper. Private hotels outside the west gate, in and around the village of **Khatia**, range from walk-in budget lodges to high-style resorts that should be booked at least five working days before arrival. It's almost always worth enquiring about a possible discount in any standard of hotel here; if the hotel is having a lean patch they will negotiate a good reduction.

MPTDC accommodation can be booked in advance either by calling into a regional MPTDC tourist office (in Delhi, Mumbai, Calcutta, Jhansi, Jabalpur (or most of the other major towns in Madhya Pradesh), or through the Central Reservations – Tours Division, MPTDC Ltd, Fourth Floor Gangotri, TT Nagar, Bhopal 462 003 (☎0755/778383). However, if you haven't booked anything, it's always worth checking room availability in Jabalpur before arriving.

Wherever you stay, make sure you tell the bus-driver to drop you off at the right place, as the hotels at Khatia and the park gates are scattered along a six-kilometre stretch of road that sees very little traffic during the day.

Indian Adventures, Khatia (book through IAWR, 257 SV Rd, Bandra, Mumbai 400 050; ☎022/640 8742, ℻640 6399. A similar "all-in" package to *Kipling Camp*, and even further from the park gate. Chalets overlooking river, library, resident experts and alfresco restaurant with occasional dance performances. Pay in dollars. ⑧–⑨

Kipling Camp, 4km from Khatia (book through Tollygunge Club Ltd, 120 DP Sasmal Rd, Calcutta 700 033; ☎033/473 3306, ℻473 1903). British-owned and -run cottage complex offering the rustic experience with five-star comfort. "Ethnic"

rooms, meals outside in a beautiful Barga-style restaurant, evenings around the fire and pleasant forest location. Full board, safari and guides included. ⑨

Krishna Jungle Resort, 4.5km from Khatia ☎0761/401263, ℻315153, ✉hotelkhrishna@hotmail.com. Another complex oozing rustic charm, but this has a swimming pool, some rooms have a/c and the ambience is very relaxing. The best food in Khatia is served here. ⑦–⑧

Machan Complex, Khatia ☎07649/77584.

Around half a kilometre before the park gate, this was the first hotel along the stretch, and is now the cheapest option. It's an old faithful among the backpacker crew with its family atmosphere and cosy log fires in the evening. Very basic, with dorms (Rs50), Jeep hire, and very cheap, home-cooked thalis or à la carte from the new, stylish menu. **❶**–**❸**

Motel Chandan, Khatia ☎ 07649/77220. Just before the barrier on the roadside. Overpriced and slightly shabby rooms with mind-bending patterned lino on the floors, but it's clean and dependable. The attached *dhaba* specializes in pancakes smothered with local honey. **❹**–**❺**

MPTDC Baghira Log Huts, Kisli. Spacious rooms in self-contained chalets in the heart of the forest. Nos 1–8 overlook a meadow where animals come to graze. Good restaurant, with a varied menu and beer. **❻**

MPTDC Youth Hostel, opposite Kisli's main gate. The "in-park" location is excellent, and there's a good-value dorm. The tariff includes a thali dinner in the evening. **❶**–**❸**

Van Vihar Backpackers Retreat, Khatia (no phone). A friendly place well off the road at Khatia Gate. The ultra-basic rooms all have attached bath and hot water, and open into a flower-filled garden. There is a little outdoor restaurant serving thalis and pancakes. Jeeps are arranged. **❷**

Bandhavgarh National Park

With Kanha becoming ever more popular, Madhya Pradesh's second national park at **BANDHAVGARH**, tucked away in the hilly northeast of the state, is receiving increasing attention from tourists. The draw is that the park has the highest relative density of **tigers** of any of India's reserves, shelters a collection of fascinating ruins, and offers the chance of trekking through the jungle on elephant-back. It's a long haul to Bandhavgarh from either Jabalpur (195km) or Khajuraho (237km), but worth it – not only to track tigers and deer but also, as all the accommodation is close to the park gates, to watch the array of bird life, without even entering the park.

Bandhavgarh may be one of India's newer national parks, but it claims a long history. Legend dates the construction of its hilltop **fort** to the time of the epic *Ramayana*, when monkey architects built Rama a place to rest on his return from his battle with the demon king of Lanka. Excavations of caves tunnelled into the rock below the fort revealed inscriptions scratched into the sandstone in the first century BC, from which time Bandhavgarh was the base for a string of dynasties. Among them were the **Chandellas**, responsible for the temples at Khajuraho, who ruled from here until the twelfth century. The **Bhagels** took over in the twelfth century, staking a claim to the region that is still held by their direct descendant, the Maharaja of Rewa. The dynasty shifted to Rewa in 1617, allowing Bandhavgarh to be slowly consumed by forest and by the bamboo and grasslands that provided prime hunting ground for the Rewa kings. The present maharaja ended his hunting days in 1968 when he donated the area to the state as parkland. In 1986, two more chunks of forest were added to the original core zone, giving the park a total area of 437 square kilometres.

The Park

Though there are flat grassy *maidans* in the south of the park, Bandhavgarh is predominantly rugged and hilly, clad in *sal* trees in the valleys, and mixed forest in the upper reaches, which shelter a diverse avian population. The park headquarters are in the tiny village of **Tala**, a stone's throw from the main gate in the north, connected to Umaria, 32km southwest, by a road slicing through the park's narrow midriff. Jeep tracks wind through the park from the north gate in Tala, circling below the central **fort** through forest and grassland, and passing watering holes and streams, good spots for viewing wildlife.

On the whole, Jeep safaris tend to stick to the core area where the chances of spotting one of the fifty or so **tigers** are high, and glimpses of deer and monkeys guaranteed. Deer species include shy but animated gazelle and small barking deer, as well as the more common *nilgai* (blue cow) and *chital* (spotted deer). Sloth bears, porcupines, sambar and muntjac also hide away in the forest, while hyenas, foxes and jackals appear occasionally in the open country. If you're very fortunate, you may catch sight of an elusive leopard.

Look out too for some very exotic **birds** – one hundred and fifty species at the last count, though no doubt you could add to the list if you stayed long enough. Regular stars include various drongos, flycatchers, bee-eaters, rollers, parakeets, eagles, vultures and two kinds of rare **hornbills**. A more novel way of game viewing is to ride **elephant-back** in the misty dawn hours, tramping through the undergrowth as the *mahawat* hacks through spider webs and overhanging branches. Elephants have been part of Bandhavgarh society for generations, and are essential in the daily dawn search for the tigers.

The crumbling ramparts of the **fort** crown a hill in the centre of the park, 300m above the surrounding terrain. The fort was off-limits to all visitors at the time of writing, but ask about the situation when you visit, as it affords spectacular views over the valley, and by far the best bird-watching. If the fort is out of bounds you can still take in a few modest temples, the rock-cut cells of monks and soldiers, and a massive stone Vishnu reclining on his cobra near a pool that dates from the tenth century and still defies the undergrowth. The exotic plant life here attracts numerous species of insects that may make your skin crawl, but not as much as the thought that tigers may be watching you as you wander the sites. They're more likely, however, to stick to the lower levels nearer their favourite prey, but the risks are real nonetheless.

Park practicalities

Bandhavgarh is **open** from November to June (6.15–10am & 2.15–5.45pm; Rs200 [Rs10], private vehicle Rs100, obligatory guide Rs90, Rs25 extra with camera, Rs200 extra with video), but the **best time to visit**, if you want to spot wildlife, is during the hotter months between March and June. This is when thirsty tigers and their prey are forced out to the waterholes and the park's three perennial streams. The heat can be trying, especially when the town's sporadic electricity supply precludes the use of fans or air-conditioning between 6am and 2pm. Visiting in the cooler months, when wildlife viewing is still excellent, is more comfortable.

Without your own vehicle, **getting there** can be tricky. The easiest option by **rail** is to catch the daily overnight *Narmada Express* #8433 which goes through Indore, Bhopal, Jabalpur and Bilaspur (if you are coming from Orissa) to **Umaria**, the nearest railhead to the park. Three daily **buses** (7.30am, 1.30pm, 6.00pm; 45min–1hr) leave Umaria for **Tala**, 33km northeast. Alternatively, a shared **Jeep** from here to Tala is Rs15 per head, or a private taxi will cost about Rs350. Approaching from Khajuraho, or Varanasi, make your way to **Satna** on the main train line and pick up a train straight to Umaria. There is currently no bus service between Satna and Umaria. If you are coming from Delhi (or Agra), the best train is the *Utkal Express* #8478, which leaves Nizamuddin station at 12.50pm and arrives in Umaria early the next day. Travelling by **rented car** either from Khajuraho or Jabalpur takes roughly five hours, and will cost upwards of Rs2500 for the round trip, plus an extra Rs250–300 for each night you stay.

To cover a reasonable distance within the park, book a **Jeep** at the headquarters at the park gate (Rs500) or through your hotel. Up to five people can share a jeep – this will lower the cost considerably – for a morning or afternoon session. **Elephant rides** can also be arranged at the park office or your hotel (Rs300 per hour, shared by a maximum of four people). However, the elephants also wait for visitors in the area where they have discovered a tiger or two lurking deep in the forest; the lure of a quick jaunt into the jungle to get a virtually guaranteed sighting is hard to resist. The charge of Rs300 still applies, although you only get about half an hour at most; your Jeep will await your return and then continue the tour.

For the serious wildlife enthusiast, there are a few very experienced naturalists in Tala, all of whom can be contacted through your hotel. S.K. Tiwari of Skay's Camp (℡07653/ 65355, ℻65309) specializes in nature photography, and has an impressive knowledge of Indian animal and bird life.

Accommodation and eating

Most of Bandhavgarh's new and established hotels, all of which are in **Tala**, cater for travellers on a higher budget, and offer "jungle-plan" prices – all-inclusive 24hr deals including meals and two Jeep safaris per person. However, there are also a few budget lodges and mid-priced hotels. The only option for **eating** outside your hotel is at one of the friendly, cheap *dhabas* on the main road.

Baghela, Umaria Road. Small, simple and slightly overpriced budget option run by a very erratic manager. ❸

Bandhavgarh Jungle Camp, Umaria Road. One of the oldest resorts, with double-roomed tents (with hot showers and dressing rooms) in the gardens of the old maharaja's lodge. Alfresco lunch between safaris, and dinner (preceded by a slide show) in the lodge. Book through Bandhavgarh Wildlife Camp & Safari, B/21 Greater Kailash Enclave II, New Delhi 110048 ℡011/685 4626, ℻686 4614. Jungle-plan arrangement only, at a rather steep $135.

Bandhavgarh Jungle Lodge, close to the river; turn left off Umaria Road. Characterful, comfortable huts finished in mud coating and tribal-style painting. Residents eat set multi-cuisine meals alfresco in the pleasant garden. Book through Tiger Resorts Ltd, Suite 206 Rakesh Deep, 11 Commercial Complex, New Delhi 110049 ℡011/685 3760, ℻686 5212. Jungle-plan $140, or accommodation only (pay in rupees). ❼

Kum Kum, Umaria Road, next to White Tiger Forest Lodge ℡07653/65324. A very friendly newcomer, with excellent-value rooms, each with tribal designs on the walls and attached bathrooms with 24hr hot water. A Rs25 unlimited thali around the fire is also hard to beat. ❸

MPTDC White Tiger Forest Lodge, Umaria Road, next to the barrier over the main road ℡07653/65308. Large complex with clean, cosy rooms, all with attached bath and hot water, and a good restaurant and bar. Rooms 17–21 are in bungalows with large verandas overlooking the river – an excellent place for bird-watching, and tigers occasionally come here to drink in the height of summer. ❻–❼

Royal Retreat, Umaria Road ℡07653/65322. The Maharajah's former lodge, aimed at independent visitors. Each room is atmospheric but simple and the bathrooms are large; the dorm is great value at Rs150. There is even a ten-percent discount for the walk-in tourist. ❻

Tiger Lodge, Umaria Road. Small, very friendly and basic lodge and *dhaba*. The bare rooms have fans, and some have attached bathrooms. ❷

Tiger Trails, 2.5km beyond Tala (book through Indian Adventures, C257, SV Rd, Bandra west, Mumbai 400 050; ℡022/6408742, ℻6432622). This place is not cheap, but it is the most tastefully decorated place in Tala. The open-air dining room overlooks a little lake that is great for bird-watching, and the cottages are comfortable and peaceful – a total escape. Pay in dollars. ❾

V Patel Jungle Resorts, close to *Nature Heritage* ℡07653/65323. Excellent-value, welcoming resort whose four clean rooms have attached bath, hot water and a communal veranda. Also has a flower-filled garden and an alfresco restaurant. Book by phone, or in Jabalpur at 212 Abhaykunj, Narmada Road (℡0761/410736). Jungle plan $155, or accommodation only. ❺

Western Madhya Pradesh

The geography of **western Madhya Pradesh** is dominated by the River Narmada, which drains westwards through a wide alluvial valley, bounded in the south by the Satpura hills and the Maharashtran border, and in the north by the rugged Vindhya Range. Forming the major trade corridor between the Ganges plains and the west coast, the region – known as **Malwa** – was for nearly a thousand years an independent princely state ruled from the sprawling hilltop fort complex at **Mandu**. The former capital, now deserted, is the area's outstanding tourist attraction, with its ruined mosques, tanks and palaces, and its spectacular panoramic views.

Most visitors travel to Mandu via the dull industrial city of **Indore**, then continue northeast to Bhopal, or south on the main Delhi–Mumbai train line towards Jalgaon, the jumping-off point for the Ellora and Ajanta caves. The sacred city of **Ujjain**, 55km north of Indore, boasts a bumper crop of modern Hindu temples, but little else. You could, nevertheless, choose to pause here on your way to or from southern Rajasthan on the Western Railway, the most direct land link with Delhi. Alternatively, you could head south to the Narmada and the fascinating Hindu pilgrimage centres of **Omkareshwar** and **Maheshwar**.

Indore and around

INDORE, the second largest city in Madhya Pradesh, is huge, modern, heavily industrialized, and generally dull. If you find yourself with time to kill en route to or from **Mandu**, 98km southwest, however, a couple of worthwhile sights lie hidden among its tangle of ferroconcrete flyovers, expressways and crowded bazaars.

Situated at the confluence of the Kham and Saraswati rivers, the city was for centuries merely an insignificant stopover on the pilgrimage trails to Omkareshwar and Ujjain, 55km north. In the eighteenth century, however, it became the capital of the **Holkar** dynasty, whose chief, Malhar Rao, had previously managed to scrounge several choice scraps of land from the Marathas during their northward advance against the Moghuls. Later, Rao's daughter-in-law, **Ahilya Bai**, took over control of the state, which at its height stretched as far as the Ganges and the Punjab. Described by a contemporary British diplomat as "the most exemplary ruler that ever lived", the rani was a kind of central-Indian Queen Victoria, who, in addition to founding the modern city of Indore, built palaces, temples, *dharamshalas* and charitable institutions all over the country. When she died in 1795, her four grandsons dragged the state into a bloody civil war. A series of skirmishes with the Marathas and East India Company followed, ending in the Treaty of 1818, which secured for the dynasty a small but rich dominion with Indore as the capital. The city's expansion gained momentum in the nineteenth century, fuelled by a lucrative trade in cotton and opium. Despite remaining loyal to the British in the Mutiny, the maverick Holkar maharajas stayed firmly under the thumb of their colonial overlords until Independence, when they were finally relieved of their powers by the Congress.

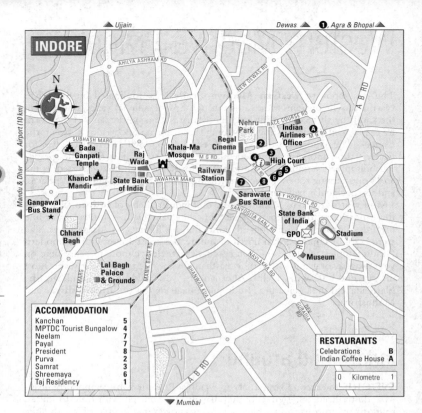

Indore, these days, is the region's biggest business and commercial centre. The nearby industrial estate of **Pithampur**, hyped as "the Detroit of India", hosts numerous giant steel and auto manufacturers, including Honda, Bajaj, Hindustan Motors and Pratap Steel. The resulting **affluence** has made a big impact: satellite dishes, luxury hotels and American-style shopping malls are popping up all over, while the nouveaux riches swan ostentatiously around town on brand-new Japanese scooters. Even the auto-rickshaws seem shinier.

The City

With the exception of Indore's **museum**, over on AB Road near the GPO, most of the city's sights lie west of the train line, in and around the bazaar. Two broad thoroughfares, MG Road and Jawahar Marg, form the north and south boundaries of this cluttered and chaotic district, which is interrupted in the east by the confluence of the Saraswati and Kham rivers – little more than trickles of black slime bordered by *bastees* and heaps of decomposing rubbish. The surrounding suburbs, by contrast, are a much more congenial prospect of detached houses, new apartment blocks and leafy gardens – home to Indore's managerial classes and a couple of old Holkar palaces.

The Lal Bagh palace

Set in its own grounds on the banks of the Kham, the **Lal Bagh palace** (Tues–Sun 10am–5pm; Rs2) is another of those extravagant Neoclassical creations so beloved of the ludicrously rich maharajas of the nineteenth and early twentieth centuries. The building took two generations of the Holkar family around thirty years to complete, and was, in its day, rivalled only by the Scindias' Jai Vilas palace in Gwalior. Granted carte blanche and a limitless budget, its British architects and interior decorators came up with a cross between Brideshead and Versailles – a vast stately home dripping with Doric columns, gilt stucco, crystal chandeliers, and piles of replica Rococo furniture. In 1987, the property was inherited by the state government, which installed an exceedingly tiny museum (one dusty cabinet) in the reception hall and renamed it the Nehru Centre.

Lal Bagh's main entrance is via a pair of grandiose wrought-iron **gates**, modelled on those at Buckingham Palace, which bear the Holkar family arms, with their motto "Success attends he who strives" inscribed in Hindi below. Note the wheat and poppies in the background, symbolizing the two main sources of the dynasty's prosperity. The ground floor of the palace consists of several large chambers: the **durbar hall**, used for royal assemblies, the state banquet hall and the ballroom, with its specially sprung herring-bone dance floor. Hanging on the wall of the billiards room nearby, a fine picture of Tukoji Rao (1902–25) – the ruler responsible for completing the palace – is encrusted with precious stones. The maharaja sent his own court artist to France to study European painting so that his portrait could be rendered in the "correct" style. The cherubs, flying nymphs, and Greek and Roman gods adorning the ceilings of the adjacent rooms are equally convincing. Also worth checking out is the underground passage leading down to the kitchens. One of the rooms hidden away in this vault contains a modest but very colourful collection of **tribal artefacts**, including terracotta votive statues, clothes, jewellery, murals and brass sculpture.

The Raj Wada

The Holkars' old palace, the **Raj Wada**, is Indore's principal landmark, presiding over a palm-fringed square in the heart of the city. Built in the style of a western Indian town house, the eighteenth-century mansion's most prominent feature is a lofty, seven-storey gateway. Its upper four floors were originally made of wood, which made it particularly prone to fire; most of the palace collapsed after the last one, in 1984. Only the facade and the family temple, immediately inside the main courtyard, survive.

The Kanch Mandir and bazaars

Tucked away deep in the bazaar district, ten minutes' walk west of Raj Wada, the Jain **Kanch Mandir**, or "Mirror Temple" (daily 10am–5pm; no photos), is one of the city's more eccentric religious monuments. Surprisingly, for a faith renowned for its austerity, the interior of the temple is decked with multi-coloured glass **mosaics**. All around the temple there are donation boxes with the bust of a man on top – put a coin in his hand then push the lever on the side to watch him eat the money. Vivid tableaux lining the sides of the entrance hall depict the horrors in store for sinners in the afterlife.

The **bazaars** in the vicinity of the Kanch Mandir and Raj Wada are great for a stroll. Rows of stalls and open-fronted shops are jammed beneath picturesque four-storeyed houses with overhanging wooden balconies. The gold and silver **jewellery market**, the Sarafa Bazaar, is Indore's best known. You'll find it around the corner from the Mirror Temple, near the massive wholesale textile market, where cloth is still sold by weight. Also worth seeking out are shops on Bajaj Khana Chowk that specialize in traditional embroidered and beadwork costumes, and the atmospheric fruit and vegetable market on the riverbank beneath the lime-green **Khala-Ma mosque**.

The Central Museum

Indore's **Central Museum** (Mon–Sat 10am–5pm) is over in the southeast of the city, near the GPO. Its large collection includes finds from nearby prehistoric sites, as well as fine Jain and Hindu sculpture from the ruined eleventh- and twelfth-century temples at Hinlajgarh. The downstairs gallery boasts a handful of priceless **Harappan terracottas** unearthed at Mohenjo Daro, in southern Pakistan. None of the exhibits is adequately labelled, but the museum attendants are happy to show you around.

Practicalities

Trains arriving in Indore on the Central Railway pull in at the main-line station in the middle of the city. The principal **bus stand**, "Sarawate" (☎0731/465688), is a short walk south from platform 1, beyond the overpass. Buses for **Mandu** use the less convenient "Gangawal" bus stand (☎0731/480688), a three-kilometre auto-rickshaw ride west towards the domestic **airport**, 10km out of town.

Moving on from Indore

Tickets for daily Indian Airlines flights to Delhi, Bhopal and Mumbai and twice-weekly ones to Gwalior (Mon and Fri) from **Indore airport** (☎0731/411758) can be booked at the office (☎0731/431595) on Race Course Road, 2km northeast of the station. There's no airport bus, but there are plenty of taxis and auto-rickshaws.

As for **trains**, two broad-gauge branches of the Western Railway connect Indore to cities in northern India. The fastest service to Delhi, the daily Indore–Nizamuddin Express #4005, leaves at 4pm and heads north via Ujjain, Kota and Bharatpur. The other branch, serviced by the daily Malwa Express #9367 (departs 12.30pm, arrives 7.50am next day), runs east to Bhopal, then north to New Delhi on the Central Railway via Jhansi, Gwalior, and Agra.

Trains to Rajasthan leave twice daily on the metre-gauge line for Chittaurgarh and Ajmer, and once to Jaipur on the Purna–Jaipur Express #9770 (9.50pm, arrives 2pm next day). Getting to Ellora and Ajanta means catching the 3.45am Jaipur–Purna Express #9769 to Kandhwa, arriving at 9.50am, in time to pick up the 11.25am Lashkar Express #1062 for Jalgaon (arrives 2.35pm). The daily 2.15pm Narmada Express #8233 is the only train to Jabalpur, for connections to Kanha and Bandhavgarh.

To get to Mandu by **bus** from Indore, take one of two daily direct services (4hr) from Gangawal bus stand; or the 3.20pm direct from the more convenient Sarawate bus stand. Failing that, take any of the frequent services from Gangawal bus stand to Dhar (2–3hr), which is connected to Mandu by half-hourly buses (1hr). Less frequent services run to Dhar from Sarawate bus stand.

MPSRTC, whose office is in Sarawate, operates "luxury" buses to Bhopal four times daily (6am, noon, 2.45pm & 9pm; 5–6hr); you have to catch the 6am if you want to make the 2.50pm daily Delhi-bound Shatabdi Express.

Reliable travel agents in town include the excellent President Travels, at *Hotel President*, 163 RNT Rd (☎0731/533472), Royal Tourist Service, 164 RNT Rd (☎0731/513471) and Taj Tours & Travels, at *Hotel Taj Regency*, near Scheme 54 (☎0731/438606).

MPTDC's helpful **information** office (daily 10am–5pm; closed 2nd and 3rd Sat of the month; ☎0731/528653), in the MPTDC Tourist Bungalow behind the R.N.Tagore Natya Griha Exhibition Hall on Rabidranath Tagore Road (RNT Road), hands out the usual glossy leaflets and a better-than-average city map. They also have a car for rent (with driver), available for two-day **tours** to Mandu and for trips to Omkareshwar and Maheshwar all charged at Rs5 per km, plus Rs250 per night halt.

The State Bank of Indore (Mon–Fri 10am–2pm, Sat 10am–noon) has a **foreign exchange** office opposite their main branch on Raj Wada. The Bank of Baroda (same hours), across town on Agra–Bombay (AB) Road, near the **GPO**, deals with Visa. There's a 24-hour **pharmacy** (☎0731/528301) in the MY Hospital compound, off AB Road. Internet cafés are rife across the city, but the best service is Dishnet, RNT Road, in Silvermall, 2nd floor (☎0731/452001) – this big centre is open around the clock, the connections are fast and there is central a/c.

The most convenient means of **getting around** is by metered auto-rickshaw; or rather more cheaply by the ancient *tempos* that ply defined routes – just stop them and ask if they will pass your destination.

Accommodation

The majority of Indore's **hotels** cater for business visitors and are scattered around the prosperous suburb of **Tukoganj**, 1km east of the railway station. Competition here is stiff, so standards tend to be high, and prices reasonable. The same cannot be said of the cheaper accommodation, most of which is in the noisy and polluted area between Sarawate and the railway station. Ignore the touts who try to drag you off to the dire lodges opposite the bus stand, and head instead for the better-value budget hotels along **Chhoti Gwaltoli**, a lane beneath the big Patel flyover. All but the absolute rock-bottom lodges levy the mandatory ten-percent **luxury tax**. The recently renovated dorms of the railway retiring rooms are cleaner and slightly more expensive than usual and handy for an early morning departure (Rs100).

Kanchan, Kanchan Bagh ☎0737/270871. A pleasant little hotel that avoids the impersonal business orientation of neighbouring mid-range hotels; the rooms are well appointed and there is a bar and a good multi-cuisine restaurant. ⑤–⑥

MPTDC Tourist Bungalow, RNT Road ☎0731/521818. Small, claustrophobic place tucked away behind the R. N. Tagore Natya Griha Exhibition Hall, with some a/c rooms. It's not up to the usual MPTDC standards, and the closest restaurant is the *Apsara* in the same compound. ④–⑤

Neelam, 33/2 Patel Bridge Corner ☎0731/464616. Despite the dingy exterior, this is good value and near the station, with clean rooms and cable TV. ②–④

Payal, 38 Chhoti Gwaltoli ☎0731/463202. One of the best deals among the row of inexpensive hotels – all rooms are smart and have attached shower-toilets. It's definitely worth shelling out an extra Rs50 for the airy deluxe rooms with Star TV. ③

President, 163 RNT Rd ☎0731/528866, ℱ512230. Comfortable, with all a/c rooms. Facilities include a health club, excellent veg restaurant, rooftop café, and reputable in-house travel agent. ⑦

Purva, 565 MG Rd ☎0731/541149. Small, friendly and spotless hotel, five minutes from the station. Although a recent tariff hike makes it a tad overpriced. ⑤–⑥

Samrat, 18/5 MG Rd ☎0731/527889. Large, modern hotel geared towards business travellers, so all rooms are comfortable with all the essential mod cons for busy people. Restaurant meals and room service are available. ⑤–⑦

Shreemaya, 12 RNT Rd ☎0731/514081. Yet another hotel servicing the business sector – its standards are deluxe, including foreign exchange and a car park. All its name signs are in Hindi, but as Indore's largest hotel, it's not hard to miss. ⑥–⑦

Taj Residency, Vijaynagar, 3km from the centre of town, just off AB Road ☎0731/557700, ℱ555354. The top hotel in Indore, aimed primarily at international business clientele with smooth and efficient staff and service, luxury rooms, a pool, fitness centre and several dining choices, including the swanky open-air terrace grill. Dollars only. ⑨

Eating

Eating out is popular among Indore's middle classes, so there are plenty of quality restaurants around the city centre to choose from. Most are located in the larger hotels, such as the *Shreemaya* and *President*, and serve the usual Indian and Chinese dishes. Thanks to the current "health food" craze, there are a couple of excellent pure-veg places as well, the classiest being *Woodlands* in the *President*. Cheaper food is available at the dingy *dhabas* and canteens around Sarawate bus stand. Stick to the ones doing a brisk trade, and you shouldn't go far wrong.

Apsara, RNT Road. Popular, inexpensive family place just in front of the *Tourist Bungalow*, serving great veg food inside and in the open air. For a snack, try their delicious stuffed naan and *kulcha* breads.

Celebrations, in the annexe to the right of *Hotel Shreemaya*. Spotlessly clean and ultramodern coffee shop serving all things naughty from cream cakes and ice cream to pizzas.

Indian Coffee House, next to Rampura Building, off MG Road. The usual south Indian snacks served by waiters in turbans and cummerbunds.

Opens at 7.30am for big breakfasts and the papers. There's another branch set in peaceful grounds behind the high court.

Status, below *Hotel Purva*, 565 MG Rd. Superb eat-till-you-burst Rajasthani lunchtime thalis, with varied veg dishes, dhal, breads and chutneys – all for Rs60. Rather disappointing vegetarian à la carte later on.

Woodlands, 163 RNT Rd. *Hotel President*'s swanky pure-veg a/c restaurant that claims to offer "scrumptious food of international fame", serves stylish but pricey south Indian specialities.

Mandu

Set against the rugged backdrop of the Vindhya hills, the medieval ghost-town of **MANDU**, 98km from Indore, is one of central India's most atmospheric historical monuments. Come here at the height of the monsoons, when the rocky plateau and its steeply shelving sides are carpeted with green vegetation, and you'll see why the Malwa sultans christened their capital **Shadiabad**, or "City of Joy". Even during the relentless heat of the dry season, the ruins make an exotic spectacle. Elegant Islamic palaces, mosques and onion-domed mausoleums crumble beside large medieval reservoirs and precipitous ravines, while below, an endless vista of scorched plains and tiny villages stretches off to the horizon. Mandu can be visited as a day-trip from Indore, but you'll enjoy it more if you spend a couple of nights, giving you time not only to explore the ruins, but to witness the memorable sunsets over the Narmada Valley.

Right from the moment you turn off the main highway on the road that winds its way up to the plateau, there are lonely mausoleums and overgrown mosques dotted among the scrub; a tantalizing taste of what is to come. Rather oddly too, there is a **fossilarium**, 5km short of Mandu, although the single most intriguing aspect of this place is the mammoth model dinosaur striding over the cliff-edge.

Some history

Archeological evidence suggests that the remote hilltop was first fortified around the sixth century AD, when it was known as Mandapa-Durga, or "Durga's hall of worship" – in time corrupted to "Mandu". Four hundred years later, the site gained in strategic importance when the powerful **Paramaras** moved their capital from Ujjain to Dhar, 35km north. The plateau's natural defences, strengthened by Raja Bhoj (see p.424), proved, however, unable to withstand persistent attacks by the Muslim invaders during the twelfth century. The fort eventually fell to the sultans of Delhi in 1305.

While the Sultanate had its hands full fending off the Mongols on their northern borders a century or so later, Malwa's Afghan governor, Dilawar Khan **Ghuri**, seized the chance to establish his own independent kingdom. He died after only four years on the throne, however, leaving his ambitious young son at the helm. During **Hoshang Shah**'s illustrious 27-year reign, Mandu was promoted from pleasure resort to royal capital, and acquired some of the finest Islamic monuments in Asia, including the Jami Masjid, Delhi Gate and the sultan's own tomb.

Mandu's golden age continued under the **Khaljis**, who took over from the Ghuri dynasty in 1436, when Mahmud Shah Khalji poisoned Hoshang Shah's grandson. Another building boom and several protracted wars later, Mandu settled down to a lengthy period of peace and prosperity under **Ghiyath Shah** (1469–1500). Famous for his love of cooking and beautiful women, Ghiyath amassed a harem of 15,000 courtesans, and a bodyguard of a thousand Turkish and Abyssinian amazons, whom he accommodated in the appropriately lavish Jahaz Mahal. The sybaritic sultan lived to a ripe old age, but was poisoned by his son shortly after his eightieth birthday. His successor, Nasir Shah, died of guilt ten years later, and Mandu, dogged by feuds and the threat of rebellion, became an easy target for the militaristic Sultan of Gujarat, who invaded in 1526. In the centuries that followed, control over the fort and its rapidly decaying monuments passed between a succession of independent rulers and the Moghuls. It never regained its former prominence, however, and was deserted by the time the Marathas annexed the region in 1732. These days, Mandu is a tranquil backwater that sees far fewer visitors than it deserves. Apart from at weekends, when busloads of exuberant day-trippers breeze in from Indore, the only people you're likely to see picking through the ruins are the Bhil villagers who farm the surrounding fields.

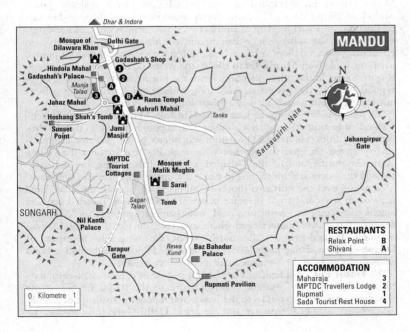

The monuments

Mandu's **monuments** derive from a unique school of Islamic architecture that flourished here, and at the region's former capital, Dhar, between 1400 and 1516. Much admired for their elegant simplicity, the buildings are believed to have exerted a considerable influence on the Moghul architects responsible for the Taj Mahal.

Mandu's platform, a 23km-square plateau, is separated from the body of hills to the north by the **Kakra Khoh**, literally "deep ravine". A narrow causeway forms a natural bridge across the gorge, carrying the present road across and up via a series of subsidiary gates to the fort's modern entrance, beside the original, and very grand Delhi Gate. From here, the road runs south past the first and main concentration of monuments, the **Royal Enclave**, to the village square, which stands in the middle of the second, or **village group**. The remaining sites lie further to the south, east of the picturesque **Sagar Talao** tank, and in a fortified enclosure overlooking the Narmada Valley known as the **Rewa Kund group**.

If you don't have your own vehicle, the most pleasant way of **getting around** the fort and its widely dispersed monuments is to rent a bicycle (Rs30 per 24hr) from the VIP Wine Shop, just off the main square, or from your hotel. Alternatively, you can squeeze into the village's decrepit old *tempo* that runs between the village square and Rewa Kund group at regular intervals, or rent one of the town's two auto-rickshaws for a complete tour.

The Royal Enclave

Reached via the lane that leads west off the village square, the **Royal Enclave** (daily 9am–5pm; Rs2, Fri free; Rs25 extra with video) is dominated by Mandu's most photographed monument, Ghiyath Shah's majestic **Jahaz Mahal**, or "Ship Palace". The name derives from its unusual shape and elevated situation on a narrow strip of land between two large water tanks. It originally housed the sultan's huge harem, and the thousand-strong all-women guard that protected them. A breezy rooftop terrace, crowned with four domed pavilions, looks over **Munja Talao** lake to the west, and the square, stone-lined **Kapur Sagar** in the other direction. From the northern balcony, you also get a good view of the geometric sandstone bathing pools where the palace's inhabitants would have whiled away their long incarceration.

The next building along the lane is the **Hindola Mahal**, or "Swing Palace" – so-called because its distinctive sloping walls supposedly look as though they are swaying from side to side. The design was, in fact, purely functional, intended to buttress the graceful but heavy stone arches that support the ceiling inside. At the far end of the T-shaped assembly hall, a long stepped ramp allowed the sultan and his retinue to reach the upper storey on elephant-back.

Sprawling over the northern shores of Munja Talao lake are the dilapidated remains of a second royal pleasure palace. The **Champa Baodi** boasts an ingeniously complex ventilation and water-supply system which kept its dozens of *tykhanas* (subterranean chambers) cool during the long Malwan summers. Immediately to the north stands the venerable **Mosque of Dilawara Khan**, dating from 1405. The chunks of Hindu temple used to build its main doorway and colonnaded hall are still very evident.

The **Hathi Pol**, or "Elephant Gate", with its pair of colossal, half-decapitated elephant guardians, was the main entrance to the Royal Enclave. Now closed, you will have to return to the bazaar and follow the road out of Mandu to reach the edge of the plateau and the grand **Delhi Gate**. Built around the same time as Dilawara Khan's mosque, this great bastion, towering over the cobbled road in five sculpted arches, is the most imposing of the twelve that stud the battlements along the fort's 45-kilometre perimeter. The views from its ramparts over Kakra Khoh, the chasm through which invading armies invariably chose to attack Mandu, are spectacular. Just before Delhi gate, you pass the "shop" of **Gada Shah**, an upstart adviser to Hoshang Shah; after he successfully defended the emperor and Mandu during an attack by the Sultan of Gujarat, he built himself a rather nice palace in the royal enclave – opposite the Jahaz Mahal, no less. He then built his so-called shop to dispense advice on all matters concerning the kingdom.

The village group

Some of the fort's best-preserved buildings are clustered **around the village** (all open daily 9am–5pm, $10 [Rs5]). Work on the magnificent pink sandstone mosque on the west side of the main square, the **Jami Masjid**, commenced during the reign of Hoshang Shah and took three generations to complete. Said to be modelled on the Great Mosque at Damascus, it rests on a huge raised plinth pierced by rows of tiny arched chambers – once used as cells for visiting clerics. A flight of steps leads up from the square to the large domed entrance porch. Beyond the ornate *jali* screens and bands of blue-glaze tiles that decorate the main doorway, you arrive in the Great Courtyard, enclosed by rows of pillars and small domes. The prayer hall at the far end is surmounted by three larger domes and houses a small pulpit and some finely carved inscriptions from the Koran.

Hoshang Shah's tomb (c. 1440), directly behind the Jami Masjid, is this group's real highlight. It stands on a low plinth at the centre of a square-walled enclosure, and is crowned by a squat central dome and four small corner cupolas. Now streaked with mildew and mud washed down from the bats' nests inside its eaves, the tomb is made entirely from milky-white marble – the first of its kind in the subcontinent. An inscription on the right door jamb records the visit, in 1659, of the Moghul emperor Shah Jahan, who brought four of his architects to admire the building before they began work on the Taj Mahal. The interior of the tomb is very plain, except for the elaborate pierced-stone windows that illuminate Hoshang's sarcophagus.

On the opposite side of the square to the Great Mosque, the **Ashrafi Mahal**, or "Palace of Coins", was a theological college (*madarasa*) that the ruler Muhammad Shah later converted into a tomb. The complex included a giant marble mausoleum and seven-storey *minar*, or victory tower, of which only the base survives.

Around the Sagar Talao

En route to the Rewa Kund, a further handful of monuments are scattered around the fields east of Sagar Talao. Dating from the early fifteenth century, the **Mosque of Malik Mughis** is the oldest of the bunch, once again visibly constructed using ancient Hindu masonry. Note the turquoise tiles and fine Islamic calligraphy over the main doorway. The high-walled building opposite was a caravanserai, where merchants and their camel trains would rest during long treks across the subcontinent.

A short way south, the octagonal tomb known as the **Dai-ki-Chhoti Bahan-ka-Mahal** looms above the surrounding fields from a raised plinth, still retaining large strips of the blue ceramic tiles that plastered most of Mandu's beautiful Afghan domes. Young couples from the nearby village creep off here during the evenings for a bit of privacy, so make plenty of noise as you approach.

The Rewa Kund group

The road to the **Rewa Kund group** (6km away from the main village) heads past herds of water buffalo grazing on the muddy foreshores of the lake, then winds its way gently through a couple of Bhil villages towards the far southern edge of the plateau. Stately old baobabs line the roadside, like giant upturned root vegetables. The bulbous-bottomed trees, natives of the African Sahel, were introduced to India by Arab traders, and are now used by the local tribespeople for their many medicinal properties.

The **Rewa Kund** itself nestles behind a rise further up the hill. Noted for its curative powers, the old stone-lined reservoir is popular with bus parties of Indian visitors, who picnic under the trees by its banks. Water from the tank used to be pumped into the cistern in the nearby **Baz Bahadur Palace** (daily 9am–5pm). Bahadur, the last independent ruler of Malwa, retreated to Mandu to study music after being trounced in battle by Rani Durgavati. Legend has it that he fell in love with a Hindu singer named Rupmati, whom he enticed to his hilltop home with an exquisite palace that she could admire from the window of her father's house on the Nirmar plains below. The couple eventually married, but did not live happily ever after. When Akbar heard of Rupmati's beauty, he dispatched an army to Mandu to capture her and the long-coveted fort. Bahadur managed to slip away from the ensuing battle, but his bride, left behind in the palace, poisoned herself rather than fall into the clutches of the attackers.

The romantic **Rupmati Pavilion** (sunrise–sunset), built by Bahadur for his bride-to-be, still rests on a ridge high above the Rewa Kund. Beneath its lofty terrace, the plateau plunges a sheer 300m to the gently undulating Narmada Valley. The view is breathtaking, especially at sunset or on a clear day, when you can just about make out the sun-bleached banks of the sacred river as it winds west towards the Arabian Sea.

The Nil Kanth Palace

Another idyllic spot for watching the sun set over the plains is the **Nil Kanth Palace**, an old Shiva temple converted by the Moghuls into a water pavilion. It clings to the top of a steep cliff at the head of a rugged ravine on the western edge of the plateau, and was used by Akbar as a royal retreat. Persian verses on the walls of one room record the emperor's military exploits in the Deccan and, in a more philosophical vein, remind readers of the transience and futility of worldly achievement. It can be reached along a track that forks right off the main road, 500m south of Mandu village square.

Practicalities

Although there are a couple of direct private **buses** to Mandu from Indore, it's often quicker to travel to Dhar and pick up the half-hourly local service to the fort from there – a 35-kilometre journey that takes over one hour. Direct services back to Indore run twice a day. **Taxis** can be arranged at all hotels in Indore (see p.499), and charge around Rs800 for the round trip from Indore, plus a hefty Rs250 waiting charge if you stay overnight – which still works out cheaper than an MPTDC rental car from their Tourist Office in Indore.

There is nowhere to **change money**; the nearest bank is in Indore. You can make **STD/ISD calls** from several booths dotted around the village square. The disorganized **post office**, on the main road near the Rama temple, is not recommended for poste restante.

Most **places to stay** inside the fort are managed by MPTDC, who advise visitors to book a couple of days in advance. Their cheapest hotel, *Travellers'*

Lodge (☎ 07292/63221; ❹), at the north end of the plateau near the SADA barrier, is friendly and attentive, with scenic views, and clean rooms with attached bath and hot water. It's a one-kilometre hike from the main square where the buses pull in, however, so ask to be dropped off en route. The adjacent *Hotel Rupmati* (☎ 07292/63270; ❹–❻) is slightly better value with all a/c rooms, each with a private balcony overlooking the dramatic ravine below; there is a decent restaurant in the garden and a bar that serves very reasonably priced cold beers. In the centre of the village, SADA's ultra-basic *Tourist Rest House* (☎ 07292/63232; ❷), opposite the Jami Masjid, has a few basic rooms with attached bath; but before you stay, you have to fork out a minimum advance of Rs200. Nearby, the temple *dharamshala* (❶) next to Ashrafi Mahal, has clean, spartan doubles with attached bathrooms. Round towards the Royal Enclave the new *Maharaja Hotel* (☎ 07292/63288; ❷) is the best budget deal, with ten simple but clean rooms and a restaurant around a courtyard. The MPTDC *Tourist Cottages* (☎ 07292/63235; ❺–❻), 2km south of the square, is Mandu's most comfortable and expensive hotel. The campus of chalets, in gardens overlooking the Sagar Talao tank, boasts twenty large rooms with attached shower-toilets, hot water and some a/c.

The *Tourist Cottages'* semi-open-air restaurant is the smartest **place to eat** in the fort, although the moderately priced menu is fairly limited to Indian veg dishes. Unlike the cafeteria in the *Travellers' Lodge*, you don't have to order your evening meal in advance. The *Shivani Hotel*, halfway between the square and the SADA barrier, serves up cheap but absolutely delicious veg thalis, *subzi* and *chapatis*. The *Relax Point* and *Krishna Hotel*, on the square, also offer chai, cold drinks, great samosas and so-so thalis. Avoid **meat and paneer**, though, as frequent power cuts mean that even places with refrigerators can have problems keeping it fresh.

Ujjain

Situated on the banks of the sacred River Shipra, **UJJAIN**, 55km north of Indore, is one of India's seven holiest cities. Like Haridwar, Nasik and Prayag (near Allahabad), it plays host every twelve years to the country's largest religious gathering, the **Kumbh Mela** (see p.329), which in 1992 drew an estimated fifteen million pilgrims here to bathe; naked *sadhus* are among the millions jamming the waterfront, waiting to wash away several lifetimes of accumulated bad karma. Outside festival times, Ujjain is a great place for people watching, as pilgrims and locals alike go about the daily business of puja, temple visiting, and chai drinking. All around the main temples, you see modern Hinduism at its most kitsch, with all types of devotional paraphernalia, gaudy lighting and plastic flower garlands on sale. Down at the *ghats*, women flap wet saris dry whilst their soapy children splash in the water, and sleepy *pujaris* ply their trade beneath the rows of orange and whitewashed riverside shrines. A mini-Varanasi this is not, but the temples rising behind the *ghats* are majestic at dusk, and with the ringing of bells and incense drifting around, this atmospheric place can feel timeless.

Some history

Excavations north of Ujjain have yielded traces of settlement as far back as the eighth century BC. The ancient city was a major regional capital under the

UJJAIN

ACCOMMODATION

Atlas	4
Chandragupta	1
Girnar	3
MPTDC Shipra	5
MPTDC Yatri Niwas	7
Rama Krishna	2
Surana Palace	6

RESTAURANTS

Ashnoi	D
Chanakya	A
New Raj Kumar	C
Sudana	B

Chousath Yogini Temple

Kalideh Mahal, Siddavath & Bhartrihari Caves

River Shipra

Govardhan Sagar

Ksheer Sagar

Scindia Statue

GOPAL MANDIR MARG

CHATTRI CHOWK

Gopal Mandir

Harsiddhi Mandir

Footbridge

Rudra Sagar

Mahakaleshwar Mandir

Ram Ghat

Khwara Shakeb Ki Masjid

Madhav Clock Tower

GPO

Dewas Bus Stand

Railway Station

LALA LAJPAT RAI MARG

ASHOK MARG

ARYA SAMAJ MARG

LAMI SAI MARG

TILAK MARG

MAHAKALESHWAR MARG

AHILYA BAI MARG

CHANDRASHEKHER AZAD MARG

VEER DURGADAS MARG

PATEL MARG

HARSIDDHI MARG

JAI SINGH PURA MARG

BHAGAT SINGH MARG

SANTA RAJA MARG

KALIDAS MARG

TATA TOPE MARG

VIKRAM MARG

DHANVANTRI MARG

WAKHWA MARG

UNIVERSITY ROAD

NARAYANAN MARG

Bhopal & Dewas

& P.D.V. Bus Stand

Vedha Shala Observatory

N

0 Metres 500

Mauryans (Ashok was governor here for a time during the reign of his father), when it was known as **Avantika** and lay on the main trade route that linked northern India with Mesopotamia and Egypt. According to Hindu mythology, Shiva later changed its name to **Ujjaiyini**, "He Who Conquers With Pride", to mark his victory over the demon king of Tripuri. Chandra Gupta II, renowned for his patronage of the arts, also ruled from here in the fourth and fifth centuries AD. Among the Nava Ratna, or "Nine Gems", of his court was the illustrious Sanskrit poet **Kalidasa**, whose much-loved narrative poem *Meghduta* (Cloud Messenger) includes a lyrical evocation of the city and its inhabitants.

Ujjain was sacked in 1234 by Iltutmish, of the Delhi Slave Dynasty, who razed most of its temples. Thereafter, the Malwan capital was governed by the sultans of Mandu, by the Moghuls, and by **Raja Jai Singh** from Jaipur, who designed, along with many renovation projects elsewhere in India, the Vedha Shala observatory (Ujjain straddles the Hindu first meridian of longitude). Ujjain's fortunes declined from the early eighteenth century onwards, except for a sixty-year renaissance between the arrival of the Scindia dynasty in 1750 and their departure to Gwalior. These days, nearby Indore sees the lion's share of the region's industrial activity, leaving Ujjain's 367,000-strong population to make its living by more traditional means.

Arrival, city transport and information

Trains arriving in Ujjain on both broad-gauge branches of the Western Railway pull in at the station in the centre of town; Ujjain is on a link line between Indore and Bhopal, with regular intercity trains shunting between the three. Two minutes' walk northeast of the station is the **Dewas Gate bus stand**, where buses for Gwalior, Agra, Rajasthan and Bhopal depart. The inconvenient **P.D.V. Bus Stand**, next to the *MPTDC Yatri Niwas,* serves Indore, Bhopal and Mandu. The city is fairly spread out, so you'll need to **get around** by auto-rickshaw or by renting a **bicycle** from the shop opposite the bus stand. Frequent **tempos**, #2 and #9, connect the station to the main temple area. **Taxis** can be arranged through the MPTDC *Hotel Shipra* (℡0734/551495), in the cantonment area, which is also the best source of **information**. The State Bank of India (Mon–Fri 10.30am–2pm, Sat 10.30am–noon) is on Udwaria Road, east of the main bazaar.

Accommodation

Most of Ujjain's limited **accommodation** is within easy walking distance of the railway station, so ignore the auto-rickshaw-wallahs when you arrive, unless you plan to stay in one of the two upmarket hotels, both 2km southeast in the cantonment area. Luxury tax of between 10 and 15 percent is charged on all rooms costing over Rs100. If you plan to stay a while, you could try an **ashram**; *Shri Ram Mandir* (❶) close to Rudra Sagar, is one of the best.

Atlas, Station Road, Indore Gate ℡ 0734/560473. Respectable, well-managed hotel with a goldfish pond in the reception area. All rooms have windows, attached bathrooms and comfortable beds. Close to the station. ❸–❺.

Chandragupta, Subhash Marg ℡0734/561600. Indifferent staff run this cell-block-style lodge opposite the station, the cheapest of the bunch with passably clean but small rooms. ❷–❸.

Girnar, Station Road, Indore Gate ℡0734/554161. Next door to the *Atlas*. Recommended, clean, quiet hotel, with comfortable, good-sized rooms, some with attached shower-toilets. ❸–❺.

MPTDC Shipra, University Road ☏0734/551495. Immaculately tidy, leafy and peaceful place, with large and comfortable rooms, some with a/c. ③–⑥.

MPTDC Yatri Niwas, off Lal Bahadur Shastri Marg ☏0734/511398. Large, institutional block almost 2km out of town, conveniently near the bus station for Mandu. The immaculate partitioned dorms (Rs80) have comfortable beds and clean sheets,

and there are four simple doubles. There's a good restaurant on site too. ③.

Surana Palace, 23 GDC Rd, Dushera Maidan ☏0734/513045. Certainly not a palace, but a large characterless block that is showing its age. However, the rooms and suites are comfortable, and there is a good restaurant. Check-out is 9am. ⑤–⑧.

The City

The Western Railway cuts straight through the centre of the city, forming a neat divide between the spacious and affluent residential suburbs to the south, and the more interesting, densely packed streets northwest of the station. Unless you spend all day wandering through the bazaar, sightseeing in Ujjain usually means treading the temple trail, with a brief foray south of the *ghats* to visit the Vedha Shala observatory.

The Mahakaleshwar Mandir and the Harsiddhi Mandir

Ujjain's chief landmark, the **Mahakaleshwar Mandir**, crowns a rise above the river, and is the logical place to start a tour of the town. Its gigantic saffron-painted sanctuary tower, a modern replacement for the one destroyed by Iltutmish in 1234, soars high above a complex of marble courtyards, water tanks and fountains, advertising the presence below of one of India's most powerful *shivalingams*.

Housed in a claustrophobic subterranean chamber, the *lingam* is mounted on a solid silver base and piled high with floral offerings left by a constant stream of worshippers. All around the sanctum, devotees prostrate themselves before the *lingam*, and the air is thick with incense and the hum of chanting. The *lingam* is one of India's twelve **jyotrilingam** – "*lingam* of light" – whose essential energy, or *shakti*, derives from the earth, rather than from the rituals performed around it, and is considered particularly potent, especially by Tantric followers, due to its unusual south-facing position. A narrow passage leads out of the sanctum to an adjacent courtyard, where several more modern accessory shrines are dedicated to Shiva's consort, Parvati, and their two sons, Ganesh and Kartikeya.

From the Mahakaleshwar Mandir, head west down the hill past the Rudra Sagar tank to another auspicious temple. Hindu mythology identifies the **Harsiddhi Mandir** as the spot where Parvati's elbow fell to earth while Shiva was carrying her burning body from the *sati* pyre. The temple has been a centre of Devi worship ever since. Its main shrine, erected by the Marathas in the eighteenth century, houses (from left to right) images of Mahalakshmi (the goddess of wealth), Annapurna (an incarnation of Durga), and Saraswati (the goddess of wisdom).

The Gopal Mandir

Standing at the end of a chaotic market square, in the heart of the bazaar, the picturesque **Gopal Mandir** was erected by one of the Scindia ranis in the early nineteenth century. With its distinctive blend of Moghul domes, Moorish arches and lofty Hindu sanctuary tower, the temple makes a fine example of late Maratha architecture. Inside, the sanctum's silver-plated doors were placed here by Mahaji Scindia, who rescued them from Lahore after they had been carried off by Muslim looters. The shrine room itself, lined with marble, silver and mother-of-pearl, contains icons of the presiding deity, Gopal (Ganesh), together with his parents, Shiva and Parvati.

The Vedha Shala

In addition to being a major religious centre, Ujjain was the birthplace of mathematical astronomy in India, research into the motion of the stars and planets having been carried out here since the time of Ashok. Later, Hindu astronomers fixed both the **first meridian** of longitude and the Tropic of Cancer here – the reason why Raja Jai Singh of Jaipur, governor of Malwa under the Moghul emperor Mohammad Shah, chose it as the site for another of his surreal open-air observatories. Built in 1725, the **Vedha Shala** (daily sunrise–sunset; free) lies 1km southwest of the railway station, overlooking a bend in the River Shipra. The complex is nowhere near as large as its more famous cousins in Delhi and Jaipur, the Janta Mantars, but remains in excellent condition with very informative guides (their service is free) and labelling. Local astronomers continue to use its five instruments, or *yantras*, to formulate ephemerides (charts predicting the positions of the planets), which you can buy at the site.

Eating

Ujjain suffers from a dearth of decent **places to eat**. Most visitors either stick to their hotel restaurant, or else chance a plate of veg curry, rice and *chapatis* in one of the cheap *dhabas* opposite the railway station.

Ashnoi, University Road. Ujjain's newest and nicest place to eat, with lots of plastic flora, wicker chairs and a/c; the moderately priced menu is excellent pure vegetarian, with a few Chinese dishes thrown in for good measure.
Chanakya, Subhash Marg. The best of several no-frills restaurants opposite the station. Spicy, inexpensive veg food, and chilled beer. The popular *Ankur* next door offers more of the same.
Nauratan, *Shipra Hotel*, University Road. Typical MPTDC restaurant offering tasty veg, Mughlai, tandoori and Chinese dishes, plus some Western options (even fish and chips) and a wide choice of beers and spirits.
New Raj Kumar, 20 Bhaktawar Ganj, Dushera Maidan. Low-priced and unpretentious pure-veg joint, tucked away down a suburban backstreet near *Surana Palace*.
White House, *Surana Palace*, 23 GDC Rd. Wide range of carefully prepared Indian and Chinese vegetarian dishes at moderate prices, served indoors or on the lawn. There's also a fast-food outlet on the premises with pizza, veggie-burgers and ice cream.

Maheshwar

Overlooking the north bank of the mighty River Narmada, 91km southwest of Indore, **MAHESHWAR** has been identified as the site of King Kartvirajun's ancient capital, **Mahishmati**, a city mentioned in both the *Mahabharata* and *Ramayana*. In the eighteenth century, Maharani **Ahilya Bhai** built a palace and several temples here, giving the town a new lease of life. Today, it's a prominent port of call on the Narmada Hindu pilgrimage circuit, but well off the region's tourist trail.

The waterfront **ghats** that line the river below an old sandstone palace, however, make a quintessentially Indian spectacle. Parties of *yatris* take holy dips, drying their clothes in the breeze blowing off the river, while *pujaris* and groups of *sadhus* sit around murmuring prayers under raffia sunshades. If you're not pushed for time, you could enjoy a fifteen-minute ferry trip across the river to the hamlet of **Navdatoli** on the far bank, where archeologists have uncovered evidence of settlement dating from the Lower Paleolithic era – not that there's much to see when you get there.

Once you've had a look at the whitewashed shrines and the **sati stones** dotted around the *ghats*, head for the flight of steps leading under the ornate sandstone facade of the palace to a raised courtyard, where you'll find a pair of eighteenth-century temples. The larger of the two, the **Ahilya Bhai Mandir**, has an overhanging balcony wrapped around its tower with a great-bird's eye view over the waterfront.

The **palace** and **fort** complex itself, further up the steps, houses the workshops of the Rewa Society, established by the maharani 250 years ago to promote the local handloom industry. Maheshwari **saris** are famous all over India for their distinctive patterns and superior quality; check out the designs for yourself by visiting the weavers' workshops (Mon–Fri 10am–5pm), which are sponsored by a German aid project. Though descendants of the old ruling family still occupy parts of the building, a couple of rooms around the entrance courtyard have been given over to a small **museum** (leave your shoes at the entrance). Exhibits include a life-size effigy of the devout Ahilya Bhai (shown seated on her throne, or *rajgadi*), a couple of moth-eaten palladins, old photographs of the Holkar dynasty, and the shrine from which Maheshwar's annual Dussehra festival begins.

Practicalities

Accommodation is limited to the *Ahilya Trust Guest House* (❶), a charitable institution near the palace, and the handful of rudimentary *dharamshalas* around the small square behind the *ghats*. This, in part, explains why many visitors prefer to visit as a day-trip. All roads to Maheshwar are in a terrible state, so allow extra time for pothole negotiation if you are in a private car – the journey from Mandu can take up to four hours, and from Indore, at least three. There is a shady car park in the fort area (Rs10), just near the entrance to the museum. **Buses** also run from Dhar (every 20min; 2hr). Buses from Indore are fairly frequent, taking three and a half hours, with a change at the market town of Dhamnod, 76km southwest of Indore on the NH-3. The nearest railhead is at **Barwaha**, 39km west.

Places to eat are thin on the ground, as the majority of visitors to the town are pilgrims who cook their own food. Try a vegetarian meal in one of the *dhabas* on the square if your digestive system is up to it.

Omkareshwar

East of the main river crossing at Barhawa, the Narmada dips southwards, sweeps north again to form a wide bend, and then forks around a two-kilometre-long wedge-shaped outcrop of sandstone. Seen from above, the island, cut by several deep ravines, bears an uncanny resemblance to the "Om" symbol. This, coupled with the presence on its sheer south-facing side of a revered *shivalingam*, has made **OMKARESHWAR**, 77km south of Indore, one of the most sacred Hindu sites in central India.

Since ancient times, pilgrims have flocked here for *darshan* and a holy dip in the river. In recent years, it has also become one of the "in" places on the freak circuit, with long-stay Westerners vying with the *sadhus* in the dreadlocks and chillum-smoking stakes. Still, if you can stomach all that, it can be an atmospheric diversion, with ruined temples, wayside shrines, bathing places and caves strung together by an old paved pilgrims' trail.

From the bus stand at the bottom of the village on the mainland, Omkareshwar's only street runs 400m uphill to a ramshackle square, where you'll find most of the *dharamshalas* and chai shops, and a handful of stalls hawking lurid *puja* paraphernalia (including the excellent stylized **maps** taken home by pilgrims as souvenirs of their visits). To get to the island itself, cross the high concrete footbridge or take one of the flat-bottomed ferries that shuttle between the *ghats* crouched at the foot of the river gorge. Once across, you're soon swallowed up by the crowded narrow lane leading to the main temple.

The prominent white *shikhara* that now soars above the **Shri Omkar Mandhata Mandir** is a relatively new addition to the dense cluster of buildings on the south side of the island. Below it, the ornate pillars in the assembly hall, or *mandapa*, are more representative of the shrine's great antiquity. Myths relating to the origins of the deity in the low-ceilinged sanctum date back to the second century BC. Another of India's twelve **jyotrilinga** ("*linga* of light"), it is said by Hindus to have emerged spontaneously from the earth after a struggle between Brahma, Vishnu and Shiva.

Around the island

Traditionally, the *parikrama* (circular tour) of Omkareshwar begins at the *ghats* below Shri Mandhata and proceeds clockwise **around the island**. The walk takes at least a couple of hours, so carry plenty of water if you plan to do the whole thing in one go.

The first section of the trail is a leisurely half-hour stroll from the footbridge to the pebble-strewn western tip of the island, where you'll find a small chai stall and a couple of insignificant shrines. The **Trivendi Sangam**, or "Three-rivers Confluence", is an especially propitious bathing place, where the Narmada forks as it merges with the Kaveri. From here, the path climbs above the fringe of fine white sand lining the northern shore until it reaches level ground. The ruins of the **Gaudi Somnath temple** stand in the middle of the plateau, surrounded by a sizeable collection of sculpture mounted on concrete plinths. The sanctuary houses a colossal *shivalingam*, attended by an equally huge Nandi bull. At this point, drop down a steep flight of steps to the village, or continue east towards the old fortified town that crowned the top of the island before it was ransacked by Muslims in the medieval era. Numerous chunks of temple sculpture, lying discarded among the rubble, include a couple of finely carved gods and goddesses, used for shade by families of black-faced langur monkeys.

After scaling the sides of a gully, the trail leads under the large ornamental archway of the **Surajkund Gate**, flanked by three-metre figures of Arjun and Bheema, two of the illustrious Pandava brothers. The tenth-century **Siddhesvara temple** stands five-minutes' walk away to the south, on a patch of flat ground overlooking the river. Raised on a large plinth decorated with rampaging elephants, it has some fine *apsaras*, or female fertility figures, carved over its southern doorway, and a donatory Sanskrit inscription.

Of the two possible routes back to the village, one takes you along the top of the plateau before dropping sharply down, via another ruined temple and the **maharaja's palace**, to the Shri Mandhata temple. The other follows a flight of steps to the river-bank, and then heads past a group of *sadhus'* caves to the main *ghats*.

Practicalities

Omkareshwar is connected by state **bus** to Khandwa (4 daily; 2hr 30min) and Indore (3 daily; 4–6hr). You can also get here by catching the Indore to Khandwa bus as far as **Omkareshwar Road**, a junction and chai stop on NH-3, from where a beaten-up local bus runs the remaining 15km. Omkareshwar Road is also the nearest railhead, but only slow passenger services stop here. Barhawa, on the north bank of the Narmada, is the closest main-line railway station.

The nearest **bank** with a foreign exchange counter is at Indore. A small **post office** on the main street, however, offers reliable poste restante.

The range of **accommodation** has expanded recently, with more lodges and the privilege of attached baths in some rooms. For those seeking the ascetic experience, the central *dharamshalas* in the mainland village, are cheap (Rs20–50), and offer close-hand experience of pilgrim culture. On the down side, *dharamshala* rooms tend to be windowless cells, with washing facilities limited to a standpipe in the yard (to encourage people to use the river) and communal toilets. One of the best is *Jat Samaj* (●), facing the river, to the right of the bridge on the main square – look for the rooftop figure on horseback. Another favourite is *Ahilya Bhai* (●), tucked away behind the Vishnu temple off the road to Mamaleshwar temple and the *ghats*. This and its close neighbour, *Tirole Kunbi Patel* (●), have great views over the river to the Om island from their balconies and roof terraces. If these are full, try the massive *Raja Pratap* (●) towering over the main square. It's the only one with a sign in English, and is fine for a night's stay.

If you can't face a spell in a *dharamshala*, there are a few alternatives. The peaceful *Yatrika Niwas* (❸), behind the bus stand, has spartan but clean rooms, some with bathrooms; the distance from the *ghats* reduces the impact of devotional music played there early each morning. Just off the square before it joins the bridge a flight of stone steps leads to *Maharajah Guest House* (℡07280/71237; ❷–❸), a delightful family house shaded by bougainvillea with ten rooms, each with an attached bath. Quiet and cosy, it is a long-established bastion for chronic hippies searching for spirituality in comfort. Alternatively, directly opposite the Shri Omkar Mandhata Mandir, the new *Hotel Ashwaria* (❷–❸) has simple, clean doubles (all non-a/c) and attached bathrooms, and a restaurant. Visitors with their own vehicle may also manage to talk their way into the large, pink, and very pukka *Irrigation Project Guest House* (❹) at the top of the hill, whose clean, comfortable rooms are normally reserved for visiting engineers.

Long-stay visitors and pilgrims tend to opt for cooking their own **meals** using stoves provided by the *dharamshalas* or bought at minimal cost in the bazaar, where you can also get basic provisions. The alternatives are the good, pure-veg restaurant at *Hotel Ashwaria*, which is a safe bet, or the cheap fiery, greasy, vegetarian dishes (no meat or eggs at this sacred spot) from the grungy chai stalls around the square. The best, which cooks dishes to order, is just by the bridge, or you could try the friendly *Jay Ambe Bhojnalaya* café by the bus stand. Don't risk eating at the food stalls on the island.

Travel details

Trains

Bhopal to: Agra (16–20 daily; 5hr 30min–10hr); Chennai (3–5 daily; 23–32hr); Delhi (18–22 daily; 7hr 45min–15hr); Goa (1 daily; 30hr); Gwalior (17–22 daily; 4hr 15min–7hr); Indore (4–6 daily; 5hr–8hr 15 min); Jabalpur (3–4 daily; 6–7hr); Jalgaon (2–3 daily; 7–9hr); Jhansi (22–26 daily; 3hr–5hr 40min); Manmad (for Aurangabad; 7–10 daily; 9hr–11hr 30min); Mumbai (4 daily; 14hr 55min–18hr); Nagpur (12–15 daily; 5hr 30min–9hr

30min); Pune (2–3 daily; 16–17hr); Sanchi (2 daily;
45–55min); Ujjain (4–6 daily; 3hr–5hr); Vidisha
(3–4 daily; 40–50min).

Gwalior to: Agra (23–26 daily; 1hr 10min–2hr
20min); Bhopal (19–24 daily; 3hr 40min–7hr);
Calcutta (4 weekly; 22hr 30min–24hr 30min);
Chennai (2–4 daily; 28–40hr); Delhi (21–25 daily;
3hr 50min–9hr); Goa (1 daily; 36hr 35min); Indore
(1daily; 13hr); Jabalpur (2 daily; 11hr 50min–13hr
20min); Jalgaon (2 daily; 12hr 30min–16hr
30min); Jhansi (22–26 daily; 1hr–2hr 45min);
Mumbai (5–6 daily; 20hr–25hr); Pune (2–3 daily;
21–24hr); Puri (1 daily; 39hr); Satna (1–2 daily;
10hr); Ujjain (1–2 daily; 13hr); Vidisha (5–6 daily;
4hr 30min–6hr).

Indore to: Agra (1–2 daily; 14hr 30min–16hr);
Ajmer (2 daily; 13hr 30min–16hr); Bhopal (2–4
daily; 4hr 45min–8hr); Calcutta (3 weekly; 34hr);
Chennai (Mon only; 34hr); Chittaurgarh (2 daily;
7hr 30min–8hr 35min); Delhi (2–3 daily;
10hr–18hr 20min); Gwalior (1–2 daily; 12hr
40min–13hr 15min); Jabalpur (1 daily; 15hr
35min); Jaipur (1–2 daily; 12–16hr); Jhansi (1
daily; 11min); Kota (1–2 daily; 6hr 30min–7hr
40min); Mumbai (1 daily; 15hr); Ujjain (4–5 daily;
1hr 30min–2hr).

Jabalpur to: Bhopal (2–3 daily; 6hr 30min–7hr
20min); Calcutta (1 daily; 23–25hr); Chennai (1–2
daily; 23hr 45min–32hr); Delhi (2 daily; 15hr
40min–19hr 40min); Gwalior (2 daily; 10–13hr);
Indore (1 daily; 15hr 45min); Jhansi (3 daily; 8hr
50min–11hr); Mumbai (3–5 daily; 18–20hr); Patna
(2–4 daily; 12hr 30min–16hr 30min); Satna (3–4
daily; 3hr); Ujjain (1 daily; 13hr); Varanasi (4–7
daily; 8hr–11hr 45min).

Ujjain to: Ahmedabad (1–2 daily; 9–11hr); Agra
(2–3 daily; 12hr 10min–16hr); Bhopal (5–6 daily;
3hr–6hr 15min); Calcutta (3 weekly; 32hr);
Chennai (6 weekly; 32hr 30min–33hr 30min);
Delhi (2–3 daily; 12hr–21hr 30min); Gwalior (1–2
daily; 10hr 40min); Indore (4–6 daily; 1hr
50min–2hr 30min); Jabalpur (1–2 daily; 10hr
40min–13hr); Jaipur (6 weekly; 8hr 45min–10hr);
Jhansi (2–4 daily; 9–10hr); Nagpur (4 weekly;
12hr); Varanasi (3 weekly; 31hr 35min).

Buses

Bhopal to: Indore (every 15min; 5–6hr); Jabalpur
(3 daily; 8–10hr); Nagpur (5 daily; 10–11hr);
Pachmarhi (4 daily; 5–6hr); Sanchi (hourly; 1hr
30min–2hr); Ujjain (hourly; 5–6hr); Vidisha (hourly;
2hr–2hr 30min).

Gwalior to: Agra (hourly; 2–3hr); Datia (every
30min; 1hr 40min–2hr); Delhi (4 daily; 8hr); Jhansi
(every 30min; 3hr); Khajuraho (4 daily; 7–9hr);
Shivpuri (every 30min; 2hr–2hr 30); Ujjain (3 daily;
12hr).

Indore to: Agra (1 daily; 16hr); Aurangabad (3
daily; 14hr); Bhopal (hourly; 5–6hr); Chittaurgarh (1
daily; 10hr); Dhar (every 30min; 2–3hr); Jaipur (3
nightly; 15hr); Kota (4 daily; 8–9hr); Mandu (3
daily; 4hr); Mumbai (2 daily; 20hr); Nagpur (1
daily; 14hr); Omkareshwar (3 daily; 4–6hr);
Udaipur (6 daily; 15hr); Ujjain (every 15min; 1hr
30min–2hr).

Jabalpur to: Khajuraho (5 daily; 7–9hr); Kisli (for
Kanha; 2 daily; 5–7hr); Mandla (hourly; 3hr);
Murwara (for Bandhavgarh; every 30min; 2hr);
Nagpur (12 daily; 7hr); Satna (6–8 daily; 8hr).

Khajuraho to: Agra (1 daily; 8hr–13hr); Bhopal (2
daily; 10hr); Gwalior (1 daily; 6hr–9hr); Jhansi (7
daily; 4–6hr); Mahoba (5 daily; 3hr); Panna (4
daily; 1hr); Satna (5 daily; 4hr); Varanasi (1 nightly;
16–18hr)

Ujjain to: Agra (2 daily; 15hr); Delhi (1 daily; 21hr);
Dhar (5 daily; 4hr); Gwalior (2 daily; 12hr); Kota (10
daily; 8hr); Maheshwar (4 daily; 5hr);
Omkareshwar (3 daily; 6–7hr).

Flights

Bhopal to: Delhi (1 daily; 1hr 10min–2hr); Gwalior
(2 weekly; 45min); Indore (1 daily; 30min);
Mumbai (1 daily; 2hr 5min).

Gwalior to: Bhopal (2 weekly; 45min); Delhi (5
weekly; 45min–1hr 5min); Indore (2 weekly; 1hr
45min); Jabalpur (3 weekly; 1hr 25min); Mumbai
(2 weekly; 3hr 20min).

Indore to: Bhopal (1 daily; 30min); Delhi (1 daily;
2hr 10min–3hr); Gwalior (2 weekly; 1hr 45min);
Mumbai (1 daily; 1hr 5min).

Jabalpur to: Delhi (3 weekly; 2hr 55min); Gwalior
(3 weekly; 1hr 30min).

Khajuraho to: Agra (1 daily; 40min); Delhi (2 daily;
1hr 50min); Varanasi (2 daily; 40min).

CHAPTER 6

Highlights

* **Narrow-gauge railway** A rattly ride through stunning mountain scenery to the Raj-era hill station of Shimla. **See p.522**

* **Rewalsar** Buddhist pilgrimage site based around a sacred lake, with monasteries, temples, caves and hermitages. **See p.539**

* **Dharamsala** This relaxing hill station, home of the Dalai Lama, is an ever-popular place for rest, meditation retreats and trekking. **See p.542**

* **Dharamsala trek** A fantastic five-day trek leading through Dhaula Dhar forest to the Indriha pass, visiting traditional villages. **See p.552**

* **Manikaran hot springs** Sacred to Sikhs and Hindus, this steamy settlement stands at the gateway to the spectacular Parvati Valley. **See p.565**

* **Manali** Travellers en route to Ladakh chill out at this honeymoon capital, enjoying Himalayan panoramas from flower-filled gardens. **See p.569**

* **Spiti valley** Tiny Tibetan villages and beautiful white *gompas* dot Spiti's lunar landscape. **See p.583**

* **Manali–Leh highway** The second-highest road in the world, passing through a vast wilderness. **See p.587**

6

Himachal Pradesh

Ruffled by the lower ridges of the Shivalik Range in the far south, cut through by the Pir Panjal and Dhauladhar ranges in the northwest, and dominated by the great Himalayas in the north and east, **HIMACHAL PRADESH** (HP) is India's most popular and easily accessible hill state. Sandwiched between the Punjab and Tibet, its lowland orchards, subtropical forests and maize fields peter out in the higher reaches where pines cling to the steep slopes of mountains whose inhospitable peaks soar in rocky crags and forbidding ice fields to heights of more than 6000m.

Together with deep gorges cut by rivers crashing down from the Himalayas, these mountains form natural boundaries between the state's separate districts. Each has its own architecture, from rock-cut shrines and *shikhara* temples to colonial mansions and Buddhist monasteries. Roads struggle against the vagaries of the climate to connect the larger settlements, which are way out-numbered by remote villages, many of which are home to semi-nomadic **Gaddi** and **Gujjar** shepherds.

An obvious way to approach the state is to head north from Delhi to the state capital, **Shimla**, beyond the lush and temperate valleys of **Sirmaur**. The former summer location of the British government, Shimla is a curious, appealing mix of grand homes, churches and chaotic bazaars, with a favourable climate and breathtaking views. The main road **northeast** from Shimla tackles a pass just north of **Narkanda**, then follows the River Sutlej east to **Sarahan**, with its spectacular wooden temple, and enters the eastern district of **Kinnaur**, most of which is accessible only to those holding **Inner Line permits** (see p.518). Alpine and green in the west, Kinnaur becomes more austere and barren as it stretches east to the Tibetan plateau, its stag-gering beauty enhanced by delicate timber houses, temples and fluttering prayer flags.

Another road from Shimla climbs slowly northwest to **Mandi**, a major stag-ing post for the state. To the north is Himachal's most popular tourist spot, the **Kullu valley**, an undulating mass of terraced fields, orchards and forests over-looked by snowy peaks. Its epicentre is the rapidly expanding tourist town of **Manali**, sixteen hours by bus from Delhi. Long a favourite hangout of Western hippies, Manali is set in idyllic mountain scenery and offers trekking, white-water rafting and relaxing hot springs in nearby **Vashisht**. The sacred site of **Manikaran** in the Parvati valley has a large Sikh Gurudwara, small Hindu temple and deliciously hot sulphur-free springs.

Beyond the Rohtang Pass in the far north of Kullu district, the high-altitude desert valleys of **Lahaul and Spiti** stretch beneath massive snowcapped peaks and remote settlements with Tibetan *gompas* dotting the landscape. **Permits** are needed for travel through to Kinnaur, but **Ki**, **Kaza**, and **Tabo** are open, as is the road through Lahaul to Leh in Ladakh.

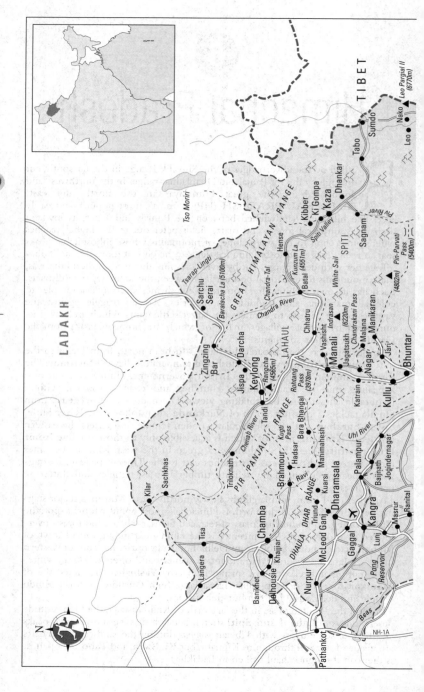

TIBET

Leo Pargial II
(6770m)

Nako

Leo

Sumdo

Tabo

Dhankar

Ki Gompa

Kaza

Kibber

Pin River

Spiti Valley

SPITI

Sagnam

Hense

Pin-Parvati
Pass
(5400m)

GREAT HIMALAYAN RANGE

Kunzum La (4551m)

Batal

White Sail

Chandrakani Pass

(4802m)

Chandra-Tal

Chatru

Indrasan
(6220m)

Chandra River

Vashisht

Jagatsukh

Malana

Manikaran

Tso Moriri

Tsarap-Lingti

Baralacha La (5100m)

Sarchu
Serai

LAHAUL

Manali

Nagar

Jari

Bhuntar

LADAKH

Darcha

Zingzing
Bar

Jispa

Keylong

Rangcha
(4565m)

Tandi

Chenab River

Rohtang
Pass
(3978m)

Katrain

Kullu

PIR PANJAL RANGE

Kugti
Pass

Bara Bhangal

Uhl River

Palampur

Bajinath

Jogindernagar

Kilar

Sachkhas

Triloknath

Brahmour

Hadsar

Manimahesh

Ravi

Kuarsi

Dharamsala

Ranital

Chamba

Tisa

Khajjiar

McLeod Ganj

Triund

DHAULA DHAR RANGE

Gaggal

Kangra

Luni

Masrur

Langera

Banikhet

Dalhousie

Nurpur

Pong
Reservoir

Beas

Pathankot

NH-1A

N

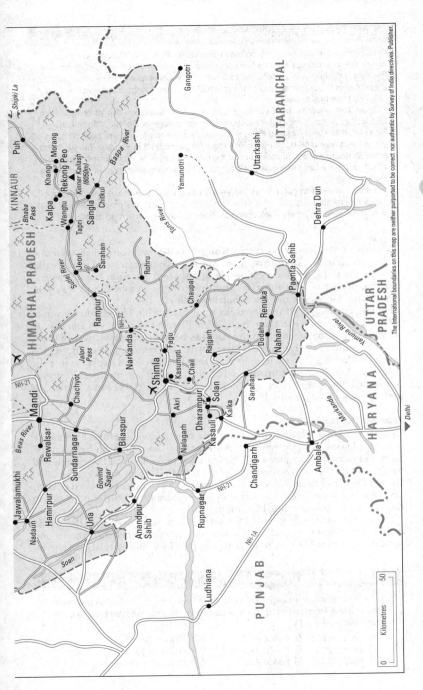

The International boundaries on this map are neither purported to be correct nor authentic by Survey of India directives. Publisher.

Foreigners travelling between between Sumdo in Spiti and Morang in Kinnaur – where the road passes within a few kilometres of Western Tibet – require **Inner Line Permits**. Officially you are required to travel in a group of four or more organized by a travel agent, but it is possible for individual travellers to obtain a permit and proceed by local bus or Jeep.

Inner Line Permits are valid for seven days and available free of charge from District Magistrates' or District Commissioners' offices in **Shimla, Manali, Kullu, Rampur, Kaza** and **Rekong Peo**. If travelling independently, you're best off applying at **Kaza** (see p.584) in Spiti or **Rekong Peo** (see p.533) in Kinnaur. You will need three photographs and photocopies of the relevant pages of your passport and visa. When you get your permit make at least four photocopies to present at checkpoints along the way.

When travelling through restricted areas, you should never take photographs of military installations or sensitive sites like bridges. Stick to the main route and you should have no problems – excepting perhaps the state of the road itself.

Visitors to the densely populated **Kangra valley** west of Manali invariably make a beeline for **Dharamsala**, whose large community of Tibetan exiles includes the Dalai Lama himself. Trekking paths lead east from here to the tea-growing district of **Palampur**, and north across the treacherous passes of the Dhauladhar mountains into the **Chamba Valley**.

Finding guides and porters for **treks** is rarely difficult. The season runs from July to late November in the west, and late October in the north and east. In **winter**, all but the far south of the state lies beneath a thick blanket of snow, enticing groups of adventurous skiers to try out remote pistes. The region north of Manali is accessible only from late June to early October when the roads are clear. Even in **summer**, when the days are hot and the sun strong, northern Himachal is beset with cold nights; always carry warm clothes, or pick up a locally made shawl.

Some history

The earliest known inhabitants of the area now known as Himachal Pradesh were the **Dasas**, who entered the hills from the Gangetic plain between the third and second millennium BC, having been pushed out of their homeland by the Indus Valley civilization that swept into India from the West. By 2000 BC the Dasas had been joined by the **Aryans**, and a number of tribal republics, known as *janapadas*, began to emerge in geographically separate regions, where they fostered separate cultural traditions.

The terrain made it impossible for one ruler to hold sway over the whole region. The **Guptas** forged inroads into the mountains between the second and fifth centuries AD, only to be ousted in turn by Vardhana rulers, then petty

Accommodation price codes

All accommodation prices in this book have been categorized using the price codes below. Prices given are for a double room, and all taxes are included. For more details, see p.51.

❶ up to Rs100   ❹ Rs300–400   ❼ Rs900–1500
❷ Rs100–200   ❺ Rs400–600   ❽ Rs1500–2500
❸ Rs200–300   ❻ Rs600–900   ❾ Rs2500 and upwards

Rana and Thakur chieftains, and ultimately the Hindu **Rajputs**. As early as 550AD Rajput families had gained supremacy over the northwestern districts of Brahmour and Chamba, just two of the many princely states created between the sixth and sixteenth centuries. Of these, the most powerful was **Kangra**, where the Katoch Rajputs held off attacks on their treasure-stocked fort from the sultans, Mahmud of Ghazni (1009 AD), and the Tughluqs (fourteenth century) before finally falling to the Moghuls in the sixteenth century.

During the medieval era, **Lahaul and Spiti** remained aloof, governed not by Rajputs, but by the Jos of Tibetan origin, who introduced Tibetan customs and architecture, and profited from trade between India, Lhasa and Samarkand. After a period of submission to Ladakh, Lahaul and Spiti came under the rajas of **Kullu**, a central princely state that reached its apogee in the seventeenth century. Further south, the region around **Shimla** and **Sirmaur** was divided into over thirty independently governed *thakurais*. In the late seventeenth century, the newly empowered **Sikh** community, based at **Paonta Sahib** (Sirmaur), added to the threat already posed by the Moghuls. By the eighteenth century, under **Maharaja Ranjit Singh**, the Sikhs had gained strongholds in much of western Himachal, and considerable power in both Kullu and Spiti.

Battling against Sikh expansion, Amar Singh Tapur, the leader of the **Gurkha** army set on extending his own Nepalese dominion, failed to take Kangra, but consolidated power in the southern Shimla hill states. The *thakurai* chiefs turned to the **British** for help, and forced the last of the Gurkhas back into Nepal in 1815. Predictably, the British assumed power over the south, thus tempting the Sikhs to battle in the **Anglo–Sikh War**. With the signing of a treaty in 1846 the British annexed most of the south and west of the state, and in 1864 pronounced Shimla, a cool retreat for British officers and their families, the summer government headquarters.

After Independence, the regions bordering present–day Punjab were integrated, named Himachal Pradesh ("Himalayan Provinces"), and administered by a chief commissioner. By 1956, HP was recognized as a Union Territory, and in 1966 the state as it exists today was formed, with Shimla as its capital.

Despite being a political unity, Himachal Pradesh is hardly culturally homogeneous. With over ninety percent of the population living outside the main towns, and many areas remaining totally isolated during the long winter months, Himachal's separate districts maintain distinct customs, architecture, dress and agricultural methods. Though Hinduism dominates, there are substantial numbers of Sikhs, Muslims and Christians, and Lahaul, Spiti and Kinnaur have been home to Tibetan Buddhists since the tenth century.

Shimla and around

Shimla, Himachal's capital, is India's largest and most famous hill station, where much of the action in Rudyard Kipling's colonial classic *Kim* took place. While the city is a favourite spot for Indian families and honeymooners, its size does little to win it popularity among Western tourists who tend to pass through on their way to Manali. It is however, a perfect halfway house if you're heading to the Kullu Valley, or back in the other direction towards the plains of Haryana and Punjab. It's also the starting post for forays into the remoter regions of Kinnaur and Spiti.

The southernmost area of the state, **Sirmaur**, is Himachal's most fertile area and enjoys an equable climate. **Nahan**, the capital, holds little of interest, but the major Sikh shrine in **Paonta Sahib** and **Renuka** wildlife sanctuary are worth visiting if you have your own transport. Southeast of Shimla, **Kausali** is a peaceful place to break your journey from Chandigarh, whilst nearby **Nalagarh Fort** has been converted into the finest hotel in the state.

Northeast of Shimla, the village of **Sarahan**, site of the famous Bhimakali temple, set against a spectacular backdrop of soaring peaks, can be visited in a two- or three-day round trip from Shimla, or en route to Spiti.

Shimla

Whether you travel by road or rail, the last stretch of the climb up to **SHIMLA** seems interminable. Deep in the foothills of the Himalayas, the hill station is approached via an unfeasibly sinuous route that winds from the plains at Kalka across nearly 100km of precipitous river valleys, pine forests, and mountainsides swathed in maize terraces and apple orchards. It's not hard to see why the British chose this inaccessible site as their summer capital. At an altitude of 2159m, the crescent-shaped ridge over which it spills is blessed with perennially cool air, crisp light, and superb **panoramas** across verdant, undulating country to the snowy peaks of the Great Himalayan range.

Named after its patron goddess, Shamla Devi (a manifestation of Kali), the tiny village that stood on this spot was "discovered" by a team of British surveyors in 1817. Shortly afterwards, groups of battle-weary army officers began to trickle up here between skirmishes with the Gurkhas in the Sutlej Valley. Glowing reports of its beauty and climate gradually filtered to the imperial capital, Calcutta, and within a decade, the ridges around Shimla were peppered with bungalows and holiday cottages. The British finally persuaded the local raja to part with the land in 1830, and the settlement became the subcontinent's most fashionable summer resort. Each year, long trains of packhorses and coolies picked their way up from the plains, bringing with them the Raj's top brass, and legions of grass-widows whose husbands were obliged to sweat it out at lower elevations. The annual migration was finally rubber-stamped in 1864, when Shimla – now an elegant town of mansions, churches and cricket pitches – was declared the Government of India's official hot-season HQ. The civil servants had to carry on business as usual, but for most of its temporary residents, the summer capital was an endless round of garden parties, formal dinners, high teas, balls, bridge games and evening promenades along the main street, the Mall. With the completion of the **Kalka–Shimla Railway** in 1903, Shimla lay only two days by train from Delhi. Its meteoric rise continued after Independence, when, following the reorganization of the Punjab in 1966, Shimla became state capital of Himachal Pradesh.

Today, Shimla is still a major holiday resort, popular mainly with nouveau riche Punjabis and Delhi-ites who flock here in their thousands during the May–June run-up to the monsoons, and then again in September and October. Its jaded colonial charm also appeals to foreigners looking for a taste

SHIMLA

▲ Kufri

N

ACCOMMODATION			
The Cecil		Sangeet	12
Chanakya		Uphar	5
Chapslee		Vikrant	3
Dreamland		White	13
Fontaine Bleau		Woodland	7
Oberoi Clarks	10	Woodville Palace	2
Pineview	14	YMCA	16
Ranjan		YWCA	8
			4
			11
			6

RESTAURANTS	
Ashiana	C
Baljee's	D
Choice	E
Devico's	A
Fascination	D
Goofa	C
Himani	G
Indian Coffee House	B
Nalini	I
New Plaza	F
Sher-e-Punjab	H

Jakhu Temple
2455m

Narkanda, Rampur & Kinnaur ◄

LAKKAR BAZAAR

Christ Church

THE RIDGE

RAJ BHAVAN ROAD

Lift

Taxi Rank

Rivoli Bus Stand

HPTDC Tourist Office

Town Hall

THE MALL

BAZAAR

Gaiety Theatre

Bank of Baroda

ANZ Grindlay's Bank

GPO

SCANDAL POINT

UCO Bank

State Bank of India

Taxis

CART RD

Main Bus Stand

Railway Station

VICTORY TUNNEL

THE MALL

Taxi Rank

Metres

0   200

Kalka, Chandigarh, Delhi & Airport ▲ (21 km)   ▲ Museum & Viceregal Lodge

The Viceroy's toy train

Until the construction of the **Kalka–Shimla railway**, the only way to get to the Shimla hill station was on the so-called **Cart Road** – a slow, winding trail trodden by lines of long-suffering porters and horse-drawn tongas. Plans for a narrow-gauge railway had been started as early as 1847, but it took the intervention of the viceroy himself, **Lord Curzon**, to get the massive undertaking off the ground.

By the time the 96-kilometre line was completed in 1897, 103 tunnels, 24 bridges, and 18 stations had been built between Shimla and the railhead at Kalka, 26km northeast of Chandigarh. These days, buses may be quicker, but a ride on the "toy train" is far more memorable – especially if you travel first-class, in one of the glass-sided rail cars. Hauled along by a tiny blue-and-white diesel locomotive, they rattle at a leisurely pace through stunning scenery, taking between five-and-a-half and seven hours to reach Shimla.

Along the route, you'll notice the guards exchanging little leather pouches with staff strategically positioned on the station platforms. The bags they receive in return contain small brass discs, which the drivers slot into special machines to alert the signals ahead of their approach. **"Neal's Token System"**, in place since the line was first inaugurated, is a fail-safe means of ensuring that trains travelling in opposite directions never meet face to face on the single-track sections of the railway.

For information about train times and ticket booking, see p.528.

of the Raj. The *burra-* and *memsahibs* may have moved on, but Shimla retains a decidedly **British feel**: pukka Indian gentlemen in tweeds stroll along the Mall smoking pipes, while neatly turned-out schoolchildren scuttle past mock-Tudor shop-fronts and houses with names like *Braeside*. At the same time, the dense, chaotic mass of corrugated iron rooftops immediately below the ridge, Shimla's **bazaar**, lends an unmistakably Indian aspect to the town, an active market and gateway for the northwestern Himalayan region.

The **best time to visit** is during October and November, before the Himachali winter sets in, when the days are still warm and dry, and the morning skies are clear. From December to late February, heavy snow is common, and temperatures hover around, or below zero. The spring brings with it unpredictability: warm blasts of air from the plains, and flurries of freezing rain from the mountains. Try to avoid the two **high seasons** (mid-April to mid-June & mid-Sept to mid-Jan), when accommodation is scarce and expensive. Whenever you come, though, bring plenty of warm clothes as the nights can get surprisingly chilly.

Arrival, information and local transport

Buses arriving on the main Chandigarh and Manali highways approach Shimla from the west, via Cart Road and pull in at the chaotic main **bus stand**, halfway around the hill. Buses from Narkanda, Rampur and Kinnaur arrive at the **Rivoli bus stand** (or "Lakkar Bazaar") on the north side of the Ridge, though some continue to the **main bus stand**. Shimla's **airport** lies 21km southeast of town on the Mandi road at Jubarhati.

The HPTDC main **tourist office** (daily: high season 9am–7pm; low season 9am–6pm; ☎0177/252561, ⊛www.hptdc.nic.in), is located on the Mall near Scandal Point. They organize whistle-stop **sightseeing tours** to destinations around Shimla, including Kufri, Chail, Narkanda and Sarahan, as well as Heritage Walks (2–3hr; Rs50) around Shimla, and helicopter rides (3 routes, prices according to route and number of passengers). To venture into the more remote and challenging regions such as Kinnaur and Spiti, check out the many mountaineering and trekking agencies on the Mall. For a list of recommended operators see p.527.

Local transport

Wherever you arrive in Shimla, you'll be mobbed by **porters**. Most of the town is pedestrianized, and seriously steep, so you may be glad of the extra help to carry your gear, but bear in mind that most porters double as touts and demand a commission which will increase the cost of your room. **Taxis**, which line up outside the Tourist Reception Centre on Cart Road, are the best way to get to the pricier hotels on the outskirts. The main Vishal Himachal Taxi Union rank (☎0177/257645) is 1km east of the bus stand, at the bottom of the **elevator** (Rs5 each way) that connects the east end of Cart Road with the Mall. The list of set fares they publish applies to high season; at other times, you should be able to negotiate discounts. Other, more central, taxi ranks can be found just above the main bus station and near the tourist office on Cart Road. The elevator, known as "the lift", consists of two stages connected by a corridor midway – keep your ticket, bought from the operator, with you for the second stage.

Accommodation

Most travellers only spend a couple of nights in Shimla – long enough to see the sights, and to book an onward ticket. There's little to detain you any longer, and **accommodation** is, in the main, phenomenally expensive. Between mid-April and mid-September, tariffs double; during May, June and July, finding anywhere at all to stay is impossible if you haven't booked in advance. At other times it's worth trying to negotiate a **discount**: a fifty percent reduction is usual from November to early April. The prices listed here are for high season.

The Cecil, the Mall ☎ 0177/204848, or reserve through Delhi ☎ 011/436 3030. A piece of Shimla's history. Bought and revamped by the Oberoi group, it is luxurious but devoid of character, with little but the facade as a reminder of its past. Rooms $225–275. **⑨**

Chanakya, Lakkar Bazaar ☎ 0177/254465. Cosy, clean and central. The cheaper rooms are good value. **④**–**⑤**

Chapslee, Lakkar Bazaar ☎ 0177/202542, ⓔ chapslee@vsnl.com. Beautiful old manor house which captures Shimla's grand past; set in its own grounds on the edge of town and stuffed with antiques. Five luxurious suites, one single room, and a library, card room, tennis court, and croquet lawn. Book in advance. Meals also available to non-guests if booked in advance. **⑨**

Dreamland, the Ridge, above the church ☎ 0177/206897. Good-value during the low season, with clean rooms, most with hot water, Star TV, and views of the Himalayas. **⑤**–**⑥**

Fontaine Bleau, below the Kali temple, near the Mall ☎ 0177/253549. Simple rooms in a friendly eccentric family house just a short walk up from the station. Don't arrive with a porter as they won't pay a commission. Good value. **②**–**③**

Oberoi Clarks, the Mall ☎ 0177/251010. Period building converted into a very comfortable, formula five-star. Rooms $132, plus 10 percent tax, with all meals included. **⑨**

Pineview, Mythe Estate, below the Mall ☎ 0177/257045. A good location facing north on the far side of the Victory tunnel, with a wide choice of comfortable rooms. **⑤**–**⑦**

Ranjan, just above the bus stand. Large white building with simple rooms, some original fittings and a sunny balcony. Good if you can't face the climb up the hill from the bus stand. **④**

Sangeet, the Mall ☎ 0177/202506–7. Friendly, comfortable, modern hotel. Good value. **⑥**–**⑦**

Uphar, the Ridge, near the *Dreamland* ☎ 0177/257670. Friendly place, large rooms some with Star TV and balcony: all have hot showers. **④**–**⑤**

Vikrant, Cart Road, near the station ☎ 0177/253602. Handy for late arrivals and early departures. Large hotel with some singles. All rooms have TV. **⑤**

White, Lakkar Bazaar ☎ 0177/256136. Centrally located and well-managed hotel, with immaculate, light rooms with views. Deluxe suites excellent. Recommended. ⑤–⑦

Woodland, Daisy Bank Estate ☎ 0177/211002. Tucked away above the eastern end of the mall in a concrete jungle – range of clean rooms, the pricier ones with bathtubs. Quiet, bazaar views and easy access to Jakhu Peak. ④–⑥

Woodville Palace, Raj Bhavan Road, ☎ 0177/223919. Twenty mintues' walk south from Christ Church, an elegant, old-fashioned 1930s mansion on the peaceful western side of town, with huge rooms, period furniture, lawns and a badminton court. Members of the former local royal family still live upstairs. Its showpiece Royal Suite is priced at Rs6000. ⑧–⑨

YMCA, the Ridge ☎ 0177/204085. Large rooms, including seven en-suites. In-house dining hall, Star TV, snooker tables (Rs50), table tennis (Rs40), and sun-terrace. West wing is more modern. There's a Rs40 membership charge and breakfast is included. Low-season rates negotiable. ③–⑥

YWCA, Constantia, the Mall ☎ 0177/203081. A large rambling old building in grounds right on top of the Ridge with great views of the distant Himalayas. Basic rooms and hot water by the bucket. ②–③

The Town

Although Shimla and its satellite districts sprawl over the flanks of five or more hills, the centre is fairly compact, on and immediately beneath a shoulder of high ground known as the "**Ridge**". From here, a tangle of roads and lanes tumbles down in stages, each layer connected to the next by precipitous stone steps. **The Mall**, the main pedestrian thoroughfare, curves around the south slope of the hill, above the warren-like bazaar. **Cart Road**, the highest road open to motor traffic, circles the base of the town.

The Ridge

Shimla's busy social scene revolves around the broad and breezy piazza that straddles **the Ridge**, overlooking rippling foothills with the jagged white peaks of the Pir Panjal and Great Himalayan ranges on the horizon. In the afternoon, when the mountains are enveloped in cloud, honeymooners and holidaymakers have their photos taken in brilliantly patterned *puttoos* (home-spun blankets), watched by the shoeshine boys and porters touting for business. During high season the Ridge is a hive of activity with entertainment provided by brass bands and ponymen offering rides. The mall in the evenings is packed with shoppers, couples ambling hand-in-hand, and young people hanging around.

The Victorian-Gothic spire of **Christ Church** is Shimla's most prominent landmark. Built to accommodate the peak-season Europeans, it was never quite able to cope with the crush: on one occasion, the vicar complained to the assembled *memsahibs* that their copious crinolines took up too much space. The **stained-glass windows**, the finest in British India, depict (from left to right) Faith, Hope, Charity, Fortitude, Patience and Humility.

At the other end of the ridge, **Scandal Point** is the focus of Shimla's famous mid-afternoon meet when crowds gather here to gossip. Watched over by a statue of the Punjabi nationalist hero Lala Lajpat Rai, the intersection takes its name from the elopement that began here of a high-ranking British official's daughter with a handsome Indian prince.

The Mall

The road up from the railway station passes ice-cream parlours, shawl shops and department stores before hitting the **Mall** at Scandal Point. The HP State Emporium is worth checking out for its Kullu shawls and felt-fronted Kinnauri caps. Flanked by a long row of unmistakeably British half-timbered buildings, Shimla's main shopping street was, until World War I, strictly out-of-bounds to all "natives" except royalty and rickshaw-pullers. These days, rickshaws, man-powered or otherwise, are banned, and non-Indian faces are few. The quintessentially colonial **Gaiety Theatre**, however, looks exactly as it did in the heyday of the Raj. The Shimla Amateur Dramatic Company still performs here, while in the gentlemen's club within the same premises, the talk revolves around cricket and share prices.

The bazaar

Walk down any of the narrow lanes leading off the Mall, and you're plunged into a warren of twisting backstreets. Shimla's **bazaar** is the hill station at its most vibrant – a maze of dishevelled shacks, brightly lit stalls, and minarets, cascading in a clutter of corrugated iron and rotting timber to the edge of Cart Road. Little has changed since the nineteenth century, when Rudyard Kipling, in his novel *Kim*, wrote: "A man who knows his way there can defy all the police of India's summer capital, so cunningly does veranda communicate with veranda, alley-way with alley-way, and bolt-hole with bolt-hole." Apart from being a good place to shop for authentic souvenirs, this is also one of the few areas of town that feels Himalayan: multicoloured Kullu caps (*topis*) bob about in the crowd, alongside the odd Lahauli, Kinnauri or Tibetan face.

The museum

Tucked away on the western edge of town, the HP state **museum** (Tues–Sun 10am–1.30pm & 2–5pm, closed 2nd Sat of month; free) is a 1500-metre hike west from the centre, but well worth the effort; its diverse collection includes contemporary and antique works of art, well displayed in an elegant colonial mansion.

The ground floor is given over largely to temple sculpture, and a gallery of magnificent **Pahari miniatures** – examples of the last great Hindu art form to flourish in northern India before the deadening impact of Western culture in the early nineteenth century. An offspring of the Moghul painting tradition, the Pahari or "Hill" school is renowned for subtle depictions of romantic love, inspired by scenes from Hindu epics.

The hike to Jakhu temple

The early-morning hike up to the Jakhu, or "monkey", temple is something of a tradition in Shimla. The top of the hill (2455m) on which it stands offers a superb panorama of the Himalayas – particularly breathtaking before the bubbles of cloud blister up later in the day. The relentlessly steep climb takes twenty to forty minutes. Visitors with mobility problems may want to arrange a horse; a couple usually hang around in the main square opposite the Gandhi statue. During the season, all you have to do is follow the crowds. The path starts just left of Christ Church.

After the hard walk up, the temple itself, a red-and-yellow-brick affair crammed with fairy lights and tinsel, comes as something of an anticlimax. The shrine inside houses what are believed to be the footprints of Hanuman, commander-in-chief of the monkey army that helped Rama in his struggle against the archdemon Ravana – the subject of the *Ramayana*. Legend has it that the monkey god, adored by Hindus for his strength and fidelity, rested on Jakhu after collecting healing Himalayan herbs for Rama's injured brother, Lakshmana. Watch out for the troupes of mangy monkeys around the temple. Pampered by generations of pilgrims and tourists, they have become a real pest; hang on to your bag and don't flash food.

Among the museum's **paintings** are dozens of Moghul and Rajasthani miniatures and a couple of fine "Company" watercolours. Produced for souvenir-hunting colonials by the descendants of the Moghul and Pahari masters, the *fakirs*, itinerant *sadhus* and mendicants they depict could have leapt straight from the pages of Kipling. Also worth checking out are the striking contemporary oils of the Himalayas, a small collection of nineteenth- and twentieth-century deity masks from Kullu (see p.561) and Sarahan (see p.531), and a remarkable collection of temple bronzes. One room is devoted to Mahatma Gandhi, packed with photos of his time in Shimla, and amusing cartoons of his political relationship with the British.

To get there, follow the Mall past the post office and downhill, passing *Dalziel* and *Classic* hotels, then take the right fork at the first intersection and left at the second, where a signpost guides you up the last, short ascent.

The Viceregal Lodge and Prospect Hill

Shimla's single most impressive colonial monument, the old **Viceregal Lodge** (Mon–Sat 10am–1pm & 1.30–5pm; Rs10), summer seat of British government until the 1940s and today home to the Institute of Advanced Studies, is a fifteen-minute walk west of the museum. Perfectly placed on the flattened wooded top of Observatory Hill, its elevated location could not have been more apt for the high seat of imperial power in British India. From here, streams trickle into the Sutlej and Arabian Sea in one direction, and down to the Jamuna, the Ganges, and the Bay of Bengal in the other.

Here is Shimla at its most British. The solid grey mansion, built in Elizabethan style with a lion and unicorn set above the entrance porch, surveys trimmed lawns fringed by pines and flowerbeds. Inside, the lodge is just as ostentatious, though only sections of the ground floor are open to the public: a vast teak-panelled entrance hall, an impressive library (formerly the ballroom), and the guest room, notable for its intricately carved walnut ceiling and period furniture. The **conference room**, hung with photos of Nehru, Jinnah and Gandhi, was the scene of crucial talks in the run-up to Independence. On the stone terrace to the rear of the building, a bronze plaque profiles and names the peaks visible in the distance.

The short hike up to **Prospect Hill** (2176m), a popular picnic spot, ties in nicely with a visit to the Lodge. By cutting through the woods to the west of the mansion, you can drop down to a busy intersection known as **Boileauganj**, from where a tarmac path climbs steeply up to the small shrine of Kamana Devi. The summit gives fine views across the entire south side of Shimla ridge, and over the hills and valleys of southern HP towards the plains of the Punjab – a murky brown haze on the horizon.

Eating

Few **restaurants** in Shimla retain the colonial ambience you might expect, and standards are generally poor and variety disappointingly lacking. Catering mainly for Indian visitors, they are heavily Punjabi-oriented, with an emphasis on rich, spicy, meat-based menus. At the top of the range, try the restaurants at *The Cecil* or *Clarks*. Several "fast food" restaurants along the Mall offer everything from *dosas* and Chinese food to Mughlai cooking; some have adjoining bars. For a really cheap and filling meal, try the fried potato patties (*tikki*) or chickpea curry and puris (*channa batura*) at one of the snack bars that line the steps opposite the Gaiety Theatre. Alternatively the bazaar is good for cheap *dhabas* – look around the upper and middle markets where you will also find some delicious samosas. The Mall's many **bakeries** and ice-cream parlours offer postprandial comfort for the sweet-toothed.

Ashiana, the Ridge. HPTDC restaurant in a converted bandstand offering mainly non-veg Indian food, including tasty chicken *makhanwalla*, pizzas and a few Chinese dishes.

Baljee's, 26 the Mall. A landmark on Shimla's culinary and social map, this hectic smart-set coffee house does a roaring trade in snacks, sweets and ice cream in the evenings, but serves no alcohol. Try the piping hot *gulab jamuns*, served to after-dinner strollers at their takeaway counter.

Choice, Middle Bazaar, 100m down from *Baljee's* on the left. Tiny, no-nonsense Chinese restaurant with an exhaustive menu of cheap and delicious dishes.

Devico's, the Mall. Western-style fast-food joint with south Indian snacks, veggie-burgers, and shakes. There's an additional restaurant downstairs and a plush bar upstairs.

Fascination, 26 the Mall. This swish à la carte restaurant at *Baljee's* (upstairs) offers a good selection of Indian and Chinese dishes, including non-veg options such as curried brains, and sausage, egg and chips.

Goofa, the Ridge. The *Ashiana's* dreary vegetarian offshoot – directly below in a cavernous basement – serves filling, moderately priced thalis.

Himani, 48 the Mall. *Baljee's* main rival has a lively (mostly male) bar on the 1st floor, and a restaurant & pool den on the top floor. Menu includes tandoori dishes and south Indian.

Indian Coffee House, the Mall. Atmospheric but grubby café with colonial ambience, offering the usual *Coffee House* package of veg snacks and attentive waiter service.

Nalini, near the lift, the Mall. Small and very popular veg restaurant that serves thalis, dosas and Chinese food; they have a great street-side sweet counter.

New Plaza, 60/1 Middle Bazaar, down the steps opposite the *Gaiety*. Popular unpretentious family restaurant. Drab decor but good-value food.

Sher-e-Punjab, Upper Bazaar. One of a string of cheap and basic dhabas just below the Mall. Hearty portions of spicy bean, chickpea, and dhal.

Listings

Airlines Indian Airlines, c/o Ambassador Travels, The Mall ☎0177/258014 and Jagson ☎0177/225188.

Banks and exchange UCO Bank, close to the GPO, ANZ Grindlay's at Scandal Point and the State Bank of India, between Scandal Point and the railway station, each exchange currencies. Visa encashments can be made at the Bank of Baroda on Cart Road, five minutes' walk east of the bus stand. Authorized agencies, such as Span Tours near Scandal Point and Sindh Tours on the Mall keep longer hours, but only change dollars and sterling.

Bookshops Maria Brother, an antiquarian bookshop on the Mall, sells old maps and etchings as well as a limited selection of new books – but don't expect a bargain. Asia Bookshop and Minerva, also on the Mall, both stock a selection of paperbacks.

Internet access *Rendez-vous* cybercafé at Scandal Point is open 10am–10pm.

Hospitals Indira Gandhi Medical College Hospital ☎0177/203073; Deen Dayal Hospital, near the ISBT ☎0177/254071.

Laundry Band Box and Whiteway, both on the Mall.

Permits for travel into the restricted "Inner Line" zone (see p.518) are issued at the District Magistrate's office ☎0177/257005 (Mon–Sat 10am–5pm; closed 2nd Sat of the month) below the Mall.

Pharmacies Indu Medical, the Mall (9am–8pm).

Post The green-painted, Swiss-chalet-style GPO (Mon–Sat 10am–7pm), with its efficient poste restante counter, is near Scandal Point on the Mall.

Travel agents Reliable operators include the adventurous Vicky Negi at Eagle Himalayan Tours, 23 Tashkent Annex, near AG Office below the Mall ☎0177/252880, and Anil Bhardwaj at Band Box, 9 the Mall, near Scandal Point ☎0177/283333, who specializes in tailor-made itineraries. Other recognized agencies are White Height Himalaya Travels ☎0177/252542 and Great Himalayan Travels ☎0177/259834. The *YMCA* ☎0177/204085 also organizes treks and safaris. In general, Jeep safaris and high-level trekking cost around $59 per head per day for a group of at least three people; low-level or "soft" trekking costs around $39 per head per day.

The **toy train** leaves Shimla for **Kalka**, where you can change onto the main broad-gauge line for **Chandigarh** and **New Delhi**. The 10.35am departure from Shimla will get you into Kalka just in time to catch the 4.50pm Himalayan Queen #4096, arriving in New Delhi just after 10pm. The other toy train services depart at 2.25pm, 5.30pm, and 5.45pm, arriving in Kalka at 8.15pm, 10.15pm, and 10.55pm respectively. **Reservations** for onward journeys from Kalka can be made at Shimla station (℡ 0177/252915; enquiries ℡ 131). Alternatively, you can catch a bus to Chandigarh and continue to Delhi by train from there.

The **main bus stand** (℡ 0177/258765), on Cart Road below the bazaar, services Chandigarh, Delhi, Mandi, Kullu, Dharamsala, Manali, and elsewhere, while the Rivoli (or Lakkar Bazaar) bus stand, reached via the path dropping behind ANZ Grindlays Bank on Scandal Point, handles departures to Narkanda, Ani, Rampur, Sarahan, and Kalpa (for Kinnaur).

Passengers for **Manali** or **Delhi** can choose between "luxury" a/c, "deluxe" non-a/c, or Himachal's standard bone-shaking state buses. Tickets for the former two should be booked a day in advance at travel agents on the Mall, while state bus tickets can be reserved at the HPTDC tourist office on Scandal Point (daily 10am–1pm & 2–4pm); alternatively, head to the counters at the main bus stand. For **Chandigarh**, services are so frequent there's no need to book. **Flights** between Delhi and Shimla (1hr 10min) are operated by Jagson Airlines (Tues, Thurs & Sat) and Archana Airways (Mon, Wed, Fri & Sun) on eight-seater planes for around $100. Tickets are available through the HPTDC tourist office.

See Travel Details at the end of this chapter for more information on journey frequencies and durations.

South of Shimla

On the border with Uttar Pradesh, the town of **Paonta Sahib**, where pastel-yellow houses are packed tightly into the cobbled streets, holds an important shrine dedicated to **Guru Gobind Singh**, the tenth Sikh guru, who lived here. Paonta Sahib provides good bus connections for travel to Shimla from points such as Mussoorie, Dehra Dun, Haridwar and Rishikesh. Should you wish to stay here, the HPTDC *Hotel Yamuna* (℡01704/22341; ❺–❻) on the banks of the River Yamuna, has pleasant rooms, and a restaurant and bar. From Punjab or Haryana, the first town on the road is **Nahan**, Sirmaur's capital, connected by bus to Ambala, 105km southwest, and the hill stations further north. Six daily buses (2hr) make the journey 45km east of Nahan to **Dodahu**, 2km from the secluded lake at **Renuka**, where a **wildlife sanctuary** protects rare deer plus a magnificent pride of Asiatic lions, introduced in the hope of creating a stable breeding population. Tropical forests reach the lakeside, along which trees and reeds shelter colonies of herons, kingfishers and bee-eaters. Carp and snub-nosed turtles swim by, free from the threat of poachers. Devotional music and chiming bells can be heard at sunrise and sunset drifting across from the nearby Hindu temples. The HPTDC *Hotel Renuka* (℡01704/8339; ❹–❻), in sloping gardens on the western shore, has rooms opening onto a shady veranda, as well as dorm beds (Rs75), and serves good food.

Kausali

Though it sees few tourists, the small, slow-paced town of **KASAULI**, cradled by pine forests 77km southwest of Shimla (3hr by bus), and with a touch of

Raj architecture, makes a good stopoff point on the way north from Delhi. Criss-crossed by spindly cobbled streets, spreading along low ridges carpeted with forests and flower-filled meadows, Kasauli abounds in gentle short strolls; the hike to the summit of nearby Monkey Point (4km) is as energetic as most tourists get.

The nearest railway station is Dharampur on the Kalka–Shimla line, from where buses travel the 11km up to Kasauli; there are also direct buses from Shimla. From Kasauli, an easy and scenic twelve-kilometre trek leads through forests to **Kalka**, railhead for the **toy train** to Shimla. There is no tourist office in Kasauli but the manager at the HPTDC *Rose Common* will provide information on paths, and train and bus times. You can **change money** at the Bank of Baroda (Mon–Fri 11am–3pm) on Lower Mall.

Accommodation and eating

Kasauli has several **hotels** catering for the mostly Indian tourists who pass through. Aside from the cheaper lodges, most hotels have high-ceilinged rooms with fireplaces, carpets and balconies, in true Raj style. Few have built-in water heaters but supply hot water in buckets. Apart from the larger hotels, **food** options are limited to *dhabas* serving *aloo mutter*, *aloo gobi* and dhal, and fresh *puris* in the morning.

Alasia, Lower Mall ☏ 01792/72008. A Raj-era house with large rooms and balconies, plus a couple of special suites facing north towards the distant mountains. One of Kasauli's better hotels. ⑥–⑦

Anchal, Post Office Road ☏ 01792/72042. Good-value option. Some rooms are poky and dim, but others have balconies and views south over the lowlands. ①–②

Gian, Post Office Road ☏ 01792/72887. Unremarkable, but homely. Some private bathrooms and balconies. ①–②

HPTDC Rose Common, Lower Mall ☏ 01792/72005. Period bungalow converted into a comfortable hotel almost 1km east of town, with beautiful gardens and silver-service tea and coffee all day. Its six well-maintained rooms are often full, so call ahead or book through HPTDC in Shimla (☏ 0177/252561) or Delhi (☏ 0177/332 5320). The restaurant has an extensive menu and, along with the lawn, is open to nonresidents. ⑥–⑦

Maurice, Lower Mall ☏ 01792/72074. Large rambling Raj house run by Osho devotees, with towering ceilings and airy balconies. ④–⑤

Nalagarh Fort

If you can afford it, the eighteenth-century **fort** of **Nalagarh** converted into probably the finest hotel in Himachal Pradesh, is an excellent place to break the journey between Delhi and Kullu. Overlooking the Punjab plains, the fort lies 60km from Chandigarh and 12km off the main Chandigarh–Mandi road. Towering above the town with the Himachal foothills rising steeply behind, the fort played a key role in the Gurkha wars of the early nineteenth century, and is today filled with memorabilia evoking its military past. An *Ayurvedic* clinic offering massage and a shop selling various health potions add to the luxury. **Accommodation** (⑧–⑨) is in beautifully maintained suites, each with period furniture, including the Raj Mahal honeymoon suite and the even more ostentatious Mansarovar suite (Rs6400). An atmospheric, period-decorated lounge bar overlooks terraced grounds with a tennis court, croquet lawn and swimming pool. Book in advance either directly (☏ 01795/23009) or through the Delhi office (☏ 011/469 0741, ☏ 463 4139).

Northeast of Shimla: from Narkanda to Sarahan

Another hill town seeing few foreign visitors is **NARKANDA** (2725m), a scruffy collection of corrugated-iron and timber houses, chai stalls, and wayside *dhabas*, 65km northeast of Shimla. This former staging post on the Hindustan–Tibet caravan route gained popularity during the Raj era for bear hunting. You won't see many bears today as much of the surrounding forests have been mercilessly logged, but there are some good rambles through the cedar forests and the **views** of the Himalayas are reward enough for coming here. Three hours' from Shimla, Narkanda makes a good resting point on the bumpy, six-hour journey to Sarahan. **Hatu Peak** (3143m), crowned by a lonely hilltop **Durga temple**, 7km east of town, looks out over the river Sutlej winding far below, and a string of white-tipped mountains to the north and east.

Narkanda acts as the roadhead and main market town for the area's widely dispersed apple and potato growers, and also as one of the state's few **skiing** resorts (Jan–March), aimed mainly at beginners. HPTDC's seven-day all-inclusive ski packages cost around Rs4000 and can be booked through their office in Shimla (☎0177/252561). Smaller groups and solo travellers should contact local mountaineer and ski instructor, Jampa Tsondu, at the High Altitude Trekking and Skiing Centre (☎01782/8466), near the bus stand.

Accommodation is limited to HPTDC's quietly situated *Hotel Hatu* (☎01782/8430; ⑥–⑦), with large well-appointed rooms, great views from the lawns, and a restaurant; the *Snow View* (no phone; ③), up the hill; and back at the bazaar, the *Himalayan Dhaba*'s owner, Mr Negi, rents out large en-suite north-facing rooms (no phone; ③) in the same building as the ski centre. For a little more comfort, *Mahamaya Palace* (☎01782/8448; ⑤) has reasonable en-suite rooms and a restaurant.

Rampur

Once over the pass at Narkanda, the highway winds steadily down the south side of the Sutlej Valley, passing through fragrant deodar and pine forests. After crossing the Sutlej river, which divides the Shimla and Kullu districts, a Jeep track follows the *nala* (tributary) north towards the village of **Ani** and the **Jalori Pass** – for centuries the principal route to the Kullu Valley. The main road, meanwhile, veers east through a grandiose, V-shaped defile towards **RAMPUR**, a major transport hub 132km northeast of Shimla. Formerly the capital of the princely state of Bhushur, the town was once a prosperous and picturesque settlement, thronging with merchants from China, Yarkhand and Tibet. Today, however, it's a gritty and cheerless cluster of concrete houses hemmed in by a forbidding wall of rock. During the local **Lavi mela** festival (late Oct or early Nov), hill-people from the remote interior gather in their finest garb to trade bundles of wool, homespun shawls, and sacks of dried fruit and nuts.

The gabled **Padam Palace** (closed to public), home of the Bahadurs, the local ruling family who trace their lineage back 123 generations to Lord Krishna, was built in 1919. The palace encloses an older Moghul-style building and a grand *durbar* hall – complete with silver throne and slits in its wood-panelled walls to allow the women of the court to spy on proceedings within.

Across the main road from the bus stand, the small Buddhist **gompa** houses a huge metal prayer wheel and a rock reputedly bearing ten million minute inscriptions of the mantra "Om Mane Padme Hum".

Practicalities

Rampur has onward **bus** connections to Rekong Peo and direct through Kinnaur all the way to Kaza in Spiti, and – when the road is open – to Kullu. **Inner Line Permits** for Kinnaur can be obtained from the District Magistrate's office, or else in Rekong Peo (see p.533).

The best of the budget **lodges** near the bus stand is the poky *Rama Guest House* (℡01782/33136; ❶). For a little more comfort head to the *Hotel Bhagavati* (℡01782/33117; ❷–❹), at the bottom of the bazaar. Back on the main road, the helpful *Highway Home* (℡01782/33063; ❶–❷) has a popular restaurant and bar. By far the most comfortable place to stay is the HPTDC *Bushehar Regency* (℡01782/33239; ❻–❽), on the Shimla-facing edge of town. For **food**, the *Café Sutluj*, 100m closer to town, is pleasantly air-conditioned with an ambitious menu, a bar and a great terrace downstairs overlooking the river. On the Kinnaur side of the bus stand, the *Hotel Narindera* (℡01782/33155; ❷–❺) is cheaper, serving good Indian food and with a range of accommodation including a dorm, basic doubles and some a/c rooms.

Sarahan

Secluded **SARAHAN**, erstwhile summer capital of the Bhushar rajas, sits astride a 2000-metre ledge above the River Sutlej, near the Shimla–Kinnaur border. Set against a spectacular backdrop, the village harbours one of the northwestern Himalaya's most exotic spectacles – **Bhimakali temple**. With its two multi-tiered sanctuary towers, elegantly sloping slate-tiled roofs, and gleaming golden spires, it is the most majestic early timber temple in the Sutlej Valley – an area renowned for housing holy shrines on raised wooden platforms. Although most of the structure dates from the early twentieth century, parts are thought to be more than eight hundred years old. The construction technique of stacking dry-stone blocks between logs gives the walls their distinctive brown and grey stripes.

Blood sacrifice in Sarahan

The **Bhima Kali** deity, a local manifestation of the black-faced, bloodthirsty Hindu goddess Kali (Durga), has for centuries been associated with **human sacrifice**. Once every decade, until the disapproving British intervened in the 1800s, a man was killed here as an offering to the *devi*. Following a complex ceremony, his newly spilled blood was poured over the goddess's tongue for her to drink, after which his body was dumped in a deep well inside the temple compound. If no victim could be found, it is said that a voice would bellow from the depths of the pit, which is now sealed up.

The tradition of blood sacrifice continues in Sarahan to this day, albeit in less extreme form. During the annual **Astomi** festival, two days before the culmination of **Dussehra**, a veritable menagerie of birds and beasts are put to the knife, including a water-buffalo calf, sheep, goat, fish, chicken, crab, and even a spider. The gory spectacle draws large crowds, and is a memorable alternative to the Dussehra procession in Kullu, which takes place at around the same time in mid-October.

A pair of elaborately decorated metal doors lead into a large courtyard flanked by rest rooms and a small carved-stone **Shiva shrine**. Visitors are to leave shoes and any leather articles at the racks, before heading up the steps to a second, smaller yard. Beyond another golden door, also richly embossed with mythical scenes, the innermost enclosure holds the two **sanctuary towers**. The one on the right houses musical instruments, flags, paladins and ceremonial weapons used in religious festivals, a selection of which is on show in the small "museum" in the corner of the courtyard. Non-Hindus who want to climb to the top of the other more modern tower to view the highly polished gold-faced deity have to don a saffron cap. On your way across the yard, note the delicate carving that surrounds the main tower's projecting wooden balconies, and the gargoyles that gape from the eaves of its gabled roof – crowned with crimson pennants to advertise the presence of the goddess within. Bhima Kali herself is enshrined on the top floor. Decked with garlands of flowers, she peers out from behind clouds of *dhoop* smoke, tended not by ordinary villagers, as is normally the case in Himachal, but by bona fide *brahmin* priests.

Practicalities

Buses from Shimla to Sangla and Rekong Peo pass through the small town of Jeori, from where several buses a day travel 20km south to Sarahan; taxis are also available. Alternatively, there's a direct bus service from Rampur. Keen walkers might fancy ambling along the well-worn mule track to Sarahan from Jeori which takes about ninety minutes. **Accommodation** at Sarahan itself is fairly limited. HPTDC's *Hotel Srikhand* (℡01782/203294; ⑤–⑨) is a concrete monster, but with a delightful garden. Rooms are clean and comfortable, though overpriced, and come with hot water and views of the valley. There's also a dorm (Rs50) and a cheaper annexe. Its restaurant offers a good veg menu in a relaxing terrace with fine views over the mountains to the north. The *Temple Rest House* (②–④), inside the Bhimakali courtyard, has clean and pleasant rooms. More luxurious rooms with attached baths in the new wing are excellent value, and there's the option of dorm accommodation (Rs50). The *Snow View* (℡01782/74260; ③) has rooms and hot water by the bucket. When the temple kitchens aren't dishing up their usual cheap and filling pilgrims' food, try one of the several *dhabas* around the square outside.

Kinnaur

Before 1992, the remote backwater of **KINNAUR** was strictly off-limits to tourists. A rugged buffer zone between the Shimla foothills and the wild western extremity of Chinese-occupied Tibet, it was considered too sensitive for foreigners to wander around unsupervised. To some extent this still holds true. Although visitors are now allowed to travel through the "**Restricted Area**", and on to Spiti, Lahaul and the Kullu Valley, permits are still required (see p.518). Other areas of Kinnaur – notably the **Baspa Valley**, and the sacred **Kinner-Kailash** massif visible from the mountain village of **Kalpa** are completely open.

Straddling the mighty River Sutlej, which rises on the southern slopes of Shiva's winter abode on the Tibetan plateau, Mount Kailash, Kinnaur has for centuries been a major trans-Himalayan corridor. Merchants travelling between China and the Punjabi plains passed through on the **Hindustan–Tibet caravan route**, stretches of which are still used by villagers and trekkers. The bulk of the traffic that lumbers east towards the frontier, however, uses the newer fair-weather road, veering north into Spiti just short of the ascent to Shipki La pass, on the Chinese border, which remains closed.

In the well-watered, mainly Hindu west of the region, the scenery ranges from subtropical to almost alpine: wood-and-slate villages, surrounded by maize terraces and orchards, nestle beneath pine forests and vast blue-grey mountain peaks. Further east, beyond the reach of the monsoons (June–Sept), it grows more austere, and glaciers loom on all sides. The hospitable Buddhist inhabitants of middle and upper Kinnaur are descendants of aboriginal peoples pushed into the mountains by the Aryan invasions of the second millennium BC. **Buddhism** arrived thanks to the tenth-century kings of Guge, who ruled what is now southwestern Tibet. **Rinchen Zangpo** (958–1055), the "Great Translator" credited with the "Second Spreading" of the faith in Guge, passed through here on his way home from the plains, where he had been sent by the ruler Yeshod to absorb the traditions of Indian Buddhism. In his wake, he left behind several monasteries, and a devotion to a pure form of the Buddhist faith that has endured here for nearly one thousand years. In the sixteenth century, after Guge had fragmented into dozens of petty fiefdoms, the **Bhushar kings** took control of Kinnaur. They remained in power throughout the British Raj, when this was one of the battlegrounds of the espionage war played out between agents of the Chinese, Russian and British empires – the "Great Game" evocatively depicted in the novels of Rudyard Kipling.

Rekong Peo

East of Jeori, the road climbs high above the Sutlej, traversing sheer ravines on cable bridges. Tiny wooden villages, each with a pagoda-roofed temple, cling to the mountain sides – many at gradients beyond which human habitation would seem impossible. At **Wangtu** bridge, the old Inner Line, and trailhead for the Kinnaur–Pin Valley–Kaza trek, the highway switches to the north bank of the river over a bridge high above the water line. Beyond the village of **Tapri**, a right fork leads to **Sangla** in the Baspa Valley, while the main highway continues to **REKONG PEO**, district headquarters of Kinnaur, 4km above the main road. Its batch of concrete houses and government buildings around a small *maidan* gives it the air of a dismal frontier settlement. The only reason to stop is to buy trekking supplies, pick up the trail to Kalpa, or obtain an "Inner Line" **permit** (see p.518) from the District Magistrate's office in the large building near the bus stop. The Mandala travel agency next to the *Mayur* hotel can provide the required letter of introduction and can also process the whole application for a fee.

The Rekong Peo **bazaar**, however, is good for crowd-watching, particularly in late afternoon when it fills up with villagers waiting for the bus home. Many of the women don traditional Kinnauri garb for their trip to town – green velvet jackets, heavy home-spun blankets with intricate borders, raw-silk cummerbunds, stacks of elaborate silver jewellery, and caps set at jaunty angles above their long black plaits. Around 2km above the bazaar behind the All India Radio complex, stands the **Mahabodhi Kinnaur Buddhist temple** with its large yellow Maitreya statue overlooking an orchard. The temple was consecrated during the Kalachakra ceremony performed here by the Dalai Lama in 1992.

Practicalities

Rekong Peo's **buses** are fairly frequent considering its relative isolation. Buses stop at the bend in the main bazaar before proceeding up the hill on the Kalpa road for 2km to the **main bus stand**. Several daily services run to Shimla, an early morning departure runs direct to Mandi and direct buses to nearby Sangla. There are even direct buses to Chandigarh and Delhi. Buses to upper Kinnaur and Spiti include two to Puh and a morning departure for Kaza. Alternatively you can flag down the Tapri–Kaza bus as it passes Poberi, the Rekong Peo turn-off on the main road. Between Shipki and Sumdo, the fragile road is frequently blocked or washed away by landslides and floods. When this happens you'll have to walk over the affected area and wait to swap buses on the other side.

Accommodation is limited to the *Hotel Fairyland* (℡01786/22477; ❸), above the main street where the buses pull in, which has modest but clean rooms, some with private baths, and views to Kinner-Kailash, and the *Shivling Guest House* (℡01786/22421; ❸), about 1500m up the road, which has clean rooms, a cheap dorm, hot showers and a good **restaurant** and bar, and is well placed for catching early buses. Filling meat-based noodle dishes, spicy veg stews, and Tibetan salt-butter tea are available around Rekong. The *Fairyland's* restaurant is justifiably popular, with great views of the busy market and the mountains towering beyond.

Kalpa (Chini)

Almost 250km northeast of Shimla and 12km along a twisting road from Rekong Peo, **KALPA** can be reached by road, or on foot along various steep tracks. Its dramatic location astride a rocky bluff, high above the right bank of the Sutlej and its narrow atmospheric lanes, make the hike worthwhile. The ancient Tibetan *gompa* here was founded by Rinchen Zangpo; there is also a small Shiva temple and the narrow lanes of the village are worth a wander to soak in the atmosphere of this once-thriving trade centre. Opposite Kalpa, the magnificent **Kinner-Kailash** massif sweeps 4500m up from the valley floor – a rugged ridge of sharp grey peaks flecked with folds of ice and snow. The mountain in the middle, Jorkaden (6473m), is the highest, followed by the sacred summit of Kinner-Kailash (6050m) to the north, and the needle point of Raldang (5499m) in the south. Up the valley you'll see remains of the Hindustan–Tibet road.

Practicalities

Kalpa is a far more attractive place to stay than Rekong Peo, although finding **accommodation** can involve some walking. HPDTC offer three options: the *Kinner Kailash Resort* (℡01786/26159; ❻–❼), the *Kinner Kailash Cottage* (❸), and the *Kinner Villa* (❸–❺), 300m from the main complex. Below *Kinner Villa*, the *Timberline Trekking Camp* (❻) offers luxurious tents and meals. Other options include the *Shivalik Guest House* (℡01786/26158; ❸), immediately below the tourist complex, and the *Forest Rest House* (❹), a splendid bungalow at the top of the village, with large rooms and superb views from its garden – head up the dirt track that turns right off the metalled road 400m below the bazaar, and follow the path past the school and Forest Department Office.

Apart from the hotels there are few **places to eat** in Kalpa other than the local *dhabas*. Transport between Rekong Peo and Kalpa includes buses, shared taxis or private taxis.

Unfrequented mountain trails criss-cross Kinnaur, offering treks ranging from gentle hikes to challenging climbs over high-altitude passes. The routes along the Sutlej Valley, punctuated with government rest houses and villages, are feasible without the aid of ponies, but away from the main road you need to be completely self-sufficient. Porters can usually be hired in Rampur, Rekong Peo and the Baspa Valley except in early autumn (Sept/Oct), when they're busy with the apple harvest.

The Kinner-Kailash circuit

The five- to seven-day *parikrama* (circumambulation) of the majestic Kinner-Kailash massif, a sacred pilgrimage trail, makes a spectacular trek, for which you won't need an Inner Line permit. The circuit starts at the village of MORANG, on the left bank of the Sutlej, served by buses from Tapri or Rekong Peo. A Jeepable track runs southeast from here to Thangi, the trailhead and continues through Rahtak, over the Charang La pass (5266m) to Chitkul in the Baspa Valley. The trail then follows the river down to the beautiful village of Sangla, from where a couple of worthwhile day hikes can be made – to Kamru fort behind the village, or the steep ascent to the Shivaling La pass, from where there are superb views of Raldang (5499m), the southernmost peak on the Kinner-Kailash massif. The final stage passes through the lower Baspa Valley, via Shang and Brua to Karcham, which overlooks the NH-22 highway. The best time for the Kinner-Kailash *parikrama* is July and August.

Wangtu to Kaza, via the Pin Valley

This challenging route across the Great Himalayan range, via the Kalang Setal glacier and the Shakarof La pass, is a dramatic approach to Spiti and the Pin Valley, and no restrictions apply. The trail, which is very steep, snow-covered, and hard to follow in places, should definitely not be attempted without ponies, porters, adequate gear, and a guide – preferably one arranged through a reputable trekking agency. It starts at WANGTU on the main highway, passing through Kafnoo village, Mulling, Phustirang (3750m), and over the Bhaba Pass (4865m), a gruelling slog through snowfields, before dropping down into the beautiful and isolated Pin Valley. Kaza (see p.584), the district headquarters of Spiti, lies a further three or four days' hike to the north. On its way to the main road, the trail winds through remote settlements including Kharo, from where the ancient Buddhist *gompa* at Khungri can be reached.

Chitkul to Har-ki-Dun

This ten-day trek to Garhwal is subject to restrictions as it passes along the edge of the Inner Line. The trek starts from Chitkul and crosses the Baspa River to Doaria. The route then climbs up a side valley to follow a lateral moraine up to the Zupika Gad and then a steep ascent – the final section of which is up a crevassed glacier – to the Borsu Pass (5300m). The other side of the pass is down a steep snow and boulder field requiring some scrambling; you arrive a few days later in the beautiful valley of Har-ki-Dun in Garhwal. You should be able to link the trek with one over the Yamunotri Pass and Dodi Tal (see p.389) to Uttarkashi but this depends on conditions around the roadhead of Har-ki-Dun and Yamunotri. A guide is essential.

The old Hindustan–Tibet road from Kalpa to the Rupa Valley

Another route to consider is the relatively easy five-day trek starting at Kalpa and following the old Hindustan–Tibet road through the remote hamlets of upper Kinnaur (permits needed), past Shi Asu to the Rupa Valley. The views along the route are superb and the villagers are extremely hospitable, inviting you to their houses and offering you local produce. The old road, now crumbling in places, is ideal for mountain biking. Although there is a route from the Rupa Valley over the Manirang Pass into Spiti, few locals know it or are willing to guide you across, as they are now wealthy apple-growers.

The Baspa Valley

Hemmed in by the pinnacles of Kinner-Kailash to the north, and the high peaks of the Garhwal range to the south, the seventy-kilometre River Baspa rises in the mountain wilderness along the Indo-Tibetan border, to flow through one of Kinnaur's most beautiful and secluded areas. Despite its comparative accessibility, the **Baspa Valley** sees few visitors and is so far unspoilt. The exquisite river valley, meandering down from the high mountains on the borders with Garhwal and Tibet, and the picturesque villages are well worth a detour from the main Rampur–Spiti road (NH-22). Although the head of the valley is closed to all tourists, there are still plenty of walking opportunities exploring side valleys rising enticingly to forgotten passes.

The valley's largest settlement, **SANGLA**, a mere 30km from Tibet, is served by daily **buses** from Shimla, Rampur, Rekong Peo and Tapri, and makes an excellent base to visit nearby **Kamru** village, forty minutes' walk above Sangla, with its warren of lanes and slate-roofed stone houses, and its wood-and-stone gable-roofed **fort**. Tibetan prayer flags flutter in the breeze and the inhabitants retain Buddhist funerary rites, although they are mostly Hindu and no longer read Tibetan. At the centre of the village is a **temple** with a very interesting mural depicting an image of the Buddhist Mahakala juxtaposed with an image of Hanuman.

You can **stay** in Sangla at the friendly *Mount Kailash Guest House* (T 01786/42390; ❶–❸), above the road and next to the school, with a great garden and a range of traditional-style rooms; the rather spartan *Baspa Guest House* (❷) on the main road near the village centre; and, during high season, the *Trekkers' Lodge* (❷), just down the road. Eating options are limited to hotel restaurants and a couple of small cafés in the centre.

Further up the Baspa Valley the scenery becomes more dramatic and 8km from Sangla there's a wonderful campsite on a bend in the river, the *Banjara Camp* (T 0551/339049; ❼), with luxurious tents and meals inclusive. At **Rakcham**, 14km and 40min by bus from Sangla, the *Rupin View* (❶–❸) has some pleasant rooms with shared baths and hot water. There is a cheap dorm and its restaurant has a limited menu. They can also organize **porters** and **guides** for treks such as the tough three-day hike to Thangi.

On a rise with dramatic views of the opening valley, **Chitkul**, 25km from Sangla, is as far up the valley as you can go without an Inner Line permit (see p.518). The village marks the start of the upper valley with several snow peaks ahead in close proximity. At the far end, a gate and checkpoint mark the start of the Inner Line that is patrolled by the army from camps scattered in the mountains above. Chitkul has no shops and the only accommodation is a basic PWD *Rest House* (❶) or the more expensive *Timberline Trekking Camp* (❻), which offers luxury tents and meals inclusive. Visible above the village, a trail winds steeply up to a huge saddle below the **Charang La pass** – the route of the Kinner-Kailash *parikrama*, or pilgrimage circuit, described on p.535. Throughout the Baspa Valley and especially past Sangla, trekkers and campers need to be self-sufficient in food and fuel so as not to overburden the local subsistence-oriented economy.

Upper Kinnaur

Inner Line Permits are required for **upper Kinnaur**, the remote region east of Kalpa (see p.534). Five to six hours by Jeep from Rekong Peo, within a day's hike of the frontier, the tiny hamlet of **Puh** is the area's main settlement, chosen by the Dalai Lama in summer 1992 as the venue for the **Kalachakra ceremony**. Evidence from inscriptions suggest that Puh was, in the eleventh century, an important trading centre that fell under the influence of the Tibetan kingdom of Guge when the Great Translator, Rinchen Zangpo travelled through the area spreading the faith. The temple here is devoted to Sakyamuni, with wooden columns supporting a high ceiling and a circumambulatory path around the altar.

The monastic village of **Kanam** off the main road, 25km before Puh, has seveal *gompas* and temples. Beyond Puh, the road bends north, crossing the Sutlej for the last time at **Khab**, near the Spiti confluence. To the northeast Kinnaur's highest peak, **Leo Pargial II** (6770m), rises in a near-vertical 4000-metre wall of cream-coloured buttresses and pinnacles which marks the border with Tibet and overlooks the old Indo–Tibet road at the **Shipki La pass** (5569m). The NH-22 continues north, following the Spiti River through the barren wastes of the Hanglang Valley – very similar to parts of Ladakh. Small settlements of dry-stone houses are piled high with fuel and fodder, and surrounded by poplars, apricot groves, and barley terraces. **NAKO**, the largest village, nestles high above the river at 2950m around a small **lake**. The eleventh-century complex of the **Nako Chokhor** in the northwest corner, is attributed to Rinchen Zangpo, and although it's in desperate need of restoration, houses exquisite paintings comparable to those of Alchi. The finest building of all is the **Serkhang** or "Golden Hall" dedicated to the Tathagatas or Supreme Buddhas. Each of the inside walls is decorated with lavish mandalas made of stucco and enhanced with fading gold leaf. There are a couple of guesthouses here – one near the bus stand and a more basic but friendlier one near the lake.

The road from Upper Kinnaur to Spiti is frequently closed by landslides between the Shipki La and Sumdo due to the notorious **Malling Slide**, a high-risk landslide zone. If travelling on public transport you can usually cross any landslide on foot and catch transport on the other side, an option not available to those in private vehicle, who should therefore check the state of the road in Kaza or Tabo before proceeding too far. Once beyond Sumdo, the rest of Spiti is open, Inner Line Permits are not required and you have more freedom to explore and get off the beaten track.

Northwest Himachal

From Shimla the main road winds west and north to the riverside market town of **Mandi**, an important crossroads in the heart of Himachal linking the Kullu Valley and the hills to **the northeast**. The rolling foothills in the northwest are warmer and more accessible than Himachal's eastern reaches, though less dramatic and considerably lower. The area however sees little tourism outside **Dharamsala**, the British hill station turned Tibetan settlement, home to His Holiness, the Dalai Lama. Dharamsala is an excellent base for treks over the soaring Dhauladhar Range to the **Chamba Valley**, harbouring uniquely styled Hindu temples in **Brahmour** and **Chamba**. South of Chamba, the fading hill station of **Dalhousie** still has a certain ex-Raj charm, and is popular with Indian tourists who arrive in droves during the hot season to enjoy the cool tree-clad heights and sublime views.

The following section traces the River Beas and NH-21 as they weave from Mandi to Dharamsala, linking a string of quiet mountain towns and villages. Just outside Mandi, sacred **Rewalsar** is great for a few days' rest, while further along the route you could stop at **Jogindernagar** to pick up the narrow-gauge train that weaves through patchwork fields and light forest to the **Kangra Valley**. The main town **Kangra**, huddles round its ancient fort, dwarfed by the sheer mountains rising behind Dharamsala, just an hour away.

Mandi to Dharamsala

The road northwest from Mandi skirts the edges of the hills, passing through thick pine forests and lush tea gardens. While most visitors make the six-hour journey to Dharamsala in one go on one of the nine daily **buses**, those with more time can pause at the small towns of **Baijnath** and **Palampur**, or pick up the narrow-gauge train as it trundles slowly through the fertile valleys between **Jogindernagar** and **Kangra** (see box p.541).

Mandi

The junction town of **MANDI**, 158km north of Shimla, straddles the River Beas, its houses clinging to the rising slopes of the gorge. Once a major trading post for Ladakhis heading south – *mandi* means market – the town boasts few sights, though the riverside *ghats*, dotted with stone temples where *sadhus* and pilgrims pray, present a colourful scene. Mandi also holds a collection of sixteenth-century Nagari-style temples above the town on **Tarna Hill**. To get there, climb the 160 steps facing the market square, or take the road which winds up from the bridge close to the Bank of Baroda. On the summit is the main Kali temple, decorated with garish paintings of the fierce mother goddess draped in skulls and blood; in the sanctuary, gold-clad walls surround a black stone Kali.

The frenetic **bus stand** is across the river on the east bank; its café does delicious veg food. There are departures every 20–30min for Kullu, Manali, Dharamsala and Shimla, as well as longer-distance services. Buses for Rewalsar leave from here, and also pick up passengers from the central square. The town has plenty of **hotels**, most an auto-rickshaw- or taxi-ride away across the river. *The* place to stay is the ramshackle *Raj Mahal* (℡01905/22401; ❷–❺), above the town square, a period-furnished palace set in spacious shady gardens, with a good restaurant and a dingy but atmospheric bar. The *Shiva* (℡01905/24211; ❷–❹) on the opposite side of the square, is less atmospheric but clean and cheap. For a bit more comfort try the *Evening Plaza* (℡01905/25123; ❷–❻) in Indira market, with a range of rooms including a/c and simple doubles. Nearer the river, below the bus stand on the east bank, the simple *Vyas Guest House* (℡01905/35556; ❷) has a few cosy doubles and the *Aryan Bungalow* (℡01905/25261; ❷–❸) in Moti Bazaar, 300m away, is also reasonable. Handy for the bus stand and right above it, HPTDC's *Hotel Mandav* (℡01905/35503; ❹–❻) is a large institutional hotel with a restaurant and a bar, where the cheaper rooms are good-value. *Café Shiraz*, at the edge of the main square, serves south Indian snacks.

Rewalsar

If you've any interest in Buddhism it's worth taking a detour 24km southeast of Mandi to **REWALSAR**, where three Tibetan monasteries (Nyingma, Drikung Kagyu and Drukpa Kagyu) mark this important place of pilgrimage. The peaceful village comprises less than a hundred low slate-roofed houses, ranged around a small sacred lake. The **monasteries**, crowned with gold-fringed pagodas, are reflected in pleasing symmetry in waters which positively teem with fish. Monks, nuns and pilgrims circumambulate the lake beneath fluttering prayer flags, and amble through lanes full of tiny shrines, chapels and sacred trees. Above Rewalsar are caves, chapels and small *gompas*, all accessible by well-trodden but very steep paths up from the lake. Beyond the ridges encircling the sacred lake many other smaller lakes glitter amongst the hills.

It's believed that Padmasambhava left many footprints and handprints in rocks and caves up in the hills around the lake and many of these caves are still used today as isolated meditation retreats. Of the three monasteries around the lake, **Tso-Pema Ogyen Heruka Gompa**, below the tourist lodge, is the most venerated and atmospheric – check out the tree planted by the Dalai Lama in 1957. Towering dramatically over the lake and visually dominating the Rewalsar setting is the large but much newer Drukpa Kagyu Zigar Gompa.

Rewalsar is also sacred to Hindus and Sikhs. For Hindus, Rewalsar is mentioned in the *Puranas* (possibly sixth-century), one of which refers to Rewalsar as the abode of the sage Lomas, for whose sake the lake was created with waters from the Ganga and Yamuna. A couple of small Hindu temples, a Nandi bull statue and lakeside ghats reflect Rewalsar's Hindu connections. On the west shore, the Sikh **gurudwara** attracts pilgrims retracing the steps of Guru Gobind Singh, who came here in 1702; this is one of the few sites associated with his life in Himachal. To the south a small **sanctuary** protects deer and Himalayan black bears.

The HPTDC *Rewalsar Inn* (℡01905/80252; ❸–❹), a short way back from the north shore, has comfortable rooms, with hot showers, and a small dorm. Visitors who plan to stay for a while may well prefer the simple but pleasant **monastery accommodation**. The Nyingma Gompa (℡01905/80226; ❶–❷) below the tourist lodge has several rooms as does the Drikung Kagyu Gompa (℡01905/80364; ❶–❷) with its views across the lake. The massive Drukpa Kagyu Gompa (℡01905/80210; ❶–❷) is the newest of the three and a little more comfortable. **Eating** is limited to several small but reasonable Tibetan restaurants near the lake which serve *thukpa*, *momos* and noodles, and the *dhabas* along the main road serving north Indian food.

Jogindernagar and Baijnath

JOGINDERNAGAR, 63km northwest of Mandi, is an uninviting little town holding little more than two streets flanked by wooden-fronted houses and a crowded bus stand. The main reasons to stop here are to pick up the Kangra Valley **trains** (8am, 12.20pm) to Pathankot, and to visit the Tibetan settlement at **BIR**, 15km to the west, where there are a couple of monasteries and a fledgling paragliding centre. Rickshaws near the bus stand cover the three-kilometre journey west to the railway station. The smart HPTDC *Hotel Uhl* (℡01908/22002; ❹–❻) is at the eastern end of town.

BAIJNATH, 30km west of Jogindernagar, is only noteworthy for its grey stone **Vaidyanath temple**, dedicated to Shiva as Lord of Physicians, whose round-edged *shikhara* is easily visible from the main road, a few hundred metres from the bus stand. Carvings on the sides depict Surya (the sun-god), Karttikeya (the god of war, Shiva's second son), and an emaciated Chamunda (a terrible form of Durga), garlanded with skulls. It's a short, steep walk to the temple from Baijnath station, just over 1km west of town. *Hotel Standard* (no phone; ❷) at the bus stand is an option if you need to stay here.

Palampur and around

Further into the Kangra Valley, tree-clad slopes give way to rolling deep-green fields, as the westbound road enters Himachal's prime tea-growing area, around the small town of **PALAMPUR**, less than 30km northwest of Baijnath. Few travellers stop here, though the area has a couple of exceptional places to stay as well as a few sights of interest. Among them, **Tashi Jong** 12km to the east just off the main highway, is a Tibetan settlement with a monastery dedicated to Shakyamuni and decorated with striking murals. Palampur is also the trailhead for walks to nearby hills and gorges, such as the short hike 2km north of the *T-Bud* to the spectacular 300-metre-wide **Neugal Gorge**, on the River Bundla, and **treks** into the Kullu and Chamba valleys.

The best of the town's **hotels** is HPTDC *Hotel T-Bud* (☏01894/31298; ❺–❻), surrounded by lawns and pine trees 1km north of town, with immaculate, spacious rooms and an excellent restaurant. Options along the main road closer to the bus stand include the reasonable *Hotel Sawhney* (☏01894/30888; ❷–❺) and the *Highland Regency* (☏01894/31222; ❸–❹) with a dorm (Rs50) and good-value doubles with balconies. To sample the delights of life on a **tea estate**, head for *Country Cottage Tea Garden Resort*, Chandpur Tea Estate

---

Trekking from Palampur district

With its lush tea gardens, alpine meadows and the harsh and rocky crags of the Dhaula Dhar range, Palampur is a good base for some lesser-known treks; the passes north of town offer unrivalled views of the Kangra Valley.

An easy four-day hike **from PALAMPUR** over **Waru Pass** (3850m), the "gateway of wind", via Satchali, Thanetar and Dhog to **Holi**; continuing for two more testing days to the sacred **Manimahesh Lake** near Brahmour. From Dhog it's possible to continue east to Barabhangal and as far as Manali.

A pleasant but difficult seven- or eight-day trek **from PALAMPUR** starts by crossing **Sunghar Pass** (4473m), then leads back across the Dhaula Dhar ranges at **Jalsu Pass** (3600m) and south to Baijnath. **Baijnath** itself, only 40km from Palampur by road, is a good trailhead for treks to Chamba or Bharabhangal, following paths that traverse glaciers, waterfalls, the high Thamsar Pass (4665m) and the River Ravi.

Treks from **Billing** lead via Rajgunda, Palachak, and over the Thansar Pass to **Marhu** from where you can continue west to **Chamba** (3 days) and **Manimahesh** (3 days), or southeast to **Manali** over the Kalihan ("black ice") Pass. The latter is a strenuous route requiring six days and is suitable only for experienced trekkers. A gradual ascent through forests and over streams and frequent ridges leads to the lofty meadows of **Sukha Parao** from where you continue to **Lama Parao** (3150m) and **Gwari** (3750m) – the last stop before the pass. The route drops to **Sanghor**, then via **Railli** (9km) to **Sangchur** (22km). From here it is an easy walk down through villages, bright valleys and pine woods along the River Beas to **Manali** (12km).

Trek & Tour Himachal, opposite the bus stand in Palampur and at the *Country Cottage Tea Garden Resort*, offer all-inclusive tailor-made packages with most equipment provided except sleeping bags.

(☎01894/30647, ☏30417; **➐**–**➑**) 4.5km to the east of Palampur, set in fifty acres of tea plantations, orchards and forest. One of the most luxurious places to stay in the region is nearby in **Taragarh**, 8km east towards Baijnath, at the *Taragarh Palace* (☎01894/63034; **➐**–**➑**) – a 1930s palace set in a fifteen-acre wooded estate, home to the Raja of Kashmir. The palace has period furnishings, a swimming pool, and a campsite geared to visiting tour groups. You should book ahead either directly or through their office in New Delhi at 15 Institutional Area, Lodhi Rd (☎011/469 2317).

Kangra

Although **KANGRA** is bypassed by most travellers on their way to Dharamsala, 18km further north, it's certainly worth a brief visit. Buses from all over the Kangra Valley and further afield pull into the bus stand 1km north of the town centre, where there are frequent connections to Dharamsala. Kangra can also be reached from Pathankot by the daily Kangra Queen narrow-gauge railway service.

Before the creation of Himachal Pradesh state, Kangra was capital of a district of the same name. For centuries, it fell prey to invasions by Sikhs and Muslims, before the British took control in 1847 and reinstated the Katoch rajas in the town they had founded in the tenth century. Amid the crowded streets, the **central bazaar** brims with puja paraphernalia – red powder, coconuts, tinsel and sugar. Behind it, against the precipitous Dhaula Dhar, the **Bajreshwari Devi temple** dominates a courtyard chequered in marble and black stone. The temple's legendary wealth invited much Muslim interest between the twelfth and fifteenth centuries; Mahmud of Ghazni, Feroz Shah Tughluq and Sikander Lodi all took their turn sacking and looting. It was finally laid low by an earthquake in 1905 – what you see today is the result of extensive rebuilding, and holds little architectural appeal.

Kangra's crumbling yet still sturdy **fort**, accessible by rickshaw, imperiously surveys the river valley from 4km south. Also damaged by the earthquake, it is a shadow of its former self, overgrown and inhabited by screeching green parrots that flit through a few simple temples still tended by priests. High gates, some British-built, span a cobbled path to the deserted ramparts. The fort (*garh*) supposedly built over the ear (*kan*) of Shiva together gave the name to town and district.

The Kangra valley railway

India has five of the twenty or so vintage "toy trains" or narrow-gauge mountain railways in the world – three in the Himalayas and two of these in Himachal Pradesh. Most famous is the Kalka–Shimla line (see p.522), but the little-known 163-kilometre Kangra Valley railway is also a magnificent engineering feat. Unlike the Kalka line, with its 103 tunnels and tortuous switchbacks, engineers of this route preferred bridges – 950 in all, many of which are still considered masterpieces – that give passengers uninterrupted views all the way from Pathankot to Jogindernagar. The Dhaula Dhar mountains, rising from the valley floor to well over 4000m, are visible for much of the journey, their snow-capped peaks towering above the fields. Although slower than the equivalent road journey the scenery is far more impressive, particularly the stretch between Kangra and Mangwal.

Trains leave Pathankot daily at 2.15am and 10.55am, and arrive in Jogindernagar at 11.25am and 6.25pm, respectively, and leave Jogindernagar at 8am and 12.30pm, arriving in Pathankot at 5.30pm and 10.30pm. The luxury Kangra Queen Pathankot (daily 8.20am and 1.45pm) travels the 128km to Palampur in just under four hours.

Places to stay include the simple *Ashoka* (☎01892/65147; ❶) and the *Maurya* (☎01892/65875; ❸–❹), both between the bus stand and town. For more comfort head for the *Raj* (☎01892/64062; ❹–❻), opposite the bus stand, with pleasant rooms, a good restaurant and bar.

Masrur

Southwest of Kangra a narrow road skirts low rippling hills for 30km to the tiny hamlet of **MASRUR**, the only place in the Himalayas with **rock-cut Hindu temples** similar to those at Ellora in Maharashtra. While nowhere near as impressive as their distant cousins, these weather-worn monoliths have survived the centuries remarkably well. Hewn out of natural rock formations during the ninth and tenth centuries, the fifteen temples devoted to Shiva, Sita, Ram and Lakshmi bear eroded carvings of meditating mendicants and buxom maidens guarding dim cavernous sanctuaries. Passages cut into the rocky mounds wind up to a flat roof above the main temple, pierced by a vast *shikhara* adorned with Hindu deities. Statues litter the site and line the low walls of a large tank but most of the best ones now sit in state museums.

If you don't have your own vehicle, you can get to Masrur from Kangra by catching a direct bus to Pir Bindu, and getting off at the tiny hamlet of Nagrota Suriyan, from where you walk 1.5km up to the temples.

Jawalamukhi

A simple whitewashed temple in the otherwise nondescript town of **JAWALAMUKHI**, 35km south of Kangra, protects one of north India's most important Hindu shrines. The sanctuary, crowned with a squat golden spire, contains a blue gas flame, revered as a manifestation of the goddess of fire, Jawalamukhi. Priests are eager to light emissions of gas in smaller chambers for expectant devotees, but only the main flame is kept alight continuously. A three-kilometre *parikrama* or circumambulation starts from the temple, climbing steeply up into the wooded hills and taking in several shrines on the way.

Accommodation includes HPTDC's *Jawalaji Hotel* (☎01970/22280; ❺–❼), a tacky, monolithic hotel with ordinary and a/c rooms, a dorm (Rs50), and a restaurant. A much cheaper option is the large *dharamshala* down the road. Several buses daily travel direct to Dharamsala, 53km east.

Dharamsala and McLeod Ganj

Home to the Dalai Lama and Tibetan government in exile, and starting point for some exhilarating treks into the high Himalayas, **DHARAMSALA**, or more correctly, its upper town **McLEOD GANJ**, is one of Himachal's most irresistible destinations. Spread across wooded ridges, beneath the stark rock faces of the Dhauladhar Range, 150km east of Pathankot and 160km northwest of Mandi, the town is divided into two distinct and separate sections, almost a thousand metres apart in altitude. Originally a British hill station, **McLEOD GANJ** has been transformed by the influx of **Tibetan refugees** fleeing Chinese oppression in their homeland. Monks and nuns stroll its narrow streets lined with trading stalls and restaurants. Tibetan influence here is very strong, their achievements including the construction of temples, schools,

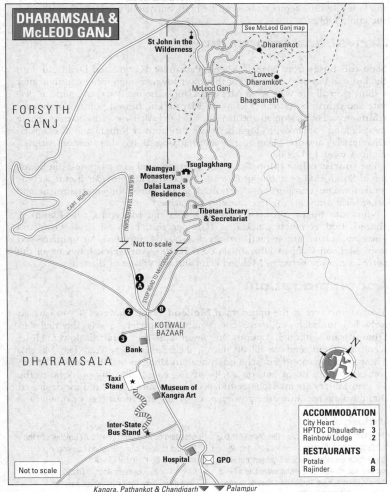

DHARAMSALA & McLEOD GANJ

Dal Lake & TCV

Triund & Indrahar Pass

St John in the Wilderness

Dharamkot

Lower Dharamkot

McLeod Ganj

Bhagsunath

See McLeod Ganj map

FORSYTH GANJ

CART ROAD

BUS ROUTE TO McLEODGANJ

Namgyal Monastery

Dalai Lama's Residence

Tsuglagkhang

Tibetan Library & Secretariat

Not to scale

STEEP ROAD TO McLEODGANJ

① Ⓐ

② Ⓑ

③

KOTWALI BAZAAR

Bank

DHARAMSALA

Taxi Stand

Museum of Kangra Art

Inter-State Bus Stand

Hospital

GPO

N

Not to scale

Kangra, Pathankot & Chandigarh ▼ ▼ Palampur

ACCOMMODATION
City Heart   1
HPTDC Dhauladhar 3
Rainbow Lodge   2

RESTAURANTS
Potala   A
Rajinder   B

monasteries, nunneries, meditation centres, and the most extensive library of Tibetan history and religion.

As well as playing host to hordes of foreign and domestic tourists, McLeod Ganj is a place of pilgrimage that attracts Buddhists and interested parties from all over the world, including Hollywood celebrities Richard Gere, Uma Thurman and Cindy Crawford. Many people visit India specifically to come here, and its relaxed and friendly atmosphere can make it a difficult place to leave.

Despite heavy snows and low **temperatures** between December and March, McLeod Ganj receives visitors all year round. Summer brings torrential rains – this being the second wettest place in India – that return in bursts for much of the year. Daytime temperatures can be high, but you'll need warm clothes for the chilly nights.

Arrival and information

State-run **buses** from Manali, Mandi, Pathankot, Kangra and Delhi pull into the bus stand in the very south of the lower town, though some continue after a short stop all the way up to McLeod Ganj – the usual arrival point for private and deluxe buses from Delhi and Manali. The nearest point of arrival for **trains** from Delhi, Punjab and Jammu Tawi is Pathankot – the narrow-gauge train linking Pathankot to Jogindernagar also stops at Kangra and at Nagrota. Dharamsala's airport, 11km to the south at Gaggal, has three Indian Airlines' flights a week to Delhi.

The **tourist office** (Mon–Sat 10am–5pm), located in a purpose-built building at South End near *Bhagsu Hotel* in McLeod Ganj, provides useful accommodation and transport information. A good source for entertainment and other local listings is the free monthly magazine *Contact*.

Numerous **buses** run between Dharamsala and McLeod Ganj (40min). A **shared taxi** is much quicker at Rs6 per seat; both McLeod Ganj and Dharamsala have unions with fixed prices clearly displayed. An ordinary taxi from McLeod Ganj to Dharamsala costs Rs100. **Auto-rickshaws** travel the fairly level route between McLeod Ganj and the village of Bhagsu.

Accommodation

Most visitors stay in the upper town **McLeod Ganj**. However if you have an early bus to catch, or arrive late, you might prefer to stay the night in **Dharamsala**, although options are fewer and the standards lower. Hotel accommodation tends to fill up during the Tibetan New Year (Feb/March). Those planning long-term stays often head to **Bhagsu** or **Dharamkot**, where you can rent rooms or huts on a self-catering basis. A handful of rooms in the Tibetan Library are available to students taking courses here, and for dedicated Buddhists, there's always the possibility of staying at a monastery or nunnery.

McLeod Ganj

Cheryton Jogibara Road, near the *Chocolate Log* ☏ 01892/21237. Cute and comfortable double-storey cottage set in a pleasant garden, but with just four rooms. Ask at the *Chocolate Log*. ❸–❹

Chonor House, near Thekchen Choeling Gompa, south end ☏ 01892/21077. Part of the Norbulingka Institute for Tibetan Culture, with very well-presented rooms decorated by artists, combining traditional Tibetan decor with modern comfort. There is also an excellent restaurant. All proceeds go to preserving Tibetan Culture. ❽–❾

Clouds End Villa, Naoroji Road ☏ 01892/22109. The luxurious home of a local raja, set in woodlands halfway between McLeod Ganj and Dharamsala, and decorated with hunting trophies. ❼

Drepung Loseling Guest House, off Jogibara Road ☏ 01892/21087. Standard lodge, plain and well maintained with good views from an open roof terrace. Upstairs rooms are best but usually occupied by long-term guests. All proceeds to the Tibetan refugee camp Drepung Loseling in Mundgod, South India. ❷–❸

Ekant Lodge, Jogibara Road ☏ 01892/21593, 1km down from the main bazaar past the *Chocolate Log*. Quiet location with views to the forest, nine good-value rooms. ❷

Glenmore Lodge, Mall Road ☏ 01892/21010. Five luxurious cottages and a main building set in picturesque woodlands around 1km above the main bazaar. ❽

Green, Bhagsu Road ☏ 01892/21200. Well kept, comfortable and popular, with valley views and a good restaurant, though sometimes suffers water shortages. The large *Green* cybercafé is adjacent. ❶–❸

Him Queen, south end ☏ 01892/21861. An ostentatious hotel with a selection of ordinary, deluxe and VIP rooms, all carpeted and with TV and balcony. ❼–❽

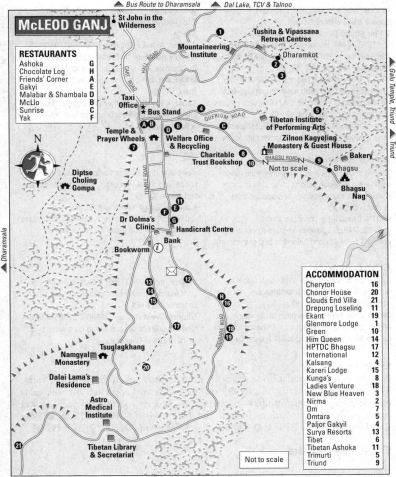

McLEOD GANJ

RESTAURANTS
Ashoka	G
Chocolate Log	H
Friends' Corner	A
Gakyi	E
Malabar & Shambala	D
McLlo	B
Sunrise	C
Yak	F

ACCOMMODATION
Cheryton	16
Chonor House	20
Clouds End Villa	21
Drepung Loseling	11
Ekant	19
Glenmore Lodge	1
Green	10
Him Queen	14
HPTDC Bhagsu	17
International	12
Kalsang	4
Kareri Lodge	15
Kunga's	8
Ladies Venture	18
New Blue Heaven	3
Nirma	2
Om	7
Omtara	5
Paljor Gakyil	4
Surya Resorts	13
Tibet	6
Tibetan Ashoka	11
Trimurti	5
Triund	9

Bus Route to Dharamsala Dal Lake, TCV & Talnoo

St John in the Wilderness

Tushita & Vipassana Retreat Centres

Mountaineering Institute

Dharamkot

Taxi Office

Bus Stand

QUERIUM ROAD

Tibetan Institute of Performing Arts

Temple & Prayer Wheels

Welfare Office & Recycling

Zilnon Kagyeling Monastery & Guest House

Bakery

Charitable Trust Bookshop

BHAGSU ROAD

Not to scale

Bhagsu

Diptse Choling Gompa

Bhagsu Nag

Dr Dolma's Clinic

Handicraft Centre

Bank

Bookworm

Namgyal Monastery

Tsuglagkhang

Dalai Lama's Residence

Astro Medical Institute

Tibetan Library & Secretariat

Not to scale

Steep Jeep Road & Walking Route to Dharamsala

Dharamsala

Galu Temple, Triund Triund

CART ROAD HALL ROAD TEMPLE ROAD JOGIBARA ROAD

HIMACHAL PRADESH | Dharamsala and McLeod Ganj

HPTDC Bhagsu, at southern extremity ℡ 01892/21091. Large flagship hotel with indifferent management but comfortable carpeted rooms and small gardens in a quiet location close to the centre. ❻–❽

International, Jogibara Road ℡ 01892/ 21476. Officially the *Kalsang Tsomo International Guest House*. Welcoming and cosy, with just 8 rooms and constant hot water. Funds to the Tibetan Govt. Staff of the legendary but now defunct *Horizon café* now run a small café here. Good value place. ❷–❸

Kalsang Guest House, TIPA Road ℡ 01892/ 21709. Simple rooms with shared bathrooms and a large roof with good views. ❷–❸

Kareri Lodge, south end ℡ 01892/21132. Five spotless rooms, two with superb balcony views, in a quiet location near *Bhagsu Hotel*. Preference given to long-term guests, who are also offered discount rates. ❹–❻

Kunga's, Bhagsu Road ℡ 01892/21180. Friendly hotel run by Nick Tenzin, with an attractive range of rooms and a great restaurant. ❷–❸

Ladies Venture, Jogibara Road ℡ 01892/21559, past the *Chocolate Log*. Well-appointed, clean rooms in a welcoming Tibetan-run hotel in a quiet location, with a garden and a small café. ❸–❹

Om, near the bus stand ℡ 01892/21313. Simple, quiet and very friendly lodge on the western edge of town, with a few homely rooms on the upper terrace and a cosy restaurant. ❶–❸

Paljor Gakyil Guest House, TIPA Road ☎01892/21443. Immaculate lodge with plain or carpeted rooms, dorm beds (Rs25) and great views over McLeod Ganj. ❷–❹

Surya Resorts, south end ☎01892/21418. Big, brash, modern hotel, with some large glass-fronted rooms facing west over the plains, with carpets and low-level double beds. ❼–❽

Tibet, Bhagsu Road ☎01892/21587. Excellent hotel, popular and central, overlooking the valley,

with a superb restaurant. Part of the Charitable Trust with all proceeds going to support orphans. ❺–❼

Tibetan Ashoka, Jogibara Road ☎01892/21763. Friendly, congenial and popular place. Rooms vary from simple with shared facilities to deluxe with hot shower en suite. Superb views from the roof patio. ❶–❹

Zilnon Kagyeling Monastery, Bhagsu Road (no phone). Single rooms with shared facilities in an active *gompa*. ❶

Dharamsala

City Heart, ☎01892/ 23761. Reasonable rooms with views. Although lacking somewhat in atmosphere, has a rooftop terrace and popular local restaurant. ❸–❺

HPTDC Dhauladhar, near bus stand ☎01892/24926. Spacious en-suite rooms with constant hot water and balconies that give superb

views over the plains to the south. Good mid-priced food in the restaurant, a bar, garden terrace and lawns. ❺–❼

Rainbow Lodge, off Kotwali Bazaar ☎01892/22647. Bit grubby but the upstairs rooms have balconies with great views towards the plains. ❸

Dharamkot

New Blue Heaven, off the main path below the teashop. Small family house with garden, but a bit tricky to get to after dark. ❷

Nirma Guest House, in the heart of the village, just off the road, with en-suite rooms. A chance to brush up your Hebrew with stoned Israeli guests. ❷

Omtara, ☎01892/ 21365. A couple of rooms in quiet friendly family house with garden in Lower Dharamkot. ❷–❸

Trimurti Guest House, ☎01892/ 21364. A few rooms in quiet family place with lawn and small shrine in Lower Dharamkot. ❷

Bhagsu

For cheap accommodation in Bhagsu ask at the row of shops or in the cafés. The *Triund* (☎01892/21122; ❺–❻), on the left as you approach the village, is one of Bhagsu's ugly modern constructions, but its rooms are spacious and comfortable. Similar options include the *Pink White* (☎01892/21209; ❸), the *Oak View* (☎01892/21084; ❸–❹) and the *Meghaven* (☎01892/21277; ❹–❻).

Dharamsala

It's easy to see why most visitors bypass Dharamsala itself, a haphazard jumble of shops, offices and houses. The only place of interest is the small **Museum of Kangra Art** (Tues–Sun 10am–5pm), with a small collection of Kangra miniatures and some modern art.

From the bus stand at the bottom of town, a road winds through the crowded bazaars and continues through 10km of hairpin bends to McLeod Ganj. On foot, the quickest route is a shorter (3km) but much steeper track winding up to McLeod Ganj's southern end from behind the vegetable market, passing the Tibetan Library and the Dalai Lama's residence. Taxis also hurtle down this treacherous road and its hairpin bends with great haste.

McLeod Ganj

The ever-expanding settlement of **McLeod Ganj** extends along a pine-covered ridge with valley views below and the near vertical walls of the Dhaula

Dhar range towering behind. Despite being named after David McLeod, the Lieutenant Governor of Punjab when the hill station was founded in 1848, little evidence of British occupation remains. Intersected by two narrow potholed roads, the focal point of McLeod Ganj is its Buddhist **temple**, ringed with spinning red and gold prayer wheels. The ramshackle buildings of the town are decked with white, red, green, blue and yellow flags, printed with prayers, that flutter constantly in the wind, and the streets are coloured with the ruby robes of monks and nuns. Today Indian residents are outnumbered by Tibetans, who still stream in after long arduous journeys across the frozen Himalayas from the Tibetan plateau. McLeod Ganj is not simply a political haven for them, but also home to their spiritual leader, the Dalai Lama, and a place where children are free to learn Tibetan language, history and religion without breaking Chinese-imposed law in Tibet. It is also the home of the Tibetan government in exile.

It's easy to find your way around McLeod Ganj. At its northern end, the road up from the lower town arrives at a small congested square that serves as the bus stand. Roads radiating from here head south to the Dalai Lama's residence and the Library of Tibetan Works and Archives, north to the village of Dharamkot, the Tushita Retreat Meditation Centre and to the Tibetan Children's Village next to Dal Lake, and east to the small hamlet of Bhagsu.

You may not notice it, but a concerted effort is being made to clean up McLeod Ganj. The **Welfare Office** in particular has initiated several schemes to tackle environmental issues, including a **Green Shop** on Bhagsu Road, which sells boiled filtered water in an effort to deal with the plague of plastic bottles.

The Residence of the Dalai Lama

The Dalai Lama settled temporarily in McLeod Ganj in 1960; four decades later he's still there, and his **residence** on the south edge of town has become his permanent home in exile. His own quarters are modest, and most of the walled compound overhanging the valley is taken up by government offices. In front of the private enclosure, Dharamsala's main Buddhist temple, **Tsug Lakhang**, shelters images of Sakyamuni (the historical Buddha), Padmasambhava (who introduced Buddhism to Tibet) and Avalokitesvara (the *bodhisattva* of compassion) seated in meditation postures, surrounded by offer-

Meeting his holiness the Dalai Lama

The Dalai Lama is in great demand. Tibetans fleeing their homeland come to him for blessing and reassurance; monks and nuns from all over India and Nepal look to him for spiritual guidance; and an ever-increasing number of Westerners arrive in Dharamsala hoping for a moment of his attention. Twenty years ago it might have been possible for people to meet His Holiness on an individual basis; now casual visitors should count on attending a **public audience**, when he greets and shakes the hands of several hundred people. These are scheduled according to demand, taking place when His Holiness has the time, and sufficient personal requests to make it worthwhile have been handed in at the Branch Office in McLeod Ganj (above the Welfare Office on Bhagsu Road).

Private audiences are granted to a select few, and can only be arranged by writing at least four months in advance. The Dalai Lama's secretary receives hundreds of such letters each day, and each case is reviewed on its merits. Spiritual enquiries are referred to a resident lama who can give advice on specific points, and secretaries and community leaders are usually able to answer queries about Tibetan issues.

ings from devotees – packets of biscuits, fruit, incense and prayer flags. After paying homage to the Buddha inside, devotees circumambulate the temple, turning the numerous prayer wheels sending prayers out in all directions. Every afternoon monks from the nearby Namgyal monastery hold fierce but disciplined debates in the courtyard opposite the temple, amid shouts, claps and gestures that make up part of the traditional way of learning. The small Namgyal café provides quality meals and snacks (Tues–Sun 11am–8.30pm).

Library of Tibetan Works and Archives

The **Library of Tibetan Works and Archives** (Mon–Sat 9am–1pm, 2–5pm; closed 2nd & 4th Sat of month; ☎01892/22467, ☏23723, ⊚ltwa@ndf.vsnl.net.in) has one of the world's most extensive collections of original Tibetan manuscripts of sacred texts and prayers, books on all aspects of Tibet, copious information on Indian culture and architecture, and a rich archive of historical photos. Decorated on the exterior with bright Tibetan motifs, it is housed in the Tibetan Central Administration compound, below the southern end of McLeod Ganj. The library is not the sole attraction – Tibetan language and philosophy **courses** are held each weekday (see Listings p.552).

On the first floor of the library, a small **museum** (Rs10) displays Buddhist statues, finely moulded bronzes, and mandalas (symmetrical images, used in meditation to symbolize inner spiritual journeys and the pattern of the universe). In front of the library, a small café serves hot drinks and cakes. An information centre in the **Tibetan Secretariat** beside the entrance to the compound provides up-to-date news about the Tibetan community in Tibet and around the world. Just outside, the small **Astro Medical Institute** (9am–1pm & 2pm–5pm) is staffed by monks who diagnose symptoms by examining the

---

The folk opera of Tibet

Lhamo originated from the masked dance drama of Tibet, dating from the sixth to ninth centuries. In the fourteenth century, Lama Thangtong Gyalpo recognized the potential of this art form to teach the morals and philosophy of Tibetan Buddhism to ordinary people. *Lhamo* performances traditionally last a whole day and are accompanied by musicians playing cymbals, drums and horns. Before each performance the arena is purified in a complex procedure involving seven Ngonpa characters in flat black masks and six dancing fairies, or Ringas. They give thanks to Thangtong Gyalpo, the patron saint of *lhamo*, and place his statue in centre stage. The narrator, Shung Shangen, then enters and offers a resumé of the opera in classical Tibetan (now understood by very few), culminating with a high shout.

The performers enter to the sound of music introducing the various characters – the **hero** (a prince or king), dressed in dragon-patterned brocade and a wide-brimmed hat; the **heroine**, draped in golden silk and wearing a hat of flowers; the **villain**, often a witch, dressed in black and hiding behind a black-and-white mask, followed by a retinue of ghoulish **demons** whose masks show wide staring eyes, blood-red lips and sharp fangs. Each character has a special dance, and sings in a drawn-out, droning manner known as *namthar* – throaty, high and resonant and so strong that the voice carries beautifully, riding clearly over the accompanying drums and cymbals. The plots revolve around tales from early Buddhist texts, re-enactments of the Buddha's life and the deeds of great Tibetan saints, or stories from the courts of the emperor Songsten Gampo, under whom Buddhism was established in Tibet. Even if you don't know what's going on, you'll catch the drift of it from the bursts of laughter and expectant faces in the audience.

eyes, pulse and urine, and prescribe pills made of herbs, precious stones and sometimes animal products, mixed on particularly auspicious lunar dates. You can also have your horoscope prepared here.

Tibetan Institute of Performing Arts

The **Tibetan Institute of Performing Arts** (℡01892/21478, ℡21033, ⊛www.tibetanarts.org) was founded in 1959 to preserve the Tibetan identity in exile. Around 120 people live on its campus in the forests above McLeod Ganj overlooking Bhagsunath, including artists, teachers, musicians and administrators. The TIPA troupe perform traditional *lhamo* operas (see box opposite) and have played a morale-building role at Tibetan refugee camps throughout India, while also sharing Tibet's rich cultural heritage with international audiences. Information on upcoming events and tours can be sought at its office (Mon–Sat 9am–12 & 1pm–5pm, closed 2nd & 4th Sat of month). *Lhamo* instructors from the institute teach the art to Tibetans in India and Nepal and also to non-Tibetans. Other traditional art forms such as literature, crafts, statue making, *thangka* painting, woodcarving and metalcraft are held in the **Norbulingka Institute** (℡01892/22664, ⊛www.norbulingkainstitute.org) near Sidpur, 30min by bus from Dharamsala. Accommodation is available at the institute guesthouse (❺).

North and east of McLeod Ganj

A minor road winds northwards from the McLeod Ganj bus stand to the **Mountaineering Institute** (℡01892/21787; Mon–Sat 10am–1.30pm & 2–5pm; closed 2nd Sat of month), where Mr Saini provides information on the region, including books and maps on the Dhaula Dhar range, and organizes trekking expeditions. Continuing up the road you approach two Buddhist retreat centres both beautifully situated in the midst of forests and most conducive for meditation and spiritual furtherment. The **Tushita** Tibetan Buddhist Centre was founded in 1972 by Lama Thubten Zopa Rinpoche, while just around the corner is **Dhamma Sikhara**, a Theravadan Vipassana centre (see Listings p.552 for details of courses at both centres). From here the road contnues to the small settlement of Dharamkot, starting point for walks to **Triund** (2975m) and treks over the high passes to the Chamba Valley. **Tabla** lessons are available at *Trimurti Niwas* (℡01892/21364) in lower Dharamkot.

The small, murky **Dal Lake**, connected to Dharamkot by a path down through the wooded slopes, is the scene of an animal fair and Shaivite festival in September. It stands behind the **Tibetan Children's Village** (TCV), a huge complex providing education and training in traditional handicrafts for around 2000 students, many of whom are orphans or have been brought to safety by parents who have returned to Tibet.

The Bhagsu road heads east from McLeod Ganj's main square, skirting the hillside for 2km before reaching the tiny village of **Bhagsunath** with its ancient Shiva temple. The last couple of years has seen massive changes here with the construction of several incongruous hotels catering primarily for the domestic tourist market. However it is still a pleasant enough place with a few cafés near the temple complex including the excellent vegetarian *Trimurti* with its roof terrace. Beyond the temple a path meanders up the boulder-strewn slopes of a small stream up to a **waterfall** where there's a small chai stall. It is inadvisable for women to walk alone between Bhagsunath and McLeod Ganj at night as there have been several attacks in the past few years.

Eating

McLeod Ganj is one of those places where sitting, chatting and philosophizing in **restaurants** is the favoured activity. Tibetan dishes such as *thukpa* and *momos* are prominent, along with Chinese egg noodles, *chow mein* and stir frys. Fresh-baked Tibetan bread and cakes are widely available, and you'll also come across omelettes, chips, toast, veggie-burgers and plenty of Israeli dishes. In **Dharamsala**, there's no shortage of snack stalls, but less choice of cuisine.

McLeod Ganj

Ashoka, Jogibara Road. Friendly place with a mellow space upstairs and a street buzz downstairs. Good Indian food and a range of beers, pricier than average.

Chocolate Log, Jogibara Road. Delicious cakes, pies and truffles plus savouries such as spinach pizza. Eat inside or laze on deckchairs in a pleasant garden. Reasonably priced (9.30am–6pm, 5pm in winter; closed Tues).

Chonor House, *Chonor* guesthouse of same name, south end (☎ 01892/21077). An excellent but expensive restaurant with a varied menu serving exquisite Tibetan food plus a sprinkling of Thai dishes and even American pies. Worth booking ahead.

Friends' Corner, Temple Road. Popular, comfortable place by the bus stop, with a range of food and beers. and a good sound system.

Gakyi, Jogibara Road. Humble and homely, with great Tibetan and Western veg dishes, and the town's best fruit muesli and Tibetan bread.

Malabar, Jogibara Road. One of a row of well-frequented traveller restaurants with a varied menu.

McLlo, Central Square. Massive neon-lit monstrosity overlooking the bus stop. Large selection of good Western food though overpriced, and second floor drinking den which is pleasant early evening but can get very rowdy later on.

Nick's Italian Kitchen, *Kunga's Hotel*, Bhagsu Road. The affable Nick is an excellent cook with a large repertoire including great pasta, banana cake and lemon-curd cake which is apparently a favourite with Richard Gere.

Om, *Om Hotel*. Friendly, comfortable restaurant jutting out over the hillside with the town's only west-facing roof terrace. Generous portions of good Tibetan and Chinese veg food and a few Western-style snacks. Great value.

Sunrise, Bhagsu Road. Small, friendly and popular travellers' café and late-night hang-out place, with a mixed menu.

Shambala, Jogibara Road. Cramped seating but good veg food, with fresh cakes and filled pancakes.

Tibet, in the hotel of the same name, Bhagsu Road. One of the best venues in Dharamsala for Tibetan and Chinese food, veg and non-veg. High prices, but worth every rupee.

Trimurti, Bhagsu. Excellent Indian vegetarian café with rooftop terrace. Great value.

Yak, Jogibara Road. Small and simple restaurant, popular with the locals, serving good Tibetan food.

Dharamsala

Your best bets for Indian and Western dishes are the *Hotel Dhauladhar* and the *City Heart* in Kotwali Bazaar. There are several cheap and cheerful *dhabas* serving decent Indian food including *Rajinder* at the main crossroads. For Tibetan food around Kotwali Bazaar, try the *Potala*, a small but clean café with a simple menu.

Listings

Banks and exchange The State Bank of India in McLeod Ganj has ceased foreign exchange transactions. There's another branch in lower Dharamsala (Mon–Fri 10am–2pm, Sat 10am–noon). The Bank of Baroda, in the lower town, issues money to Visa card holders, with one or two days' delay. There are several authorized private foreign exchange agencies in McLeod Ganj.

Bookshops The Tibetan Bookshop and Information Office is a good place to browse for books on Tibetan Buddhism, as is the friendly and informative Charitable Trust Shop, both on Jogibara Road in the main bazaar. Bookworm, opposite the Tourist Office, South End, is small but has a very good selection especially on Buddhism and also stocks secondhand books.

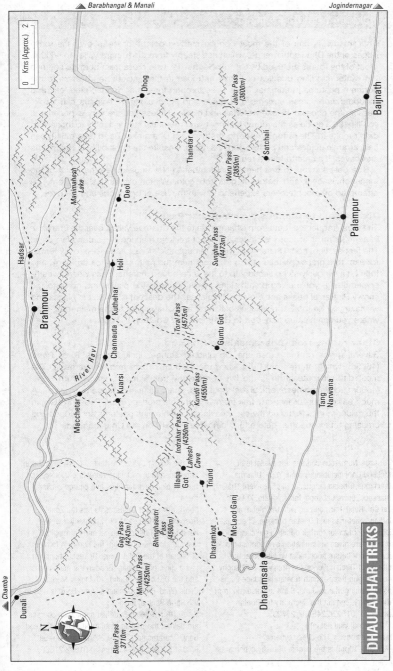

0 ‖ Kms (Approx.) ‖ 2

Baijnath

Dhog

Jalsu Pass
(3600m)

Thanetar

Satchali

Waru Pass
(3850m)

Deol

Palampur

Manimahesh Lake

Sunghar Pass
(4473m)

Hadsar

Holi

Brahmour

Kuthehar

Channauta

Toral Pass
(4575m)

Guntu Got

River Ravi

Kuarsi

Macchetar

Kundli Pass
(4550m)

Indrahar Pass
(4350m)

Illaqa
Got

Lahesh
Cave

Tang
Narwana

Triund

Bhimghasutri
Pass
(4580m)

Dharamkot

McLeod Ganj

Gag Pass
(4243m)

Minkiani Pass
(4250m)

Dharamsala

Bleni Pass
3710m

◀ Chamba

Dunali

N

DHAULADHAR TREKS

Dharamsala is one of the most popular starting points for treks over the rocky ridges of the Dhauladhar range, which rise steeply from the Kangra Valley to 4600m. Most of the routes are used by Gaddi shepherds, who cross from north to south in the winter, cradling bundles of lambs and kids in their jackets, and return to the northern pastures in summer. Trails pass through forests of deodar, pine, oak and rhododendron, cross streams and rivers and wind along vertiginous cliff tracks passing the occasional lake waterfall and glacier. Unless you are very experienced, you'll need a guide as the routes are steep and memorial stones testify to those who didn't make it. The Mountaineering Institute on Dharamkot Road (see p.549) can help arrange guides and porters and has maps. Despite the availability of rough huts and caves, it's best to take a tent.

The best season to trek here is September to November when the worst of the monsoon is over and before it gets too cold. Winter climbing should only be attempted by mountaineers experienced with the use of crampons and ice axes.

Dharamsala to Chamba over Indrahar Pass

The most frequented route from Dharamsala to the Chamba Valley, over the Indrahar Pass (4350m), is arduous in places, but most trekkers manage it in around five days. The first section, from Dharamkot, winds through thick forest and steep rocky terrain for 9km to a grassy plateau at Triund. From here the path climbs to Laqa Got, and then on a seriously steep section up to the knife-edged Indrahar Pass where, weather permitting, you'll enjoy breathtaking views south to the plains and north to the snowy Pir Panjal peaks and Greater Himalayas. The descent is difficult in places and will take you via the Gaddi villages of Kuarsi and Channauta to the main road, from where you can pick up transport to Brahmour and Chamba by road.

Other routes from Dharamsala to Chamba

Several other routes cross the Dhauladhar Range. including the Toral Pass (4575m) which starts from Tang Narwana (1150m), 10km from Dharamsala. The most difficult route north is the five- or six-day trek across Bhimghasutri Pass (4580m), covering near-vertical rocky ascents, sharp cliffs and dangerous gorges. A much easier four- or five-day trek from Dharamsala crosses Bleni Pass (3710m) in the milder ranges to the northwest, weaving through alpine pastures and woods and crossing a few streams, before terminating at Dunali, on the Chamba road.

Courses Numerous courses are available in McLeod Ganj including Iyengar Yoga, Dharma teachings, Tibetan language, Hindi, ancient Thai massage, universal yoga, tabla, karate, Xi Gung, Tai Chi, Reiki, Harmonizing with the Moon, and Indian vegetarian and Tibetan cooking. Check listings in *Contact* for further details. Free classes on *dharma* are given in translation by Buddhist monks for an hour before noon most weekdays at the Library of Tibetan Works and Archives. Philosophy courses and three-month Tibetan language courses (beginning March, June, Sept) are also run from the Library (contact the Secretary for Tibetan Studies ℡ 01892/22467, ℻ 23723, ℮ ltwa@ndf.vsnl.net.in).

Internet access The *Green* cybercafé (7.30am–10pm) is the largest of many cybercafés,

but the *Aroma Cybercafé* next to *Gakyi's* restaurant stays open until midnight. *Hotel Snow Palace* and the *Om* also have facilities and charge similar rates.

Hospitals Lower Dharamsala has the Zonal Hospital (℡ 01892/22133), but many travellers head for the Tibetan Medical and Astrological Institute, ten minutes from the library. A former physician of the Dalai Lama, Dr Yeshi Dhondhen, has a clinic off Jogibara Road in the main bazaar, and the Dr Lobsang Dolma Khangkar Memorial Clinic (Wed–Fri 9am–noon & 2pm–5pm) is next to the State Bank of India.

Meditation Tibetan Buddhist meditation courses are held at the Tushita Meditation Centre, McLeod Ganj, Dharamsala 176219, HP (office Mon–Sat 9.30–11.30am & 1–4.30pm; ℡ 01892/21866,

Ⓟ21246, Ⓔtushita@ndf.vsnl.net.in). Courses range from short retreats of eight to ten days and an intensive three-month summer purification retreat (Vajrasattva). Accommodation is available in simple rooms and dorms and there's also an excellent library. Book well in advance. The Vipassana Centre, Dhamma Sikhara, next to Tushita, follows teachings more akin to Theravada Buddhism. They run fairly austere ten-day silent retreats and daily sittings (register in person Mon–Sat 4–5pm or contact ☏01892/21309, Ⓔdsikhara@yahoo.com). Courses free for first time students and by donation for those returning.

Post office McLeod Ganj's post office on Jogibara Road (Mon–Fri 9am–5pm, Sat 9am–1pm) has a poste restante counter that holds letters for up to one month. Letters not addressed to McLeod Ganj, Upper Dharamsala, end up in the GPO in lower town. STD telephones are widely available.

Shopping Stalls and little shops along the main streets stock Tibetan trinkets, inexpensive warm clothing, incense, prayer bells, rugs and books. The large handicrafts shop on Jogibara Road sells *thangkas* of all sizes, along with prayer flags, and you can have a *bakku* (a Tibetan women's dress) stitched here for around Rs600 plus the cost of the cloth. The Green Shop, Bhagsu Road, sells recycled painted cards, hand-painted T-shirts, books on the

environment and filtered boiled water for Rs5.

Tibetan settlement For enquiries about the Tibetan settlement, call in either at the Welfare Office on Bhagsu Road in McLeod Ganj or directly at the Reception Centre below the post office, where donations of clothes, books, blankets and pens for new Tibetan arrivals are always gratefully accepted. Another good place for information is the Tibetan Bookshop and Information Office on Jogibara Road in the main market.

Teaching The Yong Ling School, Jogibara Road on the left past the post office, welcomes volunteer teachers.

Travel agents Himachal Travels, on Jogibara Road (☏01892/21428), and Katoch Travels upstairs, book local and private buses, trains from Pathankot and domestic flights, and confirm or alter international flights. You can also rent taxis for journeys within Himachal Pradesh or beyond, and enquire about treks. Ways Tours & Travels, Temple Road (☏01892/21910), is a well-organized agency that handles international flights and changes money. Yeti Trekking, the Mall (☏01892/21032), above the bazaar, offers treks and has plenty of equipment for rent. Outdoor Adventure, *Himalayan Café*, Bhagsu Road (☏01892/21578), is another reputable trekking operator.

⑥

HIMACHAL PRADESH | Dalhousie and around

Moving on from Dharamsala

Indian Airlines fly thrice weekly to Delhi (Mon, Wed, Fri 3pm). HRTC run numerous buses to destinations in Himachal Pradesh, Delhi and Chandigarh. Most travellers prefer to book "deluxe" buses through operators in McLeod Ganj near the bus stand. Try Himachal Travels (☏01892/21428) or Potala Tours & Travels, Bhagsu Road, opposite *Hotel Tibet* (☏01892/21378). Buses to Pathankot, handy for train connections and road access to Dalhousie and Chamba leave every 30min from the main bus stand in the lower town. As well as the services listed in the Travel Details on p.589, there are two or three buses a week to Leh in high season (mid-June to August). Four daily buses depart for Manali (4am, 11am, 6pm and 8.30pm), six to Delhi (5am, then five 4.30–8.30pm), all via Chandigarh, and four to Shimla (5.30am, 8.30am, 8.45pm and 9.30pm). Those heading to Manali and Shimla might consider breaking the journey in Mandi to visit Rewalsar.

See Travel Details at the end of this chapter for more information on journey frequencies and durations.

Dalhousie and around

The quiet, relaxed hill station of **Dalhousie** spreads over five low-level hills at the western edge of the Dhauladhar Range. While the town itself, interspersed with Raj-era buildings, low-roofed stalls and hotels, is unremarkable, the pine-covered slopes around it are intersected with paths and tracks ideal for short undemanding walks.

From Dalhousie the road east zigzags through forests to **Khajjiar**, a popular local day out, before descending through terraced mountain slopes to **Chamba**, perched above the rushing River Ravi. It's a slow and relaxed place with some fascinating temples and a small art museum. **Brahmour**, three hours further east by bus and the final settlement on the road into the mountains, holds more Hindu temples and both towns make good bases for **treks** into the remote **Pangi Valley**.

In the summer of 1998, the **massacre** of 34 road workers by Kashmiri separatists in a remote part of the Chamba district bordering the mountains of Doda sent shock waves through the region. The killings have fuelled a mistrust of Gujjar shepherds who apparently guided the perpetrators across remote mountain passes into Chamba. Although a one-off incident, it's worth being cautious in this area near the Jammu/Kashmir border.

Dalhousie

DALHOUSIE owes its name to Lord Dalhousie, Governor General of Punjab (1849–56), attracted by the cool climate to establish a sanitorium here for the many British, who, like himself, suffered ill health. Early in the twentieth century, it made a popular alternative to crowded, expensive Shimla, but thereafter declined. A small population of Tibetans has lived here since the Chinese invasion of Tibet in 1959; some moved to Dharamsala, but many stayed, selling sweaters, watches, bags and ornaments. Today Dalhousie is a favourite summer retreat for holidaying Punjabis, but receives only a handful of Western tourists, few of whom stay longer than a day or two.

The town is spread over a series of hills with winding roads connecting the two focal points, the **chowks**. Gandhi Chowk, with its cluster of restaurants, and post office, is the busiest section. From here the Mall and Garam Sarak dip and curve to Subhash Chowk, at the top end of the largely Muslim Sadar Bazaar. North of here, the bus stand and information office mark the main road out of town. Forest tracks snake around the hillsides connecting Gandhi and Subhash chowks passing beneath overhanging pines, and rocks painted with bold bright Tibetan Buddhist images of Tara, Guru Rinpoche and Sakyamuni and short Tibetan prayers.

Walks around Dalhousie include a short stroll south of Gandhi Chowk to **Panch Pulla**, where five bridges span a rushing stream and a drab memorial commemorates the World War II freedom-fighter Ajit Singh.

Practicalities

Dalhousie is usually approached by **bus** from Pathankot in the Punjab, 80km southwest, or Chamba, 30km north; the tortuous journeys through the Himalayan foothills from Dharamsala (7hr 30min) and Shimla (18hr) are not recommended. The **tourist information office** (Mon–Sat 10am–5pm; ☎ 01899/42136), close to the bus stand, provides transport information. A steep path leads up from the bus stand to the Mall and local Maruti taxis ply the steep winding roads. The State Bank of India at the bus stand has foreign **exchange** facilities.

Numerous **hotels** cater for Dalhousie's summer hordes, but many offer substantial **discounts** in the off-season. The *Silverton*, above the Circuit House, the Mall (☎ 01899/40674; ❻–❼) is an old-world manor house with large rooms and immaculate lawns set within private woodlands. *Aroma & Claire's*

(☎01899/42199; ❺–❼), a rambling 1930s building south of Subhash Chowk on Court Road is atmospheric, if a bit cluttered and eccentric, with a library and leafy patios. Others hotels include the Raj-esque 1920s *Grand View* (☎01899/40760; ❼–❽), up the hill from the bus stand, whose huge rooms have north-facing balconies. A cluster of mid-range hotels 500m along Sat Dhara Road, off Gandhi Chowk, include the *Hotel New Super Star* (☎01899/40051; ❻–❼) and the slightly cheaper *Moonlight Crags* (☎01899/40239). *Garam Sarak* in the Mall (☎01899/42124; ❹–❻) is a friendly family-run hotel below the road and close to Subhash Chowk. There is a large terrace and great views down to the plains. The Youth Hostel (☎01899/42189; ❷), five minutes' walk west of the bus stand, has dorm beds (members Rs20–40, nonmembers Rs100) and doubles.

Apart from the hotel restaurants, **places to eat** include the *Milan* and *Kwality's* at Gandhi Chowk, *Moti Mahal* and *Preet Palace* at Subhash Chowk, and a few Punjabi *dhabas* between Subhash Chowk and Sadar Bazaar.

Khajjiar

Heading east towards Chamba, the road descends through deodar forests to the meadows of **Khajjiar** where the small twelfth-century temple of **Khajjinag** looks down over a vast rolling green with a small lake cupped in the centre. Khajjiar is a popular day-trip from Dalhousie for Indian tourists who come to have their pictures taken and to take pony rides. If you want to stay, *Sunil Lodge* (☎01899/36321; ❶), 1km from the temple along the road to Chamba, has spacious rooms and good views from the veranda. HPTDC's *Hotel Devdar* (☎01899/36333; ❻–❼) looks down onto the meadow with comfortable rooms and two dormitories (Rs75). Beyond the meadow towards Chamba there is the *Gautam G.H.* (☎01899/36355; ❹) and the *Mini Swiss* (☎01899/36364; ❼–❾) with good food and views. The road past Khajjiar dips across denuded and terraced hillsides down towards Chamba. A tourist bus leaves Dalhousie at 9.30am for Khajjiar, returning the same day, and five buses leave daily for Chamba, each one making a chai stop at Khajjiar.

Chamba

Shielded on all sides by high mountains, and protected by forces in Kangra to the south, **Chamba** was ruled for over a millennium by kings descended from

Chamba festivals

Chamba's annual four-day **Suhi Mata Festival**, in early April, commemorates Rani Champavati, the wife of the tenth-century Raja Sahil Verman, who gave her name to the town. A curious legend relates that when water from a nearby stream failed to flow through a channel supposed to divert it to the town, local brahmins advised Raja Verman that either his son or his wife would have to sacrifice themselves. The queen obliged; she was buried alive at the head of the channel, and the water flowed freely. Only women and children participate in the festival, dancing on the *chowgan* before processing with an image of Champavati and banners of the Rajput solar emblem to the Suhi Mata temple in the hills behind the town.

Minjar, a week of singing and dancing at the start of August to celebrate the growth of maize, is also peculiar to Chamba. Its climax comes on the last day, when a rowdy procession of locals, Gaddis and Gujjars, dressed in traditional costumes, leaves the palace and snakes down to the riverbank, where bunches of maize are thrown into the water.

Raja Singh Varma, who founded it in 920 AD. Unlike Himachal states further south it was never formally under Moghul rule, and its distinct Hindu culture remained intact until the first roads were built to Dalhousie in 1870. When the state of Himachal Pradesh was formed in 1948, **CHAMBA** became the capital, and only large town of Chamba district. Today, only a handful of visitors make it out here, passing through before or after trekking, or stopping off to see the unique temples.

In summer, Gujjars, nomadic Muslim dairymen, wheel great urns of milk through the streets, and migratory Gaddi shepherds gather in Chamba before moving south to Kangra. The *chaugan*, a large green used for sports, evening strolls and festive celebrations, marks the centre of town, overlooked by the **Rang Mahal** palace, now a college. The distinctive **tribal jewellery** made of silver is sold by weight in the bazaar, while outside the Lakshmi Narayan temple complex, **coppersmiths** manufacture curved ceremonial trumpets and brass hookahs.

Treks in the Pangi valley to Lahaul

Few trekkers make it to the spectacular, all but inaccessible **Pangi Valley**, between the soaring Greater Himalayan Range in the north and the Outer Himalayan Range in the south. With its deep river gorges and barren mountain peaks, it offers a wide range of scenery and vegetation: cultivated fields give way to forests of pine, deodar, spruce and silver oak, and beyond that hardy shrubs. Inhabited by nomadic Gaddi shepherds, the valley maintains a unique village culture. Several peaks within it have never been climbed, and onward paths lead to Kashmir, Lahaul and Zanskar. The trek takes nine or ten days from **Traila** (90km north of Chamba) via Satraundhi (3500m) over the Sach pass to Killar, Sach Khas, and finishing in Purthi from where you can take a bus via Tindi to **Udaipur**. Buses run from here to Keylong, capital of Lahaul and northwards to Leh or south over the Rohtang Pass and down to Manali.

The most popular treks from Chamba lead south over the **Dhaula Dhar** via the Minkiani or Indraha pass to Dharamsala.

Treks from Brahmour

Trekking routes lead north from **Brahmour** (2130m) over the Pir Panjal range across passes covered with snow for most of the year. The challenging trek over **Kalichho Pass** (4990m), "The Abode of Kali", ends in the village of **Triloknath**, whose ancient temple to three-faced Shiva is sacred to both Hindus and Buddhists. Buses run from here to Udaipur, and on to Keylong and Manali.

Another demanding route crosses the **Kugti Pass** (5040m), "that which makes one miserable to reach". From **Hadsar**, an hour by bus from Brahmour, the path follows the River Budhil for 12km to **Kugti**, then up to **Kuddi Got**, a vast flower-filled meadow (4000m). The next stage, over the pass, requires crampons and ice axe for an incredibly taxing six-hour climb. Having enjoyed views of the towering peaks of Lahaul and Zanskar from the summit, you plummet once again to the head of a glacier at **Khardu**, continuing down to Raape, 7km from **Shansha**, which is linked to Udaipur and Keylong by road.

A delightful three-day trek to the sacred lake of Manimahesh (4183m) starts from and returns to Hadsar, host of a massive annual Hindu pilgrimage every August. The awesome Manimahesh Kailash massif, with its permanent glaciers and ice fields, overlooks the lake. Equipment can be rented and porters and guides hired in Chamba and Brahmour. Mani Mahesh Travels, near Lakshmi Narayan temples, Chamba (☎ 01899/22507), organizes and equips treks.

Lakshmi Narayan temples

The intimate complex of **Lakshmi Narayan temples**, behind Dogra Bazaar west of the *chaugan*, is of a style found only in Chamba and Brahmour. Three of its six earth-brown temples are dedicated to Vishnu and three to Shiva, all with profusely carved outer walls and curious curved *shikharas* (spires), topped with overhanging wooden canopies and gold pinnacles added in 1678 in defiance of Aurangzeb's order to destroy all Hindu temples in the hill states. Niches in the walls contain images of deities, but many stand empty, some statues lost in the earthquake of 1905 and others looted more recently.

Entering the compound, you're confronted by the largest and oldest temple, built in the tenth century. It enshrines an idol of Lakshmi Narayan (Vishnu), sculpted in Rajasthani marble. The buxom maidens flanking the entrance to the sanctuary, each holding a water vessel, represent the goddesses Ganga and Yamuna, while inside a frieze depicts scenes from the *Mahabharata* and *Ramayana*. One shows Vishnu with a lotus stem emerging from his navel that blooms with six flowers, each supporting a separate god. Temples dedicated to Shiva fill the third courtyard. Among the images on the outer walls, Shiva's consort is depicted in her various forms as Parvati, Durga, Gauri and Uma. In the inner sanctuary, once your eyes are accustomed to the dim light, you'll see sturdy brass images of Shiva, Parvati and Nandi, inlaid with silver and copper brought from mines nearby.

Other temples

Of Chamba's other temples, the most intriguing is the tenth-century **Chamunda Devi temple** high above the town in the north, a steep half-hour climb up steps that begin near the bus stand. Decorated with hundreds of heavy brass bells and protecting a fearsome image of the bloodthirsty goddess Chamunda, the temple is built entirely of wood, and commands an excellent view up the Ravi gorge and to the hills in the north. Panels cut into the wooden ceiling depict such scenes as Krishna stealing butter, four-armed Shiva wearing a tiger's skin, and comely maidens surrounded by birds.

Back in town, south of the *chaugan* near the post office, the small, lavishly carved eleventh-century **Harirai temple** contains a smooth brass image of Vaikuntha, the triple-headed aspect of Vishnu. Though often obscured by cloth and vermilion, it is a fine example of the excellent bronze-work that has become Chamba's hallmark.

Bhuri Singh Museum

The **Bhuri Singh museum** (Tues–Sun 10am–5pm; free) at the south end of the *chowgan*, holds a reasonable display of local arts and crafts. Its eighteenth- and nineteenth-century **Kangra miniature paintings**, depicting court life and amorous meetings, and men and women smoking elaborate hookahs, are much bolder than their Moghul-influenced Rajasthani equivalents. Temple statues and sculptures, pillars and lintels are displayed alongside silver jewellery, heavy bronzes from Chamba, early coins, and murals taken from the palace. Inscribed copper plates record land and property grants and temple donations from the tenth to the eighteenth century.

The museum's best feature is its small cache of **rumals**. Made by women since the tenth century, used in ceremonial exchanges to cover gifts, *rumals* are like embroidered paintings, depicting scenes from popular myth rather than the geometric and floral patterns more common elsewhere in India. Today only a few women continue this tradition, but a weaving centre in the old palace is attempting to revitalize the art.

Practicalities

Buses arrive at the cramped bus stand in the north of town, overlooked by several lodges, the best of which is the slightly shabby *Chamunda View* (℡01899/22478; ④–⑤). *Jimmy's Inn* (℡01899/24748; ②–③), opposite the bus stand, has comfortable if small rooms and hot water by the bucket. Chamba's best **hotel** is the HPTDC *Hotel Iravati* (℡01899/22671; ⑤–⑦) on the northwest edge of the *chowgan*, with comfortable carpeted en-suite rooms with bathtubs. Their cheaper annexe, *Champak* (℡01899/22774; ③), has reasonable doubles and a dorm (Rs50). Other budget options include the less salubrious but passable *Rishi* (℡01899/24343; ②–④), with some rooms overlooking the Lakshmi Narayan temples.

The best **food** can be found at the *Iravati*, though the *Rishi* and *Park View*, both on Museum Road, are decent alternatives. Try local specialities such as *madhra*, a rich, oily, and slightly bitter mix of beans and curd. The string of *dhabas* south of the *chowgan* dish up cheaper north Indian and local food in less hygienic surroundings. The **Tourist Office** (Mon–Sat 10am–5pm; ℡01899/24002) is in the round building next to the *Iravati*.

The *Orchard Hut* (℡01899/22607; ③–⑤), with meals inclusive, provides a taste of village life situated among rolling hills and terraced fields 12km from Chamba on the road to Sahu; dorm accommodation (Rs50) and three-person tents (Rs100) are also available. They also organize treks and gentler walks into the hills around Chamba. Book through Mani Mahesh Travels (℡01899/22507), near the Lakshmi Narayan complex.

A direct night bus from Chamba to **Dharamsala** departs at 9.30pm. Of the two routes from Chamba to Kangra, and beyond, via Pathankot or Laru, the latter is much quicker. For Dharamsala, take the service via Laru, get off at Gaggal (Dharamsala airport), and take local transport the final 11km; this route can save several hours.

Brahmour

BRAHMOUR is a one-horse town of shiny slate-roofed houses, apple trees and small maize fields, shadowed on all sides by high snowy peaks. The **temples**, whose curved *shikharas* dominate the large, neatly paved central square, are more dramatic and better preserved than their rivals at Chamba. The sanctuaries are unlocked only for puja in the mornings and evenings, permitting a glimpse of bold bronze images of Ganesh, Shiva and Parvati, unchanged since their installation in the seventh and eighth centuries when Brahmour was capital of the surrounding mountainous region.

The efficient Mountaineering Institute has details of local treks, reliable guides and porters, and equipment for rent (see p.549). Except during the *yatra* or pilgrimage when everywhere is booked up, you can find **accommodation** at a handful of guesthouses including *Aditya Talyka* (②–③) which is probably the best in Brahmour. If it's full, try the *Chamunda G.H.* (℡01090/25056; ①–②) with en-suite rooms, or the *Sharma* (℡01090/25025; ③–④) nearby. There isn't much choice of **food**, with a handful of stalls lining the main road between the bus stand and the square.

The Kullu Valley

The majestic **KULLU VALLEY** is cradled by the Pir Panjal to the north, the Parvati Range to the east, and the Barabhangal Range to the west. This is Himachal at its most idyllic; roaring rivers, pretty mountain villages, orchards and terraced fields, thick pine forests and high snow-flecked ridges.

Known in the ancient Hindu scriptures as **Kulanthapitha**, or "End of the Habitable World", the Kullu Valley extends 80km north from the mouth of the perilously steep and narrow **Larji Gorge**, near Mandi, to the foot of the **Rohtang Pass** – gateway to the arid mountain wastes of Lahaul and Ladakh. For centuries, it formed one of the major trade corridors between Central Asia and the Gangetic plains. Local rulers, based first at **Jagatsukh** and later at **Nagar** and Sultanpur (now **Kullu**), were able to rake off handsome profits from the through traffic, extending their kingdom as far south as Mandi, east to the Sutlej, and north into Lahaul and Spiti. This trade monopoly, however, also made it a prime target for invasion, and in the eighteenth and early nineteenth centuries, the Kullu rajas were forced to repulse attacks by both the Raja of Kangra and by the Sikhs, and finally saw their lands annexed by the British in 1847.

Over the following years, colonial families crossed the Jalori Pass from Shimla, making the most of the valley's alpine climate to grow the **apples** that, along with **cannabis** cultivation, today form the mainstay of the rural economy. The first road, built to export the fruit, wound up to Kullu in 1927. Improved communications brought greater prosperity, but spelled the end of the peace and isolation, prompting many settlers to pack up and leave long before Independence. The population expanded again in the 1950s and 1960s with an influx of **Tibetan refugees**.

In spite of the changes wrought by roads, immigration and, more recently, mass tourism, the Kullu Valley's way of life is maintained in countless timber and stone villages. Known as **paharis** ("hill people"), the locals – high-caste landowning Thakurs, and their (low-caste) sharecropping tenant farmers – still sport the distinctive Kullu cap, or *topi*. The women, meanwhile, wear colourful headscarves, and *puttoos* fastened with silver pins and chains. Venture into the lush meadows above the tree line, and you'll cross paths with nomadic **Gaddi** shepherds who follow their flocks between pastures, invariably with an orphaned lamb muffled inside their long woollen coats.

Most tourists make a beeline for **Manali** after a gruelling bus ride from either Leh or Delhi. With its vast choice of hotels, restaurants and relaxed feel, there is something here for everyone. Still an evergreen hippy hangout, it has also become India's number one honeymoon spot and place of rendezvous for young lovers. The most recent phenomenon to hit town is the trekker – striving for Himalayan highs and a momentary glimpse of enlightenment in the neighbouring Buddhist kingdoms of Zanskar, Ladakh and Spiti.

Few travellers actually stay in **Kullu town** and the only real attraction is the annual Dussehra festival in October when the town launches into festive gear. The recent introduction of **flights** from Delhi, to Bhuntur, south of Kullu, offers a welcome but weather-dependent alternative to the long overnight bus journeys. North of town, **Nagar**'s castle and ancient temples make a pleasant change from the claustrophobic concrete of modern Manali, as do **Manikaran**'s sacred hot springs, up the spectacular **Parvati Valley**. **Trekking**

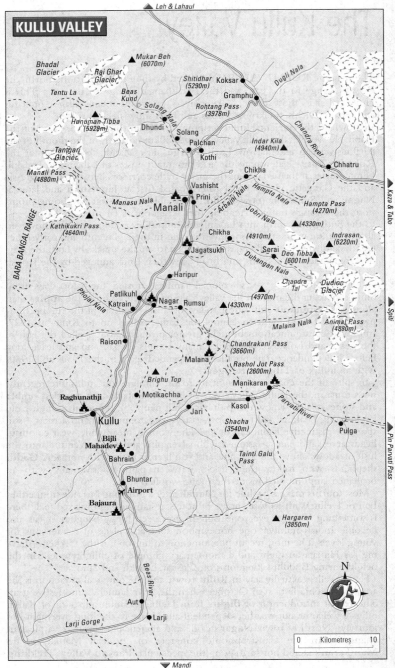

▲ Leh & Lahaul

Bhadal
Glacier

Rai Ghar
Glacier

▲ Mukar Beh
(6070m)

Shitidhar
(5290m)
▲

Koksar ●

Dugli Nala

Tentu La

Beas
Kund

Gramphu ●

Solang Nala

Rohtang Pass
(3978m)

Chandra River

Hanuman Tibba
(5928m)

Dhundi ●

Solang ●

Palchan ●

Indar Kila
(4940m) ▲

Chhatru ●

Tangari
Glacier

Kothi ●

Chikha ●

Manali Pass
(4880m) ▲

Vashisht ▲
Prini ●

Manasu Nala

Manasu Nala

Manali

Hampta Nala

Árbajni Nala

Hampta Pass
(4270m)

Kathikukri Pass
(4640m) ▲

Chikha ●

Jobri Nala

▲ (4330m)

Indrasan
(6220m) ▲

Serai
(4910m) ▲

Jagatsukh ▲

Duhangan Nala

Deo Tibba
(6001m) ▲

Haripur ●

Chandra
Tal

Dudion
Glacier

Patlikuhl ●

Nagar ●
Rumsu ●

▲ (4970m)

Katrain ●

Phojal Nala

Malana Nala

Animal Pass
(4880m)

Raison ●

▲ (4330m)

Chandrakani Pass
(3660m)

Malana ▲

Rashol Jot Pass
(2600m)

Brighu Top ▲

Manikaran ▲

Parvati River

Raghunathji ▲

Motikachha ●

Jari ●

Kasol ●

Pulga ●

Kullu ▲

Bijli
Mahadev ▲

Shacha
(3540m) ▲

Bahrain ●

Tainti Galu
Pass

Bhuntar ▲

Airport

Bajaura ▲

Hargaren
(3850m) ▲

N

Beas River

Aut ●

Larji ●

Larji Gorge

0   Kilometres   10

▼ Mandi

◀ Kaza & Tabo

◀ Spiti

◀ Pin Parvati Pass

opportunities range from day-hikes up the Beas River's side valleys, or **nalas**, to challenging long hauls over high-altitude passes and glaciers. Away from the roads, you step into a medieval time warp little altered since the days when the Kullu Valley was one of the most remote places on earth.

Kullu

KULLU, the valley's capital since the mid-seventeenth century, became district headquarters after Independence. Despite being the region's main market and transport hub it has been eclipsed as a tourist centre by Manali, 40km north. Kullu is noisy, polluted, and worlds away from the tranquil villages that peer down from the surrounding hillsides.

Most travellers pass straight through but there are several **temples** dotted around the town, some of which provide fine valley views. The night-time views are quite spectacular as lights in the surrounding hillside villages sparkle and provide a different perspective on the scale of the valley.

Patlikuhl, Footbridge & Manali

KULLU

Rupi Palace

Bus Stand
AKHARA BAZAAR

Raghunathji Temple

Bus Stand (Main)
SARVARI BAZAAR

GPO
BAZAAR

Taxi Stand

DHALPUR

N

MAIDAN

0   Metres   200

NH21

ACCOMMODATION
Bijleshwar View   4
Sarvari   5
Sheetal   1
Shobla   3
The Nest   2
RESTAURANTS
Hot Stuff   C
HPTDC Monal   B
Radha   A

Apple Valley Resort   *Bhuntar Airport (10 km), Parvati Valley & Mandi*

The temples

Kullu's most famous temple, the **Raghunathji Mandir** is home to a sacred statue of Lord Raghunathji, a manifestation of Rama, brought to Kullu by Raja Jagat Singh in the mid-seventeenth century. The Raja had been advised by his priests to install the sacred icon here and crown it king in his place, as a penance for causing the death of a local brahmin (thereby ridding himself of a punitive curse that had been turning all his food into worms). To this day, the Kullu rajas consider themselves mere viceroys of Raghunathji, the most powerful *devta* in the valley and the focus of the Dussehra procession. The temple is tucked away behind the Kullu raja's **Rupi Palace** above the bus station. Half an hour's walk further up, the paved trail leads beyond Sultanpur to a high ridge, with excellent views over the Beas to the snow peaks in the east. **Vaishno Devi Mandir**, a small cave-temple that houses an image of the goddess Kali (Durga), is a stiff 3km further on.

Another important temple stands 8km southeast of town, atop the bluff that overlooks the sacred confluence, or *sangam*, of the Beas and Parvati. Although it's far closer to Bhuntur than Kullu, you have to approach the **Bijli Mahadev Mandir** via the Akhara Bazar–Tapu suspension bridge and a well-worn track

In the Kullu region, often dubbed the "**Valley of the Gods**", the village deity reigns supreme. No one knows how many *devtas* and *devis* inhabit the hills south of the Rohtang Pass, but nearly every hamlet has one, each with its own history, foibles and temple. Legend has it that they originally descended from the Chandrakani Pass. Jamlu, the maverick god of Malana, lifted the lid of the chest in which they were all trapped, and a gust of wind scattered the small circular icons around the villages.

The part each one plays in village life depends on his or her particular **powers**; some heal, others protect the "parish" borders from evil spirits, summon the rains, or ensure the success of the harvest. Nearly all, however, communicate with their devotees by means of **oracles**. Drawn from the lower castes, the village shaman, or **gaur**, is subject to prohibitions that forbid him, among other things, to cut his hair, wear leather, or spread manure on his fields. When called upon to perform, he strips to the waist and, accompanied by the trumpets and drums of the temple band, enters a trance in which the *devta* uses his voice to speak to the congregation. The deity, carried out of the temple on a ceremonial palanquin, or *rath*, rocks back and forth on the shoulders of its bearers as the *gaur* speaks. His words are always heeded, and his decisions final; the *devta*-oracle decides the propitious dates for marriages, and for sowing crops, and arbitrates disputes.

The single most important outing for any village deity is **Dussehra**, which takes place in the town of **Kullu** every October after the monsoons. Although the week-long festival ostensibly celebrates Rama's victory over the demon-king of Lanka, Ravana (in the local dialect, *dushet hera* means "the demon killed"), it is also an opportunity for the *devtas* to reaffirm their position in the grand pecking order that prevails among them – a rigid hierarchy in which the Kullu raja's own tutelary deity Rama, alias **Raghunathji**, is king.

The Kullu Dussehra is thought to date from the seventeenth century, when the valley's Hindu rulers set out to weaken the hold of indigenous "nature cults": the worship of animist spirits residing in mountain peaks, rocks, trees, streams, and caves. Judging by the turn-out for the festival, the raja's ruse worked a treat. On the tenth day of the new, or "white" moon in October, between 150 and 200 *devtas* make their way to Kullu to pay homage to the Raghunathji. As befits a region that holds its elderly women in high esteem, the procession proper cannot begin until **Hadimba**, the grandmother of the royal family's chief god, arrives from the Dunghri temple in Manali. Like her underlings, she is borne on an elaborately carved wooden *rath* swathed in glittering silk and garlands, and surmounted by a richly embroidered parasol, or *chhatri*. Facing each of the four directions, eight or twelve gold and silver **masks** are strapped to the side of the deities, preceded by raucous trumpets, standard bearers, priests, and bare-chested *gaurs*.

Raghunathji leads the great **procession** in his six-wheeled *rath*. Hauled from the Rupi palace on long ropes by a team of two hundred honoured devotees, the palanquin lurches to a halt in the middle of Kullu's dusty *maidan*, to be circumambulated by the raja, his family, and retinue of priests. Thereafter, the festival's more secular aspect comes to the fore. **Folk dancers**, decked out in traditional Himachali dress, perform for the vast crowds; the *maidan* by this time has acquired all the trappings of an Indian funfair, with market stalls, sweet-sellers, itinerant snake charmers, astrologers, *sadhus* and tawdry circus acts, all serenaded by a deafening barrage of drumming and Hindi film music. The revelries finally draw to a close six days later on the full moon, when the customary **blood sacrifices** of a young buffalo, a goat, a cock, a fish and a crab are made to the god.

Kullu's Dussehra, now a major tourist attraction, has become increasingly staged and commercialized. Book accommodation in advance, and be prepared for a crush if you want to get anywhere near the *devtas*.

6

HIMACHAL PRADESH | Kullu

south along the left bank of the Beas. Bijli Mahadev is renowned for its extraordinary **lingam**. Bolts of lightning, conducted into the inner sanctum by means of the twenty-metre, trident-tipped pole, are said periodically to shatter the icon, which later, with the help of invocations from the resident *pujari*, magically reconstitutes itself. From the temple there are superb panoramic views of the Parvati and Kullu valleys and Himachal's highest peaks. You can **stay** in the temple rest house (donations welcome), a simple affair with a single cold tap, and no toilets, and walk down into the Parvati Valley the next day.

Practicalities

Long-distance **buses** heading up and down the valley pull in at the **main bus stand** in **Sarvari Bazaar**, on the north side of the Sarvari Nala, which flows through the town from the west. Local services heading north also drop and pick up passengers opposite the congested **Akhara Bazaar depot**, at the north end of town, and at the top of **Dhalpur maidan**, at the south end. This is closer to most of the hotels and restaurants, and the District Commissioner's office (Mon–Sat 10am–5pm, 2nd Sat of month closed; ☏01902/22727) – the place to apply for **Inner Line permits** (see p.518) for restricted areas in Spiti and upper Kinnaur. HPTDC's **tourist office** (daily 10am–7pm, ☏01902/22349) is on the west side of Dhalpur *maidan*. They can book tickets on HPTDC's deluxe buses to Delhi, Shimla and Chandigarh. **Flights** to Kullu from Delhi and Shimla arrive in **Bhuntur**, thirty minutes south of Kullu by bus. Taxis to the airport should be booked in the union office on the main road close to the tourist office. Indian Airlines are handled by Ambassador Travels (☏01902/25286) and Jagsons (☏01902/65222) who both charge foreigners $150 to fly one-way, to or from Delhi. *Sip'n'surf* internet café (☏01902/24395) is just down and round from the *Radha dhaba*.

If you're travelling on to **Nagar**, catch one of the frequent Manali-bound buses that run north along the main road, on the west side of the valley, and jump off at **Patlikuhl**, 5km north of Katrain, where you can pick up a shared taxi or local bus for the remaining 6km. Buses also run direct to Manali via Nagar, from the end of the Tapu suspension bridge, across the river from the Akhara Bazaar bus depot. This service, which leaves more or less hourly, is slower, but far more scenic.

Accommodation and eating

Kullu has a reasonable choice of **accommodation**, although during Dussehra the price of rooms rises alarmingly, quadrupling in some hotels, and most places are booked way in advance. The rates quoted below are for high season; at other times discounts of up to fifty percent may be given. Most of the hotels have small, moderately priced **restaurants**. Otherwise, there are rock-bottom *dhabas* in the bazaar: *Radha*, on the town side of the footbridge, is the cleanest. HPTDC's *Monal Café*, near the tourist office, is a pleasant place with a range of food and views of the *maidan* while *Hot Stuff* next door is livelier and popular, with a mixed menu which includes burgers, and pizzas as well as Indian food.

Apple Valley Resorts, Mohal Village ☏01902/22310, ✉aplvaley@nde.vsnl.net.in. Four-star resort between Bhuntur and Kullu with individual chalets set in landscaped gardens on the banks of the Beas. ❽
Bijleshwar View, behind the tourist office, Dhalpur ☏01902/22877. Quiet, clean, central and

friendly; large en-suite rooms with fireplaces. ❸–❺
The Nest, next to the bus stand ☏01902/22685. One of the best around the bus stand, clean, convenient, with very good-value doubles. ❷–❹
Sarvari, south of the *maidan* and up a small lane ☏01902/22471. Quiet location with wide range of

rooms in old and new deluxe block, including dorms (Rs75), and with good views down-valley. Restaurant and bar. ⑤–⑦
Sheetal, Akhara Bazaar ☎ 01902/24548. On the northern edge of town on the Manali road; a pleasant little guesthouse with cheap and immaculate rooms overlooking the river. Excellent value. ①
Shobla, Dhalpur ☎ 01902/22800. Once Kullu's top hotel but now showing its age. Large rooms, a

good mixed-cuisine restaurant, though expensive by Kullu standards – and a relaxing lawn. ⑤–⑦
Vaishali, Gandhi Nagar ☎ 01902/65675, 4km south of town next to Swami Shyam's ashram. Sizeable, comfortable rooms, a pleasant garden and a rooftop café with dramatic views of the river. ⑥–⑦

The Parvati Valley

Hemmed in by giant-pinnacled mountain peaks, the **Parvati Valley**, which twists west from the glaciers and snowfields on the Spiti border to meet the Beas at Bhuntur is the Kullu Valley's longest tributary. Picturesque hamlets perch precariously on its sides, amid lush terraces and old pine forests. Only those along the road, however, see many visitors – an incongruous combination of Western hippies and van-loads of Sikh pilgrims bound for the *gurudwara* at **Manikaran**, 32km northeast of the Beas-Parvati confluence. Crouched at the foot of a gloomy ravine, this ancient religious site, sacred to Hindus as well as Sikhs, is famous for the **hot springs** that bubble out of its stony river banks.

To make the most of Parvati's stunning scenery you'll have to **hike**. Two popular trails thread their way up the valley: one north from **Jari**, over the Chandrakani Pass to Nagar, passing through the fascinating hill village of **Malana** (see p.579); the other follows the River Parvati east to another sacred hot spring and *sadhu* hang-out, **Khirganga**. The trail continues from Khirganga to **Mantalai** with its Shiva shrine and over the awesome 5400m Pin–Parvati pass into **Spiti**. This serious snowfield is riddled with crevasses and takes several hours to cross. A guide is absolutely essential.

Parvati disappearances

In the past few years more than a dozen travellers have mysteriously **disappeared** in the Parvati Valley. Most were travelling alone, although the most recent incident in August 2000 involved three campers who were brutally attacked in their tent, thrown into the gorge and left for dead – one survived. Several theories have been put forward to explain these disappearances, from drug-related accidents on the steep and treacherous mountain trails, to attacks by bears or wolves, foul play by the numerous cannabis cultivators in the region, and even that the disappeared may have joined secret cults deep in the mountains. The most recent case suggests they have most likely been victims of bandit attacks, motivated solely by money, with the wild waters of the Parvati river conveniently placed for disposing of bodies. To add to the concern, some posters placed around Manikaran of the missing people have been ripped down and relevant pages from hotel registers have also vanished. This steamy place of pilgrimage is at the heart of the mystery, the last place most of the travellers were seen alive. Individual travellers should **take heed** and only use recognized guides on treks across the mountains. Don't attempt solo treks – even along the relatively simple trail over the Chandrakhani Pass between Nagar and Malana and the straightforward trek to the hot springs at Khirganga. There are many trekking agencies in Kullu and Manali who can put you in touch with a reputable guide.

Jari and Kasol

Spilling over the main road and down the south side of the Parvati Valley, **JARI**, 15km from Bhuntur, looks across to the precipitous Malana *nala* in the north, and to the snow-flecked needles of the Baranagh Range on the eastern horizon. It's a convenient point from which to catch the trail up to **Malana**, which starts from near the centre of the village before descending to cross the river. Like many of its lookalike cousins, the tatty settlement supports a small transient population of stoned Westerners, attracted by the top quality *charas*. The *Village Guest House* (❶), a traditional wooden-balconied house ten minutes' walk from the square and the *Ratna Guest House* (❶), a five-minute walk above the square are both popular. Other options include the *Krishna Guest House* (❷) with good views and the nearby *Om Shiva* (❶–❷), situated right next to the start of the trail to Malana.

Beyond Jari, the road winds down towards the rushing grey-green Parvati, which it meets at **KASOL**, a pleasant village straddling a mountain stream and surrounded by forest. A mere 4.5km from Manikaran and a pleasant walk along a wooded road, Kasol has grown in popularity, and now has a large resident population of *charas*-smoking Westerners. A trickle of trekkers also plod through on their way to or from the pass of Rashol Jot (2440m), a hard day's climb up the north side of the valley which provides an alternative approach to Malana and the Chandrakani route to the Kullu Valley (see boxes on trekking and Parvati disappearances on p.578–579 & p.564 respectively). **Accommodation** ranges from basic rooms in village houses and simple guesthouses to a bit more comfort at the *Rainbow Café* guesthouse (❷), with its excellent and congenial café under the trees. Other recommended places include the *Yerpa, Apple Tree, Luxmi House,* and the more expensive *Kasol Inn*.

Manikaran and around

A short distance beyond Kasol, clouds of steam billowing from the rocky riverbank herald the Parvati Valley's chief attraction. Hindu mythology identifies **MANIKARAN** as the place where the serpent king Shesha stole Parvati's earrings, or *manikara*, while she and her husband Shiva were bathing in the river. When interrogated by the god of destruction, the snake, who had slithered away to hide in his subterranean kingdom, Patala, flew into a rage and snorted the earrings out of his nose. Ever since, boiling water has poured out of the ground. The site is also venerated by Sikhs, who have erected a massive green and white onion-domed concrete *gurudwara* over the springs.

Boxed in at the bottom of a vast, sheer-sided chasm, Manikaran is a damp, dark and claustrophobic place where you're unlikely to want to spend more than a night – long enough for a soak in a hot tub, and a chat to the *babas* who congregate on the riverbank. Most of the action revolves around the springs themselves, reached via the lane that leads through the village from the footbridge. On the way, check out the finely carved pale-grey stone **Rama temple** just past the main square, and the pans of rice and dhal cooking in the steaming pools on the pavements. Down at the riverside **Shiva shrine**, a brightly painted concrete box whose accessory deities have also been left to stew in the hot springs, semi-naked **sadhus** sit in the scalding waters smoking chillums and bumming cigarettes from the curious Westerners who wander past. Sikh pilgrims, meanwhile, make their way to the nearby **gurudwara**, where they take a purifying dip in the underground pool, then congregate upstairs to listen to musical recitations from the Sikhs' holy book, the *Guru*

Granth Sahib. If you visit, keep your arms, legs and head covered; tobacco is prohibited inside the complex.

Practicalities

Buses leave Bhuntur every couple of hours for Manikaran (1hr 30min). The last bus for Kullu, via Bhuntur, leaves around 5.30pm. You can also hire Maruti-van **taxis**. Except during May and June, when Manikaran fills up with Punjabi visitors, **accommodation** is plentiful and inexpensive. All the hotels listed here have a steaming indoor hot tub but the abundance of moisture has left them feeling damp and dirty. HPTDC *Hotel Parvati* (℡01902/73735; ❺) near the Raghunath temple on the main street has large, well-furnished rooms, a restaurant, and a riverside lawn. The *Sharma Guest House* (℡01902/73742; ❶–❷), at the other end of the bazaar, near the *gurudwara*, has attached doubles and the slightly better *Padha Family Guest House* (℡01902/73728; ❶–❸) opposite has rooms around a courtyard, and a good café. On the bus stand side of the river, *Amar Palace* (℡01902/73740; ❸–❻) and the *Sharda Classic* (℡01902/73851; ❹–❺) are comfortable mid–range places catering more for domestic tourists. **Places to eat** range from the *Parvati*'s mid-priced Punjabi restaurant to the no-frills makeshift *dhabas* along the main street. The best of the tourist cafés catering for trekkers and budget travellers is the *Shiva Café*, near the springs, which serves Indian and Chinese food, plus brown bread, pizza, porridge, pancakes and apple pie. The small *O-Rest* overlooking the river is more airy, but the food is mediocre and further towards the bridge is the *Hot Spring* café.

Around Manikaran

Twelve kilometres beyond Manikaran the small village of **Pulga** has also become popular with travellers who cannot cope with the pace of Old Manali. The road now runs all the way from Manikaran to Pulga – a fact that will no doubt alter the nature of the place. Simple rooms are available in village houses and there are now a couple of tiny guesthouses, as well as some travellers' cafés and the inevitable German bakery. Back-to-nature purists who find Pulga too modern have moved even further up the valley to the last village, **Kalga**, where there are no showers, or bakeries and only one common outside toilet. Beyond all the villages, 25km from Manikaran, and situated on an alpine meadow is **Khirganga** where you can indulge yourself in more hot springs. A couple of tea houses provide basic food and there is some sheltered accommodation under canvas. Khirganga is a four-to-five-hour walk from Pulga along beautiful forest trails, but should not be attempted alone. See box on p.564.

Nagar

Stacked up the lush terraced lower slopes of the valley as they sweep towards the tree line from the left bank of the Beas, Nagar, 6km from the main road junction at Patlikuhl, is the most scenic and accessible of the hill villages between Kullu and Manali. Clustered around an old **castle**, this was the regional capital before the local rajas decamped to Kullu in the mid-1800s. A century or so later, European settlers began to move in.

Seduced by the village's ancient **temples**, tranquil setting and unhurried pace, many visitors find themselves lingering in Nagar – a far less hippified village than those further north – longer than they intended. Today, Russians inspired by the life and work of the artist-philosopher **Nicholas Roerich** flock to Nagar; some to assist with the centre named after him, others simply to paint. Numerous tracks wind up the mountain to more remote settlements, providing a choice of enjoyable **hikes**. The tranquillity of Nagar may be about to be shattered as there are plans to divert the main road from Patlikuhl to Manali along this side of the river so as to avoid the terrible landslides that plague the existing main road. The effects of change are already being felt with more and more construction eating into the orchards surrounding the village.

The castle

Since it was erected by Raja Sidh Singh (c.1700), Nagar's central **castle**, astride a sheer-sided bluff, has served as palace, colonial mansion, courthouse and school. It is now a Himachal-run hotel, but nonresidents can wander in to admire the views from its balconies. Built in the traditional "earthquake-proof" *pahari* style (layers of stone bonded together with cedar logs), the castle has a central courtyard, next to which stands a small museum, and an even smaller shrine. The **Jagti Patt temple**'s amorphous deity, a triangular slab of rock strewn with rose petals and rupee notes, is said to have been borne here from its home on the summit of Deo Tibba by a swarm of wild honeybees – the valley's *devtas* in disguise.

The Nicholas Roerich Gallery

Perched on the upper outskirts of the village and shaded by lofty palms, the **Nicholas Roerich Gallery** (Tues–Sun 9am–1pm & 2–5pm; Rs10) houses an exhibition of paintings and photographs dedicated to the memory of its former occupier, the Russian artist, writer, philosopher, archeologist, explorer and mystic. Around the turn of the twentieth century, Roerich's atmospheric landscape paintings and esoteric philosophies – an arcane blend of Eastern mysticism and *fin-de-siècle* humanist-idealism – inspired a cult-like following in France and the United States. Financed by donations from devotees, Roerich, variously compared by his admirers to Leonardo and Buddha, was able to indulge his obsession with Himalayan travel in a series of lengthy expeditions to far-flung corners of Tibet and Central Asia. He retired to Nagar in 1929, dying here eighteen years later.

The exhibition, in a small room on the ground floor, comprises a dozen or so evocative oil paintings in striking colours, reflecting Roerich's love for the mountains, and blending his Russian background with the mythological landscape of the Himalayas. The collection is complemented by a few old photos of the self-styled guru with Chinese silk robes, cossack boots and burly beard. The second-floor balcony provides excellent views of the valley and also the interior of Roerich's house, preserved exactly as it was when he lived there.

A path winds further up above the road through the forest for around 100m to **Urusvati-Himalayan Folk Art Museum** set among the large deodar trees of the forty-acre estate (same ticket applies). Founded by Madame Roerich in 1928, the museum features a collection of local folk art, costumes, more of Roerich's paintings, several paintings by his Russian followers, and a gallery of Russian folk art. A counter sells postcards and a small selection of books related to his work. Those interested in Roerich's astonishing paintings and philosophy can contact the International Centre (icr.moscow@mtu.net.ru).

The temples

The largest and most distinctive of Nagar's ancient Hindu **temples** and shrines, the wooden pagoda-style **Tripuri Sundri**, stands in a small enclosure at the top of the village, just below the road to the Roerich Gallery. Like the Dunghri temple in Manali, it is crowned with a three-tiered roof, whose top storey is circular. Animal carvings project from the eaves of the shrine, which houses an image of the Mother Goddess – "Beauty of the Triple World". Its *devta* is the focus of an annual *mela* (mid-May) in which deities from local villages are brought in procession to pay their respects.

Ten minutes' walk further up the hill – follow the stone steps that lead right from the road – brings you to a clearing where the old stone **Murlidhar** (Krishna) **Mandir** looks down on Nagar, with superb views up the valley to the snow peaks around Solan and the Rohtang Pass. Built on the ruins of the ancient town of Thawa the shrine, set in a large courtyard, is strictly off-limits to non-Hindus although the family who look after the temple are welcoming.

Finally, on your way to or from the bus stand at the bottom of the village, look out for the finely carved stone *shikharas* of the **Gaurishankar Mandir**. Set in its own paved courtyard below the castle, this Shiva temple, among the oldest of its kind in the valley, houses a living *lingam*, so slip off your shoes before approaching it.

Practicalities

Nagar is equidistant from Kullu and Manali (21km) and connected to both by regular **buses**. The direct services that ply the left-bank road, on the eastern side of the valley, are slower (1hr 30min from Manali and 1hr 30min from Kullu), but more scenic and straightforward than the more frequent services along the main highway on the opposite, west side. The latter drop at **Patlikuhl** (3km north of Katrain), from where taxis, auto-rickshaws and hourly buses cross the Beas to climb up to Nagar (6km). If you arrive in daylight and are not weighed down with bags, you can also walk from Patlikuhl on the old mule track – a hike of up to an hour. The last direct bus from Manali leaves around 5pm; if you miss it, travel on any bus on the main road to Patlikuhl and change there.

The castle, Roerich Gallery, temples, and most of Nagar's accommodation lie above the small bazaar where the buses pull in. If you have your own vehicle, you can drive all the way up to the Roerich Gallery at the top of the village.

If you are thinking of **trekking** around Nagar contact Ravi Sharma at Himalayan Mountain Treks (☎01902/47747), *Poonam Mountain Lodge,* who has equipment and can arrange porters and guides. He also arranges Jeep trips to Lahaul and Spiti. Alternatively, local guides are easy to find, but make sure that they are reputable. You are advised to use guides especially if crossing the **Chandrakhani Pass** to Malana (see p.579).

Accommodation and eating

Nagar's most popular place to **stay**, the HPTDC *Hotel Castle* (☎01902/47816; ❸–❼), offers well-furnished en-suite doubles (some with superb views from spacious wooden balconies) and dorm beds (Rs75). Book in advance at any HPTDC tourist office to secure one of the more expensive rooms in the west wing. A good fall-back is the *Sheetal Guest House* (☎01902/47750; ❷–❺), up the road, where rooms come with balconies, bathrooms and hot water, and at reduced rates off-season. The equally comfortable *Poonam Mountain Lodge* (☎01902/47747; ❸), around the corner, offers cosy doubles and has a good non-veg restaurant serving local specialities such as red rice.

The friendly *Snow View Guest House* (☎01902/47735; ❷), adjacent to the Tripuri Sundri temple, has doubles that open onto a pleasant garden, along with cheaper non-attached rooms, dorm beds and an inexpensive rooftop café.

The popular *Alliance Guest House* (**1**–**2**), halfway between the Tripuri Sundri and the Roerich Gallery has simple, clean rooms and a warm family atmosphere. Close above the bus stand, off the first bend to the castle, *Chand Kulvi* (**2**–**3**) has sizeable rooms and a garden. Near Nagar, 1km up a rough road from Katrain, the *Tree House Cottage* (☏01902/40365; **2**–**6**), set in a beautiful, quiet pomegranate and apple orchard, offers a range of accommodation including self-catering cottages. The brand new *Karbo Shin Guesthouse* (☏01902/47842; **2**–**3**) in Ghourdor village, has four rooms, a shared bathroom with hot shower, excellent food, and superb views, and also arranges local and long-distance treks. To get there take a rickshaw or taxi from Nagar or walk up the path from the bus stand past the Chand Kulvi (10–15min).

The *Cinderella Restaurant* serves good food, including grilled trout available if ordered a few hours in advance. Other **eating** options include the *Chandrakhani Café*, set in a pleasant orchard above Tripura Sundari and run by a couple of Westerners, who serve brown rice, herbal teas, hummus and tahini. Down at the main bazaar overlooking the bus stand, the *Prem Rose Café* is a favourite with locals and travellers alike. A path below the Punjab National Bank leads to the small Anthem Organics cheese factory where you can stock up on their springy Caerphilly-like cheese.

Manali and around

Himachal's main tourist resort, **MANALI**, stands at the head of the Kullu Valley, 108km north of Mandi. Despite lying at the heart of the region's highest mountain ranges, it remains easily accessible by road from the plains; after one hour on a plane and a short hop by road, or sixteen hours on a bus from Delhi, you could be staring from your hotel veranda across apple orchards and thick pine forests to the eternal snowfields of Solang Nala, which shine a tantalizing stone's throw away to the north. With the continuing troubles in Kashmir, Manali has become increasingly popular with domestic tourists, giving rise to an eclectic mix of honeymooners, holiday-makers, hippies, trekkers and traders.

The Manali that lured travellers in the 1970s has certainly changed although the majestic mountain scenery, thermal springs and quality *charas* can still be enjoyed. **Old Manali** retains some of its atmosphere and the village of **Vashisht** across the valley, with its increasing choice of guesthouses and cafés, has become a popular place to chill out. For those preferring to venture into the mountains, Manali makes an ideal **trekking** base for short hikes and serious expeditions, with plenty of opportunity to meet potential trekking companions, and to hire guides and porters. Countless agencies can help put a package together for you. The relaxing hotels in Manali's cleaner greener outskirts, and dozens of sociable cafés and restaurants, ranged around a well-stocked **bazaar**, provide a welcome relief from the rigours of the mountain trails. For more on treks around Manali and the Kullu Valley, see p.578.

Arrival and information

Buses pull in to Manali's **bus stand** in the middle of the Mall, a short walk from the helpful **tourist office** (Mon–Sat 10am–1pm & 1.30–5pm;

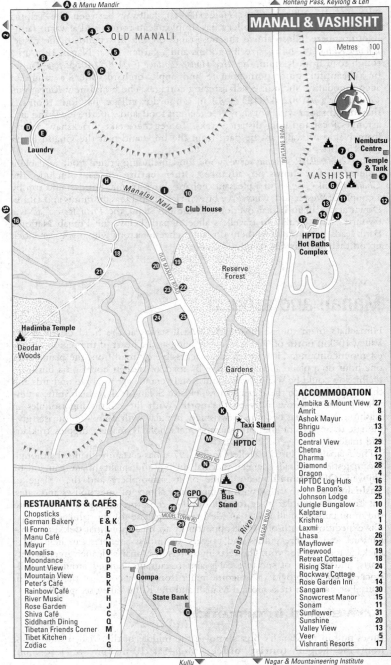

OLD MANALI

Laundry

Manalsu Nala

Club House

Reserve
Forest

Hadimba Temple

Deodar
Woods

Gardens

VASHISHT

Nembutsu
Centre

Temple
& Tank

HPTDC
Hot Baths
Complex

★ Taxi Stand

ⓘ
HPTDC

MISSION RD

GPO
P

Bus
Stand

MODEL TOWN RD

Gompa

Gompa

State Bank

OLD MANALI ROAD

ROHTANG ROAD

NAGAR ROAD

Beas River

ACCOMMODATION

Ambika & Mount View	27
Amrit	8
Ashok Mayur	6
Bhrigu	13
Bodh	7
Central View	29
Chetna	21
Dharma	12
Diamond	28
Dragon	4
HPTDC Log Huts	16
John Banon's	23
Johnson Lodge	10
Jungle Bungalow	10
Kalptaru	9
Krishna	1
Laxmi	3
Lhasa	26
Mayflower	22
Pinewood	19
Retreat Cottages	18
Rising Star	24
Rockway Cottage	2
Rose Garden Inn	14
Sangam	30
Snowcrest Manor	15
Sonam	11
Sunflower	31
Sunshine	20
Valley View	13
Veer	5
Vishranti Resorts	17

RESTAURANTS & CAFÉS

Chopsticks	P
German Bakery	E & K
Il Forno	P
Manu Café	L
Mayur	A
Monalisa	N
Moondance	O
Mount View	D
Mountain View	P
Peter's Café	B
Rainbow Café	K
River Music	F
Rose Garden	H
Shiva Café	J
Siddharth Dining	C
Tibetan Friends Corner	Q
Tibet Kitchen	M
Zodiac	I & G

(☏01902/52175). You can make reservations for the town's state-run hotels at the HPTDC offices next door. If you need to **change money**, the State Bank of India (Mon–Fri 10am–2pm, Sat 10am–noon) is on the main road 250m south of the Mall. There are also a handful of authorized private agencies open longer hours but these usually offer lower rates. The main **post office**, off Model Town Road, has a reliable poste restante counter (Mon–Sat 9am–1pm & 1.30–5pm) and there is an **internet** café next door. **Inner Line Permits** for restricted areas such as upper Kinnaur are issued at the Sub-District Magistrate's office (☏01902/54100); two photos and photocopy of passport and visa details are needed – although most people apply either in Kaza (see p.584), or if travelling south–north, in Rekong Peo (see p.533).

Accommodation

There are four quite distinct accommodation sectors in Manali. Most longer-stay budget places are clustered in **Old Manali**, where rough-and-ready family-run guesthouses nestle amidst the orchards. A *charas*-induced torpor hangs over many of them, but the peace and quiet and views from their flower gardens make the two-kilometre hike worthwhile. Tucked away behind the Mall is a cluster of identikit concrete hotels known as **Model Town**. Mostly mid-range and seriously lacking character, they are however conveniently located and can be very good value in the off-season. Most of Manali's **classic hotels** with gardens and character are dotted around the northern and western outskirts. Finally, across the Beas River, a couple of kilometres south, the expanding enclave of **New Manali** comprises several comfortable, if characterless, top-of-the-range hotels. Although Manali itself is considered safe, **women** should be wary of walking along the lane from town to Old Manali after dark, which has been the scene of several attempted **rapes** over the last few years.

All hotels are registered with the tourist authority and are obliged to display their charges at the reception. Tariffs rocket in Manali during **high season** (April–July & Sept–Nov). At other times, a fifty percent reduction on the advertised rates for more expensive hotels is standard. The few hotels that stay open in **winter** cater mainly for skiing parties. All prices listed below are for high season.

Chetna, below Hadimba temple ☏01902/52245. Spruce red and white building in a peaceful location with large, neat rooms, lawns, verandas and hot water. ③–⑤

HPTDC Log Huts, overlooking Manalsu Nala ☏01902/52407. Comfortable wooden holiday cottages with one or two bedrooms, tucked away in the woods with kitchen and most comforts including Star TV but overpriced. ⑧–⑨

Johnson Lodge, Old Manali Road ☏01902/53023. Three-star comfort in an old colonial building converted into separate cottages. Also known as *Joe Lawrence's*. ⑦

John Banon's, Old Manali Road ☏01902/52335. Old guesthouse with large though slightly run-down rooms. Pleasant orchard-cum-gardens with valley views. ⑤

Mayflower, Old Manali Road ☏01902/52104. The old wing is cheaper but the new wing overlooking pine forests, with its spacious wood-panelled rooms, is one of the best deals in Manali. ⑤–⑦

Pinewood, off Old Manali Road ☏01902/52118. Colonial building with furniture and garden to match. All rooms with balcony. Good value off-season. ⑥

Retreat Cottages, Log Hut Road ☏01902/52042. Immaculate and good-sized self-catering two- and three-bedroom suites with baths (Rs5000) in a tastefully designed building. Meals can also be ordered. ⑥

Rising Star, Hadimba temple road ☏01902/52381. Budget rooms at the back boast big verandas overlooking a leafy garden. Among the best deals in town. ③–⑤

Snowcrest Manor, above the Log Huts ☏01902/53351, ✉ushahtls@vsnl.com. New hotel occupying highest point in Manali with luxury rooms and large terrace overlooking valley. ⑧–⑨

Sunflower, Tibetan quarter ☎ 01902/52419. One of several hotels near the *gompas*; better value off-season. ❸–❹

Sunshine, off Old Manali Road ☎ 01902/52320. Old double-storey wooden building with period fur-niture, fireplaces, and magnificent views from spacious balconies. Meals served on request in the dining room. Fixed price throughout the year. ❹

Old Manali

Ashok Mayur, ☎ 01902/ 52868. Small, basic and friendly guesthouse opposite *Shiva* café, with balconies warmed by the morning sun. ❶

Dragon, ☎ 01902/ 52790. New hotel with brash exterior but comfortable and spacious en-suite rooms with hot water and balconies. ❸–❹

Jungle Bungalow, above the Club House ☎ 01902/52278. Simple but comfortable rooms, shared bathrooms and walls for graffiti. ❶

Krishna, ☎ 01902/53071. Small, friendly place with wide balconies and hot water in shared bathrooms. Connecting doors between rooms make it handy for small groups. ❷

Laxmi, ☎ 01902/53569. Large, clean and simple budget rooms surrounded by shady flower gardens and orchards. Shared bathrooms only. ❷

Rockway Cottage, 500m along a track off and above the main road in an idyllic setting (no phone). Pleasant rooms, some with wood heaters. Good food in the garden café. Well worth the effort, but bring a torch. ❷

Veer, ☎ 01902/52410. Simple place with fine views down the valley from a lovely leafy garden. Some attached bathrooms, too. ❷

New Manali

Situated a couple of kilometres south of Manali on the left bank of the Beas, the developing strip of hotels here include the *Holiday Inn* (☎01902/52262; ❽–❾), *Manali Ashok* (☎01902/53103; ❽), *Honeymoon Inn* (☎01902/53234; ❻–❽), *Imperial Palace* (☎01902/53330; ❽) and a couple of cheaper ones such as the *Evergreen* (☎01902/53038; ❻–❼) and the *Narayan* (☎01902/53133; ❺).

Model Town

A number of carbon-copy **hotels** are clustered in the grid of narrow streets immediately behind the Mall, in a quarter known as **Model Town**. Though bland and boxed-in, these mid-range places make good bases from which to hunt for other accommodation once you've found your feet. Recommended accommodation includes: *Central View* (☎01902/52319; ❹–❺), which has bath-tubs in some rooms, *Diamond* (☎01902/53058; ❹–❺), *Lhasa* (☎01902/52134; ❺), *Mount View* (☎01902/52465; ❸–❺), with rooftop terrace and views, and the *Sangam* (☎01902/53019; ❻).

The Town

Manali's main street, **the Mall**, quite unlike its namesake in Shimla, is a noisy scene of constant activity, fronted by the bus station, several shopping markets, a line of hotels and restaurants, and travel agents. Find a good window seat and watch the world go by – locals in traditional caps, Tibetan women in immaculate rainbow-striped pinafores, Nepali porters, Buddhist monks, the odd party of Zanskaris swathed in fusty woollen *gonchas*, souvenir-hunting Indian tourists and a curious mix of Westerners. Most people staying a while in Manali stick to the quieter areas, lodging in the old town, and take daily strolls through the surrounding woods and hills, where villagers at work in the fields seem untroubled by the racy pace of the Mall.

Manali's days as an authentic *pahari* bazaar ended when the mule trains were superseded by Tata trucks, but it's still great for souvenir **shopping**. Woollen goods are the town's real forte, particularly the brilliantly patterned **shawls** for which Kullu Valley is famous. The NSC (New Shopping Centre) market near

Manali's **Taxi Operators' Union kiosk** (℡01902/52450) stands on the east side of the square at the top of town, just up from the tourist office. The taxis have fixed rates which are negotiable off-season.

Weather and road conditions permitting, HPTDC (℡01902/52116), two doors down from the tourist office, run daily bus **tours** to the **Rohtang Pass** (9am–5pm; Rs175). Other tours include day-trips to **Manikaran** in the Parvati Valley (9am–6pm; Rs200). Tickets can be booked ahead at the tourist office.

Considering the fierce white water that thrashes down the Kullu Valley during spring melt, Manali's **rafting** scene is surprisingly low-key. Raft trips down the River Beas are offered between the end of May and early July, when water levels are highest, beginning at Bhuntur (just south of Kullu) and ending 14km downstream at the mouth of the Larji gorge. The price should include meals, lifejackets, helmets, and return travel; check exactly what you're paying for, as some unscrupulous operators expect you to make your own way back after the trip.

The **heli-skiing** around Manali is supposed to be great, but costs $5000 a week. Regular skiing in the Solang valley is popular from January to April. The Solang valley is also the biggest **paragliding** centre in India. **Mountain-biking** is also possible from mid-July to mid-September and you can rent bikes here.

If you're planning a trekking or rafting trip, shop around to compare prices and packages; many agencies are fly-by-night operators who make their money from mark-ups on long-distance bus tickets to Delhi, Chandigarh and Leh. Long-established, **reputable agents** include the very experienced Rup Negi at Himalayan Adventurers (℡01902/52182), opposite the tourist office, and Himanshu Sharma at Himalayan Journeys (℡01902/52365, ✉himjourn@del3.vsnl.net.in), next to the State Bank of India. They can organize rafting, mountain-biking, ski packages at Solang, and heli-skiing in the thick of winter. Other recommended agents include Chandertal Treks & Tours (℡01902/52665) and Beas Treks & Tours (℡01902/52806), both at the New Shopping Centre. Most agents also operate **Jeep safaris** to remote regions such as Spiti.

the bus stand sells a good selection. The price of a shawl depends on its size, age, quality of wool, and, most important of all, your ability to haggle. The cheapest are machine-woven, thin, and neither warm nor durable. Genuine pure-wool handloom shawls with embroidered borders start at around Rs500, but those made from finest pashmina – an exquisitely soft wool shorn from the underbelly of Himalayan goats – cost several thousand rupees. The acid test for quality pashmina is that it does not crease when crumpled. Shop around and check out the fixed-price factory shops to get an idea of what's available. The government-sponsored Bhutico on the Mall opposite the tourist office and the Bodh Shawl factory shop just off the Mall south of the bus stand are both recommended.

Elsewhere around the bazaar, innumerable stalls are stacked with handwoven goods and pillbox Kullu **topis**. Those with gaudy multicoloured up-turned flaps and gold piping are indigenous to the valley, but you can also pick up the plain-green velvet-fronted variety favoured by Kinnauris.

Manali's other speciality is **Tibetan curios** such as prayer wheels, amulets, *dorjees* (thunderbolts), masks, musical instruments, jewellery and **thangkas**. Few of the items hawked as antiques are genuine, but it takes an expert eye to spot a fake. The same applies to silver **jewellery** inlaid with turquoise and coral, which can nonetheless be attractive and relatively inexpensive. Several stalls near the bus stand are ideal for a good rummage, with counters packed with silver jewellery and semiprecious stones such as agate, amber, lapis lazuli, turquoise and coral.

The Hadimba temple

Resting on a wide stone platform in a dense stand of old deodar, fifteen minutes' walk northwest of the bazaar, the **Hadimba temple** is Manali's oldest shrine and the seat of Hadimba (or "Hirma Devi"), wife of Bhima. Legend has it that Bhima (the strongest of the five Pandava brothers of *Mahabharata* fame) fell in love with this "mountain belle", the only sister of the fierce demon Tandi, killed by Bhima in hand-to-hand combat. Considered to be an incarnation of Kali, Hadimba is worshipped in times of adversity, and also plays a key role in the Dussehra festival (see p.562). Hadimba is supposed to have given the kingdom of Kullu to the forefathers of the rajas of Kullu, and in veneration and affection the family to this day refer to her as "grandmother". Soft-drinks stands, curio stalls, yak rides and photo opportunities in a range of outlandish costumes cater for visitors while the presiding deity looks on.

The massive triple-tiered wooden pagoda crowned by crimson pennants and a brass ball and trident (Shiva's *trishul*), dates from 1553, and is a replica of earlier ones that burned down in successive forest fires. Its facade writhes with wonderful woodcarvings of elephants, crocodiles and folk deities, as well as scenes from a legend in which a raja chops the hands off the royal sculptor to prevent him from repeating his masterpiece elsewhere. Entered by a door surmounted by wild ibex horns, the gloomy **shrine** is dominated by several large boulders, one of which shelters the stone on which goats and buffalo are sacrificed during important rituals. The hollow in its middle, believed to be Vishnu's footprint, channels the blood to Hadimba's mouth.

The gompas

Manali harbours the highest concentration of **Tibetan refugees** in the Kullu Valley, hence the numer of prayer flags stringed and fluttering over the approach roads into town, and the presence, on its southern edge, of two shiny new **gompas**.

Capped with polished golden finials, the distinctive yellow corrugated-iron pagoda roof of the **Gadhan Thekchhokling gompa** is an exotic splash of colour amid the ramshackle huts of the Tibetan quarter. Built in 1969, the monastery is maintained by donations from the local community and through the sale of **carpets** handwoven in the temple workshop. When they are not looking after the **shop**, the young *lamas* huddle in the courtyard to play *cholo* – a Tibetan dice game involving much shouting and slamming of wooden *tsampa* bowls on leather pads. The brightly painted *La-khang*, or prayer hall, dominated by a large seated Shakyamuni, stands on the west side of the quadrangle and is open to visitors. Photography is permitted; leave a donation in the box as you leave. Beside the main entrance, a roll of honour recounts the names of Tibetans killed during the violent political demonstrations that wracked China in the late 1980s.

The smaller and more modern of the two *gompas* stands nearer the bazaar, in a garden that in late summer blazes with sunflowers. Its main shrine, lit by dozens of bare electric bulbs and filled with fragrant Tibetan incense, houses a colossal gold-faced Buddha, best viewed from the small room on the first floor. Downstairs, monks sit on the veranda block-printing brightly coloured prayer flags.

Old Manali

Old Manali, the village from which the modern town takes its name, lies 2km north of the Mall, on the far side of the Manalsu *nala*. Unlike its crowded, concrete offspring, the settlement retains an unhurried and traditional feel. To get there, head north up Old Manali Road, bear right at the fork in the road, and keep going through the pine woods until you reach the iron bridge across the river.

You'll pass a string of small guesthouses and cafés before reaching the village proper, clustered on top of a steeply shelving ledge of level ground above the *nala*. It is also known as **Manaligarh** after its ancient citadel – a ruined fort surrounded by a patchwork of maize terraces and deep-green orchards that fan down to the Beas. At the centre of the village is an unusual, brash new temple dedicated to **Manu**, who, as is written in the second-century BC *Manusmriti*, "the remembered utterances of Manu", laid the foundations of Hindu law that continues to today, as well as *varna* or "colour" – the basis of the caste system. Inscribed stones dating from the Middle Ages embedded into the concrete paving reveal the site's antiquity. The place of the temple was originally called Manualiya or the "home of Manu", which, according to one theory, was later shortened to "Manali".

Built in the old *pahari* style, most of the houses of Old Manali have heavy stone roofs and wooden balconies hung with bushels of drying herbs and tobacco. Handlooms holding half-woven woollen shawls stand outside doorways whose lintels are painted with folk murals, while cows chew their way through bales of sweet-smelling hay scattered across smoky courtyards. The only indication that tourism has not entirely passed Old Manali by is the bands of scruffy kids that accost you, thrusting lumps of *charas* in your face and demanding "one pen, one pen".

Eating

Manali's wide range of **restaurants** reflect the town's melting-pot credentials: Tibetan *thukpa* joints stand cheek-by-jowl with south Indian coffee houses, Gujarati thali bars, and Nepalese-run German pastry shops. Whatever their ostensible speciality, though, most offer mixed menus that include Chinese and Western dishes alongside standard north Indian favourites. For rock-bottom budget food, head for one of the *dhabas* opposite the bus stand. Virtually every café in Manali serves serious "**tourist breakfasts**" of porridge, pancakes, toast and jam; chai and omelette-wallahs appear on the Mall before dawn if you need to steel yourself for a long and bumpy bus journey.

Finally, stock up on energy-rich **trekking food** at the local produce stores and bakeries in the bazaar. The state-sponsored co-op, near the temple on the Mall, sells sacks of nuts, dried fruit and pots of pure honey at fixed prices.

Chopsticks, the Mall. Very popular Tibetan-run restaurant with a pleasant atmosphere and varied menu. Good selection of music, with interesting fusions between techno, drum and bass, and classical Indian.

German Bakery, Old Manali Road near the Mall; another in Old Manali. Both good places to indulge a sweet tooth: apple pie, strudel, lemon cake, and Western wholefood snacks.

Il Forno, Hadimba Road. A traditional building that has been successfully converted into an Italian-run restaurant serving excellent pizzas, pasta, salads and tiramisu. Good views.

Manu Café, Old Manali. A local house with a small upstairs café, which despite the usual travellers' menu is best for local food.

Mayur, Mission Road, just off the Mall. Exciting and extensive Indian menu at very reasonable prices. Candles, serviettes and classical Indian music. Recommended.

Monalisa, bazaar area. Cosy, sociable tourist café with a reasonably priced menu of Indian, Chinese and Continental dishes, desserts, soups and light snacks.

Moondance, Old Manali. Popular garden café and meeting place above the river with a varied menu that includes Mexican and Italian dishes.

Mount View, the Mall. Chinese, Japanese, and authentic Tibetan food in Chinese-style restaurant decorated with paper lanterns.

Mountain View Café, Old Manali. Set away from most of the guesthouses, with extensive views.

Simple yet varied menu; open 24hr in season or when there's sufficient demand.

Peter's Café, off Old Manali Road, near the Mall. Behind the *German Bakery*, congenial atmosphere with good breakfasts if you don't mind the whiff of *charas*.

River Music Café, the bridge, Old Manali, hang-out place with tables on terrace or floor cushion seating under shelter. Usual menu and good sound system.

Shiva Café, Old Manali. Sociable, lazy balcony, an open fire most evenings, and Chinese, Indian and pasta dishes make this popular among budget travellers.

Siddharth Dining, next to State Bank of India. Excellent Maharashtran and South Indian food. Range of popular Western food in high season.

Tibetan Friends' Corner, Siyali market, just behind the Mall. A small upstairs restaurant serv-

Moving on from Manali

Manali is well connected by bus to other Himachali towns and major cities on the plains. HPSRTC run luxury, deluxe and ordinary buses, all of which can be booked at the bus stand. During the summer, demand invariably outstrips supply, particularly for the faster services, so book as far in advance as possible, and be prepared for regular and fruitless visits to ticket offices. The numerous travel agents dotted around town also sell tickets for private "deluxe" services to Delhi, Shimla and Dharamsala. Consider breaking your journey in Mandi (for Rewalsar) or using the Kangra valley railway to reach Dharamsala, or Pathankot from where you can pick up trains for Amritsar, Delhi and Rajasthan. The Rohtang pass at the head of the Kullu valley is only open June–Oct when buses travel to Keylong, capital of Lahaul. It can be difficult to book onward transport from Keylong to Leh as buses nearly always arrive full, so either reserve a seat in advance or consider returning to Manali to book all the way through. Buses also cross the Rohtang La to Kaza, capital of Spiti from where you can continue to Shimla, although permits are required to travel beyond Tabo. Harrisons Travels (℡01902/53338), Monal Himalayan Travels (℡01902/54031), Swagatam (℡01902/52390) and Hill Tours (℡01902/52183), on the Mall, and Valleycon (℡01902/52316), at the bus stand and at *Mayur* restaurant, all sell tickets.

Transport to Leh

If you can afford to split the Rs12,000 fare, mini-vans and Maruti Gypsy taxis are the most comfortable way to get to Ladakh from Manali and you might get a cheaper deal from a returning vehicle. Backpackers usually travel the 485km to Leh by bus – an arduous, but unforgettable two-day trip (28hr), involving a night halt under canvas along the route.

HPTDC's daily "luxury" bus, bookable through the tourist office, costs around Rs1000, which includes accommodation at the tent colony near Sarchu. The journey can take three days, with two nights on the road. Otherwise, choice is limited to the beaten-up buses operated by HPSRTC and their J&K equivalents, which despite their discomfort are faster.

Officially, the Manali–Leh Highway is open from mid-June until September 15, after which the state services are suspended and emergency services aren't available for civilian traffic. Some of the private companies, however, continue to operate until the end of September, when the inflated end-of-season prices they charge encourage them to risk getting stuck in an early snowfall. Four-wheel-drive taxis continue to ply the route well into October, but again you risk getting stuck and having to spend a few extra freezing cold nights on the road.

Whenever and however you travel, avoid the bumpy back seat of the bus and take food and lots of water (at least 2–3 litres) to reduce the risk of dehydration and altitude sickness. The road traverses the 4800m to Baralacha La on the first day. Around 50km beyond Sarchu, you attain an altitude of 5000m at Lachulung La, and later the same day, 5360m at Tanglang La, the highest point on the road.

See Travel Details at the end of this chapter for more information on journey frequencies and durations.

ing good Tibetan food and decorated in Tibetan style. Japanese, Chinese and Western food also available.

Tibet Kitchen, near the Club House, Old Manali. A comfortable and popular restaurant with a mixed menu serving great Tibetan food as well as the odd Japanese dish.

Vashisht

Famous for its sweeping valley views and sulphurous hot-water springs, the ever-expanding village of **VASHISHT**, 3km north of Manali, is an amorphous jumble of traditional timber houses and modern concrete cubes, divided by

---

Treks around Manali and the Kullu valley

The Kullu Valley's spectacular alpine scenery and proximity to some of HP's most dramatic and accessible peaks make it perfect for **trekking**. The trails are long and steep, but more than repay the effort with superb views, varied flora and the chance visit remote hill stations.

Within striking distance of several major trailheads, **Manali** is the most popular place to begin and end treks. While **package deals** offered by the town's many agencies can save time and energy, it is relatively easy to organize your own trip with maps and advice from the Tourist Office and Mountaineering Institute at the bottom end of town. Porters and horsemen can be sought out in the square behind the main street. Always take a reliable **guide**, especially on less-frequented routes as you cannot rely solely on **maps**. Some trekkers have reported difficulties when descending from the Bara Bangal pass as maps don't do the terrain justice.

The optimum **season** is right after the monsoons (mid-Sept to late Oct), when skies are clear and pass-crossings easier. From June to August, you run the risk of sudden, potentially fatal snow, or view-obscuring cloud and rain.

Manali to Beas Kund

The relatively easy trek to Beas Kund, a glacial lake at the head of Solang *nala*, is the region's most popular short hike. Encircled by 5000-metre-plus peaks, the well-used campground beside the lake, accessible in two days from Manali, makes a good base for side-trips up to the surrounding ridges and passes.

From **Palchan**, a village 30min north of Manali by bus, follow the Jeep track up the valley to **Solang**, site of a small ski station, rest house, and the Mountaineering Institute's log huts. The next two hours take you through pine forests, grassy meadows and boulder chokes to the campground at **Dhundi** (2743m), Gaddi grazing land with the Hanuman Tibba massif (5928m) to the west. A more strenuous walk of 5–6hr the next day leads to **Beas Kund**. The hike up to the **Tentu La** pass (4996m) and back from here can be done in a day, as can the descent to Manali via Solang.

Manali to Lahaul, via the Hampta Pass

The three-day trek from the Kullu Valley over the Hampta Pass to Lahaul, the old caravan route to Spiti, is a classic. Rising to 4330m, it is high by Kullu standards; do not undertake it without allowing good time to **acclimatize**. **Day 1**, from the trailhead at **Prini** (near Manali) through Hampta village to the campground above **Sethen**, is an easy hike of 4–5hr up the verdant, forested sides of the valley. **Day 2**, another 5hr, brings you to **Chikha**, a high Gaddi pasture below the pass; stay put for a day or so if you're feeling the effects of altitude. The ascent (700m) on **Day 3** to the **Hampta Pass** (4330m) is gruelling, but the views from the top – of Indrasan and Deo Tibba to the south, and the moonscape of Lahaul to the north – are sublime recompense. It takes 6–7hr of relentless rock-hopping and stream-crossing to reach **Chhatru**, on the floor of the Chandra Valley. From here, you can turn east

paved courtyards and narrow muddy lanes. It is the epicentre of the local budget travellers' scene, with a good choice of guesthouses and cafés; the tranquil and traditional atmosphere is interrupted by the occasional rave that takes place in the woods, or if the weather is poor, in one or two obliging hotels.

You can get to Vashisht by road, or along the footpath that winds up the steep slope from the main highway past the HPTDC hot baths complex and rejoins the road just before the village. The **Hot Bath Complex**, with its individual bathing tubs (regular and deluxe), is currently closed due to a dispute between the villagers and the Himachal government regarding payments and the water supply that the villagers believe to be theirs by right. In the meantime, the only

towards Koksar and the **Rohtang Pass**, or west past the world's largest glacier, **Bara Shigri**, to **Batal**, the trailhead for the Chandratal–Baralacha trek (see p.582).

Nagar to Malana via the Chandrakani Pass and onwards

The trek to Jari in the Parvati Valley from Nagar, 21km south of Manali, is quintessential Kullu Valley trekking with superb scenery and fascinating villages. The round trip can be completed in three days, but you may be tempted to linger in **Malana** and explore the surrounding countryside. A **guide** is essential, as the first stage involves crossing a maze of grazing trails, and because Malana is culturally sensitive and requires some familiarity with local customs. In addition, several people have **disappeared** in the Parvati Valley over the last few years in suspicious circumstances (see p.564). Note too that the descent to the Parvati Valley is too steep for pack ponies but porters are available in Nagar through the guesthouses, including Himalayan Mountain Treks at *Poonam Mountain Lodge*.

The trail leads through the village of Rumsu and then winds through wonderful old-growth forests of mixed chestnut, walnuts, pines and huge deodar cedars. The pasture just above the tree line makes ideal camping ground. From here, a climb of 4km takes you to the **Chandrakani Pass** (3660m), which has fine views west over the top of the Kullu Valley to the peaks surrounding Solang Nala, and north to the Ghalpo mountains of Lahaul. Some prefer to reach the base of the pass on the first day and then camp below the final ascent.

The inhabitants of **MALANA**, a steep 7km descent from the pass, are known for their frostiness and staunch traditions. Although notions of **caste pollution** are not as strictly adhered to as they once were, you should observe a few basic **"rules"** in Malana: wait to be invited into the village before entering; stick to paths at all times; keep away from the temple; and above all, don't touch anybody or anything, especially not children or houses. If you do commit a cultural blunder, you'll be expected to make amends: usually in the form of a cash payment for a sacrificial offering of a young sheep or goat to the village deity, **Jamlu**, one of the most powerful Kullu Valley gods. His **temple**, open to high-caste Hindus only, is decorated with lively folk carvings, among them images of soldiers – the villagers claim to be the area's sole remaining descendants of Alexander the Great's army. *Santu Ram's* (**①**), in the middle of the Harijan quarter, is the most popular **guesthouse** here, as its owner is an authority on local trails. Part of the village headman's house also functions as a small hostel (**①**). Both offer simple meals. The official camping ground, lies 100m beyond the village spring.

The **final stage** of the trek takes you down the sheer limestone and scrub-strewn sides of Malana *nala* to the floor of the Parvati Valley – a precipitous 12km drop. From the hamlet of **Rashol**, you have a choice of three onward routes: either head east up the right bank of the river to **Manikaran** (see p.565); follow the trail southwest to the sacred **Bijli Mahadev Mandir** (see p.561); or climb the remaining 3km up to the road at **Jari**, from where regular buses leave for Bhuntur, Kullu and Manali.

place for a hot soak is in the bathing pools of Vashisht's ancient temple (free), which is far more atmospheric anyway. Divided into separate sections for men and women, they attract a decidedly mixed crowd of Hindu pilgrims, Western hippies, semi-naked *sadhus*, and gangs of local kids that splash happily about in the pungent soapy water.

Vashisht boasts two old stone **temples**, opposite each other above the main square and dedicated to the local patron saint Vashista (and guru of Raghunathji). The smaller of the two opens onto a partially covered courtyard, and is adorned with elaborate woodcarvings. Those lining the interior of the shrine, blackened by years of oil-lamp and *dhoop* smoke, are worth checking out. Above the village, the **Nembutsu Centre** (℡01902/53494) runs short- and long-term **meditation** courses.

Accommodation

Vashisht is packed with budget **guesthouses**, many of them old wooden buildings with broad verandas and uninterrupted vistas up the valley. If you don't mind primitive plumbing, grungy beds and dope smoke, the only time you'll not be spoilt for choice is during high season, when even floor-space can be at a premium. On the outskirts, a couple of larger hotels offer good value, comfortable rooms. The places below are marked on the Manali & Vashisht map on p.570.

Amrit, the uppermost hotel, tucked away behind the temple ℡1902/54209. Turquoise-painted wooden house with basic facilities. Grubby but atmospheric with rickety balconies affording fine views. **➊**

Bhrigu Hotel, below the village centre, on the roadside ℡ 01902/53414. Large hotel whose west-facing rooms all have attached bathrooms and superb views from their balconies. **➌**

Bodh, behind *Dolnath Guest House* ℡ 01902/54165. Opposite a large wooden building in heart of village with superb views from the roof terrace. Shared bathrooms. **➋**

Dharma, five minutes' walk up the lane behind the temples ℡ 01902/52354. Basic old wing and new wing with hot showers. Highest hotel in Vashisht with great views. **➊–➌**

Kalptaru, overlooking the temple tanks ℡ 01902/53443. You can't get any closer to the baths – with reasonable rooms, mostly en-suite. Small garden and veranda from which to watch the world go by. **➊**

Rose Garden Inn, next to the HPTDC baths (no phone). Two cosy chalet-style rooms with carpets and bathtubs, looking over a grassy lawn. **➊**

Sonam, just down the road from the square (no phone). Dirt cheap, cramped and grubby, but an old favourite. **➊**

Valley View, close to *Bhrigu* ℡ 01902/53420. A great terrace restaurant, reasonable rooms including some with good views, but a bit expensive. **➍–➎**

Vishranti Resorts, just above the main highway ℡ 01902/53421. A bright white building overlooking the footpath, with large, light, clean rooms, hot showers, a sunny roof terrace, garden and restaurant. Good value. **➋–➌**

Eating

As a backpacker's paradise, most of Vashisht's numerous cafés serve typical fare, including fried rice, noodles, omelettes, pancakes and lassis. In addition to the cafés, bakeries provide wholemeal bread, apple pies and a variety of sticky things. Most of the cafés are hang-out places, and several have open-air terraces with free views, but there is little to choose between them.

Rainbow Café and **Bakery**, just past *Kalptaru* hotel with views from the terrace and traveller-friendly offerings such as pancakes, pasta and spring rolls.

Rose Garden, on the main road above HPTDC baths. Tastefully decorated, expensive restaurant with a good selection of Italian food, excellent cap-

pucinos/real coffee and a pleasant garden with a wonderful kiwi-fruit vine.

Zodiac, off the square. Vashisht's most famous New-Age café – with a liberal sprinkling of older folk in a timeless, smoke-filled atmosphere. Menu includes pumpkin pie and herbal teas. Internet facilities at the *Cyberdelic* café in the same enclosure.

Lahaul and Spiti

Few places on earth can mark so dramatic a change in landscape as the **Rohtang Pass**. To one side, the lush green head of the Kullu Valley; to the other, an awesome vista of bare, chocolate-coloured mountains, hanging glaciers and snowfields that shine in the dazzlingly crisp light. The district of **Lahaul and Spiti**, Himachal's largest, is named after its two subdivisions, which are, in spite of their numerous geographical and cultural similarities, distinct and separate regions.

Lahaul

Lahaul, sometimes referred to as the Chandra-Bhaga Valley, is the region that divides the Great Himalayas and Pir Panjal ranges. Its principal river, the Chandra, rises deep in the barren wastes below the **Baralacha Pass**, a major landmark on the Manali–Leh road, from where it flows south, veering north-west around the base of the immense **Bara Shigri glacier** towards its confluence with the River Bhaga near Tandi. Here, the two rivers become the Chenab, and crash north out of Himachal to Kishtwar in Kashmir. Lahaul's **climate** is very similar to that of Ladakh and Zanskar, which border it to the north. The valley receives precious little rain, and during the summer the sun is very strong and the nights cool. Between late October and late March, heavy snow closes the passes, and seals off the region. Even so, its inhabitants, a mixture of Buddhists and Hindus, enjoy one of the highest per capita incomes in the subcontinent. Using glacial water channelled down the mountains through ancient irrigation ducts, Lahauli farmers manage to coax a bumper crop of **seed potatoes** from their painstakingly fashioned terraces. The region is also the sole supplier of **hops** to India's breweries, and harvests prodigious quantities of wild herbs, used to make perfume and medicine. Much of the profit generated by these cash crops is spent on lavish jewellery, especially seed-pearl necklaces and coral and turquoise-inlaid silver plaques, worn by the women over ankle-length burgundy or fawn woollen dresses.

Lahaul's traditional costume and Buddhism are a legacy of the Tibetan influence that has permeated the region from the east, along the course of the River Spiti.

State **buses** run from Manali up the Chandra and Bhaga valleys to Keylong and Darcha from whenever the Rohtang Pass is cleared, usually in late June, until it snows up again in late October. You can also travel through Lahaul on private Leh-bound buses if there are free seats.

Keylong

Lahaul's largest settlement and the district headquarters, **KEYLONG**, 114km north of Manali, is a good place to pause on the long road journey to Ladakh. Although of little interest itself, the village lies amid superb scenery, within a day's climb of three Buddhist **gompas**, one visible on the opposite (south) side of the grandiose Bhaga Valley. A couple of **stores** in the busy little market sell trekking supplies if you are heading off towards Zanskar.

Although the old trade routes to Ladakh and Tibet are now sealed with tarmac, most of this remote and spectacular region is still only accessible on foot. Its trails, though well frequented in high season, are long, hard and high, and punctuated by few settlements, so you must be self-sufficient and have a guide. Packhorses and provisions are most readily available in **Manali**; or **Keylong** and **Darcha** (Lahaul) and **Kaza** (Spiti) if you can afford to wait a few days. A good rope for river crossings will be useful on many of the routes, particularly in summer when the glaciers are melting and the water levels at their highest.

The **best time** to trek is July to early September, when brilliant blue skies make this an ideal alternative to the monsoon-prone Kullu Valley. By late September, the risk of snowfall deters many visitors from the longer expeditions. Whenever you leave, allow enough time to acclimatize to the **altitude** before attempting any big passes: AMS (Acute Mountain Sickness) claims victims here every season (see Basics, p.35).

The most popular trek is from **Darcha** over the **Shingo La** pass (5090m) to **Padum** in Zanskar. The trail passes through **Kargyak**, the highest village in Zanskar and follows the Kargyak valley down to its confluence with the Tsarap at Purne. There is a small café, shop, and camping ground here and it's a good base for the side trip to **Phuktal gompa**, one of the most spectacular sights in Zanskar. During the high season (July–Aug), a string of chai stall-tent camps spring up at intervals along the well-worn trail through the Tsarap valley to Padum, meaning that you can manage without a guide or ponies from here on. Do not bank on finding food and shelter here at the start or end of the season.

Lahaul's other popular trekking route follows the River Chandra north to its source at the **Baralacha Pass** (4650m), and makes a good extension to the Hampta Pass hike described on p.578–579. Alternatively, catch a Kaza bus from Manali to the trailhead at **Batal** (3960m) below the **Kunzum La** (4551m). The beautiful milky-blue **Chandratal** ("Moon") **Lake** is a relentless ascent of 7hr from Batal, with stunning views south across the world's longest glacier, **Bara Shigri**, and the forbidding north face of the **White Sail** massif (6446m). The next campground is at **Tokping Yongma** torrent. **Tokpo Yongma**, several hours further up, is the second of the two big side torrents and is much easier to ford early in the morning; from here it is a steady climb up to the **Baralacha Pass**. You can then continue to Zanskar via the Phirtse la, or pick up transport (prearranged if possible) down to Keylong and Manali or onwards to Leh.

One of the best treks in **SPITI** is up the **Pin Valley**. Starting 24km southeast of Kaza, a trail heads south along the right bank of the River Pin past a string of traditional settlements and monasteries to **Ghurguru**, where it forks in two; the northern path over the Pin-Parvati Pass (5400m) to **Manikaran** in the Parvati Valley (see p.565), and the southern one to Wangtu in **Kinnaur** via the Bhaba Pass (4865m).

Lahauli Buddhists consider it auspicious to make a clockwise circumambulation – known as the **Rangcha Parikarma** – of the sacred **Rangcha mountain** (4565m), which dominates the confluence of the Bhaga and Chandra rivers. A well-worn trail that makes a long day-hike from Keylong, the route is highly scenic, and takes in the large **Khardung gompa** along the way. Rising over 1000m from its base elevation (3348m), the trail is a hard slog if you haven't acclimatized, and should not be undertaken lightly. Carry plenty of food, water, and warm clothing, and be prepared to turn back if you start to feel dizzy and/or acutely short of breath. A rough motorable road leads to Khardung *gompa* (10km), but closer to Keylong and on the same side of the valley are two quiet and picturesque *gompas* high up the mountainside, **Shasher Gompa** (3km), run by Lama Paljor, and **Gungshal Gompa** (5km). A short but rewarding **trek** (14km) crosses the Drilbu pass on the opposite side of Keylong, and descends to the village of Gondla on the road to Rohtang Pass and Manali.

Practicalities

Keylong is connected by regular state **buses** to Manali, and (in summer) by private buses to all points north and south along the main highway. Note that onward **transport to Leh** can be difficult to arrange in high season (July & Aug), as most buses are full by the time they get there. Travellers frequently find themselves having to ride on the roof, or hitch a lift on one of the trucks that stop at the *dhabas* on the roadside above the village: neither legal, nor particularly safe. There are eight buses daily to Manali, the first one leaving at 5am.

Keylong's **hotels** can be found along the main road above the town and strung out along the Mall that runs through the bazaar below the main highway. A steep path leads down to the bazaar from the main road just past where the buses pull in. The *Tashi Deleg* (℡01900/22450; **❹–❻**) on the Mall has a range of clean and comfortable en-suite rooms with hot showers. The *Gyespa* (℡01900/22207; **❸**) also has en-suite rooms with hot showers, and a dorm (Rs40), and a small *chorten* in the garden, but isn't as clean; both hotels have views of Kardang Gompa. Hotel *Dupchen* (℡01900/22687; **❷–❸**) has an even cheaper dorm (Rs30), while the *Lamayuru* (℡01900/22202; **❷**) has just four rooms – pleasant and clean with hot showers – and the best restaurant in town. Back on the main road 2km towards Darcha, the newly opened *Circuit House and Tourist Complex* promises to be the most comfortable in town. The *Gangzala* (no phone; **❷**), on the southern edge of town, has three nice rooms with hot showers and the *Leh Dhaba* is opening a large hotel (**❷**), including dorm accommodation (Rs40), where the buses pull in, which will be convenient for early departures.

The main post office is on the main road a little way beyond the bus stand. Down on the Mall, *Snowphone* internet centre and the *Lamayuru* cybercafé offer slower and more expensive access than in Manali. There are no foreign currency facilities here.

Spiti

From its headwaters below the **Kunzum Pass**, the river Spiti drains 130km southeast to within a yak's cough of the border of Chinese-occupied Tibet, where it meets the Sutlej. The valley itself, surrounded by huge peaks and with an average altitude of 4500m, is one of the highest and remotest inhabited places on earth – a desolate, barren tract scattered with tiny whitewashed mud-and-timber hamlets and lonely lamaseries.

Until 1992, Spiti in its entirety lay off-limits to foreign tourists. Now, only its far southeastern corner falls within the **"Inner Line"** – which leaves upper Spiti, including the district headquarters **Kaza**, freely accessible from the northwest via Lahaul. If you are really keen to complete the loop through the restricted area to or from Kinnaur (see p.532), you can do so with a **permit** (see p.518).

One of the main incentives to visit the restricted zone is the chance to visit **Tabo** *gompa*, which harbours some of the oldest and most exquisite Buddhist art in the world. It is one of several *gompas* in Spiti believed to have been founded by **Rinchen Zangpo**, the "Great Translator" who imported Buddhism to western Tibet (Guge) in the tenth and eleventh centuries. The others are even further off the beaten track, tucked away in side valleys. Getting to them is half the fun: footpaths and mule tracks to the more remote areas offer some of India's best **trekking**.

Two buses a day leave Manali for Spiti every morning during the summer once the Rohtang La and Kunzum La (4550m) are clear of snow. It is also possible to hire **Jeeps** from Manali (through HPTDC or any other travel agency) and to trek in from the Kullu valley or south from the Baralacha La. Soon after crossing the Kunzum La the road passes through the tiny village of Lossar where there is a police checkpoint. Accommodation is available in a couple of basic hotels: the *Sam Song* (**❷**) and the *Serchu* (**❷**). Lossar is a convenient starting point for the trek to Chandra Tal, and has a small Tibetan *gompa*. From here Kaza is a mere 58km further down the Spiti valley. The entire road from the Rohtang La to Kaza is unsealed and makes for a bumpy, gruelling ride.

Kaza and around

KAZA, the subdivisional headquarters of **Spiti**, lies 76km southeast of the Kunzum Pass, and 201km from Manali. Overlooking the left bank of the Spiti river it is the region's main market and roadhead, and a good base from which to head off on two- or three-day treks to monasteries and remote villages such as Kibber, Kiato and Dumla in an area famed for its fossils. It is also possible to trek to Dhankar (32km) via Shichling and on to Tabo (43km) via Poh. For the less energetic, the one-day hike to Comic village and Tangyud *gompa* is well worthwhile. For those hoping to **trek** out, Kaza is a good place to pick up porters and ponymen, with rates comparable to those in Kullu. For those planning to continue on to Kinnaur and Shimla, **Inner Line Permits** can be obtained from the Additional Deputy Commissioner's office in the new town. The "Inner Line" starts at Sumdo, beyond Tabo. The road past Sumdo frequently gets blocked especially at the dreaded Malling Slide, so if you have your own vehicle check to see whether you can get through.

Of the **places to stay** in the old Spitian quarter, the best are the friendly family-run *Milarepa's* (**❷**), and for a bit more comfort, the more extensive *Sakya's Abode* (**❷–❹**) next door, which offers a wide range of rooms. Close by on the main road is the *Snow Lion* (**❷–❸**) with large pleasant rooms and a café. Down a lane near the *Snow Lion* is the homely and friendly *Mahabaudha Guest House* (**❷**), set in a delightful little garden. The *Himachal Tourism Lodge* (**❹–❺**), 500m off the main road towards the river, also has tent accommodation (**❸**).

Ki Gompa

Set against a backdrop of snow-flecked mountains and ochre and brown cliffs, **Ki Gompa**, whose white buildings stick to the steep sides of a windswept conical hillock, is a picture-book example of Tibetan architecture, and one of Himachal's most exotic spectacles. Founded in the sixteenth century, Ki is the largest **monastery** in the Spiti Valley, supporting a thriving community of *lamas* whose Rinpoche, Lo Chien Tulk from Nako village in Kinnaur (see p.537), is said to be the current incarnation of the "Great Translator" Rinchen Zangpo. His glass-fronted quarters crown the top of the complex, reached via crumbling stone steps that wind between the *lamas'* houses below. A labyrinth of dark passages and wooden staircases connect the prayer and assembly halls, home to collections of old *thangkas*, weapons, musical instruments, manuscripts, and devotional images (no photography). During the new moon towards late June or early July, Ki plays host to a large festival celebrating the "burning of the demon" when *chaam* dances are followed by a procession that winds its way down to the ritual ground below the monastery where a large butter sculpture is set on fire. Pilgrims prostrate themselves on the ground for the procession of *lamas* to walk over them.

Ki lies 12km northwest of Kaza on the road to Kibber. Ki Gompa is a steep 1km walk up from the road but some buses go to the monastery gate. To appreciate the full effect of its dramatic southern aspect, it's best to walk the last section anyway, or better still **walk** all the way along a mere 8.5km along trails. Accommodation in Ki is scant – *Hotel Gompa Heart* only operates as a restaurant, but there are several guesthouses in Kibber just 4km beyond Ki Gompa.

Kibber

KIBBER (4205m) is reputedly the highest settlement with a motorable road and electricity in the world. Jeep tracks, satellite dishes and the odd tin-roofed government building aside, its smattering of a hundred or so old Spitian houses is truly picturesque. Surrounded in summer by lush green barley fields, Kibber also stands at the head of a trail that picks its way north across the mountains, via the high **Parang La** pass (5578m) to Ladakh. Before the construction of roads into the Spiti Valley, locals used to lead ponies and yaks this way to trade in Leh bazaar. These days only the old folks in the village know the path, which is used by shepherds as a route to the pastures above. Some Manali-based trekking companies offer a seventeen-day trek from here to the lake of **Tso Moriri** in Ladakh. Shorter routes around Kibber explore the delightful villages in the area and the incredible scenery, and eventually link up with Kaza. A pathway or *kora* leads all the way round the village to a tiny walled enclosure draped in colourful fluttering prayer flags. In 1983 Lama Serkang Rinpoche (from Tabo gompa) passed away in Kibber and was cremated here. A water source erupted from the rocks at that moment and is still running. Pilgrims come from all over Spiti to drink from this sacred spring and a well-tended garden inside the enclosure defies the surrounding barren land.

Buses run from Kaza, Jeeps are available for hire, or you can walk the 16km. Trails lead down from Kibber to Ki loosely following the road and racing vehicles down is a popular sport. Four guesthouses in Kibber cater to the increasing numbers of tourists and trekkers passing through: the *Norling* (☏01906/26242; ❷–❸) and the *Rainbow* (☏01906/26234; ❷), at the entrance to the village, both have terraces, the *Resang* (☏01906/26231; ❷) and *Sargong* (☏01906/26222; ❷–❸) are a little further in.

Dhankar and the Pin Valley

Midway between Kaza and Tabo, near the meeting of the Pin and Spiti rivers, a rough road veers off to the east for 12km to the village of **DHANKAR** (3890m) or "a place in the mountains unreachable for strangers" and houses another monastery associated with the Great Translator, Rinchen Zangpo. Set against a lunar landscape of crumbling cliffs, the **Lha Opa Gompa** dates back to the twelfth century. The main interest, however, lies in the small chapel on the uppermost peak behind the village of Dhankar – the **Lhakang Gompa** – with its brilliant murals depicting the life of the Buddha. Probably painted in the seventeenth century, the dominant bright red pigment has survived especially well. Although some of the work has been vandalized, the scenes depicting the Buddha's birth in the heavenly realm, his re-birth and life in Kapilavastu and his rejection of worldly ways are spectacular. The *gompa* also affords superb views down to the confluence of the main Spiti river and the Pin tributary which flows down from the snowfields of the massive Pin Parvati pass. Keen walkers may like to check out the lake a couple of kilometres above the village. Dhankar is not on a bus route so you will have to arrange your own transport or walk from the main road.

The Pin Valley

Just before Dhankar, a small road turns off the main Kaza–Shimla highway and crosses the river Spiti at Attargu and winds around precipitous bends for 26km up-valley to the tiny settlement of Mikim (population 26) at the confluence of the Pin and Parahio rivers. On the way it passes through the village of Guling, above which stands the important Nyingma *gompa* of Gungri, believed to date back to the eighth and ninth centuries. There is a simple hotel, the *Himalaya* (❶), a couple of cafés serving *thukpa* and *momos*, and a camping ground. From here it's just 4km up to Mikim and the slightly larger settlement of Sagnam across the river. There are a couple of buses a day from Mikim to Kaza. Although there's no accommodation in Mikim, there's a PWD *Rest House* in nearby Sagnam and an opportunity to cross the river on a pulley-bridge, suspended above the waters in a tiny metal basket. The upper reaches of the valley are only accessible by trekking, and lead to the Pin–Parvati pass.

Tabo

One of the main reasons to brave the rough roads of Spiti is to get to **Tabo Gompa**, 43km east of Kaza. The mud and timber boxes that nestle on the steep north bank of the Spiti may look drab, but the multi-hued murals and stucco sculpture they contain are some of the world's richest and most important ancient Buddhist art treasures: the link between the cave paintings of Ajanta, and the more exuberant Tantric art that flourished in Tibet five centuries or so later. According to an inscription in its main assembly hall, the monastery was established in 996 AD, when **Rinchen Zangpo**, an emissary of King Yeshe Od of Guge, was disseminating *dharma* across the northwestern Himalayas. In addition to the 158 Sanskrit Buddhist texts he personally transcribed, the "Great Translator" brought with him a retinue of Kashmiri artisans to decorate the temples. The only surviving examples of their exceptional work are here at Tabo, at Alchi in Ladakh, and Toling and Tsaparang *gompas* in Chinese-occupied western Tibet.

Enclosed within a mud-brick wall, Tabo's **Chogskhar**, or "sacred enclave", contains eight temples and twenty-four *chortens* (stupas). The largest and oldest structure in the group, the **Sug La-khang**, stands opposite the main entrance. Erected at the end of the tenth century, the "Hall of the Enlightened Gods" was conceived in the form of a three-dimensional *mandala*, whose structure and elaborately decorated interior functions as a mystical model of the universe complete with deities. There are three distinct bands of detail – the lower level paintings depict episodes in the life of the Buddha and his previous incarnations; above are stucco gods and goddesses; and the top of the hall is covered with meditating Buddhas and *bodhisattvas*. The giant four-armed figure in front of the altar, lit by butter lamps, is **Vairocana**, a manifestation of the primordial Buddha.

The other temples date from the fifteenth and eighteenth centuries. Their contents illustrate the development of Buddhist iconography from its early Indian origins to the Chinese-influenced opulence of medieval Tibetan Tantricism that still, in a more lurid form, predominates in modern *gompas*. The new *gompa*, inaugurated by the Dalai Lama in 1983, houses thirty or so *lamas* and a handful of *chomos* (nuns), some of whom receive training in traditional painting techniques under a *geshe*, or teacher from eastern Tibet.

Practicalities

There are a number of **accommodation** options in Tabo. The friendly, atmospheric *Millennium Monastery Guest House* (❷–❸), outside the main monastery gates has simple rooms, with and without en suite, as well as dorm accommodation (Rs50). At the nearby *Café Kunzam-Top*, the affable Pema dishes up both Tibetan and Indian food, and also runs a small guesthouse and campsite off the main road. For a bit more comfort, try the *Himalayan Ajanta* (❸), next to the State Bank near the new temple gates, and the PWD *Rest House* (❸), with large comfortable rooms and attached bathrooms. Three **buses** a day travel to Kaza, one of which, departing early, travels all the way to Manali, a distance of 242km. Another bus passes through early in the morning to Rekong Peo in Kinnaur (via Sumdo) from where you can continue to Shima, 374km away.

The Manali–Leh Highway

Since it opened to foreign tourists in 1989, the famous **Manali–Leh highway** has deservedly replaced the old Srinagar–Kargil route as the most popular approach to Ladakh. In summer, a stream of clapped-out government buses, private minibuses and Enfield motorcycles set off from the Kullu Valley to travel along the second-highest road in the world, which reaches a dizzying altitude of 5328m. Its surface varies wildly, from fairly smooth asphalt through potholes of differing depths, to dirt tracks sliced by glacial streams, traversing a starkly beautiful lunar wilderness peopled only by nomadic shepherds, tar-covered road coolies, and the gloomy soldiers that man the isolated military checkpoints.

THE MANALI-LEH HIGHWAY

Not to scale
Distances are shown from Manali

N

ZANSKAR

Leh (3505m)
(485km)

Karu (450km)   Upshi (436km)

Tanglang La (376km)   Dibring Camp

Moray Plains

Lachuglung La (276km)   Pang (301km)

Tso Moriri

Shingo La (5100m)

Zingzing Bar   Sarchu Serai (222km)

Baralacha La (186km)

Keylong (113km) (3348m)   Darcha (145km)
Jispa
Rangcha (4565m)

Tandi (107km)   Koksar (71km)   Cbio (6227m)

Gupt Parbat (6158m)   Chandra River

Kunzum La Pass (4551m)

Rohtang Pass (51km)

Manali (1896m)   White Sail (6451m)

Spiti

Shimla & Delhi

Depending on road conditions, the 485-kilometre journey can take anything from twenty-six to thirty hours. Bus drivers cover more distance on the first day than the second, stopping for a short and chilly night in one of the overpriced **tent camps** along the route. These, however, are few and far between after September 15, when the highway officially closes. In practice, all this means is that the Indian government won't airlift you out if you get trapped in snow; some companies run regardless. For more details on **transport** between Manali and Leh, see p.577.

Manali to Keylong
Having made its way past the bleak military installations and wayside settlements above **Manali**, the road crosses the Beas to begin its long ascent of the **ROHTANG PASS**

(3978m). Buses pull in for breakfast 17km before the pass at a row of makeshift *dhabas* at Marhi (3360m). A small Tibetan temple dedicated to Palden Lhamo, reached via a flight of steps, crowns the top of a bluff from where you view a wonderful panorama of the upper Beas Valley. Though not all that high by Himalayan standards, Rohtang itself, a U-shaped defile between two 5000-metre peaks, is one of the most treacherous passes in the region. Each year, Gaddis and mountaineers are caught unawares by sudden weather changes; hence the vultures wheeling overhead, and Rohtang's name, which literally means "piles of dead bodies". An igloo-shaped brick building, actually a small Hindu temple, marks the source of the river Beas. From the pass a breathtaking vista of the dusty dark-brown mountains of **Lahaul** can be seen to the north.

The descent from Rohtang to the floor of the **Chandra Valley** affords tantalizing glimpses of the shining White Sail massif (6446m) in the east. **KOKSAR**, where the road finally reaches the river, is little more than a scruffy collection of chai stalls with a **checkpoint** where you have to enter passport details in a ledger – one of many such stops on the road to Leh.

The next few hours are among the most memorable on the entire trip. Bus seats on the left are best, as the road runs across the northern slopes of the valley through the first Buddhist settlements, hemmed in by towering peaks and hanging glaciers. A sharp descent around the base of the sacred **Rangcha** mountain brings you to the Chandra–Bhaga confluence at **Tandi**, after which the road crosses the river on a Bailey bridge and forks, west to Udaipur and north along the Bhaga Valley to **Keylong** (see p.581).

Keylong to Sarchu Serai

Beyond Keylong, the Bhaga Valley broadens, but its bare sides support very few villages. By the time you reach **Darcha**, a lonely cluster of dry-stone huts and dingy tent camps on the edge of a vast pebbly river confluence, the landscape is utterly denuded. All buses stop here for passengers to grab a hot bowl of Tibetan *thukpa* from a wayside *dhaba*. There's little else to do in Darcha, which would be the definitive one-horse frontier post were it not for all the ponies hanging around its outskirts near the Shingo La trailhead – the main trekking route north to Zanskar (see p.636). If you are not on one of the through Manali–Leh buses, you are better off stopping at **Jispa** 7km south, a pleasant little hamlet with ample camping along the river. There is a small but pleasant guesthouse (**②**) above the road, and the monolithic but comfortable, concrete *Hotel Ibex* (☎01900/33203; **❼**), which you might consider worth the luxury after a gruelling trek.

From Darcha, the road climbs steadily northeast across mountain sides of wine-red and pale-green scree. The **Baralacha La** is the first major pass, a windswept vale of red-brown rock and grit splashed with streaks of snow. The Bhaga, Chandra, and Yunan rivers fall away from its sides in different directions.

Buses stop at **Sarchu Serai** for the night where bed is a piece of lumpy ground in a tent made from army-surplus parachutes. There are several more expensive camps dotted along the road, one or two of which charge up to an exhorbitant Rs800 per person including food. HPTDC's *Tent Camp* (**❸**) serves steaming plates of rice, dhal and veg, as do a handful of similarly priced *dhabas* nearby.

Sarchu Serai to Tanglang La

Sarchu Serai packs up for the season from September 15. Northbound buses thereafter press on over **Lachuglang La** (5019m), the second highest pass on the highway, to the tent camp at **Pang** (4500m), which stays open longer.

Unfortunately, this means that the drive through one of the most dramatic stretches of the route, through an incredible canyon, is in darkness. Sarchu Seral is also 2500m higher than Manali, and travellers coming straight from Manali might suffer from the higher altitude here.

The army camp at Pang, 3km north of the *serai*, stands at the mouth of the **Pang Gorge** at the far southern end of the extraordinary **Moray Plains**: a 45-kilometre-long plateau encircled by rolling hills and, nosing up above them, brilliant white Himalayan peaks. This serene Tibetan landscape is the domain of nomadic pashmina-rearing herdsmen who migrate here from Rupsu in eastern Ladakh each summer. Look out too for wild asses, marmots, and the elusive *nabu* (blue sheep) that graze the open grassland.

After Dibring, the road starts its ascent of the fourth and final pass, the **Tanglang La**, a dizzying 5360m, the highest point on the Manali–Leh highway. Drivers pull in for a brief photo session alongside the sign exclaiming "Unbelievable! Is it not". Staring north beyond the multicoloured tangle of prayer flags across Ladakh to the Karakoram range, just visible on the horizon, you may well agree.

Travel details

Trains

Pathankot to Joginder Nagar (2 daily; 7hr 30min–9hr 10min).
Shimla to: Kalka (4 daily; 4hr 45min–5hr 45min).

Buses

Dalhousie to: Amritsar (2 daily; 5hr 30min); Jullundhar (1 daily; 6hr); Khajjiar (2 daily; 1hr); Pathankot (hourly; 3hr 30min).
Dharamsala to: Baijnath (hourly; 3hr 30min); Chamba (1 daily; 9hr); Chandigarh (6 daily; 7–8hr); Dalhousie (1 daily; 6hr–7hr); Delhi (6 daily; 12hr); Dehra Dun (1 daily; 9hr); Haridwar (1 daily; 14hr); Jawalamukhi (8 daily; 2hr 30min); Kangra (every 15min: 45min–1hr); Kullu (4 daily; 8hr); Manali (4 daily; 10hr); Mandi (7 daily; 6hr); McLeod Ganj (every 20min; 40min); Nahan (1 daily; 12hr); Pathankot (10 daily; 3hr).
Chamba to: Amritsar (1 daily; 8hr); Brahmour (7 daily; 3hr); Dalhousie (10 daily; 2hr 30min); Delhi (1 nightly; 18hr); Kangra (2 daily; 6hr); Khajjiar (3 daily; 1hr 30min); Mandi (1 daily; 15hr); Pathankot (10 daily; 5hr).
Kangra to: Delhi (every 30min; 12hr); Jawalamukhi (every 15min; 1–2hr); Mandi (4 daily; 6hr); Masrur (3 daily; 2hr); Pathankot (10 daily; 3–4hr).
Kasauli to: Chandigarh (5 daily; 2hr 30min); Delhi (3 daily; 7hr 30min); Kalka (3 daily; 1hr 30min); Solan (5 daily; 40min).
Kullu to: Amritsar (1 daily; 16hr); Bhuntur (every 10min; 30min); Chandigarh (8 daily; 6hr 30min); Dehra Dun (1 daily; 14hr); Delhi (6 daily; 14hr);

Haridwar (1 daily; 14hr); Manali (every 10min; 1hr 15min–2hr); Mandi (every 30min; 3hr); Manikaran (every 30min; 2hr); Nagar (hourly; 1hr 30min).
Manali to: Amritsar (1 daily; 16hr); Chandigarh (13 daily; 8–11hr); Dehra Dun (1 daily; 16hr); Delhi (8 daily; 16–17hr); Haridwar (2 daily; 16hr); Kangra (7 daily; 12hr); Kaza (2 daily; 12hr); Keylong (11 daily; 6hr); Mandi (every 30min; 4hr); Manikaran (every 30min; 4hr); Nagar (hourly; 1hr 30min); Pathankot (2 daily; 12hr); Udaipur, Lahaul (1 daily; 7hr).
Mandi to: Dharamsala (7 daily; 6hr); Kullu (every 30min; 3hr); Manali (every 30min; 4hr); Shimla (7 daily; 6hr).
Shimla to: Chail (4 daily; 3hr); Chandigarh (every 15min; 4hr); Dalhousie (1 daily; 14hr); Dehra Dun (3 daily; 9hr); Delhi (hourly; 10hr); Dharamsala (4 daily; 10hr); Haridwar (3 daily; 10hr); Kalka (every 30min; 3hr); Kangra (10 daily; 8hr); Kasauli (hourly; 2hr 30min); Kullu (7 daily; 7–8hr); Manali (7 daily; 9–10hr); Mandi (7 daily; 6hr); Nahan (4 daily; 6hr); Narkanda (5 daily; 3hr); Pathankot (5 daily; 13hr); Rampur (5 daily; 6hr); Rekong Peo (3 daily; 9–11hr); Sarahan (2 daily; 7hr); Solan (every 30min; 1hr 30min).

Flights

Dharamsala (Gaggal) to: Delhi (3 weekly; 1hr 30min).
Kullu to: Delhi (daily; 1hr 20min).
Shimla to: Delhi (daily; 1hr 10min); Kullu (daily; 30min).

* **Leh** Medieval streets, a Tibetan-style palace, bazaars and looming snowy peaks. See p.597

* **Tikse** Along with Lamayuru, the Indian Himalayas' most impressive monastery complex. See p.614

* **Hemis** Ladakh's largest monastery hosts its annual masked-dance ritual and *thangka* unveiling at the height of the summer. See p.615

* **Chemrey & Thak Thok** Neighbouring but strikingly different monasteries – one on a near-perfect conical hill and the other built into a catacomb. See p.616–617

* **Tso Moriri** This exquisite high-altitude lake features snow-fringed desert mountains, rare migratory birds and nomadic herders. See p.618

* **Alchi** Wonderful painted murals and stucco images are hidden behind the simple exterior of this ancient monastery. See p.625

* **Lamayuru** An awesome walled *gompa* rising above a mass of weirdly eroded rock. See p.628

* **Zanskar** Walled in by the Himalayas, Zanskar can only be reached during the winter by following the frozen river route. See p.636

7

Ladakh

LADAKH, the far-flung eastern corner of troubled Jammu and Kashmir state, is India's most remote and sparsely populated region, a high-altitude desert cradled by the Karakoram and Great Himalayas ranges, and criss-crossed by line upon line of razor-sharp peaks and ridges. To government servants and soldiers from the plains, charged with the unenviable task of guarding its fragile frontiers with China and Pakistan, this barren, breathless land is a punishment posting. In fact, in May 1999 the cross-border skirmishes with Pakistan escalated into a full-blown conflict known as the **Kargil War** (see p.623). Although the Indian government has been pursuing a policy of dialogue with disparate Kashmiri separatist groups, most backed by Pakistan, the situation remains volatile. There are signs of a possible negotiated settlement, but you are advised to consult the media and check with the tourist authorities before travelling in this area, especially if you intend to travel the highway between Srinagar and Leh through Kargil.

Despite the problems of Kashmir, for more on which see p.1498, Ladakh remains one of the most rewarding and pleasurable destinations for those tourists who do venture here as it offers the chance to experience at first hand a magical landscape and culture that, until as recently as 1974, had only been glimpsed by a few intrepid Western travellers. Far beyond the reach of the monsoons, Ladakh receives little snow, especially in the valleys, and even less rain. Only the most frugal methods enable its inhabitants to farm the thin sandy soil, frozen solid for eight months of the year and scorched by searing sun for the other four. Nourished by meltwater channelled through elaborate irrigation ditches, a single crop of barley (roasted to make the staple *ngamphe*) is sown and harvested between late June and the first October frosts. At lower altitudes, where neat terraced fields provide vivid green splashes against the bare rock and mica-flecked scree slopes, this is supplemented by fast-growing strains of wheat, garden vegetables, apricots and walnuts. Higher up, the relentless chill and steep gradients render agriculture impossible, and villagers depend on animals – yaks, goats, sheep and *dzo* (a hybrid of the yak and the domestic cow) – for wool, milk and butter to barter or sell for grain and fuel. In recent years, **global warming** has meant drier winters with even less snow; the consequent loss of snow-melt has put pressure on traditional farming and irrigation, resulting in a real fear of drought, the effects of which are now being felt in villages such as Alchi.

Variously described as "Little Tibet" or "the last Shangri-La", **La-Dags** – "land of high mountain passes" – is one of the last enclaves of Mahayana **Buddhism**, Ladakh's principal religion for nearly a thousand years, now brutally suppressed by the Chinese in its native Tibet. Except near the Kashmiri border, the outward symbols of Buddhism are everywhere: strings of multi-

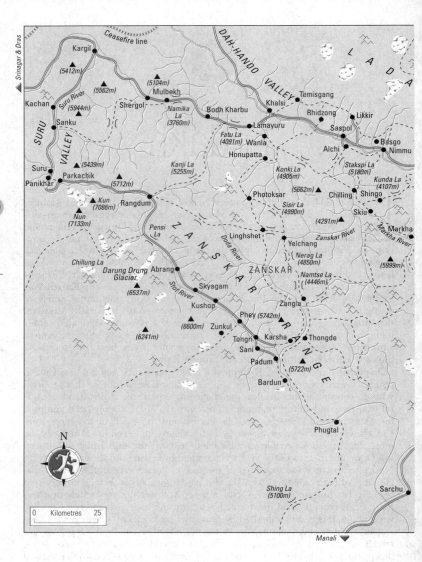

coloured prayer flags flutter from the rooftops of houses, while bright prayer wheels and whitewashed *chortens* (the regional equivalent of stupas; see p.603) guard the entrances to even the tiniest settlements. More impressive and mysterious still are Ladakh's medieval **monasteries**. Perched on rocky hilltops and clinging to sheer cliffs, **gompas** are both repositories of ancient wisdom and living centres of worship. Their gloomy prayer halls and ornate shrines harbour remarkable art treasures: giant brass Buddhas, *thangkas*, libraries of antique Tibetan manuscripts, weird musical instruments and painted walls that writhe with fierce Tantric divinities.

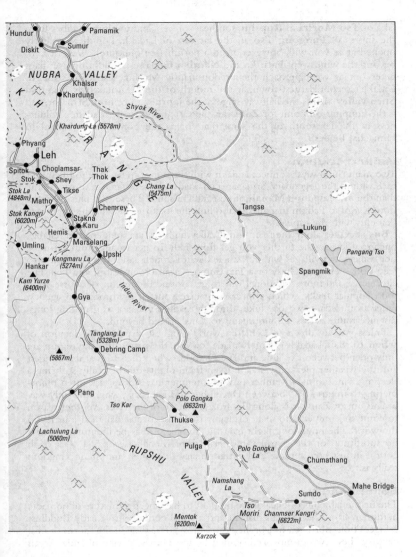

The highest concentration of monasteries is in the **Indus Valley** near **Leh**, the region's capital. Surrounded by sublime landscapes and crammed with hotels, guesthouses, and restaurants, this atmospheric little town, a staging post on the old Silk Route, is most visitors' point of arrival and an ideal base for side trips. North of Leh across one of the highest motorable passes in the world, **Khardung La**, lies the valley of **Nubra**, only accessible to foreigners since the mid-1990s, where sand dunes grace the valley floor in stark contrast to the towering crags of the Karakoram Range. With the easing of restrictions, it is now also possible to visit the great wilderness around the lake of **Tso Moriri** in **Rupshu**, southeast of Leh, and to glimpse Tibet from the shores of **Pangong Tso** in the far east of Ladakh. For these recently opened areas you will, however, need a permit (see opposite). West of Leh, beyond the windswept **Fatu La** and **Namika La** passes, Buddhist prayer flags peter out as you approach the predominantly Muslim district of **Kargil**. Ladakh's second largest town, at the mouth of the breathtakingly beautiful **Suru Valley**, marks the halfway stage of the journey to or from Srinagar, and is the jumping-off point for **Zanskar**, the vast and virtually road-free wilderness in the far south of the state that forms the border with Lahaul in Himachal Pradesh.

Visiting Ladakh

Two main "highways" connect Ladakh with the rest of India. Due to the unrest in Kashmir, the legendary Srinagar–Leh road now sees far less tourist traffic than the route up from **Manali**, almost 500km south. These two, plus the track from Kargil to Padum in Zanskar, also link the majority of Ladakh's larger settlements with the capital.

Bus services along the main Indus Valley highway are frequent and reliable, but grow less so the further you get from Leh. To get to and from off-track side-valleys and villages within a single day, it is much easier to splash out on a jeep **taxi** – either a Gipsy or a Tata Sumo – available in Kargil and Leh. The alternative, and more traditional way to get around the region, of course, is on foot. Popular **treks**, which you can organize yourself or through an agency, range from sedate two-day hikes through roadless villages, to gruelling long-distance routes across the mountains to Zanskar, and beyond.

Unless you fly direct to Leh (the world's highest airport), the decision of **when to visit** Ladakh is largely made for you: the passes into the region are only open between late June and late October, when the sun is at its strongest and the weather pleasantly warm. Even then, nights can be chilly, so bring a sleeping bag. From November onwards, temperatures drop fast, often plummeting to minus 40°C between December and February, when the only way in and out of Zanskar is along the frozen surface of the river. Another reason to come in summer is to make arguably the most spectacular road journey in the world. The hour-long flight over the Himalayas may be memorable, but is no substitute for the two-day-plus trip from Manali (see p.581) – a crash course in just how remote and extraordinary this lonely mountain kingdom really is.

Some history

The first inhabitants of Ladakh are thought to have been a mixture of nomadic herdsmen from the Tibetan plateau and a small contingent of early Buddhist refugees from northern India called the Mons. Some time in the fourth or fifth century, these two groups were joined by the **Dards**, a tribe of Indo-Aryan

---

Accommodation price codes

All accommodation prices in this book have been categorized using the **price codes** below. Prices given are for a double room, and all taxes are included. For more details, see p.51.

❶ up to Rs100	❹ Rs300–400	❼ Rs900–1500
❷ Rs100–200	❺ Rs400–600	❽ Rs1500–2500
❸ Rs200–300	❻ Rs600–900	❾ Rs2500 and upwards

Much of Ladakh is still inaccessible to the casual tourist, but with the easing of tensions along the border between India and China, parts of this incredible land, once hidden behind the political veil of the "Inner Line", are being opened up. Three areas in particular were opened to visitors in the mid-1990s: the **Nubra Valley** bordering the Karakoram Range to the north of Leh; the area around **Pangong Tso**, the lake to the east of Leh; and the region of **Rupshu** with the lake of **Tso Moriri**, to the southeast of Leh. (Dha Hanu in west Ladakh was similarly opened but, being sensitively close to the frontline of the Kargil War of 1999, has once again been closed to tourists.) Both Indian and foreign visitors need **permits** to visit these areas. In theory, permits are only issued to groups of at least four persons accompanied by a guide, and only through a local tour operator. However, in practice there are ways round this rule, and once you have your permit, the checkpoints are quite relaxed about how many of you there are in a group.

Permits are obtained from the **Collectors' Office** on the far side of the polo ground in **Leh** but the office, now in collusion with local agents, discourages any direct approach and tends to only deal through one of Leh's many **tour operators** (see p.609). Tour operators charge a **fee** – usually around Rs50 per head. As some of the areas in question are inaccessible by public transport (such as Tso Moriri), you may well find yourself using a tour operator anyway, in which case the operator will include your permit in the package. In theory, you need to submit two photographs for your permit but in practice this no longer applies; you will need two photocopies of the relevant pages of your passport and visa. Provided you apply in the morning, permits are usually issued on the same day. Once you have your permit, usually only valid for a maximum period of seven days, make at least five copies before setting off, as checkpoints like to keep a copy when you log in. Checkpoints occasionally spot-check to see the original copy of the permit.

origin who migrated southeast along the Indus Valley, bringing with them irrigation and settled agriculture.

The first independent kingdom in the region was established in the ninth century by the maverick nobleman Nyima Gon, taking advantage of the chaos after the collapse of the Guge empire of western Tibet. **Buddhism**, meanwhile, had also found its way across the Himalayas from India. Disseminated by the wandering sage-apostles such as Padmasambhava (alias "Guru Rinpoche"), dharma gradually displaced the pantheistic shamanism of the Bon cult (which still holds sway in remote villages north of Khalsi, near Lamayuru). The eastward expansion of the faith towards the Tibetan plateau continued in the tenth and eleventh centuries – the period later dubbed the **"Second Spreading"**. Among its key proselytizers was the "Great Translator" **Rinchen Zangpo**, a scholar and missionary associated with the foundation of numerous monasteries in Ladakh and in neighbouring Spiti (see p.586).

Around the fourteenth century, Ladakh passed through a dark age during which, for reasons that remain unclear, its rulers switched allegiance from Indian to Tibetan Buddhism, a form of the faith deeply invested with esoteric practices drawn from the **Tantra** texts, and possibly influenced by the animated celebrations common to Bon (see Contexts, p.1516). This coincided with the rise to prominence in Tibet of **Tsongkhapa** (1357–1419), who is accepted as founder of the **Gelug-pa** or "Yellow Hat" school. With the Dalai Lama at its head, Gelug-pa is today the most popular school in Ladakh with many more monasteries than sects such as **Kagyu**, which is closely linked with Milarepa, a Tantric practitioner (eleventh-century) whose ideas and sonnets are revered by many

Ladakhi Buddhists. Under **Tashi Namgyal** (1555–70), who reunified the kingdom, Ladakh became a major Himalayan power, and the ascent to the throne of the "Lion", **Sengge Namgyal**, in the seventeenth century, signalled further territorial gains. After being routed by the Moghul-Balti army at Bodh Kharbu in 1639, he turned his energies to civil and religious matters, founding a new capital and palace at Leh, as well as a string of monasteries that included Hemis, seat of the newly arrived **Brugpa** sect, a branch of the Kagyu school.

Sengge's building spree created some fine monuments, but it also drained the kingdom's coffers, as did the hefty annual tribute paid to the Moghuls after the Bodh Kharbu debacle. Finances were further strained when Deldan, Sengge's successor, picked a quarrel with his ally, Tibet. The fifth Dalai Lama dispatched an army of Mongolian horsemen to teach him a lesson, and three years of conflict were only ended after the Moghul governor of Kashmir intervened on Ladakh's behalf. This help, however, came at a price: Aurangzeb demanded more tribute, ordered the construction of a mosque in Leh, and forced the Ladakhi king to convert to Islam.

Trade links with Tibet resumed in the eighteenth century, but Ladakh never regained its former status. Plagued by feuds and assassinations, the kingdom teetered into terminal decline, and was an easy target for the **Dogra** general Zorawar Singh, who annexed it for the Maharaja of Kashmir in 1834. The Ladakhi royal family was banished to Stok palace, where their descendants reside to this day.

Ladakh became a part of independent India in 1948, following the first of the four Indo-Pak wars fought in the region. However, both the international frontier and the so-called **"Ceasefire Line"** that scythes through the top of Jammu and Kashmir remain "unauthenticated": even today, the two armies take periodic pot-shots at each other across the disputed Siachen Glacier in the Karakorams, 100km north. When you consider the proximity of China, another old foe who annexed a large chunk of Ladakh in 1962, it is easy to see why this is India's most sensitive border zone – and why it remained off-limits to tourists until 1974. Today, Ladakh comprises around seventy percent of the state of Jammu and Kashmir as it stands. Like the other state districts, the Kashmir Valley and Jammu, Ladakh has its own distinct culture hemmed in by boundaries formed by high mountain ranges that have ensured independent development over several centuries. Long dissatisfied with state government based in Srinagar, and after years of agitation, the Ladakhis finally saw the establishment in their region of an **Autonomous Hill Development Council** in September 1995, localizing – in theory – government control. However, the **Ladakh Buddhist Association**, the main organ of Ladakh's Buddhists, accuses the state government of continued victimization and manipulation and the purposeful mismanagement of the AHDC. Faced with a growing Muslim population, and the possibility of becoming a minority in their homeland, the LBA are calling for the dispersal of the AHDC and the recognition of Ladakh as a distinct entity to protect indigenous Ladakhi interests. The Muslims, especially those around Kargil and Drass in Western Ladakh, heavily influenced by the politics of the Kashmir Valley, are vehemently opposed to any separation of Ladakh from Jammu and Kashmir.

Relations between Ladakh's Muslims and Buddhists reached an all-time low in July 2000 when, after an unguarded comment about Islam by an official of the LBA, Kashmiri separatists shot dead three Buddhist monks outside their monastery in Rangdum in the remote region between the Suru Valley and Zanskar. A German traveller who had the misfortune of hitching a ride on the same truck as the terrorists was also executed. The shockwaves of the massacres were felt throughout Ladakh, with curfews imposed on Leh.

Most of Ladakh's Buddhist festivals, in which masked dance dramas are performed by lamas in monastery courtyards, take place in January and February, when roads into the region are snowbound. This works out well for the locals, for whom they relieve the tedium of the relentless winter, but it means that few outsiders get to experience some of the northern Himalayas' most vibrant and fascinating spectacles. Recently, however, a few of the larger *gompas* around Leh have followed the example of Hemis, and switched their annual festivals to the summer, to attract tourists. Proceeds from ticket sales go towards maintenance and restoration work, and the construction of new shrines. However, this often means that camera-toting tourists, who pay around Rs150 for a plastic bucket-chair, get the choice front-row seats.

The precise dates of these monastic events over a five-year period, which vary according to the Tibetan lunar calendar, are published in the useful local guide, *Reach Ladakh*, available from most bookshops in Leh; the description of the Hemis Festival programme is also very useful in providing an insight into the proceedings. Alternatively, the tourist office in Leh produces a listings booklet called *Ladakh Monastic Festivals*. The following festivals are held in summer but many of the important *gompas* such as Matho (mid-Feb to mid-March), Spitok (mid-Jan), Tikse (late Oct to mid-Nov) and Diskit (mid-Feb to early March) in Nubra, hold their *chaams* (dance festivals) in winter or spring. Other important festivals in Ladakh include Losar (the Tibetan/Ladakhi New Year) which falls any time between mid-December and early January.

Hemis Tsechu (June 20–21, 2002; July 9–10, 2003; June 27–28, 2004).

The largest event of its kind draws huge crowds, and is unmissable if you are within striking distance. See p.615.

Karsha Gustor (July 7–8, 2002; July 26–27, 2003; July 14–15, 2004).

Close to the town of Padum in Zanskar, the picturesque monastery holds its *chaam* in midsummer. See p.640.

Thak Thok Tsechu (July 19–20, 2002; Aug 7–8, 2003; July 27–28, 2004).

A colourful festival featuring elaborate costumes, which makes a pleasant day-trip from Leh, taking in picturesque Chemrey on the way. See p.617.

The Festival of Ladakh (late Aug to early Sept). A popular J&KTDC-sponsored two-week event held principally in Leh and designed to extend the tourist season, featuring archery contests, polo matches, Bactrian camels from Nubra and traditional Ladakhi dance accompanied by some tedious speeches.

Sani Nasjal (July 23–24, 2002; Aug 11–12, 2003; July 30–31, 2004).

If you're in the area, it's well worth catching the festival at Zanskar's oldest monastery (see p.640).

Phyang Tsedup (July 12–13, 2002; July 31–Aug 1, 2003; July 19–20, 2004).

Featuring the usual *chaam* dances, and the ritual display of a giant *thangka*. See p.624.

Leh

As you approach **LEH** for the first time, via the sloping sweep of dust and pebbles that divide it from the floor of the Indus Valley, you'll have little difficulty imagining how the old trans-Himalayan traders must have felt as they plodded in on the caravan routes from Yarkhand and Tibet: a mixture of relief at having crossed the mountains in one piece, and anticipation of a relaxing spell in one of central Asia's most scenic and atmospheric towns. Spilling out of a side-valley that tapers north towards eroded snow-capped peaks, the Ladakhi capital sprawls from the foot of a ruined Tibetan-style palace – a maze of mud brick and concrete flanked on one side by cream-coloured desert, and on the other by a swathe of lush irrigated farmland.

Leh only became regional capital in the seventeenth century, when Sengge Namgyal shifted his court here from Shey, 15km southeast, to be closer to the head of the Khardung La–Karakoram corridor into China. The move paid off: within a generation the town had blossomed into one of the busiest markets on the Silk Road. During the 1920s and 1930s, the broad bazaar that still forms its heart received more than a dozen pony- and camel-trains each day. Leh's prosperity, managed mainly by the Sunni **Muslim** merchants whose descendants live in its labyrinthine **old quarter**, came to an abrupt end with the closure of the Chinese border in the 1950s. Only after the Indo-Pak wars

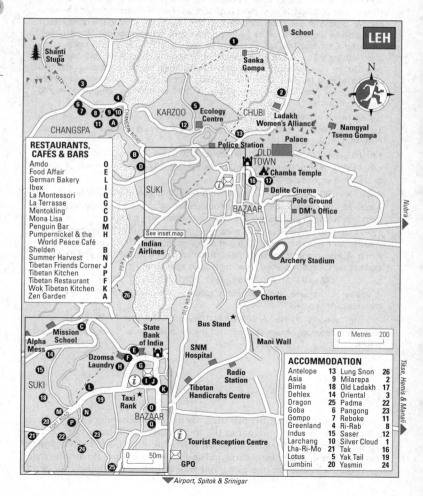

LEH

RESTAURANTS, CAFÉS & BARS

Amdo	O
Food Affair	E
German Bakery	L
Ibex	I
La Montessori	Q
La Terrasse	G
Mentokling	C
Mona Lisa	D
Penguin Bar	M
Pumpernickel & the World Peace Café	H
Shelden	B
Summer Harvest	N
Tibetan Friends Corner	J
Tibetan Kitchen	P
Tibetan Restaurant	F
Wok Tibetan Kitchen	K
Zen Garden	A

ACCOMMODATION

Antelope	13	Lung Snon	26
Asia	9	Milarepa	2
Bimla	18	Old Ladakh	17
Dehlex	14	Oriental	3
Dragon	25	Padma	22
Goba	6	Pangong	23
Gompo	7	Reboke	11
Greenland	4	Ri-Rab	8
Indus	15	Saser	12
Larchang	10	Silver Cloud	1
Lha-Ri-Mo	21	Tak	16
Lotus	5	Yak Tail	19
Lumbini	20	Yasmin	24

Airport, Spitok & Srinigar

Health in Leh: altitude sickness and dirty water

As Leh is 3505m above sea level, some travellers, and especially those who arrive by plane from Delhi, experience mild **altitude sickness**. If you develop any of the symptoms – persistent headaches, dizziness, insomnia, nausea, loss of appetite or shortness of breath – your body has not yet acclimatized to the comparative lack of oxygen in the thin Ladakhi air; don't worry, it will, probably in as little as 24 hours, though it can take longer. In the meantime, take it easy and drink plenty of fluids – 3–4 litres of water a day is recommended. In addition, lay off alcohol, and don't try to climb any hills for at least three days. For more information, see p.35, or call the hospital's **AMS** (Acute Mountain Sickness) **hotline:** ☎ 01982/52014 (daily 9am–5pm) or ☎ 01982/52360 (daily 5pm–9am).

A health problem that affects far more travellers, however, is diarrhoea. **Dirty water** is invariably the culprit – a consequence of the grossly inadequate sewage system, which can't cope with the massive summer influx of visitors. Redouble your normal health precautions while you are here: take extra care over what you drink, and avoid salads and raw vegetables unless you know they have been cleaned in sterilized water. Many hotels now filter their own water making it perfectly safe to drink, and the Dzomsa Laundry provides safe water in recycled plastic bottles (see p.607). Meat of any kind is also risky; most of it travels up from Srinagar in unrefrigerated trucks.

of 1965 and 1971, when India rediscovered the hitherto forgotten capital's strategic value, did its fortunes begin to look up. Today, khaki-clad *jawans* (soldiers) and their families from the nearby military and air force bases are the mainstay of the local economy in winter, when foreign visitors are few and far between.

Undoubtedly the most radical shake-up, however, ensued from the Indian government's decision in 1974 to open Ladakh to foreign **tourists**. From the start, Leh bore the brunt of the annual invasion, as busloads of backpackers poured up the road from Srinagar. Twenty or so years on, though the main approach is now via Himachal Pradesh rather than Kashmir, the summer influx shows no sign of abating. Leh has doubled in size and is a far cry from the sleepy Himalayan town of the early 1970s. During July and August, tourists stroll shoulder to shoulder down its main street, most of whose old-style outfitters and provision stores have been squeezed out by Kashmiri handicraft shops, art emporiums and Tibetan restaurants. A rapid increase in the number of Kashmiri traders, who have little choice but to seek business outside Kashmir, has in recent years led to unrest in Leh's bazaar, the first communal violence ever seen in normally peaceful Ladakh.

Leh has nonetheless retained a tranquil side, and is a pleasant place to unwind after a long bus journey. Attractions in and around the town itself include the former **palace** and **Namgyal Tsemo gompa**, perched amid strings of prayer flags above the narrow dusty streets of the **old quarter**. A short walk north across the fields, the small monastery at **Sankar** harbours accomplished modern Tantric murals and a thousand-headed Avalokitesvara deity. Leh is also a good base for longer **day-trips** out into the Indus Valley. Among the string of picturesque villages and *gompas* within reach by bus are **Shey**, site of a derelict seventeenth-century palace, and the spectacular **Tikse gompa**. Until you have adjusted to the altitude, however, the only sightseeing you'll probably feel up to will be from a guesthouse roof terrace or garden, from where the snowy summits of the majestic **Stok–Kangri massif** (6120m), magnified in the crystal-clear Ladakhi sunshine, look close enough to touch.

Arrival, information and local transport

A taxi from Leh **airport**, 5km southwest of town on the main Srinagar highway, will set you back a fixed fare of around Rs80 to the bazaar, or Rs125 to Changspa where many of the town's hotels are located. State and private **buses** pull into the dusty town bus stand, fifteen minutes' walk, or a short taxi ride (Rs30), south of the bazaar and most of the hotels. Manali buses terminate on Fort Road, within easy walking distance of several hotels.

J&KTDC's **tourist reception centre** (Mon–Sat 10am–4pm; ☎01982/52094), 3km from the bazaar on the airport road, is too far out of town and hardly worth visiting. The **tourist information centre** on Fort Road in the bazaar (July to mid-Sept Mon–Sat 8am–8pm; mid-Sept to June Mon–Fri 10am–4pm, Sat 10.30am–noon) is a bit more helpful. Two banks offer **moneychanging** facilities in Leh: try the efficient Foreign Exchange Service Centre of the J&K Bank, 1st Floor, Himalaya Shopping Complex, Main Bazaar (facilities may move to their new complex on Fort Road); or the State Bank of India on the main market square, who operate an infuriatingly chaotic system and don't publish daily exchange rates. Elsewhere, private licensed foreign exchange, including some hotels such as *Khangri* and travel agents around Fort Road, invariably offer rates around five percent lower but are accessible after hours and at weekends. *Khangri* also has a Foreign Exchange Bureau on the main bazaar opposite the post office.

The **taxi operators' union** rank (daily 7am–6pm; ☎01982/53309) is almost directly opposite the tourist information centre. Each driver carries a list of fixed fares to just about everywhere you might want to visit in Ladakh, taking into account waiting time, *gompa* entrance fees and night halt charges. However, these rates only apply to peak season; reductions of up to forty percent can be had at other times. Deal directly with the drivers, or their boss in the union office will take a cut (payable by you). All taxis are subject to the union's rates, and taxis hired outside the area, such as those from Manali, may earn the wrath of the union, and are sometimes made to pay a surcharge which is then passed onto the client. Prices are on the high side as the season is so short. Expect to pay around Rs60 to Changspa, Rs1700 to Hemis, and Rs6000 to Nubra with an additional Rs250 for a night's stay. Hunt around the tour operators in the bazaar and you can get cheaper deals for long-distance rides, especially if you don't mind a Maruti (Suzuki) Gypsy which is a bit more cramped and bumpy on Ladakh's rough roads.

Accommodation

Leh is absolutely glutted with **accommodation**, most of it refreshingly neat, clean and excellent value. Budget travellers in particular are in for a treat. Gone are the days of bedding down on dusty, tick-infested rooftops. Now most of the town's **cheap guesthouses** are immaculately whitewashed traditional houses, set on the leafy outskirts, with sociable garden terraces that look onto green fields. Simple double rooms go from around Rs150, even in high season. For a little more, you can often find a sunny en-suite "glass room" with a view all to yourself. Breakfasts are usually included in the price, served in the garden or at low Tibetan tables (*chogtse*) in the family kitchen, surrounded by chests full of shiny copper pots, plates and brass and wooden tea urns (*gur-gurs*). Some guesthouses now offer a wide range of accommodation, from cheap traditional rooms to comfortable new blocks.

Rooms in family houses account for the bulk of Leh's plentiful **budget accommodation**. **Karzoo** and **Suku**, northwest of the main street, are very central but become tourist ghettos during high season; if you're after peace, quiet, idyllic countryside and mountain views, head for **Changspa** village, fifteen minutes' walk west of the bazaar. More in the thick of things are the mainly Muslim houses of the **old town**. Crouched in the shadow of Leh palace, these are cheap and full of atmosphere, but finding your way home after dark through the maze of narrow, unlit and not particularly clean lanes can be a trial.

Rooms in Leh's **mid-range hotels** come with en-suite shower-toilets and piped hot water, while **upmarket** accommodation is limited and poor value for money by Indian standards. Aimed primarily at tour groups, the rates of these hotels usually include full board. The prices below are for the high season, when hotels tend to be block-booked by package tour groups. Off season, prices can be slashed by as much as sixty percent.

Antelope, Chubi ☎ 01982/52086. A short walk from the centre, this is a quiet spot, with a pleasant garden and plain rooms under the shadow of the palace. ❷–❹

Asia, Changspa ☎ 01982/53403. Large riverside guesthouse with a spanking new block. Sociable terrace-cum-café and meditation classes, but limited views. ❸–❹

Bimla, Malpak, off Fort Road ☎ 01982/52754. Central, though secluded, with nice rooms and plenty of space outside to lounge around. ❸–❹

Dehlex, Pharka ☎ 01982/52755. Simple and quiet despite its central location, with a pleasant garden. If it's full, try *Ti-Sei* behind it. ❷–❸

Dragon, south of the bazaar ☎ 01982/52139. An ersatz traditional building close to the centre, with plush Western-style rooms arranged around a central courtyard, and a good restaurant. ❽

Goba, Changspa ☎ 01982/53670. Well-maintained traditional house with a pleasant garden, sometimes used as a venue for meditation and alternative therapies. ❷–❸

Gompo, Changspa ☎ 01982/52717. Relaxed and cheap with a pleasant little garden café; if it's full, try one of several alternatives down this lane including the new block of the *Tsaro* (☎ 01982/53626) next door. ❸–❹

Greenland, Changspa ☎ 01982/53156. Old guesthouse with spacious glass rooms or smaller singles downstairs and a cosy garden. ❷–❸

Indus, Malpak, off Fort Road ☎ 01982/52502. Cheap singles and a few doubles, with some attached bathrooms and solar-heated water. Central, pleasant and open in winter. ❷–❹

Larchang, Changspa ☎ 01982/52797. Small guesthouse tucked away behind the *Asia*, with a range of doubles with attached baths, set around a pleasant shaded courtyard. ❷–❸

Lha-Ri-Mo, Old Leh Road ☎ 01982/52101. Palatial, repro mansion down Fort Road. A favourite with tour groups but now declining in favour of new establishments. Rates include all meals. ❽

Lotus, Upper Karzoo ☎ 01982/53129. Large new hotel built in traditional style with a level of comfort aimed at tour groups. Their rates include full board. ❽

Lumbini, Fort Road ☎ 01982/52182. Owned by one of the abbots of Phyang, this is the latest addition to central Leh in the luxury category; it's aimed at tour groups with rates that include full board. ❽

Lung Snon, lane opposite *Hotel Mandala*, Sheldan, 1km south of the centre past the Indian Airlines office ☎ 01982/52749. Friendly family guesthouse built around a leafy courtyard. Pleasant and worth the trek. ❷–❸

Milarepa, Lakrook, Chubi ☎ 01982/53218. Owned by a politician and quiet with an extensive garden in a pleasant setting to the north of Leh, it's well worth the walk. ❸–❺

Old Ladakh, old town ☎ 01982/52951. Ladakh's first-ever guesthouse is homely and central, and offers a choice of rooms: the kitsch "deluxe" one (pink pillows and Tibetan rugs) is a real winner. ❷–❸

Oriental, below the Shanti Stupa, Changspa Lane, Changspa ☎ 01982/53153. Congenial and popular guesthouse with spotless rooms, solar-heated water, superb views, nourishing home-cooked meals and a genuinely warm welcome even in winter. ❷–❹

Padma, Ghirghir, off Fort Road ☎ 01982/52630. There are two parts to this hotel: a traditional old building with immaculate rooms with shared baths, a beautiful kitchen, a garden and mountain views; and a modern annexe with comfortable doubles and attached baths and a rooftop restaurant. ❸–❼

Pangong, Chulung ☎ 01982/52300. Pleasant, newish hotel built around a courtyard garden with spacious, well-priced rooms, a cybercafé and an inviting balcony. ❺

Reboke, Changspa ☏01982/53230. A small, simple but friendly guesthouse which also has a couple of rooms with attached baths, at the far end of a narrow lane past the ugly *Sun & Sand*. If full try the simple rooms at *Chunka* (☏01982/52630) next door. ❷

Ri-Rab, Changspa Lane ☏01982/53108. Solid modern hotel with a local flavour, crisp cotton sheets, rooftop views and full board. A bit expensive but with money change and telephone facilities. ❻

Saser, next to the Ecology Centre ☏01982/52575. Modern hotel which successfully embraces elements of traditional architecture, with a pleasant garden courtyard and comfortable rooms with attached baths – a bargain off-season. ❺

Silver Cloud, Near Sankar *Gompa* ☏01982/53128. Excellent purpose-built family guesthouse in modern Ladakhi style, with immaculate rooms and something to suit most budgets. Well worth the trek through the fields. ❷–❼

Tak, old town. Another old favourite, but boxed in beneath the palace and very grubby. The (cheap) glass rooms are by far the best deal. ❷

Yak Tail, Fort Road ☏01982/52118. Slap in the centre of town, and with most amenities, including currency exchange and a pricey restaurant that hosts weekly culture shows. ❼

Yasmin, Changspa Lane ☏01982/52405. Sunny garden and clean and comfortable rooms in a custom-built guesthouse owned by one of Ladakh's literary figures: relaxed and attractive but a little expensive. ❺–❻

The Town

With the mighty hulk of the palace looming to the north, it's virtually impossible to lose your bearings in Leh. The broad main bazaar runs north to south through the heart of town, dividing the labyrinthine old quarter and nearby polo ground from the greener and more spacious residential districts of **Karzoo** and **Suku** to the west. **Fort Road**, the other principal thoroughfare, turns west off the main street and then winds downhill past the taxi rank, the *Hotel Dreamland*, and the arrival and departure point for Manali buses, towards the Indian Airlines office on the southern outskirts.

The bazaar and old town

After settling into a hotel or guesthouse, most visitors spend their first day in Leh soaking up the atmosphere of the **bazaar**. Sixty or so years ago, this bustling tree-lined boulevard was the busiest market between Yarkhand and Kashmir. Merchants from Srinagar and the Punjab would gather to barter for pashmina wool brought down by nomadic herdsmen from western Tibet, or for raw silk hauled across the Karakorams on Bactrian camels. These days, though the street is awash with kitsch curio shops and handicraft emporiums, it retains a distinctly Central Asian feel. Clean-shaven Ladakhi lamas in sneakers and shades rub shoulders with half-bearded Baltis from the Karakoram and elderly Tibetan refugees whirring prayer wheels, while snatches of Chinese music crackle out of the shopkeepers' transistor radios. At the bottom of the bazaar, women from nearby villages, stovepipe hats perched jauntily on their heads, sit behind piles of vegetables, spinning wool and chatting as they appraise the passers-by. Even if you're not shopping for trekking supplies, check out the **provision stores** along the street, where bright pink, turquoise, and wine-red silk cummerbunds hang in the windows. Inside, sacks of aromatic spices, dried pulses, herbs and tea are stacked beside boxes of incense, soap and spare parts for kerosene stoves.

When you've had enough of the bazaar, head past the new green-and-white-painted **Jami Masjid** at the top of the street, and follow one of the lanes that lead into the **old town**. Apart from the odd electric cable, nothing much has changed here since the warren of flat-roofed houses, crumbling *chortens*, *mani* walls (see opposite) and narrow sandy streets was laid down late in the sixteenth century – least of all the plumbing. One place definitely worth walking through the putrid-smelling puddles to visit, however, is the **Chamba temple**. It's not easy to find on your own; ask at the second row of shops on the left after the big arch for the key-keeper (*gonyer*), who will show you the way. Hemmed in by dilapidated medieval mansions, the one-roomed shrine houses a colossal image of Maitreya, the Buddha to come, and some wonderful old wall paintings.

The palace

Lording it over the old town from the top of a craggy granite ridge is the derelict **palace** (daily 7–10am & 4–6pm; Rs10) of the sixteenth-century ruler Sengge Namgyal. A scaled-down version of the Potala in Lhasa, it is a textbook example of medieval Tibetan architecture, with gigantic sloping buttressed walls and projecting wooden balconies that tower nine storeys above the surrounding houses. Since the Ladakhi royal family left the palace in the 1940s, damage inflicted by nineteenth-century Kashmiri cannons has caused large chunks of it to collapse. Bring a flashlight, and watch where you walk: in spite of restoration work, holes gape in the floors and dark staircases.

Apart from the flaking murals that decorate the ruined royal apartments and state rooms on the upper levels, very few remnants of the palace's former splendour survive. The main reason to pick your way through its gutted interior is to reach the **roof terrace**, which offers spectacular **views** over the mud-brown rooftops of the old town to the wrinkled flanks and snow-covered ridges of the Stok-Kangri mountains.

Chortens and mani walls

Among the more visible expressions of Buddhism in Ladakh are the chess-pawn-shaped **chortens** at the entrance to villages and monasteries. These are the Tibetan equivalent of the Indian stupa (see p.437) – large hemispherical burial mounds-cum-devotional objects, prominent in Buddhist ritual since the third century BC. Made of mud and stone (now also concrete), many *chortens* were erected as acts of piety by Ladakhi nobles, and like their southern cousins, they are imbued with mystical powers and **symbolic significance**: the tall tapering spire, normally divided into thirteen sections, represents the soul's progression towards nirvana, while the sun cradled by the crescent moon at the top stands for the unity of opposites, and the oneness of existence and the universe. Some contain sacred manuscripts that, like the *chortens*, wither and decay in time, illustrating the central Buddhist doctrine of impermanence. Those enshrined in monasteries, however, generally made of solid silver and encrusted with semiprecious stones, contain the ashes or relics of revered *rinpoches* (incarnate lamas). Always pass a *chorten* in a clockwise direction: the ritual of circumambulation mimics the passage of the planets through the heavens, and is believed to ward off evil spirits. The largest array is to be found in the desert east of **Shey** (see p.613), the former capital, but look out for the giant brightly painted specimen between the bus station and Leh bazaar, whose red spire stands out against the snowy Stok-Kangri mountains to the south.

A short way downhill from the big *chorten*, near the radio station, stands an even more monumental symbol of devotion. The 500-metre **Mani wall**, erected by King Deldan Namgyal in 1635, is one of several at important religious sites around Ladakh. Ranging from a couple of metres to over a kilometre in length, the walls are made of hundreds of thousands of stones, each inscribed with prayers or sacred mantras – usually the invocation *Om Mani Padme Hum*: "Hail to the Jewel in the Lotus". It goes without saying that such stones should never be removed and visitors should resist the urge to climb onto the walls to have photographs taken.

Also worth a look as you pass is the **Dukhar temple** on the fourth storey (ask the monk to unlock it for you). The gloomy shrine, whose centrepiece is a thousand-armed image of the goddess Tara, houses eerie masks, musical instruments and weapons – props for the recitals and religious ceremonies once held in the courtyard outside.

Namgyal Tsemo gompa

Once you are acclimatized to the altitude, the stiff early-morning hike up to **Namgyal Tsemo gompa** (daily 7–9am), the monastery perched precariously on the shaly crag behind Leh palace, is a great way to start the day. Two trails lead up to "the Peak of Victory", whose twin peaks are connected by giant strings of multicoloured prayer flags; the first and most popular path zigzags across its south side from the palace road, while a second scales the more gentle northern slope via the village of Chubi (the route followed by the lama from Sankar *gompa* who tends to the shrine each morning and evening). Alternatively, you could drive there along the dirt track that turns left off the main Khardung La highway, 2km north of the bus stand.

Approaching the *gompa* from the south, the first building you come to is the red-painted **Maitreya temple**. Thought to date from the fourteenth century, the shrine houses a giant Buddha statue flanked by *bodhisattvas*. However, its wall paintings are modern and of less interest than those in the **Gon-khang** (temple of protector deities) up the hill. Most famous of these, on the left of the door as you enter, is the honorary portrait of Tashi Namgyal, the temple's founder and prolific builder. In the gloomy interior, you can just make out murals of Shakyamuni (the historical Buddha) and Tsong-kha-pa, founder of the Gelug-pa sect. The veiled central deity itself sports a shiny phallus, believed to cure infertility in women.

The Shanti Stupa

A relatively new addition to the rocky skyline around Leh is the toothpaste-white **Shanti Stupa** above Changspa village, 3km west of the bazaar. Inaugurated in 1983 by the Dalai Lama, the "Peace Pagoda", whose sides are decorated with gilt panels depicting episodes from the life of the Buddha, is one of several such monuments erected around India by a "Peace Sect" of Japanese Buddhists. It can be reached by car, or on foot via a steep flight of 157 steps, which winds up from the end of Changspa Lane to the café just below the stupa – a welcome respite for those not fit or acclimatized. The site is particularly atmospheric at dusk, when the drums played at evening puja seem to set the pace of growing shadows as the sun sinks behind the mountains in the west.

The Ecology Centre

Five minutes' walk north of the main bazaar (next to the *Tsemo-La Hotel*), the **Ecology Centre** (Mon–Sat 10am–5pm; ☎01982/52646) is the headquarters of LEDeG (the Ladakh Ecological Development Group) – a local non-governmental organization that aims to counter the negative impact of Western-style "development" by fostering economic independence and respect for traditional culture. This involves promoting "appropriate" technologies such as solar energy, encouraging organic farming and cottage industries, and providing education on environmental and social issues through village drama, workshops and seminars. A garden hosts an open-air exhibition of solar gadgets, hydraulic pumps, water mills and other ingenious energy-saving devices that have proved successful throughout Ladakh. There's also a small

With limited resources at their disposal, a handful of voluntary organizations, including LEDeG, battle to protect Ladakh's delicate environment and ancient culture against the sea of change. **SECMOL** (Students' Educational and Cultural Movement of Ladakh), founded in 1988 by Ladakhi university students, strives to increase awareness of developmental issues and guide younger students through an educational system fraught with chronic inadequacies. In the hope of maintaining pride in Ladakh's traditions, SECMOL teaches local history and runs workshops on handicrafts, agriculture and technology. **Volunteer** help from TEFL-qualified visitors is especially appreciated at the summer schools run just outside Leh. If you'd like to meet members of SECMOL, either write in advance, or drop into their office on the northern outskirts of town (Mon–Sat 2–6pm; ☏01982/52421), ten minutes' walk up the hill from Ali Shah's Postcard Shop.

The **Women's Alliance of Ladakh**, another project inspired by Helena Norberg Hodge and closely aligned to the Farm Project, is a co-operative designed to reinforce traditional Ladakhi culture, also based in Chubi. The best time to visit the Alliance is during one of their fetes, where you can sample local produce, pick up handicrafts and catch exhibitions of colourful traditional costume and performances of folk dance. **LEHO** (Ladakh Environment and Health Organization) places its emphasis on the proper utilization of land and water resources and the management of livestock on a sustainable basis within the framework of Ladakh's ancient traditions. Their office and showroom is on the first floor of the Himalaya Complex, near the post office in the main bazaar (☏01982/52580).

library, and a **handicraft shop**, selling locally made clothes, *thangkas*, T-shirts, books and postcards.

Try to catch a screening of LEDeG's short **video**, *Ancient Futures: Learning From Ladakh* (Mon–Sat 4pm), shown to a minimum of ten people, which gives an insightful account of Ladakhi culture and the sweeping changes of the past thirty years, many of them direct results of tourism. The film is an excellent introduction to the civilization, traditions and severe ecological and cultural problems facing Ladakh. However, some of the political issues, including the proxy war on the borders of Jammu & Kashmir and the huge military presence in the area, are skirted, and the film has its detractors among local Ladakhis.

Helena Norberg Hodge, the Swedish-born founder of LEDeG who appears in the film, has written an excellent book on Ladakh, *Ancient Futures*, available at the handicraft shop. When in town she appears in person on Wednesdays to lead the discussion that follows the video. Norberg Hodge is also the founder of the International Society for Ecology and Culture (ISEC), devoted to promoting sustainable ways of living in both "developing" and "developed" countries. ISEC employs **volunteers** in Ladakh on the **Farm Project** to help local farmers maintain traditional farming methods.

Sankar gompa

Nestled amid the shimmering poplar coppices and terraced fields of barley that extend up the valley behind Leh, **Sankar gompa**, 3km north of the town centre, is among the most accessible monasteries in central Ladakh – hence its restricted visiting hours for tourists (daily 7–10am & 5–7pm; Rs10). You can get there either by car, or on foot: turn left at the junction above Ali Shah's Postcard Shop, and then right onto the concrete path that runs alongside the stream. Sankar appears after about twenty minutes' walk, surrounded by sun-bleached *chortens* and a high mud wall.

7

LADAKH | Leh

The monastery, a small under-*gompa* of Spitok, is staffed by twenty monks, and is the official residence of the **Kushok Bakul**, Ladkah's head of the Gelug-pa sect. Appropriately for such a high-ranking *rinpoche*, his glass-fronted penthouse enjoys pride of place on top of the main building, crowned with a golden spire and a *dharma chakra* flanked by two deer (symbolizing the Buddha's first sermon in Sarnath). A flight of steps leads from the courtyard to the **Du-khang** (main prayer hall). Beyond the Lords of the Four Quarters and Wheel of Life mandala that adorn the veranda, you enter a high-ceilinged hall whose walls writhe with lustrous multicoloured murals. Those on either side of the doorway are the most amazing: many-armed pot-bellied bovine monsters drink blood from skull cups, while the copulating *yab-yum* couples to the right are garlanded with severed heads and engulfed in swirling red and yellow flames.

Above the Du-khang stands the *gompa*'s principal deity, Tara, in her triumphant, 1000-armed form as Dukkar, or "Lady of the White Parasol", presiding over a light, airy shrine room whose walls are adorned with a Tibetan calendar and tableaux depicting "dos and don'ts" for monks – some very arcane indeed. Another flight of steps leads to the *gompa* **library** and, eventually, a roof terrace with fine views towards the north side of Namgyal Tsemo hill and the valley to the south.

Shopping

Between June and September, Leh is swamped by almost as many transient Tibetan and Kashmiri **traders** as souvenir-hungry tourists. Most of the merchandise hawked in their temporary boutiques and stalls comes from outside the region too: papier-mâché bowls, shawls and carpets from Srinagar, jewellery and miniature paintings from Jaipur, and "Himalayan" handicrafts, including *thangkas*, churned out in Nepal and by Tibetan refugees in Old Delhi. Prices tend to be high, so haggle hard, and don't be conned into shelling out for cleverly faked "antiques". Much of the "silver" on sale is in fact cheap white metal.

Tibetan and Ladakhi **curios** account for the bulk of the goods on sale in Leh's emporiums, though most of these are run by Kashmiris from the Srinagar Valley. The Ladakh Art Palace off the main bazaar, one of the very few locally run souvenir stores, is a good place to browse. Tibetan traders are also making an impact on the high street with several curio shops along Fort Road as well as the Charitable Trust Tibetan Handicrafts Emporium and the Tibetan Handicraft Emporium, both aligned to the Tibetan government and located near each other opposite the *Amdo Restaurant* in the Main Bazaar.

Among the vast array of curios are Tibetan trumpets (*thumpchen*), cymbals, brass and copper *chang* kettles, prayer wheels, thunderbolts (*dorjes*), *gur-gur* tea churners, *chaam* dance masks, *thangkas*, and coral and seed-pearl necklaces, to name but a few. During the season, temporary "Tibetan markets" run by itinerant Tibetans spring up around **Fort Road**, where you can pick up amulets, butter lamps, beads, and cheaper silver jewellery inlaid with semiprecious stones. However, the best place to head for **thangkas** and handwoven **Tibetan carpets** is the Tibetan Children's Village Handicraft Centre, up the hill from the GPO, which also has racks of cheap woollen Nepali-style jackets, waistcoats, and the whole gamut of "Free Tibet" stickers and posters.

If money is no object, you could even splash out on a **perak**, a long Ladakhi headdress, encrusted with turquoises, which cost upwards of Rs5000. **Turquoise** is sold by the *tolah* (there are eighty *tolahs* to a kilogram), and

Situated on a strategic corner between Upper Thaka Road and Old Fort Road at one end of the market square, the **Dzomsa Laundry** provides a vital service in ecology-sound washing, using biodegradable detergent and water at a safe distance from habitation. *Dzomsa*, which literally means "meeting point", also serves delicious fresh apricot juice which you can drink while sitting outside watching the world go by. If you're wondering what to do with your empty mineral water bottles, you can recycle them here and have them filled with safe drinking water.

quality and age determine the price. You'll find vendors sitting on the main road; otherwise try the locally owned Potala – an atmospheric old-world shop well worth a rummage – down Nowshara Lane, off the main road close to the Jami Masjid. Next door, Himalayan Art is also locally owned, with an extensive and well-ordered selection of curios, ranging from stones to *thangkas*.

For **authentic Ladakhi souvenirs**, try the outfitters and provision stores dotted along the main bazaar. The Lahauli-run Sonambongo Barongpa & Sons, at the top-right end of the street, sells traditional costume and religious paraphernalia at fixed prices. If you've been wondering where to find those dapper stovepipe hats (*tibi*), hand-dyed *gonchas*, raw silk cummerbunds, tie-dyed rope-soled shoes (*pabbu*), Bhutanese cross-button shirts, prayer flags, real Ladakhi incense, or even monks' robes, look no further.

The **Ecology Centre**'s handicraft shop (with a second branch at the bottom of the bazaar) is another source of good-quality traditional clothing, including hand-knitted woollen jumpers, hats and socks. Few of the **pashmina shawls** on offer in the shops along Fort Road are genuine. Although the wool from pashmina goats is gathered by nomadic herders in eastern Ladakh, most of it lands up in the Kashmir Valley for milling and weaving. However, a couple of Ladakhi co-operatives are trying to break the traditional Kashmiri monopoly of the business and are producing pashmina shawls in Ladakh itself. On the first floor of the Himalaya Shopping Complex, Main Bazaar, Ladakh Environment and Health Organization (LEHO) sell plush or plain shawls for around Rs5000. You can also try the Chang Tang Co-operative in Karzoo, five minutes' walk up the lane past the Ecology Centre run by five local women who buy wool direct from the nomadic herdsmen.

Of the **bookshops** in Leh, Artou's is one of the best, with two branches – one on the main bazaar, and another between *Tibetan Restaurant Devi* and the Ecology Centre. Both stock a fair selection of Indian Penguin classics, plus dozens of more expensive titles on Ladakh and the Himalayas. Lehling, near the post office in the Main Bazaar, has a similar selection including maps. Secondhand paperbacks are sold or part-exchanged at Prakash Stationers opposite the vegetable market. Fairdeal Stationers near the Jami Masjid, Main Bazaar Square, has only a small selection of books but is good for **newspapers**. While **postcards** are widely available, the oldest photographers in Leh, Ali Shah's Postcard Shop above the main bazaar, is worth a visit, especially for its black-and-white photographs of Ladakh.

Eating

As Leh's thriving restaurant and café scene has been cornered by the refugee community, **Tibetan food** has a high profile, alongside tourist-oriented

Chinese and European dishes. The most popular Tibetan dish is *momos* – crescent-shaped pasta shells, stuffed with meat, cheese, or vegetables, and (if you're lucky) ginger, then steamed and served with hot soup and spicy sauce. Fried *momos* are called *kothays*. *Thukpa*, another wholesome favourite, is broth made from fresh pasta strips, meat and vegetables. These, and dozens of variations, are dished up in swanky tourist restaurants but you can tuck into bigger portions of the same stuff (for a fraction of the price) at modest, although not always hygienic, backstreet "momo kitchens".

Most visitors have **breakfast** in their hotel or guesthouse, where the host family cook small round loaves of Ladakhi wheat-flour bread (*tagi shamos*), eaten piping hot with honey, or jam, and butter. For a truly authentic Leh breakfast, grab a couple of flat-breads from the clay-oven bakeries on the narrow lane at the top of the bazaar; the Tibetan restaurateurs don't mind you turning up with your own. If you fancy a change, apple-pie and chocolate-brownie **pastry shops**, most owned by the Sikh-run German Bakery chain, are dotted all over town serving filled baguettes, croissants and muesli breakfasts. A majority of tourist restaurants offer a mixed menu including some with **Continental cooking**. Several health-food outlets, including the Dzomsa Laundry, sell honey, dried fruit and nuts, but avoid fresh apricots as they are difficult to digest unless, according to local tradition, you crack the nut and eat the seed as well.

Beer is widely available in most of Leh's tourist restaurants while **chang**, a local barley brew, is harder to come by: ask at your guesthouse if they can get some in for you. A handful of bars cater to the tourist trade, including the *Ibex* near the taxi stand on Fort Road.

Amdo, Main Bazaar. Two Tibetan restaurants overlooking the main street. The one on the east side catches the morning sun and serves hearty *tsampa* porridge for breakfast.

Food Affair, Main Bazaar. A great outdoor café on the square with a mix of baked and cooked food especially good for breakfast and snacky lunches, catching up on letters or just people-watching.

German Bakery, Fort Road, Suku. Sister business to its Manali namesake, equally well stocked with home-baked chocolate cakes, apple strudel, cheese and wholemeal bread. The adjoining café is a popular hang-out.

Ibex, Fort Road (opposite taxi stand). Good for its Indian food with a bar for beer and generous measures of spirits.

La Montessori, Main Bazaar. Coir mats and minimal decor, but mouthwatering cheese *kothays* figure among the many inexpensive Tibetan dishes.

La Terrasse, Goji Complex (opposite the State Bank of India). A great rooftop location in the centre of town, good for breakfast or for a beer in the evenings. Serves Indian, Chinese and European dishes, but no local cuisine.

Mentokling, Changspa Lane, near Mission School. One of the best of the garden cafés along this road with a good all-round menu but especially strong on Indian food; a good bet when the rest of Leh is closed by strikes.

Mona Lisa, near Alpha Mess, off Changspa Lane. A legendary Ladakhi-run restaurant now re-established in a vegetable garden, serving all the usual stuff, and some ambitious international alternatives (such as Swiss cream cheese and falafels).

Penguin Bar, Fort Road. A great place for a beer, or German Bakery snacks or for a meal in a leafy garden setting. The *Dolphin* next door by the river is similar.

Pumpernickel & the World Peace Café, Main Bazaar. A long-term traveller's haunt with a useful notice board and good for breakfast, bread, pies and rolls.

Shelden, Changspa Lane. Pleasant garden restaurant in Changspa with a good all-round menu and a pleasant ambience, especially in the evenings.

Summer Harvest, Fort Road. A popular all-rounder in the centre of town, though the food is nothing to write home about.

Tibetan Friends Corner, opposite the taxi stand. Recently transformed from a dingy hole to a popular eating joint, with filling and cheap food: a big hit with local *thukpa*-slurping Tibetans.

Tibetan Kitchen, *Hotel Tso-Kar*, Fort Road. Considered by many, locals and visitors alike, to be the best Tibetan food in town but only open in high season. Large parties are advised to book.

Tibetan Restaurant, New Market, Main Bazaar Square. Friendly and popular little café with a limited menu, but convenient as a meeting point.

Wok Tibetan Kitchen, Main Bazaar. Wide choice of Tibetan and Chinese food in clean and airy first-floor restaurant. Reasonable prices.
Zen Garden, Changspa Lane. Seasonal, open-air restaurant with a barbecue under willow trees offering a varied menu with Indian, Chinese and traveller-friendly food including pasta and the usual Israeli dishes.

Arranging a trek or tour and hiring equipment

Leh offers a bewildering number of operators for the large volume of tourists who come to Ladakh to trek. Most trek and tour operators offer much the same services sharing much the same resources. Although **trekking** rates are quite uniform, you can get some cheaper deals on items such as porterage and pony hire by shopping around. You can also **rent equipment** either through the chosen agency or through places like the Traveller Shop, White House, Fort Road (☎ 01982/53048). Expect to pay Rs100 a day for a tent, Rs70 for a sleeping bag, Rs30 for a gas stove and Rs40 for an ice axe, for those intending to attempt the climb of Stok Kangri. Mero (Mountaineering Expeditions & Rescue Operations), across Fort Road (☎ 01982/53070), also supplies equipment and is cheaper but the quality of the equipment isn't so good. Both Mero and the Traveller Shop act as trek operators supplying guides, porters, transport and food. Standard rates for package treks start from around $25 per day, but for those who prefer to arrange things themselves, **pony hire** through an agent in Leh costs around Rs400 a day and a pony man, who can guide and cook, an extra Rs300. See p.610 for a list of tour operators.

Damage to the **environment** has become an issue of paramount importance in Ladakh. Although plastic bags are banned as they clog up the vital river systems that the state so depends on, shopkeepers continue to use them. Plastic mineral water bottles are a particular headache and so you are advised to bring your own filtration system (see p.32) with you; some places in Leh will refill mineral water bottles with safe water (see p.599). You are advised to leave all unnecessary packaging behind before arriving in Ladakh.

Listings

Bike rental Mountain bikes may be rented through Highland Adventures in the *Hotel Ibex* complex. Rates are around Rs250 per day plus a deposit, with discounts for longer periods. Others to try are Dreamland Trek & Tours and Wisdom Travels both on Fort Road.
Hospital Leh's overstretched, poorly equipped SNM Hospital (☎ 01982/52360 or 52014), is 1km south of the centre on the main road. For urgent medical treatment, contact a doctor through any upmarket hotel.
Internet access Despite the sporadic electricity supply (expect a trickle in the evenings), Leh has several cybercafés including Gypsy's World, Fort Road; Silk Route Travels opposite the State Bank, Main Bazaar; *Pangong Hotel* down Library Road in Chulung; and the excellent *Cyberia* at the *High Life Restaurant* on Fort Road. Charges start at Rs2 a minute, with *Cyberia* being amongst the cheapest.
Laundry If your hotel or guesthouse doesn't take laundry, the best place to have your clothes washed is Dzomsa Laundry (see the box on p.607).
Libraries The Ecology Centre's excellent library (Mon–Sat 10am–4pm) keeps books on everything from agriculture to Zen Buddhism, as well as periodicals, magazines, and files of articles on Ladakh and development issues. Students of Buddhism should check out the CIBS library in Choglamsar (Mon–Sat 10am–1pm & 2–4pm), where the helpful librarians speak English.
Meditation, yoga and alternative therapy Small classes are run by the Mahabodhi Society in Changspa which specializes in Vipassana (☎ 01982/44025; their extensive complex in Devachan (☎ 01982/44155, ⓦ www.mahabodhi@geocities.com) near Chogamsar includes a meditation centre with courses ranging from three to seven days. The *Asia Guesthouse* on Changspa Lane houses a German-run Vajrayana Meditation and Healing Arts

As befits India's remotest Himalayan town, Leh is singularly hard to get to, and even harder to leave. Fragile road and air links mean visitors all too often find themselves stranded waiting for passes to open or planes to appear. Wherever and however you travel, book your onward ticket as far in advance as possible, be prepared for delays if the weather changes, and allow plenty of time to connect with onward flights.

The quickest way out of Leh is **by plane**. During the summer, weather permitting, Indian Airlines flies to **Delhi** (2 daily), **Jammu** (Thurs & Sun), **Chandigarh** (Tues) and **Srinagar** (Sat). The rest of the year, flights are less reliable. Tickets can be booked and confirmed at the Indian Airlines/Tushita Travels office beyond *Hotel Lha-Ri-Mo* on Fort Road (Mon–Fri 10am–5pm, Sat 10am–noon; ✆01982/52076), but you may have to wait: the computer is "down" a lot more than it's "up". Excessive demand for seats also contributes to the queues, which are worse at the start and end of the tourist season before the passes open, and after the summer festival. It's often a good idea to arrive thirty minutes before the office opens - you can start queuing inside. In addition, due to the altitude of Leh airport, planes arriving here full have to leave with a lighter load (ie empty seats), so some people inevitably get stuck. If you can, have your seat confirmed as soon or even before you get to Leh. However, takeoffs require near-perfect visibility and the slightest scrap of cloud in the wrong place can result in the last-minute cancellation of the flight.

The overland route to **Manali** in Himachal Pradesh (see p.578) is officially open till September 15, but invariably a sense of panic sets in towards the end of the season, and some **bus** operators such as HPTDC fold up earlier. Private buses continue to ply the route through to early October as long as the weather holds and so do four-wheel-drive Gypsies. The 485-kilometre journey across the Himalayas takes two days, with a night halt in a tent camp en route. Tickets for HPTDC's tri-weekly "deluxe" buses can be booked at their office upstairs on Fort Road. HPTDC's fare to Manali including one night in their dank tented camp at Sarchu costs Rs800, but

Centre. Classes and sessions for yoga, reiki, shiatsu and other alternative therapies, well advertised by posters and leaflets, are held at a variety of venues, usually guesthouses.

Motorbikes Although several places now hire motorcycles with the going rate of around Rs700 a day for an Enfield, you should check the bikes carefully as you don't want to break down in places such as Khardung La. By far the most reliable of the agencies is Summer Adventures, *Hotel Zambhala* (✆01982/52651), a short walk to the north of the Main Bazaar Square towards Changspa Lane, but the selection is limited.

Pharmacy Met Ram Vinay Kumar at the top of the main bazaar sells a range of allopathic pills and potions, as well as underwear, batteries and tampons. For Tibetan medicine, try Dr Tsewang Rigzin Larje, whose clinic is by the old bus stand, south of the main bazaar.

Photography Ali Shah's Postcard Shop, two minutes' walk north of the main bazaar, stocks fresh film of all kinds, including slide film. If it's closed, try ND Dijoo & Sons on the main street. Also look around the area beside the Jami Masjid. Check the cases for expiry dates.

Police ✆01982/52018 or 52200.

Post The post office is at the Main Bazaar (Mon–Sat 10am–1pm & 2–4pm). For parcels, go to the GPO (Mon–Sat 10am–4.30pm), out of town on Airport Road, whose unreliable poste restante counter is tucked around the back. You can also receive letters through the Tourist Information Centre on Fort Road.

Sauna and massage The sauna at Thanglang House, Changspa Lane (✆01982/53350) operates on demand during the season (3pm till late) and charges Rs150; they also offer Ayurvedic massage sessions.

Telephones Though many shops have STD/ISD facilities, trunk and international telephone connections are poor, and prices higher than elsewhere in India. Most of the telephone facilities are to be found around the main bazaar and along Fort Road.

Tour operators Reliable agents recommended for trekking and Jeep safaris include: Gypsy's World Treks and Tours, Fort Road ✆01982/52935; Explore Himalayas, Chokhang Complex, Main Bazaar ✆01982/52727; Rimo Expeditions, *Hotel Kanglhachen* ✆01982/53348, another well-estab-

be prepared for the journey taking a day longer. Several agencies along Fort Road including Dreamland Trek & Tours (℡01982/52927) sell tickets for private buses to Manali. They will also help arrange a Sumo or Gypsy to Manali from Rs11,000 one-way, or find you a seat in a shared Jeep (four in all). This is by far the most comfortable option and, if you leave before dawn, there's a good chance you can avoid the tented camps and reach the relative luxury of Keylong that evening. You may be lucky and find a Jeep returning to Manali, in which case expect to pay around Rs8000. Cheaper options include the ramshackle buses run by the HPSRTC and J&KSRTC state transport corporations, bookable the day before departure at the town bus stand. Don't underestimate the Manali–Leh highway. Even when the road is in good shape, it can be a long hard haul; after it has been recently cleared of snow or landslides the journey can take three or four days. A full account of the route, starting at Manali, is given on p.587.

J&KSRTC buses to Srinagar run from mid-June to late October, albeit carrying far fewer tourists than in past years. The two-day, 434-kilometre trip is broken by an overnight stop in Kargil (see p.631), and long waits at roadblocks while interminable military and civil truck convoys lumber up the one-way sections of the road. Tickets for buses (6am daily except Sun) go on sale between 4pm and 5pm on the day before departure at J&KSRTC's office in the town bus stand. If you're heading for Srinagar, pick up a copy of Kashmir Times in the bazaar to catch up on the latest events in the troublesome valley.

If you want to hitch (unadvisable for lone women travellers) to either Manali or Srinagar, the truck park in Leh is between the old bus stand and the polo ground. Bear in mind you'll be expected to pay your way (around two-thirds of the current bus fare), and chip in for toll charges at police checkpoints. Trucks are also liable to break down more frequently than buses, and have more accidents.

For information regarding local bus services to destinations in Ladakh, see the relevant account, or consult the Travel Details on p.641.

lished operator; and Footprints, Raku Complex, Fort Road ℡01982/52512, who boast ecofriendly adventure tours. Others worth looking at are Adventure North, Hotel Dragon ℡01982/52139, and Dreamland Trek & Tours, Fort Road ℡01982/52927, while K2 Adventure, Main Bazaar Square ℡01982/53532, offers competitive rates for Jeep rent. Alternatively, you could try smaller agencies such as Oriental Travels, Oriental Lodge, below the Shanti Stupa, Changspa ℡01982/53153, for a more personalized service. Several of these agents also offer rafting on the River Indus (see p.612).

Southeast of Leh

Southeast of Leh, the Indus Valley broadens to form a fertile river basin whose lush geometrical barley fields, interspersed with a tangle of turquoise streams, contrast sharply with the bare brown snow-capped mountains that sweep up from its sides. Among the spectacular Buddhist monuments that crown the rocky knolls and razorback ridges at the edge of the flat valley floor are **Shey**, site of a ruined palace and giant brass Buddha, and the stunning monastery of **Tikse**. Both overlook the main highway and are thus served by regular buses.

With the exception of **Stok Palace**, home of the Ladakhi queen, sights on the opposite (south) side of the Indus, linked to the main road by a relatively unfrequented and partly surfaced road, are harder to reach by public transport. South of Stok, **Matho** *gompa* is more famous for its winter oracle festivals than its art treasures, but is well worth a visit, if only for the superb views from its

While water levels are high, between the end of June and late August, Leh's more entrepreneurial travel agents operate rafting trips on the River Indus. The routes are tame by comparison with Nepal's, but floating downstream in a twelve-seater rubber inflatable is a hugely enjoyable way to experience the valley's most rugged and beautiful landscape. Two different stretches of the river are used: from Spitok to the Indus-Zanskar confluence at Nimmu (3hr), and from Nimmu to the ancient temple complex at Alchi (2hr 30min). Experienced rafters may also want to try the more challenging route between Alchi and Khalsi, which takes in the kilometre-long series of rapids at Nurla. The annual multi-day expedition down the Zanskar River to the Indus is by far the most rewarding as it also includes the spectacular road approach to Padum.

Several adventure tour operators in Leh offer white-water rafting on the Indus, but all act as agents for Delhi-based operators who bring the equipment up during the season. Tickets should be booked at least a day in advance. The best established of the operators is Rimo Expeditions, *Hotel Kanglhachen* Complex (☎01982/53348), near the Ecology Centre; prices start from Rs900. Make sure when you book that the price includes transport to and from the river, rental of life jackets and helmets, and meals, and that the raft has a waterproof strongbox for valuables.

roof terrace. Further south still, either cross the Indus and rejoin the highway, calling in at **Stakna** *gompa* en route, or continue down the left bank to **Hemis**, Ladakh's wealthiest monastery and the venue for one of the few religious festivals held in summer. If you want to side-step your fellow tourists without spending a night away from Leh, head up the austerely beautiful tributary valley opposite Hemis to the *gompas* of **Chemrey** and **Thak Thok**, the latter built around a fabled meditation cave.

Further east and south, the easing of restrictions has opened up new areas. East of Thak Tok, the road crosses the Chang La and then veers east to the high mountain lake of **Pangong Tso**, most of which lies in Tibet. Far more relaxing and inviting is the vast wilderness of **Rupshu** with new trekking possibilities around the shores of **Tso Moriri**. Permits are required for all these recently derestricted areas; for full details see the box on p.595.

Stok

Just beyond the Tibetan refugee camp at **Choglamsar**, a side road turns left off the highway to cross the Indus on an iron bridge plastered with prayer flags, and then continues up towards a huge TV mast. At the top of a huge moraine of pebbles swept down from the mountains, the elegant four-storey **STOK Palace** stands under the shadow of the intrusive tower, above barley terraces studded with threshing circles and whitewashed farmhouses. Built early in the nineteenth century by the last ruler of independent Ladakh, it has been the official residence of the Ladakhi royal family since they were ousted from Leh and Shey two hundred years ago.

The present Gyalmo or "queen", Deskit Angmo, a former member of parliament, still lives here during the summer, but has converted one wing of her 77-roomed palace into a small **museum** (daily 7am–7pm; Rs20). The fascinating collection comprises some of the royal family's most precious heirlooms, including antique ritual objects, ceremonial tea paraphernalia and exquisite sixteenth-century **thangkas** illuminated with paint made from crushed rubies, emeralds and sapphires. The *pièces de résistance*, however, are the Gyalmo's **per-**

aks. Still worn on important occasions, the ancient headdresses, thought to have originated in Tibet, are encrusted with slabs of flawless turquoise, polished coral, lapis lazuli and nuggets of pure gold. Also of interest are a couple of swords whose blades were allegedly tied in knots as a demonstration of strength by King Tashi Namgyal, and several sacred **dzi stones** – "pearls of pure happiness" – said to have fallen from heaven, and worn to ward off evil spirits.

Stok gompa, five minutes' walk up the valley, boasts a collection of dance-drama masks, and some lurid modern murals painted by lamas from Lingshet *gompa* in Zanskar, the artists responsible for the Maitreya statue in Tikse (see p.614).

Buses leave Leh for Stok (40min) at 7.30am, 1pm and 4.30pm. A day in Stok is more than enough to do the museum and the *gompa* justice, and to explore the beautiful side-valley behind the village – trailhead for the Markha Valley trek (see p.634). The last bus for Leh leaves at 2pm and if you miss it or are tempted to **stay**, try the *Hotel Highland* (❹), a palatial two-storey house with fine views from its well-furnished en-suite rooms. Alternative accommodation includes the dingy nameless guesthouse (❶) just above it.

Shey

SHEY, 15km southeast of Leh and once the capital of Ladakh, is now all but deserted, the royal family having been forced to abandon it by the Dogras midway through the nineteenth century. Only a semi-derelict palace, a small *gompa* and a profusion of *chortens* remain, clustered around a bleached spur of rock that juts into the fertile floor of the Indus Valley. The ruins overlook the main highway, and can be reached on the frequent minibuses between Leh bus stand and Tikse. Alternatively, you could walk to Shey from Tikse monastery along a windy path that passes through one of Ladakh's biggest *chorten* fields with hundreds of whitewashed shrines of varying sizes scattered across the surreal desert landscape. You can get extremely dehydrated along the four-kilometre trek, so bring plenty of water and a hat.

The **palace**, a smaller and more dilapidated version of the one in Leh, sits astride the ridge below an ancient fort. Crowned by a golden *chorten* spire, its pride and joy is the colossal metal Shakyamuni Buddha housed in its ruined split-level temple (daily 6–9am). Installed in 1633 at the behest of Sengge Namgyal's son Deldan, the twelve-metre icon allegedly contains a hoard of precious stones, mandalas and powerful charms. Entering from a painted antechamber lined with shelves of ancient manuscripts, and exquisite murals which have been undergoing extensive restoration, you pass through heavy wooden doors to come face to face with the Buddha's huge feet, soles pointing upwards. The customary circumambulation leads around the base of the statue through a haze of incense smoke to total darkness behind. Upstairs, from a balcony surrounding the statue's torso, you can see the massive Buddha, painted gold with tightly curled blue hair, in better light, and inspect the magnificent paintings of Buddhas, *bodhisattvas*, *mahasiddhas* and fierce protector deities coating the temple walls. Preserved for centuries by thick soot from votary butter lamps, these are among the finest in the valley, painted in stunning detail and tinted with gold applied with smooth hair-fine brushstrokes.

Five minutes' walk across the fields from the palace, in the centre of a *chorten*-strewn plain, stands a **temple**, enshrining another massive Shakyamuni statue (daily 7–9am & 5–6pm). Best viewed from the mezzanine veranda on the first floor, it is slightly older than its cousin up the hill. The descendants of the Nepali metalworkers who made it, brought here by Sengge Namgyal, still live and work in the isolated village of **Chilling**, famous for its traditional silverware. Downstairs, the *gompa*'s Du-khang contains dusty old *thangkas* and manuscripts.

Easily missed as you whizz past on the road is Shey's most ancient monument. The **rock carving** of the five Tathagata or "Thus gone" Buddhas, distinguished by their respective vehicles (*vahanas*) and hand positions (*mudras*), appears on a smooth slab of stone on the edge of the highway; it was probably carved soon after the eighth century, before the "Second Spreading" (see p.595). The large central figure with hands held in the gesture of preaching (turning the wheel of *dharma*), is the Buddha Resplendant, Vairocana, whose image is central in many of the Alchi murals (see p.625).

Two **rooms** are available in a traditional Ladakhi house (➋) with a pleasant garden and simple home cooking, booked through the *Shilkhar Restaurant* (☎01982/47061), on the main road opposite the path leading up to the palace. The garden **restaurant** has a varied if uninspiring menu, and is the only option available in Shey. Shey is well connected to Leh with around two buses every hour; the last bus for Leh leaves around 6pm.

Tikse

Ladakh's most photographed and architecturally impressive *gompa* is at **TIKSE**, 19km southeast of Leh. Founded in the fifteenth century, its whitewashed *chortens* and cubic monks' quarters rise in ranks up the sides of a craggy sunbleached bluff, crowned by an imposing ochre- and red-painted temple complex whose gleaming golden finials are visible for miles in every direction.

A metalled road cuts up the empty west side of the hill from the main highway to the monastery's small car park. If you arrive by minibus from Leh (hourly, from the town bus stand), pick your way across the wasteground below the *gompa* and follow the footpath up through its lower buildings to the main entrance, where monks issue tickets (Rs20). Tikse's reincarnation as a major tourist attraction has brought it mixed blessings: its constant stream of summer visitors spoils the peace and quiet necessary for meditation, but the income generated has enabled the monks to invest in major refurbishments, among them the spanking new **Maitreya temple** immediately above the main courtyard. Inaugurated in 1980 by the Dalai Lama, the spacious shrine is built around a gigantic fourteen-metre gold-faced Buddha-to-come, seated not on a throne as is normally the case, but in the lotus position. The bright murals on the wall behind, painted by monks from Lingshet *gompa* in Zanskar, depict scenes from Maitreya's life. In recent years Tikse's reputation has been somewhat sullied by the diminishing reputation of the *rinpoche*, who took to politics as a member of J&K's ruling party, the Kashmiri-Muslim-dominated National Conference.

Tikse's garish modern temple may have had hours of work lavished upon it, but its dingy **Du-khang**, at the far end of the courtyard up a steep flight of steps, hasn't seen a lick of paint in centuries. Faded murals of ghoulish Tantric deities peer out of the gloom of the old prayer hall, which contrary to appearances is still in everyday use. The key-keeper will show you around the tiny chapels behind the head lama's throne, pointing out the ancient cloth-bound manuscripts stacked in wooden racks against the side walls. Before you leave the Du-khang, check out the enormous *thangkas* stored on the shelf opposite the main doorway. These are unrolled once a year during the annual autumn *chaam* dance festival, Tikse Gustor. For most foreign visitors, however, the highlight of a trip to Tikse is the view from its lofty **roof terrace**. A patchwork of barley fields stretches across the floor of the valley, fringed by rippling snow-flecked desert mountains and a string of Tolkien-esque monasteries, palaces, and Ladakhi villages: Shey and Stok to the northwest, Matho on the far side of the Indus, and Stakna crowning a knoll to the south. Come here early enough in the morning, and you'll be able to enjoy this impressive panorama accompanied by primeval groans from the *gompa's* gargantuan Tibetan trumpets – played on the rooftop at puja time.

The last **bus** back to Leh leaves at 6pm. The village's *Skalzal Chamba Hotel* (☏01982/47004; ③), run by the monastery, offers **accommodation** and flexible rates, and has a good garden restaurant with a varied menu ranging from Tibetan food to pancakes.

Matho

MATHO, 27km south of Leh, straddles a spur at the mouth of an idyllic side-valley that runs deep into the heart of the Stok-Kangri massif. Though no less interesting or scenically situated than its neighbours, the *gompa*, the only representative in Ladakh of the **Sakyapa** sect (that held political power in thirteenth-century Tibet), sees comparatively few visitors. Unlike Tikse, across the Indus, it doesn't lie on the main highway, so is less accessible by bus: services leave Leh daily at 8am and 4pm, returning at 9.30am and 5.30pm. By car, Matho also makes an ideal halfway halt on the bumpy journey along the little-used left-bank road between Stok and Hemis.

Despite its collection of four-hundred-year-old *thangkas*, the monastery is best known for its **oracle festival**, Matho Nagran, held on the twenty-fifth and twenty-sixth day of the second Tibetan month (around Feb/March). Two oracles, known as *rongzam*, are elected by lot every three years from among the sixty or so resident lamas. During the run-up to the big days, the pair fast and meditate in readiness for the moment when they are possessed by the spirit of the deity. Watched by crowds of rapt onlookers, they then perform all manner of death-defying stunts that include leaping blindfold around the *gompa's* precipitous parapets while slurping kettle-fulls of *chang*, and slashing themselves with razor-sharp sabres without drawing blood. The events are rounded off with colourful *chaam* dances in the monastery courtyard, and a question-and-answer session in which the *rongzam*, still under the influence of the deity, make prophecies about the coming year.

You can check out the costumes and masks worn by the monks during the festivals in Matho's small **museum**, tucked away behind the Du-khang. Men are also permitted to visit the eerie **Gon-khang** on the roof (strictly no photography), where the oracles' weapons and ritual garb are stored. The floor of the tiny temple lies under a deep layer of barley brought as harvest offerings by local villagers.

Hemis

Thanks to the **Hemis Tsechu** festival – one of the few held in summer (mid-July), when the passes are open – **HEMIS**, 45km southeast of Leh, is the most famous *gompa* in Ladakh. Every year in mid-July, hundreds of foreign visitors join the huge crowds of locals, dressed up in their finest traditional garb, that flock to watch the colourful two-day pageant. However, at other times, the rambling and atmospheric seventeenth-century Drugpa monastery (entrance Rs20), which oversees Stakna and Chemrey (also of the Drugpa sect, part of the Kagyu order), can be disappointingly quiet. Although Hemis is one of

Ladakh's foremost religious institutions, only a skeleton staff of monks and novices are resident off-season. Besides the occasional ritual and chanting of religious texts to the accompaniment of drumbeats, the main activity of the hallowed *gompa* seems to be playing host to the steady trickle of camera-toting tourists on day-trips from Leh.

Crouched at the foot of a narrow sinuous ravine, amid a leafy oasis of poplar and willow trees, Hemis stays hidden from view until you are virtually beside it. The only signs of the *gompa's* existence from the valley are the immense *mani* walls stretching over the rock outflow above you, pointing like giant arrows to the mouth of the gorge.

The main entrance, reached via a long flight of steps, opens onto the large rectangular courtyard where the festival **chaam dances** are performed. Accompanied by cymbal crashes, drum rolls and periodic blasts from the temple trumpets, lamas dressed in opulently brocaded silk costumes and ghoulish masks mime episodes from Buddhist mythology. Now and again, young novices scamper onto the stage to caricature the stylized gestures of the baddies, egged on by a delighted crowd. The show culminates on the second day with a frenzied dismemberment of a dummy, symbolizing the destruction of the human ego, and thus the triumph of Buddhism over ignorance and evil. Illustrating the basic teachings of Mahayana Buddhism, the dramas are also a form of popular entertainment, eagerly anticipated by Ladakhi villagers.

Once every twelve years, the Hemis festival also hosts the ritual unrolling of a giant *thangka*. The *gompa's* prize possession, which covers the entire facade of the building, was embroidered by women whose hands are now revered as holy relics. Decorated with pearls and precious stones, it will not now be on show again until 2004. Among the treasures on permanent display is an exquisite Buddha Shakyamuni, also inlaid with jewels. The serene-faced colossus sits in the Cho-khang chamber at the far end of the courtyard, along with a couple of richly inlaid silver *chortens*.

Practicalities

By car, Hemis is an easy day-trip from Leh. By **bus**, services are only frequent during the festival; at other times a single daily service leaves Leh at 9.45am and returns at 12.30pm, leaving no time to have a good look round. Another bus leaves Leh at 4pm but stays the night at Hemis, returning the next morning at 7am. **Accommodation** in Hemis is very limited with basic rooms (❶) in local houses, some let by monks (ask the ticket person or the café below the *gompa*); alternatively, ask at the *Parachute Restaurant* in the village below for possibilities in local houses. You can find free camping below the village and at the *gompa's* café, run by young *carrom*-playing monks and serving soft drinks and basic meals – a camping site here costs Rs50. The *Parachute Restaurant* has a similar menu but includes a selection of pancakes, and if you want to explore the area, will arrange day-treks into the rugged mountains enclosing Hemis.

Chemrey

Clinging like a swallow's nest to the sides of a shaly conical hill, the magnificent *gompa* of **CHEMREY** (Rs20) sees very few visitors because of its location – tucked up the side-valley that runs from Karu, below Hemis, to the Chang La pass into Pangong. If you don't have your own vehicle, you'll have to be prepared to do some walking to get here. It takes around fifty minutes to follow the dirt track down to the river and up to the monastery after the Leh–Thak Thok bus drops you off beside the main road.

Founded in 1664 as a memorial to King Sengge Namgyal, the monastery is staffed by a dwindling community of around twenty Drugpa monks and their young novices. Its main **Du-khang**, off the courtyard on the lower level, boasts a fine silver *chorten* and a set of ancient Tibetan texts whose title pages are illuminated with opulent gold and silver calligraphy. Upstairs in the revamped **Guru-La-khang**, reached via several flights of rickety wooden steps, sits a giant brass statue of Padmasambhava (founder of the Nyingmapa school), swathed in silk brocade and encrusted with semiprecious stones. Its murals, painted in the early 1980s, are the work of an artist from Nimmu village.

Thak Thok

Clustered around a lumpy outcrop of eroded rocks, 4km up the valley from Chemrey, the small *gompa* of **THAK THOK** (pronounced *Tak-Tak* and meaning "top of the rocks") above the village of **Sakti**, is the sole representative in Ladakh of the ancient Nyingmapa order. The main shrine here is a cave in which the apostle Padmasambhava is said to have meditated during his epic eighth-century journey to Tibet. Blackened over the years by sticky butter-lamp and incense smoke, the dark and mysterious grotto is now somewhat upstaged by the monastery's more modern wings nearby. As well as some spectacular thirty-year-old wall paintings, the **Urgyan Photan Du-khang** harbours a collection of multicoloured yak-butter candle-sculptures made by the head lama.

For a glimpse of "state-of-the-art" Buddhist iconography, head to the top of Thak Thok village, where a shiny new temple houses a row of huge gleaming Buddhas, decked out in silk robes and surrounded by garish modern murals.

Apart from during the annual **festivals** of Thak Thok Tse Chu (9–11 of the sixth Tibetan month; see p.597) and Viz Thak Thok Manchog (20–29 of the ninth Tibetan month), the village of Sakti is a tranquil place, blessed with serene views south over the snowy mountains behind Hemis. **Accommodation** is available in the J&KTDC *Tourist Bungalow* (❸). There are also plenty of ideal camping spots beside the river, although as ever you should seek permission before putting up a tent on someone's field. Five **buses** a day leave Leh for Sakti, the first at 8am and the last at 4pm. A couple of minibuses also ply the route up the valley from the junction at Karu on the main highway.

Pangong Tso

Pangong Tso, 154km to the southeast of Leh, is one of the largest saltwater lakes in Asia, a long narrow strip of water stretching from Ladakh east into Tibet. Only a quarter of the 130-kilometre-long lake is in Ladakh, and the Indian army, who experienced bitter losses along its shores in the war against China in 1962, jealously guard their side of the frontier. Until the mid-1990s, it was off limits to visitors, and tourists still need a permit to come here (see the box on p.595). The lake, at an altitude of 4267m, with the dramatic glacier-clad Pangong Range to its south and the Changchenmo Range reflected in its deep blue-green waters to the north, measures 4km across at its widest point. Bitter winds blow across the brackish water making it one of the coldest places in Ladakh; visitors, who are only allowed as far as the army outpost at **Spangmik** on the shore of the lake and not encouraged to linger too long, are usually glad to see the back of it. Still, the lake provides a tantalizing view of Tibet in the distance, which, along with its proximity to Leh, is the main draw for tourists.

There is little habitation in the region and even less transport. Occasional buses go as far as Tangse, but from there four-wheel vehicles are required, which is why the easiest way to get here is on a two-day **Jeep safari** organized by one of the many tour operators based in Leh (see p.610). After going past Chemrey-visible on a conical hill on the right, the road to Pangong Tso veers right before crossing the 5475-metre **Chang La** pass, and then continues to **Tangse** where there is a small *gompa* which used to be on a vital trade route.

Tour operators provide all the necessary facilities including camping and food at Luking, 15km north of the lake, and will also arrange your permit. Jeep safari prices start in the region of Rs6000 for up to four people plus a driver and guide. To add further interest to the route, take in the monasteries of Chemrey and Thak Thok as well.

Tso Moriri

Famous for the large herds of *kiang*, or wild ass, which graze on its shores, the lake of **Tso Moriri**, 210km southeast of Leh, lies in the sparsely populated region of **Rupshu**. Like Pangong Tso, Tso Moriri has only recently become accessible to visitors, and permits are needed to travel in the region (see the box on p.595). With its great trekking potential, the region is becoming a popular destination for Jeep safaris out of Leh which head to **Karzok**, the only large village in the area, located on the shores of the lake at an altitude of 4000m.

Nestling in a wide valley flanked by some of the highest peaks in Ladakh – **Lungser Kangri** (6666m) and **Chanmser Kangri** (6622m) – the twenty-kilometre-long lake is also home to flocks of migratory *nangpa* or bar-headed geese. Occasionally, large herds of pashmina goats and the camps of nomadic herders who brave the elements throughout the year, punctuate the vast emptiness. Karzok, which has a small *gompa*, home to a group of nuns, is a friendly place, but the ill effects of tourism with its accompanying litter is beginning to show. To help protect the fragile ecosystem, a new directive stipulates that no habitation can be built within 700m of the shore of the lake. Visitors should bring their own food supplies and make sure they take all their rubbish away.

With the absence of any public transport except for the odd truck, the only really feasible way to get to Tso Moriri from Leh is on a Jeep safari (see p.610 for details of tour operators in Leh). These usually follow a circular itinerary via **Upshi** and **Chumathang** to **Mahe Bridge**, 144km from Leh, before turning towards **Pulga** and over the **Namshang La** on a rough road to Karzok. To complete the round trip, the tour continues on towards the Manali–Leh Highway (see p.587) taking in the lake of **Tso Kar** and the small village of **Thukse** on the way. Some taxis travelling from Manali to Leh take this route to avoid the **Tanglang La** (5328m) on the highway when it is snowbound.

The open spaces of Tso Moriri make for some pleasant **trekking** including the relatively easy – if you are acclimatized – three-day, forty-kilometre circuit of the lake. Another route gaining popularity is the trail from Rumtse near Upshi via Tso Kar to Tso Moriri. Some trekking operators in Manali and Leh can arrange more ambitious routes such as the ancient trade routes linking **Spiti** to Tso Moriri and Leh, but restrictions on the length of validity of permits can prove a hindrance. Treks start from around $30 per person per day in a group of four. This usually includes transport, food and tents. Accommodation is also available in a tent colony at Karzok for a whopping Rs800 per head. Jeep safaris from Leh start at around Rs7000 for a two-day trip.

North of Leh: Nubra Valley

Until 1994, the lands north of Leh were off limits to tourists, and had been unexplored by outsiders since the nineteenth century. Now, the breathtaking **Nubra Valley**, unfolding beyond the world's highest stretch of motorable road as it crosses the **Khardung La** (5578m), can be visited with a seven-day **permit** (see p.595), which gives you enough time to explore the stark terrain and trek out to one or two *gompas*.

The valley's mountain backbone looks east to the Nubra River and west to the Shyok River, which weave south to meet amid silver-grey sand dunes and boulder fields. To the north and east, the mighty Karakoram Range marks the Indian border with China and Pakistan, a fierce terrain of jagged peaks and snowy passes once crossed by caravans carrying silks, spices, gems and cloth. Now a sensitive area, these heights are a lonely outpost for soldiers who brave the cold and bouts of mountain sickness in the name of duty. In the valley it's relatively mild, though **dust storms** are common, whipping up sand and light debris in choking clouds above the broad riverbeds.

It's thought that the Nubra Valley may once have been filled by a glacier more than 1000m deep. This, and the high-altitude climate, have left rocky land that is fertile only at the mouths of ravines, where villages of cosy two-storey houses and whitewashed *chortens* are overlooked by a monastery. Before the region passed into the administrative hands of Leh, Nubra's ancient kings ruled from a palace in **Charasa**, topping an isolated hillock opposite Sumur, home to the valley's principal monastery. Further up the Nubra River, the hot springs of **Panamik**, once welcomed by footsore traders, are blissfully refreshing after ten hours on a bus. By the neighbouring Shyok River, **Diskit**, surveyed by a hillside *gompa*, lies just 7km from **Hundur**, known for its peculiar high-altitude double-humped Bactrian camels.

The route north to Nubra, a steep and rough road that forces painful groans from buses and trucks, keeps Leh in sight for four hours before crossing the Khardung La, and ploughing down more gently towards the distant Karakoram Range. Due to its strategic importance as the military road to the battlefields of the Siachen Glacier, the road to Nubra is kept open all year round but conditions can be treacherous at any time. There's free chai at the pass for jeep passengers: buses don't stop until the descent into the northern valley is well under way, and you can measure your relief at the North Pullu (alp) checkpoint and chai stall by the young Shyok River. Past the village of Khardung, the road sweeps above honey-coloured canyons before dropping down towards the river valley at Khalsar, the usual lunch stop. Tourists stopping for lunch at the grotty little town on the edge of a military base have been sometimes made to pay a tax (Rs100) for the upkeep of Khalsar, which is a disappointing and misleading introduction to the Nubra.

Buses to Nubra Valley (from Rs60) leave Leh for Panamik via Sumur at 5.30am (Mon & Wed; 10hr), and to Diskit at 6am on alternate days (Sun, Tues, Thurs, Fri; 6hr). The buses return the next day to Leh and you should book your return journey on arrival in Panamik, Sumur or Diskit. Alternatively, **Jeeps** for a maximum of five people can be rented from Leh taxi rank or any tour operator (see p.610). A complete three-day itinerary, including a visit to Diskit and Panamik costs in the region of Rs9000 for the Jeep plus driver. Once in the valley, **hitching** on military or road-builders' trucks is an option, though it's unadvisable for lone travellers. The few **taxis** at Diskit charge from around Rs1000 for a day's exploration of the valley with trips to Sumur and

Panamik adding up. Buses between Diskit and Panamik travel twice weekly (Mon & Wed).

Sumur

Soon after passing Khalsar, the road crosses the confluence of the Shyok and Nubra rivers and follows the Nubra to a patch of green sloping from the river to the base of precipitous mountains. **SUMUR**, a sleepy oasis spread over a large area, is home to the valley's most influential monastery, **Samstem Ling gompa**, a pleasant forty-minute walk behind the village. Built in 1841, the *gompa* is home to over a hundred Gelug-pa monks, aged between seven and seventy. At the heart of the monastery lies the large Du-khang which is hung with *thangkas* and dominated by a huge gilded statue of Shakyamuni, accompanied by Maitreya and the protector deity Mahakala. Across the courtyard, the long, low Gon-khang is guarded by statues of fierce protector deities strung with wide-eyed skulls and figurines of the 84 *mahasiddhas*, venerated Tantric saints. Samstem Ling is linked to the *gompa* of Rhizong in the Indus Valley west of Leh (see p.627).

To catch the morning or evening pujas at the *gompa*, you'll have to **stay** in Sumur, but with a handful of places to choose from and pleasant rambles through rustic lanes and across lush, stream-fed terraced fields, this is not a bad proposition. Near the main road-crossing, *Tsewang Jorgais* has basic doubles including two with attached baths (no phone; ②–③) and a vegetarian garden, café and camping; camping is also available at *Tashi's Khangsar* (no phone; ③). A further 500m up the side road you come to *Lhamachan* (no phone; ②) with basic rooms in the old house and two new garden rooms in a pleasant setting. If it's full, try *Largail*, a small rustic house 200m up the path. However, by far the best of Sumur's cheap guesthouses is the welcoming *Stakray* (no phone; ①–③), well worth the two-kilometre walk from the main road (follow the path and veer right at the crossroads until you come to an impressive *mani* wall in a wooded section: you are now close). Set in a wonderful vegetable garden and orchard, the new block has pleasant rooms and the incredible price includes meals and hot water; the old family house has plenty of atmosphere and is cheap. For a bit more comfort, head up the Panamik road for 1km towards the road to the *gompa*, to the *Yarab Tso* at Teggar (Leh ☎01982/53153; ⑦ including full board).

Buses leave from the prayer wheel on the main road for Leh (Tues & Thurs; 8hr), Panamik (Mon & Wed; 1–2hr), and for Diskit (Thurs & Sun; 3–4hr).

Panamik

Almost two hours' bus journey (30km) up the valley from Sumur, **PANAMIK** (aka Pinchimik), a dusty hamlet overlooked by the pin-point summit of Charouk Dongchen, marks the most northerly point in India accessible to tourists. Buses stop between the **hot springs** and the only guesthouse, the *Silk Route* (②), just over 1km short of the village proper, where cobbled alleys weave between houses, prayer wheels and thorny scrubs to riverside barley fields. Splitting into wide rivulets at this point, the sapphire Nubra seems shallow and tame, but it's not – heed local advice not to ford it as there have been several reported accidents involving travellers.

After a cleansing trip to the hot springs, where two rooms each have a deep tub filled with piping hot sulphurous water, there's little to do in Panamik other than walk. A dot on the mountainside across the river, **Ensa gompa** makes an obvious excursion. The route, three hours each way, passes through the village and crosses a bridge beyond the vast boulder field 3km upstream, then joins a wide Jeep track above the river for 3–4km. The final haul up a precipitous gorge hides the *gompa* from view until you stumble upon it, couched in an unexpected valley of willow and poplar trees fed by a perennial sweetwater stream. Though the *gompa* is usually locked, the views from rows of crumbling *chortens* nearby make the climb worthwhile. If one of the few semi-resident monks is there, however, you'll be shown inside to see the old wall paintings in the temples, and the footprint of Tsong-kha-pa, allegedly imprinted at this spot when he journeyed from Tibet to India in the fourteenth century.

All **buses** passing through Sumur originate from or terminate in Panamik.

Diskit and Hundur

After passing Khalsar, buses and trucks bound for the western villages by the Shyok turn onto a flat, grey expanse of boulders and sand dunes with the Karakoram and the Ladakh ranges towering above. A dusty collection of low-roofed houses, **DISKIT**, on first impressions, feels rather dull but soon reveals its quiet charm. The more appealing **old town**, with balconied houses and wind-blown poplars, lies below the main road before the diversion to the centre. Get off at the first bus stop on the main road near where some of the guest-houses are located. From here a road runs down through the old quarter to the bazaar and another ascends to the *gompa*.

The caramel-brown hillside above the old town supports Diskit's picturesque **gompa**, built in 1420 by Changzem Tserab Zangpo, a disciple of Tsong-kha-pa. If you don't have a jeep to follow the wide track, walk beside the long *mani* wall, which continues on the other side of the road, and trace the path that winds upwards from its end to the monastery; the steep walk takes around thirty minutes.

The *gompa*'s steps climb past the monks' quarters to the first of a group of temples (Rs20; a monk may offer his services as a guide). Local legend has it that a Mongol demon, a sworn enemy of Buddhism, was slain nearby, but his lifeless body kept returning to the *gompa*. What are reputed to be his wrinkled head and hand, grey and ageless, are now clasped by a pot-bellied protector deity in the spooky **Gon-khang**, a dark and claustrophobic temple, packed with fierce gods and goddesses.

The tiny **Lachung temple**, higher up, is the oldest here. Soot-soiled murals face a huge Tsong-kha-pa statue, topped with a Gelug-pa yellow hat. In the heart of the *gompa*, the Du-khang's remarkable mural, filling a raised cupola above the hall, depicts Tibet's Tashilhunpo *gompa*, where the Panchen Lama is receiving a long stream of visitors approaching on camels, horses and carts. Finally, the Kangyu Lang (bookroom) and Tsangyu Lang temples act as store-rooms for hundreds of Mongolian and Tibetan texts, pressed between wooden slats and wrapped in red and yellow silk. Young and boisterous novice monks add to the colour of the *gompa* which is linked to Tikse near Leh (see p.614).

The flat rooftop outside the Gon-khang affords views across to Sumur to the east, the dunes and boulders of the flat southern valley, and to Kobet peak in the north. **HUNDUR**, a tiny village in a wooded valley, 7km north, is as far as one is allowed to go along this part of the Nubra Valley, at the end of a pleasant walk from Diskit. The village is most notable for its indigenous lanky Bactrian camels which you may encounter en route. The main monastery at Hundur, usually locked, lies just below the main road, near the bridge and the end of the route. The remains of another monastery are scattered along the crags a short walk above the road.

Practicalities

Buses return to Leh from Diskit (Tues, Thurs, Fri & Sun; 6hr). Make sure you buy a ticket from the bus driver when he arrives from Leh the previous day, otherwise you're unlikely to be let on. Buses stop on the main road by the prayer wheel where the road descends through the old quarter to the bazaar, and once again on the new road to the bazaar. There's a bus to Sumur and Panamik on Thursday and Sunday. If you're not alone, **hitching** is a good alternative. You can usually get a lift with one of the slow military vehicles running up and down the valley. Abdul Razzaq, an ex-teacher, organizes **camel rides** around Hundur starting around Rs400: ask at the *Snow Leopard*.

Accommodation

Accommodation in Diskit is simple, but ample. By the top bus stop close to the prayer wheel on the main road, *Olthang Guest House* (☎01980/20025; ❷–❹) has very comfortable rooms, decent washing facilities (hot water on request) including one room with an attached bath, and home-grown vegetables from the picturesque garden for dinner in the café, which doubles as a bar in the evenings. Follow the road down from the prayer wheel and along the *mani* wall on your right through a *chorten* gate in the wall to cosy *Sun Rise* (no phone; ❷) which has cheap beds, shared bathrooms and a pleasant garden. The *Karakoram* (☎01980/20024; ❷), a bit further on, is simpler but has plenty of atmosphere and a pleasant garden good for camping. Continue down the road past the basic *Khangsar Guesthouse* (no phone; ❶) near the SSB's office, to a lane behind a set of *chortens* and the very pleasant *Thechung* (☎01980/20002; ❸); it has beautiful sunny glass rooms and clean bathrooms down steps outside. Near the village centre, the comfortable *Sand Dune Guest House* (☎01980/20022; ❷–❸), run by two congenial sisters, has long been popular, boasting rooms with attached baths, a dorm (Rs50) and a garden café. All the guesthouses will provide food.

Accommodation in **Hundur** is improving, but the *Tourist Lodge* (❷) is isolated on the Diskit edge of the village and without electricity. Welcoming *Snow Leopard* (❷–❸) is by far the best option, set in a beautiful vegetable garden, with great views and some rooms with attached bathrooms. However, it is difficult to find: from below the temple on the main road turn right and follow a wide path parallel to the main road past a newly built guesthouse. Another option, the *Moonland Guest House* (❶), also known as *Nerchungpa*, 1km down from the main road veering right at the first T-junction below the *gompa* temple, is somewhat neglected.

West of Leh

Of the many *gompas* accessible by road **west of Leh**, only **Spitok**, piled on a hilltop at the end of the airport runway, and **Phyang**, which presides over one of Ladakh's most picturesque villages, can be comfortably visited on day-trips from the capital. The rest, including **Likkir** and **Rhizong** and the unmissable temple complex at **Alchi**, with its wonderfully preserved eleventh-century murals, are usually seen en route to or from **Kargil**. The 231-kilometre jour-

The Kargil war

After three years of cross-border artillery exchanges across the "Ceasefire Line", in the spring of 1999 conflict between India and Pakistan escalated into the full-blown **Kargil War**. The war was to shatter any semblance of Indo-Pakistani dialogue which seemed to be gradually improving after years of impasse, and resulted in the dramatic overthrow of the Pakistani prime minister Nawaz Sharif, and the re-establishment of military rule by General Musharraf. Pakistani intentions were to cut the Srinagar–Leh Highway and capture the Muslim-dominated areas of western Ladakh, putting further pressure on Indian Kashmir.

In early May, the Indian army realized that infiltrators across the disputed 150-kilometre Line of Control, who had followed the high ridges snaking into Indian territory, were not disparate bands of separatists but Pakistani regulars. The ensuing conflict to dislodge the Pakistanis involved intense artillery battles and raids by an initially dispirited Indian army up from the valley floors to near inaccessible positions, many on peaks in excess of 5000m. Some of the heaviest fighting, involving regiments from all over India including the newly formed Ladakh Scouts, took place in the Drass sector, where Pakistani positions came as close as 3km to the strategic highway. The battles for the peaks of Tololing and Tiger Hill above Drass proved crucial in turning the tide of a war which was the first between the neighbours to be fully televised. After nearly three months of bitter fighting the war came to a close towards the end of July 1999, with Pakistan having to retreat from the heights, by which time over a thousand Indian and Pakistani soldiers had lost their lives.

ney, taking in a couple of high passes and some mind-blowing scenery, can be completed in a single twelve-hour haul. To do this stretch of road justice, however, spend at least a week making short forays up the side-valleys of the Indus, where idyllic settlements and *gompas* nestle amid barley fields and mountains.

One of the great landmarks punctuating the former caravan route is the photogenic monastery of **Lamayuru**. Reached via a nail-biting sequence of hairpin bends as the highway climbs out of the Indus Valley to begin its windy ascent of **Fatu La**, it lies within walking distance of some extraordinary lunar-like rock formations, at the start of the main trekking route south to Padum in Zanskar. Further west still, beyond the dramatic **Namika La** pass, **Mulbekh** is the last Buddhist village on the highway. From here on, *gompas* and *gonchas* give way to onion-domed mosques and flowing *salwar kamises*.

At the time of writing the main Leh highway was open, but check out the current situation before travelling. Otherwise, **transport** along the main highway is straightforward in summer, when ramshackle state and private buses ply between Leh and Kargil. Getting to more remote spots, however, can be hard. Many travellers resort to paying for a ride on one of the countless Tata trucks that lumber past in long convoys, which may save time, but is a far more dangerous way to travel this hair-raising road. Getting a group together to rent a **Jeep** from Leh (p.611) is expensive, but saves time.

Spitok

SPITOK gompa, rising incongruously from the end of the airport runway, makes a good half-day foray from Leh, 10km up the north side of the Indus Valley. If you can't afford the taxi fare, the easiest way to get there is to stroll down to the crossroads above the GPO and J&KTDC's tourist reception centre, and then flag down any of the **buses** heading west along the main Srinagar highway. Travellers who walk the whole way invariably regret it, as the route is relentlessly dull, passing through a string of unsightly military installations hemmed in by barbed-wire fences.

By contrast, the fifteenth-century **monastery**, which tumbles down the sides of a steep knoll to a tight cluster of farmhouses and well-watered fields, is altogether more picturesque. Approached by road from the north, or from the south along a footpath that winds through Spitok village, its spacious rooftops command superb views.

The main complex, a typical mixture of dusty, dimly lit old prayer halls and vivid modern shrine rooms, is of less interest than the **Paldan Lumo** chapel, perched on a ridge above. Probably aimed at the mostly Hindu members of the Indian army posted at Leh, a sign outside warns visitors not to "deliberately mistake" the Gon-khang for a Kali temple. Offerings made to the black-faced and bloodthirsty Hindu goddess of death and destruction are, it insists, "not acceptable". The shrine to Vajra Bhairava, a Tantric guardian deity of the Gelug-pa order, is distinctly spooky. Lit by flickering butter lamps, the cluttered and cobwebbed chamber houses a row of veiled guardian deities whose ferocious faces are only unveiled once a year. After waving incense smoke before them and muttering a few mantras, the key-keeper lama will pass around handfuls of sweets newly infused with protective power. If you have a flashlight, check out the 600-year-old paintings on the rear wall of the chapel, which is Spitok's oldest building.

Phyang

A mere 24km west of Leh, **PHYANG gompa** looms large at the head of a secluded side-valley that tapers north into the rugged Ladakh Range from the Srinagar highway. Of the three daily **buses** that run here from the capital, the 8am departure (1hr 15min) is the most convenient as it allows you plenty of time to explore the monastery and the pretty nearby village. Buses return to Leh at 10am and 5.30pm; between these times, you can walk across the fields to the Kargil-bound road (30min), and hitch a lift on a truck.

The *gompa* itself, a tall buttress-walled building, houses a fifty-strong community of Brigungpa lamas, members of the larger Kagyu sect, but few antique murals of note, most having recently been painted over with brighter colours. Its only treasures are a small collection of fourteenth-century Kashmiri bronzes (locked behind glass in the modern Guru-Padmasambhava temple), and the light and airy **Du-khang**'s three silver *chortens*, one of which is decorated with a seven-eyed coffee-coloured **dzi stone**. The gem, considered to be highly auspicious, was brought to Phyang from Tibet by the monastery's former head lama, whose ashes the *chorten* encases.

Tucked away around the side, the shrine in the *gompa*'s gloomily atmospheric **Gon-khang**, lit by a single beam of dusty sunlight, houses a ferocious veiled protector deity and an amazing collection of weapons and armour plundered during the Mongol invasions of the fourteenth century. Also dangling from the cobweb-covered rafters are various bits of dead animals, including most of a vulture, an ibex skull, and several sets of yak horns, believed to be nine-hundred-year-old relics of the Bon cult (see p.595).

Phyang's annual **festival**, Phyang Tsedup, formerly held during the winter but recently switched to summer (falls between mid-July and early Aug) in order to coincide with the tourist season, is the second largest in Ladakh (after Hemis). Celebrated with the usual masked *chaam* dances, the event is marked with a ritual exposition of a giant ten-metre brocaded silk *thangka*.

Like Tikse, Phyang's recent reputation has been somewhat sullied by one of the two abbots of Phyang who has taken to politics and is now part of the

National Conference, Kashmir's Muslim-dominated ruling party. Buddhists who are suspicious of the NC's divisive intentions feel the abbot, who is now also a wealthy landlord, is being manipulated for the control of Ladakh.

Likkir

Five kilometres to the north of the main Leh–Srinagar highway, shortly before the village of Saspol, the large and wealthy *gompa* of **LIKKIR**, home to around one hundred monks, is renowned for its huge yellow statue of the Buddha-to-come which towers serenely above the terraced fields. A pleasant break from the bustle of Leh, the village of Likkir now offers a small but adequate choice of accommodation which, along with the sheer tranquillity of the surroundings, can tempt travellers to linger a few days.

Overlooking a lively and clear mountain stream, the *gompa*, 3km up the valley from the village, is also known as Lu-khyil ("water spirits circled"), a reference to *naga* spirits who are said to have once lived here. Founded in 1065 by Lama Duwang Chosje, who was given the land by Lachen Gyalpo, the fifth king of Ladakh, the *gompa* originally belonged to the Khadampa sect. In 1470 it was converted by Lawang Lotos, a monk from central Tibet, into the Gelug-pa monastery that is still here today. Extensively renovated in the eighteenth century, the *gompa* shows little sign of the antiquity related to the site. The impressive Du-khang is devoted to the three Buddhas – Marme Zat (past), Shakyamuni (present) and Maitreya (future), while the Gon-khang, decorated with lavish murals of the fiercesome deities Yamantaka and Mahakala, contains the statue of the wrathful protector, Tse-Ta-Pa.

Likkir is the starting point for the excellent and popular two-day hike to Temisgang via Rhizong, which provides a comparatively gentle introduction to trekking in Ladakh. For those with less time, several shorter walks exploring the ridges and valleys around Likkir will prove just as rewarding.

If you have missed the direct bus from Leh which leaves at 4pm, you can get dropped off on the main Leh–Kargil highway and walk the short but treeless one-kilometre road to the village; the direct bus returns for Leh at 7am next morning. The village, 3km south of the *gompa*, consisting of terraced fields scattered along the waterways that feed the oasis, now has a choice of guesthouses and camping facilities. *Gaph-Chow* (☎01982/52748; ❷–❹) in the lower village is pleasant and well organized with simple but comfortable rooms, some with attached baths, and you'll find camping facilities in the lovely vegetable garden; there is an attractive meditation room and, along with the garden café, a traditional Ladakhi kitchen as well. Of Likkir's other guesthouses, the *Norboo Spon* (❷; follow signs and your nose at the top of the village), a world away, is a traditional family home with a genuine welcome, a wonderful terrace and a choice of clean, basic accommodation including two popular glass rooms; the Ladakhi kitchen is a must.

Alchi

Driving past on the nearby Srinagar–Leh highway, you'd never guess that the cluster of low pagoda-roofed cubes 3km across the Indus from **Saspol**, dwarfed by a spectacular sweep of pale-brown and wine-coloured scree, is one of the most significant historical sites in Asia. Yet the *Chos-khor*, or "religious enclave", at **ALCHI**, 70km west of Leh, harbours an extraordinary wealth of ancient wall paintings and wood sculpture, miraculously preserved for over nine centuries inside five tiny mud-walled temples. Art historians rave about the site because its earliest murals are the finest surviving examples of a style that flourished in Kashmir during the "Second Spreading". Barely a handful of the monasteries founded during this era escaped the Muslim depredations of the fourteenth century. Alchi is the most impressive of them all, the least remote and the only one you don't need a special permit to visit. Nestled beside a bend in the milky-blue River Indus, amid some dramatic scenery, it's also a serene spot and the perfect place to break a long journey to or from the Ladakhi capital.

The *Chos-khor* consists of five separate temples, various residential buildings and a scattering of large *chortens*, surrounded by a mud-and-stone wall and a curtain of tall poplar trees. If you are pushed for time, concentrate on the two oldest buildings, the **Du-khang** and the **Sumtsek**, both in the middle of the enclosure. Entrance **tickets** (Rs15) are issued by a caretaker lama from nearby Likkir *gompa*, who will unlock the doors for you; he may even give you the key and let you look round by yourself. To make the most of the paintings' vibrant colours, you'll need a strong flashlight; but don't use a camera flash as it will damage the murals, last restored in the sixteenth century.

The Du-khang

An inscription records that Alchi's oldest structure, the **Du-khang**, was erected late in the eleventh century by Kaldan Shesrab, a graduate of the now-ruined Nyarma *gompa* near Tikse, itself founded by the "Great Translator" Rinchen Zangpo (see p.595). Approached via a walled courtyard and a path that runs under a hollow *chorten*, the square temple's wooden doorway is richly carved with meditating *bodhisattvas*. Once your eyes adjust to the gloom inside, check out the niche in the rear wall where Vairocana, the "Buddha Resplendent", is flanked by the four main Buddha manifestations that appear all over Alchi's temple walls, always presented in their associated colours: Akshobya ("Unshakeable"; blue), Ratnasambhava ("Jewel Born"; yellow), Amitabha ("Boundless Radiance"; red) and Amoghasiddhi ("Unfailing Success"; green). The other walls are decorated with six elaborate mandalas, interspersed with intricate friezes.

The Sumtsek

Standing to the left of the Du-khang, the **Sumtsek** is Alchi's most celebrated temple, and the highest achievement of early-medieval Indian-Buddhist art. Its woodcarvings and paintings, dominated by rich reds and blues, are almost as fresh and vibrant today as they were 900 years ago, when the squat triple-storey structure was built.

The resident lama leads visitors under a delicate wooden facade to the interior of the shrine, shrouded in a womb-like darkness broken only by flickering butter lamps. Scan the walls with a flashlight and you'll see why scholars have filled volumes on this chamber alone. Surrounded by a swirling mass of mandalas, Buddhas, demigods and sundry other celestials, a colossal statue of **Maitreya**, the Buddha-to-come, fills a niche on the ground floor, his head shielded from sight high in the second storey. Accompanying him are two equally grand **bodhisattvas**, their heads peering serenely down through gaps in the ceiling. Each of these stucco statues wears a figure-clinging *dhoti*, adorned with different, meticulously detailed motifs. Avalokitesvara, the *bodhisattva* of compassion (to the left), has pilgrimage sites, court vignettes, palaces and pre-Muslim style *stupas* on his robe, while that of Maitreya is decorated with episodes from the life of Gautama Buddha. The robe of Manjushri, destroyer of falsehood, to the right, shows the 84 masters of Tantra, the mahasiddhas, adopting complex yogic poses in a maze of bold square patterns.

Among exquisite **murals**, some repaired in the sixteenth century, is the famous six-armed green goddess Prajnaparamita, the "Perfection of Wisdom" central to Mahayana thought, and closely associated with Tara. Heavily bejewelled, she sits on a lotus by Avalokitesvara's gigantic left leg. Amazingly, this, and the multitude of other images that plaster the interior of the Sumtsek, resolve, when viewed from the centre of the shrine, into a harmonious whole.

Other temples

The *Chos-khor's* three **other temples** all date from the twelfth and thirteenth centuries, but are nowhere near as impressive as their predecessors. Tucked away at the far, river end of the enclosure, the **Manjushri La-khang** is noteworthy only for its relatively recent "Thousand Buddha" paintings and gilded four-faced icon of Manjushri that fills almost the whole temple. Next door the **Lotsawa La-khang**, with its central image and mural of Shakyamuni, is one of a handful of temples dedicated to Rinchen Zangpo, the "Great Translator", whose missionary work inspired the foundation of Alchi; his small droopy-eared image sits on the right of Shakyamuni. The lama may need to be cajoled into unlocking the **La-khang Soma**, the small square shrine south of the Sumtsek, which is decorated with three large mandalas and various figures including an accomplished *yab-yum*: the Tantric image of the copulating deities symbolizes the union of opposites on a material and spiritual level.

Practicalities

One **bus** per day leaves Leh for Alchi in summer (around 3.30pm), taking three hours to cover the 70km and returning at 7am next day. Other buses heading in that direction leave Leh at 5.30am (for Kargil) and 9am (for Dah-Hanoo) – you can catch one of these, get off at the turn-off past **Saspol**, and walk the remaining 4km via the motorable suspension bridge west of the village. Though there are obvious shortcuts, you may find a ride.

Of the growing selection of **guesthouses** in Alchi, the *Lotsava* (②), left of the main road as you approach the *Chos-khor*, is pleasant and simple with earth floors; the landlady serves filling breakfasts and evening meals in the small garden if you give her enough warning. Around the car park, the *Potala* (②), just above the tea stall, has simple rooms sharing common baths while the *Zimskhang Hotel* (③), near the top of the path to the temples, is a decent place to eat with a pretty garden, but the rooms are grungy and overpriced especially during the high season; their annexe, the *Royal Choskor* (③) across the path is roomier with hot water by the bucket. By far the most attractive option is the purpose-built *Sam Dubling* (③–④), a new guesthouse 100m above the taxi stand approached by following the stream behind the Potala. The *Alchi Resort* (☎01982/52520; ⑥) near the taxi stand consists of luxurious huts aimed at tour groups while the popular and friendly *Choskor* (②–③), 800m before the taxi stand on the left, is a traditional house with simple rooms and a pleasant garden with camping.

Rhizong

Blocking the head of a rocky ravine, the towering monastery of **RHIZONG** remains hidden off the main highway 72km west of Leh. A wealthy monastery, presided over by Shas Rinpoche and linked to Sumur in the Nubra, the atmospheric Rhizong is a relatively new *gompa* dating from the seventeenth century. Getting there is half the challenge as there is no public transport along the five-kilometre road leading up from the highway between Khalsi and Saspol.

The road follows a stream past a small nunnery – **Thardot Choling** – to a car park from where you walk up the ravine which can become incredibly hot in the middle of the day.

Inside the Du-khang, draped with *thangkas* and exquisite but smoky murals, stands the central image of Shakyamuni flanked by Amitaus, the Buddha of long life, and by Avalokiteshvara, otherwise known as Chenrazig – the Buddha of compassion. The struggle up to the *gompa* is further rewarded by the hospitality of the monks who are likely to offer you tea, and, if you are lucky, will invite you to one of their informal prayer meetings. With shafts of light filtering through darkened rooms and the throb of chanted prayers, a visit to Rhizong takes you to the heart of Buddhist Ladakh.

If you don't have your own **transport**, coming from Leh you will need to get off any Khalsi-bound bus at the appropriate junction and walk the rest of the way. Very basic accommodation is available at the *gompa* and women can look for a place to stay at the nunnery below. But, strictly speaking, Rhizong remains a day-trip. A new road which is being blasted up to the monastery from the car park to cope with the increasing number of visitors will cut out the climb through the ravine, but then that's half the challenge.

Lamayuru

If one sight could be said to sum up Ladakh, it would have to be **LAMAYURU gompa**, 130km west of Leh. Hemmed in by a moonscape of scree-covered mountains, the whitewashed medieval monastery towers above a scruffy cluster of tumbledown mud-brick houses from the top of a near-vertical, weirdly eroded cliff. A major landmark on the old silk route, the *gompa* numbers among the 108 (a spiritually significant number, probably legendary) founded by the Rinchen Zangpo in the tenth and eleventh centuries. However, its craggy seat, believed to have sheltered Milarepa during his religious odyssey across the Himalayas, was probably sacred long before the advent of Buddhism, when local people followed the shamanical Bon cult (see p.595). Just twenty lamas of the Brigungpa branch of the Kagyu school are left now, as opposed to the four hundred that lived here a century or so ago. Nor does Lamayuru harbour much in the way of art treasures. The main reason visitors make the short detour from the nearby Srinagar–Leh road is to photograph the *gompa* from the valley floor, or to pick up the trail to the Prikiti La pass – gateway to Zanskar – which begins here.

The footpath from the highway brings you out near the main entrance to the monastery, where you should be able to find the lama responsible for issuing entrance tickets (Rs20), and unlocking the door to the **Du-khang**. Lamayuru's newly renovated prayer hall houses little of note other than a **cave** where Naropa, Milarepa's teacher, is said to have meditated, and a rancid collection of yak-butter sculptures. If you're lucky, you'll be shown through the tangle of narrow lanes below the *gompa* to a tiny **chapel**, whose badly damaged murals of mandalas and the Tathagata Buddhas are contemporary with those at Alchi (see p.625).

Practicalities

Lamayuru lies too far from either Leh or Kargil, 107km west, to be visited in a day-trip, so you either have to call in en route between the two, or spend the night here; unfortunately the present choice of accommodation isn't great. **Buses** stop opposite the *Dehung Labrang Restaurant*, which serves simple, uninspiring meals: avoid the grubby rooms (❶). The *Monastery Hotel* (❷) currently

has two basic rooms and a dorm (Rs50) with bathrooms outside. It's a great spot overlooking the monastery; the monastery courtyard around the corner is being developed into a large mid-range hotel. Other accommodation includes the *Shangrila* (**❷**) on the motor road to the lower village, with basic grubby rooms and outside toilets, though some improvements are being made, and a great terrace. By far the best option is the welcoming family-run *Dragon Guest House* (**❶–❹**) with a range including one coveted glass room, and a pleasant garden restaurant which is the best place to eat in Lamayuru. The *Moonland* garden restaurant next door looks attractive but is dull in comparison. The regular bus service to Leh departs at 10am and the one to Kargil at noon.

Mulbekh

West of Lamayuru, the main road crawls to the top of **Fatu La** (4091m), the highest pass between Leh and Srinagar, then ascends **Namika** ("Sky-Pillar") **La**, so called because of the jagged pinnacle of rock that looms above it to the south. Once across the windswept ridge, it drops through an Arizona-esque landscape of disintegrating desert cliffs and pebbly ravines to the wayside village of **MULBEKH**. The last sizeable Buddhist settlement along the road, before the Muslim Purki settlements around Kargil, is scattered around the banks of the River Wakha, whose glacial waters flow through a lush carpet of barley fields peppered with poplars and orchards of walnut and apricot trees.

Formerly an outpost of the Zangla kingdom of western Ladakh (the deposed monarchs, King Nyima Norbu Namgyal Dey and his queen, Tashi Deskit Angmo, still live in a dilapidated four-storey mansion on the western outskirts of the village), Mulbekh would be a sleepy hamlet were it not for the endless convoys of trucks and tourist buses that thunder through while the passes are open. Those visitors who stop at all tend only to stay long enough to grab a chai at a roadside *dhaba*, and to have a quick look at the seven-metre-high **Maitreya** ("Chamba" in Tibetan) **statue** carved from the face of a gigantic boulder nearby. The precise origins of the shapely four-armed Buddha-to-be are not known, but an ancient inscription on its side records that it was carved between the seventh and eighth centuries, well before Buddhism was fully established in Tibet. The best place from which to view the bas-relief is the flat roof of the small *gompa* that partially obscures it. The single-chambered *gompa* dedicated to the 1000-armed Chenrazig (Avalokiteshvara), is decorated with particularly beautiful murals. No entrance fee is charged, but the lamas appreciate a donation.

Another incentive to prolong your stay in Mulbekh is the two village **gompas**, perched atop a smooth 200-metre rock 1km west of the Chamba statue. A steep flight of steps winds up to the whitewashed temples, one of which is occupied by a small community of young nuns. Neither houses any great treasures, but the views down the Warkha Valley from their terraces make the climb (a very stiff one if you're not yet acclimatized to the altitude) well worthwhile.

Accommodation in Mulbekh is limited to shabby rooms above the tea shops such as the *Paradise* (**❶**) and the *Tsomo Riri* (**❶**) on the main road opposite the Chamba statue, where you can get *thukpa*, dhal, rice, *momos* and butter tea; in the evenings they turn into cheap drinking dens. The *Tourist Bungalow* (**❸**), 500m down the road towards Leh, is a far better bet with attached baths, but is poorly maintained. Around 4km to the east of Mulbekh on the road to Leh, lies the small and relatively new nunnery of **Jangchup Choeling**, governed by Rhizong (see p.627), which has a school and pleasant garden courtyard, and where rooms are available for women visitors.

Kargil

Even though it is surrounded by utterly awe-inspiring scenery, few travellers find anything positive to say about **KARGIL**, capital of the area dubbed **"Little Baltistan"**, which rises in a clutter of corrugated iron rooftops from the confluence of the Suru and Drass rivers. Close to the Ceasefire Line and Pakistani positions, Kargil served as the logistics centre for 1999's Kargil War (see p.623), targeted by Pakistani artillery. The Pakistanis caused the Indian army great embarrassment by destroying the underground ammunition dump at Kargil in the early stages of the conflict. Aside from the odd building destroyed, much of the town escaped unscathed as the army bases lie on the outskirts of town: on the surface, Kargil has changed little. If you're overnight-ing on the way between Leh and Srinagar, virtually all you'll see of the town between the time the bus pulls in (around 7pm) and leaves (5am the next morning) is the grim bus stand and, as likely as not, the inside of an equally grotty hotel. If, on the other hand, you're bound for Padum in Zanskar, an eighteen-hour journey south down the Suru Valley, two or three days waiting for a bus is par for the course.

Unusually for Ladakh, the majority of Kargil's 5500 inhabitants, known as Purki, are strict **Muslims**. Unlike their Sunni cousins in Kashmir, however, the locals here are orthodox **Shias**, which not only explains the ubiquitous Iranian Ayatollah photographs, but also the conspicuous absence of women from the bazaar. Descendants of settlers and Muslim merchants from Kashmir and Yarkhand, Purkis speak a dialect called **Purig** – a mixture of Ladakhi and Balti. Indeed, had it not been for the daring reconquest of the region by India dur-ing the 1948 Indo–Pak war (the Indian army forced their Pakistani adversaries out of town after transporting an entire tank division over the Zoji La pass), Kargil would today be part of Baltistan, the region across the Ceasefire Line which it closely resembles. Prevailing Islamic laws make it advisable to dress conservatively, and women in particular should keep their arms and legs cov-ered.

Once you've found somewhere to stay, there's little to do in Kargil other than take a stroll along the main street. Formerly a major market on the old Samarkand–Srinagar caravan route, the busy **bazaar** is nowadays a run-of-the-mill string of provision stores, ironmongers, hole-in-the-wall cafés and fly-blown butchers. Among the bearded and woolly-hatted passers-by you'll also come across the odd white turban of an **Agha**. Kargil's puritanical spiritual leaders, who have banned polo and dancing in the town, still travel to Iran to receive religious training, which they follow up with bouts of study at the famously austere **Imambaras** – Shi'ite theological colleges – at the east end of the main thoroughfare.

Practicalities

Buses arriving in Kargil from Leh, Srinagar and Padum either pull in to the main bus stand, immediately below the top (west) end of the bazaar, or at the truck park above the river, two minutes' walk downhill from the main street. If you plan to head off early in the morning, check when you buy your ticket where the bus leaves from. There are only a couple of buses every day for Mulbekh but you may be able to catch a Matador – a shared minibus. The buses to Padum in Zanskar are subject to delays but run on alternate days and include A-class (Rs200) and B-class services (Rs120). A taxi is far more comfortable and rewarding but the one-way fare to Padum is Rs7000 (Rs1200).

J&KTDC's **tourist reception centre** (Mon–Sat 10am–4pm, July & Aug till 7pm; ☎ 01985/2228) is on the east side of town, around the corner from the **taxi stand** and most of the hotels. As well as the usual leaflets on Ladakh and Kashmir, they rent out Norwegian **trekking equipment**, including four-season sleeping bags, tents, coats, and boots. If you need to **change money** (or travellers' cheques), the State Bank of India (Mon–Fri 10am–2pm, Sat 10am–noon) is in the middle of the main street. Its rates are poor, but better than at the *Siachen Hotel*, which is the only place to cash currency outside bank hours.

Accommodation

If you've heard anything about Kargil, it is probably that its **hotels** are dreadful – which may be unfair on the few upmarket places, and the J&KTDC *Tourist Bungalows*, but is certainly true of the rock-bottom "guesthouses" around the bazaar. The Kashmir crisis, which reduced tourist traffic to a trickle, has aggravated the problem by squeezing half the hotels out of business. Those that remain are either geared towards tour groups, or else are total dives. What's more, room tariffs soar in July and August, when a flea-infested windowless hovel without running water can cost as much as Rs250. The rates quoted below apply to peak season; discounts are usually available at other times; most of the more salubrious hotels offer meals, with substantial discounts if you don't take the option.

Crown, near the bus stand. Rambling old budget hotel that has seen better days. Some rooms come with attached bathrooms and there is even a cheap dorm. **②**

D'Zojila, Lankore ☎ 01985/2227. Kargil's top hotel, 2km east of town, offers upmarket accommodation for wealthy trekkers; it's expensive, but the rates quoted include all meals. Phone on arrival for a courtesy bus. **⑤ –⑧**

Greenland, at the end of the lane leading off the east side of the taxi stand ☎ 01985/2324. A notch above rock-bottom, with a restaurant and reasonable rooms (some attached bathrooms); rooms on the first floor are roomier with running hot water. **② –④**

J&KTDC Tourist Bungalow no.1, a 5min walk uphill from the crossroads above the bus stand ☎ 01985/2328. Clean rooms, clean sheets and

peaceful atmosphere, with a small dining room. By far the best budget deal in town. If the *chowkidar* says it's full, get a "chit" from the tourist office. **② –③**

J&KTDC Tourist Bungalow no.2, behind the truck park above the river ☎ 01985/2266. Not a patch on its namesake across town, but still good value and convenient for early departures. **②**

Kargil Continental, Main Bazaar, past the tourist office ☎ 01985/2304. Open all year, with large comfortable rooms and a pleasant garden; it's a bit soulless and expensive, though meals are included in the price. **⑤ –⑧**

Siachen, below the west side of the taxi stand ☎ 01985/33055. Large, comfortable, and one of the best of the downtown hotels, with immaculate en-suite rooms, a restaurant, STD phones and a foreign exchange bureau. **④ –⑥**

Eating

Besides upmarket hotels like the *Siachen*, finding somewhere to **eat** in Kargil is a toss-up between the small tourist-oriented cafés on the lane from the truck park to the bazaar, or a *dhaba* on the main street. Choice is even more limited for **breakfast**; all the restaurants are closed, but hot chapatis and omelettes are served from 7am onwards at the chai stall just up from the *Naktul* (take your own plate). A couple of chai-wallahs also hang around the bus stand at the crack of dawn.

Karan Singh Punjabi Janata, east end of Main Street. One of the town's better *dhabas*: spicy Indian sauces spooned onto groaning platefuls of rice.

Kargil Darbar, *Marina Hotel*, near the Polo Ground. A versatile hotel restaurant with a reasonable menu including Chinese food.

Naktul, between the truck park and the bazaar. Fierce "Ayatollah" decor, but the food – basic Chinese and some bland Western alternatives – is OK. Generous portions and cheap, too. Try the delicious (bottled) apple juice.

Nishat, main bazaar opposite Shashila. A Kashmiri restaurant with a mixed menu including Chinese.

Ruby, main bazaar. A popular restaurant serving local specialities including *yakhani* (meat cooked in yoghurt) and *gustaba* (meat balls).

Shashila, main bazaar. *Naktul*'s main rival, with a flashy exterior; they serve Kashmiri and Chinese dishes as well as *momo thukpa*.

The Suru Valley

A spellbinding divide between two of the world's most formidable mountain ranges, the **Suru Valley** winds south from Kargil to the desolate Pensi La – the main entry point for Zanskar. Since a fair-weather road was bulldozed all the way to Padum, you can travel to the heart of this remote region by bus (albeit a clapped-out J&K state one), in a single haul of around fourteen hours. The first leg, usually undertaken in the pre-dawn darkness, leads through the broad lower reaches of the Suru Valley, whose fertile floor is strewn with Muslim villages, clustered around gleaming metal mosque domes. By the time the first rays of daylight appear, the surrounding mountains have grown vast, bare and brown, only cultivated along the narrow strip lining the river. Gradually, the pristine white ice-fields and rocky pinnacles of **Nun-Kun** (7077m) nose over the horizon. Apart from a brief disappearance behind the steep sides of the valley at **Panikhar**, this awesome massif dominates the landscape all the way to Zanskar.

Shortly after Panikhar, the Suru veers east around the base of Nun-Kun, passing within a stone's throw of the magnificent **Gangri Glacier**. Having wound across a seemingly endless boulder field, closed in on both sides by sheer mountain walls, the road emerges at a marshy open plain surrounded by snow peaks and swathes of near-vertical strata. **Juldo**, a tiny settlement whose fodder-stacked rooftops are strung with fluttering prayer flags, marks the beginning of Buddhist **Suru**.

The climb to the pass from **Rangdum gompa**, across the flat river basin from Juldo, is absolutely breathtaking. One glistening 6000-metre peak after another appears atop a series of side-valleys, many lined with gigantic folds of rock and ice. The real high point occurs shortly beyond **Pensi La** (4401m), as the road, swinging around dizzying switchbacks, overlooks the colossal S-shaped **Darung Drung Glacier**, whose milky-green meltwaters drain southeast into the Stod Valley, visible below.

Panikhar

Although by no means the largest settlement in the Suru Valley, **PANIKHAR**, three hours' bus ride south of Kargil, is a good place to break the long journey to Padum. Before the Kashmir troubles, it was a minor trekking centre, at the start of the Lonvilad Gali–Pahalgum trail. These days, the scruffy collection of roadside stalls and poor mud-brick farmhouses sees very few tourists, even in high season.

The main reason to stop is to hike to nearby **Parkachik La**, for panoramic views of the glacier-gouged north face of the mighty **Nun-Kun massif**. The **trail** up to the pass, known locally as Largo ("Nothing") La, begins on the far side of the Suru, crossed via a suspension bridge thirty minutes south of the village. It may look straightforward from Panikhar, but the four-hour round-trip climb to the ridge gets very tough indeed towards the top, especially for

The ancient footpaths that crisscross **Ladakh** and **Zanskar** provide some of the most inspiring **trekking** in the Himalayas. Threading together remote Buddhist villages and monasteries, cut off in winter behind high passes whose rocky tops bristle with windswept thickets of prayer flags, nearly all are long, hard and high – but rarely dull. The **best time** to trek is from June to September. New areas where restrictions have recently been lifted such as the Nubra Valley and Rupshu (Tso Moriri) are gradually being developed, and Leh- and Manali-based trekking agents are busy exploring new itineraries.

Whether you make all the necessary preparations yourself, or pay an agency to do it for you, **Leh** is the best place to plan a trek. **Equipment,** including high-quality tents, sleeping bags, Karrimats, boots and duck-down jackets, can be rented through one of several agencies along Fort Road (see p.609) including J&KTDC's tourist information centre. Alternatively, buy your own Indian-made kit in the bazaar and resell it again afterwards. To find **ponies** and **guides**, essential for all the routes outlined below, head for the Tibetan refugee camp at **Choglamsar**, 3km south of Leh.

Several agents in Leh advertise five-day climbing expeditions to **Stok Kangri** (6120m) via the village of Stok with a comparatively nontechnical final climb for around $35 per head per day for a group of four. However, though popular, you should be aware that these expeditions are unofficial and, strictly speaking, you should first apply for a permit to the Indian Mountaineering Foundation in Delhi, but today no one bothers.

Trekking is undoubtedly the most rewarding way to explore the region, but it can also be highly disruptive. Minimize your impact in culturally and ecologically sensitive areas by respecting the following "golden rules", set out in LEDeG's *Guidelines For Visitors To Ladakh*. Be as **self-reliant** as possible, especially with food and fuel. Buying provisions along the way puts an unnecessary burden on the villages' subsistence-oriented economies, and encourages strings of unsightly "tea shops" (invariably run by outsiders) to sprout along the trails. Always burn kerosene, never wood – a scarce and valuable resource. Refuse should be packed up, not disposed of along the route, no matter how far from the nearest town you are, and plastics retained for recycling at the Ecology Centre in Leh. Always bury your faeces and, if you can't convert to water, burn your toilet paper afterwards. Finally, do not defecate in the dry-stone huts along the trails; local shepherds use them for shelter during snow storms.

Spitok to Hemis via the Markha Valley

The beautiful **Markha Valley** runs parallel with the Indus on the far southern side of the snowy Stok–Kangri massif, visible from Leh. Passing through cultivated valley floors, undulating high-altitude grassland, and snow-prone passes, the winding trail along it enables trekkers to experience life in a roadless region without having to hike for weeks into the wilderness – as a result, it has become the most frequented route in Ladakh. This will, however, change when the new road from Chilling presently under construction is completed. Do not attempt this trek without adequate wet- and cold-weather gear: snow flurries sweep across the higher reaches of the Markha Valley even in August.

The circuit takes six to eight days to complete, and is usually followed anticlockwise, starting from the village of **Spitok** (see p.623), 10km south of Leh. A more dramatic approach, via **Stok** (see p.612), affords matchless views over the Indus Valley to the Ladakh and Karakoram ranges, but involves a sharp ascent of **Stok La** (4848m) on only the second day; don't try it unless you are already well acclimatized to the altitude.

From Spitok, the trail crosses the Indus via an iron footbridge, then follows the south bank of the river 7km west to the narrow mouth of the tree-lined Jingchen

Valley. Camp beside the stream at Jingchen village, 4km further on, or higher up the valley near the Rumbak. Day 2 takes you five hours south down a side-valley, via the picturesque village of Yurutse, to a camp at the foot of Kunda La (4907m), crossed after a long climb on Day 3. Shingo, the first settlement below the pass, is a pleasant spot to set up camp if you are doing the trek in short stages. Otherwise, press on 6km down a wild-rose- and willow-lined stream gorge to the River Markha. A boggy campsite below the village of Skiu, hidden in a side-valley 2km further upstream from the confluence, marks the end of this stage.

The next two days' walking are relatively easy, winding west along the river via a series of footbridges and small villages such as Markha, where you can visit a ruined fort and small *gompa*. Beyond Umling, 3km east, the valley widens, and the peak of Kang Yurze (6400m) rears up to the south. Hankar stands at the mouth of a side-valley which you follow up to the Nimaling plain, a rolling pasture crisscrossed by gurgling streams and grazed by the yaks, *dzos*, sheep and horses of nearby villages. The ascent of Kongmaru La (5274m), the highest pass on the route, begins shortly after Nimaling on the penultimate leg. It takes two hours if you are properly acclimatized, and is rewarded with fine views north across the Indus Valley. By the time you reach Chogdo after the steep and zigzagging descent from the ridge, you may well be more than ready to call it a day; if not, carry on through Sumda to Martselang on the main Indus Valley highway, from where a dusty trail winds up to Hemis *gompa* (see p.615). The campsite in the woods below the monastery, serviced by a couple of chai stalls, marks the end of the trek.

Likkir to Temisgang

A motorable road along the old caravan route through the hills between Likkir and Temisgang makes a leisurely two-day hike, which takes in three major monasteries (Likkir, Rhizong and Temisgang) and a string of idyllic villages. It's a great introduction to trekking in Ladakh, the perfect acclimatizer if you plan to attempt any longer and more demanding routes. Ponies and guides for the trip may be arranged on spec at either Likkir or Temisgang villages, both of which have small guesthouses and are connected by daily buses to Leh.

Lamayuru to Alchi

Albeit short by Ladakhi standards, the five-day trek from Lamayuru to Alchi is one of the toughest in the region, winding across high passes and a tangle of isolated valleys, past a couple of ancient *gompas*, and offering superb panoramic views of the wilderness south of the Indus Valley. It's very hard to follow in places, so don't attempt it without an experienced guide, ponies, and enough provisions to tide you over if you lose your way.

Day 1 follows the main Zanskar traverse (outlined below) southeast from Lamayuru (see p.628), to Wanla via the Prikit La (3810m). Shortly after the campground at Phanjila, 3hr beyond Wanla at the confluence of the Spong and Ripchar *nalas*, the trail peels away from the Padum route and heads east up Ripchar Nala to Hinju, at the foot of Konki La (4905m). Take time out here before the strenuous climb up to the pass. Once across, a zigzagging descent winds down to the head of Sumdah Chu stream gorge, and thence through the tiny hamlets collectively known as Sumdah Chunoon, where there is a small *gompa* and plenty of space to camp. Stage four, to the bottom of the high Stakspi La (5180m), takes you north up a side-valley and can be completed in eight hours. If you are fully acclimatized, the ensuing three-hour ascent should present no problems, although the steep 1000-metre drop down the other side to Alchi (see p.625) is tricky in places.

continued overleaf

continued from previous page

Padum to Lamayuru

The trek across the rugged Zanskar Range from **Padum** to **Lamayuru** on the Srinagar–Leh highway, usually completed in ten to twelve days, is a hugely popular but very demanding long-distance route, not to be attempted as a first-time trek, nor without adequate preparation, ponies and a guide. We describe the route from south to north here, but there is no reason not to follow it in the opposite direction, from Lamayuru.

Two trails from **Padum** (see p.638) cover the first half of the trek. The slightly easier one winds along the east bank of the Zanskar via **Thonde** and **Zangla** (where you can detour up to an old palace and monastery) to **Honia**. Then the route ascends **Namtse La** (4446m), crossed halfway through the third stage. Day 4 involves a long hard slog over **Nerag La** (4850m) and a steep drop to cross the Zanskar at **Nerag** village. An hour or so north of the river, you meet up near **Yelchang** village with the other path which, after following the Zanskar's west bank to **Karsha** (see p.640), has wriggled over four passes, including the 5000-metre **Hanuma La**. This second and longer route allows you to visit the spectacular **Lingshet gompa**, famous for its *thangka* artists.

From Yelchang, a single track picks its way across a sheer wall of scree to **Sengge La** (the "Lion Pass"; 5000m). **Photokasar** above the River Photang, normally reached on Day 6 or 7, marks the start of the climb up a side-valley to **Sisir La** (4990m), after which you drop sharply down to Spong Nala, thence to the campground at **Honupatta** village. Two relatively easy stages round off the trek. The trail follows the river 4km downstream to **Wanla**, and then up the Shilakung Valley and through a rocky gorge to **Prikit La**. **Lamayuru** (see p.628) nestles on the narrow floor of the Sangeluma gorge, 90min below the pass.

For an outline of the two main approach routes to Zanskar from the south, see **"Trekking in Lahaul and Spiti"** (p.582).

those not used to the altitude. However, even seasoned trekkers gasp in awe at the sight that greets them when they finally arrive at the cairns. Capped with a plume of cloud and with snow streaming from its huge pyramidal peak, Nun sails 3500m above the valley floor, draped with heavily crevassed hanging glaciers and flanked by its sisters, multi-pinnacled Kun and saddle-topped Barmal.

There are only two **places to stay** in Panikhar. The *Kayoul Hotel & Restaurant* (**1**), directly opposite the bus stand, has a couple of very basic rooms with fold-away *charpois* and shared "earth" latrines, plus a ramshackle roadside café. For a bit more comfort, try the modest J&KTDC *Tourist Bungalow* (**1**), 100m further down the road on the left, where a large en-suite room with running water and a Western toilet sets you back a mere Rs50. **Buses** to Kargil leave from the *Kayoul* at 7am and 11am. If you're looking for a lift to Padum, collar the truckers as they leave the *dhaba* after their lunch; the one-way fare costs around the same as the bus (Rs150).

Zanskar

Despite the Indian government dropping restrictions to Pangong Tso, Tso Moriri and the Nubra Valley, mountain-locked **ZANSKAR**, literally "Land of White Copper", remains the most stunning and remote corner of Ladakh accessible by road. Hemmed in by the Zanskar Range and the Great Himalayan Divide, the nucleus of the region is a Y-shaped glacial valley system drained by three main rivers. The **Stod** (or Doda) emerges by the Pensi La to flow southeast into a wide triangular plain at **Padum**, the district headquarters, where it merges with the waters of the **Tsarap** (or Lingit) to form the River **Zanskar**. This fast-flowing milky turquoise torrent surges northeast to meet the Indus at Nimmu, gouging a chasm through the jagged mountains en route.

Lying to the leeward side of the Himalayan watershed, Zanskar sees a lot more snow than central Ladakh. Even its lowest passes remain blocked for six or seven months of the year, while midwinter temperatures can drop to a bone-numbing minus 40°C. Ten thousand or so tenacious souls subsist in this bleak and treeless terrain – among the coldest inhabited places on the planet – muffled up for half the year inside their smoke-filled whitewashed crofts, a winter's-worth of fodder piled on the roof.

A little over a decade ago, anything the resourceful Zanskaris could not produce for themselves (including timber for building) had to be transported into

7

Chaddar

The giant trench worn by the **Zanskar River** as it surges from Padum to join the Indus at Saspol, 120km northeast, is one of the deepest and most spectacular canyons in the world. Passing through a vast uninhabited wilderness at the very heart of the Himalayas, it supports a greater population of wild ibex than people. Moreover, because its sides are so sheer, no road, pony track or footpath penetrates the central section. In the depths of winter, however, when temperatures plunge to minus 30°C or below, the normally fast-flowing Zanskar freezes over, usually around early January, allowing villagers from isolated settlements and the Zanskar Valley to briefly escape their snowbound homes. The journey, as perilous and extraordinary as any in the Himalayan region, is known in Ladakh as **chaddar**.

For centuries, Zanskaris have risked their lives on the frozen river to sell yak butter and collect provisions or just to relieve the tedium of the long hard winters of Zanskar. Leh, with its fancy bazaar, stores packed with goodies, cinemas and cosmopolitan crowds, provides a welcome distraction. Once the river is deemed safely frozen, they pull on a pair of white army-surplus gum boots and set off north, shouting invocations to the mountain gods and carrying little more than a week's supply of *tsampa* and tea to sustain them. If all goes well, the walk through the gorge – from Hanumil, the last village in Zanskar, to Chilling, from where a dirt road runs the remaining leg to the Indus Valley – takes three to four days. Along the way, the Zanskaris sleep in caves burning driftwood to fuel cooking fires. Aside from exposure to the searing cold, whipped up by fierce winds funnelled down the gorge, the greatest danger facing *chaddar* walkers is, ironically, a thaw which, when it comes, submerges the hard base ice under a metre or more of slush. After the slush freezes, it forms razor-sharp needles that prove painful to walk on. Occasionally it becomes necessary to climb high above the river, chancing hazardous pitches or inch-wide ledges without ropes.

Despite the fact that very few adventure-tour operators risk the frozen river, an increasing number of foreigners are attempting the route. It's not difficult to locate a **guide** and **porters**: just ask around *Lingshet Labrang* or the other Zanskari hostels opposite the main bus stand in Leh. From mid-January onwards, returning groups leave Leh daily in minibuses and you can tag along with one, or better still employ a *chaddar* specialist to travel at your own pace, as Zanskaris tend to do the trip a lot faster.

the region over 4000 to 5000-metre passes, or, in midwinter, carried along the frozen surface of the Zanskar from its confluence with the Indus at Nimmu – a twelve-day round trip that is still the quickest route to the Srinagar–Leh road from Padum. Finally, in 1980, a motorable dirt track was blasted down the Suru and over Pensi La into the Stod Valley. Landslides and freak blizzards permitting (Pensi La can be snowbound even in August), the bumpy journey from Kargil to Padum can now be completed in as little as fourteen hours.

Most visitors come to Zanskar to **trek**. Numerous trails wind their way north from Padum to central Ladakh, west to Kishtwar, and south to neighbouring Lahaul – all long hard hikes that involve strenuous ups and downs (see p.634-636). If, on the other hand, you travel down here hoping to use the district headquarters as a comfortable base from which to make short day-trips, you'll be disappointed. Only a handful of Zanskar's widely scattered *gompas* and settlements lie within striking distance of the road. The rest are hidden away in remote valleys, reached after days or weeks of walking and surrounded by a shattered wilderness of mountains, where life has altered little since Buddhism first crossed the Himalayas from Kashmir over a thousand years ago.

Improved communications may yet turn out to be a mixed blessing for Zanskar. For while it has undoubtedly brought a degree of prosperity to Padum, the new road has already forced significant changes upon the rest of the valley – most noticeably a sharp increase in tourist traffic – whose long-term impact on the region's fragile ecology and traditional culture has yet to be fully realized. Increased tourism has, in fact, done little to benefit the locals financially, as agencies in Leh, Manali, Srinagar and even Delhi pocket the money paid by trekking groups. Zanskaris, weary of seeing their region come second to Kargil (which lies in the same administrative district), have been campaigning for several years for a sub-hill council status with more control over development, a parliamentary representative in Srinagar and a road following the Zanskar river gorge to Nimmu; the road project is going ahead but painfully slowly. Buddhist concerns have also been heightened in the face of state government mismanagement and communal tensions that followed the massacre of the three monks at Rangdum in July 2000.

Padum

After a memorable trek or bus ride, **PADUM**, 240km to the south of Kargil, comes as a bit of an anticlimax. Instead of the picturesque Zanskari village you might expect, the region's administrative headquarters and principal roadhead turns out to be a desultory collection of crumbling mud and concrete cubes, oily truck parks and incongruous tin-roofed government buildings, scattered around the sides of a stony hillock. The settlement's only real appeal lies in its superb location. Nestled at the southernmost tip of a broad, fertile river basin, Padum presides over a flat patchwork of farm land fringed with grey-pebble riverbeds and enclosed on three sides by colossal walls of scree and snow-capped mountains.

Straddling a nexus of several long-distance trails, Padum is an important **trekking hub** and the only place in Zanskar where tourism has thus far made much of an impression. During the short summer season, you'll see almost as many weather-beaten Westerners wandering around its sandy lanes as locals – a mixture of indigenous Buddhists and Sunni Muslims. Even so, facilities remain very basic, limited to a small tourist office, a handful of temporary tea-shops and guesthouses, as well as the inevitable rash of Kashmiri handicraft stalls. Nor is there much to see while you are waiting for your blisters to heal or your bum to recover from the bus journey down here. Apart from a small **mosque**, the Jami Masjid, whose plate-metal roof and multicoloured minarets are Padum's most prominent feature, the only noteworthy sight within easy walking distance is a small **Tagrimo gompa**, ensconced amid the poplar trees fifteen minutes' walk to the west.

Practicalities

Arriving in Padum by **bus**, you'll be dropped in the dusty square at the far south end of the village, close to the old quarter and a couple of the cheaper guesthouses. Tickets for the trip (Rs120 & Rs200) go on sale around 2pm the day before departure at Kargil bus stand. J&KTDC's **tourist reception centre** (July–Sept Mon–Sat 10am–7pm; ☎01983/45017) lies 1km north of the square in Mane Ringmo on the side of the main road, two minutes' walk from the other main concentration of guesthouses. Unlike their branches in Leh and Kargil, this one doesn't rent out trekking gear, but is good for general advice. Due to the short season and the limited tourist trade, renting a car in Padum is expensive, with rates available through the Padum Taxi Union office near the bus stand: a trip to Karsha and back costs around Rs800.

As yet, there is nowhere in Padum to change money, although you can post letters at the **GPO** next door to the tourist complex. STD telephone facilities are available nearby at the Zanskar Telecom Service (☎01983/45046).

Basic **trekking supplies** are sold at the hole-in-the-wall stores above the bus stand. Prices are much higher than elsewhere, so it pays to bring your own provisions with you from Kargil. Most trekkers arrange **ponies** through the tourist office or guesthouse owners but you can also try Zanskar Tour & Travels (☎01983/450646) who also supply guides and other help for treks. Either way, expect to pay Rs300–350 per pony per day, depending on the time of year (ponies transport grain during the harvest, so they're more expensive in early September). If you have trouble finding a horse-wallah, ask around Pipiting village, thirty minutes' walk north across the fields from Padum, where most of them hang out. Guides and porters cost a lot more at around Rs2500–3000 a day, especially over high altitudes.

Accommodation

Accommodation in Padum is limited to a handful of grotty guesthouses and rooms in private family homes. In both cases, bathrooms are usually shared, and toilets of the "long-drop" variety. One exception is the simple but comfortable J&KTDC *Tourist Bungalow* (❷), whose well-maintained en-suite double rooms have running cold water. The *Hotel Ibex* (☎01983/45012; ❸–❺) is the best Padum has to offer–with pleasant doubles set around a courtyard; other options include the grotty *Haftal* (❷) and the more salubrious *Chorala* (☎01983/45035; ❷–❹), which offers reasonable doubles and even has a travel desk, both near the bus stand. The least shambolic of the budget guesthouses in the village proper is the *Greenland* (❶), near the mosque, which boasts a couple of light and airy rooms.

Camping is also an option and pitches at the J&KTDC site, up near the tourist reception centre, cost Rs50 per night. Trekkers arriving from Shingo La sometimes camp beside the stream in the Tsarap Valley.

Eating

Finding **food** in Padum only tends to be a problem towards the end of the trekking season; by mid-October, stocks of imported goods (virtually everything except barley flour and yak butter) are low, and even a fresh egg can be a cause for celebration. Earlier in the year, temporary teashops and cafés ensure a supply of filling and fairly inexpensive meals. The best place to eat is at the *Hotel Ibex* restaurant. For cheap Chinese and Tibetan food, try the *Changthang* near the *Tourist Bungalow*, or the *Zanskar Moonland Restaurant* nearby. Most guesthouses also provide half-board if given enough warning.

Around Padum

Public transport around the Zanskar Valley is virtually nonexistent, so unless you can afford the vastly inflated fares demanded by Padum's taxi union, you can only get as far into the sweeping plains around Padum as you can hike in a day. For all but the most athletic and determined, this leaves just two possible excursions, of which the hike across the fields to **KARSHA gompa**, Zanskar's largest Gelug-pa monastery, is easily the most rewarding. From a distance, this cluster of whitewashed mud cubes clinging to the rocky lower slopes of the mountain north of Padum looks like some strange geological formation. Only close up is it possible to pick out the individual monks' quarters and temples, which date from the tenth to the fourteenth century. Of the prayer halls, the recently renovated Du-khang and Gon-khang at the top of the complex are the most impressive, while the small *Chukshok-jal*, set apart from the *gompa* below a ruined fort on the far side of a gully, contains Karsha's oldest wall paintings, contemporary with those at Alchi (see p.625).

The quickest way to get to Karsha on foot is to head north from Padum to the cable bridge across the Stod, immediately below the monastery. Set off early in the morning; the violent icy storms that blow in from the south across the Great Himalayan Range around mid-afternoon make the ninety-minute hike across the exposed river basin something of an endurance test. Karsha is a far more pleasant place to stay than Padum and some villagers rent **rooms** to tourists. Try the wonderful glass room belonging to Thuktan Thardot in Sharling Ward just below the *gompa* (❶).

Karsha can also be reached by road, via the bridge at **Tungri**, 8km northwest of Padum. En route, you pass another large *gompa*, **SANI**, lauded as the oldest in Zanskar, and the only one built on the valley floor. Local legend attributes its foundation to the itinerant Padmasambhava (Guru Rinpoche) in the eighth century. Though the name of the **Kanishka Chorten**, behind the main temple, suggests it may have been established by the Kushan King Kanishka in the first or second century, it is more likely that it was named after the emperor centuries later. There are two small temples in the Du-khang grounds: one, in which Naropa is said to have meditated around nine hundred years ago, is permanently locked, while the other, the **La-khang**, has unique painted stucco bas-reliefs whose deep niches enshrine dusty gold-faced icons, most of them manifestations of Padmasambhava. Set apart from the temples a little to the north is a 2m-high Maitreya figure, carved out of local stone some time between the eighth and tenth centuries.

Travel details

The bus details here apply during the tourist season between July 1 and September 15 only, after which date the Manali–Leh highway is officially closed. Most other roads, including the highway from Leh to Srinagar via Kargil, remain open till the end of October. Despite heavy snow falls, the road from Leh to the Nubra Valley over the incredibly high Khardung La is kept open all year.

Buses

Leh to: Alchi (1 daily; 3hr); Chemrey (3 daily; 2hr); Diskit (Nubra) (1 weekly; 6hr); Hemis (1–2 daily; 1hr 45min); Kargil (2–3 daily; 6hr 30min); Lamayuru (2–3 daily; 6hr 30min); Likkir (1 daily; 3hr); Manali (6–8 daily; 28hr); Matho (2 daily; 1hr); Panamik & Sumur (Nubra) (2 weekly; 10hr); Phyang (3 daily; 1hr 15min); Shey (hourly; 30min); Spitok (4 hourly; 20min); Srinagar (1–2 daily except Sun; 24hr); Stok (3 daily; 40min); Temisgang (1 daily; 5hr); Thak Thok (3 daily; 2hr 30min); Tikse (hourly; 45min).

Kargil to: Drass (2–3 daily; 2hr); Leh (2–3 daily; 6hr 30min); Mulbekh (2–3 daily; 1hr 30min); Padum (3 weekly; 18hr); Panikhar (2 daily; 3hr); Sankhu (3 daily; 1hr 30min); Srinagar (1–2 daily; 12hr).

Flights

Leh to: Delhi (daily, 2 daily in high season; 1hr 15min–3hr); Chandigarh (1 weekly; 1hr)); Jammu (2 weekly; 50min); Srinagar (1 weekly; 45min).

CHAPTER 8

Highlights

❋ **Rock garden, Chandigarh** This bizarre sculpture garden, assembled from industrial debris by a local eccentric, is India's second most visited attraction, after the Taj Mahal. **See p.650**

❋ **Border ceremony, Wagha** Shorter and more colourful than a cricket match, the border ceremony is a highly charged event, especially on Sundays, when hundreds of people gather. **See p.660**

❋ **The Golden Temple, Amritsar** One of the great sights – and sounds – of India; *kirtan* (devotional songs) are performed throughout the day and into the night. **See p.660**

8

Haryana and Punjab

The prosperous states of **HARYANA** and **PUNJAB** occupy the flat and fertile tract of river plain that extends northwest from Delhi, towards the mountains of Jammu & Kashmir and the border with Pakistan. Divided by the Partition of August 1947, Punjab has been systematically shorn of its once vast territory: losing the Punjab Hills to Himachal Pradesh and later sacrificing a further chunk to create Haryana. Crossed by the five major tributaries of the **Indus**, the former British-administered region of Punjab ("Land of Five Rivers") was split down the middle at Independence. Indian Muslims fled west into Pakistan, and Hindus east, in an exodus accompanied by horrific massacres. The Sikhs, meanwhile, threw in their lot with India, which they considered a safer option than the homeland of their Muslim archenemies. In 1966, prime minister Indira Gandhi, in response to Sikh pressure, further divided the state into two semi-autonomous districts: predominantly Sikh Punjab, and 96-percent Hindu Haryana, both governed from the newly built capital of **Chandigarh**.

There is little of tourist interest in the two states other than the beautiful Golden Temple in Amritsar and the wacky rock garden of Chandigarh, but the region, known as India's "bread basket" is very important to the nation's **economy**. Punjabi farmers produce nearly a quarter of India's wheat, and one-third of its milk and dairy foods, **Ludhiana** churns out ninety percent of the country's woollen goods and the Hero factory in **Jalandhar** manufactures the world's best-selling bicycle. Helped by remittance cheques from millions of expatriates in the UK, US and Canada, the state's per capita income is now almost double the national average.

Sikh men are recognizable by their turbans and beards while the women usually wear colourful *salwar kamise*. The Sikh faith encourages economic self-reliance and strong family ties and their temples or **gurudwaras** are very welcoming, being open to all castes and creeds. Their warrior tradition, which dates from the days of resistance against the Moghuls, served the Sikhs well during the Raj, when they formed the backbone of the British–Indian army.

Although you'll see full-bearded orthodox *sardars* strolling around the **Golden Temple** in the holy city of **Amritsar**, most Sikhs today are liberal. Known as **sahajdharis**, less devout members of the faith are frequently stereotyped as *bon viveurs*, and with some justification: Punjab boasts both India's richest regional cuisine, and its highest per capita consumption of **alcohol**.

Most travellers simply pass through the region en route to Himachal Pradesh, or to the Indo-Pak border at **Wagha**, but a visit to the Golden Temple is well worth the effort. Linger longer and check out Le Corbusier's experimental city of **Chandigarh**, the Moghul monuments at **Sirhind** and **Pinjore**, the great *gurudwara* at **Anandpur Sahib**, the European-inspired **Kapurthala** or any of the countless brick villages. You'll find the inhabitants, many of whom seem to have a cousin in Toronto or Southall, extremely hospitable.

Some history

Punjab's arid Chaggar Valley, stretching south from the Shivalik Hills on the HP border to the deserts of Rajasthan, witnessed the rise of urban settlement as early as 3000 BC. Now known as the **Harappan** civilization, this string of fortified towns was invaded by the Aryans around 1700 BC. Among the Sanskrit scriptures set down in the ensuing **Vedic** age was the **Mahabharata**, whose epic battles drew on real-life encounters between the ancient kings of Punjab at **Karnal**, 118km north of Delhi. Conquered by the Mauryans in the third century BC, it saw plenty more action as various invading Moghul armies passed through on their way from the Khyber Pass to Delhi, including Babur who routed Ibrahim Lodi at **Panipat**, beside the Jamuna, in 1526.

Meanwhile, further north, **Sikhism** was beginning to establish itself under the tutelage of Guru Nanak (1469–1539). Based on the notion of a single Formless God, the guru's vision of a casteless egalitarian society found favour both with Hindus and Muslims, in spite of Moghul Emperor Aurangzeb's concerted attempts to stamp it out. Suppression actually strengthened the Sikh faith in the long run, inspiring the militaristic and confrontational tenth guru **Gobind Singh** to introduce the Five Ks, part of a rigorous new orthodoxy called the **Khalsa**, or "Community of the Pure" (see also Contexts).

Having survived repeated seventeenth-century Afghan invasions, the Sikh nation emerged to fill the power vacuum left by the collapse of the Moghuls. Only in the 1840s, after two bloody wars with the British, was the Khalsa army finally defeated. Thereafter, the Sikhs played a vital role in the Raj, helping to quash the Mutiny of 1857. The relationship only soured after the **Jallianwalla Bagh massacre** of 1919 (see p.662), which also ensured that the Punjab's puppet leaders (who hailed the general responsible as a hero) were discredited, leaving the way open for the rise of radicalism.

After the Partition era, things calmed down enough after Independence for the new state to grow wealthy on its prodigious agricultural output. As it did, militant Sikhs began to press for the creation of the separate Punjabi-speaking state they called Khalistan. A compromise of sorts was reached in 1966, when the Hindu district of Haryana and the Sikh-majority Punjab were nominally divided. However, the move did not silence the separatists, and in 1977 Indira Gandhi's Congress was trounced in state elections by a coalition that included the Sikh religious party, the **Akali Dal**.

A more sinister element entered the volatile equation with the emergence of an ultra-radical separatist movement led by **Sant Jaranil Singh Bhindranwale**. Covertly supported by the national government (who saw the group as a way to defeat the Akali Dal), Bhindranwale and his band waged a

The International boundaries on this map are neither purported to be correct nor authentic by Survey of India directives. Publisher.

Crossing Haryana and Punjab en route to, or from, Delhi, you're bound to travel, at some stage, along part of the longest, oldest and most famous highway in India. Stretching 2000km from Peshawar near the rugged Afghan–Pakistan frontier to Calcutta on the River Hooghly, NH-1, alias the **Grand Trunk Road**, was described by Kipling in his novel *Kim*, whose hero and his Tibetan lama companion set off along it in search of "The River of Arrows", as "the Big Road", and "the Backbone of all Hind".

The first recorded mention of this trade corridor dates from the fourth century BC, when it was known as the **Uttar Path** ("the North Way"). A century later, the emperor Ashoka upgraded it with paving stones and watchtowers, placing edict pillars at intervals along the route. Midway through the sixteenth century, the Afghan warlord Sher Shah Suri, who briefly usurped power from the Moghuls, added several *sarais* (staging posts) for caravan trains, including **Sirhind** near modern Chandigarh. He also stamped out highway robbery by holding village headmen accountable for crimes committed on their stretch of the road.

In the years to come, the Moghuls sank wells along the Grand Trunk Road, and the British covered it with asphalt. More recently, several sections were converted into four-lane highways, complete with crash-barriers and neat white lines that everyone ignores. However, the streams of Tata trucks and overloaded buses that now tear along NH-1 have done little to deter more traditional traffic: donkey carts (*ekkas*), rickshaws, cyclists and barefoot pilgrims still plod along the hard shoulder, watched by imperious holy cows. The *sarais*, meanwhile, have been overtaken by their twentieth-century counterpart, the roadside dhaba, where truckers can tuck into a plateful of chicken or chana dhal, and crash out on a *charpoi*. As Kipling said – "such a river of life... exists nowhere else in the world."

ruthless campaign of sectarian terror in the Punjab which came to a head in 1984, when they occupied the Golden Temple; Indira's brutal response, **Operation Blue Star** (see p.658), plunged the Punjab into another ugly bout of communal violence. Four years later, history repeated itself when a less threatening occupation of the temple was crushed by **Operation Black Thunder**. Since then, the Punjabi police have gone on to make considerable advances against the terrorists – helped, for the first time, by the Punjabi peasant farmers, the **Jats**, who had grown tired of the inexorable slaughter. Despite the occasional eruption and the murder of the chief minister of Punjab in 1995, these days the situation is calmer, and Haryana and Punjab, previously a no-go zone for tourists, is safe to travel in once again.

Chandigarh

After the 1947 Partition when the principal Punjabi city Lahore was claimed by Pakistan, the new state found itself without a capital. Premier Jawaharlal Nehru saw this as a golden opportunity to realize his vision of a city "symbolic of the future of India, unfettered by the traditions of the past, [and] an expression of the nation's faith in the future", and dispatched scouts to Europe to search for designers. When their original choice, Polish-born Mathew Nowicki, was killed in a plane crash in 1950, the controversial Swiss-French architect Charles-Edouard Jeanneret, alias **Le Corbusier** (1887–1965), was offered the job.

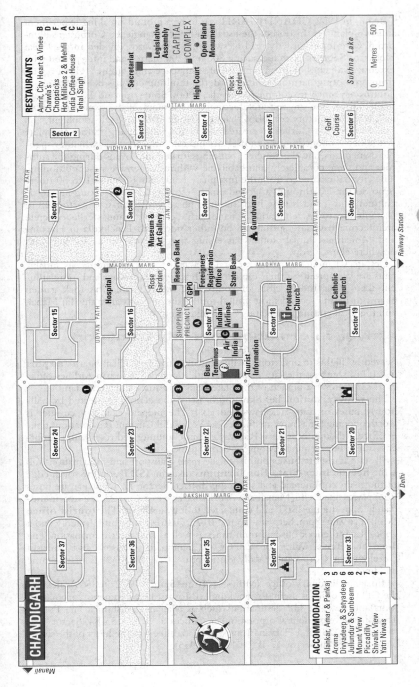

CHANDIGARH

RESTAURANTS

Amrit, City Heart & Vinee	B
Chawla's	D
Chopsticks	F
Hot Millions 2 & Mehfil	A
India Coffee House	C
Tehal Singh	E

Sector 2

Sector 11

Sector 15

Sector 24

Sector 23

Sector 3

Sector 10

Museum & Art Gallery

Hospital

Rose Garden

Reserve Bank

GPO

Foreigners' Registration Office

State Bank

SHOPPING PRECINCT

Sector 17

Indian Airlines

Air India

Bus Terminus

Tourist Information

Sector 4

Sector 9

Gurudwara

Sector 16

Sector 22

Sector 5

Sector 8

Sector 18

Protestant Church

Catholic Church

Sector 19

Sector 7

Golf Course

Sector 6

UTTAR MARG

VIDHYAN PATH

VIDHYAN PATH

VIDYA PATH

UDYAN PATH

JAN MARG

HIMALAYA MARG

SAROVAR PATH

MADHYA MARG

MADHYA MARG

Sector 21

Sector 20

SAROVAR PATH

DAKSHIN MARG

HIMALAYA MARG

Sector 37

Sector 36

Sector 35

Sector 34

Sector 33

CAPITAL COMPLEX

Legislative Assembly

Secretariat

Open Hand Monument

High Court

Rock Garden

Sukhna Lake

0	Metres	500

ACCOMMODATION

Alankar, Amar & Pankaj	3
Aroma	5
Divyadeep & Satyadeep	6
Jullundur & Sunbeam	8
Mount View	2
Piccadilly	7
Shivalik View	4
Yatri Niwas	1

Railway Station ▶

Delhi ▶

Manali ▶

8

HARYANA AND PUNJAB | Chandigarh

647

Begun in 1952, **CHANDIGARH** was to be a ground-breaking experiment in town planning. Instead of the usual amorphous tangle, Le Corbusier's blueprints were for an orderly grid of sweeping boulevards, divided into 29 neat blocks, or **Sectors**, each measuring 800 by 1200 metres, and interspersed with extensive stretches of green: a fusion of "sun, space and verdure". However, far from promoting harmony and accord, the resulting city has been a source of controversy since its completion in the 1960s. Some applaud Le Corbusier's brainchild as "the greatest architectural achievement of the twentieth century", while detractors complain that the design is flawed, self-indulgent, and "un-Indian". Le Corbusier created a city for fast-flowing traffic, complete with dozens of enormous roundabouts and car parks at a time when few people owned cars, and the concrete buildings turned into ovens during the summer and were completely uninhabitable without expensive air-conditioning. The city has expanded from the first phase comprising Sectors 1 to 30 (there is no Sector 13), through a second phase – sectors 31 to 47 eating into agricultural land – and is now into the third phase with (half-size) sectors 48 to 61. Satellite towns emulating Chandigarh's grid plan and sterile concrete architecture have also sprung up on either side, with Panchkula in Haryana and Mohali in Punjab somewhat easing the pressure on a city left with nowhere else to grow.

Despite Chandigarh's infrastructural and aesthetic shortcomings, its inhabitants are very proud of their capital, which is cleaner, greener and more affluent than other Indian cities of comparable size. Chandigarh's rock garden claims to be the second most visited tourist site in India after the Taj Mahal, and the local cuisine is deliciously rich and spicy.

Arrival, information and city transport

Served by flights to and from Delhi, Amritsar and Leh, Chandigarh's **airport** lies 11km south of the city centre. Facilities include an Indian Airlines office (☎0172/704539), a branch of the State Bank of Patiala and a taxi stand.

The **railway station** lies 8km southeast of the centre, connected by half-hourly buses or auto-rickshaws and taxis. The prepaid rickshaw counter is worth queuing for as rates are fixed. There's a useful Current Reservations ticket office, although Northern Railway's main computerized reservation counter is at the bus terminal (Mon–Sat 8am–8pm).

All state transport **buses** pull in to the main transport and information hub – the frenetic **Inter-State Bus Terminus** (aka the **ISBT**), on the south edge of the main commercial and shopping district, Sector 17. Most private buses from places like Delhi, Manali and Amritsar arrive in Sector 22, at a stop immediately opposite the ISBT and connected to it by a subway. The **tourist office** (Mon–Fri 9am–5pm, Sat 9am–1pm; ☎0172/704614) is helpful, friendly and a good place to check bus and train times as well as any other information. The Tour and Travel Wing of CITCO (Chandigarh Industry and Tourism Development Corporation; daily 8am–7pm; ☎0172/703839) is in the same building.

Himachal Pradesh's office (Mon–Sat 10am–5pm; ☎0172/708569), next to the CITCO office is useful for booking HP Tourist Development Corporation tours and buses to HP destinations such as Manali and Shimla. The Punjab Tourism Development Corporation has offices at SCO 183-84, Sector 8-C (☎0172/781138), and Haryana Tourism's head office is at the heart of the shopping complex in Sector 17-B (☎0172/702955).

City transport

Chandigarh is too spread out to explore on foot, but cycle- and auto-rickshaws cruise the streets. Auto meters are invariably "out of order" so be sure to negotiate prices first. Cycle rickshaws are much cheaper, but the drivers find the long haul up to the north end of town or to the railway station tough going, so allow plenty of time. Next to the prepaid auto-rickshaw booth behind the ISBT, the main **taxi** stand (☎0172/704621) is open 24hr. CITCO's Tour and Travel Wing at the ISBT can also arrange half- or full-day excursions and will probably get you a better price.

Accommodation

Chandigarh's sky-high property prices make its **accommodation** among the most expensive in India. Tariffs at the bottom end are particularly inflated, with no corresponding improvement in standards. If you want to spend less than Rs200, choice is limited to the railway **retiring rooms** or an airless cell in one of the many unlicensed budget guesthouses (alias "tourist bungalows"), tucked away in quiet suburbs or backstreets, which the municipality are forever trying to close down. Luxury tax is not levied in Chandigarh, but several of the pricier places slap ten-percent **service charges** on the bill.

Alankar, 803 Sector 22-A ☎0172/708801. A mid-range hotel with attached bathrooms, hot showers and TVs; clean and close to the bus stand. ⑥

Amar, 806-6 Udyog Path, Sector 22-A ☎0172/704638. Cheapest of the three identikit hotels in this block but with no single rooms. ⑤–⑥

Aroma, Himalaya Marg, Sector 22-C ☎0172/700045. An attractive two-star hotel with a restaurant, 24hr coffee shop, lawns and good value a/c rooms. ⑦–⑧

Divyadeep, 1090-91 Sector 22-B ☎0172/705191. Pleasant budget hotel run by Sai Baba devotees. Clean rooms and a large rooftop area; one of the best-value options in Chandigarh. ④–⑤

Jullundur, Udyog Path, Sector 22-B ☎0172/706777. Reasonable and comfy mid-range place built around central atrium. ⑤–⑥

Mount View, Sector 10 ☎0172/740544, ℱ742220, ⓔcitco10@chl.dot.net.in. Chandigarh's top hotel, 2km from the centre, with sauna, health club, business centre and pool. ⑨

Pankaj, Udyog Path, Sector 22-A ☎0172/709891. Slightly more expensive than the adjacent *Amar* and *Alankar* next door, but a bit more comfortable. ⑦

Piccadilly, Himalaya Marg, Sector 22-B ☎0172/707571. Upmarket business-oriented hotel close to the city centre with central a/c, classy restaurant, bar, coffee shop, and in-house travel agent. ⑧

Satyadeep, 1102-03 Sector 22-B ☎0172/703103. Run by the same management as the nearby *Divyadeep* and worth trying if the former is full. ④–⑤

Shivalik View, Sector 17 ☎0172/700001, ⓔcitco17@ch1.dot.net.in. This CITCO hotel is the largest and swankiest hotel in the centre, with a rooftop restaurant and shopping arcade. ⑧

Sunbeam, Udyog Path, Sector 22-B ☎0172/708100. Upmarket hotel opposite the ISBT with swish marble lobby, plush restaurant and bar, plus foreign exchange for guests. ⑦–⑧

Yatri Niwas, Sector 24 ☎0172/700050. Large grounds and gardens. Reasonable en-suite rooms and also an eight-bed dorm (Rs100). ⑤–⑥

The City

Chandigarh's numbered **sectors** are further subdivided into lettered blocks making route-finding relatively easy. Le Corbusier saw the city plan as a living organism, with the imposing **Capital Complex** to the north as a "head", the shopping precinct, **Sector 17**, a "heart", the green open spaces as "lungs", and the crosscutting network of roads, separated into eight different grades for use by various types of vehicles (in theory only), a "circulatory system".

The museum and art gallery

Situated in the green belt known as the Leisure Valley, five minutes by rickshaw
north of the city centre, Chandigarh's large museum and art gallery form part
of a cultural complex which includes the adjoining Rose Garden and open-air
theatre where free concerts are occasionally staged. The **museum** (Tues–Sun
10am–4.30pm; Rs1), in Sector 10, houses a sizeable and informatively displayed
collection of ancient sculpture, miniature paintings and contemporary Indian
art. Among prize pieces on the first floor are a dozen or so standing Buddhas
from Gandhara, noted for their delicately carved "wet-look" *lunghis* and distinctly Hellenic features – a legacy of Alexander the Great's conquests. Also
Greek-influenced are the beautiful terracotta heads mounted in glass cases at
the top of the main staircase; like the Buddhas, they date from the first and second centuries BC.

Art enthusiasts will find plenty to pore over in the adjacent **gallery**, where
abundant exquisite Moghul, Kangra and Rajasthani miniatures are accompanied by interpretive panels outlining the main features of the respective
schools. Modern works featured in the end room include a couple of A.N.
Tagore's atmospheric watercolours, five original Roerichs and several over-
the-top patriotic and devotional Sikh canvases.

The Capital Complex

Three blocks north of the centre, in the shadow of the Shivalik Hills, the
Capital Complex, Sector 1, is the site of some of Le Corbusier's most ambitious experiments. The concrete campus, set amid balding sun-parched lawns,
was designed to express the strength and unity of independent India. Ironically,
the area is now surrounded by barbed wire and patrolled by armed guards, and
has been indefinitely closed to casual tourists since the assassination of the chief
minister of Punjab, Beant Singh, in front of the Assembly in October 1995.
Check at the tourist office to see if guided tours have been reinstated.

The most imposing edifice in the group is the eleven-storey **Secretariat**,
Chandigarh's highest building, which houses ministerial offices belonging to
both Haryana and Punjab, and has a roof garden with good views over the city.
The resemblance of the **Legislature Assembly**, or Vidhan Sabha, just north,
to a power station is no coincidence: Le Corbusier was allegedly inspired by a
stack of cooling towers he saw in Ahmedabad. The most colourful of the three
buildings stands opposite the Secretariat. Said to incorporate elements of the
Buland Darwaza in Fatehpur Sikri, the **High Court**, whose double roof symbolizes the protective power of the law, is decorated inside with huge woollen
tapestries. The High Court is also shared between the two states of Haryana
and Punjab. North of the High Court is the black, thirteen-metre-high **Open
Hand** monument, Chandigarh's adopted emblem. Weighing all of 45 tonnes it
revolves on ball-bearings like a weather vane and stands for "post-colonial harmony and peace".

The rock garden

Close to the Capital Complex, and a refreshing counterpoint to Le Corbusier's
drab concrete cityscape, is the **rock garden** (daily 8am–6pm; Rs5), a surreal
fantasyland fashioned from fragments of shattered plates, neon strip lights, pots,
pebbles, broken bangles and assorted urban-industrial junk. The open-air exhibition is the lifelong labour of retired Public Works Department road inspector **Nek Chand Saini**, known simply as Nek Chand. Inspired by a recurrent
childhood dream, he spent seven years collecting strangely shaped rocks as well
as urban and industrial waste from the debris of 26 local villages bulldozed

down for land for redevelopment. He began construction in 1965 intending it to be just a small garden. When it was discovered by a malaria research team, clearing the jungle in 1973, it caused astonishment. Although completely illegal, the secret garden now covering 12 whole acres aroused great local interest and was recognized as a great artistic endeavour. An enlightened decision awarded Nek Chand a salary to continue his work and a workforce of fifty labourers to help. The garden opened to the public in 1976 and now covers 25 acres containing several thousand sculptures. CITCO's leaflet describes Nek Chand's toils thus:

Sitting by his hut, under the star-spangled Chandigarh sky, he used to burn cycle and auto-tires to provide him spotlight and, while his eyes profusely watered in the acrid smoke of the improvised fire... would patiently shape, stone by stone, an enchanted kingdom of his dreams.

Nek Chand, now 74, continues to expand the site, which has seen three distinct phases of increasing grandeur. While his earlier work was mostly figurative and used recycled materials, with the granting of more land he began to indulge in greater fantasy, turning the rock garden into a labyrinth of more than a dozen different enclosures, interconnected by narrow passages, arched walkways, streams, bridges, grottos, waterfalls, battlements and turrets. Teeming on weekends with excited children and parents, the complex is alive with bird, animal and human figures, whose rigid stance and transfixed facial expressions take their cue from Indian *adivasi* (tribal) art. Stick to the path, or you could end up wandering the maze of pebble palaces and mock-Moghul ramparts until the *chowkidar* finds you at closing time. Nek Chand's ideas about turning unwanted waste into a work of great imagination and beauty are promoted by the Nek Chand Foundation: contact 34 Highbury Place, London N5 1QP (T +44 020 7359 1747, @ sburns@gallery.source.co.uk).

Eating

Chandigarh has no shortage of **places to eat**, whether you just want to grab a quick snack between buses from a rough-and-ready roadside *dhaba*, try some of the new fast-food joints serving veggie burgers and ice cream, or splash out on a classy Punjabi meal. As everywhere in Punjab, Chandigarh's most popular food is chicken, cooked in a variety of ways. Pastry shops like Monica's, Sector 8-B, produce excellent cheesecake and gateau. Sai Sweets, between the *Divyadeep* and *Satyadeep* hotels, and Sindhi Sweets in Sector 17-E, are two of the best sweet shops in town. Takeaway has become very popular and not just for pizzas – most restaurants provide a service. Alcohol is widely available, and there are many bars around Sector 17 serving draught and bottled beer.

Amrit, City Heart and **Vinee**, opposite the bus stand. Cheap, clean, *dhaba*–like restaurants serving excellent food. *City Heart* is probably the best of the three and should not be confused with its sister concern *City Heart 2* which is more of a pub.
Bhoj, *Hotel Divyadeep*, #1090-1, Sector 22-B. Classy pure-veg thali joint run by Sai Baba devotees.
Chawla's, Sector 22-C. Tandoori restaurant renowned for its rich cream chicken.

Chopsticks, near *Hotel Piccadilly*, Himalaya Marg. Expensive a/c Chinese restaurant with tinted windows and an impressive menu.
Hot Millions, 1st floor, Sector 17 Piazza. Part of the successful fast-food chain, sells everything from *dosas* to pizzas. This branch also has a good salad bar, while *Hot Millions 2* in Sector 17 near *Mehfil* has a popular pub – *Down Under*.
India Coffee House, Sector 17-C. Clean budget chain with a limited but predictable menu, including *dosas*, sandwiches, and coffee.

Mehfil, Sector 17. The exclusive preserve of Chandigarh's smart set, *the* place to sample rich Mughlai and Punjabi cuisine in a/c comfort.

Tehal Singh, #1116-17 Sector 22-B. Cheap and very popular tandoori restaurant. *Singh's Chicken* right next door provides competition.

Listings

Ambulance ☎ 102
Airline offices Air India, SCO 107-108, Sector 17-B (Mon–Fri 9.30am–1pm & 2–5.30pm, Sat 9.30am–1pm; ☎ 0172/703510); British Airways, Nijhawan Travel Services, Sector 9-D ☎ 0172/741419; Indian Airlines, #171-2, Sector 17-C (Mon–Fri 10am–1pm & 2–5pm; ☎ 0172/704539); Japan Airlines, Onkar Travels, Sector 17-B ☎ 0172/704910; Jet Airways & Air Canada, Sector 9-D ☎ 0172/705092; Kuwait Airlines, Trans Air Travels, Sector 17 ☎ 0172/702833; Lufthansa, Sector 17-C ☎ 0172/702435. Bajaj Travels, SCO 96-97, Sector 17-C (☎ 0172/704500) are agents for international airlines, as well as domestic airlines Archana and Jagsons.
Banks and exchange Several of the banks ranged around Bank Square on the northwest side of Sector 17 change money, including the UCO Bank, Punjab National Bank, the State Bank of India and Andhra Bank, which also handles Visa.
Doctors Dr S.P. Bedi, 69 Sector 8 ☎ 0172/780708.
Hospitals Chandigarh's General Hospital is in Sector 16 (☎ 0172/780756), but is not as good as the PGI, Sector 12 (☎ 0172/541018).
Internet access Internet services are available at City Graphics Booth 820-B, Sector 22-A opposite the ISBT (☎ 0172/705695) and *Cyber Café 22* and *Fundooz Cyber Café* both on Himalaya Marg Sector–22.
Left luggage There is a 24hr cloakroom in the bus stand.
Optician Weldon, SCO 83, Sector 17-D, ☎ 0172/703024, provides an efficient same-day service.
Pharmacies Sahib Singh & Sons, near Sindhi Sweets, Sector 17-E ☎ 0172/742574; Bharat Medical, Sector 16 (24hr).

Moving on from Chandigarh

Chandigarh's long-distance transport connections are summarized on p.665. The railway station, 8km from the centre, has direct services to Delhi, Amritsar and Jodhpur. Regular buses run to Delhi (248km), but the journey can be made in almost half the time by taking the superfast a/c Shatabdi Express trains (#2006 & #2012 departing at 6.50am & 12.20pm). Second-class tickets cost Rs435, four times the bus price, but the journey is far more comfortable and convenient. Other useful trains include the #4096 *Himalayan Queen* (dep 5.35pm, arr New Delhi 10.30pm), the daily #4535 Kalka–Amritsar Express (dep 4.58pm, arr Amritsar 23.20pm) and the daily #4887 Kalka–Jodhpur Express (dep 22.10pm, arr Jodhpur 17.45pm next day).

Most travellers move on from the city by bus. All ordinary, a/c, deluxe and semi-deluxe state buses operate out of the frenetic Inter-State Bus Terminus (ISBT) in Sector 17. State transport buses travel to a huge number of destinations including Rekong Peo, Rishikesh, Haridwar, Dehra Dun, Chamba, Dharamsala and several places in Rajasthan – tickets can be pre-booked at the counters on the ground floor or just pay on the bus. Most private buses to Delhi, Manali, Shimla, Dharamsala and Amritsar leave from opposite the ISBT in Sector 22.

Chandigarh is an important transport hub for Shimla. The quickest way to get to Shimla is by bus (4hr–4hr 30min): either with the direct Himachal Pradesh or Haryana Roadways ordinary "express" buses or with more comfortable deluxe buses, departing every 15min from the ISBT. You can also get there on the slower but more congenial Viceroys' "Toy Train" (see p.522), from Kalka 26km to the north-east, and connected to Chandigarh by frequent buses. The scenic 75-kilometre journey from Kalka to Shimla takes around 5hr 30min (dep 4am, 5.30am, 6.30am & 11.55am). See p.528 for Shimla–Kalka times.

Indian Airlines fly to Leh, Amritsar and Delhi.

Police ☎0172/544437.

Shopping Several states run handicraft emporiums in the Sector 17 shopping complex, among them Punjab, whose Phulkari store stocks a good range of embroidered silk, woodwork and traditional pointed Punjabi shoes (*phulkari*). For quality handloom products, try the nearby UP emporium, or the Khadi Gramodyog in the Shivalik View's small arcade: both are strong on block-printed calico garments, especially *salwar kamise*. Sector 17 also has a couple of good bookshops including Capital Book Depot with a travel section.

Around Chandigarh

While Chandigarh's futuristic architecture may be of limited interest to most travellers, the ornamental Moghul gardens in **Pinjore**, on the northern outskirts of the city, have a much more universal appeal. Southwest of Chandigarh, there are further Moghul ruins at **Sirhind**, a good place to stop overnight between Delhi and Amritsar. **Anandpur Sahib**, the home of the Khalsa movement and one of Sikhism's most venerated shrines, lies just off the Chandigarh–Mandi highway and makes a worthwhile detour, especially during the festival of Holi.

Pinjore

PINJORE, 22km north of Chandigarh and 7km south of Kalka on the Shimla road, is best known for its walled **Yadavindra Gardens**, one of many sites associated with the exile of the Pandavas, chronicled in the *Mahabharata*. The gardens originally belonged to the rajas of Sirmaur, but under the Moghuls, Pinjore was taken over by Aurangzeb's foster brother, Fidai Khan, who erected three pleasure palaces for his wife amid the cypress trees. Legend tells that the raja reclaimed his summer retreat by sending a female fruit-seller with goitre to the imperial imposters. On being told that the woman's unsightly swelling was caused by the local water, the begum and her entourage fled.

These days, the walled gardens harbour a small otter sanctuary, aviary, and zoo, and are popular places for a picnic. One of the three palaces has been converted by Haryana Tourism into a comfortable hotel, the *Budgerigar* (☎01733/21877; ⑤–⑦), which boasts a range of rooms including a dorm (Rs100). Frequent local **buses** connect Pinjore with Chandigarh and Kalka.

Sirhind

Close to the Grand Trunk Road (NH-1) and Northern Railway, **SIRHIND**, 48km southwest of Chandigarh, was the capital of the Pathan Suri sultans and the site of an important *caravansarai* (the name derives from *Sir-i-Hind*, "the Head or Frontier of Hind or Hindu India"). Today, only a couple of minor-league Moghul palaces, hot baths and pleasure pavilions remain from the illustrious past, but it is still a pleasant overnight stop between Delhi and Amritsar, just as it was when the emperors and their entourages passed through.

The site of the Moghul ruins, **Aam–Khas–Bagh**, and lies 2.5km north of the town proper. Here you'll see Shimla's best-preserved monuments, encircled by the high walls of Sher Shah Suri's sixteenth-century **fort**. Approached via a tree- and fountain-lined walkway, the ruins of the old baths, or **hammam**, enclose a giant whose water was channelled into geometric bathing pools outside. Nearby stand the ruins of emperor Shah Jahan's residence, the **Daulat Khana**. Just behind the tourist complex, in much better shape, is the seventeenth-century **Sheesh Mahal** or "Palace of Mirrors". 1.5km north of the tourist complex, **Fatehgarh Sahib**, a pristine white *gurudwara*, stands in memory of Guru Gobind Singh's two youngest sons who were bricked up alive in the fort by the Moghul emperor Aurangzeb for not embracing Islam. Cover your head to enter the *gurudwara*. Next door to Fatehgarh Sahib, the fourteenth-century *dargah* (burial shrine), dedicated to a Sufi saint, attracts busloads of Muslim pilgrims and provides a sharp reminder of the intense friction caused by the proximity of religions so fundamentally opposed.

Practicalities

Regular **buses** run between Chandigarh and Sirhind, a stopping-point on the main Delhi–Amritsar **railway**. The railway station lies 5km from the tourist complex. Buses from Amritsar usually drop passengers at the Grand Trunk Road intersection, 7km south of Aam-Khas-Bagh – catch a local bus into town or take a rickshaw.

Housed in a small eighteenth-century summer palace, the **PTDC Maulsarai Tourist Complex** (℡01763/22250; ❹) overlooks gardens and the Sheesh Mahal. The Archaeological Survey has repossessed much of the building and there is just one large but shabby room left, full of character, with high ceilings and lots of peeling plaster. Inexpensive **food**, chilled beers and cold **drinks** are served in the dining room, or alfresco on the tank-side terrace. **Mosquitoes** can be a problem, so keep the insect repellent handy. The **PTDC Bougainvillea Tourist Complex** (℡01763/40170; ❸–❻) on GT Road has ordinary, air-cooled and a/c rooms, as well as a restaurant.

Anandpur Sahib

The gleaming-white, citadel-like *gurudwara* at **ANANDPUR SAHIB** ("The City of Bliss"), stands 75km north of Chandigarh. Known as the **Gurudwara Kesgarh Sahib**, it is one of the holiest Sikh shrines, commemorating the birth of the Khalsa movement by Guru Gobind Singh three hundred years ago. Its fortress-like appearance with surrounding citadels, gates and ramparts hints at its difficult past and the long years of struggle against Muslim domination and jealous Hindu kingdoms.

Guru Gobind Singh's father, Guru Tegh Bahadur, laid the foundations in 1664, but was beheaded by the zealous Moghul emperor Aurangzeb in Delhi for refusing to convert to Islam. His head was brought back to Anandpur Sahib and cremated at the spot now marked by the shrine of **Gurudwara Sis Ganj**. Guru Gobind Singh built the fortifications which withstood a string of onslaughts from hostile neighbours, and, on March 30, 1699, Guru Gobind Singh initiated five disciples into the Khalsa, whose goals were to support the poor, fight oppression, discard dogma, superstition and caste, and be warriors of their faith.

All are welcome inside the *gurudwara* (cover head and remove shoes) to listen to the devotional singing (*kirtan*) and accompanying readings by *granthis* from the Sikh holy book, the *Guru Granth Sahib*. Every year around March the festival of **Hola Mohalla** takes place below Kesgarh Sahib, attracting thousands of people. The festival celebrates Khalsa and reinterprets the Hindu festival of colour, Holi; the festivities include displays of horsemanship and swordsmanship by the *nihangs* – an orthodox sect devoted to the great guru.

Practicalities

The infrastructure of Anandpur Sahib underwent rapid development to cope with the high number of visitors attending the tricentenary celebrations of the

Khalsa in 1999 but accommodation is limited to the *gurudwara*, ITDC's new luxury hotel and further afield at the nearest town, Ropar, there's *Pinkcassia Tourist Complex*, the Boat Club, (☎01881/22097; ③–⑤), in pleasant riverside grounds 45km south on the Chandigarh–Mandi highway. Local buses run between Ropar and Anandpur Sahib, but there are plans for a new high-speed railway line between Anandpur Sahib, New Delhi and Chandigarh.

Pathankot

The dusty town of **PATHANKOT**, 270km north of Chandigarh and 101km to the northeast of Amritsar, is an important cantonment and railway junction, close to the frontier with Pakistan and near the borders with Himachal Pradesh and Jammu. Many travellers pass through to pick up bus connections to Dharamsala, Dalhousie, Chamba and Kashmir, or to take the slow train east through the picturesque Kangra Valley.

Practicalities

Pathankot can rustle up a few **hotels**, should you need to spend the night. The *Tourist Hotel* (☎0186/20660; ②–④), on Railway Road, has reasonable rooms, while the *Khalsa Hindu*, also on Railway Road (☎0186/21093; ②–③) features three nice roof-terrace rooms, though the downstairs rooms are a bit dingy. The well-kept railway retiring rooms (☎0186/20046; Rs100, Rs 200 for air-con) are good value and the a/c rooms have sofas, carpets and private bathrooms with hot water. PTDC's *Gulmohar Tourist Complex*, Shimla Pahari, Mission Road (☎0186/20292; ③–⑤), away from the hustle and bustle, has a wide choice of rooms, restaurant and bar, and pleasant gardens ideal for breakfast or a beer in the evenings; it lies 2km from the railway station. The *Venice*, Dhangu Road (☎0186/25061; ⑥–⑦), is Pathankot's top business hotel but lacks atmosphere.

Himachal Pradesh Tourism has a downbeat but friendly **tourist office** at the railway station (Mon–Sat 10am–5pm; ☎0186/20316). **Buses** to Chamba (122km) take around five hours, and to Dalhousie (80km) three and a half. Numerous buses run to Jammu, as well as trains to Jammu Tawi for those travelling through to Srinagar. The slow narrow-gauge passenger **trains** to Jogindernagar (2 daily; 7hr 30min–9hr) wind through the scenic Kangra Valley, offering grand views of the Dhauladhar Range, and make a pleasant alternative to the busy road to both Dharamsala (change at Kangra) and the Kullu valley (bus from Jogindernagar). Other useful trains include the daily #3152 Jammu–Sealdah Express terminating in Calcutta, and the daily #4805 Jammu–Jodhpur Express.

Taxis to Dharamsala cost Rs600–900 (2hr 30min) depending on the vehicle, driver and your bargaining skills.

Amritsar

The Sikh's holy city of **AMRITSAR**, site of the fabled **Golden Temple**, is the largest city in Punjab: noisy, dirty, dusty and hopelessly congested. Its one

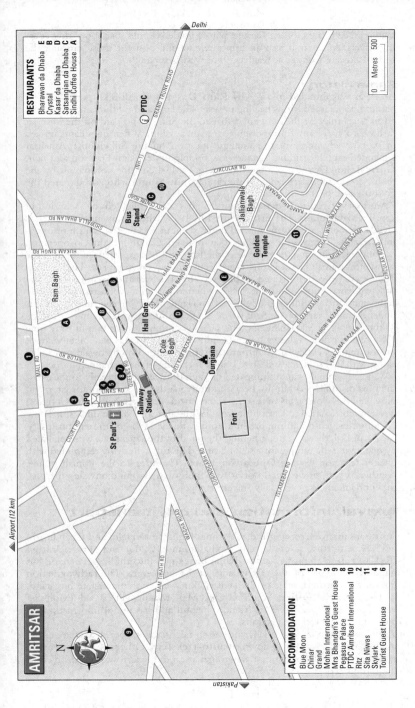

AMRITSAR

N

Airport (12 km)

Pakistan

Delhi

RESTAURANTS

Bharawan da Dhaba	E
Crystal	B
Kasar da Dhaba	D
Satsangian da Dhaba	C
Sindhi Coffee House	A

ACCOMMODATION

Blue Moon	1
Chinar	5
Grand	7
Mohan International	3
Mrs Bhandari's Guest House	9
Pegasus Palace	8
PTDC Amritsar International	10
Ritz	2
Sita Niwas	11
Skylark	4
Tourist Guest House	6

Ram Bagh

Bus Stand

Golden Temple

Jallianwala Bagh

Ramgariah Bazaar

Chatiwind Bazaar

Mukerian Bazaar

Circular Road

Hall Gate

Cole Bagh

Durgiana

Fort

Railway Station

St Paul's

GPO

PTDC

Grand Trunk Road

Inlet

City Centre Road

Circular Road

Shiwala Bhalan Rd

Hukam Singh Rd

Taylor Rd

Mall Rd

Court Rd

Queens Rd

Links Rd

Albert Rd

Wagha Road

Ram Tirath Rd

Gobindgarh Rd

Islamabad Rd

Circular Rd

Hall Bazaar

Sharifpura Mandi Bazaar

Guru Bazaar

Nimak Mandi

Lahori Bazaar

Khazana Bazaar

Petkam Bazaar

0   Metres   500

saving grace is the Golden Temple, whose golden domes soar above the teeming streets. Amritsar is also an important staging post for those crossing the Indo–Pakistani frontier at Wagha, 29km west (see p.660).

Some history

Amritsar was founded in 1577 by **Ram Das**, the fourth Sikh guru, beside a bathing pool famed for its healing powers. The land around the tank was granted in perpetuity by the Moghul Akbar to the Sikhs (who paid off the local Jat farmers to avoid any future dispute over ownership). When merchants moved in to take advantage of the strategic location on the Silk Route, Amritsar expanded rapidly, gaining a grand new temple under Ram Das' son and heir, **Guru Arjan Dev**. Sacked by Afghans in 1761, the shrine was rebuilt by the Sikhs' greatest secular leader, **Maharaja Ranjit Singh**, who also donated the gold used in its construction.

Amritsar's **twentieth–century** history has been blighted by a series of appalling **massacres**. The first occurred in 1919, when thousands of unarmed civilian demonstrators were gunned down without warning by British troops in **Jallianwalla Bagh** – an atrocity that inspired Gandhi's Non–Co-operation Movement. Following the collapse of the Raj, Amritsar experienced some of the worst communal blood-letting ever seen on the subcontinent. The Golden Temple, however, remained unaffected by the volatile politics of post-Independence Punjab until the 1980s, when as part of a protracted and bloody campaign for the setting up of a Sikh homeland, heavily armed fundamentalists under the preacher-warrior Sant Jaranil Singh **Bhindranwale** occupied the Akal Takht, symbol of Sikh militancy. The siege was brought to an end in early June 1984, when prime minister Indira Gandhi ordered an inept paramilitary attack on the temple, code-named **Operation Blue Star**. Bhindranwale was killed along with 200 soldiers, and 2000 others, including pilgrims trapped inside.

Widely regarded as an unmitigated disaster, Blue Star led directly to the assassination of Indira Gandhi by her Sikh bodyguards just four months later, and provoked the worst riots in the city since Partition. Nevertheless, the Congress government seemed to learn little from its mistakes. In 1987, Indira's son, Rajiv Gandhi, reneged on an important accord with the Sikhs' main religious party, the Akali Dal, thereby strengthening the hand of the separatists, who retaliated by occupying the temple for a second time. This time, the army responded with greater restraint, leaving **Operation Black Thunder** to the Punjab police. Neither as well provisioned nor as well motivated as Bhindranwale's martyrs, the fundamentalists eventually surrendered.

Arrival, information and city transport

Amritsar's **airport**, serving Indian Airlines flights from Delhi and Chandigarh, lies 12km northwest of the city. Taxis (around Rs200) and auto–rickshaws (Rs100) run to the town centre, while **buses** pull into the huge, frenetic bus stand off GT Road on the eastern edge of the city centre. The **railway** station lies on the northern edge of the centre, 2km west of the interstate bus stand. PTDC's **tourist office**, Youth Hostel, Mall Mandi, GT Road (Mon–Sat 9am–5pm; ☎0183/231452) is friendly, helpful and has useful information on bus and other travel connections.

Amritsar is too large and labyrinthine to negotiate on foot. If you are crossing town or in a hurry, flag down an **auto–rickshaw**. Otherwise, stick to **cycle rickshaws**, which are the best way to get around the narrow, packed streets of the old quarter.

Accommodation

Amritsar's numerous **hotels** are spread out all over the city. While mid-range and upmarket accommodation is plentiful, budget options are limited. There is the Golden Temple's *gurudwaras* (see box), the *Tourist Guest House*, on the main road between the bus stand and the railway station, which commission-hungry rickshaw-wallahs will try to tell you is full, plus a clutch of cheap Indian–oriented hotels opposite the bus stand (②–③) handy for late arrivals and for moving on.

Blue Moon, the Mall ℡0183/220416. Friendly, helpful place, much better value than its more expensive competitors. There's a decent restaurant open to nonresidents and an extraordinary miniature railway in the garden. Some economy rooms in the pipeline. ⑦

Chinar, Links Road ℡0183/564655, Clean and reasonably priced place handy for railway station; the rooms are en suite and have TV. ③–⑤

Grand, opposite the railway station ℡0183/562977. Neat, clean, convenient and central with a pleasant garden courtyard: the best in its category around the station. ⑤–⑥

Mohan International, Albert Road ℡0183/227801. One of Amritsar's top hotels but grossly overpriced. Popular for Punjabi wedding receptions which are colourful spectacles but very noisy. ⑨

Mrs Bhandari's Guest House, 10 Cantonment ℡0183/228509, ℻ 222390. Separate chalets in grounds of old colonial home. Popular with overlanders, the large lawns and gardens include a small swimming pool. "British-style" three-course meals are available for guests only. Those with tents can camp in the grounds for Rs150 per person. ⑦

Pegasus Palace, opposite the railway station ℡0183/565111. A range of reasonably clean rooms in a fading but spacious building. ③–⑥

PTDC Amritsar International, near the bus stand ℡0183/555991. Large, drab and poorly maintained government-run establishment with delusions of grandeur. ⑤–⑦

Ritz, 45 the Mall ℡0183/562836. Comfortable old hotel in a quiet suburb just north of the city centre, with lawns, gym and a pool. ⑧

Sita Niwas, near Guru Ram Das Niwas and the Golden Temple ℡0183/543092. A good and popular budget option with wide range of rooms, most en suite, and 24hr hot water. Some rooms are poky; one has a triple bed and mirrored ceiling. ③–⑥

Skylark, 79 Link Rd ℡0183/222353. One of the best options along this short road opposite the railway station; spacious rooms but expensive due to the noisy intersection. ⑥

Tourist Guest House, Hide Market, near Bhandari Bridge, GT Road ℡0183/553830. Shabby vestige of the "hippy trail" days, the guesthouse is nevertheless still popular with budget travellers. Avoid the rooms at the back next to the railway. ②–③

The Gurudwaras

Undoubtedly the most authentic places to stay in Amritsar are the Golden Temple's three **gurudwaras**. Intended for use by Sikh pilgrims, these charitable institutions also open their doors to foreign tourists, who can stay for a maximum of three nights. Lodging at *gurudwaras* is usually free, as is the Sikh custom, but donations are gratefully accepted. Of the three, the *Sri Guru Ram Das Niwas* is the larger, while the neighbouring *Sri Guru Nanak Niwas* (where Bhindranwale and his men holed up prior to the Golden Temple siege in 1984) also offers a limited number of double rooms with attached shower-toilets (①). By far the most comfortable option is the newer and clean *Guru Hargobind Niwas* (①), representing excellent value.

Apart from the inevitable dawn chorus of throat-clearing, the downside of staying in a *gurudwara* is that facilities are very basic (*charpoi* beds and communal washbasins in the central courtyard) and **security** can be a problem. During festivals, rooms and beds are at a premium and tourists are less likely to find space here.

The City

The Golden Temple stands in the heart of the **old town**: a disorientating maze of narrow lanes and bazaars. Eighteen fortified **gateways** punctuate the aptly named **Circular Road**, of which only one (to the north) is original. Skirting the edge of the old quarter, the railway line, crossed by a series of chaotic road bridges, forms a sharp divide between the bazaar and the more spacious British-built side of the city. Most of the hotels and restaurants are located in this district, around the Maginot-Line-style **railway station**. Further north, long straight tree-lined streets full of fast-moving traffic eventually peter out into leafy residential suburbs, peppered with run-down churches and colonial bungalows. The fastidiously neat military barracks of the **cantonment** form the northwestern limits of the city.

The Golden Temple

Even visitors without a religious bone in their bodies cannot fail to be moved by Amritsar's resplendent **Golden Temple**, spiritual centre of the Sikh faith and open to all. Built by Guru **Arjan Dev** in the late sixteenth century, the richly gilded **Harmandir** rises from the middle of an artificial rectangular lake, connected to the surrounding white marble complex by a narrow causeway. Every Sikh tries to make at least one pilgrimage here to listen to the sublime music (*shabad kirtan*), readings from the *Adi Granth* and also to bathe in the purifying waters of the temple tank – the **Amrit Sarovar** or "Pool of Immortality-Giving Nectar".

The best time to visit the temple is early morning to catch the first rays of sunlight gleaming on the bulbous golden domes and reflecting in the waters of the Amrit Sarovar. Sunset and evenings are an excellent time to tune in to the beautiful music performed in the Harmandir. All are welcome to sit quietly in the inner sanctum and enjoy the ambience and decor. The helpful information office (daily 8am–6.30pm) to the right of the main entrance organizes guid-

---

Bedlam at the border

Every evening as sunset approaches, the **India-Pakistan border** closes for the night with a spectacular and somewhat Pythonesque show. It takes place at a remote little place called Wagha, 27km west of Amritsar, and has become a popular tourist attraction, especially on a Sunday. Hundreds if not thousands of Indians make their way westwards to Wagha (and Pakistanis eastwards) where they congregate, eat ice cream and wait for the setting of the sun. The nearest town, 2km away, is Attari, connected by frequent minibuses to Amritsar.

Indian guards sporting outrageous moustaches and outlandish hats entertain the crowds, who watch from specially erected stands; the guards perform synchronized speed marching along a 100-metre walkway to the border gate where they turn and stomp back. Raucous cheering, clapping and much blowing of horns accompanies the spectacle. Guards on the Pakistan side then emulate their neighbours' efforts to much the same sort of cacophony on the other side of the gate. Several times the guards strut their military catwalk and then vanish into the guardhouse. Flags are simultaneously lowered, the gates slammed shut and the crowds on either side rush forward for a massive and congenial photo session. The tension dissolves and the people on both sides realize their common divided fate. Suddenly more empathy than ever occurs on a cricket pitch permeates the air, hundreds of photos are taken, and then everyone heads home – back to business as usual.

Visitors of all nationalities and religions are allowed into the Golden Temple provided they respect a few basic **rules**, enforced by patrolling guards. Firstly, tobacco, alcohol and drugs of any kind are forbidden. Before entering, you should also leave your shoes at the free cloakrooms, cover your head (cotton scarves are available outside the main entrance – or wear your Kullu hat), and wash your feet in the pool below the steps. **Photography** is permitted outside, but not inside any of the shrines.

ed tours, provides details on temple accommodation and has books and leaflets about the temple and Sikh faith.

The Parikrama

The principal north entrance to the temple, the **Darshini Deori**, leads under a Victorian **clocktower** to a flight of steps, from where you catch your first glimpse of the Harmandir, floating serenely above the glassy surface of the Amrit Sarovar. Dropping down as a reminder of the humility necessary to approach God, the steps end at the polished marble **Parikrama** that surrounds the tank, its smooth white stones set with the names of those who contributed to the temple's construction.

The shrines on the north edge of the enclosure are known as the **68 Holy Places**. Arjan Dev, the fifth guru, told his followers that a visit to these was equivalent to a pilgrimage around all 68 of India's most sacred Hindu sites. Several have been converted into a **Gallery of Martyrs**, in which paintings of glorious but gory episodes from Sikh history are displayed.

Four glass-fronted booths punctuate the Parikrama. Seated in each is a priest, or **granthi**, intoning verses from the *Adi Granth*. The continuous readings are performed in shifts; passing pilgrims touch the steps in front of the booths with their heads and leave offerings of money.

At the east end of the Parikrama, the two truncated **Ramgarhia Minars** – brick watchtowers whose tops were blasted off during Operation Blue Star – overlook the Guru-ka-Langar and the main bathing **ghats**. Hang around here long enough, and you'll see a fair cross-section of modern Sikh society parade past: families of Jat farmers, NRIs (Non-Resident Indians) on holiday from Britain and North America flaunting flash video cameras, and the odd group of fierce-looking warriors carrying lances, sabres and long curved daggers. Distinguished by their deep-blue knee-length robes and saffron turbans, the ultra-orthodox **nihangs** (literally "crocodiles") are devotees of the militaristic tenth guru, Gobind Singh.

The Guru-ka-Langar

For Sikhs, no pilgrimage to the Golden Temple is considered complete without a visit to the **Guru-ka-Langar**. The giant communal canteen, which overlooks the eastern entrance to the temple complex, provides **free food** to all-comers, regardless of creed, colour, caste or gender. Sharing meals with strangers in this way is intended to reinforce one of the central tenets of the Sikh faith, the **principle of equality**, instigated by the third guru, **Amar Das**, in the sixteenth century to break down caste barriers.

The tradition of commensality is still practised in *gurudwaras* all over India, but nowhere more forcefully reaffirmed than here at the Langar. Some 10,000 chapati and black dhal dinners are dished up each day in an operation of typical Sikh efficiency, which you can witness for yourself by joining the queues that form outside the hall at meal times (daily 11am–3pm & 7–9pm). When the doors open, up to 3000 pilgrims at a time pile in to take their places on the long coir floor mats. The meal begins only after grace has been sung with great solemnity by a volunteer, or *sevak*, and continues until everyone has eaten their fill. By the time the tin trays have been collected up and the floors swept for the next sitting, another crowd of hungry pilgrims has gathered at the gates, and the cycle starts again. Although the meals are paid for out of the temple's coffers, most visitors leave a small donation in the boxes in the yard outside.

The Akal Takht

Directly opposite the ceremonial entrance to the Harmandir, the **Akal Takht** is the second most sacred shrine in the Golden Temple complex. A symbol of God's authority on earth, it was built by Guru Hargobind in the seventeenth century and came to house the Shiroman Gurudwara Parbandhak committee, the religious and political governing body of the Sikh faith founded in 1925.

During the 1984 siege, **Bhindranwale** and his army used this golden–domed building as their headquarters, fortifying it with sandbags and machine-gun

---

The Jallianwalla Bagh massacre

Only 100m northeast of the Golden Temple, a narrow lane leads between two tall buildings to Jallianwalla Bagh memorial park (April–Sept 9am–5pm, Oct–March 10am–4pm), site of one of the bloodiest atrocities committed in the history of the British Raj.

In 1919, a series of one-day strikes, or *hartals*, was staged in Amritsar in protest against the recent Rowlatt Act, which enabled the British to imprison without trial any Indian suspected of sedition. When the peaceful demonstrations escalated into sporadic looting, the Lieutenant Governor of Punjab declared martial law and called for reinforcements from Jalandhar. A platoon of infantry arrived soon after, led by General R.E.H. Dyer.

Despite a ban on public meetings, a mass demonstration was called by Mahatma Gandhi for April 13, the Sikh holiday of Bhaisakhi. The venue was a stretch of waste ground in the heart of the city, hemmed in by high brick walls and with only a couple of alleys for access. An estimated 20,000 people gathered in Jallianwalla Bagh for the meeting. However, before any speakers could address the crowd, Dyer and his 150 troops, stationed on a patch of high ground in front of the main exit, opened fire without warning. By the time they had finished firing, ten to fifteen minutes later, the unarmed demonstrators lay dead and dying, many of them shot in the back while clambering over the walls. Others perished after diving for cover into the well that still stands in the middle of the *bagh*.

No one knows exactly how many people were killed. Official estimates put the death toll at 379, with 1200 injured, although the final figure may well have been three to four times higher. Hushed up for over six months in Britain, the Jallianwalla Bagh massacre caused an international outcry when the story finally broke. It also proved seminal in the Independence struggle, prompting Gandhi to initiate the widespread civil disobedience campaign that played such a significant part in ridding India of its colonial overlords.

Moving first-hand accounts of the horrific events of April 13, 1919, and contemporary pictures and newspaper reports, are displayed in Jallianwalla Bagh's small martyrs gallery. The well, complete with chilling bullet holes, has been turned into a memorial to the victims.

posts. When Indian paratroopers tried to storm the shrine, they were mown down in their hundreds while crossing the courtyard in front of it: the reason why the army ultimately resorted to much heavier-handed tactics to end the siege. Positioned at the opposite end of the Amrit Sarovar, tanks pumped a salvo of high-explosive squash-head shells into the delicate facade, reducing it to rubble within seconds. The destruction of the Akal Takht offended Sikh sensibilities more than any other aspect of the operation.

The shrine has been largely rebuilt and now looks almost the same as it did before June 6, 1984. Decorated with elaborate inlay, its ground floor is where the *Adi Granth* is brought each evening from the Harmandir, borne in a gold and silver paladin.

The Jubi Tree

The gnarled old **Jubi Tree** in the northwest corner of the compound was planted 450 years ago by the Golden Temple's first high priest, or *Babba Buddhaya*, and is believed to have special powers. Barren women wanting a son hang strips of cloth from its branches, while marriage deals are traditionally struck in its shade for good luck – a practice frowned upon by the modern temple administration.

The Harmandir

Likened by one guru to "a ship crossing the ocean of ignorance", the triple-storey **Harmandir**, or "Golden Temple of God" was built by Arjan Dev to house the *Adi Granth*, (Original Book), which he compiled from teachings of all the Sikh gurus; it is the focus of the Sikh faith. The temple has four doors indicating it is open to people of all faiths and all four caste divisions of Hindu society. The large dome and roof, covered with 100kg of gold leaf, is shaped like an inverted lotus, symbolizing the Sikhs' concern for temporal as well as spiritual matters.

The long causeway, or "**Guru's Bridge**", which joins the *mandir* to the west side of the Amrit Sarovar, is approached via an ornate archway, the **Darshani Deorh**. As you approach the sanctum check out the amazing Moghul-style marble inlay work and beautiful floral gilt above the doors and windows.

The **interior** of the temple – decorated with yet more gold and silver, adorned with ivory mosaics and intricately carved wood panels – is dominated by the enormous **Adi Granth**, which rests on a sumptuous throne beneath a jewel-encrusted silk canopy. Before his death in 1708, Guru Gobind Singh, who revised the *Adi Granth*, declared that he was to be the last living guru, and that the tome would take over after him – hence its full title, the *Guru Granth Sahib*. *Granthis* intone continuous readings from the text as the worshippers file past, accompanied by singers and musicians, whose ethereal performance is relayed by loudspeakers around the complex. Known as *Shri Akhand Path*, a single continuous reading of the *Guru Granth Sahib* is carried out in three-hour shifts and takes around 48 hours to complete.

Eating

Amritsar boasts a clutch of swish a/c **restaurants**, mostly located in the modern end of town north of the railway. For cheaper food, try the simple vegetarian **dhabas** around the Golden Temple and bus stand serving cheap and tasty *puris* and *chana* dhal. Some local specialities are **Amritsari fish** and *pinnies* and *matthies*, sweets made from lentils available at *Durga*'s on Lawrence Road.

Bharawan da Dhaba, near the Town Hall. One of the best *dhabas* in Amritsar, not far from the Golden Temple. Cheap, wholesome and recommended.

Crystal, Crystal Chowk. One of the city's most popular restaurants, with mid-priced Indian, Chinese and Continental dishes served in comfortable surroundings, or from "fast-food" outlets on the street.

Kasar da Dhaba, near Durgiana Temple. Another great dhaba which through its success has developed several branches throughout the city.

Prabhat, ground floor, *Hotel Pegasus Palace*, opposite the railway station. *Dhaba*–style restaurant serving generous portions. Cheap, but low on atmosphere.

Satsangian da Dhaba, 126 City Centre, right opposite bus station. Excellent cheap *parathas* and veg food and efficient service.

Sindhi Coffee House, opposite Ram Bagh. Tinted windows and tablecloths, and an exhaustive mixed-cuisine menu that includes several Sindhi specialities. Moderate to expensive.

Moving on from Amritsar

Amritsar is a major hub for traffic heading northeast to Jammu & Kashmir, southeast towards Delhi via Chandigarh (the main jumping-off place for Shimla and central HP), and west to India's only land-border crossing point with Pakistan at Wagha.

All state **buses** depart from the massive bus station located off the Delhi Road (NH-1), while private buses including a/c services leave from around Pink Plaza or Gandhi Gate. Agencies such as Sanan Travels (☎0183/223522) and Maharajah Travels (☎0183/500768), operate deluxe and a/c buses to **Delhi** (8hr) and **Chandigarh** (225km; 4–5hr). For **Pathankot** (101km) and other connections to Himachal Pradesh, you are restricted to state transport buses, but the journey is relatively painless. Delhi, 475km away, is a long tiring road journey and most travellers prefer to go by train.

The best **trains** for Delhi are the daily superfast all a/c chaircar Amritsar–New Delhi Shatabdis – the #2014 (dep 5.15am arr 10.50am) and the #2030 (dep 17.05, arr 22.50). Other trains include the Amritsar–New Delhi Express #4660 (dep 6.15am; 8hr) and the #4648 *Flying Mail* to Old Delhi (11.30am; 9hr), as well as the daily #3050 Amritsar–Howrah Express via Varanasi; the daily #1058 Amritsar–Dadar Express to Mumbai; and the twice-weekly (Wed & Sun) #9772 Amritsar–Jaipur Express. **Flights** to Delhi are run by Indian Airlines (Tues, Wed & Sat; 55min) and Air India (Wed, Sun).

For **Pakistan**, take one of the frequent buses to **Attari**, from where it's just 2km to the border at **Wagha**, or hire a taxi from Amritsar the whole way. Rickshaws are available between Attari and Wagha. You'll have to cross into Pakistan by foot – it can take up to two hours to complete formalities. Tourists just wishing to watch the bizarre border spectacle (see box p.660) can rent taxis or auto-rickshaws for the round trip but if you need to stay the night near the border, accommodation is available at the *Neem Chameli Tourist Complex* (❹), which has air-cooled rooms, restaurant and bar, or the *Niagara Falls Hotel* (☎0183/382646; ❺). Onward connections to Lahore from the Pakistani side of the frontier are generally good. Twice a week (on Mon & Thurs) the #4607 Amritsar–Lahore Samjhauta Express **train** leaves Amritsar for Lahore at 7am, reaching Wagha at 7.40am. It is then scheduled to leave Wagha at 11.30am, to reach Lahore at 4.15pm but is invariably delayed. In the other direction, the #4608 Lahore–Amritsar Express (Tues & Fri) departs at 8am, reaching Wagha at 12.30pm and is scheduled to depart from Wagha at 2.20pm, arriving in Amritsar at 3pm.

A full rundown of destinations reachable by train and bus from Amritsar is given opposite.

Listings

Airlines The main Indian Airlines office is on Court Road ☎0183/213392; Air India (☎0183/546122) is located at the *Amritsar International Hotel* complex near the bus stand.

Ambulance ☎0183/220900 or 501702.

Banks and exchange Several banks offer foreign exchange facilities including the State Bank of India, halfway between the bus stand and the Golden Temple, the Bank of Punjab, near the temple, and the Chartered Bank and ANZ Grindlays, both at Hall Bazaar. Authorized agencies such as Narang Travels at the *Amritsar International Hotel* arcade, near the bus stand, also change money.

Hospitals Kakkar Hospital, Green Avenue (☎0183/506015); Sri Guru Nanak Dev, Majhita Road (☎0183/212837); and Munilal Chopra Hospital, Mall Road (☎0183/223046) are the best in the city.

Left luggage can be left for short periods at the Golden Temple's *gurudwaras*, or at the railway station cloakroom.

Police ☎100 or 0183/228185.

Shopping *Tablas* (hand-drums), harmonia and other musical instruments are available at the shops outside the Golden Temple, where you can also buy cheap cassettes of the beautiful *kirtan* played in the shrine itself. Other possible souvenirs include a pair of traditional *Arabian Nights*-style Punjabi leather slippers – sold at stalls east of the temple's main entrance.

Swimming pools Both the *Mohan International* and *Ritz* hotels allow discretionary use of their outdoor pools (nonresidents Rs150, towels not included).

Travel agents Narang Travels, 2 *Amritsar International Hotel* (☎0183/554902) are good for most air ticketing.

Travel details

Trains

Amritsar to: Agra (2 daily; 13–16hr); Calcutta (2 daily; 37–45hr); Chandigarh (1 daily; 6hr); Delhi (11 daily; 5hr 30min–12hr); Gwalior (1 daily; 18hr); Jhansi (1 daily; 20hr 35min); Mumbai (3 daily; 31hr 25min–44hr); Pathankot (3 daily; 2hr 30min–3hr); Varanasi (2 daily; 22–26hr).

Chandigarh to: Amritsar (1 daily; 6 hr); Delhi (4 daily; 3hr 30min–6hr); Jodhpur (1 daily; 21 hr); Kalka (3 daily; 45min–1hr 10min).

Pathankot to: Amritsar (3 daily; 2hr 30min–3hr); Calcutta (Sealdah – 1 daily; 42hr); Delhi (4 daily; 10hr 30min–13hr); Jodhpur (1 daily; 20hr) Jogindernagar (2 daily; 7hr 30min–9hr); Varanasi (1 daily; 27hr).

Buses

Amritsar to: Chandigarh (30min; 5–6hr); Delhi (12 daily; 8–10hr); Dharamsala (1 daily; 7hr); Kullu (1 daily; 16hr); Pathankot (hourly; 3hr); Wagha/Attari (hourly; 45min).

Chandigarh to: Agra (1 daily; 10hr); Amritsar (every 30min; 5–6hr); Anandpur Sahib (8 daily; 3–4hr); Chamba (6 daily; 12hr); Dehra Dun (7 daily; 4hr); Delhi (every 20min; 6hr); Dharamsala (hourly; 7–8hr); Haridwar (7 daily; 6hr); Jaipur (7 daily; 11hr); Kalka (every 20min; 40min); Kasauli (5 daily; 2hr 30min); Kullu (12 daily; 6hr 30min); Manali (12 daily; 8hr); Rishikesh (2 daily; 6hr); Shimla (every 30min; 4hr–4hr 30min); Sirhind (hourly; 1hr 30min).

Pathankot to: Ambala (every 20min; 7hr); Amritsar (every 15min; 3hr); Chamba (hourly; 5hr); Dalhousie (hourly; 3hr 30min); Delhi (every 20min; 11hr); Dharamsala (12 daily; 3hr 30min); Jammu (every 10min; 3hr); Jullundhar (hourly; 3hr); Kangra (10 daily; 3–4hr); Manali (5 daily; 12hr); Mandi (5 daily; 8hr); Shimla (5 daily; 12hr).

Flights

Amritsar to: Delhi (5 weekly; 55min).

Chandigarh to: Amritsar (2 weekly; 30min); Delhi (2 weekly; 2hr); Leh (1 weekly; 1hr).

CHAPTER 9

Highlights

✱ **Ahmedabad** Superb Indo-Islamic architecture and bustling bazaars; outlying sights include Mahatma Gandhi's Sabarmati ashram. **See p.672**

✱ **Sun Temple, Modhera** A beautiful eleventh-century temple, set in peaceful gardens: the finest example of Solanki architecture. **See p.688**

✱ **Rani-ki-vav, Patan** This delicately sculpted underground edifice is the zenith of Gujarat's famous step-wells. **See p.689**

✱ **Dwarkadish temple** Important pilgrimage centre as the westernmost holy town, famed in legend as Krishna's capital. **See p.704**

✱ **Sasan Gir** The protected forest here is the last remaining habitat of the rare Asiatic lion. **See p.714**

✱ **Diu** This relaxed island is west India's most congenial beach venue, with a Portuguese flavour in its colonial architecture. **See p.715**

✱ **Palitana temples** Shatrunjaya Hill bristles with sumptuously carved marble shrines and provides stunning views. **See p.723**

✱ **Champaner** A Solanki fortress and Jain temples are among the attractions around this ancient Muslim city. **See p.729**

9

Gujarat

The western state of **GUJARAT** was tragically catapulted to international attention in January 2001 by a cataclysmic **earthquake**, its epicentre in the western region of Kutch, that left at least 30,000 dead and 250,000 homeless (see box p.693). This sudden disaster added to the woes of a state already beleaguered by severe **water shortages** following three consecutive failed monsoons. Measures adopted to combat that problem – the import of water by train and longer-term solutions like the construction of bore-wells, desalination plants and the world's largest canal system – had already taxed state coffers before the earthquake struck. Gujarat's established reputation as India's **wealthiest state**, however, places it in a better position for recovery than other parts of the country might have been.

The region's prosperity dates as far back as the third millennium BC, when the **Harappans** started trading shell jewellery and textiles. The Jain-dominated textile industry remains an important source of income to the state, as do crafts to villagers on a smaller scale. Gujarat also boasts some of the subcontinent's biggest oil refineries, and Kandla, India's **largest port**, handles one third of the country's imports. There is also a vast and lucrative shipbreaking yard at Alang; and eighty percent of the country's diamond cutting and polishing takes place in centres such as Ahmedabad and Surat.

Notwithstanding its recent tragedy, Gujarat has plenty to offer those who take time to detour from its more famous northerly neighbour Rajasthan and is free of the hard-sell and hassle that tourists often encounter there. The lure of important **temple cities forts** and **palaces** is balanced by the chance to search out unique crafts made in tribal communities whose way of life remains scarcely affected by global trends.

As so often in India, Gujarat's **architectural diversity** reflects the influences of its many different rulers – the Buddhist Mauryans, who also supported the Jain faith, Hindu rajas and Muslim emperors, who combined their skills and tastes with Hindu craftsmanship to produce remarkable mosques, tombs and palaces. **Ahmedabad**, state capital until 1970 and the obvious place to begin a tour, harbours the first mosques built in the curious **Indo-Islamic** style, as well as richly carved temples and step-wells dating to the eleventh century. Its fascinating residential areas are lined with tall wooden *havelis* (ornate mansions), carved in finest detail by prosperous merchants from the eighteenth century onwards. From Ahmedabad it's an easy trip north to the ancient capital of **Patan** and the Solanki sun temple at **Modhera**, or south to the excavated Harappan site at **Lothal**. In the northwest, the largely barren region of **Kutch** – occasionally cut off from the rest of the state by vast tracts of flooded marshland – was bypassed by Gujarat's successive waves of foreign invaders.

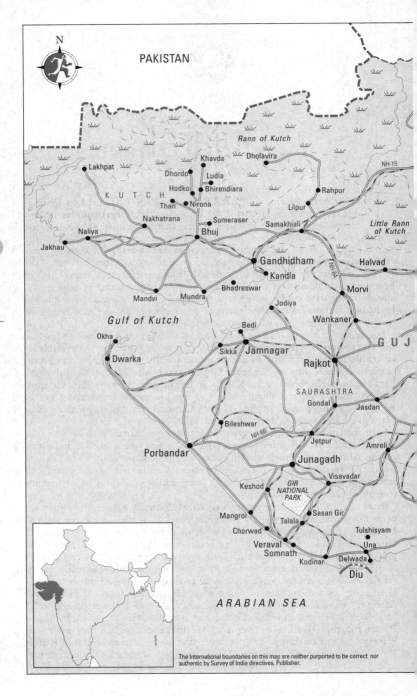

The International boundaries on this map are neither purported to be correct nor authentic by Survey of India directives. Publisher.

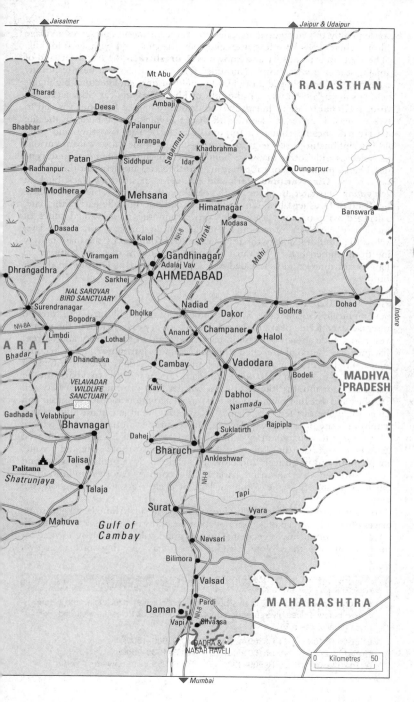

Consequently, this intriguing area, despite its recent travails, preserves a village culture where crafts long forgotten elsewhere are practised with age-old skill.

The Kathiawar peninsula, also known as **Saurashtra**, is the true heartland of Gujarat, scattered with temples, mosques, forts and palaces that bear testimony to centuries of rule by Buddhists, Hindus and Muslims. Architectural highlights include superb Jain temples on the hills of **Shatrunjaya**, near Bhavnagar, and **Mount Girnar**, close to Junagadh. The coastal temple at **Somnath** is said to have witnessed the dawn of time, and that at **Dwarka** to be built on the site of Krishna's ancient capital. At **Junagadh**, rocks bearing two-thousand-year-old inscriptions from the reign of Ashoka stand a stone's throw from curious mausoleums and Gothic mansions built by the Muslims in the nineteenth century. There's plenty of scope for spotting **wildlife**, too, in particular the lions in the forested **Gir National Park** and the herds of strutting black buck at **Velavadar**. Separated from the south coast by a thin sliver of the Arabian Sea, the island of **Diu**, actually a Union Territory and not officially part of the state, is fringed with beaches, leafy palm groves and the whitewashed spires of Portuguese churches, providing an idyllic setting for lazy sun-kissed days. Across the Gulf of Cambay, the thin coastal strip followed by the main railway line from Ahmedabad to Mumbai features a few towns of more commercial than tourist interest and the faded old Portuguese port of **Daman** in the far south.

Visiting Gujarat

Geographically Gujarat takes a little from each of its neighbours: with forested hilly tracts and fertile plains in the south and east, dry desert sands in the northwest and a wide stretch of coast, in parts sandy, and in parts rocky and barren, that includes the coral-enriched shoreline close to **Jamnagar**. It can become unbearably hot in summer, though a cool sea breeze does relieve the tension of heavy pre-monsoon days along the coast. The **best time to visit** is in the warm pleasant months (though nights can get chilly in midwinter) between October and February, when you may also encounter traditional music and dances at numerous festivals. Thanks to extensive road and train links, **travel** within the state presents few problems, but communication barriers do require a little effort to overcome (few timetables are written in English). You'll need stamina to negotiate the slow train journeys but buses, both state and private, are plentiful and not usually too crowded, while roads are generally wider and better surfaced than in many parts of the country. Another indication of Gujarat's prosperity is the complete lack of cycle rickshaws throughout the state.

You'll be hard pushed to find a luxury **hotel** outside Ahmedabad and some places offer little choice of accommodation beyond spartan lodges. As for **food**, which is predominantly vegetarian, Gujarat's good-value thalis are renowned for their size and sweetness. Note that Gujarat is India's only **dry state**: to enjoy a

---

Accommodation price codes

All accommodation prices in this book have been categorized using the price codes below. Prices given are for a double room, and all taxes are included. For more details, see p.51.

❶ up to Rs100	❹ Rs300–400	❼ Rs900–1500
❷ Rs100–200	❺ Rs400–600	❽ Rs1500–2500
❸ Rs200–300	❻ Rs600–900	❾ Rs2500 and upwards

Tattoos

If you spend any time in the rural areas of Gujarat, or come across tribal people in the cities, you'll notice the heavy blues and blacks of **tattoos** that cover the arms, hands, faces and torsos of most tribal women and many tribal men. This art, **chhundana padavava**, has been practised for centuries, and like *mehandi* – rich red henna patterns stencilled onto hands and feet – is a traditional form of beautification and identification.

For women, the typical rows and symmetrical designs of dots and simple shapes around necks, wrists and ear lobes are endowed with the power to attract men and increase chances of love at first sight, as well as ensuring fidelity in a spouse. In some regions, a woman without *chhundana* is thought to have less chance of bearing children, and runs the risk of reincarnation as a camel. Tattoos of scorpions and serpents are believed to protect from bites and stings, while images of butter-churning paddles, *ravaiyo*, guarantee a continuous flow of milk from the family cattle. Men who are initiated into the occult and practise "black magic" bear a *narmund*, a human skull, on their chest, while a weighing scale on the palm of a woman's hand indicates that she has been offered in marriage without a dowry demanded from her parents. The actual process of tattooing is often carried out amid dancing, singing and the pulsating beat of *dhola* drums.

cold beer, you'll have to head to the Union Territory enclaves of Daman and Diu or get a permit at one of the few hotels allowed to serve alcohol.

Some history

The first known settlers in what is now Gujarat were the **Harappans**, who appeared from Punjab in around 2500 BC and established over a hundred towns and cities. Their skilful craftsmanship, combined with important trade links with Africans, Arabs, Persians and Europeans, won them prosperity; despite this, the civilization fell into decline in 1900 BC, largely because of severe flooding around the Indus delta. From 1500 to 500 BC the **Yadavas**, Krishna's clan, held sway over much of Gujarat, with their capital at Dwarka on the western tip of Saurashtra.

Gujarat's political history begins in earnest with the powerful **Mauryan empire**, established by Chandragupta with its capital at Junagadh, then known as Girinagar, and reaching its peak under Ashoka. After his death in 226 BC, Mauryan power dwindled; the last significant ruler was Samprati, Ashoka's grandson, a Jain who built fabulous temples at *tirthas* (pilgrimage sites) such as Girnar and Palitana.

In the first century AD the Western **Satraps**, members of the Saka (Scythian) tribes, gained control of Saurashtra. They ruled it until soon after 388 AD, before rule passed first to the **Guptas** and then to the **Maitrakas** who established their capital at Valabhi. The ensuing centuries saw the arrival of the northern Gurjar tribes, who were to give the state its name, and the Kathi tribespeople from the northwest, who established several small independent states in Saurashtra. The rulers of Sind (now in Pakistan) meanwhile dominated western Gujarat, including Kutch.

In the eleventh and twelfth centuries Saurashtra came under the sway of the **Solanki** (or Chauhan) dynasty; their splendid Jain temples suffered during the raids of Mahmud of Ghazni in 1027, but Muslim rule was not established until the Khalji conquest in 1299. Eight years later, Muzaffar Shah's declaration of independence from Delhi marked the foundation of the **Sultanate of**

Gujarat, which lasted until its conquest by the Moghul emperor Akbar in the sixteenth century. In this period Muslim, Jain and Hindu styles were melded to produce remarkable Indo-Islamic mosques and tombs, characterized by the elaborate carvings found in Jain temples, and intersected in Hindu fashion by slender pillars meeting in delicate arches. Contrary to impressions encouraged by recent sectarian violence, particularly in Ahmedabad, Islam never eclipsed Hinduism or Jainism, and the three have lived side by side for centuries.

In the 1500s, the **Portuguese**, already settled in Goa, turned their attention to the Gujarati coast, aware of the excellent potential of its ports and its long history of trade. Having captured Daman in 1531, they took Diu four years later, building forts and typically European towns and coming to dominate the oceans with the imposition of high taxes and import duties. Fending off Arab and Muslim attacks, the Portuguese governed the ports until they were subsumed under the Indian Union in the 1960s.

The **British East India Company** set up its original Indian headquarters in Surat in 1613, and soon established their first "factory", a self-contained village for labourers' and merchants' houses and warehouses, sowing the seeds of a prospering textile industry. When British sovereignty was established in 1818, governor generals moved into some of Gujarat's main cities, though the peninsula of Saurashtra never passed into British control and remained an amalgamation of over two hundred petty states until Independence. British rule brought mixed results: while machinery upgraded textile manufacture and brought substantial wealth to the region, many manual labourers were put out of business. Their cause was valiantly fought by Gujarat-born **Mahatma Gandhi** (see box p.706), whose campaigns for Independence and social equality brought international attention to his ashram in Ahmedabad. After Partition, due to its position bordering the new Muslim state of Pakistan, Gujarat received an influx of Hindus from Sind and witnessed terrible sectarian fighting as Muslims fled to their new homeland.

In 1960, after the Marathi and Gujarati **language riots** (demonstrators sought the redrawing of state boundaries according to language, as had happened in the south), Bombay state was split and Gujarat state created. The Portuguese enclaves, along with Goa, were forcibly annexed by the Indian government in 1961. After Independence Gujarat was a staunch Congress stronghold, apart from a brief defeat by the Janata party in 1977, until the fundamentalists of the BJP took control of the state in 1991. They retained their majority by a narrow margin in the 1998 state elections but signs suggest that their increasing unpopularity will be reflected in defeat next time.

Ahmedabad

AHMEDABAD, a mass of factories, mosques, temples and high-rise offices, sprawls along the banks of the River Sabarmati some 90km from its mouth in the Bay of Cambay. First impressions can be poor: Gujarat's largest city is a dirty, polluted place, noisy with a grumbling flow of traffic. Give it a little time, however, and the mix of ancient and modern – along with the combination of thriving Hindu, Muslim and Jain communities – lends the city an appealing character that can be hard to resist. Although it suffered quite badly in the 2001 earthquake (see p.693), damage was sustained more in outlying residential areas than the parts that attract visitors.

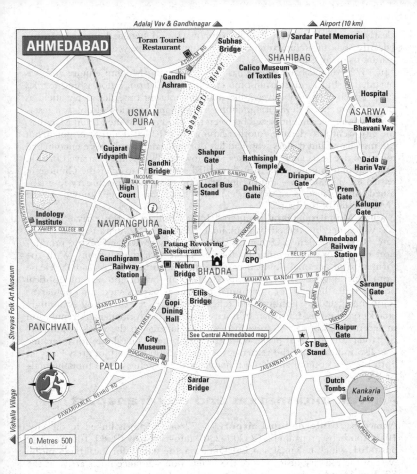

AHMEDABAD

Toran Tourist Restaurant

Subhas Bridge

Sardar Patel Memorial

SHAHIBAG

Calico Museum of Textiles

Gandhi Ashram

Hospital

USMAN PURA

ASARWA

Mata Bhavani Vav

Gujarat Vidyapith

Shahpur Gate

Hathisingh Temple

Dada Harin Vav

Gandhi Bridge

INCOME TAX CIRCLE

KASTORBA GANDHI RD

Diriapur Gate

High Court

Local Bus Stand

Delhi Gate

Prem Gate

Indology Institute

ST XAVIER'S COLLEGE RD

Kalupur Gate

NAVRANGPURA

Bank

Patang Revolving Restaurant

Ahmedabad Railway Station

RELIEF RD

Gandhigram Railway Station

Nehru Bridge

BHADRA

GPO

MAHATMA GANDHI RD (M G RD)

Sarangpur Gate

Ellis Bridge

SARDAR PATEL RD

PANCHVATI

Gopi Dining Hall

See Central Ahmedabad map

Raipur Gate

City Museum

ST Bus Stand

PALDI

JAGANNATHJI RD

Dutch Tombs

Sardar Bridge

Kankaria Lake

DAWAHARLAL NEHRU RD

LALPITHI RD

0 Metres 500

▲ Shreyas Folk Art Museum

▲ Vishalla Village

9

GUJARAT | Ahmedabad

A wander through the bazaars and *pols* (residential areas) of the bustling **old city** is rewarding enough, but Ahmedabad is also packed with a pungent diversity of architectural styles, with over fifty mosques and tombs, as well as Hindu and Jain temples and grand step-wells (*vavs*). Among the most outstanding monuments are **Sidi Sayyid's Mosque**, the hybrid **Jami Masjid**, the **Dada Harini Vav** and **Bhadra Fort**. In addition, assorted **museums** provide a good introduction to Gujarati culture: the extensive **Calico Museum of Textiles** in the northern district of Shahi Bagh rates as one of the world's finest and Mahatma Gandhi's **Sabarmati Ashram** has an exhibition on his life and the Indian Freedom Movement.

Some history

When **Ahmed Shah** inherited the Sultanate of Gujarat in 1411, he chose to move his capital from Patan to the site of Asawal village, a small settlement on the east bank of the Sabarmati, renaming it after himself. The city quickly grew as skilled artisans and traders were invited to settle. Its splendid mosques were clearly intended to assert Muslim supremacy, and heralded the new **Indo–Islamic** style of architecture, which, though best displayed here, is a marked feature of many Gujarati cities.

In 1572, Ahmedabad became part of the growing Moghul empire and was regarded as India's most handsome city. It profited from a flourishing textiles trade which exported velvets, silks and shimmering brocades as far afield as Europe. But after a devastating famine in 1630 and a period of political instability when government passed between the Muslims and the Hindu Marathas, the city went into decline. Another famine in 1812 left it almost crippled, but the merchants and traders who had left during Maratha rule were encouraged to return five years later when taxes were lowered by the newly arrived British. Trade in opium grew – the British needed something to offer the Chinese in return for silk and tea – and the introduction of modern machinery re-established Ahmedabad as a textile exporter that came to be known as the "Manchester of the East".

When **Mahatma Gandhi** entered Indian politics in the early 1900s, he was welcomed by Ahmedabad's manual labourers as a Gujarati and an advocate of self-sufficiency. Under his guidance they revitalized textile production once more and eventually formed protective trade unions. With the formation of national political parties and the imminence of India's release from British governance, the city became an important seat of political power, and a hotbed for communal tension as parties vied for popularity. Riots instigated by political and religious differences, including some ugly attacks on the tiny Christian minority, have sullied Ahmedabad's reputation in recent years but have done little lasting damage to the city's communities; today the city is at peace with itself once more. The desire for tolerance was also indicated by the return to power in 2000 of the Congress Party in both the city council and key *panchayats* at the expense of the fundamentalist BJP.

Arrival, information and city transport

Ahmedabad's **international airport** (☎079/642 5633) is linked to the city, 10km south, by prepaid taxi (Rs200–250), auto-rickshaw (Rs80–100) and city bus #101, which terminates at **Lal Darwaja**, the station for local buses in the west of the old city, near most of the hotels. Long-distance buses arrive at the **ST Bus Stand** in the southeast of the old city, 1km from the hotels, while the **railway station** is to the east, at the far end of Relief Road and MG Road. City buses to Lal Darwaja run from both the railway station (#48, #122 and #133) and the bus stand (#13/1, #32 and #52/2). Metered **taxis** and mostly unmetered auto-rickshaws are in abundance at the airport, the railway station and both bus stands.

Although most of the action is on the east bank of the Sabarmati, the efficient and welcoming main **tourist office** is across the river in HK House, just off Ashram Road, 1km north of Nehru Bridge (Mon–Sat, 10.30am–1.30pm & 2–6pm, closed 2nd & 4th Sat of month; ☎079/658 9683, ℻658 2183, ℮ahmedabad@gujarattourism.com). Provided they have more than ten takers (which isn't that often), the municipal corporation run a four-hour **city bus tour** from an office on platform #0 at Lal Darwaja (daily 9.30am & 2pm; Rs35; book a day in advance on ☎079/535 2911). They also organize a Heritage Walk of Ahmedabad – ask at the tourist office for details.

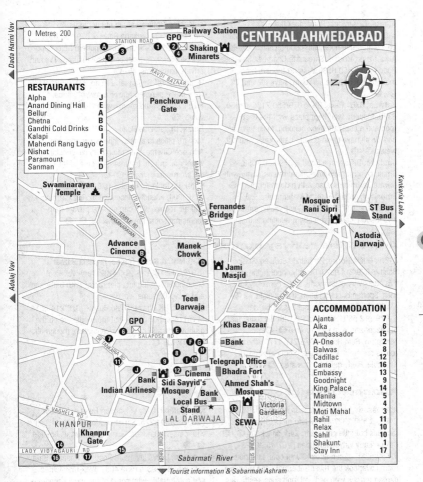

CENTRAL AHMEDABAD

0 Metres 200

Dada Harini Vav
Adalaj Vav

STATION ROAD
Railway Station
GPO
Shaking Minarets
RAVDI BAZAAR
Panchkuva Gate

RESTAURANTS

Alpha	J
Anand Dining Hall	E
Bellur	A
Chetna	B
Gandhi Cold Drinks	G
Kalapi	I
Mahendi Rang Lagyo	C
Nishat	F
Paramount	H
Sanman	D

Swaminarayan Temple

TEMPLE RD
SWAMINARAYAN
RELIEF RD / TILAK RD
MAHATMA GANDHI RD / M.G.RD

Advance Cinema

Manek Chowk

Fernandes Bridge

Mosque of Rani Sipri

ST Bus Stand

Kankaria Lake

Astodia Darwaja

Jami Masjid

Teen Darwaja

SARDAR PATEL RD

GPO
SALAPOSE RD
BP TANKARIA RD

Khas Bazaar

Bank

ACCOMMODATION

Ajanta	7
Alka	6
Ambassador	15
A-One	2
Balwas	8
Cadillac	12
Cama	16
Embassy	13
Goodnight	9
King Palace	14
Manila	5
Midtown	4
Moti Mahal	3
Rahil	11
Relax	10
Sahil	10
Shakunt	1
Stay Inn	17

Telegraph Office

Cinema

Bhadra Fort

Bank
Indian Airlines
Sidi Sayyid's Mosque
Ahmed Shah's Mosque
Bank
Local Bus Stand
LAL DARWAJA
Victoria Gardens
SEWA

K VAGHELA RD
KHANPUR
Khanpur Gate
LADY VIDYAGAURI RD

NEHRU BRIDGE
ELLIS BRIDGE

Sabarmati River

9

GUJARAT | Ahmedabad

▼ Tourist information & Sabarmati Ashram

It can be fun to amble the narrow backstreets of the old city on foot, but to cover wider distances and avoid the noise and chaos of walking along the main roads you'll need to use **public transport**. This can be stressful, as the overloaded **buses** which race round town have their numbers and destinations written in Gujarati. If in doubt, **auto–rickshaws** are abundant and open to bargaining.

Accommodation

Ahmedabad's **hotels** range from grubby adequacy to polished luxury. Most are conveniently located in the west end of the old city, within walking distance of the bazaars, the local bus station, banks, the GPO and many of the sights. Others are clustered around the railway station, while north of Nehru Bridge, in the rather classy Khanpur area, the hotels are smarter.

Ajanta, Dr Tankaria Road, near the GPO ℡ 079/550 6992, ℻ 550 6522. Colourfully decorated, comfortable hotel with good facilities. ④–⑤

Alka Guest House, Shreenath Chamber, Salapose Road ℡ 079/550 0830. A smart modern hotel, though rather sterile; all rooms have a/c and TV. ⑤–⑥

Balwas, 6751 Relief Rd ℡ 079/550 7135, ℻ 550 6320. Modern, well-kept place with the best rooms in a separate back building. Most have a/c, and TV, all have clean private bathrooms with hot water. ④–⑤

Cadillac, Dr Tankaria Road ℡ 079/550 7558. Small, colourful and low-priced rooms, some with private bathrooms. Also with a dorm for men. ❷

Embassy, behind Bank of Maharashtra, Lal Darwaja ℡ 079/550 7273. Good-value comfortable and friendly hotel in a modern building with all amenities. Optional a/c in many rooms. ⑤–⑥

Goodnight, Dr Tankaria Road ℡ 079/550 6997, ℻ 550 6998. Spick and span modern hotel opposite Sidi Sayyid's mosque. All rooms have TVs and private bathrooms. ⑤–⑥

Rahil, just off Dr Tankaria Road ℡079/551 0442. New place perched above a row of shops. Freshly decorated rooms with cable TV. Good value. ④

Relax, Dr Tankaria Road ℡ 079/550 7301. Clean modern place in a noisy side street opposite Advance Cinema, with room service, constant hot water and private bathrooms. Some of the cheapest a/c rooms in India. ❷–④

Sahil, Dr Tankaria Road ℡ 079/550 7351, ℻ 350004. Friendly place next to *Relax*. Ordinary and a/c rooms, with carpets and private bathrooms but some are windowless. ❸–⑤

Around the railway station

A-One Guest House, Fanibunda Building, Station Road ℡ 079/214 9823. Directly opposite the station, this offers very basic rooms and a dormitory for men. Spartan but clean enough for a night. ❷–❸

Manila, Lalbhai Chambers, Kapasia Bazaar ℡ 079/212 5894. Clean place with the usual marble decor and some a/c rooms. ④–⑥

Midtown, Reid Road ℡ 079/217 1775. Cheapest rooms are small and airless. Some a/c and TV available. Fairly quiet for this area. ❸–⑤

Moti Mahal Guest House, Kapasia Bazaar ℡ 079/212 1881, ℻ 214 4132. Very well-kept clean hotel offering identikit rooms with bathroom and cable TV, some a/c. ⑤

Shakunt, HK Bhavan, Reid Road ℡ 079/214 5614. Smart reception area – but the rooms are on the grubby side and have poor ventilation, though all have TV. ④–⑥

Khanpur district

Ambassador, Lady Vidyagauri Road ℡ 079/550 2490, ℻ 550 2327. Large and modern with all facilities but little character; 24hr checkout. ⑤–⑥

Cama, Lady Vidyagauri Road ℡ 079/550 5281, ℻ 550 5285, ✉ camahotel@vsnl.com. Luxurious rooms overlook the River Sabarmati, and there's a garden terrace with pool. All mod cons, restaurant, coffee shop and one of the few permit rooms in the state where you can drink alcohol. Inconvenient 9am checkout. ⑨

King Palace, Lady Vidyagauri Road ℡ 079/550 0280, ℻ 550 0275. Smart comfortable rooms, all with cable TV and a/c. Good value for this bracket. ⑥–⑧

Stay Inn, Lady Vidyagauri Road, by Khanpur Gate ℡ 079/550 3993, ℻ 550 4053. Well-maintained and comfortable with some of the most economical rooms in this area. Partial a/c and 24hr checkout. ④–⑥

The City

The historic heart of Ahmedabad is the **old city**, an area of about three square kilometres on the east bank of the river, dissected by the main thoroughfares Relief Road and Gandhi Road and reaching its northern limits at **Delhi Gate**. It's the best place to start any exploration, taking in the squat buildings of the original citadel, **Bhadra**, the **mosques** and tombs of Ahmedabad's Muslim rulers, vibrant bazaars and *pols* – labyrinths of high wooden *havelis* and narrow cul-de-sacs that still house families all belonging to the same caste or trade.

Bhadra and Sidi Sayyid's mosque

The solid fortified citadel, **Bhadra**, built of deep red stone in 1411 as Ahmedabad's first Muslim structure, is relatively plain in comparison to later mosques. The palace inside is now occupied by offices and off-limits to tourists, but you can climb to its roof via a winding staircase just inside the main gateway and survey the streets below from behind its weathered bastions. In front of the citadel is a small public garden and **Alif Shah's mosque**, gaily painted in green and white. Further east, beyond the odoriferous meat market in **Khas Bazaar**, is **Teen Darwaja**, a thick-set triple gateway built during Ahmed Shah's reign that once led to the outer court of the royal citadel. A trio of pointed arches engraved with Islamic inscriptions and detailed carving spans the busy road below and shelters cobblers and pedlars.

A prominent feature on the front of glossy city brochures, **Sidi Sayyid's mosque** (1573), famed for the ten magnificent *jali* (lattice-work) screens lining its upper walls, sits in the centre of a busy traffic circle in the northwest corner of Bhadra. The two semicircular screens high on the western wall are the most spectacular, with floral designs exquisitely carved out of the yellow stone so common in Ahmedabad's mosques. The eastern face is open, revealing a host of pillars that divide the hall into fifteen areas, each with skilfully sculpted domed ceilings. Stonework within depicts heroes and animals from popular Hindu myths – one effect of Hindu and Jain craftsmanship on an Islamic tradition that rarely allowed the depiction of living beings in its mosques. Women cannot enter this mosque, but the gardens around it afford good views of the screens.

Ahmed Shah's mosque

West of Bhadra citadel, not far from Victoria Gardens, **Ahmed Shah's** small and attractively simple **mosque** was the private place of worship for the royal household. Sections of an old Hindu temple, perhaps dating back to 1250 AD, were used in its construction – hence the incongruous Sanskrit inscriptions on some of the pillars in the sanctuary. The mihrabs are particularly ornate, the

The kites of Ahmedabad

On January 14, when Gujarat celebrates **Makar Sankrati** to mark the last harvest of winter, Ahmedabad hosts the **International Kite Festival**, the largest of its kind in the world. For weeks in advance shops brim with a splendid assortment of kites of strange and original designs, many painted with animals or the faces of gods and heroes.

India has a long tradition of kite-flying, and during the festival the city comes alive with diving and darting kites flitting through the clear blue skies as families join with enthusiasts from all over Asia and as far afield as America and Japan. On the first day of the festival, crowds of kite-flyers gather in Patang Nagar, a "kite town" – usually in the police stadium – to display models of all sizes, made of paper, cloth, bamboo and fibreglass. There's a carnival atmosphere, with food and crafts stalls and performances of dance and music late into the night. On the second day you can follow the experts to the city's roof terraces and learn to fly kites, and after dark the night sky is ablaze with *tukal* kites strung with coloured lights. The climax of the festival comes on the third day, when kite strings are coated with a lethal mixture of ground glass, egg yolk and boiled rice, and kites are played off against one another in fierce combat. Cries of "kata!" (I've cut!) fill the air as slashed kites fall stricken from the skies and come to rest limply on telegraph wires and trees.

central one carved in white and black marble. Hidden behind pierced stone screens above the sanctuary in the northeast corner, the *zenana*, or women's chamber, is entered by steps from outside the main wall.

Jami Masjid

A short walk from Teen Darwaja along Gandhi Road leads to the spectacular **Jami Masjid**, or Friday Mosque. Completed in 1424, it stands today in its entirety, except for two minarets destroyed by an earthquake in 1957. Always buzzing with people, the mosque is even busier on Fridays, when thousands converge to worship.

A wide flight of steps leads to a vast marble courtyard surrounded on three sides by shady arched cloisters, known as *dalans*. A meeting place as well as an area for prayer, the courtyard has a water tank used for ablutions in its centre, and at the west end, facing Mecca, is the sandstone *qibla*, the main prayer hall, crowned with three rows of five domes. The 260 elegant pillars supporting its roof are covered with profuse unmistakeably Hindu carvings, while close to the sanctuary's principal arch a large black slab is said to be the base of a Jain idol inverted and buried as a sign of Muslim supremacy. The *zenana* is behind finely perforated stone screens above the main sanctuary.

Manek Chowk and the Tomb of Ahmed Shah

East of the Jami Masjid, the jewellery and textiles market, **Manek Chowk** is a bustling hive of colour where jewellers work in narrow alleys amid newly dyed and tailored cloth. Immediately outside the east entrance of the mosque, the square **Tomb of Ahmed Shah I**, who died in 1442, stands surrounded by pillared verandas. Women are not permitted to enter the central chamber, where his grave, and those of his son and grandson, lie shrouded in cloth.

Further into the market area, you'll find the mausoleum of Ahmed Shah's queens, **Rani-ka-Hazira**, surrounded by the dyers' colourful stalls. Its plan is identical to Shah's own tomb, with pillared verandas clearly inspired by Hindu architectural tastes. Inside, the graves are elaborately decorated with metal inlay and mother-of-pearl, now a little faded and worn.

Swaminarayan temple

North from Rani-ka-Hazira through Temple Road, a narrow street of fabric shops, and across Relief Road, the **Swaminarayan temple** stands behind huge gates and brightly painted walls. Forming a delicate contrast to the many hard stone mosques in the city, both the temple and the houses in the courtyard surrounding it are of finely carved wood, with elaborate and intricate patterns typical of the style of the *havelis* of north and west Gujarat. The temple's main sanctuary is given over to Vishnu and his consort Lakshmi.

Mosque and Tomb of Rani Sipri

Near Astodia Darwaja in the south of the city, the small and elegant **mosque of Rani Sipri** was built in 1514 at the queen's orders. Her grave lies in front, sheltered by a pillared mausoleum. The stylish mosque shows more Hindu influence than any other in Ahmedabad, with several Hindu carvings and an absence of arches. Its pillared sanctuary has an open facade to the east and fine tracery work on the west wall.

Shaking minarets

South of the railway station, opposite the large gate of Sarangpur Darwaja, **Sidi Bashir's minars** are all that remain of the mosque popularly named after one of Ahmed Shah's favourite slaves. Over 21m high, these are the best existing example of the **"shaking minarets"** – built on a foundation of flexible sandstone, probably to protect them from earthquake damage – that were once a common sight on Ahmedabad's skyline. At least two European visitors, Robert Grindlay (1826) and Henry Cousens (1905), reported climbing to the top storey of one minaret, shaking it hard, and causing its twin to shake, but as entry is restricted you'll be lucky to be able to try this yourself, or even to get into the modern mosque beneath the *minars*.

Dada Harini Vav

Northern Gujarat abounds in remarkable step-wells – deep, with elaborately carved walls and broad flights of covered steps leading to the shaft – but **Dada Harini Vav**, in the northeast of the city just outside the old boundaries, is among the very finest. It can be reached by taking bus #111 to Asarwa; ask to be dropped nearby, and either walk or take an auto-rickshaw to the well. While it's a Muslim construction, built in 1500 for Bai Harir Sultani, superintendent of the royal harem, the craftsmen were Hindu, and their influence is clear in the lavish and sensuous carvings on the walls and pillars. The best time to visit is an hour or so before noon when the sculpted floral patterns and shapely figurines inside are bathed in sunlight. **Bai Harir**'s lofty mosque and lattice-walled tomb stand west of the well.

A couple of hundred metres north, the neglected **Mata Bhavani Vav** was probably constructed in the eleventh century, before Ahmedabad was founded. It's profoundly Hindu in character, and dedicated to Bhavani, an aspect of Shiva's consort Parvati, whose modest shrine is set in the back wall of the well shaft.

Hathi Singh temple

The Svetambara **Hathi Singh temple** (daily 10am–noon & 4–7.30pm), a few hundred metres north of Delhi Gate, is easily distinguished by its high carved column, visible from the road. Built entirely of white marble embossed with smooth carvings of dancers, musicians, animals and flowers, this serene temple is dedicated to Dharamnath, whose statue stands in the main sanctuary. He is the fifteenth *tirthankara*, or "ford-maker", one of twenty-four great teachers sanctified by the Jains. Other *tirthankaras* peer out with jewelled eyes from smaller shrines in the pillared cloisters around the courtyard.

Calico Museum of Textiles

Nobody should leave Ahmedabad without visiting the **Calico Museum of Textiles** (daily except Wed 10.30–11.30am & 2.45–3.45pm; free), in the Sarabhai Foundation, in Shahibagh, 3km north of Delhi Gate (bus #101, #101/1 & #103); it's simply the finest collection of textiles, clothes, furniture, temple artefacts and crafts in the country. It's best to arrive early so you can take your time; once inside, you'll be shown round by a guide. Colourful embroidered wall-hangings depicting Krishna legends hang from the second floor right down to ground level. Cloth decorated with tie-dye (*bandhani*), glinting mirror-work, screen prints, block prints and intricate embroidery include exquisite pieces made for the British and Portuguese and exported to Bali, while from India's royal households there's an embroidered tent and the robes of Shah Jahan, along with elaborate carpets and plump cushions that once furnished Muslim palaces.

The collection also includes some of the best examples of the *patola* saris woven in Patan (see p.689), as well as the extravagant *zari* work that gilds saris

Almost ninety percent of women who work in India are self-employed. Existing outside the protection of labour laws and the minimum wage, they are particularly subject to exploitation, often at the hands of unscrupulous banks and private lenders. Ahmedabad, however, has maintained a tradition of self-help since the days of Gandhi, and has achieved world recognition as the home base of the groundbreaking **Self-Employed Womens' Association**, SEWA (☎079/550 6444, ℻550 6446, ⊛www.sewa.org), founded in the early 1970s by Ela Bhatt. Originally set up to offer legal advice, provide training and child care, negotiate with police and local government for vendors' licences and education for members' children, it soon grew. SEWA opened its own co-operative *Mahila Bank*, the first to offer women low-interest loans, savings and deposit accounts, and insurance, thus enabling women in Ahmedabad to buy basic materials and tools, and use their income to live on rather than paying off loans.

In 1984 a major textile industry slump affected 35,000 families, most of them Harijans and Muslims. Many had to resort to rag and paper picking, collecting grimy scraps of paper, polythene and broken glass for recycling, a task which threatened their health and brought in pathetic wages. Setting up training centres in weaving, sewing, dyeing and printing, and providing efficient machinery, SEWA helped to re-establish many women in the textile labour force, and provided an outlet for their products. Contracts with government institutions guarantee a place of work for cleaners and vendors; members now provide vegetables, fruit and eggs to all government hospitals, jails and municipal schools in Ahmedabad.

SEWA also trained its members in accountancy, management and office skills, and its management committee includes farmers, rag pickers and *bidi*-makers. By the 1980s, members felt confident enough to bring their personal grievances to this approachable team, voicing complaints of verbal and sexual assault in the workplace and at home. Two thousand women registered a protest against *sati* (widow burning) in 1987. A committee was formed to investigate crimes against Muslim women, particularly *talak*, a practice sanctioned by the Koran that allows a man to divorce his wife by uttering the words "I divorce you" three times, often leaving them destitute. Verbal divorce and polygamy, still common elsewhere in India, were banned in Gujarat in 1988. SEWA also strongly opposes sex determination tests that lead to female foeticide, a widespread practice in Gujarat, and its work has now spread to several other Indian cities.

in heavy gold stitching and can bring their weight to almost nine kilos. The Jain section features statues housed in a replica *haveli* temple, along with centuries-old manuscripts and *mandalas* painted on palm leaves; note the traditional symbols such as the snake-and-ladder motif representing rebirth and karma. Among exhibits from elsewhere in India are Kashmiri shawls, Kullu embroidery, glittering silk brocades from Varanasi, folk art from the Punjab and masks and large wooden temple cars (processional vehicles) from Tamil Nadu. Tribal crafts such as Kutchi silk-and-cotton *mashru* weaving are displayed in spectacular wooden *havelis* from Patan and Siddhpur in northern Gujarat. Clearly labelled models and diagrams explain the weaving, dyeing and embroidery processes.

City Museum

Just west of Sardar Bridge in the modern Sanskar Kendra on Bhagatcharya Road, Ahmedabad's newest tourist attraction, the **City Museum** (Tues–Sun 11am–8pm; free) is well worth a visit. The nicely laid out exhibits cover such diverse subjects as the history of the city, urban growth, sociological development and the activities of Gandhi and the freedom movement. Other displays include ancient sculpture, folk and modern art, paintings of literary figures, and a fine colourful section on world religions. There are also a few kites left from the old Kite Museum that used to occupy this building.

Sardar Patel Memorial Museum

Two hundred metres north up Shahibagh Road, the **Sardar Patel Memorial Museum** (daily 9am–5.30pm; free) houses an exhibition of photos, clippings and mementoes from the life and career of the great ally of Gandhi and Nehru. The labelling is mostly in Hindi and the tribute is rather marred by an annexe of blatant propaganda for the controversial Narmanda dam project (see Contexts).

Gandhi Ashram

At the northern end of Ashram Road, set beside sublime gardens, Gandhi's **Sabarmati Ashram** (daily 7am–8.30pm; free) displays the Mahatma's letters and possessions, along with a powerful collection of photographs of his years of fighting for freedom. It was here that Gandhi lived in humble apartments from 1917 until 1930 and held meetings with weavers and Harijans as he helped them find security and re-establish the manual textile industry in Ahmedabad. In keeping with the man's uncluttered lifestyle, the collection of his personal property is modest but poignant – wooden shoes, white seamless clothes and a pair of round spectacles. A one-hour **sound and light show** telling his life story has an English-language showing three evenings a week (Sun, Wed & Fri 8pm; Rs5) except during monsoon. Tickets are sold at the door, or you can reserve on ☎079/748 3073. The ashram itself is no longer operating, but many people come here simply to sit and meditate.

Other museums

Ahmedabad's museums are strong in arts and crafts. Among them, the informative **Shreyas Folk Art Museum**, way out to the west near the city limits (Tues–Sat 3–6pm, Sun 10am–noon & 3–6pm; free; bus #41 from Lal Darwaja), displays the traditional work of Gujarat's many tribes. The **Tribal Museum** (Mon–Fri noon–5.30pm, Sat noon–5pm; free) in the northeastern corner of Gujarat Vidyapith, on Ashram Road 100m south of Income Tax Circle, is also illuminating, detailing the various peoples of the state and their customs, such as the painting of "magical" pictures by Bhils (see p.695) to ward off disaster. **N. C. Mehta Gallery**, in the Indology Institute near Gujarat University (Tues–Sun 11am–noon & 3–5pm; free; bus #55 from Lal Darwaja), has a superb collection of miniatures from all over India.

Parks and gardens

Ahmedabad's quieter spots and open spaces provide welcome relief from the chaos of the busy streets. Just south of Bhadra, the **Victoria Gardens** are suitably formal, with spacious lawns and tree-lined promenades around a pompous statue of Queen Victoria. The entrance is round the side, away from the main road. Southwest of the old city, picturesque gardens also surround the artificial 34-sided **Kankaria Lake**. Dating from 1451, the lake has a fascinating ornate sluicegate on its eastern edge, a collection of Dutch and Armenian tombs on the west bank, and an island in the centre. The cramped **zoo** is not far north of the lake. It's best to visit in the cool of the evening; bus #32 runs frequently between Kankaria and Lal Darwaja.

Vishalla village

If you're not going to make it to the more traditional Gujarati villages, don't turn your nose up at **Vishalla village** (daily 11am–2pm & 7–11pm), out on Sarkhej Road, 4km south of town (bus #31). Designed this century by Surendra Patel, Vishalla is an admirably authentic collection of traditionally decorated mud huts where potters, weavers and *paan*-makers demonstrate their skills. The **Vechaar Utensils Museum** (daily 11am–2pm & 7–10.30pm; Rs5) houses a vast collection of Gujarati metalware, including jewellery, knives and forks, and odd-looking machinery for milking camels.

The village atmosphere can also be taken in during a leisurely evening trip, when dinner is served (7.30–11pm) to the accompaniment of local dance, music or puppet shows; the menu includes Gujarati dishes, super-sweet deserts and mugs of buttermilk. Lunch is served during the earlier session, with snacks and juices available at all times.

Eating

Ahmedabad's **restaurants** are clustered around Salapose Road and Relief Road, while good stalls in Khas Bazaar serve kebabs and fresh, gloopy dhal. As usual the better hotels in all districts have restaurants offering Indian, Chinese and some Western dishes with some fine independent eateries dotted around too.

Alpha, Dr Tankaria Road. Huge menu of tasty multi-cuisine veg and non-veg in an equally spacious a/c hall. Open 8am–11pm.

Anand Dining Hall, Salapose Road, off Relief Road. Small, very inexpensive veg place, good for Gujurati thalis. Open for lunch and dinner daily, except Sun evening. A branch across the street serves south Indian snacks 8am–10pm.

Bellur, Station Road. Low-priced south Indian veg food in simple surroundings with a/c upstairs. Open 7am–11pm.

Chetna Dining Hall, Relief Road. Popular veg place for excellent cheap south Indian dishes and sumptuous Gujarati thalis. Open 10.30am–3pm & 6.30–10pm.

Food Inn, under *Hotel Goodnight*, Dr Tankaria Road. Smart, a/c restaurant with a wide variety of Indian and Chinese food, including non-veg. Open 9am–11pm, meals 11am–4pm & 6.30–11pm.

Gandhi Cold Drinks House, Khas Bazaar. Refreshing milk and ice-cream concoctions, including Indonesian-style "Royal Faluda", unique to Ahmedabad, and saffron-flavoured *kesar* milk-shake. Open 10.30am–11pm.

Gopi Dining Hall, Pritamrai Road ☎ 657 6388. Great no-smoking veg place on the west side of Ellis Bridge, with Gujarati and Punjabi thalis at unbeatable prices. Very popular, so reserve or queue. Open 10am–3pm & 6.30–10.30pm.

Kalapi, Dr Tankaria Road. A/c no-smoking restaurant opposite Advance Cinema. The best veg food in Bhadra at easily affordable prices. Open 9am–11pm, meals 11am–4pm & 6–11pm.

Mahendi Rang Lagyo Fruit Juice House, Relief Road. Large stall with a wide selection of juices and shakes made to order. Open 6am–midnight.

Moti Mahal, in *Moti Mahal* hotel, Kapasia Bazaar. A stone's throw from the railway station, this non-veg hotel restaurant and sweet centre is renowned for its service and quality. The salted *lassis* with cumin are great. Open 5am–1am.

Nishat, corner of MG Road and Khas Bazaar. Smarter new premises with a/c room upstairs, serving sumptious meat dishes and veg standards. Open 5am–11pm.

Paramount, in *Hotel Paramount*, Bhadra. Drab exterior but imaginatively decorated inside, this a/c non-veg restaurant dishes up a wide selection of excellent Indian and Chinese dishes and desserts. Open 10am–11pm, meals 11.30am–4pm & 6–11pm.

Patang, just west of Nehru Bridge ☎ 079/657 7709. Revolving restaurant, on top of a tower; well worth the expense (Rs200–300). An excellent non-veg buffet prepared by the Kashmiri chef includes a range of unusual salads, subtle sauces and delicious sweets. Book in advance.

Sanman, MG Road, opposite the Jami Masjid. Gujarati and Punjabi veg dishes, filling and inexpensive thalis and south Indian snacks. Open 9am–11pm, meals from 11am.

Toran Tourist Restaurant, opposite the Gandhi Ashram, Ashram Road. Vegetarian place serving Punjabi food and Gujarati thalis. Handy for the ashram but not worth going out of your way for. Open 7am–10pm.

Listings

Airlines, Domestic Indian Airlines, on the road from Sidi Sayyid's Mosque to Nehru Bridge ⊕079/550 3061; Jet Airways, Ashram Road opposite Gujarat Vidyapith ⊕079/754 3304.

Airlines, International Air India, off Ashram Road near the High Court ⊕079/658 5657; Air France, Paduban House near Ellis Bridge town hall ⊕079/544 2391; British Airways, Nijhawan Travel

Moving on from Ahmedabad

There are three daily express trains to Bhavnagar (5hr 25min–7hr), and two nightly to Junagadh (8hr 20min–9hr 55min) and Veraval (10hr 25min–12hr 5min), of which the Girnar Express #9946 is faster. Of the five to seven trains serving Rajkot and Jamnagar, the overnight Saurashtra Express #9215 continues to Porbandar, while the Saurashtra Mail #9005 also serves Dwarka and Okha. For Bhuj, the quickest route is to take the late-night Kutch Express #9031 to Gandhidham and pick up one of the five daily connections there. For Vadodara (2hr), there are no less than 14 trains daily, most continuing to Surat (4hr 30min), seven to Vapi (for Daman; 6hr), and seven or eight to Mumbai Central (9–10hr) – to arrive early in the morning, catch one of the evening departures, the #2902, #9144 or #9006. Alternatively, the Shatabdi Express #2010 will speed you to Mumbai in just over seven hours (daily except Friday), calling at Vadodara (1hr 35min) and Surat (3hr 30min). Of the three daily services to Delhi, the overnight Ashram Express #2915 is by far the fastest (16hr 30min) and most convenient, also calling at Jaipur very early in the morning, though the Rajdhani Express #2957 (Mon, Wed and Fri) takes over two hours less. Udaipur has an overnight express (8hr 45min), and a daytime passenger train (10hr 30min) which continues to Chittaurgarh (17hr); to Jodhpur, the best train is the nightly Suryanagari Express #4846 (9hr 5min). For fast-track services further afield the daily Navjivan Express #6045 goes all the way to Chennai (37hr 30min), the daily Ahmedabad-Howrah Express #8033 to Calcutta and there are direct trains on certain days to other destinations like Bangalore, Hyderabad and Trivandrum.

For journeys within Gujarat, it can be less hassle to opt for a bus, which at least travels at sociable hours. The ST Bus Stand serves a variety of local destinations including Gandhinagar (every 15min; 1hr), Dholka (for Lothal, half-hourly; 1hr 30min), and Nal Sarovar (1 morning departure; 2hr), Mehsana (every 10min; 2hr), and Dhrangadhra (half-hourly; 3hr). In Rajasthan, there are buses to Mount Abu, Udaipur and Jaipur (overnight). There are also overnight services to Mumbai, Indore and Bhopal, but none to Delhi. More comfortable and expensive private buses to various destinations both in Gujarat and interstate are run by Punjab Travels, 3 Embassy Mkt, off Ashram Road just north of the tourist office (⊕079/658 9200) and by any of a cluster of agencies in Paldi, just west of Sardar Bridge, from where most services leave. One agency that takes phone bookings for sleeper coaches to Bhuj and other towns is Patel Tours and Travels at 8 Schroff Chambers, Paldi (⊕079/657 6492). Other private bus operators can be found near the ST stand and the railway station.

Flights to Delhi are operated by Indian Airlines (2–3 daily) and Jet Airways (1 daily); both airlines also fly to Mumbai (3 each daily). Other destinations served by Indian Airlines are Bangalore (1 daily), Calcutta (6 weekly), Hyderabad (4 weekly), and Jaipur (3 weekly). Ahmedabad is undergoing expansion as an international airport with Air India now operating a daily flight to New York via London and on most days to Chicago via London or Frankfurt; Indian Airlines has flights to various Gulf states on most days. Express Travels, just off Ashram Road near the tourist office (⊕079/658 8602), can arrange all flights.

See Travel Details at the end of this chapter for more information on journey frequencies and durations.

Service, off Ashram Road ☎ 079/656 5957; KLM, in the Shefali Centre, Paldi ☎ 079/657 7677; Delta and Swissair, c/o Samveg, in the Surayarath Building behind the White House, Panchvati ☎ 079/640 2798; Alitalia, Cathay Pacific and Kenya Airways, c/o Ajanta Travels, off Ashram Road 300m south of Income Tax Circle ☎ 079/640 5077.

Banks and exchange Facilities for US or sterling cash and travellers' cheques are available at the Bank of India in Khas Bazaar, the Central Bank of India opposite Sidi Sayyid's Mosque, and the State Bank of India opposite Lal Darwaja bus station (all Mon–Fri 11am–3pm, Sat 11am–1pm). For Visa encashment, go to the Bank of Baroda's Ashram Road branch on the west side of the river, 300m north of Nehru Bridge. There's a branch of Thomas Cook at 208 Sakar III, off Ashram Road near the High Court (☎ 079/550 5312).

Bookshops For maps, guides and books try Sastu Kitab Ghar on Relief Road 100m east of Salapose Road, or People's Book House 100m further down. The New Order Book Co, on the west side of Ellis Bridge, sells books on Indian philosophy, architecture and crafts. Mapin, at 31 Somnath Rd, just off Ashram Road in Usmanpura, publish glossy books on Indian art and culture, and stalls under Fernandes Bridge on MG Road have a lot of tatty paperbacks among which you might find the odd gem.

Cinemas Advance Cinema on Salapose Road opposite the *Relax Hotel* and Krishna Cinema on Relief Road by the *Chetna* restaurant are very popular. The Natraj on Ashram Road often shows English films.

Internet access Facilities available at It Baag, 308 Nirman House, near the *Times of India*, Ashram Road. Turn off down a small sidestreet just south of the turning to the tourist office. A convenient outlet in Bhadra is Abrar Telelink, on Salapose Road opposite the Advance Cinema.

Hospitals VS General, Ellis Bridge (☎ 079/657 7621) is a large government hospital; for traditional treatments, try Akhandanand Ayurvedic, Akhandanand Road (☎ 079/550 7796).

Motorbikes Buy an Enfield or have one repaired at Shaik & Co Agency, round the back of Swastik Supermarket, on Ashram Road near the tourist office ☎ 079/214 9522.

Post office Salapose Road (Mon–Sat 8am–8pm, Sun 10.30am–4.30pm).

Photography Gujarat Mercantile Co, 100m south of the GPO on Salapose Road ☎ 079/550 5421; Scanner Fotoshop on the first floor, Padshah Pol, opposite Pragati Co-op Bank, Relief Road, 100m east of the *Chetna* restaurant ☎ 079/535 7358.

Shopping The SEWA craft shop (Mon–Sat 10am–7pm) on the east side of Ellis bridge, a few doors from the organization's reception centre.

Around Ahmedabad

The most obvious day-trip from Ahmedabad is north to **Adalaj**, with its impressive step-well, and perhaps on a little further to the new capital of **Gandhinagar**, which has the extraordinary Swaminarayan religious complex, but is otherwise a characterless conglomeration of landscaped grids. South of town, the lake, pavilions and mausoleums of **Sarkhej** make a pleasant break from the crowded city. Further south, beyond the **Nal Sarovar** bird sanctuary, is **Lothal**, an excavated ancient Harappan site which dates back four thousand years, giving a sense of the area's ancient past; the mosques in **Dholka** en route date back to the fourteenth century.

Adalaj Vav

One of Gujarat's most spectacular step-wells, or *vavs*, **Adalaj Vav** (daily 8am–6pm; free), stands in lovingly tended gardens about 1km from a bus stop on the route between Ahmedabad, 19km away, and Gandhinagar. Once a Hindu sanctuary, the well is now totally out of use; local women wash clothes and cooking utensils at modern water taps nearby.

The monument is best seen around noon, when sunlight penetrates to the bottom of the five-storey octagonal well shaft. Steps lead down to the cool depths through a series of platforms raised on pillars. Alive with exquisite sculptures, the walls, pillars, cornices and niches portray erotica, dancing maidens, musicians, animals and images of Shiva in his terrible aspect, Bhairava.

Stone elephants, horses and mythical animals parade around the sides of the shaft, where green parrots swoop down to rest out of the glaring sun. Before descending you'll see several Sanskrit inscriptions etched into the walls just above eye level, one of which records the building of the well by Ruda, wife of a local chief, in 1498.

Gandhinagar

The second state capital after Chandigarh to be built from scratch since Independence, the uninspiring city of **GANDHINAGAR** is laid out in thirty residential sectors in an ordered style influenced by the work of **Le Corbusier**, who designed Chandigarh and had a hand in conceiving the layout of New Delhi. Its near-symmetrical numbered streets are wide and strangely quiet, lined with a total of sixteen *lakh* trees – that's 26 per head of the city's population. There's little to warrant spending much time here, but the headquarters of the Swaminarayan sect, **Akshardam**, is worth a look. This vivacious Hindu revivalist movement, established in 1907 by Brahmaswarup Shastriji Maharaja, promotes Vedic ideals pronounced by Lord Swaminarayan (1781–1830). Born in Uttar Pradesh, the saint settled in Gujarat where he built six temples, wrote religious discourses and proclaimed that his presence would continue through a succession of saints, the most recent of whom is a Gujarati named Pramukh Swami Maharaja.

The Akshardam may advocate simplicity and poverty, but the colossal **Swaminarayan complex** on J Road, Sector 20 (daily, but most attractions closed Mon, 7.30am–9.30pm), a centre for representing the precepts and practices of the sect, is hugely extravagant. Built of pink sandstone, all six thousand tonnes of it brought from Rajasthan, with domed roofs raised on almost one hundred profusely carved pillars, it's furnished inside with Karnataka rosewood. The statues of Swaminarayan and two other prominent gurus shimmer with a gold leaf coating. The Hall of Holy Relics, containing possessions of Swaminarayan, also has a state-of-the-art display of images projected onto fourteen screens. There are three exhibition halls too (daily except Mon, Nov–Feb 9am–6.30pm, March–Oct 10am–8pm; Rs25). In Nityanand Hall, fair-complexioned figures represent themes from the great Hindu epics, while the works of Indian mystical poets such as Tulsidas and Kabir are shown and models of *sadhus* tolerantly "discuss" world religions with a view to attaining universal harmony. There's a Centre for Applied Research in Social Harmony in the landscaped gardens.

Regular **buses** run between Gandhinagar and Ahmedabad (1hr), but there's only one train a day in each direction (1hr) and the station is rather inconveniently placed, out in Sector 14. Although the town sees few tourists, it does have a **tourist office** on Gha Road in Sector 16, 200m north of Road #4. Should you want to **stay**, the *Capital Guest House*, next to the tourist office (entrance round the back, ☏02712/32651; ❸–❺), is acceptable. There's a **youth hostel** 300m behind it (☏02712/22364; ❶) with spartan dorms and a discount for cardholders, and the a/c *Hotel Haveli* (☏02712/24051, ☏24057; ❺–❼) in Sector 11, 300m behind the bus stand. Note that to telephone Gandhinagar from Ahmedabad you need to replace the ☏02712 city code with ☏82, and in the opposite direction, replace ☏079 with ☏89.

Sarkhej

Just under 10km southwest of Ahmedabad (bus #31 from Lal Darwaja), in the suburb of **Sarkhej**, is a complex of beautifully fashioned monuments arranged around an artificial lake. The square tomb of the revered saint

Sheikh Ahmed Khattu, the spiritual mentor of Ahmed Shah, who died in 1445, is the largest mausoleum in Gujarat, with scores of pillars inside supporting the domed roof. Tracery work and inlaid marble decorates the upper walls and the outer wall supports rows of arched wooden doors and brass screens. The mausoleum was constructed by Ahmed Shah's successor, Mohammed Shah, in 1446. The later Sultan Mohammed Beghada (died 1511) so deeply admired Sheikh Ahmed that he added palaces, a harem and a vast lake to the site, and finally chose to build his own tomb here as well. Sarkhej became a retreat of Gujarati Sultans, who added gardens, pavilions and tombs to the elaborate complex. While some of the buildings are falling into ruin, it remains a charming place, usually teeming with brightly dressed Gujarati holiday-makers, and has a serene beauty comparable to that of Udaipur in Rajasthan.

Nal Sarovar reserve

A visit to **Nal Sarovar**, set in 121 square kilometres of wet grasslands some 50km southwest of Ahmedabad, is best between November and February, when the reserve attracts colonies of flamingoes, cranes, storks, pelicans, ducks and geese. Nal Sarovar is seen as a valuable asset by conservationists campaigning for a reduction in road building and industrial pollution, both fast drying out Gujarat's remaining expanses of wetland.

Dholka

A 35-kilometre journey southwest of Ahmedabad by bus or train brings you to **DHOLKA**, and its three majestic ruined mosques. The modestly proportioned **Masjid of Hilal Khan Qazi** (1333), featuring detailed tracery work, and the **Tanka Masjid** (1361), decorated with elaborate Hindu carvings, are both unaffected by Islamic design. More dilapidated, the **Mosque of Alif Khan** (1453) is distinctively Persian, dominated by solid square towers on either side of the facade. Dholka village is famous for its pomegranate and guava orchards, and also has a stunning wooden *haveli* temple.

Lothal

Remains of the **Harappan** (Indus Valley) civilization that once spread across what are now western India and eastern Pakistan have been discovered in over fifty places in Gujarat. The largest excavated site is at **Lothal** (daily dawn–dusk; free), close to the mouth of the River Sabarmati, roughly 100km south of Ahmedabad, and an easy journey by bus (change at Dholka) or train (3hr). The only decent **accommodation** is 7km away at **Utelia** in the shape of the impressive *Palace Utelia*, bookable through North West Safaris in Ahmedabad (℡079/630 2019, ℗630 0692, ✉ssibal@ad1.vsnl.net.in; ➏–➐).

Foundations, platforms, crumbling walls and paved floors are all that remain of the prosperous sea-trading community that dwelt here between 2400 and 1900 BC, when a flood all but destroyed the settlement. A walk around the **central mound** reveals the old roads that ran past ministers' houses and through the acropolis, where you can see the remains of twelve baths and a sewer. The lower town, evident today from a scattering of fragmented bricks and foundations, comprised a bazaar, workshops for coppersmiths, beadmakers and potters, and residential quarters. On the eastern edge of the site, shattered walls enclosing a rectangle indicate the existence of a dock – the only one discovered of its kind, suggesting that Lothal was probably a port serving a number of Harappan towns.

Before the Mauryan empire took hold in the fourth century BC, the greatest empire in India was the **Indus Valley Civilization**. Well-planned, sophisticated settlements dating back to 2500 BC were first discovered in 1924 on the banks of the River Indus in present-day Sind (in Pakistan), at **Mohenjo Daro** (which means "mound of the dead" in Sindi). Further excavations in 1946 on the banks of the River Ravi in Punjab revealed the city of **Harappa**, dating from the same era, on which archeologists based their knowledge of the entire Indus Valley Civilization. In its prime, this great society spread from the present borders of Iran and Afghanistan to Kashmir, Delhi and southern Gujarat, covering an area larger than the Egyptian and Syrian dominions put together. It lasted until 1900 BC when a series of heavy floods swept away the towns and villages in the delta regions of major rivers in Sind, Saurashtra and southern Gujarat.

A prosperous and literate society, importing raw materials from regions as far west as Egypt and trading ornaments, jewellery and cotton cultivated in the fertile delta plains, it also had a remarkable, centrally controlled political system. Each town was almost identical, with separate areas for the ruling elite and the "workers", and all buildings built with bricks measured according to a system distinctly similar to that laid out in the Vedic *Shastras* (the earliest Hindu treatises). A uniform system of weights and measures, corresponding almost exactly to modern ounces, was used, and the complex, efficient drainage systems were unmatched by any other pre-Roman civilization.

Towns established on river deltas were perfectly placed for trade. **Lothal**, close to the Gulf of Cambay in southern Gujarat, was a major port, and also the source of shells which the Harappans made into jewellery. Some four thousand years later, Cambay is still the largest producer of shell jewellery in India, and southern Gujarati artisans make their wonderful beadwork using barely altered materials and techniques.

Although much about this complex society remains unknown – including their impenetrable script – similarities do exist between the Indus Valley Civilization and present-day India. While their most important deity appears to have been a horned god, there was also a strong custom of worshipping a mother goddess, in the same way as Hindus. The *peepal* tree is revered as it is by Buddhists today, and there is evidence, too, of phallic worship, still strong among Shaivites. Altars bearing the remains of animal sacrifice have been discovered in Lothal and, in every settlement, large baths suggest a belief in the purifying quality of water. For more about the Indus Valley Civilization and its significance in Indian history, see p.1471.

Evidence has been found here of an even older culture, perhaps dating from the fourth millennium BC, known because of its red pottery as the **Red Ware Culture**. You can see remains from this period and from the Indus Valley Civilization in the illuminating site **museum** (daily except Fri 10am–5pm; free). Among the jewellery collection, a necklace made from gold beads, each a mere 25mm in diameter, provides evidence of sophisticated skills and great wealth. Seals, delicately carved with animal motifs, were used by the Harappans to mark packages; one from Bahrain, imprinted with a dragon and a gazelle, is testimony to the extent of their trading links. A range of accurate weights and compasses testifies to the Harappans' knowledge of geometry and astronomy. From the Red Ware Culture, the museum displays bowls, jars, ceramic and terracotta pots and toys – including touchingly familiar spinning tops and marbles.

Northern Gujarat

North of Gandhinagar, the district of Mehsana was the Solanki's seat of government between the eleventh and thirteenth centuries. Some remains of their old capital – including the extraordinary **Rani-ki-Vav** step-well – still stand at **Anhilawada Patan**, just outside the modern city of **Patan**, which is home to Gujarat's last remaining *patola* weavers. From the city of **Mehsana**, at the province's centre, it's easy to get to the ancient and well-preserved sun temple at **Modhera**. Jain temples in the hills at **Taranga** and **Idar** can be reached from Mehsana, or directly from Ahmedabad.

Mehsana

The crowded residential city of **MEHSANA**, less than 100km north of Ahmedabad, doesn't merit a visit in its own right – the one building of any interest is the old **Rajmahal** palace, now used as government offices. As the only place in the area to offer a choice of **accommodation**, it does, however, make an obvious base for visiting any of the towns in northern Gujarat. The centre of town is compact, with the train and bus stations only 500m apart. *Avon Guest House* (℡02762/51394; ❶) is the best of the four cheapies opposite the former, while the *Hotel Apsara* (℡02762/51027; ❷–❹) in Janta Supermarket on Rajmahal Road, almost opposite the bus stand, has clean and simple ordinary and a/c rooms, some with balconies and all with private bath, and a food hall selling excellent and very low-priced thalis. Janta Supermarket, in fact a shopping precinct, also contains a **post office** (Mon–Sat 10am–6pm), **telegraph office** (Mon–Sat 7am–10pm, Sun 8am–4pm), and three **banks**, including the State Bank of India (Mon–Fri 11am–3pm, Sat 11am–1pm). **Trains** link Mehsana to Ahmedabad (2–3hr), Delhi (15–18hr) via Abu Road (2hr) and Ajmer (7hr), and Jodhpur (7hr 30min). There are also very slow passenger trains to Patan (2hr). **Buses** tend to be rather faster, serving Ahmedabad, Vadodara, Surat, Bhuj, Modhera, Abu Road, Ranakpur, Ajmer and Jodhpur.

Modhera

If you visit only one town in northern Gujarat, it should be **MODHERA**, where the eleventh-century **sun temple** (daily 8am–6pm; $5 [Rs5]) is the best example of Solanki temple architecture in the state. Almost a thousand years old, the temple has survived Muslim iconoclasm and nineteenth-century earthquakes; apart from a missing *shikhara* and slightly worn carvings, it remains largely intact.

The Solanki kings numbered Jains among their courtly advisers, and were probably influenced in their temple design by Jain traditions; deities and their vehicles, animals, voluptuous maidens and complex friezes adorn the sandy brown walls and pillars. Within the *mandapa*, or pillared entrance hall, twelve *adityas* set into niches in the wall portray the transformations of the sun in each month of the year – representations found only in sun temples. Closely associated with the sun, *adityas* are the sons of *Aditi*, the goddess of infinity and eternity, and represent the constraints under which the universe can exist. According to Indian convention, Modhera's sun temple is positioned so that at the equinoxes the rising sun strikes the images in the sanctuary, which at other times languish in a dim half-light. In front of the temple, a large tank with staggered steps and small shrines set into its four sides lies dry for most of the year. During the monsoon, however, it gives freshness to the temple, and the gardens around bloom with colour.

Modhera is linked by road to Mehsana (40min) and Ahmedabad (2–3hr). If you are coming from Ahmedabad by bus and want to save time, ask to get out at Mehsana highway and you can head off the hourly Modhera buses at the junction without going all the way into town. There are also direct buses from Modhera to Patan. There are **no hotels**, but the state-run *Toran Cafeteria* in the temple grounds sells thalis, snacks and ice cream.

Patan and Anhilawada Patan

Modern bustling **PATAN**, roughly 40km northwest of Mehsana, was founded in 1796. It has few monuments to speak of, but the streets of its older quarters are interesting enough, overlooked by the carved balconies and lintels of Muslim *havelis* and the marble domes and canopies of Jain temples. In an area called **Sadvi Wada** you can watch the complex weaving of silk *patola* saris, once the preferred garment of queens and aristocrats, and now made by just one family. Each sari takes from four to six months to produce, and is sold for up to Rs70,000. Silk threads are dyed in a set pattern before being woven on a complex loom, and the utmost care is taken to ensure completely even tension throughout the cloth. Patan is linked to Mehsana by six daily **trains** (2hr).

The big-city bustle of Patan is a far cry from the old Gujarati capital at **ANHILAWADA PATAN**, 2km northwest. The original city served several Rajput dynasties, including the Solankis, between the eighth and the twelfth century, before being annexed by the Moghuls. It fell into decline when Ahmed Shah moved the capital to Ahmedabad in 1411. Little remains now except traces of fortifications scattered in the surrounding fields, and the stunning step-well, **Rani-ki-Vav** (daily 8am–6pm; $5 [Rs5]), built for the Solanki queen Udaimati in 1050 and extensively restored during the 1980s. The restorations, unlike those at the sun temple in Somnath, are not obtrusively modern, and re-create as perfectly as possible the original carving.

Rani-ki-Vav is undoubtedly Gujarat's greatest step-well, with a deep octagonal shaft, wide flights of steps and exquisite figures and foliate designs etched into the dark grey stone walls and pillars. The well shaft, now home to a colony of particularly large bees, boasts most of its original decoration, and not one tiny area of stone has been missed by the *silavat* masons. There are several sun motifs dating from the era of pre-Hindu sun worship, but these are far outnumbered by sculptures of Vishnu and his various *avatars*, or incarnations.

Not far from the well is **Sashtraling Talou**, the "thousand-*lingam* tank" built at the turn of the twelfth century, but razed during Moghul raids. Only a few pillars remain of the Shiva temples that surrounded the tank. This is part of the same complex (daily 8am–6pm; free) that includes a small open-air museum displaying a modest collection of sculpture from the area. Sparse ruins of Rani Udaimati's house crumble nearby on a hill that affords excellent views over the surrounding plains. The mosques and tombs that you see are within easy walking distance, and make for interesting exploration; many were constructed using pillars from Hindu temples.

The only **accommodation** in Patan is the pleasant two-room government *Toran Tourist Centre* (☎02766/21515; ❷), which serves basic veg meals, is rarely full and makes for a quiet rural stay.

The Jain temples at Taranga and Idar

Although they're off the tourist trail, the hilltop temples at **Taranga** and **Idar** are easy to get to: 60km or so northeast of Mehsana, both can be reached by bus, and Taranga is on the railway line (though the daily train chugs up from

Mehsana at a snail's pace, taking almost three hours). Idar is also connected to Ahmedabad, over 100km south, by road.

Built during the Solanki period, **TARANGA** temples are particularly striking, and better preserved than more famous sites such as Mount Abu, Girnar and Shatrunjaya. Pilgrims and white-clad monks and nuns gather here year-round to take blessings and pray at its shrines. The **main temple**, built of durable sandstone, is dedicated to Ajitanath, the second of twenty-four *tirthankaras* who represent the great teachers of Jainism. His image, complete with the jewelled eyes that adorn all Jain statues, gazes out from the main sanctuary, sturdy and still, while the rest of the temple is alive with a frenzied tangle of voluptuous maidens and musicians in smooth carved stone round the walls, pillars and ceilings, interspersed with rollicking animals and floral patterns.

The temples at **IDAR** are less interesting, though they too are etched with numerous carvings. A plaque states that the larger **Svetambara temple** was built in 242 BC – it's more likely to date from the eleventh century, though the site itself may well have been a pilgrimage centre for centuries before. Most of what you see today is the result of recent renovation. Beside it, the **Digambara temple** is less ornate and more peaceful, decked with pictures of naked saints and ascetics who were shunned by the Svetambaras when the two sects formed. Used by Hindu and Jain meditators, the caves cut into the hills nearby are said to be sources of great spiritual power.

The **town** below the hill has a distinctly medieval feel, with few modern buildings and an abundance of delicately carved *havelis*. Now a quiet market town, it was once the home of the Maharaja of Idar and the capital of a large province; remnants of its rich past include an eerie ruined palace, twelfth-century Shiva temples overlooking a dry lake, a small dirty step-well and grand arched city gates. The adequate *Hotel Dreamland* on Highway Road (☎02778/50597; ❷), has basic, slightly grubby **rooms**.

Kutch

Bounded on the north and east by marshy flats and on the south and west by the Gulf of Kutch and the Arabian Sea, the province of **KUTCH** (also Kuchchh or Kachchha) is a place apart. All but isolated from neighbouring Saurashtra and Sind, the largely arid landscape is shot through with the colours of the heavily embroidered local dress. Kutch legends can be traced in sculpture motifs, and its strong folk tradition is still represented in popular craft, clothing and jewellery designs. Although few tourists make it out to this region, those who do are invariably enchanted. With a little effort, you can head out from the central city of **Bhuj** to villages, ancient fortresses, medieval ports and isolated monasteries.

The treeless marshes to the north and east, known as the Great and Little **Ranns of Kutch**, can flood completely during a heavy monsoon, effectively transforming Kutch into an island, though it's now several years since this last happened. Home to the rare wild ass, the Ranns are also the only region in India where flamingoes breed successfully, during July and August, out of reach of any but the most determined bird-watchers who can cross the marshes by camel. The southern district, known as **Banni**, was once among India's most fertile areas, and though drier today, still supports crops of cotton, castor-oil

Kutch is known for its distinctive traditional crafts, from embroidery to jewellery-making and carving. The northern villages of Dhordo, Khavda and Hodko are home to the few remaining communities of **leather embroiderers**, who soak hide in a solution of water, latex and lime in an underground earthen pot before stitching it with flower, peacock and fish motifs. The finished bags, fans, horse belts, wallets, cushion covers and mirror frames are sold in villages all through the region. Dhordo is also known for its **woodcarving**, while Khavda is one of the last villages to continue the printing method known as **ajrakh**. Cloth is dyed with natural pigments in a lengthy process similar to batik, but instead of wax, a mixture of lime and gum is used to resist the dye in certain parts of the cloth when new colours are added. Women in Khavda **paint terracotta** pots with dusky whites, reds and blacks, using cotton rags and brushes made from bamboo leaves.

Rogan painting is now practised only in Biber in northern Kutch. A complex process turns hand-pounded castor oil into coloured dyes which are used to decorate cushion covers, bedspreads and curtains with simple geometric patterns. Craftsmen also make melodic **bells** coated in intricate designs of copper and brass; these were once used for communication among shepherds.

Kutchi **silver engraving** is a dwindling art form, traditionally practised in Bhuj. Molten silver is poured into a mould, and, when dry, engraved by gentle taps with fine, sharp tools and small hammers. The final products, such as trays, pots, cups, pens and picture frames, are smoothed down and polished in an acid solution. Silver jewellery is common, featuring in most traditional Kutchi costumes. The anklets, earrings, nose rings, bangles and necklaces are similar to those seen in Rajasthan, since many of them are made by the Ahir and Rabari communities who live in both areas. In Kutch, the silver is mixed with zinc to make it more malleable, and converted into wires and sheets. The main centres for silver are Anjar, Bhuj, Mandiri and Mundra.

The most common form of **cloth** printing is **bandhani**, or tie-dye, practised in most villages, but concentrated in Mandvi and Anjar. Kutchi clothes are distinctive for their fine embroidery and bold designs; one design unique to the area is *mushroo*-weaving (*ilacha*), a skill practised today by less than twenty artisans. The yarn used is silk, carefully dyed before it is woven in a basic striped pattern, with a complex design woven over the top in such fine detail that it seems to be embroidered. *Ilacha* cloth, made into *cholis* (blouses) and dresses, is hard to buy now; the best place to see it is Mandvi, or in the Calico Museum in Ahmedabad (see p.679).

9

GUJARAT | Kutch

plants, sunflowers, wheat and groundnuts. Northern Kutch, on the other hand, is semidesert, with dry shifting sands and no perennial rivers; villagers rely on income drawn from traditional crafts.

Some history

Remains from the third millennium BC in eastern Kutch suggest that migrating Indus Valley communities crossed the Ranns from Mohenjo Daro in modern Pakistan to Lothal in eastern Gujarat. Traditional history recounts that Kutch belonged to the Yadavas, when it was known for the rich grasses that flourished on the ash manure that fell from heaven at the request of a wandering sage. Despite being so cut off, Kutch felt the effect of the Buddhist Mauryan empire, and later came under the control of the Greek Bactrians, the Western Satraps and the powerful Guptas. The Arab invasion of Sind in 720 AD pushed refugees into Kutch's western regions, and tribes from Rajputana and Gujarat crossed its eastern borders. Later in the eighth century the region fell under the sway of the Gujarati capital Anhilawada (now Patan), and by the tenth century the Samma Rajputs, later known as the Jadejas, had infiltrated Kutch from the west, and established themselves as rulers. Their line continued until Kutch was absorbed into the Indian Union in 1948.

When the Muslim sultans ruled Gujarat, they made repeated unsuccessful attempts to cross into Kutch. It remained separate, however, with its own customs, laws and a thriving maritime tradition. Trade with Malabar, Mocha, Muscat and the African coast brought in spices, drugs, silks, rhino hides and elephant tusks, while connections with Africa also encouraged the slave trade, already common among the Portuguese in southern Saurashtra. African deck hands and slaves arrived with merchants and sailors, and after the abolition of slavery in 1834 a small African community settled in north Bhuj. Their crafts, dances and music have been integrated into the region's traditional arts.

Bhuj

Set in the heart of Kutch, the narrow streets and old bazaars of the walled town of **BHUJ** retained a medieval flavour unlike any other Gujarati city until they were reduced to rubble in the earthquake of January 2001 (see box opposite). Very little remains of the old city and, consequently, the account below has been condensed in accordance with the latest available information.

Bhuj was established as the capital of Kutch in the mid-sixteenth century by Rao Khengarji, a Jadeja Rajput. The one interruption before 1948 in his family's continuous rule of the city was a brief period of British domination early in the nineteenth century. When the governance of the state was handed back to the rightful ruler, Maharao Desal, in 1834, the import of slaves from Africa was banned and Africans were given homes in the north of the city. With the establishment of the city of Gandhidham and the port of Kandla southeast of the capital, the economic centre of gravity shifted away from Bhuj, leaving it to carry on its traditions little affected by the modernizations of the twentieth century.

Practicalities

Transport connections to Bhuj made a swift recovery in the wake of the earthquake, with timetables resuming as normal. The **airport**, from where Indian Airlines and Jet Airways have one daily flight each to Mumbai, is 5km north of town and 15min by auto-rickshaw. **Trains** arrive at the railway station a little over 1km north of town, from where rickshaws can take you anywhere in town. The conversion of the track from metre to broad gauge is expected to be complete in 2001, so that long-distance trains can reach Bhuj; currently there are only five daily passenger trains to and from Gandhidham. The **bus stand** is on ST Station Road on the southern edge of the old city and there are frequent GSTC services to Ahmedabad, Rajkot and Jamnagar, as well as Kutchi towns like Mandvi and Mundra. More sparse connections serve Jaisalmer, Udaipur and some villages in northern Kutch.

The only two **hotels** operating in the months after the earthquake were the *Lake View* (☎02832/53422, ℱ50832; ❺–❻), on the south side of Hamirsar Tank, and the more upmarket but better-value *Prince* (☎02832/20370, ℱ50373, ℮prince@ad1.vsnl.net.in; ❻–❼), on Station Road; these establishments both have restaurants.

The Town

Bhuj is overlooked from the east by the old and crumbling fort on Bhujia Hill, while the vast **Hamirsar Tank**, with a small park on an island in its centre, stands on the western edge of town.

On the morning of Friday January 26, 2001, Gujaratis, like their compatriots all over India, were preparing to celebrate **Republic Day** with parades and family gatherings, when the world caved in on them. At 9.15am, an earthquake measuring 7.9 on the Richter scale rocked the state and, within minutes, entire towns were reduced to heaps of fallen masonry.

The epicentre was near Bhachau, east of Bhuj, which, along with other Kutchi towns, bore the brunt of devastation. The earthquake was unusually shallow and the impact movement of plates was particularly severe. In **Bhachau** alone, only 5000 of 25,000 inhabitants survived the immediate collapse of nearly all its buildings. **Anjar** was also flattened and, in more populous **Bhuj**, the historic old town was levelled along with its hospitals, leaving the injured nowhere to go for treatment. Gujarat's biggest city, **Ahmedabad**, did not escape unscathed, with well over one hundred mostly residential suburban blocks destroyed. Fatalities ran into the hundreds in Rajkot, Jamnagar and as far afield as Surat, while tremors were felt in Delhi and even parts of south India. Although the exact number of deaths is never likely to be known, it is estimated at 30,000–40,000.

In the immediate **aftermath**, the only people to be seen in the old town of Bhuj – previously home to thousands of families – were parties of security personel pulling out the dead and injured and protecting property from looters. These magnificent buildings had survived quakes in the past, but the sheer velocity and power of this one reduced them to piles of stones in seconds. In the following days, Gujaratis began to arrive from all over India to search for missing relatives and reclaim belongings. Army engineers deemed it too dangerous to enter the more precarious structures, even when bodies were thought to be still inside. Amid these scenes of trauma and desolation, some individuals undertook extremely hazardous but highly paid missions into buildings to retrieve other people's family treasures.

Unlike other natural disasters on the subcontinent, such as the Orissa cyclone, this earthquake affected every social group, meaning that those responsible for organizing help in the hardest-hit areas were either killed, injured or dealing with personal tragedy themselves. Around 250,000 homeless **survivors** slept out in makeshift camps as winter temperatures dipped to freezing at night; others who had family members outside Gujarat simply gathered whatever they could and left immediately.

Despite the speedy reaction of **international aid** organizations and the heroic work on the ground by nongovernment groups such as SEWA and Abiyan, the scale of tragedy could have been minimized had there been an effective disaster plan in place. Rescue teams found themselves hampered by officials who were unable to direct them quickly enough to the critical areas. As the situation stabilized in the following months, questions were asked about what could be done at the national level to make better provision in the future. Meanwhile, the cost of rebuilding and lost revenue in the crucial areas of trade and the textile industry was still being assessed. Many handlooms were destroyed in the villages, bringing local production to a standstill, while the big textile factories also suffered damage. The government in Delhi moved quickly in announcing a one-year two-percent tax levy on higher-bracket private earnings and on companies to assist Gujarat's recovery. In addition, a huge amount of foreign aid poured into special programmes for the long and painful process of reconstruction.

Although the networks of transport and communication were restored very quickly – phone lines were up within two weeks and rail and bus services restored – visitors to the worst-affected areas are advised to contact **Gujarati Tourism** in Ahmedabad (℡079/658 9683, ☏658 2183, ✉ahmedabad@gujarattourism.com) for an update on what tourist facilities are currently available.

9

GUJARAT | Kutch

Before the earthquake, Bhuj's **old city** was made up of an intricate maze of streets and alleyways leading to the **palace complex**, guarded by sturdy walls and high heavy gates, which enclosed the Aina and Prag Mahals. The more attractive **Aina Mahal** was built in the eighteenth century during the reign of Maharao Lakho, and after Independence turned into the **Maharao Madansinji Museum**, in which the opulence of the royal dynasty was showcased. Although parts of the building survived the earthquake, it is uncertain whether restoration is possible or how much of the collection, including furniture, costumes, jewellery, European glasswork and manuscripts, was salvaged. Also undecided is the fate of the damaged **Prag Mahal**, built nearby in the 1860s, combining Moghul, British, Kutchi and Italian architectural styles. Sadly, the Kutch Museum, which used to occupy the southeast corner of Hamirsar Tank, was completely destroyed along with all its treasures.

One building only to have suffered minimal damage is the **Sharad Bagh Palace** (daily except Fri 9am–noon & 3–6pm; Rs10, Rs20 extra with camera, Rs100 extra with video) at the southwest corner of Hamirsar Tank. Built in 1867 and the retreat of the last maharao, the small porticoed buildings are delicately proportioned and include a plush drawing room, decked with hunting trophies, photographs and old clocks, and the dining room which contains Maharao Madansinjhi's coffin, shipped over from England after his death in 1991. The palace's most appealing feature, however, is its well-tended garden, complete with pretty flower beds, giant bamboo trees, lofty palms and tennis courts.

Just south of Hamirsar Tank and west of College Road, a path leads to the 250-year-old Ramkund tank, which is made of hard grey stone and shaded by trees. Decorated with skilfully crafted images of Kali, Vishnu, Nag and Ganesh, the tank also has small niches in the walls where oil lamps would glitter in the dusk as devotees prayed at the evening puja. Nearby is a set of sixteenth-century *sati* stones.

Villages around Bhuj

Bhuj is a useful base for visiting the **outlying villages**, whether by bus or taxi. If you go by **bus**, you will have to do some walking to reach some of the most interesting Kutchi settlements, which lie a few kilometres from the nearest roads. There are regular **shared taxis** for Mandvi, Mundra and Gandhidham, but for most other Kutchi destinations you will have to charter one.

In November 2000 access to the villages of **northern Kutch** became unrestricted on a trial basis; prior to that, due to the sensitive Pakistani border, you needed a $30 permit. Many trips in this area are best made by taxi as accommodation cannot be guaranteed and bus services are infrequent. At the time of writing it was impossible to verify the extent of earthquake damage in many places around Kutch, including whether the accommodation listed below was still viable, so you are advised to check the current situation in advance with Gujarati Tourism.

Mandvi

The compact town of **MANDVI**, on the west bank of a wide tidal estuary 60km south of Bhuj, faces the Arabian Sea to the south and supports a dwindling dhow-building industry. In the late eighteenth century it was the docking point for a fleet of four hundred vessels exporting goods from a hinterland that encompassed Gujarat and the lands to the north as far as Jaisalmer. Merchants, seamen and later the British were all keen to settle in this flourish-

Kutch has the most significant and conspicuous population of tribal communities in Gujarat, most of whom migrated from east and west from the seventh century onwards. Each tribe can be identified from its costume, and gains its income from pastoral farming or crafts such as weaving, painting, woodcarving and dyeing. Traditionally, each has concentrated on different crafts, although the distinctions today are far less clear-cut.

The **Rabari** is the largest group in the Kutchi pastoral community, with three main tribes hailing from Marwad in Rajasthan. They rear cattle, buffalo, goats, sheep and camels, sell *ghee*, weave, and are known for fine **embroidery**. The men, most of whom sport a white turban, wear white cotton trousers tight at the ankle and in baggy pleats above the knee, a white jacket (*kehdiyun*) with multiple folds tucked around chest level and overlong sleeves, and a blanket thrown over one shoulder. Rabari women dress in black pleated jackets or open-backed blouses, full black skirts and tie-dyed head cloths, usually black and red, and always deck themselves with heavy silver jewellery and ivory bangles around the upper arms. Typical houses made of mud or brick are decorated inside with *gargomati* – a raised pattern of whitewashed mud and dung inlaid with mirrors. Child marriages, customary among the Rabari, are performed over a four- or five-day period in the summer; immediately upon the birth of a daughter, a mother starts embroidering cloth to form the most valuable basis of her dowry. In **Bhujodi**, near Bhuj, the Rabari weave camel wool on pit looms into blankets and shawls.

Claiming descent from Krishna, the **Bharvad** tribes infiltrated Gujarat from Vrindavan, close to Mathura in Uttar Pradesh. Their dress is similar to that of the Rabaris, though the men are distinguishable by the peacock, parrot and flower motifs sewn into their *khediyun*, and the women by their bright backless shirts, *kapadun*, rarely covered by veils. Both men and women wear a thick *bori* cloth around the waist. Mass marriages take place among the Bharvad every few years, a custom originating as a form of protection in the Muslim period when single girls were frequently victims of abduction (the kidnapping of married girls was heavily punished). In the first week of each September the Bharvads gather at the Trinetresvar temple in **Tarnetar**, 65km from Rajkot, celebrating with dances and songs and sheltering under the shade of embroidered umbrellas made especially for the occasion.

The wandering **Ahir** cattle-breeders came to Gujarat from Sind, and settled as farmers in Kutch and at Morvi in Saurashtra, where they mixed with other tribes. Baggy trousers and *khediyun* are worn by the men, together with a white loosely wound head-cloth; the women dress like the Rabaris, with additional heavy silver nose rings. The children's bright *topis*, or skull-caps, overlaid with neat fragments of mirrors, are like those common in Pakistan. During Diwali, Ahirs lead their cattle through the streets to be fed by other local communities, which bestows merit on the giver and is good for karma.

The **Charans**, the long-established bards of Gujarat, encompass in their clans the Maldharis, who raise prize cattle in southern Kutch and the Gir Forest, and the leather-workers known as Meghavals. They claim descent from a celestial union between Charan and a maiden created by Parvati, and many gain almost divine status after death. The women are often worshipped by other tribes, since their connection with Parvati links them closely to the mother goddess, Ashpura, who is popular in Kutch. The men's curses were once considered so powerful that they drove their opponents to kill themselves in the hope that the curse would be deflected upon the Charans: such "heroes" are remembered by stone monuments around Kutch depicting a man piercing his neck with a dagger.

Said to have migrated from Pakistan, the Kutchi **Jats** can be identified by their black dress. Young Jat girls have dainty plaits curving round the sides of their faces, and wear heavy nose rings. Traditionally seminomadic camel- and cattle-rearers, with houses made of reed (*pakha*) that are easily folded and carried from place to place, they have recently begun to settle more permanently.

ing port; few remained, but they left behind grand mansions, imaginatively painted and carved in a style clearly influenced by European tastes.

Mandvi has a leisurely feel, with several chai stalls set among the old houses, and cluttered shops stretching west of the estuary. The **markets** are stocked with *bandhani* and silver, and one street crashes and clanks with the noise from the iron-forgers' blackened stalls. The estuary is blocked on the south side by shifting sands, forming a long, uncrowded **beach** offering good swimming, although camel and horse rides are more popular with Indian tourists. The beach is also the site of the tall windmills that power an electricity plant. Beside the estuary you can see the dhows being hand-built from long wooden planks, with nails up to 1m long forged by local blacksmiths. Fifty men spend two years building each ship, many of which still make the long journey to ports in the west, often carrying Muslims to Mecca for the *Haj* pilgrimage. Flamingoes and other wader birds frequent the mud flats when the tide is out.

Mandvi's neglected and little-visited **Vijay Vilas Palace** (daily 8am–1pm & 2–6pm; Rs10, Rs25 extra with camera, Rs100 extra with video), 8km west of town (turn left after 4km), is a sandy-white domed building set in almost 700 acres of land, built as a summer retreat by Kutch's maharao in the 1940s. Inside, Belgian, British and Italian furniture fills the high-ceilinged carpeted rooms, hunting trophies deck the walls, and a grand stairway leads to the ladies' quarters on the first floor. Small apartments and cool marble courtyards lie open to the sky, and a pavilion projecting from the roof catches fresh sea breezes and commands excellent views.

Practicalities

Hourly **buses** run between Bhuj and Mandvi (1hr 30min); **taxis** crammed with as many people as possible make the journey when full, for Rs25 a head. Of the town's few **guesthouses**, the clean, modern *Sahara*, adjoining the city wall some 300m west of the bus stand (☎02834/20272; ❷–❸) is the best, and has a dorm (Rs50); the *Maitri Guest House* in a smartly painted building 200m further west (☎02834/20183; ❷–❸) is also good; the *Shital*, near the bridge (☎02834/21160; ❷), is cheap and cheerful. A few kilometres east of town the GTDC *Toran Beach Resort* (☎02834/30516; ❷–❻) has tents and more luxurious cabins. You can also stay in one of two guesthouses at *Vijay Vilas Palace* (☎02834/20043; ❻–❽), which although characterful are not very good value by Indian standards; meals (Rs100) are served in the aristocratic dining room. Otherwise the best bet for **food** is *Zorba the Buddha Restaurant* on KT Shah Road, west of the bus stand behind an old town gate (11am–2pm & 6–10pm), where the renowned thalis have over ten dishes, plus fresh chutneys, pickles and sweets.

Mundra

The small, lively fishing port of **MUNDRA**, 20km east of Mandvi, has few sights of particular note of its own, but it's a pleasant place to catch the sea-breeze and buy local crafts. These include batik prints, heavy silver jewellery and unusual woollen *namadas*, as well as floor coverings, wall-hangings and camel saddles dyed in earthy maroons, blues, yellows and black. A bus ride and a short walk will get you to several small Rabari and Jat villages nearby and, to the east, the Jain temples at **Bhadreswar**, decorated with immaculate white sculpture, are a focus for pilgrims from all over Gujarat.

Mundra is served by slow **buses** from Mandvi (8 daily; 1hr 30min), but it's best reached direct from Bhuj, 30km north, by bus (hourly; 1hr). The road from Bhuj runs through a dry red-brown rocky landscape, past broad fields of wheat and sunflowers, before approaching the thick walls that circle the town. Basic **rooms** are available at the *Saheb* (☎02838/22356; ❶) and the *Eshant* (☎02838/22737; ❶–❷), both near the central crossroads. The main reason to come to Mundra is to take advantage of the new **ferry crossing** (3–4hr; Rs155, Rs210 a/c) to Sikka for Jamnagar. Tickets can be booked at Rajchamunda Travels (☎02838/22511), not far from the bus stand; the boat leaves at 5pm daily and there are transfers at each end of the trip for Rs10.

Southeast to Kandla

The fifty-kilometre journey southeast from Bhuj to **KANDLA**, India's busiest port, takes you past dry scrubland. In the small village of **Bhujodi**, less than 10km out of Bhuj, Rabari men weave thick shawls and blankets on pit looms dug into the floors of squat mud houses decorated with *gargomati*. You can buy their products from a small shop run by the Bhujodi Handweaving Co-op Society.

The first main town beyond Bhuj, **ANJAR**, was the capital of Kutch until 1548. It's an important centre of bright and intricate Ahir embroidery, *band-hani*, batik and nut-cracker making, and holds busy markets once or twice a week. Further east is **GANDHIDHAM**, the city planned for Sind refugees who came to Kutch after Partition. An industrial centre, supporting the modern port of Kandla at the mouth of the Gulf of Kutch, Gandhidham holds little attraction for tourists, though it's convenient for road and rail connections to Rajasthan and Gujarat. Both towns suffered extensive damage in the earthquake. Buses run hourly between Bhuj and Gandhidham (1hr), and there are five trains a day, two continuing to Kandla.

North of Bhuj

One bus a day from Bhuj makes the journey to the craft centres of **KHAV-DA**, **HODKO** and **DHORDO**, where clusters of grass-roofed mud huts are decorated with traditional clay and whitewash patterns. You'll need to stay the night. Another popular craft centre, and an easy day-trip, is the village of **LUDIA**, though the painted mud huts are more attractive than the local embroidery, which is better at **Bhirendiara** and **Sumeraser** on the way. The area around Ludia has adopted a fairly commercial attitude towards tourists, so expect insistent sales pitches.

West of Khavda, the temple community of **THAN** is home to a small group of Hindu *sadhus* known as *Khanpata* ("split-ear") because of the heavy ornaments they wear in their ears. The order was founded by the twelfth-century saint Dharamnath who travelled to Kutch from Saurashtra and practised severe austerities for years on a nearby hill. A temple marking the spot is visited by *sadhus* year round, and may have been converted from an earlier sun temple by the Kathi tribe. The single daily bus currently leaves Bhuj at 5.15pm (3hr); you can **stay** overnight at Than's *dharamshala* in return for a donation.

Near Than, the village of **BIBER** has a temple to Rama decorated with friezes depicting scenes from the *Ramayana*, executed using a long-forgotten technique known as *kamagar*. At neighbouring **NIRONA** you can see cloth painted in the ancient *rogan* style (though only one family there still does it). There are nine daily buses between Bhuj and Nirona (1hr 30min). In the easternmost part of Kutch, it's also possible to stay overnight in a *dharamshala* at the Gandhi Ashram in **Lilpur**, or beyond that at **Rahpur**, enabling you to visit the archeological excavations at **DHOLAVIRA**, an island in the Rann where traces of the ancient Harappan civilization (see p.687) have been discovered. The bus from Bhuj to Dholavira (7hr) leaves in the morning.

Saurashtra

SAURASHTRA, also known as the **Kathiawar Peninsula**, forms the bulk of Gujarat state, a large knob of land spreading south from the hills and marshes of the north out to the Arabian Sea, cut into by the Gulf of Cambay to the east and the Gulf of Kutch to the west. This is Gujarat at its most diverse, populated by cattle-rearing tribes and industrialists, with Hindu, Jain, Buddhist and Muslim architecture, modern urban centres and traditional bazaars. Saurashtra boasts India's finest Jain temple city at **Shatrunjaya** near **Palitana**, Krishna temples at **Dwarka** and **Somnath** and Ashoka's Buddhist capital, **Junagadh**. Lions thrive in the national park in **Gir Forest**, while in the flat yellow grassland northeast of Bhavnagar, India's largest herd of black buck live in a protected sanctuary at **Velavadar**. Gandhi's birthplace is still honoured in **Porbandar**; he is also remembered by a museum in **Rajkot** where he spent some years. The best place to head for to enjoy sun, sea, beaches and beer is the formerly Portuguese island of **Diu**, just off the south coast.

Rajkot

Founded in the sixteenth century, **RAJKOT** was ruled by the Jadeja Rajputs until merging with the Union of Saurashtra after Independence, since when it has become a successful industrial centre. Best known for its associations with **Mahatma Gandhi**, who lived and worked here for some time, this quiet city has little to attract tourists except a museum and Gandhi's family home. Its central position, however, makes it a good base for trips to nearby Morvi and Wankaner.

Arrival and information

Three main roads radiate from the busy road junction at Sanganwa Chowk in the centre of Rajkot: **Dhebar Road** heads south, past the ST bus stand 100m away; **Lakhajiraj Road** goes east, through the old city; and **Jawahar Road** runs north, past Alfred High School (whose former pupils include M. K. Gandhi) and Jubilee Gardens towards **Rajkot Junction station**, 2km northeast (get off here rather than at City Station if arriving by train), and the airport 4km northwest.

Rajkot's rather redundant **tourist office** (Mon–Sat 10.30am–6pm; ☏0281/234507) is off Jawahar Road, north of Sanganwa Chowk behind the *State Bank of Saurashtra* – look for the blue ATM signs as the bank's name is in Gujarati. You'll find the **Post Office** (Mon–Sat 8am–7.30pm, Sun 10am–4pm) on Sadar Road, off Jawahar Road opposite Jubilee Gardens.

Accommodation

Rajkot has a host of **hotels** around the bus stand; the cheapest leave much to be desired so it's worth spending a little more to find welcome relief from the noise and dirt of the city. For the same reason, most places listed are on the marginally quieter back side of the stand, to the east.

Babha Guest House, Panchnath Road, off Jawahar Road just south of Alfred High School ☏0281/220861, ☏221384, ✉hotelbabha@rajkot.com. One of the cleanest budget options, with small rooms, some of which are a/c. ❸–❻

Galaxy, Jawahar Road, 100m north of Sanganwa Chowk ☏0281/222904, ☏227053, ✉galaxyhotel@wilnetonline.net. Spacious rooms – some a/c – on the third floor of a shopping complex. High standard of hygiene and service, but access is by lift only – staff claim the stairs can be unlocked "immediately" in case of fire. **6**–**7**

Govardhan, Kanak Road ⊤ 0281/240681, ⊕ 240684. Smart modern hotel with cosy rooms, all en suite with TV and some a/c. **4**–**6**

Jayshree, Kanak Road ⊤ 0281/227954. Good-value clean rooms with TV. **2**–**3**

Jyoti, Kanak Road, 200m north of the bus stand ⊤ 0281/225271. Reasonably clean but poky rooms and a dorm (Rs60). **2**

Kavery, Kanak Road ⊤ 0281/239331, ⊕ 231107. Upmarket place round the corner from the *Jyoti*.

Good comfortable rooms, some a/c, and suites. **7**–**8**

Milan, Shri Sadguru Complex, 30/37 Karanpara ⊤ 0281/235878. Large hotel very close to the noisy bus stand with relatively clean and airy rooms. **2**

Samrat International, 30/37 Karanpara ⊤ 0281/222269, ⊕ 232274. A little south of the *Milan*. Clean and businesslike, but not as smart, friendly or as good value as the *Galaxy*. **5**–**7**

The Town

In the most appealing area of Rajkot, the **old city**, typical Gujarati wooden-fronted houses, with intricately carved shutters veiling stained-glass windows, stand among more modern, faceless constructions. The Gandhis moved here from Porbandar in 1881; tucked away in the narrow streets on Ghitaka Road, off Lakhajiraj Road about 300m east of Sanganwa Chowk – the turning is marked by a blue signpost, but it's not easily spotted – the family house **Kaba Gandhi no Delo** (Mon–Sat 9am–noon & 3–6pm; free) has a small display of artefacts and photographs from the Mahatma's life.

Rajkot's chief tourist attraction is the **Watson Museum** (daily except Wed and 2nd & 4th Sat of month, 9am–12.30pm & 2.30–6pm; Rs2), in a robust nineteenth-century building in Jubilee Bagh. The museum, named after Colonel Watson, British Political Agent from 1886 to 1893, displays relics from 2000 BC to the nineteenth century, including findings from Indus Valley sites, medieval statues, manuscripts, miniatures and Rajput bronzes. On the ground floor a vast collection of portraits of Gujarat's rulers surrounds a staunch Queen Victoria, fashioned in 1899 by Alfred Gilbert who modelled Eros in London's

Moving on from Rajkot

Of Rajkot's two **train** services to Mumbai, by far the better is the Saurashtra Mail #9006, leaving late afternoon and arriving 8.10am the next morning. There are also three expresses and several passenger trains to Jamnagar (2–3hr) and Porbandar (4hr 30min–6hr), two expresses and three fast passenger trains to Dwarka (5hr 30min–7hr) and Okha (6hr 30min–8hr), an overnight fast passenger train to Bhavnagar (8hr 30min), and four trains a day (one fast) to Junagadh (3hr 15min–4hr) and Veraval (5hr 15min–6hr). For those in a hurry to get to south India, there are weekly trains to each of Secunderabad, Thiruvananthapuram, Kochi and Coimbatore, originating in Rajkot on four different days. The main station for trains in and out of Rajkot is called Rajkot Junction.

Frequent **buses** from the State Bus Terminal connect Rajkot with other Gujarati towns; private buses offer faster services for long-distance journeys and also serve places like Pune, Mumbai and Udaipur, but are invariably as full as the state buses. Book at Shri Sadguru Travels or other agents behind the bus station, where you can also pick up shared taxis to Junagadh.

The only destination accessible directly by **air** is Mumbai, served daily by Jet Airways in the morning and Indian Airlines in the evening.

See Travel Details at the end of this chapter for more information on journey frequencies and durations.

Piccadilly Circus. Next door, the **Lang Library** (daily 9–10.50am & 5–6.50pm) is a grand but seldom-used cobwebbed reading room, flanked with dusty English-language books. Unsurprisingly, most local people are more interested in the daily Gujarati newspapers.

Eating

Most **restaurants** in Rajkot serve unfailingly good Gujarati thalis with a wide range of sweet and sour tastes, often in unending supply. Western food is only found in the more upmarket hotels. Most places don't open until 10.30am, so early risers will have to survive on a cup of sweet tea and snacks until then. As you would expect, cheap *dhabas* can be found behind the bus stand and opposite the railway station.

City Fast Food, 37 Karanpura. Clean café behind the bus stand serving meals and south Indian snacks, including wonderful *dosas*.

Havmor, Jawahar Road, opposite Alfred High School. Comfortable a/c restaurant for good Punjabi, Chinese and Western options and their own-brand selection of ice creams. Probably the best non-veg place in town. Open 10am–11pm.

Kavery Hotel, Kanak Road. The *Bukara* serves quality Chinese, Punjabi and Continental veg and non-veg, while the *Woodlands* offers Mexican, Thai and Gujarati veg fare. Good service at both. Open 8–10am, 11am–3pm & 7–11pm.

Laxmi Lodge, Sanganwa Chowk. Popular dining hall serving cheap Gujarati thalis. Open 10.30am–3pm & 6.30–9.30pm.

Rainbow, Sanganwa Chowk. Small place below the *Himalaya Guest House*, with south Indian veg snacks, pizzas, and ice cream (no hot drinks). Open 10am–11pm.

Samarkand, *Samrat International Hotel*, 30/37 Karanpara. Good selection of Indian and Chinese veg in a comfortable a/c setting. Open 11.30am–3pm & 7–11pm.

Around Rajkot

The princes of Rajkot district left a rich legacy of elaborate residences whose architectural styles range from the delicate detail of the seventeenth century to bold 1930s Art Deco. The palaces at **Wankaner** and **Morvi** are easily seen in a day, while the older palace at **Halvad** a little further out can be combined with a trip to the wild ass sanctuary in the Little Rann of Kutch, accessible from **Dhrangadhra**.

Morvi

The delightful little town of **MORVI** (also spelt Morbi), two hours north from Rajkot on the banks of the River Machhu, once commanded a strategic defensive position, guarding against intrusions into the Kathiawar Peninsula from the Rann of Kutch in the north. Instability among neighbouring petty states left Morvi insecure until the mid-nineteenth century when the political climate changed and the town prospered. The eclectic **Mani Mandir**, built in 1880, married conflicting Venetian Gothic, Rajput and Saracenic styles, to produce a surprisingly fine and extremely unusual result. A suspension bridge, built in 1882, spans the river to the entrance of the palace. Closer to the main road, the later Art Deco **New Palace** (1931–44) is more imaginatively decorated than its plain two-storey granite exterior suggests. One of its fourteen bedrooms, embellished with erotic murals, lies underground, and there is a bathroom completely covered in sea shells. There are no fixed **visiting hours** for either building; Mani Mandir is now used as offices and only the courtyards are open to visitors. If you catch the caretaker of the New Palace on a good day you may be lucky enough to be permitted to see all the fascinating interior.

Wankaner

The flamboyant Ranjit Vilas Palace at **WANKANER**, 39km northeast of Rajkot, is still home to the family who once ruled the old state of the same name. Built between 1899 and 1914, the symmetrical building can be seen from far across the flat Saurashtran plains. Up close, its fancy arched facade shows a frenzy of Moghul, Italianate and Victorian Gothic styles with large windows and domed towers, and scores of hunting trophies looming from the walls. You can **stay** here, in buildings separate from the palace, one of which is an Art Deco structure with a swimming pool and a preserved step-well (☎02828/20000, ☎20002; **❼**–**❽**). Meals, taken in the palace, are included.

Dhrangadhra

The unassuming town of **DHRANGADHRA**, over 100km northeast of Rajkot, has little to detain visitors, but is the starting point for a visit to the **wild ass sanctuary** in the flat saline wilderness of the Little Rann of Kutch. The wild ass is distinguished from a common ass by the dark brown stripe down its back; you'll almost certainly see herds of them, dainty and small but very fast when they sprint over the dusty mud flats.

Permission to visit the sanctuary should be sought from the Sanctuary Superintendent in Dhrangadhra; Jeeps can be rented for Rs400 for a maximum period of five hours. It's possible to stay in the *Government Rest House* (☎0272/445068 or 448499; **❶**), which can be booked in advance from Ahmedabad.

Halvad

The seventeenth-century lakeside **palace** at **HALVAD**, an otherwise nondescript small town 20km west of Dhrangadhra, features some superb wooden carvings and, nearby, a number of intriguing **tombstone monuments** (*pallias*) commemorating acts of bravery and heroism. Certain images recur; the symbol of a raised hand or arm indicates the death of a woman who has committed *sati* or self-immolation, while a mounted spear-bearing bard records the death of a courtly poet offered by his lord as surety for a loan and driven to suicide in the case of default. Halvad's *Rest House* (**❶**) has simple **rooms**.

Jamnagar and around

Close to the northwest coast of Saurashtra, the busy, noisy city of **JAMNA-GAR** preserves some fabulous architectural surprises at its heart. Founded in the sixteenth century, the walled city was built to the east of Ranmal Lake, centring on the circular Lakhota Fort. **K.S. Ranjitsinhji**, the famously elegant cricketer who played for England alongside W. G. Grace, ruled Jamnagar for several years at the turn of the twentieth century, improving commercial contacts and replacing run-down buildings with attractive constructions that remain as testimony to a prosperous and efficient rule. The city is renowned for excellent *bandhani* (tie-dye), sold in its markets.

Arrival and information

The centre of town from a tourist's point of view is **Bedi Gate** near the shopping centre and office complex of **New Super Market**. As its name suggests, this junction was one of the gates of the old city, which lies to its south, but most of the walls have long since been demolished. Northwest of Bedi Gate, Pandit Nehru Marg leads past **Teen Bati**, an imposing triple gateway, and on towards the **railway station**, 6km out. The ST **bus stand** is 2km or so west of Bedi Gate, on the other side of **Ranmal lake**, and the **airport** 8km west of that. Auto-rickshaw is the best way into town, though you could walk from the bus stand (20min), and some buses may drop you at **Teen Bati**. The State Bank of India in New Super Market (Mon–Fri 11am–3pm, Sat 11am–1pm) will **change cash** or travellers' cheques. Savetime Travel (℡0288/553137) on Bedi Gate Road is an efficient agent for air tickets and other travel queries.

Accommodation

Acceptable **accommodation** is limited in Jamnagar. Most of the cheap places can be found in and around New Super Market, but are noisy and leave a lot to be desired. The more expensive hotels are comparatively good value, though more spread out.

Aram, Nand Niwas, Pandit Nehru Marg ℡0288/551701, ℻554957. Palatial old house with a garden restaurant 2km towards the railway station from Bedi Gate. The large a/c rooms, nostalgic for the days of the Raj and filled with European antiques, have a faded charm. ⑥–⑧

Ashiana, Third Floor, New Super Market ℡0288/559110, ℻551155. Carpeted deluxe rooms and grubbier ordinary ones; all have TVs and bathrooms with hot water. The best maintained in New Super Market, but often full. ③–⑥

Gayatri Guest House, Sumer Club Road ℡0288/564727. A five-minute walk south of the bus stand; reasonably comfy rooms, some with a/c and TV. Great value singles. ④–⑥

Kama, opposite ST bus stand ℡0288/559217, ℻558219. Set slightly back from the mayhem, this functional concrete block has the most decent

rooms in the immediate vicinity of the bus stand. ③–⑤

Lakeview, Sumer Club Road ℡0288/565311. In the same block as the *Gayatri* but slightly more upmarket. Smart, fairly plush and efficient, with all facilities. ④–⑥

President, Teen Bati ℡0288/557491, ℻558491, ℮president@wilnetonline.net. Very clean, well-managed hotel with parking, bar, restaurant and currency exchange. Credit cards accepted. ⑤–⑧

Punit, Pandit Nehru Marg, just northwest of Teen Bati ℡0288/559275, ℻550561. Friendly, clean and popular, with a small roof terrace. More centrally placed than other mid-range options. ⑤–⑧

Shital, Narayan Cottage, opposite New Super Market ℡0288/554288. Cheap and basic, with a dorm (Rs50). En-suite rooms not much more expensive than those unattached. ②

The City

The most remarkable of Ranjitsinhji's constructions is **Willingdon Crescent**, the swooping arches of its curved facade overlooking the wide streets of Chelmsford Market. In the heart of town, just off Rangit Road southwest of Bedi Gate, stands the late-nineteenth-century **Ratan Bai Mosque**. This grand domed prayer hall, its sandalwood doors inlaid with mother-of-pearl, is the unlikely neighbour to a magnificent pair of **Jain temples**, one dedicated to Adinath (the first *tirthankara*) and one built to honour Shantinath (the sixteenth). The quality and quantity of the **murals** on the walls, ceilings and pillars of the temples is extraordinary. Hazy yellows, greens, pinks, oranges and blues depict a riot of flowers, people, gods and domestic objects, while tableaux tell the life stories of Jain saints. The most spectacular of the two, **Shantinath Mandir**, is a maze of brightly coloured columns, each section of roof between them highlighted with individual designs; the marble floor beneath is emblazoned with distinctive Jain patterns in yellow, black, white and red. Above the main sanctuary, an enormous dome rises in a series of concentric circles glinting with gold. The outer side of the large dome over **Adinath Mandir** is inlaid with gold and coloured mosaic and both temples have cupolas enriched with a design of mirrors above the entrance porch.

The temples form the hub of **Chandni Bazaar**, an almost circular market area enhanced by doorways edged with mosaic panels. Small lanes flanked with the meticulously carved wooden doors and balconies of ancient homes lead off it in all directions.

Stretching west towards the bus stand, Ranmal Lake acts as a wide moat and defence for **Lakhota Fort** (daily except Wed and 2nd & 4th Sat of month, 10.30am–1pm & 3–6.30pm; Rs2), connected to solid land in both directions by a causeway but only accessible from the north side. Thick circular walls studded with gun-holes protect the inner building. On entering you'll pass a guardroom containing muskets, swords and powder flasks; the **museum** on the upper floor holds a mediocre display of paintings, sculpture, folk art and coins. South of the lake stands the solid **Bhujia Fort** (daily 8am–1pm & 5–7pm if you can find the caretaker – ask at neighbouring petrol station). To its northwest, on the edge of the old city, the **Bala Hanuman temple** has been the scene of round-the-clock nonstop chanting ("Shree Ram, Jay Ram, Jay Jay Ram") since 1964, for which feat it is cited in the Guinness Book of Records.

Eating

A fairly wide choice of good inexpensive **restaurants**, most of them clustered around Teen Bati, serve vegetarian dishes. Most places close at 10pm.

Amiras, *Hotel Ashiana*, New Super Market. Humble surroundings, but serves very tasty, great-value Punjabi and Gujarati dishes, south Indian snacks and breakfasts. Open 8am–10pm.

Kalpana, Teen Bati. Ageing decor but great cheap veg food: south Indian, Punjabi, ice cream, fruit juice and milkshakes, but no hot drinks. Open Tues–Sun, 8.30am–10pm.

Maruti, Sumer Club Road, 10min walk from the bus stand. A huge selection of well-prepared Indian and Chinese veg dishes, served in the plush a/c interior or on the airy roof terrace. Open 10am–3pm & 6–11pm.

Rangoli, 100m from New Super Market. South Indian and Punjabi dishes at higher-than-average prices. Open daily except Wed 9am–3pm & 5–11pm.

Seven Seas, *Hotel President*. A/c and dimly lit with comfortable seats. Indian, Chinese and Western dishes at moderate prices; good if you fancy a meat feast. Open 6am–11pm.

Shree Ram Dairy, Teen Bati, next to *Kalpana*. Ice cream and jelly, milkshakes and other childhood favourites: flavours include mango and *chiku*. Open daily except Tues 10am–11pm.

The marine national park

The northwest coast of Saurashtra, bordering the heavily tidal Gulf of Kutch, is fringed with more than forty small islands, whose ever depleting mangrove population gives rise to some of the richest marine life off mainland India. In 1980, 295 square kilometres of the gulf was declared a marine sanctuary, and in 1982, over half of this was officially recognized as a marine national park.

The coast off Jamnagar has always been exploited for pearl fishing, and still supports a small population of pearl oysters. Permission to take a boat from Jamnagar to Pirotan Island – where the coral is particularly rich – can be sought from the Chief Conservator of Forests and Wildlife, Koti Annexe, Vadodara or the marine national park director in Jamnagar; it may not be granted, however. Besides abundant coral, the Gulf of Kutch shelters sea-turtles, snakes, dolphins, sharks and octopuses, and attracts thousands of birds such as flamingoes, pelicans, harriers, cormorants, ibises and oyster-catchers.

Despite pressure from conservationists, the mangroves are still cut for firewood and industries along the west coast of Saurashtra continue to pollute the sea with effluents. As the mangroves disappear, so does the aquatic life they support; mud from the coastline, no longer anchored by tree roots, is pushed from the shore to smother the coral reefs, thus denying fish their natural habitat.

Dwarka

In the far west of the peninsula, fertile wheat, groundnut and cotton fields, lightly ruffled by a cool sea breeze, emerge in vivid contrast to the arid expanses further inland. According to popular Hindu legend, Krishna fled Mathura to this coastal region, declaring **DWARKA** his capital. A labyrinth of narrow winding streets cluttered with temples, the town resonates today with the bustle of eager saffron-clad pilgrims and the clatter of celebratory drums. Dwarka really comes to life during the major Hindu festivals; the most fervent are Shivratri, dedicated to Shiva (Feb/March) and Janmashtami, Krishna's birthday (Aug/Sept).

The elaborately carved tower of **Dwarkadish temple** (daily 6am–12.30pm & 5–9pm) looms proudly 50m above the town. Inside, the sixteenth-century sanctuary, voluptuously sculpted and spilling out swirls of incense and murmured prayers, is surrounded by smaller shrines nestling in chiselled corners beneath sturdy pillars. Non-Hindus can enter only on signing a form declaring, at the very least, respect for religion. Get small change for donations from the change-wallahs at the east entrance.

When Krishna came to Dwarka with the Yadava clan, he eloped with Princess Rukmini. One kilometre east of town, the small **Rukmini temple** – which local priests may tell you is 1500 years old, but in fact dates from the twelfth century – is, if anything, more architecturally impressive than the Dwarkadish temple, with carvings of elephants, flowers, dancers and Shiva in several of his aspects covering every wall.

Practicalities

Trains from Jamnagar arrive at the station north of town from where tongas ferry visitors to hotels and the temple. The **bus stand** on the road to Okha has regular services to and from Jamnagar, Porbandar and Veraval. Dwarka Darshan run **tours** (Rs25) at 8am and 2pm to Bet Dwarka and the underground *jyotrilingam* at the Nageshwar temple, 16km from Dwarka.

Accommodation in Dwarka is, for the most part, cheap and unelaborate. The well-kept *Toran Guest House* (☏02892/34013; ❶–❸), on the edge of town near the coast, offers dorms and doubles, all with mosquito nets. The clean, modern *Hotel Rajdhani* on Hospital Road (☏02892/34070; ❸–❺), just off the main road between the bus stand and the temple, has excellent-value rooms, all with TV. Very near Dwarkadish temple, *Uttam Guest House* (☏02892/34234; ❷) is homely enough, while towards the railway station *Hotel Meera* (☏02892/34031; ❷–❹) is clean and comfortable, and serves undoubtedly the best **thalis** in town. The *Kant Lodge* on the main road into town also does good thalis or, for Punjabi and Chinese dishes, try the *Milan* restaurant 100m further out of town.

Bet Dwarka

A day-trip to the tiny island of **Bet Dwarka**, also closely associated with the Krishna legend, is a must for any pilgrim to Dwarka, as its (architecturally uninspiring) temple is said to stand on the spot where Krishna died. Small, precariously full wooden dinghies transport pilgrims from the port of **OKHA**, on the westernmost point of the peninsula, to the island, where devotees scatter rupees and flowers towards Krishna's shrine and wait eagerly for the appearance of the priest who hands out *prasad*. Theoretically, you are supposed to return from Bet Dwarka on the same boat you went on after one hour. In practice, nobody seems to mind if you stay longer, allowing you to relax on the fine deserted beach clearly visible to the left of the village as you approach the island. Not surprisingly, fishing is a big source of income, but due to pollution, salt production and the destruction of mangroves, the quantity of fish is declining dangerously.

State **buses** run from Dwarka to Okha (1hr) every thirty minutes, although they sometimes terminate 20km along the road at Mithapur, 8km short of Okha, from where you can hop on a *tempo* the rest of the way. **Private buses** leave from the vegetable market and there are frequent Jeeps. There are no passenger boat services from Okha across the Gulf of Kutch at present, though there is talk of introducing a hovercraft service to Mandvi, and possibly even to Mumbai.

Porbandar

Once an international port and state capital, **PORBANDAR**, smack in the middle of the 200km of coastline between Veraval and Dwarka, is inextricably associated with the family of **Mahatma Gandhi**, who was born here. In fact, he was just one in an important political line – his uncle, father and grandfather all served as prime minister to the Maharaja of the Jethwa Rajput state. In addition, and in common with much of the southwest coast of Saurashtra, Porbandar is linked with the legends of **Krishna** – in ancient times the settlement was called Sudampuri, after one of Krishna's comrades.

Today, shrouded in a dim haze of excretions from the cement and chemical factories on its outskirts, Porbandar is grimier than ever and has little to attract regular tourists, save, of course, Gandhi's house. However, it is from this town and the surrounding area that most of Gujarat's **diaspora** originate, and "NRIs" (Non-resident Indians) from Britain, Canada and East Africa are often here on visits to family and friends.

Arrival and information

Porbandar is largely enclosed by water; by the sea to the south and by a smelly freshwater creek curving round from the north into the busy harbour on the western side of town. A path follows the coast from east to west but the **beaches** in between, used as public toilets, are rather unpleasant. Porbandar's main street, **Mahatma Gandhi (MG) Road**, runs from a fountain at its eastern end, northeast of which is the **railway station**, to a **triple gateway** at its western end, near Gandhiji's house. In the middle, at the **main square**, it is bisected by Aria Sumaj Road, which runs northwards across Jubilee Bridge, and southwards to the **GPO** (Mon–Sat 8am–6pm). Just east of that is the **ST bus stand** (connected to MG Road by ST Road) and, to its south, the main beach. **Banks** along MG Road change foreign currency and travellers' cheques. An internet service is run from the basement of the *Kuber* hotel.

Accommodation

Porbandar has an adequate range of **hotels**. Those in town are generally better quality but noisier, while the two seaside hotels have marine views to make up for their shortcomings. Checkout time is usually an inconvenient 10am.

Indraprasth, off ST Road ☎ 0286/242681, ☏ 242682. With its huge neon sign visible all over town, this large new hotel has a garden restaurant. Rooms include all mod cons, some unusually shaped beds, and are tastefully decorated with original murals by a local artist. ⑥–⑧

Kuber, off ST Road ☎ 0286/241289, ☏ 250164. Comfortable but fairly characterless hotel; Porbandar's poshest until usurped by the *Indraprasth* opposite. There is a pool hall in the complex. ⑤–⑧

Gujarat's most famous son was born **Mohandas Karamchand Gandhi** in 1869 at Porbandar on the Kathiawar peninsula. Although his family were merchants by caste – Gandhi meaning grocer – both his grandfather and father had risen to positions of political influence. Young Mohandas was shy and sickly, only an average scholar, but from early on questioned the codes of power around him and even flouted accepted Hindu practice: once eating meat for a year believing this would give him the physical edge the British appeared to possess. As a teenager, he began to develop an interest in spirituality, particularly in the Jain principle of **ahimsa** (nonviolence).

Gandhi moved to London to study law at 19, outwardly adopting the appearance and manners of an English gentleman, but also keeping to his mother's wish that he resist meat, alcohol and women. Avidly reading the Bible alongside the Bhagavad Gita, he started to view different religions as a collective source of truth from which everyone could draw spiritual inheritance.

After a brief spell back in India, Gandhi left again to practise law in South Africa, where the plight of fellow Indians – coupled with his own indignation at being ejected from a first-class rail carriage – fuelled his campaigns for racial equality. His public profile grew and he gained crucial victories for minorities against the practices of indentured labour. During this time he also opted to transcend material possessions, dressing in the handspun *dhoti* and shawl of a peasant, and he took a vow of celibacy. This turn to ascetic purity he characterized as *satyagraha*, which derived from Sanskrit ideas of "truth" and "firmness", and would become the touchstone of **passive resistance**. Returning to India with his messianic reputation well established – the poet Tagore named him "Mahatma" (Great Soul) – Gandhi travelled the country campaigning for **swaraj** (home rule). He also worked tirelessly for the rights of women and untouchables, whom he called **Harijans** (children of God), and founded an ashram at Sabarmati outside Ahmedabad where these principles were upheld (see p.681).

Gandhi stepped up his activities in the wake of the brutal massacre of protesters at Amritsar (see box p.662), leading a series of self-sufficiency drives during the 1920s, which included the public burning of imported clothes on huge pyres and culminated in the great **salt march** from Ahmedabad to Dandi in 1930. This month-long 386-kilometre journey led a swelling band of followers to the coast, where salt was made in defiance of the British monopoly on production. The march drew worldwide attention: though Gandhi was promptly imprisoned, British resolve was seen to have weakened and on release he was invited to a round-table meeting in London to discuss home rule. The struggle continued for several years and Gandhi served more time in jail – his wife Kasturbai dying by his side.

As the nationalist movement gained strength, Gandhi grew more concerned about the state of Hindu-Muslim relations. He responded to outbreaks of **communal violence** by subjecting his own body to self-purification and suffering through fasting. When Britain finally guaranteed independence in 1947 and sent Lord Mountbatten to oversee transition, it seemed that Gandhi's dream of a united and free India was possible after all. But the partition of India left him with a deep sense of failure. Once more he fasted in Calcutta in a bid to stem the violence as large numbers of Hindus and Muslims were exchanged between the new countries.

Gandhi's commitment to the fair treatment of Muslim Indians and his intention to visit and endorse Pakistan as a neighbour enraged many Hindu fundamentalists. He survived an attempt on his life on January 20, 1948, only to be shot dead from close range by a lone Hindu gunman in Delhi ten days later. Prime Minister Nehru announced the loss on national radio: "Friends and comrades, the light has gone out of our lives and there is darkness everywhere." The funeral was attended by a roll call of postwar statesmen and women. One representative of the new world order, US Senator Vandenberg, remarked that "Gandhi made humility and truth more powerful than empires".

GUJARAT | Saurashtra

9

Moon, ST Road ⊕ 0286/248380, ⊕ 250092.
Friendly and cosy hotel with immaculate small en-suite rooms, all with cable TV. **②**–**⑤**
Moon Palace, MG Road, 100m east of square
⊕ 0286/241172, ⊕ 243248,
ⓔ moonpalace@mail.com. New hotel with a wide range of rooms of varying comfort to suit all budgets. **②**–**⑦**
New Oceanic Hotel, Villa No 8, Chowpatty, by the beach ⊕ 0286/242917, ⊕ 241398. Overpriced hotel and restaurant playing on its sea view.
⑤–**⑥**
New Rajkamal Guest House, MG Road
⊕ 0286/242674. Still fairly rundown despite some renovation and very basic, but the cheapest in town, so it's often full. **①**
Sheetal, Aria Sumaj Road, opposite the GPO
⊕ 0286/247596, ⊕ 241821. Curious, plush lodge. All rooms have bathrooms, and those with a/c offer a real treat – bathtubs and padded wardrobes. **②**–**⑥**
Toran Tourist Bungalow, Chowpatty, by the beach ⊕ 0286/21476. Dilapidated and totally lacking in atmosphere, this GTDC hotel has doubles with sea-facing balconies and dorms. A simple indoor restaurant facing the sea serves tasty but unimaginative dishes. **③**–**⑤**

The Town

Mohandas Karamchand Gandhi was born in Porbandar on October 2, 1869 and lived here until he was 12. **Gandhi's birthplace** (free, but the guide will expect a donation) stands in the corner of a large courtyard in the west of town, in a narrow street entered through a large triple gateway and lined with carved wooden houses. The whole place is empty, though some of the walls in the reading and prayer rooms on the upper floors bear faded traces of paintings.

The modern temple next to the house, **Kirti Mandir** (*kirti* means age), was donated to the city in 1950 by the industrialist Nanjibhai Kalidas to commemorate Gandhi's 79 years; hence the 79 lamps adorning its 79-foot-high spire. Upstairs, a **museum** displays photographs, handmade Gujarati crafts and a bizarre collection of bottled seeds and oils, while downstairs there's a small **bookstore**. A couple of kilometres north of town (over Jubilee Bridge, then straight on, bearing left after 20m, and turning left after another 50m) the desperately old-fashioned **Planetarium**, topped by a statue of Nehru, is not worth bothering with. Directly opposite, however, set in a verdant garden, the airy pillared hall **Bharat Mandir** – another Kalidas benefaction – was built in memory of popular Hindi heroes. The figures of divinities are bright and distinct on the walls, and in the centre of the floor there's a large relief map of India.

Eating

Although Porbandar is well known in Gujarat for its **seafood**, you'll have a job finding it. Outside the hotel restaurants, there's a fairly uninspiring choice of **places to eat**; many seem to serve only a limited number of the dishes listed on the menus.

Aadarsh, MG Road, about 100m west of the main square. Popular, inexpensive veg restaurant for south Indian snacks. Open 10am–9.30pm.
Modern, off MG Road, just over 200m east of the square. Situated in a market, but clearly signposted, this is the best place in town for non-veg meals. Open 10am–10.30pm.
National, MG Road, next to the *Aadarsh*. Muslim-run place serving skimpy but ultra-cheap portions of meat and veg. Open 10.15am–2.45pm & 6.30–10.30pm.

Royal, ST Road. Tiny fish restaurant with no English-language sign (coming from MG Road, it's one block south on the right – look for the poster of Gulf fish on the wall inside). The pomfret is excellent, if rather fiery, but prices are higher than you'd expect from the look of the place. Open 11am–11pm.
Swagat, MG Road, 250m east of the main square. The best restaurant in town; softly lit and serving excellent, mid-priced Punjabi and south Indian veg dishes. Open 9am–3pm & 5.30–10pm.

Around Porbandar

Inland from Porbandar, a scattering of ancient temples are easily visited in a day. **BILESHWAR**, an hour north, is a small village built round an early seventh-century Shiva temple. Though the temple's exterior is of little interest, being coated in modern plaster, the inner sanctuary has a large monument dating from the Maitraka period (sixth to seventh century). Twenty kilometres further north, in a serene wooded valley, **GHUMLI** boasts one of Gujarat's largest step-wells, **Vikai Vav**. Dating from the early twelfth century, it is superb, with richly carved pillars and pavilions topped by peaked pyramidal roofs. At the more dilapidated (thirteenth-century) **Naulakha temple**, you can still see elaborate decorations beneath the collapsed roof. It's best to visit both villages early in the morning, as bus services back to Porbandar are poor (6 daily; 2hr–2hr 30min).

Junagadh and around

The friendly small town of **JUNAGADH** (also spelt Junagarh), around 160km from Diu (via Veraval), is an intriguing place, with a skyline broken by domes and minarets and narrow streets whose shopfronts brim with spices piled in high powdery pyramids. It's fun to amble through the town's lively bazaars, and with a mixture of Buddhist monuments, Hindu temples, mosques, bold gothic archways and mansions – not to mention the magnificent Jain temples on **Mount Girnar** – Junagadh is an exciting city to explore for anyone with an interest in architecture and a taste for history.

From the fourth century BC to the death of Ashoka (*c*. 232 BC), Junagadh was the capital of Gujarat under the Buddhist Mauryas. The short reigns of the Kshatrapas and the Guptas came to an end when the town passed into the hands of the Hindu Chudasanas, who in turn soon lost out to Muslim invaders. Muslim sovereignty lasted until Independence when, although the leaders planned to unite Junagadh with Pakistan, local pressure ensured that it became part of the Indian Union.

Because of the sanctity of Mount Girnar, the **Shivaratri festival** (Feb/March) assumes particular importance in Junagadh, when thousands of saffron-clad *sadhus* come to camp around the town and in the surrounding hills. Fireworks, processions, chanting, chillum-smoking and demonstrations of body-torturing ascetic practices continue for nine days and nights. Tourists arriving in Junagadh at this time are in for a memorable experience, but rooms are at a premium, so book well in advance.

Arrival and information

Arriving in Junagadh by bus or train, you're within easy walking distance of nearly all the hotels. From the long distance bus stand, turn right, then left at the main road and straight on across the railway tracks into the town centre; from the railway station, take a right down Station Road and a left at the end, by the petrol station. Local transport is provided by **auto–rickshaws**, though bicycles are great for getting around; with a bit of leg-work you can even cycle to the foot of Mount Girnar. Run-of-the-mill bikes can be had from a shop just west of Chittakhana Chowk, or from the *Relief Hotel*.

The best **information** on the town's sites and the religious significance of Girnar, as well as on Sasan Gir and further afield, is to be had from the friendly manager of the *Relief* hotel. The **GPO** (with poste restante) is 2km south of town; a smaller branch next to the local bus depot sells stamps and aerograms.

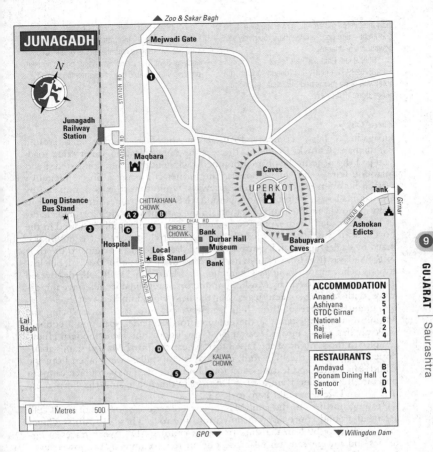

JUNAGADH

▲ *Zoo & Sakar Bagh*

Mejwadi Gate

N

Junagadh
Railway
Station

Maqbara

Caves

UPERKOT

Tank

Girnar

Long Distance
Bus Stand

CHITTAKHANA
CHOWK

DHAL RD

CIRCLE
CHOWK

Hospital

Local
★ Bus Stand

Bank
Durbar Hall
Museum

Bank

Babupyara
Caves

GIRNAR RD

Ashokan
Edicts

Lal
Bagh

KALWA
CHOWK

STATION RD

STATION RD

MAHATMA GANDHI RD

ACCOMMODATION	
Anand	3
Ashiyana	5
GTDC Girnar	1
National	6
Raj	2
Relief	4

RESTAURANTS	
Amdavad	B
Poonam Dining Hall	C D
Santoor	D
Taj	A

0 — Metres — 500

GPO ▼

▼ *Willingdon Dam*

The State Bank of India opposite the Durbar Hall Museum **changes** dollar and sterling cash; to exchange travellers' cheques, head for the nearby State Bank of Saurashtra or the Bank of Baroda in Azad Chowk Bazaar (all Mon–Fri 11am–3pm, Sat 11am–1pm). The *Cyber Café* (☎0285/628422), in the same complex as the *Ashiyana* hotel on Jayshree Road, offers internet access (Rs60/hr).

Accommodation

Junagadh offers average, simple **accommodation** with decent choices for budget travellers, but few with any claims to comfort or mod cons.

Anand, Bus Station Road ☎0285/630657. Clean and fresh with TV and some a/c rooms; they guarantee to change the sheets daily but have an awkward 9am checkout. ❸–❻

Ashiyana, Jayshree Road, just west of Kalwa Chowk ☎0285/624295. Excellent value uniform rooms with attached baths and cable TV. ❷

GTDC Girnar, Mejwadi Gate ☎0285/621201. Government-run hotel in an unattractive concrete block in the quiet northern outskirts of town; clean but impersonal with a reasonable restaurant that serves dinner from 6pm. ❹–❻

National, Kalwa Chowk ☎0285/627891. The clean and comfy non-a/c rooms are better value

than the overpriced a/c ones. Average food, fish and meat – and poor service mars the dimly lit downstairs restaurant. ❸–❺
Raj, Dhal Road, Chittakhana Chowk ☎ 0285/623961. Good-value friendly Muslim-run hotel with large rooms and attached bathrooms plus a dorm (Rs60). ❷–❸

Relief, Dhal Road, Chittakhana Chowk ☎ 0285/620280. Homely attached rooms, some with a/c. Average restaurant serves breakfast as early as 5am. The friendly manager prides himself on supplying reliable tourist information. ❷–❺

The City

Junagadh is fairly compact, focused on the busy market area around Chittakhana Chowk. To the north, near the railway station, quiet wide roads lead past the majestic Maqbara monuments while in the south congested streets surround Circle and Janta Chowks. The former comprises a fine semicircular terrace between towering Gothic gateways, while the latter is dominated by Durbar Hall with its modest museum. MG Road continues further south to Kalwa Chowk, another hub of activity. In the east the imposing fortified citadel of **Uperkot** (daily 6am–7pm; Rs1), perched on a thickly walled mound in the northeast of the city, is a peaceful place with a rich history, but is now colonized by eagles, egrets and squirrels. Legend dates the fort's origins to the time of the Yadavas (Krishna's clan) who fled Mathura to settle in Dwarka, but historians believe it was built by Chandragupta Maurya in 319 BC. Rediscovered and repaired in 976 AD by Muslim conquerors, it regained its defensive importance, withstanding sixteen sieges over the next eight hundred years.

A grand sequence of three high gateways cut into solid rock during the Muslim occupation stands at the entrance to the citadel, spanning a cobbled walkway that winds upwards past a *kund* (small pool) and some modern Hindu temples to the summit of the raised fort, where the **Jami Masjid** stands abandoned. Supporting the high roof, many of its 140 pillars were taken from the Chudasana palace and feature common Hindu motifs. The two fierce cannons opposite the mosque were used at Diu fort in defence against the Portuguese in 1530 and were brought here in 1538.

Heading north from the Jami Masjid, you come to a complex of small cells arranged around courtyards cut down into the rock. These **Buddhist Caves** ($5 [Rs5]) were built in the third or fourth century AD – worn traces of figurines and foliage can still be made out on the columns in the lower level. Nearby, more than 170 steps descend to the well **Adi Chadi Vav**, believed to have been built at the bequest of two maidservants of the royal household in the fifteenth century. The more impressive eleventh-century **Navghan Kuva**, in the southeast of the citadel, consists of a superb staircase that winds around the well shaft to the dimly lit water level over 52m below. A large tank nearby collects water from the surrounding hills to supply the town.

Below the southern wall of the fort, the **Babupyara Caves** ($5 [Rs5]), hewn from the rock between 200 BC and 200 AD, were used by Buddhists until the time of Ashoka, and then by Jains. A little to the north of Uperkot, the slightly later, plainer **Khapra Kodia caves** remain in good condition, intersected with staircases, colonnades and passages.

East of the main entrance to Uperkot, in Janta Chowk, the **Durbar Hall Museum** (daily except Wed and the 2nd & 4th Sat of each month, 9am–12.15pm & 3–6pm; Rs2) takes up part of the former palace of the nawabs. Silver chairs in the great hall stand in regal splendour around a large carpet, valuable silver clocks encase scruffy stuffed birds and huge coloured chandeliers hang from the ceiling. Surrounding rooms contain silver *howdahs* (elephant seats), weaponry, portraits and a collection of textiles, including 400-

year-old cloth embroidered with gold thread, displayed alongside royal parasols overlaid with intricate needlework.

Junagadh's chief Muslim monuments are the boldly decorated **muqbara** – quite unlike any other in Gujarat – on M G Road opposite the High Courts. Built for Muslim rulers in the nineteenth century, these squat and square mausolea are crowned with a multitude of bulbous domes. Smaller domes front the balconies overhanging the high curved arches cut into the tombs' sides. The most opulent tomb is the 1892 sepulchre of Mahabat Khan I, but more outstanding, for its complex design, is that of Vizir Sahib Baka-ud-din Bhar, completed four years later and flanked on each corner by tall minarets hugged with spiral staircases. Next to the *muqbara* is a mosque whose multicoloured pillars and gaily painted walls are oddly reminiscent of a *cassata*.

A group of smaller memorials to earlier nawabs stands in a peaceful graveyard, shielded by shops on Chittakhana Chowk and overgrown with coarse yellow grass. Delicate in both size and design, they boast fine carving on the graves and stone lattice-work cut from the walls. You'll have to scramble around the back of the shops to find the entrance: the rooftop of the adjacent *Amdavad* restaurant gives good aerial views.

Ashokan edicts

Two kilometres east of town on the road to Girnar, a rock engraved with the Buddhist **edicts of Ashoka** (daily except Wed 8.30–11am & 2–6pm; $5, Junagadh's most famous monarch, remains where it was placed in the third century BC, its impact somewhat marred by a modern shelter and concrete platform. Written in the Prakrit dialect, the worn verses etched into the granite encourage the practice of *dharma* and equality and beseech different religious sects to live in harmony and repent the evils of war. Situated on the route taken by pilgrims to the sacred hill of Girnar, the influence of Ashoka's edicts was strong: even as late as the seventh century AD there were about three thousand Buddhists in Junagadh, and over fifty convents. Sanskrit inscriptions on the same rock were added during the reigns of King Rudraman (150 AD) and Skandagupta (455 AD).

Mount Girnar

Rising to a height of over 1100m, **Mount Girnar**, a steep-sided extinct volcano 4km east of Junagadh, is a major pilgrimage centre for both Jains and Hindus, and has been considered sacred since before the third century BC. Buses leave from Junagadh's local depot hourly, dropping passengers at the mountain base from where five thousand irregular steps lead to the summit. It's best to start the ascent, which takes at least two hours, well before 7am when the scorching sun rises from behind the peak. The path climbs through eucalyptus forests before zigzagging across the sheer rock face, and there's a ready supply of chai and biscuits at stalls along the way.

On a plateau below the summit, roughly ninety minutes' climb from the base of the steps, the picturesque huddle of Jain temples has been slightly renovated since its erection between 1128 and 1500. **Neminath**, the 22nd *tirthankara* who is said to have died on Mount Girnar after seven hundred years of meditation and asceticism, is depicted as a black figure sitting in the lotus position holding a conch in the marble **Neminath temple**, the first on the left as you enter the "temple city". The temple comprises a vast complex of courtyards, cloisters and lesser shrines, and has exquisite carving on its pillars and within the domed roofs, decorated on the outside with unusual coloured mosaic. The **Mallinath temple** opposite was built by the brothers Vastupal and Tejapala, who also funded temples in Mount Abu and Shatrunjaya. Chequered black-and-white marble floors run through the three sanctuaries off the entrance porch, carved musicians and dancers adorn the ceiling of the main shrine and two smaller shrines feature images of *tirthankaras* raised on marble platforms.

It's well worth making the effort to climb the final two thousand steps to the summit of Mount Girnar; the views on the way are breathtaking. At the top, a temple dedicated to the Hindu goddess **Amba Mata** attracts both Hindu and Jain pilgrims, particularly newlyweds who come here to be blessed by the mother goddess and to pray for a happy marriage. Steps lead down from this temple and then up again along a narrow ridge towards **Gorakhnath Peak**, where a small shrine covers what are supposedly the footprints of the pilgrim Gorakhnath, and further to a third peak where the imprints of Neminath's feet are sheltered by a small canopy. At the most distant point of the ridge, a shrine dedicated to the fierce Hindu goddess **Kalika**, the eternal aspect of Durga, is a haunt for near-naked **Aghora ascetics** who express their absolute renunciation of the world by ritually enacting their own funerals, living among corpses on burial grounds, and smearing themselves with ash from funeral pyres.

Sakar Bagh

The pleasant flower-filled Sakar Bagh, 3.5km north of Junagadh, encloses the **zoo** and the small **Junagadh Museum** (daily except Wed 9am–12.15pm & 3–6.15pm; Rs10), which houses assorted prehistoric and other implements, medieval-era statues, manuscripts, ornaments and stuffed animals. The zoo, renowned for its successful breeding of endangered Asiatic lions, is home to wolves, tigers, birds and bears, all a little cramped in treeless cages, and a dim aquarium boasting nothing more impressive than goldfish.

Eating

Hotel **food halls** are supplemented by streetside stalls, and a few **restaurants**.

Amdavad, Dhal Road, just east of Chittakhana Chowk. Limited menu of veg and non-veg faves (try the chicken tikka) on an airy rooftop. Friendly service and good views of streetlife and tombs.
Poonam Dining Hall, just off Dhal Road. Excellent-value all-you-can-eat Gujarati thalis and thick *lassis*. Open 11am–11pm.

Santoor, north of Kalwa Chowk on MG Road. Excellent, reasonably priced south Indian and Punjabi dishes. Open 9.45am–3pm & 5–11pm.
Taj, Dhal Road, Chittakana Chowk. A good place for cheap meat and fish dishes with books on Gandhi to read while you wait. Open 9am–noon for breakfast, noon–2.30pm & 7–10.30pm for meals.

Moving on from Junagadh

Trains to Rajkot, Ahmedabad and the south coast call at Junagadh. The Down #352 leaves at 6am every morning for Sasan Gir (2hr 30min) and Delvada (6hr) for connections to Diu. It's slow, but more comfortable than the bus. Of the services to Rajkot, the afternoon Veraval-Rajkot Mail #9837 is the best; for Ahmedabad the overnight Girnar Express #9945 is the most convenient. There are two morning expresses to Veraval.

Buses from the long-distance bus stand, just west of Chittakhana Chowk, serve destinations around the state, although you'll have to change at Una for Diu. Bus #4 for Girnar (7 daily; 20min) leaves from the local bus stand 200m south of Chittakhana Chowk, or you can go by auto-rickshaw for Rs30–35. Agents around Kalwa Chowk such as Mahasagar Travels sell tickets for private buses, notably to Mumbai (18hr), while Raviraj Travels is good for services within Gujarat.

See Travel Details at the end of this chapter for more information on journey frequencies and durations.

Veraval and Somnath

On the Saurashtran coast, midway between Porbandar and Diu, the most lingering impression of the port of **VERAVAL** is its fishy stench. There's little to do here, unless you can endure the smells to watch the dhow-building in the docks, but Veraval is the jumping-off point for trips to **SOMNATH**, 5km east, whose temple is one of the twelve *jyotrilingas* of Shiva (see Contexts). Its shrines to Vishnu and connection with Krishna – who is said to have lived here with the Yadavas during the time of the *Mahabharata* – make it equally important for Vaishnavites.

Practicalities

Veraval is well connected by **bus** to Junagadh, Porbandar, Diu and Dwarka; the stand is west of town. **Trains**, from Junagadh (2hr), Rajkot (5hr) and Ahmedabad (12hr), pull in to the station just over 1km north of town. For long journeys by train from Veraval it's best to change at Rajkot. To get to Somnath take the **bus** (every 15–30min) – it stops a few hundred metres east of the Shiva temple. **Auto-rickshaws** are also available.

Veraval has a wider choice of **accommodation** than Somnath, though the smell and dirt may be enough to dissuade you from staying. The *Tourist Bungalow* on College Road (℡02876/20488; ❷–❺), on the outskirts near the shore and the lighthouse, offers a dorm, spacious rooms and a modest restaurant. The *Hotel Utsav* (℡02876/22306; ❸–❺), almost opposite the bus stand, is about as smart as you'll find and has decent prices on a/c rooms, although the *Hotel Chirag*, a block south of the main street, 200m east of the bus stand (℡02876/44205; ❷–❺) is also good. The dowdy *Hotel Satkar*, which overlooks the noisy street directly opposite the bus stand (℡02876/20120, ℻ 40006; ❷–❹), is basic but bearable.

In **Somnath**, *Sri Somnath Guest House* (℡02876/20212; ❶), on Triveni Road 100m back from the bus station, with a sign in Gujarati only, has inexpensive, very simple rooms; those at the modern *Mayuram* (℡02876/20286; ❸), almost immediately next door, are less spartan and cleaner. The more modern *Shiram* (℡02876/20999; ❸), tucked away in the side streets near the temple, has reasonable rooms but no a/c, despite what its sign proclaims. Twenty kilometres north along the coast, the old **summer palace** of the Junagadh nawabs at **CHORWAD** is now the GSTC *Palace Beach Resort* (℡02876/88556; ❺–❼), with separate cottages in well-tended gardens. There's nothing else to see or do here, which is a great part of its charm.

Food is unremarkable but easy to come by in both Veraval and Somnath, usually in simple form in hotels or at ordinary roadside stalls. In Veraval, the comfortable, a/c *Sagar* restaurant, opposite the *Chirag*, provides a varied vegetarian menu of Indian, Chinese and some Continental dishes, while the *Jill*, on the main road nearby, offers thalis and a limited menu and the anonymous fast-food joint below does veg pizzas and other snacks.

Somnath

SOMNATH consists of only a few streets and a bus stand – even its famed sea-facing **temple** is little to look at, despite its many-layered history. Legend has it that the site, formerly known as **Prabhas Patan**, was dedicated to Soma, the juice of a plant used in rituals and greatly praised for its enlightening and strengthening powers (and hallucinogenic effects) in the RigVeda. The temple of Somnath itself is believed to have appeared first in gold, at the behest of the sun god, next in silver, created by the moon god, a third time in wood at the command of Krishna and, finally, in stone, built by Bhimdeva, the strongest of the five Pandava brothers from the *Mahabharata* tale.

The earliest definite record, however, dates the temple to the tenth century when, rich from devotees' donations, it spilled over with precious stones and gold and rang to the sounds of musicians and dancing girls. Unfortunately, such wealth came to the attention of the brutal iconoclast Mahmud of Ghazni who captured and plundered so many of western India's cities between 1000 and 1027 AD; the temple was battered and pillaged, and its riches taken to Afghanistan. The next seven centuries saw a cycle of rebuilding and sacking, though the temple lay in ruins for over two hundred years after a final sacking by Aurangzeb before the most recent reconstruction began in 1950. Very little of the original structure remains and, although planned in the style of the Solanki period, the temple is built from unattractive modern stone. It's just possible to imagine its former glory from the height of the pillars supporting the towering *mandapa* and the fervour of the stream of devotees who pray in its airy halls. The main pujas are held at 7am, noon and 7pm.

In the small yard a little to the north, Somnath's fascinating **museum** (daily except Wed and 2nd & 4th Sat of month, 9am–noon & 3–6pm; Rs2) contains most of the architectural treasures saved from the temple – statues, lintels, sections of roof pillars, friezes and *toranas* from the tenth to twelfth centuries. It's all a bit cramped, but plans to move the collection to a new building opposite the bus stand will no doubt improve matters, and perhaps encourage the curators to invest in more explanatory labels.

Tongas and rickshaws gather outside the bus station, ready to take pilgrims to **temple sites east of Somnath**. Most important of these is **Triveni Tirth**, at the confluence of the Hiran, Saraswati and Kapil rivers as they flow into the sea: a peaceful place with a couple of unspectacular new temples. Before reaching the confluence, the road passes the ancient **Surya Mandir**, probably built during the Solanki period and now cramped by a newer temple and concrete houses built almost against its walls. Close to the sea, **Triveni Ghat** marks the place where Krishna's body was supposedly cremated after he was killed by a hunter who mistook him for a deer.

Gir National Park

The **Asiatic lion** which, thanks to hunting, forest-cutting and poaching, has been extinct in the rest of India since the 1880s, now survives in the wild in just 1150 square kilometres of the gently undulating Gir Forest. **Gir National Park** (mid-Oct or Nov to mid-June daily 7–11am & 3–5.30pm), entered from **Sasan Gir**, 60km southeast of Junagadh and 45km northeast of Veraval, holds almost three hundred Asiatic lions in its 260 square kilometres. They share the land with Maldhari cattle-breeders, whose main source of income is buffalo milk. Many families have been relocated outside the sanctuary, but those who remain are paid compensation by the government for the inevitable loss of buffalo to marauding lions. Gir also shelters two hundred **panthers**, seen more easily here than in any other Indian park.

Permits ($5 per day, $5 extra with camera, $10 extra with video) can be obtained at the **park information centre** in the grounds of the *Sinh Sadan Guest House* in Sasan Gir. You must enter the park in a Jeep ($10), hired from the information centre, which can take up to six people plus the mandatory guide ($10). Although a little unenthusiastic at times, they should know the spots where sightings are more likely, and may agree to follow any route you wish to take (maps available at information centre). Two good tracks are "Deva Danga" and "Riley's", or out to the lake near Kamelshwar, just west of the park boundary, where there's a good chance of glimpsing a marsh crocodile.

The rare **Asiatic lion** (*panthera leo persica*) is paler and shaggier than the more common African breed, with longer tail tassles, more prominent elbow tufts and a larger belly fold. Probably introduced to India from Persia, the lions were widespread in the Indo-Gangetic plains at the time of the Buddha. In 300 BC Kautilya, the minister of Chandragupta Maurya, offered them protection by declaring certain areas *abharaya aranyas*, "forests free from fear". Later, in his rock-inscribed edicts, **Ashoka** admonished those who hunted the majestic animals – the emblem of Ashoka, printed on all Indian currency notes, shows four Asiatic lions standing back to back.

Such a symbol of potency was favourite game for India's nineteenth-century rulers and by 1913, not long after it had been declared a protected species by the Nawab of Junagadh, the Asiatic lion population was reduced to twenty. Since then, Gir Forest has been recognized as a sanctuary (1969), and a national park (1975), and their number has swelled to over 250. While this is good news for the lions, they are starting to stray from the sanctuary, and recent attacks on humans and their livestock have caused justifiable concern. If plans to create a new sanctuary near Porbandar come to fruition, the lions should be assured security in their natural habitat.

Though sightings are far from certain, the lions are accustomed to human noise, and seem not to be disturbed by Jeeps, so if you see one, you should be able to watch it for a while. Summer is the best time to spot them, when they gather at waterholes to drink. For a certain guarantee, head for **Dewaliya** (daily dawn–dusk; $5), a fenced-off area of the park known as the "interpretation centre". Regular Jeeps (Rs200 return) leave from Sasan Gir; once in the centre visitors are driven in a minibus past docile lions. You get a surprisingly good impression of them "in the wild" here – they still have to hunt their food even if the deer have limited space to escape.

Practicalities

Sasan Gir village is connected by **train** to Junagadh, Veraval and Delvada, and by **bus** to Junagadh, Veraval and Una. The railway station, which also serves as a bus stand, is set back from the one main road that bisects the tiny town. You may be approached with an offer of a cheap basic **room**; if not, try asking at a stall. There are also three **hotels** in the village. Sadly, the Forest Department's delightful *Sind Sadan Guest House* (☏02877/85540; ❼–❾), in an old house amid well-kept gardens, recently hiked its prices for foreigners along with the park fees and even a dorm bed costs $5. Off the main road, past a small crocodile farm, rooms at the deluxe *Hotel Taj* (☏ & ☏02877/85528; ❾) are offered at international rates; and the new *Maneland Jungle Lodge* (☏02877/85555; ❾), several kilometres in the direction of Dewaliya, provides similar luxuries at a slightly cheaper price. You can **eat** at the stalls at the station end of the main road.

Diu

Set a little off the southern tip of Saurashtra, the island of **DIU**, less than 12km long and just 3km wide, was still under Portuguese control only forty years ago. Today, governed as a Union Territory from Delhi along with Daman, it has a relaxed atmosphere quite different from anywhere in central Saurashtra.

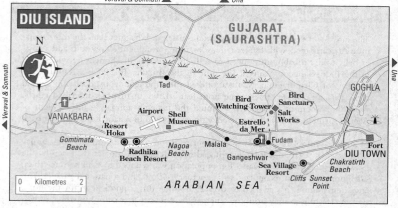

DIU ISLAND

N

GUJARAT
(SAURASHTRA)

Veraval & Somnath ◄

Tad

VANAKBARA

Airport   Shell
Museum

Resort
Hoka

Bird
Watching Tower

Bird
Sanctuary

Estrello
da Mer

Salt
Works

► Una

GOGHLA

Gomtimata
Beach

Radhika
Beach Resort

Nagoa
Beach

Malala

Fudam

Gangeshwar

Sea Village
Resort

Chakratirth
Beach

Fort

DIU TOWN

0   Kilometres   2

Cliffs Sunset
Point

ARABIAN SEA

Though its smallish beaches are nowhere near as idyllic as Goa's, most visitors stay longer than intended, idling in cafés, cycling around the island or strolling along the cliffs. The leisurely pace is also due in part to the lack of alcohol restrictions: the island's many bars can ply you with a vast array of beers and various hard liquors.

The island is easy to explore by bike. Diu Town in the east is the focus, where a maze of alleys lined with distinctive Portuguese buildings form the hub of the **old town**, where the **fort** stands on the easternmost tip of the island, looking out into the Gulf of Cambay. Along the northern coast the island's main road runs past salt pans that give way to mud flats sheltering flocks of water birds, including flamingoes that stop to feed in early spring. The route skirting the south coast passes rocky cliffs and beaches, the most popular of which is **Nagoa Beach**, before reaching the tiny fishing village of **Vanakbara** in the very west of the island.

Some history

The earliest records of Diu date from 1298, when it was controlled by the Chudasana dynasty. Soon after, like most of Gujarat, it fell into the hands of invading Muslims and by 1349 was ruled by Mohammed bin Tughluq who successfully boosted the shipbuilding industry. Diu prospered as a Gujarati harbour, and in 1510 came under the government of the Ottoman Malik Ayaz, who repelled besieging **Portuguese** forces in 1520 and 1521. Well aware of Diu's strategic position for trade with Arabia and the Persian Gulf, and having already gained a toehold in Daman on the eastern edge of the Gulf of Cambay, the Portuguese did not relent. Under the leadership of **Nuno da Cunha**, they once more tried, but failed, to take the island in 1531. In 1535 Sultan Bahadur of Gujarat agreed to sign a peace accord with Nuno da Cunha, but when the two leaders met, Bahadur was murdered and the Portuguese took control of Diu, immediately building the fort and a strong wall around the town.

While local traders and merchants thrived under the new rule, many resented paying taxes to boost Portuguese coffers already full with profits from customs duties levied on all vessels using the port. In defiance, local seamen made a series of unsuccessful raids on Portuguese ships. Moghul and Arab attacks were courageously resisted, too, but the Portuguese were finally forced out in

1961 by the Indian government which, after a swift bombing campaign, declared Diu part of India.

Arrival and information

The usual point of entry to Diu island is by road, via **Goghla**, the small fishing village on the mainland that forms the northern edge of Diu territory. The three hotels here are nothing special and most people head straight on to the island across the new bridge that links it to the northwestern edge of Diu Town. If arriving directly from points west, you may come across the other bridge in the centre of the island. **Buses** usually pull in to the stand by the bridge, from where you'll have to walk to the town. Better transport connections are found on the mainland, at **Una** (for the bus stand) and **Delvada** (for the railway station) and connected to Diu by *tempos*, auto-rickshaws and half-hourly buses. Jet Airways operates a **flight** every day but Saturday to Mumbai via Porbandar. The **tourist office** (Mon–Fri 9.30am–1.30pm & 2–6pm, Sat 9.30am–noon; ☏02875/52653), in the port opposite the main square, has maps and information. The **GPO** is on the west side of the main square, upstairs (Mon–Sat 8am–noon & 2–5pm). In the last year or two several private agencies have been authorized to **change money**; Abdul Aziz Musa opposite *Nilesh Guest House* offers slightly better rates, but they are all lower than the mainland. The State Bank of Saurashtra, near the square, (Mon–Fri 10am–2pm, Sat 10am–noon) is still the only one to do exchange but requires a photocopy of your passport's personal details page. The most common way to get around is by **bike** (Rs40–50/day), which you can rent at shops near the main square or close to the gate on the town's western edge. You can also rent well-maintained **motorbikes** (Rs100/day) from the mechanic opposite the petrol station between the square and the bus stand or at many of the hotels. Reshma Travels opposite *Nilesh Hotel* also rents cars. Auto-rickshaws are available, but if you're staying at Nagoa and want to get back from town at night expect high charges. There are several places to use the **internet** around town – the one next to the *Alishan* is most prominent – but expect to pay Rs80 per hour for very slow connections.

Accommodation

The atmosphere of Diu's **hotels**, largely concentrated in Diu Town around the central open-air markets and along Fort Road on the northeast coast, is in keeping with the leisurely pace of the island. Nearly all have a restaurant and bar, and negotiable prices for rooms most of the year. Prices below reflect the official tariff, off which you will hopefully get sizeable discounts of at least fifty percent. However, festival periods, particularly Diwali and Holi, see hotels fill and prices rocket. Some people may also be put off at such times by the rowdy atmosphere, fuelled by the freely available cheap booze.

Ankur, near the western gate ☏02875/52388, ℻53135, ✉shamal@ad1.vsnl.net.in. Clean and efficient with big airy rooms, but a bit impersonal. ⑤–⑦

Apana, Fort Road ☏02875/52112, ℻52309. Lively and fairly friendly, with adequate attached rooms, most with cable TV; the most expensive have sea-facing balconies. ⑥

Estrella Do Mar, Fudam Church, Nagoa Road ☏02875/52966. Fast becoming a favourite with those staying longer, this lovely converted church has six large basic rooms, as well as cooking facilities for residents. Fine atmosphere and setting. ①–②

Galaxy, near the bus stand ☏02875/53399. Comfortable and nicely decorated new hotel, let down by its location. ⑤–⑦

Jay Shankar, Jallandhar Beach ☏02875/52424. By far the best budget option, with a friendly atmosphere. The restaurant is better as a place for meeting people than for its basic curries and simple seafood. ①–②

Nilesh Guest House, set back from the fish market ℡ 02875/52319. Popular no-frills lodge with very basic rooms. Doubles with bath in the newer wing are not bad, but the restaurant is awful. ❷–❺

Pensão Beira Mar, Fort Road ℡ 02875/52342, ℱ 53213. Colonial mansion, totally refurbished in classical style by new owners. Its six rooms, including two huge corner suites, have a common sea-facing veranda. Maximum thirty percent discount. ❻–❼

Prince, Main Bazaar ℡ 02875/52265. Large clean rooms with balconies but not much of a view and it lacks character. Rather overpriced. The restaurant serves the usual standards. ❺–❼

Radhika Beach Resort, Nagoa Beach ℡ 02875/52554, ℱ 52553, ℮ radhikar@ad1.vsnl.net.in. The island's prime resort. All immaculate a/c deluxe and VIP rooms, set in beautifully landscaped grounds. Quality restaurant and residents-only swimming pool. ❽–❾

Resort Hoka, behind Nagoa Beach ℡ 02875/53036. The best budget place to stay outside Diu Town. Tasteful, simple rooms in a friendly rural setting. The courtyard restaurant serving travellers' staples is a little pricey. ❷–❺

Samrat, Collectorate Road ℡ 02875/52354, ℱ 52754. Diu Town's most upmarket hotel, recently spruced up. Comfortable carpeted a/c rooms with cable TV, balconies, attached bathrooms and constant hot water. ❹–❻

São Tome Retiro, St Thomas Church ℡ 02875/53137. Only five rooms of vastly different size and quality in the upstairs of the atmospheric church/museum. Regular barbecue parties in the yard open to outsiders. ❷–❸

Sea Village Resort, Sunset Point ℡ 02875/54345. Great setting but the ramshackle corrugated iron huts are rather dingy and grubby. Outdoor restaurant with fine bay view. ❹–❺

Tourist Cottages, Jallandhar Beach ℡ 02875/52654. Charming government-run a/c cottages for two or four people on the coast overlooking the Arabian Sea. ❻

Diu Town

Cosy little **Diu Town** is protected by the fort in the east and a wall in the west. **Nagar Seth's Haveli**, one of the grandest of the town's distinctive Portuguese mansions, is on Makata Road, hidden in the web of narrow streets that wind through the residential Old Portuguese District. Fisherfolk make daily trips from the north coast in wooden boats; women lay the silvery catch out on rugs to sell in the market near the mosque.

Although the Christian population is dwindling along with the old language, a few **churches** built by the former European inhabitants are still used. Portuguese Mass is celebrated beneath the high ceilings and painted arches of **St Paul's**, while the church of **St Thomas**, to the northwest, is now a museum (daily 8am–9pm; free), and that of **St Francis of Assisi**, to the south, is partly occupied by the local hospital.

Diu's serene **fort** (daily 7am–6pm; free) stands robust, resisting the battering of the sea on three sides and sheltering birds, jackals and the town jail. Its wide moat and coastal position enabled the fort to withhold attack by land and sea, but there are obvious scars from the Indian government's air strikes in 1961 – notice the hole above the altar of the church in the southwest corner. Now abandoned almost completely to nature, and littered with centuries-old cannonballs, it commands excellent views out to sea and over the island.

Around the island

Cliffs and rocky pools make up much of the southern coast of the island, giving way to the occasional sandy stretch. South of Diu Town is the small **Jallandhar Beach**; the larger **Chakratirth Beach**, overlooked by a high mound, is a little to the west, just outside the city walls. In many ways this is the most attractive beach and it's usually deserted, making it the best option for an undisturbed swim, especially for female travellers. At its western end, **Sunset Point** provides the regular spectacle of a golden disc sinking into the waves. The longest and only developed beach is at **Nagoa**, 7km west of town, where

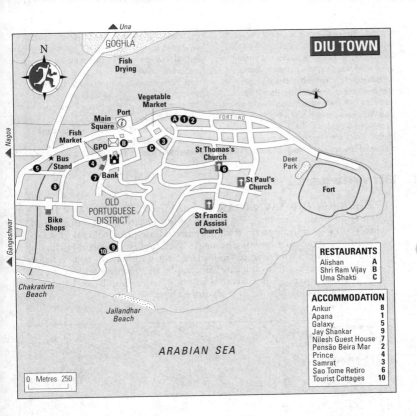

RESTAURANTS
Alishan	**A**
Shri Ram Vijay	**B**
Uma Shakti	**C**

ACCOMMODATION
Ankur	**8**
Apana	**1**
Galaxy	**5**
Jay Shankar	**9**
Nilesh Guest House	**7**
Pensão Beira Mar	**2**
Prince	**4**
Samrat	**3**
Sao Tome Retiro	**6**
Tourist Cottages	**10**

9

GUJARAT | Saurashtra

there are three hotels (avoid the grim *Gangar Sagar Rest House*) and a restaurant, as well as stalls, camel rides and the like, but sunbathers, especially women, are more likely to get hassled here by attention-seekers. Two buses a day leave Diu Town at 11am and 4pm and return from Nagoa at 1pm and 6pm. If you have a vehicle, splendid **Gomtimata Beach**, between Nagoa and Vanakbara, is invariably deserted.

Not far out of town, a turning off the Nagoa Road leads to **FUDAM**, an attractive village of Portuguese houses washed in pale yellow and sky-grey, dominated by the smooth white bell towers of its church, now a guesthouse. One small outdoor **bar**, shaded by twisted palm fronds, stands in the centre of the village. Further along the main road, on the right just before the airport, the newly opened **Shell Museum** (daily 10am–7pm; Rs10) is worth a visit, as much for the enthusiastic personal attention of the gentlemanly owner as the undoubtedly magnificent collection of rare shells from all over the world.

Eating

Sadly, the only vestige of Portuguese influence on the dining scene in Diu is the availability of alcohol. Some of the hotel **restaurants** are rather plain, but the better ones are listed below. Most bars close in the afternoon and after 9pm, although restaurants are often open later. Stalls in the main square sell snacks and mix excellent creamy lassis all day.

Alishan, Fort Road. Decent veg, meat and fish, with Chinese options.

Apana, Fort Road. Slightly posher and pricier than the *Alishan* next door, with a pleasant terrace. Good tandoori chicken and lobster is usually available if ordered in advance. Open 7am–11pm.

Ashiyana, Old Portuguese District. One of the only surviving places serving good filling thalis. Open 11am–3pm & 6–10pm.

Pensão Beira Mar, Fort Road. Attractive rooftop restaurant offering a wide range of Indian, Chinese and Continental dishes. Chicken and fish a speciality, washed down by beer or port.

Samrat, Collectorate Road. One of the best hotel restaurants, serving the earliest breakfast. Quality north Indian dishes in rich sauces are the best on offer.

Shri Ram Vijay, just off the square. Best place for cheap and delicious ice creams and shakes.

Uma Shakti, behind the market. Friendly hotel rooftop with copious portions of tasty Indian, Chinese and Western food but less musical taste.

Bhavnagar

The coastal port of **BHAVNAGAR**, founded in 1723 by the Gohil Rajput Bhavsinghji, whose ancestors came to Gujarat from Marwar (Rajasthan) in the twelfth century, is an important trading centre whose principal export is cotton. With few sights of its own, Bhavnagar does, however, boast a fascinating bazaar in the old city, and is an obvious place to stay for a night or two before heading southwest to the wonderful Jain temples of Palitana. Incidentally, it is one of the few places (Ahmedabad is another) where you'll see hand-carts being pulled by man and wife, or by women alone.

Arrival

Arriving by **train**, the way into town is straight ahead along Station Road. From the ST **bus stand**, turn right up ST Station Road for the town centre. The State Bank of Saurashtra and the Bank of India have **exchange** facilities (open usual Gujarati hours Mon–Fri 11am–3pm, Sat 11am–1pm); they're on Amba Chowk between the hotels *Shital* and *Vrindavan*. The **GPO** (Mon–Fri 10am–6pm, Sat 10am–1pm) is next to the High Court on High Court Road, with branches just off Station Road a block south of the station, and opposite the southeastern corner of the dried-up Ganga Jalia Tank. You can rent **bikes** (Rs3/hr) from a shop less than 100m south of the *Mini Hotel* on Station Road.

Accommodation

Bhavnagar has a reasonable choice of **places to stay**. There are a few budget hotels near the railway station, which also has retiring rooms; the more upmarket options are in Darbargadh, towards the bus stand, and around the bus stand itself.

Apollo, ST Station Road, opposite the bus stand ☏ 0278/425251, ⊕ 412440. Carpeted clean rooms with TV, some a/c. ⑤–⑥

Blue Hill, opposite Pil Gardens ☏ 0278/426951, ⊕ 427313. Modern well-maintained five-storey hotel with all mod cons, views over the gardens from front rooms and a roof terrace. ⑦–⑧

Jubilee, opposite Pil Gardens ☏ & ⊕ 0278/421744, ⊕ 430045. Similar to the adjacent *Blue Hill*, but not quite as smart and a little cheaper. ⑦–⑧

Mini, Station Road ☏ 0278/439149, ✉ bhv@hotelmini.com. Clean well-kept rooms, some with TV, some without windows. ②–③

Nilambagh Palace, ST Station Road ☏ 0278/424241, ⊕ 428072. The classiest hotel in Bhavnagar, in an old palace set in vast gardens west of the bus stand, with large luxurious rooms. ⑧–⑨

Satkar, Station Road ☏ 0278/423027, ⊕ 414894. Small well-maintained rooms, all with attached baths, some with cable TV. Best value near the railway station. ③–⑤

Shital, Darbargadh ☏ 0278/428773. Small basic hotel with 9am checkout and a men's dorm (Rs75). Entrance hidden round back in alley. ②–③

Vrindavan, Darbargadh ☏ 0278/518928. Immaculate but unelaborate rooms (some with TV and a/c), set in part of a massive old palace in the town centre. Best value for budget travellers. 24hr checkout. ②–⑤

The City

The focus of interest in Bhavnagar is the **old city**, its vibrant markets overlooked by delicate wooden balconies and the plush, pillared fronts of former merchants' houses. Sections of the old city are reserved for specific trades; there's a silver bazaar, a street lined with rope and tool stalls, a cloth bazaar where tailors perch like birds in tiny cubby holes above the shops, and a gold bazaar full of watchmakers and menders. Local handicrafts to look out for include *bhandani* and the elaborate beadwork characteristic of the region.

There are only a couple of formal attractions. The marble temple, **Ganga Devi Mandir**, by the dry Ganga Jalia Tank in the centre of town, has a large dome and intricate lattice-work on its walls, while the otherwise unspectacular **Takhteshwar temple**, raised on a hill in the south of town, at least affords a good view over the city to the Gulf of Cambay in the east. Southeast of the town centre, on the road to Diamond Chowk, the **Gandhi Smirti Museum** (Mon–Sat, closed 2nd & 4th Sat of month 9am–12.30pm & 2.30–6pm; free) exhibits Buddhist, Jain and Hindu statues, medieval bronzes, Harappan terracottas and a fossil display flanked by the four-metre jawbones of a sperm whale. Labels are mostly in Gujarati. Upstairs is a display devoted to Gandhi's life, and a Khadi Gramodyog shop.

Eating

Most of Bhavnagar's **restaurants** adjoin the main hotels, and offer local, national and international cuisine; the most upmarket is the *Nilambagh Palace Hotel*. An excellent unnamed place behind Police Chowk on Gandhi Road stays open all day for low-priced local thalis.

Blue Hill, opposite Pil Gardens. The hotel has two high-standard restaurants: the *Nilgiri*, with Indian, Chinese and Western; and *Gokul*, which serves Gujarati thalis, and is slightly cheaper.

Manali, *Apollo Hotel*, ST Station Road. Comfy ground-floor restaurant serving excellent meat, prawn and veg dishes. Sauces are especially rich and tasty. Open 11am–2.30pm & 7–10.30pm.

Mashoor Juice Centre, Darbargadh. Excellent range of juices at this corner stall. Open 10am–10pm.

Mini Dining Hall, *Hotel Mini*, Station Road. Supper-time Gujarati thalis at low prices. Open 8.30–10.30pm.

Vrindavan, *Hotel Vrindavan*, Darbargadh. Good Gujarati thalis and south Indian snacks in an a/c hall. Open 11am–3pm & 7–11pm.

Woodlands, in the *Jubilee Hotel*, opposite Pil Gardens. Decent pure veg place for Indian, Chinese and Western food on a pleasant terrace. Meals 11am–3pm & 7–11pm, sandwiches round the clock.

Moving on from Bhavnagar

The usual way to get anywhere from Bhavnagar is by **bus**. Services run from the ST bus stand to Ahmedabad (hourly; 5hr), Mumbai, Bhuj, Rajkot, Junagadh and Veraval, plus Vadodara (8 daily; 6hr) and Surat (3 daily; 9hr). There's no direct service to Diu but seven to Una (6hr), where you can pick up buses to Diu every half-hour. There are hourly buses to Palitana (1hr 15min) but only one daily service direct to Velavadar (1hr). **Private buses**, operated by firms such as AD Amin opposite the ST station (☎0278/421307) and Punjab Travels opposite the *Galaxy Cinema* on Kala Nala Road (☎0278/424582), serve destinations in Gujarat and interstate. Some pricier sleeper buses (with berths) are available.

Three daily express **trains** run from Bhavnagar to Ahmedabad (5hr 35min–7hr 5min), where you'll have to change for anywhere beyond. There are also three fast passenger trains to Palitana, and one overnight to Rajkot. **Flights** to Mumbai (50min) are operated four days of the week by Indian Airlines (northwest of Ganga Jalia Tank; ☎0278/426503). The airport is 5km southeast of town and best reached by auto-rickshaw for Rs35–40.

See Travel Details at the end of this chapter for more information on journey frequencies and durations.

Velavadar Black Buck Sanctuary

Outside the tiny village of **VELAVADAR**, 65km north of Bhavnagar, the **Black Buck Sanctuary** (mid-Oct to mid-July) shelters the highest concentration of this Indian antelope anywhere. Although the area was only officially declared a sanctuary in 1969, the buck were always protected by the Bishnoi tribe (see pp.193 and 226). You can see the elegant black-and-white males strutting, chasing and jousting with their magnificent curved horns to define and defend their territories, each accompanied by a group of light-coloured females. It is also possible to walk in the park and watch wolves, now rare in India, visiting the water holes.

There is only one direct **bus** to Velavadar (1hr) leaving Bhavnagar at 4.30pm and returning the following morning, so a visit to the sanctuary entails at least one night's **stay** at the small, perfectly located *Kaliyar Bhavan Forest Lodge* (❷), unless you hire a taxi for around Rs800. **Permission** to visit (Rs15 for 3 days, Rs15/day extra with camera or video, Rs5/day extra with vehicle) must be sought from Bhavnagar's Forest Office (Mon–Sat, closed 2nd & 4th Sat of month 10.30am–6pm; ☎0278/426425), in the cream and brown concrete government offices known as Multi-Storey Building, Annexe F/10, just west of the bus stand. **Food** is usually available but should be ordered in advance. **Guides** are not a necessity, but can be hired very cheaply.

Shatrunjaya and Palitana

For many visitors, the highlight of a trip to Saurashtra is a climb up the holy hill of **Shatrunjaya** (7am–7pm), India's principal Jain pilgrimage site, just outside the dull town of **PALITANA**, 50km southwest of Bhavnagar. Almost nine hundred temples – many made of marble – crown this hill, said in legend to be a chunk of the mighty Himalayas from where the Jains' first *tirthankara*, Adinath, and his chief disciple gained enlightenment. While records show that the hill was a *tirtha* as far back as the fifth century, the existing temples date only from the sixteenth century, anything earlier having been lost in the iconoclastic Muslim raids of the 1500s and 1600s.

Climbing the wide steps up Shatrunjaya takes one to two hours, depending on weather conditions and fitness, though, as with all hilltop pilgrimage centres, *dholis* (seats on poles held by four bearers) are available for those unable or unwilling to walk. The view as you ascend is magnificent; spires and towers swoop upwards, hemmed in by mighty protective walls. You should allow at least two more hours to see even a fraction of the temples.

The individual *tuks* – temple enclosures – are named after the merchants who funded them. Together they create a formidable city, laid over the two summits and fortified by thick walls. Each *tuk* comprises courtyards within courtyards chequered in black-and-white marble and several temples whose walls are exquisitely and profusely carved with saints, birds, animals, buxom maidens, musicians and dancers. Many temples are two or even three storeys high, with balconies crowned by perfectly proportioned pavilions. The looming *shikharas* (spires) are hollow on the inside, their conical ceilings swarming with carved figures that flow in concentric circles outwards from a central lotus blossom.

The largest temple, dedicated to Adinath, in the Khartaravasi *tuk* on the northern ridge, constantly hums with murmured prayers and blessings, and is usually full of masked nuns and monks, dressed in white and carrying white fly-whisks. The southern ridge and the spectacular Adishvara temple in its western corner are reached by taking the right-hand fork at the top of the path. On a clear day the view from the summit takes in the Gulf of Cambay to the south, Bhavnagar to the north and the mountain range which includes Mount Girnar to the west.

The **museum** close to the bottom of the hill displays a collection of Jain artefacts, labelled in Gujarati but well worth seeing, and an ancient clock that invites a great deal of attention every hour when a model man emerges from a hole to hit a bell.

A path leads along the ridge and down into the valley of Adipur, 13km away, but it's open for one day only, during the festival of **Suth Tera** (Feb/March). Up to 50,000 pilgrims come to Shatrunjaya for this unique display of devotion and are welcomed at the end of their *yatra* in a tented compound at Adipur with food and drink donated by Jain merchants.

Practicalities

Auto-rickshaws and tongas run from Palitana to the foot of Shatrunjaya, or it's a thirty-minute walk. **Buses to Palitana** arrive from and leave for Bhavnagar (hourly; 1hr–1hr 30min), Junagadh (2 daily; 6hr) and Una (for Diu; 1 daily; 5hr). Three daily passenger **trains** connect Palitana with Bhavnagar (2hr).

There is no **accommodation** on Shatrunjaya so you'll have to stay in Palitana, either at one of many Jain *dharamshalas* in the old part of town (all of which oblige guests to observe strict vegetarianism) or in one of the hotels on the bus stand side of town. The comfortable GTDC *Hotel Sumeru* (☎02848/2327; ❸–❺), on Station Road between the bus stand and the railway station, has ordinary and a/c rooms, and dorms (Rs50). Its restaurant serves lunchtime thalis, à la carte evening meals and simple breakfasts. Accommodation at *Hotel Shavrak* (☎02848/2428; ❷–❸), opposite the bus stand, is adequate, though less spacious; it also has inexpensive men-only dorms (Rs50). In the narrow alley next to it, the basic and very cheap *Jagurti Restaurant* serves excellent Gujarati meals and snacks, and is always busy.

Southeastern Gujarat

The seldom-visited **southeastern** corner of Gujarat, sandwiched between Maharashtra and the Arabian Sea, harbours few attractions to entice you off the road or railway line to or from Mumbai. There's little to recommend **Vadodara** (Baroda), former capital of the Gaekwad rajas, but its proximity to the old Muslim town of **Champaner** and the ruined forts and exotic Jain and Hindu temples that encrust **Pavagadh Hill**. Further south, the dairy pastures around **Anand** gradually give way to a swampy, malaria-infested coastal strip of banana plantations and shimmering saltpans cut by silty, sinuous rivers and peppered with mango trees and brick villages. The area's largest city is **Surat**, a sprawling modern industrial centre whose handful of colonial monuments are engulfed by some of the most chronically congested streets in South Asia. The historic port of **Bharuch**, overlooking the River Narmada 66km north of Surat, is not overtly picturesque but the old colonial quarter can still make a worthwhile diversion from the main route south. The only place of real interest in the far south of the state is the former Portuguese territory of **Daman**. Although nowhere near as appealing as its colonial cousins Goa and Diu, the 12km-long enclave, whose main *raison d'être* is as a watering hole for alcohol-starved Gujarati men, does boast some impressive colonial architecture, and a couple of so-so beaches.

The west coast's main **transport** arteries, the NH-8 and Western Railway, run in tandem between Mumbai and Ahmedabad. Even if you are only making short hops, stick to the trains: the highway, a graveyard of overturned buses and Tata trucks, is one of the most nail-bitingly terrifying roads in India.

Vadodara (Baroda)

The area between Ahmedabad and **VADODARA** (or Baroda) is primarily agricultural, but Vadodara itself is a heavily congested noisy industrial city. Though the old city does retain some interest, with its beautiful ancient *havelis* and various bazaars, and offers some green escapes, Vadodara has few tourist attractions. However, it does make the most convenient place to stay for a trip to the ruined city of **Champaner** and, if you are here at the time of the Navratri festival (late Sept/early Oct), you can join the throngs watching thousands of children dancing into the small hours.

Prior to Independence, Vadodara was ruled by the Gaekwad Rajputs. Unlike their Rajasthani counterparts, they were little affected by the Indian government's withdrawal of privy purses, and continue to live in lavish **palaces**.

Ahmedabad   Ahmedabad   Airport (6 km)

VADODARA

N

Indian Airlines

Baroda Museum   Health Museum

ST Bus Stand

Railway Station

SAYAJI BAGH   Zoo

Planetarium

MS University

SAYAJI GUNJ

See inset map

RC DUTT RD

Kirti Mandir

Nazarbaug Palace

RAOPURA RD   NAYA BAZAAR

Tambekarwada Haveli   Sarsagar Tank   Laheri Pura Gate   Pani Gate

DANDIA BAZAAR   M G ROAD

Yogikrupa

STATION ROAD

City Buses

TILAK ROAD

Nyaya Mandir   Mandvi Gate

Laxmi Niwas Palace

Bank

Maharaja Fateh Singh Museum

Gendi Gate

ACCOMMODATION

Ambassador	5
Delux	8
Green Hotel	2
Jagdish Hindu Lodge	4
Kalyan	7
P.M. Regency	3
Rainbow	9
Surya	6
Welcomgroup Vadodara	1

RESTAURANTS

Canara Coffee House	F
Copper Coin	D
Gokul Hotel	E
Havmor	B
Radika	A
Sun 'n' Shine	C

0   Metres   500

Surat   Surat

Arrival and information

The **railway station** and **bus stand** are very close together in the west of town, within easy walking distance of almost all the hotels. The airport is 6km northeast, or about Rs30 away by auto-rickshaw. There's a very helpful **tourist information** desk in the station (Mon–Sat 11am–5pm; ☎0265/794456), which sells a leaflet with a map and a list of the city's main sights. They also arrange **city tours** (daily except Thurs 2–6pm), if there are ten or more takers, and a tour to **Pavagadh**. Sterling and dollars cash or travellers' cheques can be **changed** at the Bank of Baroda international services branch in Sayaji Gunj behind Kadak Bazaar (Mon–Fri 11am–3pm), the Bank of South India opposite, or the State Bank of India on RC Dutt (Racecourse) Road between the *Green* and *Welcomgroup* hotels. The Trade Wings agency behind *Hotel Amity* in Sayaji Gunj also runs an efficient exchange service and is open later than the banks. The **GPO** is off Raopura Road in the centre of town. For **secondhand books**, try the stall on the corner of Tilak Road by the *Jagdish Lodge* in Sayaji Gunj. The great number of students also means there is an abundance of **cyber cafés** around Sayaji Gunj.

Accommodation

Vadodara's **hotels** are designed with business visitors in mind: there are several mid-range and upmarket places, and just a handful of inexpensive lodges which could all do with improved maintenance. Most of the hotels are grouped in the **Sayaji Gunj** area just south of the railway station.

Ambassador, Sayaji Gunj ℡0265/362726, ℻361129. Slightly grubby but spacious rooms with TV and bath. A good lower mid-range option. ❸–❺

Delux, Kadak Bazaar ℡0265/362533. Hardly lives up to its name but this small clean hotel in the heart of a lively bazaar is friendly. ❷

Green Hotel, RC Dutt (Racecourse) Road ℡0265/336111. The best low-budget option five minutes' walk from the station. The 100-year-old house has rooms (some with TV & phone) with period furniture and real character, though it lacks the modern touch. ❷–❸

Jagdish Hindu Lodge, Sayaji Gunj ℡0265/361495. Clean and friendly with decent-sized rooms, although these are only divided by wooden partitions and the place does get busy. ❶–❷

Kalyan, Sayaji Gunj ℡0265/362211. Clean and efficient hotel, with reasonably priced well-furnished rooms. ❹–❺

P.M. Regency, Sayaji Gunj ℡0265/361616, ℻363050. Smart modern multistorey with all facilities. Good value for its price range. ❻–❽

Rainbow, Commerce Centre 7th Floor, Sayaji Gunj ℡0265/363072, ℻363091. Small but spotless and well-furnished rooms with TV, phones and fantastic views. ❺–❻

Surya, Sayaji Gunj ℡0265/361361, ℻361555, ℇsales@hotelsurya.com. Smart option with spacious rooms and fine service but not quite as good value as the *P.M. Regency*. ❻–❽

Welcomgroup Vadodara, RC Dutt Road ℡0265/330033, ℻330050, ℇvadodara@itchotels.co.in. Baroda's only five-star hotel, with predictably swanky and well-maintained rooms plus all services. ❾

The City

Vadodara's chief attractions are in **Sayaji Bagh**, the large green park whose main entrance is on Tilak Road. It takes one or two hours to get round the large Indo-Saracenic **Baroda Museum and Picture Gallery** (daily 10.30am–5.30pm; Rs5), reached from University Road, which holds art and textiles from all over the world, Gujarati archeological remains and Moghul miniatures. Among the best exhibits are carved doors and lintels taken from Gujarat's *havelis* and some fine fifth-century Jain bronzes excavated nearby. Works in the Picture Gallery are mostly British and European from the seventeenth to nineteenth centuries, including Poussin's *Christ and Mary Magdalene*, a Rubens portrait and a painting by Johann Zoffany of David Garrick as Macbeth. As well as the museum, Sayaji Bagh contains a **Planetarium** (35min shows daily except Thurs in English at 5pm; Rs5), a pitiful **zoo**, a small **Health Museum** (11am–6pm; free), and a toy train running on what must be the narrowest gauge in India (10 inches).

From Sayaji Bagh, Tilak Road continues east across the river past **Kirti Mandir**, the mausoleum of Vadodara's rulers, towards the old city, the centre of which is MG Road, bounded at its western end by **Laheri Pura Gate** and **Nyaya Mandir** (literally "New Temple"), a fine Indo-Saracenic building which is now a law court. There's another gate (Pani Gate) at the eastern end of MG Road, near the late-nineteenth-century **Nazarbaug Palace** and, halfway between the two, the four-way **Mandvi Gate**, originally Moghul but much altered since. To the west of MG Road is an artificial lake, the **Sarsagar Tank** (check out *Pratap Talkies*, an over-the-top Art Deco pile at the northeastern corner), surrounded by glorious painted *havelis* and with a huge modern statue of Shiva in the middle. Other buildings worth a look include **Laxmi Niwas Palace** in the south of town, the most extravagant of Vadodara's palaces, now a heritage hotel. Glimpse it from the road or from the dull **Maharaja Fateh Singh Museum** (Tues–Sun 10.30am–5.30pm; Rs20) in the palace grounds.

Eating

With a large student population and a constant influx of business people, Vadodara has a choice of **restaurants** in all price ranges. Several upmarket hotels lay on buffet spreads; fast-food and snack joints are dotted all around the Sayaji Gunj and station areas.

Canara Coffee House, Dandia Bazaar Pukka coffee – a rarity in north India – and south Indian snacks at very low prices; a good place for breakfast. Open 7am–10pm.

Copper Coin, World Trade Centre, Sayaji Gunj. Good though not cheap variety of veg and non-veg fare in an octagonal a/c room with piped muzak. Open noon–4pm & 7–11pm.

Gokul, Koti Char Rasta. Small snack bar serving excellent south Indian, Punjabi and Gujarati thalis, and ice cream at very low prices. Open 10am–10pm.

Havmor, Tilak Road. Tasty but fairly pricey Indian, Chinese and Western food with a/c and good service. Open noon–10.45pm.

Kalyan Hotel, Sayaji Gunj. Veg canteen extremely popular with students, coffee shop specializing in Mexican snacks and restaurant; all reasonably priced. Open 7.30am–11pm.

Radika, Sayaji Gunj. Glass-fronted and very popular inexpensive thali house with a red plastic sign in Gujarati (next door to LM Kothari & Sons). Open 8am–10pm.

Sun'n'Shine, Sayaji Gunj. Breezy roof terrace with South Indian and other snacks (open 5–11pm). Behind it a huge a/c hall offers a full menu of veg and non-veg, including tasty varieties of kebab, to the mellow sound of live *ghazals* in the evening; open 11am–3pm & 7–11pm.

Surya, Sayaji Gunj. Two good moderately priced veg restaurants: the *Vega*, offering filling lunch buffets with dishes from all over the world; and the cheaper *Myra*, with delicious Gujarati thalis.

Moving on from Vadodara

Vadodara **railway station** is often rather crowded and queues for tickets can be long (the reservation office is upstairs); you can bypass the hassle for a Rs15–25 fee if you buy your ticket from Yogikrupa Travel Service opposite (daily 8am–8pm; ☏ 0265/794977). All trains travelling along the main Delhi–Mumbai line stop here. New Delhi is reached by at least ten daily trains (12–24hr), via Kota and Sawai Madhopur, with one train a day to Jaipur (11hr 50min). There are at least fourteen daily services to Ahmedabad (1hr 55min–2hr 30min), some of which continue to Rajkot, Jamnagar and Porbandar and one each to Dwarka/Okha and Gandhidam. Going south, nine stop at Vapi (for Daman, 4hr). The fastest and most expensive train in both directions is the daily Rajdhani Express #2951/2952, serving Kota (6hr 30min), New Delhi (12hr, overnight) and Mumbai Central (4hr 40min), while the other superfast Shatabdi Express #2009/2010 serves Ahmedabad (1hr 55min), Surat (1hr 50min) and Mumbai Central (5hr 30min) daily except Friday. Further afield there is the daily Navjivan Express #6045 to Chennai (32hr 50min) and on most days there is some service to other points in the far east or south of India.

The **bus stand** on Station Road, a little north, has regular, state-run services to other Gujarati towns, including Ahmedabad, Bharuch, Surat, Champaner (hourly; 1hr 30min), Bhavnagar (hourly; 6hr) and Rajkot (hourly; 8hr). Mumbai (14hr) is served by eight buses, all in the evening, but none start at Vadodara, so they may be full when they arrive - the train is far better. There are also services to Pune, Indore and Bhopal (1 daily; 16hr). Stalls selling tickets for **private buses** (to Mumbai, Rajasthan and Madhya Pradesh) line Station Road.

Indian Airlines **flies** daily to Mumbai (55min) and Delhi (1hr 25min). The office is in Fatehgunj, just north of Sayaji Bagh (☏ 0265/794747). There are also two daily flights to Mumbai (50min) with Jet Airways (☏ 0265/343441).

See Travel Details at the end of this chapter for more information on journey frequencies and durations.

Pavagadh and Champaner

The hill of **Pavagadh**, 45km northeast of Vadodara, rises 820m above the plains, overlooking the almost forgotten **Muslim city** of **CHAMPANER**. For Pavagadh, take a Jeep from Champaner, or walk up the path that ascends through battered gates and past the old walls of the Solanki fortress to a midpoint where you can get snacks, souvenirs and a welcome cup of sweet chai. From here you can proceed by chairlift (7min) – or on foot up a well-trodden path – to the summit, where a number of Jain temples lie below a Hindu temple dedicated to Mataji, with a shrine to the Muslim saint Sadan Shah on its roof. The ruined **fort** (daily 8am–6pm; $5) still has some of its vast walls and battlements but little inside to warrant the ASI entry fee. The view from the hill stretches for miles over the patchwork plains of south Gujarat and you can spot concrete barricades under construction along the Narmada canal.

In 1297 the Chauhan Rajputs made Pavagadh their stronghold, and fended off three attacks by the Muslims before eventually losing to Mohammed Begada in 1484. All the women and children committed *johar* and the men who survived the battle were slain when they refused to embrace Islam. After his conquest, Mohammed Begada set to work on Champaner, which took 23 years to build. The town was the political capital of Gujarat until the death of Bahadur Shah in 1536, when the courts moved to Ahmedabad and Champaner fell into decline.

Champaner today has a strange, time-warped atmosphere. The massive city walls with inscribed gateways still stand, encompassing several houses, exquisite mosques and Muslim funerary monuments, as well as newer Jain *dharamshalas* to accommodate and feed pilgrims visiting Pavagadh. Champaner's largest mosque, the exuberant **Jami Masjid**, is east of the walls. Towering *minars* stand either side of the main entrance, and the prayer halls are dissected by almost two hundred pillars supporting a splendid carved roof raised in a series of domes. The central dome, three times the height of the others, shelters an octagonal shaft trimmed with richly carved balconies. The *zenana*, or women's prayer section, is in the northwest corner behind perforated stone walls.

Buses from Vadodara leave hourly (via Halol; 1hr 30min) for Champaner, where there's a modest chai stall. There's also a direct service from Ahmedabad every three hours. The state-owned *Hotel Champaner* (⊕ 02676/45641; ❸–❺) halfway up Pavagadh, has adequate **rooms**, with magnificent views over the vast plains of south Gujarat and a dorm (Rs60). The **restaurant** serves veg thalis.

Bharuch

The rarely visited provincial backwater of **BHARUCH** (formerly Broach), halfway between Vadodara and Surat, stands on the marshy north bank of the Narmada, 48km short of the Arabian Sea. A thriving port and mercantile capital since the first millennium AD, its heyday was during the seventeenth century, when its ships sailed for Southeast Asia to fetch spices to trade at its now-ruined British and Dutch factories. Today, the coastal trade hurtles past on the NH-8, and only if you have a penchant for jaded colonial trading posts will you find the tumbledown European houses and forlorn old quarter worth an hour or so out of a long train journey.

Clustered onto the two-kilometre-long narrow ridge that separates the bustling modern end of Bharuch from the sleepy right bank of the Narmada, the **old quarter** lies a ten-minute ride west of the railway station and bus stand. Ask the rickshaw-wallah to head for the **Jami Masjid**, a fourteenth-century mosque hemmed in by wooden balconies and flaking colour-washed walls. Its colonnaded courtyard, pierced by three doorways and crowned with a row of thirteen shallow domes, is a giant jigsaw puzzle of intricately carved masonry plundered from a Jain temple that formerly stood on the spot. Once you've checked out the richly decorated ceilings in the sanctuary hall, head downhill until you reach the **town walls**, erected by Shivaji to replace those destroyed by Aurangzeb in 1660. A walkway runs along the top of the ramparts, giving good views over marshy mud flats, grazed by sleek grey water buffalo, to the river.

The walls veer north when they arrive at the edge of a dried-up creek, near a pale-blue Victorian clocktower, and the large colonial-style palace of an ex-nawab who frittered away his inheritance on opium. Drop down from here, and follow the riverbank west through a putrid-smelling *basti*, to come out eventually at the old **quay**, now a fishing dock. Apart from their triangular sails (a legacy of Bharuch's trading links with the Arabian Gulf), the ramshackle flat-bottomed inshore fishing dhows here, built in the roadside carpenters' yards at the top of the hill, are identical to those that still fish the saltwater lagoons of central Portugal.

Arrival and information

Bharuch is on the main NH-8 **highway** and the main **railway** line between Vadodara and Mumbai, with multiple connections to the north and south; all express **trains** stop here.

Luggage can be left at the railway station parcel office, right of the main exit, while you explore town. Most of the **places to stay** are near the railway station. The best budget option is the *Hotel Classic* (☏02642/32264; ❷–❺), tucked behind the tall buildings on the south side of Station Road, which offers ensuite doubles with carpets, cable TV and balconies, or clean, windowless wood-partition cells. The modern *Hotel President* (☏02642/31957, ☏40376; ❹–❻), right next to the station, is a reliable option, with clean rooms, all with TV. The smart *Hotel Plaza* near the bus stand (☏02642/30922; ❻) is centrally air-conditioned.

There is a hygeinic thali joint at the *Hotel Palmland*, close to the bus stand, or you could try the smartish **restaurants** at the *President* and *Plaza* hotels. Otherwise, take your pick from the lookalike veg cafés along Station Road, a little west of the *Plaza*, or grab a snack by the station.

Surat

Packed around a tight bend in the River Tapti, 19km before it dumps its silty waters into the Gulf of Cambay, sprawling **SURAT** was the west coast's principal port before the meteoric rise of Bombay. These days, it is one of India's fastest growing industrial centres but of no real interest to visitors other than business travellers or die-hard colonial history buffs. Apart from a couple of melancholic European cemeteries, Surat's most memorable feature is its **traffic** which, even by Indian standards, is appalling.

Founded by Parsi refugees in the twelfth century, Surat emerged as a minor trading post during the sixteenth century, when it was plundered and razed numerous times by the Portuguese. In 1592 it was taken by Akbar and entered a period of prosperity before the **British** took control early in the seventeenth century, having been granted trading rights by the Moghuls and seen off the Portuguese in the naval battle off "Bloody Point". The Dutch and French followed, but saw their *godowns*, or warehouses, sacked by Shivaji's Marathas in 1664. The British secured dominance by the end of the century and Surat might eventually have become west India's number one city had it not been devastated by fire and floods in 1837. Many of the Jain and Parsi merchants fled south to Bombay, precipitating a decline from which Surat has only recently recovered.

Over the past decade, the city's booming textile, chemical and diamond-cutting businesses (a legacy of the Dutch trade links) have generated a sixty percent growth in population. The resultant overcrowding and pressure on an already overtaxed infrastructure, however, are all too evident. In the winter of 1992–93, the packed commercial and Muslim districts around the main bazaar finally burst at the seams, erupting into some of the worst communal riots the state has ever seen.

Arrival and information

Surat, on the main line from Ahmedabad to Mumbai, has very good **train** connections, and is served by regular **buses** from within Gujarat and interstate. Both stations are on the eastern edge of the city centre, with the massive Ring Road stretching out leftwards from the major junction to your left as you come out of the railway station, or to your right as you come out of the bus station. Private buses tend to leave you about 50m from the railway station, so ignore rickshaw-wallahs who offer to take you there as you stagger sleepily off the overnight bus. The easiest way to **get around** town is to use auto-rickshaws. Although making reservations can be a major hassle, trains are more convenient than buses when it comes to **moving on**. Agents around the ST station offer tickets on **private buses** to destinations as far afield as Kerala but also within Gujarat and to Rajasthan and Maharashtra.

GTDC's **tourist office** (Mon–Sat, closed 2nd & 4th Sat of month 10.30am–6pm; ☏0261/476586), is hidden away at 1/847 Athugar St in Nanpura. The Rs25 auto-rickshaw ride from the railway station takes you 4km up the Ring Road to the junction called Athwa Gate (just before the elevated section), then right and up the first real street on the left, where it's 100m up on your left. They have city maps and can arrange visits to **diamond-cutting workshops**. The State Bank of India (Mon–Fri 11am–3pm, Sat 11am–1pm) is in the same street.

Accommodation

Although you are unlikely to choose to stay in Surat, there are plenty of **hotels** near the station (many of them in Sufi Baug, the street running straight ahead opposite the entrance). Finding a room is only a problem towards the end of weekday afternoons, by which time most places are booked by visiting business travellers, so avoid a protracted hunt in the heat by phoning ahead.

Diamond Plaza, 6/3014 Unapani Road ☏0261/414061, ☏413906. Five minutes' walk from the station, one block behind the main road at the far end of Sufi Baug, this spotless new hotel provides compact well-furnished rooms with phone and TV. ⑤–⑥

Embassy, to the right of Sufi Baug ☏0261/443170, ☏443173. Stylish new three-star, carpeted throughout, with a/c, bathtubs and "ozonated water around the clock". The best in its bracket. ⑦–⑧

Omkar and **Vaibhav**, Eighth Floor, Omkar Chambers, Sufi Baug, opposite the station

☏0261/419329. Two hotels with identical prices and a shared reception (with handy train timetable), attached or shared shower-toilets, room-service tea, lots of coming and going, great if not exactly picturesque views and optional Star TV. A good budget deal. ③

Sarvajanik, Station Road, opposite the station ☏0261/426434. Very good value, with spotless en-suite singles and doubles; hot water is provided 4–10pm. ③

Simla Guest House, Sufi Baug ☏0261/41164. Very friendly place with small clean rooms, some with TV. Cheap non-attached singles. ③–④

The City

Surat's two main sights are some distance apart, but can be seen in an hour if you take an auto-rickshaw between them. A good spot to start is **Chowk**, the busy riverside intersection at the foot of Nehru Bridge. Facing the old British High Court building on one side, and the incongruous steeple of an Anglican church on the other, the **castle** is the city's oldest monument, erected in 1540 on the banks of the Tapti by the Sultan of Gujarat in an attempt to curtail the trading activities of the Portuguese. It later fell to both the Moghuls and the British and these days merely houses government offices. You can wander in and scale the ramparts, from where there are views upriver and over the old walled town to the east.

The only other of Surat's historic sites worth hunting out lies fifteen minutes northeast across town beside Kataragama Road, beyond the fortified gateway of the same name. The domed mausolea of the weed-choked **English cemetery** could easily be mistaken for an oriental tomb garden. Now in a sorry state, the graveyard is locked but you can hop over the low wall behind the *peepal* tree on the pavement. Its most impressive sepulchre, a mildewing collection of pillars and arches crowned with crossed cupolas, is that of General Oxinden, who defeated the Marathas, and his brother Christopher. The smaller of the two large tombs, to the left, is believed to be the final resting place of Gerald Aungier, of Bombay fame (see p.743). Most of the other more modest graves belong to young colonial officers and their families, who succumbed to fever in this lonely malaria-infested trading post.

Eating

Most of Surat's **restaurants** are in the better hotels, while many of the cheaper lodges offer basic room-service menus. The ST bus stand refreshment room is open 24 hours.

Embassy Hotel, off Sufi Baug, opposite the railway station. Two restaurants, one serving set breakfasts and thalis, the other Indian, Chinese and Western dishes in a clean, pleasant atmosphere. Open 7am–midnight.

Mossam, *Hotel Yuvraj*, off Sufi Baug, opposite the railway station. Stylish, moderately priced Gujarati cooking and south Indian snacks in sophisticated surroundings. Open 11am–3.30pm & 7–11.30pm.

Savera, Sufi Baug. Canteen serving savoury cheap veg and non-veg north Indian food. Open 9am–10pm.

Sheer-e-Punjabi, below Omkar Chambers, Sufi Baug. Swanky and somewhat pricey tandoori house with marble floors, tablecloths and a varied mostly non-veg menu. Open 9am–1am; takeaway available.

Daman

Ask any Gujarati what they know about **DAMAN** and they'll probably say "liquor". As a Union Territory, independent of the dry state that surrounds it, Daman has liberal licensing laws and low duty on booze, making it something of a target at weekends for busloads of Gujarati men who drink themselves senseless, sway up and down the main street and then crash out in cheap hotel rooms for the night, generally being pretty obnoxious. The rest of the time Daman is quieter but disappointing on the whole, with a rather forlorn feel and a couple of uninspiring beaches, although it does offer excellent seafood, a small duty-free market and some immaculate Portuguese churches, houses and forts.

Straddling the mouth of the **Damanganga River**, which rises in the Sayadhri Range on the Deccan plateau, Daman made an obvious target for the Portuguese, who took it in 1531 from the Sultan of Gujarat's Ethiopian gov-

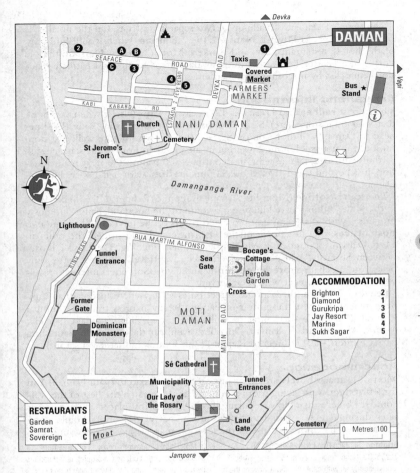

DAMAN

NANI DAMAN

- Taxis
- Covered Market
- FARMERS' MARKET
- Bus Stand
- Church
- Cemetery
- St Jerome's Fort

MOTI DAMAN

- Lighthouse
- Tunnel Entrance
- Former Gate
- Dominican Monastery
- Sea Gate
- Bocage's Cottage
- Pergola Garden
- Cross
- Sé Cathedral
- Municipality
- Our Lady of the Rosary
- Tunnel Entrances
- Land Gate
- Cemetery

RING ROAD
RUA MARTIM ALFONSO
SEAFACE ROAD
DEVKA ROAD
ESTRADA 2 FEVEREIRO
KABI KABARDA RD

▲ Devka
▶ Vapi
◀ Jampore ▼
Damanganga River

ACCOMMODATION

Brighton	2
Diamond	1
Gurukripa	3
Jay Resort	6
Marina	4
Sukh Sagar	5

RESTAURANTS

Garden	B
Samrat	A
Sovereign	C

0 Metres 100

ernor, Siddu Bapita. The governor of Goa, Dom Constantino de Bragança, cajoled the Sultan of Gujarat into ceding the territory 28 years later, after which it became the hub of the Portuguese trans-Arabian Sea trade with East Africa. The town's economic decline was precipitated by the British occupation of Sind in the 1830s, which effectively strangled its **opium** business. Colonial rule, however, survived until 1961 when, after a rather ineffective six-year barricade, Nehru lost patience with Portuguese refusal to negotiate a peaceful handover and sent in the troops.

Today Daman is administered from New Delhi as a Union Territory, along with the nearby ex-Portuguese colonies of Diu, and Dadra and Nagar Haveli. Apart from alcohol production and sales, its chief sources of income are coconuts, salt production and smuggling. In recent years, the local tourist office has also been trying to promote the area as a mini-Goa. Don't be taken in – the unbroken stretch of palm-fringed sand that runs along its twelve-kilometre coastline may look idyllic in the brochures, but on closer inspection turns out to be a grubby fishing beach.

The town of Daman is made up of two separate districts. On the north side of the Damanganga River is **Nani** ("Little") **Daman**, where you'll find most of the hotels, restaurants, bars and markets; **Moti** ("Great") **Daman**, the old Portuguese quarter, lies to the south, its Baroque churches and Latinate mansions encircled by imposing stone battlements.

Arrival and information

The nearest **railhead** to Daman is 12km east at **Vapi** (check when you book that your train stops here). Shared Ambassador **taxis** charging only Rs10 per head to Daman will drop you on Seaface Road, a five-minute walk east from most of the hotels – if none is waiting in the square in front of the station, walk to the main road, take a right and continue 500m until the next main junction. Just beyond the flyover is the ST **bus station**, with half-hourly buses to Daman. You can also get there by auto-rickshaw.

The **tourist office** (Mon–Fri 9.30am–1.30pm & 2–6pm; ☎02638/255104), in the pink administrative building just south of the bus stand, hands out glossy brochures with lots of gushing prose and **maps** of the territory. There are two **post offices**: one just north of the Damanganga Road bridge, the other in Moti Daman, opposite the Municipal Council building. On Devka Road, between Seaface Road and the river, Executive Travels & Tours is the only place you can change **foreign currency** and Cyber Soft offers internet browsing, if they can connect with their server.

Leaving Daman, there are no direct buses to anywhere further than Vapi, from where the best transport connections are by express train to Mumbai Central (9 daily; 3–4hr), Surat (9 daily; 1hr 45min–3hr), Vadodara (9 daily; 4–5hr), Ahmedabad (7 daily; 6–7hr) and even, on the overnight Saurashtra Janata Express #9017, direct to Rajkot (12hr 30min) and Jamnagar (15hr).

Accommodation

Most of Daman's **hotels** are on or just off Seaface Road in Nani Daman. Aim for a first floor west-facing room if you can, as these catch the best of the welcome sea breezes that blow in during the evenings. Most places will give lower rates during quieter weekdays. Prices are higher at the resort hotels along Dwarka beach – more because of the location than for any added comfort.

Brighton, Seaface Road ☎ 02638/251208, ℻ 255209. Good range of comfy well-furnished rooms, nearly all with cable TV and a view of the sea. ❺–❼

Diamond, near the taxi stand ☎ 02638/254235. Neat but not particularly good-value rooms in a solid, respectable hotel. Some a/c and only b/w TVs. ❹–❻

Gurukripa, Seaface Road ☎ 02638/255046, ℻ 254433. The posh place to stay in town with a roof garden, bar and quality restaurant; the spacious en-suite rooms are all a/c with Star TV. Good value. ❺–❻

Jay Resort, Moti Daman ☎ 02638/254575. Just outside the fort, east of the bridge; the only hotel in Moti Daman. Currently consists of three ramshackle detached cottages in a quiet, green setting by a small lake. Good if you want peace, so book in advance, but some way from all but its own limited restaurant/bar. ❹

Marina, Estrada 2 Fevereiro ☎ 02638/254420. Simple rooms with solid period furniture in a stylish but tatty colonial house. A bargain if you don't mind peeling plaster, dodgy plumbing and old beds. ❷–❸

Sukh Sagar, Estrada 2 Fevereiro ☎ 02638/255089. Friendly hotel on a quiet street, with good clean rooms and a decent restaurant. ❸–❺

Nani Daman

Most of the action in **Nani Daman** centres on **Seaface Road**, which runs west from the market past rows of hotels, seedy bars and IMFL (Indian Made Foreign

Liquor) stores to the **beach**. Too polluted for a comfortable swim or sunbathe, Daman's dismal strand is only worth visiting around sunset, when the local fisherwomen hang strips of filleted pomfret on wooden racks to dry. At the opposite (east) end of Seaface Road, the Portuguese **covered market** has a reputation as a purveyor of exotic contraband, although you won't find many packets of the fabled foreign cigarettes or bottles of whisky among the imported chocolate, Hindi film cassettes and cheap cotton clothes. More picturesque is the open-air **farmers' market** just behind it, where, on weekday mornings, local women squat beside piles of fresh flowers, whole spices, fruit and vegetables.

Daman's noisiest trading, however, takes place at the **riverfront**. Head down here in the morning and you'll see scores of fishing boats moored at the quay, their bows hung with garlands of marigolds for good luck. While the night's catch is being landed, coolies haul heavy blocks of ice up the gangplanks to be hacked into pieces over baskets full of glistening fish that the fisherwomen, gathered on the beach below, then sell to the assembled housewives and restaurateurs. A good place from which to watch it all is the ramparts of **St Jerome's Fort**, directly behind the quay. Erected in the early seventeenth century to counter the threat of Moghul invasion, the citadel encircles a small *maidan*, a Catholic church and a well-kept walled Portuguese graveyard.

Moti Daman

The town's most impressive monuments are across the river in the leafy colonial compound of **Moti Daman**, 2km south of Seaface Road. Once inside the huge heavily fortified walls that surround the quarter, you're a world away from the sandy cluttered streets of the new town. Elegant double-storeyed mansions with sweeping staircases, wooden shutters, verandas and colour-washed facades stand on sun-dappled courtyards. Now used as government offices, these residences were originally the homes of Portuguese nobles or *fidalgos* – the only people allowed to live inside the fort.

Moti Daman's highlights are its **churches**, which rank among the oldest and best-preserved Christian monuments in Asia. Grandest of all is the **cathedral** (Church of Bom Jesus) on the main square. Built in 1603, its gigantic gabled Baroque facade opens onto a lofty vaulted hall, at the end of which stands a gilded altar watched over by six statues of saints and a benign Madonna. On the opposite side of the square, the **Church of Our Lady of the Rosary** is crammed with ornate woodwork, notably some fine tableaux of the life of Jesus by the altar, while strings of fragrant jasmine and rose petals festoon its ceilings.

Main Road links Moti Daman's two **gates**, which were installed in the 1580s following a Moghul invasion, and passes the **Pergola Garden**, a memorial to two Portuguese police officers who died in a mythical "uprising" in Dadra and Nagar Haveli. These former Portuguese enclaves, eighty percent of whose population are "tribals", were ceded by the Marathas in 1781 as an indemnity for two Portuguese ships they had sunk. Though both India and Portugal agreed on an official version – in which the locals rose up against the Portuguese and liberated the territory in 1954 – the reality was that Indian police officers in plain clothes acting on secret orders from the Maharashtra state government entered the territory, shot the policemen, and frightened the rest away with firecrackers. It is now a Union Territory, governed by the same authority as Daman and Diu.

A small cottage next to the northern ("sea") gate was once the home of the eighteenth-century Portuguese poet Bocage, while atop the bastion facing the southern ("land") gate is the cell where prisoners condemned to death in Portuguese times spent their final days. Nearby are entrances to a couple of **tunnels**; the larger one – its destination unknown and possibly dangerously low in oxygen if you go in too far – is blocked by debris, while the smaller leads from the top to the bottom of the bastion. If you enter, take a light and beware of snakes, which hide in crevices in the walls, and may spring out if disturbed. At the western edge of the fort, a ruined **Dominican monastery** still has stellar carvings above what used to be the main altar. By the old **lighthouse** to its north, there are good views across the river.

Beaches

If you crave a beach, but are turned off by Nani Daman's drab black sands, there are a couple of more appealing spots outside town. **Devka** (or Dwarka beach), backed by coconut plantations and a string of large resort hotels, can be reached in fifteen minutes by rickshaw, or by bus from the stop on the main road near the market. At the far southern end of the territory, also fifteen minutes' rickshaw ride from Nani Daman, **Jampore** is cleaner and less frequented, but both beaches share the disadvantage of the sea receding beyond 500m of slimy mud and barnacle-encrusted rock at low tide.

Eating and drinking

The disproportionately large number of **places to eat** in Daman is due to the town's liquor laws, which oblige all bars to serve food with alcohol. Most of the "bar-restaurants" along Seaface Road are restaurants in name only, and best avoided. **Seafood**, on offer all year except during the monsoons, is especially good from late September to early November, when the fish market is glutted with fresh crabs, prawns and lobsters. Also seasonal is *papri*, a street snack consisting of beans baked in a pot with potatoes, sold with a special masala between January and April.

Though Daman is more than just a drinking centre, the abundance of cheap cold **beer** does add to the attraction of the place. **Tari** (palm wine), traditionally sold in earthenware pots, is best bought where you see the pots tied to trees to collect it; the Marwad area on the way to Devka is known for it, but the stuff sold by the beach in town is likely to be watered down.

Brighton, Seaface Road. Comfortable a/c multi-cuisine restaurant, serving veg and non-veg specialities and filling set breakfasts. Open 7am–11pm.

Garden, Seaface Road. A bar with a large terrace out back, serving reasonably priced tandoori pomfret and lobster, as well as Goan and Damanese meat and veg specialities. Open 11am–3pm & 6–11pm.

Gurukripa, Seaface Road. The place for a slap-up meal, serving veg and non-veg tandoori, seafood, pomfret stuffed with prawns, fish curries, Chinese dishes and Goan *fenni* (coconut spirit) nips. Open 7am–11pm.

Samrat, Seaface Road. Spotless roadside restaurant that specializes in inexpensive, eat-till-you-burst Gujarati thalis that come with *namkeens* (salty titbits), a couple of different dhals, and mouthwatering mild veg dishes. Strictly "pure-veg" (read "no alcohol") and excellent value. Open 11am–4pm & 7–11pm.

Sovereign, Seaface Road. South Indian snacks, side dishes and beers served indoors or alfresco on a breezy balcony. Open 6.30–10pm.

Travel details

Trains

Ahmedabad to: Abu Road (6–9 daily; 3hr 30min–4hr 30min); Ajmer (3–6 daily; 7hr 5min–10hr 55min); Bangalore (3 weekly; 35hr 55min–37hr 40min); Bhavnagar (3 daily; 5hr 25min–7hr); Calcutta (1 daily; 44hr 10min); Chennai (1 daily; 37hr 30min); Delhi (3–5 daily; 14hr 15min–33hr 35min); Dwarka (1–2 daily; 10hr 50min); Jaipur (3–5 daily; 9hr 5min–13hr 30min); Jamnagar (4–5 daily; 5hr 55min–7hr 55min); Jodhpur (2–3 daily; 9hr 5min–9hr 55min); Junagadh (2 nightly; 8hr 20min–9hr 55min);

Mumbai (7–8 daily; 7hr 10min–12hr 20min); Porbandar (1–2 daily; 10hr 25min); Rajkot (5–7 daily; 4hr 5min–5hr 35min); Surat (11–14 daily; 3hr 30min–4hr 30min); Trivandrum (2 weekly; 42hr 25min); Udaipur (1 nightly; 8hr 45min); Vadodara (14–17 daily; 1hr 35min–2hr 25min); Varanasi (3 weekly; 41hr 40min); Veraval (2 nightly; 10hr 25min–12hr 5min).

Bhavnagar to: Ahmedabad (3 daily; 5hr 35min–7hr 5min); Palitana (3 daily; 2hr).

Bhuj to: Gandhidham (5 daily; 1hr 50min).

Diu (Delvada station) to: Junagadh (1 daily; 6hr 55min); Sasan Gir (1 daily; 4hr); Veraval (1 daily; 2hr 50min).

Dwarka to: Ahmedabad (1–2 daily; 10hr 40min); Jamnagar (3–4 daily; 2hr 20min–4hr 40min); Mumbai (1 daily; 20hr 25min); Rajkot (3–4 daily; 4hr 50min–7hr 30min).

Junagadh to: Ahmedabad (1 daily; 9hr 25min); Diu/Delvada (1 daily; 6hr); Rajkot (4 daily; 3hr 20min–5hr); Sasan Gir (1 daily; 2hr 30min); Veraval (6 daily; 2hr–3hr 30min).

Porbandar to: Ahmedabad (1–2 daily; 10hr); Jamnagar (2–3 daily; 2hr 25min–4hr); Mumbai (1 daily; 23hr 30min); Rajkot (2–3 daily; 4hr 40min–6hr); Surat (1 daily; 16hr 40min); Vadodara (1 daily; 13hr 35min).

Rajkot to: Ahmedabad (3–5 daily; 4hr 20min–5hr 15min); Junagadh (4 daily; 3hr 30min–5hr 15min); Mumbai (2 daily; 14hr 35min–18hr 40min); Porbandar (2–3 daily; 4hr 30min–5hr 45min); Veraval (1 daily; 5hr 15min).

Vadodara to: Ahmedabad (14–17 daily; 1hr 55min–2hr 30min); Baruch (22–25 daily; 48min–1hr 15min); Calcutta (1 daily; 42hr); Delhi (8–10 daily; 12–24hr); Indore (1 daily; 8hr 18min); Mumbai (16–20 daily; 7hr); Porbandar (1 daily; 13hr 45min); Pune (5 weekly; 10hr 20min–11hr 5min); Surat (25–30 daily; 1hr 50min–2hr 30min).

Buses

Ahmedabad to: Abu Road (8 daily; 6hr); Ajmer (4 daily; 14hr); Bhavnagar (hourly; 5hr); Bhuj (12 daily; 8–10hr); Diu (2 daily; 11hr); Dwarka (3 daily; 11hr); Indore (1 nightly; 10hr); Jaipur (1 nightly; 16hr); Jamnagar (hourly; 7hr); Jodhpur (4 daily; 12hr); Junagadh (10 daily; 8hr); Mumbai (1 nightly; 14hr); Porbandar (6 daily; 10hr); Rajkot (hourly; 5hr); Surat (every 30min; 5hr 30min); Udaipur (hourly; 8hr); Una (4 daily; 10hr); Vadodara (every 10min; 2hr 30min); Veraval (4 daily; 10hr).

Bhavnagar to: Ahmedabad (hourly; 5hr); Bhuj (4 daily; 8hr); Junagadh (5 daily; 7hr); Mumbai (1

daily; 17hr); Palitana (hourly; 1hr 15min); Rajkot (14 daily; 4hr); Una (7 daily; 6hr); Vadodara (8 daily; 6hr).

Bhuj to: Ahmedabad (12 daily; 8–10hr); Bhavnagar (4 daily; 8hr); Gandhidham (hourly; 1hr); Jamnagar (3 daily; 7hr); Palanpur (3 daily; 8hr); Rajkot (4 daily; 7hr).

Diu to: Ahmedabad (2 daily; 11hr); Junagadh (1 daily; 5hr 30min); Rajkot (2 daily; 7hr 30min); Una (every 30min; 40min); Veraval (4 daily; 3hr).

Dwarka to: Ahmedabad (3 daily; 11hr); Jamnagar (8 daily; 3hr); Junagadh (3 daily; 5hr); Porbandar (hourly; 3hr); Veraval (hourly; 5–6hr).

Junagadh to: Ahmedabad (10 daily; 8hr); Jamnagar (hourly; 5hr); Palitana (2 daily; 6hr); Porbandar (10 daily; 3hr); Rajkot (hourly; 2hr 30min); Sasan Gir (10 daily; 1hr 30min); Una (10 daily; 4hr); Veraval (every 30min; 2hr).

Porbandar to: Ahmedabad (6 daily; 10hr); Dwarka (hourly; 3hr); Jamnagar (hourly; 2hr 30min); Rajkot (10 daily; 5hr); Una (4 daily; 6hr 30min); Veraval (6 daily; 4hr).

Rajkot to: Ahmedabad (hourly; 5hr); Jamnagar (every 30min; 2hr); Junagadh (hourly; 2hr 30min); Porbandar (10 daily; 5hr); Una (6 daily; 8hr); Vadodara (12 daily; 8hr); Veraval (hourly; 5hr).

Vadodara to: Ahmedabad (every 10min; 2hr 30min); Baruch (every 30min; 2hr); Bhavnagar (8 daily; 6hr); Indore (2 daily; 12hr); Mumbai (8 daily; 14hr); Pune (3 daily; 14hr); Rajkot (12 daily; 8hr); Surat (every 30min; 3hr).

Flights

Ahmedabad to: Bangalore (1 daily; 3hr 15min); Calcutta (6 weekly; 2hr 15min–3hr 35min); Delhi (3–4 daily; 1hr 25min–2hr 35min); Hyderabad (4 weekly; 1hr 40min); Jaipur (3 weekly; 1hr); Mumbai (5–6 daily; 1hr); Vadodara (1 daily; 30min).

Bhavnagar to: Mumbai (1–2 daily; 50min–1hr 15min).

Bhuj to: Mumbai (2 daily; 1hr 5min).

Diu to: Porbandar (6 weekly; 45min); Mumbai (6 weekly; 2hr 45min).

Jamnagar to: Bhuj (1 daily; 40min); Mumbai (1 daily; 2hr 15 min).

Porbandar to: Diu (6 weekly; 30min); Mumbai (6 weekly; 1hr 30min).

Rajkot to: Mumbai (2 daily; 50min–1hr).

Vadodara to: Delhi (1 daily; 1hr 25min); Mumbai (3 daily; 50–55min).

CHAPTER 10 Highlights

* **Victoria Terminus** A fantastically eccentric pile, perhaps the greatest railway station ever built by the British. See p.747

* **The Gateway of India** The departure-point for the last British troops leaving India, now a favourite spot for an evening stroll. See p.756

* **Fisherman's shanty town Colaba** Once a Koli village, this area is home to fishermen from all parts of India, and is one of Mumbai's most communally diverse areas. See p.757

* **Prince of Wales Museum** The main enticement is the fine collection of Indian art, including erotic Gita Govinda paintings. See p.757

* **Maidans (parks)** Where Mumbai's citizens escape the hustle and bustle to play cricket, eat lunch and hang out. See p.760

* **Elephanta Island** A magnificent rock-cut Shiva temple on an island in Mumbai harbour. See p.769

* **Nightlife** The best pubs and clubs in India and great international cuisine. See pp.776–779

* **Bollywood blockbusters** Check out the latest Hindi mega movie in one of the city centre's gigantic air-con cinemas. See p.778

Mumbai

Young, brash and oozing with the cocksure self-confidence of a maverick moneymaker, **MUMBAI** (formerly **Bombay**) revels in its reputation as India's most dynamic and Westernized city. Behind the hype, however, intractable problems threaten the Maharashtran capital, foremost among them a chronic shortage of space. Crammed onto a narrow spit of land that curls from the swamp-ridden coast into the Arabian Sea, Mumbai has, in less than five hundred years since its "discovery" by the Portuguese, metamorphosed from an aboriginal fishing settlement into a sprawling megalopolis of over sixteen million people. Whether you are being swept along broad boulevards by endless streams of commuters, or jostled by coolies and hand-cart pullers in the teeming bazaars, Mumbai always feels like it is about to burst at the seams.

The roots of the population problem lie, paradoxically, in the city's enduring ability to create wealth. Mumbai alone generates 38 percent of India's GNP, its port handles half the country's foreign trade, and its movie industry is the biggest in the world. Symbols of prosperity are everywhere, from the phalanx of office blocks clustered on Nariman Point, Maharashtra's Manhattan, to the yuppie couples nipping around town in their shiny new Maruti hatchbacks. The flip side to the success story, of course, is the city's much-chronicled poverty. Each day, hundreds of economic refugees pour into Mumbai from the Maharashtran hinterland. Some find jobs and secure accommodation; many more (around a third of the total population) end up living on the already overcrowded streets, or amid the appalling squalor of Asia's largest slums, reduced to rag-picking and begging from cars at traffic lights.

However, while it would definitely be misleading to downplay its difficulties, Mumbai is far from the ordeal some travellers make it out to be. Once you've overcome the major hurdle of finding somewhere to stay, you may begin to enjoy its frenzied pace and crowded, cosmopolitan feel. Conventional **sights** are thin on the ground. After a visit to the most famous colonial monument, the **Gateway of India**, and a look at the antiquities in the **Prince of Wales Museum**, the most rewarding way to spend time is simply to wander the city's atmospheric streets. **Downtown**, beneath rows of exuberant **Victorian-Gothic** buildings, the pavements are full of noisy vendors and office-wallahs hurrying through clouds of wood smoke from gram-sellers' braziers. In the eye of the storm, encircled by the roaring traffic of beaten-up red double-decker buses, lie other vestiges of the Raj, the **maidans**. Depending on the time of day, these central parks are peppered with cricketers in white flannels, or the bare bums of squatting pavement-dwellers relieving themselves on the parched brown grass. North of the city centre, the broad thoroughfares splinter into a

Airports ▲

NATH PAI MARG (REAY RD)

Veermata Jeejamata Museum
V J B Udyan (Victoria Gardens)

N M JOSHI MARG

Mahalakshmi Racecourse

Willingdon Golf Course

Municipal Dhobi Ghats

Maratha Mandir Cinema

State Bus Terminal
Mumbai Central

Bus Stop for Downtown

Red Light District

Chor Market

Chatrapathi Shivaji Terminus (Victoria Terminus)

Jami Masjid

CRAWFORD MARKET

Zaveri Bazaar

Metro Cinema (Buses to Goa)

Foreigners' Registration Office

Bombay Hospital, Azad Maidan

Bhuleshwar Market

Mumba Devi Temple

Opera House

Gymkhanas

Grant Rd Railway Station

Tarporevala Aquarium

Mani Bhavan (Mahatma Gandhi Museum)

Chowpatty Beach

Haji Ali's Tomb

Mahalakshmi Temple

Crossword Bookshop

Breach Candy Hospital

Towers of Silence

Bulbunath Mandir Temple

PM (Hanging) Gardens

Kamla Nehru Park

Malabar Hill

Jain Temple

Walukeshwar Temple

ARABIAN SEA

Banganga Tank

N

740

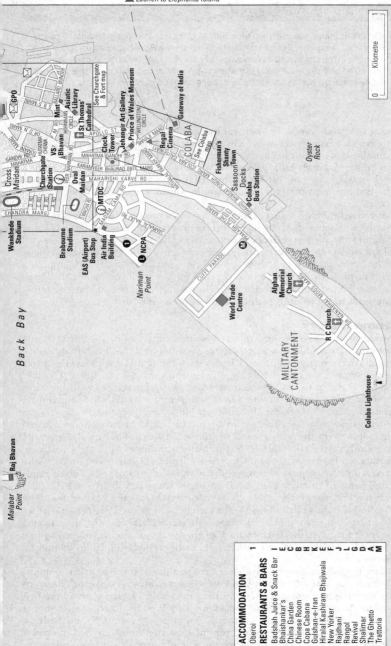

▲ *Launch to Elephanta Island*

GPO

See Churchgate
& Fort map

Mint
S B S MARG
HORNIMAN
CIRCLE
P M RD
BALLARD BUNDER
St Thomas'
Cathedral
Asiatic
Library
APOLLO ST
Jehangir Art Gallery
Prince of Wales Museum
Clock
Tower
Gateway of India
Regal
Cinema
COLABA
See Colaba
map
Fisherman's
Shanty
Town
Sassoon
Docks
Colaba
Bus Station

VS
Bhavan
MAHATMA GANDHI RD
KARAMVEER BHAURAO PATIL MARG
WELLINGTON
CIRCLE
CHHATRAPATI SHIVAJI MARG
COLABA CAUSEWAY

Cross
Maidan
Churchgate
Station
VEER NARIMAN RD
Oval
Maidan
MAHARISHI KARVE RD
MTDC
CHANDRA MARG

Wankhede
Stadium

Brabourne
Stadium

EAS (Airport)
Bus Stop

Air India
Building
NCPA

*Nariman
Point*

CUFFE PARADE

World Trade
Centre

Afghan
Memorial
Church

R C Church

MILITARY
CANTONMENT

DR NANABHAI MOOS MARG

Colaba Lighthouse

Back Bay

*Malabar
Point*
Raj Bhavan

*Oyster
Rock*

0   1
Kilometre

ACCOMMODATION
Oberoi   1

RESTAURANTS & BARS
Badshah Juice & Snack Bar   I
Bhaishankar's   E
China Garden   C
Chinese Room   B
Copa Cabana   H
Gulshan-e-Iran   K
Hiralal Kashiram Bhajiwala   E
New Yorker   F
Rajdhani   J
Rangol   L
Revival   G
Shalimar   D
The Ghetto   A
Trattoria   M

In 1996 Bombay was renamed **Mumbai**, as part of a wider policy instigated by the ultra-right-wing Shiv Sena Municipality to replace names of any places, roads and features in the city that had connotations of the Raj. Mumbai is the Marathi name of the local deity, the mouthless "Maha-amba-aiee" (Mumba for short), who is believed to have started her life as an obscure aboriginal earth goddess.

maze of chaotic streets. The **central bazaar** districts afford glimpses of sprawling Muslim neighbourhoods, as well as exotic **shopping** possibilities, while Mumbai is at its most exuberant along **Chowpatty Beach**, which laps against exclusive **Malabar Hill**. When you've had enough mayhem, the beautiful rock-cut Shiva temple on **Elephanta Island** – a short trip by launch across the harbour from the promenade, **Apollo Bunder** – offers a welcome half-day escape.

If you're heading for Goa or south India, you'll probably have to pass through Mumbai at some stage. Its international airport, **Sahar**, is the busiest in the country; the **airline offices** downtown are handy for confirming onward flights, and all the region's principal air, road and rail networks originate here. Whether or not you choose to stay for more time than it takes to jump on a train or plane to somewhere else depends on how well you handle the burning sun, humid atmosphere and perma-fog of petrol fumes, and how seriously you want to get to grips with the India of the twenty-first century.

Some history

Mumbai originally consisted of seven **islands**, inhabited by small Koli fishing communities. At different times, various dynasties held this insignificant outlying district; the city of Puri on **Elephanta** is thought to have been the major settlement in the region, until King Bimba, or Bhima, built the town of Mahim on one island, at the end of the thirteenth century. Hindus controlled the area until it was captured in the fourteenth century by the Muslim Gujarat Sultanate. In 1534, Sultan Bahadur of Ahmedabad ceded the city to the **Portuguese**, who felt the land to be of little importance, and concentrated development in the areas around Mahim and Bassein. They handed over the largest island to the English in 1661, as part of the dowry when the Portuguese infanta Catherine of Braganza married Charles II; four years later Charles received the remaining islands and the port, and the town took on the anglicized name of Bombay from the Portuguese "Buan Bahia" or Good Bay. This was the first part of India that could properly be termed a colony; elsewhere on the subcontinent the English had merely been granted the right to set up "factories", or trading posts. Because of its natural safe harbour and strategic position for trade, the **East India Company**, based at Surat, wanted to buy the land; in 1668 a deal was struck, and Charles leased Mumbai to them for a pittance.

The English set about an ambitious programme of fortifying their outpost, living in the area known today as Fort. However, life was not easy. There was a fast turnover of governors, and malaria and cholera culled many of the first settlers. A chaplain of the East India Company, Reverend Ovington, wrote at the end of the seventeenth century: "One of the pleasantest spots in India seemed no more than a parish graveyard, a charnel house... Which common fatality has created a Proverb among the English there, that two monsoons are

MUMBAI

⑩

the age of a man." **Gerald Aungier**, the fourth governor (1672–77), set out to plan "the city which by God's assistance is intended to be built", and by the start of the eighteenth century the town was the capital of the East India Company. He is credited with encouraging the mix that still contributes to the city's success, welcoming Hindu traders from Gujurat, Goans (escaping Jesuit persecution), Muslim weavers, and most visibly, the business-minded Zoroastrian **Parsis**.

Much of the British settlement in the old Fort area was destroyed by a devastating fire in 1803, and the European population remained comparatively low well into the 1800s. The arrival of the **Great Indian Peninsular Railway** in the 1850s improved communications, encouraging yet more immigration from elsewhere in India. In 1852 the first of many land-reclamation projects (still ongoing) fused the seven islands; just a year later the rail link between Bombay and the cotton-growing areas of the Deccan plateau opened. This crucial railway, coupled with the cotton crisis in America following the Civil War, gave impetus to the great Bombay cotton boom and established the city as a major industrial and commercial centre. With the opening of the Suez Canal in 1859, and the construction of enormous docks, Bombay's access to European markets improved further. **Sir Bartle Frere**, governor from 1862 to 1867, oversaw the construction of the city's distinctive colonial-Gothic buildings; the most extravagant of all, **Victoria Terminus** railway station – now officially

The Dons

Criminals have always been a part of Mumbai's life, but the 1980s saw an intensification of **organized crime** in the city. Previously, gangsters had confined their activities to small-scale racketeering in poor neighbourhoods. After the post-1970s real-estate boom however, many petty "landsharks" became powerful godfather figures, or **dons**, with drug- and gold-smuggling businesses as well as involvement in extortion and prostitution. Moreover, corrupt politicians who employed the gangs' muscle-power to rig elections had become highly placed political puppets with debts to pay – a phenomenon dubbed **criminalization**. The dividing line between the underworld and politics grew increasingly blurred during the Nineties – in 1992, no less than forty candidates in the municipal elections had criminal records.

The gangs have also become integral in the dirty war between India and Pakistan, with Karachi-based Dawood Ibrahim heavily implicated with the Pakistani security services – he is thought to be behind the bombings of 1993 (see p.745) – and Bombay's leading don Chhota Rajan with the Indian forces. In fact, many see the bungling of Rajan's recent extradition from Thailand, and his subsequent escape from a guarded hospital room (he drugged his Thai police guards and climbed out of the window using his bed sheets) as payment for services rendered.

The late Eighties saw the entrance of the dons into **Bollywood**, when the rise of video and TV made regular film financiers nervous of investing in the industry. Mob money poured in and it's an open secret that the film industry is one of the favoured forms of money-laundering with the dons – rival films mysteriously put back their release dates in order to give mob-backed movies a clear run at the box office. In 2000, however, the authorities began to take action, and Bollywood mogul Bharat Shah (who usually has around ten billion rupees invested in films at any one time) was arrested for financial links to the Dawood Ibrahim gang.

However, Mumbai is still the playground for mafia gangs, each with their own personalities and legends. If you read any newspapers while you're in the city you won't escape this phenomenon; the media revels in the shocking and bloodthirsty exploits of the gangsters, and the unfolding sagas run like a Bollywood blockbuster.

Chatrapathi Shivaji Terminus or CST – is a fitting testimony to this extraordinary age of expansion.

Not all Mumbai's grandest architecture is owed to the Raj – wealthy Jains and Parsis have also left their mark throughout the downtown area. As the most prosperous city in the nation, Bombay was at the forefront of the Independence struggle; Mahatma Gandhi used a house here, now a museum, to co-ordinate the struggle through three decades. Fittingly, the first British colony took pleasure in waving the final goodbye to the Raj, when the last contingent of British troops passed through the Gateway of India in February 1948. Since Independence, Mumbai has prospered as India's commercial and cultural capital and this period has seen the population grow tenfold to more than sixteen million.

However, as early as 1982, Mumbai's infrastructure was starting to buckle under the tensions of overpopulation. A bitter and protracted **textile strike** had impoverished tens of thousands of industrial workers, unemployment and crime were spiralling and the influx of immigrants into the city showed no signs of abating. Among the few beneficiaries of mounting discontent was the extreme right-wing Maharashtran party, the **Shiv Sena**. Founded in 1966 by Bal "the Saheb" Thackery, a self-confessed admirer of Hitler, the Sena's uncompromising stand on immigration and employment found favour with the disenchanted mass of lower-middle-class, mainly Marathi-speaking Hindus in the poorer suburbs. The party's venom, at first focused on the city's sizeable south Indian community, soon shifted to its fifteen-percent Muslim minority. Communal antagonism flared briefly in 1984, when ninety people died in riots, and again in 1985 when the Shiv Sena routed the Congress party in

Festivals in Mumbai

Mumbai has its own versions of all the major Hindu and Muslim **festivals**, plus a host of smaller neighbourhood celebrations imported by its immigrant communities. Exact dates vary from year to year; check in advance at the government tourist office.

Makar Sankranti (Jan). A celebration of prosperity, when sweets, flowers and fruit are exchanged by all, and kites are flown in the parks as a sign of happiness.

Elephanta Music and Dance Festival (Feb). MTDC-organized cultural event including floodlit performances by classical artists with the Shiva cave temple as a backdrop.

Gudi Padva (March/April). The Maharashtran New Year.

Gokhulashtami (July/Aug). Riotous commemoration of Krishna's birthday; terracotta pots filled with curd, milk-sweets and cash are strung from tenement balconies and grabbed by human pyramids of young boys.

Nowroz (July/Aug). The Parsi New Year is celebrated with special ceremonies in the Fire Temples, and feasting at home.

Ganesh Chathurthi (Aug/Sept). Huge effigies of Ganesh, the elephant-headed god of prosperity and wisdom, are immersed in the sea at Chowpatty Beach in a ritual originally promoted by freedom-fighters to circumvent British anti-assembly legislation. Recently it has seemed in danger of being hijacked by Hindu extremists such as the Shiv Sena, tingeing it more with chauvinism than celebration.

Nariel Purnima (Sept). Koli fishermen launch brightly decorated boats to mark the end of the monsoon.

Dussehra (Oct). Rama's victory over the evil king of Lanka, Ravana, is marked in Mumbai by re-enactments of scenes from the *Ramayana* on Chowpatty Beach.

municipal elections. Between December 1992 and late January 1993, two waves of **rioting** in Mumbai affected not only the Muslim ghettos and poor industrial suburbs, but, for the first time, much of downtown too. According to (conservative) official statistics, 784 people died, and around 5000 were injured – seventy percent of them Muslim.

Just as Mumbai was regaining its composure, disaster struck again. On March 12, 1993, ten massive **bomb blasts** ripped through the heart of the city, killing 317 people. No one claimed responsibility, but the involvement of "foreign hands" (ie Pakistan) was suspected. The city recovered from the explosions with astonishing speed, with hoardings erected beside the motorways ("Bombay Bounces Back!", "It's My Bombay", "Bombay, I Love You") attempting to restore the pride and ebullience with which India's most confident city had formerly gone about its business.

Arrival and information

Unless you arrive in Mumbai by train at **Chatrapathi Shivaji Terminus** (formerly Victoria Terminus), be prepared for a long slog into the centre. The international and domestic **airports** are north of the city, way off the map, and ninety minutes or more by road from the main hotel areas, while from **Mumbai Central** train or **bus station**, you face a laborious trip across town. Finding a place to stay can be even more of a hassle; phone around before you set off into the traffic.

By air

For many visitors, **Sahar** (30km), Mumbai's busy **international airport**, provides their first experience of India. The complex is divided into two "modules", one for Air India flights and the other for foreign airlines. Once through customs and the lengthy immigration formalities, you'll find a 24hr State Bank of India exchange facility, rather unhelpful government (ITDC) and state (MTDC) tourist information counters, car rental kiosks, cafés and a prepaid taxi stand in the chaotic arrivals concourse. There's also – very usefully – an **Indian Railways booking office** which you should make use of if you know your next destination; it'll save you a long wait at the reservation offices downtown. If you're on one of the few flights to land in the afternoon or early evening – by which time most hotels tend to be full – it's worth paying on the spot for a room at the **accommodation booking desk** in the arrivals hall. All of the domestic airlines also have offices outside the main entrance, and there's a handy 24hr **left luggage** "cloakroom" in the car park nearby (Rs20–50 per day, depending on the size of your bag; maximum duration 90 days).

From the domestic terminal it is less than a fifteen-minute walk (across the main road) or Rs15 auto-rickshaw ride to Vile Parle station from where **suburban trains** run every few minutes (5am–midnight; 35–40min; Rs5) to Churchgate. The international terminal lies about 3km from the next station out of town on the same line, Andheri, and linked to it by buses #308, #338 and #409 or a Rs25 rickshaw ride. This is a fast and cheap way into town, and convenient unless you are really loaded down with luggage.

Many of the more upmarket hotels, particularly those near the airport, send out **courtesy coaches** to pick up their guests. **Taxis** are comfortable and not too extravagant. To avoid haggling over the fare or being duped by the private taxi companies outside the airport, pay in advance at the taxi desk in the arrivals hall. The price on the receipt, which you hand to the driver on arrival at your destination, is slightly more than the normal meter rate (around Rs260 to Colaba or Nariman Point, or Rs93 to Juhu), but at least you can be sure you'll be taken by the most direct route. Taxi-wallahs invariably try to persuade you to stay at a different hotel from the one you ask for. Don't agree to this; their commission will be added on to the price of your room.

Internal flights land at Mumbai's more user-friendly **domestic airport**, **Santa Cruz** (26km to the north), which is divided into separate modern terminals: the cream-coloured one (Module 1A) for Indian Airlines, and the blue-and-white (Module 1B) for private carriers. If you're transferring directly from here to an international flight at Sahar, 4km northeast, take the free "fly-bus" that shuttles every fifteen minutes between the two. The Indian government and MTDC both have 24hr information counters in the arrivals hall, and there's a foreign exchange counter and accommodation desk tucked away near the first-floor exit. Use the yellow-and-black metered taxis that queue outside the exit. The touts that claim to be running a prepaid taxi system overcharge hugely – a journey to Colaba should cost around Rs250, no more.

Don't be tempted to use the **auto-rickshaws** that buzz around outside the airports; they're not allowed downtown and will leave you at the mercy of unscrupulous taxi drivers on the edge of Mahim Creek, the southernmost limit of their permitted area.

By train

Trains to Mumbai from most central, southern and eastern regions arrive at **Victoria Terminus** (officially renamed Chatrapathi Shivaji Terminus or CST), the main railway station at the end of the Central Railway line. From here it's a ten- or fifteen-minute ride to Colaba; either pick up a taxi at the busy rank outside the south exit, opposite the new reservation hall, or make your way to the main road and catch one of the innumerable buses.

Mumbai Central, the terminus for Western Railway trains from northern India, is further out from the centre; take a taxi from the main forecourt, or cross the hectic road junction next to the station and catch a BEST bus from the top of Dr DN Marg (Lamington Road); #66 and #71 run to VT (CST) and #70 to Colaba Causeway. It costs around the same to take a suburban train from Mumbai Central's local platform, across the footbridge. Four stops on is Churchgate station, the end of the line, a short taxi ride from Colaba (Rs20–30).

Some trains from south India arrive at more obscure stations. If you find yourself at **Dadar**, way up in the industrial suburbs, and can't afford a taxi (Rs120), cross the Tilak Marg road bridge onto the Western Railway and catch a suburban train into town, or take BEST bus #1 or #70 to Colaba, #66 to Central. **Kurla** station, where a few Bangalore trains pull in, is even further out, just south of Santa Cruz airport; taking a suburban train for Churchgate is the only reasonable alternative to a taxi (Rs220). From either, it's worth asking at the station when you arrive if there is another long-distance train going to Churchgate or Victoria Terminus shortly after – it's far preferable to trying to cram into either a suburban train or bus.

By bus

Nearly all interstate **buses** arrive at **Mumbai Central** bus stand, a stone's throw from the railway station of the same name. Again, you have a choice between municipal black-and-yellow taxis, the BEST buses (#66, #70 & #71),

Victoria Terminus (Chatrapathi Shivaji Terminus)

Inspired by St Pancras station in London, F.W. Stevens designed **Victoria Terminus**, the most barmy of Mumbai's buildings, as a paean to "progress". Built in 1887 as the largest British edifice in India, it's an extraordinary amalgam of domes, spires, Corinthian columns and minarets that was succinctly defined by the journalist James Cameron as "Victorian-Gothic-Saracenic-Italianate-Oriental-St Pancras-Baroque". In keeping with the current re-Indianization of the city's roads and buildings, this icon of British imperial architecture has been renamed **Chatrapathi Shivaji Terminus**, in honour of a Maratha warlord who dedicated his life to fighting the Muslim Moghuls and professing Hindu cultural identity. However, this is a bit of a mouthful and the locals mostly still use **VT** (pronounced "vitee") when referring to it, though it's always **CST** officially.

Few of the two million or so passengers who fill almost a thousand trains every day notice the mass of decorative detail. A "British" lion and Indian tiger stand guard at the entrance, and the exterior is festooned with sculptures executed at the Bombay Art School by the Indian students of John Lockwood Kipling, Rudyard's father. Among them are grotesque mythical beasts, monkeys and plants and medallions of important personages. To minimize the sun's impact, stained glass was employed, decorated with locomotives and elephant images. Above it all, "Progress" stands atop the massive central dome.

An endless frenzy of activity goes on inside: scuttling passengers; hundreds of porters in red with impossibly oversize headloads; TTEs (Travelling Ticket Examiners) in black jackets and white trousers clasping clipboards detailing reservations; spitting checkers busy handing out fines to those caught in the act; chai-wallahs with trays of tea; trundling magazine stands; crowds of bored soldiers smoking *beedis*; and the inexorable progress across the station of sweepers bent double. Amid it all, whole families spread out on the floor, eating, sleeping or just waiting and waiting.

which run straight into town from the stop on Dr DN Marg (Lamington Road), two minutes' walk west from the bus station, or a suburban train from Mumbai Central's local platform over the footbridge.

Most **Maharashtra State Road Transport Corporation** (MSRTC) buses terminate at Mumbai Central, though those from Pune, Nasik (and surrounding areas) end up at the **ASIAD** bus stand, a glorified parking lot near the railway station in **Dadar**.

Buses from Goa drop off at various points between central and downtown Mumbai. Most of the private companies currently work from the roadside in front of the Metro Cinema, at the north end of MG Road, while Kadamba (the Goan state transport corporation) buses stop nearby on the opposite (east) side of Azad Maidan, where they have a small ticket kiosk. Both places are an inexpensive taxi ride from the main hotel district.

Information

The best source of **information** in Mumbai is the excellent **Government of India tourist office** (Mon–Fri 8.30am–6pm, Sat 8.30am–2pm; ☎022/203 3144) at 123 M Karve Rd, opposite Churchgate station's east exit. The staff here are exceptionally helpful and hand out a wide range of leaflets, maps and brochures both on Mumbai and the rest of the country. There are also 24hr tourist **information counters** at Sahar International (☎022/832 5331) and Santa Cruz (☎022/615 9320) airports.

Maharashtra State Tourism Development Corporation Ltd (**MTDC**) main office, on Madam Cama Road (Mon–Sat 8.30am–7pm; ℡022/202 6731), opposite the LIC Building in Nariman Point, sells tickets for city sightseeing tours and can reserve rooms in MTDC resorts. They too have information counters at Sahar International and Santa Cruz airports, as well as at VT and Dadar railway stations and near the Gateway of India.

If you need detailed **listings**, ask at any tourist office for a free copy of the slick *Mumbai This Fortnight*, which is user-friendly and has a wealth of useful information, despite being a commercial venture. If you want to spend any time in the city, invest in a copy of the *Pocket Mumbai Guide* (Rs20), which, although badly produced, contains more detailed information on bus and local train services as well as a useful rail map.

For **what's on** you're better off checking out the "The List" section of *Mid-Day* (Mumbai's main local rag), the "Metro" page in the *Indian Express*, or the "Bombay Times" section of the *Times of India*. All are available from street vendors around Colaba and the downtown area and cost Rs2–3.

For a detailed **map** of Mumbai, look for Karmarkar Enterprise's *Most Exhaustive A–Z* street plan (Rs60). It's fiendishly hard to find in bookstores (Crossword, on Bhulabai Desai Road, usually have one or two in stock), but the pavement guidebook- and magazine-wallahs along VN Road, between Churchgate and Flora Fountain, may have copies. Otherwise, the Discover India Series has produced a good, up-to-date map and listings book called the *Road Guide to Mumbai* (Rs60), that is widely available.

City transport

Only a masochist would travel on Mumbai's hopelessly overtaxed public **transport** for fun. For much of the day, traffic on the main roads crawls along at little more than walking speed, or grinds to a halt in endless jams at road junctions. On the plus side, it might take forever to ride across town on a dusty red double-decker **bus**, but it will never set you back more than a few rupees. Local **trains** get there faster, but are a real endurance test even outside rush hours. **Rickshaws** do not run downtown. A less stressful way of seeing the historical and cultural highlights of the city is on a **walking tour** (Sun); contact the Bombay Heritage Walks Society (℡022/8344622).

Buses
BEST (Bombay Electric Supply and Transport; 24hr information line ℡022/414 3611) operates a **bus** network of labyrinthine complexity, extend-

---

Tours

Of MTDC's sightseeing **tours** around Mumbai, the "City" tour (Tues–Sun 2–6pm; Rs75) is the most popular, managing to cram Colaba, Marine Drive, the Hanging Gardens, Kamla Nehru Park and Mani Bhavan into half a day; the "Suburban" tour (Tues–Sun 9.15am–6.15pm; Rs120) takes in Kanheri caves, Krishnagiri Upavan National Park, a lion safari and Juhu in a full day. MTDC also run an hour-long evening tour of the illuminated sights on an open-top bus, departing daily at 7pm and 8.30pm (Rs70 upper deck, Rs20 lower deck). **Tickets** should be booked in advance from the MTDC office (see above) at Nariman Point (the main departure area).

ing to the furthest-flung corners of the city. Unfortunately, neither route booklets, maps nor "Point to Point" guides (which you can consult at the tourist office or at newsstands) make things any clearer. Finding out which bus you need is difficult enough. Recognizing it in the street can be even more problematic, as the numbers are written in Maharathi (although in English on the sides). Aim, wherever possible, for the "Limited" services, which stop less frequently, and avoid rush hours at all costs. Tickets should be bought from the conductor on the bus.

Useful bus routes

#1/#3/#6(Ltd)/#11(Ltd)/#103/#124 Colaba bus station to Mahatma Phule (Crawford) Market, via VT (Nagar Chowk)
#43 Colaba bus station to GPO
#70 Colaba to Dadar Station (W), via Mumbai Central
#106/#107 Colaba to Kamala Nehru Park, via Chowpatty Beach
#124 Colaba to Vatsalabai Desai Chowk, via Mumbai Central
#132 Colaba to Breach Candy, via Vatsalabai Desai Chowk
#81 Churchgate to Santa Cruz, via Vatsalabai Desai Chowk (for Haji Ali's tomb and Mahalakshmi temple)
#66 VT to Mumbai Central
#91(Ltd) Mumbai Central to Kurla station.

Trains

Mumbai would be paralysed without its local **trains**, which carry millions of commuters each day between downtown and the sprawling suburbs in the north. One line begins at VT, running up the east side of the city as far as Thane. The other leaves Churchgate, hugging the curve of Back Bay as far as Chowpatty Beach, where it veers north towards Mumbai Central, Dadar, Santa Cruz and Vasai, beyond the city limits. Services depart every few minutes from 5am until midnight, stopping at dozens of small stations. Carriages remain packed solid virtually the whole time, with passengers dangling precariously out of open doors to escape the crush, so start to make your way to the exit at least three stops before your destination. The apocalyptic peak hours are worst of all. Women are marginally better off in the "ladies carriages"; look for the crowd of saris and *salwar kamises* grouped at the end of the platform.

Taxis

With rickshaws banished to the suburbs, Mumbai's ubiquitous black-and-yellow **taxis** are the quickest and most convenient way to nip around the city centre. In theory, all should have meters and a current rate card (to convert the amount shown on the meter to the correct fare); in practice, particularly at night or early in the morning, many drivers refuse to use them. If this happens, either flag down another or haggle out a fare. As a rule of thumb, expect to be charged Rs5 per kilometre after the minimum fare of around Rs13, together with a small sum for heavy luggage (Rs5 per article). The latest addition to Mumbai's hectic roads is the **cool cab**, a blue taxi that boasts air-conditioning, and charges higher rates for the privilege.

Boats

Ferryboats regularly chug out of Mumbai harbour, connecting the city with the far shore and some of the larger islands in between. The most popular with visitors is the **Elephanta Island** launch (see p.769) which departs from the Gateway of India. Boats to **Mandve** (9 daily; 6.30am–6.15pm; 90min; Rs40), for Alibag, the transport hub for the rarely used **coastal route south**, leave from the Gateway of India.

Car rental

Cars with drivers can be rented per eight-hour day (Rs800–1000 for a non-a/c Ambassador, upwards of Rs1200 for more luxurious a/c cars), or per kilo-metre, from ITDC. They have an (occasionally) staffed counter at the Government of India tourist office and on the eleventh floor of the Nirmal Building at Nariman Point. Otherwise, go through any good travel agent (see p.783). Ramniranjan Kedia Tours and Travels (☎022/437 1112) are recom-mended if you want to book a vehicle on arrival at Sahar international airport.

Self-drive is also now available in Mumbai, though the service seems to be intended more for middle-class Indians out to impress their friends ("They'll never know it's rented!"), than tourists. You will be a lot safer if you leave the driving to someone more at home with the city's racetrack rules of the road. If you are willing to risk it, Autoriders International Ltd (in association with Hertz) at 139 Auto World, Tardeo Road (☎022/496 1714, ☎492 1172), or Avis (☎022/285 7327, ⊛www.avis.co.in) in the *Oberoi* are recommended.

Accommodation

Even though Mumbai offers all kinds of **accommodation**, finding a room at the right price when you arrive can be a real problem. Budget travellers, in par-ticular, can expect a hard time: standards at the bottom of the range are grim and room rates exorbitant. A windowless cell with wood-partition walls and no running water costs Rs300 and above, while a comfortable room in the centre of town, with an attached toilet and shower, and a window, will set you back the best part of Rs1000. The best of the relatively inexpensive places tend to fill up by noon, which can often mean a long trudge in the heat with only an overpriced fleapit at the end of it, so you should really phone ahead as soon as (or preferably well before) you arrive. Prices in upmarket places are further inflated by the state-imposed **"luxury tax"** (between four and thirty percent depending on how expensive the room is), and **"service charges"** levied by the hotel itself; such charges are included in the price symbols shown below.

Colaba, down in the far, southern end of the city, has dozens of possibilities in each price range and is where the majority of foreign visitors head first. A short way across the city centre, **Marine Drive**'s accommodation is generally a little more expensive, but more salubrious, with Back Bay and the prome-nade right on the doorstep. If you're arriving by train and plan to make a quick getaway, a room closer to **VT** station is worth considering. Alternatively, **Juhu**, way to the north near the airports, boasts a string of flashy four- and five-stars, with a handful of less expensive places behind the beach. For those who just want to crawl off the plane and straight into bed, plenty of options can be found in the suburbs around **Sahar** and **Santa Cruz** airports, a short taxi ride from the main terminal buildings.

Finally, if you would like to **stay with an Indian family**, ask at the gov-ernment tourist office in Churchgate, or at their information counters in Sahar and Santa Cruz (see p.747) about the popular "paying guest" scheme. Bed and breakfast-style accommodation in family homes, vetted by the tourist office, is available throughout the city at rates ranging from Rs500–1200.

Colaba

A short ride from the city's main commercial districts, railway stations and tourist office, **Colaba** makes a handy base. It also offers more in the way of food and entertainment than neighbouring districts, especially along its busy main thoroughfare, "**Colaba Causeway**" (Shahid Bhagat Singh – SBS – Marg). The streets immediately south and west of the Gateway of India are chock-full of accommodation, ranging from grungy guesthouses to India's most famous five-star hotel, the *Taj Mahal Intercontinental*. Avoid at all costs the nameless lodges lurking on the top storeys of wooden-fronted houses along **Arthur Bunder Road** – the haunts of not-so-oil-rich Gulf Arabs and touts who depend on commission from these rock-bottom hostels to finance their heroin habits. If, like many, you find all this sleaze a turn-off, Colaba's quieter, leafier backstreets harbour plenty of respectable mid-range hotels.

The hotels below are marked on the **map** of Colaba on p.755.

Aga Bheg's & Hotel Kishan, ground & 2nd Floor, Shirin Manzil, Walton Road ☎ 022/284 2227 or 283 8386. *Aga Bheg's* has lurid pink walls and little wooden blue beds, though it's clean, cool, and with a thankfully quiet and relaxed atmosphere. *Hotel Kishan's* more tasteful a/c rooms are incredibly good value. ❺–❻

Ascot, 38 Garden Rd ☎ 022/284 0020, ☏ 204 6449, ✉ ascothotel@vsnl.com. One of Mumbai's oldest hotels. Comfortable, spacious rooms, with cable TV and room service. ❽

Diplomat, 24–26 PK Boman Behram Marg ☎ 022/202 1661, ☏ 283 0000, ✉ diplomat@bom3.vsnl.net.in. Hemmed in by the *Taj* across the road and in need of a face-lift, but the rooms are pleasant. ❽–❾

Fariyas, 35 Arthur Rd ☎ 022/204 2911, ☏ 283 4492, 🌐 www.fariyas.com. Next on the scale down from the *Taj*. Relaxing roof garden, luxurious decor with themed suites, pool, health club, business centre, central a/c and all the trimmings. The *Tavern* pub is very popular with trendy Bombayites. Rates in dollars only. ❾

Goodwin, Jasmine Building, Garden Road ☎ 022/287 2050, ☏ 287 1592, ✉ services@vsnl.com. Top-class three-star with restaurant, bar and 24hr room service. The *Garden* (☎ 022/283 1330, ☏ 204 4290) next door, is similar but slightly inferior. Both ❾

Gulf, 4/36 Kamal Mansion, Arthur Bunder Road ☎ 022/285 6672, ☏ 283 2694, ✉ gulfhotel@hotmail.com. Seedy neighbourhood, but respectable and grandly decorated, with clean modern rooms. ❽

Harbour View, 3rd and 4th Floors, 25 PJ Ramchandani Marg ☎ 022/282 1089, ☏ 284 3020, ✉ parkview@bom3.vsnl.net.in. Decent hotel tucked away above the Strand cinema, boasting comfortable, modern standard rooms and slightly more expensive (and larger) sea-facing ones. All rooms a/c. ❽–❾

Lawrence, 3rd Floor, 33 Rope Walk Lane, off K Dubash Marg, opposite Jehangir Art Gallery ☎ 022/284 3618. Mumbai's best-value cheap hotel if you don't mind the great hike up the stairs. Six immaculate double rooms (one single) with fans, and not-so-clean shared shower-toilet. Breakfast included in the price. Best to book in advance. ❹–❺

Prosser's, 2–4 Henry Rd ☎ 022/283 4937. Noisy, with mostly wood-partitioned rooms that are clean and air-cooled. ❹–❻

Regency, 18 Lansdowne House, Mahakari Bhusan Marg, behind the Regal cinema ☎ 022/202 0292, ☏ 287 3375. Well-appointed rooms (though bathrooms need re-doing) and cheaper attic garrets with character. ❼

Regent, 8 Best Rd ☏022/287 1854, ☏202 0363, @hotelregent@vsnl.com. Luxurious, international-standard hotel on small scale, with all mod cons but smallish rooms. ❽

Salvation Army, Red Shield House, 30 Mereweather Rd, near the *Taj* ☏022/284 1824. Rock-bottom bunk beds in cramped, stuffy dorms (lockers available), large good-value doubles (some a/c), and a sociable travellers' scene. Cheap canteen food. Priority given to women, but your stay is limited to one week or less. ❶–❺

Sea Shore, 4th Floor, 1-49 Kamal Mansion, Arthur Bunder Road ☏022/287 4237. Among the best budget deals in Colaba. The sea-facing rooms with windows are much better than the airless cells on the other side. Friendly management and free, safe baggage store. Common baths only, though some rooms have a/c. If it's full you can always try the wooden-partitioned rooms at the seedy *India* (☏022/283 3769; ❹–❺) or the grubby but bear-able ones at the *Sea Lord* (☏022/284 5392; ❹–❻) in the same building. ❺–❼

Shelley's, 30 PJ Ramchandani Marg ☏022/284 0229, ☏284 0385, @www.shelleyshotel.com.

Charmingly old-fashioned hotel in the colonial mould despite renovations to the rooms. Pukka dining hall and pricier rooms with sea views. ❼–❽

Taj Mahal Intercontinental, PJ Ramchandani Marg ☏022/202 3366, ☏287 2711, @www.tajhotels.com. The stately home among India's top hotels, and the haunt of Mumbai's *beau monde*. Opulent suites in an old wing or a modern skyscraper, plus shopping arcades, outdoor pool, swish bars and restaurants. Starts at $290. ❾

Whalleys', Jaiji Mansion, 41 Mereweather Rd ☏022/282 1802. Well-established, popular hotel in a rambling colonial building, with 27 rooms (of varying sizes), shared or attached shower-toilets, pleasant veranda and some a/c. Reasonable value with breakfast included. ❼

YWCA, 18 Madam Cama Rd ☏022/202 5053, ☏202 0445, @ywcaic@bom8.vsnl.net.in. Relaxing, secure and quiet hostel with spotless dorms, doubles or family rooms. Rate includes membership, breakfast and filling buffet dinner. Dorm beds also available (Rs650). One month's advance booking (by money order) advisable. ❼

Marine Drive and Nariman Point

At the western edge of the downtown area, Netaji Subhash Chandra Marg, or **Marine Drive**, sweeps from the skyscrapers of Nariman Point in the south to Chowpatty Beach in the north. Along the way, four- and five-star hotels take advantage of the panoramic views over Back Bay and the easy access to the city's commercial heart, while a couple of inexpensive guesthouses are worth trying if Colaba's cheap lodges don't appeal. Compared with Colaba, Marine Drive and the arterial **VN Road** that connects it with Churchgate are more open and relaxed. Families and office cronies plod along the promenade in the evening, approached more often by gram- and balloon-wallahs than junkies and moneychangers.

The hotels below are marked on the **map** on p.758, apart from the *Oberoi*, which is marked on p.740.

Ambassador, VN Road ☏022/204 1131, ☏204 0004, @ambassador@vsnl.com. Luxurious four-star with excellent views from upper front-side rooms and a revolving Thai/Chinese rooftop restaurant. Dollars only. ❾

Bentley, 3rd Floor, Krishna Mahal, Marine Drive ☏022/281 1787. Run-down hotel on the corner of D Road. No lift, no a/c, no attached bath-rooms and no frills (except windows), but clean rooms, some of which have sea-facing bal-conies – at a price. 24hr checkout, and break-fast included. ❺

Chateau Windsor, 5th Floor, 86 VN Rd ☏022/204 4455, ☏202 6459, @info@chateauwindsor.com. Spotless single, double or group rooms (some on the small side), shared or attached bathrooms and

optional a/c. It's very popular, so reservations are recommended. ❼–❽

Marine Plaza, 29 Marine Drive ☏022/285 1212, ☏282 8585, @www.sarovarparkplaza.com. Glitzy pad on the seafront, with every luxury mod con, glass-bottomed swimming pool, health club, Chinese restaurant, pub and 24hr coffee-shop. ❾

Norman's, 127 Marine Drive ☏022/281 4234, ☏281 3362. Small, moderately priced ground-floor guesthouse, with neat, clean rooms, some attached shower-toilets and a/c. ❼–❽

Oberoi, Nariman Point ☏022/232 5757, ☏204 3282, @www.oberoihotels.com. The *Taj's* main com-petitor – India's most expensive hotel – is glitteringly opulent, with a pool, a Polynesian restaurant and your own personal butler. Rates start at $320. ❾

Around Victoria (Chatrapathi Shivaji) Terminus

Arriving in Mumbai at **VT** after a long train journey, you may not feel like embarking on a room hunt around Colaba. Unfortunately, the area around the station and the nearby GPO, though fairly central, has little to recommend it. The majority of places worth trying are mid-range hotels grouped around the crossroads of P D'Mello (Frere) Road, St George's Road and Shahid Bhagat Singh (SBS) Marg, immediately southeast of the post office (5min on foot from the station). VT itself also has **retiring rooms** (Rs150), although these are booked up by noon.

The hotels below are marked on the **map** on p.755.

City Palace, 121 City Terrace ☏022/261 5515, ☏267 6897. Large and popular hotel bang opposite the station. "Ordinary" rooms are tiny and windowless, but have a/c, are perfectly clean and proudly sport "electronic push button telephone instruments". **❼**

Grand, 17 Sprott Rd, Ballard Estate ☏022/269 8211, ☏262 6581, ⓦwww.grandhotelbombay.com. Solid and very comfortable with a faintly 1930s feel. Central a/c, restaurant and 24hr foreign exchange. **❽**

Lord's, 301 Adi Mazban Path, Mangalore Street ☏022/261 8310. Above *City Kitchen* restaurant, this is drab, but reasonably clean and cheap for the area. Mostly shared bathrooms. **❸–❹**

Manama, opposite George Hospital, 221/225 P D'Mello Rd ☏022/261 3412, ☏261 3860. Very friendly, clean, popular budget option with run-of-the-mill rooms, some a/c. Currently being renovated. Book ahead. **❻**

Prince, 34 Walchand Hirachand Rd, near Red Gate ☏022/261 2809, ☏265 8049. The best all-round economy deal in this area: modest, neat and respectable. Avoid the airless partition rooms upstairs. **❻**

Railway, 249 P D'Mello Rd ☏022/261 6705, ☏265 8049. Spacious, clean and friendly, and the pick of the mid-range bunch around VT, though correspondingly pricey. **❼–❽**

Ship, 3rd Floor, 219 P D'Mello Rd ☏022/261 7613. The cheapest option near VT, with cavernous, crowded dorms (including one for women) and tiny partitioned rooms which are incredibly claustrophobic unless you get one with a window – though they do come with TV. Dorm beds (Rs130) come with in-built locker underneath. **❸**

Juhu Beach

Since the early 1970s, a crop of exclusive **resort hotels** has been creeping steadily down the road that runs behind **Juhu Beach**, twenty minutes' drive from Santa Cruz airport. Most offer the predictable hermetically sealed five-star package, with bars, restaurants and a pool to lounge beside. It's hard to believe that anyone would come to India expressly for this sort of thing, but if money's no object and you want to keep well away from all the hustle, bustle and poverty, you'll be spoiled for choice. **Vile Parle** (pronounced *Vee*lay *Par*lay) is the nearest suburban railway station to Juhu. Both the hotels below lay on courtesy buses from the airports.

Centaur Juhu Beach, Juhu Tara Road ☏022/611 3040, ☏611 6343, ⓦwww.centaurhotel.com. Gigantic five-star with a palatial foyer, sea views, pool and various speciality restaurants. **❾**

Holiday Inn, Balraj Sahani Marg ☏022/670 4444, ☏620 4452, ⓦwww.holidayinnbombay.com. Overlooking the beach, this revamped five-star boasts two pools, terrace garden, shops, bars and formula furnishings. Dollars only. **❾**

Around the airports

Hotels near Sahar and Santa Cruz **airports** cater predominantly for transit passengers and flight crews, at premium rates. If you arrive in Mumbai at an inconvenient hour when most of the hotels in the city proper are closed or full, you may want to arrange less expensive accommodation in the nearby suburbs of **Santa Cruz**, **Vile Parle** or **Andheri**. Bookings can be made through the accommodation desk in the arrivals concourse at Sahar, or by phone. Nearly all the hotels below have courtesy buses to and from the terminal building.

Airport Palace, Vakola Bridge, Bull's Royce Colony Road ☎ 022/614 0057. Small, airless non-a/c rooms, but all with fresh bed linen and lockable doors. ⑤

Air View, 12th Nehru Road, Santa Cruz East ☎ 022/612 0060. Quiet hotel near rail and bus stations. Clean rooms with either fan or a/c. ⑤–⑥

Ashwin, near Marol Fire Station, Andheri Kurla Road, Andheri East ☎ 022/836 7267, ℻ 836 7258. One of several medium-sized, international-standard hotels right outside Sahar. Rooms are comfortably deluxe and there's a good multi-cuisine restaurant. ⑧

Centaur, Western Express Highway, Santa Cruz ☎ 022/615 6660, ℻ 611 6535, ℮ centaur.airport@vsnl.com. Circular building directly outside the domestic airport, with five stars, three restaurants, two bars and one pool. ⑨

Kamat's Plaza, 70-C Nehru Rd, Vile Parle ☎ 022/612 3390, ℻ 612 5974. Plush four-star with a swimming pool. ⑧–⑨

Kumaria Presidency, Andheri Kurla ☎ 022/835 2601, ℻ 837 385, Facing the international airport. One of a string of three-stars bookable through the accommodation desk in airport arrivals. ⑧

Leela, Sahar ☎ 022/691 1234, ℻ 691 1455, ℠ www.theleela.com. Ultra-luxurious, the best in the area in fact, with an art gallery, four restaurants, a nightclub and amazing sports facilities. Dollars only. ⑨

Samrat, 3rd Road, Khar, Santa Cruz East, near Khar railway station ☎ 022/648 5441, ℻ 649 3501. Another comfortable transit hotel in a quiet suburban backstreet. No courtesy bus. ⑥–⑧

Shangri-La, Nanda Parker Road, Vile Parle East ☎ 022/612 8983. Cheerful budget hotel near the domestic airport with lots of clean and basic a/c and non-a/c rooms, some refurbished. Good Chinese restaurant tacked alongside. ④–⑥

The City

Between the airports to the north and the southern tip of Mumbai lies a thirty-kilometre, seething mass of streets, suburbs and relentless traffic. Even during the relatively cool winter months, exploring it can be hard work, requiring plenty of pit stops at cold-drink stalls along the way. The best place to start is down at the far south end of the peninsula in **Colaba**, home to most of the hotels, restaurants and best-known sights, including the **Gateway of India**. Fifteen minutes' walk north takes you past the **Prince of Wales Museum** to the **Fort** area, home of all the banks and big stores, plus the cream of Mumbai's ostentatious Raj-era buildings. The extravagant Victoria Terminus (Chatrapathi Shivaji Terminus) overlooks its northern limits, close to the impressive onion dome of the **GPO**. The hub of the suburban train network, **Churchgate station**, stands 4km west, across the big maidans that scythe through the centre of town. Churchgate, and the **tourist office**, is a stone's throw from the sweeping curve of Back Bay. With **Nariman Point**'s skyscrapers at one end, lively **Chowpatty Beach** and the affluent apartment blocks of **Malabar Hill** at the other, the Bay is Mumbai at its snazziest. But the area immediately north and east is ramshackle and densely populated. The **central bazaars** extend from **Crawford Market**, beyond VT station, right up to **J Boman (JB) Behram Marg**, opposite the other main-line railway station, **Mumbai Central**.

Colaba

At the end of the seventeenth century, **Colaba** was little more than the last in a straggling line of rocky islands extending to the lighthouse that stood on Mumbai's southernmost point. Today, the original outlines of the promontory (whose name derives from the Koli who first lived here) have been submerged under a mass of dilapidated colonial tenements, hotels, bars, restaurants and handicraft shops. If you never venture beyond the district, you'll get a very dis-

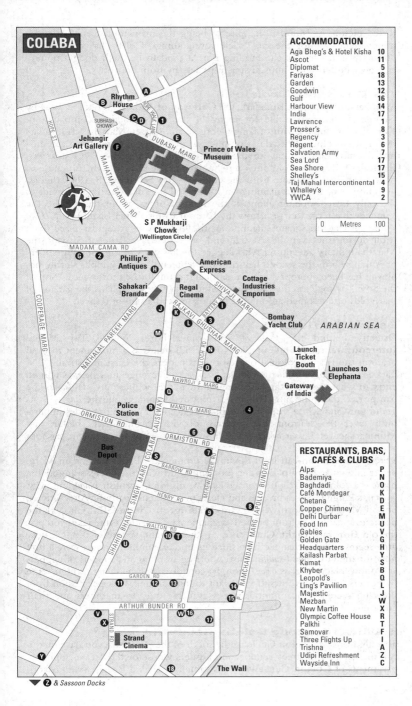

COLABA

ACCOMMODATION

Aga Bheg's & Hotel Kisha	10
Ascot	11
Diplomat	5
Fariyas	18
Garden	13
Goodwin	12
Gulf	16
Harbour View	14
India	17
Lawrence	1
Prosser's	8
Regency	3
Regent	6
Salvation Army	7
Sea Lord	17
Sea Shore	17
Shelley's	15
Taj Mahal Intercontinental	4
Whalley's	9
YWCA	2

0 Metres 100

ARABIAN SEA

RESTAURANTS, BARS, CAFES & CLUBS

Alps	P
Bademiya	N
Baghdadi	O
Café Mondegar	K
Chetana	D
Copper Chimney	E
Delhi Durbar	M
Food Inn	U
Gables	V
Golden Gate	G
Headquarters	H
Kailash Parbat	Y
Kamat	S
Khyber	B
Leopold's	Q
Ling's Pavillion	L
Majestic	J
Mezban	W
New Martin	X
Olympic Coffee House	R
Palkhi	T
Samovar	F
Three Flights Up	I
Trishna	A
Udipi Refreshment	Z
Wayside Inn	C

The Wall

Z & Sassoon Docks

torted picture of Mumbai. In spite of being the main tourist enclave and a trendy hang-out for the city's rich young things, Colaba has retained the distinctly sleazy feel of the bustling port it used to be, with dodgy money-changers, dealers and pimps hissing at passers-by from doorways.

The Gateway of India

Mumbai's most famous landmark, the **Gateway of India**, was built in 1924 by George Wittet, responsible for many of the city's grandest constructions. Commemorating the visit of King George V and Queen Mary in 1911, India's own honey-coloured Arc de Triomphe was originally envisaged as a ceremonial disembarkation point for passengers alighting from the P&O steamers. Ironically, today it is more often remembered as the place the British chose to stage their final departure from the country – on February 28, 1948, the last detachment of troops remaining on Indian soil set sail from here. Nowadays, the only boats bobbing about at the bottom of its stone staircase are the launches that ferry tourists across the harbour to Elephanta Island (see p.769).

The spruced-up square surrounding the Gateway is a popular place for a stroll during the evenings. At one end, an equestrian statue of **Shivaji**, the Maratha military adventurer who dogged the last years of the Moghul emperor Aurangzeb in the second half of the seventeenth century, looks sternly on. Shivaji has been appropriated as a nationalist symbol (the prototypical "Son of the Soil") by the extreme right-wing Shiv Sena, which explains the garland of marigolds often draped around the statue's neck as a sign of respect.

Behind the Gateway

Directly behind the Gateway, the older hotel in the **Taj Mahal Intercontinental Hotel** complex (see p.752) stands as a monument to local pride in the face of colonial oppression. Its patron, the Parsi industrialist J.N. Tata, is said to have built the old *Taj* as an act of revenge after he was refused entry to what was then the best hotel in town, the "whites only" *Watson's*. The ban proved their undoing. *Watson's* disappeared long ago, but the *Taj*, with its grand grey and white stone facade and red-domed roof, still presides imperiously over the seafront, the preserve of visiting diplomats, sheikhs and Mumbai's jet set. Lesser mortals are allowed in to sample the opulent teashops and restaurants.

From the *Taj*, you can head down the promenade, PJ Ramchandani Marg, better known as **Apollo Bunder** (nothing to do with the Greek sun god; the name is a colonial corruption of the Koli words for a local fish, *palav*, and quay, *bunda*), taking in the sea breezes and views over the busy harbour. Alternatively, Shivaji Marg heads northwest towards **Wellington Circle** (SPM Chowk), the hectic roundabout in front of the Regal cinema. The latter route takes you past the old **Bombay Yacht Club**, another idiosyncratic vestige of the Raj. Very little seems to have changed here since its smoky common rooms were a bolt hole for the city's *burra-sahibs*. Dusty sporting trophies and models of clippers and dhows stand in glass cases lining its corridors, polished from time to time by bearers in cotton tunics. If you want to look around, seek permission from the club secretary; accommodation is available only to members and their guests.

Southwards along Colaba Causeway

To walk from Wellington Circle to the south of the peninsula, you have first to run the gauntlet of street-vendors and hustlers who crowd the claustrophobic pavements of **Colaba Causeway** (this stretch of Shahid Bhagat Singh Marg).

It's hard to believe that such a chaotic city thoroughfare, with its hole-in-the-wall cafés, clothes stores and incense stalls, was reclaimed from the sea.

On the corner of the Colaba Causeway and Arthur Bunder Road you'll find the **Shree Bhid Mahadeo Mandir**, a Shiva temple built in 1923 round a sacred tree. It's a tiny place plastered with many different gods, with a small but colourful Shiva shrine by the tree; one of the Brahmins speaks English and will happily answer any questions. You can also make a puja here and they won't hassle you for big donations – Rs10 is sufficient.

Turning left down **Arthur Bunder Road**, you'll pass many Muslim perfumeries, hotels and restaurants. At the end of the road is the *Voodoo Lounge*, which in previous incarnations (it's now a gay bar) played host to a number of bands including the Stones, Led Zeppelin and Pink Floyd. Taking a right past here you'll come out by a small sea-wall which is named **The Wall** in honour of Pink Floyd. It's a nice place at sunset, when locals and transients can be found chilling out, making it a good place to meet people. From here, a short walk south will bring you into the **fisherman's shanty town**; you can wander through this communally mixed area that demonstrates a religious tolerance that does credit to the city – it's not dangerous but remember it's a residential area so have your *namastes* (greetings) ready.

From here head east back onto Colaba Causeway and a five-minute walk will bring you to the wholesale seafood market at **Sassoon Docks**, a kilometre or so south of central Colaba, which provides an unexpected splash of rustic colour amid the drab urban surroundings. Koli fisherwomen, their cotton saris hitched dhoti-style, squat beside baskets of glistening pomfret, prawns and tuna, while coolies haul plastic crates of crushed ice over rickety gangplanks to the boats moored at the quay. The stench, as overpowering as the noise, comes mostly from bundles of dried fish that are sold in bulk. **"Bombay duck"**, the salty local snack, has found its way to many a far shore, but you'll be hard pushed to find any in Colaba's own restaurants. **Photography** is strictly forbidden, as the market is close to a sensitive military area.

From the docks, hop on any bus heading south down Colaba Causeway (#3, #11, #47, #103, #123, or #125) to the **Afghan Memorial Church of St John the Baptist**, built (1847–54) as a memorial to the British victims of the First Afghan War. Hemmed in by the cantonment area, the pale yellow church, with its tall steeple and tower, would look more at home beside the playing fields of Eton than the sultry waters of the Arabian Sea. If the door is unlocked, take a peep at the marble plaques and stained-glass windows inside.

Downtown Mumbai

Aldous Huxley famously described Mumbai as "one of the most appalling cities of either hemisphere", with its "lavatory bricks and Gothic spires". The critic Robert Byron, although a wholehearted fan of New Delhi, was equally unenthusiastic, feeling moved to refer to **downtown Mumbai** in 1931 as "that architectural Sodom", claiming that "the nineteenth century devised nothing lower than the municipal buildings of British India. Their ugliness is positive, daemonic." Today, however, the massive erections of Empire and Indian free enterprise appear not so much ugly, as intriguing.

Prince of Wales Museum (Chatrapati Shivaji Museum) and Jehangir Art Gallery

Set back from Mahatma Gandhi (MG) Road in an attractive garden is the unmissable **Prince of Wales Museum of Western India** (Tues–Sun

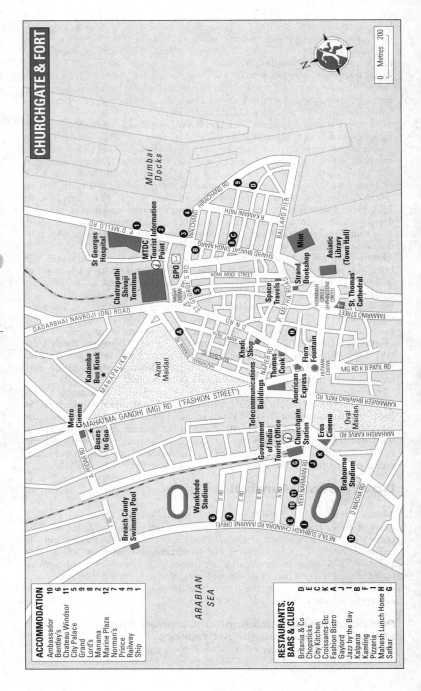

CHURCHGATE & FORT

Mumbai Docks

ARABIAN SEA

N

0 Metres 200

ACCOMMODATION

Ambassador	10
Bentley's	6
Chateau Windsor	11
City Palace	5
Grand	9
Lord's	8
Manama	2
Marine Plaza	12
Norman's	7
Prince	4
Railway	3
Ship	1

RESTAURANTS, BARS & CLUBS

Britania & Co	D
Chopsticks	E
City Kitchen	C
Croissants Etc	K
Fashion Bistro	A
Gaylord	J
Jazz by the Bay	B
Kalpana	F
Kamling	I
Pizzeria	I
Mahesh Lunch Home	H
Satkar	G

St Georges Hospital

Chatrapathi Shivaji Terminus

MTDC Tourist Information Point

GPO

NAGAR CHOWK

P. D'MELLO RD

WALCHAND HIRACHAND RD

SHAHID BHAGAT SINGH MARG

R KAMANI PATH

BALLARD PIER

Mint

Asiatic Library (Town Hall)

Strand Bookshop

St. Thomas' Cathedral

Space Travels

HOMI MODI STREET

ST GEORGE'S RD

D N RD

P. MEHTA ROAD

HARNIMAN CIRCLE (ELPHINSTONE CIRCLE)

TAMARIND STREET

DADARBHAI NAVROJI (DN) ROAD

Azad Maidan

MAHAPALIKA

Kadamba Bus Kiosk

HAZARIMAL SOMANI RD

MAHAKAVI BHUSHAN RD

AMRIT PATH

Khadi Shop

Thomas Cook

Flora Fountain

American Express

HUTAMA CHOWK

MG RD K B PATIL RD

Metro Cinema

Buses to Goa

MAHATMA GANDHI (MG) RD ("FASHION STREET")

A. PODAR RD

Telecommunications Buildings

NAPIER RD

Government of India Tourist Office

Churchgate Station

Eros Cinema

KARAMVEER BHAVRAO PATIL RD

Oval Maidan

MAHARSHI KARVE RD

Breach Candy Swimming Pool

Wankhede Stadium

D RD

C RD

B RD

A RD

VEER NARIMAN RD

Brabourne Stadium

D WACHA RD

NETAJI SUBHASH CHANDRA RD (MARINE DRIVE)

F RD

10.15am–6pm; Rs150, Rs15 extra with camera). This distinctive Raj-era building, crowned by a massive white Moghul-style dome, houses a superb collection of paintings and sculpture that you'll need several hours, or a couple of visits, to get the most out of. Its foundation stone was laid in 1905 by the future King George V, then Prince of Wales; the architect, George Wittet, went on to design the Gateway of India. The museum is undoubtedly the finest example of his work; the epitome of the hybrid **Indo–Saracenic** style, it is said to be an "educated" interpretation of fifteenth- and sixteenth-century Gujarati architecture, mixing Islamic touches with typically English municipal brickwork.

The **central hall**, overlooked by a carved wooden balcony, provides a snapshot of the collection with a few choice Moghul paintings, jade work, weapons and miniature clay and terracotta figures from the Mauryan (third century BC) and Kushana (first to second century AD) periods. From Bengal (first century BC) are horrible-looking *yakshis* (godlings or sprites) devouring lizards. Sculpture galleries on either side of the hall open onto the front garden; the one to the right houses the museum's **natural history** section, which contains a large and well-kept – if somewhat unfashionable – collection of stuffed birds, fish and animals.

The main **sculpture room** on the **ground floor** displays some excellent fourth- and fifth-century heads and figures from the Buddhist state of

Dabawallahs

Mumbai's size and inconvenient shape create all kind of hassles for its working population – not least having to stew for over four hours each day in slow municipal transport. One thing the daily tidal wave of commuters do not have to worry about, however, is finding an inexpensive and wholesome home-cooked lunch. In a city with a wallah for everything, it will find them. The members of the **Mumbai Tiffin Box Suppliers Association**, known colloquially, and with no little affection, as **"dabawallahs"**, see to that. Every day, around 4000 *dabawallahs* deliver freshly cooked food from 125,000 suburban kitchens to offices in the downtown area. Each lunch is prepared early in the morning by a devoted wife or mother while her husband or son is enduring the crush on the train. She arranges the rice, dhal, *subzi*, curd and *parathas* into cylindrical aluminium trays, stacks them on top of one another and clips them together with a neat little handle. This **tiffin box**, not unlike a slim paint tin, is the lynchpin of the whole operation. When the runner calls to collect it in the morning, he uses a special colour code on the lid to tell him where the lunch has to go. At the end of his round, he carries all the boxes to the nearest railway station and hands them over to other *dabawallahs* for the trip into town. Between leaving the wife and reaching its final destination, the tiffin box will pass through at least half a dozen different pairs of hands, carried on heads, shoulder-poles, bicycle handlebars and in the brightly decorated handcarts that plough with such insouciance through the midday traffic. Tins are rarely, if ever, lost, and always find their way home again (before the husband returns from work) to be washed up for the next day's lunch.

To catch *dabawallahs* in action, head for **VT** or **Churchgate** stations around late morning time, when the tiffin boxes arrive in the city centre. The event is accompanied by a chorus of "lafka! lafka!" – "hurry! hurry!" – as the *dabawallahs*, recognizable in their white Nehru caps and baggy khaki shorts, rush to make their lunch-hour deadlines. Most collect about one rupee for each tin they handle, netting around Rs1000 per month in total. *Daba* lunches still work out a good deal cheaper than meals taken in the city restaurants, saving precious paise for the middle-income workers who use the system, and providing a livelihood for the legions of poorer immigrants from the Pune area who operate it.

Gandhara, a former colony of Alexander the Great (hence the Greek-style stat-ues). Important Hindu sculptures include a seventh-century Chalukyan bas-relief from Aihole depicting Brahma seated on a lotus, and a sensuously carved torso of Mahisasuramaraini, the goddess Durga with tripod raised ready to skewer the demon buffalo. On the way up to the **first floor** a display on the astonishingly urban **Indus Valley Civilization** (3500–1500 BC) has models of typical settlements, mysterious seal moulds in an as-yet-undeciphered script, and jewellery. The main attraction, though, has to be the superb collection of **Indian painting**, including illustrated manuscripts and erotic Gita Govinda paintings in the pre-Moghul Sultanate style. **Moghul schools** are well repre-sented, too, with fine portraits and folios from the reign of Akbar (1556–1605), and sublime drawings of animals and birds from the Jehangir (1605–28) school. The well-known portrait of the emperor Shah Jahan (1628–57) and his fore-fathers is also on display.

Jade, porcelain and ivory can be seen on the **second floor**, along with a col-lection of **European art** that includes a minor Titian and a Constable. In the weapons collection are the swords of emperors Shah Jahan and Aurangzeb, a shield of Akbar ornamented with the zodiac, and various daggers, maces and guns. The poorly lit **Indian textiles room** showcases brocaded saris, turbans, and antique Kashmiri shawls, intricately patterned with flowers, birds, animals and abstract designs.

Technically in the same compound as the Prince of Wales Museum, though approached from further up MG Road, the **Jehangir Art Gallery** (daily 11am–7pm; free) is Mumbai's best-known venue for contemporary art, with five small galleries specializing in twentieth-century arts and crafts from around the world. You never know what you're going to find – most exhibitions last only a week and exhibits are often for sale.

Around Oval Maidan

Karmaveer Bhaurao Patil Marg's southern edge holds a statue of Dr B.R. Ambedkar (1891–1956), who though born into an outcast Hindu communi-ty, converted to Buddhism. A great number of "untouchables" followed suit; many are now part of a militant movement calling themselves *dalits*, "the oppressed", eschewing Gandhi's reconstructed name of Harijans, "god's peo-ple". Some of Mumbai's most important Victorian buildings line the eastern side of the vast green **Oval Maidan**, behind the statue, where impromptu cricket matches are held almost every day (foreign enthusiasts are welcome to take part, but should beware the maidan's demon bowlers and less-than-even pitches). Partially obscured by police huts, the dull yellow **Old Secretariat** now serves as the City Civil and Sessions Court. Indian civil servant G.W. Forrest described it in 1903 as "a massive pile whose main features have been brought from Venice, but all the beauty has vanished in transhipment". Inside, you can only imagine the originally highly polished interior, which no longer shines, but buzzes with activity. Lawyers in black gowns, striped trousers and white tabs bustle up and down the staircases, whose corners are emblazoned with expectorated paan juice, and offices with perforated swing-doors give glimpses of textbook images of Indian bureaucracy – peons at desks piled high with dusty beribboned document bundles.

Across A S D'Mello Road from the Old Secretariat, two major buildings belonging to **Mumbai University** (established 1857) were designed in England by Sir Gilbert Scott, who had already given the world the Gothic extravaganza of London's St Pancras railway station. Access through the main gates is monitored by caretakers who only allow you in if you say you're using

⑩

the library. Funded by the Parsi philanthropist Cowasjee "Readymoney" Jehangir, the **Convocation Hall** greatly resembles a church. Above its entrance, a huge circular stained-glass window features a wheel with spokes of Greek pilasters that separate signs of the zodiac. The library (daily 10am–10pm) is beneath the 79.2-metre-high **Rajabhai clock tower** which is said to be modelled on Giotto's campanile in Florence. Until 1931, it chimed tunes such as *Rule Britannia* and *Home Sweet Home*. It's worth applying for a visitor's ticket to the library (Rs5 a day, Rs10 for three days) just to see the interior. The magnificent vaulted wooden ceiling of the reading room, high Gothic windows and stained glass still evoke a reverential approach to learning.

Hutatma Chowk (Flora Fountain)

A busy five-point intersection in the heart of the Fort area, the roundabout formerly known as **Flora Fountain** has been renamed **Hutatma Chowk** ("Martyr's Square") to commemorate the freedom fighters who died to establish the state of Maharashtra in the Indian Union. The chowk centres on a statue of the Roman goddess **Flora**, erected in 1869 to commemorate Sir Bartle Frere. It's hard to see quite why they bothered – the Raj architecture expert, Philip Davies, was not being unkind when he said, "The fountain was designed by a committee, and it shows."

Facing Hutatma Chowk is a **statue of Dadabhai Naoroji** (1812–1917) showing the first Indian member of the British parliament (1892–95). You may want to tarry here a while to consult Machindra Govind Pawar, who for years has sat next to the statue daily (except Sunday) between 8am and 8pm. Signs explain his business, offering cures for "rheumatism, hair falling, piles, fistula and sex weakness". Sri Pawar, who hails from Pune, says he is a practitioner of *Ayurved*, and operates on a basis that sounds like commercial suicide: he accepts no payment until his patients are cured.

Horniman Circle and the Town Hall

Horniman Circle, formerly Elphinstone Circle, is named after a pro-Independence newspaper editor. It was conceived in 1860 as a centrepiece of a newly planned Bombay by the then Municipal Commissioner, Charles Forjett, on the site of Bombay "Green". Forjett, a Eurasian, had something of a peculiar reputation; he was fond of disguising himself in "native" dress and prowling about certain districts of the city to listen out for seditious talk. In 1857, at the time of the First War of Independence (as it is now known by Indians; the British call it the Indian Mutiny), Forjett fired two suspected revolutionaries from a cannon on the Esplanade (roughly the site of the modern maidans).

It is often said that the design of Horniman Circle was based on Tunbridge Wells or Leamington Spa in England, with elegant Neoclassical buildings centring on a garden with a fountain. East of the square, the impressive Doric **Town Hall** on SBS Marg houses the vast collection of the **Asiatic Library**.

St Thomas' Cathedral

The small, simple **St Thomas' Cathedral** (daily 6.30am–6pm), on Tamarind Street, is reckoned to be the oldest English building in Mumbai, blending Classical and Gothic styles. Governor Aungier self-righteously envisaged it with "the main design of inviting the natives to repair thereunto, and observe the gravity and purity of our own devotions". After his death, the project was abandoned; the walls stood 5m high for forty-odd years until enthusiasm was rekindled by Richard Cobbe, a chaplain to the East India Company, in the second decade of the eighteenth century. He believed the church's unfinished walls represented "a mark of derision for the natives for whose conversion they were partly raised [and] a reproach and a scandal to the English in Bombay". It was finally opened on Christmas Day 1718, complete with the essential "cannon-ball-proof roof". In those days, the seating was divided into useful sections for those who should know their place, including one for "Inferior Women".

St Thomas' whitewashed and polished brass-and-wood interior looks much the same as when the staff of the East India Company worshipped here in the eighteenth century. Lining the walls are memorial tablets to English parishioners, many of whom died young, either from disease or in battle.

Marine Drive and Chowpatty Beach

Netaji Subhash Chandra Marg, better known as **Marine Drive**, is Mumbai's seaside prom, an eight-lane highway with a wide pavement built in the 1920s on reclaimed land. Sweeping in an arc from the skyscrapers at Nariman Point in the south, Marine Drive ends at the foot of Malabar Hill and the old Chowpatty Beach. The whole stretch is a favourite place for a stroll; the promenade next to the sea has uninterrupted views virtually the whole way along, while the apartment blocks on the land side – most of which are ugly, unpainted concrete and called something-or-other Mahal – are some of the most desirable and expensive addresses in the city.

It's a great place for people-watching. Early in the morning yuppies in shorts speed-walk or jog before breakfast while street kids, mothers and babies and limbless beggars take up position at the traffic lights at major junctions to petition drivers and passengers for a rupee. Those one rung further up the social ladder have something to sell: twisted fun balloons or a newspaper. Some kids perfunctorily wipe a rag over the bodywork and do their best to wrest a few coins from momentarily captive people, ninety percent of whom stare resolutely ahead.

Evening sees servants walking their bosses' Pekinese or poodles, and children playing under the supervision of their *ayahs* (nannies). Sometime after 6pm the place magically transforms; the British called it the "Queen's Necklace". The massive red sun disappears into the sea, street lights snap on, five-star hotels glow and neon lights blink. Innumerable couples materialize to take romantic strolls down to the beach, stopping on the way to buy from a peanut vendor or to pay off a *hijra*, or eunuch, threatening to lift up his sari and reveal all.

Just beyond the huge flyover, B Bridge, are a series of cricket pitches known as **gymkhanas**, where there's a good chance of catching a match any day of the week. A number are exclusive to particular religious communities. The first doubles as a swanky outdoor wedding venue for Parsi marriages; others include the Catholic, Islamic and Hindu pitches, the last of which has a classic colonial-style pavilion.

Chowpatty Beach
Chowpatty Beach is a Mumbai institution, which really comes to life at night and on Saturday. People do not come here to swim (the sea is foul) but to wander, sit on the beach, let the kids ride a pony or a rusty Ferris wheel, have a massage, get ears cleaned or hair cut, listen to musicians, buy drugs, have a go on a rifle range, consult an astrologer, watch dreadlocked ascetics perform public austerities, get conned, and picnic on *bhel puri* and cups of kulfi. Gupta

Bhelwallas's *bhel puri* stall satisfied the discerning Mumbai palate with a secret concoction of the sunset snack for over a century; unfortunately, at the time of writing all the *bhel puri*-wallahs had been evicted from the beach in an attempt to clean the place up, but since they are a well-loved part of the scene it's hoped they will be relocated nearby soon. There are also plenty of good ice-cream bars and restaurants across Marine Drive, opposite the beach (see p.776), where you'll find Wagh's Fine Art Studio, whose curious collection of plaster figures in the window includes a much larger than life Gandhi plus Alsatian dog.

Once a year in September the **Ganesh Chathurthi** festival (see p.744) draws gigantic crowds to participate in the immersion of idols, both huge and small, of the elephant-headed god Ganesh.

Just west of Chowpatty Beach is the **Breach Candy swimming pool**, where membership is strictly restricted to the upper echelons of society. However, tourists are allowed to join for the day (Rs200), and use both the British-style indoor pool and the India-shaped outdoor pool. The complex overlooks the beach, with relaxing sun loungers and a good restaurant.

Mani Bhavan Mahatma Gandhi Museum

Mani Bhavan, 19 Laburnum Rd (daily 9.30am–6pm), was Gandhi's Bombay base between 1917 and 1934. Set in a leafy upper-middle-class road, the house is now a permanent memorial to the Mahatma with an extensive research library. Within the lovingly maintained polished-wood interior, the walls are covered with photos of historic events and artefacts from the man's extraordinary life – the most disarming of which is a friendly letter to Hitler suggesting world peace. Gandhi's predictably simple sitting room-cum-bedroom is preserved behind glass. Laburnum Road is a few streets along from the Bharatiya Vidya Bhavan music venue on KM Munshi Marg – if coming by taxi ask for the nearby Gamdevi Police Station.

Malabar Hill

Malabar Hill, the long, steep-sided promontory enfolding Chowpatty Beach at the north end of Back Bay, is Mumbai's ritziest neighbourhood. Since the eighteenth century, its lush forests, fresh sea breezes and panoramic views have made the hill an attractive location for the grand mansions and bungalows of the city's merchants and governors. These days however, high-rise, high-rent apartment blocks have squeezed out all but a handful of the old colonial buildings to make way for Mumbai's "new money" set – the in-crowd of politicians, millionaires, film stars and gangsters who flit across the glossy pages and gossip columns of India's popular magazines. Somehow, though, a few jaded remnants of the city's past have managed to weather the changes.

Before heading up the hill from the busy roundabout at the far end of Chowpatty Beach, make a short diversion through the narrow backlanes to **Balbunath Mandir**, one of Mumbai's most important Hindu temples. You'll have no trouble finding the entrance: just look for the melee of stray cattle and flower-sellers that forms here around puja times. The building itself, a clumsy modern agglomeration of towers, turquoise arches and staircases, makes a much less interesting spectacle than the stream of *pujaris* (priests) and pilgrims on the greasy stone steps leading to it.

The municipal parks and the Jain temple

From the Balbunath temple, the most pleasant and direct route up to Malabar Hill's main thoroughfare, **Ridge Road**, now renamed **Bal Gangadhar** (or

The Towers of Silence

High on the top of Malabar Hill, screened from prying eyes by an imposing wall and a dense curtain of vegetation, stand the seven Parsi **Towers of Silence**, or *dokhmas*. If you know only one thing about the Parsis, it is probably that they dispose of their dead by leaving the corpses on top of tall cylindrical enclosures for their bones to be picked clean by vultures. This ancient mortuary ritual, thought to predate the 2500-year-old faith, was advocated by the prophet Zoroaster as a means of avoiding pollution of the four sacred elements (air, water, earth and, the holiest of all, fire). Recently, Parsis have been debating whether to switch to electric cremation as a sound, and more sanitary, alternative – supposedly because scraps of human flesh discarded by the overfed vultures have been appearing on balconies, rooftops and gardens near the Towers. Whatever they decide, no one will thank you for trying to peep at the *dokhmas* themselves, which are off-limits to all living people other than the pall-bearers who put the corpses in place. Not to be put off, *Time-Life* once published a colour photograph of a funeral taken from the buildings overlooking the site. Enraged Parsis retorted by asking how the photographer would feel if he saw pictures of *his* mother's body being pecked to bits by birds?

BG) **Kher Marg**, is via the tangle of crumbling concrete paths through the woods below it. The trail emerges near a pair of dull but popular public parks. The larger, known as the "**Hanging Gardens**" (renamed "Pherozeshah Mehta Gardens") is full of loving couples smooching ostentatiously around its gravel paths and manicured flowerbeds. By contrast, the smaller **Kamala Nehru Children's Park** (across the road) is unlikely to appeal to anyone over the age of seven. The views of Back Bay are, in any case, better admired from the congenial terrace bars of the *Naaz Café* nearby.

A kilometre or so straight down the ridge from the parks stands Malabar Hill's **Jain temple**. Mumbai's Jains originally came from Gujarat in the late seventeenth century to escape persecution by the Hindu Marathas. Since then, their legendary sharp business sense has helped make these ultra-strict vegetarians one of the city's most prosperous minorities. According to an ancient dictum, Jains should, every day after bathing, walk barefoot to their local temple in a length of stitchless cloth to pray, a gesture of humility and renunciation that contrasts with the lavish decoration of the temples themselves. This temple, though on the small side, is no exception. Mirrors and colourful paintings cover the walls surrounding the approach to the central chamber, where the polished marble image of **Adinath**, the first of the 24 Jain teacher-prophets, or *tirthankaras*, is enshrined. In front of the image, devotees make rice patterns as offerings. The temple also runs a stall selling freshly baked pure-veg biscuits, sweets and cakes. It's to the left of the main entrance, near the racks where shoes and leather articles have to be deposited.

Walukeshwar Mandir and Banganga Tank

Beyond the Jain temple, Malabar Hill tapers off to a narrow spit that shelves steeply down to Back Bay on one side, and the rocky seashore on the other. **Walukeshwar Mandir**, among the few of Mumbai's ancient Hindu sites not buried under layers of conurbation, can be reached via a lane left off the main road. According to the *Ramayana*, Rama paused here during his journey south to rescue Sita from the clutches of the evil Ravana, and fashioned a lingam out of sand to worship Shiva. Over time, the Walukeshwar, or "Sand-Lord" shrine, became one of the western Indian coast's most important religious centres, venerated even by the marauding Malabar pirates who menaced the islands.

Today's temple, erected in 1715 after the original had been destroyed by the Portuguese, is unremarkable and best bypassed in favour of the more impressive **Banganga tank** below it. Hemmed in by a towering wall of apartment blocks, the spring that feeds the tank is believed to have been created by an arrow fired from Rama's own fabled bow. Today, it's a minor pilgrimage site, busy only on "white" (full-) or "black" (no-) moon days of the month. At other times, Banganga's stone ghats, numerous subsidiary shrines, and scum-covered greenish waters see little more than a trickle of bathers, drawn mostly from the slum encampments which have sprung up on the broken land lining the shore. A path picks its way past these shacks, and the washing lines of the dhobis who live in them, to the **cremation ghats** nearby.

North of Malabar Hill

Two of Mumbai's most popular religious sites, one Hindu, the other Muslim, can be reached by following Bhulabhai Desai Road **north from Malabar Hill** as far as Prabhu Chowk, through the exclusive suburb of **Breach Candy** (bus #132 from Colaba). Alternatively, make for Mumbai Central and head due northwest to **Vatsalabai Desai Chowk** (also bus #132).

Mahalakshmi Mandir is joined to Bhulabhai Desai Road by an alley lined with stalls selling puja offerings and devotional pictures. Mumbai's favourite *devi*, **Lakshmi**, goddess of beauty and prosperity – the city's most sought-after attributes – is here propitiated with coconuts, sweets, lengths of shimmering silk and giant lotus blooms. At weekends, queues for *darshan* extend right the way across the courtyard and down the main steps beyond. Gifts pile so high that the temple *pujaris* run a money-spinning sideline reselling them. Their little shop, to the left of the entrance, is a good place to buy cut-price saris and brocades infused with lucky Lakshmi-energy. While you're here, find out what your future holds by joining the huddle of devotees pressing rupees onto the rear wall of the shrine room. If your coin sticks, you'll be rich.

A temple has stood on this rocky outcrop for well over a thousand years. Not until the eighteenth century, however, when the hitherto swampy western edge of the city was drained, was the present building erected. Legend has it that the goddess herself told a contractor working on the project that unless her icon – which she said would soon reappear from the sea where it had been cast by Muslim invaders – was reinstated in a temple, the breach-wall would not hold back the waves. Sure enough, the next day a Lakshmi deity was fished out of the silt by workmen, to be installed on this small headland, where it has remained to the present day.

Another site shrouded in myth is the mausoleum of the Muslim saint, Afghan mystic **Haji Ali Bukhari**, occupying a small islet in the bay just north of the Mahalakshmi temple. Islamic lore has two legends regarding its founding, though both agree he was sailing to India after performing *Haj* at Mecca; the first says that the coffin was washed ashore on these rocks after it had, on strict instructions from the saint, been cast into the sea off the coast of what is now Pakistan. The other is that the saint, when he realized he wouldn't reach India before his death, asked his disciples – the Fazla brothers – to build his tomb where he died. The construction took the brothers one year and was completed in 1865. The tomb is said to be very effective in answering prayers and the locals say that believers of all faiths make supplications here – it's even claimed British generals gave thanks to the saint after winning battles. It's connected to the mainland by a narrow concrete **causeway**, only passable at low tide. When not immersed in water, its entire length is lined with beggars who change one-rupee pieces into ten-paise coins for pilgrims. The prime sites, closer to the snack bars that flank the main entrance, near the small mosque, and the gateway to the **tomb** itself, are allocated in a strict pecking order. If you want to make a donation, spare a thought for the unfortunates in the middle. After all the commotion, the tomb itself comes as something of a disappointment. Its white Moghul domes and minarets look a lot less exotic close up than when viewed from the shore, silhouetted against the sun as it drops into the Arabian Sea.

A couple of kilometres further up the coast, the densely packed districts of central Mumbai are broken by a huge, empty expanse of dusty brown grass. The optimistically named **Mahalakshmi racecourse**, founded in 1879, is the home of the Mumbai Turf Club and a bastion of the city's Anglophile elite. Regular meetings take place here at weekends between November and March. If you fancy a hack yourself, the Amateur Riding Club also rents out horses during the week (except Wednesdays).

The central bazaars

Lining the anarchic jumble of streets north of Lokmanya Tilak (formerly Carnac) Road, Mumbai's teeming **central bazaars** are India at its most intense. You could wander around here for months without seeing the same shop front twice. In practice, most visitors find a couple of hours mingling with the crowds in the heat and din quite enough. Nevertheless, the market districts form a fascinating counterpoint to the wide and Westernized streets of downtown, even if you're not buying.

In keeping with traditional divisions of guild, caste and religion, most streets specialize in one or two types of merchandise – a pain if you want to see a smattering of all the goods on offer in a relatively short time. If you lose your bearings, the best way out is to ask someone to wave you in the direction of **Abdul Rehman Street**, the busy road through the heart of the district, from where you can hail a cab.

Crawford Market
Crawford (aka Mahatma Phule) **Market**, ten minutes' walk north of VT station, is an old British-style covered market dealing in just about every kind of

fresh food and domestic animal imaginable. Thanks to its pompous Norman-Gothic tower and prominent position at the corner of Lokmanya Tilak Road and Dr DN Marg, the Crawford Market is also a useful landmark and a good place to begin a foray into the bazaars.

Before venturing inside, check out the **friezes** wrapped around its exterior – a Victorian vision of sturdy-limbed peasants toiling in the fields designed by Rudyard Kipling's father, Lockwood, as principal of the Bombay School of Art in 1865. The **main hall** is still divided into different sections: pyramids of polished fruit and vegetables down one aisle, sacks of nuts or oil-tins full of herbs and spices down another. Sitting cross-legged on a raised platform in front of each stall is its eagle-eyed owner, wearing starched *khadi* pyjamas and a Nehru cap, with a fresh red *tilak* smeared on his forehead.

Around the back of the market, in the atmospheric **wholesale wing**, the pace of life is more hectic. Here, noisy crowds of coolies mill about with large reed-baskets held high in the air (if they are looking for work) or on their heads (if they've found some).

One place animal-lovers should definitely steer clear of is Crawford Market's **pet** and **poultry** section, on the east side of the building. You never quite know what creatures will turn up here, cringing in rank-smelling, undersized cages. The **tobacco** market, by contrast, is altogether more fragrant. Look out for the Muslim hookah merchants selling picturesque smoking paraphernalia.

North of Crawford Market

The streets immediately **north of Crawford Market** and west of **Mohammed Ali Road**, the main drag through Mumbai's Muslim ghettos, form one vast bazaar area. Ranged along both sides of narrow **Mangaldas Lane**, the cloth bazaar, are small shops draped with lengths of bright silk and cotton. Low doorways on the left open onto a colourful **covered market** area, packed with tiny stalls where you'll be badgered to sit and take tea while merchants tempt you with dozens of different saris and scarves.

Eastwards along Mangaldas Lane from Carnac Road, the pale green-washed domes, arches and minarets of the **Jami Masjid**, or "Friday Mosque" (c.1800), mark the start of the Muslim neighbourhoods. **Memon Street**, cutting north from the mosque, is the site of the **Zaveri Bazaar**, the jewellery market.

By the time the gleaming golden spire that crowns the **Mumba Devi temple**'s cream and turquoise tower appears at the end of the street, you're deep in a maze of twisting lanes hemmed in by tall, wooden-balconied buildings. The temple is one of the most important centres of Devi worship in India. Reached via a tiny courtyard where *pujaris* regale devotees with religious songs, its shrine houses a particularly revered, and unusual, deity. Her present resting place was built early in the nineteenth century, when she was relocated from her former home to make way for VT Station. Mumba Devi's other claim to fame is that her name is the original root of the word "Bombay", as well as the newer, and more politically correct, Maharashtran version, "**Mumbai**".

Chor Bazaar, Mutton Road and the red-light district

Jump in a taxi at the Mumba Devi temple for the two-kilometre trip north to the other concentration of markets around **Johar Chowk**, just north of SP Patel Road. The most famous of these, **Chor** (literally "thieves") **Bazaar** (where vendors peevishly insist the name is a corruption of the Urdu *shor*, meaning "noisy"), is the city's largest **antiques**-cum-flea market. Friday, the Muslim holy day, is the best day to be here. From 9am onwards, the neighbourhood is cluttered with hawkers and hand-carts piled high with bric-a-brac and assorted junk being eagerly rummaged by men in skullcaps. At other times, the antique shops down on **Mutton Road** are the main attraction. Once, you could hope to unearth real gems in these dark, fusty stores, but your chances of finding a genuine bargain nowadays are minimal. Most of the stuff is pricey Victoriana – old gramophones, chamber pots, chipped china – salvaged from the homes of Parsi families on the decline. The place is also awash with **fakes**, mainly small bronze votive statues, which make good souvenirs if you can knock the price down.

Press on north through Chor Bazaar and you'll eventually come out onto **Grant Road** (Maulana Shaukatali Road). Further north and west, in the warren of lanes below JB Behram Marg, lies the city's infamous **red-light district**. **Kamathipura**'s rows of luridly lit, barred shop fronts, from where an estimated 25,000 prostitutes ply their trade, are one of Mumbai's more degrading and unpleasant spectacles. Many of these so-called **"cage girls"** are young teenagers from poor tribal areas, and from across the border in Nepal, who have been sold by desperate parents into **bonded slavery** until they can earn the money to pay off family debts. The area is definitely no place to wander around on foot.

Elephanta

An hour's boat ride from Colaba, the tranquil, forested island of **ELEPHANTA** is one of the most atmospheric places in Mumbai. Populated only by a small fishing community, it makes a wonderful contrast to the seething claustrophobia of the city, even when crowded with day-trippers at weekends. Originally known as **Gharapuri**, the "city of Ghara priests", the island was renamed in the sixteenth century by the Portuguese in honour of the carved elephant they found at the port (see p.770). Its chief attraction is its unique **cave temple**, whose massive **Trimurti** (three-faced) **Shiva sculpture** is as fine an example of Hindu architecture as you'll find anywhere.

"Deluxe" boats set off from the Gateway of India (Oct–May hourly 9am–2.30pm; Rs85 return including government guide); book through the kiosks near the Gateway of India. Ask for your guide at the caves ticket office on arrival – they take about thirty minutes. **Ordinary ferries** (Rs65 return), also from the Gateway of India, don't include guides, and are usually packed. The journey takes about an hour on either boat.

Cool drinks and souvenir stalls line the way up the hill, and at the top, the MTDC *Chalukya* restaurant offers food and beer, and a terrace with good views out to sea, but you cannot stay overnight on the island.

The Cave

Elephanta's impressive excavated eighth-century **cave** (9.30am–4pm; $5 [Rs5]), covering an area of approximately 5000 square metres, is reached by climbing more than one hundred steps to the top of the hill. Inside, the massive columns, carved from solid rock, give the deceptive impression of being structural. To the right, as you enter, note the panel of **Nataraj**, Shiva as the cosmic dancer. Though spoiled by the Portuguese who, it is said, used it for target practice, the panel remains magnificent; Shiva's face is rapt, and in one of his left hands he removes the veil of ignorance. Opposite is a badly damaged panel of Lakulisha, Shiva with a club (*lakula*).

Each of the four entrances to the simple square main **shrine** – unusually, it has one on each side – is flanked by a pair of huge fanged *dvarpala* guardians (only those to the back have survived undamaged), while inside a large *lingam* is surrounded by coins and smouldering joss left by devotees. Facing the northern wall of the shrine, another panel shows Shiva impaling the demon **Andhaka**, who wandered around as though blind, symbolizing his spiritual blindness. Shiva killed him as he attempted to steal a divine tree from heaven. The panel behind the shrine on the back wall portrays the marriage of **Shiva and Parvati**. Moving east, the next panel shows Ganghadaran, Shiva receiving the descending river Ganga, his lover, to live in his hair, while Parvati, his wife, looks on. A powerful six-metre bust of **Trimurti**, the three-faced Shiva, who embodies the powers of creator, preserver and destroyer, stands nearby, and to the west a sculpture shows Shiva as **Ardhanarishvara**, half male and half female. Near the second entrance on the east, another panel shows Shiva and Parvati on **Mount Kailasha** with Ravana about to lift the mountain. His curved spine shows the strain.

Uptown and the outskirts

Greater Mumbai has crept inexorably northwards to engulf villages and swampland in a pall of chimneys, motorways and slums. These grim industrial areas hold few attractions, but possibilities for full- or half-day excursions include the quirky **Victoria and Albert museum** and botanical gardens in Byculla, and the **beach** at Juhu. All lie within reach of a suburban railway station, although you will, in most cases, have to take a rickshaw or taxi for the last few kilometres. Beyond them to the north lie the Buddhist caves chiselled out of the hillside at **Kanheri**, and the crumbling Portuguese fort at **Bassein**.

Byculla and the Veermata Jeejamata (Victoria and Albert) museum

As the bedrock of Mumbai's once-gigantic weaving industry, **Byculla**, immediately north of the central bazaar, epitomizes the grim legacy of nineteenth-century industrialization: idle chimney stacks, overcrowding and pavements strewn with ragged, sleeping bodies. The cotton mills and sweatshops are still here, churning out cheap clothes for the massive domestic market, but few can claim the turnovers they enjoyed a hundred years ago. Today, eclipsed by their old Gujarati rivals in Surat and Ahmedabad, all but the larger nationalized mills teeter on the brink of bankruptcy.

Visitors are welcome to look around the few of Byculla's cotton mills still in business, but a more common reason to come up here is to see the **Veermata Jeejamata (Victoria and Albert) museum** (daily except Wed 10.30am–4.30pm; Rs2) on Dr Babasaheb Ambedkar Marg. Inspired by its namesake in London, this grand Victorian-Gothic building was built in 1871 to house artefacts relating to Mumbai's history and development. Engravings, photographs and old maps are displayed in a small gallery on the first floor, along with sundry *objets d'art*. Downstairs in the main hall, the exhibits are more eclectic. Among the Victorian china and modest assortment of south Indian bronzes are cases filled with papier-mâché parakeets, pickaxe heads and plastic models of vegetables. More instructive is the scale model of a Parsi Tower of Silence (see p.765), with a gruesome description of the mortuary rituals performed on the real ones on Malabar Hill.

The museum's oldest and most famous exhibit, however, is the **stone elephant** in the small garden to the rear of the building. Now somewhat forlorn and neglected in the shadows, this was the very beast that inspired the Portuguese to name the island in the harbour "Elephanta" (see p.769). The crumbling figure was brought here for safekeeping in 1863 from its original, and more fittingly prominent, site alongside the landing stage that leads up to the cave temple.

A wrought-iron gateway beyond the elephant opens onto one of Mumbai's most popular venues for an old-fashioned family day out. The peaceful and green **Victoria Gardens** (daily except Wed 8am–6pm) hold a huge collection of South Asian flora, plus Mumbai's only **zoo** (Rs4), where, after a trip around the predictably small and smelly cages, kids can enjoy an elephant or camel ride.

Both museum and botanical gardens can be reached either by BEST **bus** (#3 or #11(Ltd) from Colaba, or #19 from Flora Fountain and Crawford Market); or by suburban train to Byculla station, on the opposite (western) side of the motorway.

Juhu Beach

With its palm trees, glamorous seaside apartment blocks and designer clothes stores, **Juhu**, 30km north of downtown, is Mumbai's answer to Sunset Boulevard. Unless you're staying in one of the many five-star hotels lining its five-kilometre strip of white sand, however, this affluent suburb holds little appeal. Sunbathing and swimming are out of the question, thanks to an oily slick of raw sewage that seeps into the Arabian Sea from the slum bastis surrounding Mahim Creek to the south. A more salubrious way to enjoy Juhu is to walk along the strand after office hours, when young families turn out in droves to enjoy the sunsets and sea breezes, attracting a bevy of *bhel puri*-wallahs, sideshows, mangy camels and carts, and lads hawking cheap Taiwanese toys. The rows of brightly painted stalls along the beach whip up delicious varieties of *falooda*, a fruit, ice-cream and vermicelli milkshake unique to Mumbai.

Further north up Juhu Road, the headquarters of the International Society for Krishna Consciousness (ISKCON) deals with matters more spiritual. Its richly appointed **Krishna temple** (daily 4am–1pm & 4–9pm) draws local Hindus in their Sunday-best shirtings and saris, and well-heeled Westerners wearing kaftans, *kurtas* and *dhotis*. Rich visitors get to stay in what must surely rank as the world's most glamorous *dharamshala* – a modern, multistorey hotel complex with its own vegetarian restaurant, conference hall and theatre.

Kanheri Caves

The chief reason to make the day's excursion to the suburb of Borivli, 42km out at the northern limits of Mumbai's sprawl, is to visit the Buddhist **Kanheri Caves** (daily 9am–5.30pm; $5 [Rs5]), ranged over the hills in virtually unspoilt forest. It's an interminable journey by road, so catch one of the many **trains** (50min) on the suburban line from Churchgate (marked "BO" on the departure boards; "limited stop" trains are 15min faster) to Borivli East. When you arrive, take the Borivli East exit, where a **bus** (for Kaneri Cave via SG Parles; Rs10), **auto-rickshaw** (about Rs60) or **taxi** (about Rs90) will take you the last 15km. Bring water and food as the stalls here only sell warm soft drinks.

Kanheri may not be as spectacular as other cave sites, but some of its sculpture is superb – though to enjoy the blissful peace and quiet that attracted its original occupants you should avoid the weekend and the crowds of day-trippers. Most of the caves, which date from the second to the ninth century AD, were used simply by monks for accommodation and meditation (*viharas*) during the four months of the monsoon, when an itinerant life was impractical – the season when the forest is at its most beautiful. They are connected by steep winding paths and steps; engage one of the friendly local guides at the entrance to find your way about, but don't expect any sort of lecture as their English is limited. Due to a recent spate of muggings in some of the remoter caves, it is not advisable to venture off the beaten track alone.

In **Cave 1**, an incomplete *chaitya* hall (a hall with a stupa at one end, an aisle and row of columns at either side), you can see where the rock was left cut, but unfinished. Two stupas stand in **Cave 2**; one was vandalized by a certain N. Christian, whose carefully incised Times-Roman graffiti bears the date 1810. A panel shows seated Buddhas, portrayed as a teachers. Behind, and to the side, is the *bodhisattva* of compassion, Padmapani, while to the right the *viharas* feature rock-cut beds.

Huge Buddhas, with serenely joyful expressions and unfeasibly large shoulders, stand on either side of the porch to the spectacular **Cave 3**. Between them, you'll see the panels of "donor couples", thought to have been foreigners that patronized the community. Inside, leading to a stupa at the back, octagonal columns in two rows, some decorated with animal motifs, line the magnificent Hinayana *chaitya* hall.

The sixth-century **Cave 11** is a large assembly hall, where two long "tables" of rock were used for the study of manuscripts. Seated at the back, in the centre, is a figure of the Buddha as teacher, an image repeated in the entrance, to the left, with a wonderful flight of accompanying celestials. Just before the entrance to a small cell in **Cave 34**, flanked by two standing Buddhas, an unfinished ceiling painting shows the Buddha touching the earth. There must be at least a hundred more Buddha images on panels in **Cave 67**, a large hall. On the left side, and outside in the entrance, these figures are supported by *nagas* (snakes representing *kundalini*, yogic power).

Bassein Fort

Trundling over the rickety iron bridge that joins the northern fringes of Mumbai to the Maharashtran mainland, you could easily fail to notice the ruined fort at **Bassein** (or Vasai), 61km north of the city centre. Yet these mouldy stone walls, obscured by a carpet of palms and lush tropical foliage at the mouth of the milky-blue River Ulhas, once encompassed India's most powerful and prosperous colonial settlement. It was ceded to the Portuguese by Sultan Bahadur of Gujarat in 1534, in return for help in the Gujarati struggle against the Moghuls, and quickly became the hub of the region's maritime trade, "The Court of the North", from which the Portuguese territories at Goa, Daman and Diu were administered. In 1739, however, the **Marathas** laid siege to the city for three months, eventually wiping out the garrison, and a final death blow was dealt in 1780 by the cannons of the **British**. Bassein's crumbling remnants were left to be carried off for raw building material or reclaimed by the coastal jungle, and only a handful of weed-infested buildings still stand today.

If you don't mind spending hours in a crowded suburban **train** (around 1hr 15min from Churchgate), Bassein makes an atmospheric day-trip from the city. Only a few express trains stop at the nearest mainline station, Vasai Road, from where the onward trip (11km) involves jumping in and out of **shared auto-rickshaws** – Rs5 for each leg. These stop halfway at a busy market crossroads, where you catch another ride for the last stretch from a stand 100m up a road left from the crossroads. Ask for the "*kila*", the Marathi word for "fort". Stock up on food and drink at Vasai Road; there's nowhere very sanitary to eat in Bassein.

The **fort** is entered through a large gateway in its slanting stone battlements. Once inside, the road runs past a modern monument to the Maratha leader,

Shivaji, before heading towards the woods and the old Portuguese town. The ruins are a melancholy sight: *peepal* and tall palm trees poke through the chancels of churches and convents, while water buffalo plod listlessly past piles of rubble, and monkeys leap and crash through the canopy overhead.

By contrast, the small **fishing village**, under the archway from the rickshaw stand, is thriving. The spiritual legacy of the Portuguese has endured here longer than their architectural one, as shown by the painted Madonna shrines tucked into wall-niches and crucifixes gleaming on the singlets of the fishermen lounging in the local bar. On the **beach**, a short way down the narrow sandy footpath through the main cluster of huts, large wooden frames are hung with pungent-smelling strips of dried pomfret, while nearby, fishing boats bob around in the silt-laden estuary water.

Eating

In keeping with its cosmopolitan credentials, Mumbai (and Colaba above all) is crammed with interesting **eating places**, whether you fancy splashing out on a buffet lunch-with-a-view from a flashy five-star revolving restaurant, or simply tucking into piping-hot roti kebab by gaslight in the street.

Colaba

Colaba (see map on p.755) has even more places to eat than it does hotels. In the space of just 1km, you can sample an amazing array of **regional cuisines**: pure-veg "Hindu hotels" serving delicious Gujarati and south Indian food stand cheek-by-jowl with Muslim cafés whose menus will delight die-hard carnivores. Nearby, within a stone's throw of the *Taj* and its expensive gourmet restaurants, are Mumbai's oldest and best-loved Chinese joints. Other than during the monsoons (when choppy seas keep the fishing fleet in the polluted waters of the harbour), these offer fresh, safe **seafood** dishes of tiger prawns, crab or delicate white pomfret. Still in Colaba, traditional Iranian restaurants serve minced lamb and mutton specialities, while revamped café-bars dish up

---

Street food

Mumbai is renowned for distinctive street foods – and especially bhel puri, a quintessentially Mumbai masala mixture of puffed rice, deep-fried *vermicelli*, potato, crunchy *puri* pieces, chilli paste, tamarind water, chopped onions and coriander. More hygienic, but no less ubiquitous, is pao bhaji, a round slab of flat bread stuffed with meat or vegetables simmered in a vat of hot oil, and kanji vada, savoury doughnuts soaked in fermented mustard and chilli sauce. And if all that doesn't appeal, a pit stop at one of the city's hundreds of juice bars probably will. There's no better way to beat the sticky heat than with a glass of cool milk shaken with fresh pineapple, mango, banana, *chikoo* (small brown fruit that tastes like a pear) or custard apple. Just make sure they hold on the ice – made, of course, with untreated water.

Restaurants, bars and cafés are listed below by district. The most expensive restaurants, particularly in the top hotels, will levy "service charges" that can add thirty percent to the price of your meal. Phone numbers have been given where we recommend you reserve a table for dinner.

draught beer and reasonable Western food for tourists and local yuppies. Non-vegetarians will enjoy succulent meats, smothered in the split-lentil stew known as dhansak, in Parsi restaurants, while Goan and Mangalorean "lunch-homes" crop up everywhere too – good for a pork vindaloo or a fiery fish curry.

The majority of Colaba's cafés, bars and restaurants – among them the popular travellers' haunts, *Leopold's* and the *Café Mondegar* – are up at the north end of the Causeway. Those below are divided into **price categories** based on the cost of a main dish: inexpensive (below Rs75), moderate (Rs75–200) and expensive (above Rs200).

Inexpensive

Bademiya, behind the *Taj* on Tulloch Road. Legendary Colaba kebab-wallah serving delicious flame-grilled chicken, mutton and fish steaks, in hot tandoori *rotis*, from benches on the sidewalk.

Kamat, Colaba Causeway. Friendly little eatery serving the best south Indian breakfasts in the area.

Majestic, near Regal cinema, Colaba Causeway. Large, traditional south Indian joint patronized by off-duty taxi-wallahs, junior office staff and back-packers.

Mezban, Apollo Bunder Road, off Colaba Causeway. Cheap but delicious Arabic, Punjabi and Mughlai food in light, airy surroundings. Excellent non-veg items and the pizzas aren't bad either.

New Martin, near the Strand cinema, Strand Road. Unpromising formica booths, but famed for delicious Goan dishes such as prawn *pulao*, sausages, pork vindaloo and spicy fish curry. Also does takeaways.

Olympic Coffee House, 1 Colaba Causeway. *Fin-de-siècle* Iranian café with marble tabletops, wooden wall panels and a mezzanine floor for "ladies". Decor more alluring than the menu of greasy meat dishes, but nonetheless a good place for a lunch break, though not – strangely – coffee.

Udipi Refreshment, Colaba Causeway. One of many inexpensive south Indian and Gujarati thali joints that line the Causeway south of KP's. One will set you back only Rs20–25.

Moderate

Alps, Nawroji Fardunji Road. Trendy, ersatz American restaurant serving lamb-burgers, fries, sizzling steaks and copious "mixed-grills" to Western chart-music. Cheap beer by the pitcher, too.

Baghdadi, Tulloch Road. Male-dominated place famous for its meat: mostly mutton and chicken steeped in spicy garlic sauce. Chauffeurs pick up takeaways here for their bosses in the *Taj*.

Food Inn, 61 Colaba Causeway. Not much of a looker from the outside, but serves excellent Punjabi dishes – especially non-veg. Frequented mainly by locals who think *KP's* has lost its touch.

Kailash Parbat ("KP's"), 1 Pasta Lane, near the Strand cinema. Uninspiring on the outside, but the *alu parathas* for breakfast, pure veg nibbles, hot snacks and sweets (across the road) are worth the walk. A Colaba institution – try their famous *makai-ka* (corn) *rotis*.

Leopold's, Colaba Causeway. Colaba's most famous – and overpriced – café-bar is determinedly Western, with a clientele to match. Three hundred items on the menu from scrambled eggs to "chilly chicken", washed down with cold beer (Rs110). There's also a bar upstairs.

Expensive

Ling's Pavilion, 19/21 Lansdowne Road, behind the Regal cinema ☏022/285 0023. Swanky Chinese restaurant: soft lighting, marble floors and gourmet Cantonese cuisine.

Palkhi, Walton Road ☏022/284 0079. Over-the-top, quasi-medieval decor and traditional Mughlai cooking for the health-conscious (lighter on oil and spices). Lots of veg options too.

Tanjore, Taj Mahal ☏022/202 3366. Opulent interior, rich Mughlai cuisine and classical Indian music and dance in the evening. Expense-account prices.

Downtown

In the following list, *Britania & Co*, *City Kitchen* and *Mahesh Lunch Home* feature on the **Churchgate and Fort map** (see p.758); the others appear on the **Colaba map** (p.755).

Britania & Co, opposite the GPO, Sprott Road, Ballard Estate. Definitive Iranian/Parsi food and decor. Try their special "*berry pulao*" or Bombay duck dishes. A real find, and cheap too.

Chetana, 34 K Dubash Marg ☏022/284 4968. Painstakingly prepared Rajasthani/Gujarati food, including set thalis (Rs150) at lunchtime and numerous à la carte dishes – absolutely the last word in fine veg cuisine. Expensive, but not extravagant. Reserve for dinner.

City Kitchen, 301 SBS Marg. Highly rated hole-in-the-wall Goan restaurant. Serves all the usual dishes – mostly fish and meat simmered in coconut milk and fiery spices. Inexpensive.

Copper Chimney, 18 K Dubash Marg ☏022/204 1661. Renowned eatery with wonderful ceramic murals and stylish versions of standard north Indian dishes; the tandoori kebabs are recommended. Reservations essential at weekends. Superb but expensive.

Kalpana, 254 Shahid Bhagatsingh Road, 3min east from VT. Great place to get your bearings if you've just flopped off a train at VT. Inexpensive Punjabi dishes and great thali (veg and non-veg) served in a light, airy dining hall with comfortable seating.

Khyber (sign not in English), opposite Jehangir Art Gallery, Kala Ghoda ☏022/267 3227. Ultra-fashionable, with opulent Arabian Nights interior and uncompromisingly rich Mughlai/Punjabi cuisine.

The chicken *makhanwallah* is legendary. Reservations essential.

Mahesh Lunch Home, 8-B Cawasji Patel St, Fort. Inexpensive Keralan restaurant serving authentic veg "meals" and delicious non-veg options – chicken fried in ginger or fish masala on groaning platefuls of rice.

Café Samovar, Jehangir Art Gallery, MG Road. Very pleasant, peaceful semi-open-air café, with varying menu of food and drink: *roti kebabs*, prawn curry, fresh salads and dhansak, chilled guava juice and beer.

Trishna, 7 Ropewalk Lane, Kala Ghonda ☏022/267 2176. Visiting dignitaries and local celebs from the President of Greece and Imran Khan to Bollywood stars have eaten here (as photos attest). Wonderful fish dishes in every sauce going, and prices to match the clientele. Very small, so book in advance.

Wayside Inn, opposite Jehangir Art Gallery, K Dubash Marg. Upmarket Parsi café, with red-chequered tablecloths and solid English cooking. Nice place for a coffee after visiting the museum.

Churchgate and Nariman Point

The restaurants listed below are marked on either the **Churchgate and Fort map** on p.758 or the **Mumbai map** on pp.740-741.

Chopsticks, 90a VN Rd ☏022/204 9284. Wide choice of pricey meat, seafood and veg in fiery Szechuan and milder Cantonese style. Try the excellent *dim sum* or dishes with such inscrutable names as "ant climbing up the tree". Buffet lunch Rs200.

Croissants Etc, Industrial Insurance Building, opposite Churchgate station. Filled croissants, pricey pastries and other Western food, including delicious cakes.

Gaylord, VN Road ☏022/282 1259). Parisian-style terrace café in the heart of Mumbai. Tandoori, sizzlers and some Western food. Wholemeal bread, baguettes and sticky buns in the patisserie.

Kamling, VN Road ☏022/204 2618. Favourite for the title of oldest, best and most authentic Chinese in town. Southeast Asian flight crews and well-heeled locals tuck into delicious Cantonese dishes – try the mouthwatering "chimney soup" or the (expensive) seafood specialities.

The Outrigger, *Oberoi Hotel*, Nariman Point ☏022/202 4343. Polynesian specialities (Chinese with more fruit thrown in), tribal masks and a full-size canoe. Expensive.

The Pearl of the Orient, *Ambassador Hotel*, VN Road ☏022/291131. Revolving Oriental restaurant in glam four-star hotel with panoramic views. Reserve for dinner – expensive.

The Pizzeria, Corner of Veer Nariman and Marine Drive. Delicious freshly baked pizzas served on newly renovated terrace overlooking Back Bay, or to take away. Plenty of choice, and moderate to expensive prices.

Purohit's, VN Road ☏022/204 6241. Justly popular traditional restaurant serving a good range of mid-price Gujarati thalis, Punjabi main dishes and South Indian *chaat*.

Rangoli, inside NCPA Centre, Nariman Point ☏022/202 3366. Excellent-value Continental/Oriental buffet lunches (Rs350) are its forte, but the à la carte menu is gourmet standard though fairly pricey. Be warned that the waiters may put on a "show" in the evening.

Satkar, opposite Churchgate station's western exit. Busy pure-veg terrace restaurant: great for south Indian "fast food" and crowd-watching.

Trattoria, *Hotel President*, 90 Cuffe Parade ☏022/215 0808. Surprisingly authentic Italian cuisine. Pizza and pasta with fresh herbs, real Parmesan, bitter-chocolate ice cream, and a big buffet lunch on Sundays (noon–3pm; Rs400).

Crawford Market and the central bazaars

Badshah Juice and Snack Bar, opposite Crawford Market, Lokmanya Tilak Road. Mumbai's most famous *falooda* joint also serves delicious *kulfi*, ice creams and dozens of freshly squeezed fruit juices. The ideal place to round off a trip to the market.

Bhaishankar's, near Bhuleshwar Market, CP Tank Circle. One of Mumbai's oldest and most respected sweet shops. Try their Bengali *barfi*, cashew *kalingar* or masala milk (made with pistachio, almonds, saffron and nutmeg).

Gulshan-e-Iran, Palton Road ☎022/265183. Popular Muslim breakfast venue on the main road that does inexpensive biryanis, kebabs, chutneys and fresh bread. Open all day.

Hiralal Kashiram Bhajiwala, Kumbhar Tukda, Bhuleshwar Market. Cheap restaurant serving great *farsan* savouries, including *ponk vadas* (millet and garlic balls), *batata vadas* (made with sweet potatoes) and *kand bhajis* (deep-fried purpleyam), all with a tasty, fiery chutney.

Rajdhani, Mangaldas Road (in the silk bazaar opposite Crawford market). Outstanding, eat-till-you-burst Gujarati thalis dished up by barefoot waiters to discerning aficionados. A little more expensive than usual, but well worth it.

Shalimar, Bhindi Bazaar Junction. Outstanding Mughlai, tandoori and (not as good) Chinese food in a cool Art Deco marbelled interior. Great food and reasonable prices make it very popular with Muslim Mumbayakas.

Chowpatty Beach and Kemp's Corner

Chowpatty Beach is a popular venue for a picnic, crowded with vendors selling *kulfi* in clay cups and *bhel puri*, *kanji vada* and *pao bhaji*. **Kemp's Corner**, crouched under the hectic G Deshmukh flyover, fifteen minutes' walk north, boasts a clutch of very good places to eat – handy for visitors to Malabar Hill. The restaurants listed below feature on the **map** on p.740.

China Garden, Om Chambers, 123 August Kranti Marg ☎022/363 0841. Malabar Hill's glitterati don their finest for this place, which has expensive, authentic Chinese, Korean, Thai and Japanese food.

Chinese Room, Kwality House, Kemp's Corner ☎022/380 6771. A less expensive alternative to *China Garden*, specializing in quality Szechuan, Hunan and Cantonese cooking, with great seafood.

Gupta Bhelwalla, around Chowpatty Beach. The most legendary stall in India, where colourful variations of hot/cold, sweet/sour *bhel puri* are whipped up in front of you with flair. Utterly delicious. May take some tracking down due to the clearing of food stands on Chowpatty Beach.

New Yorker, Fulchand Niwas, 25 Chowpatty Seaface. Western food – baked potatoes, pizzas, burgers, and some Tex-Mex options – dished up in a bustling a/c café. Moderate.

Paramount, Marine Drive, near the Aquarium. Small Iranian café, which while it has a certain charm, has marble-top tables, wood-panelled and mirrored walls, applies strict rules: signs request that you "Do not spit", "Do not comb your hair", "Do not stretch legs on other pieces of furniture" and, most advisedly, "Do not sit unnecessarily a long time". Inexpensive.

Revival, above *London Pub*, Chowpatty Seaface, near the footbridge. Expensive but good-value 1930s retro restaurant serving imaginative and tasty Italian (with authentic ingredients) and Indian veg food.

Nightlife and entertainment

Mumbai never sleeps. No matter what time of night you venture out, there are bound to be others going about some business or other. The city has always led the **nightlife** scene in India and there are bars and clubs to suit every taste: jazz dens compete with salsa, tabla-dance fusions and funk. Mumbai's alternative but decidedly yuppie crowd meet at the *Ghetto Bar* before heading down to the gay, glitzy or groovy clubs around Colaba and Juhu.

Of course, Mumbai is also a cultural centre, attracting the finest **Indian classical music** and **dance** artists from all over the country; ⊛www

On the principle that laughter is the best medicine, Mumbai doctor Madan Kataria has created a new kind of therapy: hasya (laughter) yoga. There are now over 300 **Laughter Clubs** in India and many more worldwide; around 50,000 people joined the Laughter Day celebrations in Mumbai in January 2001.

Fifteen-minute sessions start with adherents doing yogic breathing whilst chanting "Ho ho ha ha," which develops into spontaneous "hearty", "silent" and "swinging" laughter. Sessions mostly take place between 6am and 7am, a time that, according to the good doctor, "keeps you in good spirits throughout the day, energizes your body and charges you with happiness". There are many clubs in Mumbai itself: to find out about them, check ⓦwww.indiabuzz.com/laughter/yogi.htm.

.dream merchants.org/theatreguide/tg.htm has good listings and includes bus routes and stations. There are frequent concerts and recitals at venues such as: Bharatiya Vidya Bhavan, KM Munshi Marg (☎022/363-0224), the headquarters of the international cultural (Hindu) organization; Cowasjee Jehangir (CJ) Hall opposite the Prince of Wales Museum (☎022/282-2457); Birla Matushri, 19 Marine Lines (☎022/203-6707); Tejpal Auditorium, 7 AK Nayak Marg (☎022/207-2061); Shanmukhananda Hall, 6 J Yagnik Marg (☎022/403-1357); and the National Centre for the Performing Arts, Narimon Point (NCPA; ☎022/288-3838) auditorium. NCPA also offers modern Gujarati, Hindi, Marathi and English-language **plays** as well as Western **chamber music**, while a smattering of platinum-selling Western rock artists appear at Mumbai stadium.

Bars and cabarets

Mumbai has an unusually easy-going attitude to **alcohol**; popping into a bar for a beer is very much accepted (for men at least) even at lunchtime. Chowpatty Beach and Colaba Causeway, where you'll find *Leopold's* and the *Café Mondegar*, form the focus of the travellers' social scene, but if you want to sample the pulse of the city's nightlife, venture up to Bandra and Juhu.

There is also a seamier side to the city's nightlife, concentrated around (illegal) late-night **cabarets** in the Grant Road area. In these dens of iniquity, women dance before men-only crowds in clothes that might in the West be considered Victorian in their propriety but would be unheard of anywhere else in India.

Café Mondegar, Colaba Causeway. Draught beer by the glass or pitcher, imported beer and deliciously fruity cocktails in a small café-bar. The atmosphere is very relaxed, the music tends towards rock classics and the clientele is a mix of Westerners and students; murals by a famous Goan cartoonist give the place a nice ambience.

Gables, Arthur Bunder Road, Colaba. Small and dark bar serving very cheap beer (from Rs45) and liquors to a tranquil male Indian clientele.

The Ghetto, 30 Bhulabhai Desai Road, near Breach Candy, Mahalakshmi (bus #132 from downtown). The alternative Mumbai scene where young arty, theatre types gather to play their music with attitude and write profound thoughts on the walls – the uniformed waiters do, unfortunately, ruin the effect. Cheap beer by the pitcher.

Jazz by the Bay, next to *The Pizzeria*, 143 Marine Drive. The official Channel V TV hang-out is a convenient place to crawl to after stuffing yourself with pizza. There's nightly live music, with both Indian and foreign artists performing, except on Sundays and Mondays when it's karaoke. Rs150 entrance; free Tues.

Leopold Pub, 1st Floor, *Leopold's*, Colaba Causeway. Swanky, self-consciously Western-style bar-nightclub, with bouncers, serving expensive beers to Mumbai's smart set. No single men admitted.

The Tavern, *Fariyas Hotel*, Colaba. Another "English-style" pub, complete with wooden beams, loud music and imported beer.

For anyone brought up on TV, it's hard to imagine the power that **movies** continue to wield in India. Every village has a cinema within walking distance and, with a potential audience in the hundreds of millions, the Indian film industry is the largest in the world, producing around 900 full-length features each year. Regional cinema, catering for different language groups (in particular the Tamil cinema of Chennai), though popular locally, has little national impact. Only Hindi film – which accounts for one-fifth of all the films made in India – has crossed regional boundaries to great effect, most particularly in the north. The home of the Hindi blockbuster, the "all-India film", is Mumbai, famously known as **Bollywood**.

To overcome differences of language and religion, the Bollywood movie follows rigid conventions and genres; as in myth, its characters have predetermined actions and destinies. Knowing a plot need not detract from the drama, and indeed, it is not uncommon for Indian audiences to watch films numerous times. Unlike the Hollywood formula, which tends to classify each film under one genre, the Hindi film follows what is known as a "masala format", and includes during its luxurious three hours a little bit of everything, especially romance, violence and comedy. Frequently the stories feature dispossessed male heroes fighting evil against all odds with a love interest thrown in. The sexual element is repressed, with numerous wet sari scenes and dance routines featuring the tensest pelvic thrusts. Other typical themes include male bonding and betrayal, family melodrama, separation and reunion and religious piety. Dream sequences are almost obligatory, too, along with a festival or celebration scene – typically Holi, when people shower each other with paint – a comic character passing through, and a depraved, alcoholic and mostly Western "cabaret", filled with strutting villains and lewd dancing.

Bollywood has moved closer to Hollywood in recent years with a rise in **budgets** of tens of millions of dollars, with foreign settings and an increase in on-screen sauciness. But, with pirate videos and a thirty-percent drop in audiences, a number of big-budget movies are failing to make money, and many now lose up to Rs100,000,000. Coupled with the recent mafia scandals involving financing (see p.743), Bollywood is in big trouble, and an overhaul of the industry is desperately needed.

Visitors to Mumbai should have ample opportunity to sample the delights of a movie. To make an educated choice, buy *Bombay* magazine, which contains extensive **listings** and reviews. Otherwise, look for the biggest, brightest hoarding, and join the queue. Seats in a comfortable air-conditioned cinema cost around Rs20, or less if you sit in the stalls (not advisable for women). Of the two hundred or so **cinemas**, only eight regularly screen **English-language** films. The most central and convenient are the Regal in Colaba, the Eros opposite Churchgate station, the Sterling, the New Excelsior and the New Empire, which are all a short walk west of CST station.

Nightclubs

The **nightclub** scene in Mumbai is the best in India and the late Nineties saw the rise of a funkier, groovier scene as the moneyed jet set began to hear the latest house, trance, fusion and funk that was hitting the decks in Goa and the West.

Most discos and clubs charge per couple on the door, and in theory have a "couples-only" policy. In practice, if you're in a mixed group or don't appear sleazy you won't have any problems. At the five-star hotels, entry can be restricted to hotel guests and members.

Copa Cabana, Marine Drive. Dark, smoky atmosphere, Latino music and lots of tequila. Free shoots for the ladies on Weds till 10pm and Thurs is 2 for 1 on Indian liquors.

Fashion Bistro, 16 Marzban Rd, next to Sterling Cinema. Mannequins display designer creations in one room, with a bar and tiny dance floor in another. Deafeningly loud Western chart-music with a

Seventies and Eighties night on Fri. Rs200–300 cover charge per couple.

Headquarters, 166 MG Rd, opposite Regal Cinema, Colaba. Great little student club with good DJs, hip decor and a storming Goa-trance night on Fri. It is, however, fairly pricey with a Rs200–400 cover charge – though couples get in free Tues, Thurs & Sun. Tues–Sun 8pm–1.30am.

The 1900s, *Taj Mahal*. Pounding disco, free to guests but otherwise for members only. If you can get in, you'll see the cream of Mumbai society at their air-kissing best.

Razzberry Rhinoceros, *Juhu Hotel*, Juhu Beach. Much UV lighting and a good-size dance floor

playing trance (Fri), drum'n'bass (alternate Wed) and the latest Western sounds (Sat & alternate Weds). Also has live rock bands on Thursdays as well as occasional blues, jazz or reggae bands on Sun. Cover charge Rs100–400 per couple and closes at 1.30am – though the coffee shop overlooking the beach stays open till 5 or 6am.

Three Flights Up, Apollo Bunder, Colaba. Used to have the longest bar in Asia and, despite moving to new (smaller) premises, is the biggest club in Mumbai. The music is Western disco, there's a no-smoking policy on the dance floor and fantastic a/c.

Shopping

Mumbai is a great place to shop, whether for last-minute souvenirs, or essentials for the long journeys ahead. Locally produced **textiles** and export-surplus clothing are among the best buys, as are **handicrafts** from far-flung corners of the country. With the exception of the swish arcades in the five-star hotels, prices compare surprisingly well with other Indian cities. In the larger shops, rates are fixed and **credit cards** are often accepted; elsewhere, particularly dealing with street-vendors, it pays to haggle. Uptown, the **central bazaars** – see p.767 – are better for spectating than serious shopping, although the **antiques** and Friday flea market in the Chor, or "thieves" bazaar, can sometimes yield the odd bargain. The **Zaveri** (goldsmiths') **bazaar** opposite Crawford Market is the place to head for new gold and silver jewellery. The city features a number of swish modern **shopping centres**, including India's largest, Crossroads, at 28 Pandit MM Rd near the Haj Ali mosque. In Colaba, there's also Sahakari Brandar which sells a range of good-value handicrafts and household goods. An attached supermarket stocks a cornucopia of dry and tinned goods.

Opening hours in the city centre are Monday to Saturday, 10am to 7pm. The Muslim bazaars, quiet on Friday, are otherwise open until around 9pm.

Antiques

The **Chor Bazaar** area, and Mutton Street in particular, is the centre of Mumbai's **antique trade**. For a full account, see p.768. Another good, if much more expensive, place to sift through the fakes for a real gem or two is **Phillip's** famous antique shop, on the corner of Madam Cama Road, opposite the Regal cinema in Colaba. This fascinating, old-fashioned store has changed little since it opened in 1860. Innumerable glass lamps and chandeliers hang from the ceiling, while antique display cases are stuffed with miniature brass, bronze and wood Hindu sculpture, silver jewellery, old prints and aquatints. Most of the stuff on sale dates from the twilight of the Raj – a result of the Indian government's ban on the export by foreigners of items more than a century old.

In the **Jehangir Art Gallery** basement, a branch of the antiques chain Natesan's Antiqarts offers a tempting selection of antique (and reproduction) sculpture, furniture, paintings and bronzes.

Clothes and textiles

Mumbai produces the bulk of India's **clothes**, mostly the lightweight, light-coloured "shirtings and suitings" favoured by droves of uniformly attired office-wallahs. For cheaper Western clothing, you can't beat the long row of stalls on the pavement of MG Road, opposite the Mumbai Gymkhana. "**Fashion Street**" specializes in reject and export-surplus goods ditched by big manufacturers, selling off T-shirts, jeans, leggings, summer dresses, and trendy sweatshirts. Better-quality cotton clothes (often stylish designer-label rip-offs) are available in shops along **Colaba Causeway**, such as Cotton World, down Mandlik Marg.

If you're looking for **traditional Indian clothes**, head for the Khadi Village Industries Emporium at 286 Dr DN Marg, near the Thomas Cook office. As Whiteaway & Laidlaw, this rambling Victorian department store used to kit all the newly arrived *burra-sahibs* out with pith helmets, khaki shorts and quinine tablets. These days, its old wooden counters, shirt and sock drawers stock dozens of different hand-spun cottons and silks, sold by the metre or made up as vests, *kurtas* or block-printed *salwar kamises*. Other items include the ubiquitous white Nehru caps, *dhotis*, Madras-check *lunghis* and fine brocaded silk saris.

Handicrafts

Regionally produced **handicrafts** are marketed in assorted state-run emporia at the World Trade Centre, down on Cuffe Parade, and along Sir PM Road, Fort. The quality is consistently high – as are the prices, if you miss out on the periodic holiday discounts. The same goes for the **Central Cottage Industries Emporium**, 34 Shivaji Marg, near the Gateway of India in Colaba, whose size and central location make it the single best all-round place to hunt for souvenirs. Downstairs you'll find inlaid furniture, wood- and metal-work, miniature paintings and jewellery, while upstairs specializes in toys, clothing and textiles – Gujarati appliqué bedspreads, hand-painted pillowcases and Rajasthani mirror-work, plus silk ties and Noel Coward dressing-gowns. **Mereweather Road**, directly behind the *Taj*, is awash with Kashmiri handicraft stores stocking overpriced papier-mâché pots and bowls, silver jewellery, woollen shawls and rugs. Avoid them if you find it hard to shrug off aggressive sales pitches.

Perfume is essentially a Muslim preserve in Mumbai. Down at the south end of Colaba Causeway, around Arthur Bunder Road, shops with mirrored walls and shelves are stacked with cut-glass carafes full of syrupy, fragrant essential oils. **Incense** is hawked in sticks, cones and slabs of sticky *dhoop* on the sidewalk nearby (check that the boxes haven't already been opened and their contents sold off piecemeal). For bulk buying, the hand-rolled, cottage-made bundles of incense sold in the Khadi Village Industries Emporium on Dr DN Marg (see above) are a better deal; it also has a handicraft department where, in addition to furniture, paintings and ornaments, you can pick up glass bangles, block-printed and calico bedspreads, and wooden votive statues produced in Maharashtran craft villages.

Books

Mumbai's excellent English-language **bookshops** and bookstalls are well stocked with everything to do with India, and a good selection of general classics, pulp fiction and travel writing. Indian editions of popular titles cost a fraction of what they do abroad and include lots of interesting works by lesser-known local authors. If you don't mind picking through dozens of trigonometry textbooks, back issues of National Geographic and salacious 1960s paperbacks, the **street stalls** between Flora Fountain and Churchgate station can also be good places to hunt for secondhand books.

Chetana, 34 Dubash Rd (Rampart Row). Exclusively religion and philosophy.

Crossword, Mahalakshmi Chambers, 22 Bhulabhai Desai Rd, Breach Candy ☏ 022/492 2458. Mumbai's largest and most reputed retailer, a bus ride (#132) from the downtown area.

Nalanda, ground floor, *Taj Mahal*. An exhaustive range of coffee-table tomes and paperback literature.

Pustak Bharati, Bharatiya Vidhya Bhavan, KM Munshi Marg. Excellent small bookshop specializing in Hindu philosophy and literature, plus details of Bhavan's cultural programmes.

Shankar Book-Stand, outside the *Café Mondegar*, Colaba Causeway. Piles of easy-reads, guidebooks, classic fiction, and most of the old favourites on India.

Strand, next door to the Canara Bank, off PM Road, Fort. The best bookshop in the city centre, with the full gamut of Penguins and Indian literature.

Music

The most famous of Mumbai's many good **music shops** are near the Moti cinema along SV Patel Road, in the central bazaar district. Haribhai Vishwanath, Ram Singh and RS Mayeka are all government-approved retailers of traditional Indian instruments, including sitars, sarods, tablas and flutes. For **cassettes and CDs** try Rhythm House, Subhash Chowk, next to the Jehangir Art Gallery. This is a veritable Aladdin's cave of classical, devotional and popular music from all over India, with a reasonable selection of Western rock, pop and jazz.

Listings

Banks and currency exchange The logical place to change money when you arrive in Mumbai is at the State Bank of India's 24hr counter in Sahar airport. Rates here are standard but you'll have to pay for an encashment certificate – essential if you intend to buy tourist-quota train tickets or an Indrail pass at the special counters in Churchgate or VT stations. All the major state banks downtown change foreign currency (Mon–Fri 10.30am–2.30pm, Sat 10.30am–12.30pm); some also handle credit cards and cash advances. Several 24hr ATMs handle international transactions, usually Visa, Delta and Mastercard – it's best to check with your bank which you can use beforehand. It's also worth noting that there's often a limit on how much you can take out: it can be as low as Rs4000. ATM machines can be found at: Air India Building, Nariman Point and 293 DN Rd, Fort (Citibank); and 52/60 MG Rd, near Hutama Chowk, Fort and Asha Mahal, Kemp's Corner Flyover, Breach Candy (HSBC). The fast and efficient American Express office (daily 9.30am–6pm; ☏ 022/204 8291), on Shivaji Marg, around the corner from the Regal cinema in Colaba, offers all the regular services (including poste restante) to travellers' cheque- and card-holders and is open to anyone wishing to change cash. Thomas Cook's big Dr DN Marg branch (Mon–Sat 9.30am–6pm; ☏ 022/204 8556), between the Khadi shop and Hutatma Chowk, can also arrange money transfers from overseas.

Airlines, domestic Alliance Air ☏ 022/611 4426; Air India ☏ 022/287 6565, ✉ www.airindia.com; Indian Airlines, Air India Building, Nariman Point (Mon–Sat 8.30am–7.30pm, Sun 10am–1pm & 1.45–5.30pm; ☏ 022/202 3031); counter at the airport ☏ 022/615 6850; Jet Airways, Amarchand Mansion, Madam Cama Road ☏ 022/285 5788; Sahara Airlines Unit 7, Ground Floor, Tulsiani Chambers, Nariman Point ☏ 022/283 5671.

Airlines, international Aeroflot, Ground Floor, Tulsiani Chambers, Free Press Journal Road, Nariman Point ☏ 022/287 1942; Air France, Maker Chambers VI, 1st Floor, Nariman Point ☏ 022/202 5021; Air India, Air India Building, Nariman Point ☏ 022/202 4142; Air Lanka, 12-D, Raheja Centre, Nariman Point ☏ 022/282 3288; Alitalia, Industrial Insurance Building, VN Road, Churchgate ☏ 022/204 5026; British Airways, 202-B Vulcan Insurance Building, VN Road, Churchgate ☏ 022/282 0888; Cathay Pacific, Bajaj Bhavan, 3rd Floor, 226, Nariman Point ☏ 022/202 9561; Delta, *Taj Mahal*, Colaba ☏ 022/288 5652; Emirates, 228 Mittal Chambers, Nariman Point ☏ 022/287 1645; Gulf Air, Maker Chamber V, Nariman Point ☏ 022/202 1626; KLM, Khaitan Bhavan, 198 J Tata Rd, Churchgate ☏ 022/283 3338; Kuwait Airways, 86 VN Rd, Churchgate ☏ 022/204 5331; Japan

Airlines, Raheja Centre, Nariman Point ☎ 022/287 4937; Lufthansa, 1st Floor, Express Towers, Nariman Point ☎ 022/202 7178; Pakistan International Airlines, Mittal Tower, B Wing, 4th Floor, Nariman Point ☎ 022/202 1373; Qantas Airways, 42 Sakhar Bhavan, Nariman Point ☎ 022/202 0343; Royal Nepal Airlines, 222, Maker Chamber V, Nariman Point ☎ 022/283 6197; SAS and Thai Airways, 15 World Trade Centre, Cuffe Parade, Colaba ☎ 022/215 5301; Saudia, Ground Floor, Express Towers, Nariman Point ☎ 022/202 0199; Scandinavian Airlines, Ground Floor, Podar House, 10 Marine Drive, Churchgate ☎ 022/202 7083; South African Airways, Podar House, 10 Marine Drive, Churchgate ☎ 022/282 3454; Swissair, Maker Chamber VI, 220 Nariman Point ☎ 022/287 2210; Syrian Arab Airlines, 7 Brabourne Stadium, VN Road, Churchgate ☎ 022/282 6043; TWA and Australian Airlines, Amarchand Mansion, M Carve Road ☎ 022/282 3080.

Ambulance ☎ 022/266 2913 or ☎ 101 for general emergencies or ☎ 105 for heart cases.

Airport enquiries Sahar International Airport ☎ 022/836 6700. Santa Cruz Domestic Airport: Terminal 1A for Indian Airlines ☎ 022/615 6633; 1B for all other airlines ☎ 022/615 6600.

Consulates and high commissions Although the many consulates and High Commissions in Mumbai can be useful for replacing lost travel documents or obtaining visas, most of India's neighbouring states, including Bangladesh, Bhutan, Burma, Nepal and Pakistan, only have embassies in New Delhi and/or Calcutta (see relevant city account). All of the following are open Monday to Friday: Australia, 16th Floor, Maker Tower "E", Cuffe Parade (9am–5pm; ☎022/218 1071); Canada, 41/42 Maker Chambers VI, Nariman Point (9am–5.30pm; ☎022/287 6027); China, 1st floor, 11 M.L. Dahanukar Marg (10am–4.30pm; ☎022/282 2662); Denmark, L & T House, Narottam Moraji Marg, Ballard Estate (10am–12.45pm; ☎022/261 4462); Germany, 10th Floor, Hoechst House, Nariman Point (9–11am; ☎022/283 2422); Republic of Ireland, Royal Bombay Yacht Club Chambers, Apollo Bunder (10am–noon; ☎022/202 4607); Netherlands, "International" Building, New Marine Lines, Cross Road, 1 Churchgate (9am–5pm; ☎022/201 6750); Norway, Navroji Mansion, 31 Nathelal Parekh Marg (10am–1pm; ☎022/284 2042); Philippines, 61 Sakhar Bhavan, Nariman Point (10am–1pm; ☎022/202 4792); Singapore, 9th Floor, 94 Sakhar Bhavan, Nariman Point (9am–noon; ☎022/204 3205); South Africa, Gandhi Mansion, 20 Altamount Rd (9am–noon; ☎022/3893725); Spain, Ador House, 3rd floor, 6 K Dubash Marg, Kala Ghoda (10.30am–1pm; ☎022/287 4797); Sri Lanka, Sri

Lanka House, 34 Homi Modi St, Fort (9.30am–11.30am; ☎022/204 5861); Sweden, 85 Sayani Rd, Subash Gupta Bhawan, Prabhadevi (9.30am–12.30pm; ☎022/288 4563); Switzerland, Maker Chamber IV, 10th floor, Nariman Point (8am–11am; ☎022/204 3003); Thailand, Malabar View, 4th floor, Dr Purandure Marg, Chowpatty Sea Face (9am–noon; ☎022/363 1404); United Kingdom, 2nd Floor, Maker Chamber IV, Nariman Point (8am–11.30am; ☎022/283 0517); USA, Lincoln House, 78 Bhulabhai Desai Rd (7am–11am; ☎022/363 3611).

Hindi lessons Kalina University, in north Mumbai, and a number of private academies run short courses. Ask at the tourist office in Churchgate (☎ 022/203 3144) for more details.

Hospitals The best hospital in the centre is the private Mumbai Hospital (☎ 022/206 7676), New Marine Lines, just north of the government tourist office on M Karve Road. Breach Candy Hospital (☎ 022/363 3651) on Bhulabhai Desai Road, near the swimming pool, is also recommended by foreign embassies.

Internet access A couple of cramped 24hr places (Rs40 per hour) can be found in Colaba, just round the corner from *Leopold's* on Nawroji F Marg, though it's worth paying the Rs5 extra at Access Infotech, located down a small alley further down Colaba Causeway on the left, which is faster and more comfortable. Near VT, several places can be found on Sahid Bhagat Singh Marg where Nikhil Communication Centre at no. 268 costs Rs40 per hour and is open till 1am. On-line is another good name and they have two cafés: 82 Veer Nariman Rd, Churchgate and 39 Sea Face, Chowpatty (both Rs50/hr).

Left luggage If your hotel won't let you store bags with them, try the cloakrooms at Sahar and Santa Cruz airports (see pp.745-746), or the one in VT station (Rs7–10 a day). Anything left here, even rucksacks, must be securely fastened with a padlock and can be left for a maximum of one month.

Libraries Asiatic Society, SBS Marg, Horniman Circle, Ballard Estate (Mon–Sat 10.30am–7pm); British Council (for British newspapers), A Wing, 1st Floor, Mittal Tower, Nariman Point (Tues–Sat 10am–6pm); Alliance Française de Mombai, Theosophy Hall, 40 New Marine Lines; Max Mueller Bhavan, Prince of Wales Annexe, off MG Road (Mon–Fri 9.30am–6pm). The KR Cama Oriental Institute, 136 Mumbai Samachar Marg (Mon–Fri 10am–5pm, Sat 10am–1pm), specializing in Zoroastrian and Iranian studies has a public collection of 22,000 volumes in European and Asian languages. Mumbai Natural History Society, Hornbill House (Mon–Fri 10am–5pm, Sat

10am–1pm, closed 1st & 3rd Sat of the month), has an international reputation for the study of wildlife in India. Visitors may become temporary members which allows them access to the library, natural history collection, occasional talks and the opportunity to join organized walks and field trips.

Pharmacies Real Chemist, 50/51 Kaka Arcade (☎022/200 2497) and Royal Chemists, M Karve Road (☎022/534 0531), both close to Mumbai Hospital, are open 24hr. Kemps in the *Taj Mahal* also opens late.

Photographic studios and equipment The Javeri Colour Lab, opposite the Regal cinema in Colaba, stocks colour-print and slide film, as do most of the big hotels. A small boutique behind the florists in the Shakhari Bunder covered market does instant Polaroid passport photographs.

Police The main police station in Colaba (☎022/285 6817) is on the west side of Colaba Causeway, near the crossroads with Ormiston Road.

Postal services The GPO (Mon–Sat 9am–8pm, Sun 9am–4pm) is around the corner from VT Station, off Nagar Chowk. Its poste restante counter (Mon–Sat 9am–6pm, Sun 9am–3pm) is among the most reliable in India, although they trash the letters after four weeks. The much less efficient parcel office (10am–4.30pm) is behind the main building on the first floor. Packing-wallahs hang around on the pavement outside. DHL (☎022/850 5050) have eleven offices in Mumbai, the most convenient being the 24hr one under the *Sea Green Hotel* at the bottom of Marine Drive.

State tourist offices: Goa, Mumbai Central Railway Station ☎022/308 6288; Gujarat, Dhanraj Mahal, Chhatrapati Shivaji Maharaj Marg, Apollo Bunder ☎022/202 4925; Himachal Pradesh, 36 World Trade Centre, Cuffe Parade ☎022/218 1123; Jammu & Kashmir, 25 World Trade Centre ☎022/218 9040; Kerala Tourism Information Counter, "Kairali", Nirmal Building, Nariman Point ☎022/202 6817; Madhya Pradesh, 74 World Trade Centre ☎022/218 7603; Rajasthan, 230 Dr DN Marg, Fort ☎022/204 4162; Tamil Nadu, G2(A), Royal Grace, Lokmanya Tilak Colony Marg No. 2, Dadar (East) ☎022/411 0118; and Uttar Pradesh, 38 World Trade Centre ☎022/218 5458.

Swimming pools The snooty sports club at Breach Candy, north of Malabar Hill, is a popular place to beat the heat. A day's membership costs around Rs200.

Telephones and faxes STD booths abound in Mumbai. For rock-bottom phone and fax rates however, head for Videsh Sanchar Bhavan (open 24hr), the swanky government telecom building on MG Marg, where you can make reverse charge calls to destinations such as the UK, US and Australia. Receiving incoming calls costs a nominal Rs10. Numbers in the city change constantly, so if you can't get through after several attempts, try directory enquiries on ☎197.

Travel agents The following travel agents are recommended for booking domestic and international flights, and long-distance private buses where specified: Ambassador Travels, 14, Embassy Centre, Nariman Point ☎022/283 1046; Cox and Kings India Ltd, 271/272, Dr DN Marg ☎022/204 3065, ⊛ www.coxkings.com; Magnum International Tours & Travels, Frainy Villa, 10 Henry Rd, Colaba ☎022/285 2343, ✉ magnum.intnal@axcess.net.in; Peerless Hotels & Travels Ltd, Ground Floor, Churchgate Chambers, 5 New Marine Lines ☎022/265 1500; Sita World Travels Pvt Ltd, 8 Atlanta Building, Nariman Point ☎022/284 0666, ✉ boml.sita@sma.springtrpg.ems.vsnl.in; Thomas Cook (see p.781)

Moving on from Mumbai

Most visitors feel like getting out of Mumbai as soon as they can. Fortunately, Mumbai is equipped with "super-fast" services to arrange or confirm **onward travel**. All the major international and domestic **airlines** have offices in the city, the railway networks operate special tourist counters in the main reservation halls, and dozens of **travel agents** and road transport companies are eager to help you on your way by **bus**.

Travel within India

Mumbai is the nexus of several major internal flight routes, train networks and highways, and is the main transport hub for traffic heading towards south India. The most travelled trails lead north up the Gujarati coast to **Rajasthan** and

Delhi; northwest into the **Deccan** via Aurangabad and the caves at Ellora and Ajanta; and south, through Pune and the hills of the Western Ghats towards **Goa** and the Malabar coast. Public transport is cheap and frequent, but book in advance and be prepared for delays.

By plane

Indian Airlines and other **domestic carriers** fly out of Santa Cruz to destinations all over India. Availability on popular routes (especially Mumbai–Goa–Mumbai) should never be taken for granted. Check with the airlines as soon as you arrive; **tickets** can be bought directly from their offices (see p.781), or through any reputable travel agent, although you'll have to pay the mandatory Rs600 **airport tax** when you get to Santa Cruz.

In theory, it is also possible to book domestic air tickets abroad when you buy your original long-haul flight. However, as individual airlines tend to have separate agreements with domestic Indian carriers, you may not be offered the same choice (or rates) as you will through agents in Mumbai. Note, too, that Indian Airlines is the only company offering 25 percent discounts (on all flights) to customers under the age of thirty.

By train

Two main networks converge on Mumbai: the **Western Railway** runs to north and west India; the **Central Railway** connects Mumbai to central, eastern and southern regions.

Nearly all services to Gujarat, Rajasthan, Delhi and the far north leave from **Mumbai Central** station, in the mid-town area. Second-class tickets can be booked here through the normal channels, but the quickest place for foreign nationals to make reservations is at the efficient tourist counter (no. 28) on the first floor of the Western Railway's booking hall, next door to the Government of India tourist office in Churchgate (Mon–Fri 9.30am–4.30pm, Sat 9.30am–2.30pm; ☏022/203 8016, extension 4577 for foreigners). This counter also has access to special **"tourist quotas"**, which are released the day before departure if the train leaves during the day, or the morning of the departure if the train leaves after 5pm. If the quota is "closed" or already used up, and you can't access the **"VIP quota"** (always worth a try), you will have to join the regular queue.

Mumbai's other "Tourist Ticketing Facility" is in the snazzy air-conditioned Central Railway booking office to the rear of VT (Mon–Sat 9am–1pm & 1.30–4pm; counter no. 22 or 21 on Sun), the departure point for most trains heading east and south. Indrail passes can also be bought here, and there's an MTDC tourist information kiosk in the main concourse if you need help filling in your reservation slips.

Just to complicate matters, some Central Railway trains to **south India**, including the fast Dadar–Madras Chennai Express #6063 to Madras, do not depart from VT at all, but from **Dadar station**, way north of Mumbai Central. Seats and berths for these trains are reserved at VT. Finally, if you're booking tickets to Calcutta, make sure your train doesn't leave from **Kurla station**, which is even more inconvenient, up near the airports. Getting to either of these stations on public transport can be a major struggle, though many long-distance trains from VT or Churchgate stop there and aren't as crowded.

By bus

The main departure point for long-distance **buses** leaving Mumbai is the frenetic **Central bus stand** on JB Behram Marg, opposite Mumbai Central

The services listed below are the most direct and/or the fastest. This list is by no means exhaustive and there are numerous slower trains that are often more convenient for smaller destinations.

Destination	Name	No.	From	Frequency	Departs	Total time
Agra	Punjab Mail	#2137/38	CST	Daily	7.10pm	21hr 30min
Aurangabad	Devgiri Express	#1003	CST	Daily	6.10pm	7hr 25min
Bangalore	Udyan Express	#6529	CST	Daily	7.55am	24hr 40min
Bhopal	Flrozpur Punjab Mail	#2137	CST	Daily	7.10pm	14hr 10min
Calcutta	Gitanjali Express	#2859	CST	Daily	6am	32hr 55min
	Mumbai–Howrah Express	#8001	CST	Daily	8.15pm	36hr
Chennai	Mumbai–Chennai Express	#6011	CST	Daily	2pm	26hr 45min
Cochin*	Kanniyakumari Express	#1081	CST	Daily	3.35pm	38hr 10min
Goa	Mumbai–Madgaon Express	#KR011	CST	Daily	10.30pm	12hr
Hyderabad	Hussainsagar Express	#7001	CST	Daily	9.55pm	15hr 15min
Jaipur	Bandra–Jaipur Express	#9707	Bandra	Daily	9.25pm	23hr
Jodhpur	Bandra–Bikaneer Express	#4708	Bandra	Daily	3.10pm	19hr 25min
New Delhi	Rajhani Express	#2951	MC	Daily	4.55pm	17hr
	Paschim Express	#2925	MC	Daily	11.35am	23hr 20min
	Golden Temple Mail	#2903	MC	Daily	9.30pm	23hr 30min
Pune	Shatabdi Express	#2027	CST	Daily	6.40pm	3hr 25min
Trivandrum	Kanniyakumari Express	#1081	CST	Daily	3.35pm	44hr 45min
Udaipur	Saurashtra Express**	#9215	MC	Daily	7.45am	24hr 40min
Varanasi	Mahanagiri Express	#1093	CST	Daily	11.55pm	28hr

*details also applicable for Ernakulam Town
**change at Ahmedabad to the Delhi Sarai Rohila Express #9944

railway station. States with bus company counters here (daily 8am–8pm; ☎022/307 6622), include Maharashtra, Karnataka, Madhya Pradesh, Goa and Gujarat. Few of their services compare favourably with train travel on the same routes. Reliable timetable information can be difficult to obtain, reservations are not available on standard buses, and most long-haul journeys are gruelling overnighters. Among the exceptions are the **deluxe buses** run by MSRTC to Pune, Nasik and Kolhapur; the small extra cost buys you more leg-room, fewer stops and the option of advance booking. The only problem is, most leave from the **ASIAD** bus stand in Dadar, thirty minutes or so by road or rail north of Mumbai Central.

Other possibilities for road travel include the "super-fast" **luxury coaches** touted around Colaba. Most are run by private companies, guaranteeing breakneck speeds and possible long waits for the bus to fill up. ITDC also operate similarly priced services to the same destinations, which you can book direct from their main offices downtown or through the more conveniently situated Government of India tourist office, 123 M Karve Rd, Churchgate. Two night buses leave Nariman Point every evening for the twelve-hour trip to **Aurangabad**, and there are morning departures to **Nasik** and **Mahabaleshwar**, which take six and seven hours respectively.

Since the inauguration of the controversial Konkan Railway, the best-value way to travel the 500km from Mumbai to Goa has been by train. However, tickets for the twelve-hour ride down the coast tend be in short supply, and virtually impossible to obtain at short notice, so it's best to try and book with an Indian Railways agent back home before setting off. Otherwise, you'll probably find yourself having to shell out for a flight. Considering how hellish the bus ride can be, and how hard getting hold of train tickets is, it's well worth paying the extra to travel by plane, ideally before you leave home, which could save you days waiting around in Mumbai.

By plane

At present, four airlines – Air India, Indian Airlines, Jet Airways and Sahara – operate daily services to Goa. Demand for seats is fierce (particularly around Christmas/New Year) and you may well have to wait several days. If you didn't pre-book when you purchased your international ticket, check availability with the airlines as soon as you arrive; tickets can be bought directly from their offices (see Listings), or through any reputable travel agent in Mumbai, although bear in mind that an agent may charge you the dollar fare at a poorer rate of exchange than that offered by the airline company.

All Goa flights leave from Chatrapathi Shivaji Domestic Airport, 30km north of the city centre. One-way fares for the forty-minute flight start at $53 with Indian Airlines, and rise to $83 with Sahara, or $93 ($72 for under-30s) with swisher Jet. In addition, Air India operates an Airbus service to Mumbai on Mondays and Thursdays for $85. Few people seem to know about this flight, so you can nearly always get a seat on it.

By train

The new Konkan Railway line runs daily express trains from Mumbai to Goa. However, these services are not always available as they are invariably booked for at least a month in advance. If you don't have a reservation, it may be possible to get a place on your planned day of travel by joining the waiting list. But by the far the best option, if

Leaving India

In spite of its prominence on trans-Asian flight routes, Mumbai is no longer the bargain basement for **international air tickets** it used to be. Discounted fares are very hard to come by – a legacy of Rajiv Gandhi's economic reforms of the 1980s. If you do need to book a ticket, stick to one of the tried and tested agents listed on p.783.

All the major airlines operating out of Mumbai have offices downtown where you can buy scheduled tickets or confirm your flight; see p.781 for a list of addresses. The majority are grouped around Veer Nariman Road, opposite the *Ambassador Hotel*, or else on Nariman Point, a short taxi ride west of Colaba.

Travel details

Trains

Direct services to: Agra (4 daily; 23hr 15min–27hr); Ahmedabad (4 daily; 7hr 10min–12hr); Aurangabad (2 daily; 7hr 20min); Bangalore (3 daily; 24hr 30min); Bhopal (4 daily; 14hr); Calcutta (4 daily; 33–40hr); Chennai (3 daily; 24–29hr); Coimbatore (1 daily; 10hr); Delhi (11 daily; 17–33hr); Hyderabad (2 daily; 15–17hr); Indore (1 daily; 14hr 35min); Jaipur (2 daily; 18–23hr); Jodhpur (1 daily; 22hr; change at Ahmedabad); Kolhapur (3 daily; 11–12hr); Nagpur (4 daily; 14–15hr); Nasik (15 daily; 4hr); Pune (25 daily; 3hr 15min–5hr); Thiruvananthapuram (2 daily; 42hr); Udaipur (1 daily; 25hr; change at Ahmedabad); Ujjain (1 daily; 12hr 25 min); Varanasi (2 daily; 29–36hr).

you know your travel dates in advance, is to book a ticket with an Indian Railways agent in your home country several months ahead; for more, see Basics on p.46.

Don't be tempted to travel "unreserved" class on any Konkan service as the journey as far as Ratnagiri (roughly midway) is overwhelmingly crushed. The most convenient of the Konkan services is the overnight Mumbai–Madgaon Express #KR0111 (10.40pm; 12hr) which departs from VT (CST). The other, only slightly faster train is the Madavi Express #KR0103, leaving CST at 5.15am.

Fares in second class cost around Rs250 (£4/$6), or Rs750 (£13/$19) for a three-tier berth in first class.

By bus

The Mumbai–Goa bus journey ranks among the very worst in India. Don't believe travel agents who assure you it takes thirteen hours. Depending on the type of bus you get, appalling road surfaces along the sinuous coastal route make eighteen to twenty hours a more realistic estimate.

Bus tickets start at around Rs290 for a push-back seat on a beaten-up Kadamba (Goan government) or MSRTC coach. Tickets for these services are in great demand in season, so book in advance at Mumbai Central or Kadamba's kiosks on the north side of Azad Maidan, near St Xavier's College (just up from CST station; ☏022/262 1043). More and more private overnight buses (around 25 daily) also run to Goa, costing around Rs375–400 for a noisy front-engined Tata bus, Rs400–450 for an a/c bus with pneumatic suspension and on-board toilet, and Rs600–675 for a service with coffin-like sleeper compartments which quickly become unbearably stuffy. Tickets should be booked at least a day in advance through a reputable travel agent (see p.783), though it's sometimes worth turning up at the car park opposite the Metro cinema, Azad Maidan, where most buses leave from, on the off-chance of a last-minute cancellation. Make sure, in any case, that you are given both your seat and the bus registration number, and that you confirm the exact time and place of departure with the travel agent, as these frequently vary between companies.

Buses

Only state bus services are listed here; for details of private buses, see p.784.

Mumbai Central to: Aurangabad (2 daily; 10hr); Bangalore (3 daily; 24hr); Bijapur (3 daily; 12hr); Goa (2 daily; 18–19hr); Indore (2 daily; 16hr); Ujjain (1 daily; 17hr).

ASIAD Dadar to: Kolhapur (4 daily; 10hr); Nasik (17 daily; 5hr); Pune (half-hourly; 4hr).

Flights

For a list of airline addresses and travel agents, see pp.781–783. In the listings below, AA represents Alliance Air, IA is Indian Airlines, JA Jet Airways, and SA Sahara Airlines.

Santa Cruz airport to: Ahmedabad (AA, IA, JA 6–7 daily; 1hr); Aurangabad (IA, JA 2 daily; 1hr 30min); Bangalore (AA, IA, JA 11 daily; 1hr 30min); Bhopal (SA, AL 2 daily; 1hr 25min); Calcutta (AA, IA, JA, SA 5–6 daily; 2hr 25min); Calicut (AA, IA, JA 2–5 daily; 1hr); Chennai (AI, JA 8–9 daily; 1hr 45min); Cochin (AA, IA, JA, 4 daily; 1hr 50min); Coimbatore (IA, JA 2 daily; 1hr 50min); Delhi (AA, AL, IA, JA, SA, 22–26 daily; 1hr 45min–2hr); Goa (AA, IA, JA, SA 3–4 daily; 1hr 55min); Hyderabad (AA, AL, IA, JA 6–8 daily; 1hr 15min); Indore (AL, JA, SA 3–4 daily; 1hr 10min); Jaipur (AL, JA, SA 7–8 daily; 1hr 35min); Jodhpur (AL 4 weekly; 2hr 20min); Madurai (IA, 1 daily; 1hr 55min); Mangalore (AL, JA 4 daily; 1hr 15min); Nagpur (AL, IA 2 daily; 1hr 55min); Pune (JA 2–3 daily; 35min); Thiruvananthapuram (AA, IA, JA 3–5 daily; 2hr); Udaipur (AA, IA, JA 2–3 daily; 1hr 45min); Varanasi (IA, SA 1–2 daily; 3hr 5min)

CHAPTER 11

Highlights

* **Ellora caves**
  Breathtaking Hindu,
  Buddhist and Jain caves
  carved from solid vol-
  canic rock. See p.806

* **Ajanta caves** Chiselled
  from a horseshoe-
  shaped ravine and
  adorned with extraordi-
  nary Buddhist and Hindu
  murals. See p.815

* **Meteorite crater near
  Lonar** A vast crater
  cradling lonely temples
  hidden in the jungle: off
  the beaten track, but
  well worth the trek.
  See p.821

* **Ambala Lake** An atmospheric holy lake near
  Ramtek, with few visitors
  and minimal exploitation.
  See p.830

* **Gandhi Ashram,
  Sevagram** Learn about
  the great man's life and
  beliefs at the ashram he
  lived in. See p.831

* **Miniature train to the
  hill station of Matheran**
  Fantastic views across
  the Western Ghats.
  See p.833

* **Konkan Coast** The scenic route from Mumbai
  to Goa, with several
  relaxing beach resorts
  along the way.
  See p.835

* **Ganapatipuli** A little-
  visited golden sandy
  beach, with a lovely
  Ganapati temple.
  See p.836

Maharashtra

Vast and rugged, the modern state of **MAHARASHTRA**, the third largest in India, was created in 1960, from the Marathi-speaking regions of what was previously Bombay State. As soon as you leave its seething port capital, **Mumbai** (formerly Bombay), developed by Europeans, and now the epitome of modern, cosmopolitan, polyglot India, you enter a different world with a different history.

Undoubtedly, Maharashtra's greatest treasures are its extraordinary **cave temples** and **monasteries**. The finest of all are found near **Aurangabad**, renamed after the Moghul emperor Aurangzeb and still home to a sizeable Muslim population (as well as the poor man's Taj Mahal, the **Bibi-Ka-Maqbara**). The busy commercial city is the obvious base for visits to the caves at **Ajanta**, with their fabulous and still-vibrant murals, and the monolithic temples of **Ellora**, where the Hindu **Kailash temple** may look like a structural building but was carved in its entirety from the rock. From the second century BC, this region was an important centre of Buddhism; artificial caves were excavated to shelter monks, and the finest artists sculpted magnificent cathedral-like halls for congregational worship.

Away from the cities, the most characteristic feature of the landscape is a plenitude of **forts** – as the western borderland between north and south India, Maharashtra's trade routes were always important, but could also bring trouble. **Inland**, parallel to the sea, and never further than 100km from it, the mighty Western Ghats rise abruptly. The areas of level ground that crowned them, endowed with fresh water, were easily converted into forts where small forces could withstand protracted sieges by large armies. Less aggressive modern visitors can scale such windswept fortified heights at Sinhagad, Pratapgarh, and **Daulatabad** – which briefly, bizarrely and disastrously replaced Delhi as capital in the fourteenth century.

During the last century, the mountains found another use. When the summer proved too much for the British in Bombay, they sought refuge in nearby **hill stations**, the most popular of which, **Mahabaleshwar**, now caters for droves of Indian holiday-makers. **Matheran**, 170km southeast of Mumbai and 800m higher, has a special attraction: quite apart from its cool, wet climate, it offers superb views and wooded paths. It is also closed to all motorized road traffic. Instead, visitors board a rickety miniature train that twists up the hill on a sinuous track. Beyond the *ghats*, the modern city of **Pune**, site of the internationally famous **Osho ashram** founded by the New-Age guru, Bagwan Rajneesh, presides over a semi-arid tableland of flat-topped hills and dusty wheat fields. Maharashtra extends 900km further east across the Deccan plateau to the geographical centre of the subcontinent, an area largely populated by several different tribal groups and where Mahatma Gandhi set up his headquarters at **Sevagram** during the Independence struggle.

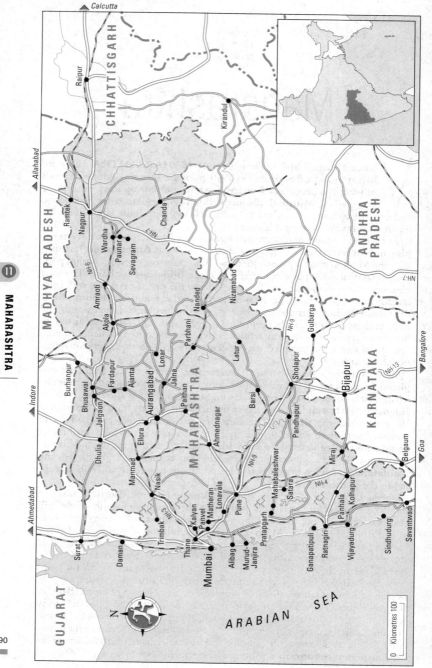

To the west, Maharashtra occupies 500km of the **Konkan coast** on the Arabian Sea, from Gujarat to Goa. The palm-fringed coast winds back and forth with countless inlets, ridges and valleys, peppered with forts. In the absence of its former seaborne traffic, this region of picturesque ports and deserted beaches is in decline as the younger generations seek to make more money in Mumbai or Goa. However, now that the Konkan railway runs down the coastline, it may well open up more tourism in the area. Close to Mumbai, sleepy, old-fashioned **Murud-Janjira** has splendid beaches and an extraordinary island fort. More determined travellers with time to zigzag their way around will find more, all the way to Goa: places such as Jaigarh, Ganapatipuli, Vijayadurg, Malvan and Sindhudurg, each with its own history and a battle-scarred fort to prove it.

For all the efforts of the Moghuls, Islam has made little impact on Maharashtra; eighty percent of the population is Hindu. Nasik, 187km northeast of Mumbai, balances modern industry alongside ancient associations with the Ramayana; one of the four sites of the Kumbh Mela, when up to four million devotees battle to bathe simultaneously in the holy River Godavari, even during less auspicious times it is a magnet for pilgrims. A short distance west, one of India's most sacred Shiva shrines lies close to the source of the Godavari, reached by a short trek from Trimbak. Finally, in the far south, the little-visited town of Kolhapur, almost at the Karnataka border, has retained plenty of old-fashioned character and makes a good place to break the long journey to Goa.

Some history

Although some Paleolithic remains have been discovered, Maharashtra enters recorded history in the second century BC, with the construction of its first Buddhist caves. These lay, and still lie, in peaceful places of great natural beauty, but could never have been created without the wealth generated by the nearby caravan trade routes between north and south India.

The region's first Hindu rulers – based in Badami, southern Maharashtra – appeared during the sixth century, but the eighth-century Rashtrakutas achieved a greater authority. Buddhism was almost entirely supplanted throughout the entire country by the twelfth century, in what has been characterized as a peaceful people's revolution attributable largely to the popular songs and teachings of poet-saints. The tradition they established continued to flourish throughout the thirteenth and fourteenth centuries, even when forced underground by Islam, reaching its zenith in the simple faith of the Ramdas, the "Servant of Rama" (1608–81).

Ramdas, ascetic and political activist, provided the philosophical underpinning behind the campaigns of Maharashtra's greatest warrior, **Shivaji** (1627–80). The fiercely independent Maratha chieftain united local forces to place insurmountable obstacles in the way of any prospective invader; so effective were their guerrilla tactics that he could even take on the mighty Moghuls. Shivaji progressively fought his way northwards, at a time when the Moghuls, who had got as far as capturing Daulatabad in 1633, were embroiled in protracted family feuds. A year after he succeeded in sacking the great port of Surat (Gujarat), in 1664, he was defeated in battle and imprisoned by Aurangzeb in Agra. He is said to have escaped by hiding in a package which the prison guards imagined was a gift intended for local Brahmins; once outside, Shivaji simply walked away disguised as a religious mendicant. By the time he died, in 1680, he had managed to unite the Marathas into a stable and secure state, funded by the plunder gleaned through guerrilla raids as far afield as Andhra Pradesh.

Back at the Moghul court the following year, Aurangzeb's son Akbar rebelled briefly against his father, then fled to Maharashtra, where he sought protection from Shivaji's son Shambhuji, before going into exile in Iran. That was the trigger for Aurangzeb to move his operations south; Bijapur (1686) and Golconda (1687) fell, and Shambhuji was captured and summarily executed in 1689. Aurangzeb must have thought that the way was now clear, but the Marathas proved impossible to subdue; he was to spend 25 years in the region, unable to leave, fighting a long series of inconclusive battles until his death at the age of 89. The Marathas had meanwhile become a confederacy whose dominion extended as far east as Orissa. By the end of the eighteenth century, however, their power had weakened and the British were able to take full control.

Maharashtra claims a crucial role in the development of a nationalist consciousness. An organization known as the Indian National Union, originally convened in Pune, held a conference in Bombay in 1885, which was thereafter known as the **Indian National Congress**. This loose aggregate of key figures from local politics around the country was to change the face of Indian politics. At first, its aim was limited to establishing a national platform to raise the status of Indians, and it remained loyal to the British. In the long term, of course, it was instrumental in the achievement of Independence 62 years later: many of Congress's factional leaders over the years were from Maharashtra.

With Independence, the Bombay Presidency, to which most of Maharashtra belonged, became known as Bombay State. Maharashtra as such was created in 1960. Its manufacturing industries, centred on Mumbai (formerly Bombay) and to a lesser extent cities such as Nagpur, Nasik, Aurangabad, Sholapur and Kolhapur, now account for a quarter of the nation's output. Textiles have long been important, but this is now also one of the premier high-tech industry regions, especially along the Mumbai-Pune corridor. However, the majority of Maharashtra's population of over 80 million are engaged in **agriculture**; main crops include sugar cane, cotton, peanuts, sunflowers, tobacco, pulses, fruit and vegetables. The western edge of the Deccan plateau has uncertain rainfall, and cultivation is concentrated close to rivers, while the southwestern monsoon sometimes halts in the mountains, leaving the rocky land to the east unwatered. Here, farmers rely on hardy staples such as millet and maize.

Northern Maharashtra

Beyond the seemingly endless concrete housing projects, petrochemical works and mosquito-infested swamplands of Greater Mumbai, a wall of bare bluish-brown hills dominates the horizon. The **Western Ghats** form a series of huge steps that march from the narrow, humid coastal strip to the edge of the **Deccan** plateau in a vast, dry tableland punctuated with ridges of weathered plateaux and plains dotted with scruffy villages and market towns. **Northern Maharashtra's** main transport arteries, the NH-3 and Central Railway line, wind in tandem through this stark landscape, following an ancient trade route that once linked the western ports with the prosperous cities further north. Over the centuries, a number of pilgrimage sites sprang up to take advantage of the lucrative through-traffic, and these form the principal points of interest in the region today.

The holy city of **Nasik** is a handy place to break journeys to or from Mumbai, four hours away by road. Amid impressive scenery, the town of **Trimbak**, 10km west at the start of a steep half-day hike to the source of the sacred River Godavari, makes a more relaxing overnight stop. Most foreign visitors, however, head straight for the regional capital, **Aurangabad**, the jumping-off point for the rock-cut **caves** at **Ellora** and **Ajanta** and the meteorite crater at **Lonar**. Among **Muslim monuments** to seek out here are Aurangabad's answer to the Taj Mahal, the **Bibi-Ka-Maqbara**, the dramatic hilltop fort at **Daulatabad**, and the tiny tomb town of **Rauza**, 5km from Ellora, where the emperor Aurangzeb is buried.

From Aurangabad, a well-beaten track cuts through the middle of Madhya Pradesh, via **Jalgaon**, towards Varanasi and Nepal. Alternatively, you could head across central India to **Wardha** and **Nagpur**, in the far northeastern corner of the state, where a couple of **Gandhi ashrams**, and the picturesque white-washed Hindu temple complex at **Ramtek** make pleasant pauses on long cross-country hauls.

Aurangabad and beyond

It's easy to see why many travellers regard **AURANGABAD** as little more than a convenient, though largely uninteresting, place in which to kill time on the way to **Ellora** and **Ajanta**. First impressions seem to confirm its reputation as an industrial metropolis: wide streets, fast traffic, ugly building sites, and gaping patches of urban wasteland merge into a featureless ferroconcrete sprawl. Yet, given a little effort, northern Maharashtra's largest city can compensate for its architectural shortcomings. Scattered around its ragged fringes, the dilapidated remains of fortifications, gateways, domes and minarets – including those of the most ambitious Moghul tomb garden in western India, the **Bibi-Ka-Maqbara** – bear witness to an illustrious imperial past; the small but fascinating crop of **rock-cut Buddhist caves**, huddled along the flanks of the flat-topped, sandy yellow hills to the north, are remnants of even more ancient occupation.

The city, originally called **Khadke**, or "Big Rock", was founded in the early sixteenth century by **Malik Amber**, an ex-Abyssinian slave and prime minister of the independent Muslim kingdom of the Nizam Shahis, based at Ahmadnagar, 112km southwest. It was a perfect spot for a provincial capital: on the banks of the **River Kham**, in a broad valley separating the then-forested Sahyadri Range to the north from the Satharas to the south, and at a crossroads of the region's key trade routes. Many of the **mosques** and palaces erected by Malik Amber still endure, albeit in ruins.

▲ Bibi-Ka-Maqbara & Aurangabad Caves ▲❶ Ajanta & Jalgaon

AURANGABAD

Shivaji Maidan

KILA ARAK

Delhi Gate

DELHI RD

Makai Gate

HARSOOL RD

Jama Masjid

Town Hall

GPO

Purwar Museum

City Chowk City "Place"

BEGUMPURA RD

PANCHAKKI RD

Dargah & Panchakki

Police Station

Juna Bazaar Chowk

GHATI RD

BAZAAR

Shah Ganj Masjid

GHATI RD

Himroo Factory

Bicycle Rental

Weekly Market Ground

Bus Stand

Bicycle Rental

Gulmandi Square

Zaffar Gate

DR AMBEDKAR RD

❸

Paithan Gate

❷

AURANGPURA

❹

❽

Trade Wings

Indian Airlines Office

❺

State Bank

❾ ❿

DR RAJENDRA PRASAD MARG

Osman Pura

Kranti Chowk

TILAK MARG

❶❷ ❶❸ ❶❹

STATION RD (WEST)

PADAMPURA

STATION RD (EAST)

JALNA RD

JALNA ROAD

❹

❻ ❼ & Airport (8 km)

◀ Ellora, Khuludabad & Daulatabad

◀ Manmad & Mumbai

Kham River

Paithan

Railway Station

0 Metres 750

ACCOMMODATION

Ajanta Ambassador	7
Ashoka	2
Devpriya	4
Great Punjab	14
Green Palace	3
MTDC Holiday Resort	13
Natraj	12
President Park	6
Printravel	5
Regal Plaza	9
Shree Maya	10
Taj Regency	1
Tourist Home	11
Youth Hostel	8

RESTAURANTS

Agra Mistan	A
Food Lovers	G
Foodwala's Bhoj	B
Foodwalla's Tandoori	F
Mingling	D
Radhika	E
The Kitchen	H
Woodland	C

Hyderabad ▶

In 1629, Shah Jahan's redoubtable army swept south across the Deccan to usher in **Moghul** rule. As **Fatehnagar**, Aurangabad became the centre of operations for their protracted military campaign. It really rose to prominence, however, towards the end of the seventeenth century, when **Aurangzeb** decamped here from Delhi to supervise the subjugation of his troublesome enemies in the region. At his behest, the impressive city walls and gates were raised in 1682 to withstand the persistent Maratha attacks that bedevilled his later years. Following his death in 1707, the city was renamed in his honour as it changed hands once again. The new rulers, the **Nizams of Hyderabad**, somehow staved off the Marathas for the greater part of 250 years, until the city finally merged with Maharashtra in 1956.

Today Aurangabad is one of India's fastest growing commercial and industrial centres, manufacturing everything from pharmaceuticals to auto-rickshaws for a voracious Mumbai market. It's a decidedly upbeat place – with plenty of interesting shops in the old city, restaurants and bars – and a peaceful one, despite the potentially uneasy combination of a local council dominated by the far-right Shiv Sena party, and a sizeable Muslim minority. Easy day-trips from Aurangabad include the dramatic fort of **Daulatabad**, a veritable warren of secret passages and strategic architecture that was briefly the fourteenth-century capital of Moghul India. Just a little further along the Ellora road is the Muslim village of **Khuldabad**, where the tomb of Emperor Aurangzeb lies under a carpet of rose petals and, in the neighbouring courtyard, a ragged curtain is drawn back to reveal a trunk containing the sacred "Robe of the Prophet".

Arrival and information

Daily flights from Delhi and Mumbai arrive at Aurangabad's **airport**, Chikal Thana, 8km east of the city. Metered **taxis** are on hand for the trip into town (around Rs150 to Station Road East or West), and courtesy **minibuses** whisk away guests booked into the nearby five-star hotels. The mainline **railway station** stands on the southwest edge of the city centre, within easy reach of most hotels, and a 2.5-kilometre ride south down Station Road (West) from the **bus stand** – the hectic arrival point for all buses.

A counter at the airport (open at flight arrival times) provides arrival information, while more detailed enquiries are fielded at the Government of India **tourist office** on Station Road West (Mon–Fri 8.30am–6pm, Sat 8.30am–1pm; ☏0240/331217) by the legendary Mr Yadav, who will go out of his way and sit down for hours to describe regional highlights, and help you arrange approved guides. The MTDC runs a tourist office inside its *Holiday Resort* hotel on Station Road East (daily 7am–9.30pm; ☏0240/331513) which is useful for booking **guided tours** of the city and Ellora and Ajanta caves or resorts – though little else. Both offices hand out glossy maps and leaflets on local attractions, although these aren't particularly informative.

The most central places to **change money** are the State Bank of India (Mon–Fri 10.30am–2pm, Sat 10am–noon) on Dr Rajendra Prasad Road at Kranti Chowk. Alternatively, a private and very efficient foreign exchange service is provided at Trade Wings (daily 8am–8pm; ☏0240/322677) on Dr Ambedkhar Road, directly opposite the *Printravel Hotel*, though they charge a Rs60 commission. There are no ATM machines that make international transactions in Aurangabad. The **GPO** (Mon–Sat 10am–5pm, speedpost 8am–7pm, registered mail and parcels 10am–2pm), and efficient poste restante counter, are at Juna Bazaar Chowk, on the north side of the old city. A sealing wax and sewing service is available outside, and stationery is on sale in the shop opposite. There's an **internet** café (daily 8.30am–10pm; Rs40/hr) opposite the *Hotel Printravel*, or try the slightly more expensive – but super-fast – service inside the *Shree Maya Hotel* (Rs60/hr).

A reliable and efficient IATA-approved **travel agent**, recommended for booking or reconfirming flights, is Welworth Travels, Dr Ambedkhar Road (☏0240/337151).

City transport

Most of Aurangabad's sights lie too far apart to take in on foot. The city is, however, buzzing with **auto-rickshaws**, which, on the whole, will happily flag their meters; longer sightseeing trips work out much cheaper if you settle on a fare in advance (taking waiting time into account). Alternatively, try the **tempos** (three-wheeled taxis), which are incredibly cheap but only ply certain

Various companies run daily guided tours of Aurangabad and the surrounding area, all operating to the same itineraries and departure times; only the prices vary. Before booking, bear in mind that the caves at Ellora and Ajanta are closed on Monday. The popular MTDC **Ellora and City** tour (depart 9.30am, return 5.30pm; Rs140 plus entrance fees) takes in the Bibi-Ka-Maqbara, Panchakki, Daulatabad fort, Aurangzeb's tomb at Rauza, and the Ellora caves (but not the Aurangabad ones), and is ridiculously rushed. The **Ajanta** tour (depart 8am, return 5.30pm; Rs180 plus entrance fees) goes to the caves only, and is a long round trip to make in a day. Both tours are on "deluxe" buses with English-speaking guides, and depart from the MTDC *Holiday Resort*. If you want to spend more time at the site, stay in the cave-side MTDC accommodation, or at Fardapur, or travel on to Jalgaon (see p.822 for both).

State Transport Corporation tours of Ellora and City (depart 8am, return 6pm; Rs74), and Ajanta (depart 8am, return 6pm; Rs137), include an English-speaking guide and visit the same sights as the MTDC ones. The tours leave from the Central bus stand and can be booked in advance (℡0240/331647) or on the day at the stand. State buses also run daily from the Central bus stand to Ellora and Ajanta on a frequent basis.

routes. Taxis can be hailed in the street or found at the railway station and **cars with drivers** can be hired through travel agents such as Classic Travel (℡0240/335598), in the lobby of MTDC's *Holiday Resort* on Station Road East, or the agency inside the *Tourist Home*. Expect to pay Rs800–900 for an eight-hour day with an additional overnight charge of around Rs150.

Much the cheapest and most satisfying way to get around the city, however, is by **bicycle**. While the busy main streets and market can be hair-raising at times, a ride out to the sights in the north of town makes an enjoyable alternative to public transport. Local women are rarely, if ever, seen cycling in Aurangabad but it is fine for foreign women to take to two-wheels – although you will most likely attract a crowd of young men eager to accompany you if you are alone. Two stalls just north of the bus stand have the best bikes (Rs20/hr [Rs5/hr]; no deposit).

Accommodation

Aurangabad's proximity to some of India's most important monuments, together with its new "boom-city" status, ensures a profusion of **hotels**. On the whole, standards tend to be high and prices very reasonable, particularly in the **budget** places, most of which are strung along Station Road East between the bus stand and the railway station, and range from extremely basic Indian lodges to more pleasant travellers' hostels. All have 24-hour checkout unless otherwise stated.

Ajanta Ambassador, Chikalthana ℡0240/485211, ℡484367. Luxurious five-star near the airport, with over-the-top ersatz traditional interior. Excellent sports facilities. ⑧–⑨

Ashoka, Tilak Marg, Paithan Gate ℡0240/329555. Right in the busy heart of the old city, if you are searching for a bit of atmosphere. The rooms are reasonably clean, if dark, and good-value. ②–③

Devpriya, near Sidharth Gardens, Dr Ambedkhar Road ℡0240/339032. Neat, clean and efficiently run family hotel. ④–⑤

Great Punjab, Station Road East ℡0240/336482. Business-oriented hotel very near the railway station. All 42 rooms have bathrooms, balconies and TVs. Bland but very good value. ④–⑤

Green Palace, opposite the bus stand on Dr Ambedkhar Road ℡0240/335501. Spartan but clean. Handy if you have just crawled off a bus and can't face a room hunt. There are a crop of good fall-backs such as the *Shangrila* nearby. ❸

MTDC Holiday Resort, Station Road East ☎0240/334259, ☎331198. Spacious, comfortable rooms, if a touch shabby. Mosquito nets over the beds. ❻

Natraj, Station Road West ☎0240/324230. Very traditional lodge run by two elderly Gujarati brothers. Spacious, clean, good-value rooms with shared bathrooms around a peaceful courtyard. No left luggage, and strictly no alcohol. ❷

President Park, Airport Road ☎0240/486201, ☎484823, ☎www.presidenthotels.com. Luxury business hotel softened by the moon-shaped pool with a sunken bar and gardens. All the rooms face onto the pool, and there is a coffee shop, health suite and good veg restaurant. ❽

Printravel, Dr Ambedkhar Road ☎0240/329707. Faintly 1950s-style building near city centre. Common balcony with easy chairs and a good restaurant. Huge rooms. ❹

Regal Plaza, Bansilal Nagar off Station Road East ☎0240/329322. Immaculate if unexciting hotel near the tourist office. Peaceful and good value. ❸–❹

Shree Maya, Bansilal Nagar, off Station Road West, near the Government of India Tourist Office ☎0240/333093, ☎shrimaya@bom4.vsnl.net.in. Friendly, well-run mid-pricer with large clean rooms (some a/c), all with attached bathrooms and TV. Has a pleasant rooftop terrace restaurant serving local and north Indian dishes. Recommended. ❸–❹

Taj Residency, Ajanta Road ☎0240/333501, ☎331328, ☎www.tajhotels.com. The newest and most impressive of the five-stars. Well out of town, but palatial, peaceful and better value than its competitors near the airport. Large swimming pool, tennis courts, gardens and health suite. ❽–❾

Tourist Home, Station Road West ☎0240/337212. Congenial travellers' hostel with neat rooms, attached shower-toilets, and a sociable terrace where evening thalis are served. Excellent value. ❷–❸

Youth Hostel, off Station Road West ☎0240/334892. Cheapest option in town: neat and clean segregated dorms (Rs20 members, Rs40 nonmembers) with mosquito nets, and reasonable private rooms. Full-board rates also available. Book in advance if possible. Checkout 9am (closed 11am–4pm). ❷

The City

Captains of industry and five-star hotels may have supplanted Moghul emperors and palaces, but Aurangabad has retained much of its Islamic feel. Head for the Muslim quarter around the **City Chowk** area of the city and you'll see women veiled in long black *burkhas*, as well as **mosques** that continue to draw large crowds on Fridays. The old walled city, laid out on a grid by Malik Amber in the sixteenth century, still forms the core of Aurangabad's large **bazaar** area. It's best approached via **Gulmandi Square** to the south, along any of several streets lined with colourful shops and stalls. The bazaar lacks the character and intensity of those in larger Indian cities, but has a pleasant, workaday feel, and you'll not be approached by too many zealous salesmen.

Keep walking north, and you'll come out on the chaotic east–west thoroughfare of Ghati Road. In a tiny backroom behind a shop on Ghati Road (another entrance on Sarafa Road) stands the **Purwar Museum** (daily 10am–1pm & 3–6pm; free). Housed in a beautiful old *haveli*, this impressive private collection of antiquities boasts a seventeenth-century Koran hand painted by Aurangzeb, superb bronzes, and a host of other wonderful objects accumulated by a retired doctor. Look for the sign above a doorway, and ask at the handicraft shop next door to be let in.

The unremarkable eighteenth-century **Shah Ganj Masjid** that presides over the main square directly east of City Chowk is surrounded on three sides by small shops and a congested roundabout-cum-racetrack. Anyone keen to see other remnants of Aurangabad's Moghul splendour should make for the city's largest and most impressive mosque, the **Jami Masjid**, 1km northwest of Shah Ganj Masjid. The present building is considerably older than its recent coat of pale-purple colourwash suggests; its amalgam of parts was begun by Malik

Marco Polo wrote of some fabric he was given in the Deccan region that it was "as fine as a spider's web, and kings and queens of any country will take pride in wearing it". The material in question could well have been woven in Aurangabad. Since well before the arrival of the Muslims in the thirteenth century, the region's weavers have skilfully combined local silk with gold thread to produce some of the most opulent and sought-after brocades in India. However, following the decline in the city's fortunes after the departure of the Moghuls, few could afford this extravagant mixture, or **kamkhab**. Cotton was therefore blended with silk to create a cheaper alternative – **Himroo**, literally "similar".

At one time Aurangabad held hundreds of Himroo handlooms. Today, only one family, the Quraishis, continue to produce the fabric in the traditional way. You can see them and their employees in action on special double-sided looms in a tiny **factory** buried deep in the narrow backstreets of the Mondhard district, near Zaffar Gate. This is also one of the few places in India where you can watch traditional **paithani saris** being made. Using designs set down more than two thousand years ago, the Quraishis take six months or more to weave these famously elaborate brocaded lengths of cloth, some of which cost tens of thousands of rupees.

The Himroo factory (daily 10am–5pm) is not easy to find, but most rickshaw-wallahs know the way. If you feel like buying some fabric as a souvenir (not an obligation), the weavers keep a counter stocked with shawls and saris, as well as inexpensive batiks featuring scenes and motifs cribbed from the murals at Ajanta – prices start at about Rs500.

Amber in 1612 and added to by Aurangzeb nearly a century later. To the east of the mosque lie the ruins of Aurangzeb's former imperial headquarters, the **Kila Arak**. Once this was a complex of palaces, battlements, gateways, tanks and gardens that housed three princes and a retinue of thousands.

Finally, every Thursday, an excellent **weekly market** is held just west of the bus stand, across the River Kham. Villagers from outlying areas pour in all morning on bullock carts, the women to set up eye-catching vegetable and spice stalls, the men to stand around in their best *dhotis* and Nehru caps while goats and glistening buffalo are put through their paces in the auction. The market gets into its stride by noon, winding up around 5pm.

The Dargah and Panchakki

On the left bank of the Kham River, on Panchakki Road, the **Dargah** of Baba Shah Muzaffar (daily sunrise–8pm; free) is a religious compound built by Aurangzeb as a memorial to his spiritual mentor, a *chisti* mystic. The principal point of interest is not so much the mosque, the modest tomb or ornamental gardens nearby, pleasant as they are, but the unusual adjoining **water mill** known as the **Panchakki**. Water pumped underground from a reservoir in the hills 6km away collects in a tank, now teeming with enormous *khol* fish, to drive a small grindstone once used to mill flour for members of the *madrasa*, or theological college, next door. Directly beneath the fish tank, sealed behind a wall at ground level by the river, is a large assembly hall supported by four rows of enormous pillars. The whole complex was an impressive engineering feat for its time, although visitors from wetter climes may regard Panchakki charms with rather less enthusiasm than the water-crazy locals. Nonetheless, the tank complex, and the nearby Bibi-Ka-Maqbara (see below) are both very lively and social places to wander around in the early evening with lots of chai shops, *mehendi* (henna hand-painting) artists and souvenir shops galore.

The Bibi-Ka-Maqbara

Were it not so flagrantly an imitation of the Taj Mahal, Aurangabad's much-maligned Moghul tomb-garden would probably attract more admiration. In spite of being one of India's most impressive Islamic monuments, however, the **Bibi-Ka-Maqbara** (daily 8am–sunset; $5 [Rs5]) is widely regarded as the definitive "also ran".

The mausoleum, completed in 1678, was dedicated by **Prince Azam Shah** to the memory of his mother **Begum Rabi'a Daurani**, Aurangzeb's wife. Originally intended to rival the Taj Mahal, lack of resources dogged the 25-year project, and the end result fell far short of expectations. The entrance to the complex is through an enormous brass-inlaid **door**, decorated with an elaborate geometric pattern said to be of Persian origin. An inscription around its edge names the maker, the year of its installation and the chief architect, **Ata Ullah**. Looking at the mausoleum from beyond the ornamental gardens and redundant fountains in front of it, you can see why commentators have been critical. The truncated minarets and ungainly entrance arch make the Bibi-Ka-Maqbara seem squat and ill-proportioned compared with the elegant height and symmetry of the Taj. The impression is not enhanced by the abrupt discontinuation of marble after the first 2m as a cost-saving measure.

Of the two entrances to the main tomb, one provides access to the inner balcony while the second leads down through another beautiful door to the **vault** itself (since a suicidal student jumped from a minaret, visitors may no longer climb them). Be sure to remove your shoes at the steps. Inside, an exquisite octagonal **lattice-screen** of white marble surrounds the raised plinth supporting Rabi'a Daurani's grave. Like her husband's in nearby Rauza, it is "open" as a sign of humility. The unmarked grave beside it is said to be that of the empress's nurse. Through a slanted window on the back wall, the rays of the rising sun illuminate the tomb for three minutes each morning.

The caves

Carved out of a steep-sided spur of the Sahyadri Range, directly overlooking the Bibi-Ka-Maqbara, Aurangabad's own **caves** (Tues-Sun 8.30am–5pm; $5 [Rs5]) bear no comparison to those in nearby Ellora and Ajanta, but their fine **sculpture** makes a worthwhile introduction to rock-cut architecture. In addition, the infrequently visited site is peaceful and pleasant in itself, with commanding views over the city and surrounding countryside.

The caves themselves, all Buddhist, consist of two groups, eastern and western, numbered 1 to 9 by the Archaelogical Survey of India. The majority were excavated between the fourth and eighth centuries, under the patronage of two successive dynasties: the **Vakatkas**, who ruled the western Deccan from Nasik, and the **Chalukyas**, a powerful Mysore family who emerged during the sixth century. All except the much earlier Cave 4, which is a *chaitya* hall, are of the *vihara* (monastery) type, belonging to the Mahayana school of Buddhism.

Unless you cycle, the only practical way of **getting to the caves** is by auto-rickshaw or taxi; you'll be expected to shell out for waiting time, or the return fare. You could also drop down on foot to the Bibi-Ka-Maqbara to pick up an auto-scooter back into town.

The western group

The **western**, and oldest, group of caves is reached via a long flight of steps leading left off the main road. The first of interest, **Cave 2**, is a sixth-century *vihara*, with a columned veranda and a doorway flanked by two *bodhisattvas*.

Inside, a small shrine containing a seated Buddha is surrounded by an unusual passage. **Cave 3** is a remarkably elaborate seventh-century *vihara*. Its most vivid friezes, depicting scenes from the lives of the Buddha, adorn the stone "beams" above the pillars in the main chamber.

Cave 4, the oldest at Aurangabad, may date from the first century AD, and is the only representative of the earlier and more austere Hinayana phase of architecture. Unlike its neighbours, the cave is a rectangular apsidal-ended *chaitya* hall, with a monolithic stupa as its focal point. The characteristic timber-style ceiling is thought to have been an imitation of earlier freestanding wooden structures.

The eastern group

If you only have time to visit one group, it should be the **eastern**, 1km further along the hillside. **Cave 6** contains some finely carved *bodhisattvas*, together with traces of painting on the ceiling of its porch, but the sculpture in **Cave 7** is the real highlight. Its veranda has columned shrines to either side, with a lotus-holding Padmapani and Shakyamuni flanked by six goddesses; a chubby Panchika (guardian of the earth's treasures) and Hariti (goddess of prosperity) stand to the right. The panel on the left of the doorway shows the *bodhisattva* Avalokitesvara (lord of compassion) encircled by the eight mortal fears: fire, the sword, chains (imprisonment), shipwreck, lions, snakes, rampant elephants and the Demon of Death. Nearby, a couple of heavy-breasted *tara* figures bear witness to the increasing preoccupation with female creative energy – *shakti* – cults during the latter part of the Buddhist epoch. Finally, to the left of the preaching Buddha in the sanctuary is Aurangabad's most celebrated panel: a frieze showing a dancer in a classical pose accompanied by six female musicians.

The small unnumbered cave next to **Cave 6** has intrigued archeologists since its rediscovery in 1961. Unusually, the central deity here is the Hindu god **Ganesh**, while on the mural to its right an image of the Buddha provides graphic evidence of the overlap of Buddhism and Brahmanism in the eighth century.

Eating and drinking

Food in Aurangabad tends to be an incongruous mixture of strictly vegetarian **Gujarati** and meat-oriented north Indian Muslim dishes. Typically, "nonveg" is synonymous with dim lights, drawn curtains and a male clientele, while the veg restaurants attract families, and are particularly popular on Sunday evenings, when booking is recommended. As elsewhere in Maharashtra, drinking is a male preserve, carried out in the many specially segregated bars (or **permit rooms**), with the exception of the larger and more tourist-oriented hotels and restaurants.

Agra Mistan, off Tilak Marg, Aurangpura. Clean, no-nonsense restaurant on the southern edge of the old town, serving authentic, moderately priced Gujarati food, mainly to visiting business people. Can be hard to find on foot, but the rickshaw drivers know where it is.

Food Lovers, Station Road East, opposite MTDC office. A kitsch wonderland of bamboo, plastic waterfalls and fishtanks – all lit by candlelight. The mid-price Indian and Chinese food is good too.

Foodwala's Bhoj, near Baba Petrol Pump, Dr Ambedkhar Road. An old favourite, pure-veg restaurant at shiny new premises. Renowned for its meticulously prepared, good-value lunchtime Gujarati thalis.

Foodwala's Tandoori, Shyam Chambers, Station Road West. Upmarket a/c bar-restaurant with numerous à la carte chicken and mutton dishes. Pricey but worth it.

The Kitchen, Station Road East, opposite MTDC office. Reasonably priced and well-run diner serving quality Indian food to a mix of Indian holidaymakers and backpackers. Features many local (mainly non-veg) dishes, a Rs30 unlimited thali and Continental or English breakfasts.
Mingling, *Rajdoot Hotel,* Jalna Road. Best Chinese in town, though a bit ostentatious and overpriced.

Radhika, *Hotel Nandanvan,* Station Road West. Justly popular, serving a large selection of inexpensive veg dishes (mainly south Indian) in garden. *Rathi* next door is equally good non-veg version, with cold beer, but dingy surroundings. Both are excellent value.
Woodland, Jalna Road, opposite *President Park Hotel.* Decidedly yuppie crowd but locally renowned for good south Indian food.

Moving on from Aurangabad

Daily flights from Aurangabad to Mumbai (40min; $75) are operated by Jet Airways (8.45pm) and Indian Airlines (5.30pm). The Indian Airlines flight also carries on to Delhi ($175). Their office is on Jalna Road (℡0240/485421).

All the state transport corporation (MSRTC) buses leave from the Central bus stand and the MTDC buses depart from the MTDC *Holiday Resort.* The MSRTC run good-value "luxury" daily night-buses to Mumbai. If you feel like a little more comfort, there are a couple of companies running more expensive a/c buses to most of the larger destinations; tickets can be booked through travel agents. Getting to Pune is easy, on MSRTC's "express" (every 30min; 5hr). Nasik buses are less frequent (5 daily; 3hr). A couple of private bus companies run buses to Indore, Nasik, Pune, Udaipur, Ahmedabad and Jalgaon which can be booked through most travel agents.

Trains to and from Aurangabad are very limited, as the city is not on the main line. The two services to Mumbai (8hr 30min) are the heavily booked Devagiri Express #1004 and Tapovan Express #7618, which leave at 9.05pm and 2.40pm, respectively. You can also get direct to Secunderabad (for Hyderabad) on the Manmad–Kacheguda Express #7663 (11hr 30min) at 7.20pm. Otherwise, the nearest main-line station, at Jalgaon, 108km north, is served by trains to Delhi, Agra, Bhopal, Calcutta and Madras.

See Travel Details at the end of this chapter for more information on journey frequencies and durations.

Daulatabad (Deogiri)

Northwest of Aurangabad, the main Ellora road runs through fertile Deccani farmland punctuated by the occasional red-brick village or Muslim tomb crumbling in shady evergreen glades. Looming on the horizon of this serene and prosperous countryside is the stark profile of one of India's most imposing fortresses. Invading armies must have stopped dead when confronted with **DAULATABAD**, 13km northwest of Aurangabad. The awesome hilltop citadel crowns a massive conical volcanic outcrop whose sides have been shaped into a sheer sixty-metre wall of granite. The fort's forbidding appearance is further accentuated by the slender victory **minaret** rising out of the ruins of the city that once sprawled from its base, like a pink finger in the face of the approaching enemy. If only for the panoramic **views** from its summit, Daulatabad makes an excellent pause en route to or from the caves at Ellora, 17km northwest.

Aside from the inevitable Buddhist and Jain hermits, occupation of the site – then known as **Deogiri**, "Hill of the Gods" – dates from its ninth-century role as bastion and capital of a confederacy of Hindu tribes. The **Yadavas** were responsible for scraping away the jagged lower slopes of the mount to form its vertical-cliff base, as well as the fifteen-metre-deep moat that still encircles the upper portion of the citadel. Their prosperity eventually aroused the interest of the acquisitive Delhi sultans, who stormed the fortress in 1294 and carried off a raja's ransom in gold, silver and precious stones.

Muslim occupation of Deogiri began in earnest with the arrival in 1327 of Ghiyas-ud-din **Tughluq**. Convinced that the fort was the perfect base for campaigns further south, the sultan decreed that his entire court should decamp here from Tughluqabad, the "third city" of Delhi (see p.1484). The epic 1100-kilometre march cost thousands of lives, the sultan's underfed and exhausted subjects dropping like flies by the wayside. Life in the new capital – which Tughluq prematurely renamed Daulatabad, or "Abode of Good Fortune" – was not much of an improvement. Within seventeen years, drought, famine and the growing threat of a full-scale Moghul invasion on his northern borders forced the beleaguered ruler to concede defeat and return to Tughluqabad. His audacious governor, Zafar Khan, seized the moment, and in 1327 mounted a rebellion to establish the **Bahmani** dynasty. Thereafter, the fortress fell to a succession of different regimes, including Shah Jahan's **Moghuls** in 1633, before it was finally taken by the **Marathas** midway through the eighteenth century.

The fortress

Daulatabad's labyrinthine **fortress** (daily 6am–6pm; $5 [Rs5]) incorporates so many ingenious ways to snuff out unwanted intruders that it's almost inconceivable anyone ever managed to penetrate the formidable outer defences, let alone fight their way up the 183 metres of ramparts, moats and dark passages to the citadel. The tone is set by the vicious, elephant-proof spikes that stick menacingly out of the main gates. Once inside, three **cannons** (two Persian and one Dutch) lie discarded in the first of several claustrophobic courtyards as reminders of the aerial bombardment which would have rained down upon the attackers. The proud **Chandminar**, or "Victory Tower", further along, was more a psychological than a military deterrent. Soaring above the heart of the old town, of which only the scantest traces now remain, the majestic pink minaret was erected by Ala-ud-din Bahmani to celebrate his conquest of the fort in 1435. The Persian blue and turquoise tiles that once plastered it in complex geometric patterns have disappeared.

The Jami Masjid, directly opposite the Chandminar, is Daulatabad's oldest Islamic monument. Built by the Delhi sultans in 1318, to chastise Deogiri's Hindu occupants for their refusal to pay annual tribute, the well-preserved mosque comprises 106 pillars plundered from the Hindu and Jain temples which previously stood on the site. The mosque was recently converted into a Bharatmata temple, much to the chagrin of local Muslims. Nearby, the large stone-lined "Elephant" **tank** was once a central component in the fort's extensive water-supply system. Two giant terracotta pipes channelled water from the hills into the Deogiri's legendary fruit and vegetable gardens.

Once beyond the open ground surrounding the tower, the main walkway heads through a series of interlocking bastions, fortified walls, moats and drawbridges before emerging to the **Chini Mahal**, or "Chinese Palace", where the last Galconda ruler Abdul Hasan Tana Shah was imprisoned in 1687 by the Moghul emperor Aurangzeb. Following thirteen years of torture, Tana Shah is said to have begged for, of all things, a pot of curd, which once eaten caused his head to explode. His corpse was then dragged behind an elephant to Rauza where it was finally entombed. The impressive ram-headed **Kila Shikan** ("Fort Breaker") cannon, inscribed with its name in Persian, rests on a stone platform nearby. From here onwards, a sequence of macabre traps lay in wait for the unwary intruder. First, a moat infested with man-eating crocodiles had to be crossed in order to reach the foot of the citadel, or **Bala Kot**. Next, the attackers had to crawl through a maze of pitch-black passageways cut from the fort's solid-rock foundations. At one point, these fork and rejoin to dupe enemy soldiers into fighting each other in the darkness. If they survived that ruse, the toxic fumes emanating from the red-hot iron cover that sealed the only exit to the underground tunnel would probably finish them off. The bodies would be dumped down the slanting chutes in the side walls, to be devoured by hungry crocodiles waiting in the moat below.

At the end of the tunnel, a broad flight of rock-cut steps climbs to an attractive twelve-pillared pavilion. The **Baradi** is thought to have been the residence of a Yadavi queen, though it was later used by the emperor Shah Jahan during his visits to Daulatabad. The **views** from the flat roof of the building are superb. Note the tombs clinging to the foot of the barren brown hills to the east, and the street plan of the old town below, just discernible through the rubble-strewn wasteground beside the Jami Masjid. An even more impressive panorama is to be had from the **look-out post** perched on the summit of the hill, where you'll find another old cannon (the "Storm Creator") and an ancient rock-cut cave, home during the Moghul period to a renowned Hindu ascetic.

Practicalities

If you're not on a guided tour, it's recommended that you hire a guide (Rs80) as the passages of the fort are pitch-black and hopelessly confusing otherwise. Although Daulatabad features on the MTDC guided **tour** of Ellora from Aurangabad (see p.796), you'll have more time to enjoy it by travelling there on one of the hourly shuttle **buses** between Aurangabad and the caves. From Daulatabad, it is easy to catch another bus onto Khuldabad and Ellora. The stop is directly opposite the main entrance to the fort, beside the string of chai and souvenir stalls and the good, small MTDC-run **restaurant**. Daulatabad holds no **accommodation** for visitors.

Khauldabad (Rauza)

As the silhouette of Daulatabad's fort recedes into the haze on the horizon, the Ellora–Aurangabad Road climbs a sun-bleached ridge called **Peepal Ghat**. Nestled on this saddle of high ground, 22km from Aurangabad and a five-kilometre ride from the caves, **KHAULDABAD**, also known as **Rauza**, is an old walled town famous for a bumper crop of tumbledown onion-domed **tombs**. Among the Muslim notables deemed worthy of a patch of earth in this most hallowed of burial grounds (**"Khauldabad"** means "Heavenly Abode"), were the emperor Aurangzeb, a couple of nizams, and a fair few of the town's *chisti* founding fathers – the seven hundred mystic missionaries dispatched by the saint Nizam-ud-din Aulia to soften up local Hindus before the Sultanate's invasion in the fourteenth century. Rauza's monuments are nowhere near as impressive as those in Delhi or Agra, but a couple harbour important **relics** and are still venerated for their miraculous properties. While they see a steady trickle of visitors, and even large crowds on festival days, the lesser mausoleums on the outskirts of the sleepy Muslim town lie deserted and all but forgotten, their old stone pavilions, bulbous domes and walled enclosures choked with weeds and grazed by herds of scruffy goats.

The Dargah of Sayeed Zain-ud-din

Khauldabad is encircled by tall granite battlements and seven fortified **gateways** raised by Aurangzeb before his death in 1707. The last of the great

Moghuls is buried inside the town's most famous **dargah**, or shrine-tomb, midway between the North and South gates. Steps lead up from the main thoroughfare through a domed porch into a peaceful courtyard surrounded by whitewashed cloisters and minarets. **Aurangzeb's tomb** lies under the arch to the left. In keeping with the teachings of Islam, the grave itself is a humble affair decorated only by the fresh flower petals scattered by visitors, open to the elements instead of sealed in stone. The devout emperor insisted that it be paid for not out of the royal coffers, but with the money he raised in the last years of life by selling his own hand-quilted white skull-caps. The pierced-marble **screen** and walls that now surround the spot were erected much later by the British viceroy, Lord Curzon, and the Nizam of Hyderabad.

Aurangzeb chose this as his final resting place primarily because of the presence, next door, of Sayeed **Zain-ud-din**'s tomb. The mausoleum of the Muslim saint, or *pir*, occupies a quadrangle separating Aurangzeb's grave from those of his wife and second son, Azam Shah. Its doors are beautifully inlaid with slabs of silver, brass and bronze, while the steps leading to it are encrusted with highly polished semiprecious stones donated by the wandering Muslim ascetics, or *fakirs*, who formerly came here on pilgrimages. Locked away behind a small door is Rauza's most jealously guarded relic. The **Robe of the Prophet** is revealed to the public once a year, on the twelfth day of the Islamic month of Rabi-ul-Awwal (usually around November), when the tomb becomes the focus of a festival attracting crowds of worshippers from all over India.

The other buildings in this *dargah* are a small **mosque** (on the west side of the main courtyard) and the **Nakkar Khanna**, or Music Hall, which, on high days and holy days, hosts performances of *qawwali*.

The Dargah of Sayeed Burhan-ud-din

Directly opposite Zain-ud-din's tomb is the **Dargah of Sayeed Burhan-ud-din**, a *chisti* missionary buried here in 1334. The shrine is said to contain hairs from the Prophet's beard which magically increase in number when they are counted each year. At the end of the fourteenth century, when a cash crisis had left the saint's disciples unable to provide for either themselves or the upkeep of the beloved *dargah*, a pair of **"silver trees"** miraculously sprouted in its central courtyard. These days, the only precious metal in the tomb is in panels set into the doors of the shrine, although for a small donation the attendant will point out the two innocuous-looking lumps in the pavement nearby where the fabled trees once stood, and which are still said to secrete the odd drop of silver.

On the road down to the Ellora caves, you pass one of Rauza's few empty tombs. Commissioned by a foreign ambassador who fell ill here in the eighteenth century, this modest mausoleum was never occupied. Shortly after it was completed, the diplomat recovered from his supposdly terminal illness and limped home to Persia, where he eventually died, leaving his tomb to lie forever idle on this peaceful, west-facing ridge.

Practicalities

MSRTC **buses** pull in every half-hour or so at Rauza's small bus stand, a short walk west of the walls, en route between Aurangabad and the Ellora caves just down the hill. There is no **accommodation** in Khauldabad, so you should press on to Ellora or Aurangabad. If the prospect of **eating** in one of the sweet shops and chai stalls in Rauza's main bazaar doesn't appeal, you'll have to wait until you get to Ellora.

Ellora

Palaces will decay, bridges will fall, and the noblest structures must give way to the corroding tooth of time; whilst the caverned temples of Ellora shall rear their indestructible and hoary heads in stern loneliness, the glory of past ages, and the admiration of ages yet to come.

Captain Seely, *The Wonders of Ellora*

Maharashtra's most visited ancient monument, the **ELLORA** caves, 29km northwest of Aurangabad, may not enjoy as grand a setting as their older cousins at Ajanta, but the amazing wealth of **sculpture** they contain more than compensates, and this is an unmissable port of call if you're heading to or from Mumbai, 400km southwest. In all, 34 Buddhist, Hindu and Jain caves – some excavated simultaneously, in competition – line the foot of the two-kilometre-long Chamadiri escarpment as it tumbles down to meet the open plains. The site's principal attraction, the gargantuan **Kailash temple**, rears from a huge, sheer-sided cavity cut from the hillside. The world's largest monolith, this vast lump of solid basalt is fashioned into a spectacular agglomeration of interconnecting colonnaded halls, galleries and sacred shrines.

The original reason why this apparently remote spot became the focus of so much religious and artistic activity was the busy **caravan route** that cut through here on its way between the prosperous cities to the north and the ports of the west coast. Profits from the lucrative overland trade fuelled a five-hundred-year spate of excavation, beginning midway through the sixth century AD at around the same time that Ajanta, 100km northeast, was abandoned. This was the twilight of the Buddhist era in central India; by the end of the seventh century, **Hinduism** had begun to reassert itself. The Brahmanical resurgence gathered momentum over the next three hundred years under the patronage of the Chalukya and Rashtrakuta kings – the two powerful dynasties respon-

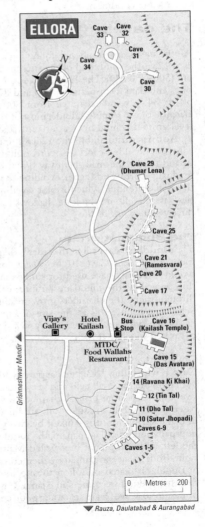

ELLORA

Cave 33 Cave 32
Cave 34
Cave 31
Cave 30
Cave 29 (Dhumar Lena)
Cave 25
Cave 21 (Ramesvara)
Cave 20
Cave 17
Vijay's Gallery   Hotel Kailash   Bus Stop   Cave 16 (Kailash Temple)
MTDC/ Food Wallahs Restaurant   Cave 15 (Das Avatara)
Grishneshwar Mandir
14 (Ravana Ki Khai)
12 (Tin Tal)
11 (Dho Tal)
10 (Sutar Jhopadi)
Caves 6–9
Caves 1–5

0   Metres   200

▼ *Rauza, Daulatabad & Aurangabad*

sible for the bulk of the work carried out at Ellora, including the eighth-century Kailash temple. A third and final flourish of activity on the site took place towards the end of the first millennium AD, after the local rulers had switched allegiance from Shaivism to the Digambara sect of the **Jain** faith. A small cluster of more subdued caves to the north of the main group stand as reminders of this age.

Unlike the isolated site of Ajanta, Ellora did not escape the iconoclasm that accompanied the arrival of the **Muslims** in the thirteenth century. The worst excesses were committed during the reign of **Aurangzeb** who, in a fit of piety, ordered the systematic destruction of the site's "heathen idols". Although Ellora still bears the scars from this time, most of its best pieces of sculpture have remained miraculously intact. The fact that they were cut from hard rock, beyond the reach of the monsoon downpours, has preserved the caves in remarkable condition.

The caves

All the **caves** are numbered, following a roughly chronological plan. Numbers 1 to 12, at the south end of the site, are the oldest, from the Vajrayana Buddhist era (500–750 AD). The Hindu caves, 17 to 29, overlap with the later Buddhist ones and date from between 600 and 870 AD. Further north, the Jain caves – 30 to 34 – were excavated from 800 AD until the late eleventh century. Because of the sloping hillside, most of the cave entrances are set back from the level ground behind open courtyards and large colonnaded verandas or porches. **Admission** to all but the Kailash temple is free.

To see the oldest caves first, turn right from the car park where the buses pull in and follow the main pathway down to Cave 1. From here, work your way gradually northwards again, avoiding the temptation to look around Cave 16, the Kailash temple, which is best saved until late afternoon when the bus parties have all left and the long shadows cast by the setting sun bring its extraordinary stonework to life.

The Buddhist group

The **Buddhist caves** line the sides of a gentle recess in the Chamadiri escarpment. All except Cave 10 are *viharas*, or monastery halls, which the monks would originally have used for study, solitary meditation and communal worship, as well as the mundane business of eating and sleeping. As you progress through them, the chambers grow steadily more impressive in scale and tone. Scholars attribute this to the rise of Hinduism and the need to compete for patronage with the more overtly awe-inspiring Shaivite cave-temples being excavated so close at hand.

Caves 1 to 5

Cave 1, which may have been a granary for the larger halls, is a plain, bare *vihara* containing eight small cells and very little sculpture. In the much more impressive Cave 2, a large central chamber is supported by twelve massive, square-based pillars while the side walls are lined with seated Buddhas. The doorway into the shrine room is flanked by two giant *dvarpalas*, or guardian figures: an unusually muscular Padmapani, the lotus-holding *bodhisattva* of compassion, on the left, and an opulent bejewelled Maitreya, the "Buddha-to-come", on the right. Both are accompanied by their consorts. Inside the sanctum itself, a stately Buddha is seated on a lion throne, looking stronger and more determined than his serene forerunners in Ajanta. Caves 3 and 4, slightly older and similar in design to Cave 2, are in rather poor condition.

The **rock-cut caves** scattered across the volcanic hills of the northwestern Deccan rank among the most extraordinary religious monuments in Asia, if not the world. Ranging from tiny monastic cells to colossal, elaborately carved temples, they are remarkable for having been hewn by hand from solid rock. Their third-century BC origins seem to have been as temporary shelters for Buddhist monks when heavy monsoon rains brought their travels to a halt. Modelled on earlier wooden structures, most were sponsored by **merchants**, for whom the casteless new faith offered an attractive alternative to the old, discriminatory social order. Gradually, encouraged by the example of the Mauryan emperor Ashoka, the local ruling dynasties also began to embrace Buddhism. Under their patronage, during the second century BC, the first large-scale monastery caves were created at **Karle**, **Bhaja** and **Ajanta**.

Around this time, the austere **Hinayana**, or "Lesser Vehicle", school of Buddhism predominated in India. In keeping with the original teachings of the Buddha, closed communities of monks had little or no interaction with the outside world. Caves cut in this era were mostly simple "worship halls", or **chaityas** – long, rectangular apsed chambers with barrel-vaulted roofs, and two narrow colonnaded aisles curving gently around the back of a monolithic **stupa** (see p.437). Symbols of the Buddha's Enlightenment, these hemispherical burial mounds provided the principal focus for worship and meditation, circumambulated by the monks during their communal rituals.

The **methods** employed to excavate the caves altered little over the centuries. First, the basic dimensions of the ornamental facade were sketched onto the cliff face. Next, gangs of stonemasons hacked out a rough hole (later to become the *chaitya*'s graceful horseshoe-shaped window), through which they chiselled deep into the rock. As they worked their way down to floor level, using heavy iron picks, the labourers left chunks of raw rock for skilled sculptors to transform into pillars, devotional friezes and stupas.

By the fourth century AD, the Hinayana school was losing ground to the more exuberant **Mahayana**, or "Greater Vehicle", school. Its emphasis on an ever-enlarging pantheon of deities and **bodhisattvas** (merciful saints who postponed their accession to nirvana to help mankind towards Enlightenment) was accompanied by a transformation in architectural styles. *Chaityas* were superseded by lavish monastery halls, or **viharas**, in which the monks both lived and worshipped, and the once-prohibited image of the Buddha became far more prominent. Occupying the circumambulatory recess at the end of the hall, where the stupa formerly stood, the colossal **icon** acquired the 32 characteristics, or **lakshanas** (including long dangling ear-lobes, cranial protuberance, short curls, robe and halo) by which the Buddha was distinguished from lesser divinities. The peak of Mahayanan art came towards the end of the Buddhist age. Drawing on the rich catalogue of themes and images contained in ancient scriptures such as the **Jatakas** (legends relating to the Buddha's previous incarnations), Ajanta's exquisite and awe-inspiring wall **painting** may, in part, have been designed to rekindle enthusiasm for the faith, which was, by this point, already starting to wane in the region.

Attempts to compete with the resurgence of **Hinduism**, from the sixth century onwards, eventually led to the evolution of another, more esoteric religious movement. The **Vajrayana**, or "Thunderbolt" sect stressed the female creative principle, **shakti**, with arcane rituals combining spells and magic formulas. Ultimately, however, such modifications were to prove powerless against the growing allure of Brahmanism.

The ensuing shift in royal and popular patronage is best exemplified by **Ellora**, where, during the eighth century, many old *viharas* were converted into temples, their shrines housing polished *shivalinga* instead of stupas and Buddhas. Hindu cave architecture, with its dramatic mythological **sculpture**, culminated in the tenth century with the magnificent **Kailash temple**, a giant replica of the freestanding structures that had already begun to replace rock-cut caves. It was Hinduism that bore the brunt of the iconoclastic medieval descent of Islam on the Deccan, Buddhism having long since fled to the comparative safety of the Himalayas, where it still flourishes.

MAHARASHTRA | Ellora

Known as the "Maharwada" cave because it was used by local Mahar tribes-people as a shelter during the monsoon, Cave 5 is the grandest single-storeyed *vihara* in Ellora. Its enormous 36-metre-long rectangular assembly hall is thought to have been used by the monks as a refectory, and has two rows of benches carved from the stone floor. At the far end, the entrance to the central shrine is guarded by two fine *bodhisattva* figures of Padmapani and Vajrapani – the "Thunderbolt Holder". The Buddha inside is seated, this time on a stool; his right hand touching the ground in the mudra denoting the "Miracle of a Thousand Buddhas", performed by the Master to confound a gang of heretics.

Cave 6

The next four caves were excavated at roughly the same time in the seventh century, and are mere variations on their predecessors. On the walls of the antechamber at the far end of the central hall in **Cave 6**, are two of Ellora's most famous and finely executed figures. **Tara**, the female consort of the *bodhisattva* Avalokitesvara, stands to the left, with an intense, kindly expression. On the opposite side, the Buddhist goddess of learning, Mahamayuri, is depicted with her emblem the peacock, while a diligent student sets a good example at his desk below. The parallels with Mahayuri's Hindu counterpart, Saraswati, are obvious (the latter's mythological vehicle is also a peacock), and show the extent to which seventh-century Indian Buddhism incorporated elements from its rival faith in an attempt to rekindle its waning popularity.

Caves 10, 11 and 12

Excavated in the early eighth century, **Cave 10** is one of the last and most magnificent of the Deccan's rock-cut *chaitya* halls. Steps lead from the left of its large veranda to an upper balcony, where a trefoil doorway flanked by flying threesomes, heavenly nymphs, and a frieze of playful dwarfs leads to an interior balcony. From here, you have a good view down into the long apsed hall, with its octagonal pillars and vaulted roof. The stone "rafters" carved out of the ceiling, imitations of the beams that would have appeared in earlier free-standing wooden structures, are the source of this cave's popular name, the **Sutar Jhopadi**, or "Carpenter's Workshop". At the far end, a seated Buddha is enthroned in front of a votive **stupa** – the hall's devotional centrepiece.

In spite of the rediscovery in 1876 of its hitherto hidden basement, **Cave 11** continues to be known as the **Dho Tal**, or "two floors" cave. Its top storey is a long columned assembly hall housing a Buddha shrine and, on its rear wall, images of Durga and Ganesh, the elephant-headed son of Shiva – evidence that the cave was converted into a Hindu temple after being abandoned by the Buddhists.

Cave 12 next door – the **Tin Tal**, or "three floors" – is another triple-storeyed *vihara* approached via a large open courtyard. Again, the main highlights are on the uppermost level, once used for teaching and meditation. The shrine room at the end of the hall, whose walls are lined with five large *bodhisattvas*, is flanked on both sides by seven Buddhas – one for each of the Master's previous incarnations. Those on the left are shown in deep meditation, while those to the right are once more depicted in the *mudra* that signifies the "Miracle of a Thousand Buddhas".

The Hindu group

Ellora's seventeen **Hindu caves** are grouped around the middle of the escarpment, to either side of the majestic Kailash temple. Excavated at the start of the Brahmanical revival in the Deccan, during a time of relative stability, the cave-temples throb with a vitality absent from their restrained Buddhist predecessors. Gone are the rows of heavy-eyed, benign-faced Buddhas and *bodhisattvas*. In their place, huge **bas-reliefs** line the walls, writhing with dynamic scenes from the Hindu scriptures. Most are connected with **Shiva**, the god of destruction and regeneration (and the presiding deity in all of the Hindu caves on the site), although you'll also come across numerous images of Vishnu, the Preserver, and his various incarnations.

The same tableaux crop up time and again, a repetition that gave Ellora's craftsmen ample opportunity to refine their technique over the years leading up to their greatest achievement, the **Kailash temple** (Cave 16). Covered separately on p.810, the temple is the highlight of any visit to Ellora, but you'll appreciate its beautiful sculpture all the more if you check out the earlier Hindu caves first. Numbers 14 and 15, immediately south, are the best of the bunch if you're pushed for time.

Cave 14

Dating from the start of the seventh century AD, and among the last of the early excavations, **Cave 14** was a Buddhist *vihara* converted into a temple by the Hindus. Its layout is similar to that of Cave 8, with the shrine room set back from the wall and surrounded by a circumambulatory passage. The entrance to the sanctum is guarded by two impressive river goddesses, Ganga and Yamuna, while in an alcove behind and to the right, seven heavy-breasted fertility goddesses, the **Sapta Matrikas**, dandle chubby babies on their laps. The female aspect of Shiva's elephant-headed son, Ganesh, sits to their right beside two cadaverous apparitions, Kala and Kali, the goddesses of death. Superb **friezes** adorn the cave's long side walls. Starting at the front, those on the left (as you face the shrine) show Durga slaying the demon buffalo Mahisa; Lakshmi, the goddess of wealth, enthroned on a lotus as her elephant attendants shower her with water; Vishnu, in the form of the boar, Vahara, rescuing the earth goddess Prithvi from the primordial flood; and finally Vishnu, shown with his two wives. On the opposite wall, the panels are devoted exclusively to Shiva. The second from the front shows him playing dice with his wife Parvati; then doing the dance of death as Nataraja; and in the fourth frieze, blithely ignoring the demon Ravana's futile attempts to shake him and his consort off their heavenly abode, Mount Kailash.

Cave 15

Like its neighbour, the two-storeyed **Cave 15**, reached via a long flight of steps, began life as a Buddhist *vihara* but was hijacked by the Hindus and became a Shiva shrine. Skip the largely uninteresting ground floor, and make for the upper level to find some of Ellora's most magnificent sculpture. The cave's name, **Das Avatara**, is derived from the sequence of panels along the right wall, which show five of **Vishnu**'s ten incarnations (*avatars*). The one nearest the entrance shows Vishnu in his fourth manifestation as the Man-Lion, **Narashima**, which he adopted to slay a demon that could not be killed "by man nor beast, by day or night, inside or outside a palace" (Vishnu got him by lying in wait at dawn inside the entrance hall to his palace). Note the demon's serene expession as he prepares to die, confident in the knowledge that he will attain salvation having been killed by a god. In the second frieze from the front, the Preserver appears as the "**Primordial Dreamer**", reclining on the coils of Anantha, the cosmic serpent of Infinity. His navel is about to sprout a lotus flower from which Brahma will emerge to begin the creation of the world.

A carved panel in a recess to the right of the antechamber shows Shiva emerging from a *lingam*. His rivals, Brahma and Vishnu, stand before the apparition in humility and supplication – symbolizing the supremacy of Shaivism in the region at the time the conversion work was carried out. Finally, halfway down the left wall of the chamber, as you're facing the shrine, the cave's most elegant piece of sculpture shows Shiva, as Nataraja, poised in a classical dance pose.

Caves 17 to 29

Only three of the Hindu caves strung along the hillside north of the Kailash temple are worth making the effort to visit. **Cave 21** – the **Ramesvara** – was excavated late in the sixth century. Thought to be the oldest Hindu cave at Ellora, it harbours some well-executed sculpture, including a fine pair of river goddesses on either side of the veranda, two wonderful door guardians and some sensuous loving couples, or *mithunas*, dotted around the walls of the balcony. Look out, too, for the superb panels featuring Shiva and Parvati. **Cave 25**, further along, contains a striking image of the sun-god **Surya** speeding in his chariot towards the dawn.

From here, the path picks its way past two more excavations, then drops steeply across the face of a sheer cliff to the bottom of a small river gorge. Once under the seasonal **waterfall**, the trail climbs the other side of the gully, to emerge beside **Cave 29**, the **Dhumar Lena**. Dating from the late sixth century, the cave boasts an unusual cross-shaped floor plan similar to the Elephanta cave in Mumbai harbour (see p.769). Pairs of rampant lions guard its three staircases, while inside, the walls are covered with huge **friezes**. Left of the entrance, Shiva skewers the Andhaka demon; in the adjacent wall panel he foils the many-armed Ravana's attempts to shake him and Parvati off the top of Mount Kailash (look for the cheeky dwarf baring his bum to taunt the evil demon). On the south side, a dice-playing scene shows Shiva teasing Parvati by holding her arm back as she prepares to throw.

The Kailash temple (Cave 16)

Cave 16, the colossal **Kailash temple** (daily 6am–6pm; Rs5), is Ellora's masterpiece. Here, the term "cave" is not only a gross understatement, but a complete misnomer. For although the temple was, like the other excavations, hewn from solid rock, it bears a striking resemblance to the freestanding structures – at Pattadakal and Kanchipuram (see p.1222) in south India – on which it was modelled. The monolith is believed to have been the brainchild of the Rashtrakuta ruler **Krishna I** (756–773). One hundred years and four generations of kings, architects and craftsmen elapsed, however, before the project was completed. Climb up the track leading along the lip of the compound's north-facing cliff, to the ledge overlooking the squat main tower, and you'll see why.

The sheer scale is staggering. Work began by digging three deep trenches into the top of the hill using pickaxes and lengths of wood which, soaked with water and stuffed into narrow cracks, expanded to crumble the basalt. Once a huge chunk of raw rock had been exposed in this way, the royal sculptors set to work. In all, a quarter of a million tonnes of chippings and debris are estimated to have been cut from the hillside, with no room for improvisation or error. The temple was conceived as a giant replica of Shiva and Parvati's Himalayan abode, the pyramidal **Mount Kailash** – a Tibetan peak, said to be the "divine axis" between heaven and earth. Today, all but a few fragments of the thick coat of white-lime plaster that gave the temple the appearance of a snowy mountain have flaked off, to expose elaborately carved surfaces of grey-brown stone beneath. Around the rear of the tower, these have been bleached and blurred by centuries of erosion, as if the giant sculpture is slowly melting in the fierce Deccani heat.

The temple

The main **entrance** to the temple is through a tall stone screen, intended to mark the transition from the profane to the sacred realms. After passing between two guardian river goddesses, Ganga and Yamuna, you enter a narrow passage that opens onto the main forecourt, opposite a panel showing **Lakshmi**, the goddess of wealth, being lustrated by a pair of elephants – the scene known to Hindus as "Gajalakshmi". Custom requires pilgrims to circumambulate clockwise around Mount Kailash, so descend the steps to your left and head across the front of the courtyard towards the near corner.

From the top of the concrete steps in the corner, all three principal sections of the complex are visible. First, the shrine above the entrance housing Shiva's vehicle **Nandi**, the bull; next, the intricate recessed walls of the main assembly hall, or **mandapa**, which still bear traces of the coloured plaster that originally coated the whole edifice; and finally, the sanctuary itself, surmounted by the stumpy, 29-metre pyramidal tower, or **shikhara** (best viewed from above). These three components rest on an appropriately huge raised platform, borne by dozens of lotus-gathering elephants. As well as symbolizing Shiva's sacred mountain, the temple also represented a giant **chariot**. The transepts protruding from the side of the main hall are its wheels, the Nandi shrine its yoke, and the two life-sized trunkless elephants in the front of the courtyard (disfigured by marauding Muslims) are the beasts of burden.

Most of the main highlights of the temple itself are confined to its side walls, which are plastered with vibrant **sculpture**. Lining the staircase that leads up to the north side of the *mandapa*, a long, lively narrative panel depicts scenes from the *Mahabharata*. Below this, you may recognize episodes from the life of **Krishna**, including one, in the bottom right corner, in which the young god suckled the poisoned breast of a wet nurse sent to kill him by his evil uncle. Krishna survived, but the poison dyed his skin its characteristic blue. Continuing around the temple in a clockwise direction, the majority of the panels around the lower sections of the temple are devoted to **Shiva**. On the south side of the *mandapa*, in an alcove carved out of the most prominent projection, you'll find the relief widely held to be the finest piece of sculpture in the compound. It shows Shiva and Parvati being disturbed by the multi-headed demon **Ravana**, who has been incarcerated inside the sacred mountain and is now shaking the walls of his prison with his many arms. Shiva is about to assert his supremacy by calming the earthquake with a prod of his toe. Parvati, meanwhile, looks nonchalantly on, reclining on her elbow as one of her handmaidens flees in panic.

At this point, make a short detour up the steps at the bottom (southwest) corner of the courtyard, to the "**Hall of Sacrifices**", with its striking frieze of the seven mother goddesses, the **Sapta Matrikas**, and their ghoulish companions Kala and Kali (shown astride a heap of corpses), or head straight up the stairs of the main assembly hall, past the animated battle scenes in the dramatic **Ramayana frieze**, to the shrine room. The sixteen-columned assembly hall is shrouded in a gloomy half-light designed to focus worshippers on the presence of the deity within. Using a portable arc light, the *chowkidar* will illuminate fragments of painting on the ceiling, where Shiva, as **Nataraja**, performs the dance of death, as well as numerous erotic *mithuna* couples. The sanctum itself is no longer a living **shrine**, although it still houses a large stone *lingam* mounted on a *yoni* pedestal, symbolizing the dual aspects of Shiva's procreative energy.

The Jain group

Ellora's small cluster of four **Jain caves** is north of the main group, at the end of a curving asphalt road. They can be reached either from Cave 29, by dropping down to the T-junction and bearing right, or directly from the Kailash temple. Either way, the two-kilometre round-trip is quite a hike in the heat, and you may feel like taking a rickshaw.

Excavated in the late ninth and tenth centuries, after the Hindu phase had petered out, the Jain caves are Ellora's swansong. After the exuberance of the Kailash temple, their modest scale and subdued interiors lack vitality and inspiration, although some of the decorative carving is very fine. Only one of the group is of any real note. **Cave 32**, the **Indra Sabha** ("Indra's Assembly Hall"), is a miniature version of the Kailash temple. The lower of its two levels is plain and incomplete, but the upper storey is crammed with elaborate stonework, notably the ornate **pillars** and the two *tirthankaras* guarding the entrance to the central shrine. The naked figure of **Gomatesvara**, on the right, is fulfilling a vow of silence in the forest. He is so deeply immersed in meditation that creepers have grown up his legs, and animals, snakes and scorpions crawl around his feet. On the opposite doorway, **Parashvanath's** protective coat of cobra heads is another mark of a spiritual superman. Note the massive lotus carved on the ceiling, and the traces of the original blue **painting** around it. The shrine houses a Buddha-like icon **Mahavira**, the twenty-fourth *tirthankara* and founder of the Jain faith.

The Grishneshwar Mandir

Rising above the small village west of the caves, the cream-coloured *shikhara* of the eighteenth-century **Grishneshwar Mandir** pinpoints the location of one of India's oldest and most sacred deities. The *lingam* enshrined inside the temple's cavernous inner sanctum is one of the twelve "self-born" **jyotrilinga** ("*linga* of light"), thought to date back to the second century BC. Non-Hindus are allowed to join the queue for *darshan*, but men have to remove their shirts before entering the shrine itself.

Ellora practicalities

Most visitors use Aurangabad as a base for day-trips to the caves, **getting to Ellora** either via the half-hourly MSRTC buses or on one of MTDC's popular guided **tours** (see p.796). These tours are very rushed, however; if you prefer to take in the caves at a more leisurely pace and climb Daulatabad Hill, either spend the night at Ellora or leave Aurangabad early in the morning. If you wish to hire a guide, official multilingual ones are on hand to take you on a tour (1hr 30min–2hr) of the most interesting caves (groups of 1–4 Rs255, groups of 5–15 Rs380).

Ellora offers a couple of decent **places to stay**. The *Hotel Kailash* (☎02437/41043, ✆41067; ❸–❻) is a small campus of self-contained chalets insensitively positioned opposite the caves, and a few cheaper rooms by the road, with a restaurant and an a/c bar. They also have a limited number of **dorm beds** (Rs150) in an adjacent wing called the *Nataraj*. The only other accommodation is *Vijay's Rock Art Gallery and Restaurant* (❷), a little down the road from the *Kailash*. The rooms and washing facilities here are very basic, but the congenial guesthouse, run by a local painter for "visiting artists, writers and thinkers", is a nice place to stay if you've come to study the caves in any detail. You can also buy wonderful reproduction paintings of the Ajanta murals.

Tasty, moderately priced **food** is available at the MTDC restaurant. In addition to the usual veg and non-veg Indian dishes, they serve Chinese, good-value lunchtime thalis and cold beer – indoors under the fan or alfresco on the shady terrace. You can also order meals and filled rolls in the *Kailash's* slightly pricier *Heritage* restaurant, but their turnover is sluggish, especially during the week. Roadside *dhabas* opposite the bus stand sell *bhajis*, pakoras and other greasy snacks as well as inexpensive rice-plates – follow the rickshaw drivers who know the best ones.

Ajanta

Hewn from the near-vertical sides of a horseshoe-shaped ravine, deep in the semi-arid hills of the Deccan, the rock-cut caves at **AJANTA** occupy a site worthy of the spectacular ancient art they contain. Less than two centuries ago, this remote spot was known only to the local Bhil tribespeople; the shadowy entrances to its abandoned stone chambers lay buried deep under a thick blanket of creepers and jungle. The chance arrival in 1819 of a small detachment of scarlet-coated East India Company troops, however, brought the caves' obscurity to an abrupt end. Their **"discovery"** reads like an Indiana Jones screenplay. Led to the top of the precipitous bluff that overlooks the gorge by a young "half-wild" scout, the tiger-hunters spied, far below, what has now been identified as the facade of Cave 10 protruding through the dense foliage.

The gung-ho British soldiers had made one of the most sensational archeological finds of all time. Further exploration revealed a total of 28 colonnaded caves chiselled out of the chocolate-brown and grey basalt cliffs lining the River Waghora. More remarkable still were the exquisite and immaculately preserved **paintings** writhing over their interior surfaces. For, in addition to the phalanxes of stone Buddhas and other **sculpture** enshrined within them, Ajanta's excavations are adorned with a swirling profusion of multicoloured murals, depicting everything from battlefields to boudoirs, sailing ships to city streets and teeming animal-filled forests to snow-capped mountains. Even if you aren't wholly *au fait* with the narratives they portray, it's easy to see why these paintings rank among India's most beautiful treasures.

In spite of its comparative remoteness, Ajanta receives an extraordinary number of visitors. If you want to enjoy the site in anything close to its original serenity, avoid coming at a weekend or public holiday – it takes a fertile imagination indeed to picture Buddhist monks filing softly around the rough stone steps when riotous schoolkids and holiday-makers are clambering over them. The best **seasons to visit** are either during the monsoon, when the river is swollen and the verdant gorge reverberates with the sound of the crashing waterfalls, or during the cooler winter months between October and March. At other times, the relentless Deccan sun beating down on the bare south-facing rock can make a trip around Ajanta a real endurance test. Whenever you come, bring a hat, some shades, a strong **flashlight** and plenty of bottled drinking water.

Some history

Located close enough to the major trans-Deccan trade routes to ensure a steady supply of alms, yet far enough from civilization to preserve the peace and tranquillity necessary for meditation and prayer, Ajanta was an ideal location for the region's itinerant Buddhist monks to found their first permanent monasteries. Donative inscriptions indicate that its earliest cave excavations took place in the second century BC.

In its heyday, Ajanta sheltered more than two hundred monks, as well as a sizeable community of painters, sculptors and labourers employed in excavat-

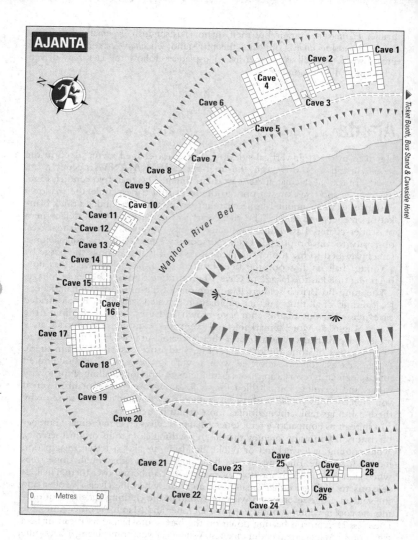

AJANTA

Cave 1
Cave 2
Cave 4
Cave 3
Cave 6
Cave 5
Cave 7
Cave 8
Cave 9
Cave 10
Cave 11
Cave 12
Cave 13
Cave 14
Cave 15
Cave 16
Cave 17
Cave 18
Cave 19
Cave 20
Cave 21
Cave 22
Cave 23
Cave 24
Cave 25
Cave 26
Cave 27
Cave 28

Waghora River Bed

N

0   Metres   50

ing and decorating the cells and sanctuaries. Some time in the seventh century, however, the site was abandoned – whether because of the growing popularity of nearby Ellora, or the threat posed by the resurgence of Hinduism, no one knows. By the eighth century, the complex lay deserted and forgotten, overlooked even by the Muslim iconoclasts who wrought such damage to the area's other sacred sites during the medieval era.

Had the fateful tiger-hunting expedition not appeared over the horizon in 1819, Ajanta might have languished under a shroud of vegetation to this day. Instead, its wonders have been pored over by more prying eyes than just about any other Indian monument outside the "golden triangle" of Delhi, Agra and Jaipur. Early attempts to document the amazing discovery, however, met with such little success that Ajanta has been associated with a sinister **curse**. In 1866, after spending 27 years faithfully copying the paintings from his field-camp nearby, the artist **Robert Gill** lost his entire collection when London's Crystal Palace burned to the ground. The same fate befell another batch of facsimiles in the 1870s, which went up in smoke with London's Victoria and Albert Museum, while the efforts of a Japanese team were dramatically foiled when their rice-paper impressions of Ajanta's sculpture were crushed in an earthquake. Even **restoration** work has been dogged with misfortune. In 1920, the Nizam of Hyderabad (who then ruled the region) employed a pair of Italian experts to patch up some of the more badly damaged paintings. Unfortunately, the varnish they used to seal the flakier fragments of plaster to the cave walls darkened and cracked over time, causing further irreparable deterioration.

Nowadays, the job of restoration has fallen to the Archaelogical Survey of India (ASI). Among measures to minimize the impact of the hundreds of visitors who daily trudge through is a ban on **flash photography**, and strict limits on the numbers allowed into a single cave at any given time – another reason to avoid weekends. Although further tourist development is being planned, the only commercialism to have hit Ajanta is the mushrooming postcard and souvenir stalls around the bus stand below the main entrance and the crystal-sellers who'll give you one as a present, then attach a hefty price tag. Just above the stand is a handy **left luggage** hut (ask for the "cloakroom") where you can stash bags while you look around, though note that the security guard knocks off at 5pm sharp.

For more information on the rock-cut caves of northwestern Deccan, see p.807.

The caves

On arrival at the Ajanta **caves**, head straight through the pack of postcard- and gem-wallahs in the small bazaar-cum-bus stand, to the admissions kiosk on the other side of the rise (daily 9am–5.30pm; Rs0.50), to buy your entry and all-important **light-tickets** (Rs5). An obvious path leads from there to the grand **Mahayana** *viharas*; if you'd prefer to see the caves in chronological order, however, start with the smaller **Hinayana** group of *chaitya* halls at the bottom of the river bend (caves 12, 10, 9 & 26), then work your way back up, via Cave 17. If you need help getting up the steps, sedan chair-porters (Rs150/hr), or *dhooli*-wallahs, stand in front of the stalls below. Official **guides** make a two-hour tour (groups of 1–4 Rs255, 5–15 Rs380) and can be arranged through the ticket office; most deliver an interesting spiel (it's difficult to follow the pictorial stories without them), but you may well feel like taking in the sights again afterwards, at a more leisurely pace.

Cave 1

Cave 1 contains some of the finest and stylistically most evolved paintings on the site. By the time work on it began, late in the fifth century, *viharas* served not only to shelter and feed the monks, but also as places of worship in their own right – hence the addition to the rows of cells lining the front and side walls of a central **shrine room**. In common with most Mahayana *viharas*, the extraordinary **murals** lining the walls and ceilings depict episodes from the birth story and former lives of the Buddha, the *Jatakas*. One of the most elaborate is the **Mahanjanaka**, which extends most of the way along the left-hand wall. This tells of a shipwrecked king who meets a solitary ascetic and decides to renounce all worldly attachments. On his return to his palace, his queen,

Cave painting techniques

The basic **painting techniques** used by the artists of Ajanta to transform the dull rock walls into lustrous kaleidoscopes of colour changed surprisingly little over the eight centuries the site was in use, from 200 BC to 650 AD. First, the rough-stone surfaces were primed with a six- to seven-centimetre coating of paste made from clay, cow-dung, and animal hair, strengthened with vegetable fibre. Next, a finer layer of smooth white lime was applied. Before this was dry, the artists quickly sketched the outlines of their pictures using red cinnabar, which they then filled in with a coating of *terre verte*. The **pigments**, all derived from natural water-soluble substances (kaolin chalk for white, lamp soot for black, glauconite for green, ochre for yellow and imported lapis lazuli for blue), were thickened with glue and added only after the undercoat was completely dry. Thus the Ajanta paintings are not, strictly speaking, frescoes (always executed on damp surfaces), but **tempera**. Finally, after they had been left to dry, the murals were painstakingly polished with a smooth stone to bring out their natural sheen.

The artists' only sources of **light** were oil-lamps and sunshine reflected into the caves by metal mirrors and pools of water (the external courtyards were flooded expressly for the purpose). Ironically, many of them were not even Buddhists, but Hindus employed by the royal courts of the day. Nevertheless, their extraordinary mastery of line, perspective and shading, which endows Ajanta's paintings with their characteristic other-worldly light, resulted in one of the great technical landmarks in Indian Buddhist art history.

with the help of a bevy of alluring dancing girls, unsuccessfully attempts to dissuade him. The last scene shows her husband leaving on a white horse, with a crowd of wailing courtesans in his wake.

Beyond the Mahanjanaka, left of the doorway into the main shrine, stands another masterpiece. **Padmapani**, the lotus-holding form of Avalokitesvara, is surrounded by an entourage of smaller attendants, divine musicians, lovers, monkeys and a peacock. His heavy almond eyes and languid hip-shot *tribhanga* (or "three-bend") pose exudes a distant and sublime calm. Opposite, flanking the right side of the doorway, is his counterpart, **Vajrapani**, the thunderbolt holder. Between them, these two *bodhisattvas* represent the dual aspects of Mahayana Buddhism: compassion and knowledge.

The real focal point of Cave 1, however, is the gigantic sculpted Buddha seated in the shrine room – the finest such figure in Ajanta. Using portable electric spotlights, guides love to demonstrate how the expression on the Buddha's exquisitely carved face changes according to where the light is held: sombre to the left, blissful to the right, and serene when the light source is shone from below. On the pedestal below the statue, look for the wheel, symbolizing *dharma*, Buddha's teachings, and the deer which stands for the sermon he preached at Sarnath (see p.355).

On the way out, you may be able to spot this cave's other famous *trompe l'oeil*, crowning one of the pillars (on the third pillar from the rear as you face the shrine): the figures of four, apparently separate stags which, on closer inspection, all share the same head.

Cave 2

Cave 2 is another, similarly impressive, Mahayana *vihara*, dating from the sixth century. Here the ceiling, which seems to sag like a tent roof, is decorated with complex floral patterns, including lotus and medallion motifs. The design clearly takes its cue from ancient Greek art – a legacy of Alexander the Great's foray into the subcontinent half a millennium earlier. Sculpted friezes in the small subsidiary shrine to the right of the main chapel centre on a well-endowed fertility goddess, **Hariti**, the infamous child-eating ogress. When the Buddha threatened to give her a taste of her own medicine by kidnapping *her* child, Hariti flew into a frenzy (upper right), but was subdued by the Buddha's teachings of compassion (upper left). Below, a schoolroom scene shows a teacher waving a cane at a class of unruly pupils.

The side walls teem with lively **paintings** of the *Jatakas* and other mythological episodes. A frieze on the left veranda shows the birth of the Buddha, emerging from under his mother's arm, and his conception when a white elephant appeared to her in a dream (bottom left). Nearby, is one of several scenes portraying the "miracle of a thousand Buddhas", in which the Buddha, to confound a party of heretics, is said to have multiplied himself a thousand times.

Caves 3 to 9

Caves 3, 4 and 7 hold little of interest, but take a quick look into **Cave 6**, a double-storeyed *vihara* with a finely carved doorjamb above its shrine room, a handful of octagonal pillars, and some peeling paintings above the entrances to its cells. Cave 8 is always closed; it contains the generator for the lights.

Cave 9, which dates from the first century BC, is the first *chaitya* you come to along the walkway. Resting in the half-light shed by a characteristic *peepal*-leaf-shaped window in the sculpted facade, the hemispherical **stupa**, with its inverted pyramidal reliquary, forms the devotional centrepiece of the 14m-long hall. The fragments of painting that remain, including the procession scene on the left wall, are mostly superimpositions over the top of earlier snake-deities – *nagarajas*.

Cave 10

Though partially collapsed, and marred by the unsightly wire meshing erected by the ASI to keep out bats, the facade of **Cave 10**, a second-century BC *chaitya* hall – the oldest and most impressive of its kind in the ravine – is still a grand sight. The cave's main highlights, however, are far smaller and more subdued. With the help of sunlight reflected from a mirror held by an attendant, you may be able to pick out the fading traces of painting along the left wall (now encased in glass). The scene in which a raja and his retinue approach a group of dancers and musicians surrounding a garlanded *bodhi* tree – a symbol of the Buddha (the Hinayanas preferred not to depict him figuratively) – is believed to be the earliest surviving Buddhist mural in India. Elsewhere on the wall is graffiti scrawled by the British soldiers who rediscovered the caves in 1819.

The apsidal-ended hall itself, divided by three rows of painted octagonal pillars, is dominated by a huge monolithic **stupa** at its far end. If there's no one else around, try out the *chaitya*'s amazing acoustics.

Cave 16

The next cave of interest, **Cave 16**, is another spectacular fifth-century *vihara*, with the famous painting known as the "**Dying Princess**" near the front of its left wall. The "princess" was actually a queen named **Sundari**, and she isn't dying, but fainting after hearing the news that her husband, King Nanda (Buddha's cousin), is about to renounce his throne to take up monastic orders. The opposite walls show events from Buddha's early life as **Siddhartha**.

Cave 17

Cave 17, dating from between the mid-fifth and early sixth centuries, boasts the best-preserved and most varied paintings in Ajanta. As with caves 1 and 2, only a limited number of visitors are allowed in at any one time. While you wait, have a look at the frescoes on the **veranda**. Above the door, eight seated Buddhas, including Maitreya, the Buddha-to-come, look down. To the left, an amorous princely couple share a last glass of wine before giving their worldly wealth away to the poor. The wall that forms the far left side of the veranda features fragments of an elaborate "Wheel of Life".

Inside the cave, the murals are, once more, dominated by the illustrations of the *Jatakas*, particularly those in which the Buddha takes the form of an animal to illustrate certain virtues. Running in a continuous frieze down the left aisle, the **Vishvantara Jataka** tells the story of a prince who was banished from the court by his father for giving away a magic rain-making elephant. Among the more poignant scenes in this long narrative is one where Vishvantara bids farewell to his queen in their four-poster bed before heading off to a hermitage in the forest. Nearby, on the wall to the left of the main shrine, is one of Ajanta's more gruesome highlights. In the **Sudasa Jataka**, a *bodhisattva* adopts the guise of a lioness to talk a prince out of eating his subjects. The artists have spared no detail, with gory illustrations of the cooking pots and chunks of human flesh being chopped up to put in them. Cannibalism is also the theme of the great **Simhala** frieze on the right-hand side of the cave. This relates the story of a merchant-adventurer and his band of mariners who, after being shipwrecked and washed ashore on a desert island, find themselves surrounded by voluptuous maidens. In a cruel twist, these beautiful women turn, by night, into a horde of blood-crazed, man-eating ogresses. Luckily for the castaways, a *bodhisattva* appears in the form of a horse to lead them into a victorious battle against the evil she-demons.

The pillar separating the *Simhala Jataka* from a smaller frieze, which shows how the Buddha tore out his eyes to give to a blind brahmin, holds an exquisite and much-celebrated portrait of a sultry, dark-skinned princess admiring herself in a mirror while her handmaidens and a female dwarf look on. The *chowkidars* will demonstrate how, when illuminated from the side, her iridescent eyes and jewellery glow like pearls against the brooding dark background.

Cave 19

Excavated during the mid-fifth century, when the age of Mahayana Buddhism was in full swing, **Cave 19** is indisputably Ajanta's most magnificent *chaitya* hall, its **facade** teeming with elaborate sculpture. On the columns flanking the walls, benign *bodhisattvas* in translucent robes are interspersed with meditating Buddhas, while on either side of the gracefully arched and pointed window, two pot-bellied, double-chinned demigods look smugly down. The penchant of the Mahayanas for theatrical luxuriance has been interpreted as a response to the concurrent rise of Brahmanism. This Hindu influence is even more manifest in the friezes that line the interior of the **porch**. On the left wall, crowned with a halo of cobra heads, the snake-king Nagaraja and his queen sit in a relaxed pose – reminiscent of the many Shiva and Parvati panels at Ellora, and of the indigenous snake-cult that formerly held sway here in the Waghora gorge.

Inside the hall, the faded frescoes are of less note than the sculpture around the tops of the pillars. The standing Buddha at the far end, another Mahayana innovation, is even more remarkable. Note the development from the stumpier stupas enshrined within the early *chaityas* (caves 9 & 10) to this more elon-

gated version. Its umbrellas, supported by angels and a vase of divine nectar, reach right up to the vaulted roof.

Caves 21 to 26

Caves 21 to 26 date from the seventh century, a couple of hundred years after the others, and form a separate group at the far end of the cliff. Apart from the unfinished **Cave 24**, whose roughly hacked trenches and pillars give an idea of how the original excavation was carried out here, the only one worth a close look is **Cave 26**. Envisaged on a similarly grand scale to the other large *chaitya*, Cave 19, this impressive hall was never completed. Nevertheless, the sculpture which the artisans had chiselled out here before they inexplicably downed tools is among the most vivid and dramatic at Ajanta. In the gloomy apse at the far end, the Buddha sits in front of a large cylindrical stupa ringed with *bodhisattvas*. In the "**Temptation of Mara**" frieze to his right (your left as you enter the cave), he appears again, this time impassively ensconced under a *peepal* tree as seven tantalizing sisters try to seduce him. Their father, the satanic Mara, watches from astride an elephant in the top left corner. The ruse to lead the Buddha astray fails, of course, eventually forcing the evil adversary and his daughters to retreat (bottom right). In contrast, the colossal image of **Parinirvarna**, Siddhartha reclining on his deathbed, along the opposite wall is a veritable pool of tranquillity. Check out the weeping and wailing mourners below, and the flying angels and musicians above, preparing to greet the sage as he drifts into nirvana. The soft sunlight diffusing gently from the doorway over Buddha's fine sensuously carved features completes the appropriately transcendent effect.

The viewpoint

The stiff thirty-minute climb to the "**viewpoint**" from where the British hunting party first spotted the Ajanta caves is well worth the effort – the panorama over the Waghora gorge and its surrounding walls of bare, flat-topped mountains is stunning. The easiest way to pick up the path is to head through the souvenir stalls outside the entrance to the caves and ford the river; alternatively, drop down the steps below caves 16 and 17 and follow the walkway until you reach a concrete footbridge. Turn left on the far side of the river, and then right when you see steps branching uphill. A right turn at the end of the bridge will take you further into the ravine, where there's an impressive waterfall. Don't attempt this during **monsoon**, though, as water levels can be dangerously high.

Ajanta practicalities

The only way of **getting to Ajanta,** unless you have your own transport, is by **bus**. Five daily MSRTC buses make the 100-minute climb into the hills from the nearest railhead at **Jalgaon**, 58km north. An equal number make the three-and-a-half hour road trip from **Aurangabad** 166km to the southwest, with a pit stop at the market town of **Shillod**. The last buses leave Ajanta for both Jalgaon and Aurangabad at 5.35pm. If you miss these, don't worry, a bus or Rs5–10 shared taxi to nearby **Fardapur** will put you on the main Aurangabad-Jalgaon bus route with half-hourly services each way. Provided you catch an early enough bus up here, it's possible to see the caves, grab a bite to eat, and then head off again in either direction. Alternatively, you could do the round trip from Aurangabad on one of the rushed **tours** (see p.796). There are also single daily services to and from Pune and Indore.

Limited **accommodation** is available in Ajanta proper – most visitors stay in Aurangabad, or Jalgaon, to catch a train early the following day. If you want to stay within striking distance of the caves, there's MTDC's heavily booked and slightly overpriced *Caveside Hotel* at the bus stand (℡02438/4226; ❸). Otherwise their *Holiday Resort* (℡02438/4230; ❹–❺), a few kilometres down the Jalgaon road in the village of **Fardapur**, has some tatty rooms with fans but no (much-needed) mosquito nets, or more expensive and comfortable modern ones; they also have a rock-bottom dorm (Rs50) if you don't mind sleeping on the floor. At the caves, the most popular places to **eat** are the two *dhabas* opposite the bus stand that serve Rs25 thalis and other snacks (both close at 7pm sharp). If they don't tickle your fancy, the only other option is the more upmarket restaurant inside the *Caveside Hotel* which serves veg and non-veg Punjabi dishes including thalis for Rs50–65.

Lonar

Few visitors get to the unique crater at **LONAR**, but those who do find this **meteorite-formed lake** an amazing and tranquil sight. Poor bus connections and limited accommodation mean that the site, although only 150km from Aurangabad, has avoided the horrors of modern tourist development that Ellora and Ajanta are beginning to suffer: ill-planned concrete tourist facilities, masses of souvenir shops, touts and car parks.

Lonar has always been a site of mystery; it is referred to as *Taratirth* in Hindu legend and was believed to have been formed by a shooting star. In fact, the **crater** was formed about 50,000 years ago when a fireball from space pierced the atmosphere and, after hitting the earth's crust at Lonar, buried itself deep below. The crater is the biggest of its kind in the world, with a diameter of 1800m and a depth of 170m, and it is also the only impact crater to occur in basalt rock. There have been a number of international scientific experiments carried out on the shallow lake and its environs in the basin of the crater, which have most notably discovered that the soil and rocks on the shores are magnetic and that the lake has a highly alkaline pH of 10.5. According to modern science, this should mean that no living organisms can exist in the water as it is too salty. However, some simple unicellular forms of blue-green algae have been identified in water samples, which potentially means that multicellular life could one day develop in the lake – evolution on earth, take two.

There is a steep **path** down to the lake beside the tourist bungalow. In the crater basin you emerge by a twelfth-century temple dedicated to Shiva after he slayed the demon Lonasura. The path turns right at the banana plantation, and follows the line of the shore to another medieval temple, home to two images of Surya (the sun god) and the daytime resting-place of herds of goats. Around the shores of the decidedly green lake, buffalo wallow, peacocks strut and other birdlife such as the greater flamingo, Indian moorhen and dusky reed warbler nestle in its reeds. Beyond the temple, the path virtually disappears but a bit of determined bush-bashing brings you out at a thirteenth-century Vaishnava shrine whose beautifully carved stone walls and pillars lie tumbledown and folorn. The path clearly climbs up by a river out of the crater at this point, past a *lingam* cast in stone to mark the place where Rama and Sita are said in the *Ramayana* to have bathed during their exile from Ayodhya.

Practicalities

The easiest way to get to Lonar is by **taxi** from Aurangabad or Jalgaon which from either costs around Rs1500 return for a day-trip or Rs2000 overnight. Otherwise, take the state **bus** either from Aurangabad to Jalna, then on to Sindkund Raja, and lastly change onto a bus for Lonar – though this takes five to eight hours. You can also go direct from Fardapur to Lonar on an early-morning bus.

The only **accommodation** at Lonar itself is at the *PWD Bungalow* (❶), where the MTDC rents out three rooms, though it may close down when their new resort opens – enquire about this at any MTDC office or resort. The MTDC *Holiday Resort* (see p.821) at Fardapur is the only other decent accommodation within striking distance.

Jalgaon

Straddling an important junction in the Central and Western Railway networks, as well as the main trans-Deccan trunk road, NH-6, **JALGAON** is a busy market town for the region's cotton and banana growers, and a key jumping-off point for travellers heading to or from the Ajanta caves, 58km south. Even though the town holds nothing of interest, you may find yourself obliged to hole up here to be well placed for a morning departure. If so, an early night with a good book should appeal considerably more than the dismal cafés and seedy permit-rooms (bars) outside the railway station.

Practicalities

Jalgaon is well served by main-line **trains** between Delhi, Calcutta and Mumbai, and convenient for most cities to the north on the Central Railway. Express services also pass through en route to join the Southeastern Railway at **Nagpur**.

Buses to Indore (257km north) and Pune (336km south) leave from the busy MSRTC bus stand, a ten-minute rickshaw ride across town from the railway station. Uncle Travels, opposite the *Amram Guest House* on Station Road, also operates luxury overnight video buses to Indore (depart 9.30pm; 8hr), Pune (depart 9.30pm; 9hr) and Mumbai (depart 9pm; 10hr 30min). If you're heading to **Ajanta**, the fastest bus is the half-hourly service to **Aurangabad**, 166km south, five of which pass through Ajanta, and the remainder stopping at **Fardapur**, a few kilometres and a Rs5 shared taxi or local bus ride away.

You shouldn't have any difficulty finding **accommodation**. If you're not too squeamish about dirty toilets and a dawn chorus of throat-clearing, you could try the **retiring rooms**, above platform 1 at the railway station. As well as the usual four- to six-bed dorms (Rs150), some more expensive but good-value rooms (❷) are tacked on the side. The rest of Jalgaon's places to stay are within easy walking distance, with a number of cheap lodges around the square at the station's entrance and along the main street, Station Road. *Amram Guest House*, Station Road (℡0257/226549; ❸) is comfortable, with reasonably clean – if cramped – singles and doubles, fresh sheets, TVs, fans and some attached shower-toilets. Left off Station Road down a little side street, the a/c *Chandan Hotel* (℡0257/226192; ❸–❹) offers plain, clean rooms. The best mid-range option, however, has to be the very spruce *Plaza Hotel*, two minutes from the station on the left side of Station Road (℡0257/227354; ❸). Its economy rooms are particularly good, with immaculate, tiled rooms, fans and 24-hour checkout; pricier rooms come with cable TV, and they'll provide tea in your room if you're leaving early in the morning. The Jain owners also act as an unofficial tourist office and have a wealth of local information, including a decent map. If these are all full, or if you're looking for more comfort, carry on to the roundabout at the end of Station Road, where the *Tourist Resort* (☎0257/225192; ❸–❻) has rooms ranging from simple economy singles to a/c suites. For rock-bottom prices, the cheapest (and scummiest) place is *Rakash's Guest House* (☎0257/221007; ❶) just past the *Plaza Hotel*.

There's no better place to **eat** than the *Anjali*, immediately outside the station on the right. This small, spotless, no-smoking restaurant opens at 7am for breakfast and does a good range of pure-veg snacks and south Indian and Punjabi meals at other times of the day, including copious thalis – though note that the food here is very spicy. If you fancy something meaty (or not as hot), the north Indian *Hotel Arya* is a five-minute walk – turn left at the roundabout at the top of Station Road, carry on past the **internet café** (Mon–Sat 8.30am–10pm; Rs30/hr) and *Arya Thali* (reasonable and inexpensive thalis), take the first left and it's on the left. For Chinese food, the *Snowbell*, opposite the *Hotel Plaza*, has the best in town, though it's only open in the evenings.

Nasik and around

Lying at the head of the main pass through the dark eroded hills of the Western Ghats, **NASIK** makes an interesting stopover on the lengthy journey to or from Mumbai, 187km southwest. From the grim barrage of industrial estates, hoardings, *dhabas* and general conurbation creeping along its ring road, you'd be forgiven for thinking the city holds no interest for anyone other than truckers and travelling salesmen. However, this is one of the four sites of the world's largest religious gatherings, the **Kumbh Mela**, held at different locations in India every three years (see p.329); Nasik holds the next one in late 2003. Millions of pilgrims will descend on the temple and *ghat*-lined banks of the **River Godavari**, to take a purifying dip at one of the most auspicious moments in the Hindu calendar.

Even outside festival times, the riverside sees plenty of action. According to the *Ramayana*, Nasik was where Rama – Vishnu in human form – his brother Lakshmana, and wife Sita lived during their exile from Ayodhya, and the arch-demon Ravana carried off Sita from here in an aerial chariot to his kingdom, Lanka, in the far south. The scene of such episodes forms the core of the busy pilgrimage circuit – a vibrant enclave packed with religious specialists, beggars, *sadhus* and street vendors touting puja paraphernalia. However, Nasik has a surprising dearth of historical buildings – even the famous temples beside the Godavari only date from the **Maratha era** of the eighteenth century. Its only real monuments are the rock-cut caves at nearby **Pandav Lena**. Excavated at the peak of Buddhist achievement on the Deccan, these two-thousand-year-old cells hark back to the days when, as capital of the powerful **Satavahana** dynasty, Nasik dominated the all-important trade routes linking the Ganges plains with the ports to the west.

Today, the city continues to prosper, though the high profile of recently relocated Mumbai businesses has done little to dampen its religious fervour. If anything, the extra cash has come as a boon for the local *pujaris*. Newly inaugurated temples, dripping with fairy lights and equipped with powerful hi-fi systems, stand cheek by jowl with glitzy sari emporia, shopping arcades and ice-cream parlours.

From Nasik, you can make an interesting day-trip to the highly auspicious village of **Trimbak**, where hordes of Shaivite Hindu pilgrims come to seek the nectar of immortality, spilt by Vishnu whilst in battle. A steep climb up from Trimbak takes you to **Brahmagiri**, the source of the holy Godavari River.

The City

After the hectic main streets of Nasik's commercial centre, the more colourful **riverbank** area comes as something of a surprise. Turn down any of the narrow back lanes behind MG Road and you'll emerge eventually from the maze of dilapidated wooden houses and balconies of the old quarter at the open ground lining the Godavari (pronounced God*av*ri) River. The small stretch on the opposite bank, between the Holkar and Santar Gardi Mahara bridges, is the focal point. In 1991, during the Kumbh Mela, an estimated 3.5 million devotees converged here to bathe; usually, however, the site plays host to more secular pursuits, as *dhobi*-wallahs gather on the *ghats* each morning to thump away at soapy bundles, and shoppers haggle over the produce piled neatly under rows of raffia sunshades at the **riverside market**.

South of the market, below the Ram Situ footbridge, lies the eighteenth-century **Naro Sankar Mandir**. Built by the Marathas, this distinctive dark-stoned Shiva temple has some lively sculpture on the roof of its *mandapa*, and a bustling *devi* shrine. Originally, it was known as the Rameshvara Mandir; the name was changed when a local warrior, Sardar Naroshakar, installed an enormous church bell which he'd plundered from the Portuguese after their defeat at the battle of Vasai (Bassein) in 1739. The now clapper-less bell is housed in a pavilion set in the wall of the western enclosure.

Ram Kund

A hundred metres further west along the riverbank, past the market and a lurid sky-blue-and-orange Hanuman, the **Ram Kund** is the reason most people come to Nasik. Surrounded by concrete viewing towers (built to alleviate the crush at the big *melas*), it looks more like an overcrowded municipal swimming pool than one of India's most ancient sacred places. Yet for the thousands of devout Hindus who avail themselves of its purifying properties each day, these murky waters are the holiest of holies.

Among the Ram Kund's more arcane attributes is its capacity to dissolve bones – a trick that has earned it the epithet of "**Astivilaya Tirth**" or "Bone Immersion Tank". Some of the more celebrated remains that have allegedly ended up here are those of King Dasharatha of Ayodhya (Rama's father), Jawaharlal Nehru, his daughter Indira Gandhi, her son Rajiv, and a host of saints, musicians and movie stars.

Kala Ram Mandir

Follow the street opposite Ram Kund up the hill, past assorted ashrams and *dharamshalas*, to arrive at the city's second most important sacred site, the area around the **Kala Ram Mandir**, or "Black Rama Temple". Among the well-known episodes from the *Ramayana* to occur here was the event that led to Sita's abduction, when Lakshmana sliced off the nose of Ravana's sister after she had tried to seduce Rama by taking the form of a voluptuous princess. Sita's cave, or **Gumpha**, a tiny grotto known in the *Ramayana* as *Parnakuti* ("Smallest Hut"), is just off the square. On removal of shoes and payment of a small donation, you can squeeze into it to see where Sita spent all those lonesome hours while the boys were off doing battle with the forces of darkness and destruction.

The **Kala Ram temple** itself, at the bottom of the square, houses unusual jet-black deities of Rama, Sita and Lakshmana; these are very popular with visiting pilgrims, as access is free from all caste restrictions. The best time to visit is around sunset, after evening puja, when a crowd, mostly of women, gathers in the courtyard to listen to a traditional storyteller recount tales from the *Ramayana* and other epics.

Pandav Lena

Halfway up one of the precipitous conical hills that overlook the Mumbai–Agra road, 8km southwest of Nasik, is a small group of 24 rock-cut caves, some dating from the first century BC. The **Pandav Lena** site is famous for its well-preserved inscriptions in the ancient Pali language, and fine ancient stone sculpture.

Access to Pandav Lena is via a steep and uneven path. The caves themselves are numbered from right to left in chronological order – start with **Cave 18**, left of the entrance. This small *chaitya* hall has a striking facade, with two leaf-shaped arches encasing auspicious Buddhist symbols. The two monastery caves, *viharas*, to either side, reached by flights of stone steps complete with their original railings, contain carved Buddhas – later additions made during the sixth century. Two further noteworthy caves are over on the other side of the group. **Caves 3** and **10**, both *viharas* dating from the second century AD, have superb stone carvings, as well as the famed **Pali inscriptions** above their doorways. These set out in elaborate detail the caves' benefactors (among them dynastic rulers, wealthy landowners, a writer and even a local Hindu worthy), as well as the complex financial provisions made for the monks who lived here.

The most straightforward way of **getting to Pandav Lena** without your own vehicle is by auto-rickshaw (less than Rs50 each way) – trying to get on one of the packed buses at the bus stand can be difficult.

Practicalities

Buses from Mumbai pull in at the **Mahamarga bus stand**, a ten-minute rickshaw ride from the city centre. Aurangabad buses terminate at the chaotic central **City bus stand**, an easy walk from several cheap hotels and restaurants. Arrival by train is more problematic, as the **railway station**, on Nasik Road, lies 8km southeast. Buses meet incoming trains, but they tend to be sporadic or packed. Luckily, there is no shortage of shared taxis and auto-rickshaws. If you plan to leave Nasik by train, particularly at a weekend when the city booking counter, off MG Road (Mon–Fri 10am–5pm) is closed, reserve your outward ticket on arrival.

Predictably for a city that sees so few foreign visitors, the MTDC **tourist office**, near the golf course on Old Agra Road (Mon–Fri 10am–5pm; ☎0752/70059) is welcoming, but not worth the trouble to find. Their daily "Darshan Tour" (7.30am–3pm; Rs80) of the city and its environs will only appeal to those with a passion for ferroconcrete temple architecture. To **change money**, the State Bank of India (Mon–Fri 10am–2pm, Sat 10am–noon) is just up from the City bus stand on Swami Vivekanand Road. The **GPO** is around the corner on Trimbak Road. **Internet** access is available at Shree Laxmi Communications (daily 8am–10pm; Rs40/hr), near the *Hotel Basera*.

Accommodation

Most of Nasik's **hotels** are pitched at middle-class Mumbai business travellers. The few noteworthy exceptions are the lodge-style budget places around the City bus stand *chowk*. These, however, tend to fill up early, soon after their noon checkout times.

Basera, Sivaji Road ☎0253/575616. Very close to the City bus stand. Airy, comfortable rooms, all with hot water and windows and some a/c. Added attractions are its astrology and palm readings. ❸–❹

Padma, Sharampur Road ☎0253/576837. Directly opposite the City bus stand. Safe, clean and convenient with attached restaurant and permit room. All rooms have attached bathrooms and hot water 6–9am. ❹

Panchavati, 430 Vakil Wadi ☎0253/578771, ℻571823. Nasik's largest hotel, right in the middle of town, including three restaurants and a "Mexican-style" saloon bar. Also equipped with Jacuzzi, sauna, foreign exchange and room service. ❻–❼

Panchavati Yatri, 430 Vakil Wadi ☎0253/579031, ℻577869. Good-value and slightly cheaper wing of the *Panchavati Hotel* with 24hr coffee shop, bar and an excellent veg restaurant. Some a/c rooms. ❺–❻

Raj Mahal Lodge, Sharampur Road ☎0253/72880. Across the road from the City bus stand. Very basic, though neat and clean. All rooms have hot water and TVs. The best-value budget hotel. ❹

Eating and drinking

By and large, Nasik's best-value **meals** are to be had in its traditional "keep it coming" thali restaurants. While they may not always be the cheapest option, for less than the price of a beer you can enjoy carefully prepared and freshly cooked food, often including such regional specialities as *bajra* (wholemeal *rotis*) and *bakri* (hot oatmeal biscuits), together with a plethora of tasty vegetable, pulse and lentil dishes. The city's religious associations tend to mean that meat and alcohol are rarer than elsewhere in Maharashtra, but most of the larger hotels have bars and restaurants with permits.

Baraka, opposite *Basera Hotel*. Decked out like the inside of a desert tent, this place has mid-price veg and especially non-veg Mughlai and northern dishes, all served in copper *baltis*. Best non-veg option within walking distance of the bus station.

Dhaba, *Panchavati Hotel*, Vakil Wadi. Classy Rajasthani-style thalis. Popular with families.

Pangat, *Panchavati Yatri Hotel*, Vakil Wadi. Mild but mouthwatering veg thalis at reasonable prices in pseudo-traditional Maharashtran ambience (mud walls and murals). Very good value.

Samrat, Swami Vivekanand Road. Well-known thali joint, five minutes from the City bus stand, doing a brisk trade in moderately priced, quality Gujarati food.

Shipla, near the *Panchavati Hotel*, Vakil Wadi. A garden restaurant that offers a small amount of peace and respite amidst the chaos; the usual range of veg and non-veg, Chinese and particularly good Punjabi tandoori items.

Suruchi, under *Basera Hotel*, Sivaji Road. Cheap, clean, no-nonsense, south Indian fast-food café that also serves spicy snacks and cold drinks. Full of crowds of office workers at lunch. Family/ladies room upstairs.

Trimbak (Trimbakeshwar)

Crouched in the shadow of the Western Ghats, 10km west of Nasik, **TRIM-BAK** – literally "Three-Eyed" in Marathi, another name for Lord Shiva – is yet another place of great significance for Hindus. This was the exact spot where one of the four infamous drops of immortality-giving *amrit* nectar fell to earth from the *kumbh* vessel during the struggle between Vishnu's vehicle Garuda and the Demons – the mythological origin of the Kumbh Mela (see p.329). Trimbak is also near the source of one of India's longest and most sacred rivers, the **Godavari**; the spring can be reached via an ancient pilgrim-trail that cuts through a cleft in an awesome, guano-splashed cliff face. En route you pass colourful wayside shrines and a ruined **fort** (see below).

Make your way down the main street, past ramshackle shops selling vermilion powder and strings of wooden beads, to the entrance of the **Trimbakeshwar Mandir**. Numbering among India's most sacred centres for Shiva worship (it houses one of the twelve "self-born" *jyotrilinga* – see Contexts), the temple is unfortunately closed to non-Hindus. Its impressive eighteenth-century *shikhara* (tower), however, can also be glimpsed from the backstreets nearby. Close to the temple, the **Kushawarth Tirth** is a small, stone-lined tank said to contain Ganges water. Its name is thought to derive from the *kush* grass used in puja ceremonies that once grew in profusion around it. Although the present *ghats* and temple date from 1750, myths relating to the Kushawarth Tirth occur in the *Puranas*, so it may have been used for 2500 years.

The Brahmagiri hike

The round trip to **Brahmagiri**, the source of the Godavari, takes between two and three hours. It's a strenuous walk, particularly in the heat, so make sure you take adequate water. From the trailhead at the bottom of the village, the way is paved and stepped as far as the first level outcrop, where there are some welcome chai stalls and a small hamlet. Beyond that, either turn left after the last group of huts and follow the dirt trail through the woods to the foot of the **rock-cut steps** (20min), or continue straight on, to the three **shrines** clinging to the base of the cliff above. The first is dedicated to the goddess Ganga, the second – a cave containing 108 *linga* – to Shankar (Shiva), and the third to the sage Gautama Rishi, whose hermitage this once was.

The steps climb 550m above Trimbak to the remains of **Anjeri Fort** – a site that was, over the years, roughed up by the armies of both Shah Jahan and Aurangzeb before it fell into the hands of Shaha-ji Raj (father of the legendary rebel-leader Sivaji). The **source** itself is another twenty minutes further on, across **Brahmagiri Hill**, in the otherwise unremarkable Gaumukhu ("Mouth of the Cow") temple. From its rather unimpressive origins this paltry trickle somehow gathers sufficient momentum to flow for nearly 1000km east across the entire Deccan plateau to the Bay of Bengal.

Practicalities

Getting to Trimbak from Nasik is easy. Hourly **buses** leave from the depot opposite the main City bus stand (45min). To return you can catch a bus (until around 8pm), or one of the shared **taxis** that wait outside Trimbak bus stand; there's no difference in price as long as the car is full.

Although Trimbak makes an easy day-trip from Nasik, it's a peaceful and atmospheric place to spend a night, with plenty of basic pilgrim **accommodation**. The MTDC *Tourist Bungalow* (☎0259/33143; ❸) opposite the start of the Brahmagiri path is the best option, with scruffy (but peaceful) doubles with attached bathrooms and cheap dorm beds. In the unlikely event of it being full, head for the equally shabby *Alpobatchet Bhavan Rest House* (②) just across the *ghat*.

For **food**, you're more or less limited to one of the two restaurants on the main street which both serve adequate thalis and north Indian dishes. There's also internet access at *RajNet Café* (8am–10pm; Rs30/hr) towards the top of the main street.

Nagpur and around

Capital of the "land of oranges" and geographically at the virtual centre of India, **NAGPUR** is the focus of government attempts to develop industry in the remote and tribal northeastern corner of Maharashtra – most foreigners in the city are there for business rather than aesthetic purposes. The trickle of visitors who do stop here tend to head straight for the Gandhian ashrams at **Sevagram** and **Paunar**, near **Wardha** only 77km southwest, for a retreat in an idyllic village or to spend some time studying the works and ideas of the Mahatma. To get really off the beaten track for a day, head for the stark white hilltop temple complex at **Ramtek**, a mere ninety-minute bus ride northeast of Nagpur.

The Town

This site, on the banks of the River Nag, was first occupied in the tenth century by aboriginal Gonds, but Nagpur itself was founded by a family of militaristic local Hindu rulers, the Bhonslas, midway through the eighteenth century. In 1853, the Bhonslas fell foul of Lord Dalhousie's "Principle of Lapse" (a grossly iniquitous law which gave the British the right to take over any native state whose ruler died without a male heir), and Nagpur became the capital of the Central Provinces. Today, it's a thriving industrial and commercial centre, with a surprisingly affluent, easy-going and uncongested feel for a city of more than a million people. Nagpur's most prominent landmark, the **Sitabuldi Fort**, stands in the heart of the city, on a saddle between two low hills above the railway station. Strengthened by the British in the wake of the 1857 Mutiny, its ramparts and monuments were later annexed by the Indian army and are now closed to the public. Further reminders of colonial days survive in the **Civil Lines** area, immediately north and west of Sitabuldi Hill. The grand civic buildings and bungalows from which the British Commissioner administered the vast Central Provinces region (except in midsummer, when he and his legions of *burra-sahibs* decamped to Pachmarhi – see p.445) today house the university and government offices.

If you have an evening to fill in Nagpur, take an auto-rickshaw out to the **Ambazari Bagh**, the large artificial lake and gardens 5km southwest of the railway station, for a row and a chai at its waterside cafés.

Practicalities

Nagpur's busy central mainline **railway station**, Nagpur Junction, is a short auto-rickshaw ride from the main hotel and market districts along Central Ave. MSRTC **buses** pull in at the State bus stand, a further 1500m southeast of the railway station. Buses to and from Madhya Pradesh use the smaller MPSRTC bus stand, five minutes' walk south down the main road outside the station.

The MTDC **tourist office** (10am–6pm; ☏0712/529325) opposite the *Hardeo Hotel* on Dr Munje Margi Road, can book other MTDC accommodation but will disappoint if you're seeking specific information relating to Nagpur. At the helpful MPTDC **tourist office**, on the fourth floor of the Lokmat Building, Wardha Road (Mon–Fri 10am–5pm; 0712/523324), you can book accommodation for Pachmarhi (see p.405) and for Kanha National Park (see p.489) – though it'll take two days unless you pay Rs50 to phone Bhopal (in which case they can do it within the hour). The **GPO** (Mon–Sat 10am–6pm) is on Palm Road, in the Civil Lines, 4km west of the centre. **Banks** that deal in foreign exchange include the State Bank of India (Mon–Fri 10.30am–2.30pm, Sat 10.30am–12.30pm) on Kingsway, near the railway station.

Accommodation

Most of Nagpur's **places to stay** are across the big railway bridge east of the station, along **Central Avenue**, or southwest of the fort around **Sitabuldi**, in the central bazaar. The station also has cheap **retiring rooms** (Rs60–80).

Blue Diamond, 113 Central Ave, Dosar Chowk ☏0712/727460, ℻559534, ℯbluediamond @nagpurkhoj.com. Cheap, dingy and near the station. All rooms have cable TV, a/c, attached bathrooms and "peep-out" balconies. 24-hour checkout. ❸–❹

Blue Moon, Central Ave ☏0712/726061, ℻727591. Nearest the station and definitely the least seedy of the cheaper hotels; cleanish and friendly with large doubles. ❸–❹

Centre Point, 24 Central Bazaar Rd ☏0712/520910, ℻523093, ℯhcpngo@nagpur.net.in. The most established of Nagpur's top hotels, with all the trimmings, including a pool. ❼

Hardeo, Dr Munje Margi Marg, Sitabuldi

☏0712/529115, ℻534885. Fairly new, three-star hotel in city centre. Quality restaurant, a/c rooms, bar and 24hr coffee shop. Recommended. ❽

Jagson's Regency, Wardha Rd ☏0712/228120, ℻224524. Modern luxury hotel next to the airport, boasting a rooftop restaurant, shopping arcade, gym and pool. 24-hour checkout. ❽–❾

Pal Palace, 25 Central Ave ☏0712/724725, ℻722337. Clean, comfortable and spacious rooms, some a/c, in slick and central three-star. Foreign exchange facility. ❻–❼

Skylark, 119 Central Ave ☏0712/724654. Close to railway station and best value in its class, with cable TV in all rooms and a good restaurant. Some credit cards accepted. ❹

Eating

While Nagpur's swish hotels, such as the *Hardeo* and *Jagson's Regency*, boast the majority of its top gourmet restaurants, a number of smaller, less pretentious **places to eat** around Central Avenue and Sitabuldi offer excellent food at a fraction of the cost.

Continental, Central Ave. Low light, lurid decor, and a good selection of inexpensive spicy (mainly meaty) Indian food and chilled beer. Some veg options too.

Naivedhyam, off Rani Jhansi Chowk, Sitabuldi. Respectable first-floor family restaurant serving delicious veg food to a background of Hindi-Hawaiian music and fish tanks.

Parnakuti, North Ambhajari Road, Daga Layout, on the outskirts near the lake. Attractive restaurant noted for rustic decor and authentic, mouthwatering mid-priced Maharashtran cooking. Hard to find but well worth it.

Shivraj, Central Avenue, near *Blue Moon*. Tasty and cheap South Indian snacks and thalis, especially good for breakfast as it opens at 7am. Recommended.

Ramtek

The picturesque cluster of whitewashed hilltop temples and shrines at **RAMTEK**, 40km northeast of Nagpur on the main Jabalpur road (NH-7), is one of those mysterious, alluring apparitions spied from afar on long journeys through central India. Few travellers take the trouble to visit here – a busy year sees just five hundred foreigners. According to the *Ramayana*, this craggy, scrub-strewn outcrop, marooned in a sea of yellowing wheat fields, was yet another spot where Rama, Sita and Lakshmana paused on their way back from Lanka. It is also allegedly the place where the greatest-ever Sanskrit poet and playwright, **Kalidasa**, penned the fifth-century *Meghdoota*, "the Cloud Messenger". Although few traces of these ancient times have survived (most of Ramtek's temples date from the eighteenth century), the site's old paved pilgrim trails, sacred lake, tumbledown shrines and fine views across the endless plains more than live up to its distant promise.

Buses from Nagpur go directly up to **Ram Mandir** (the temple complex) or stop short at Ramtek town. Ramtek's bus stand is 2km from the central market square, **Gandhi Chowk**, which is most easily reached in a shared auto-rickshaw (Rs5). Once in the bazaar, head past the sweet stalls to the lane leading out of its top right-hand corner. At the T-junction, bear right and follow the track through the houses until it reaches open grazing land, on the far side of which a flight of stone steps climbs steeply up the rocky, south-facing side of Ramtek hill. The pathway eventually brings you out at a raised courtyard in front of the main entrance to the **temple complex**. Built in 1740 by Raghoji I, the Bhonsla ruler of Nagpur, it stands on the site of an earlier structure erected between the fourth and fifth centuries, of which only three small sandstone shrines remain.

The best **views** are to be had from the small onion-domed belvederes and whitewashed pavilions that surmount the flat roofs and battlements encircling the inner courtyard. To the southwest, you look out over the cluttered jumble of Ramtek town to the shining blue irrigation tanks on its outskirts, while the panorama in the other direction takes in a vast expanse of dead-flat and dusty wheat fields peppered with the occasional coppice of trees. At puja times, this is a good vantage point from which to watch the temple *pujaris* doing their rounds of the various shrines, ringing bells and waving smoky oil lamps before the deities.

Ambala Lake

Another of Ramtek's sacred sites is **Ambala Lake**, a holy bathing tank 1500m on foot from the hilltop. To pick up the flagstone pathway that leads down to it, head along the concourse opposite the temple's main entrance porch to the edge of the plateau. From here, either turn left towards the small **Trivikarma Krishna temple**, clinging to the north slope of the hill, or continue down the main pilgrims' trail to the **lake**, which lies at the bottom of the gully, enfolded by a spur of parched brown hills. Its main attractions, at least for the shaven-headed pilgrims who make their way here in rented mini-vans for a *dhoti*-soaking dip in its holy waters, are the temples and *ghats* clinging to its muddy banks. More energetic visitors may wish to combine a look with a *parikama*, or circular **tour** of the tank, taking in the semi-derelict cenotaphs and weed-choked shrines scattered along the more tranquil north and western shores. A rickshaw (Rs15) will get you back to Gandhi Chowk – the drivers hang around by the chai shop near the entrance.

Practicalities

Direct **buses** leave **Nagpur** (MSRTC stand) every hour for the hour-long trip to Ramtek. Long-distance MPSRTC buses also pass by en route to and from **Jabalpur**, although these will dump you on the main road, 3km from town. If

11

you don't feel like hiking up to the temple, **auto-rickshaws** will whisk you up from the town bus stand via Ambala Lake for around Rs50. A pleasant alternative to these are bicycles which are available for rent near the bus stand (Rs5/hr, no deposit). Ramtek's **railway** station, 4km from the town centre, connects with Nagpur, but this service takes longer than the bus.

Apart from the mosquito-infested pilgrims' *dharamshalas* and ashrams around Ambala Lake, the only accommodation near the sights is the newly privatized MTDC *Resort* (☎07114/55620; ❷–❹) on the hill beside the main temple complex, offering simple but clean self-contained rooms and a six-person dorm (Rs70). Otherwise, there are more basic en-suite rooms just next to the bus stand towards the centre of town (no sign in English or phone; ❶). **Food** and snacks are available at the MTDC resort for residents and nonresidents alike, or there are a couple of basic *dhabas* opposite the bus stand and the *Shakti Restaurant* in Nehru Chowk (near Gandhi Chowk) which is primarily the town bar, but can eventually rustle up some food – ask what they can do straight away or you'll literally wait hours for them to get it from an out-of-town hotel.

Sevagram

SEVAGRAM, Gandhi's model "Village of Service", is set deep in the serene Maharashtran countryside, 9km from the railroad town of **Wardha**. The Mahatma moved here from his former ashram at Sabarmati in Gujarat during the monsoon of 1936, on the invitation of his friend Seth Jamnalal Bajaj. Right at the centre of the subcontinent, within easy reach of the Central Railway, it made an ideal headquarters for the national, nonviolent *Satyagraha* movement, combining seclusion with the easy access to other parts of the country Gandhi needed in order to carry out his political activities.

These days, the small settlement is a cross between a museum and living centre for the promulgation of Gandhian philosophies. Interested visitors are welcome to spend a couple of days here, helping in the fields, attending discussions and prayer meetings (daily 4.45am, 10am & 6pm; bring mosquito repellent for the last), and learning the dying art of hand-spinning. The older ashramites, or **sadhaks**, are veritable founts of wisdom when it comes to the words of their guru, Gandhiji.

The ashram
Named after the Mahatma's wife, the **Kasturba Gandhi Hospital**, on the corner of the main road, was set up by the ashram to provide cut-price health care for local farming communities. From the hospital, a short walk down the lane to the right takes you past fields and farmland to the **visitors' centre** (Sun–Fri 9am–12.30pm & 2–5.30pm), with its photos and documents relating to Gandhi's life.

The real focal point of the ashram is the main **compound** on the left side of the lane. These modest rustic huts, with two-tiered terracotta roofs, smooth mud walls and shady courtyards, have altered little since Gandhi and his disciples lived here in the last years of the Independence struggle. Elderly men and women in simple handmade cotton clothes sit crosslegged on the wide verandas, spinning thread and singing devotional songs, to the mild amusement of visitors from the city who look on with a peculiar mixture of respect for the Mahatma's memory and disdain for those who keep it alive in this way. The first hut along the path has been converted into a small shop selling *khadi* goods and books about Gandhi. Nearby, the **Adi Niwas** was the Mahatma's first home in Sevagram. The interior of the **Bapu Kuti** opposite, Gandhi's main residence, has been kept exactly as it was in the 1930s, complete with its original bed, massage table and the few luxuries Gandhi permitted himself: amongst other things, the famous pair of tiny round specs, a spittoon and his beloved three brass monkeys.

Elsewhere, the compound holds the Mahatma's **secretariat**, or correspondence room, which enshrines a phone installed by the British as a pre-Independence "hot-line"; the **Ba–Kuti**, where Kasturba lived; the **Parchure Kuti**, home of the Sanskrit scholar Shri Parchure Shashtri (the Mahatma's devotion to this close friend, a leprosy sufferer, did much to de-stigmatize the disease in India); and the **Akiri Niwas**, or "Final Home", where Gandhi stayed before leaving Sevagram for the last time.

Practicalities

Half-hourly, jam-packed local **buses** run from **Wardha** – on the Central Railway and accessible from Mumbai (759km) – to the crossroads outside the Kasturba Gandhi Hospital, from where it's a two-kilometre walk to the ashram. Do yourself a favour and catch a shared taxi (Rs10) from outside the chaotic bus stand. There are frequent "express" buses from Nagpur's MSRTC bus stand, 77km northeast, to Wardha (2hr).

Accommodation is limited to the ashram's own *Yatri Niwas* (☎07125/2172; donations) a basic but spotless hostel for those staying at the ashram – it is not really a hotel, but phone to see what they have. If you decide to stay and learn something of Gandhi and the philosphy of nonviolence, you can sleep and eat here for no charge, though you'll be expected to do a couple of hours communal work a day. The only other place to stay nearby, MTDC's *Tourist Hotel* in Wardha (☎07152/43872; ❸), has a dozen largish, self-contained rooms. 24-hour checkout; reserve in advance at any MTDC tourist office.

Paunar

Crowning a low hillock overlooking a rocky riverbank at **PAUNAR**, 10km south of Wardha on the Nagpur Road, Vinoba **Bhave's** ashram has an altogether more dynamic feel than its more famous cousin at Sevagram. Bhave, a close friend and disciple of Gandhi, best remembered for his successful Bhoondan or "**land gift**" campaign to persuade wealthy landowners to hand over farmland to the poor, founded the ashram in 1938 to develop the concept of **swarajya**, or "self-sufficiency". Consequently, organic gardening, milk production, spinning and weaving have an even higher profile here than the regular meditation, prayer and yoga sessions. Another difference between this institution and the one up the road is that the *sadhaks* here are almost all female.

The ashram's living quarters, painted the pale blue worn by most of its inhabitants, are arranged like cloisters around an attractive square courtyard. At the far end, Bhave's old **room** is now a shrine, its bare interior enlivened by fresh marigolds and incense. Stone steps lead down from the upper level to a small terrace looking out over the **ghats** where two small memorials mark the spots where a handful of Gandhi's, and later Bhave's ashes were scattered onto the river: Gandhi's is the circular plinth at the end of the long, narrow jetty, Bhave's the brass urn on the small stupa-shaped dome to the right. Every year on February 12, the *ghats*, which are immersed by floods for four months during the monsoon, are inundated with half a million people who come here to mark the anniversary of Gandhi's death.

Paunar can be reached by **bus** from either Nagpur (67km) or Wardha by jumping off at the old stone bridge near the ashram. Alternatively, you can **walk** the 3km from Sevagram. The path, a cart track that runs over the hill opposite the hospital crossroads, comes out in the roadside village 1km west of the Paunar ashram.

As with Sevagram, it is possible to **stay** at Paunar in one of the visitors' rooms or dorms (donation). These are frequently booked up during conferences or seminars, so check when you arrive. Women are given preference if space is short. **Meals**, made from organic, home-grown produce, are available on request.

Southern Maharashtra

Most tourists heading south from Mumbai skip southern Maharashtra, but if you have a little time you can break up the journey and ease the burden of covering vast distances. **Pune** retains its Maratha character, in the old quarter at least, and also boasts a unique museum; some may also be attracted by its much-derided Osho Commune. Hill stations such as **Matheran** provide coolness, wooded walks and fine views, while the **Konkan coast** has little-visited beaches and forts that make a pleasant journey down to Goa. From **Lonavala**, you can get to see the earliest Buddhist rock-cut art in the western Deccan, sometimes even in peaceful solitude, and **Kolhapur**, the last major city before Karnataka to the south, or Goa to the southwest, is a place full of character with a strange blend of Maratha and so-called Indo-Saracenic architecture.

Matheran

The little hill station of **MATHERAN**, 170km east of Mumbai, is set on a narrow north–south ridge, at an altitude of 800m in the Sahyadri Range. From viewpoints with such names as Porcupine, Monkey and Echo, at the edge of sheer cliffs that plunge into steep ravines, you can see way across the hazy plains – on a good day, so they say, as far as Mumbai. The town itself, shrouded in thick mist for much of the year, has for the moment one unique attribute: cars, buses, motorbikes and auto-rickshaws are prohibited. That, added to the journey up, on a **miniature train** that chugs its way through spectacular scenery to the crest of the hill, gives the town an agreeably quaint, time-warped feel. Brightly painted hand-pulled rickshaws trundle along dirt lanes, while monkeys crash across the rusting corrugated-iron rooftops of bungalows.

Matheran (literally "mother forest") has been a popular retreat from the heat of Mumbai since the nineteenth century, when it was an exclusive bolt hole for British families. These days, however, few foreign visitors venture up here, and those that do only hang around a couple of days, killing time before a flight, or to sample one of India's most charming colonial-style hotels, **Lord's Central Hotel**. The tourist season lasts from mid-September to mid-June (at other times it's raining or misty), and is at its most hectic between November and January (Diwali), April and May, and virtually any weekend. There's really nothing up here to do but relax, wander the woods on foot or horseback, and enjoy the fresh air and views.

As the crow flies, Matheran is only 6.5km from Neral on the plain below, but the train climbs up on 20km of track with no less than 281 curves, said to be among the sharpest on any railway in the world. From 1907, the demanding haul was handled by four complex steam engines. Sadly, they puffed their last in 1980 and were replaced by cast-off diesels from Darjeeling, Shimla and Ooty. The two-hour train ride is a treat, especially if you get a window seat; but be prepared for a squash and hard benches.

In 1974, the All India Rail Strike cut Matheran off. To combat the situation, the track was made passable for Jeeps and finally in 1984 was sealed, up to Dasturi Naka, 2km from the town. A strong lobby wants to extend it to the centre, which if successful will undoubtedly destroy Matheran's quaint character.

Practicalities

To reach Matheran by **train**, you must first get to **Neral Junction**, 21km away. This is easily done by taking the hourly suburban train from **Mumbai** (CST) to Kargat, which stops at Neral (2hr 15min; Rs133). Otherwise, the daily Deccan Express #1007 (8.45am) or Sahyadri Express #7307 (6.35am) are both considerably quicker and also leave from CST. From **Pune** (2–3hr), the 9.10am Sahyadri Express #7304 stops at Neral. If you miss this, travel to Karjat and pick up the suburban service to Mumbai.

Narrow-gauge trains up from **Neral** to **Matheran** (2hr; Rs24) depart at 8.40am, 11am and 5pm (also 4.15pm, April & May). These are timed to link up with incoming expresses, so don't worry about missing a connection if the train you're on is delayed – the toy train service should wait. Matheran **station** is in the centre of town on MG Road, which runs roughly north–south.

All **motor transport**, including shared taxis and minibuses from Neral (Rs45 per person full, Rs225 for car), parks at the taxi stand next to the MTDC *Holiday Camp* at Dasturi Naka, 2km north of the town centre. From here you can walk with a porter (Rs80), be led by horse (Rs100), many of which moonlight from the local racecourse, or take a labour-intensive rickshaw (Rs120–160). Settling on a price for any of these takes some time and it really isn't that far, so if you're happy to carry your own bags, follow the rail tracks, which cut straight to the middle of Matheran, rather than the more convoluted dirt road. There is a little halt on the miniature railway near the Dasturi Nakataxi stand, but unless you've already booked a seat, you won't be allowed on. However you arrive, you must pay a **toll** (Rs12) to enter the town.

A small **tourist information** booth (daily 10am–6pm) opposite the railway station has maps and can help you get your bearings – otherwise, you can buy maps (Rs2) of the town at *Prince's Café*. You can **change money** at the State Bank of India near the station or *Lord's Central Hotel* after hours.

Accommodation and eating

Matheran has plenty of **hotels**, though few could be termed cheap. Most are close to the railway station on MG Road and on the road behind it, Kasturba Bhavan. Reduced rates may apply for midweek or long stays, and during the rainy off-season (when many places close down). Virtually all the hotels provide **full** or **half board** at reasonable rates, but if you want to eat out, or are on a tight budget, try one of the numerous thali joints around MG Road.

Alexander, near Alexander Point, 2km south of the railway station ☎ 02148/30151 or Mumbai 022/4926610. Pleasant wooded location with rooms, slightly dilapidated cottages (some a/c) and good Gujarati restaurant. Full board only. **❼**–**❽**

Gujarat Bhavan, Maulana Azad Road ☎ 02148/30278 or Mumbai 022/2030876. Clean and comfortable pure-veg resort hotel, with a range of rooms and cottages (some a/c with TV). Full board only. **❺**–**❽**

Hope Hall, MG Road ☎ 02148/30253, opposite *Lord's Central Hotel*. The best budget option: large, clean en-suite rooms arranged around a secluded yard with badminton and table tennis at the quiet end of town. Great deals off-season, too. **❸**

Lord's Central, MG Road ☎ 02148/30228, ☞ 30595 or Mumbai ☎ 022/3867776. Matheran's most characterful landmark, near the railway station. Genteel (non-a/c) Raj-era cottages with terraces, and superb views across the Western Ghats from a relaxing garden. Excellent veg and non-veg menu including Parsi and British food. Full board only, booking recommended. **❻**–**❽**

MTDC Holiday Camp, Dasturi Naka ☎ 02148/30277, ☞ 30566 or Mumbai ☎ 022/2026713. Cottages in a large old colonial house, and a cheap dorm (Rs80), plus a simple open-air restaurant. Forty minutes' walk from the centre of town, but a good option. **❻**–**❽**

Prasanna, MG Road, opposite the railway station ☎ 02148/30258. Fairly basic room-only budget lodge; close to the station. A touch pricey for what it is. **❸**

Royal, Kasturba Road ☎ 02148/30247 or Mumbai 022/3872784. Spruce and modern, with a large terrace and a rather retro and very shiny espresso machine. Full board and vegetarian. **❼**–**❽**

Rugby, Vithalrao Kotwal Marg ☎ 02148/30291, ☞ 30252 or Mumbai ☎ 022/2021090. Two minutes' walk up the road opposite the railway station. Old hotel, recently renovated and expanded, offering a range of rooms around a garden, with a multi-cuisine restaurant (complete with Raj-era decor) and a good bakery attached. **❾**

Murud-Janjira

The Konkan coast, stretching south down the length of Maharashtra to Goa, remains unspoilt and has a distinct culture with its own dialect of Marathi and a fiery cuisine. The further you get from Mumbai the quieter and more tranquil it becomes – the towns closer to Mumbai are inundated with Mumbaiakas for much of the year, especially at weekends.

The first really nice place is the unspoilt, unhurried little coastal town of **MURUD-JANJIRA**, 165km south of Mumbai, once part of a state belonging to the Siddis of Janjira. Modern development seems to have passed this quiet backwater by, and many of its distinctive houses are largely built of wood, some brightly painted, fronted by pillared verandas with built-in benches and gates. The beach is wide and flat and safe for swimming, though 3km north in Kashid, the beach is more sandy. Nearing Murud, the undulating coast road from Mumbai passes through attractive countryside with the sea slipping in and out of view, its shore lined with casuarinas, coconut and betel palms. Inland is agricultural land used to cultivate rice and string beans, and beyond forested hills, prowled, according to locals, by leopards.

The imposing **fort** of Janjira (2km south), which until the 1970s was inhabited by descendants of the Siddis, was built on an island in the Rajpuri creek in 1515. Even the Marathas, fort fanatics as they were, failed to penetrate its fifteen-metre-high walls. Shivaji attacked in 1659, followed by his son Shambhuji, who tried digging a tunnel and even attempted to fill the channel out to the island. The trip out by local *hodka* boat (around Rs50), from the jetty at the southern end of town, makes an excellent excursion.

You can get fine views of the bay and surrounding countryside by climbing more than 200 steps up to the small hilltop **Dattatreya Temple**, dedicated to the triple-headed deity comprising Vishnu, Shiva and Brahma. It's a simple structure, with an Islamic-style tower; inside, decorative tiles cover the floor of the wood-and-brick *mandapa* with flower and peacock designs, while

European-looking angelic figures and landscapes adorn the ceiling. Left of the cell holding a Dattatreya image is a portrait of the nineteenth-century Maharashtran saint, **Gajanan Maharaj**, smoking *ganja*.

The dilapidated eighteenth-century **Nawab's Palace** – which bears more than a passing resemblance to the Addams Family residence – overlooks Janjira, 2km north of Murud. It was opened in 1991 as a museum, but soon closed due to vandalism, and today its present owner, the erstwhile Nawab Shah Siddi Mahmood Khan, lives elsewhere and visitors are considered trespassers.

Practicalities

There is a **ferry** service from the Gateway of India in Mumbai to **Rewas** (hourly 6am–5.30pm; 1hr), from where you have to get a local bus that trundles through the coastal villages from Alibag to Murud. Most direct **buses** from Mumbai Central take five hours; there are two faster ASIAD services (5.45am & 11am; 3hr 30min), which must be booked in advance. All stop on Murud's main street, Durbar Road, parallel to the coast, where you'll find the tiny post office, covered market, a handful of basic restaurants and the town's few **hotels**. The *Aman Place* on Durbar Road, near the Chowk bus stand (☎021447/4297; ❸), a few basic, clean doubles set in a private garden that runs down to the beach. If you want peace, palm trees and hammocks after the hype of Mumbai, this is the place to head for. Northwards up Durbar Road, the luxury concrete bungalows of the *Golden Swan Beach Resort* (☎021447/4078, ⊛www.goldenswan.com; ❻–❽) are inches from the virtually deserted beach, with a simple canteen-style restaurant. A good place to **eat** is the *Nest Bamboo House*, on Darbar Road south of the chowk, which serves good mid-price Indian and Chinese dishes as well as veg and non-veg thalis – also a fine choice to try out the distinctive and fiery Konkan fish dishes.

Ganapatipuli

Two hundred and fifteen kilometres south of Marud-Janjira brings you to the tiny village of **GANAPATIPULI**, which has a long, golden sandy beach and a very fine **Ganapati temple**. Although attracting thousands of Indian pilgrims each year, this sleepy place sees relatively few foreign visitors with most of the tourists being honeymooners from Mumbai. The temple is built around a Ganapati *omnar*, a naturally formed – though not strictly accurate – image of the god. Built in 1923, the temple has some very fine carvings including 47 sculptures of Ganapati variants around the outside. If you're interested, the friendly brahmin inside speaks English and can tell you all their names. Apart from the temple, there really isn't that much to do here apart from lounge on the beach or do watersports at the swanky MTDC *Resort* (☎02357/35248, ℗35328; ❹–❽) which has very comfortable and mostly a/c rooms, as well as cheaper tent accommodation – all a stones' throw from the beach. If your budget won't stretch to this, the temple also has simple pilgrim accommodation in rooms (❶), though the mattresses are hard, the bathrooms grubby and you'll need your own mosquito net. For **food**, you can sample decent Nepalese cooking at the MTDC resort, or eat less expensively at one of the *dhabas* at the bottom of the village towards the main road.

To get to Ganapatipuli, either make your way to Ratnagiri (on the Konkan railway and well connected by state and private buses) and take a local bus (10 daily; 1–1hr 30min) the last 32km, or take one of the direct MSRTC services from Mumbai, Pune or Kolhapur. All the buses stop outside the MTDC resort.

Lonavala

Just thirty years ago, the town of **LONAVALA**, 100km southeast of Mumbai and 62km northwest of Pune, was a quiet retreat in the Sahyadri hills. Since then, the place has mushroomed to cope with hordes of holiday-makers and second-home owners from the state capital, and is now only of interest as a base for the magnificent **Buddhist caves** of **Karle**, **Bhaja** and **Bedsa**, some of which date from the Satavahana period (second century BC). Frequent buses arrive at Lonavala's central **bus stand**, just off the Mumbai–Pune Road (NH-4), but the train is infinitely preferable. Lonavala is on the main railway line between Mumbai (3hr) and Pune (1hr 30min), and all express trains stop here. The **railway station** is on the south side of town, close to the centre, and you'll want to take the path right at the end of platform 1 to get there. With a car, or by taking an early train, it's just about possible to take in the caves as a day-trip from Mumbai, but it's better to allow yourself a full day to get around.

Accommodation

Lonavala has a wide range of **accommodation**, from very cheap to five-star; many of its hotels lower their rates out of season (Oct–March) or for longer stays or weekdays. Budget and mid-range places are concentrated in the centre, by the bus and railway stations.

Adarsh, behind the bus stand on Shivaji Road ☏02114/72353. Spotless a/c and non-a/c rooms, some overlooking a central courtyard. Dependable mid-range option, but the management aren't very welcoming and early mornings are noisy. ④–⑦

Chandralok, Shivaji Road ☏02114/72294. Clean, comfortable rooms with shower-toilets, 24hr hot water, friendly staff and excellent Gujarati restaurant. The economy room is especially good value. ③–⑦

DT Shahani Health Home, DJ Shahani Road ☏02114/72784. Lonavala's best budget option: large, immaculate rooms in a modern block tucked down a suburban backstreet. Full board. ④

Duke's Retreat, Mumbai–Pune Road, Khandala ☏02114/73826, ☏73836, ✉duke@ccmob.sprintsmx.cms.vsnl.net.in. Superb position overlooking a ravine, with prizewinning garden and pool (Rs150 for nonresidents). Comfortable rooms and cottages, with its own outdoor café, a/c restaurant and bar. Weekend packages include breakfast and dinner. ⑧–⑨

Kumar Resorts, Mumbai–Pune Road ☏02114/73091. One of three standard luxury motels facing each other on the main road; all rooms have a/c and are large and comfortable. Good restaurant and a swimming pool. ⑦–⑧

MTDC Karle Resort, Mumbai–Pune Road ☏02114/82230, ☏82370. On the Lonavala–Karle bus route, 3km from Malavli railway station and 7km out of town. Range of comfortable accommodation (some a/c) in cottages, suites and economy doubles in a tranquil setting. ⑤–⑧

Eating

While most of the hotels in Lonavala lay on full board or have very good **restaurants**, a number of smaller restaurants and snack bars on the main street cater for the brisk through trade. You'll also come across dozens of shops selling the local sweet speciality, **chikki** – a moreish, but dentally challenging, amalgam of dried fruit and nuts set in rock-solid honey toffee. *Super Chikki* on the main street allows you to sample the many varieties before you buy, and they giftwrap the sticky blocks in attractive old-fashioned boxes. Their main competitors, *National Chikki*, further down, is also recommended; this is also the best place to stock up on delicious deep-fried nibbles (*namkeen*), the other local speciality.

Chandralok, *Hotel Chandralok*, Shivaji Road. Wonderful and cheap "unlimited" Gujarati thalis served in a large canteen, with several kinds of bread and buttermilk dishes.

Diamond, Mumbai–Pune Road, opposite the *Kumar Resort*. Garden restaurant specializing in Punjabi and Chinese food with fairly high prices but a relaxing atmosphere – hopefully a little quieter now the new highway has been opened.

Guru Krippa, Mumbai–Pune Road. Sparkling, clean pure-veg joint on the main street: piping-hot south Indian snacks, cheese toasties, and inexpensive thalis with Chinese and Punjabi main meals. Also a good selection of ice creams, *kulfi* and full-on *faloodas*. Recommended.

Shabri, *Hotel Rama Krishna*, Mumbai–Pune Road. The well-heeled *Mumbaikas* favourite. Spacious and clean, serving the full range of north and south Indian dishes and chilled beer.

The Buddhist caves of Karle, Bhaja and Bedsa

The three cave sites of **Karle**, **Bhaja** and **Bedsa** comprise some of the finest rock-cut architecture in the northwest of the Deccan region. Though not in the same league as Ajanta and Ellora, they harbour some beautifully preserved ancient sculpture, dating from the era when this region lay on several long-distance trade routes, and are definitely worth a look if you are passing.

The three sites lie some way from each other, all to the east of Lonavala. Covering Karle and Bhaja under your own steam by bus and/or train is manageable in a day, if you are prepared for a good walk, but if you want to get out to Bedsa too, and can afford it, the easiest option is to rent an **auto-rickshaw** (around Rs250) or **car** (Rs400 for 4hr) for the day (usually found at Lonavala railway station). Finally, if you want to see the caves at their best, **avoid the weekends**, when they are inundated with bus loads of rowdy day-trippers.

For a full rundown on the history and features of rock-cut cave architecture in the Deccan, see p.807.

Karle

KARLE (also Karla and Karli) is 3km north of **Karle Caves Junction** on the Mumbai–Pune Road and 11km from Lonavala. Take any bus to the junction (from where it's a Rs15–20 rickshaw ride), or there are five daily buses (6am, 9am, 12.30pm, 3pm & 6.30pm) that head for the caves directly from Lonavala, with the last bus returning from Karle at 6.30pm.

The rock-cut Buddhist *chaitya* hall at Karle, reached by steep steps that climb 110m, is the largest and best preserved in India, dating from the first century AD. As you approach across a large courtyard, itself hewn from the rock, the enormous fourteen-metre-high facade of the hall towers above, topped by a horseshoe-shaped window and with three entrances below, one for the priest and the others for devotees. To the left of the entrance stands a *simhas stambha*, a tall monolithic column capped with four lions.

In the porch of the cave, dividing the three doorways, are panels of figures in six couples, presumed to have been the wealthy patrons of the hall. Two rows of octagonal columns with pot-shaped bases divide the interior into three, forming a wide central aisle and, on the outside, a hall that allowed devotees to circumambulate the monolithic stupa at the back. Above each pillar's fluted capital kneels a finely carved elephant mounted by two riders, one with arms draped over the other's shoulders. Amazingly, perishable remnants survive from the time when the hall was in use: teak ribs on the vaulted ceiling show that the stone was carved to resemble a wooden structural model. Surmounting the stupa are the remains of a carved wooden umbrella.

Full views of the main entrance are obscured by the much later accretion, to the right, of a Hindu shrine to **Ekviri**, a goddess-oracle revered by Koli fishing communities. Fences are often erected outside it, to regulate the flow of worshippers who seek *darshan* or to consult the goddess. When questions are addressed to Ekviri, areca nuts are placed on silver discs above the head of the image. Depending on which nut falls to the ground, right or left, the answer is "yes" or "no". Tuesdays and Fridays are the busiest times, but Karle is at its most frenetic during the annual Chaitra (March/April) festival, when the blood of sacrificed chickens is smeared on the steps up the hill.

Bhaja

Although the eighteen **caves** (daily 8.30am–6pm) at **BHAJA** may not be as elaborate as those at Karle, they are more atmospheric, giving visitors a much clearer sense of their original tranquillity (particularly during the rainy season, when monks traditionally ceased their wanderings). They lie 3km south of Karle Caves Junction, reached by following a path up from the village square near the railway station at Malavli, just 1.5km away. Regular passenger trains (hourly; Rs3) call here, and are the cheapest and most convenient way to get back to Lonavala if you're not travelling by rented rickshaw or car.

The caves at Bhaja are among the oldest in India, dating from the late second to early first century BC, during the earliest, Hinayana, phase of Buddhism. Most consist of simple halls – *vihara* – with adjoining cells that contain plain shelf-like beds; many are fronted by rough verandas. Bhaja's apsidal *chaitya* hall, **Cave 12**, which contains a stupa, but no figures, has 27 plain bevelled pillars which lean inwards, mimicking the style of wooden buildings. Sockets in the stone of the exterior arch reveal that it once contained a wooden gate or facade. Further south, the last cave, **Cave 19**, a *vihara*, is decorated with superb carvings. Mysteriously, scholars identify the figures as the Hindu gods, **Surya** and **Indra**, who figure prominently in the Rig Veda (c. 1000 BC). In Vedic mythology Surya, the sun god, is conventionally described flying through the sky as he banishes darkness; here, left of the entrance, he rides a chariot pulled by four horses and accompanied by two women who carry a parasol and fly-whisk. The chariot crushes the bodies of naked demonesses, who appear to float in the air. The panel to the right is thought to show Indra, who in the Vedas represents power, particularly lightning, thunder and rain, and thanks to the quantity of sacred soma drink that he quaffs, frequently becomes huge. In this striking sculpture, two figures are shown riding an elephant (Indra's vehicle), all of them gigantic in relation to the landscape. The elephant grasps what appears to be a little tree in his trunk.

Bedsa

It's quite possible that you won't encounter anyone else when visiting the caves at **BEDSA**, which is one of its great attractions. Once you reach the village, 12km beyond Bhaja on NH-4, or a three-kilometre bus ride from Kamshet, the nearest railway station, you'll have to ask the way to the unsigned path. The village kids hanging around might scramble up the steep hillside with you, for a fee.

Bedsa's **chaitya hall**, excavated later than that at Karle, is far less sophisticated. The entrance is extremely narrow, leading from a porch which appears to be supported, though of course it is not, by four octagonal pillars more than 7m high, with pot-shaped bases and bell capitals; bulls, horses and elephants rest on inverted, stepped slabs on top. Inside, 26 plain octagonal columns lead to an unadorned monolithic stupa.

Pune (Poona) and beyond

At an altitude of 598m, **PUNE**, Maharashtra's second largest city, lies close to the Western Ghat mountains (known here as the Sahyadri hills), on the edge of the Deccan plains as they stretch away to the east. The British chose Pune in 1820 as an alternative headquarters for the Bombay Presidency to escape the captial's summer heat and monsoon deluge. Their military cantonment in the northwest of town is still used by the Indian army, and a number of British buildings, such as the Council Hall and Deccan College, survive.

Settlement on the site is thought to date back two thousand years, when Kasba, a fortified town, lay between the River Mula to the northwest and the Nagzari Nala creek to the east. Occupying a strategic position on trade routes between the Deccan and the Arabian Sea, the town prospered during the early Hindu period. Under the sixteenth-century Marathas, Pune became the capital and military headquarters of a sovereign state, until its rulers were deposed

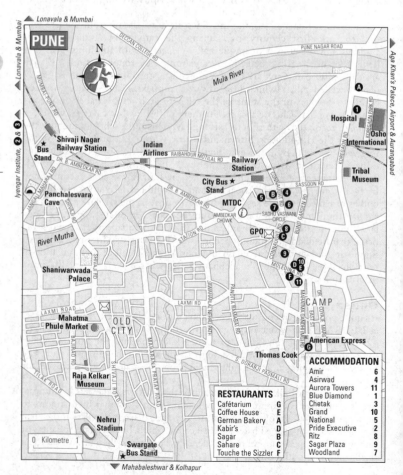

▲ Lonavala & Mumbai

PUNE

N

Lonavala & Mumbai ◀

◀ Iyengar Institute, ❷ & ❸

Aga Khan's Palace, Airport & Aurangabad ▶

DECCAN COLLEGE RD

PUNE NAGAR ROAD

Mula River

MUNDHWA-PUNE RD

Ⓐ

KOREGAON PARK RD

Hospital

Shivaji Nagar Railway Station

Bus Stand

DR. B. AMBEDKAR RD

Indian Airlines

RAIBAHADUR MOTILAL RD

Railway Station

Osho International

KOREGAON RD

DR. B. AMBEDKAR RD

City Bus Stand ★

SASSOON RD

Tribal Museum

Panchalesvara Cave

JANGLI MAHARAJ RD

SHIVAJI RD

STATION RD

MTDC ⓘ

AMBEDKAR CHOWK

SADHU VASWANI CIRCLE

CONNAUGHT RD

Ⓢ Ⓑ Ⓐ
Ⓢ Ⓗ Ⓖ

DR. AMBEDKAR RD

River Mutha

SHIVAJI RD

GPO ✉

Ⓒ

ⒹⒷ

Shaniwarwada Palace

Ⓢ
ⒹⒺ
Ⓕ
Ⓣ

DHOLE PATIL RD

MOLEDINA RD

JAWAHARLAL NEHRU PATH

LAXMI ROAD

C A M P

PANDIT TILAK MARG

MAHATMA GANDHI MARG

DR. COYAJE MARG

EAST ST

Mahatma Phule Market ✉

OLD CITY

LAXMI RD

American Express

Raja Kelkar Museum

BAJIRAO RD

SHIVAJI ROAD

MAHARANA PRATAP ROAD

S. DORABJI PADMALI RD

Thomas Cook

TILAK ROAD

Nehru Stadium

Swargate ★ Bus Stand

0   Kilometre   1

RESTAURANTS

Cafétarium	G
Coffee House	E
German Bakery	A
Kabir's	D
Sagar	B
Sahare	C
Touche the Sizzler	F

ACCOMMODATION

Amir	6
Asirwad	4
Aurora Towers	11
Blue Diamond	1
Chetak	3
Grand	10
National	5
Pride Executive	2
Ritz	8
Sagar Plaza	9
Woodland	7

▼ Mahabaleshwar & Kolhapur

by the Brahmin Peshwa family, who dominated Pune during the eighteenth century before the arrival of the British.

Since colonial days, Pune has continued to develop as a major industrial city and a centre for higher education. But to most outsiders, it is notorious as the home of the **Osho Commune International**, founded in 1970 by the charismatic Bhagwan Rajneesh, or Osho (1931–90), whose syncretic and, to many Indians, scandalous philosophy of life lured thousands of followers from Europe and America.

The vast views of the rocky Bhuleshwar mountains and valleys that greet you from the lonely hilltop fort of **Sinhagad** – a short bus ride from Pune – is reward enough after the aerobic jaunt up to the atmospheric ruins, once the scene of a dramatic siege by the Maratha warlord, Shivaji. Northeast of Pune, the hill station of **Mahabaleshwar** is where the urban masses from Mumbai and Pune head to get their countryside fix of fresh air, summer fruits and long walks.

Arrival and information

Pune's Lohagaon **airport**, 10km northeast of the centre, is served by flights from Mumbai, Delhi, Chennai, and Bangalore. Prepaid taxis (Rs200), auto-rickshaws (Rs100) and regular "Ex-Servicemen" buses (Rs20–25) are on hand for the fifteen-minute trip to the city centre. Pune is an important staging point on southern express-train routes from Mumbai (3hr 30min–4hr 30min); the main **railway station** is in the centre of town, south of the river. Auto-rickshaws and tourist taxis wait outside the station – locals often use the shared long-distance taxis to get to Mumbai. Of the three main **bus stands**, the City Bus Stand next to the railway station serves the city itself (with signs and timetables only in Marathi), and some destinations south and west, including Goa and Mumbai. Swargate Bus Stand, about 5km south, close to Nehru Stadium, services Karnataka, while the stand next to Shivaji Nagar Railway Station, 3km west of the centre, runs buses to towns in the north, including Nasik, Aurangabad and Lonavala. To establish which station you require for your destination, ask at the enquiries hatch of the City Bus Stand.

You can book city tours, make MTDC resort reservations and seek advice about bus services at the **MTDC Tourist Office** (Mon–Sat 10am–5.30pm; ☏0212/612 6846, ☏611 9434), deep within the government *babu's* (bureaucrat) citadel, inside "I" block of Central Building (enter between Ambedkar Chowk and Sadhu Vaswani Circle). You can also do this at the **Information Counter** (allegedly Mon–Fri 10am–6pm & Sat 10am–1pm; closed 2nd and 4th Sat of month) opposite the railway station's first-class booking office. The MTDC conducts a day-long **tour** of Pune (daily 9am–5.30pm; Rs85) in conjunction with the city transport system, which at least guarantees that you'll see all the sights, which can be difficult in such a sprawling city.

The best places to **change money** are at Thomas Cook, on the corner of MG Road and General Thimmaya Road (Mon–Sat 9.30am–6pm; ☏0212/648188, ☏643027); the State Bank of India on Laxmi Road will do the same, only more slowly and without the Rs30 commission. There's also an American Express office around the corner from Thomas Cook, 19 MG Rd (Mon–Sat 9.30am–6pm; ☏0212/631848 or 9) although they don't change money or travellers' cheques. The very efficient **GPO** (Mon–Sat 10am–6pm) is on Connaught Road.

Pune's premier **bookshop**, the Modern Bookshop, on General Thimmaya Road (Mon–Sat 9.30am–1pm & 4–8.30pm; ☏0212/633597), stocks an impressive array of fiction, and a good selection of Indian maps and guidebooks. You can access the **internet** in many places, including the *Cyber Café* in Ashok Vijay Complex, MG Road (Rs50/hr) and the *Crystal Cyber Café* in the Crystal Complex, MG Road (Rs40/hr); both are conveniently open 24hr.

Accommodation

Pune is well stocked with **hotels**, though in keeping with most big cities, prices are quite high for what you get. Most of the budget accommodation can be found in the area south of the railway station around Connaught Road. The station itself also has better-than-average **retiring rooms** (Rs50–80).

Amir, 15 Connaught Rd ☎ 0212/621840. Good range of dark but comfortable rooms and facilities including coffee shop, bar, and two restaurants. Checkout 5pm. ❼ –❽

Ashirwad, 16 Connaught Rd ☎ 0212/628885, ⓕ 626121. Newish hotel near the station. Some a/c rooms with balconies and TV. Good veg restaurant, room service, exchange and travel desk. ❼

Aurora Towers, 9 Moledina Rd ☎ 0212/631818, ⓕ 631826. Upper-range place 2km from railway station, with 24hr room service and coffee shop, two good restaurants, shops and pool. ❽ –❾

Blue Diamond, 11 Koregaon Rd ☎ 0212/663775, ⓕ 627755, ⓔ bluediamond.pune@sm2.sprintrpg.ems.vsnl.net. in. Five-star hotel, 2km northeast of railway station near the Osho ashram. Posh Indian and Chinese restaurants serving buffet lunches, 24hr coffee shop, swimming pool, and shops. ❽ –❾

Chetak, 1100/2 Model Colony ☎ 0212/352681, ⓕ 354078. Good-value accommodation in the suburbs. Deservedly popular with students from nearby Iyengar Institute. Book in advance. ❻ –❼

Grand, 8 Moledina Rd ☎ 0212/668728, opposite *Aurora Towers Hotel*. Single wood-partition rooms with common bathrooms, or simple but spacious en-suite doubles in an old colonial townhouse. Relaxing veranda, beer garden, restaurant and

fast-food outlet, cats and friendly management. ❸ –❹

National, 14 Sassoon Rd, two minutes' walk from the railway station ☎ 0212/68054. Rooms with wooden verandas and attached bathrooms in a dilapidated old building, while others are in basic modern "cottages". Popular with budget travellers and Ba'hai devotees. ❸ –❹

Pride Executive, 5 University Rd, Shivaji Nagar ☎ 0212/553 4567, ⓕ 553328, ⓦ www.pridegroup.com. Business hotel with comfortable modern a/c rooms and pricey multicuisine restaurant, plus bar and coffee shop. ❾

Ritz, Connaught Road ☎ 0212/622995. Former travellers' hangout revamped with swish marble interiors and prices to match. There are two restaurants – thankfully still serving their legendary Gujarati thalis – and a travel centre. ❼ –❾

Sagar Plaza, 1 Bund Garden Rd ☎ 0212/622622, ⓕ 612633, ⓔ sparkplaza@wmi.co.in. Medium-sized, flashy four-star, 1km from railway station, with ritzy restaurant, 24hr coffee shop, bar, health club, bookshop and swimming pool. ❾

Woodland, Sadhu Vaswani Circle ☎ 0212/626161, ⓕ 623131. Good-value rooms, mostly a/c, ten minutes' walk from the railway station. Veg restaurant, travel desk and foreign exchange. ❼ –❽

The City

Pune centre is bordered on the north by the **River Mula** and to the west by the **River Mutha** – the two join in the northwest to form the Mutha–Mula, at Sangam Bridge. The principal shopping area, and the greatest concentration of restaurants and hotels, is in the streets south of the railway station, particularly Connaught and, further south, **MG Road**. The old Peshwa part of town, by far the most interesting to explore, is towards the west between the fortified **Shaniwarwada Palace** and fascinating **Raja Dinkar Kelkar Museum**; old wooden *wadas*, palatial city homes, survive on these narrow, busy streets, and the Victorian, circular **Mahatma Phule Market** is always a hive of activity.

Raja Dinkar Kelkar Museum

Dinkar Gangadhar Kelkar (1896–1990), aside from being a celebrated Marathi poet, published under the name Adnyatwass, spent much of his life travelling and collecting arts and crafts from all over the country. In 1975, he donated his collection to the Maharashtran government for the creation of a museum dedicated to the memory of his son, Raja, who had died at the age of 12.

Housed in a huge old-town mansion, the **Raja Dinkar Kelkar Museum** (daily 8.30am–12.30pm & 3–6pm; Rs50, [Rs10]), on 1378 Shukrawar Peth (buses #72 or #74 from the railway station to Mahatma Phule Market), is a wonderful pot-pourri in which beauty and interest is found in both artistic and everyday objects. Kitchen utensils include a camelskin oil container and a wooden noodle-maker which, like other Indian cooking tools such as the coconut scraper, requires its operator to sit astride it. Paraphernalia associated with *paan,* the Indian passion, includes containers in every conceivable design, made from silk, wood, brass and silver; some mimic animals or fish, or are egg-shaped and in delicate filigree, others are solid heavy-duty boxes built to with-stand constant use. Lime applicators, nut-holders, and mortars are equally elab-orate and nutcrackers often take the form of a loving couple. Also on show are musical instruments, superb Marathi textiles and costumes, toys, domestic shrines and furniture, beauty accessories and a model of Shaniwarwada Palace.

Shaniwarwada Palace

In the centre of the oldest part of town, only the imposing high walls of the **Shaniwarwada Palace** (daily 8am–noon & 2–6pm; Rs2) survived three fires in the eighteenth and nineteenth centuries. The palace, founded by the Peshwa ruler Bajrao I in 1730 and the chief residence of the Peshwas until the British arrived in 1817, has little to excite interest today. Entrance is through the Delhi gate on the northside, one of five set into the perimeter wall, whose huge teak doors come complete with nasty elephant-proof spikes. Just inside, faded murals show Ganapati, Vishnu and scenes from the *Ramayana.* Court musicians (drums and double-reed wind *shehnais*) played from the balconies above, a practice that is revived three times a year: January 26 (Republic Day), May 1 (Maharashtra Workers' Day) and August 15 (Independence Day). The interior of the palace is now grassed over, the seven-storey building entirely absent. Only one of the guides, usually available in the afternoons, speaks English. Bus #3 runs the 2km southwest from the railway station to the palace.

Panchalesvara cave

The **Panchalesvara cave**, to the west of town, just across the River Mula, lies in a rather surprising urban setting at the northern end of busy Jungli Maharaj Road (buses #4, #16 or #98). Hewn from rock in the same manner as the more elaborate examples elsewhere in Maharashtra, the cave dates from the Rashtrakuta period (eighth–ninth centuries). Steps lead from the pavement to a path which ends in a square courtyard and a circular roofed Nandi enclosure. Beyond it, the roughly excavated cave, with broad, square, plain pillars, is unfin-ished, bearing numerous chisel marks, and yet appears to have been in contin-uous use for a thousand years. Locals can be seen at prayer at most times of the day, or dozing in the shade during *tiffin* breaks. The central shrine contains a *shivalingam,* while to either side subsidiary cells hold figures of Lakshmi, Ganesh, Rama, his wife Sita and brother Lakshmana.

Aga Khan Palace and Gandhi Memorial

In 1942, Mahatma Gandhi, his wife Kasturba and other key figures of the free-dom movement were interned at the **Aga Khan Palace** (daily 9am–12.30pm & 1.30–6pm; Rs2), which is set in quiet leafy gardens, across the River Mula, 5km northeast of the centre (buses #1, #158 & #156). The Aga Khan donated the palace to the state in 1969, and it is now a small Gandhi museum, typical of many all over India, with captioned photos and simple rooms unchanged since they were occupied by the freedom fighters. A memorial behind the house commemorates Kasturba, who died during their imprisonment. A small Khadi shop sells hand-loom cloth and products made by village co-operatives.

Bhagwan Rajneesh

It is thirty years or so since the first disciple was initiated into the **Bhagwan Rajneesh** cult, latterly renamed Osho Commune International, an evolving philosophy of Buddhism, Sufism, sexual liberationism, Tantric practices, Zen, yoga, hypnosis, Tibetan pulsing, disco and unabashed materialism. The first Rajneesh ashram was founded in Pune in 1974. It rapidly attracted droves of Westerners and some Indians, who adopted new Sanskrit names and a uniform of orange or maroon cottons and a bead necklace with an attached photo of the enlightened guru, in classic style, sporting long white hair and beard. This immediately identified the wearer as a *sannyasin* (borrowing from Shaivistic tradition, a renunciating mendicant who has attained a state of holiness).

Few early adherents denied that much of the attraction lay in Rajneesh's novel approach to fulfilment. His dismissal of Christianity ("Crosstianity") as a miserably oppressive obsession with guilt struck a chord with many, as did the espousal of liberation through sex. Within a few years, satellite ashrams were popping up throughout Western Europe, most notably in Germany and Italy, as well as in Japan. Rajneesh assured his devotees that material comfort was not to be shunned and making money, at least for the ashram, was no bad thing. By 1980, an estimated 200,000 devotees had liberated themselves in 600 meditation centres across 80 countries.

To protect itself from pollution, nuclear war and the AIDS virus, the organization poured money and a great deal of energy into a utopian project, **Rajneeshpuram**, on 64,000 acres of agricultural land in Oregon, USA. It was at this point that the tabloids and TV documentary teams really got interested in Rajneesh, now a multimillionaire. His predilection for Rolls-Royce cars was big news – he owned 90, yet could not drive. Baffled observers watched as hordes of tambourine-banging, ecstatic devotees lined Main Street Rajneeshpuram, paying homage to their guru, who would bestow beatific smiles as he swished by.

Infiltrators leaked stories of strange goings-on at Rajneeshpuram and before long its high-powered female executives became subject to police interest. Charges of tax evasion, drugs, fraud, arson and a conspiracy to poison several people in a neighbouring town to sway the vote in local elections provoked further sensation. Although he claimed to know nothing of this, Rajneesh pleaded guilty to breaches of US immigration laws and was deported in 1985. Following protracted attempts to resettle in 21 different countries, and now suffering complications of ME, the Valium-addicted Rajneesh returned home to Pune where he died in 1990 aged 59.

The ashram has suffered since then, beset by internal squabbles and financial trouble. At his death, Rajneesh appointed an inner circle to manage the group, though several have departed and the Osho "brand" – with 3.5 million books sold each year (supplemented by tapes, paintings and photos) – is now controlled from Zurich and New York. Pune doesn't see enough of this to meet its twenty-percent annual shortfall in revenue and relies heavily on private doations. Life at the ashram has also changed; whereas in its heyday an average stay was three to six months, today people typically stay less than two weeks and few followers live on site. This has led to a labour shortage, with non-Osho locals brought in to keep the place afloat, and a dismantling of the sense of community that was the source of its attraction.

Osho Commune International

Pune is the headquarters of the Bhagwan Rajneesh's avowedly nonreligious **Osho Commune International**, 17 Koregaon Park (℗0212/628562, ℗624181, ⓦwww.osho.net), 2km east of the railway station. Calling itself a "tasteful and classy resort", the commune celebrates the sniping of critics, proudly displaying the *Wall Street Journal's* description of it as a "spiritual Disneyland for disaffected First World yuppies".

With a considerable daily income during peak season (Dec–March) and years of dedicated help from volunteers, the commune has transformed its twenty acres into a dreamy playground of cafés, swimming pool, sauna and clinics, with a shop selling Osho's enormous list of books, videos and cassettes. The faithful have erected space-age, air-conditioned buildings, landscaped the gardens, bored tube wells for water, planted trees to improve air quality and grow organic vegetables. Courses at its Multiversity are offered in a variety of New-Age and traditional techniques, mostly one-day (Rs1600) to three-day (Rs5400). Forty-five-minute lunchtime demos and one-day inductions (Rs500) are also available if you want to try before you buy. Osho's own brand of jargon is extensive; tennis, for example, is here played as Zennis, which helps you "get out of your body's way, bring the outer and the inner together" in "a unique synthesis of tennis and meditation". There are a host of other courses ranging from primal screaming to meditation techniques and more offbeat therapies.

This ecofriendly bubble follows a strict door policy: visitors who wish to spend longer than the daily hour-long guided tours (held throughout the day, ask at reception; Rs10) must produce two passport photos and an HIV-negative certificate no less than 30 days old. If you don't have one and still want to stay there, you'll have to take an HIV test at the ashram clinic (Rs125 next-day results, Rs275 results in 3hr). Day-passes cost Rs130 and you'll also need two robes (maroon for daywear, white for evenings) which cost Rs300 inside the ashram, or Rs150 from stalls outside.

Tribal Museum

The Tribal Research and Training Institute, which runs the **Tribal Museum**, Koregan Road (daily 10am–5pm; free) 2km east of the railway station, is ded-

---

Pune's Ganesh festival

Pune's major festival, Ganapati Chaturthi, is dedicated to the elephant-headed Hindu deity Ganesh, the remover of obstacles and the most auspicious god for embarking on new endeavours. Once a domestic ritual, Ganesh Chaturthi was turned into a public rallying point for Hindus by the freedom fighter Bal Gangadhar Tilak in the late nineteenth century; both Pune and Mumbai celebrate it in extravagant style each year.

On the first day, images of Ganesh, some huge and smothered in fairy lights, are erected in homes and public places, decorated with flowers and food, and worshipped. Over the next ten days or so events include arts and crafts displays, village fairs, sports competitions and a food festival, as well as Indian classical music and dance performances, usually featuring the most illustrious names in the country. On the last day the Ganesh images are taken in procession and immersed in water, the streets teeming with singing and dancing devotees.

Needless to say, Pune is very crowded during the festival, which takes place during late August and early September. MTDC organize the event, and can help arrange accommodation and all-in packages.

icated to the protection and documentation of Maharashtra's numerous tribal groups, such as the Wagdheo, Bahiram, Danteshwari and Marai, who number more than five million. The museum's faded photos, costumes and artefacts serve as an excellent introduction to this little-known world, but the highlights are the wonderful collections of dance masks and Worli wedding paintings. Talk to the director of the museum if you're interested in guided (but culturally sensitive) **tours** to tribal areas.

Moving on from Pune

At Pune's **airport** (℡0212/6685201), Jet Airways (℡0212/6137181) and Indian Airlines (0212/6126451) service **Delhi** (daily 7.05pm & 7.20pm; 2hr). Jet also fly to **Chennai** (daily 2pm; 3hr), via **Bangalore** (45min); tickets can be purchased at their office, 39 Dr Ambedkhar Rd (℡0212/664189; reservations 0212/659939). There are also direct flights to **Mumbai** (daily 6pm; 35–45min) on East-West, *Amir Hotel*, Sadhu Vaswani Road (℡0212/665862), and Damania Airways, 17 MG Rd; (Mon–Sat 8.30am; ℡0212/640814), while NEPC fly the Pune–Bangalore–Madras route three times weekly (Tues, Thurs & Sat 4.30pm). The cheapest and most convenient way of **getting to the airport** is to take the Indian Airlines airport or "ex-armymen" bus (Rs20–25), which both leave from in front of the *Hotel Amir*.

As Pune is one of the last stops for around twenty long-distance trains bound for Mumbai, **rail services** are excellent. Many depart early morning, however, and some terminate at Dadar, so always check first – an information service is run through the Railway Enquiries Office (℡131/133). The most convenient, if crowded, options for **Mumbai CST** are Deccan Queen Express #2124 (7.15am), Pragati Express #1026 (7.45am) and Sahyadhri Express #2028 (5.35pm; 4hr) which all take around three-and-a-half hours. Direct express trains from Pune also run to Hyderabad (Mumbai–Hyderabad Express #7031; daily 4.55pm), New Delhi (Jhelum Express #1077; daily 5.35pm), Chennai (Mumbai–Chennai Express #6011; daily 6.15pm), Bangalore (Udyan Express #6529; daily noon) and Thiruvananthapuram (Kanniya Kumari Express #1081; daily 3.35pm). Reservations for all trains should be made at the new Reservation Centre next to the station (Mon–Sat 8am–2pm & 2.15–8pm, Sun 8am–2pm). There are also several **24-hour taxi** agencies near the City bus stand that drive the four hours to Dadar in Mumbai, take up to four people and charge Rs920 per car (Rs230 per person when filled).

Private luxury buses to Ahmedabad (daily 4.30pm; 18hr 30min; Rs320), Indore (daily 6.30pm; 14hr 30min; Rs350), Goa (6.30pm; 12hr 30min; Rs250), Aurangabad (3 daily; 5hr; Rs130) and Ratnagiri (daily 9.45pm; 9hr 15min; Rs220) can be booked through Prasanna Tours & Travels, Sivaji Nagar Terminus (℡0212/5539358) or Swargate Terminus (℡0212/444-4139, ⊛www.prasannatours.com). Recommended **travel agents** for the above are Abhay Travels, 42 Karve Rd (℡0212/543 6463, ℻546 6663), and Bulsara Tours & Travels, 14 Sadhu Vaswani Rd (℡0212/623137, ℻629911).

Before travelling on the uncomfortable and crowded **state buses**, seek advice from the MTDC Tourist Information Counter at the railway station or call ℡0212/626218 for the latest information on state bus services; the bus stands display no information in English. Services from the busy City stand next to the station head south, to Mahabaleshwar (10 daily; 3hr), Kolhapur (18 daily; 12hr), and Goa (4.45am, 5.30am, 4.45pm, 6.15pm, 7.15pm & 7.45pm 15hr; book in advance from the Kadamba hatch). ASIAD buses to Mumbai (4hr) also leave here every 15 minutes between 5.30am and 11.30pm, but must be booked a day or so in advance. If heading up to Lonavala or Aurangabad, you'll have to travel across the river to the Shivaji Nagar terminus.

See Travel Details at the end of this chapter for more information on journey frequencies and durations.

Eating

In addition to the hotel restaurants, there are numerous reasonably priced cafés and fast-food outlets around **Connaught** and **Moledina** roads, always busy in the evening. A sociable place to round off the day is on Dr Ambedkhar Road, running east from the GPO, where, from dusk until around 10pm, a string of pavement cafés serve up spicy snacks, cold drinks and fresh juices to young punters.

Cafétarium, Sunder Plaza, MG Road. Smart coffee shop in the atrium behind Thomas Cook, serving mid-morning until 11pm. The place for a cappuccino, light lunch or cosmopolitan meal.

Coffee House, 2 Moledina Rd, Camp. A relaxing, upmarket south Indian snack joint that serves the best coffee, *dosas* and breakfasts in Pune. It's also a/c, and a good spot to beat the heat.

German Bakery, 291 Koregan Park. One of the infamous chain of cafés providing safe Western meals, pastry snacks and home-made breads for homesick travellers and Oshoites.

Kabir's, 6 Moledina Rd. Good selection of north Indian dishes for around Rs50–90, including lots of tasty *tandoori* options. Try to get a table outside in the garden. Serves beer.

Sagar, Sassoon Road, opposite the railway station. Large and busy, serving tasty, Indian and Chinese food in clean, no-smoking surroundings. The place to head for if you are staying at the *National* or have a long wait for a train.

Sahare, 5 Connaught Rd. Outstanding Gujarati/Rajastani unlimited thalis served in spotless airy surroundings opposite the GPO. Costs a little more than the average thali, but well worth it.

Touche the Sizzler, 7 Moledina Rd, Camp. Great fast food: chicken and lamb "sizzlers" and burgers, and plenty of Punjabi-style veg dishes. Popular with Pune's bright young things, and a little pricey.

Sinhagad

The windswept, ruined fort of **SINHAGAD** (formerly Kandana), 26km southwest of Pune at the top of an almost perpendicular cliff in the Bhuleshwar mountains, can easily be visited in a day-trip from Pune by catching a #49 bus (hourly 6.30am–9.30pm; 1hr) from the Swargate bus stand. This involves a stiff two-hour climb from the foot of the hill, but with your own transport you can drive a great deal closer. In 1647 Shivaji, the greatest chief of the Marathas, on hearing that his general Tanaji had died capturing the fort, lamented "I have won the fort, but lost the lion". To commemorate Tanaji's achievement, it was renamed Sinhagad, "lion fort". Tanaji had attacked on a moonless night, on the western side; the sheer size of the cliff was seen as such a deterrent that the fort was left undefended by the forces of Udai Bhan, who were celebrating a wedding. However, according to legend, Tanaji had in his service the old campaigner Yashwanti, an iguana, which with a rope ladder tied to its tail was thrown onto the cliff face and, after three attempts, stuck securely. So strong was the iguana's grip that, before the night was out, three hundred of Tanaji's men had climbed into the fort.

Surprisingly, a few families live in simple houses within its twelve-metre-high walls. Some can serve you a cup of tea; other villagers from the plain climb up every day in the hope of selling pots of yoghurt to day-trippers.

Mahabaleshwar

MAHABALESHWAR, 250km southeast of Mumbai and the most visited hill resort in Maharashtra, is most easily reached from Pune (120km northeast). The highest point in the Western Ghats (1372m), it is subject to extraordinarily extreme **weather** conditions. The start of June brings heavy mists and a dramatic drop in temperature, followed by a deluge of biblical proportions: up to seven metres of rain can fall in the hundred days up to the end of September. As a result, tourists only come here between November and May; during April and May, at the height of summer, the place is packed. The main attraction is the network of marked **hiking trails** through the woods, leading to waterfalls and assorted vantage points, with views over the peaks and down to the plains. You can also take boats out on the central **Yenna Lake**, and shop for strawberries, raspberries, locally made jams and honey in the lively market.

For most foreign visitors, Mahabaleshwar's prime appeal is its location midway between Mumbai and Goa. However, to complete the short but rewarding walk to **Wilson's Point**, the highest spot on the ridge, you'll have to arrive well before dusk. To pick up the (driveable) trail, head south through the bazaar (away from the bus stand) and straight over the crossroads at the end past the *Mayfair* hotel; ten minutes further up the hill, you reach a red-and-white sign pointing left off the road. Wilson's Point lies another stiff ten minutes' up, crowned by a gigantic radio transmitter that is visible for miles. The sunset panoramas from here can be breathtaking.

Practicalities

The central **State bus stand** at the north end of the bazaar serves **Pune** (9 daily; 3hr), the most convenient railhead, as well as **Kolhapur** (5 daily; 7hr) and **Satara** (every two hours daily; 1hr), which is 17km from Satara Road railway station, connected to Mumbai via Pune and Miraj (for Goa). To get here from **Mumbai**, much the best option is to catch the MSRTC semi-luxury bus which departs from the Mumbai Central bus stand each morning at 7am (7hr); return buses leave at 1pm, 2.45pm and 9pm, and should be booked in advance from the reservations hatch at the far end of the concourse – there are three ordinary services during the morning each way.

As in many hill stations, despite an abundance of hotels, prices in Mahabaleshwar are well above average. The cheapest **places to stay** are on the road parallel with the main bazaar, **Murray Peth**, where, with a little haggling, you can pick up rooms for under Rs200. Accommodation is scarce during the monsoon (mid-June to mid-Sept), when most hotels close, and during peak season (Nov–May), when tariffs double.

Ashoka Inn, 289 Murray Peth ☎02168/60622. One of a string of dependable, clean and essentially characterless places on this street. Restaurant, STD phone, but no views. ⑦

Dreamland, directly below the State bus stand ☎02168/60228. Large, established resort hotel in extensive gardens. Rooms range from simple chalets ("cottages") to new a/c poolside apartments with stupendous views. The congenial garden café serves decent espresso and the restaurant fine Indian, Continental, Mexican and Chinese cooking. ⑧

Fountain, opposite Koyna Valley ☎02168/60227, ⓕ60137; also bookable in Mumbai through *Fountain's Fast Food Restaurant* ☎022/367 7182. Close to the centre with posh doubles (some a/c

with TV) and pure veg restaurant serving Indian, Western and Chinese dishes. ⑦

Grand, Woodlawn Road ☎02168/60322. Tucked away in a leafy and secluded spot, five minutes by taxi from the centre. Simpler than its name would suggest, but decent rooms with verandas and very pleasant garden. ⑥–⑦

MTDC Holiday Camp, 2km from the centre ☎02168/60318, ⓕ60300 or Mumbai ☎022/202 6713. Wide range of good-value no-frills accommodation, including cottages to sleep four, doubles and a dorm (Rs100). Simple restaurant and beer bar. ⑤–⑧

Shri Paradise, Main Road, near State bus stand ☎02168/60523. Run-of-the-mill budget lodge. ③–⑤

Pratapgarh

An hour's bus ride away from Mahabaleshwar, or a hike of 24km, the seventeenth-century **fort** of **PRATAPGARH** (daily, dawn to dusk; free) stretches the full length of a high ridge. Reached by five hundred steps, it is famously associated with the Maratha chieftain, **Shivaji**, who lured the Moghul general Afzal Khan here from Bijapur to discuss a possible truce. Neither, it would seem, intended to keep to the condition that they should come unarmed. Khan attempted to knife Shivaji, who responded by killing him with the gruesome *wagnakh*, a set of metal claws worn on the hand. Modern visitors can see Afzal Khan's tomb, a memorial to Shivaji, and views of the surrounding hills.

Kolhapur and Panhala fort

KOLHAPUR, on the banks of the River Panchaganga 225km south of Pune, is thought to have been an important centre of the Tantric cult associated with Shakti worship since ancient times. The town probably grew up around the sacred site of the present-day **Mahalakshmi temple**, still important in the life of the city, although there are said to be up to 250 other temples in the area. With a population of more than 500,000, Kolhapur has become a major industrial centre, but the city has retained enough Maharashtran character to make it worthy of a stopover.

Between the tenth and thirteenth centuries the city was ruled by the Yadavas; later it came under the Moghuls, and in 1675 it was conquered by the Maratha chief Shivaji. His descendants, the Chhatrapatis, ruled until Independence, having shifted their provincial capital here from Panhala (18km northwest) in 1708. In the late nineteenth century, Kolhapur played an important role in the development of the so-called **Indo–Saracenic** style of architecture. The architect Major Charles Mant, under the auspices of the maharaja, blended Western styles with Islamic, Jain and Hindu ones, resulting in buildings that profoundly affected the evolution of colonial architecture. Mant's work, which can be seen all over the city, includes the High School and Town Hall; the General Library; the Albert Edward Hospital; and the New Palace, now a museum. Despite this prolific output, Mant lived in constant (unfounded) terror that his buildings would collapse; he commited suicide at the age of 42 in 1881.

The **Mahalakshmi temple**, whose cream-painted sanctuary towers soar above the town, is thought to have been founded in the seventh century by the Chalukyan king Karnadeva, following damage inflicted by the Moghuls. However, what you see today probably dates from the early eighteenth century. It is built from bluish-black basalt on the plan of a cross, with the image of the goddess Mahalakshmi beneath the eastern and largest of five domed towers. The *mandapa* hallways leading to the main shrine hold figures of Garuda, Vishnu's bird *vahara* (celestial vehicle), and Ganapati, which devotees circumambulate prior to approaching the goddess, flanked by the goddesses Mahakali and Saraswati. Four-armed Mahalakshmi, in black stone, holds a mace and shield, fruit and a cup. Her head is crowned with a cobra whose hood stands over a *shivalingam*.

Presiding over the square just up the road from the Mahalakshmi temple, the **Rajwada**, or Old Palace, is still occupied by members of the Chhatrapati family. Visitors can see the entrance hall (daily 10am–6pm) by passing under a pillared porch which extends out into the town square.

Kolhapur is famous as a centre for traditional wrestling, or *kusti*. On leaving the palace gates, turn right and head through the low doorway in front of you, from where a path picks its way past a couple of derelict buildings to the sunken *motibaug*, or **wrestling ground**. Come here between 5.30am and

5.30pm, and you can watch the wrestlers training, mainly dressed in tiny thongs and caked in red dirt. The main season is between June and September, the coolest time of year, but you may see them active at other times. Hindus and Muslims train together, and it's fine to take photographs.

The maharaja's **New Palace** (Tues–Sun 9.30am–1pm & 2.30–6pm; Rs10), 2km north of the centre, was built in 1884, following a fire at the Rajwada. Designed by Major Mant, its style fuses Jain and Hindu influences from Gujarat and Rajasthan, and local touches from the Rajwada, while remaining indomitably Victorian, with a prominent clock tower. The present maharaja lives on the first floor, while the ground floor holds an absorbing collection of costumes, weapons, games, jewellery, embroidery and paraphernalia such as silver elephant saddles.

Practicalities

Two direct express **trains** leave Mumbai CST for Kolhapur via Pune (9hr) each evening: the Mahalaxmi Express #1011 (8.25pm; 12hr 15min) and the Sahyadri Express #7303 (5.45pm; 11hr 20min). Heading in the other direction, the Mahalaxmi Express, bound for Pune and Mumbai leaves Kolhapur at 7.15pm. The **railway station** is 500m from the **bus stand** on Station Road, near the centre of town. A five-minute walk from here (turn right) brings you to the **MTDC tourist office**, in the Kedar Complex on Station Road (Mon–Sat; 8.30am–6.30pm; ☎0231/692935), where you can sign up for a whistle-stop guided **tour** of Kolhapur and Panhala (Mon–Sat 10am–5.30pm; Rs50). The only place in Kolhapur to change **travellers' cheques** is at the State Bank of India (Mon–Fri 10am–2pm, Sat 10am–noon) at Dasara Chowk Bridge, near Shahamahar railway station.

There's no shortage of decent reasonably-priced **accommodation** in Kolhapur, most within easy reach of the bus stand along Station Road. *Hotel Maharaja*, 514 Station Rd (☎0231/650829; ❸) is a basic lodge, directly opposite the bus stand, with dozens of good-value, simple, clean rooms, and a veg restaurant. If it's full, try the *Hotel Parth* (☎0231/664841; ❸) next door. Near the railway station, *Hotel Tourist*, 204 E New Shahupuri, Station Rd (☎0231/650421, ℻653346; ❸–❺), is also a good bet. One of the best options, though, is in a peaceful suburb a five-minute rickshaw drive away: *Hotel Woodlands*, 204E, Tarabai Park (☎0231/650941; ℻633378; ❺–❻), with a range of a/c and non-a/c rooms with TV, 24-hour coffee shop, multi-cuisine restaurant, garden and bar.

Outside the hotels, the best **food** is to be had in *Subraya* at the top of Station Square, a comfortable, modern a/c restaurant, with a varied menu including good Maharashtran thalis, breakfast and cheaper south Indian-style snacks such as tasty *dosas*, *wada pao* and filling *pani puris*.

Panhala fort

Regular buses (30min) run between Kolhapur and **Panhala fort**, 18km northwest. Although it has legendary connections with the god Parashurama (Rama with the axe), the fort was probably founded by King Raja Bhoja in the late twelfth century. It covers a vast area, with massive perimeter walls over 7km in length and a steep slope beneath. Nevertheless, Panhala could not reasonably be described as impregnable. Over the years it has fallen to the Devagiri Yadavas, various Maratha chieftains, and, in 1489, the Adil Shahi dynasty of Bijapur, who erected the ramparts that still stand. Shivaji took Panhala in 1659, only just managing to escape with his life a year later when it was retaken by the Bijapur army. According to tradition, he was saved because one of his lieutenants posed as the leader and was killed, allowing Shivaji to make a quick exit, and regain it later. After this, the fort fell to the Moghul Aurangzeb (1700), became Maratha state capital under Tarabai until 1782, and went to the British in 1827.

The Teen Darwaza ("three door") gate meant successive doors could only be approached at an awkward angle, trapping troops in the inner courtyard and making it impossible to charge. A well in the corner was used to send word to allies; lemons with incised messages were dropped into the water, and would float to a lake outside.

A number of modern buildings have been erected within the fort, some of them palatial homes belonging, it is said, to wealthy personages such as "sugar barons" and the famous Hindi film-song artist, Lata Mangeshkar. There's a newly privatized MTDC resort (☎02328/35333; ❹–❼) if you fancy staying, or alternativly enjoy the vista from the *Hotel Hilltop* (☎02328/35054, ☎0231/660061; ❼).

Travel details

Trains

Aurangabad to: Ahmedabad (4 daily; 18hr); Delhi (5 weekly; 24hr 50min); Mumbai (20 daily; 8hr 15min).

Jalgaon to: Agra (3–4 daily; 14hr 20min–17hr 20min); Bangalore (1–2 daily; 24–26hr 30min); Bhopal (2 daily; 7–8hr 25min); Calcutta (4 daily; 28–34hr); Chennai (1 daily; 24hr); Delhi (3 daily; 18–22hr); Gwalior (3–5 daily; 13–15hr); Jhansi (3–5 daily; 11hr 15min–13hr 20min); Mumbai (9–11 daily; 7hr 40min–9hr 35min); Nagpur (5–7 daily; 7hr 45min–9hr 35min); Pune (16 daily; change at Bhusaval; 10hr); Varanasi (2–4 daily; 19hr 40min–23hr); Wardha (6–7 daily; 6–7hr 30min).

Nagpur to: Bhopal (13 daily; 5hr 30min–8hr 30min); Calcutta (4–6 daily; 18hr 40min–24hr); Chennai (2–5 daily; 15–24hr); Delhi (10–12 daily 13hr 45min–22hr 30min); Hyderabad (2–4 daily; 8hr 30min–14hr 45min); Indore (1 daily; 14hr 5min); Jabalpur (8 weekly; 9hr 15min–9hr 55min); Jalgaon (5–7 daily; 7hr 45min–9hr 35min); Mumbai (5–6 daily; 17hr 25min–15hr); Nasik (4 daily; 11–13hr); Pune (1–2 daily; 17–19hr); Varanasi (6 weekly; 19hr 15min–19hr 55min); Wardha (hourly; 2hr).

Nasik to: Agra (3–4 daily; 17hr 30min–21hr); Bhopal (4–5 daily; 10hr–12hr 20min); Calcutta (3 daily; 31hr 20min–37hr 30min); Delhi (3 daily; 21hr 10min–25hr 50min); Jabalpur (5–6 daily; 12hr 30min–14hr 45min); Mumbai (13–15 daily; 4–6hr); Nagpur (4 daily; 11–13hr).

Pune to: Bangalore (2–3 daily; 19hr 15min–22hr 15min); Chennai (3 daily; 20–25hr 45min); Delhi (3 daily; 26hr 30min–29hr); Jalgaon (16 daily; 10hr); Hyderabad (3–4 daily; 11hr 20min–13hr 15min); Kolhapur (4 daily; 7hr 30min–7hr 50min); Mumbai (20–23 daily; 3hr 25min–5hr 10min); Nagpur (1–2 daily; 17–19hr).

Buses

Aurangabad to: Ahmedabad (1 nightly; 14hr); Ajanta (hourly; 3hr); Bijapur (1 daily; 12hr); Ellora (every 30min; 40min); Indore (2 daily; 12hr); Jalgaon (hourly; 4hr); Mumbai (6 nightly; 10–12hr); Nagpur (4 daily; 12hr); Nasik (8 daily; 5hr); Pune (7 daily; 5hr).

Jalgaon to: Ajanta (4 daily direct; 1hr 40min); Aurangabad (every 30min; 4hr); Fardapur (for Ajanta; every 30min; 1hr 25min); Mumbai (1 daily; 10hr 30min); Nagpur (2 daily; 9hr); Pune (5 daily; 9hr).

Nagpur to: Aurangabad (4 daily; 12hr); Bhopal (1 daily; 7hr); Indore (4 daily; 11hr); Jabalpur (9 daily; 7hr); Jalgaon (2 daily; 9hr); Pune (5 daily; 16hr); Ramtek (hourly; 1hr 30min).

Nasik to: Aurangabad (8 daily; 5hr); Mumbai (6 daily; 4hr); Pune (every 30min; 3hr); Trimbak (hourly; 45min).

Pune to: Aurangabad (7 daily; 5hr); Bijapur (1 daily; 8hr); Goa (4 daily; 15hr); Kolhapur (4 daily; 12hr); Mahabaleshwar (9 daily; 3hr); Mumbai (hourly; 4hr 30min); Nasik (every 30min; 3hr).

Flights

Aurangabad to: Delhi (1 daily; 3hr 25min); Mumbai (1 daily; 40min).

Nagpur to: Calcutta (2 weekly; 1hr 30min); Delhi (1 daily; 2hr 25min); Hyderabad (2 weekly; 1hr); Mumbai (2 daily; 1hr 15min).

Pune to: Ahmedabad (3 weekly; 1hr); Bangalore (1 daily; 1hr 25min); Chennai (3 weekly; 2hr 50min); Delhi (1 daily; 2hr); Mumbai (3 daily; 35–45min).

CHAPTER 12 # Highlights

* **Old Goa** Belfries and Baroque church facades loom over the trees on the banks of the Mandovi, all that remains of a once splendid colonial city. See p.868

* **Beach shacks** Tuck into a fresh kingfish, tandoori pomfret or a lobster supper, washed down with *feni* or an ice-cool Kingfisher beer. See p.878

* **Flea market, Anjuna** Goa's most vibrant bazaar is the place to pick up the latest party gear, shop for touristy souvenirs, and watch the crowds go by. See p.885

* **Nine Bar, Ozran Vagator** Epicentre of hip Goa, where trance music accompanies the sunsets over Vagator beach. See p.889

* **Arambol** An alternative resort with exquisite beaches and a ramshackle fishing village. See p.895

* **Perreira-Braganza House, Chandor** The region's most impressive colonial-era mansion, crammed with period furniture and fittings. See p.901

* **Sunset stroll, Palolem** Tropical sunsets don't come much more romantic than at this idyllic palm-fringed cove in the hilly deep south. See p.908

Goa

I f one word could be said to encapsulate the essence of **GOA**, it would have to be the Portuguese *sossegarde*, meaning "carefree". The pace of life in this former colonial enclave, midway down India's southwest coast, has picked up over the past twenty years, but in spite of the increasing chaos of its capital, beach resorts and market towns, Goa has retained the laid-back feel that has traditionally set it apart from the rest of the country. Its 1.4 million inhabitants are unequivocal about the roots of their distinctiveness; while most of the subcontinent was colonized by the stiff-upper-lipped British, Goa's European overlords were the **Portuguese**, a people far more inclined to enjoy the good things in life than their Anglo-Saxon counterparts.

Goa was Portugal's first toe-hold in Asia, and served as the linchpin for a vast trade network for over 450 years. However, when the Lusitanian empire began to founder in the seventeenth century, so too did the fortunes of its capital. Cut off from the rest of India by a wall of mountains and hundreds of miles of unnavigable alluvial plain, it remained resolutely aloof from the wider subcontinent. While India was tearing itself to pieces in the run-up to Independence in 1947, the only machetes being wielded here were cutting coconuts. Not until 1961, after an exasperated Indian Prime Minister, Jawaharlal Nehru, gave up trying to negotiate with the Portuguese dictator Salazar and sent in the army, was Goa finally absorbed into India.

Those who visited in the late 1960s and 1970s, when the overland travellers' trail wriggled its way south from Bombay, found a way of life little changed in centuries: Portuguese was still very much the lingua franca of the well-educated elite, and the coastal settlements were mere fishing and coconut cultivation villages. Relieved to have found somewhere inexpensive and culturally undemanding to recover from the travails of Indian travel, the travellers got stoned, watched the mesmeric sunsets over the Arabian Sea and partied madly on full-moon nights, giving rise to a holiday culture that soon made Goa synonymous with hedonistic **hippies**.

Since then, the state has largely shaken off its reputation as a drop-out zone, but hundreds of thousands of visitors still flock here each winter, the vast majority to relax on Goa's beautiful **beaches**. Around two dozen stretches of soft white sand indent the region's coast, from spectacular 25-kilometre sweeps to secluded palm-backed coves. The level of development varies wildly; while some are lined by ritzy Western-style resorts, the most sophisticated structures on others are palm-leaf shacks and old wooden outriggers that are heaved into the sea each afternoon.

Wherever you travel in Goa, vestiges of former Portuguese domination are ubiquitous, creating an ambience that is at once exotic and strangely familiar.

MAHARASHTRA

KARNATAKA

PERNEM

Terekol
Querim
Pernem
Mandrem Arambol
Parcem
Aswem
Morjim Siolim
Chapora
Vagator
Anjuna
BARDEZ
Baga
Calangute
Candolim
Fort Aguada
Miramar
Cabo Raj Bhavan
Dona Paula
Vasco
da Gama
Mormugao

Tirakol

BICHOLIM

Bicholim

Sanquelim

SATARI

Valpoi

Chapora

Mapusa

Chorao
Island
Divar
Island

Naroa
Piedade
Old Goa

Porvorim
Betim
Reis
Magos
Mandovi
PANJIM
TISWADI

Karmali
(Carambolim)

Goa Velha
Pilar
Zuari

Mardol

BONDLA
SANCTUARY

Tamdi
Surla

PONDA
Tisk
Khandepar
Ponda

Molem

BHAGWAN
MAHAVEER
SANCTUARY

Dabolim Airport
Bogmalo

MORMUGAO

Pequeno
Island

São Jorge
Island

Cansaulim
Majorda
Betalbatim
Colva
Benaulim
Varca

Lutolim
Rachol
Margao
SALCETE

Chandor

SANGUEM
Colem
Dudhsagar
Falls

ARABIAN
SEA

Quepem
Zambaulim
Rivona

Sanguem

Cavelossim
Mobor
Betul

Dom Bosco

QUEPEM

Cabo da
Rama
Agonda
Palolem
Galjibag

Malikarjun

Chaudi

COTIGAO
SANCTUARY

Talpona

CANACONA

Polem

SAHYADRI RANGE

0   Kilometres   20

Karwar & Gokarn, Jog Falls

This is particularly true of Goan food which, blending the Latin love of meat and fish with India's predilection for spices, is quite unlike any other regional cuisine in Asia. Equally unique is the prevalence of **alcohol**. Beer is cheap, and six thousand or more bars around the state are licensed to serve it, along with the more traditional tipple, *feni*, a rocket-fuel spirit distilled from cashew fruit or coconut sap.

Travelling around the Christian heartland of central Goa, with its white-washed churches and wayside shrines, it's all too easy to forget that **Hinduism** remains the religion of more than two-thirds of the state's population. Unlike in many parts of the country, however, religious intolerance is rare here, and traditional practices mingle easily with more recently implanted ones. Faced by the threat of merger with neighbouring states, Goans have always put regional cohesion before communal differences at the ballot box. A potent stimulus for regional identity was the campaign through the 1980s to have **Konkani**, the language spoken by the vast majority of Goans, recognized as an official state language, which it eventually was in 1992. Since then, the **immigration** issue has come to dominate the political agenda. Considerably more prosperous than neighbouring states, Goa has been deluged over the past couple of decades with economic refugees, stirring up fears that the region's cultural distinctiveness will disappear. Among the main employers of migrant labour in recent years has been the **Konkan Railway**, completed in 1997 to form a super-fast land link with Mumbai – another conduit of economic prosperity that has brought lasting changes.

Which beach you opt for when you arrive largely depends on what sort of holiday you have in mind. Heavily developed resorts such as **Calangute** and **Baga**, in the north, and **Colva** (and to a lesser extent **Benaulim**), in the south, offer more "walk-in" accommodation, shopping and tourist facilities than elsewhere. Even if you don't fancy crowded bars and purpose-built hotels, it can be worth heading for these centres first, as finding places to stay in less commercialized corners is often difficult. **Anjuna**, **Vagator**, and **Chapora**, where accommodation is generally more basic and harder to come by, are the beaches to aim for if you've come to Goa to party. However, the bulk of budget travellers taking time out from tours of India end up in **Palolem**, in the far south, or **Arambol**, beyond the increasingly long reach of the charter buses. Although fast becoming resorts in their own right, these two fishing villages have largely preserved the laid-back atmosphere most people come to Goa for.

Foremost among the attractions away from the coast are the ruins of the Portuguese capital at **Old Goa**, 10km from Panjim – a sprawl of Catholic cathedrals, convents and churches that draws crowds of Christian pilgrims from all over India. Another popular day excursion is to Anjuna's Wednesday **flea market**, a sociable place to shop for souvenirs and dance wear. Further inland, the thickly wooded countryside around **Ponda** harbours numerous temples, where you can check out Goa's peculiar brand of Hindu architecture. The district of Salcete, and its main market town, **Margao**, is also littered with Portuguese mansions, churches and seminaries. Finally, wildlife enthusiasts may be tempted into the interior to visit the nature reserve at **Cotigao** in the far south.

The best **time to come** to Goa is during the dry, relatively cool winter months between late October and late March. At other times, either the sun is too hot for comfort, or the monsoon rains make life miserable. During peak season, from mid-December to the end of January, the weather is perfect, with temperatures rarely nudging above 32°C. Finding a room or a house to rent at

Accommodation price codes

All accommodation prices in this book have been categorized using the price codes below. Prices given are for a double room, and all taxes are included. For more details, see p.51.

❶ up to Rs100	❹ Rs300–400	❼ Rs900–1500
❷ Rs100–200	❺ Rs400–600	❽ Rs1500–2500
❸ Rs200–300	❻ Rs600–900	❾ Rs2500 and upwards

Some of Goa's festivals are on fixed dates each year; ask at a tourist office for dates of the others. The biggest celebrations take place at Panjim and Margao.

Festa dos Reis (Jan 6). Epiphany celebrations include a procession of young boys decked out as the Three Kings to the Franciscan chapel of Reis Magos, near Panjim on the north bank of the Mandovi, 3km east of Fort Aguada. Other processions are held at Cansaulim and Chandor.

Carnival (Feb/March). Three days of *feni*-induced mayhem, centring on Panjim, to mark the run-up to Lent.

Shigmo (Feb/March). The Goan version of Holi is celebrated with big parades and crowds; drum and dance groups compete and huge floats, which threaten to bring down telegraph wires, trundle through the streets.

All Saints (March). On the fifth Monday in Lent, 26 effigies of saints, martyrs, popes, kings, queens and cardinals are paraded around the village of Velha Goa, near Panjim. A fair also takes place.

Igitun Chalne (May). *Dhoti*-clad devotees of the goddess Lairya enter trances and walk over hot coals at the village of Sirigao, Bichloim.

Sanjuan (June 24). The festival of St John is celebrated all over Goa, but is especially important in the coastal villages of Arambol and Terekol. Youngsters torch straw dummies (representing St John's baptism, and thus the death of sin), while revellers in striped pants dive into wells after drinking bottles of *feni*.

Janmashtami (Aug). Ritual bathing in the River Mandovi, off Diwadi Island, to celebrate the birth of Krishna.

Dussehra (Sept/Oct). Nine days of festivities in which more effigies are burned on bonfires, and children perform episodes from the life of Rama.

Diwali (Oct/Nov). The five-day Hindu "festival of lights" features processions all over the region, often accompanied by fireworks, and the exchange of sweets by neighbours, regardless of their faith.

Christmas (Dec 24–25). Celebrated everywhere in Goa. Late-night Mass is usually followed by music, dancing and fireworks.

that time, however – particularly over Christmas and New Year when tariffs double, or triple – can be a real hassle.

Some history

The sheer inaccessibility of Goa by land has always kept it out of the mainstream of Indian history; on the other hand, its control of the seas and the lucrative spice trade made it a much-coveted prize for rival colonial powers. Until a century before the arrival of the Portuguese adventurer **Vasco da Gama**, who landed near Kozhikode in Kerala in 1498, Goa had belonged for over a thousand years to the kingdom of **Kadamba**. In the interim it had been successfully conquered by the Karnatakan Vijayanagars, the Muslim Bahmanis, and Yusuf Adil Shah of Bijapur, but the capture of the fort at Panjim by **Afonso de Albuquerque** in 1510 signalled the start of a Portuguese occupation that was to last 450 years.

As Goa expanded, its splendid capital (now Old Goa) came to hold a larger population than Paris or London. Though Ismail Adil Shah laid siege for ten months in 1570, and the Marathas under Shivaji and later chiefs came nail-bitingly close to seizing the region, the greatest threat was from other European maritime nations. While the Dutch made several unsuccessful attacks, the

British at first preferred the avenue of diplomacy. Their **East India Company** signed the **Convention of Goa** in 1642, granting them the right to trade with the colony, and use its harbours.

Meanwhile, conversions to **Christianity**, started by the Franciscans, gathered pace when St Francis Xavier founded the **Jesuit** mission in 1542. With the advent of the **Inquisition** soon afterwards, laws were introduced censoring literature and banning any faith other than Catholicism – even the long-established Syrian Christian community were branded heretics. Hindu temples were destroyed, and converted Hindus adopted Portuguese names, such as da Silva, Correa and de Sousa, which remain common in the region. The transnational influence of the Jesuits eventually alarmed the Portuguese government; the Jesuits were expelled in 1749, which made it possible for Indian Goans to take up the priesthood. However, standards of education suffered, and Goa entered a period of decline. The Portuguese were not prepared to help, but neither would they allow native Goans equal rights. An abortive attempt to establish a Goan Republic was quelled with the execution of fifteen Goan conspirators.

A spin-off of the British conflict with Tipu Sultan of Mysore (a French ally) at the end of the eighteenth century was the **British occupation** of Goa, which lasted sixteen years from 1797. The occupation was solely military; the

---

Police, trouble and nudism

While the vast majority of visitors to Goa never encounter any **trouble**, tourism-related crime is definitely more prevalent than in other parts of the country. **Theft** is the most common problem – usually of articles left unattended on the beach. Don't assume your valuables are safe in a padlocked house or hotel room, either. Break-ins, particularly on party nights, are on the increase. The most secure solution is to rent a deposit box in a bank, which costs around Rs100, or to opt for one of the few guesthouses with lockers.

The other eventuality to avoid, at all costs, is getting on the wrong side of the law. **Drugs** are the most common cause of serious trouble. Many travellers imagine that, because of Goa's free-and-easy reputation, drug use is legal: it isn't. Possession of even a small amount of cannabis is a criminal offence, punishable by large fines or prison sentences of up to ten years. Arrests, however, rarely result in court appearances. The Goan police tend to ensure that offenders are given the opportunity of leaving the country first, having relieved them of nearly all their spare cash and valuables. That said, Fort Aguada prison had, at the last count, half-a-dozen foreigners serving long sentences for drugs offences.

Though violent crime is rare, women should think twice before wandering down deserted beaches and dark tracks on their own. **Sexual harassment** usually takes the form of unsubtle ogling, but there have also been several incidents of **rape** in recent years. Wherever you're staying, therefore, take the same common-sense precautions as you would at home: keep to the main roads when travelling on foot or by bicycle, avoid dirt tracks and unfrequented beaches (particularly on party nights) unless you're in a group, and when you're in your house after dark, ensure that all windows and doors are locked.

Finally, remember that **nudism** is prohibited. In case tourists miss the "NO NUDISM" signs posted at the entrances to most beaches, police regularly patrol the busier resorts to ensure that decorum is maintained. If you are tempted to drop your togs, check that there are no families within eyeshot. No one is likely to object openly, but when you consider that wet Y-fronts and saris are about as risqué as beachwear gets for most Indians, you'll understand why men in G-strings and top-less women cause such a stir.

White Maruti van taxis serve as the main means of travelling between resorts. You'll find them lined up outside most charter hotels, where a board invariably displays "fixed rates" to destinations in and around the region. These fares only apply to peak season, however, and at other times you should be able to negotiate a hefty reduction.

By ferry

If auto-rickshaws are the quintessentially Indian mode of transport, flat-bottomed ferries are their Goan equivalent. Crammed with cars, buses, commuters on scooters, fisherwomen and clumps of bewildered tourists, these rusting blue-painted hulks provide an essential service, crossing the coastal backwaters where bridges have not yet been built. They're also incredibly cheap, and run from the crack of dawn until late in the evening. The most frequented river crossings in Goa are Panjim to Betim, across the Mandovi (every 15min); Old Goa to Divar Island (every 15min); Siolim to Chopdem, across the Chapora River for Arambol and Pernem (every 15min); Querim to Terekol, over the Terekol River (every 30min); and Cavelossim, in the far south of Salcete, to Assolna (every 20–30min).

By train

Following years of controversy, the Konkan Railway was completed in 1997, running down the coast from Mumbai to link with the southern rail network at Mangalore. This now serves as Goa's principal long-distance transport artery, but is rarely convenient for shorter journeys within the state. The relative infrequency of services and distance of the line from most of the resorts means you're invariably better off catching the bus.

By bus

The Goan transport corporation, Kadamba, runs long-distance services throughout the state from their main stands at Panjim, Mapusa and Margao. Private buses, serving everywhere else including the coastal resorts, are cheap, frequent, and more relaxed than many in India, although you should still brace yourself for a crush on market days and when travelling to major towns and tourist centres. Details on how to get around by bus are listed in the relevant accounts, and on p.916.

By motorcycle taxi

Goa's unique pillion-passenger motorcycle taxis, known locally as "pilots", are ideal for nipping between beaches or into town from the resorts. Bona fide opera-

Goan authorities never gave up their administration. Despite a certain liberalization, such as the restoration of Hindus' right to worship and the final banishment of the dreaded Inquisition in 1814, the nineteenth century saw widespread civil unrest. During British occupation many Goans moved to Bombay, and elsewhere in British India, to find work.

The success of the post-Independence Goan struggle for freedom owed as much to the efforts of the Indian government, who cut off diplomatic ties with Portugal, as to the work of freedom fighters such as **Menezes Braganza** and **Dr Cunha**. After a "liberation march" in 1955 resulted in a number of deaths, the state was blockaded. Trade with Bombay ceased, and the railway was cut off, so Goa set out to forge international links, particularly with Pakistan and Sri Lanka. That led to the building of Dabolim airport, and a determination to improve local agricultural output. In 1961, prime minister Jawaharlal Nehru

tors ride black bikes (usually Rajdoots) with yellow mudguards and white number plates. Fares, which should be settled in advance, are comparable with auto-rickshaw rates: roughly Rs5 per kilometre.

By rented motorcycle

Renting a motorcycle in Goa gives a lot of freedom but can be perilous. Every season, an average of one person a day dies on the roads; many are tourists on two-wheelers. Make sure, therefore, that the lights and brakes are in good shape, and be especially vigilant at night: many Goan roads are appallingly pot-holed and unlit, and stray cows and bullock carts can appear from nowhere.

Officially, you need an **international driver's licence** to rent, and ride, anything more powerful than a 25cc moped. Owners and rental companies rarely enforce this, but some local **police** use the rule to extract exorbitant baksheesh from tourists. If you don't have a licence with you, the only way around the problem is to avoid big towns such as Panjim, Margao and Mapusa (or Anjuna on market day), and only to carry small sums of money when driving. If you are arrested for not having the right papers, it's no big deal, though police officers may try to convince you otherwise; keep cool, and be prepared to negotiate. Some unlicensed operators attempt to rent out machines to unwary visitors; always make sure you get some evidence of rental and insurance.

Rates vary according to the season, the vehicle, and how long you rent it for; most owners also insist on a deposit and/or passport as security. The range is pretty standard, with the cheapest choice, a 50cc **moped**, costing Rs100 per day. These are fine for buzzing to the beach and back, but to travel further try the stalwart **Enfield Bullet 350cc**, popular mainly for its pose value (upwards of Rs250 per day); the smaller but more reliable **Honda Kinetic 100cc**, which has automatic gears and is a good first-time choice (Rs150–200/day); or the best all-rounder, the **Yamaha RD 100cc**: light, fast enough, reliable, economical and with manual gears (Rs150–225/day). The notoriously unreliable Indian makes, **Rajdoot** and **Bajaj**, are best avoided.

Tours

On paper, GTDC's guided **tours** from Panjim, Margao, Calangute and Colva seem like a good way of getting around Goa's highlights in a short time. However, they're far too rushed for most foreign tourists, appealing essentially to Indian families wishing to combine a peek at the resorts with a whistle-stop puja tour of the temples around Ponda. Most also include a string of places inland that you wouldn't otherwise consider visiting. Leaflets giving full itineraries are available at any GTDC office, where you can also buy tickets: full-day tours cost Rs95.

finally ran out of patience with his opposite number in Lisbon, the right-wing dictator Salazar, and sent in the armed forces. Mounted in defiance of a United Nations resolution, "**Operation Vijay**" met only token resistance, and the Indian army overran Goa in two days. Thereafter, Goa (along with Portugal's other two enclaves, Daman and Diu) became part of India as a self-governing **Union Territory**, with minimum interference from Delhi.

Since Independence, Goa has continued to prosper, bolstered by iron-ore exports and a booming tourist industry, but is struggling to hold its own against a tidal wave of **immigration** from other Indian states. Its inhabitants voted overwhelmingly to resist a merger with neighbouring Maharashtra in the 1980s, and successfully lobbied for Konkani to be granted official-language status in 1987, when Goa was finally declared a fully fledged state of the Indian Union. Since then, however, its political life has been dogged by chronic **insta-**

bility. In the 1990s, no less than twelve chief ministers held power over a succession of shaky, opportunistic coalitions, which saw standards of government plummet to depths hitherto unseen in the region. Elections were invariably followed by periods of deal cutting, in which old scores were settled and revenge exacted for past defections and betrayals. As a result, policy-making has been rendered nearly impossible, while **corruption** has eroded the fabric of government.

Among the main beneficiaries of the ongoing chaos have been the extreme right-wing Hindu fundamentalists, the **BJP** (Bharatiya Janata Party). In the past, their pro-merger stance made them unpopular with the Goan electorate – even Hindus – despite the party's dominance in the national arena. But at the time of writing – in the wake of the political coup of November 1999 when a Congress splinter group came to power under the leadership of Francisco Sardinha – the BJP occupied one quarter of the seats in the Goan assembly.

Panjim and central Goa

Take any mid-sized Portuguese town, add a sprinkling of banana trees and auto-rickshaws, drench annually with torrential tropical rain, and leave to simmer in fierce humid sunshine for at least one hundred and fifty years, and you'll end up with something like **PANJIM** (also known by its Maharathi name, **Panaji** – "land that does not flood"). The Goan capital has a completely different feel from any other Indian city. Stacked around the sides of a lush terraced hillside at the mouth of the River Mandovi, its skyline of red-tiled roofs, whitewashed churches, and mildewing concrete apartment blocks has more in common with Lisbon than Lucknow. This lingering European influence is most evident in the small squares and cobbled lanes of the town's old Latin quarter, **Fontainhas**. Here, Portuguese is still very much the lingua franca, the shop fronts sport names like José Pinto and de Souza, and the women wear knee-length dresses that would turn heads anywhere else in the country.

For centuries, Panjim was little more than a minor landing stage and customs house, protected by a hilltop fort, and surrounded by stagnant swampland. It only became capital in 1843, after the port at Old Goa had silted up, and its rulers and impoverished inhabitants had fled the plague. Although the last Portuguese viceroy managed to drain many of the nearby marshes, and erect imposing public buildings on the new site, the town never emulated the grandeur of its predecessor upriver – a result, in part, of the Portuguese nobles' predilection for erecting their mansions in the countryside rather than the city. Panjim expanded rapidly in the 1960s and 1970s, without reaching the unmanageable proportions of other Indian state capitals. After Mumbai, or even Bangalore, its uncongested streets seem easygoing and pleasantly parochial. Sights are thin on the ground, but the palm-lined squares and atmospheric Latin quarter, with its picturesque Neoclassical houses and Catholic churches, make a pleasant backdrop for aimless wandering.

Some travellers see no more of Panjim than its noisy bus terminal – which is a pity. Although you can completely bypass the town when you arrive in Goa, either by jumping off the train or coach at Margao (for the south), or Mapusa

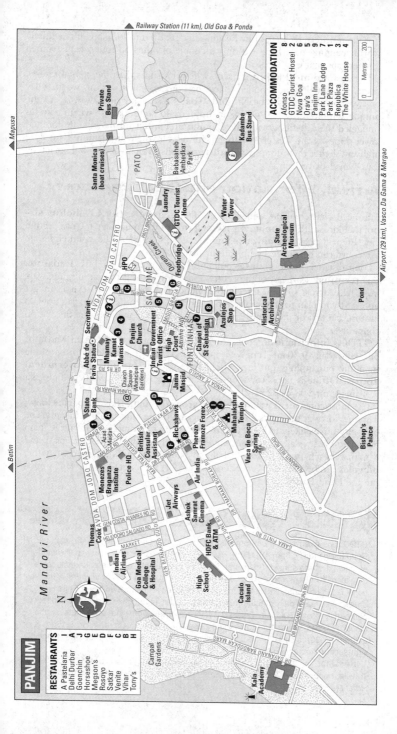

PANJIM

RESTAURANTS
A Pastelaria	I
Delhi Durbar	A
Goenchin	J
Horseshoe	G
Megson's	E
Rosoyo	D
Satkar	F
Venite	C
Vihar	B
Tony's	H

ACCOMMODATION
Afonso	8
GTDC Tourist Hostel	2
Nova Goa	6
Orav's	5
Panjim Inn	9
Park Lane Lodge	7
Park Plaza	1
Republica	3
The White House	4

Metres 0 — 200

(for the northern resorts), or by heading straight off on a local bus, it's definitely worth spending time here – if only a couple of hours en route to the ruined former capital at Old Goa.

The area **around Panjim** attracts far fewer visitors than the coastal resorts, yet its paddy fields and wooded valleys harbour several attractions worth a day or two's break from the beach. **Old Goa** is just a bus ride away, as are the unique temples around **Ponda**, an hour or so southeast, to where Hindus smuggled their deities during the Inquisition. Further inland still, the forested lower slopes of the Western Ghats, cut through by the main Panjim–Bangalore highway, shelter the impressive **Dudhsagar falls**, which you can only reach by four-wheel-drive Jeep.

Arrival, information and local transport

European charter planes and domestic flights arrive at Goa's **Dabolim airport**, 29km south of Panjim on the outskirts of Vasco da Gama, Goa's second city. Prepaid taxis into town (45min; Rs475), booked at the counter in the forecourt, can be shared by up to four people.

Long-distance and local **buses** pull into Panjim at the town's busy **Kadamba bus terminal**, 1km east of the centre in the district of Pato. Ten minutes' walk from here, across Ourem Creek to Fontainhas, brings you to several budget hotels. If you plan to stay in the more modern west end of town, flag down a motorcycle taxi or jump into an auto-rickshaw at the rank outside the station concourse.

GTDC's **information** counter, inside the concourse at the main Kadamba bus stand (daily 9.30am–1pm & 2–5pm; ☏0832/225620) is useful for checking train and bus timings, but little else. The more efficient **India Government Tourist Office** is across town on Church Square (Mon–Fri 9.30am–6pm, Sat 9.30am–1pm; ☏0832/223412).

The most convenient way of **getting around** Panjim is by **auto-rickshaw**; flag one down at the roadside or head for one of the ranks around the city. The only city **buses** likely to be of use to visitors run to Dona Paula from the main bus stand via several stops along the esplanade (including the Secretariat), and Miramar beach-front. If you feel up to taking on Panjim's anarchic traffic, **bicycles** can be rented (Mon–Sat only; Rs3/hr) from a stall up the lane opposite the Head Post Office.

Accommodation

The majority of Goa's Indian visitors prefer to stay in Panjim rather than the coastal resorts, which explains the huge number **hotels** and **lodges** crammed into the town centre. Finding a place to stay is only a problem during the festival of St Francis (Nov 24–Dec 3), Dusshera (Sept/Oct) and during peak season (mid-Dec to mid-Jan), when tariffs double. At other times, hotels try to fill rooms by offering substantial discounts. The most atmospheric options are in Fontainhas, down by Ourem Creek, and in the backstreets behind the esplanade. Standards are generally good, and even the cheapest rooms should have a window, a fan, running water and clean sheets. Most other hotels are bland places in the modern, west end of town.

Note that **checkout times** here vary wildly. Find out what yours is as soon as you arrive, or your hard-earned lie-in could end up costing you an extra day's rent.

Alfonso, St Sebastian Chapel Square, Fontainhas ☎0832/222359. Recently refurbished colonial-era house in a picturesque backstreet. Spotlessly clean, cool en-suite rooms, friendly owners and rooftop terrace with views. Single occupancy rates available. **⑤**–**⑥**

GTDC Tourist Hostel, Avda Dom Joao Castro ☎0832/223396 or 227103. Spacious rooms in a bustling government-run hotel next to the main road and river. Shops, a hair salon and tourist information in the lobby. Some a/c. **⑤**–**⑥**

Nova Goa, Dr Atmaram Borkar Road ☎0832/226231, ⓕ224958, ⓔnovagoa@goa1.dot.net.in. Panjim's brightest, newest top-class hotel in the heart of the shopping area and with the usual comforts, plus bathtubs and a pool. Popular mainly with visiting Portuguese and corporate clients. **⑧**–**⑨**

Orav's, 31 Janeiro Rd, Fontainhas ☎0832/46128. Modern building in the old quarter, with good-sized, comfortable rooms and small balconies on the front side overlooking the rooftops. **④**

Panjim Inn, E-212, 31 Janeiro Rd, Fontainhas ☎0832/226523, ⓕ228136, ⓦwww.panjiminn.com. Grand colonial-era town-house, now managed as an upmarket but homely hotel, with period furniture, sepia family photos, balconies and a common veranda, where meals and drinks are served to guests. An even more beautiful Hindu house across the road, *Panjim Pousada*, renovated by the same owner, offers the chance to sample what Panjim must have felt like

a century ago, with a leafy inner courtyard and huge breadfruit tree overhanging the rear veranda. Easily the best place in its class. **⑥**–**⑦**

Park Lane Lodge, near Chapel of St Sebastian ☎0832/220238 or 227154, ⓔpklaldg@goatelecom .com. Spotless and characterful but cramped family guesthouse in old colonial-style house. Pepper and coffee plants add atmosphere to a narrow communal terrace, and there's a TV lounge upstairs; also safe-deposit facilities, internet access, laundry service and good off-season discounts. **④**

Park Plaza, Azad Maidan ☎0832/422601–5, ⓕ225635. A newish hotel on a quiet square near the river. Close to the commercial centre, with all the usual amenities, including a restaurant, and courteous staff. Good full- and half-board packages for single travellers. **⑦**

Republica, Jose Falcao Road, near GTDC *Tourist Hostel* ☎0832/224630. Rock-bottom budget travellers' lodge with grubby rooms, attached shower-toilets and river views from a large wooden veranda. A last resort option only. **②**–**③**

The White House, PO Box 329, behind GTDC *Tourist Hostel* ☎0832/255239 or 223928. Renamed to coincide with Clinton's 2000 India visit, this quirky 1920s lodge, close to the river-front and run by a garrulous landlord, caters mainly for salesmen and the odd budget traveller. Its rooms are roughish and musty during the rainy season, but reasonably good value. **②**–**④**

The Town

Until a decade or so ago, most visitors' first glimpse of **Panjim** was from the decks of the old Bombay steamer as it chugged into dock at the now-defunct ferry ramp. These days, however, despite the recent inauguration of the Konkan Railway, the town is most usually approached by road – from the north via the huge ferroconcrete bridge that spans the Mandovi estuary, or from the south on the recently revamped NH-7, which links the capital with the airport and railhead at Vasco da Gama. Either way, you'll have to pass through the suburb of **Pato**, home of the main Kadamba bus terminal, before crossing Ourem Creek to arrive in Panjim proper. West of **Fontainhas**, the picturesque Portuguese quarter, the commercial centre's grid of long straight streets fans out west from Panjim's principal landmark, **Church Square**. Further north, the main thoroughfare, **Avenida Dom Joao Castro**, sweeps past the Head Post Office and **Secretariat** building, before bending west along the water-front.

Church Square

The leafy rectangular park opposite the India Government tourist office, known as **Church Square** or the **Municipal Garden**, forms the heart of Panjim. Presiding over its east side is the town's most distinctive and photo-genic landmark, the toothpaste-white Baroque facade of the **Church of Our Lady of the Immaculate Conception**. Flanked by rows of slender palm trees, at the head of a criss-crossing laterite walkway, the church was built in 1541 for the benefit of sailors arriving here from Lisbon. The weary mariners would stagger up from the quay to give thanks for their safe passage before pro-ceeding to the capital at Old Goa – the original home of the enormous bell that hangs from its central gable.

The Secretariat

The road that runs north from the church brings you out at the riverside near Panjim's oldest surviving building. With its sloping tiled roofs, carved-stone coats of arms and wooden verandas, the stalwart **Secretariat** looks typically colonial. Yet it was originally the summer palace of Goa's sixteenth-century Muslim ruler, the Adil Shah. Later, the Portuguese converted it into a tempo-rary rest house for the territory's governors (who used to overnight here en route to and from Europe) and then a residence for the viceroy. Today, it accommodates the Goan State Legislature, which explains the presence of so many shiny chauffeur-driven Ambassador cars outside, and the armed guards at the door.

A hundred metres east, a peculiar statue of a man holding his hands over the body of an entranced reclining woman shows **Abbé Faria** (1755–1819), a Goan priest who emigrated to France to become one of the world's first pro-fessional hypnotists.

An even more impressive edifice than the Mhamay Kamat mansion is the **Menezes Braganza Institute**, now the town's Central Library, which stands behind the esplanade, 1km west of the Secretariat past the Abbé de Faria statue. Among the colonial leftovers in this grand Neoclassical building, which was erected as part of the civic makeover initiated by the Marquis of Pombal and Dom Manuel de Portugal e Castro in the early nineteenth cen-tury, are the panels of blue-and-yellow-painted ceramic tiles, known as **azulejos**, lining the lobby of the west (Malacca Road) entrance. These larg-er-than-life illustrations depict scenes from Luis Vaz Camões' epic poem, *Os Luisiades*. The tone of the tableaux is intentionally patriotic (valiant Portuguese explorers being tossed on stormy seas and a nobleman standing defiantly before a dark-faced Raja of Calicut), but the tale was, in fact, intended as an invective against the Portuguese discoveries, which Camões rightly believed was milking his mother country dry and leaving its crown easy prey for the old enemy, Spain.

Fontainhas and Sao Tomé

Panjim's oldest and most interesting district, **Fontainhas**, lies immediately west of Pato, overlooking the banks of the oily green Ourem Creek. From the footbridge between the bus stand and town centre, a dozen or so blocks of Neoclassical houses rise in a tangle of terracotta rooftops up the sides of **Altinho Hill**. At siesta time, Vespas stand idle on deserted street corners, while women in Western clothes exchange pleasantries with their neighbours from open windows and leafy verandas. Many buildings have retained their traditional coat of ochre, pale yellow, green or blue – a legacy of the Portuguese insistence that every Goan building (except churches, which had to be white) should be colour-washed after the monsoons.

At the southern end of the neighbourhood, the pristine whitewashed **Chapel of St Sebastian** is one of many Goan churches to remain faithful to the old colonial decree. It stands at the end of a small square where Fontainhas' Portuguese-speaking locals hold a lively annual street *festa* to celebrate their patron saint's day in mid-November. The eerily lifelike crucifix inside the chapel, brought here in 1812, formerly hung in the Palace of the Inquisition in Old Goa. Unusually, Christ's eyes are open – allegedly to inspire fear in those being interrogated by the Inquisitors.

Sao Tomé ward is the other old quarter, lying north of Fontainhas on the far side of Emilio Gracia Road. This is the area to head for if you fancy a bar crawl: the narrow streets are dotted with dozens of hole-in-the-wall taverns, serving cheap, stiff measures of *feni* under strip lights and the watchful gaze of colourful Madonnas. You'll feel less conspicuous in the neighbourhood's best known hostelry, the *Hotel Venite* (see p.867).

The State Archeological Museum

The most noteworthy feature of Panjim's **State Archeological Museum** (Mon–Fri 9.30am–1.15pm & 2–5.30pm; free) is its imposing size, which stands in glaringly inverse proportion to the collections inside. In their bid to erect a structure befitting a state capital, Goa's status-obsessed bureaucrats ignored the fact that there was precious little to put in it. The only rarities to be found amid the lame array of temple sculpture, hero stones, and dowdy colonial-era artefacts are a couple of beautiful Jain bronzes rescued by Customs and Excise officials from smugglers and, on the ground floor, the infamous Italian-style table used by Goa's Grand Inquisitors, complete with its original, ornately carved tall-backed chairs. On your way out, look out too for the photos of the prehistoric rock carvings at Kajur and Usgalimal, lining the walls of the main entrance hall. Their discovery in a remote corner of the state in 1993 effectively redrew the Konkan coast's archeological map by proving that more than 12,000 years ago – well before the arrival of settled agriculturalists from the north – the region supported a population of hunter-gatherers.

Eating and drinking

Catering for the droves of tourists who come here from other Indian states, as well as more price-conscious locals, Panjim is packed with good **places to eat**, from hole-in-the-wall fish-curry-rice joints to swish air-conditioned restaurants serving top-notch Mughlai cuisine. In a week you could feasibly attempt a gastronomic tour of the subcontinent without straying more then five minutes from the Municipal Gardens. Vegetarians are best catered for at the numerous *udipi* canteens dotted around town, most of which open around 7am for blow-out **breakfasts** – great if you have just staggered into town after a night on the bus. Beer, *feni* and other spirits are available in all but the purest "pure veg" places, especially in the hole-in-the-wall taverns around Sao Tomé.

A Pasteleria, Dr Dada Vaidya Road. Panjim's best bakery does dozens of Western-style cakes, biscuits and sticky buns, including brownies and fruit loaves. Its savoury selection of tasty egg puffs, and succulent, spicy chicken or prawn patties is good too. Takeaway only.

Delhi Durbar, behind the *Hotel Mandovi*. A provincial branch of the famous Mumbai restaurant, and the best place in Panjim – if not all Goa – to sample traditional Mughlai cuisine of mainly meat steeped in rich, spicy sauces (try their superb *rogan josh* or melt-in-the-mouth chicken tikka). Most main dishes are pricey, at around Rs120, but this place is well worth a splurge.

Goenchin, off Dr Dada Vaidhya Road. Glacial a/c and dim lighting, but (along with *Sweet and Sour* in Vasco – see p.898) the best and most authentic Chinese food in Goa. Count on Rs300 per head.

Horseshoe, Rua de Ourem, Fontainhas. The town's only Portuguese-Goan restaurant, serving a limited, but very reasonably priced, menu of old standards such as *caldo verde* soup and grilled sardines. The food is so-so, but the decor and atmosphere make this a worthwhile option. Most mains around Rs50.

Megson's, next to *Moti Mahal*, 18 June Rd. The state's top deli, with a great selection of traditional Goan foods: spicy sausages, prepared meats, tangy cheese from the Nilgiris, olive oil, and the best *bebinca* you can buy (ask for Linda brand).

Rosoyo, 18 June Rd. Run by *Megson's*, this busy little fast-food joint is *the* place to sample tasty, hygienic Mumbai-style street food: crunchy *bhel puri* or delicious *pau bhaji*. They also serve wonderful Gujarati snacks such as *thepla* – chappatis griddle-cooked with curry leaves and cumin, and served with south Indian *chatni* – plus a range of shakes and ice creams. You'll be hard pushed to spend Rs50 here.

Satkar, 18 June Rd. Newest and much the most congenial of Panjim's numerous South Indian snack joints. They do a huge range of dishes,

Goan food and drink

Not unnaturally, after 450 years of colonization, Goan **cooking** has absorbed a strong Portuguese influence. Palm vinegar (unknown elsewhere in India), copious amounts of coconut, garlic, tangy tamarind and fierce local chillies all play their part. Goa is the home of the famous *vindaloo* (from the Portuguese *vinho d'alho*, literally "garlic wine"), originally an extra-hot and sour pork curry, but now made with a variety of meat and fish. Other **pork** specialities include *chouriço* red sausages, *sorpotel*, a hot curry made from pickled pig's liver and heart, *leitao*, suckling pig, and *balchao*, pork in a rich brown sauce. Delicious alternatives include vinegar chicken, spicy chicken or mutton *xacutti*, made with a sauce of lemon juice, peanuts, coconut, chillies and spices. The choice of **seafood**, often cooked in fragrant masalas, is excellent – clams, mussels, crab, lobster, giant prawns – while **fish**, depending on the type, is either cooked in wet curries, grilled, or baked in tandoor clay ovens. Try *apa de camarão*, a spicy prawn pie with a rice and semolina crust. *Sanna*, like the south Indian *iddli*, is a steamed cake of fermented rice flour, but here made with palm toddy. Sweet tooths will adore *bebinca*, a rich, delicious solid egg custard with coconut.

As for **drinks**, locally produced wine, spirits and beer are cheaper than anywhere in the country, thanks to lower rates of tax. The most famous and widespread beer is, of course, Kingfisher, which tastes less of glycerine preservative than it does elsewhere in India, but you'll also come across pricier San Miguel, brewed in Mumbai and nothing like the original. Goan port, a sweeter, inferior version of its Portuguese namesake, is ubiquitous, served chilled in large wine glasses with a slice of lemon. Local whiskies, brandies, rums, gins and vodkas come in a variety of brand names for less than Rs20 a shot, but, at half the price, local speciality *feni*, made from distilled cashew or from the sap of coconut palms, offers strong competition. Cashew *feni* is usually drunk after the first distillation, but you can also find it double-distilled, flavoured with ginger, cumin or sasparilla to produce a smooth liqueur.

including Chinese and North Indian, but most people go for their fantastic *masala dosas* and piping hot, crunchy samosas, which get the vote as the best in town.

Tony's, Emilio Gracia Road/31 Janeiro Rd, Fontainhas. A blue-painted street-stall run by a retired footballer and his wife, who serve up the freshest, tastiest and most authentic Goan food in town. Dishes (see p.866 for explanations) include sublime fish cutlets, chicken *xacuti*, chilli beef, *sorpatel* and – on Saturdays only – perfect *sanna*, made with real palm *toddi*. Around Rs30 per person for a filling meal; no veg options. Takeaway only.

Venite, 31 Janeiro Rd. Deservedly popular hotel restaurant, serving great fresh seafood, including affordable lobster and crab, along with Western dishes, desserts, *feni* and cold beers. Wooden floors, balcony seats, candles and an eclectic cassette collection add to the ambience. Good breakfasts, too. Closed Sun.

Vihar, 31 Janeiro Rd, around the corner from *Venite*. Arguably the best *udipi* in Panjim, and more conveniently situated than *Satkar*. Try their super tasty *rawa masala dosas*.

Listings

Airlines Air India, *Hotel Fidalgo*, 18 June Rd ☎0832/224081; British Airways, Shiv Tower, EDC Plaza, Patto ☎ & ℻0832/420335 or 420320; Gulf Air, Air France, Royal Jordanian, Sri Lankan Airlines, Kenyan Airways, Bimab Bangladesh, Air Seychelles, American Airlines all c/o Jetair, Rizvi Chambers, 1st Floor, H Salgado Road ☎0832/222438, 226154 or 223172; Indian Airlines, Dempo Building, Dr D Bandodkar Road ☎0832/223831; Jet Airlines, Sesa Ghor, ECD Plaza, next to GTDC *Pato Tourist Home*, Patto ☎0832/431472; KLM (also PIA), 2nd floor, Mahalaxmi Chambers ☎0832/426678, 224802 or 222633, ℻224802; Sahara Airlines, *Hotel Fidalgo*, Room 133, 18 June Rd ☎0832/230634; Swissair & Sabena, Ground Floor, Sesa Ghor, EDC Plaza, Plot #20, Patto ☎0832/422255, ℻432233.

Banks and ATMs The most efficient places in Panjim to change money are: Thomas Cook, near the Indian Airlines office, at 8 Alcon Chambers, Devanand Bandodkar Road (Mon–Sat 9am–6pm, Oct–March also Sun 10am–5pm; ☎0832/221312, ℻221313); and the Pheroze Framroze Exchange Bureau on Dr P Shirgaonkar Road (Mon–Sat 9.30am–7pm & Sun 9.30am–1pm). Unlike most private companies, the latter's rates are competitive and they don't charge commission on either currency or travellers' cheques. The HDFC Bank on 18 June Rd has a handy 24hr ATM, where you can make withdrawals using Visa or Mastercard. Changing money in the regular, government-run banks tends to take a lot longer, but the rates are invariably best: State Bank of India is opposite the *Hotel Mandovi*, Avda Dom Joao Castro; the Bank of Baroda (where you can draw money on Visa cards), is on Azad Maidan; and the Corporation Bank is on Church Square, around the corner from the Government Tourist Office.

Books The bookshops in the *Hotel Fidalgo* and the *Hotel Mandovi* stock a range of English-language fiction in paperback, and special-interest titles and coffee-table tomes on Goa.

British Consular Assistant The British High Commission of Mumbai has a Consular Assistant in Panjim: Shilpa Sarah Caldeira's office is on the third floor of 302 Manguirish Building (opposite Gulf Supermarket), 18 June Rd ☎0832/228571, ℻232828; ℮bcagoa@goa1.dot.net.in.

Hospital Panjim's largest hospital, the Goa Medical College (aka the GMC), in the west of town at the far end of Avda Dom Joao Castro, is grim and overstretched; if you're able to travel, head for the more modern and better-equipped Salgaonkar Hospital. Ambulances (☎0832/46300 or 44566) are likely to get you there a lot less quickly than a standard taxi.

Music and dance Regular recitals of classical Indian music and dance are held at Panjim's school for the performing arts, the Kala Academy in Campal, at the far west end of town on Devanand Bandodkar Road. For details of forthcoming events, consult the boards in front of the auditorium or the listings page of local newspapers.

Pharmacies Panjim's best pharmacy is Hindu Pharma (☎0832/43176), next to the *Hotel Aroma* on Church Square, which stocks Ayurvedic, homeopathic and allopathic medicines.

Police Police Headquarters is on Malaca Road, central Panjim.

Post Panjim's reliable poste restante counter (Mon–Sat 9.30am–1pm & 2–5.30pm) is in the Head Post Office, 200m west of Pato Bridge. To get your stamps franked, walk around the back of the building and ask at the office behind the second door on the right. For parcel stitching, ask at Deepak Stores on the corner of the next block

north.
Travel agents AERO Mundial, Ground Floor, *Hotel Mandovi*, Dr D Bandodkar Road ℡ 0832/223773; Menezes Air Travel, Rua de Ourem ℡ & ℱ 0832/222214. For air and Damania catamaran

tickets, try MGM International, Mamai Camotim Building (near Secretariat); or Tradewings Ltd, Mascarenhas Buildings (near Jolly Shoes), Dr Atmaram Borkar Road ℡ 0832/22243.

Old Goa

At one time a byword for splendour, with a population of several hundred thousand, Goa's erstwhile capital, **OLD GOA**, was virtually abandoned following malaria and cholera epidemics that plagued the city from the seventeenth century onwards. Today you need considerable imagination to picture the once-great capital as it used to be. The maze of twisting streets, piazzas and ochre-washed villas has gone, and all that remains is a score of extraordinarily grandiose churches and convents. Granted World Heritage Status by UNESCO, Old Goa today attracts bus loads of foreign tourists from the coast, and Christian pilgrims from around India, in roughly equal numbers. While the former come to admire the gigantic facades and gilt altars of the beautifully preserved churches, the main attraction for the latter is the tomb of **St Francis Xavier** (see p.871), the renowned sixteenth-century missionary, whose remains are enshrined in the **Basilica of Bom Jesus**.

If you are staying on the coast and contemplating a day-trip inland, this is the most obvious and accessible option. Just thirty minutes by road from the state capital, Old Goa is served by buses every fifteen minutes from Panjim's Kadamba bus stand; alternatively, hop into an auto-rickshaw, or rent a taxi. GTDC also slot the site's highlights into several of their guided coach **tours**; further details and tickets are available at any GTDC hotel or tourist office.

Arch of the Viceroys and the Church of St Cajetan

On arriving at the river landing stage to the north, seventeenth-century visitors passed through the **Arch of the Viceroys** (1597), constructed to commemorate Vasco da Gama's arrival in India and built from the same porous red laterite as virtually all Old Goa's buildings. Above it a Bible-toting figure rests his foot on the cringing figure of a "native", while its granite facade, facing the

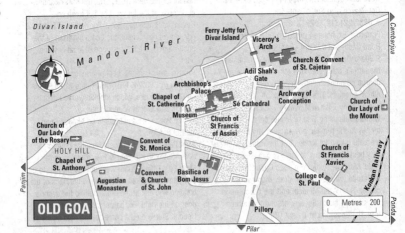

river, holds a statue of da Gama himself. It is hard to imagine today that these overgrown fields and simple streets with a few cool-drinks stands were once the focus of a lively market, with silk and gem merchants, horse dealers and carpet weavers. The one surviving monument, known as **Adil Shah's Gate**, predates the Portuguese and possibly even the Muslim period. Hindu in style, it consists simply of a lintel supported by two columns in black basalt, to which are attached the remains of perforated screens. You can find it by turning left at the crossroads immediately above the Arch of the Viceroys.

A short way up the lane from the Gate, the distinctive domed **Church of St Cajetan** (1651) was modelled on St Peter's in Rome by monks from the Theatine order, who believed in Divine Providence; they never sought charity, but simply expected it. While it does boast a Corinthian exterior, you can also spot certain non-European elements in the decoration, such as the cashew-nut designs in the carving of the pulpit. Hidden beneath the church is a crypt where the embalmed bodies of Portuguese governors were once kept in lead coffins before they were shipped back to Lisbon. Forgotten for over thirty years, the last batch (of three) was only removed in 1992 on the eve of the state visit to Goa of Portuguese President Mario Soares.

The Sé (St Catherines' Cathedral)

The Portuguese Viceroy Redondo (1561–64) commissioned the **Sé**, or **St Catherines' Cathedral**, southwest of St Cajetan's, to be "a grandiose church worthy of the wealth, power and fame of the Portuguese who dominated the seas from the Atlantic to the Pacific". Today it stands larger than any church in Portugal, although it was beset by problems, not least a lack of funds and Portugal's temporary loss of independence to Spain. It took eighty years to build and was not consecrated until 1640.

On the Tuscan-style exterior, the one surviving tower houses the **Golden Bell**, cast in Cuncolim (south Goa) in the seventeenth century. During the Inquisition, its tolling announced the start of the gruesome *auto da fés* that were held in the square outside, when suspected heretics were subjected to public torture and burned at the stake. Reconstruction of parts of the roof, which once had overhanging eaves, has damaged some paintings inside. The scale and detail of the Corinthian-style interior is overwhelming; huge pillars divide the central nave from the side aisles, and no less than fifteen altars are arranged around the walls, dedicated among others to Our Ladies of Hope, Anguish and Three Needs. An altar to St Anne treasures the relics of the **Blessed Martyrs of Cuncolim**, whose failed mission to convert the Moghul emperor Akbar culminated in their murder by Muslims, while a chapel behind a highly detailed screen holds the **Miraculous Cross**, which stood in a Goan village until a vision of Christ appeared on it. Said to heal the sick, it is kept in a box; a small opening on the side allows devotees to touch it. The staggeringly ornate gilded main **altar** comprises nine carved frames and a splendid crucifix. Panels depict episodes from the life of St Catherine of Alexandria (died 307 AD), including an interchange of ideas with the pagan Roman emperor Maxim, who wished to marry her, and her subsequent flogging and martyrdom.

The Archbishop's Palace

Adjoining the Sé Cathedral, with which it is an exact contemporary, the **Archbishop's Palace** is unique as the last surviving civil building of colonial Goa's golden era. Though in a lamentable state of disrepair, its steeply inclined roofs and white facade still perfectly embody of the solidity and imposing strength of the so-called "chã" style of architecture, derived from military constructions of the day, of which the most extreme example was the Viceroy's Fortress Palace (Palacio da Fortaleza), which has since vanished without trace. Presenting their most austere aspect to the river, these two fortified palaces formerly dominated the skyline of the waterfront, appropriately enough for a city perennially under threat of attack.

Nineteenth-century photos show that the city-facing side of the building was originally enfolded by a low wall, which surrounded a garden. This has long been dismantled, but the two grand **entrance porches** remain intact. The one on the right (as you look at the building) is original, complete with red decorative frescoes lining the side walls, among the last remaining paintings of their kind left in Goa. During the Portuguese heyday, guards in blue livery would have stood on its steps, as they did in the Viceroy's palace and most *hidalgo* houses.

The palace is officially closed to visitors so if you want to have a nose around, you'll have to bully or bribe the ASI caretaker into letting you.

The Church of St Francis of Assisi and Archeological Museum

Southwest of the Cathedral is the ruined **Palace of the Inquisition**, in operation up until 1774, while to the west stands the **Convent of St Francis of Assisi**, built by Franciscan monks in 1517 and restored in the mid-eighteenth century. Today, the core of its **Archeological Museum** (daily except Fri 10am–5pm; Rs5) is a gallery of portraits of Portuguese viceroys, painted by local artists under Italian supervision. Other exhibits include coins, domestic Christian wooden sculpture, and downstairs in the cloister, pre-Portuguese Hindu sculpture. Next door, the **Church of St Francis** (1521) features fine decorative frescoes and paintings on wood showing the life of St Francis of Assisi.

Basilica of Bom Jesus

Close to the convent of St Francis, the 1605 church of **Bom Jesus**, "Good" or "Menino Jesus" (Mon–Sat 9am–6.30pm, Sun 10am–6.30pm), is known principally for the **tomb of St Francis Xavier**. In 1946, it became the first church in India to be elevated to the status of Minor Basilica. On the west, the three-storey Renaissance facade encompasses Corinthian, Doric, Ionic and Composite styles.

The interior is entered beneath the choir, supported by columns. On the northern wall, in the centre of the nave, is a cenotaph in gilded bronze to **Dom Jeronimo Mascaranhas**, the Captain of Cochin and benefactor of the church. The main altar, extravagantly decorated in gold, depicts the infant Jesus under the protection of St Ignatius Loyola; to each side are subsidiary altars to Our Lady of Hope and St Michael. In the southern transept, lavishly decorated with twisted gilded columns and floriate carvings, stands the **Chapel and Tomb of St Francis Xavier**. Constructed of marble and jasper in 1696, it was the gift of the Medici, Cosimo III, the Grand Duke of Tuscany; the middle tier contains panels detailing the saint's life. An ornate domed reliquary in silver contains his remains; on his feast day, December 3, the saint's finger is displayed to devotees.

Holy Hill

A number of other important religious buildings, some in ruins, stand opposite Bom Jesus on **Holy Hill**. The **convent of St Monica**, constructed in 1627, destroyed by fire in 1636 and rebuilt the following year, was the only

Goan convent at the time and the largest in Asia. It housed around a hundred nuns, the Daughters of St Monica, and also offered accommodation to women whose husbands were called away to other parts of the empire. The **church** adjoins the convent on the south. As they had to remain away from the public gaze, the nuns attended Mass in the choir loft and looked down upon the congregation.

Inside, a **Miraculous Cross** rises above the figure of St Monica at the altar. In 1636, it was reported that the figure of Christ had opened his eyes, motioned as if to speak, and blood had flowed from the wounds made by his crown of thorns. The last Daughter of St Monica died in 1885, and since 1964 the convent has been occupied by the Mater Dei Institute for nuns.

Nearby, the **Convent of St John of God**, built in 1685 by the Order of Hospitallers of St John of God to tend to the sick, was rebuilt in 1953. At the top of the hill, the **Chapel of Our Lady of the Rosary**, built in 1526 in the Manueline style (after the Portuguese king Manuel I, 1495–1521), features

St Francis Xavier

Francis Xavier, the "Apostle of the Indies", was born in 1506 in the old kingdom of Navarre, now part of Spain. After taking a masters' degree in philosophy and theology at the University of Paris, where he studied for the priesthood until 1535, he was ordained two years later in Venice. He was then recruited by (Saint) **Ignatius Loyola** (1491–1556) along with five other priests into the new "Society of Jesus", which later became known as the **Jesuits**.

When the Portuguese king, Dom Joao III (1521–57), received reports of corruption and dissolute behaviour among the Portuguese in Goa, he asked Ignatius Loyola to despatch a priest who could influence the moral climate for the better. In 1541 Xavier was sent to work in the diocese of Goa, constituted seven years before, and comprising all regions east of the Cape of Good Hope. Arriving after a year-long journey, he embarked on a busy programme throughout southern India. Despite frequent obstruction from Portuguese officials, he founded numerous churches, and is credited with converting 30,000 people and performing such miracles as raising the dead and curing the sick with a touch of his beads. Subsequently he took his mission further afield to Sri Lanka, Malacca (Malaysia), China and Japan where he was less successful.

When Xavier left Goa for the last time, it was with the ambition of evangelizing in China; however, he contracted dysentery aboard ship and died on the island of San Chuan (Sancian), off the Chinese coast, where he was buried. On hearing of his death, a group of Christians from Malacca exhumed his body – which, although the grave had been filled with lime, they found to be in a perfect state of preservation. Reburied in Malacca, it was later removed and taken to Old Goa, where it has remained ever since, enshrined in the Basilica of Bom Jesus.

However, Saint Francis' incorruptible corpse has never rested entirely in peace. Chunks of it have been removed over the years by relic hunters and curious clerics: in 1614, the right arm was dispatched to the Pope in Rome (where it allegedly wrote its name on paper), a hand was sent to Japan, and parts of the intestines to southeast Asia. One Portuguese woman, Dona Isabel de Caron, even bit off the little toe of the cadaver in 1534; apparently, so much blood spurted into her mouth, it left a trail to her house and she was discovered.

Every ten years, the saint's body is carried in a three-hour ceremony from the Basilica of Bom Jesus to the Sé Cathedral, where visitors file past, touch and photograph it. During the 1995 "exposition", which was rumoured to be the last one, an estimated two million pilgrims flocked for *darshan* or ritual viewing of the corpse, these days a shrivelled and somewhat unsavoury spectacle.

Ionic plasterwork with a double-storey portico, cylindrical turrets and a tower that commands fine views across the river from the terrace where Albuquerque surveyed the decisive battle of 1510. Its cruciform interior is unremarkable, except for the marble tomb of **Catarina a Piró**, believed to have been the first European woman to set foot in the colony. A commoner, she eloped here to escape the scandal surrounding her romance with Portuguese nobleman Garcia de Sá, who later rose to be governor of Goa. Under pressure from no less than Francis Xavier, Garcia eventually married her, but only *in articulo mortis* as she lay on her deathbed. Her finely carved tomb, set in the wall beside the high altar, incorporates a band of intricate Gujarati-style ornamentation, probably imported from the Portuguese trading post of Diu.

Ponda and around

Characterless, chaotic **PONDA**, 28km southeast of Panjim and 17km north-east of Margao, is Ponda *taluka's* administrative headquarters and main market town, but not somewhere you're likely to want to stay. Straddling the busy Panjim–Bangalore highway (NH-4), the town's ugly concrete centre is perma-nently choked with traffic, and guaranteed to make you wonder why you ever left the coast. Of the few visitors who stop here, most do so en route to the nearby **Hindu temples** or **wildlife reserves** further east, or to take a look at Goa's best-preserved sixteenth-century Muslim monument, the **Safa Masjid**, 2km west on the Panjim road. Built in 1560 by the Bijapuri ruler Ibrahim Adil Shah, this small mosque, with its whitewashed walls and pointed terracotta tile roof, is renowned less for its architecture than for being one of only two Islamic shrines in Goa to survive the excesses of the Portuguese Inquisition.

Practicalities

Ponda is served by regular **buses** from Panjim (via Old Goa) and Margao, and lies on the main route east to Karnataka. The Kadamba bus stand is on the main square, next to the auto-rickshaw rank.

There are plenty of **places to stay** if you get stuck here. Best of the budget lodges is the *Padmavi* (no phone; ❶) at the top of the square. For more com-fort, try the *President* (☎0832/312287; ❸–❺), a short rickshaw ride up the Belgaum road, which has large, clean en-suite rooms, some with air condi-tioning. More upmarket is the three-star *Atash* (☎0832/313224, ℗313239; ❻), 4km northwest on the NH-4 at **Farmagudi**, whose comfortable a/c rooms have satellite TV, and there's also a restaurant and car parking facilities. However, the best mid-range deal within striking distance of Ponda has to be GTDC's *Tourist Resort* (☎0832/312932; ❸–❺), also at Farmagudi (look for the signpost on the roundabout below the Shivaji memorial), whose en-suite chalets, stacked up the side of a steep hill overlooking the highway, are spacious, clean and reasonably priced. There's also a small terrace restaurant serving a standard menu of spicy mixed cuisine.

Temples around Ponda

Scattered among the lush valleys and forests **around Ponda** are a dozen or so **Hindu temples** founded during the seventeenth and eighteenth cen-turies, when this hilly region was a Christian-free haven for Hindus fleeing persecution by the Portuguese. Although the temples themselves are fairly modern by Indian standards, their deities are ancient and held in high esteem by both local people and thousands of pilgrims from Maharashtra and Karnataka.

The temples are concentrated in two main clusters: the first to the north of Ponda, on the NH-4, and the second deep in the countryside, around 5km west of the town. Most people only manage the **Shri Manguesh** and **Shri Mahalsa**, between the villages of **Mardol** and **Priol**. Among the most interesting temples in the state, they lie just a stone's throw from the main highway and are passed by regular **buses** between Panjim and Margao via Ponda. The others are further off the beaten track, although they are not hard to find on motorbikes: locals will wave you in the right direction if you get lost.

Mardol and Priol

Although the **Shri Manguesh** temple originally stood in a secret location in Cortalim, and was moved to its present site between **MARDOL** and **PRIOL** during the sixteenth century, the structure visitors see today dates from the 1700s. A gateway at the roadside leads to a paved path and courtyard that gives onto a water tank, overlooked by the white temple building, raised on a plinth. Also in the courtyard is a seven-storey *deepmal*, a tower for oil lamps. Inside, the floor is paved with marble, and bands of decorative tiles emblazon the white walls. Flanked by large *dvarpala* guardians, embossed silver doorways with floriate designs lead to the sanctum, which houses a *shivalingam*.

Two kilometres south, the **Mahalsa Marayani** temple was also transferred from its original site, in this case Salcete *taluka* further south, in the seventeenth century. Here, the *deepmal* is exceptionally tall, with 21 tiers rising from a figure of Kurma, the tortoise incarnation of Vishnu. Original features include a marble-floored wooden *mandapa* (assembly hall) with carved pillars, ceiling panels of parakeets and, in the eaves, sculptures of the incarnations of Vishnu.

Dudhsagar waterfalls

Measuring a mighty 600m from head to foot, the famous **waterfalls** at **DUDHSAGAR**, on the Goa–Karnataka border, are some of the highest in India, and a spectacular enough sight to entice a steady stream of visitors from the coast into the rugged Western Ghats. After pouring across the Deccan plateau, the headwaters of the Mandovi River form a foaming torrent that fans into three streams, then cascades down a near-vertical cliff face into a deep green pool. The Konkani name for the falls, which literally translated means "sea of milk", derives from clouds of foam kicked up at the bottom when the water levels are at their highest. Overlooking a steep, crescent-shaped head of a valley carpeted with pristine tropical forest, Dudhsagar is set amid breathtaking **scenery** that is only accessible on foot or by Jeep; the old Vasco-Castle Rock railway actually passes over the falls on an old stone viaduct, but services along it are infrequent (See below).

Practicalities

The best time to visit Dudhsagar is immediately after the monsoons, from October until mid-December, although the falls flow well into April. Unfortunately, the train line, which climbs above the tree canopy via a series of spectacular cuttings and stone bridges, only sees two services per week in each direction (Tues & Sat; depart Margao 7.21am), neither of them returning the same day. As a result, the only practicable way to get there and back is by four-wheel-drive **Jeep** from **Colem** (reachable by train from Vasco, Margao and Chandor, or by taxi from the north coast resorts for around Rs1000). The cost of the onward thirty- to forty-minute trip from Colem to the falls, which takes you across rough forest tracks and two or three river fords, is around

Rs250–350 per person; the drive ends with an enjoyable fifteen-minute hike, for which you'll need a sturdy pair of shoes. Finding a Jeep-wallah is easy; just turn up in Colem and look for the "Controller of Jeeps" near the station. However, if you're travelling alone or in a couple, you may have to wait around until the vehicle fills up, or else fork out Rs2000 or so to cover the cost of hiring the whole Jeep yourself. Note that it can be difficult to arrange transport of any kind from Molem crossroads, where regular taxis are in short supply.

North Goa

Beyond the mouth of the Mandovi estuary, the Goan coast sweeps **north** in a near-continuous string of beaches, broken only by the odd saltwater creek, rocky headland, and three tidal rivers – two of which, the Chapora and Arondem, have to be crossed by ferry. The most developed resorts, **Calangute** and **Baga**, occupy the middle and northern part of the seven-kilometre strip of pearl-white sand that stretches from the Aguada peninsula in the south to a sheer laterite promontory in the north. Formerly, the infamous colonies of Goa hippies gathered in these two villages during their annual winter migration; now both heave during high season with British charter tourists, bus loads of trippers from out-of-state and itinerant vendors hawking fruit and trinkets on the beach. The "scene", meanwhile, has shifted northwards, to the beaches around **Anjuna**, **Vagator** and **Chapora**, where the Christmas–New Year parties take place.

Most of the tourist traffic **arriving in north Goa** from Mumbai is siphoned off towards the coast through **Mapusa**, the area's main market town. For short hops between towns and resorts, **motorcycle taxis** are the quickest and most convenient way to get around, but **buses** also run to all the villages along the coast, via the **ferry crossings** at Siolim, 7km north of Anjuna, and Querim (for Terekol).

Mapusa

The ramshackle market town of **MAPUSA** (pronounced *Map*sa) is the district headquarters of Bardez *taluka*. If you arrive by road from Mumbai and plan to stay in one of the north Goan resorts, you can jump off the bus here and pick up a local service straight to the coast, rather than continue on to Panjim, 13km south.

A dusty collection of dilapidated modern buildings scattered around the west-facing slope of a low hill, Mapusa is of little more than passing interest in itself, although on Fridays it hosts a lively **market** (hence the town's name, which derives from the Konkani words for "measure", *map*, and "fill up", *sa*). Calangute and Anjuna may be better stocked with souvenirs, but this bazaar is more authentic. Visitors who have flown straight to Goa, and have yet to experience the rest of India, wander in on Friday mornings to enjoy the pungent aromas of fish, incense, spices and exotic fruit stacked in colourful heaps on the pavements. Local specialities include strings of spicy Goan sausages (*chouriço*), bottles of *todi* (fermented palm sap) and large green plantains. You'll also encounter sundry freak shows, from run-of-the-mill snake charmers and kids dressed up as *sadhus*, to wide-eyed flagellants, blood oozing out of slashes on their backs.

Practicalities

Other than to shop, you may want to visit Mapusa to arrange **onward transport**. All buses between Goa and Maharashtra pass through, so you don't need to travel to Panjim to book a ticket to Mumbai, Pune, Bangalore or Mangalore. Reservations for private buses can be made at the numerous agents' stalls at the bottom of the square, next to where the buses pull in; the **Kadamba terminal** – the departure point for long-distance state buses and local services to Calangute, Baga, Anjuna, Vagator, Chapora, and Arambol – is five minutes' walk down the main road, on the southwest edge of town. You can also get to the coast from Mapusa on one of the **motorcycle taxis** that wait at the bottom of the square. Rides to Calangute and Anjuna take twenty minutes, and cost Rs40. **Taxis** charge considerably more, but you can split the fare with up to five people.

As soon as you step off the bus, you'll be pestered by touts trying to get you to rent a **motorbike**. They'll tell you that rates here are lower than on the coast – they're not. Another reason to wait a while is that Mapusa is effectively a "no-go zone" for rented motorbikes, especially on Friday, when the police set up roadblocks on the outskirts of town to collar tourists without international licences (see p.859).

Accommodation and eating

Nearly all long-distance buses pull in to Mapusa in the morning, leaving plenty of time to find **accommodation** in the coastal resorts nearby. If you have to spend the night here, though, there are plenty of places within easy walking distance of the Kadamba bus stand. The best budget deal is GTDC's *Tourist Hotel* (℡0832/262794 or 262694; ❺), on the roundabout below the square, which has spacious and clean rooms, a Goa **tourist information** counter, and a small Damania Shipping office. The *Vilena*, across town near the Municipality Building on Mapusa Road (℡0832/263115; ❷–❺), also offers good-value economy rooms (with or without attached bathrooms), in addition to more comfortable a/c ones, and has a dimly lit bar and small rooftop restaurant. On the north side of the main square, the *Hotel Satyaheera* (℡0832/262849 or 262949; ❺) is the town's top hotel, with mostly a/c rooms.

Mapusa's most relaxing **restaurant** is the *Ruchira*, on the top floor of the *Hotel Satyaheera*, which serves a standard Indian menu with Goan and Chinese alternatives, and cold beer. The *Hotel Vrindavan*, on the east side of the main square, dishes up Mapusa's best inexpensive south Indian snacks, along with an impressive range of ice creams and shakes. Cheaper but less salubrious Goan thali joints can be found in the streets east of the main square.

Candolim and Fort Aguada

Compared with Calangute, 3km north along the beach, **CANDOLIM** (from the Konkani *kandoli*, meaning "dykes", in reference to the system of sluices that the area's first farmers used to reclaim land from nearby marshes) is a surprisingly sedate resort, attracting mainly middle-aged package tourists from the UK and Scandinavia. Over the past five years or so, however, its ribbon development of hotels and restaurants has sprouted a string of multistorey holiday complexes, and during peak season the few vestiges of authentically Goan culture that remain here are drowned in a deluge of Kashmiri handicraft stalls, luridly lit terrace cafés and shops crammed with postcards and beachwear. Long gone are the days when this was a tranquil bolt hole for burgundy-clad *sanyasins* from the Rajneesh ashram at Pune. Now the beach where they used

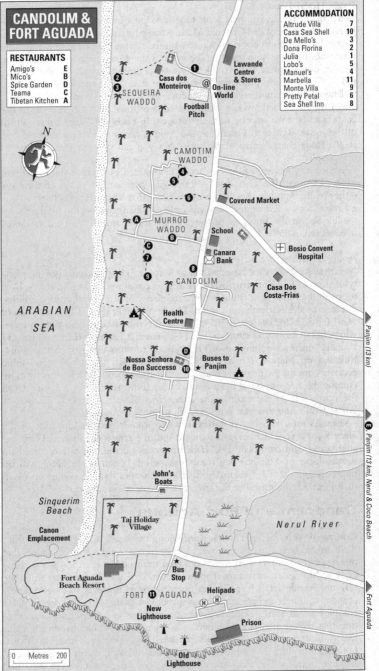

CANDOLIM & FORT AGUADA

▲ Calangute (2 km)

ACCOMMODATION
Altrude Villa	7
Casa Sea Shell	10
De Mello's	3
Dona Florina	2
Julia	1
Lobo's	5
Manuel's	4
Marbella	11
Monte Villa	9
Pretty Petal	6
Sea Shell Inn	8

RESTAURANTS
Amigo's	E
Mico's	B
Spice Garden	D
Teama	C
Tibetan Kitchen	A

N

Lawande
Centre
& Stores

Casa dos
Monteiros

@ On-line
World

SEQUEIRA
WADDO

Football
Pitch

CAMOTIM
WADDO

Covered Market

MURROD
WADDO

School

Canara
Bank

Bosio Convent
Hospital

CANDOLIM

Casa Dos
Costa-Frias

ARABIAN
SEA

Health
Centre

Nossa Senhora
de Bon Successo

Buses to
Panjim

Panjim (13 km)

Panjim (13 km), Nerul & Coco Beach

John's
Boats

Sinquerim
Beach

Taj Holiday
Village

Nerul River

Canon
Emplacement

Fort Aguada

Fort Aguada
Beach Resort

Bus
Stop

FORT AGUADA

Helipads

New
Lighthouse

Prison

Old
Lighthouse

0   Metres   200

12

GOA | North Goa

876

to hold yoga positions is lined with sun beds, parasols and shack cafés, and the surf sees more jet-skis and paragliders than fishing boats. On the plus side, Candolim has lots of pleasant places to stay, many of them tucked away down quiet sandy lanes and better value than comparable guesthouses in nearby Calangute, making this a good first stop if you've just arrived in Goa and are planning to head further north after finding your feet.

Immediately south, a long peninsula extends into the sea, bringing the seven-kilometre white sandy beach to an abrupt end. **FORT AGUADA**, which crowns the rocky flattened top of the headland, is the best-preserved Portuguese bastion in Goa. Built in 1612 to protect the northern shores of the Mandovi estuary from Dutch and Maratha raiders, it is home to several natural springs, the first source of drinking water available to ships arriving in Goa after the long sea voyage from Lisbon. On the north side of the fort, a rampart of red-brown laterite juts into the bay to form a jetty between two small sandy coves. This picturesque spot, known as **Sinquerim Beach**, was among the first places in Goa to be singled out for upmarket tourism. Taj Group's *Fort Aguada* resorts, among the most expensive hotels in India, lord it over the beach from the lower slopes of the steep-sided peninsula.

The ruins of the **fort** can be reached by road; head through the *Taj Holiday Village*, and turn right when you see the sign. Nowadays, much of the site serves as a prison, and is therefore closed to visitors. It's worth a visit, though, if only for the superb views from the top of the hill where a four-storey Portuguese **lighthouse**, erected in 1864 and the oldest of its kind in Asia, looks down over the vast expanse of sea, sand and palm trees of Calangute beach on one side, and across the mouth of the Mandovi to Cabo Raj Bhavan, and the tip of the Mormugao peninsula, on the other.

Practicalities

Buses to and from Panjim stop every ten minutes or so at the stand opposite the *Casa Sea Shell*, in the middle of Candolim. A few head south here to the *Fort Aguada Beach Resort* terminus, from where services depart every thirty minutes for the capital via Nerul village; the rest all go direct to Panjim via Nerul bridge, immediately east of the junction, or else hasten north along the main drag to Calangute. **Taxis** can be located outside any of the major resort hotels listed below, or flagged down on the road. During the season, there is often a shortage of **motorcycles for rent** here, and you may find yourself having to search for a bike in Calangute (see p.881).

Accommodation

Candolim is charter-holiday land, so **accommodation** tends to be expensive for most of the season. That said, if bookings are down you can find some great bargains here. The best place to start looking is at the end of the lane that leads to the sea opposite the Canara Bank, at the north side of the village.

Altrude Villa, Murrod Waddo ☎ 0832/277703. Large, airy rooms with attached tiled bathrooms and private verandas. The larger ones on the first floor have sea views. ❺–❼

Casa Sea Shell, Fort Aguada Road, near *Bom Successo* ☎ 0832/277879. A new block, identical to *Sea Shell Inn*, but with its own pool, picturesquely situated beside a small chapel. The rooms are large, with spacious tiled bathrooms, and the staff and management welcoming and courteous. Arguably the best choice in this class. ❻

De Mello's, Monteiro's Road ☎ 0832/277395. Gaudy pink-and-orange place in the dunes that takes the overspill from the (pricier) *Dona Florina* next door. Smallish rooms with not very private balconies, but only a stone's throw from the beach and very quiet. ❺

Dona Florina, Monteiro's Road ☎ 0832/275051 or 277398, ☎ 276878. Large, ten-year-old guesthouse in superb location, overlooking the beach in the most secluded corner of the village. Sanyasins from the Rashneesh ashram from Pune have long been its mainstay, hence the higher than usual rates – worth paying if you want idyllic sea views. No vehicle access. ⑥–⑦

Julia, Escrivao Waddo ☏0832/277219. At the north end of the village. Comfortable en-suite rooms, tiled floors, balconies, a relaxing, sociable garden, and easy access to the beach. ④

Lobo's, Camotim Waddo ☏0832/279165. In a peaceful corner of the village, this is a notch up from *Manuel's*, opposite, with larger rooms, a long common veranda on the ground floor and very friendly owners. ④

Manuel's, Camotim Waddo ☏0832/277729. Small family guesthouse that's been around for years and is welcoming, clean and cheap, although somewhat boxed in by other buildings. All rooms have fans and attached shower-toilets. ③–④

Marbella, Sinquerim ☏0832/275551, ℻276509. Individually styled suites and spacious rooms (from Rs1000) in a beautiful house built to resemble a traditional Goan mansion. The decor, fittings and furniture are gorgeous, especially in the top-floor "Penthouse" (Rs2000), and the whole place is screened by greenery. Unashamedly romantic and well worth splashing out on. ⑦

Monte Villa, Murrod Waddo ☏0832/276344, ℮montvila@goatelecom.com. Seven lovely en-suite rooms, 2min from the beach, recently revamped by friendly Gulf returnees. Scrupulously clean and with some sea views. Ask for "M5", which has a breezy corner balcony. Internet access available. ④–⑤

Pretty Petal, Camotim Waddo ☏0832/276184. Not as twee as it sounds: very large, modern rooms, all with fridges and balconies, and relaxing, marble-floored communal areas overlooking lawns. Their top-floor apartment (#113), with windows on four sides and a huge balcony, is the best choice, though more expensive. ⑥

Sea Shell Inn, Fort Aguada Road, opposite the Canara Bank ☏0832/276131. Homely, immaculately clean rooms in a roadside hotel featuring safe-deposit lockers, laundry facility and a popular terrace restaurant. The tariff includes use of a nearby pool – a very good deal. ⑤

Eating and drinking

Candolim's numerous beach **cafés** are a cut above your average seafood shacks, with pot plants, state-of-the-art sound systems and prices to match. Basically, the further from the *Taj* complex you venture, the more realistic the prices become.

Amigo's, 3km east of Candolim at Nerul bridge. Well off the beaten track and rarely patronized by tourists, this rough-and-ready riverside shack, tucked away under the bridge, is famous locally for its superb fresh seafood, served straight off the boats on no-nonsense stone tables. Fish curry and rice is their stock in trade, but they also do stuffed pomfret, calamari chilli-fry, red snapper and, best of all, Jurassic-sized crabs in butter-garlic sauce. Count on Rs150 for the works, with drinks.

Casa Sea Shell, in *Casa Sea Shell* hotel. This is the place to head for top-notch tandoori and North Indian dishes, although they also offer a good choice of Chinese and European food. Excellent service and moderate prices.

Mico's, Murrod Waddo. Succulent barbecued meats and seafood are the speciality of this stylish but unpretentious new restaurant, set around a beautifully renovated Portuguese-era house just off the main road. They also serve a range of tasty, healthy starters (including great satay chicken, hummus and tzatziki), tender steak in whisky sauce and a great Thai-style curry made with fresh coconut, lemongrass and ginger. Main courses from Rs90 (for Indian veg),to Rs500 (for a grilled fresh lobster).

Sea Shell, at the *Sea Shell Inn*, Fort Aguada Road. A congenial terrace restaurant that cooks seafood and sizzling meat meals to order – also good for vegetarians and anyone fed up with spicy Indian food. Try one of their delicious cocktails.

Spice Garden, opposite Canara Bank. The food here is not up to much, but the live music is well worth dropping in for. A local guitarist does singa-long numbers (and beautiful Konkani wedding songs if cajoled), interspersed with Tom Jones covers from the owner, complete with dramatic gestures and heavy vibrato: a must.

Teama, Murrod Waddo, opposite *Altrude Villa*. One of the best places in the area to sample authentic Goan food. Try their prawn-curry-and-rice house speciality, or milder fish *caldin*. Most of the main meals cost around Rs120–175, and they have a good breakfast menu. Occasional live music during the season.

Tibetan Kitchen, Murrod Waddo. A swish offshoot of the established Calangute restaurant, serving filling and tasty (but non-spicy) Tibetan and Chinese specialities, and a good range of Western dishes, in comfortable surroundings behind the dunes. Most main dishes under Rs100.

Calangute

A mere 45-minute bus ride up the coast from the capital, **CALANGUTE** is Goa's busiest and most commercialized resort, and the flagship of the state government's bid for a bigger slice of India's package-tourist pie. In the 1970s and early 1980s, this once-peaceful fishing village epitomized Goa's reputation as a haven for hedonistic hippies. Indian visitors flocked by the bus load from Bombay and Bangalore to giggle at the tribes of dreadlocked Westerners lying naked on the vast white sandy beach, stoned out of their brains on local *feni* and cheap *charas*. Calangute's flower-power period, however, has long passed. Hoteliers today joke about the days when they used to rent out makeshift shacks on the beach to backpackers. Now many of them manage tailor-made tourist settlements, complete with air-conditioned rooms, swimming pools and lush lawns, for groups of suitcase-carrying fortnighters.

The charter boom, combined with a huge increase in the number of Indian visitors, for whom this is Goa's premier resort, has placed an impossible burden on Calangute's rudimentary infrastructure. Each year, as another crop of construction sites blossoms into resort complexes, what little charm the village has retained gets steadily more submerged under ferroconcrete and heaps of garbage. The pollution problems are compounded by an absence of adequate provision for waste disposal and sewage treatment, and ever-increasing water-consumption levels. One worrying sign that Calangute has already started to stew in its own juices has been a dramatic rise in **malaria** cases: virex, and the more serious falciparum strain, are now both endemic here, and rife during the early part of the season.

The town and beach

The road from the **town** to the beach is lined with Kashmiri-run handicraft boutiques and Tibetan stalls selling Himalayan curios and jewellery. The quality of the goods – mainly Rajasthani, Gujarati and Karnatakan textiles – is generally high, as are the prices. Haggle hard and don't be afraid to walk away from a heavy sales pitch – the same stuff crops up every Wednesday at Anjuna's flea market. The **beach** itself is nothing special, with steeply shelving sand, but is more than large enough to accommodate the huge numbers of high-season visitors. Most of the action centres on the beachfront below GTDC's unsightly *Tourist Resort*, where crowds of Indian women in saris and straw hats stand around watching their sons and husbands frolic in the surf. Nearby, stray cows nose through the rubbish left by the previous bus party, while an endless stream of ice-cream- and fruit-sellers, *lunghi*-wallahs, ear cleaners and masseurs work their way through the ranks of trippers.

To escape the melee of the main beachfront area, head fifteen minutes or so south, towards the rows of old wooden boats moored below the dunes at Maddo Waddo (literally "toughies' quarter", referring to the fishermen, who used to be very tough indeed before the relatively recent advent of the outboard motor).

At the other end of the village's social hierarchy, one of Calangute's wealthiest families in the early eighteenth century built an extraordinary mansion, the **Casa dos Proença**, which still stands just north of the market area, beyond the Bank of Baroda. Its most distinctive feature is a wonderful tower-shaped veranda whose sides are covered in screens made from oyster shells (*carepas*). The gallery is surmounted by a grand pitched roof, designed to funnel the air entering the room through the windows and other openings (now glazed) – an ingenious natural air-conditioning system that was in time adopted all over the Portuguese empire.

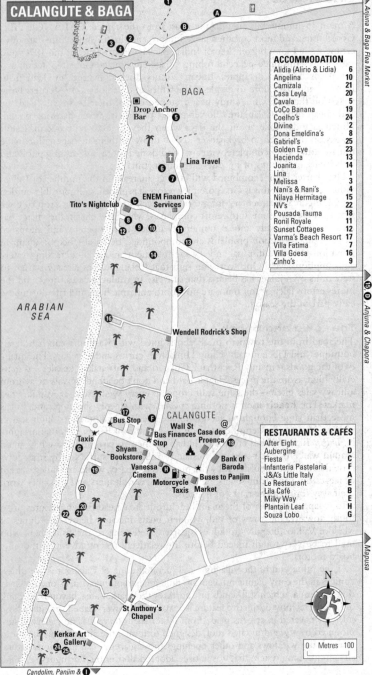

CALANGUTE & BAGA

❶
Ⓐ
Ⓑ
❸ ❷
❹

BAGA

Drop Anchor Bar
❺

✝ Lina Travel
❻
❼

Ⓒ ENEM Financial Services

Tito's Nightclub
❽
⑫ ❾ ❿
⓫
⓭

⑭

ARABIAN SEA

Ⓔ

⑯
Wendell Rodrick's Shop

@

⑰
Bus Stop
CALANGUTE
Ⓕ
Wall St
Bus Finances
Stop
@
Casa dos Proença
⑱
Taxis ★
Ⓖ
Shyam Bookstore
Bank of Baroda
⑲
Vanessa Cinema Ⓗ
Motorcycle Taxis
Buses to Panjim
Market
@
⑳
㉒ ㉑

㉓

St Anthony's Chapel

Kerkar Art Gallery
㉔ ㉕

▲ Anjuna

▶ Anjuna & Baga Flea Market

▶ ⑮ Ⓓ, Anjuna & Chapora

▶ Mapusa

▼ Candolim, Panjim & ❶

ACCOMMODATION

Alidia (Alirio & Lidia)	6
Angelina	10
Camizala	21
Casa Leyla	20
Cavala	5
CoCo Banana	19
Coelho's	24
Divine	2
Dona Emeldina's	8
Gabriel's	25
Golden Eye	23
Hacienda	13
Joanita	14
Lina	1
Melissa	3
Nani's & Rani's	4
Nilaya Hermitage	15
NV's	22
Pousada Tauma	18
Ronil Royale	11
Sunset Cottages	12
Varma's Beach Resort	17
Villa Fatima	7
Villa Goesa	16
Zinho's	9

RESTAURANTS & CAFÉS

After Eight	I
Aubergine	D
Fiesta	C
Infantaria Pastelaria	F
J&A's Little Italy	A
Le Restaurant	E
Lila Café	B
Milky Way	H
Plantain Leaf	G
Souza Lobo	

0 Metres 100

N

Practicalities

Buses from Mapusa and Panjim pull in at the small bus stand-cum-market square in the centre of Calangute. Some continue to Baga, stopping at the crossroads behind the beach en route. Get off here if you can (as the main road veers sharply to the right); it's closer to most of the hotels. **Motorcycle taxis** hang around opposite the temple in the market area, and around the little sandy square behind GTDC's *Tourist Resort*, next to the steps that drop down to the beach-front. Ask around here if you want to rent a **motorcycle**. Rates are standard; the nearest **petrol station** (or "pump") is five minutes' walk from the beach, back towards the market on the right-hand side of the main road. **Bicycles** are also widely available for around Rs50 per day.

There's a State Bank of India on the main street, but the best place to **change money** and travellers' cheques is Wall Street Finances (Mon–Sat 8.30am–7pm, Sun 10am–2pm), opposite the petrol pump and in the shopping complex on the beach-front. If they are closed, try the fast and friendly ENEM Finances in Baga, who open late (daily 8am–9pm), but offer poorer rates. For Visa encashments, go to the Bank of Baroda, just north of the temple and market area; a commission fee of Rs100, plus one percent of the amount changed, is levied on all Visa withdrawals.

Accommodation

Calangute is chock-full of **places to stay**. Demand only outstrips supply in the Christmas–New Year high season, and at Diwali (Sept/Oct), when the town is inundated with Indian tourists; at other times, haggle a little over the tariff, especially if the place looks empty.

Even the cheapest rooms tend to have a veranda or a balcony, and an attached bathroom; nowhere is far from the shore, but sea views are more of a rarity. The top hotels are nearly all gleaming white, exclusive villa complexes with pools, and direct beach access. High-season rates in such places can be staggeringly steep, as they cater almost solely for package tourists.

Camizala, 5-33B Maddo Waddo ☎0832/279530 or 276263. Lovely, breezy little place with only four rooms, common verandas and sea views. About as close to beach as you can get, and the ward is very quiet (see *Casa Leyla* review below). Cheap considering the location. ❸

Casa Leyla, Maddo Waddo ☎&℗0832/276478. A great place if you're a family looking for somewhere with plenty of space for a let of at least one week. The rooms are huge and well furnished, with fridges, kid-friendly beds and chairs, and basic self-catering facilities, while the house itself, whose upper storey sits up in the palm canopy, is set deep in the secluded fishing ward, behind the quietest stretch of the beach. ❹–❺

CoCo Banana, 1195 Umta Waddo ☎&℗0832/276478, down the lane past *Meena Lobo's* restaurant. Very comfortable, spacious chalets, all with bathrooms, mosquito nets, extralong mattresses and verandas, around a central garden. Run by a very sorted Swiss-Goan couple that have been here for years. ❺–❻

Coelho's, just south of *Golden Eye*, near the ice factory, Gaura Waddo ☎0832/277646. Twelve very spacious rooms in a large new house, on the peaceful (sea-facing) side of the village, 2min from the beach. Individual balconies, and a wonderful roof terrace with sea views. ❹–❺

Gabriel's, next door to *Coelho's*, Gauro Waddo ☎0832/279486, ℗277484. A congenial, quiet guesthouse midway between Calangute and Candolim, run by a gorgeous family who go out of their way to help their guests, many of whom return year after year. Shady garden, pleasant views from rear side across the *toddi* dunes, top little restaurant and very close to the beach. ❹

Golden Eye, A-1/189 Gaura Waddo ☎0832/277308, ℗276187. Large rooms, balconies, sea views and a terrace restaurant, all smack on the beach. One of the first purpose-built hotels in Calangute. ❻

NV's, south Calangute ☎0832/279749 or 281334, ℗nv-goa@hotmail.com. Homely, traditional Goan guesthouse right on the beach, run by a fisher family and holding its own despite proximity of a large package resort. Eleven rooms, four with breezy common balcony. A good budget option. ❸–❺

GOA | North Goa

881

Pousada Tauma, Porba Waddo ☎ 0832/279061, ⓕ 279064, ⓦ www.pousada-tauma.com. New luxury resort complex, comprising double-storey laterite villas ranged around a pool, in the middle of Calangute, but screened from the din by lots of vegetation. Understated decor, and a very exclusive atmosphere, preserved by five-star prices. Their big draw is a first-rate Keralan Ayurvedic health centre (open to nonresidents). ❾

Varma's Beach Resort, 2min east of GTDC *Tourist Resort* ☎ 0832/276077, ⓕ 276022. Attractive a/c rooms, with balconies overlooking a leafy garden. Close to the centre of the village, but secluded. ❽

Villa Goesa, Cobra Waddo ☎ 0832/277535, ⓕ 276182, ⓔ alobo@goatelecom.com. A stone's throw from the beach and very swish, set around a lush garden of young palms and lawns. Occasional live music and a cocktail bar. All rooms have balconies. ❼

White House, 185/B Gaura Waddo, near *Goan Heritage* ☎ 0832/277938, ⓕ 276308. Immaculate, large rooms in modern block close to the beach, with balconies, bathrooms and some views. If full, try the equally comfortable *Dona Cristalina* along the lane (☎ 0832/297012). ❺ –❻

Eating and drinking

Calangute's **bars** and **restaurants** are mainly grouped around the entrance to the beach and along the Baga road. As with most Goan resorts, the accent is firmly on **seafood**, though many places tack on a few token veg dishes. Western breakfasts (pancakes, porridge, muesli, eggs) also feature prominently.

After Eight, Gauro Waddo, midway between Calangute and Candolim, down a lane leading west off the main road, between the Lifeline Pharmacy and a small chapel. Superb gourmet restaurant run by two ex-Taj (Mumbai) whizz kids, in a quiet garden. Steaks are their most popular dish, but chef Chakraborthy has a sublime touch with seafood, served with original, delicate sauces. Most main courses around Rs250.

Gabriel's, in *Gabriel's* guesthouse, Guara Waddo. Authentic Goan cooking (pork *sorpotel*, chicken *xacuti*, stuffed squid and prawn masala), and very popular Italian dishes (with home-made pasta) served on a cosy roof terrace well away from the main road. A tiny bit pricier than average (most mains around Rs80) but worth it, and they do real espresso coffee.

Infantaria Pastelaria, next to St John's Chapel, Baga Road. Roadside terrace café that gets packed out at breakfast time for its piping hot croissants, freshly baked apple pie and real coffee. During the season they do full-on breakfast buffets too, with cereals and fresh fruit (Rs80 including

drinks). Indian-Continental dinner menu served upstairs in the evening. Takeaways from the street-facing counter.

NV's, south Calangute. A ten-minute trek down the beach, but well worth it for no-nonsense platefuls of grilled fish, calamari and crab, all fresh from the family boat and at rock-bottom prices.

Plantain Leaf, near Vanessa Cinema, market area. The best *udipi* restaurant outside Panjim, serving the usual range of delicious dosas and other spicy snacks in a clean, cool, marble-lined canteen, with relentless background *filmi* music. Try their tasty *idly-fry* – south India's answer to chips – or the filling thalis (Rs35).

Souza Lobo, on the beachfront. One of Goa's oldest restaurants and deservedly famous for its superb seafood, served on crisp gingham tablecloths by legions of fast-moving waiters in matching Madras-checked shirts. Blow-out fish sizzlers and mouthwatering tiger prawns or lobsters are the house specialities, but they do a mean stuffed avocado for veggies. Get there early, and avoid weekends. Most main dishes Rs100–150.

Nightlife

Calangute's **nightlife** is surprisingly tame for a resort of its size. All but a handful of the bars wind up by 10pm, leaving punters to prolong the short evenings back at their hotels, find a shack that's open late, or else head up to Baga (see opposite). The other places that consistently work into the wee hours are a couple of dull hippy hang-outs in the woods to the south of the beach road: *Pete's Bar*, a perennial favourite next door to the *Angela P. Fernandes Guest House*, is generally the most "lively", offering cheap drinks, backgammon sets and relentless Bob Marley. Further afield, *Bob's Inn*, between Calangute and Candolim, is another famous old bar, renowned above all for its extrovert owner, who claims with some justification to have been Goa's first hippy.

Finally, don't miss the chance to sample some pukka Indian culture while you are in Calangute. The **Kerkar Art Gallery**, in Gaurwaddo, at the south end of town (☎0832/276017), hosts evenings of **classical music and dance** (Tues 6.45pm; Rs250 on door or in advance), held in the back garden on a sumptuously decorated stage, complete with incense and evocative candlelight. The recitals, performed by students and teachers from Panjim's Kala Academy, are kept comfortably short for the benefit of Western visitors, and are preceded by a short introductory talk.

Baga

BAGA, 10km west of Mapusa, is basically an extension of Calangute; not even the locals agree where one ends and the other begins. Lying in the lee of a rocky, wooded headland, the only difference between this far northern end of the beach and its more congested centre is that the scenery here is marginally more varied and picturesque. A small river flows into the sea at the top of the village, below a broad spur of soft white sand, from where a dirt track strikes across an expanse of paddy fields towards Anjuna.

Until the early 1990s, few buildings stood at this far northern end of the beach other than a handful of old red-tiled fishers' houses nestling in the dunes. Since the package boom, however, Baga has developed more rapidly than anywhere else in the state and today looks less like a Goan fishing village than a small-scale resort on one of the Spanish Costas, with a predominantly young, charter-tourist clientele to match. But if you can steer clear of the lager louts and bar brawls, Baga boasts distinct advantages over its neighbours: a crop of excellent restaurants and a nightlife that's consistently more full-on than anywhere else in the state, if not all India.

Accommodation

Accommodation is harder to arrange on spec in Baga than in Calangute, as most of the hotels have been carved up by the charter companies; even rooms in smaller guesthouses tend to be booked up well before the season gets under way. If you're keen to stay, you may have to hole up further down the beach for a night while you hunt around for a vacancy. The rough-and-ready places dotted around the fishing village usually have space; look for signs on the main square. Cheap houses and rooms for rent are also available on the quieter north side of the river, although these are like gold dust in peak season. If you come then, beware of "compulsory gala dinner supplements" or some similarly named ruse to slap stiff surcharges (typically Rs750 per head) on to your room tariff.

Alidia (Alirio & Lidia), Baga Road, Saunta Waddo ☎0832/276835 or ☎&℗279014, ℮alidia@goaworld .com. Attractive modern chalet rooms with good-sized verandas looking onto the dunes. Double or twin beds. Quiet, friendly and the best deal in this bracket. ❹–❻

Angelina, near *Tito's*, Saunta Waddo ☎0832/279145. Spacious, well-maintained rooms with large tiled bathrooms and big balconies, off the road but still in the thick of things. A/c available. ❸–❺

Cavala, on the main road ☎0832/277587 or 276090, ℗277340, ℬwww.cavala.com. Modern hotel in tastefully traditional mould; simple rooms, and separate balconies, but a little close to the road for comfort. ❻–❼

Divine, near *Nani's & Rani's*, north of the river ☎0832/279546. Run by fervent Christians (the signboard features a burning cross and bleeding heart), the rooms are on the small side, but clean; some have attached shower-toilets. ❸

Dona Emeldina's, Saunta Waddo
0832/276880. Pleasantly old-fashioned cottages with verandas opening onto lawns, run by a garrulous Portuguese-speaking lady. A bargain in low and mid-season (Rs550–650), but pricey over Christmas, due to its proximity to the party enclave – a dubious distinction. If she's fully booked, check out her other place, the cheaper but less appealing *Baga Queen* nearby. ❼

Hacienda, Baga Road 0832/277348. Nothing special but good value, with big, airy rooms, balconies, running hot water and a neat little garden. ❺–❻

Joanita, Baga Road 0832/277166. Clean, airy rooms with attached baths and some double beds, around a quiet garden. A good choice if you want to be in the village centre but off the road. ❸–❹

Lina, north of the river 0832/281142. Baga's most secluded guesthouse, deep in a peaceful palm grove on the edge of dense woodland. Quiet, with only four simple en-suite rooms, and cheap for the area. ❸

Melissa, 620 Anjuna Rd 0832/279583. Eight recently built rooms in a clean, quiet block on the north side of the river, all with attached shower-toilets. Good off-season discounts, too. ❸

Nani's and Rani's, north of the river
0832/276313 or 277014. A handful of red-tiled, whitewashed budget cottages in a secluded garden behind a huge colonial-era house. Fans, some attached bathrooms, well-water, outdoor showers and internet facility. ❷–❹

Nilaya Hermitage, Arpora Bhati
0832/276793–4 or 275187–8, 276792, nilaya@goa1.dot.net.in. Set on the crest of a hilltop 6km inland from the beach, with matchless views over the coastal plain, this place ranks among India's most exclusive hotels, patronized by a very rich international jet set. On site are a steam room, gym, clay tennis court, and a restaurant that's open to lesser mortals who can't afford to stay here. Rooms from around $245 for two, including meals and airport transfers. ❾

Ronil Royale, Baga Road 0832/276101, 276068. Baga's most upmarket hotel, a ten-minute walk from the beach, has Portuguese-style apartments overlooking two small pools, with a swish restaurant. ❾

Sunset Cottages, Saunta Waddo 0832/276802, 275001. The best mid-budget choice in this generally overpriced area below *Tito's*. In season it's rammed with beery Brits, but the smallish rooms are well kept and the management friendly. ❺–❻

Villa Fatima, Baga Road 0832/277418. Thirty-two attached rooms in a large, three-storey back-packers' hotel centred on a sociable garden terrace. Their rates are reasonable, varying with room size. All attached bathrooms. ❹–❻

Zinho's, 7/3 Saunta Waddo 0832/277383. Tucked away off the main road, close to *Tito's*. Half a dozen modest-size, clean rooms above a family home. Near to the beach and good value. ❹

Eating

Baga has the best range of **restaurants** in Goa, from standard beach shacks to swish pizzerias and terrace cafés serving real espresso coffee. Because of the stiff competition, prices are generally reasonable and the quality of cooking high. Even if they wouldn't be seen dead here during the day, many old Goa hands come to Baga to eat in the evenings. For a splurge, splash out on a candle-lit dinner at *J&A's Little Italy*, or a romantic Italian meal at *Fiesta*.

Aubergine, 3km inland at Arpora. Sophisticated, intimate garden restaurant created by Goan designer Wendell Rodricks. The Norman chef, Patrick Le Clerc, aims to provide simple, wholesome dishes that blend Indian ingredients with French flair – try the wonderful *Papillotte de Poisson Farci Beurre Nantais* (fish fillet with prawn stuffing steamed in banana leaf with white wine and butter). And his chocolate mousse is unmissable. Mains Rs135–225; real Cuban cigars Rs90–440.

Fiesta, Tito's Lane. Baga's most extravagantly decorated restaurant enjoys a perfect spot at the top of a long dune with sea views. The menu's Mediterranean, with a generous measure of Portuguese. Most mains around Rs180; wine Rs70 per glass, or by the bottle (Rs550).

J&A's Little Italy, Baga Creek. Mouthwatering, authentic Italian food (down to the imported Parmesan and olive oil) served in the riverside garden of an old fisherman's cottage. Cooked in a wood-fired oven, their pizzas are delicious (try the amazing "smoked beef" house speciality), and dishes of the day include fresh lasagne. Count on Rs250–300 per head for the works; extra for wine (Rs60 per glass).

Le Restaurant, Baga Road. Hot contender for the title of best restaurant in Goa, as much for its classic French cooking as the reasonable prices and fun atmosphere, whipped up by the three Gallic partners against a backdrop of classy red curtains and Christmas lights. Steaks are the chef's forte, but they offer plenty of seafood and veg alternatives. Main courses around Rs150.

Lila Café, Baga Creek. Laid-back bakery-cum-snack-bar, run by a German couple who've been here for years. Their healthy home-made breads and cakes are great, and there's an adventurous lunch menu featuring spinach à la crème, aubergine pâté and smoked water buffalo ham, rounded off with real espresso coffee. Open 8am–8pm.

Milky Way, midway between Calangute and Baga. Baga's best breakfast venue (occupying the same garden as *Le Restaurant*), serving mountainous bowls of fresh fruit and home-made curd, as well as pancakes, muesli and omelettes.

Nani's and Rani's, at *Nani's and Rani's* guesthouse on the north side of the river. Friendly family-run restaurant serving unremarkable but inexpensive, tasty food on a sociable veranda overlooking the river. Popular with budget travellers.

Nightlife

Nightlife revolves around *Tito's*, on a sandy hillock above the beach. Women are allowed in for free; "unaccompanied" men have to pay Rs100–250, depending on the crowd. Be warned, however, that in recent years this has become something of a pick-up joint, frequented by groups of so-called "rowdies" from Delhi and Mumbai, with the lager-fuelled antics you'd find in a rough British nightclub. A marginally more sedate option, run by the same owners is *Mambo's*, further down the hill, where karaoke is the big attraction. At the far end of Baga beach, *Drop Anchor* is deservedly the most popular place for a quiet drink. Also owned by the *Tito's* family, it serves up cocktails in addition to the usual range of beers and spirits, and has a terrace with easy chairs on the sand.

Anjuna

With its fluorescent-painted palm trees and infamous full-moon parties, **ANJUNA**, 8km west of Mapusa, is Goa at its most "alternative". Fractal patterns and Day-Glo Lycra may have superseded cotton kaftans, but most people's reasons for coming are the same as they were in the 1970s: drugs, dancing and lying on the beach slurping tropical fruit. Depending on your point of view, you'll find the headlong hedonism a total turn-off or heaven-on-sea. Either way, the scene looks here to stay, despite government attempts to stamp it out, so you might as well get a taste of it while you're in the area, if only from the wings, with a day-trip to the famous **flea market**.

One of the main sources of Anjuna's enduring popularity as a hippy hangout is its superb **beach**. Fringed by groves of swaying coconut palms, the curve of soft white sand is safer for bathing than most of the nearby resorts, especially at the more peaceful southern end, where a rocky headland keeps the sea calm and the undertow to a minimum. North of the market ground, the beach broadens, running in an uninterrupted kilometre-long stretch of steeply shelving sand to a low red cliff. The village bus park lies on top of this high ground, near a crop of small cafés, bars and Kashmiri handicraft stalls. Every lunchtime, tour parties from Panjim pull in here for a beer, before heading home again, leaving the ragged army of sun-weary Westerners to enjoy the sunset.

The season in Anjuna starts in early November, when most of the long-staying regulars show up, and peters out in late March, when they drift off again. During the Christmas and New Year rush, the village is inundated with a mixed crowd of round-the-world backpackers, refugees from the British club scene and revellers from all over India, lured by the promise of the big beach parties. A large contingent of these are young Israelis fresh out of the army and

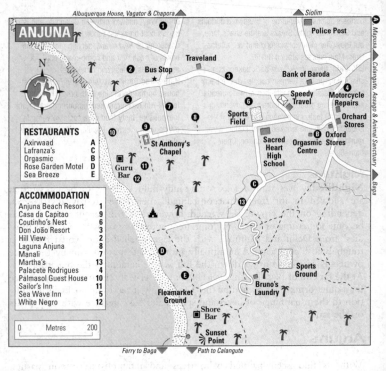

ANJUNA

Police Post

N

Bus Stop ★

Traveland

Bank of Baroda

Speedy Travel

Motorcycle Repairs

Orchard Stores

Sports Field

RESTAURANTS

Axirwaad	A
Lafranza's	C
Orgasmic	B
Rose Garden Motel	D
Sea Breeze	E

St Anthony's Chapel

Sacred Heart High School

Orgasmic Centre

Oxford Stores

Guru Bar

ACCOMMODATION

Anjuna Beach Resort	1
Casa da Capitao	9
Coutinho's Nest	6
Don João Resort	3
Hill View	2
Laguna Anjuna	8
Manali	7
Martha's	13
Palacete Rodrigues	4
Palmasol Guest House	10
Sailor's Inn	11
Sea Wave Inn	5
White Negro	12

Sports Ground

Bruno's Laundry

Fleamarket Ground

Shore Bar

Sunset Point

| 0 | Metres | 200 |

full of devil-may-care attitudes to drugs and other people's sleep. Outside peak season, however, Anjuna has a surprisingly simple, unhurried atmosphere – due, in no small part, to the shortage of places to stay. Most visitors who come here on market day or for the raves travel in from other resorts.

Whenever you come, keep a close eye on your valuables. **Theft**, particularly from the beach, is a big problem. Party nights are the worst; if you stay out late, keep your money and papers on you, or lock them somewhere secure (see p.857). Thieves have even been known to break into local houses by lifting tiles off the roof.

Practicalities

Buses from Mapusa and Panjim drop passengers at various points along the tarmac road across the top of the village, which turns right towards Chapora at the main Starco's crossroads. If you're looking for a room, get off here as it's close to most of the guesthouses. The crossroads has a couple of small **stores**, a **motorcycle taxi** rank, and functions as a de facto village square and **bus stand**.

The *Manali Guesthouse* and Oxford Stores **change money** (at poor rates). The Bank of Baroda on the Mapusa road will make encashments against Visa cards, but doesn't do foreign exchange, nor is it a good place to leave valuables, as thieves have previously climbed through an open window and stolen a number of "safe custody" envelopes. The **post office**, on the Mapusa road, 1km inland, has an efficient poste restante counter. *Manali Guest House* also offers **internet access** (Rs60/hr), but Colours, next to Speedy Travel, has a much faster connection and a/c for the same price.

The Anjuna flea market

Anjuna's Wednesday **flea market** is the hub of Goa's alternative scene, and *the* place to indulge in a spot of souvenir shopping. A decade or so ago, the weekly event was the exclusive preserve of backpackers and the area's semi-permanent population, who gathered here to smoke *chillums*, and to buy and sell clothes and jewellery they probably wouldn't have the nerve to wear anywhere else: something like a small pop festival without the stage. These days, however, everything is more organized and mainstream. Pitches are rented out by the metre, drugs are banned and the approach roads to the village are choked solid all day with a/c buses and Ambassador cars ferrying in tourists from resorts further down the coast.

The range of goods on sale has broadened, too, thanks to the high profile of migrant hawkers and stallholders from other parts of India. Each region or culture tends to stick to its own corner. At one end, Westerners congregate around racks of New-Age and dance gear, batik and designer beachwear. Nearby, hawk-eyed Kashmiris sit cross-legged beside trays of silver jewellery and papier-mâché boxes, while Tibetans, wearing jeans and T-shirts, preside over orderly rows of prayer wheels, turquoise bracelets and sundry Himalayan curios. Most distinctive of all are the Lamani women from Karnataka, decked from head to toe in traditional tribal garb, and selling elaborately woven multicoloured cloth, which they fashion into everything from jackets to money belts, and which makes even the Westerners' party gear look positively funereal. Elsewhere, you'll come across dazzling Rajasthani mirror-work and block-printed bedspreads, Keralan woodcarvings and a scattering of Gujarati appliqué.

What you end up paying for this exotic merchandise largely depends on your ability to **haggle**. Lately, prices have inflated as tourists not used to dealing in rupees will part with almost anything. Be persistent, though, and cautious, and you can usually pick things up for a reasonable rate. Even if you're not spending, the flea market is a great place to sit and watch the world go by. Mingling with the sun-tanned masses are bands of strolling musicians, itinerant beggars, performing monkeys and snake-charmers, as well as the inevitable hippy jugglers, clad in regulation waistcoats and billowing pyjama trousers.

Accommodation

Most of Anjuna's very limited **accommodation** consists of small unfurnished houses, although finding one is a problem at the best of times – in peak season it's virtually impossible. By then, all but a handful have been let to long-staying regulars who book by post several months in advance. If you arrive hoping to sort something out on the spot, you'll probably have to make do with a room in a guesthouse at first, although most owners are reluctant to rent out rooms for only one or two days at a time. Basically, unless you mean to stay for at least a couple of months, you're better off looking for a room in Calangute, Baga or nearby Vagator or Chapora.

Anjuna Beach Resort, De Mello Waddo ⓣ 0832/274499, ⓔ fabjoe@goa1.dot.net.in. Fifteen spacious, comfortable rooms with balconies, fridges, attached bathrooms and solar hot water in a new concrete building. Those on the upper floor are best. Good value. ❻

Casa da Capitao, near St Anthony's Chapel ⓣ 0832/273832. Three basic but spruce, purple-painted rooms amid lots of greenery, and with large sitouts. ❹

Coutinho's Nest, Soronto Waddo ⓣ 0832/274386. Small, very respectable family guesthouse on the main road. Their immaculately clean rooms are among the village's best budget deals. Shared shower-toilets only. ❸

Don João Resort, Soronto Waddo ⓣ 0832/274325, ⓕ 273447, ⓦ www.goacom.com/hotels/donjoao.html. An unsightly multistorey hotel, slap in the middle of the village, and aimed squarely at the charter market, with a poolside restaurant, fridges in the rooms and inflated rates; precisely the kind of place Anjuna could do without. ⑧

Hill View, De Mello Waddo ⓣ0832/273235. One of the newer and more pleasant budget places, run by a landlady who puts Israeli guests into a separate "unbreakable" block. Quiet location, and good value. ③

Hilton, on the main road near the bus park ⓣ0832/274432 or 273477. Five double rooms in a characterless outbuilding, 500m behind the beach. Some attached shower-toilets. ④

Laguna Anjuna, De Mello Waddo ⓣ0832/274305. Recently opened "alternative designer" resort, in a similar mould to the famous *Nilaya* at Arpora (see p.884), but somewhat less expensive ($120 in peak season). It comprises 25 colourfully decorated laterite "cottages", grouped behind a convoluted pool, with a restaurant, pool room and bar. ⑨

Manali, south of *Starco's* ⓣ0832/274421, ⓔmanali@goatelecom.com. Anjuna's best all-round budget guesthouse has simple rooms opening onto a yard, fans, safe deposit, money-changing, library, internet connection, a sociable terrace-restaurant and shared bathrooms. Very good value, so book in advance. ②

Martha's, 907 Montero Waddo ⓣ0832/273365. Eight immaculate en-suite rooms, including two pleasant houses, run by a warm and friendly fami-ly. Basic amenities include kitchen space, fans and running water. ⑤

Palacete Rodrigues, near *Oxford Stores* ⓣ0832/273358, ⓕ274310. Two-hundred-year-old residence converted into an upmarket guesthouse. Carved wood furniture, and a relaxed, traditional Goan feel. Single occupancy available. ⑥

Palmasol Guest House, Praia de St Anthony, behind middle of beach ⓣ0832/273258, ⓕ222261. Huge, comfortable rooms in an immaculately kept old house very near the beach. The larger ones have running water, verandas, cooking space and a relaxing garden; cheaper alternatives in the back yard. ④–⑥

Sailor's Inn, southwest of St Anthony's Chapel ⓣ0832/273439. Four plain, clean rooms, very close to the sea shore, and with spacious sitouts, in a quiet spot, although you pay for proximity to the beach. ⑤–⑥

Sea Wave Inn, De Mello Waddo ⓣ0832/274455. Smart, spacious, high-ceilinged rooms in a new block. Tiled bathrooms and balconies. Not the best location, but good value at this price. ⑥

White Negro, 719 Praia de St Anthony, south of the village ⓣ0832/273326, ⓔmjanets@goa1.dot.net.in. A row of fourteen spotless back-to-back chalets catching the sea breeze, all with attached bathrooms and 24hr running water. Also a lively restaurant and friendly management. Good value. ⑦

Water shortages

Because of the extra inhabitants it attracts over the winter, Anjuna has become particularly prone to water shortages. These tend not to affect many visitors, as the drought only begins to bite towards the end of March when the majority have already left. For the villagers, however, the problem causes genuine hardship. Use well water very sparingly and avoid water toilets if possible – traditional dry ("pig") ones are far more ecologically friendly.

Eating and drinking

Anjuna is awash with good **places to eat and drink**. The beach shacks tend to be overpriced by comparison with those elsewhere in the state (especially on flea market days, when they hike their prices) but many will feel the location is worth paying for. Responding to the tastes of its many "alternative" visitors, the village also boasts a crop of quality wholefood cafés serving healthy veg dishes and juices. The most sophisticated restaurant in the area, however, has to be the *Axinwaad*, 4km inland at Assagao.

Axinwaad, 483 Rua de Boa Vista, Bouta Waddo, Assagao. Located 4km east along the main Mapusa road, this atmospheric restaurant occupies a lofty old Portuguese-era *palacio*, decked out and lit with blue colours and textiles to create an underwater ambience. The menu (mains around Rs150) blends East and West, and all points in between. On Thursdays, it metamorphoses into a "Lounge Groove Space", serving tapas and Arab mezes, with guest DJs.

Lafranza's, south end of village on the road to the market ground. The budget travellers' choice: big portions of tasty fresh fish and fries, with plenty of veg options.

Martha's Breakfast Home, at *Martha's* guesthouse, 907 Montero Waddo. Secluded, ultra-friendly breakfast garden serving fresh Indian coffee, crêpes and delicious waffles.

Orgasmic, near Oxford Stores. Gaudily decorated with coloured pea lights and flouro paints, this is where the Anjuna's wealthy, healthy alternative clique like to dine on gourmet vegetarian food. If you're hankering for safe, adventurous salads, you'll be spoilt for choice (Rs100 for a big bowl). They also do great tofu dishes and even sushi.

Rose Garden Motel, on the beach south of the *Shore Bar*. Not to be confused with the *Rose Garden Restaurant* in the village. The exhaustive menu here features superb, reasonably priced seafood sizzlers and tasty Indian veg dishes.

Sea Breeze, market ground. Does a roaring trade in cold beer and snacks on Wednesdays. At other times the vast tandoori fish selection is tasty and good value, especially for groups; order in advance.

Sun 'n' Sand, market ground. Renowned for its whopping fresh-fruit salads served with crumbled coconut and curd. Great for inexpensive, healthy breakfasts.

Nightlife

Thanks to a recent ban on amplified music after 10pm, Anjuna no longer deserves the reputation it gained through the 1980s as a legendary rave venue, but big **parties** do still take place here from time to time, especially around the Christmas–New Year full-moon period. Smaller events may also happen whenever the organizers can muster the increasingly large pay-offs demanded by local police.

At other times, **nightlife** centres on the *Nine Bar*, above Vagator beach, where big trance sounds attract a fair-sized crowd for sunset. On Wednesdays after the flea market, the *Shore Bar*, in the middle of Anjuna beach, offers more of the same on a larger scale, with hundreds of foreigners making the most of the police-free zone on the bar's steps. The music gains pace as the evening wears on, winding up around 10pm, when there's an exodus over to the *Primrose Café* in Vagator, which stays open until after midnight. *Axinwaad* in Assagao is the place to be on Thursday nights, when the restaurant becomes a cool lounge club, with cutting-edge fusion from visiting DJs.

Vagator

Barely a couple of kilometres of cliff-tops and parched grassland separate Anjuna from the southern fringes of its nearest neighbour, **VAGATOR**. A desultory collection of ramshackle farmhouses and picturesque old Portuguese bungalows scattered around a network of leafy lanes, the village is entered at the east via a branch off the Mapusa road, which passes a few small guesthouses and restaurants before running down to the sea. Dominated by the red ramparts of Chapora fort, Vagator's broad white sandy beach – **Big Vagator beach** – is undeniably beautiful, spoiled only by the daily deluge of whisky-swilling tour parties that spill across it at lunchtimes.

Far better, then, to head to the next cove south. Backed by a steep wall of crumbling palm-fringed laterite, **Ozran** (or "Little") **Vagator beach** is more secluded and much less accessible than either of its neighbours. To get there, walk ten minutes from Big Vagator, or drive to the end of the lane off the main Chapora–Anjuna road, from where a footpath drops sharply down to a wide stretch of level white sand (look for the mopeds and bikes parked at the top of the cliff). At this southern end of the beach (dubbed "Tel Aviv Beach"), a row of makeshift **cafés** provides shade and sustenance (and relentless trance music) for a predominantly Israeli crowd. In spite of the Goan nudism laws, topless bathing is the norm; not that the locals, nor the odd

The dark side of the moon

Hedonism has figured prominently in European images of Goa from the mid-sixteenth century, when mariners and merchants returned to Lisbon with tales of unbridled debauchery among the colonists. The French traveller François Pyrard was first to chronicle this as moral decline, in a journal peppered with accounts of wild parties and sleaze scandals.

Following the rigours of the Inquisition, a semblance of morality was restored, which prevailed through the Portuguese era. But traditional Catholic life in Goa's coastal villages sustained a rude shock in the 1960s with the first influx of hippies to Calangute and Baga beaches. Much to the amazement of the locals, the preferred pastime of these would-be *sadhus* was to cavort naked on the sands together on full-moon nights, amid a haze of *chillum* smoke and loud rock music blaring from makeshift PAs. The villagers took little notice of these bizarre gatherings at first, but with each season the scene became better established, and by the late 1970s the Christmas and New Year parties, in particular, had become huge events, attracting thousands of foreign travellers.

In the late 1980s, the local party scene received a dramatic face-lift with the coming of acid house and techno. Ecstasy became the preferred dance drug as the dub-reggae scene gave way to rave culture, with ever greater numbers of young clubbers pouring in for the season on charter flights. Goa soon spawned its own distinctive brand of psychedelic music, known as Goa Trance. Distinguished by its multilayered synth lines and sub-bass rhythms, the hypnotic style combines the darkness of hard techno with an ambient sentiment. Cultivated by artists such as Juno Reactor and Hallucinogen, the new sound was given wider exposure when big-name DJs Danny Rampling and Paul Oakenfold started mixing Goa Trance in clubs and on national radio back in the UK, generating a huge following among music lovers who previously knew nothing of the place which had inspired it.

In spite of the growing interest in Goa Trance, the plug was pulled on the state's party scene in 1994–95. For years, drug busts and bribes provided the notoriously corrupt local cops with a lucrative source of baksheesh. But after a couple of drug-related deaths, a series of sensational articles in the local press and a decision by Goa Tourism to promote upmarket over backpacker tourism, the police began to demand impossibly large bribes – sums that the organizers could not hope to recoup. Although the big New Year and Christmas events continued unabated, smaller parties, hitherto held in off-track venues such as "Disco Valley" behind Middle Vagator beach, started to peter out, much to the dismay of local people, many of whom had become financially dependent on the raves and the punters they pulled in to the villages.

Against this backdrop, news of the Y2K amplified-music ban between 10pm and 7am seemed to sound the death knell for Goa's party scene. At the time, locals and expats alike still believed the ruling would have little impact – that the police would simply use it as a pretext to extort still larger bribes from bar owners and party organizers. But they were wrong. Since winter 1999–2000, the nights on Goa's coast have, with a few notable exceptions, been silent. Only a handful of cafés and clubs can muster large enough payoffs to stay open through the small hours, and most of these are mainstream venues in Baga.

So if you've come to Goa expecting an Indian equivalent of Ko Pha Ngan or Ibiza-on-the-Arabian Sea, you'll be sorely disappointed. Only over Christmas and New Year, when tourist numbers ensure organizers can recoup the massive outlay on bribes, do parties take place, and these are a far cry from the free-and-easy events that once filled the beaches on full-moon nights.

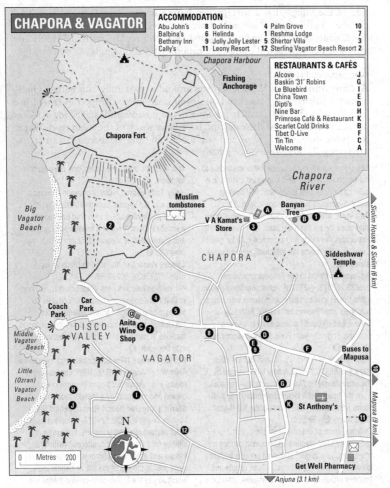

CHAPORA & VAGATOR

ACCOMMODATION

Abu John's	8	Dolrina	4	Palm Grove	10
Balbina's	6	Helinda	1	Reshma Lodge	7
Bethany Inn	9	Jolly Jolly Lester	5	Shertor Villa	3
Cally's	11	Leony Resort	12	Sterling Vagator Beach Resort	2

RESTAURANTS & CAFÉS

Alcove	J
Baskin '31' Robins	G
Le Bluebird	I
China Town	E
Dipti's	D
Nine Bar	H
Primrose Café & Restaurant	K
Scarlet Cold Drinks	B
Tibet O-Live	F
Tin Tin	C
Welcome	A

Chapora Harbour

Fishing Anchorage

Chapora Fort

Big Vagator Beach

Muslim tombstones

V A Kamat's Store

Chapora River

Banyan Tree

CHAPORA

Siddeshwar Temple

Coach Park

Car Park

Anita Wine Shop

DISCO VALLEY

Middle Vagator Beach

Little (Ozran) Vagator Beach

VAGATOR

Buses to Mapusa

St Anthony's

Get Well Pharmacy

0 Metres 200

N

Siolim House & Siolim (6 km)

Mapusa (9 km)

Anjuna (3.1 km)

12

GOA | North Goa

groups of inebriated men that file past around mid-afternoon, seem in the least perturbed.

Like Anjuna, Vagator is a relaxed, comparatively undeveloped resort that appeals, in the main, to budget travellers with time on their hands. Accommodation is limited, however, and visitors frequently find themselves travelling to and from Baga every day until a vacancy turns up in one of the guesthouses.

Practicalities

Buses from Panjim and Mapusa, 9km east, pull in every fifteen minutes or so at the crossroads on the far northeastern edge of Vagator, near where the main road peels away towards Chapora. From here, it's a one-kilometre walk over the hill and down the other side to the beach, where you'll find most of the village's accommodation, restaurants and cafés. The *Primrose Café*, on the south side of the village, has a **foreign exchange** licence (for cash and travellers' cheques) but their rates are well above those on offer at the banks in Mapusa and Calangute. If you need medical attention, contact Dr Jawarhalal Henriques at Zorin, near the petrol pump in Chapora (☎0832/274308).

Accommodation

Accommodation in Vagator revolves around a few family-run budget guest-houses, a pricey resort hotel and dozens of small private properties rented out for long periods. The usual charge for a house is between Rs2000 and Rs4500 per month; ask around the cafés and back lanes south of the main road. **Water** is in very short supply here, and you'll be doing the villagers a favour if you use it frugally at all times (see p.888).

Abu John's, halfway between the crossroads and the beach (no phone). Self-contained chalets in a quiet garden, all with bathrooms and running water. A comfortable mid-range option. ❺

Balbina's, Menndonca Waddo (no phone). Cosy little place below the main road, with views of the fort across the valley and a terrace café for guests. Quiet, and the rooms (all attached) are well maintained. ❸

Bethany Inn, next to the Chapora crossroads ☎0832/273973, ℱ273731, ℮bethany@goatelecom.com. Seven immaculately clean rooms with fridges, balconies and attached bathrooms. Tastefully furnished, and efficiently managed by two young brothers, originally from Pune. Internet access available. ❺–❻

Cally's, near St Anthony's Church, behind Bella Bakery ☎0832/273704. A new block owned by the same family as *Dolrina*, twenty minutes back from the beach, with clean tiled bathrooms and views from relaxing verandas across the fields. Good value. ❷–❸

Dolrina, north of the road near the beach ☎0832/273382. Nestled under a lush canopy of trees, Vagator's largest and most popular budget guesthouse is run by a friendly Goan couple and features attached or shared bathrooms, a sociable common veranda, individual safe deposits and roof

space. Single occupancy rates, and breakfasts available. ❺

Jolly Jolly Lester, halfway between the crossroads and Big Vagator beach ☎0832/273620. Eleven pleasant doubles with tiled bathrooms, plus a small restaurant, set in a lovingly kept garden and surrounded by woodland. Single occupancy possible. ❺

Leoney Resort, on the road to Disco Valley ☎0832/273634, ℱ273595, ℮romi@goatelecom.com. Smart chalets and pricier (but more spacious) octagonal "cottages" on sleepy side of village, ranged around a pool. Restaurant, laundry, lockers and foreign-exchange facilities. A comfortable option. No advance bookings Dec–Jan. ❼

Reshma Lodge (Mrs Bandobkhar's), next to the Anita Wine Shop ☎0832/273568. Inexpensive rooms in a newish building with running water, owned and managed by a friendly local lady. ❹

Sterling Vagator Beach Resort, behind Big Vagator beach ☎0832/274377. Upmarket resort hotel pitched at wealthy Indians, but extremely shabby for the price. A/c "cottages" (with TVs, fridges and attached bathrooms) grouped around a large pool at the top of the hill, or behind the beach at sea level; two multi-cuisine restaurants, safe deposit and moneychanging. ❾

Eating, drinking and nightlife

Vagator boasts an eclectic batch of **restaurants**, with wildly varying menus and prices, and an equally dramatic turnover of chefs. Western tourists tend to stick to the pricier ones lining the road through the village, while Indian visitors frequent the more impersonal, cheaper places down on the beach itself. The bar to head to for a sundowner is *Nine Bar* (formerly *Ram Das Swami's*), on the cliff-top above Ozran beach, where alternative Goa struts its stuff, accompanied by a wall of techno. When it closes (at 9pm), everyone makes their way over to the *Primrose Café*, which offers much the same atmosphere, without the views.

Alcove, next to *Ram Das Swami's*, above Ozran beach. This unsightly cliff-top complex enjoys the best location for miles, with spellbinding sea views

through the palms. The food is also a cut above the competition, and the service slick. Try their fish dish of the day, washed down with a cocktail.

Baskin "31" Robbins, near *Primrose Café*. Thirty-one flavours of melt-in-the-mouth American ice-cream. The nut crunch is to die for.

Le Bluebird, on the road out to *Nine Bar*. Tucked away in the most appealing corner of the village is Vagator's famous French-run restaurant, which serves classier-than-average Continental food at traveller-friendly prices. Seafood is their strong point, but they offer a better range of veg dishes than you'd find in a real French restaurant, as well as crêpes, Bordeaux claret and champagne (around Rs2000 per bottle).

China Town, next to *Bethany Inn*. For the past few seasons, this small roadside restaurant, tucked away just south of the main drag, has been the village's most popular budget place to eat, serving particularly tasty seafood dishes in addition to a large Chinese selection, as well as all the usual Goa-style travellers' grub.

Dipti's, on the Mapusa road. Extraordinary magic-mushroom plastic art meets Ajanta-mural decor is the hallmark of this cosy bar, which serves a full Indian-Goan-Chinese-Continental menu. It's also a friendly place for a quiet cocktail.

Jolly Jolly Lester, halfway between the village crossroads and Big Vagator beach. Not to be confused with *Julie Jolly's*, near the *Primrose Café*. This one's smaller, offering a better selection of inexpensive seasonal seafood, salads and tasty Western-style veg dishes.

Nine Bar, above Ozran beach. Boasting a crystal trance sound system, this cliff-top café enjoys a prime location, with fine sea views from its terrace through the palm canopy, where Nepali waiters serve up cold beer and the usual range of budget travellers' grub to a generally spaced-out clientele. They've recently enlarged the place to accommodate a dance floor and chill-out area.

Primrose Café and Restaurant, on the southern edge of the village. Goa's posiest café-bar livens up around 8pm and serves tasty German whole-food snacks, light meals and cakes, as well as drinks.

Tibet O-Live, east side of the village, on the main road. Run by a team of friendly young lads from Darjeeling, this place shuttles between Manali in the summer and Goa in the winter, and has earned a strong reputation in both for its ultra-tasty, inexpensive pizzas. They also serve mouth-watering fried *momos* (the spinach and cheese ones are best).

Tin Tin, west side of the village, near the cliff-top car park. The kind of theme bar that makes you wonder why you ever left home: large and lavishly decorated, and crammed with a mainly young package-tourist clientele, hence the higher-than-average prices, which the expat British co-owner justifies with a popular "big portions" policy. The menu is exhaustive, but best bets are the dishes of the day chalked on boards.

Chapora

Crouched in the shadow of a Portuguese fort on the opposite, northern side of the headland from Vagator, **CHAPORA**, 10km from Mapusa, is a lot busier than most north-coast villages. Dependent on fishing and boat-building, it has, to a great extent, retained a life of its own independent of tourism. The workaday indifference to the annual invasion of Westerners is most evident on the main street, lined with as many regular stores as travellers' cafés and restaurants. It's unlikely that Chapora will ever develop into a major resort; tucked away under a dense canopy of trees on the muddy southern shore of a river estuary, it lacks both the space and the white sand that have pulled crowds to Calangute and Colva.

If you have your own transport, however, Chapora is a good base from which to explore the region: Vagator is on the doorstep, Anjuna is a short ride to the south, and the ferry crossing at Siolim – gateway to the remote north of the state – is barely fifteen minutes away by road. The village is also well connected by bus to Mapusa, and there are plenty of sociable bars and cafés to hang out in. The only drawback is that accommodation tends, again, to be thin on the ground. Apart from the guesthouses along the main road, most of the places to stay are long-stay houses in the woods.

Chapora's chief landmark is its venerable old **fort**, most easily reached from the Vagator side of the hill. At low tide, you can also walk around the bottom of the headland, via the anchorage and the secluded coves beyond it to Big

Vagator, then head up the hill from there. The red-laterite bastion, crowning the rocky bluff, was built by the Portuguese in 1617 on the site of an earlier Muslim structure (thus the village's name – from *Shahpura*, "town of the Shah"). Deserted in the nineteenth century, it lies in ruins today, although the **views** up and down the coast from the weed-infested ramparts are still superb.

Practicalities

Direct **buses** arrive at Chapora three times daily from Panjim, and every fifteen minutes from Mapusa, with departures until 7pm. **Motorcycle taxis** hang around the old banyan tree at the far end of the main street, near where the buses pull in. Air, train, bus and catamaran **tickets** may be booked or reconfirmed at Soniya Tours and Travels, next to the bus stand.

If you want to check into a cheap guesthouse while you sort out more permanent **accommodation**, try the basic *Shertor Villa* (℡0832/424335; ❷–❸), off the west side of the main street. Nearly all its rooms, ranged around a sheltered back yard, come with fans and running water. If this place is full, try the *Helinda* (℡0832/274345; ❷–❸), at the opposite end of the village, which has rock-bottom options and a couple of more comfortable rooms with attached shower-toilets, as well as a good restaurant. The only luxury place hereabouts is the *Siolim House* (℡0832/272138 or 272942, ℻272323, ⓦwww .siolimhouse.com; ❾), 5km inland from Chapora along the south bank of the river, in Siolim village. Housed in a recently restored *palacio*, the hotel captures the period feel of the Portuguese era, with elegant, simply furnished rooms ranged around a central pillared courtyard. It also has a twelve-metre pool in the garden, and an unobtrusive restaurant serving fine Goan food.

Finding cheap **meals** in Chapora itself is easy: just take your pick from the crop of inexpensive little cafés and restaurants on the main street. The popular *Welcome*, halfway down, offers a reasonable selection of cheap and filling seafood, Western and veg dishes, plus relentless reggae and techno music, and backgammon sets. If you're suffering from chilli-burn afterwards, *Scarlet Cold Drinks* and the *Sai Ganesh Café*, both a short way east of the main street, knock up deliciously cool fresh fruit milkshakes.

Pernem and the far north

Sandwiched between the Chapora and Arondem rivers, the predominantly Hindu *taluka* of **Pernem** – in the *Novas Conquistas* area – is Goa's northernmost district and one of its least explored regions. Apart from the fishing village of **Arambol**, which attracts a trickle of backpackers seeking a rougher, less pretentious alternative to the resorts south of the River Chapora, the beautiful Pernem coastline of long sandy beaches, lagoons and coconut plantations has few settlements equipped to cope with visitors. However, the picturesque, if bumpy, journey north from Arambol to **Terekol fort**, on the Maharashtran border, provides ample incentive to spend a day away from the beach.

Heading to Pernem from Anjuna, Vagator, or Chapora, you have to travel a few kilometres inland to pick up the main Calangute road, as it runs north over a low ridge of laterite hills, to the river crossing at **Siolim**. Pending the completion of the road bridge currently being built here, the two **car ferries** that chug back and forth across the river remain the only dependable link, and one of the high points of the journey north.

Once across the river, head straight on until you reach a fork in the road, where a sign pointing right to "Harmal/Terekol" marks the quick route to Arambol.

Arambol (Harmal)

The largest coastal village in Pernem district, and the only one really geared up for tourism, is **ARAMBOL** (or Harmal), 32km northwest of Mapusa. If you're happy with basic amenities but want to stay somewhere lively, this might be your best bet. The village's two beaches are beautiful and still relatively unexploited – thanks to the locals, who a few years back managed to block proposals put forward by a local landowner to site a sprawling five-star resort here. Parties do occasionally happen, drawing revellers across the river from Anjuna and Vagator, but these are rare intrusions into an otherwise tranquil, out-of-the-way corner of the state.

The one unpleasant aspect of Arambol is **crime**. The rate of thefts has gone through the roof here over the past few seasons. Dozens of travellers lose their passports and money each season, mostly from rented houses, so make sure your valuables are secure when you go out, especially after dark.

Modern Arambol is scattered around an area of high ground west of the main coast road, where most of the buses pull in. From here, a bumpy lane runs downhill, past a large school and the village church, to the more traditional end of the village, clustered under a canopy of widely spaced palm trees. The main **beach** lies 200m further along the lane. Strewn with dozens of old wooden fishing boats and a line of tourist café-bars, the gently curving bay is good for bathing, but much less picturesque than its neighbour around the corner.

To reach **"Paradise beach"**, follow the track over the headland to the north. Beyond a rather insalubrious smelling, rocky-bottomed cove, the trail emerges to a broad strip of soft white sand hemmed in on both sides by steep cliffs. Behind it, a small freshwater lake extends along the bottom of the valley into a thick jungle. Hang around the banks of this murky green pond for long enough, and you'll probably see a fluorescent-yellow human figure or two appear from the bushes at its far end. Fed by boiling hot springs, the lake is lined with sulphurous mud, which, when smeared over the body, dries to form a surreal, butter-coloured shell. The resident hippies swear it's good for you and spend much of the day tiptoeing naked around the shallows like refugees from some obscure tribal initiation ceremony – much to the amusement of Arambol's Indian visitors.

Practicalities

Buses to and from Panjim (via Mapusa) pull into Arambol every half-hour until noon, and every 90min thereafter, at the small bus stand on the main road. A faster private **minibus** service from Panjim arrives daily opposite the chai stalls at the beach end of the village. **Boats** leave here every Wednesday morning for the ninety-minute trip to the flea market at Anjuna. Tickets should be booked in advance from the *Welcome Restaurant* by the beach (Tues–Sun 8–9am & 8–9pm; Rs150), which also rents out motorcycles and scooters. The **post office**, next to the church, has a poste restante box; there are also several places offering **internet access** in the village, the cheapest and newest of them just past the junction on the main road. Reliable **moneychangers** include: Delight, on the east side of the main road, and Tara Travel, directly opposite, where you can also reconfirm and book air and catamaran tickets.

Apart from a couple of purpose-built chalets on the edge of the village, most of Arambol's **accommodation** consists of simple houses in the woods behind the beach. Some of the more expensive places have fully equipped kitchens and showers, but the vast majority are standard-issue bare huts, with "pig" toilets and a well in the back garden. Long-stay visitors either bring their own bedding and cooking stuff, or kit themselves out at Mapusa market. Good places to start room-hunting when you've just arrived are the *Villa Oceanic* (℡0832/292296; ❷–❸), in the middle of the village, and the nearby *Ave Maria* (℡0832/29764; ❸), the closest Arambol has to bona fide guesthouses.

The choice of **places to eat** has broadened impressively over the past few years. Pick of the bunch is the excellent *Double Dutch Bakery Café*, tucked away among the *toddi* trees in a clearing just below the main street (look for the yellow signboard). Run by an expat Dutch couple, it serves a tempting selection of delicious, healthy breakfasts, and home-made snacks, cakes and pastries during the day. They've also recently started offering evening meals of a standard not yet matched in the village, including great Indonesian dishes and a sumptuous Mughlai chicken. Arambol's other outstanding restaurant is the *Relax Inn*, north of the main entrance to the beach, through a gap in the bushes. Frequented by the village's resident German paragliding fraternity, it dishes up generous portions of fresh Goan-style seafood, with fries and copious salads. You generally have to wait longer than usual to be served, because they prepare each dish to order, sauces included. For inexpensive Indian rice-based meals, best bets are the no-nonsense chai stalls at the bottom of the village. *Sheila's* and *Siddi's* tasty thalis both come with *puris*, and they have a good travellers' breakfast menu of pancakes, eggs and curd. *Dominic's*, also at the bottom of the village (near where the road makes a sharp ninety-degree bend), is renowned for its fruit juices and milkshakes, while *Sai Deep*, a little further up the road, does generous fruit salads with yoghurt.

Terekol

North of Arambol, the sinuous coast road climbs to the top of a rocky, undulating plateau, then winds down through a swathe of thick woodland to join the River Arondem, which it then follows for 4km through a landscape of vivid paddy fields, coconut plantations and temple towers protruding from scruffy red-brick villages. The tiny enclave of **TEREKOL**, the northernmost tip of Goa, is reached via a clapped-out car ferry (every 30min; 5min) from the hamlet of Querim, 42km from Panjim.

After the long and scenic drive, the old **fort** that dominates the estuary from the north is a bit of an anticlimax. Hyped as one of the state's most atmospheric historic monuments, it turns out to be little more than a down-at-heel country house recently converted into a low-key luxury hotel. If your visit coincides with the arrival of a guided tour, you may get a chance to look around the gloomy interior of the **Chapel of St Anthony**, in the fort's claustrophobic cobbled square; at other times it's kept locked.

Practicalities

The few visitors that venture up to Terekol tend to do so by motorbike, heading back at the end of the day to the relative comfort of Calangute or Baga. If you run out of fuel, the nearest service station is at Arambol. One of GTDC's daily **tours** from Panjim (see p.859) comes up here, as does one daily Kadamba **bus** from the capital; alternatively, the 7am bus from Siolim, on the Chapora River, pulls in at the Querim ferry an hour later.

Accommodation is limited to the posh *Hotel Tirakhol Fort Heritage* (℡0832/782240, ℻782326; ❼), whose rooms are pleasant and comfortable, but way overpriced at Rs800 for the no-frills (windowless) options, and around Rs2000 (plus taxes) for a luxury suite with sea views. The **restaurant** downstairs, kept busy in the daytime by bus parties, offers seafood, Indian and Chinese dishes, as well as beer.

South Goa

Beyond the unattractive port city of **Vasco da Gama**, and its nearby airport, the southern reaches of the state harbour some of the region's finest **beaches**, with attractive Portuguese-style villages nestled in a hilly interior. Many visitors base themselves initially at **Benaulim**, 6km west of Goa's second city, **Margao**. The most traveller-friendly resort in the area, Benaulim stands slap in the middle of a spectacular 25-kilometre stretch of pure white sand, backed by a broad band of coconut plantations. Although increasingly carved up by Mumbai time-share companies, low-cost accommodation here is plentiful and of a consistently high standard. Nearby **Colva**, by contrast, has degenerated over the past five or six years into an insalubrious charter resort, frequented by huge numbers of day-trippers. More polluted and far less relaxing than its neighbours, it's not somewhere you'd choose to hole up for a beach holiday.

With the gradual spread of package tourism down the coast, **Palolem**, a couple of hours' south of Margao down the main highway, has emerged as most budget travellers' first choice, despite its relative inaccessibility. Set against a backdrop of forest-cloaked hills, its beach is spectacular and development relatively low-key.

Vasco da Gama

VASCO DA GAMA (commonly referred to as "Vasco"), 29km by road southwest of Panjim, sits on the narrow western tip of the Mormugao peninsula, overlooking the mouth of the Zuari River. Acquired by the Portuguese in 1543, this strategically important site was formerly among the busiest ports on India's west coast. It remains a key shipping centre, with container vessels and iron-ore barges clogging the choppy river mouth, but holds nothing of interest for visitors, particularly since the completion of the Konkan Railway,

Dabolim airport

Dabolim, Goa's airport, lies on top of a rocky plateau, 4km southeast of Vasco da Gama. A large new civilian terminal was recently constructed at this naval aerodrome to accommodate Goa's rapidly increasing air traffic, but long delays are still common – so if you're catching a flight from here, aim to check in well in advance.

Facilities in the terminal buildings include State Bank of India foreign exchange desks (open for flights), post office counters, and counters for domestic airlines. There's also a handy prepaid taxi counter outside the main exit. Fixed fares to virtually everywhere in the state are displayed behind the desk; pay here and give the slip to the driver when you arrive.

Facilities in Dabolim's first-floor departures hall include another pint-size State Bank of India (Mon, Tues, Thurs & Fri 10.30am–1.30pm, Sat 10.30am–noon), a sub-post office and branches of several domestic airlines: Indian Airlines (daily 7.15am–2pm; ☎ 0832/512788), Gujarat Airways (daily 9.30am–5pm; ☎ 0832/516060), Sahara Airlines (daily 9.30am–5pm; ☎ 0832/510043) and Jet (daily 9.30am–5pm; ☎ 0832/511005). There's a very ordinary and overpriced cafeteria, too, but it doesn't open in time for early morning domestic departures, so if you're looking for a filling breakfast, head across the road from the front of the terminal building to the staff canteen, where you can grab piping hot *bhaji pao* and *batata wada* for a few rupees. Finally, don't forget that if you're leaving Goa by international charter you have to pay Rs300 airport tax at the State Bank counter before you check in.

GOA | South Goa

when Goa's main railhead shifted from here to Margao. The only conceivable reason you might want to come to Vasco is to catch a bus to **Dabolim airport**, 4km southeast.

Practicalities

Vasco is laid out in a grid, bordered by Mormugao Bay to the north, and by the railway line on its southern side. Apart from the cluster of oil storage tanks, the town's most prominent landmark is the **railway station** at the south end of the main Dr Rajendra Prasad Avenue. **Arriving by bus** from Panjim or Margao, you'll be dropped off at the inconveniently situated interstate Kadamba terminus, 3km east of the town centre. Local **minibuses** ferry passengers from here to the more central market bus stand, at the top of the square, where buses from Dabolim airport also pull in. **Auto-rickshaws**, and Ambassador and motorcycle **taxis**, hang around on the corner of Swatantra Path and Dr Rajendra Prasad Avenue, near the station and the small **cycle rental** stall. If you need to **change money**, head for the State Bank of India (Mon–Fri 10am–2pm, Sat 10am–noon) at the north end of F L Gomes Road. GTDC's **tourist information** counter is in the lobby of their *Tourist Hostel* (daily 9.30am–5pm).

Thanks to its business city status, Vasco boasts a better-than-average batch of **hotels**. Most are plush mid-range places, although there are several no-frills lodges near the railway station. Best of the budget bunch is the neat and clean *Annapurna*, on Dattatreya Deshpande Road (T0832/513375 or 513715; ③). If it's full try the GTDC *Tourist Hostel*, off Swatantra Path near the station (T0832/510829 or 513119; ③–⑤). Moving upscale, the *Citadel*, Pe Jose Vaz Road (T0832/513190 or 512222, F513036; ⑤), currently offers the best value for money among Vasco's many modern mid-range places. At the other end of town opposite Hindustan Petroleum, the *Maharaja* (T0832/513075–8, F512559; ⑥–⑦) has similar tariffs and spotless rooms, but dismal views over the refinery. Finally, for fully air-conditioned comfort, complete with plush bars, restaurants and a gym, check in to Vasco's top hotel, the *La Paz*, on Swatantra Path (T0832/512121, F513302; Wwww.hotellapazgardens.com; ⑥).

All of the hotels listed above have **restaurants**, but for traditional Indian snacks and thalis, the *Annapurna*'s ground-floor vegetarian cafeteria is hard to beat. At the other end of the centre, next door to *Hotel La Paz*, the excellent *Welcome Restaurant,* a more modern snack bar, serves a huge selection of dosas, as well as the usual range of bhajis and a full Punjabi menu; most main dishes cost between Rs30 and Rs50.

Margao (Madgaon) and around

MARGAO, the capital of prosperous Salcete *taluka*, is regarded as Goa's second city, even though it's marginally smaller than Vasco da Gama, 30km northwest. Surrounded by fertile farmland, the town has always been an important agricultural market, and was once a major religious centre, with dozens of wealthy temples and *dharamshalas* – however, most of these were destroyed when the Portuguese absorbed the area into their Novas Conquistas ("New Conquests") during the seventeenth century. Today, Catholic churches still outnumber Hindu shrines, but Margao has retained a distinctly cosmopolitan feel, largely due to a huge influx of migrant labour from neighbouring Karnataka and Maharashtra. The resultant overcrowding has become a real problem in the town centre, whose 1950s municipal buildings and modern concrete blocks stew under a haze of traffic pollution.

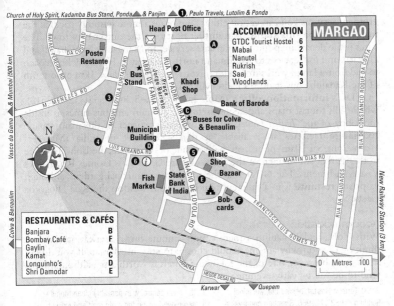

Church of Holy Spirit, Kadamba Bus Stand, Ponda & Panjim, Paulo Travels, Lutolim & Ponda

MARGAO

Head Post Office

ACCOMMODATION	
GTDC Tourist Hostel	6
Mabai	2
Nanutel	1
Rukrish	5
Saaj	4
Woodlands	3

Poste Restante

Bus Stand

Praça Jorge Barreto

RUA DA PADRE MIRANDA

Khadi Shop

Bank of Baroda

Buses for Colva & Benaulim

Municipal Building

Music Shop

Bazaar

MARTIN DIAS RD

Fish Market

State Bank of India

Bob-cards

RAFAEL PEREIRA RD

DA COSTA RD

M. MENEZES RD

MIGUEL LOYOLA FURTADO RD

ABBE DE FARIA RD

LUIS MIRANDA RD

JINACIO DE LOYOLA RD

FRANCISCO LUIS GOMES RD

RUA DE CONSTANCIO ROQUE DA COSTA

RUA DA SAUDADES

New Railway Station (3 km)

BHARATKAR

HEGDE DESAI RD

Vasco da Gama & Mumbai (500 km)

Colva & Benaulim

N

RESTAURANTS & CAFÉS	
Banjara	B
Bombay Café	F
Gaylin	A
Kamat	C
Longuinho's	D
Shri Damodar	E

0   Metres   100

Karwar   Quepem

If you're arriving in Goa on the Konkan Railway from Mumbai or South India, you'll almost certainly have to pause in Margao to pick up onward transport by road. The other reason to come here is to shop at the town's excellent **market**. Stretching from the south edge of the main square to within a stone's throw of the old railway station, the bazaar centres on a labyrinthine covered area that's a rich source of authentic souvenirs, and a good place to browse. While you're here, take a short rickshaw ride north to the stately **Church of the Holy Spirit**, in the heart of a dishevelled but picturesque colonial enclave. Presiding over the dusty Largo de Igreja square, the church, built by the Portuguese in 1675, is one of the finest examples of late-Baroque architecture in Goa, boasting a pristine white facade and an interior dripping with gilt, crystal and stucco.

For a taste of Goa's wonderful vernacular colonial architecture, you'll have to head inland where a scattering of picturesque farming villages **around Margao** harbour a crop of decaying old Portuguese *palacios*, as well as a handful of idiosyncratically Goan Hindu temples.

Practicalities

Margao's new **railway station**, the only stop in Goa for most long-distance express services on the Konkan Railway, lies 3km south of the centre. The reservation office (Mon–Sat 8am–4.30pm, Sun 8am–2pm) is divided between the ground and first floor; bookings for the superfast Rajdhani Express to Delhi are made at the hatch to the left of the main entrance. Tickets for trains to Mumbai are in short supply, so make your reservation as far in advance as possible, get here early in the day to avoid agonizingly long queues, and bring a book. Several of the principal trains that stop in Margao do so at unsociable times of night, but there's a 24hr information counter (⊕0832/712790), and a round-the-clock prepaid auto-rickshaw stand outside the exit.

Local private buses to Colva and Benaulim leave from in front of the *Kamat Hotel*, on the east side of Margao's main square. Arriving on long-distance government services you can get off either here or (at a more leisurely pace) at the main **Kadamba bus stand**, 3km further north, on the outskirts of town. The latter is the departure point for interstate services to Mangalore, via Chaudi and Gokarn, and for services to Panjim and north Goa. Paulo Travel's deluxe coach to and from Hampi works from a lot next to the *Nanutel Hotel*, 1km or so south of the Kadamba bus stand on Padre Miranda Road.

GTDC's **information office** (Mon–Fri 9.30am–5.30pm; ☎0832/222513), which sells tourist maps and keeps useful lists of train and bus times, is inside the lobby of the *Tourist Hostel*, on the southwest corner of the main square. **Exchange** facilities are available at the State Bank of India (Mon–Fri 10am–2pm, Sat 10am–noon), off the west side of the square; the Bobcard office in the market sub-branch of the Bank of Baroda, on Luis Gomes Road, does Visa encashments. The **GPO** is at the top of the municipal gardens, although its **poste restante** is in a different building, 200m west on the Rua Diogo da Costa.

Accommodation

With Colva and Benaulim a mere twenty-minute bus ride away, it's hard to think of a reason why anyone should choose to **stay** in Margao. If you do get stuck here, however, one of the following hotels is worth a try, although most tend to be full by early evening.

GTDC Tourist Hostel, behind the Municipal Building ☎0832/721966. Standard good-value government block, with en-suite rooms (some a/c) and a restaurant. A safe budget option. ❺

Mabai, 108 Praca Jorge Barreto ☎0832/721658. The *Woodlands'* only real competitor is frayed around the edges, but clean and central. Some a/c. ❹

Nanutel, Padre Miranda Road ☎0832/733176, ☎733175. The town's top hotel, pitched at visiting businesspeople, with 55 centrally a/c rooms, pool, bookshop, travel desk and a quality restaurant. ❻–❼

Rukrish, opposite the Municipal Building ☎0832/721709. Best of the rock-bottom lodges in

the town centre, with passably clean rooms – some overlooking the main road and market. ❶–❷

Saaj, Miguel Loyola Furtado Road ☎0832/711757. A newcomer that's marginally brighter and cheaper than its main competitor, the nearby *Woodlands*. ❸–❺

Woodlands, Miguel Loyola Furtado Road ☎0832/721121. Margao's most popular mid-range hotel, around the corner from the *Tourist Hostel*. Its bargain "non-deluxe" rooms are often booked up. Reservations recommended. Some a/c. ❸–❺

Eating and drinking

After a browse around the bazaar, most visitors make a beeline for *Longuinho's*, the long-established hang-out of Margao's English-speaking middle classes. If you are on a budget, try one of the South Indian-style pure-veg cafés along Francisco Luis Gomes Road. A couple of these, notably the *Bombay Café*, open early for breakfast.

Banjara, De Souza Chambers ☎0832/722088. This swish basement restaurant is the classiest north Indian joint outside Panjim, specializing in rich Mughlai and tandoori dishes. Tasteful wood and oil-painting decor, unobtrusive *ghazaal* background music, imported liquors and slick service. Most main courses around Rs100.

Bombay Café, Francisco Luis Gomes Road. Popular with office workers and shoppers for its cheap veg snacks, served on tin trays by young

lads in grubby cotton uniforms.

Gaylin, behind Grace Church. Smart, air-conditioned Chinese restaurant serving a good selection of Cantonese and Szechuan dishes (mostly steeped in hot red Goan chilli paste). Count on around Rs150–200 for three courses; extra for drinks.

Kamat, Praça Jorge Barreto, next to the Colva/Benaulim bus stand. The town's busiest *udipi* canteen, serving the usual South Indian selection, as well as hot and cold drinks. Their *masala dosas* are the best for miles.

Longuinho's, opposite the *Tourist Hostel*, Rua Luis Miranda. Relaxing, old-fashioned café serving a reasonable selection of moderately priced meat, fish and veg mains, freshly baked savoury snacks, cakes and drinks. The food isn't up to much these days, and the old Goan atmosphere has been marred by the arrival of satellite TV, but it's a pleasant enough place to catch your breath over a beer.

Shri Damodar, opposite Gandhi Market, Francisco Luis Gomes Road. One of several inexpensive cafés and ice-cream parlours ranged around the temple square. This one is the cleanest, and has an air-cooled "family" (read "women's") room upstairs.

Lutolim

Dotted around the leafy lanes of **LUTOLIM**, 10km northeast of Margao, are several of Goa's most beautiful **colonial mansions**, dating from the heyday of the Portuguese empire when this was the country seat of the territory's top brass. Lying just off the main road, the village is served by eight daily **buses** from Margao, which drop passengers off on the square in front of a lopsided-looking church. The cream of Lutolim's houses lie within walking distance of here, nestled in the woods, or along the road leading south. However, you shouldn't turn up at any of them unannounced; visits have to be **arranged in advance** through the Margao tourist office.

Pick of the crop in Lutolim is **Miranda house**, a stone's throw from the square. Fronted by a plain classical facade, the mansion was built in the 1700s, though renovated later following raids by a clan of rebel Rajput bandits. Today, it is occupied by a famous Goan cartoonist and his family, direct descendants of the wealthy areca planters who originally owned the surrounding estate. **Roque Caetan Miranda house**, two minutes' walk south of the square, and **Salvador Costa house**, tucked away on the western edge of the village, are other mansions worth hunting out; the latter is occupied by an elderly lady who only welcomes visitors by appointment.

Lutolim's other attraction is the quirky model village-cum-heritage centre, a short way east of the square, called **Ancestral Goa** (daily 9am–6pm; Rs20). Set up to show visitors a cross-section of local village life as it was a hundred years ago, it's a well-meaning but ultimately dull exhibition of miniature houses and dressed dummies.

Chandor

Thirteen kilometres east of Margao across the fertile rice fields of Salcete lies sleepy **CHANDOR** village, a scattering of tumbledown villas and farmhouses ranged along shady tree-lined lanes. The main reason to venture out here is the splendid **Perreira-Braganza/Menezes-Braganza house** (daily except holidays; recommended donation Rs50), regarded as the grandest of Goa's colonial mansions. Dominating the dusty village square, the house, built in the 1500s by the wealthy Braganza family for their two sons, has a huge double-storey facade, with 28 windows flanking its entrance. Braganza de Perreira, the great-grandfather of the present owner, was the last knight of the king of Portugal; more recently, Menezes Braganza (1879–1938), a famous journalist and freedom fighter, was one of the few Goan aristocrats to actively oppose Portuguese rule. Forced to flee Chandor in 1950, the family returned in 1962 to find their house, amazingly, untouched. The airy tiled interiors of both wings contain a veritable feast of **antiques**. Furniture enthusiasts, and lovers of rare Chinese porcelain, in particular, will find plenty to drool over, while anyone interested in religious relics should request a glimpse of St Francis Xavier's diamond-encrusted toenail, recently retrieved from a local bank vault and enshrined in the east wing's tiny chapel. The house's most famous feature, however, is its ostentatiously grand ballroom, or **Great Salon**, where a pair of matching high-backed chairs, presented to the Perreira-Braganzas by King Dom Luís of Portugal, occupy pride of place.

Visitors generally travel to Chandor by taxi, but you can also get there by bus from Margao (8 daily; 45min). It's generally fine to turn up without an appointment, but to ensure someone from the family is in to receive you, phone ahead (☎0832/784227 or 9822/160009).

Colva

A hot-season retreat for Margao's moneyed middle classes since long before Independence, **COLVA** is the oldest and largest – but least appealing – of south Goa's resorts. Its leafy outlying *vaddos*, or wards, are pleasant enough, dotted with colonial-style villas and ramshackle fishing huts, but the beachfront is dismal: a lacklustre collection of concrete hotels, souvenir stalls and fly-blown snack bars strewn around a bleak central roundabout. The atmosphere is not improved by heaps of rubbish dumped in a rank-smelling ditch that runs behind the beach, nor by the stench of drying fish wafting from the nearby village.

Practicalities

Buses leave Margao (from outside the *Kamat Hotel* on Praça Jorge Barreto) every thirty minutes for Colva, dropping passengers at the main beach-front, and at various points along the main road. Auto-rickshaws charge Rs100 from the railway station.

To rent a **motorcycle**, ask around the taxi rank, or in front of *Vincy's Hotel*, where 100cc Yamahas are on offer at the usual rates. **Petrol** is sold by the

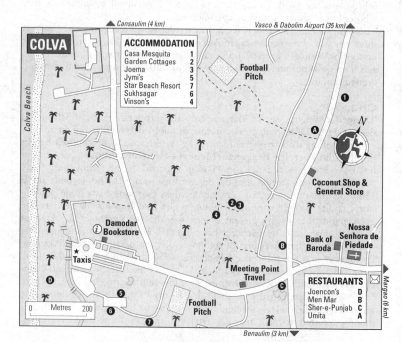

Bisleri bottle from a little house behind the Menino Jesus College, just east of *William's Resort*. This is the only petrol stop in Colva, but the stuff sold may well be adulterated.

Meeting Point Travel (☎0832/723338, ☎732004), between *William's Resort* and the crossroads, exchanges **travellers' cheques** and **cash** at a little under bank rates, and Sanatan Travels, 200m east of the church does encashments on Visa and Mastercard. Both also book and reconfirm domestic and international flights, and arrange deluxe bus, catamaran and train tickets to other parts of India.

The **post office**, opposite the church in the village, has a small but reliable poste restante box. Damodar Book Store, on the beach-front, stocks a good selection of reasonably priced secondhand paperbacks in English. They also do part-exchange, and have the best range of postcards in Colva.

Accommodation

Mirroring the village's rapid rise as a package-tour resort, Colva's plentiful **accommodation** ranges from bare cockroach-infested cells to swish campuses of chalets and swimming pools, with a fair selection of good-value guesthouses in between. Most of the budget rooms lie amid the more peaceful palm groves and paddy fields north of here: the quarter known as Ward 4, which is accessible via the path that winds north from *Johnny Cool's* restaurant, or from the other side via a lane leading west off the main Colva–Vasco road.

Casa Mesquita, 194 Vasco Rd, Ward 3 ☎0832/788173. Large rooms, with rickety four-poster beds (if you're lucky) but no fans or attached shower-toilets, in fading old colonial-style house. Mosaic-floored verandas add to the old-world atmosphere. Western water-toilet, and some cheap dorm beds available on request. A touch grubby, but cheap and full of period feel. ❶–❷

Garden Cottages, Ward 4 (no phone). Immaculately maintained, attractive budget guest-house in Colva's most tranquil quarter. Spacious twin-bedded en-suite rooms with fans, and a garden. ❷–❸

Joema, Ward 4 (no phone). Established in 1973, which probably makes this the oldest guesthouse in Colva. They've since added four small and simple but scrupulously clean attached rooms around the back. Easy, friendly Goan family atmosphere, with kids and pigs charging around, and a relaxing café-restaurant from mid-November. ❷–❸

Jymi's, opposite *Sukhsagar* ☎0832/788016. Large, long-established budget travellers' hotel,

with passable en-suite rooms. A good place to hole up until you find somewhere nicer, as it usually has vacancies. ❹

Star Beach Resort, near Football Ground ☎0832/788166 or 780092, ✉resortgoa@yahoo.com. Spacious rooms in new complex, with a large (crystal clear) pool, in-house generator, Ayurvedic health centre and inexpensive a/c. Not such a great deal at the beginning of the season, but they only increase their rates by Rs100 over Christmas. ❼

Sukhsagar, opposite the *Penthouse* restaurant ☎0832/721888, ✉731666. Nothing special from the outside, but its en-suite rooms are clean, light and airy, and the best deal in this price range. There's also a pleasant palm-shaded garden to relax in. Some a/c. ❻

Vinson's, Ward 4; no phone. The newest of this ward's good-value cheapos. Quiet and secluded. ❷–❸

Eating and drinking

When the season is in full swing, Colva's beachfront sprouts a row of large seafood **restaurants** on stilts, some of them very ritzy indeed, with tablecloths, candles and smooth music. The prices in these places are top-whack, but the portions are correspondingly vast, and standards generally high. Budget travellers are equally well catered for, with a sprinkling of **shack-cafés** at the less-frequented ends of the beach, and along the Vasco road.

Joencon's, second restaurant south from the beach-front. The classiest of Colva's beach restaurants. Agonizingly slow service and pricey, but the food is superb: try their flamboyant fish sizzlers, mouthwatering tandoori sharkfish or Chinese and Indian veg specialities.

Men Mar, Vasco Road. Their lassis, prepared with fresh fruit and home-made curd, are delicious. Open for breakfast.

Sher-e-Punjab, near the main crossroads, between the beach-front and church. Offshoot of the popular Panjim Punjabi joint, serving an exhaustive menu of inexpensive, deliciously spicy Indian food. Butter chicken is their signature dish, but there are plenty of tasty vegetarian options, including rich *dhal makhani*, and their naan bread is possibly the best in the village.

Umita, Vasco Road. Down-to-earth Goan and Indian veg cooking served up by a friendly Hindu family. Try their blow-out "special" thalis or whopping fresh fruit and curd breakfasts. Opens early.

Nightlife

Catering for an uncomfortable mixture of boozy Indian men from out-of-state and young European charter tourists, Colva's **nightlife** is less than enticing these days, despite the presence at the south end of the beach of Goa's few surviving "discos". *Splash* boasts a big MTV satellite screen and music to match, with a late bar and dance floor that livens up around 10pm. Less sophisticated than *Mambo's* and *Tito's* in Baga, however, it can be unpleasant for women. In theory, single men ("stags") aren't allowed on the dance floor, but this doesn't stop them trying their luck. If you'd prefer to get plastered somewhere cheaper and less pretentious, try *Johnny Cool's*, midway between the beach and Colva crossroads. *Men Mar*, on the Vasco Road, also serves beers, snacks and lassis until around 10.30pm.

Cobra warning

You'll rarely see a villager in Colva or Benaulim crossing a rice field at night. This is because paddy is prime territory for snakes, especially **cobras**. If you do intend to cut across the fields after dark, take along a strong flashlight, make plenty of noise and hit the ground ahead of you with a stick to warn any lurking serpents of your approach.

Benaulim

According to Hindu mythology, Goa was created when the sage Shri Parasurama, Vishnu's sixth incarnation, fired an arrow into the sea from the top of the Western Ghats and ordered the waters to recede. The spot where the shaft fell to earth, known in Sanskrit as Banali ("place where the arrow landed") and later corrupted by the Portuguese to **BENAULIM**, lies in the dead centre of Colva Beach, 7km west of Margao. Fifteen years ago, this atmospheric fishing and rice-farming village, scattered around the coconut groves and paddy fields between the main Colva–Mobor road and the dunes, had barely made it onto the backpackers' map. Since the completion of the nearby Konkan railway, however, huge numbers of big-spending middle-class Indians have started to holiday here, in the rash of gigantic luxury resorts and time-share apartment blocks that now fill the rice fields. As a result, the village's famously *sossegarde* feel, which previously made it the number-one choice for independent travellers, is only discernible amid the scruffier fishers' quarters and along some of the back lanes leading to Colva.

Nevertheless, if you time your visit well (avoiding Diwali and the Christmas peak season), Benaulim is still hard to beat as a place to unwind. The seafood

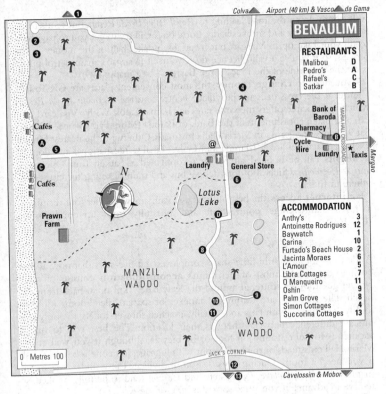

BENAULIM

RESTAURANTS

Malibou	D
Pedro's	A
Rafael's	C
Satkar	B

Bank of
Baroda

Pharmacy

Cycle
Hire   Laundry ★ Taxis

Cafés

Cafés

Prawn
Farm

Laundry   General Store

Lotus
Lake

MANZIL
WADDO

MARIA HALL CROSSROADS

Margao

ACCOMMODATION

Anthy's	3
Antoinette Rodrigues	12
Baywatch	1
Carina	10
Furtado's Beach House	2
Jacinta Moraes	6
L'Amour	5
Libra Cottages	7
O Manqueiro	11
Oshin	9
Palm Grove	8
Simon Cottages	4
Succorina Cottages	13

VAS
WADDO

0 Metres 100

JACK'S CORNER

Cavelossim & Mobor ▼

is superb, accommodation and motorbikes cheaper than anywhere else in the state, and the beach breathtaking, particularly around sunset time, when its brilliant white sand and churning surf reflect the changing colours to magical effect. Shelving away almost to **Cabo da Rama** on the horizon, the beach is also lined with Goa's largest, and most colourfully decorated, fleet of wooden outriggers, and these provide welcome shade during the heat of the day. Hawkers, itinerant masseurs and fruit-wallahs appear at annoyingly short intervals, but you usually escape them by renting a bike and pedalling south on the hard tidal sand beyond the *Taj Exotica*, where tourism has made less of an impact.

Practicalities

Buses from Margao, Colva, Varca, Cavelossim and Mobor roll through Benaulim every half-hour, dropping passengers at the Maria Hall crossroads. Ranged around this busy junction are two well-stocked **general stores**, a couple of **café-bars**, a **bank**, **pharmacy** and the taxi and auto-rickshaw rank, from where you can pick up **transport** to the beach 2km west.

Signs offering **bicycles** and **motorbikes** for rent are dotted along the lane leading to the sea: rates are standard, descending in proportion to the length of time you keep the vehicle. Worth bearing in mind if you're planning to continue further south is that motorbikes are much cheaper to rent (and generally in better condition) here than at Palolem, where there's a relative shortage of vehicles. **Petrol** is sold by the litre from a table at the roadside, two minutes' walk south down the road leading to *Royal Palm Beach Resort*, but tends to be laced with solvent and smokes badly. Local boys will try to get you to pay them to fill your bike up in Margao, but invariably pocket half of the money in the process, so if you've a valid licence do it yourself (Margao's main petrol pump is on the west side of the Praça Jorge Barreto – see map p.899).

If you need to **change money**, the most convenient places are GK Tourist Centre, at the crossroads in the village centre, and the *L'Amour Beach Resort*, which in principle offers the same rates as Thomas Cook. With a Visa card, you can also make encashments at the Bank of Baroda (Mon–Fri 9.30am–2.30pm, Sat 9.30am–12.30pm), on Maria Hall crossroads. Otherwise, the nearest foreign exchange facilities are at Margoa and Colva. Finally, international and domestic **flights** can be booked, altered or reconfirmed at Sarken Tour Operators, and at *L'Amour*, which also does deluxe bus and train ticketing for cities elsewhere in India.

For **internet access**, the best outfit is GK Tourism, who offer four terminals, a faster-than-average connection and blissfully cool air-conditioning (Rs60/hr).

Accommodation

Aside from the unsightly time-share complexes and five-stars that now all but encircle the village, most of Benaulim's **accommodation** consists of small budget guesthouses, scattered around the leafy lanes 1km or so back from the beach. The majority are featureless annexes of spartan tiled rooms (dubbed locally "cottages"), with fans and, usually, attached shower-toilets; the only significant difference between them is their location. The best way to find a vacancy is to hunt around on foot or by bicycle, although if you wait at the Maria Hall crossroads or the beachfront with luggage, someone is bound to ask if you need a room. During peak season, the village's few mid-range hotels (namely *L'Amour*, *Failaka*, *Palm Grove* and *Carina*) tend to be fully booked, so reserve in advance if you want to stay in one of these.

Anthy's, Sernabatim ☎0832/733824. Technically in Colva, but one of the few places hereabouts actually located in the dunes. Well-maintained rooms, with tiny bathrooms, breezy verandas and the beach on your doorstep. ③–⑤

Antoinette Rodrigues, near Jack's Corner, 1695 Vas Waddo ☎0832/731735. Large new block backing onto the soccer pitch just before the fishers' quarter, named after and run by its friendly owner. The rooms are pleasant, with separate balconies and green views; best is the pricier corner one, which is larger, has a lockable steel cupboard and a fridge – well worth the extra Rs50. ④

Baywatch, Sernabatim ☎0832/730075. An unfortunate name, but very pleasant little complex in the dunes between Benaulim and Colva, with immaculate rooms opening onto a deep common veranda. Among the best places in its category if prices and standards are maintained. ③–⑤

Carina, Tamdi-Mati, Vas Waddo ☎0832/734166, ☎711400, ✉carinabeachresort@yahoo.com. This good-value upmarket hotel lies in a tranquil location on the south side of Benaulim and offers a pool, bar-restaurant, foreign exchange facilities and room service. Some a/c. ⑥–⑦

Furtado's Beach House, Sernabatim ☎0832/705265 or 770043. Not to be confused with *Furtado's* in the village proper. This one is slap on the beach, with en-suite rooms and road access. Very popular, mainly with refugees from Colva's charter hotels. The best fallback if nearby *Anthy's* is full. ③

Jacinta Moraes, 1608/A Vas Waddo ☎0832/770187. Half-a-dozen largish clean rooms, and two new family apartments behind the main block, all with fans, attached shower-toilets, sound plumbing and Western toilets. Friendly and central, though some will consider it too close to the *Royal Palms* resort for comfort. ②

L'Amour, on the beach-front ☎0832/733720. Benaulim's longest-established hotel is a comfortable thirty-room cottage complex, with terrace restaurant, travel agent, moneychanging and some a/c. No single occupancy. ⑥–⑦

Libra Cottages, Vas Waddo ☎0832/731740. In much the same mould as *Jacinta Moraes*, only a bit brighter, with a couple more rooms, including two economy options around the back. Very good value. ❸

O Manqueiro, Vas Waddo ⌖ 0832/734164. Dependable budget guesthouse in the secluded south of the village, run by a family with a predilection for plastic fruit. Their best rooms (Rs400 per double) are in the recently constructed "Millennium" block, which have small balconies, but new beds and mattresses – as opposed to rooms above the family house next door (Rs200), which are very basic indeed (rickety beds, old mattresses, common toilets and wood partition walls). ❷–❹

Oshin, Mazil Waddo ⌖ 0832/770069. Large, triple-storey complex set well back from the road, with views from balconies over the tree tops from top-floor rooms. Spacious and clean, with en-suite bathrooms. A notch above most places in this area, and good value. ❹

Palm Grove, Tamdi-Mati, 149 Vas Waddo ⌖ 0832/722533, ⓔ palmgrovecottages@yahoo.com. Secluded hotel surrounded by beautiful gardens, with a luxurious new block around the back, some a/c, a pleasant terrace restaurant and friendly management. A bike-ride back from the beach-front, but by far the most pleasant place in its class. ❹–❼

Simon Cottages, Sernabatim Ambeaxir ⌖ 0832/734283. Currently among the best budget deals in Benaulim: large rooms, all with shower-toilets and sitouts, opening onto a sandy courtyard in a secluded spot at the unspoilt north side of the village. You can book through Silver Stores at Maria Hall crossroads during shop hours. ❷–❸

Succorina Cottages, House 1711/A, Vas Waddo ⌖ 0832/712072. Immaculate rooms in a new house, 1km south of the crossroads in the fishing village, with glimpses of the sea across the fields. You'll need at least a bicycle to stay here, but it's a perfect place to get away from the tourist scene. ❷–❸

Eating and drinking

Benaulim's proximity to Margao market, along with the presence of a large Christian fishing community, means its **restaurants** serve some of the most succulent, competitively priced seafood in Goa. The best shacks flank the beach-front area, where *Johncy's* catches most of the passing custom. However, you'll find better food at lower prices in the smaller joints further along the beach, which seem to change owners and chefs annually; the only way to find out which ones offer the best value for money is to wander past and see who has the most customers.

Malibou, on the lane leading south through Vas Waddo, near *Palm Grove*. Cosy little corner café-restaurant that's a popular late-night drinking spot. Attentive service, fresh seafood and they have a tandoor to bake pomfret, kebabs and spicy chicken.

Pedro's, on the beach-front. Long waits, but the food – mostly fish steaks served with delicious home-made sauces – is freshly cooked, tasty and inexpensive (Rs50 for a generous cut of kingfish).

Rafael's, on the beach-front. Rough-and-ready beach café serving all the usual stuff, plus fried rice, salads and deliciously stodgy oven-hot coconut pudding. Worth patronizing if only because it's the oldest café in the village, and hasn't changed a jot since it opened.

Palm Grove, at hotel of same name, Tamdi-Mati, Vas Waddo. Mostly Goan seafood, with some

Indian and Continental options, dished up alfresco in cosy garden café-restaurant that's lit with fairy lights.

Satkar, Maria Hall crossroads. No-frills locals' *udipi* canteen on the crossroads that's the only place in the village where you can order regular Indian snacks – samosas, *masala dosas*, pakoras and spicy chickpea stew (*channa*) at regular Indian prices. And the *bhaji pao* breakfast here is a must.

L'Amour, at hotel of same name on the beach-front. Just about the slickest restaurant in Benaulim, serving an exhaustive multi-cuisine dinner menu (mains Rs80–125), as well as drinks. With background noise limited to chinking china and hushed voices, it's also a relaxing place for breakfast: fresh fruit, muesli, yoghurt and pancakes.

Cavelossim and Mobor

Sleepy **CAVELOSSIM**, straddling the coast road 11km south of Colva, is the last major settlement in southwest Salcete: its only claim to fame. A short way beyond the village's picturesque church square, a narrow lane veers left (east) across an open expanse of paddy fields to the Cavelossim–Assolna **ferry cross-**

ing (last departures: 8.30pm from Cavelossim, 8.45pm from Assolna), near the mouth of the Sal River. Make the crossing at low tide, and you'll probably see scores of men wading up to their necks in the water, collecting clams, mussels and oysters from the river silt. The discovery that the bed of the Sal between here and nearby Betul was phenomenally rich in **shellfish** was only made a couple of years back. Present stocks are expected to last for another three or four years, although the boom may be brought to a premature end if the Directorate of Fisheries (whose job is ostensibly to promote the welfare of local fishermen) press ahead with plans to dredge the river. If you're heading south to Canacona, turn *left* off the ferry – not right as indicated on local maps – and continue as far as Assolna bazaar, clustered around a junction on the main road. A right turn at this crossroads puts you on track for Palolem and Canacona.

Carry straight on at the junction just past the square in Cavelossim, however, and you'll eventually arrive at **MOBOR**, where Colva beach fades into a rounded sandy spur at the mouth of the Assolna River. This would be an exquisite spot if it weren't the site of south Goa's largest, and most obtrusive, package-tourist enclave. Crammed together onto a narrow spit of dunes between the surf and estuary, the controversial *Leela Palace*, *Holiday Inn* and *Dona Sylvia* resort hotels combine to create a holiday camp ambience that has as little to do with Goa as their architecture. Moreover, most have at some time been served writs by the region's green lobby for infringing environmental laws. Unless you've hundreds of dollars to waste on the hugely inflated tariffs they charge walk-in customers, look for accommodation elsewhere.

The far south: Canacona

Ceded to the Portuguese by the Raja of Sund in the Treaty of 1791, Goa's **far south – Canacona district** – was among the last parts of the territory to be absorbed into the Novas Conquistas, and has retained a distinctly Hindu feel. The area also boasts some of the state's most outstanding scenery. Set against a backdrop of the jungle-covered Sahyadri hills (an extension of the Western Ghat range), a string of pearl-white coves and sweeping beaches scoop its indented coastline, enfolded by laterite headlands and colossal piles of black boulders.

With the exception of the village of **Palolem**, whose near-perfect beach attracts a steady flow of day-trippers and longer-staying travellers during high season, the coastal settlements hereabouts remain rooted in a traditional fishing and *toddi*-tapping economy. However, the red gash of the **Konkan Railway** threatens to bring its days as a tranquil rural backwater to an end. For the last year or two, it has been possible to reach Canacona by direct "super-fast" express trains from Mumbai, Panjim and Mangalore: the developers' bulldozers and concrete mixers are sure to follow.

The region's main transport artery is the NH-17, which crawls across the Sahyadri and Karmali Ghats towards Karnataka via the district headquarters, **Chaudi**. Bus services between here and Margao are frequent; off the highway, however, bullock carts and bicycles far outnumber motor vehicles. The only way to do the area justice, therefore, is by motorcycle, although you'll have to rent one further north (Benaulim's your best bet for this) and drive it down here as few are available *in situ*.

Palolem

PALOLEM, 35km south of Margao, pops up more often in glossy holiday brochures than any other beach in Goa, not because the village is a major package-tour destination, but because its crescent-shaped bay, lined with a swaying

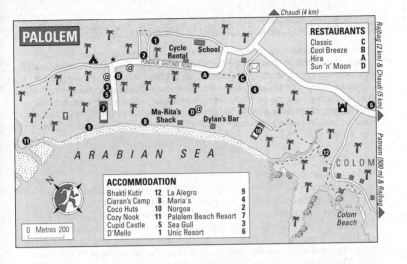

Chaudi (4 km)

Cycle Rental   School

PUNDALIK GAITONDI ROAD

Ma-Rita's Shack   Dylan's Bar

A R A B I A N   S E A

Rajbag (2 km) & Chaudi (5 km)

Panem (500 m) & Rajbag

COLOM

Colom Beach

RESTAURANTS

Classic	C
Cool Breeze	B
Hira	A
Sun 'n' Moon	D

ACCOMMODATION

Bhakti Kutir	12	La Alegro	9
Ciaran's Camp	8	Maria's	4
Coco Huts	10	Norgoa	2
Cozy Nook	11	Palolem Beach Resort	7
Cupid Castle	5	Sea Gull	3
D'Mello	1	Unic Resort	6

0 Metres 200

curtain of coconut palms, is irresistibly photogenic. Hemmed in by a pair of wooded headlands, it forms a perfect curve of white sand, arcing north from a pile of gargantuan boulders to the spur of **Sahyadri Ghat**, which tapers into the sea, draped in thick forest and studded with large black rocks. Beyond it, a narrow causeway runs through the shallows to a islet whose only permanent inhabitants are a colony of black-faced langur monkeys.

Until relatively recently, this idyllic spot was south Goa's best-kept secret. Over the past five or six years, however, Palolem has become a fully fledged resort, with shack-restaurants and palm-leaf huts lining the entire beach. Around 1500 visitors stay here in peak season at any one time, most of them independent travellers seeking an escape from the more commercial tourist scene further north. Their ranks are swollen by droves of day-trippers, both domestic and foreign, who travel down in minibus taxis or pleasure boats, and disappear again around sunset.

That this overwhelming seasonal influx has not entirely spoilt the village is a tribute to the enlightened attitude of the local community, which has consistently resisted plans to develop Palolem. The local municipality strictly forbids any concrete construction in the palm groves behind the beach – hence all the leaf huts, tents and bamboo platforms. Because of this relative independence of the charter trade, Palolem's season is considerably longer than normal. While Benaulim and Colva's shack owners are busily building their shelters in early November, Palolem's have usually been up and running for weeks. Even so, outside December and January, it remains peaceful here, with the pace of life set more by the traditional rhythms of *toddi* tapping than the arrival and departure of tourists.

Long before foreign sun worshippers started to show up here, Palolem's *raison d'être* was its home distilleries, and **coconut feni** remains the main cottage industry. Once each week, the telltale roar of stills emanates from little shacks at the less-frequented corners of the village. Head down to the beach the next morning, and you'll see the fruits of this work being loaded onto boats for "export" to Karnataka. The locals keep plenty of the best stuff for themselves, though, both for consumption at home and in the little bars dotted around the groves behind the beach.

Water shortages in Palolem

The vast increase in visitor numbers in Palolem has been blamed for the severe water shortages that have afflicted Canacona district over the past three years. The municipality seems unwilling or unable to do anything about the problem, so the onus falls on tourists to **use as little water as possible** during their stay. One of the most effective ways you can do this is to **avoid water-toilets**, which dump a colossal quantity of untreated sewage into often poorly manufactured septic tanks below the ground. Traditional pig loos, still common in the village, are a far cleaner, greener option.

Arrival and information

Frequent **buses** run between Margao and Karwar (in Karnataka) via Chaudi (every 30min; 2hr), where you can pick up an **auto-rickshaw** (Rs50) or **taxi** (Rs80) 2km west to Palolem. Alternatively, get off at the Char Rostay ("Four-Way") crossroads, 1.5km before Chaudi, and walk the remaining kilometre or so to the village. Regular buses also go all the way to Palolem from Margao; these stop at the end of the lane leading from the main street to the beach-front. The last bus from Palolem to Chaudi/Margao leaves at around 4.30pm; check with the locals for the precise times, as these change seasonally. **Bicycles** may be rented from a stall halfway along the main street for the princely sum of Rs5 per hour (with discounts for longer periods).

The village has several **public telephones**: avoid the one in the *Beach Resort*, which charges more than double the going rate for international calls, and head for the much cheaper ISD/STD booths 100m down the lane (next to the bus stop). This is also where you'll find the best **internet cafés** in the village. Several agents in Palolem are licensed to **change money**; Sarken Tours inside the *Nature Restaurant* and LKP Forex in the *Beach Resort* offer the best rates.

Accommodation

Local resistance to large-scale development explains why – with the exception of the *Beach Resort*'s tent camp, *Bhakti Kutir* in nearby Colom (see below) and a handful of small budget guesthouses – most of the village's **accommodation** consists of simple palm-leaf huts. Costing anywhere between Rs100 and Rs350 per night, they vary in size and standards of comfort, but tend to have shared showers and toilets. The other option is to look for a room in a family home. Most, although not all, of these also have limited shared washing facilities and pig toilets. The easiest way to find a place is to walk around the palm groves behind the beach with a rucksack; sooner or later someone will approach you. Rates vary from Rs100 to Rs200 per night, depending on the size of the room, and the time of year.

The cheapest places, however, are to be found in Colom, around the headland south of Palolem village, where Hindu fishing families rent the odd room out to tourists. Further south still, behind Patnem beach, the shack owners erect rudimentary leaf huts slap on the beach.

Bhakti Kutir, on the headland above Colom fishing village ☏ 0832/643460 or 643472, ☏ 643469, ✉ bhaktikutir@yahoo.com. Homely, ecofriendly thatched village huts equipped with Western amenities (including completely biodegradable chemical toilets), in a secure, leafy compound five minutes' walk from the south end of Palolem

beach. Beautifully situated and sensitively designed to blend with the landscape by German-Goan owners. ❹–❻

Ciaran's Camp, middle of the beach ☏ 0832/643477 or 644074, ✉ johnciaran@hotmail.com. One of Palolem's longest established hut camps: twenty structures, sharing five toilets,

equipped with fans, mozzie nets, mirrors and tables. Free library, laundry, bar, restaurant and safe lockers. ❸

Coco Huts, south end of Palolem beach ☎ 0832/643104. Thai-style bamboo and palm-thatch huts on stilts, lashed to *toddi* trees around a sandy clearing, slap on the beach. The "rooms" have fans, electric lights and safe lockers, but toilets are shared, and the leaf walls offer little privacy. ❹–❺

Cozy Nook, north end of the beach, near the island ☎ 0832/643550. After *Bhakti Kutir*, this is the most attractively designed setup in the village, comprising 25 bamboo huts (sharing 7 toilets, but with good mattresses, mozzie nets, safe lockers and fans) opening onto the lagoon on one side and the beach on the other – an unbeatable spot, which explains the higher than average tariffs. ❸–❹

Cupid Castle, on the road to the beach-front ☎ 0832/643326. An original name, but these recently built rooms are characterless, and a little too close to the beach-front for comfort. Nonetheless, they're clean, spacious, and have attached bathrooms. ❹

D'Mello, Pundalik Gaitondi Road ☎ 0832/643057. A mix of attached and non-attached rooms on three storeys, some in a concrete annexe set back from the main road. ❹

La Alegro, north side of the beach ☎ 0832/643498. En-suite rooms slap on the beach. Very basic and not all that well maintained, but the location's great. The same owner also has

five more (cheaper) identikit rooms around the back. ❸

Maria's, south of the village, near the *Classic* restaurant ☎ 0832/643732 or 643856, ✉ selvin16@yahoo.com. Five simple rooms opening onto an orchard of banana, fruit and spice trees. All with attached shower-toilets, and very friendly management. Nice little bar-restaurant, ISD phone and internet access on site. A good deal. ❷

Norgoa, Gaitondi Road (no phone). Half a dozen basic rooms of varying size, with shared shower-toilets, on the main road through the village. They also have six budget-priced bamboo "huts" in the front garden. ❶–❸

Palolem Beach Resort, on the beach-front ☎ 0832/643054, ℻ 643054, ✉ yogesh@goa1.dot.net.in. Twin-bedded canvas tents, each with their own locker, lights and fans, grouped under a shady *toddi* grove in a walled compound. In addition, there's a handful of small en-suite rooms. The big drawback here is noise from the busy terrace restaurant. ❸–❺

Sea Gull, next door to *Cupid Castle* ☎ 0832/643978. Dark but serviceable rooms with attached shower-toilets behind a bar near the beach-front area. ❸

Unic Resort, Tembi Waddo ☎ 0832/643059. A relative newcomer that, strictly speaking, is in Colom, a 10min walk inland from the beach; you can also get here via the backroad to Chaudi. The rooms are plain but clean, with fans and en-suite bathrooms, and there's a secluded German-run restaurant on an adjacent terrace. ❹

Eating and drinking

With the beach now backed by brightly lit shack cafés, finding somewhere to **eat** in Palolem is not a problem. Finding quality cooking, however, can be a hit-and-miss business, mainly because most of the fresh fish has to bought in from Margao and Karwar (the locals only catch mackerel in their hand-nets). Currently the most popular places among travellers, and a cut above the competition, are *Sun 'n' Moon*, just behind the beach, and *Cool Breeze*, on the beach road; after hours, die-hard drinkers head through the palm trees to bars, which stay open until the last customer has staggered home. Travellers on tight budgets should note the row of tiny **bhaji stalls** outside the *Beach Resort*, and also the *Hira Restaurant* in the village proper, where you can order tasty and filling breakfasts of *pao bhaji*, fluffy bread rolls, omelettes and chai for next to nothing.

Beach Resort, Palolem beach-front. The one place to definitely avoid: indifferent, overpriced food and grating background music.

Bhakti Kutir, between Palolem beach and Colom fishing village. Laid-back terrace café-cum-restaurant with sturdy wooden tables and a German-bakery style menu. Cooked dishes here are pricey (mains around Rs100), but delicious (their omelettes are made with imported cheese), and

the ingredients are usually local and organically produced.

Classic (aka "German Bakery"), south of the centre. Former German-Bakery-owned establishment that's lost its franchise and gone downhill as a result. Service standards have dropped over the past few seasons and several lapses in hygiene have been reported (they seem to hold on to some of their pastries too long).

Cool Breeze, beach road. Co-run by a British couple, this is currently the classiest restaurant in the village. Their tandoori chicken and seafood, in particular, have set new standards for Palolem, and the prices are reasonable. Come early, or you could face a long wait for a table.

Cozy Nook, far north end of the beach. Wholesome Goan-style cooking served on a small terrace that occupies a prime position opposite the island. Their filling set four-course dinners (7–9pm; Rs110) are deservedly popular, offering imaginative and carefully prepared dishes such as pan-fried fish, aubergine with shrimps and fresh beans. They also do a tasty veg equivalent (Rs90), as well as a full seafood, north Indian curry and snack menu.

Hira, Pundalik Gaitondi Road. Tiny locals' café at the south end of the village, serving "cheap and best" *bhaji*–bread breakfasts, good south Indian-style filter coffee and freshly fried samosas, with a complimentary *Navhind Times* passed around if you're lucky.

Maria's, south side of the village, near *Classic* restaurant. Authentic Goan food, such as chicken vindaloo, fried calamari and spicy vegetable side dishes, prepared entirely with local produce and served alfresco on a terrace. Maria's garrulous husband, Joseph, serves a mean *feni*, too, flavoured with cumin, ginger or lemongrass.

Sun 'n' Moon, Palolem beach. This small restaurant, tucked away in the palm grove behind the beach, gets packed out in the evenings, thanks to the consistently good, inexpensive food, and the attentive service of the owner, Sanjay, and his mum. Mountainous seafood sizzlers are the house speciality, but they also do tasty tandoori meat, fish and vegetarian dishes. There's even an internet booth these days.

Chaudi

CHAUDI (aka Chauri, or Canacona), 33km south of Margao, is Canacona district's charmless headquarters. Packed around a noisy junction on the main Panjim–Mangalore highway, it is primarily a transport hub, of interest to visitors only because of its proximity to Palolem, 2km west. Buses to and from Panjim, Margao, and Karwar in Karnataka *taluka* trundle in and out of a scruffy square on the main street, from where taxis and auto-rickshaws ferry passengers to the villages scattered across the surrounding fields. The area's only **pharmacy** stands just off the crossroads, handy if you're staying in Palolem.

If you spend much time in Palolem, you're sure to nip into Chaudi to shop for provisions, or simply soak up its gritty Indian atmosphere, which comes as a bit of a shock after the dreamy beaches nearby. The small covered **market** is an essential source of fresh fruit and vegetables; several stalls sell stoves, cooking equipment and other hardware, while the excellent **Udipi Hotel**, a short way south of the main crossroads, is one of the few places for miles where you can eat pukka South Indian food: try their filling Rs15 thalis, or spicy fried pakora and samosas – all freshly prepared, and piping hot if you come around 5pm. They also do delicious lassis, sweetened with traditional syrups.

Agonda

AGONDA, 10km north of Chaudi, can only be reached along the sinuous coast road connecting Cabo da Rama with NH-14 at Chaudi. No signposts mark the turning and few of the tourists that whizz past en route to Palolem pull off here, but the beach, fringed along its entire length by *toddi* trees, is superb. Its remote location is not the only reason this three-kilometre spread of white sand has been bypassed by the bulldozers. Villagers here are opposed to any kind of tourist development. In 1982, when a group of absentee landlords sold off a chunk of the beach to a Delhi-based hotel chain, the locals refused to vacate the plot, insisting the proposed five-star hotel and golf course would ruin their traditional livelihoods. Faced with threats of violent resistance, and protracted legal battles, the developers eventually backed down, and the unfinished concrete hulk they left behind is today the only unsightly structure for miles.

This acrimonious episode may in part explain the relative scarcity in Agonda of facilities for visitors. At present, there are only two **places to stay**, both sit-

Wherever possible, try and book plane tickets directly through the **airline** as private agents charge the dollar fare at poor rates of exchange; addresses of airline offices in Panjim are listed on p.867. Seats on all **Konkan Railway** services can be booked at the KRC reservation office on the first floor of Panjim's Kadamba bus stand (Mon–Sat 8am–8pm, Sun 8am–2pm), or at KRC's main reservation hall in Margao station (Mon–Sat 8am–4.30pm, Sun 8am–2pm; ☏0834/712780). Make your bookings as far in advance as possible, and try to get to the offices soon after opening time – the queues can be horrendous. Seats on the Konkan Railway from Goa to Mumbai are in notoriously short supply as the lion's share of the quotas goes to longer-distance travellers from Kerala, with the result that peak periods tend to be reserved up to two months in advance. Book Kadamba **bus tickets** at their offices in Panjim and Mapusa bus stands (daily 9–11am & 2–5pm); private companies sell theirs through the many travel agents immediately outside the bus stand in Panjim, and at the bottom of the square in Mapusa. **Information** on all departures and fares is available from Goa Tourism's counter inside Panjim's bus stand.

For a full rundown of destinations reachable from Goa by bus, train and plane, see Travel Details at the end of this chapter.

To Mumbai

If you're heading north to **Mumbai**, the quickest and easiest way is **by plane**. Between three and six planes leave Goa's Dabolim airport daily. One-way fares for the forty-minute flight range from $53 with Indian Airlines, or $83 with Sahara, to $93 ($72 for under 30s) with swisher Jet. In addition, Air India operate an Airbus service to Mumbai on Mondays and Thursdays. Few people seem to know about this flight, so you can nearly always get a seat on it; the one drawback is that you have to check in three hours before departure as Air India is an international carrier. Wherever possible, try to book tickets directly through the airline (for addresses see Listings on p.867). Private agents charge you the dollar fare at poor rates of exchange, although when you take into account the cost of the taxi and hassle involved in travelling to the airline office, the net saving of booking direct may seem irrelevant.

Since the inauguration of the **Konkan Railway** in 1996, journey times to Mumbai from Goa have been slashed from twenty-four to twelve hours. Two services run daily, the most convenient of them being the Konkan–Kanya Express (#0112), which departs from Margao at 6.15pm, arriving at CST (still commonly known as "Victoria Terminus", or "VT") at 6.35am the following day. The other fast train from Margao to Mumbai CST is the Madgaon-Mumbai Express (#0104).

The cheapest, though most nightmarish, way to get to Mumbai is by **night bus** (see p.787), which takes fourteen to eighteen hours, covering 500km of rough road at often terrifying speeds. Fares vary according to levels of comfort, and luxury buses arrive two or three hours sooner. Book Kadamba bus tickets at their offices in the Panjim and Mapusa bus stands (daily 9–11am & 2–5pm); private companies sell theirs through the many travel agents immediately outside the bus stand in Panjim, and at the bottom of the square in Mapusa. The most popular private service to Mumbai, and the most expensive, is the 24-seater run by a company called Paulo Travels. A cramped berth on this bus (which bizarrely you may have to share) costs Rs600, and it is worth pointing out that women travellers have complained of harassment during the journey. For tickets, contact Paulo Holiday Makers, near the Kadamba bus stand, Panjim (☏0832/223736) or at *Hotel Nanutel*, opposite *Club Harmonia*, Margao (☏0834/721516). Information on all departures and fares is available from Goa Tourism's counter inside Panjim's bus stand (see Arrival, information and local transport, p.862).

To Hampi

Two or three clapped-out government **buses** leave Panjim's Kadamba stand (platform 9) each morning for Hospet, the last one at 10.30am. Brace yourself for a long, hard slog; all being well, it should take nine or ten hours, but delays and breakdowns are frustratingly frequent. **Tickets** for Kadamba and KSRTC (Karnatakan State Road Transport Corporation) services should be booked at least one day in advance at the hatches in the bus stand.

From Margao, you can also travel to Hampi on a swish new **night bus**, complete with pneumatic suspension and berths. The service, operated by a firm called Paulo Travels, leaves from a lot next to the *Nanutel Hotel* on Margao's Rua da Padre Miranda, at 6pm, arriving in Hampi early the next morning. Tickets cost around Rs375 and can be bought from most reputable travel agents around the state. Although the coach is comfortable enough, the coffin-like berths can get very hot and stuffy, making sleep very difficult; moreover, there have been compaints from women of harassment during the night on this service.

A much less stressful option than the bus is the twice-weekly **train** service, which leaves from Vasco (at 6.50am) and Margao (7.21am) stations on Tuesdays and Saturdays, arriving in Hospet just over eight and a half hours later at 4pm. Tickets can be bought on the day at either point of departure. This is a wonderful rail journey, taking you one of the wildest stretches of the Western Ghats, including the Dudhsagar Falls area (see p.873). Travelling in the other direction, trains leave Hospet at 10.45am on Mondays and Fridays, and arrive in Margao at 6.45pm.

To Gokarna, Mangalore and southern Karnataka

From Goa, the fastest and most convenient way to travel down the coast to Gokarn is via the **Konkan Railway**. At 2.10pm, train #KR001 leaves Margao, passing through Chaudi at 3pm en route to Gokarn Road, the town's railhead, where it arrives at around 4.20pm. The station lies 9km east of Gokarn itself, but buses and rickshaws are on hand to shuttle passengers the rest of the way. As this is classed as a passenger service, you don't have to buy tickets in advance; just turn up at the station 30–45min before the departure time and pay at the regular ticket counter. As ever, it is a good idea to **check timings** in advance, through any tourist office or travel agent.

Buses take as much as two-and-a-half hours longer to cover the same route. A direct service leaves Margao's interstate stand in the north of town daily at 1pm. You can also get there by catching any of the services that run between Goa and Mangalore, and jumping off either at **Ankola**, or at the Gokarn junction on the main highway, from where frequent private minibuses and tempos run into town.

The Konkan highway is straightforward by **motorcycle**, with a better-than-average road surface, and frequent fuel stops along the way. Travelling on a rented bike also gives you the option of heading down sandy side lanes to explore some of the gorgeous beaches glimpsed from the road. Aside from the obvious dangers involved in motorcycling on Indian highways, the main drawback is **crossing the border**, which can involve a baksheesh transaction.

To Delhi

The Konkan Railway has also improved train services to **Delhi**, which can now be reached on the superfast Rajdhani Express #2431 in a little under 26 hours (Tues & Thurs only). A slower daily service, the Mangala Lakshadweep Express #2617, takes nearly 38 hours to cover the same distance. Alternatively, you can fly to the capital with Indian Airlines or Jet in 2hr 45min from around $245 one-way.

uated at the far (south) end of the beach. The better of the pair is the *Dunhill Beach Resort* (℡0832/647328; ❷–❸), which has twelve simple en-suite rooms with small verandas opening onto a sandy enclosure. It's a clean and peaceful place, and the family who run it serve spicy Goan-fried mackerel, calamari, rice and curry to order on their small terrace. If they're full, *Caferns* (℡0832/647235; ❷) down the road is a good fall-back.

Cotigao Wildlife Sanctuary

The **Cotigao Wildlife Sanctuary**, 10km southeast of Chaudi, was established in 1969 to protect a remote and vulnerable area of forest lining the Goa–Karnataka border. Encompassing 86 square kilometres of mixed deciduous woodland, the reserve is certain to inspire tree-lovers, but less likely to yield many wildlife sightings: its tigers and leopards were hunted out long ago, while the gazelles, sloth bears, porcupines, panthers and hyenas that allegedly lurk in the woods rarely appear. You do, however, stand a good chance of spotting at least two species of monkey, a couple of wild boar and the odd *gaur* (the primeval-looking Indian bison). Best visited between October and March, Cotigao is a peaceful and scenic park that makes a pleasant day-trip from Palolem, 12km northwest. Any of the buses running south on the NH-14 to Karwar via Chaudi will drop you within 2km of the gates. However, to explore the inner reaches of the sanctuary, you really need your own transport. The wardens at the reserve's small **Interpretative Centre** will show you how to get to a 25m-high tree-top watchtower, overlooking a **waterhole** that attracts a handful of animals around dawn and dusk. Written permission for an overnight **stay**, either in the watchtower or the Forest Department's small *Rest House* (❶), must be obtained from the Deputy Conservator of Forests, 3rd Floor, Junta House, Panjim (℡0832/45926), as far in advance of your visit as possible. If you get stuck, however, the wardens can arrange a tent, blankets and basic food.

Travel details

Trains

Margao to: Chaudi (3 daily; 50min); Colem (2 weekly; 55min); Delhi (1–2 daily; 26–35hr); Ernakulam/Kochi (2 daily; 12–15hr 40min); Gokarn (1 daily; 2hr 10min); Hospet (2 weekly; 8hr 40min); Hubli (2 weekly; 5hr 30min); Mangalore/Kanakadi (5 daily; 4–6hr); Mumbai (2 daily; 12hr); Thiruvananthapuram (2 daily; 16hr 15min); Udupi (4 daily; 3hr 40min); Vasco da Gama (2 weekly; 30min).

Buses

Panjim to: Arambol (12 daily; 1hr 45min); Aurangabad (1 daily; 16hr); Baga (every 30min; 45min); Bijapur (7 daily; 10hr); Calangute (every 30min; 40min); Candolim (every 30min; 30min); Chaudi (hourly; 2hr 15min); Gokarna (2 daily; 5hr 30min); Hampi (2 daily; 9–10hr); Hospet (3 daily; 9hr); Hubli (hourly; 6hr); Hyderabad (1 daily; 18hr); Kolhapur (hourly; 8hr); Mahabaleshwar (1 daily;

12hr); Mangalore (4 daily; 10hr); Mapusa (every 15min; 25min); Margao (every 15min; 55min); Mumbai (6 daily; 14–18hr); Mysore (2 daily; 17hr); Old Goa (every 15min; 20min); Ponda (hourly; 50min); Pune (7 daily; 12hr); Vasco da Gama (every 15min; 45min–1hr).

Mapusa to: Anjuna (hourly; 30min); Arambol (12 daily; 1hr 45min); Baga (hourly; 30min); Calangute (hourly; 45min); Chapora (every 30min; 30–40min); Mumbai (6 daily; 13–17hr); Panjim (every 15min; 25min); Vagator (every 30min; 25–35min).

Margao to: Agonda (4 daily; 2hr); Benaulim (every 30min; 15min); Chaudi (every 30min; 1hr 40min); Cavelossim (8 daily; 30min); Chandor (hourly; 45min); Colva (every 15min; 20–30min); Gokarna (1 daily; 4hr 30min); Hampi (1 nightly; 10hr); Karwar (every 30min; 2hr); Lutolim (8 daily; 30min); Mangalore (5 daily; 7hr); Mapusa (10 daily; 2hr 30min); Mobor (8 daily; 35min); Mumbai

(2 daily; 16–18hr); Panjim (every 30min; 50min); Pune (1 daily; 12hr).

Vasco da Gama to: Bangalore (1 daily; 16hr); Colva (2 daily; 30min); Mangalore (2 daily; 11hr); Margao (every 15min; 40min); Panjim, via Sao Jacinto (every 15min; 45min–1hr); Pilar (every 15min; 30min).

Benaulim to: Cavelossim (hourly; 20min); Colva (every 30min; 20min); Margao (every 30min; 15min); Mobor (hourly; 25min).

Chaudi to: Panjim (hourly; 2hr 15min); Gokarna (1 daily; 3hr); Karwar (every 30min; 1hr); Margao (every 30min; 1hr 40min); Palolem (2 daily; 15min).

Flights

Dabolim airport (Vasco da Gama) to: Bangalore (2 daily; 1hr 30min–2hr 25min); Chennai (Madras) (2 weekly; 3hr); Cochin (2 weekly; 1hr); Delhi (4 weekly; 2hr 25min); Hyderabad (4 weekly; 2hr 55min); Mumbai (3–6 daily; 40min).

GOA | Travel details

CHAPTER 13

Highlights

✳ **Victoria Memorial** A monument to the British Empire in Calcutta that is a dizzying blend of Moghul and Italian architecture. See p.937

✳ **Eden Gardens** Enjoy the chaos and spectacle of a match at Calcutta's famous cricket ground. See p.940

✳ **Sunderbans** A mangrove forest that is home to a profusion of wildlife, including Bengal tigers. See p.961

✳ **Shantiniketan** This tranquil university town exudes the spirit of its founder, the mystic and philospher Rabindranath Tagore. See p.964

✳ **Toy Train** Small-gauge steam-driven railway, which takes nine hours to loop though stunning scenery to Darjeeling. See p.970

✳ **Darjeeling** A charming hill station with spectacular views and famously fine tea. See p.973

✳ **Singalila Trek** This Darjeeling trek features unforgettable mountain vistas, especially beautiful in April and May, when the rhododendrons are in bloom. See pp.980–981

✳ **Kalimpong** Orchids grow in profusion around this backwater hill station. See p.986

13

Calcutta and West Bengal

nique among Indian states in stretching all the way from the Himalayas to the sea, **WEST BENGAL** is nonetheless explored in depth by few travellers. That may have something to do with the exaggerated reputation of its capital, **CALCUTTA**, which is actually a sophisticated and friendly city that belies its popular image as poverty-stricken and chaotic. Certainly the rest of Bengal holds an extraordinary assortment of landscapes and cultures, ranging from the dramatic hill station of **Darjeeling**, within sight of some of the highest mountains in the world, to the vast mangrove swamps of the **Sunderbans**, prowled by man-eating Royal Bengal tigers who share the seas with sharks and crocodiles. The narrow central band of the state is cut across by the huge River Ganges as it pours from Bihar into Bangladesh; the **Farrakha Barrage** feeds south-flowing channels such as the River Hooghly, the lifeline of Calcutta.

At the height of British rule, in the nineteenth and early twentieth centuries, Bengal flourished both culturally and materially, nurturing a vibrant creative blend of West and East. The **Bengali Renaissance** produced thinkers, writers and artists such as Raja Ram Mohan Roy, Bankim Chandra Chatterjee, and above all **Rabindranath Tagore**, whose collective influence still permeates Bengali society a century later.

Not all of Bengal, however, is Bengali; the recent Nepalese-led separatist movement for the creation of a semi-autonomous "Gurkhaland" in the Darjeeling area has highlighted sharp differences in culture. Although the Hindu Nepalese largely displaced the indigenous tribal groups of the north during the nineteenth century, a new influx of Tibetans has revitalized the traditions of lama-ism. In the southwest, on the other hand, tribal groups such as the Santals

CALCUTTA AND WEST BENGAL

Accommodation price codes

All accommodation prices in this book have been categorized using the price codes below. Prices given are for a double room, and all taxes are included. For more details, see p.51.

① up to Rs100	④ Rs300–400	⑦ Rs900–1500
② Rs100–200	⑤ Rs400–600	⑧ Rs1500–2500
③ Rs200–300	⑥ Rs600–900	⑨ Rs2500 and upwards

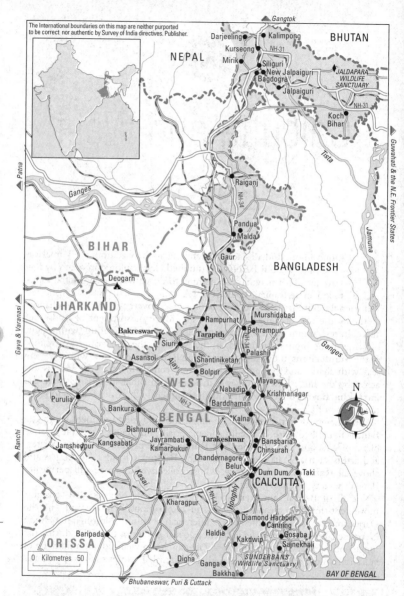

and the Mundas still maintain a presence, and itinerant Baul **musicians** epitomize the region's traditions of song and dance. The Bauls are most often heard around Tagore's university at **Shantiniketan**, where his own musical form, *Rabindra Sangeet*, is a popular amalgam of influences including folk and classical. Other historical specialities of Bengal include the erection of ornate and delicate **terracotta temples**, as seen at Bishnupur, and the manufacture of **silk**, concentrated around Murshidabad, the last independent capital of Bengal.

Bengal's own brand of Hinduism emphasizes the **mother goddess**, who appears in such guises as the fearsome Kali and Durga, the benign Saraswati, goddess of learning, and Lakshmi, the goddess of wealth. The most mysterious of all is Tara, an echo of medieval links with Buddhism; her temple at Tarapith is perhaps the greatest centre of Tantrism in the entire country. In recent years, however, the prayer flags have given way to red flags, and the new religion of politics.

Some history

Although Bengal was part of the Mauryan empire during the third century BC, it first came to prominence in its own right under the Guptas, in the fourth century AD. So dependent was it on trade with the Mediterranean that the fall of Rome caused a sharp decline, only reversed with the rise of the Pala dynasty in the eighth century.

After a short-lived period of rule by the highly cultured Senas, based at **Gaur**, Bengal was brought under Muslim rule at the end of the twelfth century by the first Sultan of Delhi, Qutb-ud-din-Aibak. Sher Shah Suri, who usurped power from the Moghuls in the mid-sixteenth century, achieved much in Bengal; it was thanks to him that the Grand Trunk Road took its most developed form, running all the way to the Northwest Province on the borders of his native Afghanistan. Akbar took back the territory in 1574, just in time to face the advent of the Europeans.

The Portuguese, who were the first to set up a trading community beside the Hooghly, were soon joined by the British, Dutch and French and many others. Rivalry between them – all received some degree of sanction from the Moghul court – eventually resulted in the ascendancy of the **British**, with the only serious indigenous resistance coming from the tutelary kingdom of **Murshidabad**, led by the young Siraj-ud-Daula. His attack on the fledgling British community of Calcutta in 1756 culminated in the infamous **Black Hole** incident, when British prisoners, possibly in error, were incarcerated in a tiny space that caused many to suffocate to death. Vengeance, in the form of a British army from Madras under **Robert Clive**, arrived a year later. The defeat of Siraj-ud-Daula at the Battle of Plassey heralded the start of British domination of the entire subcontinent. Bengal became the mainstay of the British East India Company, and its lucrative trading empire, until the company handed over control to the Crown in 1854.

Until 1905, Bengal encompassed Orissa and Bihar; then it was split down the middle by Lord Curzon, leaving East Bengal and Assam on one side and Orissa, Bihar and West Bengal on the other. That aroused bitter resentment, and the rift it created between Hindus and Muslims was a direct cause of the second Partition, in 1947, when East Bengal became East Pakistan. During the war with Pakistan in the early 1970s that resulted in the creation of an independent **Bangladesh**, up to ten million refugees fled into West Bengal; most have now returned. Shorn of its provinces, and with the capital moved from Calcutta to Delhi in 1911, the story of West Bengal in the twentieth century was largely a chronicle of decline.

Economically, the **rice** grown in the paddy fields of the lowlands remains West Bengal's most important cash crop, though **tea** comes a close second. The introduction of tea was largely the work of the British, who cleared the forests of the Himalayan foothills; they brought tea plants from China, but local Darjeeling tea soon developed a reputation of its own. The other great nineteenth-century industry, **jute**, has not fared so well. Most was grown in East Bengal – now Bangladesh – while the mills themselves were located along the

River Hooghly around Calcutta. As a result, after 1947, the mills found it hard to obtain supplies; however, new jute-growing regions have since been developed.

Politics permeates almost every aspect of life in West Bengal today. After a couple of decades of relative calm under the **Communist Party of India (Marxist)**, lead by the enigmatic Jyoti Basu, political turmoil is once again threatening. The state was all but brought to its knees in the 1960s and 1970s, when the **Naxalites** (Communist Party of India – Marxist-Leninists) launched an abortive but bloody attempt at revolution. After a bitter three-way struggle between the CPI(M), the Congress and the Naxalites, the CPI(M) finally emerged victorious. Under Jyoti Basu, the CPI(M) somehow succeeded in balancing rhetoric and old-fashioned socialism with a prudent practicality, and their strong rural base has enabled them to weather the collapse of world communism. But the CPI(M) has been unable to stem industrial decay and long gradual decline, and today West Bengal is slowly slipping into the "backward" category of states. The rise of the **Trinamul Congress** under the energetic leadership of Mamata Bannerjee has challenged the CPI(M)'s power base, leading to violent clashes between the parties, resulting in regular fatalities. To compound the turmoil, political elements to the north of the state are now calling for independence from West Bengal.

Calcutta (Kolkata) and around

One of the four great urban centres of India, **CALCUTTA** is to its proud citizens the equal of any city in the country in charm, variety and interest. Like Mumbai and Chennai, it is not an ancient city; its roots lie in the European expansion of the seventeenth century. The showpiece capital of the British Raj, this was the greatest colonial city of the Orient. Descendants of the fortune-seekers who flocked from across the globe to participate in Calcutta's eighteenth- and nineteenth-century trading boom remain conspicuous in its cosmopolitan blend of communities. Despite this, there has been a recent rise in Bengali nationalism, which has resulted in the renaming of the city as **KOLKATA** – the Bengali pronunciation and official new name – which has yet to be universally embraced.

Since Indian Independence mass migrations of dispossessed refugees, occasioned by twentieth-century upheavals within the subcontinent, have tested the city's infrastructure to the limit. The resultant suffering – and the work of Mother Teresa in drawing attention to its most pathetic victims – has given Calcutta a reputation for **poverty** that its residents consider ill-founded. They argue that the city's problems are no longer as acute as those of Mumbai or other cities across the world, and that the slum scenes familiar from the book and film *City of Joy* are distortions of the truth. In fact, though Calcutta's mighty Victorian buildings lie peeling and decaying, and its avenues have long been choked by its inability to expand any further, Calcutta exudes a warmth that leaves few visitors unmoved. The opening of India's first underground system in 1984 was seen as the first portent of a new economic beginning, but there is little denying that, over the years, the city has lost much ground to newly emerging commercial centres elsewhere in the country.

The Bengalis of Calcutta like to see themselves as the **intelligentsia** of India; a long-standing maxim states that "what Bengal does today, India will do tomorrow." This is a city where artistic endeavour is held in higher esteem than political and economic success, home to a multitude of **galleries** and huge Indian classical **music** festivals, with a thriving Bengali-language **theatre** scene and a tradition of **cinema** brought world renown by Satyajit Ray. Adding to the chaos and colour, Calcutta has a wonderful tradition of political posters and graffiti. Witty and flamboyant slogans compete with a forest of advertising hoardings to festoon every available surface.

Though Marxists may rule from the chief bastion of imperialism, the **Writers Building**, and the site of the notorious Black Hole of Calcutta, now obscured by the main post office, visitors still experience Calcutta first and foremost as a colonial city. Grand edifices in a profusion of styles include the imposing **Victoria Memorial** and the gothic **St Paul's Cathedral**, while the eclectic **Indian Museum**, one of the largest museums in Asia, ranges from natural history to art and archeology. Among numerous venerable Raj institutions to have survived are the racecourse, the polo ground, the reverence for cricket and several exclusive gentlemen's clubs.

In terms of **climate**, Calcutta is at its best during its short winter, when the daily maximum temperature hovers around 27°C, and the markets are filled with vegetables and flowers. Before the monsoons, the heat hangs unbearably heavy; the arrival of the rains in late June brings relief, but usually also heavy floods that turn the streets into a quagmire. After a brief period of post-monsoon heat, October and November are quite pleasant; this is the time of the city's biggest festival, **Durga Puja**.

Some history

By the time the remarkable **Job Charnock** established the headquarters of the **East India Company** at **Sutanuti** on the east bank of the Hooghly in 1690, the riverside was already dotted with trading communities from European countries. Besides the British, previously based at Hooghly on the west bank, there were the French at Chandernagore, the Dutch and Armenians at Chinsurah, the Danes at Serampore, the Portuguese at Bandel, and even Greeks at Rishra and Prussians at Bhadeshwar.

Supported by Armenian funds, the East India Company bought land around Sutanuti, and in 1699 completed their first fort in the area – **Fort William**. A few years later the East India Company amalgamated Sutanuti and two other villages to form the town of **Calcutta**. Although several theories exist, the name may well derive from *Kalikutir*, the house or temple of Kali – a reference to the temple of **Kalighat**. Job Charnock, the town's first governor, married an Indian woman who had been rescued from committing *sati* on her first husband's funeral pyre. With trading success came ambitious plans for development; in 1715 a delegation to the Moghul court in Delhi negotiated trading rights, along with several villages and towns on both banks of the Hooghly, to create a territory that was around 15km long. The company built a moat around the perimeter to ward off possible Maratha attacks; known as the **Maratha Ditch**, it is marked by today's Circular Road. Later, the company

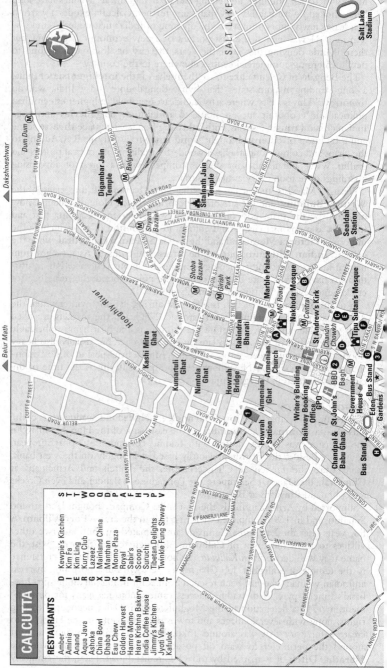

CALCUTTA

RESTAURANTS

Amber	S
Aminia	I
Anand	T
Aqua Java	R
Ashoka	G
China Bowl	X
Dhaba	U
Eau Chew	C
Golden Harvest	N
Hamro Momo	P
Hare Krishna Bakery	M
India Coffee House	B
Jimmy's Kitchen	L
Jyoti Vihar	K
Kafulok	T
Kewpie's Kitchen	D
Kim Fa	I
Kim Ling	E
Kurry Club	R
Lazeez	G
Mainland China	X
Manthan	U
Momo Plaza	C
Royal	N
Sabir's	P
Scoop	F
Suruchi	H
Tibetan Delights	J
Twinkle Fung Shway	P
	V

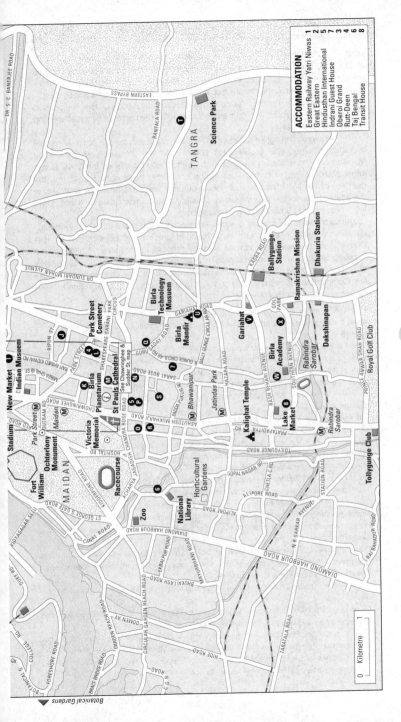

Botanical Gardens ▲

ACCOMMODATION

Eastern Railway Yatri Niwas	1
Great Eastern	2
Hindusthan International	5
Indrani Guest House	7
Oberoi Grand	3
Rutt-Deen	4
Taj Bengal	6
Transit House	8

Science Park

TANGRA

EASTERN BYPASS

BANTALA ROAD

DR S C BANERJEE ROAD

Stadium

New Market

Indian Museum

Park Street

Maidan

OUTRAM RD

Park Street Cemetery

Birla Technology Museum

GARIAHAT ROAD

GARIAHAT ROAD

Birla Mandir

Gariahat

Ballygunge Station

Dhakuria Station

Ramakrishna Mission

Dakshinapan

KASBA ROAD

DR SUNDARI MOHAN AVENUE

Birla Planetarium

St Pauls Cathedral

See Chowringhee & Sudder St. map

SHAKESPEARE SARANI

PARK CIRCUS

BALLY GUNGE CIRCULAR ROAD

GUNGE CIRCULAR ROAD

SARAT BOSE ROAD

ASHUTOSH MUKHERJI ROAD

AJC BOSE ROAD

GURU SADAY ROAD

HAZRA ROAD

Birla Academy

Rabindra Sarobar

SOUTHERN AVENUE

RASH BEHARI AVENUE

Jatindas Park

Bhawanipur

Kalighat Temple

Lake Market

Rabindra Sarobar

PRATAPADITYA RD

Victoria Memorial

Fort William

MAIDAN

Racecourse

HOSPITAL RD

ACHARYA JAGADISH CHANDRA BOSE ROAD

KIDDERPORE ROAD

ST GEORGE'S GATE ROAD

CANAL ROAD

National Library

Zoo

Horticultural Gardens

GOPAL NAGAR RD

ALIPORE ROAD

CHETLA CRG

STATION ROAD

DIAMOND HARBOUR ROAD

TOLLYGUNGE ROAD

Tollygunge Club

Royal Golf Club

PRINCE ANWAR SHAH ROAD

N R SARKAR AVENUE

DIAMOND HARBOUR ROAD

BHUKAILASH ROAD

MAYURBHANJ ROAD

FEBALPUR ROAD

GARDEN REACH ROAD

CIRCULAR GARDEN REACH ROAD

BRACE BRIDGE ROAD

DUKE RD

DOMEN AV

HIDE ROAD

TARATALA ROAD

TARATALA ROAD

RAJ BAHADUR ROAD

C.G.R ROAD

FORESHORE RD

COLLEGE RD

BOTANICAL G RD

VIDYASAGAR SETU

0 Kilometre 1

The festivals of Calcutta

Most of Calcutta's Hindu **festivals** are devoted to forms of the mother goddess, **Shakti**. As one of the last centres of north Indian Buddhism, Bengal reflects a unique blend of traditions; **Tantric** Hinduism, closely related to Vajrayana Buddhism, continues to be evident in the devotion to mysterious deities such as **Tara** (see p.822). Calcutta's own deity, the black goddess **Kali**, is an emanation of **Durga**, the consort of Shiva. Kali is depicted with four arms, standing on the prostrate Shiva after killing the demon Raktviya.

The two-week **Durga Puja** (Sept/Oct) is the most lavish festival of all. A symbol of victory, **Durga**, wife of Shiva, is shown with ten arms slaying the demon Mahisasura, who assumed the shape of a buffalo and threatened the gods. Durga either sits on a lion, or is accompanied by one. Other pujas honour **Lakshmi**, the goddess of wealth, whose festival falls in autumn, and **Saraswati**, the goddess of the arts and learning, who is shown as a beautiful fair woman sitting on a lotus playing a sitar-like instrument known as the *veena*.

During the festivals, images of straw, papier-mâché, or *sola pith*, originally moulded as voluptuous women with large rounded breasts and physical detail, then clothed and decorated, are carried in noisy procession to makeshift altars called *pandals*. Supported by donations from businesses and local residents, *pandals* often block off small streets and blare popular music through distorting loudspeakers. Competition between *pandals* can lead to street fights, when the image is taken for immersion to the river after puja.

Joydeb Mela (early Jan) Commemorating Joydeb, the author of the *Gita Govinda* revered by Bauls, and held in the village of Kenduli near Shantiniketan; the place to hear Baul minstrels in their element.

Ganga Sagar Mela (mid-Jan) During the winter solstice of Makar Sankranti, hundreds of thousands of Hindu pilgrims travel through Calcutta for a three-day festival at Sagar Dwip, 150km south at the mouth of the Hooghly where the Ganges meets the sea. Many of the *sadhus* drawn to the *mela* stay at the Shiva temple at Nimtolla Ghat, north of Howrah Bridge.

Saraswati Puja (Jan/Feb) Important *pandal* festival to the goddess of learning, celebrated throughout the city.

Chinese New Year (Jan/Feb) Celebrated with a week-long festival of dragon dances, firecrackers and fine food, concentrated around the suburb of Tangra.

Shivratri (late Feb) The nationwide Shiva festival is celebrated all over the city.

Bakrid (Feb/March) Large parts of the Maidan are converted into a gigantic prayer ground when thousands of Muslims pray at the end of Ramadan.

Dol Purnima or **Holi** (Feb/March) The spring festival, when anyone foolhardy enough to go out is liable to be splashed and powdered in bright colours, is especially popular with Calcutta's Biharis.

Muharram (May/June) Shi'ite Muslims mark the anniversary of the martyrdom of Hussein by severe penance including processions during which they flagellate themselves.

Vishvakarma Puja (Sept) Dedicated to the god of creation; craftsmen and artists decorate their tools with images of the deity.

Durga Puja (Sept/Oct) At the onset of winter, Durga Puja is the Bengali equivalent of Christmas. It climaxes on Mahadashami, the tenth day, when images are taken to the river for immersion. Elsewhere, the festival is known as Dussehra.

Lakshmi Puja (Oct/Nov) Held five days after Mahadashami on the full moon, to honour the goddess of wealth.

Diwali & Kali Puja (Oct/Nov) Two weeks after Lakshmi Puja, Kali Puja is held on a moonless night when goats are sacrificed. Kali Puja coincides with Diwali, the festival of light.

Christmas (Dec 25) Park Street and the New Market are adorned with fairy lights and the odd Christmas tree. Plum pudding is sold at confectioners, and Midnight Mass is well attended.

Posh Mela (late Dec) Held in Shantiniketan just after Christmas, the *mela* attracts Bauls, the wandering minstrels who perform to large audiences (too large for some tastes).

entangled itself in the web of local power politics, with consequences both unforeseen – as with the Black Hole (see p.939) – and most assiduously desired – as when the Battle of Plassey in 1758 made the British masters of Bengal. Recognized by parliament in London in 1773, the company's trading monopoly led it to shift the capital of Bengal here from Murshidabad, and Calcutta became a clearing house for a vast range of commerce, including the lucrative export of opium to China.

At first, the East India Company brought young bachelors out from Britain to work as servants. Referred to as "writers", they lived in spartan conditions in communal mud huts, until the **Writers' Building** was eventually erected for their convenience. As they took to indigenous ways, and cohabited with local women, they were responsible for the emergence of the new **Eurasian** community. In time, parliament rescinded the company's monopoly; when the doors of trade were thrown open, merchants and adventurers flocked in from far and wide, including Parsis, Baghdadi Jews, Afghans and Indians from other parts of the country. By 1857, such splendid buildings as the Court House, Government House and St Paul's Cathedral, had earned Calcutta the sobriquet "City of Palaces". In reality, the humid and uncomfortable climate, putrefying salt marshes and the hovels that grew haphazardly around the city created unhygienic conditions that were a constant source of misery and disease.

The city's affluent elite – Bengali merchants included – came to be known as the **"bhadra log"**, the good people. Although the term was lampooned by Kipling in his depiction of the *Bandar Log* or "Monkey People" in *The Jungle Book*, they were responsible for the great flowering of cultural and artistic expression known as the **Bengali Renaissance** (see box on p.936). The decline of Calcutta as an international port came with the opening of the Suez Canal in 1869, the emergence of Bombay, and the end of the opium trade. In 1911, the days of glory came to a definitive end; the imperial capital of India was transferred to Delhi.

Arrival and information

Calcutta's **airport**, 20km north of the city centre, is served by international flights – although only a small proportion of visitors actually enter India here – as well as services from throughout the country. Officially "Netaji Subhash Bose International Airport", it is still universally known by its old name of **Dum Dum** – a name that became infamous during the Boer War, when the notorious (and now banned) exploding bullet was manufactured in a nearby factory. The dreary **international terminal** has moneychanging facilities, a **prepaid taxi booth** and a Government of India tourist information counter but little else. In complete contrast, the modern **domestic terminal**, 500m to the south, has a much better range of amenities including an accommodation booking counter, tourist information, restaurants, bookshops, a railway reservation desk and a prepaid taxi booth. Booked here, a **taxi** to the central Sudder Street area costs around Rs130. Alternatively, an airport **bus** travels down Chowringhee (officially renamed Jawaharlal Nehru Road) to the Indian Airlines office and passes the western end of Sudder Street. **Minibuses** run to BBD Bagh, but these can get crowded and prove to be an unwelcome introduction to the city. Another possibility is to take a taxi to the end of the **Metro** at Dum Dum, 6km away, and then take the underground line (Rs5) to Park

While Calcutta struggles to maintain its position as a world city, a strong parochial trend in recent years has been to replace all English eventually with Bengali – the most obvious result has been the renaming of the city as Kolkata. The shedding of the city's colonial past began decades ago in the Sixties and Seventies when many of the old British street names were officially changed, but Calcutta is slow to change and, three decades or so later, some of the original names continue to be widely used in tandem. The most important of these is Chowringhee or Jawaharlal Nehru Road (which we continue to call Chowringhee). Other name changes to note are Rabindranath Tagore Street (although everyone still calls it Camac Street), BBD Bagh (still often referred to by its old name, Dalhousie Square or simply "Dalhousie"), Indira Gandhi Road (everyone calls it Red Road), Lenin Sarani (Dharamtala), Mirza Ghalib Street (Free School Street), Bepin Bihari Ganguly Street (Bowbazar Street), Rabindra Sarani (Chitpore Road), Ho Chi Minh Sarani (Harrington Street), Dr Mohammed Ishaque Road (Kyd Street), AJC Bose Road (Lower Circular Road), Muzaffar Ahmed Street (Ripon Street), Shakespeare Sarani (Theatre Road) and Rafi Ahmed Kidwai Street (Wellesley Street)

Street, the nearest station to Sudder Street. Fairlie Place station on the railway (see p.924) is good for BBD Bagh.

Of Calcutta's two main **railway stations**, neither of which is on the Metro system, **Howrah Station** – the point of arrival for major trains from the south and west, such as the Rajdhani Express from Delhi – stands on the far bank of the Hooghly a couple of kilometres west of the centre. To reach the central downtown area, traffic has to negotiate **Howrah Bridge** – the definitive introduction to the chaos of the city, especially during rush hours, which start late in the mornings. Long queues form at Howrah's **taxi rank** outside the station building, when main trains pull in. Avoid touts and taxis who break the rank and invariably ask astronomical prices to avoid using the meter – and head straight for the prepaid taxi booth; a prepaid taxi to Sudder Street costs Rs43. **Minibuses** and **buses** (#S5, #S6, #S7 and #41A) also operate from Howrah, but tend to be very crowded. The best alternative is to follow the signs from the station gate and take a **ferry** ride (Rs3) across the Hooghly with great views of the bridge, to Babu Ghat or the adjacent Chandpal Ghat, close to BBD Bagh, and pick up a metered taxi, bus or minibus from there.

Sealdah Station, used by trains from the north, is on the eastern edge of the centre, and much more convenient as you don't have to get across the river. There is a convenient **prepaid taxi booth** in the car park. Long-distance **buses** from the south terminate at **Babu Ghat Bus Stand**, not far from Fort William on the east bank, while some luxury buses, such as the *Rocket* from Darjeeling, arrive at **Esplanade Bus Stand**, less than 1km north of Sudder Street.

Information

The efficient and friendly **Government of India Tourist Office**, 4 Shakespeare Sarani (Mon–Fri 9am–6pm, Sat 9am–1pm; ☏033/282 5813 or 282 1457, ✉ caltour@cal2.vsnl.net.in) is your best bet for information on Calcutta, West Bengal and destinations further afield, and can assist with itineraries and booking tours. The **Government of West Bengal Tourist Bureau**, 3/2 BBD Bagh East (☏033/248 8271), arranges tours of Calcutta and package trips around West Bengal. They also issue permits and book tours and accommodation at the Sunderbans and Jaldapara wildlife parks. **Tourist informa-tion counters** at the airport and Howrah Station offer the same services.

English-language **newspapers** such as the *Statesman*, *Telegraph* and *Hindusthan Standard* remain the primary source for information on **what's on** but the monthly *CalCalling* (Rs240), also found in some hotel rooms, is excellent for listings and general information on the city. *Calcutta This Fortnight* is a free leaflet, available from both the West Bengal and Government of India tourist offices.

City transport

Virtually all the different modes of transport that clog the streets of Calcutta – trams, buses, rickshaws, metered taxis, and minibuses – add to the problem of congestion. However, the **Metro**, India's first and Calcutta's pride and joy, provides a fast, clean and efficient way to get around. It's also very easy to use, as it consists of just the one line running on a north–south axis.

The **river** is also used for transport, with the *ghats* near Eden Gardens at the hub of a **ferry** system. The most pleasant way to beat the traffic is to take one of the very regular ferries from Chandpal Ghat to Howrah Station; other sailings head downriver from Armenian, Chandpal or Babu *ghats* to the Botanical Gardens, although the running of this route is erratic. Of more use to commuters than tourists, a **circular railway** loops south from Sealdah before moving upriver along the Strand and Princep Ghat, past Howrah Bridge and eventually to Dum Dum. While using public transport, be wary of **pickpockets**, especially on crowded buses.

The Metro

Despite a couple of small fires in recent years, Calcutta's Russian-designed **Metro**, inaugurated in 1984, is every bit as good as its inhabitants proudly claim, a spotless contrast to the streets above, with trains operating punctually every few minutes. Services run from 7am to 9.30pm Monday to Saturday and from 2.30pm to 9.30pm on Sundays. Tickets are very cheap – you can travel the entire length of the line from Dum Dum in the north to Tollygunge in the south for just Rs7. The line follows Calcutta's main arteries including Chowringhee Road, with convenient stations such as Park Street, Kalighat, Esplanade and Rabindra Sadan.

City tours

City tours (around Rs100) are organized both by the Government of India Tourist Office and the West Bengal Tourist Bureau (see opposite), leaving from their respective premises around 7.30–8.30am and returning around 5pm. Although you don't get much time anywhere they give you a good feel for the city.

An even better way to explore the sprawl of Calcutta is to hire your own **taxi and guide**, arranged through the Government of India Tourist Office. For a group of three to four people, it works out reasonably cheap (half-day tours from Rs250 and full-day tours from Rs350).

Walking tours provide a great insight into the historic heart of the city and start from BBD Bagh; contact Footsteps (☏ 033/337 5757) for more information.

Buses and minibuses

Calcutta supports a vast and complicated **bus** network, in operation each day between roughly 5am and 11pm, and subject to overcrowding and attendant pickpocketing problems. The profusion of bus routes, many privately run, is best explained in the dark-blue pocket guide, *Calcutta & Howrah* by DP Publications (Rs9) and available through roadside magazine and book vendors and at railway-station bookshops. Once the mainstay of Calcutta Transport Corporation – **CTC** – today just a handful of red double-decker buses are to be seen still in service. Useful bus routes include: **#8** from Howrah via Esplanade and Gariahat Road to Gol Park; **#S17**, from Chetla near Kalighat via Esplanade; and **#5** and **#6**, which both travel via Howrah and the Esplanade-Chowringhee area, and stop at the Indian Museum at the head of Sudder Street. The **#C6** travels via Chowringhee, passing the top of Park Street before crossing the Vidyasagar Setu, the second Hooghly Bridge, to the Botanical Gardens. Buses with an "S" prefix denote special express buses charging marginally more. Of the three Executive bus routes, the **#E3** runs from Esplanade to the airport.

In addition, private brown-and-yellow **minibuses** travel at inordinate speeds on ad-hoc routes; their destinations are usually painted boldly in Bengali and English on their sides, and conductors shout them out at bus stops or major junctions.

Don't be fooled by empty buses – they are either about to stop for a few hours or will fill up in a few seconds; be careful getting on and off buses as they tend to stop in the middle of the road.

Taxis

Taxis in Calcutta prove to be extremely good value, especially on long journeys such as to and from the airport (around Rs130 for a twenty-kilometre ride), but a few drivers can be unwilling to go anywhere for less than Rs50, even for short journeys. Sudder Street's taxi touts are particularly averse to haggling, and you're better off walking around the corner and flagging down a cab. Alternatively, you could use the **prepaid taxi** service behind *Trincas Restaurant* on Park Street, in the parking lot of the *Park Hotel* (other such services are found at the main railway stations and the airport). Most cabs have working **meters** and tend to use them in conjunction with the conversion charts they are obliged to carry. To complicate matters, there are two meter systems operating simultaneously. New digital meters (located inside the cab) start on Rs10 but add on another twenty percent. Old meters (located on the outside) start on Rs5 but the fare will be charged at double what the meter says plus another twenty percent. When fare rises are announced, the Taxi Association finds it cheaper to issue the conversion charts rather than reset each and every meter. Note there is a small additional charge for placing your luggage in the boot, which is invariably dusty and filled with oily rags.

Trams

Calcutta's cumbersome **trams**, barely changed since they started operating in 1873, are on their way out; their inability to deviate from fixed rails to cope with the city's crazy traffic makes them more of a nuisance than anything else. However, for all their grime and general dilapidation, they do have an odd quirky charm, and provide an interesting way of seeing the city; women travellers may well be glad of the rush-hour women-only coaches. Routes include **#21**, Howrah Bridge to Park Circus via BBD Bagh, Esplanade and Rafi

Ahmed Kidwai Road; **#20**, Howrah Bridge via Sealdah to Park Circus (**#26** follows the same route but continues, via Gariahat, to Ballygunge Station); **#25**, BBD Bagh to Ballygunge via Rafi Ahmed Kidwai Road, Park Circus and Gariahat; and **#32**, Howrah Bridge to Tollygunge via BBD Bagh, Esplanade, the Maidan and Kalighat.

Rickshaws, auto-rickshaws and cycle rickshaws

Calcutta is the only city in India to have **human-drawn rickshaws**, which are only available in the central areas of the city, especially around New Market where many drivers supplement their meagre income by acting as pimps. Rickshaws come into their own during the monsoons, when the streets get flooded to hip height and the rickshaw-men can extract healthy amounts of money for their pains. If you take one, take care not to lean back as your weight will unbalance the driver. Most of the rickshaw-pullers are Bihari pavement-dwellers, who live short and very hard lives. Haggle for a realistic price but feel free to give a handful of baksheesh too.

    Auto-rickshaws, rare in the centre of town, are used as shared taxis on certain routes and link with Metro stations in suburbs such as Rashbehari and Gariahat; try to avoid a share of the front cab as accidents do happen. **Cycle rickshaws**, banned from much of the city, are only available in outlying suburbs.

Accommodation

As soon as you arrive in Calcutta, taxi-drivers are likely to assume that you'll be heading for central **Sudder Street**, east of Chowringhee Road. As the main travellers' hub in the city, the area is a sociable place to stay with numerous small to mid-sized hotels; in fact, many visitors spend most of their time in this one enclave. Most Sudder Street hotels are in the budget or mid-range brackets. The cheaper options are generally small and grubby so it may well be worth spending a few rupees more for a hotel with a terrace or courtyard.

    The many **guesthouses** now on offer all over Calcutta – usually comfortable private houses or flats, with the use of a "cook-cum-bearer" – provide mid-budget travellers with an alternative to Sudder Street. Be sure to clarify the food arrangements and all costs at the start of your stay. The Guest Agency, a division of Travel & Cargo Service, 23 Shakespeare Sarani (℡033/247 9662), represents guesthouses throughout the city. The Government of India Tourist Office, 4 Shakespeare Sarani (℡033/282 5813 or 282 1402) also runs a **paying guest** scheme which costs Rs300–500 per night.

    Some of the city's very **top hotels** are slightly further afield; the luxurious *Taj Bengal* for example is in Alipore to the south.

    Well-heeled travellers might also consider a stay at Calcutta's most exclusive **club**, considered one of the best in the world, the Tollygunge Club, at the southern end of the Metro line, at 120 Deshapran Sasmal Rd (℡033/473 2316, ℡473 1903; ❻–❽). Accommodation, with a choice of exclusive cottages or rooms in one of two newish blocks, includes temporary membership and the use of an eighteen-hole golf course, plus riding, swimming, tennis and squash facilities, as well as open-air and indoor restaurants and a good bar. You will need to contact the secretary well in advance to reserve a room as the club is extremely popular and often full.

Sudder Street, Park Street and Chowringhee

Astoria, Sudder Street ☏033/245 1514. Mid-range alternative with old-fashioned rooms for those who've slummed it once too often. ❼–❽

Centrepoint Guest House, 20 Mirza Ghalib St ☏033/244 8184. Friendly and popular, though cramped, with a range of rooms (some a/c) and two cheap clean and cramped dorms (Rs70) – one for men and one for women. ❸–❹

Crystal, 11/1 Kyd Street (Dr Mohammed Ishaque Road) ☏033/226 6400, Ⓔhotelcrystal@caltiger.com. Friendly hotel with decent-sized rooms – some with a/c – and hot showers. ❺–❼

Dolphin, 8 A K Mohammed Siddique Lane ☏033/244 2248. Ten minutes' walk from Sudder Street, tucked away down a tiny lane. Small clean rooms with TV and cold showers. ❸

Fairlawn, 13A Sudder St ☏033/245 1510, ⓌWww.fairlawnhotel.com. A famous old-fashioned hotel with exudes a decadent and eccentric Raj atmosphere, chock-full of memorabilia. Non-residents can sample a drink in the lush garden. From $57. ❾

Galaxy, 3 Stuart Lane ☏033/246 4565. Small hotel with just a few rooms all with TV. Clean and good value. ❺

Lindsay, 8A/B Lindsay St ☏033/245 2237. You couldn't get closer to New Market. A somewhat dull mid-range option with a forex bureau, restaurant and a bizarre coffee shop. ❼–❽

Lytton, 14 Sudder St ☏033/249 1872, ⓌWww.lyttonhotel.com. The most modern and comfortable hotel on the street with central a/c but otherwise lacking in character. Facilities include a bar and a couple of good restaurants. ❽

Maria, 5/1 Sudder Street ☏033/245 0860. Old building with high ceilings and good-sized budget rooms which are often full; there is also a dorm (Rs70), a good cybercafé and a pleasant terrace upstairs. ❸

Modern Lodge, 1 Stuart Lane ☏033/244 4960. Cramped but reasonably priced hotel with a relaxing roof terrace, popular since the 1960s with budget travellers. ❷–❸

Neelam, 11 Dr Mohammed Ishaque St ☏033/226 9198. Pleasant hotel a couple of blocks from the main drag with reasonably sized rooms. ❹

New Kenilworth, 1 & 2 Little Russell St ☏033/282 8394, ⓌWww.kenilworthhotels.com. Comfortable and plush place with better value in the new block; it has a reputation for good service and comes with a good restaurant, a coffee shop, two bars and a multigym with steam bath and sauna. From $110. ❾

Oberoi Grand, 15 Chowringhee Rd ☏033/249 2323, ⓌWww.oberoihotels.com. With its white Victorian facade which harks back to the Raj, this completely revamped central hotel is very much part of the fabric of the city. Very luxurious with a swimming pool, and Thai and Indian restaurants. From $250. ❾

Oriental, 9A Marquis St, off Mirza Ghalib St ☏033/245 9936. Small clean rooms away from all the touts, with cable TV and cold showers. ❹

Paragon, 2 Stuart Lane ☏033/244 2445. Dark and dingy downstairs rooms but nevertheless a popular and traveller-friendly place; slightly better rooms are around the rooftop courtyard. ❷–❹

Park, 17 Park St ☏033/249 3121, ⓌWww.theparkhotels.com. Modern five-star hotel in a good location on a cosmopolitan street, with all amenities including swimming pool, multigym, late checkout and good food at the hotel's two restaurants. Comfortable if characterless, with a bar that's lively at weekends. From $250. ❾

Peerless Inn, 12 Chowringhee Rd ☏033/228 0301, ⓌWww.peerlessinn.com. An expensive four-star hotel with a very upmarket Bengali feel. The restaurant specializes in local cuisine, and there is also a 24hr coffee shop. From $95. ❾

Plaza, 10 Sudder St ☏033/244 6411. Friendly, clean and popular with visiting businessmen. ❺–❼

Salvation Army Red Shield Guest House, 2 Sudder St ☏033/245 0599. Good budget option, which is often booked up and has changed little over the years. Dorms (from Rs60) and a few doubles including a couple of a/c; passing through its large gate is a welcome relief from the noise and pollution outside. ❸–❻

Shilton, 5A Sudder St ☏033/245 1512. Large old building set behind a gateway. Reasonable rooms popular with visiting Bangladeshis. ❹

Times Guest House, Sudder Street, near the *Blue Sky Café* ☏033/245 1796. Small, friendly place with a dorm (Rs60) and a few cramped double rooms. ❸

Timestar, 2 Tottee Lane ☏033/245 0028. Fair-sized rooms in old villa with a/c and hot water by the bucket. TVs in some rooms. ❸

VIP International, 51 Mirza Ghalib St ☏033/229 0345. Good location and decent-sized carpeted rooms with cable TV, but expensive. ❼–❽

YMCA, 25 Chowringhee Rd ☏033/249 2192. Once a grand nightclub near the Indian Museum, now a faded but popular meeting place with a range of rooms, some with a/c, on a half-board basis. Temporary membership (Rs40) allows access to a well-kept snooker table and table tennis. ❺–❻

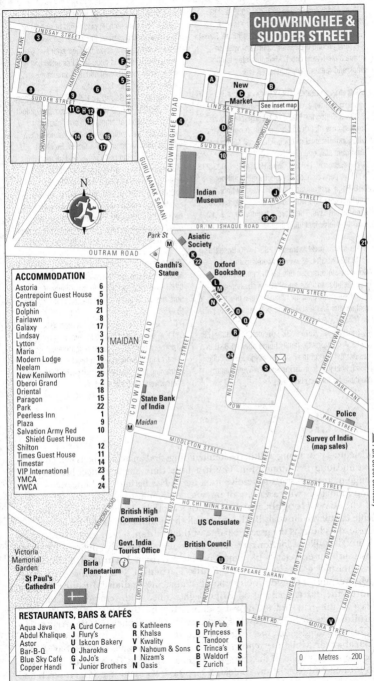

CHOWRINGHEE & SUDDER STREET

LINDSAY STREET

MADGE LANE

HARTFORD LANE

MIRZA GHALIB STREET

SUDDER STREET

CHOWRINGHEE LANE

New Market

See inset map

CHOWRINGHEE ROAD

LINDSAY STREET

MADGE LANE

HARTFORD LANE

SUDDER STREET

Indian Museum

CHOWRINGHEE LANE

MARQUIS STREET

MIRZA GHALIB STREET

MARKET STREET

DR. M. ISHAQUE ROAD

GURU NANAK SARANI

Park St

Asiatic Society

Oxford Bookshop

Gandhi's Statue

OUTRAM ROAD

ACCOMMODATION

Astoria	6
Centrepoint Guest House	5
Crystal	19
Dolphin	21
Fairlawn	8
Galaxy	17
Lindsay	3
Lytton	7
Maria	13
Modern Lodge	16
Neelam	20
New Kenilworth	25
Oberoi Grand	2
Oriental	18
Paragon	15
Park	22
Peerless Inn	1
Plaza	9
Salvation Army Red Shield Guest House	10
Shilton	12
Times Guest House	11
Timestar	14
VIP International	23
YMCA	4
YWCA	24

MAIDAN

CHOWRINGHEE ROAD

RUSSEL STREET

PARK STREET

RIPON STREET

ROYD STREET

RATT AHMED KIDWAI ROAD

PARK LANE

State Bank of India

Maidan

MIDDLETON STREET

MIDDLETON ROW

Police

PARK STREET

Survey of India (map sales)

SHORT STREET

WOOD STREET

CATHEDRAL ROAD

LITTLE RUSSEL STREET

HO CHI MINH SARANI

RABINDRANATH TAGORE STREET

British High Commission

US Consulate

Govt. India Tourist Office

British Council

SHAKESPEARE SARANI

Victoria Memorial Garden

St Paul's Cathedral

Birla Planetarium

LORD SINHA RD

PRETORIA ST

HUNGERFORD STREET

OUTRAM STREET

LAUDON STREET

ALBERT RD

MOIRA STREET

► Park Street Cemetery

13

CALCUTTA AND WEST BENGAL | Calcutta

RESTAURANTS, BARS & CAFÉS

Aqua Java	G	Curd Corner	A	Kathleens	G	Oly Pub	F
Abdul Khalique	J	Flury's	R	Khalsa	L	Princess	D
Astor	U	Iskcon Bakery	O	Kwality	V	Tandoor	Q
Bar-B-Q	O	Jharokha	P	Nahoum & Sons	C	Trinca's	K
Blue Sky Café	G	JoJo's	T	Nizam's	I	Waldorf	S
Copper Handi	T	Junior Brothers	N	Oasis	E	Zurich	H

0   Metres   200

933

YWCA, Middleton Row ☎ 033/229 7033 & 229 0260. For women who plan to stay in town a while, there is no better place. Just off Park Street, it is built around a pleasant courtyard with an immaculate tennis court. Minimum stay is one week and meals are included. ⑤–⑥

Elsewhere in the city

Eastern Railway Yatri Niwas, Howrah Station ☎ 033/323 3561 & 660 1742. Large place with small dorms (Rs80) and a/c suites, for travellers with long-distance or upper-class rail tickets only. Maximum stay one night. ②–④

Great Eastern, 1-3 Old Court House St ☎ 033/248 2311, ⓔ geh@vsnl.com. Famous old hotel near BBD Bagh, patronized by Mark Twain, where the marble floors and wood-panelled corridors have seen better days. There are a handful of cheaper, non-a/c rooms including singles for under Rs600. ⑦–⑧

Hindusthan International, 235/1 AJC Bose Rd ☎ 033/247 2394, ⓦ www.hhihotels.com. Comfortable business hotel with indifferent service. Facilities include an arcade with shops and travel services, plus an Indian Airlines office, restaurants and a swimming pool open to the public for a fee. From $165. ⑨

Indrani Guest House, 3B Lovelock St ☎ 033/475 7712. A comfortable family home offering B&B in a residential part of the city off Ballygunge Circular Road, with just four rooms so book well ahead; suitable for longer stays. ⑥

Rutt-Deen, 21B Loudon St ☎ 033/240 2389, ⓔ ruttdeen@vsnl.com. Popular with businesspeople and wedding parties, this place features comfortable rooms (now showing their age) and a pleasant garden, plus good facilities including currency exchange. It's well situated on a leafy avenue just off Park Street. ⑧

Taj Bengal, 24B Belvedere Rd, Alipore ☎ 033/223 3939, ⓕ 223 1766, ⓦ www.tajhotels.com. Opulent, showpiece hotel, attempting to amalgamate Bengali features with the usual *Taj* grandeur but without the character of the *Grand*. Excellent Chinese and Indian restaurants and all mod cons including a pool and a disco. From $245. ⑨

Transit House, 11A Raja Basanta Roy Rd ☎ 033/466 3481, ⓔ transit1@vsnl.net. Excellent, comfortable guesthouse with a reputation for being safe for women travellers on their own; away from the centre but in an interesting location close to markets and the lakes. ⑥–⑦

At the airport

Airways Lodge, no. 2 Airport Gate ☎ 033/552 8280. The cheapest place in the vicinity of the airport; handy for early departures and late arrivals. ③–④

ITDC Airport Ashok, Calcutta Airport ☎ 033/551 9111, ⓦ www.theashokgroup.com. Handy for the airport but not the city; a large featureless government-run luxury hotel with a health club and swimming pool. There are now several cheaper alternatives along VIP Road. ⑨

The City

Calcutta's crumbling weatherbeaten buildings and anarchic streets can create an intimidating first impression. Given a little time and patience, however, the huge metropolis starts to resolve itself into a fascinating conglomerate of styles and influences with a variety of impressive skylines to match.

The **River Hooghly**, which was until recently only spanned by the remarkable cantilever Howrah Bridge, is not all that prominent in the life of the city. Instead its heart is the green expanse of the **Maidan**, which attracts Calcuttans from all walks of life for recreation, sports, exhibitions and political rallies. At its southern end stands the white-marble **Victoria Memorial**, and close by rise the tall gothic spires of **St Paul's Cathedral**. Next to the busy **New Market** area alongside looms the all-embracing **Indian Museum**. Further north, the district centred on BBD Bagh is filled with reminders of the heyday of the East India Company, dominated by the bulk of the **Writers' Building** with **St Andrew's Kirk** nearby; a bit further out, the **Armenian Church** stands on the edge of the frenetic, labyrinthine markets of **Barabazaar**, while the renowned and influential temple of **Kalighat** is away to the south, in one of the city's more congested areas. **Tangra**, or Chinatown, is located 3km east of the Maidan. Calcutta's two main stations, **Howrah** and

Sealdah, are 4km apart, both north of the Maidan and on opposite sides of the Hooghly River.

The Maidan, New Market and Park Street

The **Maidan** – literally "field" – which stretches from the area known as Esplanade in the north to the racecourse in the south, and is bordered by **Chowringhee Road** to the east and the Strand and the river to the west, is one of the largest city-centre parks in the world. This vast area of open space stands in utter contrast to the chaotic streets of the city that surrounds it, big enough to swallow up several clubs, including the Calcutta Ladies Golf Club, and the immaculate greens of the Calcutta Bowling Club. It was created when the now-inconspicuous **Fort William** was laid out near the river in 1758, and Robert Clive cleared tracts of forest to give its guns a clear line of fire. Originally it was a haven for the elite, with a strictly enforced dress code. Now, early each morning, ordinary citizens come to exercise, shepherds graze their flocks, and riders on horseback canter along the old bridleways. In the late afternoons, it plays host to scores of impromptu cricket and football matches, as well as games of kabadi (see p.71).

Esplanade

The 46-metre column of **Shahid Minar** (Martyrs' Memorial) towers over busy tram and bus terminals and market stalls at the northeast corner of the Maidan, known as Esplanade. As the **Ochterlony Monument**, it was built in 1828 to commemorate the memory of David Ochterlony, who led the East India Company troops to victory in the Nepalese Wars of 1814–16. Further northeast, in the small **Curzon Park** among the trees and fenced-off patches of greenery beyond the tram terminus, a colony of rats has burrowed a warren of holes. Local office workers spend their lunch hours feeding the fat and complacent rodents.

New Market and Chowringhee

Beneath its Gothic red-brick clock tower, the single-storey **New Market**, in the centre of cosmopolitan Calcutta, can have changed little since it opened in 1874. Its real name is Sir Stuart Hogg Market; supposedly, the ghost of Sir Stuart haunts the market, roaming the corridors at night crying out for peace. It would be easier to imagine that he was bemoaning the antics of its coolies, who drag willing and unwilling customers into the various shops in search of commission, and also double as black-market touts. At the north end of the market, a characterless multistorey building has been erected to replace sections gutted by a fire in 1985.

The market itself stocks a vast array of household goods, luggage, ready-made garments, jewellery, curio shops, bookshops, textiles, and kitchenware, as well as meat, vegetables and fruit. Among shops that stand out from the rest, Chamba Lama sells Tibetan curios and antique items such as silver jewellery and new bronzes. The **Symphony** music store has a good selection of classical and popular Indian music, while **Sujata's** is known for its silk, and **Nahoum & Sons** is a Jewish bakery. Further up the corridor, condiment stalls offer cheese from Kalimpong, miniature rounds of salty Bandel cheese, and *amshat*, blocks made up of sheets of dried mango.

The formerly elegant colonnaded front of Chowringhee Road, with its long line of colonial villas and palaces, is now in a sorry state of decay and perpet-

Although a rich tradition of poetry existed in India long before the arrival of the Europeans – even scientific manuscripts were written in rhyming couplets – **prose** was all but unknown. Thus the foundation by the British of **Fort William College** in 1800 – primarily intended to assist administrators to learn Indian languages by commissioning prose in Bengali, Urdu and Hindi – had the unexpected side effect of helping to create a vital new genre in indigenous literature. Bankim Chandra Chatterjee (1838–99), a senior civil servant who wrote novels of everyday life, became known as the father of Bengali literature, while Michael Madhusudan **Dutt** (1829–73) introduced European poetic conventions into Bengali poetry. Simultaneously, Westernization began to sweep Bengali middle-class society, as people grew disenchanted with their culture and religion.

A leading figure in the new intelligentsia was **Raja Ram Mohan Roy** (1774–1833), born an orthodox Hindu, who travelled in Tibet before joining the East India Company, and eventually died in England as the ambassador of the Moghuls. Roy founded the **Brahmo Samaj**, a socio-religious movement that believed in a single god and set out to purge Hinduism of its idol worship and rituals, advocating the abolition of *sati* and child marriage. **Keshab Chandra Sen**'s Navabidhan (New Dispensation), a synthesis of all the world's major religions, created a split in 1866 over its emphasis on universal Unitarianism and the downplaying of the role of Hinduism. A reformer of boundless energy and a renowned orator, Keshab Sen travelled to Britain to lecture, commanding huge audiences and even meeting Queen Victoria.

No single figure epitomized the **Bengali Renaissance** more than **Rabindranath Tagore**, a giant of Bengali art, culture and letters, and a Brahmo, who received the Nobel Prize for Literature in 1913. As well as writing several hymns, he set out the principles of the Brahmo Samaj movement in *The Religion of Man*. The intellectual and cultural freedom of the Brahmo Samaj earned it an important influence over the Bengali upper classes that endures to this day, but in recent years extreme Bengali reformists have attacked the movement for having been a corrupting influence on Bengali society.

During and following the period of the Renaissance, Bengal saw a resurgence of Hindu thought through religious leaders such as **Ramakrishna** (1836–86), a great Kali devotee whose message was carried as far as North America by his disciple **Vivekananda**. Having spent some time in London as a student, **Sri Aurobindo** (1872–1950) returned to India to become a freedom fighter and, finally, emerged as one of the most influential philosophers of twentieth-century India. Aurobindo, who went on to establish his own ashram in Pondicherry, preached a return to a reformed esoteric Hinduism.

ually crowded with hawkers and shoppers. The only one of its grand institutions to survive relatively unscathed is the Victorian **Grand Hotel** which, after endless renovations and changes of management remains a haven of colonialism, with its palm court inspired by the famous *Raffles* of Singapore.

Indian Museum

At the corner of Chowringhee and Sudder streets, the stately **Indian Museum** (Tues–Sun: March–Nov 10am–5pm; Dec–Feb 10am–4.30pm; Rs150 [Rs10]) is the oldest and the largest museum in India, founded in 1814. Built around a central courtyard, the present high-ceilinged building was opened to the public in 1878, and is one of the largest museums in Asia, housing a huge variety of exhibits from sculpture to natural history.

Visitors come to the museum in their thousands, many of them villagers who bring offerings to the *jadu ghar* or "house of magic". The main showpiece is a collection of **stone and metal sculptures** obtained from sites all over India, which centres on a superb Mauryan polished sandstone **lion capital**, dating from the third century BC. One gallery houses the impressive remains of the second-century BC Buddhist **stupa from Bharhut** in Madhya Pradesh, partly re-assembled to display posts, capping stones, railings and gateways all made from red sandstone. Carvings depict human and animal figures, as well as scenes from the *Jataka* tales of the Buddha's many incarnations. There is also a huge collection of Buddhist schist sculptures, dating from the first to the third century, from the Gandhara region. Relics in the Prehistory Gallery are supposed to be those of the Buddha. You'll also see stone sculpture from **Khajuraho** and Pala bronzes, plus copper artefacts, Stone-Age tools and terracotta figures from other sites.

Along with an excellent exhibit of Tibetan *thangkas*, the museum holds Kalighat *pats* (see p.946) and paintings by the **Company School**, a group of mid-nineteenth-century Indian artists who emulated Western themes and techniques for European patrons. Finally, there's a spectacular array of fossils and stuffed animals, most of which look in dire need of a decent burial.

Park Street

Just around the corner from the museum, the **Asiatic Society** at 1 Park St, established in 1784 by Orientalists including Sir William Jones, houses a huge collection of around 150,000 books and 60,000 ancient manuscripts, some of which date back to the seventh century. The society has a **reading room** open to the public (Mon–Fri 10am–8pm, Sat & Sun 10am–5pm; free) and a **gallery** of art and antiquities with paintings by Rubens and Reynolds, a large collection of coins and one of Ashoka's stone edicts.

Around 2km along Park Street from the Maidan, the disused but recently restored **Park Street Cemetery** is one of the city's most haunting memorials to its imperial past. Inaugurated in 1767, it is the oldest in Calcutta, holding a wonderful concentration of pyramids, obelisks, pavilions, urns and headstones, under which many well-known Brits lie buried. The epitaphs make fascinating reading.

Fort William

A road leads west through the Maidan from the top of Park Street to the gates of **Fort William**. As the fort functions as the military headquarters of the Eastern Command, entry is restricted and the public is only allowed into certain sections on special occasions. Built on the site of the old village of Govindapur, and commissioned by the British after their defeat in 1756, the fort was completed in 1781 and named after King William III. A rough octagon, about 500m in diameter, whose massive but low bunker-like battlements are punctuated by six main gates, the fort was designed to hold all the city's Europeans in the event of attack. To one side it commanded a view of the Maidan, cleared to give a field of fire; to the other it dominated the river and its crucial shipping lanes. Water from the river was diverted to fill its surrounding moat. Eighteenth- and nineteenth-century structures inside include the Church of St Peter's (now a library), barracks and stables, an arsenal, strong rooms and a prison. Today, the army still controls the Maidan and any special construction or activity must be approved by them.

Victoria Memorial and the Calcutta Gallery

The dramatic white marble **Victoria Memorial** (Tues–Sun: March–Oct 10am–4pm; Nov–Feb 10am–5pm; Rs5) at the southern end of the Maidan, with its formal gardens and water courses, continues to be Calcutta's pride and joy. Other colonial monuments and statues throughout the city have been renamed or demolished, but the popularity of Queen Victoria seems to endure for ever; thirty years of attempts to change the name of the "VM" have come to nothing.

This extraordinary hybrid building, with Italianate statues over its entrances, Moghul domes in its corners, and tall elegant open colonnades along its sides, was conceived by Lord Curzon to commemorate the empire at its peak. Designed by Sir William Emerson, it was completed in 1921. Flanked by two ornamental tanks, a sombre statue of Queen Victoria gazes out towards the Maidan from a pedestal lined with bronze panels and friezes. Faced with Makrana marble from Jodhpur, the building itself is capped by a dome bearing a revolving five-metre-tall bronze figure of Victory.

The main entrance, at the Maidan end, leads into a tall chamber beneath the dome. The 25 galleries inside burst with mementoes of British imperialism – statues and busts of Queen Mary, King George V and Queen Victoria; paintings of Robert Clive and the Queen (again); a huge canvas of the future Edward VII entering Jaipur in 1876; French guns captured at the Battle of Plassey in 1758; and the black marble throne of a nawab defeated by Robert

Satyajit Ray

India's most highly acclaimed film director, Satyajit Ray (1921–92), was a Calcuttan through and through but won more plaudits abroad than he did in his homeland. Fascinated by film-making from an early age, Ray studied painting at Rabindranath Tagore's university at Shantiniketan where he came into contact with pastoral life, an experience which was to influence much of his work. Later, with the help of his friend, Bansi Chandra Gupta, a painter who shared many of his interests in films, Ray launched the Calcutta Film Society in 1947.

While working for a British advertising agency as an illustrator and designer, Ray stumbled upon the Bengali novel by Bibhuti Bhusan Bannerji called *Pather Panchali* (*Song of the Little Road* – the story of a brahmin family in rural Bengal), and fell in love with the book. A couple of years later Ray befriended the celebrated French film director Jean Renoir, who was in Calcutta looking for locations and actors to film Rumer Godden's book *The River*. Renoir provided an essential impetus by encouraging Ray to go ahead with the making of a film of *Pather Panchali*. Ray started shooting in October 1952 in the village of Gopalnagar, Bannerji's birthplace; after numerous hurdles, mostly financial, the film was finally completed in 1955.

Pather Panchali's premier in New York was a great success, "a triumph of imaginative photography" in the words of one critic, but the Calcutta preview met with a cool reception, leaving Ray despondent. However, the film soon went on to high acclaim and an award at the Cannes Film Festival, establishing Ray as an international director of repute. After *Pather Panchali* came *Aparajito* (1956) and *Apur Sansar* (1959), which completed the "Apu Trilogy", still considered Ray's finest work. He went on to make 36 films, the last one being *Agantuk* (*The Stranger*) in 1991. Ray also wrote fourteen novels, five screenplays, and numerous books of movie criticism and made several documentaries including one on Rabindranath Tagore. A number of musical recordings have been released of Ray's film soundtracks, including the music to the Apu Trilogy by Ravi Shankar and the film score to *Jalsaghar* (*The Music Room*) by Vilayat Khan, another of India's great classical musicians. Satyajit Ray was honoured with an Oscar for his lifetime achievement in the film industry and in India was awarded the prestigious Bharat Ratna.

Clive. One air-conditioned chamber, converted and renamed the **Calcutta Gallery**, is dedicated to the Indians of the city and the Independence struggle. The evening **Sound and Light** show (Tues–Sun 7.15–8pm; Rs20) concentrates on the same theme.

Admission to the Victoria Memorial's popular gardens is free during the day. After they close at dusk, the Maidan in front of the gates is transformed. A seething mass of people come to enjoy the breeze, roadside snacks, and pony and *tikka* (open carriage) rides, and to watch the garish **musical fountains**.

St Paul's Cathedral and around

The gothic **St Paul's Cathedral**, a little way along from the Victoria Memorial, was erected by Major W.N. Forbes in 1847. Measuring 75m by 24m, its iron-trussed roof was then the longest span in existence. For improved ventilation, the lancet windows inside extend to plinth level, and tall fans hang from the ceiling. The most outstanding of the many well-preserved memorials and plaques to long-perished imperialists is the stained glass of the west window, designed by Sir Edward Burne-Jones in 1880 to honour Lord Mayo, assassinated in the Andaman Islands. The original steeple was destroyed in the 1897 earthquake; after a second earthquake in 1934 it was remodelled on the Bell Harry Tower at Canterbury Cathedral.

Immediately north of the cathedral, the **Birla Planetarium** (daily 12.30–6.30pm; Rs15), one of the largest in the world and certainly the largest in Asia, holds several shows every day (in English 1.30pm & 6.30pm; in Bengali 3.30pm & 5.30pm; in Hindi 12.30pm, 2.30pm & 4.30pm).

South of the cathedral, the **Academy of Fine Arts** (Tues–Sun 3–8pm; Rs5) on Cathedral Road is a showcase for Bengali contemporary arts. As well as temporary exhibitions, it holds permanent displays of the work of artists such as Jamini Roy and Rabindranath Tagore. A café and pleasant grounds add to the appealing ambience. Rabindra Sadan, the large auditorium close by, regularly features programmes of Indian classical music and next door, **Nadan**, designed by Satyajit Ray, is a large and lively film centre with archives, library and auditoria.

Around the corner on Chowringhee, the small **Nehru Children's Museum**, 94/1 Chowringhee Rd (Tues–Sun noon–8pm; Rs10, under-12s Rs2), places a strong emphasis on the Hindu classics, illustrating the *Ramayana* and the *Mahabharata* with toys, puppets and picture shows.

Central Calcutta

The commercial and administrative hub of both Calcutta and West Bengal is **BBD Bagh**, which die-hard Calcuttans still insist on referring to as **Dalhousie Square**. The new official name, in a fine piece of official rhetoric, commemorates three revolutionaries hanged for trying to kill Lieutenant-Governor General Lord Dalhousie. In the centre of the square is the large Lal Dighi tank, or artificial pond.

Built in 1868 on the site of the original Fort William – destroyed by Siraj-ud-Daula in 1756 – the **GPO** on the west side of the square hides the supposed site of the **Black Hole of Calcutta**. On a hot June night in 1756, 146 English prisoners were forced by Siraj-ud-Daula's guards into a tiny chamber with only the smallest of windows for ventilation; most suffocated to death by the next morning. By all accounts, the guards were unaware of the tragedy unfolding and, on hearing the news, Siraj-ud-Daula was deeply repentant. A memorial to the victims that formerly stood in front of the Writers' Building was removed in 1940 to the grounds of St John's Church south of the GPO. When Robert Clive regained control of Calcutta, he had learned his lesson. Fort William was not rebuilt in this virtually undefendable location in a built-up area, but in its current location on the Maidan, with clear visibility in all directions.

Now the seat of the West Bengal government, the **Writers' Building** to the north of the square was built in 1780 to replace the original structure used to house the clerks or "writers" of the East India Company. No official tours take in the building, but wandering in to any department reveals a world of endless corridors and vast chambers, desks piled high with dusty old files and clerks in a state of advanced apathy.

West of the Writers' Building, beyond the headquarters of Eastern Railways on Netaji Subhash Road, you come to the heart of Calcutta's **commercial district**, clustered around the Royal Stock Exchange at the corner of Lyon's Range. The warren of buildings, erected along the same lines as the contemporary business districts of Shanghai, houses all sorts of old colonial trading companies; Scottish names in particular still seem to be very much in evidence. One of its most extraordinary sights is **Exchange Lane**, where stockbrokers sit in brightly painted wooden cubicles armed with telephones and carry on business with punters on the street.

A further symbol of Calcutta's Scottish traditions is the grey spire of **St Andrew's Kirk**, which rises in the middle of the road at the northeast end of BBD Bagh. This Scottish church was built in 1818, in the face of intense opposition from Church of England representatives. To the east, the oldest street in the city, formerly known as Mission Row but now called RN Mukherjee Road, holds the **Old Mission Church**, founded in 1770 by the Swedish missionary Johann Kiernander. South of the GPO, **St John's Church** was erected in 1787. Inside, along with memorials to British residents and to the first Bishop of Calcutta, Bishop Middleton, hangs an impressive painting of *The Last Supper* by Johann Zoffany, in which prominent Calcuttans are depicted as apostles. In the grounds, Calcutta's first graveyard holds the tomb of Job Charnock.

Dominating this area south of BBD Bagh, **Government House** (only open to the public with prior permission) overlooks the north end of the Maidan and the ceremonial Red Road, which was once used as an airstrip and is the only thoroughfare in the city without potholes. Until 1911, this was the residence of the British governors-general and the viceroys of India; now the official home of the Governor of Bengal, it is known as **Raj Bhavan**. When built at the very end of the eighteenth century, it was intended to be a palace, modelled on Kedleston Hall in Derbyshire. Sealed off by tall iron fencing from the rest of the city, Government House is approached through four ornamental gateways guarded by lions and sphinxes. Along with a throne room once used by George V, and a spectacular chandeliered ballroom, the interior holds Calcutta's first lift, introduced by Lord Curzon and still in working condition. Trophies littered around the formal grounds include a large bronze cannon mounted on a winged dragon, captured at Nanking during the Opium Wars, and brass cannons from the Afghan campaigns.

Nearby, opposite the **Assembly House** (Rajya Sabha) of West Bengal's Legislative Council, are the All India Radio building, and the sports complex of **Eden Gardens**, site of the huge world-famous **cricket** ground (officially known as the Ranji Stadium), which occasionally suffers riots and fires started by overzealous fans, especially when their team is seen to be losing. Watching a test match here is an unforgettable experience as the 100,000-seat stadium resounds to the roar of the crowd and the sound of crackers thrown indiscriminately; if you want to avoid the missiles, sit in the covered sections. West of the sports complex, at the northwest corner of the Maidan, an ornamental park offers an artificial lake, a Burmese pagoda, and pleasant walks along palm-strewn paths. Nearby, at Fairly Place Jetty, the ornamental **Millennium Park** (daily 1–8pm; Rs5) is a pleasant riverside garden.

North Calcutta

The sprawling and amorphous area of **north Calcutta** was long part of the "native" town rather than the European sectors, and was where the city's prosperous nineteenth-century Bengali families created their little palaces. Today its markets continue to thrive unchanged, and the occasional church stands as a reminder of days gone by.

North of BBD Bagh, the area known as **Barabazaar** has played host to a succession of trading communities; the Portuguese were here even before Job Charnock landed at the fishing village that stood close by, and it later became home to Marwari and Gujarati merchants. The small and hectic lanes south of MG Road are lined with shops and stalls that sell everything from glass bangles to textiles.

At the northwest corner of Barabazaar, near Howrah Bridge, is Calcutta's oldest church, the **Armenian Church of Our Lady of Nazareth**. Founded in 1724 by Cavond, an Armenian from Persia, it was built on the site of an Armenian cemetery in which the oldest tombstone dates to 1630. The Armenian community, drawn from both Armenia and Persia, was already highly influential at the courts of Bengal by the time the British arrived, and played an important role in the early history of the East India Company. Later they went on to help start the lucrative jute industry. Just around the corner on MG Road at Murghihatta, the "Chicken Market", stands the Portuguese **Roman Catholic Cathedral**, built in 1797.

East of Barabazaar on Rabindra Sarani (formerly Chitpore Road), the huge red **Nakhoda Masjid**, whose two lofty minarets rise to 46m, is the great Jami Masjid (Friday mosque) of the city. Completed in 1942, it was modelled on Akbar's Tomb at Sikandra near Agra; its four floors can hold ten thousand worshippers. The traditional Muslim market that flourishes all around the mosque sells religious items along with clothes, dried fruit and sweets such as *firni*, made of rice. Down the road is the *Royal*, a renowned Muslim restaurant that has seen better days. North along Rabindra Sarani, musical instrument-makers specialize in sitars, harmoniums and *tanburas*.

Until relatively recently, the chaotic jumble of streets to the south along Rabindra Sarani housed a thriving **Chinatown**, opium dens and all. Chinese families continue to live around Chhatawala Gully, where a small early-morning street market offers home-made pork sausages, noodles and jasmine tea. But the stalls serving *wonton* and *dim sum* are rapidly disappearing and the legendary *Nanking* restaurant, once one of the most elegant in the city, has finally closed its doors. Today, the best Chinese restaurants can be found in the east of the city, in the new Chinatown in Tangra.

North of MG Road, on the tiny Muktaram Babu Street off Chittaranjan Avenue, the extraordinary **Marble Palace** (Tues, Wed & Fri–Sun; free; no photography) preserves its lavish, sensuous treasures in somewhat cramped and dilapidated conditions. Visitors should obtain passes to join a guided tour from the tourist offices at BBD Bagh or Shakespeare Sarani. Built in 1835 by Raja Rajendro Mullick Bahadur, a wealthy *zamindar* (landowner) educated by an

English tutor, the colonnaded mansion epitomizes the incredible profusion of influences of the period, and is still maintained by the raja's descendants, who live here. The palace earns its name from its ornate marble-paved chambers, which hold statues, European antiques, Belgian glass, chandeliers, mirrors and Ming vases. There are paintings by Rubens, Titian, Sir Joshua Reynolds and Gainsborough. Look out for two paintings by Ravi Varma – a portrait of a woman whose eyes gaze back at you from wherever you view the painting, and a picture of five galloping horses which seem to change direction as you walk past. Other quirks include a bronze gorilla, a four-metre-high rosewood statue of Queen Victoria, a large red glass chalice from Belgium which detects poisoned food, and Venus statues in every nook and cranny.

North of Marble Palace is the city's main red-light area, **Sonagachi**. This is not a district in which travellers are particularly welcome; the police here have been known to arrest foreigners. If curiosity gets the better of you and you want to explore the area, leave your valuables behind.

On Dwarkanath Tagore Lane, a short walk northeast of the Marble Palace, the small campus of Rabindranath Tagore's liberal arts university, **Rabindra Bharati**, preserves the house where he was born and died. Now the **Rabindra Bharati Museum** (Mon–Fri 10am–5pm, Sat 10am–1.30pm; free), currently undergoing restoration, it holds a large collection of his paintings. Next door, Bichitra Bhavan is used, as it was by Tagore himself, to stage theatrical performances. In September, it is the scene of a festival commemorating the Nobel Laureate.

Further east, **College Street** stretches along the edge of Calcutta University. Established in 1857 as the pride of Bengali learning, it still has one of the largest student bodies in the world. Senate House, one of its earliest buildings, was gutted during the turbulent days of the early Seventies. College Street deals exclusively in books and supplies for students; its pavement stalls and shops are an excellent hunting ground for secondhand books, if not genuine antiques. Adjoining Albert Street, the famous **India Coffee House**, although now a bit jaded, continues to attract students and the intelligentsia. The small **Ashutosh Museum of Indian History** (Mon–Fri 10.30am–4.30pm, Sat 10.30am–2pm; free), at the Centenary Building on College Street, has a good collection of Bengali art, handicrafts and fabrics as well as rare Buddhist manuscripts and statues.

North Calcutta has two large **Jain temples**. One, in **Belgachia** next to the bridge and the Metro station, is a simple red-sandstone structure set in

Pollution and floods

With no controls on the emissions of its armada of diesel-engined vehicles, Calcutta is cursed with heavy atmospheric **pollution** – as any visitor to the city soon learns. For its residents, lung problems are part of everyday life. Rush hours are especially noxious, with grey fumes frequently obscuring the sunset. During the long months when the city holds its breath and waits for the monsoons to hit, the still and heavy air can be unbearable; and when the rains finally roll in at the end of June, Calcutta becomes a swamp. Being obliged to wade thigh-deep through filthy water, along roads riddled with pot-holes and open manholes, contributes to further health problems. Calcutta's **water table** is contaminated to a depth of over 6m, and gastric disease is endemic. Anyone who can afford it equips their home with its own purification systems or tube well. On top of all that, the Calcutta Corporation is hopelessly unequal to the task of keeping the city clean; streets are strewn with litter and rubbish tips pile shoulder high.

manicured lawns, dedicated to the Digambara sect. The other, at **Manicktolla**, known as the **Parasnath** Jain temple, consists of a group of temples set in an ornate garden which holds ponds full of carp. It honours **Sitalnath**, the lord of water and the tenth in the line of 24 *tirthankaras* (crossing-makers) that culminated with Mahavira, born in Vaishali in 599 BC. Neoclassical marble and alabaster statues grace the grounds while the main temple, another architectural hybrid, is crowned by an ornate cupola. Inside the chamber the image of Sitalnath is surrounded by glitzy marble-work studded with silver. An odd mixture of Venetian and post-Moghul, its assorted multi-hued chandeliers are offset by the surrounding glass and mirrors. Along with an information centre, the temple area has several Jain shrines and boarding houses.

Howrah and the River Hooghly

Although **Howrah** is technically a separate town, as the home of much of Calcutta's industry, as well as Howrah Station, it forms an integral part of the city. Until recently, antiquated **Howrah Bridge** was the only road link across the River Hooghly; since the opening of the tall and elegant **Vidyasagar Setu**, the second Hooghly bridge, a few years ago, the west bank of the river is changing rapidly. Vidyasagar Setu (also referred to as the New or Natun Bridge) provides easy access to Shibpur and the beautiful **Botanical Gardens**, and onwards southwest to the open highways towards Orissa.

Across the river from central Calcutta, **Howrah Station**, built in 1906, is a striking red-brick building, topped by eight square towers and used by millions of passengers each day. During the war in Bangladesh in the early Seventies, it found itself sheltering thousands of refugees in horrific conditions.

Until silting rendered it impractical for large ships, the **River Hooghly**, a distributary of the Ganges, was responsible for making Calcutta a bustling port. Unlike those at Varanasi, the *ghats* that line its east (Calcutta) bank have no great esoteric significance; they simply serve as landings and places for ritual ablutions. Around 1.5km north of Howrah Bridge, **Nimtolla Ghat**, one of the city's main cremation grounds, is sealed off from the public gaze. The large steps alongside, and a Shiva temple, attract strange *sadhus* as they head through the city on their way to January's Ganga Sagar Mela (see p.926). A little further north, behind **Kumartuli Ghat**, a warren of lanes is home to a community of artisans who specialize in making the clay, straw and pith images of deities used for the major festivals. In the days leading up to the great pujas, especially that of Durga, **Kumartuli** is a fascinating hive of activity. As you walk north, you come next to **Baghbazaar Ghat**, where overloaded barges of straw arrive for the craftsmen of Kumartuli. Baghbazaar, the Garden Market, stands on the original site of Sutanuti, its grand but decaying turn-of-the-twentieth-century mansions epitomizing the long-vanished lifestyle of the Bengali gentry, the *bhadra log*.

South of Howrah Bridge, but right in its shadow, the large **Armenian Ghat** is at its most animated soon after dawn, when traditional gymnasts and wrestlers, devotees of Hanuman the monkey god, do their morning practice, and a flower market is in full swing. Nearby, vehicles, from trams to handcarts, battle inch by inch to gain access to the Howrah Bridge. As the cobbled and much-potholed Strand heads south, it passes several warehouses on the way beyond Fairly Place to another cluster of *ghats*. **Babu Ghat** here, identified by its crumbling colonnade, is used for early-morning bathing, attended by *pujaris* (priests) and heavy-handed masseurs. Nearby, Babu Ghat's Bus Stand is one of

Howrah Bridge

One of Calcutta's most famous landmarks, **Howrah Bridge** – officially Rabindra Setu, though few use this new name – is 97m high and 705m long, spanning the river in a single giant leap to make it the world's largest cantilever bridge. It was erected during World War II in 1943 to give Allied troops access to the Burmese front, replacing an earlier pontoon bridge that opened to let river traffic through. Looking like a giant version of something a child might make using a construction set, it was the first bridge to be constructed using rivets and is still the world's busiest bridge, used by millions of commuters daily. Its eight lanes are perpetually clogged with vehicles, and in the 1980s became so worn out that a man pushing his broken-down car is said to have fallen through a hole and disappeared. Don't let that put you off; the bridge has been undergoing major repairs, and joining the streams of perspiring pedestrians who walk across it each day is a memorable experience.

Vidyasagar Setu, the second Hooghly bridge, built 3km south to relieve the strain, was 22 years in the making. It's a vast toll bridge, high enough to let ships pass below, and with spaghetti-junction-style approaches. Despite the reluctance of many to use the new bridge, a one-way system that governs the use of Howrah Bridge is at last forcing traffic to swallow the Rs7 toll.

Calcutta's main cross-country terminuses, while ferries from **Chandpal Ghat**, a couple of hundred metres north, provide an easy alternative to Howrah Bridge.

Further south, past Eden Gardens, the Strand opens out into the promenades near Fort William, where people come to enjoy the cool evening river breezes. An ice-cream parlour overlooks the river and snack vendors are everywhere. A short boat trip to the new bridge and back costs around Rs40.

Botanical Gardens

The **Botanical Gardens** at Shibpur lie 10km south of Howrah Station on the west bank of the Hooghly. Although they were created in 1786 to develop strains of Indian tea, Calcuttans have only started to appreciate these 109 hectares once again since the opening of the second bridge. Populated by countless bird species, such as waders, cranes, and storks, the huge gardens are best seen in winter and spring and early in the mornings, when they're free from the grime of the metropolis. Their single most famous feature is the **world's largest banyan tree**, 24.5m high and an astonishing 420m in circumference. Now over 240 years old, a survivor of cyclones in 1864 and 1867 that eventually caused it to lose its main trunk, its 1825 aerial roots drop from the overhead branches to create the effect of a small forest. Elsewhere, palm trees abound around the lakes, ponds and ornamental footbridges, and especially the brooding, atmospheric Palm House. The Orchid House, the Herbarium and the Fern Houses are also worth seeing, and there's an attractive riverside promenade.

The gardens are accessible as a tedious road trip from Esplanade, by minibus or the ordinary ash-coloured #C6 bus. The #T9 runs from Park Street and #6 minibus runs from Dharamtala via Howrah. Taxis from the central Sudder Street area cost around Rs80–100 one way and are by far the easiest way to get there. Getting back is no problem as several buses start from outside the gardens and head for the Esplanade and Park Street; alternatively you could pay a taxi to wait for you. If and when the erratic **ferry** service is running from

Chandpal or Babu Ghat, this is by far the most pleasant way of getting to the gardens.

South Calcutta

South of the Maidan and Park Street, Calcutta spreads towards **suburbs** such as Alipore and Ballygunge, both within easy distance of the centre. The thoroughfare that starts life as Chowringhee proceeds south from Esplanade past **Kalighat** to **Tollygunge**, following the Metro line which terminates near the luxurious Tollygunge Club, the mansion of an indigo merchant now surrounded by immaculate golfing fairways and bridle paths. Northeast of Tollygunge, beyond a white-tiled mosque built in 1835 by descendants of Tipu Sultan, the vast open area around the Rabindra Sarobar lakes leads to **Ballygunge**, the home of Calcutta's Bengali middle classes.

Alipore

Around 3km south of Park Street, the crumbling nineteenth-century splendour of **Alipore** is slowly being engulfed by a forest of multistorey buildings. Not far from the racecourse, opposite the luxury *Taj Bengal* hotel, the extremely popular **Calcutta Zoo** (daily 6am–5pm; Rs2) houses such weird and wonderful animals as a tigon, a cross between a lion and a tiger; a litigon, a cross between a tigon and a lion; a litatitigon . . . and so forth. Now threatened with closure, the zoo also has white tigers from Rewa, a reptile house, an aquarium (Rs1), a children's zoo and four restaurants. Although many of the cages are clean, their surroundings are notably litter-strewn.

Elegant triple-arched gates just south of the zoo lead to **Belvedere**, the former residence of the Lieutenant-Governor of Bengal, now the **National Library** (Mon–Fri 10am–6pm; separate periodical and newspaper reading room on Esplanade Mon–Fri 9am–2pm, Sat & Sun 10am–6pm; free). Presented to Warren Hastings by Mir Jafar, the building's original simplicity was enhanced by double columns and the sweeping staircase that leads to the Durbar Hall. When the capital shifted to Delhi, this library was left behind; today it houses a huge and extensive collection of books, periodicals and reference material, as well as rare documents in an air-conditioned chamber.

Half a kilometre south, Alipore's small **Horticultural Gardens** (Tues–Sun 6–10am & 2–5pm; Rs1), popular with early morning walkers, cherish a wide assortment of plants and flowers. The flower show here at the start of February is well worth a visit.

Kalighat

Calcutta's most important temple, **Kalighat**, 5km south of Park Street along Ashutosh Mukherjee Road, an extension of Chowringhee Road, stands at the heart of a congested and animated area. This plain but typically Bengali temple, built of brick and mortar in 1809 but capturing the sweeping curves of a thatched roof, is dedicated to Kali, the black goddess and form of Shakti. According to legend, Shiva went into a frenzy after the death of his wife Sati, dancing with her dead body and making the whole world tremble. The gods had attempted to stop him in various ways before Vishnu took his solar discus and chopped the disintegrating corpse into 51 bits. The spot where each piece fell became a *pitha*, or pilgrimage site, for worshippers of the female principle of divinity – Shakti. The shrine here marks the place where her little toe fell.

The temple is open all hours, and is always a frenzied hive of activity. Unless you manage to leave your shoes yourself at the entrance, greedy priests grab

Mother Teresa, Calcutta's most famous citizen (1910–97), was born Agnes Gonxha Bojaxhiu to Albanian parents, and grew up in Skopje in the former Yugoslavia. After joining the Sisters of Loreto, an Irish order, she was sent as a teacher to Darjeeling, where she took her vows in May 1931 and became Teresa. In her work at St Mary's School in Calcutta, she became aware of the incredible poverty around her; in 1948, with permission from Rome, she put aside her nun's habit to clothe herself in the simple blue-bordered white sari that became the uniform of the **Missionaries of Charity**.

The best known of their many homes and clinics is **Nirmal Hriday**, a hospice for destitutes. In the face of local resistance, Mother Teresa chose its site at Kalighat – Calcutta's most important centre of Hinduism – in the knowledge that many of the poor specifically come here to die, next to a holy *tirtha* or crossing-place. Mother Teresa's simple piety and single-minded devotion to the poor won her international acclaim, including the Nobel Peace Prize in 1979. Subsequently she also attracted a fair share of controversy, with her fierce anti-abortion stance, giving rise to accusations of fundamentalist Catholicism. She was also accused by her detractors of disregarding modern advances in medicine in favour of saving the souls of the dying and destitute. Censure, however, seems iniquitous in the light of her immense contribution to humanity.

If you're interested in working for the Missionaries of Charity, they can be contacted at Mother House, 54A AJC Bose Rd (☎ 033/249 7115). However, they do occasionally have to turn casual **volunteers** away; it's not always possible to make constructive use of all the would-be helpers who arrive unannounced.

hold of them and whisk you downstairs to confront the dramatic monolithic image of the terrible goddess in the basement, with her huge eyes and bloody tongue.

The courtyard beyond the main congregational hall is used for sacrificing goats, especially during festivals such as Durga Puja and Kali Puja; supposedly, humans were formerly sacrificed here to appease the fertility goddess. To the north of the compound, a *lingam* is worshipped by women praying for children, while shops all around cater for pilgrims. Musical instrument-makers around Kalighat Bridge specialize in tablas and other percussion instruments, while the area in general is infamous for its prostitution, pickpockets and beggars. **Nirmal Hriday**, Mother Teresa's home for the destitute and dying, is nearby.

Kalighat paintings

Early in the nineteenth century, Kalighat was in its heyday, drawing pilgrims, merchants and artisans from all over the country. Among them were the **scroll painters** from elsewhere in Bengal, who developed the distinctive style now known as **Kalighat pats** (paintings). Adapting Western techniques, they used paper and water-based paints instead of tempera, and gradually moved away from religious themes to depict contemporary subjects. By 1850, Kalighat *pats* had taken on a dynamic new direction, satirizing the middle classes in much the same way as today's political cartoons. As a result, their work serves as a witty record of the period, filled with images of everyday life. Kalighat *pats* can now be found in galleries and museums around the world, and in the Indian Museum as well as the Birla Academy here in Calcutta (see opposite).

Ballygunge and the lakes

Two kilometres southeast of St Paul's Cathedral, the **Birla Industrial and Technological Museum** (Tues–Sun 10am–5pm; Rs5) on Gurusaday Road is dedicated to Indian technology. Its large pleasant galleries are set out to attract children in particular, with working models such as miniature mining scenes. A short walk further south on Gariahat Road – also known here as Old Ballygunge Road – is the lavish Hindu temple, the **Birla Mandir** (daily 6–11.30am & 4.30–9pm), built by the same family over 22 years and finally completed in the early 1990s. Best seen in the evenings when lights give the entire structure a dramatic effect, the chandeliered temple, clad with marble and ornate sculpture from Rajasthan, encompasses several styles of classic temple architecture.

Less than 2km further south lies the intersection of **Gariahat Mor** at the heart of a Bengali shopping precinct, especially good for traditional cotton saris and *kurta* pyjamas, that comes alive in the evenings and positively animated during festival periods such Durga Puja. Adjacent **Gariahat Market** also has a distinct Bengali flavour, packed with food vendors. Further west, Rashbehari Avenue leads to another interesting shopping area, **Lake Market**, 1.5km from Gariahat Mor, renowned for its south Indian community and good for recorded music. Past the busy roundabout of **Gol Park**, 400m south of Gariahat Mor, the road branches southwest to the **Rabindra Sarobar** lakes. These man-made lakes, with their tree-lined walkways, are the base of Calcutta's flourishing rowing clubs.

A multistorey building on Southern Avenue houses the **Birla Academy of Art and Culture**, also funded by the industrial Birla family (Tues–Sun 4–8pm; Rs5). Its small auditorium hosts concerts and theatre, while galleries hold exhibitions of contemporary art, plus an eclectic collection of Indian art through the ages covering folk art, bronzes, stone sculptures, terracotta, miniatures, textiles and Kalighat paintings. Among artists of the Bengali Renaissance represented here are the trio of Tagores – Rabindranath, Abanindranath and Gaganendranath. In addition, there are Indian classical dance classes and art classes. The **Lake Kali Bari** alongside has grown in three decades from a small roadside Kali shrine to a major temple.

East Calcutta

The **Eastern Bypass**, a ring road that eventually connects to the VIP road leading to the airport, has helped open up the eastern limits of Calcutta, allowing the city to spread. Sprawling suburbs like Salt Lake have become desirable and, close by, the **Netaji Subhash Bose Stadium** (also known as the Salt Lake Stadium) hosts occasional football tournaments and national events. A kilometre north of the stadium is **Nicco Park** (daily 10am–8pm; Rs25), extremely popular especially at the weekends, where the fee allows entry to ten rides including the water-coaster; most of the rides, however, are tame. Just to the east is Calcutta's latest pleasure complex, **Aquatica** (daily 8am–6pm; from Rs25; families only at weekends), which boasts a massive wave pool complete with beach, plus water rides like the Black Hole.

On the junction of the bypass and JBS Halden Avenue near Tangra, a large and somewhat dusty dinosaur greets visitors to **Science City** (9am–9pm; Rs10) which has faint echoes of Disney's Epcot centre in Florida, combining picnic areas with informative, interactive exhibits on different aspects of science and technology. Close to the airport in a rustic environment, **Arts Acre** (11am–5pm; free), 3km off the VIP Road, Kaikhali Junction, provides workshops for artists in a range of disciplines from ceramics to painting; you can see artists at work or visit the gallery.

Eating and drinking

Although Calcuttans love to **dine out**, traditional Bengali cooking is generally restricted to the home. Authentic Chinese cuisine, available in areas such as **Tangra** (closes early around 10pm) on the road to the airport, is the most popular option, though rich Muslim cooking can be sampled at places like the *Amina*, and Tibetan cafés fill the area around Rabindra Sadan Metro.

The most cosmopolitan strip of the city for **bars** and restaurants is the western end of **Park Street**, where incongruous names such as *Blue Fox* and *Moulin Rouge* date back to the 1960s and 1970s when the street was the centre of a small but thriving pop, jazz and cabaret scene; some restaurants and bars continue to put on live music. Restaurants and cafés around Sudder Street cater for Western travellers staying in the local hotels.

New Market and Sudder Street

Some of the best food and certainly the best chai in this area can be enjoyed from the numerous **street vendors**. You can get spicy Indian breakfasts and strong sweet chai to kickstart the day at a fraction of restaurant prices. The food is fresh and the wooden benches provided make excellent viewpoints. Behind New Market are several **Muslim restaurants**, mostly serving meat dishes, but a couple do excellent vegetarian samosas.

Aaheli, *Peerless Inn*, 12 Chowringhee Rd ☎ 033/243 0222. Excellent Bengali food and good atmosphere.

Abdul Khalique, 32 Marquis St. Cheap Muslim café near the corner of Stuart Lane, serving good *kati* and egg rolls.

Aminia, 6A SN Banerjee Rd, behind New Market & opposite Elite Cinema. Superb and inexpensive Mughlai cooking; the biryanis are excellent but rich.

Aqua Java, Third Millennium New Empire, New Market. Trendy café serving great coffee and snacky meals including pizzas; there is another one at 79 SN Pandit St, Bhowanipur.

Astor, 15 Shakespeare Sarani ☎ 033/242 9950. Bar and several restaurants including the multi-cuisine *Serai* and the *Banyan Tree* serving Bengali food, but the best is *Kebab-e-Que* in the garden, which serves excellent tandoori food.

Blue Sky Café, Sudder Street. On a corner, halfway down the strip. Budget travellers' haunt providing all the old favourites. Clean, well run and a popular meeting place.

Curd Corner, Sudder Street. One-table café offering curd, fresh fruit juice, coffee and street scenes.

JoJo's, 6 Sudder St. Upstairs a/c restaurant packed at lunchtime, with a good flexible menu including travellers' fare.

Kathleens, 12 Mirza Ghalib St. Justifiably popular bakery and patisserie with several other branches.

Khalsa, Madge Lane. Simple but enduringly popular *dhaba* serving basic cheap food.

Lytton, 14 Sudder St. Along with a bar, the hotel has two good restaurants including the *Dynasty* serving Chinese food and *Gaylords* serving Indian and Western.

Nahoum & Sons, F20, New Market. Long-standing family confectioners selling delicious fruitcake, cashew macaroons, *chola* (Jewish braided bread), cheese straws, chicken patties and bagels with cream cheese.

Nizam's, 22–25 Hogg Market. Legendary if somewhat faded place behind New Market to the north, which specializes in the *kati roll*. These spicy *sheesh kebabs*, rolled into a *paratha* of white flour, are now sold throughout the city. Take away or eat in cubicles around the central halls.

Oberoi Grand, 15 Chowringhee Rd ☎ 033/249 2323. Although expensive, *Ban Thai* produces by far the best Thai cooking in town.

Oasis, 2 Madge Lane. Small a/c multi-cuisine restaurant between Sudder Street and New Market. Pricey but popular lunchtime restaurant with a/c and a mixed menu. Closed Thurs.

Park, 17 Park St ☎ 033/249 3121. *Zen* is an upmarket "Oriental" restaurant serving dishes from Thailand, China, Japan and Indonesia; *Saffron* specializes in Indian cuisine.

Princess, 12 Mirza Ghalib St. Around the corner from Sudder Street, this smart but affordable place is good for tandoori, ice cream, teas and cold beer. Closed Thurs.

CALCUTTA AND WEST BENGAL | Calcutta

Waldorf, Park Street, opposite the Post Office. Quality Chinese restaurant which has had a chequered history but is now on the up.

Zurich, 3 Sudder St. Near the *Blue Sky Café* and similarly pitched at travellers; more comfortable and restaurant-like, with good food and a relaxed atmosphere.

Around Park Street

Bar-B-Q, 43 Park St. Good Indian and Chinese food in pleasant surroundings, with a bar downstairs.

Copper Handi, 77/1 Park St. Mid-priced multi-cuisine restaurant best for its *dum-pukht* (slow bake) Lakhnavi (Lucknow) cooking.

Flury's, 18 Park St. Calcutta landmark, on the corner with Middleton Row. A legendary teashop now well past its sell-by-date with rumours of its impending conversion to a *Mcdonald's*. Still good for cakes, patties and Swiss pastries – try the rum balls. They also make their own chocolates.

Jharokha, 42A Park Mansions, Free School Street. Excellent, clean and cheap vegetarian snack bar and sweet counter with a restaurant upstairs good for a range of Indian cooking.

Junior Brothers, 18B Park St. Highly recommended and reasonably priced vegetarian Indian cooking.

Kwality, 17 Park St. Comfortable, plush and airy, one of Park Street's best restaurants, with a range of food as well as ice cream. Bar and snacks only on Thurs.

Tandoor, 55 Park St. As the name suggests, it specializes in tandoori food.

Trinca's, 17B Park St. Multi-cuisine restaurant, strong on Indian food but with a good Chinese annexe. Once a popular nightspot, it's now a bit faded, but still puts on live music with Indian film songs in the evenings and Western covers after 9pm.

South Calcutta

Aqua Java, 79 SN Pandit St, Bhowanipur. Trendy café serving great coffee and snacky meals including pizzas.

China Bowl, Southern Avenue, Gol Park. Dimly lit a/c Chinese restaurant which would otherwise be quite ordinary but for its location near the lakes.

The Dhaba, Ballygunge Phari. Sikh-run café, where the core menu of good Punjabi cooking in the mid-range restaurant upstairs has been extended to cover middle-class tastes.

Hamro Momo, Suburban Hospital Road (lane off Chowringhee, opposite Rabindra Sadan Metro). One of a handful of good Tibetan food cafés on this street.

Kurry Club, 176 Sarat Bose Rd. Close to the lakes and, despite the name, serves a sprinkling of Italian, Mexican as well as Indian food.

Lazeez, Shambhu Nath Pandit Street, Bhowanipur. Comfortable, mid-range, good for both Indian and Western cooking.

Momo Plaza, 2A Suburban Hospital Rd. Another good Tibetan café, specializing in *shyabhaley* – large flat *momos*.

Radhu's, Lake Market. Once renowned snack bar serving fried fish, cutlets and Bengali *alu dam* (steamed potatoes).

Taj Bengal, 24B Belvedere Rd, Alipore ☎033/223 3939. Smart and beautifully presented, the *Chinoiserie* offers some of Calcutta's best Chinese food; *Sonargaon* (Bengali for "Golden Town") serves local delicacies and north Indian food; the *Coffee Shop* is open all hours and also serves meals; and the pool-side barbecue prepares kebabs and griddle-based dishes.

Tibetan Delights, down a lane just off Suburban Hospital Road. Similar to *Momo Plaza* but with a better ambience. Chicken *momos* are popular.

Twinkle Fung Shway, 1/1 Dover Lane, close to Gariahat Mor. Small Thai restaurant with an upbeat ambience; the food spiced for Bengali tastes.

Tangra (China Town)

Kafulok, 47 South Tangra Rd ☎033/329 4130. Versatile and reliably good restaurant with a good all-round menu.

Kim Fa, 47 South Tangra Rd ☎033/329 2895. One of Tangra's best and most-established Chinese restaurants – Thai soup, garlic prawns and chilli king prawns which can be quite potent.

Kim Ling, South Tangra Road. Good family-run restaurant – try the honey chicken, or the chicken with black mushrooms and baby corn.

Elsewhere in the city

Amber, 11 Waterloo St ☏033/248 6520. Quality restaurant serving absolutely superb Mughlai and tandoori cooking. Plush and dimly lit, it covers three floors, and has a bar downstairs.

Anand, 19 Chittaranjan Ave. South Indian snacks as well as veggie-burgers and milkshakes.

Eau Chew, P-32 Mission Row Extension, Ganesh Chandra Avenue ☏033/237 8260. A Chinese family-run restaurant above a petrol station. Excellent food but the best dishes like the *Chimney Soup* are off the menu and best ordered in advance.

Golden Harvest, 11/1 Sarat Bose Rd near Minto Park ☏033/247 0294. Upmarket restaurant serving excellent Chinese and Indian food from lunchtime till late.

Hare Krishna Bakery, ISKCON, 3C Albert Rd. A great little bakery run by the Hare Krishna sect; serves good brown bread.

India Coffee House, College Street. Atmospheric historic café in the heart of the university area where students and intellectuals continue to meet.

Jimmy's Kitchen, AJC Bose Road and Shakespeare Sarani crossing. An old favourite and a justifiably popular Chinese restaurant with specialities such as mandarin fish.

Jyoti Vihar, 3A Ho Chi Minh Sarani. Inexpensive and deservedly popular a/c south Indian café near the US Consulate, which gets packed at lunchtime.

Kewpie's Kitchen, 2 Elgin Lane ☏033/475 9880. A home with a restaurant annexe. A Bengali feast fit for the *jamai babu* (son-in-law) first entering his wife's home – try their *lucci* (puris) and the fish and prawn preparations including *rui kalia*, *ilisher bhapa*, *malai chingri* (prawns in cream) and *daber-chingri* (prawns in a green coconut).

Mainland China, Uniworth House, 3A Gurusaday Rd ☏033/287 2006. Popular new restaurant serving excellent Chinese food in plush surroundings; it's being expanded to include a disco. Book ahead.

Manthan, 3 Waterloo St. Versatile mid-priced restaurant somewhat overshadowed by its illustrious neighbour, *Amber*, down the road.

Royal, near Nakhoda Masjid, Rabindra Sarani. Although it has seen better days, this legendary restaurant still serves up good Muslim cuisine; try the chicken *champ* (Thursdays only) and *rumali roti* or the biryani.

Sabir's, Chandni Chowk. Traditional, tasty but very rich Muslim cooking behind the market. Try their *razala* – an aromatic meat curry.

Scoop, 71 Strand Rd, Man-o-War Jetty. The pleasant riverside location rather than the food recommends this snack bar; renowned for its extravagant ice creams, it also serves pizzas. Crowded in the evenings and at weekends.

Suruchi, 89 Elliot Rd. Run by the All Bengal Women's Union – a charity for rehabilitated prostitutes and their children – and one of the few places you can sample authentic Bengali cooking. Unpretentious atmosphere and very reasonable prices; highly recommended. Look out for *macher jhol* (fish stew). Closed Sat and Sun evenings.

Sweet shops

Milk-based sweets such as the small and dry *sandesh* are the Bengali speciality. Though confections such as the white *rosogulla*, the brown (deep-fried) *pantua* and the distinctive black *kalojam*, all in syrup, are found elsewhere in north India, nowhere are they as good as in Calcutta. Try also *lal doi* – a delicious red steamed yoghurt made with jaggery – or plain white *mishti doi* made with sugar. Sweet shops often serve savoury snacks in the afternoons such as *nimki* (literally salty), deep-fried light pastry strips; *shingara*, a delicate Bengali samosa; and *dhal puri*, paratha-like bread made with lentils.

Bhim Chandra Nag, Surya Sen Street, off College Street. Best of several good sweet shops in the area.

Ganguram, 46C Chowringhee Rd. Legendary sweet shop near Victoria Memorial with branches all over the city; try *mishti doi* (sweet steamed yoghurt) and *sandesh*.

Girish Chandra Dey, 167N Rashbehari Ave. One of several good shops in the Gariahat area; good *sandesh*.

Jadav Chandra Das, 127A Rashbehari Ave. Another popular outlet in Gariahat.

KC Das, 11 Esplanade East and 1/433 Gariahat Rd. One of the city's most famous sweet shops; try their *rosogolla*.

Sen Mahasay, 171H Rashbehari Ave. Next to Gariahat Market, renowned for its *sandesh*.

Bars and nightclubs

The tense all-male atmosphere of Calcutta's **bars** is slowly changing with a young new clientele and a small but lively music scene. For a relaxed atmosphere try the big hotels, some of which also have discos, such as the lively *Anticlock* at the *Hotel Hindusthan* and *Pink Elephant* at the *Grand*. The *Park Hotel* is currently the trendiest spot in town.

Amber, 11 Waterloo St. On the ground floor of a superb restaurant (see opposite), with strong a/c and low lights.

Ashoka, 3B Chowringhee Rd. Adjacent to the Esplanade, and good for a cold beer; *New Cathay* next door is similar.

Bar-B-Q, 43 Park St. Below the restaurant; one of the better bars on the strip.

Chowringhee Bar, *Oberoi Grand*, Chowringhee Road. Plush and well presented but pricey.

Oly Pub 21 Park St. Formerly the *Olympia*, a basic marble-floored downstairs bar, and a more comfortable "family room" upstairs. Renowned for its steaks.

Someplace Else, *Park Hotel*, 17 Park St. A pleasant, dimly lit bar which gets especially jumping in the evenings when live bands belt out familiar covers. Open every day (noon–midnight) and longer on Saturdays (till 2am).

Sunset Bar, *Lytton Hotel*, Sudder Street. Friendly and relaxed bar, popular with travellers.

Tantra, *Park Hotel*, 17 Park St. The liveliest disco in Calcutta, where the action starts at 8.30pm (Tues–Sat) and 5pm (Sun); Rs250 cover for a couple midweek, Rs400 weekends.

Culture and entertainment

Calcutta's lively arts scene is well known for its **music** and Bengali theatre, though the latter is of limited access to most tourists as performances are in Bengali. A handful of galleries hold exhibitions of fine art, and the cultural centres of the various consulates (listed on p.955) also play an important role in the life of the city. Of the many nonreligious festivals each year, the **Ganga Utsav**, held over a few weeks around the end of January at Diamond Harbour, involves music, dance and theatrical events. **Rabindra Sadan** is Calcutta's theatre and concert hall district, with numerous venues including **Nandan** next door on AJC Bose Road, the city's leading art-house cinema. *Calcutta This Fortnight* (see p.929), is a useful source for **listings** or look up *Cal Calling* or local papers.

Music and dance

Calcuttan **music** audiences have a reputation as the most discerning in the country. The main concert season is winter and spring, with the huge week-long **Dover Lane Music Festival**, held under a marquee in south Calcutta around the end of January and early February, attracting many of India's best musicians. Other popular venues for single- and multi-day festivals include Rabindra Sadan on the junction of AJC Bose Road and Cathedral Road and Kala Bhavan on Theatre Road (Shakespeare Sarani). **Sangeet Research Academy**, near Tollygunge Metro Station, one of India's leading north Indian classical music research institutes, offers long-term courses in various music forms and holds free Wednesday-evening concerts. **All India Radio Calcutta** is a good source for Indian classical music, folk music and *Rabindra Sangit*, the songs of Rabindranath Tagore.

Cinemas

Cinemas that show English-language films three or four times each day can be found along Chowringhee near Esplanade and New Market. All are air-conditioned; some, like the Lighthouse on Humayan Place, are fine examples of Art Deco. Names to look for include Elite, SN Banerjee Road; Globe, Lindsay Street; and Chaplin, Chowringhee Place. Nandan (☎033/223 1310), behind Rabindra Sadan on AJC Bose Road, is the city's leading art-house cinema with library, archives and three auditoria. The Jamuna on Marquis Street, and the Globe on Madge Lane are the closest cinemas to Sudder Street.

Galleries

Bengal has a proud and lively tradition of contemporary art, with its few **galleries** showing a high standard of work.

Academy of Fine Arts, Cathedral Road. Showplace for local artists and venue for international exhibitions of contemporary art. Permanent exhibitions include works by Rabindranath Tagore and Jamini Roy as well as sculpture. Tues–Sun 3–8pm; Rs5.

Birla Academy of Art and Culture, Southern Avenue. Ancient and modern art with regular exhibitions of contemporary Indian artists. Tues–Sun 4–8pm; Rs5.

CIMA (Centre of International Modern Art), 2nd Floor, Sunny Towers, 43 Ashutosh Chowdhury Ave.

Prestigious Ballygunge gallery, showing work by contemporary artists.

Gallery Katayun, Jassal House, Auckland Square. Close to Lower Circular Road and the Rawdon Street crossing, with frequent exhibitions of contemporary art.

Oxford Bookshop Gallery, 17 Park St. Recently renovated bookshop with a gallery holding special exhibitions on the mezzanine floor.

Shopping

Unlike Delhi, Calcutta is not geared towards tourism – a fact which is reflected, with one or two exceptions, by its **shops**. However, it does hold many characterful **markets**, including the wide-ranging **New Market** (see p.935), and local institutions such as **Gariahat** in the south (see p.947) and **Barabazaar** to the north (see p.941). Modern **shopping complexes** – good for bookshops, clothes, leather and jewellery – are cropping up all over the city; these include the Emami Shoppers City at Lord Sinha Road, the brand new Metro Shopping Centre at 1 Ho Chi Minh Sarani, good for clothes and leather goods, and the Shree Ram Arcade, opposite the Lighthouse near New Market.

Among typical Bengali handicrafts to look out for are **metal** *dokra* items from the Shantiniketan region northwest of the city, in which objects such as animals and birds are roughly cast by a lost-wax process to give them a rough, wiry look. Long-necked, pointy-eared terracotta horses from Bankura, in all sizes, have become something of a cliché. *Kantha* **fabrics** display delicate line stitching in decorative patterns, while Bengali **leatherwork** features simple patterns dyed in subtle colours.

Books

The month-long **Calcutta Book Fair**, held on the Maidan near Park Street in January and February, is now among the biggest of its kind in the country, and provides a good opportunity to pick up books at a discount.

Classical Books, Middleton Row. Small, friendly and well worth a browse.

Dey Bros, B47 New Market. One of several bookshops in this part of the market selling popular books on India and a selection of novels.

Family Book Shop, 1A Park St. On the Chowringhee end of Park Street, this place is small but crammed full of books.

Landmark, Emami Shoppers City, 3 Lord Sinha Rd. Modern and extensive bookshop in a popular new shopping complex.

Oxford Book & Stationery, 17 Park St. Completely and tastefully revamped with a/c, an art gallery and a music section; a limited collection of fiction, coffee-table books, maps, guides, magazines, stationery and postcards. There's a cybercafé as well as a tea counter – the *Cha Bar* – but both are expensive, Occasional book launches are held here.

Seagull, 31A SP Mukerjee Rd, Bhowanipur, near Indira Cinema. A modern bookshop owned by the publishing house of the same name: good browsing with interesting titles covering a wide range and strong on the arts.

Emporia

Good selections of most handicrafts, including lace, can be found in various **state emporia**, many of which are located in the large **Dakshinapan** shopping complex south of Dhakuria Bridge near Gol Park. Offering fixed (if slightly high) prices, these are the simplest places to start shopping.

Aavishkar, 20K Park St. Popular shop on the corner with Middleton Row, stocking stationery and cards, music, pottery by local artists, and garden-fresh Darjeeling and Assam teas.

Assam, 8 Russell St. As part of Assam House, the emporium sells handicrafts and textiles from Assam including fabrics in *pat* and *moga*, two techniques of silk manufacturing.

Bengal Home Industries, officially 57 Chowringhee Rd but actually just around the corner on AJC Bose Road. Very strong on furnishings and fabrics, plus Bengali handicrafts including terracotta artefacts.

Central Cottage Industries, 7 Chowringhee Rd, Esplanade. Part of the national chain, selling handicrafts from all over India. Along with fabrics, leather, papier-mâché from Kashmir and furnishings, there is a small but interesting collection of silver jewellery, with some tribal bracelets.

Gujari, Dakshinapan complex, near Gol Park. An outstanding selection of Gujarati textiles, including handloom and mirrored cushion covers.

Manipur, 15L Lindsay St, opposite New Market. A selection of souvenirs from Manipur, the northeast hill state bordering Myanmar.

Nagaland, 13 Shakespeare Sarani. A fine assortment of Naga shawls, with red bands and white and blue stripes on black backgrounds. As with Scots tartan, certain patterns denote particular tribes.

Orissa Handicrafts, Dakshinapan complex, near Gol Park. Very strong on silk and *ikat* cloth.

Saroj, 3A Camac Street ☏033/229 1002. For the serious collector, a wonderful if expensive collection of art and antiquities including paintings, prints, maps and furniture.

Shyam Ahuja, 10 Azimganj House, 7 Camac St. Upmarket ethnic and designer fabrics and furnishings and an international name in dhurries.

Fabrics and clothing

Calcutta's dress sense, in general, is conservative, and the choice of ready-made garments is not very exciting. However, a wide range of fabrics is available, and all outlets should be able to point you towards a very good (and very cheap) **tailor**; there are several around Mirza Ghalib Street and Sudder Street. A handful of upmarket boutiques such as Burlingtons and Benetton, both on Mirza Ghalib Street, cater for the city's wealthy. You can still get shoes made to order at one of the many Chinese shoe shops around Chittaranjan Avenue.

Balaram Saha, 14/6 Gariahat Rd. Tangail, Baluchari and Kantha saris from Bengal.

Handloom House, 2 Lindsay St. Near New Market, a government-run, co-operative shop with a wide range of textiles including cotton and raw silks at reasonable fixed prices.

Henry's, New Market. One of Calcutta's better-known Chinese shoe shops.

Indian Silk House, AC Market, 1 Shakespeare Sarani. Lots of printed silks.

Jaggi & Sons, Lindsay Street. One of several good tailors in the city with a long tradition of formal men's tailoring.

Kolhapuri Centre, Gariahat Road, Ballygunge Phari. Dedicated to selling Kolhapuri sandals and shoes – painful at first, but very comfortable if you persist; there's another branch on College Street.

Musical instruments

Calcutta is renowned for its sitar and sarod makers – expect to pay upwards of Rs5000 for a decent instrument. Shops around Sudder Street are strongest on Western instruments but their traditional instruments are invariably of inferior quality and may be beyond tuning; **Rabindra Sarani** (Chitpore Road) has several shops but quality is suspect. Calcutta must produce more tabla players than any other Indian city, with Anindo Chatterjee being the most highly acclaimed at present; tabla-makers can be found at **Kalighat**, next to Kalighat Bridge and at **Keshab Sen Street** off College Street.

Hemen Roy & Sons, Rashbehari Avenue, Triangular Park. Once master instrument-makers to Ali Akbar Khan, the sarod maestro, but they have lost their crown to competition in recent years. They now make sitars and *tanburas* as well.
Hiren Roy & Son, Rashbehari Avenue, Gariahat. The most famous sitar-maker in the country whose clients include Imrat Khan, Vilayat Khan and Ravi Shankar; off-the-shelf instruments available.
Manoj Kumar Sardar & Bros, 8A Lalbazaar St, opposite Lalbazaar Police Station. Ashok Sardar makes very good sitars and sarods to order, with a

small selection of off-the-shelf instruments; he also sells Indian-made guitars.
Mridangam, 114/10A Hazra Road, Kalighat. Best of the three tabla-making businesses a few minutes' walk from the Kali temple.
Naskar & Sons, 14 Ganga Prasad Mukherji Rd, Bhowanipur. Behind the busy market of Jhagu Bazaar off S P Mukherjee Road, Naskar makes good sitars but is especially renowned for his *tanburas*, the drone instruments used to accompany singing.

⑬ Sports

Calcuttans are big sports fans. **Football** matches, especially those between the two leading clubs, Mohan Bagan and East Bengal, and **cricket** test matches draw huge crowds. There are two major stadium complexes, the **Ranji Stadium** at Eden Gardens and the new **Salt Lake Stadium** on the edge of the city.

The **Maidan**, home to the Calcutta Bowling Club and the Ladies Golf Club, is a favourite venue for impromptu cricket and football matches, and the scene in winter and spring of regular race meetings. These are run by the Calcutta Turf Club, and bets can also be placed at their premises on Russell Street. Also in winter, army teams play **polo** at the grounds at the centre of the racecourse. The curious sport of **kabadi**, a fierce form of tag played by two teams on a pitch the size of a badminton court, can also be seen around the Maidan.

The easiest **swimming pool** for visitors to use is Calcutta Swimming Club, 1 Strand Rd (☎033/248 2894) where you can apply for temporary membership. The *Hindusthan Hotel*, 235-1 AJC Bose Rd (☎033/247 2394) allows non-residents to use their pool on a fee-paying daily basis. Across the road from the superbly equipped Tollygunge Club, where with the right connections you might get to use the pool and tennis courts, the elite Royal Calcutta Golf Club is the world's second-oldest golf club, after St Andrews in Scotland.

Listings

Airlines, domestic
Indian Airlines 39 Chittaranjan Ave ☎ 033/236 0810 or 236 0870 (24hr with a tourist counter); also at *Hotel Hindusthan International*, 235/1 AJC

Bose Rd ☎ 033/247 2394 and *Great Eastern Hotel*, 1 Old Court House St ☎ 033/ 248 2311; airport office enquiries ☎ 033/511 9846, flight enquiries: general ☎ 141, recorded ☎ 140, arrival ☎ 142, departure ☏143. Jet Airways 18D Park St ☏033/229 2227 & 229 2237; airport enquiries ☏033/5511 9894; Sahara Indian Airlines 2A Shakespeare Sarani ☏033/282 7686.

Airlines International * *International airlines with flights in and out of Calcutta.* Airline/flight enquiries: ☏033/511 8787 & 511 9721; Aeroflot 58 Chowringhee Rd ☏033/282 3765*; Air Canada Chitrakoot Bldg, 230A AJC Bose Rd ☏033/247 7783; Air France 41 Chowringhee Rd ☏033/240 8646 & 242 6161; Air India 50 Chowringhee Rd ☏033/242 2356*; Air Lanka East Anglia House, 3C Camac St ☏033/229 2092; Alitalia 228 AJC Bose Rd ☏033/280 5695; American Airlines Chitrakoot Bldg, 230 AJC Bose Rd ☏033/280 1335; Austrian Airlines Vasundhara Bldg, 2/7 Sarat Bose Rd ☏033/474 5091; Bangladesh Biman 30C Chowringhee Rd ☏033/229 2843*; British Airways 41 Chowringhee Rd ☏033/288 3451*; Canadian Pacific IGAT, Vasundhara, 2/7 Sarat Bose Rd ☏033/475 0226; Cathay Pacific 1 Middleton St ☏033/240 3211; Continental Airlines Stic Travels, East Anglia House, 3C Camac St ☏033/229 2092; Druk Air Tivoli Court, 1A Ballygunge Circular Rd ☏033/240 2419*; Gulf Air Chitrakoot Bldg, 230A AJC Bose Rd ☏033/247 7783; Japan Airlines 35A Chowringhee Rd ☏033/246 8363; KLM Royal Dutch Airlines 1 Middleton St, Jeevan Deep ☏033/240 3151*; Kuwait Airlines Chitrakoot Bldg, 230 AJC Bose Rd ☏033/247 4697; Lufthansa Airlines 30A/B Chowringhee Rd ☏033/229 9365; Malaysian Airlines Stic Travels, East Anglia House, 3C Camac St ☏033/229 2092; North West Airlines 1 Middleton St, Jeevan Deep ☏033/240 3151; Qantas 58 Chitrakoot Bldg, 230 AJC Bose Rd ☏033/247 0718; Royal Brunei East Anglia House, 3C Camac St ☏033/229 2092*; Royal Jordanian Airlines Vasudhara Building, 2/7 Sarat Bose Rd ☏033/475 1261*; Royal Nepal Airlines 41 Chowringhee Rd ☏033/288 8534*; SAS Landmark Building, 228A AJC Bose Rd ☏033/240 5178; Singapore Airlines 1 Lee Rd ☏033/280 9898; Swissair 46C Chowringhee Rd ☏033/288 4643; Tarom Romanian Landmark Building, 2/7 Sarat Bose Rd ☏033/240 3171*; Thai Airways International 8th floor, Crescent Tower, 229 AJC Bose Rd ☏033/280 1630*.

Ambulance Ambulance services are provided by Dhanwantary Clinic, 1 National Library Ave (☏033/479 2290) and Emergency Doctors' Service, A 165 Lake Gardens (☏033/473 0604).

Banks and currency exchange Calcutta Airport has a 24hr branch of the State Bank of India, as well as Thomas Cook at the international terminal. Major banks, concentrated either in the vicinity of BBD Bagh or scattered around Chowringhee Road, include Bank of America, 8 India Exchange Place; Bank of Tokyo, 2 Brabourne Rd; Banque Nationale de Paris, 4a BBD Bagh East; Citibank, 43 Chowringhee Rd; Hong Kong & Shanghai, 8 Netaji Subhas Rd (24hr service); Standard Chartered, 4 Netaji Subhas Rd; State Bank of India, Middleton Street and Calcutta airport; and Standard Chartered Grindlays, 41 Chowringhee Rd and 19 Netaji Subhas Rd (Rs200 per exchange transaction). The ATM machines at some banks (such as most Standard Chartered and Grindlays as well as HSBC and the Citibank at 43 Chowringhee Rd) take Mastercard and Visa. Other currency exchange bureaus include: Thomas Cook, Chitrakoot Building, 230 AJC Bose Rd (☏033/247 5378) and American Express, 21 Old Court House St near the West Bengal Tourist Office (☏033/248 8464). Private foreign exchange bureaus offer the convenience of longer hours and less bureaucracy despite their slightly poorer rates. There are several along Sudder Street; a convenient one in *Hotel Lindsay* opposite the New Market; Maneek Lal Sen in New Market, RR Sen, 18 Chowringhee Rd; LKP Forex, 41-A Park Mansions, Mirza Ghalib Street (Free School Street) just off Park Street; and American Express at Tata Finance, 75C Park St, near the post office.

Car rental Car Cab, 2 Manook Lane (off Ezra Street) ☏033/235 3535; Car Rent Services, 233–4A AJC Bose Rd ☏033/441285; Durgapur Automobiles, 113 Park St ☏033/294044; Europcar, Vins Overseas India Ltd, 4th Floor, ITC Centre, 4 Russel St ☏033/245 4910; New Lakshmi Travels, 296 Rashbehari Ave ☏033/440 5317; Sona International, 17 Surya Sen St ☏033/241 6186; Wentz International, Airport ☏033/511 8783 & 219 Kamalalaya Centre, 56a Lenin Sarani ☏033/247 9345; 24hr.

Consulates Australia, 19 Netaji Subhas Rd ☏033/220 8346; Bangladesh, 9 Circus Ave ☏033/247 5208; Indonesia, Mukti Chambers, Ground Floor, 4 Clive Row ☏033/210 2653; Nepal, 1 National Library Ave, Alipore ☏033/479 1224; Philippines, Industry House, 19th Floor, 10 Camac Street ☏033/242 4721; Singapore, 7/1 Lord Sinha Rd ☏033/282 4106; Sri Lanka, Nicco House, 2 Hare St ☏033/248 5102; Thailand, 12B Mandeville Gardens ☏033/440 7836; UK, 1 Ho Chi Minh Sarani ☏033/242 5171 & 288 5172; USA, 5/1 Ho Chi Minh Sarani ☏033/282 3611.

Cultural centres Cultural representatives of overseas countries in Calcutta, typically with reading rooms and facilities for performances and film shows, include: the British Council, 5 Shakespeare Sarani ☏033/242 5370 & 282 5944; the Russian

Gorky Sadan, Gorky Terrace, near Minto Park; and the German Max Mueller Bhavan, 8 Pramathesh Barua Sarani ☎ 033/475 9398. Similar facilities can be found at the Ramakrishna Mission Institute of Culture in Gol Park, and USIS, American Centre, 38A Chowringhee Rd ☎ 033/245 1221.

Hospitals Cheap, government-run hospitals (notoriously mismanaged) include Calcutta Hospital &

Moving on from Calcutta

By air

For information about flights from Calcutta Airport, call ☎ 033/511 8787 or 511 9721; otherwise call the individual airlines listed on pp.954-955 to confirm departure and arrival. Remember that return flights must be confirmed at least 72 hours in advance. Besides a good network of domestic flights, Calcutta is served by several short- and long-haul international flights. Major domestic routes from Calcutta are summarized in the Travel Details on p.990. For details on getting to the Andaman Islands from Calcutta, see opposite.

By rail

Information on train connections is available around the clock: ☎ 033/220 3535-3544 or ☎ 131. Making reservations to leave Calcutta by train is easy, with computerized booking offices throughout the city. The best place to book train tickets is at the tourist office on the first floor of the South Eastern Railways office, in the northwest corner of BBD Bagh at 6 Fairlie Place (Mon–Sat 10am–1pm & 1.30–5pm, Sun & hols 10am–2pm; ☎ 033/242 2789 or 220 4025). You'll need to bring proof of encashment to reserve a berth if paying in rupees. Reservations up to sixty days in advance can be made for most trains out of the city.

Other booking offices (same hours) include the South Eastern Railway Booking & Information Centre, Esplanade Mansions, opposite Raj Bhavan (☎ 033/248 9530); Booking Office for Eastern and South Eastern Railways, Alexandra Court, 61 Chowringhee Rd, Rabindra Sadan; Howrah Station, 1st Floor; Computerized Booking Office, 3 Koilaghat St (☎ 033/248 0257); New Koilaghat, 14 Strand Rd (☎ 033/220 3496); Sealdah Station, 1st Floor (☎ 033/350 3496).

Among major trains departing from hectic Howrah Station are the a/c Rajdhani Express #2301 which covers the 1145km to Delhi in under 18hr, stopping at Mughal Serai (change for Varanasi), Allahabad and Kanpur en route; on Thursdays and Sundays as #2305 it travels via Patna as does the Howrah–New Delhi Purva Express #2303 (Mon, Tues, Fri & Sat). The same train, the Howrah–New Delhi Purva Express, as #2381 travels via Gaya instead (Wed, Thurs & Sun) and Varanasi on the way to Delhi. The Kalka Mail #2311 follows a similar route to Old Delhi before proceeding on to Kalka in Himachal Pradesh, while the Doon Express #3009 travels via Gaya, Varanasi and Lucknow to Dehra Dun and Uttaranchal, but is nearly always late. Other trains through Patna include the Amritsar Mail #3005. For Mumbai, 1968km southwest, the best trains are the Gitanjali Express #2860, which takes over 33hr, and the slightly slower early-morning Howrah–Mumbai Mail #8002. Going south, the Puri Express #8007 leaves in the evening from Howrah's new complex and heads via Bhubaneshwar to arrive at Puri early in the morning; the Howrah–Bhubaneshwar Dhauli Express #2821 departs early in the morning and gets to Bhubaneshwar around 1.30pm; the Coromandel Express #2841 departs early afternoon and takes around 28hr to cover the 1663km to Chennai via Bhubaneshwar. By far the best train for Bolpur, the station for Shantiniketan, is the Shantiniketan Express #3015 that leaves Howrah at 9.55am.

Several trains head towards Darjeeling, including the early-morning Kanchenjunga Express #5657 from Sealdah, which pulls into New Jalpaiguri (NJP)

Medical Research Institute, 7–2 Diamond Harbour Rd ☎033/456 2674; Medical College Hospital, 88 College St ☎033/241 4091; SSKM Hospital, 244 AJC Bose Rd ☎033/223 6242. Private medical care, if expensive by comparison, is infinitely superior to the service at government hospitals. Try the Belle Vue Clinic, 9 Dr UN Brahmachari St ☎033/247 2321; Tibetan Medical & Astro Institute,

just too late in the evening to get by road to Darjeeling or Gangtok: it continues to Guwahati. The Kamrup Express #5659 leaves Howrah at 5.35pm arriving at NJP at 7am before proceeding to Guwahati. The Howrah–Guwahati Express #3045 leaves at 10pm, stopping at NJP at 9.25am and arriving at Guwahati at 4pm. Best of the night trains, the Darjeeling Mail #3143, leaves Sealdah at 7.15pm and is scheduled to arrive at NJP at 8.30am, to connect with the Toy Train to Darjeeling. (See p.970 for more details on the Toy Train.).

There is a direct service between Howrah and Raxaul (Bihar) for Nepal. The #3021 Mithila Express departs at 4pm arriving the following day at 9am.

By road

The most famous of the main roads out of the city are the Grand Trunk Road (see p.646), which runs via Varanasi and Delhi all the way to Peshawar in Pakistan, and the Mumbai Trunk Road.

Normally, you have to reckon on an average speed on Bengal's notoriously poor highways of around 30kph, but the buses to Siliguri – handy for Darjeeling and Sikkim – cover the 560km journey overnight, if not in any great comfort (around 8pm; Rs260 and Rs400 a/c). ITDC and Rocket Bus are a couple to try at the Esplanade Bus Stand.

Frequent buses for Bhubaneshwar and Puri in Orissa leave the Babu Ghat Bus Stand, where Orissa Roadways and West Bengal State Transport have booths. Buses from Babu Ghat also head to Namkhana, en route to Bakkhali, and there's an early-morning local service for Basanti and the Sunderbans. Buses leave both Babu Ghat and Esplanade for the beach at Digha.

From Calcutta to Bangladesh

Calcutta is the main gateway to Bangladesh from India; you can reach Bangladesh by air, train or road. The Bangladesh Consulate is at 9 Circus Ave (☎033/247 5208 or 240 5111); visas must be obtained in advance.

There are at least two flights daily from Calcutta to Dhaka and a return ticket costs around $100. Biman flies daily to Calcutta and twice weekly to Chittagong. Indian Airlines have five flights a week to Dhaka and two to Chittagong.

Although there is no direct line from Calcutta into Bangladesh, trains from Sealdah take you as far as Bongaon. From here you can take an auto-rickshaw to Haridaspur, 5km away, and then a rickshaw to Benapal on the border where you can find cheap accommodation. After a refreshing night's sleep take a bus to Dhaka via Jessore which will take around eight hours. Buses run from Esplanade bus stand to Bongaon every hour on the hour from 7am to 4pm (3hr).

From Calcutta to Andaman Islands

Alliance Air (Indian Airlines) fly to Port Blair five times a week but if you want to take a ship (leaving every two weeks) you'll need to book through the Shipping Corporation of India, 13 Strand Rd (☎033/284 2354). Although theoretically you need a permit before buying your ticket, the Foreigners Regional Registration Office at 237 AJC Bose Rd (☎033/247 3300) has informed travellers to get their permits on arrival in Fort Blair; check in advance. There are four classes starting with bunk beds (from around Rs1000) to a/c dorms and cabins; the journey takes three to four days, so bring plenty to read and some food to supplement the dull meals.

9 East Rd, Jadavpur; Metropolitan Laboratory and Nursing Home, 18 Shakespeare Sarani ☎033/432487; Park Nursing Home, 4 Victoria Terrace ☎033/244 3586; and Woodlands Nursing Home, 8/5 Alipore Rd ☎033/456 7075. ARMS (Asia Rescue & Medical Services), 42B Park Mansions, 57 Park Street (Free School Street ☎033/229 2922, ⊛www.armsindia.com), targeted at foreign visitors, offers 24hr medical assistance through a well-equipped surgery but at a price designed for travel insurance claims.

Internet Internet access (from Rs30 an hour) is easily available but the smaller hole-in-the-wall places do not always have fast leased lines or ISDN; in some cases their connections are also suspect. The British Council library, 5 Shakespeare Sarani, is the most reliable and The Amazone, 8 Bowbazar St, with its rainforest theme, is friendly with free tea and coffee. Of the many around Sudder Street, try the *Hotel Palace* on Chowringhee Lane, while *Hotel Maria* is one of the best. Around the corner on Free School Street, near the Kyd Street intersection, try Cyber World. A little further, BQ's, 53D Free School Street, has a lot more elbowroom above a popular new pool hall. The *Junction* is a well-run chain with several cybercafés including ones at 22A Royd St, 20 Park St and Gariahat Phari. Others include *The Emerge*, 59B Park St, and Dishnet, Park Plaza, 71 Park St.

Libraries Asiatic Society Library, 1 Park St; British Council Library, 5 Shakespeare Sarani (Rs100 for a month – borrow books, use the reference section and enjoy cheap internet rates); National Library, 1 Belvedere Rd; Ramakrishna Mission Library, Gol Park; University of Calcutta library, College Square.

Opticians Lawrence & Mayo, 20E Park St ☎033/229 8310 and 11 Government Place East ☎033/248 1818 same-day delivery service); Stephens Opticians, 23 Chowringhee Rd ☎033/291895.

Permits The Foreigners' Registration Office is at 237 AJC Bose Rd (☎033/247 3300). Apply here for permits if you plan to go to the Andaman Islands by boat.

Pharmacies Blue Print, 1 Old Court House St; Dey's Medical Stores, 20A Nelly Sengupta Sarani and 55 Gariahat Rd; King & Co (Homeopath), 29 Shyama Prasad Mukherjee Rd; Singh & Roy, 4–1 Sambhunath Pandit St (daily, 24hr Wed–Sun); Sterling & Co (Homeopath), 91-C Elliot Rd; Welmed, 4–1 Sambhunath Pandit St (daily, 24hr Mon & Tues).

Photography Camera Craft, Park Centre, 1st floor, 24 Park St, for camera repairs; Narains's Photo Cine Centre, 20H Park St; North East Colour Photo, 14 Sudder St near New Market, offers one-hour processing. Madan Street between SN Banerji

Road and Dharamtala is good for all kinds of film, but non-refrigerated.

Police ☎100. The central police station is on Lal Bazaar Street, BBD Bagh (☎033/235 3024).

Postal services Calcutta's imposing GPO, on the west side of BBD Bagh, houses the poste restante and has a philatelic department. The Central Telegraph Exchange is nearby at 8 Red Cross Place, close to Telephone Bhavan, the headquarters for Calcutta Telephones. If you're staying in the Sudder Street area, the New Market Post Office, Mirza Ghalib Street, is much more convenient. Sending parcels is easiest from the large and friendly post office on Park Street, where enterprising individuals will handle the entire process for you for a negotiable fee.

State tourist offices The most useful of the many tourist offices representing other states in Calcutta are those that cover the northeastern states, and issue whichever permits may be necessary (details of permit requirements can be found on p.1043), and that of the Andaman and Nicobar islands. Andaman and Nicobar, 3A Auckland Place ☎033/247 5084; Arunachal Pradesh, 41B Chowringhee Place ☎033/228 6500; Assam, 8 Russell St ☎033/229 5094; Manipur, 26 Rowland Rd ☎033/474 7087; Meghalaya, 9 Russell St ☎033/229 0797; Mizoram, 24 Old Ballygunge Rd ☎033/475 7887 & 475 7034; Nagaland, 11 Shakespeare Sarani ☎033/242 5269 & 282 5247; Orissa, 41 Lenin Sarani ☎033/216 4556; Sikkim, 5/2 Russell St ☎033/246 7516 & 246 8983; Tripura, 1 Pretoria St ☎033/242 5703.

Telephones Overseas phone calls can easily be made from the city's numerous STD/ISD booths and some also have fax facilities; most are now digitalized with LED monitors showing the duration and charge of each call. Inland calls can be made from the same booths but getting a line can take forever, especially after 7pm when rates become cheaper.

Travel agents American Express Travel Related Services, 21 Court House St (☎033/248 9584) and Thomas Cook, Chitrakoot Building, 230 AJC Bose Rd (☎033/247 5378) deal with inbound tours and international flights. Miles 'n' More opposite *Blue Sky Café*, 2/1 Sudder St (☎033/246 4991) and Star Travels, 10 Sudder St (☎033/245 1655) book domestic and international flights. Travel Media, 40H Mirza Ghalib St (☎033/244 8353) is a multi-purpose shop selling international and domestic airline tickets as well as making railway bookings. Warren Travels, 31 Chowringhee Rd (☎033/226 6178) is a well-established service dealing with international and domestic flights, hotel bookings, group tours, and travel documents; so is Sita World Travels, 3B Camac St (☎033/247 5420).

Around Calcutta

The River Hooghly served for centuries as a lifeline for foreign traders; north of Calcutta, its banks are dotted with the remains of tiny European settlements such as **Serampore** and **Chandernagore**. All these sites, together with the Hindu temples of **Dakshineshwar**, **Belur Math** and **Kalna**, and even the great Vaishnavite centres of **Nabadip** and Mayapur further north, can be taken in as day-trips on local trains from Calcutta's Sealdah and Howrah stations. Simple hotels are always available should you want to stay.

Dakshineshwar and Belur Math

At the outermost edge of Calcutta, 20km north of Esplanade on the east bank of the river, the popular temple of **DAKSHINESHWAR** stands in the shadow of Bally Bridge. Built in 1855 by Rani Rashmoni, a wealthy widow, it was a product of the Bengali Renaissance, consecrated at a time when growing numbers of middle-class Hindus were rejecting their faith. As the rani was not a brahmin, she found it hard to employ a priest, but one of those she eventually contracted became renowned as the saint **Ramakrishna** who, despite his simplicity, went on to become a powerful influence on Bengali religious thinking. Set in a vast courtyard and ringed by a band of blood-red paint, the white-washed Kali temple is an ornate variation on the typical Bengali hut design, with a curved roof and second storey capped by nine *chhatris*, each with a bee-hive cupola, in the *nava-rattan* ("nine-jewelled") style. Ramakrishna's former room, beside the main gate, now preserves his personal effects.

Along the riverfront, perched above the *ghats*, twelve identical small temples contain *shivalinga*, while another temple houses images of Radha and Krishna. In the small park outside the complex, visitors feed tribes of rhesus monkeys.

Also in Dakshineshwar, not far from the main temple, **Yogoday Satsanga Math** is the headquarters of the Self-Realization Fellowship, founded in California in 1925 by the author of *Autobiography of a Yogi*, Paramahansa Yogananda.

Across Bally Bridge from Dakshineshwar, 3km south along the west bank of the Hooghly, the massive riverfront temple at **BELUR MATH** was erected by a disciple of Ramakrishna, Swami Vivekananda, in 1938. A symbol of the resurgence in Bengali Hinduism, it incorporates elements from several world religions; the gate is inspired by early Buddhist sculpture, the windows by Islamic architecture, and the ground plan is based on the Christian cross.

Local trains run from Sealdah to Dakshineshwar, and from Howrah to Belur Math.

Serampore

In 1799, the Englishman William Carey set up a press in Danish **SERAMPORE**, 25km north of Calcutta, and began to produce Bengali and Sanskrit bibles. He also pioneered Indian-language dictionaries, and established the Serampore College in 1819, which later became Asia's first modern university. Built on a high bank overlooking the river, the large Neoclassical building houses a small museum dedicated to Carey's life and work. Books in the accompanying library date back to the eighteenth century.

Chandernagore, Hooghly and Bandel

Around 35km north of Howrah, the former French outpost of **CHANDER-NAGORE** still bears traces of its colonial masters, who left in 1949 and officially ceded the town to India in 1952. Crumbling buildings along its grand riverside promenade, formerly the Quai Dupleix and now **the Strand**, include what was once the Hotel de Paris, while the Eglise du Sacré Coeur, set back from the river, houses an image of Joan of Arc. Nearby, the eighteenth-century mansion of the French administrator serves as the **Institut de Chandernagore**, with a library, a French-language school and an interesting museum of documents, antiques, art and sculpture (Mon–Wed & Fri 4–6.30pm, Sun 11am–5pm; free).

The next significant community as you continue north from Chandernagore is the former Armenian township of **Chinsurah**. A kilometre beyond that, **HOOGHLY** was a major East India Company trading post. Packed with Islamic monuments, it was devastated in turn by the Moghuls and the Marathas before being retaken by Robert Clive. Both Chandernagore and Hooghly lie on the busy suburban train network from Howrah.

Eight kilometres out of Chandernagore, the grounds of the **Church of Our Lady of the Bandel**, one of eastern India's oldest churches and still a major centre of Catholic pilgrimage, sweep down to the river. Consecrated by Portuguese Augustinian friars in 1599, it was destroyed by the Moghuls in 1640 but rebuilt in 1660. A cross marks the spot where an image known as Our Lady of Happy Voyages, which had been lost in the river during the siege, miraculously reappeared some years later. There is a large hall devoted to St Augustine, a grotto and a cloistered courtyard.

Trains from both Howrah and Sealdah pass within 2km of the church, stopping at Nainati, where cycle rickshaws are available.

Nabadip and Mayapur

Pilgrims come in their thousands to the pleasant little town of **NABADIP** (or Nawadip), on the west bank of the Hooghly, around 100km north of Howra. Although it was the eleventh-century capital of Bengal under the Sen dynasty, and the home of **Sri Chaitanya** (1486–1533), a Hindu sage, few of the many temples clustered around its Mayapur Ghat are of any great antiquity. The most important are **Gauranga Mahapur** and **Sonar Gauranga**, but the courtyards of virtually all are alive with devotees singing *kirtan* (devotional song). A fifty-kilometre *padakrama*, or foot pilgrimage, links Chaitanya with various sites spread across nine islands. Although a Vaishnava town, Nabadip's most atmospheric temple is the **Kali Bari** at Poramatolla, dedicated to the goddess, tucked into the folds of one of the most impressive banyan trees you are ever likely to see.

Nabadip's twin town **MAYAPUR** lies across the river, a short, often overcrowded ferry ride away, with the conspicuous massive stupa-like temple belonging to ISKCON, the Hare Krishna sect, clearly visible across the water. The labyrinthine temple – a symbol of the contemporary face of Vaishnavism – stands in the middle of an ornamental park and is extremely popular, especially at weekends when the whole place takes on a festive atmosphere, with visitors crowding the walkways ushered along a multi-tiered one-way system. Nearby, the old temple and hermitage of **Gauriya Math** lies almost forgotten in tranquil surroundings. The controversy regarding the antiquity of Mayapur versus Nabadip lingers on but certainly Nabadip has the older feel.

Trains from Howrah run to Nabadip, 2.5km from the main Boral *ghat* (Rs15 by cycle rickshaw), from where ferries (Rs2) leave regularly for Mayapur. Suburban trains from Sealdah serve Krishnagar with buses travelling the 18km to Mayapur; the connecting medium-gauge train to Nabadip Ghat is sporadic but if you do get it you will need to catch a ferry to either Mayapur or

Nabadip from the adjacent Swarupganja Ghat. Mayapur is also serviced by direct CSTC **buses**, departing from Esplanade in Calcutta. ISKCON (3C Albert Rd, Calcutta ☏033/247 8242) runs day-trips starting at 6am and returning at 8.30pm for Rs125 each way.

If you want to **stay** in Nabadip, the *Trimurti* (☏03472/40170; ❸–❹) on Bazaar Road, Poramatolla is friendly and clean with comfortable rooms in the heart of the market. ISKCON's own *Guest House* (☏03472/45711, Calcutta reservations: ☏033/463 4959; ❶–❸) in Mayapur is a massive, well-organized complex with three lodges, including a dorm (Rs10), and can be booked through their centre in Calcutta. Their *prasad* (lunch Rs30, dinner Rs15) served at their *Gada* lodge, is a treat but you will have to join the long orderly lines on the floor. The alternative is the *Janhabi Tirtha Hotel* (❷–❹) nearby, poorly run but with a frontage on the river.

Coastal Bengal

The coast of West Bengal consists of two very distinct sections, on either side of the **River Hooghly**. To the east are the **Sunderbans**, one of the largest estuarine deltas in the world covering an area of 2500 square kilometres. Here you'll find the **Sunderbans Tiger Reserve** and the seaside resort of **Bakkhali**. On the west side of the Hooghly, an unbroken line of beaches goes all the way to **Digha**, the last resort before the coastline of Orissa begins.

Sajnekhali and the Sunderbans Tiger Reserve

The cluster of mangrove-covered islands known as the **Sunderbans**, or "beautiful forest", lie in the Ganges Delta, stretching east from the mouth of the Hooghly to Bangladesh. They are home to the legendary **Royal Bengal tiger**, a ferocious man-eater which has adapted remarkably well to this watery environment, and swims from island to island – covering distances of as much as 40km in one day. Other wildlife includes wild boar, spotted deer, Olive Ridley sea turtles, sharks, dolphins and large estuarine crocodiles. Among the people who find themselves sharing this delicate ecosystem with the mighty cats are honey collectors, woodcutters and fisherfolk. All, regardless of their official religion, worship Banbibi, the goddess of the forest; their occupations are so hazardous that wives take off all their married ornaments when their husbands go out to the forest, becoming widows until they return. As the tigers like to creep up from behind, the honey collectors and woodcutters wear masks at the back of their heads. Meanwhile, the women and children drag nets along the estuary shores to catch prawns – no less hazardous, considering they have to deal with crocodiles and sharks as well as tigers.

The main camp of the **Sunderbans Tiger Reserve**, at **SAJNEKHALI**, is sealed off from the jungle by wire fencing (though tigers still stray into the compound); permits are meticulously checked as you pass through. Guests stay in the *Sajnekhali Tourist Lodge* (☎ 03463/52699; ❸–❺), a large ramshackle forest **lodge** built on stilts; the price includes meals. The Project Tiger complex has a mini zoo, a small museum and a watchtower. Food is left out for the wild animals in the late afternoons, which invariably attracts deer and monkeys but rarely tigers. However, the cats have been known to jump the fence and it's advised not to venture out after dark. Other Sunderbans watchtowers stand at Sudhannyakhali, Haldi and Netidhopani, near the ruins of a four-hundred-year-old temple approached via caged pathways meant to protect you from the very real threat of tiger attack.

All transport within the reserve is by **boat**, which can be rented with the help of the staff at the lodge for around Rs80 an hour or Rs500 for a whole day. You have to take along a Project Tiger guide. The loud diesel motors of the boats tend to scare wildlife away, but when they cut their engines the silence is awesome.

Practicalities

The **best time to visit** is in winter and spring. Getting to the Sunderbans **from Calcutta** is a laborious process. First you need to pick up a special **permit** from the West Bengal Tourist Office in BBD Bagh East, where you can also reserve **accommodation** in Sajnekhali or sign up for a two-day **tour** by bus and launch. The tours run at weekends only, leaving Calcutta at 6.30am Saturday morning and returning at 9pm Sunday, and cost from Rs1200 with food, sleeping on the boat (Rs1500 for sleeping on dry land). Long-weekend trips of two nights (three days) are laid on during holidays. The main disadvantage of joining a group tour is that the general chatter reduces the likelihood of seeing any animals. Alternatively, you could arrange a tour through the Royal Sunderbans Tour Centre at **Canning** (☎ 03463/52699, mobile ☎ 9118 55594) who arrange launches, boats and luxury tours.

Whether you travel by **train** (from Sealdah; the route is outlined in reverse, below) or by **bus**, the journey from Calcutta to the Sunderbans by public transport is complicated. To go by road, start by catching a bus from Babu Ghat to **Basanti** (4 daily; 3hr); aim for the one at 7am. From Basanti, you cross by ferry to **Gosaba**, an hour-long trip through the delta rendered far more pleasant if you sit well away from the belching diesel engines. **Sajnekhali**, which comprises a Government Guest House (closed to the public) and a Forest Department complex but little else, is a six-kilometre cycle rickshaw ride from Gosaba, along a road that passes through some lovely flower-bedecked villages. Finally, to reach the Project Tiger compound itself, and the *Tourist Lodge*, you have to cross the estuary again, on a country boat from the further back and less likely looking of the two *ghats*, or jetties. There isn't usually a lot of traffic around here, so you may well have to wait or appeal to local boatmen.

When you go **back to Calcutta**, allow plenty of time to make all the connections; the last bus leaves Basanti around 4pm. Alternatively, shared autoscooters from Basanti can take you to **Doc Ghat** (30min), to pick up a boat across the river to **Canning**, and then a local train to Sealdah via Ballygunge station. If you're unlucky enough to find that the tide is out when you get to Canning, you're faced with a laborious 500-metre wade through calf-deep squelchy mud; follow the locals by rolling up your trousers and walking slowly so as to avoid splashing. A short walk through the town brings you to the station, where there are taps to wash off the mud. Your reward is the train ride itself, infinitely faster and more comfortable than the bus.

Along the Hooghly to the sea

As the Hooghly bends south on its way to the sea, it becomes larger and larger; when it reaches the Bay of Bengal at **Diamond Harbour**, 50km south of Calcutta, it is very wide indeed. The harbour was used by the East India Company, and a ruined fort is said to date back to Portuguese pirates. The trip down here from the city, by bus or train from Sealdah station, is a popular day's excursion for Calcuttans, though it's also possible to stay the night at the *Sagarika Tourist Lodge* (℡03174/55246; ❷–❺), which has some a/c rooms. Book through the tourist office on BBD Bagh.

Sagardwip, at the mouth of the Hooghly and accessible by ferry or bus from Diamond Harbour, is revered by Hindus as the point where the Ganges meets the sea. The actual confluence is venerated at the **Kapil Muni Temple**, on an island that bears the brunt of the savage Bay of Bengal cyclones and is gradually being submerged. On Makar Sankranti (mid-Jan), during the **Sagar Mela**, hundreds of thousands of pilgrims from all over India descend on the island, cramming into the water to bathe. A selection of ashrams, *dharamshalas* and hotels provide **accommodation**.

The beach resorts

The popular seaside resort of **DIGHA**, 175km southwest of Calcutta and almost halfway to Puri in Orissa, with its immense silted hard beach, was originally conceived as a health sanatorium. Direct buses run from the Esplanade terminus in Calcutta; trains from Howrah station run to Kharagpur from where you can take a bus. Alternatively you can get here on a WB tourist bureau bus.

If anything, the casuarina-lined beach at **BAKKHALI**, 80km south of Diamond Harbour on the east side of the Hooghly, is even harder than the one at Digha. However, it's much less developed and far more attractive, and at high tide gets some impressive surf. From Esplanade, Gol Park or Babu Ghat in Calcutta take an early bus either direct via a ferry crossing to **Fraserganj** or change at Namkhana; you could also take a train to Diamond Harbour and then continue by bus. Buses terminate at Fraserganj, 1km from Bakkhali, where there's a WB Tourism **Tourist Lodge** (❸).

Central Bengal

Central Bengal offers little in the way of major sights to tempt tourists off the Calcutta–Darjeeling route. It is a low-lying rural region where the pace of life is in stark contrast to that of its frenetic capital, Calcutta. **Shantiniketan**, built on the site of Rabindranath Tagore's father's ashram, is a haven of peace, and a must for anyone interested in Bengali music, art and culture. The other highlights of the region include a cluster of exquisite terracotta temples in **Bishnupur**, the ruins of **Gaur**, the region's seventh-century capital, and the palaces of **Murshidabad**, capital of Bengal's last independent dynasty, supplanted by the British.

Bishnupur

The tranquil and attractive backwater of **BISHNUPUR**, around 150km northwest of Calcutta, is a famous centre of Bengali learning, renowned above all for its exquisite **terracotta temples**. It was the capital of the Malla rajas, under whose patronage one of India's greatest schools of **music** developed. Largely beyond the sphere of Muslim influence in Bengal, Bishnupur's long tradition of temple-building had its roots in the basic form of the domestic hut. Translated into temple architecture, built of brick, as stone was rarely available, and faced with finely carved terracotta decoration (often depicting scenes from the *Ramayana*), the temples combine striking simplicity of form with vibrant texture.

Several temples stand within the enclosure of the later Muslim fort which lies a few kilometres from the *Tourist Lodge*. **Raas Mancha**, built around 1600 by Bir Hambir in a unique pyramidal style, is used to display the images of Krishna and Radha during the annual Raas festival. The tenth-century **Mrinmoyee temple** encloses the auspicious *nababriksha*, nine trees growing as one. An early example of the *pancharatna* design, **Shyam Rai** was built in 1643, with five (*panch*) brick spires and extensive decoration. The **Madan Mohan**, with its domed central tower, is one of the largest, dating from the late seventeenth century. Its facade panels depict scenes from the life of Krishna. The remains of the **Pathar Darwaza**, the laterite gate to the old Malla fort, can be seen, along with the remains of the strategically placed *bundhs* or reservoirs that doubled as moats.

Three express **trains** a day connect Bishnupur to Calcutta's Howrah Station; if you miss these, local trains connect to Kharagpur on the busy Howrah–Jamshedpur–Puri line and **buses** run to Tarakeshwar, linked to Howrah on the local EMU railway network. **Accommodation** options in Bishnupur are limited with the pleasant *Tourist Lodge* (❸–❺) set by a large tank, reasonably comfortable and best located for the temples. Alternatives include the basic *Tarama* and *Rangini* lodges (both ❷) in Satyepirtola, in the market.

Shantiniketan and around

A world away from the clamour and grime of Calcutta, **SHANTINIKETAN** is another peaceful haven, 136km northwest of the city. Founded by **Rabindranath Tagore** in 1921 on the site of his father's ashram, both the settlement, and its liberal arts university **Vishwa Bharati**, were designed to promote the best of Bengali culture. Towards the end of the Bengali Renaissance, Tagore's vision and immense talent inspired a whole way of life and art; the university and school still operate under this momentum.

Centred around the **Uttarayan** complex of buildings, designed by Tagore, the university remains in perfect harmony with its surroundings, despite its recent growth as Calcuttans have settled or built holiday homes nearby. Well-known graduates include Indira Gandhi and Satyajit Ray, and departments such as **Kala Bhavan** (art) and **Sangeet Bhavan** (music) still attract students from all over the world. **Chini Bhavan** – the China Department – is the largest of its kind in India; its superb collection of manuscripts was for years locked away due to tensions between India and China. **Kala Bhavan Gallery** (daily except Wed 1–5pm; free) houses twentieth-century Bengali sculpture and painting including works by eminent artists such as Abanendranath and Gaganendranath Tagore and Nandalal Bose. The **Vichitra museum** (daily except Wed 10am–1.30pm

Rabindranath Tagore

The Bengali poet and literary giant, **Rabindranath Tagore** (1861–1941), has inspired generations of artists, poets and musicians. He developed an early interest in theatre, and set his poems to music – now, as *Rabindra Sangeet*, one of the most popular musical traditions in Bengal. Introduced to England and the West by the painter William Rothenstein and the poet W.B. Yeats, Tagore had his collection of poems *Gitanjali* first published in translation in 1912, and the following year was awarded the Nobel Prize for Literature. Though he preferred to write in Bengali, and encouraged authors in other Indian languages, he was also a master of English prose. Not until he was in his seventies did his talent as an artist and painter emerge, developed from scribblings on the borders of his manuscripts. Tagore was an enormous inspiration to many, including his student, the illustrious painter Nandalal Bose, and later the film-maker Satyajit Ray (see p.938) who based several of his films on the works of the master.

& 2–4.30pm, Tues 1.30–4pm; Rs2) captures the spirit of Tagore's life and work with a collection of his paintings, manuscripts and personal effects.

The centre of **Surul**, a village 4km from Shantiniketan (a 20min cycle-rickshaw ride), holds several small but delightful **terracotta temples**. These are scattered near the Rajbari, or "the house of the zamindar" – a sort of manor house with a large courtyard.

The large fair of **Posh Mela** (also known as Posh Utsav), is held between December 22 and 25 to commemorate the initiation of Rabindranath Tagore's father, Maharshi Debendranath Tagore, into the Brahmo Samaj. Posh Mela features sports, dances and music, all with a strong Shantal and folk influence, but is most renowned for the Bauls, Bengal's wandering minstrels who have created their own unique style of folk music.

Across the railway track, roughly 4km east of Shantiniketan, the small Kali temple of **Kankalitala**, unusual in having an oil painting of Kali as its central image, makes a pleasant day out, especially if you arrange your own bicycle. Unfortunately, in recent years, the calm has been shattered by noisy picnickers, especially at weekends, who leave the place strewn with litter. Behind the temple there's a *smashana* – cremation ground – used by Tantrics.

Practicalities

Bolpur, 3km south of Shantiniketan, is the nearest **railway** station, on the main line between Calcutta and Darjeeling, and also served by local trains running between Burddhaman (or Burdwan) and Rampurhat. The best train to get to Bolpur **from Calcutta** is the Shantiniketan Express #3015, which leaves Howrah at 9.55am and terminates at Bolpur at 12.30pm. Sometimes a fancy first-class lounge coach, decorated with terracotta, is attached, but even then it's more fun to travel second-class, as Baul singers occasionally get on and busk. The Rampurhat Express #3017 leaves Howrah at 6.05am and passes through Bolpur at 8.54am; the same train (#3018) is the last returning train departing Bolpur at 6.30pm and arriving in Howrah at 9.45pm. Other day trains to consider are the Kanchenjunga Express (#5657, leaves Sealdah 6.25am) and the Teesta Torsha Express (#3141, leaves Sealdah 1.40pm).

If you're heading on from Shantiniketan **to Darjeeling**, the best of the many express trains is the Darjeeling Mail, which is timetabled to stop at 10.32pm in Bolpur and to arrive in New Jalpaiguri (NJP) at 8.15am the next morning. Alternatively, the Kanchenjunga departs at 9.35am and arrives at NJP at

6.10pm, which means a night's stay in the Siliguri area before moving on to Darjeeling. **Reservation quotas** from Bolpur are tiny, so book early; there's another reservations counter near the post office in Shantiniketan.

Local **buses** from Bolpur use either the Bolpur bus stand, next to the station, or the Shantiniketan bus stand at Jamboni, 2km west towards Surul. Cycle rickshaws are the chief means of transport in the area. The best way to experience Shantiniketan is to cycle – ask at your hotel or at one of the cycle shops along the main road.

Accommodation and eating

The Shantiniketan area holds a reasonable amount of **accommodation**, with the university's *International Guest Houses* ideal if you're planning a medium or long-term stay. The *Tourist Lodge*'s restaurant is popular for its simple wholesome cooking while the rooftop *Paschimi*, run by a Indo-British couple, is especially good in the evenings, serving Mediterranean food including pasta.

Bolpur Lodge, Bolpur ☎03463/52662. Although it may look like a hostel, the large lodge set off the main road has a pleasant leafy courtyard, a/c rooms and a restaurant. ❷–❺

Bonpulak, Shyambati ☎03463/53193. Three wonderful airy rooms in a pleasant family home with a small colourful garden and meals by prior arrangement. ❸–❹

Camellia, Prantik, near the railway station ☎03463/55044. A concrete intrusion in a disappearing rustic landscape near Prantik station. Comfortable with a good restaurant and swimming pool open to nonresidents (from Rs75). ❼–❾

Chhuti, 241 Charu Palli, Jamboni ☎03463/52692. Comfortable and well-laid-out complex, with thatched cottages, some a/c, and a good restaurant. The most luxurious option around Shantiniketan; credit cards accepted. ❺–❼

International Guest House, Shantiniketan. The university runs two of these large guesthouses –

the *Old* and the *New*, although the old one looks newer. Large simple rooms and a cheap restaurant. ❶–❷

Khelaghar, 135 Purva Palli ☎03463/52544. A quiet leafy garden with comfortable cottages that need to be booked ahead. ❻

Khushi Lodge, Ratan Palli ☎03463/53876. Popular and welcoming guesthouse with a Japanese connection but small rooms; the rooftop restaurant – *Paschimi* – serves Western food and is great in the evenings. ❷–❹

Surabhi Lodge, Shantiniketan Road ☎03463/52636. One of a handful of similar small lodges along this stretch of the main road from Bolpur. Plain rooms and poor location. For more comfort try *Sathi* around the corner. ❷–❸

Tourist Lodge, Bolpur Tourist Lodge Road ☎03463/52699. Large and rather institutional, but otherwise not too bad. A/c rooms, cottages, dorm (Rs80), a garden and a decent restaurant. ❸–❼

Tarapith

One of the most important centres of Tantric Hinduism, **TARAPITH**, lies 8km from **Rampurhat** railway station. The temple and cremation ground, in a grove beside the river, are popular with Tantric *sadhus*, and it is not uncommon to witness rituals involving skulls and cremation ashes. The temple itself is a simple building in the *bankura* style dedicated to *shakti* as the mysterious and feared goddess Tara who appears here with a silver face and large eyes; shrines litter the area, and the grove is populated by vociferous monkeys. Tarapith has a handful of hotels like *Sathi* (☎03461/53287; ❸–❻), simple guesthouses and a pleasant *dharamshala* near the temple. The Rampurhat Express, which departs from Howrah at 6am arrives at 10.20am, while the 5.10pm train from Rampurhat gets back to Shantiniketan at 6.23pm. Several Expresses also stop here but usually at inconvenient hours.

Kendubilwa

The town of **KENDUBILWA**, also known as **Kenduli**, on the bank of a wide shallow river 42km from Shantiniketan, is the birthplace of **Jaidev**, the author of *Gita Govinda*, and the spiritual home of the Bauls. Its small terracotta temple is engulfed each year in mid-January when the **Jaidev Mela** attracts streams of pilgrims, as well as an interesting collection of *yogis* and *sadhus* who gather amongst the folds of the tall banyan trees to hear the Bauls perform through the night. Over the years the *mela* has grown to include a wide range of stalls and even a funfair. During the *mela*, special buses leave regularly from Bolpur (2hr).

Bakreswar

A quiet but important temple town on the edge of the Chotanagpur plateau, 58km northwest of Shantiniketan, **BAKRESWAR** is considered, along with Kalighat in Calcutta (see p.945), to be one of the 51 Sati *pithas*. The temple of **Mahishamardini** commemorates the spot where a part of Shakti's forehead fell, cut by Vishnu as the distraught and destructive Shiva carried her dead body. Shiva himself is venerated by the **Bakranath** temple. Nearby **hot springs** such as Agnikund, or "fire spring", have a high sulphur content, reach temperatures of 67°C, and are considered to have great therapeutic value. **Buses** for Bakreswar depart from the Jamboni bus stand to the west of Shantiniketan; change at Suri.

Murshidabad

Set in the brilliant green landscape of rural Bengal, historic **MURSHID-ABAD** lies close to the bustling commercial town of **Behrampur**, 200km north of Calcutta. Several eighteenth-century monuments along the banks of the Hooghly stand as reminders of its days as the last independent capital of Bengal. Established early in the eighteenth century by the **Nawab Murshid Quli Khan**, Murshidabad was soon eclipsed when the forces of Siraj-ud-Daula were defeated by Robert Clive at the Battle of Plassey in 1757, as a result of which the British came to dominate Bengal from the new city of Calcutta. Clive described Murshidabad as equal to London, with several palaces and seven hundred mosques; now it's not even a city and most of its past glory lies in ruins, though it is still renowned for cottage industries, especially silk weaving.

Murshidabad's intriguing mixture of cultures is reflected in its architectural styles, which range from the Italianate **Hazarduari** (daily except Fri 10am–4.30pm; $5 [Rs5]) the nawab's palace, designed by General Duncan Macleod of the Bengal Engineers, to the **Katra Mosque**, built by Murshid Quli Khan in the style of the mosque at Mecca. The palace, with its mirrored banqueting hall, circular *durbar* room, armoury and library of fine manuscripts is now a museum – some of the paintings are in dire need of restoration but the portrait collection is excellent. Its gardens and riverside promenade are a popular recreational area.

A large oxbow lake, the **Moti Jheel** or **Pearl Lake**, guards the desolate ruins of Begum Ghaseti's palace where Siraj-ud-Daula reigned before his defeat, and which was subsequently occupied for a while by Clive. To the south, across the river, **Khushbagh**, the **Garden of Delight**, holds the tombs of many of the nawabs, including Alivardi Khan and Siraj-ud-Daula.

Accommodation in Murshidabad is limited, with the friendly and welcoming *Hotel Manjusha* near Hazardwari (☎03482/70321; ④–⑤) offering rooms with balconies and a colourful flower garden on the river. **Behrampur**, easily accessible by auto-rickshaw (Rs10 shared) or bus 12km away, lies on the busy north–south highway and has far more amenities, including the *Tourist Lodge* (☎03482/50439; ③–⑤) which has some a/c rooms; the *Behrampore Lodge*,

30/31 RN Tagore Rd (☎03482/50500; ❷–❻) is welcoming and serves meals. There's another cheaper branch at 5 RN Tagore Rd (❷–❸). The *Samrat* (☎03482/50439; ❷–❼), on the main highway some 3km south of the centre at Panchanantatala is handy for the Murshidabad turnoff, with a wide range of accommodation from dorms (Rs50) to carpeted a/c rooms. The most luxurious around, it also has a garden, a good restaurant and an a/c restaurant-bar.

A handful of **trains** run here from Calcutta (Sealdah station; 4–6hr), including the Bhagirathi Express and the Lalgola Passenger; the latter also stops at Murshidabad. **Buses** (5hr) depart from Behrampur station for Calcutta's Esplanade – ITDC leaves at 10pm and the better ABC Travels leaves at 11pm (Rs70); purchase tickets before 5pm.

Malda and around

The large, unattractive commercial town of **MALDA**, 340km north of Calcutta, straddles the highway to the north and is renowned for its local mango harvest. A natural port, at the confluence of two rivers, it was once a prosperous trading post for silk and cotton; in the seventeenth and eighteenth centuries it housed Dutch, French and English factories. Little of interest has survived from that period, but Malda makes a good base to explore the historic sites of **Gaur** and **Pandua**, both earlier capitals of Bengal. which can be reached by either bus or tonga.

Malda is on the main line between Calcutta and Darjeeling, served by **trains** such as the Gaur Express, Kanchenjunga Express and the Darjeeling Mail. **Accommodation** includes *Manohar*, a good budget option on Station Road (❷–❸) with small rooms, attached baths and a restaurant; while *Pratapaditya* (☎03512/68104; ❸–❼) a short distance down Station Road, offers a lot more luxury with some a/c rooms and a good restaurant. *Purbanchal* (☎03512/66183; ❸–❻) at 420 Mor, New Banshbari, an old mid-range favourite, has a good restaurant, bar and travel service and is often full. The *Malda Tourist Lodge*, Rathbari, English Bazaar (☎03512/66183; ❷–❻), doubles as the local **tourist office** and is currently being expanded. **Taxis** for both Gaur and Pandua charge Rs600 for the day.

Gaur

Spread across a landscape of lush paddy fields, 16km south of Malda on the border with Bangladesh, **GAUR** was the seventh-century capital of King Sasanka, and then successively belonged to the Buddhist Pals and the Hindu Senas. The latter, the last Hindu kings of Bengal, were violently displaced by the Muslims at the start of the thirteenth century. The city was eventually sacked in 1537 by Sher Shah Suri, and its remaining inhabitants were wiped out by plague in 1575.

Deserted and overgrown, Gaur today is hard to relate to the city of one million inhabitants described by the Portuguese historian, Faria-y-Souza. Nothing remains of the pre-Muslim period apart from large tanks, such as the **Sagar Dighi**, built in 1126 and almost 1500m long, and the embankments of the old city, which extend for several kilometres through the verdant rural landscape. **Dakhil Darwaza**, an impressive gateway built in 1425 of small red bricks, leads through the embankments surrounding the **Fort**, in the southeast corner of which a colossal twenty-metre-high wall encloses the ruins of the old palace. Nearby are the **Qadam Rasul Mosque**, built in 1531 to contain the Prophet's footprint in stone, and the seventeenth-century tomb of Fateh Khan, one of Aurangzeb's generals, in Bengali hut

⑬

style. Other remains of interest include the elegant **Tantipara Mosque**, with its finely detailed terracotta decoration, the Lattan or **Painted Mosque**, where traces remain visible of the enamelled bricks that gave it its name, and the massive **Bara Sona Masjid**, "Great Golden Mosque", northeast of the Fort.

Pandua

The splendid **Adina Masjid** at **PANDUA**, 18km north of Malda, built by Sikander Shah around 1370, was in its day the largest mosque in the subcontinent. It now lies in ruins but these still betray the origin of much of the building materials – carved basalt masonry from earlier Hindu temples was used to support 88 brick-built arches and 378 identical small domes, the design following that of the great eighth-century mosque of Damascus.

Other monuments include the **Eklakhi mausoleum** – one of the first square brick tombs in Bengal with a carved Ganesh on the doorway; and **Qutb Shahi Masjid**, or the Golden Mosque, built to honour saint Nur Qutbul-Alam whose ruined shrine is nearby together with that of Saint Hazrat Shah Jalal Tabrizi.

North Bengal

NORTH BENGAL, where the Himalayas soar from the flat alluvial plains towards Nepal, Sikkim and Bhutan, holds some magnificent mountain panoramas, and also some of India's best **hill stations**. Most visitors pass as quickly as possible through **Siliguri** en route to **Darjeeling**, **Kalimpong** and the small state of Sikkim. For anyone with a bit of time on their hands, the **Jaldapara Wildlife Sanctuary**, home to the one-horned rhino, bison and wild boar, east of Siliguri near the Bhutanese border, makes a worthwhile detour.

Besides the occasional strike, few travellers will notice, but today the region is wracked by **political turmoil**, with the Gurkhaland movement, centred around Darjeeling, and the Kamtapuri Liberation Front, which purports to represent most of North Bengal south to Malda, calling for a complete break from the state of West Bengal. To compound matters, Bodo and ULFA insurgents have rendered unsafe the borders with Bangladesh and the forested frontier with Bhutan to the far northeast.

Siliguri and New Jalpaiguri

A major commercial hub and Bengal's second city, the bustling and dusty town of **SILIGURI** has a thriving tea-auction centre and serves as the gateway to Darjeeling, Kalimpong, Sikkim and Bhutan. Together with its main railway station, **NEW JALPAIGURI** – commonly referred to as NJP – and the airport at **Bagdogra**, it forms an unavoidable link between the rail and air connections to Calcutta and Delhi, and the roads up into the mountains. The border with Nepal at **Kakarbitta** nearby is open to tourists, though the bus journey from there to Kathmandu is an arduous one.

Most tourists pass straight through Siliguri, but travel connections may mean that you have to stop overnight. There is little of interest to see apart from a small Tibetan enclave 1km or so beyond *Hotel Cindrella* on Sevoke Road, where you'll find **Tashi Gomang Stupa**, established by His Eminence Kalu Rinpoche (5am–noon & 1–5pm). At the end of a small lane next to the *Sona Hotel*, delicious fragrances rise as Tibetan medicine-makers pound fresh herbs and spices; top quality Tibetan healing and meditation incense is available for sale here. There is also a Tibetan Astro Institute nearby.

Practicalities

Bagdogra airport, 12km west of Siliguri and served by flights from Delhi, Calcutta and Guwahati, is connected not only with Siliguri itself, but also directly to Darjeeling as well as to Gangtok in Sikkim by **helicopter**. There

---

The Darjeeling Himalayan railway: the toy train

Completed in 1881, the small-gauge (2ft or 610mm) Darjeeling Himalayan Railway was designed as an extension of the North Bengal State Railway, climbing from New Jalpaiguri, via Siliguri, for a tortuous 88km up to Darjeeling. Given World Heritage status by UNESCO in 1999, the Toy Train – as it is affectionately called – follows the Hill Cart Road, which was designed so that even bullock carts could travel up its gradual incline from the plains, crossing it at regular intervals and even sharing it with traffic.

No longer an essential mode of transport, the Toy Train, pulled by endearing, ancient blue steam engines, some over 75 years old, had, in recent years, fallen on hard times. Efforts to improve the service by introducing diesel engines to share the line with the old steam locomotives, have helped to quicken timetables but have taken away some of the charm. Some of the new engines proved too powerful and the result was several derailments but, at leisurely speeds, none were serious.

Weather permitting, first-class coaches with large viewing windows provide magnificent views as the six-hour journey from the plains progresses and the scenery gradually unfolds; second class can be fun but crowded. At the high pass at Jorebungalow near Ghoom (2438m), 7km short of Darjeeling, the dramatic panorama of the Kanchenjunga Range is suddenly revealed. Just beyond Ghoom, the train does a complete circle at the Batasia Loop – the most dramatic of the three loops encountered along the way; another method used to gain rapid height is the reversing stations where the track follows a "Z" shape.

A word of warning though: some travellers find this claustrophobic and painfully slow ride a real test of endurance, especially after an overnight journey from Calcutta to Siliguri. An alternative, more relaxing, way to experience the Toy Train is to take a short ride from Darjeeling to Ghoom just 7km down the track where you can visit a few monasteries and either walk, hitch, bus or even take the train back to Darjeeling.

For more information on the Toy Train, contact the Darjeeling Himalayan Railway Society c/o Marilyn Metz, 80 Ridge Rd, London N8 9NR (@ www.dhrs.org; @ m.metz@pro-net.co.uk), or contact the *Windamere Hotel* (see p.977) in Darjeeling.

have been difficulties with the runway at Bagdogra which means flights get suspended for weeks at a time – check in advance.

Most **buses** arriving at Siliguri terminate in or around the **Tenzing Norgay Bus Terminal** on Tenzing Norgay Road – Siliguri's central artery.

Siliguri does have its own railway station, used by the Toy Train, but the **New Jalpaiguri** (NJP) station, 4km east, is the main railway junction in the region with trains to and from Calcutta, Delhi and Assam. Auto- and cycle rickshaws ply the route battling through the often-gridlocked market; taxis travel along the circuitous route on a twelve-kilometre detour.

The Government of West Bengal's **tourist office** (Mon–Fri 10.30am–4pm, Sat 10.30am–noon; ☏0353/431974), opposite *Hotel Vinayak* on Hill Cart Road, provides information and organizes weekend excursions to Jaldapara Wildlife Sanctuary. They also have branch offices at Jalpaiguri station (daily 7–10am & 4–7pm; ☏0353/421118) and at the airport (☏0353/450714). Opposite the bus stand, the **Sikkim Tourist Information Centre** (☏0353/432646), SNT Colony, in the same compound as the Sikkim Nationalized Transport stand, provides information and **Sikkim permits**. Facilities for **changing money** are erratic. The State Bank of India, Mangaldeep Building, Hill Cart Road (☏0353/431361) only accepts American Express travellers' cheques in US dollars; some of the upmarket hotels also have change facilities and so does *Mainak Tourist Lodge*. There are **post offices** on Bidhan Road, close to the Central **Railway Booking Office**, near Kanchenjunga Stadium, and near the Tenzing Norgay Bus Terminal.

Accommodation and eating

The best restaurants are located in hotels and Hill Cart Road has the greatest choice.

Apsara, 18 Patel Rd, opposite Tenzing Norgay Bus Terminal ☏0353/524252. Down a lane parallel to the main road, this is a friendly and helpful Tibetan-run hotel close to all amenities. ❸–❹

Chancellor, Sevoke Mor, corner of Sevoke and Hill Cart roads ☏0353/432360. Welcoming and central Tibetan-run hotel with a quiet block at the back; good Tibetan, Chinese and Indian food is served in the restaurant. ❷–❹

Cindrella, Sevoke Road, 3rd mile ☏0353/547136, ⊛www.cindrellahotels.com. Five kilometres from the bus station. Large and comfortable with spacious grounds, a sauna, Jacuzzi and swimming pool, travel services, a restaurant and internet access. ❽–❾

Holydon, NJP Station Road ☏0353/423558. Friendly and cheap hotel, convenient for the main railway station; one of a handful of similar places along this road. ❸

Manila, Hill Cart Road, opposite Tenzing Norgay Bus Terminal ☏0353/518813. Part of a new breed of comfortable mid-range hotels coming up around Siliguri, with a good tandoori restaurant and a bar. ❺–❻

Sinclairs, Pradhan Nagar ☏0353/522674, ⊛www.sinclairshotels.com. Upmarket hotel which has bounced back after a bad patch, with comfortable rooms, money exchange, swimming pool and a reasonable restaurant. ❼–❽

Sona, Sevoke Road, Salugara ☏0353/590269. Pleasant lodge in the Tibetan area with en-suite rooms. The nearby *Dorje* is a bit more basic. ❸

Tourist Service Agency (TSA Guest House, Pradhan Nagar ☏0353/430872. On a quiet street opposite the bus terminal, this is a friendly, helpful and good-value option; they also have a travel agency down the road. ❸–❻

Vinayak, Hill Cart Road ☏0353/431130. A good mid-range hotel with a choice of rooms including some a/c. The restaurant downstairs serves good Indian food. ❹–❼

WBTD Mainak Tourist Lodge, Pradhan Nagar ☏0353/430986. Set in large grounds with friendly, welcoming staff, comfortable rooms, a restaurant and bar and internet. Car rental available. ❺–❼

Both Indian Airlines and Jet Airways fly to Calcutta, Delhi and Guwahati. The Indian Airlines' office is in the *Hotel Mainak* Complex, Hill Cart Road (℡0353/431509); Jet Airways is in the *Hotel Vinayak*, Hill Cart Road (℡0353/431495). At the time of going to press, flights to and from Bagdogra had been suspended due to runway repairs.

All major trains, most terminating or starting at Guwahati, use NJP station, not Siliguri. Reservations can be made at NJP Railway Station or the Central Railway Booking Office (daily 8am–4pm), Bidhan Road, near Kanchenjunga Stadium in Siliguri. The main trains to Calcutta include the Darjeeling Mail #3143/3144, the Kanchenjunga Express #5657/5658 and the Kanchenkanya Express #3149/3150 (3 weekly), all of which terminate at Sealdah; as well as the Kamrup Express #5659/5660 which terminates at Howrah. Trains to Delhi include the efficient Rajdhani Express #2423/2424 (22hr), the North East Express #5651/5652 (29hr) and the Brahmaputra Mail #4055/4056 (30hr), all of which pass through Patna with con-nections for Gaya and Bodhgaya. The Mahananda Link Express #4083/4084 stops at Mughal Sarai, convenient for Varanasi. The Trivandrum Express #5627/5628 runs to Guwahati (13hr) and Trivandrum (52hr), and the Dadar Express #5647/5648 to Guwahati (13hr) and Mumbai (52hr).

The easiest way to get to Darjeeling is by shared Jeep. Jeeps depart from in front of the station as soon as they are full (11 people), take 3–5 hours and cost Rs50 one way. Other options include the Toy Train (leaving NJP at 9am, arriving Darjeeling 3.30pm), or a bus from Siliguri's Tenzing Norgay Bus Terminal. Regular buses and shared Jeeps also run to Kalimpong and to Gangtok.

Overnight buses to Calcutta (12hr), such as the Rocket Bus and ITDC, are much cheaper than the train (Rs260 non-a/c, Rs400 a/c), and have the advantage of depositing you in Esplanade, near the central Sudder Street area. Whatever you're promised, be it a "luxury bus" or a "two by two", be prepared for a severe rattling. North Bengal State Transport Corporation buses run to Calcutta, Patna and Guwahati.

If you're heading for Kathmandu in Nepal, you can share a taxi (Rs35), arrange an auto-rickshaw (Rs180) or taxi (Rs250) or catch a bus to the border at Kakarbitta and make your own arrangements there. Pick up a Nepalese visa for $25 in cash on the Indian side at Paniktanki from where cycle rickshaws are available to cross the border. The advantage of a pause in Kakarbitta is that it gives you a greater choice of onward buses; overnight buses leave around 4pm each day, arriving in Kathmandu around 9am the next morning. You could also book a bus ticket all the way through to Kathmandu at various agencies in Siliguri including the Tourist Service Agency (TSA), in the lane opposite the bus terminal, Pradhan Nagar (℡0353/531219; ℮tsaslg@dte.vsnl.net.in). For a lot more luxury take one of several flights from Bhadrapur in Nepal to Kathmandu (US$109); taxis charge around Rs375 for the 45-minute journey from Kakarbitta to Bhadrapur and airport tax is Rs110. Bookings can be made through agencies like the TSA. The helpful TSA also books helicopter flights to Gangtok (Rs1500) which leave from Bagdogra, connecting with incoming Indian Airlines and Jet Airways flights.

Sikkim Nationalized Transport, Pradhan Nagar, Tenzing Norgay Road and Booking Office (daily 10am–4pm; ℡0353/421496), runs a good service to Gangtok and various other points in Sikkim (departing 7am–2.30pm). Sikkim per-mits (see p.975), can be obtained at SNT, and shared Jeeps are also available from here.

Buses also run to Phuntsoling, on the border of Bhutan, just 160km away, and to Thimpu the capital, 176km further on, as well as to Guwahati in Assam, although the train is far more comfortable.

Jaldapara Wildlife Sanctuary

Apart from Darjeeling and the hills, most of North Bengal is well off the beaten track; few travellers venture off the Darjeeling–Sikkim–Nepal road. Probably the best reason to do so is to visit the small **Jaldapara Wildlife Sanctuary**, roughly 124km east of Siliguri. The sanctuary was established in 1943 to help protect wildlife against the encroachment of tea cultivation. Consisting of tracts of tall elephant grass on the banks of the River Torsa, and set against the backdrop of forested foothills, it now shelters around fifty highly endangered greater **one-horned rhinoceroses**, wild elephants, sambar and hog deer.

Jaldapara is open from November to the end of April, with March being the best month to view animals, as they graze on new shoots. Much the best way to explore it is on elephant back (Rs140 [Rs70]). The easiest way to get here is on a package **tour** organized by the WB Tourist Office in Siliguri (☎0353/431974), bookable in Siliguri, Darjeeling or Calcutta, which leaves Siliguri at noon on Saturday and returns early evening on Sunday. However, it is also possible to travel by train or bus from Siliguri to the town of **Madarihat**, 7km from the sanctuary, from where taxis run to **Hollong** in the heart of the forest for around Rs150. **Accommodation** and **food** are available at the *Jaldapara Tourist Lodge* at Madarihat (❻) or at the *Hollong Forest Lodge* (❺–❻) where foreigners pay more – both of which must be booked through the WB tourist offices in Siliguri, Darjeeling or Calcutta.

Darjeeling

Part Victorian holiday resort, part major tea-growing centre, **DARJEELING** (from *Dorje Ling*, "the place of the thunderbolt") straddles a ridge 2200m up in the Himalayas and almost 600km north of Calcutta. Fifty years after the British departed, the town remains as popular as ever with holiday-makers from the plains, and promenades such as the Mall and the Chowrasta still burst with life. Although the infrastructure created under the Raj is now struggling to cope with the ever-expanding population and Darjeeling is plagued by acute shortages of water and electricity, it's a fascinating and cosmopolitan place. The greatest appeal for visitors has to be its stupendous mountain vistas – with Kanchenjunga, the third-highest mountain in the world, dominating the northern horizon. The town also has a considerable Tibetan presence and like Dharamsala in Himachal Pradesh offers great opportunities to study Tibetan culture. The best seasons to visit – and to attempt the magnificent trek to Sandakphu to see Everest – are after the monsoons and before winter (late Sept to late Nov), and spring (mid-Feb to May).

Until the nineteenth century, Darjeeling belonged to **Sikkim**. However, in 1817, after a disastrous war with Nepal, Sikkim was forced to concede the right to use the site as a health sanatorium to the **British**, who had helped to broker a peace settlement. Darjeeling soon became the most popular of all hill resorts, especially after the Hill Cart Road was built in 1839 to link it with Siliguri. **Tea** arrived a few years later, and with it an influx of Nepalese labourers, and the virtual disappearance of the forests that previously carpeted the hillsides. The town's growing economic significance led Britain to force a treaty

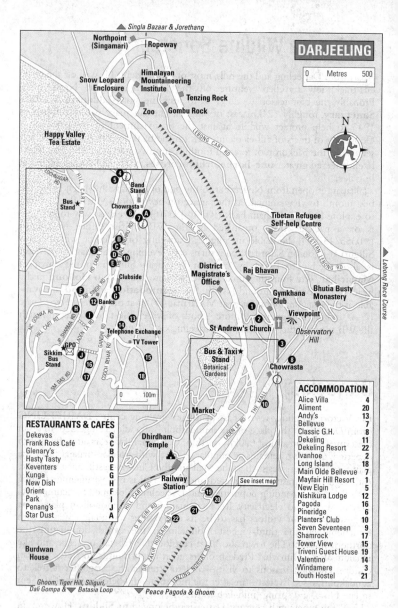

▲ Singla Bazaar & Jorethang

DARJEELING

0 — Metres — 500

Northpoint
(Singamari) | Ropeway

Snow Leopard
Enclosure

Himalayan
Mountaineering
Institute

Tenzing Rock

Zoo | Gombu Rock

Happy Valley
Tea Estate

LEBONG CART RD

N

Band
Stand

Chowrasta

Bus
Stand

HILL CART RD

COCHNAGAR RD

Tibetan Refugee
Self-help Centre

HILL CART RD

WESTERN LEBONG RD

District
Magistrate's
Office

Raj Bhavan

Gymkhana
Club

Bhutia Busty
Monastery

Clubside

Banks

Telephone Exchange

TV Tower

Viewpoint

St Andrew's Church

Observatory
Hill

GPO

Sikkim
Bus
Stand

Bus & Taxi ★
Stand

Botanical
Gardens

Chowrasta

0 — 100m

HILL CART RD

NR GOENKA RD

DR SHARMA RD

GANDHI RD

LADEN LA RD

COOCH BEHAR RD

SM DAS RD

Market

THE MALL

LADEN LA RD

See inset map

RESTAURANTS & CAFÉS

Dekevas	G
Frank Ross Café	C
Glenary's	B
Hasty Tasty	D
Keventers	E
Kunga	G
New Dish	H
Orient	F
Park	I
Penang's	J
Star Dust	A

Dhirdham
Temple

Railway
Station

D B GIRI RD

HILL CART RD

DR ZAKIR HUSSAIN RD

Burdwan
House

ACCOMMODATION

Alice Villa	4
Aliment	20
Andy's	13
Bellevue	7
Classic G.H.	8
Dekeling	11
Dekeling Resort	22
Ivanhoe	2
Long Island	18
Main Olde Bellevue	7
Mayfair Hill Resort	1
New Elgin	5
Nishikura Lodge	12
Pagoda	16
Pineridge	6
Planters' Club	10
Seven Seventeen	9
Shamrock	17
Tower View	15
Triveni Guest House	19
Valentino	14
Windamere	3
Youth Hostel	21

▼ Ghoom, Tiger Hill, Siliguri,
Dali Gompa & ▼ Batasia Loop

▼ Peace Pagoda & Ghoom

▶ Lebong Race Course

on the Sikkimese in 1861, thereby annexing Darjeeling and Kalimpong. Part of the aim was to develop trade via the two towns with Tibet; when the Tibetans demurred, Colonel Younghusband was despatched into the mountains, where his troops pulverized the ill-equipped and archaic Tibetan army at Gyantse in 1904. In the early 1900s, Darjeeling had a reputation for being one of the most glamorous and far-flung outposts of the British empire, attracting socialites and adventurers in equal numbers.

After Independence, the region joined West Bengal, administered from Calcutta, but calls for autonomy grew, taking shape in the **Gurkhaland** movement of the 1980s. Led by the **Gurkha National Liberation Front** (GNLF) under the leadership of Subhash Ghising, a long and frequently very violent campaign ended in the early 1990s in what some see as a compromise. Today, the GNLF controls the Darjeeling Hill Council, still under the aegis of the West Bengal government, but running vital services such as tourism and transport. After a decade of relative calm, the peace was violently shattered in February 2001 when Ghising was seriously wounded in an attempt on his life, probably by the opposing Gurkha Liberation Organization who accuse Ghising of a sellout. The uncertain days of politically motivated wildcat strikes once more threaten to cripple Darjeeling, but the boom in tourism looks set to continue.

Arrival, information and transport

Virtually all travellers arriving in Darjeeling from the plains come via Siliguri, whether by the Toy Train, shared Jeep or bus. Jeeps and buses stop at the **bus stand** in the lower half of the town from where it's a bit of an uphill trek to the main hotel area. Taxis and some Jeeps will take you up to **Clubside** near the **Mall**, at the upper end of town; porters are available (from Rs20), but be careful as some act as touts so you could end up paying more for your room. Darjeeling is best explored on foot – in fact much of it, such as the Mall and the Chowrasta, is closed to all vehicles.

Darjeeling's **Tourist Bureau**, 1 The Mall (Mon–Fri 10am–4.30pm; ☏0354/54050), on **Chowrasta** above the Indian Airlines office, can organize transport for local sightseeing, and sells tickets for DGHC buses during the season to Siliguri and to Bagdogra to connect with flights (Rs65). **DGHC Tourism**, in the same office (☏0354/54214), also assists with arranging tours, transport and booking trekkers' huts; their main office at Silver Fir, Bhanu Sarani (daily; ☏0354/54879) is open at the weekends. DGHC also arrange white-water rafting on the River Teesta (from Rs350).

If you're planning to head on to **Sikkim**, you'll have to get a **permit**; travelling to Gangtok, you can get a two-day permit instantly at the border checkpoint at **Rangpo** and extend it in Gangtok – check to see whether you can do the same at the border crossing at Naya Bazaar for West Sikkim. Restrictions on visiting Sikkim are easing up, and from Darjeeling you can travel directly to West Sikkim on a breathtaking 27-kilometre road descending through tea plantations to Jorethang via Naya Bazaar, or via Singtam to Gangtok. If you need to get your permit in Darjeeling, pick up a form from the **District Magistrates Office** (Mon–Fri 10am–4pm) on Hill Cart Road near Loreto Convent; take it to be stamped at the **Foreigners' Registration Office** (daily 10am–6pm) on Laden La Road, then return to the DM's office for the final stamp. The process is a formality and quite easy but it does involve legwork.

Accommodation

Darjeeling has no shortage of **hotels**; in fact new ones spring up all the time, placing further strains upon the infrastructure. The main thing to establish before you check in anywhere is the **water** situation; many cheaper places only provide water in buckets, and charge extra if you like it hot. Off-season (late June to Sept & late Nov to April) **discounts** can be as much as fifty percent. The prices given below are for peak season.

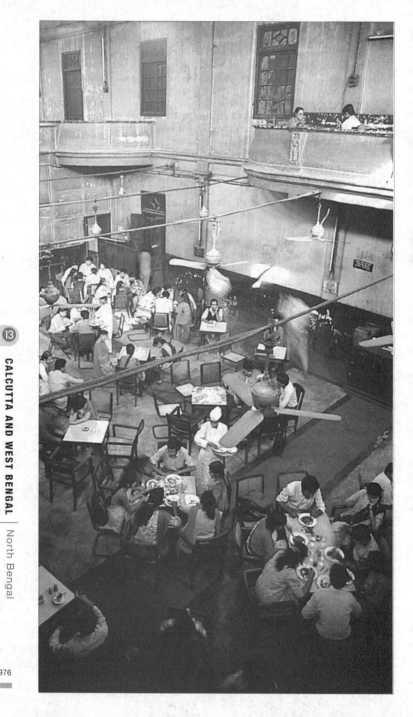

Alice Villa, 41 HD Lama Rd ☎0354/54181. At the crossroads just below Chowrasta, a quaint Victorian hotel and a modern annexe with spacious but characterless rooms. ⑥

Aliment, 40 Dr Zakir Hussein Rd ☎0354/55068. Cheap and very popular travellers' hang-out with a wonderful top-floor café and friendly management but poky rooms. ②

Andy's, 102 Zakir Hussein Rd ☎0354/53125. Best of the ridge-top guesthouses with immaculate rooms and great views towards Kalimpong and Bhutan; closed in winter. ⑥

Bellevue, the Mall ☎0354/54075. Above the tourist bureau, and dominating Chowrasta; not as grand as it once was, but still pleasant enough with low-key service but airy wood-lined rooms and a pleasantly situated bar and restaurant. ⑥–⑦

Classic G.H., CR Das Road ☎0354/54106. Clean comfortable rooms with bathrooms and veranda. A couple of minutes below Chowrasta with great views. ⑦

Dekeling, 51 Gandhi Rd, above the popular *Dekevas* restaurant ☎0354/54159, @www.dekeling.com. *Dekeling* offers great central location, a range of comfortable rooms with running hot water – the timber rooms upstairs are warm and charming – and good off-season discounts. The owners Norbu and Sangay are especially welcoming and helpful. Recommended. ⑥–⑦

Dekeling Resort, Hawk's Nest, 2 AJC Bose Rd ☎0354/53092, @www.dekeling.com. Four luxury suites with fireplaces and tasteful Tibetan decor in a delightful old Tibetan-owned colonial villa; well worth the short walk out of town. Good home cooking also available. ⑧

Ivanhoe, 4 Franklyn Prestage Rd ☎0354/56082. Renovated old colonial villa with seven spacious rooms. Dark but atmospheric and convenient, only five minutes' walk beyond Chowrasta. ⑥

Long Island, 11/A/2 Dr Zakir Hussein Rd ☎0354/52043. Just beyond the *Tower View* and above the road. Friendly, with a pleasant café and some of the best budget rooms on the ridge top. Views towards Bhutan. ②

Main Olde Bellevue, Behind Bellevue, 1 & 5/1 Nehru Rd ☎0354/54178. A dull new block or the rambling old manor hotel gradually being renovated, with creaky wooden corridors, large rooms and ancient plumbing. ⑥–⑦

Mayfair Hill Resort, below Government House ☎0354/56376. Once a maharaja's summer retreat, this offers ostentatious luxury with additional cottages, good facilities and an immaculate garden. ⑨

New Elgin, 32 HD Lama Rd ☎0354/54114, ℱ54267, @www.elginhotels.com. A premier hotel, opulent and well maintained with an old-fashioned formal atmosphere and good facilities. Rates include all meals. From $90. ⑨

Nishikura Lodge, 43 Laden La Rd ☎0354/52978. Central with pleasant, well-maintained rooms, especially the triples which face out with balconies. Rather expensive for what's on offer though. ⑤

Pagoda, 1 Upper Beechwood Rd ☎0354/53498. A quiet central spot, close to Laden La Road and the post office, with keenly priced rooms and a fire in the lounge; this area is no longer the haunt of budget travellers. ③

Pineridge, the Mall ☎0354/54074. Well situated next to Chowrasta and part of a large mansion with spacious old-fashioned rooms but little atmosphere. Open fires for use in winter and healthy off-season discounts. ⑤–⑥

Planters' Club, also known as the Darjeeling Club ☎0354/54348. A Darjeeling landmark with old-fashioned rooms, coal fires, a billiard room, bar, restaurant and library. Guests have to take temporary membership (Rs50). ⑤–⑧

Seven Seventeen, HD Lama Road ☎0354/55099. Extensive, well-run hotel with comfortable airy rooms, despite the location just above the bazaar. Exchange facilities and credit cards are accepted for un-discounted rooms. ⑦

Shamrock, Upper Beechwood Road ☎0354/56387. Atmospheric and friendly Bhutanese-run budget hotel with a cosy kitchen, where communal evening meals are served. ②–③

Tower View, 8/1 Dr Zakir Hussein Rd ☎0354/54452. A friendly place near the TV tower with good views, internet access and a great restaurant. Good budget option with cheap cubbyholes plus a couple of pleasant wood-lined rooms. ②

Triveni Guest House, 85/1 Dr Zakir Hussein Rd ☎0354/53114. Plain and roomier than the *Aliment* opposite, but not as popular. Friendly with a great restaurant and a good internet café. Nice views from the sun deck. ②

Valentino, 6 Rockville Rd ☎0354/52228. Modern Chinese-run place situated above the telephone exchange. Boasts clean and comfortable rooms, well worth their price, with breakfast included. Also a great restaurant and bar. ⑥–⑦

Windamere, Observatory Hill ☎0354/54041 ℱ54043, @www.windamerehotel.com. The most celebrated of Darjeeling's hotels, which has accommodated a pantheon of rich and famous guests. Old-fashioned self-contained cottages with Raj memorabilia. Expensive, but well worth a visit

for tea on the lawn or the occasional concert. From $120. ⑨
Youth Hostel, 16 Zakir Hussein Rd ☏ 0354/56794. Plain budget rooms on top of the ridge with wonderful views. The staff can advise

you on trekking in the area, but someone walked off with the original trekkers' log book. Five- and eight-bed dorms (Rs40) as well as a couple of double rooms with attached baths. ❷–❸

The Town

The heart of Victorian Darjeeling is the **Chowrasta** (four roads), a square above the busy bazaar on Hill Cart Road. A small group of interesting curio shops line one side, with a bandstand at the northern end and ponymen offering rides to tourists who often outweigh the emaciated beasts. One of the four main roads that meet at the Chowrasta is **the Mall**, lined on one side by shops and restaurants and on the other by less permanent market stalls, which descends from Chowrasta to Clubside, the area below the prestigious **Planters' Club**. Established in 1868, and otherwise known as the **Darjeeling Club**, this venerable institution was once the centre of Darjeeling high society. Not much seems to have changed since the days when tea planters from all over the territory rode here to attend social occasions. Visitors who take temporary membership are welcome to stay, and facilities such as the bar and snooker room are available for a day-use fee.

Darjeeling tea

Although the original appeal of Darjeeling for the British was as a hill resort with easy access from the plains, inspired by their success in Assam they soon realized its potential for growing tea. As the British East India Company first cleared the forests to introduce Chinese tea, they discovered that some of the plants they were discarding were indigenous strains. Today, Darjeeling continues to flourish, producing China Jat, China Hybrid and Hybrid Assam. A combination of factors, including altitude and sporadic rainfall, have resulted in a relatively small yield – only three percent of India's total – but Darjeeling is a delicate black tea that is considered to be one of the finest in the world. It is also one of the most expensive; the world record is held by a grade from Castleton, an estate near Kurseong, which sold at auction a few years ago for an astronomical Rs13,500 a kilo.

Grades such as Flowery Orange Pekoe (FOP) or Broken Orange Pekoe (BOP) are determined by quality and length of leaf during a production process that includes withering, crushing, fermenting and drying. The word Pekoe comes from the Chinese *pa-kho* and alludes to the soft down of a child's cheek, thought to resemble the fine down on one side of new tea leaves which appear as flushes. The plucking season (March–Dec) in Darjeeling produces two flushes, the best of which is the second. Then comes a monsoon tea of inferior quality, and finally, a vintage autumnal. If you're interested in learning how tea is dried and processed, call in at the **Happy Valley Tea Estate** (Tues–Sat 8am–noon & 1–4.30pm, Sun 8am–noon; free) beyond the Botanical Gardens.

As for **buying tea**, vendors with good reputations include R.N. Agarwal, who have a stall on the Mall, and Nathmull's on Laden La Road, a large shop where they are only too happy to sit and explain the virtues, vices and vicissitudes of various teas. Such vendors usually trade in unblended tea, bought directly from tea gardens. Being independent, they are able to pick and choose according to quality and do not necessarily stock tea from the same garden every year. The typical cost of a kilo of good middle-grade tea is around Rs500. Nathmull's are happy to ship tea home for you.

Taking the right fork from the northern end of the Chowrasta, near the bandstand, brings you to the **viewpoint** from where you can survey the Kanchenjunga massif and almost the entire state of Sikkim. From near the *Windamere Hotel* steps, ascend the pine-covered hillside to **Observatory Hill**, another viewpoint and the site of the monastery which gave Darjeeling its name. Decorated with streams of Buddhist prayer flags, the shrine at the summit, dedicated to the wrathful Buddhist deity Mahakala, whom Hindus equate with Shiva, has been influenced by Hinduism, creating a garish hybrid of styles.

A steep road leads down from the Chowrasta opposite the Darjeeling Stores and next to *Star Dust* café, to **Bhutia Busty Monastery**, the focus of Darjeeling's community of Bhutias, a people of Tibetan origin. This small Nyingma *gompa* with its beautifully painted facade was founded at the end of the nineteenth century as a branch of Phodang in Sikkim, but is now almost empty.

Another Raj-era institution, now in sad decline, stands near Observatory Hill. The **Gymkhana Club** hit rock bottom during the Gurkhaland movement when a paramilitary outfit set up camp in its skating hall. It's now once again possible for visitors to drop in and play billiards, snooker, badminton, table tennis, tennis, squash and even to roller-skate; there is also a small library, a bar and bridge tables. On rare occasions such as New Year, the Gymkhana's dance floor comes alive and live bands beat out familiar covers, reminiscent of heady days gone by.

Below the club, the dreary **Natural History Museum** (daily except Thurs 10am–4pm; Rs5) holds a huge but somewhat faded assortment of stuffed animals and birds. Further away from Chowrasta, and a steep drop down from Government House, the extensive **Tibetan Refugee Self-Help Centre** stands above the road leading to the disused Lebong racecourse. Founded in 1959, it houses around seven hundred refugees, most of whom make carpets or

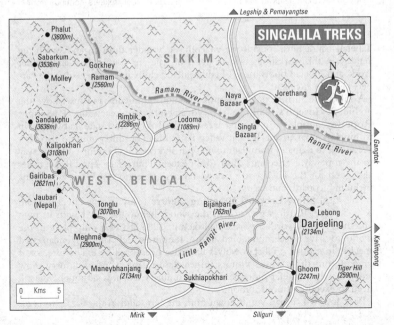

SINGALILA TREKS

▲ Legship & Pemayangtse

Phalut (3600m)

Sabarkum (3536m) — Gorkhey

Molley — Ramam (2560m)

SIKKIM

Ramam River

Naya Bazaar — Jorethang

N

Sandakphu (3636m) — Rimbik (2286m) — Lodoma (1089m) — Singla Bazaar

Kalipokhari (3108m)

Rangit River

Gairibas (2621m)

WEST BENGAL

Jaubari (Nepal) — Tonglu (3070m) — Bijanbari (762m) — Lebong

Darjeeling (2134m)

Meghma (2900m)

Little Rangit River

Maneybhanjang (2134m) — Sukhiapokhari — Ghoom (2247m) — Tiger Hill (2590m) ▲

0 Kms 5

Mirik ▼   Siliguri ▼

▶ Gangtok

▶ Kalimpong

The single ridge of the Singalila Range rises near Darjeeling and extends all the way to the summit of Kanchenjunga. Unfortunately, although some longer trails have been opened in Sikkim (see p.1019) for package groups armed with the right permits, there is no provision yet of linking them to the relatively easy trails along the initial sections of the ridge to Sandakphu (3636m) and Phalut (3600m). Easily accessible from Darjeeling, the Sandakphu–Phalut trail provides magnificent views of the higher ranges and lightweight expeditions are possible as there are trekking huts (though the quilts provided are inadequate when it gets cold) and simple food stalls along the way. Several organizations (see p.983) arrange itineraries and porters (Rs250 a day) as well as guides (Rs350); DGHC Tourism and Trek-Mate in Darjeeling both rent equipment (sleeping bags cost Rs30, plus Rs1500 deposit). If you plan to venture out alone, check out the log book at the *Youth Hostel* in Darjeeling for tips from others who have done the treks.

Views from the Sandakphu–Phalut trail take in four of the five highest mountains in the world – Everest, Kanchendzonga, Makalu and Lhotse. To keep the panorama in sight rather than behind you, trek north from Sandakphu towards Phalut. The best time to trek is after the monsoons (Oct & Nov), and during spring (Feb–May). It gets hot at the end of April and into May, but this is an especially beautiful season, with the rhododendrons in bloom.

Maneybhanjang, a small town and roadhead 27km from Darjeeling, is the usual starting point for the route. Foreigners are expected to register with the police at Sukhiapokhari and Maneybhanjang, though they don't check. Taking a taxi or the early-morning bus (7am; 90min) to Maneybhanjang from Darjeeling enables you to start the trek the same day, otherwise you can stay in the basic *Pradhans* (❶), the *Goperna Lodge* (❷), or the simple but comfortable rooms above *Wangdi Tibetan Restaurant* (❶). The steep trail as far as Sandakphu is wide enough for a Jeep to pass so it is in fact possible to drive along this first section of the route.

Assuming you start from Maneybhanjang, DAY 1 begins with a sharp climb to Meghma, then eases to the hut at Tonglu (3070m). Most trekkers continue from

Tibetan handicrafts. Tourists are welcome to wander through and watch the activity in the workshops; among items on sale are clothes, hats and leather work, and Tibetan boots made of embroidered cloth and leather soles; the carpets here are excellent.

A kilometre further north towards the high mountains and just above the gothic **St Joseph's College** (or Northpoint), you reach the **Passenger Ropeway**, a cable car providing access to the Tukvar Tea Estate halfway down to Singla Bazaar in the Rangit Valley far below. The thirty-minute trip runs according to demand from 9am to 4.30pm and costs Rs55 return. On the way to the ropeway, Darjeeling's **Zoo** (daily except Thurs 8am–4pm; Rs10, ticket also good for the HMI – see below) houses a selection of Himalayan fauna including leopards and bears.

The small **Snow Leopard Breeding Centre** (daily except Thurs 9–11am & 2–3.30pm; Rs10), segregated in the woods below the HMI with its own entrance, is well worth a visit. Established in 1986, it is the only place in the world to have successfully bred **snow leopards** (officially an endangered species) in captivity; Tibetan wolves have also been bred here. The director, if present, sometimes allows visitors to get close to the wonderful, furry snow leopards which are far more benign than ordinary leopards, although you still need to exercise utmost caution.

Back in town, a road winds down from the bus stand in the bazaar to enter

Meghma to the small town of Jaubari in Nepal, with its handful of small cheap lodges such as the *Everest Lodge* (❶), *Indira Lodge* (❶) and *Teacher's Inn* (❶); there are also places to eat. Officials, well-used to trekkers passing through, look the other way. On **DAY 2**, the Jaubari trail rejoins the main one at **Gairibas**, continues to **Kalipokhari** and **Bikhebhanjang**, then rises steeply to **Sandakphu** (3636m), which has a trekkers' hut with blankets, a small friendly lodge near the memorial stone, and a couple of PWD bungalows.

The panorama opens out as you leave Sandakphu on **DAY 3**, and the trek follows the ridge to **Sabarkum**. There's no shelter or food there, but you can find both by dropping down to the right for thirty minutes to **Molley**, where there's an inhospitable DGHC trekkers' hut. On **DAY 4**, retrace your steps to Sabarkum and continue along the ridge to **Phalut** (3600m) where you'll find a trekkers' lodge. The panorama from here is particularly impressive. Either retrace your steps to Sandakphu on **DAY 5**, or follow the trail from Phalut via **Gorkhey**, which has a trekkers' hut, to **Rammam** (2560m), home of the comfortable and welcoming *Sherpa Lodge* (❺) and a DGHC trekkers' hut.

The final day, **DAY 6**, leads to **Rimbik** (2286m); check with locals before setting off as the route is confusing. Accommodation options in Rimbik include the friendly but cramped *Shiva Pradhan* (❶), which has hot water but an unflattering location; warm and cosy *Sherpa Lodge* (❸), where they'll help arrange bus tickets to Darjeeling; the *New Sherpa Tenzing* (❸) with shared baths and hot water by the bucket; and a DGHC trekkers' hut. Rimbik is a roadhead served by buses and taxis heading to Darjeeling, or you can set off on another (long) day's walk to **Bijanbari**, which also has transport to Darjeeling.

There are several other trekking routes including: Darjeeling–Maneybhanjang–Tonglu–Sandakphu and back to Darjeeling on the same route (118km; 4 days); Darjeeling–Maneybhanjang–Tonglu–Sandakphu–Phalut and back on the same route (160km; 6 days); Darjeeling–Maneybhanjang–Sandakphu–Phalut–Ramam–Rimbik and back (130km; 6 days); and Darjeeling–Maneybhanjang–Sandakphu–Rimbik and back (128km; 4 days).

the **Botanical Gardens**, where pines, willows and maples cover the hillside and pleasant walks zigzag down to the slightly dilapidated central greenhouses, filled with ferns and orchids. One final prominent sight you're bound to notice is the multi-roofed **Dhirdham Temple**, below the railway station, built as a replica of the great Shiva temple of Pashupatinath on the outskirts of Kathmandu.

The **Toy Train** (see p.970), has a tourist service to **Ghoom** driven by lovingly preserved ancient steam locomotives, departing Darjeeling at 10.30am and returning two hours later (Rs200). If you want to see Ghoom's monasteries (see p.985) at leisure, you could take the train up and take alternative transport or walk back.

The Himalayan Mountaineering Institute

The **Himalayan Mountaineering Institute**, reached via the zoo and covered by the same ticket, is one of India's most important training centres for mountaineers, holding numerous courses (Indians only) throughout the year. Its first director was **Sherpa Tenzing Norgay**, the conqueror of Everest, who lived and died in Darjeeling; although he claimed to be a Sherpa, a recent book has instigated controversy by tracing his roots to Tibet. Most of the instructors are still Sherpa or Bhutia mountain men. In the heart of the beautiful leafy complex are two fascinating exhibition halls (daily except Thurs 9am–4.30pm).

The **HMI Museum** is dedicated to the history of mountaineering, with equipment old and new, a relief map of the Himalayas, and a collection of costumes of different hill people, while the **Everest Museum** tells the fascinating and moving story of the conquest of the highest mountain in the world. Photographs from early expeditions include pictures of the third British Everest Expedition in 1924 when Irvine and Mallory were last seen "going strong for the top", and of Tenzing and Hillary's successful climb in 1953. Other photos include one of Tashi Tenzing who followed his grandfather's footsteps to the top of Everest on May 23, 1997, and of the Nepali climber Kaji Sherpa who set a new world record in October 1998 by scaling Everest from base camp to summit in 20 hours 24 minutes without supplementary oxygen. Opposite the museum entrance, a small path leads up to Tenzing Norgay's resting place and a memorial unveiled by Sir Edmund Hillary in 1997, to honour both Tenzing Norgay and "those attributes of human endeavour and continued perseverance."

Eating and drinking

Darjeeling has plenty of choice for **eating out**. The more touristy of its restaurants are around the top of town. Many of the hotels, such as the *Windamere* and *New Elgin*, have good multi-cuisine restaurants. The *Aliment* has an excellent budget-traveller-friendly menu (you can have a meal for Rs40–100) while *Triveni* opposite is similar and the *Tower View* produces excellent home cooking. The *New Embassy* restaurant at the Chinese-owned *Valentino* is well worth the splurge. For **drinks** or light meals, try *Joey's Pub*, a friendly place on Dr SM Das Road with good atmosphere, or *Beni's Café* on the same road, which does excellent snacks and Indian sweets.

Dekevas, 51 Gandhi Rd. A relaxed ambience popular with travellers and locals alike, with the usual mixed menu including a wide range of Tibetan dishes and a very good-value breakfast. *Kungas* next door is similar.

Frank Ross Café, 14 the Mall. Vegetarian snack bar serving sandwiches and pizzas and an incredible range of *dosas*; a pity about the coffee.

Glenary's, the Mall. For years Darjeeling's most reputable eating place, now completely revamped with a restaurant-cum-bar serving the best tandoori in town, and a great coffee shop and patisserie below.

Hasty Tasty, the Mall. Indian fast food. Cheese *dosas*, cheesy music, and superb veg thalis. Very popular with Indian holidaymakers.

Keventers, Clubside. A landmark café serving toasted sandwiches and fried breakfasts including bacon and ham. The terrace above the crossroads is excellent for people-watching, even if the service is poor.

New Dish, JP Sharma Road. Excellent Chinese food in dour surroundings; it's owned by the former chef to the Bhutan royal family.

Orient, JP Sharma Road. Chinese, Indian and good local food served at tables or in private cubicles; the decor is gaudy.

Park, opposite the State Bank of India, Laden La Road. Plush new restaurant serving good Indian and Chinese food.

Penang's, opposite the GPO, Laden La Road. Cheap, grubby but popular local haunt serving *momos* and *thukpa*.

Star Dust, Chowrasta. Open-air restaurant serving coffee and snacks; the great terrace makes up for the dull food.

Listings

Banks and exchange The State Bank of India (Mon–Fri 10am–2pm, Sat 10am–noon; Rs25 per transaction), Laden La Road, is slow and only accepts American Express or Thomas Cook travellers' cheques in US$ and UK£. Standard Chartered Grindlays (Mon–Fri 10am–1.30pm, Rs200 per transaction), Laden La Road, only changes US$ and Australian dollar travellers'

The nearest **airport** to Darjeeling is **Bagdogra**, 100km to the south (see p.970), but at the time of going to press was closed for repairs. A DGHC bus leaves the *Tourist Lodge* and Clubside around 8am each day to connect with flights; tickets for the bus can be booked at the Tourist Bureau. Indian Airlines (℡0354/54230) have an office on the Mall at Chowrasta and Jet Airways tickets are available at Pineridge Travels (℡0354/53912), a few metres away also on the Mall or at Clubside Tours and Travels, JP Sharma Road (℡0354/54646). Pineridge Travels also handles all flights (several airlines) from **Bhadrapur** in Nepal to **Kathmandu** ($109); taxis charge around Rs375 for the 45-minute journey from the border town of Kakarbitta to Bhadrapur, and airport tax is Rs110.

Buses and minibuses (Rs350) run every thirty minutes or so to **Siliguri** from the bus stand at the bazaar; shared taxis charge Rs60. Buses for **Mirik** leave every thirty minutes between 8am and 9am (2hr). Two minibuses run each day to **Gangtok** (4–5hr; Rs75) – a private bus at 7.30am and SNT (Sikkim Nationalized Transport) at 1pm. One minibus leaves every day for **Kalimpong** (3hr; Rs38) at 8am.

Jeeps run to **Gangtok**, **Siliguri**, **Mirik**, **Kalimpong** and **Jorethang** (for west Sikkim), and, though slightly more expensive than buses, are by far the most efficient and comfortable way to travel, especially if you pay more to book a front seat. Book in advance if you can at the Jeep stand (next to the bus stand); each route has its own syndicate and some have two or three. Gangtok services (3–4hr; Rs110) run frequently between 7am and 2pm.

The **Toy Train** (see p.970) runs to **Siliguri** and **New Jalpaiguri**, weather and landslides permitting, but takes an angst-inducing six-and-a-half hours; the train leaves at 8.30am. **Railway reservations** (daily 10am–noon & 2–4pm) for selected **main-line trains** out of NJP can be made at Darjeeling's station a couple of days before departure. They have tourist quotas for trains to Delhi, Calcutta, Bangalore, Cochin and Thiruvananthapuram.

Although it's possible to buy bus tickets for **Kathmandu**, you still have to change buses at Siliguri and most travellers prefer to make their own arrangements.

Travel, trek and tour operators

Clubside Tours and Travels JP Sharma Road ℡ 0354/54646. Established and reliable company dealing with airline tickets, tours and trekking.

DGHC Tourism Silver Fir Building ℡0354/54214. Arranges transport, manages trekking huts and organizes white-water rafting on the River Teesta.

Diamond Travels 37B Old Super Market (℡0354/53467). Trekking, transport to Kathmandu, Calcutta and Guwahati.

Greenland Tours & Travels 21 Beechwood, Laden La Road ℡ 0354/53011. Low-key, friendly travel, tour and trek operator, with a book exchange, up the steps above the post office.

Himalayan Adventures Das Studios, 15 Nehru Rd ℡0354/54004; dastrek@ozemail .com.au. Established Indo-Australian company which runs upmarket treks and tours.

Himalayan Travels 18/1 Gandhi Rd ℡ 0354/52254. A major trek operator in west Sikkim as well as Sandakphu.

Juniper Tours and Travels Laden La Road ℡ 0354/52095, Established travel agent on main thoroughfare.

Kanchenjunga Treks & Tours DB Giri Road ℡ 0354/52095. An efficient, international organization run by Tenzing Norgay's son: excellent for trekking and mountaineering.

Pineridge Travels, *Pineridge Hotel*, The Mall ℡ 0354/53912. Efficient, modern agency that arranges Jet Airways tickets as well as flights from Bhadrapur (Nepal) to Kathmandu.

Trek-Mate Singalila Arcade, Nehru Road ℡0354/74092, odyssey@dte.vsnl.net.in. Helpful agency which arranges treks to Sandakphu and west Sikkim. Also provides guides and porters and rents out sleeping bags, down jackets and day packs.

cheques. Licensed private foreign exchange vendors are a bit more flexible but charge around four percent more than the bank rate. Amongst these, the *Hotel Mohit* is marginally more expensive than *Hotel Seven Seventeen*, both on HD Lama Road; Pineridge Travels, *Pineridge Hotel*, the Mall charges Rs2 for every US$ changed.

Bookshops Oxford Books & Stationery, Chowrasta. Excellent selection of novels and coffee-table books.

Car rental Darjeeling Transport Corporation, Laden La Road (①0354/52074) is one of the more established operators; others are centred around Clubside.

Hospital Try Planters' Hospital, Planter's Club, the Mall ①0354/54327; Mariam Nursing Home, the Mall ①0354/54327. The Tibetan Medical & Astro Institute, *Hotel Seven Seventeen*, 26 HD Lama Rd ①0354/54735 is part of the Dalai Lama's medical organization, Men-Tsee-Khang, and has a clinic and a well-stocked dispensary. There is also a Women's Clinic (Mon–Sat 1.30–5pm, Sun 10am–1pm), under *Hotel Springburn*, 70 Gandhi Rd, run by Dr Gupta Singh.

Internet access Compuset Centre, Das Colour Lab, Gandhi Road; Cyber Café, Triveni Guest House, 85/1 Dr Zakir Hussein Rd; Cyber Café, 1st floor, *Hotel Red Rose*, 37 Laden La Rd; Darjlink, *Hotel Pradhan*, 57 Gandhi Rd. These places charge around Rs90 per hour.

Pharmacies Frank Ross & Co, the Mall; there are several pharmacies clustered around Sadar Hospital above the bus stand.

Photography Das Studios and Darjeeling Photo Stores, both on the Mall.

Post office The main post office (Mon–Sat 10am–5pm is located on Laden La Road.

Thangka painters Dawa Gyentshe Bhutia, Kamal Bhavan, below Botanical Garden, PB Gurung Road; Lama Tsondu Sangpo, the School of Tibetan Thangka Painting, Gonjan Monastery, Rongbul.

Tibetan studies The Manjushree Centre of Tibetan Culture, 8 Burdwan Rd (①0354/54159 or 52354, ⑩www.kreisels.com/manjushree), founded in 1988 to preserve and promote Tibetan culture, offers both part-time Tibetan language classes (Mon–Sat 4–5.30pm) and more intensive three-, six- and nine-month courses (from $150). The centre also has a library with lending facilities ($20 deposit), and holds regular seminars, talks, video shows and exhibitions. The Chakpori Medical School at Thurbo (en route to Teesta) runs excellent long courses in Tibetan medicine.

Visas and permits The Foreigners' Regional Registration Office, Laden La Road, is opposite the State Bank of India (daily 10am–6pm); the District Magistrate's Office is on Hill Cart Road, near Loreto Convent (Mon–Fri 10am–4pm).

Around Darjeeling

One really unmissable part of the Darjeeling experience is the early-morning mass exodus to **Tiger Hill**, to watch the sunrise. This can easily be combined with a visit to the old monastery of **Ghoom**, and the huge monastery at **Sonada** on Hill Cart Road towards Siliguri. The picturesque lake at **Mirik** near the Nepal border attracts weekend crowds from Darjeeling and makes for an easy day-trip.

Tiger Hill

Jeeps and taxis packed with tourists leave from Clubside in Darjeeling around 4am each morning, careering 12km through Ghoom and the woodlands to catch the sunrise at **TIGER HILL**. This incredible viewpoint (2585m) provides an unparalleled 360° Himalayan panorama, with the steamy plains bordering Bangladesh to the south, the Singalila Range with Everest beyond to the west, Kanchenjunga and Sikkim to the north, and the Bhutan and Assam Himalayas trailing into the distance to the northeast. From left to right, the **peaks** include: Lhotse (which actually looks larger than Everest); Everest itself; Makalu; then, after a long gap, the rocky summit of Kang on the Sikkim–Nepal divide; the prow of Jannu in Nepal; Rathong; tent-like Kabrus south and north; Talung; Kanchenjunga main, central and south; Pandim; Simvo; horned

Narsing; and the fluted pyramid of Siniolchu. As the sun rises from the plains, it lights each one in turn; not yet obscured by the haze of the day, they are bathed in pastel hues. In peak season up to 500 Jeeps leave Darjeeling daily, transporting more than 5000 people to the viewpoint. Tour operators in Darjeeling offer tours for Rs50 (Rs400 for a reserved Jeep) including a stop at one of **Ghoom's** gompas, and the **Batasia Loop** and Gurkha War Memorial for which there is an additional fee of Rs5.

The **viewing tower** provides a warmer space for those who wish to see the sunrise from behind the safety of glass and costs Rs5 for the top floor or Rs10 for the VIP lounge below (includes a cup of coffee). Viewing is followed by the entertaining post-sunrise game of "find your Jeep".

It's also possible to walk up Tiger Hill during the day and camp for the night near the top. The *Tourist Bungalow* (Rs100), on the plain below the summit, offers cheap **accommodation** in dorm beds, and dinner.

Ghoom and other monasteries

Often obscured in cloud, **GHOOM** (2438m), with its charming little railway station and tiny bazaar on the edge of Jorebangla, has several interesting monasteries, the most venerated of which is **Yiga Choling**, or the Old Ghoom Monastery tucked off the main thoroughfare, above the brash new *Sterling Resort*. From Ghoom railway station, head back towards Darjeeling for 200m and turn left into the side road (signposted) and continue through the small market for 500m. Built in 1850 by Sharap Gyatso, a renowned astrologer, the monastery comprises a single chambered temple, with a few residential buildings and an outhouse. Inside the prayer hall is a huge statue of Maitreya, the Buddha of the future. Adorned with *katas* (ceremonial scarves), this statue is of an exceptionally high standard of workmanship with fine detail above and around the bronze face. A painting of the Mahakala is hidden under red cloth as it is considered too fierce to be looked at directly. The monastery has had a recent face-lift with the murals repainted by local Darjeeling *thangka* artists under the guidance of master painter Dawa Gyentshe Bhutia. A short walk past the monastery lies the small open cemetery with wonderful views all around.

The new monastery, **Samten Choling**, on a bend in the main road to Darjeeling, is sometimes included on the Jeep tours to Tiger Hill. It's a small but colourful *gompa;* you may prefer to spend more time looking around it when the Jeeps have all returned to Darjeeling, and the atmosphere is more conducive to taking in the murals and chatting to the few monks who live here.

In the small hamlet of Rongbul, south of Ghoom and below Hill Cart Road, next to the small Nyingmapa **Gonjan Monastery**, the School of Tibetan Thangka Painting is run by the artist Lama Tsondu Sangpo, and worth checking out if you are interested in Tibetan art.

Further down Hill Cart Road, the influential **Sonada Monastery**, founded in the 1960s, was the seat of **Kalu Rinpoche** who developed a large American and French following. It has recently been extensively renovated to house Kalu Rinpoche's young *tulku* or reincarnation. Rooms (❶) are available for retreat and you can dine with the monks for a nominal fee.

Halfway between Ghoom and Darjeeling on the main road stands the imposing **Thupten Sanga Choeling**, otherwise known as the **Dali Gompa**, inaugurated by the Dalai Lama in 1993. This is a very active **Drukpa Kagyu** *gompa* with two hundred monks, including several young *rinpoches*. The huge meditation hall is richly decorated with exquisite murals and ceiling mandalas.

Five larger-than-life statues represent, from left to right, Guru Rinpoche, Chenrezig, Sakyamuni, Tara and the fourth Drukpa Kagyu lama, Padme Karpo.

Ghoom is the highest point on the Toy Train railway, just 7km from Darjeeling. A steam-driven tourist train (Rs200), leaving Darjeeling at 10.30am, travels up to Ghoom but doesn't leave enough time to take in the monasteries at your leisure. The regular 8.30am service from Darjeeling is much cheaper and arrives here at 9.15am. You could take alternative transport back to Darjeeling or take the top road for a quiet, traffic-free walk back, taking in the stupendous views along the way with a visit to the **Peace Pagoda** in the woods above the Dali Gompa.

Mirik

MIRIK, 45km southwest of Darjeeling near the border with Nepal, is the region's newest resort, primarily geared up for domestic tourists. There is a large and lively **Gelug-pa** or "yellow hat" monastery above the picturesque central lake, but most of the tourism is centred around boating on the lake. Surrounded by large tea estates and pine forests, Mirik is a pleasant enough place and can be visited as a long day-trip from Darjeeling or as a stopover on an alternative route down to Siliguri.

Most of the **accommodation** is restricted to the newer **Krishnagar** settlement at the southern end of the lake. At the bottom of the road leading to the *gompa* is *Imny's Lodge* (☎0354/43505; ❸), a pleasant budget option. Comfortable *Jagjeet* (☎0354/43231; ❻–❽) has a good restaurant; *Sadhbhawana* (☎0354/43651; ❷–❹) is pleasant and roomy but reasonable; and there's new and comfortable *Mhelung* (☎0354/43231; ❺), which doesn't serve food. The choice of **eating places** includes *Sukh Sagar*, a good Sikh-run vegetarian restaurant by the lake. Buses and shared Jeeps (last at 3pm) run to and from Darjeeling and Siliguri.

Kalimpong and around

Though it may seem quite grubby at first, the quiet hill station of **KALIMPONG**, 50km east of Darjeeling, has much to offer including an extraordinary profusion of orchids and other flowers, plus great views of the Kanchenjunga, several monasteries and lots of potential for walks in the surrounding hills, which are still home to the tribal **Lepcha community**. Unlike Darjeeling, this was never a tea town or resort, but a trading town on the vital route to Tibet, and it was this very access to the borders which meant that Kalimpong was virtually out of bounds for tourists for a couple of decades following the Sino-Indian conflict of the early 1960s. Despite the large military presence, Kalimpong's recent history has been a sad one of neglect leading to major water shortages and a general decay in the infrastructure. A deep-rooted dissatisfaction has its political voice in the **Gurkha Liberation Organization**, a shadowy, radical movement committed to the cause of **Gurkhaland** and freeing the Darjeeling Hills from the state of West Bengal, with violence if necessary. The GLO, based in Kalimpong and led by Chhatri Subha, is fundamentally opposed to the GNLF who they accuse of a sellout. Despite occasional threats of political violence and wildcat strikes, this under-developed town with its leafy avenues comes as a breath of fresh air after the razzmatazz of Darjeeling.

Kalimpong spreads along a curving ridge to either side of its main **market area**, known as **Tenth Mile**. There are none of the curio and tourist shops so abundant in Darjeeling but the silk brocade, jewellery, and Tibetan cloth available in local shops is cheaper and better quality here than in either Darjeeling or Gangtok. On Wednesdays and Saturdays, Tenth Mile gets very lively as villagers flock in from the surrounding areas for the principal weekly markets. Below the *Silver Oaks Hotel*, the **Gangjong Paper Factory** on Printam Road (Mon–Sat 9am–4.30pm) welcomes visitors to their handmade paper workshop and shop.

Rinkingpong Hill, which looms above the town to the southwest, was once a surveying point; hence the local name *Durpin Dara*, which means "binocular ridge". It is now firmly in the hands of the army, who allow tourists through in taxis but occasionally stop those on foot. At its highest point, entirely surrounded by the army, **Zong Dog Palri Phodrang Monastery**, built in 1957 to house three copper statues brought from Tibet in the 1940s, was modelled on Guru Rinpoche's mythical pure realm palace and consecrated by the Dalai Lama. There is a large image of Guru Rinpoche (in Sanskrit: Padma Sambhava), the patron saint and founder of the Nyingmapa order, as well as some impressive frescoes, and an excellent collection of *thangkas* (not always on display). Upstairs there's an image of the thousand-armed Chenrezig (or Avalokitesvara) and an ornate wooden mandala. In 1983 a scholastic institute was set up with funding from Bhutanese royalty to teach Buddhist philosophy. The monastery is a scenic 4km hike from the centre of town.

At the other end of town, half an hour's walk up Deolo Hill brings you to the **Tharpa Choling Gompa**, a Gelug-pa monastery, founded in 1892 but

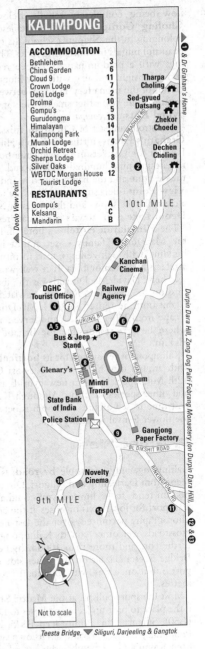

KALIMPONG

ACCOMMODATION
Bethlehem	3
China Garden	6
Cloud 9	11
Crown Lodge	7
Deki Lodge	2
Drolma	10
Gompu's	5
Gurudongma	13
Himalayan	14
Kalimpong Park	11
Munal Lodge	4
Orchid Retreat	1
Sherpa Lodge	8
Silver Oaks	9
WBTDC Morgan House Tourist Lodge	12

RESTAURANTS
Gompu's	A
Kelsang	C
Mandarin	B

Deolo View Point

& Dr Graham's Home

Tharpa Choling

K.D. PRADHAN RD

Sed-gyued Datsang

Zhekor Choede

Dechen Choling

10th MILE

RISHI ROAD

Kanchan Cinema

DGHC Tourist Office

Railway Agency

GURUNG RD

Bus & Jeep Stand

ONGDEN RD

MAIN ROAD

HL DIKSHIT ROAD

Glenary's

Mintri Transport

Stadium

State Bank of India

Police Station

Gangjong Paper Factory

BL DIKSHIT ROAD

RINKINGPONG RD

Novelty Cinema

9th MILE

N

Not to scale

Teesta Bridge, ▼ *Siliguri, Darjeeling & Gangtok*

Durpin Dara Hill, Zong Dog Palri Fobrang Monastery (on Durpin Dara Hill),

⑫ & ⑬

now being completely rebuilt. Below and closer to town is **Dechen Choling Gompa**, a small Bhutanese monastery founded in 1692 and belonging to the Nyingma school. Its two meditation halls are covered with beautiful murals in contrasting styles. The lower hall has extremely old paintings with a predominance of deep red pigments, whilst the shrine room above is bright and airy, with new murals in pastel shades depicting the main deities of the monastery. Halfway between these two monasteries just off the main road lie two other smaller Gelugpa *gompas*, **Zhekar Choede** and **Sedgyued Datsang** *gompa*.

The strong impact of **Christian missionaries** in the area is evident in **Dr Graham's Home**, further up Deolo Hill. Founded in 1900 by a Scotsman, the Rev Dr John Anderson Graham, as a home for six orphans, this school today has around nine hundred students, and has inspired several similar schools for the destitute and the handicapped in India. Above Dr Graham's Home, **Deolo View Point** offers superb views of the town, the **Teesta Valley** below, and on a clear day, the snows and the passes of Nathula and Jelepla into Tibet. Nearby **Deolo Lake** is the town's inadequate reservoir.

The **Himalayan Hotel** – a hotel and a "museum" as well as the home of the MacDonald family – set amidst landscaped gardens, is an impressive building with oak ceilings, teak furniture and a large collection of Tibetan artefacts and memorabilia. It is well worth a visit even if you can't afford to stay here. David MacDonald was the interpreter on Francis Younghusband's mission to Lhasa in 1904 and was later posted to Tibet as a British Trade Agent until he retired in 1924. MacDonald helped the 13th Dalai Lama to escape from Tibet in 1910, and served as British Political Officer in Sikkim where he was responsible for Britain's relations with Tibet, Bhutan and Sikkim.

Kalimpong is renowned for its **horticulture** and especially its orchid culture with around fifty nurseries such as Sri Ganesh Mani Pradhan, Ganesh Villa, 12th Mile, specializing in new hybrids as well as cacti, amaryllis, palms, ferns and other species of plants. Although Kalimpong blossoms all year long, the best time to see orchids in bloom is between mid-April and mid-May, when the flower festival is usually held.

Practicalities

Kalimpong, only accessible by **road**, is served by regular buses, taxis and Jeeps from Darjeeling and Siliguri. Direct transport to and from Gangtok in Sikkim tends to be limited; you could also connect from Gangtok–Siliguri transport for local taxis or buses at the crossroads near the Teesta Bridge (no photography permitted) over the fast-flowing River Teesta. A sign near the crossroads welcomes you to Kalimpong although the town itself is 15km further on, and more than 1000m higher up. Since the advent of the new Bridge, Teesta Bazaar on the other side of the river is no longer the transport hub it once was, with the Siliguri road bypassing it by a couple of kilometres.

Most transport pulls in at the **Motor Stand** in the central market area. This is the place to pick up Jeeps and buses to Darjeeling (2hr 30min–4hr; Jeep from Rs50), Siliguri (2hr 30min; Jeep Rs45, bus Rs30). and Gangtok (3hr; Jeep Rs50, van Rs85); each route has its own syndicate and ticket office. Moving on from Kalimpong, remember the last reliable transport links are around mid-afternoon. Kalimpong's **DGHC tourist office**, Damber Chowkh (Mon–Sat 9am–4pm; ☎03552/57992, ⊛www.kalimpong.org) is good for general information and leaflets; they also arrange white-water rafting on the Teesta (from Rs450). The Central Bank on Main Road changes money and the **post office** is close to the centre of town, above the bazaar area just behind the police station.

Accommodation and eating

Kalimpong's acute **water** shortages are likely to influence your choice of **accommodation** – few of the lower-range options have running water. The market area (Tenth Mile) and the area around the Motor Stand are where you will find most budget hotels.

The best **restaurants** are in the hotels – the *Kalimpong Park*, *Crown* and *China Garden*. Other options include the legendary *Gompu's* bar and restaurant at Dambar Chowk which serves great *momos*; the *Mandarin*, a Chinese restaurant at the Motor Stand; and the basic but friendly *Kelsang*, tucked around the corner from the Motor Stand serving curd and Tibetan food.

Bethlehem, Rishi Road, 10th Mile ☎03552/55185. Comfortable with hot running water and clean bathrooms; if full try *Norling* next door with its beautifully painted Tibetan restaurant. ④

China Garden, Lal Gulli, Motor Stand ☎03552/55945. Chinese-run hotel and restaurant with some of the cleanest rooms in the bazaar, features include attached bathrooms, hot water and good Chinese food. ④–⑤

Cloud 9, Next to *Kalimpong Park Hotel*, Ringkingpong Road ☎03552/57304. New hotel with five spacious rooms above a restaurant and bar especially lively when the owner Binodh is around, with guitar jams and Beatles covers. ⑥

Crown Lodge, 100m down from the Motor Stand ☎03552/55846. Large, clean but characterless. The *Crown* restaurant next door is very good. ④–⑤

Deki Lodge, Tripai Road, 10th Mile ☎03552/55095. Ten minutes' walk from the Motor Stand, this is a clean and very welcoming family-run budget hotel. There's running hot water and a pleasant open-air café. ②–⑤

Droima, Evening Side, 9th Mile, below *Novelty Cinema* (buses and Jeeps stop here). ☎03552/58404 & 55968. A family hotel with a special place in Tibetan history – run by Jigme Shakabpa, grandson of Tsepon Shakabpa, the last finance minister of free Tibet. Boasts a wide range of rooms, from the beautiful Tibetan suite down to simple doubles, and a pleasant garden with great views. ③–⑥

Gompu's, Dambar Chowk ☎03552/55818. Friendly, legendary hotel in the heart of the market, with atmospheric wooden rooms which have seen better days. Now more popular for its bar and restaurant. ③

Gurudongma, below Hill Top ☎03552/55204. The immaculate family home of General Jimmy Singh, with just two rooms in the house and a very pleasant cottage in the picturesque garden; book ahead. ⑦–⑧

Himalayan ☎03552/55248, @himhotl@cte.vsnl.net.in. Historic and comfortable hotel full of Tibetan memorabilia, set amid exquisite gardens; the modern blocks are luxurious but lack the ambience. Price includes meals. ⑧–⑨

Kalimpong Park, Ringkingpong Road ☎03552/55304. The main building is old and quaint, but most guest rooms are in the spacious but characterless modern block behind. They accept credit cards, and there's a helpful travel desk and a good restaurant. ⑦

Munal Lodge, Malli Road ☎03552/55404. Down from *Gompu's*, airy and clean rooms with excellent views from the terrace. ③

Orchid Retreat, 12th Mile ☎03552/57217, @thakro@vsnl.com. Fabulous horticultural garden and nursery with comfortable rustic cottages amongst the palms and ferns; simple luxury which must be booked ahead. ⑧

Sherpa Lodge, Ongden Road ☎03552/55159. Basic but friendly hotel, overlooking the stadium; the rooms at the back are cheaper. ③

Silver Oaks ☎03552/55296, ☎55368, @www.elginhotels.com. Comfortable and plush, Kalimpong's premier (four-star) hotel with full amenities; its rather drab grey-brick and glass exterior conceal Raj-era charm. From $90. ⑨

WBTDC Morgan House Tourist Lodge, Durpin Hill ☎03552/55384. Grand grey lodge, around 4km from town, set in fabulous gardens and built for a British jute merchant. The equally beautiful annexe, the *Tashiding Tourist Lodge*, belonged to Jigme Dorji, a premier of Bhutan whose murder still remains a mystery. ⑧

Around Kalimpong

Although the **Lepchas**, the original inhabitants of the area, have lost their traditional way of life in most other parts of Darjeeling and Sikkim, their lifestyle has remained relatively untouched in the unspoilt forest-covered hills and deep river valleys to the south of Kalimpong. Lying on an old trade route to Bhutan, the small hamlet of **LAVA**, 35km from Kalimpong and accessible by shared Jeep, makes an ideal base for exploring the nature trails of **Neura National Park**, abundant with orchids, birds and other wildlife. Lava is also convenient for approaching the **Rachela Pass** (3152m) on the Sikkim–Bhutan border which provides excellent views of the Chola Range including Chomalhari (7314m), the sacred mountain of Bhutan on its border with Tibet. Basic **accommodation** in Lava includes the *Forest Rest House* ①, which should be booked through the Forest Department in Kalimpong. Pleasant trails lead west from Lava towards **Budhabare**, a weekly-market town in the Git River Valley which has a sprinkling of Lepcha, Gurkha and Bhutia villages. The track continues through forest to **Kafer** which has a comfortable *Tourist Bungalow* ⑤ with a dorm (Rs50). At nearby **Lolegaon**, there's the *Forest Rest House* ①, and alternative accommodation in village houses; the trail north from here crosses the Relli River near the village of the same name and returns directly to Kalimpong. Gurudongma, Hill Top, Kalimpong (☎03552/55204, ⊛www.adventuresikkim.com), a well-organized, upmarket trek and tour operator, arranges treks in the region from their *Farm House* ⑧–⑨, a rustic but luxurious development on the beautiful Samthar Plateau, 80km from Kalimpong.

Travel details

Trains

Calcutta to: Agra (1 daily; 30hr); Ahmedabad (1 daily; 44hr); Bhubaneshwar (10 daily; 8–12 hr); Chennai (5 daily; 27–35hr); Delhi (7 daily; 18–34hr); Guwahati (3 daily; 20–25hr); Gwalior (2 weekly; 26hr); Haridwar (1 daily; 30hr); Jabalpur (1 daily; 21hr); Jaipur (1 daily; 30hr); Jalgaon (3 daily; 28–34hr); Lucknow (3 daily; 18hr); Mumbai (3 daily; 33–42hr); Nagpur (4 daily; 19–25hr); Patna (5 daily; 7–10hr); Puri (2 nightly; 11–12hr); Ranchi (1 daily; 10hr); Shantiniketan (6–7 daily; 2hr 30min–4hr); Siliguri NJP (6–7 daily; 12–14hr); Thiruvananthapuram (1 weekly; 49hr); Ujjain (2 weekly; 33hr 40min); Varanasi (5–8 daily; 8hr 30min–20hr).

Shantiniketan (Bolpur) to: Calcutta (6–7 daily; 2hr 30min–4hr); Siliguri (NJP) (5–6 daily; 8hr 35min–9hr 15min).

Siliguri (New Jalpaiguri (NJP) to: Calcutta (6–7 daily; 12–14hr); Delhi (4–5 daily; 21hr 15min–31hr 10min); Guwahati (7–8 daily; 8hr 40min–10hr 50min); Patna (4–5 daily; 8hr 25min–11hr 10min); Shantiniketan (Bolpur) (5–6 daily; 8hr 35min–9hr

15min); Varanasi (Mughal Sarai) (3–4 daily; 12hr–18hr 36min).

Buses

Calcutta to: Bhubaneshwar (4 daily; 8–10hr); Puri (2 daily; 12hr); Siliguri NJP (4 daily; 12hr).
Siliguri to: Calcutta (4 daily; 12hr).

Flights

Any disparities in length of flight times are due to stopovers operating on certain flights only. In the listings below, AA represents Alliance Airways (Indian Airlines), AI Air India, BB Bangladesh Biman, DA Druk Air, IA Indian Airlines, JA Jet Airways, S is Sahara and TA is Thai Airways.

Calcutta to: Agartala (AA, IA 2 daily; 50min); Ahmedabad (AA 6 weekly; 2hr); Bagdogra/Siliguri (IA, JA 8 weekly; 55min); Bangkok (IA, DA, KL, TA 10 weekly; 1hr 20min); Bhubaneshwar (AA 6 weekly; 55min); Chennai (IA, JA 2 daily; 2hr 5min); Delhi (AA, IA, JA 5 daily; 2hr 5min); Dhaka (BB IA, 2 daily; 1hr 10min); Guwahati (IA, JA 2 daily; 1hr 10min–3hr 15min); Hyderabad (AA, JA 2 daily; 1hr

50min–3hr 15min); Imphal (AA, IA, JA 1 daily; 1–2hr); Jaipur (AA 6 weekly; 2hr 30min); Kathmandu (IA 5 weekly; 1hr 35min–2hr 15min); Lucknow (AA, S 2 daily; 2hr 20min); Mumbai (AI, IA, JA, S 5 daily; 2hr 30min); Nagpur (AA 3 weekly; 1hr 30min); Paro (Bhutan; DA 2 weekly; 1hr 20min); Patna (AA, S 1 daily; 1hr–2hr 30min); Port Blair (AA 5 weekly; 2hr); Varanasi (S 3 weekly; 1hr 30min); Yangon (Rangoon) (IA 2 weekly; 2hr 20min).

Bagdogra (Siliguri) to: Calcutta (IA, JA 8 weekly; 55min); Delhi (IA, JA 3 weekly; 2–4hr); Guwahati (IA 3 weekly; 2–3hr). Check to see whether Bagdogra flights are operating as the airport has been shut for repairs.

CHAPTER 14

Highlights

* **Sonepur Mela** Held in
  early November and
  lasting for a whole
  month, this festival and
  cattle fair sees a great
  gathering of pilgrims and
  sadhus. See p.999

* **The Bodhi Tree** A cutting from the tree under
  which Buddha was
  enlightened provides the
  focus of Bodhgaya's
  renowned Mahabodhi
  Temple. See p.1005

* **Rajgir** A dusty Buddhist
  pilgrimage town full of
  shrines and host to
  India's best sushi restaurant. See p.1009

* **Palamau National Park**
  This national park covers
  1000 square kilometres
  of hills in remote western
  Bihar, and offers
  elephant rides through
  tiger country.
  See p.1012

14

Bihar and Jharkhand

BIHAR and **JHARKHAND** occupy the flat eastern Ganges basin, south of Nepal between Uttar Pradesh and West Bengal. Now desperately poor and troubled, the region's glory days came early, when this was the land of the Buddha – born in Lumbini in Nepal, he spent much of his life wandering through the kingdoms of the Ganges. In his quest for truth during the sixth century BC, Prince Gautama visited **Vaishali** and **Rajgir**, before moving on to **Bodhgaya** and gaining enlightenment under the Bodhi Tree. Only during the nineteenth century was it demonstrated that the major events of the Buddha's life took place in identifiable sites here in north India, and the region now draws Buddhist pilgrims from all over the world. As well as being the first centre of Buddhism in north India, Bihar was its last bastion; the university of **Nalanda** stands as a poignant reminder of the extent of the faith.

During the sixth century BC, this was the heartland of the **Magadhas**, whose king, Bimbisara, was converted by the Buddha at his capital of Rajagriha (now Rajgir). Shortly after the Magadhas shifted their capital to Patna, they were overthrown around 321 BC by the dynamic **Chandragupta Maurya**, said to have met Alexander the Great. The next major dynasty to rule the area was the **Guptas**, around the fourth century AD, whose advent marked the return of Hinduism. Extraordinarily, even after the Muslim Sultanate swept the region at the end of the twelfth century, and the Moghuls came to rule all northern India from Delhi three hundred years later, the Buddhist centre of Bodhgaya continued to thrive. Bihar was incorporated into Bengal in 1764, soon fell under British jurisdiction, and eventually became a province and finally a state of modern India. Following agitation by the tribal majority in the south, the new state of Jharkhand was hewn out of Bihar in 2000.

Accommodation price codes

All accommodation prices in this book have been categorized using the price codes below. Prices given are for a double room, and all taxes are included. For more details, see p.51.

- ❶ up to Rs100
- ❷ Rs100–200
- ❸ Rs200–300
- ❹ Rs300–400
- ❺ Rs400–600
- ❻ Rs600–900
- ❼ Rs900–1500
- ❽ Rs1500–2500
- ❾ Rs2500 and upwards

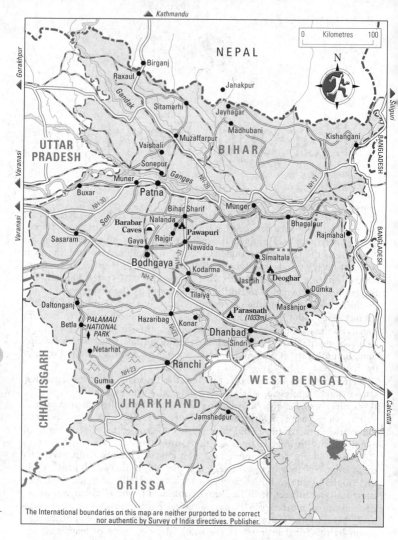

The International boundaries on this map are neither purported to be correct nor authentic by Survey of India directives. Publisher.

After torrential monsoons hit the Himalayas, much of Bihar is annually sub-merged with the River Kosi bursting its banks, and the Ganges in full flow, and yet at other times the area is racked by drought. Jharkhand, in the red hills of the Chotanagpur plateau to the south, has large tracts of forest; the remote southwestern region holds the wildlife sanctuary of Palamau National Park. Due to poverty, inter-caste violence and general lawlessness, Bihar and Jharkhand have a reputation as the worst-run states in the country (see box). Although the ordinary visitor or Buddhist pilgrim is usually unaffected by the frequent kidnappings, murders and acts of banditry, no one chooses to travel the roads at night.

"Good, bad and Bihar" ran a recent magazine headline that listed Bihar last of India's states in every index of development, from literacy to GDP. Even Buddhist pilgrims who race to the holy towns that are pumped with Japanese investment cannot but notice the decline: roads are appalling, buses and trains are ancient and jammed and in the capital itself there are no street lights and no one goes out at night. Yet Bihar is blessed with ample resources of coal and iron and large tracts of arable land. Its appalling condition is due largely to criminal misgovernance.

For most of the years since Independence, Bihar was ruled by a mafia of high-caste landowners who bled the state's coffers and kept the region entrenched in the feudal values of the "cow belt". No lower caste was allowed to catch the eye of his social superior or to sit on a chair in his presence. All that seemed about to change in 1991 when a rabble-rouser from the lowly caste of buffalo milkers, Laloo Prasad Yadav, united the backward castes, the Muslims and the untouchables – seventy percent of the electorate – under the banner of social justice, and won the election by a landslide. The charismatic earthy figure who willingly drank tea with the lowest of the low, the caste of rat-eaters, and promised "a lantern for every home", seemed like the new broom the state needed. In power, Laloo delighted with his common touch; he spontaneously unclogged traffic congestion by walking the streets with a loud-hailer and filled the grounds of his official residence with buffalo.

Unfortunately Laloo proved at least as bad as his predecessors. His cabinet of caste brethren included men wanted for murder and kidnap. Any distinction between criminals and politicians disappeared as violence became the usual route to political success. One hopeful candidate said, "without one hundred men with guns you cannot contest an election in Bihar." Much of the countryside degenerated into civil war as the upper castes, lower castes, Maoist guerrillas, police and private armies clashed in massacre and counter-massacre, leaving their enemies beheaded, or "shortened" as the locals say.

Laloo's career looked to be over when in 1997 he was imprisoned for embezzling billions of rupees from the state's animal husbandry department. He responded by getting his illiterate wife proclaimed chief minister and ruling through her from prison. He is currently free, but increasingly embroiled in scandal, and she remains officially in power.

Commentators who wrote Bihar off as a feudal irrelevance have been proved wrong as the state's social revolution has been repeated across India's poorer regions: everywhere the socially divisive brahminical order is under siege. Yet ballot rigging is no longer unusual, criminals fill the parliaments and, in Bihar, they could still do with a few more lanterns.

Patna and around

The capital of Bihar, **PATNA**, dates back to the sixth century BC, which makes it one of the oldest cities in India. Today, it's a nice enough place, but one which holds only the barest of indications of its former glory as the centre of the Magadhan and Mauryan empires. The sprawling metropolis hugs the south bank of the Ganges, stretching for around 15km in a shape that has changed little since Ajatasatru (491–459 BC) shifted the Magadhan capital here from Rajgir.

The first Mauryan emperor, **Chandragupta**, established himself in what was then **Pataliputra**, in 321 BC, and pushed the limits of his empire as far as the

PATNA

Sonepur, Vaishali, Muzaffarpur & Nepal ▲

Nalanda & Rajgir ▲

ACCOMMODATION
Akash	8
Chanakya	11
Kautilya Vihar Tourist Bungalow	10
Mamta	5
Maurya Patna	1
Mayur	9
Pataliputra Ashok	6
Rajasthan	3
Samrat International	7
Shyama	4
Youth Hostel	2

RESTAURANTS
Bansi Vihar	C
Madras	A
Mayfair	B
Paljï	D

River Ganges

Mahatma Gandhi Bridge

Old Opium Warehouse

Catholic Church

Har Mandir Sahib

Sher Shahi Mosque

Qila House

Gulzar Bagh Railway Station

Kumrahar Excavations

NEW BYPASS RD

Saif Khan's Mosque

Mahendra Ghat Ferry Terminal

Khuda Baksh Oriental Library

Khapi Emporium

Rajendra Nagar Railway Station

ASHOK RAJ PATH

BARI RD

OLD BYPASS RD

State Bank of India

EXHIBITION RD

HOTEL LANE

Patna Junction Railway Station

FRAZER RD

DAK BUNGALOW RD

BUDDHA MARG

Patna Museum

BAILEY RD

BEER CHAND PATEL PATH

GPO

Bus Stand

Bus Stand

British Library

Golghar

Gandhi Maidan

Indian Airlines

State Bank of India

Patna Junction Railway Station

Patna Museum

Harding Road Bus stand

GPO

DINAPORE RD

0 Metres 200

0 Metres 500

Muner & Varansi ▲

Airport ▲

Gaya ▲

N

Indus; his grandson **Ashoka** (274–237 BC), among the greatest of all Indian rulers, held sway over even greater domains. To facilitate Indo-Hellenic trade, the Mauryans built a Royal Highway from Pataliputra to Taxila in Pakistan, which later became the Grand Trunk Road, and similar highways reached towards the Bay of Bengal and along the east coast. The city experienced two later revivals. The first Gupta emperor, also named **Chandra Gupta**, made Patna his capital early in the fourth century AD, and a thousand years later it was rebuilt by the brilliant Afghan ruler Sher Shah Suri (1540–45), who constructed the Sher Shahi Mosque in the east of the city. Nearby, the beautiful *gurudwara* of **Har Mandir** was built to honour the birthplace of the tenth and most militant Sikh Guru – guru Gobind Singh. In his honour, the old quarter of the city is often referred to as **Patna Sahib**.

Arrival and information

Patna has three **stations** but all main-line train services arrive at Patna Junction, in the west of the city. Fraser Road (now Mazharul-Raq Path), immediately north of the station, is the main drag, with as much glamour as the state can muster – though even here you'll see rag pickers living on the pavement. Patna's **airport** lies 5km to the west, linked to town by taxis and Indian Airlines buses. A few hundred metres west of the station, the chaotic **Harding Park bus stand** runs services to and from Gaya, Varanasi, and the Nepal border at Raxaul (gate 6). North of Fraser Road, between Gandhi Maidan and the River Ganges, the **Gandhi Maidan bus stand** is the terminus for Bihar State Transport and serves destinations throughout Bihar. Cycle rickshaws and auto-rickshaws are the most common means of transport; shared Vikram auto-rickshaws cross the city east to west for around Rs10 with a change at Gandhi Maidan for Patna Sahib.

The **Bihar Tourist Office**, cunningly disguised as the *Silver Oak Bar* on Fraser Road (Mon–Fri 9am–6pm, Sat 9am–1pm; ☏0612/225295), provides scant information and organizes weekend tours, taking in Patna, Nalanda, Rajgir and Pawapuri. The inconveniently located **Government of India Tourist Office**, close to the railway bridge at Sudama Place, Kankar Bagh Road (Mon–Fri 9am–6pm, Sat 9am–1pm; ☏0612/345776), runs a guide service and is more helpful. A number of agents (see p.1000) also organize tours and arrange **car rental**, but many drivers refuse to take visitors to the more isolated areas as the roads are so bad. The State Bank of India, on West Gandhi Maidan (☏0612/226134), handles **foreign exchange**, and the **GPO** is on Buddha Marg. For **internet** access, visit Cybercity (8am–7pm; Rs 50/hr) close to the *Bansi Vihar Restaurant* on Fraser Road.

Accommodation

Patna has plenty of **accommodation**, although curiously most of it is fully booked most of the time. The cheaper hotels can be found on "Hotel Lane" at the station end of Fraser Road opposite the *Samrat*. The top end of Exhibition Road also has a cluster of cheap to mid-range hotels, while Patna's number-one hotel the *Maurya* is at the top of Fraser Road near the *maidan*. The railway station **retiring rooms** are good value at Rs100.

Akash, Hotel Lane, off Fraser Road
☏0612/239599. Better than most in the lane, with smallish but clean rooms. ❸–❹

Chanakya, Beer Chand Patel Marg
☏0612/223141. Comfortable three-star hotel with a couple of restaurants. ❽

Kautilya Vihar Tourist Bungalow, Beer Chand Patel Path ☎ 0612/225411. Spacious but badly maintained place run by Bihar Tourism, offering a/c rooms and a restaurant. ❺

Mamta, intersection of Fraser Road and Dak Bungalow Chowk ☎ 0612/221311. Large rooms with attached bath, plus the excellent *Anarkali* restaurant. ❺

Maurya Patna, Fraser Road, South Gandhi Maidan ☎ 0612/222061. The only luxury hotel in town with numerous facilities and a nice location. Boasts a pleasant bar, multi-cuisine restaurant, travel agency and swimming pool. ❾

Mayur, Fraser Road ☎ 0612/224149. A reasonable restaurant, a large dimly lit bar and affordable if ordinary rooms with hot water in the mornings. ❹–❺

Pataliputra Ashok, Beer Chand Patel Path ☎ 0612/226270. Large, comfortable chain hotel with friendly staff. Swimming pool, restaurant and travel agency. ❾

Rajasthan, Fraser Road ☎ 0612/225102. A friendly and well-managed old Indian-style hotel with some a/c rooms and a recommended vegetarian restaurant. ❺–❻

Samrat International, Fraser Road ☎ 0612/220560. The fanciest hotel in this part of town. Close to amenities, with comfortable rooms (some a/c) with satellite TV and a few restaurants including a rooftop one open in winter. Expensive for what you get – there isn't even constant hot water – but you may end up here by default as it's the only hotel near the station that isn't usually full. ❼

Shyama, Exhibition Road ☎ 0612/655539. One of the better budget hotels on this busy road, with cheap rooms and attached baths. ❷–❸

Youth Hostel, near the *Maurya Patna* at top end of Fraser Road (no phone). The usual restrictions apply, but it's only Rs40 for a dorm bed. Clean and well run, it's the best budget option in town, but you have to be a member of the YHA.

The Town

Patna's most remarkable monument dates from the British era. This huge grain storage house known as **Golghar**, the "round house" – now a symbol of the city, was built in 1786 by John Garstin at the behest of the then administrator, Warren Hastings, in the hope of avoiding a repetition of the terrible famine of 1770. Mercifully it never needed to be used. Overlooking the river and the *maidan*, it looks like the upper half of a giant off-white Easter egg, decorated with two sets of stairs that spiral their way to the summit, 29m above the road. These were designed so that coolies could carry grain up one flight, deliver their load through a hole at the top, and descend the other stairs. Constructed with stone slabs, the base of the structure is 125m wide, with 3.6-metre-thick walls. Sightseers now clamber up for views of the mighty river and the town.

Within walking distance, close to the new Indira Gandhi Planetarium, the **Patna Museum** (Tues–Sun 10am–4.30pm; Rs2), though faded and run-down, has an excellent collection of sculpture. Among its most famous pieces is a polished sandstone female attendant or *yakshi*, holding a fly-whisk, found at Didarganj and dating from the third century BC. Some Jain images from the Kushana period, and a group of Buddhist *bodhisattvas* from the Gandhara region (northwest Pakistan), belong to the second and third centuries AD. Amongst the natural-history exhibits are several stuffed animals, including a few freakishly deformed ones, and a gigantic fossilized tree thought to be 200 million years old. The museum also houses Chinese art, and the second floor is devoted to some superb Tibetan *thangkas* (scroll paintings), in dire need of restoration.

Founded in 1900, the **Khuda Bhaksh Oriental Library**, east of Gandhi Maidan, has a remarkable selection of books from all over the Islamic world, all gathered by one man. Besides rare Persian and Arabic manuscripts, it houses Moghul and Rajput miniatures, and manuscripts rescued from the Moorish University at Córdoba in Spain. One of its more unusual exhibits is a tiny Koran measuring just 25mm in width.

Har Mandir Sahib and beyond

In the most interesting area of Patna – the older part of town, 10km east of Gandhi Maidan – filthy congested lanes crammed with vehicles of all kinds lead to **Har Mandir Sahib**, the second holiest of the four great Sikh shrines known as *takhts* (thrones), and dedicated to Guru Gobind Singh, born in Patna in 1660. The dazzling white onion-domed marble temple is set in an expansive courtyard off the main road. Visitors are welcome to roam around the courtyard and even venture inside where more than likely there will be some devotional music playing. A free shoe locker service is provided at the edge of the courtyard; remove your shoes and cover your head before entering. Shared auto-rickshaws cost around Rs5–10 from Gandhi Maidan.

A little way north, the private **Qila House** (or Jalan Museum) on Jalan Avenue holds a fine collection of art including Chinese paintings and Moghul filigree work in jade and silver (call ahead for permission from the Jalan family; ☎0612/225070). Among the antiques are porcelain that once belonged to Marie Antoinette, and Napoleon's four-poster bed. Further west, the **Old Opium Warehouse** at **Gulzaribagh**, now a printing press, gives you the chance to see the former warehouses where the East India Company stored opium for trade on behalf of the British government. A couple of kilometres west stands **Saif Khan's Mosque** or the "mosque of stone", built by Parwez Shah, son of the great Moghul emperor Jahangir, during his time in charge of Bihar.

Eating

Fraser Road features several good **restaurants**, such as the *Bansi Vihar*, a good-value south Indian veg place – though wrap up warm as the air-conditioning is fierce – and the excellent *Anarkali* in *Hotel Mamta*. Reasonable *Palji* at Krishna Chowk near the railway station is popular with locals, and the *Mayfair* at the end of Hotel Lane is cheap, cheerful and always busy. The *Madras* does good south Indian food and the *Rajasthan* hotel nearby has a quality vegetarian restaurant. Many of the a/c restaurants along this stretch double as bars and have two shifts – families are served earlier in the evening; later the custom is all male.

Around Patna

Patna makes a popular base for exploring Nalanda and Rajgir, as well as Vaishali to the north, but there are also places of interest closer at hand. The fabulous *dargah* – Sufi mausoleum – at **Muner**, on the road to Varanasi, is the prime attraction, but if you're in the area between early November and early December, don't miss the **Sonepur Mela**, an enormous month-long **cattle fair** held across the huge Gandhi Bridge, 25km north of Patna at the confluence of the Gandak and Ganges. Cattle, elephants, camels, parakeets and other animals are brought for sale, pilgrims combine business with a dip in the Ganges, *sadhus* congregate, and festivities include song and dance performances as well as a large funfair with stalls and a circus. Incidentally, Sonepur town claims to have the longest railway platform in the world, though it's not one that would win any prizes for maintenance.

Bihar Tourism (see p.997) organizes tours and maintains a tourist village at Sonepur during the Mela, with a bungalow and several huts providing a range of accommodation (➊–➍).

Patna Junction is the most important **railway** station in the region, connected to Gaya, Delhi, Varanasi, Darjeeling (NJP), Calcutta, Mumbai and Chennai. There is a foreigners' reservation counter on the first floor of the booking office. The best train to **Calcutta** (Howrah) is the fast Rajdhani Express #2306 (Tues & Sat); other principal trains to Calcutta are the Poorva Express #2304 (Mon, Thurs, Fri & Sun) and the Howrah–Amritsar Express #3050. The Patna–Delhi–Shramjeevi Express #2401 also stops at Varanasi and most major trains stop at **Mughal Sarai**, not far from Varanasi. Among others, the Rajdhani Express #2305 and the Poorva Express #2303 travel to Delhi. The Guwahati Dadar Express #5646 travels to Mumbai and in the other direction, on its way to **Guwahati**, stops at **New Jalpaiguri**, handy for Darjeeling and Sikkim; more convenient trains to the northeast include the NE Express #5622. The Patna–Puri Express #8450 (Wed) travels to **Puri** on the Orissa coast, while the #2816 New Delhi–Puri train (Mon, Wed, Thurs & Sat) is more regular, but passes through Gaya not Patna; take the 9.50am Patna Hatia Express #8625 for the short journey to Gaya. Travelling to the deep south, the weekly Cochin–Patna Express #6310 leaves on Thurs and the Patna–Chennai Express #6044 leaves twice a week (Thurs & Sat).

Patna Airport is linked by Indian Airlines, at City Office, South Gandhi Maidan (☏ 0612/222554), to Calcutta, Ranchi, Delhi and Lucknow; Sahara Indian Airlines, East Gandhi Maidan (☏ 0612/661109) flies three times a week (Mon, Wed & Fri) to Delhi (via Varanasi) and the same days to Mumbai via Lucknow. Necon Air (☏ 0612/224511) flies to Kathmandu three times a week (Tues, Thurs & Sun) and can be booked through Mamta Travels (see below).

Travel companies offer bus tickets to **Kathmandu** with a voucher for the bus across the border although it is just as easy and often wiser to make your own arrangements. Although Harding Road bus stand is a 200-metre stretch of chaos with few signs and no central booking office, there are plenty of vociferous touts who will guide you to your bus. Around eighteen buses a day leave for the six-hour ride to the Nepalese border at Raxaul (see p.1002) from gate 6 starting at 4am and timetabled until 1am, although it's best to stick to services running during daylight hours. **Buses** to Gaya, Vaishali and via Muner to Varanasi leave from Harding Road – some services to Vaishali also depart from the Gandhi Maidan bus stand. There are no direct buses to Rajgir, Nalanda and Pawapuri; services run via Bihar Sharif.

Reliable **travel agents** include: Ashok Travel & Tours, in the *Hotel Pataliputra Ashok*; Inter Travel Shop, Fraser Road (☏ 0612/221337); Travel Corporation of India, Maurya Patna Complex (☏ 0612/221699); and Mamta Travels, *Mamta Hotel*, Fraser Road (☏ 0612/220383), who are also agents for Necon Air.

Muner

The imposing but neglected red-sandstone **mausoleum** of the Sufi saint Yahia Muneri overlooks a lake 27km west of Patna on the busy Varanasi road, 1km west of **MUNER** – an easy bus ride from the city. The shrine itself, built in 1605 by Ibrahim Khan, the governor of Gujarat under Jahangir, stands atop a hillock; the beautifully maintained gardens below are the responsibility of the devout and traditionalist Sufi caretakers. Every year, around February, a three-day *urs* or festival in the saint's honour attracts pilgrims from far and wide, including *qawwals*, the renowned Sufi minstrels of the Chistia orders of Delhi and Ajmer. If you do come to Muner, it's worth knowing that the town is famous for its **sweets**, and especially *ladoos*, made of lentils.

North Bihar

The one area of Bihar capable of growing reliable crops is the fertile agricultural belt along the Himalayan foothills north of the Ganges. Other than passing through en route to Nepal via the large town of **Muzaffarpur**, most visitors only pause to explore the remains of the abandoned Buddhist city of **Vaishali**, although the region also holds a handful of shrines and temple towns associated with the *Ramayana*.

Vaishali

Set amid paddy fields 55km north of Patna, the quiet hamlet of **VAISHALI** is significant to both Buddhists and Jains. Archeological excavations are still in progress and only a fraction of this ancient city, buried in the silt of the River Gandak and dating from the sixth century BC, has yet been unearthed. This was where the Buddha preached his last sermon before he died in Kushinagar around 483 BC.

Named after King Visala, who is mentioned in the *Ramayana*, Vaishali is believed by some historians to have been the first city state in the world to practise a democratic, republican form of government. After leaving Nepal and renouncing the world and his family, Prince Gautama studied here, but eventually rejected his master's teachings and found his own path to enlightenment and Buddhahood. He returned to Vaishili three times and on his last visit announced his final liberation – *Mahaparinirvana* – and departure from the world. One hundred years later, in 383 BC, the Second Buddhist Council was held in Vaishali and two stupas were erected. For a further thousand years, under Pataliputra (Patna) as capital, Vaishali continued to prosper.

A small but well-presented **archeological museum** (daily except Fri 10am–5pm; free) provides a glimpse into the ancient Buddhist world. A short path next to the **Coronation Tank** (Abhishekh Pushkarni) leads off to the remains of the stupa, now covered by a roof, where the supposed ashes of the Buddha were found in a silver urn.

Two kilometres north at **Kolhua** stands the remarkably well-preserved **Ashokan Pillar**, erected by the Mauryan emperor (273–232 BC) to commemorate the site of the Buddha's last sermon. Known locally as Bhimsen-ki-lathi (Bhimsen's Staff), the 18.3-metre-high pillar, made of polished red sandstone, is crowned by a lion sitting on an inverted lotus, which faces north towards Kushinagar. Jains of the Svetambara sect, who believe that the last *tirthankara*, Mahavira, was born in Vaishali in 599 BC, have erected a shrine in the fields 1km east of Kolhua.

Travel agents in Patna can arrange **transport** to Vaishali or you can take a bus as far as Sonepur or Hajipur, and change onto one of the overcrowded local shared taxis. Direct buses leave from Gandhi Maidan but are few and far between. Most people take in Vaishali as a day-trip from Patna, but there is a tourist bungalow (❶–❷) and a youth hostel (❶) here, both run by Bihar Tourism (☎0612/225295).

The road to Nepal

Travellers heading from Patna towards **Nepal** have to cross the border at **Raxaul**, six hours away by bus. If you want to break the journey at **Muzaffarpur** you'll find limited **accommodation** near the bus stand and in

Jitwarpur, a village on the outskirts of the small town of Madhuban, in the district of Mithila in north Bihar, is the home of a vibrant tradition of Indian folk art. Madhubani paintings started out as decorations for the outside of village huts, executed by women using natural dyes. Illustrations of mythological themes, incorporating images of local deities as well as Hindu gods and goddesses, the paintings were eventually transferred onto handmade paper, often using bright synthetic primary colours to fill the strong black line drawings. You do see plain black and white pictures, but more familiar now are paintings dominated by reds, pinks and blues and offset by yellow on a white background. Fabrics printed with Madhubani designs have become very chic; these days they tend to be professionally made elsewhere, and are sold in the expensive boutiques of India's major cities.

Buses connect Patna to Madhubani (5hr 30min) where there is some basic accommodation; rickshaws can take you on to Jitwarpur.

the town centre near the railway station. You can then continue to Raxaul by bus or train.

RAXAUL itself is an unattractive, grubby town with limited amenities, infested with mosquitoes and flies, so you're better off staying at Birganj across the Nepal border. If you have **to stay**, the clean **retiring rooms** are the best bet, but guests have to have a rail ticket and pay a small fee. The *Ajanta* on Ashram Road (**2**) is the best that Raxaul has to offer, with some a/c rooms, attached baths and meals prepared to order, or there's the more basic *Asia*, also on Ashram Road (**1–2**). **Cafés** along the main road include one at the cinema, serving a local delicacy of kebab and *muri* (puffed rice).

The border itself, between Raxaul and the Nepalese town of **Birganj**, 5km away (a Rs20 rickshaw ride), is open 24hr for foreigners, but in practice the Nepal side is often left unmanned and closes from 7pm to 5am. If you don't already have a visa, you'll be expected to pay in cash ($30). Early-morning buses and one at night run from Birganj to Kathmandu (12hr) and Pokhara (10hr). Minibuses (8hr) cost slightly more – reserve a seat in advance of departure if you can. The foreign exchange facility in Raxaul will only change Indian to Nepalese rupees, but Birganj has facilities to change travellers' cheques and US dollars.

Central Bihar

South of the Ganges and north of the hills of the Chotanagpur plateau, **Central Bihar** contains some of north India's most important Buddhist sites. The greatest shrine of all, a focus for Buddhists from around the world, is the Bodhi Tree at **Bodhgaya** where the Buddha gained enlightenment.

Gaya

The flyblown and densely packed town of **GAYA**, 100km south of Patna, serves as an essential transit point for visitors to **Bodhgaya**, 13km away. Far from appealing in itself, it is however of great significance to Hindus, who come here to honour their parents a year after death by offering *pind* – a gift of funeral cakes – at the massive **Vishnupad temple**, where non–Hindus are forbidden. After the monsoon, when the river is in spate, pilgrims bathe in the river and present offerings. During the dry season, they have to content themselves with holes dug into the riverbed to the water level.

Practicalities

Most people arrive at Gaya by **train** and are met by a bewildering array of touts offering rickshaws, auto-rickshaws, taxis and tongas; all of them assume that you are heading for Bodhgaya. The best option is take a cycle rickshaw to Kacheri bus stand from where you can continue to Bodhgaya by auto-rickshaw or bus. If you arrive after dark, plan to stay the night in Gaya as the route between the two is dangerous bandit territory. There is precious little to do in Gaya and tourist facilities and information are appalling given the large numbers of tourists passing through.

Accommodation and eating

Most of Gaya's **hotels** are along Station Road near the railway station, and there's little to choose between them. The *Ajatsatru* has the widest range of rooms, while the *Siddhartha International* is the only luxury hotel in town. The **railway retiring rooms** are clean, some with a/c (Rs 1000).

Ajatsatru, opposite the station ☎ 0631/21514. Wide range of rooms with attached bathrooms. Also has its own restaurant. ❷–❺

Ajit Rest House, Station Road ☎ 0631/420198. Standard budget option near the station. ❶–❷

Pal, off Station Road down a short alley ☎ 0631/436953. Reasonable budget place, quieter than those on the main road. ❶–❷

Siddhartha International, Station Road ☎ 0631/436243. The best in Gaya with a/c rooms, foreign exchange and a plush restaurant. ❾

Moving on from Gaya

Moving on from Gaya is a high priority for most foreign visitors, who usually only wish to travel 13km to the sanctuary of Bodhgaya. However Gaya is an important transport centre and a major junction on the main railway line between Calcutta, Varanasi and New Delhi. Trains to Calcutta include the Poorva Express #2382, the Dehra Dun Express #3010 and the faster but less convenient Rajdhani Express #2302, which departs very early in the morning. The New Delhi–Puri Express #2816 runs on Mon, Wed, Thurs and Sat to Puri on the Orissa coast. Trains to New Delhi include the Rajdhani Express #2301 (Mon, Tues, Thurs, Fri & Sat) and the Poorva Express #2381 (Wed, Thurs & Sun).

Bihar Roadways runs services from the Gandhi Maidan bus stand to Patna, Ranchi, Varanasi and Calcutta. Buses to Rajgir leave from the Gaurakshini bus stand across the river on the outskirts of town (hourly; 2hr 30min). Three buses to Patna (7am, 8am & 3pm) pick up passengers from the train railway. Buses to Bodhgaya leave from the Kacheri bus stand, from where you can also pick up shared auto-rickshaws.

Bodhgaya

BODHGAYA, 13km south of Gaya beside the River Phalgu, is sacred to Buddhists as the place where the Buddha gained enlightenment. A giant Buddhist resort of international monasteries and temples has grown up around the imposing **Mahabodhi temple**, which holds the world's most revered tree, an offshoot of the original Bodhi tree under which the Buddha supposedly sat.

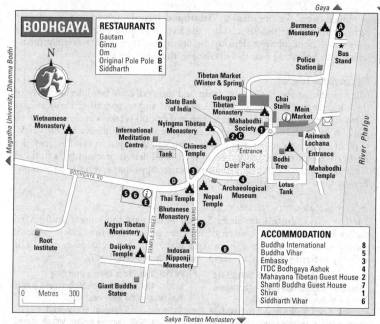

Sakya Tibetan Monastery ▼

Bodhgaya is by far the most important and significant of the four holy sites of Buddhism – the other three being Buddha's birthplace, Lumbini in Nepal; Sarnath near Varanasi, where he preached his first sermon ("The Turning of the Wheel of Dharma"); and Kushinagar near Gorakhpur, Uttar Pradesh, where he passed away.

Although the site dates back to the period immediately following the Buddha's passing, the temple complex probably began to take its present shape in the seventh century AD, around the time the Chinese pilgrim Xuan Zhang visited it. Even after the sack of Nalanda and the virtual demise of Buddhism in north India, it continued to flourish during the Muslim period. After the sixteenth century it began to decline, falling into the hands of brahmin Hindu priests, who professed to be baffled by its origins when the first British archeologists turned up here early in the nineteenth century. Once excavations had shown the site's true provenance, it was rejuvenated by overseas Buddhists, and is now the most important pilgrimage site of international Buddhism, with all Buddhist nations represented in its many scattered monasteries, temples and shrines.

From November to February, Bodhgaya is the home of an animated community of exiled **Tibetans**, sometimes including the Dalai Lama himself, as well as a stream of shaven-headed international Tibetophiles. During this time a huge canvas city emerges on the grounds next to the Gelugpa monastery. Hinayana and Mahayana meditation courses attract others, while large monasteries from places like Darjeeling bring their international followers to attend ceremonies and lectures under the Bodhi Tree, where Buddhists from around the world rub shoulders. In summer, from mid-March to mid-October, long after the Dalai Lama's official and unofficial entourage has left for the hills, the region becomes oppressively hot, and Bodhgaya returns once again to its quiet ways.

Unfortunately all is not wholly peaceful at this holiest of holy shrines. The Mahabodhi temple is also sacred to Hindus, who see the Buddha as an incarnation of Vishnu, and, strangely, the committee that looks after it is controlled by a Hindu majority, despite strong protests from the Buddhist world. The resultant differences of approach are exacerbated by contrasting forms of worship – while the Buddhists continue a solitary inward approach, Hindus tend towards spectacle and noisy ceremony.

The Mahabodhi Temple and the Bodhi Tree

The elegant single spire of the **Mahabodhi temple**, rising to the lofty height of 55m above the trees of its leafy compound at the centre of Bodhgaya, is visible from all over the surrounding countryside. Within the temple complex, which is liberally sprinkled with small stupas and shrines, the main brick temple stands in a hollow encircled by a stone railing dating from the second century BC. Only three-quarters of the railing remains in place; other sections are in the site museum and museums in Calcutta and London.

Unlike most popular temples in India, the Mahabodhi temple exudes an atmosphere of peace and tranquillity. Extensively renovated during the nineteenth century, it is supposed to be a replica of the seventh-century structure that in turn stood on the site of Ashoka's original third-century shrine. Its busy detail includes niches and short towers on all four corners. Inside the temple, a single chamber holds a large gilded image of the Buddha, while upstairs are a balcony and a small plain meditation chamber.

At the rear of the temple to the west, the large **Bodhi Tree** grows out of an expansive base, in pleasant grounds that attract scholars and meditators. For all its holiness, this is in fact only a distant offshoot of the original tree under which the Buddha gained enlightenment as the actual tree was destroyed by Ashoka before his conversion to the faith. His daughter Sanghamitta took a sapling to Sri Lanka, and planted it at Anuradhapura, where its offshoots were nurtured, and a sapling was brought back and replanted here. Pilgrims tie coloured thread to its far-reaching branches, decorated by prayer flags, and Tibetans accompany their rituals with long lines of butter lamps. A sandstone slab with carved sides next to the tree is believed to be the **Vajrasana** or "thunder-seat" upon which the Buddha sat facing east (towards the temple).

The small white **Animesh Lochana temple** to the right of the compound entrance – a miniature version of the main one – marks the spot where the Buddha stood and gazed upon the Bodhi Tree in gratitude. It now obscures the view of the tree, but not the long raised platform known as the **Chankramana** along the northern wall where the Buddha paced in meditation. Remains of a row of columns suggest that it may once have been covered. Numerous ornate stupas from the Pala period (seventh–twelfth centuries AD) are littered around the grounds. Next to the temple compound to the south is the rectangular Lotus Pool where the Buddha may have bathed.

Entry to the temple compound (daily 6am–6.30pm) is from the east; shoes are tolerated within the grounds but not inside the temple, and can be left here. There is a Rs5 camera and Rs100 video camera tax.

Temples and monasteries

Incongruous modern monasteries and temples transform the arid landscape into Buddhaworld. Some are very simple and others, like the **Thai** temple, complete with its unmistakeable roof, elaborate confections. They are all open from around 7am to noon and from 2pm to 6pm. The Gelugpa **Tibetan** monastery, or *gompa*, is located within the Tibetan quarter northwest of the main shrine. Built over the last four decades, the complex includes a central prayer hall, a large prayer wheel and residential buildings. Each winter, this area of Bodhgaya is transformed by its annual influx of Tibetans, who erect a small market and set up restaurants and cafés. The bigger of the two other Tibetan monasteries further west belongs to the **Kagyu** sect; its spacious main prayer hall is decorated with beautiful modern murals, Buddha images and a large *Dharma Chakra* or Wheel of Law. The other two major Tibetan schools also have monastic representation here – there's a new **Nyingma** *gompa* next to the Chinese temple and a small **Sakya** *gompa* beyond *Hotel Buddha International*.

Next to the Kagyu monastery, the Daijokyo monastery captures in concrete some elements of a traditional Japanese temple and belongs to the **Nichiren** sect. Opposite that, the **Indosan Nipponji temple** has an elegant and simple hut-like roof and a beautiful image of Buddha inside its main hall. Next door, the exquisite **Bhutanese Monastery** features finely painted murals and ceiling mandalas. In a decorative garden at the end of the road, the 25-metre

Meditation courses in Bodhgaya

Especially during the winter high season, short- and long-term meditation courses are available in either of two distinct traditions of Buddhism – Mahayana (the Great Vehicle), epitomized by the various forms of Tibetan Buddhism which spread across China and Japan evolving along the way, and Hinayana (or Theravada), as practised in Sri Lanka, Thailand and other parts of Southeast Asia. Check noticeboards in the various cafés, and ask at the Root Institute or the Burmese Vihar.

The Root Institute for Wisdom Culture (☎0631/400714, ⊛ www.rootinst@nda.vsnl.net.in) is a real haven, a semi-monastic *dharma* centre 2km west of the main temple with pleasant gardens, a shrine room, library and accommodation, all enclosed in its own grounds. It organizes seven- and ten-day residential courses, focusing on the Mahayana tradition. An eight-day course costs Rs2600 including food. Single rooms, some with bathrooms and verandas, are available from Rs225–350, and the pleasant dorm is Rs125 a day. Breakfast is included. Practitioners can take on rooms for retreats of up to three months, but these should be booked well in advance. The institute is always looking for volunteers, for general tasks and to help in its charitable school and polio clinic. All are funded by the Foundation for the Preservation of the Mahayana Tradition. FPMT runs ninety Buddhist meditation and retreat centres throughout the world including one in Kopan near Kathmandu, Nepal, and is involved in the ambitious Maitreya Project to construct a 128-metre Buddha.

The Dhamma Bodhi International Meditation Centre (☎0631/400437), one of many Vipassana centres in India, lies a few kilometres out of town near Magadha University on Dobi Road. It organizes regular ten- and twenty-day courses throughout the year (except June). Details of all Vipassana courses are available from the International Academy in Maharashtra (☎02553/84076). Alternatively, you can contact the Dhamma Dipa Centre in England (Harewood End, Hereford HR2 8JS; ☎01989/730234).

The International Meditation Centre (☎0631/400707), a couple of hundred metres behind the Chinese temple, is run by Dr Rastrapal Mahathera and holds ten-day beginners' Vipassana courses and thirty-day courses for the more experienced. A typical day begins at 4.30am and features six hours of group meditation with various breaks in between. Donations are accepted as there are no fixed fees.

Another centre of activity is the Burmese Vihar. Although not currently running meditation courses they have some useful information and are involved with voluntary social work projects including schools. Western volunteers are always welcome. The Thai temple also runs occasional meditation courses in the Theravada tradition. Friends of the Lotus Mission just behind the Chinese temple offer Zen instruction.

Japanese-style **Giant Buddha Statue** was consecrated by the Dalai Lama in 1989. The Sri-Lankan-based **Mahabodhi Society** (☏0631/400742), responsible for reviving Bodhgaya in the nineteenth century, maintains a small complex northwest of the Mahabodhi temple and has staff willing to offer advice on accommodation and courses.

Bodhgaya's **Archeological Museum** (daily except Fri 10am–5pm; free), a short way west of the Deer Park near the *Ashok Hotel*, holds a collection of locally discovered sculpture, and ninth-century Pala bronzes of Hindu and Buddhist deities.

Practicalities

Buses connecting Bodhgaya and Gaya leave from outside Gaya train station and more frequently from the Kacheri bus and auto-rickshaw stand a couple of kilometres south of the station. Shared auto-rickshaws are quicker, even more frequent and cost just a little more. You'll need to travel back to Gaya to pick up most onward services from Bodhgaya, although two buses a day run directly to Patna departing from the Bihar Tourism Complex at 7am and 2pm, and a direct bus also leaves for Varanasi at 5am.

All buses turn round on the main road north, by the Burmese Vihar and 600m before the pedestrianized temple zone, while auto-rickshaws drop off at the end of the road. The pedestrian area in front of the main Mahabodhi temple has numerous souvenir stalls and travel agents, a small tourist office and throngs of expectant beggars and buskers who greet you with salutations and empty bowls. The main **tourist office** (Mon–Fri 9am–6pm, Sat 10am–1pm) is in the Bihar Tourist Complex a couple of hundred metres past the Thai temple. The State Bank of India (Mon–Fri 10.30am–2.30pm, Sat 10.30am–12.30pm) in front of the *Mahayana Tibet Guest House* has a tiny **foreign-exchange** room. There is also a Bank of India in the *Embassy Hotel* building. Tours of the area and car rental can be arranged by any of the numerous **travel agents** in Bodhgaya bearing predictable names such as Buddha Tours, Middle Way Tours and Potala Tours.

Recent building activity has resulted in several new, mediocre and overpriced **hotels**. Pilgrims usually stay in their respective temples, monasteries or pilgrim guesthouses. Most of the monastery guesthouses welcome tourists, but expect them to adhere to the same rules and regulations as the pilgrims, in particular no smoking, alcohol or sex. They are much cheaper than the hotels and provide opportunities to chat to the monks and join in the *pujas*. Wherever you stay, make sure they provide a mosquito net or put up your own.

Accommodation: monasteries

Bhutanese Monastery. Old guesthouse, next to the monastery, and full of character. Singles and family rooms. ❷–❹

Burmese Monastery (Vihar), Gaya Road. Set in a pleasant garden, this is a long-time favourite with Westerners. It is very spartan, cramped but cheap, and the absence of fans and a/c and the prevalence of biting insects will test your Buddhist indifference to personal comfort. ❶

Daijokyo Temple, near the Giant Buddha Statue ☏0631/400747. Beautifully maintained Japanese Nichiren Buddhist hotel for pilgrims and tour groups; others are allowed to stay by discretion – telephone first. An excellent kitchen specializes in Japanese

cuisine. Currently running on a donations basis.

Gelugpa Tibetan Monastery. At the end of the pedestrian zone, this popular accommodation stands right in the heart of it all. ❷–❸

Kagyu Tibetan Monastery. On the road to the big Buddha, this is a friendly low-cost, chilled-out place. ❶

Mahabodhi Society Pilgrim Rest House (*Sri Lankan Guest House*, ☏0631 400742), Mahabodhi Society. Popular with pilgrims and often full. There's a dorm and a handful of rooms, plus a reasonable vegetarian canteen. ❶–❸

Nyingma Tibetan Monastery. New accommodation block overlooking the monastery. Large rooms

with shared bathrooms, but excellent value. ❶
Root Institute, past the Thai temple
☎ 0631/400714. Meditation centre which offers
accommodation in two comfortable new blocks as
well as detached rooms for retreats. A peaceful
environment with well-maintained gardens (see

p.1006). Breakfast included. ❸ –❹
Sakya Tibetan Monastery, on the edge of town
past the *Buddha International* hotel. Quiet,
basic and cheap, and it has just been refurbished. ❶

Accommodation: hotels

Buddha International ☎ 0631/400506. In the
south of town near the Indosan Japanese temple.
With an impressive lobby and nice lawn it's pleasant but pricey. ❼ –❽
Buddha Vihar, Bihar Tourist Complex
☎ 0631/400445. Cheap three- four- and six-bed
dorm accommodation. ❶
Embassy, opposite the Nepalese temple
☎ 0631/400711. Reasonable rooms and rooftop
views, but a little expensive for what you get. ❻ –❽
ITDC Bodhgaya Ashok, near the museum
☎ 0631/400700. Comfortable bungalow-type
accommodation with a pleasant lawn, an upmarket restaurant and several in-house facilities
including a travel desk. ❽ –❾

Mahayana Tibetan Guest House, 200m from the
Gelugpa Monastery. This huge hotel is new, spotless and a little bland. ❸ –❹
Shanti Buddha Guest House, just past the
Sujata, south of the museum. Reasonable, but
pricy en-suite rooms. ❻ –❽
Shiva, opposite Mahabodhi Temple,
☎ 0631/400425. Central, small and new with a
range of comfortable a/c rooms, a traveller-style
restaurant and internet access. ❺ –❼
Siddharth Vihar, Bihar Tourist Complex
☎ 0631/400445. Double rooms with attached bath
and carpets. ❸ –❺

Eating

There are several small **cafés** in the Mahabodhi temple market complex. The
friendly and informative *Ginza* restaurant opposite the Thai temple serves stan-
dard travellers' favourites as well as Tibetan bread and Japanese food. Opposite
the Burmese Vihar, you'll find excellent cinnamon rolls and apple strudel at the
Gautam tent restaurant. The various *Pole Pole* restaurants nearby have similar
Western-oriented menus and all claim to have been the first; the *Original Pole
Pole* is the most pleasant, with good coffee. *Om Restaurant* opposite the Deer
Park has standard traveller food and does a good veg Manchurian. During the
Tibetan influx (Nov–Feb), Tibetan cafés spring up in the temporary tented
market area across the road from the Gelugpa Tibetan Monastery. *Fujiya Green*,
which sets up just west of the monastery, serves cheap and nourishing Tibetan
and Chinese food in a surprisingly salubrious tent.

Around Bodhgaya: Mahakala Caves

The **Mahakala** (or Dungeshwari) **Caves**, in remote, almost desert-like surroundings on the far side of the Phalgu 18km northeast of Bodhgaya, are where
the Buddha did the severe penance that resulted in the familiar image of him
as a skeletal, emaciated figure. After years of extreme self-denial at Mahakala,
he realized its futility and walked down to Bodhgaya, where he received rice
as a gift. A short time later, after a final battle with temptation, he achieved nirvana under the Bodhi Tree. A short climb from the base of the impressive cliff
leads to a Tibetan monastery and the small caves themselves. A Buddhist shrine
inside the main cave is run by Tibetans, although a Hindu priest has recently
set himself up in competition. Few tourists make it here and the occasional car
or bus that does arrive gets mobbed by urchins and beggars. Offers by international Buddhist communities to help build roads and some sort of infrastructure have been rejected by the Bihar government.

Rajgir

Eighty kilometres northeast of Bodhgaya, the small market town of **RAJGIR** nestles in the rocky hills that witnessed the meditations and teachings of both the Buddha and Mahavira. The capital of the Magadha kingdom before Pataliputra, this was where King Bimbisara converted to Buddhism. Today the picturesque and quiet environs, visited by international pilgrims, are also enjoyed as a health resort because of the local **hot springs**. The pools are always open, but can get unpleasantly crowded.

Several sites bear witness to the Buddha's many visits. A Japanese shrine at **Venuvana Vihara** marks the spot where a monastery was built for the Buddha to live in, while it was at **Griddhakuta** (Vulture's Peak) that the Buddha set in motion his second Wheel of Law. Each year, during the three-month rainy season, he preached to his disciples here. The massive modern **Peace Pagoda** built by the Japanese dominates the hill and can be reached by a rather tricky little chairlift, 3km from the centre of Rajgir, which takes fifteen minutes round-trip (daily 8.15am–1pm & 2pm–5pm, last ticket 4.30pm; Rs15). Only "physically fit and mentally sound persons are allowed to enjoy the lift". Griddhakuta is actually halfway down the hill, so you may prefer to wander down from here rather than climb back up to take the chairlift. Look out for the 26 Jain shrines on top of these hills, reached by a challenging trek attempted almost solely by Jain devotees. On an adjacent hill, in the **Saptaparni cave**, the first Buddhist council met to record the teachings of the Buddha after his death.

Rajgir is connected by **bus** to Gaya, Bodhgaya and Patna, which usually involves a change at Bihar Sharif, 25km away. You can also visit Rajgir as part of a long and tiring day-trip including Nalanda and Pawapuri from either Patna or Bodhgaya.

The Centaur Hokke hotel

Japanese interest in Rajgir is not only evident in the huge Peace Pagoda, but also in the altogether more curious Centaur Hokke hotel. Designed by a Japanese architect, its strange shape and corridors act like a giant air-conditioning unit, with circulating air keeping temperatures down. The hotel also has its own shrine room – cylindrical, roofless and 18m high. There are twenty-six rooms in all, twenty Japanese-style and six Western-style, but it's the restaurant that takes the biscuit. The *Lotus* without doubt provides the finest Japanese food in Rajgir, and possibly the whole of India. Guests are greeted with iced cologne-soaked flannels in the summer and steaming flannels in the cool season. Fresh fish and prawns are flown in daily from Calcutta, special Japanese rice is grown near Kathmandu by select farmers, vegetables are also brought in from Nepal, and to sample state-of-the-art Japanese haute cuisine in the middle of India's badlands costs from just $1.

Accommodation

Ajatshatru, near the hot springs ℡ 06119/25273. A basic place run by Bihar Tourism, where it costs Rs100 to stay in a dorm.

Anand, a couple of hundred metres up the road opposite the bus station ℡ 06119/25030. Nice terrace and cosmic blue paint. ❶

Centaur Hokke, 4km from the bus station and 2km from Kund market, at the end of a dusty road leading from the hot springs ℡ 06119/25245. An ugly concrete exterior plays host to an extraordinary Japanese restaurant and comfortable rooms (see box). Worth a visit just to try the seaweed sandwiches. ❾

Gautam Vihar, 300m from the bus station on the road to Nalanda ℡ 06119/25273. Spacious old building with conference facilities. Large rooms with pleasant verandas and attached bath. Run by Bihar Tourism. ❸–❺

Rajgir, round the corner from the *Anand* ☏06119/25266. Pleasant garden, reasonable rooms and restaurant. ❶–❷

Siddharth, Kund Market ☏06119/25216. Cheerful and popular hotel, a couple of kilometres from the town centre – it's best to take a rickshaw. Carpets and attached bath. ❸–❺

Tathagat Vihar, 1km from the hot springs on the road to the *Centaur Hokke* ☏06119/25273. Run by Bihar Tourism. ❸

Nalanda

The richly adorned towers and the fairy-like turrets, like the pointed hill-tops, are congregated together . . . The stages have dragon projections and coloured eaves, the pearl-red pillars carved and ornamented, the richly adorned balustrades, and the roofs covered with tiles that reflect the light in a thousand shades. These things add to the beauty of the place.

Hiuen Tsang, who spent twelve years at Nalanda as student and teacher.

Founded in the fifth century AD by the Guptas, the great monastic **Buddhist university** of **NALANDA** flourished, with thousands of international students and teachers, until it was sacked by the Afghan invader Bhaktiar Khilji in the twelfth century. Excavations have revealed nine levels of occupation on the site, dating back to the time of the Buddha and the Jain founder Mahavira, in the sixth century BC. Most of it is now in ruins, but the orderliness and scale of what remains is staggering evidence of the strength of Buddhist civilization in its prime. Nalanda is now part of the modern Buddhist pilgrimage circuit, but even the casual tourist will appreciate taking the time to walk through the extensive site, or climb its massive 31-metre **stupa** for commanding views. The site is strewn with the remains of stupas, temples and eleven monasteries, their thick walls impressively intact.

Courses taught at Nalanda included the study of scriptures of the Mahayana and Hinayana Schools of Buddhism, Brahmanical and Vedic texts, philosophy, logic, theology, grammar, astronomy, mathematics and medicine. Education was provided free, supported by the revenue from surrounding villages, and by benefactors such as the eighth-century king of Sumatra. Informative booklets available at the ticket booth render the numerous and solicitous guides unnecessary. A small alfresco bar inside the grounds serves tea, coffee and soft drinks without the hassle of the touts and beggars at the entrance.

Nalanda Museum (daily except Fri 10am–5pm; free) houses antiquities found here and at Rajgir, including Buddhist and Hindu bronzes and a number of undamaged statues of the Buddha. Other sculptures produced here during the eighth- to tenth-century Pala period are displayed at the Indian Museum in Calcutta, the National Museum in New Delhi and the Patna Museum. **Nava Nalanda Mahavihara**, the Pali postgraduate research institute, houses many rare Buddhist manuscripts, and is devoted to study and research in Pali literature and Buddhism.

Shared **Jeeps** ply regularly between Bihar Sharif and Rajgir, stopping at the turning to Nalanda from where an assortment of transport, including shared tongas, is available for the remaining 2km to the gates of the site. An old colonial villa 300m past the site is now run as a PWD **rest house** (❶) and exudes an evocative air of the decaying Raj, offering large double rooms with veranda, lounge and gardens. Simple food and soft drinks are available.

Jasidih and Deogarh

JASIDIH, a small industrial town 220km southeast of Patna on the main line to Calcutta, has started to attract travellers due to the international popularity of the ascetic Swami Satyananda and his Rikhya Yoga Ashram, 12km from the centre. Note, however, that the ashram is open to the public only a few select days every year; visitors are expected to donate clothing and medicine. Yoga courses are run by his disciple Niranjan within the walls of the old fort at Monghyr, 60km to the north (nearest train station, Jamalpur) and 180km east of Patna. For information, write to Bihar Yoga Bharati, Ganga Darsham Fort, Monghyr, Bihar 811201.

Baidyanath Dham, the Shiva temple at **DEOGARH**, 6km to the east on the Ganges, has been an important pilgrimage centre for centuries; legend has it that this is where the evil Ravana rested on his way to Lanka after abducting Sita. Deogarh's tranquillity is shattered during the annual *mela*, held during the monsoon month of Shravan (July/Aug) when around 100,000 pilgrims visit the temple every day.

Practicalities

Almost midway between Patna and Calcutta (Howrah), Jasidih is easily accessible by **train**, and several **buses** link Monghyr, Jamalpur and Jasidih. Jasidih's small selection of **hotels** includes the reasonable *Yatrik* (❸), the vast *Arog Bhavan* (❶–❺), with a very cheap dorm as well as a/c rooms, and the amazing *Mitra Garden* (❹–❺), offering a/c rooms, a restaurant and indoor and outdoor pools – the proprietor will have you picked up from the station and also organizes trips to nearby Santal villages. Options near the ashram include the *Sita* (❸) and *Dreamland* (☎06432/22299; ❸). In Deogarh, the *Yatrik* (☎06432/22299; ❸–❺) and the *Baidyanath* (☎06432/23112; ❸–❹) have very reasonably priced a/c rooms.

The best **food** is in the hotel restaurants – *Mitra Garden's* is the best – although in Jasidih, the excellent vegetarian meals at *Neelkamal* are also worth a try.

Jharkhand

On the eastern extremities of the Vindhya hills, at the northern fringes of the Deccan, lie the forested hills and escarpments of the rugged **Chotanagpur plateau**. The area became a new state, **JHARKHAND**, in 2000, after years of agitation by its largely tribal population, though it seems unlikely that its extreme poverty and lawlessness can be dealt with by creating a slew of new government positions and changing some names.

The state capital is **Ranchi**, although **Jamshedpur** in the southeast corner is one of eastern India's most important industrial towns, the headquarters of the steel conglomerate TISCO. The forests that surround Jamshedpur, at the edge of the plateau, are home to aboriginal tribes such as the Santals, Oraon and Munda, who amount to around sixty percent of the region's population. Christian missionaries have had a strong impact here, and some Munda villages display shrines to the Virgin, but much of the area is **unsafe** for travellers as it is patrolled by bandits and left-wing guerrilla groups.

This area was formerly renowned for its **wildlife**. Sadly, the beautiful forests of the **Palamau** or **Betla National Park**, on the southwest edge of Chotanagpur, have been damaged by years of drought and its tigers are now severely endangered.

Ranchi and around

RANCHI, at the heart of the Chotanagpur plateau, is ugly and poor and it's hard to believe that it was once the summer capital of Bihar, full of tea-gardens. The only reason to come here is to visit one of its ashrams such as the extensive Yogoda Math Ashram.

Several major **trains** – connecting with, among other places, Calcutta, Delhi, Patna, Daltonganj, Dhanbad, Jasidih and Jamshedpur – either call at Ranchi station, near the southern end of the Main Road, or terminate at Hatia, 7km away. **Indian Airlines** has daily flights between Ranchi and Delhi, while there are twice-weekly flights (Tues & Sat) for Patna and Calcutta. Their offices are at 4 Welfare Centre Enclave, and Jawan Bhavan, both on Main Road (⊕0651/206160). From the **main bus stand** near the railway station, regular Nagar Seva buses travel to **Gaya** (8hr), Hazaribagh, Netarhat, Jamshedpur, and to **Daltonganj**, headquarters of the Palamau (Betla) National Park, 160km to the west. Ranchi's **Tourist Office**, in the Tourist Complex, *Hotel Birsa Vihar*, Main Road (Mon–Sat 8am–8pm; ⊕0651/314826), is friendly but offers little more than dusty brochures. They also have an information booth at the railway station. Holiday Travellers, Patel Chowkh (⊕0651/300573) offers organized **tours** to the waterfalls around Ranchi, Betla and Netarhat.

Accommodation and eating

Most of Ranchi's **hotels** are along, or just off, the long Main Road. If you'd rather not eat in your hotel, *Friends Restaurant*, Station Road, is a cheap and basic café serving south Indian snacks, while *Suttor*, on Club Road, is a good multi-cuisine restaurant. One of the best places is *Kaveri*, Church Complex, Main Road, a very reasonably priced vegetarian restaurant despite its upmarket ambience, while *Krishna*, downstairs, is a bit cheaper. The *Maharaja* Chinese restaurant also serves good food.

Embassy, Station Road ⊕0651/314764. One of the better budget hotels along this stretch; reasonably clean with attached baths. ③–④

Highland Inn, Old Hazaribagh Road ⊕0651/309537. Old-world, simple bungalow, with atmospheric if faded rooms, within walking distance of the railway station and bus stand. ③

Kwality Inn, Station Road ⊕0651/305469. Justifiably popular with central a/c and smart, comfortable rooms, and one of the best restaurants in town – the *Nook*. ⑥–⑦

Ranchi Ashok, Doranda district ⊕0651/500441. Ranchi's most prestigious, with central a/c, and all facilities including a bar and an expensive restaurant; it's part of a poorly run government chain. ⑧–⑨

South Eastern Railway, Station Road ⊕0671/208048. Capturing that Raj atmosphere, with pleasant gardens, and bungalows with sizeable rooms and pillared verandas. ⑤–⑥

Yuvraj, Main Road, Doranda district ⊕0651/300403. Popular hotel with some a/c rooms and a good restaurant. ③–⑥

Palamau (Betla) National Park

In a remote and lawless corner of the state, 170km west of Ranchi, the beautiful forests of the **PALAMAU NATIONAL PARK** (also known as Betla), cover around 1000 square kilometres of hilly terrain rising south towards Madhya Pradesh. Part of the **Project Tiger** scheme (see Contexts, p.1532), Palamau has been hard hit by drought, and even optimistic estimates of its tiger population stand at a mere sixty. Tiger sightings, more common in the hot season, are proudly announced on a noticeboard at the park offices.

Like many national parks, Palamau consists of a buffer zone, open to visitors, surrounding a core area which is not; the tigers are known to roam around 20km a day, but tend to concentrate in the core area. The fact that several villages are located within the park boundaries has not helped the protection of animals, despite a scheme of compensation for owners of cattle killed by tigers. Other animals found in the park include wild elephants, best seen after the monsoons, *nilgai* (antelope), leopard, gaur (bison), Indian wolf, wild boar and wild dogs. The best way to see the park is from the back of an **elephant**, and the earlier in the morning you go the more animals you're likely to spot.

Practicalities

The official headquarters of the park, **Daltonganj**, 25km from Betla, are served by direct buses and a branch railway line from Ranchi. Five buses each morning and three each afternoon (first at 7.30am; last at 4.30pm) run from Daltonganj to Betla, which is 6km off the main Ranchi–Daltonganj road. If you're coming from Ranchi, you could try to change buses at the turn-off and get to Betla without going through Daltonganj. This is a fairly lawless corner of the state, so it's best to avoid night travel.

Next to the **Betla** gates, the main park entrance, a small complex holds administration offices, rest houses and an **information centre**, where entry tickets, elephant rides and accommodation in any of the Forest Department's rest houses can be arranged. All arrangements, including car or Jeep rental and accommodation, can also be made at Daltonganj through the Director, Project Tiger, Jail Compound.

Forest Department Rest Houses in Betla itself include the main one (❷), which prioritizes visiting civil servants and is comfortable with attached baths, and the very cheap and basic *Janata* and *Shyama* lodges (❶).

There are also a couple of **hotels**. The privately run *Naihar* (❶–❹), 300m from the park gates, has a nice garden, a dorm, a/c rooms and a reasonable restaurant serving Chinese and Indian food, while the grand-looking *Van Vihar* (☎06562/822111; ❷–❹), recently opened by Bihar Tourism, offers spacious rooms (some a/c) and also has a restaurant. Simple **cafés** can be found opposite the gates at Betla.

Travel details

Trains

Gaya to: Allahabad (4 daily; 4hr 20min–6hr 30min); Calcutta (6 daily 6–9hr); Dehra Dun (1 daily; 26hr); Delhi (9 daily; 12–15hr); Haridwar (1 daily; 23hr); Kalka (1 daily; 27hr); Lucknow (3 daily; 10–13hr); Mughal Sarai (13 daily; 3–5hr); Mumbai (1 daily; 31hr); Patna (4 daily; 2hr 30min); Puri (3 weekly; 17–40hr); Ranchi (3 daily; 8hr 20min); Sasaram (10 daily; 1–3hr); Varanasi (3 daily; 4hr–5hr 30min).

Patna to: Agra (1 daily; 17hr 35min); Allahabad (8 daily; 6–8hr); Calcutta (6 daily; 7hr 30min–12hr); Chennai (2 weekly; 44hr); Delhi (8 daily; 12–24hr); Gaya (4 daily; 2hr 30min); Guwahati (3 daily); Lucknow (3 daily; 9–14hr); Mumbai (3 daily; 33–36hr); Puri (1 daily; 19hr); Ranchi (3 daily; 11–14hr); Varanasi (3 daily; 4–6hr).

Ranchi to: Allahabad (2 weekly; 16hr); Calcutta (Howrah; 1 daily; 11hr); Daltonganj (1 daily; 7hr 30min); Delhi (2 weekly; 23–26hr); Dhanbad (2 daily; 5hr 30min); Gaya (2 daily; 7hr 20min); Jasidih (2 daily; 9hr); Patna (3 daily; 10–14hr).

Buses

Bodhgaya to: Gaya (hourly; 45min); Patna (2 daily; 5hr); Ranchi (daily; 12hr); Varanasi (1 daily; 6–7hr).

Gaya to: Bodhgaya (hourly; 45min); Mughal Sarai (6 daily; 5hr); Patna (hourly; 3hr); Ranchi (8 daily; 8hr); Sasaram (8 daily; 3hr); Varanasi (6 daily; 5hr 30min).

Patna to: Gaya (hourly; 3hr); Ranchi (4 daily; 12–14hr); Raxaul (18 daily; 6hr); Vaishali (2 daily; 3hr); Varanasi (4 daily; 6hr 30min).

Ranchi to: Bodhgaya (1 daily; 21hr); Calcutta (Howrah; 2 weekly; 2hr 20min); Daltonganj (4 daily; 8hr); Delhi (2 daily; 1hr 40min); Dhanbad (6 daily; 5hr); Gaya (8 daily; 8hr); Patna (daily; 12–14hr).

Flights

Patna to: Calcutta (1 daily; 1hr 20min); Delhi (3 daily; 1hr 30min); Lucknow (1 daily; 1hr); Mumbai (1 daily; 2hr 15min); Ranchi (1 daily; 45min); Varanasi (1 daily; 35min).

CHAPTER 15

Highlights

* **Rumtek** One of Sikkim's most venerated monasteries, Rumtek is home to the Black Hat sect, and hosts a spectacular festival in February. See p.1027

* **Maenam mountain** A day-trek through an ancient forest to the summit of the mountain; you may be lucky enough to spot deer and red panda. See p.1028

* **Pemayangtse** A wonderful seventeenth-century monastery perched on a high ridge facing Darjeeling. See p.1031

* **Pelling** This sleepy town has gentle walks to nearby monasteries, and stunning views of Kanchenjunga. See p.1033

* **Dzongri Trail** Trek through rhododendrons and across high alpine meadows close to Khangchendzonga, the third-highest mountain in the world. See pp.1036–1037

* **Tashiding** A monastic complex on a conical hill with marvellous views. See p.1038

15

Sikkim

The tiny and beautiful state of **SIKKIM** lies just south of Tibet, sandwiched between Nepal to the west and Bhutan to the east. Though measuring just 65km by 115km, it ranges from sweltering deep valleys a mere 300m above sea level to lofty snow peaks such as Kanchenjunga (Kanchendzonga to the locals), which, at 8586m, is the third-highest mountain in the world. The capital city, **Gangtok**, at 1870m, follows the extreme contours of the land and all roads snake around its precarious slopes. It has good facilities and magnificent post-monsoon views. Permits for restricted areas can only be obtained in Gangtok and there are many **trekking** agents based here. As yet few roads penetrate this rugged Himalayan wilderness and every monsoon they take a massive battering, with large and frequent landslides disrupting communications and providing plenty of muddy repair work for the locals.

For centuries, until war with China in the early 1960s led the Indian government to see it as a crucial corridor between Tibet and Bangladesh, Sikkim was an isolated, independent Buddhist kingdom. As a result of its annexation by India in 1975, it has experienced dramatic changes. Now a fully fledged Indian state, it is predominantly Hindu, with a population made up of 75 percent **Nepalese Gurungs**, and less than twenty percent **Lepchas**, its former rulers. Smaller proportions survive of **Bhutias**, of Tibetan stock, and **Limbus**, also possibly of Tibetan origin, who gave the state its name – *sukh-im*, "happy homeland". Nepali is now the lingua franca and the Nepalese are socially and politically the most dominant people in the state. The ruling minority in neighbouring Bhutan, having observed this transition with alarm, has adopted an intransigent and aggressive stance towards the Nepalese, with ugly violence on both sides and the final expulsion of all ethnic Nepalese from Bhutan.

Sikkim continues to hold a special status within the Indian union, exempt from income tax and attracting government subsidy. Although only Sikkimese can hold major shares in property and businesses, partnerships with Indian

15

SIKKIM

Accommodation price codes

All accommodation prices in this book have been categorized using the price codes below. Prices given are for a double room, and all taxes are included. For more details, see p.51.

- ① up to Rs100
- ② Rs100–200
- ③ Rs200–300
- ④ Rs300–400
- ⑤ Rs400–600
- ⑥ Rs600–900
- ⑦ Rs900–1500
- ⑧ Rs1500–2500
- ⑨ Rs2500 and upwards

The International boundaries on this map are neither purported to be correct nor authentic by Survey of India directives. Publisher.

(non-Sikkimese) entrepreneurs, and subsidies to indigenous Sikkimese light industry have led to a prosperity evident as soon as you cross the border from West Bengal.

Historically, culturally and spiritually, Sikkim's strongest links are with **Tibet**. For those visitors who now make their way here, **trekking** and **monasteries** are the main reasons to come. There are over two hundred monasteries, mostly belonging to the ancient **Nyingmapa** sect. **Pemayangtse** in west Sikkim is the most important historically and houses an extraordinary wooden mandala depicting Guru Rinpoche's Heavenly Palace. **Tashiding**, built in 1717, is another important and active Nyingmapa monastery, surrounded by prayer flags and *chortens* and looking across to snow-capped peaks. **Rumtek**, 23km from Gangtok, the seat of the **Gyalwa karmapa**, head of the **Karma Kagyu** lineage, is probably the most influential monastery in Sikkim.

Though foreigners need to obtain a permit to visit Sikkim, getting one is a mere formality. The easiest way is to request a permit when applying for your Indian visa. They are usually valid for two weeks from entry into the state, which allows enough time to visit the towns and villages at a fairly leisurely pace but places constraints on time if trekking; permits are usually renewable for a further two weeks. The permit covers the main southern belt from Gangtok across to Pemayangtse. Two-day permits are available instantly at the Sikkim border at Rangpo, and the checkpoints at Melli and Naya Bazaar/Jorethang may soon begin to issue them.

Certain areas in central Sikkim (the Lepcha heartland) and the sensitive border regions with Tibet remain completely off limits to foreigners. Other parts of Sikkim are open for tourism but not included in the regions covered by your permit. For those areas you require an endorsement of your permit, a free service which is provided quickly at the tourist information office in Gangtok. Extensions and trekking permits for certain regions can similarly be obtained in Gangtok while Sikkim permit extensions are also available through the Superintendent of Police at Gangtok, Mangan, Gyalzing and Namchi. Certain restricted areas, like Changu (Tsangu, Tsomgo) Lake, Yumthang and Dzongri, only allow foreigners in groups (usually a minimum of four), accompanied by representatives of approved travel agents. Despite all these regulations, Sikkim is slowly opening up and the trend looks set to continue.

Areas covered by Sikkim permit
Central and Eastern Sikkim: Gangtok, Rumtek, and if on a tour, Changu Lake.
Northern Sikkim: Phodong, Labrang, Mangan up to Singhik.
Western Sikkim: Jorethang, Naya Bazaar, Legship, Ghezing, Pelling and Pemayangtse.

Areas requiring permit endorsement
Western Sikkim: Tashiding, Yoksum, Khecheopalri Lake.
Eastern Sikkim: Changu Lake (day-permits for Nathu La are available for Indian visitors but not foreigners).

Restricted areas open only to group tours
Northern Sikkim: Chungthang, Lachung, Yumthang, Yume Samdang, Lachen, Guru Dongmar and Thanggu and the trek to Green Lake. The route from Lachen over the Goecha La to Dzongri is now open for mountaineering expeditions and takes three weeks plus – regulations are different for mountaineering expeditions than for ordinary tour groups who only have the standard two-week permit.
Western Sikkim: Dzongri, Singalila Range.

Offices in India issuing permits
Airport immigration, at the four main entry points – Delhi, Mumbai, Calcutta, Chennai.
Foreigners Regional Registration Offices, in Delhi, Mumbai, Calcutta and Chennai.
Foreigners Regional Registration Office, Laden La Road, Darjeeling (see Darjeeling section for details).
Resident Commissioner, Sikkim House, 14 Panchsheel Marg, Chanakyapuri, New Delhi ☏ 011/611 5346.
Sikkim Tourist Centre, SNTC Bus Stand, Hill Cart Road, Siliguri ☏ 0354/432646.
Sikkim Tourist Information Centre, 4C Poonam Building, 5 Russell St, Calcutta ☏ 033/249 9935.

15

SIKKIM

Sikkim is where the monsoons that rush in off the Bay of Bengal hit the Himalayas; its gigantic mountain walls and steep wooded hillsides, drained by torrential rivers such as the **Teesta** and the **Rangit**, are a botanist's dream. The lower slopes abound in **orchids**; sprays of cardamom carpet the forest floor, and the land is rich with apple orchards, orange groves and terraced paddy fields (to the Tibetans, this was **Denzong**, "the land of rice"). At higher altitudes, monsoon mists cling to huge tracts of lichen-covered forests, where countless varieties of rhododendron carpet the hillsides and giant magnolia trees punctuate the deep verdant cover. Higher still, approaching the Tibetan plateau, dwarf rhododendron provide vital fuel for yak herders. All over Sikkim, forests and wilderness areas are inhabited by elusive snow leopards, tahr (wild ass on the Tibet plateau), *bharal* or blue sheep, and the symbol of Sikkim – the endangered **red panda**.

The **best time to visit** Sikkim is between mid-March and June but especially March, April and May, when the rhododendrons and orchids bloom – although temperatures can be high, especially in the valleys. Any earlier than that, and lingering winter snow can make trekking too difficult. During the monsoons, from the end of June until early September, rivers and roads become impassable, though plants nurtured by the incessant rain erupt again into bloom towards the end of August. October, when orchids bloom once again, and November, tend to have the clearest weather of all. As December approaches, it gets bitterly cold at high altitudes, and remains that way until early March, despite long periods of clear weather.

Some history

No one knows quite when or how the **Lepchas** – or the Rong, as they call themselves – came to Sikkim, but their roots can be traced back to the animist Nagas of the Indo-Burmese border. **Buddhism**, which arrived from Tibet in the thirteenth century, took its distinctive Sikkimese form four centuries later, when three Tibetan monks of the old Nyingmapa order, disenchanted with the rise of the reformist Gelug-pas, migrated south and gathered at Yoksum in western Sikkim. Having consulted the oracle, they sent to Gangtok for a certain Phuntsog Namgyal, whom they crowned as the first **chogyal** or "righteous king" of Denzong in 1642. Both the secular and religious head of Sikkim, he was soon recognized by Tibet, and set about sweeping reforms. His domain was far larger than today's Sikkim, taking in Kalimpong and parts of western Bhutan.

Over the centuries, territory was lost to the Bhutanese, the Nepalese and the **British**. Sikkim originally ceded Darjeeling to the East India Company as a spa in 1817, but was forced to give up all claim to it in 1861 when the kingdom was declared a protectorate of the British. **Tibet**, which perceived Sikkim as a vassalage, objected and invaded in 1886. A small British force sent in 1888 to Lhasa helped the British consolidate their hold on Sikkim and later, in 1903, Francis Younghusband led a military expedition through Sikkim to Lhasa to force concessions from Tibet, but returned a changed man after a powerful mystical experience when crossing the high Himalayas. By importing workers from Nepal to work in the tea plantations of Sikkim, Darjeeling and Kalimpong, the British sought to diminish the strong Tibetan influence and helped alter the ethnic make-up of the region, with the new migrants soon outnumbering the indigenous population.

After Indian Independence, the reforming and intensely spiritual eleventh chogyal, **Tashi Namgyal**, strove hard until his death in 1962 to prevent the dissolution of his kingdom. Officially Sikkim was a protectorate of India, and the

Although the potential is huge, **trekking** in Sikkim, confined to certain routes in the west and recently opened areas in the north, remains restricted. The fact that trekking permits do not extend your total stay in Sikkim places a great constraint on time, while high charges, payable in US dollars, ensure that only the well-heeled get to see certain areas.

Trekking permits are only available from the Sikkim tourism offices in Gangtok and Delhi. Trekking or tour operators in Gangtok (see p.1025) can make the necessary arrangements; if they do, check the papers before you set off, as the slightest error can lead to problems later on. Trekking parties usually consist of at least four people – numbers are normally concocted (for the purposes of the permit) by operators, who charge an official daily rate of $35–50 per head.

The two high-altitude treks currently on offer are the **Dzongri–Goecha La** route and the Singalila ridge, both detailed on pp.1036-1037. Although mountains such as Tangchung Khang (6010m) and Jopuno (5935m) were designated as "trekking peaks", bureaucratic wrangles mean that permission is still not forthcoming. At the moment Dzongri bears the brunt of the trekking industry in the state, and the pressure is beginning to tell severely on the environment (see p.1034).

The Mountain Institute, based in Nepal, has launched the **Sikkim Biodiversity and Ecotourism Network** in order to develop tourism, while protecting natural resources and the environment. Their aims include support of local communities and the development of a sustainable and healthy infrastructure. For more information, contact them at PO Tadong, NH-31A, Gangtok ☎03592/31046, ⓔ tmisikk@dte.vsnl.net.in, or The Mountain Institute, Dogwood & Main Street, Franklin WV26807, USA ☎1-304-358-2401, ⓔ summit@mountain.org.

---

role of India became increasingly crucial, with the Chinese military build-up along the northern borders that culminated in an actual invasion early in the 1960s. His son **Palden Thondup**, the last chogyal, married as his second wife an American, Hope Cook, whose reforms as gyalmo (queen) did not prove popular and also came to irritate the Indian government. The embattled chogyal eventually succumbed to the demands of the Nepalese majority, and Sikkim was **annexed** by India in 1975 after a referendum with an overwhelming 97-percent majority. The chogyal remained as a figurehead until his death in 1981, by which time Hope Cook had abandoned him and returned to the United States with their children. Some of the chogyal's family still live in seclusion in Gangtok. The state continues to be treated with care by the Indian government, partly through a lingering sense of unease amongst the disaffected Sikkimese minority, but more importantly because Sikkim is still a bone of contention between India and China. Today, the **Sikkim Democratic Front** forms the government of Sikkim and, while life in Sikkim remains generally contented, mismanagement is creeping in, effecting the state's infrastructure.

Gangtok

The capital of Sikkim, the overgrown hill town of **GANGTOK** (1870m), occupies a rising ridge in the southeast of the state, on what used to be a busy trade route into Tibet. Due to rapid development and new wealth, it now retains only a few traditional Sikkimese elements; there's an ugly assortment of

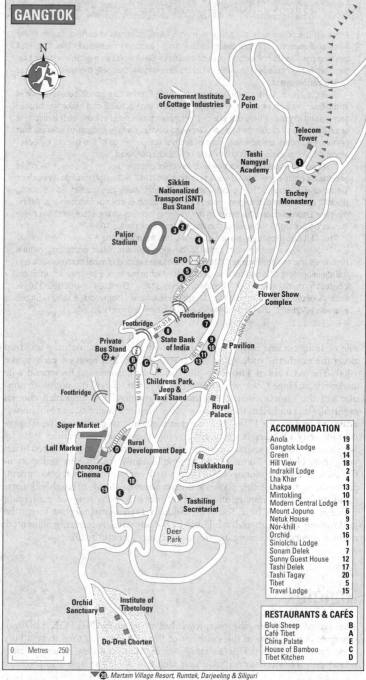

GANGTOK

N

Tashi View Point, Phodong & Mangan

Changu Lake, Hanuman Tok & Nathu La

Government Institute of Cottage Industries

Zero Point

Telecom Tower

Tashi Namgyal Academy

Enchey Monastery

Sikkim Nationalized Transport (SNT) Bus Stand

Paljor Stadium

GPO

PALJOR STADIUM ROAD

Flower Show Complex

RIDGE ROAD

Footbridges

Footbridge

NH-31A

State Bank of India

Pavilion

Private Bus Stand

TIBET RD

BHANU PATH

Childrens Park, Jeep & Taxi Stand

Footbridge

M G MARG

Royal Palace

Super Market

Lall Market

Rural Development Dept.

Tsuklakhang

Denzong Cinema

Tashiling Secretariat

Deer Park

Orchid Sanctuary

Institute of Tibetology

Do-Drul Chorten

0   Metres   250

20, Martam Village Resort, Rumtek, Darjeeling & Siliguri

15

SIKKIM | Gangtok

ACCOMMODATION

Anola	19
Gangtok Lodge	8
Green	14
Hill View	18
Indrakill Lodge	2
Lha Khar	4
Lhakpa	13
Mintokling	10
Modern Central Lodge	11
Mount Jopuno	6
Netuk House	9
Nor-khill	3
Orchid	16
Siniolchu Lodge	1
Sonam Delek	7
Sunny Guest House	12
Tashi Delek	17
Tashi Tagay	20
Tibet	5
Travel Lodge	15

RESTAURANTS & CAFÉS

Blue Sheep	B
Café Tibet	A
China Palate	E
House of Bamboo	C
Tibet Kitchen	D

concrete multistorey buildings which is growing, virtually unchecked, all the time. However, a short amble soon leads you away from the hectic central market area, while longer walks out into the surrounding countryside provide glimpses of the full grandeur of the Himalayas. On a good day, you can see Kanchenjunga and the fluted pyramid of Siniolchu.

Although modern Gangtok epitomizes the recent changes in Sikkimese culture and politics, its Buddhist past is the root of its appeal for visitors, evident in the collection at the **Institute of Tibetology** and the charming **Enchey Monastery**, as well as the impressive **Rumtek Monastery** 24km east of town. However, the **Palace** used by the chogyals between 1894 and 1975 is now out of bounds, occupied by the new regime and not acknowledged as part of Sikkimese heritage. Sikkim's pride and joy, the **orchid**, is nurtured at several sites in and around Gangtok, and celebrated every spring in a flower show held near **White Hall**, the governor's residence on the ridge above town.

Arrival and information

Gangtok is not served directly by rail; most travellers arrive by **Jeep** from **Siliguri** in West Bengal (4hr 30min; see p.72), the transport centre for the railhead at **New Jalpaiguri** and for **Bagdogra** airport. Shared Jeeps also run from **Darjeeling** and **Kalimpong**. A **helicopter** service (Rs1500) connects Bagdogra airport with Gangtok, run in conjunction with Sikkim Tourism and designed to meet passengers arriving on Indian Airlines and Jet Airways flights. At the time of writing, though, both airlines had temporarily suspended flights to Bagdogra due to ongoing repairs to the runway.

All **buses** run by **Sikkim Nationalized Transport** (SNT), the state carrier, use the **SNT bus stand** on Paljor Stadium Road, but passengers may prefer to be dropped off earlier at the main crossing on MG Marg near the State Bank of India, which is more convenient for the **tourist office**. Non-SNT buses stop at the **private bus stand**, located on a small sliproad just off the National Highway, a couple of hundred metres before the crossing where there is a selection of hotels. Shared taxis and Jeeps from Kalimpong and Darjeeling also stop here or along MG Marg; Jeeps and taxis from other destinations in Sikkim terminate at a stand at **Childrens Park**, just above MG Marg. For transport details to, from and around Sikkim – all subject to disruption during the monsoons – see p.1039.

Sikkim Tourism's **tourist information centre**, MG Marg (mid-March to early June & mid-Sept to Nov daily 9am–7pm; mid-June to mid-Sept & Dec–Feb Mon–Sat 10am–4pm; ☎03592/22064), provides maps and will advise on arranging transport. This is also the place to pick up **West Sikkim permits** (available Mon–Sat 10am–4pm) to cover Tashiding, Khecheopalri and Yoksum. For details of **trekking permits**, see p.1019. Sikkim Tourism also sell tickets for their spectacular **helicopter flights** (Rs1200–5000), including flights to west Sikkim, Yumthang, Gangtok and, the most breathtaking of them all, a ninety-minute Kanchendzonga trip up the Zemu Glacier.

Changing money is limited to the State Bank of India (SBI) near the tourist office at the junction of NH-31A and MG Marg, and a couple of licensed private bureaus including Silk Route Tours & Travels at the *Green Hotel* on MG Marg and Namgyal Treks & Tours off Tibet Road. While the SBI restricts itself to changing dollars and sterling, Namgyal and Silk Route, which charge around 1.5 percent of the transaction, will change several currencies; **credit card** facilities in Gangtok are limited, with only the main ones accepted and only in select places.

The main **post office** lies down Paljor Stadium Road just beyond the *Hotel Tibet*. The town is brimming with **email** services for around Rs60 per hour; try the Centre for Computer Communications and Technology (CCCT) in the Tashiling Secretariat near the King's Palace and Royal Chapel, *Green Hotel* on MG Marg, Electra also on MG Marg, Gokula in the Yama Building on MG Marg, the *Blue Sheep Café* at the tourist centre and Komputech on Paljor Stadium Road.

Accommodation

Gangtok's **hotels** are expensive in high season – broadly speaking April to June and September to November – but at other times offer discounted rates. Many hotel rooms have excellent views of Kanchenjunga and operate a viewing tax, which makes them slightly more expensive. As the town spreads so does the choice of accommodation, with good hotels springing up along the highway at Deorali and Tadong.

Central Gangtok

Anola, MG Marg, New Market ☏ 03592/23238, ⊜ anola@mailcity.com. Comfortable and well-maintained Sikkimese-run hotel which has a reputation for quality; the restaurant serves excellent Sikkimese food. ❻ – ❼

Gangtok Lodge, NH-31A near junction with MG Marg ☏ 03592/26562. Overlooking the crossroads, this place is central, friendly and good value, if a bit cramped. ❹

Green, MG Marg ☏ 03592/23354. A wide range of rooms, most without views. Popular restaurant downstairs. ❸ – ❺

Hill View, MG Marg, New Market ☏ 03592/23545. Quietly situated in a charming little garden compound above the road. Airy rooms and friendly staff. ❺ – ❻

Indrakill Lodge, Paljor Stadium Road ☏ 03592/29173. Just below the road, the *Indrakill* is small and cheap but reasonable, with hot water by the bucket. ❸ – ❺

Lha Khar, Opposite SNT, Paljor Stadium Road ☏ 03592/25708. Immaculate rooms in a well-run guesthouse convenient for the bus stand; its restaurant has a reputation for good Sikkimese cooking. ❺

Lhakpa, Tibet Road ☏ 03592/23002. Cheap, atmospheric hotel-restaurant above the main bazaar. A bar as much as a restaurant, it serves Indian, Tibetan and Sikkimese food with prior notice. ❸ – ❹

Mintokling, Bhanu Path (Tashiling Road), ☏ 03592/24226, ⊜ mintokling@hotmail.com. Old Sikkimese family home with twelve wonderful rooms and a lovely garden quietly situated near the palace high above the market. ❻

Modern Central Lodge, Tibet Road ☏ 03592/24670. Friendly and popular hotel geared

towards backpackers, with useful information but some visitors feel pressured to join their tours. Boasts running hot water, a restaurant and even snooker. ❹ – ❺

Mount Jopuno, Paljor Stadium Road ☏ 03592/23502. New hotel/Institute of Hotel Management Training Centre. Featuring twelve rooms with hot water and attached bathroom, and a rooftop terrace, it is well-maintained and offers good value. ❻ – ❼

Netuk House, Tibet Road ☏ 03592/26778, ⊜ netuk@sikkim.org. A family home with a comfortable hotel annexe, warm and atmospheric with full Sikkimese decor and a pleasant roof terrace; meals are included in the price. ❾

Nor-khill, Paljor Stadium Road ☏ 03592/25637, ⊛ www.elginhotels.com. Luxurious former guesthouse of the Chogyal. All facilities including a good restaurant and large plush rooms, with all mod cons but a poor location overlooking the sports stadium; rooms start at $129. ❾

Orchid, NH-31A ☏ 03592/23151. An old favourite with nice enough rooms, especially those that look across the town and valley. Good restaurant, too, with cheap Chinese and Tibetan food. ❸ – ❹

Sonam Delek, Tibet Road ☏ 03592/22566. High above the bazaar, with a range of comfortable clean rooms with balconies and excellent views across the valley to the mountains. Pleasant and relaxing garden and a good restaurant – the *Oyster*. ❺ – ❻

Sunny Guest House, near private bus stand, NH-31A ☏ 03592/22179. There are no single rooms but it is pleasant and has great triples on the rooftop. ❺

Tashi Delek, MG Marg, New Market ☏ 03592/22991, ⊛ www.hoteltashidelek.com. An easily missed entrance off the market area hides one of Gangtok's most prestigious addresses – a plush, extensive but unremarkable complex with comfortable rooms (some a/c). The multi-cuisine *Blue Poppy* restaurant and adjoining rooftop café, with fabulous views, serve Sikkimese and Tibetan dishes, and club sandwiches. **❾**

Tibet, Paljor Stadium Road ☎03592/22523 or 23468. Award-winning hotel with Tibetan decor. All deluxe rooms have Kanchenjunga views but the roadside rooms are overpriced. The *Snow Lion* restaurant is arguably the best place in town to eat out. **❼–❾**

Travel Lodge, Tibet Road ☎03592/23858. Pleasant hotel, run on an annual contract basis. Most rooms are carpeted, with balconies and hot running water; the best rooms are on the top two floors and have good views. **❸–❻**

Around Gangtok

Martam Village Resort ☎03592/23314, ✉martam31@hotmail.com. Five kilometres beyond Rumtek in the midst of beautiful rice terraces, the resort, offering traditional Sikkimese food and hospitality, boasts eleven landscaped en-suite cottages with thatched roofs, hot water, verandas and views. Mountain bikes are available for hire and there are easy walks to visit nearby villages. Rates include meals. Recommended. **❽**

Shambala Mountain Resort, Rumtek ☎03592/52240, ✉sikkim@ahmedindia.com. A pleasant garden resort at Rumtek (see p.1028).

Siniolchu Lodge, high above Gangtok, near the Enchey monastery ☎03592/22074. A badly run government lodge with incredible location: good value if you don't mind the Rs50 taxi ride up from the bazaar (or the steep 30min walk). Best views in town and recommended if you want to get away from it all. **❸–❹**

Tashi Tagay, NH-31A, near State Bank of India, Tadong ☎03592/31631. Small, welcoming Tibetan family-run hotel 5km from Gangtok. Clean, homely atmosphere, with a good restaurant popular with locals. It's a steep fifteen-minute walk up to Do Drul *chorten* and central Gangtok is an easy Rs10 taxi ride away; recommended. **❹–❻**

The Town

Though central Gangtok – which means "the hilltop" – is concentrated immediately below the palace, its unchecked urban sprawl begins almost as soon as the road rises from the valley floor at Ranipool, 10km southwest. Most of the town itself looks west; one explanation for the lack of development east of the ridge is that tradition dictates that houses face northwest, towards Kanchenjunga, Sikkim's guardian.

The town's best shopping areas are the **Main Market**, stretching for a kilometre along MG Marg, with workshops such as the Sakya Metal Works specializing in bronzes and silver jewellery, and the local produce bazaar of **Lall Market**, where stalls sell dried fish, yak's cheese (*churpi*), and yeast for making the local beer (*tomba*). At the huge complex run by the **Government Institute of Cottage Industries**, on the National Highway north of the centre, visitors can watch rural Sikkimese create carpets, hand-loomed fabrics, *thangka* paintings and wooden objects, and buy their work, at fixed prices, in a showroom. Curio shops on MG Marg and on Paljor Stadium Road sell turquoise and coral jewellery, plus religious objects such as silver ritual bowls and beads.

Right at the top of town just below a colossal telecom tower, 3km from the centre of town and reached by several roads (the most picturesque follow the west side of the ridge), **Enchey Monastery** is a small two-storey Nyingmapa *gompa*. It was built in the mid-nineteenth century on a site blessed by the Tantric master Druptob Karpo who was renowned for his ability to fly. Visitors are welcome; the best time to visit is between 7am and 8am, when the monastery is busy and the light is good. Surrounded by tall pines, and housing over a hundred monks, it's a real gem of a place. Built by the chogyal, on traditional Tibetan lines, its beautifully painted porch holds murals of protective deities and the wheel of law, while the conch shells that grace the doors are auspicious Buddhist symbols. Enchey holds an annual *chaam*, or masked lama dance, each December or January according to the lunar calendar.

The walk down from Enchey leads to the **Flower Shoe Complex** (daily 8am–5pm; Rs5) at the northern end of Ridge Road near White Hall, where a large well-maintained greenhouse has a good collection of orchids and other Himalayan plants laid out around a set of water features. The complex, with a shop selling seeds, plants and bulbs, comes alive in March and April during the annual flower festival.

Although in theory guards deny entry to the **Royal Palace** to anyone without permission, visitors not carrying cameras are occasionally granted access to **Tsuk-lakhang**, the yellow-roofed royal chapel at its far end, to see its impressive murals, Buddhist images and vast collection of manuscripts. Here too there's a lama dance, known as *kagyat*, at the end of December, during which the main gates are open to the public; some years the *kagyat* takes place in Pemayangtse instead (see p.1031).

Beyond the chapel the road meanders down to the small **Deer Park** (Mon–Sat 8–11am & Sun 8am–5pm) and beyond to Deorali, 3km from the centre on the National Highway, where, set in wooded grounds, is the museum-cum-library of the **Institute of Tibetology** (daily 10am–4pm; Rs5). Here you can see an impressive collection of books and rare manuscripts, as well as religious and art objects such as exquisite *thangkas* (scrolls). It's hard to believe that the adjacent **Orchid Sanctuary** boasts 200 species as it is so poorly maintained. The blooms are best seen in April and May (daily 8am–4pm).

A couple of hundred metres beyond the Institute on the brow of the hill, an imposing whitewashed *chorten* (see p.603), known as the **Do-Drul Chorten** and one of the most important in Sikkim, dominates a large lively monastery. The *chorten* is capped by a gilded tower, whose rising steps signify the thirteen steps to nirvana; the sun and moon symbol at the top stands for the union of opposites and the elements of ether and air. The 108 prayer wheels that surround it – each with the universal prayer *Om mani padme hum*, "Hail to the jewel in the lotus" – are rotated clockwise by devotees as they circle the stupa. Nearby, a prayer hall houses a large image of **Guru Rinpoche** (Padmasambhava) who brought Buddhism to Tibet at the request of King Trisong Detsen in the eighth century AD. He later travelled through Sikkim hiding precious manuscripts (*termas*) in caves, for discovery at a future date by *tertons*. Curiously, part of the head of the image projects into the ceiling protected by a raised section of roof; belief has it that the image is slowly growing.

Eating and drinking

Sikkimese food is a melange of Nepalese, Tibetan and Indian influences; rice is a staple, and dhal is readily available, while *gyakho* is a traditional soup served on special occasions. Sikkimese delicacies include *ningro* (fern rings), *shisnu* (nettle soup), *phing* (glass noodles) and *churpi* (yak cheese) cooked with chillies. Some of the best eating is in the restaurants of hotels such as the *Tibet* and *Anola*, and there are now several fast food places and patisseries, like *Porky's* and *Café Tibet*, to choose from.

Most restaurants serve **alcohol**. "Foreign" liquor such as brandy and beer is cheap enough, but look out for **tomba**, a traditional drink consisting largely of fermented millet, with a few grains of rice for flavour, served in a wooden or bamboo mug and sipped through a bamboo straw. The mug is occasionally topped up with hot water; once it's been allowed to sit for a few minutes, you're left with a pleasant milky beer. *Tomba* is usually found in less salubrious places although most hotels will provide it on request. Note that the Sikkimese have alcohol-free days during full moon.

The busiest route in and out of Sikkim is the road between Gangtok and Siliguri in West Bengal, site of the nearest airport and railway station (see p.972). Flights from Bagdogra can be booked at the Indian Airlines office on Tibet Road in Gangtok (☏ 03592/23099) and at either Josse & Josse, MG Marg (☏ 03592/24682), agents for Jet Airways, or through Silk Route Tours and Travels, first floor, *Green Hotel*, MG Marg (☏ 03592/23354), who also sell tickets for the various airlines flying from Biratnagar (2hr from Siliguri) in eastern Nepal to Kathmandu. Sikkim Tourism sell tickets for the helicopter flight (Rs1500) to Bagdogra to connect with Indian Airlines and Jet flights. Train reservations from New Jalpaiguri can be made at the SNT complex on Paljor Stadium Road (☏ 03592/22016 & 22014), but the reservations quota for Gangtok is highly inadequate so it is better to book in Siliguri.

Shared Jeeps are the most popular and efficient mode of transport, though buses are slightly cheaper. Jeeps to Siliguri (Rs90), Kalimpong (Rs65), Darjeeling (Rs100) and Pelling (Rs150) leave from the private bus stand on NH-31A. Jeeps to Rumtek leave from Lall Bazaar, while Jeeps to other destinations within Sikkim such as Legship, Ghezing, Pelling and Jorethang, depart from the children's park transport stand just above the tourist office. These services are timetabled and require advance booking (from the counters in the corner).

Those determined to suffer the buses – although those to Siliguri are not that bad – can choose between SNT (Sikkim Nationalized Transport) or the ever-growing number of private operators. The SNT bus stand is on NH-31A beyond the *Tibet* hotel and the private bus stand is also on NH-31A just past the *Orchid*. Buses run to Kalimpong, Darjeeling and Siliguri in West Bengal and Ravangla, Legship, Ghezing, Pelling, Jorethang and Phodong in Sikkim. SNT run buses to Bagdogra to coincide with flights, and private buses also travel the route.

Trekking and tour operators

All high-altitude treks in Sikkim have to be conducted in groups and arranged through travel agents. Prices may vary a little between agents: high altitude treks for three to five people cost $40–70 per person per day, while low-altitude treks for three to four people cost around $30 per person per day, rising to $35 per person for groups of two to three people.

Blue Sky Tours & Travels Tourism Building, MG Marg ☏ 03592/25113, ⓔ blueskytours@usa.net. Very helpful agency which specializes in Jeep tours and will point you in the right direction for your other travel needs.

Namgyal Treks & Tours Tibet Road ☏ 03592/23701, ⓔ trekking@dte.vsnl.net.in. Namgyal Sherpa is a highly capable high-altitude trek and expedition operator (and there aren't many in Gangtok), and also a Nepal specialist.

Potala Tours & Treks Paljor Stadium Road ☏ 03592/22041. One of several near-identical agents along this stretch opposite the *Tibet* hotel, specializing in Yumthang and Dzongri.

Sikkim Tours & Travels offices on Church Road and Super Market ☏ 03592/22188, ⓦ www.sikkiminfo.com/stt. The owner Lukendra is an extremely helpful and experienced travel operator who specializes in nature tours and photography, bird-watching and treks.

Tashila Tours and Travels NH-31A ☏ 03592/22979, ⓔ tashila@sikkim.org. Experienced operator offering trekking and two-hour to three-day river-rafting expeditions from Singtam to Rangpo (Rs700–7000). Also yak safaris, angling, and monastery tours.

Yak and Yeti Travels *Hotel Superview Himalchuli*, Zero Point ☏ 03592/24643, ⓔ yakyeti@mailcity.com. Friendly and reliable service run by Satish Bardewa who has experience in mountaineering and mountain bike expeditions.

Blue Sheep, MG Marg, next to the Tourist Information Office. A relaxed and fairly priced option with good Indian and Chinese food and a bar.

Café Tibet, NH-31A, past the hospital, run by the *Tibet* hotel. Popular with students, the café serves pizzas and burgers, croissants, cakes and ice cream. It's spotlessly clean and has great views.

China Palate, MG Marg, New Market. A combination of a bar and a restaurant serving Tibetan and local cuisine – try their Sikkimese combo (Rs70) which includes *shisnu* and *ningro*; the hotel *Anola* opposite also has a reputation for its wonderful Sikkim cooking.

Green, *Green Hotel*, MG Marg. A popular restaurant serving Indian and Chinese food, for around Rs50.

House of Bamboo, MG Marg. A popular and congenial café-cum-bar that's one of the best in town. Especially lively in the early evenings.

Modern Central Lodge, Tibet Road. Good travellers' choice for hearty breakfasts, including muesli and delicious pancakes.

Oyster, *Sonam Delek Hotel*, Tibet Road ☏03592/22566. Excellent Sikkimese, Tibetan and Indian food that's well worth the extra rupees. Prices start from around Rs70.

Snowlion, *Tibet Hotel*, Paljor Stadium Road ☏03592/22523 or 23468. Probably the best restaurant in Gangtok. The superb Tibetan and Indian food with a selection of Sikkimese and Japanese dishes comes highly recommended.

Tibet Kitchen, MG Marg, New Market. A lively café-cum-bar with decor where James Dean meets the Dalai Lama; their flexible menu ranges from breakfasts to *momos*, Chinese, Tibetan and Indian.

Around Gangtok

The most obvious destinations for day-trips from Gangtok are the great Buddhist monasteries of **Rumtek** to the southwest, and **Phodong** to the north. Towering above the town of **Ravangla** to the west of Gangtok, the forested peak of **Maenam** is famous for its plants and the tremendous view from its summit; the trek could be done as a short excursion or en route to West Sikkim.

Closer to Gangtok there are three popular viewing points offering panoramas of the **Kanchenjunga Range**. The most accessible is **Ganesh Tok**, a steep walk from the TV tower and Enchey monastery. A small Ganesh shrine and views of Gangtok and the mountains reward those that make the climb. **Hanuman Tok** (2300m), 7km out of town on the road to Changu Lake, is the site of a Hanuman temple, and the cremation ground of the Royal Family, with *chortens* containing relics of the deceased. On the road to Phodong, **Tashi View Point**, 6km out of Gangtok, provides views of the eastern aspects of Kanchenjunga, whose tent-like appearance here is radically different from the way it looks from Darjeeling, and the snowy pyramid of Siniolchu (6888m), which the pioneering mountaineer Eric Shipton ranked among the most beautiful in the world.

Changu Lake, 35km northeast of Gangtok (3780m) and just 20km from the Tibetan border at **Nathu La** is an extremely beautiful place with a small Shiva shrine. It is possible to visit the Kyongnosla Alpine Sanctuary (3350m) where a profusion of wild flowers bloom between May and August and migratory birds stop over in winter on their annual pilgrimage from Siberia to India. Long popular with Indian visitors as an accessible and easy opportunity to sample the high-mountain environment and experience snow, it's now open to foreigners, but due to its location can only be visited as part of a group tour. Many of Gangtok's travel agents, including Yak and Yeti, Bayul, Hangu and Sikkim Tours, run excursions and some hotels will arrange tours at the request of their guests. Foreigners are not permitted up to Nathu La but Indians can travel up in groups on day-trips to take a peek at the Chinese lines.

Rumtek

Visible from Gangtok, a 24-kilometre road trip southwest of the capital, the large *gompa* of **RUMTEK** is the main seat of the **Karma Kagyu** lineage – also known as the **Black Hat** sect – founded during the twelfth century by the first Gyalwa karmapa, Dusun Khyenpa (1110–93). Dusun Khyenpa established the Tsurphu monastery in central Tibet near Lhasa, which became the headquarters of the Karma Kagyu for eight centuries until the Chinese invasion of Tibet in 1959. The sixteenth **karmapa**, Rangjung Rigpe Dorje, fled Tibet for Sikkim where he was invited to stay at the old Rumtek *gompa*. Within a couple of years the karmapa had begun the work of building a new monastery at Rumtek to become his new seat, on land donated by the Sikkimese king Chogyal Tashi Namgyal. One of the great Tibetan figures of the twentieth century, the sixteenth karmapa was very influential in the spread of Tibetan Buddhism to the West, setting up over 200 Karma Kagyu centres and raising funds for the rebuilding of Tsurphu. When he died in 1981, the sixteenth karmapa left behind a wealthy monastery with an international reputation, but one bitterly divided by squabbling over his successor (see p.1517).

The new Rumtek, now heavily guarded against possible raids by feuding parties, is a large and lavish complex consisting of the main temple, golden stupa, and the Karma Shri Nalanda Institute, with a few smaller shrines and a guesthouse outside the monastery courtyard. The monastery is dominated by a **main temple** with its ornate facade covered with intricate brightly painted wooden lattice work, overlooking the expansive **courtyard**. Large red columns support the high roof of the **prayer hall**, where the walls are decorated with murals and *thangkas*. Visitors can attend daily rituals, when lines of monks sit chanting. A chamber off the hall, used for Tantric rituals, is painted with gold against a black background and depicts wrathful protective deities (no photography).

During Losar, the Tibetan New Year (in February), the main courtyard stages *chaam* dance spectacles, in which ceremonial **Black Hat dancers** in colourful costumes spin and move to the magical and ponderous sounds of horns, drums and clashing cymbals.

The **Karma Shri Nalanda Institute of Buddhist Studies**, behind the main temple, built in 1984 in traditional Tibetan style, is the most ornate of all the buildings of Rumtek. Monks spend a minimum of nine years studying here followed by an optional three-year period of isolated meditation. The main hall on the third floor is decorated with magnificent murals, and holds images including the Buddha Shakyamuni – the historic Buddha – and the sixteenth karmapa.

The ashes of the sixteenth karmapa are contained in a gilded four-metre-high *chorten* or stupa, studded with turquoise and coral in the **Golden Stupa** hall opposite the Institute. Behind the stupa is a central statue of Dorje Chang (Vajradhara) flanked by Tilopa, Naropa, Marpa and Milarepa, the four great Kagyu teachers. Statues of the previous sixteen karmapas line the side walls. The door to the hall and *chorten* is kept closed so you will need to knock loudly or find a monk to take you in.

Half a kilometre beyond the new monastery and Rumtek village, a path leads to the simple original Rumtek *gompa*, founded in 1740 and recently renovated, in an attractive wooded clearing and surrounded by empty outbuildings in traditional Sikkimese alpine style, with latticed wooden windows. Behind the statues in the main prayer hall on the right side is a small shrine room dedicated to the Karma Kagyu protector Mahakala, an image so fierce that it is kept veiled.

If you don't arrange your own transport there, the best way to get to Rumtek is by shared Jeeps that leave Gangtok from Lall Bazaar when full and cost Rs25 per head. There's also one SNT bus from Gangtok each day, which leaves at 4pm and returns the next morning. Noodles and chai are available at the teashops clustered near the monastery gate and the checkpoint where foreigners are requested to give passport details.

Accommodation

There's a limited choice of accommodation in Rumtek. The monastery's own hotel, *Kunga Delek* (no phone; ❶–❷), opposite the entrance to the courtyard, has small clean rooms with attached bathroom; there are good views and basic food is available. Just below the Kunga Delek and next to a couple of stalls is the atmospheric but basic *Sangay* (no phone; ❷), with six doubles, one single and a traditional restaurant with great views. *Sun-Gay Rumtek Guesthouse* (no phone; ❷–❸), close to the main gate of the monastery, is by far the best of the budget options. It is a friendly place, despite the vicious guard dogs thankfully tethered during the day, and boasts clean rooms in a new block with views. A traditional smoke-blackened wooden kitchen churns out banana pancakes and other favourites. A couple of hundred metres before the main gate, the new *Shambhala Mountain Resort* (℡03592/52240, ✉ sikkim@ahmedindia.com; ❼–❽), is set in a pleasant garden complex with doubles and comfortable cottages, some in local ethnic style; the main block is comfortable but characterless. The most luxurious accommodation in the area, however, is *Martam Village Resort* (see p.1023).

Phodong and Labrang

Phodong, 38km north of Gangtok on the Mangan road, is another living monastery, but a far less ostentatious one. Lying on a spur of the hill 1km above the main road, and commanding superb views, it consists of a simple square main temple, plus several outhouses and residential quarters. Built in the early eighteenth century, this was Sikkim's pre-eminent Kagyu monastery until the growth of Rumtek in the 1960s. It too hosts colourful lama dances, similar to the *chaam* of Rumtek, each December. A rough road leads a further 4km up to another renovated old monastery – the unusual octagonal **Labrang**. A cluster of *chortens* between these two monasteries marks the ruins of **Tumlong**, Sikkim's capital city for most of the nineteenth century.

Two kilometres beyond the Phodong monastery turn-off in the hamlet on the main road, *Yak & Yeti* (no phone; ❶–❷) and the slightly more comfortable *Northway* (no phone; ❷–❸), which has a restaurant, offer clean budget accommodation in idyllic rural settings. The bus to Gangtok stops at the hamlet around 4pm; shared Jeeps also ply the route.

Ravangla

Spread across a high saddle, 65km west of Gangtok and 52km east of Pelling, the sleepy market town of **RAVANGLA** makes for a convenient stopover, especially for those who would like to trek through one of the last remaining **rhododendron forests** in south-central Sikkim. Under threat of desecration from a new road designed to allow in Jeep-loads of tourists, the fabulous **Maenam Sanctuary** still remains a botanist's dream, covering the flanks of the gigantic forested peak which looms over the town.

Rising to an altitude of 3235m, the summit of **Maenam** with its small chapel to Guru Rinpoche (Padma Sambhava), a good stiff climb of around 1000m in ascent and around 10km in distance from the bazaar, boasts superlative views from the summit, weather permitting. Due to the mountain's position on the watershed between the Teesta and the Rangit river systems, overcast weather can veil the dramatic views of the distant plains to the south, and of the Kanchenjunga range and especially the horned summit of Narsing (5825m). Feasible as a day-trek, the **ascent** of Maenam (2hr 30min–4hr) starts with steps rising from the bazaar up to the small *gompa* (usually shut) before trailing off the road and rising at first gently and then quite steeply through the sanctuary. Besides locals and the occasional Indian trekker, few come this way, and you may even be lucky enough to glimpse some wildlife including deer, the elusive red panda, black bear and a variety of birds. If you want to catch the sunrise from the summit, take a good sleeping bag, food and water, as there is a dilapidated shelter in which to huddle from the elements but little else. Locals, who occasionally camp up here, scour the forests for firewood; deforestation is a real worry so use your discretion and bring down your rubbish.

The route through the forest is not all that obvious (especially in descent when a wrong turn can dump you on the wrong side of the mountain) and you may want to take a local guide (Rs350) arranged through hotels in Ravangla. The small, friendly **tourist information office** (Mon–Sat 9am–4pm; ☎03595/60863) in the main bazaar on the Legship road, is run by an NGO to help promote the area and can also assist with arranging a guide. Ravangla has a small Tibetan refugee community 1km above town which is mostly out of bounds for tourists, except for the **Kheunpheling Carpet Centre** with a factory and a small carpet shop. Monasteries in the vicinity of Ravangla include the old and the new gompas at **Ralang**, 13km to the north, with shared Jeeps travelling the route on demand. The old *gompa*, Karma Rabtenling, is linked to the ninth karmapa and founded in 1768. The new Ralang monastery, built in 1995 in much the same style as Rumtek, and also part of the Kagyu order, is one of the largest temple buildings in Sikkim.

Buses and shared **Jeeps** leave from the stand at the crossroads towards the southern end of the market, for Gangtok as well as Legship where you will need to change for Pelling; you can't be assured of transport much after midday. The shortest route to Darjeeling is via Namche where you may have to change for a Jeep or bus to Jorethang and then change for Darjeeling.

Ravangla now features a reasonable choice of **accommodation**, all closely grouped. *Meanamla* on Kewzing Road (the Legship Road) (☎03595/60666; ➏) offers a modest degree of comfort with attached baths, hot water, a restaurant and a good bar. *Meanamla* is flanked by the *New Dzongri* (☎03595/60707; ➎) on one side, with smaller rooms as well as running hot water and a restaurant; on the other side, the *Swallow's Nest* (☎03595/60847; ➍) is a bit cheaper and pokier (no phone; ➊). *Babyla*, opposite, is far more basic but has a restaurant serving local food. Near the taxi stand, *Hotel 10Zing* (☎03595/60705; ➍) is a friendly place with clean rooms over a popular restaurant serving excellent food, including *gyathuk* and *momos*; they also run a reliable travel service.

Western Sikkim

This beautiful land, characterized by great tracts of virgin forest and deep river valleys, offers ancient monasteries such as **Pemayangtse** and **Tashiding** and the attractive but rapidly developing hamlet of **Pelling**. The old capital,

Yoksum, lies at the start of the trail towards Dzongri and Kanchenjunga. On the far west, along the border with Nepal, the watershed of the Singalila Range rises along a single ridge, with giants such as Rathong and Kabru culminating in Kanchenjunga itself. Although only two high-altitude trails are currently available, and these are subject to restrictions and high charges, several low-altitude treks provide opportunities to enjoy the terraced landscapes, waterfalls and forests at your leisure.

Permit restrictions (see p.1017) mean that trekkers can only follow well-beaten trails and within a limited period of time. If you are coming from Darjeeling and arrange permits and itineraries in advance you could enter Sikkim at **Jorethang** and go directly to Pelling or Yoksum, saving precious permit time.

Jorethang and Legship

The most important town in western Sikkim, **JORETHANG**, lies in the very south of the state, just across the River Rangit from Singla Bazaar in West Bengal and a mere 30km north of Darjeeling, just visible across the tea plantations. Set on an extensive shelf, which makes it feel oddly flat despite the huge hills that rise in every direction, it's a surprisingly pleasant and well-ordered place, with a good market and a couple of decent budget **hotels**. The *Namgyal* (☎03595/76118; ❸) next to the Darjeeling taxi stand has good-value doubles with running hot water, some with river views; it also has the best restaurant in town and an a/c bar. *Hotel Walk-In* (no phone; ❷), in the middle of the market around the corner from the bus stand, has more basic doubles but a reasonable restaurant.

Jorethang is well connected by **bus** with the rest of Sikkim, and there are direct buses to Siliguri (7am, 8am & 9am), but no buses cross the border due south into West Bengal, although **Jeeps** make the extraordinarily steep 25-kilometre journey to Darjeeling. Buses for Gangtok leave at 7am and 1pm, for Pelling at 1pm, and for Ghezing at 8.30am and 12.30pm, connecting with the 2pm departure for Tashiding and Yoksum. Shared Jeeps ply regularly to Legship (change here for Pelling, Yuksom and Tashiding) and to Namche for those travelling to Ravangla. The territory around Singla Bazaar south of the river from Naya Bazaar, Jorethang's twin town, is not particularly safe, and vehicles are occasionally forced to pay an unofficial road tax by militant tea-pickers. Few Jeeps leave Jorethang after 1pm.

LEGSHIP, in the deep Rangit Valley 26km north of Jorethang, is the first town you come to if you approach western Sikkim from Gangtok, just under 100km west. It's an important regional road junction and one where you could find yourself with an hour or so to spare, but not an interesting destination. *Trishna* (no phone; ❷–❸) at the crossroads, has a few rooms and a restaurant. Jeeps and buses connect Legship with Gangtok, Jorethang, Ravangla, Ghezing and Pelling as well as Yoksum via Tashiding.

Ghezing

The unattractive market town of **GHEZING** (which sometimes appears as **GYALSHING**), 110km west of Gangtok, is the administration centre and transport hub of western Sikkim. It's a good place to stock up on provisions, and has a handful of basic **hotels** around the main square, including the *Kanchanzonga* (no phone; ❷), which has a restaurant; the *Mayalu* (no phone; ❶); and the *Chopstick* (no phone; ❷), with lighter and brighter rooms and views across the valley to Ravangla. The most comfortable place in the centre of town is the *Attri* (☎03595/50602; ❺–❻) at the top end of Ghezing with a/c double rooms. But for a bit of luxury head for the dramatically situated *Tashigang Resort* at Deecheling (☎03595/50340; ❼–❽), where doubles come with balconies and sweeping views, and the landscaped garden harbours traditional Sikkim cottages. A small monastery, **Hin Shan** *gompa*, home to a handful of Bhutanese monks, is thirty minutes' walk up out of town and offers excellent views of Kanchenjunga.

Shared **Jeeps** leave for Gangtok, Siliguri (tickets in advance from the counter near the playground ☎03595/50121) and Pelling (just turn up) and other local destinations from the main square. A reserved Jeep to Yoksum will cost Rs800–1200 depending on the season. The SNT office (6.30am–3.30pm) is at the bottom of town next to a small Tibetan *gompa*. A bus to Siliguri (via Jorethang) leaves at 7am daily, and other buses to Jorethang leave at 9.30am, 1pm and 3.30pm – change there for Darjeeling and Siliguri. A daily bus for Gangtok departs at 7am and a daily service to Khecheopalri Lake at 2.30pm, passing through Pelling. At 2pm there's a service for Yoksum, via Legship and Tashiding.

Pemayangtse

Perched at the end of a ridge parallel to (and visible from) that of Darjeeling, the haunting monastery of **PEMAYANGTSE**, 118km from Gangtok and a mere 2km from Pelling, is poised high above the River Rangit, which snakes towards its confluence with the Teesta on the West Bengal border. It's a nine-kilometre journey along the main road from Ghezing; or you can take a steep, four-kilometre short cut through the woods past a line of *chortens* and the otherwise uninteresting ruins of Sikkim's second capital, **Rabdantse**.

"Perfect Sublime Lotus", founded in the seventeenth century by Lhatsun Chempo, one of the three lamas of Yoksum, and extended in 1705 by his reincarnation, is the most important *gompa* in Sikkim and belongs to the Nyingma school. Expansive views of the Kanchenjunga massif and the surrounding woods create an atmosphere of meditative solitude. Surrounded by exquisite outhouses, with intricate woodwork on the beams, lattice windows and doors, the main *gompa* itself is plain in comparison. Built on three floors, it centres around a large hall which contains images of Guru Rinpoche and Lhatsun Chempo (the latter was an enigmatic Tibetan lama who is the patron saint of Sikkim), and an exquisite display of *thangkas* and murals. On the top floor, a magnificent wooden sculpture carved and painted by Dungzin Rinpoche, a former abbot of Pemayangtse, depicts Sang Thok Palri, the celestial abode of Guru Rinpoche, rising above the realms of hell. The extraordinary detail includes demons, animals, birds, Buddhas and *bodhisattvas*, *chortens* and flying dragons, and took him just five years to complete. An annual *chaam* – masked dance – is held here during the Tibetan New Year (Feb), and attracts visitors from all over Sikkim.

In 1980, the **Denjong Padma Choeling Academy** was set up by the monastery to provide a home and education to destitute children and orphans, and there are currently around 200 children being housed, clothed, fed and educated here. The curriculum has a strong cultural base and is also vocational. Generous donations have enabled further building and the setting up of a yak and *dri* dairy project near Dzongri, a tea garden and carpet-weaving. The volunteer teachers, more of whom are always welcome, receive free accommodation in the monastery, opportunities to study meditation and Buddhism,

and to learn local crafts. The monastery also runs courses at the International Heritage Meditation centre where nine well-furnished rooms are available to students of Buddhism or anyone wanting to experience monastic life. Contact Sonam Yongda at Pemayangste Gompa, West Sikkim 737 113; ☏03595/50760 or 50141, ℗03592/24802.

Pelling and around

The laid-back, scenic, but rapidly swelling hamlet of **PELLING**, situated 2085m above sea level only 2km beyond Pemayangtse, looks north towards the glaciers and peaks of Kanchenjunga. High above forest-covered hills, in an amphitheatre of cloud, snow and rock, the entire route from Yoksum over Dzongri La to the Rathong Glacier can be seen. Pelling itself consists of little more than a road junction, helicopter pad and numerous hotels – most of which have been built in the last few years, creating the so-called "Bengali Boulevard", a strip of highly unimaginative identikit concrete blocks. Luckily, this is not enough to detract from the charm of Pelling: numerous attractive walks and hotel terraces allow you to gaze in awe at the world's third-highest peak. A four-kilometre trail rises from the playing fields just above Pelling to reach the small but highly venerated monastery of **Sanga Choling**, one of the oldest *gompas* in Sikkim. This *gompa* is another of Lhatsun Chenpo's creations, and is held in high esteem among the Nyingmapa. Gutted by fire, it has been rebuilt and houses some of the original clay statues.

For those with permit endorsements to visit Khecheopalri Lake, Yoksum and Tashiding, a scenic low-altitude **trek** along trails and roads starts from Pelling (see below). Public transport runs from both Yoksum and Tashiding back to Legship from where you can continue to Ghezing, and eventually back to Pelling.

Shared **Jeeps** travel regularly (6am–4pm) between Pelling and Ghezing; twice daily for Gangtok via Ravangla (6am & noon); and once a day for Siliguri (6am). There is no direct service to Yoksum from Pelling but a daily **bus** leaves Ghezing and travels via Legship and Tashiding. One bus leaves Ghezing daily for Khecheopalri Lake and passes through Pelling (3.30pm) but the service is erratic, and two leave Pelling for Ghezing (8am & 9am). The road from Pelling via Rimbi to Yuksom is too poor for buses but is being slowly repaired and upgraded. There is a small **post office** in Upper Pelling next to the Sikkim Tourist Centre and **email** facilities for Rs1.50 per minute at Cyberia in *Hotel Phamrong*. Although there are no official facilities for **changing money** in Pelling, the Sikkim Tourist Centre will change small amounts of cash in US dollars only. The Sikkim Tourist Centre also houses Help Tourism, an unofficial **information** centre and travel and tour operator with an emphasis on ecotourism. For trekking information consult the books at *Hotel Garuda*.

Accommodation

Garuda, at the crossroads ☏03595/58319. A popular travellers' haunt and good meeting place, this well-run family hotel offers a range of singles, doubles and dorms (Rs50), and useful comment books have the latest trekking information. The restaurant boasts excellent food and low-key service. ❸–❺

Kabur, 200m before the crossroads ☏03595/58504. A friendly place, though not quite as atmospheric as *Garuda*. Has doubles with car-

pets and hot water, one cheap four-bed room and a pleasant rooftop terrace. ❸

Ladakh, Upper Pelling. A traditional, rustic Sikkimese house with one double, two triples and a dorm (Rs40); the common bathrooms are outside but the family-run lodge is being upgraded to add comfort and two new wooden rooms. ❷

Mount Pandim, just below Pemayangtse monastery ☏03595/50756. Extensive and comfortable government hotel, beautifully located with magnificent

views and a reasonable restaurant. ❻–❼
Pelling , "Bengali Boulevard", Lower Pelling
☏ 03595/50707. Brightly painted place in
Sikkimese style. Rooms with balconies. ❸–❺
Phamrong , Upper Pelling ☏ 03595/58218,
✉ hotelphamrong@hotmail.com. A new hotel with
a wide range of comfortable, clean rooms, running
hot water and attentive service; there's a pleasant
restaurant and great views from some of the more
expensive rooms. Email is also available. ❻–❼
Samtenling , "Bengali Boulevard", Lower Pelling
☏ 03595/50689. Atmospheric old-world place surviving in the midst of the new; their good restaurant serves *tomba*. ❹

Sikkim Tourist Centre , above the crossroads
☏ 03595/50788. Running hot water and attached
baths, but overpriced. A useful list in reception
describes local package tours and places of interest. ❺
Sister Family Guesthouse , a short walk down
from the *Garuda*, towards Lower Pelling
☏ 03595/50569. This quiet option offers eight
rooms, hot water by the bucket and a cosy restaurant. ❸
View Point , near the helipad ☏ 03595/50638. A
recently improved and extended hotel with comfortable doubles and running hot water; the views
from the terrace are wonderful. ❸–❹

Khecheopalri Lake

Surrounded by dense forests and hidden in a mountain bowl (2000m) 33km to
the northwest of Pelling, **Khecheopalri Lake**, known as the "Wishing Lake", is
sacred to the Lepchas. Legend has it that if a leaf drops onto the lake's surface a
guardian bird swoops down and picks it up, thereby maintaining the purity of the
water. Another tale tells that Khecheopalri Lake and Kathok Lake in Yoksum are
female and male counterparts and were once neighbours. However, villagers gave
more importance to Kathok and neglected Khecheopalri, dumping rubbish
there and destroying her sanctity, causing her to relocate in a huff to a more salubrious and less inhabited area. Public transport runs along the Pelling–Yuksom
road (only when conditions allow) to the Khecheopalri turn-off known as zero
point, from where it's an eleven-kilometre hike up a rough but motorable road
with only occasional Jeeps travelling the route (landslides permitting) to the lake.
The Pelling bus, if it is running, leaves Pelling at 3pm, stays overnight and returns
at 7am. If you want to trek to Khecheopalri, a shortcut leads down to the river
valley, steeply up to the Pelling Yuksom road and then up to the lake (allow 5hr);
you can continue the circuit to Yuksom (see opposite).

Conservation and the Kanchenjunga National Park

Set up in 1996 with the help of the Sikkim Biodiversity and Ecotourism Network
(see p.1019), the **Khangchendzonga Conservation Committee** (KCC), a com-
munity-based NGO based in Yuksom, aims to promote **ecological awareness** to
locals and visitors alike. The KCC's main concern is the impact of tourism on the
fabric of the **Kanchenjunga National Park**, and their methods include planting
trees, mobilizing local participation in the planning of **ecotourism** and organizing
clean-up campaigns.

In 1997 the KCC's programme to clean the trails produced 400kg of tins and other
rubbish including 100kg of plastic, from the Yoksum, Dzongri and Thangsing areas
alone. The waste – a tiny fraction of what is still up there – was brought down for
landfill and incineration. Other KCC programmes include publishing information
leaflets to promote eco-awareness, training local workers including porters and guides
in the ecotourism industry and educating villagers on alternative sources of income
generation such as vegetable production. Although they have had some success, the
KCC continues to meet stern opposition and hostility from certain quarters and
especially government agencies, which have tried to hinder their plans to clean the
litter off the trails. For more information on the KCC, contact their co-ordinator
Chewang Bhutia at the *Hotel Wild Orchid*, Yuksom (✉ kcc_sikkim@hotmail.com).

Khecheopalri village and the *gompa* 2km from the lake on top of the ridge provide excellent views of Mount Pandim (6691m), and several sacred caves are scattered through the hills. **Guides** to these caves and to Yoksum, Tashiding and Pelling can be arranged through *Trekker's Hut* (no phone; ●), one of the few **accommodation places** at Khecheopalri, a friendly but very basic option which serves simple meals such as rice and dhal, noodles and Tibetan bread. It also has some very useful information on the local area and a definitive list for bird-watchers. Another option is the tiny *Pilgrim's Rest House* (no phone; ●) nearer the lake, which has a shrine room and chapel sometimes used by visiting monks. A small tea stall next to the *Pilgrim's Rest House* serves chai and simple meals. The trail to Yoksum is 18km long and takes around four hours. Stock up on snacks from Ghezing market or some of the small stalls in Pelling. The *Garuda* hotel in Pelling can also provide food and information on the trail.

Yoksum

The sleepy, spread-out hamlet of **YOKSUM**, which occupies a large shelf at the entrance to the Rathong Chu gorge, 40km north of Pemayangtse at the end of the road, holds a special place in Sikkimese history. This was the spot where three lamas converged to enthrone the first religious king of Sikkim, Chogyal Phuntsog Namgyal, in 1642. Named the "Great Religious King" he established Tibetan Buddhism in Sikkim. This meeting of three lamas coming from different directions across the Himalayas was predicted by Guru Rinpoche nine centuries earlier. Lhatsun Chenpo is supposed to have buried offerings in Yoksum's large white **Norbugang Chorten** built with stones and earth from different parts of Sikkim. From here a path branches left through the village to a small grove and the simple stone throne of the first chogyal. In front of the throne an impressive footprint embedded in a rock by one of the lamas no doubt impressed the king too. High above the town, prayer flags announce the site of the Nyingma **Dubdi Monastery**, built in 1701. From the end of the road at the hospital, a path threads past water wheels and a small river and rises through the forest to arrive at the dramatically situated *gompa*, looking out over Yoksum. Unless you've made prior arrangements, however, there's unlikely to be anyone around to let you have a look inside. **Kathok Lake**, a small scummy pond at the top end of town has nothing of the pristine beauty of sister-lake Khecheopalri, but has views of the snowcapped peaks in the distance.

Yoksum's main role these days is as the start of the **Dzongri Trail**. Visitors with West Sikkim permits are welcome in Yoksum, but unless you have a Dzongri Trek permit you're not supposed to venture any further. The police are quite vigilant, so there's not much chance of a surreptitious high-mountain trek, but so long as you're not carrying a backpack they may allow a day-trip along the main trail to the Parekh Chu and its confluence with the Rathong Chu – a 28-kilometre round trip. You won't see the high Himalaya, but you do pass through some beautiful forest scenery (visibly being eroded to feed the increasing demands of the trekking industry). Yaks – or rather *dzo*, a more manageable cross between yak and domestic cattle – travel this route, with supplies for trekking parties and isolated communities.

Practicalities

The road to Yuksom is in shocking condition, which means that the daily **bus**, which usually leaves from outside the *Dzongrila* (see below), for Ghezing via Tashiding (90min) and Legship (2hr) doesn't always quite make it to Yuksom.

When this is the case, the bus usually leaves from Gerathang, 5km down the road, at 7am. A couple of seriously overcrowded **Jeeps** depart at around 6.30am to Tashiding and Legship and occasionally on to Jorethang on demand.

Accommodation in Yuksom is improving, with several budget options around the small market area including: *Demazong* (no phone; ❷–❹), where some rooms come with attached baths; *Wild Orchid* (no phone; ❷), an attractive traditional house; and the plain *Dzongrila* (no phone; ❶), which also has a cheap dorm (Rs40). The *Arpan* (no phone; ❶), on the outskirts of Yuksom, has three rooms and a small restaurant serving noodles and dhal. A little closer to Yuksom's tiny market, *Pemathang* (no phone; ❸–❹) is a pleasant place with

---

West Sikkim high-altitude treks

Two **high-altitude treks** are currently allowed in Sikkim. The first, from **Yoksum** to **Dzongri**, in the very shadow of Kanchenjunga, passes through huge tracts of forest and provides incredible mountain vistas. The second, the **Singalila ridge**, explores the high pastures of the Singalila frontier range with breathtaking views of the massif. Trekkers for either of the two must have special **permits** (see p.1019), travel in groups organized by authorized agencies (see p.1025), complete with largely superfluous guides and a liaison officer, and pay a daily rate of $40–70. Check your permit carefully and that the food arrangements before you set off – both should be included in the cost. Bring adequate clothing – including protective headgear to cope with the heat of the river valleys – boots and sleeping bags. For general advice on trekking equipment and health issues, see Basics.

The Dzongri Trail

Although Dzongri is the junction of several trails, the prescribed route onwards leads to **Goecha La** via Zemanthang and Samiti Lake. Well-marked and dotted with basic accommodation, the trail, also used by yak herders, is at its best in May when the rhododendrons bloom.

DAY 1 It takes approximately 6hr to climb the 16km from **Yoksum** (1780m) to **Tsokha** (3048m). The trail begins gently and soon reaches deep forest cover before arriving at the Parekh Chu above its confluence with the Rathong. The next 3–4km involve a knee-grinding ascent past the rambling *Forest Rest House* at **Bakhim** (2684m). You have now entered the lichen zone and cloud forests. **Tsokha**, 1.5km further on and 300m higher, settled by Tibetan yak herders, has a couple of huts including the *Trekkers Hut* as well as several rustic houses, where guests are offered Tibetan tea – a salty brew made with rancid butter. Their kitchen rafters are blackened by smoke and hung with slowly curing chunks of yak meat.

DAY 2 can be spent acclimatizing yourself to the altitude at Tsokha, perhaps with a short trek of around 5km towards Dzongri, to a watchtower which (weather permitting) has superb views of Kanchenjunga.

DAY 3 The eleven-kilometre section from **Tsokha** to **Dzongri** (4024m) takes 4–5hr, rising through beautiful pine and rhododendron forests to **Phedang Meadows** (3450m), before continuing to the hut on the meadows of Dzongri.

DAY 4 Once again, it's worth staying around Dzongri for further acclimatization. That gives you the opportunity to climb Dzongri Hill above the hut, for early-morning and early-evening views of Kanchenjunga's craggy south summit. Look out for the black tooth of Kabur, a forbidding-looking holy mountain that towers above Dzongri La. Several trails meet at the meadows at Dzongri – one descends to cross the Rathong Chu and rises again to the demanding pass of Kang La into Nepal; another crosses Dzongri La (4400m), descends around 450m and rises again to the HMI base camp 12km away at Chaurikhang and the Rathong Glacier.

attached baths and a small picturesque garden; neighbouring *Yangri Gang* (no phone; ❷) is not nearly as attractive but is traveller-friendly with a restaurant and basic but acceptable rooms. The *Tashi Gang* (☏03593/58289; ❼) a large, pink and somewhat incongruous building, is the plushest of Yoksum's hotels and the only place with running hot water; it also has a restaurant and the only telephone in town. At the other end of the scale, the abysmally maintained *Trekker's Hut* (no phone; ❶) has plain wooden rooms, outhouse toilets and allows camping.

Besides hotel restaurants, the only other **places to eat** are the cafés along the main drag which serve basic meals such as rice and dhal; the *Yak* is the friendliest and is a good place to meet the locals.

DAY 5 The eight-kilometre trek from Dzongri to Thangsing (3841m) takes around 4hr, descending against an incredible backdrop of peaks to a rhododendron forest, crossing a bridge and continuing through woods to the *Trekkers Hut* at Thangsing at the end of a glacial valley.

DAY 6 The ten-kilometre short, sharp shock up to Samiti Lake (4303m) takes around 3hr. The trail follows a stream and alpine meadows past a yak herders' hut, then traverses glacial moraine, crosses meadows and a rocky landscape before arriving at the emerald-green Samiti Lake (local name Sungmoteng Tso). The camping ground here is next to a giant boulder, which provides some shelter from cold winds or storms. If you are still going strong, you could continue to Zemanthang (4453m) where there's a *Trekkers Hut*.

DAY 7 Very much the climax of the trek, and also by far its most difficult section – not because of any technicalities, but simply due to its high altitude. From Samiti Lake the fourteen-kilometre round-trip climb takes around 4hr up to Goecha La and 2–3hr back down again. Leaving Samiti Lake, the trail follows glacial moraine, drops to a dry lake at Zemanthang, then makes a final grinding rise alongside cairns decorated with the occasional prayer flag to the defile at Goecha La (4940m). Kanchenjunga South is clearly visible above the pass, while to the left glaciers tumble off Kabru Dome.

DAY 8 Most of the long 24-kilometre hike from Samiti Lake back to Tsokha is downhill and takes around 8hr, involving a short cut to avoid Dzongri. Crossing the bridge and following the path to a junction signed to the left puts you back above Tsokha, to rejoin the trail to Yoksum.

The Singalila ridge

The Singalila ridge has been recently opened for trekkers who come armed with the right permits and guides, with itineraries ranging between ten and fourteen days. The section of the ridge for trekkers stretches from the roadhead at Uttarey (1965m), 28km to the west of Pelling, and ascends to Chewa Bhanjang (3170m) on the Sikkim-Nepal frontier. Thereafter, the trail rarely descends below 3500m, crossing steep rocky hillsides and high alpine meadows above the tree line with spectacular views of the looming Kanchenjunga massif; the highest point of the trail is the Dafey Bhir pass at 4400m. Several lakes such as Lampokhari, all considered holy, are encountered along the route, and here and there dwarf rhododendron forests bring a blaze of colour. After Dafey Bhir the route dips steeply to Gomathang (3725m), a yak herders' shelter on the banks of the Boktochu; the route then passes through a delightful forest of silver fir and rhododendron before arriving at the welcome sight of the bungalow at Dzongri. You could descend from here via Tsokha to Yuksom or continue to Goecha La, thus completing a grand and rewarding traverse.

Tashiding

The beautiful *gompa* of **TASHIDING** occupies the point of a conical hill 19km southeast of Yoksum, high above the confluence of the Rangit and the Rathong. "The Devoted Central Glory" was built in 1717, after a rainbow was seen to connect the site to Kanchenjunga. A wide path leaves the main road near an impressive *mani* wall (painted green and inscribed in silver paint with the mantra *Om mani padme hum*: "Hail the jewel in the lotus") and leads steeply past rustic houses and fields up to the monastery compound. The large complex consists of a motley collection of buildings, *chortens*, several chapels and the unassuming main temple, which was recently rebuilt using some of the features and wooden beams of the original. At the far end of the temple complex is an impressive array of *chortens* containing relics of Sikkim's chogyals and lamas. On the fifteenth day of the first month of the Tibetan New Year, devotees from all over Sikkim gather in Tashiding for the **Nyingmapa Bhumchu festival** where they are blessed with the holy water from an ancient bowl said by legend never to dry up. Oracles consult the water's level to determine the future.

Around 2km below the *gompa*, Tashiding's tiny bazaar is situated near a saddle that separates the mountainside from the monastery hill. Basic **accommodation** in the bazaar includes the friendly and cosy *Blue Bird* (no phone; ❶), complete with restaurant serving simple wholesome food, and the more spacious, slightly more expensive *Mount Siniolchu Guesthouse* (no phone; ❶) further up the hill. A daily **bus** from Yoksum passes through Tashiding at around 8.30am and continues via Legship to Ghezing. In the other direction the bus leaves Ghezing at 2pm, passing through Tashiding (at approximately 3.30pm) on its way up to Yoksum or Gerathang, 5km short of Yoksum, if the road, as it usually is, is down. One or two timetabled Jeeps and a handful of unscheduled Jeeps and trucks also connect Yoksum to Tashiding and Legship. Trails through the forests and along stretches of the main road make trekking an alternative option to public transport; the route to Legship takes around two and a half hours.

North Sikkim

Most of spectacular **north Sikkim** is closed to visitors. Until 1993 no one was allowed to venture past Phodong, but now groups armed with special permits, arranged through travel and tour operators in Gangtok (see p.1025), are allowed as far as **Yume Samdang** and **Thanggu**, at the edge of the Tibetan plateau. Every year throughout the monsoon, **landslides** take out stretches of road, severely disrupting transport, and areas get cut off from Gangtok and the rest of the country. Teams of local villagers are drafted in to clear boulders, rebuild and shore up the cliffs.

The road north of Gangtok follows the deep Teesta gorge past Phodong across what is said to be the highest bridge in Asia (no photography allowed), before reaching the quiet little town of **MANGAN**, administrative centre for north Sikkim. There is little of interest here but a few basic hotels and cafés on the main road providing "food and lodging". The *Himalayan* (no phone; ❹) has the biggest rooms in town and its own restaurant while the *Lachen Valley* (no phone; ❸), *Ganga* (no phone; ❸) and *North Point Lodge* (no phone; ❸) offer much the same on a smaller scale. The drive down to **Namprikdang**, a popular angling spot at the confluence of the Rangit and Teesta, is both spectacular and hair-raising. A small *gompa* 5km north of Mangan – the northernmost point for those tourists not travelling in a group – **Singhik** provides incredible views, especially early in the morning, of the huge east face of Kanchenjunga. The new *Tourist Lodge* (no phone; ❸) at Singhik takes advantage of the location widely considered to be the best viewpoint in all Sikkim. Although a magnificent valley branches northwest from Mangan towards Kanchenjunga, this area is reserved as the Lepcha heartland where non-Lepchas are not allowed.

A further 40km north lies **CHUNGTHANG**, a dark and grubby town, set in a deep valley at the confluence of the Lachen and Lachung rivers, with a large military presence. There is a large Public Works Department bungalow here; although it's generally used for PWD employees tourists can stay if there's room. There are also a couple of basic hotels including the *Neelam* (no phone; ❷) on the main road, with a decent but simple restaurant.

Beyond Chumthang the valleys fork. These are border areas and the military, who maintain the rough roads, are very sensitive – photography, even of harmless monasteries, is not tolerated. The road to the right climbs rapidly to the small settlement of **LACHUNG**, the "big pass", a mere 15km west of Tibet. Across the river, **Lachung Monastery** is a two-storey Tibetan-style *gompa* belonging to the Nyingmapa sect. Most of the accommodation here, inclusive of meals, will be booked through your tour operator in Gangtok, such as *Lecoxy Tours & Travels* (see p.1025). Alternatives include the *Apple Valley Inn* (no phone; ❹) and the more basic *Alpine Resort* (no phone; ❷–❸).

Twenty-four kilometres further north, the valley becomes even more spectacular. Craggy snow-bound peaks rise as high as 6000m to either side above **YUMTHANG**, which has hot sulphur springs but no accommodation. *Yaksey Lodge* (no phone; ❹), halfway between Lachung and Yumthang, provides a base from which to discover the valley.

Several interesting **high-altitude treks** are now open to group tours in this isolated region, including the popular Lachen–Green Lake trek which takes approximately five days (one-way) and offers great views of Mount Siniolchu (6687m) across the Zemu glacier. Green Lake is the base for climbing expeditions attempting the many 6000–7000m peaks in the region. One such route from Green Lake crosses the Zemu and Talung glaciers, and reaches Goecha La (4940m) and Dzongri La before it finally descends into Western Sikkim, but this is only for experienced mountaineers. Another extremely challenging route to Green Lake begins at Thanggu, 28km beyond Lachen. Trekking permits for the north must be sought through Sikkim Tourism in Delhi and mountaineering permits through the Indian Mountaineering Foundation also in Delhi.

Travel details

Jeeps

Jeeps tend to go when full, except for the Gangtok–Ghezing and Pelling services, which depart once daily. There are no train or plane services available and the helicopter service from Gangtok only operates to meet flights at Bagdogra. Buses cost a few rupees less than the Jeeps but they are much slower and tend to be a lot more uncomfortable.

Gangtok to: Darjeeling (5–6hr); Ghezing (4–5hr); Kalimpong (3–4hr); Pelling (5–6hr); Mangan (2–3hr); Siliguri (5–6hr).
Ghezing to: Gangtok (5–6hr); Jorethang (2hr 30min –3hr); Pelling (30min); Yoksum (2hr 30min–3hr).
Jorethang to: Darjeeling (2hr); Gangtok (4–5hr); Ghezing (2hr); Legship (1hr).

CHAPTER 16

Highlights

* **Kamakhya Temple, Guwahati** An important Tantric fertility temple with distinctive Assamese architecture. See p.1048

* **Kaziranga National Park, Assam** Encounter the rare one-horned rhino on a dawn elephant ride. See p.1052

* **Shillong** This former British Raj hill station with its bustling market

bazaar is the gateway for trips to Cherrapunjee. See p.1061

* **Tawang Monastery, Arunachal Pradesh** A spectacular Tibetan Buddhist monastery in one of the most remote locations imaginable. See p.1082

* **Kohima** Proud capital of Nagaland, with a superb museum of Naga life. See p.1085

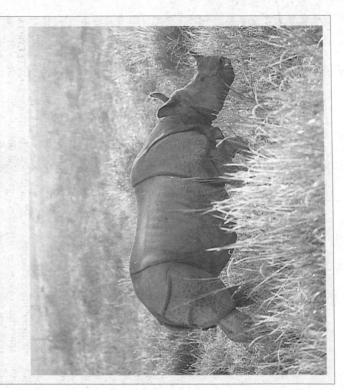

The Northeast

C ertainly the least explored and arguably the most beautiful region of India, the **NORTHEAST**, connected to the rest of India by a very narrow stretch of land between Bhutan and Bangladesh, has long been all but sealed from the outside world. Arunachal Pradesh shares an extremely sensitive northern border with Chinese-occupied Tibet and together with Nagaland, Manipur and Mizoram, a 1600-kilometre border with Myanmar. Insurgency has plagued the region since Independence, with tribal groups pushing for various degrees of autonomy and independence as well as fighting each other. A huge influx of Bengalis into the region and consequent displacement of many tribal people has created further tension, particularly in the northernmost reaches. However, government restriction of access permits eased up considerably in 2000, and despite ongoing tensions, this fascinating region continues to open up both for tour groups and independent travellers.

Until the 1960s the region comprised just two states, the North East Frontier Agency (NEFA), now known as Arunachal Pradesh, and Assam, but separatist pressures further divided it into seven states, known as "the seven sisters". **Assam** consists of the low-lying valley of the Brahmaputra, while the other states occupy the surrounding hills. Situated on the banks of the Brahmaputra, Assam's capital **Guwahati**, boasts two of India's most important ancient temples, and acts as a gateway to the entire region; all the other states depend heavily on the transport routes of the Assam Valley.

Each hill state has its own distinctive character, forged by the landscape, climate and peoples. **Meghalaya**, is home to the wettest place on earth, and is populated by the colourful Jaintia, Khasi and Garo tribes. Its capital, **Shillong**, retains some of the colonial atmosphere from its time as the summer capital of East India. **Tripura** was cut off from the Bangladeshi plains during the 1947 Partition, and still feels more like India proper than the rest of the region. Highlights include the water palace of Neermahal and the rock sculptures at Unakoti.

Accommodation price codes

All accommodation prices in this book have been categorized using the price codes below. Prices given are for a double room, and all taxes are included. For more details, see p.51.

❶ up to Rs100
❷ Rs100–200
❸ Rs200–300
❹ Rs300–400
❺ Rs400–600
❻ Rs600–900
❼ Rs900–1500
❽ Rs1500–2500
❾ Rs2500 and upwards

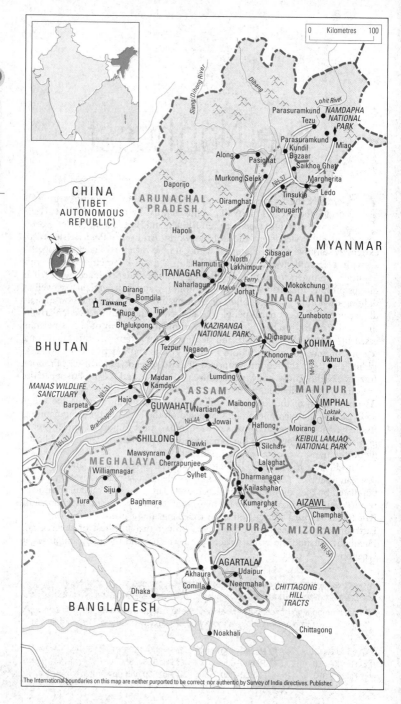

The International boundaries on this map are neither purported to be correct nor authentic by Survey of India directives. Publisher.

The other four states all require **permits** to visit (see below). The Mizo, Manipuri and Naga peoples live in divided homelands bisected by the border of India and Myanmar. **Mizoram**, in the Lushai hills, is currently the most peaceful state, predominantly Christian due to intensive missionary work under the British and with one of the highest literacy rates in India. Neighbouring **Manipur**, once an independent princely kingdom, is at the heart of the cultural crossroads where the subcontinent and Southeast Asia meet. The people are more closely related to the neighbouring Burmese than to the Aryans from the west, and speak languages quite unrelated to Hindi or

Access and permits

Although the region is increasingly opening up for tourism, regulations can change according to the current state of security. Check with the Indian Embassy or tourist office before travelling and again with state representatives in India.

Assam, Meghalaya and Tripura are completely open; you can enter by any route and travel freely within. Foreigners require Restricted Area Permits to visit Manipur, Mizoram, Nagaland and Arunachal Pradesh and are officially required to travel in groups of at least four. Individual travellers should have permits endorsed at the Foreigners' Registration Office in the state capitals. Indian nationals require Inner Line Permits for Arunachal Pradesh and Nagaland.

Due to the sensitive border with Tibet, visitors to Arunachal Pradesh must travel with a recognized tour operator and pay a $50 fee. Although few of the northeast hill states pose any particular danger to tourists, it's best to check the current situation before travelling and follow local advice. For a history of the troubles and further background information, see the box on p.1056.

Permits

Foreigners can apply for Restricted Area Permits directly to the state government representatives of Manipur, Mizoram, Nagaland and Arunachal Pradesh in the Chanakyapuri enclave of New Delhi or in Calcutta, but unusual cases should be directed to the Ministry of Home Affairs, Foreigners' Division, Lok Nayak Bhavan, near Khan Market in New Delhi. Permit applications should be made at least four weeks in advance of your desired travelling dates; expect to make several visits before any permit is granted. Permits can also be requested at the Indian Embassy or High Commission in your own country; apply three months in advance if possible. An invitation from someone in one of the states will make either process quicker and more certain.

To obtain Inner Line Permits, Indian citizens should apply with two passport photographs to representatives of the state governments concerned. Applications should only take a day to process and are valid for a week in the first instance but can be extended for up to six months in the relevant state capital.

State Government representatives

Arunachal Pradesh Arunachal Bhawan, Kautilya Marg, Chanakyapuri, Delhi ☏011/301 3915; 4B Chowringee Rd, Calcutta ☏033/248 6500.

Manipur Manipur Bhawan, 2 Sardar Patel Marg, Chanakyapuri, Delhi ☏011/687 3311; Manipur Bhawan, 26 Rowland Rd, Calcutta ☏033/474 7087.

Mizoram Mizoram Bhawan, Circular Rd (behind the Sri Lankan Embassy), Chanakyapuri, Delhi ☏011/301 5951; Mizoram House, 24 Old Ballygunge Rd, Calcutta ☏033/475 7034.

Nagaland 29 Aurangzeb Rd, Delhi ☏011/301 2296; Nagaland House, 12 Shakespeare Sarani, Calcutta ☏033/242 5269.

Assamese. Outside the relative calm of the capital **Imphal**, intertribal disputes involving village raids, arson and killings are common, and visitors are advised not to venture beyond Loktak Lake. To the north, the lush mountains of **Nagaland** are home to fourteen major tribal groups, each with a strong sense of identity and history. A progressive tourist policy has seen Kohima and the surrounding villages opening up, and some of the further-flung tribal capitals can also be visited. **Arunachal Pradesh** is one of the most remote states in India and is home to a vast array of different peoples, many of whom are of Tibetan origin. The Himalayas here rise to 6500m and in the far northwestern corner, surrounded by an awesome circle of mountains, is the huge Buddhist monastery of Tawang, one of the largest in Asia.

The main attractions in the northeast are the extraordinary diversity of peoples and the spectacular **landscapes**. One of the wettest monsoon belts in the world, most of the region was, until recently, rich in teak forests and wild elephants. It has an astounding array of flora and fauna – estimated at fifty percent of India's entire biodiversity. Of the region's many **wildlife sanctuaries**, the most famous are **Kaziranga** in Assam, home to the Indian one-horned rhino; **Namdapha** in the furthest corner of Arunachal, which ranges from 400m to 6500m; and **Manas**, home of Project Tiger. The recommended **time to visit** is from November to April, although Tawang is extremely cold by December. It rains heavily from May to the end of September.

Travelling through this region demands a considerable amount of **time**, energy and perseverance. Bureaucracy, language barriers and interminably long daytime bus journeys provide a challenge which, though frustrating at times, can be richly rewarding. In ten days you could travel from West Bengal to Guwahati, Shillong, and Kaziranga, while three weeks would be enough to cover the main sights of the "open" states of Assam, Meghalaya and Tripura; incorporating the more distant, permit-required states would take considerably longer. One of the main barriers to travel is that there are few **entry and exit points**, although a couple more airports have opened with domestic flights to Guwahati and Calcutta. The State Bank of India also recently withdrew **foreign exchange** services across the northeast, except for Guwahati and Shillong.

Assam

The state of **ASSAM** is dominated by the mighty **River Brahmaputra**, whose lush seven-hundred-kilometre valley is sandwiched between the Himalayan foothills to the north and the hills and plateau of Meghalaya to the south. Although much of the valley is under cultivation, large tracts of woodland make this one of the most forested states in India.

Assam produces more than half of India's **tea**. Most of its eight hundred tea estates were laid down by the British, who created a basic infrastructure of roads, as well as one golf club for every fifteen estates, to relieve the tedium and loneliness of the planters. It is also one of India's few **oil** regions, home to the first oil refinery in Asia at **Digboi** in Upper Assam.

Political violence has racked Assam over the last two decades. In 1979, a campaign against Bangladeshis voting in a by-election led to strikes and protests against their community, largely organized by the All-Assam Students' Union (AASU). The unrest culminated in a boycott of the 1983 State Assembly elections and a series of riots that left more than 3000 dead. Two years later the

Ahom and Bodos

Migration of people has played a major role in the history of the northeastern hill states. The **Ahom**, originally called the Shan, were Buddhists from Thailand who invaded in 1228 and settled in the northeast corner of the valley of the Brahmaputra. Establishing their capital at Sibsagar, they named the region Assam, "undulating land". By the end of the sixteenth century the fiery and tenacious Ahoms had displaced the Kacharis and Koche of northeastern Bengal and western Assam, and they later repelled several Muslim invasions from Bengal.

Intermingling with the mostly Bengali Aryans of the lowlands, they became accomplished cultivators and, as they adopted Hindu socio-religious traditions, a new Assamese identity emerged. In the eighteenth century, the formal conversion of the Ahom chief to Hinduism prompted a rebellion, which was quelled with the help of the Burmese, who then absorbed the entire kingdom, marking the end of Ahom rule. The kingdom was united with India when the Burmese eventually ceded it to the British in 1826.

The term **Bodo**, derived from Bhotia (another name for Tibet), describes several trans-Himalayan tribes, including the Monpas, Nishing and Mishmis of Arunachal Pradesh, groups in the Cachar hills of Tripura, and the Garos of Meghalaya. The Bodos have recently come to be regarded as a single ethnic group, and a campaign for Bodo autonomy has grown over the last decade. The major insurgency groups at present are the Bodo Liberation Tiger Force and the National Democratic Front of Bodoland.

United Liberation Front of Asom (**ULFA**) began an armed struggle for independence. Kidnappings and murders became common, and the targeting of wealthy tea plantation managers almost closed down the industry until, in 1991, the Indian army's Campaign Rhino struck at the ULFA, forcing them to the negotiating table. Some cadres, however, refused to give up the struggle or the income it generated, and the problem remained unresolved. At the same time, Assamese nationalism sparked opposition from Bodos, Cachars and other ethnic minorities, giving rise to further insurgence.

The capital of Assam, **Guwahati**, is a busy town and continues to be the main communication centre for the whole northeast. It is also the site of one of India's most important Kali temples, **Kamakhya**, and the temple of **Navagraha**, once a great centre of astrology and astronomy. Within easy access of Guwahati, the bountiful grasslands of the wildlife sanctuary at **Kaziranga** are renowned for their one-horned **rhinos** – the state symbol.

Guwahati and around

Once known as Pragjyotishpura (Light of the East), the most striking feature of **GUWAHATI** (or Gauhati), the capital of Assam, is the **Brahmaputra**, whose swollen sandy channel is so wide that the far shore is often rendered invisible. Of its many atmospheric temples, **Kamakhya** and **Navagraha** both occupy commanding hilltop positions, while **Umananda** sits on a small island in the middle of the Brahmaputra.

Guwahati's main business, **tea**, is booming. The Assam Tea Auction Centre (Tues & Wed 9.30am–1pm & 2.30–6pm) in the outlying suburb of Dispur holds auctions of a scale that previously took place in Calcutta and London. The busy downtown market area contrasts sharply with the rural riverside northeast of the centre, and the surrounding hills rising beyond the coconut palms give Guwahati a scenic backdrop.

GUWAHATI

RESTAURANTS

Gauhati Dairy	C
Madras Cabin	F
Ming Room	E
Paradise	D
Ramble	B
The Dhaba	A
Woodlands	G

ACCOMMODATION

Ananda Lodge	5
Belle Vue	1
Brahmaputra Ashok	2
Dynasty	6
Nandan & Chilarai	10
President	3
Raj Mahal	7
Tibet	8
Tourist	9
Tourist Lodge	4

Zoo & Shillong

Hospital, Dispur, Basistha & Shillong

Hajo, Airport (18 km), Saraighat Bridge & Madan Kamdev

Arrival, information and city transport

The **railway station** lies in the centre of town, with the **state bus stand**, which operates a left-luggage service (4.30am–10.30pm), right behind. The back of the railway station leads into the hectic Paltan Bazaar area, from which most of the private bus companies operate. Guwahati **airport**, 18km east of the centre, is served by taxis (from outside the *Nandan Hotel*) and airport buses, including those run by Indian Airlines.

The Assam government **tourist office** in the *Tourist Lodge* on Station Road (Mon–Sat 10am–5pm; closed 2nd & 4th Sat of month; ☏ 0361/544475) organizes **day-trips** and longer **tours**; their day- and overnight-packages to Kaziranga National Park are particularly good value. Branch offices in the railway station and at the airport keep the same hours. The **ITDC Tourist Office**, GL Publication Complex, GS Road (Mon–Fri 9am–5pm, Sat 10am–1pm; ☏ 0361/547407), provides information on the entire northeast.

Guwahati has an efficient and extensive system of **minibuses**, which can be flagged down by the roadside, and **cycle rickshaws** are readily available. The main terminal for river **ferries** to Umananda Island is at **Sukreswar Ghat**.

Accommodation

Guwahati has a good selection of **places to stay**. In addition to the budget options in Paltan Bazaar, several new hotels compete for the business market. Alternatively, railway station **retiring rooms** can be booked at the information desk.

Ananda Lodge, MN Road, Pan Bazaar ☏ 0361/544832. Good-value budget lodge, with a clean courtyard and pleasant atmosphere, but dingy rooms. Food is available. ❶–❷

Belle Vue, MG Road, opposite Raj Bhavan ☏ 0361/540847. On a wooded hill overlooking the river, away from the noise of the bazaars. Although showing age, it still has charm. Some of the larger rooms have balconies. ❼

Brahmaputra Ashok, MG Road ☏ 0361/541064. The top hotel in Guwahati, near the river and 2km from the railway station. Car rental and foreign exchange facilities for guests only. ❾

Chilarai Regency, off GS Road, Paltan Bazaar ☏ 0361/546877. Comfortable hotel next door to the *Nandan*, with a children's playground. ❻–❼

Dynasty, SS Road, Fancy Bazaar ☏ 0361/510496. In the heart of the market area, a top-range hotel with two good restaurants. ❾

Nandan, GS Road, Paltan Bazaar ☏ 0361/521476. Large three-star near the bus stand with comfortable en-suite rooms and a restaurant, bar and email facilities. ❽

President, GNB Road, Pan Bazaar ☏ 0361/544979. Mid-range accommodation with attached bathrooms and TV, fifteen minutes' walk from the railway station. ❻–❼

Raj Mahal, AT Road, Paltan Bazaar ☏ 0361/522478–83. Four-star comfort with all mod cons including travel and airline agencies. ❽

Tibet, GS Road, Paltan Bazaar, opposite bus station ☏ 0361/639600. One of the best budget options, with rooms ranging from comfortable – mostly with attached bathrooms and TV – to very comfortable. ❸–❻

Hotel Tourist, opposite the bus stand, Paltan Bazaar ☏ 0361/610190. Noisy and fairly basic, but convenient for late arrivals and early departures. ❷

Tourist Lodge, Station Road ☏ 0361/544475. Grubby and overpriced but convenient for the railway station. The government tourist office is based here. ❹

The Town

Paltan Bazaar, **Pan Bazaar** and **Fancy Bazaar**, Guwahati's main shopping areas, are bunched in the centre on either side of the railway, with the older residential areas north of the tracks. Most of the bazaars deal simply in provisions; **silk** and other Assamese crafts are sold at several good shops on GNB Road east of ANZ Grindlays Bank.

Archeological and ethnographic displays in Assam's **State Museum**, near the centre of town (Tues–Sat 10am–4.15pm, Sun 9am–1pm; closed 2nd & 4th Sat of month; Rs2), include stone and copper plate inscriptions dating from the fifth century, a twelfth-century sculpture of Surya, terracotta and costumes.

The Shiva temple of **Umananda** stands on an island bluff in the middle of the Brahmaputra. Its location, at the top of a steep flight of steps up from the beach, is, however, more dramatic than the temple itself. A couple of shops sell offerings at the temple gates but there are no chai or food stalls. Ferries and motor launches leave from behind the Deputy Commissioner's Court on MG Road.

On the commanding Nilachal Hill, overlooking the river 8km west of the centre, the important Kali temple of **Kamakhya**, with its beehive-shaped *shikhara*, is a fine example of the distinctive Assamese style of architecture. As one of the *shakti pithas*, it marks the place where Sati's *yoni* (vulva) landed when her body fell to earth in 51 pieces, and is one of the three most important Tantric temples in India. Small shops selling offerings line the long avenue leading up to the temple entrance, and every morning it bustles with saffron-robed priests and pilgrims. Inside, the temple is richly scented with incense, and highly charged as the crowds jostle their way towards the inner sanctum where iron-rich water flows through a cleft in the rock. Animal sacrifice is very much a part of the ritual here and kid goats are bathed in the ceremonial tank before being led to slaughter behind the temple hall. The temple is best visited early in the morning with hundreds of pilgrims creating quite a lively atmosphere. A short walk up the hill brings you to a smaller temple with wonderful views of Guwahati and the Brahmaputra. Buses leave from the small stand a couple of hundred metres up from the *Tourist Lodge* and can be picked up along MG Road.

East of the town centre, atop another hill, is the atmospheric **Navagraha** temple – the "temple of the nine planets", an ancient seat of astrology and astronomy – with wonderful acoustics. Housed in a single red dome, in classic Assamese beehive style, the central *lingam* is encircled by a further eight representing the planets, each lit by clusters of candles. Although limited by the lack of telescopes, Indian astronomers managed to discern six planets including the moon. A small Ganesh shrine guards the entrance to the inner sanctum and the *lingams* represent, clockwise: the moon (Chandra), Mars (Mangala), the Dragon's Head (Rahu), Saturn (Sani), the Dragon's Tail (Ketu), Jupiter (Brhaspati), Mercury (Buddha) and Venus (Sukra).

Further from the centre, the **Srimanta Sankaradeva Kalakshetra**, on Shillong Road in the Panjabari district, celebrates the cultural identity of the Assamese in dance, drama, music and art. **Sankaradeva** was a saint, poet, scholar, social reformer and preacher largely responsible for the fifteenth-century Assamese renaissance. It houses a museum, art gallery, open-air theatre and traditional Vaishnavite temple. Guwahati's leafy and well-managed **Zoo** and **Botanical Gardens** (daily except Fri: April–Sept 7am–5pm; Oct–March 8am–4pm; Rs3, Rs5 extra with camera, Rs250 extra with video) are 5km east of the centre. Animals include the one-horned rhino, the state symbol of Assam, as well as tigers and leopards.

Eating

Most of Guwahati's mid-range and more expensive hotels have bars and multi-cuisine **restaurants** concentrating on Mughlai and Chinese food. Only the *Paradise* specializes in Assamese cuisine – pleasantly mild, and reminiscent of Bengali food in its emphasis on fish. For breakfast, various places around the bus stand open early for tea and omelettes.

The Dhaba, GNB Road, Silpukhuri. Good, moderately priced north Indian meat dishes and tarka dhal, served amid traditional Assamese decor of cane and bamboo. Open noon–10.30pm.

Dynasty, SS Road, in the *Dynasty Hotel*. Two quality restaurants serving north Indian, tandoori, Chinese and Western fare.

Gauhati Dairy, MN Road, Pan Bazaar. Excellent snacks including samosas, delicious sweets and fresh curd. Open 7.30am–8pm.

Madras Cabin, AT Road, Paltan Bazaar. Tasty, cheap, south Indian food; very handy for breakfast before catching an early morning bus or train. Open 4.30am–10pm.

Ming Room, Chandmari, next to the flyover, just south of the railway track. Bit of a walk from the centre but serves best Chinese food in town, at higher prices than elsewhere. Open noon–10pm.

Paradise, GNB Road, Silpukhuri. Excellent Assamese restaurant, especially good for lunch, with thalis, meat curries and Chinese food. Open 10am–3.30pm & 6–9.30pm.

Ramble, HB Road, Pan Bazaar. Dependable Assamese and Chinese dishes, including meat curries and fish. Open 10am–9.30pm.

Woodlands, GS Road, Ulubari. Great north and south Indian veg restaurant, serving thalis, *masala dosas* and real coffee. Open 8am–9pm.

Listings

Airlines British Airways, c/o Pelican Travels, *Brahmaputra Ashok Hotel* (℡0361/630123); Indian Airlines, GS Road, Ganeshguri Charili, near Assam

Assembly, Dispur (℡0361/564420 or 564421); Jet Airways, GNB Road, Silpukhuri (℡0361/520255); Air India, c/o Aryna Travels, on GS Road,

---

Moving on from Guwahati

Many routes follow narrow, steep-twisting mountain roads, making progress painfully slow and onward travel daunting. State-run buses from the ASTC stand in AT Road (℡0361/510984) go to Shillong (hourly, 6am–5pm; 4hr); Tezpur (hourly 6am–4pm; 4–5hr); Kaziranga (14 daily; 4hr); Jorhat (9 daily, via Kaziranga; 7hr); Silchar (2 daily, 6am & 5pm; 12hr); Itanagar (2 daily; 12hr); Siliguri (3 daily; 12hr); Agartala (1 daily; 24hr); and Imphal (1 daily; 19hr). The Imphal service travels via Dimapur and Kohima.

Private companies run the same routes, charge a little more and tend to be more comfortable; most have booths in Paltan Bazaar just behind the railway station. Blue Hill (℡0361/547911); Network (℡0361/522007); Assam Valley (℡0361/546133); and Green Valley (℡0361/544636) run services throughout the region. Buses for Hajo (6 daily; 1hr 15min) run from Machkowa bus stand off MG Road southwest of the centre.

Several daily trains link Guwahati to Delhi – the North-East Express #5621 to New Delhi (departs 8.30am; 36hr); the Brahmaputra Mail #4055 to Old Delhi (departs noon; 41hr); the Avadh–Assam Express #5609 (departs 8pm; 44hr). The speedy Rajdhani Express #2423 runs thrice weekly (Mon, Thurs & Fri; departs 6am; 28hr). For Calcutta, the daily Kanchenjunga Express #5658 to Sealdah station (departs 10pm; 22hr 35min) and the daily Kamrup Express #5960 (departs 7am; 23hr 30min) are two of the best. Hardened train travellers heading south can take the weekly Guwahati–Trivandrum Express #5628 (Wed 5am) to Chennai (54hr), Bhubaneshwar (31hr) and Trivandrum (75hr). Alternatively, take the Guwahati–Bangalore Express #5626 (Tues & Sun 5am; 63hr) via Bhubaneshwar (31hr). Within the hill states, there are services to Lumding (3 daily; 4–6hr), two of which continue to Dimapur (7hr). On the metre-gauge line, the daily Arunachal Express #5813 serves Rangapara (7hr) North Lakhimpur (13hr) and Murkong Selek (19hr).

Indian Airlines flies to Agartala (3 weekly; Tues, Sat & Sun; 40min); Calcutta (daily; 1hr 10min); Delhi (daily 2hr 25min); and Imphal (Thurs & Sun; 50min). Jet Airways fly from Guwahati to Calcutta (daily), Delhi (daily), Imphal (2 weekly) and Bagdogra (3 weekly); Sahara (℡0361/547808) flies daily to Delhi and Dibrugarh. Pawan Hans helicopter service (℡0361/840311) flies to Shillong (1–2 daily), Tura (4 weekly), and Naharlagun in Arunachal Pradesh (4 weekly).

See Travel Details at the end of this chapter for more information on journey frequencies and durations.

Bhangagarh, 3km from the centre (℡ 0361/561881); Sahara, GS Road, Uluwari, near Bara petrol station (℡ 0361/547808).

Banks and exchange ANZ Grindlays on GNB Road (Mon–Fri 10am–3pm; Sat 10am–12.30pm), opposite the State Museum changes US and Australian dollars, or pounds sterling, and cashes travellers' cheques. The State Bank of India (Mon–Fri 10am–2pm, Sat 10am–noon) on MG Road, 50m west of ARB Road, cashes travellers' cheques and changes foreign currencies.

Bookshops There are a number of bookshops in Pan Bazaar, notably Western Book Depot, Josovanta Road just off HB Road, with a good selection of fiction, and titles on the northeast; the Advanced Study Centre on MN Road opposite *Ananda Lodge*; and the Modern Book Depot on HB Road near MN Road.

Internet access Internet Club opposite *Ananda Lodge*; Net Vision Cyber Park, Pan Bazaar near Gauhati dairy, both on GS Road.

Hospital Downtown Hospital ℡ 0361/331003; Guwahati Medical College Hospital ℡ 0361/529457.

Pharmacy Life Pharmacy on GS Road, just south of B Barua Road, is open 24 hours.

Photography New Frontier Colour Lab, SS Road, Lakhtokia, 50m west of Pan Bazaar; S Ghoshal, HB Road, Pan Bazaar near *Ramble* restaurant.

Post office ARB Road, just round the corner from the State Bank of India (Mon–Sat 10am–6pm). The telegraph office is nearby and is open 24 hours.

Travel agents Jungle Travels, GNB Road, Silpukhuri (℡ 0361/524121), agents for American Express (no currency services), book domestic and international flights. Raj Mahal Travel and Tours, based at the *Raj Mahal Hotel*, represent Indian Airlines, Jet Airways and Sahara. Air tickets out of Guwahati can also be booked through Rhino Travels, MN Road, Pan Bazaar (℡ 0361/540666), and buses run to the airport from their office. Travelaid (℡ 0361/544770) at the Brahmaputra Ashok can book all domestic airlines.

Around Guwahati

Beside a picturesque waterfall 11km southeast of Guwahati, two small red-domed temples at **BASISTHA**, in Assamese beehive style, commemorate Vasistha Muni, author of the *Ramayana*. Nestling within an impressive copse of trees, with rock carvings in the stream to add to the air of antiquity, Basistha is popular with pilgrims and picnickers alike. City buses for Basistha can be picked up from outside the library by the junction of GNB Road and Station Road, or indeed anywhere down GNB Road as far as the flyover, and beyond on RG Baruah Road.

The small town of **HAJO**, 32km northwest of Guwahati, is sacred to Buddhists, Hindus and Muslims and attracts pilgrims of each. A long palm tree-lined stone stairway climbs a hill to the small Hindu temple of **Hayagriba Madhab** where, locals claim, the Buddha entered nirvana. Praying at the mosque of **Pao Mecca** nearby grants Muslims a quarter (*pao*) of the spiritual benefit of Mecca. Hajo is easily accessible from Guwahati's Machkowa bus stand (6 daily; 1hr 15min). The nearby village of **Sualkuchi** is known for the production of golden *muga* silk.

Some 40km north of Guwahati, **MADAN KAMDEV** was the site of a Tantric temple to Shakti (Durga) dating back to the Pallava dynasty in the eleventh and twelfth centuries. The temple, mentioned in the Tantric scriptures as the *Yogini Tantra*, is no more, but the **museum** preserves many figures in various erotic postures, which some archeologists claim are only rivalled by Khajuraho (see p.468) for expressiveness of erotica. Buses run the 35km to Baihata Chariali on NH-52, from where it's a five-kilometre walk or rickshaw ride.

Tezpur and around

Amid tea gardens and military cantonments on the north bank of the Brahmaputra, 181km northeast of Guwahati, the busy little town **TEZPUR** stands on the ancient site of **Sonitpur** (City of Blood). According to legend, this was the scene of a terrible battle involving Krishna himself, who journeyed here from Gujarat to rescue his grandson, imprisoned by the local ruler, King Asura, for secretly marrying the king's daughter. Despite opposition from Shiva, who Asura revered, Krishna won the day and the lovers were reunited. In more recent fighting, Tezpur was almost captured by the Chinese army as they swept down through Arunachal Pradesh in 1962.

Nehru Maidan, the triangular green behind the *Tourist Lodge*, features a pretty little church and the small **District Museum** (Tues–Sun 10am–4.30pm; free), with old manuscripts and sculptures from both ancient and modern times (notably a very Assamese-looking Gandhi), labelled in Assamese and English. Opposite the *Tourist Lodge*, **Chitralekha Udyan** (daily 8am–8pm; Rs5, Rs10 extra with camera), with its central lake (paddleboats Rs20 for 15min), was established by a British deputy commissioner in the 1800s to house remnants of Asura's palace. The park is at its best in the early evening when the fairylights and pathways are lit up. The main market, **Chowk Bazaar**, is on MC Road roughly 1km north of the *Tourist Lodge*, with the ancient **Mahabhairav temple**, dedicated to an incarnation of Shiva, still further north. One kilometre east along the river, the hill of **Agnigarh** commands great views over the town and river, and is known as the place where Asura imprisoned his daughter, Usha. There is little left of **Da-Parbatia temple**, 6km west of town, except its finely carved door frame depicting Ganga and Yamuna, said to be the oldest specimen of religious art in Assam.

Practicalities

Tezpur's ASTC state **bus stand** is on Kabarkhana (KK) Road, 500m north from the **tourist office** (Mon–Sat 10am–4.30pm; ☏03712/21016) in the *Tourist Lodge* on KP Agarwalla Road in the town centre. The **GPO** (Mon–Fri 10am–6pm, Sat 10am–2pm) is on Head Post Office Road, parallel to the main road. The State Bank of India does not change foreign currency here. Flights on Indian Airlines and Jet Airways can be booked through Anand travels (☏03712/30693) at the *Luit* hotel.

Tezpur's top hotel, the *Luit* (☏03712/22083; ❹–❼), a large white building 100m north of the state bus stand on Ranu Singh Road, offers hot showers and

Moving on from Tezpur

The state bus stand has ASTC buses to Guwahati (13 daily; 4hr 30min); Jorhat (4 daily; 4hr) via Kaziranga (1hr 30min), continuing to Tinsukia (1 daily) or Dibrugarh (3 daily). Other services run to Sibsagar (2 daily; 5hr 30min), Shillong (1 daily; 9hr) and Siliguri (1 daily; 16hr). APSTS buses run to Itanagar (8hr) and Bomdila (7hr) via Bhalukpong (1hr 30min). Private bus companies, such as Blue Hill and Green Valley, operate luxury buses from opposite the state bus stand to the same destinations once or twice daily; they are faster, more comfortable and more expensive.

Himalayan Holidays (☏03712/24162), Shambhala Tours & Travels (☏03712/52108), and Seven Sisters Safari (☏03712/23580), all on Kabarkhana (KK) Road, run daily Tata Sumo 4WD services from Tezpur to Tawang, a mere twelve hours away. Sumos are a good way to travel, much quicker and more comfortable than the buses. Other destinations include Rupa, Bomdila and Itanagar. The railway station, a little way beyond the private bus stand, sees little action other than the termination of the #5716 Samastipur–Tezpur train. Indian Airlines flies to and from Calcutta (Thurs, Sun; 2hr 5min) via Dimapur (30min). Their office is two doors down from the *Tourist Lodge*. See Travel Details at the end of this chapter for more information on journey frequencies and durations.

a/c rooms in its new wing and cheaper rooms in an older wing. The *Durba* (☏03712/24276; **❹–❻**) on KK Road is good value, while the *Tourist Lodge* (☏03712/21016; **❸**) has five rooms and a cheap fifteen-bed dorm (Rs30). Other options include the *Meghdoot* on KK Road, 500m north of the ASTC bus stand near Chowk Bazaar (☏03712/20714; **❷–❸**), and the *Tawang* (☏03712/30686; **❷**) on MC Road, with small basic rooms. The *Raj Chinese Hotel* on Nehru Maidan serves excellent Chinese **food**.

Around Tezpur

Tezpur is an ideal base for a trip to the small, rarely visited wildlife sanctuary of **Orang**, 65km away. The Eco Camp at Potosali – a joint venture between the Forestry and Wildlife departments and the Assam Anglers – lies a few kilometres before the Arunachal border checkpoint on the Bhoroli river. They can arrange fishing trips to pit your wits and strength against the mighty mahseer, as well as jungle treks, rafting and visits to local villages. Accommodation is in double-bed tents with thatched covers and a four-bed dorm. Fishing trips can be booked through the Assam Angling Association in Guwahati (☏0361/545847) or Tezpur (☏03712/20004). The *Assam Tourist Lodge* (no phone; **❷**), virtually the last building on the Assamese side of the border, towards the river, can also arrange fishing trips.

The wildlife sanctuaries

Most of Assam's magnificent **wildlife sanctuaries** are in the Brahmaputra Valley, where the large tracts of grasslands on the flood plains are home to the Indian one-horned rhino, and a host of other animals, sightings of which are almost guaranteed.

The most famous park, **Kaziranga**, is renowned for its elephant grass and rhino, but also incorporates some forest areas. Close to the Bhutanese border, **Manas** is also populated with rhinos and elephants, and is Assam's sole tiger project.

Kaziranga

Covering an area of 430 square kilometres on the southern bank of the Brahmaputra, **Kaziranga National Park**, 217km east of Guwahati, occupies the vast valley floor against a backdrop of the forest-covered Karbi Anglong hills. Rivulets and *bhils* (shallow lakes), and the semi-evergreen forested "Highlands", just out of reach of the Brahmaputra's annual floods, blend into marshes and flood plains covered with tall elephant grass. Rhinos, deer and herds of wild buffalo graze nonchalantly close to the park entrance at **Kohora**. The rich bird life includes egrets, herons, storks, fish-eating eagles and a grey pelican colony. Few tracks penetrate this sea of grass, however, and the wild elephants seldom venture into it, preferring to remain in the forested Highlands, while tigers are incredibly elusive. With grasslands bordering onto cultivated fields and domestic cattle encroaching on the sanctuary and introducing epidemics, the wild animals are under increasing threat. Poaching is rife, with rhino horns fetching astronomical prices as aphrodisiacs.

Kaziranga's one-horned **rhino**, numbering over a thousand, the largest concentration in the subcontinent – is best seen from the back of an elephant, early on a winter's morning. **Elephant rides** (5.30am & 7am) last around one hour, and should be booked the previous evening at the park offices in Kohora. Although the elephants do not penetrate far into the sanctuary and only travel in a three- or four-kilometre circle, it is incredible how much wildlife can be seen in this

small area. The rhinos seem oblivious to camera-clicking tourists, although like the unpredictable wild buffalo, they're equipped with lethal horns and are potentially ferocious. Although **Jeeps** (arranged through the Deputy Director of Tourism at Kohora, or *Wild Grass*; see opposite) will take you deeper into the forest than the elephants, they cannot get nearly as close to the wildlife.

Kaziranga is open from mid-November to early April. During the monsoons (June–Sept), the Brahmaputra bursts its banks, flooding the low-lying grasslands and causing animals to move from one area to another within the park. Deer and even leopard often cross the main road, heading for the hills until the waters recede.

Kaziranga practicalities

The main gate for Kaziranga, at **Kohora** on the NH-37 (AT Road), consists of a handful of cafés and a small local market. ASTC and private **buses** stop here on their way to and from Guwahati, Tezpur and Upper Assam; some private buses retain a seat quota for Kaziranga passengers. The most convenient way to visit Kaziranga is on one of the Assam tourist office **tours** which leave from Guwahati (see p.1047) at 9am, arriving in Kaziranga around 2pm. The tour includes overnight accommodation in the *Bonoshree Lodge*, meals, an elephant ride and return transport to Guwahati.

The **Directorate of Tourism** (☎03776/62423) is hidden a few hundred metres off the road to the north in the *Bonani Lodge*. All visitors have to sign in

The mighty Brahmaputra

One of the great rivers of Asia, the **Brahmaputra** commences its 3000-kilometre journey to the Bay of Bengal from the slopes of Kailash in western Tibet, a mountain venerated by Hindus and Buddhists alike as the incarnation of Meru, the core of the universe. As Tibet's great river, the Tsangpo, it traverses east across the high-altitude Tibetan plateau north of the Great Himalayan Range, carving out myriad channels and sandbanks on its way. As it tumbles from the Himalayan heights towards the plains of the subcontinent it twists back on itself, cutting a deep – and still unnavigated – gorge, until finally turning south to emerge in Arunachal Pradesh as the Dihang. Just beyond Pasighat, the Dibang and Lohit rivers merge with it and it becomes the Brahmaputra. Now an enormous wash of silt-laden water so wide in places that you cannot see the far bank, it passes through the heart of Assam, creating an ever-fluctuating pattern of sandbanks and islands on its way, skirts the hills of Meghalaya before entering Bangladesh, and finally heads due south, spreading across the plains and merging with sea in the Bay of Bengal.

The river is both a blessing and a curse to the people of Assam. Every year during the monsoon it bursts from its wide, shallow channel into the flood plain, wreaking destruction and havoc, then leaving wonderfully fertile land in its wake. Decades of uncontrolled logging in Tibet by the Chinese have caused irreparable environmental damage: topsoil and water cascades down the denuded slopes into the Brahmaputra. Environmental historians have noticed an alarming trend in the records: after just four major floods in three hundred years, the region flooded in 1950 following a massive earthquake in Assam, and suffered widespread flooding twelve more times in the next fifty years, culminating in the 1998 disaster, which surpassed previous floods in its fury and relentlessness. Five million people were affected in Assam, with damage to crops and homes, and more than five hundred animals perished in Kaziranga Park, 22km from the river. Having devastated Assam, all of this water still had to drain away, and the plains and people of Bangladesh all but disappeared underwater for three months.

here, before making for the **park headquarters** alongside, where you can book elephant and Jeep rides and **accommodation** in nearby lodges. *Aranya* (☎03776/62429; **❹–❺**) is the largest and most comfortable, with en-suite a/c rooms, private balconies, room service and the best restaurant. *Bonani* is smaller, also with a/c and a restaurant (**❸–❺**), while *Bonoshree* (**❷**) has eight doubles and a four-bedded room, all with bath. The budget option, *Kunjaban*, offers both private rooms (**❶**) and dorms (Rs30), with bed linen for a few rupees extra.

A kilometre and a half off the road, 4km east of Kohora, is the highly rated *Wild Grass* (☎03776/62437; **❻**), a **luxury resort** at the foot of the Karbi hills on the River Diring. Endorsed by the Worldwild Fund for Nature and Project Tiger, it can book Jeep safaris and elephant rides in the park and **fishing trips** to the Eco Camp at Potosali (see p.1052). In summer, when the park is closed, they compensate with a swimming pool, wildlife tours from the park boundary, rafting and elephant rides. Reserve through *Wild Grass*, PO Kaziranga, Dist Golaghat 785109, or Barua Bhavan, 1st Floor, 107 MC Road, Uzanbazar, Guwahati (☎0361/546827, ☎541186).

Most people staying in the park take the inexpensive **meals** provided at fixed times in *Bonani Lodge* (order in advance), although better food at more flexible times can be had at *Aranya Lodge*.

Visiting Kaziranga independently can be expensive due to the two-tier price system, with different **entry costs** for Indian nationals (Rs10) and foreigners (Rs175). There are separate charges for elephant rides (Rs100/525) and Jeeps (Rs350) from the lodges to the park entrance, as well as a complex system of camera fees.

Manas

Bordering Bhutan, on the banks of the River Manas 176km west of Guwahati, **MANAS**, Assam's only **Project Tiger** sanctuary (Dec–April), is a spellbinding place. As it emerges from the jungle-covered Himalayan foothills onto the plains, the snow-fed river is one of the best fishing grounds for the legendary mahseer, a pike-like game fish renowned as a fighter. Manas became a UNESCO World Heritage Site in 1985, was extended by 500 square kilometres in 1990, and is now home to the tiger, leopard, rhino, wild elephant, water buffalo, the rare hispid hare and the pygmy hog.

The Forest Department offers accommodation at the park entrance **Bansbari Gate** (two double rooms in the Inspection Bungalow) and **Mothanguri** (2 bungalows, a cottage and a dorm), 20km into the park, either of which can be booked through the Field Director (☎03666/33413), Deputy Director (☎03666/32289) or Research Officer (☎03666/62609) of Project Tiger in Barpeta Road. Meals are not served, so bring your own **food**. The nearest **bus stop** and **railway station** are at **Barpeta Road**, where there is an information office and *Tourist Lodge* (**❸**) run by Assam Tourism. The park entrance is 20km further on and there is no public transport; taxis charge around Rs1000 each way.

Upper Assam

Jorhat is the main centre for the region, with an airport and road connections, and acts as the gateway to Kaziranga, Nagaland and northern Arunachal Pradesh. Although not particularly attractive to tourists in itself, Jorhat makes a good base for exploring the unique Vaishnavite culture of **Majuli**, the largest river island in the world, and **Sibsagar**, former capital of the Ahoms and home to numerous tombs, temples and palaces.

JORHAT, 310km east of Guwahati, has research establishments dedicated to the tea industry, and an annual tea festival. The town is not of great interest, but you will probably have to stop here if coming to or from Majuli. **Buses** stop on the main thoroughfare, AT Road, part of the NH-37 highway. The ASTC terminal is half a block north of the private companies' offices and bus stops. Assam Tourism's **tourist office** is at the *Tourist Lodge* on MG Road, 300m south of AT Road (Mon–Sat, closed 2nd & 4th Sat of month, 10am–4pm; ☏0376/321579). The **GPO** is on Post Office Road, between the ASTC stand and MG Road. There are no foreign exchange facilities here.

The *Tourist Lodge* (☏0376/321579; ❸) has large and comfortable carpeted **rooms**, as does *Hotel Paradise* (☏0376/321521; ❺–❻), down a lane off AT Road 30m, past the ASTC bus station. Other mid-range hotels on this lane include the *Dilip* (☏0376/321610; ❸–❺), the *Neera* (☏0376/322618; ❸), and the slightly cheaper *Janata Paradise* (☏0376/320610; ❷–❹).

You can **eat** at each of these hotels; other options include the *Oasis* on MG Road and *Treats* on KB Road (Mon–Sat), both of which serve local and

Trouble in the northeast

Since Independence, the northeastern states have been dogged by conflict and insurgence that has made this one of the more unstable regions in India. Much of the trouble stems from competing desires for autonomy, statehood and independence. The northeast has long suffered national political neglect from Delhi, and the hill tribes have been marginalized further by the dominant state of Assam. Both these factors have given rise to separatist movements and the contempt with which these wishes have been met has turned them into violent uprisings.

Another ingredient in the troubles has been ethnic rivalry, especially in Manipur and parts of Assam, between hill tribes and plains people. The biggest conflicts, however, stem from the influx of Bengalis, putting pressure on a region where land is already scarce. Bangladesh's massive overpopulation and land shortages have caused continuous and large-scale illegal migration into Tripura and beyond. Bengalis are now the majority group, and within Bangladesh, Bengali Muslims have displaced the mainly Buddhist Chakmas of the Chittagong Hill Tracts, whose ever-increasing numbers as refugees, along with Bhutanese Nepalis, place further strain on land resources in the northeast.

The United Liberation Front of Asom (ULFA), one of the region's largest and most powerful insurgent groups, started by demanding the expulsion of Bengalis, but gradually became a group fighting for Assamese independence. ULFA's history illustrates well many of the features of local insurgence. It has formed links with other militants in the region, most importantly with the National Socialist Council of Nagaland (NSCN), the region's oldest insurgent group, and also with groups in Myanmar; together they have shared experience, training and arms.

In the hope of weakening India's hold on the northeast, the governments of Pakistan, China and Bangladesh often turn a blind eye to separatist rebels training within their borders, and have supplied training, arms and funds. Even within India, local political parties and state authorities maintain links with the insurgents; the ULFA and the NSCN in particular have had strong connections both at state and local political level.

Agreements between insurgents and state governments often fail to work. When their leadership makes a deal, extremists within the group typically break away and a cycle of insurgency continues, as in Nagaland in 1975 and ULFA in 1992. Only in Mizoram have the extremist factions fizzled out.

Chinese food. The *Food Hut* near the *Tourist Lodge* does Assamese thalis as do most of the hotel restaurants. The *Cherry Garden* bakery on KB Road has excellent cakes and savoury snacks, including pizza.

ASTC **buses** run to Guwahati (every 30min; 6–7hr), Tezpur (5 daily; 4hr), Sibsagar (every 15min; 1hr 30min), Tinsukia (hourly; 5–6hr), Dimapur (1 daily; 5hr) and Itanagar (daily; 9hr). Kaziranga (2hr 30min) is served by buses to Guwahati and Tezpur. **Private companies** such as Blue Hill, Green Valley, Assam Valley and Network all run services to Guwahati, Sibsagar, Tinsukia and Dimapur. There are also buses to Mariani, the nearest main-line railway station, where the #5606 Jorhat–Guwahati Express leaves every evening at 8.05pm, calling at Dimapur and Lumding, and arriving in Guwahati at 7.30am.

Indian Airlines (⊕0376/320011) on AT Road offer flights to Calcutta (Tues, Sat; 2hr 5min) via Dimapur (25min). Jet Airways (⊕0376/325652) – office at *Hotel Paradise* – flies to Calcutta (2 weekly) and Imphal (2 weekly). The airport, 5km out of town, can be reached by rickshaw, auto-rickshaw or Indian Airlines buses.

Majuli

Ferries run twice a day from **Nimatighat**, 12km north of Jorhat, to **MAJULI**, the largest river island in the world, with its unique Vaishnavite *sattras* (monasteries). The population contains a wide mix of tribal peoples, including Ahoms, Kacharis, Mising and Deori.

Ferries leave from the ferry station, the exact location of which shifts according to the water level and course of the river, and the crossing takes between an hour and a half and two hours. There are morning and afternoon ferries, but it's virtually impossible to visit Majuli as a day-trip as the timings only give you an hour or so on the island. Buses run on the island to the village of **Kamalabari** (6 daily, roughly 5km), and beyond to the island's "capital" at **Garamur**. There are 22 **sattras** (see bo below) on the island, including those in Garamur and Kamalabari. The *sattra* at **Auniati**, 4km west, keeps royal artefacts from the Ahom kingdom and has an interesting collection of Assamese handicrafts and jewellery. **Bengenati**, 4km east, was built in the early seventeenth century. **Shamaguri**, 6km beyond Bengenati, is renowned for the making of clay and bamboo masks – used for traditional festivals and performances. Other *sattras* include **Bongaori**, 8km beyond Shamaguri, and **Dakhinpat** 5km further south. Majuli has been recommended as a UNESCO World Heritage Site.

Assamese Vaishnavism

Vishnu worship was established in Assam in the seventh century, and by the fifteenth century had eclipsed Shaivism. Its distinctive Assamese form was developed by Srimanta Sankardeva (1449–1569), a poet, playwright, musician, composer and theologian, who saw Vishnu as the quintessential cosmic force

The main institution of Assamese Vaishnavism is the sattra. The first one was founded by Sankardeva at his birthplace Bardowa, but is no more – destroyed by the ever-changing watercourse of the Brahmaputra. The *sattra* is a temple, monastery, school and centre for the arts where poetry, folk music, literature, sculpture and dance are explored, often in combination – as in *dhulia*, a masked theatrical dance relating episodes from the *Ramayana* and *Mahabharata*. Sattras consist of a prayer hall (*namghar*) surrounded by living quarters for devotees, and *ghats* for bathing.

Although distances are short, public transport is limited to the occasional bus, with taxis and auto-rickshaws more expensive options. For those with plenty of time, the most relaxing way to take in the *sattras* is on foot over a couple of days.

Most visitors **stay** at the *Circuit House* in Garamur (☎03775/74439; **①**). In Kamalabari it is possible to stay at the *sattra* (☎03775/73302) for a donation. Arrangements for **food** are best made where you are staying.

From Majuli there is a morning and afternoon ferry. The journey from Garamur to Jorhat takes around five hours. It is also possible to travel north from Majuli, with two daily ferries from Luhitghat, 3km north of Garamur, to Khabalughat on the north bank, from where there are buses to North Lakhimpur, and thence buses to Itanagar or Tezpur, and even a train to Guwahati. Allow yourself plenty of time.

Sibsagar

The former capital of the Ahoms and one of the oldest towns in Assam, **SIB-SAGAR** – "The Ocean of Shiva" – lies 60km northeast of Jorhat and 369km from Guwahati. Its cluster of monuments from six centuries of Ahom rule are still of significance to modern Assamese culture. A huge tank, constructed by Queen Madambika in 1734, lies at the heart of the complex. Rising from its southern shore, the massive, plain, 32-metre-high **Shivadol** is the tallest Shiva temple in India, flanked by smaller temples dedicated to Durga and Vishnu. The dome has wonderful acoustics should you be lucky enough to chance upon a puja with chanting and prayers. On the western shore of the lake next to a park, the **Tai Ahom Museum** (Mon–Thurs & Sat, 10.30am–3.30pm; free) contains a few ancient artefacts.

Temples and palaces in varying degrees of abandonment dot the local area, including the **Rang Ghar**, a two-storey oval pavilion 6km from town built by King Pramatta Singha in the eighteenth century to stage elephant fights and other sporting events. In 1979, it was the scene of a secret meeting that led to the foundation of ULFA. Nearby, isolated in flat, bare countryside, are the ruined eighteenth-century palaces of the **Kareng Ghar** and the **Talatal Ghar**, with another at **Gargaon**, 13km east of Sibsagar. *Maidams* (tombs) of the early Ahom kings can be found at their original thirteenth-century capital of **Charaideo**, 28km east of Sibsagar, and there are further tank and temple complexes like Sibsagar's at **Rangpur**, **Rudrasagar** and **Gaurisagar**, all within a twelve-kilometre radius of Sibsagar.

The *Tourist Bungalow* on the southwest corner of the tank is currently occupied by the Indian army, leaving the *Hotel Kareng* (☎03842/22713; **③**) as the best option, on Temple Road, 100m in front of the Shivadol temple, with a pleasant bar and restaurant. Alternatively, the *Annapurna Lodge* (☎03842/22218; **②–③**), 200m behind the cinema opposite the bus station, also has reasonable rooms.

The **post office** is south of the lake, opposite the Durga temple. There are no foreign exchange facilities. The ASTC **bus stand** has services to Jorhat (every 15min; 1hr 30min), Kaziranga (9 daily; 4hr), Guwahati (7 daily; 8hr), Tezpur (2 daily; 6hr) and Tinsukia (4 daily; 3hr 30min). Private bus companies ply the same routes and charge more for the comfort they offer.

South Assam

South Assam, ridged by the Cachar hills, is the crossing point for the surrounding states of Meghalaya, Tripura, Mizoram, and Manipur. While the main town, **Silchar**, contains little of interest, places further afield, notably the low-key hill station of **Haflong**, are far more appealing.

Silchar

The nondescript town of **SILCHAR** is south Assam's main transport nexus. There's little to do here but wait for a bus or train out, but you may find yourself having to **stay** the night. The top hotel in town is the *Sudakshina* (☏03842/30156; ❺–❻), on Shillong Patty, with comfortable carpeted rooms, hot water and cable TV. The excellent-value *Hotel Siddharth* (☏03842/32473; ❸–❺), just round the corner on Narshingtola, has clean rooms with showers, filtered water and TV. Other options include the reasonable *Swagat* on Central Road (☏03842/30667; ❷–❸) and the *Geetanjali* (☏03842/31738; ❸–❺) on Club Road, which has large rooms, hot water and one of the best **restaurants** in town. A group of Tibetan traders run a small wool market next to the *Swagat* during the winter months – worth a visit for its clothing, carpets and friendly atmosphere.

Silchar transport connections

The **state bus stand**, near the Devdoot cinema, is the terminus for Assam, Meghalaya and Tripura state services. Buses leave for Guwahati, Shillong, Agartala and Aizawl. The road to Imphal is not recommended due to its numerous army checkpoints and long delays. There are also buses to Haflong (2 daily; 6hr). Most **private bus companies** including Sagar, Capital, Tania and Network run the same services and have numerous agents all over town. Sumos have recently been introduced on some routes and come recommended as they are considerably quicker on the winding mountainous roads.

The **railway station** is 3km out of town in Tarapur, with trains to Haflong and Lumding from where you can pick up connections to Guwahati. The #5802 Silchar–Lumding Cachar Express (daily, 6.30pm) reaches Haflong at 11.55pm and Lumding at 5.15am. The #5812 Silchar–Lumding Barak Express (daily, 7.30am) reaches Haflong at 1.30pm and Lumding at 6.45pm. Silchar's **airport**, 13km away, can be reached by shared taxi from outside the Indian Airlines office on Club Road; Moti Travels on Hospital Road (☏03842/33716) is a ticket agent. Indian Airlines (☏03842/20072) flies to Calcutta (daily Mon–Sat; 1hr) and Imphal (Tues, Thurs, Sat; 30min).

Haflong and around

The scenic hill resort of **HAFLONG**, 84km north of Silchar, is the seat of the North Cachar Hills Autonomous District Council, where members of several ethnic groups including Dimasas, Hmars, Nagas and Mizos, belonging to different religious denominations – Christian, Hindu and Buddhist – live together in apparent harmony. Give or take, that is, the odd ruction in support of statehood or at least further autonomy, and the odd consignment of arms or militants en route to Manipur or Nagaland.

Haflong's **market** is at its best and most colourful on Saturday when it's overflowing with rice-beer (*dju*) and other local produce. Private **buses** pull in on Main Road, 100m above the market by the Hamringdi cinema, with departures early morning and midday for Silchar (5hr), plus one overnight departure to Guwahati (9hr). ASTC has morning and noon departures to Silchar. The railway station – at Lower Haflong is 3km from town. The best train to Lumding is the #5812 which leaves at 1.40pm arriving five hours later. The best train to Silchar is the #5811 which leaves at 11.50am and takes six hours. **Accommodation** options include the *Elite, Joyeswary Eastern* and *Rahamaniya*, all of which have basic **restaurants**, though the *Elite* (7am–9pm), is probably the best. There are no exchange facilities in Haflong.

Nine kilometres south of Haflong on the Silchar road, **Jatinga** is famed in local folklore as the place where birds commit mass suicide. The more brutal truth is that on certain foggy, moonless nights in autumn, local migrant birds can become disorientated while flying up the valley over the saddle of the hill and are attracted with lights by local people, who clobber them with bamboo poles and eat them. There is a **bird-watching centre** in Jatinga, where you can stay with permission from the District Forestry Office in Haflong. Buses to Silchar pass through, or you can make a day-trip from Haflong by auto-rickshaw.

Meghalaya

MEGHALAYA, one of the smallest states in India, occupies the plateau and rolling hills between Assam and Bangladesh. Its people, predominantly Christian and belonging to three main ethnic groups, the Khasis, Jaintias and Garos, are strikingly different from those of Assam, as is its landscape. Much of Meghalaya ("land of the rain-clouds"), is covered with lush forests, rich in orchids. These "blue hills" catch the main force of the monsoon-laden winds off the Bay of Bengal, and are among the wettest places on earth. Stupendous waterfalls can be seen near the capital, **Shillong**, but the most dramatic plummet from the plateau to the south, around **Cherrapunjee**. The hills of Meghalaya rise to just under 2000m, which makes for a pleasant year-round climate, a welcome refuge from the steamy valleys of Assam. On January 21, 1972, after an eighteen-year struggle for autonomy from Assam, it became a fully fledged state. Meghalaya has a high literacy rate and teaching is in English.

Khasis, Garos and Jaintias

Meghalaya is home to three different tribal groups. The Khasis have Mongoloid and Proto-Australoid features and their language belongs to the Mon-Khmer group, suggesting that they have origins in Southeast Asia, possibly in present-day Cambodia. Their religion is monotheistic in the belief in a formless creator and life after death, and they have no temples as the earth itself is considered sacred enough. Curiously, the Khasi word for "stone" is *men*, as in the ancient European *dolmen* and *menhir*. The Jaintias, who inhabit the eastern regions of the state around Jowai, share a similar ancestry.

The Garos trace their origins to Tibet and their language belongs to the Tibeto-Burman linguistic group, though physically they bear little resemblance to Tibetans. The cultural and religious practices of the Garos also differ greatly from Buddhist Tibet. As animists, their belief system centres on the spirit world and they once performed human sacrifice to ensure good harvests. However, fervent evangelization introduced in colonial times has seen Christianity become dominant here, and animism has had to adapt with it.

The Khasi, Jaintia and Garo tribes are all matrilineal societies, with property and land being inherited by the daughters or the mothers' family, and children take their mothers' names.

Shillong and around

With its rolling hills and tall elegant pines, **SHILLONG** was known to the British as "the Scotland of the East". The impression is first brought to mind by **Barapani**, the loch-like reservoir on its fringes, although the chilly nights may also seem reminiscent. At an altitude of around 1500m, Shillong became a popular hill station for the British, who built it on the site of a thousand-year-old Khasi settlement and made it the capital of Assam in 1874. Much of the original Victorian town is still evident – the large gardens around **Ward Lake** and the buildings surrounding it conjure up images of a colonial past. The eighteen-hole golf course, founded in 1898 by a group of enthusiastic British civil servants, is the oldest golf course in Asia.

Away from the centre, Shillong hasn't worn well: an acute water shortage and a general lack of planning have resulted in haphazard growth, and the sur-

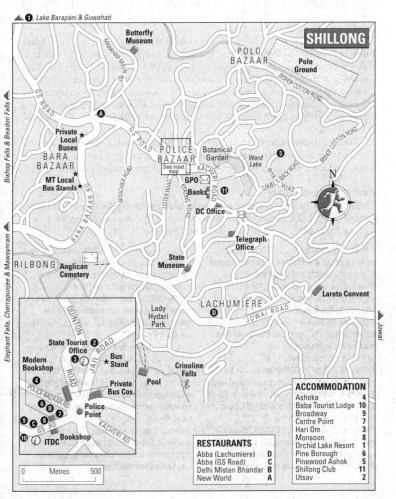

SHILLONG

1, Lake Barapani & Guwahati

Butterfly Museum

POLO BAZAAR

Polo Ground

BISHOP COTTON ROAD

MAWKHAR MAIN RD

GS ROAD

Private Local Buses

BARA BAZAAR

MT Local Bus Stands

BOUCHER ROAD

BARA BAZAAR RD

LISTER ROAD

KEATING ROAD

POLICE BAZAAR

See inset map

Botanical Garden

Ward Lake

GPO

Banks

KACHERI ROAD

RITA'S BACK ROAD

CAMEL'S BACK ROAD

BISHOP COTTON ROAD

DC Office

N

Telegraph Office

State Museum

RILBONG

Anglican Cemetery

Lady Hydari Park

LACHUMIERE

Lareto Convent

JOWAI ROAD

Jowai

Bishop Falls & Beadon Falls

Elephant Falls, Cherrapunjee & Mawsynram

QUINTON

JAIL ROAD

State Tourist Office

Modern Bookshop

Bus Stand

Crinoline Falls

Pool

Private Bus Cos.

POLICE BAZAAR RD

Police Point

GS RD

ITDC

Bookshop

KACHERI RD

0   Metres   500

RESTAURANTS

Abba (Lachumiere)   D
Abba (GS Road)   C
Delhi Mistan Bhandar   B
New World   A

ACCOMMODATION

Ashoka   4
Baba Tourist Lodge 10
Broadway   9
Centre Point   7
Hari Om   3
Monsoon   8
Orchid Lake Resort 1
Pine Borough   6
Pinewood Ashok   5
Shillong Club   11
Utsav   2

rounding hills have been subjected to severe deforestation. The influx of settlers from the plains and the strain this has placed on natural resources has led to occasional outbreaks of communal violence.

Arrival and information

In the absence of auto-rickshaws, black and yellow wasp-like taxis buzz around the town, competing with city buses both on routes and numbers of passengers carried (the record is 15) and generally adding to the chaos. Central Shillong can easily be explored on foot. Buses from outside the state pull in at the **Police Bazaar** area at the heart of town. The state **tourist office**, on Jail Road opposite the main bus station (Mon–Sat 7.30am–5pm, Sun 7.30–11am; ☎0364/226220), is the place to make reservations for guided city **tours** (8.30am–2.30pm; Rs80), or out to Cherrapunjee (8am–4.30pm; Rs100, minimum 15 people), while the ITDC **tourist office** is nearby on GS Road (Mon–Fri 9.30am–5.30pm, Sat 9.30am–2pm; ☎0364/225632). The Modern Book Depot, opposite the ITDC office on GS Road, stocks town maps and **books** on the northeastern region.

The **GPO** is on Kacheri Road, opposite the *Shillong Club*, as is the **State Bank of India**, where there are foreign exchange facilities; the branch in Police Bazaar does not exchange money. *Khattu Cyber Cafe* in the SMS Complex, next to Hotel Monsoon on GS Road, provides internet access.

Those interested in exploring Meghalaya's awesome **caves** can contact the Meghalaya Adventurers Association at the Mission Compound near the Synod Complex (☎0364/224465 or 243059), or through *Hotel Centre Point* in the Police Bazaar.

Cultural Pursuits Adventures, based at the Shillong golf course *Barking Deer Café*, runs several tours in Meghalaya and Assam, including a fifteen-day festival special in October and November, and can also arrange tailor-made itineraries.

Accommodation

Shillong has a healthy range of **accommodation**, with older hotels clustered around Ward Lake, newer ones springing up in the congested Police Bazaar area, and several more basic options along Quinton Road.

Ashoka, Police Bazaar Road ☎0364/223690. Basic but cheap with common bathrooms, geared for domestic tourists and budget travellers. ❷

Baba Tourist Lodge, GS Road ☎0364/211285. Friendly, clean and very good value, with a/c and hot water by the bucket. ❸–❹

Broadway, GS Road ☎0364/226996. Comfortable mid-range hotel, all rooms a/c, with an attached restaurant at street level. ❹–❺

Centre Point, Police Bazaar Road ☎0364/225210, ℮225239. Plush hotel in the heart of town, with all mod cons and a good range of facilities, including restaurant, *La Galerie*. ❻–❼

Hari Om, Quinton Road ☎0364/227231. Basic veg hotel with common bathrooms. ❶

Monsoon, GS Road ☎0364/227106. Friendly hotel opposite the ITDC Tourist Office, by far the nicest in Shillong. All rooms have hot shower, colour TV and a/c. Recommended. ❺

Orchid Lake Resort, ☎0364/570258. Seventeen kilometres from Shillong on Barapani Lake, with twenty rooms overlooking the lake. ❻

Pine Borough, Police Bazaar Road ☎0364/227523. Large hotel with reasonable rooms, with attached bathrooms and TV. The *Mikado* restaurant serves Indian and Chinese food, and there's a bar. ❹

Pinewood Ashok, Rita Road, European Ward ☎0364/223116, ℮224176. A grand old hotel, straight out of the Raj, built in 1917 for British tea planters. Dotted around the landscaped grounds are cottages with Burma teak panels, carpeted wooden floors, fireplaces, bathtubs and a billiard room. ❼–❽

Shillong Club, Kacheri Road ☎0364/226938, ℮227497. One of India's famous old clubs, offering accommodation in its residential quarters. Large rooms with balconies, hot showers, cable TV

and partial views of the lake. Prices include temporary membership. ⑤–⑥
Utsav, Jail Road, opposite main bus stand ☎ 0364/503268. Homely place with smallish rooms and hot water by the bucket. Make sure your room has a window because about half the rooms don't have them. ③

The Town

Life in Shillong used to revolve around the decorative **Ward Lake**. In the exclusive European Ward next to it, the large bungalows set in generous pine-shadowed gardens include Government House, the official residence of the governor. The ambience here is in stark contrast to the bustle around **Police Bazaar**, where the narrow streets are packed with vendors trading in local handicrafts, Khasi women wearing toga-like *jainsem*, in checked gingham and tartan designs, and Khasi men smoking roughly chiselled pipes. **Bara Bazaar**, further west, is even more hectic, attracting locals and hill-people to its warren of stalls and shops. Primarily, it is a produce and provisions market – vegetarians and those with fragile constitutions would do well to avoid the meat section – but you may come across interesting jewellery and handicrafts. Bara Bazaar is the scene of Meghalaya's oldest and most important market, **Iewduh**, which is held every eight days, although it's exceedingly busy and crowded every day.

Meghalaya's **State Museum**, in Lachumiere, has exhibits depicting tribal customs, and a weaker collection of ancient sculptures from elsewhere in India (Mon–Sat: summer 10am–4.30pm; winter 10am–4pm, closed 2nd & 4th Sat of the month; free). More unusual is the tiny **Butterfly Museum**, based in the home of Mr Wankhar, in the Riatsamthiah area, which holds an extensive collection of (dead) rare butterflies and moths (Mon–Fri 10am–4pm, Sat 10.30am–1pm; Rs5). Since 1939, Mr Wankhar has run a breeding farm in the Khasi hills to the south, shipping eggs and cocoons all over the world.

Although Shillong's **Botanical Gardens**, below the lake, across a viaduct, are not really worth a visit, **Lady Hydari Park** is an attractive ornamental park, modelled on a Japanese garden. A small forestry museum, a mini-zoo and a deer enclosure are tucked away among the pines. Lovers of old churchyards will enjoy the **Anglican cemetery** in Rilbong, with gravestones dating back to the last century, including those of soldiers killed in the Lushai campaign in Mizoram. **Shillong Peak**, 10km away, rises to 1960m and on a clear day both the Himalayas and the plains of Bangladesh can be seen from the top.

Eating

There are plenty of places in **Police Bazaar** to pick up a snack. **Bara Bazaar** also has a few simple restaurants and cafés. Most of the hotels also have restaurants or room service.

Abba, GS Road. The best Chinese restaurant in Shillong, with another branch on the main Jowai Road, Malki Point, Lachumiere. Both closed on Sundays.
Broadway, *Broadway Hotel*, GS Road. Attractive and very reasonably priced restaurant specializing in Indian and Chinese food. Recommended.
Delhi Mistan Bhandar, Police Bazaar Road. Classic Indian snacks and sweets. Very cheap,

always full, and recommended for its excellent breakfasts.
La Galerie, *Hotel Centre Point*, Police Bazaar. One of Shillong's plushest restaurants serving fine Indian and Chinese food.
New World, GS Road, at Bara Bazaar junction. A local favourite, serving good Chinese food including spicy Szechuan dishes.

Moving on from Shillong

Local buses run to Cherrapunjee (2 daily; 2hr), Mawsynram (2 daily; 3hr), and Jowai (every 30min; 1hr 30min) from Bara Bazaar. For Smit take the Jowai bus and walk from the main road. **Jeeps** leave from outside the *Anjalee* cinema for the same destinations when full. **State buses** leave from the bus stand on Jail Road for Guwahati (hourly; 3–4 hr); Silchar at 7am and 7pm (10hr); and Tura at 7am and 5pm (12hr). **Private bus** firms such as Blue Hill, Network and Assam Valley run services all over the northeast and there are ticket agents all around Police Point. The journey to Agartala is a tortuous 24 hours. For Aizawl you may prefer to travel to Silchar and then continue by Jeep. Services to Nagaland and Manipur go via Guwahati, so again you might prefer to break the journey. Evergreen Travels next to Sheba Travels (Police Point) run frequent Tata Sumo services to Guwahati (3hr) – just turn up and book. The border crossing to **Bangladesh** at Dawki, southeast of Cherrapunjee, is served by private buses from Bara Bazaar, and a fleet of Tata Sumos which park near the *New World* restaurant.

There are no passenger flights out of Meghalaya's Umroi airport, but bookings on Indian Airlines and Sahara can be made through Sheba Travels, Police Bazaar Point (℡0364/226222). Jet Airways have an agency at Police Point on Jail Road and in Hotel Centre Point. There are also 2–3 **helicopter** flights daily (Mon–Sat) to Guwahati (℡0364/223200 or 222864).

See Travel Details at the end of this chapter for more information on journey frequencies and durations.

Smit

The cultural heart of the Khasi people, the small village of **SMIT** is situated high on an exposed plateau 15km east of Shillong. In the centre of the village stands a traditional thatched palace from where the king ruled his subjects. Every year in mid-November Smit hosts the important Khasi festival of Pomblang Nongkrem, a five-day celebration during which the locals air their colourful festive attire. The hillock behind the village offers good views of the surrounding countryside. Although there is no accommodation, the village has a couple of simple *dhabas* where you can enjoy a chai and watch the world go by. Taxis run between Shillong and Smit, though you may be surprised at the local concept of "full". All buses to Jowai pass the Smit turn-off from where it is a pleasant four-kilometre walk into the village.

Cherrapunjee and around

The important market town of **CHERRAPUNJEE**, 56km south of Shillong, achieved fame as the wettest place on earth. The highest daily rainfall ever recorded fell here in 1876 – 104cm in 24 hours – but Cherrapunjee now shares its watery crown with nearby Mawsynram, whose overall annual rainfall recently pipped it at the post. Cherrapunjee's numerous falls are most impressive during the steamy monsoon season when awesome torrents of water plunge down to the Bangladeshi plains. Noh Kalikai, the fourth-highest falls in the world, was named after Kalikai, a poor local woman, who in Khasi legend was tricked into eating her daughter by a jealous and evil second husband and then threw herself from the top of the falls after recognizing some fingers in her betel-nut basket.

Cherrapunjee is divided into upper and lower sections, spread out over several kilometres. The upper town consists of a few poky buildings built around

The wettest place on earth

The residents of Cherrapunjee not only have to put up with 1080cm annual rainfall, but have suffered the loss of their crown as the wettest place on earth to Mawsynram, a small town just a few kilometres away. To add insult to injury, locals are now having to cope with serious droughts as well.

Between June and September the monsoon clouds strike the huge escarpment that separates Meghalaya and Bangladesh and shed their loads with a vengeance. Little of the water remains in the area, however, much of it draining straight into the porous limestone, or cascading from cliffs in a spectacular array of waterfalls. Logging and deforestation has further reduced the ability of the soil to hold water, and a large population increase has exacerbated the problem. From October to March, the area suffers severe drought, and local people have to trek miles to collect water from springs, with cans of water costing up to Rs20 in the long dry season.

the Ramakrishna Mission, and has a couple of **restaurants**, the *Diengdoh* and the *Raindrop*. The lower part has all the civil offices from the days when it served as administrative capital for the region, and a couple of churches. The various points of interest – the Noh Kalikai waterfall, Bangladesh viewpoint, and Mawsmai village and cave – are each a few kilometres in different directions out of Cherrapunjee; the easist and most comfortable way of seeing them all is to join the Meghalaya Tourism day-trip (daily 8am–4.30pm; Rs80). State buses and Jeeps run from Shillong if you prefer to do it on your own, but there is no accommodation available. Buses leave from the *Anjalee Cinema* bus stand in Shillong at 7am and the last bus returns at 2.30pm. Shared taxis and Jeeps are more readily available on the day of the market (every eight days, and four days after the Iewduh in Shillong) famous for its local orange honey and tribal jewellery.

A one-day jungle trek along the David Scott trail from Mawphlang to Cherrapunjee can be arranged through Impulse Inc, NGO Network, near Horseshoe Building, Lower Lachumiers in Shillong (☎0364/500587). The trail was constructed during the nineteenth century to facilitate transport of goods. Maswphlang is the site of an ancient sacred grove from which the sacred fruits could be eaten but never taken away.

Mawsynram and Jakrem

MAWSYNRAM, now officially the "world's wettest place", is just 12km away from Cherrapunjee as the crow flies, but there is no direct transport between the two – you will have to come back at least as far as Upper Shillong. Buses from Shillong leave from Bara Bazaar. Mawsynram's main attraction is **Mawjinbuin Cave**, where a stalagmite resembling a Shiva-lingam is perpetually bathed by water dripping from a breast-shaped stalactite above. The only **accommodation** in Mawsynram is the Inspection Bungalow (❶); you need permission from the Deputy Commissioner's Office in Shillong to stay there. **JAKREM**, 64km west of Shillong, has hot sulphur springs blessed with medicinal properties.

Dawki

Ninety-six kilometres south from Shillong, **DAWKI** is the most important of the Meghalaya–Bangladesh border crossings and has excellent views of the Khasi Hills and Bangladesh below. A regular Jeep service from Bara Bazaar serves Dawki. The equivalent border town in Bangladesh is Tamabil, just two-

and-a-half hours from Sylhet. There is no Bangladesh visa office in Meghalaya, so you will need to possess a valid visa before entering the state – Calcutta has a consulate. There is also a Bangladesh Embassy in Agartala, Tripura and a border crossing into Bangladesh from there (see p.1070). If you are arriving at Dawki from Bangladesh, the last bus to Shillong departs around 11.30am. Accommodation is available, including an Inspection Bungalow, bookable at the police station.

Jaintia Hills

The **Jaintia Hills** in the east of the state are fairly easy to access, with regular buses and taxis leaving from Shillong's Bara Bazaar to **Jowai**, the main market town of the region. The marketplace is hectic and colourful, especially on main market day. A walk along the river Myntdu will take you to the memorial tomb of U Kiang Nangbah, a Jaintia patriot who was hanged by the British in 1862 for leading a revolt against their rule. **Accommodation** is limited to the *Circuit House* above the town (❶–❷), with good views; it's best to reserve through the Deputy Commissioner's Office in Shillong first, or ring ahead (☎03652/22365), as it's often booked by officials. Turn left at the main T-junction and head up the hill. Alternatively, at the bottom end of town, the basic *New Broadway* (❷) has dingy rooms.

Jowai makes a good base for visiting **Nartiang**, 24km to the north, and 65km northeast of Shillong. This was once the summer capital of the Jaintia kings, and features ancient monoliths – the tallest of which stands eight metres – dating back to the megalithic Hynniewtrep people, and in folklore erected by the Jaintia giant Mar Phalyngki. Nartiang also has a fifteenth-century Durga temple.

From Jowai, you can also visit **Krem Kotsati–Umlawan**, 60km southeast, which at 21km is the longest cave system in mainland Asia, and which attracts caving enthusiasts from all over the world.

Meghalayan festivals

The Khasis have two main festivals – Pomblang Nongkrem and Shad Suk Mynsiem. Nongkrem is a five-day harvest thanksgiving which takes place in November in the village of Smit. An important part of this festival is the *pomblang* or decapitation of goats, which are then offered to the Syiem of Khryim (head of the Khasi State). A range of folk dances in full Khasi costume follow the ritual. Shad Suk Mynsiem ("dance of the happy soul"), is a thanksgiving to the Khasis' God for past blessings and prayers for more of the same in future years. It takes place in April or May and unlike the *pomblang* there are no sacrifices, just lots of dancing.

For the Jaintias, Behdienkhlam is the most important festival, celebrated at the conclusion of the sowing period in July. Jowai is the best place to watch the proceedings. Traditionally the men of the village beat ("behdien") the roof of every house in the village with bamboo poles to drive away evil spirits ("khlam"), while the women prepare sacrificial food for the ancestors. The festival ends with games involving mud, balls and sticks.

The Garos celebrate their harvest with the festival of Wangala, held in honour of Saljong, the sun god of fertility, which and usually takes place in October. Also known as the hundred-drum festival, resounding rhythms accompanied by flutes and gongs set the scene for the energetic dancers. Wine and meat in good measure accompany the proceedings. The Garos have a plethora of fascinating dance routines including Doregata, in which the women have to knock their partners' turbans off using their heads, and Chambil Mesara, a whirling dance involving a pomelo.

Tripura

Tucked away in a corner of the northeast, surrounded by Bangladesh on three sides, the lush green mountains and valleys of **TRIPURA** have attracted many different peoples over the centuries. It became part of the Indian Union in 1949; since then its fate has been entwined with that of Bengal. The Partition of India and subsequent creation of East Pakistan (now Bangladesh) in 1948, followed by war, famine and military regimes drove millions of Bangladeshis to flee into Tripura, where they now outnumber the indigenous people by four to one, leaving many of the original inhabitants feeling that their land and resources have been stolen and exploited. Tripura is more like India proper than the other northeast hill states and its connections with the Bangladeshi plains are strong. The Tripuris are the biggest tribal group, accounting for more than half the tribal population, and the Reangs, originally from the Chittagong Hill Tracts, are the second biggest tribe.

Agartala, the state capital, is a laid-back city with a palace and a few temples, from which easy day-trips can be made to **Udaipur** and the fairy-tale palace at **Neermahal**. It's also the jump-off point for an adventurous trip to the extraordinary rock-cut sculptures at **Unakoti**, in the north. Tripura's **forests** were once famed for their elephants, praised by the Moghul chronicler Abu Fazal in his *Ain-e-Akbari*. Sadly, due to the widespread and uncontrolled practice of slash-and-burn agriculture, and to general pressure on the land, wildlife has come under severe threat. A handful of sanctuaries such as Gumti, Rowa, Trishna, and **Sepahijala** strive to protect the few forests that remain.

The **history** of the kingdom of Tripura and its Manikya rulers, who claimed descent from far-off Rajput *kshatryas*, is told in a curious Bengali poem, the *Rajmala*. Udai Manikya (1585–96) founded the city of **Udaipur** on the site of the old capital of Rangamati, adorning it with beautiful tanks, buildings and temples. The Tripura Sundari temple here is one of India's most important *shakti pithas*. After staving off the Muslim rulers of Bengal, the Manikyas finally submitted to the Moghuls, but continued to rule the kingdom until it was eventually subsumed into British India. Maharaja Birchandra Manikya, who came to the throne in 1870 and was heavily influenced both culturally and spiritually by Bengal – and by his close relationship with Bengali poet, author

Trouble in Tripura

Although Tripura is now completely open to tourism, insurgency and ethnic conflict remain a problem, particularly in the north. For this reason buses from Silchar to Agartala travel in convoy with a military escort from Kumarghat as far as Teliamura. Although you're unlikely to meet trouble in the tourist spots, it's sensible to keep your ear to the ground and heed the advice of local people.

The NLFT (National Liberation Front of Tripura) and the ATTF (All Tripura Tiger Force) are fighting for tribal rights, autonomy, independence and the expulsion of Bengalis. Other insurgents have a financial agenda. In the run-up to elections, kidnapping and extortion help raise large sums of money which can then buy political clout: a successful group may promise to step down from the election in exchange for payments from the competing political parties. Another common event is the mass surrender of militants after elections – followed by their appointment in well-paid jobs. The UBLF (United Bengal Liberation Front) recently joined the fray with vicious reprisals against tribals to quell the activities of the other two groups.

and painter Rabindranath Tagore – established Bengali as the language of the court. You will also see lots of quite graphic clay sculptures of **Kali**, Bengal's favourite goddess, made by households for their monthly pujas. English is not widely spoken here.

Agartala and around

AGARTALA, the capital of Tripura, is a laid-back administrative centre very reminiscent of the low-level towns of Bangladesh, whose border is just 2km away. Its main monument of interest is the gleaming white **Ujjayanta Palace**, completed in 1901. Set amid formal gardens and artificial lakes, this huge building, whose main block now houses the State Legislative Assembly, covers an area of around eight hundred acres. One of many temples nearby and open to the public, the **Jagannath** temple with its orange tower rises from an octagonal plinth across the road. It contains some fascinating and very colourful sculptures depicting various episodes in Krishna's life. Other temples of interest include **Ummaneshwar** temple on the other side of the palace tanks and the Buddhist **Venuban Vihar** (7–11am & 4–7pm), 1km north on Airport Road. **Gedu Mian Mosque** near the bus and taxi stand is encrusted with a mosaic of broken crockery pieces.

Most of Agartala's amenities, bazaars, bus stands and administrative offices are concentrated in the centre, immediately south of the palace. Opposite the GPO, the **State Museum** displays interesting ethnographic and archeological

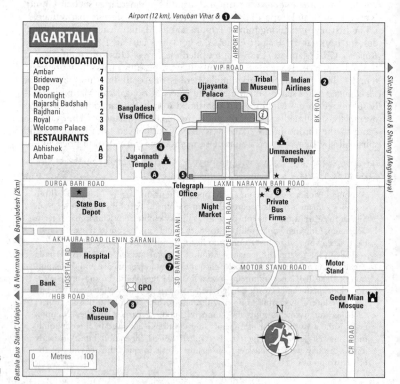

exhibits (Mon–Sat 10am–5pm; free), with one gallery devoted to the excavations at Unakoti in the forests of northern Tripura. The Tribal Cultural Research Institute and Museum (11am–1pm) at Supari Bagan lies well hidden in the backstreets of Krishna Nagar district, near the Jagannath temple. Those wishing to access the internet should head to Star Graphics, on BK Road, 50m past the *Rajdhani* hotel, or to Cyber Masti, on Durga Bari Road, next to the Telegraph office.

Five kilometres east of the modern town, **Old Agartala**, or Puran Haveli, the previous capital of Tripura, holds the unusual **Chaturdas Devata** or "fourteen deities" temple. This otherwise unassuming temple's tribal roots are revealed in July every year, when the festival of Karchi Puja draws people from all over the region. It can be reached by auto-rickshaw, or by bus to Khayerpur, from where it's a short walk.

Practicalities

Arriving by bus, you'll probably be dropped off at one of the private company offices on Laxmi Narayan Bari (LN Bari) Road, or at the state bus depot at Krishna Nagar. If arriving at the airport, buses and taxis ply the 12km to the centre of town. The local **tourist office** (Mon–Sat 10am–5pm, Sun 3–5pm; ☎0381/225930) can be found in a wing of the palace, which in theory is the only part of the palace open to the public, but they may be able to get you a visitor's pass for the main part if you're interested. They also organize **tours** and arrange transport for sightseeing.

The **post office** (Mon–Sat 7am–6pm) is at Post Office Chowmuhani. Note that there are currently no foreign exchange facilities here. Cycle **rickshaws** and auto-rickshaws are plentiful, and **Jeeps** can be chartered at the bus stand.

Accommodation and eating

Agartala has a small but good selection of **hotels** – nothing fancy, but something for everyone. All places listed provide mosquito nets. Choices for **eating** are more limited: *Abhishek* on Durga Bari Road (10am–9pm) is the best in town, with indoor and garden tables; *Ambar*, next to the hotel of the same name, is another option.

Ambar, SD Barman Sarani ☎0381/228439. Central location with reasonably priced rooms. **②**

Brideway, JB Road, near the west side of the palace ☎0381/207298. Friendly place. Reasonable rooms with large attached bathrooms. **②–④**

Deep Guest House, LN Bari Road ☎0381/204718. Small hotel on main road. Carpets and attached bathrooms, though the single rooms lack windows. **③**

Moonlight, LNB Road ☎381/200813. Basic and friendly with attached bathrooms and a good cheap veg restaurant. **①**

Rajarshi Badshah, Airport Road ☎0381/201034. A couple of kilometres out of town through the north gate. Pleasant, peaceful rooms, lawn, gardens and restaurant. **④–⑤**

Rajdhani, BK Road, near Indian Airlines office ☎0381/223387. Comfortable mid-range hotel near the palace. **③–⑥**

Royal Guest House, Palace Compound West ☎0381/225652. Down a side street near the palace. Roomy and comfortable, with a good restaurant. **⑤**

Welcome Palace, HGB Road ☎0381/224940. New hotel and the best in town. Their *Kurry Klub* restaurant serves Thai, Chinese and Indian food. **④–⑥**

Around Agartala

On the border with Bangladesh, 27km south of Agartala, the large lake of **Kamala Sagar** is overlooked by a small but important Kali Temple. Its twelfth-century sandstone image of Mahisa-Mardini, a form of Durga, has a *shivalingam* in front of it. Buses leave from Battala bus stand in Agartala to the lake (5 daily; 1hr).

On the road to Udaipur, 33km south of Agartala, the nature reserve at

Sepahijala extends over eighteen square kilometres, with a lake, zoo and botanical gardens, and is home to primates including the Hoolock gibbon and golden langur and around 150 species of birds. The beautiful *Abasarika Bungalow* (**❶**) offers comfortable rooms in jungle surroundings which you can book in advance at the Forestry Office (℡0381/222224) in Agartala, 2km up Airport Road on the left. All buses to Udaipur travel past the park gate.

Moving on from Agartala

State buses leave from the terminus on the corner of Hospital Road and LN Bari Road for the gruelling stop-start convoy to Silchar, Shillong and Guwahati. It's well worth paying extra for the more comfortable private buses run by Network, Capital, Tania, Green Valley and Sagar which depart from LN Bari Road, 100m east of the palace. The private services each offer virtually identical prices, timing and standard. All buses heading north from Agartala have to travel in twice-daily army-escorted convoys from Teliamura to Kumarghat, leaving at the same times – 6am and 12 noon. Buses to Udaipur (every 15min; 2hr), Melaghar (for Neermahal; every 30min; 2hr) and Kamala Sagar (5 daily; 1hr) run from Battala bus stand at the western end of HGB Road, as do shared Jeeps – faster but more cramped – for the same destinations. Kumarghat, seven hours away, is the nearest railhead to Agartala.

Agartala's airport, 12km north of the centre, can be reached by bus or taxi from the motor stand, by bus from the beginning of Airport Road, or by auto-rickshaw. Indian Airlines, on VIP Road, just west of BK Road (℡0381/225470), flies to Calcutta (1–2 daily; 50min) and Guwahati (Tues, Sat, Sun; 40min).

Agartala is just 2km from the border with Bangladesh, and you can easily walk or take a rickshaw to the checkpoint on Akhaura Road. Rickshaws on the Bangladeshi side can take you to Akhaura Junction, 4km away, from where there are trains to Comilla, Sylhet and Dhaka (2hr 30min). Although there are seven official border crossings from Tripura to Bangladesh, this one is the most convenient.

The Bangladeshi Embassy (Mon–Thurs 8.30am–1pm & 2–4.30pm; Fri 8.30am–noon & 2–4.30pm; ℡0381/224807) next to the *Brideway* hotel issues visas on the spot. Two passport photos are needed and prices vary according to nationality; UK passport holders pay £40 and US citizens $45.

See Travel Details at the end of this chapter for more information on journey frequencies and durations.

Udaipur

The former capital of the Manikyas, **UDAIPUR** retains an atmosphere of antiquity not found in the metropolis of Agartala. An important market town, it is surrounded by paddy fields and low forested hills. On the southwest bank of **Jagannath Dighi** tank stand the ruins of the **Jagannath** temple, while the seventeenth-century **Moghul Masjid** marks the furthest outpost of the Moghal Empire. **Tripura Sundari**, the most important temple in the area, stands 5km outside Udaipur, on a small hillock in front of a holy lake which teems with carp and turtles. Built in typical Bengali-hut style with a square sanctum and large meeting hall in front, this is one of the 51 *shakti pithas* sacred to the Tantras, marking the spot where Sati's right leg is supposed to have fallen when Shiva was carrying her body from the funeral pyre. Animal sacrifices are performed here daily.

Most people visit Udaipur on a long day-trip from Agartala, but **accommodation** is available at the *Pantha Niwas Tourist Lodge* (**❶–❷**). There's also a small tourist office (☎0381/22432). **Buses** run to Agartala (every 15min; 2hr) and Melaghar (for Neermahal; every 30min; 30min), as well as frequently departing shared **Jeeps**.

Neermahal

The fairy-tale water palace of **NEERMAHAL**, in the middle of **Rudrasagar Lake**, 55km south of Agartala, was built in 1930 as a summer residence for Maharaja Bir Bikram Kishore Manikya. Inspired by Moghul architecture, the palace (daily 9am–6pm) is rather derelict inside, but the exterior and gardens have been restored, and the sight of the domes and pavilions reflected in the lake, especially under the early evening floodlights, is impressive. You can rent boats to cross the lake to the palace from just opposite the tourist lodge (motorboats Rs125 per hour; punts Rs60 per half hour), a very pleasant journey among lily pads, dragonflies, ducks and cormorants.

The lake is 1km from the town of **Melaghar**, from where buses run to Agartala (every 30 min; 2hr) and Udaipur (every 30min; 30min). Neermahal can be visited together with Udaipur as a day-trip from Agartala, provided you're steeled for a long hard day – the round trip covers 130km along seriously pot-holed roads. Should you prefer to break up the journey, the lakeside *Sagarmahal Tourist Lodge* (☎0381/64418; ❷) has large rooms, some affording great views across the lake, along with seven-bedded dorms (Rs30). Food is available at the lodge and at a nearby **restaurant** run by the local fishermen's co-operative.

North Tripura

In the northwest corner of Tripura, 20km from Dharmanagar and 180km from Agartala, **UNAKOTI** is one of the most intriguing archeological sites in the region. The site consists of several gigantic rock-cut images scattered across a hillside. Although most of the images are as yet unexplained, it is considered an eighth-century Shaivite site. Certainly Shiva, Durga and Vishnu, as well as a particularly enormous Ganesh, can be discerned, and a palpable Buddhist influence there too.

The nearest accommodation at **Kailashahar**, the District Headquarters for North Tripura, lies 10km away. Neither the *Forest Rest House* (❶) nor *Dak Bungalow* (❶) are really intended for tourists; you'll need to seek permission from the local Forestry Office (☎03824/22224) for the former, and the local Deputy Commissioner's Office for the latter. Kailashahar connects by bus to Agartala (2 daily; 7hr) and to the nearest railhead at **Dharmanagar** (7 daily; 1hr 30min). From there, a tortuously slow night train runs to Lumding (17hr) via Karimganj (4hr 40min) and Haflong (11hr), and an afternoon train for Silchar (6hr 15min). **Kumarghat**, 140km north of Agartala, is a seven-hour bus ride away, with the afternoon bus meeting the train to Lumding which starts here.

Mizoram

Heading south from Assam into the hills of **MIZORAM**, "the land of the highlanders", forests and bamboo-covered hills suddenly take the place of green

The uprising that ended

Mizoram's two main species of bamboo flower every fifty years (one eighteen years after the other), attracting hordes of rats and boosting their fertility rate fourfold. The rats devour crops in the fields, leaving famine in their wake. The first time this happened, in 1959, unpreparedness and apparent callousness on the part of the newly independent governments in Delhi and Assam led **Laldenga**, a clerk on the District Council, to found the **Mizo Famine Front** (MFF). Set up initially to combat famine, it transformed to become the **Mizo National Front** (MNF), a guerrilla group fighting for secession. The government's heavy-handed response in 1967, rounding up Mizos from their homes into guarded villages under curfew, not only boosted support for the MNF, but also sought to wipe out the traditional Mizo way of life at a stroke. Bangladeshi independence was a bitter blow to the MNF, who had relied on Pakistani support, and moderates on both sides eventually brought the MNF to the negotiating table, where statehood was granted in 1986 in return for an end to the insurgency. Laldenga became chief minister of the new state, but his administration lost to Congress in the following elections. For the last few years, Mizoram has been the most peaceful of the "seven sisters."

paddy fields and tea estates – the winding mountain road is scenic, but the journey long. Despite the difficult terrain, Mizoram is a gentle pastoral land, and the **Mizos** are a friendly and welcoming people. Whitewashed Christian churches dot the landscape, giving it more of a Central America feel than a state squashed between Myanmar and the Chittagong Hill Tracts of Bangladesh.

The Mizos, who migrated to the area from the Chin hills of Burma, were regularly raiding tea plantations in the Assam Valley right into the late nineteenth century; only in 1924 did the British administration finally manage to bring about some semblance of control. They opened up what was then the **Lushai hills** to missionaries, who with great zest and zeal converted much of the state to Christianity. **Aizawl**, its busy and cosmopolitan capital, is a large sprawling city built on impossibly steep slopes which have necessitated stilted housing. In the heart of the state, traditional Mizo communities occupy the crests of a series of ridges, each village dominated by its chief's house and *zawl-buk*, or bachelors' dormitory. An egalitarian people, without sex or class distinctions, the Mizos remain proud of their age-old custom of *Tlawmgaihna*, a code of ethics which governs hospitality. Among surviving traditions are the **Cheraw**, "bamboo dance", performed for mothers who die in childbirth to welcome them to *Pialral*, the realm of the dead, and the weaving of local costumes such as the *puan*, characterized by white, black and red stripes.

Tourism remains restricted due to the sensitive border with Myanmar, and permits are still required, but the opening of the new airport at Lengpui has already made the state far more accessible, a trend that looks certain to continue.

Aizawl

One of India's remotest state capitals, **AIZAWL** perches precariously on the steep slopes of a sharp ridge, straddling the watershed between the Tlawng and the Tuirial river valleys and given a comfortable year-round climate by its altitude of 1250m. Although the views are of hills rather than snowy mountains, it has something of the feel of a Himalayan hill station. There's little to see in the way of monuments and temples, but the markets are interesting, and the rural surroundings are within easy reach by bus or on foot.

The road from the north makes a dramatic entrance through a deep cleft in the rocky ridge, emerging from the shadows to provide a first glimpse of Aizawl. A white cross stands guard at the entrance of the pass.

Due to its precipitous setting, much of Aizawl does not see the sun for significant parts of the day, and the new multistorey concrete edifices clinging to the hillsides only increase the depth of the shade. However, there are many vantage points offering great views of the lush green hills surrounding Aizawl, stretching out in every direction and dotted with church spires and villages. **Chaltlang Hill**, high above Chandmari in the north, and the Theological College perched above the dramatic cleft on the road into Aizawl are two of the best.

Zarkawt is the main downtown area, where you'll find a host of cheap hotels on the upper of two parallel streets which form part of Aizawl's complex and largely one-way road network. They are connected by a series of ridiculously long and steep stairways which run haphazardly between the shops, markets and offices. The lower road runs to Treasury Square, the administrative area, and the upper road leads back to Chandmari and Chaltlang. **Bara Bazaar** sells wares ranging from recordings of Mizo music to bespoke shoes made by Chinese cobblers. Further up the hill, Solomon's Cave in **Zodin Square** is an indoor market selling fabrics, garments and music; traditional stuff is notably absent. The District Industries Centre in Upper Bazaar stocks local handicrafts such as shawls and bags. The **Mizoram State Museum**, on MacDonald Hill (Mon noon–4pm; Tues–Fri 10am–4pm; free), has a small but interesting collection of Mizo costumes and implements.

The Durtlang hills immediately north of Aizawl, and Luangmual, 7km west, provide pleasant walking country – both easy day-trips from the centre, and you may prefer the idyllic setting of the Luangmual Tourist Lodge to the hotels in the centre of town. Buses leave for Luangmual from outside the Salvation Army Temple.

Practicalities

Of the **minibuses** that run between central Aizawl and the suburbs, the most useful head from the top of town near the GPO and Zodin Square to Chandmari in the north – otherwise a tiring two-kilometre walk.

The friendly and hospitable staff of the state **tourist office**, in the Chandmari district (Mon–Fri 9am–5pm; ☎0389/341227), provide advice, information and transport, and can book tourist lodges throughout Mizoram – including the one here in Aizawl. The landmark **post office** is on Treasury Square. The State Bank of India has a **foreign exchange** counter but is somewhat reticent. Don't bank on it.

Accommodation and eating

Several **hotels** in Aizawl are geared towards budget and mid-range travellers, and simple cafés, especially around Bara Bazaar, serve **Mizo food**. Lentils, fish, rice and bamboo shoots are popular; the mild dishes can be a welcome change from most north Indian cooking. There are several cheap and cheerful local *dhabas* on Zodin Square.

Ahimsa, Zarkawt ☎0389/341133. One of Aizawl's better hotels. Central, with comfortable rooms, rooftop views and a popular restaurant. ⑤
Berawtlang Tourist Complex, Zemabawk ☎0389/342067. Seven hilltop cottages with great views in a rural setting. ⑤

Capital Guest House, Zarkawt ☎0389/341721. Below Capital Travels. Clean rooms and hot water by the bucket. ③–④
Chawlhna, Zarkawt ☎0389/342292. Popular budget hotel – the cheapest of the budget options along this stretch – with canteen-like restaurant. ②–③

Chief, Zarkawt ☏ 0389/346418. Reasonable rooms in a central location, but slightly overpriced. ⑤
Luangmual Tourist Home, ☏ 0389/332263. A few kilometres out of town on a bus route, very friendly with clean rooms around a garden court-yard. Dorm accommodation also available. Recommended for its views and ambience. ②
Ritz, Bara Bazaar, near Machhunga Point ☏ 0389/326247. Comfortable business hotel with some en-suite rooms. Excellent restaurant and rooftop views. ④ –⑤

State Guest House, Bawngkawn ☏ 0389/340131. One of the smartest hotels, with all mod cons and a restaurant with a good reputation for Indian and Chinese cooking. ③ –⑤
Tourist Lodge, Chaltlang ☏ 0389/341083. Perched on a sharp ridge with a terrace providing great views. Large but slightly run-down rooms. A steep walk from the centre. Dorm accommodation available (Rs50). ③

Moving on from Mizoram

The only recommended road out of Mizoram leads to Silchar, 180km north in Assam. Tata Sumos are the quickest and most comfortable way to travel, taking around 6–7 hours. There are several Sumo agents around Zarkawt including Chungnungi (☏ 0389/344616). Several private bus companies run services to Silchar (12hr) including Capital Travels (☏ 0389/340166) and Jagannath Travels (☏ 0389/350113), also based in Zarkawt. Sumo and bus services are also available direct to Shillong and Guwahati. Mizoram State Transport offer cheaper, slower and less comfortable rides. For Manipur and Nagaland, the best option is to fly from Aizawl to Imphal. Flights to Imphal are also available from Silchar, but the road from Silchar to Imphal is not recommended, due to numerous military checkpoints.

Aizawl's new airport at Lengpui, 90min north handles flights to Calcutta (Mon, Wed, Fri; 55min) and Imphal (Mon, Wed, Fri; 30min). Book through Quality Tour & Travels (☏ 0389/341265), A–51, Chanmari who also run an airport bus service. Their office is just a couple of minutes walk down from the tourist office.

Manipur

The state of **MANIPUR**, stretching along the border with Myanmar, centres on a vast lowland area watered by the lake system south of its capital **Imphal**. This almost forgotten region is home to the **Meithei**, who have created in iso-lation their own fascinating version of Hinduism. Though the area around Imphal is now all but devoid of trees, the outlying hills are still forested, and shelter such exotic birds and animals as the spotted linshang, Blyth's tragopan, the curiously named Mrs Hume's bar-backed pheasant, slow loris, Burmese pea-fowl and the beautifully marked clouded leopard, as well as numerous unclassified varieties of orchids. The unique natural habitat of **Loktak Lake**, with its floating islands of matted vegetation, is home to the sangai deer.

Manipur's **history** can be traced back to the founding of Imphal in the first century AD. Despite periodic invasions from Burma, it enjoyed long periods of independent and stable government until the end of the Indo–Burmese war in 1826 when it was incorporated into India. It came under British rule in 1891 after the Battle of Kangla. During World War II, most of Manipur was occu-pied by the Japanese, with 250,000 British and Indian troops trapped under siege in Imphal for three months. Thanks to a massive RAF air-lift operation from Agartala, they held out, and when Japanese troops received the order to end the Imphal campaign it was in effect the end of the campaign to conquer India. Manipur became a fully fledged Indian state in 1972. Since then it has seen waves of violence as a result of self-rule campaigns and a brutal conflict

The festivals and performing arts of Manipur

Manipuri dance, like the associated colourful traditions of Myanmar, Indonesia and Thailand, is replete with Hindu themes and influences. Now recognized as one of India's main classical dance forms, it centres around the story of Krishna cavorting with the *gopis* (milkmaids). Here the *gopis* are dressed in elaborate crinoline-like skirts, while the accompanying music includes energetic group-drumming, with large barrel drums suspended across the players' shoulders. The Jawaharlal Nehru Manipur Dance Academy, North AOC, Imphal, Manipur's premier dance institution, arranges occasional recitals and hosts an annual dance festival.

The **martial arts** of Manipur are currently going through something of a revival with performances by men and women being choreographed for the stage. **Thang-Ta** is a dynamic form utilizing *thang*, the sword and *ta*, the spear. Fast, furious and seemingly extremely dangerous, performances take place each May during **Lai Haraoba**, a ritual dance festival held at Moirang (see p.1077).

Finally, the annual **Heikru Hitongba Boat Race** is held every September as part of a celebration to commemorate the founding of the two major Vaishnavite temples of Imphal, Bijoy Govinda and Govindjee. Two teams of rowers, standing in long dugout canoes, race on the Thangapat moat near the Bijoy Govinda temple.

---

between the Kukis and Nagas. Disturbances are still common and tourists are advised not to venture too far from the capital. For permit requirements see p.1043.

Imphal and around

Circled by distant hills, the capital of Manipur, **IMPHAL**, lies on a plain at an altitude of 785m. Though it lacks dramatic monuments, its broad avenues give it an open feel. Imphal feels closer to Southeast Asia than India, and visitors encounter the problem of a **language** barrier as many of the locals speak neither English nor Hindi.

Langthabal, set on a small hillock 8km south of Imphal on the road to Burma overlooking the University of Manipur, has remains of an old palace, together with a few temples and ceremonial houses. The **Khonghampat Orchidarium**, 12km north of Imphal on NH-39 (the Dimapur road), displays over a hundred varieties of orchids which bloom in April and May in a riot of colours.

The Town

Imphal's small centre is sandwiched between the stately avenue of Kanglapat to the east and the somewhat stagnant River Nambu to the west. The town's **Polo Ground** dominates the area; according to popular legend, the Manipuri game of *Sagol Kangjei* is the original form of the modern game of polo. In one corner, the **Shaheed Minar** memorial commemorates the Meithei revolt against British occupation in 1891, while just southeast, the **Manipur State Museum** (Tues–Sun 10am–4.15pm; Rs2) focuses on tribal costumes, jewellery and weapons along with geological, archeological and natural history displays.

At the heart of Imphal, along Kangchup Road, the fascinating daily market of **Khwairamband** – also known as *Nupi Keithel* and *Ima Bazaar* (mothers' market) – is run by more than 3000 Meithei women, making it the largest of its kind in Asia. One section is devoted to textiles – shawls and fabrics including the *moirangphee*, the traditional Meithei dress. This striped skirt comes in two pieces, which for a small fee will be stitched together on the spot with amazing speed. Across the road, the other section of the market sells local fish, vegetables, and other provisions. Smaller markets nearby sell handicrafts including cane and wicker. If you prefer not to haggle, there are a few fixed-price shops around including Sangai Handloom and Handicrafts, at GM Hall, near the clock tower, and the Handloom House in Paona Bazaar.

South of the old palace complex, the golden dome of **Shri Govindjee**, Manipur's pre-eminent Vaishnavite temple, can be seen amongst the palm trees. The temple has a large prayer hall and pleasant ambience; the early morning pujas, complete with conch blowing, drumming and procession, are well worth attending – aim to be there by 7.30am. The **British War Cemetery**, 500m north of the *Tourist Lodge*, is the resting place of British and Indian soldiers killed during the Burma campaign and is beautifully maintained by the Commonwealth War Graves Commission.

Practicalities

State **buses** arrive at the stand next to the Polo Ground and private buses at their individual offices, most of which are along MG Avenue, 200m north of Khwairamband Bazaar. Manipur's **tourist office** (Mon–Sat 9.30am–5pm, Oct–March 4.30pm; closed 2nd Sat of month; ☎0385/320337) is based at *Hotel Imphal* north of the palace on the main Dimapur road. The ITDC tourist office, on Jail Road (Mon–Sat 9.30am–5.30pm; ☎0385/221131), provides information and maps. The **GPO** (Mon–Sat 9am–5pm) is on Secretariat Road, at the southern end of the palace complex. Individual travellers can get permits endorsed at the **Foreigners Registration Office**, along from the GPO. The State **Bank** of India on MG Ave has closed its foreign exchange services. Internet facilities are available at Millennium Link, Paona Bazaar, opposite Jeevan Opticals (☎0385/220579).

Auto- and cycle rickshaws are the main means of **transport** within Imphal. The rickshaw-wallahs wear hats, shades and scarves to protect their faces from the dust and fumes, all of which make them look rather intimidating and don't help to bridge the language gap.

Moving on from Imphal

Imphal's **airport**, 6km south of town, is connected by Indian Airlines to Calcutta (daily; 1–2hr), Silchar (Tues, Thurs, Sat; 30min), Delhi (Thurs, Sun; 3hr 50min) via Guwahati (50min) and Aizawl (Mon, Wed, Fri; 30min). The Indian Airlines office is on MG Avenue (☎0385/220999) and Jet Airways in Room 201, *Hotel Nirmala* on the same road.

Bus connections with Guwahati are good, but the 579-kilometre journey takes around eighteen hours. Several private bus companies, including Manipur Golden Travels, Green Valley, Network and Kangleipak, operate from MG Avenue near the State Bank of India, and also have stands on DM Road outside *Hotel Tampha*. National Highway 39 – "The Burma Road" – links Imphal to Kohima in Nagaland and continues to Dimapur, the nearest railhead 215km away. You will need a valid permit for Nagaland to travel this route. Buses to Dimapur (6hr) leave daily at 6am and will drop off passengers at Kohima, but on the edge of town, not at the central bus stand. For those heading to Silchar, the 200-kilometre road journey via the border point of Jiribam may look tempting, but military checkpoints and bus searches make it a nightmare trip of around fourteen hours. The thrice-weekly 30-minute flight is recommended.

See Travel Details at the end of this chapter for more information on journey frequencies and durations.

Accommodation and eating

Imphal has a few simple **hotels** in the market area, and a handful of mid-range ones further out. Similarly the choice of **restaurants** is small – the best in town being the *Host* in the *Anand Continental* hotel. There are no **bars** – this is a dry state.

Anand Continental, Khoyathong Road ☏0385/223422. Best in town with carpets, hot showers, TV in all rooms and excellent restaurant. **❻**

ITDC Imphal, North AOC, Dimapur Road ☏0385/220459. Resplendent government-run hotel with large rooms, lawns and restaurant. **❹–❻**

Mass, Assembly Road ☏0385/222797. Reasonable-sized doubles some with balconies and attached bathrooms. Central location. **❷–❹**

Nirmala, MG Avenue ☏0385/229014. A good-

value option with carpeted rooms and hot showers – soap and towels provided. **❹–❻**

Pintu, North AOC, Dimapur Road ☏0385/224172. Large pink building next to the cinema. Clean and friendly, with a restaurant whose advert declares that "slightly hurried food" is served here. **❸–❹**

Tampha, North AOC, Dimapur Road ☏0385/221486. Basic accommodation near small *dhabas* and the bus stand. **❶–❷**

White Palace, MG Avenue ☏0385/220599. Reasonable hotel with fair-sized rooms near the main markets. **❸–❹**.

Loktak Lake

South of Imphal, the huge and complex body of water known as **Loktak Lake**, fed by numerous rivers and dotted with islands, is home to a unique community of fishermen who live on large rafts made of reeds. Rare and endangered sangai, brow-antlered "dancing" deer, live on the floating vegetation that covers much of the lake, sharing their habitat with other species including the hog deer. Much of the lake is taken up by the **Keibul Lamjao National Park**, 53km from Imphal, which attracts a host of waterfowl and migratory birds between November and March. A forty-room hilltop *Tourist Bungalow* on **Sendra Island**, 48km from Imphal, provides a good vantage point from which to view the lake and can be booked through the tourist office in Imphal.

On the more populated western shore of Loktak, the small town of **MOIRANG**, 45km south of Imphal, is the traditional centre of Meithei culture, with a temple devoted to the pre-Hindu deity **Thangjing**. In April 1944, the Indian National Army under Netaji Subhas Chandra Bose planted its flag here, having fought alongside the Japanese against the British Indian Army for the cause of Independence. A **memorial** and **museum** commemorating the event includes several photos and Japanese-issued rupee notes from 1943. Guided tours of Loktak usually take in Moirang, or you can take a bus (1hr) from the private stand at Keishampat on Jail Road, near the centre of Imphal. The *Moirang Tourist Home* is currently occupied by the Indian army, so travellers will have to return to Imphal for accommodation.

Arunachal Pradesh

ARUNACHAL PRADESH, "the land of the dawn-lit mountains", is one of the last unspoilt wildernesses in India. In a state where almost every major river valley is home to a different tribe, Arunachal has a wealth of fascinating cultures and peoples, though much is still off limits for foreigners. There is a wealth of biodiversity too, with a dazzling array of flora and fauna, including more

Arunachal's numerous and inaccessible mountain valleys have developed distinct micro-cultures often in very small areas. The **Monpas**, who have a strong affinity with the Bhutanese, occupy the valleys north of Bomdila; their largest town, Dirang, with its *dzong* (fort), is just before the pass at Sela. Although they practise Buddhism, focused around the great monastery of Tawang, they retain many of their original animist-shamanist beliefs, and wear distinctive five-pointed yak-hair skullcaps.

The **Sherdukpens** live south of the Bomdila Range, in Rupa and the valleys of the Tengapani. Traditionally, the Sherdukpen men wear a sword in a scabbard around their waist. Although they have a reverence for Tibetan Buddhism, their religious beliefs are a curious blend of Buddhism and shamanism, with *jijis*, or priests, practising witchcraft to counteract malevolent spirits.

Further southeast are the **Akas**, literally "painted", who colour their faces with resin and charcoal. East of Kameng, the menfolk of the sturdy hill people known as the **Nishing** wear a distinctive wicker helmet surmounted by the red-dyed beak of a hornbill. Protruding in front of their foreheads is a bun of plaited hair called *podum*, skewered horizontally with a large brass pin. The Nishing trace their descent from Abo Teni, a mythical primeval man, as do the neighbouring **Apatanis** who are the best known of all the tribal groups. Occupying a 26-square-kilometre plateau around Hapoli, the Apatanis are experts at terraced rice cultivation. They too wear a hat and *podum* on their foreheads but do not sport the distinguishing yellow ribbon of the Nishing.

In the northeastern extremes bordering Myanmar and Nagaland are the **Nocte** and **Wancho** tribes with striking facial tattoos.

than five hundred species of orchids, in a habitat that combines glacial terrain, alpine meadows and subtropical rainforests.

Despite its beauty, tourism in Arunachal Pradesh has been discouraged due to the extremely sensitive border with Chinese-occupied Tibet in the north and Myanmar in the east. In 1962 the Chinese invaded Arunachal Pradesh, reaching Tezpur in Assam, a 300-kilometre incursion which India has never forgotten. Since then a strong military stance has been adopted in the area and consequently all visitors need **permits** (see p.1043 for details).

The new capital city of **Itanagar** is located north of the Brahmaputra across from Jorhat and Majuli island. In the far west of the state, the road to **Tawang**, one of Arunachal's highlights, runs through rugged hills, covered by dense primeval forests. Starting at **Bhalukpong** on the Assamese border it climbs steadily up to the pleasant market town of **Bomdila** (2460m), with its Tibetan monasteries, before crossing the bleak and dramatic 4300-metre **Sela pass** from where it eventually zigzags down into Tawang. In the far northeast of Arunachal, **Namdapha National Park** is home to snow leopards, tigers, bears and elephants. Eight other **wildlife sanctuaries** are dotted throughout the state. **Tezu**, also in the northeast corner, is the gateway to one of India's most important and least accessible Hindu pilgrimage sites, **Parasuramkund**, where a dip not only relieves pilgrims of the dirt and grime of getting there but also washes away the sins of a lifetime.

Itanagar

The town of **ITANAGAR**, just under 400km northeast of Guwahati, has been developed as the capital of Arunachal Pradesh largely because of its convenient location near the road and rail arteries alongside the Brahmaputra, but holds little to interest visitors. Surrounded by densely forested hills, the town itself is little more than a four-kilometre stretch of road running between Zero Point, where the two top-range hotels are located, and Ganga Market, the main bazaar area where you can find cheaper accommodation around the bus stand.

The small **Tibetan Buddhist temple** consecrated by the Dalai Lama reflects the extensive Tibetan influence in this frontier land and provides good views of Itanagar and the surrounding countryside. The **Jawaharlal Nehru State Museum** (Tues–Sat 9.30am–5pm; Rs1) describes the festivals, dances and lifestyle of the main local tribes, and houses an extensive ethnographic collection, displaying woodcarvings, musical instruments, textiles and model houses. A workshop behind the museum specializes in traditional cane manufacture and the adjacent salesroom sells tribal handicrafts. The murky brown waters of **Gyakar Sinyi** (Ganga Lake) and lush jungle surrounding it are straight out of *Jurassic Park* and provide a taste of the magnificent scenery of the whole state; the lake is a ten-kilometre taxi ride or walk from Itanagar. A 2.5-kilometre concrete path around the lake becomes a serious jungle trek on its far side, with creepers, vines, brambles and touch-sensitive tentacles adding to the fun; sturdy footwear is recommended. There are no chai stalls or shops so bring a supply of water and food.

Practicalities

The nearest **airport** 67km away at **Lilabari** in Assam is served by NEPC flights to and from Guwahati (2hr 20min) and flights to, but not from, Dibrugarh (45min). There is also a thrice-weekly Pawan Hans **helicopter** service between Itanagar and Guwahati from **Naharlagun** just 10km away. **Trains** from Guwahati run as far as Harmuti, 33km away in Assam. Overnight **buses** (Blue Hill, Network, Taara etc) connect Itanagar with Guwahati (11hr), and Arunachal State Transport run an extensive but basic service throughout the state. As there's no bridge across the Upper Brahmaputra, services to Tinsukia, Jorhat and Dibrugarh go via Tezpur. Recently introduced Tata Sumos have greatly reduced travel times; destinations include Hapoli (5hr), Bomdila (7hr 30min), Pasighat (6hr 30min) and Along (10hr). Several agents around Ganga Market sell tickets. The main **tourist office** (☎0360/244115) is in Naharlagun. Taxis, shared taxis and cycle rickshaws can be picked up around town.

The best bet for **accommodation** is Itanagar: the *Donyi-Polo Ashok* (☎0360/212626, ☎212611; ⑧) above Zero Point is the top hotel, while the *Arun Subansiri* (☎0360/212806; ⑥) below Zero Point provides some competition. Several mid-range and budget options can be found in Ganga Market. *Hotel Samsara* (☎0360/211266; ③) in the Akash Deep complex is friendly with a large relaxing rooftop space and indoor and outdoor restaurants. The *Blue Pine* (☎0360/212042; ②–⑤) on APST Road, *Alpine* (☎0360/213253; ②) and *Himalaya* (☎0360/212210; ②) are similar alternatives. For **eating**, try the *Dragon Restaurant*, at 1st Floor Akash Deep, which offers Chinese, Indian and some Western dishes or *Hotel Jimsi* on the main drag at Ganga Market. Should you get stuck in Naharlagun, *Hotel Arunachal* (☎0360/244960; ④–⑥) and the *Simang* (☎0360/245111; ③–④) are both central.

West Arunachal

Bordered by Bhutan and Tibet, the isolated hills and valleys of western Arunachal climb to some of the remotest glaciers and peaks in the Himalayas. With the exceptions of **Gori Chen** (6858m) and **Nyegi Kangsang** (7047m), most of the 6000-metre-plus mountains remain completely unknown. The solitary road serving the region runs from Tezpur in Assam to **Tawang**, ending bone-shakingly high in the mountains at one of Asia's largest monasteries. On the way you pass through the small friendly market town of **Bomdila**, set haphazardly on a steep hillside and home to three Tibetan monasteries, and **Dirang**, an ancient-looking fortress town a couple of hours up the valley.

Bhalukpong

The river **Kameng**, famed for its fighting mahseer fish, emerges from a deeply forested valley at **Bhalukpong**. The Kameng Angling Association (☎03782/23224) can help you pit your wits against the river life and can also arrange white-water rafting. All public transport services from Tezpur to Bomdila stop here for border formalities and refuelling. Accommodation is available at the *Aama Yangri* (☎03782/34507; ❸–❹) or just across the state border at the *Assam Tourist Lodge* (☎03872/23224). **Tipi**, seven kilometres north of Bhalukpong, has an orchidarium with five hundred different species of orchid. From here, the narrow highway winds up through dense and beautiful mountain forests to Bomdila, 100km away.

Bomdila

Bomdila is a picturesque and peaceful town (2530m) set amidst apple orchards on a spur of the Thagla Ridge, the dividing line between rainforests to the south and subalpine valleys to the north.

Bomdila's three **Tibetan Buddhist monasteries** reflect the origins and culture of the local people and its proximity to Tibet. The largest of these, a Gelugpa *gompa* high above the town, was inaugurated by the Dalai Lama in October 1997. The caretaker monk will show you round. A small suite of rooms make up the Dalai Lama's private residential quarters. The rooftop offers superb views of the town and surrounding mountains. The older *gompa* below houses a large blue statue of the Medicine Buddha – Sangye Menhla. The third *gompa* is at the end of the main market street in the middle of the town.

The police station and **foreigners' registration office**, where independent travellers should get their permits endorsed, are a couple of hundred metres above the sports ground in the upper part of town. A few kilometres beyond Bomdila on the Tawang road the snow-covered peaks of Gorichen (6488m) and Kangto (7042m) come into view. Himalayan Holidays (☎03782/22017), on the main market street, offer a friendly service and can also arrange local sightseeing trips. They also lead **treks** in the region, including one to Gorichen base camp. Wanges Computer World next door is Bomdila's sole cybercafé.

Practicalities

There are just two **routes** out of Bomdila: onward and upward towards Tawang, and back down towards the Assamese border. State buses run from the bus station in the lower part of town to **Tezpur** (1 daily; 7–8hr) and **Tawang** (3 weekly; 8hr). **Private buses** run by Akama depart from outside Himalayan Holidays for Tezpur (1 daily; 6–7hr). Tata Sumos are the best way to negotiate these steep switchback roads and are quicker, more comfortable, though more expensive. Daily services run to Tezpur, via Rupa and Tawang.

The majority of the **hotels** are in the middle part of town, near the main market, although there are a couple of basic places in the lower town near the bus station. The top hotel is in upper Bomdila, opposite the sports ground. **Restaurants** in the middle part of town include the *Dragon* and *Denzong* in the main street and there are *dhabas* dotted around, selling simple food.

Chushi Gangtok, main market street (no phone). Three dirt-cheap five-to-seven-bed dorms in large wooden building. ❶

Dawa, lower town ☏ 03782/22360. Friendly place just up from the bus stand, with a few basic rooms and outside toilets. ❶

La, opposite sports ground, upper town ☏ 03782/22097. Small pleasant rooms with or without attached bathrooms. ❸

Passang, main market road, middle town ☏ 03782/22627. The pick of the bunch along this stretch, the most central and convenient, with simple clean rooms and attached bathrooms. ❷–❸

Siphiyang Phong, opposite the sports ground, upper town ☏ 03782/22286. Top hotel in town; carpeted rooms with TV and hot water, and its own generator. ❻

Tourist Lodge, above the police station, upper town ☏ 03782/22049. Spacious rooms with hot showers and wood-burning stoves (wood Rs40 per bundle). ❷–❹

Rupa and beyond

The small picturesque settlement of **RUPA**, 17km below Bomdila, is the centre of the Sherdukpen people who occupy the hills that stretch all the way to Bhutan. They practise a mixture of Tibetan Buddhism and animism, and their two main annual festivals reflect this duality. Rupa has an attractive Tibetan *gompa* and a colourful riverside *lhakang* (chapel) a little further up the valley. A small roadside Guru Rinpoche cave graces the entrance to the town. Places to stay include the *Arohee* (❸) and the *Sawme* (❶–❷). Views of Bomdila way up on the ridge can be enjoyed from various vantage points around Rupa.

Another 55km beyond Rupa lies the large and influential Tibetan refugee settlement of **Tenzingang**. The Gelugpa monastery here houses nearly four hundred lamas and is one of only two Tantric Gelugpa centres in India. The original monastery, founded in 1474 by Jetsun Kunga Thondrup near Xegar in central Tibet, was destroyed by the Chinese during the Cultural Revolution. It has been reconstructed here on land donated by neighbouring villages. Behind the throne is a large statue of Cho, a rare manifestation of Sakyamuni Buddha crowned by Je Tsong Khapa, who is seated on his right. There is a large Guru Rinpoche shrine at the entrance of the monastery complex. Another 15km beyond Tenzingang lies the tiny end-of-the-road settlement of Kalaktang surrounded by densely forested hills dotted with villages and close to the Bhutanese border. The small Nyingma Zangdo Peri *gompa* houses some wacky sculptures.

Dirang and beyond

Ninety minutes beyond Bomdila and halfway to the Sela Pass lies the ancient fortress of Dirang. Although most of the original fort lies in ruins, the village itself is worth checking out and there's a five-hundred-year-old *gompa* above the village. New Dirang is 5km further on. The only accommodation consists of the brand-new *Hotel Pemaling* (❹), with attached bathrooms, hot showers and a restaurant, and the adjacent *Tourist Lodge* (❹), halfway between the *gompa* and the new town, and with great views over the latter.

Soon after crossing the Sela Pass, you reach the **Jaswant Singh Memorial**, where buses and Sumos make a brief stop. It is dedicated to the Indian soldier who held off the invading Chinese army single-handedly for several days in 1962 by racing from bunker to bunker firing at Chinese positions, creating the illusion that the position was held by a substantial Indian garrison. He was eventually captured and killed by the Chinese, who continued virtually all the way to Tezpur before retreating to Tibet. Chinese mule tracks were discovered in a remote corner of Arunachal Pradesh in the autumn of 2000, sending waves of concern throughout Arunachal and India as a whole.

Tawang

Another 180km east from Bomdila along mountainous switchback road, and cut off from the rest of Arunachal by a high ridge breached by the dramatic Sela Pass, the great Buddhist monastery of **Tawang**, the largest in India, dominates the land of the Monpas. Perched at around 3500m, it looks out onto a semicircle of peaks, snowcapped for much of the year, and seemingly close enough to touch. Tawang feels very much like the end-of-the-road place that it is and there are few luxuries to be enjoyed here.

The **monastery** is a couple of kilometres beyond the town. It was established in the seventeenth century when this area was part of Greater Tibet, and was the birthplace of the sixth Dalai Lama. The magnificent fortress-like complex houses around 500 monks in 65 residential buildings, and is renowned for its collection of manuscripts and *thangkas*. The main shrine room is richly decorated and houses several statues including a beautiful 1001-armed Chenresig (or Avalokitesvara). Two *ani gompas* (nunneries) are visible from the main gate, clinging to the steep mountain slopes in the distance. They can be reached by foot in a couple of hours or by vehicle from the centre of town. Beyond Tawang and very close to the border of Tibet lies the lake district of Bangachangsa. Dotted with pristine high-altitude lakes, small *gompas* and Guru Rinpoche caves, it is sacred to Tibetan Buddhists and also to Sikhs – Guru Nanak visited the region twice, hence the small Sikh *gurudwara*. There is no public transport but Jeep taxis are available for the journey.

Practicalities

Independent travellers should register at the **foreigners' registration office**, above and behind the state bus stand. Arunachal State Transport run **buses** to Bomdila and there are also private buses, but the daily Tata Sumo services are by far the best mode of transport if you're willing to pay the extra rupees. Book in advance from ticket agents in the bus stand square.

The few **restaurants** in town offer basic Tibetan food – *momos* (meat or veg dumplings), *thukpa* (thick noodle soup) – and simple Indian dishes. The *Masaang Norling* restaurant opposite the *Masaang* hotel bakes delicious Tibetan bread with home-churned butter and also sells Meakins 10,000 – a superstrong lager brewed in Uttar Pradesh and available only in Arunachal. There are a couple of decent mid-range **hotels**, which are mostly basic yet clean. As the sun sets the temperature here plummets; shops and restaurants close at around 5pm.

Arunachal Tourist Lodge, above the main market road, halfway along ☏037824/22359. The most comfortable and spacious hotel in town with rooms ranging from basic to large with running hot water. ❷–❻

Drema (no phone). Fairly basic, but with the luxury of hot water. ❷–❸

Gori Chen, overlooking the large Tibetan arch on the main road (no phone). Impressive exterior, but fairly basic inside, with double and triple rooms. ❷–❸

Masaang, 200m from the bus stand (no phone). Basic, but clean and friendly place, with attached bathrooms. ❶

Paradise, just before the large arch on the main market road (no phone). Large, en-suite rooms with sofas, TV and hot water by the bucket. ❹–❺

Shangri La, next door to the *Masaang* (no phone). Clean and basic rooms with bathrooms attached. ❶

Central and East Arunachal

The picturesque hill station of **Hapoli** (formerly Ziro), 1780m above sea level on the Apatani plateau, is 150km north of Itanagar. Although there is little to see in the town itself, there's lively activity in the market area. There are several villages dotted around the plateau, some of which are within walking distance. **Old Ziro** is a scenic seven-kilometre walk from the centre of Hapoli, or you can take one of the half-hourly buses. Accommodation is available in Hapoli at the pleasant *Arunachal Guest House* (☎03788/24196; ❷–❸), a couple of minutes above the main road behind the army barracks and administration offices; the *Jumalhari* (no phone; ❸) on the main road; and the *Hotel Blue Pine* (☎03788/24812; ❺), at the Pai Gate turning on the edge of town on the right – the only place with hot showers, but 2km from the town centre. Tata Sumo services run to Itanagar, Daporijo, Along and Pasighat, and can be booked in advance with any of the agents on the main road.

To the north and east, **Along** and **Pasighat**, the district headquarters of West and East Siang respectively, offer trekking and angling and can be reached from Itanagar, North Lakhimpur, or from Dibrugarh via ferry to Oiramghat. Accommodation in both is available at the local *Circuit House* (❶–❷). Pasighat also has a handful of private hotels and the option of a visit to the **Dr D Ering Memorial Wildlife Sanctuary**, home to buffalo, tiger, deer and a variety of bird life.

In eastern Arunachal, the remote valleys of the **Dibang** and **Lohit** rivers, inhabited by tribes such as the Mishmis, descend from snow-covered passes through subtropical forests to the plains of the Brahmaputra. The sacred Hindu site of **Parasuramkund**, on the banks of the River Lohit, is mentioned in the *Kalika Purana* as the place where Parasuram washed away his act of matricide. Thousands of pilgrims make the arduous journey here on Makar Sankranti (mid-Jan), the most auspicious day of the year to take a dip as it's said to wash away all negative karma accumulated in this lifetime. The nearest town, **Tezu**, acts as the gateway to the site, with accommodation available at the *Circuit House* (no phone; ❶) and *Inspection Bungalow* (no phone; ❶). The nearest railhead is at Tinsukia, 120km to the southwest.

Namdapha National Park (Oct–April) is unique for its massive range of altitude (200–4500m). Close to the Myanmar border, it is home to tigers, leopards (clouded and snow), as well as red pandas. The park headquarters are at **Miao**, where a *Tourist Lodge* (no phone; ❶) provides transport. Accommodation is also available at the *Forest Inspection Bungalow* (no phone; ❶). Buses to and from Miao pass through **Margherita**, 64km southwest, and **Tinsukia**, 40km further on. Tinsukia has three daily trains to Guwahati all via Dimapur (7hr) and Lumding (9–10hr 30min). From **Dibrugarh**, 47km beyond Tinsukia, daily flights serve Delhi and Guwahati with Sahara Airlines, and Calcutta (4 weekly) with Indian Airlines. Daily trains run to Guwahati including the #5960 Howrah Kamrup Express which terminates in Calcutta and the #4055 Brahmaputra Mail which goes to Delhi.

Nagaland

On the border with Myanmar, south of Arunachal Pradesh and east of Assam, **NAGALAND** is physically and conceptually at the very extremity of the subcontinent. Many of its hills and valleys, home to the fiercely independent Nagas, were uncharted until recently, and the eastern regions remain far beyond the reach of the skeletal road network, despite the fact that the forested mountains rarely exceed 3000m in height. Today this remains the most **politically sensitive** of the northeastern hill states. The two factions of the

National Socialist Council of Nagaland (NSCN) are locked in battle for independence against the Indian army and often against each other as well. The capital **Kohima** is safe, but shuts down at sunset, after which it is eerily silent. A progressive tourism policy has recently eased permit restrictions and opened up the regional capitals of Mokokchung and Phek.

When the British arrived in neighbouring Assam they initially chose to leave the fierce warrior tribes of Nagaland well alone. After continued Naga raids on Assamese villages, the British, in their commitment to protecting colonial subjects, sought to push the Nagas back into the hills, sparking a series of battles during the mid-nineteenth century. The Angami warriors defeated the British twice, but were finally defeated in 1879 by the numbers and superior technology of the British. A truce was declared with the British agreeing not to penetrate beyond certain boundaries within Nagaland. A commissioner stationed in Khonoma toured the territories collecting taxes, sorting disputes, and came to hold a certain authority among the various tribes. The Nagas remained loyal to the British, joining the fight against the Japanese invaders during World War II. At the time of Indian Independence, the Nagas pleaded with the British to grant them an independent homeland, but instead found their homeland divided into two with the larger area falling to Burma. After Independence, Gandhi asked the Nagas to remain within the new-found union for ten years promising them choice of destiny thereafter. Gandhi was assassinated, his promise never fulfilled, and fifty years on the Nagas are still fighting for a homeland they believe is their inherent right.

The Nagas

There are fourteen main tribal groups in Nagaland, most of them inhabiting villages perched high on mountain ridges. Naga warriors have long been feared and respected throughout the northeast and head-hunting was practised within living memory, but the state is now ninety percent Christian. The Nagas originally lived in northeast Tibet, then moved through southwest China into Myanmar, Malaya and Indonesia, as well as eastern Assam. The Angami, Ao, Chakhesang, Chang, Khamniungan, Konyak, Lotha, Phom, Pochury, Rengma, Sangtam, Sumi, Yimchunger and Zeliangrong all have distinct cultural traits yet share a common "Naga identity". They are skilful farmers, growing up to twenty different species of rice according to altitude and aspect of the terraces.

Traditionally, Nagas differentiate between the soul, a celestial body, and the spirit, a supernatural being. The human soul resides in the nape of the neck, while the spirit, being in the head, holds great power and brings good fortune. Heads of enemies and fallen comrades were once collected to add to those of the community's own ancestors. Some tribes decorated their faces with tattoos of swirling horns to mark success in head-hunting. The heads were kept in the men's meeting house (*morung*) of each village, which also served as the boys' dormitory, and was decorated with fantastic carvings of animals, elephant heads and tusks. The Nagas also constructed megalithic monuments which lined the approaches to villages personifying those who erected them after death. Menhirs stand in pairs, or in long double rows, to honour fame and generosity or enhance the fertility of a field. The Angamis were never ruled by chiefs; the closest equivalent is the *Thevo*, a descendant of the founder of the village and mediator between the community and the supernatural world. Every village was subdivided into *khels*, which often had independent intertribal policies, and through which disputes could be settled in bloody fights. Traditionally, relations between the sexes were conducted with great openness and equality.

Although each tribe has its own dialect, a hybrid language drawn from various Naga languages and Assamese has developed into the common Nagamese tongue.

Kohima

Founded by the British in the nineteenth century, **KOHIMA**, the capital of Nagaland, was built alongside the large Angami village of Kohima, solely for administrative purposes. The town continues in this role – for a more intimate glimpse of traditional Naga life you'll need to wander up to the old village, or visit **Khonoma**, 20km beyond Kohima, the Nagas' once impregnable stronghold, sacked by the British in 1879 and again by the Indian army in 1956. Jakhema, a few kilometres south on the road to Manipur, with terraced fields surrounding the village, is also worth visiting for its traditional feel.

The Town

Spread loosely over a saddle joining two large hills, Kohima forms a pass that played a strategic role during World War II. The highway from Imphal to Dimapur – the route along which the Japanese hoped to reach the plains of India – crosses the saddle at the foot of the **Second World War Cemetery**, which dominates the town. Its immaculate gardens stand as memorial to the Allies who died at this very spot during the three-month Battle of Kohima, which ended in April 1944 after claiming the lives of over 10,000 soldiers.

Below the cemetery in central Kohima, bustling markets sell local produce and a variety of colourful Naga shawls, bags, decorative spears and other handicrafts. Weaving is a traditional handicraft here and each Naga tribe has distinctive shawls such as the black, red and green of the local Angamis.

The large Angami settlement of **Kohima Village** is set on a high hill overlooking modern Kohima. Only a few of its buildings are traditional with pitched roof and crossed "house-horns" on the gable, but its tightly knit labyrinth of lanes and houses gives the village a definite Naga feel. Carved heads to signify family status, grain baskets in front of the houses, and troughs used to make rice beer are among the distinctive features. The grunts, squeals and other bodily effects from the myriad pigs – virtually every family keeps them – add to the bucolic atmosphere.

The fascinating **State Museum** (Mon–Sat 9.30am–2.30pm, closed every 2nd Sat; Rs1) in Bayavu Hill Colony, a pleasant twenty-minute walk from Centre Point, houses an excellent collection of Naga jewellery, dominated by yellow, red and dark-blue beads, and figures displaying costumes of the various Naga tribes. Upstairs is a small modern art gallery. The museum grounds include a couple of huts, an impressive gateway and a huge log drum, traditionally used in religious rites, during festivals and for sending messages across the hills.

Practicalities

Most private buses from Imphal are through services to Dimapur and don't go into the centre of town – ask the driver to drop you off on the main highway just below the *Japfu* hotel. State buses arrive and leave from the bus stand in the centre of town.

Taxis and minibuses are the main forms of public transport around the town although the central area is small enough to explore on foot. The **tourist office** (Mon–Fri 10am–4pm; ☏0370/222214) is on the National Highway, below the *Japfu*.

Kohima has few **accommodation** choices, though standards aren't bad. Kohima's showpiece hotel is the *Japfu* (☏0370/222721; ❻–❼), on PR Hill at the top end of town, with spacious rooms and a restaurant. The popular *Pine*, on Phool Bari (no phone; ❹–❺) has decent doubles but no singles. The *Valley*

View (**2**) next to the bus station is friendly and helpful but fairly basic and the *Capital* (⊤0370/224365; **2**–**3**), opposite, has rooms ranging from grim to good.

Naga food is fairly simple – rice, boiled vegetables, chicken and pork, with ginger and chilli the main spices. Chinese food is also widely available at the basic cafés on Main Bazaar and around Centre Point. Most restaurants and *dhabas* close at 5pm but if you want to eat a bit later, the *Abu Hotel*, a tiny Indian *dhaba* 100m from Centre Point on the road to upper town, stays open until 6pm.

Moving on from Kohima

From Kohima, roads lead south to Imphal and west to the railhead and airport at Dimapur. There are state and private buses for both destinations and state buses run from the bus stand in the centre of town. Tickets for private buses can be bought from agents in the centre of town and on Phool Bari. State buses to Dimapur run hourly from 6am–4pm and daily early-morning services run to Mokokchung and Zunheboto. From Mokokchung the road continues to Jorhat in Upper Assam. Frequent Tata Sumo services depart for Dimapur when full from the taxi stand 200m up from the bus station.

Khonoma

The beautiful Angami village of **KHONOMA**, 20km northwest from Kohima, holds a special place in Naga history as the place where Angami warriors made their final stand against the British in 1879. Magnificent rice terracing surrounds the village, irrigated by a complex system of bamboo water pipes, and twenty different types of rice are grown here, each specifically suited to the elevation, soil and aspect of the terraces. A flight of steps, approached through a traditional carved gate, leads up to the highest point of the village from where excellent views take in the hills and the neighbouring villages of Mezoma and Secuma. Khonoma is divided into three *khels* – Merhumia, Semomia and Thevomia, which holds the *Hiekha Khwehu* (large meeting circle).

Over the densely forested ridge behind the village lies the scenic Dzoukou valley, part of the Khonoma Nature Conservation and Tragopan Sanctuary. Guides can be hired in Khonoma for the popular four-day trek to the heart of the sanctuary, which is graced with waterfalls and offers wonderful views. Public transport is limited to the daily village bus which leaves Kohima around 2pm below the *Japfu* hotel and returns to Kohima early the following morning but, as there are no hotels in Khonoma, hiring a taxi is the best way to make a day-trip there.

Dimapur

DIMAPUR, the "city of the river people", 74km northwest of Kohima, is Nagaland's largest and most industrialized town – and the only one not located in hill country. It bears little resemblance or affinity to the rest of Nagaland and functions for visitors primarily as a gateway to the state. It's a noisy polluted city and the mushroom-like monuments – fertility symbols dating back to the Kachari Kingdom – are the main point of interest, standing on the riverside edge of town.

The sole railhead in Nagaland, Dimapur, is served by **trains** to Simaluguri (for Sibsagar), Tinsukia and Dibrugarh in Upper Assam. The best service for Guwahati is the daily overnight Kamrup Express #5960, which leaves at 10.35pm, arriving in Guwahati at 6.30am. **Buses** run to Guwahati and towns throughout the northeastern hill states. State and private buses run to Kohima (3hr) from the Nagaland bus stand as do Tata Sumos (2hr–2hr 30min) from the main drag outside. Private buses to Jorhat, Guwahati and Itanagar leave from the Assam bus stand in Golaghat Road across the railway tracks. Dimapur's **airport**, 6km out of town on the Kohima road, has four weekly flights to Calcutta and Guwahati.

If you have to spend the night here, **accommodation** options include the *Tourist Lodge* (☎03862/26355; ❷), next to the Nagaland bus stand; the *Fantasy* (☎03862/32013; ❸–❺) next door; *Hotel Senti* at the end of Golaghat Road (☎03862/29656; ❸–❻); and *Hotel Tragopan* (☎03862/30291; ❻–❼) near the overbridge.

Travel details

Trains

Guwahati to: Calcutta (2–3 daily; 23–24hr); Chennai (6 weekly; 54hr); Delhi (4 daily; 28–41hr); Dibrugarh (2 daily; 14–15hr); Dimapur (2 daily; 6hr); Jorhat (1 daily; 12hr); Mughalsarai (2–3 daily; 23–29 hrs); Mumbai (3 weekly; 43–46 hr).
Jorhat to: Guwahati (1 daily; 12 hours).

Kohima to: Dimapur (10 daily; 3hr); Guwahati (1 daily; 12–14hr).
Shillong to: Agartala (1 daily; 24hr); Aizawl (3 weekly; 22hr); Cherrapunjee (2 daily; 2hr); Guwahati (12 daily; 3–4hr); Silchar (2 daily; 11hr); Tura (2 daily; 12hr).

Buses

Agartala to: Guwahati (1 daily; 24hr); Neermahal (every 30min; 2hr); Shillong (1 daily; 20hr); Silchar (2 daily; 11hr); Udaipur (every 15min; 2hr).
Aizawl to: Silchar (2 daily; 12hr).
Guwahati to: Agartala (1 daily; 24hr); Imphal (1 daily; 18hr); Itanagar (2 daily; 11hr); Jorhat (12 daily; 6–7hr); Kaziranga (12 daily; 4hr 30min); Kohima (1 daily; 12–14hr); Shillong (12 daily; 3–4hr); Silchar (2 daily; 13hr); Siliguri (3 daily; 12hr); Tezpur (12 daily; 4hr).
Imphal to: Dimapur (2 daily; 9hr); Guwahati (1 daily; 18hr); Kohima (2 daily; 6hr).
Jorhat to: Dimapur (1 daily; 3hr 30min); Guwahati (12 daily; 6–7hr); Tezpur (5 daily; 4hr); Tinsukia (6 daily; 4hr 30min).

Flights

Guwahati to: Agartala (3 weekly; 40min); Calcutta (2–3 daily; 1hr 10min); Delhi (3 daily; 2hr 25min); Imphal (4 weekly; 50min).
Imphal to: Calcutta (1–2 daily; 1–2hr); Delhi (2 weekly; 3hr 50min); Jorhat (2 weekly; 40 min); Silchar (3 weekly; 30min).
Jorhat to: Calcutta (4 weekly; 2hr 5min); Dimapur (2 weekly; 25min).
Aizawl to: Calcutta (3 weekly; 55 min); Imphal (3 weekly; 30 min).
Agartala to: Calcutta (1–2 daily; 50min).
Dibrugarh to: Calcutta (4 weekly; 1hr 30 min).
Dimapur to: Calcutta (4 weekly; 1hr 10 min).

CHAPTER 17

Highlights

* **Bhubaneswar** Hidden in the city's suburbs are five hundred or so temples, with unique architecture and elaborate sculptures. See p.1096

* **Pipli** Small village famous for its big and bold appliqué; the main street is a riot of colour with parasols, tablecloths and clothing in every store. See p.1107

* **Puri** Pilgrims flock to the vast temple devoted to Lord Jagannath, particularly during the frenetic midsummer Car Festival. See p.1113

* **Konarak** An elegant thirteenth-century Hindu temple sitting astride a huge stone chariot. See p.1123

* **Olive Ridley turtles** These endangered creatures find their way to Gahirmatha beach for one night in February to lay eggs – an unforgettable scene. See p.1127

Orissa

D espite being one of India's poorest regions, **ORISSA** boasts a distinctive and rich cultural heritage. From a backdrop of thickly forested mountains, where *adivasi* communities continue a very traditional way of life, the mighty Mahanandi and Brahmani rivers meander down to the fertile alluvial plains that run along the coast of the Bay of Bengal.

Any visitor to Orissa cannot fail to notice the glaring contrast throughout the region, between the overwhelming vibrancy of the temples and monuments of powerful former dynasties and the desperately impoverished, drought-prone, paddy-field economy of Orissa today. Despite the seemingly idyllic existence of villages with their thatched roofs and whitewashed temple towers dotted among palm groves and surrounded by green fields, villagers face a constant struggle against the devastating and unpredictable tropical and cyclonic weather conditions and equally unstable politics.

The coastal plains claim the highest concentration of historical and religious monuments – Orissa's principal tourist attractions. **Puri**, site of the famous **Jagannath temple** and one of the world's most spectacular devotional processions, the *Rath Yatra*, combines the heady intensity of a Hindu pilgrimage centre with the more hedonistic pleasures of the beach. Just a short hop off the main Calcutta–Chennai road and railway, Puri sees its fair share of backpackers, who are enticed by plenty of budget accommodation near the beach and a laid-back social scene. **Konarak**, a short hop up the coast, has the ruins of Orissa's most ambitious medieval temple. Hidden for years under a gigantic sand dune, its surfaces writhe with exquisitely preserved sculpture, including some eyebrow-raising erotica. The ancient rock-cut caves and ornate sandstone temples of **Bhubaneswar**, the state capital – all too often skipped by visitors – hark back to an era when it ruled a kingdom stretching from the Ganges delta to the mouth of the River Godavari.

Away from the central "golden triangle" of sights, foreign visitors are few and far between; not so the Bengalis, who travel in family groups throughout

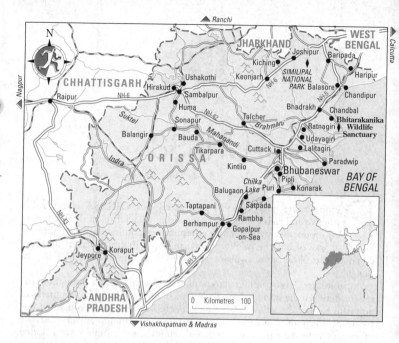

coastal Orissa. Those who come to the region tend to have a specialist interest, such as bird or animal life, temples or tribal culture. In these outlying districts, you certainly need such passions to brave the rigours of minimal infrastructure and overtaxed public transport. The **Simlipal National Park**, deep in the *sal* forests of the far northeast, boasts some spectacular scenery, as well as wild tigers, elephants and hundreds of other species of animals, birds and reptiles that have all but disappeared from more populated areas. In winter, the small islands dotted around **Chilika Lake**, a huge salt-water lagoon south of Bhubaneswar, become a bird-watcher's paradise. Further north, the **Bhita Kanika Sanctuary** at the end of Orissa's river delta, a remote stretch of beach is the nesting site for a school of giant Olive Ridley marine turtles that migrate here in February and March from the South American coast.

From the number of temples, pilgrims and wayside shrines in Orissa, you'd be forgiven for thinking Hinduism was its sole religion. In fact, almost a quarter of the population are **adivasi**, or "tribal" (literally "first") people, thought to have descended from the area's pre-Aryan aboriginal inhabitants. In the more inaccessible corners of the state, such as the tract of near-impenetrable hill country running the length of the interior, many of these groups have retained unique cultural traditions and languages. However, the scourge of "ethnic" tourism is the latest development to encroach on the *adivasis'* way of life after dam builders, missionaries and "advancement programmes" initiated by the state government. Hotels and travel agents throughout Puri offer "tribal tours" for lots of dollars, none of which ever trickles down into the *adivasi* villages.

Orissa enjoys a fairly congenial **climate** for most of the year, with average temperatures ranging from 17°C between November and March, to a bearable-if-humid 32°C in summer. The monsoon blows in around mid-June, just in time for the festival of *Rath Yatra*. The cool winter months are the **best time to visit**, particularly around *Makar Sankranti*, in January, when Orissan villages celebrate the end of the harvest with colourful festivals.

Getting around presents few practical problems if you stick to the more populated coastal areas. National Highway 5 and the Southeast Railway, which cut in tandem down the coastal plain via Bhubaneswar, are the main arteries of the region. A metre-gauge branch line also runs as far as Puri, connecting it by frequent, direct express **trains** to Delhi, Calcutta and Chennai. Elsewhere, **buses** are the best way to travel. Regular government and ever-expanding private services cover all the main routes and most of the more remote stretches.

Some history

Other than scattered fragmentary remains of prehistoric settlement, Orissa's earliest archeological find dates from the fourth century BC. The fortified city of **Sisupalgarh**, near modern Bhubaneswar, was the capital of the **Kalinga** dynasty, about which little is known except that its power was founded on domination of the lucrative land and maritime trade routes leading south. The existence of such rich pickings so close to his frontiers was too strong an enticement for the ambitious Mauryan emperor **Ashoka**. In the third century BC, he descended on ancient Kalinga with his imperial army, and routed the kingdom in a battle so bloody that the carnage was supposed to have inspired his legendary conversion to **Buddhism**. Rock edicts erected around the empire extol the virtues of the new faith, *dharma*, as well as the principles that Ashoka hoped to instil in his vanquished subjects. With the demise of the Mauryans, Kalinga enjoyed something of a resurgence. Under the imperialistic **Chedi** dynasty, which followed the Jain faith, vast sums were spent expanding the capital and on carving elaborate monastery caves into the nearby hills of **Khandagiri** and **Udaigiri**. In the course of the second century BC, however, the kingdom gradually splintered into warring factions and entered a kind of Dark Age. The influence of Buddhism waned, Jainism all but vanished, and **Brahmanism**, disseminated by the teachings of the Shaivite zealot Lakulisa, started to resurface as the dominant religion.

By the seventh century, Orissa's rise to prominence was well under way. Over the next five hundred years, a succession of powerful and prosperous Hindu dynasties ruled the region, creating some of the finest artistic and architectural achievements in the history of south Asia. When the **Eastern Gangas** took control early in the twelfth century, this "golden age" reached its zenith. Fuelled by the gains from a thriving trade network (extending as far east as Indonesia), the Ganga kings erected magnificent **temples** at Bhubaneswar, Puri and Konarak, in which the Shiva worship and arcane Tantric practices espoused by earlier Orissan rulers were replaced by new forms of devotion to Vishnu. The shrine of the most popular royal deity of all, Lord Jagannath at Puri, was by now one of the four most hallowed religious centres in India.

With the exception of a brief incursion by Firuz Sultan in the fourteenth century, Hinduism in Orissa came through the Muslim occupation of Bihar and Bengal comparatively unscathed. Such good fortune, however, was not to last. In the fifteenth century, the **Afghans of Bengal** swept south to annexe the region, with Man Singh's **Moghul** army hot on their heels in 1592. That even a few medieval Hindu monuments escaped the excesses of the ensuing iconoclasm is miraculous; thankfully some did, though **non-Hindus** have never since been allowed to enter the most holy temples in Puri and Bhubaneswar. In 1751 the **Maharathas** from western India ousted the Moghuls as the dominant regional power. The East India Company, mean-

Chances of coinciding with a festival while in Orissa are good, since the region celebrates many of its own as well as all the usual Hindu festivals. See p.1129 for additional details of Mayurbhunj festivals.

Makar Mela (mid-Jan). Pilgrims descend on a tiny island in Chilika Lake to leave votive offerings in a cave for the goddess Kali.

Adivasis Mela (Jan 26–Feb 1). Bhubaneswar's "tribal" fair is a disappointing cross between Coney Island and an agricultural show, though it does feature good live music and dance.

Magha Saptami (Jan & Feb). During the full moon phase of Magha, a small pool at Chandrabhaga beach, near Konarak, is swamped by thousands of worshippers in honour of Surya, the sun god and curer of skin ailments.

Panashankanti (early April). In various regions, on the first day of Vaisakha, saffron-clad penitents carrying peacock feathers enter trances and walk on hot coals.

Chaitra Parba (mid-April). Santals (the largest of Orissa's many *adivasi* ethnic groups) perform *Chhou* dances at Baripada in Mayurbhunj district, northern Orissa. Some fishing castes also hold "horse-dances" involving wooden horse costumes, drumming and processions through the streets.

Ashokastami (April & May). Bhubaneswar's own Car Festival (procession of temple chariots), when the Lingaraj deity takes a dip in the Bindu Sagar tank.

Sitalasasthi (May & June). Celebration of the marriage of Shiva and Parvati, celebrated in Sambalpur and Bhubaneswar.

Rath Yatra (June & July). The biggest and grandest of Orissa's festivals. Giant images of Lord Jagannath, his brother Balabhadra and his sister Subhadra make the sacred journey from the Jagannath temple to Gundicha Mandir in Puri.

Badi Yatra (Nov & Dec). Commemorates the voyages made by Orissan traders to Indonesia. Held at full moon on the banks of the River Mahanadi in Cuttack.

Konarak Festival (early Dec). A festival of classical dance featuring Orissan and other regional dance forms in the Sun Temple at Konarak.

while, was also making inroads along the coast, and 28 years after Clive's victory at Plassey in 1765, Orissa finally came under **British rule**.

Since **Independence**, the state has sustained rapid **development**. Discoveries of coal, bauxite, iron ore and other minerals have stimulated considerable industrial growth and improvements to infrastructure. Despite such urban progress, however, Orissa remains a poor rural state, heavily dependent on agriculture to provide for the basic needs of its 32 million inhabitants. Orissa did not move smoothly into the new millennium; recent political instability and a "super cyclone" in October 1999 (see p.1119), which ripped through the northern and central coastal plains, have together left a trail of destruction and despair.

Bhubaneswar

At first impression, **BHUBANESWAR** may strike you as surprisingly dull for a city with a population approaching half a million and a history of settlement stretching back over two thousand years. Featureless Fifties architecture and rows of rapidly decaying concrete shopping arcades stand where you might expect exotic bazaars, while long tree-lined avenues diffuse the usual intensity of a busy state capital. Beyond the confines of the modern planned city, however, things improve considerably. Hidden among the backstreets and wastegrounds of the southern suburbs are the remnants of some of India's finest medieval **temples**, evidence of a much earlier and infinitely more inspired building boom than the one that followed Independence. These are indisputably the main attractions, made all the more atmospheric by the animated religious life that continues to revolve around them, particularly at festival times.

Bhubaneswar first appears in history during the fourth century BC, as the capital of ancient **Kalinga**. It was here that Ashoka erected one of the subcontinent's best-preserved rock edicts – still in place 5km south of **Dhauli**. Under the **Chedis**, ancient Kalinga gained control over the thriving mercantile trade in the region and became the northeast seaboard's most formidable power. The elaborate sculpture adorning a complex of Jain caves cut from the hillsides of **Khandagiri** and **Udaigiri**, which overlook the capital, provides a taste of the military might and opulent royal lifestyles enjoyed by its rulers.

Not until the fifth century AD, long after the Chedis had disappeared, did Bhubaneswar re-emerge as a regional force. As home to the revolutionary Pasupata sect, the city, known by this time as **Ekamrakshetra**, became a key centre for the promulgation of Shaivism – worship of Shiva and his female

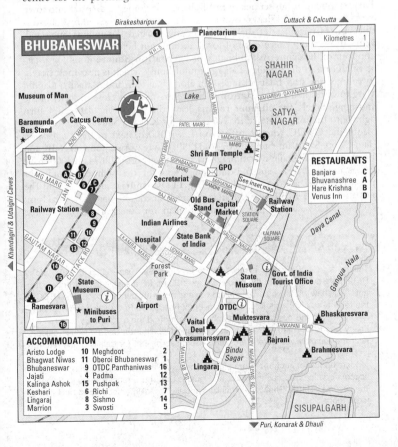

counterpart Shakti. When the **Sailodbhavas** made it their capital in the seventh century, wealth and power were coupled with the mounting religious fervour and Bhubaneswar embarked in earnest upon its "golden age". Nothing is so expressive of the prosperity and self-confidence of this era as its religious architecture. Between the seventh and twelfth centuries, some 7000 sandstone temples are said to have been erected around the **Bindu Sagar**. Intended both as offerings to the gods and as symbols of authority, the temples evolved from the relatively modest proportions favoured by the Bhauma-Karas and Somavamsis to the Gangas' gigantic creation, the **Lingaraj** – home of **Tribhubaneshwara**, or "lord of three worlds", from which the city eventually took its name. Their passion for architecture did not, however, prevent Bhubaneswar's medieval rulers from retaining an army strong enough to hold off the eastward advance of Islam until the end of the fifteenth century. When the Moghuls did eventually take the city, they made up for lost time by razing all but a few of the temples. Thereafter, Bhubaneswar was consigned to relative obscurity. Only after Independence, when the nearby city of Cuttack reached bursting point, was it officially declared the new state capital.

Arrival, information and city transport

There's no regular bus service from Bhubaneswar domestic **airport** into town but taxis and auto-rickshaws cover the 2–3km journey to the centre. Long-distance **buses** terminate at the inconveniently situated Baramunda bus stand, 5km out on the western edge of town, though not before making a whistle-stop tour of the centre. Ask to be dropped at **Station Square** (look for a statue of a horse in the middle of a large roundabout), which is near most hotels. If you miss the stop, frequent buses run along Raj Path and Mahatma Gandhi Marg towards the **railway station** in the centre of town, close to many of the mid-range hotels. For **cheaper rooms**, leave the station via platform 4, turn right onto the main Cuttack road and head for Kalpana Square, 1km south.

Both the **OTDC tourist office** on Lewis Road, next to the *Panthaniwas Hotel* (Mon–Sat 10am–5pm; ☏ 0674/431299, ⓦ www.orissa-tourism.com), and the counters at the railway station (24hr) and the airport (☏ 0674/404006) have leaflets and local area maps, and can arrange taxis for local sightseeing and assist in getting hotel and train bookings. The **ITDC tourist office** behind the museum at B-21 BJB Nagar (Mon–Fri 9am–1pm & 1.30–6pm, Sat 9am–1pm; ☏ 0674/432203) also stocks leaflets and city plans for other parts of the country.

Tours

Tickets for OTDC's rather rushed city tours (Tues–Sun 9am–5.30pm; Rs95, a/c Rs120) are available from the office on Lewis Road; for a slightly higher price, an auto–rickshaw will let you avoid the crowds and move at your own pace. The OTDC trip to Puri and Konarak (Mon–Sat 9am–6pm; Rs105, a/c Rs150) also involves too much time on the bus and not enough looking around the sights. They also run a luxury bus to Berhampur via Chilika Lake and Gopalpur-on-Sea from their office near the *Panthaniwas Hotel* (7am–2pm; Rs60; see p.1134 for details of the return journey).

More upmarket package tours of Bhubaneswar, Puri and Konarak, with four-star accommodation, a/c car transport and guides, can be arranged through Swosti Travels (see p.1103). They also organize specialist "wildlife", "tribal" and "architectural" tours.

Modern Bhubaneswar is too spread out to explore on foot and is best seen by auto- or cycle **rickshaw**. Sights outside the city, such as Dhauli or the Udaigiri and Khandagiri caves, can reached by local **buses**, from the old city bus stand near Capital Market, by auto-rickshaw or on one of OTDC's **luxury bus tours**. Cycle rickshaw-wallahs will also make the trip but the journey can be painfully slow. Private Ambassador **taxis** can be arranged through most travel agents and upmarket hotels (Rs800 per day), although far better value are the taxis at the OTDC tourist office (Rs250 half-day, Rs410 full day), or at large hotels such as the *New Kenilworth* or the *Kalinga Ashok*, and cost around Rs800 for a full day.

Accommodation

As state capital, Bhubaneswar offers the typical range of accommodation from luxurious five-stars to the filthiest of lodges. While the better-class hotels are spread out all over the city, the inexpensive places tend to be grouped around the **railway station**, or near the busy **Kalpana Square** junction at the bottom of Cuttack Road, a five-minute rickshaw ride away. The railway station also has **retiring rooms** if you're really stuck. Reservations must be made in advance at the counter in the main hall.

Aristo Lodge, Kalpana Square ⊤0674/417963. Very basic, but friendly; some rooms have TV and all have attached bath. ❶

Bhagwat Niwas, 9 Buddha Nagar, ⊤0674/417708, right behind the *Pushpak*. Managed by an Aurobindo devotee, the hotel is safe and welcoming. A range of simple, clean rooms, some with balcony and a/c; there's an in-house ISD booth and a good restaurant. ❷–❺

Bhubaneswar, Cuttack Road ⊤0674/416977. Behind the swish exterior, the budget rooms are exceedingly dingy but the more expensive rooms are cleaner and some have a/c. There is a small, dim restaurant. ❷–❹

Jajati, MG Marg ⊤0674/400352. This modern hotel at the top end of Station Square is a little frayed around the edges, but the a/c rooms are comfortable and good value. ❸–❺

Kalinga Ashok, Gautam Nagar ⊤0674/431055, Ⓕ 432066. Popular with tour groups, this friendly hotel strives to celebrate Orissan culture, from organizing dance displays to the decor. Large rooms, restaurant, coffee shop and a bar. ❼–❽

Keshari, Station Square ⊤0674/534994. Over-eager to please, but very close to the railway station. The rooms are dark but clean and comfortable, and the restaurant serves local specialities. ❻–❽

Lingaraj, Old Station Bazaar, near the platform 4 railway station exit ⊤0674/416342. Extremely convenient for early trains: the rooms are spotless but soulless. ❷–❹

Marrion, 6 Janpath ⊤0674/502328. Upmarket and welcoming hotel with a pool, foreign exchange, travel agent and two good restaurants, one serving Chinese food. The bar has intriguing frescos around the walls, and is open to nonresidents. ❽–❾

Meghdoot, 5-B Sahid Nagar ⊤0674/505802. Some distance away in the north of town, but well appointed. All rooms, from high-quality doubles to luxurious suites, have bathtubs and colour TV. Good restaurant, coffee shop and foreign exchange. ❽

Oberoi Bhubaneswar, Nayapalli ⊤0674/418198, Ⓕ 301302. Indisputably the city's top hotel, in the north of town. Exquisitely furnished using antique textiles, stone and metalwork; facilities include an excellent restaurant, an efficient travel centre, foreign exchange, internet access, and a pool. ❾

OTDC Panthaniwas, Lewis Road ⊤0674/432515. Institutional government hotel close to the museum and temples. Nothing fancy, but the rooms are large and comfortable, with TV in the a/c rooms, room service and three restaurants. ❹–❻

Padma, Kalpana Square ⊤0674/416626. A busy little place with cheap and simple rooms; a good fall-back if others are full. No restaurant. ❷

Pushpak, Kalpana Square ⊤0674/310185. Popular with businessmen; the large rooms have attached bathrooms and balconies. There's a separate bar and multi-cuisine restaurant downstairs. Slightly overpriced and not a place for single women. ❸–❻

Richi, Station Square ⊤0674/534619. Large efficient place opposite the station, with hot showers and cable TV in all rooms. The price includes bed chai and breakfast. ❹–❻

Sishmo, 86/A-1 Gautam Nagar ℡ 0674/433600. Plush five-star in the centre of town with pleasant rooms, a bar, pool, 24hr coffee shop and excellent restaurant. ⑨

Swosti, 103 Janpath ℡ 0674/534178, fax 534524. Grand four-star hotel bang in the centre of town. Luxurious rooms, all with cable TV; travel agency, two top-class restaurants and a bar. ⑨

The temples

Of the five hundred or so **temples** that remain in Bhubaneswar, only a handful are of interest to any but the most ardent templo-phile. They are all in the south of the city and quite spread out, but it's possible to see the highlights in a day thanks to the city's ubiquitous rickshaw-wallahs. A tour of the main temples in an auto-rickshaw should cost Rs150–200 (including waiting time).

Most visitors see the temples in a historically chronological order. Apart from giving a sense of the development of Orissan architecture over the years, this also leaves the most impressive monuments until last. The majority are active places of worship, so dress appropriately, remove your shoes (and any leather items) at the entrance and seek permission before taking photographs, particularly inside the buildings. The resident brahmin will expect a donation if he's shown you around, of course, but don't necessarily believe the astronomical amounts recorded in the ledgers you'll be shown.

The central group

The compact **central group**, just off Lewis Road, beyond the museum and OTDC *Panthaniwas Hotel*, includes some of Bhubaneswar's most celebrated temples. In order to see the oldest first, follow the footpath from the main road past the more recent Muktesvara Mandir and its adjacent water tank, as far as a small square lined with cold-drink stalls and souvenir shops.

Parasumaresvara Mandir

The best preserved and most beautiful of Bhubaneswar's early temples, the lavishly decorated **Parasumaresvara Mandir** stands in the shade of a large *banyan* tree just beyond the square, and was built around 650 AD. Art historians rave about this temple, which, with its plain, rectangular assembly hall (*jagamohana*), simple stepped roof and squat beehive-shaped tower (*deul*), typifies the predominant style of late seventh-century Orissa. In addition to the sheer quality of its exterior sculpture, Parasumaresvara is significant in marking the then-recent transition from Buddhism to Hinduism. The brahmin may point out panels depicting **Lakulisha**, the proselytizing Shaivite whose sect was largely responsible for the conversion of Orissa to Hinduism, in the fifth century. On the east side of the tower he appears with four disciples at his feet, while on the west, above the relief showing Shiva as Nataraj (Lord of the Dance), he adopts the full-blown lotus position, looking every bit the meditating Buddha. Around the corners of the *deul* are even more blatant assertions of Hindu supremacy. Look for the **rampant lions** with their heads thrown back, crouched or standing above elephants, symbols of the beleaguered Buddhist faith.

Elsewhere, the sculpture concentrates mainly on the Hindu pantheon and scenes from mythological narratives. In the far corner of the courtyard, an intriguing *lingam*, the **Sahasralingam**, is decorated with a thousand miniature versions of itself.

Muktesvara Mandir

Back towards the main road, the **Muktesvara Mandir**, often described as the "gem" of Orissan architecture, dates from the middle of the tenth century, and

Orissan temples constitute one of the most distinctive regional styles of religious architecture in south Asia. To make sense of the buildings, you need to be able to identify the conventional features, many of which have endured for thousands of years. These are recorded in the **Shilpa Shastras** – Sanskrit canonical texts that set out, in meticulous detail, ancient building specifications and their symbolic significance.

Unlike Christian churches or Muslim mosques, Hindu temples are not simply places of worship, but are objects of worship in themselves – re-creations of the "Divine Cosmic Creator-Being" or the particular deity enshrined within them. For a Hindu, to move through a temple is akin to entering the very body of the god to be glimpsed in the shrine room during the moment of *darshan*, or ritual viewing of the deity – the culmination of an act of worship. In Orissa, this concept also finds expression in the technical terms used in the *Shastras* to designate the different parts of the structure: the foot (*pabhaga*), shin (*jangha*), torso (*gandi*), neck (*kantha*), head (*mastaka*) and so forth.

Most temples are made up of two main sections. The first and most impressive of these is the **deul**, or sanctuary tower. A soaring, curvilinear spire with a square base and rounded top, the *deul* symbolizes Meru, the sacred mountain at the centre of the universe. Its intricately ribbed sides, which in later buildings were divided into rectangular projections known as *raths*, usually house images of the accessory deities, while its top supports a lotus-shaped, spherical *amla* (a motif derived from an auspicious fruit used in Ayurvedic medicine as a purifying agent). Above that, the vessel of immortality, the *kalasha*, is crowned by the presiding deity's sacred weapon, a wheel (Vishnu's *chakra*) or trident (Shiva's *trishul*). The actual deity occupies a chamber inside the *deul*. Known in Oriya as the **garbha griyha**, or inner sanctum, the shrine is shrouded in a womb-like darkness intended to focus the mind of the worshipper on the image of God.

The **jagamohana** ("world delighter"), which adjoins the sanctuary tower, is a porch where the congregation gathers for readings of religious texts and other important ceremonies. Its pyramidal roof, made up of layers of receding steps, contrasts sharply with the gently curving lines of the tower. Larger temples, such as the Lingaraj in Bhubaneswar and the Jagannath in Puri, also have structures that were tacked on to the main porch when music and dance were more commonly performed as part of temple rituals. Like the *jagamohana*, the roofs of the **nata mandir** (the dancing hall) and **bhoga-mandapa** (the hall of offerings) are pyramidal. The whole structure, along with any smaller subsidiary shrines (often earlier temples erected on the same site), is usually enclosed in a walled courtyard.

Over the centuries, as construction techniques and skills improved, Orissan temples became progressively grander and more elaborate. It's fascinating to chart this transformation as you move from the earlier buildings in Bhubaneswar to the acme of the region's architectural achievement, the stunning Sun Temple at **Konarak**. Towers grow taller, roofs gain extra layers, and the **sculpture**, for which the temples are famous all over the world, attains a level of complexity and refinement unrivalled before or since.

is set in its own low-walled courtyard. On the way in you will pass the murky green waters of the small **Marichi Kund** tank, believed to cure infertility – which doesn't altogether explain its popularity with noisy adolescent boys.

The Muktesvara was constructed two hundred years after the Parasumaresvara, and represents the new, more elaborate style that had evolved in Bhubaneswar. The *jagamohana* here has the complex pyramidal roof normally associated with Orissan temples, while the *deul*, though similar in shape to its predecessor, places more emphasis on vertical rather than horizontal lines. Once again, the sandstone **sculpture** is the most striking feature. Directly in front of the main entrance, the ornamental **torana** (gateway), topped by two reclining female figures, is the Muktesvara's masterpiece. The grinning lions and dwarfs around the windows on the side of the porch, known as the *bho* motif, come a close second. The temple brahmin can show you the irreverent lice-picking monkeys around the latticed windows, and a clever little panel hidden among the ornamentation covering the base platform: when you block out some of the peripheral detail, it reveals three separate dancing nymphs. Tucked into the alcove wall between the *deul* and the *jagamohana* there is an intriguing panel of a horse-type animal rearing up as if to crush a crouched figure below. The animal actually comprises nine different mammals, if you can make them out.

Nearby, on the edge of Muktesvara's terrace stands an example of the mature phase of Orissan temple building. The unfinished **Siddhesvara** was erected at more or less the same time as the Lingaraj, in the eleventh century, but is nowhere near as impressive. The lesser deities around the tower, Ganesh and Karttikeya (Shiva's sons), and the inordinate number of shrieking resident bats are about its only remarkable points.

The eastern group

To reach the first of the more scattered **eastern group** of temples, ten to fifteen minutes' walk from Muktesvara, head back up Lewis Road as far as the crossroads, turn right down Tankapani Road, and keep going until you reach the park on the right.

Rajrani Mandir

Even though it was never completed, the twelfth-century **Rajrani Mandir** (sunrise–sunset daily; Rs2) is among the very finest of Bhubaneswar's later temples. The name refers to the particular *rajarania* (yellow-pink) sandstone used in the construction of the temple. From the far end of the well-watered gardens in which it stands, the profile of the *deul*, with its successive tiers of projections rising to form an elegant eighteen-metre tower, is the building's most unusual feature. Closer up, you can make out the profusion of sculpted figures for which Rajrani is equally famous. The best are about 3m off the ground surrounding the sides of the tower. The **dikpalas** ("guardians of the eight directions") are the deities who "protect" the main shrine. Surrounded by their respective vehicles and attributes, they form a marked contrast to the languid and alluring poses of the exquisite female figures (*nayikas*) that stand between them.

Compared to the sanctuary tower, the Rajrani's porch looks plain and unfinished. Of considerably more interest to some may be the **palm-leaf manuscripts** being hawked in the temple gardens. Spurred on no doubt by Khajuraho's money-spinning example, enterprising local artists have tried to make up for Bhubaneswar's comparative lack of erotic sculpture by applying this most ancient of Orissan skills to illustrating the *Kama Sutra*. The results sometimes verge on the surreal.

Brahmesvara Mandir

From Rajrani, a fair walk leads up Tankapani Road to the turn-off for the **Brahmesvara Mandir**, 500m on the right. Along the way you cross a canal, originally dug by King Kharavela in the first century BC, and an open stretch of ground to the left of the road with the oddly shaped temple of

Bhaskaresvara in the middle. The temple is unfinished, but has an interesting three-metre *lingam*, or phallus, enshrined in its double-storeyed interior, which archeologists claim was formerly a Mauryan column.

Unlike most of its neighbours, the eleventh-century Brahmesvara temple itself, at the end of the dirt lane opposite the entrance to the Bhaskaresvara, still houses a living deity, as indicated by the saffron pennant flying from the top of the sanctuary. The gateway in the high enclosure wall brings you out opposite a small cloth-covered image of Lakshmi. Here too you can see the *dikpalas* on the corners, and a fierce Chamunda on the western facade (shown astride a corpse and holding a trident and severed head). Curvaceous maidens admire themselves in mirrors or, in the panels around the tower, respond with some abandon to the advances of their male consorts. An inscription, now lost, records that one Queen Kovalavati once made a donation of "many beautiful women" to this temple – proof perhaps that **devadasis**, the dancers–cum–prostitutes who were to become a prominent feature of Orissan temple life in later years, made an early appearance here. Unfortunately, the temple brahmins are reluctant to allow non-Hindus into the strongly atmospheric shrine room for *darshan*, or a view of the *shivalingam*. There's a majestic Nandi, Shiva's bull, with testicles well polished by years of worshippers giving them a propitious rub on the way in; and an inner sanctum, richly carved and lit by butter lamps, which is filled with incense smoke and the heady scent of oil-soaked flowers left as puja offerings.

The Bindu Sagar group

By far the largest group of temples is clustered around the **Bindu Sagar** ("ocean drop tank"), 2km south of the city centre. This small artificial lake, mentioned in the *Puranas*, is itself a place of great religious importance. Said to contain nectar, wine and water drawn from the world's most sacred rivers, the tank is the main bathing place both for pilgrims visiting the city and for the Lingaraj deity, who is taken to the pavilion in the middle once every year during Bhubaneswar's annual **Car Festival** (Ashokastami) for his ritual purificatory dip. The hours around sunrise and sunset are the most evocative time for a stroll here, when the residents of the nearby *dharamshalas* file through the smoky lanes to pray at the *ghats*.

Lingaraj Mandir

Immediately south of the Bindu Sagar stands the most stylistically evolved temple in all Orissa. Built early in the eleventh century by the Ganga kings, one hundred years before the Jagannath temple at Puri, the mighty **Lingaraj Mandir** has remained very much a living shrine. The small square in front of the main gateway still throngs with pilgrims clutching bananas and coconuts bought at the colourful stalls nearby to be offered as *prashad* to Tribhubaneshwara, the local deity. Foreign visitors cannot enter the temple, but there is a **viewing platform** overlooking the north wall, around the corner from the main entrance. From this vantage-point you can see all four of the principal sections of the building. The two nearest the entrance, the *bhoga-mandapa* (Hall of Offering) and the *nata mandir* (Hall of Dance, associated with the rise of the *devadasi* system – see p.1121) are both later additions to the complex. If you have binoculars you may just be able to pick out some of the beautiful **sculpture**, depicting the music and dance rituals that would once have taken place inside.

Even more than the huge *jagamohana*, loaded with fancy stonework, and the characteristic pyramidal roof, the immense 45-metre *deul* is the literal and aesthetic high point of the Lingaraj. Notice the rampant lion projecting from the curved sides of the tower, and the downtrodden elephant beneath him – again, the triumph of Hinduism over Buddhism. On the top, the typical Orissan motif of the flattened, ribbed sphere (*amla*) supported by gryphons, is crowned with Shiva's trident. As in the Brahmesvara temple, the long saffron pennant announces the living presence of the deity below.

The **shrine** inside is very unusual. The powerful 2.5-metre-thick Svayambhu (literally "self-born") *lingam* that it contains, one of the twelve *jyotrilinga* in India, is known as "Hari-Hara" because it is considered half Shiva, half Vishnu – an extraordinary amalgam that is thought to have resulted from the ascendancy of Vaishnavism over Shaivism in the twelfth and thirteenth centuries. Unlike other *linga*, which are bathed every day in a concoction prepared from hemlock, Svayambhu is offered a libation of rice, milk and *bhang* by the brahmins. Another peculiar feature of the shrine room is that it lacks a ceiling. Instead, the roof reaches right to the top of the tower.

Vaital Deul Mandir

Head left from the Lingaraj viewing platform and up the main street to **Vaital Deul**, one of the group's oldest buildings and a real feast of Tantric art. The temple was built in around 800 AD in a markedly different style from most of its contemporaries in Bhubaneswar, drawing heavily on earlier Buddhist influences (the south Indian-style tower, called *kakhara* after an Orissan pumpkin, resembles the distinctive *chaitya* arches found in rock-cut caves). Vaital Deul also boasts some very accomplished stonework. Among the panels of Hindu deities encrusting its outer walls, you may occasionally come across examples of some of India's earliest **erotic sculpture**, thought to catalogue positions used in the Tantric rituals that took place inside.

Once your eyes adjust to the darkness of the **interior**, or if you've brought a torch, you swiftly realize that this was no ordinary temple. Even if you missed the telltale post outside the entrance (a four-faced *lingam* used for tethering the sacrificial offerings), the grotesque images adorning the walls of the *jagamohana* graphically convey the macabre nature of the esoteric rites once performed here. Durga, in her most terrifying aspect as **Chamunda**, peers out of the half-light from behind the grille at the far end of the hall – her withered body, garlanded with skulls and flanked by an owl and a jackal, stands upon a rotting corpse. In front of her, to the right of the door, an even more nightmarish figure of a man picks himself up from the floor, having filled his skull-cup with blood from the decapitated body nearby. The whole gruesome frieze is littered with severed heads and jackals gnawing at corpses.

Around the town

The **Orissa State Museum**, in a large modern building at the top of Lewis Road (Tues–Sun 10am–5pm, entry times 10am–1pm & 2–4pm; Rs1), has a collection of "tribal" artefacts, illuminated manuscripts and various archeological finds. On display in the downstairs galleries are pieces of religious sculpture, including pre-twelfth-century Buddhist statues, coins and donative inscriptions on stone and copper plates salvaged from the city's temples. The upstairs rooms feature ethnographic material from indigenous Orissan societies. As well as heavy jewellery, musical instruments, weapons, tools and motheaten traditional costumes, there are reproductions of **chitra muriya**, the folk murals seen on walls and floors in village houses around Puri. The museum's real highlight, however, has to be its collection of antique **painting** and illuminated **palm-leaf manuscripts** (see p.1104). Only the National Museum in New Delhi holds finer examples of this traditional Orissan art form.

Hidden away on the northwestern edge of town, close to Baramunda bus stand on NH-5, is the Tribal Research Institute's anthropological **Museum of Man** (Mon–Sat 10am–5pm; free). The distinctive cultures and art of the 62 different tribal groups spread throughout Orissa, mostly in the southern hinterlands, are exhibited in a brand new complex of galleries. The garden outside is filled with the houses of the *adivarsi* groups portrayed here, and while most of the houses are over-idealized versions of the real thing, the murals decorating their walls are more authentic. Tucked behind the main institute building, a library holds an extensive and very dusty, but nonetheless fascinating, collection of all the books and journals ever compiled on the *adivasi* groups of Orissa.

The largest **cactus collection** in Asia (daily 10am–5pm; free) is housed on the opposite side of the highway to the Museum of Man, in Acharya Vihar. This state-funded initiative is a truly exotic foray into the little-known world of the cactus. Throughout the year, many of the 1050 types of cactus grown here are in bloom, a spectacular show of lurid colour mixes and prickly texture. The resident botanists will proudly show you unique hybrid varieties, and demonstrate experiments both on the plants and in their top-notch laboratories. They have recently discovered that the humble cactus can cure elephantiasis, a disease that causes huge swelling in the limbs and affects a great number of the paddy farmers across Orissa; this natural remedy has been tested with great success but has yet to hit the market.

Capital Market, situated in a residential area along Janpath, is the place to buy typical Orissan handlooms, handicrafts and jewellery. All the material shops claim to be the official government outlet, so the prices for lengths of beautifully woven cloth and ready-made garments are very competitive. Tucked in a corner of Unit Two East, next to a large fast-food joint, is a treasure-trove of tribal and village crafts and jewellery and materials, all at bargain prices. Ask to look in the dusty cupboards and you may well stumble across an antique mask or two.

Eating

Eating out in Bhubaneswar is basically limited to a choice between the predictable five-star food dished up in the a/c comfort of places such as the *Sishmo*, or the cheap and chilli-ful south Indian dishes served in the rather less salubrious cafes such as the *Vineeth* or the *Swosti*; both are opposite the railway station and open for breakfast. The one or two restaurants that make an effort to include traditional **Orissan cuisine** on their menus are worth seeking out (you will have to order at least eight hours in advance); seafood dishes combining prawns or delicate pomfret (a white fish) with rice, fresh vegetables, coconut, yoghurt and spices are common in the coastal villages, but you rarely see them in the city. One traditional delicacy you're sure to come across, however, is the **coconut milk** sold by street vendors – just make sure the straws are as fresh as the fruit. Look out for an Orissan speciality – yummy cheesecake stuffed with almonds.

Banjara, 109 Station Square. Smart interior and reasonable prices. Serves Indian and Chinese food, specializing in tandoori dishes.

Bhuvanashree, top of Station Square next to the *Jajati* hotel. Excellent, clean veg restaurant with some south Indian food, a choice of thalis and good coffee. Closed Tues.

Fahien, Mohini and **Parijat**, *OTDC Panthaniwas*, Lewis Road. *Fahien* and *Mohini* offer identical menus of standard Indian, Chinese and Western food; the former being the more comfortable. *Parijat* is south Indian; its unlimited breakfast buffet (6.30–9.30am) is undeniably good value at Rs15.

Hare Krishna, Janpath, just north of the junction with MG Road, entrance up a flight of stairs in a small market. Quite expensive, with waiters in dinner jackets rather than *dhotis*, but the food is strictly ISKCON-style (the Hare Krishna movement's unique cuisine, without garlic or onions): vegetarian and delicious.

Sishmo, *Sishmo Hotel*. High-quality food with unusual Indian dishes in classy surroundings. Pricey, but not as expensive as it looks.

Swosti, *Swosti Hotel*. Ultra-reliable place for good, moderately priced nosh, and authentic Orissan dishes, such as the mouthwatering *dahi machho* (river fish in yoghurt sauce).

Venus Inn, Cuttack Road. Very popular place serving up delicious south Indian fare.

Listings

Airlines Indian Airlines' main booking office is on Raj Path, near New Market (Mon–Fri 10am–5.30pm, bookings until 4.15pm; ☏0674/402380). Air India is on Janpath (☏0674/516668).

Banks and exchange The State Bank of India (Mon–Fri 10am–2pm, Sat 10am–noon) on Raj Path has an efficient foreign exchange counter and accepts all major currencies.

Bookshops The Modern Book Depot at the top of Station Square has a rack of pulp fiction. The Bookshop, across the square in Ashoka Market, stocks a wide range of Western literature, Indian literature in translation, as well as books on politics, religion and history.

Dance Visits or lessons can be arranged through the Orissa Dance Academy, 64 Kharwal Nagar, Unit 3. The Rabindra Mandap auditorium on Sachivalaya Marg (☏0674/417677) runs regular music, dance and drama events.

Internet access Com Cyber Tech, 1st floor, Ashoka Market Building, Station Square. Internet

use Rs3 per minute. Many places around the city offer email, but actually achieving access to Hotmail or Yahoo! is really a matter of chance here in Bhubaneswar.

Hospital The Capital Hospital and Homeopathic Clinic (☏0674/401983) is near the airport. For casualty, call ☏0674/400688. There's an Ayurvedic hospital between the *Panthaniwas* hotel and the Rameswara temple (☏0674/432347). For a Red Cross ambulance, call ☏0674/402389.

Music The *Sishmo* and *Meghdoot* stage regular performances of Indian classical music and *ghazals*.

Photography Unicolor Photo Lab, 133 Ashok Nagar, 1st floor, Janpath. Fotomakers, 28 West Tower, New Market.

Post office On the corner of Mahatma Gandhi Marg and Sachivalaya Marg (Mon–Fri 9am–5pm, Sat 9am–1pm). For poste restante ask at "enquiries" on the middle counter. A pan-wallah by the main entrance packs and seals parcels.

Police station Raj Path, near the State Bank of India (☏0674/401232).

Moving on from Bhubaneswar

Bhubaneswar is on the main Howrah–Chennai line with many trains passing through daily, including the Coromandel Express #2841/42. Also heading south, the weekly Guwahati–Cochin Express #5624 (Fri) and the twice-weekly Guwahati–Bangalore Express #5626 (Tues & Sun) call here. Trains to Delhi include the Rajdhani Express #2421 on Wed and Sun, and a daily service from Puri on either the New Delhi Express #2815 or the Neelachal Express #8475 (Tues, Fri & Sun). Trains to Calcutta include the Sri Jagannath Express #8410 and the Puri–Howrah Express #8008, both daily.

Orissa State Transport runs regular buses from Baramunda bus stand to Berhampur, Chilika, Cuttack, Konarak, Puri (every 20min) and Sambalpur. Interstate buses serve Calcutta, 480km away. You can pick up buses to Puri, Pipli and Cuttack from Jayadev Nagar opposite the *Kalinga Ashok* hotel, and from near the railway station. Minibuses run to Puri (Rs10 per person) as soon as they are full, but they become extremely overloaded and drive dangerously fast. There are regular Indian Airlines flights to Calcutta, Chennai, Delhi, Hyderabad and Mumbai.

See Travel Details at the end of this chapter for more information on journey frequencies and durations.

17

Around Bhubaneswar

A number of places around Bhubaneswar are worth combining with a day-trip to the city. Fifteen minutes by auto-rickshaw out of the centre, the second-century BC caves at **Khandagiri** and **Udaigiri** offer a glimpse of the region's history prior to the rise of Hinduism. **Dhauli**, just off the main road to Puri, boasts an even older monument: a rock edict dating from the Mauryan era, commemorating the battle of c.260 BC that gave the emperor Ashoka control of the eastern seaports, and thus enabled his missionaries to export the state religion across Asia. **Pipli**, 20km south, is famous for its appliqué work and colourful lampshades.

Udaigiri and Khandagiri caves

Six kilometres west of Bhubaneswar, beyond the leafy avenues of its exclusive suburbs, a pair of low hills rise from the coastal plain. More than two thousand years ago, caves chiselled out of their malleable yellow sandstone were home to a community of **Jain monks**. Nowadays, they lie virtually deserted, left for troupes of black-faced langur monkeys and occasional parties of tourists to clamber over. Though by no means in the same league as the caves of the Deccan, **Udaigiri** and **Khandagiri** (daily 8am–6pm; Rs5) rank, nevertheless, among Orissa's foremost historical monuments.

Inscriptions show that the **Chedi** dynasty, which ruled ancient Kalinga from the first century BC, was responsible for the bulk of the work. There are simple monk's cells for meditation and prayer, as well as royal chambers where the hallways, verandas and facades outside several caves are encrusted with **sculpture** depicting court scenes, lavish processions, hunting expeditions, battles, dances and a host of domestic details from the daily life of Kalinga's cool set. The later additions (from medieval times, when Jainism no longer enjoyed royal patronage in the region) are more austere, showing the twenty-four heroic Jain prophet-teachers, or *tirthankaras* ("crossing-makers").

Every year, Udaigiri and Khandagiri play host to a **sadhu convention**. For a week or so in late January, the caves and surrounding woodland are claimed by dozens of itinerant holy men, resplendent in their saffron robes and coiled dreadlocks, who gather on the hillside to intone verses from the **Gita** into crackly PA systems.

From Bhubaneswar, the caves are approached via a road that follows the route of an ancient **pilgrimage path** (leading, archeologists believe, to a now-vanished stupa). As you face the hills with the highway behind you, Khandagiri ("Broken Hill") is on your left and Udaigiri ("Sunrise Hill") on your right. It's best to begin with the latter, which has the finest of the early stonework.

Udaigiri

The **Udaigiri** caves occupy a fairly compact area around the south slope of the hill. **Cave 1** (Rani Gumpha or "Queen's Cave"), off the main pathway to the right, is the largest and most impressive of the group. A long frieze across the back wall shows rampaging elephants, panicking monkeys, sword fights and the abduction of a woman, perhaps illustrating episodes from the life of Kalinga's King Kharavela. **Caves 3** and **4** contain sculptures of a lion holding its prey and elephants with snakes wrapped around them, and pillars topped by pairs of peculiar winged animals. **Cave 9**, up the hill and around to the right, houses a damaged relief of figures worshipping a long-vanished Jain symbol. The crowned figure is thought to be the Chedi king, Vakradeva, whose donative inscription can still be made out near the roof. Inside the sleeping cells of all the caves, deep grooves in

Orissan art and artists

Few regions of India retain as rich a diversity of traditional art forms as Orissa. While a browse through the bazaars and emporia in Puri and Bhubaneswar provides a good idea of local styles and techniques, a trip out to the villages where the work is actually produced is a much more memorable way to shop. On the whole, different villages specialize in different crafts – a division that harks back to the origins of the caste system in Orissa. Patronage from the nobility and wealthy temples during medieval times allowed local artisans, or *shilpins*, to refine their skills over generations. As the market for arts and crafts' expanded, notably with the rise of Puri as a pilgrimage centre, guilds were formed to control the handing down of specialist knowledge and separate communities established to carry out the work. Today, the demand for souvenirs, particularly easily transportable ones, has given many old art forms a new lease of life.

• **Stone sculpture** With modern temples increasingly being built out of reinforced concrete, life for Orissa's stone sculptors is getting tougher. Nevertheless, the work of a few small communities remains on a par with that of their illustrious forebears at Konarak and Bhubaneswar. At Lalitgiri, the Buddhist monument northeast of Cuttack, families of sculptors claim to own tools used by their ancestors to build the eighth- and ninth-century monasteries nearby. In the Santal villages near Lulung, in the Simlipal National Park, they have lately had to diversify from stone phalluses to pressure cookers to stay in business. However, in Pathuria Sahi ("Stonecarvers' Lane") and the famous Sudarshan Workshop in Puri, master-craftsmen and apprentices still fashion Hindu deities and other votive objects according to specifications laid down in ancient manuals.

• **Painting** *Patta chitra*, classical Orissan painting, is closely connected with the Jagannath cult. Traditionally, artists were employed to decorate the inside of the temples in Puri and to paint the deities and chariots used in the Rath Yatra. Later, the same vibrant colour schemes and motifs were transferred to lacquered cloth or palm leaves and sold as sacred souvenirs to visiting pilgrims. In the village of Raghurajpur near Puri, where the majority of the remaining artists, or *chitrakaras*, now live, business is still booming. Outside each house, young men sit painting, surrounded by coconut shells of the special paint, all made from the powders of local mineral stones. It was here that the much-lauded artist Silpaguru Mohapatra (1919–98) refined the previously crude technique of *Patta Chitra* painting to produce painstakingly detailed depictions of Hindu mythology. Specialities include devotional images of Lord Jagannath, scenes from the *Gita Govinda* and sets of gan-jiffa – small round cards used to play a trick-taking game based on the struggle between Rama and the demon Ravana, as told in the *Ramayana*.

• **Palm-leaf manuscripts** Palm leaves, or *chitra pothi*, have been used as writing materials in Orissa for centuries, and the basic techniques have changed little. Using a sharp stylus called a *lohankantaka*, the artist first scratches the text or design onto the surface of palm leaves, then applies a paste of turmeric, dried leaves, oil and charcoal. When the residue is rubbed off, the etching stands out more clearly. On many, palm-leaf flaps are tied onto the structure so an innocent etching of an

the stone wall at the back and in the floor were specially designed to carry rainwater down from the roof as an early air-conditioning system.

To reach **Cave 10**, return to the main steps and climb towards the top of the hill. Its popular name, Ganesh Gumpha, is not derived from the elephants in front of the cave, but from the appearance of the elephant-headed Ganesh on the rear wall of the cell on the right. From here, follow the path up to the ledge at the very top of Udaigiri Hill for good views and the ruins of an old **chaitya hall**. This was probably the main place of worship for the Jain monks who lived

animal or deity can be lifted to reveal *Kamasutra* action. Some scholars claim that the rounded Oriya script may have developed to cope with the problems of writing on palm leaves, the straight lines of other Indian languages being more likely to pierce the leaf. Today, *Patta Chitra* artists in **Raghurajpur** bind strips of palm leaves together to make canvases, and in the **Raghunandan Library** in Puri students diligently copy old manuscripts to sell to tourists. The best places to see genuine antique palm-leaf books, however, are the national museum in New Delhi or the state museum in Bhubaneswar.

• **Textiles** Distinctive textiles woven on handlooms are produced throughout Orissa. Silk saris from **Berhampur** and **Sambalpur** are the most famous, combining bands of rich colours and brocade with traditional geometric and figurative designs, though **ikat**, which originally came to Orissa via the ancient trade links with Southeast Asia, is also typical. It is created using a tie-dye-like technique known as *bandha* in which bundles of thread are wrapped and dyed in different colours, and the pattern emerges automatically when they are woven together. The same principle is employed by weavers from the village of **Nuapatna**, 70km from Bhubaneswar, who produce silk *ikats* covered in verses from the scriptures for use in the Jagannath temple.

• **Appliqué** The village of **Pipli** (see p.1107), between Bhubaneswar and Puri, has the monopoly on appliqué, another craft rooted in the Jagannath cult. Geometric motifs and stylized birds, animals and flowers are cut out of brightly coloured cloth and sewn onto black backgrounds. Pipli artists are responsible for the chariot covers used in the Rath Yatra as well as for the small canopies, or *chhatris*, suspended above the presiding deity in Orissan temples. These days, the more entrepreneurial among them are turning their hands to garish secular goods, with wall-hangings, bedspreads, lampshades, handbags, beach brollies and heart-shaped shields (*tarasa*) among the current favourites.

• **Metalwork** *Tarakashi* (literally "woven wire"), or silver filigree, is Orissa's best-known metalwork technique. Using lengths of wire made by drawing strips of silver alloy through small holes, the smiths create distinctive ornaments, jewellery and utensils for use in rituals and celebrations. The designs are thought to have come to India from Persia with the Moghuls, though the existence of an identical art form in Indonesia, with whom the ancient Orissan kingdoms used to trade, suggests that the technique itself may be even older. *Tarakashi* is now only produced in any quantity in **Cuttack** and it's becoming a dying art form, thanks to a preference among Hindus for gold jewellery rather than silver, and a reluctance on the part of the artisans to change their designs with the times.

• **Dhokra** The *dhokra* (lost-wax) metal-casting technique practised by *adivasi* communities in Mayurbhunj and Keonjhar districts has done very well out of the recent revival of interest in "ethnic" art. You can spot *dhokra* objects – usually figurines depicting animals or tribal deities – by the distinctive woven-wire patterns that are used to decorate them. The effect is achieved by adding threads to the original wax image, before it is covered with a clay mould which is then filled with molten metal.

below and may even once have housed the legendary **Kalinga Jina**, a kind of votive cult object-cum-Holy Grail that Kharavela recovered after it had been removed by the King of Magadha (south Bihar).

Below the ruins are **Cave 12**, shaped like the head of a tiger, and **Cave 14**, the Hathi Gumpha, known for the long **inscription** in ancient Magadhi carved onto its overhang. This relates in glowing terms the life history of King Kharavela, whose exploits, both on and off the battlefield, brought in the fortune needed to finance the cave excavation. Guides take great delight in pointing out the hole in the rear wall that they insist was "the queen's shitting place" – scatological conjecture perhaps, but the channels next to it do seem to lead from ruined reservoirs on the hill above.

Khandagiri

The caves on the opposite hill, **Khandagiri**, can be reached either by the long flight of steps leading from the road, just up from the main entrance to the Udaigiri caves, or by cutting directly across from Hathi Gumpha via the steps that drop down from Cave 17. The latter route brings you out at **Caves 1** and **2**, known as Tatowa Gumpha ("Parrot Caves") for the carvings of birds on their doorway-arches. Cave 2, excavated in the first century BC, is the larger and more interesting. On the back wall of one of its cells, a few faint lines in red *Brahmi* script are thought to have been scrawled two thousand years ago by a monk practising his handwriting. The reliefs in **Cave 3**, the Ananta Gumpha ("Snake Cave") – serpents decorate the doorways – contain the best of the sculpture on Khandagiri hill, albeit badly vandalized in places. **Caves 7** and **8**, left of the main steps, were former sleeping quarters, remodelled in the eleventh century as sanctuaries. Both house reliefs of *tirthankaras* on their walls as well as Hindu deities which had become part of the Jain pantheon by the time conversion work was done. **Cave 9**, the last of any real note, was also reconverted in medieval times. It too contains *tirthankaras*, though only the three standing images of Rishabanatha (in black chlorite stone) are any good.

From the nineteenth-century **Jain temple** at the top of the hill there are clear views across the sprawl of Bhubaneswar to the white dome of Dhauli.

Dhauli

The gleaming, white **Vishwa Shanti Stupa** on **Dhauli Hill**, 8km south of Bhubaneswar on the Pipli road, was built by Japanese Buddhists in 1972. It overlooks the spot where the Mauryan emperor **Ashoka** defeated the Kalingas in the decisive battle of 265 BC, and slightly eclipses the older memorial stupa. Apart from bringing the prosperous Orissan kingdom to its knees, the victory also led the emperor, allegedly overcome by remorse at having slain 150,000 people, to renounce the path of violent conquest in favour of the spiritual path preached by Gautama Buddha. Ever since, there has been a unique tradition in Orissa for its military leaders to construct a place of worship as a symbol of kinship and victory rather than a fort, as was the custom in Rajasthan and Maharashtra, for example. The stupa at Dhauli is a memorial to Ashoka's legendary change of heart. Panels around the sides illustrate episodes from the life of the emperor (below) and the Buddha (above), while the umbrella-like projections on the top symbolize the five cardinal Buddhist virtues of faith, hope, compassion, forgiveness and nonviolence.

After his enlightened realization, Ashoka set about promoting the maxims of his newly found faith in **rock edicts** installed at key sites around the empire (see History in Contexts). One such inscription, in ancient **Brahmi**, the ancestor of all non-Islamic Indian scripts, still stands on the roadside at the foot of Dhauli Hill. The translation gives some idea of its contents: a typically colourful mixture of rambling philosophical asides, discourses on animal rights and tips on how to treat your slaves. The Dhauli edict also includes the famous "All men are my children . . ." line, but diplomatically omits the account that crops up elsewhere describing how many Kalingas Ashoka had put to the sword before he finally "saw the light".

Alongside the stupa there's a recently renovated Shiva temple – the **Dhabaleshwara Mandir**. The terrace on top of Dhauli Hill offers great **views** of the geometrically patterned rice fields, especially through the early morning mists.

If you don't have your own vehicle and are not on a tour, **getting to Dhauli** involves a two-kilometre walk. Ask to be dropped off the bus at Dhauli Chowk, the junction on the main Puri–Bhubaneswar road, and make your way along the avenue of cashew trees to the rock edict. The road to the stupa begins its short climb up the hill here, ending at a small car park surrounded by postcard and chai stalls.

Pipli

Fifteen minutes or so beyond Dhauli, on the Puri road, splashes of bright colour in the shop fronts ranged alongside the main street announce your arrival in **PIPLI**, Orissa's **appliqué** capital (see box p.1105). Much of what the artisans produce here nowadays on their hand-powered sewing machines is shoddy kitsch compared with the painstaking work traditionally undertaken for the Jagannath temple. The shops do not open early; the best time to wander around is in the evening when gas lamps, lots of devotional music and gentle bargaining make the experience much more atmospheric. Express enough interest, though, and you'll be shown some of the better-quality pieces for which Pipli is justly famed. Bedspreads, wall-hangings and small *chhatris* (awnings normally hung above household and temple shrines) are about the most authentic goods on offer – though who's to say Lord Jagannath doesn't use letter-holders and napkins.

Puri and around

A true-hearted pilgrim does not fear to measure kingdoms with his feeble footsteps.

Old Hindu saying

As the state's premier temple town, **PURI** is swathed in an aura of mysticism and frenetic pilgrim activity. It is the site of the famous **Jagannath temple** – which soars out of the narrow packed streets and colonial suburbs like some kind of misplaced space rocket – as well as the location of one of India's most spectacular religious festivals, the annual **Rath Yatra**. Puri is engaging outside festival times too, with the fanatical devotion to the daily needs of Lord Jagannath, and the mass of wonderfully creative commercial celebrations of the deity, including rickshaw hoods, puppets and beedi packets. The town emerged remarkably unscathed from the 1999 cyclone (see box p.1119), which is all the more incredible if you have just driven past the environmental devastation along the coastal road between Puri and Konnark.

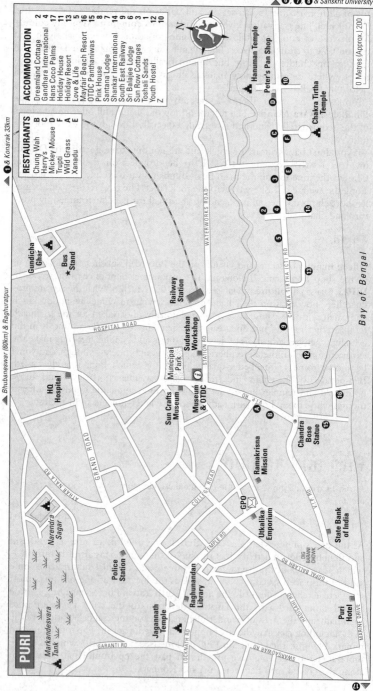

PURI

◀ Bhubaneswar (60km) & Raghuratpur

◀ Markandesvara Tank

Narendra Sagar

Jagannath Temple

Raghunandan Library

Police Station

HQ Hospital

Gundicha Ghar

★ Bus Stand

Railway Station

Sudarshan Workshop

Sun Crafts Museum

Museum & OTDC

Municipal Park

Ramakrisna Mission

GPO

Utkalika Emporium

Chandra Bose Statue

State Bank of India

Puri Hotel

Hanuman Temple

Peter's Pan Shop

Chakra Tirtha Temple

Bay of Bengal

▲ ❶ & Konarak 33km

▲ ❻, ❼, ❽ & Sanskrit University

GARANTI RD
LOCKNATH RD
ATHARA NALA RD
GRAND ROAD
TEMPLE RD
COLLEGE ROAD
HOSPITAL ROAD
STATION RD
WATERWORKS ROAD
CHAKRA TIRTHA (CT) RD
VIP RD
GOPAL BALLABH RD
HARIDASHPUR RD
SWARGADWAR RD
MARINE DRIVE
BADANI CHOWK

N

0 Metres (Approx.) 200

RESTAURANTS

Chung Wah	B
Harry's	C
Mickey Mouse	D
Trupti	F
Wild Grass	A
Xanadu	E

ACCOMMODATION

Dreamland Cottage	2
Gandhara International	4
Hans Coco Palms	17
Holiday House	11
Holiday Resort	13
Love & Life	5
Mayfair Beach Resort	16
OTDC Panthaniwas	15
Pink House	8
Santana Lodge	7
Shankar International	14
South East Railway	9
Sri Balajee Lodge	6
Sun Row Cottages	3
Toshali Sands	1
Youth Hostel	12
Z	10

Three distinct types of visitors come to Puri: middle-class Bengalis lured by the combined pleasures of the promenade and a puja in the nearby temple; young Western and Japanese visitors keen to discover Puri's small **travellers' scene**; and the thousands of pilgrims who flock in to worship Lord Jagannath. Over the years the three have staked out their respective ends of town and stuck to them. It all makes for a rather bizarre and intoxicating atmosphere, where you can be transported from the maelstrom of religious devotion to the sea and back to the relative calm of your hotel veranda at the turn of a bicycle wheel.

Puri **town** isn't particularly attractive – a mixture of pastiches of colonial buildings and new multistorey hotels – but the palm trees and lack of traffic make for a laid-back atmosphere. The travellers' scene here is relatively mellow – no techno raves or beach parties, and everything shuts down early – but it has a charm of its own and a certain timelessness. The town **beach** is pretty grim and becoming increasingly swallowed up by new hotels, but it's easy to cycle or walk to cleaner stretches.

Some history

The early history of Puri, before its rise to prominence as a Hindu religious centre, is rather obscure. It's known that the surrounding forests were once the territory of the Sabaras, a pre-Aryan group, and that the sacred Buddhist site of **Dantapura** ("town of the tooth"), where one of the Buddha's teeth was enshrined, may also have been here, but few traces of these ancient times have survived.

Until the seventh and eighth centuries, Puri was little more than a provincial outpost along the coastal trade route linking eastern India with the south. Then, thanks to its association with the Hindu reformer **Shankaracharya** (Shankara), the town began to feature on the religious map. Shankara made Puri one of his four *mathas*, or centres for the practice of a radically new, and more ascetic form of Hinduism. Holy men came here to debate the new philosophies – a tradition carried on in the town's temple courtyards to this day. With the arrival of the **Gangas** at the beginning of the twelfth century, this religious and political importance was further consolidated. In 1135, Anantavarman Chodaganga founded the great temple in Puri, and dedicated it to **Purushottama**, one of the thousand names of Vishnu – an ambitious attempt to integrate the many feudal kingdoms recently conquered by the Gangas. Under the Gajapati dynasty in the fifteenth century Purushottama's name changed to **Jagannath** ("Lord of the Universe"). Henceforth **Vaishnavism** and the devotional worship of Krishna, an incarnation of Vishnu, was to hold sway as the predominant religious influence in the temple. Puri is nowadays one of the four most auspicious pilgrimage centres, or *dhams*, in India. It's impossible to estimate the exact number of people who travel here each year, but in high season as many as five thousand pour daily through the bus and railway stations, while during the annual *Rath Yatra* or "Car Festival", the population temporarily swells to nearly a million.

By comparison, Western-style leisure **tourism**, centred firmly on the town's long sandy beach, is a new phenomenon. The British were the first to spot Puri's potential as a resort. When they left, the Bengalis took over their bungalows, only to find themselves sharing the beach with an annual migration of young, *chillum*-smoking Westerners attracted to the town by its abundant hashish. Today, few vestiges of this era remain. Thanks to a concerted campaign by the municipality to clean up Puri's image, the "scene" has dwindled to little more than a handful of cafés, and is a far cry from the swinging hippy paradise some still arrive here hoping to find. The current spate of hotel development, mostly multistorey concrete edifices rising high above the surrounding palm trees, has further affected the ambience.

Arrival, information and city transport

Trains arriving at Puri's end-of-line **station**, in the north of town, are greeted by fired-up cycle rickshaw-wallahs sprinting alongside in the race to catch a foreigner. You'll encounter similar "rickshaw rage" at the main bus station and the Jagannath temple, caused by competition for the commission offered by the aggressively touting hotels. The bus stand is further in the north of the city, a ten-minute rickshaw ride from the centre through the bumpy back-streets.

The OTDC **tourist office** on Station Road (Mon–Sat 10am–5pm, closed 2nd Sat of the month; ☎06752/22664) is friendly and helpful; the 24-hour counter at the railway station is a waste of time. Train travel arrangements are best made or checked directly with the station itself or else through a travel agent.

Puri is fairly spread out but flat, so **bicycles** (approximately Rs15 per day) are ideal for getting around and exploring the maze of streets around the Jagannath temple. There are several places to rent them on Chakra Tirtha (CT) Road, in the travellers' enclave. **Auto-rickshaws** are thin on the ground, though one or two are always hanging around the railway station. **Mopeds** (Rs150 per day) and Enfield **motorbikes** (Rs250 per day) are rented out by a couple of travel agents and shops along CT Road for full or half-days and are useful for trips up the coast to Konarak. In-house **travel agents** at the larger hotels can help with all transport arrangements, though the most reliable all-round place for ticket booking, flights and car/motorcycle/bike rental is Heritage Tours, based at the *Mayfair Beach Resort* (☎06752/23656).

Accommodation

Virtually all Puri's **hotels** stand on or near the beach, where a strict distinction is observed: the hotels pitched at domestic tourists are lined up behind Marine Drive, the promenade on the west end of the beach, while budget-conscious Westerners are sandwiched further east between the high-rise, upmarket resort hotels and the fishing village. This latter district around CT Road, known as **Pentakunta**, has become a real backpacker enclave, with numerous identikit hotels offering dorms, simple doubles, hot water and midget verandas. The less expensive hotels are quiet during the summer months, but the pricier accommodation tends to be booked solid well in advance over Rath Yatra, which coincides with the Bengali holiday season – make reservations as early as possible. Checkout is 8am for all hotels in Puri due to the influx of early trains on the town, although in the monsoon period this rule is less rigidly enforced.

Dreamland Cottage, off CT Road
☎06752/24122. Not exactly roses around the door, but homely and relaxed, with a leafy secluded garden dotted with birdcages. Five rooms all with attached bath, but no a/c. ❶

Gandhara International, CT Road
☎06752/24623. Good value for the budget traveller, with cheap clean rooms and dorms (Rs40) around a courtyard, and a new upmarket block

behind with a/c rooms, hot showers and TV. Two roof terraces and a restaurant serving authentic Japanese food on request. Internet, travel service and free poste restante also avaliable. ❷–❻

Hans Coco Palms, Marine Drive ☎06752/22638. Modern complex in a superb setting 2km west of the centre; all rooms overlook the sea and the beach is pleasant here. Central a/c, bar and restaurant. ❹–❽

Holiday House, CT Road ☎ 06752/23782. Clinical but comfortable Western-style hotel with 44 rooms, some with balconies overlooking the beach; its restaurant is not recommended. ❸–❹

Holiday Resort, CT Road ☎ 06752/22440. Somewhat incongruous five-storey hotel, but it's clean and well maintained with a good restaurant, beach access and a large lawn. All rooms have huge beds, TV and a sea view. ❻–❼

Love and Life, CT Road ☎ 06752/24433. Popular with the many young Japanese visitors to Puri, with an easy-going atmosphere and a good restaurant. The clean rooms all have an attached bath, and are either in the main block or in cottages in the garden. The dorm is Rs30 per bed. ❷–❺

Mayfair Beach Resort, off CT Road ☎ 06752/24041. Luxury chalets and rooms looking down through palm trees to a pool and the beach. Five-star facilities, including a massage parlour, a bar and an excellent restaurant. Recommended. ❽–❾

OTDC Panthaniwas, off CT Road ☎ 06752/22562. A good-value hotel; some of the plain but spacious rooms catch sea breezes; the old Raj-era building has more atmosphere. There is a pleasant restaurant, a bar and children's playground. ❺–❽

Pink House, off CT Road right on the beach ☎ 06752/22253. Laid-back, pinky-red pad, at the edge of the fishing village with its very own travellers' scene and an adjacent restaurant. ❶–❷

Santana Lodge, at the very end of CT Road ☎ 06752/23491. Small, pleasant hotel geared up for travellers; especially popular with the

Japanese. Prices include breakfast and communal dinner. ❶–❷

Sri Balajee Lodge, CT Road ☎ 06752/23388. Some way beyond most of the other hotels, this small lodge has simple rooms around a colourful courtyard. ❷–❹

Sun Row Cottages, CT Road, just past *Gandhara International* ☎ 06752/23259. Little cottages, each with a private veranda, big cane chairs and attached bath. Current renovations will improve the facilities. Rent becomes cheaper for a longer stay. ❶–❷

Shankar International, off CT Road ☎ 06752/22696. Slightly old-fashioned, though well run, with rooms at assorted prices on three floors, sea views and a lawn with wicker chairs. ❸–❺

South Eastern Railway Hotel, CT Road ☎ 06752/22063. Nothing has changed here since it was the premier bolt-hole for Calcutta's *burra-* and *memsahibs*. Turbaned bearers with big belts pad barefoot around the wide verandas; some of the rooms even have two bathrooms, one Western-style, the other Indian. A must for Raj-ophiles, even if only for dinner. ❻

Toshali Sands, Konarak Road ☎ 06752/23571. Self-styled "ethnic village" 9km north of town, consisting of a/c cottages grouped around a garden and pool. Good restaurant, gym and sauna; ideal for families. ❽–❾

Youth Hostel, off CT Road ☎ 06752/22424. Segregated dorms (Rs40) with three, seven or ten beds, and an 11pm curfew. There's a camping area and parking for vehicles. ❶

Pandas

Few non-Hindu visitors to Puri are aware of the world of the **yatri panda**, or "pilgrimage priest". The *panda*'s job is basically to "look after" the pilgrims during their stay: to fix them up with board and lodging, to make sure they take in all the sites in the correct order, and, as brahmins, to offer prayers for them at the temple. In return, the pilgrims are expected to leave a generous goodbye tip, or **bidagi**, when they leave. Apart from bringing "good luck" in the next life, the *bidagi* system is also, needless to say, highly lucrative for the *pandas*.

No surprise then that each *panda*, and the *dharamshala* to which he is connected, holds his own exclusive rights to the rich pickings. Every town and village in the country is carved up according to long-established links recorded in special **ledgers**. The first thing the *pandas* have to ascertain from the new arrivals, therefore, is their place of birth, family name and caste. Once these are established, the pilgrims are ushered from the station back to the appropriate *dharamshala* and shown the records of visits made by previous generations from their village or family. Woe betide anyone who tries to poach clients. When they're not relieving hapless *yatris* of their rupees or indulging in that time-honoured Puri tradition of drinking *bhang* (a sugar and milk-based preparation containing ground cannabis leaves), *pandas* spend their days **wrestling** in Puri's old-style gyms.

Z, CT Road ☎ 06752/22554. An institution, the *Z* (pronounced "jed") made its name by providing cheap, clean and comfortable rooms. Prices are higher now, but the rooms are still pleasant and there are plenty of communal areas, including a large garden and a common room with TV. Women-only dorm (Rs60) also available. ❷–❹

The Jagannath temple

The mighty **Jagannath temple** in Puri is one of the four holy *dhams*, or "abodes of the divine", drawing pilgrims, or *yatris*, here to spend three auspicious days and nights near Lord Jagannath, the presiding deity. The present temple structure, modelled on the older Lingaraj temple in Bhubaneswar, was erected by the Ganga ruler Anantavarman Chodaganga, at the start of the twelfth century.

Non-Hindu visitors, despite the temple's long-standing "caste no bar" rule, are obliged to view proceedings from the flat roof of the **Raghunandan Library** (Mon–Sat 10am–noon & 4–8pm), directly opposite the main gate. One of the librarians, wielding a long stick to fend off the monkeys, will show you up the stairs via their collection of dusty tomes and **palm-leaf manuscripts**, to the vantage point overlooking the East Gate. You should make a donation for this service – but don't believe the large sums written in the ledger.

From the rooftop you have a fine view of the immense **deul**, at 65m by far the loftiest building in the entire region. Archeologists have removed the white plaster from the tower to expose elaborate **carving** similar to that on the Lingaraj. Crowning the very top, a long scarlet pennant and the eight-spoked wheel (*chakra*) of Vishnu announce the presence of Lord Jagannath within.

The pyramidal roofs of the temples' adjoining halls, or *mandapas*, rise in steps towards the tower like a ridge of mountain peaks. The one nearest the sanctuary, the *jagamohana* (Assembly Hall), is part of the original building, but the other two, the smaller *nata mandir* (Dance Hall) and the *bhoga-mandapa* (Hall of Offerings) nearest the entrance, were added in the fifteenth and sixteenth centuries. These halls still see a lot of action during the day as worshippers file through for *darshan*, while late every night they become the venue for devotional music. Female and transvestite dancers (*maharis* and *gotipuras*) once performed episodes from Jayadev's *Gita Govinda*, the much-loved story of the life of Krishna, for the amusement of the Lord Jagannath, his brother Balabhadra and sister Subhadra. Nowadays, piped songs have replaced the reverential dramatics.

Outside the main building, in the walled compound surrounding the temple, stand dozens of subsidiary shrines that the pilgrims can also honour during their visit. Nearby, on the left of the enclosure, are the **kitchens**. The food prepared here, known as *mahaprashad*, is blessed by Lord Jagannath himself before being eaten. It's said to be so pure that even a morsel taken from the mouth of a dog and fed to a brahmin by a Harijan (an "untouchable") will cleanse the body of sin. Everywhere, devotees mill around carrying pieces of broken pots full of dhal and rice; they can only offer food to the deity from an imperfect pot as Lord Jagannath is the only perfection in this world. Among the ten thousand or so daily recipients of the *mahaprashad* are the six thousand employees of the temple itself. These **servants** are divided into 96 hereditary and hierarchical orders known as *chhatisha niyoga*, and include the priests who minister to the needs of the deities (teeth cleaning, dressing, feeding, getting them ready for afternoon siesta, and so forth), as well as the teams of craftspeople who produce all the materials required for the daily round of rituals.

Stand on any street corner in Orissa and you'd be hard pushed not to spot at least one image of the black-faced **Jagannath deity**, with his brother **Balabhadra** and sister **Subhadra**. This faintly grotesque family trio, with glaring eyes, stumpy legless bodies, and undersized arms protruding menacingly from heavily garlanded heads, seems to crop up everywhere – from buses and cycle rickshaws, to *bidi* wrappers and bags of nuts.

The origins of this peculiar national symbol are shrouded in **legend**. One version relates that the image of Lord Jagannath looks the way it does because it was never actually finished. King Indramena, a ruler of ancient Orissa, once found the god Vishnu in the form of a tree stump washed up on Puri beach. After performing all the necessary prostrations, he carried the lump of wood to the temple and, following instructions from Brahma, called the court carpenter Visvakarma to carve out the image. Visvakarma agreed to perform the task on condition that no one so much as set eyes on the deity until it was completed. The king, however, unable to contain his excitement, peeped through a crack in the door of the carpenter's workshop during the night to see how the job was progressing. Visvakarma spotted him, downed tools just as he had promised and cast a spell on the deity so that no one else could finish it.

These days, new versions have to be produced about every twelve years (they rot in the humidity) by specially trained temple priests in a sacred ceremony known as **Nava Kalebara**, literally "new embodiment". The culmination of this highly secret, nocturnal ritual takes place when the "divine essence" of the old Lord Jagannath is removed from his hollowed-out chest and placed inside that of the new incumbent.

The Jagannath deities are also the chief focus of Puri's annual "Car Festival", the **Rath Yatra**. For a couple of weeks in midsummer, the town is saturated with visitors who come to witness the procession of the colossal Jagannath chariots, or *raths*, down Puri's Grand Road. Rath Yatra is just one episode in a long cycle of rituals that begins in the full moon phase of the Oriya month of Djesto (June & July). In

A good place to sample the atmosphere of the temple is in front of the main gate on the east side. The elaborate doorway is usually jammed with groups of *yatris*, some newly alighted from special buses, others making their way barefoot through the crowds from nearby *dharamshalas*. In front of the gateway, its base splashed with vermilion and flowers, is a **column** that once stood before the Surya temple in Konarak. It was brought here in the eighteenth century by the Maharathas and is topped by a figure of Aruna, the charioteer of the sun god.

Around the temple

The crowded streets **around the Jagannath temple** are buzzing with activity – commercial as much as religious. **Grand Road**, Puri's broad main thoroughfare, is lined with a frenetic **bazaar**, many of its stalls specializing in *rudraksha malas* (Shaivite "rosaries" made of 108 beads), Ayurvedic cures and the ubiquitous images of Lord Jagannath. Look out too for the wonderful "religious maps" of Puri. Hindu mythology traditionally represents the pilgrimage site in the form of a conch shell made up of seven concentric layers, with the deities' platform as the innermost core and the outer third under the sea. Not much help for finding your way around, but a superb souvenir.

Leading south from the main square in the temple surrounds, the dingy **Swargadwar** ("Cremation") **Road** plunges you into a world of acrid smells,

the first of these, the **Chandan Yatra**, special replicas of the three temple deities are taken to the **Narendra Sagar** where for 21 consecutive days they are smeared with *chandan* (sandalwood paste) and rowed around in a ceremonial, swan-shaped boat. At the end of this period, in a ceremony known as **Snana Yatra**, the three go for a dip in the tank, after which they head off for fifteen days of secluded preparation for Rath Yatra.

The Car Festival proper takes place during the full moon of the following month, Asadho (July & Aug). Lord Jagannath and his brother and sister are placed in their chariots and dragged by 4200 honoured devotees through the assembled multitudes to their summer home, the **Gundicha Ghar** ("Garden House"), 1.5km away. If you can find a secure vantage point and escape the crush, it's an amazing sight. The immense chariots are draped with brightly coloured cloth and accompanied down Grand Road by elephants, the local raja (who sweeps the chariots as a gesture of humility and equality with all castes) and a cacophony of music and percussion. Each has a different name and a different-coloured cover, and is built anew every year to rigid specifications laid down in the temple's ancient manuals. Balabhadra's *rath*, the green one, leads; Subhadra is next, in black; and lastly, in the thirteen-metre-tall chariot with eighteen wheels and a vivid red and yellow drape, sits Lord Jagannath himself. It takes eight hours or more to haul the *raths* to their resting place. After a nine-day holiday, the sequence is performed in reverse, and the three deities return to the temple to resume their normal lives.

Conventional wisdom has it that the procession commemorates Krishna's journey from Gokhul to Matheran; historians cite the similarity between the *raths* and temple towers to claim it's a hangover from the time when temples were made of wood. Whatever the reason for the Car Festival, its devotees take it very seriously indeed. Early travellers spoke of fanatics throwing themselves under the gigantic wheels as a short cut to eternal bliss (whence the English word "**Juggernaut**", meaning an "irresistible, destructive force"). Contemporary enthusiasts are marginally more restrained, but like most mass gatherings in India the whole event teeters at times on the brink of complete mayhem.

tea stalls and heaps of oily sweets swarming with flies. For most of the day the entire length of the lane is lined with beggars sitting in front of rice and ten-paise coins tossed by passing pilgrims. You're also likely to see bare-chested brahmins from the temple performing their ablutions, sacred threads tucked safely over their ears to preserve purity (the ear is the purest part of the body in Hinduism, being associated with the source of the Ganges). Keep going down Swargadwar Road for long enough and you eventually surface to the glaring sunshine and sea breezes of the main promenade. The cremation ground itself, situated well beyond the south corner of the beach, is among India's most auspicious mortuary sites. Inquisitive tourists, especially those wielding cameras, are definitely not welcome.

A more enjoyable foray from the main square is the trip up to the **sacred tanks** in the north of town (best attempted by bicycle). Follow the north wall of the Jagannath temple up to the little road junction in the far corner, then turn right and stick to the same narrow twisting backstreet for about a kilometre until you arrive at the **Markandesvara tank**. This large, steep-sided bathing place is said to have been the spot where Vishnu once resided in the form of a *neem* tree while his temple was buried deep under a sand dune. There's no sign of the tree, but the temples on the south side are worth a look, particularly the smaller of the group, which contains images of the Jagannath trio.

If you retrace your route from here back down the lane as far as the first road junction, then bear left and continue for another kilometre or so, you'll emerge at the **Narendra Sagar**, Puri's most holy tank. A small temple stands in the middle, joined to the *ghats* by a narrow footbridge. During the annual **Chandan Yatra** (swimming festival), a replica deity of Lord Jagannath, Mandan Mohan, is brought here every day for his dip. The temple itself is plastered with vivid **murals** that you can photograph on payment of the set fee listed nearby. The list also advertises the range of services offered by the temple *pujaris*, including the unlikely sounding "throw of bone" and "throw of hair" – references to the tank's role as another of Puri's famous mortuary ritual sites.

Museums and the Sudarshan workshop

The **Sun Crafts Museum** (daily 10am–6pm; free), on the crossroads of VIP Road and Station Road, is an intriguing little foray into the more commercial side of the Lord Jagannath phenomenon. Run by a Hare Krishna devotee, this museum is an extensive collection of every kitsch interpretation of the deity and his siblings. There is also a workshop where countless little wooden versions are painstakingly painted, stone is carved and garish outfits are made to dress the gods. These are sent off to ISKON centres around the world. The museum also has the sole remaining copy of a very controversial interpretation of Lord Jagannath mounted on the centre of a Christian crucifix. This was a symbolic demand for religious tolerance in light of growing hostility between Hindus and Christians in Orissa recently. If you ask, the crucifix will be discreetly shown to you.

Puri's small **museum** (Tues–Sun 10am–5pm; free), tucked away above the tourist office on Station Road, houses tacky reproductions of the Jagannath deities' ceremonial garb, along with models of the *raths* used in the Car Festival. You won't find much information, but the handful of displays are clearly labelled and supplemented by photos.

Further down the road towards the railway station, close to the Shinto shrine, the **Sudarshan workshop** is one of the few traditional stone-carvers' yards left in Puri. For once, the sculptors and their apprentices seem more interested in pursuing their art than selling it to tourists, but gladly point potential customers in the direction of the factory **shop** next door. Most of the pieces here are large religious icons beautifully carved out of khondalite – the multi-coloured stone used in the Sun Temple at Konarak.

The beach

If a peaceful swim and a lie in the sun are your top priorities, you may be disappointed with **Puri beach**. It's not just the constant stream of hawkers that's the problem – the stretch of beach in front of the fishing village has become a three-kilometre-long open-air toilet and rubbish dump. Although it's a cheaper and perhaps more natural way of dealing with sewage than pumping it into the ocean, it does tend to get between your toes on the beach. If you want to swim and sunbathe, the stretch of beach beyond the Sanskrit University, 3km to the east, is cleaner and quieter.

In the west end of town, along **Marine Parade**, the atmosphere is more akin to a Victorian holiday resort, with a row of hotels looking across the parade to the beach. This stretch is very much the domain of the domestic tourist industry and the beach is much cleaner here. It's a pleasant place to stroll and becomes highly animated after sunset when the nightly market gets going, even though many of the stalls sell nothing other than kitsch souvenirs. Fast-food outlets line the street, and there are numerous chai stalls and small restaurants just inland.

Local fishermen patrol the beach as **lifeguards**; recognizable more by their triangular straw hats and *dhotis* than their strapping physiques, they wade with their punters into the surf and literally hold their hands to keep them on their feet. This may seem a little excessive to anyone used to choppier water, but the **undertow** claims victims every year, so weak swimmers should be careful. When not saving lives, the fishermen are busy at the CT Road end of the beach, engaged in the more traditional industries of mending nets and boats. The **fishing village** is one of the biggest in Orissa, with dozens of tiny triangular sails tacking to and fro off the coast during the day. Once landed, the catch is transferred to baskets for women to carry to the **fish market** in the village, and the heavy boats dragged up the beach. The best time to pay a visit is around dawn, when the sight of the little fleet putting out towards the sun rising over the sea can make Puri seem truly exotic after all.

Eating

Inexpensive eating options around Pentakunta are limited to the handful of cafés along CT Road, most of which are of the "write your own order" ilk, with typically unexciting, spiced-down travellers' menus. Most of the restaurants do thalis, some better than others, and there's good **fresh fish** to be had. Better food can be found in the restaurants at the nearby resort hotels. Most serve a reasonable range of veg and non-veg Indian dishes, including fish, with a few Chinese alternatives thrown in.

Chung Wah, *Hotel Lee Gardens*, VIP Road. Popular restaurant serving inexpensive Chinese food.

Gandhara, *Gandhara International Hotel*, CT Road. Primarily for hotel guests, but non residents can book in advance for excellent and authentic Japanese meals. You can take a cold beer up onto the high roof terrace and enjoy the sea view.

Harry's, CT Road. One of the most popular budget places with good fish, freshly pressed fruit juices and a pleasant garden area out back.

Holiday Resort, CT Road. Classy a/c restaurant at hotel of the same name. The upmarket Western decor is less appealing than the food, which includes superb Bengali thalis (lunch only) and is not too expensive.

Love and Life, CT Road, at the eponymous hotel. Traveller-oriented place serving the staple Western favourites as well as more costly Japanese dishes with the accent on fresh fish. There is a barbecue area in the garden to grill your own fish.

Mayfair, *Mayfair Beach Resort*, off CT Road. Sophisticated and delicious. A top-class chef whips up an unusually adventurous menu, including Orissan specialities (order 8hr in advance), making this the best place for an extravagant evening away from dhal and rice.

Mickey Mouse, CT Road. The loudest music and the most original lampshades. Very laid-back service and chess sets provided. A popular place for a late-night drink.

South East Railway, CT Road, at hotel of the same name. Idiosyncratic colonial charm, with checked tablecloths, silver butter dishes and waiters in *pukka* turbans. The poor-value set menus are less memorable. Nonresidents should give a couple of hours' warning.

Trupti, CT Road. Indian veg restaurant serving a good range of regional thalis. Especially busy at lunchtime.

Wild Grass, corner of VIP Road and College Road, 2km from the CT Road ghetto. Popular with the locals, serving excellent *tandoori*, seafood, vegetarian and Orissan dishes at very reasonable prices, with tables spread around a beautiful leafy garden. Open for lunch and dinner. Recommended.

Xanadu, CT Road. Easily the best of the cheapies with a pleasant garden and extensive menu, including a special children's breakfast. Its special claim is that "we cook only in low cholesterol" – great for those who have had one samosa too many.

Listings

Bicycle rental Along CT Road between the *Gandhara* and *Love and Life*; places include *Mickey Mouse* and Unique Tours.

Banks and exchange The State Bank of India, beyond the *Nilachal Ashok Hotel*, on VIP Road

(Mon–Fri 10am–2pm, Sat 10am–noon), will change American Express travellers' cheques and cash in US and Australian dollars, Deutschmarks and sterling, but doesn't give cash on credit cards. You can also change money at a branch of the

Allahabad Bank, on Temple Road, 200m up from the GPO towards the temple, and Trade Wings, above the *Travellers Inn* on CT Road.

Bookshops Loknath Bookshop next to *Raju's* restaurant on CT Road. Books bought and sold, or you can use the extensive library upon paying a deposit of Rs300, with books lent at Rs10 per day. Selection of postcards and stationery.

Hospitals Puri's main "HQ" hospital (℡ 06752/23742) is well outside the town centre on Grand Road. Hotels such as the *Panthaniwas*, or Heritage Tours at the *Mayfair*, can help find a doctor in an emergency.

Internet access Service at the *Gandhara* is the best value at Rs1.50 per min. Otherwise try *Harry's Café* also along CT Road, though it's expensive at Rs5 per min.

Police The main station is on Grand Road, near the Jagannath temple.

Post office The GPO is on Kacheri Road (Mon–Fri 10am–5pm, Sat 10am–noon). For poste restante (Mon–Fri 9am–noon & 4–6pm, Sat 9am–noon), use the side door on the left side of the building.

Shopping and markets Utkalika and the other hand-loom emporiums, just up from the GPO on Temple Road, stock a good range of local crafts at fixed prices. Surdarshan on Station Road (close to the OTDC tourist office) is the best place to buy traditional stone sculpture. For reproductions of the Jagannath deity, look in the bazaar around the temple. For classical Orissan paintings visit the Patta Chitra Centre on Nabakalebar Road. There's a lively market on the beach off Marine Drive, south of *Puri Hotel*, open every evening until around 10pm.

Tours OTDC runs tour buses from in front of the *Panthaniwas* to nearby attractions including Bhubaneswar and environs (Tues–Sat 6.30am–7.00pm; Rs110, a/c Rs150), and Chilika

Moving on from Puri

Puri is joined to the main Calcutta–Chennai routes by a branch line of the busy South East **Train** network and a good metalled road through Bhubaneswar, so it's well connected with most other major Indian cities. Travel agents at major hotels can also book tickets.

The Puri–New Delhi Express #2815 leaves at 9.05am (Mon, Wed, Thurs & Sat), calling at **Bhubaneswar, Gaya** and **Mughalsarai** (for Varanasi), and arrives in **Delhi** at 5pm the following day. The slower Neelachal Express #8475 (Tues, Fri & Sun) leaves Puri at the same time stopping at the same stations, but arrives in Delhi at 9.25pm. Avoid the evening Kalinga–Utkal Express #8477 between Puri and Delhi; it's much slower and frequently late. The quickest and most convenient train to **Calcutta** is the Jagannath Express #8410, which leaves Puri at 9.15pm for the 11hr overnight trip. For central Indian destinations such as Jabalpur or Nagpur, take the Kalinga–Utkal Express #8477 as far as Bilaspur and change there. Getting to **Mumbai** involves changing at Bhubaneswar and a total journey time of more than 40hr.

If you're heading for **south India**, it's also best to change at Bhubaneswar or Khurda Road, 44km from Puri, where you can pick up any of a number of daily trains to **Chennai** (22hr), including the daily Coromandel Express #2841 and twice-weekly Guwahati–Bangalore Express #5426 (Tues & Sun). There are two trains through to Thiruvananthapuram in Kerala: the Howrah–Trivandrum Express #6234 (Tues & Sun; 49hr) and the weekly Guwahati–Trivandrum Express #5628 (Wed; 43hr). Computerized reservations can be made at the main station (Mon–Sat 8am–3pm, Sun 8am–1pm; ℡ 06752/22056) or through Puri's many travel agents.

There are hourly buses, although **minibuses** are the easiest way to travel, between Puri and Bhubaneswar (both Rs15). Services are fast (1hr) and frequent until 5pm, but make sure that it's "non-stop" before you get on. The same applies to Konarak minibuses (Rs10), which also leave when full from the main city bus stand in the east of town, near the Gundicha Ghar. **Jeeps** ply the same route hourly for the same price, departing from the bus stand when full.

If you plan to head south by road along the Orissan coast, a luxury bus to Satapada on Chilika Lake leaves every thirty minutes during the day from the main bus stand.

See Travel Details at the end of this chapter for more information on journey frequencies and durations.

Lake (daily 6.30am–7.30pm; Rs85). Gandhara
Travel does tours and ticketing and organizes trips
to Konarak during the dance festival. Heritage Tours
(℡06752/23656), based at the *Mayfair Beach
Resort*, are well established and reliable and offer
6- to 10-day tribal tours in Orissa, as well as
special interest tours such as bird-watching and
archeology. Imperial Tours on CT Road also
arranges tribal village tours.

Around Puri

Back inland among the coconut palms, rice paddies, muddy lakes and rivers,
are many traditional brahmin villages, most of them Vaishnavite. Two such
places, about 12km from Puri just off the main Bhubaneshwar road, are
BIRAPRATAPUR and **GANGANARAYANPUR**, where you can see
thatched houses of baked clay and wood, many painted with bright designs,
and small temples fronted by stone frames used for suspending the deity during festivals. You may even chance upon the house of an astrologer and have
your fortune told. For those not quite up to puffing around the area by bike,

The Orissa cyclone

Orissa is no stranger to the "super cyclone". Records dating from 1885 show that
winds of up to 250km per hour left about 5000 people dead, and cyclones have
since hit the Bay of Bengal with alarming regularity. All day on October 28, 1999,
the winds were picking up but, as there had been no cyclone warning, villagers
continued to work in the paddy fields that stretch along the alluvial plains of
Orissa's coastline. In port, just northeast of Bhubaneswar, the harbour master had
tracked the path of a cyclone on a US Navy website. The pinpoint accuracy of the
charts showed it to be heading straight for his office; he immediately ordered all
ships in the bay to head out to sea, away from the course of destruction.

The cyclone hit land the following day. For 36 hours, winds blew up to 300km
per hour, and a five-metre tidal wave washed 20km inland over Paradwip and
Konarak districts, drew back, and then spread over the land again. Mud and dung
houses, sheltering whole families and their livestock, were swept away, along with
roads, telephone lines, electricity cables and train tracks. Around twenty purpose-
built cyclone shelters were each able to accommodate 1500 people standing up,
though as many as 3000 squeezed into some. Many villagers refused to leave their
houses, thinking this was just another monsoon storm; to leave would mean a loss
of precious earnings, and their belongings would be vulnerable to looting.

On the third day the winds finally dropped and the flood-levels lowered, but
many people remained stranded in trees. They were starving, in shock, without
clean water, and all around them bodies of victims and livestock began to decom-
pose. Luckily, a much-feared epidemic of cholera or typhoid was avoided, but the
toll from the cyclone and the lack of immediate rescue response left a death toll
close to 15,000, although the official government figure is 10,000.

Similarly affected states such as Andhra Pradesh and West Bengal, as well as
Bangladesh, have suffered disasters of similar scale, although potentially huge death
tolls have been significantly reduced by effective preparation, such as warning systems throughout the villages and the construction of community cyclone shelters.
Orissa, by contrast, paid the maximum price as its government had not implemented recommendations from the 1984 National Cyclone Review.

Two years on, and the damage wrought on the lush casuarina and palm plantations along the once tropical and beautiful coastline between Konarak and Puri is
still very much in evidence – the area is now a wasteland of fallen and stripped
trees. While villages have been rebuilt and livelihoods restored, Orissa's cyclone survivors continue to live with the terrible consequences of those few days.

Heritage Tours (☎ 06752/23656) in Puri arrange **guided tours** of a couple of villages for around Rs700 per car, including food.

Konarak and around

Time runs like a horse with seven reins,
Thousand-eyed, unageing, possessing much seed.
Him the poets mount; His wheels are all beings.

The *Artharva Veda*

If you visit only one temple in Orissa, it should be **KONARAK**. Standing imperiously in its compound of lawns and casuarina trees, 35km north of Puri on the coast road, this majestic pile of oxidizing sandstone is considered to be the apogee of Orissan architecture and one of the finest religious buildings anywhere in the world.

The temple is all the more remarkable for having languished under a huge mound of sand since it fell into neglect three hundred or so years ago. Not until early this century, when the dune and heaps of collapsed masonry were cleared away from the sides, did the full extent of its ambitious design become apparent. In 1924, the earl of Ronaldshay wrote of the newly revealed temple as "one of the most stupendous buildings in India which rears itself aloft, a pile of overwhelming grandeur even in its decay". A team of seven galloping horses and twenty-four exquisitely carved wheels found lining the flanks of a raised platform showed that the temple had been conceived in the form of a colossal chariot for the sun god **Surya**, its presiding deity. Equally sensational was the rediscovery among the ruins of some extraordinary **erotic sculpture**. Konarak, like Khajuraho (see p.468), is plastered with loving couples locked in ingenious amatory postures drawn from the **Kamasutra** – a feature that may well explain the comment made by one of Akbar's emissaries, Abdul Fazl, in the sixteenth century: "Even those who are difficult to please," he enthused, "stand astonished at its sight."

Apart from the temple, a small **museum** and a fishing **beach**, Konarak **village** has little going for it. In recent years, a few cafés and hotels have mushroomed around its dusty bus stand to service the stream of bus parties that buzz in and out during the day, spilling out crowds of day-trippers to clamber over the ruins in their best silk saris and shirtings. Sundays and public holidays in particular are best avoided if you're hoping for some peace and quiet. In any case, aim to be around at sunset after most of the tour groups have left, when the rich evening light works wonders on the natural colours in the khondalite sandstone.

Some history

As with all important temples, Konarak has its own popular **origin myth**. Samba, one of Krishna's sons, was caught spying on his stepmothers while they were bathing in the river. Enraged by his son's prurience, Krishna is said to have cursed him with leprosy and expelled him from the palace. Twelve years of penances later, Surya (who is also the divine healer of skin complaints) took pity on the boy and cured him of the disease, in return for which Samba built a temple dedicated to the sun god nearby.

History, as ever, has a different version of events. Inscription plates attribute the founding of the temple to the thirteenth-century Ganga monarch

1120

Narashimadeva, possibly to commemorate his military successes against the Muslim invaders. Whatever the truth, the temple projects an aura of power, perhaps due to the two very powerful magnets said to have been built into the tower, with the poles placed in such a way that the throne of the king was suspended in mid-air.

The mighty sun temple, with its seventy-metre tower, was a landmark for European mariners sailing off the shallow Orissan coast, who knew it as the "**Black Pagoda**", and the frequent incidence of shipping disasters along the coast was blamed on the effect of the aforesaid magnets on the tidal pattern. The tower also proved to be an obvious target for raids on the region. In the fifteenth century Konarak was sacked by the Yavana army; though unable to raze the temple or destroy its deity, which had been smuggled away by the

Odissi dance

Even visitors who don't normally enjoy classical dance cannot fail to be seduced by the elegance and poise of Orissa's own regional style, **Odissi**. Friezes in the Rani Gumpha at Udaigiri (see p.1103) attest to the popularity of dance in the Orissan courts as far back as the second century BC. By the time the region's Hindu "golden age" was in full swing, it had become an integral part of religious ritual, with purpose-built dance halls, or *nata mandapas*, being added to existing temples and corps of dancing girls employed to perform in them. **Devadasis**, literally "wives of the god", were handed over by their parents at an early age and symbolically "married" to the deity. They were trained to read, sing and dance and, as one disapproving early nineteenth-century chronicler put it, to "make public traffic of their charms" with male visitors to the temple. Gradually, ritual intercourse (a legacy of the Tantric influence on medieval Hinduism) degenerated into pure prostitution, and dance, formerly an act of worship, grew to become little more than a form of commercial entertainment. By the colonial era, Odissi was all but lost, its secrets frozen in ancient sculpture or absorbed into the popular traditions of musical plays that toured provincial towns and villages.

This would probably have heralded the end of Odissi altogether, had it not been for the rediscovery in the 1950s of the **Abhinaya Chandrika**, a fifteenth-century manual on classical Orissan dance. Like Bharatanatyam, India's most popular dance style, Odissi has its own highly complex language of poses and steps. Based on the *tribhanga* "hip-shot" stance, movements of the body, hands and eyes convey specific emotions and enact episodes from well-known religious texts – most commonly the Gita Govinda (the Krishna story). Using the *Abhinaya* and temple sculpture, dancers and choreographers were able to reconstruct this grammar into a coherent form and within a decade Odissi was a thriving performance art once again. Today, dance lessons with a reputed guru have become *de rigueur* for the young daughters of Orissa's middle classes – an ironic reversal of its earlier associations.

Few types of dance match Odissi for sheer style. The dancers deck themselves out in extravagant costumes of pleated silk brocades, silver jewellery, bells, jasmine flowers and distinctive *dhotis*, while in front of the stage, musicians and singers recite hypnotic *talas* – cycles of devotional poetry set to music. Unfortunately, catching a live performance is largely a matter of being in the right place at the right time. The only regular recitals take place in the Jagannath temple. If, however, you're not a Hindu, the annual festival of dance at Konarak, in the first week of December, is your best chance of seeing Orissa's top performers. While the atmosphere might not be as authentic as in the temple, the dancing is superb and the floodlit backdrop spectacular. Failing that, the state television station broadcasts Odissi quite regularly, especially on public holidays. If you're keen to learn, a number of dance academies in Bhubaneswar run intensive courses for beginners (see p.1102).

priests to Puri, the marauding Muslims nevertheless managed to damage it sufficiently to allow the elements to get a foothold. As the sea receded, sand slowly engulfed the building and salty breezes set to work on the spongy khondalite, eroding the exposed surfaces and weakening the superstructure.

According to local legend, the removal of the magnets would cause the temple to crumble. Indeed, by the end of the nineteenth century, the tower had disintegrated completely, and the porch lay buried up to its waist, prompting one art historian of the day to describe it as "an enormous mass of stones studded with a few peepal trees here and there".

Restoration only really began in earnest at the start of the twentieth century. After putting an end to the activities of the local raja, who had been plundering the ruins for masonry and sculpture to use on his own temple, government archeologists set about unearthing the immaculately preserved hidden sections of the building and salvaging what they could from the rest of the rubble. The porch was shored up with rocks and sand, large chunks of the walls were rebuilt, and chemicals applied to the stonework to prevent further deterioration. Finally, trees were planted to shelter the compound from the corrosive winds, and a museum opened to house what sculpture was not shipped off to Delhi, Calcutta and London. Today, Konarak is one of India's most visited ancient monuments, and the flagship of Orissa Tourism's bid to promote the area as an alternative to the "golden triangle" of Delhi, Agra and Jaipur.

Practicalities

The easiest way to get to Konarak from Puri, 33km down the coast, is by **bus** or **Jeep**. There are regular services in both directions and the journey only takes an hour or so, which makes it possible to do the round trip in a day – the last bus back to Puri leaves at 6.30pm. Buses from Bhubaneswar are much less frequent and take between two and four hours to cover the 65km (with a change at Pipli), depending on whether you catch the one direct express "tourist" bus, which leaves from the town stand at 10am. Alternatively, you could join one of OTDC's **tours** which leave from the *Panthaniwas* (Tues–Sun 6.30am–7pm; Rs110, a/c Rs150), with stops at Konarak, Bhubaneswar and Dhauli. The OTDC **tourist office** is in the *Yatri Niwas* hotel.

With Puri only an hour down the road, few people end up staying in Konarak. If, however, you want to enjoy the temple at a more leisurely pace or just fancy spending the night somewhere a little more peaceful, there is **accommodation** in the village. Not far from the main entrance to the monuments, the OTDC *Panthaniwas* (℡06758/36831; ❷–❹) has dark but clean and reasonably priced rooms with a/c and hot water. They also run the reasonable *Travellers' Lodge* (℡06758/36823; ❸–❹), tucked behind the pleasant OTDC *Yatri Niwas* (℡06758/36820; ❷–❸), which has mosquito nets (essential), a restaurant and coloured fountains in the gardens. The manager here has an impressive knowledge of local history and the temple itself. Most of the "hotels" clustered around the main entrance to the temple have "no lodging – only fooding". The *Labanya Lodge* (℡06758/36824; ❶), a little out of the village on the beach road, is the most backpacker-friendly place and has a small garden.

For **food** you have a choice between the row of thali and tea stalls opposite the temple or a more substantial meal in one of the hotel restaurants. The *Panthaniwas'* very popular and inexpensive *Geetanjali* café serves the usual range of veg and rice dishes. The *Yatri Niwas* is also open to nonresidents and is likely to be packed out at lunchtime with tour parties, all tucking into a good Orissan thali. The *Sun Temple Hotel* is the best of the *dhabas*.

The temple

The main entrance to the **temple** complex on its eastern, sea-facing side brings you out directly in front of the **bhoga-mandapa**, or "hall of offerings". Ornate carvings of amorous couples, musicians and dancers decorating the sides of its platform and stocky pillars suggest that the now roofless pavilion, which was a later addition to the temple, must originally have been used for ritual dance performances.

To get a sense of the overall scale and design, stroll along the low wall that bounds the south side of the enclosure before you tackle the ruins proper. As a giant model of Surya's war chariot, the temple was intended both as an offering to the Vedic sun god and as a symbol for the passage of time itself – believed to lie in his control. The seven **horses** straining to haul the sun eastwards in the direction of the dawn (only one is still intact) represent the days of the week. The **wheels** ranged along the base stand for the twelve months, each with eight spokes detailed with pictures of the eight ideal stages of a woman's day. Originally, a **stone pillar** crowned with an image of Aruna, Surya's charioteer, also stood in front of the main door, though this has since been moved to the eastern gateway of the Jagannath temple in Puri.

With the once-lofty **sanctuary tower** now reduced to little more than a clutter of sandstone slabs tumbling from the western wing, the **porch**, or *jago-mohana*, has become Konarak's real centrepiece. Its impressive pyramidal roof, rising to a height of 38m, is divided into three tiers by rows of uncannily life-like statues – mostly musicians and dancers serenading the sun god on his passage through the heavens. Among the figures on the bottom platform are a four-headed, six-armed Shiva, garlanded with severed heads and performing the dance of death. Though now blocked up, the huge cubic **interior** of the porch was a marvel of medieval architecture. The original builders ran into problems installing its heavy ornamental ceiling, and had to forge ten-metre iron beams as support – a considerable engineering feat for the time.

Amazingly elaborate **sculpture** embellishes every nook and cranny of the outside of the porch – and most other parts of the temple – in a bewildering profusion of deities, animals, floral patterns, mythical beasts and aquatic monsters. This is what attracts the majority of visitors to Konarak – above all, the infamous **erotica**. Look at any carved surface for long enough and you're sure to come across a voluptuous maiden striking an alluring pose or a richly bejewelled couple sharing a tender moment. Some of Konarak's most beautiful erotic pieces are to be found in the niches halfway up the walls of the porch, where a keen eye may be able to spot the telltale pointed beards of *sadhus*, clearly making the most of a lapse in their vows of chastity. Bawdier scenes also appear in miniature along the sides of the platform and around the two remaining intricate doorframes on the main building – just look for the groups of tittering teenagers. Though sculpture of this kind is not uncommon in India, only rarely does it run to such rampant excesses. Many theories have been advanced over the years to explain the phenomenon. In Konarak's case, it seems likely that the erotic art was meant as a kind of metaphor for the ecstatic bliss experienced by the soul when it fuses with the divine cosmos – a notion central to **Tantra** and the related worship of the female principle, **shakti**, which were prevalent throughout medieval Orissa.

Moving clockwise around the temple from the south side of the main staircase, the intricately worked faces of the **platform** are what first grab most people's attention. Check out the detail on the **wheels**, and the extraordinary **friezes** that run in narrow bands above and below them. These depict military processions (inspired by King Narashimadeva's tussles with the Muslims) and hunting scenes, and feature literally thousands of rampaging elephants. If you want to keep any children busy for a while, tell them to find the giraffe which crops up on the top frieze along the south side of the platform – proof that trade with Africa took place during the thirteenth century.

Once past the porch you arrive at a double staircase that leads up to a shrine containing a **statue of Surya**. Carved out of top-quality green chlorite stone, this serene image – one of three around the base of the ruined sanctuary tower – is a real masterpiece. Notice his characteristic tall riding boots and the little figure of Aruna, the charioteer, holding the reins of the seven horses at his feet. The other two statues in the series are also worth a look, if only to compare their facial expressions which, following the progress of the sun around the temple, change from wakefulness in the morning (south) to heavy-eyed weariness at the end of the day (north). Before working your way around the far side of the porch, you can also climb down into the remains of the **sanctum sanctorum** where the deity was once enshrined. At the foot of the western wall there's an altar-like platform covered with carving: the kneeling figure in its central panel is thought to be King Narashimadeva, the donor of the temple.

Power cuts permitting, the sun temple is **floodlit** most evenings (May–Sept 7–10pm; Oct–April 5.30–9.30pm). In early December it also hosts one of India's premier **dance festivals**, drawing an impressive cast of both classical and folk dance groups from all over the country. For the exact dates, line-up and advance bookings, contact OTDC in Bhubaneswar (℡0674/432515) or Delhi (℡011/344580).

Elsewhere in the compound

The first and largest of the two small **shrines** in the southwest corner, the **Mayadevi temple** (formerly dedicated to Surya's wife, the shadow goddess), is the most interesting of the other sites in the compound. Positioned at the north and south ends of the compound, now occupying their own separate pedestals, are the impressive **colossi** that once guarded the temple entrances: harnessed elephants to the north and rearing war-horses led by soldiers to the south. The lions that used to flank the eastern gateway have been moved to a spot near the "Hall of Offerings".

Around Konarak

Some way outside the compound, near the *Yatri Niwas* hotel, the **archeological museum** (daily 9am–5pm; Rs5) has lost most of its juicy pieces to Delhi, but there is a brave attempt to reconstruct a platform wall and a chariot wheel of the temple using fragments of the original sculpture and lurid pink plaster. The rest of the galleries are a bawdy show of the ancient variety – the sheer number of "celestial beauties", fragments of busts, curvaceous hips and couples locked in Tantric poses, is a real feast. Outside, a small shed in the northeast corner of the enclosure houses a stone architrave inside, bearing images of **nine planet deities**, the Navagrahas, which originally sat above one of the temple's ornamental doorways and is now kept as a living shrine.

Unless you like beaches, few attractions **around Konarak** are likely to tempt you. Konarak's own **beach** was once picturesque but is now thoroughly windswept and forlorn due to the impact of the cyclone in October 1999 (see p.1119). Only 3km from the temple along the Puri road, it's hard to believe that the obvious storm damage somehow left the Sun temple without a scratch. The beach area still a good place to wander in the evening, and to watch the local fishing fleet at work, but far from ideal for swimming or sunbathing. For more privacy, catch a local bus heading south and jump off after a couple of kilometres when you see a track leading from the main road through the woods and dunes to the sea. Chances are you'll have long stretches of white sand to yourself. To get back again, flag down a bus or Jeep from the roadside.

A stone's throw away from Konarak beach lies the sacred pond where Samba was cured of leprosy – the miracle that allegedly inspired the founding of the sun temple. For a couple of days every year during the full or "white" moon phase of Magha (Jan & Feb), **CHANDRABHAGA** is also the site of a big religious festival, the **Magha Saptami Mela**. Thousands of pilgrims converge on the pool during the small hours to take a holy dip in its curative waters, then shuffle off to the beach where, in accordance with an age-old custom mentioned in the *Puranas*, they watch the sun rise over the sea.

Cuttack

After the comparative serenity of the surrounding countryside, **CUTTACK** comes as something of a shock. Orissa's former capital and most densely populated city is a crowded, noisy place packed onto a narrow island amid a tangle of tributaries and sandbanks in the River Mahanandi. As the major river crossing for the busy north–south land trade route and a nexus for the canals that connect the Orissan interior with the sea, the island developed into a strategic site.

In the sixteenth century, Orissa's last independent Hindu ruler, Mukunda Harichandan, built a grand nine-storey palace on site of the defensive **Barbati Fort**. Under the **Marathas**, Cuttack's lucrative trade with the British on the coast financed the construction of new temples and, thanks to a particularly liberal administration, **mosques** for the city's sizeable Muslim minority. When the British finally merged the region's 26 princedoms, Cuttack was a logical choice as state capital. Its prominence, however, was shortlived; constant floods and chronic overcrowding ensured that the capital had eventually to be moved to the drier and far less constricted site at Bhubaneswar.

The town centre's narrow streets are congested and chaotic, packed with busy shops and stalls and hindered by a complex network of canals. The most interesting area is atmospheric **old quarter** with its bazaars and jewellery shops specializing in **Chandni,** the silver filigree work unique to Cuttack and practised here for many centuries. The nearby **Kadam-i-Rasul**, a complex of domed mosques and shrines, is one of the few interesting buildings. The sparse ruins of **Barbati Fort** lie on the northwest of the stadium overlooking the Mahanadi River. After Barbati, the road follows the riverbank out as far as **Chahata Ghat**, on the westernmost point of the island.

Practicalities

Cuttack's **railway station** lies east of the city centre, in the middle of the island. **Buses** in both directions turn west off NH5, which runs parallel with the railway line, towards the city bus stand, 2km further up Link Road. Halfway between the two, the run-down Arunodhya Market building houses the ineffectual OTDC **tourist office** (daily 10am–5pm; ☎0671/61225), which also has a counter at the railway station.

The majority of the cheap **hotels** are near the silver bazaar in Choudury Bazaar but for a little more money you can get a much better deal. The OTDC *Panthaniwas* (☎0671/621867; ④–⑤) on Buxi Bazaar has a range of simple, clean rooms, all with hot water, and a reasonable restaurant. The best hotels in town are the *Akbari Continental* on Haripur Road (☎0671/623251; ⑦–⑧) which has central a/c, a good restaurant, bar and foreign exchange and the *Ashoka* on Ice Factory Road, near College Square and the railway station, which has a/c rooms (☎0671/613508; ③). These two, and the *Panthaniwas*, are also by far the best **places to eat** in Cuttack.

North of Cuttack

As you head **north from Cuttack** and the Mahanandi, the profile of the Eastern Ghats recedes temporarily into the haze on the horizon leaving a flat expanse of paddy fields, palm trees and mud-walled villages. This area was particularly affected by the cyclone, leaving houses and livelihoods destroyed. The main railway line and NH5 twisting alongside it follow the path of the famous **pilgrim trail**, the Jagannath Sadak, that once led from Calcutta to Puri. Until the end of the nineteenth century this now hectic route was no more than a mud track. Then, following the 1865 famine that wiped out nearly a quarter of Orissa's population, the British were pressured into completing a road and rail link with more prosperous parts of the country. With the addition of iron bridges in the 1960s, the highway became the endless stream of trucks, ramshackle old buses, *dhabas* and chai-stalls it is today.

Balasore

The first town of any note along the way, **BALASORE** (literally "town of the young lord" – Krishna) was one of the earliest British outposts in India. In 1636, it was given by the emperor Shah Jahan to a British surgeon, Gabriel Broughton, after he had successfully cured a Moghul princess of burns (her clothes had caught fire during a sea voyage). If the port hadn't silted up in the eighteenth century, Balasore might well have become Calcutta. As it is, the sea is now 13km away and the town is little more than a collection of market stalls grouped around a crossroads and a railway station, although it's useful for transport connections.

The centrally located **bus stand**, with services to Baripada, Bhubaneswar, Cuttack and Chandipur, is a ten-minute cycle rickshaw ride from the railway station. **Accommodation** is plentiful, but avoid the dives around the station unless you're catching an early morning train. The hotels on Sahadevkhunta Road, just up from the bus stand on the other side of the tracks, are a better deal. The well-run *Hotel Swarnachuda* (☎06782/363440; ②–⑥) has a range of rooms, some a/c, with a small restaurant and bar. Further down, the identical *Hotel Suraj* (☎06782/363630; ②–④) has more rooms for the budget-conscious. There's nowhere in Balasore to **change money**.

Chandipur

From the main market square in Balasore, a narrow surfaced road winds its way out through the remnants of the old town to the open fields and picturesque

Every year around February and March, a strip of beach at the end of Orissa's central river delta witnesses what must surely be one of the world's most extraordinary natural spectacles, although recent environmental changes are threatening its future. Having swum right across the Pacific and Indian oceans, 200,000 female **Olive Ridley marine turtles** crawl onto the sand; each looks for a safe spot, then sets about digging a hole with its hind flippers in which to lay its annual batch of eggs. Twenty minutes later, after a quick breather, they're off again into the surf to begin the journey back to their mating grounds on the other side of the world.

No one knows quite why they travel such distances, but for local villagers the arrival of the giant turtles has traditionally been something of a boon. Turtle soup for breakfast, lunch and tea . . . and extra cash from market sales. Over the years the annual slaughter began to turn into something of a green gold rush, and turtle numbers plummeted drastically until a special wildlife reserve was set up to protect them at the personal behest of Indira Gandhi. Today, the Bhitarakanika Sanctuary on **Gahirmatha beach**, 130km northeast of Bhubaneswar, is a safe haven for the creatures. Weeks before the big three- or four-day invasion, coastguards monitor the progress of the schools as they approach the Orissan shoreline and armed rangers ensure that poachers are kept at bay. For wildlife enthusiasts it's a field day. Thanks to the fact that during their labour the preoccupied turtles are not surprisingly oblivious to the presence of humans, you can watch the whole sequence at close range.

In recent years, however, environmental changes have threatened the turtles' habitat. Several hundred local families have begun to cultivate land within the sanctuary, water quality has been threatened by the growth of illegal prawn farms and in 1997 more than one hundred trawlers were caught illegally fishing in the area without "turtle excluder devices" (TEDs). The Worldwide Fund for Nature is monitoring the area, but in the last two years, there have been very few turtles nesting on Gahirmatha beach.

Visits to Gahirmatha are allowed, though you should ask at the OTDC tourist office in Bhubaneswar to find out exactly when – or if – the turtles are expected. **Permits, transport, food** and **accommodation** can be a problem unless you are prepared to rough it or to pay through the nose for a rental car, as the sanctuary is well off the beaten track.

---

villages beyond. After running along 16km of flood-proof embankment it eventually arrives at the seaside settlement of **CHANDIPUR** with its white sandy beach. Frequent blasts can be heard from the highly protected military base next door; among other explosive ammunition, the Indian army tests their land-to-air missiles here. Thankfully, the village itself is peaceful and friendly, sprawled out along the coast. At low tide the sea retreats 3km, something of a godsend to the locals who, with their dugouts and hand nets, are able to fish the parts the big fleets down the coast daren't reach. There's not a great deal to do in Chandipur other than paddle in silty water but it's a relaxing enough place and one that rarely attracts more than a handful of visitors.

Five daily **buses** run from Balasore, or you can take an auto-rickshaw, though expect to have to pay the return fare. Apart from during public holidays, when Chandipur is swamped with trippers from Calcutta, finding somewhere to **stay** is also relatively easy. Away from the beach, the *Larica Yatri Niwas* (☎06782/370034; **②–③**) has modern rooms around a courtyard, some cheaper dorms (Rs60) and a restaurant. On the road that turns down to the beach, you'll find good rooms at the *Shubham* (☎06782/370025; **④–⑤**) which also has a restaurant and boasts an attractive garden with playground for children. In a colonial building directly overlooking the beach, the OTDC *Panthaniwas* (☎ 06782/370051; ❹–❺) has atmospheric rooms with private balconies, with additional rooms in a newer block behind. There's a dorm (Rs70) and a good restaurant serving delicious fresh fish (if given advance notice) and a decent eggy breakfast. *Hotel Golden* (no phone; ❷) has four spartan but clean rooms each with a bathroom and a shared veranda, but no restaurant. For very cheap, fresh seafood and thalis, head for the friendly *Hotel Graharaj* up the road from the beach, open from 6am to 11pm. **Tours** of the area's attractions (that are hard to visit without your own transport) include some off-the-beaten-track **temples** and day-trips to Simlipal National Park and can be arranged at the OTDC *Panthaniwas*. Maharaja Tours, a private company based in the village, also run sightseeing trips from Chandipur.

Baripada

A little way north of Balasore, the highway crosses the River Burhabalanga and splits in two, the right fork towards the Bengal border and the left towards the hills of the Orissan interior. Further inland, the intensively cultivated alluvial plains of the coastal strip gradually give way to patches of deciduous forest and red-laterite soil, punctuated by termite mounds and neatly thatched villages. The district is the traditional home of the **Santal** tribe. Comprising around seventy percent of the local *adivasi* population, the Santals are predominantly settled agriculturalists who practise a blend of ancestor worship and Hinduism. They're known for having developed a written form of their tribal language, Olchikki, and for their festivals and dances. The town of **BARIPADA**, is head-quarters of **Mayurbhunj** district (pronounced "marvunj") and the main gate-way to the nearby Simlipal National Park (see opposite), which you reach after about ninety minutes' drive.

As the main **market** town for some widely scattered farming communities, Baripada is a good place to get an idea of small-town Orissan life. The town was the focus of world attention in 1999, when an Australian missionary and his two young sons were murdered whilst attending a prayer meeting; Hindu fundamentalists blamed the missionary for forcing conversions in the *adivasi* communities. Amid local support, the mission continues today with an impressive leprosy hospital.

The **town** itself is a typically Indian mixture of tumbledown shops and hous-es, with a whitewashed **Jagannath temple**, a miniature of Puri's. The quietly decaying bungalows and grand but time-worn civic buildings were erected by the local maharaja during the days of the Raj. Mayurbhunj was among the last of the princely states to join independent India. For centuries it remained under the **Bhanja** kings, a reputedly "progressive" ruling family favoured by the British, whose present incumbent still lives in an incongruous Neoclassical mansion overlooking the river in the north of town.

Practicalities

Arriving in Baripada, **buses** pass the temple at the bottom of the broad main street and then head up the hill to the bus stand and market. From here it's a five-minute walk to the most central **hotels**: the simple *Bishram* (☎ 06792/53535; ❶) and the *Hotel Ambika* (☎ 06792/52557; ❷–❹) are both shabby but adequate places with variously priced rooms, all with attached baths and frames for the much-needed mosquito nets. Baripada's best **restaurant** is on the ground floor of the *Ambika*. The surroundings look none too salubri-

In addition to celebrating all the usual Hindu festivals, which have in many cases been distinctively adapted by the *adivasi* population, the Mayurbhunj district also has its own totally unique festivals, rarely experienced by outsiders. The dates vary from year to year in accordance with the astrological calendar, so enquire in advance at a tourist office or consult an Oriya calendar at a newspaper stall.

Karam Puja (mid-Jan). A harvest festival celebrated by the Mahanta (*kshatriya*) caste and *munda* tribals. Large gatherings, plus a procession to the river where women plant seeds in the sand, with music and dance.

Chaitra Parbar (mid-April). This Hindu end-of-spring bash is marked by tribal *Chhou* dancing, a form of dance developed from pre-battle warm-up routines.

Rath Yatra (June & July). Baripada's very own Car Festival is lively and memorable, albeit upstaged by Puri's. Subhadra's (Jagganath's sister) chariot is pulled exclusively by women.

Damorda Yatra (Sept & Oct). Tribal ancestor-worship ritual, which involves the immersion of a deceased relative's ashes in the local tank.

Tusu Parbar (Nov & Dec). Unmarried girls carry an effigy of a local (anti-Moghul) resistance heroine to the tank and submerge it, while crowds of men tear apart a chicken thrown from the town *neem* tree.

---

ous but they serve a good selection of Indian veg and non-veg and above-average Chinese dishes. A rather less convenient option is the *Durga* (℡06792/53438; ❷–❹), in an old British-style building 3km out of town past the temple. The OTDC **tourist office** (Mon–Fri 10am–5pm) is five minutes' walk from the bus stand in the opposite direction. The manager at the *Ambika* can arrange transport to Simlipal or rent out **bicycles** and **Jeeps**.

Simlipal National Park

West of Baripada, the landscape suddenly changes from open fields to the thickly wooded slopes and ridges of the Eastern Ghats. At more than 1000m, **Khairbhuru**, the peak visible from the outskirts of town, is the highest in the region and one of the last true wildernesses in eastern India. The mixed decid-uous forests, perennial streams and glades of savannah grasslands draped around its flanks have allowed for an uncommonly rich diversity of flora and fauna.

In 1979 the whole area (2750 square kilometres) around the mountain was declared a wildlife sanctuary – primarily in an attempt to revive its dwindling population of **tigers** (see Wildlife Contexts). Prior to this it had been the exclusive preserve of the Maharaja of Mayurbhunj, who used the woods as a private hunting ground and source of timber (the narrow-gauge railway run-ning from Baripada to the main line on the coast was built to carry the lum-ber out). Six years later **SIMLIPAL** was officially designated a national park, and the following year became the site of one of India's first Project Tiger reserves.

Simlipal deserves to be one of eastern India's major attractions. The fact that it isn't has less to do with the amount of wildlife within its borders – abundant by any standards – than with its comparative **inaccessibility**. Unlike its coun-terparts in neighbouring states, transport to and around the park is a real prob-lem and accommodation is rudimentary. If you overcome these obstacles, how-ever, the rewards more than compensate. Apart from the elusive tigers – park rangers, perhaps a touch optimistically, claim they number almost one hundred – the reserve boasts leopards, langurs, barking and spotted deer, gaur, sloth bears, mongoose, flying squirrels, porcupines, turtles, monitor lizards, pythons and the very rare **mugger crocodile**. Herds of wild **elephant** are also common (too common for the unfortunate villagers, who have to spend nights in tree houses waiting to scare rampaging pachyderms away from their crops) and there are reportedly 231 species of **birds** flying around. All this with a backdrop of beautiful granite hills and as tranquil and pristine an old-growth forest as you're likely to find anywhere. No less than 1076 species of plant have been recorded here, including an impressive 87 different varieties of orchid.

Park practicalities

The park is **open** from November to mid-June (daily 6am–noon; visits extended to 2pm on prior arrangement ☏06792/52593), but the ideal visiting season ends in February. The majority of the ninety-odd tigers are supposed to hang out in the 845-acre "core zone" which is mostly out of bounds. There are two main **entrances**: one at Joshipur in the west (convenient if you're driving from Calcutta, and close to most of the lodges), and one at Pithabata near Baripada on the eastern side. You have to pay a daily **entry fee** (Rs100 [RS10]) plus Rs100 per vehicle and Rs100 camera charge). From the gates, unsurfaced but driveable roads link up the lodges with the numerous waterfalls, panoramas, grazing areas and water holes in the buffer zone.

The easiest way to visit Simlipal is on an organized **tour**. Heritage Tours in Puri (☏06752/278000 or 278001) and Swosti Travels in Bhubaneswar (☏0674/534178) are reputable. They will arrange permits, transport, accommodation and guides at very short notice and charge reasonable rates. Without your own vehicle, the only alternative way to **get around** the park is to rent a **Jeep**. This can be arranged through the manager at the *Ambika* in Baripada, or through the less reliable taxi-wallahs hanging around the bus stand. In either case, expect to pay up to Rs1000 per day. Another way to cut costs is to use **JOSHIPUR** as an alternative base for visiting the park; closer to most of the points of interest than Baripada, it also features a couple of extremely basic lodges, and Jeeps are available for rent. For more information contact the Joshipur wildlife warden (☏06797/2224).

Accommodation

Advance booking is officially required for all but one lodge, the *Aranya Niwas*, through the Field Director of Project Tiger, Baripada 757002, Mayurbhunj district, Orissa ☏06792/52593. It is not possible to pay for any accommodation using foreign currency or traveller's cheques.

Where to go in Simlipal is largely dictated by the location of the **lodges**. There are six dotted around the park, but the best from the point of view of spotting wildlife is **Chahala** (83km from Baripada) – one of the maharaja's former hunting lodges, just inside the core zone near a salt-lick where animals congregate in the evenings. As with all accommodation in the park, facilities are very basic. You have to take in your own **food** and all utensils are provided, although the *chowkidar* will cook for you. The other lodges are Barheipani (73km), a small wooden lodge on stilts with wide verandas, near a waterfall with impressive views; Newana (60km), which is in a "frost-prone valley"; Gudugudia (25km from Joshipur), said to be particularly good for bird-watching; and Joranda (64km from Baripada), which has a bit of everything and a waterfall. The only lodge not requiring advance permission is the *Aranya Niwas* (❹) at **Lulung**, on the Baripada side (Rs150 by Jeep from Baripada). You're unlikely to see much wildlife here, but the rooms are pleasant; there's a cheap dorm (❶) and a restaurant, and the compound, surrounded by an elephant-proof ditch, is right in the heart of the forest.

Southern Orissa

Long stretches of dishevelled roadside settlements and rural stations along the National Highway do not inspire much excitement about the stretch of coast between Puri and Andhara Pradesh. However, there are a couple of scenic detours that may tempt you to break a long journey. Three hours south of the capital, at the foot of a barren, sea-facing spur of the Eastern Ghats – which creep up to the coast here – is India's largest salt-water lake. **Chilika**'s main attractions are the one million or so migratory birds that nest here in winter, and leisurely boat trips to its islands. Seventy kilometres further on, **Gopalpur-on-Sea** is sufficiently remote to have remained a decidedly low-key beach town. Out of season, the only people are families from the local fishing community. **Berhampur**, 16km inland, is southern Orissa's biggest market town, and the main transport hub for the sinuous route west through the hills to the tribal districts of **Koraput** and **Jeypore**.

Chilika Lake

Were it not for its glass-like surface, **CHILIKA LAKE**, Asia's largest lagoon, could easily be mistaken for the sea. From its mud-fringed foreshore you can barely make out the narrow strip of marshy islands and sand-flats that separate the 1100-square-kilometre expanse of brackish water from the Bay of Bengal. Come here between December and February, though, and you'll see dozens of **migratory bird species** from as far afield as Siberia and Iran, including avocets, ruffs, pelicans, ospreys, flamingoes and rare cranes. Chital and black buck can also sometimes be spotted on the shore, and schools of little dolphins surround the boats. Elsewhere around the lake, several **islands** (some inhabited by small subsistence fishing communities, others deserted) are popular destinations for daily **boat trips**. By and large, the fishing villages and fabled island "kingdom" of **Parikud** on the eastern side of the lake, home to one of India's wackier maharajas, are passed up in favour of the *devi* shrine on **Kalijai** island. Legend has it that a local girl once drowned here on the way to her wedding across the lake. Since no suitable male member of the family could be found to accompany the girl on the journey, her father stepped in at the last minute – a serious breach of Hindu custom. En route, a retributory storm blew in from the sea and overturned the boat. When they had all but given up the search for survivors, some fishermen claimed to have heard the girl's voice calling from under the water that she had become a goddess and that a shrine should be inaugurated in her name. Over the years the miracle has become associated with **Kali** (Shiva's consort Durga in her terrifying aspect) and the place it occurred something of a sacred site. Each year at *makar sankrati*, after the harvest, pilgrims flock to the tiny island from all over Orissa and West Bengal to leave votive offerings in the cave where the deity was enshrined.

Practicalities

The best **place to stay** on the lake is the excellent value *Yatri Niwas* (**❷**) at **Satapada** on the coastal side, just 45km from Puri and linked by several daily buses. Some rooms have private balconies and the well-tended gardens run down to the lake; the restaurant prepares delicious thalis and fresh seafood if given advance notice. Rooms can be booked from Puri's tourist office. There's a cheap and accessible OTDC *Panthaniwas* (⊕06810/57346; **❹–❻**), near the railway station at **Rambha**, 135km from Bhubaneswar, but it's lacklustre and best avoided. The only plus is that it's well placed for walks around the more

Prawns and politics

Global demand for the delicate translucent flesh of the humble **prawn** has led to a boom in intensive prawn cultivation in many places in Asia. But although demand has pushed up prices and attracted much-needed hard currency, the benefits have often been outweighed by heavy environmental and social costs.

In the late 1980s, the Orissan government gave one of India's largest corporations permission to cultivate prawns at the edge of Chilika Lake and sell them exclusively for export. The opposition denounced the initiative and campaigned against it. When it was voted in at the next state election, however, it promptly signed the deal anyway. The High Court subsequently nullified the decision, deciding that the traditional way of life of the local people – fishing and rice cultivation – was more important than satisfying distant foreign palates. Despite the block on the big corporations, an unofficial **prawn mafia** moved in and carried on regardless, quashing local protest by greasing a few official palms, and intimidating local villagers by bombing their fishing grounds and stealing their nets.

The **environmental consequences** have been disastrous. Artificial banks have been built to separate the prawn ponds from the lake, creating widespread drainage problems, and the artificial feed and chemicals used have left a permanent residue, polluting the waters and poisoning native fish. Every year the illegal prawn farmers are extending their farms by encroaching on the lake during the dry season, fencing off the dry lake margins and commencing production when the rains come.

As catches have become smaller, many locals have lost their livelihoods as fishermen. Some have moved into the towns looking for work while others have ended up in distant states, working on the roads for a pittance. Back in the villages they left behind, there have been serious social and economic problems. Despite the prawn's rising value on the international market, little if any of the new money comes through to local pockets, and the villagers are slipping deeper into poverty.

---

scenic southern corner of the lake. The OTDC *Panthaniwas* (☏06756/20488; ④–⑥) at **Barkul**, 34km north of Rambha, is a collection of shabby pink chalets, but rooms come with bath and mosquito nets (you won't get a wink of sleep without one) and the food is reasonable. If you plan to visit between September and March, it is best to book ahead in the Bubaneswar OTDC tourist office. To get there, take a bus from Puri or Bhubaneswar towards Berhampur and get off at **Balugaon**, where you can get an auto-rickshaw for the remaining 7km to Barkul. Alternatively, Gandhara Travels in Puri runs **daytrips** to Chilika on Mondays and Fridays for Rs100 per head.

OTDC motor launches, and rowing boats manned by local villagers, operate **boat trips** from Barkul and Satapada; prices are about Rs450 per hour for a seven-seater motor launch, or Rs650 for a place in a twenty-seater boat if you don't mind noisy crowds. The round trip to **Kalijai island**, the most popular option with domestic tourists, takes around two hours, while the bird sanctuary of **Nalabana island** takes four. The manager at the Barkul *Panthaniwas* can arrange seats. Rowing boats also depart from Rambha, though the fishermen who run them seem to be more intent on attending to their nets than ferrying passengers to the islands.

Gopalpur-on-Sea

Two thousand or more years ago, when the Kalingas were piling up wealth from the pearl and silk trade with southeast Asia, **GOPALPUR-ON-SEA**, formerly the ancient port of Paloura, must have been a swinging place. Today, the only time you're likely to encounter much action is during the monsoon, when the village is temporarily inundated with Bengali holiday-makers. For the rest of the year, its desultory collection of crumbling bungalows and seafront hotels stands idle, left to the odd backpacker blown off-course by the promise of an undiscovered beach paradise, and the armies of industrious fishermen hauling in hand nets on Gopalpur's endless empty shoreline. Paradise it certainly isn't, but if you're looking for a spot along the coast to unwind and enjoy the warm sea breezes, this could be just the place.

The village has plenty of accommodation, much of it heavily discounted in the off-season, and there's a reasonable choice of places to eat. Despite appearances to the contrary, Gopalpur's long white sandy **beach** is far from an ideal place to swim and sunbathe. For the local fishing community (*katias*), the rare spectacle of a white (read "rich and apparently insane") person strolling half-naked through their workplace is a major distraction; a swim in the sea, let alone a discreet doze in the sun, is a veritable crowd-puller. Still, if you don't mind being the centre of attention and are content to watch the locals fish, dressed in their traditional pointed straw bonnets and bright saris, the beach is an enjoyable place to while away a few hours.

Getting there is easiest via Berhampur, from where frequent minibuses and Jeeps depart from the central bus stand for the sixteen-kilometre trip. You'll be dumped at the top of Gopalpur's "main street", ten minutes' walk from the seafront and most of the hotels.

Accommodation and eating

Gopalpur's many **rooms** tend to cost considerably more than elsewhere, and you may well feel inclined to haggle. Only during holiday times, however, are they liable to be booked up in advance. The rates below all refer to the off-season between March and October. As for **eating**, there's a surprising dearth of seafood in Gopalpur, though some restaurateurs can be cajoled into cooking the odd pomfret, given sufficient warning.

Holiday Home, on corner of promenade and main road ☎0680/242049. A relaxed establishment in an old colonial building. The rooms are all large and colourful, each with access to the communal veranda. Food is prepared on request. ❸–❺

Holiday Inn, near the lighthouse. Couldn't be less like its North American namesake – a handful of very basic rooms around a yard with bucket baths and no running water. The friendly family allow guests to use their kitchen. ❶

Mermaid, on the north side of the beach ☎0680/242050. Friendly place pitched at wealthy Calcuttans, with plain rooms and private sea-facing balconies. With advance notice, nonresidents can enjoy the delicious Bengali thalis prepared here for the discerning palate. ❻–❼

Oberoi Palm Beach, ☎0680/242021. Cosy, characterful five-star, with chalets around a central lawn, a jogging track, a tennis court, lots of palm trees and easy access to the beach. The congenial restaurant serves plush, expensive buffet spreads and delicious seafood; the bar has a good wine selection and is reasonably priced. ❾

Panthaniwas, to the right, along the seafront ☎0680/242088. Unfortunately there are no sea-facing rooms, but this new hotel has clean rooms, each with attached bath, and a dorm (Rs70); the excellent chef will whip up tasty Indian dishes and breakfast on demand. ❹–❺

Rosalin, on the seafront ☎0680/242071. Chaotic family-run establishment with basic small rooms around a small garden-courtyard and a very informal restaurant for standard omelette, tea and toast breakfasts or dhal, veg and rice dinners. Cheap and cheerful. ❶–❷

Sea Side Breeze, north side of the beach ☎0680/82075. Simple, but pleasant enough, with spacious neat rooms. ❷–❹

Berhampur

BERHAMPUR is the last major Orissan town before Andhra Pradesh. There is little of tourist interest except perhaps the **weavers' quarter** around the temple where the town's famous silk saris are still produced using traditional hand looms. Moving on is most people's priority.

The main **bus** routes from Berhampur are north to Bhubaneswar (4hr; the OTDC luxury bus leaves at 2.30pm); west past Taptapani (every 15min; Rs15) towards Rayagada and Koraput; and east to Gopalpur-on-Sea. Private buses leave from the new bus stand, some way across town, while the state transport company works out of the more central bus stand in the square. The main-line **railway station** is a ten-minute rickshaw ride to the south.

There are a few decent **places to stay** should you get stuck here; if it's not too late, it's far better to head down the road to Gopalpur-on-Sea for the night. The rambling old *Government Rest House* (℡0680/200466; ❷–❸) opposite the cricket ground is the best value – basic but cheap and central. Just around the corner *Hotel Moti* (℡0680/203641; ❸–❻) is overpriced and dingy, with some a/c rooms and a restaurant. If all else fails the **railway retiring rooms** at the station will do for a night. For **food**, the *Moti* has a decent, if very dark, restaurant.

Taptapani

One possible foray from Berhampur, if you're tempted by the lure of the nearby hills and scenes of Orissan countryside at its most rural, is the trip up to **TAP-TAPANI**, a spa village nestled in the *ghats* 51km to the west. The road leads out through Berhampur's hectic commercial district to a broad, flat-bottomed river valley strewn with huge black granite boulders and poor-looking villages. Along the way, patches of rice paddy and red-brown soil are enlivened by glimpses of local women hard at work in their blue and green cotton saris. Paddy workers and cowherders are noticeable by the conical woven hats with extremely wide brims that they carefully balance on their heads. An hour or so out, the increasingly bumpy road gradually narrows and loses most of its traffic, the hills and *sal* forest begin to close in and the bus, stuffed full with villagers heading upcountry, starts to crawl around the hairpins towards the pass. Among the passengers you're likely to see a number of **Tibetans** from the Chandragiri refugee camp, 45km off the main road beyond Taptapani. Following the Chinese invasion in 1957 the refugees were given land by the Orissan government on which to settle and have lived there ever since, weaving carpets and breeding ferocious guard dogs for a living.

After the journey up the valley, Taptapani itself is little more than a line of dingy snack stalls and mildewed bungalows deep within dense forest – the kind of place to which government servants pray not to be posted. Pilgrims come here for the legendary **hot springs**, believed to cure infertility. The boiling sulphurous water bubbles out of a cleft in the mountainside and is piped into a small pool, where jutting little rocks smeared with vermilion and hibiscus petals mark the presence of the living deities believed to reside in the water. It is prohibited to dip any part of the body in the pool. Behind, a plain tank contains the spring water for people to paddle in; it's not so clean but the temperature is soothing. Women seeking to avail themselves of its curative effects are supposed to grope under the surface for seeds that fall off the tree overhanging the pond – an act of endurance that can take days to accomplish.

If you choose to **stay** in Taptapani, you can enjoy the water in the privacy of your own hotel; it's pumped into capacious sunken bathtubs in some of the more expensive rooms at the atmospheric and peaceful OTDC *Panthaniwas* (℡06814/49531; ❹–❺). It is a short way down the hill from the springs, and commands fine views over the trees and valley to the hills in the distance. Although the *Panthaniwas* is rarely full, there's absolutely nowhere else to stay for miles around, so it's safest to reserve a room through an OTDC office or hotel in advance. The decent **restaurant** at the *Panthaniwas* serves inexpensive and delicious Indian food.

Beyond Taptapani

Beyond Taptapani, you're soon worlds away from the congested roads and towns of Orissa's coastal plains. Traffic dries up, villages become even poorer and less frequent and rice cultivation is squeezed out by thick forest. The appearance of pots attached to sago palms and windowless mud huts with low thatched roofs indicate that you've arrived in Orissa's *adivasi* heartland. The pass above Taptapani is the start of the **Saora**'s traditional land. Further west around the Koraput and Jeypore area live the **Dongria Kondh**, the **Koya** and the **Bondas**.

Officially, you're not allowed into the district without first obtaining a **permit** from the state government. Paranoia about **Naxalites** hiding out in the forests along the Andhra Pradesh border, coupled with a marked reluctance to allow foreigners into tribal zones, make these notoriously difficult to obtain. It's still possible to move freely around the various towns and villages in Orissa's wild west, though it's hard to know which, if any, are worth the hassle of minimal infrastructure, rudimentary accommodation and infrequent transport. If you're really keen to visit *adivasi* villages, the best, though far from the cheapest, way is to arrange a trip through a specialist **travel agent** in Bhubaneswar or Puri. They'll take care of the permits, sort out food and rooms and, if they're any good, have local contacts to make sure you behave appropriately in the villages and markets. Heritage Tours (☏06752/27800 or 278001) in Puri arrange six- to ten-day trips for roughly Rs1200 (or the dollar equivalent) per person per day and make every effort not to intrude where outsiders are not welcome. However, *adivasi* villages see no share of the spoils, a situation they feel justifiably angry about, and you may well receive a very frosty reception. Whichever way you look at it though, turning up in an isolated and culturally sensitive place with an Ambassador car and a camera has got to be a pretty unsound way of "meeting" the locals.

Travel details

Trains

Bhubaneswar to: Agra (1–2 daily; 29–37hr 30min); Balasore (10 daily; 4hr); Bangalore (2 weekly; 31hr); Berhampur (7 daily; 2hr 30min–3hr); Calcutta (6–8 daily; 8–13hr); Chennai (2–4 daily; 20hr 45min–26hr); Cochin (4 weekly; 36–38hr); Cuttack (11 daily; 30–55min); Delhi (3–4 daily; 25–43hr); Hyderabad (3 daily; 20–24hr); Mumbai (1 daily; 38hr); Puri (7 daily; 2–3hr); Varanasi (3 weekly; 23hr).
Puri to: Agra (1 daily; 38hr 40min); Balasore (5–6 daily; 4hr 30min–6hr); Bhubaneswar (5–6 daily; 1hr 30min–2hr); Calcutta (2 daily; 11hr 30min); Delhi (3 daily; 32–44hr); Varanasi (3 weekly; 22hr).
Balasore to: Bhubaneswar (7–9 daily; 3hr 45min–6hr); Calcutta (6–8 daily; 4–5hr); Puri (5–6 daily; 6–7hr).

Buses

Bhubaneswar to: Balasore (every 30min; 3hr 30min–5hr); Berhampur (6–8 daily; 3hr); Calcutta (4

nightly; 10hr); Cuttack (every 15min; 45min–1hr); Konarak (1 daily; 1hr 30min–2hr); Pipli (every 15min; 30min); Puri (every 15min; 2hr).
Puri to: Bhubaneswar (every 20min; 2hr); Calcutta (2 daily; 12hr); Chilika Lake (1 daily; 2–3hr); Konarak (every 30min; 40min–1hr).
Balasore to: Baripada (every 20min; 1hr); Bhubaneswar (6–8 daily; 3hr 30min–5hr); Calcutta (5 daily; 5–7hr); Chandipur (5 daily; 30min); Puri (4–6 daily; 5–7hr).
Berhampur to: Bhubaneswar (6–10 daily; 3hr); Gopalpur-on-Sea (every 15min; 30min); Koraput (1 daily; 13hr); Rayagada (1 daily; 3hr); Taptapani (hourly; 1hr 15min).

Flights

Bhubaneswar to: Calcutta (1 daily; 55min); Chennai (4 weekly; 2hr 30min); Delhi (daily; 2hr 10min); Hyderabad (3 weekly; 1hr 45min); Mumbai (3 weekly; 2hr); Visakhapatnam (4 weekly; 55min).

CHAPTER 18

Highlights

✱ **Hyderabad** This predominately Islamic city offers a compelling combination of monuments, museums and lively bazaars. **See p.1139**

✱ **Golconda Fort** Set in a lush landscape just west of Hyderabad, the capital of the Qutb Shahi dynasty boasts a dramatic fort. **See p.1144**

✱ **Warangal** Features two important Hindu monuments: the medieval fort and a thousand-pillared Shiva temple. **See p.1148**

✱ **Nagarjunakonda** Ancient Buddhist sculptures and stupas, dotted around an island in Nagarjuna Sagar lake. **See p.1149**

✱ **Amaravati** At this village on the banks of the Krishna, fine carvings surround the remains of a great stupa. **See p.1152**

✱ **Tirumala Hill, Tirupati** The most visited pilgrimage centre in the world, Tirumala Hill is crowned by the Venkateshwara Vishnu temple. **See p.1155**

✱ **Puttaparthy** Sai Baba's main ashram attracts modern pilgrims from all over the world, and forms the centrepiece of a thriving community. **See p.1157**

18

Andhra Pradesh

Although **ANDHRA PRADESH** occupies a great swathe of eastern India, stretching for more than 1200km along the coast from Orissa to Tamil Nadu and reaching far inland from the fertile deltas of the Godavari and Krishna rivers to the semi-arid Deccan Plateau, it's not a place that receives many tourists. Most foreign travellers pass through en route to its more attractive neighbours, which is understandable as places of interest are few and far between. However, the sights that Andhra Pradesh does have to offer are absorbing and well enough connected to warrant at least a few stops on a longer tour of south India.

The state capital, **Hyderabad**, although run-down in parts, is an undoubtedly atmospheric city dating from the late sixteenth century. Its endless bazaars, eclectic Salar Jung museum and the mighty **Golconda Fort** nearby make it an enticing place to spend a day or two. Outlying areas are home to the spanking new towers of hi-tech companies. By contrast, its modern twin, commercial **Secunderabad**, excels only in characterlessness. **Warangal**, 150km northeast of Hyderabad, has both Muslim and Hindu remains from the twelfth and thirteenth centuries, while the region's Buddhist legacy – particularly its superb sculpture – is preserved in museums at sites such as **Nagarjunakonda** (south of Hyderabad) and **Amaravati**, the ancient Satavahana capital. In the east, the big cities of **Vishakapatnam** and **Vijayawada** have little to recommend them, though the latter makes a convenient access point for Amaravati. However, the temple town of **Tirupati** in the far southeast – best reached from Chennai in Tamil Nadu – is one of India's great Hindu phenomena, a fascinating and impossibly crowded pilgrimage site, said to be more popular even than Mecca. In the southwest of the state, the small town of **Puttaparthy** attracts a more international pilgrim crowd, drawn here by the prospect of *darshan* from spiritual leader Sai Baba.

Although modern industries have grown up around the capital, and shipbuilding, iron and steel are important on the coast, most people in Andhra Pradesh remain poor. Away from the Godavari and Krishna deltas, where the

---

Accommodation price codes

All accommodation prices in this book have been categorized using the price codes below. Prices given are for a double room, and all taxes are included. For more details, see p.51.

① up to Rs100   ④ Rs300–400   ⑦ Rs900–1500
② Rs100–200   ⑤ Rs400–600   ⑧ Rs1500–2500
③ Rs200–300   ⑥ Rs600–900   ⑨ Rs2500 and upwards

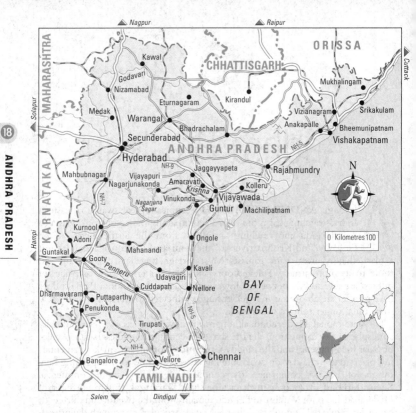

soil is rich enough to grow rice and sugar cane, the land is in places impossible to cultivate.

Some history

Earliest accounts of the region, dating back to the time of **Ashoka** (third century BC), refer to a people known as the Andhras. The **Satavahana dynasty** (second century BC–second century AD), also known as the Andhras, came to control much of central and southern India from their second capital at Amaravati on the Krishna. They enjoyed extensive international trade with both eastern Asia and Europe, and were great patrons of Buddhism. Subsequently, the Pallavas from Tamil Nadu, the Chalukyas from Karnataka, and the Cholas all held sway. By the thirteenth century, the Kakatiyas of Warangal were under constant threat from Muslim incursions, while later on, after the fall of their city at Hampi, the Hindu Vijayanagars transferred operations to Chandragiri near Tirupati.

The next significant development was in the mid-sixteenth century, with the rise of the Muslim **Qutb Shahi dynasty**. In 1687, the son of the Moghul emperor Aurangzeb seized Golconda. Five years after Aurangzeb died in 1707, the viceroy of Hyderabad declared independence and established the Asaf Jahi dynasty of **nizams**. In return for allying with the British against Tipu Sultan of Mysore, the nizam dynasty was allowed to retain a certain degree of autonomy even after the British had come to dominate all India.

During the struggle for Independence, harmony between Hindus and Muslims in Andhra Pradesh disintegrated. **Partition** brought matters to a climax, as the Nizam desired to join other Muslims in the soon-to-be-created state of **Pakistan**. In 1949 the capital erupted in riots, the army was brought in and Hyderabad state was admitted to the Indian Union. Andhra Pradesh state was created in 1956 from Telegu-speaking regions (although Urdu is widely spoken in Hyderabad) that had previously formed part of the Madras Presidency on the east coast and the princely state of Hyderabad to the west. Today almost ninety percent of the population is Hindu, with Muslims largely concentrated in the capital.

Hyderabad/Secunderabad

A melting-pot of Muslim and Hindu cultures, the capital of Andhra Pradesh comprises the twin cities of **HYDERABAD** and **SECUNDERABAD**, with a combined population of around six million. Secunderabad, of little interest to visitors, is the modern administrative city founded by the British, whereas Hyderabad, the old city, with its seething **bazaars**, **Muslim monuments** and **Salar Jung Museum** has heaps of charm. Despite this, Hyderabad went into decline after Independence with tensions often close to the surface due to lack of funding – the old city only received 25 percent of the budget despite having 45 percent of the population. In recent years, however, the area has received a new lease of life from the computer industry, and Hyderabad is now at the forefront of software training, rivalling Bangalore as the south's hi-tech capital. This upturn has increased the optimism of Hyderabadis, whether they are reaping direct benefits or not; they now gleefully refer to their city as "Cyberabad".

Hyderabad was founded in 1591 by **Mohammed Quli Shah** (1562–1612), beside the River Musi, 8km east of Golconda, the fortress capital of the Golconda empire which by now was suffering from overcrowding and a serious lack of water. Unusually, this new city was laid out on a grid system, with huge arches and stone buildings that included Hyderabad's most famous monument, **Charminar**. At first it was a city without walls; these were only added in 1740, as defence against the Marathas. Legend has it that a secret tunnel linked the spectacular **Golconda Fort** with the city, dotted with dome-shaped structures at suitable intervals to provide the unfortunate messengers who had to use it with the opportunity to come up for fresh air.

For the three hundred years of Muslim reign, there was harmony between the predominantly Hindu population and the minority Muslims. Hyderabad

Hyderabad addresses

Hyderabadis appear to have a deep mistrust of logical, consistent road-naming, mapping and **addresses**. One road merges into another, some addresses refer to nothing more specific than a locality and others identify themselves as being opposite buildings that no longer exist. Just as confusing are those that have very specific addresses consisting of a string of hyphenated numbers referring to house and plot numbers, incomprehensible to anybody other than town surveyors. All this is somewhat ironic in a city that is home to one of the major sections of the Survey of India.

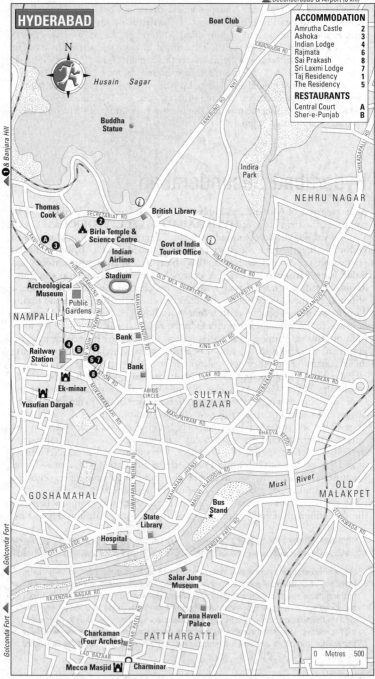

was the most important focus of Muslim power in south India at this time; the princes' fabulous wealth derived primarily from the fine gems, particularly diamonds, mined in the Kistna Valley at Golconda. In the 1600s, Golconda was the diamond centre of the world. The famous **Koh-i-Noor** diamond was found here – the only time it was ever captured was by Moghul Emperor Aurangzeb, when his son seized the Golconda Fort in 1687. It ended up, cut, in the British royal crown.

Arrival and information

The old city of **Hyderabad** straddles the River Musi. Most places of interest lie south of the river, while much of the accommodation is to the north. Further north, separated from Hyderabad by the Husain Sagar Lake, is the modern twin city of **Secunderabad**, where some long-distance trains terminate, and where all through trains deposit passengers. If you do have to get off at Secunderabad, your ticket is valid for any connecting train to Hyderabad; and if none is imminent, many buses including #5, #8 and #20 ply between both stations. Hyderabad **airport**, 8km north of the city at Begumpet, is served by auto-rickshaws, taxis, and buses #9M or #10 via Nampally station, and a number of routes including #10, #45, #47 and #49 from Secunderabad. **Hyderabad railway station** (also known as Nampally) is close to all amenities and offers a fairly comprehensive service to major destinations. The well-organized **long-distance bus stand** occupies an island in the middle of the Musi River, 3km southeast of the railway station.

The main **tourist office** in Hyderabad is the **APTDC office** (daily 7am–7pm) on Secretariat Road just before it becomes Tank Bund, opposite a large public building known as the BRK (℡040/345 3036, ℻345 3086, ✉apttdc@satyam.net.in); the other APTDC office, at Yatri Nivas, Sardar Patel Road, Secunderabad (℡040/781 6375), is of little use unless you want to book one of their tours. The **Government of India tourist office**, Sandozi Buildings, Himayatnagar Road, Hyderabad (Mon–Fri 9am–5pm; ℡040/763 0037), offers a few brochures. However, the best source of local information is the monthly **magazine**, *Channel 6*, widely available from bookstalls for Rs12.

Guided tours

APTDC operates a number of guided tours. All times quoted below are when the tours set off from the Secunderabad office; pick-up time in Hyderabad is 45min later.

The better of the two city tours (daily 8am–5.15pm; Rs130) includes Husain Sagar, the Birla temple and planetarium, Qutb Shahi tombs (not Fri), Salar Jung Museum (not Fri), Charminar and Golconda. There are also shorter morning and afternoon city tours and one to Golconda Fort's sound and light show (daily 4.15–9.15pm; Rs100 including entrance fee), which also drives past Hi-Tech City. Ramoji Film City, 35km south, also has its own tour (daily 7.45am–6pm; Rs350 including entry).

The Nagarjuna Sagar tour (daily 6.30am–9.30pm; Rs225) covers 360km in total, and is rather rushed, but is a convenient way to get to this fascinating area (see p.1149). The longer tours to Tirupati/Tirumala, more conveniently reached from Chennai and further afield in south India, are not worth considering.

Accommodation

The area in front of **Hyderabad railway station** (Nampally) has the cheapest accommodation, but you're unlikely to find anything basic for less than

Rs200. The grim little enclave of five lodges with "Royal" in their name is usually full and best avoided. The real **bargains** are more in the mid- to upper-range hotels, which offer better facilities for lower rates than in other big cities. About 2km north of Secunderabad railway station, decent places line **Sarojini Devi Road**, near the Gymkhana Ground.

Hyderabad

Amrutha Castle, Secretariat Road, Saifabad ⊤040/329 9899, ⊕324 1850, ⓔamruthacastle@pol.net.in. Affiliated to *Best Western*, this extraordinary hotel, designed like a fairy castle with round turret rooms, offers full international facilities at fair prices. With its rooftop swimming pool, it's a good place to splash out. ❽–❾

Ashoka, 6–1–70 Lakdi-ka-Pul ⊤040/323 0105, ⊕323 3739. Standard mid-range hotel with a variety of clean attached rooms, including cable TV and some a/c. ❺–❻

Indian lodge, Nampally station ⊤040/657 3840. The best of the basic lodges in the station area. All rooms en suite, with TV. ❸

Rajmata, Nampally High Road, opposite railway station ⊤040/320 1000. Set back from the road in the same compound as the various *Royal* lodges. Large, clean non-a/c deluxe rooms. Their adjacent *Lakshmi* restaurant offers good south Indian veg food. ❺

The Residency, Nampally High Road ⊤040/320 4060, ⊕320 4040, ⓔreservations@theresidency-hyd.com Swish, modern hotel belonging to the *Quality Inn* group; the most upmarket option near the station. The restaurant serves good veg food, beautifully presented in plush surroundings. ❼–❾

Sai Prakash, Station Road ⊤040/461 1726, ⊕461 3355. A modern hotel, complete with capsule lift, less than 5min walk from the station. Features comfortable, carpeted rooms (all with cable TV) set around an atrium. High standards (non-a/c in particular), and very popular. Good restaurants and bar. ❻–❼

Sri Laxmi lodge, Gadwal Compound, Station Road ⊤040/320 1551. Quiet place with clean attached rooms down a lane opposite the *Sai Prakash*. Very good value. ❷

Taj Residency, Road No. 1, Banjara Hills ⊤040/339 3939, ⊕339 2218, ⓔtrhres.hyd@tajhotels.com One of three Taj Group hotels in the vicinity with the usual top-notch facilities, overlooking a lake, 4km from the centre of Hyderabad. Cheapest room around $100. Good restaurant and coffee shop. ❾

Secunderabad

National Lodge annexe, opposite Secunderabad Railway station ⊤040/770 5572. No-frills lodge, but the best of the bunch if you need to catch an awkwardly timed train. To the left of the older *National* as you come out from the station. ❷

Parklane, 115 Park Lane ⊤040/784 0466, ⊕784 0599. Large rooms (ordinary and deluxe), with views onto other buildings, very clean bathrooms, Star TV, restaurant and friendly staff. ❺–❻

Ramakrishna, St. John's Road ⊤040/783 4567, ⊕782 0933. Comfy mid-range option in a large concrete block opposite the railway reservation complex. Some a/c rooms, and it's the smartest place in the station area. ❺–❻

Taj Mahal, 88 Sarojini Devi Rd ⊤040/812105. Clean and efficient but old-fashioned hotel with character, built in 1949, but bearing no detectable relation to the Taj Mahal. Rooms are clean, comfortable and spacious, although a bit dark. Veg restaurant with snacks and spicy Andhra meals. No bar. ❹–❻

The City

Hyderabad is divided into three: **Hyderabad**, the old city; **Secunderabad**, the new (originally called Husain Shah Pura); and **Golconda**, the old fort. The two cities are basically one big sprawl, separated by a lake, **Husain Sagar**, which was created in the 1500s and named after Husain Shah Wali, who had helped Ibrahim Quli Qutb Shah recover from a serious illness. A huge stone Buddha stands in the centre of the lake. The main hi-tech and film industry centres lie quite some distance to the west and south of this triangle.

The most interesting area, south of the River Musi, holds the **bazaars**, **Charminar** and the **Salar Jung Museum**. It must be a long time since the Musi amounted to very much. Even after the rains the river is about a tenth the width of the bridge; most of the area under the bridge is grassed over, some planted with palms and paddy. North of the river, the main shopping areas are centred around Abids Circle and the Sultan Bazaar (ready-made clothes, fruit, veg and silk), ten minutes' walk east of the railway station. Abids Circle is connected to MG Road, which runs north to join Tankbund Road at Husain Sagar and on to Secunderabad, while to the south it metamorphoses into Nehru Road.

Salar Jung Museum

The unmissable **Salar Jung Museum** (daily except Fri 10am–5pm; Rs150), on the south bank of the Musi, houses part of the huge collection of Salar Jung, one of the nizam's prime ministers, and his ancestors. A well-travelled man of wealth, with an eye for objets d'art, he bought whatever took his fancy from both the East and West, from the sublime to, in some cases, the ridiculous. His extraordinary hoard includes Indian jade, miniatures, furniture, lacquer-work, Moghul opaque glassware, fabrics, bronzes, Buddhist and Hindu sculpture, manuscripts, and weapons. There are also good examples of *bidri*, decorated metalwork cast from an alloy of zinc, copper and tin, that originated in Bidar in northern Karnataka. Avoid visiting the museum at the weekend, when it gets very crowded.

Charminar, Lad Bazaar and the Mecca Masjid

A maze of bazaars teeming with people, the old city has at its heart the **Charminar**, or Four Towers, a triumphal arch built at the centre of Mohammed Quli Shah's city in 1591 to commemorate an epidemic. As its name suggests, it features four graceful minarets, each 56m high, housing spiral staircases to the upper storeys. Although a secular building, it has a mosque (now closed) on the roof; the oldest in Hyderabad, it is said to have been built to teach the royal children the Koran. The yellowish colour of the whole building is thanks to a special stucco made of marble powder, gram and egg yolk.

Charminar marks the start of the fascinating **Lad Bazaar**, as old as the town itself, which leads to Mahboob Chowk, a market square featuring a mosque and Victorian clocktower. Lad Bazaar specializes in everything you could possibly need for a Hyderabadi marriage; it's full of bangle shops, old stores where you can buy rosewater, herbs and spices, exotic materials and more mundane *lunghis*. You'll also find silver filigree jewellery, antiques and *bidri*-ware, as well as boxes, plates, hookah-paraphernalia and the like, delicately inlaid with silver and brass. Hyderabad is the centre of the pearl trade; **pearls**, so beloved of the nizams that they not only wore them but apparently liked nothing more than having them ground into powder to eat, can be bought in the markets near the Charminar. Southeast of Lad Bazaar, the complex of **Royal Palaces** includes Chaumahalla, four palaces set around a central courtyard.

Southwest, behind the Charminar, is **Mecca Masjid**, the sixth-largest mosque in India, constructed in 1598 by the sixth king, Abdullah Qutb Shah, from locally hewn blocks of black granite. Small red bricks from Mecca are slotted over the central arch. The mosque can hold 3000 followers with up to 10,000 in the courtyard; on the left of the courtyard are the tombs of the nizams. Outside the mosque is a stall where they will change your torn, cut rupee bills at good rates.

The **Charkaman**, or Four Arches, north of Charminar, were built in 1594 and once led to the parade ground of royal palaces (now long gone). The surrounding narrow streets spill over with interesting small shops; through the western arch, **Doulat-Khan-e-Ali** (which originally led to the palace), stores sell lustrous brocade and old saris. The arch itself is said to have once been hung with rich gold tapestries.

North of the river

The **Yusufian Dargah**, with a striking bulbous yellow dome, is set in a leafy courtyard not far south of the railway station (follow the road that runs down from the Ek-minar mosque and look for an alley on the right). It is the shrine of a seventeenth-century Sufi saint of the venerable Chisti order and you can enter with covered head and circle the flower-decked tomb. About a kilometre north of the station, set in Hyderabad's tranquil public gardens, the **AP state museum** (daily except Fri 10.30am–5pm; Rs2) displays a modest but well-labelled collection of bronzes, prehistoric tools, copper inscription plates, weapons, household utensils and even an Egyptian mummy. There's a gallery of modern art in the new extension, too. The nearby **health museum** (Mon–Sat 10.30am–1.30pm & 2–5pm; free) is dowdy and uninspiring.

The **Birla Venkateshwara temple** (daily 7am–noon & 3–9pm), on Kalabahad ("black mountain") Hill, north of the Public Gardens, is open to all, irrespective of caste, creed or nationality. Constructed in Rajasthani white marble in 1976 by the Birla Trust, it was set up by the wealthy industrialist Birla family. Although the temple itself is not of great interest, it affords fine views. Nearby, and built by the same organization, is the **planetarium** (shows are in English: Mon–Sat 11.30am, 4pm & 6pm; Sun & hols 11.30am, 3.45pm & 6pm; Rs10) and a brand new **science centre** (daily 10.30am–8.30pm; Rs10) with lots of satellite hardware and photos, machines demonstrating sensory perceptions and a small dinosaur display.

Husain Sagar

Husain Sagar, the large expanse of water separating Hyderabad from Secunderabad, lends a welcome air of tranquility to the busy conurbation. People come here to stroll along Tank Bund, the road that runs around the eastern side of the lake, and to relax in the small parks dotted along the water's edge. In the centre of the lake stands an enormous, modern stone statue of the **Buddha Purnima** or "Full Moon Buddha", which was eventually erected onto its plinth in 1992, after spending a while underwater when it sank at the first attempt to transport it there. Regular **boats** chug out to the statue from Lumbini Park, just off Secretariat Road.

Golconda Fort and the tombs of the Qutb Shahi kings

Golconda, 122m above the plain and 11km west of old Hyderabad, was the capital of the seven Qutb Shahi kings from 1518 until the end of the sixteenth century, when the court moved to Hyderabad. Well preserved and set in thick green scrubland, it is one of the most impressive forts in India. The citadel boasted 87 semicircular bastions and eight mighty gates, four of which are still in use, complete with gruesome elephant-proof spikes.

To get **to the fort**, bus #119 runs from Nampally. Both the #66G direct bus from Charminar and #80D from Secunderabad stop outside the main entrance. **For the tombs**, take #123 and #142S from Charminar. From Secunderabad the #5, #5S, and #5R all go to Mehdipattanam, where you should hop onto #123. Or, of course, you could take a rickshaw and spare yourself the bother (agree a waiting fee in advance). Set aside a day to explore the fort, which covers an area of around four square kilometres; it's well worth hiring one of the many guides who gather at the entrance, or at least buying one of the handy little pamphlets, including map, sold by vendors.

Entering the **fort** (daily 9am–5pm; $5 [Rs5]) by the Balahisar Gate, you come into the Grand Portico, where guards clap their hands to show off the

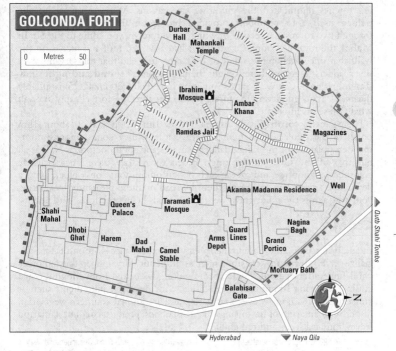

GOLCONDA FORT

0 Metres 50

Durbar Hall
Mahankali Temple
Ibrahim Mosque
Ambar Khana
Ramdas Jail
Magazines
Akanna Madanna Residence
Well
Shahi Mahal
Queen's Palace
Taramati Mosque
Dhobi Ghat
Harem
Dad Mahal
Camel Stable
Arms Depot
Guard Lines
Grand Portico
Nagina Bagh
Mortuary Bath
Balahisar Gate

Qutb Shahi Tombs

Hyderabad   Naya Qila

fort's acoustics; the claps can be clearly heard at the Durbar Hall. To the right is the **mortuary bath**, where the bodies of deceased nobles were ritually bathed prior to burial. If you follow the arrowed anticlockwise route, you then pass along a straight walled path before coming to the two-storey residence of ministers Akkana and Madanna, and starting the proper ascent to the Durbar Hall. Halfway along the steps, which pass assorted water channels and wells, you arrive at a small dark cell named after the court cashier **Ramdas**, who while incarcerated here produced the clumsy carvings and paintings that litter the gloomy room. Nearing the top, you come across the small, pretty mosque of Ibrahim Qutb Shah; beyond here, set beneath two huge granite stones, is an even tinier temple to Durga in her manifestation as Mahakali.

The steps are crowned by the three-storey **Durbar Hall** of the Qutb Shahs, on platforms outside which the monarchs would sit and survey their domains. Their accompaniment was the lilting strains of court musicians, as opposed to today's cacophony of incessant clapping from far below. As you head back down to the palaces and harems, you pass the tanks that supplied the fort's water system.

The ruins of the **queen's palace**, once elaborately decorated with multiple domes, stand in a courtyard centred on an original copper fountain that used to be filled with rosewater. You can still see traces of the "necklace" design on one of the arches, at the top of which a lotus bud sits below an opening flower with a cavity at its centre that once contained a diamond. Petals and creeper leaves are dotted with tiny holes that formerly gleamed with rubies and diamonds; parrots, long gone, had rubies for their eyes. Today visitors can only speculate how splendid it must all have looked, especially at night, when flaming torches illuminated the glittering decorations. At the entrance to the **palace** itself, four chambers provided protection from intruders. Passing through two rooms, the second of which is overgrown, you come to the **Shahi Mahal**, the royal bedroom. Originally it had a domed roof and niches on the walls that once sheltered candles or oil lamps. It is said that the servants used silver ladders to get up there to light them. Golconda's **sound and light** show (English: March–Oct Wed, Sat & Sun 7pm; Nov–Feb 6.30pm; Rs25) is suitably theatrical. It's a good way for foreigners to get into the fort cheaply, though what you see is limited.

There are 82 **tombs** (daily except Fri 9.30am–4.30pm; Rs2) about 1km north of the outer wall. Set in peaceful gardens, they commemorate commanders, relatives of the kings, dancers, singers and royal doctors, as well as all but two of the Qutb Shahi kings. Faded today, they were once brightly coloured in turquoise and green; each has an onion dome on a block, with a decorative arcade. You can reach them by road or, more pleasantly, by picking your way across the quiet grassy verges and fields below the fort's battlements.

Eating

In addition to the hotel restaurants, plenty of "meals" places around town specialize in **Hyderabadi cuisine**, such as authentic biryanis, or the famously chilli-hot Andhra cuisine. Hyderabadi cooking is derived from Moghul court cuisine, featuring sumptuous meat dishes with northern ingredients such as cinnamon, cardamom, cloves and garlic, and traditional southern vegetarian dishes with an array of flavourings like cassia buds, peanuts, coconut, tamarind leaves, mustard seeds and red chillies.

Akbar, 1-7-190 MG Rd, Secunderabad. Hyderabadi cuisine at moderate prices.

Amrutha Castle, Secretariat Road, Saifabad. Dine at the ground-floor *Hare and Hound*, presided over by suits of armour. Great-value evening buffet with a delicious range of soups, meat, fish, veg and sweets for around Rs200.

Ashoka, 6-1-70 Lakdi-ka-Pul. Hotel with a/c *Saptagiri* cafeteria serving good-value south Indian snacks and some north Indian dishes.

Central Court, Lakdi-ka-Pul. The hotel's *Touch of Class* restaurant offers good Hyderabadi non-veg plus some veg options and barbecue kebabs on a small patio; also Mughlai, Western and Chinese food. There's a good-value lunch buffet at Rs55–75, and in the evenings a pricier buffet and à la carte.

Paradise-Persis, MG Road, Secunderabad. Very popular multi-restaurant complex bashing out fine Hyderabadi cuisine at moderate prices.

Sai Prakash, Station Road. The *Woodlands* serves good-value veg south Indian snacks and north Indian dishes. *Rich'n'Famous*, in the same hotel, is much posher and pricier, with comfy chairs and imaginative daily specials including crab, prawns and specialities from both Hyderabad and further afield.

Sher-e-Punjab, corner of Nampally High Road and station entrance. Basic basement restaurant with good tasty north Indian food at bargain prices.

Taj Residency, Road No. 1, Banjara Hills. The *Dakhni* restaurant inside the hotel serves excellent, pricey, authentic south Indian cuisine, and Hyderabadi specialities.

Listings

Airlines Air France, Gupta Estate lst floor, Basheerbagh ☏ 040/323 0947; Air India, 5-9-193 HACA Bhavan, opposite Public Garden Saifabad ☏ 040/323 2747; British Airways, Nijhawan Travel Services, 5-9-88/4 Ainulaman Fateh Maidan Rd ☏ 040/324 1661; Delta/Sabena/Swissair/Singapore Airlines, GSA: Aviation Travels, Navbharat

Chambers, 6-3-1109/1 Raj Bhavan Rd ☏ 040/331 2380; Gulf Air/TWA/Bangladesh Biman/Air Canada/Royal Jordanian, Jet Air, Flat 202, 5-9-58 Gupta Estate, Basheerbagh ☏ 040/324 0870; Indian Airlines, opposite Assembly Saifabad (office ☏ 040/329 9333; general flight information ☏ 140;

pre-recorded flight info ☎142; Jet Airways, 6-3-1109/1 GF Nav Bharat Chambers, Raj Bhavan Road ☎040/330 1222; Lufthansa, 3-5-823 Shop #B1–B3, Hyderaguda ☎040/323 5537; Qantas, Transworld Travels, 3A lst floor, 5-9-93 Chapel Rd ☎040/329 8495.

Banks and exchange Oddly for a state capital, most banks still don't do foreign exchange, two exceptions being the State Bank of Hyderabad, MG Road, and Federal Bank, 1st floor, Orient Estate, MG Road. Both are open Mon–Fri 10.30am–2.30pm, the latter also Sat 10.30am–12.30pm. It's better to head for an agency such as Thomas Cook ☎040/329 6521 at Nasir Arcade, Secretariat Road; or L.K.P. Forex ☎040/321 0094 on Public Gardens Road, only ten minutes' walk north of Nampally station. Both are open Mon–Sat 9.30am–5.30pm. In Secunderabad try the Allahabad Bank, next to *Park Lane* hotel.

Bookshops Higginbothams, 1 Lal Bahadur Stadium, Hyderabad; Gangarams, 62 DSD Rd, near *Garden Restaurant* in Secunderabad; and Kalaujal, Hill Fort Road, opposite the Public Gardens, which specializes in art books. Both shops offer a wide selection of literature, nonfiction titles and reference books.

Car rental Air Travels in Banjara Hills (☎040/335 3099, ☏335 5088) and Classic Travels in Secunderabad (☎040/775 5645) both provide a 24hr service, with or without driver.

Crafts Leepakshi, the AP state government emporium at Gunfoundry on MG Road, stocks a wide range of handicrafts, including Bidri metalwork, jewellery and silks. Utkalika (Government of Orissa handicrafts), House no. 60-1-67, between the Ravindra Bharati building and *Hotel Ashoka*, has a modest selection of silver filigree jewellery, handloom cloth, *ikhat* tie-dye, Jagannath papier-mâché

Moving on from Hyderabad

Daily **train** services from **Hyderabad railway station (Nampally)** include: the Charminar Express #2760 to Chennai (7pm; 14hr); the Hyderabad–Cochin Express #7030 (noon; 27hr); the Andhra Pradesh Express #2723 to Delhi (6.40am; 26hr); the Hyderabad–Mumbai Express #7032 (8.40pm; 17hr); the East Coast Express #7046 to Calcutta (7am; 33hr) via Vijayawada (6hr), Vishakapatnam (13hr 30min) and Bhubaneswar (23hr); and the Rayasaleema Express #7429 to Tirupati (5.30pm; 15hr 30min). All northeast-bound services call at Warangal and most at Vijayawada. **From Secunderabad**, there are some originating services and many through trains in all directions. Useful services include the Konarak Express #1020 to Mumbai (10.50am; 17hr 30min), Secunderabad–Bangalore Express #7085 (5.40pm; 13hr 35min), the Kacheguda–Mandad Express #7664 to Aurangabad (6pm; 14hr 20min) and the Secunderabad–Varanasi Express #7091 (Mon & Wed 10.30pm; 30hr 15min).

The **railways reservations office** at Hyderabad (Mon–Sat 8am–2pm & 2.30–8pm, Sun 8am–2pm) is to the left as you enter the station. Counter #211 (next to enquiry counter) is supposedly for tourist reservations, but it's also used for group bookings and lost tickets. Foreign visitors can make bookings at the Chief Reservation Inspector's Office on platform 1 (daily 9am–5pm). The **Secunderabad reservation complex** is by the major junction with St. John's Road over 400m to the right as you exit the station. Counter 134 is for foreigners.

From the Central Bus Stand, **regular bus services** run to Amaravati, Bangalore, Bidar, Chennai, Mumbai, Nagarjuna Sagar, Tirupati, Vijayawada and Warangal. Also various **deluxe and video buses** depart for Bangalore, Chennai, Mumbai and other major destinations, from outside Nampally station, where you will find a cluster of private agencies.

Between them, Indian Airlines and Jet Airways offer three **daily flights** to Bangalore, at least seven to Mumbai, three to Delhi, three or four to Chennai, two to Vishakapatnam, at least one to Tirupati and one or two to Calcutta, via Bhubaneswar on three of those days. Flights also depart for Ahmedabad and Cochin on some days. Indian Airlines runs at least one flight daily to one or other of the Gulf states and Air India also has flights to Mumbai, and a new service twice weekly direct to Singapore (2hr 30min).

See Travel Details at the end of this chapter for more information on journey frequencies and durations.

figures and buffalo bone carvings. Cheneta Bhavan is a modern shopping complex a little south of the railway station, stuffed with hand-loom cloth shops from various states, including Tamil Nadu, Uttar Pradesh, Rajasthan, Madhya Pradesh and Andhra Pradesh. For silks and saris, try Meena Bazaar, Pochampally Silks and Sarees, and Pooja Sarees, all on Tilak Road.

Cycles Bicycles can be rented for Rs20 per day at a friendly stall on the right as you approach Hyderabad station from Nampally High Road.

Hospitals The government-run Gandhi Hospital is in Secunderabad ☎ 040/770 2222; the private CDR Hospital is in Himayataagar ☎ 040/322 1221; and there's a Tropical Diseases Hospital in Nallakunta ☎ 040/766 7843.

Internet access The most convenient internet access is available from Satyam Online at Modern Xerox (daily 9am–10pm; ☎ 040/460 3894, near

the Ek-minar mosque, behind Nampally station, for Rs35 per hour. Other outlets are to be found in the Abids area.

Library The British Library, Secretariat Road (Tues–Sat 11am–7pm; ☎ 040/323 0774) has a wide selection of books and recent British newspapers. Officially you must be a member or a British citizen to get in.

Pharmacies Apollo Pharmacy ☎ 040/323 1380 and Health Pharmacy ☎ 040/331 0618 are both open 24hr.

Police ☎ 040/323 0191.

Travel agents General agents for airline and private-bus tickets include: Travel Club Forex ☎ 040/323 4180, Nasir Arcade, Saifabad, close to Thomas Cook; and Kamat Travels, in the *Hotel Sai Prakash* complex ☎ 040/461 2096. There's a host of private-bus agents on Nampally High Road outside Hyderabad railway station.

Around Hyderabad

As you head north from Hyderabad towards the borders of Maharashtra and Madhya Pradesh, the landscape becomes greener and more hilly, sporadically punctuated by attractive black-granite rock formations. There is little to detain visitors here except the small town of **Warangal**, conveniently situated on the main railway line as it loops across to the east, which warrants a stop to visit the nearby medieval fort and Shiva temple. South of the capital, vast swathes of flat farmland stretch into the centre of the state, where the Nagarjuna Sagar dam has created a major lake with the important Buddhist site of **Nagarjunakonda**, now an island, in its midst.

Warangal

WARANGAL – "one stone" – 150km northeast of Hyderabad, was the Hindu capital of the Kakatiyan empire in the twelfth and thirteenth centuries. Like other Deccan cities, it changed hands many times between the Hindus and the Muslims – something that is reflected in its architecture and the remains you see today.

Warangal's **fort** (4km south) is famous for its two circles of fortifications: the outer made of earth with a moat, and the inner of stone. Four roads into the centre meet at the ruined temple of **Svayambhu** (1162), dedicated to Shiva. At its southern, freestanding gateway, another Shiva temple, from the fourteenth century, is in much better shape; inside, the remains of an enormous *lingam* came originally from the Svayambhu shrine. Also inside the citadel is the **Shirab Khan**, or **Audience Hall**, an early eleventh-century building very similar to Mandu's Hindola Mahal (see p.502).

The largely basalt Chalukyan-style **"thousand-pillared" Shiva temple** (daily 10am–6pm; $5), just off the main road, beside the slopes of Hanamkonda Hill (6km north), was constructed by King Rudra Deva in 1163. A low-roofed building, on several stepped stages, it features superb carvings and three shrines to Vishnu, Shiva and Surya the sun god. They lead off the *mandapa* whose numerous finely carved columns give the temple its name. In front, a polished Nandi bull was carved out of a single stone. A Bhadrakali temple stands at the top of the hill.

Practicalities

If you make an early start, it's just about possible to visit Warangal in a day-trip from Hyderabad. Frequent buses and trains run to the town (roughly 3hr). Warangal's **bus stand** and **railway station** are opposite each other, served by local buses, auto- and cycle rickshaws. The easiest way to cover the site is to **rent a bicycle** from one of the stalls on Station Road. As you follow Station Road from the station, if you are heading for the fort turn left just beyond the post office, under the railway bridge and left again at the next main road. For Hanamkonda turn right onto JPN Road at the next main junction after the post office, left at the next major crossroads onto MG Road, and right at the end onto the Hanamkonda main road. The temple and hill are on the left.

   Accommodation is limited: *Hotel Ashok* on Main Road, Hanamkonda, 6km from the railway and bus stand (℡08712/85491; ❹–❻), has a/c rooms, a restaurant and bar and is rather more upmarket than *Hotel Ratna* (℡08712/60645, Ⓕ60096; ❸–❻), 2km from the station on MG Road. Basic lodges nearer the station include *Vijaya* (℡08712/25851; ❷–❸) on Station Road, which is the closest and best value, and *Urvasi* (℡08712/61760; ❷–❹) at the junction of Station and JPN roads, which has some a/c rooms. Several decent **eating places** line Station Road – the upstairs *Titanic*, halfway along on the right, serves good tandoori and other non-veg dishes. Internet facilities are available at *Grace@Net* on JPN Road for Rs30 per hour.

Nagarjunakonda

NAGARJUNAKONDA, or "Nagarjuna's Hill", 166km south of Hyderabad and 175km west of Vijayawada, is all that now remains of the vast area, rich in archeological sites, submerged when the huge Nagarjuna Sagar Dam was built across the River Krishna in 1960. Ancient settlements in the valley were first discovered in 1926; extensive excavations carried out between 1954 and 1960 uncovered more than one hundred sites dating from the early Stone Age to late medieval times. Nagarjunakonda was once the summit of a hill, where a fort towered 200m above the valley floor; now it's just a small oblong island near the middle of Nagarjuna Sagar Lake, accessible by boat from the mainland. Several Buddhist monuments have been reconstructed, in an operation reminiscent of that at Abu Simbel in Egypt, and a **museum** exhibits the more remarkable ruins of the valley. **VIJAYAPURI**, the village on the shore of the lake, overlooks the colossal dam itself, which stretches for almost 2km. Torrents of water flushed through its 26 floodgates produce electricity for the whole region, and irrigate an area of almost 800 square kilometres. Many villages had to be relocated to higher ground when the valley was flooded.

The island and the museum

Boats arrive on the northeastern edge of **Nagarjunakonda island**, unloading passengers at what remains of one of the gates of the fort, built in the fourteenth century and considerably renovated by the Vijayanagar kings in the mid-sixteenth century. Low, damaged, stone walls skirting the island mark the edge of the fort, and you can see ground-level remains of the Hindu temples that served its inhabitants.

Well-kept gardens lie between the jetty and the museum, beyond which nine Buddhist monuments from various sites in the valley have been rebuilt. West of the jetty, there's a reconstructed bathing *ghat*, built entirely of limestone during the reigns of the Ikshvaku kings (third century AD). A series of levels and steps leads to the water's edge; boards etched into some of its slabs were probably used for dice games.

The **maha-chaitya**, or stupa, constructed at the command of King Chamtula's sister in the third century AD, is the earliest Buddhist structure in the area. It was raised over relics of the Buddha – said to include a tooth – and has been reassembled in the southwest of the island. Nearby, a towering **statue** of the Buddha stands draped in robes beside a ground plan of a monastery that enshrines a smaller stupa. Other **stupas** stand nearby; the brick walls of the *svastika chaitya* have been arranged in the shape of swastikas, common emblems in early Buddhist iconography.

In the **museum** (daily except Fri 9am–5pm), **Buddhist sculptures** include large stone friezes decorated with scenes from the Buddha's life: his birth; his mother's vision of an elephant and a lotus blossom; his renunciation, and his subversion of evil as he meditated and realized enlightenment under the *bodhi* tree. Twelve statues of standing Buddhas – one of which reaches 3m – show the Buddha in various postures of teaching or meditation. Many pillars are undamaged, profusely carved with Buddha images, bowing devotees, elephants and lotus medallions.

Earlier artefacts include stone tools and pots from the Neolithic age (third millennium BC), and metal axe heads and knives (first millennium BC). Among later finds are several inscribed pillars from Ikshvaku times, recording in Prakrit or Sanskrit the installation of Buddhist monasteries and statues. The final phase of art at Nagarjunakonda is represented by medieval sculptures: a thirteenth-century *tirthankara* (Jain saint), a seventeenth-century Ganesh and Nandi, and a set of eighteenth-century statues of Shiva and Shakti, his female consort. Also on display is a model showing the excavated sites in the valley.

Practicalities

Organized **APTDC tours** from Hyderabad to Nagarjunakonda (see p.1141) – taking in the sites and museum, the nearby Ethiopothala Waterfalls and an engraved third-century Buddhist monolith known as the Pylon – can be a bit rushed: if you want to spend more time in the area you can take a bus from Hyderabad (4hr; all the regular Macherla services stop at Vijayapuri) or Vijayawada (6hr; a direct service runs daily at 11am and frequent services leave from Guntur). It can be quicker to change at Macherla.

Accommodation at Vijayapuri is limited, and you need to decide in advance where you are going to stay in order to know where to get off the bus, as there are two distinct settlements 6km apart on either side of the dam. For easy access to the sites it is better to stay near the jetty on the right bank. Ask the bus to leave you at the launch station. The drab-looking concrete *Nagarjuna Motel Complex* (☎08642/78188; ❷) has adequate rooms and some a/c. Five hundred metres away in the village, the *Golden Lodge* (☎08642/78148; ❶) is much more basic. Both APTDC places are on the other side of the dam as you approach the lake from the direction of Hyderabad. The APTDC *Vijay Vihar Complex* (☎08680/77362; ❺), which has spacious rooms with balconies and a good restaurant, is 2km further up the hill from the APTDC *Project House* (☎08680/76540; ❸–❺) in the left-bank village. However, if you want to stay in these more comfortable surroundings, there is a frequent shuttle bus to the right bank and it is a pleasant walk to the dam and lake shore.

Tickets for **boats** to the island (daily 9am & 1.30pm; 45min) are on sale 25 minutes before departure (Rs25). Each boat leaves the island ninety minutes after it arrives, which allows enough time to see the museum and walk briskly round the monuments, but if you want to take your time and soak up the pleasant atmosphere without the crowds from the boat, take the morning boat and return in the afternoon. A cafeteria on the island serves drinks and occasionally biscuits, but only opens when the boat is in, so take provisions.

Eastern Andhra Pradesh

Perhaps India's least visited area, **eastern Andhra Pradesh** is sandwiched between the Bay of Bengal in the east and the red soil and high peaks of the Eastern Ghats in the north. Its one architectural attraction is the ancient Buddhist site of **Amaravati**, near the city of **Vijayawada**, whose sprinkling of historic temples is far overshadowed by impersonal, modern buildings. Some 350km north, the major port of **Vishakapatnam** is not as grim as it first seems, but it's not a place to linger long. For anyone with a strong desire to explore, however, pockets of natural beauty along the coast and in the hills of eastern Andhra Pradesh can offer rich rewards. In this sleepy landscape, little affected by modernization, bullocks amble between swaying palms and the rice fields are iridescent against rusty sands. Unless you have the patience to endure the excruciatingly slow public transport system, your own vehicle is essential.

Vijayawada and around

Almost 450km north of Chennai, a third of the way to Calcutta, **VIJAYAWA-DA** is a bustling commercial centre on the banks of the Krishna delta, hemmed in by bare granite outcrops 90km from the coast. This mundane city, alleviated by the mountain backdrop and some urban greenery, is seldom visited by tourists, but does, however, make the obvious stop-off point for visits to the third-century Buddhist site at **Amaravati**, 60km west.

A handful of **temples** in Vijayawada merit a quick look. The most important, raised on the low Indrakila Hill in the east, is dedicated to the city's patron goddess **Kanaka Durga** (also known as Vijaya), goddess of riches, power and benevolence. Though it is believed to be thousands of years old, with the exception of a few pillared halls and intricate carvings, what you see today is largely renovated (and freshly whitewashed). Across the river, roughly 3km out of town, there's an ancient, unmodified cave temple at **Undavalli**, a tiny rural village set off the main road, easily reached on any Guntur-bound bus, or the local #13 service. The temple is cut out of the granite hillside in typical Pallava style: simple, solid and bold. Each of its five levels contains a deep low-roofed hall, with small rock-cut shrines to Vishnu, Shiva and Parvati, and pillared verandas guarded by sturdy grey statues of gods, saints and lions. Views from the porches take in a sublime patchwork of rivulets, paddy fields and banana plantations.

Practicalities

Vijayawada's **railway station**, on the main Chennai–Calcutta line, is in the centre of town. Buses arriving from Vishakapatnam, Guntur, Amaravati and as far afield as Hyderabad and Chennai pull into the **bus stand** further west.

Specific ticket offices cater for each service, and a **tourist office** (℡0866/523966) has details on local hotels and sights. APTDC also has an office in the centre of town at Hotel Ilapuram Complex, Gandhi Nagar (℡0866/570255). You can **change money** at Zen Global Finance, 40–6–27 Krishna Nagar in Labbipet. Between the bus stand and railway station, Ryes Canal flows through the heart of town.

Vijayawada is a major business centre, with a good selection of mid-range **hotels**, all less than 2km from the railway station and bus stand. Most have reasonably priced restaurants serving Andhra thalis and à la carte items. Budget options include *Monika Lodge* (℡0866/571334; ❷–❸), just off Elluru Road about 500m from the bus stand: very simple, and slightly grubby. Two better-value places, both on Atchutaramaiah Street, which links the railway station to Elluru Road, are the *Hotel Narayana Swamy* (℡0866/571221; ❸), and the *Sri Ram* (℡0866/579377; ❹–❻) with spotless rooms, some a/c and all with cable TV. A posher option is the modern *Hotel Swarna Palace* on Elluru Road at the junction with Atchutaramaiah Street (℡0866/577222, ℻574602; ❺–❻). The rooms are comfortably furnished, with cable TV. The fourth-floor restaurant provides large portions of Indian, Chinese and Continental food with city views and something of a disco appearance without the music. The *Raj Towers* (℡0866/571311, ℻571317; ❹–❼), also on Elluru Road, is a tall modern block with good mid-range rooms.

Guntur

Another sprawling and bustling commercial city 30km southwest of Vijayawada, **GUNTUR** has no merits of its own but makes an even more convenient jumping-off point for Amaravati than Vijayawada, especially if you are coming from the area of Nagarjuna Sagar. There are buses every ten to fifteen minutes to Vijayawada (45min–1hr), and every half-hour to Amaravati from the old bus stand (adjacent to the main bus stand). If you decide to spend the night here, there are some perfectly adequate **lodges** right opposite the bus stands. *Annapurna Lodge* (℡0863/356493; ❷–❹) has decent-sized clean rooms and some a/c; *Padmasri Lodge* (℡0863/223813; ❷–❹) also has a/c and cheaper singles.

Amaravati

AMARAVATI, a small village on the banks of the Krishna 30km west of Vijayawada, is the site of a Buddhist settlement, formerly known as Chintapalli, where a stupa larger than those at Sanchi (see p.435) was erected over relics of the Buddha in the third century BC, during the reign of Ashoka. The stupa no longer stands, but its great size is evident from the large mound that formed its base. It was originally surrounded by grey stone railings with a gateway at each of the cardinal points, one of which has been reconstructed in an open courtyard. Its decoration, meticulously carved and perfectly preserved, shows the themes represented on all such Buddhist monuments: the Buddha's birth, renunciation and life as an emaciated ascetic, enlightenment under the Bodhi tree (see p.1005), his first sermon in the Deer Park, and *parinirvana*, or death. Several foundation stones of monastic quarters remain on the site.

Exhibits at the small but fascinating **museum** (daily except Fri 10am–5pm; $5 [Rs5]) range in date from the third century BC to the twelfth century AD. They include statues of the Buddha, with lotus symbols on his feet, a head of tightly curled hair, and long ear lobes, all traditional indications of an enlightened teacher. Earlier stone carvings represent the Buddha through such symbols as the *chakra* (wheel of *dharma*), a throne, a stupa, a flaming pillar or a *bodhi* tree, all being worshipped. The lotus motif, a central symbol in early Buddhism, is connected with a dream the Buddha's mother had shortly after conception, and has always been a Buddhist symbol of essential purity: it appears repeatedly on railings and pillars. Later sculptures include limestone statues of the goddess Tara and *bodhisattva* Padmapani, both installed at the site in medieval times when the community had adopted Mahayana teachings in place of the earlier Hinayana doctrines. What you see here are some of the finer pieces excavated from the site – other remains have been taken to the Chennai Government Museum and the British Museum in London.

Practicalities

Theoretically **buses** run hourly from Vijayawada to Amaravati but the service seems to be unreliable, so it's best to take a bus to Guntur (every 15min; 45min–1hr), where you can pick up a connection to Amaravati (1hr–1hr 30min). Buses return to Guntur every half-hour. Organized **boat tours** run from the APTDC *Krishnaveni Motel*, next to the main bridge, on the south bank of the Krishna in Vijiyawada, to Amaravati and back for Rs50 when the river is high enough, not often in recent years. The excavated site and museum are roughly 1km from the bus stand. Trishaws – miniature carts attached to tricycles and brightly painted with chubby film stars – take tourists to the site and the riverbank, where there are several drink stalls. APTDC has two small guest houses on the banks of the Krishna beside the attractive Sri Amareshwara Swamy temple at the far end of the main street: the *Dharani* (℡08645/55332; ❷), which also has cheap dorm beds (Rs50); and the slightly more comfortable *Poonami* (℡08645/65332; ❸). Their canteen provides basic meals and snacks.

Visakhapatnam and around

One of India's most rapidly growing industrial cities, and its fourth-largest port, **VISAKHAPATNAM** (also known as Vizag), 350km north of Vijayawada, is a big unpleasant city choked with the smells and dirt of a busy shipbuilding industry, an oil plant and a steel factory. Such is its sprawl that it has overtaken and polluted much of the neighbouring town of Waltair, once a health resort. Although there's little to warrant a stop at Vishakapatnam, the district of Waltair with its uncrowded tree-lined roads and seafront make for a pleasant stroll. If you head that way, you can visit the modest collection of art and sculpture at the **Visakha Museum** (Tues–Sun 4–8pm; Rs1.50) on Beach Road near the *Hotel Park*. The beach around here is far enough from the port for the sea to be reasonably clean, though the best beach for swimming is at Kalshagiri further north, reached by regular buses from the RTC complex.

Various traces of older civilizations lie within a day's journey of the city. At **Bheemunipatnam**, 30km north, you can see the remains of a Dutch fort and a peculiar cemetery where slate-grey pyramidal tombs are abandoned to nature. **Borra**, 70km inland on a minor road that winds through the Eastern Ghats and the Araku forests, boasts a set of eerie limestone **caves** whose darkness is pierced with age-old stalactites and stalagmites (daily 8am–noon & 2–5pm; Rs12). You'll need a car to get to **Mukhalingam**, 100km north of Bheemunipatnam, where three Shaivite temples, built between the sixth and twelfth centuries, rest in low hills. Their elaborate carvings and well-preserved towering *shikharas* display slight local variations to the otherwise standard Orissan style (see p.1097). There's nowhere to stay in Mukhalingam.

Practicalities

Vishakapatnam's **railway station**, on the Chennai–Calcutta coastal route, is in the old town, towards the port. The ride to Delhi takes a tedious two days. The **bus stand**, known as RTC Complex, is in a newer area, 3km from the coast. There's an **airport**, 12km west of town, with daily connections to Hyderabad and Mumbai, and several weekly to Calcutta and Bhubaneswar; bus #38 runs from the airport to the centre. Irregular **ships** make the three-day crossing to Port Blair on the Andaman Islands roughly once a month.

The **tourist office** (Mon–Sat 10.30am–5pm; ☎0891/596761) at the Srimukh Complex, Dwaraka Nagar, is difficult to find and only of use if you want to book a City (daily 8.30am–6pm; Rs90) or Borra Caves (daily 8.30am–6pm; Rs250 including lunch) tour, though this can be done more easily in any case at the APTDC booth in the RTC complex. The Andhra Bank near the RTC complex will **change money**.

If you arrive late by bus, head for the well-maintained **retiring rooms** (Rs100) in the bus stand. Otherwise, most **hotels** are in the old town, near the railway station; turn right out of the station and walk for a few minutes. The best is *Hotel Karanths*, 33-1-55 Patel Marg (☎0891/502048; ❸–❺), whose spotless rooms have balconies, pressed sheets, colour TV and attached bathrooms. The downstairs restaurant serves unbeatable thalis and tiffin at low prices. Next door, *Dakshayani* (☎0891/561798; ❷) offers simple grotty rooms, some with private bathrooms. Round the corner in Bowdara Road, the *Sri Ganesh Hotel* (☎0891/563274; ❷) is a better budget option with simple clean rooms. Vishakapatnam's nicest upmarket hotel, the *Park* on Beach Road (☎0891/554488; ❺), has luxurious rooms, a swimming pool, a bar and restaurant, and access to the beach. Adjacent to the *Park* is the smart *Palm Beach* (☎0891/554026; ❻), which also offers full amenities.

Southern Andhra Pradesh

The further south you travel from the fertile lands watered by the great Krishna and Godavari rivers, the less hospitable the terrain becomes, especially in the rocky southwest of the state. For Hindus, the main attraction in southern Andhra Pradesh is the tenth-century **Venkateshvara temple**, outside **Tirupati**, the most popular Vishnu shrine in India, where several thousand pilgrims come each day to receive *darshan*. **Puttaparthy**, the home town of the spiritual leader Sai Baba, is the only other place in the region to attract significant numbers of visitors. Both Tirupati and Puttaparthy are closer to Bangalore in Karnataka and Chennai in Tamil Nadu than to other points in Andhra Pradesh, and for many tourists, constitute their only foray into the state.

Tirupati

Set in a stunning position, surrounded by wooded hills capped by a ring of vertical red rocks, the **Shri Venkateshvara temple** at Tirumala, an enervating drive 700m up in the Venkata hills, 11km from **TIRUPATI** and 170km northwest of Chennai, is said to be the richest and most popular place of pilgrimage in the world, drawing more devotees than either Rome or Mecca. With its many shrines and *dharamshalas* the whole area around Tirumala Hill provides a fascinating insight into contemporary Hinduism practised on a large scale. If you are not particularly keen on waiting in line for hours at a time, choose the day of your visit with care; avoid weekends, public and school holidays, and particularly special festivals, as you are likely to meet at least 10,000 other visitors.

Govindarajaswamy temple

Just a five-minute walk from the railway station, the one temple in Tirupati itself definitely worth a visit is **Govindarajaswamy**, whose modern grey *gopura* is clearly visible from many points in town. Begun by the Nayaks in the sixteenth century, it is an interesting complex with large open courtyards decorated with lion sculptures and some ornate wooden roofs. It also houses the Venkateshvara Museum of Temple Arts. The inner **sanctum** is open to non-Hindus and contains a splendid large black reclining Vishnu, coated in bronze armour and bedecked in flowers. The *sanadarsanan* (daily 9.30am–12.30pm; Rs5) will let you in to glimpse the deity, and participate in fire blessings at the main and subsidiary shrines. The temple's impressive tank lies 200m to the east.

Tiruchanur Padmavati temple

Between Tirupati and Tirumala Hill, the **Tiruchanur Padmavati temple** is another popular pilgrimage halt. A gold *vimana* tower with lions at each corner surmounts the sanctuary, which contains a black stone image of goddess Lakshmi with one silver eye. At the front step, water sprays to wash the feet of the devotees. A Rs20 ticket allows you to jump the queue to enter the sanctuary. If you'd like to donate a sari to the goddess, you may do so, upon payment of Rs1200. Cameras are prohibited.

Tirumala Hill, the Venkateshvara temple and Kapilateertham

There's good reason for the small shrine to Ganesh at the foot of **Tirumala Hill**. The journey up is hair-raising and it's worth saying a quick prayer when embarking on it, but at least separate routes up and down preclude head-on crashes. Overtaking is strictly forbidden, but drivers do anyway; virtually every bend is labelled "blind" and every instruction to drive slowly is blithely ignored. The fearless sit on the left for the best views; the most devout, of course, climb the hill by foot. When you get to the top, you will see barbers busying themselves giving pilgrims tonsures as part of their devotions. Non-Hindus are permitted to enter the inner sanctum, but for everyone, *darshan*, a view of the god, is the briefest of brief experiences. Temple funds support a university, hospital, orphanages and schools at Tirupati as well as providing cheap, and in some cases free, accommodation for pilgrims.

The **Venkateshvara temple** dedicated to **Vishnu** and started in the tenth century, has been recently renovated to provide facilities for the thousands of pilgrims who visit daily; a rabbit warren of passages and waiting rooms wind their way around the complex in which pilgrims interminably shuffle towards the inner sanctum. Unless your visit is intended to be particularly rigorous, on reaching the temple you should follow the signs for the special *darshan* that costs Rs50 (daily 6–10am ex Fri & noon–9pm). This will reduce the time it takes to get inside by hours, if not days. You have to sign a declaration of faith in Lord Venkateshvara and give your passport number. There is a seated waiting area.

Once inside, you'll see the somewhat incongruous sight of brahmins sitting at video monitors, observing the goings-on in the inner sanctum; the constant to-ing and fro-ing includes temple attendants bringing in supplies, truckloads of oil and other comestibles, and huge cooking pots being carried across the courtyard. You may also catch deities being hauled past on palanquins to the accompaniment of *nagesvaram* (a south Indian oboe-like double-reed wind instrument) and *tavil* drum, complete with an armed guard. At the entrance is a colonnade, lined with life-sized statues of royal patrons, in copper or stone. The *gopura* gateway leading to the inner courtyard is decorated with sheets of embossed silver; a gold *stambha* (flagstaff) stands outside the inner shrine next to a gold upturned lotus on a plinth. Outside, opposite the temple, is a small museum, the **Hall of Antiquities** (daily 8am–8pm). Your special *darshan* ticket entitles you to enter the museum via a shorter queue opposite the exit and to pick up two free *laddu* sweets. **Kapilateertham**, a temple at the bottom of the hill, has a gaily painted little Hindu pleasure garden at the entrance; after the rains, a powerful waterfall crashes into a large tank surrounded by colonnades, and everyone piles in for a bath, ensuing in typically good-natured pilgrim bedlam.

Chandragiri Fort

In the sixteenth century, **Chandragiri**, 11km southwest of Tirupati, became the third capital of the Vijayanagars, whose power had declined following the fall of the city of Vijayanagar (Hampi) in Karnataka. It was here that the British negotiated the acquisition of the land to establish Fort St George, the earliest settlement at what is now Chennai. The original fort (daily except Fri 10am–5pm; $5), thought to date from c.1000 AD, was taken over by Haider Ali in 1782, followed by the British in 1792. A small **museum** of sculpture, weapons and memorabilia is housed in the main building, the Indo-Saracenic Raja Mahal. Another building, the **Rani Mahal**, stands close by, while behind that is a hill with two freestanding boulders that was used as a place of public execution during Vijayanagar times. A little temple from the Krishna Deva Raya period and a freshwater tank stand at the top of the hill behind the Raja Mahal. In the evening there is a 45-minute **sound and light** show (English version: Nov–Feb 7.30pm, March–Oct 8pm; Rs20).

Practicalities

The best way of **getting to Tirupati** is by train from Chennai; the trip can be done in a day if you get the earliest of the three daily services (3hr 30min). From Hyderabad it takes sixteen hours. An APTDC counter at the **railway station** (daily 7.30am–7pm; ☏08574/56877) is accessible from the entrance hall and platform 1, where there's a 24hr left-luggage office and a self-service veg refreshment room. Stands sell English copies of TKT Viraraghava Charya's *History of Tirupati*, and there's a Vivekananda religious bookshop next door. Tirupati's APSRTC Central **bus station** – also with 24hr left-luggage – is about 1km east of the railway station. Frequent express services run from Chennai (4hr), but the train is far more comfortable. However, if you're travelling south and want to avoid Chennai, there are hourly buses to Kanchipuram (5hr), three of which continue to Mahabalipuram (7hr). In addition, a useful daily train stops at the Tamil Nadu temple towns of Tiruvannamalai, Chidambaram, Thanjavur and Trichy. Local transport is provided by beautifully decorated **cycle rickshaws**, with silver backs, colourfully painted, and some covered by appliquéd cloth, as well as auto-rickshaws.

A special section at the back of the bus stand has services every few minutes **to Tirumala** and the Venkateshvara temple. You shouldn't have to queue too long unless it's a weekend or festival. An easier option is to take a **taxi**, best organized through the APTDC **tourist counter** at the railway station; avoid the unlicensed taxis outside the station as they could be stopped by the Tirumala police. The tourist office also run a tour (10am–5.30pm; Rs125 not including entrance tickets) which takes in Chandragiri **Fort** (except Fri) and a number of temples, but does not include the Venkateshvara temple owing to the long queues.

Accommodation and eating

Unless you're a pilgrim seeking accommodation in the *dharamshalas* near the temple, all the decent **places to stay** are in Tirupati, near the railway and bus stand: there's a vast array of hotels and lodges to suit all budgets. **Eating** is recommended in the bigger hotels; there are, of course, cheap "meals" places in town and near the temple.

Bhimas Deluxe, 34-38 G Car St, near railway station ☏ 08574/25521, ℻ 25471, ℮ bhimas-deluxe@bhimas.com Decent, comfortable rooms (all have optional a/c). The *Maya* veg restaurant serves south Indian snacks in the morning, and north Indian plus some Chinese dishes in the evenings. ⑤ –⑥

Bhimas Paradise, Renigunta Road ☏ 08574/25747, 25568. This and the sister *Bhimas Residency* next door offer clean functional rooms, some a/c, with tiny balconies. Star TV, pool, garden and 24hr coffee shop. Ugly location on main road. The restaurant, *Bharani*, is clean and dark, serving veg south Indian snacks, thalis and north Indian dishes. ⑤ –⑦

Indira Rest House, Tiruchanur Road ☏ 08574/23125. Basic, no-nonsense lodge, a few minutes' walk behind the railway lines from the bus stand. Some new a/c rooms ❷ –⑤

Maurya, 149 TP Area ☏ 08574/24894, ℻ 53859. Well-maintained hotel east of the temple tank with some a/c rooms, and cable TV. Good value. ❸ –⑤

Mini Bhimas, 191 Railway Station Rd ☏ 08574/25930. Very basic but cleanish en-suite rooms. ❷

Raghunadha, 191 Railway Station Rd ☏ 08574/23130. Good, simple, clean lodge; one of the better cheap places. Cable TV in all rooms and some a/c. ❷ –⑥

Sindhuri Park, beside bathing tank ☏ 08574/56430. Sparkling new all a/c hotel with excellent facilities and great views of the tank and temple; the smartest place in the centre. The basement *Vrinda* restaurant serves quality veg food, including a range of thalis. ⑥ –⑦

Puttaparthy

Deep in the southwest of the state, amid the arid rocky hills bordering Karnataka, a thriving community has grown up around the once insignificant village of **PUTTAPARTHY**, birthplace of spiritual leader Sai Baba, whose followers believe him to be the new incarnation of God. Centring on **Prasanthi Nilayam**, the ashram where Sai Baba resides from July to March, the town has schools, a university, a hospital and sports centre which offer up-to-date and free services to all. There's even a small airport. The **ashram** itself is a huge complex with room for thousands, with canteens, shops, a museum and library, and a vast assembly hall where Sai Baba gives *darshan* twice daily (6.40am & 3pm). Queues start more than an hour before the appointed time, and a lottery decides who gets to sit near the front. The **museum** (daily 10am–noon) contains a detailed, fascinating display on the major faiths with illustrations and quotations from their sacred texts, punctuated by Sai Baba's comments.

Practicalities

Puttaparthy is most accessible from Bangalore in Karnataka (see p.1396), from where seven daily **buses** (4hr) run to the stand outside the ashram entrance. The town is also connected to Hyderabad (3 daily; 10hr) and Chennai (1 nightly; 11hr). Regular buses make the 42-kilometre run to **Dharmavaram**,

Shri Satya Sai Baba

Born **Satyanarayana Raju** on November 23, 1926 in Puttaparthy, then an obscure village in the Madras Presidency, Satya is reported to have shown prodigious talents and unusual purity and compassion from an early age. His apparently supernatural abilities initially caused some concern to his family, who took him to Vedic doctors and eventually to be exorcized. Having been pronounced to be possessed by the divine rather than the diabolical, at the age of 14 he calmly announced that he was the new incarnation of **Sai Baba**, a saint from Shirdi in Maharashtra who died eight years before Satya was born.

Gradually his fame spread, and a large following grew. In 1950 the **ashram** was inaugurated and a decade later Sai Baba was attracting international attention; today he has millions of devotees worldwide, a considerable number of whom turn out for his birthday celebrations in Puttaparthy, when he delivers a message to his devotees. Just 5ft tall, with a startling Hendrix-style Afro, his smiling, saffron-clad figure is seen on posters, framed photos and murals all over south India. Though his **miraculous powers** reportedly include the ability to materialize *vibhuti*, sacred ash, with curative properties, Sai Baba claims this to be an unimportant activity, aimed at those firmly entrenched in materialism, and emphasizes instead his message of **universal love**. In recent years a number of ex-followers have made serious accusations about coercion and even sexual abuse on the part of the guru himself, which have been vehemently denied. Whatever your feelings about the divinity of Sai Baba, the atmosphere around the ashram is undeniably peaceful, and the growth of such a vibrant community in this once-forgotten backwater is no small miracle in itself.

the nearest **railhead**, which has good services north and south. There are also two **flights** a week from Mumbai.

Most visitors **stay** at the ashram in large bare sheds or smaller rooms if available. Except in the case of families, accommodation is strictly segregated by sex. Costs are minimal, and though you can't book in advance, you can enquire about availability at the secretary's office (℡08555/87583). Outside the ashram, many of the basic lodges are rather overpriced. However, the *Sai Ganesh Guest House* near the police station (℡08555/87079; ❷) is friendly and a good cheap option. The new *Sri Sai Sadam* at the far end of the main street is great value; all rooms have fridge, TV and balcony with views of the countryside or the ashram, and there's a meditation room and rooftop restaurant (℡08555/87507; ❸–❹). At the top end, the all a/c *Sai Towers*, near the ashram entrance (℡0855/87270; ❼) charges a lot for its smallish rooms, but has a good restaurant downstairs. Even nonresidents can **eat** in the ashram canteen, and there are simple snack stalls along the main street.

Travel details

Trains

Hyderabad/Secunderabad to: Aurangabad (1 daily; 12hr 22min); Bangalore (3–4 daily; 11hr 45min–15hr 50min); Bhubaneswar (3 daily; 19hr 50min–22hr 55min); Calcutta (2 daily; 27hr 40min–33hr 15min); Chennai (2 daily; 14hr 5min–14hr 15min); Delhi (2–3 daily; 22hr 10min–32hr 50min); Mumbai (3 daily; 15hr 35min–17hr 40min); Tirupati (3–4 daily; 14hr–15hr 30min); Varanasi (2 weekly; 30hr 15min); Vijayawada (12–13 daily; 5hr 10min–7hr 45min); Vishakapatnam (5–6 daily; 11hr 30min–19hr 10min); Warangal (9–10 daily; 2hr 8min–3hr 18min).

Tirupati to: Chennai (3 daily; 3hr 15min); Hyderabad/Secunderabad (3–4 daily; 13hr 20min–17hr 10min); Tiruchirapalli (1 daily; 14hr 15min); Varanasi (1 daily; 36hr); Vijayawada (3–6 daily; 6hr 25min–8hr 45min); Vishakapatnam (2–3 daily; 13hr 25min–19hr 5min).

Vijayawada to: Calcutta (5–7 daily; 21hr 55min–33hr 20min); Chennai (7–12 daily; 5hr 45min–8hr 50min); Delhi (4–6 daily; 23hr 10min–32hr 50min); Hyderabad/Secunderabad (12–13 daily; 5hr 15min–8hr 10min); Tirupati (3–6 daily; 6hr 25min–8hr 15min); Vishakapatnam (12–16 daily; 6hr 5min–12hr 30min).

Vishakapatnam to: Bhubaneswar (5–7 daily; 6hr 45min–9hr 50min); Calcutta (5–7 daily; 15hr 15min–23hr); Chennai (2–4 daily; 12hr 45min–15hr 55min); Delhi (1–2 daily; 34hr 40min–39hr 45min); Hyderabad/Secunderabad (5–6 daily; 11hr 50min–15hr 40min); Tirupati (2–3 daily; 14hr 30min–16hr 50min); Vijayawada (12–16 daily; 5hr 55min–11hr 10min).

Buses

Hyderabad to: Amaravati (2 daily; 7hr); Bangalore (hourly; 13hr); Bidar (19 daily; 4hr); Chennai (1 daily; 16hr); Mumbai (8 daily; 17hr); Puttaparthy (3 daily; 10hr); Tirupati (7 daily; 12hr); Vijayapuri (10 daily; 4hr); Vijayawada (every 15min; 6hr); Warangal (every 15–30min; 3hr).

Tirupati to: Chennai (every 30min; 3hr 30min–4hr); Kanchipuram (hourly; 3hr 30min); Hyderabad (7 daily; 12hr); Mahabalipuram (3 daily; 5hr 30min); Puttaparthy (1 daily; 10hr).

Vijayawada to: Amaravati (hourly; 2hr); Guntur (every 15min; 1hr–1hr 30min); Hyderabad (every 15min; 6hr).

Flights

Hyderabad to: Ahmedabad (4 weekly; 1hr 40min); Bangalore (2–3 daily; 1hr); Calcutta (1–2 daily; 2–3hr); Chennai (3–4 daily; 1hr–1hr 45min); Cochin (2 weekly; 2hr 40min); Delhi (3 daily; 2hr–2hr 10min); Mumbai (6–7 daily; 1hr 15min–3hr); Tirupati (1–2 daily; 55min–1hr 20min); Vishakapatnam (2 daily; 1hr–1hr 30min).

Puttaparthy to: Mumbai (2 weekly; 1hr 20min).

Vishakapatnam to: Bhubaneswar (4 weekly; 55min); Calcutta (4 weekly; 2hr 20min); Chennai (4 weekly; 1hr 5min); Delhi (4 weekly; 3hr 35min); Hyderabad (2 daily; 1hr–1hr 30min); Mumbai (1 daily; 2hr 45min).

CHAPTER 19

Highlights

✳ **Scuba-diving** Beautiful coral reefs teem with vivid underwater life.
See p.1167

✳ **Port Blair** The Cellular Jail stands as a reminder of the hilly Andaman capital's bleak colonial past. See p.1171

✳ **Wandoor** The white sandy beach and islets of the Mahatma Gandhi National Marine Park are the archipelago's most popular day-trip destination, and a good appetizer for more remote parts. See p.1175

✳ **Havelock Island** Cruise by boat to the Andamans' most popular holiday hang-out, very laid-back, friendly and great for diving.
See p.1177

✳ **North Andaman** The long haul on the road from Port Blair is worthwhile for the backdrop of thick rainforest and the dazzling tropical beaches when you get there.
See p.1181

19

The Andaman Islands

T he **ANDAMAN ISLANDS**, comprising India's most remote state, are situated 1000km off the east coast in the middle of the Bay of Bengal, connected to the mainland by flights and ferries from Calcutta, Chennai and Vishakapatnam. Thickly covered by deep green tropical forest, the archipelago supports a profusion of wildlife, including some extremely rare species of bird, but the principal attraction for tourists lies offshore, around the pristine reefs ringing most of the islands. Filled with colourful fish and kaleidoscopic corals, the crystal-clear waters of the Andaman Sea feature some of the world's richest and least spoilt marine reserves – perfect for **snorkelling** and **scuba diving**. Potential visitors may, however, consider that the expense and effort required to get there, the lack of infrastructure and certain increased health risks, as well as ethical concerns about ecological and tribal issues, rather outweigh the benefits of a trip.

For administrative purposes, the Andamans are grouped with the **Nicobar Islands**, 200km further south but, as yet, strictly off limits to foreigners. Approximately 200 islands make up the Andaman group and nineteen the Nicobar. They are islands of varying size, the summits of a submarine mountain range stretching 755km from the Arakan Yoma chain in Burma to the fringes of Sumatra in the south. All but the most remote of these are populated in parts by **indigenous tribes** whose numbers have been slashed dramatically as a result of nineteenth-century European settlement and, more recently, rampant **deforestation**. Today felling is supposed to be restricted, and 86 percent of the islands' forests are officially "protected". Nevertheless, *padauk* and teak are still extensively used for building materials, furniture and tourist knick-knacks, and those areas of woodland still open to the lumberjacks are being stripped of valuable foreign-currency-earning timber ahead of the all-out ban on extraction expected in the next few years.

Foreign tourists are only permitted to visit certain parts of the Andaman group, separated by the deep Ten Degree Channel from the Nicobar Islands.

Accommodation price codes

All accommodation prices in this book have been categorized using the price codes below. Prices given are for a double room, and all taxes are included. For more details, see p.51.

❶ up to Rs100	❹ Rs300–400	❼ Rs900–1500
❷ Rs100–200	❺ Rs400–600	❽ Rs1500–2500
❸ Rs200–300	❻ Rs600–900	❾ Rs2500 and upwards

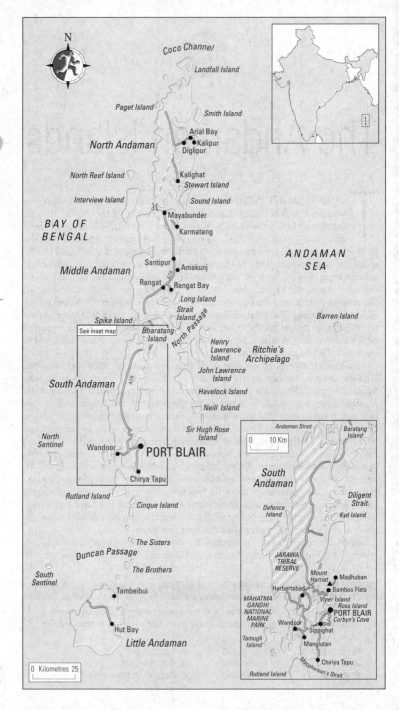

0 Kilometres 25

The point of arrival for boats and planes is **South Andaman**, where the predominantly Tamil and Bengali community in the small but busy capital, **Port Blair**, accounts for almost half the total population. **Permits** obtainable on the mainland or on arrival by air are granted for a stay of one month. The most beautiful beaches and coral reefs are found on outlying islands. A healthy get-up-and-go spirit is essential if you plan to explore these, as connections and transport can be erratic, frequently uncomfortable and severely limited, especially on the smaller islands. Once away from the settlements, you enter a Coca-Cola-free zone where you'll need your own camping supplies and equipment. It's also worth pointing out that a surprising number of travellers fall sick in the Andamans. The dense tree cover, marshy swamps and high rainfall combine to provide the perfect breeding ground for mosquitoes, and **malaria** is endemic in even the most remote settlements. Sandflies are also ferocious in certain places and **tropical ulcer** infections from scratching the bites is a frequent hazard.

The **climate** remains tropical throughout the year, with temperatures ranging from 24° to 35°C and humidity levels never below seventy percent. By far the best time to visit is between January and May. From mid-May to October, heavy rains flush the islands, often bringing violent cyclones that leave west-coast beaches strewn with fallen trees, while in November and December less severe rains arrive with the northeast monsoon. Despite being so far east, the islands run on Indian time, so the sun rises as early as 4.30am in summer and darkness falls soon after 5pm.

Some history

The earliest mention of the Andaman and Nicobar islands is found in **Ptolemy's** geographical treatises of the second century AD. Other records from the Chinese Buddhist monk I'Tsing some five hundred years later and Arabian travellers who passed by in the ninth century depict the inhabitants as fierce and cannibalistic. **Marco Polo** arrived in the thirteenth century and could offer no more favourable description of the natives: "The people are without a king and are idolaters no better than wild beasts. All the men of the island of Angamanian have heads like dogs . . . they are a most cruel generation, and eat everybody they catch . . ." It is unlikely, however, that the Andamanese were cannibals, as the most vivid reports of their ferocity were propagated by Malay pirates who held sway over the surrounding seas, and needed to keep looters well away from trade ships that passed between India, China and the Far East.

During the eighteenth and nineteenth centuries **European missionaries** and trading companies turned their attention to the islands with a view to colonization. A string of unsuccessful attempts to convert the Nicobaris to Christianity was made by the French, Dutch and Danish, all of whom were forced to abandon their plans in the face of hideous diseases and a severe lack of food and water. Though the missionaries themselves seldom met with any hostility, several fleets of trading ships that tried to dock on the islands were captured, and their crews murdered, by Nicobari people.

In 1777 the British Lieutenant Blair chose the South Andaman harbour now known as **Port Blair** as the site for a **penal colony**, based on the deportation of criminals that had proved successful in Sumatra, Singapore and Penang. Both this scheme, and an attempt to settle the Nicobar Islands in 1867, were thwarted by adverse conditions. However, the third go at colonization was more successful, and in 1858 Port Blair finally did become a penal settlement, where political activists who had fuelled the Mutiny in 1857 were made to clear land and build their own prison. Out of 773 prisoners, 292 died, escaped or were hanged in the first two months. Many also lost their lives in attacks by Andamanese tribes who objected to forest clearance, but the settlement continued to fill with people from mainland India, and by 1864 the number of convicts had grown to 3000. In 1896 work began on a jail made up of hundreds of tiny solitary cells, which was used to confine political prisoners until 1945. The prison still stands and is one of Port Blair's few "tourist attractions".

In 1919, the British government in India decided to close down the penal settlement, but it was subsequently used to incarcerate a new generation of freedom fighters from India, Malabar and Burma. During World War II the

Native people of the Andaman and Nicobar Islands

Quite where the **indigenous population** of the Andaman and Nicobar islands originally came from is a puzzle that has preoccupied anthropologists since Radcliffe-Brown conducted his famous field work among the Andamanese at the beginning of this century. Asian-looking groups such as the Shompen (see below) may have migrated here from the east and north when the islands were connected to Burma, or the sea was sufficiently shallow to allow transport by canoe, but this doesn't explain the origins of the black populations, whose appearance suggests African roots. Wherever they came from, the survival of the islands' first inhabitants has been threatened by traders and colonizers, who introduced disease and destroyed their territories by widespread felling. Thousands also died from addiction to alcohol and opium, which the Chinese, Japanese and British exchanged for valuable shells. Of perhaps 5000 aborigines in 1858, from six of the twelve native tribal groups, only five percent remain.

On the Nicobar Islands, the distinctly Southeast Asian **Nicobaris**, who claim descent from a Burmese prince and were identified as *lojenke* (naked people) by I'Tsing, have integrated to some extent with recent settlers, following widespread conversion by Christian missionaries. While they continue to live in small communities of huts raised on stilts, most have adopted modern agricultural methods, raising pigs and cultivating fruit and vegetable gardens rather than hunting. One of the largest communities of Nicobaris is at John Richardson Bay, near the town of Hut Bay on Little Andaman. The **Shompen** of Great Nicobar, on the other hand, have not assimilated, and less than two hundred survive, living predominantly on the coast, where they barter in honey, cane and nuts with the Nicobaris.

The indigenous inhabitants of the Andamans, divided into *eramtaga* (those living in the jungle) and *ar-yuato* (those living on the coast), traditionally subsisted on fish, turtles, turtle eggs, pigs, fruit, honey and roots. Although the largest group when the islands were first colonized, less than thirty **Great Andamanese** remain, forcibly settled on Strait Island, north of South Andaman as a "breeding centre" and reliant on the Indian authorities for food and shelter. In the 1860s, the Rev. H. Corbyn set up a "home" for them to learn English on Ross Island, insisting that they wear clothes and attend reading and writing classes. Five children and three adults from Corbyn's school were taken as curiosities to Calcutta in 1864, where they were shown around the sights. The whole experience, however, proved more fascinating for the crowds who'd come to ogle the "monkey men" than for the Andamanese themselves, who, one of the organizers of the trip, ruefully remarked "...never evinced astonishment or admiration at anything which they beheld, however wonderful in its novelty we might suppose it would appear to them". From the foreign settlers the Andamanese tragically contracted diseases such as syphilis, measles, mumps and influenza, and fell prey to opium addiction. Within three years almost the entire population had died.

The **Jarawas**, who shifted from their original homes when land was cleared to build Port Blair, now live on the remote western coasts of Middle and South

islands were occupied by the **Japanese**, who tortured and murdered hundreds of indigenous islanders suspected of collaborating with the British, and bombed the homes of the Jarawa tribe. British forces moved back in 1945, and at last abolished the penal settlement.

After **Partition**, refugees, mostly low-caste Hindus from Bangladesh and Bengal, were given land in Port Blair and North Andaman, where the forest was clear-felled to make room for rice paddy, cocoa plantations and new industries. Since 1951, the population has increased more than ten-fold, further swollen by repatriated Tamils from Sri Lanka, thousands of Bihari labourers, ex-

Andaman, hemmed in by the Andaman Trunk Road which since the 1970s has cut them off from hunting grounds and freshwater supplies. Over the past two decades, encroachments on their land by loggers, road builders and Bengali settlers have met with fierce resistance. Dozens, possibly hundreds, of people have died in skirmishes. In one incident a party of Burmese were caught poaching on Jarawa land; of the eleven men involved, six limped out with horrific injuries, two were found dead, and the other three were never seen again. Most of the incidents have occurred on or near the Andaman Trunk Road, which is why armed escorts board the buses at several points during the journey north from Port Blair to Mayabunder.

Some contact with the Indian government used to be made through gift exchanges at each full moon, when consignments of coconuts, bananas and red cloth were taken to a friendly band of Jarawas on a boat, but the initiative was later cancelled. The damage may well have been done though, for some Jarawas have become curious about what "civilization" has to offer and since 1997 have taken to holding their hands out for goodies to passing vehicles and even visiting Indian settlements near their territory. When the initially generous reception waned, their visits evolved into surreptitious raids and there was an attack on a police outpost in March 1998. So tensions remain high and government plans in the pipeline for the permanent settlement and "development" of the Jarawas does not bode well for the independent survival of some of the planet's last hunter-gatherers.

Aside from a couple of violent encounters with nineteenth-century seamen (seventy were massacred on first contact in 1867), relations with the **Onge**, who call themselves **Gaubolambe**, have been relatively peaceful. Distinguished by their white-clay and ochre body paint, they continue to live in communal shelters (*bera*) and construct temporary thatched huts (*korale*) on Little Andaman. The remaining population of around one hundred retain their traditional way of life on two small reserves. The Indian government has erected wood and tin huts in both, dispatched a teacher to instruct them in Hindi, and encouraged coconut cultivation, but to little avail. Contact with outsiders is limited to an occasional trip into town to purchase liquor, and visits from rare parties of anthropologists. The reserves are strictly off limits to foreigners, but you can learn about the Onge's traditional hunting practices, beliefs and rituals in Vishvajit Pandya's wonderful ethnography study, *Above the Forest*.

The most elusive tribe of all, the **Sentinelese**, live on North Sentinel Island west of South Andaman. Some contact was made with them in 1990, after a team put together by the local administration had left gifts on the beaches every month for two years, but subsequent visits have invariably ended in a hail of arrows. Since the early 1990s, the AAJVS, the government department charged with tribal welfare, have effectively given up trying to contact the Sentinelese, who are estimated to number around eighty. Flying in or out of Port Blair, you pass above their island, ringed by a spectacular coral reef, and it is reassuring to think that the people sitting at the bottom of the plumes of smoke drifting from the forest canopy have for so long resisted contact with the outside world.

servicemen given land grants, economic migrants from poorer Indian states, and the legions of government employees packed off here on two-year "punishment postings". This replanted population greatly outnumbers the Andamans' indigenous people, who currently comprise around half of one percent of the total. Contact between the two societies is limited, and is not always friendly. In addition, there exists within Port Blair a clear divide between the relatively recent incomers and the so-called **"pre-42s"** – descendants of the released convicts and freedom fighters whose families settled here before the major influx from the mainland. This small but influential minority, based at the exclusive Browning Club in the capital, has been calling for curbs on immigration and new property rules to slow down the rate of settlement. While doubtless motivated by self-interest, their demands nevertheless reflect growing concern for the future of the Andamans, where rapid and largely unplanned development has wreaked havoc on the natural environment, not to mention on the indigenous population.

With the days of the timber-extraction cash cow now numbered, the hope is that **tourism** will replace tree felling as the main source of revenue. However, the extra visitor numbers envisaged are certain to overtax an already inadequate infrastructure, aggravating seasonal water shortages and sewage disposal problems. Given India's track record with tourism development, it's hard to be optimistic. Perhaps the greatest threat is the plan to extend the airport runway in 2002, which will allow long-haul flights from Southeast Asia to land here. In the meantime, smaller charter planes from Bangkok and Singapore may start arriving by the end of 2001. If only a trickle of the tourist traffic flooding between Thailand and India is diverted through the Andamans, the impact on this culturally and ecologically fragile region could be catastrophic.

Getting to the Andaman Islands

Port Blair, on South Andaman, is served by Indian Airlines **flights** from Calcutta (daily except Wed & Fri) and Chennai (Mon, Wed, Fri & Sun); Jet Airways now runs a daily flight from Chennai, which means that availability is a lot easier than it used to be on that sector. Tickets for the two-hour flights remain expensive though, at around $200 one way, unless you qualify for a discount.

It's also possible to get to Port Blair by **ship**. Services to and from Chennai have stabilized and can now be reasonably relied upon to leave in each direction every Friday. Those from Calcutta departing every two weeks and Vishakapatnam once every month are still somewhat erratic. Although far cheaper than flying, the crossings are long (3–4 days), uncomfortable and often delayed by bad conditions and bureaucracy. Those wishing to travel to the Andaman Islands by ship from Vishakapatnam should contact the Foreigners' Regional Registration Office, SP Police, Rajaram Mohanroy Rd (℡0891/562709) for a permit and A.V. Banojirow & Co, PO Box 17, opposite Port Main Gate (℡0891/565597, ℻566507), for ticket and sailing information.

Tourists arriving by plane can pick up the **permit** necessary to visit the islands on arrival at Port Blair airport; passengers travelling on a ship should obtain one at a foreigners' registration office before leaving India, but check the current situation – you may be able to get it in Port Blair. Refer to the relevant chapters for full details on obtaining permits from Chennai (see p.1209), Calcutta (p.957) and Vishakapatnam (p.1154). Permits are usually extendable for fifteen days beyond the original thirty but the authorities sometimes only allow you to stay in Port Blair for that period; not an appealing prospect.

The seas around the Andaman and Nicobar islands are some of the world's most unspoiled. Marine life is abundant, with an estimated 750 species of fish existing on one reef alone. Parrot, trigger and angel fish live alongside manta rays, reef sharks and loggerhead turtles. Many species of fish and coral are unique to the area and fascinating life-systems exist in ash beds and cooled lava based around the volcanic Barren Island (see p.1184).

For a quick taste of marine life, you could start by **snorkelling**; most hotels can supply masks and snorkels, though some equipment is in dire need of replacement. The only way to get really close, however, and venture out into deeper waters, is to **scuba dive** (see p.73). The experience of weaving in and out of coral beds, coming eye to eye with fish or swimming with dolphins and barracudas is unforgettable.

At present, the islands only have three proper **dive centres**. Two are based in the Port Blair area, reputable and PADI registered, but far from cheap: **Samudra** (☏ 01392/33159, ☏ 31824) occupies a former Japanese bunker at the *Sinclair Bay View Hotel* (see p.1171); while the Swiss-run **Andaman Divers** (☏ 01392/33461 or 6–9pm 35771, ☏ 33463) have an office in the *Peerless Resort* at Corbyn's Bay. Both charge qualified divers around Rs2500 for two local dives and Rs3200 for trips to Wandoor and beyond. Beginners can do introductory dives with basic training at Rs1800/2800 for a half/full day. For a hefty Rs15,000, you can also do a three- or four-day PADI open-water course. When booking dives with either, check which sites they use: Cinque Island offers arguably the best diving in the area, and is worth shelling out a little extra to visit as it is otherwise difficult to reach. It is best to avoid the occasional fly-by-night unregistered operations that pop up offering cut-price diving trips, as neither their equipment nor expertise can be counted on.

The most congenial and cheapest of the bona fide centres is the **Andaman Scuba Club** (☏ info@AndamanScubaClub.com) on Havelock Island (see p.1178). Run by a friendly Swiss duo and their Indian partner, all PADI-certified instructors, they offer dives at prime sites in the area to those qualified at Rs1000 each plus Rs500 daily for equipment rental, open-water courses at Rs12,900 and advanced courses at Rs10,000. "Discover Scuba" theory, training and intro dives cost Rs2500 and they allow unlimited free snorkelling trips to anyone who has dived with them. They are reliable, safe and fun to dive with, and will accept foreign currency or travellers' cheques as payment.

Underwater in the Andamans, it is not uncommon to come across schools of reef sharks, which rarely turn hostile, but one thing to watch out for and avoid is the **black-and-white sea snake**. Though the snakes seldom attack – and, since their fangs are at the back of their mouths, would find it difficult to get a grip on any human – their bite is twenty times more deadly than that of the cobra.

Increased tourism inevitably puts pressure on the delicate marine ecosystem, and poorly funded wildlife organizations can do little to prevent damage from insensitive visitors. You can ensure your presence in the sea around the reefs does not harm the coral by observing the following **Green Coral Code** while diving or snorkelling:

• Never touch, or walk on, living coral or it will die.

• Try to keep your feet away from reefs while wearing fins; the sudden sweep of water caused by a flipper kick can be enough to destroy coral.

• Always control the speed of your descent while diving; enormous damage can be caused by divers' landing hard on a coral bed.

• Never break off pieces of coral from a reef, and remember that it is illegal to export dead coral from the islands, even fragments you may have found on a beach.

19

THE ANDAMAN ISLANDS

South Andaman: Port Blair and around

South Andaman is today the most heavily populated of the Andaman Islands – particularly around the capital, **Port Blair** – thanks in part to the drastic thinning of tree cover to make way for settlement. Foreign tourists can only visit its southern and east central reaches – including the beaches at **Corbyn's Cove** and **Chiriya Tapu**, the fine reefs on the western shores at **Wandoor**, 35km southwest of Port Blair and the environs of **Madhuban** and **Mount Harriet** on the east coast across the bay from the capital.

With your own transport it's easy to find your way along the narrow bumpy roads that connect small villages, weaving through forests and coconut fields, and skirting the swamps and rocky outcrops that form the coastline.

Port Blair

PORT BLAIR, a characterless cluster of tin-roofed buildings tumbling towards the sea in the north, east and west and petering into fields and forests in the south, merits only a short stay. There's little to see here – just the **Cellular Jail** and a few small **museums** – but as the point of arrival for the islands, and the only place with a bank, tourist offices and hotels, it can't be avoided. If you plan to head off to more remote islands, this is also the best place to stock up on supplies and buy necessary equipment.

Arrival and information

Port Blair has two jetties: **boats** from the mainland moor at **Haddo Jetty**, nearly 2km northwest of **Phoenix Jetty**, arrival point for inter-island ferries. The Director of Shipping Services at Phoenix Jetty has the latest information on boats and ferries, but you can also check the shipping news column of the local newspaper, the *Daily Telegrams*, for details of forthcoming departures. Advice on booking ferry tickets appears in the box on p.1172.

The smart new **airport** terminal is 4km south of town at Lamba Line. Entry **permits** are issued to foreigners from the immigration counters as you enter the arrivals hall. **Taxis** are on hand for short trips into town (Rs40–50), but if you have booked a room in any of the middle- or upper-range hotels or do so at the counter in the airport, you should find a shuttle bus waiting outside.

The counter at the airport (℡03192/32414) hands out a useful brochure, but the main **A&N tourist office** (Mon–Sat 10am–5pm; ℡03192/32694) is situated in a modern building, diagonally opposite Indian Airlines on the southern edges of the town. Unless you want to book accommodation in an ANI-IDCO hotel or a seat on one of their tours (such as to Wandoor, see p.1170), it's hard to think of a reason to go there; they don't keep transport timetables or any useful information about the rest of the archipelago. North of the centre on Junglighat Main Road, the **Government of India Tourist Office** (Mon–Fri 8.30am–5pm; ℡03192/33006) is little better.

Road names are not used much in Port Blair, with most establishments addressing themselves simply by their local area. The name of the busiest and most central area is **Aberdeen Bazaar**, where you'll find the superintendent of police (for permit extensions), the SCI office for onward bookings by sea (℡03192/33590), and the State Bank of India (Mon–Fri 9am–1pm, Sat 9–11am). Some hotels will change travellers' cheques, but you'll get faster service and better rates at Island Travels (℡03192/33034; Mon–Sat 2–5pm), which has a licence to change money, and is just up the road from the clocktower in

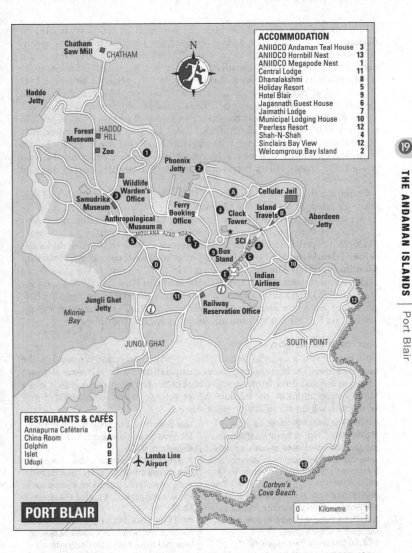

ACCOMMODATION

ANIIDCO Andaman Teal House	3
ANIIDCO Hornbill Nest	13
ANIIDCO Megapode Nest	1
Central Lodge	11
Dhanalakshmi	8
Holiday Resort	5
Hotel Blair	9
Jagannath Guest House	6
Jaimathi Lodge	7
Municipal Lodging House	10
Peerless Resort	12
Shah-N-Shah	4
Sinclairs Bay View	12
Welcomgroup Bay Island	2

RESTAURANTS & CAFÉS

Annapurna Caféteria	C
China Room	A
Dolphin	D
Islet	B
Udupi	E

PORT BLAIR

Aberdeen Bazaar. You can email or use the internet for Rs60 per hour at Kembu's NetJoint (☎03192/34949) on Moulana Azad Road near *Jagannath Guest House*. There is also a Net café in the *Hotel Blair* complex.

Local transport and tours

Walking is tiring and time-consuming in hilly Port Blair – even taking into account the minimal amount of sightseeing the place offers – making transport essential. Yellow-top **taxis** gather opposite the bus stand. They all have meters, but negotiating the price before leaving is usual practice. Expect to pay Rs50 for a trip from the centre of town to Corbyn's Cove. In 1999 the islands received their first fleet of **auto-rickshaws**, but they tend to charge almost as much as taxis.

Local **buses** run infrequently from the bus stand in central Port Blair to Wandoor and Chiriya Tapu, and can be used for day-trips, though it's best to rely on your own transport to get around South Andaman. **Bicycles** can be rented from Aberdeen Bazaar, at Rs5 per hour, but the roads to the coasts are most easily covered on a **Vespa** or **motorcycle**, both available for rent at TSG Travels (Mon–Sat 8.30am–7pm; ☎ 03192/32894) on Moulana Azad Road behind Phoenix Bay. They require a licence and Rs500 deposit. Singh Travels at the Singh cloth store near the Aberdeen Bazaar clocktower have a few old scooters with gears. They are less fussed about showing a licence but ask for a Rs1000 deposit. Rental rates at both places are Rs120 per day. The petrol pump is on the crossroads west of the bus stand, and there's another on the road towards the airport. Fill up before you leave town, as petrol is hard to come by elsewhere.

Cramming the island's few interesting sights together with a string of dull destinations, most of the ANIIDCO **tours** are a complete waste of time; you're better off renting a scooter or taxi and taking in the jail and museums at your own pace. However, more worthwhile are their **harbour cruises** (daily 3–5pm; Rs20) that depart from Phoenix Jetty for fleeting visits to the floating docks and **Viper Island** (see p.1174), and the day-trips to **Wandoor** and the **Mahatma Gandhi National Marine Park** (see p.1175). The bus tour to Wandoor (8am; Rs75) connects with the 10am boat to the islands of Red Skin (Rs90) and Jolly Buoy (Rs125). You can also spend an evening cruising the harbour with a buffet dinner and entertainment on the *Atlantis*, ANIIDCO's floating restaurant (daily 7pm; Rs225), but it's primarily aimed at wealthy Indian visitors.

Accommodation

Port Blair boasts a fair selection of places to stay. Concentrated mainly in the centre of town, the bottom-range **accommodation** can be as dour as any port town on the mainland. More comfortable hotels occupy correspondingly more salubrious locations on the outskirts. Wherever you intend to stay, it's definitely worth booking ahead during peak season.

ANIIDCO Andaman Teal House, Delanipur ☎ 03192/34060. High on the hill above Haddo port this place offers great views, spacious and pleasant rooms, and is very good value, although can be inconvenient without your own transport. ❸–❹

ANIIDCO Hornbill Nest, 1km from Corbyn's Cove ☎ 03192/34305. Clean, roomy cottages on a hillside by the coast. Great location, catching the sea breezes, but transport to and from town is a problem unless you rent a scooter. ❸

ANIIDCO Megapode Nest, Haddo Hill ☎ 03192/33659, ☏ 32702. A&N Tourism's upscale option has 25 comfortable rooms, and pricier self-contained "cottages", ranged around a central lawn, with good views, and a quality restaurant. ❼

Central Lodge, Middle Point ☎ 03192/33632. Ramshackle wooden building situated in a secluded top corner of town. A rock-bottom option, offering basic rooms or garden space for hammocks. ❶

Dhanalakshmi, Aberdeen Bazaar, Port Blair ☎ 03192/33952. Friendly, clean and very good value but not particularly good value. The rooms are all en suite and tiled, but can get stuffy (you have to

keep the front windows closed because of traffic noise, and the back ones shut to keep out the mosquitoes). ❺–❼

Holiday Resort, Premnagar, a fifteen-minute walk from the centre ☎ 03192/30516. This is the best mid-price deal in the town centre; it's clean and spacious, with some a/c, a bar and a TV lounge. ❺–❻

Hotel Blair, HSKP Complex, five minutes from the bus stand ☎ 03192/38109, ☏ 34062. Reasonable-value modern hotel with large clean rooms in a fairly quiet location. Airy rooftop restaurant. ❺–❼

Jagannath Guest House, Moulana Azad Road ☎ 03192/32148. One of the best-value basic lodges: clean, central and convenient for the jetty. The front-side rooms are the nicest, though marginally more expensive. No telephone bookings taken. ❸

Jaimathi, Moulana Azad Rd ☎ 03192/33457. Popular lodge with both Westerners and Indians. Large fairly clean rooms with communal balconies. Slightly cheaper than the *Jagannath* next door and more likely to have availability. ❷–❸

Municipal Lodging House, opposite Municipal Swimming Pool ☏ 03192/34919. Port Blair's best budget deal: clean rooms with good beds, fans, bathrooms, balconies and sea views, but it's often booked up with Bengali tourists and inter-island travellers. ❷

Peerless Resort, Corbyn's Cove ☏ 03192/33461, ℱ 33463. Perfect setting amid gardens of palms, jasmine and bougainvillea, opposite a white sandy beach. Balconied a/c rooms, cottages, bar, and a mid-priced restaurant where the evening buffet doesn't always match up to what is served in simpler places elsewhere. Ideal for families. ❾

Shah-N-Shah, Mohanpura, near the bus stand ☏ 03192/33696. Set between the bus stand and the boat jetty, this is basic but comfortable, with en-suite rooms and a sociable terrace. ❸–❹

Sinclair Bay View, on the coast road to Corbyn's Cove ☏ 03192/33159, ℱ 31824, ℮ sinclairs@vsnl.com. Clifftop hotel offering spotless carpeted rooms, balconies, en-suite bathrooms, dramatic views, bar and restaurant, in-house diving school and airport shuttle bus. ❽

Welcomgroup Bay Island, Marine Hill, Port Blair ☏ 03192/20881. Port Blair's swishest hotel; elegant, airy and finished with polished dark wood. All rooms have carpets and balconies overlooking Phoenix Jetty (the less expensive ones are a little cramped). There's a quality restaurant, gardens and open-air sea-water swimming pool, though tariffs are decidedly steep at over $100 per double. ❾

The Town

Port Blair's only firm reminder of its gloomy past, the sturdy brick **Cellular Jail** (Mon–Sat 9am–noon & 2–7pm), overlooks the sea from a small rise in the northeast of town. Built between 1896 and 1905, its tiny solitary cells were quite different and far worse than the dormitories in other prison blocks erected earlier. Only three of the seven wings that originally radiated from the central tower now remain. Visitors can peer into the cells (3m by 3.5m), and imagine the grim conditions under which the prisoners existed. Cells were dirty and ill-ventilated, drinking water was limited to two glasses per day, and the convicts were expected to wash in the rain as they worked clearing forests and building prison quarters. Food, brought from the mainland, was stored in vats where the rice and pulses became infested with worms; more than half the prison population died long before their twenty years' detention was up. Protests against conditions led to hunger strikes in 1932, 1933 and 1937, resulting in yet more deaths, and frequent executions took place at the gallows that still stand in squat wooden shelters in the courtyards, in full view of the cells. The **Sound and Light Show** (daily in English 7.15pm; in Hindi 6pm; not during the rainy season of May–Sept & Nov; Rs10) outlines the history of the prison, and a small **museum** by the entrance gate (same hours as the jail) exhibits lists of convicts, photographs and grim torture devices.

South of the jail near the Water Sports Complex, you can see tanks full of fish and coral from the islands' reefs at the **Aquarium** (daily 9am–1.30pm & 2–5.30pm; free). In the Haddo area in the west side of town, exhibits in the **Anthropological Museum** (Mon–Sat 9am–noon & 1–4pm; free), devoted to the Andaman and Nicobar tribes, include weapons, tools and also rare photographs of the region's indigenous people taken in the 1960s. Among the most striking of these is a sequence featuring the Sentinelese, taken on April 26, 1967, when a party of Indian officials made the first contact with the tribe. After scaring the aborigines, the visitors marched into one of their hunting camps and made off with the bows, arrows and other artefacts now displayed in the museum. The anthropologist charged with documenting the expedition noted afterwards that "the whole atmosphere was that of conquering hordes over-running conquered territory".

Further northwest in Delanipur opposite ANIIDCO's *Teal House* hotel, the **Samudrika Naval Maritime Museum** (Tues–Sun 9am–noon & 2–5.30pm;

Rs10) is an excellent primer if you're heading off to more remote islands, with a superlative shell collection and informative displays on various aspects of local marine biology. One of the exhibits features a cross-section of the different corals you can expect to see on the Andamans' reefs, followed up with a run-down of the various threats these fragile plants face, from mangrove depletion and parasitic starfish to clumsy snorkellers.

Wildlife lovers are advised to steer clear of the grim little **zoo** (Tues–Sun 8am–5pm; Rs1), further down towards Haddo, whose only redeeming feature is that it has successfully bred rare crocodiles and monkeys for release into the wild. The adjoining **Forest Museum** (Mon–Sat 8am–noon & 2–5pm; free) is an equally dismal spectacle, feebly attempting to justify the Indian Forest Service's wholesale destruction of the Andamans' forests with a series of lacklustre photographs of extraction methods. However, if you really want to confront the grim reality of the local timber industry, press on north to **Chatham Sawmill** (daily 7am–2.30pm), at the end of the peninsula marking the northernmost edge of Port Blair. One of the oldest and largest wood-processing plants in Asia, it seasons and mills rare hard-

Moving on from Port Blair

Port Blair is the departure point for all flights and ferry crossings to the Indian mainland; it is also the hub of the Andamans' inter-island bus and ferry network. Unfortunately, booking tickets (especially back to Chennai, Calcutta or Vishakapatnam) can be time-consuming, and many travellers are obliged to come back here well before their permit expires to make reservations, before heading off to more pleasant parts to kill their remaining days.

To the mainland

If you've travelled to the Andamans by ship, you'll know what a rough ride the sixty-hour crossing can be in bunk class, and how difficult tickets are to come by (see p.1166). It's also a good idea to talk to fellow travellers about current conditions, which vary from year to year and vessel to vessel. The one factor you can be sure about is that the ship offers the cheapest route back. The downside is that schedules can be erratic, and accurate information about them difficult to obtain – annoying when you only have a one-month permit. For Chennai, whose weekly service on Fridays run by the DSS is the most reliable, you'll have to head down to the ticket office at Phoenix Jetty. Basically, the only sure way of finding out when the next ship is leaving and securing a ticket to Calcutta and Vishakapatnam is to join the "queue" outside the SCI office (☎03192/33590), opposite the *Dhanalakshmi* hotel in Aberdeen Bazaar. In theory, tickets are supposed to go on sale a week in advance of departure, but don't bank on it. Bear in mind, too, if you're reading this a couple of days' journey away from the capital, and with only a week or less left on your permit, that the local police can get heavy with foreigners who outstay their allotted time.

Returning to the mainland by plane in just two hours instead of sixty can save lots of time and hassle, but at $200 one-way, air tickets to Chennai and Calcutta are far from cheap. With the introduction of Jet Airways' daily service on top of Indian Airlines four flights a week, tickets to Chennai are usually easy to obtain at short notice apart from peak times like Diwali or Christmas. Booking on one of the five weekly IA flights to Calcutta needs more advance planning but if you're in a hurry polite persistence at their office can work wonders as they often don't know exactly how many seats are available till the last minute because of strict payload limits. The IA office (☎03192/34744) is diagonally opposite the ANIIDCO office, while Jet Airways (☎03192/36911) is on the first floor at 189 Main Rd, Junglighat, next to the GITO office.

woods taken from various islands – a sad testimony to the continued abuse of international guidelines on tropical timber production. Photography is prohibited.

Eating

Between them, Port Blair's **restaurants** offer dishes from north and south India, Burmese specialities, and a wide variety of seafood. For rock-bottom budget travellers, there are roadside stalls selling plates of grilled fish at Rs10, in addition to the usual crop of cheap but run-of-the-mill "meals" cafés in the main bazaar: of these, the *Majestic*, *Gagan* and *Milan* on AB Road are the best, but you should steer clear of the *Dhanalakshmi's* notoriously dreadful canteen.

In Port Blair, as throughout the Andamans, attitudes to **alcohol** lag somewhat behind the mainland, and you'll be lucky to find a cold beer outside the upscale hotels. For the usual range of IMFLs, you'll have to join the drunken scrum at the seedy state liquor shop, tucked away down the alley running alongside the *Shah-N-Shah* hotel.

On the day of your flight, be sure to check in at least ninety minutes before the scheduled departure time (security formalities can be protracted), and expect to have to "click" your camera to prove it is just that. Note, too, that Indian law strictly forbids the removal of coral from the Andamans. Get caught with any in your luggage and you'll lose your flight, and probably have to pay a hefty bribe to the police.

Travellers intending to catch onward **trains** from their port of arrival on the mainland should note that Port Blair has an efficient computerized Southern Railways reservation office near the Secretariat (Mon–Sat 8.30am–1pm & 2–4pm).

Inter-island services

Buses connect Port Blair with most major settlements on South and Middle Andaman, mainly via the Andaman Trunk Road. From the crowded, disorganized bus stand at the bottom of town, one daily government service at 5am runs via Rangat (6hr) as far as **Mayabunder** (9hr), from where you have to catch a boat across the straits to **Kalighat** on North Andaman in order to press on north to **Diglipur** and **Ariel Bay**. There's another daily service to Rangat at 6am. Several private companies including Geetanjali Travels (tickets at *Tillai* teashop by the bus stand) and the cheaper Ananda (℡ 03192/33252) run deluxe or video coach (earplugs essential) services, which leave from the road outside the bus stand also at 5am.

Most of the islands open to foreign tourists, including **Neill**, **Havelock**, **Middle** and **North Andaman**, are also accessible by **boat** from Phoenix Jetty. Details of forthcoming departures are posted in the shipping news columns of the local newspapers, but the most reliable source of information is the office on the first floor of the Harbour Authority building, Phoenix Jetty, where you can also book tickets in advance. Schedules change frequently but you can expect a boat most days to Havelock, roughly four weekly to Neill and Rangat and twice weekly to Diglipur. If possible, try to travel on a newer vessel like the *Ramanujam*. The journeys on older boats can be a lot longer and more uncomfortable than you might expect. From 9am onwards, the heat on board is intense, with only corrugated plastic sheets for shade, while the benches are highly uncomfortable and the toilets generally dismal. You should take adequate supplies of food and water with you; only biscuits and simple snacks are sold on the boats. More details of boat services to destinations outside the capital appear in the relevant accounts.

Annapurna Caféteria, Aberdeen Bazaar, towards the post office. Far and away Port Blair's best south Indian joint, serving the usual range of huge crispy *dosas*, north Indian and Chinese plate meals, delicious coffee, and wonderful *pongal* at breakfast. The lunchtime thalis are also great.

China Room, on the hill above the Phoenix Jetty ☎03192/30759. The most tourist-oriented restaurant in town, run by a Burmese-Punjabi couple whose roots are vividly reflected in the chilli-and-ginger-rich cuisine. Particularly recommended for seafood, which comes in a range of tasty sauces. There's a roomy courtyard, but reserve a table inside if it's rainy.

Dolphin, Marthoma Church Complex, Golghar. Pleasantly decorated new restaurant serving carefully prepared dishes. Mostly Indian and Chinese but some Continental and a few house specialities involving chicken and seafood.

Islet, below the Cellular Jail. A safe option for non-veg north Indian tandoori, especially chicken, although they offer a good selection of vegetarian dishes, too. Snappy service and good views of the bay from the window seats or balcony.

New India Cafe, Moulana Azad Road. In the basement of *Jaimathi* lodge, this cheap restaurant is popular with Westerners and Indians alike. Wide menu of veg and meat dishes but expect to wait if you order anything that's not already prepared.

Udupi, near Post Office. North and South Indian standards served on a pleasant covered terrace. Good cheap thalis, including some with fish.

Waves, *Peerless Resort*, Corbyn's Cove. Pricey, but very congenial alfresco hotel restaurant under a shady palm grove, and one of the few places in town you can order a beer with your meal. Most dishes around Rs100.

Around Port Blair

At some point, you're almost certain to find yourself killing time in Port Blair, waiting for boats to show up or tickets to go on sale. Rather than wasting days in town, it's worth exploring the **coast** of South Andaman which, although far more densely populated than other islands in the archipelago, holds a handful of easily accessible beauty spots and historic sites. Among the latter, the ruined colonial monuments on **Viper** and **Ross islands** can be reached on daily harbour cruises or regular ferries from the capital. For **beaches**, head southeast to **Corbyn's Cove**, or cross South Andaman to reach the more secluded **Chiriya Tapu**, both of which are easily accessible on day-trips if you rent a moped or taxi. By far the most rewarding way to spend a day out of town, however, is to catch the tourist boat from **Wandoor** to **Jolly Buoy** or **Red Skin islands** in the **Mahatma Gandhi National Marine Park** opposite, which boasts some of the Andamans' best snorkelling. The other area worth visiting is **Mount Harriet** and **Madhuban** on the central part of South Andaman, north across the bay from Port Blair.

Viper and Ross islands

First stop on the harbour cruise from Port Blair (daily 3–5pm; Rs20) is generally **Viper Island**, named not after the many snakes that doubtless inhabit its tangled tropical undergrowth, but a nineteenth-century merchant vessel that ran aground on it during the early years of the colony. Lying a short way off Haddo Wharf, it served as an isolation zone for the main prison, where escapees and convicts (including hunger strikers) were sent to be punished. Whipping posts and crumbling walls, reached from the jetty via a winding brick path, remain as relics of a torture area, while occupying the site's most prominent position are the original gallows.

No less eerie are the decaying colonial remains on **Ross Island**, at the entrance to Port Blair harbour, where the British sited their first penal settlement in the Andamans. Originally cleared by convicts wearing iron fetters (most of them sent here in the wake of the 1857 Mutiny, or First War of Independence), Ross witnessed some of the most brutal excesses of British colonial history, and was the source of the prison's infamy as **Kalapani**, or Black Water. Of the many convicts transported here, distinguished by their branded foreheads, the majority perished from disease or torture before the clearance of the island was completed in 1860. Thereafter, it served briefly as the site of Rev. Henry Corbyn's **"Andaman Home"** – a prison camp created with the intention of "civilizing" the local tribespeople – before becoming the headquarters of the revamped penal colony, complete with theatre hall, tennis courts, swimming pool, hospitals and grand residential bungalows. Rather ambitiously dubbed "the Paris of the East", the settlement typified the stiff-upper-lipped spirit of the Raj at its most cruel: while the *burra-* and *memsahibs* dressed for dinner and sang hymns in church, convicts languished in the most appalling conditions only a kilometre away. In the end, the entry of the Japanese into World War II, hot on the heels of a massive earthquake in 1941, forced the British to evacuate, and in the coming years most of the buildings were dismantled by the new overlords, who themselves founded a POW camp here.

Little more than the hilltop Anglican church, with its weed-infested graveyard, has survived the onslaught of tropical creepers and vines, and the island makes a peaceful break from Port Blair. To get here, jump on one of the regular launches from Phoenix Jetty (daily except Wed; departing 8.30am, 10.30am & 12.30pm and returning 8.45am, 10.45am & 12.40pm; Rs15).

Corbyn's Cove and Chiriya Tapu

The best beach within easy reach of the capital lies 10km southeast at **Corbyn's Cove**, a small arc of smooth white sand backed by a swaying curtain of palms. There's a large hotel here (see p.1171), but the water isn't particularly clear, and bear in mind that lying around scantily clothed will bring you considerable attention from crowds of local workers.

For more isolation, rent a moped or take a taxi 30km south to **Chiriya Tapu** ("Bird Island"), at the tip of South Andaman. The motorable track running beyond this small fishing village leads through thick jungle overhung with twisting creepers to a large bay, where swamps give way to shell-strewn beaches. Other than at lunchtime, when it often receives a deluge of bus parties, the beach offers plenty of peace and quiet, forest walks on the woodcutters' trails winding inland from it, and easy access to an inshore reef. However, the water here is nowhere near as clear as at some spots in the archipelago, and serious snorkellers and divers may be tempted to try for a boat out to volcanic **Cinque Island** (see p.1184), a couple of hours' further south. Groups from the big hotels in Port Blair use inflatables with outboard motors to reach Cinque, but it is also possible to charter your own fishing boat here; ask around the bar in the village, and expect to pay around Rs3000 per boat for the return trip.

Wandoor and the Mahatma Gandhi National Marine Park

Much the most popular excursion from Port Blair is the boat ride from **Wandoor**, 30km southwest, to one or other of the fifteen islets comprising the **Mahatma Gandhi National Marine Park**. Although set up purely for tourists, the trip is worth doing, gaining you access to one of the richest coral reefs in the region. Boats depart from Wandoor at 10am (daily except Mon; Rs90–125, plus Rs10 entry permit to the park); you can get there on A&N Tourism's **tour** (Rs75) or by local bus, but it is more fun to rent a moped and ride down to meet the boat yourself.

The long white **beach** at Wandoor is littered with the dry, twisted trunks of trees torn up and flung down by annual cyclones, and fringed not with palms, but by dense forest teeming with bird life. You should only snorkel here at high tide. From the jetty, the boats chug through broad creeks lined with dense mangrove swamps and pristine forest to either **Red Skin Island** or, more commonly, **Jolly Buoy**. The latter, an idyllic deserted island, boasts an immaculate shell-sand beach, ringed by a bank of superb coral. The catch is that the boat only stops for around an hour, which isn't nearly enough time to explore the shore and reef. While snorkelling off the edges of the reef, however, beware of **strong currents**.

Mount Harriet and Madhuban

The richly forested slopes of **Mount Harriet** make for decent exercise and can easily be done as a day-trip from Port Blair. You can take one of the hourly passenger ferries from Chatham to **Bamboo Flats** or, if you want to have your own transport on the other side, there are five daily vehicle ferries from Phoenix Bay. From Bamboo Flats it's a pleasant seven-kilometre stroll east along the coast and north up a path through trees hung with thick vines and creepers to the 365-metre summit, which affords fine views back across the bay. An intermittent bus service runs between Bamboo Flats and Hope Town, where the path starts, and saves you 3km. Alternatively, Jeeps and taxis are available to take you all the way to the top but they charge at least Rs200. There's a Rs10 charge to enter Mount Harriet National Park but the checkpost is on the road so you probably won't be asked if you take the path. If you have your own wheels or strong legs you can reach **Madhuban** on the coast northeast of the mountain. You'll find a decent beach here and the area is still used for training logging **elephants**, so you stand a good chance of seeing them learning their trade.

Islands north of Port Blair

Printed on the permit card you receive on arrival in the Andamans is a list of all the other **islands** you're allowed to visit in the archipelago. The majority of them are north of Port Blair. Given the great distances involved, not to mention the often erratic connections between them (and the time limit imposed by the one-month permit), it definitely pays to know where to head for as soon as you arrive rather than drift off on the first promising ferry out of Phoenix Jetty. The best way of doing this is to talk to fellow travellers arriving back in the capital. The following accounts will give you a good idea of what to expect upcountry, but new islands are opened up to tourists each year and these may well offer the kind of wilderness experience you're here for.

Having travelled all the way to the Andamans, it is surprising how many visitors make a beeline for the only two developed islands in the group, **Neill** and **Havelock**, both within easy reach of Port Blair. To get further north, where tourism of any kind has thus far had very little impact, you can take a ferry from Havelock to ramshackle **Rangat**, at the south end of **Middle Andaman**, or bypass the whole east coast by catching a bus from Port Blair direct to **Mayabunder**, the main market town for the central and north Andamans. Either way, you'll be lucky not to be marooned from time to time in some truly grim little settlements, interspersed with a few long hard slogs up the infamous **Andaman Trunk Road** (or "ATR").

On Middle and North Andaman, and their satellite islands, **accommodation** is scarce, to say the least. Aside from a handful of ANIIDCO hotels (bookable in advance in Port Blair), the only places to stay are APWD rest houses set aside for government officials and engineers. To stay in these it is best to get a letter of recommendation from the APWD office in Port Blair but you have to give specific dates. Just turning up is not guaranteed to meet with success even if rooms are free. Settlements such as Rangat, Mayabunder and Diglipur, in the far north, also have very rudimentary lodges. To escape the settled areas you have to be prepared to rough it, travelling on in-shore fishing dugouts, sleeping on beaches and cooking your own food. The rewards, however, are great. Backed by dense forest filled with colourful birds and insects, the beaches, bays and reefs of the outer Andamans teem with wildlife, from gargantuan crabs, pythons and turtles, to dolphins, sharks, giant rays and the occasional primeval-looking dugong.

Essential **kit** for off-track wanderings includes a sturdy mosquito net, mats to sleep on (or a hammock), a large plastic container for water, some strong antiseptic for cuts and bites (sandflies are a real problem on many of the beaches) and, most importantly, **water purification** tablets or a water purifier – bottled water is virtually nonexistent. Wherever you end up, preserve the goodwill of local people by packing your rubbish out – carrying it in your backpack – or burning it, and being sensitive to scruples about dress and nudity, especially in areas settled by conservative Bengali or Tamil Hindus.

Neill

Tiny, triangular-shaped **Neill** is the most southerly inhabited island of **Ritchie's Archipelago**, three hours' ferry ride northeast of Port Blair. The source of much of the capital's fresh fruit and vegetables, its fertile centre, ringed by a curtain of stately tropical trees, comprises vivid patches of green paddy dotted with small farmsteads and banana plantations. The beaches are mediocre by the Andamans' standards, but worth a day or two en route to or from Havelock. **Boats** leave Port Blair four or five times each week for Neill, continuing on to Havelock and Rangat.

Neill boasts three **beaches**, all of them within easy cycling distance of the small bazaar just up the lane from the hotel (you can rent **cycles** from one or other of the stallholders from Rs20–30 per day). The best place to swim is **Neill Kendra**, a gently curving bay of white sand, which straddles the jetty and is scattered with picturesque wooden fishing boats. A more secluded option, **Lakshmangar**, lies a little over 3km north: head right at the ANIIDCO hotel (see below) and follow the road for around twenty minutes until it dwindles into a surfaced track, then turn right. Wrapped around the headland, the beach is a broad spur of white shell sand with shallow water offering good snorkelling. Exposed to the open sea and thus prone to higher tides, **Sitapur** beach, 6km south at the tip of the island, is less appealing, but the ride across Neill's central paddy land is pleasant.

The island now has three **accommodation places**. From the jetty, a two-minute walk brings you to the ANIIDCO *Hawabill Nest* (☎ 03192/82630; **④**–**⑥**), a dozen or so clean, carpeted rooms with sitouts, ranged around a central courtyard and restaurant, best booked in advance from Port Blair. The two private options are both at Lakshmangar: the *Pearl Park Hotel* (☎ 03192/82510; **②**–**⑦**) has some small huts and posher a/c bungalows, while the *Tango* (no phone; **①**–**②**) offers much more basic bamboo huts. Apart from the **restaurants** at these three establishments and a few stalls around the jetty, the only other place to eat is the highly recommended *Gyan*, halfway along the road to Lakshmangar.

Havelock

Havelock is the largest island in Ritchie's Archipelago, and the most intensively cultivated, settled like many in the region by Bengali refugees after Partition. Thanks to its regular ferry connection with the capital, it is also visited in greater numbers than anywhere else in the Andamans. In peak season, as many as three hundred tourists may be holed up here, and at such times Havelock's much-photographed Radhnagar beach, often touted as the most beautiful in India, can feel overwhelmed. Party lovers from Goa have also turned up over the past few winters, complete with rave gear and full-on sound systems, so the writing may well be on the wall for Havelock. On the plus side, the boat journey here from Neill, skirting a string of uninhabited islets with shadowy views of South Andaman to the west, is wonderful, and wildlife – both on land and in the sea – remains abundant despite intensive settlement and deforestation.

Havelock's main **jetty** is on the north side of the island, at the village known as **Havelock #1**. There are three small **lodges** as you turn right from the jetty, on the mangrove-lined outskirts of the village. Best of these is the friendly *Maya Sea View* (☏03192/82367; ❶–❸), which has attached and non-attached rooms as well as a couple of open bamboo shacks. Further along is the similar seafront *M.S. Guest House* (☏03192/82439; ❶–❷) and the *U.S. Lodge* is a fall-back. You'll find basic **restaurants** at the lodges and snacks to be had at stalls in the village. Otherwise, rent a **moped** (Rs150 per day) or **cycle** (Rs50 per day) for a few days and head straight inland to the bazaar, 2km to the south. Further accommodation listed below is available at beaches #2 to #5, really one long unbroken strand, which you get to by turning left at the main junction, or at Radhnagar (aka #7 beach), 12km southwest, reached by turning right. An intermittent bus service also covers these routes, but you could find yourself waiting all day for it and missing out on a room.

The first place to stay on the **east coast** is *Eco Villa* (no phone; ❸) at beach #2, whose ten huts are not the best value but the cook is famous for concocting rare culinary delights. At beach #3 is the base of the excellent **Andaman Scuba Club** (see p.1167 for details). Next up is the *Sunrise* (☏03192/82387; ❷), with more huts set in a picturesque palm grove, followed by the rather overpriced cottages of ANIIDCO's *Dolphin Yatri Niwas* (☏03192/82411, ☏82444; ❸–❼) at beach #5. This is also the only place on the island to **change money** in an emergency but the rates are dire. The last and best of the places along this stretch is the *Coconut Grove* (☏03192/82427; ❷), which has sturdy huts of varying sizes and the most sociable restaurant.

Heading past a string of thatched villages hemmed in by banana groves and paddy fields, the road towards **Radhnagar** drops through some spectacular woodland to a kilometre-long arc of perfect white sand, backed by stands of giant *mowhar* trees. The water is a sublime turquoise colour, and although the coral is sparse, marine life here is diverse and plentiful, especially among the rocks around the corner from the main beach (to get there on foot, backtrack along the road and follow the path through the woods and over the bluff). Radhnagar has two **places to stay**: ANIIDCO's *Tent Camp* (no phone; ❷–❺), rows of canvas tents of varying size and comfort and a toilet block, and the upmarket *Jungle Resort* (☏03192/37656, ☏37657; ❸–❼), run by a Swiss-Andaman family, who offer luxurious wood-and-thatch cottages and a few more basic huts in a clearing behind the beach. They also have a good restaurant and there is a string of basic food shacks lining the road down to the beach, of which *Travellers* is justifiably the most popular. As the nesting site for a colony of Olive Ridley **turtles**, Radhnagar is strictly protected by the Forest Department, whose wardens ensure tourists do not light fires or sleep on the beach.

Long Island

Just off the southeast coast of Middle Andaman, **Long Island** is dominated by an unsightly plywood mill, but don't let this put you off. Served by only two boats per week from the capital (usually Wed & Sat), and two daily lumber launches from Rangat, it sees far fewer visitors than either Neill or Havelock, but boasts a couple of excellent beaches, at **Marg Bay** and **Lalaji Bay**, both of which are most easily reached by chartering a fisherman's dinghy from the jetty. The latter beach is earmarked as the site of a new private tented accommodation enterprise, which should be running by late 2001. Otherwise, you could try your luck at the APWD *Rest House* (**❷**), or camp. This is a good island to head for if you want to sidestep the hordes at Havelock, but don't have time to tackle the long trip north.

Middle Andaman

For most travellers, **Middle Andaman** is a charmless rite of passage to be endured en route to or from the north. The sinuous Andaman Trunk Road, hemmed in by walls of towering forest, winds through miles of jungle, crossing the strait that separates the island from its neighbour, Baratang Island, by means of rusting flat-bottomed ferry. The island's frontier feeling is heightened by the presence on the buses of armed guards, and the knowledge that the impenetrable forests west of the ATR are the **Jarawa Tribal Reserve** (see p.1164). Of its two main settlements, the more northerly **Mayabunder** is slightly more appealing than characterless inland **Rangat** because of its pleasant setting by the sea, but neither town gives any reason to dally for long.

Rangat and around

At the southeast corner of Middle Andaman, **RANGAT** consists of a ramshackle sprawl around two rows of insanitary chai shops and general stores divided by the ATR, which in the monsoon degenerates into a fly-infested mud slick, churned at regular intervals by overladen buses. However, as a major staging post on the journey north, it's impossible to avoid; just don't get stranded here if you can help it.

Ferries to and from Port Blair (9hr) dock at **Rangat Bay** (aka **Nimbutala**), 8km east; some stop at Havelock Island (4 weekly) and Long Island (2 weekly), and there are also two daily lumber boats to Long Island. In addition, the village is served by two daily government **buses** to Port Blair (7–8hr) as well as some private services, which pass through in the morning en route from Mayabunder. The APWD *Rest House* (☎03192/74237; **❷**), pleasantly situated up a winding hill from the bazaar with views across the valley, is the best **place to stay** and eat, providing good filling fish thalis. Otherwise, the most bearable lodge is the *Avis* (☎03192/27554; **❷**) on Church Road. The town's best **restaurant** is the *Hotel Vijay*, whose amiable proprietor serves up copious thalis and, if the boat is in, crab curry, along with the usual range of soft drinks and mineral water.

If you do get stuck here, rather than staying put in Rangat jump on a bus heading north, or find a Jeep to take you to **Amakunj beach** aka Cuthbert Bay, 9km along the road from Nimbutala to Mayabunder. On the right of the road just beyond the helipad, a Forest Department signboard saying "Sand Collection Point" marks the start of a track running the remaining 500m to the sea. The beach has little shade to speak of, but the snorkelling is good and, best of all, there's the very comfortable ANIIDCO *Hawksbill Nest* (☎03192/79022; **❸–❹**) **hotel** on the main road, which is invariably empty.

Mayabunder

About two hours further north by road, perched on a long promontory right at the top of the island and surrounded by mangrove swamps, is **MAYABUN-**

DER, springboard for the remote northern Andaman Islands. The village, which is home to a large minority of former Burmese **Karen** tribal people who were originally brought here as cheap logging labour by the British, is more spread out and more appealing than Rangat, but again there is little to hold your interest for long. At the brow of the hill, before it descends to the jetty, a small hexagonal wooden structure houses the **Forest Museum/Interpretation Centre** (Mon–Sat 8am–noon & 1–4pm; free), which holds a motley collection of turtle shells, snakes in formaldehyde, dead coral, a crocodile skull and precious little information. Next door, the APWD *Rest House* (☏03192/73211; ❶–❷) is large and very comfortable, with a pleasant garden and gazebo overlooking the sea, and a dining room serving good set meals. The only other reasonable **accommodation** nearby is back in the centre of the bazaar at the *S&S Lodge* (☏03192/73449; ❶), which has clean but unattached rooms; the dilapidated and cockroach-infested *Lakshminarayan Lodge* should be avoided at all costs. Further afield at **Karmateng beach**, 14km southeast, there's another ANIIDCO hotel, the *Swiftlet Nest* (☏03192/73495; ❸–❹) but nothing else. Two buses are supposed to go there daily, failing which there are taxis or auto-rickshaws.

Moving on from Mayabunder

Until the last stretch of the Andaman Trunk Road and a bridge across the narrow strait to North Andaman Island just west of Mayabunder are completed in 2002, the shortest crossing is the ferry ride to **Kalighat** (2 daily; 3hr). The first departure of the day leaves at 9.30am, on a boat that's hopelessly small and cramped, so come prepared for hours of relentless sun (or torrential rain in the monsoons). That said, the journey is very memorable, especially towards its latter stages when the mangrove-lined sides of the creek close in as you approach Kalighat. The other boat leaves at 3pm when the early morning buses from Port Blair have arrived, making it possible to get all the way from the capital to North Andaman in a day, though it's a back-breaking journey to attempt in one go.

Heading in the opposite direction, **buses to Port Blair** are regular but it is advisable to book ahead, with tickets for the daily government departure (at 6am) going on sale from 3pm the previous day at the bus stand, 2km from the jetty near the bazaar. Of the private services, the fastest and most comfortable is the one operated by Geetanjali Travels, which links up with the arrival of the first ferry from Kalighat, leaving the jetty at 7.30am (you can buy tickets on the bus). The trip takes nine to ten hours, depending on how long you have to wait at the two ferry crossings along the way. There are also four or five additional services to **Rangat**, the first at 8.30am from the bus stand.

Interview Island

Mayabunder is the jumping-off place for **Interview Island**, a windswept nature sanctuary off the remote northwest coast of Middle Andaman. Only opened to tourists in 1997, it's large and mainly flat, and completely uninhabited save for a handful of unfortunate forest wardens, coastguards and policemen, posted here to ward off poachers. As foreigners aren't permitted to spend the night on the island, few tourists ever make it to Interview, but those that do are rarely disappointed. If you've come to the Andamans to watch **wildlife**, this should be top of your list.

The only way to reach Interview is to charter a private fishing dinghy from Mayabunder jetty. Arrange one the day before and leave at first light.

Approaching the island, you'll be struck by its wild appearance, particularly noticeable on the northwest where the monsoon storms have wrecked the shoreline forest. If you can, however, get your boatman to pull up onto the **beach** at the southern tip of the island, which has a perennial freshwater pool inside a low cave; legend has it that the well, a nesting site for white-bellied **swifts**, has no bottom. At the forest post, where you have to sign an entry ledger, ask the wardens about the movements of Interview's feral **elephants**, descendants of trained elephants deserted here by a Calcutta-based logging company after its timber operation failed in the 1950s. When food (or potential mates) are scarce, the elephants take to the sea and swim to other islands (sometimes, it is said, all the way to Mayabunder).

North Andaman

Shrouded in dense jungle, **North Andaman** is the least populated of the region's large islands, crossed by a single road linking its scattered Bengali settlements. Timber extraction is proceeding apace here, despite a promise by the Island Development Authority to phase out logging by the year 2000, but the total absence of motorable roads into northern and western areas has ensured blanket protection for a vast stretch of convoluted coastline, running from Austin Strait in the southeast to the northern tip, Cape Price. Even if it were physically possible to reach this region, you wouldn't be allowed to, but it's reassuring to know at least one extensive wilderness survives in the Andamans. That said, the imminent completion of the ATR's final section, which will connect the far north to Mayabunder, may herald the start of a new settlement influx, with the same disastrous consequences for the environment as have been seen elsewhere.

Kalighat

Until the new road is finished, **KALIGHAT**, where the river becomes un-navigable and the ferryboat from Mayabunder turns around, serves as the main entry point to North Andaman. A cluttered little bazaar unfolds from the top of the slipway, hemmed in by dense mangrove swamps, and when you arrive you should hope a bus is standing here to take you to Diglipur. If there isn't, head for one of the village's dismal little chai stalls and dig in for a wait, or turn right to see if there's space in the three-roomed *Government Rest House* (no phone; ❷) on the hill overlooking the end of the street. The *chowkidar* in this quaint wooden house is friendly, but refuses to cook for tourists so you'll have to chance the chai stalls for a meal.

The one worthwhile place to visit in this area is **Radhnagar**, 10km out of town and served by hourly buses, where there's a beautiful sandy beach backed by unspoilt forest where camping is feasible. Try to rent a **cycle** from one of the stalls in Kalighat though, as the beach is 2km outside Radhnagar bazaar, providing the nearest source of fresh water.

In principle, four **buses** per day run north from Kalighat to **Diglipur** (12.30pm, 1pm, 3pm & 5.30pm); they're crammed full, but the trip only takes 45 minutes. Look out for logging elephants beside the road shortly after leaving Kalighat. Heading south, the **boat** leaves at 5am for Mayabunder. If you're continuing on to **Port Blair**, buy a through bus ticket for Geetanjali Travels' express video coach at PVL Sharma's grocery store, in the bazaar; this service is timed to leave just after the boat arrives from Kalighat. If you take the second boat at 12.30pm, you can get no further than Mayabunder or Rangat the same day.

Diglipur and Arial Bay

Known in the British era as Port Cornwallis, **DIGLIPUR**, North Andaman's largest settlement, is another disappointing market where you're only likely to pause long enough to pick up a local bus further north to the coast. On the hill above the bus stand, the APWD *Rest House* (☎03192/72203; ❶) offers the village's only **accommodation**, but the *chowkidar* is less than welcoming and you're better off pressing on 9km to **ARIAL BAY**, where a smaller but much more congenial APWD *Rest House* (no phone; ❶) stands on a hillock overlooking the settlement's small bazaar. Better still, continue another 9km to **Kalipur**, served by several daily buses, where ANIIDCO recently opened what must rank among the region's biggest white elephants. Occupying a perfect spot on a hilltop, with superb views inland and to sea, the *Turtle Resort*; (☎03192/72553; ❸–❹), an unfeasibly large concrete hotel for such a remote location, has spacious, clean rooms with fans and a restaurant (residents only). Only five minutes' walk from the hotel down the path by the sharp bend in the road there's an excellent deserted beach, backed by lush forest and covered in photogenic driftwood. Swimming is best at high tide because the water recedes across rocky mudpools.

The staff at the hotel claim it's possible to walk from here to **Saddle Peak**, at 737m the highest mountain in the Andamans, which rises dramatically to the south, swathed in lush jungle. Permission to make the three- to four-hour climb must be obtained from the Range Officer at Arial Bay, but don't attempt the hike without a guide and plenty of drinking water. The majority of tourists who find their way up here, however, do so in order to explore the various **islands** dotted around the gulf north of Arial Bay, particularly **Smith** (see below).

The best **place to eat** in this area is the *Mohan Restaurant*, at the far end of the bazaar in Arial Bay, which serves cold drinks and huge portions of fresh local seafood against a surreal backdrop of lurid cherubs and a poster of the racehorse Red Rum. From Arial Bay, the **boat** that has made its way up from the capital returns direct (Wed & Sat 4pm; 13–14hr) to Port Blair overnight.

Smith Island

Over recent years **Smith Island** has become one the most popular escapes for travellers wishing to live out their Robinson Crusoe fantasies. Although it has not yet been included on the list printed on foreign tourist permits, it has achieved semi-official status and Rs10 permits are issued at the port authority in Arial Bay because of its proximity to the protected wildlife reserve at **Ross Island** (not to be confused with the one near Port Blair). The typically densely forested island has a small settlement at the ferry jetty, about thirty minutes' journey from Arial Bay.

There are no roads, but a walking trail (2hr) leads across to the main beach, where up to thirty Westerners may be camping at any one time. There's a freshwater spring behind the beach but no food and only basic rice, vegetables and fruit are available at the village so all camping gear and other provisions must be taken along from the mainland. It is likely, however, that permanent rentable tents and even huts may appear soon. Fishing boats will ferry people direct to the beach for around Rs50 per head, as long as they've got a few takers. At low tide Smith is connected to Ross by a sandbar which people walk across, though they are not strictly allowed onto the protected island.

Other islands

The remaining islands open to foreign tourists in the Andaman group are all hard to get to and, with the exception of **Little Andaman** – where a vestigial population of Onge tribespeople have survived a massive influx of Indian Tamils and native Nicobars – uninhabited. Two hours' boat ride south of Chiriya Tapu on South Andaman, **Cinque Island** offers superlative diving, outshone only by distant **Barren Island**, whose volcanic sand beds teem with marine life.

Cinque Island

Cinque actually comprises two islets, joined by a spectacular sand isthmus, with shallow water either side that covers it completely at high tide. The main incentive to come here is the superlative diving and snorkelling around the reefs. However, heaps of dead coral on the beach attest to damage recently wreaked by the Indian navy during the construction of the swish air-conditioned "cottages" overlooking the beach. Rumour has it that these were built for the visit of a Thai VIP in 1996, but local government officials now use them as bolt holes from Port Blair.

Although there are no **ferries** to Cinque, it is possible to arrange dinghies from Chiriya Tapu village on the mainland (see p.1175). The two dive centres in Port Blair also regularly come here with clients. Currently, your permit only allows you to spend the day on the island; overnight stays are prohibited.

Barren Island

The most intriguing island open to tourists in the Andaman group has to be **Barren Island**, twenty hours' sea voyage east of Port Blair. India's only active **volcano**, the arid brown mountain blew its top in May 1991 after lying dormant for 188 years, and has done so on two occasions since in 1994 and 1995. The only living creatures on Cinque are a herd of **goats**, released in 1891 by the British to provide sustenance for any shipwrecked sailors. There are no ferries to the island, but diving expeditions regularly make the trip as the seas around Barren are the richest in the region.

Little Andaman

Little Andaman is the furthest point south in the archipelago you can travel to on a standard one-month tourist permit. Located ten hours by sea from Port Blair, most of the island has been set aside as a tribal reserve for the **Onge** (see p.1165) and is thus off limits. The only areas you're allowed to visit lie on either side of the main settlement, Hut Bay, which sits halfway down the east coast. The northern part of this stretch has been mercilessly clear-felled, leaving a stark wasteland flanking the main road to the largest beach at **Butler Bay**, 16km from Hut Bay, while the coast to the south boasts few beaches to compare with those further north in the Andamans. Given the discomfort involved in getting here (the boat journey can be a hideous experience), it's not hard to see why so few travellers bother.

Those that do rarely venture far out of **Hut Bay**, a scruffy agglomeration of chai shacks, hardware and provision stores ranged along Little Andaman's single surfaced road. The only remarkable features of this insalubrious, unwelcoming place are an extraordinarily high incidence of cerebral **malaria** and the most ferocious **sandflies** in all the islands – more reasons not to come here. Unfortunately, the late-afternoon arrival time of the ferry means that unless you're kitted out to camp and have enough provisions, you'll have to spend at least a night in town (see below). As soon as you can, though, head north to Butler Bay or south down the coast, beyond the Christian Nicobari settlements around **John Richardson Bay** (3km), to the island's only other accessible **beaches**; be prepared for sandflies and long walks to water sources, and try not to wander into the Onge's reserve, which begins at the lighthouse.

Practicalities

Boats leave Port Blair for Little Andaman around twice a week; the service to aim for is the one that continues south to Car Nicobar, capital of the Nicobar Islands, as the ferry is larger and marginally more comfortable. Both arrive at the main jetty (specially enlarged for the full-on logging operation still under way here), a 3km plod from the bazaar, where you'll find the island's only established **accommodation**. Before leaving Port Blair, it's worth making a reservation at head office for the APWD *Rest House* (no phone; ❷), 1km north of the shops behind the **hospital**, which has clean and spacious en-suite rooms. Otherwise your only option is the bleak *GM Lodge* (no phone; ❶) in the bazaar, whose rooms wouldn't look out of place in Port Blair's Cellular Jail. If you find yourself having to sleep here, take your mattress and mosquito net onto the roof as constant power cuts render the fans useless. At the time of writing, basic huts were being knocked up at Butler Bay.

Travel details

Flights

Port Blair to: Calcutta (5 weekly; 2hr); Chennai (1–2 daily; 2hr).

Rangat Bay to: Havelock Island (4 weekly; 4–5hr); Long Island (1–2 daily; 1hr 30min–2hr); Neill Island (2 weekly; 5–6hr); Port Blair (4 weekly; 8–10hr).

Boats

Arial Bay to: Port Blair (2 weekly; 12–14hr); Smith Island (1–2 daily; 30min).
Havelock to: Long Island (2 weekly; 2–3hr); Neill Island (4 weekly; 1hr–1hr 30min); Port Blair (6 weekly; 4–6hr); Rangat Bay (4 weekly; 4–5hr).
Mayabunder to: Kalighat (2 daily; 2hr 30min–3hr)
Port Blair to: Arial Bay (2 weekly; 12–14hr); Calcutta (1 every 2 weeks; 60hr); Chennai (1 weekly; 60hr); Havelock Island (6 weekly; 4–6hr); Little Andaman (2 weekly; 9–10hr); Long Island (2 weekly; 7hr 30min–9hr); Neill Island (4 weekly; 3–4hr); Rangat Bay (4 weekly; 8–10hr); Vishakapatnam (1 monthly; 56hr).

Buses

Diglipur to: Arial Bay (every 1–2hr; 20min); Kalighat (4 daily; 45min); Kalipur (5 daily; 40min).
Mayabunder to: Karmateng beach (2 daily; 30min); Port Blair (3–5 daily; 9–10hr); Rangat (5 daily; 2hr–2hr 30min).
Port Blair to: Chiriya Tapu (3 daily; 1hr 15min); Mayabunder (3–5 daily; 9–10hr); Rangat (5 daily; 7–8hr); Wandoor (4 daily; 1hr 15min).
Rangat to: Mayabunder (5 daily; 2hr–2hr 30min); Port Blair (5 daily; 7–8hr).

CHAPTER 20 # Highlights

✳ **Mamallapuram** Stone-carvers' workshops, a long sandy beach and a bumper hoard of Pallava monuments have made this the state's principal tourist attraction.
See p.1211

✳ **Pondicherry** Former French colony that has retained the ambience of a Gallic seaside town: croissants, a promenade and gendarmes wearing *képis*. See p.1229

✳ **Thanjavur** Home to some of the world's finest Chola bronzes, this town is dominated by the colossal shrine tower of the Brihadishwara Temple.
See p.1244

✳ **Madurai** This major temple, the love-nest of Shiva and his consort Meenakshi, hosts a constant round of festivals.
See p.1256

✳ **Kanniyakumari** Sacred meeting point of the Bay of Bengal, Indian Ocean and Arabian Sea, at the tip of the subcontinent.
See p.1272

✳ **The Ghats** The spine of southern India, where you can trek through forested mountains and tea plantations from the refreshingly cool hill stations of Ooty, Conoor and Kodaikanal.
See p.1274

Tamil Nadu

W hen Indians refer to "the South", it's usually **TAMIL NADU** they're talking about. While Karnataka and Andhra Pradesh are essentially cultural transition zones buffering the Hindi-speaking north, and Kerala and Goa maintain their own distinctively idio-syncratic identities, the peninsula's massive Tamil-speaking state is India's Dravidian Hindu heartland. Traditionally protected by distance and the mili-tary might of the southern Deccan kingdoms, the region has, over the cen-turies, been less exposed to northern influences than its neighbours. As a result, the three powerful dynasties dominating the south – the Cholas, the Pallavas and the Pandyans – were able, over a period of more than a thousand years, to develop their own unique religious and political institutions, largely unmolest-ed by marauding Muslims. The most visible legacy of this protracted cultural flowering is a crop of astounding **temples**, whose gigantic gateway towers, or *gopuras*, still soar above just about every town large enough to merit a railway station. It is the image of these colossal wedge-shaped pyramids, high above the canopy of dense palm forests, or against patchworks of vibrant green paddy fields, which Edward Lear described as "stupendous and beyond belief"; indeed, the garishly painted gods, goddesses and mythological creatures cling-ing onto the towers linger in the memory of most travellers.

The great Tamil temples are merely the largest landmarks in a vast network of **sacred sites** – shrines, bathing places, holy trees, rocks and rivers – inter-connected by a web of ancient pilgrims' routes. Tamil Nadu harbours 274 of India's holiest Shiva temples, and 108 are dedicated to Vishnu. In addition, five shrines devoted to the five Vedic elements (Earth, Wind, Fire, Water and Ether) are to be found here, along with eight to the planets, as well as other places revered by Christians and Muslims. Scattered from the pale orange crags and forests of the Western Ghats, across the fertile deltas of the **Vagai** and **Kaveri** rivers to the Coromandel coast on the Bay of Bengal, these sites were cele-brated in the hymns of the Tamil saints, composed between one and two thou-

Accommodation price codes

All accommodation prices in this book have been categorized using the price codes below. Prices given are for a double room, and all taxes are included. For more details, see p.51.

❶ up to Rs100	❹ Rs300–400	❼ Rs900–1500
❷ Rs100–200	❺ Rs400–600	❽ Rs1500–2500
❸ Rs200–300	❻ Rs600–900	❾ Rs2500 and upwards

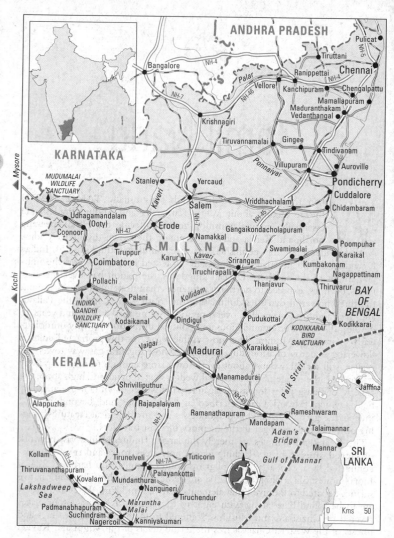

sand years ago. Today, so little has changed that the same devotional songs are still widely sung and understood in the region.

The Tamils' living connection with their ancient Dravidian past has given rise to a strong **nationalist movement**. With a few fleeting lapses, one or other of the pro-Dravidian parties have been in power here since the 1950s, spreading their anti-brahmin, anti-Hindi proletarian message to the masses principally through the medium of movies. Indeed, since Independence, the majority of Tamil Nadu's political leaders have been drawn from the state's prolific **cinema** industry. Indians from elsewhere in the country love to caricature their southern cousins as "reactionary rice growers" led by "fanatical film stars". While such stereotypes should be taken with a pinch of salt, it is undeniable that the Tamil way of life, which has evolved along a distinctive and unbroken path since prehistoric times, sets it apart from the rest of the subcontinent. This remains, after all, one of the last places in the world where a classical culture has survived well into the present.

Despite its seafront fort, grand mansions and excellence as a centre for the performing arts, the state capital **Chennai** (formerly **Madras**) is a hot, chaotic, noisy Indian metropolis that still carries faint echoes of the Raj. However, it is a good base for visiting **Kanchipuram**, a major pilgrimage and sari-weaving centre, filled with reminders of an illustrious past.

Much the best place to start a temple tour is nearby in Mamallapuram, a seaside village that – quite apart from some exquisite Pallava rock-cut architecture (fifth–ninth centuries) – boasts a long stretch of beach. Further down the coast lies Pondicherry, a former French colony and home to the famous Sri Aurobindo ashram; nearby, the campus of Auroville has carved a role as a popular "New Age" centre. The road south from Pondicherry puts you back on the temple trail, leading to the tenth-century Chola kingdom and the extraordinary architecture of Chidambaram, Gangaikondacholapuram, Kumbakonam and Darasuram. For the best Chola bronzes, however, and a glimpse of the magnificent paintings that flourished under Maratha rajas in the eighteenth century, travellers should head for Thanjavur. Chola capital for four centuries, the city boasts almost a hundred temples and was the birthplace of Bharatanatyam dance, famous throughout Tamil Nadu.

In the very centre of Tamil Nadu, **Tiruchirapalli**, a commercial town just northwest of Thanjavur, held some interest for the Cholas, but reached its heyday under later dynasties, when the temple complex in neighbouring **Srirangam** became one of south India's largest. Among its patrons were the Nayaks of **Madurai**, whose erstwhile capital further south, bustling with pilgrims, priests, pedlars, tailors and tourists, is an unforgettable destination.

Rameshwaram, on the long spit of land reaching towards Sri Lanka, and **Kannyakumari**, at India's southern tip (the auspicious meeting point of the Bay of Bengal, the Indian Ocean and the Arabian Sea) are both important pilgrimage centres, with the added attraction of welcome cool breezes and vistas over the sea.

While Tamil Nadu's temples are undeniably its major attraction, the hill stations of **Kodaikanal** and **Ooty** in the west of the state are popular destinations on the well-beaten tourist trail between Kerala and Tamil Nadu. The verdant cool hills offer mountain views and gentle trails wind through the forests and tea and coffee plantations. You can stay in the teak forests of **Mudumalai Wildlife Sanctuary** and trek in **Anamalai Sanctuary**, situated near Kodaikanal in the Palani Hills, although due to recent terrorist activity the core areas of both sanctuaries have been closed to the public for the last few years. To get close to any real wildlife, you'll have to head for the coast, where areas of wetland provide perfect resting places for migratory birds, whose numbers dramatically increase during the winter monsoon at **Vedanthangal**, near Chennai, and **Point Calimere**.

Visiting Tamil Nadu

Temperatures in Tamil Nadu, which usually hover around 30°C, peak in May and June, when they often soar above 40°C, and the overpowering heat makes anything but sitting in a shaded café exhausting. The state is barely affected by the southwest monsoon that pounds much of India from June to September: it receives most of its **rain** between October and December, when the odd cyclone may well make an appearance. The cooler, rainy days, however, bring their own problems: widescale flooding can disrupt road and rail links and imbue everything with an all-pervasive dampness.

Accommodation throughout the state is good and plentiful; all but the smallest towns and villages have something for every budget. Most hotels have their own dining halls which, together with local restaurants, usually serve sumptuous and unlimited thalis, tinged with tamarind and presented on banana leaves. **Indigenous dishes** are almost exclusively vegetarian; for north Indian or Western alternatives, head for the larger hotels or more upmarket city restaurants.

Some history

Since the fourth century BC, Tamil Nadu has been shaped by its majority **Dravidian** population, a people of uncertain origins and physically quite different from north Indians. Their language developed separately, as did their social organization; the difference between high-caste brahmins and low-caste workers has always been more pronounced here than in the north – caste divisions that continue to dominate the state's political life. The influence of the powerful *janapadas*, established in the north by the fourth and third centuries BC, extended as far south as the Deccan, but they made few incursions into **Dravidadesa** (Tamil country). Incorporating what is now Kerala and Tamil Nadu, it was ruled by three dynasties: the **Cheras**, who held sway over much of the Malabar coast (Kerala), the **Pandyas** in the far south, and the **Cholas**, whose realm stretched along the eastern Coromandel coast. Indo-Roman trade in spices, precious stones and metals flourished at the start of the Christian era, when **St Thomas** arrived in the south, but dwindled when trade links began with Southeast Asia.

In the fourth century, the **Pallava** dynasty established a powerful kingdom centred in **Kanchipuram**. By the seventh century, the successors of the first Pallava king, Simhavishnu, were engaged in battles with the southern Pandyas and the forces of the Chalukyas, based further west in Karnataka. However, the centuries of Pallava dominion are not marked simply by battles and territorial expansion; this was also an era of social development. **Brahmins** became the dominant community, responsible for lands and riches donated to temples. The emergence of *bhakti*, devotional worship, placed temples firmly at the centre of religious life, and the inspirational *sangam* literature of saint-poets fostered a tradition of dance and music that has become Tamil Nadu's cultural hallmark.

In the tenth and eleventh centuries, the Cholas experienced a period of profound expansion and revival; they soon held sway over much of Tamil Nadu, Andhra Pradesh and even made in-roads into Karnataka and Orissa. In the spirit of such glorious victories and power, the Cholas ploughed their new wealth into the construction of splendid and imposing temples, such as those at Gangaikondacholapuram, Kumbakonam and Thanjavur.

The **Vijayanagars**, who gained a firm footing in Hampi (Karnataka) in the fourteenth century, resisted Muslim incursions from the north and spread to cover most of south India by the sixteenth century. This prompted a new phase of architectural development: the building of new temples, the expansion of older ones and the introduction of colossal *gopuras*, or towers. In Madurai, the Vijayanagar governors, **Nayaks**, set up an independent kingdom whose impact spread as far as Tiruchirapalli.

Simultaneously, the south experienced its first significant wave of **Europeans**. First came the Portuguese, who landed in Kerala and monopolized Indian trade for about a century before being joined by the British, Dutch and French. Though mostly on cordial terms with the Indians, the Western powers soon found themselves engaged in territorial disputes. The most marked were between the French, based in **Pondicherry**, and the British, whose stronghold since 1640 had been Fort St George in **Madras**. After battles at sea and on land, the French were confined to Pondicherry, while British ambitions reached their apex in the eighteenth century, when the East India Company occupied Bengal (1757) and made firm its bases in Bombay and Madras.

As well as rebellions against colonial rule, Tamil Nadu also saw anti-brahmin protests, in particular those led by the Justice Party in the 1920s and 1930s. **Independence** in 1947 signalled the need for state boundaries, and by 1956 the borders had been demarcated on a linguistic basis; Andhra Pradesh and Kerala were formed, along with Mysore state (later Karnataka) and **Madras Presidency**. In 1965, Madras Presidency became **Tamil Nadu**, the latter part of its name coming from the Chola agrarian administrative units known as *nadus*.

Since Independence, Tamil Nadu's industrial sector has mushroomed. The state was a Congress stronghold until 1967, when the **DMK** (Dravida Munnetra Kazhagam), championing the lower castes and reasserting Tamil identity, won a landslide victory. Anti-Hindi and anti-central government rule, the DMK flourished until the film star "**MGR**" (MG Ramachandran) broke away to form the **All India Anna Dravida Munnetra Kazhagam** (AIADMK), and won an easy victory in the 1977 elections. Virtually deified by his fans-turned-supporters, MGR remained successful until his death in 1987, when the Tamil government fell back into the hands of the DMK. Soon after, the AIADMK were reinstated, led by **Sri Jayalalitha Jayaram**, an ex-film star and dancer once on close terms with MGR (see p.1195). The AIADMK are now back in power and the DMK is skulking around in the background while former Chief Minister Karunanidni fights his ground over corruption charges; the tussle for power continues.

Chennai (Madras)

In the northeastern corner of Tamil Nadu on the Bay of Bengal, **CHENNAI** (still commonly referred to by its former British name, **Madras**) is India's fourth largest city, with a population nudging six million. Hot, fast, congested and noisy, it is the major transportation hub of the south – the international airport makes a marginally less stressful entry point to the subcontinent than Mumbai or Delhi – and most travellers stay just long enough to book a ticket for somewhere else. The attractions of the city itself are sparse, though it does boast fine specimens of **Raj architecture**, pilgrimage sites connected with the apostle **Doubting Thomas**, superb **Chola bronzes** at its state museum, and plenty of **classical music** and **dance** performances.

As capital of Tamil Nadu, Chennai is, like Mumbai and Calcutta, a comparatively modern creation. It was founded by the **British East India Company** in 1639, on a five-kilometre strip of land between the Cooum and Adyar rivers, a few kilometres north of the ancient Tamil port of **Mylapore** and the Portuguese settlement of San Thome, established in 1522. The site had no natural harbour; it was selected by Francis Day, the East India Company agent, in part because he enjoyed good relations with the Nayak governor Dharmala Ayyappa, who could intercede with the Vijayanagar Raja of Chandragiri, to whom the ter-

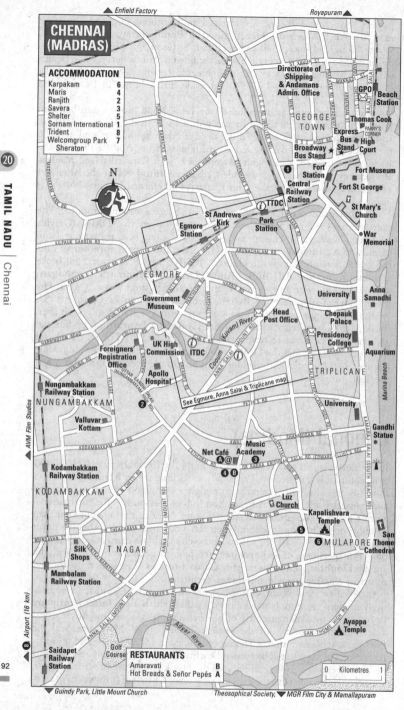

CHENNAI
(MADRAS)

▲ Enfield Factory   Royapuram ▲

ACCOMMODATION

Karpakam	6
Maris	4
Ranjith	2
Savera	3
Shelter	5
Sornam International	1
Trident	8
Welcomgroup Park	7
Sheraton	

N

Directorate of
Shipping
& Andamans
Admin. Office

GPO

Beach
Station

GEORGE
TOWN

Thomas Cook

Express
Bus
Stand

PARRY'S
CORNER

High Court

Broadway
Bus Stand

Fort
Station

Fort Museum

Central
Railway
Station

Fort St George

TTDC

St Mary's
Church

St Andrews
Kirk

Park
Station

War
Memorial

Egmore
Station

KILPAUK GARDEN RD

EGMORE

University

Anna
Samadhi

Government
Museum

Head
Post
Office

Chepauk
Palace

Presidency
College

Aquarium

Foreigners
Registration
Office

UK High
Commission

ITDC

Coovm (Kuvam) River

TRIPLICANE

Apollo
Hospital

See Egmore, Anna Salai & Triplicane map

Nungambakkam
Railway Station

NUNGAMBAKKAM

University

Valluvar
Kottam

Gandhi
Statue

KODAMBAKKAM HIGH RD

Net Café

Music
Academy

Kodambakkam
Railway Station

KODAMBAKKAM

Luz
Church

Kapalishvara
Temple

San
Thome
Cathedral

Silk
Shops

T NAGAR

MULAPORE

Mambalam
Railway Station

Saidapet
Railway
Station

Golf
Course

Adyar River

Ayappa
Temple

RESTAURANTS

| Amaravati | B |
| Hot Breads & Señor Pepés | A |

0   Kilometres   1

▼ Guindy Park, Little Mount Church   Theosophical Society, ▼ MGR Film City & Mamallapuram

▲ AVM Film Studios   ▲ Airport (16 km)

ritory belonged. In addition, the land was protected by water on the east, south and west; cotton could be bought here 20 percent cheaper than elsewhere; and, apparently, Day had acquired a mistress in San Thome. A fortified trading post, completed on St George's Day in 1640, was named **Fort St George**. By 1700, the British had acquired neighbouring territory including **Triplicane** and **Egmore**, while over the course of the next century, as capital of the **Madras Presidency**, which covered most of south India, the city mushroomed to include many surrounding villages. The French repeatedly challenged the British, and finally in 1746, managed to destroy most of the city. **Robert Clive** ("Clive of India"), then a clerk, was taken prisoner, an experience said to have inspired him to become a campaigner. Clive was among the first to re-enter Chennai when it was retaken by the British three years later, and continued to use it as his base. Following this, fortifications were strengthened and the British survived a year-long French siege in 1759, completing the work in 1783. By this time, however, Calcutta was in the ascendancy and Madras lost its national importance.

The city's renaissance began after Independence, when it became the centre of the Tamil **movie industry**, and a hotbed of **Dravidian nationalism**. Rechristened as Chennai in 1997 (to reassert its precolonial identity), the metropolis has boomed since the Indian economy opened up to foreign investment under Rajiv and Rao (former prime ministers) in the early 1990s. The flip side of this rapid economic growth is that the city's infrastructure has been stretched to breaking point; poverty, oppressive heat and pollution are more likely to be your lasting impressions of Chennai than the conspicuous affluence of its modern marble shopping malls.

Arrival

Chennai airport in Trisulam, is comprehensively served by international and domestic flights; the two terminals are a minute's walk from each other, 16km southwest of the city centre on NH-45. Out in the main concourse, you'll find a 24hr post office, Thomas Cook and State Bank of India foreign-exchange

---

Name changes

The city's former name, "Madras", is not the only one to have been weeded out over the last few years by pro-Dravidian politicians. Several major roads in the city have also been renamed as part of an ongoing attempt to **"Dravidify"** the Tamil capital (most of the new names immortalize former nationalist politicians). However, far from all of Chennai's inhabitants are in favour of the recent changes, while some (notably a large contingent of auto-rickshaw-wallahs) seem completely oblivious to them. The confusing result of this is that both old and new names remain in use. We have used the new ones throughout the chapter. Thus Mount Road, the main shopping road through the centre of town, is now **Anna Salai**; to the east, Triplicane High Road, near *Broadlands Hotel*, has become **Quaide Milleth Salai**; Poonamallee High Road, running east–west across the north of the city is **Periyar EVR High Road**; North Beach Road, along the eastern edge of George Town is known as **Rajaji Salai**; South Beach Road, the southern stretch of the coastal road, is **Kamaraj Salai**; running west, Edward Elliot's Road has been renamed **Dr Radha Krishnan Salai**; Mowbray's Road is also known as **TTK Road**, and Nungabamkkam High Road is now **Uttamar Gandhi Salai**.

Although, for the sake of political correctness, we've adopted the new names, it's safe to say that the old ones are still more commonly understood, and that using them will not cause offence – unless, of course, you happen to be talking to a pro-Dravidian activist.

One notable difference between the Chennai movie industry and its counterpart in Mumbai is the influence of **politics** on Tamil films – an overlap that dates from the earliest days of regional cinema, when stories, stock themes and characters were derived from traditional folk ballads about low-caste heroes vanquishing high-caste villains. Already familiar to millions, such Robin Hood-style stereotypes were perfect propaganda vehicles for the nascent Tamil nationalist movement, the Dravida Munnetra Kazhagam, or **DMK**. It is no coincidence that the party's founding father, **C.N. Annadurai**, was a top screenplay and script writer. Like prominent Tamil Congress leaders and movie-makers of the 1930s and 1940s, he and his colleagues used the two popular film genres of the time – "mythologicals" (movie versions of the Hindu epics) and "socials" (dramas set around caste conflicts) – to convey their political ideas to the masses. Audiences were actively encouraged by party workers to boo the villains and cheer each time the proletarian hero, or DMK icons and colours (red and black), appeared on the screen. From this tradition were born the **fan clubs**, or *rasigar manrams*, that played such a key role in mobilizing support for the nationalist parties in elections.

The most influential fan club of all time was the one set up to support the superstar actor Marudur Gopalamenon Ramachandran, known to millions simply as "**MGR**". By carefully cultivating a political image to mirror the folk-hero roles he played in films, the maverick matinee idol generated fanatical grass-roots support in the state, especially among women, and rose to become chief minister in 1977. His eleven-year rule is still regarded by liberals as a dark age in the state's history, as chronic corruption, police brutality, political purges and rising organized crime were all rife during the period. Even the fact that his bungled economic policies penalized precisely the rural poor who voted for him never dented MGR's mass appeal. When he suffered a paralytic stroke in October 1984, 22 people cut off limbs, toes and fingers as offerings to pray for his recovery, while more than a hundred followers attempted to burn themselves to death. For the next three years he was barely able to speak let alone govern effectively, yet the party faithful and fan club members still did not lose faith in his leadership. When he died in 1987, two million people attended his funeral and 31 grief-stricken devotees committed ritual suicide. Even today, MGR's statue, sporting trademark

counters, several STD telephones, and a couple of snack bars. It's by no means certain that anyone will be staffing the **Government of Tamil Nadu Tourist Information Centre** booth at the arrivals exit, but if you're lucky you may be able to fix up accommodation from here, or at the "Free Fone" desk nearby. If you plan to leave Chennai by train, Southern Railways have a computerized **ticket reservation** counter (daily 10am–5pm), immediately outside the domestic terminal exit.

To get away from the airport, there are prepaid minibus and taxi counters at the exit in the international arrivals hall. **Taxis** cost around Rs200–250 for the 35-minute ride to the main hotels or railway stations; rickshaws charge around Rs150–175, but you'll have to lug your gear out to the main road as they're not allowed to park inside the airport forecourt. A taxi to **Mamallapuram** costs in the region of Rs450. Shuttle **buses** (Rs50) run to Egmore and Central stations and Thiruvalluvar (Express) bus stand, but they call at several upmarket hotels en route, and are certainly not "Express". The cheapest way to get downtown is to walk to the main road and take any bus marked Broadway from the near side. Ask to be let off at the central LIC (Life Insurance Company) stop, close to hotels, restaurants and tourist information.

sunglasses and lamb's-wool hat, is revered at tens of thousands of wayside shrines across Tamil Nadu.

MGR's political protégé, and eventual successor, was a teenage screen starlet called **Jayalalitha**, a convent-educated brahmin's daughter whom he spotted at a school dance and, despite an age difference of more than thirty years, recruited to be both his leading lady and mistress. The couple would star opposite each other in 25 hit films, and when MGR eventually moved into politics, Jayalalitha followed him, becoming leader of the AIADMK (the party MGR set up after being expelled from the DMK in 1972), after a much publicized power struggle with his widow. Larger than life in voluminous silver ponchos and heavy gold jewellery, the now portly Puratchi Thalavi ("Revolutionary Leader") has taken her personality cult to extremes brazen even by Indian standards. On her forty-sixth birthday in 1994, Rs50,000 of public money was spent on giant cardboard cut-outs depicting her in academic and religious robes, while 46 of her more fervent admirers rolled bare-chested along the length of Anna Salai. Jayalalitha's spell as chief minister, however, was brought to an ignominious end at the 1996 elections, after allegations of fraud and corruption on an appropriately monumental scale. Despite being found guilty by the High Court, she still managed to bring down the national government and force a general election in 1999 (by withdrawing AIADMK support from Prime Minister Vajpayee's shaky, BJP-led coalition) and later ousted her arch rival, **M. Karunanidhi**, leader of the DMK, to regain her old job as Chief Minister of Tamil Nadu. One of her first acts was to exact revenge on Karunanidhi, throwing him and one thousand of his supporters into prison on corruption charges.

The intermingling of Tamil politics and cinema is now so established in the state that it's almost inconceivable for anyone to attain high office without some kind of movie credentials. Distinguished among Chennai's huge roadside hoard-ings by his MGR-style shades and yellow shawl, the previous chief minister was another former screenwriter, while the wavy-haired megastar of the 1980s, **Rajnikanth**, ended years of speculation a few years back when he threw his lot in with Congress (I) party. As a typecast villain rather than eternal do-gooder, his screen image differs wildly from MGR's but if he manages to galvanize his fan club, the complexion of Tamil politics could be totally transformed for the first time in decades.

Trains run every ten to fifteen minutes (4.30am–11pm) from **Trisulam** Station, 500m from the airport on the far side of the road, to Park, Egmore and North Beach stations, taking roughly 45 minutes.

By train

Arriving in Chennai by train, you come in at one of two **long-distance rail-way stations**, 1.5km apart on Periyar EVR High Road, towards the north of the city. **Egmore Station**, in the heart of the busy commercial Egmore dis-trict, is the arrival point for most trains from Tamil Nadu and Kerala. On the whole, all the others pull in at **Central Station**, further east, on the edge of George Town, which has a 24hr left-luggage office, and STD phone booths outside the exit. Information kiosks at both stations are poorly staffed and badly equipped, but both have plenty of metered taxis and auto-rickshaws.

By bus

Buses from elsewhere in Tamil Nadu arrive at two bus stands – **Express** and **Broadway** – which are opposite each other in George Town, near the High Court complex off NSC Bose Road. Both stations are crowded but Broadway, which also

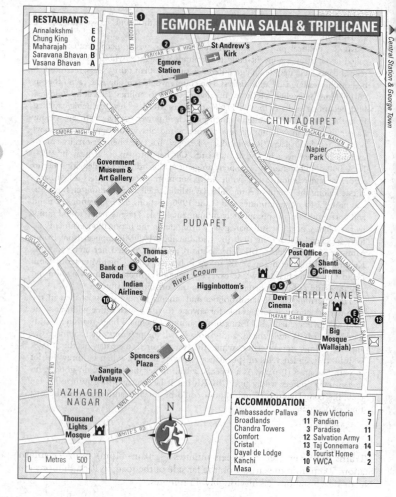

EGMORE, ANNA SALAI & TRIPLICANE

RESTAURANTS

Annalakshmi	E
Chung King	C
Maharajah	D
Saravana Bhavan	B
Vasana Bhavan	A

St Andrew's Kirk

Egmore Station

CHINTADRIPET

Napier Park

EGMORE HIGH RD

Government Museum & Art Gallery

PUDAPET

Head Post Office

Shanti Cinema

Bank of Baroda

Thomas Cook

River Cooum

Higginbottom's

Devi Cinema

TRIPLICANE

Indian Airlines

THAYAR SAHIB ST

Big Mosque (Wallajah)

Spencers Plaza

BUNNY RD

Sangita Vadyalaya

AZHAGIRI NAGAR

N

WHITE'S RD

Thousand Lights Mosque

0 Metres 500

ACCOMMODATION

Ambassador Pallava	9	New Victoria	5
Broadlands	11	Pandian	7
Chandra Towers	3	Paradise	11
Comfort	12	Salvation Army	1
Cristal	13	Taj Connemara	14
Dayal de Lodge	8	Tourist Home	4
Kanchi	10	YWCA	2
Masa	6		

sees services from Karnataka, Kerala and Andhra Pradesh, is also extremely confusing: it's little more than a dirty, chaotic, potholed yard, and a nightmare to negotiate with luggage. You have to walk out of the bus stands to the main road to pick up a rickshaw. For details of buses to **Mamallapuram** from Broadway, see p.1211.

Information

At the highly efficient and very helpful **Government of India Regional Tourist Office** (GOIRTO) at 154 Anna Salai (Mon–Fri 9.15am–5.45pm, Sat 9am–1pm; ☎044/846 0285 or 846 1459, ⑩www.tourismindia.com), you can pick up maps and leaflets, and arrange accommodation. They also supply the names of reliable tour agents for car rental, and keep a list of approved **guides** you can arrange for a private tour of the city, either for a full day (Rs350–750), or half-day (Rs250–500).

The **Tamil Nadu Tourism Development Corporation** (TTDC), 4 EVR Periyar Rd (Mon–Fri 10am–5pm; ☏044/536294, ⓦwww.tamilnadutourism .com), outside Park Station, a ten-minute walk northeast of Anna Salai, can only book accommodation in their own hotels across the state. Advance bookings for

The Chennai festival and the sabhas

The sabhas of Chennai – the city's arts societies and venues, of which the most illustrious is the Chennai Music Academy – stage regular public performances of Carnatic classical music and Bharatanatyam dance. Here, ambitious artists have to undergo the scrutiny of a fanatical audience and a less-than-generous bevy of newspaper critics, whose reviews can make or break a career.

Musicians are expected to interpret correctly the subtleties of any given composition, *raga* or *tala*. The sets of notes that make up a *raga* occupy a place midway between melody and scale; they must be played imaginatively in improvisation, but in strict sequences and with correct emphasis. The worst crime, the sign of an amateur, is to slip accidentally into a different *raga* that might share the same scale. *Tala*, the rhythmic cycle and bedrock of the music, will often be demonstrated by someone on stage, and consists of a series of claps and waves; unlike in north India, this element is overt in the south and the audience delights in clapping along to keep the often-complex time signatures. The pleasure is heightened during percussion improvisations on the barrel-shaped *mridangam* drum or *ghatam* clay pot that accompany many performances.

During the annual Chennai Festival, held from December 15 until January 1, up to five hundred events are staged, primarily at the Music Academy (☏044/ 8112231) on T.T.K. Road. It's a real orgy of classical music and dance recitals, in which many of India's greatest artistes – from all over the country – can be seen at work.

Female vocalists to look out for include Mani Krishnaswamy, Charumathi Ramachandran, Sudha Raghunathan and Bombay Jayashree; duos such as the Mumbai and Hyderabad Sisters are also popular. Top-ranking male singers, K.V. Narayanaswamy, B. Rajam Iyer and younger artists like Thrissur Ramachandran and T.N. Seshagopalan should not be missed. Among the best of the instrumentalists are E. Gayatri and Rama Varma on the gentle melodic *vina*, a stringed instrument unique to the south; Ramani on the flute; violinists such as T.N. Krishnan and D. Ananda Raman; and N. Ravikiran on the *gottuvadyam*, a rare member of the *vina* family, laid flat on the floor and played much like a slide guitar. Carnatic music's answer to John Coltrane is Kadri Gopalnath, whose soaring saxophone and flamboyant dress have made him one of the most distinctive figures on the circuit. Former child prodigy, U. Sriniwas, is the electric mandolin maestro. Cassettes and CDs of all the above artistes are available at *Music World* in Spencer Plaza. For addresses of good musical instrument shops in the city, see Listings on p.1208.

The predominant dance style is Bharatanatyam, as performed by stars such as Alarmail Valli, and the Dhananjayans. Dance dramas are also staged by the Kalakshetra Academy, a school of dance and music set in a beautiful 100-acre compound near the sea in Tiruvanmiyur, on the southern outskirts of the city.

To find out about all performances of music and dance, ask at the government tourist office on Anna Salai, consult the listings pages of local papers such as the *Hindu*, or have a look in *Chennai: This Fortnight*, available at hotels and bookshops. You may also like to pay a visit to the Sangita Vadyalaya, behind the HDF Bank on Anna Salai (Mon–Fri 9.15am–5.45pm), which displays an impressive array of Indian musical instruments. The centre was set up to preserve and restore antique pieces, but resident artisans also revive rare instruments which are no longer commonly played. You can try your hand at a few of them, and experiment with an amazing array of old percussion pieces.

ITDC hotels across the whole country can be made, and tours of the city, state and country arranged, at the **India Tourist Development Corporation** (ITDC) office at 29 Victor Crescent, C-in-C Road (Mon–Sat 6am–8pm, Sun 6am–2pm; ℡044/827 8884, ✉itdc.ros@gems.vsnl.net.in). Tourist offices for other states, including Himachal Pradesh, Kerala, Rajasthan and Uttar Pradesh, are at 28 C-in-C Rd. *Hallo! Chennai* (see below) has full details of these and other state offices, as does the GOIRTO on Anna Salai.

The long-established *Hallo! Chennai* (monthly; Rs10) is an accurate directory to all the city's services, with full moon dates (useful for estimating temple festivals), a guide to Tamil Nadu for tourists, exhaustive flight and train details, and an outline of Chennai bus timetables. Alternatively, there's a new, even more comprehensive bi-monthly directory called *Madura Welcome, Chennai* (Rs30), which lists every bus service and route in Chennai, and from Chennai to other towns in the state. Both are available at all book and stationery shops. Unfortunately, neither have a "What's On" section; for forthcoming music and dance performances, consult the events column on page three of the *Hindu*, ask at the tourist office, or try and get hold of a copy of *Chennai: This Fortnight*, available free from all moderate to expensive hotels.

City transport

The offices, sights, railway stations and bus stands of Chennai are spread over such a wide area that it's impossible to get around without using some form of **public transport**. Most visitors jump in auto-rickshaws, but outside rush hours you can travel around comfortably by **bus**, or suburban **train**.

Buses

To ride on a bus in most Indian cities you need to be incredibly resilient and a master of the art of hanging on to open doorways with two fingers. **Buses** in Chennai, on the other hand, are regular, inexpensive, and only cramped during rush hours. On Anna Salai, buses have special stops, but on smaller streets you have to flag them down, or wait with the obvious crowd. Buses in Egmore gather opposite the railway station. Numbers of services to specific places of interest in the city are listed in the relevant accounts, or for a full directory of bus routes, buy *Madura Welcome, Chennai* (see above).

Trains

If you want to travel south from central Chennai to Guindy (Deer Park), St Thomas Mount or the airport, the easiest way to go is by **train**. Services run every fifteen minutes (on average) between 4.30am and 11pm, prices are minimal, and you can guarantee a seat at any time except rush hour (9am & 5pm). First-class carriages substitute padded seats for wooden slatted benches, and are a little cleaner; buy a ticket before boarding.

City trains travel between: North Beach (opposite the general post office), Fort, Park (for Central), Egmore, Nungambakkam, Kodambakkam, Mambalam (for T Nagar and silk shops), Saidapet (for Little Mount Church), Guindy, St Thomas Mount and Trisulam (for the airport).

Taxis and rickshaws

Chennai's yellow-top Ambassador **taxis** gather outside Egmore and Central railway stations and at the airport. All have meters, but drivers often prefer to set a fixed price before leaving, and invariably charge a return fare, whatever

One good way to get around the sights of Chennai is on a TTDC **bus tour**; bookings are taken in the relevant offices. They're good value, albeit rushed, and the guides can be very helpful.

The **TTDC half-day tour** (daily 8am–1pm or 1.30pm–6.30pm; Rs105 non a/c, or Rs150 a/c) starts at their office on EVR Periyar Salai. It takes in Fort St George, the Government Museum, the Snake Park, Kapalishvara Temple and Elliot's Beach and Marina Beach (on Friday, the Government Museum is closed, so the tour goes to the Birla Planetarium instead).

TTDC also offer good-value **day-trips**, including visits to Mamallapuram, Kanchipuram, and Pondicherry; meals are included in the tariff.

the destination. At around Rs150 from Central Station to Triplicane, they're practically pricing themselves out of business.

Flocks of auto- and cycle rickshaws wait patiently outside tourist hotels, and not so patiently outside railway stations. **Auto-rickshaw** drivers in Chennai are notorious for their demand for high fares from locals and tourists alike. A rickshaw from Triplicane to either of the bus stations, plus Egmore and Central railway stations should cost no more than Rs40. All rickshaws have meters; a few drivers use them if asked, but in many cases you'll save a lot of frustrating bargaining by offering a small sub above the meter-reading (a driver may offer you a rate of "meter plus 5", meaning Rs5 above the final reading). If you need to get to the airport or station early in the morning, book a rickshaw and negotiate the price the night before (the driver may well sleep in his vehicle outside your hotel).

Only take **cycle rickshaws** on the smaller roads; riding amid Chennai traffic on a fragile tricycle seat can be extremely hair-raising.

Car, motorcycle and bike rental

Car rental, with driver, is available at many of the upmarket hotels, or the Government of India Tourist Office can supply you with a list of approved, safe drivers. It's a great, relatively stress-free way to get about if you can afford it; Ambassadors cost Rs600–700 per day (or Rs1100–1200 for a/c).

Anyone brave enough to rent a **moped** or **motorcycle** for short rides around the city, or tours of Tamil Nadu, should head for U-Rent Services, at 36, IInd Main Rd, Poonamallee High Road (Mon–Sat; ☏044/441 1985). You'll need an international driving licence. Prices range from Rs150 to Rs350 per day, and you have to pay a flat Rs250 annual membership fee regardless of how long you rent a bike for.

Bicycles may be rented by the hour from dozens of stalls around the city, but you'll have to keep your wits about you riding through the centre, especially on Anna Salai.

Accommodation

Finding a **place to stay** in Chennai can be a problem, as hotels are often full by noon. Demand has pushed prices up, so only a couple of places offer anything for less than Rs200; if you are on a budget, it is advisable to phone and book in advance, at least from the railway station or airport.

The main concentration of mid-range and inexpensive hotels is located around the railway station in **Egmore**, and further east in **Triplicane**, a characterful, busy market and Muslim residential district. The bulk of the top hotels are in the south of the city and several offer courtesy buses to and from the airport. Almost all hotels have at least one south Indian/multi-cuisine restaurant attached to their premises.

There are **Southern Railway retiring rooms** in both Central and Egmore stations. Dorm beds cost Rs50, and spacious if run-down doubles are presided over by a stern matron in a regulation blue sari. The latter are excellent value, so they tend to fill up quickly.

Due to frequent shortages, visitors should use **water** as sparingly as possible.

Egmore

The accommodation listed below is marked on the Egmore, Anna Salai and Triplicane **map** on p.1196.

Chandra Towers, 9 Gandhi Irwin Rd ☎ 044/823 3344, ℻ 825 1703. The plushest hotel in the area; all the comforts you'd expect at this price, including central a/c, foreign exchange, 24hr coffee shop, bar and rooftop restaurant. ❼–❽
Masa, 15/1 Kennet's Lane ☎ 044/825 2966. Variously priced rooms with attached bathrooms in a very clean, modern building, close to the station. Good value. ❷–❹
New Victoria, 3 Kennet's Lane ☎ 044/825 3638. All rooms a/c with hot showers and some with balconies. Nonresidents can use the bar (11am–11pm) and internet centre (Rs40/hr) while waiting for a train. Rate includes breakfast. ❼–❽
Pandian, 9 Kennet's Lane ☎ 044/825 2901, ℻ 825 8459. Pleasant, clean and modern mid-scale place within walking distance of the railway station. Ask for a room on the Church Park side of the building for green views. Some rooms are a/c. ❻–❼
Salvation Army Red Shield Guest House, 15 Ritherdon Rd ☎ 044/532 1821. A friendly and

helpful Sally Army lodge tucked away in a leafy backstreet behind the station. All extremely basic with several dorms (Rs70; not advised for single women), a four-bed room (Rs350) and doubles with attached baths (some a/c). ❸–❺
Tourist Home, 21 Gandhi Irwin Rd ☎ 044/825 0079. Popular hotel directly opposite the railway station. Rooms (some a/c) have showers, telephones, clean sheets and towels; there are also three and six-bedded rooms. Ask for a back room, as the place suffers badly from early morning noise. Good value but often full. ❹–❻
YWCA International Guest House, 1086 Periyar EVR High Rd ☎ 044/532 4234, ℻ 532 4263. Attractive hotel in quiet gardens behind Egmore station. Spotless, spacious rooms, safe-deposit and a good restaurant. A highly recommended safe and friendly place; book in advance. The rates include a buffet breakfast. ❺–❻

Anna Salai and Triplicane

The accommodation listed below is marked on the Egmore, Anna Salai and Triplicane **map** on p.1196.

Ambassador Pallava, 30 Montieth Rd ☎ 044/855 4476, ℻ 855 4492. Colossal four-star, close to Anna Salai, with great views from its upper storeys. Amid all the cool, white marble and gold-plated mirrors there is a pool, disco and health club. ❾
Broadlands, 16 Vallabha Agraham St, Triplicane ☎ 044/854 5573. An old whitewashed house, with crumbling stucco and stained glass, ranged around a leafy courtyard; the kind of budget travellers' enclave you either love or loathe. It has a large roof terrace and clean rooms, a few with attached bathrooms, private balconies and views of the mosque. Inexpensive left-luggage facility is available, but a reprehensible "No Indians" policy is very strictly enforced. ❸–❹

Comfort, 22 Vallabha Agraham St, Triplicane ☎ 044/858 7661. A chaotic place with yards of dimly lit corridors; rooms are clean but on the small side, all with attached bathrooms. ❹–❺
Cristal, 34 CNK Rd, Triplicane ☎ 044/858 5605. A safe and friendly place run by a team of brothers; the reception is busy with locals sipping coffee in the reception all day. Rooms are tiled and clean, all with attached showers in a modern building off Quaide Milleth Salai. There is no restaurant. ❷
Kanchi, 28 C-in-C Rd ☎ 044/827 1100, ℻ 827 9000. Indifferent staff and a soulless skyscraper, redeemed by superb views from its spacious rooms, two excellent restaurants (one rooftop) and bar. ❻–❼

Paradise, 17/1 Vallabha Agraham St, Triplicane ☏044/854 1542. Next door to *Broadlands*, and a dependable choice if you're after an inexpensive room with an attached shower-toilet. *Paradise* features seating on a large roof terrace, and room service. ❸–❹

Taj Connemara, Binny Road ☏044/852 0123, ☏852 3361. Dating from the Raj era, this white-washed Art Deco five-star hotel is a Chennai insti-

tution situated near Anna Salai. The best rooms are the big, "heritage" ones, each with Victorian decor, a dressing room and veranda overlooking the pool. The "standard" rooms, by contrast, are modern, overpriced and disappointing: they catch unpleasant smells from a polluted river nearby. There is a pool, several good restaurants, a shopping arcade, and a bar. ❾

Outside the centre

The accommodation listed below is marked on the Chennai (Madras) **map** on p.1192.

Karpakam, 41 South Mada St, Mylapore ☏044/494 2987. Very ordinary, slightly dingy place whose only outstanding feature is its location overlooking the Kapalishvara Temple; it's also on the right side of the city for the airport, 12km away. ❺–❻

Maris, 9 Cathedral Rd ☏044/827 0541, ☏825 4847. A 1970s concrete block right next to the *Sheraton* and near the Music Academy. Their a/c rooms are a particularly good deal for the area, but there is a distinct lack of atmosphere. You can book TTDC city tours here. ❻–❼

Ranjith, 9 Nungambakkam High Rd ☏044/827 0521. Spotless en-suite rooms (some a/c) with cable TV. Veg and non-veg restaurants, bar and travel agent. ❻–❼

Savera, 69 Dr Radha Krishnan Salai Rd ☏044/827 4700, ☏827 3475. Slightly older than the other upmarket hotels in the locality, but boasting all mod cons, including a pool, good pastry shop, bar, excellent south Indian speciality restaurant, and rooftop restaurant with great views. ❽–❾

Shelter, 19–21 Venkatesa Agraharam St, Mylapore ☏044/495 1919, ☏493 5646. Sparklingly clean,

centrally a/c luxury hotel that's a stone's throw from the Kapalishvara Temple, and better value than most upscale places at this price. ❽–❾

Sornam International, 11 Stringer St ☏044/535 3060. The best of a generally ropy bunch around Central Station; clean and respectable enough, but really only worth considering if you can't face an auto-rickshaw ride across town or have an early train to catch. There is a veg restaurant. ❸

Trident, 1/24 GST Rd ☏044/234 4747, ☏234 6699. Comfortable five-star hotel in lovely gardens with luxurious rooms and swimming pool. Near the airport (3km), but a long (12km, albeit complimentary) drive into town. Good restaurants, one of which serves Thai cuisine. ❾

Welcomgroup Park Sheraton, 132 TTK Rd ☏044/499 4101, ☏499 7101. The last word in American-style executive luxury, with bow-tied valets and in-room fax machines, yet somehow not too ostentatious. Three excellent restaurants, a 24hr coffee shop and other five-star facilities. Recommended choice for business travellers. ❾

The City

Chennai divides into three main areas. The northern district, separated from the rest by the River Cooum, is the site of the first British outpost in India, **Fort St George**, and the commercial centre, **George Town**, which developed during British occupation. At the southern end of Rajaji Salai is **Parry's Corner**, George Town's principal landmark – look for the tall grey building labelled *Parry's* – it's a major bus stop.

Central Chennai is sandwiched between the Cooum and Adyar rivers, and crossed diagonally by the city's main thoroughfare, **Anna Salai**, the modern, commercial heart of the metropolis. To the east, this gives way to the atmospheric old Muslim quarters of **Triplicane** and a long straight **Marina** where fishermen mend nets and set small boats out to sea, and hordes of Indian tourists hitch up saris and trousers for a quick paddle. South of here, near the coast, **Mylapore**, inhabited in the 1500s by the Portuguese, boasts

Kapalishvara Temple and San Thome Cathedral, both tourist attractions and places of pilgrimage. Further out, south of the Adyar, is the Portuguese church on St Thomas Mount.

Fort St George

Quite unlike any other fort in India, **Fort St George** stands amid state offices facing the sea in the east of the city, just south of George Town on Kamaraj Salai. It looks more like a complex of well-maintained colonial mansions than a fort; indeed many of its buildings are used today as offices, a hive of activity during the week as people rush between the Secretariat and State Legislature.

The fort was the first structure of Madras town and the first territorial possession of the British in India. Construction began in 1640, but most of the original buildings were replaced later that century, after being damaged during French sieges. The most imposing structure is the eighteenth-century colonnaded **Fort House**, coated in deep-slate-grey and white paint. Next door, in the more modestly proportioned **Exchange Building** – site of Madras' first bank – is the excellent **Fort Museum** (daily except Fri 10am–5pm; $5 [Rs5]). The collection within faithfully records the central events of the British occupation of Madras with portraits, regimental flags, weapons, coins minted by the East India Company, medals, stamps and thick woollen uniforms that make you wonder how the Raj survived as long as it did. The squat cast-iron cage on the ground floor was brought to Madras from China, where for more than a year in the nineteenth century it was used as a particularly sadistic form of imprisonment for a British captain. The upper floor, once the public exchange hall where merchants met to gossip and trade, is now an **art gallery**, where portraits of prim officials and their wives sit side by side with fine sketches of the British embarking at Chennai in aristocratic finery, attended by Indians in loincloths. Also on display are etchings by the famous artist **Thomas Daniells**, whose work largely defined British perceptions of India at the end of the eighteenth century.

South of the museum, past the State Legislature, stands the oldest surviving Anglican church in Asia, **St Mary's Church** (daily 9am–5pm), built in 1678, and partly renovated after the battle of 1759. Constructed with thick walls and a strong vaulted roof to withstand the city's many sieges, the church served as a store and shelter in times of war. It's distinctly English in style, crammed with plaques and statues in memory of British soldiers, politicians and their wives. The grandest plaque, made of pure silver, was presented by Elihu Yale, former governor of Fort St George (1687–96), and founder of Yale University in the USA. A collection of photographs of visiting dignitaries, including Queen Elizabeth II, is on display in the entrance porch. Nearby, **Robert Clive's house** is in a rather sorry state, used by the Archaeological Survey of India as offices.

George Town

North of Fort St George, the former British trading centre of **George Town** (reached on bus #18 from Anna Salai) remains the focal area for banks, offices and shipping companies. This confusing – if well-ordered – grid of streets harbours a fascinating medley of architecture: eighteenth- and nineteenth-century churches, Hindu and Jain temples, and a scattering of mosques, interspersed with grand mansions. In the east, on Rajaji Salai, the **General Post Office** occupies a robust earth-red Indo-Saracenic building, constructed in 1884. George Town's southern extent is marked by the bulbous white domes and sandstone towers of the **High Court**, and the even more opulent towers of the **Law College**, both showing strong Islamic influence.

Government Museum

It's well worth setting aside at least half a day to explore the Chennai **Government Museum** (daily except Fri 9.30am–5pm; Rs3, Rs20 extra with camera); to get there, hop on bus #11H from Anna Salai for Pantheon Road, south of Egmore railway station. It has remarkable archeological finds from south India and the Deccan, stone sculptures from major temples, and an unsurpassed collection of Chola bronzes.

A deep red circular structure, fronted by Italian-style pillars and built in 1851, the **main building** stands opposite the entrance and ticket office. The first gallery is devoted to archeology and geology, with tools, pots, jewellery and weapons from the Stone and Iron ages, and maps of principal excavations. Later exhibits include a substantial assortment of dismantled panels, railings and statues from the second century AD stupa complex at **Amaravati** (see p.1152). Depicting episodes from the Buddha's life and scenes from the *Jataka* stories from ancient Hinayana Buddhist texts, these sensuously carved marble reliefs are widely regarded as the finest achievements of early Indian art, outshining even the Sanchi *toranas*. Sadly, they are poorly lit and inadequately labelled; some have even been defaced with graffiti, while others are blackened and worn from constant rubbing. To the left of the Amaravati gallery, high, arcaded halls full of stuffed animals lead to the **ethnology gallery** (currently under renovation, so it may be closed to the public) where models, clothes and weapons, along with photographs of expressionless faces in orderly lines, illustrate local tribal societies, some long since wiped out. A fascinating display of wind and string instruments, drums and percussion includes the large predecessor of today's sitar and several very old tablas. Nearby, a group of wooden doors and window frames from Chettinad, a region near Madurai, are exquisitely carved with floral and geometric designs much like those found in Gujarati *havelis*.

The museum's real treasure, however, is the modern, well-lit gallery, left of the main building, which contains the world's most complete and impressive selection of **Chola bronzes** (see p.1248). Large statues of Shiva, Vishnu and Parvati stand in the centre, flanked by glass cases containing smaller figurines, including several sculptures of Shiva as **Nataraja**, the Lord of the Dance, encircled by a ring of fire, and standing with his arms and legs poised and head provocatively cocked. One of the finest models is **Ardhanarishvara**, the androgynous form of Shiva (united with Shakti in transcendence of duality); the left side of the body is female and the right male, and the intimacy of detail is astounding. A rounded breast, a delicate hand and tender bejewelled foot are counterpoints to the harsher sinewy limbs and torso, and the male side of the head is crowned with a mass of matted hair and serpents.

A **children's museum** demonstrates the principles of electricity and irrigation with marginally diverting, semi-functional models, while the magnificent Indo-Saracenic **art gallery** houses old British portraits of figures such as Clive and Hastings, plus Rajput and Moghul miniatures, and a small display of ivory carvings.

St Andrew's Kirk

Just northeast of Egmore Station, off Periyar EVR High Road, **St Andrew's Kirk**, consecrated in 1821, is a fine example of Georgian architecture. Modelled on London's St Martins-in-the-Fields, it is one of just three churches in India which has a circular seating plan, laid out beneath a huge dome painted blue with gold stars and supported by a sweep of Corinthian columns. Marble plaques around the church give a fascinating insight into the kind of people that left Britain to work for the imperial and Christian cause. A staircase leads onto the flat roof, surrounding the dome, from where you can climb further up into the steeple past the massive bell to a tiny balcony affording excellent views of the city.

Marina

One of the longest city beaches in the world, the **Marina** (Kamaraj Salai) stretches 5km from the harbour at the southeastern corner of George Town, to San Thome Cathedral. The impulse to transform Chennai's "rather dismal beach" into a Marina, styled "from old Sicilian recollections" to function as a "lung" for the city, was conceived by Mountstuart Elphinstone Grant-Duff (governor 1881–86) who had otherwise won himself the reputation for being "feeble, sickly" and a "failure". Over the years, numerous buildings, some of which undoubtedly would not have figured in memories of Sicily, have sprung up, among them surreal modern memorials to Tamil Nadu's chief political heroes and freedom fighters.

Today the **beach** itself is a sociable stretch, peopled by idle paddlers, picnickers and pony-riders; every afternoon crowds gather around the beach market. However, it suffers miserably from being just a little downstream from the port, which belches out waste and smelly fumes, as well as being the local toilet around the areas where the fishermen hang out. Unsurprisingly, swimming and sunbathing are neither recommended nor approved. At the northern end is the **MG Ramachandran Samadhi**, where Tamil tourists flock in droves to pay their respects at the shrine of the state's most illustrious movie actor and chief minister "MGR" (see p.1194). Just to the south lies one of the oldest of the city's university buildings: **Senate House** (1879), an uncharacteristically Byzantine-influenced design by Robert Fellowes Chisholm (1840–1915). He was one of the British leaders in developing the Indo-Saracenic hybrid style, incorporating Hindu, Jain and Muslim elements along with solid Victorian British brickwork.

Going south, past the Indo-Saracenic **Presidency College** (1865–71), a number of stolid Victorian university buildings include the **Lady Willingdon Teacher Training College**. Next door, the college's hostel, a huge lump of a building with a semicircular frontage painted white and yellow, was formerly the Madras depot of the Tudor Ice Company. From 1840 to 1870, imported ice from the northeast US was shipped here in clippers, caked in pine sawdust to prevent it from melting, and hauled ashore to be sold from this building, known at that time, and for years after, as the **Ice House**. At the height of the trade, 150,000 tons were imported each year, but the bottom fell out of the business when a rival company set up a steam-powered ice factory in the city in 1874. The Ice House's other claim to fame is that it hosted the inauguration of the Ramakrishna movement in south India, after Swami Vivekananda stayed in it for nine days following his return from Europe in 1897.

Mylapore

Long before Madras came into existence, **Mylapore**, south of the Marina (reached by buses #4, #5 or #21 from the LIC building on Anna Salai), was a major settlement; the Greek geographer Ptolemy mentioned it in the second century AD as a thriving port. During the Pallava period (fifth to ninth centuries) it was second only to Mamallapuram (see p.1211).

An important stop – with Little Mount and St Thomas Mount – on the St Thomas pilgrimage trail, **San Thome Cathedral** (daily 6am–8pm) marks the eastern boundary of Mylapore, lying close to the sea at the southern end of the

Marina. Although the present neo-Gothic structure dates from 1896, San Thome stands on the site of two earlier churches (the first possibly erected by Nestorian Christians from Persia during the tenth century) built over the tomb of St Thomas; his relics are kept inside. Behind the church, a small **museum** (Mon–Sat 10am–5pm) houses stones inscribed in Tamil, Sanskrit (twelfth-century Chola) and early Portuguese, and also a map of India dated 1519.

The large **Kapalishvara temple** sits less than 1km west of the San Thome Cathedral. Seventh-century Tamil poet-saints sang its praises, but the present structure, dedicated to Shiva, probably dates from the sixteenth century. Until then, the temple is thought to have occupied a site on the shore; sea erosion or demolition at the hands of the Portuguese led it to be rebuilt inland. The huge (40m) *gopura* towering above the main east entrance, plastered in stucco figures, was added in 1906. Surrounding an assortment of busy shrines, where priests offer blessings for devotees and non-Hindus alike, the courtyard features an old tree where a small shrine to Shiva's consort, Parvati, shows her in the form of a peahen (*mayil*) worshipping a *lingam*. This commemorates the legend that she was momentarily distracted from concentrating on her lord by the enchanting dance of a peacock. Shiva, miffed at this dereliction of wifely duty, cursed her, whereupon she turned into a peahen. To expiate the sin, Parvati took off to a place called Kapalinagar, and embarked upon rigorous austerities.

A little further west, before you come to TTK Road, the **Luz Church**, on Luz Church Road, is thought to be the earliest in Chennai, built by the Portuguese in the sixteenth century. Its founding is associated with a miracle; Portuguese sailors in difficulties at sea were once guided to land and safety by a light which, when they tried to find its source, disappeared. The church, dedicated to Our Lady of Light, was erected where the light left them.

Little Mount Caves

St Thomas is said to have sought refuge from persecution in the **Little Mount Caves**, 8km south of the city centre (bus #18A, #18B, or #52C from Anna Salai), now 200m off the road between the Maraimalai Adigal Bridge and the residence of the governor of Tamil Nadu. Entrance to the caves is beside steps leading to a statue of Our Lady of Good Health. Inside, next to a small natural window in the rock, are impressions of what are believed to be St Thomas' handprints, created when he made his escape through this tiny opening.

Behind the new circular church of Our Lady of Good Health, together with brightly painted replicas of the *Pietà* and Holy Sepulchre, is a natural **spring**. Tradition has it that this was created when Thomas struck the rock, so the crowds that came to hear him preach could quench their thirst; samples of its holy water are on sale.

St Thomas Mount

According to legend, St Thomas was speared to death (or struck by a hunter's stray arrow) while praying before a stone cross on **St Thomas Mount**, 11km south of the city centre, close to the airport (take a suburban train to Guindy railway station, and walk from there). **Our Lady of Expectation Church** (1523) is reached by 134 granite steps marked at intervals with the fourteen Stations of the Cross. At the top of the steps, a huge old banyan tree provides shade for devotees who come to fast, pray and sing. Inside the church, St Thomas' cross is said to have bled in 1558; above the altar which marks the spot of the Apostle's death, a painting of the Madonna and Child is credited to St Luke. A memento stall stands nearby and cool drinks are available in the adjacent Holy Apostle's Convent.

The Theosophical Society Headquarters

The **Theosophical Society** was established in New York in 1875 by American Civil War veteran Colonel Henry S. Olcott, a failed farmer and journalist, and the eccentric Russian aristocrat Madame Helena Petrovna Blavatsky, who claimed occult powers and telepathic links with "Mahatmas" in Tibet. Based on a fundamental belief in the equality and truth of all religions, the society in fact propagated a modern form of Hinduism, praising all things Indian and shunning Christian missionaries. Needless to say, its two founders were greeted enthusiastically when they transferred their operations to Madras in 1882, establishing their headquarters near Elliot's Beach in Adyar (buses #5, #5C or #23C from George Town/Anna Salai). Even after Madame Blavatsky's psychic powers were proved to be bogus, the society continued to attract Hindus and Western visitors, and its buildings still stand today, sheltering several shrines and an excellent **library** (Mon–Sat 8.30–10am & 2–4pm) of books on religion and philosophy. The collection, begun by Olcott in 1886, comprises 165,000 volumes and nearly 200,000 palm-leaf manuscripts, from all over the world. A selection is housed in an exhibition room on the ground floor. This includes 800-year-old scroll pictures of the Buddha; a seventeenth-century treatise from London on embalming bodies; rare Tibetan xylographs written on bark paper; exquisitely illuminated Korans; a giant copy of Martin Luther's *Biblia* printed in Nuremberg three hundred years ago; and a Bible in seven languages that's the size of a thumbnail.

The 270 acres of woodland and gardens surrounding the society's headquarters make a serene place to sit and restore spirits away from the noise and heat of the city streets. In the middle of the grounds, a vast 400-year-old **banyan tree**, said to be the second-largest in the world, provides shade for up to 3000 people at a time. J. Krishnamurthi and Maria Montessori have both given talks under its tangle of pillar-like root stems, whose growth Theosophists see as symbolizing the spread of the society itself.

The Enfield factory

India's most stylish home-made motorcycle, the **Enfield Bullet**, is manufactured at a plant on the outskirts of Chennai, 18km north of Anna Salai (bus #1 from LIC Building or Parry's Corner). With its elegant tear-drop tank and thumping 350cc single-cylinder engine, the Bullet has become a contemporary classic – in spite of its propensity to leak oil and break down. Bike enthusiasts should definitely brave the long haul across town to see the **factory**, which is as much a period piece as the machines it turns out. Guided tours, which last around ninety minutes and are free (Mon–Fri 9.30am–5.30pm; ☎ 044/543 3000), have to be arranged in advance by telephoning the Enfield's marketing general manager, Mr K Muralidharan. You can do this yourself, or through the Government of India Tourist Office on Anna Salai.

Eating

Chennai runs on indigenous fast-food **restaurants** and "meals" (thali) joints, in particular the legendary *Saravana Bhavan* chain, which serves superb south Indian food for a fraction of the cost of a coffee at one of the five-stars. That said, a minor splurge at *Annalakshmi* on Anna Salai or the *Park Sheraton* on TTK Road is well worth considering.

The restaurants listed below are marked on either the Egmore, Anna Salai and Triplicane **map** on p.1192 or the Chennai **map** on p.1196.

Annalakshmi, 804 Anna Salai ⊕044/8525109. A nonprofitmaking venture run voluntarily by devotees of Swami Shivenanda; you choose one of several set menus (each with different Ayurvedic properties). You'll enjoy a leisurely and expensive meal in beautiful surroundings, then all your money goes to charitable works in the community. Recommended.

Amaravati, corner of Cathedral/TKK Road. Just one place in a complex of four good regional speciality restaurants, south of the downtown area. This one does excellent Andhran food, including particularly tasty biryanis.

Chung King, Anna Salai, Down an alleyway to the left of *Buhari* restaurant. Genuine Chinese cuisine prepared by a pukka Chinese chef.

Geetham, *Kanchi Hotel*, 28 C-in-C Rd. Circular glass-sided restaurant on rooftop of nine-storey tower block. The multi-cuisine menu is surprisingly inexpensive, and the views superb. Open 11am–noon & 7–10pm only.

Hot Breads, opposite *Hotel Maris*, Cathedral Road. Wholewheat breads, baguettes, fresh quiches, and an impressive range of cakes, biscuits and pastries. Decent espresso coffee, too. Eat in or take away.

Maharaja, 307 Quaide Milleth Salai. Excellent vegetarian restaurant, popular with budget travellers. Great-value set meals, flavourful and spicy vegetable dishes and a good range of cheap and filling snacks (try their great *uttapams* or huge paper *dosas*); also ice creams, lassis and good coffee. Open till midnight.

Saravana Bhavan, Thanigai Murugan Rathinavel Hall, 77 Usman Rd, T Nagar. This famous south Indian fast-food chain is an institution among the Chennai middle class, with branches opposite the bus stand in George Town, and in the forecourt of the Shanti cinema (at the top of Anna Salai). Try their delicious *rawa iddlis*, or range of thalis rounded off with some freshly made *ladoo* or *barfi* from the sweets counter outside.

Se–or (Don) Pepés, 1st floor, above *Hot Breads*, Cathedral Road. Swish a/c Tex-Mex joint, serving a predictable menu of fajitas, enchiladas, tortillas, burritos plus so-so pasta dishes (dubbed "Euro-Mex"). Main courses about Rs120.

Vasana Bhavan, 20 Gandhi Irwin Rd. Easily the best "meals" joint among many around Egmore station, with ranks of attentive waiters and delicious pure veg food – just Rs24 for an unlimited thali. It's busy, spotlessly clean, and their coffee and sweets are delicious.

Verandah, *Taj Connemara*, Binny's Road ⊕044/852 0123. The ideal venue for a posh Sunday morning breakfast buffet (Rs236): crisp newspapers and fresh coffee served in silver pots. The blow-out lunchtime buffets (Rs413) are also recommended, and they serve à la carte Italian food in the evening (around Rs350 per head). *The Rain Tree* is the second Taj eatery, with great Chettinad (south Indian) specialities included in the weekend dinner buffets (about Rs400). Reserve in advance.

Welcomgroup Park Sheraton, 132 TTK Rd ⊕044/499 4101, ⊕499 7101. More – extremely good – upmarket hotel restaurants. Best of all is the *Dakshin*, one of the country's top south Indian restaurants offering an excellent choice of unusual dishes from the four southern states, including seafood and fish in marinated spices, Karnataka mutton biryani and piping-hot *iddliappam* and *appam* made on the spot. There is live Carnatic music; expect to pay around Rs600 per head with beer.

Listings

Airline offices (most Mon–Fri 10am–5pm, Sat 10am–1pm), include: Air India, 19 Marshalls Rd ⊕044/855 4477, airport ⊕044/234 7400; Air France, Thaper House, 43–44 Montieth Rd ⊕044/855 4899; Air Lanka, Nagabrahma Towers, 76 Cathedral Rd ⊕044/826 1535; British Airways, Khaleeli Centre, Montieth Road ⊕044/855 4680; Gulf Air, 52 Montieth Rd ⊕044/855 3091; Indian Airlines, 19 Marshalls Rd (office open round the clock, but for bookings daily 8am–5pm; ⊕044/855 3039, ⊕855 5208; Jet Airways, Thaper House, 43–44 Montieth Rd ⊕044/855 5353; Lufthansa, 167 Anna Salai ⊕044/852 5095; KLM, *Taj Connemara*, Binny's Road ⊕044/852 0123; Malaysia Airlines, Karumuttu Centre, 498 Anna Salai ⊕044/434 9632; Qantas, Eldorado Building, 112 Nungambakkam High Rd ⊕044/827 8680; Sahara, Lokesh Towers, 18 Kodakkakkam High Rd ⊕044/828 3180; Singapore Airlines, 108 Dr Radha Krishnan Salai ⊕044/852 2871; Swissair, 191 Anna Salai ⊕044/852 2541; Thai International, GSA, Malavikas Centre, 144 Kodambakkam High Rd, Nungambakkam ⊕044/822 6149. For American, Air Canada, Biman, Philippine, Royal Jordanian and TWA, contact Jet Airways, Apex Plaza, 3 MG Rd ⊕044/826 2409.

Banks and currency exchange Tourists have few difficulties changing money in Chennai: there are plenty of banks, and the major hotels offer exchange facilities to residents only. A conveniently central option is American Express, G-17, Spencer Plaza, 769 Anna Salai (Mon–Fri 9.30am–5.30pm, Sat 9.30am–2.30pm). Thomas Cook (Mon–Sat 9am–6pm) have offices at the Ceebros Centre, 45 Montieth Rd, Egmore, at the G-4 Eldorado Building, 112 Nangambakkam High Rd and also at the airport (open to meet flights). For encashments on Visa cards, go to Bobcards, next door to the Bank of Baroda on Montieth Road, near the *Ambassador Pallava Hotel*. You can use Visa and Mastercard at the 24hr ATM at Citibank, 766, Anna Salai.

Bookshops the original Higginbothams on Anna Salai is Chennai's oldest bookshop, with a vast assortment of Indian and Western titles, and a few maps at rupee rates. Its main competitor, Bookpoint, at 160 Anna Salai, has a more up-to-date selection of fiction, and handy free publicity newsletters with reviews of the latest Indian releases. Serious bookworms, however, head for the hole-in-the-wall Giggles, in the *Taj Connemara Hotel*, where, stacked in precariously high piles, you'll find a matchless stock of novels, academic tomes on the region and coffee-table books. Unlike other bookstores in the city, this one will take credit cards and post purchases abroad for you for nominal charges.

Cinemas The Abhirami and Lakshmi along Anna Salai show English-language films, but for the full-on Tamil film experience, take in a show at the Shanti, off the top of Anna Salai, which boasts the city's biggest screen and a digital stereo sound-system. Nearby, the equally massive Devi hosts the latest Bollywood blockbusters.

Consulates Canada, 3rd Floor Dhun Bldg, 827 Anna Salai ☎ 044/852 9828; France, Kothari Bldg, 114 Nungambakkam High Rd ☎ 044/472131; Germany, 22 C-in-C Rd ☎ 044/827 1747 (9am–noon); Indonesia, 5 North Leith Castle Rd, San Thome ☎ 044/245 1095; Netherlands, 738 Anna Salai ☎ 044/811566; Norway, Royal Parry House, 43 Moore St ☎ 044/517950 (10am–5pm); Sri Lanka, 9-D Nawab Habibullah Rd ☎ 044/827 0831; Sweden, 6 Cathedral Rd ☎ 044/827 5792 (9.30am–1pm); UK, 24 Anderson Rd, Nungambakkam ☎ 044/827 3136; USA, 220 Anna Salai ☎ 044/827 3040 (Mon–Fri 8am–5.15pm).

Cultural institutions Alliance Française, 3/4-A College Rd, Nungambakkam ☎ 044/827 2650; British Council, 737 Anna Salai ☎ 044/826 9402 (Mon–Fri 10am–5pm); Max Mueller Bhavan, 13 Khadar Nawaz Khan Rd ☎ 044/826 1314.

Hospitals The best-equipped private hospital in Chennai is the Apollo, 21/22 Greams Rd ☎ 044/827 7447. For an ambulance, try ☎ 044/102, but it's usually quicker to jump in a taxi.

Internet access is easily available throughout the city, albeit at wildly varying rates. The snazziest option, is Net Café, at 101/1 Kanakasri Nagar, down an alleyway off Cathedral Road (daily 7am–midnight) – look for the neon "@" sign, but rates are high and they're reluctant to let you compose offline. SRIS Netsurfing Café on the first floor of Spencer Plaza is a cheaper, though smaller, alternative. Gee Gee Net in Triplicane is next door to *Hotel Comfort*, open 24hr and charges only Rs15 per hour between 11pm and 1pm, or Rs25 between 1pm and 11pm. Otherwise, head for *Hotel Himalaya* on Quaide Milleth Salai, also open 24hr (Rs25/hr).

Left luggage Counters at Egmore and Central railway stations store bags for Rs7 per day; they usually require you to chain and padlock your baggage and you must show your train ticket. Some hotels also guard luggage at a daily rate.

Music stores Musee Musical, 67 Anna Salai (☎ 044/849380), stocks sitars, percussion, flutes and the usual shoddy selection of Hofner/Gibson-copy guitars. For the best range of concert quality Indian instruments, including *vinas*, check out Saptaswara Music Store, on Raipetha Road, Mylapore (☎ 044/499 3274). Music World, on the first floor of Spencer Plaza, has the best selection of contemporary Indian and Western music in the city.

Photographic equipment Dozens of stores around town offer film and developing services on modern machines (Konica studios are particularly reliable), but the only Kodak-approved Q-Lab in the city (recommended for transparency processing) is Image Park, GEE Plaza, 1 Craft Rd, Nungambakkam (☎ 044/827 6383). Reliance Opticals, at 136 Anna Salai, stocks Fuji Provia and Sensia II. For camera repair, your best bet is Camera Crafts, 325/8A Quaide Milleth Salai, Triplicane, near *Broadlands Hotel*. Delhi Photo Stores, in an arcade directly behind the big Konica shop on Wallajah Road, is crammed with spare parts and other useful Indian-made bits and bobs for cameras.

Postal services Chennai's main post office is on Anna Salai (daily 8am–8pm). If you're using it for poste restante, make sure your correspondents mark the envelope "Head Post Office, Anna Salai", or your letters could well end up across town at the GPO, north of Parry's Corner on Rajaji Salai (same hours). The post office on Quaide Milleth Salai, in Triplicane (Mon–Sat 7am–3pm) is convenient if you're staying at *Broadlands*.

Telephones and faxes The easiest way to make a local or international phone call is at one of the thousands of orange-yellow booths across the city offering PCO/STD/ISD, all of which charge a set government rate. Most of these places offer fax and photocopy services also, or can point you to one that can. If you need to send a telegram, the main post office offers the most efficient service. **Travel agents** Reliable travel agents include American Express, G-17 Spencer Plaza, 768/769 Anna Salai ☎044/852 3592; Diana World Travels, 45 Montieth Rd ☎044/826 1716; PL Worldways, G-11 Ground Floor, Spencer Plaza ☎044/852 1192; Surya Travels, F-14 1st Floor, Spencer Plaza ☎044/855 0285; Thomas Cook, Chebroos Centre, Montieth Road, Egmore ☎044/827 3092.

Moving on from Chennai

Transport connections between Chennai and the rest of India are summarized on p.1289. If you're short of time, consider employing one of the **travel agents** listed above to book your plane, train or bus ticket for you. This doesn't apply to boat tickets for the Andaman Islands, which have to be booked in person.

By air

Chennai's domestic airport stands adjacent to the international terminal, 16km southwest of the centre at **Meenambakkam**. The easiest way to get there is by taxi or auto-rickshaw, but if you're not too weighed down with luggage you can save money by jumping on a suburban train to **Trisulam station**, 500m from the airport.

Indian Airlines flies from Meenambakkam to seventeen destinations around the country, including several daily flights to Mumbai, Delhi, Hyderabad, Calcutta and Bangalore. In addition, Jet Airways operates services to Bangalore, Coimbatore, Delhi, Hyderabad, Mumbai, Pune and Thiruvananthapuram. Both airlines fly several times a week to Port Blair. A full summary of flights appears on p.1291.

By train

Trains to Tiruchirapalli (Trichy), Thanjavur, Pudukottai, Rameshwaram, Kodaikanal Road, Madurai, and most other destinations in south Tamil Nadu leave from **Egmore Station**. All other trains leave from **Chennai Central**. Left of the main building, on the first floor of the Moore Market Complex, the efficient **tourist reservation counter** (Mon–Sat 8am–8pm, Sun 8am–2pm) sells tickets for trains from either station. The booking office at Egmore, up the stairs left of the main entrance (same hours), also handles bookings for both stations, but has no tourist counter. Check fares and up-to-date timetables at ⓦ www.southernrailways.com.

By boat

Boats leave Chennai every week to ten days for **Port Blair**, capital of the **Andaman Islands**. However, getting a ticket and the relevant permit can be a rigmarole, compounded by the absence of a regular schedule. The first thing you'll need to do is head up to the Chennai Port Trust, next to the Directorate of Shipping on Rajaji (North Beach) Road, George Town, where a small hut houses the Andaman Administration Office. A chalkboard on the wall advertises details of the next sailing, and you buy a ticket from the hatch around the corner, at the front of the main building. There are no ticket sales on the day of sailing.

The authorities may demand that you register at the **Foreigners' Registration Office** (Mon–Fri 9.30am–5pm), a twenty-minute auto-rickshaw ride southwest across town on Haddow's Road (between the UK High Commission and French Consulate). You are also required to buy a **permit** to

Recommended trains from Chennai

Destination	Name	No.	From	Departs	Total time
Bangalore	Shatabdi Express*	#2007	Central	6am**	4hr 45min
	Bangalore Mail	#6007	Central	10.10pm	7hr 15min
Bhubaneswar	Coromandel Express	#2843	Central	9.05am	20hr 10min
	Howrah Mail	#6004	Central	10.30pm	23hr 45min
Calcutta	Coromandel Express	#2842	Central	9.05am	28hr 15min
	Howrah Mail	#6004	Central	10.30pm	32hr 25min
Coimbatore	Shatabdi Express*	#2023	Central	3.10pm	6hr 50min
	Kovai Exp	#2675	Central	6.15am	7hr 35min
Delhi	Tamil Nadu Express	#2621	Central	10pm	33hr
	Grand Trunk Express	#2615	Central	11pm	36hr 45min
Hyderabad	Charminar Express	#2759	Central	6.10pm	14hr 15min
Kanyakumari	Kanyakumari Express	#6721	Central	1pm	17hr 15min
Kochi/Ernakulam	Alleppey Express	#6041	Central	7.35pm	13hr
	Trivandrum Mail	#6319	Central	6.55pm	12hr
	Kodaikanal Pandyan Express	#6717	Egmore	7.30pm	10hr
Madurai	Madurai Express	#6717	Egmore	7.30pm	11hr 20min
Mettuppalayam (for Ooty)	Nilgiri Express	#6605	Central	8.15pm	12hr 15min
Mumbai	Mumbai Express	#6012	Central	11.45am	27hr 20min
	Chennai Express	#1064	Central	6.60am	24hr 15min
Mysore	Shatabdi Express*	#2007	Central	6am**	4hr 45min
	Mysore Express	#6222	Central	10.30pm	11hr 20min
Rameshwaram	Sethu Express	#6701	Egmore	8.25pm	18hr 10min
Thanjavur	Cholan Express	#6153	Egmore	8am	9hr 15min
	Sethu Express	#6701	Egmore	8.15pm	9hr 30min
Tirupathi	Saptagiri Express	#6057	Central	6.25am	3hr
Thiruvananthapuram	Trivandrum Mail	#6319	Egmore	6.55pm	17hr
Varanasi	Ganga Kaveri Express**	#6039	Central	5.30pm	38hr 30min

*A/c only   **Mon & Sat only

visit the Andamans, which can be obtained from the Foreigners' Registration Office in Chennai, Delhi, Mumbai, Calcutta, or now you can even get it on arrival in Port Blair. Bear in mind, however, that the permit is only valid for one month, from the date of purchase. To get the permit, you have to fill in a form and supply three passport photos; hand it in before lunch and you should be able to pick up the permit later that same day.

The three- to four-day crossing gets mixed reviews. Conditions, especially in the rock-bottom bunk class at Rs1150, can be hot and squalid; go for the most expensive ticket you can afford. Cabin fares (per bed) are Rs2700 for B-class (six-berth, shared bathroom) and Rs3420 for a first class (four-berth en suite). For Rs4140 you get a deluxe two-berth cabin with a private bathroom. Unvarying meals of dhal, rice and vegetables are served for around Rs100 per day; it's a good idea to take a good supply of snacks and fruit.

By bus

Most long-distance **buses** leave from the **Express Bus Stand** on Esplanade Road, near Parry's Corner, George Town. It's a well-organized, if crowded, place with a computerized **reservations** hall on the first floor (7am–9pm;

State Express Transport Corporation (SETC) services, as well as interstate buses
to neighbouring Andhra, Kerala and Karnataka. A full rundown of these, giving frequency and journey times, appears in Travel Details on p.1290.

If you're heading to Mamallapuram, Pondicherry or Chidambaram via the
fast new coastal highway, you'll have to jump on an unreserved bus from the
much more chaotic **Broadway Bus Stand**, on the opposite side of Prakasm
Road. Gangs of kids will pull you towards your bus for a few rupees; they provide a useful service as there are no signs in English and they will get you on
the correct bus.

The fastest services to **Mamallapuram** are #188, #188A and anything
marked "East Coast Express" (every 30min; less than 2hr); #19A, #19C, #119
and #119A all take an hour longer.

The northeast

Fazed by the fierce heat and air pollution of Chennai, most visitors escape as
fast as they can, heading down the Coromandel coast to India's stone-carving
capital, **Mamallapuram**, whose ancient monuments include the famous Shore
Temple and a batch of extraordinary rock sculptures. En route, it's well worth
jumping off the bus at **Dakshina Chitra**, a new folk museum 30km south of
Chennai, where traditional buildings from across south India have been beautifully reconstructed. Further inland, **Kanchipuram** is an important pilgrimage and silk-sari-weaving town from where you can loop southwest to
Tiruvannamalai, a wonderfully atmospheric temple town clustered at the
base of the sacred mountain, Arunachala. The sprawling ruins of **Gingee** stand
midway between here and the coast, where you can breakfast on croissants and
espresso coffee in the former French colony of **Pondicherry**. A short way
north, **Auroville**, the Utopian settlement founded by followers of the Sri
Aurobindo Ghose's spiritual successor, The Mother, provides a New-Age haven
for soul-searching Westerners and an economy for the local population.

Both Mamallapuram and Pondicherry are well connected to Chennai by
nail-bitingly fast bus services, running along a smooth new coastal highway
that was recently completed with World Bank funding. Take care to use state
buses where possible; their safety record is far better than the private buses. You
can also get to Pondicherry by train, but this involves a change at the junction
town of **Villupuram**, from where services are slow and relatively infrequent.

Mamallapuram (Mahabalipuram)

Scattered around the base of a colossal mound of boulders, is the small seaside
town of **MAMALLAPURAM** (aka Mahabalipuram), 58km south of
Chennai. From dawn till dusk, the rhythms of chisels chipping granite resound
down its sandy lanes – evidence of a stone-carving tradition that has endured
since this was a major port of the Pallava dynasty, between the fifth and ninth
centuries. Little is known about life in the ancient city, and it is only possible
to speculate about the purpose of much of the boulder sculpture, which
includes one of India's most photographed monuments, the **Shore Temple**. It
does appear, however, that the friezes and shrines were not made for worship
at all, but rather as a showcase for the talents of local artists. Due in no small

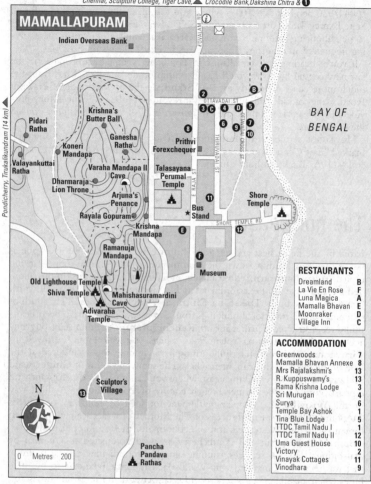

MAMALLAPURAM

Indian Overseas Bank

Krishna's Butter Ball

Pidari Ratha

Ganesha Ratha

Koneri Mandapa

Valayankuttai Ratha

Varaha Mandapa II Cave

Dharmaraja Lion Throne

Arjuna's Penance

Rayala Gopuram

Krishna Mandapa

Ramanuja Mandapa

Old Lighthouse Temple

Shiva Temple

Mahishasuramardini Cave

Adivaraha Temple

Prithvi Forexchequer

Talasayana Perumal Temple

Bus Stand

Museum

Shore Temple

BAY OF BENGAL

Sculptor's Village

Pancha Pandava Rathas

N

0 Metres 200

RESTAURANTS

Dreamland	B
La Vie En Rose	F
Luna Magica	A
Mamalla Bhavan	E
Moonraker	D
Village Inn	C

ACCOMMODATION

Greenwoods	7
Mamalla Bhavan Annexe	8
Mrs Rajalakshmi's	13
R. Kuppuswamy's	13
Rama Krishna Lodge	3
Sri Murugan	4
Surya	6
Temple Bay Ashok	1
Tina Blue Lodge	5
TTDC Tamil Nadu I	1
TTDC Tamil Nadu II	12
Uma Guest House	10
Victory	2
Vinayak Cottages	11
Vinodhara	9

part to the maritime activities of the Pallavas, their style of art and architecture had wide-ranging influence, spreading from south India as far north as Ellora (see p.805), as well as to Southeast Asia. This international cultural importance was recognized in 1995 when Mamallapuram was granted World Heritage Site status by UNESCO.

Mamallapuram's monuments divide into four categories: open-air **bas-reliefs**, structured **temples**, man-made **caves** and **rathas** ("chariots" carved *in situ* from single boulders to resemble temples or the chariots used in temple processions). The famous bas-reliefs, **Arjuna's Penance** and the **Krishna Mandapa**, adorn massive rocks near the centre of the village, while the beautiful **Shore Temple** presides over the beach. Sixteen man-made caves, in different stages of completion, are scattered through the area, but the most complete of the nine *rathas* are in a group, named after the five Pandava brothers of the *Mahabharata*.

Given the coexistence of so many stunning archeological remains with a long white-sand **beach**, it was inevitable this would become a major destination for Western travellers. Over the past two decades, Mamallapuram has certainly oriented its economy to the needs of tourists, with the inevitable presence of Kashmiri trinket sellers, bus-loads of city dwellers at the weekends, massage-wallahs and hawkers on the beach, burgeoning budget hotels and little fish restaurants. The Shore Temple is now sadly a shadow of the exotic spectacle it used to be when the waves lapped its base, though the atmosphere generated by the stone-carvers' workshops and ancient rock-art backdrop is unique in India.

Arrival, information and getting around

Numerous daily **buses** ply to and from Chennai, Thiruvannmalai, Kanchipuram and Pondicherry. The bus stand is in the centre of the village.

The nearest **railway station**, at Chengalpattu (Chingleput), 29km northeast on the bus route to Kanchipuram, is on the main north–south line, but not really a convenient access point. A **taxi** from Chennai costs around Rs500 (or Rs450 from the airport); book through the tourist office, or the prepaid taxi booth at Chennai airport. Mamallapuram suffers badly from aggressive touting by a small number of hotels. There is a list of accredited hotels on a board at the bus stop – the hotel recommendations given below are all on this list.

The **Government of Tamil Nadu Tourist Office** (Mon–Sat 9.45am–5.45pm; ☏04114/42232) is one of the first buildings you see in the village; on your left as you arrive from Chennai. It is a good place to find out about local festivals, pukka hotels, and bus times.

Unless you're staying at one of the upscale hotels, there are only two official places to **change money** in the village: the Indian Overseas Bank, on TK Kunda Road, or the more efficient Prithvi Forexchequer, 55 East Raja St, opposite *Mamalla Bhavan Annexe*. The most reputable **travel agent** in the village is J.R.S. Travels on East Raja Street (look for the aeroplane and train painted on the outside window): otherwise head into Chennai.

Mamallapuram itself comprises little more than a few roads. By far the best way to get to the important sites is by **bicycle**, which you can rent from shops on E Raja Street, opposite the entrance to the *Temple Bay Ashok Beach Resort*, or MK Cycle Centre, 28 Ottavadai St, for around Rs20 per day. **Scooters** and Enfield **motorcycles** are also available for Rs200–350 a day, from Poornima Travels, next to *Moonraker* restaurant.

Accommodation

With more than twenty years' experience of tourism, Mamallapuram is not short of **accommodation**. The bulk of cheap and mid-range lodges are within the village, some distance from the beach, which is the preserve of the more expensive places. Large hotels of varying standards sit side by side along a six-kilometre stretch of coast. Without a taxi or bike, getting to these can prove a bit of a hassle; it's easy enough to take a rickshaw out there from the village, but not in the other direction. However, the walk back into Mamallapuram along the beach is pleasant – if you're not carrying luggage.

Long-term lodgings can be arranged in the sculptors' village behind the workshops on the way to the Pancha Pandava *rathas*. The two oldest established guesthouses are *R. Kuppuswamy's* and *Mrs Rajalaxmi's* next door, but there are plenty of new homes that do not use commission touts. They're all pretty basic, with thatched roofs and common shower-toilets in the yard, but have fans and are clean and homely. At around Rs350 per week, they're also just about the cheapest places to stay in the area.

Golden Sun, 3km from town, 59 Kovalam Rd ☏04114/4985246, ☏498 2669. Not as smart as the *Ideal*, but the gardens are attractive – the sea-facing rooms offer the best value. Health club, restaurant and pool. ⑥–⑧

Greenwoods, Ottavadi Cross Street ☏04114/43318. A very friendly family-run place set in a lush garden, lovingly tended by the numerous ladies of the house. There are a/c or non-a/c rooms a stone's throw from the beach, each with a little thatched balcony. Boasts a good internet café (Rs60/hr). ③–④

Ideal Beach Resort, 4km from town, Kovalam Road ☏04114/42240, ☏42243. Lots of comfortable cottages, near the Tiger Cave. Large pool, and pleasant alfresco restaurant. Popular with overland tour groups, so book well ahead during the high season. ⑧–⑨

Mamalla Bhavan Annexe, E Raja Street ☏04114/42260, ☏42160. Efficient and modern hotel on the main plaza through the village, with spotless comfortable rooms (mostly a/c) overlooking a courtyard. Non-a/c rooms have mosquito nets. Unfortunately it's a way from the beach, but there's a very good restaurant to compensate. ④–⑥

Rama Krishna Lodge, 8 Ottavadai St ☏04114/42331. Clean, well-maintained rooms in the heart of the tourist enclave, all with bathrooms but no a/c, set round a courtyard filled with pot plants; the newest ones are on the top storey, and have sea views. There's a back-up generator, too, and they often have vacancies when everywhere else is full. The thatched rooftop restaurant has an excellent German bakery. ①–②

Sri Murugan Guest House, Ottavadai Street ☏04114/42552. New, good-value place next door to the *Ramakrishna*. Small and peaceful, with courteous service and clean rooms; one of the nicest options in the area. ③–④

Surya, Thirukula Street ☏04114/42292. Lakeside hotel set in a leafy compound, dotted with broken sculpture. Run by a retired archeologist, the hotel seems rather peripheral to his sculpture school and gallery (open to the general public), which share the same space. There is a range of rooms, some with a/c and balconies; mosquito nets are available and, considering the proximity of the lake, essential. Features a new pool, though bathtub is probably a more apt description. ②–⑥

Taj Fisherman's Cove, Covelong Beach, 30min drive north from Mamallapuram ☏04114/04128.

Four-star hotel, with bar and restaurants. Rooms in main building overlook a beachside garden, while circular cottages stand at the ocean's edge. ⑨

Temple Bay Ashok (ITDC) Beach Resort ☏04114/42251, ☏42257. A great location – on the beach near the village, with views of the Shore Temple, geared towards tour group bookings. Thatched, basic cottages on the beach all have sea-facing balconies, and there are huge rooms in the main building, plus a swimming pool and restaurant. ⑨

Tina Blue Lodge, Ottavadi Street ☏04114/42319. A real family business, this is a well-established place with pleasant, simple turquoise and white-washed rooms, mosquito nets and attached bathrooms. Upstairs, the blue roof terrace is a great airy space with eclectic music and a good restaurant (see p.1220). ②–③

TTDC Hotel Tamil Nadu Beach Resort, Kovalam Road ☏04114/42235, ☏42268. A predictably overpriced, dilapidated state-run place made up of huge split-level cottages (some non-a/c) with sea-facing "sitouts", a very large pool, bar and multi-cuisine restaurant plus a camping ground. ⑤–⑦

TTDC Hotel Tamil Nadu Unit II Camping Site, Shore Temple Road ☏04114/42287. Just behind the beach, adjacent to the village tank. The site is slightly rundown, but has cheap dorm (Rs50 per bed), as well as new a/c rooms, and shabbier standard non-a/c. ⑤–⑦

Uma Guest House, 11 Ottavadi Cross St ☏04114/42697. A new, quiet and spotless hotel, run by a quiet man who goes by the unlikely name of "Lion". If your budget can stretch to it, its worth paying that bit more for the a/c rooms that have breezy, private balconies (but no sea view). ③–⑥

Victory, 5 Ottavadai St ☏04114/42179. A small, popular European-run guesthouse with comfortable rooms and a congenial restaurant with good music. ③

Vinayak Cottages, 68 E Raja St ☏04114/42445. Four spacious thatched cottages set in a leafy garden, a stone's throw from the bus stand but a bit far from the beach atmosphere. Offers Western toilets, and tables outside. ③–④

Vinodhara, 4 Ottavadi Cross St ☏04114/42694. A large place opposite *Lakshmi Lodge*. Immaculately tiled, all non-a/c but the cool rooms catch sea breezes, and you can see the Shore Temple from the top floor. Great value for the price. ②–③

The Krishna Mandapa and Arjuna's Penance

A little to the west of the village centre, the enormous bas-relief known as the **Krishna Mandapa** shows Krishna raising Mount Govardhana aloft in one hand. The sculptor's original intention must have been for the rock above

Krishna to represent the mountain, but the seventeenth-century Vijayanagar addition of a columned *mandapa*, or entrance hall, prevents a clear view of the carving. Krishna is also depicted seated milking a cow, and standing playing the flute. Other figures are *gopas* and *gopis*, the cowboys and girls of his pastoral youth. Lions sit to the left- one with a human face and above them is a bull.

Another bas-relief, **Arjuna's Penance** (also referred to as the "Descent of the Ganges") is a few metres north, opposite the modern Talasayana Perumal Temple. The surface of this rock erupts with detailed carving, most notably the endearing and naturalistic renditions of animals. A family of elephants dominates the right side, with tiny offspring asleep beneath a great tusker. Further still to the right, separate from the great rock, is a freestanding sculpture of an adult monkey grooming its young.

On the left-hand side, Arjuna, one of the Pandava brothers and a consummate archer, is shown standing on one leg. He is looking at the midday sun through a prism formed by his hands, meditating on Shiva, who is represented by a nearby statue, fashioned by Arjuna himself. The *Shiva Purana* tells that Arjuna made the journey to a forest on the banks of the Ganges to do penance, in the hope that Shiva would part with his favourite weapon, the *pashupatashastra*, a magic staff or arrow. Shiva eventually materialized in the guise of Kirata, a wild forest-dweller, and picked a fight with Arjuna over a boar they both claimed to have shot. Arjuna only realized he was dealing with the deity after his attempts to drub the wild

The temples of Tamil Nadu

No Indian state is more dominated by its **temples** than Tamil Nadu, where temple architecture catalogues the tastes of successive dynasties, and testifies to the centrality of religion in everyday life. Most temples are built in honour of Shiva and Vishnu and their consorts; all are characterized not only by their design and sculptures, but by constant activity – devotion, dancing, singing, pujas, festivals and feasts. Each is tended by brahmin priests, recognizable by their *dhotis* (loincloths), a sacred thread draped over the right shoulder, and marks on the forehead. One to three horizontal (usually white) lines distinguish Shaivites; vertical lines (yellow or red), often converging into a near-V shape, are common among Vaishnavites.

Dravida, the temple architecture of Tamil Nadu, first took form in the **Pallava** port of **Mamallapuram**. A step-up from the cave retreats of Hindu and Jain ascetics, the earliest Pallava monuments were **mandapas**, shrines cut into rock faces and fronted by columns. The magnificent **bas-relief** at Mamallapuram, Arjuna's Penance, shows the fluid carving of the Pallavas at its most exquisite. This sculptural skill was transferred to freestanding temples, **rathas**, carved out of single rocks and incorporating the essential elements of Hindu temples: the dim inner sanctuary, the *garbhagriha*, capped with a modest tapering spire featuring repetitive architectural motifs. In turn, the Shore Temple was built with three shrines, topped by a **vimana** similar to the towering roofs of the *rathas*; statues of Nandi, Shiva's bull, later to receive pride of place, surmount its low walls. In the finest structural Pallava temple, the Kailasanatha Temple at **Kanchipuram**, the sanctuary, again crowned with a pyramidal *vimana*, stands within a courtyard enclosed by high walls. The projecting and recessing bays of the walls, carved with images of Shiva, his consort and ghoulish mythical lions, *yalis*, were the prototype for later styles.

Pallava themes were developed in Karnataka by the Chalukyas and Rashtrakutas, but it was the Shaivite **Cholas** who spearheaded Tamil Nadu's next architectural phase, in the tenth century. In **Thanjavur**, Rajaraja I created the Brihadeshvara Temple principally as a status symbol; its proportions far exceed any attempted by the Pallavas. Set within a vast walled courtyard, the sanctuary, fronted by a small pil-man proved futile; narrowly escaping death at the playful hand of Shiva, he was finally rewarded with the weapon. Not far away, mimicking Arjuna's devout pose, an emaciated (presumably ascetic) cat stands on hind legs, surrounded by mice.

To the right of Arjuna, a natural cleft represents the **Ganges**, complete with *nagas* – water spirits in the form of cobras. Near the bottom, a fault in the rock that broke a *naga* received a quick fix of cement in the 1920s. Evidence of a cistern and channels remain at the top, which at one time must have carried water to flow down the cleft, simulating the great river. It's not known if there was some ritual purpose to all this, or whether it was simply an elaborate spectacle to impress visitors. You may see sudden movements among the carved animals: lazing goats often join the permanent features.

A little way north of Arjuna's Penance, precipitously balanced on the top of a ridge, is a massive, natural, almost spherical boulder called **Krishna's Butter Ball**. Picnickers and goats often rest in its perilous-looking shade.

Ganesha ratha and Varaha Cave

Just north of Arjuna's Penance a path leads west to a single monolith, the **Ganesha ratha**. Its image of Ganesh dates from this century; some say it was installed at the instigation of England's King George V. The sculpture at one end, of a protecting demon with a tricorn headdress, is reminiscent of the Indus Valley civilization's 4000-year-old horned figure known as the "proto-Shiva".

lared hall (*mandapa*), stands beneath a sculpted *vimana* that soars over 60m high. Most sculptures once again feature Shiva, but the *gopuras*, or towers, each side of the eastern gateway to the courtyard, were an innovation, as were the lions carved into the base of the sanctuary walls, and the pavilion erected over Nandi in front of the sanctuary. The second great Chola Temple was built in **Gangaikondacholapuram** by Rajendra I. Instead of a mighty *vimana*, he brought new elements, adding subsidiary shrines and placing an extended *mandapa* in front of the central sanctuary, its pillars writhing with dancers and deities.

By the time of the thirteenth-century **Vijayanagar** kings, the temple was central to city life, the focus for civic meetings, education, dance and theatre. The Vijayanagars extended earlier structures, adding enclosing walls around a series of **prakaras**, or courtyards, and erecting freestanding *mandapas* for use as meeting halls, elephant stables, stages for music and dance, and ceremonial marriage halls (*kalyan mandapas*). Raised on superbly decorated columns, these *mandapas* became known as **thousand-pillared halls**. Tanks were added, doubling as water stores and washing areas, and used for festivals when deities were set afloat in boats surrounded by glimmering oil lamps.

Under the Vijayanagars, the *gopuras* were enlarged and set at the cardinal points over the high gateways to each *prakara*, to become the dominant feature. Rectangular in plan, and embellished with images of animals and local saints or rulers as well as deities, *gopuras* are periodically repainted in pinks, blues, whites and yellows, a sharp and joyous contrast with the earthy browns and greys of halls and sanctuaries beyond. **Madurai** is the place to check out Vijayanagar architecture, and experience the timeless temple rituals. Dimly lit halls and sun-drenched courtyards hum with murmured prayers, and regularly come alive for festivals in which Shiva and his "fish-eyed" consort are hauled through town on mighty wooden chariots tugged by hordes of devotees. Outside Tiruchirapalli, the temple at **Srirangam** was extended by the Vijayanagar Nayaks to become south India's largest. Unlike that in Madurai, it incorporates earlier Chola foundations, but the ornamentation, with pillars formed into rearing horses, is superb.

Behind Arjuna's Penance, southwest of the Ganesha ratha, is the **Varaha Mandapa II Cave**, whose entrance hall has two pillars with horned lion-bases and a cell flanked by two *dvarpalas*, or guardians. One of four **panels** shows the boar-incarnation of Vishnu, who stands with one foot resting on the *naga* snake-king as he lifts a diminutive Prithvi – the earth – from the primordial ocean. Another is of Gajalakshmi, the goddess Lakshmi seated on a lotus being bathed by a pair of elephants. Trivikrama, the dwarf brahmin who becomes huge and bestrides the world in three steps to defeat the demon king Bali, is shown in another panel, and finally a four-armed Durga is depicted in another.

The Shore Temple

East of the village, a distinctive silhouette above the crashing ocean, Mamallapuram's **Shore Temple** (daily sunrise–sunset; $10 [Rs10]) dates from the early eighth century and is considered to be the earliest stone-built temple in south India. The design of its two finely carved towers was profoundly influential: it was exported across south India and eventually abroad to Southeast Asia. Today, due to the combined forces of wind, salt and sand, much of the detailed carving has eroded, giving the whole temple a soft, rounded appearance.

The taller of the towers is raised above a cell that faces out to sea – don't be surprised to see mischievous monkeys crouching inside. Approached from the west through two low-walled enclosures lined with small Nandi (bull) figures, the temple comprises two *lingam* shrines (one facing east, the other west), and a third shrine between them housing an image of the reclining Vishnu. Recent excavations, revealing a tank containing a structured stone column thought to have been a lantern, and a large Varaha (boar incarnation of Vishnu) aligned with the Vishnu shrine, suggest that the area was sacred long before the Pallavas chose it as a temple site.

The lighthouses and the Mahishasuramardini Cave

At the highest point in an area of steep paths, unfinished temples, ruins, scampering monkeys and massive rocks, south of Arjuna's Penance, the **New Lighthouse** affords fine views east to the Shore Temple, and west across paddy fields and flat lands littered with rocks. Next to it, the **Olakanesvara** ("flame-eyed" Shiva), or **Old Lighthouse Temple**, used as a lighthouse until the beginning of the twentieth century, dates from the Rajasimha period (674–800 AD) and contains no image.

Nestling between the two lighthouses is the **Mahishasuramardini Cave**, whose central image portrays Shiva and Parvati with the child Murugan seated on Parvati's lap. Shiva's right foot rests on the back of the bull Nandi, and Parvati sits casually, leaning on her left hand. On the left wall, beyond an empty cell, a panel depicts Vishnu reclining on the serpent, his attitude of repose contrasted with the weapon-brandishing demons, Madhu and Kaithaba. Other figures seek Vishnu's permission to chase them. Opposite, an intricately carved panel shows the eight-armed goddess Durga as Mahishasuramardini, the "crusher" of the buffalo demon Mahishasura. The panel shows Durga riding a lion, in the midst of the struggle. Accompanied by dwarf *ganas*, she wields a bow and other weapons; Mahishasura, equipped with a club, can be seen to the right, in flight with fellow demons.

The tiny **Archaeological Survey of India Museum** (daily 9am–1pm & 2–5pm; Rs2, camera Rs10) on W Raja Street, near the lighthouse, has a rather motley collection of unlabelled Pallava sculpture found in and around Mamallapuram.

Pancha Pandava rathas

In a sandy compound 1.5km south of the village centre stands the stunning group of monoliths known for no historical reason as the **Pancha Pandava rathas** (daily sunrise–sunset; entrance only by $10 [Rs10] ticket, obtainable at Shore Temple) the five chariots of the Pandavas. Dating from the period of Narasimhavarman I (c.630–670 AD), and consisting of five separate freestanding sculptures that imitate structured temples plus some beautifully carved life-size animals, they were either carved from a single gigantic sloping boulder, or from as many as three distinct rocks.

The "architecture" of the *rathas* reflects the variety of styles employed in temple building of the time, and stands almost as a model for much subsequent development in the **Dravida**, or southern, style. The Arjuna, Bhima and Dharmaraja *rathas* show strong affinities with the Dravidian temples at Pattadakal in Karnataka and caves 32 and 16 at Ellora in Maharashtra (see p.805). Carving was always executed from top to bottom, enabling the artists to work on the upper parts with no fear of damaging anything below. Any unfinished elements there may be are always in the lower areas.

Intriguingly, it is thought that the *rathas* were never used for worship. A Hindu temple is only complete when the essential pot-shaped finial, the *kalasha*, is put in place – which would have presented a physical impossibility for the artisans, as the *kalasha* would have had to have been sculpted first. *Kalashas* can be seen next to two of the *rathas* (Dharmaraja and Arjuna), but as part of the base, as if they were perhaps to be put in place at a later date.

The southernmost and tallest of the *rathas*, named after the eldest of the Pandavas, is the pyramidal **Dharmaraja**. Set on a square base, the upper part comprises a series of diminishing storeys, each with a row of pavilions. Four corner blocks, each with two panels and standing figures, are broken up by two pillars and pilasters supported by squatting lions. Figures on the panels include Ardhanarishvara (Shiva and female consort in one figure), Brahma, the king Narasimhavarman I, and Harihara (Shiva and Vishnu combined). The central tier includes sculptures of Shiva Gangadhara holding a rosary with the adoring river goddess Ganga by his side and one of the earliest representations in Tamil Nadu of the dancing Shiva, Nataraja, who became all-important in the region. Alongside, the **Bhima** *ratha*, the largest of the group, is the least complete, with tooling marks all over its surface. Devoid of carved figures, the upper storeys, like in the Dharmaraja, feature false windows and repeated pavilion-shaped ornamentation. Its oblong base is very rare for a shrine.

The Arjuna and Draupadi *rathas* share a base. Behind the **Arjuna**, the most complete of the entire group and very similar to the Dharmaraja, stands a superb unfinished sculpture of Shiva's bull Nandi. **Draupadi** is unique in terms of rock-cut architecture, with a roof that appears to be based on a straw thatched hut (a design later copied at Chidambaram; see p.1236). There's an image of Durga inside, but the figure of her lion vehicle outside is aligned side-on and not facing the image, a convincing reason to suppose this was not a real temple. To the west, close to a life-size carving of an elephant, the *ratha* named after the twin brothers **Nakula** and **Sahadeva** is, unusually, apsidal ended. The elephant may be a visual pun on this, as the Sanskrit technical name for a curved ended building is *gajaprstika*, "elephant's backside".

The road out to the *rathas* resounds with incessant chiselling from sculptors' workshops. Much of their work is excellent, and well worth a browse – the sculptors produce statues for temples all over the world and are used to shipping large-scale pieces. Some of the artists are horrifyingly young; children often do the donkey work on large pieces, which are then completed by master craftsmen.

Eating

Mamallapuram is crammed with small restaurants, most of them specializing in **seafood** – tiger prawns, pomfret, tuna, shark and lobster – usually served marinated and grilled with chips and salad. The upmarket hotels charge a lot more for the same variety of dishes, and lack the atmosphere of the village. Wherever you eat, avoid a nasty shock at the end of your meal by establishing exactly how much your fish, or lobster, is going to cost in advance.

As this is a traveller's hangout, there is the usual array of pasta, pancakes, brown bread and bland Indian dishes. If you want to enjoy real Indian food – including full-on fiery fish curry – head over to the bus stand where there are some good joints serving excellent, spicy thalis and *dosas*. Likewise for breakfast, you can get a plate of steaming *iddlis* from the carts at the station for less than Rs10.

Beer is widely available, but it's on the pricey side (Rs75) and you will have to be discreet, as there are periodic police raids and few places have a licence.

Dreamland, Ottavadi Street. Run as part of a local youth-training initiative, the delightful Swami and Ganesh duo make this place the most welcoming and relaxed place to sit and chill out all day. The filter coffee is superb and comes in a huge glass, and the food – a pasta, fish, pancake menu – is predictable but always tasty and fresh.

Golden Palette, *Mamalla Bhavan Annexe*, E Raja Street. Blissfully cool café with a/c and tinted windows, serving the best veg food in the village Rs50 thalis at lunchtime, north Indian tandoori in the courtyard in the evenings – and wonderful ice-cream sundaes. Worth popping in just for a coffee to beat the heat.

La Palais Croisette, *Ramakrishna Hotel*, Ottavadi Street. A popular new German Bakery place with delicious croissants, several different set breakfasts, and variations on lasagne, pasta, pizza and moussaka.

La Vie En Rose, next to the sculpture museum at the south end of the village. Upstairs on a pleasant balcony overlooking the bustle and workshops below, it features a Westerner-oriented menu, plus a few unusual salads, pasta dishes (their spaghetti's great) and chicken specialities.

Luna Magica, beyond Ottavadai Street. Slap on the beach with top-notch seafood, particularly tiger prawns and lobster, which are kept alive in a tank. The big specimens cost a hefty Rs600–800, but are as tasty as you'll find anywhere, served in a rich tomato, butter and garlic sauce. They also do passable sangria, made with sweet Chennai red wine, and cold beer, with plenty of less expensive dishes – including a good fish curry and "sizzlers" – for budget travellers.

Mamalla Bhavan, opposite the bus stand, Shore Temple Road. The best no-frills, pure-veg and delicious "meals" joint for miles, and invariably packed. Equally good for *iddli-wada* breakfasts, and evening *dosas* and other snacks. Unlimited thalis cost Rs20.

Moonraker, Ottavadai Street. Cool jazz and blues sounds, great fresh seafood, chess sets and slick service ensure this place is filled year round with foreign tourists; the owners will try and entice you in every single time you pass by.

Tina Blue Lodge, Ottavadai Street. Think deep blue and sea green, cane furniture, eclectic music, karam boards, good beach views and beer. This is what draws people all day, as well as their excellent honey-banana pancakes.

Village Inn, Thirukula Street. Now in a new location, this little thatched eatery is still as popular as ever, and serves up seafood, grilled on a charcoal fire, as well as an established favourite – their superb butter-fried chicken in a tomato-garlic sauce (Rs55).

Around Mamallapuram

The sandy hinterland and flat estuarine paddy fields around Mamallapuram harbour a handful of sights well worth making forays from the coast to see. A short way north along the main highway, the **Government College of Sculpture** and elaborately carved **Tiger Cave** can easily be reached by bicycle. To get to the **Crocodile Bank**, where rare reptiles from across south Asia are bred for release into the wild, or **Dakshina Chitra**, a museum devoted to south Indian architecture and crafts, you'll need to jump on and off buses or rent a moped for the day. Finally, a good target for a day-trip inland is the hilltop temple at **Tirukalikundram**, west of Mamallapuram across a swathe of unspoilt farmland.

Government College of Sculpture

A visit to the **Government College of Sculpture**, 2km north of Mamallapuram on the Kovalam (Covelong) Road (☎04114/42261) gives a fascinating insight into the processes of sculpture training. You can watch anything from preliminary drawing, with its strict rules regarding proportion and iconography, through to the execution of sculpture, both in wood and stone, in the classical Hindu tradition. Contact the college office to make an appointment.

Tiger Cave

Set amid groves close to the sea, 5km north from Mamallapuram on the Kovalam (Covelong) Road, the extraordinary **Tiger Cave** contains a shrine to Durga, approached by a flight of steps that passes two subsidiary cells. Following the line of an irregularly shaped rock, the cave is remarkable for its elaborate exterior, which features multiple lion heads surrounding the entrance to the main cell.

Crocodile Bank

The **Crocodile Bank** (Tues–Sun 8am–5.30pm; Rs15, camera Rs10) at Vadanemmeli, 14km north of town on the road to Chennai, was set up in 1976 by the American zoologist Romulus Whittaker, to protect and breed indigenous crocodiles. The bank has been so successful (from fifteen crocs to five thousand in the first fifteen years) that its remit now extends to saving endangered species, such as turtles and lizards, from around the world.

Low-walled enclosures in its garden compound house hundreds of inscrutable crocodiles, soaking in ponds or sunning themselves on the banks. Breeds include the fish-eating, knobbly-nosed gharial, and the world's largest species, the saltwater *crocodylus porosus*, which can grow to 8m in length. You can watch feeding time at about 4.30pm each Wednesday. The temptation to take photos is tempered by the sight of those hungry saurians clambering over each other to snap up the chopped flesh, within inches of the top of the wall.

Another important field of work is conducted with the collaboration of local Irula people, whose traditional expertise is with snakes. Cobras are brought to the bank for **venom collection**, to be used in the treatment of snakebites. Elsewhere, snakes are repeatedly "milked" until they die, but here at the bank only a limited amount is taken from each snake, enabling them to return to the wild. Coastal route buses #117 and #118 stop at the entrance.

Dakshina Chitra

Occupying a patch of sand dunes midway between Chennai and Mamallapuram, **Dakshina Chitra** (daily except Tues 10am–6pm; Rs5), literally "Vision of the South", is one of India's best-conceived folk museums, devoted to the rich architectural and artistic heritage of Kerala, Karnataka, Andhra Pradesh and Tamil Nadu. The museum, set up by the Chennai Craft Foundation, exposes visitors to many disappearing traditions of the region which you might otherwise not be aware of, from tribal fertility cults and *Ayyannar* field deities to pottery and leather shadow puppets.

A selection of traditional buildings from across peninsular India has been painstakingly reconstructed using original materials. Exhibitions attached to them convey the environmental and cultural diversity of the south, most graphically expressed in a wonderful textile collection featuring antique silk and cotton saris from various castes and regions. Catch any of the buses heading north to Chennai or rent a moped from Mamallapuram (see p.1213).

Tirukalikundram

The village of **TIRUKALIKUNDRAM**, 16km east on the road to Kanchipuram, is locally famous for its hilltop Shiva Temple, where a pair of white neophran vultures, believed to be reincarnated saints on their way between Varanasi and Rameswaram, used to swoop down at noon to be fed by the priests. No one knew how long these visits had been going on, or why, in 1994, the vultures suddenly stopped coming. Their absence, however, was taken as a bad omen, and, sure enough, that year massive cyclones ravaged the Tamil Nadu coast.

Four hundred hot stone steps need to be scaled to reach the top, but don't let that – or the effort required to disabuse various individuals, including the priests, of the impression that you need their multifarious services and paid company – deter you. Once on the hilltop, the views are sublime, especially at sunset.

Regular **buses** run to Tirukalikendra from Mamallapuram, en route to Kanchipuram, but it's more fun to rent a moped or motorcycle for the trip (see p.1213). You could conceivably pedal out here, too (the route is flat all the way), but you'll need to start out early in the day to avoid the worst of the heat.

Kanchipuram

Ask any Tamil what **KANCHIPURAM** (aka "Kanchi") is famous for, and they'll probably say silk saris, shrines and saints – in that order. A dynastic capital throughout the medieval era, it remains one of the seven holiest cities in the subcontinent, sacred to both Shaivites and Vaishnavites, and among the few surviving centres of goddess worship in the south. Year round, pilgrims pour through for a quick puja stop on the Tirupati tour circuit and, if they can afford it, a spot of shopping in the sari emporia. For non-Hindu visitors, however, Kanchipuram holds less appeal. Although the temples are undeniably impressive, the town itself is unremittingly hot, with only basic accommodation and amenities. You'll enjoy its attractions a whole lot more if you come here on a **day-trip** from Chennai or Mamallapuram, both a two-hour bus ride east.

Established by the **Pallava** kings in the fourth century AD, Kanchipuram served as their capital for five hundred years, and continued to flourish throughout the Chola, Pandya and Vijayanagar eras. Under the Pallavas, it was an important scholastic forum, and a meeting point for Jain, Buddhist and Hindu cultures. Its **temples** dramatically reflect this enduring political prominence, spanning the years from the peak of Pallava construction to the seventeenth century, when the ornamentation of the *gopuras* and pillared halls was at its most elaborate (for more on Tamil Nadu's temples, see p.1216). All can be easily reached by foot, bike or rickshaw, and shut daily between noon and 4pm.

Ekambareshvara Temple

Kanchipuram's largest temple and most important Shiva shrine, the **Ekambareshvara Temple** – also known as Ekambaranatha – is easily identified by its colossal whitewashed *gopuras*, which rise to almost 60m, on the north side of town. The main temple contains some Pallava work, but was mostly

constructed in the sixteenth and seventeenth centuries, and stands within a vast walled enclosure beside some smaller shrines and a large fish-filled water tank.

The entrance is through a high-arched passageway beneath an elaborate *gopura* in the south wall. It leads to an open courtyard and a majestic "thousand-pillared hall", or *kalyan mandapa*. This faces the tank in the north and the sanctuary in the west that protects the emblem of Shiva (here in his form as **Kameshvara**, Lord of Desire), an "earth" *lingam* that is one of five *lingams* in Tamil Nadu that represent the elements. Legend connects it with the goddess **Kamakshi** (Shiva's consort, "Wanton-Eyed"), who angered Shiva by playfully covering his eyes and plunging the world into darkness. Shiva reprimanded her by sending her to fashion a *lingam* from the earth in his honour; once it was completed, Kamakshi found she could not move it. Local myths tell of a great flood that swept over Kanchipuram and destroyed the temples, but did not move the *lingam*, to which Kamakshi clung so fiercely that marks of her breasts and bangles were imprinted upon it.

Behind the sanctum, accessible from the covered hallway around it, an eerie bare hall lies beneath a profusely carved *gopura*, and in the courtyard a venerable **mango tree** represents the tree under which Shiva and Kamakshi were married. This union is celebrated during a festival each April, when many couples are married in the *kalyan mandapa*.

Sankaramandam

Kanchipuram is the seat of a line of holy men bearing the title **acharya**, whose line dates back perhaps as far as 1300 BC to the saint Adi Sankaracharya. The

68th acharya, the highly revered Sri Chandrasekharendra Sarasvati Swami, died in January 1994 at the age of 101. Buried in the sitting position, as is the custom for great Hindu sages, his mortal remains are enshrined in a *samadhi* at the **Sankaramandam**, a *math* (monastery for Hindu renouncers) down the road from the Ekambreshvara Temple. The present incumbent, the 69th acharya, has his quarters on the opposite side of a marble meditation hall to the shrine, and gives *darshan* to the public during the morning and early evening, when the *math*'s two huge elephants are given offerings. Lined with old photographs from the life of the former swami, with young brahmin students chanting Sanskrit verses in the background, it's a typically Tamil blend of simple sanctity and garish modern glitz.

Kailasanatha Temple

The **Kailasanatha Temple**, the oldest structure in Kanchipuram and the finest example of Pallava architecture in south India, is situated among several low-roofed houses just over 1km west of the town centre. Built by the Pallava King Rajasimha early in the eighth century, its intimate size and simple carving distinguish it from the town's later temples. Usually quieter than its neighbours, the shrine becomes the focus of vigorous celebrations during the **Mahashivratri festival** each March. Like its contemporary, the Shore Temple at Mamallapuram, it is built of soft sandstone, but its sheltered position has spared it from wind and sand erosion, and it remains remarkably intact, despite some rather clumsy recent renovation work.

Kamakshi Amman Temple

Built during Pallava supremacy and modified in the fourteenth and seventeenth centuries, the **Kamakshi Amman Temple**, northwest of the bus stand, combines several styles, with an ancient central shrine, gates from the Vijayanagar period, and high, heavily sculpted creamy *gopuras* set above the gateways.

This is one of India's three holiest shrines to Shakti, Shiva's cosmic energy depicted in female form, usually as his consort. The goddess Kamakshi, a local form of Parvati, shown with a sugar-cane bow and arrows of flowers, is honoured as having lured Shiva to Kanchipuram, where they were married, and thus having forged the connection between the local community and the god. In February or March, deities are wheeled to the temple in huge wooden "cars", decked with robed statues and swaying plantain leaves.

Vaikuntha Perumal Temple

Built shortly after the Kailasanatha Temple at the end of the eighth century, the smaller **Vaikuntha Perumal Temple**, a few hundred metres west of the railway station, is dedicated to Vishnu. Its lofty carved *vimana* (towered sanctuary) crowns three shrines containing images of Vishnu, stacked one on top of the other. Unusual scenes carved in the walls enclosing the temple yard depict events central to Pallava history, among them coronations, court gatherings and battles with the Chalukyas who ruled the regions to the northwest. The temple's pillared entrance hall was added by Vijayanagar rulers five centuries later, and is very different in style, with far more ornate sculpting.

Varadarajaperumal Temple

The Vaishnavite **Varadarajaperumal Temple** stands within a huge walled complex in the far southeast of town, guarded by high gates topped with *gopuras*. The inner sanctuary boasts superb carving and well-preserved paintings, but non-Hindus only have access to the outer courtyards, and the elaborate sixteenth-century pillared hall close to the western entrance gate. The outer columns of this *mandapa* are sculpted as lions and warriors on rearing horses, to celebrate the military vigour of the Vijayanagars, who believed their prowess was inspired by the power of Shakti.

Practicalities

Flanked on the south by the River Vegavathi, Kanchipuram lies 70km southwest of Chennai, and about the same distance from the coast. **Buses** from Chennai, Mamallapuram and Chengalpattu stop at the stand in the town centre on Raja Street. The sleepy **railway station** in the northeast sees only five daily passenger services from Chengalpattu (one of them, #161, originating in Chennai) and two from Anakkonam.

As most of the main roads are wide and traffic rarely unmanageable, the best way to **get around** Kanchi is by **bicycle** – available for minimal rates (Rs2/hour) at stalls west and northeast of the bus stand. The town's vegetable markets, hotels, restaurants and bazaars are concentrated in the centre of town, near the bus stand.

Note that unless you have some used dollars and are happy to chance the black market, there is nowhere in the town to **change money**; the nearest official foreign-exchange places are in Chennai and Mamallapuram.

Accommodation and eating

There's not a great choice of **accommodation** in Kanchipuram, but the hotels are sufficient for a night. The less expensive lodges offer minimal comfort, while the pricier places, if not exactly elaborate, are clean and comfortable and generally serve good south Indian dishes in their own **restaurants**. The most highly rated place to eat in town, however, is **Saravana Bhavan** on Gandhi Road, an offshoot of the famous Chennai chain of pure vegetarian restaurants, which offers superb Rs30 "meals" at lunchtime, and a long list of south Indian snacks the rest of the day. They open at 6am for breakfast, and there's a cool a/c annexe inside. It's also marginally less like bedlam than the other main meals joints in the centre, which tend to get swamped by shaven-headed pilgrims from Tirupati.

Baboo Surya, 85 E Raja Veethi St ☎ & ☎04112/22555. Kanchi's top hotel: large and modern with immaculate a/c and non-a/c rooms, glass lift and a good veg/tandoori restaurant. Ask for a room with "temple view". ❺–❻

Jaybala International, 504 Gandhi Rd ☎04112/24348. Slightly more old-fashioned than the *Baboo Surya*, but with huge rooms and lower tariffs. They also offer excellent-value single occupancy rates, and *Saravana Bhavan* (see above) is on the doorstep. Some a/c. ❹–❺

Sri Kusal Lodge, 68C Nellukkara St ☎04112/22356. Very friendly, marble-lined lodge; the best of the bunch, though the rooms open onto a rather dismal corridor. Good English is spoken here. ❷

Sri Rama Lodge, 21 Nellukkara St ☎04112/22435. Good, fairly clean budget lodge with attached bathrooms and some a/c rooms. Best bet if *Sri Kusal* is booked. ❷–❸

Sri Vela Lodge, Railway Station Road ☎04112/21504. Another run-of-the-mill lodge, across town from the bus stand. Larger than average rooms, with attached shower-toilets and fans, but still airless. Busy "meals" restaurant downstairs. ❷

TTDC Tamil Nadu, Railway Station Road ☎04112/22553. A friendly and dependable place, although rather overpriced; rooms are large and clean enough if a little shabby. The restaurant has a snazzy new menu card, but it is still undeniably dingy and best avoided. ❺–❼

Vedanthangal

One of India's most spectacular bird sanctuaries lies roughly 1km east of the village of **VEDANTHANGAL**, a cluster of squat, brown houses set in a patchwork of paddy fields 30km from the east coast and 86km southwest of Chennai. It's a tiny, relaxed place, bisected by one road and with just two chai stalls.

The **sanctuary** (daily dawn–dusk) a low-lying area less than half a kilometre square, is at its fullest between December and February, when it is totally flooded. The rains of the northeast monsoon, sweeping through in October or November, bring indigenous water birds ready to nest and settle until the dry season (usually April), when they leave for wetter areas. Abundant trees on mounds above water level provide perfect nesting spots, alive by January with fledglings. Visitors can watch the avian action from a path at the water's edge, or from a watchtower (fitted out with strong binoculars). Try to come at sunset, when the birds return from feeding. Common Indian species to look out for are openbill storks, spoonbills, pelicans, black cormorants, and herons of several types. You may also see ibises, grey pelicans, migrant cuckoos, sandpipers, egrets, which paddle in the rice fields, and tiny, darting bee-eaters. Some migrant birds pass through and rest on their way between more permanent sites; swallows, terns and redshanks are common, while peregrine falcons, pigeons and doves are less regularly spotted.

Practicalities

Getting to Vedanthangal can present a few problems. The nearest town is Maduranthakam, 8km east, on NH-45 between Chengalpattu and Tindivanam. Head here to wait for the hourly buses to the sanctuary, or catch one of the four daily services from Chengalpattu. Taxis make the journey from Maduranthakam for Rs200–250, but cannot be booked from Vedanthangal.

Vedanthangal's only accommodation is the two-roomed **forest lodge** (❶) near the bus stand, school and chai stall. Rooms, spacious and comfortable with attached bath, have to be booked through the Wildlife Warden, 50, 4th Main Gandhi Nagar, Adyar, Chennai (℡ 044/413947) – if you turn up on spec, it may well be full, especially in December and January. They'll prepare food if given enough notice.

Tiruvannamalai

Synonymous with the fifth Hindu element of fire, **TIRUVANNAMALAI**, 100km south of Kanchipuram, ranks, along with Madurai, Kanchipuram, Chidambaram and Trichy, as one of the five holiest towns in Tamil Nadu. Its name, meaning "Red Mountain", derives from the spectacular extinct volcano, **Arunachala**, which rises behind it, and which glows an unearthly crimson at dawn. This awesome natural backdrop, combined with the presence in the centre of town of the colossal **Arunachaleshvara Temple**, makes Tiruvannamalai one of the region's most memorable destinations. Well off the tourist trail, it is a perfect place to get to grips with life in small-town Tamil Nadu. The countless shrines, sacred tanks, ashrams and paved pilgrim paths scattered around the sacred mountain (not to mention the legions of dreadlocked *babas* who line up for alms outside the main sites) will keep anyone who is interested in Hinduism absorbed for weeks.

Mythology identifies Arunachala as the place where Shiva asserted his power over Brahma and Vishnu by manifesting himself as a *lingam* of fire, or **agnilingam**. The two lesser gods had been disputing their respective strengths when Shiva pulled this primordial pyro-stunt, challenging his adversaries to locate the top and bottom of his blazing column. They couldn't (although Vishnu is said to have faked finding the head) and collapsed on their knees in a gesture of supreme submission. The event is commemorated each year at the rising of the full moon in November/December, when a vast vat of ghee and paraffin is lit by priests on the summit of Arunachala. This symbolizes the fulfilment of Shiva's promise to reappear each year to vanquish the forces of darkness and ignorance with firelight.

The sacred Red Mountain is also associated with the famous twentieth-century saint, **Sri Ramana Maharishi**, who chose it as the site for his twenty-three-year meditation retreat. A crop of small ashrams have sprung up on the edge of town below Sri Ramana's Cave, some of them more authentic than others, and the ranks of white-cotton-clad foreigners floating between them have become a defining feature of Tiruvannamalai over the past five or six years.

Arunachaleshvara Temple

Known to Hindus as the "Temple of the Eternal Sunrise", the enormous **Arunachaleshvara Temple**, built over a period of almost a thousand years, consists of three concentric courtyards whose gateways are topped by tapering *gopuras*, the largest of which cover the east and north gates. The best spot from which to view the precinct, a breathtaking spectacle against the sprawling plains and lumpy, granite Shevaroy hills, is the path up to Sri Ramana Maharishi's meditation cave, Virupaksha (see below), on the lower slopes of Arunachala. To enter the temple, however, head for the huge eastern gateway, which leads through the thick outer wall carved with images of deities, local saints and teachers. In the basement of a raised hall to the right before entering the next courtyard is the Parthala *lingam*, where Sri Ramana Maharishi is said to have sat in a state of Supreme Awareness while ants devoured his flesh.

The caves and Sri Ramanasram ashram

Opposite the western entrance of the temple complex, a path leads up a holy hill (15min) to the **Virupaksha Cave**, where Ramakrishna stayed between 1899 and 1916. He personally built the bench outside and the hill-shaped *lingam* and platform inside, where all are welcome to meditate in peace. When this cave became too small, constantly crowded with relatives and devotees, Ramana shifted to another, hidden away in a clump of trees a few minutes further up the hill. He named this one, and the small house built onto it, **Skandasraman**, and lived there between 1916 and 1922. The inner cave here is also set aside for meditation, and the front patio affords splendid views across the temple, town and surrounding plains.

The caves can also be reached via the pilgrims' path winding uphill from the **Sri Ramanasram ashram**, 2km south of the temple along the main road. This simple complex is where the sage lived after returning from his retreat on Arunachala, and where his body is today enshrined (Hindus customarily bury saints in the sitting position rather than cremate their bodies). The *samadhi* has become a popular place for Sri Ramana's devotees on pilgrimage, but interested visitors are welcome to stay in the dorms here. There's also an excellent bookshop stocking a huge range of titles on the life and teachings of the guru, as well as quality postcards, calendars and religious images.

Pradakshana

During the annual Kartiggai festival, Hindu pilgrims are supposed to perform an auspicious circumambulation of Arunachala, known as the **Pradakshana** (*pra* signifies the removal of all sins, *da* the fulfilment of desires, *kshi* freedom from the cycle of rebirth, and *na* spiritual liberation). Along the way, offerings are made at a string of shrines, tanks, temples, *lingams*, pillared meditation halls, sacred rocks, springs, trees, and caves related to the Tiruvannamalai legends. Although hectic during the festival, the paved path linking them all together is quiet for most of the year, and makes a wonderful day-hike, affording fine views of the town and its environs.

Practicalities

Tiruvannamalai is served by regular buses from Vellore, and by eleven daily services from Pondicherry. Coming from the coast, it's easiest to make your way there on one of the numerous buses from Tindivandum. The town bus stand is 2km north of the temple on the main road to Gingee. Half a kilometre north of there, the **railway station** is on the line between Tirupati and Madurai, with a daily service in each direction.

Amazingly, you can access the **internet** from Tiruvannamalai, at the Image Computer Centre, 52 Car St (daily 10am–10pm).

Accommodation and eating

For such an important pilgrimage place, Tiruvannamalai has surprisingly few decent **hotels**. If your budget can stretch to it, stay at the two-star *Trisul*, a couple of minutes' walk from the main temple entrance at 6 Kanakaraya Mudali St (⊕ 04175/22219; ❺–❻), which has huge, immaculately clean rooms (some of them with a/c), courteous staff and a good restaurant. Its only drawback is that it gets booked for long periods by Westerners studying at one or other of the ashrams. The next best option, and excellent value for money, is *NS Lodge*, facing the Arunachaleshvara Temple's south entrance at 47 Thiruvoodal St (⊕ 04175/25388; ❷–❹). Its rooms are neat and clean, some have a/c and all have cable TV and attached shower-toilets; there's also a great view of the temple towers from the roof. Moving down the scale, pick of the budget lodges is the *Sri Durgalakshmi*, just west of the bus stand at 73 Chinnakadai St (⊕ 04174/26041; ❷). If it's full, try the shabbier *Prakasam* next door (⊕ 04175/26041; ❶–❷), owned by the same family. Otherwise, a reliable option is further into town towards the temple: the *Park* (⊕ 04175/22471; ❷–❺), 26 Kosmadam St, just northeast of the main temple entrance. It boasts a range of rooms from basic but clean to a/c and comfortable and there's a busy vegetarian canteen on the ground floor.

For **food**, you've a choice of a dozen or so typical south Indian "meals" joints, of which the *Udipi Brindhavan Hotel*, just off the bottom of Car Street, is the most traditional (though not the most hygienic). Delicious hot ghee chapatis are served here all afternoon, as well as all the usual rice specialities. The other commendable *udipi* restaurant in town is the *Deepam*, also on Car Street opposite the temples' east entrance, which boasts a cooler "deluxe" wing next door (same name), where you can order ice creams and milk shakes; both branches serve excellent *parottas* for under Rs10. If you feel like a change from south Indian, head for the *Trisul*, whose posh ground-floor restaurant serves a north Indian buffet for around Rs100, as well as a full tandoori menu.

Gingee

An epic landscape of huge boulder hills, interspersed by lush splashes of rice paddy and banana plantations, stretches east of Tiruvannamalai towards the coast. The scenery peaks at **GINGEE** (pronounced "*Shinjee*"), 37km east of the Red Mountain along the Pondicherry highway, where the ruins of Tamil Nadu's most spectacular **fort** sprawl over a vast swathe of sun-scorched granite.

Dissected by the main Tiruvannamalai–Pondicherry road, Gingee fort (whole complex, including palace: daily sunrise–sunset; $10 [Rs10]) comprises three separate citadels, crowning the summits of three dramatic hills: Krishnagiri to the north, Rajagiri to the west, and Chandrayandurg to the southeast. Connecting them to form an enormous triangle, 1.5km from north to south, are twenty-metre-thick walls, punctuated by bastions and gateways that give access to the protected zones at the heart of the complex. It's hard to imagine such defences ever being overrun, but they were, on numerous occasions following the fort's foundations by the Vijayanagars in the fifteenth century. The Muslim Adil Shahis from Bijapur, Shivaji's Maharathas, and the Moghuls all conquered Gingee, using it to consolidate the vulnerable southern reaches of their respective empires. The French also took it in 1750, but were ousted by the British after a bloody five-week siege eleven years later.

From the road, head south to the main **east gate**, where a snaking passage emerges, after no less than four changes of direction, inside the **palace** enclave. Of the many structures unearthed by archeologists here, the most distinctive is the square seven-storey **Kalyana Mahal tower**, focal point of the former governor's residence, featuring an ingenious hydraulic system that carried water to the uppermost levels, crowned by a tapering pyramidal tower. Continue west through a gateway, and you'll pick up the path to **Rajagiri**, Gingee's loftiest citadel; at 165m above the surrounding plain, it's a very stiff climb in the heat, but the views are well worth the effort.

Practicalities

Gingee is easily accessible by **bus** from Tiruvannamalai, 37km west, and Pondicherry, 68km southeast. You can either alight at the site itself, 2km west of **Gingee** town, or, if you intend to spend the night there, dump your bags at the hotel and continue to the ruins by auto-rickshaw. The only **accommodation** to speak of (and the only dependable place to leave luggage while you visit the fort), is the *Shivasand* hotel, on MG Road, opposite the main bus stand (℡04145/22218; ❸–❺), whose *Vasantham* south Indian restaurant is Gingee's classiest place to eat. From the town centre, auto-rickshaws charge Rs80–90 for the return trip to the fort; you'll have to settle an additional fee for waiting time. Note that there are no refreshments, not even drinking water, available at the site, so take your own, or wander 500m back down the road towards town to the small roadside chai stall in the village.

Pondicherry and Auroville

First impressions of **PONDICHERRY**, the former capital of French India, can be unpromising. Instead of the leafy boulevards and *pétanque* pitches you might expect, its messy outer suburbs and bus stand are as cluttered and chaotic as any typical Tamil town. Closer to the seafront, however, the atmosphere grows tangibly more Gallic, as the bazaars give way to rows of houses whose shuttered windows and colourwashed facades wouldn't look out of place in Montpellier. For anyone familiar with the British colonial imprint, it can induce culture shock to see richly ornamented Catholic churches, French road names and policemen in De Gaulle-style *képis*, not to mention hearing French spoken in the street and seeing *boules* played in the dusty squares.

Known to Greek and Roman geographers as "Poduke", Pondicherry was an important staging post on the second-century maritime trade route between Rome and the Far East (a Roman amphitheatre has been unearthed at nearby Arikamedu). When the Roman empire declined, the Pallavas and Cholas took

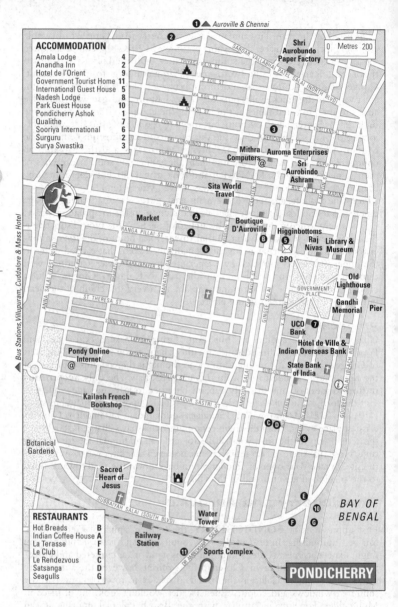

ACCOMMODATION

Amala Lodge	4
Anandha Inn	2
Hotel de l'Orient	9
Government Tourist Home	11
International Guest House	5
Nadesh Lodge	8
Park Guest House	10
Pondicherry Ashok	1
Qualithe	7
Sooriya International	6
Surguru	2
Surya Swastika	3

RESTAURANTS

Hot Breads	B
Indian Coffee House	A
La Terasse	F
Le Club	E
Le Rendezvous	C
Satsanga	D
Seagulls	G

PONDICHERRY

control, followed by a succession of colonial powers, from the Portuguese in the sixteenth century to the French, Danes and British, who exchanged the enclave several times after the various battles and treaties of the Carnatic Wars in the early eighteenth century. Pondicherry's heyday, however, dates from the arrival of **Dupleix**, who accepted the governorship in 1742 and immediately set about rebuilding a town decimated by its former British occupants. It was he who instituted the street plan of a central grid encircled by a broad oblong boulevard, bisected north to south by a canal dividing the "Ville Blanche", to the east, from the "Ville Noire", to the west.

Although relinquished by the French in 1954 – when the town became the headquarters of the **Union Territory of Pondicherry**, administering the three other former colonial enclaves scattered across south India – Pondicherry's split personality still prevails. West of the canal stretches a bustling Indian market town, while to the east, towards the sea, the streets are emptier, cleaner and decidedly European. The seaside promenade, **Goubert Salai** (formerly Beach Road), has the forlorn look of an out-of-season French resort, complete with its own white Hôtel de Ville. Tanned sun-worshippers share space with grave Europeans in white Indian costume, busy about their spiritual quest. It was here that **Sri Aurobindo Ghose** (1872–1950), a leading figure in the freedom struggle in Bengal, was given shelter after it became unwise to live close to the British in Calcutta. His **ashram** attracts thousands of devotees from all around the world, most particularly from Bengal.

Ten kilometres north, the Utopian experiment-in-living **Auroville** was inspired by Aurobindo's disciple, the charismatic Mirra Alfassa, a Parisian painter, musician and mystic better known as "The Mother". Today this slightly surreal place is populated by numbers of expats and visited by long-stay Europeans eager to find inner peace.

The Town

Pondicherry's beachside promenade, **Goubert Salai**, is a favourite place for a stroll; there's little to do, other than watch the world go by. The Hôtel de Ville, today housing the Municipal Offices building, is still an impressive spectacle, and a four-metre-tall Gandhi memorial, surrounded by ancient columns, dominates the northern end. Nearby, a French memorial commemorates French Indians who lost their lives in World War I.

Just north of the Hôtel de Ville, a couple of streets back from the promenade, is the leafy old French-provincial-style square now named **Government Place**. On the north side, the impressive, gleaming white **Raj Nivas**, official home to the present lieutenant governor of Pondicherry Territory, was built late in the eighteenth century for Joseph Francis Dupleix, who became governor of French India.

The **Pondicherry Museum** (Tues–Sun 10am–5pm) is on Ranga Pillai Street, opposite Government Place. The archeological collection includes Neolithic and 2000-year-old remains from Arikamedu, a few Pallava (sixth- to eighth-century) and Buddhist (tenth-century) stone sculptures, bronzes, weapons and paintings. Alongside these are displayed a bizarre assembly of French salon furniture and bric-a-brac from local houses, including a velvet S-shaped "conversation seat".

The **Sri Aurobindo Ashram** on rue de la Marine (daily 8am–noon & 2–6pm; no children under 3; photography with permission) is one of the best-known and wealthiest ashrams in India. Founded in 1926 by the Bengali philosopher-guru, Aurobindo Ghosh, and his chief disciple, personal manager and mouthpiece, "The Mother", it serves as the headquarters of the Sri Aurobindo Society, or SAS. Today the SAS owns most of the valuable property and real estate in Pondicherry, and wields what many consider to be a disproportionate influence over the town (note how many of the shops and businesses have "auro" somewhere in their name). The **samadhi**, or mausoleum, of Sri Aurobindo and "The Mother" is covered daily with flowers and usually surrounded by supplicating devotees with their hands and heads placed on the tomb. Inside the main building, an incongruous and very bourgeois-looking

Western-style room complete with three-piece suite, is where "The Mother" and Sri Aurobindo chilled out. Make sure not to tread on the Persian carpet, as devotees prostrate here also. A bookshop in the next room sells tracts, and frequent cultural programmes are presented in the building opposite.

In the southwest of town, near the railway station, you can hardly miss the huge cream-and-brown **Sacred Heart of Jesus**, one of Pondicherry's finest Catholic churches, built by French missionaries in the 1700s. Nearby, the shady **Botanical Gardens** established in 1826 offer many quiet paths to wander (daily 8.45am–5.45pm). The French planted 900 species here, experimenting to see how they would do in Indian conditions; one, the *khaya senegalensis*, has grown to a height of 25m. You can also see an extraordinary fossilized tree, found about 25km away in Tiravakarai.

Practicalities

All buses – long and short distance – pull into **New Bus Stand**, which lies on the west edge of town; for a summary of routes, see the Travel Details on p.1291. From here, a rather precarious cycle-rickshaw ride into the main hotel district should cost about Rs20, and an auto-rickshaw Rs30. Pondicherry's **railway station** is in the south, five minutes' walk from the sea; on a branch line, it's connected by four daily trains to the main line at Villupuram.

The newly refurbished **Pondicherry Tourism Development Corporation** office is on Goubert Salai (daily 8.45am–1pm & 2–5.30pm; ℡0413/339497). The staff are extremely helpful, providing leaflets and a city map, and information about Auroville; they can also book you onto their **city tour** (half-day 2–5.30pm; Rs52.50) and arrange **car rental** (Rs1300 per day, including fuel). Recommended places to **change money** include: the Indian Overseas Bank, in the Hôtel de Ville; Sita World Travels, 124 Mission St; the State Bank of India on Surcouf Street; and UCO Bank, rue Mahe de Labourdonnais. The **GPO** is on Ranga Pillai Street (Mon–Sat 10am–7.30pm).

The cheapest **internet access** in Pondicherry is offered by Mithra Computers, at 55 Canteen St, one block east of Mission Street in the northeast of town (daily 7am–9.30pm), although a more comfortable option is the air-conditioned Pondy Online, 125 Candappa St (Mon–Sat 9.30am–12.30pm & 4–9pm).

Pondicherry is well served with both auto- and cycle rickshaws, but for **getting around** most tourists rent a **cycle** from one of the many stalls dotted around town (Rs20 per day, plus Rs200 refundable deposit). If you're staying at the *Park Guest House*, use one of theirs (they're all immaculately maintained). The tourist office (see above) also rent out good bikes from their *Lake Café* on the seafront promenade, but at the rather expensive rate (Rs5/hr). For trips further afield (to Auroville, for example), you may want to rent a **moped** or **scooter**. Of the rental firms operating in town, Auroma Enterprises, 9 Sri Aurobindo St (℡0413/36179) is the cheapest and has the best reputation, with new Honda Kinetics for Rs100 per day. You'll have to pay a Rs500 deposit and leave your passport as security.

Accommodation

Pondicherry's **basic lodges** are concentrated around the main market area, Ranga Pillai Street and rue Nehru. Guesthouses in Pondicherry belonging to the **Sri Aurobindo Ashram** offer fantastic value for money, but come with a lot of baggage apart from your own (regulations, curfews and overpowering "philosophy of life" notices). Although supposedly open to all, they are not keen on advertising, or on attracting misguided individuals indulging in "spiritual tourism".

Amala Lodge, 92 Ranga Pillai St ☎0413/338910. A leafy little budget place off MG Road, hemmed in by "Job Typing" offices. The rooms are simple but acceptably clean, some with attached bath, otherwise there are communal facilities. A good fallback but you can get better value for the same price elsewhere. ❷

Anandha Inn, Sardar Vallabhai Patel Road ☎0413/330711, ⓕ331241. Seventy luxurious rooms, two restaurants and a pastry shop, in a gleaming white building. Good value and popular with tour groups, so book well in advance. ❼

Government Tourist Home, Dr Ambedkhar Salai, Uppalam ☎0413/36376. Charmless, neon-lit concrete block, at the bottom end of town and within earshot of the railway line, but an unbelievable bargain (doubles only Rs30). All rooms with attached shower-toilets and there are two ultra-cheap a/c rooms. ❶

International Guest House, Gingee Salai, near the GPO ☎0413/336699. The largest Aurobindo establishment, with dozens of very large, clean rooms, some a/c. Recommended as a budget option, and safe for single women. ❷–❹

Nadesh Lodge, 539 Mahatma Gandhi Rd, near Small Market Clock Tower ☎0413/339221. A welcoming and popular backpackers' lodge in a bustling neighbourhood bazaar. Twenty simple rooms fronting an elongated courtyard. In-house camera repair-wallahs, small library and walls of pot plants. ❷

Hotel de l'Orient, 17, Rue Romain Rolland ☎0413/343067, ⓕ227829. A beautiful, UNESCO heritage-accorded French house with ten rooms, individually decorated with French antiques, tiled balconies and long shuttered windows overlooking a leafy courtyard restaurant. Wonderfully romantic. ❽–❾

Park Guest House, at the south end of Goubert Salai ☎0413/334412. Another Sri Aurobino Society pad, with very comfortable, spotless rooms, slap on the seafront, with new mozzie nets and "sitouts" overlooking a well-watered garden. Cycle rental, laundry and cafeteria. ❹

Pondicherry Ashok, Chinnakalapet, 12km from Pondicherry on the old coastal road to Mamallapuram, near Auroville ☎0413/655160, ⓕ655140. Comfortable rooms in a quiet, breezy location on the seashore. Children's park, restaurant, barbecue and bar. Generous discounts for stays of three days or more. ❽

Qualithe, 3, Rue Mahe de Labourdonnais ☎0413/334325. Despite the row of wine shops and dingy bar downstairs, this is Pondy's most characterful budget lodge in a slightly rickety old French building. Upstairs, big, spotless rooms lead off a pleasant balcony with wicker chairs and great views over Government Place. ❹

Sooriya International, 55 Ranga Pillai St ☎0413/338910. Very large, immaculate rooms in a central hotel. An ostentatious exterior, but the tariffs are reasonable. ❻

Surguru, 104 Sardar Vallabhai Patel Salai (North Boulevard) ☎339022, ⓕ334377. Best value among Pondy's mid-price hotels. Spruce, spacious rooms, brisk service and most mod cons, including an excellent veg restaurant (see below). ❺–❻

Surya Swastika, 11 ID Koil St ☎0413/343092. Traditional Tamil guesthouse in a quiet corner of town, with nine basic rooms around a central courtyard that doubles as a pilgrims' canteen at lunchtime. Incredibly cheap, and cleaner than most of the bazaar lodges. ❶

Eating

If you've been on the road for a while and are hankering for healthy salads, fresh coffee, crusty bread, cakes and real pastry, you'll be spoilt for choice in Pondicherry. Unlike the traveller-oriented German–Bakery-style places elsewhere in the country, the Western **restaurants** here cater for a predominantly expatriate clientele, with discerning palettes and fat French-franc pay cheques. Pick of the bunch has to be the sophisticated *Le Club*, but you can eat well for a lot less at the more atmospheric *Satsanga*. **Beer** is available just about everywhere except the SAS-owned establishments.

Anugraha, *Hotel Surguru*, 104 Sardar Vallabhai Patel Salai (North Blvd). Widely rated as the best lunchtime "meals" restaurant in town (Rs30 for the full works), but they also serve superb *dosa-iddli* breakfasts and filter coffee, and a full tandoori menu in the evening. The only downside is the dingy basement location.

Hot Breads, 42 Ambour Salai. Crusty croissants,

fresh baguettes, and delicious savoury pastry snacks, served in a squeaky-clean French *boulangerie*-café full of French expats. Opens at 7.30am for breakfast and cappuccino.

Indian Coffee House, rue Nehru. Not their cleanest branch, but the coffee is good, and the waiters are as picturesque as usual in ice-cream-wafer hats.

La Terrasse , 5 Subbiah Salai (closed Wed). The most popular French restaurant for the European backpacker crew to hang out at, opening at 8.30am for croissants and coffee alfresco in the garden. Excellent prawn dishes start at Rs55, and there are crepes, pizzas and a variety of salads on offer all day, to sustain the postcard-writing clientele.

Le Club , 33 Dumas St (closed Mon). Beyond the pocket of most travellers, not to mention locals, but far and away the town's top restaurant complex. The predominantly French menu features their famous coq au vin, steak au poivre, plenty of seafood options and a full wine list, rounded off with cognac at Rs200 a shot. Count on Rs300 per head (if you foresake the shorts). There is also a cheaper bistro that is great for Sunday brunch, a tapas and cocktail bar, and a Vietnamese and Southeast Asian restaurant (open Mon).

Le Rendezvous , 30 rue Suffren. Filling seafood sizzlers, fantastic pizza and tandoori brochettes are specialities of this popular expat-oriented restaurant. They also serve fresh croissants and

espresso for breakfast, indoors, or up on the more romantic thatched rooftop, with jazz sounds and chilled beer in discreet ceramic jugs. Most main dishes Rs80–120.

Satsanga , Lal Bahadur Sastri Street. If you only eat once in Pondy, it should be here. Served on the colonnaded veranda of an old colonial mansion, the menu (devised by the French patron) is carefully prepared and exactly the kind of thing you dream about elsewhere in India: organic salads with fresh herbs, tzatziki and garlic bread, sauté potatoes, *tagliatelle alla carbonara*, and mouthwatering pizzas washed down with chilled Kingfisher. Check their *plat du jour* for fresh fish dishes. Around Rs300 per head for three courses, with drinks.

Seagulls Restaurant and Bar , Damas St. Reasonably priced, open-air rooftop restaurant in breezy spot right next to the sea, new pier and cargo harbour. Huge menu, with veg dishes, meat, seafood, Indian, Chinese and even some Italian (pizza, risotto, spaghetti). Inexpensive.

Auroville

The most New Age place anywhere in India must surely be **AUROVILLE**, the planned "City of Dawn", 10km north of Pondicherry, just outside the Union Territory in Tamil Nadu. Founded in 1968, Auroville was inspired by "The Mother", the spiritual successor of Sri Aurobindo. Around 1350 people live in communes (two-thirds of them non-Indians), with such names as Fertile, Certitude, Sincerity, Revelation and Transformation, in what it is hoped will eventually be an ideal city for a population of 50,000. Architecturally experimental buildings, combining modern Western and traditional Indian elements, are set in a rural landscape of narrow lanes, deep red earth and lush greenery. Income is derived from agriculture, handicrafts, alternative technology, educational and development projects and Aurolec, a computer software company.

Although the avowed aim is to live in harmony, the place has had its ups and downs, not least of which have been the **disputes** between the community and the Sri Aurobindo Society (SAS) over ownership since "The Mother's" death in 1973. The power struggle erupted into full-blown violence on a couple of occasions, before the police were called in. Eventually, the High Court handed over responsibility for the administration of the settlement to a seven-member council, with representatives from the state government, the SAS and Auroville itself.

Considering how little there is to see here, Auroville attracts a disproportionately large number of day-trippers – much to the chagrin of its inhabitants, who rightly point out that you can only get a sense of what the settlement is all about if you stay a while. Interested visitors are welcomed as paying guests in most of the communes (see below), where you can work alongside permanent residents.

Begun in 1970, the space-age **Matri Mandir** – a gigantic, almost spherical, hi-tech meditation centre at the heart of the site – was conceived as "a symbol of the Divine's answer to man's inspiration for perfection". Earth from 126 countries was symbolically placed in an urn, and is kept in a concrete cone, from which a speaker can address an audience of 3000 without amplification, in the amphitheatre adjacent to Matri Mandir. In accordance with "The Mother's" instructions, this is open to all (daily 4–4.45pm; arrive at least 1hr in advance; closed if there is rain), although the Aurovillians' reluctance to admit outsiders is palpable. After a long wait for tickets to be issued, accompanied by strict instructions on how to behave while inside, visitors are ushered in silence to the Matri Mandir's ramped entrance for a fleeting glimpse of the seventy-centimetre crystal ball that forms its focal point.

Practicalities

Auroville lies 10km north of Pondicherry on the main Chennai road; you can also get there via the new coastal highway, turning off at the village of Chinna Mudaliarchavadi. **Bus** services are frequent along both routes but – as Auroville is so spread out, covering some fifty or so square kilometres – it's best to come with your own transport, at the very least a bike. Most people rent a scooter or **motorcycle** from Pondicherry and ride up. Alternatively, book on to Tamil Nadu Tourism's daily **tour** from Pondicherry (depart 2pm, return 5.30pm; Rs52.50).

For a pre-visit primer, call in at the **visitor centre** (daily 9.30am–5.30pm), bang in the middle of the site near the Bharat Niwas, which holds a permanent exhibition on the history and philosophies of the settlement. You can also pick up some inexpensive literature on Auroville in the adjacent bookshop and check out a notice board for details of **activities** in which visitors may participate (these typically include yoga, reiki and Vipassana meditation, costing around Rs50 per session). In addition, there's a handicrafts outlet and several pleasant little vegetarian cafés serving snacks, meals and cold drinks.

The information desk at the visitor centre is also the place to enquire about **paying guest accommodation** in Auroville's thirty or so communes. Officially there's no lower limit on the time you have to stay, but visitors are encouraged to stick around for at least a week, helping out on communal projects; tariffs range from Rs100–500 per day, depending of levels of comfort. Alternatively, you can arrange to stay in one of four **guesthouses**, offering simple non-a/c rooms from $5 (payable in rupees). Beds in these, and the communes, are always in short supply, especially during the two peak periods of December to March and July to August, when it's advisable to book well in advance (c/o Auroville Guest Programmes, Auroville 605 101, Tamil Nadu, ☎0413/622704, ✉avguests@auroville.org.in). Otherwise, the only rooms in the area are just outside Auroville in the village of Chinna Mudaliarchavadi. The *Palm Beach Cottage Centre* (❶) is nothing of the kind (the sea is fifteen minutes' walk away), but has passably clean rooms with shared toilets and a small garden, where meals are served. Nearby, the *Cottage Guest House* (❷–❸) offers a little more comfort in thatched huts or a recently built block boasting en-suite rooms. For **food**, you won't do better than the simple, filling vegetarian meals served in Auroville itself.

Central Tamil Nadu: The Chola heartland

To be on the banks of the Cauvery listening to the strains of Carnatic music is to have a taste of eternal bliss

Tamil proverb

Continuing south of Pondicherry along the Coromandel coast, you enter the flat landscape of the **Kaveri** (aka Cauvery) **Delta**, a watery world of canals, dams, dykes and rivulets that has been intensively farmed since ancient times.

Only a hundred miles in diameter, it forms the verdant rice-bowl core of Tamil Nadu, crossed by more than thirty major rivers and countless streams. The largest of them, the **River Kaveri**, known in Tamil as *Ponni*, "The Lady of Gold" (a form of the Mother Goddess), is revered as a conduit of liquid *shakti*, the primordial female energy that nurtures the millions of farmers who live on her banks and tributaries. The landscape here is one endless swathe of green paddy fields, dotted with palm trees and little villages of thatched roofs and market stalls; it comes as a rude shock to land up in the hot and chaotic towns.

This mighty delta formed the very heartland of the **Chola** empire, which reached its apogee between the ninth and thirteenth centuries, an era often compared to classical Greece and Renaissance Italy, both for its cultural richness and the sheer scale and profusion of its architectural creations. Much as the Cholas originally intended, every visitor is immediately in awe of their huge temples, not only at cities such as **Chidambaram**, **Kumbakonam** and **Thanjavur**, but also out in the countryside at places like **Gangaikondacholapuram**, where the magnificent temple is all that remains of a once-great city.

Exploring the area for a few days will bring you into contact with the more delicate side of Chola artistic expression, such as the magnificent **bronzes** of Thanjavur.

Chidambaram

CHIDAMBARAM, 58km south of Pondicherry, is so steeped in myth that its history is hard to unravel. As the site of the *tandava*, the cosmic dance of Shiva as **Nataraja**, King of the Dance, it is one of the holiest sites in south India. A visit to the **Sabhanayaka Temple** affords a fascinating glimpse into ancient Tamil religious practice and belief. The legendary king **Hiranyavarman** is said to have made a pilgrimage here from Kashmir, seeking to rid himself of leprosy by bathing in the temple's Shivaganga tank. In thanks for a successful cure, he enlarged the temple. He also brought 3000 brahmins, of the Dikshitar caste, whose descendants are to this day the ritual specialists of the temple, distinguishable by top-knots of hair at the front of their heads.

Few of the fifty *maths*, or monasteries, that once stood here remain, but the temple itself is still a hive of activity and hosts numerous **festivals**. The two most important are ten-day affairs, building up to spectacular finales: on the ninth day of each, temple chariots process through the four Car streets (**"car festival"**), while on the tenth, **abhishekham**, the principal deities in the Raja Sabha (thousand-pillared hall) are anointed. For exact dates (one is in May/June, the other in Dec/Jan), contact any TTDC tourist office and plan well ahead, as they are very popular. Other local festivals include fire-walking and *kavadi* folk dance (dancing with decorated wooden frames on the head) at the Thillaiamman Kali (April/May) and Keelatheru Mariamman (July/Aug) temples.

The town also has a hectic market, and a large student population, based at Annamalai University to the east, a centre of Tamil studies. Among the simple thatched huts in the surrounding countryside, the only solid-looking structures are small roadside temples, most of which are devoted to Aiyannar, the village deity who protects borders, and are accompanied by *kudirais*, brightly painted terracotta or wooden figures of horses.

Sabhanayaka Nataraja Temple

For south India's Shaivites, the **Sabhanayaka Nataraja Temple** (daily 4am–noon & 4pm–10pm), where Shiva is enthroned as Lord of the Cosmic

Dance (Nataraja), is the holiest of holies. Its huge *gopuras*, whose lights are used as landmarks by sailors far out to sea in the Bay of Bengal, soar above a fifty-five-acre complex, divided by four concentric walls. The oldest parts now standing were built under the Cholas, who adopted Nataraja as their chosen deity and crowned several kings here. The rectangular outermost wall, of little interest in itself, affords entry on all four sides, so if you have the time the best way to tackle the complex is to work slowly inwards from the third enclosure in clockwise circles. **Guides** are readily available but tend to shepherd visitors towards the central shrine too quickly. Frequent **ceremonies** take place at the innermost sanctum, the most popular being at noon and 6pm, when a fire is lit in the inner sanctum, great gongs are struck and devotees rush forward to catch a last glimpse of the *lingam* before the doors are shut. On Friday nights before the temple closes, during a particularly elaborate puja, Nataraja is carried on a palanquin accompanied by music and attendants carrying flaming torches and tridents. At other times, you'll hear ancient devotional hymns from the *Tevaram*.

The western *gopura* is the most popular entrance, as well as being the most elaborately carved and probably the earliest (c.1150 AD). Turning north (left) from here, you come to the colonnaded **Shivaganga tank**, the site of seven natural springs. From the broken pillar at the tank's edge, all four *gopuras* are visible. In the northeast corner, the largest building in the complex, the **Raja Sabha** (fourteenth- to fifteenth-century) is also known as "the thousand-pillared hall"; tradition holds that there are only nine hundred and ninety-nine actual pillars, the thousandth being Shiva's leg. During festivals the deities Nataraja and Shivakamasundari are brought here and mounted on a dais for the anointing ceremony, *abhishekha*.

The importance of **dance** at Chidambaram is underlined by the reliefs of dancing figures inside the east *gopura* demonstrating 108 *karanas* (a similar set is to be found in the west *gopura*). A *karana* (or *adavu*, in Tamil) is a specific point in a phase of movement prescribed by the extraordinarily comprehensive Sanskrit treatise on the performing arts, the *Natya Shastra* (c.200 BC–200 AD) – the basis of all classical dance, music and theatre in India. A caption from the *Natya Shastra* surmounts each *karana* niche. Four other niches are filled with images of patrons and *stahapatis* – the sculptors and designers responsible for the iconography and positioning of deities.

To get into the square **second enclosure**, head for its western entrance (just north of the west *gopura* in the third wall) which leads into a circumambulatory passageway. Once beyond this second wall it's easy to become disorientated, as the roofed inner enclosures see little light and are supported by a maze of colonnades. The atmosphere is immediately more charged, reaching its peak at the very centre.

The innermost **Govindaraja shrine** is dedicated to Vishnu – a surprise in this most Shaivite of environments. The deity is attended by non-Dikshitar brahmins, who, it is said, don't always get along with the Dikshitars. From outside the shrine, non-Hindus can see through to the most sacred part of the temple, the **Kanaka Sabha** and the **Chit Sabha**, adjoining raised structures, roofed with copper and gold plate and linked by a hallway. The latter houses bronze images of Nataraja and his consort Shivakamasundari. Behind and to the left of Nataraja, a curtain, sacred to Shiva and strung with rows of leaves from the bilva tree, demarcates the most potent area of all. Within it lies the **Akashalingam**, known as the *rahasya*, or "secret", of Chidambaram: made of the most subtle of the elements, Ether (*akasha*) – from which Air, Fire, Water and Earth are born – the *lingam* is invisible. This is said to signify that God is nowhere, only in the human heart.

A crystal *lingam*, said to have emanated from the light of the crescent moon on Shiva's brow, and a small ruby Nataraja are worshipped in the Kanaka Sabha. They are ritually bathed in the flames of the priests' camphor fire or oil lamps six times a day. This inner area is where you're most likely to hear **oduvars**, hereditary singers from the middle, non-brahmin castes, intoning verses of ancient Tamil poetry. The songs with which they regale the deities at puja time, drawn from compilations such the *Tevaram* or earlier *Sangam*, are believed to be more than a thousand years old.

Practicalities

Chidambaram revolves around the Sabhanayaka Temple and the busy market area that surrounds it, along North, East, South and West Car streets. Though little more than a country halt, the **railway station**, 2km southeast of the centre, has good connections both north and south, and boasts retiring rooms and, on platform 1, a **post office** (Mon–Sat 9am–1pm & 1.30–5pm). Frequent buses from Chennai, Thanjavur, Mamallapuram, and Madurai pull in at the **bus stand**, also in the southeast, but nearer the centre, about 1km from the temple.

Staff at the TTDC **tourist office**, next to TTDC *Tamil Nadu* hotel on Railway Feeder Road, are charming and helpful, but only have a small pamphlet to give visitors. None of the **banks** in Chidambaram change money.

Accommodation and eating

To cope with the influx of tourists and pilgrims, Chidambaram abounds in budget **accommodation**, but there are few upper-bracket options beyond the *Saradharam* hotel, near the bus stand, and the *Aksha Plaza*, a brand new place on South Car Street between the bus stand and temple. The **railway retiring rooms** offer the best deal in town, with huge clean rooms, though the bathrooms are a little dilapidated; ask at the Station Master's Office on platform 1 (Rs150).

As for **eating**, there are plenty of basic, wholesome "meals" places on and around the Car streets – the *Sri Ganesa Bhavan*, on West Car Street, gets the locals' vote. For quality, inexpensive south Indian food you can't beat the *Pallavi*, at the *Saradharam* hotel, which is packed at lunchtimes for its good-value thalis. The *Annu Pallai* behind it is an equally commendable, though somewhat dingy, non-veg alternative. There's also a small *Indian Coffee House*, on Venugopal Pillai Street, that's a pleasant breakfast venue or place to peruse the papers over coffee.

Akshaya, 17/18 East Car St ☎ 04144/20192. Pleasant, clean mid-range hotel, backing onto the temple wall. Three a/c rooms, although non-a/c is better value. ❷–❺

Mansoor Lodge, 91 East Car St ☎ 04144/21072. Walls are on the grubby side, but otherwise a good, friendly cheapie: spotless, tiled floors and clean bathrooms. ❷

Raja Rajan, 162 West Car St ☎ 04144/22690. Neat and clean rooms close to the temple, with tiled bathrooms and low tariffs; the a/c ones are good value. ❷–❹

Sabanayagam, 22 East Sannathi, off East Car Street ☎ 04144/20896. Despite a flashy exterior, this is a run-of-the-mill budget place. Ask for a room with a window, preferably on the second floor overlooking the temple entrance. There's a good veg restaurant downstairs. Some a/c. ❷–❺.

Saradharam, 19 Venugopal Pillai St, opposite the bus stand ☎ 04144/21336, ☏ 22656. Large, clean and well-kept rooms (some a/c) in modern buildings, with internet access, two decent restaurants, a pizza restaurant, small garden, bar, laundry and foreign exchange. ❹–❼

TTDC Hotel Tamil Nadu, Railway Feeder Road, located between the railway station and bus stand ☎ 04144/38056. Friendly, but some rooms are shabby: check the bedding is clean, and if the a/c works. Also dorm beds (Rs50), Indian-Chinese restaurant, bar, *iddli* shop and tourist office. ❺–❻

Kumbakonam

Sandwiched between the Kaveri (Cauvery) and Arasalar rivers is **KUM-BAKONAM**, 74km southwest of Chidambaram and 38km northeast of Thanjavur. Hindus believe this to be the place where a water pot (*kumba*) of *amrita* – the ambrosial beverage of immortality – was washed up by a great deluge from atop sacred Mount Meru in the Himalayas. Shiva, who just happened to be passing through in the guise of a wild forest-dwelling hunter, for some reason fired an arrow at the pot, causing it to break. From the shards, he made the *lingam* that is now enshrined in **Kumbareshwara Temple**, whose *gopuras* today tower over the town, along with those of some seventeen other major shrines. A former capital of the Cholas, who are said to have kept a high-security treasury here, Kumbakonam is the chief commercial centre for the Thanjavur region. The main bazaar, **Big Street**, is especially renowned for its quality costume jewellery.

The main reason to stop in Kumbakonam is to admire the exquisite sculpture of the **Nageshwara Swami Shiva Temple**, which contains the most refined Chola stone carving still in situ. The town also lies within easy reach of the magnificent Darasuram and Gangaikondacholapuram temples, both spectacular ancient monuments that see very few visitors. In addition, the village of Swamimalai, only a bike ride away, is the state's principal centre for traditional **bronze casting**.

The Town

Surmounted by a multicoloured *gopura*, the east entrance of Kumbakonam's seventeenth-century **Kumbareshwara Temple**, home of the famous *lingam* from where the town derived its name, is approached via a covered market selling a huge assortment of cooking pots, a local speciality, as well as the usual

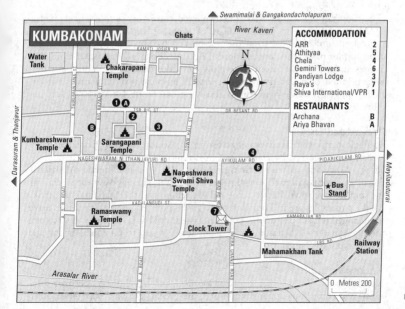

glass bangles and trinkets. At the gateway, you may meet the temple elephant, with a painted forehead and necklace of bells. Beyond the flagstaff, a *mandapa* houses a fine collection of silver *vahanas*, vehicles of the deities, used in festivals, and *pancha loham* (compound of silver, gold, brass, iron and tin) figures of the 63 Nayanmar poet–saints.

The principal and largest of the Vishnu temples in Kumbakonam is the thirteenth-century **Sarangapani Temple**, entered through a ten-storey pyramidal *gopura* gate, more than 45m high. The **central shrine** dates from the late Chola period with many later accretions. Its entrance, within the innermost court, is guarded by huge *dvarpalas*, identical to Vishnu whom they protect. Between them are carved stone *jali* screens, each different, and in front of them stands the sacred, square *homam* fireplace. During the day, rays of light from tiny ceiling windows penetrate the darkness around the sanctum, designed to resemble a chariot with reliefs of horses, elephants and wheels. A painted cupboard contains a mirror for Vishnu to see himself when he leaves the sanctum sanctorum.

The small **Nageshwara Swami Shiva Temple**, in the centre of town, is Kumbakonam's oldest temple, founded in 886 and completed a few years into the reign of Parantaka I (907–c.940). First impressions are unpromising, as much of the original building has been hemmed in by later Disney-coloured accretions, but beyond the main courtyard, occupied by a large columned *mandapa*, a small *gopura*-topped gateway leads to an inner enclosure where the earliest Chola shrine stands. Framed in the main niches around its sanctum wall are a series of exquisite stone figures, regarded as the finest surviving pieces of **ancient sculpture** in south India. With their languid stance and mesmeric, half-smiling facial expressions, these modest-sized masterpieces far outshine the more monumental art of Thanjavur and Gangaikondacholapuram. The figures show Dakshinamurti (Shiva as a teacher; south wall), Durga and a three-headed Brahma (north wall) and Ardanari, half-man, half-woman (west wall). Joining them are near-life-size voluptuous maidens believed to be queens or princesses of King Aditya's court.

The most famous and revered of many sacred **water tanks** in Kumbakonam, the **Mahamakham** in the southeast of town, is said to have filled with ambrosia (*amrit*) collected from the pot broken by Shiva. Every twelve years, when Jupiter passes the constellation of Leo, it is believed that water from the Ganges and eight other holy rivers flows into the tank, thus according it the status of *tirtha*, or sacred river crossing. At this auspicious time, as many as four million pilgrims come here for an absolving bathe; the last occasion was on February 18, 1992.

Practicalities

Kumbakonam's small **railway station**, in the southeast, 2km from the main bazaar, is well served by trains both north and south, and has a left-luggage office (24hr) and decent **retiring rooms** (Rs100). The hectic **Moffussil** (local) and **Aringannar** (long-distance) bus stands are opposite each other in the southeast of town, between the railway station and the Mahamakham tank. All the timetables are in Tamil, but there's a 24-hour enquiry office. Buses leave for Gangaikondacholapuram, Pondicherry, and Thanjavur every five to ten minutes, many via Darasuram. Frequent services run to Chennai, Trichy and several daily to Bangalore.

Accommodation

Kumbakonam is not a major tourist location, and has limited **accommodation**, with only one upper-range hotel, the *Sterling Swamimalai*, 10km southeast of town on the outskirts of Swamimalai village (see p.1242). The good news for budget travellers is that most of the inexpensive places are clean and well-maintained.

ARR, 21 TSR Big St ☎0435/421234. Fifty large, clean rooms (some a/c), on five floors, all with windows, and TVs on request. Bland, but comfortable enough, with an a/c restaurant and bar. **④–⑥**

Athityaa, Nageshwaram N (Thanjavur) Road ☎0435/421794, ℗430194. This place was once smart but is now is rather worn and grubby, especially for the price, although the rooms are spacious – ask for one on the west side, facing the temple. **④–⑥**

Chela, 9 Ayikulam Rd ☎0435/430336, ℗431592. Another large mid-range place, between the bus stand and centre, distinguished by its horrendous mock-classical facade. Soap, fresh towels and TVs are offered as standard. They also have a bar and back-up generator. **④–⑤**

Gemini Towers, 18 Ayikulam Rd ☎0435/423559. Across the road from the *Chela*; a grand name for a very run-of-the-mill budget lodge, but the place is welcoming and all the rooms are tidy and good value (though non-a/c). **②**

Pandiyan Lodge, 52 Sarangapani E Rd ☎0435/430397. The fairly acceptable single rooms in this small lodge have windows, but the dingier doubles open onto corridors. **②**

Raya's, 28–29 Head Post Office Rd ☎0435/432170, ℗422479. Central, well maintained with clean, comfortable rooms, although they are a little small for the price. The saucy "Royal Suite" (**⑥**) has mirrors on all four walls and ceiling. Conveniently near the sights. **④–⑤**

Shiva International/VPR Lodge, 101/3 TSR Big St ☎0435/424013. After the temple *gopuras*, these huge co-owned, adjacent lodges are the largest buildings in town. *VPR* offers rock-bottom rates for cleanish rooms and a prison-block atmosphere; *Siva* is altogether more pleasant, with very spacious, airy doubles. Their standard non-a/c is a bargain (ask for #301, which has great views on two sides). You can climb up on the roof for incredible views of sunset and dawn behind the *gopuras*. **②–④**

Eating

There's nothing very exciting about **eating out** in Kumbakonam, and most visitors stick to their hotel restaurant. For a change of scene, though, a few places stand out.

Archana, Big Bazaar Street. Right in the thick of the market. Popular among shoppers for its good-value south Indian "meals", and great *uttapams*, although it can get hot and stuffy inside. Foreigners appear to cause quite a stir here, but are made very welcome.

Ariya Bavan, TSR Big Street. Convenient if you're staying in *VPR/Siva* two doors down, and a dependable all-rounder, serving the usual south Indian menu, with tasty biriyani, and piping hot chapatis. Opens at 6.30am for *pongal-vadai* breakfasts.

Arogya, ground floor of the *Athityaa* hotel, Thanjavur Road. By general consent, the best veg restaurant in town. No surprises on the menu, but their lunchtime "unlimited meals" (Rs30) are excellent, and they serve north Indian tandoori in the evenings. No alcohol.

Around Kumbakonam

The delta lands around Kumbakonam are scattered with evocative vestiges of the Cholas' golden age, but the most spectacular has to be the crumbling Airavateshwara Temple at **Darasuram**, 6km southwest. Across the fields to the north, the bronze-casters of **Swamimalai** constitute a direct living link with the culture that raised this extraordinary edifice, using traditional "lost wax" techniques, unchanged since the time when Darasuram was a thriving medieval town, to create graceful Hindu deities.

You can combine the two sights in an easy half-day trip from Kumbakonam. The route is flat enough to cycle, although you should keep your wits about you when pedalling the main Thanjavur highway, which sees heavy traffic. To reach Swamimalai from Darasuram, return to the main road from the temple and ask directions in the bazaar. Swamimalai is only 3km north, but travelling between the two involves several turnings, so expect to have to ask a local to wave you in the right direction at regular intervals. From Kumbakonam, the route is more straightforward; cross the Kaveri at the top of Town Hall Road (north of the centre), turn left and follow the main road west through a ribbon of villages.

Darasuram

The **Airavateshwara Temple**, built by King Rajaraja II (c.1146–73), stands in the village of **DARASURAM**, an easy five-kilometre bus or cycle ride (on the Thanjavur route) southwest of Kumbakonam. This superb, if little-visited, Chola monument ranks alongside those at Thanjavur and Gangaikondacholapuram; but while the others are grandiose, emphasizing heroism and conquest, this is far smaller, exquisite in proportion and detail and said to have been decorated with *nitya-vinoda*, "perpetual entertainment", in mind. Shiva is called Airavateshwara here because he was worshipped in this temple by Airavata, the white elephant belonging to the king of the gods, Indra.

Darasuram's finest pieces of sculpture are the Chola black basalt images adorning wall niches in the *mandapa* and inner shrine. These include images of Nagaraja, the snake-king, with a hood of cobras, and Dakshinamurti, the "south-facing" Shiva as teacher, expounding under a banyan tree. Equally renowned is the unique series of somewhat gruesome panels, hard to see without climbing onto the base, lining the top of the basement of the closed *mandapa*. They illustrate scenes from Sekkilar's *Periya Purana*, one of the great works of Tamil literature. The poem tells the stories of the Tamil Shaivite saints, the Nayanmars, and was commissioned by King Kulottunga II, after the poet criticized him for a preoccupation with erotic, albeit religious, literature. Sekkilar is said to have composed it in the Raja Sabha at Chidambaram and when it was completed the king sat every day for a year to hear him recite it.

Swamimalai

SWAMIMALAI, 8km west of Kumbakonam, is revered as one of the six sacred abodes of Lord Murugan, Shiva's son, whom Hindu mythology records became his father's religious teacher (*swami*) on a hill (*malai*) here. The site of this epic role reversal now hosts one of the Tamils' holiest shrines, the **Swaminatha Temple**, crowning the hilltop of the centre of the village, but of more interest to non-Hindus are the hereditary **bronze-casters**' workshops dotted around the bazaar and the outlying hamlets.

Known as **sthapathis**, Swamimalai's casters still employ the "lost wax" process (*madhuchchishtavidhana* in Sanskrit) perfected by the Cholas to make the most sought-after temple idols in south India. Their finished products are displayed in numerous showrooms along the main street, from where they are exported worldwide, but it is more memorable to watch the *sthapathis* in action, fashioning the original figures from beeswax and breaking open the moulds to expose the mystical finished metalwork inside. For more on Tamil bronze casting, see p.1248.

The nearby hamlet of **Thimmakkudy**, 2km back towards Kumbakonam, is the site of the area's grandest **hotel**, the *Sterling Swamimalai* (℗ 0435/420044, Ⓕ 421705; ➒), a beautifully restored nineteenth-century brahmins' mansion kitted out with mod cons, such as fans and fridges. They also have an in-house yoga teacher, Ayurvedic massage room, and lay on a lively culture show in the evenings.

Gangaikondacholapuram

Devised as the centrepiece of a city built by the Chola king Rajendra I (1014–42) to celebrate his conquests, the magnificent **Brihadishwara Temple** stands in the tiny village of **GANGAIKONDACHOLAPURAM**, in Trichy District, 35km northeast of Kumbakonam. The tongue-twisting name means "the town of the Chola who took the Ganges". Under Rajendra I, the Chola empire did indeed stretch as far as the great river of the north, an unprecedented achievement for a southern dynasty. Aside from the temple and the rubble remains of Rajendra's palace, 2km east at Tamalikaimedu, nothing of the city remains. Nonetheless, this is among the most extraordinary archeological sites in south India, outshone only by Thanjavur, and devoid of visitors most of the time, which gives it a memorably forlorn feel.

Buses run here from Kumbakonam every five minutes and it is also served by some between Trichy and Chidambaram; to move on, buses back to Kumabakonam pass through the village every ten minutes. Be sure not to get stuck here between noon and 4pm when the temple is closed. Facilities are minimal, with little more than a few cool drinks stands. Parts of the interior are extremely dark, and a torch is useful.

Brihadishwara Temple

Dominating the village landscape, the **Brihadishwara Temple** (daily 6am–noon & 4–8pm) sits in a well-maintained, grassy courtyard, flanked by a closed *mandapa* hallway. Over the sanctuary, to the right, a massive pyramidal tower (*vimana*) rises 55m in nine diminishing storeys. Though smaller than the one at Thanjavur, the tower's graceful curve gives it an impressive refinement. At the gateway you are likely to meet the ASI caretaker, who is worth taking as a guide, especially if you'd like to climb up onto the roof for views of the vicinity and the tower.

Turning left (east) inside the courtyard, you pass a small shrine to the goddess **Durga**, containing an image of Mahishasuramardini (the slaying of the buffalo demon). Just beyond, steps climb from a large seated lion, known as Simhakinaru and made from plastered brickwork, to a well. King Rajendra is said to have had Ganges water placed in it to be used for the ritual anointing of the *lingam* in the main temple. The lion, representing Chola kingly power, bows to the huge Nandi respectfully seated before the eastern entrance of the temple, in line with the Shiva *lingam* contained within.

Directly in front of the eastern entrance to the temple stands a small altar for offerings. Two parallel flights of stairs ascend to a porch, the *mukhamandapa*, where a large pair of guardian deities flank the entrance to the long pillared *mahamandapa* hallway.

Immediately inside the temple a guide can show you the way to the tower, up steep steps. On either side of the temple doorway, sculptures of Shiva in his various benevolent (*anugraha*) manifestations include him blessing Vishnu, Devi, Ravana and the saint Chandesha. In the northeast corner an unusual square stone block features carvings of the nine planets (*navagraha*). A number of **Chola bronzes** (see p.1248) stand on the platform; the figure of Karttikeya, the war god, carrying a club and a shield, is thought to have had particular significance.

The base of the main temple sanctuary is decorated with lions and scrollwork. Above this decoration, running from the southern to the northern entrance of the *ardhamandapa*, a series of sculpted figures in plastered niches portray different images of Shiva. The most famous is at the northern entrance,

showing Shiva and Parvati garlanding the saint Chandesha, who here is sometimes identified as Rajendra I. For more on the temples of Tamil Nadu, see
p.1216.

Two minutes' walk east along the main road (turn right from the car park),
the tiny **Archeological Museum** (daily except Fri 10am–1pm & 2–5.45pm)
contains Chola odds and ends, discovered locally. The finds include terracotta
lamps, coins, weapons, tiles, bronze, bangle pieces, palm-leaf manuscripts and an
old Chinese pot.

Thanjavur

One of the busiest commercial towns of the Kaveri delta, **THANJAVUR** (aka
"Tanjore"), 55km east of Tiruchirapalli and 35km southwest of Kumbakonam,

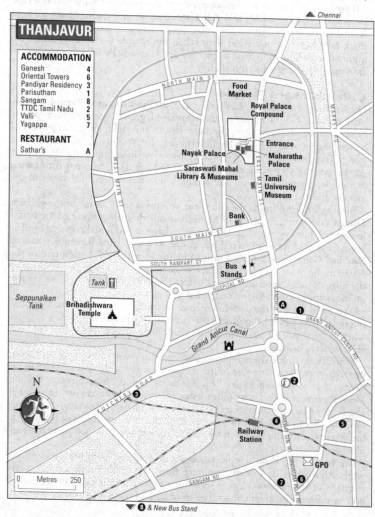

THANJAVUR

ACCOMMODATION
Ganesh   4
Oriental Towers   6
Pandiyar Residency   3
Parisutham   1
Sangam   8
TTDC Tamil Nadu   2
Valli   5
Yagappa   7

RESTAURANT
Sathar's   A

is often overlooked by travellers. However, its history and treasures – among them the breathtaking **Brihadishwara Temple**, Tamil Nadu's most awesome Chola monument – give it a crucial significance to south Indian culture. The home of the world's finest Chola bronze collection, it holds enough of interest to keep any visitors who stay here enthralled for at least a couple of days, and is the most obvious base for trips to nearby Gangaikondacholapuram, Darasuram and Swamimalai.

Thanjavur is roughly split in two by the east–west **Grand Anicut Canal**. The **old town**, north of the canal and once entirely enclosed by a fortified wall, was between the ninth and the end of the thirteenth century chosen as the capital of their extensive empire by all the Chola kings save one. None of their secular buildings survives, but you can still see as many as ninety temples, of which the Brihadishwara most eloquently epitomizes the power and patronage of Rajaraja I (985–1014), whose military campaigns spread Hinduism to the Maldives, Sri Lanka and Java. Under the Cholas, as well as the later Nayaks and Marathas, literature, painting, sculpture, Carnatic classical music and Bharatanatyam dance all thrived here. Quite apart from its own intrinsic interest, the Nayak **royal palace compound** houses an important library and museums including a famous collection of bronzes.

Of major local **festivals**, the most lavish celebrations at the Brihadishwara Temple are associated with the birthday of King Rajaraja, in October. An eight-day celebration of **Carnatic classical music** is held each January at the Panchanateshwara temple at **Thiruvaiyaru**, 13km away, to honour the great Carnatic composer-saint, Thyagaraja.

Arrival, information and orientation

Buses from Chennai, Pondicherry, Madurai and Tiruchirapalli pull in at the long-distance State Bus Stand, opposite the City Bus Stand, in the south of the old town. Other services from Tiruchirapalli, and those to and from local destinations such as Kumbakonam, stop at the New Bus Stand, inconveniently located 4km southwest of the centre, in the middle of nowhere. Rickshaws into town from here cost Rs40–50, or you can jump on one of the efficient "city buses" (Rs2) that shuttle to and from the centre every few minutes.

The **railway station**, just south of the centre, has a new computerized system (Mon–Sat 8am–2pm & 3–5pm, Sun 8am–2pm) for booking trains to Chennai, Tiruchirapalli and Rameshwaram. There are also several fast passenger services daily to Thiruvarur, Nagapattinam and Nagore. The red-and-cream station itself has an antiquated air, with its decorated columns in the main hall, and sculptures of dancers and musicians. Luggage can be left in the Parcel Office.

The **GPO** and most of the hotels and restaurants lie on or around **Gandhiji Road** (aka Train Station Road), which crosses the canal and leads to the railway station in the south. The **TTDC Tourist Office** (Mon–Fri 10am–5.45pm; ☎04362/30984), opposite the post office, is a good source of local information; there's a smaller, less efficient branch in the compound of TTDC *Tamil Nadu* hotel on Gandhiji Road (daily 8am–4pm).

You can **change money** at Canara Bank on South Main Street and, with a bit of gentle persuasion, the *Parishutham* hotel – useful out of banking hours, although the rates are not always favourable. The Government **hospital** is on Hospital Road, and there are plenty of pharmacies on Gandhiji Road.

For **internet access**, head for Gemini Soft, on the first floor of the *Oriental Towers* hotel, Srinivasam Pillai Road. As you pass through the main gate, take the white external staircase on your left.

Accommodation

Most of Thanjavur's **hotels** are concentrated in the area between the railway station and bus stands. They tend to charge higher rates than you'd pay elsewhere in the state, and there's very little choice at the bottom of the market; if you're travelling on a tight budget, this may be somewhere to consider treating yourself to an upgrade. For the **railway retiring rooms**, contact Matron on the first floor of the railway station; they comprise six big, clean double rooms opening out onto a large communal veranda, overlooking station approach. Great value, as ever, though invariably booked (Rs150).

Ganesh, 314 Srinivasam Pillai Rd, Railady ⊕ 04362/31113. Its selling point is that it is "very, very near the railway station", but it is also on a very, very noisy road. The rooms are not overly large, but they're clean, and there's a good veg restaurant downstairs. Some rooms are a/c. ❷–❺

Oriental Towers, 2889 Srinivasam Pillai Rd ⊕ 04362/31467, ⓕ 30770. Huge hotel-cum-shopping complex, with small swimming pool on the fourth floor and luxurious rooms. Although it is good value at this price and has all modern facilities, including internet access, it's not as slick as the starred hotels. ❼–❽

Pandiyar Residency, 14 Kutchery Rd ⊕ 04362/31801. Across the canal from the Brihadishwara Temple, next to a busy flyover; it's shabby and the rooms are small for the price, but the a/c deluxe options have good temple views. ❹–❺

Parishutham, 55 Grand Anicut Canal Rd ⊕ 04362/31801, ⓕ 30318. Plush hotel with spacious, centrally a/c rooms, a large palm-fringed pool (residents only), multi-cuisine restaurant, craft shop, foreign exchange and a travel agent. Popular with tour groups, so book ahead. ❾

Sangam, Trichy Road ⊕ 04362/34151 or 34026,

ⓕ 36695. Thanjavur's newest luxury hotel is 2km southwest of the centre. International four-star standards, with comfortable a/c rooms, excellent restaurant, pool and beautiful Tanjore paintings (the one in the lobby is worth a trip here in itself). ❼–❽

TTDC Tamil Nadu, Gandhiji Road, 10min from the bus and railway stations ⊕ 04362/31421. Once the raja's guesthouse, but now a typically dilapidated state-run hotel, with more character than modern alternatives. Large, comfortable carpeted rooms (some with a/c), set around a leafy enclosed garden. ❹–❺

Valli, 2948, M.K.M. Road ⊕ 04362/31584. An exceptionally friendly place with super-clean rooms (some a/c) opening onto bright green corridors; rooms range around a leafy courtyard, and there's a popular, busy canteen downstairs. The best budget option in town. ❷–❺

Yagappa, Trichy Road ⊕ 04362/30421 or 33548. Offering spacious, well-appointed rooms with "sitouts", large, tiled bathrooms and friendly staff, there's also a bar and restaurant. Reception features intriguing furniture made from coffee roots. The twenty-percent discount for all foreigners makes this place particularly good value. ❸–❺

Shopping in Thanjavur

In an old house in the suburb of Karanthattangudi, ten minutes by auto-rickshaw from the centre of Thanjavur, V.R. Govindarajan's shop at 31 Kuthirakkatti St (⊕ 04362/30282) contains an amazing array of **antiques**, including brass pots, betel nut boxes, oil lamps, coins and Tanjore paintings. Small, modern and simple examples cost around Rs500, while large, recently made pictures with 24-carat gold decoration may cost as much as Rs20,000, and for a fine hundred-year-old painting you can expect to part with Rs80,000 or more. Upstairs, seven artists work amid a chaotic collection of clocks and bric-a-brac, and you can watch the various stages in the process of Tanjore painting.

The owner of the small craft shop at the *Parishutham* hotel is very knowledgeable about local craftsmen producing Tanjore paintings, copper "art plates" and musical instruments like the classical *vina*. A branch of the government chain, Poompuhar Handicrafts, on Gandhiji Road (next to the *TTDC Tamil Nadu* hotel), stocks copper Thanjavur "art plates", brass oil lamps and sandalwood carvings, and there's a co-operative handicrafts shop above the Sangeeta Mahal concert hall in the Royal Palace compound.

Brihadishwara Temple

Thanjavur's skyline is dominated by the huge tower of the **Brihadishwara Temple**, which for all its size lacks the grandiose excesses of later periods. The site has no great significance; the temple was constructed as much to reflect the power of its patron, King Rajaraja I, as to facilitate the worship of Shiva. Profuse **inscriptions** on the base of the main shrine provide incredibly detailed information about the organization of the temple. They show it to have been rich, both in financial terms and in ritual activity. Among recorded **gifts** from Rajaraja, from booty acquired in conquest, are the equivalent of 600lb of silver, 500lb of gold, and 250lb of assorted jewels, plus income from agricultural land throughout the Chola empire, set aside for the purpose. No less than four hundred female dancers, **devadasis** (literally "slaves to the gods", married off to the deity), were employed, and each provided with a house. Other staff – another two hundred people – included dance teachers, musicians, tailors, potters, laundrymen, goldsmiths, carpenters, astrologers, accountants and attendants for all manner of rituals and processions.

Entrance to the complex is on the east, through two **gopura** gateways some way apart. Although the outer one is the larger, both are of the same pattern: massive rectangular bases topped by pyramidal towers with carved figures and vaulted roofs. At the core of each is a monolithic sandstone lintel, said to have been brought from Tiruchirapalli, over 50km away. The outer facade of the inner *gopura* features mighty fanged *dvarpala* door guardians, mirror images of each other, and thought to be the largest monolithic sculptures in any Indian temple.

Once inside, the gigantic **courtyard** gives plenty of space to appreciate the buildings. The **main temple**, constructed of granite, consists of a long pillared *mandapa* hallway, followed by the *ardhamandapa*, or "half-hall", which in turn leads to the inner sanctum, the *garbha griha*. Above the shrine, the pyramidal *vimana* tower (at just under 61m high, the largest and tallest in India when it was built in 1010) rises in thirteen diminishing storeys, the apex being exactly one third of the size of the base. Such a design is quite different from later temples, in which the shrine towers become smaller as the *gopura* entranceways increasingly dominate – a desire to protect the sanctum sanctorum from the polluting gaze of outsiders. This *vimana* is an example of a "structured monolith", a stage removed from the earlier rock-cut architecture of the Pallavas, in which blocks of stone are assembled and then carved. As the stone that surmounts it is said to weigh eighty tonnes, there is considerable speculation as to how it got up there; the most popular theory is that the rock was hauled up a six-kilometre-long ramp. Others have suggested the use of a method comparable to the Sumer Ziggurat style of building, in which logs were placed in gaps in the masonry and the stone raised by leverage. The simplest answer, of course, is that perhaps it's not a single stone at all.

The black *shivalingam*, over 3.5m high, in the **inner sanctum** is called Adavallan, "the one who can dance well" – a reference to Shiva as Nataraja, the King of the Dance, who resides at Chidambaram and was the *ishtadevata*, chosen deity, of the king. The *lingam* is not always on view, but during puja ceremonies (8 & 11am, noon & 7.30pm), a curtain is pulled revealing the god to the devotees.

Outside, the walls of the courtyard are lined with **colonnaded passageways** – the one along the northern wall is said to be the longest in India. The one on the west, behind the temple, contains 108 *lingams* from Varanasi and (heavily graffitied) panels from the Maratha period.

In the southwest corner of the courtyard, the small **Archeological Museum** (daily 9am–1pm & 4–6pm) houses an interesting collection of sculpture, including an extremely tubby, damaged Ganesh, before-and-after photos detailing restoration work to the temple in the 1940s and displays about the Cholas. You can also buy the excellent ASI booklet, *Chola Temples*, which gives detailed accounts of Brihadishwara and the temples at Gangaikondacholapuram and Darasuram. For more on Tamil Nadu's temples, see p.1216.

Chola bronzes

Originally sacred temple objects, **Chola bronzes** are the only art form from Tamil Nadu to have penetrated the world art market. The most memorable bronze icons are the **Natarajas**, or dancing Shivas. The image of Shiva, standing on one leg, encircled by flames, with wild locks caught in mid-motion, has become almost as recognizably Indian as the Taj Mahal, and few Indian millionaires would feel their sitting rooms to be complete without one.

The principal icons of a temple are usually stationary and made of stone. Frequently, however, ceremonies require an image of the god to be led in procession outside the inner sanctum, and even through the streets. According to the canonical texts known as *Agamas*, these moving images should be made of metal. Indian bronzes are made by the **cire-perdu** ("lost-wax") process, known as *madhuchchishtavidhana* in Sanskrit. Three layers of clay mixed with burned grain husks, salt and ground cotton are applied to a figure crafted in beeswax, with a stem left protruding at each end. When that is heated, the wax melts and flows out, creating a hollow mould into which molten metal – a rich five-metal alloy (*panchaloha*) of copper, silver, gold, brass and lead – can be poured through the stems. After the metal has cooled, the clay shell is destroyed, and the stems filed off, leaving a unique completed figure, which the caster-artist, or *sthapathi*, remodels to remove blemishes and add delicate detail.

Knowledge of bronze-casting in India goes back at least as far as the Indus Valley Civilization (2500–1500 BC), and the famous "**Dancing Girl**" from Mohenjo Daro. The earliest produced in the south was made by the Andhras, whose techniques were continued by the Pallavas, the immediate antecedents of the Cholas. The few surviving **Pallava** bronzes show a sophisticated handling of the form; figures are characterized by broad shoulders, thick-set features and an overall simplicity that suggests all the detail was completed at the wax stage. The finest bronzes of all are from the **Chola** period, in the late ninth to the early eleventh century. As the Cholas were predominantly Shaivite, Nataraja, Shiva and his consort Parvati (frequently in a family group with son Skanda) and the 63 Nayanmar poet-saints are the most popular subjects. Chola bronzes display more detail than their predecessors. Human figures are invariably slim-waisted and elegant, with the male form robust and muscular and the female graceful and delicate.

The design, iconography and proportions of each figure are governed by the strict rules laid down in the **shilpa shastras**, which draw no real distinction between art, science and religion. Measurement always begins with the proportions of the artist's own hand and the image's resultant face-length as the basic unit. Then follows a scheme which is allied to the equally scientific rules applied to classical music, and specifically *tala* or rhythm. Human figures total eight face-lengths, eight being the most basic of rhythmic measures. Figures of deities are *nava-tala*, nine face-lengths.

Those bronzes produced by the few artists practising today invariably follow the Chola model; the chief centre is now **Swamimalai**, 8km west of Kumbakonam (see p.1242). Original Chola bronzes are kept in many Tamil temples, but as temple interiors are often dark it's not always possible to see them properly. Important **public collections** include the Nayak Durbar Hall Art Museum at Thanjavur, the Government State Museum at Chennai and the National Museum, New Delhi.

TAMIL NADU | Central Tamil Nadu

20

The Royal Palace Compound

The **Royal Palace Compound**, where members of the erstwhile royal family still reside, is on E Main Street (a continuation of Gandhiji Road), 2km northeast of Brihadishwara Temple. Dotted around the compound are several reminders of Thanjavur's past under the Nayaks and the Marathas, including an exhibition of oriental manuscripts and a superlative museum of **Chola bronzes**. The dusty and run-down **Tamil University Museum** contains coins and musical instruments, while near the entrance to the complex, the rambling **Royal Museum** (daily 9am–6pm; Rs1, camera Rs20) houses a sadly disintegrating and badly displayed collection of costumes, portraits, musical instruments, weapons, manuscripts and courtly accessories.

Just after the ticket office for the Royal Museum, there's a new collection – the **H.H.Raja Serfoji II Memorial Hall and Museum** (daily 9am–6pm; Rs1, Rs20 extra with camera), the outcome of a lifetime investigation into the turbulent eighteenth-century reign of Serfoji II by his grandson. Unfortunately, the result is a rather thin selection of ivory desk sets and silverware, inept royal portraits, and decaying finery in a damp upper room of the palace.

The palace buildings have been in a sorry state for years; hopes were raised for their preservation when the responsibility for maintenance passed in 1993 to the Indian National Trust for Cultural Heritage (INTACH), but almost immediately some suffered extensive damage in storms. The Sarja Madi, "seven-storey" bell tower, built by Serfoji II in 1800, is closed to the public due to its unsafe condition.

Work on the palace began in the mid-sixteenth century under Sevappa Nayak, the founder of the Nayak kingdom of Thanjavur; additions were made by the Marathas from the end of the seventeenth century onwards. Remodelled by Shaji II in 1684, the **Durbar Hall**, or hall of audience, houses a throne canopy decorated with the mirrored glass distinctive of Thanjavur. Although damaged, the ceiling and walls are elaborately painted. Five domes are striped red, green and yellow, and on the walls, friezes of leaf and pineapple designs, and trumpeting angels in a night sky show European influence.

Saraswati Mahal Library Museum

The **Saraswati Mahal Library**, one of the most important oriental manuscript collections in India, is closed to the public, but used by scholars from all over the world. More than 80 percent of its 44,000 manuscripts are in Sanskrit, many on palm leafs, and some very rare or even unique. The Tamil works include treatises on medicine and commentaries on works from the Sangam period, the earliest literature of the south.

A small **museum** (daily except Wed 10am–1pm & 2–5pm; free) displays a bizarre array of books and pictures from the collection. Among the palm-leaf manuscripts is a calligrapher's *tour de force*, in the form of a visual mantra, where each letter in the inscription "Shiva" comprises the god's name repeated in microscopically small handwriting. Most of the Maratha manuscripts, produced from the end of the seventeenth century, are on paper; they include a superbly illustrated edition of the *Mahabharata*. Sadists will be delighted to see the library managed to hang on to their copy of the explicitly illustrated **Punishments in China**, published in 1804. Next to it, full rein is given to the imagination of French artist, **Charles Le Brun** (1619–90), in a series of pictures on the subject of physiognomy. Animals such as the horse, bullock, wolf, bear, rabbit and camel are drawn in painstaking care above a series of human faces which bear an uncanny, if unlikely, resemblance to them. You can buy postcards of this scientific study and exhibits from the other palace museums in the **shop** next door.

A magnificent collection of **Chola bronzes** – the finest of them from the Tiruvengadu hoard unearthed in the 1950s – fills the **Nayak Durbar Hall Art Museum** (daily 9am–1pm & 2–5pm; Rs1), a high-ceilinged audience hall with massive pillars, dating from 1600. The elegance of the figures and delicacy of detail are unsurpassed. A tenth-century statue of Kannappa Nayannar (#174), a hunter-devotee, shows minutiae right down to his embroidered clothing, fingernails and the fine lines on his fingers. The oldest bronze, four cases left of the main doorway (#58) shows Vinadhra Dakshinamurti ("south-facing Shiva") who, with a deer on one left hand, would have originally been playing the *vina* – the musical instrument has long since gone. However, the undisputed masterpiece of the collection shows Shiva as Lord of the Animals (#86), sensuously depicted in a skimpy loin cloth, with a turban made of snakes. Next to him stands an equally stunning Parvati, his consort (#87), but the cream of the female figures, a seated, half-reclining Parvati (#97), is displayed on the opposite side of the hall.

The **Rajaraja Cholan Museum** (same hours) houses Chola stone sculpture and small objects excavated at Gangaikondacholapuram (see p.1243) such as tiny marbles, games boards, bangles and terracotta pieces. Two illuminated maps show the remarkable extent of the Chola empire under the great kings Rajaraja I and his son, Rajendra I. Towering over these buildings is the Nayak-period **arsenal**, cunningly designed to resemble a temple *gopura*, with fine views of Thanjavur from the top.

Eating and drinking

For **food**, there's the usual crop of "meals" canteens dotted around town, the best of which are *Annantha Bhavan* and the *Sri Venkantan*, both on Gandhiji Road near the textile stores. The *Sangam* hotel's swish *Thillana* restaurant is a lot pricier, but worth it for the live Carnatic music. *King's* in the *Yagappa* hotel is the best choice for a quiet beer.

Annam, *Pandiyar Residency*, 14 Kutchery Rd. Small, inexpensive and impeccably clean veg restaurant that's recommended for its cut-above-the-competition lunchtime thalis (Rs25), and evening south Indian snacks (especially the delicious cashew *uttapams*). A safe option for women travellers.

King's, *Yagappa*, Trichy Road. Seven kinds of beer are served in the usual dimly lit room, or on the "lawn" (read: "sandy back yard"), where decor includes stuffed lizard and plastic flowers in fish tanks. They also serve tasty chicken and *pakora* plate snacks.

Sathar's, Gandhiji Road. This is the town's most popular non-veg restaurant, and a pretty safe place to eat chicken (because of the constant turnover) – seating is downstairs, or on a covered terrace. Dishes are around Rs60–80. There's a mostly male clientele.

Thillana, *Sangam*, Trichy Road. Swish multi-cuisine restaurant that's renowned for its superb lunchtime south Indian thalis (11am–3pm; Rs75). Evenings fea-

Moving on from Thanjavur

Travelling to Trichy, it's best to catch a bus (from the less crowded new bus stand, 4km southwest of the centre) rather than the train, as most services from Thanjavur junction are slower passenger ones that frequently run late. The same applies to buses for Kumbakonam and Pondicherry. There's no direct train service to Chennai from Thanjavur – the best route is to take a bus to Trichy, then hop on one of the frequent daily express trains. In the opposite direction, the daily overnight Sethu Express #6714 (leaves 9.50pm) runs as far as Rameshwaram. For Madurai, you either have to travel direct by bus, or take a bus to Trichy and pick up a train from there.

Kodikkarai (Point Calimere)

On a small knob of land jutting out into the sea, 65km south of Nagapattinam and 80km southeast of Thanjavur, **Kodikkarai Bird Sanctuary** plays host to around 250 species in a 17-square-kilometre area of tidal swampland, known as "the great swamp", and dry evergreen forest. On the way to the sanctuary, you pass through 50,000 acres of salt marshes around **Vedaranyam**, the nearest town, 11km north. Vast salt fields, traditionally the mainstay of the local economy, line the road, the salt drying in thatched mounds. During the Independence struggle this was an important site for demonstrations in sympathy with Gandhi's famous salt protest (see p.706). Over the last few years, however, salt has been pushed into second place by prawn cultivation, which brings a good income, but has necessitated widespread forest clearance and has reduced the numbers of birds visiting Kodikkarai.

The **best time** to visit the sanctuary is between November and February, when migratory birds come, mostly from Iran, Russia and Poland, to spend the winter. The rarest species include black bittern, barheaded goose, ruddy shelduck, Indian blackcrested baza and eastern steppe eagle. During December and January the swamps host spotted billed pelicans and around 10,000 flamingos – who live on tiny shrimp (the source of the lurid pink colouring of their plumage), and whose numbers have dropped from the 30,000 that wintered here in the days before prawn production took off. The deep forest is the home of one of the most colourful birds in the world, the Indian pitta (*pitta brachyura*).

Prodigiously well-informed local **guides**, equipped with powerful binoculars, can take you to key wildlife haunts. The Forest Department works with the Mumbai Natural History Society to ring birds and trace their migrating patterns, and occasionally the BNHS organizes **field trips** around the area.

From the jetty, you might be lucky enough to spot a school of **dolphins**. To do so, however, you need to seek permission from the Navy Command – Kodikkarai is only 40km across the Palk Strait from Jaffna, and from the grounds of the *Rest House* (see below) the navy monitors all seaborne activity between Sri Lanka and the Indian coast.

Practicalities

Kodikkarai can only be reached (by regular bus) via Vedaranyam, connected by **bus** to Nagapattinam, Thanjavur, Trichy, Chennai and Ramanathapuram (for Rameshwaram). The nearest **railway station** is 30km away at Tiruthuraipondi.

The only **accommodation** in the area, the Forest Department's exceptionally inexpensive *Poonarai Rest House* (reserve through DFO, 281/1846 W Main Street, Thanjavur, ✆04362/613 009, or the wildlife warden in Nagapattinam; ❶), has ten plain, spacious rooms, each with chairs, desk, fan, bedding, bath and balcony. Apart from in January, when the rest house is invariably full, it's usually possible to turn up without a reservation. **Food** is limited to a couple of chai shops outside the gate, although staff will bring it in if asked. If you need to eat in **Vedaranyam** turn left out of the bus stand, and again at a T-junction, into the main bazaar, Melai Street. The best place is the simple *Karaivani*, on the left-hand side, which serves veg "leaf" meals.

Tiruchirapalli and around

TIRUCHIRAPALLI – more commonly referred to as **Trichy** – stands in the plains between the Shevaroy and Palani hills, just under 100km north of Madurai. Dominated by the dramatic Rock Fort, it's a sprawling commercial centre with a modern feel; the town itself holds little attraction, but pilgrims flock through en route to the spectacular **Ranganathaswamy Temple** in **Srirangam**, 6km north.

The precise date of Trichy's foundation is uncertain, but though little early architecture remains, it is clear that between 200 and 1000 AD control of the city passed between the Pallavas and Pandyas. The Chola kings who gained supremacy in the eleventh century embarked upon ambitious building projects, reaching a zenith with the Ranganathaswamy Temple. In the twelfth century, the Cholas were ousted by the Vijayanagar kings of Hampi, who then stood up against Muslim invasions until 1565, when they succumbed to the might of the sultans of the Deccan. Less than fifty years later the Nayaks of Madurai came to power, constructing the fort and firmly establishing Trichy as a trading city. After almost a century of struggle against the French and British, who both sought lands in southeast Tamil Nadu, the town came under British control until it was declared part of Tamil Nadu state in 1947.

Arrival, information and orientation

Trichy's **airport**, 8km south of the centre, has flights to and from Chennai (daily except Thurs & Sun), Cochin (Tues, Thurs & Sat) and Calicut (Wed & Sun). The journey into town, by taxi (Rs100) or bus (#7, #28, #59, #63, #122 or #K1) takes less than half an hour; for enquiries and bookings go to Indian Airlines, 4A Dindigul Rd (℡0431/480233). There are also flights (4 weekly) from **Colombo** on Air Lanka, based in the *Femina* hotel; ℡0431/460844.

Trichy's main railway station, **Trichy Junction** – which has given its name to the southern district of town – provides frequent rail links with Chennai, Madurai and the eastern coastline. From here you're within easy reach of most hotels, restaurants and banks, as well as the **bus stands**. There are two stands – **Central** and **State Express** – opposite each other, but no fixed rules about where a particular bus will depart from; you just have to keep asking. State Express buses run frequently to major towns such as Madurai, Kodaikanal and Pondicherry, right around the clock. Private buses, if you really want to risk their manic and dangerous driving, line up along Rockins Road and hussle people aboard. The efficient local city service (#1) that leaves from the platform on Rockins Road, opposite the *Shree Krishna* restaurant, is the most convenient way of getting to the Rock Fort, the temples and Srirangam. **Rickshaws** are also widely available.

The **tourist office** (Mon–Fri 10am–5.45pm; ℡0431/460136), which proffers travel information but no maps, is opposite the State Express bus stand, just outside the *Tamil Nadu* hotel. **Banks** for foreign exchange include the State Bank of India on Dindigul Road, but will only change American Express (dollars only) or Thomas Cook (sterling only) travellers' cheques. Far more efficient is the forex dealer (Mon–Sat 10am–6pm) in the Jenney Plaza Building, a mall just beyond the *Jenney's Residency* hotel, where you can change travellers' cheques or currency, but credit cards aren't accepted.

Email can be sent from the Grace Soft Netcafé, on the ground floor of Jenney's Plaza (Mon–Sat 9.15am–11pm, Sun 5pm–10pm; Rs35/hr).

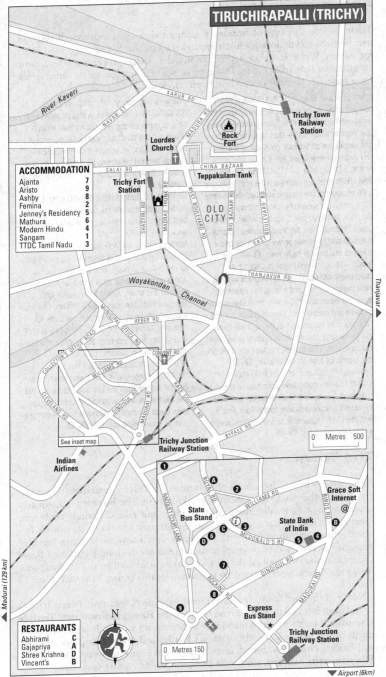

▲ Srirangam & Chennai (315 km)

TIRUCHIRAPALLI (TRICHY)

River Kaveri

KARUR RD

NAVAB ST

MADURA RD

Rock Fort

Trichy Town Railway Station

Lourdes Church ✝

SALAI RD

CHINA BAZAAR

Trichy Fort Station

Teppakulam Tank

ACCOMMODATION

Ajanta	7
Aristo	9
Ashby	8
Femina	2
Jenney's Residency	5
Mathura	6
Modern Hindu	4
Sangam	1
TTDC Tamil Nadu	3

SHASTRI RD

MADRAS TRUNK RD

WEST BOULEVARD RD

BIG BAZAAR RD

OLD CITY

EAST BOULEVARD RD

EAST BOULEVARD

Woyakondan Channel

THANJAVUR RD

Thanjavur ▶

MUNICIPAL OFFICE ROAD

HEBER RD

COLLECTOR'S OFFICE ROAD

CONVENT RD ✝

WILLIAMS RD

CLEVELAND RD

DINDIGUL RD

MADURAI RD

RACE COURSE RD

BYPASS RD

See inset map

Trichy Junction Railway Station

| 0 | Metres | 500 |

Indian Airlines

▲ Madurai (129 km)

❶

ROYAL RD

Ⓐ

❷

WILLIAMS RD

Grace Soft Internet @

State Bus Stand

RACQUET COURT LANE

ⓘ ❸

Ⓒ

MCDONALD'S RD

State Bank of India

BIRDS RD

Ⓑ

❻ Ⓓ

❺ ❹

DINDIGUL RD

MADURAI RD

❼

ROCKINS RD

❽

❾

Express Bus Stand ✦

Trichy Junction Railway Station

| 0 | Metres | 150 |

N

RESTAURANTS

Abhirami	C
Gajapriya	A
Shree Krishna	D
Vincent's	B

20

TAMIL NADU | Tiruchirapalli and around

1253

▼ Airport (6km)

Accommodation

Trichy has no shortage of **hotels** to accommodate the thousands of pilgrims that visit the town; dozens cluster around the bus stands and offer good value for money. While most are rather characterless lodges, there are a few more comfortable upmarket hotels. Traffic noise is a real problem in this area, so ask for a room at the back of any hotel you check into.

Ajanta, Rockins Road ℡ 0431/415504. A huge, 86-room complex centred on its own Vijayanagar shrine, and with an opulent Tirupati deity in reception. Popular with middle-class pilgrims; rooms (the singles are particularly good value) are plain and clean, some with a/c. ❷–❹

Aristo, 2 Dindigul Rd ℡ 0431/415858. A jaded off-beat 1960s hotel, set back from the road in its own quiet compound. The bargain standard rooms have a fair amount of superficial grime, but are huge for the price, and open onto a deep common veranda. Cosier "cottages" are the honeymooners' alternative, with pebble-strewn verandas, wacky colour schemes and mouldy bathrooms. ❸–❺

Ashby, 17A Junction Rd ℡ 0431/460652. An atmospheric old-fashioned Raj-era place which is most foreign tourists' first choice. The rooms are large and impeccably clean, with fresh towels, soap, cable TV and mozzie coils. There's decent bar and a little courtyard restaurant that the staff will press you to use (only eat here if the place is doing brisk business, otherwise its likely the food has been sitting around for a while). Great value. ❷–❸

Femina, 14C Williams Rd ℡ 0431/414501, ℻ 410615. Well-maintained place east of the state bus stand. A sprawling block of rooms and suites, some with balconies looking to the Rock Fort, features plush restaurants, travel services, shops and a 24hr coffee bar. ❺–❼

Jenney's Residency, 3/14 McDonald's Rd ℡ 0431/461301, ℻ 461451. A slightly jaded marble and mirrors place with comfortable rooms. Boasts a "Wild West" bar, and two good restaurants – including an upmarket Chinese place – cocktail bar and swimming pool (open to nonresidents for Rs100). It's certainly not cheap at $55 a night. ❾

Mathura, 9C Rockins Rd ℡ 0431/414737. Large, modern hotel opposite the bus stand. One of the best budget deals in the area, but noisy – ask for a back room. ❷–❸

Modern Hindu, 6B McDonald's Rd ℡ 0431/417858. Best of the rock-bottom lodges: an old-fashioned place, with very basic rooms (those on the top floor open onto a large common veranda and shady wall of trees), some with attached bath. The rules include "no bad character women". Single occupancy rates available. ❷

Sangam, Collector's Office Road ℡ 0431/464700. Trichy's top hotel boasts all the facilities of a four-star, including an excellent pool. ❽

TTDC Tamil Nadu, McDonald's Road ℡ 0431/414346. One of their better hotels, and just far enough from the bus stand to escape the din. Best value are the non-a/c doubles, though even these are dowdier than most of the competition; all rooms have cable TV. ❷–❻

The Town

Although Trichy conducts most of its business in **Trichy Junction**, the southern district, the main sights are at least 4km north. The **bazaars** immediately north heave with locally made cigars, textiles and fake diamonds made into inexpensive jewellery and used for dance costumes. Thanks to the town's frequent, cheap air connection with Sri Lanka, you'll also come across boxes of smuggled Scotch and photographic film. Head north along Big Bazaar Road (a continuation of Dindigul Road) and you're confronted by the dramatic profile of the **Rock Fort**, topped by the seventeenth-century Vinayaka (Ganesh) Temple.

North of the fort, the River Kaveri marks a wide boundary between Trichy's crowded streets and its more serene temples; the **Ranganathaswamy Temple** is so large it holds much of the village of Srirangam within its courtyards. Also north of the Kaveri is the elaborate **Sri Jambukeshwara Temple**, while several British **churches** dotted around town make an interesting contrast. The **Shantivanam ashram**, a bus ride away, is open to visitors year round.

The Rock Fort

Trichy's **Rock Fort** (daily 6am–8pm; Rs1; Rs10 extra with camera), looming incongruously above the bazaars in the north of town, is best reached by bus (#1) from outside the railway station, or from Dindigul Road; rickshaws will try to charge you Rs50 or more for the five-minute ride.

The massive sand-coloured rock on which the fort rests towers to a height of more than 80m, its irregular sides smoothed by wind and rain. The Pallavas were the first to cut into it, but it was the Nayaks who grasped the site's potential as a fort, adding only a few walls and bastions as fortifications. From the entrance, at the north end of China Bazaar, a long flight of red-and-white painted steps cuts steeply uphill, past a series of Pallava and Pandya rock-cut temples (closed to non-Hindus), to the **Ganesh Temple** crowning the hilltop. The views from its terrace are spectacular, taking in the Ranganathaswamy and Jambukeshwara temples to the north, their *gopuras* rising from a sea of palm trees, and the cubic concrete sprawl of central Trichy to the south.

Srirangam: Ranganathaswamy Temple

The **Ranganathaswamy Temple** at **Srirangam**, 6km north of Trichy, is among the most revered shrines to Vishnu in south India, and also one of the largest and liveliest. Enclosed by seven rectangular walled courtyards and covering more than sixty hectares, it stands on an island defined by a tributary of the River Kaveri. This location symbolizes the transcendence of Vishnu, housed in the sanctuary reclining on the coils of the snake Adisesha, who in legend formed an island for the god, resting on the primordial Ocean of Chaos.

Frequent **buses** from Trichy pull in and leave from outside the southern gate. The temple is approached from the south. A gateway topped with an immense and heavily carved *gopura*, plastered and painted in bright pinks, blues and yellows, and completed as recently as 1987, leads to the outermost courtyard, the latest of seven built between the fifth and seventeenth centuries. Most of the present structure dates from the late fourteenth century, when the temple was renovated and enlarged after a disastrous sacking in 1313. The outer three courtyards, or *prakaras*, form the hub of the temple community, housing ascetics, priests, and musicians.

At the fourth wall, the entrance to the temple proper, visitors remove footwear before passing through a high gateway, topped by a magnificent *gopura* and lined with small shrines to teachers, hymn-singers and sages. In earlier days, this fourth *prakara* would have formed the outermost limit of the temple, and was the closest members of the lowest castes could get to the sanctuary. It contains some of the finest and oldest buildings of the complex, including a temple to the goddess **Ranganayaki** in the northwest corner where devotees worship before approaching Vishnu's shrine. On the eastern side of the *prakara*, the heavily carved "thousand pillared" *kalyan mandapa*, or hall, was constructed in the late Chola period.

The pillars of the outstanding **Sheshagiriraya Mandapa**, south of the *kalyan mandapa*, are decorated with rearing steeds and hunters, representing the triumph of good over evil.

To the right of the gateway into the fourth courtyard, a small **museum** (daily 10am–noon & 3–5pm) houses a modest collection of stone and bronze sculptures, and some delicate ivory plaques. For Rs5, you can climb to the roof of the fourth wall and take in the view over the temple rooftops and *gopuras*, which increase in size from the centre outwards. The central tower, crowning the holy sanctuary, is coated in gold and carved with images of Vishnu's incarnations, on each of its four sides.

Inside the gate to the third courtyard – the final section of the temple open to non–Hindus – is a pillared hall, the **Garuda Mandapa**, carved throughout in typical Nayak style. Maidens, courtly donors and Nayak rulers feature on the pillars that surround the central shrine to Garuda, the man-eagle vehicle of Vishnu.

The dimly lit innermost courtyard, the most sacred part of the temple, shelters the image of Vishnu in his aspect of Ranganatha, reclining on the serpent Adisesha. The shrine is usually entered from the south, but for one day each year, during the **Vaikuntha Ekadasi festival**, the north portal is opened; those who pass through this "doorway to heaven" can anticipate great merit. Most of the temple's daily festivals take place in this enclosure, beginning each morning with *vina*-playing and hymn-singing as Vishnu is awakened in the presence of a cow and an elephant, and ending just after 9pm with similar ceremonies.

For more on Ranganathaswamy and Tamil Nadu's other great temples, see p.1216.

Eating

To **eat** well in Trichy, you won't have to stray far from the bus stand, where the town's most popular "meals" joints do a day-long roaring trade. For more atmosphere, stroll further up McDonald's to *Vincent's*, where you can eat alfresco.

Abhirami, 10 Rockins Rd, opposite the bus stand. Trichy's most famous south Indian serves up unbeatable value lunchtime "meals" (Rs20), and the standard range of snacks the rest of the day. They also have a "fast food" counter where you can get *dosas* and *uttapams* at any time. It opens at 6.30am for piping hot *wada-pongal* breakfasts.

Gajapriya, on the ground floor of the *Gajapriya* hotel, Royal Road. Non-veg north Indian and noodle dishes are specialities of this small, but blissfully cool and clean a/c restaurant. A good place to chill out over coffee; there's a separate "family" room for women.

Shree Krishna, 9C Rockins Rd, opposite the bus stand. Delicious and very filling American or South Indian "set breakfasts" (Rs23), specialities from all over the south after 6.30pm, and unlimited banana-leaf thalis (Rs20), all served with a big smile.

Vincent's Restaurant, next door to the bakery, Dindigul Road. An "Oriental" theme restaurant, set back from the road in its own terrace, with mock pagodas, concrete bamboo, and a multi-cuisine menu that includes tasty chicken tikka and other tandoori dishes. A bit shabby now, but it's an escape from the hectic bus stand area. No alcohol; opens at 5pm.

Madurai

One of the oldest cities in south Asia, **MADURAI**, on the banks of the River Vaigai, has been an important centre of worship and commerce for as long as there has been civilization in south India – indeed, it has long been described as "the Athens of the East". Not surprisingly then, when the Greek ambassador Megasthenes came here in 302 BC, he wrote of its splendour, and described its queen, Pandai, as "a daughter of Herakles". Meanwhile, the Roman geographer Strabo complained at how the city's silk, pearls and spices were draining the imperial coffers of Rome. It was this lucrative trade that enabled the **Pandyan** dynasty to erect the mighty **Meenakshi–Sundareshwarar Temple**. Although today surrounded by a sea of modern concrete cubes, the massive *gopuras* of this vast complex, writhing with multicoloured mythological figures and crowned by golden finials, remain the greatest man-made spectacle of the south. Any day of the

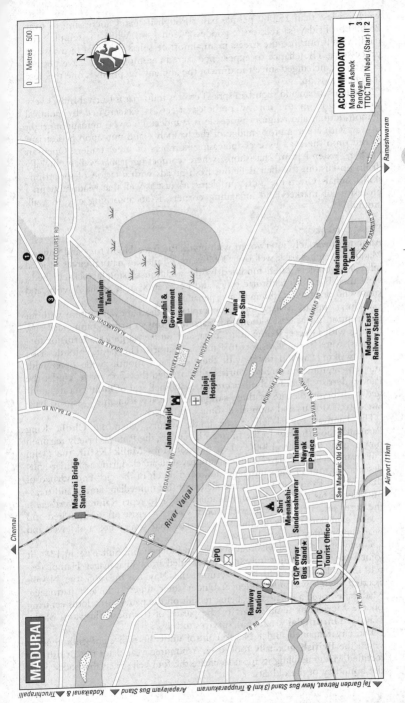

MADURAI

ACCOMMODATION
Madurai Ashok	1
Pandyan	3
TTDC Tamil Nadu (Star) II	2

Racecourse Rd
Tallakulam Tank
Alagarkovil Rd
Gokale Rd
Gandhi & Government Museums
Pt Rajiv Rd
Tamukkan Rd
Panakal Hospitali Rd
Anna Bus Stand
Jama Masjid
Kodaikanal Rd
Rajaji Hospital
Madurai Bridge Station
River Vaigai
GPO
Shri Meenakshi-Sundareshwarar
Thirumalai Nayak Palace
STC/Periyar Bus Stand
TTDC Tourist Office
Railway Station
See Madurai: Old City map
Munichalai Rd
Palayu
Old Kosavar Rd
Ramnad Rd
Mariamman Tepparulam Tank
New Ramnad Rd
Madurai East Railway Station
TPK Rd
TB Rd

◄ Chennai
◄ Taj Garden Retreat, New Bus Stand (3 km) & Tiruparakunram
◄ Arapalayam Bus Stand
◄ Kodaikanal & Tiruchirapalli
▼ Airport (11km)
▼ Rameshwaram

0 Metres 500
N

week no less than 15,000 people pass through its gates; increasing to over 25,000 on Friday (sacred to the goddess Meenakshi), while the temple's ritual life spills out into the streets in an almost ceaseless round of festivals and processions. The chance to experience sacred ceremonies that have persisted largely unchanged since the time of the ancient Egyptians is one that few travellers pass up.

Madurai's urban and suburban sprawl creates traffic jams to rival India's very worst. Chaos on the narrow, potholed streets is exacerbated by political demonstrations and religious processions, wandering cows – demanding right of way with a peremptory nudge of the haunch – and put-upon pedestrians forced onto the road by ever-increasing numbers of street traders. Open-air kitchens extend from chai-shops, where competing *parota*-wallahs literally drum up custom for their delicious fresh breads with a tattoo of spoon-on-skillet signals. Given the traffic problems, it's just as well that Madurai, with a profusion of markets and intriguing corners, is an absorbing city to walk around.

Some history

Although invariably interwoven with myth, the traceable history and fame of Madurai stretches back well over 2000 years. Numerous natural **caves** in local hills, and boulders, often modified by the addition of simple rock-cut beds, were used both in prehistoric times and by ascetics, such as the Ajivikas and Jains, who practised withdrawal and penance.

Madurai appears to have been the capital of the Pandyan empire without interruption for at least a thousand years. It became a major commercial city, trading with Greece, Rome and China, and *yavanas* (a generic term for foreigners) were frequent visitors to Pandyan seaports. The Tamil epics describe them walking around town with their eyes and mouths wide open with amazement, much as foreign tourists still do when they first arrive. Under the Pandya dynasty, Madurai also became an established seat of Tamil culture, credited with being the site of three **sangams**, "literary academies", said to have lasted 10,000 years and supported some 8000 poets.

The Pandyas' capital fell in the tenth century, when the **Chola** King Parantaka took the city. In the thirteenth century, the Pandyas briefly regained power until the early 1300s, when the notorious **Malik Kafur**, the Delhi Sultanate's "favourite slave", made an unprovoked attack during a plunder-and-desecration tour of the south, and destroyed much of the city. Forewarned of the raid, the Pandya king, Sundara, fled with his immediate family and treasure, leaving his uncle and rival, Vikrama Pandya, to repel Kafur. Nevertheless, the latter returned to Delhi with booty said to consist of "six hundred and twelve elephants, ninety-six thousand *mans* of gold, several boxes of jewels and pearls and twenty thousand horses".

Shortly after this raid Madurai became an independent Sultanate; in 1364, it joined the Hindu **Vijayanagar** empire, ruled from Vijayanagar/Hampi (see p.1442) and administered by governors, the **Nayaks**. In 1565, the Nayaks asserted their own independence. Under their supervision and patronage, Madurai enjoyed a renaissance, being rebuilt on the pattern of a lotus centring on the Meenakshi Temple. Part of the palace of the most illustrious of the Nayaks, **Thirumalai** (1623–55), survives today.

The city remained under Nayak control until the mid-eighteenth century when the **British** gradually took over. A hundred years later the British de-fortified Madurai, filling its moat to create the four Veli streets that today mark the boundary of the old city.

Arrival and information

Madurai's small domestic **airport** (℡ 0452/671333, or 670433), 12km south of the city, is served by flights to and from Chennai, Mumbai and Thiruvananthapuram. Theoretically you should be able to get information at the **Government of Tamil Nadu Tourist Information Centre** booth by the exit, but it's not always open to meet flights. Very simple snack meals ("bread-omelette") are served at the **restaurant** (daily 9am–5pm). There's also a bookshop and a branch of Indian Bank, but they can't change money. **Taxis** into the city charge a fixed rate of around Rs200. City Bus #10A leaves frequently from near the exit and will drop you at Periyar Bus Stand in town.

Arriving in Madurai by **bus**, you come in at one of five stands, all served by long-distance and city buses. In the centre, only local city buses operate from either **STC bus stand**, or **Periyar stand** next door. Both are on W Veli Street in the west of the old city, and are very close to the railway station and most accommodation. **Arapalayam bus stand** is in the northwest, close to the south bank of the river, about 2km from the railway station; it serves all state buses to and from towns in the west, including Kodaikanal and Coimbatore, and Kerala. **New bus stand** is in the southwest, 5km from the centre, and is where all State Express buses stop; it serves all major long-distance destinations, including Trichy, Kanniyakumari, Chennai, Kerala, Bangalore, Karnataka and Andhra Pradesh. **Anna bus stand**, for points north, such as the Chola cities and Rameshwaram, lies 5km out in the northeast, north of the Vaigai. Wherever you arrive, the easiest and cheapest way in is to take one of the frequent city buses into a central bus stand, then jump in an auto-rickshaw to your hotel. From W Veli Street stands, though, it's feasible to reach most of the budget places on the west side of town by cycle rickshaw or on foot.

Madurai's clean and well-maintained **railway station** is just west of the centre off W Veli Street. You can leave your luggage at the cloakroom (24hr) next to the **reservations office** (Mon–Sat 8am–2pm & 2.15pm–8pm, Sun 8am–2pm) in the main hall, where you'll also find a very helpful branch of **Tourism Department Information Centre** (daily 6.30am–8.30pm). There's a good veg **canteen** on Platform 1, and, unusually, a **prepaid auto-rickshaw** and **taxi booth** outside the main entrance, open to coincide with train arrivals.

The **Tourist Dept Main Office** is on W Veli Street (Mon–Fri 10am–5.45pm, sometimes Sat 10am–1pm; ℡ 0452/734757). However, its staff are less helpful than those at the **railway station office** (see above), which is the best place for general information and maps about Madurai and the surrounding areas, and they provide details of **car rental**. They will also arrange, with a little notice, **city tours** (7am–noon or 3pm–8pm; Rs100 per head) in a minibus with one of the government-approved **guides**, who can otherwise usually be found at the southern entrance to the temple. Find out their names first at the tourist office as they usually speak better English and are reliable. Unregistered guides may be cheaper but you may well find yourself being dragged around commission-paying shops rather than the sights. Official guided city tours, for one to four visitors, cost around Rs250 for a half-day, and Rs350 for up to eight hours. The fee for a temple tour is negotiable. If you want to rent a **taxi** to see the outlying sights, the rank at the main railway station abides by government set rates; a full-day city tour will cost Rs550.

Madurai's **post office** is at the corner of Scott Road and N Veli Street. For postal services, enter on the Scott Road side (Mon–Sat 8am–7.30pm, Sun & hols 9am–4.30pm; speedpost 10am–7pm). For **poste restante** (Mon–Sat

9.30am–5.30pm), go to the Philatelic Bureau on the southwest corner of the building, and remember to take along your passport.

Internet access is offered everywhere, but by far the most efficient is at Net Tower, 13/8 Kaka Thoppu St, in the side street by *Hotel International*, and 60/42 West Tower St, just in front of *West Tower* hotel. Both have rows of private cubicles, charge an extremely cheap Rs20 per hour, and are open 8am–midnight every day.

The best place in Madurai to **change money** is Alagendran Forex Services, 168 N Veli St, opposite the Head Post Office (Mon–Sat 9am–6.30pm), which offers more or less the same rates as the State Bank of India, 6 W Veli St. Mastercard and Visa are accepted at the Andhra Bank on W Chitrai Street, but no currency or travellers' cheques. If you get caught out by a public holiday or need to change money in the night, head for the *Supreme* hotel, whose 24hr foreign exchange desk is open to non-visitors.

Bike rental at low rates is available at SV, W Tower Street, near the west entrance to the temple, or the stall on W Veli Street, opposite the *Tamil Nadu* hotel.

Accommodation

Madurai has a wide range of **accommodation**, from rock-bottom lodges to good, clean mid-range places that cater for the flocks of pilgrims and tourists. There's a cluster of hotels on **W Perumal Maistry Street**. Upmarket options lie a few kilometres out of the town centre, north of the Vaigai. The **railway retiring rooms** (Rs150), 1st floor, stairway on platform 1 (turn right from the main entrance hall), are huge and cleanish, some with a/c, but often booked.

Aarathy, 9 Perumalkoil, W Mada Street ☎0452/731571. Great location, overlooking the Kudalagar Temple near the STC bus stand. All rooms with TV, some with a/c and a balcony. Their busy open-air restaurant is especially popular when the temple elephant, Mahalakshmi, is led through each morning. Usually full of foreigners so book ahead, but ask to see your room before checking in, as not all of them are up to standard. ❹–❺

Duke, 6 N Veli St, close to the junction with W Veli Street ☎0452/741154. A modern hotel, with larger-than-average non-a/c rooms; ask for one on the "open side", with a window. Good value. ❸

International, 46 W Perumal Maistry St ☎0452/741553. Newly renovated, this place is a rather chaotic lodge with laid-back service, but the rooms are decent and all have 72-channel cable TV, in case you get templed-out. ❸–❺

Madurai Ashok, Alagarkoil Road ☎0452/537531, ⊕537530. Plush hotel on the northern outskirts, with 24hr room service, bar, currency exchange, craft shops and a pleasant swimming pool. ❾

New College House, 2 Town Hall Rd ☎0452/742971. Currently undergoing a major refit, this is a huge maze with more than 200 rooms (a few with a/c), and one of the town's best "meals" canteens on the ground floor (see p.1268). The

very cheapest rooms are decidedly grimy, but they are likely to have vacancies when everywhere else is full. ❷–❺

Padman, 1 Perumal Tank West St ☎0452/740702, ⊕743629. The views from the front-side rooms of this modern hotel, overlooking the ruined Perumal tank, are worth paying extra for. Clean, comfortable and central with a rooftop restaurant. Again, another popular place with a foreign crowd, so book in advance. ❺

Pandyan, Race Course, north of the river ☎0452/537090, ⊕533424. A comfortable, centrally a/c hotel with a good restaurant, bar, exchange facilities, travel agency, bookstores and several craft shops. Nice garden, too. ❽–❾

Prem Nivas, 102 W Perumal Maistry St ☎0452/742532, ⊕743618. From the outside this place looks a lot swankier than it is, but the spacious rooms make it among the best mid-price deals in the city. ❹–❺

Sri Devi, 20 W Avani Moola St ☎0452/747431. Good-value, spotless non-a/c doubles right next to the temple mean this place is always filled with foreigners. There have been recent complaints about indecent behaviour of staff towards women. Also, keep your corridor-facing bathroom window tightly closed. For a romantic splurge, splash out on their "deluxe" a/c rooftop room (❻), which has matchless views over the western *gopura*. No restaurant, but they will order in food and beer for you. ❷

Supreme, 110 W Perumal Maistry St ☏0452/743151, ℗742637. A large, swish and central hotel, with a great rooftop restaurant (see p.1268) for sundowners. Boasts a 24hr forex desk, internet facilities and travel counter. A "duplex" room gets you views of Yanna Malai hill range. Book in advance. ❺–❻

Taj Garden Retreat, Pasumalai hills ☏0452/601020. Madurai's most exclusive hotel; a beautifully refurbished colonial house in the hills overlooking the city and temples, albeit 6km out. There are three kinds of rooms: "Standard" ($120); "Superior", in the period block ($145); and "Deluxe" modern cottages with the best views ($160). Facilities include gourmet restaurant, pool, bar and tennis court. ❾

TM, 50 W Perumal Maistry St ☏0452/741651. Despite the rather unfriendly reception and institutional atmosphere, this is an immaculately clean option, with spotless attached bathrooms; the top-floor rooms are the airiest. It's one of the best of the budget bunch on this street. ❸–❺

TTDC Hotel Tamil Nadu I, W Veli Street ☏0452/737471, ℗731945. Somewhat on a limb, away from the atmosphere of the temples and the bazaar, but newly refurbished with spacious rooms overlooking a leafy courtyard. The cheapest rooms are especially good value. ❷–❺

TTDC Tamil Nadu II (Star), Alagarkoil Road ☏0452/537461, ℗533203. Another government hotel, even further from the temples, 5km north of the centre. Good-sized rooms (some a/c) and a veg restaurant, though service can be rather half-hearted. ❹–❺

West Tower, 60 W Tower St ☏0452/746908. The selling point is its proximity to the temple, and the great views from the rooftop (but not from the rooms), where there's a pleasant little thatched terrace. However, the rooms are extremely basic and very overpriced; some have a/c. ❹–❻

The City

Although considerably enlarged and extended over the years, the overall layout of Madurai's **old city**, south of the River Vaigai, has remained largely unchanged since the first centuries AD, comprising a series of concentric squares centred on the massive **Meenakshi Temple**. Aligned with the cardinal points, the street plan forms a giant *mandala*, or magical diagram, whose sacred properites are believed to be activated during mass circumambulations of the central temple, always conducted in a clockwise direction.

North of the river, Madurai becomes markedly more mundane and irregular. You're only likely to cross the Vaigai to reach the city's more expensive hotels, the Gandhi Museum, and the Anna bus stand.

Sri Meenakshi-Sundareshwara Temple

Enclosed by a roughly rectangular six-metre-high wall, in the manner of a fortified palace, the **Meenakshi-Sundareshwarar Temple** (daily 5am–12.30pm & 4–9.30pm) is one of the largest temple complexes in India. Much of it was constructed during the Nayak period between the sixteenth and eighteenth centuries, but certain parts are very much older. The principal shrines (closed to non-Hindus) are those to Sundareshwar (Shiva) and his consort Meenakshi (a form of Parvati); unusually, the goddess takes precedence and is always worshipped first.

For the first-time visitor, confronted with a confusing maze of shrines, sculptures and colonnades, and unaware of the logic employed in their arrangement, it's very easy to get disorientated. However, if you're not in a hurry, this should not deter you. Quite apart from the estimated 33,000 sculptures to arrest your attention, the life of the temple is absolutely absorbing, and many visitors find themselves drawn back at several different times of the day. Be it the endless round of puja ceremonies, loud *nagaswaram* and *tavil* music, weddings, brahmin boys under religious instruction in the *Vedas*, the prostrations of countless devotees, the glittering market stalls inside the east entrance, or, best of all, a fes-

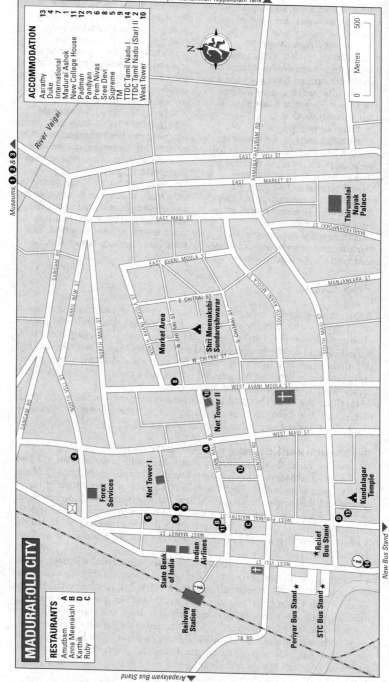

MADURAI: OLD CITY

RESTAURANTS

Amutbam	A
Anna Meenakshi	B
Karthik	D
Ruby	C

ACCOMMODATION

Aarathy	13
Duke	4
International	7
Madurai Ashok	1
New College House	11
Padman	12
Pandyan	3
Prem Nivas	6
Sree Devi	8
Supreme	5
TM	9
TDC Tamil Nadu I	14
TTDC Tamil Nadu (Star) II	2
West Tower	10

Vandiyur Mariamman Teppakulam Tank ▲

River Vaigai

RAMANATHAPURAM RD

EAST VELI ST

EAST MARKET ST

EAST MASI ST

EAST AVANI MOOLA ST

E CHITRAI ST

Shri Meenakshi Sundareshwarar

N CHITRAI ST

S CHITRAI ST

W CHITRAI ST

Market Area

SOUTH AVANI MOOLA ST

MANJANKARA ST

MAHLYADAMPOKKI ST

Thirumalai Nayak Palace

SANGAM RD

VAKIL NEW ST

NORTH VELI ST

NORTH MASI ST

NORTH AVANI MOOLA ST

SOUTH MASI ST

WEST AVANI MOOLA ST

WEST MASI ST

Net Tower II

DINIGUL RD

Kundalagar Temple

Net Tower I

TOWN HALL RD

WEST PERUMAL MAISTRY ST

WEST MARKET ST

Forex Services

State Bank of India

Indian Airlines

Railway Station

WEST VELI ST

★ Relief Bus Stand

Periyar Bus Stand ★

STC Bus Stand ★

TB RD

New Bus Stand ▶

Arapalayam Bus Stand ▲

N

0   Metres   500

tival procession, something is always going on to make this quite simply one of the most compelling places in Tamil Nadu.

Approximately fifty priests work in the temple, and live in houses close to the north entrance. They are easily identified – each wears a white *dhoti* (*veshti* in Tamil) tied between the legs; on top of this, around the waist, is a second, coloured cloth, usually of silk. Folded into the cloth, a small bag contains holy white ash. The bare-chested priests invariably carry a small towel over the shoulder. Most wear earrings and necklaces including *rudraksha* beads, sacred to Shiva. As Shaivite priests, they place three horizontal stripes of white ash on the forehead, arms, shoulders and chest and a red powder dot, sacred to the goddess, above the bridge of the nose. Most also wear their long hair tied into a knot, with the forehead shaved. Inside the temple they also carry brass trays holding offerings of camphor and ash.

Madurai takes the **gopura**, so prominent in other southern temples, to its ultimate extreme. The entire complex has no less than twelve such towers; set into the outer walls, the four largest reach a height of around 46m, and are visible for miles outside the city. Each is covered with a profusion of gaily painted stucco gods and demons, with the occasional live monkey scampering and chattering among the divine images. After a referendum in the 1950s, the *gopuras*, which had become monochrome and dilapidated, were repainted in the vivid greens, blues, and bright reds you can see today; they have to be completely redone every ten years or so (the last repaint was in the mid-1990s). It is sometimes possible, for a small fee, to climb the southern and tallest tower, to enjoy superb views over the town; for permission, enquire with the guards at one of the gateways.

The most popular **entrance** is on the east side, where the *gopura* gateway has reopened after a period of closure following the inauspicious suicide of a temple employee who leapt from the top. You can also enter nearby through a towerless gate which is directly in line with the Meenakshi shrine deep inside. In the **Ashta Shakti Mandapa** ("Eight Goddesses Hallway"), a sparkling market sells puja offerings and souvenirs, from fat garlands of flowers to rough-hewn sky-blue plaster deities. Sculpted pillars illustrate different aspects of the goddess Shakti, and Shiva's sixty-four miracles at Madurai. Behind this hall, to the south, are stables for elephants and camels.

If you continue straight on from here, cross E. Ati Street, and go through the seven-storey **Chitrai gopura**, you enter a passageway leading to the eastern end of the **Pottamarai Kulam** ("Tank of Golden Lotuses"), where Indra bathed before worshipping the *shivalingam*. From the east side of the tank you can see the glistening gold of the Meenakshi and Sundareshwarar *vimana* towers. Steps lead down to the water from the surrounding colonnades, and in the centre stands a brass lamp column. People bathe here, prior to entering the inner shrines, or just sit, gossip and rest on the steps.

The ceiling paintings in the corridors are modern, but Nayak murals around the tank illustrate scenes from the *Gurur Vilayadal Puranam* which describes Shiva's Madurai miracles. Of the two figures located halfway towards the Meenakshi shrine on the north side, one is the eighth-century king Kulashekhara Pandyan, said to have founded the temple; opposite him is a wealthy merchant patron.

On the west side of the tank is the entrance to the **Meenakshi shrine** (closed to non-Hindus), popularly known as **Amman Koyil**, literally the "mother temple". The immoveable green stone image of the goddess is contained within two further enclosures that form two ambulatories. Facing Meenakshi, just past the first entrance and in front of the sanctum sanctorum, stands Shiva's bull-vehicle, Nandi. At around 9pm, the moveable images of the god and goddess are carried to the **bed chamber**. Here the final puja ceremony of the day, the **lalipuja**, is performed, when for thirty minutes or so the priests sing lullabies (*lali*), before closing the temple for the night.

The corridor outside Meenakshi's shrine is known as the **Kilikkutu Mandapa** ("Parrot Cage Hallway"). Parrots used to be kept just south of the shrine as offerings to Meenakshi, a practice discontinued in the mid-1980s as the birds suffered due to "lack of maintenance". Sundareshwarar and Meenakshi are brought every Friday (6–7pm) to the sixteenth-century **Oonjal Mandapa** further along, where they are placed on a swing (*oonjal*) and serenaded by members of a special caste, the Oduvars. The black and gold, almost fairground-like decoration of the *mandapa* dates from 1985.

Across the corridor, the small **Rani Mangammal Mandapa**, next to the tank, has a detailed eighteenth-century ceiling painting of the marriage of Meenakshi and Sundareshwar, surrounded by lions and elephants against a blue background. Sculptures in the hallway portray characters such as the warring monkey kings from the *Ramayana*, the brothers Sugriva (Sukreeva) and Bali (Vahli), and the indomitable Pandava prince, Bhima, from the *Mahabharata*, who was so strong that he uprooted a tree to use as a club.

Walking back north, past the Meenakshi shrine, through a towered entrance, leads you to the area of the Sundareshwarar shrine. Just inside, is the huge

Meenakshi the fish-eyed goddess

The goddess **Meenakshi** of Madurai emerged from the flames of a sacrificial fire as a three-year-old child, in answer to the Pandyan king Malayadvaja's prayer for a son. The king, not only surprised to see a female, was also horrified that she had three breasts. In every other respect, she was beautiful, as her name, Meenakshi ("fish-eyed"), suggests – fish-shaped eyes are classic images of desirability in Indian love poetry. Dispelling his concern, a mysterious voice told the king that Meenakshi would lose the third breast on meeting her future husband.

In the absence of a son, the adult Meenakshi succeeded her father as Pandyan monarch. With the aim of world domination, she then embarked on a series of successful battles, culminating in the defeat of Shiva's armies at the god's Himalayan abode, Mount Kailasah. Shiva then appeared at the battlefield; on seeing him, Meenakshi immediately lost her third breast. Fulfilling the prophecy, Shiva and Meenakshi travelled to Madurai, where they were married. The two then assumed a dual role, firstly as king and queen of the Pandya kingdom, with Shiva assuming the title Sundara Pandya, and secondly as the presiding deities of the Madurai temple, into which they subsequently disappeared.

Their shrines in Madurai are today the focal point of a hugely popular fertility cult; centred on the gods' coupling, temple priests maintain that it ensures the preservation and regeneration of the Universe. Each night, the pair are placed in Sundareshwara's bedchamber together, but not before Meenakshi's nose ring is carefully removed so that it won't cut her husband in the heat of passion. Their celestial lovemaking is consistently earth-moving enough to ensure that Sundareshwara remains completely faithful to his consort (exceptional for the notoriously promiscuous Shiva). Nevertheless, this fidelity is never taken for granted, and has to be ritually tested each year when the beautiful goddess Cellattamman is brought to Sundareshwara "to have her powers renewed". After she is spurned, she flies into a fury that can only be placated with the sacrifice of a buffalo – one among the dozens of arcane ceremonies that make up Madurai's round of temple rituals.

monolithic figure of Ganesh, **Mukkuruni Vinayaka**, believed to have been found during the excavation of the Mariamman Teppakulam tank (see below). Chubby Ganesh is well-known for his love of sweets, and during his annual **Vinayaka Chathurti festival** (Sept), a special *prasad* (gift offering of food) is concocted from ingredients including 300 kilos of rice, 10 kilos of sugar and 110 coconuts.

Around a corner, a small image of the monkey god **Hanuman**, covered with *ghee* and red powder, stands on a pillar. Devotees take a little with their finger for a *tillak*, to mark the forehead. A figure of Nandi and two gold-plated copper flagstaffs face the entrance to the **Sundareshwarar shrine** (closed to non-Hindus). From here, outsiders can just about see the *shivalingam* beyond the blue-and-red neon "Om" sign (in Tamil).

Causing a certain amount of fun, north of the flagstaffs are figures of Shiva and Kali in the throes of a dance competition. A stall nearby sells tiny **butter balls** from a bowl of water, which visitors throw at the god and goddess "to cool them down". If you leave through the gateway here, on the east, you'll find in the northeast corner the fifteenth-century **Ayirakkal Mandapa**, or thousand-pillared hall, now transformed into the temple's **Art Museum** (daily 10am–5.30pm; Rs1, Rs20 extra with camera). In some ways it is a great shame, as screens have been erected and dusty educational displays replace a clear view of this gigantic hall. However, there's a fine, if rather dishevelled, collection of wood, copper, bronze and stone sculpture, and an old nine-metre-high teak temple door. Throughout the hall, large sculptures of strange, scary creatures and cosmic deities rear out at you from the broad stone pillars; it is said that if you tap the columns, every single one produces a different musical tone.

For more on the temples of Tamil Nadu, see p.1216.

Vandiyur Mariamman Teppakulam tank and the floating festival

At one time, the huge **Vandiyur Mariamman Teppakulam** tank in the southeast of town (bus #4 or #4A; 15min) was full with a constant supply of water, flowing via underground channels from the Vaigai. Nowadays, thanks to a number of accidents, it is only filled during the spectacular Teppam **floating festival** (Jan/Feb), when pilgrims take boats out to the goddess shrine in the centre. Before their marriage ceremony, Shiva and Meenakshi are brought in procession to the tank, where they are floated on a raft decorated with lights, which devotees pull by ropes three times, encircling the shrine. The boat trip is believed to be the overture to a seduction that reaches its passionate conclusion later that night in the temple. This traditionally makes the Teppam the most auspicious time of year to get married.

During the rest of the year the tank and the central shrine remain empty. Accessible by steps, the tank is most often used as an impromptu cricket green, and the shade of the nearby trees makes a popular gathering place. Tradition states that the huge image of Ganesh, Mukkuruni Vinayaka, in the Meenakshi Temple, was uncovered here when the area was originally excavated to provide bricks for the Thirumalai Nayak Palace.

Thirumalai Nayak Palace

Roughly a quarter survives of the seventeenth-century **Thirumalai Nayak Palace** (daily 9am–1pm & 2–5pm), 1.5km southeast of the Meenakshi Temple. Much of it was dismantled by Thirumalai's grandson, Chockkanatha Nayak, and used for a new palace at Tiruchirapalli. What remains today, was renovated in 1858 by the governor of Chennai, Lord Napier, and again in

1971 for the Tamil World Conference. The palace originally consisted of two residential sections, plus a theatre, private temple, harem, royal bandstand, armoury and gardens.

The surviving building, the **Swargavilasa** ("Heavenly Pavilion"), is a rectangular courtyard, flanked by 18m-tall colonnades. As well as occasional live performances of music and dance, the Tourism Department arranges a nightly **Sound and Light Show** (in English 6.45–7.30pm; Rs5), which relates the story of the Tamil epic, *Shilipaddikaram*, and the history of the Nayaks. Some find the spectacle edifying, and others soporific – especially when the quality of the tape is poor. In an adjoining hall, the **Palace Museum** (same hours as the palace) includes unlabelled Pandyan, Jain and Buddhist sculpture, terracottas and an eighteenth-century print showing the palace in a dilapidated state.

All that remains of the **Rangavilasa**, the palace where Thirumalai's brother, Muthialu, lived are just ten pillars wedged in a tiny backstreet. Take Old Kudiralayam Street, right of the palace as you face it, pass the Archaeological Department Office and turn right into Mahal Vadam Pokki Street. The third turning on the left (opposite the New India Textile Shop) is the unmarked Ten Pillars South Lane. One pillar contains a **shivalingam**, which is worshipped by passers-by.

Tamukkam Palace: the Gandhi and Government museums

Across the Vaigai, 5km northeast of the centre near the Central Telegraph Office, stands **Tamukkam** (bus #2, #3, #4, or #26; 20min), the seventeenth-century multi-pillared and arched palace of Queen Rani Mangammal. Built to accommodate such regal entertainment as elephant fights, Tamukkam was taken over by the British, used as a courthouse and collector's office, and in 1955 became home to the Gandhi and Government museums.

Madurai's **Gandhi Memorial Museum** (daily 10am–1pm & 2–5.30pm; free), far better laid out than most of the species, charts the history of India since the landing of the first Europeans, viewed in terms of the freedom struggle. Generally the perspective is national, but where appropriate, reference is made to the role played by Tamils. Wholeheartedly critical of the British, it states its case clearly and simply, quoting the Englishman, John Sullivan: "We have denied to the people of the country all that could raise them in society, all that could elevate them as men; we have insulted their caste; we have abrogated their laws of inheritance; we have seized the possessions of their native princes and confiscated the estates of their nobles; we have unsettled the country by our exactions, and collected the revenue by means of torture." One chilling artefact, kept in a room painted black, is the bloodstained *dhoti* the Mahatma was wearing when he was assassinated. Next door to the museum, the **Gandhi Memorial Museum Library** (daily except Wed 10am–1pm & 2–5.30pm; free) houses a reference collection, open to all, of 15,000 books, periodicals, letters and microfilms of material by and about Gandhi.

Opposite, the small **Government Museum** (daily except Fri 9am–5pm; closed 2nd Sat each month; free) displays stone and bronze sculptures, musical instruments, paintings (including examples of Tanjore and Kangra styles) and folk art such as painted terracotta animals, festival costumes and hobbyhorses. There's also a fine collection of shadow puppets, said to have originated in the Thanjavur area and probably exported to Southeast Asia during the Chola period. A small house in which **Gandhi** once lived stands in a garden within the compound.

Old Madurai is crowded with **textile and tailors' shops**, particularly in W Veli, Avani Moola and Chitrai streets and Town Hall Road. Take up the offers you're bound to receive to go into the shops near the temple, where locally produced textiles are generally good value, and tailors pride themselves on turning out faithful copies of favourite clothes in a matter of hours. Many shops in the immediate vicinity also offer an incentive by allowing visitors to climb up to their roofs for views over the Meenakshi complex. S Avani Moola Street is packed with **jewellery**, particularly gold shops, while at 10 N Avani Moola St, you can plan for the future at the Life & Lucky Number Numerology Centre.

Madurai is also a great place to pick up south Indian **crafts**. Among the best outlets are All India Handicrafts Emporium, 39–41 Town Hall Rd; Co-optex, W Tower Street, and Pandiyan Co-op Supermarket, Palace Road, for handwoven textiles; and Surabhi, W Veli Street, for Keralan handicrafts. For souvenirs such as sandalwood, temple models, carved boxes and oil lamps head for Poompuhar, 12 W Veli St (T0452/25517), or Tamilnad Gandhi Smarak Nidhi Khadi Gramodyog Bhavan, W Veli Street, opposite the railway station, which sells crafts, oil lamps, Meenakshi sculptures and *khadi* cloth and shirts.

The old purpose-built, wooden-pillared fruit and vegetable market, between N Chitrai and Avani Moola streets, provides a slice of Madurai life that can't have changed for centuries. Beyond it, on the first floor of the concrete building at the back, the **flower market** (24hr) is a riot of colour and fragrance; weighing scales spill with tiny white petals and plump pink garlands hang in rows. Varieties such as orange, yellow or white marigolds (*samandi*), pink jasmine (*arelli*), tiny purple spherical *vanameli* and holy *tulsi* plants come from hill areas such as Kodaikanal and Kumili. These are bought in bulk and distributed for use in temples, or to wear in the hair; some are made into elaborate wedding garlands (*kalyanam mala*). The very friendly traders will show you each and every flower, and if you've got a camera will more than likely expect to be recorded for posterity. It's a nice idea to offer to send them a copy of any photograph you take.

Eating

As with accommodation, the range of places to eat in Madurai is gratifyingly wide, and standards are generally high, whether you're eating at one of the many utilitarian-looking "meals" places around the temple, or in an upscale hotel. When the afternoon heat gets too much, head for one of the **juice bars** dotted around the centre, where you can order freshly squeezed pomegranate, pineapple, carrot or orange juice for around Rs15 per glass. To make the most of Madurai's exotic skyline, though, you'll have to seek out a **rooftop restaurant** – another of the modern city's specialities. Rock-bottom-budget travellers should try the street-side stalls at the bottom of W Perumal Maistry Street, where old ladies dish up filling leaf plates of freshly steamed *iddli* and spicy fish masala for Rs10 per portion.

Aarathy, *Aarathy Hotel*, 9 Perumalkoil, W Mada Street. Tasty tiffin (*dosas*, *iddlis* and hot *wada sambar*), served on low tables in a hotel forecourt, where the temple elephant turns up at 6am and 6pm. For more filling, surprisingly inexpensive main meals, step into their blissfully cool a/c annexe.

Amutbam, 30 Town Hall Rd. A huge menu featuring everything from full-on chicken sizzlers to Western-style snacks, via the usual range of noodles, north Indian and veg dishes. Ask for a table in their a/c section, where you can chill out for an extra Rs2 per head.

Anna Meenakshi, opposite *TM Lodge*, W Perumal Maistry Street. An upmarket branch of *New College House's* more traditional canteen, serving top tiffin to a discerning, strictly vegetarian clien-

By air

Indian Airlines flies daily to **Mumbai** via **Chennai**. Their office at 7a W Veli St, near the post office (℡ 0452/741234/6), is efficient and helpful. To get to the airport, catch a taxi for around Rs200, or take city bus #10A from Periyar bus stand.

By bus

At the last count, five different stations operated **long-distance buses** from Madurai (see p.1259); if you are still unsure which one you need, ask at the tourist office in the railway station, and ignore the unscrupulous hustlers hanging around the STC bus stand.

From the New Bus Stand, numerous government buses leave day and night to Chennai (11hr). Destinations in **Karnataka** include Bangalore, for which there are nineteen TTC (first 6am, last 10.15pm) and two KSRTC (7.45am & 10.30pm) buses. Night services also leave for Mysore (depart 4pm; 10hr). For Kerala there are three JJTC and two PRC buses a day to Ernakulam/Kochi (10hr), via Kottayam. This stand also serves **northern** destinations, such as Thanjavur, Tiruchirapalli and Kumbakonam, **Rameshwaram** (every 30min; 4hr), **Kanniyakumari** (every 30min; 6hr) and **Thiruvananthapuram**.

There are no direct services from Madurai to Ooty, but buses to **Coimbatore** (6hr) leave from the Arapalayam stand, 3km west of the centre, every 30min during the day. **Kodaikanal** (4hr) is equally well served with departures from here every 15min or so. You can also get buses to **Kumily** (for Periyar Wildlife Sanctuary) every 30min, and one a day to **Palakaad** (9hr).

By train

Madurai is on the main broad-gauge line and well connected to most major towns and cities in south India.

---

tele. This one's smaller and brighter, with shiny marble tables and an ornate bell metal lamp in the doorway. Arguably the most hygienic, best-value food in the centre. Opens 6am–9.30pm; absolutely delicious coconut or lemon "rice meals" and cheap banana-leaf thalis are served between 10.30am–4pm.

Apollo 96, *Supreme Hotel*, 110 W Perumal Maistry St. Boasting 75,000 flashing diodes and a punchy sound system, south India's most hi-tech bar looks like the set from a low-budget 1970s sci-fi movie. Beers cost Rs75. Closes at 11pm sharp. It's altogether a surreal experience.

Karthik, W Perumal Maistry Street (around the corner from the *Aarathy Hotel*, near the relief bus stand). Run-of-the-mill from the outside, but this pure veg "meals" joint is famous for its delicious *iddli-fry-masala* – mini *iddlies* turned in a spicy chilli paste (served late afternoon and evening only). Eat in or ask for a "parcel".

New College House, 2 Town Hall Rd. Huge meals-cum-tiffin hall in old-style hotel. Lunch-time, when huge piles of pure veg food are served on banana leaves to long rows of locals, is a real deep-south experience; and the coffee's pure Coorg.

Ruby, W Perumal Maistry Street. Ignore the "Alcohol Strictly Prohibited" note on the menu card: this is essentially an unlicensed bar, periodically raided by the police but a popular meeting place for foreign travellers. Cold beers (Rs60) are served in a leafy courtyard or in more claustrophobic compartments indoors, and they do hot snacks and dishes, including a fiery "Chicken 65", noodles and biriyani.

Supreme, *Supreme Hotel*, 110 W Perumal Maistry St. Arguably Madurai's best and breeziest rooftop restaurant, with sweeping views of the city and temple, and an eclectic multi-cuisine menu; the ideal venue for a sundowner. Open 4pm–midnight.

For **reservations** (Mon–Sat 8am–2pm & 2.15pm–8pm, Sun 8am–2pm), ask for a reservation form at the enquiry counter, then join the long queues in the forecourt at the station; the best time to book trains is in the evening or early morning. For **timetable** details, ask the Tourism Department Information Centre, to the right of the ticket counters.

It is possible to reach the railhead for Kodaikanal by train, but the journey is much faster by Express bus. For **Thiruvananthapuram** and **Alleppey**, head over to **Coimbatore** (see table below), and then catch the super fast New Delhi–Trivandrum Express #2626 (departs daily at 5.55am). For **Ooty**, catch any train to Coimbatore, where you should spend the night in order to pick the early morning Nilgiri Express to Mettapalayam, departure point for the Blue Mountain Railway (see p.1279).

Recommended trains from Madurai

The following daily express trains are recommended, although conversion work on the line will adversely affect many main-line services; check the current situation when booking.

Destination	Name	No.	Departs	Total time
Bangalore	Madurai–Bangalore Express	#6731	8pm	12hr
Chennai	Vaigai Express	#2636	5.20am	9hr 40min
	Pandyan Express	#6718	7.35pm	11hr 15min
Coimbatore (Ooty)	Madurai–Coimbatore Fast Passenger	#778	2.30pm	5hr 20min
Kanyakumari	Madurai–Kanyakumari Express	#6721	12.30am	5hr 45min
Rameshwaram	Coimbatore–Rameshwaram Express	#6115	6am	4hr 50min
Trichy	Vaigai Express	#2636	5.20am	2hr 45min

Rameshwaram

The sacred island of **RAMESHWARAM**, 163km southeast of Madurai and less than 20km from Sri Lanka across the Gulf of Mannar is, along with Madurai, south India's most important pilgrimage site. Hindus tend to be followers of either Vishnu or Shiva, but Rameshwaram brings them together, being where the god Rama, an incarnation of Vishnu, worshipped Shiva in the *Ramayana*. The **Ramalingeshwara Temple** complex, with its magnificent pillared walkways, is the most famous on the island, but there are several other small temples of interest, such as the **Gandhamadana Parvatam**, sheltering Rama's footprints, and the **Nambunayagi Amman Kali Temple**, frequented for its curative properties. **Danushkodi**, "Rama's bow", at the eastern end of the peninsula, is where Rama is said to have bathed, and the boulders that pepper the sea between here and Sri Lanka, known as "Adam's Bridge", are the stepping stones used by Hanuman in his search for Rama's wife, Sita, after her abduction by Ravana, the demon king of Lanka.

Rameshwaram is always crowded with day-trippers, and ragged mendicants who camp outside the Ramalingeshwara and the **Ujainimahamariamman**, the small goddess shore temple. An important part of their pilgrimage is to bathe in the main temple's sacred tanks and in the sea; the narrow strip of beach is shared by groups of bathers, relaxing cows and mantra-reciting *swamis* sitting next to sand *lingams*. As well as fishing – prawns and lobsters for packaging and export to Japan – shells are a big source of income in the coastal villages.

The heavy military presence along the approach roads to Rameshwaram reminds you of the proximity of the **war in Sri Lanka**, a short boat ride east across the Palk Strait. If you do plan to make a trip here, it is important to check the current political situation first; if there is a fresh outburst of fighting in Sri Lanka, avoid this area altogether.

Ramalingeshwara Temple

The core of the **Ramalingeshwara** (or Ramanathaswamy) **Temple** was built by the Cholas in the twelfth century to house two much-venerated **shivalingams** associated with the *Ramayana*. After rescuing his wife Sita from the clutches of Ravana, Rama was advised to atone for the killing of the demon king – a brahmin – by worshipping Shiva. Rama's monkey lieutenant, Hanuman, was despatched to the Himalayas to fetch a *shivalingam*, but when he failed to return by the appointed day, Sita fashioned a *lingam* from sand (the *Ramanathalingam*) so the ceremony could proceed. Hanuman eventually showed up with his *lingam* and in order to assuage the monkey's guilt Rama decreed that in future, of the two, Hanuman's should be worshipped first. The *lingams* are now housed in the inner section of the Ramalingeshwara, not usually open to non-Hindus. Much of what can be visited dates from the 1600s, when the temple received generous endowments from the Sethupathi rajas of Ramanathapuram.

High walls enclose the temple, forming a rectangle with huge pyramidal *gopura* entrances on each side. The gateways lead to a spacious closed ambulatory, flanked to either side by continuous platforms with massive pillars set on their edges. These **corridors** are the most famous attribute of the temple, their extreme length – 205m, with 1212 pillars on the north and south sides – giving a remarkable impression of receding perspective. Delicate scrollwork and brackets of pendant lotuses supported by *yalis*, mythical lion-like beasts, adorn the pillars.

Before entering the inner sections, pilgrims are expected to bathe in water from each of the 22 **tirthas** (tanks) in the temple; hence the groups of dripping-wet pilgrims, most of them fully clothed, making their way from one tank to the next to be doused in a bucket of water by a temple attendant. Each tank is said to have special benefits: the Rama Vimosana Tirtha provides relief from debt, the Sukreeva Tirtha gives "complete wisdom" and the attainment of *Surya Loka*, the realm of the Sun, and the Draupadi Tirtha ensures long life for women and "the love of their spouses".

Monday is Rama's auspicious day, when the Padilingam puja takes place. **Festivals** of particular importance at the temple include **Mahashivaratri** (ten days during Feb/March), **Brahmotsavam** (ten days during March/April), and **Thirukalyanam** (July/Aug), celebrating the marriage of Shiva to Parvati.

Minor temples

The **Gandhamadana Parvatam** (daily 6–11am & 3.30–6.30pm), on a hill 2km north of Rameshwaram town centre, is a venerable shrine housing Rama's footprints. On some days, ceremonies are conducted here after the 5.30am puja at the Ramalingeshwara Temple, encouraging pilgrims to climb the hill to continue their devotions. From the roof, fine views extend over the surrounding country and on clear nights you can see the lights of Jaffna.

Three kilometres east of town towards the old fishing village of Dhanushkodi, the small **Nambunayagi Amman Kali Temple**, set in a quiet sandy grove 200m off the main road, attracts people in search of cures for illnesses. Inside a banyan tree next to it is a shrine dedicated to the spirit Retatalai, "the two-headed". A pair of wooden sandals with spikes, said to belong to the spirit, are left in the shrine and locals say they can hear them clip-clopping at night when Retatalai chooses to wander. Pieces of cloth are tied to the branches of the tree to mark thanks for such boons as pregnancy after barrenness and the healing of family feuds. The bus terminates at Dhanushkodi, from where you can walk along the ever-narrowing spit of sand until the sea finally closes in and the island peters out, tantalizingly short of Sri Lanka.

Practicalities

The NH-49, the main road from Madurai, connects Rameshwaram with Mandapam on the mainland via the impressive 2km-long Indira Gandhi Bridge, originally built by the British in 1914 as a railway link, and reopened in 1988 by Rajiv Gandhi for road traffic. Armed guards at checkpoints at either end keep a watchful eye on foreign travellers. **Buses** from Madurai (via Ramnad), Trichy, Thanjavur, Kanniyakumari and Chennai pull in at the bus stand, 2km west of the centre. The **railway station**, 1km southwest of the centre, is the end of the line for trains from Chennai, Coimbatore, Thanjavur, Madurai and Ramnad, and boasts decent **retiring rooms**, a veg restaurant and a left-luggage office (5.30am–10pm).

Red-and-white city buses run every ten minutes from the stand to the main temple; otherwise, **local transport** consists of unmetered cycle and auto-rickshaws that gather outside the bus stand. Jeeps are available for rent near the railway station, and bicycles can be rented from shops in the four Car streets around the temple. There is no **ferry service** to and from Sri Lanka, due to the troubles there.

The tiny TTDC **tourist office**, 14 E Car St (Mon–Fri 10am–5pm; ☎ 04573/21371), gives out information about guides, accommodation and boat trips. TTDC also have a counter at the railway station (to coincide with arriving trains; ☎ 04573/21373), and a small booth at the bus stand (daily except holidays 10am–5.45pm). The **post office** is on Pamban Road, the road next to the bus stand.

Accommodation

Apart from the TTDC hotels, **accommodation** in Rameshwaram is restricted to basic lodges, mostly in the Car streets around the temple. The temple authorities have a range of rooms for pilgrims; ask at the Devasthanam Office, E Car Street (☎ 04573/21262). The **railway retiring rooms** consist of six large double and three triple rooms, generally cleaner (and quieter) than town lodges for the same price, plus a dorm (Rs40).

Chola Lodge, N Car Street ☎ 04573/21307. A basic pilgrim place in the quietest of the Car streets. ❷

Maharaja's, 7 Middle St ☎ 04573/21271. Located next to the temple's west gate. Good clean rooms with attached bathrooms, two with a/c and TV; there are temple views from balconies. There's no restaurant, although management will bring restaurant food in. ❸ –❺

TTDC Hotel Tamil Nadu, near the beach ☎ 04573/21064. The best place in Rameshwaram,

in a pleasant location and with bar and restaurant. They offer comfortable, sea-facing rooms, some a/c; along with a cheap dorm (Rs60). However, it's often full, so book in advance from another TTDC hotel or office. ❷ –❺

TTDC Hotel Tamil Nadu II, near the railway station on Railway Feeder Road ☎ 04573/20171. New hotel, far cheaper than the above, but in a far less attractive location and decidedly grubby, and all the rooms are non-a/c but have attached bathrooms. ❷

Eating

Eating in Rameshwaram is more about survival than delighting the taste buds. Most places serve up fairly unexciting "meals".

Arya Bhavan and **Kumbakonam**, W Car Street. Both places are run by the same family and dish up standard, inexpensive veg "meals".

Ashok Bhavan, W Car Street. Offers cheap, regional varieties of thalis.

TTDC Hotel Tamil Nadu, near the beach. Gigantic, noisy, high-ceilinged glasshouse near the sea, serving good south Indian snacks and "meals" – many items on the menu are unavailable, however.

Kanniyakumari

KANNIYAKUMARI, at the southernmost extremity of India, is almost as compelling for Hindus as Rameshwaram. It is significant, not only for its association with a virgin goddess, Kanya Devi, but also as the meeting point of the Bay of Bengal, Indian Ocean and Arabian Sea. Watching the sun rise and set from here is the big attraction, especially on full-moon day in April, when it's possible to see both the setting sun and rising moon on the same horizon. Although Kanniyakumari is in the state of Tamil Nadu, most foreign visitors arrive on day-trips from Thiruvananthapuram, the capital of Kerala, 86km northwest. While the place is of enduring appeal to pilgrims, others may find it bereft of atmosphere, its magic obliterated by ugly concrete buildings and hawkers selling shells and trinkets.

The Town

The seashore **Kumari Amman Temple** (daily 4.30–11.30am & 5.30–8.30pm) is dedicated to the virgin goddess **Kanya Devi**, who may originally have been the local guardian deity of the shoreline, but was later absorbed into the figure of Devi, or Parvati, consort of Shiva. One version of Kanya Devi's story relates how she did penance to win the hand of Shiva. The god was all in favour and set out from Suchindram for the wedding, due to take place at midnight. The celestial *devas*, however, wanted Kanya Devi to remain a virgin, so that she could retain her full quota of *shakti* or divine power, and hatched a plot. Narada the sage assumed the form of a cock and crowed; on hearing this, Shiva, thinking that it was dawn and that he had missed the auspicious time for the ceremony, went home. The image of Kanya Devi inside the temple wears a diamond nose stud of such brilliance that it's said to be visible from the sea. Male visitors must be shirtless and wear a *dhoti* before entering the temple; non-Hindus are not allowed in the inner sanctum. It is especially auspicious for pilgrims to wash at the bathing *ghat* here.

Resembling a prewar British cinema, the **Gandhi Mandapam** (daily 6.30am–12.30pm & 3–7.30pm), 300m northwest of the Kumari Amman Temple, was actually conceived as a modern imitation of an Orissan temple. It was designed so that the sun strikes the auspicious spot where the ashes of Mahatma Gandhi were laid, prior to their immersion in the sea, at noon on his birthday, October 2.

Possibly the original sacred focus of Kanniyakumari are two rocks, about 60m apart, half-submerged in the sea 500m off the coast, which came to be known as the Pitru and Matru *tirthas*. In 1892 they attracted the attention of the Hindu reformer Vivekananda (1862–1902), who swam out to the rocks to meditate on the syncretistic teachings of his recently dead guru, Ramakrishna

Paramahamsa. Incorporating elements of architecture from around the country, the 1970 **Vivekananda Memorial** (daily except Tues; 7–11am & 2–5pm), reached by the Poompuhar ferry service from the jetty on the east side of town (every 30min; same hours), houses a statue of the saint. The footprints of Kanya Devi can also be seen here, at the spot where she performed her penance.

For more on the life and teachings of Vivekananda, visit the **Wandering Monk Museum (Vivekananda Puram)**, just north of the tourist office at the bottom of town (daily 8am–noon & 4–8pm; free). A sequence of forty-one panels (in English, Tamil and Hindi) recount the *swami*'s odyssey around the subcontinent at the end of the nineteenth century.

Practicalities

Trains from Thiruvananthapuram, New Delhi, Mumbai, Bangalore and even Jammu – at 86hr, the longest rail journey in India – stop at the **railway station** in the north of town, 2km from the seafront. **From Madurai**, the best service is the #6721 Tuticorin Express, which leaves Madurai Junction at 12.30am, and arrives at 6.15am the following morning, just in time for sunrise. You can leave **luggage** in the generator room behind the ticket office for Rs5 per item.

The new and well-organized Thiruvalluvar **bus stand**, near the lighthouse west of town, is served by regular buses from Thiruvananthapuram, Kovalam, Madurai, Rameshwaram and Chennai. Taxis and auto-rickshaws provide **local transport**.

Accommodation

As Kanniyakumari is a "must-see" for Indian tourists and pilgrims, **hotels** can fill up early. However, recent developments have raised standards, and relieved the pressure on space.

Kerala House, seafront ☎04652/71257. A large colonial-era building, converted into a rest house for Keralan civil servants, whose cavernous doubles (two of them are a/c) have dressing rooms and bathrooms; some rooms have sea views. Book in advance through the Political Department of the State Secretariat in Thiruvananthapuram. ❸–❹
Lakshmi Tourist Home, E Car Street ☎04652/71333. The rooms are smart, some are sea-facing and have swish a/c. There's an excellent non-veg restaurant. ❹–❼
Maadhini, E Car Street ☎04652/71787, ☏716570. Large, newly built hotel right on the seafront above the fishing village. It has fine sea views, comfortably furnished rooms and one of the best restaurants in town. ❸–❻

Manickam Tourist Home, N Car Street ☎04652/71387. Spacious and modern rooms, some with a/c and sea views. Faces the sunrise and the Vivekananda rock. Good value. ❸–❻
Samudra, Sannathi Street ☎04652/71162. Smart new hotel near the temple entrance, with well-furnished deluxe rooms facing the sunrise. Facilities include satellite TV and a veg restaurant. ❹–❻
TTDC Hotel Tamil Nadu, seafront ☎04652/46257. Cottages (some are a/c) and clean rooms (a/c on the first floor), most with sea view. There are cheaper and very basic "mini" doubles at the back and a youth hostel dorm (Rs50). Good square meals are served in functional surroundings. ❷–❼

Eating

Aside from the usual "meals" places and hotel dining rooms, there are a few popular veg and non-veg **restaurants** in the centre of town, most of them attached to one or another of the hotels.

Archana, *Maadhini Hotel*, E Car Street. An extensive veg and non-veg multi-cuisine menu served inside a well-ventilated dining hall, or alfresco on a sea-facing terrace (evenings only).

They also serve the town's best selection of ice creams.
Saravana, just north of the Kamari Amman Temple, on the main bazaar. Arguably

The Ghats

Sixty or more million years ago, what we know today as peninsular India was a separate land mass drifting northwest across the ocean towards central Asia. Current geological thinking has it that this mass must originally have broken off the African continent along a fault line that is today discernible as a north–south ridge of volcanic mountains, stretching 1400km down the west coast of India, known as the **Western Ghats**. The range rises to a height of around 2500m, making it India's second-highest mountain chain after the Himalayas.

Forming a natural barrier between the Tamil plains and coastal Kerala and Karnataka, the *ghats* (literally "steps") soak up the bulk of the southwest monsoon, which drains east to the Bay of Bengal via the mighty Kaveri and Krishna river systems. The massive amount of rain that falls here between June and October (around 2.5m) allows for an incredible **biodiversity**. Nearly one-third of all of India's flowering plants can be found in the dense evergreen and mixed deciduous forests cloaking the *ghats*, while the woodland undergrowth supports the subcontinent's richest array of wildlife.

It was this abundance of game, and the cooler temperatures of the range's high valleys and grasslands, that first attracted the sun-sick British, who were quick to see the economic potential of the temperate climate, fecund soil and plentiful rainfall. As the forests were felled to make way for tea plantations, and the region's many tribal groups – among them the Todas – were forced deeper into the mountains, permanent **hill stations** were established. Today, as in the days of the Raj, these continue to provide welcome escapes from the fierce summer heat for the fortunate middle-class Tamils, and foreign tourists, who can afford the break.

Much the best known of the hill resorts – in fact better known, and more visited, than it deserves – is **Udhagamandalam** (formerly Ootacamund, still often "Ooty"), in the **Nilgiris** (from *nila-giri*, "blue mountains"). The ride up to Ooty, on the **miniature railway** via Coonoor, is fun, and the views breathtaking, but in general, unless you have the means to stay in the best hotels, the town itself comes as a rude shock. The other main hill station, founded by American missionaries, is **Kodaikanal**, further south near Madurai.

Accessed via the hill stations, the forest areas lining the state border harbour Tamil Nadu's principal wildlife sanctuaries, **Annamalai** and **Mudumalai** which, along with Wayanad in Kerala, and Nagarhole and Bandipur in Karnataka, form the vast **Nilgiri Biosphere Reserve**, the country's most extensive tract of protected forest. Unfortunately, the activities of a notorious sandalwood smuggler-cum-bandit, "**Veerapan**", have led to the parks being indefinitely closed to the public. As the main route between Mysore and the cities of the Tamil plains wriggles through the Nilgiris, however, you may well find yourself pausing for a night or two along the way, if only to enjoy the cold air and serene landscape of the tea terraces. Whichever direction you're travelling in, a stopover at the dull textile city of **Coimbatore** is hard to avoid, even if only to change buses.

Kodaikanal

Perched on top of the Palani range, around 120km northwest of Madurai, **KODAIKANAL**, also known as **Kodai**, owes its perennial popularity to the hilltop position of the town, which, at an altitude of more than 2000m, affords breathtaking views over the blue-green reaches of the Vagai plain. Raj-era bungalows and flower-filled gardens add atmosphere, while short walks out of the centre lead to rocky outcrops, waterfalls and dense *shola* forest. With the more northerly wildlife sanctuaries and forest areas of the *ghats* now officially closed to visitors, Kodai's outstandingly scenic hinterland also offers south India's best **trekking** terrain. Even if you're not tempted by the prospect of the open trail and cool air, the jaw-dropping **bus ride** up here from the plains makes the detour into this easternmost spur of the *ghats* an essential one.

Kodaikanal's history, with an absence of wars, battles for leadership and princely dominion, is uneventful, and the only monuments to its past are the neat British bungalows that overlook the lake and Law's Ghat Road on the eastern edge of town. The British first moved here in 1845, to be joined later by members of the American Mission who set up schools for European children. One remains as Kodai International School; despite the name, it has an almost exclusively Indian student population. The school lays a strong emphasis on music, particularly guitar playing, and occasionally holds workshops, and concerts on the green just east of the lake.

After a while in the plains of south India a retreat to Kodai's cool heights is more than welcome. However, in the height of summer (June–Aug), when temperatures compete with those in the lowlands, it's not worth the trip – nor is it a good idea to come during the monsoon (Oct–Dec), when the town is shrouded in mists and drenched by heavy downpours. In late February and

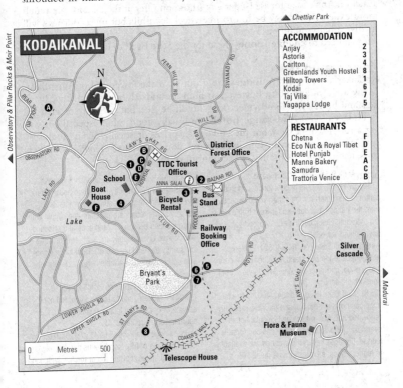

KODAIKANAL

ACCOMMODATION

Anjay	2
Astoria	3
Carlton	4
Greenlands Youth Hostel	8
Hilltop Towers	1
Kodai	6
Taj Villa	7
Yagappa Lodge	5

RESTAURANTS

Chetna	F
Eco Nut & Royal Tibet	D
Hotel Punjab	E
Manna Bakery	A
Samudra	C
Trattoria Venice	B

▲ Chettiar Park

◀ Observatory & Pillar Rocks & Moir Point

District Forest Office

TTDC Tourist Office

School

Boat House

Bicycle Rental

Bus Stand

Lake

Railway Booking Office

Bryant's Park

Silver Cascade

Flora & Fauna Museum

▶ Madurai

Coaker's Walk

Telescope House

0 Metres 500

early March the nights are chilly; the **peak tourist season** therefore, is from April to June, when prices soar.

Arrival, information and orientation

The **buses** from Madurai and Dindigul that climb the spectacular road up the steep hillside to Kodai from the plains below pull in at the stand in the centre of town. Unless you're coming from as far as Chennai or Tiruchirapalli, the bus is much more convenient than the train: the nearest **railhead**, Kodaikanal Road – also connected to Dindigul (30min) and Madurai (50min) – is three hours away by bus. Note, too, that **the road from Palani** is by far the most spectacular approach, although the least travelled (except during the monsoons when the other is invariably blocked). If you plan to spend a few days in Kodai, it's worth visiting Palani, an atmospheric destination in itself, as a day-trip just to travel this route.

Tickets for onward rail journeys from Kodaikanal Road can be booked at an office above the *Hilltop Inn* restaurant next to the *Hilltop Towers* hotel on Club Road (Mon–Sat 9am–1pm & 1.30–5pm, Sun 1.30–5pm). King Tours and Travels on Woodville Road reserves trains, buses and planes within south India. The **tourist office** (daily 10am–5.30pm), on the main road, Anna Salai (Bazaar Road), offers little except unclear sketch maps of the area. For **email**, *Alpha Net* (daily 9am–9pm; Rs60/hr) is next to *Royal Tibet* restaurant, on P.T. Road.

Taxis line Anna Salai in the centre of town, offering sightseeing at high fixed rates. Most tourists, however, prefer to amble around at their own pace. Kodaikanal is best explored on foot, or by **bicycle**, which you can rent from a stall on Anna Salai for Rs10 per day (those on offer at the lakeside are much more expensive); it may be fun to freewheel downhill, but most journeys will involve a hefty uphill push too.

If you need to **change money**, head for the State Bank of India on Anna Salai.

Accommodation

Kodaikanal's inexpensive **lodges** are grouped at the lower end of Anna Salai. Many are dim and poky, however, so hunt around. Always ask whether blankets and hot water are provided (this should be free, but you may be charged in budget places) **Mid-range hotels** are usually good value, especially if you get a room with a view, but they hike their prices drastically during high season (April–June). For its stunning location alone, *Greenland's Youth Hostel* offers unbeatable value for money at the bottom of the range.

Anjay, Anna Salai, near the bus stand ☎04542/41089. Simple budget lodge slap in the centre, it has smarter rooms than you'd expect from the outside, but does suffer from traffic noise. If they're full, check out the equally good value *Jaya* behind. ❷–❸

Astoria, Anna Salai ☎04542/40524. Well-kept hotel opposite the bus stand, with homely rooms and a good, mid-priced restaurant. No views, but comfortable enough. ❻

Carlton, off Lake Road ☎04542/40071. The most luxurious hotel in Kodaikanal. Spacious, tastefully renovated and well-maintained colonial house overlooking the lake, with a bar and comfortable lounge. Cottages within the grounds are available at higher prices; all rates include meals. ❾

Greenland's Youth Hostel, St Mary's Road ☎04542/41099. Attractive old stone house offering unrivalled views and sunsets from its deep verandas. The rooms are pleasant and simple with huge wooden beds, open fireplaces and attached bathrooms. Unfortunately, the staff are surly and constantly demand baksheesh. Trekking information and guides are available here. Book ahead. ❷–❸

Hilltop Towers, Club Road ☎04542/40413, ⓕ40415. Modern, comfortable rooms and good service. Very near the lake and school, with two south Indian restaurants. ❻–❼

Kodai, Noyce Road ☎04542/41301, ⓕ42108. Large campus of fifty incongruous but very pleasant chalets situated at the top of the hill, with good views of the town, and a quality restaurant. **⑤-⑥**

Taj Villa, Coaker's Walk, off Club Road
⌖04542/40940. Comfortable old stone house, with more character than most, in lovely gardens with superb views. All rooms have attached bathrooms, but you'll have to get hot water by the bucket. A touch overpriced, but the sunset is fabulous. Email is available here. **⑤-⑥**

Yagappa Lodge, Noyce Road, off Club Road
⌖04542/41235 or 42116. Small, clean lodge in old buildings ranged around a dusty courtyard. Good views, and the best budget deal after *Greenland's Youth Hostel*. Features a great little bar with wicker chairs and a tiny whitewashed restaurant with gingham tablecloths, serving veg meals and breakfast. **③-④**

The Town

Kodai's focal point is its **lake**, sprawling like a giant amoeba over a full 24 hectares just west of the town centre. This is a popular place for strolls, or bike rides along the five-kilometre path that fringes the water's edge, and pedal- or rowing boats can be rented on the eastern shore (Rs40 for 30min, plus Rs10 if you require an oarsman). Horse riding is also an option down by the lake, but it's rather pricey and tame at Rs80 to be led along the lakeside. Shops, restaurants and hotels are concentrated in a rather congested area of brick, wood and corrugated iron buildings east and downhill from the lake. To the south is **Byrant's Park**, with tiered flowerbeds on a backdrop of pine, eucalyptus, rhododendron and wattle, which stretches southwards to Shola Road, less than 1km from the point where the hill drops abruptly to the plains. A path, known as **Coaker's Walk**, skirts the hill, winding from the *Taj Villa* to *Greenland's Youth Hostel* (10min), offering remarkable views that on a clear day stretch as far as Madurai.

One of Kodai's most popular natural attractions is the **Pillar Rocks**, 7km south of town, where a series of granite cliffs rise more than 100m above the hillside. To get there, follow the westbound Observatory Road from the northernmost point of the lake (a steep climb) until you come to a crossroads. The southbound road passes the gentle **Fairy Falls** on the way to Pillar Rocks. Observatory Road continues west to the **Astrophysical Observatory**, perched at Kodai's highest point (2347m). Visitors can't go in, but a small **museum** (daily 10am–noon & 2–5pm; Fri only outside peak season) displays assorted instruments. Closer to the north shore of the lake, **Bear Shola Falls** are at their strongest early in the year, just after the monsoon.

East of the town centre, about 3km south down Law's Ghat Road (towards the plains), the **Flora and Fauna Museum** (Mon–Sat 10am–noon & 3–5pm; Rs1) has a far from inviting collection of stuffed animals. However, the orchid house is spectacular, and well worth a look on the way to **Silver Cascade** waterfalls, a further 2km along the road.

Chettiar Park, on the very northwest edge of town, around 3km from the lake at the end of a winding uphill road, flourishes with trees and flowers all year round, and every twelve years is flushed with a haze of pale-blue **Kurinji blossoms** (the next flowering will be in 2006). These unusual flowers are associated with the god Murugan, the Tamil form of Karttikeya (Shiva's second son), and god of Kurinji, one of five ancient divisions of the Tamil country. A temple in his honour stands just outside the park.

Eating

If you choose not to eat in any of the **hotel restaurants**, head for the food stalls along **PT Road** just west of the bus stand. Menus include Indian, Chinese, Western and Tibetan dishes, and some cater specifically for vegetarians. Look out, too, for the **bakeries**, with their wonderful, fresh, warm bread and cakes each morning.

Kodai has become something of a low-key trekking centre in recent years. Wandering around town, **guides** continually approach you offering their services on day-hikes to local viewpoints and beauty spots, or for longer trips involving night halts in villages. Scrutinize their recommendation books for comments by other tourists, and before you employ anyone, go for a coffee to discuss the possible routes, costs and nature of the walks they're offering. While most are relatively straightforward, some tackle unstable paths and steep climbs for which you'll need sturdy footwear. You should also clarify accommodation and food arrangements, transport costs and fees, in advance.

Generally, simple meals and tiffin are available at villages along the routes of longer hikes, so you don't need to carry much more than a sleeping bag, water, emergency food supplies and warm clothes for the evening. **Maps** of the area tend to be hopelessly inaccurate, but the one featured in the booklet *Beauty in Wilderness* (Rs10), available from the DFO (District Forest Office) near the *Hotel Tamil Nadu* (☎04542/40287), gives you a rough idea of distances, if not the lie of the land. While at the DFO, get permission to stay in the **Forest Rest Houses**, which provide rudimentary accommodation for around Rs25–50 per night; most have fireplaces, but bear in mind that any wood you might burn contributes to the overall **deforestation** of the Palanis. Local environmental groups are concerned about the potential long-term impact of trekking on the economy and ecology of the range, and as a result encourage walkers to pack out rubbish, bury their faeces where toilets are not available, and use purification tablets rather than bottled water.

If you'd prefer to hike without a guide, the following **route** is worth considering; most of it follows forest roads, and there are settlements at regular intervals, many of them connected to Kodai by daily bus services. You don't get to explore the wild tops of the range, but the views and countryside throughout are beautiful, with patches of indigenous *shola* forest accessible at various points.

First head out of town on the **Pillar Rocks** road towards Berijam; if you can hitch a ride, you'll avoid the horn-beeping that otherwise accompanies your progress as far as the end of the road at **Moir Point**. **Berijam** (23km), where there is a picturesque lake surrounded by dense pine and acacia forest, is little more than an outpost for forest wardens. From here, however, you can follow quiet back-country roads, taking local herders' and wood gatherers' paths that cut between the bends, to **Kavunji**, which is served by six daily buses to Kodai – handy if you're short of time. This sleepy Palani village is the home of a small NGO that promotes childrens' health projects, run by S.A. Iruthyaraj (look for the house with a white chicken painted on the wall), who is highly knowledgeable about local *shola* forests and off-track routes in the area. Further along the trail at **Polur** (8km) are some spectacular **waterfalls**. The locals say it is impossible to get close to them, but you can, by scrambling down the hillside via a muddy overgrown cattle path – and it's well worth it for the refreshing shower.

For more information on environmentally friendly trekking in the Kodai area, contact the **Palani Hills Conservation Council (PHCC)**, Amarville House, Lower Shola Road, Kodaikanal 62410 (☎04542/40711). This excellent environmental organization also welcomes foreign volunteer workers to help with their various campaigns and grass-roots projects in the Palanis.

Chetna, next to the *Charlton* hotel, by the lake. A minuscule place with a sweet pink attic and flower-filled balcony. Run by an enthusiastic and health-conscious couple from Rajasthan, who dish up simple thalis (Rs25), coffee, sweets and snacks.

Carlton, *Carlton Hotel*, off Lake Road. Splash out on a buffet spread at Kodai's top hotel (Rs300), rounded off with a *chhota* peg of IMFL scotch in the bar.

Eco Nut, J's Heritage Complex, PT Road. One of south India's few bona fide Western-style wholefood shops and a great place to stock up on trekking supplies: muesli, home-made jams, breads, pickles and muffins, high-calorie "nutri-balls" and delicious cheeses from Auroville.

Hotel Punjab, PT Road. Top north Indian cuisine and reasonably priced tandoori specialities; try their great butter chicken and hot naan.

Manna Bakery, Bear Shola Road. The fried breakfasts, pizzas and home-baked brown bread and cakes served in this eccentric, self-consciously ecofriendly café-restaurant are great, but some might find the bare concrete dining hall dingy.

Royal Tibet, PT Road. The better of the town's two Tibetan joints, with dishes ranging from thick home-made bread to particularly tasty *momos* and noodles, and some Indian and Chinese options.

Samudra, PT Road. Moderately priced seafood specialities, trucked in weekly by freezer lorry from Kochi and served in an attractive raffia and fishing-net filled dining room. Try their tandoori pomfret or filling "fish fry" budget option; the tiger prawns are the thing for a splurge, but they do plenty of chicken dishes, too steeped in tasty Chinese sauces.

Trattoria Venice, PT Road. Warming minestrone, fresh home-made pastas and pizzas and delicious tiramisu, all finished up with a cappuccino made with home-grown coffee. If this isn't enough, come for the endlessly amusing performance by the eccentric manager-entertainer-chef-waiter, Ganesh.

Coimbatore

Visitors tend only to use the busy industrial city of **COIMBATORE** as a stopover on the way to Ooty, 90km northwest. Once you've climbed up to your hotel rooftop to admire the blue, cloud-capped haze of the Nilgiris in the west, there's little to do here other than kill time wandering through the nuts-and-bolts bazaars, lined with lookalike textile showrooms, "General Traders" and shops selling motor parts.

Practicalities

Coimbatore's two main **bus stands**, Central and Thiruvalluvar, are close together towards the north of the city centre; the busy town bus stand is sandwiched in between. From Central bus stand, on Dr Nanjappa Road, buses leave for Ooty every fifteen minutes. Buses to Bangalore and Mysore can be booked in advance at the **reservation office** (9am–noon & 1–8pm). There are also frequent services to and from Madurai, Chennai and Tiruchirapalli (Trichy). A third stand, Ukkadam bus stand, serves local towns and destinations in northern Kerala, such as Pollachi, Palghat, Munnar, Trissur and Kannur; it's 4km from the others, in the southwest of the city next to the lake.

The **railway station**, 2km south of two central bus stands, is well-connected to major southern destinations. To catch the Nilgiri Blue Mountain Railway to **Ooty** (see p.1287), join the #6005 Nilgiri Express **from Chennai**, which leaves Coimbatore at 5.30am (1hr), and change onto the narrow-gauge steam railway at **Mettupalayam**, from where a train departs at 7.30am. The other connection leaves Coimbatore at 10.50am, to meet up with the 1.15pm from Mettupalayam. If you're catching the early service, try to stay near the railway station, or arrange transport the night before, as auto-rickshaws are few and far between at this early hour of the morning. Alternatively, jump on a bus to Mettupalayam from the Central bus stand before 6am, which will get you to the head of the narrow-gauge line in time for the 7.30am departure.

Coming **from Ooty**, you'll get into Mettupalayam at either 12.45pm or 6.30pm, leaving you plenty of time to grab something to eat and catch onward overnight trains from Coimbatore to Chennai and Madurai (if you intend to do this, reserve tickets in advance at Ooty). Of the overnight services to **Chennai**, the Cheran Express #2674 (daily 11.05pm; 9hr) is marginally quicker than the Nilgiri Express #6606 (daily 8.40pm; 9hr 35min), but nowhere near as smart and fast as the swish #2024 Shatabdi Express

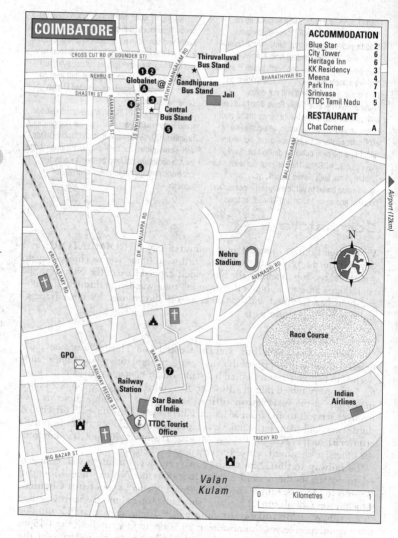

(daily 7.25am; 6hr 35min). The daily #6115 Rameshwaram Express leaves at 11.25pm for **Rameshwaram** via **Madurai** (arrive 6am). For Cochin, catch the daily #6865 Tiruchi Express (departs 12.45am; 5hr 30min). The best train for **Mangalore** is the #6627 West Coast Express (daily departs 7.55pm; 9hr).

From Coimbatore **airport**, 12km northeast and served by buses to and from the town bus stand (taxis charge around Rs175), Indian Airlines and Jet Airways fly daily to Mumbai, Chennai, Kozhikode and Bangalore, and twice a week to Cochin. Indian Airlines' office is 2km northeast of the railway station on Trichy Road (☎0422/399833 or 399821); Jet Airways is 4km along the same road (☎0422/212036).

You can **change money** at the State Bank of India and Bank of Baroda, near the railway station or, more quickly and efficiently, at TT Travels, #102 A-Block Raheja Centre, Avanashi Road (℡0422/212854), a five-minute rickshaw ride northeast of the railway station. The latter is the only one open on Sundays (daily 9.30am–5.30pm). **Internet** booths are springing up all over Coimbatore, where you can send and receive **email** for around Rs30. Two of the most convenient places are: Globalnet, on the first floor of the *Krishna Towers*, on the corner of Nehru Street and Sathyamangalam Road, just north of the bus stands; and the STD place directly opposite the *Blue Star* hotel.

Accommodation and eating

Most of Coimbatore's **accommodation** is concentrated around the bus stands. The cheapest places line Nehru Street and Shastri Road, but whatever you do avoid the rock-bottom places facing the bus stand itself, which are plagued with traffic noise from around 4am onwards.

As for **eating**, your best bets are the bigger hotels such as the *City Tower*, whose excellent rooftop restaurant, *Cloud 9*, serves a top-notch multi-cuisine menu to a predominantly business clientele. The *Malabar*, on the first floor of the *KK Residency*, is a less pricey option, popular with visitors from across the Ghats for its quality non-veg Keralan cuisine. For vegetarian south Indian food, however, you won't do better than the ultramodern *Chat Corner*, opposite the *Blue Star* hotel on Nehru Street, which has a squeaky clean "meals" restaurant, open-air terrace, and an excellent little juice bar. The food here is superb, and only marginally pricier than average.

Blue Star, 369 Nehru St ℡0422/230635. Impeccably clean rooms, all with balconies, quiet fans and bathrooms, in a modern multistorey building five minutes' walk from the bus stands. The best mid-price place in this area. ❸–❹

City Tower, Sivaswamy Road, just off Dr Nanjappa Road, a two-minute walk south of the Central bus stand ℡0422/230681, ℻230103. A smart upscale hotel situated in the city centre with modern interiors (heavy on leatherette and vinyls); the "Executive" rooms are more spacious. Some rooms are a/c. ❻–❼

Heritage Inn, 38 Sivaswamy Rd ℡0422/231451, ℻233223. Coimbatore's top hotel, featuring more than sixty centrally a/c rooms, a couple of quality restaurants and foreign exchange. Credit cards accepted. ❼–❽

KK Residency, 7 Shastri St ℡0422/232433. Large tower-block hotel around the corner from the main bus stands; very clean rooms and a couple of good restaurants. ❹–❺

Meena, 109 Kalingarayan St ℡0422/235420. Tucked away off the main drag, but handy for the bus stand. The rooms are clean, with attached shower-toilets and small balconies. A good choice for budget travellers. ❷

Park Inn, 21 Geetha Hall Rd ℡0422/301284, ℻301291. Business-oriented hotel that's the smartest option around the railway station. Immaculate, quiet and good value; room rates include breakfast. ❺–❼

Srinivasa, 365 Nehru St, next door to *Blue Star* ℡0422/230116. Near the bus stands and the cleanest of the cheap lodges in this area, which isn't saying much. ❷

TTDC Tamil Nadu, Dr Nanjappa Road ℡0422/236311. Opposite Central bus stand; convenient, clean and reliable. Better than most in the chain with a/c and non-a/c rooms. It is often fully booked, so phone ahead. ❹–❻

Coonoor

COONOOR, a scruffy bazaar and tea-planters' town on the Nilgiri Blue Mountain Railway (see p.1287) lies at the head of the Hulikal ravine, 27km north of Mettupalayam and 19km south of Ooty, at an altitude of 1858m, on the southeastern side of the Dodabetta mountains. Thanks to its proximity to its more famous neighbour, Coonoor has avoided Ooty's over-commercialization, and can make a pleasant place for a short stop.

Coonoor loosely divides into two sections, with the bus stand (regular services to Mettupalayam, Coimbatore and elsewhere in the Nilgiris) and railway station in **Lower Coonoor**, as well as an atmospheric little hill market, specializing in leaf tea and fragrant essential oils. In **Upper Coonoor**, there's a fine sprinkling of old Raj-era bungalows along the narrow lanes edged with flower-filled hedgerows. At the top lies **Sim's Park**, a fine botanical garden on the slopes of a ravine with hundreds of rose varieties (daily 8am–6.30pm; Rs5).

Around the town, rolling hills and valleys, carpeted with spongy green tea bushes and stands of eucalyptus and silver oak, offer some of the most beautiful scenery in the Nilgiris, immortalized in many a Hindi movie dance sequence. Cinema fans from across the south flock here to visit key locations from their favourite blockbusters, among them **Lamb's Nose** (5km) and **Dolphin's Nose** (9km), former British picnicking spots with paved pathways and dramatic views of the Mettupalayam plains. Buses run out here from Coonoor every two hours. It's a good idea to catch the first one at 7am, which gets you to Dolphin's Nose before the mist starts to build up, and walk the 9km back into town via Lamb's Rock – an enjoyable amble that takes you through tea estates and dense forest.

Visible from miles away as tiny orange or red dots amid the green vegetation, **tea-pickers** work the slopes around Coonoor, carrying wicker baskets of fresh leaves and bamboo rods that they use like rulers to ensure that each plant is evenly plucked. Once the leaves reach the factory, they're processed within a day, producing seven grades of tea. **Orange Pekoe** is the best and most expensive; the seventh lowest grade, a dry dust of stalks and leaf swept up at the end of the process, will be sold on to make instant tea. To visit a tea or coffee plantation, contact UPASI (United Planters' Association of Southern India), "Glenview" House, Coonoor.

Practicalities

When it comes to finding somewhere to **stay** or **eat**, there's not a lot of choice in Coonoor, and it's not a good idea to leave it too late in the day to be looking for a room. By and large the hotels are dotted around Upper Coonoor, within 3km of the station; you'll need an auto-rickshaw to find most of them. As ever, ignore any rickshaw-wallahs who state that the hotel you want to go to is "full" or "closed". The correct fare from the bus stand to Bedford Circle/*YWCA* is Rs20–25.

If you're staying at the *YWCA*, or one of the upmarket hotels, your best bet is to eat there. In the bazaar, the only commendable **restaurants** are *Hotel Tamizhamgam* (pronounced "Tamirangum"), on Mount Road near the bus stand, which is Coonoor's most popular vegetarian "meals"-cum-tiffin joint. For good-value non-veg north Indian tandoori and Chinese food, try the *Greenland* hotel, up the road.

The Travancore Bank, on Church Road in Upper Ooty, near Bedford Circle, **changes currency**, but not always travellers' cheques. Otherwise, the nearest place is the State Bank of India in Ooty (see p.1285).

Accommodation

The tariffs included here are for the low season, as high-season prices may increase by anywhere between twenty and a hundred percent, depending on the tourist influx.

Blue Hills, Mount Road ☎0423/230103. Located 1km up from the bus stand, this place offers clean doubles, complete with Formica furnishing. The concrete building is an eyesore and its popularity among all-male holiday groups means it's not recommended for female travellers, but it's cheap and the non-veg restaurant is good. ③–⑤

La Barrier Inn, Coonoor Club Road ℡0423/232561. Located way up above the bazaar, with great views of surrounding hills (and cricket nets). The rooms are spotless and very large, opening onto flower-filled balconies. This is a comfortable mid-range option. ❺

Taj Garden Retreat, Hampton Manor ℡0423/230021, ℱ232775. Colonial-era hotel with cottage accommodation, tea-garden lawns and spectacular views, plus a good range of sports and activities on offer – including freshwater fishing. Luxurious, but way overpriced, especially for foreigners, who pay 30 percent more. The restaurant serves spectacular lunchtime buffets. ❾

Venlan (Ritz), Ritz Road, Bedford ℡0423/230632, ℱ230600. Recently refurbished, this luxury hotel is in a great location on the outskirts. Very spacious with carpeted rooms, deep balconies and fine views. Much better value than the *Taj Garden Retreat* but rather lacking in charm. ❼–❽

Vivek, Figure of Eight Road, nr Bedford Circle ℡0423/230658 or 232318. Catch a town bus to Bedford Circle and walk from there. Managed by a very amiable lady, offering clean rooms (some with tiny balconies overlooking the tea terraces) and a great value dorm (Rs40). Just beware of the "monkey menace". ❷–❸

YWCA Guest House, Wyoming, near the hospital ℡0423/234426. A characterful Victorian-era house on a bluff overlooking town, with flower garden, tea terraces and fine views from relaxing verandas. There are five double rooms and two singles, plus yoga lessons and superb home-cooked meals at very reasonable rates (Rs70 non-veg; Rs40 veg). This is amongst the most congenial budget hotels in south India. No alcohol. ❹

Udhagamandalam (Ootacamund)

When John Sullivan, the British *burrasahib* credited with "discovering" **UDHAGAMANDALAM** – still more commonly referred to by its anglicized name, **Ootacamund** – first clambered into this corner of the Nilgiris through the Hulikal ravine in the early nineteenth century, the territory was the traditional homeland of the pastoralist **Toda** hill tribe. Until then, the Todas had lived in almost total isolation from the cities of the surrounding plains and Deccan plateau lands. Sullivan quickly realized the agricultural potential of the area, and acquired tracts of land for Rs1 per acre from the Todas, and set about planting flax, barley and hemp, as well as potatoes, soft fruit and, most significantly of all, **tea**, which all flourished in the mild climate. Within twenty years, the former East India Company clerk had made a fortune. Needless to say, he was soon joined by other fortune-seekers, and a town was built, complete with artificial lake, churches and stone houses that wouldn't have looked out of place in Surrey or the Scottish Highlands. Soon "**Ooty**", as the town was fondly called by the *burra-* and *memsahibs* of the south, was the "Queen of Hill Stations" and had become the most popular hill retreat in peninsular India.

Of the Todas, little further note was made beyond a couple of anthropological monographs, references to their *munds*, or settlements, in the *Madras Gazette*, and the financial transactions that deprived them of the traditional lands. Christianized by missionaries and uprooted by tea-planters and forest clearance, they retreated with their buffalo into the surrounding hills and wooded valleys where, in spite of hugely diminished numbers, they continued to preserve a more-or-less traditional way of life.

By a stroke of delicious irony, the Todas outlived the colonists whose cash crops originally displaced them – but only just. Until the mid-1970s "Snooty Ooty", continued to be "home" to the notoriously snobby British inhabitants who chose to "stay on" after Independence. They eked out their last days on tiny pensions that only here would allow them to keep a lifestyle to which they had become accustomed. Over the past two decades, travellers have continued to be attracted by Ooty's cool climate and peaceful green hills, forest and grassland. However, if you come in the hope of finding quaint vestiges of the Raj, you're likely to be disappointed; what with indiscriminate development and a deluge of holiday-makers, they're few and far between.

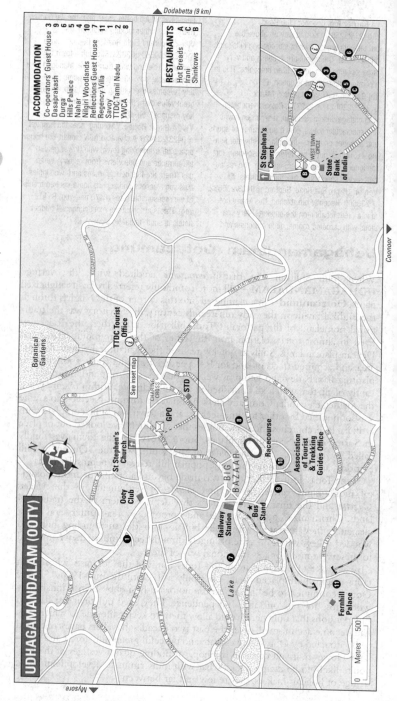

▲ Dodabetta (9 km)

UDHAGAMANDALAM (OOTY)

N

St Stephen's
Church

Ooty Club

Botanical
Gardens

TTDC Tourist
Office

See inset map

Charing
Cross

GPO

STD

BIG
BAZAAR

Racecourse

Association
of Tourist
& Trekking
Guides Office

Railway
Station

Bus
Stand

Lake

Fernhill
Palace

0   500
Metres

ACCOMMODATION

Co-operators' Guest House	3
Dasaprakash	9
Durga	6
Hills Palace	5
Nahar	4
Nilgiri Woodlands	10
Reflections Guest House	7
Regency Villa	11
Savoy	1
TTDC Tamil Nadu	2
YWCA	8

RESTAURANTS

Hot Breads	A
Irani	C
Shinkows	B

St Stephen's Church

WEST TOWN
CIRCLE

State
Bank
of India

CHARING CROSS

COMMERCIAL RD

◀ Mysore

Coonoor ▶

The **best time to come** is between January and March, thereby avoiding the high-season crowds (April–June & Sept–Oct). In May, the summer festival brings huge numbers of people and a barrage of amplified noise; worlds away from the peaceful retreat envisaged by the *sahibs*. From June to September, and during November, it'll be raining and misty, which appeals to some. From October or November to February it can get really cold.

Arrival, information and orientation

Most visitors arrive in Ooty either by bus from Mysore in Karnataka (the more scenic, if steeper, route goes via Masinagudi), or on the **miniature mountain railway** from Coonoor and Mettupalayam. The bus and railway stations are fairly close together, at the western end of the big bazaar and racecourse. **Local transport** consists of auto–rickshaws and taxis, which meet incoming trains and gather outside the bus stand and on Commercial Road around Charing Cross. You can **rent bikes** but the steep hills make cycling very hard work.

The **TTDC tourist office** (Mon–Sat 10am–5.45pm; ☎0423/443977) on the corner of Kelso Road and Woodhouse Road, is eager to help, but information is not always reliable. You can book tours here, among them one that takes in Ooty, Pykara and Mudumalai (daily 9am–7.30pm; Rs150), and calls at Pykara dam, falls and boathouse and Mudumalai Wildlife Sanctuary, making a very long day. There's a less strenuous tour of just Ooty and Coonoor (daily 9am–6pm; Rs80), which goes to Sim's Park, the Botanical Gardens, the lake, Dodabetta Peak, Lamb's Rock and Dolphin's Nose. If you get caught out by a Sunday, there's a private tourist office (daily 8am–8.30pm) in Charing Cross that gives out leaflets and advice on hotels, sightseeing and restaurants.

Ooty's **post office**, northwest of Charing Cross at West Town Circle, off Spencers Road and near St Stephen's Church, has a **poste restante** counter (enquiries and stamps Mon–Fri 9am–5pm; parcels Mon–Fri 9am–3pm & Sat 9am–2pm). For **email**, there are now numerous outlets across town, especially around Charing Cross, all charging Rs50–60 per hour for a frustratingly slow and unreliable service.

The only **bank** in Ooty that changes travellers' cheques and currency is the very *pukka* State Bank of India, on West Town Circle. While you're waiting for your cash, check out the photos in the hallway connecting the old and new blocks, dating from the era when this was the "Imperial Bank of India": stalwart, stiff-backed *burra-sabibs* pose with pipes, wives and mandatory Scottish terriers in front of the old bank building.

Accommodation

Accommodation in Ooty is a lot more expensive than in many places in India; during April and May the prices given below can rise by thirty to a hundred percent. It also gets very crowded, so you may have to hunt around to find what you want. The best by far are the grand old Raj-era places; otherwise, the choice is largely down to average hotels at above-average prices. In **winter** (Nov–Feb), when it can get pretty cold, most hotels provide extra blankets and buckets of hot water on request, but a few sharks may quietly add a charge for these services onto your final bill, so check beforehand.

Co-operators Guest House, Charing Cross ☎0423/444046. Slightly back from the main road so it's relatively quiet. An L-shaped Raj-era building with clean rooms and turquoise balconies looking down to a courtyard. Unfortunately the place has become somewhat cramped by a huge new concrete block next door. Cheap and central. ❷

Dasaprakash, south of the racecourse ☎0423/442434. This option's a solid, old-style Indian hotel, clean and reasonably quiet, overlooking the racecourse. Their cheapest ("deluxe") rooms are a bit gloomy, but the "first class" doubles are fine. There is an excellent and inexpensive south Indian veg restaurant and a travel agent. ④–⑤

Durga, Ettines Road ☏ 0423/443837. This is the best deal among the many mid-range places around Charing Cross. It's clean, comfortable and central, but the constant noise of buses stopping outside creates a lot of unwelcome noise and dust. ④–⑤.

Hills Palace, Commercial Road ☏ 0423/442239, ☏ 443430. Spanking new place that's just below the main bazaar, but secluded, quiet and spotlessly clean inside. Great value in the low season. ④

Nahar, Commercial Road, Charing Cross ☏ 0423/442173, ☏ 445173. One of Ooty's smartest hotels, offering spacious, well-furnished rooms in the centre (the best rooms are in the modern building at the back) and two veg restaurants. A favourite with large Indian family holiday parties, so book ahead. ⑦

Nilgiri Woodlands, Racecourse Road, 1km from bus stand and railway station ☏ 0423/442451, ☏ 442530. A grand Raj-era building, with a wood-panelled lobby, hunting trophies and bare, clean rooms that are particularly good value in winter. The little cottages around the garden are worth the extra. Friendly, helpful staff and a good restaurant. ④–⑦

Reflections Guest House, North Lake Road ☏ 0423/443834. Homely, relaxing guesthouse by the lake, five minutes' walk from the railway station, with rooms opening onto a small terrace. Easily the best budget option in Ooty, but it's small and fills up quickly, so book in advance. ②

Regency Villa, Fernhill ☏ 0423/443097. The maharaja of Mysore's former guesthouse, now a rather run-down, atmospheric old hotel. If you're here for faded traces of the Raj, this is the place. The palatial suites (⑥) in the main block are locked in a time warp, with frayed nineteenth-century furniture, original bathtubs, and old sepia photos of the Ooty hunt. By contrast, the second and third-rate rooms, in separate blocks, are cheerless and not at all good value. Even if you can't afford to stay here, come out for a nose around and coffee on the lawn. ⑤–⑦

Savoy, 77 Sylkes Road ☏ 0423/444142. Long-established pukka Taj-group hotel. Immaculate and chintzy old-world wooden cottages with working fireplaces around a manicured garden, and there is a pleasant restaurant and bar. You'll have to pay a pricey $75 to stay. ⑨

TTDC Hotel Tamil Nadu, Unit I & II, Unit I is in the northwest corner above Charing Cross, reached by a flight of stairs, and Unit II in the northeast corner ☏ 0423/444371, ☏ 444369 (same details for both). Two identical large, characterless complexes in the centre of town, but with good-value restaurants, a bar and billiards rooms. ②–⑥

YWCA "Anandagiri", Elk Hill Road ☏ 0423/442218. Charming 1920s building, set in spacious grounds near the racecourse. Seven varieties of rooms and chalets are on offer, all immaculate, with bucket hot water and bathrooms. There is a dining room and you can while away the evening in the cosy "English parlour", or by the piano. Excellent value, and very safe. An inexpensive laundry facility is available. Book ahead. ②–④

The Town

Ooty sprawls over a large area of winding roads and steep climbs. The obvious focal point is **Charing Cross**, a busy junction on dusty **Commercial Road**, the main, relatively flat, shopping street that runs south to the big bazaar and municipal vegetable market. Goods on sale range from fat plastic bags of cardamom and Orange Pekoe tea to presentation packs of essential oils (among them citronella, which is a highly effective natural mosquito repellent). A little way northeast of Charing Cross, the **Botanical Gardens** (daily 8am–6.30pm; Rs5, Rs5 extra with camera, Rs25 extra with video), laid out in 1847 by gardeners from London's Kew Gardens, consist of twenty hectares of immaculate lawns, lily ponds and beds, with more than a thousand varieties of shrubs, flowers and trees. There's a refreshment stand inside, and shops outside sell candyfloss, peanuts and snacks.

Northwest of Charing Cross, the small gothic-style **St Stephen's Church** was one of Ooty's first colonial structures, built in the 1820s on the site of a Toda temple; timber for its bowed teak roof was taken from Tipu Sultan's palace at Srirangapatnam and hauled up here by elephant. The area around the church gives some idea of what the hill station must have looked like in the days of the Raj. To the right of the church is the rambling and rather dilapidated **Spencer's store**, which opened in 1909 and sold everything a British home in the colonies could ever need; it is now a computer college. Nearby, in the same compound as the post office, gowned lawyers buzz around the red-brick **Civil Court**, a quasi-Gothic structure with leaded diamond-shaped windows, corrugated iron roofs and a clock tower capped with a weather vane. Over the next hill (west), the snootiest of Ooty's institutions, the **Club**, dates from 1830. Originally the house of Sir William Rumbold, it became a club in 1843 and expanded thereafter. Its one claim to fame is that the rules for snooker were first set down here (although the members of Jabalpur Club in Madhya Pradesh are supposed to have originated the game in the first place). Entry is strictly restricted to members and their guests or members of affiliated clubs. Further along Mysore Road, the modest **Government Museum** (daily except Fri & second Sat of month 9am–1pm & 2–5pm) houses a few paltry tribal objects, sculptures and crafts.

West of the railway station and racecourse (races mid–April to mid–June), the **lake**, constructed in the early 1800s, is one of Ooty's main tourist attractions, despite being heavily polluted (most of the town's raw sewage gets dumped here – worth bearing in mind if you're tempted to venture out on it). You can go boating (8am–6pm; rowing, paddle and motor Rs30–120) and horse riding (short rides Rs30–75, or Rs100 per hour).

Fernhill Palace, not far from the southeast end of the lake, and once the summer residence of the maharaja of Mysore, is now a smart hotel. It's an extraordinary pile, built in the fullest expression of Ooty's characteristic Swiss-chalet style, with carved wooden bargeboards and ornamental cast-iron balustrades. Among the compound of firs, cedars and monkey puzzle trees, a bizarre church-like building was erected as an indoor badminton court.

The Nilgiri Blue Mountain Railway

The famous narrow-gauge **Nilgiri Blue Mountain Railway** climbs up from Mettupalayam on the plains, via Hillgrove (17km) and Coonoor (27km) to Udhagamandalam, a journey of 46km passing through sixteen tunnels, eleven stations and nineteen bridges. It's a slow haul of four-and-a-half hours or more – sometimes the train moves little faster than walking pace, and always takes at least twice as long as the bus – but the **views** are absolutely magnificent, especially along the steepest sections in the Hulikal ravine.

The line was built between 1890 and 1908, paid for by the tea-planters and other British inhabitants of the Nilgiris. It differs from India's two comparable narrow-gauge lines, to Darjeeling and Shimla, for its use of the so-called **Swiss rack system**, by means of which the tiny locomotives are able to climb gradients of up to 1 in 12.5. Special bars were set between the track rails to form a ladder, which cogs of teeth, connected to the train's driving wheels, engage like a zip mechanism. Because of this novel design, only the original locomotives can still run the steepest stretches of line, which is why the section between Mettupalayam and Coonoor has remained one of South Asia's last functioning **steam routes**. The chuffing and whistle screeches of the tiny train, echoing across the valleys as it pushes its blue-and-cream carriages up to Coonoor (where a diesel locomotive takes over) rank among the most romantic sounds of south India, conjuring up the determined gentility of the Raj era. Even if you don't count yourself as a train spotter, a bone-shaking ride on the Blue Mountain Railway should be a priority while traversing the Nilgiris between southern Karnataka and the Tamil plains.

Timetable details for the line appear in the account of Coimbatore (see p.1279), and in the "Moving on from Ooty" box on p.1288.

Eating

Many of the mid-range hotels serve up good south Indian food, but Ooty has yet to offer a gourmet **restaurant**. The *Regency Villa*, however, is well worth checking out for its colonial ambience. For an *udipi* breakfast, just head for one of the restaurants around Charing Cross serving *idlli-dosa* and filter coffee.

Chandan, *Nahar Hotel*, Commercial Road, Charing Cross ☎ 0423/442173. Carefully prepared north Indian specialities (their *paneer kofta* is particularly good), and a small selection of tandoori vegetarian dishes, served inside a posh restaurant or on a lawnside terrace. They also do a full range of *lassis* and milkshakes.

Dashprakash, *Hotel Dashprakash*, south of the racecourse ☎ 0423/442434. Congenial and inexpensive tiffin café, serving unlimited, tasty thalis (Rs45; lunch and dinner) *dosas*, and excellent *uttapams* (the coconut chutney is sublime). A sister outlet in Charing Cross has a more varied menu, including north Indian dishes and thalis.

Hot Breads, Charing Cross. French-established franchise selling the usual range of quality pastries, cheesy and plain breads and savouries from a bakery outlet downstairs, as well as pizzas and other tasty snacks in a wood-lined first-floor café.

Irani, Commercial Road. A gloomy old-style Persian joint run by Baha'is. Uncompromisingly non-veg (the menu's heavy on mutton and liver), but an atmospheric coffee stop, and a popular hang-out for both men and women.

Nilgiri Woodlands, Racecourse Road, 1km from bus stand and railway station ☎ 0423/42551, ☏ 42530. There is an à la carte menu, but the inexpensive lunchtime and evening thalis (Rs45) are good too. Checked tablecloths and cane chairs give it the look of a village hall. No alcohol.

Shinkows, 42 Commissioners Rd ☎ 0423/442811. Good-value, authentic Chinese restaurant serving up good-sized portions on the spicy and pricey side – a main course will set you back about Rs130.

Moving on from Ooty

Ooty railway station has a reservation counter (10am–noon & 3.30–4.30pm) and a booking office (6.30am–7pm), where you can buy tickets for the Nilgiri Blue Mountain Railway, as well as onwards services to most other destinations in the south. From Ooty, four trains run along the narrow-gauge line to Coonoor each day, with two (depart 9.15am and 2.30pm) continuing down to Mettupalayam, on the main broad-gauge network. If you are heading to Chennai, take the second service, which meets up in Mettupayalam with the fast #6606 Nilgiri Express (depart 7.25pm; 10hr 30min).

You can also book buses in advance, at the reservation offices for both state buses (daily 9am–12.30pm & 1.30–5.30pm) and the local company, Cheran Transport (daily 9am–1pm & 1.30–5.30pm) at the bus stand. A combination of stop-start local and express "super-deluxe" state buses serve Bangalore and Mysore (half-hourly buses to both pass through Mudumalai), Kodaikanal, Thanjavur, Thiruvananthapuram and Kanniyakumari, as well as Kotagiri, Coonoor and Coimbatore nearer to hand. Private buses to Mysore, Bangalore and Kodaikanal can be booked at hotels, or agents in Charing Cross; even when advertised as "super-deluxe", many turn out to be cramped minibuses.

Mudumalai Wildlife Sanctuary

Set 1140m up in the Nilgiri hills, **Mudumalai Wildlife Sanctuary** is one of the most accessible in the south, covering 322 square kilometres of deciduous forest, split by the main road from Ooty (64km) to Mysore (97km). Unfortunately, the park has been **closed** to visitors for the past couple of seasons amid fears that the sandalwood smuggler, Veerapan, may abduct tourists or Forest Department wardens. You can, however, still stop here en route to or from Mysore to sample the peace and fresh air of the Nilgiri forest after the bus parties of day-trippers from Ooty have all gone home.

Coming from Ooty, the approach to Mudumalai is spectacular, twisting and turning down 36 hairpin bends, through wooded hills and past waterfalls (in season). Monkeys dart and play in the trees, and you may glimpse a tethered elephant from the camp at **Kargudi**, where wild elephants are tamed for work in the timber industry. Mudumalai has one of the largest populations of elephants in India, along with wild dogs, gaur (Indian bison), common and Nilgiri langur and bonnet macaque (monkeys), jackal, hyena and sloth bear – even a few tigers and panthers.

Practicalities

Until the Forest Department relax restrictions on trekking in the remote woodland areas around Mudumalai, you can only reach the park by road. The fastest and most spectacular route, via Sighur Ghat, is not negotiable by large vehicles, but private minibuses and a regular Cheran Transport **bus** service run to Masinagudi (1hr) from Ooty. Travelling on the longer, less steep route via Gudalur, standard buses to Mysore and Bangalore from Ooty take 2hr 30min to reach Theppakkadu, which is connected to Masinagudi, 8km away, by bus and Jeep. You can also walk this route, but should beware of animals, especially wild elephant.

Theppakkadu is the main access point to the sanctuary. The big event of the day (now that the van tours of the park have been suspended) is an **Elephant Camp show** (daily 6pm; Rs20) – if you're into seeing put-upon pachyderms performing puja or playing soccer to a Boney M accompaniment.

Accommodation

Standards in Mudumalai are generally high, with most of the hotels in gorgeous, peaceful settings. The best of them are up to 5km off the main road from Masinagudi in **Bokkapuram**, although two budget options overlook the main road. Book in advance, and arrange for your hosts to pick you up from the bus stop – taxis or Jeeps are rare in the village. Most places expect guests for full board, as Masinagudi only has a few simple restaurants.

Bamboo Banks Guest House, 2km from the main road, Masinagudi ☎ 0423/56222. Two rooms, and four cottages in a beautiful environment; delicious meals are served alfresco in the garden. ⑥–⑦

Chitral Walk (Jungle Trails), near Valaitotam village, 7km southeast of Masinagudi ☎ 0423/56256. The most remote and atmospheric option, it's well off the beaten track with comfortable rooms. By far the best place in this price category. ⑥

Dreamland, next to the Masinagudi crossroads ☎ 0423/56127. This is the cheapest option within reach of the park; it lacks atmosphere but is clean and safe. ❸

Jungle Hut, 5km from the road, Bokkapuram, Masinagudi ☎ & ℗ 0423/56240. The park's most expensive option: twelve very comfortable cottages and a swimming pool. ⑦

TTDC Hotel Tamil Nadu, Theppakkadu ☎ 0423/56249. Functional place, with clean four-bed rooms and a very cheap dorm (Rs50 weekdays, Rs75 weekends). Meals are by arrangement and there's a seven-night maximum stay. Officially, you should book at the TTDC office in Ooty, but you may be lucky on spec if they're not full. ❶–⑥

Travel details

Trains

* Trains from Egmore; all others from Central.
Chennai to: Bangalore (7 daily; 4hr 45min–8hr 10min); Bhubaneswar (7 daily; 20hr 10min–24hr); Calcutta (2–3 daily; 28hr 15min–32hr 50min); Coimbatore (2 daily; 6hr 50min–8hr 55min); Chengalpattu (5 daily*; 1hr); Delhi (3 daily; 29–43hr); Dindigul (5 daily*; 5hr 45min–9hr); Hyderabad (2 daily; 14–15hr); Kanniyakumari (1–2 daily; 15hr 45min–17hr 15min); Kochi (5 weekly; 10–13hr); Kodaikanal Road (4 daily*; 9hr); Kumbakonam (3 daily*; 7hr 20min); Madurai (5–6

daily*; 8hr–11hr 20min); Mumbai (3 daily; 24hr 15min–31hr 30min); Mysore (2 daily; 4hr 45min–11hr 20min); Pune (3 daily; 20hr–25hr 30min); Rameshwaram (2–3 daily*; 14hr 30min–24hr); Salem (10 daily; 4–6hr); Thanjavur (3 daily*; 8hr–9hr 30min); Thiruvananthapuram (1–2 daily; 16hr 45min–20hr); Tiruchirapalli (7–8 daily*; 5hr 20min–7hr); Tirupati (3 daily; 3hr); Vijayawada (12 daily; 7–8hr).

Chidambaram to: Chengalpattu (4 daily; 5hr 40min–8hr); Kumbakonam (3 daily; 2hr); Rameshwaram (2 daily; 12hr); Thanjavur (4 daily; 3hr); Tiruchirapalli (4 daily; 4–5hr); Tirupati (1 daily; 11hr 15min); Tiruvannamalai (1 daily; 4hr 40min).

Coimbatore to: Bangalore (2 daily; 7hr); Calcutta (4 weekly; 38hr–39hr 30min); Delhi (1–2 daily; 35–43hr); Chennai (5–6 daily; 7hr 15min–9hr 10min); Hyderabad (1 daily; 20hr 50min); Kanniyakumari (3 daily; 12hr–13hr 30min); Kochi (7 daily; 5hr–6hr 30min); Madurai (2 daily; 5–6hr); Mumbai (1 daily; 35hr); Ooty (2 daily; 5hr); Rameshwaram (1 daily; 14hr 20min); Salem (13–14 daily; 2hr 15min–3hr); Tiruchirapalli (2 daily; 5hr 30min–8hr 50min) Thiruvananthapuram (3 daily; 9hr 50min–11hr).

Kanniyakumari to: Chennai (1–2 daily; 15hr 45min–17hr 15min); Coimbatore (2 daily; 13hr 25min–16hr 45min); Delhi (Fri only; 58hr); Kochi (2–3 daily; 7hr 30min–9hr); Madurai (1–2 daily; 4hr 45min–5hr 15min); Mumbai (1 daily; 48hr); Salem (1 daily; 15hr); Tiruchirapalli (1–2 daily; 8hr 25min–9hr 30min);Thiruvananthapuram (2–3 daily; 2hr–2hr 30min).

Madurai to: Bangalore (1 daily; 12hr); Chengalpattu (4–5 daily; 9hr); Chennai (5–6 daily; 7hr 45min–11hr 15min); Coimbatore (2 daily; 5hr 20min–7hr); Kanniyakumari (1–2 daily; 5hr 45min–6hr 10min); Kodaikanal Road (4–5 daily; 23min–51min); Rameshwaram (2 daily; 4hr 50min–7hr) Tiruchirapalli (5–6 daily; 2hr 20min–4hr); Tirupati (2 weekly; 11hr 20min).

Tiruchirapalli to: Bangalore (1 daily; 9hr 30min); Chengalpattu (5–6 daily; 5hr 50min); Chennai (7–8 daily; 5–7hr); Cochin (1 daily; 10hr 50min); Coimbatore (2 daily; 5hr 30min–6hr); Kanniyakumari (1–2 daily; 10hr); Kodaikanal Road (5 daily; 2hr 40min); Madurai (5–6 daily; 3hr 10min–4hr 40min);Thanjavur (4 daily; 1hr 40min); Villupuram (1 daily; 6hr 55min).

Buses

Chennai to: Bangalore (29 daily; 8–11hr); Chengalpattu (60 daily; 1hr 30min–2hr); Chidambaram (20 daily; 5–7hr); Coimbatore (9

daily; 11–13hr); Dindigul (10 daily; 9–10hr); Hyderabad (1 daily; 18–20hr); Kanchipuram (every 20min; 1hr 30min–2hr); Kanniyakumari (9 daily; 16–18hr); Kodaikanal Road (10 daily; 14–15hr); Kumbakonam (17 daily; 7–8hr); Madurai (37 daily; 10hr); Mamallapuram (every 10min; 2–3hr); Pondicherry (every 10min; 4–5hr); Rameshwaram (5 daily; 14hr); Salem (20 daily; 5–7hr); Thanjavur (18 daily; 8hr 30min); Thiruvananthapuram (9 daily; 20hr); Tindivanam (every 20min; 3–4hr); Tiruchirapalli (every 30min; 8–9hr); Tirupati (every 20min; 4–5hr); Tiruvannamalai (every 20min; 4–6hr); Udhagamandalam (Ooty) (3 daily; 15hr); Vedanthangal (3 daily; 2–3hr); Vellore (every 30min; 2–4hr); Vijayawada (1 daily; 13–16hr).

Chidambaram to: Chengalpattu (20 daily; 4hr 30min–5hr); Chennai (10 daily; 5–6hr); Coimbatore (5 daily; 7hr); Kanchipuram (8–10 daily; 7–8hr); Kanniyakumari (3 daily; 10hr); Kumbakonam (every 10min; 2hr 30min); Madurai (8 daily; 8hr); Pondicherry (every 20min; 2hr); Thanjavur (every 20min; 4hr); Tiruchirapalli (every 30min; 5hr); Tiruvannamalai (15 daily; 3hr 30min); Vellore (5 daily; 4hr 30min).

Coimbatore to: Bangalore (10 daily; 8–9hr); Chennai (15 daily; 10–12hr); Kanchipuram (3 daily; 9–10hr); Kanniyakumari (3 daily; 14hr); Kodaikanal Road (10 daily; 6hr); Madurai (25 daily; 5–7hr); Pondicherry (6 daily; 7hr); Rameshwaram (2 daily; 14hr); Salem (40 daily; 3–4hr); Thiruvananthapuram (10–15 daily; 12hr); Tiruchirapalli (every 30min; 4–6hr).

Kanchipuram to: Chennai (every 10min; 1hr 30min–2hr); Coimbatore (4 daily; 9–10hr); Madurai (4 daily; 10–12hr); Pondicherry (12–15 daily; 7hr); Tiruchirapalli (6 daily; 7–8hr);Tiruvannamalai (15–20 daily; 3hr); Vellore (every 10min; 2hr 30min).

Kanniyakumari to: Chennai (11 daily; 14–16hr); Kovalam (10 daily; 2hr); Madurai (every 30min; 6hr); Pondicherry (10–12 daily; 12–13hr); Rameshwaram (4 daily; 9–10hr); Thiruvananthapuram (20 daily; 2hr 45min–3hr 30min); Tiruchirapalli (every 30min; 10hr).

Madurai to: Bangalore (21 daily; 8–9hr); Chengalpattu (37 daily; 9hr); Chennai (hourly; 11hr); Chidambaram (5 daily; 7–8hr); Coimbatore (every 30min; 6–10hr); Kanchipuram (6–7 daily; 10–12hr); Kanniyakumari (hourly; 6hr); Kochi (8 daily; 10hr); Kodaikanal Road (11 daily; 4hr); Mysore (5 daily; 10hr); Pondicherry (14 daily; 11–13hr); Rameshwaram (26 daily; 4hr); Thanjavur (every 30 min; 4–5hr); Thiruvananthapuram (18 daily; 7hr); Tiruchirapalli (every 30min; 4–6hr); Tirupati (6 daily; 15hr).

Pondicherry to: Bangalore (4 daily; 10–12hr); Chennai (every 30min; 2hr 30min–3hr); Chidambaram (every 20min; 2hr); Coimbatore (10 daily; 10hr); Kanchipuram (8 daily; 3–4hr); Kanniyakumari (15–20 daily; 12–13hr); Madurai (hourly; 11–13hr); Mamallapuram (every 20min; 3hr); Thanjavur (20 daily; 5hr); Tiruchirapalli (every 30min; 5–6hr); Tiruvannamalai (every 20min; 2hr).

Tiruchirapalli to: Chengalpattu (every 20min; 7–8hr); Chennai (hourly; 5–6hr); Coimbatore (every 30min; 4–6hr); Kanchipuram (2 daily; 6–7hr); Kanniyakumari (15–20 daily; 10–12hr); Kodaikanal Road (8–12 daily; 5hr); Pondicherry (20 daily; 5–6hr); Madurai (every 30min; 4–6hr); Thanjavur (every 10min; 1hr–1hr 30min); Tiruvannamalai (5 daily; 6hr).

Flights

Chennai to: Bangalore (2–4 daily; 45min); Bhubaneswar (4 weekly; 2hr 30min); Calcutta (2 daily; 2hr 5min); Coimbatore (2–3 daily; 55min–1hr 55min); Delhi (3–4 daily; 2hr 30min); Hyderabad (2–3 daily; 1hr); Kochi (1–2 daily; 1hr–2hr 15min); Madurai (1 daily; 55min); Mumbai (3–4 daily; 1hr 45min); Port Blair (1 daily; 2hr 5min); Thiruvananthapuram (1–2 daily; 1hr 10min); Tiruchirapalli (5 weekly; 50min); Tirupati (2 weekly; 25min).

Coimbatore to: Bangalore (1 daily; 40min); Chennai (1–2 daily; 1hr 5min–1hr 55min); Kochi (2 weekly; 30min); Mumbai (1 daily; 1hr 50min).

CHAPTER 21

Highlights

* **Varkala** Sit on the cliffs and watch dolphins swim, or eat south Indian snacks near the busy temple tank. See p.1317

* **The backwaters** The waterways of this dense-ly populated coastal strip can be explored by boat; local ferries chug though some of the most diverse corners. See p.1326

* **Plantations** Head into the lush hills of Thekaddy, where the air is heady with the smell of cloves, cardamom and coffee. See p.1337

* **Fort Cochin** This atmos-pheric little island, strung with Chinese fishing nets, draws on Jewish, Portuguese, British and Keralan culture. See p.1351

* **Kathakali performance** An essential part of the Kerala experience, this noisy and colourful ritu-alized drama is stunning; arrive early to watch the characters come alive as intricate make-up is applied. See p.1355

* **Thrissur** April/May sees the spectacular festival of Puram, involving caparisoned elephants, huge bands of drum-mers, fireworks and dra-matic costumes. See p.1362

Kerala

A sliver of dense greenery sandwiched between the Arabian Sea and the forested Western Ghat mountains, the state of **KERALA** runs down the southwest coast of India, around 550km long and 120km wide at its broadest point. It is blessed with unique geographical and cultural features and the overpowering tropical landscape, with 41 rivers and countless waterways, fed by two annual monsoons, intoxicates every newcomer. Equally, Kerala's arcane rituals and spectacular festivals stimulate even the most jaded imagination, continuing centuries of tradition that has never strayed far from the realms of magic.

Travellers weary of daunting metropolises will find that Kerala's cities are small-scale and more relaxed than elsewhere. For visitors, the most popular is undoubtedly the great port of **Kochi** (Cochin), where Kerala's extensive history of peaceable foreign contact is evocatively evident in the atmospheric old quarters of Mattancherry and Fort Cochin, hubs of a still-thriving tea and spice trade. The capital, **Thiruvananthapuram** (Trivandrum), almost as far south as you can go and a gateway to the nearby palm-fringed beaches of **Kovalam**, provides visitors with varied opportunities to sample Kerala's rich cultural and artistic life.

However, more so than anywhere in India, the greatest joy of exploring Kerala is the actual travelling – above all, by **boat**, in the spellbinding Kuttanad region, near historic **Kollam** (Quilon) and **Alappuzha** (Alleppey). Vessels, from cruisers to wooden longboats, ply the **backwaters** in day-long voyages, well worth taking for the chance of a close-up view of village life in India's most densely populated state. Furthermore, it's always easy to escape the heat of the lowlands by taking off to the **hills**. Roads through a landscape dotted with churches and temples pass spice, tea, coffee and rubber plantations, and natural forest, en route to wildlife reserves such as **Peppara** or **Periyar**, roamed by herds of mud-caked elephants.

Kerala is short on the historic monuments prevalent elsewhere in India, mainly because wood is the building material of choice. Moreover, what

Accommodation price codes

All accommodation prices in this book have been categorized using the price codes below. Prices given are for a double room, and all taxes are included. For more details, see p.51.

❶ up to Rs100	❹ Rs300–400	❼ Rs900–1500
❷ Rs100–200	❺ Rs400–600	❽ Rs1500–2500
❸ Rs200–300	❻ Rs600–900	❾ Rs2500 and upwards

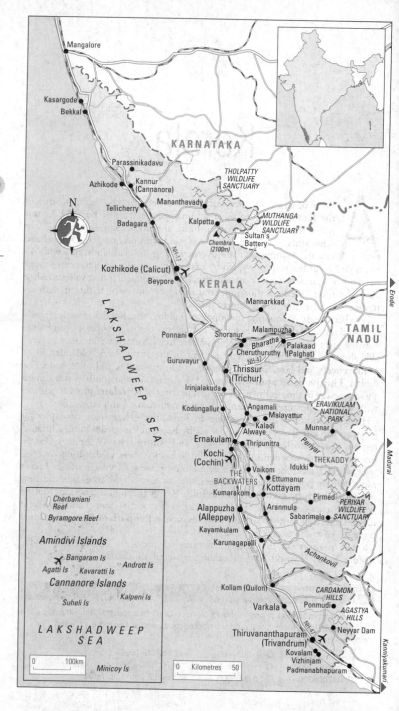

ancient temples there are remain in use, and more often than not are closed to non-Hindus. Nonetheless, distinctive buildings throughout the state eschew grandiosity in favour of elegant understatement. Following an unwritten law, few buildings, whether houses or temples, are higher than the surrounding trees; from high ground in urban areas this can create the miraculous illusion that you're surrounded by forest. Typical features of both domestic and temple architecture include long, sloping tiled and gabled roofs that minimize the excesses of both rain and sunshine, and pillared verandas; the definitive example is **Padmanabhapuram Palace**, just south of the border in neighbouring Tamil Nadu and easily reached from Thiruvananthapuram.

Phenomenal amounts of money are lavished upon many, varied, and often all-night **entertainments** associated with Kerala's temples. Fireworks rend the air, while processions of gold-bedecked elephants are accompanied by some of the loudest (and deftest) drum orchestras in the world. The famous **Puram** festival in Thrissur is the most astonishing, but smaller events take place throughout the state – often outdoors, with all welcome to attend.

Theatre and **dance** styles abound in Kerala; not only the region's own female classical dance form, **Mohiniattam** ("dance of the enchantress"), but also the martial-art-influenced **Kathakali** dance drama, which has for four centuries brought gods and demons from the *Mahabharata* and *Ramayana* to Keralan villages. Its 2000-year-old predecessor, the Sanskrit drama **Kutiyattam**, is still performed by a handful of artists, while localized rituals known as **Teyyattam**, in which dancers wearing nine-metre-tall masks become "possessed" by temple deities, continue to be a potent ingredient of village life in the north. Few visitors ever witness these extraordinary all-night performances first hand, but between December and March, you could profitably spend weeks hopping between village festivals in northern Kerala, experiencing a way of life that has altered little in centuries.

Some history

The god Parashurama, "Rama with the battle-axe", the sixth incarnation of Vishnu, is credited with creating Kerala. Born a brahmin, he set out to re-establish the supremacy of the priestly class, whose position had been usurped by arrogant *kshatryas*, the martial aristocracy. Brahmins were forbidden to engage in warfare, but he embarked upon a campaign of carnage, which only ended when Varuna, the all-seeing god of the sea, gave him the chance to create a new land from the ocean, for brahmins to live in peace. Its limits were defined by the distance Parashurama could throw his axe; the waves duly receded up to the point where it fell. Fossil evidence suggests that the sea once extended to the Western Ghats, so the legend reflects a geological truth.

Ancient Kerala is mentioned as the land of the **Cheras** in a third-century BC Ashokan edict, and also in the *Ramayana* (the monkey king Sugriva sent emissaries here in search of Sita), and the *Mahabharata* (a Chera king sent soldiers to the Kurukshetra war). The Tamil *Silappadikaram* ("The Jewelled Anklet") was composed here and provides a valuable picture of life around the time of Christ. Early foreign accounts, such as in Pliny and Ptolemy, testify to thriving trade between the ancient port of Muziris (now known as Kodungallur) and the Roman Empire.

Little is known about the early history of the Cheras; their dominion covered a large area, but their capital Vanji has not been identified. Other contemporary rulers included the Nannanas in the north and the Ay chieftains in the south, who battled with the Pandyas from Tamil Nadu in the eighth century. At the start of the ninth century, the Chera king Kulashekhara Alvar – a poet-saint of the Vaishnavite *bhakti* movement known as the *alvars* – established his own dynasty. His son and successor, Rajashekharavarman, is thought to have been a saint of the parallel Shaivite movement, the *nayannars*. The great Keralan philosopher Shankaracharya, whose *advaitya* ("non-dualist") philosophy influenced the whole of Hindu India, lived at this time.

Eventually, the prosperity acquired by the Cheras through trade with China and the Arab world proved too much of an attraction for the neighbouring **Chola** empire, who embarked upon a hundred years of sporadic warfare with the Cheras at the end of the tenth century. Around 1100, the Cheras lost their capital at Mahodayapuram in the north, and shifted south to establish a new capital at Kollam (Quilon).

When the **Portuguese** ambassador/general **Vasco da Gama** and his fleet first arrived in India in 1498, people were as much astounded by their recklessness in sailing close to Calicut during monsoon, as by their physical and sartorial strangeness. Crowds filled the streets of Calicut to see them, and a Moroccan found a way to communicate. Eager to meet the king, whom they believed to be a Christian, the Portuguese were escorted over 29km in torrential rain to his palace. However, da Gama soon found that the gifts he had brought from the king of Portugal had not made a good impression. The zamorin (raja) wanted silver and gold, not a few silk clothes and a sack of sugar.

Vasco da Gama, after such diplomatic initiatives as the kidnapping, mutilation and murder of assorted locals, nevertheless came to an agreement of sorts with the zamorin, and then pressed on to demand exclusive rights to the spice trade. He was determined to squeeze out the Keralan Muslim (*Mappila*) traders who for centuries had been a respected section of the community, acting as middlemen between local producers and traders in the Middle East. Exploiting an already existing enmity between the royal families of Cochin and Calicut, da Gama turned to Cochin, which became the site of India's first Portuguese fortress in 1503. The city's strategic position enabled the Portuguese to break the Middle Eastern monopoly of trade with western India. Unlike previous visitors, they introduced new agricultural products such as cashew and tobacco, and for the first time turned coconut into a cash crop, having recognized the value of its by-products, coir rope and matting.

The rivalry between Cochin and Calicut allowed other colonial powers to move in; both the Dutch, who forcibly expelled the Portuguese from their forts, and the British, in the shape of the East India Company, established themselves early in the seventeenth century. During the 1700s, first Raja Martanda Varma and then Tipu Sultan of Mysore carved out independent territories, but the defeat of Tipu Sultan by the British in 1792 left the British in control right up until Independence.

Kerala today can claim some of the most startling **radical** credentials in India. In 1957 it was the first state in the world democratically to elect a communist government and despite having one of the lowest per capita incomes in the country it has the most equitable land distribution, due to uncompromising reforms made during the 1960s and 1970s. In 1996, the Left Democratic Front, led by CPI(M) retook the state from the Congress-led United Democratic Front, who had been in power for five years. Poverty is not absent, but it appears far less acute than in other parts of India. Kerala is also justly proud of its reputation for health care and education, with a literacy rate that stands, officially at least, at 100 percent. However, industrial development is negligible, with potential investors from outside tending to fight shy of dealing with a politicized workforce. Too many graduates and too little investment has led a significant proportion of the male workforce to seek lucrative employment overseas in the Gulf states; it's now hard to find a family who does not have at least one relative sending substantial wealth back to Kerala. As you explore the state, you cannot fail to notice the most obvious status symbol of remittance culture – the vast pink-and-white mansions sprawling incongruously on the outskirts of every village.

Thiruvananthapuram

Kerala's capital, the coastal city of **THIRUVANANTHAPURAM** (still widely and more commonly known as **Trivandrum**), is set on seven low hills, 87km from the southern tip of India. Despite its administrative importance – demonstrated by wide roads, multistorey office blocks and gleaming white colonial buildings – it's a decidedly easy-going city, with an attractive mixture of narrow backstreets, traditional red-tiled gabled houses and acres of palm trees and parks breaking up the bustle of its modern concrete centre.

Although it has few monuments as such, Thiruvananthapuram is an ideal first stop in the state, as a window on Keralan culture. The oldest most interesting part of town is the **Fort** area in the south, around the **Shri Padmanabhaswamy temple** and **Puttan Malika palace**, while important showcases for painting, crafts and sculpture, the **Shri Chitra Art Gallery** and **Napier Museum**, stand together in a park in the north. In addition, schools specializing in the martial art Kalarippayat and the dance/theatre forms of Kathakali and Kutiyattam offer visitors an insight into the Keralan obsession with physical training and skill.

Most travellers choose to pass straight through Thiruvananthapuram, lured by the promise of Kovalam's palm-fringed beaches (see p.1305). A mere twenty-minute bus ride south, this popular resort is close enough to use as a base to see the city, although the recent upsurge in package tourism means it's far from the low-key, inexpensive travellers' hang-out it used to be.

The city of the snake Anantha

Thiruvananthapuram was the capital of the kingdom of Travancore from 1750 until 1956, when the state of Kerala was created. Its name (formally readopted to replace "Trivandrum"), derives from *thiru-anantha-puram* – "the holy city of Anantha", the coiled snake on which the god Vishnu reclines in the midst of the cosmic ocean.

Vishnu is given a special name for this non-activity – *Padma-nabha*, "lotus-navel" – and is invariably depicted lying on the sacred snake with a lotus growing umbilically from his navel. The god Brahma sits inside the lotus, which represents the beginning of a new era. Padmanabha is the principal deity of the royal family of Travancore, and of Thiruvananthapuram's **Shri Padmanabhaswamy temple**.

Arrival and information

The international **airport** (connected to most major Indian cities, as well as Sri Lanka, the Maldives and the Middle East), with tourist information and foreign exchange facilities, is 6km southwest of town and serviced by an airport bus and bus #14 to and from the City bus stand. Auto-rickshaws will run you

Kollam, Kochi & NH-47

THIRUVANANTHAPURAM

VELLAYAMBALAM

RESTAURANTS
Amma	G
Anand Bhavan	E
Arya Niwas	F
Indian Coffee House I	A
Indian Coffee House II &	B
Hot Breads	
Indian Coffee House III	H
Kalavara	D
Kerala House	C

Natural History Museum
Sri Chitra Art Gallery
Kanakakumu Palace
Air India
Indian Airlines
Zoo
MUSEUM RD
Napier Museum, Open Air Theatre & Natural History Museum

Museum of Science & Technology
Library

Stadium

VAZHUTHACUD

KUNNUKUZHI

Connemara Market

Forest Museum

ACCOMMODATION
Greenland Lodging	11
Hazeen	8
Highland	10
Horizon	5
Jas	9
KTDC Chaithram	12
KTDC Mascot	1
Lucia Continental	13
Manacaud	7
Pankaj	4
Prasanth	6
South Park	2
YWCA	3

SPENCER JCTN
BAKERY JCTN
Air Lanka
DC Books
Secretariat
Foreigners Registration Office
Telegraph Office
Aries Travel
PRESS RD
Chachu Nehru Children's Museum
VANCHIYUR
THYCAUD
Swastik Tours
GPO
Ayurveda College
COLLEGE JCTN
ARISTO ROAD
New Theatre
Tourist Reception Centre
KSRTC Bus Stand
STATION RD
THAMPANOOR
THAKARAPARAMBU RD
Railway Station
PADMAVILASAM RD
POWER HOUSE RD
FORT
Tank
City & Local Bus Stand
CHENTITTA
Sri Padmanabhaswamy Temple
Wall Street Finances
Buses to Kovalam
CHALAI
CHAL BAZAR RD
Puttan Malika Palace

Airport (6 km) ◀ Kochi
Airport (6 km) ◀
CHETTIKULANGARA RD

N

0   Metres   250

Kovalam & Kanniyakumari

into the centre for around Rs40 and there's also a handy prepaid taxi service. If you're heading straight out to Kovalam, you may find that a prepaid taxi is almost as cheap as an auto-rickshaw.

The long-distance KSRTC **Thampanoor bus stand** (℡0471/323886) and **railway station** (℡0471/329246 or 132) face each other across Station Road in the southeast of the city, a short walk east of Overbridge Junction, where Thiruvananthapuram is bisected by the long north–south MG Road. **Local buses** (to Kovalam for example) depart from **City bus stand**, East Fort, fifteen minutes' walk south from the KSRTC and railway stations. **Auto-rickshaws**, whose drivers don't always use their meters, also run to Kovalam, from the centre, for around Rs60–100. **Taxis** charge around Rs150.

Information and tours

All the **tourist offices** at the **airport** are open during flight times. The Government of India's counter (℡0471/501498) offers general information regarding Kerala and the adjacent states, while the Government of Kerala has two counters, one at the domestic terminal (℡0471/501085) and the other at the international terminal (℡0471/502298), offering Kerala-specific information including, for example, on backwater cruises. The Government of Kerala also has an office in the main block at the **Thampanoor bus stand** (Mon–Sat 10am–5pm; ℡0471/327224) which is good for general information and maps and sells tickets for backwater cruises between Kollam and Alappuzha. They have another counter at the **railway station** (℡0471/334470).

The **Kerala Tourist Development Corporation** (KTDC), the best organized of all the Indian state tourist corporations, is designed primarily to sell its own products and promote cultural events (check out Ⓦwww.keralatourism .com and Ⓦwww.ktdc.com). The KTDC's main visitor centre, opposite the Government Museum at Park View (℡0471/321132), can book accommodation in their good-value **hotel** chain, and they sell tickets for various **guided tours**. Most of these, including the city tour (daily 8am–7pm; Rs95), are far too rushed, but if you're pushed for time try the **Cape Comorin** tour (daily 7.30am–9pm; Rs230), which takes in Padmanabhapuram Palace (except Mon), Kovalam, Suchindram temple, and Kanniyakumari. They also offer their own **backwater cruises** (see p.1326) with flexible itineraries; for further information contact their head office at Mascot Square (℡0471/318976, ℻314406, Ⓔktdc@vsnl.com). Several small companies are also starting backwater cruises within striking distance of Thiruvananthapuram for those without the time to explore the much more rewarding Kuttanad region; try Island Queen at Pazhikkara, Pachalloor (℡0471/481559).

Accommodation

Thiruvananthapuram's mid-range and expensive **hotels** are, in general, cheaper than in most state capitals, but are not concentrated in any one district. Budget hotels are grouped mainly in the streets around **Central Station Road**. Good areas to start looking are **Manjalikulam Road**, five minutes' walk west from the railway station, or the lanes off **Aristo Junction**; note that the best of the budget places tend to be full by late afternoon. If you prefer to base yourself at the beach, head for **Kovalam** (see p.1305).

Greenland Lodging, Aristo Road, Thampanoor ℡0471/328114. Large, efficient and spotless budget lodge and the best there is within a stone's throw of both the bus stand and the railway sta-

tion; 24hr checkout, but get there early. ❷
Hazeen, off Aristo Road ℡0471/325181. Very clean budget lodge within easy reach of the railway station; sports the usual green-walled rooms,

but the bed linen is fresh and tiled bathrooms immaculate. ❷

Highland, Manjalikulam Road ☏ 0471/333200. Dependable mid-range option: clean, well run and a short walk from the stations. In a multistorey block, it's also the easiest place in the area to find. ❹–❻

Horizon, Aristo Road, 10min by taxi north of the railway station (☏ 0471/326888, ☏ 324444). Plush and efficient business hotel with pricey non-a/c rooms and a/c suites. Features two restaurants – one on the leafy rooftop – and a bar. The tariff includes breakfast. ❼–❽

Jass, Thycaud, Aristo Junction ☏ 0471/324881, ☏ 324443. Reasonable two-star in a quiet central location near the stations. A range of pleasant rooms, all with cable TV and Western toilets. ❺–❽

KTDC Chaithram, Station Road ☏ 0471/330977. Large tower-block hotel opposite the railway station and adjacent to Thampanoor bus stand, with spacious rooms (some a/c), a/c veg restaurant, bank, travel agent, car rental, beauty parlour, cybercafé, bookshop and bar. Good value at this price. ❺–❼

KTDC Mascot, near Indian Airlines at Mascot Junction (☏ 0471/318990). Atmospheric period building with long corridors and huge rooms, plus there's a swimming pool, bar and restaurant, and it's conveniently located near all the museums. ❼–❽

Lucia Continental, East Fort ☏ 0471/463443, ☏ 463347. A swish complex near the temple, with

104 deluxe rooms plus "fantasy suites". Boasts a restaurant, coffee shop, disco, swimming pool and a travel agent. ❾

Manacaud, Manjalikulam Road ☏ 0471/330360. Nothing special, but the best maintained of several hotels on this lane. Attached bathrooms, but the windows are small and there are no balconies. Quieter, but not as good value as identical lodges on Aristo Road. ❸

Pankaj, opposite Secretariat, MG Road ☏ 0471/464645. Stylish, well-maintained, three-star hotel. Some rooms have beautiful views over trees, as does the good Keralan restaurant. Tariff includes breakfast; foreigners pay in dollars. ❾

Prasanth Tourist Home, Aristo Road, opposite *Horizon Hotel* ☏ 0471/327180. One of a crop of rock-bottom and very basic guesthouses around a courtyard near the station. Reputable and family-run. The *Satil* and *Salvha*, next door, are similar. ❷

South Park, MG Road ☏ 0471/333333, ☏ 331861. Comfortable, business-oriented Welcomgroup four-star with a/c rooms, efficient travel agency, multi-cuisine restaurant and 24hr coffee shop. Popular with tour groups and flight crews, so book in advance. Pay in dollars. ❾

YWCA, Spencer Junction ☏ 0471/477308. Spotless en-suite doubles in modern block. Friendly, safe and central with neat rooms, but the puritanical order and quiet is slightly overwhelming and the place is locked at 10.30pm sharp. For women and married couples only, and single rates are available. ❸

The City

The historical and spiritual heart of Thiruvananthapuram is in the **Fort area**, at the southern end of **MG Road**, which encloses the Shri Padmanabhaswamy Vishnu temple. Following MG Road north leads you through the main shopping district, which is busy all day, and especially choked when one of the frequent, but generally orderly, political demonstrations converges on the grand colonial **Secretariat** building halfway along. The whole centre can be explored easily on foot, though you might be glad of a rickshaw ride (Rs15–20) back from the museums and parks, close to the top end of the road.

Fort area

A solid but unremarkable fort gateway leads from near the Kovalam bus stand at East Fort to the **Shri Padmanabhaswamy temple**, which is still controlled by the Travancore royal family. Unusually for Kerala it is built in the Dravidian style of Tamil Nadu, with a tall *gopura* gateway, but it's surrounded by high fortress-like walls, and is closed to non-Hindus; little can be seen from outside, apart from the seven-storey *gopura*.

Most of the temple buildings date from the eighteenth century, added by Raja Marthanda Varma to a much older shrine. According to legend, the temple was founded after Vishnu, disguised as a beautiful child, merged into a huge tree in the forest, which immediately crashed to the ground. There it transformed into an image of the reclining Vishnu, a full 13km long. Divakara, a sage who witnessed this, was frustrated by his limited human vision, and prayed to Vishnu to assume a form that he could see in its entirety. Vishnu complied, and the temple appeared. The area in front of the temple, where devotees bathe in a huge tank, is thronged with stalls selling religious souvenirs, shell necklaces, puja offerings, jasmine and marigolds, along with the ubiquitous plaster-cast models of Kathakali masks. As you approach, the red-brick CVN Kalari Sangam, a **Kalarippayat martial arts** gymnasium, is on the left. From 6.30am to 8am (Mon–Sat) you can watch the students practising Kalarippayat fighting exercises. Foreigners may join courses in the gym, arranged through the head teacher, although prior experience of martial arts and/or dance is a prerequisite; three-month courses are also available, but the fee of Rs500 does not cover accommodation. You can also come here for a traditional **Ayurvedic massage**, and to consult the gym's expert Ayurvedic doctors (Mon–Sat 10am–1pm & 5–7.30pm, Sun 10am–1pm).

A path along the north side of the tank leads past the north, west and southern entrances to the temple. It's an atmospheric walk, particularly in the early morning and at dusk, when devotees make their way to and from prayer (a closed iron gate bars the northern side, but everybody climbs through the gap). These neat little streets, in the old days of Kerala's extraordinary caste system, would have been a "no go" area, possibly on pain of death, to some members of the community.

Behind the temple on West Fort, set back from the road across open ground, the Margi school of **Kathakali** dance drama and **Kutiyattam** theatre (see p.1369) is housed in Fort High School. With prior notice you can watch classes; this is the place to ask about authentic Kathakali performances.

Puttan Malika Palace

The **Puttan Malika palace** (daily 8.30am–12.30pm & 3.30–5.30pm; Rs20, Rs25 extra with camera), immediately southeast of the temple, became the seat of the Travancore rajas after they left Padmanabhapuram at the end of the nineteenth century. To generate funds for much-needed restoration, the royal family has opened the palace to the public for the first time in more than two hundred years. Although much of it remains off limits, you can wander around some of the most impressive wings, which have been converted into a **museum**. Cool chambers, lined with delicately carved wooden screens and highly polished plaster floors, house a crop of dusty Travancore heirlooms. Among the predictable array of portraits, royal regalia and weapons are some genuine treasures, such as a solid crystal throne given by the Dutch, and some fine murals. The real highlight, however, is the typically understated, elegant Keralan architecture. Beneath sloping red-tiled roofs, hundreds of wooden pillars carved into the forms of rampant horses prop up the eaves, with airy verandas projecting onto the surrounding lawns.

The royal family have always been keen patrons of the arts, and the tradition is maintained with an open-air **Carnatic music festival**, held in the grounds during the festival of Navaratri (Oct/Nov). Performers sit on the palace's raised porch, flanked by the main facade, with the spectators seated on the lawn. For details, ask at the KTDC tourist office.

MG Road: markets and shopping

An assortment of **craft shops** along **MG Road** north of Station Road sell sandalwood, brass and Keralan bell-metal oil lamps (see p.1364). The Gandhian

Khadi Gramodyog, between Pazhavangadi and Overbridge junctions, stocks hand-loom cloth (dig around for the best stuff), plus radios and cassette machines manufactured by the Women's Federation. **Natesan's Antique Arts**, further up, is part of a chain that specializes in paintings and temple woodcarvings. Prices are high, but they usually have some beautiful pieces, among them some superb reproductions of Thanjur paintings and traditional inlaid chests for Kathakali costumes.

At first glance most of the **bookstores** in the area seem largely intended for exam entrants, but some, such as the a/c **Continental Books** on MG Road, stock a good choice of titles in English, mostly relating to India and with a fair selection of fiction. Smaller but with an equally wide array of English-language fiction and assorted subjects such as philosophy, history and music, **DC Books** on Statue Road, on the first floor of a building above Statue Junction, is well worth a browse. Other bookshops along MG Road include the south Indian chain store **Higginbothams** and **Paico Books**.

Almost at the top of MG Road, on the right-hand side, the excellent little **Connemara Market** is the place to pick up essentials like plastic buckets, dried and fresh fish, fruit, vegetables, coconut scrapers, exotic *bindis*, crude wooden toys, coir, woven winnowing baskets and Christmas decorations. It also holds the workshops of several **tailors**.

Public Gardens, Zoo and museums

A minute's walk east from the north end of MG Road, opposite the KTDC Visitors Centre, you come to the entrance to Thiruvananthapuram's **Public Gardens** (Tues & Thurs–Sun 10am–5pm, Wed 1–5pm; cover ticket for all museums in complex Rs5, available only outside the Biotechnology Museum, to the left of the Government Museum). As well as serving as a welcome refuge from the noise of the city – its lawns usually filled with courting couples, students and picnicking families – the park holds the city's best museums. The **Zoo** (Tues–Sun 10am–5pm; Rs4, Rs5 extra with camera) is in a nice enough setting, just inside the gate on the left, but the depressing state of the inmates, and the propensity of some visitors to get their kicks by taunting them, make it eminently missable.

To the east of the zoo, the extraordinary **Government (Napier) Museum** of arts and crafts was completed in 1880. An early experiment in what became known as the "Indo-Saracenic" style, the building has tiled double-storey gabled roofs, garish red-, black- and salmon-patterned brickwork, tall slender towers, and, above the main entrance, a series of pilasters forming Islamic arches. The spectacular interior is dimly lit through stained-glass windows, and the wooden ceiling features loud turquoise, pink, red and yellow stripes. The architect, Robert Fellowes Chisolm (1840–1915), set out to incorporate Keralan elements into colonial architecture; the museum was named after his employer, Lord Napier, the governor of the Madras Presidency. Highlights include fifteenth-century Keralan woodcarvings from Kulathupuzha and Thiruvattar, gold necklaces and belts, minutely detailed ivory work, a carved temple chariot (*rath*), wooden models of Guruvayur temple and an oval temple theatre (*kuttambalam*), plus twelfth-century Chola and fourteenth-century Vijayanagar bronzes.

The attractive **Shri Chitra Art Gallery**, opposite, with its curved veranda and tiled roof, houses some splendid paintings from the Rajput, Moghul and Tanjore schools, as well as China, Tibet and Japan. The oil paintings by Raja Ravi Varma (1848–1906), who is widely credited with having introduced oil painting to India, have been criticized for their sentimentality and Western influence, but his treatment of Hindu mythological themes is both dramatic and beautiful. Also on display are the paintings of the Russian artist-philoso-

The annual **Nishangandi Dance and Music festival** (February 22–27) is held at Kanakakannu Palace, originally built as a cultural venue for the maharajas of Tiruvananthapuram. A large amphitheatre in the formal gardens is a pleasant place to take in an evening of classical dances and music by artists invited from all over India (ask at a KTDC Tourist Office for details).

The **Arattu** festival, centred around the Shri Padmanabhaswamy temple, takes place biannually, in Meenam (March/April) and Thulam (Oct/Nov). Each time, ten days of festivities inside the temple (open to Hindus only) culminate in a procession through the streets of the city, taking the deity, Padmanabhaswamy, to the sea for ritual immersion. Five caparisoned elephants, armed guards, a *nagasvaram* (double-reed wind instrument) and *tavil* drum group are led by the maharaja of Travancore, in his symbolic role as *kshatrya*, the servant of the god. Instead of the richly apparelled figure that might be anticipated, the maharaja wears a simple white *dhoti*, with his chest bare save for the sacred thread. Rather than riding, he walks the whole way, bearing a sword. To the accompaniment of a 21-gun salute and music, the procession sets off from the east gate of the temple at around 5pm, moving at a brisk pace to reach Shankhumukham Beach at sunset, about an hour later. The route is lined with devotees, many of whom honour both the god and the maharaja. After the seashore ceremonies, the cavalcade returns to the temple at about 9pm, to be greeted by another gun salute. An extremely loud firework display rounds off the day.

For ten days in March, Muslims celebrate **Chandanakudam Maholsavam** at the Beemapalli mosque, 5km southwest of the city on the coastal road towards the airport. The Hindu-influenced festival commemorates the anniversary of the death of Beema Beevi, a woman revered for her piety. On the first and most important day, pilgrims converge on the mosque carrying earthenware pots decorated with flowers and containing money offerings. Activities such as the sword form of *daharamuttu* take place inside the mosque, while outside there is dance and music. In the early hours of the morning, a flag is brought out from Beema Beevi's tomb and taken on a procession, accompanied by a *panchavadyam* drum-and-horn orchestra and caparisoned elephants, practices normally associated with Hindu festivals. Once more, the rest of the night is taken up with fireworks.

The great festival of **Onam** (late August or September), takes place throughout the state over ten days during the coolest time of year, when Keralans remember the reign of King Mahabali, a legendary figure who, it is believed, achieved an ideal balance of harmony, wealth and justice during his tenure. Unfortunately, the gods became upset and envious at Mahabali's success and so Vishnu came to pack him off to another world. However, once a year the king was allowed to return to his people for ten days, and Onam is a joyful celebration of the royal visit. Families display their wealth, feasts and boat races are held and, in Tiruvananthapuram, there's a week-long cultural festival of dance and music culminating in a colourful street carnival (ask at a KTDC office for details).

pher and mystic, Nicholas Roerich, who arrived in India at the turn of the twentieth century. His paintings amalgamate the deep and strong colours of his Russian background with the mythical landscape of the Himalayas where he died in 1947.

Away from the centre

The **Chachu Nehru Children's Museum** (Tues–Sun 10am–5pm), in Thycaud in the east of the city, serves as a rather dusty testament to the enthusiasm of some anonymous donor, presumably back in the 1960s. One room contains ritual masks, probably from Bengal, Rajasthan and Orissa, but the rest of the place is taken up with stamps, health education displays, and more than 2000 dolls featuring figures in Indian costume, American presidents, Disney characters and British Beefeaters.

Also on the eastern side of town, visitors can by arrangement watch classes at the PS Balachandran Nair Kalari **martial arts gymnasium**, Kalariyil, TC 15/854, Cotton Hill, Vazhuthakad (daily 6–8am & 6–7.30pm). Built in 1992 along traditional lines, in stone, the *kalari* fighting pit is overlooked from a height of 4m by a viewing gallery. Students (some as young as eight) train in unarmed combat and in the use of weapons. Traditionally, the art of battle with long razor-blade-like *urumi* is only taught to the teacher's successor. The school arranges short courses in Kalarippayat, and can also provide guides for forest trekking.

Eating

Thiruvananthapuram offers menus for all tastes and budgets, although smart **restaurants** specializing in Keralan cuisine are thin on the ground. Most of the mid- to top-range hotels include a few local dishes in their pretty uniform multi-cuisine menus, and the *Pankaj* and *Horizon* both have pleasant rooftop restaurants. If you want to experience full-flavoured Keralan "meals" or need a cheap *dosa*-type snack, just head for one of the dozens of crowded, formica-tabled "meals" houses at lunchtime.

Amma, Central Station Road. Blissful a/c and conveniently near the stations, offering the usual south Indian snacks menu and no less than seven different types of *uttappam* (rice pancake).

Anand Bhawan, opposite Secretariat, MG Road. Cheap, simple restaurant near the *Pankaj*, offering hot, fresh regional veg "meals".

Arya Nivaas, Aristo Junction, Thumpanoor. Spotless vegetarian restaurant in a new hotel where you can get "meals" for less than Rs30 and an assortment of dishes such as biriyani.

Hot Breads, Anna's Arcade, Spencer Junction, MG Road. Yummy fresh and hot savoury and sweet breads, pastries and snacks, including pizzas, cheese rolls and croissants.

Indian Coffee House (I), LMS Junction. Opposite the entrance to the Public Gardens, this is a clean and efficient place to down a refreshing cold coffee after sightseeing: omelettes, south Indian snacks and meals are available all day.

Indian Coffee House (II), Spencer Junction, MG Road. Small, colonial-style building, set back from the road and a sociable place to meet local students. Serves good-value snacks, meals and real filter coffee.

Indian Coffee House (III), Central Station Road.

Next to the bus station and unbeatable for breakfast or a quick snack. Turbaned waiters serve *dosas*, *wadas*, omelettes and hot drinks in a bizarre spiral building designed by an eccentric British architect. Obligatory pit stop.

Kalavara, Press Road (lane opposite the GPO). Past several bookshops, an upstairs restaurant above a fast-food counter, which features a mixed menu plus local cuisine including pork and beef dishes. Expect to pay around Rs70.

Kerala House, next to DC Books, Statue Road. Full of atmosphere, popular and highly recommended by locals as the place to get Kerala cuisine "as mamma makes it". Lunch is "meals" and dinner is à la carte – the fish curry and steamed tapioca is particularly good.

KTDC Chaithram, Central Station Road. Two restaurants: one pure veg and the other north Indian Mughlai-style. The former, a tastefully decorated air-cooled place, is the best, offering a few good-value Keralan specialities. Recommended.

Sandha, *Pankaj Hotel*, opposite Secretariat, MG Road. Fifth-floor restaurant with a mixed menu and good-value lunch buffet and spiced-down Keralan cuisine; the ground-floor restaurant opens for breakfast.

Listings

Ayurvedic health centres Ayurvedic treatment in one form or another is to be found throughout Kerala, but for more information contact the

Ayurvedic Medical College Hospital, MG Road ☎0471/460823; for Kayachikistsa or traditional Ayurvedic massage and foot therapy contact

Agastheswara, Ayurvedic Health Centre, Jiji Nivas, Killi, Kattakkada ☎0471/291270.

Banks and exchange The State Bank of India, near the Secretariat on MG Road (Mon–Fri 10am–2pm, Sat 10am–noon) accepts only travellers' cheques and currency. The State Bank of Travancore (Mon–Fri 10am–2pm, Sat 10am–noon) at Statue Junction and the domestic airport recognizes travellers' cheques, currency, Visa and Mastercard. Wall Street Finances (Mon–Sat 10am–6pm; ☎0471/450659) is located behind the *Lucia Continental Hotel* in East Fort, and the Central Reserve Bank, in the lobby of the KTDC *Chaithram Hotel*. American Express cashes travellers' cheques and advances money on credit cards through The Great Indian Tour Company, Mullassery Tavern, Vanross Junction (☎0471/331516), east off MG Road. Thomas Cook has a counter at the airport and an office at Tourindia, MG Road (☎0471/330437).

Car rental Inter-Car, Ayswarya Buildings, Press Road ☎0471/330964; Nataraj Travels, Thampanoor ☎0471/323034; The Great Indian Tour Company, Mullassery Towers, Vanross Jctn ☎0471/331516; Travel India, opposite the Secretariat, MG Road ☎0471/478208.

Dance and drama For Kathakali and Kutiyattam check with the Margi School (see p.1369), or the tourist office on Station Road, which organizes free dance performances at the open-air Nishagandhi Auditorium (Sept–March Sat 6.45pm).

Hospitals General Hospital, near Holy Angels Convent, Vanchiyur ☎0471/443874; Ramakrishna Mission Hospital, Sastamangalam ☎0471/322123.

Internet access is widely available in Thiruvananthapuram, but on the pricey side (as is internet throughout southern Kerala) at Rs60–80 per hour. The most efficient place is at *Hotel Chaithram* (Rs60/hr). Alternatively, try Megabyte on MG Road and Tandem Communications at Statue Junction.

Pharmacies Central Medical Stores, amongst others, at Statue Junction, MG Road.

Post office in Vanchiyur district, a short distance west of MG Road (daily 8am–6pm), with poste restante counter.

Telephones the Telegraph Office, opposite the Secretariat on MG Road, is open 24hr.

Travel agents Aries Travels (specialists for tours to the Maldives), Ayswarya Bldg, Press Road ☎0471/330964; Swastik Tours and Travel, Puthenchantai, MG Road ☎0471/331691, ☎331270; The Great Indian Tour Company, Mullassery Towers, Vanross Jctn ☎0471/331516; Airtravel Enterprises (good for air tickets), New Corporation Building, MG Road, Palayam ☎0471/323900; Tourindia (pioneering cruise and tour operators), MG Road ☎0471/330437; Travel India, opposite the Secretariat, MG Road (☎0471/478208).

Yoga The Sivananda Yoga Ashram at 37/1929 Airport Road, Palkulangara, West Fort (☎0471/450942) holds daily classes at various levels, which you can arrange on spec. Better still, head for Neyyar Dam, 28km east of town, where their world-famous Dhanwanthari ashram offers excellent two-week introductory courses amid idyllic mountain surroundings (see p.1315 for more).

Around Thiruvananthapuram

Although for virtually its entire 550-kilometre length the **Keralan coast** is lined with sandy beaches, rocky promontories and coconut palms, **Kovalam** is one of the only places where swimming in the sea is not considered eccentric by locals, and which offers accommodation to suit all budgets. When it gets too hot at sea level, **Ponmudi**, a bus ride away in the Cardamom hills through forest, spice and tea plantations, makes a refreshing break. Another easy excursion from Thiruvananthapuram is its predecessor as capital of Travancore, **Padmanabhapuram**, site of a magnificent palace.

Kovalam and around

The coastal village of **KOVALAM** may lie just 10km south from Thiruvananthapuram, but as Kerala's most developed **beach resort** it's becoming ever more distanced from the rest of the state. Each year greater numbers of Western visitors – budget travellers and jet-setters alike – arrive in search of sun, sea and palm-fringed beaches. For many travellers it has become, with Goa

Thiruvananthapuram is the main transport hub for traffic along the coast and cross-country. Towns within a couple of hours of the capital – such as Varkala and Kollam – are most quickly and conveniently reached by bus. For longer hauls though, you're better off travelling by train as both the private and state (KSRTC) buses tend to hurtle along the recently upgraded coastal highway at terrifying speeds; they're also more crowded.

For an overview of travel services to and from Thiruvananthapuram, see Kerala Travel Details on p.1378.

By air

Thiruvananthapuram's airport sees daily Jet Airways' and Indian Airlines' flights to Chennai, Cochin and Bangalore. Indian Airlines also fly daily to Mumbai and twice daily to Delhi. Air India has departures to Mumbai seven days a week to connect with international flights. Indian Airlines fly five times a week to Malé in the Maldives and Air Maldives flies the same route daily with additional flights on Fridays and Sundays. Indian Airlines (2 weekly) and Air Lanka (6 weekly) both fly to Colombo in Sri Lanka.

Indian Airlines have offices at Air Centre, Mascot Jctn (℡0471/316870), and the airport (℡0471/451537) while Jet Airways is at Akshaya Towers, 1st Floor, Sasthamangalam Jctn (℡0471/321018). Air India is at Museum Road, Vellayambalam Circle (℡0471/310310 or 501205), and the airport (℡0471/501426), while Air Lanka is based at Spencer Bldg, Palayam, MG Road (℡0471/322309) and has an office at the airport (℡0471/501147). Gulf Air, which operates regular flights to various Gulf states, is across town in Vellayambalam (℡0471/328003 or 501205); and Air Maldives is also on Spencer Road (℡0471/463531) with an office at the airport (℡0471/501344). Other Middle East airlines include Saudi Arabian Airlines at Baker Junction (℡0471/321321) and Oman Airways at Sasthamangalam (℡0471/328137). British Airways is at Vellayambalam (℡0471/326604) and KLM at Spencer Junction (℡0471/463531).

By bus

From the long-distance KSRTC Thampanoor bus stand (℡0471/323886), frequent services run north through Kerala to Kollam and Ernakulam/Kochi via Alappuzha (3hr 15min). Three buses a day go up to Kumily for the Periyar Wildlife Reserve and there is one bus hourly to Kanniyakumari. Most buses running east and south are operated by the Tamil Nadu State Road Transport Corporation (TNSRTC); these include regular services to Madurai and Chennai. Tickets for all the services listed above may be booked in advance at the reservations hatch on the main bus stand concourse; note that TNSRTC have their own counter.

and Mamallapuram, the third essential stop on a triangular tour of tropical south Indian "paradises" – or indeed just another leg of the trail along the coasts of South Asia.

Europeans have been visiting Kovalam since the 1930s, but not until hippies started to colonize the place some thirty years later were any hotels built. As the resort's popularity began to grow, more and more paddy fields were filled and the first luxury holiday complexes sprang up. These soon caught the eye of European charter companies scouting for "undiscovered" beach hideaways to supplement their Goa brochures, and by the mid-1990s plane-loads of package tourists were flown here direct from the UK. This latest influx has had a dramatic impact on Kovalam. Prices have rocketed, rubbish lies in unsightly piles at the roadsides, and in high season the beach – recently enlarged to make way for even more cafés, souvenir stalls and fish restaurants – is packed nose-to-tail.

By train

Kerala's capital is well connected by train with other towns and cities in the country, although getting seats at short notice on long-haul journeys can be a problem. Reservations should be made as far in advance as possible from the efficient computerized booking office at the station (Mon–Sat 8am–2pm & 2.15–8pm, Sun 8am–2pm). Sleepers are sold throughout Kerala on a first-come, first-served basis, not on local stations' quotas.

Recommended trains from Thiruvananthapuram

Destination	Name	No.	Frequency	Departs	Total time
Bangalore	Kanniyakumari–Bangalore Express	#6525	daily	9.10am	19hr 25min
Calcutta	Trivandrum–Howrah Express*	#6323	Wed & Sat	12.45pm	48hr
	Trivandrum–Guwahati Express*	#5627	Sun	12.45pm	47hr
Chennai	Trivandrum–Chennai Mail*	#6320	daily	1.30pm	17hr 45min
	Trivandrum–Guwahati Express*	#5627	Sun	12.45pm	18hr 55min
Delhi	Rajdhani Express**	#2431	Fri & Sat	7.30pm	44hr 30min
	Kerala Express	#2625	daily	11am	52hr 30min
Ernakulam/Kochi	Kerala Express	#2625	daily	11am	4hr 30min
Kanniyakumari	Kanniyakumari Express	#1081	daily	7.15am	2hr 15min
Kollam	Kanniyakumari Express**	#1082	daily	7.30am	1hr 30min
Kozhikode	Trivandrum–Cannanore Express	#6347	nightly	9pm	9hr 50min
Mangalore	Trivandrum–Mangalore Parasuram Express***	#6349	daily	6am	16hr 20min
	Malabar Express***	#6329	daily	5.40pm	17hr 25min
Mumbai	Trivandrum–Mumbai Express	#6332	Fri	4.20am	40hr
	Kanniyakumari Express*	#1082	daily	7.30am	45hr 35min

* via Kollam, Kottayam, Ernakulam, Palakkad and Chennai
** a/c only
*** via Varkala, Kollam, Kottayam, Ernakulam, Thrissur, Kozhikode, Kannur and Kasargode

Add to this a backdrop of rapidly deteriorating concrete hotels, and you can see why Kovalam's detractors call it "the Costa del Kerala".

Arrival, information and getting around

Heading along the upgraded approach road from the capital (now littered with publicity hoardings), the frequent #9 **bus** from Thiruvananthapuram (East Fort; 20min) loops through Kovalam, and stops at the gates to the *Ashok* complex, at the northern end of the middle bay. Anyone carrying heavy bags who wants to stay by the sea (and not at the *Ashok*), should alight earlier, either at the road to the lighthouse, or the road leading down to the *Sea Rock* hotel. It's also possible to take an **auto-rickshaw** or **taxi** all the way from Thiruvananthapuram; auto-rickshaws cost between Rs60 and Rs100 but will try to get away with a lot more, while taxis charge around Rs150.

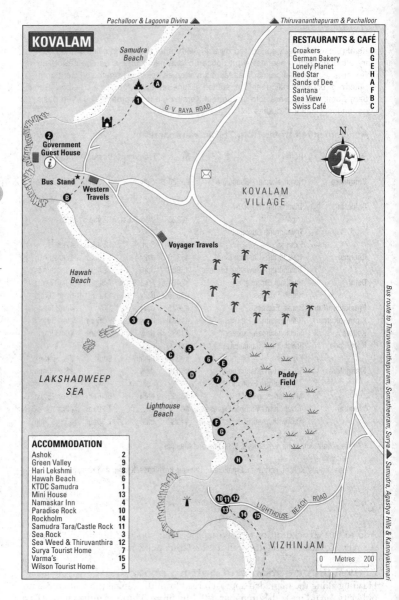

KOVALAM

Samudra Beach

G V RAYA ROAD

2 Government Guest House

Bus Stand

Western Travels

KOVALAM VILLAGE

Hawah Beach

Voyager Travels

LAKSHADWEEP SEA

Paddy Field

Lighthouse Beach

VIZHINJAM

Pachalloor & Lagoona Divina ▲   ▲ Thiruvananthapuram & Pachalloor

Bus route to Thiruvananthapuram, Somatheeram, Surya ▲ Samudra, Agastha Hills & Kanniyakumari

RESTAURANTS & CAFÉ

Croakers	D
German Bakery	G
Lonely Planet	E
Red Star	H
Sands of Dee	A
Santana	F
Sea View	B
Swiss Café	C

ACCOMMODATION

Ashok	2
Green Valley	9
Hari Lekshmi	8
Hawah Beach	6
KTDC Samudra	1
Mini House	13
Namaskar Inn	4
Paradise Rock	10
Rockholm	14
Samudra Tara/Castle Rock	11
Sea Rock	3
Sea Weed & Thiruvanthira	12
Surya Tourist Home	7
Varma's	15
Wilson Tourist Home	5

0   Metres   200

The friendly **tourist facilitation centre** (daily 10am–5pm, closed Sun in low season; ☎0471/480085), just inside the gate to the *Ashok Hotel*, is a new place with plenty of leaflets to give out and up-to-date advice about cultural events. They also run a small **reading room** next door (same hours) that stocks British and American newspapers, as well as novels.

There are now several places to **change money** at Kovalam but private exchange rates tend to vary so it's best to do some research first. Of the **banks**,

Ayurveda in Kovalam

Ayurvedic massage is advertised everywhere in Kovalam, and you'll constantly be approached by men professing to be well-qualified Ayurvedic practitioners – they even show you impressive certificates. They offer cheap massages, usually costing Rs150–500. However, most of the so-called "Ayurvedic centres" along Lighthouse Beach are seasonal, as are the "doctors" and "masseurs"; there have been an increasing number of complaints about sexual harassment during sessions and serious skin reactions to dodgy Ayurvedic oils.

If you're interested in benefiting from an Ayurvedic massage, the only centres in Kovalam that currently hold official state approval are at the *Ashok Hotel* and the KTDC *Samudra*, which both charge from Rs600 a session. Alternatively, contact the Ayurveda College in Thiruvanathapuram (℡0471/460823).

the Central Bank of India (Mon–Fri 10am–2pm, Sat 10am–noon) is at the *Ashok* and there is a branch of the Andhra Bank at the KTDC *Samudra* complex near the main gates (same hours). Among other places, you can also change money at *Wilson's Hotel* any time (the most competitive rates), at Great Indian Travel Services, Lighthouse beach (℡0471/481110), and at Western Travels, at the bus stand (℡0471/481334).

Opposite the bus stand, Western Travels (daily 8am–8pm; ℡0471/481334) is a reliable agent for flight confirmations and ticketing, and can arrange **car rental**. Great Indian Travel Service, another all-round agency, also arranges **motorbike rental** (a Bullet costs around Rs550 per day and a scooter Rs350). Voyager Travels, near the police station (℡0471/481993) specializes in all two-wheeler hire at competitive rates.

Dozens of places offer **internet** services with charges of around Rs60 per hour, but the most efficient place with super-fast connections is at *Croakers Restaurant*, Lighthouse Beach. Kovalam doesn't have a major **bookshop**, but the German Bakery has a reasonable selection for rent or for sale and there's a noticeboard to find out what is on.

Kovalam's beaches

Kovalam consists of three main beaches; the southernmost, known for obvious reasons as **Lighthouse beach**, is where most visitors spend their time. Roughly ten minutes' trudge through the sand from end to end (none of it is paved), it's bordered with cheek-to-cheek low-rise concrete guesthouses and restaurants. The red-and-white **lighthouse** stands on the promontory at the southern end of the beach, but is closed to the public.

Hawah, the middle beach, overlooked from a rocky headland by the five-star *Ashok* resort, functions each morning as a base for local fishermen, who drag a massive net through the shallows to scoop up thrashing multi-hued minnows,

Warning: swimming safety

Due to unpredictable rip currents and a strong undertow, especially during the monsoons, swimming from Kovalam's beaches is not always safe. The recent introduction of lifeguards (noticeable by their blue shirts) has reduced the annual death toll, but at least a couple of tourists still drown here each year, and many more get into difficulties. Follow the warnings of the safety flags at all times and keep a close eye on children. There's a first-aid post midway along Lighthouse beach.

singing and coiling endless piles of coir rope as they work. North of the *Ashok*, though in full view of its distinctive sloping terraces, the final, northernmost beach, **Samudra**, is the least affected of all by the changing times, dotted with a few rudimentary wooden fishing vessels.

Accommodation

Kovalam is crammed with **accommodation**, ranging from standard budget rooms with just a double bed and bathroom to five-star hilltop chalets. Only rock-bottom rooms are hard to find, as all but a handful of the many budget travellers' guesthouses have been recently upgraded to suit the standards of the large number of package tourists that flock here over Christmas. This also means that hotels are often block-booked weeks in advance; it pays to phone around and reserve a room before you arrive, which also saves you from the menace of the touts that hang around the bus stand. If you do follow a tout, remember that their "commission" is tacked onto your tariff. The main concentration of mid-range hotels is around the lively **Lighthouse beach** area, while quieter **Samudra beach** has a couple of upmarket hotels and few simple ones. The best of the resorts such as *Lagoona Davina* (see p.1312) and *Surya Samudra* (see p.1313) require transport.

Prices are extortionate compared with the rest of Kerala, soaring in peak season (Dec to mid-Jan), when you'll be lucky to find a basic room for less than Rs250. At other times, haggling should bring the rate down by twenty to fifty percent, especially if you stay for more than a week. Rates quoted below are for the high season.

Ashok, Kovalam beach ℡0471/480101, ℱ481522. Four complexes of chalets and "cottages" in Charles Correa's award-winning hilltop block. Bars, restaurants, pools, yoga centre and tennis courts make this Kovalam's swankiest option, but it's plagued by VIP security personnel and tour groups. **❾**

Green Valley, Lighthouse beach ℡0471/480636. Set amid the paddy fields, this is one of the best budget places in Kovalam, with pleasant en-suite rooms ranged around leafy and secluded courtyards and an inexpensive restaurant. However, the proximity to the paddy fields means there is a mozzie problem. **❸**

Hari Lekshmi, behind Lighthouse beach ℡0471/481341. Run by a very pleasant English lady, this little guesthouse offers four spotless white rooms with attached bathrooms, and there's a relaxing communal veranda and a kitchen. Fantastic value and highly recommended. **❷**

Hawah Beach, behind *Croaker's Restaurant* ℡0471/480431. Rather a prison block feel to the corridor with small, basic rooms and there are no views. The price and proximity to the beach is the main incentive to stay here. **❷**

KTDC Samudra, Kovalam beach ℡0471/480089, ℱ480242. Posh government-run three-star set away from other hotels overlooking its own cove. Deluxe rooms, manicured grounds, a lovely swimming pool, a good Ayurvedic massage centre,

restaurant and friendly but slow service. **❾**

Mini House, Lighthouse Road ℡0471/485198. Two large rooms with balconies and a great location right over the rocks and breaking sea, but don't underestimate the relentless noise; the third room without the view is much cheaper. **❻–❼**

Namaskar Inn, Hawah beach ℡0471/481903. Tucked in by *Sea Face Hotel*, this place has two prize rooms, each occupying an entire floor and filled with sunlight, tastefully decorated with a huge carved bed, wooden floorboards and two walls of windows looking out to sea. The other rooms are standard doubles with no sea views. **❺–❼**

Paradise Rock, Lighthouse Road ℡0471/480658. Variously priced large en-suite rooms overlooking the main beach; for Rs200 extra you get a sea-facing balcony. Clean and welcoming. **❸–❹**

Rockholm, Lighthouse Road ℡0471/480636. A range of well-appointed rooms ranged along the cliff top, some of which have great views. Popular with tour groups. **❼**

Samudra Tara/Castle Rock, Lighthouse Road ℡0471/481608. Three-storey concrete block set above the beach, with comfortable rooms and good private balconies. **❹–❼**

Sea Breeze, in the coconut grove behind Lighthouse beach ℡0471/480024. Gaudily painted pink and blue block, with huge sunny balconies overlooking a tropical garden. The rooms are clean and simple with attached bathrooms. Quiet and secluded; recommended. ❸

Sea Rock, Hawah beach ☏0471/480422. One of Kovalam's oldest established hotels, this is a concrete block slap on the seafront, with standard double rooms (a sea view costs extra) and a popular restaurant. ❽

Sea Weed, Lighthouse Road ☏0471/480391. Neat, clean and breezy hotel that claims to "get away from the madness". Some of the rooms ranged around the leafy central courtyard have a/c and, as usual, those with views cost extra. There is a pleasant rooftop restaurant. ❻–❼

Surya Tourist Home, Lighthouse beach ☏0471/481012. One of a clutch of identikit, no-frills places tucked behind the main beach, with small but clean rooms, and no sea views. Avoid the restaurants in the hotels along this row; they attract very few customers and so the ingredients may not be fresh. ❸

Thiruvathira, Lighthouse beach ☏0471/480787. Attached rooms with private verandas and a limited sea view, though boxed in. The rooms at the back are cheap and offer good value, unlike the expensive a/c option available. ❸–❽

Varma's, Lighthouse Road ☏0471/480478. The most attractive of the upper-range options along Lighthouse beach; it's modern, but the large rooms are furnished in traditional Keralan style with sea-facing balconies. The management is very friendly and helpful. ❼–❽

Wilson Tourist Home, behind the *Neelkantha Hotel* ☏0471/480051. Popular place worth the extra for spacious en-suite rooms, balconies (some with swinging chairs), garden, friendly staff and proximity to the beach. They do foreign exchange. ❹–❼

Eating and nightlife

Lighthouse beach is lined with sandy laid-back cafés and restaurants including *Garzia*, *Croaker's* and *Coral Reef*, all specializing in **seafood**, although chicken, pasta and veg options are widely available. If you want seafood, pick from the fresh fish, lobster, tiger prawns, crab and mussels on display, which are then weighed, grilled over a charcoal fire, and served with salad and chips. Meals are pricey by Indian standards – typically around Rs150 per head for fish, and double that for lobster or prawns – and the service is often painfully slow, but the ambience of the beachfront terraces is convivial enough. Beer, spirits and local *feni* (distilled palm wine) are also served – albeit very discreetly due to tight liquor restrictions – to a background of soft reggae or Pink Floyd (the rave scene has yet to hit Kovalam). For **breakfast** you can choose from any number of typical trans-Asia budget-traveller cafés serving up the usual brown bread and muesli.

Nightlife in Kovalam is pretty laid-back, revolving around the beach, where Westerners lounge about drinking and playing backgammon until the wee hours. A couple of restaurants also offer **video nights**, screening pirate copies of the latest American hits. You may well be offered *charas*, but bear in mind cannabis is illegal in Kerala, as everywhere else in India, and that the local police regularly arrest foreigners for possession.

German Bakery, Lighthouse beach. Breezy rooftop terrace at the south end of the beach, serving tasty (mostly healthy) Western food and lots of tempting cakes (try the waffles with chocolate sauce) and great fruit lassis. Breakfasts include a "full English" and "French" (croissants with espresso and a cigarette).

Lonely Planet, behind Lighthouse beach, near the *White House Hotel*. Congenial, generally inexpensive veg restaurant tucked away in the paddy fields by a little pond (bring mozzie repellent in the evening). The place to come if you're pining for Indian food, and it's one of the few places you can get *iddlis* for breakfast.

Red Star, Lighthouse beach, near the Lighthouse. A shack right on the beach, popular with those in search of food with local flavour and more than a tiny pinch of spice. The cook whips up inexpensive south Indian snacks, lassis, good Keralan "meals" at lunchtime for Rs30, as well as fiery fish curries.

Sands of Dee, Samudra beach. Run-of-the-mill, but here on the less developed Samudra beach it is the best of the few seafood restaurants and organizes a beach party and a bonfire on Sunday evenings. They have rooms as well.

Santana, Lighthouse beach. The best of the seafood joints on the beach, with a great barbecue and tandoori fish and chicken, plus good music. Stays open later than most.

Sea View, Lighthouse beach. Congenial atmosphere and good for a snack lunch or for a seafood dinner in the evenings when the day's catch may include lobster and huge king prawns.

Swiss Café, Lighthouse beach. Hip and very chic, with an excellent sound system and rustic ambience; the place is packed at sunset during "happy hour". Offers European food to rich European cus-

tomers. An elaborate menu of healthy, fresh food, lots of fish and *rösti* is served with everything; Goan fish curry is available for the mildly adventurous. A main meal will set you back Rs350–700, and light lunch dishes about Rs100.

Pozhikkara beach and Pachalloor village

Heading north along Samudra for around 4km you'll pass through a string of fishing hamlets before eventually arriving at a point where the sea merges with the backwaters to form a salt-water lagoon. Although only thirty minutes' walk from the *Ashok*, the sliver of white sand dividing the two, known as **Pozhikkara beach**, is a world away from the headlong holiday culture of Kovalam. Here, the sands are used primarily for landing fish and fixing nets, while the thick palm canopy shelters a mixed community of Hindu fishermen and Christian coir makers.

The tranquil village of **PACHALLOOR**, behind the lagoon, is a good alternative base to Thiruvananthapuram or Kovalam. There are two guesthouses here, including the original and idyllic *Lagoona Davina* (℡0471/380049, ℻462935, ✉davina@india.com; ❾, full board available), whose six individually decorated en-suite rooms open onto the water. Two cheaper cottages ($65 in high season) lie behind; lazing in a hammock under the palms, you can watch villagers paddling past in their long dug-outs, and sand-wallahs diving to fill buckets with silt. The guesthouse also organizes its own **backwater trips** (Rs350 per head for 2hr). The **food** served at *Lagoona* is exceptional – a fusion of authentic Keralan village dishes and European *nouvelle cuisine*. You can also have an Ayurvedic massage or take yoga lessons with the resident doctor, and there's a boutique with exquisite outfits made by Davina herself. If you book in advance, you'll be met at the airport, or take an auto-rickshaw 6km along the highway towards Kovalam, bearing right along the "by-pass" where the road forks (just after the Thiruvallam Bridge). After another 1km or so, a sign on the right of the road points through the trees to the guesthouse. The other guesthouse at Pachalloor, the *Beach and Lake Resort* (℡0471/381055; ❼–❽), lies across the water from *Lagoona* on the beach side, and has five rooms, but no restaurant and little atmosphere.

South of Kovalam: Vizhinjam (Vilinjam)

The unassuming village of **VIZHINJAM** (pronounced Virinyam), on the opposite (south) side of the headland from Lighthouse beach, was once the capital of the Ay kings, the earliest dynasty in south Kerala. During the ninth century the Pandyans intermittently took control, and it was the scene of major Chola–Chera battles in the eleventh century. A number of small simple shrines survive from those times, and can be made the focus of a pleasant afternoon's stroll along shady paths through coconut groves. They're best approached from the village centre, beyond a fishing community, rather than via the coast road. However, if you do walk along the coast road from Kovalam to the north side of Vizhinjam, you can't fail to be struck by the contrast; from the conspicuous consumption of a tourist resort you find yourself in a poor fishing village. A huge modern pink **mosque** on the promontory overlooks a bay of tightly packed thatched huts.

On the far side of the fishing bay in the village centre, 50m down a road opposite the police station, a small unfinished eighth-century rock shrine features a carved figure of Shiva with a weapon. The **Tali Shiva** temple, reached by a narrow path from behind the government primary school, may mark the original centre of Vizhinjam. The simple shrine is accompanied by a group of *naga* snake statues, a reminder of Kerala's continuing cult of snake worship that survives from pre-brahminical times.

The grove known as **Kovil Kadu** ("temple forest") lies near the sea, ten minutes' walk from the main road in the village along Hidyatnagara Road. Here a small enclosure contains a square Shiva shrine and a rectangular one dedicated to the goddess **Bhagavati**. Thought to date from the ninth century, these are probably the earliest structural temples in Kerala, although the Bhagavati shrine has been renovated.

Accommodation south of Kovalam

Two of the most luxurious of Kovalam's resorts lie around 8km to the south by road, and they benefit from long stretches of golden beach, as opposed to the unattractive black sand of Kovalam. The German-run *Surya Samudra* at **PULINKUDI** (℡0471/480413, ℱ481124; ⑨) consists of beautifully presented antique Keralan wood cottages (all non-a/c), which spread discreetly along a rocky hillside and look down onto two small beaches. There is an Ayurvedic centre and an extraordinary swimming pool cut into the rock that is open to nonresidents, but for a price (Rs400). Nearby, *Somatheeram* at **CHOWERA** (℡0471/481601, ℱ462935; ⑨) was formerly an Ayurvedic hospital and now offers high-quality massage and Ayurvedic medical treatment in four-star surroundings; comfortable cottages and apartments in exquisite Keralan houses spill down its landscaped hillside to a private beach. If it's full, try their sister

Kalam ezhuttu

The tradition of kalam ezhuttu (pronounced "kalam-*erroo*-too") – detailed and beautiful ritual drawings in coloured powder, of deities and geometric patterns (mandalas) – is very much alive all over Kerala. The designs usually cover an area of around thirty square metres, often outdoors and under a *pandal*, a temporary shelter made from bamboo and palm fronds. Each powder, made from rice flour, turmeric, ground leaves and burnt paddy husk, is painstakingly applied using the thumb and forefinger as a funnel. Three communities produce *kalams*; two come from the temple servant (*amblavasi*) castes, whose rituals are associated with the god Ayappa (see p.1335) or the goddess Bhagavati; the third, the *pullavans*, specialize in serpent worship. Iconographic designs emerge gradually from the initial grid lines and turn into startling figures, many of terrible aspect, with wide eyes and fangs. Noses and breasts are raised, giving the whole a three-dimensional effect. As part of the ritual, the significant moment when the powder is added for the iris or pupil, "opening" the eyes, may well be marked by the accompaniment of *chenda* drums and *elatalam* hand-cymbals.

Witnessing the often day-long ritual of drawing is an unforgettable experience. The effort expended by the artist is made all the more remarkable by the inevitable destruction of the picture shortly after its completion; this truly ephemeral art cannot be divorced from its ritual context. In some cases, the image is destroyed by a fierce-looking vellichapad ("light-bringer"). He is a village oracle who can be recognized by shoulder-length hair, red *dhoti*, heavy brass anklets and the hooked sword he brandishes either while jumping up and down on the spot (a common sight), or marching purposefully about to control the spectators. At the end of the ritual, the powder, invested with divine power, is thrown over the onlookers. *Kalam ezhuttu* rituals are not widely advertised, but check at tourist offices.

concern around the corner, *Manaltheeram* (☎0471/481610, ℱ481611; ◉), which has marginally cheaper cottages, and shares the same Ayurvedic facilities.

For a bit of quiet, head south to **POOVAR** at the mouth of the River Neyyar, 20km south of Kovalam (taxis charge Rs200). Here, the *Treasure Island* (☎0471/212063, ℱ210019; ◉), which should be pre-booked through *Wilson Tourist Home* in Kovalam (☎0471/480051), occupies a secluded spot on a palm-studded island with pleasant cottages in a coconut plantation, and a swimming pool.

Ponmudi and Peppara Wildlife Sanctuary

In the tea-growing region of the **Cardamom** (or Ponmudi) **hills**, about 60km northeast of Thiruvananthapuram and 77km from Kovalam, at an altitude of 1066m, is the hill station of **PONMUDI**. It is not a town, or even a village, but merely some accommodation along a ridge, commanding breathtaking views out across the range as far as the sea.

The main reason anyone comes up here is that it serves as the only practical base for visits to the 53 square kilometres of forest set aside as **Peppara Wildlife Sanctuary**, which protects elephants, sambar, lion-tailed macaques, leopard, and assorted birds. Although Peppara is theoretically open all year, the main season is from January until May; check before you go with the District Forest Officer, Thiruvananthapuram Forest Division, Thiruvananthapuram (☎0471/320674).

The beautiful drive up, via the small towns of Nedumangad and Vithura, runs along very narrow roads past areca nut, clove, rubber and cashew plantations, with first the Kavakulam and then the Kallar River close at hand. The bridge at **Kallar Junction** marks the start of the real climb. Twenty-two hairpin bends (numbered at the roadside) lead slowly up, firstly in the foothills, past great lumps of black rock and thick clumps of bamboo (*iramula*), then through the Kallar teak forest. You finally emerge into tea plantations; the temperature is noticeably cooler and, once out of the forest, the views across the hills and the plains below become truly spectacular – on a clear day you can see the sea. There really is nothing to do up here but the high ridges and tea estates make good rambling country.

Practicalities

Four daily **buses** run from Thiruvananthapuram to Ponmudi, via Vithura; the first is at 5.30am and the last at 10.15am. There are many more buses back from Ponmudi to Thiruvananthapuram, starting at 6am until 6.30pm. The nearest **tourist office** is currently in Thiruvananthapuram, where information on Ponmudi is readily available, although a snazzy new tourist information office should be open in Ponmudi by 2002.

The *Government Guest House* (☎0472/890230; ◉–◉) has 24 **rooms**, and seven cottages, all with hot water. The simple and inexpensive but delicious meals have to be ordered a couple of hours in advance, otherwise the cold drinks and snacks shop is open daily until 4pm, or you can walk down the road to the teashop on the bend (400m). The main building, which originally belonged to the Raja of Travancore, has lost any charm it may once have possessed, and the huge plate-glass windows of its canteen-like restaurant rattle disconcertingly in the wind, but views across the hills and misty valleys from the terrace make up for all that. Weekends get lively, thanks to the beer parlour (open 10am–6pm).

Sivananda Yoga Vedanta Dhanwantari

Located amid the serene hills and tropical forests around Neyyar Dam, 28km east of Thiruvananthapuram, the Sivananda Yoga Vedanta Dhanwantari is one of India's leading yoga ashrams. It was founded by Swami Sivananda – dubbed the "Flying Guru" because he used to pilot light aircraft over war-stricken areas of the world scattering flowers and leaflets calling for peace – as a centre for meditation, yoga and traditional Keralan martial arts and medicine. Sivananda was a renowned exponent of Advaitya Vedanta, the philosophy of non-duality, as espoused by the Upanishads and promoted later by Shankara in the eleventh century.

Aside from training teachers in advanced raja and hatha yoga, the ashram offers excellent introductory courses for beginners. These comprise four hours of intensive tuition per day (starting at 5.30am), with background lectures that provide helpful theory. During the course, you have to stay at the ashram and comply with a regime that some Western students find disconcertingly strict (smoking, alcohol, drugs, sex and even "rock music" are prohibited, the diet is pure veg, and you have to get up at the crack of dawn). However, if you are keen to acquire the basic techniques and knowledge of yoga, this is a good place to start. For more details, contact the ashram itself (℡0471/290493), or their branch in Thiruvananthapuram (37/1929 Airport Rd, West Fort; ℡0471/450942). For more information look at their publication, *Sivananda Yoga Life*, published by the Sivananda Yoga Vedanta Centre, 51 Felsham Rd, London SW15 1AZ (℡020/ 8780 0160, ✉siva@dial.pipex.com).

Padmanabhapuram

Although now officially in Tamil Nadu, **PADMANABHAPURAM**, 63km southeast of Thiruvananthapuram, was the capital of Travancore between 1550 and 1750, and therefore has a far more intimate connection with the history of Kerala. Unusually, it is administered by the government of Kerala. For anyone with even a minor interest in Keralan architecture, this small palace is an irresistible attraction. However, **avoid weekends**, when the complex gets overrun with bus parties. Occasionally parts of the palace are closed to visitors for restoration.

Set in neat gravelled grounds in a quiet location away from the main road, the predominantly wooden **Padmanabhapuram Palace** (Tues–Sun 9am–4.30pm; Rs6, Rs10 extra with camera) epitomizes classical Keralan architecture. It is reached by crossing the main road from the bus station (see below), turning left, and then following a road on the right for a pleasant ten- or fifteen-minute walk through the paddy fields. The substantial walls of the palace compound delimit a small village.

Against a backdrop of steep-sided hills, the exterior of the palace – parts of which date back to the town's earliest days – displays a perfect combination of clean lines and gentle angles, with the sloping tiled roofs of its various interconnecting buildings broken by triangular projecting gables enclosing delicately carved screens. All visitors have to be shown around by the informative **guides** who do not charge a fee but expect a tip. At busy times they will rush you through the palace, especially if there are few of you, in order to catch the next group.

In the **entrance hall** (a veranda), a brass oil lamp hangs from an ornate teak, rosewood and mahogany ceiling carved with ninety different lotus flowers. Beautifully ornamented, the revolving lamp inexplicably keeps the position in which it is left, seeming to defy gravity. The raja rested from the summer heat on the cool polished granite bed in the corner. On the wall is a collection of *onamvillu*, ceremonial bows painted with reclining Vishnus (or more properly Padmanabha), which local chieftains would present to him during the Onam festival.

Directly above the entrance, on the first floor, is the **mantrasala** or council chamber, gently illuminated through panes of coloured mica. Herbs soaking in water were put into the boxed bench seats along the front wall, as a natural cooling system. The highly polished black floor was made from a now-lost technique using burnt coconut, sticky sugar-cane extract, egg whites, lime and sand.

The oldest part of the complex is the **Ekandamandapam** – "the lonely place". Built in 1550, it was used for rituals for the goddess Durga that typically employed *kalam ezhuttu*, elaborate floor paintings (see p.1313). A loose ring attached to a column is a *tour de force* of the carpenter: both ring and column are carved from a single piece of jackwood. Nearby is a *nalekettu*, the four-sided courtyard found in many Keralan houses, open to the sky and surrounded by a pillared walkway. A trapdoor once served as the entrance to a secret passageway leading to another palace, since destroyed.

The Pandya-style stone-columned **dance hall** stands directly in front of a shrine to the goddess of learning, Saraswati. The women of the royal household had to watch performances through screens on the side, and the staff through holes in the wall from the gallery above. Typical of old country houses, steep wooden ladder-like steps, ending in trapdoors, connect the floors. Belgian mirrors and Tanjore miniatures of Krishna adorn the chamber forming part of the **women's quarters**, where a swing hangs on plaited iron ropes. A four-poster bed, made from sixteen kinds of medicinal wood, dominates the **raja's bedroom**. Its elaborate carvings depict a mass of vegetation, human figures, birds and as the central motif, the snake symbol of medicine, associated with the Greek physician Asclepius.

The **murals** for which the palace is famous – alive with detail, colour, graceful form and religious fervour – adorn the walls of the **meditation room**, used by the raja and the heirs apparent, directly above the bedroom. Unfortunately, this is now closed – allegedly because the stairs are shaky, but in fact to preserve the murals, which have been severely damaged by generations of hands trailing along the walls.

Further points of interest in the palace include a **dining hall** intended for the free feeding of up to 2000 brahmins, and a 38-kilo stone which, it is said, every new recruit to the raja's army had to raise above his head 101 times.

Travancore and the servants of Vishnu

In front of a depiction of the god in the meditation, or prayer room, at Padmanabhapuram Palace lies a sword. In 1750, **Raja Marthanda Varma** symbolically presented this weapon to Padmanabha, the god Vishnu, who reclines on the sacred serpent Anantha in the midst of the cosmic ocean, and thereby dedicated the kingdom of Travancore to Vishnu. From that day, the raja took the title of Padmanabhadasa ("servant of Padmanabha"), and ruled as a servant of the god.

Thus Travancore belonged to Vishnu, and the raja was merely its custodian – a spiritual, and presumably legal, loophole that is said to have proved invaluable in restricting the power of the British in Travancore to install a British resident.

Practicalities

Frequent **buses** run to Padmanabhapuram from Thiruvananthapuram's Thampanoor station; hop on any service heading south towards Nagercoil or Kanniyakumari and get off at **Thakkaly** (sometimes written Thuckalai). If you're determined to see Padmanabhapuram, Kanniyakumari and Suchindram in one day, leave the city early to arrive when the palace opens at 9am. Note that two express buses leave Thakkaly at 2.30pm and 3.30pm for Thiruvananthapuram. Another way to see Padmanabhapuram is on KTDC's Kanniyakumari tour which starts at Thiruvananthapuram (Tues–Sun 7.30am–9pm; Rs230) and can be picked up at Kovalam where it stops en route.

The area around the bus station, being on NH-47, is noisy and dirty. It's better to get **refreshment** from the *chaiya*-cum-food and "cool drinks" shops inside the outer walls of the palace; look for the barrows selling delicious fried *kappa* (tapioca) chips. Just outside the inner gate you can usually find tender **coconuts**.

Varkala

Long known to Keralans as a place of pilgrimage, **VARKALA**, 54km northwest of Thiruvananthapuram and 20km southeast of Kollam, is drawing more and more foreign visitors, who see the beautiful beach and cliffs 1500m beyond the village as a quiet, unspoiled alternative to Kovalam. Centred on a clifftop row of budget guesthouses and palm-thatch cafés, the tourist scene has so far been relatively low-key despite the arrival of the Taj Group's luxury resort and the occasional package tour group. Varkala is developing, albeit slowly, so enjoy it while you can; this tranquil spot could well go the same way as Kovalam. The best time to get here is between October and early March; during the monsoons the beach is virtually unusable.

Arrival and information

Varkala's railway station, 2km east of the village, is served by express and mail **trains** from Thiruvananthapuram, Kollam (hourly; 45min), and most other Keralan towns on the main line. An auto-rickshaw to the beach costs around Rs20–30. Regular **buses** also run from Thiruvananthapuram's Thampanoor stand, and from Kollam (1hr–2hr 30min). A few go all the way to the beach, but most stop in the village centre, a five-minute auto-rickshaw ride away. If you can't get a direct bus, take any "superfast" or "limited stop" bus along the main highway, NH-47, and change at Kallamballam from where you can hop onto a local bus to Varkala (11km) or resort to an auto-rickshaw (Rs70) or a taxi (Rs100).

The new **DTPC tourist information centre** (daily 8am–6pm) next to the helipad on the clifftop is very welcoming and informative and you avoid all the problems of agency middlemen, who are very prevalent in Varkala. The DTPC office will also book taxis at the official government rate, which is useful if you need to leave at night or early in the morning to avoid soaring rates. You can hire **two-wheelers** everywhere in Varkala; the going rate for a scooter is Rs200, Rs300 for a motorbike and Rs300–450 for an Enfield. **Elephant rides** are the big tourist attraction in Varkala; travel agents will offer you expensive day-long elephant rides in a nearby forest. However, when you get there you will find that you are only allowed a trundle for an hour. The official government rate is Rs250 per hour per person, and a taxi to the forest costs Rs50 return.

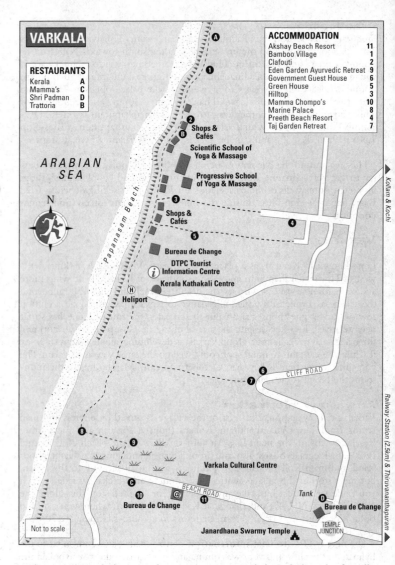

VARKALA

RESTAURANTS

Kerala	A
Mamma's	C
Shri Padman	D
Trattoria	B

ACCOMMODATION

Akshay Beach Resort	11
Bamboo Village	1
Clafouti	2
Eden Garden Ayurvedic Retreat	9
Government Guest House	6
Green House	5
Hilltop	3
Mamma Chompo's	10
Marine Palace	8
Preeth Beach Resort	4
Taj Garden Retreat	7

ARABIAN SEA

Papanasam Beach

Shops & Cafés

Scientific School of Yoga & Massage

Progressive School of Yoga & Massage

Shops & Cafés

Bureau de Change

DTPC Tourist Information Centre

Kerala Kathakali Centre

Heliport

CLIFF ROAD

Varkala Cultural Centre

BEACH ROAD

Tank

Bureau de Change

Bureau de Change

Janardhana Swarmy Temple

TEMPLE JUNCTION

Not to scale

Kollam & Kochi

Railway Station (2.5km) & Thiruvananthapuram

There are several places to **change money** in Varkala including the friendly and versatile Bureau de Change outlets on the corner of Temple Junction (aka Holy Cross) in the centre of town, on Beach Road, and on the southern end of the cliff top, next to the Tourist Information Office.

Internet centres all around Varkala charge approximately Rs50 to 60, with a Rs15 minimum charge.

Accommodation

Varkala has a fair choice of **places to stay**, from basic rooms with shared (or outside) shower-toilets to establishments offering a bit more comfort. If you're on a tight budget, head first for the cliff-top area (rickshaws can make it up there), where there are several family-run guesthouses in the coconut trees behind the row of cafés; on the way, it's worth stopping to see if the wonderful *Government Guest House* has vacancies. Accommodation is tight in **peak season** (late Nov–Jan), when you should call ahead.

Akshay Beach Resort, Beach Road, Papanasam ☎0472/602668. Clean guesthouse with en-suite rooms (some with a/c), massage and helpful management. A dull location, with no sea views, but handy for the beach and village (early bus departures). ❸–❻

Bamboo Village, North Clifftop. Four lovely, airy bamboo huts on stilts with little balconies and dinky attached bathrooms. They are very popular and have a congenial social scene of their own, as well as being great value. There is no phone so you have to turn up on spec and hope one is free. ❷–❸

Clafouti, North Clifftop ☎0472/601414. Spotless tiled rooms ranged around a courtyard, each with private balconies; the more expensive ones have sea views. A cheaper row of cottages faces the *Trattoria* restaurant. The only danger is proximity of the excellent French pastries on sale at the restaurant here (see p.1321). ❹–❺

Eden Garden Ayurvedic Retreat, off Beach Road ☎0472/603910. Pleasantly marooned in the paddy fields behind the beach, with slightly rundown en-suite rooms around a fishpond with relaxing stilted sitouts (beware of mosquitoes) and offering Ayurvedic treatment including massage and food. There is a German Bakery on site. ❸–❹

Government Guest House, five minutes' walk north of the temple, near the *Taj* hotel ☎0472/602227. Former maharaja's holiday palace, converted into a characterful guesthouse, with eight enormous rooms and meals available on request. Superb value, but a bit run-down. For more comfort try the new *Tourist Bungalow* next door and part of the same complex, where the large plain rooms are excellent value. ❷

Green House, behind Yoga School, cliff-top area ☎0472/604659. Secluded and only two minutes from the cliff edge behind a small temple, in an unhurried and friendly hamlet. Rooms are basic and cheaper ones share a communal bathroom. Popular with the backpacker crew, but there are plenty of similarly priced fall-backs nearby (try *White House* or *Red House*). ❷

Hilltop, north end of cliff ☎0472/601237. A great spot, with pleasant, breezy rooms, attached shower-toilets and relaxing terrace restaurant. The cheaper rooms are at the back, while the upstairs rooms, which are quite a bit more expensive, have sea views. Good value. ❺–❻

Mamma Chompos, Beach Road ☎0472/603995. Run by an Italian couple on a converted farm compound with reasonable rooms and communal bathrooms. Further up the hill, a new block of rooms nestles amongst the palm trees. There's a great Italian restaurant on site. ❹

Marine Palace, behind the beach ☎0472/603204. En-suite rooms in a rather dilapidated pale green building near the sea. Pricier front rooms have sea views and balconies; the thatched annexe is cheaper and the restaurant is congenial. ❹–❻

Preeth Beach Resort, cliff-top area ☎0472/600942. Large well-maintained complex shaded by a palm grove, with a range of well-appointed rooms (some a/c), each with a private balcony. There's a good restaurant in the leafy courtyard. ❻–❽

Taj Garden Retreat, near the *Government Guest House* ☎0472/603000, ℻602296. Very comfortable and central a/c rooms, a good restaurant and bar, a fitness and Ayurveda centre and a pleasant swimming pool, but all a bit ostentatious for a laidback place like Varkala. The tariff includes breakfast and dinner. ❾

The village

Known in Malayalam as Papa Nashini ("sin destroyer"), Varkala's beautiful white-sand beach, **Papanasam beach**, has long been associated with ancestor worship. Devotees come here after praying at the **Janardhana Swamy** temple (said to be more than 2000 years old) to bring the ashes of departed relatives for "final rest". Unlike in many temples in Kerala, non-Hindus are welcome. A small government hospital at its north end, opened by Indira Gandhi in 1983, was set up to benefit from three **natural springs**, and take advantage of the sea air, said to boost the health of asthma sufferers.

Backed by sheer red-laterite cliffs and drenched by rolling waves off the Arabian Sea, Papa Nashini is imposingly scenic and still a relatively peaceful place to soak up the sun, with few hawkers and only the odd group of ogling men. Its religious significance means attitudes to (female) public nudity are markedly more conservative than at other coastal resorts in Kerala; bikinis don't necessarily cause offence, but you'll attract a lot less attention if you wear a full-length cotton sarong while bathing.

Few of Varkala's Hindu pilgrims wander up to the **clifftop area**, reached by several steep footpaths, or the more gradual path up from behind the *Marine Palace* restaurant, and by the metalled road from the village that was built to service a helipad in advance of Mrs Gandhi's visit. Up here, the faintly cheesy New Age scene centres on the small Scientific School of Yoga & Massage, which offers **Ayurvedic massage** at Rs300 per session, meditation courses, "lifetime" courses in yoga (Rs750 for an unlimited number of lessons), and fortnight-long courses in massage ($100). Their small shop, Prakruthi Stores, stocks honey, essential oils, herbs and handmade soaps, as well as books on yoga, meditation and massage. The Progress Yoga Centre also offers massage sessions (Rs250–400) and seven- or ten-day-long yoga and Ayurvedic massage courses.

Sivagiri Hill, at the eastern edge of the village, harbours a more traditional **ashram** that attracts pilgrim devotees of Shri Narayana Guru, a saint who died here in 1922. Born into the low *ezhava* caste, he fought orthodoxy with a philosophy of social reform ("one caste, one religion, one God for man") which included the consecration of temples with an open-door policy to all castes, and had a profound effect on the "upliftment" of the untouchables.

Aimed unashamedly at the tourist market, the Varkala Cultural Centre (℡0472/603612) near the tank, a few metres down Beach Road from Temple Junction, holds **Kathakali** (as well as Bharatanatyam) dance performances most evenings in season (6.30pm–8pm). Alternatively, the DTPC have just started their own nightly show at the Kerala Kathakali Centre, just behind the helipad on the cliff top; tickets are available on the day from the DTPC Tourist Information Office. The Rs125 admission fee that applies to either performance, includes sitting in on the fascinating process of applying Kathakali make-up (daily 5pm–6.30pm). Although in a real performance the make-up process is much more elaborate and usually takes much longer, the session that precedes a performance here provides an insight into the art. For those who would like to learn more, the centres also offer short courses on make-up.

Eating

Seafood lovers will do well in Varkala's increasingly sophisticated clifftop café-restaurants, some of which have upper storeys raised on stilts for better sea views. Prices are quite high and the service slow, but the superb location more than compensates, especially in the evenings when the sea twinkles with the lights of countless fishing boats. Most of the restaurants offer identical menus with fresh fish, including shark, on display. Apart from Kerala, it's increasingly hard to find a menu that gives Indian cuisine any recognition, as more restaurants cater to homesick European tastebuds – pizza is rapidly taking over as the local dish.

Due to Kerala's antiquated licensing laws, which involve huge amounts of tax, **beer** is discreetly available, but at a price (Rs75–90), as none of the cafés are supposed to sell it and periodically get raided, resulting in official or unofficial fines. One alternative is to retire to the comforts of the *Taj Garden Retreat*'s bar and superb restaurant, but you will have to pay through the nose.

Clafouti, North Clifftop. Little tables under rustling palm trees, and a wonderful French bakery counter stacked with croissants, *pain-aux-raisins*, baguettes, and sweet pies. In the evening they dish up a set three-course menu (about Rs150) which is changed daily.

Kerala, North Clifftop. As the name suggests, this place serves up *iddli-dosa* breakfasts, unlimited "meals" at lunch (Rs30) and thalis, *barottas* and *dosas* in the evening. Although nowhere as spicy as the real thing, this place is about as authentic as you'll hope to get in the cliff-top area.

Mammas, Beach Road. You are greeted with the vigorous kneading of fresh dough and the wonderful smell of pizzas cooking in the traditional wood-fired oven. Relaxed and popular, and the food's delicious.

Shri Padman, next to temple, Varkala village. The large rear terrace of this unpromising, grubby-looking "meals" joint is the main travellers' hang-out in Varkala. The (Indian veg) food is cheap and delicious (try the coconut-rich *navrattan*, deep-fried cheese, garlic chapatis, or filling biriyanis), and the location atmospheric, especially at break-fast time, when villagers come to the tank to bathe.

Trattoria, North Clifftop. If you can ignore the trop-ical climate, you could be in Italy, as large groups of friends and families enjoy long lunches around tables covered with red-and-white checked table-cloths and generous bowls of pasta. The menu has fish, calamari, mussels and prawn dishes amongst the pizza and pasta – only the wine is missing.

Kollam (Quilon) and around

One of the oldest ports of the Malabar coast, **KOLLAM** (pronounced "Koillam" and previously known as Quilon), 74km northwest of Thiruvananthapuram and 85km south of Alappuzha, was once at the centre of the international spice trade. The sixteenth-century Portuguese writer Duarte Barbossa described it as a "very great city with a right good haven", which was visited by "Moors, Heathen and Christians in great numbers", and stated that "a great store" of pepper was to be found there. In fact, the port flourished from the very earliest times, trading amicably with the Phoenicians, Arabs, Persians, Greeks, Romans and Chinese.

Nowadays, Kollam is chiefly of interest as one of the entry or exit points to the backwaters of Kerala (see p.1326), and most travellers simply stay overnight en route to or from Alappuzha. The **town** itself, sandwiched between the sea and Ashtamudi ("eight inlets") Lake, is less exciting than its history might sug-gest. It's a typically sprawling Keralan market community, with a few old tiled wooden houses and winding backstreets, kept busy with the commercial inter-ests of coir, cashew nuts (a good local buy), pottery, aluminium and fishery industries. The missable ruins of **Tangasseri** fort (3km from the centre) are the last vestiges of colonial occupation.

Practicalities

The **railway station** is on the east of town, a three-kilometre auto-rickshaw ride (Rs15-20) from the jetty. Numerous daily trains each way run from Ernakulam and Thiruvananthapuram and beyond. On platform 4, the tiny District Tourism Promotion Council (DTPC) **tourist information count-er** (Mon–Sat 9am–12.30pm & 1.30–5pm) will book hotels for travellers; you have to pay one night in advance, but the only extra charge is for the phone calls. They also have a tourist office (Mon–Sat 9am–5.30pm; ☏ 0474/742558) at the **boat jetty** (for boat details, see below for boat details), but will only provide details on their own tourist ferry service. By contrast, the local **Allepuzha Tourism Development Council** (ADTC) office on the oppo-site side of the road is very friendly and dispenses unbiased information about

1321

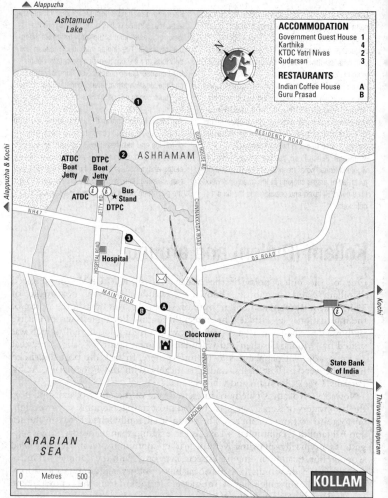

Ashtamudi
Lake

ACCOMMODATION
Government Guest House	**1**
Karthika	**4**
KTDC Yatri Nivas	**2**
Sudarsan	**3**

RESTAURANTS
Indian Coffee House	**A**
Guru Prasad	**B**

RESIDENCY ROAD

ASHRAMAM

GUEST HOUSE RD.

CHINNAKKADA ROAD

ATDC
Boat
Jetty

DTPC
Boat
Jetty

ATDC

Bus
Stand

DTPC

JETTY RD.

NH47

HOSPITAL ROAD

Hospital

OS ROAD

MAIN ROAD

Clocktower

CHINNAKKADA ROAD

State Bank
of India

BEACH RD.

ARABIAN
SEA

0	Metres	500

KOLLAM

▶ Kochi

▶ Thiruvananthapuram

both tourist and local ferry services; they also have a good number of rice boats available for backwater cruises. Both outfits operate a daily cruise from Kollam to Alappuzha, which departs at 10.30am and takes eight hours (Rs150) with stops for lunch and tea. While the cruise is popular, many visitors feel that you get a far better impression of backwater life by hopping between villages on the very cheap local ferries. Tickets for both the DTPC and ATDC ferries can be bought on the morning of the trip in the respective tourist offices; tickets for the local ferries are purchased at the booth on the jetty. Note that the ATDC ferry leaves from a pier 100m to the west of the main jetty.

The jetty and KSRTC **bus stand** are close together on the edge of Ashtamudi Lake. Bookable express **buses** are available south to Thiruvananthapuram (1hr 30min) and north to Kochi (3hr) via Alappuzha (1hr 15min).

Accommodation and eating

The most congenial **places to stay** are outside the town, across Ashtamudi Lake from the main jetty (easy to get to by auto-rickshaw, but more difficult to return from). The **railway retiring rooms** on the first floor of the railway station are spacious, clean, and very cheap (Rs150).

Apart from the hotel restaurants, other places to **eat** include the *Indian Coffee House* on Main Road, and *Guru Prasad*, a little way along, which serves great south Indian veg "meals". The best of the hotel restaurants can be found in the *Sudarsan*, which has a good-value "meals" restaurant along with its more upmarket a/c restaurant.

Government Guest House, 3km north of town, by Ashtamudi Lake ☎ 0474/743620. Characterful Euro-Keralan building, once the British Residency, with curved tiled roof and gracious verandas, in a vast compound. Ye olde British furniture in cavernous spaces, but there are just five rooms. Simple meals are served by arrangement, although most people head over to the *Yatri Nivas* to eat. You can reserve backwater cruise tickets here. Book in advance – some travellers come to Kollam purely to stay here. ❷–❹.

Karthika, off Main Road, near the Mosque ☎ 0474/751821. A large and popular budget hotel with clean, plain rooms (some a/c), ranged around a courtyard in which the centrepiece is, rather unexpectedly, three huge nude figures; very handy for the railway station and the jetty. You can hire cable TV for a night (Rs20). ❸

KTDC Yatri Nivas, across from the jetty ☎ 0474/745538. Modern, clean rooms (two a/c) with attached bathrooms and nice balconies, in a great location overlooking the lake; the best fallback if the *Government Guest House* is full. The restaurant is very popular with travellers, serving good barbecue lake fish, and there's a beer parlour. ❸–❹

Palm Lagoon, Vellimon West ☎ 0474/523974. In a beautiful location on Ashtamudi Lake but a good 15km from town. Pleasant thatched cottages and with breakfast or full board, good Ayurvedic treatment facilities, and the opportunity to explore the backwaters. Book directly or through DTPC for directions and a discount. ❻

Sudarsan, Parameswar Nagar ☎ 0474/744322. Central and popular, but definitely not as palatial as the posh foyer would lead you to believe, this place features a wide range of rooms, some with a/c and cable TV. A busy, dark a/c restaurant with a white plaster *Last Supper* at one end and a TV at the other dishes up Indian and Chinese food, and there's a bar. ❺–❽

Around Kollam: Kayamkulam and Karunagapalli

KAYAMKULAM, served by (non-express) buses between Kollam and Alappuzha, was once the centre of its own small kingdom, which after a battle in 1746 came under the control of Travancore's king Marthanda Varma. In the eighteenth century, the area was famous for its spices, particularly pepper and cinnamon. The Abbé Reynal claimed that the Dutch exported some two million pounds of pepper each year, one-fifth of it from Kayamkulam. At this time, the kingdom was known also for the skill of its army, made up of 15,000 Nayars (Kerala's martial caste).

Set in a tranquil garden, the eighteenth-century **Krishnapuram Palace** (Tues–Sat 10am–4.30pm; Rs2) is imbued with Keralan grace, constructed largely of wood, with gabled roofs and rooms opening out onto internal courtyards. It's now a museum, but unlike the palace at Padmanabhapuram (see p.1315), with which it shares some similarities, the whole place is in great need of restoration and the collection inside is poorly labelled and neglected.

A display case contains puja ceremony utensils and oil lamps, some of which are arranged in an arc known as a *prabhu*, placed behind a temple deity to provide a halo of light. Fine miniature *panchaloha* ("five-metal" bronze alloy, with gold as one ingredient) figures include the water god Varuna, several Vishnus, and a minuscule devotee deep in worship. Small stone columns carved with serpent deities were recovered from local houses.

The prize exhibit is a huge **mural** of the classical Keralan school, in muted ochre-reds and blue-greens, which covers more than fourteen square metres. It depicts **Gajendra Moksha**– the salvation of Gajendra, king of the elephants. In the tenth century Sanskrit *Bhagavata Purana*, the story is told of a Pandyan king, Indrayumna, a devotee of Vishnu cursed by the sage Agastya to be born again as an elephant. One day, while sporting with his wives at the edge of a lake, his leg was seized by a crocodile whose grip was so tight that Gajendra was held captive for years. Finally, in desperation the elephant called upon his chosen deity Vishnu, who immediately appeared, riding his celestial bird/man vehicle, Garuda, and destroyed the crocodile.

The centre of the painting is dominated by a dynamic portrayal of Garuda about to land, with huge spread wings and a facial expression denoting *raudra* (fury), in stark contrast to the compassionate features of the multi-armed Vishnu. Smaller figures of Gajendra, in mid-trumpet, and his assailant are shown to the right. As with all paintings in the Kerala style, every inch is packed with detail. Bearded sages, animals, mythical beasts and forest plants surround the main figures. The outer edges are decorated with floriate borders which, at the bottom, form a separate triptych-like panel showing Balakrishna, the child Krishna, attended by adoring females.

At a quiet spot just outside the small town of **KARUNAGAPALLI**, 23km north of Kollam on NH-47 towards Alappuzha, it's possible to watch the construction of traditional **kettu vallam** ("tied boats"). These long cargo boats, a familiar sight on the backwaters, are built entirely without the use of nails. Each jackwood plank is **sewn** to the next with coir rope, and then the whole is coated with a caustic black resin made from boiled cashew kernels. With careful maintenance they last for generations.

Karunagapalli is best visited as a day-trip from Kollam; regular **buses** pass through on the way to Alappuzha. One daytime **train**, #6525, leaves Kollam at 11.55am, arriving at Karunagapalli at 12.30pm, but you have to get a bus back. On reaching the bus stand or railway station, ask an auto-rickshaw to take you to the boatyard of the *vallam asharis*, the boat carpenters (4km northwest). The boatbuilders are friendly and willing to let visitors watch them work. In the shade of palm trees at the edge of the water, some weave palm leaves, others twist coir strands into rope, and craftsmen repair the boats. Soaking in the shallows nearby are palm leaves, to use for thatch, and coconut husks for coir rope. If you want to buy a *vallam* you'll need around two *lakh* (200,000) rupees; a far cheaper alternative is to hire these boats by the day or on longer overnight trips (see p.1327).

Alappuzha

Under its former appellation of Alleppey, **ALAPPUZHA**, roughly midway between Kollam (85km south) and Kochi (64km north), is another romantic and historic name from Kerala's past. It was one of the best-known ports along the Malabar coast, and tourist literature is fond of referring to it as "Venice of the East", but while it may be full of interconnecting **canals**, there the resemblance ends. Alappuzha is a bustling, messy town of ramshackle wood and cor-

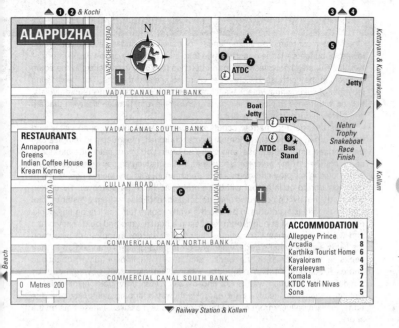

rugated iron-roofed houses, chiefly significant in the coir industry, which accounts for much of the traffic on its oily green-brown waterways.

Despite its insalubrious canals, Alappuzha is prominent on the tourist trail as one of the major centres for **backwater boat trips**, served by ferries to and from Kollam and Kottayam in particular. Most visitors stay just one night, catching a boat or bus out early the next morning. However, a short distance north the centre, the congestion eases. You can walk along the **lakeside** under a shady canopy of palm trees, enjoying the extraordinarily slow pace of Keralan village life.

Alappuzha really comes alive on the second Saturday of August, in the depths of the rainy season, when it serves as the venue for one of Kerala's major spectacles – the **Nehru Trophy snakeboat race**. This event, first held in 1952, is based on the traditional Keralan enthusiasm for racing magnificently decorated longboats, with raised rears designed to resemble the hood of a cobra. More than enthusiastically powered by up to 150 singing and shouting oarsmen, scores of boats take part, and Alappuzha is packed with thousands of spectators. Similar races can be seen at Aranmula (p.1333), and at Champakulam, 16km by ferry from Alappuzha. The ATDC information office (see below) will be able to tell you the dates of these events, which change every year.

Practicalities

The shambolic KSRTC **bus stand**, on the east of town, is served by half-hourly buses to Kollam, Thiruvananthapuram and Ernakulam; less frequent buses run to Kottayam, Thrissur and Palakkad. The **boat jetty** is just one minute's walk west from the bus stand. As the backwaters prevent **trains** from continuing south beyond Alappuzha, only a few major daily services and a handful of passenger trains depart from the **railway station**, 3km southwest of

One of the most memorable experiences for travellers in India – even those on the lowest of budgets – is the opportunity to take a boat journey on the backwaters of Kerala. The area known as Kuttanad stretches for 75km from Kollam in the south to Kochi in the north, sandwiched between the sea and the hills. This bewildering labyrinth of shimmering waterways, composed of lakes, canals, rivers and rivulets, is lined with dense tropical greenery, and preserves rural Keralan lifestyles that are completely hidden from the road.

Views change from narrow canals and dense vegetation to open vistas and dazzling green paddy fields. Homes, farms, churches, mosques and temples can be glimpsed among the trees, and every so often you might catch the blue flash of a kingfisher, or the green of a parakeet. Pallas fishing eagles cruise above the water looking for prey and cormorants perch on logs to dry their wings. If you're lucky enough to be in a boat without a motor, at times the peace will be broken only by the squawking of crows and the occasional film song from a distant radio. Day-to-day life is lived on and beside the water. Some families live on tiny pockets of land, with just enough room for a simple house, yard and boat. They bathe and wash their clothes – sometimes their buffaloes too, muddy from ploughing the fields – at the water's edge, while you often pass villagers standing up to their necks in water, far from the banks and busy with impenetrable subaquatic chores. Traditional Keralan longboats, *kettu vallam*, glide past, powered both by gondolier-like boatmen with poles and by sail. Often they look on the point of sinking, laden with heavyweight cargo with water lapping perilously over the edge. Fishermen work from rowing boats or operate massive Chinese nets on the shore.

Coconut trees at improbable angles form shady canopies, and occasionally you pass under simple curved bridges. Here and there basic drawbridges can be raised on ropes, but major bridges are few and far between; most people rely on boatmen to ferry them across the water to connect with roads and bus services, a constant criss-crossing of the waters from dawn until dusk (a way of life beautifully represented in the visually stunning film *Piravi*, by Keralan director Shaji). Poles sticking out of the water indicate dangerous shallows.

The African moss that often carpets the surface of the narrower waterways may look attractive, but it is actually a menace to small craft traffic and starves underwater life of light. It is also a symptom of the many serious ecological problems currently affecting the region, whose population density ranges from between two and four times that of other coastal areas in southwest India. This has put growing pressure on land, and hence a greater reliance on fertilizers, which eventually work their way into the water causing the build up of moss. Illegal land reclamation, however, poses the single greatest threat to this fragile ecosystem. In a little over a century, the total area of water in Kuttanad has been reduced by two-thirds, while mangrove swamps and fish stocks have been decimated by pollution and the spread of towns and villages around the edges of the backwater region.

Routes and practicalities

There are numerous backwater routes to choose from, on vessels ranging from local ferries, through chauffeur-driven speedboats offered by the KTDC, to customized *kettu vallam* and rice boat cruises. The most popular excursion is the full-day journey between Kollam and Alappuzha; you can cover part or all of the route in a day, returning to your original point of departure by bus during the evening, or, more comfortably, staying the night at either end. All sorts of private hustlers offer their services, but the basic choice lies between boats run by the Alleppey Tourism Development Co-op (ATDC) and the District Tourism Promotion Council (DTPC). The double-decker boats leave from both Kollam and Alappuzha daily, departing at 10.30am (10am check-in); tickets cost Rs150 and can be bought in advance or on the day, only at the ATDC/DTPC counters on either of the jetties (beware of unauthorized vendors selling fake tickets). Both companies make three stops during the 8hr journey, including one for lunch, and another at the renowned Mata Amritanandamayi Mission at Amritapuri. Foreigners are welcome to stay at the ashram, which is the home of the renowned female guru, Shri Amritanandamayi Devi, known as the "hugging Mama" because she gives each of her visitors and devotees a big, power-imparting hug during the daily *darshan* sessions.

Although it is by far the most popular backwater trip, many tourists find the Alappuzha–Kollam route too long and at times uncomfortable, with crowded decks and intense sun. There's also something faintly embarrassing about being cooped up with a crowd of fellow tourists madly photographing any signs of life on the water or canal banks, while gangs of kids scamper alongside the boat screaming "one pen! . . . one pen! . . .". You can sidestep the tourist scene completely by catching local ferries. These are a lot slower, and the crush can be worse, but you're far less conspicuous than on the ATDC/DTPC boat and you gain a more intimate experience of life on the backwaters. The trip from Alappuzha to Kottayam (11 daily; Rs6) is particularly recommended; the first ferry leaves at 7.30am and the last at 9.30pm. Arrive early so you can get a place on the bow, which affords uninterrupted views. There are also numerous daily ferries that ply routes between local villages, allowing you to hop on and off as you like. The scenery on these routes is more varied than between Alappuzha and Kollam, beginning with open lagoons and winding up on narrow canals through densely populated coconut groves and islands; the tickets cost one tenth of the price of the tourist boats. Whichever boat you opt for, take a sun hat and plenty of water, and check the departure times in advance, as these can vary from year to year.

Groups of up to ten people can charter a *kettu vallam* moored at Karunagapalli for a day's cruise on the backwaters. The boat has comfortable cane chairs and a raised central platform where passengers can laze on cushions; there's a toilet on board and cool drinks are available. Sections of the curved roof of wood and plaited palms open out to provide shade and allow uninterrupted views. Whether powered by local gondoliers or by sail, the trip is as quiet and restful (at least for the passengers) as you could possibly want. At around Rs3000 for the day, including lunch, the luxury is well worth it. For longer trips you take a *kettu vallam* that has been converted into a houseboat with one/two bedrooms and a kitchen. A cook will also be provided. To book either, call Tourindia, MG Road, Thiruvananthapuram (℡ 0471/331057).

Almost every mid- to top-range hotel situated near the backwaters has its own private *kettu vallum* boat available for residents to hire. Alternatively, DTPC (℡0477/251796) and ATDC (℡ 0477/243462, ⊛ www.atdcalleppey.com) operate fleets (ATDC has fifteen rice boats available, DTPC only three) from Alleppey, and there are dozens of private *kettu vallam* operators in both Alleppey and Kollam who will arrange a trip if you turn up on spec. However, overnight *kettu vallam* cruises are not cheap, at Rs3000–5000 for two people for a two- to three-day cruise. Competition is stiff, and private agencies charge very similar prices, although you may be able to haggle the price down slightly, especially in the low season.

As a word of warning, as simple as the life in the backwaters appears to be, take care of your belongings at all times; there have been recent reports of theft, especially during the night when the crew sleep on dry land and the large windows are open. If possible, lock your valuables away (or put them under the bed), and keep belongings away from the windows.

the jetty. Among these are the Bokaro/Tata Express #8690 at 6am, the Trivandrum–Mumbai CST Express #6332 at 7.20am and the Alleppey–Chennai Express #6042 at 3pm; all three stop at Ernakulam Junction before continuing to Thrissur and Palakkad. For points further north along the coast including Mangalore, you should take an early train and change at Ernakulam, as the Alleppey–Cannanore Express #6307, which continues to Kozhikode and Kannur, arrives at those destinations far too late at night. The best train south to Thiruvananthapuram is the Ernakulam–Trivandrum Express #6341(departs 7.25am); most of the other express trains in this direction leave at inconvenient hours.

Alappuzha has several rival **tourist departments**. The main ATDC tourist information office (daily 8am–8pm; ℡0477/243462, ⓦwww.atdcalleppey .com) is opposite the jetty, next to Canara Bank, and they have a smaller office on the other side of the canal, just off Komala Road. The DTPC office (daily 7.30am–9pm; ℡0477/251796), at the DTPC jetty, handles **hotel bookings** for all KTDC and private hotels throughout Kerala and in other parts of south India for the charge of the telephone call and on receipt of one night's room rate. ATDC and DTPC both sell tickets for their **ferries**, **backwater cruises** and charter boats (maximum twenty people) – good for group excursions into less visited backwaters. The Government of Kerala's tourist office, at the DTPC jetty (Mon–Sat 10am–5pm; ℡0477/260722) is good for travel information. Other ferry and charter organizations include Kerala Backwaters at Choondapally Buildings, near the Nehru Trophy finishing point (℡0477/241693), Tour Kerala, Muttal Building, Nehru Trophy Ward (℡0477/242955) and Alappuzha Tour & Co, Punchiri Building, Jetty Road (℡0477/242040).

Moneychanging facilities are available at the Bank of India on Mullakal Road and the Indian Bank on Mullakal Road, which accepts Visa and Mastercard as well as currency and travellers' cheques. The State Bank of India is on Beach Road, and Canara Bank is next to the Zion Food Shop, near the jetty; it accepts travellers' cheques and Visa, but not currency. For **internet** access, Seiki internet café opposite the *Komala Hotel* (Rs40/hr) offers by far the fastest service, or try the Zion Food Shop opposite the main jetty (Rs60/hr).

Accommodation

If you need to stay near the town centre, Alappuzha's choice of **lodgings** is uninspiring, but there are some great places to stay if you are willing to travel into the outskirts. For a traditional atmosphere, try *Sona* or the *Keraleeyam*, which specializes in Ayurvedic treatment. The *Alleppey Prince*, which has a pool, is an old favourite and within striking distance of town, while the luxurious *Kayaloram* on the southern edge of the lake ranks amongst Kerala's finest settings.

Alleppey Prince, AS Road (aka Ernakulam Road or NH-47), 2km north of the jetty ℡0477/243752. The poshest option close to the town centre, all rooms a/c. Private backwater trips, and classical music or Kathakali staged by the pool. Book ahead. ➐–➑

Arcadia, by the KSRTC bus station ℡0477/241354. Soulless place with corridors of clean rooms (some a/c) close to the jetty; the restaurant serves excellent fish. Overpriced but popular as it's so convenient for the ferry. ➍–➏

Karthika Tourist Home, Kathiyani Road, across the canal, opposite the jetty ℡0477/251354. Plain rooms, some with attached bathrooms and wicker chairs. Room 31 has large bay windows. Try this place if the *Komla* is full. ➋

Kayaloram, Punnamada Kayal ℡0477/232040, ℻252918. An incredible location in a grove of palms with views onto the lake; the twelve wood cottages are built in Keralan style with open-to-the-sky baths, and ranged around a great pool. Ayurvedic treatment courses and daily sunset

cruises are available. Book through their city office at Punchiri Buildings, Jetty Road (℡ 0477/262931) and you will be taken there by boat from the Nehru Trophy jetty. ❾

Keraleeyam, Nehru Trophy Road, Thathampally ℡ 0477/231468, ℻ 251068. Traditional Keralan house with oodles of character that has been an Ayurvedic centre for sixty years. Elegant rooms are arranged around a communal living area, and there's a delightful cottage. A resident Ayurvedic doctor is on hand, and rejuvenation courses are individually arranged, including a special diet. Right on Punnamada Kayal, the Nehru Trophy channel, and you can get here by boat from the jetty. ❼

Komala, Zilla Court Ward, north of the jetty canal, 5min by rickshaw from the bus stand

℡ 0477/243631. Large efficient hotel, easily the best in the budget and mid-range classes, and with the town's nicest south Indian restaurant. A good range of rooms, some a/c. ❷–❻

KTDC Yatri Nivas, AS Road, near *Alleppey Prince* ℡ 0477/244460. Brand new complex with good-value, sizeable rooms (some a/c and with cable TV). There is a restaurant and a beer parlour next door at their *Aaram Motel*. ❸–❻

Sona, lakeside, Thathampally ℡ 0477/235211. Beautiful old Keralan home which once belonged to a Swiss woman, with a beautiful garden and four rooms with mosquito nets and plenty of family atmosphere and home-cooking; it's the place to discover fascinating local history on the town and backwaters. Recommended. ❺

Eating

One of the most popular places to eat in Alappuzha is *Komala Hotel's Arun* **restaurant**, but there are plenty of other decent, and cheaper, places including the *Zion Food Shop* snack bar at the DTPC jetty. For a splurge, slip on some clean clothes and catch a rickshaw out to the *Alleppey Prince*, whose a/c *Vembanad* restaurant offers the town's classiest menu, and beer by the pool. The KTDC *Aaram Motel* around the corner is a lot cheaper and also serves beer.

Annapoorna, opposite the DTPC jetty. A very good cheap vegetarian "meals" restaurant; the "meals" at lunchtime include a number of coconutty Keralan veg curries.

Arun, *Komala Hotel*, Zilla Court Ward. Tasty Chinese noodles and Indian veg (including delicious *dhal makhini, malai kofta* and *subzis*), but avoid the Continental food. If it's busy, settle in for a wait.

Greens, Cullan Road, off Mullakal Road. Alappuzha's popular new veg restaurant is cheap and clean with a little garden out front. Fresh south Indian snacks and unlimited "meals" all the way – the excellent coconut *uttappam* and a lime soda will set you back just Rs17.

Indian Coffee House, Mullakal Road. Part of the all-India chain of co-operatives with a predictable menu of reliable filter coffee, omelettes, *dosas* and *iddlis*, but with the addition of meat dishes.

Kream Korner, Mullakal Road. Non-veg restaurant-cum-ice-cream parlour. Mostly chicken and mutton, with a selection of snacks, milkshakes and ice creams.

Thoppi, *Karthika Hotel*. Very modest but clean and friendly place with an ambitious, inexpensive Indian and Chinese menu. They open early for standard "omelette-bread-butter-jam" breakfasts.

Kottayam and around

The busy commercial centre of **KOTTAYAM** is strategically located between the backwaters to the west and the spice, tea and rubber plantations, forests, and the mountains of the Western Ghats to the east, 76km southeast of Kochi and 37km northwest of Alappuzha. Most visitors come here on the way somewhere else – foreigners take short backwater trips to Alappuzha or set off to **Periyar Wildlife Sanctuary**, while Ayappa devotees pass through en route to the for-est temple at Sabarimala (see p.1335).

Kottayam's long history of **Syrian Christian** settlement is reflected by the presence of two thirteenth-century churches on a hill 5km northwest of the centre, which you can get to by rickshaw. Two eighth-century Nestorian stone crosses with Pahlavi and Syriac inscriptions, on either side of the elaborately decorated altar of the **Valliapalli** ("big") church, are probably the earliest solid evidence of Christianity in India. The visitors' book contains entries from as far back as the 1890s, including one by the Ethiopian king, Haile Selassie, and a British viceroy. The interior of the nearby **Cheriapalli** ("small") church is covered with lively, unskilled paintings, thought to have been executed by a Portuguese artist in the sixteenth century. If the doors are locked, ask for the key at the church office (9am–1pm & 2–5pm).

Practicalities

Kottayam's KSRTC **bus stand**, 500m south of the centre on TB Road (not to be confused with the private stand for local buses on KK Road, aka Shastri Road), is an important stop on routes to and from major towns in south India. Four of the frequent buses to Kumily/Periyar (3–4hr) each day go on to Madurai, in Tamil Nadu (7hr), and there are regular services to Thiruvananthapuram, Kollam and Ernakulam. The **railway station** (2km north of the centre) sees a constant flow of traffic between Thiruvananthapuram and points north. **Ferries** from Alappuzha and elsewhere dock at the weed-clogged jetty, 3km south of town. For details of backwater trips from Kottayam, see p.1327.

Surprisingly, there is no adequate source of tourist information in Kottayam. The Canara Bank (Mon–Fri 10am–2pm, Sat 10am–noon) on KK Road, opposite the *Anjali Hotel*, is the only place to **change money** and travellers' cheques, while cash advances are issued on Visa and Mastercard.

Accommodation and eating

Kottayam has a good choice of mid-range **hotels** but if you are in search of utter luxury, head out to one of the five-star resorts that nestle on the banks of the nearby Vembanad lake (see p.1332) in Kumarakom. You'll be hard pushed to find a decent budget hotel here, apart from the *Ambassador*.

There are basic "meals" **restaurants** in the centre of Kottayam, such as the *Black Stone*, close to the bus station on TB Road, and a fairly dingy *Indian Coffee House* on TB Road, but the best is the vegetarian thali restaurant at *Homestead Hotel*. For an evening out, the lovely lakeside *Vembanad Lake Resort*, where you eat on a *kettu vallam* rice boat, definitely wins, although for elegant dining try the *Anjali*.

Aida, Aida Junction, MC Road ☏ 0481/568391. A large friendly hotel with a good range of rooms including some a/c and reasonably priced singles; facilities include two restaurants, a bar, Star TV, moneychanging and tours arranged on request. ❺

Ambassador, KK Road ☏ 0481/563293. A well-run economy hotel with clean rooms; the a/c ones are very good value. ❷–❸

Anjali, KK Road, 2km from railway station, close to the square, downtown ☏ 0481/563669. Dark but comfortable Casino Group business hotel in the centre of town, with international and Chinese restaurants and bar. All a/c. ❼–❽

Green Park, Kurian Uthup Road, Nagampadam, near station and private bus stand ☏ 0481/563331. Modern and efficient business hotel. Good value, with decent rooms, a bar and two restaurants. ❺–❻

Homestead Hotel, opposite *Manorama*, KK Road, 1km from the station ☏0481/560467. Well-appointed central hotel with a range of options from clean budget to comfortable a/c rooms. Their thali vegetarian restaurant does excellent "meals". ❹–❻

Vembanad Lake Resort, Kodimatha, 5min walk from ferry and 2km from town and bus station ☏ 0481/564866, ☏ 561633. Western-style motel, with large, simply furnished modern chalets (five a/c) in pleasant gardens beside an inlet of Lake Vembanad. The restaurant has good Indian, Western and Chinese dishes, including seafood. Eat outside in a lakeside garden or on a moored *kettu vallam* longboat – gorgeous at night. ❻

Windsor Castle/ Lake Village, Kodimatha ☎0481/303622, ℱ303624. Ignore the white tower block of characterless luxury rooms in the "castle" part of the hotel, and head round the back for the second part of the hotel, the "Lake Village". This is set alongside a lagoon with comfortable Keralan-style chalets and a very pleasant open-air restaurant that specializes in Keralan cuisine. There are two swimming pools, a theatre for dance performances, an Ayurvedic centre, and dugout boat rides through the substantial gardens. ❽–❾

Around Kottayam

Some of Kerala's most attractive scenery lies within easy access of Kottayam. The beautiful **Kumarakom** bird sanctuary, in the backwaters to the west, is best visited at dawn before the hoards of day-trippers arrive. **Aranmula** to the south is one of the last villages still making *kannady* metal mirrors, and has a Krishna temple that organizes a ritual "non-competitive" boat race. The Mahadeva temple at **Ettumanur**, a short way north of Kottayam, is known to devotees as the home of a dangerous and wrathful Shiva, and to art-lovers as a sublime example of temple architecture, adorned with woodcarvings and murals.

Kumarakom

KUMARAKOM, 16km west of Kottayam, is technically an island on Vembanad Lake. Although right in the thick of a tangle of lush tropical waterways, it can be reached quite easily by bus from Kottayam (every 10min). The peak time to visit the **Bird Sanctuary**, which is no longer negotiable by boat since the channels have been choked by African moss, is between November and March when it serves as a winter home for many migratory birds, some from as far away as Siberia. Species include the darter or snake bird, little cormorant, night heron, golden-backed woodpecker, crow pheasant, white-breasted water hen and tree pie. Enthusiasts should visit the sanctuary at dawn, which is the quietest and best time for viewing, and the early rays of sunlight falling through the lush tropical canopy are beautiful. Although the island is quite small, a guide is useful; you can arrange one through the KTDC *Water Scapes* or another of the luxury hotels.

Next to the sanctuary, set in waterside gardens, a refurbished colonial bungalow that once belonged to a family of Christian missionaries and rubber planters forms the nucleus of a luxury **hotel**, *The Taj Garden Retreat* (☎0481/524377; ❾). There are a couple of dozen "cottages" and a *kettu vallam* longboat grouped around a landscaped garden and direct water access to the lake. However, it's not nearly as impressive as the very friendly and understated *Coconut Lagoon Hotel* (☎0481/524491, ℱ524495; ❾), 1km northwest and reached by launch (you can telephone for the boat from a kiosk at the canal side). Superbly crafted from fragments of ruined Keralan palaces, with beautiful woodcarvings and brass work, the building alone merits a visit. It was designed in traditional Keralan style, and its air of low-key elegance is set off perfectly by the location on the edge of Vembanad Lake. Even if you can't afford to stay here, consider eating Keralan specialities at the **restaurant**.

A new rival has emerged, the *Kumarakom Lake Resort*, 3km from the village and just before the *Taj* (☎0481/524900, ℱ524987; ❾). This ostentatious place takes the concept of a heritage resort to the extreme with two beautiful 300-year-old palaces recovered and reconstructed on site, ultra-luxurious cottages made up from bits of old Keralan houses, each with an outdoor bathroom hidden in a little lush garden behind. The Ayurveda centre has two doctors, four massage rooms, and the swimming pool has a Jacuzzi whose water laps the edge of the lake. Nearby, the slightly cheaper KTDC's *Water Scapes* right on the lake (℡0481/525861, ℻525862; ❾) consists of comfortable a/c cottages built on stilts. Unfortunately, very few of the cottages have a decent view over the lake and there are too many ugly metal walkways and buildings on the lakefront; it is however, very convenient for the bird sanctuary. Alternatively, you can drift across the lake on one of their luxury *kettu vallams* moored here (book through *Water Scapes*; ❾). If you are on a budget, take advantage of the excellent *Moolappura Guest House*, just 200m before the bus stand at the *Taj* (℡0481/525980; ❺), which has just two simple rooms with attached bathrooms in the family house. The family is very warm and welcoming: they offer rides on their dugout boats, and can even boast of a professional chef among their number, who whips up delicious Keralan and Continental dishes.

Besides the hotels, the only other place to eat is KTDC's uninspiring café at the *Tourist Complex* near where the bus from Kottayam pulls in, close to the *Taj* gates.

Aranmula

The village of **ARANMULA** is another appealing day-trip – so long as you start early – from Kottayam, 30km south of the town and 10km beyond Chengannur. Its ancient temple is dedicated to Parthasarathy, which was the

---

Christianity in Kerala

The history of Kerala's **Christians** – who today represent 21 percent of the population – is said to date back to the first century AD, some three centuries before Christianity received official recognition in Europe. These days, the five main branches among a bewildering assortment of churches are the **Nestorians** (confined mainly to Thrissur and Ernakulam), the **Roman Catholics** (found throughout Kerala), the **Syrian Orthodox Church** (previously known as the Jacobite Syrians), the evangelical and reformist **Mar Thoma Syrians** (a splinter group of the Syrian Orthodox), and the Anglican **Church of South India**.

A legend, widely believed in Kerala but the object of academic scepticism, states that St Thomas the Apostle – "Doubting Thomas" – landed on the Malabar coast in AD 52, where he converted several brahmins and others, and founded seven churches. Muziris, his first port of call, has been identified as Kodungallur (see p.1365); the traditional accounts of Jews who arrived there in AD 68 state that they encountered a Christian community. Their number was augmented in the fourth century by an influx of Syrians belonging to seven tribes from Baghdad, Nineveh and Jerusalem, under the leadership of the merchant Knayi Thoma (Thomas of Cana).

Christians gradually came to the forefront as traders, and eventually gained special privileges from the local rulers. The early communities followed a liturgy in the **Syriac language** (a dialect of Aramaic). Latin was introduced by missionaries who visited Kollam in the Middle Ages; once the Catholic Portuguese turned up, in 1498, a large community of **Latin Christians** developed, particularly on the coast, and came under the jurisdiction of the Pope. In the middle of the seventeenth century, with the ascendancy of the Dutch, part of the Church broke away from Rome, and local bishops were appointed through the offices of the Jacobite Patriarch in Antioch.

During the nineteenth century, the Anglican Church amalgamated with certain "free" churches, to form the Church of South India. At the same time, elements in the Syrian Church advocated the replacement of Syriac with the local language of Malayalam. The resultant schism led to the creation of the new Mar Thoma Syrian Church.

Christmas is an important festival in Kerala; during the weeks leading up to Dec 25, innumerable star-shaped lamps are put up outside shops and houses, illuminating the night and identifying followers of the faith.

name under which Krishna acted as Arjuna's charioteer during the bloody Kurekshetra war recorded in the *Mahabharata*, and the guise in which he expounded the *Bhagavad Gita*. Each year towards the end of the Onam festival (Aug/Sept), when a **Snakeboat Regatta** is celebrated as part of the temple rituals, crowds line the banks of the River Pampa to cheer on the thrusting longboats (similar to those seen at Alappuzha; see p.1325).

Aranmula is also known for manufacturing extraordinary *kannady* **metal mirrors**, produced, using the "lost wax" technique, with an alloy of copper, silver, brass, lead and bronze. Once a prerequisite of royal households, these ornamental mirrors are now exceedingly rare; only two master craftsmen, Subramanian and Arjun Asary, and their families, still make them. The most modest models cost in the region of Rs300, while custom-made mirrors can cost as much as Rs50,000.

The **Vijana Kala Vedi Cultural Centre** offers ways of "experiencing traditional India through the study of art and village life". Introductory courses are offered in Kathakali, Mohiniattam and Bharatanatyam dance, woodcarving, mural painting, cooking, Kalarippayat, Ayurvedic medicine, and several Indian languages. Courses cost upwards of $200 per week; book by writing to the Director, Vijana Kala Vedi Cultural Centre, Tarayil Mukku Junction, Aranmula, Kerala 689533.

Ettumanur

The magnificent Mahadeva temple at **ETTUMANUR**, 12km north of Kottayam on the road to Ernakulam, features a circular shrine, fine woodcarving and one of the earliest (sixteenth-century) and most celebrated of Keralan **murals**. The deity is Shiva in one of his most terrible aspects, described as *vaddikasula vada*, "one who takes his dues with interest" and is "difficult to please". His predominant mood is *raudra* (fury). Although the shrine is open to Hindus only, foreigners are allowed to see the painting, which may be photographed only after obtaining a camera ticket from the hatch to the left of the main *gopura* entranceway. The four-metre mural depicts Nataraja – Shiva – executing a cosmic *tandava* dance, trampling evil underfoot in the form of a demon. Swathed in cobras, he stands on one leg in a wheel of gold, with his matted locks fanning out amid a mass of flowers and snakes. Outside the wheel, a crowd of celestials are in attitudes of devotion. Musical accompaniment is courtesy of Krishna on flute, three-headed Brahma on cymbals, and, playing the copper *mizhavu*, the holiest and most ancient of Keralan drums, Shiva's special rhythm expert Nandikesvara.

Ettumanur's ten-day **annual festival** (Feb/March; ask at any KTDC office for details) reflects the wealth of the temple, with elaborate celebrations including music. On the most important days, the eighth and tenth, priests bring out figures of elephants, fashioned from 460kg of gold, presented in the eighteenth century by Marthanda Varma, the raja of Travancore.

Periyar Wildlife Sanctuary

One of the largest and most visited wildlife reserves in India, the **Periyar Wildlife Sanctuary** occupies 777 square kilometres of the Cardamom hills region of the Western Ghats. The majority of its many visitors come in the hope of seeing **tigers** and **leopards** – and most leave disappointed, as the few

During December and January, Kerala is jam-packed with crowds of men in black or blue *dhotis*, milling about railway stations and filling trains on their way to the Shri Ayappa forest temple (also known as Hariharaputra or Shasta) at Sabarimala, in the Western Ghat mountains, around 200km from both Thiruvananthapuram and Kochi. The Ayappa devotees can seem disconcertingly ebullient, chanting "*Swamiyee Sharanam Ayappan*" (give us protection, god Ayappa) in a call and response style reminiscent of Western sports fans.

Although he is primarily a Keralan deity, Ayappa's appeal has spread phenomenally in the last thirty years across south India, to the extent that this is said to be the second largest pilgrimage in the world, with as many as a million devotees each year. A curious story relates to the birth of Ayappa. One day, when the two male gods, Shiva and Vishnu, were together in a pine forest, Shiva asked to see Vishnu's famed female form Mohini, the divine enchantress. Vishnu refused, having a fair idea of what this could lead to. However, Shiva was undeterred, and used all his powers of persuasion to induce Vishnu to transform. As a result of the inevitable passionate embrace, Vishnu became pregnant, and the baby Ayappa emerged from his thigh.

Pilgrims however, are required to remain celibate, abstain from intoxicants, and keep to a strict vegetarian diet for a period of 41 days prior to setting out on the four-day walk through the forest from the village of Erumeli (61km, as the crow flies, northwest) to the shrine at Sabarimala. Rather less devoted devotees take the bus to the village of Pampa, and join the five-kilometre queue. When they arrive at the modern temple complex – a surreal spread of concrete sheds and walkways in the middle of the jungle – pilgrims who have performed the necessary penances may ascend the famous eighteen gold steps to the inner shrine. There they worship the deity, throwing donations down a chute that opens onto a subterranean conveyor belt, where the money is counted and bagged for the bank. In recent years, the mass appeal of the Ayappa cult has brought in big bucks for the temple, which now numbers among India's richest, despite being open for only a few months each year. Funds also pour in from the shrine's innumerable spin-off businesses, such as the sale of coconut oil and milk (left by every pilgrim) to a soap manufacturer.

The pilgrimage reaches a climax during the festival of Makara Sankranti when massive crowds of over 1.5 million congregate at Sabarimala. On January 14, 1999, 51 devotees were buried alive when part of a hill crumbled under the crush of a stampede. The devotees had gathered at dusk to catch a glimpse of the final sunset of *makara jyoti* (celestial light) on the distant hill of Ponnambalamedu.

Although males of any age and even of any religion can take part in the pilgrimage, females between the ages of nine and fifty are barred. This rule, still vigorously enforced by the draconian temple oligarchy, was contested in 1995 by a bizarre court case. Following complaints to local government that facilities and hygiene at Sabarimala were substandard, the local collector, a 42-year-old woman, insisted she be allowed to inspect the site. The temple authorities duly refused, citing the centuries-old ban on women of menstrual age, but the High Court, who earlier upheld the gender bar, was obliged to overrule the priests' decision. The collector's triumphant arrival at Sabarimala soon after made headline news, but she was still not allowed to enter the shrine proper.

For advice on how to visit Sabarimala, via a back route beginning at Kumily near the Periyar Wildlife Sanctuary, see p.1340.

that remain very wisely keep their distance, and there's only a slight chance of a glimpse even at the height of the dry season (April/May). However, there are plenty of other animals: elephant, sambar, wild pig, Malabar flying squirrel, gaur, stripe-necked mongoose and over 260 species of birds including Nilgiri wood pigeon, blue-winged parakeet, white-bellied tree pie, laughing thrushes and flycatchers. Located close to the Kerala–Tamil Nadu border, the park makes a convenient place to break the long journey across the Ghats between Madurai and the coast. It's also a good base for day-trips into the Cardamom hills, with a couple of tea factories, spice plantations, the trailhead for the Sabarimala pilgrimage (see p.1336), and viewpoints and forest waterfalls within striking distance.

Periyar lies at cool altitudes of 900m to 1800m with temperatures between 15°C and 30°C, just over 100km east of Kottayam, and centres on a vast artificial **lake**, created by the British in 1895 to supply water to the drier parts of neighbouring Tamil Nadu, around Madurai. The royal family of Travancore, anxious to preserve favourite hunting grounds from the encroachment of tea plantations, declared it to be a Forest Reserve, and built the Edapalayam Lake Palace to accommodate their guests in 1899. It expanded as a wildlife reserve in 1933, and once again when it became part of **Project Tiger** in 1979 (see Contexts).

Seventy percent of the protected area, which is divided into core, buffer and tourist zones, is covered with evergreen and semi-evergreen forest. The **tourist zone** – logically enough, the part accessible to casual visitors – surrounds the lake, and consists mostly of semi-evergreen and deciduous woodland interspersed with grassland, both on hilltops and in the valleys. Although excursions on the lake are the standard way to experience the park, you can get much more out of a visit by **walking** with a local guide in a small group, or, especially, staying in basic accommodation in the sanctuary away from the crowd. However, avoid the period immediately after the monsoons, when **leeches** make hiking virtually impossible. The **best time to visit** is from December until April, when the dry weather draws animals from the forest to drink at the lakeside.

Getting to Periyar

The pothole-filled road that winds through the undulating hills up to **Kumily** from Ernakulam and Kottayam makes for a very long, slow drive, but it gives wonderful views across the Ghats. The route is dotted with grand churches among the trees, and numerous jazzy roadside shrines to St Francis, St George or the Virgin Mary – a charming Keralan blend of ancient and modern. Once you've climbed through the rubber-tree forests into Idukki District, the mountains get truly spectacular, and the wide-floored valleys are carpeted with lush tea and cardamom plantations.

Travellers heading for the **Periyar Wildlife Sanctuary** have first to make their way to the village of Kumily, 4km short of the barrier at **Thekkady** park entrance, on the northwest of the reserve. Kumily, which boasts a tea and spice market, is served by state and private **buses** from Kottayam (every 30min; 4hr), Ernakulam (10 daily; 6hr), and Madurai in Tamil Nadu (frequent service; 5hr 30min); most of these terminate at the scruffy bus stand east of Kumily bazaar. From here a minibus (Rs4) shuttles visitors to the park gate, although some continue through to the KTDC *Aranya Nivas*, at Thekaddy inside the sanctuary. **Auto-rickshaws** will also run you from the bus stand to the *Aranya Nivas* for Rs25 plus Rs5 park entry, but if you are arriving late remember the gates close at 6pm, after which you will have to show proof of your accommodation booking before they will let you in. If you are staying at the KTDC *Lake Palace*, the last boat is officially at 4pm but they will arrange a boat during daylight hours. The **entrance fee** to the park is Rs10 for Indians and Rs50 for foreigners, both valid for one day only; if you are staying inside the park you must go to the Forest Information Centre by the jetty each day to buy a new pass.

KTDC runs hectic and uncomfortable **weekend tours** to Periyar from Kochi, calling at Kadamattom and Idukki Dam en route; Sat 7.30am–Sun 8pm), and an even more rushed tour from Thiruvananthapuram. Unless you love being cooped up for days in video buses, give them a miss. Numerous tour operators in Thiruvananthapuram, Kovalam and Kochi also offer tailor-made packages.

Kumily

As beds inside the sanctuary are in such short supply, most visitors end up staying in or near **Kumily**, 2km north of the park gates. Kumily is a growing town where tourism seems to be slowly replacing the spice trade as the main source of income. However, the spice industry is alive and well and several agencies offer tours to plantations. Almost every shop on Thakkady Road sells freshly collected spices; just to walk along the street and breathe in the air filled with the scent of cloves, nutmeg, cinnamon and cardamom is a heady experience. In the middle of the melee of the bazaar stands the main **cardamom auction** area, where you can watch tribal women sifting and sorting the fragrant green pods in heart-shaped baskets.

Idduki's DTPC has a low-key **tourist office** (Mon–Sat 10am–5pm; ☏0486/322620) on the first floor of the Panchayat Building, Thekkady Junction. Besides offering information on the district itself, they organize conducted tours, including a *Spice Valley* tour (6.30am–9.30pm; Rs200) that takes in Munnar and several spice plantations. The other source of information is the **tourism police**, with an office at the bus stand and the main office at Ambady Junction. Their prime purpose is to maintain law and order, though they also offer information. However, there have been reports that they only provide details about hotels, tea factories, homestays and plantations that pay them commission, which will later be added to your bill.

Tea factory and **spice plantation tours** are the big tourist attraction in the area; aside from every hotel offering a tour of a farm, you will also be besieged by tourist agencies in Kumily all offering the same package at very competitive rates. Unfortunately, some places such as Abraham's Plantation have become heavily commercialized and expensive as a result of tourism; the best way to organize a tour is to ask at your hotel – most of the staff will have a relative who has a good plantation. At the time of research, Rs300–350 was the going rate for a three-hour tour, including a guide and Jeep hire.

Both the State Bank of Travancore (☏0486/322041), near the bus stand, and the Central Bank of India, KK Road (☏0486/322053), **change money**. For **internet** facilities try Rissas Communications/Media at Thekkady Junction (Rs45/hr). Although hilly, this is good cycling territory; **bicycle rental** is available from stalls in the market for around Rs30 per day.

Kumily accommodation and eating

Kumily has **accommodation** to suit all pockets and new hotels and "resorts" emerge each season. Thankfully, most of the accommodation lies well outside the bazaar area, dotted along the Thekkady Road leading to the park. Homestays such as *Green Garden* are a popular option – ask around the bazaar and you'll soon be pointed in the right direction; most charge about Rs300 and offer plantation tours and home-cooked food.

Nearly every establishment has its own café-restaurant, ranging from the *Taj Garden Retreat's* smart à la carte, to the more traveller-oriented *Coffee Inn*. The brand new *Pepper Garden Coffee House* is hidden in the lush plantation en route to *Claus Garden Home*. This inexpensive place serves up wonderful coffees, teas (both grown in the garden) and excellent breakfasts, including steamed *puttu* with mung beans and bananas; in the evening there is a bonfire and live *tabla* and flute and it's open until midnight. However, if you're on a really tight budget, the best place to eat in Kumily bazaar is the *Hotel Saravana*, one of several no-frills "meals" joints on the main bazaar. Their thalis, served on plantain leaves, are tasty, cheap and always freshly cooked, and they serve up deliciously crisp *dosas*.

Ambadi, next to turn-off for Mangaladevi temple, Thekkady Road ☎ 0486/322193. Pleasant hotel which has seen better times. Decent rooms sporting coir mats and woodcarvings, and the non-a/c "cottages" are good value. The restaurant serves good chicken. ❺–❼

Claus Garden Home, five minutes' walk south of the main bus stand (no phone) behind the *Taj*. Difficult to find, but worth the effort. Simple rooms in a cosy house with sociable verandas and mandala murals, surrounded by pepper plantations. Self-catering only. ❷

Coffee Inn, Thekkady Road (no phone). Surly staff but good budget accommodation: a handful of simple rooms (one en suite) around a covered terrace and garden. Their "Wild Huts" annexe has six rooms (and two raffia tree houses) with shared shower and toilet, and a spacious enclosed garden with a pond. The café, serving delicious homemade Western food including fresh bread, is a popular place for breakfast after the early-morning boat ride in the sanctuary. ❷–❸

Green Garden Cottage, next door to Claus Garden Home ☎ 0486/322935. One of the best organized of the homestay options with four spotless and large cottages in the family compound, each with attached bathrooms. Pleasant, quiet and great value. ❸

Kumily Gate, behind the bus stand ☎ 0486/322279. Greenish modern block with large, clean rooms and a restaurant and popular, noisy bar on site. Expensive for what it is, but good

for late arrivals and it is quite acceptable to haggle here. ❼

Maliackal Tourist Home, KK Road ☎ 0486/322589. Good clean rooms, handy for the bus stand. The most expensive rooms have cable TV and balconies (but no views). ❸–❹

Shalimar Spice Garden, Murikaddy ☎ & ☎ 0486/322132. Approached by a suspension bridge, in a secluded spot on the edge of a cardamom and pepper estate, 5km from Kumily (Rs50 by Jeep). Beautiful and tranquil place run by an Italian, with lovely cottages built using traditional Keralan teak structures; there's a pool and good restaurant ❾

Spice Village, Thekkady Road ☎ 0486/322315, ☎ 322317. Thatched huts and traditional Keralan wood cottages spread through a well-planted spice garden with a fine restaurant and a pool. You can join master classes in Keralan cookery, and there are lots of activities on offer each day. Popular with tour groups so book ahead. ❾

Taj Garden Retreat, Ambalambika Road ☎ 0486/322273. Luxurious, pseudo-rustic cottages and a main building built to emulate a jungle lodge with great views. Features an elegant restaurant and a pool. ❾

Woodlands, Thakkady Road ☎ 0486/322077. One of the cheapest places to stay in Kumily, and very rudimentary, although clean enough for a short stay, and with friendly management. Campfires can be arranged, a campsite is available, and there's a kitchen for self-catering. ❷

Into the sanctuary

Tickets for the **boat trips** (daily 7am, 9.30am, 11.30am, 2pm & 4pm; 2hr; Rs40 for lower deck, Rs80 for upper deck) on the lake are sold through the Forest Department at their hatch just above the main **visitor centre** in Thekkady, above the jetty. If you're on a tight budget, ask at the centre if there are any spaces on the Forestry Commission boat (Rs15), but you'll have to go on the lower deck.

Although it is unusual to see many animals from the boats – engine noise and the presence of a hundred other people make sure of that – you might spot a family group of elephants, wild boar and sambar deer by the water's edge. The upper deck is best for game viewing, although the seats are invariably block-booked by the upscale hotels. Turn up half-an-hour early, however, and you may be allocated any no-show places. To maximize your chances of seeing anything, take the 7am boat (wear something warm). At this hour, the mist rises over the lake and hills as you chug past dead trees – now bird perches – never cleared when the valley was flooded. Note that after heavy rain, chances of good sightings are very slim as the animals only come to the lake when water sources inside the forest have dried up.

Trekking in the sanctuary is possible (3hr; Rs350 per group, maximum five people), arranged either through the visitor centre (start 7am) or you can hire private guides, who operate on a more flexible time basis. They'll approach you in Kumily or near the park gates at Thekkady. Guides point out anything of interest, and reassure you that the fresh elephant dung on the path is nothing to worry about. The Forest Department also offers overnight trips and more elaborate week-long programmes. **Elephant rides** into the park cost Rs30 per head (30min); book at the Forest Department Centre.

Accommodation and eating in the sanctuary

The star attraction of Periyar has to be the prospect of staying in the Forest Department **watchtowers**, reached by boat from Thekkady and the best way to get a hands-on experience of the jungle. For the *Lake Palace*, *Periyar House* and the *Aranya Nivas* you should book in advance at the KTDC offices in Thiruvananthapuram or Ernakulam – essential if you plan to come on a weekend, a public holiday, or during **peak season** (Dec–March), when rooms are often in short supply.

Forest Department Rest House, Edappalayam. Very basic accommodation in the woods on the far side of the lake (you have to catch the 4pm boat and then hike, so a guide is recommended). Bring your own food and bedding. Reserve in advance at the Forest Department's Visitors Centre in Thekkady; you'll be lucky to get in at a weekend or in December. Expensive, but it's an unforgettable experience. ❹

Forest Department Watchtowers, Edappalayam and Manakkavala. Even more primitive than the *Rest House*, but the best way of sighting game: the towers overlook waterholes in the buffer zone. Book through the Visitors Centre, and take along food, candles, matches, a torch and a sleeping bag and warm clothes. Again, you have to catch the 4pm boat and trek from the jetty, so a guide is useful. Don't consider this if it's been raining, when leeches plague the trail. ❷

KTDC Aranya Nivas, just above the boat jetty, Thekkady ☎0486/322023, ☏322282. Plusher than *Periyar House*, a colonial manor with some

huge rooms, a pleasant garden, a great swimming pool, an excellent multi-cuisine restaurant, and a cosy bar. Upper deck tickets for two boat trips are included in the tariff. ❾

KTDC Lake Palace, across the lake (booked through *Aranya Nivas*). The sanctuary's most luxurious hotel with six suites in a converted maharaja's game lodge surrounded by forest, with wonderful views. Charming old-fashioned rooms, great dining and a lovely lawn. This has to be one of the few places in India where you stand a chance of spotting tiger and wild elephant while sipping tea on your own veranda. Full-board only. ❾

KTDC Periyar House, midway between the park gates and the boat jetty, Thekkady ☎0486/322026, ☏322526. Comfortable hotel close to the lake, with a restaurant, bar, and balcony overlooking the monkey-filled woods leading down to the waterside. Not as nice a location as its neighbour *Aranya Nivas*, but then a lot cheaper. Ask for a lake-facing room. ❼–❽

Around Periyar and Kumily:

the Cardamom hills

Nestled amid soaring, mist-covered mountains and dense jungles, Periyar and Kumily are convenient springboards from which to explore Kerala's beautiful **Cardamom hills**. Guides will approach you at Thekkady with offers of trips by Jeep taxi; if you can get a group together, these work out as good value. Among the more popular destinations is the **Mangaladevi temple**, 14km east of Kumily. The rough road to this tumbledown ancient ruin deep in the forest is sometimes closed due to flood damage, but when it is open the round trip takes about five hours. With a guide, you can also reach remote waterfalls and mountain viewpoints, offering panoramic vistas of the Tamil Nadu plains. Rates vary according to the season, but expect to pay around Rs500 for the taxi, and an additional Rs150 for the guide.

Of places that can be visited under your own steam, the fascinating **High Range Tea Factory** (⊕04868/77038 or 77043) lies at Puttady (pronounced "Poo-*tee*-dee"), 19km north and a rewarding diversion on the road to Munnar. Regular buses leave from Kumily bus stand; get down at Puttady crossroads, and pick up a rickshaw from there to the factory. Driven by whirring canvas belts, old-fashioned English-made machines chop, sift, and ferment the leaves, which are then dried by wood-fired furnaces and packed into sacks for delivery to the tea auction rooms in Kochi. The affable owner, Mr P.M. James, or one of his clerks, will show you around; you don't have to arrange the visit, but it's a good idea to phone ahead to check they are open.

The other possible day-trip from Kumily, though one that should not be undertaken lightly (or, because of Hindu lore, by pre-menopausal women), is to the Sri Ayappan forest shrine at **Sabarimala** (see p.1335). This remote and sacred site can be reached in a long day, but you should leave with a pack of provisions, as much water as you can carry, and plenty of warm clothes in case you get stranded. Jeep taxis wait outside Kumily bus stand to transport pilgrims to the less frequented of Sabarimala's two main access points, at a windswept mountain top 13km above the temple (2hr; Rs50 per person if the Jeep is carrying ten passengers). Peeling off the main Kumily–Kottayam road at **Vandiperiyar**, the route takes you through tea estates to the start an of appallingly rutted forest track. After a long and spectacular climb, this emerges at a grass-covered plateau where the Jeeps stop. You proceed on foot, following a well-worn path through superb old-growth jungle – complete with hanging creepers and monkeys crashing through the high canopy – to the temple complex at the foot of the valley. Allow at least two hours for the descent, and an hour or two more for the climb back up to the roadhead, for which you'll need plenty of drinking water. Given the very real risks involved with missing the last Jeep back to Kumily (the mountain is prime elephant and tiger country), it's advisable to get a group together and rent a 4WD for the day (about Rs600 plus waiting time).

Munnar

MUNNAR, 130km east of Kochi and four-and-a-half hours by bus north of Periyar, is the centre of Kerala's principal tea growing region. Although billed in tourist bumf as a "hill station", it is less a Raj-style resort than a scruffy, workaday settlement of corrugated iron-roofed cottages and factories, surrounded by vast swathes of rolling green **tea plantations**. All the same, it's easy to see why the pioneering Scottish planters that first developed this hidden valley in the 1900s felt so at home here. At an altitude of around 1600m, the town enjoys a refreshing climate, with crisp winter mornings and relentlessly heavy rain during the monsoons. Hemmed in by soaring mountains – including peninsular India's highest peak, **Anamudi** (2695m) – it also boasts a spectacular setting; when the river mist clears, the surrounding summits form a wild backdrop to the carefully manicured plantations carpeting the valley floor and sides.

Munnar's greenery and cool air draw mainly well-heeled honeymooners from Mumbai and Bangalore. However, more and more foreigners are stopping here for a few days, enticed by the spellbinding bus ride from Periyar, which runs across the high ridges and lush tropical forests of the Cardamom hills, or by the equally spectacular climb across the Ghats from Madurai. The town itself may be dull, but the **hiking** and **cycling** are excellent, with all gradients on offer, from gentle rambles through the tea fields to mountain climbing.

The Town and around

Raj-ophiles will enjoy the prospect of verandaed British bungalows clinging to the side of the shallow valleys, and the famous **High Range Club** on the southeast edge of town, with its manicured lawns and golf course (open to nonresidents). Beyond the club sprawl some of the valley's 37 thousand-acre plantations, most of which are owned by the industrial giant, Tata. Their regional headquarters in the centre of town is the place to arrange visits to **tea factories** in the area (☎0486/530561).

Munnar has become popular with young travellers who head up here for the excellent **off-road cycling**. There are no official routes, just miles and miles of hills to climb up and speed down. You can rent gearless bicycles in the market for about Rs4 per hour; if you want proper mountain bikes, ask at the DTPC office (Rs50 per day) or at KTDC *Tea County* (see p.1343) – their top-notch bikes are officially for residents but its worth enquiring if any are available.

Encompassing 100 square kilometres of moist evergreen forest and grassy hilltops in the Western Ghats, the **Eravikulam National Park** (daily 7am–6pm; foreigners Rs50, Indians Rs10; cars/taxis Rs10, auto-rickshaws Rs5), 13km northeast of Munnar (autos charge Rs150 return). It is the last stronghold of one of the world's rarest mountain goats, the **Nilgiri tahr**. Its innate friendliness made the tahr pathetically easy prey during the hunting frenzy of the colonial era. During a break in his campaign against Tipu Sultan in the late 1790s, the future Duke of Wellington reported that his soldiers were able to shoot the unsuspecting goats as they wandered through his camp. By Independence the tahr was virtually extinct; today, however, numbers are healthy, and the animals have regained their tameness, largely thanks to the efforts of the American biologist, Cifford Rice, who studied them here in the early 1980s. Unable to get close enough to properly observe the creatures, Rice followed the advice of locals and attracted them using salt. Soon, entire herds were congregating around his camp. The tahrs' salt addiction also explains why so many hang around the park gates at **Vaguvarai**, where visitors – despite advice from rangers – slip them salty snacks.

The park gates mark the start of an excellent **hike** up the most accessible of the Anamudi massif's three peaks, for which you'll need sturdy footwear, plenty of water, a fair amount of stamina and a head for heights. Due to past environmental erosion, you now need to purchase a permit before setting off, available from the Wildlife DFO in Munnar (☎0486/530487). To start the trek, follow the road as it winds through the sanctuary, cutting across the switchbacks until you reach the pass forming the Kerala–Tamil Nadu border (auto-rickshaws and Jeep taxis will drive you this far, although you can enter the park by paying the extra vehicle fee). Leave the road here and head up the ridge to your right; the path, which becomes very steep, peters out well before you reach the summit, and many hikers find the gradient too hair-raising to continue. But the panoramic views from the top are well worth the effort, and you may be rewarded with a glimpse of tahr grazing the high slopes.

Another popular excursion is the 34-kilometre uphill climb by bus through the subcontinent's highest tea estates to **Top Station**, a tiny hamlet on the Kerala–Tamil Nadu border with superb views across the plains. It's renowned for the very rare **Neelakurunji plant** (*Strobilatanthes*), which grows in profusion on the mountainsides but only flowers once every twelve years, when crowds descend to admire the cascades of violet blossom spilling down the slopes. Top Station is accessible by **bus** from Munnar (8 daily starting at 5.30am; 1hr), and taxi-Jeeps will do the round trip for Rs600.

Practicalities

Munnar can be reached by **bus** from Kochi, Kottayam, Kumily and Madurai, either directly or with a change at Tehni. State-run and private services pull into the stand in the bazaar at the north end of town, near the river confluence and Tata headquarters. For most hotels you should ask to be dropped off at Old Munnar, 2km south of the centre, near the ineffectual DTPC **tourist office** (Mon–Sat 10am–5pm; ☏0486/530679). If you need **information** on transport, accommodation and day-trips, including to Eravikulam, seek out the helpful **Joseph Iype**, who runs the Free Tourist Information Service (☏0486/530349) from a small office in the main bazaar. Immortalized in Dervla Murphy's book *On a Shoestring to Coorg*, this self-appointed tourist officer has become something of a legend, but the accommodation he has on offer is disappointing. In addition to handing out useful **maps** and newspaper articles, he'll arrange **auto-rickshaws** and **taxis** for excursions, and bombard you with background on the area. You can **change money** at the State Bank of Travancore or the State Bank of India.

Accommodation and eating

Munnar has plenty of **accommodation**, although budget options are limited and are unfortunately too close to the bus station for a peaceful sleep. Upmarket visitors generally **eat** in their hotels; the *Royal Retreat*'s plush à la carte restaurant is particularly recommended, with an eclectic menu and attentive service, while *Gurus*, in the old bazaar opposite the government high school is a characterful old-style coffee shop serving south Indian snacks. For tasty, filling and cheap meals, however, you can't beat the *Poopada*, whose small, no-frills restaurant is open to nonresidents. *Saravana* in the main market serves good vegetarian "meals" while the *East End's* plush mid-priced restaurant is the best in the town centre, with a very varied menu.

Copper Castle, Bison Valley Road, Kannan Devan hills ☏0486/530633, ☏530438. Comfortable hotel wedged into the side of a hill high above the valley; the deluxe rooms and restaurant boast excellent views. Unless you have your own car, this place is inconveniently far from town. ❽–❾

East End, Temple Road, across the river from the bus stand ☏0486/530451, ☏530227. Immaculate upmarket hotel close to the centre of town, with Raj-style "cottages" in a big garden, and a recommended mid-priced multi-cuisine restaurant with a good varied menu. ❺–❼

Government Guest House, Mattupatty Road, near the main bazaar, on the far side of the river ☏0486/530385. Characterful old British bungalow with well-refurbished and comfortable rooms; meals are provided by arrangement. The tariff appears to fluctuate daily, so you may well be able to negotiate a good discount. ❼

Hilltop Lodge, on corner of Temple Road and Thekkady Road ⊕0486/530616. Popular with the mountain biking crew, but you'll have to try and ignore the constant racket of traffic outside. This place offers the best budget deal with small, clean rooms, all with attached bathrooms (but no hot water). ❷

KTDC Tea County, Top Station Road ⊕0468/530460, ⊕530970. The grandest address in Munnar, with a range of luxurious chalet-style rooms and suites ranged along a hilltop, affording views across the valley. There's a good Indian restaurant, a bar, and a range of sporting and adventure activities, including paragliding and rock climbing. ❼–❽

Poopada, Kannan Devan hills, on the Manukulam Road ⊕0486/530223. The front looks a tad dilapi-dated but the good-sized, en-suite rooms are in fine condition. This place has about the best cheap eating in town, along with fine valley views and secluded location. Booking recommended at weekends. ❻–❼

Royal Retreat, Kannan Devan hills ⊕0486/530240. Pleasant sunny yellow complex at the south end of town; spacious and comfortable rooms, some with brick fireplaces and cane furni-ture. ❼–❽

Shree Narayana ("SN") Tourist Home, Kannan Devan hills, on the main road near the tourist office ⊕0486/530212. A popular and cheerful lodge set in forested grounds by a river, with slightly shabby rooms. Unfortunately, a recent price hike means this place isn't such good value anymore. ❺–❻

Kochi (Cochin) and Ernakulam

The venerable city of **KOCHI** (long known as Cochin), is Kerala's hottest tourist spot, spreading across islands and promontories in a stunning location between the Arabian Sea and backwaters. Its main sections – modern **Ernakulam**, in the east, and the old districts of **Mattancherry** and **Fort Cochin** on a peninsula in the west – are linked by a complex system of fer-ries, and distinctly less romantic bridges. Although most visitors end up stay-ing in Ernakulam, Fort Cochin and Mattancherry are the focus of interest, where the city's extraordinary history of foreign influence and settlement is reflected in an assortment of architectural styles. During a wander through their narrow lanes, you'll stumble upon spice markets, Chinese fishing nets, a synagogue, a Portuguese palace, India's first European church, Dutch homes, and a village green that could have been transported from England's Home Counties. The city is also one of the few places in Kerala where, at any time of year, you can be assured of seeing **Kathakali dance**, either in one of sev-eral special tourist theatres, or at a more authentic performance by a temple-based company.

Kochi was born in 1341, when a flood created a natural safe port that swift-ly replaced Muziris (Kodungallur, 50km north) as the chief harbour on the Malabar coastline. The royal family transferred here from Muziris in 1405, after which the city grew rapidly, attracting Christian, Arab and Jewish settlers from the Middle East. Its name probably derives from *kocchazhi*, meaning the new, or small, harbour.

The history of **European** involvement in Kochi from the early 1500s onwards is dominated by the aggression of, successively, the Portuguese, Dutch and British, competing to control the port and its lucrative spice trade. From 1800, the state of Cochin was part of the British Madras Presidency; from 1812 until Independence in 1947, its administration was made the responsibility of a series of *diwans*, or finance ministers. In the 1920s, the British expanded the port to make it suitable for modern ocean-going ships; extensive dredging created Willingdon Island, between Ernakulam and Fort Cochin.

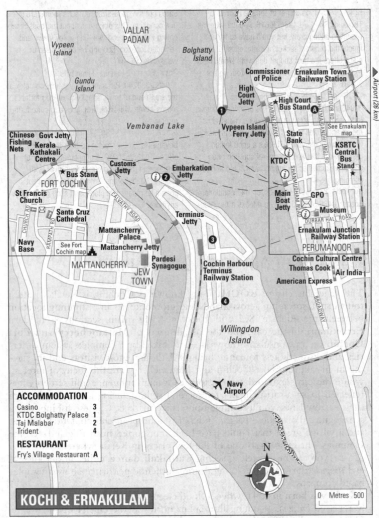

ACCOMMODATION

Casino	3
KTDC Bolghatty Palace	1
Taj Malabar	2
Trident	4

RESTAURANT

| Fry's Village Restaurant | A |

KOCHI & ERNAKULAM

0   Metres   500

▼ *Alappuzha & Thiruvananthapuram*

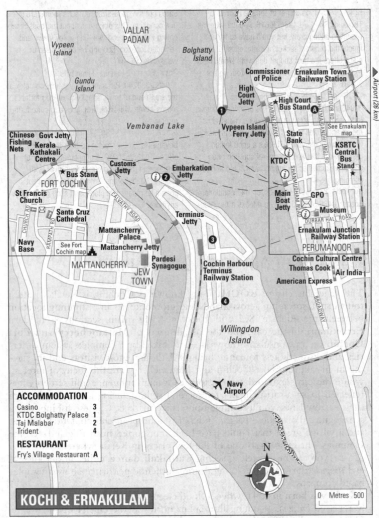

(map labels) VALLAR PADAM · *Vypeen Island* · Bolghatty *Island* · *Gundu Island* · Commissioner of Police · Ernakulam Town Railway Station · High Court Jetty · High Court Bus Stand · *Vembanad Lake* · Vypeen Island Ferry Jetty · State Bank · KTDC · KSRTC Central Bus Stand · Chinese Fishing Nets · Govt Jetty · Kerala Kathakali Centre · Customs Jetty · Embarkation Jetty · Main Boat Jetty · GPO · Bus Stand · FORT COCHIN · St Francis Church · Santa Cruz Cathedral · Terminus Jetty · Museum · Ernakulam Junction Railway Station · PERUMANOOR · Navy Base · See Fort Cochin map · Mattancherry Palace · Mattancherry Jetty · MATTANCHERRY · Pardesi Synagogue · JEW TOWN · Cochin Harbour Terminus Railway Station · Cochin Cultural Centre · Thomas Cook · Air India · American Express · *Willingdon Island* · Navy Airport · Airport (26 km) · See Ernakulam map · CAVALRY ROAD · CHURCH RD · RAMPATH RD · MARINE DRIVE · SHANMUGHAM ROAD · DURBAR HALL ROAD · BROADWAY · CHITTOOR RD · MAHATMA GANDHI (MG) RD · N

Arrival and local transport

Kochi's brand new **international airport** is at Nedumbassery, near Alwaye (aka Alua), 26km to the north of Ernakulam. Kochi is served by daily flights from **Mumbai**, **Bangalore**, **Thiruvananthapuram** and **Delhi**, and six each week from **Chennai**. Two weekly flights depart from **Goa**, **Hyderabad**, **Kozhikode**, and **Coimbatore**, as well as the **Lakshadweep Islands** and the Gulf States of **Doha**, **Dubai**, **Kuwait**, **Sharjah** and **Muscat**. There are three **railway stations** – **Ernakulam Junction** (☎131), closest to the centre, is the most important; Ernakulam Town lies 4km to the north. No trains run to Fort Cochin or Mattancherry. The Cochin Harbour Terminus, on Willingdon

Island, is useful only for people staying in one of the luxury hotels on the island.

The KSRTC **Central bus stand** (℡0484/372033), beside the rail line a short way east of MG Road and north of Ernakulam Junction, is the principal and most convenient stand for long-distance buses. There are two bus stands for private buses, which are not officially permitted to use the state highways; these buses, which have been responsible for several horrendous accidents, stop more frequently and compete with each other, overtake very dangerously, and tend to be more crowded than KSRTC buses. The **Kaloor stand** (rural destinations to the south and east) is across the bridge from Ernakulam Town railway station on the Alwaye Road, and the **High Court stand** (buses to Kumily, for Periyar Wildlife Reserve, and north to Thrissur, Guruvayur and Kodungallur) is opposite the High Court ferry jetty.

Although **auto-rickshaws** are plentiful and reliable in Ernakulam, and to a slightly lesser extent across the water in Mattancherry and Fort Cochin, everyone uses Kochi's excellent **ferry system**. **Bicycles** for exploring Mattancherry and the rest of old Kochi can be rented from a small shop on Bazaar Road between *Hotel Seagull* and Fort Cochin or from *Adams Old Inn* (Rs5 per hour).

Tours and backwater trips

KTDC's half-day **Kochi boat cruise** (daily 9am–12.30pm & 2–5.30pm; Rs50) is a good way to orient yourself. However, it doesn't stop for long in either Mattancherry or Fort Cochin, so give it a miss if you are pushed for time. Departing from the High Court Jetty on Shanmugham Road, Ernakulam, it calls at the synagogue, Mattancherry Dutch Palace, St Francis Church, the Chinese fishing nets, and Bolghatty Island. Book at the KTDC Reception Centre on Shanmugham Road (℡0484/353234).

KTDC, the Tourist Information Centre, and a couple of private companies also operate popular **backwater trips** (see p.1326) out of Kochi. Taking in a handful of coir-making villages north of the city, these are a leisurely and enjoyable way to experience rural Kerala from small hand-punted canoes. KTDC's daily tours cost Rs315, including the car or bus trip to the departure point, 30km north, and a knowledgeable guide. Better value is a similar trip run by the tourist desk at the Main Boat Jetty (daily depart 9am, return 1.30pm, or depart 2pm, return 6.30pm; Rs275; ℡0484/371761). Reserve at least a day in advance for either tour. Both also offer *kettu vallam* **houseboat** cruises along the backwaters of Cochin district, charging Rs3500–4500 per couple for a 24hr trip, including all meals.

Information

If you are based on Willingdon Island, head for the helpful Government of India **tourist office** (Mon–Fri 9am–5.30pm, Sat 9am–noon; ℡0484/668352), between the *Taj Malabar Hotel* and Tourist Office Jetty. They offer information on Kerala and beyond, can provide reliable guides and also have a desk at the airport. KTDC's **reception centre**, on Shanmugham Road, Ernakulam (℡0484/353234), reserves accommodation in their hotel chain and organizes sightseeing and backwater tours (see above). Another KTDC counter can be found at the airport, and there's a DTPC desk at the Old Collectorate, Park Avenue, Ernakulam (℡0484/371488). The tiny independent **tourist desk** (daily 8am–7pm; ℡0484/371761), at the entrance to the Main Boat Jetty in Ernakulam, is extremely helpful and friendly, and the best place to check ferry

Half the fun of visiting Kochi is getting about on the cheap local ferries. When it's not downright impossible, catching a bus, rickshaw or taxi the long way round to most parts of the city takes much longer and is far less interesting.

The map opposite shows Ernakulam's four jetties. Theoretically, the routes below should work in reverse. However, play safe, and don't rely on getting the last boat. A pamphlet giving the exact ferry timings is available from the ticket hatches by the jetties, and from the helpful tourist desk at the Main Boat Jetty in Ernakulam.

Ernakulam to Mattancherry
From Ernakulam (Main Jetty), via Fort Cochin (Customs Jetty), for Chinese fishing nets, St Francis Church, Dutch Cemetery; Willingdon Island (Terminus Jetty); and Mattancherry Jetty for Jewish Synagogue and Dutch Palace. Journey time 20min.
First boat 6am, last 9.10pm.

Ernakulam to Vypeen
From Ernakulam (Main Jetty). This frequent service has two routes: one via Willingdon Island (Embarkation Jetty; 25min), and a fast one to Vypeen (Govt Jetty; 15min).
First boat 7am, every 30min until 9.30pm.

Fort Cochin to Vypeen
From Fort Cochin (Government Jetty) to Vypeen (Government Jetty). Journey time 15 minutes.
First boat 6.30am, every 10min until 9pm.

Willingdon Island to Fort Cochin
From the Tourist Office Jetty (Willingdon Island) to Customs Jetty (Fort Cochin). Journey time 15min.
First boat 6.30am, every 30min until 6.15pm.

Ernakulam to Bolghatty Island
From Ernakulam (High Court Jetty). Journey time 10min.
First boat 6.30am, last 9pm; there are also speedboat taxis (Rs20; free if you are staying at Bolgatty Palace hotel)

Ernakulam to Varapuzha
A local ferry service that provides a chance to see the backwaters (see p.1326) if you can't travel further south than Kochi.
Six boats daily, starting at 7.40am until 6.45pm; 2hr each way. There's little to see at Varapuzha, apart from paddy fields and coconuts, so it makes sense to take the 2.30pm boat and stay on it, returning to Ernakulam just after dusk at 6.30pm.

and bus timings and you can pick up free city and state maps. A mine of information on ritual theatre and temple festival dates around the state, the award-winning office also publishes a useful south India information guide and offers daily boat tours and houseboats at very competitive rates, as well as running a fantastic guesthouse near Cannore (see p.1377).

Useful **publications** include the *Jaico Timetable* (Rs7) and the bimonthly *Cochin Shopper's Digest* (free), both of which are not exhaustive but list details of bus, train, ferry and flight times. KTDC publish an excellent walking tour map and guide to Fort Cochin (free; available from all KTDC tourist offices), which describes the fascinating histories of many of the buildings you will see in the Fort area.

The city's **tourist police** have a counter at the railway station and are on hand to answer queries and assist if you get into difficulties.

Accommodation

The romantic atmosphere of **Fort Cochin** is being exploited, and a growing number of budget guesthouses and upmarket hotels is drastically altering the face of this quaint town; property developers with little interest in restoration and conservation are creating eyesores such as the *Park Avenue* hotel. The biggest crisis however, is the **clean water shortage** that has hit the locals very hard, especially in the high season; if you do stay in Fort Cochin, try and keep your daily water consumption to a minimum. To help preserve the fort area, you could opt to stay in **Ernakulam**, which lacks the old-world ambience, but it is far more convenient for travel connections. The eighteenth-century Dutch palace on the tip of **Bolghatty Island** is a congenial three-star complex, although after years of renovation it now possesses little of its once very grand charm.

Ernakulam
Ernakulam has plenty of accommodation, although its guesthouses and hotels tend to fill up by late afternoon, so **book** in advance.

Abad Plaza, MG Road ☎0484/381122. Comfortable and pleasant business-style high-rise, with restaurant and bar, swimming pool and a well-equipped health club, in the centre of Ernakulam. ❽
Aiswarya, Jos Junction ☎0484/364454. Caters to most mid-range budgets, where the cheaper rooms are excellent value and there is a good restaurant downstairs serving "meals" and *molee* (fish in coconut sauce). The a/c rooms on the top floors come with balconies. ❺–❻
Avenue Regent, MG Road ☎0484/372662, ☏370129. Very comfortable, centrally a/c four-star, close to the railway station and main shopping area; boasts a restaurant, 24hr coffee shop and bar. Expect only the highest standards, as this place doubles as a well-respected hotel-management training college. ❽
Basoto Lodge, Press Club Road ☎0484/352140. Dependable backpackers' lodge with twelve basic rooms and no restaurant. Two rooms have small balconies. ❷
Bharat, Gandhi Square, Durbar Hall Road ☎0484/353501, ☏370502. Large modern hotel heavily endowed with the ethnic tribal look. Comfortable rooms, 24hr coffee shop and three restaurants. ❻–❼
Biju's Tourist Home, corner of Canon Shed and Market roads ☎0484/381881. Pick of the budget bunch, with thirty clean and spacious rooms, some with a/c, close to the main boat jetty. TVs may be rented, and they have an inexpensive same-day laundry service. Friendly, very popular and recommended. ❹–❺

Cochin Tourist Home, opposite railway station ☎0484/364577. Cleanest of the cheap hotels lined up outside Ernakulam Junction, but often full of noisy family and pilgrim groups. There's a resident astro-palmist. ❸–❺
Deepak Lodge, Market Road ☎0484/353882. One of a handful of well-maintained and inexpensive lodges along this road with big, very basic rooms and communal bathrooms; an extra Rs20 gets you a huge attached bathroom. ❷
Grand, MG Road ☎0484/382061. A slightly kitsch place with a 1950s feel: lots of lino and varnished wood. All the rooms are well appointed and have cable TV, and there's a multi-cuisine restaurant and bar. ❼–❽
Hakoba, Shanmugham Road ☎0484/369839. Conveniently midway between Main and High Court jetties. Dowdy, but all rooms have cable TV, and both the a/c and front rooms overlooking the street and harbour are excellent value. There's a good "meals" joint on the ground floor. ❸–❺
Maple Guest House, XL/271 Canon Shed Road ☎0484/355156. After *Biju's*, this is the best deal in the district. The rooms are spartan, but clean, cheap and central and there are some a/c. Don't be pushed into paying the extra Rs100 for a deluxe room: all you get is a rather unnecessary carpet. ❸
Metropolitan, near Ernakulam Junction railway station ☎0484/369931. Smart business hotel good for late-night arrivals or early-morning trains, but a bit too far from all the tourist attractions. Features a multicuisine restaurant, 24hr coffee shop and bar. ❼

Modern Guest House, XL/6067, Market Road ⊕ 0484/352130. Popular place with simple rooms above (noisy) Keralan veg restaurant, all en suite and with fans. If full try their annexe, the *Modern Rest House* (⊕ 0484/361407), which has sixteen plain but pleasant rooms that are slightly more expensive. ❷

Paulson Park, Carrier Station Road ⊕ 0484/382179. Close to Ernakulam Junction. Good value, with large, well-appointed rooms, some with a/c, and a ground-floor restaurant featuring a surreal fake rock garden. ❺ –❻

Sangeetha, 36/1675 Chittoor Road, near stations ⊕ 0484/368736. Well-appointed rooms, if small for the price; the non-a/c ones can be stuffy. Complimentary tea and breakfast is included in the tariff. Very convenient for the 24hr bus station next door, and they operate left-luggage facilities and foreign exchange. ❻

Sealord, Shanmugham Road ⊕ 0484/382472, ⓕ 370135. Centrally a/c high-rise near High Court jetty. Standard rooms are excellent value; the best are on the top floor. Rooftop restaurant, bar and foreign exchange. ❼

Taj Residency, Marine Drive ⊕ 0484/371471, ⓕ 371481. Ernakulam's top business hotel, with luxury rooms and a pleasant open-air restaurant; it enjoys a prime location overlooking the harbour. If you want a pool and more space though, head over to the *Taj Malabar* on Willingdon Island (see opposite). ❾

Woodlands, Woodlands Junction, MG Road ⊕ 0484/382051. A central, chic Indian-style place with cosy a/c and non-a/c rooms and spotless marble bathrooms. Next door there's a new more upmarket sister outfit with central a/c and lots of glitz. Checkout at 8am. ❻

Fort Cochin

Adams Old Inn, Burgher Street ⊕ 0484/217595. Great little family-run guesthouse in a well-restored period building; the rooms are modern and just one has a/c. There is a rooftop dorm (Rs100). ❸

Brunton Boatyard, next to Fort Cochin Jetty ⊕ 0484/215461. A new Casino group hotel, built on the site of an eighteenth-century British boatyard; the look is Keralan carved wood and whitewash, with beautifully designed breezy rooms and balconies overlooking bay. Features three speciality restaurants and the pool edges onto the lake. ❾

Chiramel Residency, 1 Lilly St ⊕ 0484/217310. A great seventeenth-century heritage-accorded guesthouse, with five carefully restored rooms around a congenial communal sitting room; the lofty rooms all have teak floors, some with a balcony and modern bathrooms. The welcoming and warm family live downstairs. ❺

Delight, opposite the Parade Ground ⊕ 0484/217658. Beautiful home with distinctive blue latticework. Six spacious, airy rooms around a leafy courtyard, run by a friendly and very helpful family, whose conservation and restoration efforts are admirable. Breakfast available. Book ahead. ❸ –❺

Elite, Princess Street ⊕ 0484/215733. Several floors of basic but clean and cheap rooms with attached bathrooms, in a friendly guesthouse above a popular restaurant. ❷ –❸

Fort House, 2/6A Calvathy Road ⊕ 0484/226103. Rooms and cheaper bamboo huts ranged around an interesting if eccentric compound, littered with pots and statues with a good café and a brilliant jetty. None of the rooms look onto the water, however. ❻

Malabar House Residency, 1/268 Parade Rd ⊕ 0484/217099. Beautiful, historic mansion renovated with a highly successful mix of old-world charm and bright and brash European designer chic. The Keralan temple-style pool in the minimalist courtyard is stunning. Tariff includes breakfast. Recommended. ❾

Tharavadu Tourist Home, Quinose Street (the road behind the post office), Fort Cochin ⊕ 0484/216897. Eight simple, clean rooms (two without bathrooms) in an old Dutch house; breakfast and cool drinks are available and there's a cheap laundry service. They do not always honour advance bookings. ❷ –❹ .

The Old Courtyard, Princess Street ⊕ 0484/216302. Owned by the Casino family group, this is the latest heritage hotel to hit the scene. The rooms have been expertly restored with antique Dutch furniture, solid teak floorboards and beams and modern bathrooms; all rooms look down on a courtyard with a pleasant restaurant under a mango tree. ❻ –❽

Willingdon and Bolghatty islands

Casino, Willingdon Island, 2km from airport, close to Cochin Harbour Terminus railway station ⊕ 0484/668221, ⓕ 668001. Deluxe and efficient

place, but utterly characterless and shut in by the grey docks. Small pool, travel agent, foreign exchange, and a choice of excellent restaurants.

Very popular with tour groups. ⑨

KTDC Bolghatty Palace, Bolghatty Island ☎0484/ 525862, ℱ354879. Extensively renovated palace in a beautiful location, a short hop from High Court Jetty. The main building, built by the Dutch in 1744 and later home to the British resident, has huge deluxe rooms, as does the modern annexe. "Honeymoon" cottages stand on stilts right on the water's edge. Reserve through any KTDC tourist office, and come armed with mosquito repellent. At weekends, the adjacent KTDC canteen and bar is noisy with day-trippers. ⑧

Taj Malabar, Willingdon Island, by Tourist Office Jetty (20min ferry from Ernakulam), near Cochin

Harbour Terminus railway station ☎0484/666811, ℱ668297. In a superb location on the tip of the island with sweeping views of the bay; the old wing and pool have been extensively refurbished, and the whole place oozes style and quality. ⑨

Trident, Bristow Road, Willingdon Island ☎0484/669595, ℱ669393. Despite the grey dockyard environs, this new hotel is the most intimate and congenial of the five stars on the island, with interesting displays of Keralan tribal and household artefacts, a pool in a tropical oasis, two restaurants, a bar and a range of luxurious rooms. Recommended. ⑨

Mattancherry

With high-rise development restricted to Ernakulam, across the water, the old-fashioned character of **Mattancherry** and nearby Fort Cochin remains intact. Within an area small enough to cover on foot, bicycle or auto-rickshaw, glimpses of Kochi's variegated history greet you at virtually every turn. As you approach by ferry (get off at Mattancherry Jetty), the shoreline is crowded with tiled buildings painted in pastel colours – a view that can't have changed for centuries.

Despite the large number of tourists visiting daily, trade is still the most important activity here. Many of the streets are busy with barrows loaded with sacks of produce trundling between *godowns* (warehouses) and little shops where dealers do business in tea, jute, rubber, chillies, turmeric, cashew, ginger, cardamom and pepper.

Jew Town

The road heading left from Mattancherry Jetty leads into the district known as **Jew Town**, where N.X. Jacob's tailor shop and the offices of J.E. Cohen, advocate and tax consultant, serve as reminders of a once-thriving community. Nowadays many of the shops sell antiques, Hindu and Christian woodcarvings, oil lamps, wooden jewellery boxes and other bric-a-brac.

Turning right at the India Pepper & Spice Trade Building, usually resounding with the racket of dealers shouting the latest spice prices, and then right again, brings you into Synagogue Lane. The **Pardesi (White Jew) Synagogue** (daily except Sat 10am–noon & 3–5pm) was founded in 1568, and rebuilt in 1664. Its interior is an attractive, if incongruous, hotchpotch; note the floor, paved with hand-painted eighteenth-century blue-and-white tiles from Canton, each unique, depicting a love affair between a mandarin's daughter and a commoner. The nineteenth-century glass oil-burning chandeliers suspended from the ceiling were imported from Belgium. Above the entrance, a gallery supported by slender gilt columns was reserved for female members of the congregation. Opposite the entrance, an elaborately carved Ark houses four scrolls of the Torah (the first five books of the Old Testament) encased in silver and gold, on which are placed gold crowns presented by the maharajas of Travancore and Cochin, testifying to good relations with the Jewish community. The synagogue's oldest artefact is a fourth-century copper-plate inscription from the Raja of Cochin.

An attendant is usually available to show visitors around, and answer questions; his introductory talk features as part of the KTDC guided tour (see

The Jews of Kochi

According to tradition, the Myuchasim Jews, who were the first to arrive on the Malabar coast, were fleeing from the occupation of Jerusalem by Nebuchadnezzar, in 587 BC. However another legend claims that the Jews initially came in the eleventh century BC, as part of a trade fleet that belonged to King Solomon. Whatever the truth, the Jews settled in Cranganore, just north of Cochin, to trade in spices. They remained respected members of Keralan society and even had their own ruler, until the Portuguese embarked upon a characteristic "Christian" policy of persecution of nonbelievers, early in the sixteenth century.

At that time, when Jews were being burned at the stake in Goa, and forced to leave their settlements elsewhere on the coast, the raja of Cochin gave them a parcel of land adjoining the royal palace in Mattancherry. A new Jewish community was created in the area now known as Jew Town, and a synagogue was built. The Jews were in demand as they spoke Malayalam, and trading was in their blood; the community thrived during the great trading period under the more liberal and supportive Dutch and later British rule.

There were three distinct groups of Jews in Kerala. The Black Jews were employed as labourers in the spice business, and their community of some thousands resulted from the earliest Jewish settlers marrying and converting Indians; Brown Jews are thought to have been slave converts. White Jews considered both groups inferior to themselves; they were orthodox and married only among their number. However, by the early 1950s, most of Kochi's Jews disappeared, when they were given free passage to Israel, where they could more easily uphold their customs and rules. The remaining White Jews are on the verge of extinction as they are determined to stay racially pure. At the time of writing only seven families survive, a total of 22 people with just enough males over the age of thirteen to perform the rituals in the synagogue – and no rabbi.

p.1345). Outside, in a small square, several antique shops are well worth a browse, but don't expect a bargain.

Mattancherry Palace

Mattancherry Palace (daily except Fri 10am–5pm) stands on the left side of the road a short walk from the Mattancherry Jetty in the opposite direction to Jew Town. The gateway on the road is, in fact, its back entrance and it remains inexplicably locked. In the walled grounds behind the gate stands a circular, tiled Krishna temple (closed to non-Hindus).

Although known locally as the **Dutch Palace**, the two-storey palace was built by the Portuguese as a gift to the Cochin raja, Vira Keralavarma (1537–61), and the Dutch were responsible for subsequent additions. While its appearance is not particularly striking, squat with whitewashed walls and tiled roof, the interior is captivating.

The **murals** that adorn some of its rooms are among the finest examples of Kerala's much underrated school of painting; friezes illustrating stories from the *Ramayana*, on the first floor, date from the sixteenth century. Packed with detail and gloriously rich colour, the style is never strictly naturalistic; the treatment of facial features is pared down to the simplest of lines for the mouths, and characteristically aquiline noses. Downstairs, the women's bedchamber holds several less complex paintings, possibly dating from the 1700s. One shows Shiva dallying with Vishnu, who has assumed a female form as the enchantress Mohini; a second portrays Krishna holding aloft Mount Govardhana; another features a reclining Krishna surrounded by *gopis*, or cowgirls. His languid pose belies the activity of his six hands and two feet, intimately caressing adoring admirers.

While the paintings are undoubtedly the highlight of the palace, the collection also includes interesting Dutch maps of old Cochin, coronation robes belonging to past maharajas, royal palanquins, weapons and furniture. Without permission from the Archaeological Survey of India, **photography** is strictly prohibited.

Fort Cochin

Moving northwest from Mattancherry Palace along Bazar Road, you pass wholesale emporia where owners, sitting behind scales surrounded by sacks of spices, may well be prepared to talk about their wares. Keep walking in a northerly direction, over the canal and then westwards into **Fort Cochin**. The architecture of the quiet streets in this enclave is very definitely European, with fine houses built by wealthy British traders, and Dutch cottages with split farmhouse doors. At the water's edge there's a bus stand, boat jetty and food and drinks stalls. This area and nearby Princess Street (which has a few budget hotels) attract backpackers and the consequent local hustlers.

Fort Cochin is home to a unique community of Eurasians, commonly known as "Anglo-Indians", who have developed a distinct and lively culture. However,

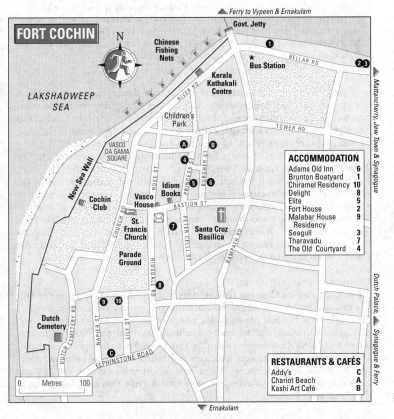

FORT COCHIN

N

LAKSHADWEEP SEA

Ferry to Vypeen & Ernakulam

Govt. Jetty

Chinese Fishing Nets

Bus Station

BELLAR RD

Kerala Kathakali Centre

RIVER RD

Children's Park

TOWER RD

VASCO DA GAMA SQUARE

New Sea Wall

ROSE ST

PRINCESS ST

BURGHER ST

Idiom Books

Vasco House

BASTION ST

CHURCH RD

Cochin Club

St. Francis Church

PETER CELLI ST

Santa Cruz Basilica

RAMPART RD

Parade Ground

RIDSDALE RD

DUTCH CEMETERY RD

NAPIER ST

LILY ST

Dutch Cemetery

ELPHINSTONE ROAD

0   Metres   100

ACCOMMODATION

Adams Old Inn	6
Brunton Boatyard	1
Chiramel Residency	10
Delight	8
Elite	5
Fort House	2
Malabar House Residency	9
Seagull	3
Tharavadu	7
The Old Courtyard	4

RESTAURANTS & CAFÉS

Addy's	C
Chariot Beach	A
Kashi Art Café	B

Mattancherry, Jew Town & Synagogue

Dutch Palace, Synagogue & Ferry

Ernakulam

Keralan murals

The quality and unique style of the murals at Mattancherry Palace in old Kochi (see p.1350), along with those in as many as sixty other locations in Kerala, are probably the best-kept secrets in Indian art. Most are on the walls of functioning temples; they are not marketable, transportable, or indeed even *seen* by many non-Hindus. Few date from before the sixteenth century, depriving them of the aura of extreme antiquity; their origins may go back to the seventh century, probably influenced by the Pallava style of Tamil Nadu, but only traces in one tenth-century cave temple survive from the earliest period. Castaneda, a traveller who accompanied Vasco da Gama on the first Portuguese landing in India, described how he strayed into a temple, supposing it to be a church, and saw "monstrous-looking images with two inch fangs" painted on the walls, causing one of the party to fall to his knees exclaiming, "if this be the devil, I worship God".

Technically classified as Fresco-Secco, Kerala murals employ vegetable and mineral colours, predominantly ochre reds and yellows, white and blue-green, and are coated with a protective sheen of pine resin and oil. Their ingenious design, strongly influenced by the canonical text, *Shilparatna*, incorporates intense detail with clarity and dynamism in the portrayal of human (and celestial) figures; subtle facial expressions are captured with the simplest of lines, while narrative elements are always bold and arresting. In common with all great Indian art, they share a complex iconography and symbolism.

Non-Hindus can see fine examples in Kochi, Padmanabhapuram (see p.1315), Ettumanur (see p.1334) and Kayamkulam (see p.1323). Visitors interested in how they are made should head for the Mural Painting Institute at Guruvayur. A paperback book, *Murals of Kerala*, by M.G. Shashi Bhooshan (Kerala Govt Dept of Public Relations) serves as an excellent introduction to the field.

---

with the development of tourism and in particular the construction of numerous guesthouses, the changes to Fort Cochin are threatening the fragile infrastructure of this community and altering the face of the area. Fort Cochin was being preserved as a **"Heritage Zone"** with the help of a grant by US Aid, but this was unfortunately cut as a result of India's nuclear tests in 1998.

One of the best ways of seeing Fort Cochin as well as Mattanchery and Jew Town, is by bicycle, available from *Adams Old Inn* on Burgher Street (Rs5/hr). Fort Cochin has a small but active arts scene with two **galleries**, one at the very hip and eco-conscious *Kashi Art Café* (Mon–Sat 8.30am–6.30pm, Sun 8.30am–2pm) on Burgher Street and the other at *Draavidia* on Jew Street in Mattancherry; both places have an emphasis on contemporary art. *Draavidia* puts on daily live Indian **classical music** programmes called Sadhana (6–7pm), with admission on a membership basis for Rs100, and the Kashi Art Gallery holds live sitar performances twice a week during the high season.

Chinese fishing nets

The huge, elegant **Chinese fishing nets** that line the northern shore of Fort Cochin add grace to an already characterful waterside view, and are probably the single most familiar photographic image of Kerala. Traders from the court of Kublai Khan are said to have introduced them to the Malabar region. Known in Malayalam as *cheena vala*, they can also be seen throughout the backwaters further south. The nets, which are suspended from arced poles and operated by levers and weights, require at least four men to control. You can buy fresh fish from the tiny market here and have it grilled on the spot at one of the ramshackle stalls.

St Francis Church

Walking on from the Chinese fishing nets brings you to a typically English village green. In one corner stands the church of **St Francis**, the first European church in India. Originally built in wood and named Santo Antonio, it was probably associated with Franciscan friars from Portugal. Exactly when it was founded is not known, but the stone structure is likely to date from the early sixteenth century; the land was a gift of the local raja, and the title deeds, written on palm leaf, are still kept in the church today. The facade, with multi-curved sides, became the model for most Christian churches in India. Vasco da Gama was buried here in 1524, but his body was later removed to Portugal.

Under the Dutch, the church was renovated and became Protestant in 1663, then Anglican with the advent of the British in 1795 and since 1949 has been attached to the Church of South India. Inside, various tombstone inscriptions have been placed in the walls, the earliest of which is from 1562. One hangover from British days is the continued use of *punkahs*, large swinging cloth fans on frames suspended above the congregation; these are operated by people sitting outside pulling on cords.

The interior of the twentieth-century **Santa Cruz Cathedral**, south of St Francis church, will delight fans of the colourful – verging on the downright gaudy – Indo-Romano-Rococo school of decoration.

Ernakulam

ERNAKULAM presents the modern face of Kerala, with more of a city feel than Thiruvananthapuram, but small enough not to be daunting. Other than the fairly dull **Parishath Thamburan Museum** (Tues–Sun 9.30am–noon & 3–5.30pm) in Darbar Hall Road, there's little in the way of sights. Along the busy, long, straight **Mahatma Gandhi (MG) Road**, which more or less divides Ernakulam in half 500m back from the sea, the main activities are shopping, eating and movie-going. Here you can email and phone to your heart's content, and choose from an assortment of great places to eat Keralan food. This area is particularly good for cloth, with an infinite selection of colours; if there's a jazzy style in *lunghis* this year, you'll get it on MG Road.

An eight-day annual **festival** at the Shiva temple in Ernakulam (Jan/Feb) features elephant processions and *panchavadyam* (drum and trumpet groups) out in the street. As part of the festival, there are usually night-time performances of Kathakali, and the temple is decorated with an amazing array of electric lights: banks of coloured tubes and sequenced bulbs imitating shooting stars.

Thripunitra

The small suburban town of **THRIPUNITRA**, 12km southeast of Ernakulam, is worth a visit for its dilapidated colonial-style **Hill Palace** (Tues–Sun 9am–12.30pm & 2–4.30pm), now an eclectic museum a short auto-rickshaw ride from the busy bus stand. The royal family of Cochin ("Honour is our family treasure") at one time maintained around forty palaces. This one was confiscated by the state government after Independence, and has slipped into dusty decline over the past decade.

One of the museum's finest exhibits is an early-seventeenth-century wooden *mandapa* removed from a temple in Pathanamthitta, featuring excellent carvings of the coronation of the monkey king Sugriva and other themes from the Ramayana. Of interest too are the silver filigree jewel boxes, gold and silver ornaments, and ritual objects associated with grand ceremonies. The epig-

High Court Jetty   Ernakulam Town Railway Station ▲ & International Airport (26 km)

ERNAKULAM

N

Sealord Boat Jetty

KTDC Tourist Office ℹ

Tourist Police

Vembanad Lake

Main Boat Jetty ℹ

Tourist Desk

Buses to ★ Fort Cochin & Thripunitra

GPO

Mymoon Cinema

KSRTC Central Bus Stand

Ernakulam Junction

Pai & Co. Books

Krishnan Nair Bros

Parishath Thamburan Museum

Durbar Hall Ground

Indian Airlines

TDM ('Durbar') Hall

Buses to ★ Fort Cochin & Thripunitra

Dr Devan's Kathakali

0   Metres   200

ACCOMMODATION

Abad Plaza	3
Aiswarya	16
Avenue Regent	18
Basoto Lodge	6
Bharat	15
Biju's Tourist Home	8
Cochin Tourist Home	17
Deepak Lodge	7
Grand	10
Hakoba	4
Maple Guest House	9
Metropolitan	13
Modern Guest House	2
Paulson Park	12
Sangeetha	14
Sealord	1
Taj Residency	5
Woodlands	11

RESTAURANTS

Bimbi's	A & H
Caravan	C
Domino's Pizza	D
Four Foods	B
Indian Coffee House	E & G
Pandhal	F

Cochin Cultural Centre ▼

raphy gallery contains an eighth-century Jewish Torah, and Keralan stone and copperplate inscriptions. Sculpture, ornaments and weapons in the bronze gallery include a *kingini katti* knife, whose decorative bells belie the fact that it was used for beheading, and a body-shaped cage in which condemned prisoners would be hanged while birds pecked them to death. Providing the place isn't crowded with noisy school groups here to see the nearby deer park, the garden behind the palace is a peaceful spot to picnic beneath the cashew trees.

Performances of theatre, classical music and dance, including consecutive all-night **Kathakali** performances, are held over a period of several days during the annual festival (Oct/Nov) at the **Shri Purnatrayisa temple**, on the way to the palace. Inside the temple compound, both in the morning and at night, massed drum orchestras perform *chenda melam* in procession with fifteen

Kochi is the only city in the state where you are guaranteed the chance to see live **Kathakali**, the uniquely Keralan form of ritualized theatre (see p.1368). Whether in its authentic setting, in temple festivals held during the winter, or at the shorter tourist-oriented shows that take place year round, these mesmerizing dance dramas are an unmissable feature of Kochi's cultural life.

Four venues in the city hold daily recitals. Beginning at 6.30pm, the hour-long shows are preceded by an introductory talk. You can also watch the dancers being made-up if you arrive an hour or so early. Tickets cost Rs100 and can be bought on the door. Most visitors only attend one show, but you'll gain a much better sense of what Kathakali is all about if you take in at least a couple. Ideally, you should also aim to catch an all-night recital at a temple festival, or at least one of the recitals given by the *Ernakulam Kathakali Club* (for either contact the Tourist Desk at the Main Boat Jetty, Ernakulam) held once a month. Keen photographers should arrive well before the start to ensure a front-row seat.

Cochin Cultural Centre, Souhardham, Manikath Road (☏0484/367866). The least commendable option: the dancing at this a/c theatre ("sound-proof, insect-proof, and dust-proof") is accomplished, but performances are short (daily 7pm), with only two characters, and you can't see the musicians. Worst of all, large tour groups monopolize the front seats, and the PA speakers at the back are excruciatingly loud.

Kerala Kathakali Centre, Cochin Aquatic Club, River Road (near the bus stand; (☏0484/809810), Fort Cochin waterfront. Performed by a company of young graduates of the renowned Kalamandalam Academy (see p.1370), and hugely enjoyable. What the actors may lack in expertise they make up for with enthusiasm, and the small, dilapidated performance space, whose doors open onto the water, adds to the atmosphere. You also get to see three characters, and the music is particularly good.

Dr Devan's Kathakali, See India Foundation, Kalathiparambil Lane, near Ernakulam railway station (☏0484/369471 or 371759). The oldest-established tourist show in the city, introduced by the inimitable Dr Devan, who steals the stage with his lengthy discourse on Indian philosophy and mythology. Entertaining maybe, but there is too much chat and not enough Kathakali. Daily performance 6.45pm–8pm, although you can watch the make-up session from 6pm.

Art Kerala, Kannanthodathu Lane, Valanjambalam (☏0484/366238). Near to the See India Foundation, the daily Kathakali performances (make-up 6pm, performance at 7pm) focus on scenes from the big epics such as the *Ramayana* and the *Mahabharatha*, which have proved popular with large tour groups so expect a crowd.

caparisoned elephants. At night, the outside walls of the sanctuary are covered with thousands of tiny oil lamps. Although the temple is normally closed to non-Hindus, admittance to appropriately dressed visitors is usually allowed at this time.

Eating

Unusually for Keralan cities, Kochi offers a wide choice for **eating out**, from the delicious fresh-cooked fish by the Chinese fishing nets at Fort Cochin, to the sophistication of the *Brunton Boatyard*. Between the two extremes, various popular, modest places in Ernakulam serve real Keralan food. The ferries run all evening, and so it is possible to enjoy a meal on one of the more atmospheric islands before heading back to Ernakulam at about 9pm.

Ernakulam

Bimbi's, Shanmugham Road and Jos Junction. Brisk new Indian-style fast-food joints. Hugely popular for inexpensive Udupi, north Indian and Chinese snacks and meals, and the tangiest *wada-sambars* in town. They also do a great selection of shakes and ice creams.

The Brasserie, *Taj Residency*, Marine Drive. Luxury coffee shop serving pricey snacks and a particularly good range of Western cakes (Dundee, plum, palmettes and fudge).

Caravan, Broadway, near the KTDC tourist office. A/c ice-cream parlour that's a good place to chill out over a banana split or milkshake. Open until midnight so you can nip in for a late dessert.

Domino's, Esplanade Complex, Canal Road (free delivery ℡ 1600-111-123). Pizzas here all come with extra chilli and the topping options reflect Keralan cuisine. They will deliver to your hotel. *Baskin Robbins* ice-cream parlour is in the same complex if you want to go the whole hog.

Four Foods, Shanmugham Road. Busy, clean and popular roadside restaurant serving veg and non-veg meals, including blow-out thalis and good-value "dish of the day". For dessert, try their Mumbai-style *faloodas*, vermicelli steeped in syrup with dry fruits and ice cream.

Fry's Village Restaurant, adjacent to Mymoor Cinema, Chittoor Road. Moderately priced, ultra-spicy Keralan and "ethnic" specialities you rarely find served in such style, including the Calicut Muslim delicacy *patthri*, wafer-thin rice pancakes, *idliappam* dumplings, and *puthoo*, steamed rice cakes.

Indian Coffee House, corner of MG Road and Durbar Hall Road. The usual excellent coffee (ask for "pot coffee" if you don't want it with sugar) and simple snacks such as *dosa* and scrambled egg. There's another branch at the corner of Canon Shed Road and Park Ave.

Lotus Cascades, *Woodlands Hotel*, Woodlands Junction, MG Road. Classy veg Indian food, with plenty of *tandoori* options, at bargain prices. Great service, too. Recommended.

Pandhal, MG Road. Very smart upmarket restaurant, serving excellent Keralan fish dishes as well as good north Indian cuisine and a sprinkling of Continental food.

Sealord, Shanmugham Road. Pricey rooftop restaurant serving good Chinese, Indian and sizzlers – but the portions are not too generous, and the view is not what it was since the shopping centre opposite was built. Great for a beer, though.

Utsav, *Taj Residency*, Marine Drive. Expensive à la carte Indian restaurant. The Rs200 lunchtime buffets are better value and you get a matchless view over the harbour and bay at noon. At night, the twinkling lights make this the place for a very romantic dinner.

Fort Cochin

Addy's, Elphinstone Road. Open 8am until midnight, in a lovely rambling seventeenth-century house, with lanterns, gingham cloths and loads of family atmosphere. The place gets enthusiastic reviews, with a high entertainment rating and praise for the meat dishes in particular, although Keralan dishes and fresh fish are also on the menu.

Brunton Boatyard, next to Fort Cochin Jetty. The expensive menu comprises a wonderful collection of dishes designed to reflect all the cultural influences that that have played a part in the history of Cochin: Lebanese, Portuguese, British Raj, Dutch, Jewish, and of course, Keralan. Unfortunately, it is à la carte and you end up just wanting to try everything.

Chariot Beach, Princess Street. Huge seafood and Chinese menu, at reasonable prices, and you can eat alfresco on their small terrace.

Elite, Princess Street. Popular and lively haunt for both travellers' and locals as it's so cheap. However, as a place to eat, the café has had mixed reviews.

Kashi Art Café, Burgher Street. Great café and exhibition space in a restored old building with a cosmopolitan yet Zen-like atmosphere. A good place to check the notice boards, learn about local campaigns, and just find some tranquil space. Healthy light meals, cakes, an excellent breakfast and wonderful coffees are served all day.

Seagull, Calvetty Road. Average restaurant, in good location overlooking the water. Their seafood in Chinese sauces is particularly tasty, but be prepared for a long wait. Serves beer and spirits.

Willingdon Island

Fort Cochin, *Casino Hotel*, Willingdon Island ℡ 0484/668 8421. This seafood restaurant is considered to be one of the best in India. You choose from the catch of the day and then you choose the style of cooking, which is all done in front of you. Delicious maybe, but it's very expensive, claustrophobic, and the decor is dull.

Taj Malabar, Willingdon Island ℡0484/666811. Two restaurants: the *Jade Pavilion* for Chinese, and *Rice Boats* serving Western, north Indian and Keralan dishes in a beautiful waterside location. The food is excellent and prices reflect this; the Rs200 lunchtime buffet is varied and good value.

Listings

Airlines, domestic: Indian Airlines, Durbar Hall Road (daily 9.45am–1pm & 1.45–4.45pm; ☏ 0484/370242 or 141); Jet Airways, Bab Chambers, Atlantis, MG Road ☏ 0484/369423; Alliance NEPC in the Chandrika Building, also on MG Road (☏ 0484/367720).

Airlines, international: Air India, 35/1301 MG Road, Ravipuram ☏ 0484/351295; British Airways, c/o Nijhawon Travels, MG Road ☏ 0484/364867; Air France, Alard Building, Wariam Road (☏ 0484/361702); Egypt Air, c/o ABC International, Old Thevara Road ☏ 0484/353457; Gulf Air, Bab Chambers, Atlantice Junction, MG Road ☏ 0484/369142; Kuwait Airways, c/o National Travels, Pulinat Building, MG Road ☏ 0484/360123; PIA, c/o ABC International, Old Thevara Road ☏ 0484/353457; Saudi Arabian Airlines, c/o Arafat Travels, MG Road ☏ 0484/352689; Singapore Airlines & Swissair, Aviation Travels, 35/2433 MG Road, Ravipuram ☏ 0484/367911. Spencer & Co, Arya Vaidya Sala Buildings, 35/718 MG Road ☏ 0484/362064 are the local agents for Air Maldives, Cathay Pacific, KLM and Northwest Airlines.

Ayurvedic treatment Although widely advertised all over town, the following two come particularly recommended – Kerala Ayurveda Pharmacy, Warriom Road, off MG Road (☏ 0484/361202; Rs350–400 for 1hr 30min) with trained doctors, and PNVM Shanthigiri, Thrikkakara (☏ 0484/558879) on the northern outskirts.

Banks and exchange Banks along MG Road in Ernakulam include ANZ Grindlays; State Bank of India, which also has a branch opposite the main KTDC tourist office on Shanmugham Road; the efficient Andhra Bank, which also advances money on Visa cards; and the State Bank of Travancore – virtually the only place in the state where you can trade in torn banknotes – which has an evening counter (4–6pm). However, to cash travellers' cheques, the best place is Thomas Cook (Mon–Sat 9.30am–6pm; ☏ 0484/369729) near the Air India Building at Palal Towers, MG Road; or try the Surana Financial Corporation next door. There's a new 24hr ATM (Visa, Mastercard) in the HDFC building on the junction of MG Road and Ravipuram Road, just south of Thomas Cook.

Bookshops Bhavi Books, Convent Road ☏ 0484/354003; Higginbothams, TD Road ☏ 0484/368834; Pai & Co, MG Road ☏ 0484/355835, Broadway ☏ 0484/361020, New Road ☏ 0484/225607. Idiom, opposite the Synagogue, Jew Town, Mattancherry and on Bastion Street, Fort Cochin (☏ 0484/220432) is a wonderful place to browse for books on travel, Indian and Keralan culture, flora and fauna, art, anthropology and there's an excellent range of nonfiction.

Cinemas Sridhar Theatre, Shanmugham Road, near the *Hotel Sealord*, screens English-language movies daily; check the listings pages of the *Indian Express* or *Hindu* (Kerala edition) to find out what's on. For the latest Malayalam and Hindi releases, head for the comfortable a/c Mymoon Cinema at the north end of Chitoor Road, or the Saritha Savitha Sangeetha, at the top of Market Road.

Handicrafts CI Company, Broadway ☏ 0484/352405. On MG Road try Kairali ☏ 0484/354507; Khadi Bhavan ☏ 0484/355279; Khataisons Curio Palace ☏ 0484/369414; Surabhi Kerala State Handicrafts (☏ 0484/382278). Carpets can be found at Coirboard Showroom; for good quality Keralan, Portuguese and Dutch antiques head over to Jew Street, Mattancherry, although you will have to bargain hard.

Hospitals General, Hospital Road ☏ 0484/360002; City, MG Road ☏ 0484/368970; Government, Fort Cochin ☏ 0484/224444.

Internet Email is widely available in the area around Princess Street in Fort Cochin (Rs60/hr); connections are slow. In Ernakulam, the most efficient and speedy internet point is on the third floor, Pepta Menaka Complex, Shanmugham Road (Rs30/hr).

Music stores Sargam, XL/6816 GSS Complex, Convent Road, opposite Public Library ☏ 0484/374216, stocks the best range of music tapes in the state, mostly Indian (Hindi films, and lots of Keralan devotional music), with a couple of shelves of Western rock and pop. Music World, MKV Building, MG Road ☏ 0484/355632, is Cochin's answer to a music superstore with Western pop, classical, compilations, world music, and *filmi* music. Sound of Melody, DH Road, near Ernakulam Junction station, also has a good selection of traditional south Indian and contemporary Western music, while Sea Breeze, 248, GCDA Complex, Marine Drive (☏ 0484/363536) is a smart upmarket shop with a strong emphasis on Western music.

Musical instruments Manual Industries, Bannerji Road, Kacheripady Jnct (☏ 0484/352513) is the best for Indian classical instruments. For traditional Keralan drums, ask at Thripunitra bazaar (see p.1354).

Photography City Camera, Lovedale Building, Padma Junction, MG Road, repair cameras and come recommended; Krishnan Nair Bros, Convent

For an overview of travel services to and from Kochi/Ernakulam, see Travel Details on p.1378.

By air

The new international airport (℡0484/610050, 610115, or 610116) at Nedumbassery near Alwaye (aka Alua), 26km to the north of Ernakulam, has been designed to attract international flights especially from the Gulf. Jet Airways has two flights a day to Mumbai, and Indian Airlines operates daily flights to Mumbai, Bangalore, Delhi, and Thiruvananthapuram. Indian Airlines flies six days a week to Chennai, and twice weekly to Goa, Coimbatore, Hyderabad and Calicut. If you want to fly to the Lakshadweep Islands, contact *Casino Hotel*, Willingdon Island (℡0484/666821; see p.1348). Indian Airlines flies twice each week to Doha, Sharjah, Kuwait and Muscat. For details of airlines and travel agents, see Listings on p.1357.

The Indian Airlines "red eye" flight to Mumbai every Tuesday at 2.30am gets you there in time for the 7.10am Air India flight direct to New York or London.

By bus

Buses leave Ernakulam's KSRTC Central bus stand for virtually every town in Kerala, and some beyond; most, but not all, are bookable in advance at the stand (reservation enquiries ℡0484/372033). Travelling south, dozens of buses per day run to Thiruvananthapuram; most go via Alappuzha and Kollam, but a few travel via Kottayam. It's also possible to travel all the way to Kanniyakumari (9hr). However, for destinations further afield in Karnataka and Tamil Nadu, you're much better off on the train: both KSRTC's "super express" and private "luxury" buses travel to these destinations, but you have to cope with the extremely fast, dangerous driving. Travelling to Mysore, go early to book a seat on the 8pm bus (10hr).

By train

Kochi lies on Kerala's main broad-gauge line, and sees frequent trains down the coast to Thiruvananthapuram, via Kottayam, Kollam and Varkala. Heading north, plenty of services run to Thrissur, and thence northeast across Tamil Nadu to Chennai, but only a couple run north to Mangalore, where a poorly served branch line veers inland to Hassan and Mysore in Karnataka.

Although most long-distance express and mail trains depart from Ernakulam Junction, a short way southeast of the city centre, a couple of key services leave

---

Road, stock the best range of camera film, including black-and-white, Kodak and Fuji, and professional colour transparencies. Several others are located along MG and Shanmugham roads.
Post office The Head Post Office (Mon–Fri 8.30am–8pm, Sat 9.30am–2.30pm & 4–8pm, Sun 10am–4pm) is on Hospital Road, not far from the Main Jetty. The city's poste restante is at the GPO, behind St Francis Church in Fort Cochin.

Tour and travel agents Clipper Holidays, 40/6531 Convent Rd ℡0484/364443. Experienced agents good for wildlife and adventure tours in Kerala and Karnataka. Other all-round travel agents specializing in tours and air-ticketing include Travel Corporation of India, MG Road (℡0484/351646), Princy World Travels, Marine Drive (℡0484/352751), Trade Wings, MG Road (℡0484/367938) and Pioneer Travels, Bristow Road (℡0484/666148).

Thrissur

The breezy bazaar town of **THRISSUR** (Trichur), roughly midway between Kochi (74km south) and Palakkad (79km northeast) on NH-47, is an obvious

from Ernakulam Town, 2km north. To confuse matters further, some also start at Cochin Harbour station, on Willingdon Island, so be sure to check the departure point when you book your ticket. The computerized reservation office – good for trains leaving all three stations – is at Ernakulam Junction (℡131 for general enquiries).

The trains listed below are recommended as the fastest and/or most convenient services from Kochi. If you're heading to Alappuzha for the backwater trip to Kollam, take the bus, as the only train that can get you there in time invariably arrives late. With the opening of the Konkan Railway, only a handful of superfast trains travel along the coast to Goa and beyond.

Recommended trains from Kochi/Ernakulam

Destination	Name	Number	Station	Frequency	Departs	Total time
Bangalore	Kanniyakumari–Bangalore Express	#6525	ET	daily	4.40pm	14hr
Mumbai	Kanniyakumari–Mumbai Express	#1082	ET	daily	12.35pm	40hr
Delhi	Rajdhani Express*	#2431	EJ	Fri & Sat	11.40pm	40hr 30min
	Kerala Express	#2625	EJ	daily	3.50pm	48hr 45min
Goa	Rajdhani Express*	#2431	EJ	daily	11.40pm	12hr 35min
	Mangala Lakshadweep Express	#2617	EJ	daily	12.15pm	16hr 18min
Chennai	Trivandrum–Chennai Mail	#6320	ET	daily	7.05pm	13hr
Mangalore	Malabar Express	#6329	ET	daily	10.53pm	10hr 30min
	Parasuram Express	#6349	ET	daily	10.50am	10hr
Thiruvananthapuram	Parasuram Express	#6350	EJ	daily	1.55pm	4hr 55min
Varkala	Parasuram Express	#6350	EJ	daily	1.55pm	3hr 43min

EJ = Ernakulam Junction
ET = Ernakulam Town
* = a/c only, Fri & Sat

base for exploring the cultural riches of central Kerala. Near the Palghat (Palakkad) Gap – an opening in the natural border made by the Western Ghat mountains – it presided over the main trade route into the region from Tamil Nadu and Karnataka. For years Thrissur was the capital of Cochin State, controlled at various times by both the zamorin of Kozhikode and Tipu Sultan of Mysore. Today, it justifiably prides itself on being the cultural capital of Kerala and is home to several influential art institutions. The town centres on Kerala's largest temple complex, **Vadakkunatha**, surrounded by a *maidan* (green) that sees all kinds of public gatherings, not least Kerala's most extravagant, noisy and sumptuous festival, **Puram**.

Arrival and information

Thrissur's **railway station** is 1km southwest of Round South, near the KSRTC **long-distance bus stand**. **Priya Darshini** (also known as "North", "Shoranur" and "Wadakkancheri") bus station, close to Round North, serves

Palakkad and Shoranur. The **Shakthan Thampuran** stand, on TB Road, 2km from Round South, serves local destinations south such as Irinjalakuda, Kodungallur and Guruvayur.

The DTPC **tourist office** (Mon–Sat 10am–5pm) is on Palace Road, opposite the Town Hall (five minutes' walk off Round East). Run on a voluntary basis, its primary purpose is to promote the elephant festival, but they also give out maps of Thrissur. KTDC have a small information counter at the *Yatri Niwas* hotel, Stadium Road (℡0487/332333). If you need to **change money**, the main branch of the State Bank of Travancore (Mon–Fri 10am–2pm, Sat 10am–noon) on the second floor next to the Paramekkavu temple, Round East, accepts American Express travellers' cheques, but not Thomas Cook or Mastercard. Opposite the same temple, the State Bank of India (same hours) changes dollars and sterling as well as travellers' cheques and the Canara Bank on South Road also changes money. The **GPO** is on the southern edge of town, near the *Casino Hotel* off TB Road. **Internet** facilities are available at the excellent Internet Thrissur.Com, 2nd floor, City Centre Shopping Complex, Round West (daily 9am until 10pm; Rs45/hr).

Accommodation

Thrissur has a fair number of mid-price **hotels**, but there's a dearth of decent budget places, except the palatial *Government Rest House*, which offers star-hotel comfort at economy-lodge rates, but the constant stream of government officials get first priority. Almost all of Thrissur's hotels follow a 24hr check-out policy.

Casino, TB Road, near the railway station ℡0487/424699, ℗442037. Once Thrissur's poshest hotel, but it has seen better days; the rooms are decent (non-a/c and a/c) and there's a multicuisine restaurant, bar and foreign exchange for residents. ⑤–⑦

Elite International, Chembottil Lane, off Round South ℡0487/421033. Pronounced *Ee-light*. A big tower block of standard rooms – some balconied rooms overlook the green – with friendly staff and a good restaurant. It's booked months ahead for Puram, when rates are ten times higher than normal. ④–⑦

Gurukripa Lodge, Chembottil Lane, off Round South ℡0487421895. Lots of rooms (including several great-value singles) in a large compound, all painted in blue; the rooms are all large and simple with cool tiled floors and have attached bathrooms. Recommended. ②

KTDC Yatri Niwas, off Museum Road ℡0487/332333. Clean and reasonable place with spotless rooms (some a/c and with cable TV), a beer parlour and south Indian restaurant good for a "meal". The best budget option after the *Rest House*. ②–④

Luciya Palace, Marar Road ℡0487/424731, ℗427290. Recently revamped Neoclassical/traditional Keralan fantasy; a highly rated mid-range choice. Some a/c rooms, but the standard non-a/c rooms, with coir mats and cane furniture, are the best deals. Single occupancy rates available. ⑤–⑦

Manapuram, Kuruppam Road ℡0487/440933. Modern and efficient two-star business hotel in the heart of the lively market. A good range of rooms with cable TV, some are a/c and a few singles, and two restaurants; credit cards accepted. ⑤–⑦

Ramanilayam Government Rest House, Palace Road ℡0487/332016. Very good-value, huge, clean, comfortable suites with balconies; non-a/c rooms are a mere Rs45 while a/c doubles cost Rs275. It's officially for VIPs, and they're not obliged to give you a room, but smart dress will help. It's hugely popular, and often full; the rate doubles after five nights. Breakfast is served; other meals by advance order only. ②–④

Siddartha Regency, Veliyannur Road, Kokkalai ℡0487/424773. Centrally a/c and comfortable Indian-oriented hotel in the southwestern corner of town, near the railway, KSRTC and Shakthan Thampuran bus stands. Features a restaurant, a bar and gardens. ⑥–⑦

The Town

The principal point of orientation in Thrissur is the **Round**, a road subdivided into North, South, East and West, which encircles the Vadakkunatha temple and *maidan* at the centre. Once you've established which side of the Round you're on, you can save yourself long walks along the busy pavement by striking out across the green.

The **State Art Museum** and **Zoo** (both Tues–Sun 10am–5pm) stand together on Museum Road, ten minutes' walk from Round East, in the northeast of town (turn right at the end of Palace Road and walk 200m down the right-hand side). Although small, the museum has excellent local bronzes, jewellery, fine woodcarvings of fanged temple guardians and a profusion of bell-metal oil lamps. The zoo, however, houses a miserable set of tenants, although it can be grimly fascinating to observe the variety of snakes that slither locally (king cobra, krait, and viper).

Next door to the *Yatri Niwas* hotel, the **Kerala Sangeet Natak Academy** (℡0487/332548) features a large auditorium that hosts occasional music and dance concerts as well as Keralan theatre, which has an enthusiastic following and tends to be heavily political. Around the corner is the **Kerala Lalitha Kala Akademi** (℡0487/333773), which often holds exhibitions of contemporary Indian art.

One of the most important churches for Thrissur's large Christian population is the Syrian Catholic **Lourdes Cathedral**, just over 1km east of the Medical College Hospital on Round East, along St Thomas College Road. Three daily masses serve a regular congregation of nine hundred. Like many of Kerala's Indo-Gothic churches, the exterior of dome and spires is more impressive than the interior, with its unadorned metal rafters and corrugated iron ceiling. Steps lead down from the altar to the crypt, a rather dilapidated copy of the grotto in Lourdes.

Vadakkunatha temple

Vadakkunatha temple (closed to non-Hindus), is a walled complex of fifteen shrines, dating from the twelfth century and earlier, the principal of which is dedicated to Shiva. Inside the walls, the grassy compound is surprisingly quiet and spacious, with a striking apsidal shrine dedicated to Ayappa (see p.1335). Sadly, many of the temple's treasures, such as the woodcarvings and murals, are not as well maintained as they might be.

Once an essential ingredient of the temple's cultural life, but now underused and neglected, the long, sloping-roofed **Kuttambalam theatre** with carved panels and lathe-turned wooden pillars, is the venue for the ancient Sanskrit performance forms Chakyar Kuttu and Kutiyattam (closed to non-Hindus).

Shopping

Thrissur is a great place to pick up distinctive Keralan **crafts**. The main shopping area is on the Round; on Round West, the **Kerala State Handicraft Emporium** specializes in wood, while a few doors along, a small branch of **Khadi Gramodyog** sells a limited range of hand-loom cloth. A far better selection of hand-loom can be found in **Co-optex** at the top of Palace Road (a one-minute walk from Round East). At **Chemmanur's**, Round South, near the *Elite Hotel*, you'll find the usual carved wooden-elephant-type souvenirs, and, on the ground floor, a high-kitsch Aladdin's Cave of nodding dogs, Jesus clocks, Mecca table ornaments and parabolic nail-and-string art. **Sportsland**, further west on Round South, aside from sports equipment, also sells crudely painted wooden toys, such as buses and cars. **Alter Media** at Utility Building, Nehru Bazaar, Nayarangadi, is a small but interesting bookshop, devoted to women's studies. **Cosmos Books**, on Round West, is a treasure trove of frilly

Puram

Thrissur is best known to outsiders as the venue for Kerala's biggest festival, Puram, which takes place on one day in April/May. Introduced by the Kochi (Cochin) raja, Shaktan Tampuran (1789–1803), Puram is today the most extreme example of the kind of celebration seen on a smaller scale all over Kerala, whose main ingredients invariably include caparisoned elephants, drum music and fireworks.

On this day, at the hottest time of year, the centre of Thrissur fills to capacity with a sea of people gravitating towards Round South, where a long wide path leads to the southern entrance of the Vadakkunatha temple complex. Two processions, representing the Tiruvambadi and Paramekkavu temples in Thrissur, compete to create the more impressive sights and sounds. They eventually meet, like armies on a battlefield, facing each other at either end of the path. Both sides present fifteen tuskers sumptuously decorated with gold ornaments, each ridden by three brahmins clutching objects symbolizing royalty: silver-handled whisks of yak hair, circular peacock feather fans, and orange, green, red, purple, turquoise, black, gold or patterned silk umbrellas fringed with silver pendants. At the centre of each group, the principal elephant carries an image of the temple's deity. Swaying gently, the elephants stand still much of the time, ears flapping, seemingly oblivious to the mayhem engendered by the crowds, bomb-like firework explosions and the huge orchestra that plays in front of them.

Known as chenda melam, this quintessentially Keralan music, featuring as many as a hundred loud, hard-skinned, cylindrical *chenda* drums, crashing cymbals and wind instruments, mesmerizes the crowd while its structure marks the progress of the procession. Each kind of *chenda melam* is named after the rhythmic cycle (*tala* or, in Malayalam, *talam*) in which it is set. Drummers stand in ranks, the most numerous at the back often playing single beats. At the front, a line of master drummers, the stars of Keralan music, try to outdo each other with their speed, stamina, improvisational skills and showmanship. Facing the drummers, musicians play long double-reed, oboe-like *kuzhals* (similar to the north Indian *shehnai*) and C-shaped *kompu* bell-metal trumpets. The fundamental structure is provided by the *elatalam* –

novels, die-hard academic criticism and books on art, drama and culture; you can even buy the latest edition of *Vogue* – at a price.

Kuruppam Road, which leads south towards the railway station from the western end of Round South, is one of the best places in Kerala to buy **bell-metal** products, particularly oil lamps made in the village of Nadavaramba, near Irinjalakuda (see p.1364). **Nadavaramba Krishna & Sons** and **Bell-metal Craft** both specialize in brass, bronze and bell metal. Lamps cost Rs80–25,000, and "superfine" bell metal is sold by weight, at over Rs250 per kilo. Continuing south on Kuruppam Road to the next junction with Railway Station Road, you'll find a number of small shops selling cheap Christian, Muslim and Hindu pictures etched on metal, and places that supply festival accessories, including umbrellas similar to those used for Puram (see box above).

Eating and drinking

Thrissur's big **hotels** offer Indian, Western and Chinese food, and Keralan lunches, while several quality, inexpensive "meals" places are clustered near **the Round**. Late at night, on the corner of Rounds South and East, opposite the Medical College Hospital, you'll find a string of chai and omelette stalls, frequented by auto-rickshaw-wallahs, hospital visitors, itinerant mendicants, Ayappa devotees and student revellers.

medium-sized, heavy, brass hand-cymbals that resolutely and precisely keep the tempo, essential to the cumulative effect of the music. Over an extended period, the *melam* passes through four phases of tempo, each a double of the last, from a majestic dead slow through to a frenetic pace.

The arrival of the fastest tempo is borne on a wave of aural and visual stimulation. Those astride the elephants stand at this point, to manipulate their feather fans and hair whisks in co-ordinated sequence while behind, unfurled umbrellas are twirled in flashes of dazzling colour and glinting silver in the sun. Meanwhile, the cymbals crash furiously, often raised above the head, requiring extraordinary stamina (and causing nasty weals on the hands). The master drummers play at their loudest and fastest, frequently intensified by surges of energy emanating from single players, one after another; a chorus of trumpets, in ragged unison, make an ancient noise.

All this is greeted by firework explosions and roars from the crowd; many people punch the air, some fairly randomly much like heavy-metal fans in the West, while others are clearly *talam branthans*, rhythm "madmen", who follow every nuance of the structure. When the fastest speed is played out, the slowest tempo returns and the procession edges forward, the *mahouts* leading the elephants by the tusk. Stopping again, the whole cycle is repeated. At night, the Vadukannatha temple entrances are a blaze of coloured lights and a spectacular firework display takes place in the early hours of the morning.

If you venture to Thrissur for Puram, be prepared for packed buses and trains. Needless to say, accommodation should be booked well in advance. An umbrella or hat is recommended. Unfortunately, Puram has become an excuse for groups of Indian men to get very drunk and act in an unpleasant manner; women are advised only go in the morning, or to watch from a safe distance.

Similar but much smaller events take place, generally from September onwards, with most during the summer (April & May). Enquire at a tourist office or your hotel, or ask someone to check a local edition of the newspaper, *Mathrabhumi*, for local performances of *chenda melam*, and other drum orchestras such as *panchavadyam* and *tyambaka*.

Bharata Lodge, Chembottil Lane, next door to *Elite Hotel*. Inexpensive, good-quality south Indian breakfasts, evening snacks and Keralan "meals" at lunchtime.

Bimbi's, *Hotel Manapuram*. A branch of the popular Cochin south Indian fast-food joint; dependably fresh food, hot meals, snacks, ice creams, sweets and a good sociable atmosphere.

Hot Breads, Ground Floor, City Centre Shopping Complex, Round West. A pukka branch of the excellent bakery chain with a chic café, selling delicious stuffed savoury croissants, fresh breads and doughy pizzas.

Indian Coffee House, Round South. The better of two in town; very busy, serving snacks and the usual excellent filter coffee. The branch on Station

Road is very run-down.

Kerala Bhavan, Railway Station Road. Recommended for breakfast and cheap Keralan "meals". A 10min walk south of Round South (most rickshaw-wallahs know where it is).

Ming Palace, Pathan Building, Round South. Inexpensive "Chindian", serving chop suey, noodles and lots of chicken and veg dishes; dim lighting and cheesy muzak.

Pathan's, Round South. Deservedly popular veg restaurant, with a cosy a/c family (female) annexe and a large canteen-like dining hall. Generous portions and plenty of choice, including *koftas*, *kormas* and lots of tandoori options, as well as Keralan thalis and wonderful Kashmiri naan.

Around Thrissur

The chief appeal of exploring the area around Thrissur is for the chances it provides to get to grips with Kerala's cultural heritage. Countless festivals, at their peak before the monsoon hits in May, enable visitors to catch some of the best drummers in the world, **Kathakali** dance drama and **Kutiyattam**, the world's oldest surviving theatre form.

Irinjalakuda

The village of **IRINJALAKUDA**, 20km south of Thrissur, has a unique temple, five minutes' walk west from the bus stand, dedicated to **Bharata**, the brother of Rama. Visitors are usually permitted to see inside (men must wear a *dhoti*), but as elsewhere, the inner parts of the temple are closed to non-Hindus. It boasts a superbly elegant tiled *kuttambalam* **theatre** within its outer courtyard, built to afford an unimpeded view for the maximum number of spectators (drawn from the highest castes only), and known for excellent acoustics. A profusion of painted woodcarvings of mythological animals and stories from the epics decorate the interior. On the low stage, which is enclosed by painted wooden columns and friezes of female dancers, stand two large copper *mizhavu* drums, for use in the Sanskrit drama Kutiyattam (see p.1369), permanently installed in wooden frames into which a drummer climbs to play. Traditionally, *mizhavus* were considered sacred objects; Nandikeshvara, Shiva's rhythm expert and accompanist, was said to reside in them. The drama for which they provided music was a holy ritual, and in the old days the instrument was never allowed to leave the temple and only played by members of a special caste, the Nambyars. Since then, outsiders have learned the art of *mizhavu* playing; some are based near the temple, but the orthodox authorities do not allow them to play inside.

Natana Kairali is an important cultural centre dedicated to the performance, protection and documentation of Kerala's lesser-known, but fascinating and vibrant theatre arts, including Kutiyattam, Nangiar Koothu (female monoacting), shadow and puppet theatres. Left of the Bharata temple as you leave, it is based in the home of one of Kerala's most illustrious acting families, Ammanur Chakyar Madhom (cite this name when you ask for directions). Natana Kairali's director, Shri G.Venu (☏0488/825559), is a mine of information about Keralan arts, and can advise on forthcoming performances.

Irinjalakuda is best reached by **bus** from the Shakthan Thampuran stand at Thrissur rather than by train, as the railway station is an inconvenient 8km east of town.

Nadavaramba bell-metal oil lamps

Keralan nights are made more enchanting by the use of **oil lamps**; the most common type, seen all over, is a slim floor-standing metal column surmounted by a spike that rises from a circular receptacle for coconut oil, and using cloth or banana plant fibre wicks. Every classical theatre performance keeps a large lamp burning centre-stage, all night. The special atmosphere of temples is also enhanced by innumerable lamps, some hanging from chains; others, *deepa stambham*, are multi-tiered and stand metres high.

The village of Nadavaramba, near Irinjalakuda, is an important centre for the manufacture of oil lamps and large cooking vessels, known as *uruli* and *varppu*. Alloys made from brass, copper and tin are frequently used, but the best are from bell metal, said to be eighty percent copper, and give a sonorous chime when struck. Shops in Thrissur that specialize in Nadavaramba-ware arrange visits to see the craftsmen at work.

Kodungallur

Virtually an island, surrounded by backwaters and the sea, the small country town of **KODUNGALLUR** (Cranganore), 35km south of Thrissur, is rich in Keralan history. The typically dusty and nondescript modern town contrasts sharply with tales of its illustrious past. Kodungallur has been identified as the site of the ancient cities of **Vanji**, one-time capital of the Chera kingdom, and **Muziris**, described in the first century AD by the Roman traveller, Pliny, as *Primum Emporium Indiae*, the most important port in India. Other accounts describe the harbour as crowded with great ships, warehouses, palaces, temples and *Yavanas* (a generic term for foreigners) who brought gold, and left with spices, sandalwood, teak, gems and silks. Its life as a great port was curtailed in 1341 by floods that silted up the harbour, leading to the development of Kochi (Cochin).

Kodungallur is also reputed to be the site where the Apostle Thomas – **Doubting Thomas** – landed in 52 AD, bringing Christianity to the subcontinent. Jews fleeing the fall of Jerusalem arrived in 69 AD and established themselves as the dons of the spice trade. By the seventh century, the region had long enjoyed peaceable relations with the Arab world, thanks to its sea trade, so it was unsurprising when **King Cheraman Perumal** converted to Islam, abdicated, and emigrated to Mecca. It is said that he founded the **Cheraman Juma Masjid** here, making it the earliest mosque to be built in India.

The town is best visited in a day-trip by **bus** from Thrissur's Shakthan Thampuran stand (90min), or en route between Thrissur and Kochi. If you want **to stay** at Kodungallur, the *Hotel Indraprastham* close to the town centre (⊕ 0488/602678; ❷–❹) has ordinary and competitively priced a/c rooms as well as a run-of-the-mill "meals" restaurant and an a/c "family" restaurant; they also have a bar.

The town

Standing on a large piece of open ground at the centre of Kodungallur, the ancient and typically Keralan **Kurumba Bhagavati temple** is the site of an extraordinary annual event that some residents would prefer didn't happen at all. The **Bharani** festival, held during the Malayalam month of Meenom (March/April), attracts droves of devotees, both male and female, mainly from "low caste" communities previously excluded from the temple. Their devotions consist in part of drinking copious amounts of alcohol and taking to the streets to sing Bharani *pattu*, sexually explicit songs about, and addressed to, goddess Bhagavati, which are considered to be obscene and highly offensive by many other Keralans. On Kavuthindal, the first day, the pilgrims run en masse around the perimeters of the temple three times at breakneck speed, beating its walls with sticks. Until the mid-1950s, chickens were sacrificed in front of the temple; today, a simple red cloth symbolizes the bloody ritual. An important section of the devotees are the crimson-clad village oracles, wielding scythe-like swords with which they sometimes beat themselves on the head in ecstatic fervour, often drawing blood. Despite widespread disapproval, the festival draws plenty of spectators.

Cheraman Juma Masjid, 1500m south of Kodungallur centre on NH-17, is thought to be the earliest mosque in India, founded in the seventh century. The present building, which dates from the sixteenth century, was until recently predominantly made of wood, of a style usually associated with Keralan Hindu temples. Unfortunately, due to weather damage, it has recently had to be partly rebuilt, and the facade, at least, is now rather mundane, with concrete minarets. The wooden interior remains intact, however, with a large Keralan oil lamp in the centre. Introduced five centuries ago for group study of the Koran, the lamp has taken on great significance to other communities, and Muslims, Christians and Hindus alike bring oil for the lamp on the auspicious occasion of major family events. In an anteroom, a small mausoleum is said to be the burial place of Habib Bin Malik, an envoy sent from Mecca by the convert king Cheraman Perumal. Women are not allowed into the mosque at any time.

The **Mar Thoma Pontifical Shrine**, fronted by a crescent of Neoclassical colonnades at Azhikode (pronounced "Arikode") Jetty (6km) marks the place where the Apostle Thomas is said to have arrived in India, soon after the death of Christ. Despite the ugly waterside promenade and the tacky visitors' centre, it is a moving spot, on the edge of the backwaters, but not worth a detour unless you're desperate to see the shard of the saint's wrist bone enshrined within the church.

Guruvayur

Kerala's most important Krishna shrine, the high-walled temple of **GURU-VAYUR**, 29km northwest of Thrissur, attracts a constant flow of pilgrims, second only in volume to Ayappa's at Sabarimala (see p.1335). Its deity, **Guruvayurappan**, has inspired numerous paeans from Keralan poets, most notably Narayana Bhattatiri who wrote the *Narayaniyam* during the sixteenth century, when the temple, whose origins are legendary, seems to have first risen to prominence.

One of the richest temples in Kerala, **Guruvayar temple** (3am–1pm & 4–10pm; closed to non-Hindus) is from very early morning to late at night awash with pilgrims in their best white clothes, often trimmed with gold. The bazaar outside the perimeter wall is full of glitter and trinkets such as two-rupee plastic Guruvayurappan signet rings, and there is a palpable air of excitement, particularly when events inside spill out into the streets. A temple committee stall outside the main gates auctions off the gifts, including bell-metal lamps, received at the shrine but, according to superstition, if you buy any of these items they must be returned to the temple as gifts.

Of the temple's 24 **annual festivals**, the most important are Ekadashi and Ulsavam. During the eighteen days of Ekadashi, in the month of Vrischikam

The founding of Guruvayur temple

The founding of the Guruvayur temple is associated with the end of Krishna's life. After witnessing the massacre of family and compatriots, Krishna returned to his capital, Dvarka, in Gujarat, to end his earthly existence. However, knowing that Dvarka would disappear into the sea on his death, he was concerned that the form of Vishnu there, which he himself worshipped, should be spared its fate.

Krishna invited Brihaspati, also known as Guru, the preceptor of the gods, and a pupil, Vayu, the god of wind, to help him select a new home for Vishnu. By the time they arrived at Dvarka, the sea (Varuna) had already claimed the city, but the wind managed to rescue Vishnu. Krishna, Guru and Vayu travelled south, where they met Parashurama, who had just created Kerala by throwing his axe into the sea (see p.1295). On reaching a beautiful lake of lotuses, Rudratirtha, they were greeted by Shiva and Parvati who consecrated the image of Vishnu; Guru and Vayu then installed it, the temple was named after them, and so the deity received the title Guruvayurappan ("Lord of Guruvayur").

(Nov/Dec), marked by processions of caparisoned elephants outside the temple, the exterior of the building may be decorated with the tiny flames of innumerable oil lamps. On certain days (check dates with a KTDC office) programmes staged in front of the temple attract the cream of south Indian classical-music artists.

During Ulsavam, in the month of Kumbham (Feb/March), when Tantric rituals are conducted inside, an **elephant race** is run outside on the first day and elephant processions take place during the ensuing six days. On the ninth day, the Palivetta, or "hunt" occurs; the deity, mounted on an elephant, circumambulates the temple accompanied by men dressed as animals, who represent human weaknesses such as greed and anger, and are vanquished by the god. The next night sees the image of the god taken out for ritual immersion in the temple tank; devotees greet the procession with oil lamps and throw rice. It is considered highly auspicious to bathe in the tank at the same time as the god.

The Punnathur Kotta Elephant Sanctuary

When they are not involved in races and other arcane temple rituals, Guruvayur's tuskers hang out at the **Punnathur Kotta Elephant Sanctuary** (daily 9am–6pm; Rs5; Rs25 extra with camera), 4km north of town. Forty elephants, aged from 6 to 93, live here, munching for most of the day on specially imported piles of fodder and cared for by their three personal *mahouts*, who wash and scrub them several times a week in the sanctuary pond – a great photo opportunity. Avoid the bulls on heat – the *mahouts* will warn you which ones they are – as they become aggressive and unpredictable; only approach an elephant if a *mahout* allows you.

All the animals are the personal possession of Lord Guruvayur, given to the temple by wealthy patrons from as far afield as Bihar and Assam; apart from the most elderly, who are allowed an honourable retirement, the elephants are gainfully employed in local temples, especially at the Guruvayur temple itself. All temples demand pretty elephants for their elaborate festivals, and the competition to rent a particularly favoured beast can become a bitter auction between villages: the standard daily charge of Rs3500 per elephant once reached a record Rs75,000.

Practicalities

Buses from Thrissur (40min) arrive at the main **bus stand** at the top end of E Nada Street, five minutes east of the temple. **Accommodation** is concentrated along this street; it's often packed to the gills with pilgrims, but the two KTDC hotels are usually good bets. The pilgrim-oriented KTDC *Anjanam*, near the entrance of the Krishna temple (☏ 0487/552408; ❷) has basic double rooms and a devotional atmosphere. The one-star deluxe, KTDC *Nandanam*, near the railway station (☏ 0487/556266; ❸–❺), offers creature comforts and some rooms have a/c. The town is crammed with pure veg "meals" **restaurants**, and there's an *Indian Coffee House* on the southern side of E Nada Street that serves south Indian snacks.

Cheruthuruthy

The village of **CHERUTHURUTHY** is an easy day-trip 32km north of Thrissur through gently undulating green country. It consists of a few lanes and one main street, which runs south from the bank of Kerala's longest river, the **Bharatapuzha** (pronounced Bharatapura). Considered holy by Hindus, the great river has declined in recent years, leaving a vast expanse of sand. Although

Among the most magical experiences a visitor to Kerala can have is to witness one of the innumerable ancient rituals, ritualized theatre or dance styles that play such an important and unique role in the cultural life of the region. The dance drama Kathakali is the best known; other less publicized forms, which clearly influenced its development, include the classical Sanskrit Kutiyattam and the village hero-worship ritual Teyyattam.

Many Keralan forms share broad characteristics. A prime aim of each performer is to transform the mundane to the world of gods and demons; his preparation is highly ritualized, involving other-worldly costume and mask-like make-up. In Kathakali and Kutiyattam, this preparation is a rigorously codified part of the classical tradition, whereas the much wilder appearance of Teyyattam differs from village to village. One-off performances of various ritual types take place throughout the state, building up to fever pitch during April and May before pausing for the monsoon (June–Aug). Finding out about such events requires a little perseverance, but it's well worth the effort; enquire at tourist offices, or buy a Malayalam daily paper such as *Mathrabhumi* and ask someone to check the listings for temple festivals, where most of the action invariably takes place. Tourist Kathakali is staged daily in Kochi (see p.1355) but to find authentic performances, contact performing arts schools such as Thiruvananthapuram's Margi (see p.1305) and Cheruthuruthy's Kerala Kalamandalam; Kutiyattam artists work at both, as well as at Natana Kairali at Irinjalakuda (see p.1364).

Kathakali

Here is the tradition of the trance dancers, here is the absolute demand of the subjugation of body to spirit, here is the realization of the cosmic transformation of human into divine.

Mrinalini Sarabhai, classical dancer

Kathakali dance drama, Kerala's most popular theatre form, is recognized as one of the four major classical Indian styles. The image of a Kathakali actor in a magnificent costume with extraordinary make-up and a huge gold crown has become Kerala's trademark, seen on anything from matchboxes to TV adverts for detergents. Traditional performances, of which there are still many, usually take place on open ground outside a temple, beginning at 10pm and lasting until dawn, illuminated by the flickers of a large brass oil lamp centre stage. Virtually nothing about Kathakali is naturalistic, because it depicts the world of gods and demons; both the male and female roles are played by men.

Standing at the back of the stage, two musicians play driving rhythms, one on a bronze gong, the other on heavy bell-metal cymbals; they also sing the dialogue. Actors appear and disappear from behind a hand-held curtain and never utter a sound, save the odd strange cry. Learning the elaborate hand gestures, facial expressions and choreographed movements, as articulate and precise as any sign language, requires rigorous training which can begin at the age of eight and last ten years. At least two more drummers stand left of the stage; one plays the upright chenda with slender curved sticks, the other plays the *maddalam*, a horizontal barrel-shaped hand drum. When a female character is "speaking", the *chenda* is replaced by the hourglass-shaped *ettaka*, a "talking drum" on which melodies can be played. The drummers keep their eyes on the actors, whose every gesture is reinforced by their sound, from the gentlest embrace to the gory disembowelling of an enemy.

Although it bears the unmistakeable influences of Kutiyattam and indigenous folk rituals, Kathakali, literally "story-play", is thought to have crystallized into a distinct theatre form during the seventeenth century. The plays are based on three major sources: the Hindu epics the *Mahabharata*, *Ramayana* and the *Bhagavata Purana*. While the stories are ostensibly about god-heroes such as Rama and Krishna, the most popular characters are those that give the most scope to the actors – the villainous, fanged, red-and-black-faced, *katti* ("knife") anti-heroes; these types, such as the kings Ravana and Duryodhana, are dominated by lust, greed, envy and violence. David Bolland's *Guide to Kathakali*, widely available in Kerala, gives invaluable scene-by-scene summaries of the most popular plays and explains in simple language a lot more besides.

When attending a performance, arrive early to get your bearings before it gets dark, even though the first play will not begin much before 10pm. (Quiet) members of the audience are welcome to visit the dressing room before and during the performance. The colour and design of the mask-like make-up, which specialist artists take several hours to apply, reveal the character's personality. The word *pacha* means both "green" and "pure"; a green-faced *pacha* character is thus a noble human or god. Red signifies *rajas*, passion and aggression, black denotes *tamas*, darkness and negativity, while white is *sattvik*, light and intellect. Once the make-up is completed, elaborate wide skirts are tied to the waist, and ornaments of silver and gold are added. Silver talons are fitted to the left hand. The transformation is complete with a final prayer and the donning of waist-length wig and crown. Visitors new to Kathakali will almost undoubtedly get bored during such long programmes, parts of which are very slow indeed. If you're at a village performance, you may not always find accommodation, so you can't leave during the night. Be prepared to sit on the ground for hours, and bring some warm clothes. Half the fun is staying up all night to witness, just as the dawn light appears, the gruesome disembowelling of a villain or a demon *asura*.

Kutiyattam

Three families of the Chakyar caste and a few outsiders perform the Sanskrit drama **Kutiyattam**, the oldest continually performed theatre form in the world. Until recently it was only performed inside temples and then only in front of the uppermost castes. Visually it is very similar to its offspring, Kathakali, but its atmosphere is infinitely more archaic. The actors, eloquent in sign language and symbolic movement, speak in the bizarre, compelling, intonation of the local brahmins' Vedic chant, unchanged since 1500 BC.

A single act of a Kutiyattam play can require ten full nights; the entire play takes forty. A great actor, in full command of the subtleties of expression through gestures, can take half an hour to do such a simple thing as murder a demon, berate the audience, or simply describe a leaf fall to the ground. Unlike Kathakali, Kutiyattam includes comic characters and plays. The ubiquitous **Vidushaka**, narrator and clown, is something of a court jester, and traditionally has held the right openly to criticize the highest in the land without fear of retribution.

Teyyattam

In northern Kerala, a wide range of ancient ritual "performances", loosely known as **Teyyattam**, are performed between October and May. They might include *bhuta* (spirit or hero worship), trance dances, the enactment of legendary events, and oracular pronouncements. The role of *teyyam* (performer) passes from father to son; they are usually from low castes, but during the ritual, a brahmin will honour the deities they represent, so the status of each individual is reversed. During a performance several *teyyam* will be involved, but only one at a time may sit on the chair of the deity and become possessed.

Although Teyyattam performances can now be seen in government-organized cultural festivals, the powerful effect is best experienced in an all-night ceremony

continued overleaf

continued from previous page

in the courtyard of a house or temple, in a village setting. Some figures, with intricately painted faces and bodies, are genuinely terrifying; costumes include metres-high headgear, sometimes doubling as a mask, and clothes of banana leaves and bark. You may be lucky enough to stumble upon a very rare performance involving fire rituals. Amid frantic drumming, a *teyyam* will volunteer to demonstrate the demonic power temporarily held within him, either by walking on red-hot coals or by rapidly dancing around the fire and throwing himself on it, an auspicious 52 times. Each time the *teyyam* allows the demon to drive his body onto the fire, the temple brahmins pull the possessed *teyyam* back.

of little consolation to locals, who have to deal with the problems of a depleted water supply, it has produced a landscape of incomparable beauty.

Cheruthuruthy is famous as the home of **Kerala Kalamandalam**, the state's flagship training school for Kathakali and other indigenous Keralan performing arts, which was founded in 1927 by the revered Keralan poet Vallathol (1878–1957). At first patronized by the Raja of Cochin, the school has been funded by both state and national governments and has been instrumental in the large-scale revival of interest in Kathakali, and other unique Keralan art forms. Despite conservative opposition, it followed an open–door recruitment policy, based on artistic merit, which produced "scheduled caste", Muslim and Christian graduates along with the usual Hindu castes, something that was previously unimaginable. Kalamandalam artists perform in the great theatres of the world, many sharing their extraordinary skills with outsiders; luminaries of modern theatre, such as Grotowski and Peter Brook, are indebted to them. Nonetheless, many of these trained artists are still excluded from entering, let alone performing in, temples, which are popular venues for Hindu art forms, and in particular music.

Non-Hindus can see *Kathakali*, *Kutiyattam* and *Mohiniattam* performed in the school's superb theatre, which replicates the wooden, sloping-roofed traditional theatres, known as *kuttambalams*, found in Keralan temples. If you're interested in how this extraordinary technique is taught, don't miss the chance to sit in on the rigorous training sessions, which have to be seen to be believed (Mon–Fri 4.30am–5pm; closed on public holidays). A handful of foreigners each year also come to the Kalamandalam academy to attend full-time **courses** in Kathakali and other traditional dance and theatre forms. Those interested should first apply in writing. Short courses last for a minimum of one month, or there are condensed courses of between three and six months. Full courses usually last between four and six years and foreign students, with the necessary student visas, are allowed to attend for a maximum of four years. Applications may be made from abroad (write to the Secretary, Kerala Kalamandalam, Vallathol Nagar, Cheruthuruthy, Thrissur Dist, Kerala 679 531), but it's a good idea to visit before committing yourself. The students' lot here is not an easy one – to say the least. For information contact the school office (☎0488/462418, ℉ 462019).

A good time to visit is during their annual week-long festival starting on Christmas Day. Held at the *kuttambalam* and at their original riverside campus amongst the trees, the festival presents all the art forms of Kerala and is free – although the limited accommodation can be a problem. A short walk past the old campus leads to a small but exquisite **Shiva temple** in classic Keralan style, where the early evening worship, when the exterior is lit with candles, is particularly rewarding.

Practicalities

Cheruthuruthy's **accommodation** is limited, with some students staying as guests in private accommodation or at the new on-site, self-catering *International Hostel* (❼). The village has a couple of simple guesthouses and the atmospheric *Government Rest House* (☎0488/462760; ❶), a short distance along the Shoranur road from Kalamandalam, has eight vast and very basic rooms, some with Western-style toilets, and all sharing a veranda. The bustling and unattractive town of Shoranur has more options but none that could capture the charm of Cheruthuruthy and its environs. **Food** may be available by arrangement, and there are simple "meals" shops in the village; of these, the *Mahatma*, serving vegetarian food, is by far the best; if you want meat try the *Shalimar* close by. **Buses** heading to Shoranur from Thrissur's Wadakkancheri stand stop outside Kalamandalam, just before Cheruthuruthy. The nearest **railway** station is Shoranur Junction, 3km south. It's on the main line and served by express trains to and from Mangalore, Chennai and all major stations south of here on the coastal route through Kerala.

Palakkad

PALAKKAD (Palghat), surrounded by paddy fields, lies on NH-47 between Thrissur (79km) and Coimbatore, Tamil Nadu (54km), and on the railway line from Karnataka and Tamil Nadu. Historically, thanks to the natural 20km-wide Palakkad Gap in the Western Ghats, this area has been one of the chief entry points into Kerala. The environs are beautiful, but the town itself doesn't warrant a stop, other than to break a journey. Arriving from Tamil Nadu, Palakkad, with its dry, Deccan-like landscape, unlike most of the state, gives a misleading first impression of Kerala. The well-preserved **fort**, built in 1766 by Haider Ali of Mysore, is the nearest thing to a "sight"; it gets plenty of visitors at weekends, despite having little to offer. However, many travellers in search of **Kathakali** and **Teyyattam** performances find themselves directed here. Particularly during April and May, hundreds of one-off events take place in the area. The local Government Carnatic Music College has an excellent reputation, and a small open-air amphitheatre next to the fort often hosts first-class music and dance performances. Ask at the tourist office (see below) for details. The landscaped gardens and amusement park at **Malampuzha** (10km north; Rs80, includes all rides), watered by the large adjacent dam, is a great attraction during the weekends when crowds come to ride the cable car (known as the "ropeway"). In the same grounds, the fantasy rock garden created by the artist Nek Chand of Chandigarh fame (see p.646) is illuminated on Saturday and Sunday nights (open until 9pm).

Practicalities

Palakkad is well connected to the rest of Kerala and most of the main express trains travelling through to Chennai, Bangalore and points further north stop at Palakkad's **railway station**, 6km to the northeast. The KSRTC **bus stand** is slap in the centre of town; most **accommodation**, in budget Indian-style lodges, is nearby. The *Ammbadi*, on TB Road, opposite the town bus stand and 500m from the KSRTC bus stand (☎0491/531244; ❸–❺), has comfortable rooms, some a/c, and the restaurant serves Indian and Chinese food. Far more upmarket, the modern *Hotel Indraprastha*, English Church Road (℡0491/534641, ℻ 539531; ❻–❾), boasts large rooms, some with a/c, a gloomy but blissfully cool a/c restaurant serving a mixed menu of Indian, Western and Chinese cuisine, a bar and a pleasant lawn. *Fort Palace*, W Fort Road (℡0491/534621; ❺–❼), is also reasonable, with some a/c rooms, a bar and a restaurant serving good Indian food. Another alternative is to head out to KTDC's *Garden House* at Malampuzha (℡0491/815217; ❺–❻) which has a range that includes large, ordinary doubles as well as some comfortable a/c rooms.

Around the corner from the *Indraprastha*, the DTPC's **tourist office** is at Fort Maidan (Mon–Sat 10am–5.30pm; ℡0491/538996). They offer colourful leaflets but not much else, though you can coax them for travel information. Both the *Indraprastha* and the *Fort Palace* **change money** for residents and, in theory, so can the State Bank of India, next door to the *Indraprastha*.

Kozhikode (Calicut)

The busy coastal city of **KOZHIKODE** (Calicut), 225km north of Kochi, occupies an extremely important place in Keralan legend and history. It is also significant in the story of European interference in the subcontinent, as Vasco da Gama first set foot in India at Kozhikode in 1498. However, as a tourist destination, it's a dud, with precious few remnants of its historic past. The few foreigners that pause here invariably do so only to break the long journey between Mysore and Kochi.

Kozhikode's roots are shrouded in myth. According to Keralan tradition, the powerful king Cheraman Perumal is said to have converted from Hinduism to Islam and left for Mecca "to save his soul", never to return. Before he set sail he divided Kerala between his relatives, all of whom were to submit to his nephew, who was given the kingdom of Kozhikode and the title zamorin, equivalent to emperor. The city prospered and, perhaps because of the story of the convert king, became the preferred port of Muslim traders from the Middle East in search of spices, particularly pepper. During the Raj, it was an important centre for the export of printed Indian cotton, whence the term "calico", an English corruption of the name Calicut – itself an anglicized version of the city's original Malayalam name, which has now been reinstated. Today, due to strong ties with the Gulf where numerous sons of the city work, Kozhikode is flourishing with the injection of new wealth.

Arrival and information

The **railway station** (℡0495/701234), served by a handful of coastal expresses and several passenger trains, is close to the centre. Trains heading north on the Konkan Railway include the fast, all a/c Rajdhani Express #2431 (Fri & Sat) which stops at Madgaon (Goa) on the way to Delhi, but the most convenient, in terms of departure time, is the Netravati Express #6636 (daily 9.45am). Neither trains stop at Mangalore but at a nearby town, Kankanadi. Trains south include the Mangala Lakshadweep Express #2618 (daily 7.35am) to Ernakulam and the overnight Malabar Express #6330 (daily 10.40pm) to Thiruvananthapuram. Of the three **bus stands**, the most important is the KSRTC stand, Mavoor Road (aka Indira Gandhi Road), from where buses run daily to destinations as far afield as Bangalore, Mysore, Ooty, Madurai,

Coimbatore and Mangalore. From the New Mafussil private stand, 500m away, on the other side of Mavoor Road, you can get local buses and services to northern Kerala. The Palayam stand is for city and infrequent long-haul buses and destinations further south, such as Palakkad, Thrissur, and Guruvayur. Private deluxe buses to Thiruvananthapuram or Kochi leave from in front of the KSRTC bus stand.

Kozhikode's **airport** (nearly always referred to as Calicut in timetables) lies at Karippur, 23km south of the city. Taxis cost Rs300, or take an **auto-rickshaw** to the Kozhikode–Palakkad highway, from where you can catch a bus. Indian Airlines **flies** twice a day to **Mumbai**, daily to **Delhi** and **Coimbatore**, and twice a week to **Chennai**; Jet Airways also flies twice a week to Mumbai. Indian Airlines flies twice a week (Mon & Fri) to **Goa** and has several international flights to Sharjah, Kuwait and Bahrain in the **Gulf**. Air India also flies to Abu Dhabi, Dubai and Muscat. For airline tickets try Century Travels, Bank Road (☎0495/766522); or directly at Indian Airlines, Eroth Centre, 5/2521 Bank Rd (☎0495/753966) or Jet Airways, 29 Mavoor Rd (☎0495/356518). Air India is also at Eroth Centre (☎0495/673001).

The friendly Government of Kerala **tourist information** booth (Mon–Sat 10am–5pm; ☎0495/700097), at the railway station, can tell you about travel connections and sites around Kozhikode. KTDC Information Centre (☎0495/722391) in their *Malabar Mansion Hotel*, at the corner of SM Street, can supply only limited information about the town and area. There is a **left-luggage** facility at the railway station but, as is always the case, they only accept locked luggage. With so much Gulf money floating around, you shouldn't have any difficulty **changing money** in Kozhikode. A good place to change any currency or travellers' cheques is at PL Worldways, 3rd Floor, Semma Towers, Mavoor Road (☎0495/722564). Banks that change money include the Standard Chartered Bank on Town Hall Road and the State Bank of India at Manachira Park. **Internet** facilities are available on the first floor (10am–10pm daily), in the block to the right of *Nandhiniee Sweets*, MM Ali Road, at Rs30 per hour.

For **backwater cruises** in the Kozhikode region try the small, friendly and efficient Malabar House Boats at either of their three city offices including 1/335 Purakkatri, Thalakalthur (☎0495/452045, ☎ 765066). Their *kettu vallam* cruises start at Purakkatri, 12km north of the city but they will arrange transport to the boat with prior notice. A 24hr cruise costs Rs6250 for two people, including meals; a day cruise will set you back Rs3000 for up to six people.

The City

Few traces remain of the model city laid out in the fourteenth century, which followed a Hindu grid formula based on a sacred diagram containing the image of the cosmic man, Purusha. The axis and energy centre of the city was dictated by the position of the ancient **Tali Shiva temple** (closed to non-Hindus) which survives to this day. Everything, and everybody, had a place in the scheme. The district around the port in the northwest was reserved for foreigners. Here, a Chinese community lived in and around Chinese Street (now Silk Street) and, later, the Portuguese, Dutch and British occupied the area. Keralan Muslims (Mappilas) lived in the southwest. The northeast of the city was a commercial quarter, and in the southeast stood the Tali temple. Here too was a palace and fort; all the military *kalaris*, martial art gymnasia, that stood around the perimeter have now gone.

Considering its history, there is very little to see in Kozhikode, though it is quite good for **shopping**. Around SM Street, many good fabric and ready-made clothes shops sell the locally produced plain white cotton cloth. You cannot fail to be dazzled by the sheer number of gold jewellery shops, full of ladies spending lavish amounts of the money faithfully sent by relatives in the Gulf. This district is also a good place to try the local *halva* sweets, especially popular with the large Mappila community. Some shops also specialize in piping-hot banana chips, straight from the frying pan.

Locals enjoy a promenade on or near the **beach** (3km from the centre) in the late afternoon and early evening. Although not suitable for swimming, it's a restful place, where you can munch on roasted peanuts sold in the many stalls while scanning the seas for jumping dolphins. After dark it's difficult to find an autorickshaw to take you back into town, but on the land side of the road regular buses run into the centre. You will have to travel to find better beaches such as the historic beach of **Kappad**, 16km to the north, where Vasco da Gama is said to have landed in 1498 with a hundred and seventy sailors; a small memorial marks the spot. A gentle and partly rocky beach with cottage accommodation at the *Kappad Beach Resort* (℡0496/683760; ❼–❽) nearby, Kappad lies 4km from Thiruvangoor on the Kozhikode–Badagara route serviced by numerous buses.

The **Pazhassirajah and Krishnamenon Museums and Art Gallery** (daily 10am–12.30pm & 2pm–5pm, except Wed 2.30–5pm only) stand together 5km from the centre on East Hill. The Pazhassirajah collection includes copies of murals, coins, bronzes and models of the umbrella-shaped, stone megalithic remains peculiar to Kerala, while the museum houses a collection of memorabilia associated with the left-wing Keralan politician VK Krishnamenon, and a gallery of works by Indian artists.

Accommodation and eating

Kozhikode's reasonably priced city-centre **hotels**, most of which operate a 24-hr check-out, can fill up by evening, especially during conventions. The beach area is a quiet alternative. Your best bet for a proper **meal** is to eat at your hotel, though you can get south Indian snacks in town at the dependable *Indian Coffee House* on Kallai Road. The open-air *Park Restaurant*, by Mananchira tank, makes an appealing city centre oasis in the evenings. *Mezban* at the Asma Tower on Mavoor Road is comfortable with a tasteful a/c section where you can get Continental and local breakfasts. The strong menu includes excellent local Malabari cuisine – try the fish. *Nandhiniee Sweets*, on MM Ali Road, is an ultra-hygienic sweets, nuts and savoury snacks pit stop, where you can also get great fresh-fruit cocktails, *badam* milk and *falooda* shakes.

Alakapuri Guest House, MM Ali Road, near the railway station, 1km from KSRTC bus stand ℡0495/723451. Built around a courtyard, some rooms have huge bathtubs, polished wood and easy chairs; the cheaper, non-a/c, options are rather spartan. The first-floor café serves great south Indian food all day; in the evening go down to the restaurant out in the courtyard garden. Single rates available. ❸–❻

Beach Hotel, Beach Road ℡0495/365363. Built in 1890 as the Malabar English Club, this well-conserved and atmospheric building has been a hotel since the 1940s. Comfortable rooms overlooking the beach have teak floors and large verandas; cheaper rooms surround a garden at the back. A restaurant serves Malabari and seafood dishes. ❺–❼

Imperial, Kallai Road ℡0495/753966. Large hotel around a courtyard with plain and cheap rooms and a very good vegetarian restaurant; not recommended for single women. ❶

Kalpaka Tourist Home, Corner of SM Road and Town Hall Road ℡0495/720222. Five storeys ranged around a weirdly shaped courtyard-cum-sari store make for a space-stationesque interior, which is now ageing. The views from the eastern side are best. Some a/c rooms, and 24hr check-out. ❸–❻

KTDC Malabar Mansion, SM Street ℡0495/722391. Modern high-rise hotel, near the railway station at the top of the main street. Huge a/c suites, reasonable non-a/c rooms, beer parlour and a good south Indian restaurant. Good value. ❸–❺

Sasthapuri, MM Ali Road ⊕0495/723281. Small budget place with well-maintained rooms and a decent roof-garden restaurant and a bar. It's tucked away down a side street to the right of Palayam bus station. ②–⑤

Taj Residency, PT Usha Road ⊕0495/765354, ⑤ 7664480. The grandest hotel in town but it lacks the ubiquitous *Taj* style; nonetheless, the rooms are well appointed and comfortable and there's a pool, coffee shop, multi-cuisine restaurant, and health and Ayurvedic centre. Breakfast is included in the tariff. ⑨

North of Kozhikode

The beautiful coast of Kerala, **north of Kozhikode**, is a seemingly endless stretch of coconut palms, wooded hills and virtually deserted beaches; the towns hold little of interest for visitors, most of whom bypass the area completely. However, then you miss out on the fun of a search through the villages for **Teyyattam**, the extraordinary masked trance dances that take place throughout the region during winter.

Kannur (Cannanore) and around

KANNUR (Cannanore), 92km north of Kozhikode, was for many centuries the capital of the Kolathiri rajas, who prospered from the thriving maritime spice trade through its port. In the early 1500s, after Vasco da Gama passed through, the Portuguese took it and erected an imposing bastion, **St Angelo's fort**, overlooking the harbour, but today this is occupied by the Indian army and closed to visitors. If you come to Kannur at all, it will probably be on the trail of **Teyyattam**, spectacular spirit-possession rituals that are an important feature of village life in the area from late October until May (see p.1369). Locating them is not always easy, but if you ask at the local tourist office or telephone the tourist desk in Cochin (⊕0484/371761), they should be able to point you in the right direction, and it's well worth heading out to the daily ritual at **Parassinikadavu** (see below). The popular town beach can get quite crowded and so for a bit more quiet head down to the small **Baby beach** (4km) which, lying in the army's cantonment area of large bungalows set in leafy gardens, is protected by restricted access (9am–5pm).

A popular weekend day-trip destination from Kannur is the **fort** at Bekal (daily 9am–5.30pm; Rs2, Fri free), which stands 45km to the north on a promontory between two long, classically beautiful palm-fringed **beaches**. Although this is one of the largest forts in Kerala and has been under the control of various powers including Vijayanagar, Tipu Sultan and the British, it's nothing to get excited about. The bastion's commanding position, with views across the bays to north and south, is impressive enough, but only four watch-towers and the outer walls survive. An adjacent Hindu temple, next to the gates, with garish stucco images of the gods, draws a steady stream of visitors while others clamber along the battlements or climb down to the beach through hidden passages. A short walk south of the main gates you'll find the Bekal Resorts' visitor centre where the café and shops only open at the weekends.

Practicalities

Straddling the main coastal transport artery between Mangalore and Kochi/Thiruvananthapuram, Kannur is well connected by **bus** and **train** to most major towns and cities in Kerala. In addition buses also travel to Mysore turning inland at Thalassery (aka Tellychery) and climbing the beautiful wooded ghats to Virajpet in Kodagu.

Decent budget **accommodation** is available at *Plaza Tourist Home* (℡0497/360031; ❷), close to the railway station gates on Fort Road, which has reasonable rooms and an *Indian Coffee House* **restaurant** downstairs. A few metres up the road lies *Madan* (℡0497/768204; ❷), a sunny friendly budget lodge set in a courtyard with simple rooms. *Swadeshi Woodlands Lodge* a few minutes away on Aarat Road (℡0497/701434; ❷) is a quiet old hotel with character in a large yard with basic rooms and a reasonable south Indian restaurant. More upscale is the plush a/c, business-oriented *Kamala International* (℡0497/766910; ❸), in the town centre on SM Road, which is undergoing major renovations. They also have a rooftop garden restaurant. The excellent-value *Government Guest House*, cantonment area (℡0497/706426; ❷), stands on the crest of a cliff overlooking the sea; the huge, simple rooms that catch the breezes are primarily for visiting VIPs, but there are usually a few spare rooms. The brilliantly located *Mascot Beach Resort* (℡0497/708445; ❻–❽), 300m

The islands of Lakshadweep

Visitors to Kochi who really want to get away from it all, and have time and a lot of money to spare, could do no better than to head for **LAKSHADWEEP**, the "one hundred thousand islands", which lie between 200 and 400km offshore in the deep blue of the Arabian Sea.

The smallest Union Territory in India consists of lagoons, reefs, sandbanks and 27 tiny coconut-palm-covered coral islands. Only ten are inhabited, with a total population of just over 50,000, the majority of whom are Malayalam-speaking Sunni Muslims, said to be descended from seventh-century Keralan Hindus who converted to Islam. The main sources of income are fishing, coconuts and related products. Fruit, vegetables and pulses are cultivated in small quantities but staples such as rice and many other commodities have always had to be imported. The Portuguese, who discovered the value of coir rope, a by-product of the coconut, controlled Lakshadweep during the sixteenth century; when they imposed an import tax on rice, locals retaliated by poisoning some of the forty-strong Portuguese garrison. Terrible reprisals followed. As Muslims, the islanders enjoyed friendly relations with Tipu Sultan of Mysore. That naturally aroused the ire of the British, who moved in at the end of the eighteenth century and remained until Independence, when Lakshadweep became a Union Territory.

Bangaram

Accommodation is available for nonresidents of India on only two of the islands. The teardrop-shaped uninhabited 128-acre islet of **BANGARAM** welcomes a limited number of foreign tourists, and expects them to pay handsomely for the privilege. Bangaram is the archetypal tropical paradise and a scuba diver's dream, edged with pristine white sands and sitting in a calm lagoon where the average water temperature stays around 26°C. Beyond the lagoon lies coral reef and the technicolour world of the deep, home to sea turtles, dolphins, eagle rays, lionfish, parrotfish, octopus and predators like barracudas and sharks. Islanders come to Bangaram and its uninhabited neighbours, which are all devoid of animal and bird life, to fish and to harvest coconuts.

It's theoretically possible to visit Bangaram all year round; the hottest time is April and May, when the temperature can reach 33°C; the monsoon (May–Sept) attracts approximately half the total rainfall seen in Kerala, in the form of passing showers, not a deluge, although seas are rough. The island remains staggeringly peaceful, and (compared to other resorts), attempts to minimize the ecological

before Baby beach, perches on a rocky shoreline with large well-appointed rooms with views across the cove to the lighthouse, foreign exchange and they serve great food in their restaurant, but there is no bar.

However, for a total escape, head 10km south to the very warm and welcoming *Costa Malabari* in **Tottada village**; book through the tourist desk at Ernakulam (☎0484/371761; ❻–❼). Hidden deep in the cashew and coconut groves, the informal house has four airy and comfortable rooms, and you are served outstanding home-cooked Malabari cuisine and seafood. Five minutes walk away are two very private golden beaches, where you can swim out to the mussel fishermen and dolphins. This is an ideal base if you want to catch some local temple rituals; you can be collected from the station with prior arrangement (Rs120).

Parassinikadavu

The easiest place to catch a glimpse of Teyyattam (see p.1369) is the village of **PARASSINIKADAVU**, 20km north of Kannur beside the River

impact of tourism. *Bangaram Island Resort* (❾) accommodates up to thirty couples in simple thatched cottage rooms, each with a veranda; cane tables and chairs sit outside the restaurant on the beach, and a few hammocks are strung up between the palms. There's no air-conditioning, TV, radio, telephone, newspapers or shops, let alone discos. The tariff, if expensive for India, compares favourably with other exotic holiday destinations. During the peak season (Dec 21 to Jan 20) it rises to $350 full board for a double room; in low season (April–Sept except Aug) it may be as much as 25 percent less. Facilities include scuba diving (from $45 per dive; lessons with qualified instructor); glass-bottomed boat trips to neighbouring uninhabited islands; and deep-sea fishing (Oct to mid-May; $50–75). Kayaks, catamarans and a sailing boat are available free. Day-trips are possible to the inhabited island of **KADMAT**, the only other island where foreigners are allowed to stay and one that, along with Kavarattu and Minicoy, is being developed as a tourist destination for well-heeled Indian visitors.

Getting to the islands

At present, the only way for foreigners to reach Bangaram is on the expensive flights on small aircraft run by Indian Airlines out of **Kochi** (1 daily, except Sun) and **Goa** (Mon, Wed & Fri) and bookable through the *Casino Hotel* on Willingdon Island (see below). Foreigners pay $300 for the round trip, which takes ninety minutes. Flights arrive in Lakshadweep at the island of **Agatti**, 8km southwest, from where the connecting boat journey to Bangaram takes two hours, picking its way through the shallows to avoid the corals. During the monsoon (May 16–Sept 15), helicopters are used so as to protect the fragile coral reefs that lie just under the surface. All arrangements, including flights, accommodation and the necessary entry permit, are handled by the *Casino Hotel*, Willingdon Island, Kochi (☎0484/668221, ℻668001). Some foreign tour operators, however, offer all-in packages combining Lakshadweep with another destination, usually Goa.

The Society for Promotion of Recreational Tourism and Sports (SPORTS) on IG Road, Willingdon Island (☎0484/668387, ℻668155) organizes six-day package cruises on one of two ships, the *Tipu Sultan* or the *Bharat Seema*. You spend two days at sea and four days lying on the beach. SPORTS will arrange all permits and the package is for full board ($450 for non-a/c, $500 for a/c), although foreigners who take the package have to stay on Kadmat, whereas fellow Indian visitors can explore two other islands nearby.

Valapatanam, where the head priest, or *madayan*, of the **Parassini Madammpura** temple performs every day during winter before assembled devotees. Elaborately dressed and accompanied by a traditional drum group, he becomes possessed by the temple's presiding deity – Lord Muthappan, Shiva in the form of a *kiratha*, or hunter – and enacts a series of complex offerings. The two-hour ceremony culminates when the priest/deity dances forward to bless individual members of the congregation. Even by Keralan standards, this is an extraordinary spectacle, and well worth taking time out of a journey along the coast for.

Regular local **buses** leave Kannur **for Parassinikadavu** from around 7am, dropping passengers at the top of the village, ten minutes on foot from the temple. However, if you want to get there in time for the dawn Teyyattam (4am–8am), you'll have to splash out on one of the Ambassador taxis that line up outside Kannur bus stand. The cabbies sleep in their cars, so you can arrange the trip on the spot by waking one up; you can also arrange a taxi through one of the more upmarket hotels. Alternatively, head out to Parassinikadavu for the early afternoon ritual, which starts around 2pm, allowing you plenty of time to get there and back by bus, with thirty minutes or so to browse the temple bazaar (whose stalls do a great line in kitsch Lord Muthappan souvenirs). Note that the performances do not always take place, so it's a good idea to phone in advance (℡0497/780722). Otherwise, if you are there between October and March, ask around or check the local newspaper, as there's sure to be a local village Teyyattam performance in the area.

Travel details

For details of ferry services on the backwaters – primarily between Alappuzha and Kollam – see p.1326.

Trains

Kochi/Ernakulam to: Alappuzha (3–5 daily; 1hr 20min); Bangalore (1 daily; 14hr); Chennai (3–5 daily; 12hr 45min–14hr 40min); Coimbatore (3–4 daily; 4hr 45min–5hr 30min); Delhi (2 daily; 40hr 30min–49hr); Kanniyakumari (2–3 daily; 8hr); Kollam (8–9 daily; 3–4hr); Kottayam (8–9 daily; 1hr 5min); Kozhikode (6–7 daily; 3hr 20min–6hr 20min); Mumbai (2–3 daily; 28hr 20min–40hr 25min); Palakkad (5–6 daily; 3hr 20min); Thiruvananthapuram (9–11 daily; 4hr 20min–5hr); Thrissur (12–14 daily; 1hr 30min–2hr).
Kozhikode to: Kochi (6–7 daily; 4hr 30min–5hr 10min); Mangalore (3–4 daily; 5hr 40min–6hr); Mumbai (2–3 daily; 16hr 20min–23hr); Thiruvananthapuram (4–6 daily; 8hr 35min–13hr 20min).
Thiruvananthapuram to: Alappuzha (2 daily; 3hr); Bangalore (1–2 daily; 18hr 40min–19hr 20min); Calcutta (3 weekly; 49hr); Chennai (1–3 daily; 18–19hr); Delhi (1–2 daily; 52hr 35min–56hr 30min); Kanniyakumari (1–2 daily; 2hr 15min); Kochi (8 daily; 3hr 30min–5hr); Kollam (hourly; 1hr 30min–1hr 50min); Kozhikode (3 daily; 8hr–11hr

30min); Margao (for Goa; 4 weekly; 16hr 25min–20hr 30min); Mumbai (1–2 daily; 24hr 20min–46hr 40min); Thrissur (5–6 daily; 6–7hr); Varkala (6 daily; 38–55min).
Thrissur to: Chennai (3–4 daily; 12hr 5min–12hr 30min); Kochi (10–12 daily; 1hr 30min–2hr 10min); Thiruvananthapuram (9–10 daily; 5hr 15min–7hr 20min).

Buses

Kochi/Ernakulam to: Alappuzha (every 30min; 1hr 30min); Kanniyakumari (6 daily; 9hr); Kollam (every 30min; 3hr); Kottayam (every 30min; 1hr 30min–2hr); Kozhikode (hourly; 5hr); Periyar (10 daily; 6–7hr); Thiruvananthapuram (every 30min; 4–6hr); Thrissur (every 30min; 2hr).
Periyar to: Kochi (8 daily; 6–7hr); Kottayam (every 30min; 3–4hr); Kozhikode (hourly; 8hr); Madurai (10 daily; 5hr 30min); Munnar (4 daily; 4hr 30min); Thiruvananthapuram (10–12 daily; 8–9hr).
Thiruvananthapuram to: Alappuzha (every 30min; 3hr 15min); Chennai (8 daily; 17hr); Kanniyakumari (12 daily; 2hr); Kochi (every 30min; 4–6hr); Kollam (every 30min; 1hr 30min);

Kottayam (every 30min; 4hr); Madurai (10 daily; 7hr); Periyar (5 daily; 8hr); Ponmudi (4 daily; 2hr 30min); Varkala (hourly; 1hr 30min).

Thrissur to: Kochi (every 30min; 2hr); Guruvayur (10 daily; 40min); Chennai (1 daily; 14hr); Mysore (2 daily; 10hr); Palakkad (6 daily; 2hr); Thiruvananthapuram (15 daily; 6–7hr).

Flights

Kochi/Ernakulam to: Bangalore (1 daily; 55min); Chennai (1–2 daily; 1hr–2hr 15min); Coimbatore (2 weekly; 30min); Delhi (1 daily; 4hr 10min); Goa (2 weekly; 55min); Hyderabad (2 weekly; 1hr 40min);

Lakshadweep (1 daily, except Sun; 1hr 30min); Mumbai (1–2 daily; 1hr 45min–3hr 5min); Thiruvananthapuram (3 weekly; 40min).

Kozhikode to: Chennai (4 weekly; 1hr–2hr 15min); Coimbatore (1 daily; 30min); Delhi (1 daily; 5hr 40min); Goa (2 weekly; 1hr 5min); Kochi (2 weekly; 30min); Mumbai (2 daily; 1hr 40min–3hr).

Thiruvananthapuram to: Bangalore (1 daily; 2hr 5min); Chennai (1 daily; 1hr 10min); Colombo (Sri Lanka) (2 weekly; 1hr 25min); Delhi (2 daily; 4hr 35min–5hr 20min); Malé (Maldives) (5 weekly; 40min); Mumbai (1 daily; 1hr 55min).

CHAPTER 22

Highlights

* **Mysore** The sandalwood city has bundles of old-fashioned charm and lots to see, including the opulent Maharaja's Palace. See p.1398

* **Halebid & Belur** Two wonderfully ornate Hoysala temples, set in the slow-paced Karnataka countryside. See p.1413 & p.1416

* **Udupi** A coastal town which, as well as boasting an important Krishna temple that attracts thousands, is the home of the *masala dosa*. See p.1431

* **Jog Falls** India's highest waterfalls offer fresh air, superb views and the chance to take a dip after the downhill hike. See p.1433

* **Gokarn** A quiet Hindu holy town, blessed with a series of exquisite crescent beaches, ideal for serious unwinding. See p.1435

* **Hampi** The remains of the Vijayanagar kingdom, scattered among fertile plantations bisected by the Tungabadra and punctuated by weird rock formations. See p.1442

* **Bijapur** Known as the "Agra of the South" for its splendid Islamic architecture, most famously the vast dome of the Golgumbaz. See p.1457

Karnataka

C reated in 1956 from the princely state of Mysore, **KARNATAKA** – the name is a derivation of the name of the local language, Kannada, spoken by virtually all of its 46 million inhabitants – marks a transition zone between northern India and the Dravidian deep south. Along its border with Maharashtra and Andhra Pradesh, a string of medieval walled towns, studded with domed mausoleums and minarets, recall the era when this part of the Deccan was a Muslim stronghold, while the coastal and hill districts that dovetail with Kerala are quintessential Hindu south India, profuse with tropical vegetation and soaring temple *gopuras*. Between the two are scattered some of the peninsula's most extraordinary historic sites, notably the ruined Vijayanagar city at Hampi, whose lost temples and derelict palaces stand amid an arid, boulder-strewn landscape of surreal beauty.

Karnataka is one of the wettest regions in India, its **climate** dominated by the seasonal monsoon, which sweeps in from the southwest in June, dumping an average of 4m of rain on the coast before it peters out in late September. Running in an unbroken line along the state's palm-fringed coast, the **Western Ghats**, draped in dense deciduous forests, impede the path of the rain clouds east. As a result, the landscape of the interior – comprising the southern apex of the triangular Deccan trap, known here as the **Mysore Plateau** – is considerably drier, with dark volcanic soils in the north, and poor quartzite-granite country to the south. Two of India's most sacred rivers, the Tungabhadra and Krishna, flow across this sun-baked terrain, draining east to the Bay of Bengal.

Broadly speaking, Karnataka's principal attractions are concentrated at opposite ends of the state, with a handful of lesser-visited places dotted along the coast between Goa and Kerala. Road and rail routes dictate that most itineraries take in the brash state capital, **Bangalore**, a go-ahead, modern city that epitomizes the aspirations of the country's new middle classes, with glittering malls, fast-food outlets and a nightlife unrivalled outside Mumbai. The state's other

Accommodation price codes

All accommodation prices in this book have been categorized using the price codes below. Prices given are for a double room, and all taxes are included. For more details, see p.51.

❶ up to Rs100	❹ Rs300–400	❼ Rs900–1500
❷ Rs100–200	❺ Rs400–600	❽ Rs1500–2500
❸ Rs200–300	❻ Rs600–900	❾ Rs2500 and upwards

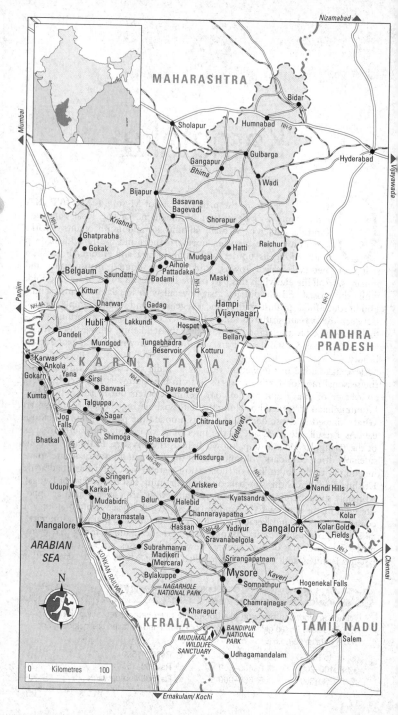

MAHARASHTRA

Nizamabad ▲

Mumbai ▲

Panjim ▲

GOA

NH-4A

NH-4

Sholapur
Humnabad
Bidar
Gulbarga
Gangapur
Bhima
Wadi
Hyderabad
Vijayawada ▲
NH-9
Bijapur
Basavana
Bagevadi
Shorapur
Krishna
Ghatprabha
Gokak
Mudgal
Hatti
Raichur
Belgaum
Saundatti
Aihole
Pattadakal
Badami
Maski
NH-13
Kittur
Dharwar
Gadag
Hampi
(Vijaynagar)
ANDHRA
PRADESH
Hubli
Lakkundi
Hospet
Bellary
Dandeli
Mundgod
Tungabhadra
Reservoir
Kotturu
K A R N A T A K A
Karwar
Ankola
Yana
Gokarn
Sirsi
Banvasi
Davangere
Kumta
NH-4
Talguppa
Sagar
Jog
Falls
Shimoga
Bhadravati
Chitradurga
Vedavati
Bhatkal
NH-17
NH-206
Hosdurga
NH-13
NH-7
Sringeri
Ariskere
Nandi Hills
Udupi
Karkal
Belur
Halebid
Kyatsandra
NH-4
Mudabidri
Channarayapatna
Kolar
Mangalore
Dharamastala
Hassan
Yadiyur
Bangalore
Kolar Gold
Fields
NH-48
Sravanabelagola
ARABIAN
SEA
Subrahmanya
Madikeri
(Mercara)
Srirangapatnam
NH-7
Chennai ▲
Bylakuppe
Mysore
Kaveri
Somnathpur
Hogenekal Falls
N
*NAGARHOLE
NATIONAL PARK*
Chamrajnagar
Kharapur
KERALA
*BANDIPUR
NATIONAL
PARK*
TAMIL NADU
Salem
*MUDUMALAI
WILDLIFE
SANCTUARY*
Udhagamandalam
KONKAN RAILWAY

0   Kilometres   100

▼ Ernakulam/ Kochi

major city, **Mysore**, appeals more for its old-fashioned ambience, nineteenth-century palaces and vibrant produce and incense markets. It also lies within easy reach of several important historical monuments. At the nearby fortified island of **Srirangapatnam** – site of the bloody battle of 1799 that finally put Mysore State into British hands, by defeating the Muslim military genius **Tipu Sultan** – parts of the fort, a mausoleum and Tipu's summer palace survive.

A clutch of other unmissable sights lie further northeast, dotted around the dull railway town of **Hassan**. Around nine centuries ago, the Hoysala kings sited their grand dynastic capitals here, at the now middle-of-nowhere villages of **Belur** and **Halebid**, where several superbly crafted temples survive intact. More impressive still, and one of India's most extraordinary sacred sites, is the eighteen-metre Jain colossus at **Sravanabelgola**, which stares serenely over idyllic Deccani countryside.

West of Mysore, the Ghats rise in a wall of thick jungle cut by deep ravines and isolated valleys. You can either traverse the range by rail, via Hassan, or explore some of its scenic backwaters by road. Among these, the rarely visited coffee- and spice-growing region of **Kodagu (Coorg)** has to be the most entrancing, with its unique culture and lush vistas of misty wooded hills and valleys. Most Coorgi agricultural produce is shipped out of **Mangalore**, the nearest large town, of little interest except as a transport hub whose importance can only increase now the new Konkan Railway is more or less operating to its full potential. Situated midway between Goa and Kerala, it's also a convenient – if uninspiring – place to pause on the journey along Karnataka's beautiful **Karavali coast**. Interrupted by countless mangrove-lined estuaries, the state's 320-kilometre-long red-laterite coast has always been difficult to navigate by land, and traffic along the recently revamped highway remains relatively light. Although there are plenty of superb beaches, facilities are, with rare exceptions, nonexistent, and locals often react with astonishment at the sight of a foreigner. Again, that may well change with the impact of the Konkan Railway – with as-yet-unguessable consequences for the fishing hamlets, long-forgotten fortresses and pristine hill and cliff scenery along the way. For now, few Western tourists visit the famous Krishna temple at **Udupi**, an important Vaishnavite pilgrimage centre, and fewer still venture into the mountains to see India's highest waterfall at **Jog Falls**, set amid some of the region's most spectacular scenery. However, atmospheric **Gokarn**, further north up the coast, is an increasingly popular beach hideaway for budget travellers. Harbouring one of India's most famous *shivalinga*, this seventeenth-century Hindu pilgrimage town enjoys a stunning location, with a high headland dividing it from a string of exquisite beaches.

Winding inland from the mountainous Goan border, NH-4A and the rail line comprise sparsely populated **northern Karnataka**'s main transport artery, linking a succession of grim industrial centres. This region's undisputed highlight is the ghost city of Vijayanagar, better known as **Hampi**, scattered around boulder hills on the south banks of the Tungabhadra River. The ruins of this once splendid capital occupy a magical site, while the village squatting the ancient bazaar is a great spot to hole up for a spell. The jumping-off place for Hampi is **Hospet**, from where buses leave for the bumpy journey north across the rolling Deccani plains to **Badami**, **Aihole** and **Pattadakal**. Now lost in countryside, these tiny villages were once capitals of the **Chalukya** dynasty (sixth to eighth centuries). The whole area is littered with ancient rock-cut caves and finely carved stone temples.

Further north still, in one of Karnataka's most remote and poorest districts, craggy hilltop citadels and crumbling wayside tombs herald the formerly troubled buffer zone between the Muslim-dominated northern Deccan and the Dravidian-Hindu south. The bustling walled market town of **Bijapur**, capital of the Bahmanis, the Muslim dynasty that oversaw the eventual downfall of Vijayanagar, harbours south India's finest collection of Islamic architecture, including the world's second-largest freestanding dome, the Golgumbaz. The first Bahmani capital, **Gulbarga**, site of a famous Muslim shrine and theological college, has retained little of its former splendour, but the more isolated **Bidar**, where the Bahmanis moved in the sixteenth century, definitely deserves a detour en route to or from Hyderabad, four hours east by bus. Perched on a rocky escarpment, its crumbling red ramparts harbour Persian-style mosaic-fronted mosques, mausoleums and a sprawling fort complex evocative of Samarkand and the great silk route.

Some history

Like much of southern India, Karnataka has been ruled by successive Buddhist, Hindu and Muslim dynasties. The influence of Jainism has also been marked; India's very first emperor, **Chandragupta Maurya**, is believed to have converted to Jainism in the fourth century BC, renounced his throne, and fasted to death at Sravanabelgola, now one of the most visited Jain pilgrimage centres in the country.

During the first millennium AD, this whole region was dominated by power struggles between the various kingdoms, such as the Vakatakas and the Guptas, who controlled the western Deccan and at times extended their authority as far as the Coromandel coast, now in Tamil Nadu. From the sixth to the eighth centuries, only interrupted by thirteen years of Pallava rule, the **Chalukya** kingdom included Maharashtra, the Konkan coast on the west, and the whole of Karnataka. The **Cholas** were powerful in the east of the region from about 870 until the thirteenth century, when the Deccan kingdoms were overwhelmed by General Malik Kafur, a convert to Islam.

By the medieval era, Muslim incursions from the north had forced the hitherto warring and fractured Hindu states of the south into close alliance, with the mighty **Vijayanagars** emerging as overlords. Founded by the brothers Harihara and Bukka, their lavish capital, Vijayanagar, ruled an empire stretching from the Bay of Bengal to the Arabian Sea and south to Cape Comorin. The Muslims' superior military strength, however, triumphed in 1565 at the Battle of Talikota, when the **Bahmanis** laid siege to Vijayanagar, reducing it to rubble and plundering its opulent palaces and temples.

Thereafter, a succession of Muslim sultans held sway over the north, while in the south of the state, the independent **Wadiyar rajas** of Mysore, whose territory was comparatively small, successfully fought off the Marathas. In 1761, the brilliant Muslim campaigner Haider Ali, with French support, seized the throne. Haider Ali, and his son Tipu Sultan, turned Mysore into a major force in the south, before Tipu was killed by the British at the **battle of Srirangapatnam** in 1799.

Following Tipu's defeat, the British restored the Wadiyar family to the throne. They kept it until riots in 1830 led the British to appoint a Commission to rule in their place. Fifty years later, the throne was once more returned to the Wadiyars, who remained governors until Karnataka was created by the merging of the states of Mysore and the Madras Presidencies in 1956. In the years since its creation the state has been spared the excesses of communal and political unrest although the scene can be volatile. Long a Congress stronghold, the party of the Gandhi dynasty was routed in the Nineties, first by a reunited Janata Dal and more recently by the fundamentalist BJP alliance, who have held the local balance of power since 1998, though there are signs of the national resurgence of Congress here too.

Bangalore and around

Once across the Western Ghats, the cloying air of Kerala and the Konkan coast gradually gives way to the crisp skies and dry heat of the dusty **Mysore Plateau**. The setting for E.M. Forster's acclaimed Raj novel, *A Passage to India*, this southern tip of the Deccan – a vast, open expanse of gently undulating plains dotted with wheat fields and dramatic granite boulders – formed the heartland of the region's once powerful princely state. Today it remains the political hub of the region, largely due to the economic importance of **BANGALORE**, Karnataka's capital, which, with a population racing towards eight million, is one of the fastest growing cities in Asia. A major scientific research centre at the cutting edge of India's technological revolution, Bangalore has a trendy high-speed self-image that ensures it is quite unlike anywhere else in south India.

In the 1800s, Bangalore's gentle climate, broad streets, and green public parks made it the "Garden City". Until well after Independence, senior citizens, film

The silicon rush

It comes as a surprise to many visitors to learn that India is the second-largest exporter of computer software after the US. Generating sales of around $720 million per year, the apex of this hi-tech boom was the Electronic City Industrial Park on the outskirts of Bangalore, dubbed Silicon Valley by the Indian press. Today, due to the meteoric rise of Hyderabad in neighbouring Andhra Pradesh as the new computer capital of India, and due to Bangalore's own growth pangs, the city is losing some of its attraction to new investors.

Bangalore's rapid industrial rise began in the early 1980s. Fleeing the crippling costs of Mumbai and Delhi, a clutch of hi-tech Indian companies relocated here, lured by the comparatively cool climate, and an untapped pool of highly skilled, English-speaking labour (a consequence of the Indian government's decision to concentrate its telecommunications and defence research here in the 1960s). Within a decade, Bangalore had become a major player in the software market, and a magnet for multinationals such as Motorola and Texas Instruments (who have their own satellite link with head office in Dallas).

For a while, Bangalore revelled in a spending frenzy that saw its centre sprout gleaming skyscrapers, swish stores and shopping malls. Soon, however, the price of prosperity became apparent. At the height of the boom, millions of immigrants poured in, eager for a slice of the action; it is estimated that in less than five years the population more than doubled to 7.5 million. However, too little municipal money was invested in infrastructure, and today Bangalore is buckling under the weight of numbers, with rocketing levels of traffic pollution. Although power cuts, which became routine in the late Nineties, have been cut back by increasing the output of the city's power grid, the new-found problems have had an adverse effect on business and industry. Some multinationals are now moving out as quickly as they moved in, forcing the city's big-spending expats and computer whizz kids to leave with them. Old Bangaloreans, meanwhile, wonder what became of their beloved "Garden City".

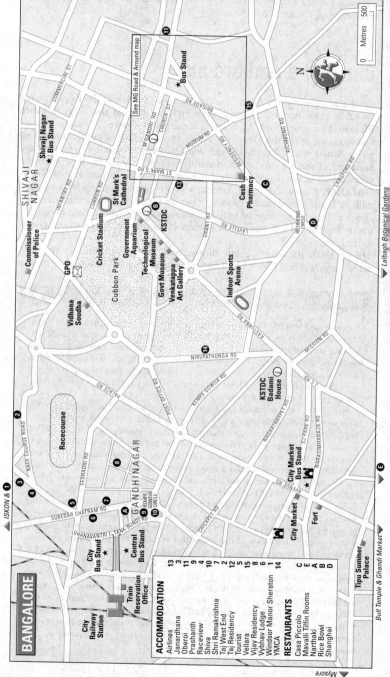

BANGALORE

ACCOMMODATION

Airlines	13
Janardhana	3
Oberoi	11
Prashanth	9
Raceview	4
Shiva	10
Shri Ramakrishna	7
Taj West End	2
Taj Residency	12
Tourist	5
Vellara	15
Vijay Residency	8
Vybhav Lodge	6
Windsor Manor Sheraton	1
YMCA	14

RESTAURANTS

Casa Piccolo	C
Mavalli Tiffin Rooms	E
Narthaki	A
Rice Bowl	B
Shanghai	D

Chennai & Airport (13 km)

& Whitefield Ashram

Metres 500

Bus Stand

Shivaji Nagar Bus Stand

SHIVAJI NAGAR

Commissioner of Police

St Mark's Cathedral

Cricket Stadium

Government Aquarium

KSTDC

Technological Museum

Govt Museum

Venkatappa Art Gallery

Indoor Sports Arena

Cash Pharmacy

Cubbon Park

GPO

Vidhana Soudha

Lalbagh Botanical Gardens

Racecourse

GANDHINAGAR

NIRUPATHUNGA RD

KSTDC Badami House

City Market Bus Stand

City Market

Fort

Tipu Summer Palace

Dhanavantri / Tank Bund Rd

SUBEDAR CHATRAM RD

KEMPE GOWDA CIRCLE

City Bus Stand

Central Bus Stand

Train Reservation Office

City Railway Station

Bull Temple & Ghandi Market

Mysore

ISKON &

stars and VIPs flocked to buy or build dream homes amid this urban idyll, which offered such unique amenities as theatres, cinemas, and a lack of restrictions on alcohol. However, during the last decade or so, Bangalore has undergone a massive transformation. The wide avenues, now dominated by tower blocks, are teeming with traffic, and water and electricity shortages have become the norm. Even the climate has been affected and pollution is a real problem.

Many foreigners turn up in Bangalore without really knowing why they've come. Some pass through on their way to see Satya Sai Baba at his ashram in **Puttaparthy** in Andhra Pradesh, or at his temporary residence at the **Whitefield** ashram on the outskirts of the city. What little there is to see is no match for the attractions elsewhere in the state, and the city's very real advantages for Indians are two-a-penny in the West. That said, Bangalore is a transport hub, especially well served by plane and bus, and there is some novelty in a Westernized Indian city that not only offers good shopping, eating and hotels, but also is the only place on the subcontinent to boast anything resembling a pub culture. The lack of cows in large parts of the city is another indication of its Western orientation. For dusty and weary travellers, Bangalore can offer a few days in a relaxed cosmopolitan city that has a reputation as a safe haven.

Some history

Bangalore began life as the minor "village of the half-baked *gram*"; to this day *gram* (beans) remain an important local product. In 1537, Magadi **Kempe Gowda**, a devout Hindu and feudatory chief of the Vijayanagar empire, built a mud fort and erected four watchtowers outside the village, predicting that it would, one day, extend that far; the city now, of course, stretches way beyond. During the first half of the seventeenth century, Bangalore fell to the Muslim Sultanate of Bijapur; changing hands several times, it returned to Hindu rule under the Mysore Wadiyar rajas of Srirangapatnam. In 1758, Chikka Krishnaraja Wadiyar II was deposed by the military genius Haider Ali, who set up arsenals here to produce muskets, rockets and other weapons for his formidable anti-British campaigns. Both he and his son, **Tipu Sultan**, greatly extended and fortified Bangalore, but Tipu was overthrown by the British in 1799. The British set up a cantonment, which made the city an important military station, and passed the administration over to the Maharaja of Mysore in 1881. After Independence, the erstwhile maharaja became governor of Mysore state. Bangalore was designated capital in 1956, and retained that status when Karnataka state was created in 1973.

Arrival, information and getting around

Recently expanded and revamped to accommodate the increased traffic and planned international flights, **Bangalore airport**, 13km north of the city centre, serves cities throughout south India and beyond; for details of departures, see p.1396. The **KSTDC desk** in the arrivals hall (daily 7.30am–1.30pm & 2–7.30pm; ☏080/526 8012) stocks leaflets on Karnataka and can book hotel rooms. Branches of the State Bank of Mysore (daily 8am–7pm) and Vijaya Bank (daily 8.30am–12.30pm) both **change money**. You can get into the city by **taxi** (Rs150; book at the prepaid desk), by the **auto-rickshaws** (Rs50) that gather outside, or by **bus** – numerous local services run along the main road only several hundred metres from the terminal.

Bangalore City railway station is east of the centre, near Kempe Gowda Circle, and across the road from the main bus stands (for the north of the city, get off at Bangalore Cantonment station). As you come into the entrance hall from the platforms, the far left-hand corner holds an **ITDC booth** (daily 7am–5.30pm; ℡080/220 4277), where you can rent cars and book tours; they will book you a hotel for a fee of ten percent of the day's room rate. The **KSTDC tourist information office** (daily 7am–10pm; ℡080/287 0068), to the right, also books tours and can provide useful advice. You'll find a rank of metered taxis outside or alternatively, prepaid auto-rickshaws charge Rs25–40 to travel to MG Road, depending on the time of day.

Innumerable **long-distance buses** arrive at the big, busy **Central** (KSRTC) **stand**, opposite the railway station. A bridge divides it from **City stand**, used by local services and by long-distance private operators.

Information

For information on Bangalore, Karnataka and neighbouring states, go to the excellent **Government of India tourist office** (Mon–Fri 9.30am–6pm, Sat 9am–1pm; ℡080/558 5417, ⊚goitoblr@satyam.net.in), in the KSFC Building, 48 Church St (parallel to MG Road between Brigade and St Mark's roads). You can pick up a free city map here and the staff will help you put together tour itineraries.

Apart from the desks at the City railway station and airport (see above), **Karnataka State Tourist Development Corporation** has two city offices: one at Badami House, NR Square (℡080/227 5883), where you can book the tours outlined below, and the head office on the second floor of 10/4 Mitra Towers, Kasturba Road, Queen's Circle (Mon–Sat except closed second Sat of month; ℡080/221 2901). For up-to-the-minute information about **what's on**, plus restaurants and shops, check the trendy and ubiquitous free listings paper *Bangalore This Fortnight* and their monthly magazine *Bangalore* that features articles and reviews. The monthly *Bangalore Trail Blazer* is another good source of information, with a directory and a short listings and review section.

If you want to visit any of Karnataka's **national parks**, try the Wildlife Office, Forest Department, Aranya Bhavan, Malleswaram (℡080/334 1993) or, better still, approach the Jungle Lodges & Resorts, Floor 2, Shrungar Shopping Centre, (off) MG Road (℡080/559 7021, ℻558 6163, ⊚jungle@giasbg01 .vsnl.net.in). A quasi-government body, Jungle Lodges promotes "ecotourism" through several upmarket forest lodges including the much lauded *Kabini River Lodge* near Nagarhole. Amongst their other properties are the *Cauvery Fishing*

Tours

KSTDC operates a string of guided **tours** from Bangalore. Though rushed, these can be handy if you're short of time. The twice-daily City Tour (7.30am–1.30pm or 2–7.30pm; Rs75), calls at the museum, Vidhana Soudha, Ulsoor Lake, Lalbagh Gardens, Bull temple and Tipu Sultan's palace and winds up with a long stop at the Government handicrafts emporium. There are other local tours featuring more obscure temples, mainly aimed at devotees, or alternative sights such as the ISKCON temple, planetarium and musical fountain. **"Outstation" tours** include a long day-trip to Srirangapatnam and Mysore (daily 7.15am–11pm; Rs230 or a/c Rs300), and a weekend tour to Hampi (Fri 8pm–Sun 10pm; Rs775). Their day-trip to Belur, Halebid and Sravanabelgola is not recommended unless you're happy to spend more than eight hours on the bus. Other tours on offer include a three-day trip to Jog Falls, five days to Goa, Gokarna and Jog Falls and similar length outings to various Tamil Nadu temple towns.

Camp at Bheemeshwari, the *Biligiri Rangaswamy Camp* at BR Hills, the *Kali Wilderness Camp* at Dandeli, and the *Devbagh Beach Resort* at Karwar. You should book all these through their Bangalore office.

Getting around

The easiest way of getting around Bangalore is by metered **auto-rickshaw**; fares start at Rs9 for the first kilometre and Rs4 per kilometre thereafter. Most meters do work and drivers are usually willing to use them, although you will occasionally be asked for a flat fare, especially during rush hours.

Bangalore's extensive **bus** system, run by the Bangalore Metropolitan Transport Corporation, radiates from the City (Kempe Gowda) bus stand (☏080/222 2542), near the railway station. Most buses from platform 17 travel past MG Road. Along with regular buses, BMTC also operates a deluxe express service, Pushpak, on a number of set routes (#P109 terminates at Whitefield ashram) as well as a handful of night buses. Other important city bus stands include the KR Market bus stand (☏080/670 2177) to the south of the railway station and Shivajinagar (☏080/286 5332) to the north of Cubbon Park – the #P2 Jayanagar service from here is handy for the Lalbagh Botanical Gardens.

You can book **chauffeur-driven cars and taxis** through several agencies including the Cab Service, Sabari Complex, 24 Residency Rd (☏080/558 6121) and the 24hr Dial-a-Car service (☏080/526 1737, ✉dialacar@hotmail.com). Typical rates for car rental are around Rs150 per hour, Rs400 for four hours (which includes 40km) and Rs550 for eight hours (80km); the extra mileage charge is around Rs5 per kilometre. Most taxi companies start calculating their time and distances from when the car leaves their depot. If you need a taxi for a one-way journey, be prepared to pay for the return fare as well. A metered taxi system is planned for the future which will make hiring a cab simpler. See Listings, p.1395, for details of self-drive car rental.

Accommodation

Arrive in Bangalore towards the end of the day, and you'll be lucky to find a room at all, let alone one at the right price, so book at least a couple of days ahead or phone around as soon as you arrive. **Budget accommodation** is concentrated around the railway station (which itself has good-value, but often full, retiring rooms; Rs100–400) and the Central bus stand. Standards in this area can be very low; the better options are on the east side, dotted around Dhanavanthri (Tank Bund) Road and parallel Subedar Chatram Road. **Mid-range** and **expensive hotels** are more scattered; some are around the Racecourse, a short rickshaw trip northeast of the station; of the many near MG Road, the *Victoria* is definitely the most characterful.

Around the railway station and Central bus stand

Prashanth, 21 E Tank Bund Rd ☏080/287 4041. Among the better lodges opposite the Central bus stand. All rooms with windows and shower-toilets. The *Mayura* nearby is the best fall-back. ❹–❺

Shiva, 14 Dhanavantri Rd ☏080/228 1778. The poshest option in the immediate vicinity of the bus stand. Balconies cost extra. ❺–❻

Shri Ramakrishna, Subedar Chatram Road ☏080/226 3041. Modern mega-lodge with 250 simple (en-suite) rooms in a colossal concrete block, set round a courtyard, with a good south Indian restaurant. ❸

Tourist, Ananda Rao Circle ☏080/226 2381. A short walk from the station, one of Bangalore's best all-round budget lodges, with small rooms, long verandas, and friendly family management. No reservations and it fills up quickly. ❷

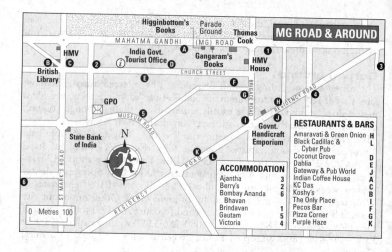

RESTAURANTS & BARS

Amaravati & Green Onion	H
Black Cadillac &	L
Cyber Pub	
Coconut Grove	D
Dahlia	E
Gateway & Pub World	J
Indian Coffee House	A
KC Das	C
Koshy's	B
The Only Place	I
Pecos Bar	F
Pizza Corner	G
Purple Haze	K

ACCOMMODATION

Ajantha	3
Berry's	2
Bombay Ananda	6
Bhavan	
Brindavan	1
Gautam	5
Victoria	4

Vijay Residency, 18 3rd Cross, Main Road ℡080/220 3024. A chain hotel and the most plush and comfortable – if a bit ostentatious. Within striking reach of the railway station, with foreign exchange and restaurant. ❼–❽

Vybhav Lodge, 60 Subedar Chatram Rd ℡080/287 3997. Good clean budget lodge offering small attached rooms with TV, dotted around a little courtyard. Very good value. ❸

Around the Racecourse and Cubbon Park

Janardhana, Kumara Krupa Road ℡080/225 4444, ℻225 8708. Neat, clean and spacious rooms with balconies and baths. Well away from the chaos and good value at this price (despite hefty service charges). ❺

Raceview, 25 Race Course Rd ℡080/220 3401. Run-of-the-mill mid-range hotel whose upper front rooms overlook the racecourse. Safe deposit, foreign exchange and some a/c. ❺–❻

Taj West End, Race Course Road ℡080/225 5055, ℻220 0010, ℮westend. bangalore @tajhotels.com Dating back to 1887 with fabulous gardens and long colonnaded walkways. The most characterful rooms are in the old wing, where deep verandas overlook acres of grounds. ❾

Windsor Manor Sheraton, 25 Sankey Rd ℡080/226 9898, ℻226 4941. Ersatz palace run by Welcomgroup as a luxurious five-star, mainly for businesspeople. Facilities include voice mail, modems, gym, Jacuzzi and pool. ❾

YMCA, Nirupathanga Road, Cubbon Park, midway between the bus stand and MG Road ℡080/221 1848. Large, clean rooms and cheaper dorm beds for men. Rock-bottom rates, but often full. ❷–❹

Around MG Road

Airlines, 4 Madras Bank Rd ℡080/227 3783. Respectable hotel in its own grounds, with lively terrace restaurant. Not particularly good value but usually has availability. A bizarre "amenities" charge is added. Some a/c. ❺–❼

Ajantha, 22-A MG Rd ℡080/558 4321, ℻558 4780. Good value, with larger than average en-suite rooms. Located down a quiet lane but close to shops. Often booked up days in advance. ❹–❻

Berry's, 46 Church St ℡080/558 7211, ℻558 6931. Not the best deal with large but rather tatty rooms. The views are great though and there are nearly always vacancies. ❻

Bombay Ananda Bhavan, 68 Vittal Mallya ℡080/221 4583, ℻227 7705, ℮anandabhavan @satyam.net.in. Family-run, Raj-era mansion in a lovely garden, with large characterful rooms (shutters and stucco ceilings). Recommended, so book well in advance. ❺–❻

Brindavan, 40 MG Rd ℡080/558 4000. Old-style mid-range hotel with some a/c rooms and an excellent south Indian "meals" restaurant. A little dowdy, but still reasonable value for money, especially for singles. ❹–❼

Goutam, 17 Museum Rd ℡080/558 8764. Large, faceless concrete block south of MG Road. The biggest of the "economy" hotels in this area, so more likely than most to have vacancies, the only reason to consider it. Overpriced and the service is poor. ❺

Oberoi, 37–9 MG Rd ℡080/558 5858, ℻558 5960, ℮unitresvn@oberoiblr.com Ultra-luxurious five-star, with a clutch of swish restaurants, beautiful landscaped garden and a pool. ❾

Taj Residency, 41/3 MG Rd ☎080/558 4444, ℻558 4748, ℮residency.bangalore@tajhotels.com Not quite in the same league as the *Oberoi*, but a fully fledged five-star, with all the trimmings. ⑨

Vellara, 283 Brigade Rd, opposite Brigade Towers ☎080/556 9116. Good-value rooms from no-frills "standard", to light and airy "deluxe" on the top floor (with sweeping city views). ④–⑤.

Victoria, 47–8 Residency Rd ☎080/558 4077, ℻558 4945. Set in its own leafy compound in the centre of town, with heaps of old-world style and a popular garden restaurant-cum-bar, serving English brekky. Single rooms are good value, the doubles adequate, while a "deluxe" buys you a veranda. Book well ahead. ⑦

The City

The centre of modern Bangalore lies about 5km east of Kempe Gowda Circle and the bus and railway stations. On **MG Road** you'll find most of the mid-range accommodation, restaurants, shops, tourist information and banks. Leafy **Cubbon Park**, and its less than exciting museums, lie on its eastern edge, while the oldest, most "Indian" part of the city extends south from the railway station, a warren of winding streets at their most dynamic in the hubbub of the **City** and **Gandhi markets**. Bangalore's tourist attractions are spread out: monuments such as **Tipu's Summer Palace** and the **Bull Temple** are some way south of the centre. Most, if not all, can be seen on a half-day tour but if you explore on foot, be warned that Bangalore has some of the worst pavements in India.

Cubbon Park and museums

A welcome green space in the heart of the city, shaded by massive clumps of bamboo, **Cubbon Park** is entered from the western end of MG Road, presided over by a statue of Queen Victoria. On Kasturba Road, which runs along its southern edge, the poorly labelled and maintained **Government Museum** (Tues–Sun 10am–5pm; Rs4) features prehistoric artefacts, Vijayanagar, Hoysala and Chalukya sculpture, musical instruments, Thanjavur paintings and Deccani and Rajasthani miniatures. It includes the adjacent **Venkatappa Art Gallery**, which exhibits twentieth-century landscapes, portraits, abstract art, wood sculpture, and occasional temporary art shows. Next door, the **Technological and Industrial Museum** (daily 10am–6pm; Rs10) is geared towards kids, while further towards the junction with MG Road, the octagonal **Government Aquarium** (Tues–Sun & closed second Tues of month 10am–5.30pm; Rs2) contains a few murky tanks downstairs and some more visible tropical fish upstairs.

Vidhana Soudha

Built in 1956, Bangalore's vast State Secretariat, **Vidhana Soudha**, northwest of Cubbon Park, is the largest civic structure of its kind in the country. K. Hanumanthaiah, chief minister at the time, wanted a "people's palace" that, following the transfer of power from the royal Wadayar dynasty to a legislature, would "reflect the power and dignity of the people". In theory its design is entirely Indian, combining local models from Bangalore, Mysore and Somnathpur with features from Rajasthan and the rest of India, but its overall effect is not unlike the bombastic colonial architecture built in the so-called Indo–Saracenic style.

Lalbagh Botanical Gardens

Inspired by the splendid gardens of the Moghuls and the French botanical gardens at Pondicherry in Tamil Nadu, Sultan Haider Ali set to work in 1760 laying out the **Lalbagh Botanical Gardens** (daily 8am–8pm; Rs2 before 6pm), 4km south of the centre. Originally covering forty acres, just beyond his fort – where one of Kempe Gowda's original watchtowers can still be seen – the gardens were expanded under Ali's son Tipu, who introduced numerous exotic species of plants and today the gardens house an extensive horticultural seedling centre. The British brought in gardeners from Kew in 1856 and – naturally – built a military bandstand and a glasshouse, based on London's Crystal Palace, which hosts wonderful flower shows. Now spreading over 240 acres, the gardens are pleasant to visit during the day, but tend to attract unsavoury characters after 6pm. Great sunsets and views of the city to the north are to be had from the central hill of very old rock, topped by a small shrine.

Tipu's Summer Palace

A two-storey structure built in 1791, mostly of wood, **Tipu's Summer Palace** (daily 9am–5pm; $5 [Rs5]), southwest of the City Market and 3km from MG Road, is similar to the Daria Daulat Palace at Srirangapatnam (see p.1407), but in a far worse state, with most of its painted decoration destroyed. Next door, the **Venkataramanaswamy temple**, dating from the early eighteenth century, was built by the Wadiyar rajas. The *gopura* entranceway was erected in 1978.

Bull Temple

Lying 6km south of the City bus stand (bus #34 & #37), in the Basavanagudi area, Kempe Gowda's sixteenth-century **Bull Temple** (open to non-Hindus; daily 7.30am–1.30pm & 2.30–8.30pm) houses a massive monolithic Nandi bull, its grey granite made black by the application of charcoal and oil. The temple is approached along a path lined with mendicants and snake charmers; inside, for a few rupees, the priest will offer you a string of fragrant jasmine flowers.

ISKCON temple

A hybrid of ultramodern glass and vernacular south Indian temple architecture, ISKCON's (International Society of Krishna Consciousness) gleaming new temple – **Sri Radha Krishna Mandir**, Hare Krishna Hill, Chord Road (daily 7am–1pm & 4–8.30pm), 8km north of the centre, is a fantastic and lavish showpiece crowned by a gold-plated dome. Barriers, designed with huge crowds in mind, guide visitors on a one-way journey through the huge, well-organized complex to the inner sanctum with its images of the god Krishna and his consort Radha. Collection points throughout, and inescapable merchandising on the way out, are evidence of the organization's highly successful commercialization. Regular **buses** to the temple depart from both the City and Shivajinagar bus stands.

Eating

With unmissable sights thin on the ground, but tempting cafés and restaurants on every corner, you could easily spend most of your time in Bangalore **eating**. Nowhere else in south India will you find such gastronomic variety. Around **MG Road**, pizzerias (including *Pizza Hut*), ritzy ice-cream parlours and gourmet French restaurants stand cheek by jowl with regional cuisine from Andhra Pradesh and Kerala, Mumbai *chaat* cafés and snack bars where, in true Bangalorean style, humble thalis from as little as Rs25 masquerade as "executive mini-lunches".

Amaravati, Residency Road Cross, MG Road. Excellent Andhra cooking with "meals" served on banana leafs and specialities including biriyanis and fried fish. Hectic at lunchtime but well worth any wait.

Casa Piccolo, Devata Plaza, 131 Residency Rd. A dozen different tasty pizzas and big portions of *wienerschnitzel*, steaks, fried chicken and ice cream but no alcohol. Tables outside and flower baskets give the place a European ambience. Patronized by the well-heeled, sunglasses-wearing studeny set and travellers.

Coconut Grove, Church Street ☎ 080/558 8596. Mouthwatering and moderately priced gourmet Keralan coastal cuisine: vegetarian, fish and meat preparations served in traditional copper thalis on a leafy terrace; try their tender coconut juice cocktail, *thala chickory bom*. Recommended.

Dahlia, Brigade Gardens, Church Street. Japanese café tucked in a modern business complex, serving authentic dishes from further east at reasonable prices.

Gateway, 66 Residency Rd ☎ 080/558 4545. The *Northern Gate* serves a fairly undistinguished selection of Mughlai and other north Indian dishes, while the *Karavalli* specializes in west coast dishes from Goa to Kerala, including seafood and veg. Very attractive room in traditional southern style with wooden ceiling – plus tables outside under an old tamarind tree. Reservations essential. Expensive.

Green Onion, Next door to the *Amaravati*, this small modern triangular-shaped establishment offers a tasty range of kebabs, curries, Chinese and sweets at fair prices in a café-style atmosphere.

Indian Coffee House, MG Road. The usual cheap south Indian snacks, egg dishes and good filter coffee, served by waiters in turbans and cummerbunds. Best for breakfast.

KC Das, 38 Church St (corner of St Mark's Road). Part of the legendary chain of Bengali sweet shops serving traditional steam-cooked sweets, many soaked in syrup and rosewater. Try their definitive *rasgullas*. Eat in or take away.

Koshy's, St Mark's Road, next to British Library. Spacious old-style café with cane blinds, pewter teapots and cotton-clad waiters. Bangalore's most congenial meeting place. Serves full meals, snacks and alcohol.

Mavalli Tiffin Rooms, Lalbagh Road. Indian fast-food restaurant, serving superb-value set menus (4–8.30pm), and good snacks (including the best *masala dosas* in Bangalore) during the day. Also pure fruit juices and lassis sweetened with honey.

Narthaki, just off Subedar Chatram Road. The best restaurant in the station/bus stand area. Filling Andhra meals are served on the first floor. On the second there is a restaurant-bar with a full menu of Indian and Chinese dishes. The chicken chilli is a belter.

The Only Place, Mota Royal Arcade, Brigade Road. Highly rated Western food, including a near-legendary lasagne, pizzas and great apple pie, at reasonable prices.

Pizza Corner, Brigade Road. Most central location of this bright new chain. Quality pizza with great "lunch munch" specials and unlimited coke refills. Some of the profits go to charity.

Rice Bowl, 40/2 Lavelle Rd. Plush air-conditioned Chinese restaurant, one of the best in town; try their chop suey and, for dessert, the lychees with ice cream.

Shanghai, G3–4 Shiva Shankar Plaza, 19 Lalbagh Rd, Richmond Circle. Among the city's top Chinese restaurants. Excellent bean curd veg soup and Hunan peppered fish, deep-fried with ginger, garlic and spring onions in a black pepper sauce.

Nightlife

The big boom may be over, but Bangalore's bright young things still have money to spend, and **nightlife** in the city is thriving. A night on the town generally kicks off with a bar crawl along **Brigade Road**, **Residency Road** or **Church Street**, where there are scores of swish **pubs**, complete with MTV, lasers and thumping sound systems. But if you persevere, you can get away from the noise and have a quiet drink. Drinking alcohol does not have the seedy connotations here it does elsewhere in India; you'll even see young Indian women enjoying a beer with their mates. There is, however, a ban on alcohol sales between 2.30 and 5.30pm, imposed in 1993 because of the number of schoolkids skipping school to booze. Pubs close at 11pm but once in you generally get served till later. For quiet, elegant drinking head for the bars of five-star **hotels** such as the *Jockey Club* at the *Taj Residency* or its competition, the *Polo Club* at the *Oberoi*, and for a taste of colonial grandeur, the *Colonnade* at the *Taj West End*.

Check the listings magazines to catch Bangalore's small but steady stream of **live music** and **theatre**, some of which is home-grown, and there are a handful of **discos**, which usually follow a couples-only policy.

Bangalore is also a major centre for **cinema**, with a booming industry and dozens of theatres showing the latest releases from India and abroad. Check the listings page of the *Deccan Herald*, the *Evening Herald*, the free listings monthly *Trail Blazer* and *Bangalore This Fortnight*, to find out what's on. Western movies are often dubbed into Hindi, although their titles may be written in English; check the small print in the newspaper. Cinema fans should head for **Kempe Gowda Circle**, which is crammed with posters, hoardings and larger-than-life cardboard cut-outs of the latest stars, strewn with spangly garlands. To arrange a visit to a **movie studio** phone Chamundeshwari Studio (℡080/226 8642) or Shree Kanteera Studio (℡080/337 1008).

Pubs and clubs

B-52, Cha Che Towers, 50 Residency Rd. Thumping high-rise pub with karaoke, disco and pool tables. Booze with a view.

Black Cadillac, 50 Residency Rd. Long-term favourite theme pub with some tables outside that also attract families.

The Club, Mysore Road ℡080/337 1008. The talk of the town, 14km from the centre, and popular with a wealthy young crowd. Features regular discos and the occasional live gig with a few big names passing through. You'll need to take a taxi.

Cyber Pub, above *Black Cadillac*, Residency Road. If you think you can cope with extremely loud music in a hi-tech bar while surfing the web, head up here for a unique experience.

Down Town, next to *Galaxy Cinema*, Residency Road. Large pub that also serves food and wine, and has a couple of pool tables at the back.

Guzzlers Inn, 48 Rest House Rd, off Brigade Road. Popular and established pub offering MTV, Star Sport, snooker, pool and draught beer.

JJ's, MSIL Building, Airport Road Cross ℡080/526 1929. A café which offers a varied evening programme including discos, folk dance and live jazz on Sunday nights led by the musician owner.

Nasa, 1/4 Church St. Karaoke and sci-fi decor with lasers in a mock space shuttle. The usual combination of big-screen MTV and in-your-face music.

Oasis, Church Street. Low light and unobtrusive sound system: the chill-out option.

Pecos, Rest House Road, off Brigade Road. Small and relaxed pub on two floors with Sixties and Seventies music; popular with a mixed arty set.

A Pinch of Jazz, The Central Park, 47 Dickenson Rd ℡080/558 4242. Upmarket jazz café serving Cajun cuisine and live soft-jazz covers.

Pub World, opposite *Galaxy Cinema*, Residency Road. A well-presented newish place popular with trendy young professionals. Actually four pubs from different regions under one roof. The usual high-volume music.

Purple Haze, opposite *Black Cadillac*, Residency Road. Still one of the trendiest of the downtown pubs with a smart but jumping upstairs bar sporting Jimi Hendrix-themed graphics. More chance of decent rock here than most places.

Shopping

Bangalore has many fine shops, particularly if you're after **silk**. A wide range of silk is available at Karnataka Silk Industries Corporation and Vijayalakshmi Silk Kendra, both on Gupte Market, Kempe Gowda Road, and at Deepam Silk Emporium on MG Road. **Handicrafts** such as soapstone sculpture, brass, carved sandalwood and rosewood are also good value; emporia include Central Cottage Industries Emporium, 144 MG Rd; the expensive Cottage Industries Exposition Ltd, 3 Cunningham Rd; Gulshan Crafts, 12 Safina Plaza, Infantry Road; and Karnataka's own state emporium, Cauvery at the MG Road and Brigade Road crossing. For **silver**, try looking on and around Commercial Street (north of MG Road) and at KR Market on Residency Road. At Jewels de Paragon between MG Road and Kasturba Road there is a dazzling array of **gold** items at "Mumbai prices". At 64 MG Rd, the renowned Natesan's Antiqarts sells antiques and beautifully made reproduction sculpture, furniture and paintings, at international art house prices. If you want to take a look at expensive Indian *haute couture* try Ffolio at Embassy Chamber, Vittal Mallya Road, which features several well-known Indian designers.

Bangalore is also a great place for **bookshops**. The first floor of Gangarams, 72 MG Rd, offers a wide selection on India (coffee-table art books and academic) plus the latest paperback fiction, and a great selection of Indian greetings cards. Higginbotham's, 68 MG Rd, is also good, while you can browse amongst a wide range of subjects in air-conditioned comfort at LB Publishers, 91 MG Rd. Premier, 46/1 Church St, around the corner from the ITDC office, crams a huge number of books into a tiny space. The shop belonging to renowned publishers Motilal Banarsidas, 16 St Mark's Rd, close to the junction with MG Road, offers a superb selection of heavyweight Indology and philosophy titles. Sankars at 15/2 Madras Bank Rd is an airy new shop with a good range of fiction, art, education and religion titles. The best **music** shops in the city centre, selling Indian and Western tapes, are HMV, on Brigade Road or St Mark's Road where you can pick up an excellent four-cassette pack introducing south Indian or Carnatic music, and Rhythms, at 14 St Mark's Rd, beneath the *Nahar Heritage* hotel.

Listings

Airlines domestic: Indian Airlines, Cauvery Bhavan, Kempe Gowda Road ☏080/221 1914, airport 526 6233; Jet Airways, 1-4 M Block, Unity Building, JC Road ☏080/227 6620, airport 526 6898; Sahara Airlines, 35 Church St ☏080/558 4457, airport 526 2531.

Airlines international: Air Canada, Sunrise Chambers, 22 Ulsoor Rd ☏080/558 5394; Air France, Sunrise Chambers, 22 Ulsoor Rd ☏080/558 9397;
Air India, Unity Building, JC Road ☏080/227 7747; Alitalia, 44 Safina Plaza, Infantry Road ☏080/559 1936; American Airlines, Sunrise Chambers, 22 Ulsoor Rd ☏080/559 4240; British Airways, 7 St Mark's Rd ☏080/227 1205; Delta/Sabena/Swiss Air/Singapore Airlines, Park View, 17 Curve Rd, Tasker Town ☏080/286 7868; Gulf Air, Sunrise Chambers, 22 Ulsoor Rd ☏080/558 4702; KLM, *Taj West End*, Race Course Road ☏080/226 8703; Lufthansa, 44/2 Dickenson Rd ☏080/558 8791; Malaysian Airlines, Richmond Circle ☏080/221 3030; Pakistan International Airlines, 108 Commerce House, 911 Cunningham Rd ☏080/226 0667; Qantas, Westminster, Cunningham Road ☏080/226 4719; Royal Brunei, Stic Travels, Imperial Court, Cunningham Road ☏080/226 7613; Thai Airlines, G-5 Imperial Court, Cunningham Road ☏080/225 6194; United Airlines, Richmond Towers, 12 Richmond Rd ☏080/224 4625.

Banks and exchange A reliable place to change money is Thomas Cook, 55 MG Rd, on the corner of Brigade Road, though if it's busy Weizmann Forex Ltd, 56 Residency Rd, near the other end of Brigade Road, is just as efficient and quieter (both Mon–Sat 9.30am–6pm); the slower State Bank of India is at 87 MG Rd (Mon–Fri 10.30am–2.30pm & Sat 10.30am–12.30pm). ANZ Grindlays at Raheja Towers on MG Road (same hours) changes money and advances cash on credit cards or alternatively, try the fast and efficient Wall Street Finances, 3 House of Lords, 13/14 St Mark's Rd (Mon–Sat 9.30am–6pm; ☏080/227 1812). Also for Visa and Mastercard advances – but not travellers' cheques – go to Bank of Baroda, 70 MG Rd (same hours as banks above).

Car rental You can find self-drive car rental at Avis, *The Oberoi*, 37–39 MG Rd ☏080/558 3503, ℮crs@avisdel.com; Europcar, Sheriff House, 85 Richmond Rd; ☏080/221 9502, ℮299 0453; and Hertz, 167 Richmond Rd, near Trinity Circle ☏080/559 9408. Charges are from Rs900 per day. For long-distance car rental and tailor-made itineraries, try Gullivers Tours & Travels, South Black 201/202 Manipal Centre, 47 Dickenson Rd ☏080/558 8001; Clipper Holidays, 406 Regency Enclave, 4 Magrath Rd ☏080/559 9032; any KSTDC office; and the ITDC booth at the railway station.

Hospitals Victoria, near City Market ☏080/670 1150; Sindhi Charitable, 3rd Main St, S R Nagar ☏080/223 7318.

Internet access At the last count Bangalore had a staggering 700 email/internet bureaus – most charge Rs20–30 per hour and offer half-hour or shorter slots. The Cyber Café, 13–15 Brigade Rd (☏080/550 0949) is the most obvious and the most popular; you'll need to get a ticket at the

Bangalore is south India's principal transport hub. Fast and efficient computerized booking facilities make moving on relatively hassle-free, although availability of seats should never be taken for granted; book as far in advance as possible. For an overview of travel services to and from Bangalore, see Travel Details on p.1468.

Bangalore's recently upgraded airport is the busiest in south India, with international and domestic departures and plans for more. The most frequent flights are to Mumbai, operated by Air India, Jet Airways, Indian Airlines and Sahara Indian, and there are also seven daily flights to Delhi. Jet Airways and Indian Airlines operate several flights a day to Chennai and at least one daily flight each to Calcutta, Goa, Cochin, Hyderabad and Pune. There is also one daily flight to Mangalore (Jet) and Trivandrum (IA). Finally, Indian Airlines has several weekly international flights to destinations in Southeast Asia and the Gulf States, while Air India operates a route to New York via London on most days.

Most of the wide range of long-haul buses from the Central stand can be booked in advance at the computerized counters near Bay 13 (7.30am–7.30pm). Aside from KSRTC, state bus corporations represented include Andhra Pradesh, Kerala, Maharashtra, Tamil Nadu and the Kadamba Transport Corporation, a Government of Goa undertaking. Timings and ticket availability for the forthcoming week are posted on a large board left of the main entrance. For general enquiries, call ⊕080/287 3377. Several private bus companies run luxury coaches to destinations such as Mysore, Bijapur, Ooty, Chennai, Kochi/Ernakulam, Trichur, Kollam and Trivandrum. Agencies opposite the bus stand sell tickets for private coach companies such as Sharma (c/o MM Travels, ⊕080/209 4099), National (⊕080/225 7202) and Shama, which advertise overnight deluxe buses to Goa (Rs250) as well as sleeper coaches (Rs400) and services to Mumbai for Rs350–450. The most reliable of the private bus companies is Vijayananda Travels at Sri Saraswathi Lodge, 3rd Main 2nd Cross, Gandhinagar (⊕080/228 7222) with several other branches in Bangalore, who operate their distinctive yellow-and-black luxury coaches to destinations such as Mangalore and Hospet for Hampi.

While Southern Railways convert to broad gauge, some rail routes in Karnataka continue to suffer disruption especially along the route from Hassan to Mangalore.

door to book your slot on the machines and there is coffee, but they don't encourage more than one person per computer. Alternatives include Cyber Inn, Residency Road and Brigade Road Cross ⊕080/559 9962; Cyber Craft, 33 Rest House Rd ⊕080/558 8341; and Cyber Den, first floor, S112A Manipal Centre, Dickenson Road ⊕080/558 6671. Take2Net, Brigade Gardens, Church Street has Rs10 per hour rates before 11am and after 9pm.
Libraries The British Council (English-language) library, 39 St Mark's Rd (Tues–Sat 10.30am–6.30pm; ⊕080/221 3485), has newspapers and magazines that visitors are welcome to peruse in a/c comfort, as does the Alliance Française (French), 16 GMT Rd (⊕080/225 8762), and Max Mueller Bhavan (German), 3 Lavelle Rd (⊕080/227 5435).
Pharmacies Open all night: Al-Siddique Pharma Centre, opposite Jama Masjid near City Market; Janata Bazaar, in the Victoria Hospital, near City Market; Sindhi Charitable Hospital, 3rd Main S R

Nagar. During the day, head for Santoshi Pharma, 46 Mission Rd.
Photographic equipment Adlabs, Mission Road, Subbaiah Circle, stocks transparency film. GG Welling, 113 MG Rd and GK Vale, 89 MG Rd sell transparency and Polaroid film.
Police ⊕100.
Post office on the corner of Raj Bhavan Road and Cubbon Street, at the northern tip of Cubbon Park, about ten minutes' walk from MG Road (Mon–Sat 10am–7pm, Sun 10.30am–1.30pm).
Swimming pools Five-star hotel pools open to nonresidents include the *Taj Residency* (Rs500 includes sauna, Jacuzzi and health club) and *Taj West End* (Rs500).
Travel agents For flight booking and reconfirmation and other travel necessities, try Gullivers Tours & Travels, South Black 201/202 Manipal Centre, 47 Dickenson Rd ⊕080/558 8001; Merry Go Round Tours, 41 Museum Rd, opposite *Berry's Hotel* ⊕ & ⊕080/558 6946; Marco Polo Tours, Janardhan

Check the situation when you arrive. Bangalore City station's reservations office (Mon–Sat 8am–2pm & 2.15–8pm, Sun 8am–2pm; reservations ☏132) is in a separate building, east of the main station (to the left as you approach). Counter 14 is for foreigners. If you have an Indrail Pass, go to the Chief Reservations Supervisor's Office on the first floor (turn left at the top of the stairs), where "reservations are guaranteed". If your reservation is "waitlisted", or you are required to confirm the booking, you may have to go on the day of departure to the Commercial Officer's office, in the Divisional Office – yet another building, this time to the west, accessible from the main road. There are two 24hr telephone information lines; one handles timetable enquiries (☏131), the other reels off a recorded list of arrivals and departures (☏133).

Recommended trains from Bangalore
The following trains are recommended as the fastest and/or most convenient from Bangalore:

Destination	Name	No.	Departs	Total time
Delhi	Rajdhani Express*	#2429	4 weekly 6.35pm	34hr 30min
	Karnataka Express	#2627	daily 6.25pm	41hr 40min
Chennai	Shatabdi Express*	#2008	daily except Tues 4.25pm	5hr
	Lalbagh Express	#2608	daily 6.30am	5hr 25min
Hospet (for Hampi)	Hampi Express	#6592	daily 10pm	9hr 50min
Hyderabad	Rajdhani Express*	#2429	4 weekly 6.35pm	11hr 55min
(Secunderabad)	Secunderabad Express	#7086	daily 5.05pm	13hr 25min
Kochi (Ernakulam)	Kanniyakumari Express	#6526	daily 9pm	12hr 50min
Mumbai	Udyan Express	#6530	daily 8.30am	23hr 55min
Mysore	Shatabdi Express*	#2007	daily except Tues 11am	2hr
	Chennai–Mysore Express	#6222	daily 7.10am	2hr 50min
	Tipu Express	#6206	daily 2.15pm	2hr 30min
	Chamundi Express	#6216	daily 6.15pm	2hr 55min
Trivandrum	Kanniyakumari Express	#6526	daily 9pm	16hr 10min

*= a/c only

Towers, 2 Residency Rd ☏080/227 4484, ☞223 6671; and Sita Travels, 1 St Mark's Rd ☏080/558 8892.

Visa extensions Commissioner of Police, Infantry Road (Mon–Sat 10am–5.30pm; ☏080/225 6242).

Around Bangalore

Many visitors to Bangalore are on their way to or from Mysore. The **Janapada Loka Folk Arts Museum**, between the two, gives a fascinating insight into Karnataka culture, while anyone wishing to see or study classical dance in a rural environment should check out **Nrityagram Dance Village**.

Janapada Loka Folk Arts Museum
The **Janapada Loka Folk Arts Museum** (daily 9am–6pm; free), 53km southwest of Bangalore on the Mysore road, includes an amazing array of Karnatakan agricultural, hunting and fishing implements, weapons, ingenious household gadgets, masks, dolls and shadow puppets, carved wooden *bhuta* (spirit-worship) sculptures and larger-than-life temple procession figures, manuscripts, musical instruments and *Yakshagana* theatre costumes. In addition, 1600 hours of **audio and video recordings** of musicians, dancers and rituals from the state are available on request.

To get to the museum, take one of the many slow Mysore buses (not the nonstop ones) from Bangalore. After the town of Ramanagar, alight at the 53-kilometre stone by the side of the road. A small **restaurant** serves simple food, and dorm **accommodation** (❶) is available. For more details contact the Karnataka Janapada Trust, 7 Subramanyaswami Temple Rd, 5th Cross, 4th Block, Kumara Park West, Bangalore.

Nrityagram Dance Village

NRITYAGRAM DANCE VILLAGE is a delightful, purpose-built model village, 30km west of Bangalore, designed by the award-winning architect Gerard de Cunha and founded by the late Protima Gauri, who tragically died in an avalanche during a pilgrimage to Kailash in Tibet in 1998. Gauri, who had left Nrityagram sometime before her death, had a colourful career in media and film, and eventually came to be renowned as an exponent of Odissi dance (see p.1121). The school continues without her and attracts pupils from all over the world. It hosts regular performances and lectures on Indian mythology and art, and also offers courses in different forms of Indian dance. **Guided tours** of the complex cost Rs250 (Tues–Sun 10am–5pm). **Accommodation** for longer stays (❼) promises "oxygen, home-grown vegetables and fruits, no TV, telephones, newspapers or noise". Contact their Bangalore office (℡080/846 6313, ⊛www.allindia.com/nritya).

Mysore

A centre of sandalwood-carving, silk and incense production, 159km southwest of Bangalore, **MYSORE**, the erstwhile capital of the Wadiyar rajas, is one of south India's most popular attractions. Considering the clichés that have been heaped upon the place, however, first impressions can be disappointing. Like anywhere else, you are not so much greeted by the scent of jasmine blossom or gentle wafts of sandalwood when you stumble off the bus or train, as by a cacophony of careering auto-rickshaws and noisy buses, bullock carts and tongas. Nevertheless, Mysore is certainly a charming, old-fashioned and undaunting town, dominated by the spectacular **Maharaja's Palace**, around which the boulevards of the city radiate. Nearby, the city centre with the colourful and frenetic **Devaraja Market** is an inviting stroll. On the outskirts of Mysore, Srirangapatnam still harbours architectural gems from the days of the great Indian hero, Tipu Sultan, and the magnificent Hoysala temple of Somnathpur lies little more than an hour's drive away.

In the tenth century Mysore was known as "Mahishur" – "the town where the demon buffalo was slain" (by the goddess Durga). Presiding over a district of many villages, the city was ruled from about 1400 until Independence by the Hindu **Wadiyars**, its fortunes inextricably linked with those of Srirangapatnam (see p.1406), which became headquarters from 1610. Their rule was only broken from 1761, when the Muslim Haider Ali and son Tipu Sultan took over. Two years later, the new rulers demolished the labyrinthine old city to replace it with the elegant grid of sweeping, leafy streets and public gardens that survive today. However, following Tipu Sultan's defeat in 1799 by the British colonel, Arthur Wellesley (later the Duke of Wellington), Wadiyar power was restored. As the capital of Mysore state, the city thereafter dominated a major part of southern India. In 1956, when Bangalore became capital of newly formed Karnataka, its maharaja was appointed governor.

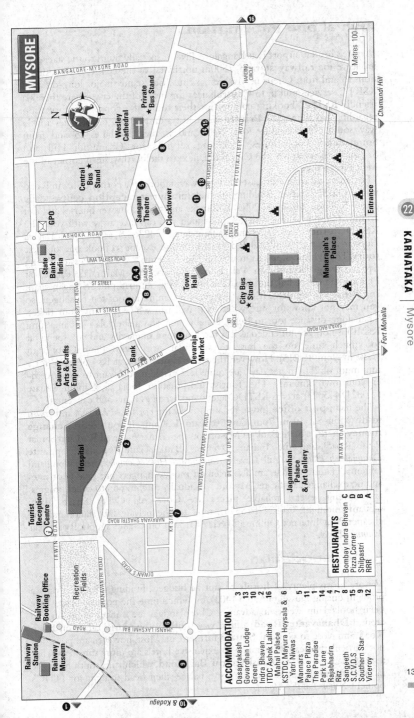

MYSORE

N

0   Metres   100

BANGALORE-MYSORE ROAD

Wesley Cathedral

Private Bus Stand ★

Central Bus Stand ★

Sangam Theatre

GPO

ASHOKA ROAD

State Bank of India

UMA TALKIES ROAD

ST STREET

KH HOSPITAL ROAD

KT STREET

Cauvery Arts & Crafts Emporium

Bank

SAYAJI RAO ROAD

Devaraja Market

Gandhi Square

Town Hall

Clocktower

HARDING CIRCLE

Chamundi Hill

VICTORIA-ALBERT ROAD

SRI HARSHA ROAD

NEW STATUE CIRCLE

Maharajah's Palace

Entrance

City Bus Stand ★

KR CIRCLE

SAYAJI RAO ROAD

Fort Mohalla

DHANAVANTHRI ROAD

Hospital

VINIBAHA (SYARAMPETT ROAD)

DEVARAJ URS ROAD

RAMA ROAD

Jaganmohan Palace & Art Gallery

NARAYANA SHASTRI ROAD

DIWAN'S ROAD

KH STREET

Tourist Reception Centre

IRWIN ROAD

Recreation Fields

DHANAVANTHRI ROAD

JHANSI LAKSHMI BAI ROAD

Railway Station

Railway Booking Office

Railway Museum

Kodagu

ACCOMMODATION

Dasaprakash	3
Govardhan Lodge	13
Green	10
Indra Bhavan	2
ITDC Ashok Lalitha	16
Mahal Palace	
KSTDC Mayura Hoysala &	6
Yatri Niwas	
Mannars	5
Palace Plaza	11
The Paradise	14
Park Lane	4
Rajabhadra	7
Ritz	8
Sangeeth	15
S.C.V.D.S	9
Southern Star	
Viceroy	12

RESTAURANTS

Bombay Indra Bhavan	C
Pizza Corner	D
Shilpastri	B
RRR	A

Arrival and information

Mysore's nearest airport is at Bangalore. Five or six daily trains to the state capital leave the **railway station**, 1500m northwest of the centre, with connections to and from Chennai. Mysore has three **bus** stands: major long-distance KSRTC services pull in to **Central**, near the heart of the city, where there's a friendly KSTDC booking counter for their tours, also good for information regarding bus times. The **Private** stand, just a dusty patch of road, lies a little way south, opposite the *Ritz Hotel*, and is used by buses to and from Somnathpur. Local buses, including services for Chamundi Hill and Srirangapatnam, stop at the **City** stand, next to the northwestern corner of the Maharaja's Palace.

Five minutes' walk southeast of the railway station, on a corner of Irwin Road in the Old Exhibition Building, the helpful **tourist reception centre** (daily 10am–5.30pm; ℡0821/422096) will make an effort to answer queries and can arrange transport, though there's not much you can take away with you. The **KSTDC office** (daily 7.30am–8.30pm; ℡0821/423652), at the hotel *Mayura Hoysala*, 2 Jhansi Laxmi Bai Rd, is of little use except to book one of their **tours**. The whistle-stop city tour (7.30am–8.30pm; Rs115) makes for a long day, covering Jaganmohan Palace Art Gallery, the Maharaja's Palace, St Philomena's Cathedral, the Zoo, Chamundi Hill, Somnathpur, Srirangapatnam and Brindavan Gardens. It only leaves with a minimum of ten passengers, so you may not know for sure whether it will run when you buy your ticket. Their long-distance tour to Belur, Halebid and Sravanabelgola (7.30am–9pm; Rs210) is not recommended as it is too long for a single day and you spend far too much time on the bus; it's a similar story with their Ooty tour (7.30am–9pm; Rs215). However, their **car rental** rates, at Rs4 per km (for a minimum of 250km per day), are quite reasonable if you want to put together your own itinerary. The Tourist Corporation India at Gandhi Square (℡0821/443023) acts as KSTDC agent and arranges tours and car rental.

The main **post office** (poste restante) is on the corner of Ashoka and Irwin roads (Mon–Sat 10am–7pm, Sun 10.30am–1.30pm). If you need to **change money**, there's a State Bank of Mysore on the corner of Sayaji Rao and Sardar Patel Road, and the Indian Overseas Bank, Gandhi Square, opposite *Dasaprakash Hotel*. Seagull Travels, *Ramanashri Hotel Complex*, near Woodland Cinema, Harding Circle are also licensed moneychangers but give poor rates and no exchange certificates. Mysore is gradually catching on to cyber progress and among several reliable places are Coca-cola Cyber Space (daily 6.30am–midnight; ℡0821/515574), next to the private bus stand, and the cheaper 24hr Internet Online (℡0821/421536) on Chandragupta Road near *Mannars Hotel*.

Accommodation

Mysore boasts plenty of **hotels** to suit all budgets. Finding a room is only a problem during Dussehra (see p.1403), by which time the popular places have been booked up weeks in advance. Cheap lodges are concentrated on and around **Dhanavantri Road**, a little way south of the tourist office on Irwin Road, and close to **Gandhi Square** further east. Most, however, are poky and not particularly clean. Mid-range to expensive hotels are more spread out, but a good place to start is **Jhansi Laxmi Bai Road**, which runs south from the railway station. If you're looking for a palace, then head straight for ITDC's opulent *Ashok Lalitha Mahal*.

Inexpensive

Govardhan, opposite the Opera cinema, Sri Harsha Road ☎0821/434118, ☏420998. Basic budget rooms close to Gandhi Square. Frayed around the edges, but clean enough. ②–③

Indra Bhavan, Dhanavantri Road ☎0821/423933, ☏422290, ✉hotel_Indra_bhavan@rediffmail.com Dilapidated and characterful old lodge popular with Tibetans, with en-suite singles and doubles. Their "ordinary" rooms are a little grubby, but the good-value "deluxe" have clean tiled floors and open onto a wide common veranda. ②–④

KSTDC Yatri Niwas, 2 Jhansi Laxmi Bai Rd ☎0821/423492. The government-run *Mayura Hoysala*'s economy wing: simple rooms around a central garden, with beer garden and terrace restaurant next door, and dorm beds for Rs70. ①–③

Mannars, Chandragupta Road ☎0821/448060. Budget hotel near the bus stand and Gandhi Square. No frills, though deluxe rooms have TV. Deservedly popular with backpackers. ②–③

Park Lane, Sri Harsha Road ☎0821/434340. Eight pleasant clean rooms backing onto a popular beer-garden/restaurant. One of the best deals at this price, but can get noisy and has some dodgy plumbing. Avoid room 8 (it's next to the generator). ②

Rajabhadra, Gandhi Square ☎0821/443023. Best value of several look-a-like lodges on the square. The front rooms are great if you don't mind being in the thick of things. Some singles. ②

Ritz, Bangalore–Nilgiri Road ☎0821/422668. Wonderful colonial-era hotel, a stone's throw from the Private bus stand. Only four rooms, so book ahead. ④

Sangeeth, 1966 Narayana Shastry Rd, near the Udipi Krishna temple ☎0821/424693. One of Mysore's best all-round budget deals: bland and a bit boxed in, but central, friendly and very good value. ②–③

Moderate to expensive

Dasaprakash, Gandhi Square ☎0821/442444, ☏443456. Slightly faded large hotel complex round a spacious courtyard: busy, clean and efficient, though lacking character. Some a/c rooms, cheap singles and a veg restaurant. ③–⑥

Green, Chittaranjan Palace, 2270 Vinoba Rd, Jayalakshmipuram ☎0821/512536, ☏516139. On the western outskirts, a former royal palace refurbished as an elegant, eco-conscious two-star, in large gardens, awarded the prize for best garden in Mysore in 1998. Spacious rooms, lounges, verandas, a croquet lawn and well-stocked library. All profits go to charities and environmental projects. Their auto-rickshaw will pick you up with prior arrangement and they can also be contacted through the Charities Advisory Trust in London ☎020/7431 3739. ⑥–⑧

ITDC Ashok Lalitha Mahal Palace, T Narasipur Road ☎0821/571265, ☏571770. On a slope overlooking the city in the distance, and visible for miles around, this white, Neoclassical palace was built in 1931 to accommodate the maharaja's foreign guests. Now it's a Raj-style fantasy, popular with tour groups and film crews. Tariffs are astronomical by Indian standards, ranging from $70 to $740 per night for the "Viceroy Suite". The tea lounge, restaurant and pool (Rs130) are open to nonresidents. Free snooker table in bar. ⑨

KSTDC Mayura Hoysala, 2 Jhansi Laxmi Bai Rd ☎0821/425349. Reasonably priced rooms and suites in a colonial-era mansion. Terrace restaurant and beer garden. Good value but the food is uninspiring and there is no room service. ④–⑥

Palace Plaza, Sri Harsha Road ☎0821/430034, ☏421070. A modern multistorey block close to all amenities where the cheaper rooms are poky but reasonable value. There are also a few a/c deluxes with extraordinary round beds and mirrored ceilings – no doubt meant for honeymooners. The restaurant is good. ④–⑥

The Paradise, 104 Vivekananda Rd, Yadavgiri ☎0821/410366, ☏514400, ✉paradise@blr.vsnl.net.in. *Dasaprakash*'s upmarket hotel; new and modern with luxurious rooms and all facilities including an excellent south Indian vegetarian restaurant. ⑥–⑧

S.C.V.D.S., Sri Harsha Road ☎0821/421379, ☏426297. Spanking new lodge with cable TV in most rooms and some a/c. Very friendly and offers Rs50 discount to foreigners. ③–⑥

Southern Star, Vinobha Road ☎0821/426426, ☏421689, ✉southernstar@vsnl.com. Modern and comfortable monolithic hotel, affiliated to *Quality Inn*, with all facilities including two restaurants, a bar and a swimming pool. ⑨

Viceroy, Sri Harsha Road ☎0821/428001, ☏433391. Snazzy new business-oriented hotel, with most mod cons and views over the park to the palace from front rooms. Mostly a/c. Quality restaurant on ground floor. ⑥–⑧

The City

In addition to its official tourist attractions, Mysore is a great city simply to stroll around. The characterful, if dilapidated, pre-Independence buildings lining market areas such as **Ashok Road** and **Sayaji Rao Road** lend an air of faded grandeur to the busy centre, teeming with vibrant street life. Souvenir stores spill over with the famous **sandalwood**; the best place to get a sense of what's on offer is the Government Cauvery Arts and Crafts Emporium on Sayaji Rao Road (closed Thurs), which stocks a wide range of local crafts that can be shipped overseas. The city's famous **Devaraja Market** on Sayaji Rao Road is one of south India's most atmospheric produce markets: a giant complex of covered stalls groaning with bananas (the delicious *nanjangod* variety), luscious mangoes, blocks of sticky *jaggery*, and conical heaps of lurid *kunkum* powder.

Maharaja's Palace

Mysore centre is dominated by the walled **Maharaja's Palace** (daily 10.30am–5.30pm; Rs10), a fairytale spectacle topped with a shining brass-plated dome surmounting a single tower. It's especially magnificent on Sunday nights and during festivals, illuminated by no less than 5000 lightbulbs. Designed in the hybrid "Indo-Saracenic" style by Henry Irwin, the British consultant architect of Madras state, it was completed in 1912 for the twenty-fourth Wadiyar raja, on the site of the old wooden palace that had been destroyed by fire in 1897. After a lengthy judicial tussle, in 1998 the courts decided in favour of formally placing the main palace in the hands of the Karnataka state government but the royal family, who still hold a claim, are set to appeal. Twelve temples surround the palace, some of them of much earlier origin. Although there are six gates in the perimeter wall, entrance is on the south side only. Shoes and cameras must be left at the cloakroom inside.

An extraordinary amalgam of styles from India and around the world crowds the lavish **interior**. Entry is through the Gombe Thotti or **Dolls' Pavilion**, once a showcase for the figures featured in the city's lively Dussehra celebrations and now a gallery of European and Indian sculpture and ceremonial objects. Halfway along, the brass **Elephant Gate** forms the main entrance to the centre of the palace, through which the maharaja would drive to his car park. Decorated with floriate designs, it bears the Mysore royal symbol of a double-headed eagle, now the state emblem. To the north, past the gate, are dolls dating from the turn of the twentieth century, a wooden *mandapa* glinting with mirror-work, and at the end, a ceremonial wooden elephant *howdah* (frame to carry passengers). Elaborately decorated with 84kg of 24-carat gold, it appears to be inlaid with red and green gems – in fact the twinkling lights are battery-powered signals that let the *mahout* know when the maharaja wished to stop or go.

Walls leading into the octagonal **Kalyana Mandapa**, the royal wedding hall, are lined with a meticulously detailed frieze of oil paintings illustrating the great Mysore Dussehra festival of 1930, executed over a period of fifteen years by four Indian artists. The hall itself is magnificent, a cavernous space featuring cast-iron pillars from Glasgow, Bohemian chandeliers, and multicoloured Belgian stained glass arranged in peacock designs in the domed ceiling. A mosaic of English floor-tiles repeats the peacock motif. Beyond here lie small rooms cluttered with grandiose furniture, including a pair of silver chairs and others of Belgian cut-crystal made for the maharaja and Lord Mountbatten, the last viceroy of India. One of the rooms has a fine ceiling of Burma teak carved by local craftsmen.

Climbing a staircase with Italian marble balustrades, past an unnervingly realistic life-size plaster of Paris figure of Krishnaraja Wadiyar IV, lounging comfortably with his bejewelled feet on a stool, you come into the **Public Durbar Hall**, an orientalist fantasy often compared to a setting from *A Thousand and*

Mysore Dussehra festival

Following the tradition set by the Vijayanagar kings, the ten-day festival of **Dussehra** (Sept/Oct), to commemorate the goddess Durga's slaying of the demon buffalo, Mahishasura (see p.67), is celebrated in grand style at Mysore. Scores of cultural events include concerts of south Indian classical (Carnatic) music and dance performances in the great Durbar Hall of the **Maharaja's Palace**. On Vijayadasmi, the tenth and last day of the festival, a magnificent procession of mounted guardsmen on horseback and caparisoned elephants – one carrying the palace deity, Chaamundeshwari, on a gold *howdah* – marches 5km from the palace to Banni Mantap. There's also a floating festival in the temple tank at the foot of **Chamundi Hill**, and a procession of chariots around the temple at the top. A torchlit parade takes place in the evening, followed by a massive firework display and much jubilation on the streets.

One Nights. A vision of brightly painted and gilded colonnades, open on one side, the massive hall affords views out across the parade ground and gardens to Chamundi Hill. The maharaja gave audience from here, seated on a throne made from 280kg of solid Karnatakan gold. These days, the hall is only used during the Dussehra festival, when it hosts classical concerts. Paintings by the celebrated artists Shilpi Siddalingaswamy and Raja Rama Varma, from the Travancore (Kerala) royal family, adorn the walls. The whole is crowned by white marble, inlaid with delicate floral scrolls of jasper, amber and lapis lazuli in the Moghul style. Somewhat out of sync with the opulence, a series of ceiling panels of Vishnu, painted on fireproof asbestos, date from the 1930s. The smaller **Private Durbar Hall** features especially beautiful stained glass and gold-leaf painting. Before leaving you pass two embossed silver doors – all that remains of the old palace.

Nearby, behind the main palace building but within the same compound, a line of tacky souvenir shops leads to a small **museum** run by the royal family which shows paintings from the Thanjavur and Mysore schools, some inlaid with precious stones and gold leaf.

Jaganmohan Palace: Jayachamarajendra Art Gallery

Built in 1861, the **Jaganmohan Palace** (daily 8am–5pm; Rs5; no cameras), 300m west of the Maharaja's Palace, was used as a royal residence until it was turned into a picture gallery and museum in 1915 by Maharaja Krishnaraja Wadiyar IV. Most of the "contemporary" art on show dates from the 1930s, when a revival of Indian painting was spearheaded by E.B. Havell and the Tagore brothers Abandrinath and Ganganendranath in Bengal.

On the ground floor, a series of faded black-and-white photos of ceremonial occasions shares space with elaborate imported clocks. Nineteenth- and twentieth-century paintings dominate the first floor; amongst them the work of the pioneering oil painter Raja Ravi Varma who, although not everyone's cup of tea, has been credited for introducing modern techniques to Indian art. Inspired by European masters, Varma gained a reputation in portraiture and also depicted epic Indian themes from the classics, such as the demon king Ravana absconding with Rama's wife Sita. Games on the upper floor include circular *ganjeeb* playing cards illustrated with portraits of royalty or deities, and board games delicately inlaid with ivory. There's also a cluster of musical instruments, among them a brass *jaltarang* set and glass xylophone, harmonicas and clarinet played by Krishnaraja Wadiyar IV himself. Another gallery, centring on a large wooden Ganesh seated on a tortoise, is lined with paintings, including Krishnaraja Wadiyar sporting with the "inmates" of his *zenana* (women's quarter of the palace) during Holi.

Chamundi Hill

Chamundi Hill, 3km southeast of the city, is topped with a temple to the chosen deity of the Mysore rajas; the goddess Chamundi, or Durga, who slew the demon buffalo Mahishasura (see p.67). It's a pleasant, easy bus trip (#201 from the City stand) to the top; the walk down, past a huge Nandi, Shiva's bull, takes about thirty minutes. Pilgrims, of course, make the trip in reverse order. Take drinking water to sustain you, especially in the middle of the day – the walk isn't very demanding, but by the end of it, after more than 1000 steps, your legs are likely to be a bit wobbly.

Seats to the left of the bus give the best views of the plain surrounding Mysore. Don't be surprised if, at the top of the hill, dominated by the temple's forty-metre *gopura*, you're struck by a feeling of déja vu – one of the displays at the **Godly Museum** states that "5000 years ago at this time you had visited this place in the same way you are visiting now. Because world drama repeats itself identically every 5000 years." Another exhibit goes to the heart of our "problematic world: filthy films, lack of true education, blind faith, irreligiousness, bad habits and selfishness". Suitably edified, you can proceed along a path from the bus stand, past trinket and tea stalls, to the temple square. Immediately to the right, at the end of this path, are four bollards painted with a red stripe; return here for the path down the hill.

Non-Hindus can visit the twelfth-century **temple** (daily 8am–noon & 5–8pm; leave shoes opposite the entrance), staffed by friendly priests who will plaster your forehead in vermillion paste. The Chamundi figure inside is solid gold; outside, in the courtyard, stands a fearsome, if gaily coloured, statue of the demon Mahishasura. On leaving, if you continue by the path instead of retracing your steps, you can return to the square via two other temples and various buildings storing ceremonial paraphernalia and animal figures used during Dussehra. You'll also come across loads of scampering monkeys, and the odd dreadlocked *sadhu* who will willingly pose for your holiday snaps, for a consideration. The magnificent five-metre **Nandi**, carved from a single piece of black granite in 1659, is an object of worship himself, adorned with bells and garlands and tended by his own priest. Minor shrines, dedicated to Chamundi and the monkey god Hanuman among others, line the side of the path; at the bottom, a little shrine to Ganesh lies near a chai shop. From here it's usually possible to pick up an auto-rickshaw or bus back into the city, but at weekends the latter are often full. If you walk on towards the city, passing a temple on the left, with a big water tank (the site of the floating festival during Dussehra), you come after ten minutes to the main road between the *Lalitha Mahal Palace* and the city; there's a bus stop, and often auto-rickshaws, at the junction.

Eating

Mysore has scores of **places to eat**, from numerous south Indian "meals" joints dotted around the market to the opulent *Lalita Mahal*, where you can work up an appetite for a gourmet meal by swimming a few lengths of the pool. To sample the renowned Mysore *pak*, a sweet, rich crumbly mixture made of *ghee* and maize flour, queue at *Guru Sweet Mart*, a small stall at KR Circle, Savaji Rao Road, which is considered the best sweet shop in the city. Another speciality from this part of the world is *malligi iddli*, a delicate light fluffy *iddli* usually served in the mornings and at lunch at several of the downtown "meals" restaurants.

Akshaya, *Hotel Dasaprakash*, Gandhi Square. Very good south Indian veg "meals" joint, serving various thalis (try the "special"), ice creams and cold drinks. Low on atmosphere, but the food is delicious and cheap.

Bombay Indra Bhavan, Savaji Rao Road. Comfortable and popular veg restaurant that serves both south and north Indian cuisine and sweets. Their other branch on Dhanavantri Road (see Accommodation) is equally, if not more, popular and also has an a/c section.

Gopika, *Govardhan Lodge*, Sri Harsh Road. Inexpensive "meals" restaurant on the ground floor of a busy hotel; opens early for Indian breakfasts of *iddlis*, *wada*, *pakora* and big glasses of hot-milk coffee.

Lalitha Mahal, T Naraispur Road. Sample the charms of this palatial five-star with an expensive

Moving on from Mysore

If you're contemplating a long haul, the best way to travel is by train, usually with a change at Bangalore. Six or seven express services leave Mysore each day for the Karnatakan capital, taking between 2hr and 3hr 30min to cover the 139km. The fastest of these, the a/c Shatabdi Express (#2008, daily except Tues 2.20pm) continues on to Chennai (7hr 5min); most of the others terminate in Bangalore, where you can pick up long-distance connections to a wide range of Indian cities (see p.1397), though the daily Mysore–Thanjavur Express (#6232) swings round south to Thanjavur (3.30pm; 14hr 50min), and every Friday the Swamajayanti Express goes all the way to Hazrat Nizamuddin in Delhi (4.20pm; 53hr). Reservations can be made at Mysore's computerized booking hall inside the station (Mon–Sat 8am–2pm & 2.15–8pm, Sun 8am–2pm). There's no tourist counter; take a good book. Due to continuing work upgrading the line, trains to Hassan are subject to disruption but theoretically there are four passenger trains a day (3–4hr), though it's better to take the bus unless you verify that they are running properly.

Reservations are not required for Bangalore (except on the Shatabdi Express), so you shouldn't ever have to do the trip by bus, which takes longer and is a lot more terrifying. If you do have to take a bus, KSRTC services leave at least every 30min from Central Bus stand, but there are few private coaches on the route. Most destinations within a day's ride of Mysore can only be reached by road. Long-distance services operate out of the Central bus stand, where you can book computerized tickets up to three days in advance. English timetables are posted on the wall inside the entrance hall, and there's a helpful enquiries counter in the corner of the compound. Regular buses leave here for Hassan, jumping-off place for the Hoysala temples at Belur and Halebid, and for Channarayapatna/Sravanabelgola (every 30min; 2–3hr). Heading south to Ooty (5hr), there's a choice of eight buses, all of which stop at Bandipur National Park. Direct services to Hospet, the nearest town to Hampi (the overnight bus leaves at 7pm and takes 10hr), and several cities in Kerala, including Kannur, Kozhikode and Kochi, also operate from Mysore and there is the option of deluxe private buses on these routes too. The only way to travel direct to Goa is on the 4pm overnight bus that arrives at Panjim at 9am. Most travellers, however, break this long trip into stages, heading first to Mangalore (12–15 daily; 7hr), and working their way north from there, usually via Gokarn – which you can also reach by direct bus (1 daily; 14hr) – or Jog Falls. Mangalore-bound buses and coaches tend to pass through Madikeri, capital of Kodagu (Coorg), which is also served by hourly buses, most of which travel through the Tibetan enclave of Bylakuppe. For details of services to Somnathpur and Srirangapatnam, see the relevant accounts below.

Mysore doesn't have an airport (the nearest one is at Bangalore), but you can confirm and book Indian Airlines flights at their office in the KSTDC *Mayura Hoysala* (Mon–Sat 10am–1.30pm & 2.15–5pm; ☎0821/421846).

hot drink in the atmospheric tea lounge, or an à la carte lunch in the grand dining hall, accompanied by live sitar music. The old-style bar also boasts a full-size billiards table.

Park Lane, Sri Harsha Road. Congenial courtyard restaurant-cum-beer garden (see Accommodation), with moderately priced veg and non-veg food (meat sizzlers are a speciality), pot plants and live Indian classical music every evening. Popular with travellers, but they actively discourage Indians and foreigners from sitting together.

Pizza Corner, Bangalore-Nilgiri Road, near Harding Circle. New branch of the Bangalore chain serving high-quality pizza in bright plastic Western decor.

Ritz, Bangalore–Nilgiri Road. Central and secluded hotel restaurant, and a nice escape from the city streets for a drink, or veg and non-veg meals. The best tables are in the courtyard at the back. Opens at 8.30am for "omelette-bread-butter-jam" breakfasts.

RRR, Gandhi Square. A plain "meals" restaurant in front with a small but plush a/c room at the back which gets packed at lunchtimes and at weekends. Well worth the wait for its excellent set menus on banana leaves, chicken biriyani and fried fish.

Shilpastri, Gandhi Square. Quality north Indian-style food, with particularly tasty tandoori (great chicken tikka). Plenty of good veg options, too, including lots of dhals and curd rice. Serves alcohol.

Around Mysore

Mysore is a jumping-off point for some of Karnataka's most popular destinations. At **Srirangapatnam**, the fort, palace and mausoleum date from the era of Tipu Sultan, the "Tiger of Mysore", a perennial thorn in the side of the British. The superb **Hoysala temples** (see p.1414) of **Somnathpur**, and further out, **Belur** and **Halebid**, are architectural masterpieces. Also near Hassan, the Jain site of **Sravanabelgola** attracts busloads of pilgrims and tourists to see the monolithic naked statue of Gomateshvara.

If you're heading south towards Ooty, **Bandipur National Park**'s forests and hill scenery offer another possible escape from the city, although your chances of spotting any rare animals are slim. The same is true of **Nagarhole National Park**, three hours southwest of Mysore in the Coorg region.

Srirangapatnam

The island of **Srirangapatnam**, in the River Kaveri, 14km northeast of Mysore, measures 5km by 1km. Long a site of Hindu pilgrimage, it is named

Wildlife sanctuaries around Mysore

Mysore lies within striking distance of three major wildlife sanctuaries – Bandipur, Nagarhole, and Mudumalai, across the border in Tamil Nadu – all of which are part of the vast Nilgiri Biosphere Reserve. In recent years, however, all three have been affected by the presence of the bandit Veerapan (see p.1502) and large parts of these forest tracts are often closed to visitors. If you are thinking of going there, check with the tourist office to see which parts are open. In early 2001 a curfew during the hours of darkness even extended to the Mysore–Ooty road while an army operation to flush Veerapan out was in progress. You will require a good deal of forward planning if you want to get the most out of the sanctuaries. A few upmarket private "resorts" on the edge of the parks and one or two tourist complexes allow visitors to experience some of the delights in an area renowned for its elephants. Forest Department accommodation at Bandipur (see p.1410) and Nagarhole (see p.1410) must be booked as far in advance as possible through the Chief Warden, Aranya Bhavan, Ashokapuram (⊕0821/480901), 6km south of the centre of Mysore, on bus #61 from the City stand. To arrange accommodation at Mudumalai, you'll need to phone ahead (see p.1288). Note that the Forest Department's rest houses can only be booked in Ooty.

after its tenth-century Sriranganathaswamy Vishnu temple, which in 1133 served as a refuge for the philosopher Ramanuja, a staunch Vaishnavite, from the Shaivite Cholas in Tamil Nadu. The Vijayanagars built a fort here in 1454, and in 1616 it became the capital of the Mysore Wadiyar rajas. However, Srirangapatnam is more famously associated with **Haider Ali**, who deposed the Wadiyars in 1761, and even more so with his son **Tipu Sultan**. During his seventeen-year reign – which ended with his death in 1799, when the future Duke of Wellington took the fort at the bloody battle of "Seringapatnam" – Tipu posed a greater threat than any other Indian ruler to British plans to dominate India.

Tipu Sultan and his father were responsible for transforming the small state of Mysore into a major Muslim power. Born in 1750, of a Hindu mother, Tipu inherited Haider Ali's considerable military skills; unlike his illiterate father, he was also an educated, cultured man who introduced radical agricultural reforms. His burning life-long desire to rid India of the hated British invaders naturally brought him an ally in the French. He obsessively embraced his popular name of the **Tiger of Mysore**, surrounding himself with symbols and images of tigers; much of his memorabilia is decorated with the animal or its stripes, and, like the Romans, he is said to have kept tigers for the punishment of criminals. Tipu's Srirangapatnam was largely destroyed by the British, but parts of the fort area in the northwest survive, including gates, ramparts, arsenals, the grim dungeons (where chained British prisoners were allegedly forced to stand neck-deep in water), and the domed and minareted Jami Masjid mosque.

The former summer palace, the **Daria Daulat Bagh** (daily except Fri 9am–5pm; $5 [Rs5]), literally "wealth of the sea", 1km east of the fort, was used to entertain Tipu's guests. At first sight, this low, wooden colonnaded building set in an attractive formal garden fails to impress, as most of it is obscured by sunscreens. However, the superbly preserved interior, with its ornamental arches, tiger-striped columns and floral decoration on every inch of the teak walls and ceiling, is remarkable. A much-repainted mural on the west wall relishes every detail of Haider Ali's victory over the British at Pollilore in 1780. Upstairs, a small collection of Tipu memorabilia, European paintings, Persian manuscripts on handmade paper and a model of Srirangapatnam are on show.

An avenue of cypresses leads from an intricately carved gateway to the **Gumbaz mausoleum** (daily except Fri 9am–5pm; free), 3km further east. Built by Tipu Sultan in 1784 to commemorate Haider Ali, and later also to serve as his own resting place, the lower half of the grey-granite edifice is crowned by a dome of whitewashed brick and plaster, spectacular against the blue sky. Ivory-inlaid rosewood doors lead to the tombs of Haider Ali and Tipu, each covered by a pall (tiger stripes for Tipu), and an Urdu tablet records Tipu's martyrdom. The interior walls are also painted in striking tiger colours.

At the heart of the fortress, the great temple of **Sriranganathaswamy** still stands proud and virtually untouched by the turbulent history that has flowed around it, and remains, for many devotees, the prime draw. Developed by succeeding dynasties, the temple consists of three distinctive sanctuaries and is entered via an impressive five-storeyed gateway and a hall that was built by Haider Ali. The innermost sanctum, the oldest part of the temple, contains an image of the reclining Vishnu.

Practicalities

Frequent **buses** from Mysore City bus stand (including #316) and all the Mysore–Bangalore **trains** pull in near the temple and fort. Srirangapatnam is

Some 2km southwest of Srirangapatnam, the **Ranganathittu Bird Sanctuary** (daily 9am–6pm; Rs100) is a must for ornithologists, especially during October/November, when the lake, fed by the River Kaveri, attracts huge flocks of migrating birds. At other times it's a tranquil spot to escape the city, where you can enjoy boat rides through the backwaters to look for crocodiles, otters and dozens of species of resident waders, wildfowl and forest birds. The easiest way to get there is by **rickshaw** from Srirangapatnam.

a small island, but places of interest are quite spread out; tongas, auto-rickshaws and bicycles are available on the main road near the bus stand. The KSTDC **hotel**-cum-restaurant, *Mayura River View* (℡0821/52114; ➍–➏), occupies a pleasant spot beside the Kaveri, 3km from the bus stand, and another good option is the smart and elegant *Fort View Resorts* (℡08236/52777; ➏–➐), set in its own grounds not far from the fort entrance.

Somnathpur

Built in 1268 AD, the exquisite **Keshava Vishnu temple** (daily 9am–5pm; $5 [Rs5]), in the sleepy hamlet of **SOMNATHPUR**, was the last important temple to be constructed by the Hoysalas; it is also the most complete and, in many respects, the finest example of this singular style (see p.1414). Somnathpur itself, just ninety minutes from Mysore by road, is little more than a few neat tracks and some attractive simple houses with pillared verandas.

Like other Hoysala temples, the Keshava is built on a star-shaped plan, but, as a triple shrine, represents a mature development from the earlier constructions. ASI staff can show you around and also grant permission to clamber on the enclosure walls, so you can get a marvellous bird's-eye view of the modestly proportioned structure. It's best to do this as early as possible, as the stone gets very hot to walk on in bare feet.

The temple is a *trikutachala*, "three-peaked hills" type, with a tower on each shrine – a configuration also seen in certain Chalukya temples, and three temples on Hemakuta hill at Vijayanagar (Hampi; see p.1442). The shrines, sharing a common hallway, are all dedicated to a different form of Vishnu. In order of "seniority" they are Keshava in the central shrine, Venugopala to the right and Jagannath to the left. The Keshava shrine features a very unusual *chandrasila*, "moonstone" step at its entrance, and, diverging from the usual semicircular Hoysala style, has two pointed projections.

The Keshava's high plinth (*jagati*) provides an upper ambulatory, which on its outer edge reproduces the almost crenellated shape of the structure and allows visitors to approach the upper registers of the profusely decorated walls. Among the many superb images here are an unusually high proportion of Shaivite figures for a Vishnu temple. As at Halebid, a lively frieze details countless episodes from the *Ramayana*, *Bhagavata Purana* and *Mahabharata*. Intended to accompany circumambulation, the panels are "read" (there is no text) in a clockwise direction. Unusually, the temple is autographed; all its sculpture was the work of one man, named Malitamba.

Outside the temple stands a *dvajastambha* column, which may originally have been surmounted by a figure of Vishnu's bird vehicle Garuda. The wide ground-level ambulatory that circles the whole building is edged with numerous, now mostly empty, shrines.

Practicalities

There are no direct **buses** from Mysore to Somnathpur. Buses from the Private stand run to T Narasipur (1hr), served by regular buses to Somnathpur (20min). Everyone will know where you want to go, and someone will show you which scrum to join. Alternatively, join one of KSTDC's guided tours (see p.1400).

You can stay at the government-owned but privately run *Tourist Rest House* (no phone; ❶), but the ultra-basic rooms are grubby and cannot be booked in advance. Also the only **food** available is in the shape of biscuits or maybe a samosa at one of the chai stalls or fruit from a street-seller; you'll have to go back to the cheap "meals" hotels at T Narasipur for anything more substantial.

Bandipur National Park

Situated among the broken foothills of the Western Ghat mountains, **Bandipur National Park**, 80km south of Mysore, covers 880 square kilometres of dry deciduous forest, south of the River Kabini. The reserve was created in the 1930s from the local maharaja's hunting lands, and expanded in 1941 to adjoin the Nagarhole National Park to the north, and Mudumalai and Wynad sanctuaries to the south in Tamil Nadu. These now collectively comprise the huge **Nilgiri Biosphere Reserve**, one of India's most extensive tracts of protected forest. However, access to the park is currently severely restricted (see p.1406), although parts such as Gopalswamy Betta remain open to visitors who have their own vehicles. In any case, Bandipur, in spite of its good accommodation and well-maintained metalled Jeep tracks, is a disappointment as a tourist destination. Glimpses of anything more exciting than a langur or spotted deer are rare outside the core area, which is off limits to casual visitors, while the noisy diesel bus laid on by the Forest Department to transport tourists around the accessible areas of park scares off what little fauna remains. If you're hoping to spot a tiger, forget it.

On the plus side, Bandipur is one of the few reserves in India where you stand a good chance of sighting wild **elephants**, particularly in the wet season (June–Sept), when water and forage are plentiful and the animals evenly scattered. Later in the monsoon, huge herds congregate on the banks of the Kabini River, in the far north of the park, where you can see the remnants of an old stockade used by one particularly zealous nineteenth-century British hunter as an elephant trap. Bandipur also boasts some fine scenery: at **Gopalswamy Betta**, 9km from the park HQ, a high ridge looks north over the Mysore Plateau and its adjoining hills, while to the south, the **Rolling Rocks** afford sweeping views of the craggy, 260-metre-deep **Mysore Ditch**.

Practicalities

The **best time to visit** is during the rainy season (June–Sept); unlike neighbouring parks, Bandipur's roads do not get washed out by the annual deluge, and elephants are more numerous at this time. By November/December, however, most of the larger animals have migrated across the state border into Mudumalai, where water is more plentiful in the dry season. When open, **avoid weekends**, as the park attracts bus loads of noisy day-trippers.

Getting to Bandipur by bus is easy; all the regular KSRTC services to Ooty from Mysore's Central bus stand (12 daily; 2hr 30min) pass through the reserve (the last one back to Mysore leaves at 5pm), stopping outside the Forest Department's reception centre (daily 9am–4.30pm). If you miss the last bus from Mysore you can change at Gundulapet, 18km away, from where you can also take a taxi to the main reception centre (Rs200).

KSTDC's *Mayura Prakruthi* at Melkamanahally (℡08229/7301; ❹–❺), 4km before Bandipur, has pleasant cottages with large, comfortable rooms and a restaurant. If the park is officially open, you can confirm accommodation bookings within the sanctuary at their Forest Department's reception centre. The rooms on offer are basic, but good value, ranging from the "VIP" *Gajendra Cottages* (❸), which have en-suite bathrooms and verandas, to beds in large, institutional dorms. The *chowkidars* will knock up simple meals by arrangement. Upmarket options include *Tusker Trails*, a **resort** run by members of the royal family of Mysore, at Mangala village, 3km from Bandipur (bookable through their office at Hospital Cottage, Bangalore Palace, Bangalore; ℡080/353 0748, ℻334 2862; ❾), which has cottages, a swimming pool and a tennis court and organizes trips into the forest. *Bush Betta*, off the main Mysore highway (booked through Gainnet, Raheja Plaza, Richmond Road, Bangalore; ℡080/551 2631; ❾), offers comfortable cottages and guided tours. Beds in the park are very limited, and it is essential to book accommodation in advance through the **Forest Department** office in Bangalore (Aranya Bhavan, 18th Cross, Malleswaram; ℡080/334 1993), or at Mysore (Project Tiger, Aranya Bhavan, Ashokapuram; ℡0821/480901).

Unless you have your own vehicle, the only **transport around the park** is the hopeless Forest Department bus, which makes two tours daily (7.30am & 4.30pm; 1hr). You may see a deer or two, but nothing more, on the half-hour **elephant ride** around the reception compound. Visitors travelling to Gopalswamy Betta should note that car rental is not available at Bandipur, but at Gundulapet, from where they will try and charge a lot more than the official Rs500. You must exit the park before nightfall.

Nagarhole National Park

Bandipur's northern neighbour, **Nagarhole** ("Snake River") **National Park**, extends 640 square kilometres north from the Kabini River, dammed in 1974 to form a picturesque artificial lake. During the dry season (Feb–June), this perennial water source attracts large numbers of animals, making it a potentially prime spot for sighting wildlife. The forest here is of the moist deciduous type – thick jungle with a thirty-metre-high canopy – and more impressive than Bandipur's drier scrub.

However, disaster struck Nagarhole in 1992, when friction between local pastoralist "tribals" and the park wardens over grazing rights and poaching erupted into a spate of arson attacks. Thousands of acres of forest were burned to the ground. The trees have grown back in places, but it will be decades before animal numbers completely recover. An added threat to the fragile jungle tracts of the region is a notorious female gang of wood smugglers from Kerala, who have developed a fearsome and almost mythical reputation. Meanwhile, Nagarhole is only worth visiting at the height of the dry season, when its muddy riverbanks and grassy swamps, or *hadlus*, offer better chances of sighting gaur (Indian bison), elephant, *dhole* (wild dog), deer, boar, and even the odd tiger or leopard, than any of the neighbouring sanctuaries.

Practicalities

Nagarhole is open year-round, but avoid the monsoons, when floods wash out most of its dirt tracks, and leeches make hiking impossible. To get there from Mysore, catch one of the two daily **buses** from the Central stand to **Hunsur** (3hr), 10km from the park's north gate, where you can pick up transport to the Forest Department's two rest houses (❷–❺). The **rest houses** have to be booked well in advance through the Forest Department offices in Mysore or Bangalore (see Bandipur, above). Turn up on spec, and you'll be told accommodation is "not available". It is also essential to arrive at the park gates well before dusk, as the road through the reserve to the lodges closes at 6pm, and is prone to "elephant blocks". The Nagarhole **visitor centre** is open 24 hours and charges foreigners a Rs150 [Rs10] entrance fee plus Rs10 per camera. They do not organize elephant rides, but schedule four bus tours – two in the morning starting at 6am, and two in the afternoon – for a minimum of two people.

Other **accommodation** around Nagarhole includes the highly acclaimed and luxurious *Kabini River Lodge* (book through Jungle Lodges & Resorts in Bangalore; ☎080/559 7021; ❾), approached via the village of Karapura, 3km from the park's south entrance. Set in its own leafy compound on the lakeside, this former maharaja's hunting lodge offers expensive all-in deals that include transport around the park with expert guides. It's impossible to reach by public transport, so you'll need to rent a car to get there and you will also have to book well in advance. Another upmarket option but not quite in the same league, the *Jungle Inn* at Veerana Hosahalli (☎08222/52781; ❾; bookable through their Bangalore office ☎080/224 3172), is close to the park entrance and arranges wildlife safaris, with a very hefty surcharge for foreign visitors. Some tour groups prefer the luxury of *Orange County* (see p.1425) near the town of Siddapura in Kodagu 75km to the north, despite the long drive.

Hassan and around

The unprepossessing town of **HASSAN**, 118km northwest of Mysore, is visited in disproportionately large numbers because of its proximity to the Hoysala temples at **Belur** and **Halebid**, both northwest of the town, and the Jain pilgrimage site of **Sravanabelgola**, southeast. Some travellers end up staying a couple of nights, killing time in neon-lit thali joints and dowdy hotel rooms, but with a little forward planning you shouldn't have to linger here for longer than it takes to get on a bus somewhere else. Set deep in the serene Karnatakan countryside, Belur, Halebid and Sravanabelgola are much more congenial places to stay.

Practicalities

Hassan's **KSRTC bus stand** is in the centre of town, at the northern end of Bus Stand Road which runs south past the post office to **Narsimharaja Circle**. Here you'll find the State Bank of Mysore, where you can change money, but not Thomas Cook travellers' cheques, and also most of the town's accommodation. Local auto-rickshaws operate without meters and charge a minimum of Rs8. Winding its way east–west via the Narsimharaja Circle, is the Bangalore–Mangalore Road (BM Road) along which you'll find the **tourist office** (1km) at Wartah Bhavan (Mon–Sat 10am–5.30pm; ☎08172/68862), good for information on bus and railway timings and the usual clutch of booklets, but not much else. The **railway station**, served in theory by four slow passenger trains a day to Mysore, is a further 2km down the road. Note that at the time of going to press, the route from here across the Ghats to Mangalore on the coast was suspended due to engineering work involved with upgrading the line.

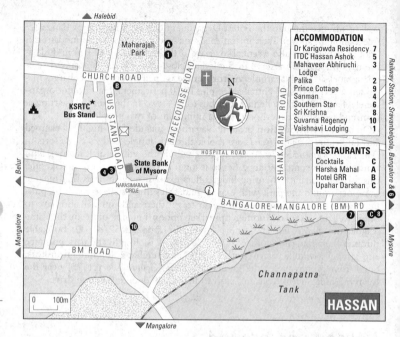

Accommodation

Considering the number of tourists who pass through, Hassan is oddly lacking in good accommodation. Most of the budget options are of a pitiful standard: the few exceptions are within walking distance of the bus stand, around **Narsimharaja Circle**. Wherever you stay, call ahead, as most hotels tend to be full by early evening.

DR Karigowda Residency, BM Road, 1km from railway station ☏ 08172/64506, ☎ 63222. Immaculate mid-range place: friendly, comfortable and amazing value. Single occupancy possible; no a/c. ❸

ITDC Hassan Ashok, BM Road, near Narsimharaja Circle ☏ 08172/68731, ☎ 68324. On the left as you approach from the railway station. Overpriced hotel for tour groups and VIPs. Uninspiring but comfortable veg and non-veg restaurant, craft shops and bar. ❽–❾

Mahaveer Abhiruchi Lodge, BM Road, near Narsimharaja Circle ☏ 08172/68885. Cleanish rooms (most with TVs and mosquito nets) and good but dilapidated veg restaurant, the *Abhiruchi*. ❷–❸

Palika, Race Course Road ☏ 08172/67145. Large, somewhat characterless, block with sizeable rooms; the cheaper ones are good value. ❹

Prince Cottage, BM Road, behind *Bhanu Theatre* ☏ 08172/65385. Small, neat guesthouse tucked away off the main road. Good value and handy for

the railway station. ❷

Sanman, Municipal Office Road ☏ 08172/68024. Above a busy restaurant, decent rooms with squeaky-clean white-tiled floors, frames for mozzie nets, attached bath, and small balconies looking onto main bazaar. ❷

Sri Krishna, BM Road ☏ 08172/63240, ☎ 60195. A large new hotel with some a/c rooms. The spacious non-a/c rooms are a great deal and the restaurant downstairs produces excellent south Indian cooking. ❺–❻

Southern Star, BM Road, 500m from train station ☏ 08172/51816, ☎ 68916, ✉ sshassan@vsnl.com. New hotel with all mod cons belonging to the *Quality Inn* chain but better value than most. Smartest place in town. ❼–❽

Suvarna Regency, PB 97, BM Road ☏ 08172/64006, ☎ 63822. Smart place with lots of lights, shiny marble lobby, comfortable rooms and a rooftop barbecue. Good value and a better choice than the *Ashok*. Some a/c. ❺–❻

Vaishnavi Lodging, Harsha Mahal Road

⌚08172/63885. Hassan's best budget lodge, with big clean rooms and veg restaurant. Reservations essential. Turn left out of the bus stand, right onto Church Road and it's on the corner of the first left turn. ❷

Eating

Most of the **hotels** listed above have commendable restaurants, or you can take your pick from the string of cheap snack bars and thali joints outside the bus stand.

Cocktails, BM Road near *Krishna*. A new multi-storey development with a terraced restaurant and bar offering a run-of-the-mill but varied menu.

Golden Gate, *Suvarna Regency*, PB 97, BM Road. Plush restaurant and bar with a garden extension, and the best Hassan has to offer; the varied menu is not cheap.

Harsha Mahal, below *Harsha Mahal Lodge*, Harsha Mahal Road. No-nonsense veg canteen

that serves freshly cooked *iddli* and *dosa* breakfasts from 7.30am.

Hotel GRR, opposite the bus stand. Traditional, tasty and filling "mini-meals" served on plantain leaves, with a wide choice of non-veg dishes and some ice creams.

Upahar Darshan, BM Road. A cheap south Indian restaurant serving good "meals" and fresh *dosas* and *iddlis*.

Moving on from Hassan

Hassan is well connected to most points in southwest Karnataka with frequent buses to Mysore from the KSRTC bus stand. Hassan lies midway on the main bus route between Mangalore (180km) and Bangalore (187km) serviced by several ordinary and occasional luxury buses, and more comfortable private buses, of which Vijayananda Travels, *Suvarna Regency*, PB 97, BM Road (⌚08172/65807), which runs the VRL service, is by far the best.

Apart from taking a tour, the only way to see Sravanabelgola (53km), Belur (37km) and Halebid (30km) in one day is by car, which some visitors share; most of the hotels can fix this up (around Rs1000 per day or Rs4 per kilometre for a minimum of 250km). Travelling by bus, you'll need at least two days. Belur and Halebid can be comfortably covered in one day; it's best to take the first (6am) of the hourly buses to Halebid (1hr) and move on to Belur (30min; 16km), from where services back to Hassan during the evening are more frequent (6.30am–6.15pm; 1hr 10min). Sravanabelgola, however, is in the opposite direction, and not served by direct buses; you have to head to Channarayapatna aka "CR Patna" (from 6.30am; 1hr) on the main Bangalore highway and pick up one of the regular buses (30min) or any number of minibuses from there. If you want to get to Sravanabelgola in time to visit the site and move on the same day (to Mysore or Bangalore), aim to catch one of the private luxury buses to Bangalore that leave from the road just below the *Vaishnavi Lodge* before dawn (5.30–6am); they all stop briefly in Channarayapatna. Bear in mind, too, that there are places to stay in both Belur and Halebid; arrive in Hassan early enough, and you can travel on to the temple towns before nightfall, although you should phone ahead to check rooms are available.

Halebid

Now little more than a scruffy hamlet of brick houses and chai stalls, **HALEBID**, 32km northwest of Hassan, was once the capital of the powerful Hoysala dynasty, who held sway over south Karnataka from the eleventh until the early fourteenth centuries. Once known as **Dora Samudra**, the city was renamed *Hale-bidu*, or "Dead City", in 1311 when Delhi Sultanate forces under the command of Ala-ud-din-Khalji swept through and reduced it to rubble.

The Hoysala dynasty ruled southwestern Karnataka between the eleventh and thirteenth centuries. From the twelfth century, after the accession of King Vishnu Vardhana, they built a series of distinctive temples centred primarily at three sites: Belur and Halebid, close to modern Hassan, and Somnathpur, near Mysore.

At first sight, and from a distance, Hoysala temples appear to be modest structures, compact and even squat. On closer inspection, however, their profusion of fabulously detailed and sensuous sculpture, covering every inch of the exterior, is astonishing. Detractors are prone to class Hoysala art as decadent and overly fussy, but anyone with an eye for craftsmanship is likely to marvel at these jewels of Karnataka art.

The intricacy of the carvings was made possible by the material used in construction: a soft steatite soapstone that on oxidization hardens to a glassy, highly polished surface. The level of detail, similar to that seen in sandalwood and ivory-work, became increasingly freer and more fluid as the style developed, and reached its highest point at Somnathpur. Beautiful bracket figures, often delicate portrayals of voluptuous female subjects, were placed under the eaves, fixed by pegs top and bottom. A later addition (except possibly in the Somnathpur temple), these serve no structural function.

Another technique more usually associated with wood is the unusual treatment of the massive stone pillars: lathe-turned, they resemble those of the wooden temples of Kerala. They were probably turned on a horizontal plane, pinned at each end, and rotated with the use of a rope. It may be no coincidence that, to this day, wood turning is still a local speciality. Only the central shaft of each pillar seems to have been turned; in the base and capitals, a less precise, presumably handworked imitation of turning is evident.

The architectural style of the Hoysala temples is commonly referred to as vesara, or "hybrid" (literally "mule"), rather than belonging to either the northern, nagari, or southern Dravidian styles. However, they show great affinity with nagari temples of western India, and represent another fruit of contact, like music, painting and literature, facilitated by the trade routes between the north and the south. All Hoysala temples share a star-shaped plan, built on high plinths (jagati) that follow the shape of the sanctuaries and mandapas to provide a raised surrounding platform. Such northern features may have been introduced by the designer and artists of the earliest temple at Belur, who were imported by Vishnu Vardhana from further north in Andhra Pradesh. Also characteristic of the Hoysala style is the use of ashlar masonry, without mortar. Some pieces of stones are joined by pegs of iron or bronze, or mortise and tenon joints. Ceilings inside the mandapas are made up of corbelled domes, looking similar to those of the Jain temples of Rajasthan and Gujarat; in the Hoysala style, they are only visible from inside.

Despite the sacking, several large Hoysala temples (see above) survive, two of which, the **Hoysaleshvara** and **Kedareshvara**, are superb, covered in exquisite carvings. A small **archeological museum** (daily except Fri 10am–5pm) next to the Hoysaleshvara temple houses a collection of Hoysala art and other finds from the area.

The Hoysaleshvara temple

The **Hoysaleshvara** temple (daily 9am–5pm; $5 [Rs5]) was started in 1141, and after some forty years of work remained incomplete; this possibly accounts for the absence here of the type of towers that feature at Somnathpur, for example. It is no longer known which deities were originally worshipped, though the double shrine is thought to have been devoted at one time to Shiva and his consort. In any event, both shrines contain *shivalinga* and are adjoined by two linked, partly enclosed *mandapa* hallways in which stand Nandi bulls.

Like other Hoysala temples, the whole is raised on a high plinth (*jagati*) which follows the star-shaped plan and provides an upper ambulatory; the *mandapas* are approached by flights of steps flanked by small freestanding, towered shrines. Inside, the lower portions of the black polished stone pillars were lathe-turned, though the upper levels appear to have been hand carved to reproduce the effect of turning.

Hoysaleshvara also features many Vaishnavite images. The **sculptures**, which have a fluid quality lacking in the earlier work at Belur, include Brahma aboard his goose vehicle Hamsa, Krishna holding up Mount Govardhana, another where he plays the flute, and Vishnu (Trivikrama) bestriding the world in three steps. One of the most remarkable images is of the demon king **Ravana** shaking Shiva's mountain abode, Mount Kailash, populated by numerous animals and figures with Shiva and Parvati seated atop. Secular themes, among them dancers and musicians, occupy the same register as the gods, and you'll come across the odd erotic tableau featuring voluptuous, heavily bejewelled maidens. A narrative frieze, on the sixth register from the bottom, follows the length of the Nandi *mandapas* and illustrates scenes from the *Bhagavata* and Vishnu *Puranas*, *Mahabharata* and *Ramayana*.

The Jain bastis and the Kedareshvara temple

Some 600m south of the Hoysaleshvara, a group of Jain *bastis* (temples) stand virtually unadorned; the only sculptural decoration consists of ceiling friezes inside the *mandapas* and elephants at the entrance steps, where there's an impressive donatory plaque. The thirteenth-century temple of **Adi Parshwanatha** marked by a large entrance *mandapa* is dedicated to the twenty-third *tirthankara*, Parshvanath, while the newer **Vijayanatha** built in the sixteenth century, easily recognized by its predominant *manasasthamba* pillar in front, is dedicated to the sixteenth *tirthankara*, Shantinath. The *chowkidar* at the Parshwanatha temple will demonstrate various tricks made possible by the carved pillars' highly polished surfaces; some are so finely turned they sound metallic when struck.

To the east, there's a smaller Shiva temple, **Kedareshvara** (1217–21), also built on a stellate plan. Unfortunately, due to instability, it's not possible to go inside. Many fine images decorate the exterior, including an unusual stone Krishna dancing on the serpent demon Kaliya – more commonly seen in bronze and painting.

Practicalities

Frequent **buses** run between Halebid (the last at 6.15pm) and Hassan, and to Belur (the last at 8.30pm). The private minibuses that work from the crossroads outside the Hoysaleshvara temple take a lot longer and only leave when crammed to bursting.

The monuments lie within easy walking distance of each other, but if you fancy exploring the surrounding countryside, rent a **bicycle** from the stalls by the bus stand (Rs3 per hour). The road running south past the temples leads through some beautiful scenery, with possible side-hikes to hilltop shrines, while the road to Belur (16km) makes for another pleasant bicycle ride. **Accommodation** in the village is limited to KSTDC *Mayura Shantala* (℡08177/73224; ❷) opposite the main temple and set in a small garden by the road. They offer two comfortable doubles with verandas, plus a four-bedded room – all should be booked in advance. Plans are afoot to construct a larger complex further south; ask at any KSTDC tourist office.

After 6pm, when the chai stalls at the crossroads are closed, the only place to **eat** is at the KSTDC *Mayura Shantala* where the food, including thalis, is uninspiring but the garden is pleasant.

Belur

BELUR, 37km northwest of Hassan, on the banks of the Yagachi, was the Hoysala capital prior to Halebid, during the eleventh and twelfth centuries. Still active (7.30am–8.30pm; open to non-Hindus; $5 [Rs5]), the **Chennakeshava temple**, a fine and early example of the singular Hoysala style, was built by King Vishnuvardhana in 1117 to celebrate his conversion from Jainism, victory over Chola forces at Talakad and his independence from the Chalukyas. Today, its grey-stone *gopura*, or gateway tower, soars above a small, bustling market town – a popular pilgrimage site from October to December, when busloads of Ayappan devotees stream through en route to Sabarimala (see p.1340). The **car festival** held around March or April takes place over twelve days and has a pastoral feel, attracting farmers from the surrounding countryside who conduct a bullock cart procession through the streets to the temple. If you have time to linger, Belur, with marginally better facilities than those found at Halebid, is a far better place to base yourself in order to explore the Hoysala region.

Built on a star-shaped plan, Chennakeshava stands in a huge walled courtyard, surrounded by smaller shrines and columned *mandapa* hallways. Lacking any form of superstructure, terminating at the first floor, it appears to have a flat roof. If it ever had a tower, it would have disappeared by the Vijayanagar (sixteenth-century) period – above the cornice, a plain parapet, presumably added at the same time as the east entrance *gopura*, shows a typically Vijayanagar Islamic influence. Both the sanctuary and *mandapa* are raised on the usual plinth (*jagati*). Double flights of steps, flanked by minor towered shrines, afford entry to the *mandapa* on three sides; this hallway was originally open, but in the 1200s, pierced stone screens, carved with geometric designs and scenes from the *Puranas*, were inserted between the lathe-turned pillars. The main shrine opens four times a day for worship (8.30–10am, 11am–1pm, 2.30–5pm & 6.30–8.30pm) and it's worth considering using one of the guides who offer their services at the gates (Rs30) to explain the intricacies of the carvings.

The quantity of **sculptural decoration**, if less mature than in later Hoysala temples, is staggering. Carvings on the plinth and lower walls, in successive and continuous bands, start at the bottom with elephants, each different, and then garlands and arches with lion heads; stylized vegetation with dancing figures, birds and animals; pearl garlands; projecting niches containing male and female figures and seated *yakshas*, or spirits; miniature pillars alternating with female figures dressing or dancing; miniature temple towers interspersed with dancers, and above them lion heads. Above the screens, a series of 42 bracket figures, added later, shows celestial nymphs hunting, playing music, dancing and beautifying themselves.

Columns inside, each unique, feature extraordinarily detailed carving, with more than a hundred deities on the central **Narasimha pillar**. The inner sanctum contains a black image of Chennakeshava, a form of Krishna who holds a conch (*shankha*, in the upper right hand), discus (*chakra*, upper left), lotus (*padma*, lower right) and mace (*gada*, lower left). He is flanked by consorts Shri Devi and Bhudevi. Within the same enclosure, the **Kappe Channigaraya temple** has some finely carved niche images and a depiction of Narasimha (Vishnu as man-lion) killing the demon Hiranyakashipu. Further west, fine sculptures in the smaller **Viranarayana** shrine include a scene from the *Mahabharata* of Bhima killing the demon Bhaga.

Practicalities

Buses from Hassan and Halebid pull into the small bus stand in the middle of town, ten minutes' walk along the main street from the temple. Some through buses do not bother to pull into the bus stand, but stop on the highway next to it. There are auto-rickshaws available, but a good way to explore the area, including Halebid, is to rent a **bicycle** (Rs3 per hour) from one of the stalls around the bus stand. The **tourist office** (Mon–Sat 10am–5pm) is located within the KSTDC *Mayuri Velapuri* compound near the temple. They have all the local bus times, and sometimes the tourist officer is available as a guide – his knowledge of the temples is quite remarkable.

The KSTDC *Mayuri Velapuri* (☎08177/22209; ❷) is the best **place to stay**, with immaculately clean and airy rooms in its new block, or dingy ones in the older wing. The two dorms are rarely occupied (Rs35 per bed), other than between March and May, when the hotel tends to be block-booked by pilgrims. Down the road, the *Annapurna* (☎08177/22039; ❷) has adequate if dull rooms over an uninspiring restaurant; the *Swagath Tourist Home* (☎08177/22159; ❶), further up the road towards the temple, is extremely basic, boxed in and does not have hot water, but is fine as a fall-back. Of the hotels around the bus stand, the *Vishnu Lodge* (☎08177/22263; ❷–❸) above a restaurant and sweet shop, is the best bet, with spacious rooms (some with TV) but tiny attached bathrooms where hot water is only available in the mornings.

The most salubrious **place to eat** is at KSTDC *Mayuri Velapuri's* newly built restaurant, but the menu is limited. There are several other options, many located beneath hotels strung along the main road, in addition to the veg *dhabas* by the temple, and the *Indian Coffee House* on the main road by the temple gates. If you have a weakness for Indian sweets, head for *Poonam's* below the *Vishnu Lodge*.

Sravanabelgola

The sacred Jain site of **SRAVANABELGOLA**, 49km southwest of Hassan and 93km north of Mysore, consists of two hills and a large tank. On one of the hills, Indragiri (also known as Vindhyagiri), stands an extraordinary eighteen-metre-high monolithic statue of a naked male figure, **Gomateshvara**. Said to be the largest freestanding sculpture in India, this tenth-century colossus, visible for miles around, as well as the nearby *bastis* (Jain temples) make Sravanabelgola a key pilgrimage centre, though surprisingly few Western travellers find their way out here. Spend a night or two in the village, however, and you can climb Indragiri Hill before dawn to enjoy the serene spectacle of the sun rising over the sugar cane fields and outcrops of lumpy granite that litter the surrounding plains – an unforgettable sight.

Sravanabelgola is linked in tradition with the Mauryan emperor Chandragupta, who is said to have starved himself to death on the second hill in around 300 BC, in accordance with a Jain practice. The hill was renamed Chandragiri, marking the arrival of Jainism in southern India. At the same time, a controversy regarding the doctrines of Mahavira, the last of the 24 Jain **tirthankaras** (literally "crossing-makers", who assist the aspirant to cross the "ocean of rebirth"), split Jainism into two separate branches. *Svetambara*, "white-clad" Jains, are more common in north India, while *digambara*, "sky-clad", are usually associated with the south. Truly ascetic *digambara* devotees go naked, though few do so away from sacred sites.

All the *tirthankaras* are represented as naked figures, differentiated only by their individual attributes: animals, inanimate objects (such as a conch shell), or symbols (such as the *svastika*). Each of the 24 is also attached to a particular *yaksha* (male) or *yakshi* (female) spirit; such spirits are also evident in Mahayana Buddhism, suggesting a strand of belief with extremely ancient origins. *Tirthankaras* are represented either sitting cross-legged in meditation – resembling images of the Buddha, save for their nakedness – or *kayotsarga*, "body upright", where the figure stands impassive; here Gomateshvara stands in the latter, more usual posture.

The monuments at Sravanabelgola probably date from no earlier than the tenth century, when a General Chamundaraya is said to have visited Chandragiri in search of a Mauryan statue of Gomateshvara. Failing to find it, he decided to have one made. From the top of Chandragiri he fired an arrow across to Indragiri Hill; where the arrow landed he had a new Gomateshvara sculpted from a single rock.

Indragiri Hill

Gomateshvara is approached from the tank between the two hills by 620 steps, cut into the granite of **Indragiri Hill**, which pass numerous rock

Gomateshvara and Mahamastakabhisheka

Gomateshvara, or Bahubali, who was the son of the legendary King Rishabdev of Ayodhya (better known as Adinath, the first *tirthankara*), had a row with his elder brother, Bharat, over their inheritance. After a fierce fight, he lifted his brother above his head, and was about to throw him to the ground when he was gripped by remorse. Gently setting Bharat down, Gomateshvara resolved to reject the world of greed, jealousy and violence by meditating until he achieved *moksha*, release from attachment and rebirth. This he succeeded in doing, even before his father.

As a *kevalin*, Gomateshvara had achieved *kevalajnana*, "sole knowledge" acquired through solitude, austerity and meditation. While engaged in this nonactivity, he stood "body upright" in a forest. So motionless was he that ants built their nest at his feet, snakes coiled happily around his ankles, and creepers began to grow up his legs.

Every twelve years, at an auspicious astrological conjunction of certain planets, the Gomateshvara statue is ritually anointed in the **Mahamastakabhisheka ceremony** – the next one is scheduled for some time between September and December of 2005 (the precise date has yet to be announced). The process lasts for several days, culminating on the final morning when 1008 *kalashas* (pots) of "liberation water", each with a coconut and mango leaves tied together by coloured thread, are arranged before the statue in a sacred diagram (*mandala*), on ground strewn with fresh paddy. A few priests climb scaffolding, erected around Gomateshvara, to bathe him in milk and *ghee*. After this first bath, prayers are offered. Then, to the accompaniment of temple musicians and the chanting of sacred texts, a thousand priests climb the scaffold to bathe the image in auspicious unguents including the water of holy rivers, sandal paste, cane juice, saffron and milk, along with flowers and jewels. The ten-hour 1993 ceremony reached a climax when a helicopter dropped 20kg of gold leaf and 200 litres of milk on the colossus, along with showers of marigolds, gemstones and multi-hued powders. The residue formed a cascade of rainbow colours down the statue's head and body, admired by *lakhs* of devotees, Jain *sadhus* and *sadhvis* (female *sadhus*), and the massed cameras of the world. A satellite township, Yatrinagar, provides accommodation for 35,000 during the festival, and eighteen surrounding villages shelter pilgrims in temporary *dharamshalas*.

inscriptions on the way up to a walled enclosure. Shoes must be deposited at the stall to the left of the steps, and you can leave bags at the site office nearby. Anyone unable to climb the steps can be carried up by chair known as *doli*. Take plenty of water especially on a hot day, as there is none available on the hill. Entered through a small wagon-vaulted *gopura*, the **temple** is of the type known as *betta*, which instead of the usual *garbhagriha* sanctuary consists of an open courtyard enclosing the massive sculpture. Figures and shrines of all the *yaksha* and *yakshi* spirits stand inside the crenellated wall, but the towering figure of Gomateshvara dominates. With elongated arms and exaggeratedly wide shoulders, his proportions are decidedly non-naturalistic. The sensuously smooth surface of the white granite "trap" rock is finely carved: particularly the hands, hair and serene face. As in legend, ant-hills and snakes sit at his feet and creepers appear to grow on his limbs.

Bhandari Basti and monastery (math)

The road east from the foot of the steps at Chandragiri leads to two interesting Jain buildings in town. To the right, the **Bhandari Basti** (1159), housing a shrine with images of the 24 *tirthankaras*, was built by Hullamaya, treasurer of the Hoysala Raja Narasimha. A high wall encloses the temple, forming a plain ambulatory which contains a well. Two *mandapa* hallways, where naked *digambara* Jains may sometimes be seen discoursing with devotees clad in white, lead to the shrine at the back. Pillars in the outer *mandapa* feature carvings of female musicians, while mythical beasts adorn the entrance to the inner, *navaranga*, hallway.

At the end of the street, the *math* (monastery) was the residence of Sravanabelgola's senior *acharya*, or guru. Thirty male and female monks, who also "go wandering in every direction", are attached to the *math*; normally a member of staff will be happy to show visitors around. Among the rare palm-leaf manuscripts in the library, some more than a millennium old, are works on mathematics and geography, and the *Mahapurana*, hagiographies of the *tirthankaras*. Next door, a covered walled courtyard contains a number of shrines; the entrance is elaborately decorated with embossed brass designs of *yali* mythical beasts, elephants, a two-headed eagle and an image of Parshvanath, the 23rd *tirthankara*, here shown as Padmavati. Inside, the courtyard is edged by a high platform on three sides, on which a chair is placed for the *acharya*. A collection of tenth-century bronze *tirthankara* images is housed here, and vibrant murals detail the various lives of Parshvanath. The hills where the *tirthankaras* stood to gain *moksha* are represented in a model, somewhat resembling a jelly mould, with tacked-on footprints.

Chandragiri Hill

Leaving your shoes with the keeper at the bottom, take the rock-cut steps to the top of the smaller **Chandragiri Hill**. Miraculously, the sound of radios and rickshaws down below soon disappears. Fine views stretch south to Indragiri and, from the north on the far side, across to a river, paddy and sugar cane fields, palms and the village of **Jinanathapura**, where there's another ornate Hoysala temple, the Shantishvara *basti*.

Rather than a single large shrine, as at Indragiri, Chandragiri holds a group of *bastis* in late Chalukya Dravida style, within a walled enclosure. Caretakers, who don't speak fluent English, will take you around and open up the closed shrines. Save for pilasters and elaborate parapets, all the temples have plain exteriors. Named after its patron, the tenth-century **Chamundaraya** is the largest of the group, dedicated to Parshvanath. Inside the **Chandragupta** (twelfth century), superb carved panels in a small shrine tell the story of Chandragupta and his teacher Bhadrabahu. Traces of painted geometric designs survive and the pillars feature detailed carving. Elsewhere in the enclosure stands a 24m-high *manastambha*, "pillar of fame", decorated with images of spirits, *yakshis* and a *yaksha*. No fewer than 576 inscriptions dating from the sixth to the nineteenth century are dotted around the site, on pillars and the rock itself.

Practicalities

Sravanabelgola, along with Belur and Halebid, features on **tours** from Bangalore and Mysore (see p.1388 & p.1400). However, if you want to look around at a civilized pace, it's best to come independently. The **tourist office** (Mon–Sat 10am–5.30pm) at the bottom of the stairs has little to offer and the management committee office next door only serves to collect donations and hand out tickets for the *dolis*.

If you want **accommodation**, there are plenty of **dharamshalas**, managed by the temple authorities, offering simple, scrupulously clean rooms, many with their own bathrooms and sitouts, ranged around gardens and courtyards, and most costing around Rs125 per night. The 24hr accommodation office (℡ 08176/57258), where you will be allocated a room, is located inside the *SP Guest House*, next to the bus stand (look for the clock tower). The *Yatri Niwas* (❸), close by and also booked through the accommodation office, is about as expensive as it gets but is only marginally better than the best of the guesthouses. *Hotel Raghu*, opposite the main tank, houses the best of the many small local **restaurants**.

Crisscrossed by winding back roads, the idyllic (and mostly flat) countryside around Sravanabelgola is perfect cycling terrain. **Bicycles** are available for rent (Rs3 per hour) at Saleem Cycle Mart, on Masjid Road, opposite the northeast corner of the tank or stalls on the main road. If you're returning to Hassan, you'll have to head to **Channarayapatna** aka "CR Patna" by bus or in one of the shared vans that regularly ply the route and depart only when bursting; change at CR Patna for a bus to Hassan.

Kodagu (Coorg)

The hill region of **Kodagu**, formerly known as **Coorg**, lies 100km west of Mysore in the Western Ghats, its eastern fringes merging with the Mysore Plateau. Comprising rugged mountain terrain interspersed with cardamom jungle, coffee plantations and swathes of lush rice paddy, it's one of south India's most beautiful areas. Little has changed since Dervla Murphy spent a few months here with her daughter in the 1970s (the subject of her classic travelogue, *On a Shoestring to Coorg*) and was entranced by the landscape and people, whose customs, language and appearance set them apart from their neighbours.

Today tourism is still virtually nonexistent, and the few travellers that pass through rarely venture beyond **Madikeri** (Mercara), Kodagu's homely capital. However, if you plan to cross the Ghats between Mysore and the coast, the route through Kodagu is definitely worth considering. Some coffee plantation owners open their doors to visitors – to find out more contact the Codagu Planters Association, Mysore Road, Madikeri (℡ 08272/29873). A good time to visit is during the festival season in early December or during the **Blossom**

The Kodavas

Theories abound as to the origins of the **Kodavas**, or **Coorgis**, who today comprise less than one sixth of the hill region's population. Fair-skinned and with their own language and customs, they are thought to have migrated to southern India from Kurdistan, Kashmir and Rajasthan, though no one knows exactly why or when. One popular belief holds that this staunchly martial people, who since Independence have produced some of India's leading military brains, are descended from Roman mercenaries who fled here following the collapse of the Pandyan dynasty in the eighth century; some even claim connections with Alexander the Great's invading army. Another theory is that the Kodavas were originally from Arabia, having been pushed out by the early Muslims and made to flee into exile. Whatever their origins, the Kodavas have managed to retain a distinct identity apart from the freed plantation slaves, Moplah Muslim traders and other immigrants who have settled here. More akin to Tamil than Kannada, their language is Dravidian, yet their religious practices, based on ancestor veneration and worship of nature spirits, differ markedly from those of mainstream Hinduism. Land tenure in Kodagu is also quite distinctive, with taxation based on type of land; unlike in some other traditional societies, women have a right to inheritance and ownership and are also allowed to remarry. Kodava martial traditions are grounded in the family where, according to custom, one son was raised to work the land while another joined the army, and even today they are allowed to carry weapons without licence.

Spiritual and social life for traditional Kodavas revolves around the **Ain Mane**, or ancestral homestead. Built on raised platforms to overlook the family land, these large, detached houses, with their beautiful carved wood doors and beaten-earth floors, generally have four wings and courtyards to accommodate various branches of the extended family, as well as shrine rooms, or **Karona Kalas**, dedicated to the clan's most important forebears. Key religious rituals and rites of passage are always conducted in the *Ain Mane*, rather than the local temple. However, you could easily travel through Kodagu without ever seeing one, as they are invariably away from roads, shrouded in thick forest.

You're more likely to come across traditional Kodava **costume**, which is donned for all auspicious occasions, such as marriages, funerals, harvest celebrations and clan get-togethers. The men wear dapper knee-length coats called *kupyas*, bound at the waist with a scarlet and gold cummerbund, and daggers (*peechekathis*) with ivory handles. Most distinctive of all, though, is the unique flat-bottomed turban; sadly, the art of tying these is dying, and most men wear ready-made versions (which you can buy in Madikeri bazaar). Kodava women's garb of long, richly coloured silk saris, pleated at the back and with a *pallav* draped over their shoulders, is even more stunning, enlivened by heaps of heavy gold and silver jewellery, and precious stones. Women also wear headscarves, in the fields as well as for important events, tying the corners behind the head, Kashmiri style.

The Kodava **diet** is heavily carnivorous, their favourite meat being pork which is an important dish at festive occasions, where it is often served as a dryish dish known as *pandi curry*, but sometimes substituted by *nooputtakoli curry* made with chicken, and usually accompanied with a rice preparation, *tumbuttu pandi*. Their traditional breakfasts, consisting of a type of chapati known as *aki oti* served with honey and *pajji*, a chutney, is far lighter.

Like all traditional Indian cultures, this one is on the decline, not least because young Kodavas, predominantly from well-off landowning families, tend to be highly educated and move away from home to find work, weakening the kinship ties that have for centuries played such a central role in the life of the region. However, in recent years there has been a rekindling of Kodava pride, and calls have been made for a state separate from Karnataka.

Showers around March and April when the coffee plants bloom with white flowers – some people, however, find the strong scent overpowering.

Kodagu is relatively undeveloped, and "sights" are few, but the countryside is idyllic and the climate refreshingly cool, even in summer. With the help of local operators, there is now a growing trickle of visitors who come to Kodagu to **trek** through the unspoilt forest tracts and ridges that fringe the district. On the eastern borders of Kodagu on the Mysore Plateau, large **Tibetan settlements** around Kushalnagar have transformed a once barren countryside into fertile farmland dotted with busy monasteries, some housing thousands of monks.

Some history

Oblique references to Kodagu crop up in ancient Tamil and Sanskrit scriptures, but the first concrete evidence of the kingdom dates from the eighth century, when it prospered from the salt trade passing between the coast and the cities on the Deccan Plateau. Under the Hindu **Haleri rajas**, the state repulsed invasions by its more powerful neighbours, including Haider Ali and his son Tipu Sultan, the infamous Tiger of Mysore. A combination of hilly terrain, absence of roads (a deliberate policy on the part of defence-conscious Kodagu kings) and the tenacity of its highly trained army, ensured Kodagu was the only Indian kingdom never to be conquered.

Peace and prosperity prevailed through the 1700s, when the state was ruled by a line of eccentric rajas, among them the paranoid Dodda Vira (1780–1809), who reputedly murdered most of his relatives, friends, ministers and palace guards. The monarchy was more accountable during the reign of his successor, Chickaviraraja Rajendra, known as **Vira Raja**, but eventually lapsed into decadence and corruption. Emulating his father's brutal example, Vira Raja imprisoned or assassinated his rivals and indulged his passion for women and spending. The king's ministers eventually appealed to the British resident in Mysore for help to depose the despot. Plagued by threats from Vira Raja, the colonial administration was eager for an excuse to intervene; they got it in 1834, when the unruly raja killed his cousin's infant son. Accusing him of maladministration, the British massed troops on the border and forced a short siege, at the end of which Vira Rajah (and what remained of his family) fled into exile.

Thereafter, Kodagu became a princely state with nominal independence, which it retained until the creation of Karnataka in 1956. During the Raj, **coffee** was introduced and, despite plummeting prices on the international market, this continues to be the linchpin of the local economy, along with pepper and cardamom. Although Kodagu is Karnataka's wealthiest region, and provides the highest revenue, it does not reap the rewards and this, coupled with the distinct identity and fiercely independent nature of the Kodavas, has resulted in the Kodagu freedom movement, known as **Kodagu Rajya Mukti Morcha**, seeking its own statehood. Methods used by the KRMM include cultural programmes and occasional strikes, known as *bandhs*, designed to close down all commercial activity in protest; traditionally they rarely use violence though a new order is emerging within the movement which has left some of the older members disgruntled.

Madikeri (Mercara) and around

Nestling beside a curved stretch of craggy hills, **MADIKERI** (**Mercara**), capital of Kodagu, undulates around 1300m up in the Western Ghats, roughly midway between Mysore and the coastal city of Mangalore. Few foreigners travel up here, but it's a pleasant enough town, with red-tiled buildings and undulating roads that converge on a bustling bazaar.

The **Omkareshwara Shiva** temple, built in 1820, features an unusual combination of red-tiled roofs, Keralan Hindu architecture, gothic elements and Islamic-influenced domes. The fort and palace, worked over by Tipu Sultan in 1781 and rebuilt in the nineteenth century, now serve as offices and a prison. Also worth checking out are the huge square **tombs of the rajas** which, with their Islamic-style gilded domes and minarets, dominate the town's skyline. **St Mark's Church** holds a small **museum** of British memorabilia, Jain, Hindu and village deity figures and weapons (Tues–Sun 9.30am–1.30pm & 2.30pm–5.30pm; free). At the western edge of town, **Rajas' Seat**, next to *Hotel Valley View*, is a belvedere, said to be the Kodagu kings' favoured place to watch the sunset.

Madikeri is the centre of the lucrative coffee trade, and although auto-rickshaws will take you there and back for around Rs150, a walk to **Abbi Falls** (8km) is a good introduction to coffee-growing country. The pleasant road, devoid of buses, winds through the hill country past plantations and makes for a good day's outing. At the littered car park at the end of the road, a gate leads through a private coffee plantation sprinkled with cardamom sprays and pepper vines, to the bottom of the large stepped falls that are most impressive during the monsoons.

Practicalities

You can only reach Madikeri by road, but it's a scenic three-hour **bus** ride via **Kushalnagar** from **Mysore**, 120km southeast (unless you mistakenly get on one of the few buses that goes via Siddapura, which take more than an hour longer). Regular services, including deluxe buses, also connect Madikeri with **Mangalore**, 135km northwest across the Ghats. The KSTRC state **bus stand** is at the bottom of town, below the main bazaar; private buses from villages around the region pull into a parking lot at the end of the main street.

The small local **tourist office** (Mon–Sat 10.30am–5.30pm; ☎08272/28580) stands five minutes' walk along the Mysore road, below Thimaya Circle, next to the *PWD Travellers' Bungalow*, and can suggest itineraries, but is otherwise quite limited. If you're thinking of **trekking** in Kodagu, contact Ganesh Aiyanna at the *Hotel Cauvery* (☎08272/25492) who is very helpful and organizes itineraries and trips for around Rs500 per day. Coorg Travels at *Vinayaka Lodge* (☎08272/25817) is also flexible and friendly and will help put together a tour. For information on Kodagu's **forests** and forest bungalows contact the Conservator of Forests, Deputy Commissioner's Office at the fort (☎08272/25708). Netraiders.com (☎08272/21131) near Chowk in the heart of the bazaar offers internet access for Rs40 per hour.

Accommodation and eating

Accommodation in Madikeri can be hard to come by, particularly in the budget range, most of which is concentrated around the bazaar and bus stand. The better-class and some of the budget hotels generally have **restaurants**. The moderately expensive restaurant at *Rajdarshan* is one of the best; surprisingly, they do not serve coffee although they do have a good bar. The *Choice Hotel* on School Road is a restaurant only, serving breakfast items and a decent range of veg and non-veg dishes. There are a couple of "meals" joints on the main road and in the centre of town, and *Veglands* is a good and highly popular vegetarian restaurant.

Capitol Village ☎ 08272/25975. Six kilometres from the centre and booked through the *Hotel Cauvery* in Madikeri, this is the best place to stay in the area, but you'll need your own transport. The "village" consists of a cottage complex surrounded by a splendid variety of horticulture on the edge of a coffee plantation. It's quiet and secluded and excellent value. ❻

Cauvery, School Road ☎ 08272/25492, ℗ 25735. Below the Private bus stand, this large and friendly place is almost hidden behind their *Capitol* restaurant. ❹

Chitra, School Road ☎ 08272/25372, ℗ 25191. Best value in town. Neat well-kept rooms, the slightly pricier ones with cable TV. Excellent non-veg restaurant-cum-bar downstairs. ❸–❹

Coorg International, Convent Road ☎ 08272/28071, ℗ 28073. Ten minutes by rickshaw from the centre, this is one of the few upmarket options. It's a large but slightly characterless hotel with comfortable Western-style rooms, a multi-cuisine restaurant, exchange facilities, and shops. ❼

East End, General Thimaya Road (aka Mysore Road; ☎ 08272/29996. A large, plain, tiled-roof colonial bungalow turned into a hotel with a hint of character, but more renowned for its popular bar and restaurant. ❸

KSTDC Hotel Mayura Valley View ☎ 08272/28387. Well away from the main road, past Rajas' Seat, and with excellent views. The rooms are huge and the restaurant serves beer. Hail a rickshaw to get there, as it's a stiff twenty-minute uphill walk from the bus stand. ❺

Rajdarshan ☎ 08272/29142. A modern and salubrious place with a landscaped garden, restaurant and bar, just down the hill on the left from the *Hotel Mayura Valley View*. ❻–❼.

Tibetan settlements and coffee plantations

Madikeri provides an excellent base from which to explore the delights of Kodagu including the **Tibetan settlements** that straddle the district border to the east. Co-operatives line the Madikeri–Mysore highway and maroon–clad monks ride tractors to work the fields around the town of **Kushalnagar**, 22km from Madikeri, and the Tibetan villages, known as "camps", scattered around **Bylakuppe**, 6km across the Kodagu border. Although the term "camp" suggests a sense of transition, the local Tibetans who first settled here as refugees in the 1960s, represent one of the largest settlements outside their homeland and have adapted remarkably well to a starkly different environment.

Today, several key monasteries punctuate the landscape. Chief amongst them is the great *gompa* of **Sera Je**, 5km to the south of the main highway. A huge complex which acts as a university for around 2000 monks, Sera centres on a large main hall built on three floors, designed to accommodate a vast congregation of monks who gather here for instruction and ceremony. Despite the colossal image of the Buddha Shakyamuni at the head of the hall, there is nothing especially attractive about the monastery, which has more of a functional air to it; the village, however, has a buzz and the monks are welcoming. Two other monasteries nearer the main road are also well worth a visit; **Nyingmapa** has peaceful grounds around a huge colourful prayer hall housing three enormous gilt Buddhas and two startling dragon columns, while the newer **Namdroling** sports a dazzling golden temple.

Sera Je's new and welcoming *Guest House* (❷), which serves to raise funds, and has pleasant clean rooms and a café, is one of the few places to stay and eat around **BYLAKUPPE**. The best place to eat is at the *Tibet Restaurant*, popular with young monks, which is due to move in late 2001 from Kushalnagar to halfway along the Sera Je road. Namgyal, the proprietor, and his brother are welcoming and a fount of local information, plus they serve great *thukpas, momos, shabhaleys, mothuk* and fried rice. The only transport to and from the main highway is by shared **auto–rickshaws** that regularly ply the route; the turn-off to Sera Je is midway between Bylakuppe and Kushalnagar. If you're arriving by bus from Mysore, ask to be let down at Bylakuppe, recognizable by the Tibetan farm co-operatives. If you're coming from the west, however, you'll reach Kushalnagar first, where there are more auto-rickshaws available at the bus stand. If you want an auto-rickshaw all to yourself, it'll cost Rs30 to Sera.

There's more **accommodation** at **KUSHALNAGAR**, but nothing wonderful. The most comfortable of the hotels is the *Kannika International* (⊕08276/74728, ⊕73318; ⑤–⑥) set back from the main road near the bus stand, with its own garden, restaurant and bar with tables on the porch, and airy rooms with televisions. Cheaper options on the main road around the bus stand include the basic *Radhakrishna Lodge* (⊕08276/74822; ❶) with adequate budget rooms and the *Ganesh* (⊕08276/74528; ❷). For a bit more quiet follow the lane along the side of the bus stand past the communications tower to the *Mahalaxmi Lodge* (⊕08276/74622; ❷). Kushalnagar is also well connected **by bus** to Mangalore (via Madikeri), Bangalore, Mysore and Hassan as well as to several destinations in Tamil Nadu. Bus times are posted in English and deluxe and express buses stop here as well.

The sleepy coffee town of **SIDDAPURA**, on the banks of the Cauvery River, lies 32km to the south of Madikeri in the heart of coffee country. You can stay on a plantation here, but at a price. Across the river, the **Dubare Reserve Forest** makes for good short exploratory treks with the chance of seeing wildlife and the occasional elephant; contact the Conservator of Forests, Deputy Commissioners Office, the Fort, Madikeri (⊕08272/25708) for more information, and take a guide. Alternatively, the resort of *Orange County* at Karadigodu, 3km from Siddapura (⊕08274/58485, code 914 from Madikeri; ⑨), arranges forest walks for guests. Approached by a small road that winds through lush plantations where tall trees provide essential cover for the coffee plants, *Orange County* lies at the edge of a wealthy estate and is the most luxurious place to stay in the whole of Kodagu. Booked through their Bangalore office (⊕080/558 2380), *Orange County* offers mock-Tudor cottages set within a manicured estate where activities include treks and horse riding and there's a pleasant pool (for residents only) and a good restaurant serving Kodava dishes as part of a varied menu. Popular with affluent Indians, some who come on a time-share basis, and tour groups, *Orange County* can provide a base from which to visit Nagarhole National Park 75km to the south (see p.1410), and should be booked in advance.

Bhagamandala and Talakaveri

A good bus excursion from Madikeri takes you to the quiet village of **Bhagamandala** (35km west), and from there to the sacred site of **Talakaveri** (9km), said to be the source of the holy Kaveri (Cauvery) River. The hill scenery is superb, and you can opt to walk part of the way on blissfully quiet country roads.

Wear something warm, and take the 6.30am bus from Madikeri's private stand to **BHAGAMANDALA**. You should arrive around 8am, with just enough time to grab a good breakfast of *parathas* and local honey at the *Laxmi Vilas* teashop, next to the bus stop from where the bus to Talakaveri leaves at 8.30am. At Bhagamandala, the holy spot where the Kaveri merges with two streams, Kanike and Sujyothi, the **Bhagandeshwara temple** is a fine example of Keralan-style architecture, with tiled roofs and courtyards.

At **TALAKAVERI** the bus stops on the slopes of Brahmagiri Hill by the entrance to the sacred tank and **temple**. During **Kaveri Shankrama** in October, thousands of pilgrims come here to witness a spring, thought to be the goddess Kaveri, known as Lopamudra, the local patron deity, suddenly spurting into a small well; to bathe in the tank at this time is considered especially sin-absolving. The belief is that if one year the spring dries up then all the rivers of southern India will dry up too. Whenever you come you're likely to find wild-haired *sadhus* and bathing pilgrims, the surrounding walls swathed in drying *dhotis* and saris. Two small shrines stand at the head of the tank, one containing an image of Ganesh and the other a metal *lingam* with *naga* snake canopy. Steep granite steps to the right lead up to the peak of **Brahmagiri Hill**, which affords superb 360° views over Kodagu.

Mangalore

Many visitors only come to **MANGALORE** on their way somewhere else. As well as being fairly close to Madikeri and the Kodagu (Coorg) hill region, it's also a stopping-off point between Goa and Kerala, and is the nearest coastal town to the Hoysala and Jain monuments near Hassan, 172km east.

Mangalore was one of the most famous ports of south India. It was already famous overseas in the sixth century, as a major source of pepper, and the fourteenth-century Muslim writer Ibn Batuta noted its trade in pepper and ginger and the presence of merchants from Persia and the Yemen. In the mid-1400s, the Persian ambassador Abdu'r-Razzaq saw Mangalore as the "frontier town" of the Vijayanagar empire (see p.1442) – which was why the Portuguese captured it in 1529. In Haider Ali's time, during the eighteenth century, the city became a shipbuilding centre. Nowadays, the modern port, 10km north of the city proper, is principally known for the processing and export of coffee and cocoa (much of which comes from Kodagu), and cashew nuts (from Kerala). It is also a centre for the production of *bidi* cigarettes. Mangalore's heady ethnic mix lived more or less in harmony until 1998, when communal riots saw sections of the city's large Christian community attacked by right-wing Hindu fundamentalists.

Arrival, information and city transport

Mangalore's busy KSRTC **bus stand** (known locally as the "Lal Bagh" bus stand) is 2km north of the town centre, Hampankatta, at the bottom of Kadri Hill. Private buses arrive at the much more central stand near the Town Hall. **Bajpe airport**, 22km north of the city (bus #22 or #47A, Indian Airlines city bus or taxis for Rs250), is served by both Indian Airlines and Jet Airways from Mumbai and Bangalore. The **railway station**, on the south side of the city centre, sees daily services from cities all over India, including Delhi, Agra, Hyderabad, Bangalore, Chennai, and Thiruvananthapuram.

Hampankatta, close to the facilities of Light House Hill Road, acts as the traffic hub of the city from where you can catch **city buses** to most destinations or **auto-rickshaws**, although their drivers prefer not to use their meters. The **tourist office** (Mon–Sat 10am–1.30pm & 2.30–5.30pm; ☏ 0824/442926) on the ground floor of the *Hotel Indraprashta* on Light House Hill Road is helpful for general information and some bus times, but carries no information on trains, for which you will need to go to the railway station.

You can **change money** at Trade Wings, Light House Hill Road (Mon–Sat 9.30am–5.30pm; ☏ 0824/426817) who cash travellers' cheques, and at TT Forex (same hours; ☏ 0824/421717), 1st Floor, Utility Royal Towers, KS Rao Road. The State Bank of India (Mon–Fri 10.30am–2.30pm & Sat 10.30am–12.30pm), near the Town Hall on Hamilton Circle, is somewhat slower.

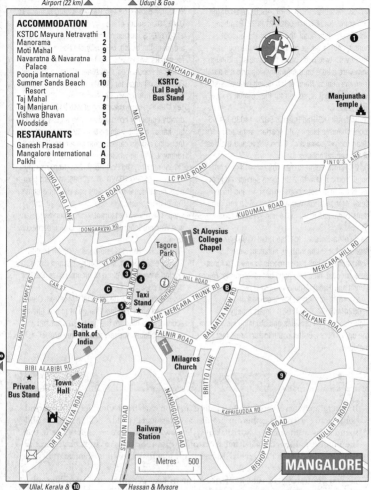

Mangalore's **GPO** (Mon–Sat 10am–7pm, Sun 10.30am–1.30pm) is a short walk from the centre, at Shetty Circle. For **email** try the friendly and popular Kohinoor Computer Zone, Plaza Towers, Light House Hill Road (Mon–Sat 8am–2am; ☎0824/429340) down the road from the tourist office, or Cyber Zoom, 1st Floor, Utility Royal Towers, KS Rao Road (Mon–Sat 9.30am–6.30pm; ☎0824/449213).

Accommodation

Mangalore's **accommodation** standards are forever improving; it even has a modern five-star hotel. The main area for hotels, **KS Rao Road**, runs south from the bus stand and has an ample choice to suit most pockets. You can also stay out of town by the beach in **Ullal**.

KSTDC Mayura Netravathi, 1500m east of the bus stand, Kadir Hill ☎ 0824/211192. Rambling, old government hotel, the best of the budget bunch, with large, good-value en-suite rooms (most with twin beds and mozzie nets), although some are a little on the grubby side and it's a trek from the centre. None of the rickshaw-wallahs knows where it is, so ask for the "Circuit House", next door. ❷

Manorama, KS Rao Road ☎ 0824/440306. A 65-room concrete block with spartan, large and very clean rooms (some a/c). Good value, and the best of the central options. ❸–❻

Moti Mahal, Falnir Road ☎ 0824/441411. Large hotel (some a/c) with 24hr room service and coffee shop, bar, pool, shops, exchange and travel desk. *Mangala* non-veg and *Madhuvan* veg restaurants serve Indian, Chinese and Western food. ❻–❼

Navaratna Palace, KS Rao Road ☎ 0824/441104. Shares a reception with its adjacent sister *Navaratna* but has better rooms (some a/c) for little extra cost. Also two good a/c restaurants: *Heera Panna* and *Palimar* (pure veg). ❹–❼

Poonja International, KS Rao Road ☎ 0824/440171, ℱ 441081. Smart mostly a/c high-rise with all facilities and stunning views from the upper floors. Buffet south Indian breakfast included. ❻–❽

Summer Sands Beach Resort, Chota Mangalore, Ullal, 10km south of the city ☎ 0824/467690, ℱ 467693. Spacious rooms and cottages (some a/c) near the beach, originally built as a campus for expats, with a pool, and a bar-restaurant serving local specialities, Indian and Chinese food. Foreign exchange for guests. Recommended. Take bus #44A from town. ❻–❽

Taj Mahal, Hampankatta ☎ 0824/421751. Large dowdy economy hotel overlooking a busy crossing but handy for the train station; the restaurant, including a plain canteen and an a/c section, is renowned for its wholesome thalis. ❸–❻

Taj Manjarun, Old Port Road, 2km from railway station ☎ 0824/420420, ℱ 420585. Modern business hotel; some rooms with sea view and all a/c. Travel desk, exchange, pool, bar and 24hr coffee shop. The pricey restaurant, *Galley*, serves Indian and Western food; *Embers* is a poolside barbecue. ❼–❽

Vishwa Bhavan, KS Rao Road ☎ 0824/440822. Cheap, plain rooms, some with attached baths, around a courtyard close to all amenities. Best of the real cheapies. ❶

Woodside, KS Rao Road ☎ 0824/440296. Old-fashioned hotel offering a range of rooms (their economy doubles are the best deal), but "no accommodation for servants". Some a/c. ❸–❻

Kambla

If you're anywhere between Mangalore and Bhatkal from October to April and come across a crowd gathering around a waterlogged paddy field, pull over and spend a day at the races – Karnatakan style. Few Westerners ever experience it, but the unique and spectacular rural sport of **Kambla**, or **bull racing**, played in the southernmost district of coastal Karnataka (known as Dakshina Kannada), is well worth seeking out.

Two contestants, usually local rice farmers, take part in each race, riding on a wooden plough-board tethered to a pair of prize bullocks. The object is to reach the opposite end of the field first, but points are also awarded for style, and riders gain extra marks – and roars of approval from the crowd – if the muddy spray kicked up from the plough-board splashes the special white banners, or *thoranam*, strung across the course at a height of 6 to 8m.

Generally, race days are organized by wealthy landowners on fields specially set aside for the purpose. Villagers flock in from all over the region, as much for the fair, or *shendi*, as the races themselves: men huddle in groups to watch cockfights (*korikatta*), women haggle with bangle sellers, and the kids roam around sucking sticky *kathambdi goolay*, the local bonbons. It is considered highly prestigious to be able to throw such a party, especially if your bulls win any events or, better still, come away as champions. Known as *yeru* in Kannada, racing bulls are thoroughbreds who rarely, if ever, are put to work. Pampered by their doting owners, they are massaged, oiled and blessed by priests before big events, during which large sums of money are often won and lost.

The City and beaches

Mangalore's strong Christian influence can be traced back to the arrival further south of St Thomas (see p.1333). Some 1400 years later, in 1526, the Portuguese founded one of the earliest churches on the coast close to the old port. Today's **Most Holy Rosary Church**, however, with a dome based on St Peter's in Rome, dates only from 1910. Fine restored fresco, tempera and oil murals by an Italian artist, Antonio Moscheni, adorn the Romanesque-style **St Aloysius College Chapel**, built in 1885 on Lighthouse Hill, near the centre.

At the foot of Kadri Hill, 3km north, reached by a host of city buses, Mangalore's tenth-century **Manjunatha temple** is an important centre of the Shaivite and Tantric **Natha–Pantha cult**. Thought to be an outgrowth of Vajrayana Buddhism, the cult is a divergent species of Hinduism, similar to certain cults in Nepal. Enshrined in the sanctuary, a number of superb **bronzes** include a 1.5-metre-high seated Lokeshvara (Matsyendranatha), made in 958 AD and considered the finest southern bronze outside Tamil Nadu. To see it close up you'll have to visit at *darshan* times (6am–1pm & 4–8pm), although the bronzes can be glimpsed through the wooden slats on the side of the sanctuary. If possible, time your visit to coincide with *mahapooja* at 8am, noon or 8pm, when the priests give a fire blessing to the accompaniment of raucous music. Manjunatha's square and towered sanctuary, containing an unusual *lingam*, is surrounded by two tiled and gabled colonnades with louvred windows, showing strong affinity with the temple complexes further south in Kerala. Nine water tanks adjoin the temple. Opposite the east entrance, steps lead via a laterite path to a curious group of minor shrines. Beyond this complex stands the **Shri Yogishwar Math**, a hermitage of Tantric *sadhus* set round two courtyards, one of which contains shrines to Kala Bhairava (a form of Dakshinamurti, the southern aspect of Shiva and deity of death), Durga and god of fire, Agni. Nearby, cut into the side of the hill, a tiny unadorned cave is credited with being one of the "night halts" for the Pandava brothers from the *Mahabharata*.

If you're looking to escape the city for a few hours, head out to the village of **ULLAL**, 10km south, whose long sandy **beach**, backed by wispy fir trees, stretches for miles in both directions. It's a deservedly popular place for a stroll, particularly in the evening when families and courting couples come out to watch the sunset, but a strong undertow makes swimming difficult, and at times unsafe. You're better off using the pool at the excellent *Summer Sands Beach Resort* (see opposite), immediately behind the beach (Rs60 for nonresidents). A further 2km past the *Summer Sands*, a banyan-lined road leads to the Shiva temple of **Someshwar**, built in Keralan style, overlooking a rocky promontory, and another popular beach which is subject to crowds of gawking youths. Towards the centre of Ullal, and around 700m from the main bus stand, is the *dargah* (burial shrine) of **Seyyid Mohammad Shareeful Madani**, a sixteenth-century saint who is said to have come from Medina in Arabia and floated across the sea on a handkerchief. The extraordinary nineteenth-century building with garish onion domes houses the saint's tomb, which is one of the most important Sufi shrines in southern India. Visitors are advised to follow custom and cover their heads and limbs and wash their feet before entering. Local **buses** (#44A) run to Ullal from the junction at the south end of KS Rao Road. As you cross the Netravathi River en route, look out for the brick chimney stacks clustered on the banks at the mouth of the estuary. Using quality clay shipped downriver from the hills, these factories manufacture the famous terracotta red **Mangalorean roof tiles**, which you see all over southern India.

Eating

The best **places to eat** are in the bigger hotels. If you're on a tight budget, try one of the inexpensive café-restaurants opposite the bus stand, or the excellent

---

Moving on from Mangalore

Mangalore is a major crossroads for tourist traffic heading along the Konkan coast between Goa and Kerala, and between Mysore and the coast. The city is also well connected **by air** to **Mumbai**, **Bangalore** and **Chennai**. Jet Airways flies to Mumbai (1–2 daily) and to Bangalore (daily), while Indian Airlines flies to Mumbai (daily) and Chennai via Bangalore (3 weekly). The Indian Airlines office is at Airlines House, Hathill Road, Lalbagh (℡ 0824/454669) and the Jet Airways office at DS Ram Bhavan Complex, Kodiabail (℡ 0824/441181).

With the inauguration of the single-track coastal **Konkan Railway**, services have opened up to Goa and Mumbai and by 2001 all but one of the planned trains were operating. One passenger train #KR2 departs Mangalore at 7.10am, travelling north along the coast and takes 6hr 20min to travel to **Margao (Goa)** via Udupi and **Gokarn**. The Matsyagandha Express (#2620), which departs at 2.50pm, is the fastest service to Goa (4hr 50min), but does not stop at Gokarn. Until the through service is introduced you have to change at Margao for **Mumbai**. The service south is more established and if you're travelling to Kerala, the **train** is far quicker and more relaxing than the bus. Two services leave Mangalore station every day for **Trivandrum**, via **Kozhikode**, **Ernakulam/Cochin**, **Kottayam** and **Kollam**. Leaving at the red-eyed time of 3.15am, the Parsuram Express (#6350) is the faster of the two but the Malabar Express (#6330), which leaves at 4.30pm, is convenient as an overnight train to Trivandrum, arriving there at 9.35am. A better choice of train connections for the coastal run south can be had from **Kasargode**, an easy bus ride across the Kerala border. For those travelling to **Chennai**, the overnight Mangalore–Chennai Mail (#6602) departs at 11.15am and follows the Kerala coast till Shoranur where it turns east to **Palakaad** before journeying on to **Erode** and arriving at Chennai at 6.20am. The West Coast Express (#6628) departs Mangalore at 8.10pm. and follows the same route but also stops at **Coimbatore**.

The traditional way to travel on to **Goa** was always by **bus**, though that is now being usurped by the Konkan Railway. Six buses leave the KSRTC Lal Bagh stand daily, taking around 10hr 30min to reach Panjim. You can jump off at Chaudi (for Palolem) en route, and some buses also go via Margao (for Colva beach), but it's best to check, as most travel direct to the Goan capital. Tickets should be booked in advance (preferably the day before) at KSRTC's well-organized computer booking hall (daily 7am–8pm), or from the Kadamba office on the main concourse. The Goa buses are also good for **Gokarn**; hop off at **Kumta** on the main highway, and catch an onward service from there. The only direct bus to Gokarn leaves Mangalore at 1.30pm. There are plenty of buses to **Udupi** and several south along the coast to **Kasargode** and **Kannur** in Kerala. Many private services also plough up and down the coast to these destinations and some head inland to **Jog Falls**, as well as Bangalore and other major towns.

For **Mysore**, **Bangalore**, **Hassan** and **Madikeri**, it's best to take the bus as the train service inland to Hassan is slow and still disrupted due to work on the line. The best private bus service to Bangalore is on the distinctive yellow luxury coaches of VRL; two buses leave at night (10pm; 8hr; Rs220) and tickets are available through Vijayananda Travels, PVS Centenary Building, Kodiyalbail, Kudmulranga Rao Road (℡ 0824/493536). Agents along Falnir Road include Kohinoor Travels (℡ 0824/426400) and Ideal Travels (℡ 0824/424899) who also run luxury buses to Bangalore and a bus to **Ernakulam** (9pm; 9hr; Rs270). Bangalore-bound luxury buses travel through Madikeri and there are hourly KSRTC buses to Mysore.

canteen inside the bus stand itself, which serves great *dosas* and other south Indian snacks. Also recommended for delicious, freshly cooked and inexpensive "meals" is the *Ganesh Prasad*, down the lane alongside the *Vasanth Mahal*. The rooftop *Palkhi* on Mercara Trunk Road is an airy family restaurant with a wide menu. For something a little more sophisticated, head for the a/c *Xanadu*, at the *Woodside Hotel*, also on KS Rao Road, which offers classy non-veg cuisine and alcohol. It's too dingy for lunch, but fine for dinner, when its kitsch fish tanks and resident duck are illuminated. One of the best of the hotel restaurants, however, is the *Moghul Darbar* at the *Mangalore International* also on KS Rao Road, which has both a plush a/c and a comfortable and non-a/c section. Although they do not serve alcohol, they offer an excellent mixed menu – if you order a vegetarian thali and add fish to it, you have a feast.

North of Mangalore: coastal Karnataka

Whether you travel the **Karnatakan (Karavali) coast** on the newly operational Konkan Railway or along the busy NH-14, southern India's smoothest highway, the route between Goa and Mangalore ranks among the most scenic anywhere in the country. Crossing countless palm- and mangrove-fringed estuaries, the railway line stays fairly flat, while the recently upgraded road, dubbed by the local tourist board as "The Sapphire Route", scales several spurs of the Western Ghats, which here creep to within a stone's throw of the sea, with spellbinding views over long, empty beaches and deep blue bays. Highlights are the pilgrim town of **Udupi**, site of a famous Krishna temple, and **Gokarn**, a bustling village that provides access to exquisite unexploited beaches. A couple of bumpy back roads wind inland through the mountains to **Jog Falls**, India's biggest waterfall, most often approached from the east. Infrequent buses crawl from the coast through rugged jungle scenery to this spectacular spot, but you'll enjoy the trip more by motorbike; it is possible to rent one in Goa and ride down the coast from there, stopping off at secluded beaches, falls and viewpoints en route.

Udupi

UDUPI (also spelt Udipi), on the west coast, 58km north of Mangalore, is one of south India's holiest Vaishnavite centres. The Hindu saint **Madhva** (1238–1317) was born here, and the **Krishna temple** and *maths* (monasteries) he founded are visited by *lakhs* of pilgrims each year. The largest numbers congregate during the late winter, when the town hosts a series of spectacular **car festivals** and gigantic, bulbous-domed chariots are hauled through the streets around the temple. Even if your visit doesn't coincide with a festival, Udupi is a good place to break the journey along the Karavali coast. Thronging with *pujaris* and pilgrims, its small sacred enclave is wonderfully atmospheric, and you can take a boat from the nearby fishing village of **Malpé beach** to **St Mary's Island**, the deserted outcrop of hexagonal basalt where Vasco da Gama erected a crucifix prior to his first landfall in India.

Incidentally, Udupi also lays proud claim to being the birthplace of the nationally popular **masala dosa**; these crispy stuffed pancakes, made from fermented rice flour, were first prepared and made famous by the Udupi brahmin hotels. Certainly, the food in Udupi is excellent.

Practicalities

Udupi's three **bus stands** are dotted around the main street in the centre of town: the "City" stand handles private services to nearby villages, including Malpé, while the adjacent "Service" stand is for long-distance private buses including numerous services to Mangalore. The KSRTC stand is for long-distance government buses to and from Mangalore, Bangalore, Gokarn, Jog Falls and Goa, and other towns along the coastal highway. Udupi's **railway station** is at Indrali on Manipal Road 3km from the centre and there are four or five trains in each direction daily. Money can be **exchanged** at the KM Dutt branch of Canara Bank on the main road just south of the bus stands. **Email** facilities are available at nearby Netpoint, one of several such outlets.

Udupi has a good choice of **places to stay and eat**. The *Hotel Sharada International* (℡08252/22910; ❸–❺), 1km out of town on the highway, has a range of rooms from singles to carpeted a/c, as well as veg and non-veg restaurants and a bar. *Kediyoor*, near the Service bus stand (℡08252/22381, 🖷22380; ❹–❻) is much the same, but with three restaurants – the a/c *Janata* serves excellent thalis, while the *Janardhana*, close to the KSRTC stand (℡08252/23880, 🖷23887; ❸–❻) is a little simpler with clean rooms, some a/c. The *Classic* restaurant in the building next door offers great seafood (chowder for example), meat and veg dishes in a classy upstairs lounge and their *Wild Rain* bar is a lively place for a drink. A couple of minutes' walk east of the main road, the *Hotel Swadesh Heritage*, Maruthi Vethika (℡08252/29605, 🖷20205, Ⓔswadesh-vip@zetainfotech.com; ❹–❼) is Udupi's most luxurious hotel, at least until the nearby *Sriram International* opens, with complimentary breakfasts, reasonable a/c rooms and two restaurants and a bar. Their vegetarian thalis are excellent. If you're looking for somewhere cheaper, try the basic but friendly and clean *Vyavahar Lodge*, on Kankads Road (℡08252/22568; ❷), between the bus stand and temple, or, better still, try and get one of the great-value front rooms overlooking the tank and temple at the new *Sri Vidyasamudra Chatra* (℡08252/20820; ❶).

The Krishna temple and maths

Udupi's **Krishna temple** lies five minutes' walk east of the main street, surrounded by the eight **maths** founded by Madhva in the thirteenth century. Legend has it that the idol enshrined within was discovered by the saint himself after he prevented a shipwreck. The grateful captain of the vessel concerned offered Madhva his precious cargo as a reward, but the holy man asked instead for a block of ballast, which he broke open to expose a perfectly formed image of Krishna. Believed to contain the essence (*sannidhya*) of the god, this deity draws a steady stream of pilgrims, and is the focus of all but constant ritual activity. It is cared for by *archaryas*, or pontiffs, from one or other of the *maths*. The only people allowed to touch the idol, they perform *pujas* (5.30am–8.45pm) that are open to non-Hindus; men are only allowed into the main shrine bare-chested. As the *acharya* approaches the shrine, the crowd divides to let him through, while brahmin boys fan the deity with cloths, accompanied by a cacophony of clanging bells and clouds of incense smoke.

A stone tank adjacent to the temple, known as the **Madhva Sarovara**, is the focus of a huge festival every two years (usually Jan 17/18), when a new head priest is appointed. Preparations for the **Paryaya Mahotsava** begin thirteen months in advance, and culminate with the grand entry of the new *acharya* into the town, at the head of a huge procession. Outside in the street, a window in the wall affords a view of the deity; according to legend, this is the spot where a Harijan, or "untouchable" devotee, denied entry due to his caste, was worshipping Krishna from outside when the deity turned to face him. A statue of the devotee stands opposite. Nearby, there's a magnificent gold-painted temple chariot (*rath*), woodcarved in the distinctive Karnatakan style, its onion-shaped tower decked with thousands of scraps of paper, cloth and tinsel.

At the **Regional Resources Centre for the Performing Arts**, in the MGM College, staff can tell you about local festivals and events that are well off the tourist trail; the collection includes film, video and audio archives. The pamphlet *Udupi: an Introduction*, on sale in the stalls around the sacred enclave, is another rich source of background detail on the temple and its complex rituals.

Malpé, Thottam and St Mary's Island

Udupi's weekend picnic spot, **Malpé beach**, 5km north of the centre, is disappointing, marred by a forgotten concrete block that was planned to be a government-run hotel. After wandering around the smelly fish market at the harbour you could haggle to arrange a boat (Rs800) to take you out to **St Mary's Island**, an extraordinary rockface of hexagonal basalt. Vasco da Gama is said to have placed a cross here in the 1400s, prior to his historic landing at Kozhikode in Kerala. From a distance, the sandy beach at **Thottam**, 1km north of Malpé and visible from the island, is tempting; in reality it's an open sewer.

Jog Falls

Hidden in a remote, thickly forested corner of the Western Ghats, **Jog Falls**, 240km northeast of Mangalore, are the highest **waterfalls** in India. These days, they are rarely as spectacular as they were before the construction of a large dam upriver, which impedes the flow of the River Sharavati over the sheer redbrown sandstone cliffs. However, the surrounding scenery is stunning at any time, with dense scrub and jungle carpeting sparsely populated, mountainous terrain. The views of the falls from the scruffy collection of chai stalls on the opposite side of the gorge is also impressive, unless, that is, you come here during the monsoons, when mist and rain clouds envelop the cascades. Another reason not to come here during the wet season is that the extra water, and abundance of leeches at this time, make the excellent **hike** to the floor valley dangerous. So if you can, head up here between October and January, and bring stout footwear. The trail starts just below the bus park and winds steeply down to the water. Confident hikers also venture further downriver, clambering over boulders to other pools and hidden viewpoints, but you should keep a close eye on the water level and take along a local **guide** to point out the safest path.

Practicalities

Getting to and from Jog Falls by public transport is not easy but should be soon with the completion of the NH-240 across the Ghats, which will cut the journey time from **Kumta** to three hours. Currently there are two **buses** daily from the Falls to Udupi and on to Mangalore (7.30am & 8.15pm; 7hr), one to Karwar (11.30am; 6hr), one to Gokarn (5.30pm; 5hr) and hourly services to Shimoga, from where you can change onto buses for Hospet and Hampi. Better connections can be had at nearby Sagar (30km southeast) with buses to Shimoga, Udupi, Mysore, Hassan and Bangalore. Of the two direct buses to Bangalore from Jog Falls, the "semi-deluxe" departs at 7.30pm (9hr) and the ordinary at 8.30am. The **tourist office** at *Tunga Tourist Home* (Mon–Sat 10am–5.30pm) is good for bus times and advice in case you need to rent a **car** or a Jeep, both available at Jog Falls. With a car or motorbike, you can approach

the falls from the coast along one of several scenic routes through the Ghats. The easiest and best maintained of these heads inland from Bhatkal to Jog Falls, but for a truly unforgettable experience, risk the tortuous, bumpy back route from **Kumta**, which takes you through some breathtaking landscape. There are very few villages, and no fuel stops, along the way, so stock up beforehand, and make sure your vehicle is in good shape.

Accommodation is limited. If you can get in, the *PWD Inspection Bungalow* (❶), on the north side of the gorge, has great views from its spacious, comfortable rooms, but is invariably full and has to be booked in advance from the Assistant Engineer's office in Siddapur. Across the falls on the main side of the settlement, the large concrete complex of the KSTDC *Mayura Gerusoppa* (T 08186/44732; ❷–❸), located past the nonfunctioning public swimming pool, has vast rooms with fading plaster and bathrooms with rickety plumbing, but the staff are friendly and there's an adequate restaurant plus good views. Their annexe, the KSTDC *Tunga Tourist Home* at the bus stand is more basic (❷) and doesn't have the garden or view. On the opposite side of the road the Karnataka Power Corporation also let their four comfy a/c rooms (T 08186/44742; ❺) when available. The youth hostel (❶), ten minutes' walk down the Shimoga road, has basic facilities but recent renovations have made it more appealing. Most travellers make do with a raffia mat on the floor of one of the houses behind the chai stalls.

The KSTDC canteen next to the *Tunga Tourist Home* at the bus stand serves reasonable south Indian vegetarian **food** including *iddlis* and *dosas*. The KSTDC *Mayura Gerusoppa* has a more comfortable restaurant with a varied menu but still manages to remain uninspiring while the chai stalls around the square serve basic thalis and (eggy) snacks.

Gokarn

Set behind a broad white-sand beach, with the forest-covered foothills of the Western Ghats forming a blue-green backdrop, **GOKARN** (also spelled Gokarna), seven hours by bus north of Mangalore, is among India's most scenically situated sacred sites. Yet this compact little coastal town – a Shaivite centre for more than two millennia – remained largely "undiscovered" by Western tourists until the early 1990s, when it began to attract dreadlocked and didjgeridoo-toting travellers fleeing the commercialization of Goa. Now, it's firmly on the tourist map, although the Hindu pilgrims pouring through still far outnumber the foreigners that flock here in winter.

Even if you're not tempted to while away weeks on isolated beaches, Gokarn is well worth a short detour from the coastal highway. Like Udupi, it is an old-established pilgrimage place, with a markedly traditional feel: shaven-headed brahmins sit crosslegged on their verandas murmuring Sanskrit verses, while Hindu pilgrims file through a bazaar crammed with religious paraphernalia to the sea for a holy dip.

Arrival and information

The new KSRTC **bus stand**, 300m from Car Street and within easy walking distance of Gokarn's limited accommodation, means that buses no longer have to negotiate the narrow streets of the bazaar. Gokarn's **railway station**, served by one daily passenger train in each direction, is at Madanageri, from where buses and *tempos* are available to take you the 9km into town.

You can **change money** at the *Om Hotel* near the new bus stand but the best rates to be had are at the Pai STD booth on the road into town near the bus

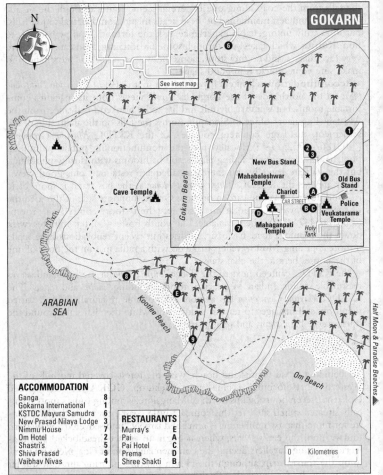

ACCOMMODATION

Ganga	8
Gokarna International	1
KSTDC Mayura Samudra	6
New Prasad Nilaya Lodge	3
Nimmu House	7
Om Hotel	2
Shastri's	5
Shiva Prasad	9
Vaibhav Nivas	4

RESTAURANTS

Murray's	E
Pai	A
Pai Hotel	C
Prema	D
Shree Shakti	B

0   Kilometres   1

stand, one several licensed dealers. The tiny Om bureau almost opposite is the best of the various **internet** joints but none have very reliable connections. **Bicycles** are available for rent from a stall next to the *Pai Restaurant*, for Rs3 per hour or Rs30 for a full day. However, due to the roughness of the tracks you will find it near impossible to cycle to beaches other than the town beach, or along the long route to Om beach.

Accommodation

Gokarn has a couple of bona fide **hotels** and a small but reasonable choice of **guesthouses**. As a last resort, you can nearly always find a bed in one of the pilgrims' hostels, or **dharamshalas**, dotted around town. With dorms, bare, cell-size rooms and basic washing facilities, these are intended mainly for Hindus, but Western tourists are welcome if there are vacancies: try the *Prasad Nilaya*, just down the lane from *Om Hotel*. After staying in the village for a couple of days, however, many visitors strike out for the **beaches**, where there is very limited accommodation (see p.1438). Some people end up sleeping rough on the beaches, but the nights can be chilly and robberies are common. Leave your luggage and valuables behind in Gokarn (most guesthouses will store your stuff for a fee), and if you plan to spend any time on the beaches, consider investing in a cheap mattress from the bazaar – you can always sell it on when you leave.

Gokarna International, on main road into town ☎ 08386/56622. Gokarna's newest and smartest hotel, which is friendly and offers unbeatable value. Good range of rooms from cheap singles to deluxe a/c; some have bathtubs, TV and balconies overlooking the palms. Also features two good restaurants, one with bar. ➋–➏ .

KSTDC Mayura Samudra, high on a bald hill above Gokarn (look for the sign on the left as you arrive) ☎ 08386/56236. Only three large rooms with crumbling plaster and bathrooms with rickety plumbing, each with sitout and garden overlooking the coast and out to sea. The staff are friendly and helpful and serve meals to order. A good option if you have transport or are willing to tackle the short but steep hike up from the bazaar past the police barracks. ➋

New Prasad Nilaya Lodge, near the new bus stand ☎ 08386/57135. A relatively new place with clean, bright spacious rooms with attached baths and food to order. Very reasonable. ➋–➌

Nimmu House, a minute's walk from the temples towards Gokarn beach ☎ 08386/56730. Gokarn's best budget guesthouse, run by the friendly and helpful lady whose name it bears, with clean rooms (some attached). The new block has very reasonable doubles; there's a reliable left-luggage facility and peaceful yard to sit in. ➊–➋

Om Hotel, near the new bus stand ☎ 08386/56445. Conventional economy hotel pitched at middle-class Indian pilgrims, with plain, good-sized en-suite rooms, some a/c, and a dingy bar-cum-restaurant. ➋–➎

Shastri Guest House, 100m from the new bus stand ☎ 08386/56220. The best of the uniformly drab and run-down guesthouses lining the main street, this is a quiet place offering some rooms with attached bath, and rock-bottom single occupancy rates. ➋

Vaibhav Nivas, off the main road, five minutes from the bazaar ☎ 08386/56714. Friendly, cheap and justifiably popular place despite the tiny rooms, most with shared bathrooms. The new extension includes some rooms with attached bathrooms. You can eat here, too, and leave luggage if you're heading off to the beaches (Rs5 per locker including a shower on return). ➊–➋

The Town

Gokarn **town**, a hotchpotch of wood-fronted houses and red terracotta roofs, is clustered around a long L-shaped bazaar, its broad main road – known as **Car Street** – running west to the town beach, a sacred site in its own right. Hindu mythology identifies it as the place where Rudra (another name for Shiva) was reborn through the ear of a cow from the underworld after a period of penance. Gokarn is also the home of one of India's most powerful *shivalinga* – the **pranalingam**, which came to rest here after being carried off by Ravana, the evil king of Lanka, from Shiva's home on Mount Kailash in the Himalayas. Sent by the gods to reclaim the sacred object, Ganesh, with the help of Vishnu, tricked Ravana into letting him look after the *lingam* while he prayed, knowing that if it touched the ground it would take root and never be moved. When Ravana returned from his meditation, he tried to pick the *lingam* up, but couldn't, because the gods had filled it with "the weight of three worlds".

The *pranalingam* resides in Gokarn to this day, enshrined in the medieval **Shri Mahabaleshwar temple**, at the far west end of the bazaar. It is regarded as so auspicious that a mere glimpse of it will absolve a hundred sins, even the murder of a brahmin. Local Hindu lore also asserts that you can maximize the *lingam*'s purifying power by shaving your head, fasting, and taking a holy dip in the sea before *darshan*, or ritual viewing of the deity. For this reason, pilgrims traditionally begin their tour of Gokarn with a walk to the beach. They are aided and instructed by their personal *pujari* – one of the bare-chested priests you see around town, wearing sacred caste threads, and with single tufts of hair sprouting from their shaven heads – whose job it is to guide the pilgrims. Next, they visit the **Shri Mahaganpati temple**, a stone's throw east of Shri Mahabaleshwar, to propitiate the elephant-headed god Ganesh. Sadly, owing to some ugly incidents involving insensitive behaviour by a minority of foreigners, tourists are now banned from the temples, though you can still get a good view of proceedings in the smaller Shri Mahaganpati from the entrance. En route, check out the splendid **rath**, or chariot, that stands at the end of the bazaar next to the Mahaganpati temple. During important festivals, notably Shiva's "birthday", **Shivratri** (Feb), deities are installed inside this colossal carved-wood cart and hauled by hand along the main street, accompanied by drum bands and watched by huge crowds.

The beaches

Notwithstanding Gokarn's numerous temples, shrines and tanks, most Western tourists come here for the beautiful **beaches** situated south of the more crowded town beach, beyond the lumpy laterite headland that overlooks the town. The hike to them takes in some superb coastal scenery, but be sure to carry plenty of water and wear a hat.

To pick up the trail, head along the narrow alley opposite the south entrance to the Mahaganpati temple, and follow the path uphill through the woods. After twenty minutes, you drop down from a sun-baked rocky plateau to **Kootlee beach** – a wonderful kilometre-long sweep of pure white sand sheltered by a pair of steep-sided promontories. Despite appearances, locals consider the water here to be dangerous. The palm-leaf chai stalls and seasonal cafés that spring up here during the winter offer some respite from the heat of the midday sun, and some of them offer very basic accommodation in bamboo shacks. Two places have more solid, lockable brick or mud huts but are likely to be booked out by long-term visitors; the *Ganga*, to the right as you first approach the beach (☏08386/57195; **●**); and *Shiva Prasad* at the far end (☏08386/57150; **●**). *Murray's Tea Shop* (aka the "Spanish teashop" after his wife) set behind a line of neatly planted palms midway down the beach, serves good pasta, sandwiches, sweets and creamy lassis in a relaxed atmosphere, and a couple of the other cafés now offer seafood and other more substantial meals. Freshwater has been a perennial problem but bottled water is widely available.

It takes around twenty minutes to hike from Kootlee to the next beach, scaling the headland to the south and following the steep gravel path as it zigzags down the other side to the sea. The views along the way are stunning, especially when you first glimpse exquisite **Om beach**, so named because its distinctive twin crescent-shaped bays resemble the auspicious Om symbol. During the Nineties this was the all-but-exclusive preserve of a hard-core hippy fringe, many of whom spend months here wallowing in a *charas*-induced torpor. However, the overall increased popularity of the area means it is now frequented by a more diverse crowd and the arrival of a dirt road from Gokarn (7km), combined with the recent acquisition of the land by developers, may slowly transform the scene into more of a resort. As it is, hammocks and basic huts still populate the palm groves and about a dozen chai houses provide ample food, drink and occasional other substances.

If the concrete mixers do descend, it's unlikely they'll ever reach Gokarn's two most remote beaches, which lie another forty- to sixty-minute walk over the hill. Tantalizingly inaccessible, **Half-Moon** and **Paradise** beaches, reached via difficult dirt paths across a sheer hillside, are, despite the presence of one or two chai houses on each and the occasional shack, mainly for intrepid sun-lovers happy to pack in their own supplies. If you're looking for near-total isolation, this is your best bet.

Eating

Gokarn town offers a good choice of **places to eat**, with a crop of busy "meals" joints along Car Street and the main road. Most popular, with locals and tourists, is the brightly lit *Pai Restaurant*, which dishes up fresh and tasty veg thalis, *masala dosas*, crisp *wadas*, teas and coffees until late. The other commendable "meals" canteen, around the corner on Car Street, is also called the *Pai Hotel*; it's much smaller, but their snacks are excellent, and the milk coffee delicious. *Shree Shakti Cold Drinks*, also on Car Street, serves mouthwatering fresh cheese, hygienically made to an American recipe and served with rolls, garlic and tomato; the friendly owner also makes his own peanut butter, and serves filling toasties and lassis. Round this off with an ice cream, either here or at any number of places along the road.

Every café does its own version of *gad-bads*, several layers of different ice creams mixed with chopped nuts and chewy dried fruit. One of the best is served at the tiny *Prema Restaurant* opposite the Mahabaleshwar temple's main gates, which has a traveller-friendly menu. The new *Gokarna International* hotel has two fine eateries: the non-veg *Downtown* offers a range of tasty meat dishes and a full bar, while the smaller *Purohit* serves south Indian veg staples. The restaurant bar at the *Om* does good fish and is more pleasant if you can find a seat in the small courtyard rather than the dingy interior.

Moving on from Gokarn

Gokarn is well connected by direct daily bus to Goa (5hr), and several towns in Karnataka, including Bangalore (13hr), Hospet/Hampi (10hr) and Mysore (14hr), via Mangalore (7hr) and Udupi (6hr). Although there are only three direct buses north along the coast to Karwar (2hr) close to the border with Goa, you can change at Ankola on the main highway for more services. For more buses to Hospet and Hampi and the best connections to Jog Falls, change at Kumta; tempos regularly ply the route between Gokarn and Kumta (32km) as well as Ankola. The KSRTC counter in the new bus stand is helpful for current bus timings.

You'll get the best train connections to Goa, Mangalore, Udupi and Kerala by going first to either Kumta or Ankola, though in the near future Gokarna Road station is due to have more services than the current one in each direction; for now, only the #KR2 passenger train to Margao at 11.30am and #KR1 to Mangalore at 3.56pm make a stop here.

Hospet

Charmless **HOSPET**, about ten hours from both Bangalore and Goa, is of little interest except as a transport hub: in particular, it is the jumping-off place for the extraordinary ruined city of Vijayanagar (Hampi), 13km northeast. If you arrive late, or want somewhere fairly comfortable to sleep, it makes sense to stay here and catch a bus or taxi out to the ruins the following morning. Otherwise, hole up in Hampi, where the setting more than compensates for the basic facilities.

Hospet's **railway station**, 1500m north of the centre, is served by the overnight Hampi Express #6592 from Bangalore and services from

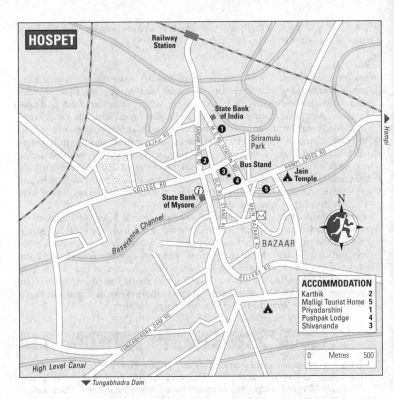

HOSPET

Railway Station

State Bank of India ❶

Sriramulu Park

RAJAJI RD

SARDAR PATEL RD

M.G. RD (STATION) RD

COLLEGE RD

❷

❸ ★ ❹

Bus Stand

❺

HAMPI CROSS RD

Jain Temple

State Bank of Mysore ℹ

OLD BUS STAND RD

MAIN BAZAAR RD

BAZAAR

N

Basavanna Channel

BELLARY RD

Hampi ▸

TUNGABHADRA DAM RD

High Level Canal

▾ Tungabhadra Dam

ACCOMMODATION

Karthik	2
Malligi Tourist Home	5
Priyadarshini	1
Pushpak Lodge	4
Shivananda	3

0   Metres   500

Hyderabad, via Guntakal Junction. The line continues west to Hubli for connections to the coast and Goa. For connections to Badami and Bijapur, travel to Gadag and change onto the slow single track running north. Auto-rickshaws are plentiful or you can get into town by cycle rickshaw (Rs10) or by foot if unencumbered.

The **long-distance bus stand** is in the centre, just off MG (Station) Road, which runs south from the railway station. The most frequent services are from Bangalore and Hubli, and there are daily arrivals from Mysore, Badami, Bijapur, Hassan, Gokarn (via Kumta), Mangalore and Goa. For a summary of services see Travel Details on p.1468. **Bookings** for long-distance routes can be made at the ticket office on the bus stand concourse (daily 8am–noon & 3–6pm), where there's also a **left-luggage** facility.

The **tourist office** at the Rotary Circle (Mon–Sat: June–March 10am–5.30pm; April & May 8am–1.30pm; ☏08394/28537) offers limited information and sells tickets for the KSTDC conducted tours (see below). You can **exchange** travellers' cheques and cash at the State Bank of Mysore (Mon–Fri 10.30am–2.30pm & Sat 10.30am–12.30pm), next to the tourist office, and cash only at the State Bank of India (same hours) on Station Road. Full exchange facilities are available at the *Hotel Malligi*, while Neha Travels (☏08394/25838) at the Elimanchate Complex, next to the *Hotel Priyadarshini* on MG Road, also changes any currency and travellers' cheques, and advances money on credit cards. They also have branches in Hampi and book airline and train tickets and cars, and run private **luxury buses to Goa**. Their sleeper coach departs at 7pm, costs Rs400 and takes fourteen hours. Luxury buses are also available for Bangalore (10hr; Rs200) departing between 10pm and 11pm at night. You can also buy tickets for these buses at Malleshwara Travels (℡08394/25696) opposite the bus stand.

Accommodation and eating

Accommodation in Hospet, concentrated around MG Road, ranges from budget to mid-price. By far the most popular place to stay is the incredibly versatile *Malligi Tourist Home*, with something to suit most budgets, but the *Priyadarshini* is also good value and nearer the railway station.

There's little to do in Hospet, so you'll probably pass a fair amount of time **eating** and **drinking**. Many of the hotels have good dining rooms, but in the evening, the upscale though affordable *Waves*, a terrace restaurant in the *Malligi* complex, is the most congenial place to hang out, serving tandoori and chilled beer from 7pm to 11pm (bring lots of mosquito repellent). *Shanbhog*, an excellent little Udupi restaurant next to the bus station, is a perfect pit stop before heading to Hampi, and opens early for breakfast.

Karthik, Pampa Villa, off MG Road ℡08394/24938, ℻20028. A new, characterless block featuring unremarkable rooms but with a surprise around the back in the form of an extraordinary nineteenth-century stone villa housing two huge suites. ❸–❼

Malligi Tourist Home, 6/143 Jambunatha Rd, 2min walk east of MG Road (look for the signs) and the bus stand ℡08394/28101, ℻27038. Friendly, well-managed hotel with cheaper, clean, comfortable rooms (some a/c) in the old block and two new wings across the immaculate lawn, with luxurious air-conditioned rooms. There is also a great new swimming pool (Rs25/hr for nonresidents) in their Waves complex beneath the restaurant/bar. They sell the otherwise hard-to-find journal *Homage to Hampi*, and offer foreign exchange. The alfresco *Madhu Paradise* restaurant/bar in the

old block serves great veg food and they have an efficient travel service. ❷–❽

Priyadarshini, MG Road, up the road from the bus stand, towards the railway station ℡08394/28838. Rooms from rock-bottom singles to doubles with TV and a/c (some balconies). Large, and bland, but spotless and very good value. They have two good restaurants: the veg *Naivedyam* and, in the garden, non-veg *Manasa*, which has a bar. Their travel service handles bus and train tickets. ❷–❻

Pushpak Lodge, near bus stand, MG Road ℡08394/21380. With basic but clean attached rooms, this is the best rock-bottom lodge. ❷

Shivananda, beside bus stand, ℡08394/20700. Well-maintained hotel with spotless rooms, all attached with cable TV and some a/c. Very good value. ❸–❺

Getting to Hampi

KSTDC's daily guided **tour** only stops at three of the sites in Hampi and spends an inordinate amount of time at the far less interesting Tungabhadra Dam. Even so, it can be worth it if you're short of time. It leaves from the tourist office at Rotary Circle (Taluk Office Circle), east of the bus station (9.30am–5.30pm; Rs80 including lunch).

Frequent **buses to Hampi** run from the bus stand between 6.30am and 7.30pm; the journey takes thirty minutes. If you arrive late, either stay in Hospet, or take a taxi (Rs100–150) or one of the rickshaws (Rs60–80) that gather outside the railway station. It is also possible to catch a bus to **Kamalpura**, at the south side of the site, and explore the ruins from there, catching a bus back to Hospet from Hampi Bazaar at the end of the day. **Bicycles** are available for rent at several stalls along the main street, but the trip to, around, and back from the site is a long one in the heat. Auto-rickshaws, best arranged through hotels such as the *Malligi* or *Priyadarshini*, will also take you to Hampi and back and charge up to Rs200. For the adventurous, Bullet **motorbikes** are available to rent (or sale) from Bharat Motors

(☎ 08394/24704) near *Rama Talkies*. Finally, some hotels in Hospet can also organize for you to hook up with **trained guides** in Hampi; ask at the *Malligi* or *Priyadarshini*.

Hampi (Vijayanagar)

The city of Bidjanagar [Vijayanagar] is such that the pupil of the eye has never seen a place like it, and the ear of intelligence has never been informed that there existed anything to equal it in the world. . . . The bazaars are extremely long and broad. . . . Roses are sold everywhere. These people could not live without roses, and they look upon them as quite as necessary as food. . . . Each class of men belonging to each profession has shops contiguous the one to the other; the jewellers sell publicly in the bazaars pearls, rubies, emeralds and diamonds. In this agreeable locality, as well as in the king's palace, one sees numerous running streams and canals formed of chiselled stone, polished and smooth. . . . This empire contains so great a population that it would be impossible to give an idea of it without entering into extensive details.

Abdu'r-Razzaq, the Persian ambassador, who visited Vijayanagar in 1443.

The ruined city of **Vijayanagar**, "the City of Victory" (also known as **HAMPI**, the name of a local village), spills from the south bank of the Tungabhadra River, littered among a surreal landscape of golden-brown granite boulders and leafy banana fields. According to Hindu mythology, the settlement began its days as Kishkinda, the monkey kingdom of the *Ramayana*, ruled by the monkey kings Vali and Sugriva and their ambassador, Hanuman; the weird rocks – some balanced in perilous arches, others heaped in colossal, hill-sized piles – are said to have been flung down by their armies in a show of strength.

Between the fourteenth and sixteenth centuries, this was the most powerful Hindu capital in the Deccan. Travellers such as the Portuguese chronicler Domingo Paez, who stayed for two years after 1520, were astonished by its size and wealth, telling tales of markets full of silk and precious gems, beautiful, bejewelled courtesans, ornate palaces and joyous festivities. However, in the second half of the sixteenth century, the dazzling city was devastated by a six-month Muslim siege. Only stone, brick and stucco structures survived the ensuing sack – monolithic deities, crumbling houses and abandoned temples dominated by towering *gopuras* – as well as the sophisticated irrigation system that channelled water to huge tanks and temples.

Thanks to the Muslim onslaught, most of Hampi's monuments are in disappointingly poor shape, seemingly a lot older than their four or five hundred years. Yet the serene riverine setting and air of magic that lingers over the site, sacred for centuries before a city was founded here, make it one of India's most extraordinary locations. Even so, mainstream tourism has thus far made little impact: along with streams of Hindu pilgrims, and tatty-haired *sadhus* who hole up in the more isolated rock crevices and shrines, most visitors are budget travellers straight from Goa. Many find it difficult to leave, and spend weeks chilling out in cafés, wandering to whitewashed hilltop temples and gazing at the spectacular sunsets.

The **best time to come** to Hampi, weather-wise, is from October to March, when daytime temperatures are low enough to allow long forays on foot through the ruins. It does start to get busy over Christmas and New Year, however, and from early January for a month or so the site is swamped by an

VIJAYANAGAR / HAMPI

Hanuman Temple

Tungabhadra River

ANEGONDI

Coracle Jetty

Virupapuragadda

Vitthala
Temple

King's
Balance

See Hampi
Bazaar map

Agni Temple &
Kotalinga Complex

Sacred
Ford

Virupaksha
Temple

Bus
Stand

Narasimha
Temple

HAMPI
BAZAAR

Rama
Temple

Achutya Bazaar

Hemakuta
Hill

Matanga
Hill

Achutharaya
Temple

Narashima
Statue

Krishna Temple

Guards'
Quarters

Gateway

Palace

Elephant Stables

Hazara Rama
Temple

Madhava Temple

Yellamma Temple

'Underground'
Temple

Palace

Hall of
Justice

Mahanavami-
Dibba

Queen's
Bath

Jain
Temple

Bhima's
Gate

Not to scale

N

ACCOMMODATION

KSTDC Mayura Bhuvaneshwari	3
Umashankar Lodge	2
Vijayanagar	1

RESTAURANT

| Goan Corner | A |

Museum

KAMALAPURAM

Kamalapuram
Bus Stand

Hospet

▼ Hospet

exodus of travellers from Goa that has been increasing dramatically over the past few years; there have even been Anjuna-style full-moon parties, complete with techno sound systems and busloads of ravers most of whom come from Israel. The influx also attracts its share of dodgy characters, and crime has become a problem in the village at this time; so if you want to enjoy Hampi at its best, come outside peak season.

Some history

This was an area of minor political importance under the Chalukyas; the rise of the **Vijayanagar empire** seems to have been a direct response, in the first half of the fourteenth century, to the expansionist aims of Muslims from the

Police, thieves and mosquitoes

Hampi is generally a safe site to wander around, but a spate of armed attacks on tourists over the past few years means that you ought to think twice before venturing on your own, especially after dark, to a number of known trouble spots. Foremost among these is Matanga Hill, to the east of Hampi Bazaar, dubbed by local guides as "sunrise point" because it looks east. Muggers have been known to jump Westerners on their way to the temple before dawn here, escaping with their cameras and money into the rocks. Although there have been fewer such incidents in the last couple of years, it's still advisable to go in a group, and to leave valuables behind. Incredibly, photographs of known rogues are posted by the police at lodges and one must wonder, as the thieves are familiar to them, why the culprits are allowed to be at large in the first place. As some precaution, the police request foreigners to register with them at the Hampi Police Outpost (℡ 08394/41240) at the Virupaksha temple.

The other hassle to watch out for in Hampi is the police themselves, who are not averse to squeezing the odd backhander from tourists. You'll see chillums smoked in the cafés, but possession of hashish (*charas*) is a serious offence in Karnataka, liable to result in a huge bribe, or worse. There have also been reports of local cops arresting and extracting baksheesh from Western men who walk around shirtless. Another reason to stay fully dressed in Hampi, particularly in the evenings, is that it is a prime malaria zone. Sleep under a mosquito net if you have one, and smother yourself in insect repellent well before sunset.

north, most notably Malik Kafur and Mohammed-bin-Tughluq. Two Hindu brothers from Andhra Pradesh, Harihara and Bukka, who had been employed as treasury officers in Kampila, 19km east of Hampi, were captured by the Tughluqs and taken to Delhi, where they supposedly converted to Islam. Assuming them to be suitably tamed, the Delhi sultan despatched them to quell civil disorder in Kampila, which they duly did, only to abandon both Islam and allegiance to Delhi shortly afterwards, preferring to establish their own independent Hindu kingdom. Within a few years they controlled vast tracts of land from coast to coast. In 1343 their new capital, Vijayanagar, was founded on the southern banks of the River Tungabhadra, a location long considered sacred by Hindus. The city's most glorious period was under the reign of **Krishna Deva Raya** (1509–29), when it enjoyed a near monopoly of the lucrative trade in Arabian horses and Indian spices passing through the coastal ports.

Thanks to its natural features and massive fortifications, Vijayanagar was virtually impregnable. In 1565, however, following his interference in the affairs of local Muslim sultanates, the regent Rama Raya was drawn into a battle with a confederacy of Muslim forces, 100km away to the north, which left the city undefended. At first, fortune appeared to be on the side of the Hindu forces, but there were as many as 10,000 Muslims in their number, and loyalties may well have been divided. When two Vijayanagar Muslim generals suddenly deserted, the army fell into disarray. Defeat came swiftly; although members of his family fled with untold hoards of gold and jewels, Rama Raya was captured and suffered a grisly death at the hands of the sultan of Ahmadnagar. Vijayanagar then fell victim to a series of destructive raids, and its days of splendour were brought to an abrupt end.

Arrival and information

Buses from Hospet terminate close to where the road joins the main street in Hampi Bazaar, halfway along its dusty length. A little further towards the

Virupaksha temple, the **tourist office** (Mon–Sat 10am–5.30pm; ☎08394/41339) can put you in touch with a **guide** – ask for Shankar – but not much else. Shankar runs a convenience store just behind the office. Most visitors coming from Hospet organize a guide from there (see p.1442).

Rented **bicycles**, available from stalls near the lodges, cost Rs5 per hour or Rs50 for a 24hr period. Bikes are really only of use if you're planning to explore Anegondi across the river – accessible by **coracle** for Rs5 – you can also rent bicycles at Kamalapuram for Rs50 per day. You can rent a motorbike for Rs300 per day not including fuel from Neha Travels who have three outlets in Hampi; the main office is at D131/11 Main Street (daily 9am–9pm; ☎08394/41590). They can also **change money** (including travellers' cheques) but at lowish rates, advance cash on credit cards and they book airline and **train tickets** as well as run **luxury buses** to Bangalore and luxury sleeper coaches to Goa; although these drop people off right in Hampi Bazaar, you have to pick them up from Hospet thanks to the powerful taxi/rickshaw mafia.

Run by Shri Swamy Sadashiva Yogi, the Shivananda Yoga Ashram overlooking the river, past the site of the new footbridge and coracle crossing, offers courses in **yoga** and **meditation** as well as homeopathic treatment, magnetotherapy and **Ayurvedic treatment**, in particular for snakebites.

Accommodation

If you're happy to make do with basic amenities, Hampi is a far more enjoyable place to stay than Hospet, with around fifty congenial **guesthouses** and plenty of cafés to hang out in after a long day in the heat. As you wander through the lanes, you may find yourself solicited by local residents offering rooms in their own homes. Staying in the village also means you can be up and out early enough to catch the sunrise over the ruins – a mesmerizing spectacle. Some travellers shun Hampi Bazaar for the burgeoning community of lodges at **Virupapuradadda** across the river or at the more comfortable *Kiskinda Resorts* at Hanomana Halli, 2km from Anegondi, which has been the scene of several raves. Outside of **high season**, which lasts for six weeks starting around Christmas, you may well get a substantial discount on the room rates quoted below.

Gopi Guest House, a short walk down the lanes behind *Shanti* ☎08394/41695. There's a pleasant rooftop café here, and all ten rooms have attached baths. ❷

KSTDC Mayura Bhuvaneshwari, Kamalapuram, 2.5km from Hampi Bazaar ☎08394/41574. The only remotely upscale place to stay within reach of the ruins. The modern block with clean en-suite rooms and competitively priced a/c rooms is agreeable enough. There's a pleasant garden, a good restaurant and a bar serving cold beers, but it feels detached from Hampi Bazaar and the village lacks charm. ❹–❺

Laxmi, just behind the main drag ☎08394/41728. A friendly guesthouse with clean rooms with shared baths. ❶

Rahul Guest House, south of Main Street, near the bus stand ☎08394/41648. Now has some new attached rooms in addition to the small and spartan old ones, which share rudimentary wash-ing and toilet facilities, along with a pleasant shaded café. ❶–❸

Shambu, around the corner from the *Gopi Guest House*. Comparable to the *Gopi*, but slightly cheaper. ❷–❸

Shanti Guest House, just north of the Virupaksha temple ☎08394/41568. Follow the lane around the side of the temple enclosure, and the lodge is 30m further on the right. Run by the affable Shivaram, this is still the most popular place to stay, comprising a dozen or so twin-bedded cells ranged on two storeys around a leafy inner courtyard. It's basic (showers and toilets are shared), but spotless, and all rooms have fans and windows. Roof space is also available if the lodge is fully booked. ❷

Shri Rama Guest House, next to the Virupaksha temple ☎08394/41219. Rock-bottom attached rooms mainly for Hindu pilgrims, but foreigners are also welcome. ❶

Umashankar Lodge, Virupapuragadda (no phone). One of the better places to stay across the river. Small but clean attached rooms set round a lush lawn. ❷.

Vicky's, at the end of the lane furthest northeast from the temple ☎ 08394/41694. Small clean rooms, some attached. Friendly and especially popular for its rooftop restaurant. ❶–❷

Vijayanagar, above coracle jetty, Virupapuragadda ☎ 08394/77640. Very cheap and rather poky cells with mattresses on the floor and shared bathrooms. Laid-back restaurant. ❶.

The site

Although spread over 26 square kilometres, the ruins of Vijayanagar are mostly concentrated in two distinct groups: the first lies in and around **Hampi Bazaar** and the nearby riverside area, encompassing the city's most sacred enclave of temples and *ghats*; the second centres on the **royal enclosure** – 3km south of the river, just northwest of **Kamalapuram** village – which holds the remains of palaces, pavilions, elephant stables, guardhouses and temples. Between the two stretches a long boulder-choked hill and swathe of banana plantations, fed by ancient irrigation canals.

Frequent buses run from Hospet to Hampi Bazaar and Kamalapuram, and you can start your tour from either; most visitors prefer to set out on foot or bicycle from the former. After a look around the soaring **Virupaksha temple**, work your way east along the main street and riverbank to the beautiful **Vitthala temple**, and then back via the **Achyutaraya** complex at the foot of Matanga Hill. From here, a dirt path leads south to the royal enclosure, but it's easier to return to the bazaar and pick up the tarred road, calling in at **Hemakuta Hill**, a group of pre-Vijayanagar temples, en route.

On KSTDC's whistle-stop **guided tour** (see p.1441), it's possible to see most of the highlights in a day. If you can, however, set aside at least two or three days to explore the site and its environs, crossing the river by **coracle** to **Anegondi** village, with a couple of side hikes to hilltop viewpoints: the west side of Hemakuta Hill, overlooking Hampi Bazaar, is best for sunsets, while **Matanga Hill**, though plagued by thieves in recent years, offers what has to be one of the world's most exotic sunrise vistas.

Hampi Bazaar, the Virupaksha temple and riverside path

Lining Hampi's long, straight main street, **Hampi Bazaar**, which runs east from the eastern entrance of the Virupaksha temple, you can still make out the remains of Vijayanagar's ruined, columned bazaar, partly inhabited by today's lively market. Landless labourers live in many of the crumbling 500-year-old buildings.

Dedicated to a local form of Shiva known as Virupaksha or Pampapati, the functioning **Virupaksha temple** (daily 8am–12.30pm & 3–6.30pm; Rs2) dominates the village, drawing a steady flow of pilgrims from all over southern India. Also known as **Sri Virupaksha Swami**, the temple is free for all who come for *arati* (worship; daily 6.30–8am & 6.30–8pm) when the temple has the most atmosphere. The complex consists of two courts, each entered through a towered *gopura*. The larger gateway, on the east, is approximately 56m high, each storey with pilastered walls and sculptures flanking an open window. It is topped by a single wagon vault and *kalasha*, pot-shaped finial. In the southwest corner a water channel runs along a large columned *mandapa*.

A colonnade surrounds the inner court, usually filled with pilgrims dozing and singing religious songs. On entering, if the temple elephant is around, you can get him to bless you by placing a rupee in his trunk. In the middle the

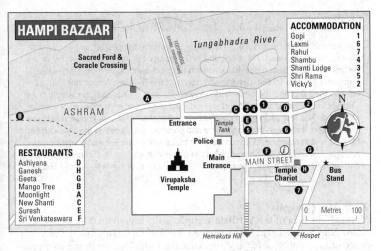

HAMPI BAZAAR

ACCOMMODATION

Gopi	1
Laxmi	6
Rahul	7
Shambu	4
Shanti Lodge	3
Shri Rama	5
Vicky's	2

Tungabhadra River

Sacred Ford &
Coracle Crossing

FOOTBRIDGE
(under construction)

ASHRAM

Entrance

Temple
Tank

Police

Main
Entrance

MAIN STREET

Virupaksha
Temple

Temple
Chariot

Bus
Stand

N

RESTAURANTS

Ashiyana	D
Ganesh	H
Geeta	G
Mango Tree	B
Moonlight	A
New Shanti	C
Suresh	E
Sri Venkateswara	F

0   Metres   100

Hemakuta Hill ▼   ▼ Hospet

principal temple is approached through a *mandapa* hallway whose carved columns feature rearing animals. Rare Vijayanagar-era paintings on the *mandapa* ceiling include aspects of Shiva, a procession with the sage Vidyaranya, the ten incarnations of Vishnu, and scenes from the *Mahabharata*; the style of the figures is reminiscent of local shadow puppets. Faced by a brass image of Nandi, a *shivalingam* is housed in the small sanctuary, its entrance decorated with painted *makaras*, semi-aquatic mythical animals whose bodies end with foliage instead of a tail. Blue water spouts from their mouths, while above them flicker yellow flames. Just outside the main temple's wall, immediately to the north, is a small earlier temple, thought to have been the "ancestor" of the Virupaksha.

The sacred **ford** in the river is reached from the Virupaksha's north *gopura*; you can also get there by following the lane around the impressive temple **tank** and past *Shanti Lodge*. A *mandapa* overlooks the steps that originally led to the river, now some distance away. Although threatened by a new footbridge, **coracles** ply from this part of the bank, just as they did five centuries ago, ferrying villagers to the fields and tourists to the popular *Uma-Shankar Café* on the other side. The path through the village also winds to an impressive ruined bridge, and on to the hilltop Hanuman shrine – a recommended round walk described on p.1449.

To reach the Vitthala temple, walk east from the Virupaksha along the length of Hampi Bazaar. At the end, a path on the left, staffed at regular intervals by conch-blowing *sadhus* and an assortment of other ragged mendicants, follows the river past a café and numerous shrines, including a Rama temple – home to hordes of fearless monkeys. Beyond at least four Vishnu shrines, the paved and colonnaded **Achutya Bazaar** leads due south to the **Tiruvengalanatha temple**, whose beautiful stone carvings – among them some of Hampi's famed erotica – are being restored by the ASI. Back on the main path again, make a short detour across the rocks leading to the river to see the little-visited waterside **Agni temple** – next to it, the Kotalinga complex consists of 108 (an auspicious number) tiny *linga*, carved on a flat rock. As you approach the Vitthala temple, to the south is an archway known as the **King's Balance**, where the rajas were weighed against gold, silver and jewels to be distributed to the city's priests.

Vijayanagar's main festivals include, at the Virupaksha temple, a Car Festival with street processions each February, and in December the marriage ceremony of the deities, which is accompanied by drummers and dances. The Hampi Festival, organized by the tourist department, takes place in early November – usually between the 3rd and the 5th – and involves classical music and dance from both Carnatic and Hindustani (north Indian) traditions performed on temple stages and at Anegondi. The festival, which is beginning to attract several well-known musicians and dancers, has been growing in size and prestige, and hotels in the area can get booked well in advance. Unfortunately, the traditional music festival, Purandaradas Aradhana (Jan/Feb), which is usually held at the Vitthala temple and celebrates the birth anniversary of the poet-composer Purandaradasa, is currently suspended.

Vitthala temple

Although the area of the **Vitthala temple** (daily 6am–6pm; $10 [Rs10]; ticket also valid for the Lotus Mahal on the same day) does not show the same evidence of early cult worship as Virupaksha, the ruined bridge to the west probably dates from before Vijayanagar times. The bathing *ghat* may be from the Chalukya or Ganga period, but as the temple has fallen into disuse it seems that the river crossing (*tirtha*) here has not had the same sacred significance as the Virupaksha site. Now designated a World Heritage Monument by UNESCO, the Vitthala temple was built for Vishnu, who according to legend was too embarrassed by its ostentation to live there. The tower of the principal Vishnu shrine is made of brick – unusual for south India – capped with a hemispherical roof; in front is an enclosed *mandapa* with carved columns, the ceiling of which has partly collapsed. Two doorways lead to a dark passageway surrounding the sanctuary.

The open *mandapa* features slender monolithic granite **musical pillars** which were constructed so as to sound the notes of the scale when struck. Today, due to vandalism and erosion from being repeatedly beaten, heavy security makes sure that no one is allowed to touch them. Guides, however, will happily demonstrate the musical resonance of other pillars on an adjacent structure. Outer columns sport characteristic Vijayanagar rearing horses, while friezes of lions, elephants and horses on the moulded basement display sculptural trickery – you can transform one beast into another simply by masking one portion of the image.

In front of the temple, to the east, a stone representation of a wooden processional **rath**, or chariot, houses an image of Garuda, Vishnu's bird vehicle. Now cemented, at one time the chariot's wheels revolved. The three *gopura* entrances, made of granite at the base with brick and stucco multistorey towers, are now badly damaged.

Anegondi and beyond

With more time, and a sense of adventure, you can head across the Tungabhadra to **ANEGONDI**, a fortress town predating Vijayanagar and the city's fourteenth-century headquarters. The most pleasant way to go is to take a *putti*, a circular rush-basket coracle, from the ford 1500m east of the Vitthala temple; the *puttis*, which are today reinforced with plastic sheets, also carry bicycles.

Forgotten temples and fortifications litter Anegondi village and its quiet surroundings. The ruined **Huchchappa-matha temple**, near the river gateway, is worth a look for its black stone lathe-turned pillars and fine panels of dancers. **Aramani**, a ruined palace in the centre, stands opposite the home of the descendants of the royal family; also in the centre, the **Ranganatha temple** is still active.

A huge wooden temple chariot stands in the village square. To complete a five-kilometre loop back to Hampi from here (best attempted by bicycle), head left (west) along the road, winding through sugar cane fields towards the sacred **Pampla Sarovar**, signposted down a dirt lane to the left. The small temple above this square bathing tank, tended by a *swami* who will proudly show you photos of his pilgrimage to Mount Kailash, is dedicated to the goddess Lakshmi and holds a cave containing a footprint of Vishnu. If you are staying around Anegondi, this quiet and atmospheric spot is best visited early in the evening during *arati* (worship).

Another worthwhile detour from the road is the hike up to the tiny white-washed **Hanuman temple**, perched on a rocky hilltop north of the river, from where you gain superb views over Hampi especially at sunrise or sunset. The steep climb up to it takes around half an hour. Keep following the road west for another 3km and you'll eventually arrive at an impressive old **stone bridge** dating from Vijayanagar times. The track from the opposite bank crosses a large island in the Tungabhadra, emerging after twenty minutes at the sacred ford and coracle jetty below the Virupaksha temple. This rewarding round walk can, of course, be completed in reverse, beginning at the sacred ford. With a bike, it takes around three hours, including the side trips outlined above; allow most of the day if you attempt it on foot, and take plenty of water.

Hemakuta Hill and around

Directly above Hampi Bazaar, **Hemakuta Hill** is dotted with pre-Vijayanagar temples that probably date from between the ninth and eleventh centuries (late Chalukya or Ganga). Three are of the *trikutachala*, "three-peaked hills", type, with three shrines facing into a common centre. Aside from the architecture, the main reason to clamber up here is to admire the **views** of the ruins and surrounding countryside. Looking across swathes of boulder-covered terrain and banana plantations, the sheer western edge of the hill is Hampi's number-one sunset spot, attracting a crowd of blissed-out tourists most evenings, along with a couple of entrepreneurial chai-wallahs.

A couple of interesting monuments lie on the road leading south towards the main, southern group of ruins. The first of these, a walled **Krishna temple complex** to the west of the road, dates from 1513. Although dilapidated in parts, it features some fine carving and shrines. On the opposite side of the road, a fifty-metre-wide processional path leading east through what's now a ploughed field, with stray remnants of colonnades straggling on each side, is all that remains of an old market place.

Hampi's most-photographed monument stands just south of the Krishna temple in its own enclosure. Depicting Vishnu in his incarnation (*avatar*) as the Man-Lion, the monolithic **Narashima** statue, with its bulging eyes and crossed legs strapped into meditation pose, is one of Vijayanagar's greatest treasures.

The southern and royal monuments

The most impressive remains of Vijayanagar, the city's **royal monuments**, lie some 3km south of Hampi Bazaar, spread over a large expanse of open ground. Before tackling the ruins proper, it's a good idea to get your bearings with a visit to the small **Archeological Museum** (daily except Fri 10am–5pm; free) at Kamalapuram, which can be reached by bus from Hospet or Hampi. Turn right out of the Kamalapuram bus stand, take the first turning on the right, and the museum is on the left – two minutes' walk. Among the sculpture, weapons, palm-leaf manuscripts and painting from Vijayanagar and Anegondi, the high-light is a superb scale model of the city, giving an excellent bird's-eye view of the entire site.

To walk into the city from the museum, go back to the main road and take the nearby turning marked "Hampi 4km". After 200m or so you reach the partly ruined massive **inner city wall**, made from granite slabs, which runs 32km around the city, in places as high as 10m. The outer wall was almost twice as long. At one time, there were said to have been seven city walls; coupled with areas of impenetrable forest and the river to the north, they made the city virtually impregnable.

Just beyond the wall, the **citadel area** was once enclosed by another wall and gates of which only traces remain. To the east, the small *ganigitti* ("oil-woman's") fourteenth-century **Jain temple** features a simple stepped pyramidal tower of undecorated horizontal slabs. Beyond it is **Bhima's Gate**, once one of the principal entrances to the city, named after the Titan-like Pandava prince and hero of the *Mahabharata*. Like many of the gates, it is "bent", a form of defence that meant anyone trying to get in had to make two 90° turns. Bas-reliefs depict such episodes as Bhima avenging the attempted rape of his wife, Draupadi, by killing the general Kichaka. Draupadi vowed she would not dress her hair until Kichaka was dead; one panel shows her tying up her locks, the vow fulfilled.

Back on the path, to the west, the plain facade of the fifteen-metre-square **Queen's Bath** belies its glorious interior, open to the sky and surrounded by corridors with 24 different domes. Eight projecting balconies overlook where once was water; traces of Islamic-influenced stucco decoration survive. Women from the royal household would bathe here and umbrellas were placed in shafts in the tank floor to protect them from the sun. The water supply channel can be seen outside.

Continuing northwest brings you to **Mahanavami-Dibba** or "House of Victory", built to commemorate a successful campaign in Orissa. A twelve-metre pyramidal structure with a square base, it is said to have been where the king gave and received honours and gifts. From here he watched the magnificent parades, music and dance performances, martial arts displays, elephant fights and animal sacrifices that made celebration of the ten-day Dussehra festival famed through-out the land (the tradition of spectacular Dussehra festivals is continued at Mysore; see p.1403). Carved reliefs of dancers, elephant fights, animals and figures decorate the sides of the platform. Two huge monolithic doors on the ground nearby may have once been part of a building atop the platform, of which no signs remain. To the west, another platform – the largest at Vijayanagar – is thought to be the basement of the **King's Audience Hall**. Stone bases of a hundred pillars remain, in an arrangement that has caused speculation as to how the building could have been used; there are no passageways or open areas.

The two-storey **Lotus Mahal** (daily 6am–6pm; $10 [Rs10]; ticket also valid for the Vitthala temple on the same day), a little further north and part of the **zenana enclosure**, or women's quarters, was designed for the pleasure of Krishna Deva Raya's queen: a place where she could relax, particularly in summer. Displaying a strong Indo-Islamic influence, the pavilion is open on the ground floor, whereas the upper level (no longer accessible by stairs) contains windows and balcony seats. A moat surrounding the building is thought to have provided water-cooled air via tubes.

Beyond the Lotus Mahal, the **Elephant Stables**, a series of high-ceilinged, domed chambers, entered through arches, are the most substantial surviving secular buildings at Vijayanagar – a reflection of the high status accorded to elephants, both ceremonial and in battle. An upper level, with a pillared hall, capped with a tower at the centre, may have been used by the musicians who accompanied the royal elephant processions. Tender coconuts are usually for sale under the shade of a nearby tree. East of here, recent archeological excavations have revealed what are thought to have been the foundations of a series of Vijayanagar administration offices, which until 1990 had remained buried under earth deposited by the wind.

Walking west of the Lotus Mahal, you pass two temples before reaching the road to Hemakuta Hill. The rectangular enclosure wall of the small **Hazara Rama** ("One thousand Ramas") temple, thought to have been the private palace temple, features a series of medallion figures and bands of detailed friezes showing scenes from the *Ramayana*. The inner of two *mandapas* contains four finely carved, polished, black columns. Many of the ruins here are said to have been part of the Hazara Rama Bazaar, which ran northeast from the temple. Much of the so-called **Underground Temple**, or Prasanna Virupaksha, lies below ground level and spends part of the year filled with rainwater. Turning north (right) onto the road that runs west of the Underground Temple will take you back to Hampi Bazaar, via Hemakuta Hill.

Eating

During the season, Hampi spawns a rash of travellers' cafés and temporary tiffin joints, as well as a number of laid-back snack bars tucked away in more secluded corners. Among the many **restaurants** in the bazaar, firm favourites with Western tourists on Main Street, serving a predictable selection of pancakes, porridge, omelettes and veggie food, include *Welcome*, *Geeta* and *Sri Vendateswara*. The *New Shanti Restaurant* opposite *Shanti Lodge* (but not owned by the same people), is another typical travellers' joint, renowned for its fresh pasta and soft cheese. Steer clear of the latter if there have been lots of power cuts. The friendly *Suresh*, behind the *Shri Rama Tourist Home*, serves delicious *shak-shuka* on banana leaves and is a good place for breakfast.

You can also get filling thalis and a range of freshly cooked snacks in the *Rahul Guest House*; other lodges with restaurants include *Vicky's* and *Gopi*. The *Moonlight*, a thatched café overlooking the river and the coracle jetty, offers bland but wholesome veg food and has a pleasant location a short walk past the *Shanti*. However, the prize for Hampi's best all-round café has to go to the *Mango Tree*, hidden away in the banana plantations beyond the coracle jetty and the Shivananda Yoga Ashram. The food is fairly run-of-the-mill, but the relaxing riverside location is hard to beat. Across the river in Virupapuradadda the most popular place, especially with Israelis, is *Goan Corner*, perched on the ridge to the left of the coracle jetty, it churns out pasta, bland curries and Israeli favourites.

You can get authentic Western-style bread and **cakes** through *Shanti Lodge*; place your order by early evening, and the cakes and pies are delivered the following day.

Monuments of the Chalukyas

Now quiet villages, **Badami**, **Aihole** and **Pattadakal**, in northwest Karnataka, were once the capital cities of the **Chalukyas**, who ruled much of the Deccan between the fourth and eighth centuries. The astonishing profusion of **tem-**

ples in the area beggars belief, and it is hard to imagine the kind of society that can have made use of them all. Most visitors use Badami, which can offer a few basic lodges, as a base; Aihole boasts a single rest house, and no rooms are available at Pattadakal. The **best time to visit** is between October and early March; in April and May, most of this part of northwest Karnataka becomes much too hot and all government offices only work between 8am and 1pm.

Badami and Aihole's cave temples, stylistically related to those at Ellora (see p.805), are some of the most important of their type. Among the many structural temples are some of the earliest in India, and uniquely, it is possible to see both northern (*nagari*) and southern (Dravida) architectural styles side by side. Clearly much experimentation went on, as several other temples (commonly referred to, in art historical terms, as "undifferentiated") fit into neither system. None is now thought to date from before the late sixth century, but at one time scholars got very excited when they believed the famous Lad Khan temple at Aihole, for example, to be even older.

Although some evidence of **Buddhist** activity around Badami and Aihole exists, the earliest cave and structural temples are assigned to the period of the Chalukya rise to power in the mid-sixth century, and are mostly **Hindu**, with a few Jain examples. The first important Chalukyan king was Pulakeshin I (535–66), but it was Pulakeshin II (610–42) who captured the Pallava capital of Kanchipuram in Tamil Nadu and extended the empire to include Maharashtra to the north, the Konkan coast on the west and the whole of what is now Karnataka. Although the Pallavas subsequently, and briefly, took most of his territory, including Badami, the capital at the end of his reign, Pulakeshin's son, Vikramaditya I (655–81) later recovered it, and the Chalukyas continued to reign until the mid-eighth century. Some suggest that the incursion of the Pallavas accounts for the southern elements seen in the structural temples.

Badami and around

Surrounded by a yawning expanse of flat farm land, **BADAMI**, capital of the Chalukyas from 543 AD to 757 AD, extends east into a gorge between two red sandstone hills, topped by two ancient fort complexes. The south is riddled with cave temples, and on the north stand early structural temples. Beyond the village, to the east, is an artificial lake, Agastya, said to date from the fifth century. Its small selection of hotels and restaurants makes Badami an ideal base from which to explore the Chalukyan remains at Mahakuta, Aihole and Pattadakal as well as the temple village of **Banashankari** 5km to the southeast. Dedicated to Shiva's consort Parvati, the shrine, accompanied by a large bathing tank, is the most important living temple of the region and attracts a steady stream of devotees, especially during the chariot festival held according to the lunar calendar sometime between January and February each year. Although of little architectural interest, but worth a visit for the atmosphere, the temple is supposed to date back to the sixth century; much of it, however, was built during the Maratha period of the eighteenth century. The whole Badami area is also home to numerous troupes of monkeys, especially around the monuments, and you are likely to find the cheeky characters all over you if you produce any food.

Practicalities

Badami **bus stand** – in the centre of the village on Main (Station) Road – sees daily services to Gadag (2hr), Hospet (5hr), Hubli (3hr), Bijapur (4hr) and Kolhapur, and frequent buses to Aihole and Pattadakal. The **railway station** is

5km north, along a road lined with *neem* trees; tongas (Rs30 or Rs5 per head shared) as well as buses and auto-rickshaws are usually available for the journey into town. A slow metre-gauge line connects Badami to Bijapur to the north, and to Gadag in the south from where you can change for trains or buses to Hospet and Hampi.

The new and friendly **tourist office** (Mon–Sat: June–March 10am–5.30pm; April–May 8am–1pm; ☏08357/20414) on Ramdurg Road next to KSTDC *Hotel Mayura Chalukya*, can put you in touch with a **guide**. If you need to **change money**, *Hotel Mookambika* opposite the bus stand will change US dollars and sterling, but no travellers' cheques; the other place to try is the *Hotel Badami Court*.

Ambika Tours & Travels at *Hotel Mookambika* runs **tours** taking in Badami, Mahakuta, Aihole and Pattadakal in Ambassador taxis for a reasonable Rs600. One of the best ways of exploring the closer sites, including Mahakuta and the temple village of Banashankari, is to rent a **bicycle**, available at Rs3 per hour from stalls in front of the bus stand, but cycling to Aihole and Pattadakal will prove challenging.

Accommodation and eating

Of Badami's handful of **places to stay** and **eat**, by far the most comfortable is the *Hotel Badami Court* (☏08357/20230; ❼–❽), 2km west of town towards the railway station. Ranged around a garden on two storeys, its 27 en-suite rooms are plain, but spacious; they serve meals and expensive beer. Their swimming pool is open to nonresidents for Rs80 per hour. Far cheaper, the KSTDC *Hotel Mayura Chalukya* (☏08357/65046; ❷), at the south side of town on Ramdurg Road, has ten basic rooms with decrepit plumbing and peeling plaster, but a new wing is nearing completion and, despite fearless scavenging monkeys, the gardens are pleasant and there's a restaurant. Opposite the bus stand, the *Mookambika Deluxe* (☏08357/65067; ❹–❼) is the best option in the centre of town, but is rather overpriced from its simple doubles on the ground floor to comfortable new a/c rooms upstairs. Their plain upstairs restaurant and livelier *Kanchan* bar and restaurant next door share the same kitchen and provide a wide menu of excellent veg and non-veg Indian and Chinese food. Other options include the grungy budget lodges opposite the bus stand, among them the *Satkar* (☏08357/20417; ❷) and the *Shri Laxmi Vilas* (☏08357/20077; ❷), which has a reasonable restaurant.

For food and especially breakfast, try the *Geetha Darshini*, 100m south of the bus stand; it's a south Indian fast-food restaurant without seating, but there are counters to stand at. The *iddlis*, *vadas* and *dosas* are out of this world. Otherwise the *Mookambika Deluxe*'s plain upstairs restaurant and livelier *Kanchan* bar and restaurant next door share the same kitchen and provide a wide menu of excellent veg and non-veg Indian and Chinese food.

Southern Fort cave temples

Badami's earliest monuments, in the Southern Fort area, are a group of sixth-century **caves** (daily sunrise to sunset; $5 [Rs5]) cut into the hill's red sandstone, each connected by steps leading up the hillside. About 15m up the face of the rock, **Cave 1**, a Shiva temple, is probably the earliest. Entrance is through a triple opening into a long porch raised on a plinth decorated with images of Shiva's dwarf attendants, the *ganas*. Outside, to the left of the porch, a *dvarpala* door guardian stands beneath a Nandi bull. On the right is a striking 1.5m-high image of a sixteen-armed dancing Shiva. He carries a stick-zither-type *vina*, which may or may not be a *yal*, a now-extinct musical instrument, on which the earliest Indian classical music theory is thought to have been developed. In the antechamber, a panel on the left shows Harihara (Shiva and Vishnu combined), accompanied by consorts Lakshmi and Parvati and the gods' vehicles Nandi and Garuda. On the right, Ardhanarishvara (Shiva combined with Parvati; half male, half female) is accompanied by Nandi and the skeleton Bringi. Ceiling panels include a coiled Naga snake deity, flying couples, and Shiva and Parvati. Inside, a columned hall, divided into aisles, leads to a small, square sanctuary at the back, containing a *lingam*.

A little higher, the similar **Cave 2**, a Vishnu shrine, is approached across a courtyard with two *dvarpala* door guardians at the end. The porch contains a panel, to the left, of Varaha, the boar incarnation of Vishnu, and, to the right, Trivikrama, Vishnu as a dwarf brahmin who inflates in size to cross the earth in three steps. On the ceiling nearby, Vishnu is shown riding his bird Garuda. A central square of the ceiling features a lotus encircled by sixteen fish; other decoration includes *svastika* designs and flying couples. Traces of painting show how colourful the caves originally were.

Steps and slopes lead on upwards, past a natural cave containing a smashed image of the Buddhist *bodhisattva*, Padmapani (he who holds the lotus), and steps on the right in a cleft in the rock lead up to the fort. **Cave 3** (578 AD) stands beneath a 30m-high perpendicular bluff. The largest of the group, with a facade measuring 21m from north to south, it is also considered to be the finest, for the quality of its sculptural decoration. Eleven steps lead up to the plinth decorated with dwarf *ganas*. Treatment of the pillars is extremely elaborate, featuring male and female bracket figures, lotus motifs and medallions portraying amorous couples.

To the east of the others, a Jain temple, **Cave 4**, overlooks Agastya Lake and the town. It's a much simpler shrine, dating from the sixth century. Figures, both seated and standing, of the 24 *tirthankaras*, mostly without their identifying emblems, line the walls. Here, the rock is striped.

After seeing the caves you can climb up to the fort and walk east where, hidden in the rocks, a carved panel shows Vishnu reclining on the serpent Adisesha, attended by a profusion of gods and sages. Continuing, you can skirt the gorge and descend on the east to the Bhutanatha temples at the lakeside. Before you get to them, there's another rock carving of a reclining Vishnu and his ten incarnations.

North Fort

North of Agastya Lake a number of structural temples can be reached by steps. The small **Archeological Museum** (daily except Fri 10am–5pm; Rs2) nearby contains sculpture from the region. Although now dilapidated, the **Upper Shivalaya temple** is one of the earliest Chalukyan buildings. Scenes from the life of Krishna decorate the base and various images of him can be seen between pilasters on the walls. Only the sanctuary and tower of the **Lower Shivalaya** survive. Perched on a rock, the **Malegitti Shivalaya** (late seventh century) is the finest southern-style early Chalukyan temple. Its shrine is adjoined by a pillared hallway with small pierced stone and a single image on each side: Vishnu on the north and Shiva on the south.

Mahakuta

Another crop of seventh-century Chalukyan temples lies 15km out of Badami on the route to Pattadakal at **Mahakuta**. Four buses a day and the occasional shared *tempo* run to the site, but the two- to three-hour walk there, via an ancient paved pilgrims' trail, is well worthwhile. Take plenty of water and an umbrella to keep off the sun. The path starts a short way beyond the museum (before you reach the first temple complex and tank). Peeling left up the hill, it winds past a series of crumbling shrines, gateways and old water courses, and peters out into the flat plateau. The turning down to Mahakuta is easy to miss: look for a stone marker post that reads "RP", which leads you to a steep, roughly paved stairway. At the bottom, the main temple complex, ranged around a crystal-clear spring-fed tank popular with bathers, and a shady court-yard dominated by a huge banyan tree, centres on the whitewashed **Mahakutesvara temple** with its silver-crowned *lingam*, around whose base are wrapped some fine stone friezes. Those on the southwest corner, depicting Shiva and Parvati with Ravana, the demon-king of Lanka, are particularly accomplished. More carvings adorn the entrance and ceilings of the **Mallikarjuna temple** on the opposite side of the tank, while in the clearing outside the nearby **Sangameshwar temple** stands a gigantic stone-wheeled chariot used during the annual festival in May.

A living Shiva temple, attracting local devotees, pilgrims and a sprinkling of *sadhus* who spend a few days amongst the scattered monuments, Mahakuta may be in the minor league of Chalukyan architecture, but has, with its brooding banyan trees, a timeless, captivating atmosphere. Unlike the other more famous sites, Mahakuta is not a museum but is, instead, run by a temple committee. There are a couple of teashops but no guesthouse; however, if want to stay, you may be able to negotiate one of the very basic rooms outside the temple gates.

Aihole

No fewer than 125 temples, dating from the Chalukyan and the later Rashtrakuta periods (sixth–twelfth centuries), are found in the tiny village of **AIHOLE** (Aivalli), near the banks of the River Malaprabha. Lying in clusters within the village, in surrounding fields and on rocky outcrops, many of the temples are remarkably well preserved, despite being used as dwellings and cat-tle sheds. Reflecting both its geographical position and spirit of architectural experimentation, Aihole boasts northern (*nagari*) and southern (Dravida) tem-ples, as well as variants that failed to survive subsequent stylistic developments.

Two of the temples are **rock-cut caves** dating from the sixth century. The Hindu **Ravanaphadigudi**, northeast of the centre, a Shiva shrine with a triple entrance, contains fine sculptures of Mahishasuramardini, a ten-armed Nateshan (the precursor of Shiva Nataraja) dancing with Parvati, Ganesh and the Sapta Matrikas ("seven mothers"). A central lotus design surrounded by mythical beasts, figures and foliate decoration adorns the ceiling. Near the entrance is Gangadhara (Shiva with the River Ganga in his hair) accompanied by Parvati and the skeleton Bringi. A two-storey cave, plain save for decoration at the entrances and a panel image of Buddha in its upper veranda, can be found partway up the hill to the southeast, overlooking the village. At the top of that hill, the Jain **Meguti** temple, which may never have been completed, bears an inscription on an outer wall dating it to 634 AD. The porch, *mandapa* hallway and upper storey above the sanctuary, which contains a seated Jain image, are later additions. You can climb up to the first floor for fine views of Aihole and surrounding country.

The late seventh–early eighth century **Durga temple** (daily 6am–6pm; $5 [Rs5]), one of the most unusual, elaborate and large in Aihole, stands close to others on open ground in the Archaeological Survey compound, near the cen-tre of the village. It derives its name not from the goddess Durga but from the Kannada *durgadagudi*, meaning "temple near the fort". Its apsidal-ended sanctuary shows influence from earlier Buddhist *chaitya* halls; another example of this curved feature, rare in Hindu monuments, can be seen in one of the *rathas* at Mamallapuram in Tamil Nadu. Here the "northern"-style tower is probably a later addition, and is incongruously square-backed. The temple is raised on a plinth featuring bands of carved decoration. A series of pillars – many featuring amorous couples – forming an open ambulatory continue from the porch around the whole building. Other sculptural highlights include the decoration on the entrance to the *mandapa* hallway and niche images on the outer walls of the now-empty semicircular sanctum. Remains of a small and early *gopura* gateway stand to the south. Nearby, a small **Archeological Museum** (daily except Fri 10am–5pm) displays early Chalukyan sculpture and sells the booklet *Glorious Aihole*, which includes a site map and accounts of the monuments.

Further south, beyond several other temples, the **Ladh Khan** (the name of a Muslim who made it his home) is perhaps the best known of all at Aihole. Now thought to have been constructed at some point between the end of the sixth century and the eighth, it was dated at one time to the mid-fifth century, and was seen as one of the country's temple prototypes. The basic plan is square, with a large adjoining rectangular pillared porch. Inside, twelve pillars support a raised clerestory and enclose a further four pillars; at the centre stands a Nandi bull. A small sanctuary containing a *shivalingam* is next to the back wall. Both *lingam* and Nandi may have been later additions, with the original inner sanctum located at the centre.

Practicalities

Six daily **buses** run to Aihole from Badami (1hr 30) via Pattadakal (45min) from 5.30am to 9pm; the last bus returns around 6pm. The only place to **stay and eat** (apart from a few chai shops) in Aihole is the small, clean and spartan KSTDC *Tourist Rest House* (T 08351/34541; ❷) about five minutes' walk up the main road north out of the village, next to the ASI offices. They have a "VIP" room, two doubles with bath plus two doubles and four singles without. Simple, tasty food is available by arrangement – and by candlelight during frequent power cuts. The *Kiran Bar* on the same road, but in the village, serves beer and spirits and has a restaurant.

Pattadakal

The village of **PATTADAKAL**, on a bend in the River Malaprabha 22km from Badami, served as the site of Chalukyan coronations between the seventh and eighth centuries; in fact it may only have been used for such ceremonials. Like Badami and Aihole, Pattadakal boasts fine Chalukyan architecture, with particularly large mature examples; and as at Aihole, both northern and southern styles can be seen. Pattadakal's main group of monuments (daily 6am–6pm; $10 [Rs10]) stand together in a well-maintained compound, next to the village, and have recently attained the status of a World Heritage Site.

Earliest among the temples, the **Sangameshvara**, also known as **Shri Vijayeshvara** (a reference to its builder, Vijayaditya Satyashraya; 696–733), shows typical southern features, such as the parapet lined with barrel-vaulted miniature roof forms and walls divided into niches flanked by pilasters. To the south, both the **Mallikarjuna** and the enormous **Virupaksha**, side by side, are in the southern style, built by two sisters who were successively the queens of Vikramaditya II (733–46). The temples were inspired by the Pallava Kailashanatha temple at Kanchipuram in Tamil Nadu, complete with enclosure wall with shrines and small *gopura* entranceway. Along with the Kanchi temple, the Virupaksha was probably one of the largest and most elaborate in India at the time. Interior pillars are carved with scenes from the *Ramayana* and *Mahabharata*, while in the Mallikarjuna the stories are from the life of Krishna. Both temples have open Nandi *mandapa* hallways and sanctuaries housing black polished stone *linga*.

The largest northern-style temple, the **Papanatha**, further south, was probably built after the Virupaksha in the eighth century. It features two long pillared *mandapa* hallways adjoining a small sanctuary with a narrow internal ambulatory. Outside walls feature reliefs (some of which, unusually, bear the sculptors' autographs) from the *Ramayana*, including, on the south wall, Hanuman's monkey army.

About 1km south of the village, a fine **Rashtrakuta** (ninth–tenth century) **Jain temple** is fronted by a porch and two *mandapa* hallways with twin carved elephants at the entrance. Inexplicably, the sanctuary contains a *lingam*. In the first *mandapa*, on the right, a stone staircase leads up to the roof, where there's a second, empty sanctuary. The porch is lined with bench seats interspersed with eight pillars; the doorway is elaborately decorated with mythical beasts.

Pattadakal is connected by regular state **buses** and hourly private buses to Badami (45min) and Aihole (22km, 45min). Aside from a few teashops, cold drinks and coconut stalls, there are no facilities. For three days at the end of January, Pattadakal hosts an annual **dance festival** featuring dancers from all over the country.

Bijapur and the north

Boasting some of the Deccan's finest Muslim monuments, **BIJAPUR** is often billed as "The Agra of the South". The comparison is partly justified: for more than three hundred years, this was the capital of a succession of powerful rulers, whose domed mausoleums, mosques, colossal civic buildings and fortifications recall a lost golden age of unrivalled prosperity and artistic refinement. Yet there the similarities between the two cities end. A provincial market town of just 210,000 inhabitants, modern Bijapur is a world away from the urban frenzy of Agra. With the exception of the mighty **Golgumbaz**, which attracts bus loads of day-trippers, its historic sites see only a slow trickle of tourists, while the ramshackle town centre is surprisingly laid-back, dotted with peaceful green spaces and colonnaded mosque courtyards. The best **time to come** here is between November and early March; in summer Bijapur gets unbearably hot and in April and May offices shut at 1pm. In the first week of February Bijapur hosts an annual **music festival** which attracts several renowned musicians from both the Carnatic (south Indian) and the Hindustani (north Indian) classical music traditions.

Some history

Bijapur began life in the tenth century as **Vijayapura**, the Chalukyas' "City of Victory". Taken by the Vijayanagars, it passed into Muslim hands for the first time in the thirteenth century with the arrival of the sultans of Delhi. The Bahmanis administered the area for a time, but it was only after the local rulers, the **Adil Shahis**, won independence from Bidar by expelling the Bahmani garrison and declaring this their capital that Bijapur's rise to prominence began.

BIJAPUR

N

Sholapur ◀

Gulbarga ▲

Sholapur ◀

Railway Station

Paderah Gate

Gadag ▶

Golgumbaz

Bahmani Gate

Stadium

Jama Masjid

Astar Mahal

Hospet ▶

Bara Kaman

Mithari Mahal

Fateh Gate

GPO

Gagan Mahal

Sat Manzil

CITADEL

GANDHI CHOWK

Cycle Rental

KSRTC Bus Stand

Badami, Belgaum & Hubli ▶

Bank

Sharpur Gate

Upli Buruj

Malik-e-Maidan

AZAD ROAD

Atike Gate

Ibrahim Rauza

0   Metres   500

RESTAURANTS

Mysore   B
Niyaz   C
Shrinidhi   A
Surabhi   D

ACCOMMODATION

Godavari	1
KSTDC Mayura Adil Shahi	7
KSTDC Mayura Adil Shahi Annexe	3
Madhuvan	4
Megharaj	5
Rajdhani	6
Sagar Deluxe	2
Samrat	8
Sanman	9

Burying their differences for a brief period in the late sixteenth century, the five Muslim dynasties that issued from the breakdown of Bahmani rule – based at Galconda, Ahmednagar, Bidar and Gulbarga – formed a military alliance to defeat the Vijayanagars. The spoils of this campaign, which saw the total destruction of Vijayanagar (Hampi), funded a two-hundred-year building boom in Bijapur during which the city acquired its most impressive monuments. However, old enmities between rival Muslim sultanates on the Deccan soon resurfaced, and the Adil Shahi's royal coffers were gradually squandered on fruitless and protracted wars. By the time the British arrived on the scene in the eighteenth century, the Adil Shahis were a spent force, locked into a decline from which they and their capital never recovered.

Practicalities

State and interstate **buses** from as far afield as Mumbai and Aurangabad (see Travel Details on p.1468), pull into the KSRTC bus stand on the southwest edge of the town centre; ask at the enquiries desk for exact timings, as the timetables are all in Kannada. Most of the Bangalore buses travel through Hospet including two overnight super-deluxe coaches. Other services run to Hyderabad, along with several to Gulbharga and Bidar and to Badami to the south. Most visitors head off to their hotel in (unmetered) auto-rickshaws, though there are also horse-drawn tongas for about the same price. Just a stone's throw away from the Golgumbaz, outside the old city walls, the **railway station**, 3km northeast of the bus stand, is a more inspiring point of arrival. However, only five passenger trains per day pass through in either direction: south to Badami and Gadag, where you can change for Hospet, Bangalore or the west coast, and north to Sholapur, for Mumbai and most points north. The only reliable source of information on train departures is the station itself, although most hotels keep a timetable in reception.

Besides the usual literature, the **tourist office** (Mon–Sat 10am–5.30pm; ☏08352/50359) behind the *Hotel Adil Shahi* annexe on Station Road can help with arranging itineraries and guides. If you need to **change money** (or travellers' cheques), the most reliable service is at Girikand Tours and Travels (☏08352/20510) on the first floor at Nishant Plaza, Rama Mandir Road; you can also use the Canara Bank, a short walk north up the road from the vegetable market, but service is painfully slow and you will need to take photocopies of the relevant pages of your passport. **Internet** services are available at Cyber Park, opposite the post office.

Bijapur is flat, compact, relatively uncongested, and generally easy to negotiate by **bicycle**; rickety Heros are available for rent from several stalls outside the bus stand for around Rs2 per hour. **Auto-rickshaws** don't have meters and charge a minimum of Rs10; although most of Bijapur is covered by a fare of Rs30, they are a much more expensive way of getting around the monuments, when they charge around Rs200 for a four-hour tour. **Taxis**, available from near the bus stand, charge Rs5 per kilometre.

Moving on from Bijapur is getting easier with efficient private companies such as VRL, recognizable by their distinctive yellow-and-black luxury coaches, travelling to Bangalore (3 buses from 7pm) and operating other overnight services to Mangalore via Udupi and Mumbai. VRL can be booked through Vijayanand Travel, Terrace floor, Shastri Market, Gandhi Circle (☏08352/51000) or their other branch just south of the bus stand. KSRTC also runs deluxe buses to Bangalore, Hubli, Mumbai and Hyderabad (via Sholapur). The five trains to Gadag depart between 4.15am and 6.25pm, while those to Sholapur leave between 3.30am and 9.05pm.

Accommodation and eating

Accommodation standards are pretty low in Bijapur, although finding a room is rarely a problem. Most budget tourists head for the KSTDC *Mayura Adil Shahi*, which, despite its shabbiness, has a certain charm; it's also cheap and central. **Eating** is largely confined to the hotels, with the odd independent establishment. At Gandhi Chowk, the *Shrinidhi Hotel* and the *Mysore Hotel* both serve good south Indian vegetarian food, while the basement *Niyaz* opposite the *Sagar Deluxe* hotel serves meat. The *Hotel Megharaj* and *Surabhi*, both on Station Road, serve good cheap vegetarian "meals".

Godavari, Athani Road ☎08352/53105, ℻56225. This monolithic modern but fading hotel is something of a landmark, and its prices have been pegged back to reflect its very average status. ❷–❺

KSTDC Mayura Adil Shahi, Anand Mahal Road ☎08352/50934. Stone-floored rooms ranged around a leafy courtyard-garden could be a lot nicer; all have slightly grubby attached bathrooms and tatty mozzie nets but clean sheets and towels. Hot and cold drinks are served on the verandas by helpful staff. The food at the restaurant– a standard mix of veg- and non-veg Indian, with some Chinese and Continental dishes – is ordinary, but they do serve chilled beer and it's pleasant to eat in the garden. ❷

KSTDC Mayura Adil Shahi Annexe, Station Road ☎08352/50401. Almost as dowdy as the main wing, but with larger, cleaner rooms, all a/c with TV and individual sitouts. No restaurant. ❺

Madhuvan, Station Road ☎08352/55571. The cleanest and best-appointed place in town, with a variety of rooms, from ordinary doubles to more comfortable a/c "deluxe" options, but expensive for what it is. The restaurant, however, serves good-value thalis at lunchtime. Can change money for residents. ❻–❼

Megharaj, Station Road ☎08352/51458. Run by the affable ex-wrestler Sundara, who unfortunately doesn't speak a word of English, the hotel has good-value doubles upstairs and even some a/c rooms. The vegetarian restaurant in the basement is cheap and good. ❷–❺

Rajdhani, opposite Laxmi Talkies, near Old Head Post Office, Station Road ☎08352/53468. Most bearable of the rock-bottom lodges in the centre, with clean rooms and a 24hr checkout. Sandwiched between two cinemas. ❷

Sagar Deluxe, next to *Bara Kaman*, Busreshwar Chowk ☎08352/59234. Centrally located hotel with unremarkable but cheap doubles and some deluxe and a/c rooms. ❷–❻.

Samrat, Station Road ☎08352/51620. Newish lodge at the east end of town. Institutional, and not all that neat, but a fall-back if the *Mayura Adil Shahi* is full. However, you can do better and the restaurant is best avoided. ❷–❸

Sanman, opposite the Golgumbaz, Station Road ☎08352/51866. Best value among the budget places, and well placed for the railway station. Good-sized rooms with mozzie nets and clean attached shower-toilets. The Udupi canteen is a stop for the bus parties, so their south Indian snacks are all freshly cooked; try the popular *puri korma* or delicious *sadar masala dosas*. ❷

The town and monuments

Unlike most medieval Muslim strongholds, Bijapur lacked natural rock defences and had to be strengthened by the Adil Shahis with huge **fortified walls**. Extending some 10km around the town, these ramparts, studded with cannon emplacements (*burjes*) and watchtowers, are breached in five points by *darwazas*, or strong gateways, and several smaller postern gates (*didis*). In the middle of the town, a further hoop of crenellated battlements encircled Bijapur's **citadel**, site of the sultans' apartments and durbar hall, of which only fragments remain. The Adil Shahis' **tombs** are scattered around the outskirts, while most of the important **mosques** lie southeast of the citadel.

It's possible to see Bijapur's highlights in a day, although most people stay for two or three nights, taking in the monuments at a more leisurely pace. Our account covers the sights from east to west, beginning with the **Golgumbaz** – which you should aim to visit at around 6am, before the bus parties descend – and ending with the exquisite **Ibrahim Rauza**, an atmospheric spot to enjoy the sunset.

The Golgumbaz

The vast **Golgumbaz** mausoleum (daily 6am–6pm; $5 [Rs5]), Bijapur's most famous building, soars above the town's east walls, visible for miles in every direction. Built towards the end of the Adil Shahis' reign, the Golgumbaz is a fitting monument to a dynasty on its last legs – pompous, decadent and ill-proportioned, but conceived on an irresistibly awesome scale.

The cubic tomb, enclosing a 170-square-metre hall, is crowned with a single hemispherical **dome**, the largest in the world after St Peter's in Rome (which is only 5m wider). Spiral staircases wind up the four, seven-storey octagonal towers that buttress the building to the famous **Whispering Gallery**, a three-metre-wide passage encircling the interior base of the dome from where, looking carefully down, you can get a real feel of the sheer size of the building. Get here just after opening time and you can experiment with the extraordinary acoustics; by 7am, though, the cacophony generated by bus loads of whooping and clapping tourists means you can't hear yourself think, let alone make out whispering 38m away. A good antidote to the din is the superb **views** from the mausoleum's ramparts, which overlook the town and its monuments to the dark-soiled Deccan countryside beyond, scattered with minor tombs and ruins.

Set on a plinth in the centre of the hall below are the gravestones of the ruler who built the Golgumbaz, **Mohammed Adil Shahi**, along with those of his wife, daughter, grandson and favourite courtesan, Rambha. At one corner of the grounds stands the simple gleaming white shrine to a Sufi saint of the Adil Shahi period, **Hashim Pir** which, around February, attracts *qawwals* (singers of devotional *qawwali* music) to the annual *urs*, which lasts for three days.

The Jami Masjid

A little under 1km southwest of the Golgumbaz, the **Jami Masjid** (Friday Mosque) presides over the quarter that formed the centre of the city during Bijapur's nineteenth-century nadir under the Nizam of Hyderabad. It was commissioned by Ali Adil Shahi, the ruler credited with constructing the city walls and complex water supply system, as a monument to his victory over the Vijayanagars at the battle of Talikota in 1565, and is widely regarded as one of the finest mosques in India. As it is a living mosque, you should not enter improperly dressed.

Approached via a square *hauz*, or ablutions tank, the main **prayer hall** is surmounted by an elegantly proportioned central dome, with 33 smaller shallow domes ranged around it. Simplicity and restraint are the essence of the colonnaded hall below, divided by gently curving arches and rows of thick plaster-covered pillars. Aside from the odd geometric design and trace of yellow, blue and green tile work, the only ornamentation is found in the mihrab, or west- (Mecca-) facing prayer niche, which is smothered in gold leaf and elaborate calligraphy. The marble floor of the hall features a grid of 2500 rectangles, known as *musallahs* (after the *musallah* prayer mats brought to mosques by worshippers). These were added by the Moghul emperor Aurangzeb, allegedly as recompense for making off with the velvet carpets, long golden chain and other valuables that originally filled the prayer hall.

The Mithari and Astar Mahals

Continuing west from the Jami Masjid, the first monument of note is a small, ornately carved gatehouse on the south side of the road. Although of modest size, the delicate three-storey structure, known as the **Mithari Mahal**, is one of Bijapur's most beautiful buildings, with ornate projecting windows and minarets crowning its corners. Once again, Ali Adil Shahi erected it, along with the mosque behind, using gifts presented to him during a state visit to Vijayanagar. The Hindu rajas' generosity, however, did not pay off. Only a couple of years later, the Adil Shahi and his four Muslim allies sacked their city, plundering its wealth and murdering most of its inhabitants.

The lane running north from opposite the Mithari Mahal brings you to the dilapidated **Asar Mahal**, a large open-fronted hall propped up by four green-painted pillars and fronted by a large stagnant step-well. Built in 1646 by Mohammed Adil Shahi as a Hall of Justice, it was later chosen to house hairs from the Prophet's beard, thereby earning the title **Asar-i-Sharif**, or "place of illustrious relics". In theory, women are not permitted inside to view the upper storey, where fifteen niches are decorated with mediocre, Persian-style pot-and-foliage murals, but for a little baksheesh, one of the girls who hang around the site will unlock the doors for you.

The citadel

Bijapur's **citadel** stands in the middle of town, hemmed in on all but its north side by battlements. Most of the buildings inside have collapsed, or have been converted into government offices, but enough remain to give a sense of how imposing this royal enclave must once have been.

The best-preserved monuments lie along, or near, the citadel's main north–south artery, Anand Mahal Road, reached by skirting the southeast wall from the Asar Mahal, or from the north side via the road running past KSTDC's *Mayura Adil Shahi Hotel*. The latter route brings you first to the **Gagan Mahal**. Originally Ali Adil Shahi's "Heavenly Palace", this now-ruined hulk later served as a durbar hall for the sultans, who would sit in state on the platform at the open-fronted north side, watched by crowds gathered in the grounds opposite. West off Anand Mahal Road, the five-storeyed **Sat Manzil** was the pleasure palace of the courtesan Rambha, entombed with Mohammed Adil Shahi and his family in the Golgumbaz. In front stands an ornately carved water pavilion, the **Jal Mandir**, now left high and dry in an empty tank.

Malik-i-Maidan and Upli Buruj

Guarding the principal western entrance to the city is one of several bastions (*burje*) that punctuate Bijapur's battlements. This one, the Burj-i-Sherza ("Lion Gate") sports a colossal cannon, known as the **Malik-i-Maidan**, literally "Lord of the Plains". It was brought here as war booty in the sixteenth century, and needed four hundred bullocks, ten elephants and an entire battalion to haul it up the steps to the emplacement. Inscriptions record that the cannon, whose muzzle features a relief of a monster swallowing an elephant, was cast in Ahmednagar in 1551.

A couple more discarded cannons lie atop the watchtower visible a short walk northwest. Steps wind around the outside of the oval-shaped **Upli Burj**, or "Upper Bastion", to a gun emplacement that affords unimpeded views over the city and plains.

The Ibrahim Rauza

Set in its own walled compound less than 1km west of the ramparts, the **Ibrahim Rauza** represents the high watermark of Bijapuri architecture (daily 6am–6pm; $5 [Rs5]). Whereas the Golgumbaz impresses primarily by its scale, the appeal of this tomb complex lies in its grace and simplicity. Beyond the reach of most bus parties, it's also a haven of peace, with cool colonnaded verandas and flocks of iridescent parakeets careening between the mildewed domes, minarets and gleaming golden finials.

Opinions differ over whether the tomb was commissioned by Ibrahim Adil Shah (1580–1626), or his favourite wife, Taj Sultana, but the former was the first to be interred here, in a gloomy chamber whose only light enters via a series of exquisite pierced-stone (*jali*) windows. Made up of elaborate Koranic inscriptions, these are the finest examples of their kind in India. More amazing stonework decorates the exterior of the mausoleum, and the equally beautiful **mosque** opposite, the cornice of whose facade features a stone chain carved from a single block. The two buildings, bristling with minarets and domed cupolas, face each other from opposite sides of a rectangular raised plinth, divided by a small reservoir and fountains. Viewed from on top of the walls that enclose the complex, you can see why its architect, Malik Sandal, added a self-congratulatory inscription in his native Persian over the tomb's south doorway, describing his masterpiece as " ... A beauty of which Paradise stood amazed".

Gulbarga

GULBARGA, 165km northeast of Bijapur, was the founding capital of the Bahmani dynasty and the region's principal city before the court moved to Bidar in 1424. Later captured by the Adil Shahis and Moghuls, it has remained a staunchly Muslim town, and bulbous onion domes and mosque minarets still soar prominently above its ramshackle concrete-box skyline. The town is also famous as the birthplace of the *chisti*, or saint, Hazrat Bandah Nawaz Gesu Daraz (1320–1422), whose tomb, situated next to one of India's foremost Islamic theological colleges, is a major shrine.

In spite of Gulbarga's religious and historical significance, its **monuments** pale in comparison with those at Bijapur, and even Bidar. Unless you're particularly interested in medieval Muslim architecture, few are worth breaking a journey to see. The one exception is the tomb complex on the northeast edge of town, known as **the Dargah**. Approached via a broad bazaar, this marble-lined enclosure, plastered in mildew-streaked limewash, centres on the tomb of Hazrat Gesu Daraz, affectionately known to his devotees as "**Bandah Nawaz**", or "the long-haired one who brings comfort to others". The saint was spiritual mentor to the Bahmani rulers, and it was they who erected his beautiful double-storeyed mausoleum, now visited by hundreds of thousands of Muslim pilgrims each year. Women are not allowed inside, and must peek at the tomb – surrounded by a mother-of-pearl-inlaid wooden screen and draped with green silk – through the pierced-stone windows. Men, however, can enter to leave offerings and admire the elaborate mirror-mosaic ceiling. The same gender bar applies to the neighbouring tomb, whose interior has retained its exquisite Persian paintings. The *Dargah's* other important building, open to both sexes, is the **Madrasa**, or theological college, founded by Bandah Nawaz and enlarged during the two centuries after his death. The syllabus here is dominated by the Koran, but the saint's own works on Sufi mysticism and ethics are also still studied.

After mingling with the crowds at the *Dargah*, escape across town to Gulbarga's deserted **fort**. Encircled by sixteen-metre-thick crenellated walls, fifteen watchtowers and an evil-smelling stagnant moat, the great citadel now lies in ruins behind the town's large artificial lake. Its only surviving building is the beautiful fourteenth-century **Jami Masjid**, whose elegant domes and arched gateways preside over a scrubby wasteland. Thought to have been modelled by a Moorish architect on the great Spanish mosque of Córdoba, it is unique in India for having an entirely domed prayer hall.

Practicalities

Daily KSRTC **buses** from Bijapur, Bidar and Hospet pull in to the state bus stand on the southwest edge of town. Private minibuses work from the road-side opposite, their conductors shouting for passengers across the main concourse. Don't be tempted to take one of these to Bidar; they only run as far as the fly-blown highway junction of Humnabad, 40km short, where you'll be stranded for hours. Gulbarga's main-line **railway station**, with services to and from Mumbai, Pune, Hyderabad, Bangalore and Chennai, lies 1.5km east of the bus stand, along **Mill Road**. **Station Road**, the town's other main artery, runs due north of here past three hotels and the lake to the busy **Chowk** crossroads, at the heart of the bazaar.

Gulbarga's main sights are well spread out, so you'll need to get around by **auto-rickshaw**; fix fares in advance. For medical help, head for the town **hospital**, east of the centre next door to the *Hotel Santoosh*, which has a well-stocked pharmacy. There is nowhere in Gulbarga to change money.

Accommodation and eating

Gulbarga is well provided with good-value **accommodation**, and even travellers on tight budgets should be able to afford a clean room with a small balcony. The one place to avoid is the grim and neglected KSTDC *Mayura Bahmani*, set in the public gardens, more of a drinking den than a hotel, and plagued by mosquitoes.

All the hotels listed below have **restaurants**, mostly pure-veg places with a no alcohol rule. *Kamat*, the chain restaurant, has several branches in Gulbarga including a pleasant one at Station Chowk, specializing in vegetarian "meals" as well as *iddlis* and *dosas*; try *joleata roti*, a local bread cooked either hard and crisp or soft like a chapati. The restaurant-only *Punjab Hotel*, at Station Chowk, has a varied Indian and Chinese veg menu, while carnivores can indulge at *Shree Nagarjuna*, just south of Mill Road at the first junction from Station Chowk, which also has a bar.

Adithya, 2-244 Main Rd, opposite Public Gardens ⊕08472/24040, ⊕26617. Unbeatable value economy doubles, or posher a/c options, in a new building. Their impeccably clean pure-veg Udupi restaurant, *Pooja*, on the ground floor, does great thalis and snacks. ❸–❻

Pariwar, Station Road, ten minutes' walk from the station ⊕08472/21522, ⊕22039. One of the town's smarter hotels, but not especially great value unless you get an economy room, which fill up by noon, so book ahead. The *Kamakshi Restaurant* (6am–10pm) serves quality vegetarian south Indian food, but no beer. Some a/c. ❹–❻

Raj Rajeshwari, Vasant Nagar, Mill Road ⊕08472/25881. Just 5min from the bus stand, friendly and better value than the *Pariwar*. Well-maintained modern building with large en-suite

rooms with balconies, plus a reasonable veg restaurant (strictly no alcohol). ❸–❻

Santosh, Bilgundi Gardens, University Road ⊕08472/22661. Upscale, efficient chain hotel peacefully located on the eastern outskirts, with big, comfortable rooms (some a/c), sitouts, veg-and non-veg restaurants and a bar. Recommended. ❸–❻

Savita Lodge, Mill Road ⊕08472/21560. Best of the basic bunch right by the bus stand. Small but wholesome attached rooms. ❷

Southern Star, near the Fort, Super Market ⊕08472/24093. New and comfortable with two restaurants and a bar and some a/c rooms; the rooms at the back look onto the ramparts of the fort but across the stagnant and putrid moat. ❷–❻

Bidar

In 1424, following the break-up of the Bahmani dynasty into five rival factions, Ahmad Shah I shifted his court from Gulbarga to a less constricted site at **BIDAR**, spurred, it is said, by grief at the death of his beloved spiritual mentor, Bandah Nawas Gesu Daraz. Revamping the town with a new fort, splendid palaces, mosques and ornamental gardens, the Bahmanis ruled from here until 1487, when the Barid Shahis took control. They were succeeded by the Adil Shahis from Bijapur, and later the Moghuls under Aurangzeb, who annexed the region in 1656, before the Nizam of Hyderabad finally acquired the territory in the early eighteenth century.

Lost in the far northwest of Karnataka, Bidar, 284km northwest of Bijapur, is nowadays a provincial backwater, better known for its fighter-pilot training base than the monuments gently decaying in, and within sight of, its medieval walls. Yet the town, half of whose 140,000 population are still Muslim, has a gritty charm, with narrow red-dirt streets ending at arched gates and open vistas across the plains. Littered with tile-fronted tombs, rambling fortifications and old mosques, it merits a visit if you're travelling between Hyderabad (150km east) and Bijapur, although expect little in the way of Western comforts, and more than the usual amount of curious approaches from locals. Lone women travellers, especially, may find the attention more hassle than it's worth.

Bidar's sights are too spread out to be comfortably explored on foot. However, auto-rickshaws tend to be thin on the ground away from the main streets, and are reluctant to wait while you look around the monuments, so it's a good idea to rent a **bicycle** for the day (Rs2 per hour) from Rouf's, only 50m east of the bus stand next to the excellent *Karnatak Juice Centre*.

Practicalities

Bidar lies on a branch line of the main Mumbai–Secunderabad–Chennai rail route, and can only be reached by slow passenger **train**. The few visitors that come here invariably arrive **by bus**, at the KSRTC bus stand on the far northwestern edge of town, which has hourly direct services to Hyderabad (3hr 30min) and Gulbarga (3hr), and several a day to Bijapur (7hr) and Bangalore (12hr). There is no tourist office or exchange facility but there are signs of Bidar's entry into the twenty-first century (and proximity to Hyderabad) in the shape of several **internet** outlets such as Swamy's Cyber Café, 100m southeast of the bus stand on Udgir Road.

Most **places to stay** are an auto-rickshaw ride away in the centre, so it makes sense to opt for the new *Hotel Mayura* (℡08482/28142; ❷–❺) opposite the bus stand, which is one of the two best in Bidar and has large rooms with optional air-conditioning. The other decent hotel is its older sister the *Ashoka* (℡08482/26249; ❷–❺), 1500m from the bus stand past Dr Ambedkar Chowk, which is comfortable with good-value deluxe rooms, some with a/c. The KSTDC *Mayura Barid Shahi* (℡08482/26571; ❷) on Udgir Road, less than 1km from the bus stand, remains very shabby despite some renovation and none of the handful of grim central lodges is worth considering.

Finding somewhere good to **eat** is not a problem in Bidar, again thanks to the restaurants at the *Mayura* and *Ashoka*, which both offer a varied selection of north Indian veg and meat dishes (try the *Mayura*'s pepper chicken) and serve cold beer. The open-air garden restaurant of the *Mayura Barid Shahi* is a lot nicer than its interior and serves mostly north Indian (try the veg *malai kofta*, or chicken tikka) with a handful of Chinese options plus chilled beer and ice cream. Also recommended, and much cheaper, is the popular *Udupi Krishna* restaurant, five minutes east of the *Mayuri Barid Shahi*, overlooking the *chowk*, which serves up unlimited pure-veg thalis for lunch; they have a "family room" for women, too, and open early (around 7.30am) for piping hot south Indian breakfasts.

The old town

The heart of Bidar is its medieval **old town**, encircled by crenellated ramparts and eight imposing gateways (*darwazas*). This predominantly Muslim quarter holds many Bahmani-era mosques, *havelis* and *khanqahs* – "monasteries" set up by the local rulers for Muslim cleric-mystics and their disciples – but its real highlight is the impressive ruins of **Mahmud Gawan's Madrasa**, or theological college, whose single minaret soars high above the city centre. Gawan, a scholar and Persian exile, was the *wazir*, or prime minister, of the Bahmani state under Mohammed Bahmani III (1463–82). A talented linguist, mathematician and inspired military strategist, he oversaw the dynasty's expansion into Karnataka and Goa, bequeathing this college as a thank-you gift to his adoptive kingdom in 1472. The distinctively Persian-style building, originally surmounted by large bulbous domes, once housed a world-famous library. However, this burnt down after being struck by lightning in 1696, while several of the walls and domes were blown away when gunpowder stored here by Aurangzeb's occupying army caught fire and exploded. Today, the *madrasa* is little more than a shell, although its elegant arched facade has retained large patches of the vibrant Persian glazed tile-work that once covered most of the exterior surfaces. This includes a beautiful band of Koranic calligraphy, and striking multicoloured zigzags wrapped around the base of the one remaining *minar*, or minaret.

Bidri

Bidar is renowned as the home of a unique damascene metalwork technique known as **bidri**, developed by the Persian silversmiths that came to the area with the Bahmani court in the fifteenth century. These highly skilled artisans engraved and inlaid their traditional Iranian designs onto a metal alloy composed of lead, copper, zinc and tin, which they blackened and polished. The resulting effect – swirling silver floral motifs framed by geometric patterns and set against black backgrounds – has since become the hallmark of Muslim metalwork in India.

Bidri objets d'art are displayed in museums and galleries all over the country. But if you want to see pukka *bidri*-wallahs at work, take a walk down Bidar's **Siddiq Talim Road**, which cuts across the south side of the old town, where skull-capped artisans tap and burnish vases, goblets, plates, spice boxes, betel-nut tins, and ornamental hookah pipes, as well as less traditional objects – coasters, ashtrays and bangles – that crop up (at vastly inflated prices) in silver emporiums as far away as Delhi and Calcutta.

The fort

Presiding over the dark-soiled plains from atop a sheer-faced red-laterite escarpment, Bidar's **fort**, at the far north end of the street running past the *madrasa*, was founded by the Hindu Chalukyas and strengthened by the Bahmanis in the early fifteenth century. Despite repeated sieges, it remains largely intact, encircled by 10km of ramparts that drop away in the north and west to 300-metre cliffs. The main southern entrance is protected by equally imposing man-made defences: gigantic fortified gates and a triple moat formerly crossed by a series of drawbridges. Once inside, the first building of note (on the left after the third and final gateway) is the exquisite **Rangin Mahal**. Mahmud Shah built this modest "Coloured Palace" after an unsuccessful uprising of Abyssinian slaves in 1487 forced him to relocate to a safer site inside the citadel. The palace's relatively modest proportions reflect the Bahmanis' declining fortunes, but its interior comprises some of the finest surviving Islamic art in the Deccan, with superb woodcarving above the door arches and Persian-style mother-of-pearl inlay on polished black granite surfaces. If the doors to the palace are locked, ask for the keys at the nearby ASI **museum** (daily 8am–1pm & 2–5pm; free), which houses a missable collection of Hindu temple sculpture, weapons and Stone Age artefacts.

Opposite the museum, an expanse of gravel is all that remains of the royal gardens. This is overlooked by the austere **Solah Khamb** mosque (1327), Bidar's oldest Muslim monument, whose most outstanding feature is the intricate pierced-stone *jali* calligraphy around its central dome. From here, continue west through the ruins of the former royal enclosure – a rambling complex of half-collapsed palaces, baths, *zenanas* (womens' quarters) and assembly halls – to the fort's west walls. You can complete the round of **the ramparts** in ninety minutes, taking time out to enjoy the views over the red cliffs and across the plains.

Ashtur: the Bahmani tombs

As you look from the fort's east walls, a cluster of eight bulbous white domes floats alluringly above the trees in the distance. Dating from the fifteenth century, the mausoleums at **Ashtur**, 3km east of Bidar (leave the old town via Dulhan Darwaza gate), are the final resting places of the Bahmani sultans and their families, including the son of the ruler who first decamped from Gulbarga, Alauddin Shah I. His **remains** by far the most impressive tomb, with patches of coloured glazed tiles on its arched facade, and a large dome whose interior surfaces writhe with sumptuous Persian paintings. Reflecting sunlight onto the ceiling with a small pocket mirror, the *chowkidar* picks out the highlights, among them a diamond, barely visible among the bat droppings.

The tomb of Allaudin's father, the ninth and most illustrious Bahmani Sultan, Ahmad Shah I, stands beside that of his son, decorated with Persian inscriptions. Beyond this are two more minor mausoleums, followed by the partially collapsed tomb of Humayun the Cruel (1458–61), cracked open by a bolt of lightning. Continuing along the line, you can chart the gradual decline of the Bahmanis as the mausoleums diminish in size, ending with a sad handful erected in the early sixteenth century, when the sultans were no more than puppet rulers of the Barid Shahis.

Crowning a low hillock halfway between Ashtur and Bidar, on the north side of the road, the **Chaukhandi of Hazrat Khalil Ullah** is a beautiful octagonal-shaped tomb built by Allaudin Shah for his chief spiritual adviser. Most of the tiles have dropped off the facade, but the surviving stonework and calligraphy above the arched doorway, along with the views from the tomb's plinth, deserve a quick detour from the road.

The Badrid Shahi tombs

The **tombs of the Badrid Shahi** rulers, who succeeded the Bahmanis at the start of the sixteenth century, stand on the western edge of town, on the Udgir road, 200m beyond and visible from the bus stand. Although not as impressive as those of their predecessors, the mausoleums, mounted on raised plinths, occupy an attractive site. Randomly spaced rather than set in a chronological row, they are surrounded by lawns maintained by the ASI. The most interesting is the tomb of **Ali Barid** (1542–79), whose Mecca-facing wall was left open to the elements. A short distance southwest lies a mass-grave platform for his 67 concubines, who were sent as tribute gifts by vassals of the Deccani overlord from all across the kingdom. The compound is only officially open for afternoon promenading (daily 4.30–7.30pm; Rs2) but the gateman may let you in earlier if he's around.

Travel details

When this book went to press, the changeover from metre- to broad-gauge track was still disrupting some train services in Karnataka and in particular those to Hassan; check the current situation with Indian Railways.

Trains

Bangalore to: Ahmedabad (3 weekly; 34hr 30min–38hr 45min); Calcutta (2 weekly; 38hr 15min); Chennai (5–7 daily; 5hr–7hr 35min); Delhi (1–2 daily; 34hr 30min–49hr 50min); Gulbarga (2–3 daily; 11hr 35min–12hr 15min); Hospet (1 daily; 9hr 50min); Hubli (2–4 daily; 8hr 30min–13hr); Hyderabad (Secunderabad) (1–3 daily; 11hr 55min–15hr 50min); Kochi (Ernakulam) (1–2 daily; 12hr 50min–13hr 5min); Mumbai (2–3 daily; 23hr 55min–25hr 55min); Mysore (6–7 daily; 2–3hr); Pune (2–4 daily; 19hr 25min–21hr 20min); Trivandrum (1–2 daily; 18hr 5min–18hr 10min).

Bijapur to: Badami (5 daily; 4hr); Gadag (5 daily; 6hr); Sholapur (5 daily; 3hr 30min).

Hassan to: Mangalore (1 daily, but subject to disruptions in service; 8hr); Mysore (3 daily; 3–4hr).

Hospet to: Bangalore (1 daily; 8hr 15min); Gadag (3 daily; 1hr 15min–1hr 30min); Hubli (3 daily; 2hr 30min–3hr).

Mangalore to: Chennai (2 daily; 19hr 5min–19hr 25min); Kochi (Ernakulam) (2 daily; 10hr 35min–11hr 15min); Goa (5 daily; 4hr 50min–6hr 30min); Gokarn (1 daily; 4hr 20min); Kollam (2 daily; 14hr 5min–15hr 5min); Kozhikode (2 daily; 5hr 35min–6hr 10min); Trivandrum (2 daily; 15hr 40min–17hr 5min).

Mysore to: Bangalore (6–7 daily; 1hr 55min–3hr 30min); Hassan (3 daily; 3–4hr).

Buses

Bangalore to: Bidar (2 daily; 16hr); Bijapur (5 daily; 13hr); Chennai (14 daily; 8hr); Coimbatore (2 daily; 9hr); Goa (5 daily; 14hr); Gokarn (2 daily; 13hr) Gulbarga (6 daily; 15hr); Hassan (every 30min; 4hr); Hospet (3 daily; 8hr); Hubli (3 daily; 9hr); Hyderabad (5 daily; 16hr); Jog Falls (1 nightly; 8hr); Karwar (3 daily; 14hr); Kodaikanal (1 nightly; 13hr); Kochi (Ernakulam) (6 daily; 12hr); Kozhikode (Calicut) (6 daily; 9hr); Madikeri (9 daily; 6hr); Madurai (2 daily; 12hr); Mangalore (19 daily; 8hr); Mumbai (2 daily; 24hr); Mysore (every 15min; 3hr); Ooty (6 daily; 7hr); Pondicherry (2 daily; 9hr).

Bijapur to: Aurangabad (4 daily; 12hr); Badami (4 daily; 4hr); Bangalore (5 daily; 13hr); Bidar (4 daily; 8hr); Gulbarga (hourly; 4hr); Hospet (15 daily; 5hr); Hubli (hourly; 6hr); Hyderabad (5 daily; 10hr); Mumbai (10 daily; 12hr); Pune (10 daily; 8hr); Sholapur (every 30min; 2hr 30min).

Hassan to: Channarayapatna (hourly; 1hr); Halebid (hourly; 1hr); Hospet (1 daily; 10hr); Mangalore (hourly; 4hr); Mysore (every 30min; 3hr).

Hospet to: Badami (2 daily; 5hr); Bangalore (3 daily; 8hr); Bidar (2 daily; 10hr); Gokarn (3 daily; 10hr); Hampi (every 30min; 30min); Hyderabad (6 daily; 12hr); Mangalore (1 daily; 12hr); Mysore (2 daily; 10hr); Panjim (3 daily; 10hr); Vasco da Gama (3 daily; 10–11hr).

Mangalore to: Bangalore (19 daily; 8hr); Bijapur (1 daily; 16hr); Chaudi (6 daily; 8hr); Gokarn (3 daily; 7hr); Kannur (6 daily; 4hr); Karwar (9 daily; 8hr); Kasargode (hourly; 1hr); Kochi (Ernakulam) (1 daily; 9hr); Madikeri (hourly; 4hr); Mysore (hourly; 7hr); Panjim (6 daily; 10–11hr); Udupi (every 10 min; 1hr).

Mysore to: Bangalore (every 15min; 3hr); Channarayapatna (every 30min; 2hr); Jog Falls (via Shimoga) (every 90min; 7hr); Kannur (5 daily; 7hr); Kochi (5 daily; 12hr); Kozhikode (5 daily; 5hr); Madikeri (hourly; 3hr); Mangalore (hourly; 7hr); Ooty (8 daily; 5hr); Srirangapatnam (every 15 min; 20min).

Flights

Bangalore to: Calcutta (2 daily; 2hr 25min–3hr 30min); Chennai (6–8 daily; 45min–1hr 5min); Delhi (7 daily; 2hr 30min); Goa (2 daily; 55min–1hr 30min); Hyderabad (2–3 daily; 1hr); Kochi (Ernakulam) (2–3 daily; 50–55min); Mangalore (1–2 daily; 40min–1hr 5min); Mumbai (11–12 daily; 1hr 30min); Pune (2 daily; 1hr 20min); Trivandrum (1 daily; 2hr 5min).

Mangalore to: Bangalore (1–2 daily; 40min–1hr 5min); Chennai (3 weekly; 1hr 55min); Mumbai (2–3 daily; 1hr 15min).

contexts

contexts

History 1471–1503

Religion...1504–1523

Indian women..1524–1530

Wildlife..1531–1540

Developement and green issues................................1541–1548

Music..1549–1560

Books 1561–1568

Language...1569–1572

Glossary 1573–1579

History

India is the product of a complex and tumultuous past. Its climate and fertile soil, which have supported settled agriculture for at least 9000 years, have also given rise to countless regional dynasties, perennially covetous of their neighbours' land and wealth. For as long as written histories of India have existed this same fecundity has also lured invaders across the deserts, oceans and mountains that border the subcontinent. Successive waves of armed colonists, from the Aryan tribes to the British, have poured down the peninsula, assimilating indigenous traditions and implanting their own. Scholars of history, archeology and religon are still trying to make sense of the extraordinary wealth of historic monuments they left behind, and what follows is necessarily only the broadest of outlines. For a fuller overview, dip into one of the recent histories of India recommended in Books, p.1561.

Prehistory

The earliest human activity in the Indian subcontinent can be traced back to the Early, Middle and Late Stone Ages (400,000–200,000 BC). Implements from all three periods have been found around the country, from Rajasthan and Gujarat in the west to Bihar in the east, from the northwest of what's now Pakistan to the tip of the peninsula; and rock paintings of hunting scenes can be seen in the Narmada Valley and elsewhere in central India.

These Paleolithic peoples were seminomadic **hunters and gatherers** for many millennia. Indeed, some isolated hill tribes continued to be hunters and gatherers or to practise the transitional "slash and burn" type of agriculture into the twentieth century. Five main peoples are known to have been present when the move to an agricultural lifestyle took place, in the middle of the eighth millennium BC: the **Negrito** race, believed to be the earliest; the **Proto-Australoid**; the **Mediterranean** peoples; the **Mongoloid** elements (confined to the north and northeast); and the western **Brachycephals** or **Alpine** peoples.

The first evidence of **agricultural settlement**, at Mehrgarh on the western plains of the Indus, is roughly contemporaneous with similar developments in Egypt, Mesopotamia and Persia. Village settlements in western Afghanistan, Baluchistan and the Sind gradually developed over the next five thousand years as their inhabitants began to use copper and bronze, domesticate animals, make pottery and trade with their western neighbours.

The distinct styles of pottery discovered at Nal and Zhob in the Brahui hills of Baluchistan, Kulli on the Makran coast and the lower Indus, and Amri in the Sind indicate the development of several independent cultures. **Terracotta figurines** of goddesses, bulls and phallic emblems echo the fertility cults and Mother Goddess worship found in early agricultural communities in the Mediterranean region and the Middle East; they also prefigure elements which were to re-emerge as aspects of the religious life of India.

The first great Indian civilization

From the start of the fourth millennium BC, the individuality of early village cultures began to be replaced by a more homogeneous style of pottery at a large number of sites throughout the **Indus Valley**; by the middle of the third millennium, a uniform culture had developed at settlements spread across nearly 1,280,000 square kilometres, including parts of the Punjab, Uttar Pradesh, Gujarat, Baluchistan, the Sind and the Makran coast. Two great cities on the Indus, **Harappa** in the north and **Mohenjo Daro** in the south, were supported by the agricultural surplus produced by such settlements. Recent archeological research has unearthed further sites, almost as large as the first two and designed on the same plan, at Kalibangan, on the border of India and Pakistan, at Kot Diji east of Mohenjo Daro, at Chanhu Daro further south on the Indus, and at Lothal in Gujarat.

The emergence of the first great Indian civilization, around 2500 BC, is almost as remarkable as its stability for nearly a thousand years. All the cities were built with baked bricks of the same size; the streets were laid out in a grid with an elaborate system of covered drains; and the houses, some with more than one storey, are large. Vast granaries and a citadel built on higher ground with a gigantic adjoining bath at Mohenjo Daro, together with the absence of royal palaces and the large numbers of religious figurines, suggest that it was a theocratic state of priests, merchants and farmers.

By now, farmers had domesticated various **animals**, including hump-backed (Brahmani) cattle, goats, water buffaloes and fowls. They cultivated wheat, barley, peas and sesamum, and were also probably the first to grow and make clothes from **cotton**. Excavations at Lothal have uncovered a **harbour**; merchants were certainly involved in extensive trading by both sea and land, for they imported metals, including gold, silver and copper, and semiprecious stones from the Indian peninsula, Persia, Afghanistan, Central Asia and Mesopotamia. While the main export was probably cotton yarn or cloth, they may have exported surplus grain as well. Indus seals found at Ur confirm the continuity of trading links with Sumer between 2300 and 2000 BC.

The sheer quantity of **seals** discovered in the Indus cities suggests that each merchant or mercantile family had its own. They're usually square, and made of steatite (a kind of soapstone), engraved and then hardened by heating. All bear inscriptions, which remain undeciphered, although nearly 400 different characters have been identified. The emblems beneath the inscriptions – iconographic scenes and animals, such as the bull, buffalo, goat, tiger and elephant – are more enlightening. One of the most notable depicts a horned deity sitting cross-legged in an ithyphallic posture, surrounded by a tiger, an elephant, a rhinoceros, a water buffalo and two deer. He appears on two other seals, and it seems certain that he was a fertility god; indeed, he has been called a "**proto-Shiva**" because of the resemblance to Pashupati, the Lord of the Beasts, a major representation of the fully developed Hindu god, Shiva. Other seals provide evidence that certain trees, especially the peepal, were worshipped, and thus anticipate their sacred status in the Hindu and Buddhist religions.

No monumental sculpture survives, but large numbers of human figurines have been discovered, including a steatite bust of a man thought to be a priest, a striking bronze "dancing girl", brilliantly naturalistic models of animals, and countless terracotta statuettes of a Mother Goddess. This goddess is thought to have been worshipped in nearly every home of the common people, but the crude style of modelling suggests that she was not part of the cult of the priestly elite.

The sudden demise of the Indus civilization in the last quarter of the second millennium BC used to be explained by invasions of barbarian tribes from the northwest; but recent research has established that tectonic upheavals in about 1700 BC caused a series of floods, and these are now considered primarily to blame.

The Vedic Age 1500–600 BC

The written history of India begins with the invasions of the charioteering **Indo-European** or **Aryan** tribes, which spelt the final collapse of the Indus civilization. This period takes its name from the earliest Indian literature, the **Vedas**, collections of hymns (*samhitas*) composed in Vedic Sanskrit. Though composed between 1500 and 1000 BC, the *Rig Veda* was not written down until as late as 900 or 800 BC. Essentially a religious text, in use to this day, it sheds great light on the social and political life of the period.

The Aryans belonged to the barbarian tribes, who broke out of the vast steppeland that stretches from Poland to Central Asia to maraud and eventually colonize Europe, the Middle East and the Indian subcontinent from the start of the second millennium BC. They probably entered the Punjab via the Iranian plateau in successive waves over several hundred years; the peaceful farmers of the Indus would have been powerless against their horse-drawn chariots. Aryan culture was diametrically opposed to the Indus civilization, and Vedic literature relates how their war god, Indra, destroyed hundreds of urban settlements.

Seminomadic hunters and pastoralists when they first settled the region known as the *Sapta-Sindu* or seven "Induses" (from Kabul to the desert of Rajasthan), as the Aryans spread eastwards into the plain between the upper Ganges and the Yamuna, known as the Doab, they adopted the techniques of settled farming from the peoples they had conquered. The tribes began to organize themselves into village communities, governed by tribal councils (*sabha* and *samiti*) and warrior chiefs (*raja*), who offered protection in return for tribute; the sacrifices of the chief priest or *purohita* secured their prosperity and martial success.

The hymns describe the intertribal conflicts characteristic of the period, but there was an underlying sense of solidarity against the indigenous peoples, known as Dasas. Originally a general term for "enemies", it came to denote "subjects" as they were colonized within the land of the Aryans (*aryavarta*). The Dasas are described as negroid phallus worshippers, who owned many cattle and lived in fortified towns or villages (*pur*). The Aryans began to emphasize the purity of blood as they settled among the darker aboriginals, and their original class divisions of nobility and ordinary tribesmen were hardened to exclude the Dasas. At the same time, the priests, the sole custodians and extrapolators of the increasingly complex oral traditions of the sacrificial religion, began to claim high privileges for their skill and training.

By 1000 BC, a fourfold division of society had been given religious sanction in a hymn, which describes how the four classes (**varnas**, literally "colour") emanated from the mouth, arms, thighs and feet of the primeval man (*purusha*). The *varnas* of priest, warrior, peasant and serf (brahmin, *kshatrya*, *vaishya* and *shudra*) have persisted as the fundamental structure of society to the present day. The first three encompassed the main divisions within the Aryan tribes, which later assumed the status of "twice-born" (*dvija*); the Dasas and other non-Aryan peoples became the *shudras*, who served the three higher classes.

During the later Vedic period, between 1000 and 600 BC, the centre of Aryan culture and power shifted from the Punjab and the northwest to the Doab, whence their influence continued to spread eastwards and southwards. The sacred texts of the *Sama*, *Yajur* and *Atharva Vedas*, the *Brahmanas* and the *Upanishads* all originate in this period. Like the *Rig Veda*, they tell us much about developments in religious life, but only offer glimpses of the Aryanization of the subcontinent.

One of the *Brahmanas* relates how Agni, the Aryan fire-god, travelled eastwards destroying the jungle until his advance was arrested by the River Gandak. The Aryans refused to cross the river because Agni had not purified the land beyond until the fire-god ordered a warrior called Videgha Mathava to transport him across the river. The story provides an insight into how colonization occurred, both in terms of the gradual progress eastwards of Aryan culture, represented by the fire-god, and of the manner in which the jungle was cleared as the migrating tribes established new settlements.

The great epic poems, the **Mahabharata** and the **Ramayana**, and the *Puranas* claim to relate to this period. Though they are unreliable as historical sources, being overlaid with accretions from later centuries, it's possible to extract some of the facts entwined with the martial myths and legends.

The account of **Hinduism** on p.1504 includes more about the *Mahabharata*, the *Ramayana*, and the development of caste divisions.

The great battle of **Kurukshetra** – the central theme of the *Mahabharata* – is certainly historical, and took place near modern Delhi some time in the ninth and eighth centuries BC. It was the culmination of a dynastic dispute among the Kurus, who, with their neighbours the Panchalas, were the greatest of the Aryan tribes. Archeological evidence has been found of the two main settlements mentioned in the epic, Indraprastha (Delhi) and Hastinapura, further north on the Ganges; the latter was the capital of the Kurus, two of whose kings, Parikshit and Janamejaya, are described as mighty conquerors in the Vedic literature.

By the time of Kurukshetra, the Aryans had advanced into the mid-Gangetic valley to establish **Kosala**, with its capital at **Ayodhya** – according to the *Ramayana*, the realm of Rama, the god-hero. Vedic literature mentions neither Rama nor his father Dasharatha, but does refer to Rama's father-in-law, Janaka of Videha. Certainly the extension of Aryan influence to south India, reflected in the myth of Rama's invasion of Sri Lanka to rescue Sita, did not occur until much later. At this time, the megalithic cultures of Madras, Kerala and Mysore remained untouched by the Aryan invaders. The Aryanization of north India, however, continued throughout the period, and began to penetrate central India as well.

The migrating tribes pushed east beyond Kosala to found the kingdoms of **Kashi** (the region of Varanasi), **Videha** (east of the River Gandak and north of the Ganges), and **Anga** on the border of Bengal. The **Yadava** tribe settled around Mathura, on the Yamuna; a branch of the Yadavas is said later to have colonized Saurashtra in modern Gujarat. Further east, down the Yamuna, the **Vatsa** kingdom established its capital at Kaushambi. Other tribes pushed southwards down the River Chambal to found the kingdom of **Avanti**; some penetrated as far as the Narmada, and by the end of the period Aryan influence probably extended into the northwest Deccan.

This territorial expansion was assisted by significant developments in Aryan civilization. When they arrived in India Aryan knowledge of **metallurgy** was limited to gold, copper and bronze, but later Vedic literature mentions tin, lead, silver and iron. The use of iron, together with the taming of elephants, facilitated the rapid clearance of the forests and jungles for settlement. They now grew a large range of crops, including rice; specialized trades and crafts grew considerably, and merchants re-established trade with Mesopotamia, curtailed since the days of the Indus civilization.

Vedic culture and society was transformed by mutual acculturation between the Aryans and indigenous peoples. By the end of the Vedic period, the Aryan tribes had consolidated into little kingdoms, each with its capital city. Some were republics, but generally the power of the tribal assemblies was dwindling, to be replaced by a new kind of politics centred on a **king**, who ruled a geographical area. His relatives and courtiers formed a rudimentary administrative system – known as "Jewel Bearers" (*ratnins*), they included the chief priest, the chamberlain and palace officials.

Kingship was becoming more absolute, limited only by the influence of the priesthood – a relationship between temporal and sacred power that became crucial. The *Brahmana* literature, compiled by the priests, contains instructions for the performance of sacrifices symbolizing royal power, such as the royal consecration ceremonies (*rajasuya*) and the horse sacrifice (*ashvamedha*). Thus, the priests sustained belief in the association of kingship with divinity through their rituals and assisted new political institutions to emerge.

Not all religious specialists were committed to these political developments, and the evolution of Aryan civilization in the late Vedic period also involved a degree of introspection and pessimism. The disintegration of tribal identity created a profound sense of insecurity, which combined with doubts as to the efficacy of sacrificial rituals led to the emergence of nonconformists and ascetics. Their teachings were set down in the metaphysical literature of the *Upanishads* and the *Aranyakas*, which laid the foundations for the various philosophical systems developed in later periods.

The age of the Buddha 600–321 BC

The age of the **Buddha** was marked by great intellectual endeavour and spiritual agitation. Though mystics and ascetics rejected the norms of Vedic society, major political and commercial developments continued; the emergence of kingdoms and administrative systems encouraged rulers to think in terms of empire.

By 600 BC, the association of tribes with the territories they had colonized had resulted in the consolidation of at least sixteen republics and monarchies, known as **mahajanapadas** (territories of the great clans). Some, like **Kuru** and **Panchala**, represented the oldest and earliest established kingdoms; others, like **Avanti**, **Vatsa** and **Magadha** had come into existence more recently. The hereditary principle and the concept of divinely ordained kings tended to preserve the status quo in the monarchies, while the republics provided an atmosphere in which unorthodox views were able to develop. The **founders** of the "heterodox" sects of **Buddhism** and **Jainism** were both born in small republics of this kind.

The consolidation of the *mahajanapadas* was based on the growth of a stable agrarian economy and the increasing importance of **trade**, which led to the use of coins and a script (*Brahmi*, from which the current scripts of India, Sri Lanka, Tibet, Java and Myanmar derive) and encouraged the emergence of towns, such as Kashi (Varanasi), Ayodhya, Rajagriha (first capital of Magadha), Kaushambi in the Ganges Valley, and Ujjain on the Narmada. The resultant prosperity stimulated conflict, however, and by the fifth century BC the four great kingdoms of Kashi, Koshala, Vatsa and Magadha and the republic of the Vrijjis between them held sway over all the others.

Eventually, **Magadha** emerged supreme, under Bimbisara (543–491 BC), a resolute and energetic organizer, and Ajatashatru (491–461 BC), who conquered Kashi and Koshala, broke up the Vrijji confederacy, and built a strong administration. Both kings set out to control the trade of the Ganges Valley and its rich deposits of copper and iron.

Magadha expanded over the next hundred years, moving its capital to **Pataliputra** (Patna) and annihilating the other kingdoms in the Ganges Valley or reducing them to the status of vassals. In the middle of the fourth century BC, the **Nanda** dynasty usurped the Magadhan throne; Mahapadma Nanda conquered Kalinga (Orissa and the northern coastal strip of Andhra Pradesh) and gained control of parts of the Deccan. The disputed succession after his death coincided with significant events in the northwest; out of this confusion the first and perhaps greatest of India's empires was born.

Darius I, the third Achaemenid emperor of Persia, had claimed Gandhara in the northwest as his twentieth satrapy, and advanced into the Punjab near the end of the sixth century BC; but a second invasion in the fourth century BC was more significant. **Alexander the Great** defeated Darius III, the last Achaemenid, crossed the Indus in 326 BC, and overran the Punjab. He was in India for just two years and although he left garrisons and appointed satraps to govern the conquered territories, his death in 323 BC made their position untenable. Chandragupta Maurya was quick to take advantage of the political vacuum.

The Mauryan Empire 321–184 BC

The accession to the throne of **Chandragupta Maurya**, who overthrew the last of the Nanda dynasty of Magadha about 321 BC, marked the beginnings of the first Indian empire. He is said to have met Alexander the Great and was probably inspired by his exploits; his 500,000-strong army drove out the Greek garrisons in the northwest, and annexed all the lands east of the Indus, and when Seleucus Nicator, Alexander's general, attempted to regain control of Macedonian provinces in India, Chandragupta defeated him too, and forced the surrender of territories in what is now Afghanistan as a reward.

According to tradition, Chandragupta was assisted by an unscrupulous brahmin adviser called Kautilya or Chanakya, the reputed author of the *Arthashastra*, a famous treatise on political economy. The Mauryan empire developed a highly bureaucratic state administration, which controlled economic life and employed a very thorough secret service system.

From about 297 BC onwards, Chandragupta's son Bindusara extended the empire as far south as Mysore, before being succeeded in around 269 BC by his son, **Ashoka** – the noblest ruler of India, whom the Buddhists called a universal emperor (*chakravartin*). Ashoka's political pragmatism and imperial vision, complemented by his humanity, practical benevolence and tolerance, mark him out as a statesman and reformer far ahead of his time. He ruthlessly consolidated his power for the first eight years of his reign, before invading and subduing the tribal kingdom of Kalinga (Orissa), his last campaign of violent conquest, in 260 BC. Two and a half years later, his conversion to **Buddhism** caused Ashoka to espouse nonviolence (*ahimsa*), and consequently to abandon territorial aggression in favour of conquest by the **Law of Righteousness** (*dharma*). The fourteen **edicts** in which he laid down its principles were engraved in the *Brahmi* script on eighteen great rocks and thirty polished sandstone pillars throughout the empire, the most famous and accessible of which can be found at Sarnath in Uttar Pradesh (see p.355) and Dhauli in Orissa (see p.1106).

Ashoka sought to neutralize the regional pluralism within the empire by his proclamation of the *dharma*, a code of conduct designed to counteract the social tensions created by the *varna* distinctions of class, sectarian conflicts and economic differences. It inculcated social responsibility, encouraged socio-religious harmony, sought to ensure human dignity and expressed a paternal concern for his subjects' wellbeing and happiness. His social reforms included the restriction of animal slaughter and the prohibition of animal sacrifices in Pataliputra – which encouraged vegetarianism, the cultivation of medicinal herbs and the establishment of healing centres. The system of communications was improved by planting roadside fruit trees and by the construction of wells and rest houses. He also replaced the annual royal hunt with a pilgrimage of righteousness (*dharma yatra*), which gave him the opportunity to visit the distant corners of the empire personally and exhibit himself as the living symbol of imperial unity.

His adoption of Buddhism and this new ethical system, however, did not interfere with his imperial pragmatism, and despite his avowed remorse after the Kalinga campaign he continued to govern the newly acquired territory, retained his army without reduction and warned the wilder tribesmen that he would use force to subjugate them if they continued to raid the civilized villages of the empire.

Ashoka's empire extended from Assam to Afghanistan and from Kashmir to Mysore; only the three Dravidian kingdoms of the Cholas, Cheras and Pandyas in the southernmost tip of the subcontinent remained independent. Diplomatic relations were maintained with Syria, Egypt, Macedonia and Cyrene, and all the states on the immediate borders. The Mauryan empire was built on military conquest and a centralized administration – its well-organized revenue department ensured a strong fiscal base – but Ashoka's imperial vision, his shrewdness, and above all the force of his personality and the loyalty he inspired, held it all together.

After Ashoka's death in 232 BC, the empire began to fall apart. While princes contested the throne, the provincial governors established their independence. Interregional rivalries and further invasions from Central Asia exacerbated matters, and in 184 BC the last of the Mauryans, Brihadratha, was assassinated by his brahmin general, Pushyamitra Shunga. The Mauryans had ruled India for nearly 140 years; Ashoka's importance was recognized more than two thousand years later, when Nehru adopted the lion capital of his Sarnath pillar as the emblem of the newly independent India.

The age of invasions 184 BC–320 AD

Although economic prosperity and cultural enrichment endured for five hundred years after the death of Ashoka, India became politically fragmented. Successive **invasions**, and the emergence of regional monarchies in the south, reduced Magadha to one of many quasi-feudal kingdoms struggling for regional power. Though it still included Bengal, Bhopal and Malwa within its boundaries, the Punjab and the northwestern territories had been lost. A dynasty founded by Pushyamitra Shunga, an orthodox brahmin under whose Shunga successors Buddhism continued to be generously patronized, with elaborate stone stupas being erected at Sanchi and Bharhur, ruled Magadha until 72 BC, when the last Shunga monarch was deposed by his servant Vasudeva Kanva.

The **Bactrian Greeks**, who had asserted their independence from the Seleucids of Syria and recaptured Gandhara (the Peshawar region of Pakistan) in 190 BC, were the first invaders. When the Mauryan empire collapsed, the Indo-Greek rulers occupied the Punjab and extended their control as far as

Mathura in Uttar Pradesh. One Indo-Greek king, Milinda or Menander, who ruled the Swat Valley and the Punjab from Sagala (Sialkot) between 155 and 130 BC, became famous for his conversion to Buddhism by the philosopher Nagasena. Another example of acculturation is found on the Garuda pillar at Besnagar (Bhilsa), by Heliodorus, the Greek envoy to the Shunga court, to commemorate the Bactrian conquests of northwestern India. Its inscription proclaimed Heliodorus to be a worshipper of Vasudeva, a god later identified with Krishna, the Lord of the Bhagavad Gita.

The next wave of invasions, in the first centuries BC and AD, saw Parthians (Pahlavas) from Iran take control of Bactria. Soon large-scale movements of Central Asian Yueh-Chi nomads had precipitated the migration of the Scythians (Shakas) from the Aral Sea area, who displaced the Parthians. During the first century AD, the Kushan branch of the Yueh-Chi in turn drove the Shakas out of northwestern India into Gujarat and Malwa around Ujjain, where they settled and became Indianized, while Kujula Kadphises established the **Kushan** dynasty in the northwest.

The third and greatest of the Kushan kings, **Kanishka**, who reigned for more than twenty years around 100 AD, extended his rule as far east as Varanasi and as far south as Sanchi. Kanishka's empire prospered through control of trade routes between India, China and the West, and his court attracted artists and musicians as well as merchants. Ashvaghosha, one of the first classical Sanskrit poets, wrote a *Life of the Buddha* (*Buddha Charita*) and is credited with converting the emperor to Buddhism.

The south

While the tribal republics of northern and central India absorbed invaders from the northwest, and the kingdoms of Ayodhya and Kaushambi continued to be important in the Gangetic valley, the first great kingdom of **southern India** was flexing its muscles. Between the second century BC and the second century AD the **Andhra** or **Satavahana** dynasty, which originated in the region between the rivers Godavari and Krishna, spread its control across much of south and central India.

Having unsuccessfully challenged the Shakas in Malwa and Gujarat, they brought the northwest Deccan under their control and created a capital at Paithan on the Godavari, northeast of Pune in Maharashtra. The Satavahanas overthrew the Kanva dynasty of Magadha in 27 BC and pushed south to the Tungabhadra and Krishna rivers. Their second capital, at **Amaravati** on the Krishna, prospered on trade with Rome and Southeast Asia, but by the middle of the third century the Satavahana kingdom had collapsed. The Pallavas took control of their territories in Andhra Pradesh, while the Vakatakas gained supremacy in the central and northwestern regions of the Deccan in the latter half of the third century, only to be subsumed within the Gupta empire by the end of the fourth century.

Further south, the three kingdoms of the **Cheras** on the Malabar coast in the west, the **Pandyas** in the central southern tip of the peninsula, and the **Cholas** on the east coast of Coromandel – together comprising much of present-day Tamil Nadu and Kerala – had been developing almost completely independently of north India. **Madurai**, the Pandyan capital, and still one of the major temple cities of the south, had become a centre of Tamil culture. Between 300 BC and 200 AD, colleges or academies (**sangam**) of poets produced a body of literature which describes an indigenous Tamil culture and society only gradually being influenced by the Aryan traditions of the north. The early kingdoms were matriarchal, and the Dravidian kinship system was endogamous, being based on cross-cousin marriage, in sharp contrast to the Indo-Aryan system of exogamy, which prescribed marriage to outsiders. Society was divided into groups based on the geographical domains of hills, plains, forest, coast and desert rather than class or *varna*, though brahmins did command high status. Although agriculture, pastoralism and fishing were the main occupations, trade in spices, gold and jewels with Rome and Southeast Asia underpinned the region's prosperity.

The three kingdoms initially balanced individual struggles for political hegemony with alliances to withstand the aggression of their northern neighbours; but after the middle of the first century BC conflicts between themselves became more frequent. This enervating warfare rendered them vulnerable; early in the fourth century AD, the **Pallavas** overran the Chola capital of Kanchipuram, and by 325 AD they were in control of Tamil Nadu. The Pallavas remained a dominant power in the south until the ninth century AD, and thus became one of the longest ruling dynasties in Indian history.

Trade and society

Despite the disintegration of the Mauryan empire and the proliferation of fiercely rival kingdoms from 200 BC to 300 AD, this was also a period of unprecedented economic wealth and cultural development. The growing importance of the mercantile community encouraged the monetization of the economy and stimulated the growth of urban centres all over India. Merchants and artisans organized themselves into guilds (*shreni*), which, along with the ruling dynasties, minted their own coins.

External **trade**, overland and maritime, opened up lines of communication with the outside world. The main highway from Pataliputra to Taxila gave India access to the old **Silk Road**, the most important trade route of the time, linking China to the Mediterranean via Central Asia. Maritime trade traversed the coastal routes between the seaports in Gujarat and southern India and as far as south Arabia; and Indian merchants established trading communities in various parts of south Asia.

The invasion of foreign peoples, the growth of trade and urbanization together had a considerable impact on the structure of society. Foreign conquerors and traders, who had to be integrated within the *varna* system; the burgeoning importance of the *vaishya* class of merchants and artisans; and the influence of urban liberalism, all presented serious challenges to law and social order. The Law Books (*Dharma Shastras*) were composed in this period in an attempt to accommodate these changes and redefine social, economic and legal rights and duties. Important developments in India's religions can also be linked to socio-economic changes. Radical schisms occurred in both Buddhism and Jainism, and may be attributed to the increasing participation and patronage of the *vaishyas*; while the Vedic religion, which had been the exclusive domain of the brahmins and *kshatryas*, underwent fundamental transformations to widen its social base.

The Classical Age 320–650

The era of the imperial Guptas (320–550 AD) and the reign of Harsha Vardhana (606–647 AD) of Kanauj, during which north India was reunified, comprises the **Classical Age** of Indian history.

Chandra Gupta I (no relation to the Mauryan Guptas) struck coins in 320 AD to celebrate his coronation and marriage to Princess Kumaradevi of the Licchavi tribe, which had re-established itself in the neighbouring territory of

Vaishali, north of the Ganges. Chandra Gupta I thus established a powerful kingdom, centred on Magadha, Koshala and Ayodhya, in the Gangetic plain, which controlled the vital East–West trade route, and claimed the title of Great King of Kings (Maharajadhiraja).

His son and heir, Samudra Gupta (c.335–376 AD), expanded the frontiers of the realm from Punjab to Assam; an inscription in Allahabad claimed that he "violently uprooted" nine kings of northern India, humbled eleven more in the south and compelled another five to pay tribute as feudatories. The martial tribes of Rajasthan and the Shakas, who had ruled Malwa and Gujarat for over two hundred years, never did more than pay homage; but Samudra had built the foundations for the second largest empire in pre-medieval India, which reached its apogee under his successor.

Chandra Gupta II (376–415 AD) finally subjugated the Shakas in Gujarat to secure access to the trade of the western coast at the end of the fourth century AD, and reunified the whole of northern India, with the exception of the northwest. He extended his influence by marrying Kuvera, a queen of the Nagas, and marrying his daughter Prabhavati to Rudrasena II of the Vakatakas, whose kingdom included parts of modern Madhya Pradesh, Maharashtra and northwestern Andhra Pradesh.

Fa Hsien, a Chinese Buddhist monk who visited India during the reign of Chandra Gupta II, noted the palaces and free hospitals of Pataliputra and the fact that all respectable Indians were vegetarian. He also mentions discrimination against the untouchables, who carried gongs to warn passers-by of their polluting presence; but generally, he describes the empire as prosperous, happy and peaceful. The Guptas performed Vedic sacrifices to legitimize their rule, and patronized popular forms of Hinduism, such as devotional religion (*bhakti*) and the worship of images of Vishnu, Shiva and the goddess Shakti in temples, which were crystallizing during the period; but Buddhism continued to thrive and Fa Hsien mentions thousands of monks dwelling at Mathura as well as hundreds in Pataliputra itself.

Patronage of art and literature under the Guptas facilitated the development of a classical idiom that became the exemplar for subsequent creative endeavours. Secular **Sanskrit literature** reached its perfection in the works of Kalidasa, the greatest Indian poet and dramatist, who was a member of Chandra Gupta II's court. The cave paintings of **Ajanta** and **Ellora** inspired Buddhist artists throughout Asia, and Yashodhara's detailed analysis of painting in the fifth century prescribed the classical conventions for the new art form. In **sculpture**, the images of the Buddha produced in Sarnath and Mathura embodied the simple and serene quality of classicism, while there were also the voluptuous mother goddesses of Hinduism.

The formative stages of the northern style of **Hindu temple**, which became India's classic architectural form, also occurred in this era; a fine example survives at **Deogarh**, near Jhansi in central India. Early Hindu temples were comparatively small and simple: an inner sanctuary (*garbha griha*) housing the deity was connected to a larger hall (*mandapa*), where the devotees could congregate to worship. This prototype of the northern Hindu temple has persisted from Gupta times to the present day, but these humble origins subsequently evolved into extravagantly ornate structures.

The era of the Guptas produced great thinkers as well: six systems of **philosophy** (*Nyaya, Vaisheshika, Sankhya, Yoga, Mimamsa* and *Vedanta*) evolved, which refuted Buddhism and Jainism. **Vedanta** has continued as the basis of all philosophical studies in India to this day. In the fifth century, the great **astronomer**, Aryabhata, argued that the earth rotated on its own axis while revolving around the sun, and his terse commentary on an anonymous mathematical text assumes an understanding of the decimal system of nine digits and a zero, with place notation for tens and hundreds. The Arabs acknowledged their debt to the "Indian art" of mathematics, and many Western European discoveries and inventions would have been impossible if they had remained encumbered by the Roman system of numerals.

Though the Gupta empire remained relatively peaceful during the long reign of Kumara Gupta, who succeeded Chandra Gupta II, by the time Skanda Gupta came to the throne in 454 AD, western India was again threatened by invasions from Central Asia. Skanda managed to repel White Hun raids, but after his death their disruption of Central Asian trade seriously destabilized the empire. By the end of the fifth century, the Huns had wrested the Punjab from Gupta control, and further incursions early in the sixth century were the death blow to the empire, which had completely disintegrated by 550 AD. Also in the sixth century another wave of Central Asian tribes, including the Gurjaras, displaced the older tribes in Rajasthan and became the founders of the **Rajput** dynasties.

After the demise of the Guptas, northern India again split into rival kingdoms, but the Pushpbhutis of Sthanvishvara (Thanesvar, north of Delhi) had established supremacy by the time **Harsha Vardhana** came to the throne in 606 AD. He reigned for 41 years over an empire that ranged from Gujarat to Bengal, including the Punjab, Kashmir and Nepal, and moved his capital to **Kanauj** in the wake of his eastern conquests. Even the king of Assam acknowledged his influence, but his attempts to advance into the Deccan were emphatically repulsed by Pulakeshin II of the Chalukyas. Harsha possessed considerable talent as well as untiring energy; in addition to his martial achievements and ceaseless touring, he wrote three dramas and found time to indulge a love of philosophy and literature. The life of Harsha (*Harshacharita*) by Bana, his court poet, is the first historically authentic Indian biography.

Harsha's empire was essentially feudal, with most of the defeated kings retaining their thrones as vassals, and when he died without heirs in 647 AD north India once again fragmented into independent kingdoms.

Kingdoms of central and south India 500–1250

After the collapse of Harsha's empire, significant events took place in the Deccan and Tamil Nadu. Aryan influences were assimilated into Dravidian culture throughout the era of the **Pallavas**, which began when they captured Kanchipuram early in the fourth century and lasted until they were overthrown by a revived Chola dynasty in the ninth century. The upper strata of society increasingly adopted Aryan ideas, but as the indigenous culture reacted to assert itself among the lower strata, a distinctive Tamil culture emerged from the synthesis.

The history of the period was dominated by conflicts between three major kingdoms. The **Pandyas** of Madurai had their own regional kingdom by the sixth century; the **Chalukyas** of Vatapi (Badami in Mysore) had expanded their kingdom into the Deccan when the Vakataka dynasty collapsed in the middle of the sixth century; and the **Pallavas** had supplanted the Satavahanas in the Andhra region and made Kanchipuram their capital.

Under Mahendravarman I, a contemporary of Harsha at the start of the seventh century, the Pallavas came into conflict with the Chalukyas over the region of Vengi in the Krishna-Godavari valley. They remained at war until the middle of the eighth century, intermittently harassed by the Pandyas further south. Both the Pallavas and the Chalukyas enlisted the support of other kingdoms at different times during the protracted struggle – the **Cheras** of Kerala, who made alliances with both sides, avoided direct involvement in the conflict – but their military strength was so evenly matched that neither was able to gain the ascendancy. Eventually the Chalukya dynasty was overthrown in 753 by a feudatory, Dantidurga, the founder of the Rashtrakuta kingdom. The Pallavas survived their archenemies by about a hundred years, then succumbed to a combined attack of the Pandyas and the Cholas.

The **Rashtrakutas** exploited the instability in the north by attempts to capture the trade routes of the Ganges Valley, and Indra III gained possession of Kanauj for a brief period, but ultimately the campaigns drained the kingdom's resources.

Meanwhile, the **Cholas** were gaining ground in Tamil Nadu; they conquered the region of Thanjavur in the ninth century, and Parantaka I, who came to power in 907 AD, captured Madurai from the Pandyas. The Cholas were defeated by the Rashtrakutas in the middle of the tenth century, who were themselves replaced by the revived "Later" Chalukyas in 973 AD, allowing the Cholas to regain lost territories and expand further during the eleventh and twelfth centuries.

Rajaraja I campaigned against the allied powers of Kerala, Ceylon and the Pandyas to break their control of western trade and combat competition from the Arab traders, who were supported by Kerala. **Rajendra I**, who succeeded his father in 1014 AD, annexed the southern territories of the Chalukyas, renewing the campaigns against Kerala and Ceylon, and initiating a northern offensive, which reached the banks of the Ganges. Rajendra did not hold his northern conquests for long, but was successful in protecting Indian commercial interests in southeast Asia.

By the end of the eleventh century the Cholas were supreme in the south, but incessant campaigning had exhausted their resources. Ironically, their destruction of the Chalukyas laid the seeds of their own downfall. Former Chalukya feudatories, such as the **Yadavas** of Devagiri in the northern Deccan and the **Hoysalas**, around modern Mysore, set up their own kingdoms; the latter attacked the Cholas from the west while the Pandyas directed a new offensive from the south. By the thirteenth century, the **Pandyas** had superseded the Cholas as south India's major power; the Yadavas and the Hoysalas controlled the Deccan until the advent of the Turkish sultans of Delhi in the fourteenth century.

Despite constant political conflicts this period was very much the classical age of the south. The ascendancy of the Cholas was complemented by the crystallization of Tamil culture; the religious, artistic, and institutional patterns of this period dominated the culture of the south and influenced developments elsewhere in the peninsula. In the sphere of religion for instance, the great philosophers **Shankara** and Ramanuja, as well as the Tamil and Maharashtran saints, had a significant impact on Hinduism in north India.

Regional kingdoms in north India 650–1250

In north India, Harsha's death was followed by a century of confusion, with assorted kingdoms competing to control the Gangetic valley. In time, the **Pratiharas**, descendants of the Rajasthani Gurjaras, and the **Palas** of Bihar and Bengal emerged as the main rivals.

The Pala king Dharmapala (770–810) was the first to gain the initiative, by taking Kanauj; however, the Pratiharas wrested it back soon after his death.

They remained in the ascendant during the ninth century, but were weakened by repeated incursions from the Deccan by the **Rashtrakutas**, who briefly occupied Kanauj in 916. The Pratiharas regained their capital, but the tripartite struggle sapped their strength and they were unable to repel the Turkish invasion of Kanauj in 1018. At the start of the eleventh century the Palas again pushed west as far as Varanasi, but had to abandon the campaign to defend their homelands in Bengal against the Chola king Rajendra.

The struggle for possession of Kanauj depleted the resources of the three competing powers and resulted in their almost simultaneous decline. In northern India, just as in the south, the tendency of feudatories of large kingdoms to assert their independence brought several small states into being. Kingdoms such as Nepal, Kamarupa (Assam), Kashmir, Orissa, the eastern Chalukyas and the Gangas of the east coast developed their own cultural identities. Regional histories and dynastic genealogies were written, local customs and literature were patronized, and the kingdoms competed to outdo each other in building temples.

In **Orissa**, small kingdoms in the Mahanadi and Brahmani valleys had co-existed for nearly five hundred years when the Somavamshi dynasty united western and central Orissa in the eleventh century, and established its capital at **Bhubaneswar**. The temples they constructed demonstrate a notable continuity from the earliest days in the eighth century, to the magnificent Lingaraja temple, dated around 1000 AD. The royal cult of Jagannath (Vishnu), with its "juggernaut" car festival and the gigantic temple at **Puri** were cultural manifestations of the political unification completed by the eastern Gangas of Kalinga in the twelfth century. The stunning chariot temple dedicated to the sun god Surya at **Konarak** in the thirteenth century represents the aesthetic climax of these regional developments.

The **Rajputs**, so influential in the culture and politics of medieval India, were descended from the sixth-century Central Asian invaders. They attained respectability in keeping with the Puranic traditions by acquiring solar or lunar genealogies and adopting *kshatrya* status. By the tenth century, the most important clans, like the Parihars (a branch of the Pratiharas) of south Rajasthan, the Chamanas or Chauhans of Shakambhari and Ajmer, and the Chalukyas or Solankis of Kathiawar, had all established regional kingdoms. Rajput clans in western and central India included the **Chandellas** of Bundelkhand, who produced the magnificent group of temples at **Khajuraho**, the Guhilas of Chittaurgarh, the Tomaras in Haryana, and the Kalachuris of Tripuri near Jabalpur.

The Rajputs fought among each other incessantly, however, and failed to grasp the significance of a new factor, which entered the politics of north India at the start of the eleventh century. **Mahmud**, a Turkish chieftain who had established a powerful kingdom at Ghazni in Afghanistan, made seventeen plundering raids into the plains of India between 1000 and 1027. Mathura, Thanesvar, Kanauj and Somnath in Saurashtra were all looted to enhance the greatness of Ghazni and only the astuteness of the Chandellas of Bundelkhand, who agreed to pay tribute, saved the temples of Khajuraho from destruction.

The three most powerful Rajputs of northern India, Prithviraja Chamana, Jahacchandra Gahadavala and Paramardideva Chandella, were in a state of three-way war when Mohammed of Ghur supplanted the line of Mahmud, seized the Ghaznavid possessions in the Punjab at the end of the twelfth century, and focused his attention on the wealthy lands further east. **Prithviraja III**, the legendary hero of the Chauhans, patched together an alliance to defeat the Turkish warlord at **Tarain** (near Thanesvar) in 1191; but Mohammed returned the next year with a superior force, defeated the Rajputs, and had Prithviraja executed, before returning home, leaving his generals to complete the conquest and establish what became known as the **Slave Dynasty**.

The Delhi Sultanate 1206–1526

The **Delhi Sultanate** was to be the major political force in north India from the thirteenth to the sixteenth century, its power and territories fluctuating with the abilities of successive rulers. Although it never succeeded in welding together an all-India empire, the impact of Islam on Indian culture reverberated for centuries throughout the subcontinent.

Mohammed was assassinated in 1206 within a few years of his return to Ghur. His empire disintegrated, to leave his Turkish slave general, **Qutb-ud-din-Aiback**, as the autonomous ruler of the Indian territories and founder of the first "slave dynasty" of the sultanate. Aiback died four years later – before the Qutb Minar, his victory tower, in Delhi could be completed – and his son-in-law **Iltutmish** (1211–36) inherited the task of securing the sultanate's tenuous hold on northern India. When Genghis Khan annihilated the world from which the ancestors of Iltutmish had come, it gave him an added incentive to consolidate his power base in India. Iltutmish had extended the sultanate's territories from the Sind to Bengal by the time he died in 1236, but the subsequent three decades were critical. His daughter, Sultana Raziyya, succeeded but was murdered in 1240, and not until Balaban, Raziyya's chief huntsman and member of her father's palace guard, took control in 1266 did the sultanate attain any degree of stability.

Meanwhile, the **Mongols** had returned in 1241. Although internecine strife within the Mongol empire from 1260–61 offered a temporary reprieve, the accession of the Khalji dynasty in 1290 coincided with a renewed threat from the Chaghatai Mongols. Their raids extended beyond the Punjab and they even laid siege to Delhi for two months in 1303. Nevertheless, **Ala-ud-din-Khalji** (1296–1315) energetically enforced Islamic rule over the autonomous Hindu states, which were a constant source of aggravation. Having conquered Gujarat and the Rajput fortresses of Ranthambor, Chittaurgarh, Sevana and Jalor in a series of expeditions between 1299 and 1311, he turned his attention to the Deccan and the south where he exacted tribute from the Yadavas of Devagiri, the Kakatiyas of Telengana, and the Pandyas. His aspirations to build a stable empire were dashed, however, when Gujarat, Chittaurgarh and Devagiri all reasserted their independence before his death in 1315.

A fresh imperial impetus came from the **Tughluq** dynasty, which succeeded the Khaljis in 1320. Under **Mohammed bin Tughluq** (1325–51), the sultanate reached its maximum extent, comparable in size to Ashoka's empire. Unfortunately, Mohammed weakened the empire by his attempts to finance his ambitions. He provoked a peasant uprising in the Doab by increasing the revenue demand to pay for an expedition to Khurasan in Central Asia, and later tried to introduce a token currency to pay the troops, which had to be withdrawn. He then made a controversial and abortive attempt to relocate his capital in a more central position at Devagiri (renamed Daulatabad) in the Deccan. Revolts signalled the first phase in the collapse of the Delhi Sultanate: Malabar, Bengal and Telengana all seceded between 1334 and 1339. The Bahmani dynasty became the autonomous rulers of the Deccan in 1347, and the new Hindu kingdom of **Vijayanagar** took advantage of the decline of the sultanate's authority to extend its influence. From its capital near Hampi, Vijayanagar dominated the region south of the Krishna and Tungabhadra rivers between the middle of the fourteenth century and 1565, when an alliance of Muslim kingdoms brought it down.

Firoz Shah Tughluq (1351–88), who re-established the capital at Delhi, stemmed the tide to some extent with the comparative mildness of his rule. He is credited with an impressive list of public works, including the building of mosques, colleges, reservoirs, hospitals, public baths, bridges and towns – especially **Jaunpur**, near Varanasi, which became a major centre of Islamic culture. However, by reverting to a decentralized administrative system he fostered the rise of semi-independent warlords, who became increasingly antagonistic under the last of the Tughluqs.

Family squabbles over the throne after Firoz Shah's death in 1388 further weakened the sultanate, and the degeneracy of his successors made it vulnerable to external predators. After **Timur**, the Central Asian conqueror known to the West as Tamburlaine, sacked Delhi in 1398, autonomous sultanates emerged in Jaunpur, Malwa and Gujarat; the Hindu kingdoms of Marwar and Mewar were established in Rajasthan; and small principalities even nearer the capital appeared at Kalpi, Mahoba and Gwalior. The Delhi Sultanate had been reduced to just one of several competing Muslim states in northern India.

After the death of the last Tughluq, Delhi was seized by Khizr Khan (1414–21), who had been an officer of the governor of Multan and Lahore appointed by Timur before he left India. In 37 years, Khizr's **Sayyid** dynasty lost Multan and was repeatedly harassed by the Sharqi sultans of Jaunpur. The sultanate experienced a modest revival under the more energetic rule of the Afghan Lodis, especially **Sikander Lodi** (1489–1517), who annexed Jaunpur and Bihar; but his successor, Ibrahim, was unable to overcome the dissension among his Afghan feudatories. Eventually, one enlisted the support of Babur, the ruler of Kabul, who defeated Ibrahim at Panipat in 1526.

By the time of the sultanate, India had considerable experience of assimilating foreigners; Greeks, Scythians, Parthians and Huns had all been absorbed over the centuries, politically, socially and culturally. However, the sultanate brought its own theologians and social institutions. **Islam** presented a new pattern of life, far less easy for the xenophobic Hindu social system to accommodate. Nonetheless, a process of mutual acculturation did slowly evolve. Despite the Muslims' iconoclastic zeal, Hinduism found common ground with some aspects of Islam: elements of Sufi mysticism and Hindu devotionalism were combined in the teachings of many saints. **Kabir** (1440–1518), in particular, denied any contradiction between Muslim and Hindu conceptions of god, preached social egalitarianism and was claimed by adherents of both creeds as their own. The replacement of Sanskrit by Persian as the official language of the administration encouraged regional languages; **Urdu** resulted from a fusion of Hindi and Persian using an Arabic script. A stylistically unified architecture began to develop, which flourished under the **Moghuls**; and new social ideas were introduced which became integral to Indian life.

The Moghul Empire 1526–1761

Babur, a descendant of both Timur and Genghis Khan, had gained control of Delhi and Agra by defeating Ibrahim, but found his position threatened by the Rajput confederacy, led by Rana Sanga of Mewar, south of Agra, and the Afghan chiefs, who had united under the Sultan of Bengal. Babur reacted vigorously by declaring a religious war (*jihad*) against the rana, annihilating the Mewar forces at the battle of Kanwaha in 1527, before turning his attention to the Afghan uprisings in the east. Although he crushed the allied armies of the Afghans and the Sultan of Bengal in 1529, his failing health forced him to retire to Lahore, where he died in 1530.

Babur possessed many talents: as well as a brilliant military campaigner, he was a skilful diplomat, a poet and a man of letters. He constructed a loosely knit empire, extending from Badakshan and Kabul to the borders of Bengal, in just four years – his personal magnetism commanding loyalty and inspiring his warrior chiefs to fresh endeavours when they yearned to depart the hot and dusty plains of India for the cool mountains of their homeland. His very readable memoirs reveal a man of sensibility, taste and humour, who loved music, poetry, sport and natural beauty.

Humayun, his son and successor, was by contrast a volatile character, alternating between bursts of enthusiastic activity and indolence. He subdued Malwa and Gujarat, only to lose both while he "took his pleasure" in Agra. **Sher Khan Sur** of south Bihar soon assumed the leadership of the Afghan opposition and after two resounding defeats Humayun had to seek refuge in Persia in 1539. A much cleverer politician than the hot-headed Humayun, Sher Khan was quick to consolidate his territorial gains in the northwest, setting up an administrative centre in Delhi, from where he waged audacious and successful campaigns in Punjab and Sind. He later subjugated several of the Rajput dynasties which had proved troublesome for the Moghuls, and it was during a siege against the toughest of these at Kalinjar that the Afghan was killed, when a rocket rebounded off the fort's walls and exploded a pile of weapons next to him. With Sher Khan's death in 1545 Humayun took advantage of the ensuing chaos to stage a return. His armies, led by Bairam Khan and Prince Akbar, crushed Sikander Sur at Sirhund in 1555; but Humayun died the following year after a fall in the Purana Qila in Delhi leaving **Akbar**, his major contribution to the Moghul empire, to succeed where he had failed.

Akbar, aged only 13, was lucky to have Bairam Khan as guardian and regent to help him survive the crisis of the first four years. Bairam, a loyal general and an experienced politician, overcame the challenge of the Hindu general Hemu at the second battle of Panipat in 1556, recovered Gwalior and Jaunpur, and handed over a consolidated kingdom of north India to Akbar in 1560. The young emperor quickly established his own control of the government in dramatic fashion. First Bairam Khan was provoked into a revolt by religious adversaries of the Moghuls and killed. Then challenges to Akbar's rule by a group centred around Adham Khan, the son of his former wet nurse, were systematically snuffed out. In 1562 the emperor discovered Adham Khan himself attempting to murder the chief minister, and executed his young adversary by throwing him from the palace walls.

Securing the empire

Akbar's first military campaigns were against the **Rajputs**; and within a decade he had secured the flank of the Moghul bases at Delhi and Agra by subduing all the Rajput domains except Mewar (Udaipur). Akbar possessed the personal magnetism of his grandfather and was a brilliant general, who above all had the gift of rapid mobilization. In 1573 he marched his army 1000 kilometres in nine days to defeat astonished insurgents in Gujarat. He had secured Bengal, the richest province, by 1576, and by the end of his reign in 1605 he controlled a broad sweep of territory north of the River Godavari, which reached from the Bay of Bengal to Kandahar and Badakshan, with the exception of Gondwana and Assam.

Akbar was as clever a politician and administrator as he was a successful general. After subduing the Rajputs, he diplomatically bestowed imperial honours on their chiefs by making them military commanders and provincial governors. By giving them autonomy within their own states, he made the Rajputs partners in the empire and thereby secured the acquiescence of the whole Hindu community. His marriage to a Jaipur princess was an important symbolic statement of this partnership.

The imperial service, in which Akbar involved both Moghuls and Rajputs, was carefully crafted to ensure that the nobility were hereditary as an aristocratic class but not as individuals. His officers – *mansabdars*, holders of commands – were arranged in grades that indicated how many troops they were obliged to maintain for imperial service. A commander of 5000 was both an important state official and a noble; but the titles were not hereditary, being conferred by appointment and promotion, and the *mansabdars'* salaries were paid in cash so that they lacked a territorial basis for insurrection.

The creation of an administrative framework, which sustained the empire by its efficient collection of revenue, was one of Akbar's most enduring achievements. He collected information about local revenue, productivity and price variations to arrive at a schedule, acceptable to the peasant farmers but also generating maximum profit for the state. Akbar recruited leaders of local communities and holders of land rights (*zamindars*) to collect the revenue in cash.

In addition to involving Hindu *zamindars* and nobles in economic and political life, Akbar adopted a conscious policy of religious toleration aimed at widening the base of his power. In particular, he abolished the despised poll tax on non-Muslims (*jizya*), and tolls on Hindu pilgrimages. A mystical experience in about 1575 inspired him to instigate a series of discussions with orthodox Muslim leaders (*ulema*), Portuguese priests from Goa, Hindu brahmins, Jains and Zoroastrians at his famous house of worship (*ibadat khana*) in Fatehpur Sikri. The discussions culminated in a politico-religious crisis and a revolt, organized by the alienated *ulema*, which Akbar ruthlessly crushed in 1581. He subsequently evolved a theory of divine kingship incorporating the toleration of all religions, and thereby restored the concept of imperial sanctity with which the early Hindu emperors had surrounded themselves, while declaring his nonsectarian credentials.

Akbar was a liberal patron of the arts and his eclecticism encouraged a fruitful Muslim-Hindu dialogue. Music, which he loved, was especially enriched by this mutual appreciation. Akbar ranks alongside Ashoka as one of the great statesmen of the world, and his reign laid the foundations for a century of stable government under the succeeding Moghuls.

The height of Moghul power

The reigns of **Jahangir** (1605–27) and **Shah Jahan** (1628–57) together represent the great age of the Moghuls, whose reputation for magnificence, pomp and luxury did not escape the notice of Europe and is recorded in the writings of Bernier and Dryden. It was a time of brisk economic activity notable for artistic and architectural splendour, as well as the excesses of imperial indulgence.

Despite his reputation for drunken cruelty, Jahangir was a connoisseur of art. It was under his patronage that the art of the **miniature**, imported from Persia, reached its perfection in Moghul painting before being further evolved and enriched by Hindu artists, especially in Rajasthan. Jahangir is best remembered for his great devotion to Nur Jahan, which he celebrated with a special issue of gold coins (*mohur*). Nur Jahan commissioned the building of the beautiful Itmad-ud-Daulah, a magnificent tomb for her parents in Agra, sometimes said to be the blueprint for the Taj Mahal.

In the political sphere, Jahangir settled the conflict with Mewar, extended the empire by subjugating the last of the Afghan domains in east Bengal and Orissa, and restrained the threat from the Deccan by defeating the combined forces of the Nizamshahi kingdom and the Adilshahis of Bijapur in 1620. However, the combination of failing health and political intrigues involving his beloved Nur Jahan prevented him from completing his Deccan campaign, and Persia's capture of Kandahar in 1622 dented the empire's prestige.

When Shah Jahan, Jahangir's son, came to power in 1628, he ruthlessly executed all the male descendants of his brothers and uncles. He displayed all the imperial qualities of administrative and military ability and, like his predecessors, was a great lover and patron of the arts, especially architecture. Delhi's **Red Fort** and **Jami Masjid**, Agra Fort, and the splendid **Taj Mahal**, the mausoleum he created for his wife Mumtaz, are the results of his personal inspiration and artistic direction. Thus he actively participated in the apogee of Indo-Persian culture, although his political achievements were less notable.

Shah Jahan attempted to deal with the ascendancy of the Marathas in the Deccan by conquering the Nizamshahi kingdom in 1636. Six years later, he sent his third son, **Aurangzeb** to govern the province. Regarding territorial gains in the region as the most promising route to the Moghul throne, the ambitious young prince, a devout Muslim and experienced military campaigner in his mid-thirties, forged an alliance with the wealthy Persian adventurer, **Mir Jumla**, to mount an attack on the latter's former employer, the sultan of **Galconda**. The two-pronged invasion met with quick success, overwhelming Hyderabad. However, just as Aurangzeb's army was poised to storm the great fort, word came from Delhi to withdraw. Behind the scenes, **Dara Shikoh**, Shah Jahan's eldest son, had persuaded his father to thwart his brother's venture, recognizing that it could impede his chances of succession. Exactly the same thing happened the following year, when Aurangzeb laid siege to Bijapur.

The battle lines were now drawn for an eventual **civil war** between the two brothers, which erupted in 1657 when Shah Jahan fell seriously ill. He recovered, but not before Aurangzeb had seen off Dara Shikoh, wiping out his army in a series of encounters that culminated in a rout at Ajmer, and eliminated a son and nephew. The thirty-year reign of the ailing emperor ended ignominiously. Aurangzeb had him incarcerated in Agra fort, where he lived out his remaining days in an opium-induced stupor gazing wistfully down the Yamuna at the mausoleum of his beloved Mumtaz.

Though lacking the charisma of Akbar or Babur, Aurangzeb evoked an awe of his own and proved to be a firm and capable administrator, who retained his grip on the increasingly unsettled empire until his death at the age of 88. In contrast to the pomp of the other Moghuls, his lifestyle was pious and disciplined. In later life the ruthless statesman became an austere sage, who fasted and spent long hours in prayer.

In the first 23 years of his rule, Aurangzeb maintained a continuity with Shah Jahan's administration and ostensibly contained disruptive elements; but he failed to solve the problems which eventually erupted after his death and caused the dissolution of the empire. The **Maratha** chief, **Shivaji**, who humiliated the Moghul army early in Aurangzeb's reign, was a constant threat. Although defeated by the Rajput Jai Singh and forced to visit the Moghul court in 1666, Shivaji made a daring escape from Agra, rallied his resources, and was soon again the master of a compact and well-organized kingdom in western India, to which the Muslim kingdoms of Bijapur and Golconda were eager to ally themselves against the imperialism of Aurangzeb.

The militant separatism of the **Sikhs** was brutally suppressed when Guru Tegh Bahadur was executed in 1675 for refusing to embrace Islam; but his son, Guru Gobind, transformed the religious community into a military sect which became increasingly powerful in the Punjab. Aurangzeb's confrontation with the Rajputs over the Jodhpur succession in 1678 resulted in another war, and the alienation of most of the Rajput partners in the empire.

Meanwhile, religious and economic discontent turned the passive support of the Hindu community, cultivated by Akbar, into indifference, disdain and even armed conflict. Aurangzeb aligned himself with the orthodox Sunni Muslims of the *ulema*, who rejected the syncretism encouraged by Akbar's nonsectarian policies. Hindu places of worship were again the object of iconoclasm, the tax on non-Muslims (*jizya*) was reintroduced, religious fairs were banned, and discriminatory duties were imposed on Hindu merchants. The Jats and the Satnamis of the Agra–Delhi region rebelled over insufferable increases in land revenue demands, and elsewhere peasant farmers rallied behind Maratha, Sikh and Rajput landholders to oppose imperial exploitation.

Aurangzeb crushed the agrarian rebellions and turned his attention to expansion. He transferred his base to the Deccan in 1681 and spent the rest of his life overseeing the subjugation of the Bijapur and Golconda kingdoms and trying to contain the Maratha rebellion. In 1689, he succeeded in capturing and executing Shivaji's son, Shambhuji, and by 1698 the Moghuls had overrun almost the whole of the peninsula. The Marathas had been suppressed, but they re-emerged under the Peshwa leadership in the eighteenth century to harass the remnants of Moghul power and even to challenge the political ambitions of the British.

Aurangzeb did manage to extend the empire during his long reign of over 48 years, but the newly acquired lands in the south were difficult to administer, his nobles were divided by factionalism, and the disruptive consequences of his policies were to be critical in the eighteenth-century collapse of the empire.

The decline of the Moghuls

Bahadur Shah, Aurangzeb's son, succeeded in 1707 and briefly restored the situation, but after his death in 1712 the disintegration of the empire and power struggles between would-be successors dominated events. By the 1720s the nizam of Hyderabad and the nawabs of Avadh and Bengal were effectively independent; the Marathas overwhelmed the rich province of Malwa in 1738; Hindu landholders everywhere were in revolt; and Nadir Shah of Persia dealt a serious blow to the empire's prestige when he invaded India, defeated the Moghul army and sacked Delhi in 1739.

The **Maratha** kingdom had by now been transformed into a confederacy under the leadership of a hereditary brahmin minister, called the Peshwa. By 1750 the Marathas had spread right across central India to Orissa, had attacked Bengal, and were insinuating themselves into the imperial politics of Delhi. When Delhi was again looted in 1757, this time by an independent Afghan force led by Ahmad Shah Abdali, distraught Moghul ministers called in the Marathas to rescue the situation. The Marathas drove the Afghans back to the Punjab; but Ahmad Shah advanced again in 1761 and overwhelmed them at the third battle of Panipat. Any designs he had on the imperial throne were dashed, however, when his soldiers mutinied over arrears of pay.

New centres of Moghul culture developed, notably at Murshidabad, Lucknow, Hyderabad, and Faizabad, but the political strength of the empire had fragmented and north India was left in a power vacuum for the next forty years. It was against this background that the European trading companies, and the East India Company in particular, were able to establish their trading posts and develop their ambitions.

The East India Company 1600–1857

The prosperity of foreign trade in India attracted European interest as early as 1498, when **Vasco da Gama** landed on the Malabar coast. During the ensuing hundred years Portuguese, Dutch, English, French and Danish companies all set up coastal trading centres, exporting textiles, sugar, indigo and saltpetre.

The **East India Company**, established by eighty London merchants in 1599 and chartered by Queen Elizabeth I on December 31, 1600, arrived in Surat in 1608. Within thirty years 27 trading posts had been established, including **Fort George** on the Coromandel coast, out of which Madras developed. The enclave of Bombay, part of Catherine of Braganza's dowry in her marriage to Charles II, became crown property in 1665, was leased to the Company from 1668, and soon replaced Surat as its headquarters. The Moghul emperor permitted the Company to establish a new settlement at **Fort William**, which grew into Calcutta, and in 1701 the British received a grant of the revenues of the Twenty-Four Parganas near Calcutta from Aurangzeb, in recognition of the growing importance of their trade in the economy of Bengal.

It was in the **south**, however, that European trading initiatives first took on a political significance, after the onset of the War of the Austrian Succession in 1740. Armed conflict between the French and English trading companies along the Carnatic coast developed into a war over the succession of the nizam of Hyderabad. The British victory and the Peace of Paris in 1763 eclipsed French ambitions in India. Meanwhile, **Robert Clive**'s defeat of the rebellious young nawab of Bengal at Plassey in 1757 had decisively augmented British power; by 1765 the enervated Moghul emperor legally recognized the Company as an Indian potentate by granting the revenue management (*diwani*) of Bengal, Bihar and Orissa to Lord Clive.

The governor-generals

Ironically, the East India Company's mastery of the rich province soon brought it to the brink of bankruptcy, provoking parliamentary intervention in its affairs. The **Regulating Act** of 1773 appointed a **governor-general** of the Company's three provinces in Calcutta, Bombay and Madras; and in 1784 the India Act established a President of the Board of Control in London to oversee the governor-general in Calcutta.

Warren Hastings, the first governor-general, made the Company's colony in Bengal politically viable, successfully defending it against the jealous governors of Bombay and Madras, and the internal dissent of his Council in England. His major achievement was to protect Bombay and Madras against the assaults from a coalition of Marathas, the nizam of Hyderabad and Haidar Ali, the sultan of Mysore; but he also laid the foundations of British administration in India by replacing the Indian revenue-collecting deputies with a Board of Revenue in Calcutta and English collectors in the districts. **Lord Cornwallis** completed the reforms by fixing the land revenues in the Permanent Land Settlement of 1793; by dividing Company service into separate political and commercial branches; and by a further Europeanization of the administration.

The governor-generals were charged with nonaggression and administrative reform until the end of the eighteenth century, but the Napoleonic Wars allowed **Lord Wellesley** to follow his imperial instincts. His swift defeat of **Tipu Sultan** of Mysore, the company's best-organized and most resolute enemy, a confrontation with the Marathas, and the subjugation of the Nizam of Hyderabad resulted in the annexation of considerable territories in Andhra Pradesh, Tamil Nadu, Mysore, the Upper Doab, Gujarat and Maharashtra; nearly all the other rulers in India recognized British suzerainty by 1805. There was a brief respite in the expansion until Napoleon's defeat in 1815, but the last vestiges of Maratha opposition were crushed by 1823, and the absorption of Sind, the Sikh kingdom of the Punjab, Kashmir, Assam, Chittagong and Lower Burma by 1852 established **British supremacy** in India.

The new British colony, however, was in a state of social and economic collapse as a result of the almost incessant conflicts of the previous hundred years. High revenue assessments had depressed the condition of both peasants and *zamindars*; peasants deserted their lands, land revenue receipts were falling, and there were local revolts and grain riots in the 1830s. Gangs of robbers (*dacoits*) had reached epidemic proportions, and their activities curtailed commerce between states and towns. The cult of the **thugs**, who robbed and murdered in honour of the goddess Kali, spread terror all over central and northern India.

Inspired by Burke's ideas, Utilitarianism and the Radical Humanism in Europe, **Lord William Bentinck**'s reforms as governor-general did little, however, to alleviate the situation. The campaign against the thugs received general approval, but his suppression of the practice of widows joining their husbands on funeral pyres (*sati*) was seen as an attack on the values of traditional Hindu society.

The Company's policy of government patronage for Indian learning was replaced after 1835 by a resolution to promote "European literature and science". Schools and colleges imparting Western knowledge through the medium of the English language were established, and English replaced Persian as the official state language. The educated elite and intellectuals like Ram Mohan Roy had already adopted Western ideas, but such cultural imperialism aggravated the unrest and distrust of the majority.

James Andrew Broun Ramsey, governor-general between 1848 and 1856, was a firm believer in the benefits of **Westernization**. He promoted Western education by initiating plans for the first three Indian universities with Sir Charles Wood, and embarked on a series of public works, including the development of the railway and telegraph systems. These were commendable achievements, but their Westernizing influence increased social tension. His controversial policy of annexing dependent but autonomous states, which brought **Oudh**, two Maratha kingdoms and five other states under direct administration, caused considerable resentment among the dispossessed and alarm among the Indian ruling classes.

The First War of Independence

Against this general background of unease, discontent had been growing in the army, which had been increasingly deployed overseas during the previous two decades – a practice resented on religious grounds by the many brahmins it contained. The cows' and pigs' grease on the cartridges of the new Enfield rifle, polluting to both Hindus and Muslims, convinced the soldiers that there was a conspiracy against their religious beliefs and sparked the revolt. The **Indian Mutiny** – the "First War of Independence" – started with a rising at Meerut on May 10, 1857, and Delhi was seized the next day. The last Moghul emperor Bahadur Shah in Delhi, the dispossessed court at Lucknow, and the exiled members of the Maratha court at Kanpur all supported the cause and some landlords participated in the rebellion.

The British authorities were caught by surprise. The Crimean War had reduced the number of their regiments in India, and their forces were concentrated around Calcutta or the Punjab. However, the revolt failed to cut their lines of communication, and crucially the **Sikh** regiments in the Punjab remained loyal. Delhi was retaken by a column from the Punjab in late September, **Kanpur** (Cawnpore) was relieved in the same month, and the final recapture of **Lucknow** in March 1858 effectively broke the back of the Mutiny. The rebels fought on under the leadership of Tantia Topi, and the valiant rani of Jhansi in central India, until they too were crushed in June 1858. The governing powers of the East India Company were abolished and the British crown assumed the administration of India through an appointed viceroy in the same year. Henceforth, British India was no longer merely a massive trade operation, but a fully fledged independent kingdom, or Raj – the term which would over time come to denote the period of British rule in the subcontinent.

The Raj and Indian nationalism 1857–1947

India played a key role in the politics of **British imperialism**, especially in the rivalry with France and Russia during this period. Its army became an instrument of British foreign policy: in the Afghan Wars, attempting to create a buffer state to block Russia's advance in Central Asia, and in the Anglo-Burmese Wars to check the French expansion in Indo-China. It was also used to protect British interests beyond the Indian subcontinent as far afield as Abyssinia and Hong Kong.

As a British colony, India assumed a new position in the world economy. Its trade benefited from the British development of the railways, and Indian businessmen began to invest in a range of industries, including the manufacture of textiles, iron and steel; but India subsidized the British economy as a source of cheap raw materials and as a market for manufactured goods. Its own economy and agriculture remained underdeveloped, and the growth of the gross national product was outstripped by increases in population.

British civil servants dominated the higher echelons of the administration, imposing Western notions of progress on the indigenous social structure. Tenurial systems based on ownership rather than land use, irrigation schemes, the suppression of social customs offensive to humanist ideals, the railways and the introduction of a Western judiciary often involved policies contrary to existing Indian interests. At the same time, the propagation of the English language and the Western knowledge to which it gave access resulted in the emergence of a new **middle class** of civil servants, landlords and professionals, whose consciousness of an Indian national identity steadily increased.

Within thirty years of the Mutiny, the history of the British in India becomes essentially a chronicle of the struggle for **Independence**. By the start of the twentieth century the British conception of empire involved a contradiction between liberal rhetoric and the fact of territorial, economic and intellectual expansion. By World War I, the imperial incentive had been swept away by the realization that Indian independence was unavoidable; the only problem remaining was how to relinquish suzerainty.

Awareness of national identity first found expression in local associations and public demonstrations about specific issues; but when the liberalism of Gladstone was confronted by a growing Indian disaffection while Lord Ripon was viceroy, the British showed their willingness to conciliate the Indian educated classes by giving their official blessing to the foundation of the first all-

India political organization, the **Indian National Congress**, in 1885. It began modestly with only seventy affluent public men as delegates, who advocated limited reforms and a consolidation of union with Britain; but by 1900 Gopal Krishna **Gokhale** and Bal Gangadhar **Tilak**, both Maratha brahmins, had emerged as leaders of the moderates and the extremists respectively. By 1905 Tilak had persuaded Congress to adopt self-government as a political aim.

Lord Curzon, a romantic imperialist, who believed that it was Britain's duty to protect India's past and educate it for the future, began his second term of office as viceroy by sending the Younghusband expedition to Lhasa in 1904. When he decided on the equally controversial partition of Bengal in 1905, it precipitated the first major confrontations with the government. There were widespread protests: Tilak proposed a no-tax campaign and a boycott of British goods, and when the government crushed the protests Bengali terrorists employed even more radical tactics including bombings and assassinations.

In 1906, concerns about the predominantly Hindu interests of Congress led to the foundation of the **All-India Muslim League** to represent the Muslims, who made up a quarter of India's population. A Liberal landslide in Great Britain produced the Morley-Minto Reforms in 1909, which paved the way for Indian participation in provincial executive councils and made allowance for separate Muslim representation. Tilak was imprisoned that year for incitement to violence. The reversal of the partition of Bengal was announced at the **Great Durbar** of 1911, held in honour of the new king George V and his queen, and the capital was moved to **Delhi**.

During World War I, the British conflict with the sultan of Turkey – still considered to be the spiritual head (*khalifa*) of Indian Muslims – provoked further demonstrations. Tilak returned to found a **Home Rule League** in 1916, and made the Lucknow Pact with the Muslims in support of their *khalifa* movement. The British responded with the Royal Proclamation of 1917, which promised a gradual development of dominion-style self-government; and two years later the Montagu-Chelmsford Reforms attempted to implement the declaration. However, legislation authorizing internment without trial, also passed in 1919, seemed to contradict these promises; the Muslim population were alarmed by the collapse of Turkey and the masses were becoming more restless.

Gandhi and Independence

At this point, **Mohandas Karamchand Gandhi** – hailed as the Mahatma or "Great Soul" – took up the initiative. The Indian-style one-day strike (*hartal*) he proposed was organized in all the major cities, but feelings ran so high that there were riots, which were mercilessly crushed by the government. In particular, General Dyer dispersed the Jallianwalla Bagh meeting in **Amritsar** on April 13, 1919 by firing on the unarmed crowd, killing 379 and wounding 1200 (see p.660 for more details). The racial bitterness invoked by the atrocity inspired Gandhi's **Non-Co-operation Movement**, but by 1922 further acts of violence induced him to call off the campaign just before he was imprisoned.

Mahatma Gandhi, born in Porbander in Gujarat, had been educated as a lawyer in England. Over the years he was influenced by Christian, Hindu, Jain, liberal and humanitarian ideas; but the doctrine of nonviolence (*ahimsa*) and the pursuit of truth (*satya*) became the philosophical cornerstones of his endeavours to achieve a united independent India. His belief in the rights of man, and especially his championing of the untouchables, whom he renamed the Children of God (*Harijan*), put him in opposition to brahmin orthodoxy;

but he won the hearts of the people when he discarded European clothes for the homespun cotton *dhoti* and shawl, to identify with the masses. His personal charisma and all-India appeal inspired the Independence movement throughout the period, whether he was in prison, organizing the rejection of imported cloth in his *swadeshi* campaign, leading acts of civil disobedience, or fasting to bring about the cessation of Hindu-Muslim community violence.

Gandhi was released from prison in 1924. Despite liberal concessions by the British, by 1928 Congress was demanding complete Independence (*purna swaraj*). The government offered talks, but the more radical elements in Congress, now led by the young **Jawaharlal Nehru**, were in a confrontational mood. Their declaration of Independence Day on January 26, 1930 forced Gandhi's hand; he responded with a well-publicized 240-mile march from his ashram in Sabarmati to make **salt** illegally at Dandi in Gujarat. This demonstration of nonviolent civil disobedience (**satyagraha**) caught the people's imagination, leading to more processions, strikes, and the imprisonment of 100,000 of his followers by the end of the year. Abortive round-table talks, the Irwin-Gandhi truce, Gandhi's trip to London for further talks, and more civil disobedience culminated in the **Government of India Act** in 1935, which still fell short of aspirations for complete Independence. Congress remained suspicious of British intentions, and despite Gandhi's overtures refused to accommodate Muslim demands for representation.

The idea of a **separate Muslim state** was first raised in 1930 by the poet Sir Mohammed Iqbal and Chaudhuri Rahmat Ali, and a group of fellow students at Cambridge coined the name **Pakistan**, literally meaning "Land of the Pure". **Mohammed Ali Jinnah**, a lawyer from Bombay who assumed the leadership of the Muslim League in 1935, initially promoted Muslim-Hindu co-operation, but he soon despaired of influencing Congress and by 1940 the League passed a resolution demanding an independent Pakistan.

Confrontations between the government, Congress and the Muslim League continued throughout World War II. Mahatma Gandhi introduced the "**Quit India**" slogan and proposed another campaign of civil disobedience; the government immediately responded by imprisoning the whole Working Party of Congress in Pune. Jinnah, meanwhile, preached his "two nations" theory to the educated, and inspired mass Muslim support with his rhetoric against "Hinduization". A spate of terrorist activities left 1000 dead and 60,000 imprisoned; by the end of the war, the government accepted that complete Independence would have to be negotiated.

British attempts to find a solution that would preserve a united India and allay Muslim fears after the war disintegrated in the face of continued intransigence from both sides, and they gradually realized that Partition was inevitable. In 1946 Jinnah provoked riots in Calcutta with his call for Direct Action, and Hindus retaliated with atrocities against Muslims in Bihar and Uttar Pradesh. The British cabinet appointed **Lord Mountbatten** as viceroy to supervise the handover of power in 1948; Mahatma Gandhi desperately sought to avert the escalating Hindu-Muslim violence and find a resolution to secure a united India; and Nehru was persuaded that a separate Pakistan would be preferable to the anarchy of communal killings.

Lord Mountbatten brought Independence forward, the subcontinent was **partitioned** on August 15, 1947 and Pakistan came into existence, even though several princely states had still to decide which of the two new countries they would join. The new boundaries cut through both Bengal and the Punjab; Sikhs, Muslims and Hindus who had been neighbours became enemies overnight. Five million Hindus and Sikhs from Pakistan, and a similar number of Muslims from India, were involved in the ensuing two-way exodus, and the atrocities cost half a million lives. Mahatma Gandhi, who had devoted himself to ending the communal violence after Partition, was **assassinated** in January 1948 by Hindu extremists antagonized by his defence of the Muslims. India had lost its "Great Soul", but the profound shock of the Mahatma's last sacrifice at least contributed to the gradual cessation of the violence.

Independent India

Jawaharlal Nehru, India's first and longest-running prime minister, proved to be a dynamic, gifted and extremely popular leader during his seventeen years of premiership. He built the foundations of a democratic, secular state, and guided the first stages of its agricultural and industrial development. Nehru's first task, however, was to consolidate the Union.

His able deputy prime minister, **Sardar Vallabhai Patel**, was made responsible for incorporating the 562 princely states within the federal Union. The nizam of **Hyderabad**, who resisted even though the majority of the state's population was Hindu, had to be persuaded by an invasion of Indian troops. The Hindu maharaja of **Kashmir** also prevaricated, as three quarters of his subjects were Muslims, and by October 1947 he had to appeal to India for help against a tribal invasion supported by Pakistan. Kashmir's accession to India resulted in the first outbreak of hostilities between the two countries; the United Nations intervened in 1949 to enforce a ceasefire line. The **French** enclaves at Pondicherry and Chandernagar were incorporated in the 1950s, but the **Portuguese** refused to accept the new situation and in 1961 Nehru had to annex **Goa**. The **Naga** people were brought within the federal Union as the Nagaland state in the same year.

The Constitution for India's "Sovereign Democratic Republic and Union of States" became law on January 26, 1950, the twentieth anniversary of "Independence Day". The franchise was made universal for all adults, and with 173 million eligible to vote in 1951 India became the **world's largest democracy**. Hindi was designated the "official language of the Union"; but south India, in particular, was adamant in its opposition to Hindi, and Nehru realigned the several state borders on linguistic principles. By 1961 the Union consisted of sixteen states and six centrally administered territories. The Punjabi-speaking Sikhs had to wait until 1966 for their state to be separated from Hindu-dominated Haryana.

Nehru sought to achieve the constitutional aims of justice, liberty, equality and fraternity with a vigorous programme of social and economic reforms. He redressed the iniquities of caste by abolishing "untouchability" in 1955 and radically improved the status of women. National average literacy was increased to 23.7 per cent by 1961 and free elementary education became more readily available, although it still fell short of aspirations.

On the **economic** front, Nehru engineered the first three of India's **Five-Year Plans** to improve production capability and eradicate poverty. Population growth and the failures of the monsoon in 1952 and 1953 eroded the mainly agricultural aims of the first plan (1951–56), but food grain production increased from 52 million to over 65 million tons by 1956, and to 80 million tons by the end of the second plan (1956–61), which also injected capital into industry. Under the third plan (1961–66), a nuclear energy programme was inaugurated, and foreign aid and technical assistance secured to speed up industrialization.

Foreign policy was Nehru's biggest disappointment. He adopted a policy of nonaligned peaceful coexistence, but **China** threatened his aim of promoting

Asian unity. He attempted to dispel the tensions created by the Chinese invasion of Tibet in 1950 by concluding a trade treaty with China in 1954, which included a declaration of mutual respect for each other's territories; but this did not deter the Chinese from building a road across a remote area of Ladakh in 1957, and India sustained losses during a confrontation in 1959. In 1962, sporadic conflicts in the Northeast Frontier Agency (**Assam**) escalated into a war; the Chinese army proved to be far superior and advanced unhindered over India's northeast frontier. Their unilateral decision to withdraw, on November 21, 1962, added humiliation to defeat and spelt the end of India's policy of nonalignment. Nehru immediately made a defence treaty with the US, and set about creating a new elite Border Security Force.

Indira Gandhi 1966–1984

The whole nation, loyal throughout the China crisis, mourned Nehru's death in 1964, which prevented him from witnessing the restoration of India's military prestige in the **Second Indo-Pakistan War** of 1965. Indian tanks had advanced to within five kilometres of a virtually defenceless Lahore when the UN ceasefire was agreed on September 23. Lal Bahadur **Shastri**, who had led the interim government, died shortly after in January 1966 leaving Nehru's daughter, **Indira Gandhi**, to establish her superiority as leader of the Congress left, over Morarji Desai's right wing of the party.

Mrs Gandhi swiftly secured American financial support for India's fourth Five Year Plan (1966–71), but her devaluation of the rupee in June 1966 aroused considerable opposition and elections the next year radically reduced her majority. Two years later, Congress split under the pressure of internal dissent. Mrs Gandhi embraced the socialist principle by nationalizing the banks, and enlisted the support of the Communists, the Sikhs and the Dravidian Progressive Federation (DMK) to form a coalition government. By this time, India had made a spectacular agricultural breakthrough with its **Green Revolution**, as a result of the introduction of high-yield grains, and in 1969 industrial growth was over seven percent. Mrs Gandhi pressed on with her socialist reforms, abolishing the former maharajas' privy purses and privileges after she had consolidated her mandate in fresh elections in 1971.

Meanwhile, Yahya Khan's brutal repression of the struggle for independence in **East Pakistan** had caused a mass exodus of refugees, and by April 1971 Bengali civilians were pouring across into India at the rate of 60,000 a day. Mrs Gandhi astutely waited until she had the moral support of the international community, signed a Treaty of Peace, Friendship and Co-operation with the Soviet Union, and launched simultaneous attacks in West and East Pakistan on December 4. India had total air superiority, as well as the support of the East Pakistan population, and by December 15 the Pakistani general capitulated and signed the Instrument of Surrender of "all Pakistan armed forces in Bangla Desh".

If the liberation of Bangla Desh was the crowning glory of Mrs Gandhi's premiership, her abandonment of the democratic ideals so dear to her father was its lowest ebb. After widespread agrarian and industrial unrest against the rate of inflation and corruption within the Congress in 1974, the clamour of protest rose to a crescendo in June 1975, and when the opposition coalition under the joint leadership of J.P. Narayan and Morarji Desai threatened to oust India's "iron lady", she declared a **State of Emergency** on June 26, which suspended all civil rights, including habeas corpus, and silenced all opposition by internment and strict censorship of the press.

Her administrative and economic reforms had the desired effect of cutting inflation and curbing corruption, but the enforced sterilization of men with two or more children, and brutal slum-clearances in Delhi supervised by her son **Sanjay**, alienated millions of her supporters. When she finally released her opponents and called off the Emergency in January 1977, the bitterness she had engendered resulted in her ignominious defeat in the March elections. The ensuing **Janata** coalition under **Morarji Desai** fell apart within two years, and his premiership was terminated by a vote of no confidence in 1979. Mrs Gandhi, who had rebuilt her Congress (I) Party with Sanjay's help, swept back into office in January 1980. Sanjay died in a plane crash a few months later; four years afterwards, Mrs Gandhi made the second, fatal, mistake of her career.

A group of terrorists demanding a separate "nation" – Khalistan – for Sikhs, took control of the **Golden Temple** in Amritsar early in 1984, and organized a campaign of violence from its precincts. Hundreds of Hindus and moderate Sikhs fell victim to terrorist attacks, and the whole nation was calling for positive action to end the atrocities. Indira sent in her tanks in June 1984, but two days of raging combat desecrated the Sikhs' holiest shrine as well as generating the first martyrs of Khalistan. In October that year, her Sikh bodyguards avenged their brotherhood and faith by assassinating Mrs Gandhi at her house in Delhi.

Communal conflict 1984–1995

Rajiv Gandhi came to power in December 1984 on a wave of sympathy boosted by his reputation as "Mr Clean", given added meaning by the **Bhopal** gas tragedy just two weeks before the elections (see p.428). The honeymoon was short-lived; the political accords he reached with the Punjab, Assam and Mizoram deteriorated into armed conflict; more than two years of "peacekeeping" by the Indian army failed to disarm Tamil guerrillas in Sri Lanka; and allegations of corruption tarnished his image. By the end of the 1980s the opposition had rallied under the leadership of **V.P. Singh**, a former Congress minister. The December 1989 elections did not give V.P. Singh's Janata Party a majority, but he managed to form a coalition government with the support of the "Hindu first" Bharatiya Janata Party (**BJP**), led by **L.K. Advani**.

Singh was immediately confronted by problems in the Punjab and Kashmir, as well as upper-caste Hindu protests against his planned implementation of proposals for a sixty percent reservation of civil service jobs for lower castes and former "untouchables"; but it was an even more emotive issue which brought down his government in less than a year. Advani had assumed the leadership of a popular Hindu revivalist movement, which was demanding that the Babri Masjid mosque in **Ayodhya**, built by Babur in the sixteenth century, should be replaced by a Hindu temple on the supposed site of the birthplace of Rama, god-hero of the epic *Ramayana*.

Singh, utterly committed to secularism, pleaded with Advani to desist but, undeterred, Advani set off towards Ayodhya in October 1990, seated on a golden chariot pushed by his followers and thousands of devout Hindus, with the avowed intention of destroying the mosque. Singh ordered Advani's arrest and the inevitable withdrawal of the BJP from his coalition government resulted in a vote of no confidence on November 7, 1990. Rajiv Gandhi declined the offer to form an interim government, hopeful that he could improve his party's position in an election. His campaign went well and it was assumed that Congress would win, until on a tour of Tamil Nadu in May 1991, he was assassinated by Tamil Tigers seeking revenge for India's active opposition to their "freedom fight" in Sri Lanka.

P.V. Narasimha Rao skilfully steered the Congress Party through the elections, and formed a government with the support of the Muslim League, the

Communist "Left Front" and Tamil Nadu's most powerful party (AIADMK). At the same time, the BJP ominously increased its seats in the Lok Sabha (the Lower House of Parliament) from 80 to 120, Advani became leader of the opposition, and the enormous popular support for the rebuilding of Rama's temple in Ayodhya encouraged the Vishwa Hindu Parishad to take up the crusade. V.P. Singh countered by leading a march of five hundred secularists to

Jammu and Kashmir

The main, if not only, reason why India and Pakistan remain bitter enemies after more than fifty years of Independence is **Kashmir**. This tiny region in the far north of the country has been gripped by a bloody civil war that has, since its escalation in the late 1980s, claimed an estimated 25,000 lives. With both countries now fully fledged nuclear states, Kashmir has become one of the world's most dangerous geopolitical flashpoints.

The roots of the conflict go back to Independence in 1947. Threatened by aggressive Baluchi and Pathan tribals from the west, the Hindu maharaja of Kashmir decided at the eleventh hour to throw his lot in with India instead of the Islamic homeland carved out by Jinnah, in spite of the fact that ninety percent of his subjects were Muslims. Since then, Pakistan has regarded Kashmir as the "unfinished business of Partition".

Agitation for the autonomy guaranteed to Kashmir under Article 370 of the Indian Constitution has intensified gradually over time, but all-out violence may have been averted had it not been for a series of blunders by New Delhi, foremost among them Indira Gandhi's decision to depose the Kashmiri chief minister, **Farooq Abdullah**, for petty political reasons in 1984. Congress-led election rigging further inflamed opposition to Indian rule, as Pakistani-backed paramilitary groups began to target government buildings and personnel, as well as army and police posts.

The catalyst that converted political dissent into full-scale insurgency, however, occurred in 1990, when unarmed Kashmiris protesting against the heavy-handed tactics of security forces in the valley were gunned down from both sides of the **Gawakadal Bridge** in the capital, Srinagar. A hundred people died in the massacre, watched by the world's press. By the following year violence and human rights abuses had become endemic, both in the valley and further south around Jammu. Armed and trained by Libya and Pakistan, guerrillas from at least nineteen Muslim countries flooded in to fight what was now regarded as *jihad*, or Holy War. Total curfews became routine, and thousands of suspected militants were detained without trial, amid innumerable accusations of torture, systematic rape of Kashmiri women by troops, disappearances of countless boys and men, and summary executions.

The war intensified through the 1990s, with a series of bloody clashes between the militants and Indian forces. The first of these was the **Sopone massacre**, when security forces, in retaliation for a grenade attack on an army barracks, shot dead fifty militants. Then, in November 1993, a rerun of the Golden Temple fiasco seemed inevitable as heavily armed militants occupied one of the region's holiest shrines, the **Hazratbal mosque**. This siege, however, ended with a government climb-down (the militants were allowed safe passage out of the mosque), although 22 protesters were shot by the army in its wake.

After the Hazratbal siege, there ensued a period of relative calm; curfews were suspended and the Jammu & Kashmir Liberation Front (JKLF)'s leader, Javed Mir, was captured. With pressure being brought to bear on India by the US for a speedy resolution of the crisis, the peace seemed likely to result in long-awaited elections, until yet another stand-off between troops and militants stalled negotiations. In May 1995, a Muslim shrine near Srinagar, the **Char-e-Sharief**,

Ayodhya, but the BJP had won control of the Uttar Pradesh state government, making them responsible for law and order, and this time it was Singh who found himself arrested and imprisoned.

In December 1992, when the situation came to a head again, the central government could not prevent extremists inciting the crowds of fanatical devotees to tear down the mosque in a blaze of publicity (see p.328). The demolition of

was burned down while surrounded by the army, killing twenty Kashmiris and sparking off riots in the capital. For the first time tourists were targeted as a means of internationalizing the independence struggle. An attempt to abduct and incarcerate three Westerners in Delhi was foiled by police but, shortly afterwards, a group of foreign Muslim extremists, **Al-Faran**, kidnapped five tourists; one, a Norwegian, was beheaded and it's assumed that the other four suffered a similar fate. A return to relative stability finally allowed Jammu & Kashmir to hold elections to the Lok Sabha in December 1997, but the results were inconclusive due to widespread boycotting.

Less than two years later, the crisis brought India and Pakistan to the verge of yet another all-out war. While the world was preoccupied with NATO's bombing of Belgrade, at least 800 Pakistani fighters crept across the so-called Line of Control (the de facto border) overlooking the Srinagar–Leh road near **Kargil** and Dras. India's response was to move thousands of troops and heavy artillery into the area, swiftly followed up with an aerial bombardment. Within days the two countries were poised on the brink of all-out war, only months after both had successfully tested long-range nuclear missiles. In the event the conflict was contained, but Pakistan took a bloody nose from the encounter, and by July 1999 the Indian army had retaken all the ground previously lost to the militants. An estimated 700 Pakistani and 330 Indian soldiers died before Pakistani premier, Nawaz Sharif, bowed to international pressure and withdrew his forces.

Kashmir was top of President Clinton's agenda when he visited India in March 2000, but the start of his five-day tour was marred by the massacre of 36 unarmed Sikhs in the village of **Chattisingpora**, the first attack on the region's Sikh minority since the start of the troubles. Following a now predictable formula, Hizbul Mujhedin, the main militant group in the valley, denied responsibility for the killings, claiming it was a "preplanned act of Indian intelligence to defame the Kashmiri freedom struggle". The Indian cabinet, for its part, saw the Sikh massacre as a "Pakistan-backed attempt to internationalize the Kashmir conflict" at a time when the world's media attention was focused on the subcontinent.

The same pattern of allegations and counter-allegations accompanied the dramatic upsurge in violence in Kashmir the following August, when a series of appalling massacres were sparked off by the gunning down of 32 Hindu pilgrims by a so-called "suicide squad" at **Pahalgam**, during the annual Armanarth Yatra. The ensuing army crackdown effectively dashed all hopes that the unilateral ceasefire, announced by **Hizbul Mujhedin** only ten days before, would pave the way for peace talks. Bombings, ambushes, suicide raids and further killings of both soldiers and civilians punctuated the troubled summer of 2000.

What little support or moral authority the Indian government could claim in the mid-1980s long ago evaporated. Now, all sections of Kashmiri society support the freedom struggle in some form, from poor farmers to top judges. After more than twelve years of unremitting violence, peace seems a long way off. One of the reasons often advanced for this is the rise to power of the pro-Hindu BJP, for whom talking tough on Kashmir wins votes. At the time of writing, however, hopes were high that the *rapprochement* between India and Pakistan in the wake of the 2001 earthquake, in which both countries sustained appalling loss of life, may pave the way to constructive dialogue and reconciliation.

the Babri Masjid was followed by terrible **riots** in many parts of the country, especially Bombay and Gujarat, where Muslim families and businesses were targeted. A few months later, in retaliation against the extreme Hindu violence, **bombs** were planted in Bombay (see p.742) by underground Muslim groups. As a result of the Babri Masjid episode, the BJP-led state governments of UP, Himachal Pradesh, Madhya Pradesh, Rajasthan and Delhi were suspended. Elections in these states in late 1993 showed that the popularity of the BJP, and its call for the creation of **Hindutva**, a Hindu homeland, was fading. They re-asserted control of Delhi, which has always been a stronghold of the Hindu right, barely hung on in Rajasthan, and lost the rest.

The electoral results provided a much needed boost for Narashima Rao, whose grip over the leadership of the Congress Party seemed to be slipping. Accused by the opposition and press of lacking decisive policies, and dogged by allegations that he had accepted a suitcase of money as a bribe from a prominent businessman (the so-called "Harsha scandal"), the prime minister was under increasing pressure to step down. However, he weathered an unsuccessful no-confidence motion mounted by the BJP, and the surprise election victories in November temporarily silenced his rivals, among them minister Arjun Singh, who would later engineer a split in the Congress Party in an attempt to wrest power from Rao.

National morale during this post-Ayodhya period was shaky. After a year blighted by bomb blasts, riots and the rise of religious extremism, it seemed as if India's era as a secular state was doomed. To rub salt in the wounds, 15,000 people died in a massive **earthquake** around the northwestern Maharashtran city of Latur, and soon after, Surat, in southern Gujarat, was at the centre of an outbreak of a disease ominously resembling bubonic **plague**. Thousands fled the city and the international community panicked, cancelling export orders and axing flights. The "plague" turned out to be a flash in the pan, but the damage to India's self-image was done.

Against this backdrop of uncertainty, the rise of right-wing Hindu-fundamentalist parties gathered pace. Temporarily cowed by the Babri Masjid debacle, the BJP took advantage of the power struggle in the Congress Party to rekindle regional support. Expediently sidelining the contentious *Hindutva* agenda, the new rallying cry was **Swadeshi** – a campaign against the Congress-led programme of **economic liberalization** and, in particular, the activities of multinationals such as Coca Cola, Pepsi and KFC (one of whose branches was forced to close by the BJP-controlled Delhi municipality). Bal Thackeray's proto-fascist **Shiv Sena** party also made ground in Maharashtra, eventually winning the State Assembly elections there in March 1995.

The rise of the BJP 1996–1999

After the **general election** of May 1996, the political landscape altered at national level, too. Polling 194 of the Lok Sabha's 534 seats, the BJP emerged as the single largest party and attempted to form a government. Despite much behind-the-scenes wheeling and dealing, however, they were unable to muster a majority and were ousted a couple of weeks later, outmanoeuvred by a hastily formed coalition, the **Unified Front**, led by **H.D. Deve Gowda**. Ironically, the UF had to rely on the support of the Congress (I) Party – the principal opponent of many of its thirteen constituent parties – to establish a working majority. The shaky coalition could not last, and by April 1997, Gowda lost a no-confidence vote over his leadership and was speedily replaced by his foreign minister, **I.K. Gujral**. Despite maintaining good relations with America and leading the Indian market away from socialism, Gujral was much criticized by conservatives for his leftist leanings and for sporting a Lenin-style goatee.

Gujral led the United Front until its defeat in the **general election** of March 1998, after which the **BJP** struggled to power as the head of a new conservative coalition government under **Atal Behari Vajpayee**. This time, the party managed to stay in office for thirteen months, as opposed to the thirteen days of its previous spell in government. The BJP had promised change and the restoration of national pride and one of its early acts in government was to conduct five underground **nuclear tests** in May 1998, provoking Pakistan to respond in kind. There was a chorus of world criticism, and US-led financial **sanctions** were imposed on both nations. BJP activists blamed the West for being hypocritical over the whole affair while in many people's eyes, the tests made the Kashmir issue more of a flashpoint – and now a potentially nuclear one. Within a couple of months of the tests, the Americans were leading the way in trying to persuade both countries to sign up to nuclear nonproliferation in the Comprehensive Test Ban Treaty (CTBT). In sharp contrast to increased tension over security issues, Vajpayee visited Pakistan in person in early March 1999, the first time an Indian prime minister had crossed the border in a decade. However, this atmosphere of seemingly warming relations between the two countries received a jolt when the Indian government tested an **Agni II missile**, capable of carrying nuclear warheads into Pakistan. Again, Pakistan matched this within days, testing their own long-range, nuclear-capable missiles.

On the domestic front, the BJP ran into a crisis in the summer of 1998 over – of all things – the **price of onions**. India, it turned out, had allowed too many onions to be exported to Central Asia at a time when they were running into short supply at home. Shoppers were left to battle in the markets for onions that rose to six times their normal price. Since they're a staple ingredient, the issue became a major political embarrassment for the BJP. It was also accused of wilful inaction in the face of a spate of **attacks on Christians** during its term in office. Particularly shocking was the burning alive of an Australian missionary and his two young sons as they slept in a car at a religious gathering in Orissa.

Following its defeat in the 1998 elections, the Congress Party emerged as a stronger political force with **Sonia Gandhi**, the Italian-born widow of the former prime minister Rajiv Gandhi, at the helm. Congress collaborated with the Jayalalitha's AIADMK to bring about the downfall of the BJP in April 1999 (see "Of Movie Stars and Ministers", p.778), but were unable to form a coalition government. As a consequence, India faced a third **general election** in as many years.

The 1999 election

At the start of the campaign, Congress hopes were high that with a Gandhi once again as party leader, it could revive the popular support lost after years of infighting and corruption scandals. Moreover, to compound the BJP's problems, Vajpayee's caretaker government was saddled with a worsening financial deficit, deteriorating relations with Pakistan and a welter of domestic difficulties, foremost among them the political fallout from an horrific **train crash** in West Bengal, in which 260 people died.

The wave of **patriotism** that swept India after the Kargil victory (see box on p.1499) was a godsend for Vajpayee (cynics argued it may well have been the hidden policy behind the army's uncompromising response to the crisis). Riding high on the feel-good factor, his party inflicted the biggest defeat

Congress had sustained since it first came to power in 1947. Vajpayee's majority was far from as large as he might have hoped, and the BJP-led National Democratic Alliance (NDA) coalition was fractured and tenuous, but Sonia's second election defeat seemed to herald, at last, the end of dynastic politics in India (in spite of the entrance onto the political stage of her charismatic 26-year-old daughter, Priyanka).

The election results also showed a clear swing of public support away from New Delhi towards smaller regional parties. Tired of corrupt police, unsafe drinking water, inadequate rubbish disposal, electricity provision, sewer and road maintenance, the emerging middle classes voted out almost half of their incumbent MPs in a spirit of exasperation which led the news magazine *Outlook* to run a lead story questioning whether India actually needs a central government at all.

The NDA's post-election party was short lived. On October 30, 1999, a massive **super-cyclone** with 175mph winds struck the north coast of Orissa. Estimates of the death toll ranged from 10,000 to 20,000, around 1.5 million villagers lost their homes and thousands more died in the following weeks from cholera, typhoid and other diseases. International aid agencies were quick to criticize the Indian government, saying the relief operation was hampered by poor co-ordination and bickering between New Delhi and the state government in Orissa.

The new millennium

The start of the new millennium saw no let-up in headline-making events. **South India** was gripped by a dramatic news story which, in spite of its relative geopolitical irrelevance, attracted massive media attention. On July 30, the Tamil sandalwood smuggler and notorious bandit, **Veerapan**, kidnapped 72-year-old matinee idol, **Raj Kumar**, A succession of negotiators were dispatched to secure a release, but to no avail. Riots broke out in the actor's home state, Karnataka, and one ardent fan even set himself on fire in protest at the abduction. It took nearly four months of secret talks to end the deadlock before the bandit, wanted for 120 murders, set the film star free, with various rumours surrounding what deal had been done and including the possibility of payment of a vast ransom.

The Veerapan scandal once again reaffirmed the extent of political corruption in Tamil Nadu where, the previous February, the larger-than-life AIADMK leader, former film starlet **Jayalalitha** was imprisoned for accepting bribes from businessmen. 5000 demonstrators were arrested in the riots that followed, as supporters set fire to a bus full of students, killing three innocent women – an incident filmed and broadcast by Star TV news.

India's political problems, however, were temporarily eclipsed by a succession of catastrophic **natural disasters** which wracked the country in mid-2000. In the arid zones of Rajasthan and Gujarat, high May temperatures compounded the third failure of the monsoons in as many years, forcing tens of thousands of poor farming families off their land in search of fodder and drinking water. Once again, the government was heavily criticized for failing to respond quickly enough, and only after pictures of emaciated refugees and their bony cattle appeared on TV did Prime Minister Vajpayee make a televised appeal for donations and announce a Rs9.5 billion relief package for victims of the **drought**.

While the 2000 monsoon, when it finally broke, made little impact on the parched northwest, **record rainfalls** wreaked havoc in Andhra Pradesh, West Bengal and low lying areas of Uttar Pradesh. An estimated 12 million were left marooned or homeless as river levels rose by as much as 4m in places. With transport and communications at a standstill for weeks, food distribution and rescue efforts all but ground to a halt. Riots broke out in camps set up by the army for **flood** victims, as supplies of food and plastic sheets ran out.

An even worse tragedy, however, lay in store for millions of Gujaratis when, in the morning of Jan 26, 2001 – Indian Independence Day – a massive **earthquake** measuring 7.9 on the Richter scale levelled a vast area in the northwest of the state.

One of the few positive repercussions of the earthquake was a slight thaw in relations with Pakistan, whose new president, General Pervez Musharraf, phoned Prime Minister Vajpayee to offer condolences and support, paving the way for possible peace talks on the Kashmir issue.

Meanwhile, internal pressures – regional and caste differences, and corruption scandals – continued to add to New Delhi's woes in the spring of 2001. Among the most dramatic concessions to the regionalist coalition partners who had helped the BJP to power was the **creation of three new states**: Jharkhand, Chattisgarh and Uttaranchal, made up of parts of Bihar, Madhya Pradesh and Uttar Pradesh.

While national security issues have tended since Independence to be dominated by relations with Pakistan, and to a lesser extent China, India seems to be increasingly aware of the threat to its integrity posed by **secessionism**. Shadowing protracted political instability of the centre, calls for greater autonomy have been intensifying at state level, particularly in the northeast, where old ethnic tensions pose a perennial threat of insurgency. Even normally peaceful Darjeeling has been plagued by civil unrest in recent years, as Gurkha factions compete for power. In the deep south, Tamil nationalism has also been on the rise, with some of its Dravidian parties forming firmer links with the Liberation Tigers of Tamil Eelam (LTTE), fighting a deadly war of liberation across the water in Sri Lanka.

Behind the steady growth of regionalism over the past few years has been a marked weakening of New Delhi's grip as the nation's political capital. Incapable of raising adequate tax revenue, and rotten to its core with **corruption**, the centre no longer commands the respect and power it used to. Chronic political instability has also taken its toll. The absence of consistent policies has meant that big business and the affluent classes have increasingly had to look after themselves, which has conspicuously widened the gap between the haves and the have nots.

As it struggles to balance the ambitions of its privileged elite with the basic needs of its poor, Indian society at the start of the twenty-first century is rife with ironies. The country recently chosen by Bill Gates as the site of Microsoft's new **Hi-Tech City**, capable of sending satellites and nuclear rockets into space, is unable to provide clean drinking water, adequate nutrition and basic education for millions of its inhabitants. Its capacity to close this yawning gap will depend on the extent to which India's politicians are able to deliver stable government, and curb the corruption and self-interest which have come to dominate public life.

Religion

For the majority of Indians, Hinduism permeates every aspect of life, from commonplace daily chores to education and politics. The vast pantheon of Hindu deities is manifest everywhere – not only in temples, but in shops, rickshaws and even on *bidi* packets and matchboxes. Beside Hindus, Muslims are the most prominent religious group; they have been an integral part of Indian society since the twelfth century, and mosques are almost as common as temples. Though Jains and Buddhists now make up a tiny fraction of the population, their impact is still felt, and their magnificent temples are among the finest in India. Both these ancient faiths, like the more recently established Sikh community, formed in reaction to the caste laws and ritual observances of Hinduism. In addition, there are small communities of Zoroastrians, descended from Iranians, and Christians, here since the first century (see p.1522). Hindu practices, such as caste distinction, have crept into most religions, and many of the festivals – see p.67 – that mark each year with music, dance and feasting, are shared by all communities. Each has its own pilgrimage sites, heroes, legends and even culinary specialities, which all combine to give India its unique religious diversity.

Hinduism

Contemporary **Hinduism** – the religion of over 85 percent of Indians – is the product of several thousand years of evolution and assimilation. It has no founder or prophet, no single creed, and no single prescribed practice or doctrine; it takes in hundreds of gods, goddesses, beliefs and practices, and widely variant cults and philosophies. Some are recognized by only two or three villages, others are popular right across the subcontinent. Hindus (from the Persian word for Indians) call their beliefs and practices *dharma*, which envelops natural and moral law to define a way of living in harmony with a natural order, while achieving personal goals and meeting the requirements of society.

Early developments

The foundations of Hinduism were laid by the **Aryans**, seminomads who entered northwest India during the second millennium BC, and mixed with the indigenous Dravidian population (see p.1473). With them they brought a belief in gods associated with the elements, including **Agni**, the god of fire and sacrifice, **Surya**, the sun-god, and **Indra**, the chief god. Most of these deities faded in later times, but Indra is still regarded as the father of the gods, and Surya, eternally present in his magnificent chariot-temple in **Konarak** (Orissa), was widely worshipped until the medieval period.

Aryan beliefs were set out in the **Vedas**, scriptures "heard" (*shruti*) by "seers" (*rishis*). Transmitted orally for centuries, they were finally written, in Sanskrit, between 1000 BC and 500 AD. The earliest were the Samhitas, or hymns; later came the *Brahmanas*, sacrificial texts, and *Aranyakas*, or "forest treatises".

The earliest and most important Samhita, the **Rig Veda**, contains hymns to deities and *devas* (divine powers), and is supplemented by other books detailing rituals and prayers for ceremonial use. The **Brahmana** stress correct ritual performance, drawing heavily on concepts of **purity and pollution** that persist today, and concentrating on sacrificial rites. Pedantic attention to ritual soon supplanted the importance of the *devas*, and they were further undermined by a search for a single cosmic power thought to be their source, eventually conceived of as **Brahma**, the absolute creator, personified from earlier mentions of Brahman, an impersonal principle of cosmic unity.

The **Aranyakas** focused upon this all-powerful godhead, and reached their final stage in the **Upanishads**, which describe in beautiful and emotive verse the mystic experience of unity of the soul (*atman*) with Brahma, ideally attained through asceticism, renunciation of worldly values and meditation. In the *Upanishads* the concepts of **samsara**, a cyclic round of death and rebirth characterized by suffering and perpetuated by desire, and **moksha**, liberation from *samsara*, became firmly rooted. Fundamental aspects of the Hindu world view, both are accepted by all but a handful of Hindus today, along with the belief in **karma**, the certainty that one's present position in society is determined by the effect of one's previous actions in this and past lives.

Hindu society

The stratification of Hindu society is rooted in the **Dharma Shastras** and **Dharma Shutras**, scriptures written from "memory" (*smriti*) at the same time as the *Vedas*. These defined four hierarchical classes, or **varnas**, each assigned specific religious and social duties known as **varnashradharma**, and established Aryans as the highest social class. In descending order the *varnas* are: **brahmins** (priests and teachers), **kshatryas** (rulers and warriors), **vaishyas** (merchants and cultivators) and **shudras** (menials). The first three classes, known as "twice-born", are distinguished by a sacred thread worn from the time of initiation (see p.1509), and granted full access to religious texts and rituals. Below all four categories, groups whose jobs involve contact with dirt or death (such as undertakers, leather-workers and cleaners) were classified as **untouchables**. Though discrimination against untouchables is now a criminal offence, in part thanks to the campaigns of Gandhi – he renamed untouchables Harijans, "Children of God" – the lowest stratum of society has by no means disappeared.

Within the four *varnas*, social status is further defined by **jati**, classifying each individual by family and precise occupation (for example, a *vaishya* may be a jewellery seller, cloth merchant, cowherd or farmer). A person's *jati* determines his **caste**, and lays restrictions on all aspects of life from food consumption, religious obligations and contact with other castes, to the choice of marriage partners. In general, Hindus marry members of the same *jati* – marrying someone of a different *varna* often results in ostracism from both family and caste, leaving the couple stranded in a society where caste affiliation takes primacy over all other aspects of individual identity. There are almost 3000 *jatis*; the divisions and restrictions they have enforced have become, time and time again, the subject of reform movements and the target of critics.

A Hindu has three aims in life: **dharma**, fulfilling one's duty to family and caste and acquiring religious merit (*punya*) through right living; **artha**, the lawful making of wealth; and **karma**, desire and satisfaction. These goals are linked with the four traditional stages in life. The first is as a child and student, devoted to learning from parents and guru. Next comes the stage of householder, expected to provide for a family and raise children, especially sons. That accomplished, he or she may then take up a life of celibacy and retreat into the forest to meditate alone, and finally renounce all possessions to become a homeless ascetic, hoping to achieve the ultimate goal of *moksha*. The small number

The *Ramayana* epic is the story of **Rama**, the seventh of **Vishnu's** ten incarnations. Although possibly based on a historic figure, Rama is seen essentially as a representation of Vishnu's heroic qualities.

Rama is the oldest of four sons born to Dasaratha, the king of **Ayodhya**, and heir to the throne. At the time of Rama's coronation, **Kaikeya**, one of the king's three wives, seizes the moment to ask the king to grant her two favours, as he had promised in a moment of rash appreciation. Her first request is for her son **Bharata** to be crowned instead of the rightful Rama; her second is for Rama to be banished to the forest for fourteen years. In an exemplary show of filial piety, Rama accepts the demands and leaves the city with his wife **Sita** and brother **Laksmana**.

One day, **Suparnakhi**, the sister of Rama's bitter enemy **Ravana**, spots Rama in the woods and instantly falls in love with him. As an ideal husband, Rama rebuffs her advances, but Suparnakhi attempts to avenge herself on Sita, seeing her as the obstacle to Rama's heart. Laksmana intervenes, cutting off Suparnakhi's nose and ears in retaliation. She then flees to her demon brother, who mobilizes fourteen giants against Rama. After Rama destroys them single-handedly, Ravana dispatches a further 14,000 warriors, who are treated in similar fashion. Thwarted by Rama's prowess, Ravana's advisers suggest that he should kidnap Rama's beloved Sita instead, causing him to die of a broken heart. Sita is successfully captured and flown by chariot to one of Ravana's palaces on the island of **Lanka**.

Determined to find Sita, Rama enlists the help of **Hanuman**, the monkey god. Hanuman leaps across the strait to Lanka and makes his way surreptitiously into Ravana's palace where he hears the evil king trying to persuade Sita to marry him. If not, he threatens, "my cooks shall mince thy limbs with steel and serve thee for my morning meal" – a choice of consummation or consumption. Hanuman reports back to Rama, who gathers an army and prepares to attack. Monkeys form a bridge across the straits allowing the invading army to cross. After much fighting, Sita is rescued and reunited with her husband.

On the long journey back to Ayodhya, Sita's honour is brought into question. To prove her innocence, she asks Laksmana to build a funeral pyre and steps into the flames, praying to Agni, the fire god. Agni walks her through the fire into the arms of a delighted Rama. They march into Ayodhya guided by a trail of lights laid out by the local people. Today, this illuminated homecoming is commemorated by Hindus all over the world during **Diwali**, the festival of lights. At the end of the epic, Rama's younger brother gladly steps down, allowing Rama to be crowned as the rightful king.

---

of Hindus, including some women, who follow this ideal life assume the final stage as **sannyasis**, saffron-clad **sadhus** who wander throughout India, begging for food, and retreat to isolated caves, forests and hills to meditate. They're a common feature in most Indian towns, and many stay for long periods in particular temples. Not all have raised families: some assume the life of a *sadhu* at an early age as *chellas*, pupils, of an older *sadhu*.

The popular deities

Alongside the *Dharma Shastras* and *Dharma Shutras*, the most important works of the *smriti* tradition, thought to have been completed by the fourth century AD at the latest, were the **Puranas**, long mythological stories focused on the Vedic gods and their heroic actions, and Hinduism's two great epics, the **Mahabharata** and **Ramayana**. Through these texts, the main gods and goddesses became firmly embedded in the religion. Alongside **Brahma**, the creator, **Vishnu** was acknowledged as the preserver, and **Shiva** ("auspicious, benign"), referred to in the *Rig Veda* as Rudra, was recognized for his destructive powers. The three are often depicted in a trinity, *trimurti*, but in time Brahma's importance declined, and Shiva and Vishnu became the most popular deities.

Other gods and goddesses who came alive in the mythology of the *Puranas*, each depicted in human or semihuman form and accompanied by an animal "**vehicle**", are still venerated across India. River goddesses, ancestors, guardians of particular places, and protectors against disease and natural disaster are as central to village life as the major deities.

Philosophical trends

The complications presented by Hinduism's view of deities, *samsara, atman* (the human soul) and *moksha* naturally encouraged philosophical debate, and led eventually to the formation of six schools of thought, known as the **Darshanas**. Each presented a different exposition of the true nature of *moksha* and how to attain it.

Foremost among these was the **Advaita Vedanta** school of **Shankara** (c.788–850 AD), who interpreted Hinduism as pure monotheism verging on monism (the belief that all is one: in this case, one with God). Drawing on Upanishadic writings, he claimed that they identified the essence of the human soul with that of God (*tat tvam asi*, "that thou art"), and that all else – the phenomenal world and all *devas* – is an illusion (*maya*) created by God. Shankara is revered as saint-philosopher at the twelve **jyotrilinga**: sacred Shaivite sites associated with the unbounded *lingam* of light, which as a manifestation of Shiva once persuaded both Brahma and Vishnu to acknowledge Shiva's supremacy.

Another important Darshana centred around the age-old practice of **yoga** (literally "the action of yoking [to] another"), elucidated by **Patanjali** (second century BC) in his *Yoga Sutras*. Interpreting yoga as the yoking of mind and body, or the yoking of the mind with God, Patanjali detailed various practices, which used in combination may lead to an understanding of the fundamental **unity** of all things. The most common form of yoga known in the West is *hatha* yoga, whereby the body and its vital energies is brought under control through physical positions and breathing methods, with results said to range from attaining a calm mind to being able to fly through the air, enter other bodies or become invisible. Other practices include *mantra* yoga, the recitation of formulas and meditation on mystical diagrams (*mandalas*), *bhakti* yoga (devotion), *jnana* yoga (knowledge) and *raja*, or royal, yoga, the highest form of yoga when the mind is absorbed in God.

Practice

The primary concern of most Hindus is to reduce bad karma and acquire merit (*punya*), by honest and charitable living within the restrictions imposed by caste, and by worship, in the hope of attaining a higher status of rebirth. Strict rules address purity and pollution, the most obvious of them requiring high-caste Hindus to limit their contact with potentially polluting lower castes. All bodily excretions are polluting (hence the strange looks Westerners receive when they blow their noses and return their handkerchiefs to their pockets). Above all else, **water** is the agent of purification, used in ablutions before prayer, and revered in all rivers, especially Ganga (the Ganges).

In most Hindu homes, a chosen deity is worshipped daily in a shrine room, and scriptures are read. Outside the home, worship takes place in temples, and

CONTEXTS | Religion

Eight times as long as the *Iliad* and *Odyssey* combined, the **Mahabharata** is the most popular of all Hindu texts. Written around 400 AD, it tells of a feuding *kshatrya* family in upper India (Bharata) during the fourth millennium BC. Like all good epics, the *Mahabharata* recounts a gripping tale, using its characters to illustrate moral values. In essence it attempts to elucidate the position of the warrior castes, the *kshatryas*, and demonstrate that religious fulfilment is as accessible for them as it is for brahmins.

The chief character is **Arjuna**, a superb archer, who with his four brothers – Yudhishtra, Bhima, Nakula and Sahadeva – represents the **Pandava** clan, upholders of righteousness and supreme fighters. Arjuna won his wife **Draupadi** in an archery contest, but wishing to avoid jealousy she agreed to be the shared wife of all five brothers. The Pandava clan are resented by their cousins, the evil **Kauravas**, led by Duryodhana, the eldest son of Dhrtarashtra, ruler of the Kuru kingdom.

When Dhrtarashtra handed his kingdom over to the Pandavas, the Kauravas were far from happy. Duryodhana challenged Yudhishtra (known for his brawn but not his brain) to a gambling contest. The dice game was rigged; Yudhishtra gambled away not only his possessions, but also his kingdom and his shared wife. The Kauravas offered to return the kingdom to the Pandavas if they could spend thirteen years in exile, together with their wife, without being recognized. Despite much scheming, the Pandavas succeeded, but on return found that the Kauravas would not fulfil their side of the bargain.

Thus ensued the great battle of the *Mahabharata*, told in the sixth book, the **Bhagavad Gita** – immensely popular as an independent story. Vishnu descends to earth as **Krishna**, and steps into battle as Arjuna's charioteer. The Bhagavad Gita details the fantastic struggle of the fighting cousins, using magical weapons and brute force. Arjuna is in a dilemma, unable to justify the killing of his own kin in pursuit of a rightful kingdom for himself and his brothers. Krishna consoles him, reminding him that his principal duty, his *varnashradharma*, is as a warrior. What is more, Krishna points out, each man's soul, or *atman*, is eternal, and transmigrates from body to body, so Arjuna need not grieve the death of his cousins. Krishna convinces Arjuna that by fulfilling his *dharma* he not only upholds law and order by saving the kingdom from the grasp of unrighteous rulers, he also serves the gods in the spirit of devotion (*bhakti*), and thus guarantees himself eternal union with the divine in the blissful state of *moksha*.

The Pandavas finally win the battle, and Yudhishtra is crowned king. Eventually Arjuna's grandson, Pariksit, inherits the throne, and the Pandavas trek to Mount Meru, the mythical centre of the universe and the abode of the gods, where Arjuna finds Krishna's promised *moksha*.

consists of **puja**, or devotion to god – sometimes a simple act of prayer, but more commonly a complex process when the god's image is circumambulated, offered flowers, rice, sugar and incense, and anointed with water, milk or sandalwood paste (which is usually done on behalf of the devotee by the temple priest, the *pujari*). The aim in *puja* is to take **darshan** – glimpse the god – and thus receive his or her blessing. Whether devotees simply worship the deity in prayer, or make requests – for a healthy crop, a son, good results in exams, a vigorous monsoon or a cure for illness – they leave the temple with *prasad*, an offering of food or flowers taken from the holy sanctuary by the *pujaris*.

Communal worship and get-togethers en route to pilgrimage sites are celebrated with *kirtan* or *bhajan*, singing of hymns, perhaps verses in praise of Krishna taken from the *Bhagavad Purana*, or repetitive cries of "Jai Shankar!" (Praise to Shiva). Temple ceremonies are conducted in Sanskrit by *pujaris* who tend the image in daily rituals that symbolically wake, bathe, feed and dress the god, and finish each day by preparing the god for sleep. The most elaborate is the evening ritual, **arthi**, when lamps are lit, blessed in the sanctuary, and passed around devotees amid the clanging of drums, gongs and cymbals. In many villages, shrines to *devatas*, village deities who function as protectors and may bring disaster if neglected, are more important than temples.

Each of the **great stages** in life – birth, initiation (when boys of the three twice-born *varnas* are invested with a sacred thread, and a mantra is whispered into their ear by their guru), marriage, death and cremation – is cause for fervent prayer, energetic celebration and feasting. The most significant event in a Hindu's life is **marriage**, which symbolizes ritual purity, and for women is so important that it takes the place of initiation. Feasting, dancing, and singing among the bride and groom's families, usually lasting for a week or more before and after the marriage, are the order of the day all over India. The actual marriage is consecrated when the couple walk seven times round a sacred fire, accompanied by sacred verses read by an officiating brahmin. Despite efforts to reduce the importance of a **dowry**, a valuable gift from the bride's family to the groom, dowries are still demanded, and among wealthier families may include televisions, videos, and cars in addition to the more common items of jewellery and money. Deaths in kitchen "accidents" of wives whose dowry is below expectations are still known to occur, see p.1526.

Festivals and pilgrimages

Life transitions are by no means the only cause for celebration among Hindus, whose year is marked by **festivals** devoted to deities, re-enacting mythological stories and commemorating sacred sites. The grandest festivals are held at places made holy by association with gods, goddesses, miracles, and great teachers, or rivers and mountains; throughout the year these are important **pilgrimage** sites, visited by devotees eager to receive *darshan*, glimpse the world of the gods, and attain merit. The journey, or *yatra*, to a pilgrimage site is every bit as significant as reaching the sacred location, and bands of Hindus (particularly *sadhus*) often walk from site to site. Modern transport, however, has made things easier, and every state lays on pilgrimage tours, when buses full of chanting families roar from one temple to another, filling up with religious souvenirs as they go.

Perhaps India's single most sacred place is the ancient city of **Varanasi** (also known as Benares or Kashi), on the banks of the Ganges. The river has been sacred since the time of the earliest Aryan settlements, and is personified as the beneficent goddess Ganga. At Varanasi it holds the redeeming quality common to all rivers, but bathing in its waters, and more particularly, dying or being cremated there, guarantees entering heaven (*svarga*) and achieving release from rebirth. *Ghats*, steps leading to the water's edge, are common in all river- or lakeside towns, the abode of priests who offer *puja* to a devotee's chosen deity.

The source of the Ganges, high in the mountains of western Uttar Pradesh at **Gangotri**, is held in great reverence, as are the five ancient temples nearby, known as **Panch Kedar**, deep in the Himalayas. Equally important are **sangams**, or **tirthas**, the points where two rivers meet. Every twelve years, when India's largest festival, the **Kumbh Mela**, is held at Allahabad, the *sangam* of the Ganges and the Yamuna, the *ghats* turn into a seething mass of bodies, overrun by near-naked ascetics who are the first of millions to bathe in the holy waters. The 2001 Kumbh Mela was seen as particularly auspicious astrologically, and attracted 75 million people, making it the largest ever gathering of humanity. Lesser *melas* are held at three-yearly intervals at the *tirthas* of Haridwar, Nasik, and Ujjain.

Vishnu

The chief function of **Vishnu**, "pervader", is to keep the world in order, preserving, restoring and protecting. With four arms holding a conch, discus, lotus and mace, Vishnu is blue-skinned, and often shaded by a serpent, or resting on its coils, afloat on an ocean. He is usually seen alongside his half-man-half-eagle vehicle, Garuda.

Vaishnavites, often distinguishable by two vertical lines on their foreheads, recognize Vishnu as supreme lord, and hold that he has manifested himself on earth nine times. These incarnations, or *avatars*, have been as fish (Matsya), tortoise (Kurma), boar (Varaha), man-lion (Narsingh), dwarf (Vamana), axe-wielding brahmin (Parsuram), Rama, Krishna and Balaram (though some say that the Buddha is the ninth *avatar*). Vishnu's future descent to earth as Kalki, the saviour who will come to restore purity and destroy the wicked, is eagerly awaited.

The most important *avatars* are Krishna and Rama. **Krishna** is the hero of the *Bhagavad Gita*, in which he proposes three routes to salvation (*moksha*): selfless action (*karmayoga*), knowledge (*jnana*), and devotion to god (*bhakti*), and explains that *moksha* is attainable in this life, even without asceticism and renunciation. This appealed to all castes, as it denied the necessity of ritual and officiating brahmin priests, and evolved into the popular *bhakti* cult that legitimized love of God as a means to *moksha*, and found expression in emotional songs of the quest for union with the divine. Through *bhakti*, Krishna's role was extended, and he assumed different faces: most popularly he is the playful cowherd who seduces and dances with cowgirls (*gopis*), giving each the illusion that she is his only lover. He is also pictured as a small, chubby, mischievous baby, known for his butter-stealing exploits, who inspires tender motherly love in women. Like Vishnu, Krishna is blue, and often shown dancing and playing the flute. Popular legend has it that Krishna was born in **Mathura**, today a major pilgrimage centre, and sported with his *gopis* in nearby **Vrindavan**. He also established a kingdom on the far western coast of Gujarat, at **Dwarka**.

Rama, Vishnu's seventh incarnation, is the chief character in the *Ramayana*, the epic detailing his exploits in exile (see p.1506).

Shiva

Shaivism, the cult of **Shiva**, was also inspired by *bhakti*, requiring selfless love from devotees in a quest for divine communion, but Shiva has never been incarnate on earth. He is presented in many different aspects, such as **Nataraja**, Lord of the Dance, **Mahadev**, Great God, and **Maheshvar**, Divine Lord, source of all knowledge. Though he does have several terrible forms, his role extends beyond that of destroyer, and he is revered as the source of the whole universe.

Shiva is often depicted with four or five faces, holding a trident, draped with serpents, and bearing a third eye in his forehead. In temples, he is identified with the *lingam*, or phallic symbol, resting in the *yoni*, a representation of female sexuality. Whether as statue or *lingam*, Shiva is guarded by his bull-mount, Nandi, and often accompanied by a consort, who also assumes various forms, and is looked upon as the vital energy, **shakti**, that empowers him. Their erotic exploits were a favourite sculptural subject between the ninth and twelfth centuries, most unashamedly in carvings on the temples of **Khajuraho**, in Madhya Pradesh.

While Shiva is the object of popular devotion all over India, as the terrible **Bhairav** he is also the god of the Shaivite **ascetics**, who renounce family and caste ties and perform extreme meditative and yogic practices. Many, though not all, smoke ganja, Shiva's favourite herb; all see renunciation and realization of God as the key to *moksha*. Some ascetic practices enter the realm of **Tantrism**, in which confrontation with all that's impure, such as alcohol, death, and sex, is used to merge the sacred and the profane, and bring about the profound realization that Shiva is omnipresent.

Other gods and goddesses

Chubby and smiling, elephant-headed Ganesh, the first son of Shiva and Parvati, is invoked before every undertaking (except funerals). Seated on a throne or lotus, his image is often placed above temple gateways, in shops and houses; in his four arms he holds a conch, discus, bowl of sweets (or club) and a water lily, and he's always attended by his vehicle, a rat. Credited with writing the *Mahabharata* as it was dictated by the sage Vyasa, Ganesh is regarded by many as the god of learning, the lord of success, prosperity and peace.

Durga, the fiercest of the female deities, is an aspect of Shiva's more conservative consort, Parvati (also known as Uma), who is remarkable only for her beauty and fidelity. In whatever form, Shiva's consort is *shakti*, the fundamental energy that spurs him into action. Among Durga's many aspects, each a terrifying goddess eager to slay demons, are Chamunda, Kali and Muktakeshi, but in all her forms she is Mahadevi (Great Goddess). Statues show her with ten arms, holding the head of a demon, a spear, and other weapons; she tramples demons underfoot, or dances upon Shiva's body. A garland of skulls drapes her neck, and her tongue hangs from her mouth, dripping with blood – a particularly gruesome sight on pictures of Kali. Durga is much venerated in Bengal; in all her temples, animal sacrifices are a crucial element of worship, to satisfy her thirst for blood and deter her ruthless anger.

The comely goddess Lakshmi, usually shown sitting or standing on a lotus flower, and sometimes called Padma (lotus), is the embodiment of loveliness, grace and charm, and the goddess of prosperity and wealth. Vishnu's consort, she appears in different aspects alongside each of his *avatars*; the most important are Sita, wife of Rama, and Radha, Krishna's favourite gopi. In many temples she is shown as one with Vishnu, in the form of Lakshmi Narayan.

Though some legends claim that his mother was Ganga, or even Agni, Karttikeya is popularly believed to be the second son of Shiva and Parvati. Primarily a god of war, he was popular among the northern Guptas, who worshipped him as Skanda, and the southern Chalukyas, for whom he was Subrahmanya. Usually shown with six faces, and standing upright with bow and arrow, Karttikeya is commonly petitioned by those wishing for male offspring.

India's great monkey god, Hanuman, features in the *Ramayana* as Rama's chief aide in the fight against the demon-king of Lanka. Depicted as a giant monkey clasping a mace, Hanuman is the deity of acrobats and wrestlers, but is also seen as Rama and Sita's greatest devotee, and an author of Sanskrit grammar. As his representatives, monkeys find sanctuary in temples all over India.

The most beautiful Hindu goddess, Saraswati, the wife of Brahma, with her flawless milk-white complexion, sits or stands on a water lily or peacock, playing a lute, sitar or *vina*. Associated with the River Saraswati, mentioned in the *Rig Veda*, she is revered as the goddess of music, creativity and learning.

Closely linked with the planet Saturn, Sani is feared for his destructive powers. His image, a black statue with protruding blood-red tongue, is often found on street corners; strings of green chillies and lemon are hung in shops and houses each Saturday (Saniwar) to ward off his evil influences.

Mention must also be made of the sacred cow, Khamdenu, who receives devotion through the respect shown to all cows, left to amble through streets and temples all over India. The origin of the cow's sanctity is uncertain; some myths record that Brahma created cows at the same time as brahmins, to provide *ghee* (clarified butter) for use in priestly ceremonies. To this day cow dung and urine are used to purify houses (in fact the urine keeps insects at bay), and the killing or harming of cows by any Hindu is a grave offence. The cow is often referred to as mother of the gods, and each part of its body is significant: its horns symbolize the gods, its face the sun and moon, its shoulders Agni (god of fire) and its legs the Himalayas.

CONTEXTS | Religion

Not only river confluences are auspicious: at Kanniyakumari, the southern tip of India, the waters of the Indian Ocean, the Bay of Bengal and the Arabian sea are thought to merge. Pilgrimages here are often combined with visits to the great temples of **Tamil Nadu**, where Shaivite and Vaishnavite saints established cults, and India's largest temples were constructed. Madurai, Thanjavur, Chidambaram and Srirangam are major pilgrimage centres, representing the pinnacle of the architectural development that began at Mamallapuram. Their festivals often involve the tugging of deities on vast wooden chariots through the streets, a practice most vigorously played out at **Puri**, in Orissa, when Lord Jagannath is taken from the temple during *Rath Yatra* for a foray through the town.

As well as specific temples sacred to particular gods – Brahma in **Pushkar**, Kali at **Calcutta**, or Shiva at the twelve *jyotrilinga* – historical sites, such as the caves of **Ellora**, and the former Vijayanagar capital at **Hampi**, remain magnets for pilgrims. More than a common ideology, it is this sacred geography, entwined with popular mythology, that unites hundreds of millions of Hindus, who have also been brought together in nationalistic struggles, particularly in response to Christian missionaries and Muslim and British domination.

Islam

Indian society may be dominated by Hindus, but **Muslims** – some ten percent of the population – form a significant presence in almost every town, city and village. The belief in only one god, Allah, the condemnation of idol worship, and the observance of their own strict dietary laws and specific festivals set Muslims apart from their Hindu neighbours, with whom they have coexisted for centuries. Such differences have often led to communal fighting, most notably during Partition, and in 1993 riots all over north India followed the destruction by Hindus of the Babri Masjid mosque in Ayodhya.

Islam, "submission to God", was founded by **Mohammed** (570–632 AD), regarded as the last in a succession of prophets, who transmitted God's final and perfected revelation to mankind through the writings of the divinely revealed "recitation", the **Koran** (Qur'an). This, the authoritative scripture of Islam, contains the basis of Islamic belief: that there is one god, Allah (though he is attributed with 99 names), and his prophet is Mohammed.

The true beginning of Islam is dated at 622 AD, when Mohammed and his followers, exiled from Mecca, made the *hijra*, or migration, north to Yathrib, later known as Medina, "City of the Prophet". The *hijra* marks the start of the Islamic lunar calendar: the Gregorian year 2000 was for Muslims 1421 AH (*Anno Hijra*).

From Medina, Mohammed ordered raids on caravans heading for Mecca, and led his community in battles against the Meccans, inspired by *jihad*, or "striving" on behalf of God and Islam. This concept of holy war was the driving force behind the incredible expansion of Islam – by 713 Muslims had settled as far west as Spain, and on the banks of the Indus in the east. When **Mecca** was peacefully surrendered to Mohammed in 630, he cleared the sacred shrine, the Ka'ba, of idols, and proclaimed it the pilgrimage centre of Islam.

Mohammed was succeeded as leader of the *umma*, the Islamic community, by Abu Bakr, the prophet's representative, or caliph, the first in a line of caliphs who led the orthodox community until the eleventh century AD. However, a schism soon emerged when the third caliph, Uthman, was assassinated by followers of Ali, Mohammed's son-in-law, in 656 AD. This new sect, calling them-selves **Shi'as**, "partisans" of Ali, looked to Ali and his successors, infallible imams, as leaders of the *umma* until 878 AD, and thereafter replaced their reli-gious authority with a body of scholars, the *ulema*.

By the second century after the *hijra* (ninth century AD), orthodox, or **Sunni**, Islam had assumed the form in which it endures today. A collection of traditions about the prophet, **Hadith**, became the source for ascertaining the **Sunna**, customs, of Mohammed. From the Koran and the Sunna, seven major **items of belief** were laid down: the belief in God, in angels as his messengers, in prophets (including Jesus and Moses), in the Koran, in the doctrine of predestination by God, in the Day of Judgement, and in the bod-ily resurrection of all people on this day. Religious practice was also stan-dardized under the Muslim law, **Sharia**, in the **Five Pillars of Islam**. The first "pillar" is the confession of faith, *shahada*, that "There is no god but God, and Mohammed is his messenger". The other four are prayer (*salat*) five times daily, almsgiving (*zakat*), fasting (*saum*), especially during the month of Ramadan, and, if possible, pilgrimage (*haj*) to Mecca, the ultimate goal of every practising Muslim.

The first Muslims to settle in India were traders who arrived on the south coast in the seventh century, probably in search of timber for shipbuilding. Later, in 711, Muslims entered Sind, in the northwest, to take action against Hindu pirates, and dislodged the Hindu government. Their presence, however, was short-lived. Much more significant was the invasion of north India under **Mahmud of Ghazni**, who rampaged through the Punjab in search of temple treasures, and in the spirit of *jihad*, engaged in a war against infidels and idol-aters. More Turkish raids followed in the twelfth century, resulting in the col-onization of India and the provision of a homeland for refugees pushed out of Persia by the Mongols. The Turks set themselves up in Delhi as **sultans**, the forerunners of the **Moghuls** (see p.1484).

Many Muslims who settled in India intermarried with Hindus, Buddhists and Jains, and the community spread. A further factor in its growth was missionary activity by **Sufis**, who emphasized abstinence and self-denial in service to God, and stressed the attainment of inner knowledge of God through meditation and mystical experience. In India, Sufi teachings spread among Shaivites and Vaishnavites, who shared their passion for personal closeness to God. Their use of music (particularly *qawwali* singing) and dance, shunned by orthodox Muslims, appealed to Hindus, for whom kirtan (singing) played an important role in religious practice. One *qawwali*, relating the life of the Sufi saint Waris Ali Shah, draws parallels between his early life and the childhood of Krishna – an outrage for orthodox Muslims, but attractive to Hindus, who still flock to his shrine in Deva Sharief near Lucknow. Similar shrines, or *dargars*, all over India bridge the gap between Islam and Hinduism.

Muslims are enjoined to pray five times daily, following a routine of utter-ances and positions. They may do this at home or in a **mosque** – always full at noon on Friday, for communal prayer. (Only the Druze, an esoteric sect based in Mumbai, hold communal prayers on Thursdays.) Characterized by bulbous domes and high minarets, from which a *muezzin* calls the faithful to prayer, mosques always contain a mihrab, or niche indicating the direction of prayer (to Mecca), a *mimbar* or pulpit, from which the Friday sermon is read, a source of water for ablutions, and a balcony for women. Firm reminders of Muslim dominance, mosques all over India display a bold linear grandeur quite different to the delicacy of Hindu temples. India's largest mosque is the Jami Masjid ("Friday Mosque") in **Delhi**, but magnificent structures, including tombs, schools and substantial remains of cities are scattered throughout north India and the Deccan, with especially outstanding examples in Hyderabad, Jaunpur, Agra and Fatehpur Sikri.

Muslim women

The position of **women** in Islam is a subject of great debate. It's customary for women to be veiled, though in larger cities many women don't cover their heads, and in strictly orthodox communities most wear a *burkha*, usually black, that covers them from head to toe. Like other Indian women, Muslim women take second place to men in public, but in the home, where they are often shielded from men's eyes in an inner courtyard, they wield great influence. In theory, education is equally available to boys and girls, but girls tend to forgo learning soon after sixteen, encouraged instead to assume the traditional role of wife and mother. Contrary to popular belief, polygamy is not widespread; while it does occur, and Mohammed himself had several wives, many Muslims prefer monogamy, and several sects actually stress it as a duty. In marriage, women receive a dowry (Hindu women must provide one) as financial security.

Buddhism

For several centuries, **Buddhism** dominated India, with adherents in almost every part of the subcontinent. However, having reached its height in the fifth century AD, it was all but eclipsed by the time of the Muslim conquest. Today Buddhists are a tiny fraction of the population, but superb monuments such as the caves of Ajanta and Ellora in Maharashtra, and the remarkable stupas of Sanchi in Madhya Pradesh, are fine reminders of this once flourishing culture. Outside the numerous Tibetan refugee camps, only Ladakh and Sikkim now preserve a significant Buddhist presence.

The founder of Buddhism, **Siddhartha Gautama**, known as the **Buddha**, "the awakened one", was born into a wealthy *kshatrya* family in Lumbini, north of the Gangetic plain in present-day Nepal, around 566 BC. Brought up in luxury as a prince and a Hindu, he married at an early age, and renounced family life when he was thirty. Unsatisfied with the explanations of worldly suffering proposed by Hindu gurus, and convinced that asceticism did not lead to spiritual realization, Siddhartha spent years in meditation, wandering through the ancient kingdom, or *janapada*, of Magadha. His enlightenment (*bodhi*) is said to have taken place under a *bodhi* tree in **Bodhgaya** (Bihar), after a night of contemplation during which he resisted the worldly temptations set before him by the demon, Mara. Soon afterwards he gave his first sermon in **Sarnath**, now a major pilgrimage centre. For the rest of his life he taught, expounding **Dharma**, the true nature of the world, human life and spiritual attainment. Before his death (c.486 BC) in Kushinagara (UP), he had established the **Sangha**, a community of monks and nuns, who continued his teachings.

Although frequently categorized as a religion, many scholars and practitioners understand Buddhism to be the science of mind. Buddhism has no god in the monotheistic sense; the deities of Tibetan Buddhism and the Buddha statues in temples are not there for worship as such – but rather as symbols to aid and deepen spiritual awareness. The Buddha's view of life incorporated the Hindu concepts of *samsara* and karma, but remodelled the ultimate goal of religion, calling it **nirvana**, "no wind". Indefinable in worldly terms, since it is by nature free from conditioning, nirvana represents a clarity of mind, pure understanding and unimaginable bliss. Its attainment signals an end to rebirth, but no communion of a "soul" with God; neither has independent existence. The most important concept outlined by the Buddha was that all things are subject to the inevitability of **impermanence**. There is no independent inherent self due to the interconnectedness of all things, and our egos are the biggest obstacles on the road to enlightenment.

Practice

Disregarding caste and priestly dominance in ritual, the Buddha formulated a teaching open to all. His followers took refuge in the three jewels: Buddha, Dharma, and Sangha. The teachings became known as **Theravada**, or "Doctrine of the Elders". By the first century BC the **Tripitaka**, or "Three Baskets" (a Pali canon in three sections), had set out the basis for early Buddhist practice, proposing *dana*, selfless giving, and *sila*, precepts which aim at avoiding harm to oneself and others, as the most important guidelines for all Buddhists, and the essential code of practice for the lay community.

Carried out with good intentions, *sila* and *dana* maximize the acquisition of good karma, and minimize material attachment, thus making the individual open to the more religiously oriented teachings, the **Four Noble Truths**. The first of these states that all is suffering (*dukkha*), not because every action is necessarily unpleasurable, but because nothing in the phenomenal world is permanent or reliable. The second truth states that *dukkha* arises through attachment, the third refers to nirvana, the cessation of suffering, and the fourth details the path to nirvana. Known as the **Eightfold Path** – right understanding, thought, speech, action, livelihood, effort, mindfulness and concentration – it aims at reducing attachment and ego and increasing awareness, until all four truths are thoroughly comprehended, and nirvana is achieved. Even this should not be clinged to – those who experience it are advised by the Buddha to use their understanding to help others to achieve realization.

The Sanskrit word **bhavana**, referred to in the West as **meditation**, translates literally as "bringing into being". Traditionally meditation is divided into two categories: **Samatha**, or calm, which stills and controls the mind, and **Vipassana**, or insight, during which thought processes and the noble truths are investigated, leading ultimately to a knowledge of reality. Both methods are taught in Buddhist centres across India.

At first, Buddhist iconography represented the Buddha by symbols such as a footprint, *bodhi* tree, parasol or vase. These can be seen on stupas (domed monuments containing relics of the Buddha) built throughout India from the time of the Buddhist emperor Ashoka (see p.1476), and in ancient Buddhist caves, which served as meditation retreats and *viharas* (monasteries). The finest are at **Ellora** and **Ajanta** (see p.814); like the remarkable stupas at **Sanchi**, they incorporate later designs which depict the Buddha in human form, standing and preaching or sitting in meditation, distinguished by characteristic marks, and indicating his teaching by hand gestures, or *mudras*.

This artistic development coincided with an increase in the devotional side of Buddhism, and a recognition of **bodhisattvas** – those bound for enlightenment who delayed self-absorption in nirvana to become teachers, spurred by selfless compassion and altruism.

The importance of the *bodhisattva* ideal grew as a new school, the **Mahayana**, or "Great Vehicle", emerged. By the twelfth century it had become fully established and, somewhat disparagingly, renamed the old Theravada school "Hinayana" (Lesser Vehicle). Mahayanists proposed emptiness, *sunyata*, as the fundamental nature of all things, taking to extremes the belief that nothing has independent existence. The **wisdom** necessary to understand *sunyata*, and the **skilful means** required to put wisdom into action in daily life and teaching, and interpret emptiness in a positive sense, became the most important qualities of Mahayana Buddhism. Before long *bodhisattvas* were joined in both scripture and art by female consorts who embodied wisdom.

Theravada Buddhism survives today in Sri Lanka, Myanmar, Thailand, Laos and Cambodia. Mahayana Buddhism spread from India to Nepal and Tibet and from there to China, Korea and ultimately Japan. In many places further evolution saw the adoption of magical methods, esoteric teachings, and the full use of sensory experience to bring about spiritual transformation, resulting in a separate school known as **Vajrayana** based on texts called *tantras*. Vajrayana encourages meditation on *mandalas* (symbolic diagrams representing the cosmos and internal spiritual attainment), sexual imagery, and sometimes sexual practice, as a means of raising energies and awareness for spiritual goals.

Tibetan Buddhism

Buddhism was introduced to **Tibet** in the seventh century, and integrated to a certain extent with the indigenous **Bon** cult, before emerging as a faith considered to incorporate all three vehicles – Hinayana, Mahayana and Vajrayana. Practised largely in Ladakh, along with parts of Himachal Pradesh and Sikkim, Tibetan Buddhism recognizes a historical Buddha, known as Sakyamuni, alongside previous Buddhas and a host of *bodhisattvas* and protector deities. These "gods" are not worshipped as such, rather they represent various emotions or states of being. The various **pujas** (ceremonies) are not so much prayers as ways of confronting or manifesting these states. For instance, to develop the quality of compassion in one's own life one may meditate and make offerings to Chenrezig, (Avalokitesvara in Sanskrit), the Buddha of compassion, or to Tara, the equivalent female embodiment. Many pujas involve elaborate rituals, and incorporate music and dance. There is a heavy emphasis on teachers, lamas (similar to gurus), and reincarnated teachers, known as *tulkus*. The **Dalai Lama**, the head of Tibetan Buddhism, is the fourteenth in a succession of incarnate *bodhisattvas*, the representative of Avalokitesvara, and the leader of the exiled Tibetan community whose headquarters are in Dharamsala (HP). With over 100,000 Tibetan **refugees** now living in India, including the Dalai Lama and Tibetan government in exile, Tibetan Buddhism is probably the most accessible and flourishing form of Buddhism in India, and there are numerous opportunities for study (see Basics, p.75).

For Buddhist monks and nuns, and some members of the lay community, meditation is an integral part of religious life. Most lay Buddhists concentrate on *dana* and *sila*, and on auspicious days, such as *Vesak* (marking the Buddha's birth, enlightenment and death), make **pilgrimages** to **Bodhgaya**, **Sarnath**, **Lumbini** and **Kushinagar**. After laying offerings before Buddha statues, devotees gather in silent meditation, or join in chants taken from early Buddhist texts. *Uposathas*, full-moon days, are marked by continual chanting through the night when temples are lit by glimmering butter lamps, often set afloat on lotus ponds, among the flowers that represent the essential beauty and purity to be found in each person in the thick of the confusing "mud" of daily life.

Among Tibetan communities, devotees hang prayer flags, turn prayer wheels, and set stones carved with mantras (religious verses) in rivers, thus sending the word of the Buddha with wind and water to all corners of the earth. Prayers and chanting are often accompanied by horns, drums and cymbals.

On January 5, 2000, 14-year-old **Orgyen Trinley Dorji**, the seventeenth **Gyalwa Karmapa**, finally reached Dharamsala after an exhausting journey across the Himalayas in a well-planned escape from under the noses of his Chinese minders. Joy within the Tibetan community was widespread but not quite universal. While the Dalai Lama had given his blessing to the choice of Orgyen Trinley, chosen as the reincarnation by the influential regent Tai Situpa Rimpoche, the main protagonists, led by a senior abbot of Rumtek monastery in Sikkim, favour their own candidate, Thasey Dorje. To compound matters, a third contender, Dawa Zangpo Dorjee Sherpa, has twice tried to take Rumtek by force, claiming that he is the real Karmapa. Much of the controversy is fuelled by the monastery's great wealth and the vast influence of the office of the Karmapa, who is considered third in the Tibetan hierarchy after the Dalai and Panchen lamas.

His detractors claim that Orgyen Trinley Dorji, born in Tibet and officially enthroned in Tsurphu in 1992, is actually Chinese and that his escape and Tai Situpa's collusion were not without Chinese blessing. Certainly, the controversy has proved divisive for the Tibetan and Himalayan Buddhist communities, a factor which may have played into the hands of the Chinese. But by all indications his choice was a popular one, and was blessed by the Tibetan government in exile. Orgyen Trinley is still confined to a monastery near Dharamsala, well guarded by Tibetan and Indian security. The Indian government has not yet allowed him to enter Sikkim, partly because the state is still a bone of contention between India and China. Orgyen Trinley Dorji has now been given refugee status, which many see as the first move towards his official entry into Sikkim and his enthronement in Rumtek. His family, in the meantime, remains under guard in Tibet.

Jainism

Though the **Jain** population in India is relatively small – accounting for less than one percent of the population – it has been tremendously influential for at least 2500 years. A large proportion of Jains live in Gujarat, and all over India they are commonly occupied as merchants and traders. Similarities to Hindu worship, and a shared respect for nature and nonviolence, have contributed to the decline of the Jain community through conversion to Hinduism, but there is no antagonism between the two sects.

Focused on the practice of **ahimsa** (nonviolence), Jains follow a rigorous discipline to avoid harm to all **jivas**, or "souls", which exist in humans, animals, plants, water, fire, earth and air. They assert that every *jiva* is pure, omniscient, and capable of achieving liberation, or *moksha*, from existence in this universe. However, *jivas* are obscured by **karma**, a form of subtle matter that clings to the soul, is born of action, and binds the *jiva* to physical existence. For the most orthodox Jain, the only way to dissociate karma from the *jiva*, and thereby escape the wheel of death and rebirth, is to follow the path of asceticism and meditation, rejecting passion, wrong view, attachment, carelessness and impure action.

The Jain doctrine is based upon the teachings of **Mahavira**, or "Great Hero", the last in a succession of 24 **tirthankaras** ("crossing-makers") said to appear on earth every 300 million years. Mahavira (c.599–527 BC) was born as Vardhamana Jnatrputra into a *kshatrya* family near modern Patna, in northeast India. Like the Buddha, Mahavira rejected family life at the age of thirty, and spent years wandering as an ascetic, renouncing all possessions in an attempt to conquer attachment to worldly values. Firmly opposed to sacrificial rites and caste distinctions, after gaining complete understanding and detachment, he began teaching others, not about Vedic gods and divine heroes, but about the true nature of the world, and the means required for release, *moksha*, from an endless cycle of rebirth.

His teachings were written down in the first millennium BC, and Jainism prospered throughout India, under the patronage of kings such as Chandragupta Maurya (third century BC). Not long after, there was a schism, in part based on linguistic and geographical divisions, but mostly due to differences in monastic practice. On the one hand the **Digambaras** ("sky-clad") believed that nudity was an essential part of world renunciation, and that women are incapable of achieving liberation from worldly existence. The ("white-clad") **Svetambaras**, however, disregarded the extremes of nudity, incorporated nuns into monastic communities, and even acknowledged a female *tirthankara*. Today the two sects worship at different temples, but the number of naked Digambaras is minimal. Many Svetambara monks and nuns wear white masks to avoid breathing in insects, and carry a "fly-whisk", sometimes used to brush their path; none will use public transport, and they often spend days or weeks walking barefoot to a pilgrimage site.

Practising Jain householders vow to avoid injury, falsehood, theft (extended to fair trade), infidelity and worldly attachment. Jain **temples** are wonderfully ornate, with pillars, brackets and spires carved by *silavats* into voluptuous maidens, musicians, saints, and even Hindu deities; the *swastika* symbol commonly set into the marble floors is central to Jainism, representing the four states of rebirth as gods, humans, "hell beings", or animals and plants. Worship in temples consists of prayer and *puja* before images of the *tirthankaras*; the devotee circumambulates the image, chants sacred verses and makes offerings of flowers, sandalwood paste, rice, sweets and incense. It's common to fast four times a month on *parvan* (holy) days, the eighth and fourteenth days of the moon's waxing and waning periods. While reducing attachment to the body, this emulates the fast to death (while in meditation), or *sallekhana*, accepted by Jain mendicants as a final rejection of attachment, and a relatively harmless way to end worldly life.

To enter a monastic community, lay Jains must pass through eleven *pratimas*, starting with right views, the profession of vows, fasting and continence, and culminating in renunciation of family life. Once a monk or nun, a Jain aims to clarify understanding through meditational practices, hoping to extinguish passions and sever the ties of karma and attachment, entering fourteen spiritual stages, *gunasthanas*, to emerge as a fully enlightened, omniscient being. Whether pursuing a monastic or lay lifestyle, however, Jains recognize the rarity of enlightenment, and religious practice is, for the most part, aimed at achieving a state of rebirth more conducive to spiritual attainment.

Pilgrimage sites are known as **tirthas**, but this does not refer to the literal meaning of "river crossing", sacred to Hindus because of the purificatory nature of water. At one of the foremost Svetambara *tirthas*, **Shatrunjaya** in Gujarat, over nine hundred temples crown a single hill, said to have been visited by the first *tirthankara*, Rishabha, and believed to be the place where Rama, Sita and the Pandava brothers (incorporated into Jain tradition) gained deliverance. An important Digambara *tirtha* is **Shravan Belgola** in Karnataka, where a seventeen-metre-high image of Bahubali (recognized as the first human to attain liberation), at the summit of a hill, is anointed in the huge *abhisheka* festival every twelve years.

In an incredibly complicated process of philosophical analysis known as **Anekanatavada** (many-sidedness), Jainism approaches all questions of existence, permanence, and change from seven different viewpoints, maintaining that things can be looked at in an infinite number of valid ways. Thus it claims to remove the intellectual basis for violence, avoiding the potentially damaging result of holding a one-sided view. In this respect Jainism accepts other religious philosophies, and it has adopted, with a little reinterpretation, several Hindu festivals and practices.

Sikhism

Sikhism, India's youngest religion, remains dominant in the Punjab, while its adherents have spread throughout northern India, and several communities have grown up in Britain, America and Canada.

Guru Nanak (1469–1539) was the movement's founder. Born into an orthodox Hindu *kshatrya* family in Talwandi, a small village west of Lahore (in present-day Pakistan), he was among many sixteenth-century poet-philosophers, sometimes referred to as *sants*, who formed emotional cults, drawing elements from both Hinduism and Islam. Nanak declared "God is neither Hindu nor Muslim and the path which I follow is God's"; he regarded God as **Sat**, or truth, who makes himself known through gurus. Though he condemned ancestor worship, astrology, caste distinction, sex discrimination, auspicious days, and the rituals of brahmins, Nanak did not attack Islam or Hinduism – he simply regarded the many deities as names for one supreme God, and encouraged his followers to shift religious emphasis from ritual to meditation.

In common with Hindus, Nanak believed in a cyclic process of death and rebirth (*samsara*), but he asserted that liberation (*moksha*) was attainable in this life by all women and men regardless of caste, and religious practice can and should be integrated into everyday practical living. He contested that all people are characterized by *humai*, a sense of self-reliance that obscures an understanding of dependence on God, encourages attachment to temporal values (*maya*), and consequently results in successive rebirths. For Sikhs, the only way to achieve release from human existence is to conquer *humai*, and become centred on God (*gurmukh*). God is seen as both absolute (*nirgun*) and personal (*sargun*), and besides being the creator of all things, is truth, beauty and eternal goodness. In their embodiment of *sargun*, the Sikh gurus are the only beings who have realized the ultimate truth, and as such, provide essential guidance to their disciples.

Guru Nanak was succeeded by a disciple, Lehna, known as **Guru Angad** ("limb"), who continued to lead the community of Sikhs ("disciples"), the **Sikh Panth**, and wrote his own and Nanak's hymns in a new script, **Gurumukhi**, which is today the script of written Punjabi.

After Guru Angad's death in 1552, eight successive gurus acted as leaders for the Sikh Panth, each introducing new elements into the faith and asserting it as a separate and powerful religious movement. Guru Ram Das (1552–74) founded the sacred city of **Amritsar**; his successor, Guru Arjan Dev, compiled the gurus' hymns in a book called the **Adi Granth**, and built the Golden Temple to house it; Arjan Dev became Sikhism's first martyr when he was executed at the hands of Jahangir. Throughout their history, the Sikhs have had to battle to protect their faith and their people, especially against the Moghuls; Guru Teg Bahadur was beheaded by Aurangzeb in 1675, an event that heralded the era of his son and successor, **Guru Gobind Singh**, who was to revolutionize the entire movement.

Gobind Singh, the last leader, was largely responsible for moulding the community as it exists today. In 1699, he founded the brotherhood of the **Khalsa** by baptizing five disciples using a sword dipped in *amrit* (the nectar of immortality). The aims of the Khalsa, as defined by Guru Gobind Singh, are to assist the poor and fight oppression, to have faith in one god and abandon superstition and dogma, to worship God, and to protect the faith with steel. The Khalsa requires members to renounce tobacco, halal meat and sexual relations with Muslims, and to adopt the **five Ks**: *kesh* (unshorn hair), *kangha* (comb), *kirpan* (sword), *kara* (steel wristlet) and *kachch* (short trousers). This code, assumed at initiation, together with the replacement of caste names with Singh ("lion") for men and Kaur ("princess") for women, and the wearing of turbans by men, created a distinct cultural identity.

Guru Gobind Singh also compiled a standardized version of the *Adi Granth*, which contains the hymns of the first nine gurus as well as poems written by Hindus and Muslims, and installed it as his successor, naming it **Guru Granth Sahib**. This became the Sikh's spiritual guide, while political authority rested with the Khalsa, or *sangat*.

Demands for a separate Sikh state – **Khalistan** – and fighting in the eighteenth century, and later after Independence, have burdened Sikhs with a reputation as military activists, but Sikhs regard their religion as one devoted to egalitarianism, democracy and social awareness. Though to die fighting for the cause of religious freedom is considered to lead to liberation, the use of force is officially sanctioned only when other methods have failed. Due to their martial traditions and emphasis on valour, Sikhs continue to provide an essential element of the Indian army.

Practice

The main duties of a Sikh are *nam japna*, *kirt karni*, and *vand chakna*; keeping God's name in mind, earning honest means, and giving to charity. Serving the community (*seva*) is a display of obedience to God, and the ideal life is uncontaminated by the **five evil impulses**: lust, covetousness, attachment, anger and pride.

Sikh **worship** takes place in a **gurudwara** ("door to the guru") or in the home, providing a copy of the *Adi Granth* is present. There are no priests, and no fixed time for worship, but congregations often meet in the mornings and evenings, and always on the eleventh day (*ekadashi*) of each lunar month, and on the first day of the year (*sangrand*). During **Kirtan**, or hymn singing, a feature of every Sikh service, verses from the *Adi Granth* or *Janam Sakhis* (stories of Guru Nanak's life), are sung to rhythmic clapping. The communal meal, *langar*, following prayers and singing, reinforces the practice laid down by Guru Nanak that openly flaunted caste and religious differences. The egalitarian nature of Sikhism is nowhere better exemplified than in the **Golden Temple** in Amritsar, the holiest of all Sikh shrines. The four doors are open to the four cardinal directions, welcoming both devotees and visitors from other faiths.

Gurudwaras – often schools, clinics or hostels as well as houses of prayer – are generally modelled on the Moghul style of Shah Jahan, considered a congenial blend of Hindu and Muslim architecture; usually whitewashed, and surmounted by a dome, they are always distinguishable by the *nishan sahib*, a yellow flag introduced by Guru Hargobind (1606–44). As in Islam, God is never depicted in pictorial form. Instead, the representative symbol Il Oankar is etched into a canopy that shades the *Adi Granth*, which always stands in the main prayer room. In some *gurudwaras* a picture of a guru is hung close to the *Adi Granth*, but it's often difficult to distinguish between the different teachers:

artistically they are depicted as almost identical, a tradition that unites the ten gurus as vehicles for God's words, or *mahalas*, and not divine beings.

Important occasions for Sikhs, in addition to naming of children, weddings and funerals, are **Gurpurbs**, anniversaries of the birth and death of the ten gurus, when the *Adi Granth* is read continuously from beginning to end.

Zoroastrianism

Of all India's religious communities, Western visitors are least likely to come across – or recognize – **Zoroastrians**, who have no distinctive dress, and few houses of worship. Most live in Mumbai, where they are known as **Parsis** (Persians) and are active in business, education, and politics. Zoroastrian numbers (roughly 90,000) are rapidly dwindling, due to a falling birth rate and absorption into wider communities.

The religion's founder, **Zarathustra** (Zoroaster), lived in Iran around the sixth or seventh century BC, and was the first religious prophet to expound a dualistic philosophy, based on the opposing powers of good and evil. For him, the absolute, wholly good and wise God, **Ahura Mazda**, together with his holy spirit and six emanations present in earth, water, the sky, animals, plants and fire, is constantly at odds with an evil power, **Angra Mainyu**, who is aided by **daevas**, or evil spirits.

Mankind, whose task on earth is to further good, faces judgement after death, and depending on the proportion of good and bad words, thoughts and actions, will find a place in heaven, or suffer the torments of hell. Zarathustra looked forward to a day of judgement, when a saviour, **Saoshyant**, miraculously born of a seed of the prophet and a virgin maiden, will appear on earth, restoring Ahura Mazda's perfect realm and expelling all impure souls and spirits to hell.

The first Zoroastrians to enter India arrived on the Gujarati coast in the tenth century AD, soon after the Arabian conquest of Iran, and by the seventeenth century most had settled in Bombay. Zoroastrian practice is based on the responsibility of every man and woman to choose between good and evil, and to respect God's creations. Five daily prayers, usually hymns (*gathas*), uttered by Zarathustra and standardized in the **Avesta**, the main Zoroastrian text, are said in the home or in a temple, before a fire, which symbolizes the realm of truth, righteousness and order. For this reason, Zoroastrians are often, incorrectly, called "fire-worshippers".

Members of other faiths may not enter Zoroastrian temples, but one custom that is evident to outsiders is the method of disposing of the dead. A body is laid on a high open rooftop (or isolated hill) known as *dakhma* (often referred to as a "tower of silence"), for the flesh to be eaten by vultures, and the bones cleansed by sun and wind. Recently, some Zoroastrians, by necessity, have adopted more common methods of cremation or burial; in order not to bring impurity to fire or earth, they only use electric crematoria, and shroud coffins in concrete before laying them in the ground.

No Ruz, or "New Day", held in mid-March, celebrating the creation of fire and the ultimate triumph of good over evil, is the most popular Zoroastrian festival; the oldest sacred fire in India, in **Udwada**, just north of Daman in south Gujarat, is an important pilgrimage site.

Christianity

For many, the diminutive figure of Mother Teresa was the quintessential icon of **Christianity** in India, but foreign nuns, however revered, are far from the only Christians in the country. In total, Christians are reckoned to number around two million people, the majority among *adivasi* (tribal) and *dalit* (untouchable) peoples.

Early history

The **Apostle Thomas** is said to have arrived in Kerala in 54 AD to convert itinerant Jewish traders living in the flourishing port of Muziris, following the death of Jesus. There are many tales of miracles by "Mar Thoma", as he is known in Malayalam. One legend tells how he approached a group of brahmins from Palur (now Malabar) who were trying to appease the gods by throwing water into the air. If the gods had accepted the offerings, the saint said, the droplets would have remained suspended. Throwing water in the air himself, it miraculously hung above him, leading most of the brahmins to convert to Christianity. The southern tradition holds that Thomas was martyred on December 21, 72 AD at Mylapore in **Madras** (the name comes from the Syriac *madrasa*, meaning "monastery"). The tomb has since become a major place of pilgrimage, and in recognition of this, the Portuguese built the gothic **San Thome Cathedral** on the site in the late nineteenth century. By oral tradition, the Church of San Thome is the oldest Christian denomination in the world, but documentary evidence of Christian activity in the subcontinent can only be traced to the sixth century, when immigrant Syrian communities were granted settlement rights by royal charter.

Arrival of the Europeans

From the sixteenth century onwards, the history of the Church in India is linked to the spread of foreign Christians across the subcontinent. In 1552, St Francis Xavier arrived in the Portuguese trading colony of **Goa** to establish missions to reach out to the Hindu "untouchables"; his tomb and alleged relics are retained in the Basilica of Bom Jesus in Old Goa to this day. In 1559, at the behest of the Portuguese king, the Inquisition arrived in Goa. Jesuit missionaries carried out a bloody and brutal campaign to "cleanse" the small colony of Hindu and Muslim religious practice. Early British incomers took the attitude that the subcontinent was a heathen and polytheistic civilization waiting to be proselytized. Later, they were less zealous in their conversion efforts, being content to provide social welfare and build very English-looking churches in their own cantonments.

The proximity of the entry-port at Calcutta to the **tribal regions** of the northeastern hill states drew the attention of Protestant missionaries during the Raj, whose fervent evangelism covered virtually all of Mizoram Nagaland, and much of Meghalaya. Muslim immigrants from Bangladesh have changed the balance in bordering areas, while other tribal districts, in Madhya Pradesh, Bihar, Karnataka and Gujarat in particular, have drawn both Catholic and Protestant missionaries. As Christianity is intended to be free of caste stigmas, it can be attractive to those seeking social advancement.

In early 1999, Christian communities in some areas, notably in Gujarat and Orissa, were subject to forced "reconversions" and attacks. These were allegedly carried out by Hindu extremists incensed by proselytizing evangelists targeting low-caste Hindus. Following an international outcry, the government said that they would be taking measures to protect the rights of minority religions – including Hindus in Christian areas.

The strong sense of regional history and culture has distinctly influenced the appearance of **Indian churches**. The St Thomas Christians of the south congregate in small white churches decorated with colourful pictures and statues of figures from the New Testament. The great twin-steepled churches of Goa and Chennai (Madras) are very different, with their heavy gold interiors and candlelit shrines to the Virgin Mary. Other churches are more syncretistic: **St John's** in south Delhi has an Anglican nave, a Hindu *chhapra* (tower) and monastic cloisters spanning out from each side. In the Himalayan part of Bengal, the influence of Buddhism is very strong. Beautiful wooden chapels are painted with scenes from the life of Christ using Buddhist symbols and Nepali-looking characters.

The Hindu influence

The **Hindu influence** on Christianity is marked too. Christian festivals in Tamil Nadu are highly structured, along caste lines, and Christians there never eat beef or pork, which are considered polluting. By contrast, Christians in Goa eat both beef and pork as a feature of their Portuguese heritage. In many churches you can see devotees offering the Hindu *arati* (a plate of coconut, sweets and rice), and women wearing *tilak* dots on their foreheads. In the same way that Hindus and Muslims consider pilgrimage to be an integral part of life's journey, Indian Christians have numerous devotional sites, including St Jude's Shrine in **Jhansi** and the Temple of Mother Mary in **Mathura**. On anniversaries of the death of a loved one, Christians carry plates of food to the graves, in much the same manner as Hindus. This sharing of traditions works both ways however. At Christmas you can't fail to notice the brightly coloured paper stars and small Nativity scenes glowing and flashing outside schools, houses, shops and churches throughout India.

Indian women

The Constitution of India adopted shortly after Independence, granted women the vote, guaranteed equality between the sexes and called on its citizens to "renounce practices derogatory to the dignity of women". However, it took until the mid-1950s for Nehru to pass most of the laws defining the legal position of women in India and, half a century later, rates of income, literacy, health and life-expectancy among women still lag well behind those of men in the subcontinent. Moreover, violence against women, notably dowry-related crimes and rape, has shown a steady increase over the past couple of decades. Most recently, it has emerged that in states such as Kerala, renowned for its exemplary record in female education and health care, the rate of female abuse in the home environment is rising. It would appear that while gender equality and respect is becoming more acceptable in Indian society as a whole, women's empowerment in the household still has a long way to go.

While individual women have succeeded in almost every branch of Indian life, the enduring expectation that a woman should pass directly from her family into marriage means that the majority, particularly in rural India, remain dependent on others for their financial security. This not only allows them few options when confronted with domestic violence, but also contributes to the widespread perception of women as a financial burden, which is in turn exacerbated by the practice of dowry.

Efforts to improve the situation have consistently brought legislators and women's groups into conflict with traditional ideals of female behaviour. The picture is further complicated by the manifold differences in regional, religious and caste identity throughout the subcontinent. Many groups, from Muslims and Christians to the hundreds of culturally distinct tribal (*adivasi*) peoples across India, have some degree of cultural autonomy underpinned by the Constitution, and most regard their own version of the role of women as central to their group identity.

Pativrata: the ideal woman

The roots of much of the prejudice directed against women in contemporary India can be traced to writings attributed to the Hindu lawgiver, **Manu**, dated between 200 BC and 200 AD. He ascribed a subordinate status to women in relation to religion, property and marriage, and included various damning depictions of the female personality.

Contained in the *Manu-Smrti* texts were prescriptions on how both men and women should best fulfil their *dharma*, or duty. According to the concept of **stri-dharma**, a code of conduct specifically for women, a woman's chief responsibility was to serve and worship her husband like a god. In this way she would become a **pativrata**, a devoted wife completely immersed in her husband's being: "If her husband should be happy, if he is sad, she should also be sad, and if he is dead she should also die" (*Shudditattva*). However, this merging of identities did not extend to "bad" behaviour, which remained the exclusive preserve of men: "Though destitute of good qualities or seeking pleasure elsewhere, a husband must be constantly worshipped as a god" while "a wife's marital duty does not come to an end even if the husband were to sell or abandon her". (Manu). Fulfilment of *stri-dharma* was complicated by a number of other requirements, not least a variety of physical attributes which needed to be present, or absent, before a girl was considered fit for marriage. These included not having red hair, too much body hair or even a sallow complexion.

In addition, the ways in which a woman could lose her honour (and thus her status as a *pativrata*) were subject not only to her own behaviour, but also to that of men. If sexually abused, for example, a woman would be considered "spoiled goods" in terms of the feminine ideal. It would also be incumbent on her, as it often is in Indian courts today, to prove that she had not provoked the action in any way – no easy task when the laws defining a respectable woman were so stringent. Precedent for this appears in the hugely popular Hindu epic, the *Ramayana*, where Sita was required by her husband, Rama, to pass an ordeal by fire to prove she had maintained her chastity during her forced abduction by Rama's adversary, the multi-headed demon, Ravana. Sita is only one among many female goddesses and mythological figures who submitted to this injustice with good grace, and whose image sustains the ideal even today.

Ideals of feminine behaviour were further reinforced by **purdah** in its various forms. Originally prescribed by Islam, the practice involved the confinement of women within the family home or, in less extreme cases, behind a veil. This fitted with the prevailing attitude that women needed to be controlled, and also offered a convenient means of enhancing a family's status by demonstrating that it was able to support its dependent womenfolk. In this way it emphasized the image of woman as a financial burden while removing her freedom to be anything else.

Cultural cross-fertilization between Islam and Hinduism has meant that purdah is common to both religions today. It remains a controversial issue among women, with some refusing to wear clothes that imply a state of purdah, and others seeing it as a mark of cultural identity or as the only way of avoiding sexual harassment.

Dowry and marriage

Thanks to the practice of **dowry** (the transfer of wealth from the bride's family to that of the groom after betrothal), **marriage** in India is an institution with potential both for increasing a family's status and for weakening it financially. While the ancient texts dictated that a woman should leave her family upon her marriage and denied her the right to inherit property (from either her own or her husband's family), they did allow her to take a portion of her family's moveable wealth with her as a "gift". This provided the bride with an element of security, but it also meant her marriage was inextricably linked with the destiny of her family's resources, leading to the popular definition of a daughter as "another man's wealth". One way a family could compensate itself, of course, was to use her marriage as a means of increasing their status through an impressive match.

The advent of a bureaucracy, set up by the British but staffed largely by Indians, saw the entry of market forces into the equation and the beginnings of dowry in its present form. As the families of high-caste brides began to compete for a limited supply of husbands with prestigious positions in the new system, the families of bridegrooms were able to wait for the most lucrative dowry offer.

As with many other status-enhancing practices, the giving and taking of dowry spread down the caste system, even to those least capable of paying the high prices. Meanwhile, the shame attached to being an unmarried woman consolidated the bargaining power of the families of bridegrooms.

Dowry

Officially banned in 1961, **dowry** is increasingly seen as a social evil but continues to be almost universally practised. From its origins as a means of providing women with a share of their family wealth, the custom has come to imply the transfer from the bride's to the groom's family of anything from blankets and household appliances to cars, exotic holidays and huge bundles of cash. For a woman, the ignominy of remaining single is such that the families of brides will often struggle to meet demands even in the face of financial ruin. At the same time, the bargaining power of the bridegroom's family is strengthened to such an extent that their demands will often start again once the marriage has taken place.

The phenomenon of **"dowry deaths"** in which women are murdered, usually through being burned in a "kitchen fire" within the family home, has been directly linked to the increasing importance of dowry. Such deaths invariably follow protracted harassment of a woman by her husband and in-laws, with demands for further payments. However, the public shame attached to leaving one's husband after marriage, added to the fact that this would almost certainly jeopardize the marriage prospects of any unmarried sisters, means that many women choose, or are forced, to remain with their in-laws, even after death threats have been made.

A 1975 survey of independent newspaper reports on dowry deaths suggested that at least one dowry murder was committed each day in Delhi alone. By 1983, this figure had almost doubled, while official figures for 1988 and 1990 showed an increase in dowry deaths from 2209 to 4835 over those two years. These figures are almost certainly conservative: being a domestic crime, dowry death often goes unreported and the police are notoriously unwilling to investigate such cases. Among women who survive, many are afraid to testify for fear of reprisals from their families.

The relation of dowry to other crimes against women is now widely accepted. Pressure on women to bear a son can lead to harassment or rejection by in-laws, and female infanticide is still practised. Over the past decade or so, it has also emerged that amniocentesis is being widely used as a sex test by families wanting a boy, and by those fearful of the financial damage a girl child will incur. Its connection with dowry is made explicit in the advertising slogans of entrepreneurial doctors, whose advice to potential customers is "Better pay Rs50 now than Rs50,000 later". An indication of the extent to which this advice is heeded can be seen in the disproportionate number of female foetuses aborted in areas where amniocentesis tests are available.

Marriage

Around 95 percent of Indian **marriages** are arranged. While the role of rural women before marriage is largely that mapped out by traditional expectations, among the middle classes it is not uncommon for the potential couple to spend some time together and be given the chance to refuse a marriage partner. Urban middle-class women are also likely to have spent a considerable amount of time in **education** which, in the ubiquitous personal columns of national newspapers where the existence of eligible young men and women is advertised by their parents, is now as much a criterion for suitability as caste, and for this reason is increasingly seen as an investment.

Education is rarely likely to take precedence over marriage however, and women will often drop their studies once a suitable match has been found. Many women have little quarrel with this, and they themselves see education as a means of obtaining a wealthier, or more interesting husband.

The **roles** demanded of women after marriage tend to diminish differences in background, and the ideal of the *pativrata*, although lived out in and modified by vastly different worlds, begins to reassert itself. The expectation that a woman will prioritize her husband over herself, often passed from mother to daughter and enforced by mothers-in-law, still has a strong place in the popular imagination. The impact this has on a woman's health and wellbeing was seen as sufficiently detrimental for the government to launch a TV campaign during the 1990s. It showed women in a variety of traditional roles – feeding her son more than her daughter or plying a husband with food while existing on only dry *rotis* herself, for example – while a voice in the background told women to attend to their own needs as well.

More often than not, apparent differences in lifestyle between traditional and modern families hide underlying philosophies that are basically the same.

Widowhood and sati

Widowhood is problematic in a country that still considers marriage as the most important aspect of a woman's life. The loss of one's husband, especially while young, was traditionally seen as a calamity so great that it could only be explained by sins committed in a past life. All would be forgiven and great honour achieved, however, if a woman decided to throw herself on her husband's funeral pyre in an act of ritual self-immolation known as **sati**. The alternative was a life of atonement and perpetual humiliation.

Although to die when one's husband dies may no longer be seen as part of a wife's duty, the treatment many widows receive today is based on strictures dating from a time when it was. Even a relatively liberated wife will break her glass bangles (symbols of marriage) and throw the pieces, together with her marriage necklace, onto her husband's cremation pyre. Thereafter, her participation in many areas of social life, especially weddings, is abruptly curtailed (widows generally have to watch the marriage of their sons or daughters from the back of the hall, if they attend the ceremony at all). In stricter families, people will also avoid any physical contact with widows, including being served food by them.

Other **prohibitions** still widely practised by Hindu widows today include the wearing of any adornment (such as rings, the scarlet vermilion powder married women smear on their hair-partings, and *bindi* marks on the forehead), dyed clothing (white saris remain the most prevalent and visible symbol of widowhood), eating any foods other than those listed in the scriptures and even sleeping on a bed. Certain castes in parts of rural India further require women to have their head shaved, and to remove their sari blouse.

The extent to which women are still subjected to such treatment – despite modern laws requiring their families to support them – can be seen by the numbers of widows present in holy cities such as **Vrindavan** in UP (see p. 000). Here they seek refuge in almshouses and *ashrams* and live by begging. According to the 1981 census, out of 23 million widows in the country, between 20,000 and 60,000 were estimated to be destitute in **Varanasi** alone. The fact that many more (an estimated 80,000 of the 1981 census total) were under twenty years old partly explains the thriving prostitution business that often exists in the cities where widows go to beg.

A more recent phenomenon illustrating the ill-treatment of dependent widows was seen during the 2001 Kumbh Mela gathering at Allahabad, where millions of families came together to wash away the sins of previous lives. Many widows were "accidentally" separated from their children in the crowds; too scared or confused to remember their family name and address, they had to

CONTEXTS | Indian women

accept their fate and begin begging, or seek charitable assistance for a roof and food.

Faced with such a bleak future, many widows in the past chose to commit *sati*. It used to be commonly believed that an honourable death was their chief motive, but court records dating from 1829, when *"suttee"* was banned by the British, show that women offered a less humiliating alternative – a small amount of maintenance for example – could often be dissuaded. It is a telling fact that the Jain religion, which permits women to become nuns, has seen hardly any incidence of *sati*.

Though rare today, the custom still exerts a powerful hold over the imagination in India. The isolated burnings that have occurred in recent times have drawn crowds of thousands and the sites remain pilgrimage places long after the event. One family of leading industrialists, the Birlas, have paid for a temple to be built commemorating a *sati* at **Jhunjhunu** in Rajasthan (see p.192), and until it was banned in 1988, an annual fair at the site attracted up to 200,000 people.

The controversial *sati* of eighteen-year-old Roop Kanwar, who died in 1987 in the Rajasthani village of Deorala, is only the most widely publicized case in recent years. Thousands of supporters, including the chief minister of Rajasthan, opposed attempts to investigate the incident, and many interpreted measures to prevent the site from becoming a shrine as interference in freedom of religion and regional culture.

Divorce

All the major religions have laws governing **divorce**, while separate regulations exist regarding inter-faith marriages. Although accepted in law, there is still a lot of stigma attached to divorce. The traditional ideal that a wife should serve her husband no matter how adulterous or abusive he is, continues to inform harsher judgements of divorced women than divorced men, and many women have difficulty being accepted back into society.

The financial implications are also more serious for women. Although there is some form of public assistance for single mothers in most urban areas, many women do not know of its existence. Their families may be unwilling to take on the economic burden of a divorced daughter, feeling their obligations to her ended after they had arranged and paid for her marriage.

The presence of a divorced woman will invariably lower the status of the household and is also seen as a danger to the marriage prospects of other single women within the family. Divorced women are often expected to take on lowly household tasks and may not be treated as full family members.

Current movements

The 1990s were earmarked by the Indian government for a **"National Action Plan for the Girl Child"**, with the aim of improving education and ending discrimination against women. A scheme launched in 1997, on Mahatma Gandhi's birthday, targets those families least able to bear the financial burden of a female child, by paying Rs500 for the birth of every girl; further financial incentives are also given to help with her education.

The underlying causes of discrimination, however, continue to be tackled most effectively by projects initiated by women themselves. The diversity of such projects reflects the vast differences between the lives of women from different castes and classes; with a rough divide between grassroots movements benefiting women from the poorest communities, and efforts by educated urban women to challenge prejudice through research and campaigning. These groups amass under the unifying banner of the **Indian Women's Movement** (IWM).

Originally, **grassroots organizations** were begun by those disillusioned by the failure of post-Independence politics to improve the situation of women, or to follow the Gandhian ideals of equality that had formed such an important part of the nationalist movement prior to Independence. Two of the best-known are SEWA, or the Self-Employed Women's Association, and the Working Women's Forum (WWF). Both were set up in response to the fact that women are particularly open to abuse from the mainstream employment system; invariably paid less than men, women are usually the first to be laid off, giving them no alternative but the precarious life of self-employment. By providing women with small loans and a banking system that enables them to save money rather than have it appropriated by their families, these organizations give women a measure of independence and the freedom to develop and maintain small businesses. In enabling them to exert greater control over their family's resources, such schemes also benefit the family as a whole.

The success of these organizations encouraged their organizers to spread into other areas, such as family planning, literacy and personal skills development. Having allowed women to see themselves as something other than wives and mothers, such projects have indirectly led to the weakening of traditional tensions – the pressure to bear sons or meet demands for dowry, for example – that have forced women into conflict with each other within the family.

Of the campaigning groups set up by poor women themselves, **the Chipko movement**, in the Himalayan foothills, is perhaps the most well known. Initially set up in protest against the appropriation of their land by developers, the movement involves peaceful resistance in the form of sit-ins and of "hugging" the trees marked for felling. As with their opposition to the World Bank-funded Narmada Dam project (see p.1546), the focus of the Chipko movement and other rural campaigning groups is also to highlight local concern for the fate of the environment and natural resources. As the family members responsible for finding water, cooking fuel and animal fodder, it is women who are most closely concerned with these issues.

Other mass movements have been seen in the villages of Bihar, where private "armies", hired to protect the interests of landowners against claims from peasant farmers for fairer wages and more secure tenancies, have been opposed by groups of women. While these movements deal with issues of concern to the whole community, in each case it is women who have organized themselves to protest. In areas where protests have succeeded, further displays of solidarity are often seen, with neighbours intervening to prevent wife-beating and other injustices within the family.

Urban elite movements include protest groups that organize demonstrations over issues such as *sati,* and particularly dowry harassment, which is most prevalent among the middle classes as greater access to the consumer goods increases the expectations of the size and contents of the dowry gift. Achieving press coverage is an important part of the work of the movements, and it was groups such as the Delhi-based *Saheli* who were largely responsible for the *sati* of **Roop Kanwar** becoming a matter for national debate.

In the face of ineffectual laws and police indifference, women's groups are increasingly taking the debate onto the streets: turning to public shaming of those responsible for crimes against women, and demonstrating outside the houses of families where dowry deaths have occurred. Such confrontational tactics represent an important step forward for the IWM. They effectively force a confrontation between modern notions of basic human rights and traditional views of female behaviour that have, for many years, allowed neighbours and other family members to remain passive when they were aware of threats to women in their communities.

The major, long-running issue affecting all women's groups is the Women's Seat Reservation Bill, which aims to introduce increasing numbers of women into positions of influence and policy-making at *panchayat* (local government), state and national level across India through a "seat quota" system. This Bill – adopted by a few states such as Karnataka and Maharashtra since the early 1990s – aims to reinforce the work of all the grassroots organizations to ensure radical and permanent change in the lives of Indian women and public attitudes. The Bill has been challenged repeatedly by those in the IWM, who perceive the quotas for women to be a token effort, and they will go largely unfilled because all the female candidates have to be well educated. They also have to be able to secure a big electoral vote, including men, and to achieve anything female representatives have to hold the respect of their male colleagues in office. Paradoxically, these attributes will be hard to come by until there are more women at the top in India.

Women's voices

Women's issues are increasingly part of mainstream debate in Indian society and are a growing area of research and study. Several universities have departments for women's studies and a small but influential research institute, The Centre for Women's Development Studies, has been established in Delhi by the academic and activist, Vina Mazumdar.

A well-established publishing house, **Kali for Women**, produces books by women, and the independent, English-language journal, **Manushi** carries articles by women on issues such as the crisis in Kashmir and India's nuclear policy as well as debates on issues such as dowry and marriage. The journal has an international readership, and its **website** (@freespeech.org/manushi) serves as a gateway to information on women's issues and organizations throughout south Asia.

By Vicki Maggs

Wildlife

From the arid Himalayan plateau to the swamps of Bengal, and from the deserts of Rajasthan to the tropical backwaters of Kerala, the breadth of India's range of habitats is only equalled by the biodiversity that it supports. Around 65,000 species of fauna are to be found here, among them 2000 different kinds of fish, 1200 birds and 340 mammals, while a staggering 13,000 varieties of flowering plants have been recorded. India is also the only country in the world where you can see both wild lions and tigers.

The Himalayas run across the breadth of the north, providing a wealth of intermingling ecosystems. Bears and black bucks range the lush deodar and rhododendron forests of the foothills, while the fabled snow leopard and yak inhabit the higher mountains. In the hills and forests of the extreme northeast, the tiger and the one-horned rhinoceros struggle to survive in beautiful – and rarely visited – sanctuaries, pitted against a biannual monsoon, severe floods and inadequate funding for protection from poachers. Down on the Gangetic Plain, a rich array of bird-life is sustained by the warm climate, the forests and the many rivers and lakes. The Ganges falls away through paddy fields in the heart of India to the Sunderbans mangrove swamps in the east, famous for their population of tigers that – most unusually – swim. Camels, both wild and domesticated, can be found in the parched Thar desert in Rajasthan; elsewhere in the west the dry climate supports spotted deer, wild asses, and the famous Asiatic lion in its last bastion of the Gir Forest. Further south, the dry Deccan plateau is thick with sandalwood forests, the home of wild elephants, while on the weathered cliffs of the Western Ghats the civet cat prowls in the abundant fern growth. In the very southern tip of India you'll find elephants, butterflies and jewel-like birds under the canopy of the teak and rosewood rainforest.

Animals

The Indian **elephant**, distinguished from its African cousin by its long front legs and smaller ears and body, is still widely used as a beast of burden in the great teak and mahogany forests. Elephants have worked and been tamed in India for three thousand years, but it is through the battle legends of the sixteenth and seventeenth centuries that they earned their loyal and stoic reputation, both as great mounts in the imperial armies of the Moghuls and as bejewelled bearers of rajas and nawabs. Elephants are also of religious significance – they're a common sight in temple processions and ceremonies, often sporting a brightly painted trunk and forehead, and throughout the subcontinent stone elephants stand guard with bells in their trunks as a sign of welcome in medieval forts and palaces. The popular Hindu elephant-headed god Ganesh, who represents success and prosperity, is supposed to have written the *Mahabharata* epic.

In the wild, there is still a sizeable population of roughly 19,000 elephants, but they have been included under the **Endangered Species Protection Act** due to the huge reduction of their natural forest habitat. Disaster still looms for the hulking animals: each adult eats roughly two hundred kilos of vegetation and drinks a hundred litres of water a day, and their search for sustenance often brings them into conflict with neighbouring rural communities. The wild elephant is now only naturally found in four areas – the southern tip of Tamil

Feared, adored, immortalized in myth and used to endorse everything from breakfast cereals to petrochemicals, few animals command such universal fascination as the tiger. India is one of the very few places where this rare and enigmatic big cat still be glimpsed in the wild, stalking through the teak forests and terai grass – a solitary predator, with no natural enemies save one.

As recently as the turn of the last century, up to 100,000 tigers still roamed the subcontinent, even though *shikar* (tiger hunting) had long been the "sport of kings". An ancient dictum held it auspicious for a ruler to notch up a tally of 109 dead tigers, and nawabs, maharajas and Moghul emperors all indulged their prerogative to devastating effect. But it was the trigger-happy British who brought tiger hunting to its most gratuitous excesses. Photographs of pith-helmeted, bare-kneed *burra-sahibs* posing behind mountains of striped carcasses became a hackneyed image of the Raj. Even Prince Philip (now president of the Worldwide Fund for Nature) couldn't resist bagging one during a royal visit.

In the years following Independence, demographic pressures nudged the Indian tiger perilously close to extinction. As the human population increased in rural districts, more and more forest was cleared for farming, depriving large carnivores of their main source of game and of the cover they needed to hunt. Forced to turn on farm cattle as an alternative, tigers were drawn into direct conflict with humans; some animals, out of sheer desperation, even turned man-eater and attacked human settlements.

Poaching has taken an even greater toll. The black market has always paid high prices for live animals – a whole tiger can fetch up to $100,000 – and for the various body parts believed to hold magical or medicinal properties. The meat is used to ward off snakes, the brain to cure acne, the nose to promote the birth of a son and the fat of the kidney – applied liberally to the afflicted organ – as an antidote to male impotence.

Nadu; the central zone of Orissa, Bihar and West Bengal; the Himalayan lowlands of Uttar Pradesh; and the Northeastern Hill States.

Another pachyderm, the lumbering **one-horned rhinoceros**, retains a tenuous foothold in the northeast of the country. Due to deforestation and the depredations of unhindered poachers cashing in on widespread oriental beliefs in the spiritual and healing properties of various parts of the rhino's anatomy, the rhino population had dropped to barely one hundred by the 1960s. Since then, numbers have risen again, and around 1100 live in the protected Manas and Kaziranga wildlife sanctuaries in Assam.

Indian tigers are fast becoming extinct in the wild (see box), but you still stand a reasonable chance of coming across one in a national park. Sightings are regularly recorded at Kanha and Bandhavgarh in Madhya Pradesh (Bandhavgarh p.492/Kanha p.489); Ranthambore in Rajasthan (see p.205); Corbett and Dudhwa in Uttar Pradesh (see p.407); Manas and Kaziranga in Assam (see p.1052); and Bandipur in Karnataka (see p.1409).

Big cats

The other **big cats** have fared worse than the tiger. Once the maharaja of Indian wildlife, the **Asiatic lion** (see box on p.000) now clings on in just one tiny patch of Gujarat, even though the proud three-headed lion emblem of the Ashokan period is still the national symbol of India. The ghostly grey- and black-spotted **snow leopard** of the Himalayas is so rare as to be almost legendary. Only the plains-dwelling **leopard** (also known as the panther) can still

By the time an all-India moratorium on tiger shooting was declared in the 1972 Wildlife Protection Act, numbers had plummeted to below 2000. A dramatic response geared to fire public imagination came the following year, with the inauguration of **Project Tiger**. At the personal behest of Indira Gandhi, nine areas of pristine forest were set aside for the last remaining tigers. Displaced farming communities were resettled and compensated, and armed rangers employed to discourage poachers. Demand for tiger parts did not end with Project Tiger, however, and the poachers remained in business, aided by organized smuggling rings. In August 1993, undercover investigators recovered a 400-kilo haul of tiger bones, together with forty fresh carcasses, from a team of Tibetan smugglers in Delhi which had promised to supply 1000kg more on demand. Unfortunately, such exposure is rare and perpetrators are most likely to get off with bail, free to return to their trade. The maximum punishment for tiger poaching is a $125 fine, or one year in prison. Well-organized guerrilla groups thus operate with virtual impunity out of remote national parks, where inadequate numbers of poorly armed and poorly paid wardens offer little more than token resistance, particularly as increased use of poison is making it more and more difficult to track poachers. Project Tiger officials are understandably reluctant to jeopardize lucrative tourist traffic by admitting that sightings are getting rarer, but the prognosis looks very gloomy indeed.

Today, though there are 23 Project Tiger sites, numbers continue to fall. Official figures optimistically claim a **population** of up to 3000–3500, but independent evidence is more pessimistic, putting the figure at under 2000. The population rise indicated by counts based on pug marks – thought to be like human fingerprints, unique to each individual – that gave such encouragement in the early 1990s has been declared inaccurate. It was estimated in 1996 that one tiger was being poached every eighteen hours and the situation is believed to be just as depressing today. The most pessimistic experts even claim that at the present rate of destruction, India's most exotic animal could face extinction early on in the new millennium.

be commonly found, especially in forested places near human settlement where domestic animals make easy prey. Other indigenous felines include the rare multicoloured marbled cat, the miniature leopard cat, the jungle cat (with a distinct ridge of hair running down its back), the fishing cat, and a kind of lynx called the caracal. The cheetah is now extinct in India.

Deer

Deer and antelope, the larger cats' prey, are much more abundant. The often solitary sambar is the largest of the **deer**, weighing up to 300kg and bearing antlers known to reach 120cm long. Smaller and more gregarious are chital (spotted deer), usually seen in herds skulking around langur monkey or human habitats looking for discarded fruit and vegetables. In a tiger reserve you may well hear the high-pitched call of the chital and the gruff reply bark of the langur warning of the presence of a tiger in the vicinity. Other deer include the elusive mountain-loving muntjac (barking deer) and the para (hog deer), which fall victim annually to flooding in the low grasslands. The smallest deer in India is the nocturnal chevrotain, known from its size (only 30cm high) as the mouse deer. The swamp deer is rarer, while the hangul (Kashmiri red deer) and musk deer are now endangered species. **Antelopes** include the nilgai ("blue cow"), the endangered black buck, revered by the Bishnoi caste who inhabit the fringes of the Thar desert around Jodhpur in central Rajasthan, and the unique forest-dwelling four-horned chowsingha (swamp deer), which has successfully been saved from near-extinction. The desert-loving gazelle is known as the *chinkara* ("the one who sneezes") due to the sneeze-like alarm call it makes.

Monkeys

The most common **monkeys** are the feisty red-bottomed Rhesus macaque and the black-faced "Hanuman" langurs, often found around temple areas. Monkeys are protected by the Hindu belief in their divine status as noble servants of the gods, a sentiment that derives from the epic *Ramayana*, where the herculean Hanuman leads his monkey army to assist Rama in fighting the demon Ravana (see p.1506). Wild monkeys live in large troupes in the forests. The Assamese macaque and the pig-tailed macaque prefer the northern hills, while the bonnet macaque dwells in the steamy tropical jungles of the south. Langurs, such as the noisy Nilgiri langur and the extremely rare golden langur, are more elusive, preferring to remain hidden in treetop foliage.

Other mammals

Among other wild animals you might hope to see in India, the shaggy **sloth bear** is hard to spot in the wild, although you may see it being forced to dance on busy roadways near tourist sites. Other bears include the black and brown bears, distinguishable by the colour of their fur. Of the **canines**, the scavenging striped hyena and the small pest-eating Indian fox are fairly common. The Indian wolf lives in the plains and deserts, and is under threat of extinction due to vigorous culling by humans protecting their domestic animals. The wild **buffalo** has a close genetic relationship with the common domesticated water buffalo: wild male buffalo prefer to mate with domestic females. More exotic members of the cow family are the hill-loving **gaur**, an Indian bison which stands 2m across at the shoulders, and the nimble, mountain-dwelling **yak**. Asia's answer to the armadillo is a scaly anteater called a **pangolin**, whose tough plate-like scales run the length of its back and tail; this armour is believed to contain magical healing properties, for which the pangolin is hunted. Around urban environments, you're likely to see the triple-striped **palm squirrel**, said to have been marked as such by the gentle stroke of Rama. Like European squirrels, they are very common, and always busy running up trees and carrying food from place to place. **River dolphins** can be seen leaping in the Ganges, especially at Varanasi.

Reptiles

The 238 species of **snake** (of which fifty are poisonous) in India extend from the 10cm-long worm snake to nest-building king cobras and massive pythons. While the mangy and languid cobra or python wrapped around the snake-charmer's neck is tame and nonvenomous, poisonous snakes you might meet in the wild are the majestically hooded cobra, the yellow-brown Russel's viper, the small krait (especially common in south India) and the saw-scaled viper. **Lizards** are common, with every hotel room seeming to have a resident gecko to keep the place free of insects. The colourful garden lizard and Sita's lizard are both found throughout India. Freshwater Olive Ridley **turtles** (see box on p.1127) nest at remote beaches along the east and southwest coasts, the most famous being Bhitarakanika Sanctuary on **Gahirmatha beach**, 130km north of Bhubaneswar, where 200,000 females come each year to lay their eggs. Similar, though much smaller, nesting sites are to be found at Morjim and Galjibag in Goa. **Crocodiles** are common throughout the subcontinent.

Birds

You don't have to be an aficionado to enjoy India's abundant **bird-life**. Travelling around the country, you'll see breathtaking birds regularly flash between the branches of trees or appear on overhead wires at the roadside.

The spectacular varieties, both resident and migratory, can be attributed to the diverse range of climates and habitats sweeping down the Indian peninsula. The extremely rare **Siberian crane** makes an annual pilgrimage to Bharatpur in Rajasthan and a wealth of different aquatic feeding and nesting habitats draws exotic waterfowl such as flamingoes, spoonbills and pelicans. Stately **eagles** swoop among the Himalayas and majestic peacocks flounce around forts and palaces.

Three common species of **kingfisher** frequently crop up amid the paddy fields and wetlands of the coastal plains. Other common and brightly coloured species include the grass-green, blue and yellow **bee-eaters** (*Merops*), the stunning **golden oriole** (*Oriolus oriolus*), and the **Indian roller** (*Coracias bengalensis*), famous for its brilliant blue, flight feathers and exuberant aerobatic mating displays. **Hoopoes** (*Upupa epops*), recognizable by their elegant black-and-white tipped crests, fawn plumage and distinctive "hoo...po...po" call, also flit around fields and villages, as do several kinds of **bulbuls, babblers** and **drongos** (*Dicrurus*), including the fork-tailed black drongo (*Dicrurus adsimilis*) – a winter visitor that can often be seen perched on telegraph wires. If you're lucky, you may also catch a glimpse of the **paradise flycatcher** (*Tersiphone paradisi*), which is widespread and among the subcontinent's most exquisite birds, with a thick black crest and long silver, tail streamers.

Paddy fields, ponds and saline mud flats are teeming with water birds. The most ubiquitous of these is the snowy white **cattle egret** (*Bubulcus ibis*), which can usually be seen wherever there are cows and buffalo, feeding off the grubs, insects and other parasites that live on them. Look out too for the mud-brown **paddy bird**, India's most common heron, distinguished by its pale green legs, speckled breast and hunched posture.

Common birds of prey such as the **brahminy kite** (*Haliastur indus*) – recognizable by its white breast and chestnut head markings – and the **pariah kite** (*Milvus migrans govinda*) – a dark-brown buzzard with a fork tail – are widespread around towns and fishing villages, where they vie with raucous gangs of house **crows** (*Corvus splendens*) and **white-eyed jackdaws** (*Corvus monedula*) for scraps. Gigantic pink-headed **king vultures** (*Sarcogyps clavus*) and the **white-backed vulture** (*Gyps bengalensis*), which has a white ruff around its bare neck and head, also show up whenever there are carcasses to pick clean, although in recent years a mysterious virus has decimated numbers.

Among India's abundant **forest birds**, one species every enthusiast hopes to glimpse is the magnificent **hornbill**, with its huge yellow beak with a long curved casque on top. Several species of **woodpecker** also inhabit the interior woodlands, among them the rare Indian great black woodpecker, which makes loud drumming noises on tree trunks between December and March.

A bird whose call is a regular feature of the Western Ghat forests, particularly in teak areas, is the wild ancestor of the domestic chicken – the **jungle fowl**. The more common variety is the secretive but vibrantly coloured, red jungle fowl (*Gallus gallus*), which sports golden neck feathers and a metallic black tail. You're most likely to come across one of these scavenging for food on the verges of forest roads.

Wildlife viewing

Although you can expect to come across many of the species listed above on the edges of towns and villages, a spell in one or other of India's nature reserves offers the best chance of **viewing wild animals**. Administered by poorly funded government bodies, they're a far cry indeed from the well-organized and well-maintained national parks you may be used to at home. Information

Selected wildlife parks and sanctuaries

India boasts 560 protected wildlife reserves and 80 national parks – if you include the various islets of the Andaman and Nicobar islands. What follows is a selection (listed in alphabetical order) of those we found most rewarding, both in terms of their wildlife and the natural environment. Bear in mind that, at the time this book went to press,

Park	State	Habitat
Bandhavgarh NP	Madhya Pradesh	sal forest
Corbett NP	Uttar Pradesh	hilly sal forest
Dudhwa Tiger Reserve	Uttar Pradesh	sal forest, grassland, wetlands
Gir Lion Sanctuary	Gujarat	teak woodland, grassland
Hazaribagh Sanctuary	Bihar	sal forest
Jaldapara Sanctuary	West Bengal	Himalayan foothills, forest, rivers
Kanha Tiger Reserve	Madhya Pradesh	teak and sal forest, maidan
Kaziranga NP	Assam	valley floodplain
Keoladeo Ghana Bird Sanctuary (Bharatpur)	Rajasthan	semi-arid scrubland, marsh
Little Rann of Kutch Sanctuary (Dhangadhra)	Gujarat	marshy mud flats
Manas Tiger Reserve	Assam	evergreen and deciduous forest, grassland
Nagarhole and Bandipur NPs	Karnataka	jungle and grassy woodland
Nal Sarovar Bird Sanctuary	Gujarat	wetland, lake
Periyar Tiger Reserve and NP	Kerala	hills surrounding lake; woodland
Point Calimere Sanctuary	Tamil Nadu	scrub, thorn jungle, tidal creeks, sandy coastal strip
Ranthambore Reserve	Rajasthan	deciduous forest, lakes
Sariska Tiger Reserve and NP	Rajasthan	valley grassland
Sunderbans Tiger Reserve	West Bengal	mangrove swamp and delta forest
Valley of Flowers NP	Uttar Pradesh	alpine

can be frustratingly hard to come by and the staff manning them can be less than helpful.

That said, at the larger, more easily accessible wildlife reserves a reasonable infrastructure exists to **transport** visitors around, whether by Jeep, minibus, coach or, in some cases, boat. Don't, however, expect to see much if you stick to these standard excursion vehicles laid on by the park authorities. Most of the rarer animals wisely keep well away from noisy groups of trippers. Wherever

those in the Western Ghats were closed pending the surrender or capture of the sandalwood smuggler Veerapan (see p.1502). Before heading into the countryside, therefore, check with the local tourist office to ensure the park you hope to visit is currently accessible.

Animals	When to go	Accommodation
tiger, leopard, jungle cat, black buck, chausingha	Dec–June	3 forest camps
tiger, wild elephant, chital, sambar, marsh crocodile, leopard, black bear	Nov–June	tourist camps inside, hotels outside park
tiger, barasingha, leopard, hispid hare, rhino, owl, storks	Nov–June	forest huts, hotels outside park
Asiatic lion, panther, wild cat, chausingha, chinkara, sambar	March to mid-June	hotels outside park
nocturnal sambar, nilgai, wild boar, leopard, sloth bear	Oct–April	2 rest houses
rhino, leopard, sloth bear, civet, jackal, wild elephant, swamp deer	Dec–April	tourist lodge, forest bungalows, youth hostel
swamp deer, tiger, gaur, chital, leopard, black buck, sambar, mouse deer, nilgai	Dec–June	forest bungalow, 2 tourist camps, 2 lodges
rhino, wild buffalo, elephant, tiger, leopard, leopard cat, black bear, Malayan sun bear	Nov–March	forest lodge, 4 tourist bungalows
heron, stork, iris, crane, jacana, cormorant, egret, gull, cuckoo, bee-eater, kingfisher	July–Nov (nesting); Nov–Feb (breeding)	2 forest lodges, hotels outside park
wild ass	Dec–May	forest rest house, hotels outside
tiger, wild buffalo, rhino, hispid hare, golden langur, swamp deer, clouded leopard	Nov–March	3 tourist lodges
wild elephant, dhole, tiger, leopard, muntjac, mouse deer, chausinha, sambar, chital, gaur	Oct–June	many tourist lodges
geese, duck, flamingo	Nov–Feb	forest lodge
tiger, wild elephant, leopard, squirrels, birdlife	Sept–May	forest rest houses, hotels outside park
black buck, jackal, wild boar, dolphins, pelicans, flamingoes	Dec–April	forest rest house
tiger, leopard, carcal, sambar, hyena, sloth bear, marsh crocodile	Oct–Feb	3 forest lodges, hotels outside park
tiger, leopard, dhole, chausingha, chinkara, nilgai, chital, birds of prey	Nov–June	2 tourist bungalows, hotels outside park
royal Bengal tiger, Ridley sea turtle, leopard, fishing cat, estuarine crocodile	Dec–Feb	forest lodge
incredible variety of flora and birds, musk deer, leopard	mid-July to mid-Aug	2 rest houses, no camping allowed

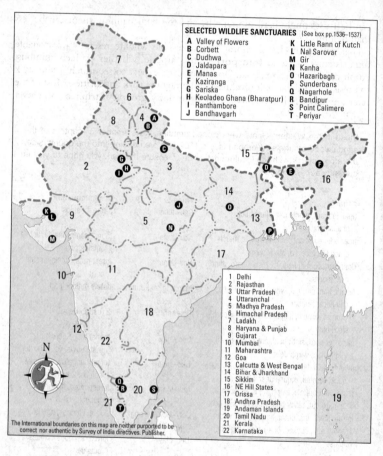

SELECTED WILDLIFE SANCTUARIES (See box pp.1536–1537)

A Valley of Flowers
B Corbett
C Dudhwa
D Jaldapara
E Manas
F Kaziranga
G Sariska
H Keoladeo Ghana (Bharatpur)
I Ranthambore
J Bandhavgarh

K Little Rann of Kutch
L Nal Sarovar
M Gir
N Kanha
O Hazaribagh
P Sunderbans
Q Nagarhole
R Bandipur
S Point Calimere
T Periyar

1 Delhi
2 Rajasthan
3 Uttar Pradesh
4 Uttaranchal
5 Madhya Pradesh
6 Himachal Pradesh
7 Ladakh
8 Haryana & Punjab
9 Gujarat
10 Mumbai
11 Maharashtra
12 Goa
13 Calcutta & West Bengal
14 Bihar & Jharkhand
15 Sikkim
16 NE Hill States
17 Orissa
18 Andhra Pradesh
19 Andaman Islands
20 Tamil Nadu
21 Kerala
22 Karnataka

The International boundaries on this map are neither purported to be correct nor authentic by Survey of India directives. Publisher.

possible, try to organize **walking safaris** with a reliable, approved guide in the forest, while bearing in mind that not all guides may be as knowledgeable and experienced as they claim, and that an untrained, unconfident guide may actually lead you into life-endangering situations; before parting with any money, ask to see recommendation books.

   Accommodation is generally available at all but the most remote sanctuaries and reserves, although it may not always be very comfortable. Larger parks tend to have a batch of luxurious, Western-style resort campuses for tour groups. In all cases, you'll find reviews of the accommodation on offer in the descriptions of individual parks featured in the Guide section of this book, along with full details of how to travel to, from and around the site. Our accounts will also advise you on the best times of year to visit in each case, and indicate the kind of wildlife present.

Myth and religion

The early **Harappa** civilization of the Indus Valley portrayed mythical creatures, bulls, elephants and tigers on their terracotta seals, amulets and toys. The itinerant **Aryan tribes** that subsequently settled in India worshipped Brahma the bull, who lay with his bovine consort to create horned **cattle** to farm the earth.

The imagery of gentle, yet strong and fertile cows and oxen is still central to the **Hindu** religion: Shaivite temples usually sport a well-reddened statue of a bull to represent Nandi, Shiva's vehicle (*vahan*), and Krishna is often depicted as a cow-herder. The *Mahabharata* epic warns that the eating of beef or wearing of leather is taboo; transgressions of this law can only be absolved by the gift of a cow to a temple. Another sin may be harder to avoid – you'll notice cows wandering freely around towns, usually when your bus swerves to avoid hitting one. Often, these are injured or old animals which the owner has released so that they can die a natural death. To touch the rump of a cow ensures fertility and prosperity.

As Brahmanical Hinduism gradually absorbed India's countless indigenous regional deities and cults, animals became a more important part of the Hindu pantheon: **Vishnu** emerged as a fish, a tortoise and a boar, an elephant head was placed on **Ganesh** (when he was mistakenly beheaded by his father, Shiva), and **Hanuman** was the loyal monkey-servant of Rama. The hooded cobra was revered as a god of the northeastern Naga tribe, and was later absorbed into the more mainstream mythological realm as the protector of Shiva and Vishnu. In fact, there are few animals and birds that do not have a spiritual association, as each of the millions of deities have to mount an animal **vahan** (vehicle) to travel between earth and heaven. Brahma rides a swan, Kartika, the god of war, sits astride a proud peacock, Ganesh is carried by a rat and Indra rides an elephant. The close link between vehicles and animals is most obvious on the roads of modern-day India, where every truck and rickshaw is liberally covered with garishly painted peacocks, cows, snakes or other animals.

The natural habitat has also played a significant role in **Buddhist** legend. Most Mahayana Buddhists recognize the ten principal Hindu deities, their animal forms and traditional *vahana*. Buddha himself is believed to have been conceived when a four-tusked white elephant entered his mother's dreams. Some legends even hold that the Buddha took on the forms of different animals during his life.

In **Jainism**, respect for all living things has led to a doctrine of vegetarianism and pacifism. Some ascetics even go naked, while others wear gauze masks over their mouths and only walk on concrete paths, gently brushing the ground in front of them to avoid killing even the smallest of insects.

As animals, plants and geographical features have come to be symbolically associated with the characteristics they display, the landscape of India and its produce has become imbued with **sacred associations** through offerings and festivals. Coconuts yield milk and succulent flesh given as a symbolic food offering (*prasad*) at the beginning of a *puja* ceremony. The unchanging womb-like form of the lotus (*padma*) has led to its strong association with "mother creation". In yoga, the "lotus position" promotes health and wisdom, while lotus flowers bearing candles are set afloat on the Ganges as a sunset *arati* offering to summon divine blessing.

The common **deer** is sacred to both Hinduism and Buddhism. The Buddha is supposed to have preached his first sermon in a deer park, and according to Hindu law, the docile and graceful creature is so holy that even the ground that it treads should be worshipped. The **peacock** is symbolically associated with fertility for its instinctive ability to sense and dance at the approach of rain.

ⓦwww.indev.nic.in/wwf
Home page of the Worldwide Fund for Nature, India, dedicated to conservation and environmental protection in the subcontinent. Useful primarily as a source for volunteer work and news.

ⓦwww.5tigers.org
Everything you ever wanted to know about tigers, and more besides.

ⓦhttp://environment:123india.com
Features, safaris reviews and the latest wildlife news from across the country.

ⓦwww.camacdonald.com/birding/asiaindia.htm
Exhaustive reviews of India's birdwatching hotspots, online resources and printed material, with dozens of pretty pics and reports from recent field trips by bona fide enthusiasts.

ⓦwww.nbs.it/tiger/
Background on India's disappearing big cat, including detailed poaching statistics – depressing reading indeed.

Development and green issues

In 1947, on the eve of Independence, serious doubts existed as to whether the emerging Indian nation would be able to feed itself. Little more than fifty years later, India is the world's tenth largest industrial power, boasting its own "Silicon Valley" (in Bangalore), nuclear missiles, communications satellites and an annual GDP increasing steadily at a rate of six to seven percent. However, while the country's elite enjoys the benefits of the consumer revolution, life for the vast majority of Indians has improved little, if at all, since Independence.

For the sixty- to seventy percent of Indians who live below the poverty line, fundamental needs are met primarily by the natural environment: water is obtained from rivers and wells, fodder and food from fields, and fuel from trees and dung. For this reason, green issues assume a significance which is difficult for people in more developed parts of the world to appreciate. When land is eroded or flooded, water polluted and forests depleted, rural livelihoods are invariably destroyed, forcing people off the land. It has been estimated that 40 million people have been displaced in India by dam schemes alone since Independence. Most of those uprooted have little option but to seek wage labour in the cities, where they join the ever-swelling slums and ranks of pavement dwellers.

Time and again, you'll hear "population" advanced as the root of India's poverty. But the real causes of the mass exodus from the countryside, of the overwhelmingly high rates of female illiteracy and infant mortality, of malnutrition and of perennially poor health among India's most disadvantaged citizens, are a lot more complex.

Population and poverty

Some time in late 2000 – demographers are still arguing over exactly when – India's **population** topped the **1 billion** mark. At the current rate of growth (which will see the population of India double in approximately 34 years), there will be more Indians than Chinese by midway through this century, or possibly before.

Huge efforts have been made by successive governments to curb India's population, yet 15.5 million babies are born every year in India (one every two seconds or so). Two generations have grown up with the family-planning mantra "*Hum do, hamare do*" ("We are two, and we have two", often corrupted on the tail-gates of Indian trucks to "We 2 are 1"). Indeed, during the most autocratic days of Indira Gandhi's rule in the 1970s, a programme of **forced sterilization** was embarked upon. By 1992, the government claimed that 45 percent of couples were "protected against pregnancy", chiefly through voluntary sterilization.

However, repeated initiatives have failed to bring down the rate of growth. In part this is due to increased life expectancy in India; fewer babies are being born, but they live longer. It is also, however, a reflection of attitudes to **birth**

control among the poor, for whom, with **infant mortality** averaging between one in nine, having lots of children represents security in old age. One recent study estimated that an average Indian couple must produce 6.3 children to give a 95 percent chance of producing a son who will live until his father is 65 years old.

The lowering of India's birth rate (as against its overall rate of population growth) derives primarily from progress in more **prosperous states**, for example Kerala, where standards of health care, female literacy and womens' rights are higher. In states such as Rajasthan, Bihar and Madhya Pradesh, which lag well behind the national average on most social indicators, the number of children being born annually remains more or less at pre-Independence levels.

Population increases rather than mismanagement of natural resources is seen by many educated Indians as the main factor inhibiting prosperity. Though this has been repeatedly rejected by studies on the subject, it is symptomatic of the wider problems arising from the traditional caste system. Further underpinning India's extreme social inequalities is an economic credo known as the **trickle-down** theory. The dominant force in the country's economic thinking since Independence, it holds that prosperity is generated from the top, filtering down to help those beneath. To some extent, the dramatic expansion of the economy in the 1990s showed that this can indeed happen, but it also proved that the benefits of prosperity at the top don't necessarily reach those most in need.

The environment

How far the wealthy and powerful interests in Indian society may be oblivious to the needs of the country's poor has been repeatedly demonstrated by the **environmental** debates that have come to the fore over the past two or three decades.

The Indian economy remains to a large extent dependent on raw materials: minerals, water, wood, cotton and other plants. Although the *raison d'être* of rapid economic growth has always been that it will create prosperity for all, the exploitation of India's environment has all too often had precisely the opposite result.

Land

India has a quarter of the world's farmers – around 700 million people, 85 percent of whom live off subsistence-oriented smallholdings. The remaining 15 percent are engaged in the kind of industrial-scale farming that powered the **Green Revolution** of the 1970s, when India changed from being the world's largest importer of food grains to a self-sufficient country.

The secret of this success was an expensive combination of imported high-yield crops, fertilizers, pesticides, irrigation methods and new machinery. Three decades down the line, however, the miraculous transformation in agricultural practices that saw off a national drought in 1988 (and even enabled India to donate food aid during the African famines of the 1980s) is increasingly regarded with considerable ambivalence. As a result of the Green Revolution, production of high-protein foodstuffs and cereals – staple food sources – has plummeted, while whole swathes of cultivable land have been degraded by overuse of chemicals. Moreover, the large-scale engineering projects required to supply farmers with the ever-increasing amounts of water the new crops needed, has led to the displacement of millions.

Another change that has had serious implications for Indian farmers over the past decade or so has been the government's relationship with the International Monetary Fund (IMF) and its sister organization, the World Bank. In order to qualify for a £90 billion loan in the late 1980s, India was obliged to end its programme of **subsidies** to farmers, who for years had been entitled to free or cheap electricity, diesel, fertilizers and pesticides. According to the World Trade Organization, such state aid constituted "interference with the free market", and was illegal.

The Seed Satyagraha

In a country of 700 million farmers, **seed** is a powerfully emotive subject. Traditionally, around eighty percent of the total quantity of seed produced in India is collected, resown, watched over and prayed for at every stage of its development. Saving, replanting and sharing seed are considered among the most fundamental of freedoms.

The power wielded by international agro-science and seed companies, and the endorsement of that power by a battery of legal impositions handed down by the World Trade Organization (WTO), has put those freedoms in jeopardy, provoking the formation of a resistance movement of a size not seen since Gandhi's non-violent "Quit India" campaign against the British. For many, the struggle is against a new form of colonialism initiated by seed companies. A spokesperson for Monsanto, for example, told the UK's *Guardian* newspaper in 1998 that the company's mission was "to consolidate the whole food chain."

Central to this process is the genetic **patenting of seeds**, giving rights over them to a specific company and thereafter making it illegal for ordinary farmers to use or collect seed without paying whatever price the company demands. Basmati rice, turmeric, black pepper and the neem tree have all been patented by US companies. In addition, under the international system of free-trade agreements, farmers are pressurized into growing cash crops (see overleaf). The required expenditure, hidden at the outset, is more than most farmers can afford, and has rapidly forced countless numbers into debt. Blocked by patent laws from returning to earlier ways of life, many have ended up destitute.

The resistance movement makes explicit the connection with the anticolonial struggle by using the name **satyagraha** – chosen by Gandhi for his campaign of nonviolent civil disobedience. Already supported by thousands of grassroots farmers organizations, its opposition to Monsanto's latest development, the so-called "terminator gene", was what finally won it the support of government.

This technology allows the production of plants that yield sterile seeds (ie ones that cannot be resown, and which thus protect the patent of the production company). It is widely feared that cross-pollination would render other crops sterile, resulting in complete dependence on foreign companies. To draw attention to this risk, a coalition of ten million Karnatakan farmers, the KRSS, mounted "Operation Cremate Monsanto", pulling up cotton crops at test sites and organizing mass rallies against the WTO. Its leader, the maverick **Professor Najundasmamy**, also staged a much-publicized laugh-in, when 6000 farmers laughed all day outside the town hall in Bangalore at their elected representatives, for "subverting democracy". The government, meanwhile, has both banned the technology and required all exporting countries to guarantee that seeds entering India are "terminator free".

Farmers were instead encouraged by a raft of incentives and publicity drives to grow **cash crops** such as cotton, which offered the additional benefit of generating foreign currency (needed to repay the IMF loans). Using newly developed high-yield seeds and chemicals, improved harvests and profits were assured, and within a couple of years, huge chunks of the country (as much as sixty percent of farm land in Andhra Pradesh) had been given over to the "White Gold".

The advertising campaigns mounted by the multinational seed and pesticide manufacturers, however, failed to warn that cotton prices might suddenly drop; that pests might develop immunities to the chemicals; that the new hybrid seeds didn't always grow; or that much greater quantities of water would be needed to cultivate them. When all these disasters struck at once, as they did a few years back, millions of farmers in India were ruined. Their only option was to borrow money from the *aarthis*, or moneylenders, who had sold them the seeds and chemicals in the first place. In Andhra Pradesh alone, around 500 farmers committed suicide by drinking the useless insecticide before lying down to die amid their failed crops.

The bio-tech giants such as Monsanto claim technology is the answer to the problems of **sustainable agricultural production**. Others, such as the permaculture-influenced Deccan Development Society, insist that self-reliance can only be attained by blending the best practices of the past with those of the present. Working with 8000 women in some of central India's poorest villages, on chronically eroded land, the DDS has promoted traditional techniques of composting, water saving, rotational farming methods and soil fertility. The growers are encouraged to plant nine or more crops at once, a system refined in India over centuries, using plants that protect each other from pests, and to provide plenty of backups if some fail. In twelve or so years, the DDS has rendered large areas of degraded farm land productive, increased average yields by as much as fifty percent, and pesticide use is declining. Initiatives such as this provide compelling support for a controversial report published in 1993 by the New Delhi-based Centre for Science and the Environment, which concluded that India's fertile land, if properly managed, could supply a population of more than double what it does today.

Deforestation

Fuel for cooking fires is one of the main causes of **deforestation**, an environmental issue which the appalling floods, droughts and cyclones suffered by India in recent years has once again brought to the forefront of the environmental agenda. Today, true forest covers around ten percent of the total land area of India. Studies in Karnataka have shown a variety of reasons for the ongoing loss, thought to be mirrored countrywide. The extension of cultivation is the most damaging factor, although mining, hydroelectric projects and the resettlement of displaced people play significant parts.

The depletion of India's tree cover has been both socially and environmentally damaging. Less woodland means more work for women, who have to spend hours each day collecting fuel. It also increases the risk of **soil erosion** and landslides. The forests cloaking the Himalayas have for millenia acted as a giant sponge for the monsoon rains, soaking them up and releasing them gradually through the countless streams and rivers flowing into the Indian plains. With the dramatic recession of the tree line this century, rainwater now runs much more quickly off the hill country, laden with precious topsoil. The severe flooding that has now become a near annual inevitability for inhabitants of riverine regions such as Bengal, is believed to be a direct consequence of deforestation. India's forests are also extraordinarily rich in **biodiversity** and, as well as absorbing rainwater, soak up carbon dioxide, one of the main greenhouse gases.

The first coherent attempts to halt deforestation in the Himalayas, and in India generally, date from an era before its potential impact was fully understood. In 1973, the now world-famous **Chipko movement** was born when the peasants of Mandal, a village high in the Garhwal Himalayas, prevented logging operations in a nearby forest by threatening to "hug" the trees. Popular feeling has also led to notable changes in state forestry policy, such as the abandonment of programmes for the clear-felling of natural forests in order to replace them with economically useful exotic species. Indeed, the strength of public opinion on forest issues was among the major factors leading to the creation of a new state, Uttaranchal, out of the hill tract of Uttar Pradesh.

Although campaigners stress the importance of returning control of the forests to their inhabitants, it has to be pointed out that a major factor in forest loss is the use of timber to fuel **domestic fires**. By extension, sheer pressure of population means that the forests are being used up faster than they can hope to regenerate, despite programmes to introduce fast-growing species.

Many of India's **mines** are located in forested regions, and the extraction of minerals such as iron ore, bauxite, copper, zinc, gypsum and limestone is increasingly carried out at the expense of forest cover. Even more directly, the Indian paper industry – India is one of the twenty largest producers of paper in the world – requires the annual felling of several million trees.

With forests dwindling by an estimated 15,000 square kilometres per year, **competition for living space** between the human population and forest animals is intensifying. Alarm bells are already sounding for some of the better-known forest creatures. Since the 1930s, the density of the human population per square kilometre has trebled, while the number of tigers has declined to an estimated eight percent of its peak. The many forest national parks may be well protected, but they have become island oases amid intensively farmed land. On occasion, larger forest animals such as elephants and tigers explicitly threaten the livelihood of farmers. In parts of rural south and eastern India, for example, elephants driven from their forest by fires often blunder through fields, villages and small towns, occasionally trampling villagers to death. For many forest creatures, avoiding humans is becoming increasingly difficult.

Indian farmers traditionally view such encroachment onto their land with mistrust. Anti-animal feelings run high: deer are poached, and tigers have been poisoned. Attempts to involve local people with the protection of the forests and their creatures have been encouraged in some areas through the growth of new organizations. In northern India, the **Ranthambore Foundation**, originally set up to protect the park's tigers, has developed compensatory schemes for local people living on the park margins, offering training in the more efficient management of livestock, the planting of trees and the improvement of local livelihoods.

Water

Drought remains one of the most pressing problems facing India and is the subject of heated debate at every level of society. An estimated 200 million people are thought not to have access to clean drinking water, one of the main reasons thousands are forced to head for the major cities each year. The other, ironically, is displacement by huge **dam and canal schemes** designed to remedy the situation.

Traditionally, the design of Indian villages has always revolved around **water storage**. Even in the poorest regions, a complex system of wells, channels and

The great Indian dam scam

The perfect symbol of a modern, technologically advanced state providing for its citizens, dams have been equated with nation-building in India since Independence. Half a century on, many of their original advocates are admitting that large dams cause more problems than they solve. In 1999 the government's Planning Commission suggested that the number of people displaced by the creation of dams may be as high as forty million.

Although a proportion of the displaced are designated **Project Affected People** (PAPs), and so qualify for rehabilitation, the land available for resettlement is not guaranteed to be cultivable and there have been incidences of other people being displaced to make way for them, and of several groups being allocated the same piece of land. These, together with the millions of others who slip through the net, have nowhere to go but the shantytowns outside cities, where for the vast majority there will be no work, no support and no chance of self-sufficiency.

The most controversial scheme to date has been in the **Narmada Valley**, running through Gujarat, Maharashtra and Madhya Pradesh, where a series of 30 megadams, 135 medium and 3000 small dams is being constructed. Up to half a million people are expected to be displaced by the project and the lives of a further 21 million who depend on the ecology of the valley will also be affected.

Although the government insists that the end result will be access to clean drinking water for millions of villagers, the cost of the thousands of kilometres of pipes and pumps needed to get water to these areas has not been budgeted for now most of the biggest investors have pulled out. Environmentalists claim that the money saved by stopping construction at this stage could be used to fund local water-harvesting projects for every village in the country.

The World Bank, which originally pledged a $450 million loan, staged an unprecedented withdrawal in 1993 on the evidence of an independent report acknowledging what the dams' detractors had been claiming for years – that "the resettlement and rehabilitation of all those displaced by the projects is not possible under prevailing circumstances and their environmental impacts have not been properly considered or adequately addressed". Despite this, the Supreme Court voted in October 2000 to remove a stay on construction of the largest dam, the **Sardar Sarovar**, that had been in place since 1994. This decision will allow a further 245 villages to be flooded, and many of their inhabitants have pledged to drown when the waters are finally released.

Narmada Bachao Andolan (NAM, @www.sardarsarovardam.com) is the opposition movement co-ordinating thousands of village-level groups in their efforts at peaceful resistance. It has now turned its attention to the **Maheshwar dam**, upstream from the Sardar Sarovar, where construction has been interrupted several times by occupation of the site by thousands of villagers. The novelist **Arundhati Roy** is one of the organization's most outspoken supporters, and in 1999 she donated her Booker Prize money for *The God of Small Things* to their cause. Soon after, she published a typically impassioned essay on India's dam building schemes, entitled *The Greater Common Good*, in which she depicted the government's plans as a kind of holocaust, prompting angry reactions from supporters of the project in Gujarat and a threat by the local municipality to demolish her second home in the central Indian hill station of Pachmarhi. Despite the intervention of India's most acclaimed novelist, with so many big businesses and political futures tied up in the Narmada project, prospects for the millions of dispossesed and relocated villagers look as bleak now as they ever have.

huge rectangular tanks has enabled villagers to withstand the driest months. Other adaptations – such as growing crops suited to the climate – ensured that demand did not exceed supply. Although modern phenomena such as deforestation and the exigences of the Green Revolution have put water resources under immense strain, experts believe the abuse and mismanagement of existing systems to be the real cause of many shortages.

All over India, creeping **privatization** of communal water sources has led to the poorest sections of society having to cope with drought conditions, even in areas with relatively high rainfall. Those with enough money (dubbed "Water Lords" in some areas) either buy pumps, thereby undermining the wells of those without, or construct bore wells, sometimes even in the bed of communal tanks, and lay claim to existing groundwater, charging for or denying access as they choose. The result is the familiar cycle of dependency, poverty, ill-health and ultimately migration to the cities.

Drought tends to be presented as the result of purely natural phenomena in the media, and this is the way many in the urban centres, including policy-makers, see it. Aid efforts often concentrate on emergency relief rather than longer-term solutions and, once the contractors and consultants have taken their cut, there is often not enough to fulfil even the original good intentions, as the recent spate of droughts in Rajasthan demonstrate.

Dam and large-scale canal construction, the favoured solutions of a succession of governments and international funders (notably the World Bank), are now widely acknowledged as the causes of lowering water-table levels in areas from which rivers and tributaries are diverted. Where vast areas of forest are submerged rainfall levels drop, and there is even mounting evidence which connects dams to earthquakes.

Air

The form of environmental degradation to which travellers in India are most likely to be exposed, and which is having the most dramatic impact on Indians' overall health, is **air pollution**.

Until a little over a decade ago, only the most privileged minority in India owned vehicles and traffic congestion was more likely to be caused by bullock carts than cars. Almost overnight, however, the opening up of the economy to foreign manufacturers brought within reach of a vast number of people the possibility of two-wheeler ownership. Scooters and 125cc motorcycles (bearing Indian names, but actually Japanese products made in India, with cheaper, inferior materials) flooded the streets, and in the big cities Japanese hatchbacks suddenly started to outnumber the old Ambassadors.

The transport revolution – coupled with the low quality of India's oil refineries, which manufacture poor-grade, highly polluting fuel – has had disastrous consequences for the subcontinent's air quality. Delhi, Mumbai and Calcutta now number among the five worst-polluted metropolitan areas in the world. Most affected of all has been **Delhi**, whose roads carry more than three times the number of vehicles they did a decade ago. On windless days during the dry season, pollution levels at major intersections in the city centre soar to fifty times or more above World Health Organization (WHO) recommended maximums.

India's traffic pollution has been compounded by the proliferation of **heavy industry**. In Delhi alone, factories have been estimated to disgorge 3000 tonnes of pollutants into the air every day, with serious implications for the health of its inhabitants. One study carried out in 1998 showed that around

8000 people a year die prematurely in the capital from pollution-related illnesses. Children under the age of 12 are especially vulnerable; one in four now has asthma, while half suffer dangerous levels of lead in their blood.

Confronted with the imminent prospect of an uninhabitable city, Delhi municipality has implemented drastic measures to curb local pollution, closing over 100,000 industrial units in residential areas, and banning all public transport vehicles not fuelled by compressed natural gas, or CNG. The scheme has been highly controversial and its long-term benefits have yet to be assessed, the only impact so far being a political backlash against the authorities which instigated the measures.

However, while the attention of legislators has tended over the past decade to focus on traffic and industry-generated "ambient" air pollution, respiratory illnesses are spiralling in rural areas due to a more traditional menace. In a recent study, the World Bank calculated that between 4 and 6 percent of deaths in India (7 to 9 percent of deaths among women and children) are attributable to **indoor pollution**, caused by the noxious cocktail of kerosene, wood and dung most Indians use for cooking. The report concluded that at least half a million children under the age of five die every year from diseases related to inhaling smoke at home; out of these, at least 300,000 have not even reached their first birthday.

Charities and NGOs working in India

For more information on charities and Non-Governmental Organizations (NGOs) working in India, see ⓦwww.indianNGOs.com.

Music

The origin of north Indian (Hindustani) classical music is shrouded in obscurity. There is a tendency in India to attribute the invention of any ancient art form to one of the many Hindu deities, and the resulting synthesis of myth and legend is often taken as literal truth. But in reality north Indian classical music as it exists today is the result of a long process of integrating many diverse cultural influences. Not only is there a rich and varied tradition of regional folk music, but all through its history India has absorbed the culture and traditions of foreign invaders, the most influential being the Muslim Moghuls.

The introduction of Turko-Persian musical elements is what primarily distinguishes north Indian classical music from its predecessor, Carnatic, now restricted to southern India. The latter is a complex, rich and fascinating musical tradition in its own right, and even an untrained ear can usually distinguish between the two.

Teachers and pupils

In the north, both Hindu and Muslim communities have provided outstanding artists. While music recognizes no religious differences – indeed it is something of a religion in its own right – distinguished musicians of Hindu origin customarily take the title of *pandit* (and become known as gurus), while their Muslim counterparts add the prefix *ustad* (meaning "master") to their names. An *ustad* may teach anything – not only his own particular art or instrument. It is not unusual for sitar maestros to teach sarod or vocal techniques to their pupils.

The **teaching** of north Indian classical music is a subject in itself. One thing that strikes a Westerner is the spiritual link between teacher and pupil. Quite often the two may be blood relations anyway, but where they are not, a spiritual relationship is officially inaugurated in a ceremony in which the teacher ties a string to the wrist of the pupil to symbolize the bond between them.

Apart from actual musical form and content, north Indian music has various extra-musical traditions and rituals, usually taught through musical families and **gharanas** ("schools"). Traditionally, Indian music is taught on a one-to-one basis, often from father to son. Many academies and colleges of music now follow the modern style, but traditionalists still adhere to the *gharana* system, and great importance is still attached to membership of a musical family or an impressive lineage. A *gharana*, which may be for singing, for any or all kinds of instruments, or for dance, is more a school of thought than an institution. It suggests a particular belief, or a preference for a certain performance style. *Gharanas* differ not only in broad terms, but also in minute details: how to execute a particular combination of notes, or simply the correct way to hold an instrument. They are usually founded by musicians of outstanding ability, and new styles and forms are added by exceptionally talented musicians who may have trained with one particular *gharana* and then evolved a style of their own.

Scales of purity and imagination

Singing is considered to be the highest form of classical music, after which instruments are graded according to their similarity to the human voice. The

Features on music, dance and performing arts, scattered throughout this book, include:

Qawwali p.133

The Performing Arts of Lucknow p.320

Bollywood p.778

Odissi Dance p.1121

Keralan Ritualized Theatre p.1368

two main vocal traditions are *dhrupad*, the purest of all, devoid of all embellishment and entirely austere in its delivery, and *khayal*, which has a more romantic content and elaborate ornamentation and is the more popular today. Less abstract vocal forms include the so-called light classical *dadra*, *thumri* and *ghazal* as well as *qawwali*, the religious music of the Sufi tradition. The degree of musical purity is assigned according to a scale which has music at one extreme and

Musical instruments

String instruments

The best-known instrument is the sitar, invented by Amir Khusrau in the thirteenth century and played with a plectrum. Of the six or seven main strings, four are played and the other two or three supply a drone or a rhythmic ostinato. There can also be between eleven and nineteen sympathetic strings. The two sets of strings are fitted on different bridges. Twenty brass frets fastened to the long hollow neck can be easily moved to conform to the scale of a particular *raag*, and their curvature allows the player to alter the pitch by pulling the string sideways across the fret to provide the gliding portamento so characteristic of Indian music.

The surbahar ("spring melody"), effectively a bass sitar, is played in the same way. Developed by Sahibdad Khan, the great-grandfather of Vilayat and Imrat Khan, it produces a deep, dignified sound. The neck is wider and longer than that of the sitar but its frets are fixed. Thanks to its size, and longer strings, the sound can be sustained for longer, and the range of the portamento is wider.

The sarod is a descendant of the Afghani rebab. Smaller than a sitar, it has two resonating chambers, the larger made of teak covered with goatskin, and the smaller, at the other end of the metal fingerboard, made of metal. Ten of its 25 metal strings are plucked with a fragment of coconut shell. Four of these carry the melody; the others accentuate the rhythm. The rest are sympathetic strings, underneath the main strings. The sarod was hugely improved by Ustad Allaudin Khan, whose pupils Ustad Ali Akbar Khan and Ustad Amjad Ali Khan are now its best-known exponents.

The sarangi is a fretless bowed instrument with a very broad fingerboard and a double belly. The entire body of the instrument – belly and fingerboard – is carved out of a single block of wood and the hollow covered with parchment. There are three or four main strings of gut and anything up to forty metal sympathetic strings. Some claim it is the most difficult musical instrument to play in the world. Certainly the technique is highly unusual. While the right hand wields the bow in the normal way, the strings are stopped not by the fingertips of the left hand, but by the nails. The *sarangi* is capable of a wide range of timbres and its sound is likened to that of the human voice, so it is usually used to accompany vocal recitals. Originally this was its only function, but in recent years it has become a solo instrument in its own right, thanks mainly to the efforts of Ustad Sultan Khan and Pandit Ram Narayan.

words at the other. As words become more audible and thus the meaning of lyrics more important, so the form is considered to be musically less pure.

Indian musicologists talk about two **kinds of sound** – one spiritual and inaudible to the human ear, the other physical and audible. The inaudible sound is said to be produced from the ether, and its function is to liberate the soul. But to feel it requires great devotion and concentration which the average person can never really attain. Audible sound, on the other hand, is actually "struck" and is said to have an immediate and pleasurable impact.

Indian music always has a **constant drone** in the background, serving as a reference point for performer and listener alike. In north Indian music this drone is usually played on the four-stringed tambura. The privilege of accompanying a teacher's performance on the tambura is often accorded to advanced students.

Indian music does not so much describe a mood (as some European music does) as help to create that mood, and then explore it to its depths. Where Western classical music starts at a particular point and then progresses from it,

The **santoor**, a hammered zither of trapezoid shape and Persian origin, has only recently been accepted in classical music. It has over a hundred strings, pegged and stretched in pairs, parallel to each other. Each pair passes over two bridges, one on each side of the instrument. The strings are struck by two curving wooden sticks. Its most notable exponent is Pandit Shiv Kumar Sharma.

The **surmandal** resembles a zither, and is used by vocalists to accompany themselves in performance. Even though its primary function is to provide the drone, singers sometimes also play the basic melody line on this instrument.

Wind instruments

The **shehnai**, the traditional instrument for wedding music, is a double-reed, oboe-type instrument with up to nine finger holes, some of which are stopped with wax for fine tuning to the scale of a particular *raag*. It demands a mastery of circular breathing and enormous breath control. A drone accompaniment is provided by a second *shehnai*.

The word **bansuri** refers to a wide variety of bamboo (*banse*) flutes, most end-blown, but some, such as Krishna's famous *murli*, are side-blown. Despite offering a range of less than two octaves, it now appears as a solo concert instrument.

Drums

The **tabla** is a set of two small drums played with the palms and fingertips to produce an incredible variety of sounds and timbres, in a range of one octave. Its name is short for *tabla-bayan* – the *tabla* is on the right and the *bayan* ("left") on the left. Its invention is attributed to Amir Khusrau, creator of the sitar. Both drum heads are made of skin, with a paste of iron filings and flour in the centre, but while the body of the *tabla* is all wood, the *banay* is metal. The *tabla* is usually tuned to the tonic, dominant or subdominant notes of the *raag* by knocking the tuning-blocks, held by braces on the sides of the instrument, into place.

Predating the tabla, the **pakhavaj** is nearly a metre long and was traditionally made of clay, although now wood is more popular. It has two parchment heads, each tuned to a different pitch, again by knocking the side blocks into place. A paste of boiled rice, iron filings and tamarind juice is applied to the smaller head and a wheat flour paste on the larger helps produce the lower notes.

The *pakhavaj* has a deep mellow sound and is used to accompany *dhrupad* singing and *kathak* dancing. A smaller version of the *pakhavaj*, the *mridangam*, is widely used in south Indian music.

Hindustani music

Nikhil Banerjee *The Hundred-minute Raga: Purabi Kalyan* (Raga Records, US). Banerjee, one of the finest sitar players of recent years, is famed for the purity and elegance of his style. This recording finds him on top form.

Vishwa Mohan Bhatt *Guitar à la Hindustan* (Original Music Impressions, India). One of Hindustani music's most famous sons, Bhatt reworked and redesigned the Spanish guitar until it emerged as a new mutant instrument cannily called the "Mohanvina". Along with Water Lily's *Gathering Rain Clouds*, this is a perfect place to begin an exploration of Bhatt's classical repertoire.

Hariprasad Chaurasia *Hari-Krishna: In Praise of Janmashtami* (Navras, UK). North Indian flautist Chaurasia is one of India's most successful ambassadors on any instrument. This three-album set captures an intimate annual tradition when the maestro, joined by his family and a few close associates, plays through the night in front of a Krishna altar in his Mumbai home. A quietly momentous album.

Ali Akbar Khan *Signature Series Volumes 1 and 2* (AMMP, US). Sarod player and master melodist Ali Akbar Khan is hailed as one of the greatest musicians on the planet, irrespective of genre. Accompanied here by one of the finest tabla players of his generation, Mahapurush Misra.

Bismillah Khan *Live In London Volumes 1 and 2* (Navras, UK). Two marvellous albums recorded in London in 1985. One of Hindustani music's foremost virtuosi, Bismillah Khan is the acknowledged master of the *shehnai*.

Imrat Khan *Ajmer* (Water Lily Acoustics, US). This 1990 recording features Khan's virtuoso performances on the sitar and its bass-voiced equivalent, the *surbahar*.

Sultan Khan *Sarangi* (Navras, UK). *Sarangi* player Sultan Khan first came under the international spotlight touring with Ravi Shankar and George Harrison, and consolidated his international career with work on the soundtrack to Gandhi. This 1992 release from a dizzy-making London concert in 1990 reveals eloquent insights that few can match.

Vilayat Khan *Sitar* (India Archive Music, US). Studio recording from the greatest living sitar player alongside – not after – Ravi Shankar. Performed with such flair and compassion that the senses tingle.

Kamalesh Maitra *Tabla Tarang – Melody on Drums* (Smithsonian Folkways, US). Compelling performance by the acknowledged master of the rare tabla tarang, a set of tablas tuned to play *raags*.

Ram Narayan *The Art of the Sarangi* (Ocora, France). "I cannot separate the *sarangi* from Ram Narayan, so thoroughly fused are they, not only in my memory but in the fact of this sublime dedication of the great musician to an instrument which is no longer archaic because of the matchless way he had made it speak." (Yehudi Menuhin)

Alla Rakha *Maestro's Choice – Tabla* (Music Today, India). A recital with Zakir Hussain illustrating the potency of Hindustani rhythm, exploring *matta taal* (a 9-beat cycle) and *jai taal* (a 13-beat cycle) with a concluding number in pashto (7 beats). Sultan Khan supports melodically on *sarangi*. Their 67-minute *Tabla Duet* (Moment, US), with Ramesh Misra on *sarangi* is also highly recommended.

Ravi Shankar *Ravi Shankar & Ali Akbar Khan In Concert 1972* (Apple, UK). Sitar and sarod pyrotechnics and profundity recorded in New York. The concert took place weeks after the death of their mutual guru Allauddin Khan, and was dedicated to him.

Various *Call of the Valley* (EMI/Hemisphere, UK). Probably the most influential Hindustani album ever made, using various time-related *raags* to depict the passage of a Kashmiri day.

Various *Inspiration – India* (EMI, UK). A selection of instrumental and tabla duos and *jugulbandi* duets giving a varied introduction to Hindustani music.

Various *The Rough Guide to the Music of India and Pakistan* (World Music Network, UK). A digestible introduction to the music of north India, with flautist Dr N. Ramani the only southerner represented. A good survey of classical, semi-classical and folk styles.

Carnatic music

Kadri Gopalnath *Sax Melodies – Naadagaambheeryam* (Sangeetha, India/US). Golpanath typifies the duality of Carnatic music in playing a modern instrument in a tradition that goes back centuries. The saxophone harks back to the older sound of the *nagaswaram*. On this album Gopalnath is accompanied by violin, *ghatam*, *mri-dangam* and *morsing*.

The Karnataka College of Percussion *River Yamuna* (Music of the World, US). Despite the ensemble's name, KCP also features the voice of the Ramamani and melody instruments such as *vina*, violin and solos. This 1997 album, a reworked version of their classic *Shiva Ganga* (1995), ranks among the most accessible introduction for beginners to the deep space of Carnatic music.

Shankar *Raga Aberi* (Music of the World, US). A spectacular *ragam-tanam-pallavi* performance featuring the growling low notes of Shankar's extraordinary ten-string double violin. The performance also features spectacular vocal percussion and solos.

L. Subramaniam *Electric Modes* (Water Lily Acoustics, US). A two-CD set, one volume of which consists of original compositions, the second of which focuses on traditional *raags*. Subramaniam is one of the most recorded Carnatic artists in the West and has regularly played in non-Carnatic contexts.

Song forms

Najma Akhtar *Qareeb* (Triple Earth). Having one track on the soundtrack of acclaimed British film *Sammy And Rosie Get Laid* assisted, but it is the lyrical gift, innovative arrangements and fine instrumental playing (including violin, sax and *santur*) that sets *Qareeb* ("Nearness") apart. A modern *ghazal* classic.

Asha Bhosle *Legacy* (AMMP/Triloka, US). A remarkable collaboration of Bhosle and great sarod player Ali Akbar Khan in a collection of classical and light-classical vocal gems.

Mehdi Hassan *Live in Concert* (Navras, UK). This triple CD, recorded live in London in 1990, captures the feel of a classical *ghazal* concert, or *mushaira* (gathering), with interjections of *thumri*, *dadra* and folk song for variety.

Bade Ghulam Ali Kham *Raga Piloo, Raga Bhairavi* & *Raga Rageshree* (Multitone Prestige, UK). These live *thumri* recordings have *sarangi*, tabla and *tanpura* accompaniment, and the artist's son as the second vocalist.

Jagjit & Chitra Singh *The Golden Collection* (Gramophone Company of India, India). The names of this husband-and-wife team are synonymous with *ghazal*. These 29 solo and duo tracks over two CDs are terrific, with tasteful *sarangi* and tabla work.

Folk

Various *Ganga: The Music of the Ganges* (EMI/Virgin Classics, France). A wonderful introduction to Indian folk and devotional music, evoking the location and context. The three CDs trace the course of the river from the Himalayas to the Bay of Bengal and feature sounds of the river alongside performances beautifully recorded in temples, at the water's edge, on boats and so on. Much of the music is devotional, but other highlights include snake charmer's music, a festival percussion ensemble, a virtuoso toy-seller's song, *bauls* and a great *shehnai dhun* performance at dawn.

Various *Bauls of Bengal* (Cramworld, Belgium). An appealing and representative introduction to the music of the *bauls*, with good instrumental playing. Recorded in Belgium in the early 90s.

continued overleaf

continued from previous page

Fanfare de Calcutta (Mehbooba Band) *Signature* (France Musiques). Recorded in a Calcuttan back alley, this 2001 album perfectly captures the anarchic sound of the north Indian wedding brass band, complete with wailing clarinets, bumpy euphonium bass, raucous cornet and trumpet calls, big cymbal clashes, and jaunty, Punjabi *Bhangra*-influenced folk rhythms.

Purna Das Baul *Bauls of Bengal* (Cram World). A compelling introduction to the wild devotional music of the *bauls*, mystical wayfaring minstrels from Bengal whose ecstatic sounds have inspired figures as diverse as Rabindranath Tagore, Alan Ginsberg and Bob Dylan. Lutes, flutes and driving *khamak* percussion underscore the joyful vocals on this, India's top-selling folk release.

Various *Inde: Rajasthan* (Ocora, France). The most varied compilation to date of folk music from north and west Rajasthan, featuring a cross-section of the region's specialist music castes.

Indian classical music revolves around the point, probing it from every angle, yet maintaining a dignified restraint. It is this restraint that distinguishes Indian classical music from the carefree abandon of Indian pop and film music.

Raags and rhythms

The mainstay of all north Indian classical music is the **raag** (or *raga*), an immensely intricate system of scales and associated melodic patterns. Each of the 200 main *raags* is defined by its unique combination of scale-pattern, dominant notes, specific rules to be obeyed in ascending or descending and associated melodic phrases. While Indian classical music is renowned for improvisation, this only takes place within the strictly defined boundaries of a particular *raag*. If the improviser wanders away from the main musical form of the *raag* his or her performance ceases to be regarded as "classical" music. The mark of a good performer is the ability to improvise extensively without abandoning the set of defining rules.

Some *raags* are linked with particular seasons; there is a *raag* for rain, and one for spring; *raags* can be "masculine" or "feminine"; and musicologists may categorize them according to whether they are best suited to a male or female voice. Each *raag* is allotted a time of day, a time identified with the spiritual and emotional qualities of the *raag*. *Raags* are specifically allocated to early morning (either before or after sunrise), mid-morning, early afternoon, late afternoon, early evening (either before or after sunset), late evening, late night and post-midnight. This system causes a few problems in northern latitudes, for there is some argument as to whether a *raag* should be heard by clock-time or sun-time. Purists adhere to the archaic tradition of a "*raag* timetable" even if they're only listening to records.

The performance of a *raag*, whether sung or played on a sitar, sarod or *sarangi*, follows a set pattern. First comes the *alaap*, a slow, meditative "mood-setter" in free rhythm which explores the chosen *raag*, carefully introducing the notes of the scale one by one. The *alaap* can span several hours in the hands of a distinguished performer, but may only last a matter of minutes; older aficionados allege that most present-day listeners cannot sustain the attention required to appreciate a lengthy and closely argued *alaap*. As a result, performers have felt under pressure to abbreviate this section of the *raag*, to reach the faster middle and end sections as soon as possible. This became customary in the recording studio, although the advent of the CD, which does not force the music to fit into 25 minutes as the LP did, has initiated a move back to longer performances.

In the next two sections, the *jorh* and the *jhala*, the soloist introduces a rhythmic element, developing the *raag* and exploring its more complex variations. Only in the final section, the *gath*, does the percussion instrument – usually the tabla or *pakhavaj* – enter. The soloist introduces a short, fixed composition to which he or she returns between flights of improvisation. In this section rhythm is an important structural element. Both percussionist and soloist improvise, at times echoing each other and sometimes pursuing individual variations of rhythmic counterpoint, regularly punctuated by unison statements of a short melody known as "the composition". The *gath* itself is subdivided into three sections: a slow tempo passage known as *vilambit*, increasing to a medium tempo, called *madhya*, and finally the fast tempo, *drut*.

Just as the *raag* organizes melody, so the rhythm is organized by highly sophisticated structures expressed through cycles known as *taals*, which can be clapped out by hand. A *taal* is made up of a number of beats (*matras*), each beat defined by a combination of rhythm pattern and timbre. It is the unique set of patterns (*bols*) available within a particular *taal* that define it. There are literally hundreds of *taals*, but most percussionists use the same few favourites over and over again, the most common being the sixteen-beat *teentaal*.

The most unfamiliar aspect of *taal* to the Western ear is that the end of one cycle comes not on its last beat, but on the first beat of the following one, so that there is a continual overlap. This first beat is known as *sum*, a point of culmination which completes a rhythmic structure, and performers often indicate it by nodding to each other when they arrive at it. Audiences do the same to express satisfaction and appreciation.

Among smaller, more discerning audiences, verbal applause such as "Wah!" (Bravo!), or even "Subhan-Allah" (Praise be to God!), is considered the standard form of appreciation. Only in Western-style concert halls, where such exclamations would be inaudible, has hand-clapping come to replace these traditional gestures of approval.

Light classical music

Many concerts of classical music end with the performance of a piece in one of the styles collectively referred to as "light classical". Although they obey the rules of classical music with respect to *raag* and *taal*, they do so less rigorously than is required for a performance of *dhrupad*, *khayal* or other pure classical styles. The *alaap* is short or nonexistent, and the composition is frequently derived from a folk melody. Indeed, it could be said that light classical music is essentially a synthesis of folk and classical practice. The two most important and widespread types are *thumri* and *ghazal*.

Thumri

The origin of **thumri** is popularly ascribed to Nawab Wajid Ali Shah, who governed Lucknow (Avadh) from 1847 to 1856. Although little interested in matters of state, he was a great patron of the arts and during his reign music, dance, poetry, drama and architecture flourished. *Thumri* employs a specific set of *raags* and is particularly associated with *kathak* dance; the graceful movements of the dancer are echoed in the lyricism of the musical style. Although classical instrumentalists in concert frequently perform a *thumri* to relax from the intensity of the pure classical style, most *thumri* is vocal, and sung in a language known as Braj Bhasha, a literary dialect of Hindi. The singer is always accompanied by the tabla, as well perhaps as the tambura, the *sarangi* or the *surmandal*, and sometimes the violin or harmonium.

The lyrics of *thumri* deal with romance. Love songs, written from a female perspective, they stress themes like dressing up for a tryst, the heartache of absence and betrayal, quarrels and reconciliation, and the joyful return from a meeting with a husband or lover. Such themes are often expressed metaphorically, with references in the lyrics to the (suggestive) flute-playing of the god Krishna, the symbol of young love. Despite the concentration on the woman's point of view, some of the greatest singers of *thumri* have been men, notably Ustad Bade Ghulam Ali Khan. As male singers are frequently middle-aged and overweight, there is a certain initial incongruity about the spectacle of this depiction of the gentle and delicate emotions of a beautiful young woman. Yet a fine artist, fat and balding though he may be, can make a song like this one infinitely affecting: "My bracelets keep slipping off/My lover has cast a spell on me/He has struck me with his magic/What can a mere doctor do?" Her bracelets have slipped off because, while pining for her absent lover, she has starved herself to the point of emaciation.

Ghazal

Still more song-like than the *thumri* is the **ghazal**. In some ways the Urdu counterpart of *thumri*, the *ghazal* was introduced to India by Persian Muslims and is mainly a poetic rather than a musical form. Although some *ghazal* tunes are based on the *raag* system, others do not follow any specific mode. The *taals* are clearly derived from folk music; at times the *ghazal* shades into the area of sophisticated pop song. Indeed, at the more commercial end of the scale – the so-called film *ghazal* – sophistication gives way to mere charm. The *ghazal* has played an important part in the cultures of India, Pakistan and Afghanistan since the early eighteenth century, when it was one of the accomplishments required of a courtesan. Modern *ghazal* singers usually come from a more "respectable" background.

While *thumri* singers take on a female persona, emotions in the *ghazal* are almost always expressed from the male point of view. Some of the finest performers of *ghazals* are women – Begum Akhtar and Shobha Gurtu among them. Many favourite *ghazals* are drawn from the works of great Urdu poets.

A patriotic poem by Faiz Ahmed Faiz, *Mujhse Pehli Si Muhabbat Mere Mehboob Na Maang* (Do not ask me my love, to love you the way I used to love you), proved a milestone in the advance of art poetry into the realm of the film *ghazal*. Sung by the popular Pakistani singer Noor Jehan in her inimitable style, her interpretation is said to have so impressed the poet Faiz that he formally relinquished all claims to it in her favour.

Tales of the golden age

Ghazals can be heard every day on the radio or in films either in India or Pakistan or in Asian communities abroad, but pure classical music is most often heard in concert – a far cry from the golden age of Indian classical music, when its chief patrons were nawabs, maharajas and zamindar landlords. At this time Indian classical music was essentially court music, and its forms and practices, perfected within this framework, were clearly aimed at a leisured elite able to appreciate the subtleties that the musicians were developing.

Many traditional tales tell of this period. For instance, the **Prince of Mysore** would take his court musicians to a neighbouring district, inhabited by deadly snakes. The performers would then play the *poongi*, a kind of wind instrument. As the sounds grew louder, the snakes would venture from their holes and slide towards the musicians. The snakes would encircle the players completely and sway in perfect rhythm, as if intoxicated by the sound. As soon as the music stopped, they would glide away quietly without biting anyone. Another story is that of **Tan-Sen**, the greatest singer that India ever produced and court musician to the emperor Akbar. Tan-Sen was said to have such extraordinary power over his music that one day, when he began singing a late-night *raag* at noon, the world was plunged into darkness.

If another story is to be believed, there was a singer even greater than Tan-Sen. One day, as Tan-Sen sang the fiery *Raag Deepak*, the whole palace went up in flames. A young water-carrying maiden who happened to be passing by saw the flames, and taking a deep breath began to sing the *Raag Megh* (associated with rain). She sang with such emotion and sincerity that the heavens poured forth torrents and the flames caused by the great Tan-Sen were extinguished. Even in modern times, skilful performers are often credited with averting famine by singing *Raag Megh*. But *Raag Deepak* is superstitiously avoided these days.

Nearly every Indian musician has such tales attached to his or her name. Another one relates to **Ustad Imdaad Khan**, court musician at Indore and exponent of the *surbahar*. One night, as he accompanied the maharaja's entourage on a tiger hunt, there was concern about a mad elephant on the rampage. As night set in and everyone prepared to settle down and remain quiet for fear of the elephant, Imdaad upset the whole party by getting his *surbahar* out for his usual practice. When he had been playing a while, a most unusual sight was seen outside his tent – a huge elephant, swaying to the sound of the *surbahar* as though hypnotized. From then on, all through the hunt, Imdaad was ordered to play the *surbahar* each night in order to keep the elephant quiet.

Sound of the south

Southern India's **Carnatic** classical music is essentially similar to Hindustani classical music in outlook and theoretical background but differs in many details, usually ascribed to the far greater Islamic influence in the north. To the Western ear, Carnatic music is emotionally direct and impassioned, without the sometimes sombre restraint that characterizes much of the north's music. For instance the **alaapaana** section, although it introduces and develops the notes of the *raag* in much the same way as the *alaap* of north Indian music, interrupts its stately progress with sparkling decorative flourishes. Often, too, the *alaapaana* is succeeded by a set of increasingly complex elaborations of a basic melody in a way that is more easily grasped than the abstract, sometimes severe improvisations of the Hindustani masters. Compositions, both of "themes" and the set variations upon them, play a much greater role in Carnatic musical practice than in Hindustani.

The *raags* of Carnatic music, like those of Hindustani music, are theoretically numbered in the thousands and musicians are expected to be familiar with them all. In practice, however, there are only two hundred main *raags* ever played, and probably only fifty or sixty are in common use.

Song is at the root of south Indian music, and forms based on song are paramount, even when the performance is purely instrumental. The vast majority of the texts are religious, and the temple is frequently the venue for performance. The most important form is the *kriti*, a devotional song, hundreds of which were written by the most influential figure in the development of Carnatic music, the singer **Tyagaraja** (1767–1847). He was central to the music, not only for his compositions but also for the development of techniques of rhythmic and melodic variations. Southern India's biggest music festival, held annually near Thanjavur on the banks of the River Kaveri, is named after him.

Although the vocal tradition is central to this music, its singers are perhaps less well known in the West than instrumentalists. M.S. Subbulakshmi and Dr M. Balamurali Krishna are among the famous names, but the most celebrated is probably Ramnad Krishnan, who has taught in America.

The instruments of Carnatic music include the **vina**, which resembles the sitar but has no sympathetic strings (Carnatic musicians appear not to like the somewhat hollow timbre that they give to the instrument), the *mridangam* double-headed drum, and the enormous *nadasvaram*, a type of oboe just over a metre long which takes great experience and delicacy to play. The violin is widely used – listen to the playing of Dr L. Subramaniam or his brother L. Shankar, better known for his fusion experiments with guitarist John McLaughlin than for his classical recordings. The mandolin is growing in popularity and the saxophone has made a strikingly successful appearance in the hands of Kadri Gopalnath. Among *vina* players look out for S. Balachander and K.S. Nayaranaswami.

Percussion is very important, perhaps more so than in Hindustani music, and percussion ensembles frequently tour abroad. In addition to the *mridangam*, percussion instruments include the *ghatam*, a clay pot played with tremendous zest and sometimes tossed into the air in a burst of high spirits. "Vikku" Vinayakram is its best-known player.

New paths

In earlier times the job of musician was more or less hereditary: would-be musicians began their musical education at the age of four, and music (as a profession) was considered beneath the dignity of the well-to-do and the academic classes. However, in recent years traditional restrictions have been relaxed, and music is no longer the province of a few families. Many educated Indians are becoming involved in both performance and composition, and as public performance loses its stigma the requirement for musicians to begin their training at a very early age becomes less forceful. Women instrumentalists too are making their mark – a startling innovation in a male-dominated musical culture. Two women with particularly high reputations are violinist Sangeeta Rajan and tabla player Anuradha Pal, both of whom have recorded in India. Several *gharanas* have been set up abroad, notably the one in California run by sarod player **Ali Akbar Khan**, who is probably Indian music's most influential living figure, and there is a steady trickle of Westerners who are willing to subject themselves to the disciplines of study.

However, the importance of the old families is barely diminished. Among the younger generation of players are such names as sarod player Brij Narayan, son of Ram Narayan, Nikil Banerjee, who studied sitar with his father Jitendra Nath Banerjee, and Krishna Bhatt, who studied with Ravi Shankar and also comes from a family of musicians. Other important figures to listen out for are sitar player Rais Khan and vocalist Rashid Khan. These, like the other names mentioned, bear witness to the remaining vitality and richness of the classical music tradition in India and abroad.

Folk music of India

There are many kinds of **Indian folk music**, but the main regional strands are those of Uttar Pradesh, Rajasthan, the Punjab (spread across both India and Pakistan), and Bengal (including Bangladesh). Kashmir produces its own distinctive folk sound, and the music of many of India's tribal peoples more closely resembles that of Southeast Asia or even Borneo than anything else in the subcontinent. Apart from obvious linguistic differences, the folk songs of each region have their own distinct rhythmic structures and are performed on or accompanied by different musical instruments. Some classical instruments are used, but the following are mostly associated with less formal folk occasions.

In **Rajasthan**, music is always played for weddings and theatre performances, and often at local markets or gatherings. There is a whole caste of professional musicians who perform this function, and a wonderful assortment of earthy-sounding stringed instruments like the *kamayacha* and *ravanhata* that accompany their songs. The *ravanhata* is a simple, two-stringed fiddle that, skilfully played, can produce a tune of great beauty and depth. Hearing it played by a fine street musician behind the city walls of Jaisalmer, it seems the perfect aural background for this desert citadel.

The *satara* is the traditional instrument of the desert shepherds. A double flute, it has two pipes of different lengths, one to play the melody, the other to provide the drone, rather like bagpipes without the bag. The bag is the musician himself, who plays with circular breathing. Local cassettes of these instruments are available in small stores across Rajasthan.

As well as drums, India boasts a variety of tuned **percussion instruments**. The most popular in this category is the *jaltarang* – a water-xylophone – consisting of a series of porcelain bowls of different sizes, each containing a prescribed amount of water. The bowls are usually struck with a pair of small sticks, but sometimes these are abandoned as the player rubs the rims of the bowls with a wet finger. The small brass, dome-shaped cymbals called *manjira* or *taal* are the best known of the many kinds of bells and gongs.

Folk and film

There are songs for all kinds of work and play in India, and almost every activity is represented in song, and there is an extensive repertoire of dance music. Inevitably, **film music** has drawn heavily from this folk tradition, but sadly has also become a relatively effortless substitute for most of it. In some instances, "pop" adaptations of traditional folk music have served to revitalize and add a fresh lease of life to the original form – *bhangra*, the folk music of Punjab, is a very good example of this. British "*bhangra*-rock" has created a fresh interest in the original *bhangra* of the Punjabi farmers.

Marching bands

Spend any time in northern India, particularly during the winter wedding season, and you're almost certain to come across at least a couple of **marching bands**. First introduced to India by the British Army in the early nineteenth century and later adopted as a folk idiom right across the north and centre of the country (where they replaced the old *shehnai*-and-drum *naubat* troupes of the Moghul era), brass bands have become an essential ingredient of working-class weddings and religious processions. Decked out in ill-fitting, mock-military uniforms (complete with tinsel epaulettes, plastic-peaked caps and buckled gaiters), the musicians (band-wallahs) are most often called upon to accompany a bridegroom's party (*baraat*) in its procession to the bride's house. The music itself – a cacophony of squealing clarinets and crowd-stopping blasts of brass played over snare and *dholok* tattoos – is invariably at odds with the mood of the groom, sitting astride a hired white horse on his way to married life with a stranger. But no one seems to care, least of all the members of the *baraat*, hip-thrusting and strutting along like Bollywood's best to the stream of Hindi film hits, folk tunes, popular *raags* and patriotic songs.

Folk music is now beginning to awaken greater interest, particularly with non-Indian record companies, and largely as a result of the growing Western interest in different kinds of Indian music. Perhaps this overseas interest has come just in time, for although it is still practised in the old way in more traditional settings and for particular rituals – weddings, births, harvest time and so on – folk music on the whole, if it is to be defined as the "music of the people", has largely been eclipsed by the output of the Indian film industry.

Whereas in the past traditional wedding songs would have been sung by the neighbourhood women all through the festivities, it is now more usual to hear film songs blaring away at Indian weddings. Nonetheless, fears that traditional music is vanishing altogether seem unwarranted: in Pakistan the unique sound of the *sohni* bands – clarinet-led brass bands which play at weddings – fills the air with wild melody, and in Rajasthan members of the traditional musicians' castes still make their living by playing at ceremonies and for entertainment. The radio and cassette player are by no means all-conquering.

This piece, by Jameela Siddiqi, David Muddyman, Ken Hunt and Kim Burton, was taken from the *Rough Guide to World Music*.

Books

The following list is a personal selection of the books that proved most useful or enjoyable during the preparation of this guide. Most of them are available in India itself, as are countless inexpensive editions of Indian and English classics. Books tagged with the ⊠ symbol are particularly recommended.

History

⊠ **Jad Adams and Phillip Whitehead** *The Dynasty: The Nehru-Gandhi Story* (Penguin). A brilliant and intriguing account of India's most famous – or infamous – family and the way its various personalities have shaped post-Independence India, although Sonia Gandhi's recent prominence rather begs an update.

A.L. Basham *The wonder that was India* (South Asia Books). Learned survey of Indian history, society, music, art and literature from 400 BC to the coming of the Muslims. Volume II, by S A Rizvi, brings it up to the arrival of the British.

Judith M. Brown *Gandhi and Civil Disobedience* (Yale). Pragmatic view of Gandhi's politics, which, refreshingly, doesn't resort to hagiography.

Larry Collins and Dominique Lapierre *Freedom at Midnight* (HarperCollins). Readable, if shallow, account of Independence, highly sympathetic to the British and, particularly, to Mountbatten, who was the authors' main source of information.

⊠ **Patrick French** *Liberty or Death* (Flamingo). The definitive account (and a damning indictment) of the last years of the British Raj. Material from hitherto unreleased intelligence files shows how Churchill's "florid incompetence" and Atlee's "feeble incomprehen-

sion" contributed to the debacle that was Partition.

⊠ **Bamber Gascoigne** *The Great Moghuls* (Constable, London). By far the most interestingly written account of lives of the first six Great Moghuls, richly illustrated with photos of the surviving monuments and details from original art works. Essential reading if you plan to explore Agra and Delhi in any depth.

Richard Hall *Empires of the Monsoon* (Harper Collins). An impeccably researched account of early colonial expansion into the Arabian Sea and Indian Ocean, tracing the web of trade connections binding Europe, Africa and the sub-continent.

Lawrence James *Raj: the Making and Unmaking of British India* (Abacus, UK). A door-stopping 700-page history of British rule in India, drawing on recently released official papers and private memoirs. The most up-to-date, erudite survey of its kind, and unlikely to be bettered as a general introduction.

⊠ **John Keay** *India: a History* (HarperCollins). In this, the most recent of his five consistently excellent books on India, John Keay manages to coax clear, impartial and highly readable narrative from 5000 years of fragmented events, spiced up with a liberal dose of fascinating snippets. Arguably the

best single-volume history currently in print.

Romila Thapar *History of India
Volume I* (Penguin). Concise paper-
back account of early Indian histo-
ry, ending with the Delhi Sultanate.
Percival Spear's *History of India
Volume II* covers the period from
the Moghul era to the death of
Gandhi.

Mark Tully and Satish Jacob
Amritsar: Mrs Gandhi's Last Stand
(Penguin India). Aptly named exami-
nation of the storming of the
Golden Temple and the prime min-
ister's eventual assassination.

Society

Trevor Fishlock *India File* (John
Murray). The latest edition of this
now classic analysis of contemporary
Indian society includes essays on the
Golden Temple siege and the rise of
Rajiv Gandhi. Recommended as an
all-round introduction.

Zia Jaffrey *The Invisibles*
(Weidenfeld & Nicolson). An investigation into the hidden world of
Delhi's *hijras*, or eunuchs. Using
anthropological and journalistic
research techniques, Jaffrey unravels
the layers of myth and mystique surrounding this secretive subculture.

⭐ **Pramila Jayapal** *Pilgrimage*
(Penguin). Sensitive account of
diverse social situations and problems
in far-flung parts of India by Jayapal,
an academic and development
expert. Also provides insight into the
experience of a Westernized Indian
returning after most of her life
abroad.

⭐ **Gita Mehta** *Karma Cola*
(Minerva). Satirical look at the
psychedelic 1970s freak scene in
India, with some hilarious anecdotes, and many a wry observation
on the wackier excesses of spiritual
tourism. Mehta's latest book, *Snakes
and Ladders* (Vintage), is a brilliant
overview of contemporary urban
India in the form of a pot-pourri
of essays, travelogues and interviews.

Prafulla Mohanti *Changing Village,
Changing Life* (Penguin). Entertaining
portrait of life in an east Indian village through the eyes of an anglicized expat. Essential reading if you
plan to visit Orissa.

Geoffrey Moorhouse *Calcutta, the
City Revealed* (Phoenix). Fascinating,
if politically out of date, anatomy of
the great city in the early 1970s.

⭐ **V.S. Naipaul** *A Million Mutinies
Now* (Penguin). A superbly
crafted mosaic of individual lives
from around the subcontinent, producing a sympathetic and rounded
portrait of the country in one of the
best books on India ever written. In
sharp contrast, his earlier work, *A
Wounded Civilisation*, is a bleak political travelogue, researched and written during and shortly after the
Emergency.

⭐ **Mark Tully** *No Full Stops in
India* (Penguin). Earnest but
highly readable dissection of contemporary India by the former BBC
correspondent, incorporating anecdotes and first-hand accounts of
political events over the past twenty
years.

Various *India* (Granta). To commemorate the fiftieth anniversary of
Indian Independence, Granta published this mixed bag of new fiction,
comment, poetry, reportage and

memoirs from an impressive cast of Indian and foreign contributors. Among its many highlights are notes from the diary of V.S. Naipaul and Sebastião Salgado's photographic essay on Mumbai.

Travel

Bill Aitken *Nanda Devi Affair* (Penguin). Slow but deeply personal account of the author's long-standing love of the Indian Himalayas and his constant ambition to climb the elusive Nanda Devi peak.

⭐ **William Dalrymple** *City of Djinns* (Flamingo). Dalrymple's award-winning account of a year in Delhi sifts through successive layers of the city's past. Each is vividly brought to life with a blend of inspired historical sleuth work and encounters with living vestiges of different eras: Urdu calligraphers, Sufi clerics, eunuchs, Persian-style pigeon fanciers and the last surviving descendant of the Moghul emperors. A real gem. His most recent book, *The Age of Kali* (published in India as *In the Court of the Fish-Eyed Goddess*) is a collection of essays drawn from ten years' travel.

Trevor Fishlock *Cobra Road* (John Murray, UK). Former *Times* correspondent Fishlock's 1999 travelogue looks set to become a classic all-round introduction to the subcontinent. Sympathetic yet balanced, it looks at many of the ironies and absurdities inherent in modern India, whilst retaining a sense of humour and adventure.

⭐ **Alexander Frater** *Chasing the Monsoon* (Penguin). Frater's wet-season jaunt up the west coast and across the Ganges plains took him through an India of muddy puddles and grey skies: an evocative account of the country as few visitors see it, and now something of a classic of the genre.

Jonathan Gregson *Bullet Up The Grand Trunk Road* (Sinclair-Stevenson). Former journalist's motorcycle journey from Calcutta to the northwest frontier, with comment on contemporary issues along the way.

Norman Lewis *A Goddess in the Stones* (Picador). Veteran English travel writer's typically idiosyncratic account of his trip to Calcutta and around the backwaters of Bihar and Orissa, with some vivid insights into tribal India.

Geoffrey Moorhouse *Om* (Sceptre). Not Moorhouse's strongest offering, but absorbing nevertheless. Following the death of his daughter, the author journeys round south India's key spiritual centres, providing typically well-informed asides on history, politics, contemporary culture and religion.

Dervla Murphy *On a Shoestring to Coorg* (Flamingo). Murphy stays with her young daughter in the little-visited tropical mountains of Coorg, Karnataka. Arguably the most famous modern Indian travelogue, and a manifesto for single-parent budget travel.

⭐ **Eric Newby** *Slowly down the Ganges* (Picador). Newby has always regarded his mammoth journey from Haridwar to the mouth of the Hooghly as the most memorable of his many adventures. Though dated in places – it was written in the 1960s – his elegant prose and wry humour evoke the timeless allure of the subcontinent's holiest river.

Tahir Shah *Sorcerer's Apprentice* (Weidenfeld & Nicolson). A journey through the weird underworld of occult India. Travelling as an apprentice to a master conjurer and illusionist, Shah encounters hangmen, baby renters, skeleton dealers, *sadhus* and charlatans.

Mark Shand *Travels on My Elephant* (Penguin). Award-winning account of a 600-mile ride on an elephant from Konarak in Orissa to Bihar, accompanied by a drunken mahout, among others; full of incident, humour and pathos. For the sequel, *Queen of the Elephants*, Shand teams up with an Assamese princess who's the country's leading elephant handler.

Aglaja Stirn & Peter van Ham *The Seven Sisters of India* (Prestel).

Definitive coffee-table book on northeastern India. Rich anthropological detail in the text is illustrated with superb photographs.

Heather Wood *Third-Class Ticket* (Penguin). A party of elderly Bengalis leave their home village for the first time to tour the subcontinent by train. Absorbing and poignant, though the ersatz fictional style grates after a while.

Michael Wood *The Smile of Murugan* (Viking). An erudite and affectionate portrait of Tamil Nadu and its people in the mid-1990s, centred on a video-bus pilgrimage tour of the state's key sacred sites. One of the most enlightening books on south India ever written, though less interesting if you're not familiar with the region.

Fiction

Anita Desai *Feasting and Fasting* (Vintage). This, the most recent novel by one of India's leading female authors, eloquently portrays the frustration of a sensitive young woman stuck in the stifling atmosphere of home while her spoilt brother is packed off to study in America.

E.M. Forster *A Passage to India* (Longman). Forster's most acclaimed novel, a withering critique of colonialism set in the 1920s. Memorable as much for its sympathetic portrayal of middle-class Indian life as for its insights into cultural misunderstandings.

Clive James *The Silver Castle* (Picador). Delightful story of a street urchin's rise from the roadside slums of outer Mumbai to the bright lights of Bollywood.

Ruth Prawer Jhabvala *Out of India* (Penguin). One of many short-story

collections that shows India in its full colours: amusing, shocking and thought-provoking. Other titles include *How I Became a Holy Mother*; *Like Birds, Like Fishes*; *Heat and Dust*; and *In Search of Love and Beauty*.

Rudyard Kipling *Kim* (Penguin). Cringingly colonialist at times, of course, but the atmosphere of India and Kipling's love of it shine through in this subtle story of an orphaned white boy. Kipling's other key works on India are two books of short stories: *Soldiers Three* and *In Black and White*.

Dominique Lapierre *City of Joy* (Arrow). Melodramatic story of a white man's journey into Calcutta's slums, loaded with anecdotes about Indian religious beliefs and customs.

Rohinton Mistry *A Fine Balance* (Faber). Two friends seek promotion from their low-caste rural lives to the opportunities of the big smoke. A compelling and savage triumph-of-the-human-spirit novel detailing the evils of the caste system and of Indira Gandhi's brutal policies during the Emergency. Mistry's *Such a Long Journey* (Faber) is an acclaimed account of a Bombay Parsi's struggle to maintain personal integrity in the face of betrayals and disappointment.

★ **R.K. Narayan** *Gods, Demons and Others* (Vintage, India). Classic Indian folk tales and popular myths told through the voice of a village storyteller. Many of Narayan's beautifully crafted books, full of touching characters and subtle humour, are set in the fictional south India territory of Malgudi.

★ **Arundhati Roy** *The God of Small Things* (Minerva). Haunting Booker Prize-winner about a well-to-do south Indian family caught between the snobberies of high caste tradition, a colonial past and the diverse personal histories of its members. Seen through the eyes of two children, the assortment of scenes from Keralan life are as memorable as the characters themselves, while the comical and finally tragic turn of events say as much about Indian history as the refrain that became the novel's catchphrase: "things can change in a day".

★ **Salman Rushdie** *Midnight's Children* (Everyman). This story of a man born at the very moment of Independence, whose life mirrors that of modern India itself, won Rushdie the Booker Prize and the enmity of Indira Gandhi, who had it banned in India. Set in Kerala and

Bombay, *The Moor's Last Sigh* (Jonathan Cape), was the subject of a defamation case brought by Shiv Sena leader Bal Thackeray.

★ **Vikram Seth** *A Suitable Boy* (Phoenix). Vast, all-embracing tome set in UP shortly after Independence; wonderful characterization and an impeccable sense of place and time make this an essential read for those long train journeys.

Manohar Shetty (ed) *Ferry Crossing* (Penguin). A "must read" if you are heading for Goa; broadly themed and colourful short stories woven around the local landscape and people.

Kushwant Singh *Train to Pakistan* (Ravi Dayal, Delhi). A chillingly realistic portrayal of life in a village on the Partition line, set in the summer of 1947. Singh's other works include *Delhi: A Novel*, a series of voices from the city's past interrupted by an old man's quest for sexual satisfaction in the present and *Sex, Scotch and Scholarship*, a collection of wry short stories.

William Sutcliffe *Are You Experienced?* (Penguin). Hilarious easy read sending up a "typical" backpacker trip round India.

Mark Tully *The Heart of India* (Penguin). The loyalties and deceptions of village life in UP, revealed through a series of short stories by an old India hand and former BBC correspondent. Hardly the best fiction to have come out of the country, but there are few more accessible anatomies of conflict-ridden modern India.

Biography and autobiography

J.R. Ackerley *Hindoo Holiday* (Penguin). During the 1920s, a gay

and eccentric pal of E.M. Forster steps into the bizarre world of an even more gay and eccentric maharaja seeking a tutor for his eighteen-month-old son.

Charles Allen *Plain Tales from the Raj* (Abacus). First-hand accounts from erstwhile *sahibs* and *memsahibs* of everyday British India, organized thematically.

James Cameron *An Indian Summer* (Penguin). Affectionate and humorous description of the veteran British journalist's visit to India in 1972, and his marriage to an Indian woman. Somewhat dated, but an enduring classic.

Gayatri Devi *A Princess Remembers* (Rupa, India). Nostalgic reminiscences of life as Maharani of Jaipur and as a politician by "one of the world's most beautiful women".

★ **M.K. Gandhi** *The Story of My Experiments with Truth* (Penguin). Gandhi's fascinating records of his life, including the spiritual and moral quests, changing relationship with the British Government in India, and gradual emergence into the fore of politics.

H.H. the Dalai Lama *Freedom in Exile* (Harper). Moving autobiography, full of humility and wisdom, and account of the Tibetan situation, told with dignity, beauty and clarity.

Paramahansa Yogananda *Autobiography of a Yogi* (Self Realization Fellowship). Uplifting account of religious awakening and spiritual development by one of the most influential Hindu masters to leave India and bring her teachings to the West.

Women

★ **Elizabeth Bumiller** *May You Be the Mother of a Hundred Sons* (Fawcett Books/Penguin India). Lucid exploration of the Indian woman's lot, drawn from dozens of first-hand encounters by an American journalist.

Sashi Deshpande *The Binding Vine* (Virago). Disturbing story of one woman's struggle for independence, and her eventual acceptance of the position of servitude traditionally assumed by an Indian wife.

Anees Jung *The Night of the New Moon* (Penguin). Revealing and poetic stories woven around interviews with Muslim women from all sectors of Indian society. Jung's *Unveiling India* is a compelling account of the life of a Muslim woman who has chosen to break free from orthodoxy.

Sarah Lloyd *An Indian Attachment* (Eland Books). Life in a Punjabi plains village through the eyes of a young Western woman, whose relationship with an opium-addicted Sikh forms the essence of this honest and enlightening book.

★ **Vrinda Nabar** *Caste as Woman* (Penguin India). Conceived as an Indian counterpart to Greer's *The Female Eunuch*, a wry study of the pressures brought to bear during the various stages of womanhood. Drawing on scripture and popular culture, Nabar looks at issues of identity and cultural conditioning.

Sakuntala Narasiman *Sati: A Study of Widow Burning in India* (Harper Collins). Definitive and engaging exploration of *sati* and its significance throughout history, including an account of the infamous Roop Kanwar case.

Sebasti L. Raj (ed) *Quest for Gender Justice* (TR Publications, Chennai). Collection of articles on the status of women in modern India by academics, activists and a couple of High Court judges.

Mala Sen *India's Bandit Queen* (HarperCollins). Journalistic account of the life of Phoolan Devi, the legendary bandit leader and subject of Shekar Kapur's film *Bandit Queen*.

Virama, Josiane Racine & Jean-Luc Racine *Virama: Life of an Untouchable* (Verso). Unique autobiography of an untouchable woman told in her own words (transcribed by French anthropologists) over a fifteen-year period, offering frank, often humorous insights into India, the universe and everything.

Development and the environment

Julia Cleves Mosse *India: Paths to Development* (Oxfam). Concise analysis of the economic, environmental and political changes affecting India, focusing on the lives of ordinary poor people and the exemplary ways some have succeeded in shaping their own future. The best country brief on the market, but only available through Oxfam, and now somewhat out of date.

⭐ Helena Norberg-Hodge *Ancient Futures: Learning From Ladakh* (Rider). An overview of Ladakh's traditional, ecologically balanced way of life, followed up by an analysis of the ways in which modern developments (notably tourism) have impinged upon it.

⭐ Jeremy Seabrook *Notes from Another India* (Pluto Press). Life

histories and interviews – compiled over a year's travelling and skilfully contextualized – reveal the everyday problems faced by Indians from a variety of backgrounds, and how grassroots groups have tried to combat them. One of the soundest, and most engaging, overviews of Indian development issues ever written.

⭐ Palagummi Sainath *Everybody Loves a Good Drought* (Penguin, India). A classic report on India's poorest districts, telling the stories of individual villages that are usually lost in a maze of development statistics. Its harrowing case studies caused uproar in the capital, galvanizing the government into some drastic aid programmes. A polished view on an India few visitors see.

The arts and architecture

Roy Craven *Indian Art* (Thames & Hudson). Concise general introduction to Indian art, from Harappan seals to Moghul miniatures, with lots of illustrations.

Mohan Khokar *Traditions of Indian Classical Dance* (Clarion Books,

India). Detailing the religious and social roots of Indian dance, this lavishly illustrated book, with sections on regional traditions, is an excellent introduction to the subject.

George Michell *The Hindu Temple* (University of Chicago Press). A fine primer, introducing Hindu temples, their significance, and architectural development.

Bonnie C. Wade *Music in India: The Classical Traditions* (Manmohar, India). A scrupulous catalogue of Indian music, outlining the most commonly used instruments, with illustrations and musical scores.

Stuart Cary Welch *India: Art and Culture 1300–1900* (Prestel). Originally produced for an exhibition at New York's Metropolitan Museum, this exquisitely illustrated and accessibly written tome covers every aspect of India's rich and varied culture. Highly recommended.

Religion

★ **Diana L. Eck** *Banaras – City of Light* (o/p). Thorough disquisition on the religious significance of Varanasi; a good introduction to the practice of Hindu cosmology. Her latest book, *Encountering God*, uses Christianity as a reference point for an exploration of the common ground between Hinduism and Buddhism.

★ **Dorf Hartsuiker** *Sadhus: Holy Men of India* (Inner Traditions International). The weird world of India's itinerant ascetics exposed in glossy colour photographs and erudite but accessible text.

J.R. Hinnelle (ed) *A Handbook of Living Religions* (Penguin). The beliefs, practices, iconography and historical roots of all India's major faiths explained in accessible language, with full bibliographies to back up each chapter. Deservedly the most popular book of its kind in print, and an ideal in-depth introduction.

★ **Roger Housden** *Travels through Sacred India* (o/p). A gazetteer of

holy places, listings of ashrams and lively essays on temples, *sadhus*, gurus and sacred sites. Hudson derives much of his material from personal encounters, which bring the subjects to life. Includes sections on all India's main faiths, and an excellent bibliography.

Christmas Humphries *Buddhism* (Penguin). Dated, and short on rituals and practices, but still the clearest, most readable work on the philosophy and beliefs of the various strands of Buddhism.

Wendy O'Flaherty (transl.) *Hindu Myths* (Penguin). Translations of key myths from the original Sanskrit texts, providing an insight into the foundations of Hinduism.

Charlie Pye-Smith *Rebels and Outcasts: A Journey through Christian India* (Penguin). An Englishman's encounters with clerics, congregations and NGOs from the full gamut of denominations. The most up-to-date survey on the subject, although unlikely to appeal to non-Christians.

Language

No less than eighteen major languages, officially recognized by the constitution, numerous minor ones and over a thousand dialects are spoken across India. When independent India was organized, the present-day states were largely created along linguistic lines, which at least helps the traveller make some sense of the complex situation. Considering the continuing prevalence of English, there is rarely any necessity to speak a local language but some theoretical knowledge of the background and having at least a few words of one or two can only enhance your visit.

The main languages of northern India, including the country's eastern and western extremities, are all Indo-Aryan, the easternmost subgroup of the Indo-European family that is thought to have originated somewhere between Europe and Central Asia several millennia BC, before tribal movements spread its progeny in all directions. The oldest extant subcontinental language is Sanskrit, one of the three "big sisters" (along with Latin and Greek) upon which philologists have created the model of proto-Indo-European language. It's known to have been spoken early in the second millennium BC, although it was not written down until much later, and is the vehicle for all the sacred texts of Hinduism. Sanskrit remained the language of the educated until around 1000 AD and is still spoken to some extent by the priestly class today, but over the centuries it gradually developed into the modern tongues of northern India: Hindi, Urdu, Bengali, Gujarati, Marathi, Kashmiri, Punjabi and Oriya.

North India

Hindi, the first language of over 200 million natives of north India, and **Urdu**, predominant among Muslims and across the border in Pakistan, are very closely related and prime examples of New Indo-Aryan languages. They developed in tandem around the markets and army camps of Delhi (the term Urdu derives from the Turkish word for "camp") during the establishment of Muslim rule around the start of the second millennium AD. Whereas Hindi later returned to the Sanskrit roots of its Hindu speakers, however, and adopted the classical **Devanagari** syllabary, Urdu became culturally more closely linked with Islam and is written in **Perso-Arabic** script. The vocabulary of each also reflects these cultural and religious ties. The scripts of Punjabi, Bengali and Gujarati are among those that have developed out of Devanagari and still bear some resemblance to it.

South India

In **south India** the picture changes completely. The four most widely spoken languages, Tamil (Tamil Nadu), Telugu (Andhra Pradesh), Kannada (Karnataka) and Malayalam (Kerala) all belong to the **Dravidian** family, the world's fourth largest group. These and related minor languages grew up quite separately among the non-Aryan peoples of southern India over thousands of years and the earliest written records of **Tamil** date back to the third century AD. The exact origins of the Dravidian group have not been established but it is possible that proto-Dravidian was spoken further north in prehistoric times before the people were driven south by the Aryan invaders. The beautiful flowing scripts, especially the exquisite curls of **Kannada**, add a constant aesthetic quality to any tour of the south.

Greetings

Greetings	*Namaste* (said with palms together at chest height as in prayer – not used for Muslims)
Hello	*Namaskar* (not used for Muslims)
Greetings	(to a Muslim) *Aslaam alequm* in reply – *ale qum aslaam*
We will meet again	*phir milenge* (goodbye)
Goodbye (to a Muslim)	*Khudaa Haafiz* (may God bless you)
How are you? (formal)	*Ap kaise hain*
How are you? (familiar)	*Kya hal hai*
Brother (a common address to a stranger)	*bhaaii* or *bhaayaa*
Sister	*didi*
Sir	*Hazuur* (Muslims only)
Sir (Sahib)	*Saaheb*

Basic words

Yes	*haan*
OK	*achhaa*
No	*nahin*
Me	*main*
You (formal)	*ap*
You (familiar)	*tum*
And/More	*aur*
How	*kaise*
How much	*kitna*
Thank-you	*dhanyavad/shukriya*
Good	*achhaa*
Bad	*kharaab*
Big	*baraa*
Small	*chhotaa*
Hot	*garam*

Cold	*thandaa*
Hot (spicy)	*jhaal*
Clean	*saaf*
Dirty	*gandaa*
Open	*khulaa*
Expensive	*mehngaa*
Come	*aao*
Please come	*aaiiye*
Go	*jaao*
Run (also "take a run" or "scram")	*bhaago*

Basic phrases

My name is . . .	*Mera nam . . . hai*
What is your name? (formal)	*Aapka naam kya hai*
What is your name? (familiar)	*Tumhara naam kya hai*
I (male) come from . . .	*Main . . . se aa rahaa hun*
I (female) come from . . .	*Main . . . se aa rahii hun*
Where do you come from?	*Kahan se aate hain*
I don't know	*Maalum nahin*
I don't understand	*Samaj nahin aayaa*
I understand	*Samaj gayaa*
I don't speak Hindi	*Main Hindi nahin bol sakta hun*
Please speak slowly	*Aaiste se boliye*
Please forgive me (I am sorry)	*Mujhe maaf kiijiiye*
It is OK	*Thiik hai*
How much?	*Kitna paisa?*
How much is this?	*Iskaa daam kyaa hai?*
What work do you do?	*Kya kaam karte hain?*
Do you have any brothers or sisters?	*Bhaai behan hai?*

Getting around

Where is the . . . ?	*. . . kahaan hai?*

Post Independence

With **Independence** it was decided by the government in Delhi that Hindi should become the **official language** of the newly created country. Interestingly, the idea of using Hindustani, a more recent colloquial hybrid of Hindi

I want to go to . . .	Main . . . jaanaa chaataa hun.	Four	char
Where is it?	Kahaan hai?	Five	panch
How far?	Kitnaa duur?	Six	chhe
Which is the bus for Gwalior?	Gwalior kaa bas kahaanhai?	Seven	saat
		Eight	aath
What time does the train leave?	Gaarii kab chhutegii?	Nine	nau
		Ten	das
Stop	ruko	Eleven	gyaara
Wait	thero	Twelve	baarah
		Thirteen	terah

Accommodation

		Fourteen	chaudah
I need a room	Mujhe kamraa chaahiye	Fifteen	pandrah
		Sixteen	solah
How much is the room?	Kamraa kaa bhaaraa kyaa hai?	Seventeen	satrah
		Eighteen	athaarah
I am staying for one night	Main ek raat ke liiye tehr rahaa hun	Nineteen	unniis
		Twenty	biis
		Thirty	tiis

Medicinal

		Forty	chaaliis
I have a headache	Sir me dard hai	Fifty	pachaas
		Sixty	saatha
I have a pain in my stomach	Meraa pet me dardhai	Seventy	sathar
		Eighty	assii
The pain is here	Dard yahaan hai	Ninety	nabbe
Where is the doctor's surgery?	Daaktarkhaanaa kahaan hai?	One hundred	ek sau
		One thousand	ek hazaar
		One hundred thousand	ek lakh
Where is the hospital?	Haspitaal kahaan hai?		
		Ten million	ek crore
Where is the pharmacy?	Dawaiikhaanaa kahaa hai?	Today	aaj
		Tomorrow/yesterday	kai
Medicine	dawaaii	Day	din
Ill	bimar	Afternoon	dopahar
Pain	dard	Evening	shaam
Stomach	pet	Night	raat
Eye	aankh	Week	haftaa
Nose	naakh	Month	mahiinaa
Ear	kaan	Year	saal
Back	piit	Monday	somvaar
Foot	paao	Tuesday	mangalvaar
		Wednesday	budhvaar
		Thursday	viirvaar

Numbers and time

Zero	sayfar	Friday	shukravaar
One	ek	Saturday	shanivaar
Two	do	Sunday	ravivaar
Three	tin		

and Urdu, popular with Gandhi and others in an effort to encourage communal unity during the fight for freedom, was never pursued; this was due to a mixture of political reasons following Partition and the fact that the language lacked the necessary refinement. A drive to teach Hindi in all schools followed and over half the country's population are now reckoned to have a decent working knowledge of the language. However, there has always been strong **resistance** to the imposition of Hindi in certain areas, especially the **Tamil-led** Dravidian south, and the vast majority of people living below the Deccan plateau have little or no knowledge of it.

This is where English, the language of the ex-colonists, becomes an important means of communication. Not surprisingly, given India's rich linguistic diversity – there are also minority tribal languages and dialects of Sino-Tibetan that do not belong to the main groups mentioned above – **English** remains a **lingua franca** for many people. It is still the preferred language of law, higher education, much of commerce and the media, and to some degree political dialogue. For many educated Indians, not just those living abroad, it is actually their first language. All this explains why the Anglophone visitor can often soon feel surprisingly at home despite the huge cultural differences. It is not unusual to overhear everyday contact between Indians from different parts of the country being conducted in English, and stimulating conversations can often be had, not only with students or businesspeople, but also with chai wallahs or shoeshine boys.

Indian English

Over the period of the British Raj, **Indian English** developed its own characteristics, which have survived to the present day. The lilting stress and intonation patterns are owing to crossover from the Indian languages, as is the sometimes bewildering pace of delivery. Likewise, certain **vowel sounds**, for example the lack of distinction between the pronunciation of "cot" and "caught", and the utterance of some consonants, such as the common retroflex nature of "p" and "t" with the tongue touching the soft palate, are also due to strong local linguistic features.

Indian languages have contributed a good deal of **vocabulary** to everyday English as well, including words like veranda, bungalow, sandal, pyjamas, shampoo, jungle, turban, caste, chariot, chilli, cardamom and yoga. The traveller to India soon becomes familiar with other terms in common usage that have not spread so widely outside the subcontinent: *dacoit, dhoti, bandh, panchayat, lakh* and *crore* are but a few (see Glossary opposite for definitions).

Perhaps the most endearing aspect of Indian English is the way it has preserved forms now regarded as highly **old-fashioned** in Britain. Addresses such as "Good sir" and questions like "May I know your good name?" are commonplace, as are terms like "tiffin", "cantonment" or "top-hole". This type of usage reaches its apogee in the more flowery expressions of the media which regularly feature in the vast array of daily newspapers published in English. Thus headlines often appear such as "37 perish in mishap", referring to a train crash, or passages like this splendid report of a bank robbery: "The miscreants absconded with the loot in great haste. They repaired immediately to their hideaway, whereupon they divided the iniquitous spoils before vanishing into thin air."

Glossary

ACHARYA religious teacher

ADIVASI official term for tribal person

AGARBATI incense

AHIMSA nonviolence

AKHANDPATH continuous reading of the Sikh holy book, the *Adi Granth*

AMRITA nectar of immortality

ANGREZI general term for Westerners

ANNA coin, no longer minted (16 annas to one rupee)

APSARA heavenly nymph

ARAK liquor distilled from rice or coconut

ARATA evening temple *puja* of lights

ASANA yogic seating posture; small mat used in prayer and meditation

ASHRAM centre for spiritual learning and religious practice

ASURA demon

ATMAN soul

AVATAR reincarnation of Vishnu on earth, in human or animal form

AYAH nursemaid

AYURVEDA ancient system of medicine employing herbs, minerals and massage

BABA respectful term for a *sadhu*

BAGH garden, park

BAITHAK reception area in private house

BAKSHEESH tip, donation or alms, occasionally means a bribe

BANDH general strike

BANDHANI tie-dye

BANIYA another term for a *vaishya*; a moneylender

BANYAN vast fig tree, used traditionally as a meeting place, or shade for teaching and meditating. Also, in south India, a cotton vest

BASTEE slum area

BAUL Bengali singer

BAZAAR commercial centre of town; market

BEGUM Muslim princess; Muslim women of high status

BETEL leaf chewed in *paan*, with the nut of the areca tree: loosely applies to the nut, also

BHAJAN song

BHAKTI religious devotion expressed in a personalized or emotional relationship with the deity

BHANG pounded marijuana, often mixed in lassis

BHOTIA Himalayan people of Tibetan origin

BHUMI earth, or earth goddess

BIDI tobacco rolled in a leaf; the "poor man's puff"

BINDU seed, or the red dot (also *bindi*) worn by women on their foreheads as decoration

BODHI TREE/BO TREE peepal tree, associated with the Buddha's enlightenment (*ficus religiosa*)

BODHI enlightenment

BODHISATTVA Buddhist saint

BRAHMIN a member of the highest caste group; priest

BUGYAL summer meadow

BUNDH general strike

BURKHA body-covering shawl worn by orthodox Muslim women

BURRA-SAHIB colonial official, boss or a man of great importance

CANTONMENT area of town occupied by military quarters

CASTE social status acquired at birth

CHAAT snack

CHADDAR large head-cover or shawl

CHAKRA discus; focus of power; energy point in the body; wheel, often representing the cycle of death and rebirth

CHANDAN sandalwood paste

CHANDRA moon

CHANG Ladakhi beer made from fermented millet, wheat or rice

CHAPPAL sandals or flip-flops (thongs)

Note that a separate glossary of architectural terms appears on p.1578; many religious terms are explained in detail in the section which begins on p.1504; and musical instruments on p.1549 onwards.

CHARAS hashish

CHARPOI string bed with wooden frame

CHAURI fly whisk, regal symbol

CHELA pupil

CHIKAN Lucknow embroidery

CHILLUM cylindrical clay or wood pipe for smoking *charas* or *ganja*

CHOLI short, tight-fitting blouse worn with a sari

CHOR robber

CHOULTRY quarters for pilgrims adjoined to south Indian temples

CHOWGAN green in the centre of a town or village

CHOWK crossroads or courtyard

CHOWKIDAR watchman/caretaker

COOLIE porter/labourer

CRORE ten million

DABBA packed lunch

DACOIT bandit

DALIT "oppressed", "out-caste". The term, introduced by Dr Ambedkar, is preferred by so-called "untouchables" as a description of their social position

DANDA staff, or stick

DARSHAN vision of a deity or saint; receiving religious teachings

DAWAN servant

DEG cauldron for food offerings, often found in *dargahs*

DEVA god

DEVADASI temple dancer

DEVI goddess

DEVTA deity from Himachal Pradesh

DHABA food hall selling local dishes

DHAM important religious site, or a theological college

DHARAMSHALA rest house for pilgrims

DHARMA sense of religious and social duty (Hindu); the law of nature, teachings, truth (Buddhist)

DHOBI laundry

DHOLAK double-ended drum

DHOLI sedan chair carried by bearers to hilltop temples

DHOOP thick pliable block of strong incense

DHOTI white ankle-length cloth worn by males, tied around the waist, and sometimes hitched up through the legs

DHURRIE woollen rug

DIGAMBARA literally "sky-clad": a Jain sect, known for the habit of nudity

among monks, though this is no longer commonplace

DIKPALAS guardians of the four directions

DIWAN (*dewan*) chief minister

DOWRY payment or gift offered in marriage

DRAVIDIAN of the south

DUPATTA veil worn by Muslim women with *salwar kamise*

DURBAR court building; government meeting

DZO domesticated half-cow half-yak

EVE-TEASING sexual harassment of women, either physical or verbal

FAKIR ascetic Muslim mendicant

FENI Goan spirit, distilled from coconut or cashew fruits

GADA mace

GADI throne

GANDA dirty

GANDHARVAS Indra's heavenly musicians

GANJ market

GANJA marijuana buds

GARI vehicle, or car

GHAT mountain, landing platform, or steps leading to water

GHAZAL melancholy Urdu songs

GHEE clarified butter

GONCHA ankle-length woollen robe worn by Ladakhi women

GOONDA ruffian

GOPI young cattle-tending maidens who feature as Krishna's playmates and lovers in popular mythology

GURU teacher of religion, music, dance, astrology etc

GURUDWARA Sikh place of worship

HAJ Muslim pilgrimage to Mecca

HAJJI Muslim engaged upon, or who has performed, the *haj*

HARIJAN title – "Children of God" – given to "untouchables" by Gandhi

HARTAL one-day strike

HIJRA eunuch or transvestite

HINAYANA literally "lesser vehicle": the name given to the original school of Buddhism by later sects

HOOKAH water pipe for smoking strong tobacco or marijuana

HOWDAH bulky elephant-saddle, sometimes made of pure silver, and often shaded by a canopy

IDGAH area laid aside in the west of town for prayers during the Muslim festival Id-ul-Zuhara

IMAM Muslim leader or teacher

IMFL Indian-made foreign liquor

ISHWARA God; Shiva

JAGHIDAR landowner

JANAPADAS small republics and monarchies; literally "territory of the clan"

JATAKAS popular tales about the Buddha's life and teachings

JATI caste, determined by family and occupation

JAWAN soldier

JHUTA soiled by lips: food or drink polluted by touch

-JI suffix added to names as a term of respect

JIHAD striving by Muslims, through battle, to spread their faith

JINA another term for the Jain *tirthankaras*

JOHAR old practice of self-immolation by women in times of war

JYOTRILINGA twelve sites sacred by association with Shiva's unbounded *lingam* of light

KAILASA or **KAILASH** A mountain in western Tibet: Shiva's abode and the traditional source of the Ganges and Brahmaputra; the earthly manifestation of the "world pillar", Mt Meru

KALAM school of painting

KAMA satisfaction

KAMISE women's knee-length shirt, worn with salwar trousers

KARMA weight of good and bad actions that determine status of rebirth

KATCHA the opposite of *pukka*

KAVAD small decorated box that unfolds to serve as a travelling temple

KHADI home-spun cotton; Gandhi's symbol of Indian self-sufficiency

KHAN honorific Muslim title

KHEJRI small tree found in the Thar desert in Rajasthan

KHOL black eye-liner, also known as *surma*

KHUD valley side

KIRTAN hymn-singing

KOTWALI police station

KSHATRYA the warrior and ruling caste

KUMKUM red mark on a Hindu woman's forehead (widows are not supposed to wear it)

KUND tank, lake, reservoir

KURTA long men's shirt worn over baggy pajamas

LAKH one hundred thousand

LAMA Tibetan Buddhist monk and teacher

LATHI heavy stick used by police

LINGAM phallic symbol in places of worship representing the god Shiva

LOKA realm or world, eg devaloka, world of the gods

LUNGHI male garment; long wraparound cloth, like a *dhoti*, but usually coloured

MADRASA Islamic school

MAHA- great or large

MAHADEVA literally "Great God", and a common epithet for Shiva

MAHALLA neighbourhood

MAHARAJA (Maharana, Maharao) king

MAHARANI queen

MAHATMA great soul

MAHAYANA "Great Vehicle": a Buddhist school that has spread throughout Southeast Asia

MAHOUT elephant driver or keeper

MAIDAN large open space or field

MALA necklace, garland or rosary

MANDALA religious diagram

MANDI market

MANDIR temple

MANI STONE stone etched with Buddhist prayers by Tibetans and laid in piles or set in streams

MANTRA sacred verse, often repeated as an aid to meditation

MARG road

MASJID mosque

MATAJI female *sadhu*

MATH Hindu or Jain monastery

MAUND old unit of weight (roughly 20kg)

MAYUR peacock

MEHENDI henna

MELA festival

MEMSAHIB respectful address to European woman

MITHUNA sexual union, or amorous couples in Hindu and Buddhist figurative art

MOKSHA blissful state of freedom from rebirth aspired to by Hindus and Jains

MOR peacock

MUDRA hand gesture used in Vedic rituals, featuring in Hindu, Buddhist and Jain art and dance, and symbolizing teachings and life stages of the Buddha

MUEZZIN man behind the voice calling Muslims to prayer from a mosque

MULLAH Muslim teacher and scholar

MUTT Hindu or Jain monastery

NADI river

NAGA mythical serpent; alternatively a person from Nagaland

NALA stream gorge in the mountains

NATAK dance

NATYA drama

NAUTCH performance by dancing girls

NAWAB Muslim landowner or prince

NILGAI blue bull

NIRVANA (aka *NIBBANA*) Buddhist equivalent of *moksha*

NIZAM title of Hyderabad rulers

NULLAH stream gorge in the mountains

OM (aka *AUM*) symbol denoting the origin of all things, and ultimate divine essence, used in meditation by Hindus and Buddhists

PAAN betel nut, lime, calcium and aniseed wrapped in a leaf and chewed as a digestive. Mildly addictive

PADMA lotus; another name for the goddess Lakshmi

PAISE there are a hundred paisa in a rupee

PAJAMA men's baggy trousers

PALI original language of early Buddhist texts

PANCHAYAT village council

PANDA pilgrims' priest

PARIKRAMA ritual circumambulation around a temple, shrine or mountain

PARSI Zoroastrian

PIND mourning ceremony on the thirteenth day after the death of an aged parent

PIR Muslim holy man

POL residential quarters, common in Gujarat

PRANAYAMA breath control, used in meditation

PRASAD food blessed in temple sanctuaries and shared among devotees

PRAYAG auspicious confluence of two or more rivers

PUJA worship

PUJARI priest

PUKKA correct and acceptable, in the very English sense of "proper"

PUNYA religious merit

PURDAH seclusion of Muslim women inside the home, and the general term for wearing a veil

PURNIMA full moon

PUROHIT priest

QAWWALI devotional singing popular among Sufis

RAAG or RAGA series of notes forming the basis of a melody

RAJ rule; monarchy; in particular the period of British Imperial rule 1857–1947

RAJA king

RAJPUT princely rulers who once dominated much of north and west India

RAKSHASA demon (demoness: *rakshasi*)

RANGOLI geometrical pattern of rice powder laid before houses and temples

RAWAL chief priest (Hindu)

RINPOCHE literally "precious one", a highly revered Tibetan Buddhist lama, considered to be a reincarnation of a previous teacher

RISHI "seer"; philosophical sage or poet

RUDRAKSHA beads used to make Shiva rosaries

RUMAL handkerchief, particularly finely embroidered in Chamba state (HP)

SADAR "main"; eg *sadar bazaar*

SADHAK a person who is engaged in an all-encompassing course in spirituality to achieve realization of the self and God

SADHU Hindu holy man with no caste or family ties

SAGAR lake

SAHIB respectful title for gentlemen; general term of address for European men

SALABHANJIKA wood nymph

SALWAR KAMISE long shirt and baggy ankle-hugging trousers worn by Muslim women

SAMADHI final enlightenment; a site of death or burial of a saint

SAMBAR a small Asian deer

SAMSARA cyclic process of death and rebirth

SANGAM sacred confluence of two or more rivers, or an academy

SANGEET music

SANNYASIN homeless, possessionless ascetic (Hindu)

SARAI resting place for caravans and travellers who once followed the trade routes through Asia

SARI usual dress for Indian women: a length of cloth wound around the waist and draped over one shoulder

SATI one who sacrifices her life on her husband's funeral pyre in emulation of Shiva's wife. No longer a common practice, and officially illegal

SATSANG teaching given by a religious figurehead

SATYAGRAHA Gandhi's campaign of nonviolent protest, literally "grasping truth"

SCHEDULED CASTES official name for "untouchables"

SEPOY an Indian soldier in European service

SETH merchant or businessman

SEVA voluntary service in a temple or community

SHAIVITE Hindu recognizing Shiva as the supreme god

SHANKHA conch, symbol of Vishnu

SHASTRA treatise

SHIKAR hunting

SHISHYA pupil

SHLOKA verse from a Sanskrit text

SHRI respectful prefix; another name for Lakshmi

SHUDRA the lowest of the four *varnas*; servant

SHULAB public toilet

SINGHA lion

SOMA medicinal herb with hallucinogenic properties used in early Vedic and Zoroastrian rituals

STHALA site sacred for its association with legendary events

SURMA black eyeliner, also known as khol

SURYA the sun, or sun god

SUTRA (aka *sutta*) verse in Sanskrit and Pali texts (literally "thread")

SVETAMBARA "white-clad" sect of Jainism, that accepts nuns and shuns nudity

SWAMI title for a holy man

SWARAJ "self rule"; synonym for independence, coined by Gandhi

TALA rhythmic cycle in classical music; in sculpture a *tala* signifies one face-length

TALUKA district

TANDAVA vigorous, male form of dance; the dance of Shiva Nataraja

TANDOOR clay oven

TANPURA The twangy drone which accompanies all classical music.

TAPAS literally "heat": physical and mental austerities

TEMPO three-wheeled taxi

TERMA precious manuscript (Tibetan Buddhist term)

TERTON one who discovers a *terma*. Usually an enlightened being who will be able to understand the benefit of the *terma* in the era of its discovery (Tibetan Buddhist term)

THAKUR landowner

THALI combination of vegetarian dishes, chutneys, pickles, rice and bread served, especially in south India, as a single meal; the metal plate on which a meal is served

THANGKA Tibetan religious scroll painting

THERAVADA "Doctrine of the Elders": the original name for early Buddhism, which persists today in Sri Lanka and Thailand

THUG member of a north Indian cult of professional robbers and murderers

TIFFIN light meal

TIFFIN CARRIER stainless steel set of tins used for carrying meals

TILAK red dot smeared on the forehead during worship, and often used cosmetically

TIRTHA river crossing considered sacred by Hindus, or the transition from the mundane world to heaven; a place of pilgrimage for Jains

TIRTHANKARA "ford-maker" or "crossing-maker": an enlightened Jain teacher who is deified – 24 appear every 300 million years

TOLA the weight of a silver rupee: 180 grains, or approximately 116g

TONGA two-wheeled horse-drawn cart

TOPI cap

TRIMURTI the Hindu trinity

TRISHULA Shiva's trident

TULKU reincarnated teacher of Tibetan Buddhism

UNTOUCHABLES members of the lowest strata of society, considered polluting to all higher castes

URS Muslim saint's day festival

VAHANA the "vehicle" of a deity: the bull Nandi is Shiva's *vahana*

VAISHYA member of the merchant and trading caste group

VARNA literally "colour"; one of four hierarchical social categories: brahmins, *kshatryas*, *vaishyas* and *shudras*

VEDAS sacred texts of early Hinduism

-WALLAH suffix implying occupation, eg: dhobi-wallah, rickshaw-wallah

WAZIR chief minister to the king

YAGNA Vedic sacrificial ritual

YAKSHA pre-Vedic folklore figure connected with fertility and incorporated into later Hindu iconography

YAKSHI female yaksha

YALI mythical lion

YANTRA cosmological pictogram, or model used in an observatory

YATRA pilgrimage

YATRI pilgrim

YOGI *sadhu* or priestly figure possessing occult powers gained through the practice of yoga (female: *yogini*)

YONI symbol of the female sexual organ, set around the base of the *lingam* in temple shrines

YUGA aeon: the present age is the last in a cycle of four *yugas*, *kali-yuga*, a "black-age" of degeneration and spiritual decline

ZAMINDAR landowner

Architectural terms

AMALAKA repeating decorative motif based on the fluted shape of a gourd, lining and crowning temple towers: a distinctive feature of northern architecture

ANDA literally "egg": the spherical part of a stupa

BAGH garden

BAOLI step-well in Gujarat and western India

BHAWAN (also bhavan) building, house, palace or residence

BHUMIKA storey

BIRADIRI summer house; pavilion

CELLA chamber, often housing the image of a deity

CENOTAPH ornate tomb

CHAITYA Buddhist temple

CHARBAGH garden divided into quadrants (Moghul style)

CHAUMUKH image of four faces placed back to back

CHHATRI tomb; domed temple pavilion

CHORTEN monument, often containing prayers, texts or relics, erected as a sign of faith by Tibetan Buddhists

CUPOLA small delicate dome

DARGAH tomb of a Muslim saint

DARWAZA gateway; door

DEUL Orissan temple or sanctuary

DIWAN-I-AM public audience hall

DIWAN-I-KHAS hall of private audience

DU-KHANG main temple in a *gompa*

DUKKA tank and fountain in courtyard of mosque

DURBAR court building, hall of audience, or government meeting

DVARPALA guardian image placed at sanctuary door

FINIAL capping motif on temple pinnacle

GARBHA GRIHA temple sanctuary, literally "womb-chamber"

GARH fort

GODOWN warehouse

GO-KHANG temple in a *gompa* devoted to protector (*gon*) deities

GOMPA Tibetan, or Ladakhi, Buddhist monastery

GOPURA towered temple gateway, common in south India

HAMMAM sunken hot bath, Persian style

HAVELI elaborately decorated (normally wooden) mansion, especially in Rajasthan

IMAMBARA tomb of a Shi'ite saint

INDO-SARACENIC overblown Raj-era architecture that combines Muslim, Hindu, Jain and Western elements

IWAN the main (often central) arch in a mosque

JAGAMOHANA porch fronting the main sanctuary in an Orissan temple

JALI latticework in stone, or a pierced screen

JANGHA the body of a temple

KABUTAR KHANA pigeon coop

KALASHA pot-like capping stone characteristic of south Indian temples

KANGYU LANG book house in a gompa storing sacred Tibetan texts and manuscripts

KOT fort

KOTHI residence

KOTLA citadel

KOVIL term for a Tamil Nadu temple

LIWAN cloisters in a mosque

MAHAL palace; mansion

MAKARA crocodile-like animal featuring on temple doorways, and symbolizing the River Ganges. Also the vehicle of Varuna, the Vedic god of the sea

MANDAPA hall, often with many pillars, used for various purposes: eg *kalyana mandapa* for wedding ceremonies and *nata mandapa* for dance performances

MEDHI terrace

MIHRAB niche in the wall of a mosque indicating the direction of prayer (to Mecca). In India the *mihrab* is in the west wall

MIMBAR pulpit in a mosque from which the Friday sermon is read

MINARET high slender tower, characteristic of mosques

PADA foot, or base, also a poetic meter

PAGODA multistoreyed Buddhist monument

POLE fortified gate

PRADAKSHINA PATHA processional path circling a monument or sanctuary

PRAKARA enclosure or courtyard in a south Indian temple

QABR Muslim grave

QILA fort

RATH processional temple chariot of south India

REKHA DEUL Orissan towered sanctuary

SHIKHARA temple tower or spire common in northern architecture

STAMBHA pillar, or flagstaff

STUPA large hemispherical mound, representing the Buddha's presence, and often protecting relics of the Buddha or a Buddhist saint

TALA storey

TANK square or rectangular water pool in a temple complex, for ritual bathing

TORANA arch, or freestanding gateway of two pillars linked by an elaborate arch

TUK fortified enclosure of Jain shrines or temples

VAV step-well, common in Gujarat

VEDIKA railing around a stupa

VIHARA Buddhist or Jain monastery

VIMANA tower over temple sanctuary

ZENANA women's quarters; segregated area for women in a mosque

index

and small print

Index

Map entries are in colour.

Key to index		
Andaman Islands (AI)	Haryana and Punjab	Northeast (NE)
Andhra Pradesh (AP)	(H&P)	Orissa (O)
Bihar and Jharkhand	Himachal Pradesh (HP)	Rajasthan (R)
(B&J)	Karnataka (Kar)	Sikkim (S)
Calcutta and West	Kerala (K)	Tamil Nadu (TN)
Bengal (C&WB)	Ladakh (L)	Uttar Pradesh (UP)
Delhi (D)	Madhya Pradesh (MP)	Uttaranchal (U)
Goa (Goa)	Maharashtra (M)	
Gujarat (G)	Mumbai (MI)	

A

accommodation 51
Agartala (NE Hills) 1068
Agartala 1068
Agonda (Goa) 913
Agra (UP) 283
Agra 294
Agra Fort (UP) 293
Ahmedabad (Guj) 672
Ahmedabad 673, 675
Ahoms and Bodos
   (NE Hills) 1045
AIDS 36
Aihole (Kar) 1455
airline offices
   in Australia and New
      Zealand 21
   in Britain 11
   in North America 17
Aizawl (NE Hills) 1072
Ajanta (M) 813
Ajanta 814
Ajmer (Raj) 208
Ajmer 209
Alappuzha (Ker) 1324
Alappuzha 1325
Alchi (L) 625
alcohol 63
Allahabad (UP) 329
Allahabad 330
Alleppey (Ker) 1324
Almora (U) 412
altitude sickness 35
Alwar (Raj) 198
Amar Sagar (Raj) 239
Amaravati (AP) 1152
Amber (Raj) 184
Amritsar (H&P) 656
Amritsar 657
Anamudi (Ker) 1341
Anandpur Sahib (H&P) .655

ANDAMAN ISLANDS
(AI) 1161
Andaman Islands 1162
ANDHRA PRADESH
(AP) 1137
Andhra Pradesh 1138
Anegondi (Kar) 1448
Anjar (Guj) 697
Anjuna (Goa) 885
Anjuna 886
antiques 84
Arambol (Goa) 895
Aranmula (Ker) 1333
architectural terms 1578
Arial Bay (AI) 1182
Arunachal Pradesh
   (NE Hills) 1077
ashrams 75
Asiatic Lion, The 714
Assam (NE Hills) 1044
Assamese Vaishnavism
   (NE Hills) 1057
ATMs 39
Auli (U) 399
Aurangabad (M) 793
Aurangabad 794
Auroville (TN) 1234
auto-rickshaws 50
Ayappa cult (Ker) 1335
Ayodhya (UP) 327
Ayurvedic medicine 37

B

Babri Masjid (UP) 328
Badami (Kar) 1452
Badrinath (U) 399
Baga (Goa) 883
Bageshwar (U) 416
Baijnath (HP) 539
Baijnath (U) 416

Bakkhali (C&WB) 963
Bakreswar (C&WB) 967
Balasore (Ori) 1126
Banaras (UP), see Varanasi
Bandhavgarh National Park
   (MP) 492
Bandipur National Park
   (Kar) 1409
Bangalore (Kar) 1385
Bangalore 1386
Bangalore MG Road ..1390
banks 40
Baralacha La (HP) 588
bargaining 81
Baripada (Ori) 1128
Barmer (Raj) 240
Baroda (Guj) 725
Barren Island (AI) 1184
Barsana (UP) 314
Basistha (NE Hills) 1050
Baspa Valley (HP) 536
Bassein (MI) 772
Bedsa (M) 839
beggars 41
Belur (Kar) 1416
Belur Math (C&WB) 959
Benares (UP), see Varanasi
Benaulim (Goa) 904
Benaulim 905
Bengali Renaissance ...936
Berhampur (Ori) 1133
Besnagar (MP) 443
Bhagamandala (Kar) ..1425
Bhagwan Rajneesh 844
Bhaja (M) 839
Bhalukpong (NE Hills) ....
  1080
Bharatpur (Raj) 201
Bharatpur 202
Bharuch (Guj) 729
Bhavnagar (Guj) 720
Bhavnagar 720

Bheraghat (MP) 486
Bhimbetka (MP) 444
Bhojpur (MP) 443
Bhopal (MP) 424
Bhopal 425
Bhopal gas tragedy 428
Bhubaneswar (Ori) 1092
Bhubaneswar 1093
Bhuj (Guj) 692
Biber (Guj) 697
bicycles in India 50
Bidar (Kar) 1464
Bidri 1466
BIHAR AND JHARKHAND
  (B&J) 993
Bihar and Jharkhand ...994
Bijapur (Kar) 1457
Bijapur 1458
Bikaner (Raj) 242
Bikaner 243
Bileshwar (Guj) 708
Bindevasani (U) 381
Binsar (U) 414
Birapratapur (Ori) 1119
Bishnupur (C&WB) 964
Bithur (UP) 318
Black Hole of Calcutta .939
Bodhgaya (B&J) 1003
Bodhgaya 1004
Bollywood 778
BOMBAY, see Mumbai
Bomdila (NE Hills) 1080
books 1561
Brahma Kumaris 254
Brahmour (HP) 558
Braj (UP) 309
Buddhism 1514
Bundelkhand (UP) 335
Bundi (Raj) 276
Bundi 277
buses 48
Bylakuppe (Kar) 1424

C

Calangute (Goa) 879
Calangute and Baga.....880
CALCUTTA (C&WB) ....
 922–991
Calcutta 924–925, 933
  Academy of Fine Arts 939
  accommodation 932
  airline offices 954
  airlines 954
  Armenian Church 941
  arrival 927
  banks and currency
    exchange 955

Barabazaar 941
Bengali renaissance 936
Birla Academy of art and
  culture 947
Birla Planetarium 939
Black Hole of Calcutta 939
Botanical Gardens 944
Calcutta Gallery 937
Calcutta Zoo 945
Chowringhee and Sudder
  Street 933
city tours 929
city transport 929
College Street 942
consulates 955
culture and entertainment 951
Dalhousie Square 939
eating and drinking 948
Eden Gardens 940
Esplanade 935
festivals of Calcutta 926
Fort William 937
Gariahat 947
history 923
Horticultural Gardens 945
Howrah Bridge 944
Indian Museum 936
internet access 958
Kalighat 945
Kalighat paintings 946
Kumartuli 943
listings 954
mail 958
Marble Palace 941
Mother Teresa 946
moving on from Calcutta ..956
Nakhoda Masjid 941
Nandan 939
National Library 945
New Market and
  Chowringhee 935
Nicco Park 947
Old Mission Church 940
pollution and floods 943
poste restante 958
Rabindra Bharati 942
Rabindra Sarobar 947
Roman Catholic Cathedral ...
 941
Satyajit Ray 938
shopping 952
St Andrew's Kirk 940
St John's Church 940
St Paul's Cathedral 939
tourist information 928
travel agents 958
Victoria Memorial 937
Writers' Building 940
Calicut (Ker) 1372
camel breeding farm
  (Raj) 249
camel safaris from
  Bikaner 244
camel safaris in Jaisalmer
  (Raj) 236
camping 53

Canacona (Goa) 908
Candolim (Goa) 875
Candolim and Fort
  Aguada 876
Cannanore (Ker) 1375
car rental 48
Cardamom Hills (Ker) .1339
carpets 82
cave-painting 816
Cavelossim (Goa) 907
caving 73
Chamba (HP) 555
Champaner (Guj) 729
Chandernagore (C&WB) ....
 959
Chandigarh (H&P) 646
Chandigarh 647
Chandipur (Ori) 1126
Chandor (Goa) 901
Chandrabhaga (Ori) ...1125
Chapora (Goa) 893
Chapora and Vagator ..891
Char Dham (U) 386
charities 90
charter flights from
  Britain 13
Chatrapathi Shivaji
  Terminus (MI) 747
Chaudi (Goa) 913
Chemrey (L) 616
CHENNAI (TN) ..1191–1211
Chennai 1192
  accommodation 1199
  airline offices 1207
  arrival 1193
  banks and currency
    exchange 1207
  car, motorcycle and bike
    rental 1199
  Chennai festival and
    sabhas 1197
  city transport 1198
  consulates 1208
  eating 1206
  Egmore, Anna Salai and
    Triplicane 1196
  Enfield motorcycle factory .....
   1206
  Fort St George 1202
  George Town 1202
  Government Museum 1203
  information and
    communications 1196
  internet access 1208
  Kamaraj Salai 1204
  Kapalishvara Temple 1205
  listings 1207
  Little Mount Caves 1205
  Luz Church 1205
  Madras 1191
  Marina 1204
  movie stars and
    ministers 1195

moving on from Chennai 1209
Mylapore 1204
post and telephone ....
post offices 1208
publications 1198
recommended trains from
  Chennai 1210
San Thome Cathedral 1204
St Andrew's Kirk 1203
St Mary's Church 1202
St Thomas Mount 1205
Theosophical Society 1206
tours 1198
travel agents 1209
Cherrapunjee (NE Hills) ......
 1064
Cheruthuruthy (Ker) ...1367
Chidambaram (TN) 1236
Chila (U) 381
children, travelling with ..89
Chilka Lake (Ori) 1131
Chini (HP), see Kalpa ...535
Chirya Tapu (AI) 1175
Chitkul (HP) 536
Chitrakut (UP) 339
Chittaurgarh (Raj) 271
Chittor (Raj), see
  Chittaurgarh
Chola Bronzes (TN) 1248
chortens and mani walls
  (L) 603
Chowera (Kera) 1313
Christianity 1521
Christianity in Kerala
  (Ker) 1333
Chunar (UP) 358
Chungthang (Sik) 1039
Cinque Island (AI) 1184
climate xi
clinics...........................36
Cochin (Ker) 1343
Coimbatore (TN) 1279
Coimbatore 1280
Colaba (MI) 754
Colva (Goa) 902
Colva 902
communications 64
Coonoor (TN) 1281
Coorg (Kar) 1420
Corbett, Jim 409
Corbett National Park
  (U) 407
Corbett National Park...408
Corbyn's Cave (AI) 1175
Cotigao Wildlife Sanctuary
  (Goa) 916
credit cards 39
cricket 70
crime 76
Crocodile bank (TN) 1221
Curzon Trail, The (U) 402

Cuttack (Ori) 1125

D

daba-wallahs 759
Dabolim airport (Goa) ..897
Dakshina Chitra (TN) ..1221
Dakshineshwar
  (C&WB) 959
Dalai Lama, Meeting the
  (HP) 547
Dalhousie (HP) 553
Daman (Guj) 732
Daman 733
Darasuram (TN) 1242
Darcha (HP) 588
Darjeeling (C&WB) 973
Darjeeling 974
Darjeeling Himalayan
  Railway, the 970
Darjeeling Tea
  (C&WB) 978
Datia (MP) 461
Daulatabad (M) 801
Dawki (NE Hills) 1065
Deeg (Raj) 200
Dehra Dun (U) 369
DELHI 97–156
Delhi 98–99
  accommodation 151
  arrival 103
  Baha'l Temple 135
  banks 149
  Connaught Place 118
  eating 138
  history 100
  Humayun's tomb 133
  Jami Masjid 126
  Jantar Mantar 117
  listings 148
  Lodi tombs 131
  moving on 152
  museums 120
  nightlife 146
  Nizamuddin 132
  Old Delhi 123
  Paharganj 110
  Purana Qila 130
  Qutb Minar 136
  Raj Path 115
  Red Fort 123
  Safdarjang's tomb 134
  shopping 142
  tourist information 105
  transport 105
  Tughluqabad 136
Deogarh (B&J) 1011
Deogiri (M) 801
Deshnok (Raj) 249
Dhankar (HP) 585

Dharamsala (HP) 542
Dharamsala and McLeod
  Ganj............................543
Dhauladhar treks 551
Dhauli (Ori) 1106
Dhikala (U) 410
Dholavira (Guj) 697
Dholka (Guj) 686
Dhordo (Guj) 697
Diamond Harbour
  (C&WB) 963
diarrhoea 34
Digha (C&WB) 963
Diglipur (AI) 1182
Dilwara temples (Raj) ...255
Dimapur (NE Hills) 1086
Dirang (NE Hills) 1081
disabled travellers 88
discount ticket agents
  in Australia and
    New Zealand 21
  in Britain 13
  in USA 17
diseases 33
Diskit (L) 621
Diu (Guj) 715
Diu island 716
Diu town 719
diving 73, 1167
Dr D. Ering Memorial
  Wildlife Sanctuary (NE
  Hills) 1083
Drangadhra (Guj) 701
dress codes 79
drought in Rajasthan ...166
drugs 77
Dudhsagar waterfalls
  (Goa) 873
Dunlod (Raj) 191
Dwarka (Guj) 704
dysentery 35
Dzongri Trail, The
  (Sik) 1035

E

eating and drinking 54
Eklingji (Raj) 267
electricity 91
Elephanta Island (MI) ...769
Ellora (M) 805
Ellora 805
email 65
Enfield motorbikes 50
Eravikulam National Park
  (Ker) 1341
Ernakulam (Ker) 1353
Ernakulam..................1354